THE GREEK NEW TESTAMENT

═══

UBS4

with

NRSV & NIV

John R. Kohlenberger III
Editor

Foreword by Bruce M. Metzger

ZondervanPublishingHouse
Academic and Professional Books
Grand Rapids, Michigan

A Division of HarperCollinsPublishers

The Greek New Testament: UBS4 with NRSV and NIV
Copyright © 1993 by John R. Kohlenberger, III

Requests for information should be addressed to:
Zondervan Publishing House
Academic and Professional Books
Grand Rapids, Michigan 49530

Library of Congress Cataloging in Publication Data

Bible. N.T. Greek. 1993.
    The Greek New Testament : UBS4 with NRSV and NIV / John R. Kohlenberger, III,
general editor ; preface by Bruce M. Metzger.
        p.   cm.
    ISBN 0-310-41400-8
    1. Bible. N.T.–Interlinear translations, English.   I. Kohlenberger, John R.   II.
United Bible Societies.   III. Bible. N.T. English. New Revised Standard. 1993.   IV.
Bible. N.T. English. New International, 1993.   V. Title.
    BS1965.51993
    225.4'8–dc20   93-27438
                                                CIP

Cover design by John M. Lucas

Printed in the United States of America

93 94 95 96 97 98 99 / DC / 10 9 8 7 6 5 4 3 2 1

This edition is printed on acid-free paper and meets the American National Standards Institute Z39.48 standard.

TABLE OF CONTENTS

The Greek New Testament With UBS⁴, NRSV and NIV

DEDICATION

To the recipients of the
Edward W. Goodrick Memorial Award
for Excellence in Biblical Language Study.

This award is bestowed annually by Multnomah Bible College
in Portland, Oregon, on the graduating student
who has displayed the highest excellence in
biblical language study over the entire course
of the college's biblical languages program.

The award honors the memory of Dr. Edward W. Goodrick,
who in his thirty-five-year tenure at Multnomah Bible College
introduced thousands to the biblical languages and
helped prepare hundreds of pastors, teachers,
missionary translators and scholars
for Christian ministry.

FOREWORD

This edition of the United Bible Societies' Greek New Testament, flanked on each side by a modern English translation, brings together into one volume the materials ordinarily found in three separate volumes. With consummate skill the editor has managed to lay out on each page three parallel accounts of the same section of text.

The two English versions presented here offer the reader an opportunity to compare two techniques of translation. Basically the difference between the two, as St. Jerome pointed out in a letter to his friend Pammachius (*Epistle* 57.5-6), involves making a rendering either *verbum ad verbum* or *sensus ad sensum*. According to the Preface of the New International Version, the Committee has "striven for more than a word-for-word translation," and has introduced "frequent modifications in sentence structure." The aim, in short, was to produce a rendering that would be "idiomatic but not idiosyncratic, contemporary but not dated." By contrast, according to the statement in the prefatory "To the Reader," the Standard Bible Committee followed the maxim, "As literal as possible, as free as necessary." Consequently the New Revised Standard Version is "essentially a literal translation. Paraphrastic renderings have been adopted only sparingly, and then chiefly to compensate for a deficiency in the English language—the lack of a common gender third person pronoun." Each of these two methods of translation is legitimate, and no position is taken here as to which is preferable.

Neither committee followed its stated procedure slavishly, and so the careful reader can occasionally find what appears to be a violation of the declared aim of the translators. It is not, however, by hunting for such infractions that the user will gain the most benefit from consulting this volume. On the contrary, by making a careful and detailed comparison back and forth between the Greek text and the two translations the student will be able to discriminate between what the passage means and what the passage says. Attention given to such matters will enlarge one's understanding of the translation process as well as the problems and difficulties that confront the conscientious translator.

Besides using the volume to make a comparison of the respective techniques of translation, such study will enable the reader also to appreciate still more fully the riches of holy Scripture. For truly, as the translators of the King James Version declared in memorable words, "Translation it is that openeth the window, to let in the light; that breaketh the shell, that we may eat the kernel; that putteth aside the curtain, that we may look into the most Holy place" (The Translators to the Reader).

The Latin dictum that Johannes Albrecht Bengel printed in the Preface of his edition of the Greek New Testament is as appropriate today as it was in 1734—

"Apply yourself totally to the text:
    apply the text totally to yourself."

Bruce M. Metzger
Princeton Theological Seminary

ACKNOWLEDGMENTS

Thanks to Stan Gundry, vice president and editor-in-chief, and Bruce Ryskamp, president of Zondervan Publishing House, for allowing me to do this book. To retiring CEO Jim Buick for the incredible corporate support and personal interest shown to me and to the late Ed Goodrick during our many years of developing biblical reference works for Zondervan.

Special thanks to Dr. Bruce M. Metzger, co-editor of the United Bible Societies' *Greek New Testament* and chair of the Translation Committee for the New Revised Standard Version, for his Foreword and for taking time from his busy schedule to review materials and answer technical questions from his unique inside perspective.

Thanks to the United Bible Societies for the use of their *Greek New Testament*, Fourth Revised Edition. To Harold P. Scanlin, translation adviser to the United Bible Societies, for his role in granting permission to use the UBS text and for answering questions regarding the text and its features.

Thanks to the National Council of the Churches of Christ in the U.S.A. for the use of the New Revised Standard Version. Thanks to the International Bible Society and to Zondervan Bible Publishers for the use of the New International Version. To Paul Woods, theological editor for Zondervan Bible Publishers, for overseeing a careful proofreading of the NIV.

Thanks to editor Ed van der Maas for coordinating editing and production.

Thanks to Dr. Walter W. Wessel of Bethel Seminary West for interacting with text-critical questions relating to the NIV.

Thanks to Mark Rice of Hermeneutika for providing a copy of BibleWorks™ for Windows™ from which an electronic copy of the UBS text was extracted for assistance in proofreading the Greek, and for providing the Graeca font which was used to typeset the UBS text.

Special thanks to James A. Swanson for both electronically and manually proofreading the UBS text and the Greek footnotes.

As always, special thanks to my wife, Carolyn, and to my children, Sarah and Joshua, for their love and encouragement.

To the Reader of the NRSV

This preface is addressed to you by the Committee of translators, who wish to explain, as briefly as possible, the origin and character of our work. The publication of our revision is yet another step in the long, continual process of making the Bible available in the form of the English language that is most widely current in our day. To summarize in a single sentence: the New Revised Standard Version of the Bible is an authorized revision of the Revised Standard Version, published in 1952, which was a revision of the American Standard Version, published in 1901, which, in turn, embodied earlier revisions of the King James Version, published in 1611.

The need for issuing a revision of the Revised Standard Version of the Bible arises from three circumstances: (*a*) the acquisition of still older Biblical manuscripts, (*b*) further investigation of linguistic features of the text, and (*c*) changes in preferred English usage. Consequently, in 1974 the Policies Committee of the Revised Standard Version, which is a standing committee of the National Council of the Churches of Christ in the U.S.A., authorized the preparation of a revision of the entire RSV Bible.

For the New Testament the Committee has based its work on the most recent edition of *The Greek New Testament*, prepared by an interconfessional and international committee and published by the United Bible Societies (1966; 3rd ed. corrected, 1983; information concerning changes to be introduced into the critical apparatus of the forthcoming 4th edition was available to the Committee). As in that edition, double brackets are used to enclose a few passages that are generally regarded to be later additions to the text, but which we have retained because of their evident antiquity and their importance in the textual tradition. Only in very rare instances have we replaced the text or the punctuation of the Bible Societies' edition by an alternative that seemed to us to be superior. Here and there in the footnotes the phrase, "Other ancient authorities read," identifies alternative readings preserved by Greek manuscripts and early versions. Alternative renderings of the text are indicated by the word "Or."

As for the style of English adopted for the present revision, among the mandates given to the Committee in 1980 by the Division of Education and Ministry of the National Council of Churches of Christ (which now holds the copyright of the RSV Bible) was the directive to continue in the tradition of the King James Bible, but to introduce such changes as are warranted on the basis of accuracy, clarity, euphony, and current English usage. Within the constraints set by the original texts and by the mandates of the Division, the Committee has followed the maxim, "As literal as possible, as free as necessary." As a consequence, the New Revised Standard Version (NRSV) remains essentially a literal translation. Paraphrastic renderings have been adopted only sparingly, and then chiefly to compensate for a deficiency in the English language—the lack of a common gender third person singular pronoun.

During the almost half a century since the publication of the RSV, many in the churches have become sensitive to the danger of linguistic sexism arising from the inherent bias of the English language towards the masculine gender, a bias that in the case of the Bible has often restricted or obscured the meaning of the original text. The mandates from the Division specified that, in references to men and women, masculine-oriented language should be eliminated as far as this can be done without altering passages that reflect the historical situation of ancient patriarchal culture. As can be appreciated, more than once the Committee found that the several mandates stood in tension and even in conflict. The various concerns had to be balanced case by case in order to provide a faithful and acceptable rendering without using contrived English. In the vast majority of cases, however, inclusiveness has been attained by simple rephrasing or by introducing plural forms when this does not distort the meaning of the passage. Of course, in narrative and in parable no attempt was made to generalize the sex of individual persons.

It will be seen that in prayers addressed to God the archaic second person singular pronouns (*thee, thou, thine*) and verb forms (*art, hast, hadst*) are no longer used. Although some readers may regret this change, it should be pointed out that in the original languages neither the Old Testament nor the New makes any linguistic distinction between addressing a human being and addressing the Deity. Furthermore, in the tradition of the King James Version one will not expect to find the use of capital letters for pronouns that refer to the Deity — such capitalization is an unnecessary innovation that has only recently been introduced into a few English translations of the Bible. Finally, we have left to the discretion of the licensed publishers such matters as section headings, cross-references, and clues to the pronunciation of proper names.

This new version seeks to preserve all that is best in the English Bible as it has been known and used through the years. It is intended for use in public reading and congregational worship, as well as in private study, instruction, and meditation. We have resisted the temptation to introduce terms and phrases that merely reflect current moods, and have tried to put the message of the Scriptures in simple, enduring words and expressions that are worthy to stand in the great tradition of the King James Bible and its predecessors. It is the hope and prayer of the translators that this version of the Bible may continue to hold a large place in congregational life and to speak to all readers, young and old alike, helping them to understand and believe and respond to its message.

For the Committee,
BRUCE M. METZGER

Preface to the NIV

THE NEW INTERNATIONAL VERSION is a completely new translation of the Holy Bible made by over a hundred scholars working directly from the best available Hebrew, Aramaic and Greek texts. It had its beginning in 1965 when, after several years of exploratory study by committees from the Christian Reformed Church and the National Association of Evangelicals, a group of scholars met at Palos Heights, Illinois, and concurred in the need for a new translation of the Bible in contemporary English. This group, though not made up of official church representatives, was transdenominational. Its conclusion was endorsed by a large number of leaders from many denominations who met in Chicago in 1966.

Responsibility for the new version was delegated by the Palos Heights group to a self-governing body of fifteen, the Committee on Bible Translation, composed for the most part of biblical scholars from colleges, universities and seminaries. In 1967 the New York Bible Society (now the International Bible Society) generously undertook the financial sponsorship of the project—a sponsorship that made it possible to enlist the help of many distinguished scholars. The fact that participants from the United States, Great Britain, Canada, Australia and New Zealand worked together gave the project its international scope. That they were from many denominations—including Anglican, Assemblies of God, Baptist, Brethren, Christian Reformed, Church of Christ, Evangelical Free, Lutheran, Mennonite, Methodist, Nazarene, Presbyterian, Wesleyan and other churches—helped to safeguard the translation from sectarian bias.

How it was made helps to give the New International Version its distinctiveness. The translation of each book was assigned to a team of scholars. Next, one of the Intermediate Editorial Committees revised the initial translation, with constant reference to the Hebrew, Aramaic or Greek. Their work then went to one of the General Editorial Committees, which checked it in detail and made another thorough revision. This revision in turn was carefully reviewed by the Committee on Bible Translation, which made further changes and then released the final version for publication. In this way the entire Bible underwent three revisions, during each of which the translation was examined for its faithfulness to the original languages and for its English style.

All this involved many thousands of hours of research and discussion regarding the meaning of the texts and the precise way of putting them into English. It may well be that no other translation has been made by a more thorough process of review and revision from committee to committee than this one.

From the beginning of the project, the Committee on Bible Translation held to certain goals for the New International Version: that it would be an accurate translation and one that would have clarity and literary quality and so prove suitable for public and private reading, teaching, preaching, memorizing and liturgical use. The Committee also sought to preserve some measure of continuity with the long tradition of translating the Scriptures into English.

In working toward these goals, the translators were united in their commitment to the authority and infallibility of the Bible as God's Word in written form. They believe that it contains the divine answer to the deepest needs of humanity, that

it sheds unique light on our path in a dark world, and that it sets forth the way to our eternal well-being.

The first concern of the translators has been the accuracy of the translation and its fidelity to the thought of the biblical writers. They have weighed the significance of the lexical and grammatical details of the Hebrew, Aramaic and Greek texts. At the same time, they have striven for more than a word-for-word translation. Because thought patterns and syntax differ from language to language, faithful communication of the meaning of the writers of the Bible demands frequent modifications in sentence structure and constant regard for the contextual meanings of words.

A sensitive feeling for style does not always accompany scholarship. Accordingly the Committee on Bible Translation submitted the developing version to a number of stylistic consultants. Two of them read every book of both Old and New Testaments twice—once before and once after the last major revision—and made invaluable suggestions. Samples of the translation were tested for clarity and ease of reading by various kinds of people—young and old, highly educated and less well educated, ministers and laymen.

Concern for clear and natural English—that the New International Version should be idiomatic but not idiosyncratic, contemporary but not dated—motivated the translators and consultants. At the same time, they tried to reflect the differing styles of the biblical writers. In view of the international use of English, the translators sought to avoid obvious Americanisms on the one hand and obvious Anglicisms on the other. A British edition reflects the comparatively few differences of significant idiom and of spelling.

As for the traditional pronouns "thou," "thee" and "thine" in reference to the Deity, the translators judged that to use these archaisms (along with the old verb forms such as "doest," "wouldest" and "hadst") would violate accuracy in translation. Neither Hebrew, Aramaic nor Greek uses special pronouns for the persons of the Godhead. A present-day translation is not enhanced by forms that in the time of the King James Version were used in everyday speech, whether referring to God or man.

For the Old Testament the standard Hebrew text, the Masoretic Text as published in the latest editions of *Biblia Hebraica*, was used throughout. The Dead Sea Scrolls contain material bearing on an earlier stage of the Hebrew text. They were consulted, as were the Samaritan Pentateuch and the ancient scribal traditions relating to textual changes. Sometimes a variant Hebrew reading in the margin of the Masoretic Text was followed instead of the text itself. Such instances, being variants within the Masoretic tradition, are not specified by footnotes. In rare cases, words in the consonantal text were divided differently from the way they appear in the Masoretic Text. Footnotes indicate this. The translators also consulted the more important early versions—the Septuagint; Aquila, Symmachus and Theodotion; the Vulgate; the Syriac Peshitta; the Targums; and for the Psalms the *Juxta Hebraica* of Jerome. Readings from these versions were occasionally followed where the Masoretic Text seemed doubtful and where accepted principles of textual criticism showed that one or more of these textual witnesses appeared to provide the correct reading. Such instances are footnoted. Sometimes vowel letters and vowel signs did not, in the judgment of the translators, represent the correct vowels for the original consonantal text. Accordingly some words were read with a different set of vowels. These instances are usually not indicated by footnotes.

The Greek text used in translating the New Testament was

an eclectic one. No other piece of ancient literature has such an abundance of manuscript witnesses as does the New Testament. Where existing manuscripts differ, the translators made their choice of readings according to accepted principles of New Testament textual criticism. Footnotes call attention to places where there was uncertainty about what the original text was. The best current printed texts of the Greek New Testament were used.

There is a sense in which the work of translation is never wholly finished. This applies to all great literature and uniquely so to the Bible. In 1973 the New Testament in the New International Version was published. Since then, suggestions for corrections and revisions have been received from various sources. The Committee on Bible Translation carefully considered the suggestions and adopted a number of them. These were incorporated in the first printing of the entire Bible in 1978. Additional revisions were made by the Committee on Bible Translation in 1983 and appear in printings after that date.

As in other ancient documents, the precise meaning of the biblical texts is sometimes uncertain. This is more often the case with the Hebrew and Aramaic texts than with the Greek text. Although archaeological and linguistic discoveries in this century aid in understanding difficult passages, some uncertainties remain. The more significant of these have been called to the reader's attention in the footnotes.

In regard to the divine name *YHWH*, commonly referred to as the *Tetragrammaton*, the translators adopted the device used in most English versions of rendering that name as "Lord" in capital letters to distinguish it from *Adonai*, another Hebrew word rendered "Lord," for which small letters are used. Wherever the two names stand together in the Old Testament as a compound name of God, they are rendered "Sovereign Lord."

Because for most readers today the phrases "the Lord of hosts" and "God of hosts" have little meaning, this version renders them "the Lord Almighty" and "God Almighty." These renderings convey the sense of the Hebrew, namely, "he who is sovereign over all the 'hosts' (powers) in heaven and on earth, especially over the 'hosts' (armies) of Israel." For readers unacquainted with Hebrew this does not make clear the distinction between *Sabaoth* ("hosts" or "Almighty") and *Shaddai* (which can also be translated "Almighty"), but the latter occurs infrequently and is always footnoted. When *Adonai* and *YHWH Sabaoth* occur together, they are rendered "the Lord, the Lord Almighty."

As for other proper nouns, the familiar spellings of the King James Version are generally retained. Names traditionally spelled with "ch," except where it is final, are usually spelled in this translation with "k" or "c," since the biblical languages do not have the sound that "ch" frequently indicates in English—for example, in *chant*. For well-known names such as Zechariah, however, the traditional spelling has been retained. Variation in the spelling of names in the original languages has usually not been indicated. Where a person or place has two or more different names in the Hebrew, Aramaic or Greek texts, the more familiar one has generally been used, with footnotes where needed.

To achieve clarity the translators sometimes supplied words not in the original texts but required by the context. If there was uncertainty about such material, it is enclosed in brackets. Also for the sake of clarity or style, nouns, including some proper nouns, are sometimes substituted for pronouns, and vice versa. And though the Hebrew writers often shifted back and forth between first, second and third personal pronouns without change of antecedent, this translation often makes them

uniform, in accordance with English style and without the use of footnotes.

Poetical passages are printed as poetry, that is, with indentation of lines with separate stanzas. These are generally designed to reflect the structure of Hebrew poetry. This poetry is normally characterized by parallelism in balanced lines. Most of the poetry in the Bible is in the Old Testament, and scholars differ regarding the scansion of Hebrew lines. The translators determined the stanza divisions for the most part by analysis of the subject matter. The stanzas therefore serve as poetic paragraphs.

As an aid to the reader, italicized sectional headings are inserted in most of the books. They are not to be regarded as part of the NIV text, are not for oral reading, and are not intended to dictate the interpretation of the sections they head.

The footnotes in this version are of several kinds, most of which need no explanation. Those giving alternative translations begin with "Or" and generally introduce the alternative with the last word preceding it in the text, except when it is a single-word alternative; in poetry quoted in a footnote a slant mark indicates a line division. Footnotes introduced by "Or" do not have uniform significance. In some cases two possible translations were considered to have about equal validity. In other cases, though the translators were convinced that the translation in the text was correct, they judged that another interpretation was possible and of sufficient importance to be represented in a footnote.

In the New Testament, footnotes that refer to uncertainty regarding the original text are introduced by "Some manuscripts" or similar expressions. In the Old Testament, evidence for the reading chosen is given first and evidence for the alternative is added after a semicolon (for example: Septuagint; Hebrew *father*). In such notes the term "Hebrew" refers to the Masoretic Text.

It should be noted that minerals, flora and fauna, architectural details, articles of clothing and jewelry, musical instruments and other articles cannot always be identified with precision. Also measures of capacity in the biblical period are particularly uncertain (see the table of weights and measures following the text).

Like all translations of the Bible, made as they are by imperfect man, this one undoubtedly falls short of its goals. Yet we are grateful to God for the extent to which he has enabled us to realize these goals and for the strength he has given us and our colleagues to complete our task. We offer this version of the Bible to him in whose name and for whose glory it has been made. We pray that it will lead many into a better understanding of the Holy Scriptures and a fuller knowledge of Jesus Christ the incarnate Word, of whom the Scriptures so faithfully testify.

The Committee on Bible Translation

June 1978
(Revised August 1983)

Names of the translators and editors may be secured from the International Bible Society, translation sponsors of the New International Version, P.O. Box 62970, Colorado Springs, Colorado 80962-2970 U.S.A.

INTRODUCTION

The first printed Greek New Testament was completed in 1514. However, it was not published until 1520 or 1522 after the Complutensian Polyglot, of which it a part, received papal sanction. The first published Greek testament was that of Desiderius Erasmus in 1516. Both of these landmark editions were diglots, presenting the New Testament in parallel columns of Greek and Latin. Both had the goal of assisting students and scholars in their reading and research of the original language by associating the Greek with the (then) more familiar Latin Vulgate.

The Greek New Testament With UBS⁴, NRSV and NIV (hereafter *Greek NT*) has a similar presentation and a similar function to the first printed Greek texts. While Greek of course remains the original language of the New Testament, English has replaced Latin as the most widely used language in biblical scholarship. Thus this volume presents the now standard *Greek New Testament* of the United Bible Societies, in its new fourth revised edition, paralleled by two of the most widely used and respected English versions, the New Revised Standard Version (NRSV) and the New International Version (NIV).

The Greek Text

The Greek text represented in the center column is the fourth revised edition of the United Bible Societies' *Greek New Testament* (UBS⁴, 1993). When its first edition appeared in 1966, it joined Nestle's regularly revised *Novum Testamentum Graece* (then in its twenty-fifth edition) as a favorite choice of students and scholars. Because of the significant involvement of Kurt Aland and the Institute for New Testament Textual Research in both the third edition of the United Bible Societies' text (UBS³, 1975; corrected 1983) and in the twenty-sixth edition of the Nestle-Aland text (NA²⁶, 1979), these two testaments have become identical in text. The texts still differ in typography and paragraphing, in Old Testament citation, and in some points of punctuation. Most differences are in their critical apparatuses, where NA²⁶ cites more individual variants in a concise and highly abbreviated apparatus, while UBS⁴ cites more extensive evidence for fewer variants.

Features of UBS⁴ Reflected in the *Greek NT*

The text of the *Greek NT* faithfully reproduces the text, typography, bracketing, paragraphing and punctuation of UBS⁴, which remains unchanged from the text of UBS³ (1983 corrected edition). Three separate computer databases of UBS³ and NA²⁶ were electronically compared by the editor and James A. Swanson, with all differences corrected by consulting the printed edition of UBS⁴. (Incidentally, the only differences discovered involved punctuation, capitalization and paragraphing.) The paragraphing, poetic indentation, and bolding of OT citations were verified page-by-page against the printed edition of UBS⁴. Even the Greek font used (Graeca™ by Linguist's Software Inc.) is practically identical to UBS⁴.

The Critical Apparatus of the *Greek NT*

The most obvious difference between the center column of the *Greek NT* and UBS⁴ is in the critical apparatus. Sometimes accounting for more than half the page, the apparatus of UBS⁴ covers 1437 sets of variant readings with extensive listings of witnesses. The *Greek NT* is not intended to replace or compete with the scholarly critical editions, but to provide a handy, useful and portable edition of three standard NT texts. Thus the apparatus of the *Greek NT* is limited to offering only those variants that are indicated in the footnotes of the NRSV and NIV, as well as selected variants reflected in the texts of the NRSV and NIV. Further, the apparatus has no listing of witnesses or evaluation of evidence. It is assumed that the student or scholar who wishes further documentation on any listed variant will turn to UBS⁴ or NA²⁶ for assistance. All variants are documented in NA²⁶; most are in UBS⁴. Any variant *not* in UBS⁴ is marked with a dagger (†).

The apparatus was developed in two stages. First, all the footnotes of the NRSV and NIV were carefully examined. Those that reflected variant readings were documented from UBS⁴. If UBS⁴ did not document a variant, the relevant information was taken from NA²⁶ and the note was marked with a dagger (†). Second, the editor drew from a database all of the textual differences between the reconstructed NIV Greek text and UBS[4]. This database was developed by Edward W. Goodrick and the editor in the course of creating *The NIV Exhaustive Concordance* (Zondervan, 1990).

Because no translation committee has published the Greek text that underlies their version since R. V. G. Tasker's *Greek New Testament*, based on the New English Bible (Cambridge, 1964), the variant readings represented in the apparatus of the *Greek NT* do not officially represent the NRSV or NIV. The editor is very grateful for valuable input and interaction from Dr. Bruce M. Metzger, chair of the Translation Committee for the NRSV, and Dr. Walter W. Wessel, an NIV translator; however, the responsibility for the content of the apparatus is solely the editor's.

Conventions and Symbols Used in the Apparatus

Each of the 620 footnotes is keyed to the Greek text by a superscript English letter. Letter and verse number are both indicated at the start of the footnote. As the numbering of each chapter starts over with the letter *a*, there are sometimes two footnotes on a page that use the same letter (e.g., p. 5), but never two notes that match letter *and* verse number. Because NRSV footnotes do not indicate the verse number they relate to, the Greek footnotes refer to NRSV footnotes by their letter. Please note that no two editions of the NRSV use exactly the same letters in their footnotes. Therefore, the cross-reference system used in the critical apparatus relates to this volume only and not to any other edition of the NRSV.

The apparatus accounts for three kinds of variants discussed in the footnotes to the NRSV and NIV: changes in, additions to and omissions from the text.

1. Changes to a word or phrase noted in the NRSV or NIV follow one of three conventions:

NRSV text: he sent word by his[i] disciples (Mt 11:2, p. 20)
NRSV note: [i] Other ancient authorities read *two of his*
Greek note: [a]2 NRSV note i δύο τῶν μαθητῶν

NIV text: Beelzebub,[c] (Mt 10:25, p. 19)
NIV note: [c]25 Greek *Beezeboul* or *Beelzeboul*
Greek note: [c]25 NIV note Βεεζεβοὺλ †

NRSV text: Gadarenes,[w] (Mt 8:28, p. 15)
NRSV note: [w] Other ancient authorities read *Gergesenes*; others, *Gerasenes*
NIV text: Gadarenes,[d]
NIV note: [d]28 Some manuscripts *Gergesenes*; others *Gerasenes*
Greek note: [c]28 NIV/NRSV notes Γεργεσηνῶν or Γερασηνῶν

2. Additions to the text noted in the NRSV or NIV similarly follow one of three conventions:

NRSV note: [g] Other ancient authorities add *openly* (Mt 6:4, p. 9)
Greek note: [b]4 NRSV note g adds ἐν τῷ φανερῷ

NIV note: [i]44 Some late manuscripts *enemies, bless those who curse you, do good to those who hate you* (Mt 5:44, p. 9)
Greek note: [d]44 NIV note adds εὐλογεῖτε τοὺς καταρωμένους ὑμᾶς, καλῶς ποιεῖτε τοῖς μισοῦσιν ὑμᾶς

NRSV note: [y] . . . other ancient authorities add *without cause* (Mt 5:22, p. 8)
NIV note: [b]22 Some manuscripts *brother without cause*
Greek note: [a]22 NIV/NRSV notes add εἰκῇ

3. Omissions from the text noted in the NRSV or NIV are generally not noted in the Greek apparatus. This is because the reader needs no additional information in order to understand the differences between the English and Greek texts. For example:

NRSV text: utter all kinds of evil against you falsely[v] (Mt 5:11, p. 7)
NRSV note: [v] Other ancient authorities lack *falsely*
Greek text: εἴπωσιν πᾶν πονηρὸν καθ' ὑμῶν [ψευδόμενοι]

Here it is clear that the note refers to the bracketed word *[ψευδόμενοι]*, so no further information is needed.

Nevertheless, some footnotes do not make it clear that their alternate rendering involves an omission. In such cases as these, a Greek note is supplied:

NRSV text: for the gate is wide and the road is easy[s]   (Mt 7:13, p. 12)
NRSV note: [s] Other ancient authorities read *for the road is wide and easy*
Greek text: ὅτι πλατεῖα ἡ πύλη[b] καὶ εὐρύχωρος ἡ ὁδὸς
Greek note: [b]13 NRSV note s omits ἡ πύλη

The apparatus also accounts for variants between the NIV Greek text and UBS[4] that are not noted in the footnotes. Such notes fall into the same three categories previously discussed and always include the phrase "NIV text":

[c]14 NIV text ὅτι δε   (Mt 7:14, p. 12)
[a]10 NIV text adds ὀπίσω μου   (Mt 4:10, p. 5)
[a]16 NIV text omits αὐτῷ   (Mt 3:16, p. 5)

Sometimes such undocumented NIV variants coincide with NRSV notes:

[b]10 NIV text and NRSV note d Ἀμών, Ἀμὼν
     (Mt 1:10, p. 1)
[d]16 NIV text and NRSV note w omit Ἰησοῦν
     (Mt 27:16, p. 59)

On occasion, the NIV and NRSV do not precisely follow UBS[4] versification. These differences are also noted in the Greek apparatus:

[c]15 NIV/NRSV texts read εὐθέως in verse 16
     (Mt 25:15, p. 52)

As stated above, this brief apparatus is meant to be used with the fuller apparatuses of UBS[4] and NA[26]. Also indispensable is Bruce M. Metzger's *A Textual Commentary on the Greek New Testament* (UBS, 1971).

The English Versions

The New Revised Standard Version

Of the many attempts to provide a well executed and widely accepted alternative to the King James Version in the late eighteenth and early twentieth centuries, none met with more success than the Revised Standard Version (RSV). The NT first appeared in 1946, the OT in 1952, and the Apocrypha in 1957. The second edition of the NT was published in 1971, an expanded Apocrypha in 1977. Combining classic ecclesiastical language with modern critical scholarship, the RSV won an instant and lasting audience and remained the standard version of English biblical scholarship until the appearance of its own revision.

The revision of the RSV began in 1974. Its main goals were to accommodate the language of the RSV to more contemporary English, to update its scholarship, and to eliminate gender-biased language. The NRSV was published in 1989 to strong praise and wide acceptance. Already it has become the base text of several major study Bibles and reference books on both academic and popular levels.

Three major characteristics of the NRSV commend its use, especially to students and communicators: its translation style, its footnotes and its careful use of gender-inclusive language. The revisers followed the maxim, "As literal as possible, as free as necessary." As a result, the NRSV is essentially a "formal equivalent," or word-for-word, translation. This translation style is often preferred by students and scholars who desire their English version to reflect the wording and grammatical structure of the Greek, without adversely affecting English clarity.

The NRSV has 6,266 footnotes, 1,822 of which are in the NT. Most of the NT footnotes reflect alternate translations and alternate textual readings and thus are invaluable to careful readers. About 500 notes offer alternate renderings of words or phrases, thus showing a significant range of meaning or nuance. Notes of this type include suggesting "Christ" in place of "Messiah" (Mt 1:1, 16, 17, 18, etc.), "temptation" for "time of trial" (Mt 6:13, etc.), or "seventy times seven" for "seventy-seven times" (Mt 18:22).

More than 500 notes document variant readings in ancient biblical manuascripts and translations, such as are documented in the Greek notes of the *Greek NT* and are discussed in the previous section. Many of these notes include familiar passages from the KJV which are not well attested in the earliest manuscripts and thus are not in the NRSV or in most other modern versions. These include such passages as the "doxology" to the Lord's prayer (Mt 6:13) and the "three witnesses" of 1 John 5:7–8. By contrast, the NRSV uses a combination of double brackets (⟦ ⟧) and footnotes to point out similar passages that have been retained in the text, but are generally regarded to be later additions to the original manuscripts (e.g., Mk 16:9-20 and Jn 7:53-8:11). Most of the textual notes reflect well-attested variants over which scholars are divided as to which is original. *Please note, however, that no matter of Christian doctrine or practice is affected by any of these variant readings.*

Nearly 800 notes present a more formal equivalent or technical translation of the Greek. Many of these include the stylistic interchange of a noun and pronoun (e.g., "Jesus" for "he" in Mt 4:12, 23, etc.). Significant in this category are notes that document the rendering of gender-inclusive Greek terms with gender-inclusive English. For example, when the Greek word ἀδελφός does not specifically refer to a male relative, it is usually rendered "brother(s) and sister(s)" (Mt 5:22, 27, etc.) or "friend(s)" (Lk 6:42, etc.). The NRSV is the first major version to reflect this change in preferred English usage and for this reason alone is widely commended for public reading and proclamation.

For further information, see "To the Reader of the NRSV" on page vii and *The Making of the New Revised Standard Version* (Eerdmans, 1991).

The New International Version

The NIV had its formal beginning in 1965, following several years of exploratory study by committees from the Christian Reformed Church and the National Association of Evangelicals, who concurred on the need for a translation of the Bible into contemporary English. The work was committed to 115 biblical scholars and English stylists representing the entire English-speaking world. Each book produced by a team of translators then passed through three successive committees for rigorous evaluation and revision. The NT was published in 1973. So well accepted was the NIV that the first printing of the complete Bible in 1978 was 1.2 million. As of 1993, more than 85 million testaments and whole Bibles of the NIV are in circulation, making it the most widely

accepted English version since the KJV.

The difference between the translation style of the NIV and the NRSV is more a matter of degree than of kind. The NIV uses a less formal English style and a smaller vocabulary: 14,462 words to 16,529. And although the NIV is essentially a formal equivalent translation, it resorts to "dynamic equivalent," or meaning-for-meaning, translation more regularly than does the NRSV. The NIV is possibly the best-balanced translation for both academic and popular use.

The NIV has 3,403 footnotes, 855 in the NT. As with the NRSV, most reflect alternate translations and textual readings. More than 300 begin with the key word "Or" or "That is" and offer alternate renderings of words and phrases. Notes of this type include suggesting "Messiah" in place of "Christ" (Mt 1:17; 2:4, etc.), "seventy times seven" for "seventy-seven times" (Mt 18:22), or "only begotten son" for "one and only Son" (Jn 3:16, 18, etc.). Others offer a more technical or formal equivalent rendering, or an explanation of technical terms such as "Decapolis" (Mt 4:25, etc.) or "phylacteries" (Mt 23:5).

About 130 notes document variant readings in ancient biblical manuscripts and translations, such as are documented in the Greek notes of the *Greek NT* and are discussed in the previous section. As in the NRSV, many of these notes include familiar passages from the KJV which are not well attested in the earliest manuscripts. These include such passages as the "doxology" to the Lord's prayer (Mt 6:13) and the "three witnesses" of 1 John 5:7–8. The questioned originality of the "longer ending" of Mark (16:9–20) and the account of the adulteress in John 7:53–8:11 are noted in subheads rather than in notes.

Unique to the NIV, among the versions reproduced in this volume, is the documentation of every OT quotation in the NT. Thus, whenever text is in bold type in the Greek column, as in Matthew 1:23; 2:6, 15 and 18, the NIV column will have the OT reference. About 365 OT quotations are cited in the NIV notes.

For further information, see "The Preface to the NIV" on pages viii-ix and *The NIV: The Making of a Contemporary Translation* (Zondervan, 1986).

NRSV

The Genealogy of Jesus the Messiah

1 An account of the genealogy[a] of Jesus the Messiah,[b] the son of David, the son of Abraham.

2 Abraham was the father of Isaac, and Isaac the father of Jacob, and Jacob the father of Judah and his brothers, 3and Judah the father of Perez and Zerah by Tamar, and Perez the father of Hezron, and Hezron the father of Aram, 4and Aram the father of Aminadab, and Aminadab the father of Nahshon, and Nahshon the father of Salmon, 5and Salmon the father of Boaz by Rahab, and Boaz the father of Obed by Ruth, and Obed the father of Jesse, 6and Jesse the father of King David.

And David was the father of Solomon by the wife of Uriah, 7and Solomon the father of Rehoboam, and Rehoboam the father of Abijah, and Abijah the father of Asaph,[c] 8and Asaph[c] the father of Jehoshaphat, and Jehoshaphat the father of Joram, and Joram the father of Uzziah, 9and Uzziah the father of Jotham, and Jotham the father of Ahaz, and Ahaz the father of Hezekiah, 10and Hezekiah the father of Manasseh, and Manasseh the father of Amos,[d] and Amos[d] the father of Josiah, 11and Josiah the father of Jechoniah and his brothers, at the time of the deportation to Babylon.

12 And after the deportation to Babylon: Jechoniah was the father of Salathiel, and Salathiel the father of Zerubbabel, 13and Zerubbabel the father of Abiud, and Abiud the father of Eliakim, and Eliakim the father of Azor, 14and Azor the father of Zadok, and Zadok the father of Achim, and Achim the father of Eliud, 15and Eliud the father of Eleazar, and Eleazar the father of Matthan, and Matthan the father of Jacob, 16and Jacob the father of Joseph the husband of Mary, of whom Jesus was born, who is called the Messiah.[e]

17 So all the generations from Abraham to David are fourteen generations; and

ΚΑΤΑ ΜΑΘΘΑΙΟΝ

1 Βίβλος γενέσεως Ἰησοῦ Χριστοῦ υἱοῦ Δαυὶδ υἱοῦ Ἀβραάμ.

2 Ἀβραὰμ ἐγέννησεν τὸν Ἰσαάκ, Ἰσαὰκ δὲ ἐγέννησεν τὸν Ἰακώβ, Ἰακὼβ δὲ ἐγέννησεν τὸν Ἰούδαν καὶ τοὺς ἀδελφοὺς αὐτοῦ, **3** Ἰούδας δὲ ἐγέννησεν τὸν Φάρες καὶ τὸν Ζάρα ἐκ τῆς Θαμάρ, Φάρες δὲ ἐγέννησεν τὸν Ἑσρώμ, Ἑσρὼμ δὲ ἐγέννησεν τὸν Ἀράμ, **4** Ἀρὰμ δὲ ἐγέννησεν τὸν Ἀμιναδάβ, Ἀμιναδὰβ δὲ ἐγέννησεν τὸν Ναασσών, Ναασσὼν δὲ ἐγέννησεν τὸν Σαλμών, **5** Σαλμὼν δὲ ἐγέννησεν τὸν Βόες ἐκ τῆς Ῥαχάβ, Βόες δὲ ἐγέννησεν τὸν Ἰωβὴδ ἐκ τῆς Ῥούθ, Ἰωβὴδ δὲ ἐγέννησεν τὸν Ἰεσσαί, **6** Ἰεσσαὶ δὲ ἐγέννησεν τὸν Δαυὶδ τὸν βασιλέα.

Δαυὶδ δὲ ἐγέννησεν τὸν Σολομῶνα ἐκ τῆς τοῦ Οὐρίου, **7** Σολομῶν δὲ ἐγέννησεν τὸν Ῥοβοάμ, Ῥοβοὰμ δὲ ἐγέννησεν τὸν Ἀβιά, Ἀβιὰ δὲ ἐγέννησεν τὸν Ἀσάφ[a], **8** Ἀσάφ[a] δὲ ἐγέννησεν τὸν Ἰωσαφάτ, Ἰωσαφὰτ δὲ ἐγέννησεν τὸν Ἰωράμ, Ἰωρὰμ δὲ ἐγέννησεν τὸν Ὀζίαν, **9** Ὀζίας δὲ ἐγέννησεν τὸν Ἰωαθάμ, Ἰωαθὰμ δὲ ἐγέννησεν τὸν Ἀχάζ, Ἀχὰζ δὲ ἐγέννησεν τὸν Ἑζεκίαν, **10** Ἑζεκίας δὲ ἐγέννησεν τὸν Μανασσῆ, Μανασσῆς δὲ ἐγέννησεν τὸν Ἀμώς, Ἀμὼς[b] δὲ ἐγέννησεν τὸν Ἰωσίαν, **11** Ἰωσίας δὲ ἐγέννησεν τὸν Ἰεχονίαν καὶ τοὺς ἀδελφοὺς αὐτοῦ ἐπὶ τῆς μετοικεσίας Βαβυλῶνος.

12 Μετὰ δὲ τὴν μετοικεσίαν Βαβυλῶνος Ἰεχονίας ἐγέννησεν τὸν Σαλαθιήλ, Σαλαθιὴλ δὲ ἐγέννησεν τὸν Ζοροβαβέλ, **13** Ζοροβαβὲλ δὲ ἐγέννησεν τὸν Ἀβιούδ, Ἀβιοὺδ δὲ ἐγέννησεν τὸν Ἐλιακίμ, Ἐλιακὶμ δὲ ἐγέννησεν τὸν Ἀζώρ, **14** Ἀζὼρ δὲ ἐγέννησεν τὸν Σαδώκ, Σαδὼκ δὲ ἐγέννησεν τὸν Ἀχίμ, Ἀχὶμ δὲ ἐγέννησεν τὸν Ἐλιούδ, **15** Ἐλιοὺδ δὲ ἐγέννησεν τὸν Ἐλεάζαρ, Ἐλεάζαρ δὲ ἐγέννησεν τὸν Ματθάν, Ματθὰν δὲ ἐγέννησεν τὸν Ἰακώβ, **16** Ἰακὼβ δὲ ἐγέννησεν τὸν Ἰωσὴφ τὸν ἄνδρα Μαρίας, ἐξ ἧς ἐγεννήθη Ἰησοῦς ὁ λεγόμενος Χριστός.

17 Πᾶσαι οὖν αἱ γενεαὶ ἀπὸ Ἀβραὰμ ἕως Δαυὶδ γενεαὶ δεκατέσσαρες, καὶ

NIV

The Genealogy of Jesus

1 A record of the genealogy of Jesus Christ the son of David, the son of Abraham:

2Abraham was the father of Isaac,
 Isaac the father of Jacob,
 Jacob the father of Judah and his brothers,
3Judah the father of Perez and Zerah,
 whose mother was Tamar,
 Perez the father of Hezron,
 Hezron the father of Ram,
4Ram the father of Amminadab,
 Amminadab the father of Nahshon,
 Nahshon the father of Salmon,
5Salmon the father of Boaz, whose mother was Rahab,
 Boaz the father of Obed, whose mother was Ruth,
 Obed the father of Jesse,
6and Jesse the father of King David.

David was the father of Solomon, whose mother had been Uriah's wife,
7Solomon the father of Rehoboam,
 Rehoboam the father of Abijah,
 Abijah the father of Asa,
8Asa the father of Jehoshaphat,
 Jehoshaphat the father of Jehoram,
 Jehoram the father of Uzziah,
9Uzziah the father of Jotham,
 Jotham the father of Ahaz,
 Ahaz the father of Hezekiah,
10Hezekiah the father of Manasseh,
 Manasseh the father of Amon,
 Amon the father of Josiah,
11and Josiah the father of Jeconiah[a] and his brothers at the time of the exile to Babylon.

12After the exile to Babylon:
 Jeconiah was the father of Shealtiel,
 Shealtiel the father of Zerubbabel,
13Zerubbabel the father of Abiud,
 Abiud the father of Eliakim,
 Eliakim the father of Azor,
14Azor the father of Zadok,
 Zadok the father of Akim,
 Akim the father of Eliud,
15Eliud the father of Eleazar,
 Eleazar the father of Matthan,
 Matthan the father of Jacob,
16and Jacob the father of Joseph, the husband of Mary, of whom was born Jesus, who is called Christ.

17Thus there were fourteen generations in all from Abraham to David, fourteen

---

a Or *birth*   b Or *Jesus Christ*   c Other ancient authorities read *Asa*   d Other ancient authorities read *Amon*
e Or *the Christ*   e Or *the Christ*

a7-8 NIV text and NRSV note c Ἀσά, 8 Ἀσά
b10 NIV text and NRSV note d Ἀμών, Ἀμὼν

a11 That is, Jehoiachin; also in verse 12

NRSV

from David to the deportation to Babylon, fourteen generations; and from the deportation to Babylon to the Messiah,[e] fourteen generations.

The Birth of Jesus the Messiah

18 Now the birth of Jesus the Messiah[f] took place in this way. When his mother Mary had been engaged to Joseph, but before they lived together, she was found to be with child from the Holy Spirit. [19]Her husband Joseph, being a righteous man and unwilling to expose her to public disgrace, planned to dismiss her quietly. [20]But just when he had resolved to do this, an angel of the Lord appeared to him in a dream and said, "Joseph, son of David, do not be afraid to take Mary as your wife, for the child conceived in her is from the Holy Spirit. [21]She will bear a son, and you are to name him Jesus, for he will save his people from their sins." [22]All this took place to fulfill what had been spoken by the Lord through the prophet:

23   "Look, the virgin shall conceive and
     bear a son,
   and they shall name him
     Emmanuel,"

which means, "God is with us." [24]When Joseph awoke from sleep, he did as the angel of the Lord commanded him; he took her as his wife, [25]but had no marital relations with her until she had borne a son;[g] and he named him Jesus.

The Visit of the Wise Men

2 In the time of King Herod, after Jesus was born in Bethlehem of Judea, wise men[h] from the East came to Jerusalem, [2]asking, "Where is the child who has been born king of the Jews? For we observed his star at its rising,[i] and have come to pay him homage." [3]When King Herod heard this, he was frightened, and all Jerusalem with him; [4]and calling together all the chief priests and scribes of the people, he inquired of them where the Messiah[e] was to be born. [5]They told him, "In Bethlehem of Judea; for so it has been written by the prophet:

6   'And you, Bethlehem, in the land of
     Judah,
   are by no means least among the
     rulers of Judah;
   for from you shall come a ruler

Greek

ἀπὸ Δαυὶδ ἕως τῆς μετοικεσίας Βαβυλῶνος γενεαὶ δεκατέσσαρες, καὶ ἀπὸ τῆς μετοικεσίας Βαβυλῶνος ἕως τοῦ Χριστοῦ γενεαὶ δεκατέσσαρες.

18 Τοῦ δὲ Ἰησοῦ Χριστοῦ ἡ γένεσις οὕτως ἦν. μνηστευθείσης τῆς μητρὸς αὐτοῦ Μαρίας τῷ Ἰωσήφ, πρὶν ἢ συνελθεῖν αὐτοὺς εὑρέθη ἐν γαστρὶ ἔχουσα ἐκ πνεύματος ἁγίου. **19** Ἰωσὴφ δὲ ὁ ἀνὴρ αὐτῆς, δίκαιος ὢν καὶ μὴ θέλων αὐτὴν δειγματίσαι, ἐβουλήθη λάθρα ἀπολῦσαι αὐτήν. **20** ταῦτα δὲ αὐτοῦ ἐνθυμηθέντος ἰδοὺ ἄγγελος κυρίου κατ' ὄναρ ἐφάνη αὐτῷ λέγων, Ἰωσὴφ υἱὸς Δαυίδ, μὴ φοβηθῇς παραλαβεῖν Μαριὰμ τὴν γυναῖκά σου· τὸ γὰρ ἐν αὐτῇ γεννηθὲν ἐκ πνεύματός ἐστιν ἁγίου. **21** τέξεται δὲ υἱόν, καὶ καλέσεις τὸ ὄνομα αὐτοῦ Ἰησοῦν· αὐτὸς γὰρ σώσει τὸν λαὸν αὐτοῦ ἀπὸ τῶν ἁμαρτιῶν αὐτῶν. **22** Τοῦτο δὲ ὅλον γέγονεν ἵνα πληρωθῇ τὸ ῥηθὲν ὑπὸ κυρίου διὰ τοῦ προφήτου λέγοντος,

23 Ἰδοὺ ἡ παρθένος ἐν γαστρὶ ἕξει
    καὶ τέξεται υἱόν,
   καὶ καλέσουσιν τὸ ὄνομα αὐτοῦ
    Ἐμμανουήλ,

ὅ ἐστιν μεθερμηνευόμενον **Μεθ'** ἡμῶν ὁ **θεός**. **24** ἐγερθεὶς δὲ ὁ Ἰωσὴφ ἀπὸ τοῦ ὕπνου ἐποίησεν ὡς προσέταξεν αὐτῷ ὁ ἄγγελος κυρίου καὶ παρέλαβεν τὴν γυναῖκα αὐτοῦ, **25** καὶ οὐκ ἐγίνωσκεν αὐτὴν ἕως οὗ ἔτεκεν υἱόν[c]· καὶ ἐκάλεσεν τὸ ὄνομα αὐτοῦ Ἰησοῦν.

2 Τοῦ δὲ Ἰησοῦ γεννηθέντος ἐν Βηθλέεμ τῆς Ἰουδαίας ἐν ἡμέραις Ἡρῴδου τοῦ βασιλέως, ἰδοὺ μάγοι ἀπὸ ἀνατολῶν παρεγένοντο εἰς Ἱεροσόλυμα **2** λέγοντες, Ποῦ ἐστιν ὁ τεχθεὶς βασιλεὺς τῶν Ἰουδαίων; εἴδομεν γὰρ αὐτοῦ τὸν ἀστέρα ἐν τῇ ἀνατολῇ καὶ ἤλθομεν προσκυνῆσαι αὐτῷ. **3** ἀκούσας δὲ ὁ βασιλεὺς Ἡρῴδης ἐταράχθη καὶ πᾶσα Ἱεροσόλυμα μετ' αὐτοῦ, **4** καὶ συναγαγὼν πάντας τοὺς ἀρχιερεῖς καὶ γραμματεῖς τοῦ λαοῦ ἐπυνθάνετο παρ' αὐτῶν ποῦ ὁ Χριστὸς γεννᾶται. **5** οἱ δὲ εἶπαν αὐτῷ, Ἐν Βηθλέεμ τῆς Ἰουδαίας· οὕτως γὰρ γέγραπται διὰ τοῦ προφήτου·

6 Καὶ σὺ Βηθλέεμ, γῆ Ἰούδα,
   οὐδαμῶς **ἐλαχίστη** εἶ ἐν τοῖς
    ἡγεμόσιν Ἰούδα·
   ἐκ σοῦ γὰρ ἐξελεύσεται ἡγούμενος,

NIV

from David to the exile to Babylon, and fourteen from the exile to the Christ.[b]

The Birth of Jesus Christ

[18]This is how the birth of Jesus Christ came about: His mother Mary was pledged to be married to Joseph, but before they came together, she was found to be with child through the Holy Spirit. [19]Because Joseph her husband was a righteous man and did not want to expose her to public disgrace, he had in mind to divorce her quietly.

[20]But after he had considered this, an angel of the Lord appeared to him in a dream and said, "Joseph son of David, do not be afraid to take Mary home as your wife, because what is conceived in her is from the Holy Spirit. [21]She will give birth to a son, and you are to give him the name Jesus,[c] because he will save his people from their sins."

[22]All this took place to fulfill what the Lord had said through the prophet: [23]"The virgin will be with child and will give birth to a son, and they will call him Immanuel"[d]—which means, "God with us."

[24]When Joseph woke up, he did what the angel of the Lord had commanded him and took Mary home as his wife. [25]But he had no union with her until she gave birth to a son. And he gave him the name Jesus.

The Visit of the Magi

2 After Jesus was born in Bethlehem in Judea, during the time of King Herod, Magi[a] from the east came to Jerusalem [2]and asked, "Where is the one who has been born king of the Jews? We saw his star in the east[b] and have come to worship him."

[3]When King Herod heard this he was disturbed, and all Jerusalem with him. [4]When he had called together all the people's chief priests and teachers of the law, he asked them where the Christ[c] was to be born. [5]"In Bethlehem in Judea," they replied, "for this is what the prophet has written:

6" 'But you, Bethlehem, in the land of
    Judah,
   are by no means least among the
    rulers of Judah;
   for out of you will come a ruler

---

[e] Or *the Christ*   [f] Or *Jesus Christ*   [g] Other ancient authorities read *her firstborn son*   [h] Or *astrologers*; Gk *magi*   [i] Or *in the East*

[c]25 NRSV note g τὸν υἱὸν αὐτῆς τὸν πρωτότοκον

[b]17 Or *Messiah*. "The Christ" (Greek) and "the Messiah" (Hebrew) both mean "the Anointed One."   [c]21 *Jesus* is the Greek form of *Joshua*, which means *the LORD saves.*   [d]23 Isaiah 7:14   [a]1 Traditionally *Wise Men*   [b]2 Or *star when it rose*   [c]4 Or *Messiah*

NRSV

who is to shepherd[j] my people
    Israel.' "

7 Then Herod secretly called for the wise men[h] and learned from them the exact time when the star had appeared. 8Then he sent them to Bethlehem, saying, "Go and search diligently for the child; and when you have found him, bring me word so that I may also go and pay him homage." 9When they had heard the king, they set out; and there, ahead of them, went the star that they had seen at its rising,[i] until it stopped over the place where the child was. 10When they saw that the star had stopped,[k] they were overwhelmed with joy. 11On entering the house, they saw the child with Mary his mother; and they knelt down and paid him homage. Then, opening their treasure chests, they offered him gifts of gold, frankincense, and myrrh. 12And having been warned in a dream not to return to Herod, they left for their own country by another road.

The Escape to Egypt

13 Now after they had left, an angel of the Lord appeared to Joseph in a dream and said, "Get up, take the child and his mother, and flee to Egypt, and remain there until I tell you; for Herod is about to search for the child, to destroy him." 14Then Joseph[l] got up, took the child and his mother by night, and went to Egypt, 15and remained there until the death of Herod. This was to fulfill what had been spoken by the Lord through the prophet, "Out of Egypt I have called my son."

The Massacre of the Infants

16 When Herod saw that he had been tricked by the wise men,[m] he was infuriated, and he sent and killed all the children in and around Bethlehem who were two years old or under, according to the time that he had learned from the wise men.[m] 17Then was fulfilled what had been spoken through the prophet Jeremiah:
18 "A voice was heard in Ramah,
    wailing and loud lamentation,
    Rachel weeping for her children;
    she refused to be consoled, because
      they are no more."

The Return from Egypt

19 When Herod died, an angel of the Lord suddenly appeared in a dream to Joseph in Egypt and said, 20"Get up, take

ὅστις ποιμανεῖ τὸν λαόν μου
    τὸν Ἰσραήλ.

7 Τότε Ἡρῴδης λάθρᾳ καλέσας τοὺς μάγους ἠκρίβωσεν παρ᾽ αὐτῶν τὸν χρόνον τοῦ φαινομένου ἀστέρος, **8** καὶ πέμψας αὐτοὺς εἰς Βηθλέεμ εἶπεν, Πορευθέντες ἐξετάσατε ἀκριβῶς περὶ τοῦ παιδίου· ἐπὰν δὲ εὕρητε, ἀπαγγείλατέ μοι, ὅπως κἀγὼ ἐλθὼν προσκυνήσω αὐτῷ. **9** οἱ δὲ ἀκούσαντες τοῦ βασιλέως ἐπορεύθησαν καὶ ἰδοὺ ὁ ἀστήρ, ὃν εἶδον ἐν τῇ ἀνατολῇ, προῆγεν αὐτούς, ἕως ἐλθὼν ἐστάθη ἐπάνω οὗ ἦν τὸ παιδίον. **10** ἰδόντες δὲ τὸν ἀστέρα ἐχάρησαν χαρὰν μεγάλην σφόδρα. **11** καὶ ἐλθόντες εἰς τὴν οἰκίαν εἶδον τὸ παιδίον μετὰ Μαρίας τῆς μητρὸς αὐτοῦ, καὶ πεσόντες προσεκύνησαν αὐτῷ καὶ ἀνοίξαντες τοὺς θησαυροὺς αὐτῶν προσήνεγκαν αὐτῷ δῶρα, χρυσὸν καὶ λίβανον καὶ σμύρναν. **12** καὶ χρηματισθέντες κατ᾽ ὄναρ μὴ ἀνακάμψαι πρὸς Ἡρῴδην, δι᾽ ἄλλης ὁδοῦ ἀνεχώρησαν εἰς τὴν χώραν αὐτῶν.

13 Ἀναχωρησάντων δὲ αὐτῶν ἰδοὺ ἄγγελος κυρίου φαίνεται κατ᾽ ὄναρ τῷ Ἰωσὴφ λέγων, Ἐγερθεὶς παράλαβε τὸ παιδίον καὶ τὴν μητέρα αὐτοῦ καὶ φεῦγε εἰς Αἴγυπτον καὶ ἴσθι ἐκεῖ ἕως ἂν εἴπω σοι· μέλλει γὰρ Ἡρῴδης ζητεῖν τὸ παιδίον τοῦ ἀπολέσαι αὐτό. **14** ὁ δὲ ἐγερθεὶς παρέλαβεν τὸ παιδίον καὶ τὴν μητέρα αὐτοῦ νυκτὸς καὶ ἀνεχώρησεν εἰς Αἴγυπτον, **15** καὶ ἦν ἐκεῖ ἕως τῆς τελευτῆς Ἡρῴδου· ἵνα πληρωθῇ τὸ ῥηθὲν ὑπὸ κυρίου διὰ τοῦ προφήτου λέγοντος, Ἐξ Αἰγύπτου ἐκάλεσα τὸν υἱόν μου.

16 Τότε Ἡρῴδης ἰδὼν ὅτι ἐνεπαίχθη ὑπὸ τῶν μάγων ἐθυμώθη λίαν, καὶ ἀποστείλας ἀνεῖλεν πάντας τοὺς παῖδας τοὺς ἐν Βηθλέεμ καὶ ἐν πᾶσι τοῖς ὁρίοις αὐτῆς ἀπὸ διετοῦς καὶ κατωτέρω, κατὰ τὸν χρόνον ὃν ἠκρίβωσεν παρὰ τῶν μάγων. **17** τότε ἐπληρώθη τὸ ῥηθὲν διὰ Ἰερεμίου τοῦ προφήτου λέγοντος,
18 Φωνὴ ἐν Ῥαμὰ ἠκούσθη,
    κλαυθμὸς καὶ ὀδυρμὸς πολύς·
    Ῥαχὴλ κλαίουσα τὰ τέκνα αὐτῆς,
    καὶ οὐκ ἤθελεν παρακληθῆναι,
    ὅτι οὐκ εἰσίν.

19 Τελευτήσαντος δὲ τοῦ Ἡρῴδου ἰδοὺ ἄγγελος κυρίου φαίνεται κατ᾽ ὄναρ τῷ Ἰωσὴφ ἐν Αἰγύπτῳ **20** λέγων, Ἐγερθεὶς παράλαβε τὸ παιδίον καὶ

NIV

who will be the shepherd of my
    people Israel.'[d]"

7Then Herod called the Magi secretly and found out from them the exact time the star had appeared. 8He sent them to Bethlehem and said, "Go and make a careful search for the child. As soon as you find him, report to me, so that I too may go and worship him."

9After they had heard the king, they went on their way, and the star they had seen in the east[e] went ahead of them until it stopped over the place where the child was. 10When they saw the star, they were overjoyed. 11On coming to the house, they saw the child with his mother Mary, and they bowed down and worshiped him. Then they opened their treasures and presented him with gifts of gold and of incense and of myrrh. 12And having been warned in a dream not to go back to Herod, they returned to their country by another route.

The Escape to Egypt

13When they had gone, an angel of the Lord appeared to Joseph in a dream. "Get up," he said, "take the child and his mother and escape to Egypt. Stay there until I tell you, for Herod is going to search for the child to kill him."

14So he got up, took the child and his mother during the night and left for Egypt, 15where he stayed until the death of Herod. And so was fulfilled what the Lord had said through the prophet: "Out of Egypt I called my son."[f]

16When Herod realized that he had been outwitted by the Magi, he was furious, and he gave orders to kill all the boys in Bethlehem and its vicinity who were two years old and under, in accordance with the time he had learned from the Magi. 17Then what was said through the prophet Jeremiah was fulfilled:

18"A voice is heard in Ramah,
    weeping and great mourning,
    Rachel weeping for her children
    and refusing to be comforted,
    because they are no more."[g]

The Return to Nazareth

19After Herod died, an angel of the Lord appeared in a dream to Joseph in Egypt 20and said, "Get up, take the child and his

---

h Or astrologers; Gk magi   i Or in the East   j Or rule
k Gk saw the star   l Gk he   m Or astrologers; Gk magi

d6 Micah 5:2   e9 Or seen when it rose   f15 Hosea 11:1
g18 Jer. 31:15

the child and his mother, and go to the land of Israel, for those who were seeking the child's life are dead." [21]Then Joseph[1] got up, took the child and his mother, and went to the land of Israel. [22]But when he heard that Archelaus was ruling over Judea in place of his father Herod, he was afraid to go there. And after being warned in a dream, he went away to the district of Galilee. [23]There he made his home in a town called Nazareth, so that what had been spoken through the prophets might be fulfilled, "He will be called a Nazorean."

The Proclamation of John the Baptist

3 In those days John the Baptist appeared in the wilderness of Judea, proclaiming, [2]"Repent, for the kingdom of heaven has come near."[n] [3]This is the one of whom the prophet Isaiah spoke when he said,

"The voice of one crying out in the
        wilderness:
'Prepare the way of the Lord,
    make his paths straight.' "

[4]Now John wore clothing of camel's hair with a leather belt around his waist, and his food was locusts and wild honey. [5]Then the people of Jerusalem and all Judea were going out to him, and all the region along the Jordan, [6]and they were baptized by him in the river Jordan, confessing their sins.

7 But when he saw many Pharisees and Sadducees coming for baptism, he said to them, "You brood of vipers! Who warned you to flee from the wrath to come? [8]Bear fruit worthy of repentance. [9]Do not presume to say to yourselves, 'We have Abraham as our ancestor'; for I tell you, God is able from these stones to raise up children to Abraham. [10]Even now the ax is lying at the root of the trees; every tree therefore that does not bear good fruit is cut down and thrown into the fire.

11 "I baptize you with[o] water for repentance, but one who is more powerful than I is coming after me; I am not worthy to carry his sandals. He will baptize you with[o] the Holy Spirit and fire. [12]His winnowing fork is in his hand, and he will clear his threshing floor and will gather his wheat into the granary; but the chaff he will burn

---

τὴν μητέρα αὐτοῦ καὶ πορεύου εἰς γῆν Ἰσραήλ· τεθνήκασιν γὰρ οἱ ζητοῦντες τὴν ψυχὴν τοῦ παιδίου. **21** ὁ δὲ ἐγερθεὶς παρέλαβεν τὸ παιδίον καὶ τὴν μητέρα αὐτοῦ καὶ εἰσῆλθεν εἰς γῆν Ἰσραήλ. **22** ἀκούσας δὲ ὅτι Ἀρχέλαος βασιλεύει τῆς Ἰουδαίας ἀντὶ τοῦ πατρὸς αὐτοῦ Ἡρῴδου ἐφοβήθη ἐκεῖ ἀπελθεῖν· χρηματισθεὶς δὲ κατ᾽ ὄναρ ἀνεχώρησεν εἰς τὰ μέρη τῆς Γαλιλαίας, **23** καὶ ἐλθὼν κατῴκησεν εἰς πόλιν λεγομένην Ναζαρέτ· ὅπως πληρωθῇ τὸ ῥηθὲν διὰ τῶν προφητῶν ὅτι Ναζωραῖος κληθήσεται.

3 Ἐν δὲ ταῖς ἡμέραις ἐκείναις παραγίνεται Ἰωάννης ὁ βαπτιστὴς κηρύσσων ἐν τῇ ἐρήμῳ τῆς Ἰουδαίας **2** [καὶ] λέγων, Μετανοεῖτε· ἤγγικεν γὰρ ἡ βασιλεία τῶν οὐρανῶν. **3** οὗτος γάρ ἐστιν ὁ ῥηθεὶς διὰ Ἠσαΐου τοῦ προφήτου λέγοντος,

Φωνὴ βοῶντος ἐν τῇ ἐρήμῳ·
Ἑτοιμάσατε τὴν ὁδὸν κυρίου,
εὐθείας ποιεῖτε τὰς τρίβους
αὐτοῦ.

4 Αὐτὸς δὲ ὁ Ἰωάννης εἶχεν τὸ ἔνδυμα αὐτοῦ ἀπὸ τριχῶν καμήλου καὶ ζώνην δερματίνην περὶ τὴν ὀσφὺν αὐτοῦ, ἡ δὲ τροφὴ ἦν αὐτοῦ ἀκρίδες καὶ μέλι ἄγριον. **5** τότε ἐξεπορεύετο πρὸς αὐτὸν Ἱεροσόλυμα καὶ πᾶσα ἡ Ἰουδαία καὶ πᾶσα ἡ περίχωρος τοῦ Ἰορδάνου, **6** καὶ ἐβαπτίζοντο ἐν τῷ Ἰορδάνῃ ποταμῷ ὑπ᾽ αὐτοῦ ἐξομολογούμενοι τὰς ἁμαρτίας αὐτῶν.

7 Ἰδὼν δὲ πολλοὺς τῶν Φαρισαίων καὶ Σαδδουκαίων ἐρχομένους ἐπὶ τὸ βάπτισμα αὐτοῦ εἶπεν αὐτοῖς, Γεννήματα ἐχιδνῶν, τίς ὑπέδειξεν ὑμῖν φυγεῖν ἀπὸ τῆς μελλούσης ὀργῆς; **8** ποιήσατε οὖν καρπὸν ἄξιον τῆς μετανοίας **9** καὶ μὴ δόξητε λέγειν ἐν ἑαυτοῖς, Πατέρα ἔχομεν τὸν Ἀβραάμ. λέγω γὰρ ὑμῖν ὅτι δύναται ὁ θεὸς ἐκ τῶν λίθων τούτων ἐγεῖραι τέκνα τῷ Ἀβραάμ. **10** ἤδη δὲ ἡ ἀξίνη πρὸς τὴν ῥίζαν τῶν δένδρων κεῖται· πᾶν οὖν δένδρον μὴ ποιοῦν καρπὸν καλὸν ἐκκόπτεται καὶ εἰς πῦρ βάλλεται. **11** ἐγὼ μὲν ὑμᾶς βαπτίζω ἐν ὕδατι εἰς μετάνοιαν, ὁ δὲ ὀπίσω μου ἐρχόμενος ἰσχυρότερός μού ἐστιν, οὗ οὐκ εἰμὶ ἱκανὸς τὰ ὑποδήματα βαστάσαι· αὐτὸς ὑμᾶς βαπτίσει ἐν πνεύματι ἁγίῳ καὶ πυρί· **12** οὗ τὸ πτύον ἐν τῇ χειρὶ αὐτοῦ καὶ διακαθαριεῖ τὴν ἅλωνα αὐτοῦ καὶ συνάξει τὸν σῖτον αὐτοῦ εἰς τὴν ἀποθήκην, τὸ δὲ ἄχυρον κατακαύσει

---

mother and go to the land of Israel, for those who were trying to take the child's life are dead."

[21]So he got up, took the child and his mother and went to the land of Israel. [22]But when he heard that Archelaus was reigning in Judea in place of his father Herod, he was afraid to go there. Having been warned in a dream, he withdrew to the district of Galilee, [23]and he went and lived in a town called Nazareth. So was fulfilled what was said through the prophets: "He will be called a Nazarene."

John the Baptist Prepares the Way

3 In those days John the Baptist came, preaching in the Desert of Judea [2]and saying, "Repent, for the kingdom of heaven is near." [3]This is he who was spoken of through the prophet Isaiah:

"A voice of one calling in the desert,
'Prepare the way for the Lord,
    make straight paths for him.' "[a]

[4]John's clothes were made of camel's hair, and he had a leather belt around his waist. His food was locusts and wild honey. [5]People went out to him from Jerusalem and all Judea and the whole region of the Jordan. [6]Confessing their sins, they were baptized by him in the Jordan River.

[7]But when he saw many of the Pharisees and Sadducees coming to where he was baptizing, he said to them: "You brood of vipers! Who warned you to flee from the coming wrath? [8]Produce fruit in keeping with repentance. [9]And do not think you can say to yourselves, 'We have Abraham as our father.' I tell you that out of these stones God can raise up children for Abraham. [10]The ax is already at the root of the trees, and every tree that does not produce good fruit will be cut down and thrown into the fire.

[11]"I baptize you with[b] water for repentance. But after me will come one who is more powerful than I, whose sandals I am not fit to carry. He will baptize you with the Holy Spirit and with fire. [12]His winnowing fork is in his hand, and he will clear his threshing floor, gathering his wheat into the barn and burning up the

---

NRSV

with unquenchable fire."

The Baptism of Jesus

13 Then Jesus came from Galilee to John at the Jordan, to be baptized by him. [14]John would have prevented him, saying, "I need to be baptized by you, and do you come to me?" [15]But Jesus answered him, "Let it be so now; for it is proper for us in this way to fulfill all righteousness." Then he consented. [16]And when Jesus had been baptized, just as he came up from the water, suddenly the heavens were opened to him and he saw the Spirit of God descending like a dove and alighting on him. [17]And a voice from heaven said, "This is my Son, the Beloved,[P] with whom I am well pleased."

The Temptation of Jesus

4 Then Jesus was led up by the Spirit into the wilderness to be tempted by the devil. [2]He fasted forty days and forty nights, and afterwards he was famished. [3]The tempter came and said to him, "If you are the Son of God, command these stones to become loaves of bread." [4]But he answered, "It is written,

'One does not live by bread alone,
   but by every word that comes from
      the mouth of God.' "

5 Then the devil took him to the holy city and placed him on the pinnacle of the temple, [6]saying to him, "If you are the Son of God, throw yourself down; for it is written,

'He will command his angels
   concerning you,'
  and 'On their hands they will bear
    you up,
so that you will not dash your foot
   against a stone.' "

[7]Jesus said to him, "Again it is written, 'Do not put the Lord your God to the test.' "

8 Again, the devil took him to a very high mountain and showed him all the kingdoms of the world and their splendor; [9]and he said to him, "All these I will give you, if you will fall down and worship me." [10]Jesus said to him, "Away with you, Satan! for it is written,

'Worship the Lord your God,
   and serve only him.' "

[11]Then the devil left him, and suddenly angels came and waited on him.

Greek

πυρὶ ἀσβέστῳ.

13 Τότε παραγίνεται ὁ Ἰησοῦς ἀπὸ τῆς Γαλιλαίας ἐπὶ τὸν Ἰορδάνην πρὸς τὸν Ἰωάννην τοῦ βαπτισθῆναι ὑπ᾽ αὐτοῦ. **14** ὁ δὲ Ἰωάννης διεκώλυεν αὐτὸν λέγων, Ἐγὼ χρείαν ἔχω ὑπὸ σοῦ βαπτισθῆναι, καὶ σὺ ἔρχῃ πρός με; **15** ἀποκριθεὶς δὲ ὁ Ἰησοῦς εἶπεν πρὸς αὐτόν, Ἄφες ἄρτι, οὕτως γὰρ πρέπον ἐστὶν ἡμῖν πληρῶσαι πᾶσαν δικαιοσύνην. τότε ἀφίησιν αὐτόν. **16** βαπτισθεὶς δὲ ὁ Ἰησοῦς εὐθὺς ἀνέβη ἀπὸ τοῦ ὕδατος· καὶ ἰδοὺ ἠνεῴχθησαν [αὐτῷ][a] οἱ οὐρανοί, καὶ εἶδεν [τὸ] πνεῦμα [τοῦ] θεοῦ καταβαῖνον ὡσεὶ περιστερὰν [καὶ] ἐρχόμενον ἐπ᾽ αὐτόν· **17** καὶ ἰδοὺ φωνὴ ἐκ τῶν οὐρανῶν λέγουσα, Οὗτός ἐστιν ὁ υἱός μου ὁ ἀγαπητός, ἐν ᾧ εὐδόκησα.

4 Τότε ὁ Ἰησοῦς ἀνήχθη εἰς τὴν ἔρημον ὑπὸ τοῦ πνεύματος πειρασθῆναι ὑπὸ τοῦ διαβόλου. **2** καὶ νηστεύσας ἡμέρας τεσσεράκοντα καὶ νύκτας τεσσεράκοντα, ὕστερον ἐπείνασεν. **3** Καὶ προσελθὼν ὁ πειράζων εἶπεν αὐτῷ, Εἰ υἱὸς εἶ τοῦ θεοῦ, εἰπὲ ἵνα οἱ λίθοι οὗτοι ἄρτοι γένωνται. **4** ὁ δὲ ἀποκριθεὶς εἶπεν, Γέγραπται,

Οὐκ ἐπ᾽ ἄρτῳ μόνῳ ζήσεται ὁ
   ἄνθρωπος,
ἀλλ᾽ ἐπὶ παντὶ ῥήματι ἐκπορευ-
   ομένῳ διὰ στόματος θεοῦ.

5 Τότε παραλαμβάνει αὐτὸν ὁ διάβολος εἰς τὴν ἁγίαν πόλιν καὶ ἔστησεν αὐτὸν ἐπὶ τὸ πτερύγιον τοῦ ἱεροῦ **6** καὶ λέγει αὐτῷ, Εἰ υἱὸς εἶ τοῦ θεοῦ, βάλε σεαυτὸν κάτω· γέγραπται γὰρ ὅτι

Τοῖς ἀγγέλοις αὐτοῦ ἐντελεῖται
   περὶ σοῦ
καὶ ἐπὶ χειρῶν ἀροῦσίν σε,
μήποτε προσκόψῃς πρὸς λίθον τὸν
   πόδα σου.

7 ἔφη αὐτῷ ὁ Ἰησοῦς, Πάλιν γέγραπται, Οὐκ ἐκπειράσεις κύριον τὸν θεόν σου. **8** Πάλιν παραλαμβάνει αὐτὸν ὁ διάβολος εἰς ὄρος ὑψηλὸν λίαν καὶ δείκνυσιν αὐτῷ πάσας τὰς βασιλείας τοῦ κόσμου καὶ τὴν δόξαν αὐτῶν **9** καὶ εἶπεν αὐτῷ, Ταῦτά σοι πάντα δώσω, ἐὰν πεσὼν προσκυνήσῃς μοι. **10** τότε λέγει αὐτῷ ὁ Ἰησοῦς, Ὕπαγε[a], Σατανᾶ· γέγραπται γάρ,

Κύριον τὸν θεόν σου προσκυνήσεις
καὶ αὐτῷ μόνῳ λατρεύσεις.

11 Τότε ἀφίησιν αὐτὸν ὁ διάβολος, καὶ ἰδοὺ ἄγγελοι προσῆλθον καὶ διηκόνουν αὐτῷ.

NIV

chaff with unquenchable fire."

The Baptism of Jesus

[13]Then Jesus came from Galilee to the Jordan to be baptized by John. [14]But John tried to deter him, saying, "I need to be baptized by you, and do you come to me?" [15]Jesus replied, "Let it be so now; it is proper for us to do this to fulfill all righteousness." Then John consented.

[16]As soon as Jesus was baptized, he went up out of the water. At that moment heaven was opened, and he saw the Spirit of God descending like a dove and lighting on him. [17]And a voice from heaven said, "This is my Son, whom I love; with him I am well pleased."

The Temptation of Jesus

4 Then Jesus was led by the Spirit into the desert to be tempted by the devil. [2]After fasting forty days and forty nights, he was hungry. [3]The tempter came to him and said, "If you are the Son of God, tell these stones to become bread."

[4]Jesus answered, "It is written: 'Man does not live on bread alone, but on every word that comes from the mouth of God.'[a]"

[5]Then the devil took him to the holy city and had him stand on the highest point of the temple. [6]"If you are the Son of God," he said, "throw yourself down. For it is written:

" 'He will command his angels
   concerning you,
  and they will lift you up in their
    hands,
so that you will not strike your foot
   against a stone.'[b]"

[7]Jesus answered him, "It is also written: 'Do not put the Lord your God to the test.'[c]"

[8]Again, the devil took him to a very high mountain and showed him all the kingdoms of the world and their splendor. [9]"All this I will give you," he said, "if you will bow down and worship me."

[10]Jesus said to him, "Away from me, Satan! For it is written: 'Worship the Lord your God, and serve him only.'[d]"

[11]Then the devil left him, and angels came and attended him.

P Or my beloved Son

[a]16 NIV text omits αὐτῷ   [a]10 NIV text adds ὀπίσω μου

[a]4 Deut. 8:3   [b]6 Psalm 91:11,12   [c]7 Deut. 6:16
[d]10 Deut. 6:13

NRSV

Jesus Begins His Ministry in Galilee

12 Now when Jesus[q] heard that John had been arrested, he withdrew to Galilee. 13He left Nazareth and made his home in Capernaum by the sea, in the territory of Zebulun and Naphtali, 14so that what had been spoken through the prophet Isaiah might be fulfilled:

15 "Land of Zebulun, land of Naphtali,
on the road by the sea, across the
    Jordan, Galilee of the Gentiles—
16 the people who sat in darkness
    have seen a great light,
and for those who sat in the region
    and shadow of death
    light has dawned."

17From that time Jesus began to proclaim, "Repent, for the kingdom of heaven has come near."[r]

Jesus Calls the First Disciples

18 As he walked by the Sea of Galilee, he saw two brothers, Simon, who is called Peter, and Andrew his brother, casting a net into the sea—for they were fishermen. 19And he said to them, "Follow me, and I will make you fish for people." 20Immediately they left their nets and followed him. 21As he went from there, he saw two other brothers, James son of Zebedee and his brother John, in the boat with their father Zebedee, mending their nets, and he called them. 22Immediately they left the boat and their father, and followed him.

Jesus Ministers to Crowds of People

23 Jesus[s] went throughout Galilee, teaching in their synagogues and proclaiming the good news[t] of the kingdom and curing every disease and every sickness among the people. 24So his fame spread throughout all Syria, and they brought to him all the sick, those who were afflicted with various diseases and pains, demoniacs, epileptics, and paralytics, and he cured them. 25And great crowds followed him from Galilee, the Decapolis, Jerusalem, Judea, and from beyond the Jordan.

The Beatitudes

5 When Jesus[q] saw the crowds, he went up the mountain; and after he sat down, his disciples came to him. 2Then he began to speak, and taught them, saying:

3 "Blessed are the poor in spirit, for theirs

Greek

12 Ἀκούσας δὲ ὅτι Ἰωάννης παρεδόθη ἀνεχώρησεν εἰς τὴν Γαλιλαίαν. 13 καὶ καταλιπὼν τὴν Ναζαρὰ ἐλθὼν κατῴ κησεν εἰς Καφαρναοὺμ τὴν παραθαλασσίαν ἐν ὁρίοις Ζαβουλὼν καὶ Νεφθαλίμ· 14 ἵνα πληρωθῇ τὸ ῥηθὲν διὰ Ἡσαΐου τοῦ προφήτου λέγοντος,

15 Γῆ Ζαβουλὼν καὶ γῆ Νεφθαλίμ,
    ὁδὸν θαλάσσης, πέραν τοῦ
        Ἰορδάνου, Γαλιλαία τῶν
        ἐθνῶν,
16 ὁ λαὸς ὁ καθήμενος ἐν σκότει
        φῶς εἶδεν μέγα,
    καὶ τοῖς καθημένοις ἐν χώρᾳ καὶ
        σκιᾷ θανάτου
    φῶς ἀνέτειλεν αὐτοῖς.

17 Ἀπὸ τότε ἤρξατο ὁ Ἰησοῦς κηρύσσειν καὶ λέγειν, Μετανοεῖτε· ἤγγικεν γὰρ ἡ βασιλεία τῶν οὐρανῶν.

18 Περιπατῶν δὲ παρὰ τὴν θάλασσαν τῆς Γαλιλαίας εἶδεν δύο ἀδελφούς, Σίμωνα τὸν λεγόμενον Πέτρον καὶ Ἀνδρέαν τὸν ἀδελφὸν αὐτοῦ, βάλλοντας ἀμφίβληστρον εἰς τὴν θάλασσαν· ἦσαν γὰρ ἁλιεῖς. 19 καὶ λέγει αὐτοῖς, Δεῦτε ὀπίσω μου, καὶ ποιήσω ὑμᾶς ἁλιεῖς ἀνθρώπων. 20 οἱ δὲ εὐθέως ἀφέντες τὰ δίκτυα ἠκολούθησαν αὐτῷ. 21 Καὶ προβὰς ἐκεῖθεν εἶδεν ἄλλους δύο ἀδελφούς, Ἰάκωβον τὸν τοῦ Ζεβεδαίου καὶ Ἰωάννην τὸν ἀδελφὸν αὐτοῦ, ἐν τῷ πλοίῳ μετὰ Ζεβεδαίου τοῦ πατρὸς αὐτῶν καταρτίζοντας τὰ δίκτυα αὐτῶν, καὶ ἐκάλεσεν αὐτούς. 22 οἱ δὲ εὐθέως ἀφέντες τὸ πλοῖον καὶ τὸν πατέρα αὐτῶν ἠκολούθησαν αὐτῷ.

23 Καὶ περιῆγεν ἐν ὅλῃ τῇ Γαλιλαίᾳ διδάσκων ἐν ταῖς συναγωγαῖς αὐτῶν καὶ κηρύσσων τὸ εὐαγγέλιον τῆς βασιλείας καὶ θεραπεύων πᾶσαν νόσον καὶ πᾶσαν μαλακίαν ἐν τῷ λαῷ. 24 καὶ ἀπῆλθεν ἡ ἀκοὴ αὐτοῦ εἰς ὅλην τὴν Συρίαν· καὶ προσήνεγκαν αὐτῷ πάντας τοὺς κακῶς ἔχοντας ποικίλαις νόσοις καὶ βασάνοις συνεχομένους [καὶ] δαιμονιζομένους καὶ σεληνιαζομένους καὶ παραλυτικούς, καὶ ἐθεράπευσεν αὐτούς. 25 καὶ ἠκολούθησαν αὐτῷ ὄχλοι πολλοὶ ἀπὸ τῆς Γαλιλαίας καὶ Δεκαπόλεως καὶ Ἱεροσολύμων καὶ Ἰουδαίας καὶ πέραν τοῦ Ἰορδάνου.

5 Ἰδὼν δὲ τοὺς ὄχλους ἀνέβη εἰς τὸ ὄρος, καὶ καθίσαντος αὐτοῦ προσῆλθαν αὐτῷ οἱ μαθηταὶ αὐτοῦ· 2 καὶ ἀνοίξας τὸ στόμα αὐτοῦ ἐδίδασκεν αὐτοὺς λέγων,

3 Μακάριοι οἱ πτωχοὶ τῷ πνεύματι,

NIV

Jesus Begins to Preach

12When Jesus heard that John had been put in prison, he returned to Galilee. 13Leaving Nazareth, he went and lived in Capernaum, which was by the lake in the area of Zebulun and Naphtali—14to fulfill what was said through the prophet Isaiah:

15"Land of Zebulun and land of Naphtali,
    the way to the sea, along the Jordan,
    Galilee of the Gentiles—
16the people living in darkness
    have seen a great light;
on those living in the land of the
        shadow of death
    a light has dawned."[e]

17From that time on Jesus began to preach, "Repent, for the kingdom of heaven is near."

The Calling of the First Disciples

18As Jesus was walking beside the Sea of Galilee, he saw two brothers, Simon called Peter and his brother Andrew. They were casting a net into the lake, for they were fishermen. 19"Come, follow me," Jesus said, "and I will make you fishers of men." 20At once they left their nets and followed him.

21Going on from there, he saw two other brothers, James son of Zebedee and his brother John. They were in a boat with their father Zebedee, preparing their nets. Jesus called them, 22and immediately they left the boat and their father and followed him.

Jesus Heals the Sick

23Jesus went throughout Galilee, teaching in their synagogues, preaching the good news of the kingdom, and healing every disease and sickness among the people. 24News about him spread all over Syria, and people brought to him all who were ill with various diseases, those suffering severe pain, the demon-possessed, those having seizures, and the paralyzed, and he healed them. 25Large crowds from Galilee, the Decapolis,[f] Jerusalem, Judea and the region across the Jordan followed him.

The Beatitudes

5 Now when he saw the crowds, he went up on a mountainside and sat down. His disciples came to him, 2and he began to teach them, saying:

3"Blessed are the poor in spirit,

---

is the kingdom of heaven.

4 "Blessed are those who mourn, for they will be comforted.

5 "Blessed are the meek, for they will inherit the earth.

6 "Blessed are those who hunger and thirst for righteousness, for they will be filled.

7 "Blessed are the merciful, for they will receive mercy.

8 "Blessed are the pure in heart, for they will see God.

9 "Blessed are the peacemakers, for they will be called children of God.

10 "Blessed are those who are persecuted for righteousness' sake, for theirs is the kingdom of heaven.

11 "Blessed are you when people revile you and persecute you and utter all kinds of evil against you falsely[v] on my account. [12]Rejoice and be glad, for your reward is great in heaven, for in the same way they persecuted the prophets who were before you.

Salt and Light

13 "You are the salt of the earth; but if salt has lost its taste, how can its saltiness be restored? It is no longer good for anything, but is thrown out and trampled under foot.

14 "You are the light of the world. A city built on a hill cannot be hid. [15]No one after lighting a lamp puts it under the bushel basket, but on the lampstand, and it gives light to all in the house. [16]In the same way, let your light shine before others, so that they may see your good works and give glory to your Father in heaven.

The Law and the Prophets

17 "Do not think that I have come to abolish the law or the prophets; I have come not to abolish but to fulfill. [18]For truly I tell you, until heaven and earth pass away, not one letter,[w] not one stroke of a letter, will pass from the law until all is accomplished. [19]Therefore, whoever breaks[x] one of the least of these commandments, and teaches others to do the same, will be called least in the kingdom of heaven; but whoever does them and teaches them will be called great in the kingdom of heaven. [20]For I tell you, unless your righteousness exceeds that of the scribes and Pharisees, you will never enter

ὅτι αὐτῶν ἐστιν ἡ βασιλεία τῶν οὐρανῶν.

4 μακάριοι οἱ πενθοῦντες, ὅτι αὐτοὶ παρακληθήσονται.

5 μακάριοι οἱ πραεῖς, ὅτι αὐτοὶ κληρονομήσουσιν τὴν γῆν.

6 μακάριοι οἱ πεινῶντες καὶ διψῶντες τὴν δικαιοσύνην, ὅτι αὐτοὶ χορτασθήσονται.

7 μακάριοι οἱ ἐλεήμονες, ὅτι αὐτοὶ ἐλεηθήσονται.

8 μακάριοι οἱ καθαροὶ τῇ καρδίᾳ, ὅτι αὐτοὶ τὸν θεὸν ὄψονται.

9 μακάριοι οἱ εἰρηνοποιοί, ὅτι αὐτοὶ υἱοὶ θεοῦ κληθήσονται.

10 μακάριοι οἱ δεδιωγμένοι ἕνεκεν δικαιοσύνης, ὅτι αὐτῶν ἐστιν ἡ βασιλεία τῶν οὐρανῶν.

11 μακάριοί ἐστε ὅταν ὀνειδίσωσιν ὑμᾶς καὶ διώξωσιν καὶ εἴπωσιν πᾶν πονηρὸν καθ' ὑμῶν [ψευδόμενοι] ἕνεκεν ἐμοῦ. 12 χαίρετε καὶ ἀγαλλιᾶσθε, ὅτι ὁ μισθὸς ὑμῶν πολὺς ἐν τοῖς οὐρανοῖς· οὕτως γὰρ ἐδίωξαν τοὺς προφήτας τοὺς πρὸ ὑμῶν.

13 Ὑμεῖς ἐστε τὸ ἅλας τῆς γῆς· ἐὰν δὲ τὸ ἅλας μωρανθῇ, ἐν τίνι ἁλισθήσεται; εἰς οὐδὲν ἰσχύει ἔτι εἰ μὴ βληθὲν ἔξω καταπατεῖσθαι ὑπὸ τῶν ἀνθρώπων. 14 Ὑμεῖς ἐστε τὸ φῶς τοῦ κόσμου. οὐ δύναται πόλις κρυβῆναι ἐπάνω ὄρους κειμένη· 15 οὐδὲ καίουσιν λύχνον καὶ τιθέασιν αὐτὸν ὑπὸ τὸν μόδιον ἀλλ' ἐπὶ τὴν λυχνίαν, καὶ λάμπει πᾶσιν τοῖς ἐν τῇ οἰκίᾳ. 16 οὕτως λαμψάτω τὸ φῶς ὑμῶν ἔμπροσθεν τῶν ἀνθρώπων, ὅπως ἴδωσιν ὑμῶν τὰ καλὰ ἔργα καὶ δοξάσωσιν τὸν πατέρα ὑμῶν τὸν ἐν τοῖς οὐρανοῖς.

17 Μὴ νομίσητε ὅτι ἦλθον καταλῦσαι τὸν νόμον ἢ τοὺς προφήτας· οὐκ ἦλθον καταλῦσαι ἀλλὰ πληρῶσαι. 18 ἀμὴν γὰρ λέγω ὑμῖν· ἕως ἂν παρέλθῃ ὁ οὐρανὸς καὶ ἡ γῆ, ἰῶτα ἓν ἢ μία κεραία οὐ μὴ παρέλθῃ ἀπὸ τοῦ νόμου, ἕως ἂν πάντα γένηται. 19 ὃς ἐὰν οὖν λύσῃ μίαν τῶν ἐντολῶν τούτων τῶν ἐλαχίστων καὶ διδάξῃ οὕτως τοὺς ἀνθρώπους, ἐλάχιστος κληθήσεται ἐν τῇ βασιλείᾳ τῶν οὐρανῶν· ὃς δ' ἂν ποιήσῃ καὶ διδάξῃ, οὗτος μέγας κληθήσεται ἐν τῇ βασιλείᾳ τῶν οὐρανῶν. 20 λέγω γὰρ ὑμῖν ὅτι ἐὰν μὴ περισσεύσῃ ὑμῶν ἡ δικαιοσύνη πλεῖον τῶν γραμματέων καὶ Φαρισαίων, οὐ μὴ εἰσέλθητε

for theirs is the kingdom of heaven. [4]Blessed are those who mourn, for they will be comforted. [5]Blessed are the meek, for they will inherit the earth. [6]Blessed are those who hunger and thirst for righteousness, for they will be filled. [7]Blessed are the merciful, for they will be shown mercy. [8]Blessed are the pure in heart, for they will see God. [9]Blessed are the peacemakers, for they will be called sons of God. [10]Blessed are those who are persecuted because of righteousness, for theirs is the kingdom of heaven.

[11]"Blessed are you when people insult you, persecute you and falsely say all kinds of evil against you because of me. [12]Rejoice and be glad, because great is your reward in heaven, for in the same way they persecuted the prophets who were before you.

Salt and Light

[13]"You are the salt of the earth. But if the salt loses its saltiness, how can it be made salty again? It is no longer good for anything, except to be thrown out and trampled by men.

[14]"You are the light of the world. A city on a hill cannot be hidden. [15]Neither do people light a lamp and put it under a bowl. Instead they put it on its stand, and it gives light to everyone in the house. [16]In the same way, let your light shine before men, that they may see your good deeds and praise your Father in heaven.

The Fulfillment of the Law

[17]"Do not think that I have come to abolish the Law or the Prophets; I have not come to abolish them but to fulfill them. [18]I tell you the truth, until heaven and earth disappear, not the smallest letter, not the least stroke of a pen, will by any means disappear from the Law until everything is accomplished. [19]Anyone who breaks one of the least of these commandments and teaches others to do the same will be called least in the kingdom of heaven, but whoever practices and teaches these commands will be called great in the kingdom of heaven. [20]For I tell you that unless your righteousness surpasses that of the Pharisees and the teachers of the law, you will

the kingdom of heaven.

Concerning Anger

21 "You have heard that it was said to those of ancient times, 'You shall not murder'; and 'whoever murders shall be liable to judgment.' 22But I say to you that if you are angry with a brother or sister,y you will be liable to judgment; and if you insultz a brother or sister,a you will be liable to the council; and if you say, 'You fool,' you will be liable to the hellb of fire. 23So when you are offering your gift at the altar, if you remember that your brother or sisterc has something against you, 24leave your gift there before the altar and go; first be reconciled to your brother or sister,c and then come and offer your gift. 25Come to terms quickly with your accuser while you are on the way to courtd with him, or your accuser may hand you over to the judge, and the judge to the guard, and you will be thrown into prison. 26Truly I tell you, you will never get out until you have paid the last penny.

Concerning Adultery

27 "You have heard that it was said, 'You shall not commit adultery.' 28But I say to you that everyone who looks at a woman with lust has already committed adultery with her in his heart. 29If your right eye causes you to sin, tear it out and throw it away; it is better for you to lose one of your members than for your whole body to be thrown into hell.b 30And if your right hand causes you to sin, cut it off and throw it away; it is better for you to lose one of your members than for your whole body to go into hell.b

Concerning Divorce

31 "It was also said, 'Whoever divorces his wife, let him give her a certificate of divorce.' 32But I say to you that anyone who divorces his wife, except on the ground of unchastity, causes her to commit adultery; and whoever marries a divorced woman commits adultery.

Concerning Oaths

33 "Again, you have heard that it was said to those of ancient times, 'You shall not swear falsely, but carry out the vows you have made to the Lord.' 34But I say to you, Do not swear at all, either by heaven,

y Gk a brother; other ancient authorities add without cause   z Gk say Raca to (an obscure term of abuse)   a Gk a brother   b Gk Gehenna   c Gk your brother   d Gk lacks to court

---

εἰς τὴν βασιλείαν τῶν οὐρανῶν.

21 Ἠκούσατε ὅτι ἐρρέθη τοῖς ἀρχαίοις, **Οὐ φονεύσεις·** ὃς δ᾽ ἂν φονεύσῃ, ἔνοχος ἔσται τῇ κρίσει. 22 ἐγὼ δὲ λέγω ὑμῖν ὅτι πᾶς ὁ ὀργιζόμενος τῷ ἀδελφῷ αὐτοῦa ἔνοχος ἔσται τῇ κρίσει· ὃς δ᾽ ἂν εἴπῃ τῷ ἀδελφῷ αὐτοῦ, Ῥακά, ἔνοχος ἔσται τῷ συνεδρίῳ· ὃς δ᾽ ἂν εἴπῃ, Μωρέ, ἔνοχος ἔσται εἰς τὴν γέενναν τοῦ πυρός. 23 ἐὰν οὖν προσφέρῃς τὸ δῶρόν σου ἐπὶ τὸ θυσιαστήριον κἀκεῖ μνησθῇς ὅτι ὁ ἀδελφός σου ἔχει τι κατὰ σοῦ, 24 ἄφες ἐκεῖ τὸ δῶρόν σου ἔμπροσθεν τοῦ θυσιαστηρίου καὶ ὕπαγε πρῶτον διαλλάγηθι τῷ ἀδελφῷ σου, καὶ τότε ἐλθὼν πρόσφερε τὸ δῶρόν σου. 25 ἴσθι εὐνοῶν τῷ ἀντιδίκῳ σου ταχύ, ἕως ὅτου εἶ μετ᾽ αὐτοῦ ἐν τῇ ὁδῷ, μήποτέ σε παραδῷ ὁ ἀντίδικος τῷ κριτῇ καὶ ὁ κριτὴς τῷ ὑπηρέτῃ καὶ εἰς φυλακὴν βληθήσῃ· 26 ἀμὴν λέγω σοι, οὐ μὴ ἐξέλθῃς ἐκεῖθεν, ἕως ἂν ἀποδῷς τὸν ἔσχατον κοδράντην.

27 Ἠκούσατε ὅτι ἐρρέθη, **Οὐ μοιχεύσεις.** 28 ἐγὼ δὲ λέγω ὑμῖν ὅτι πᾶς ὁ βλέπων γυναῖκα πρὸς τὸ ἐπιθυμῆσαι αὐτὴν ἤδη ἐμοίχευσεν αὐτὴν ἐν τῇ καρδίᾳ αὐτοῦ. 29 εἰ δὲ ὁ ὀφθαλμός σου ὁ δεξιὸς σκανδαλίζει σε, ἔξελε αὐτὸν καὶ βάλε ἀπὸ σοῦ· συμφέρει γάρ σοι ἵνα ἀπόληται ἓν τῶν μελῶν σου καὶ μὴ ὅλον τὸ σῶμά σου βληθῇ εἰς γέενναν. 30 καὶ εἰ ἡ δεξιά σου χείρ σκανδαλίζει σε, ἔκκοψον αὐτὴν καὶ βάλε ἀπὸ σοῦ· συμφέρει γάρ σοι ἵνα ἀπόληται ἓν τῶν μελῶν σου καὶ μὴ ὅλον τὸ σῶμά σου εἰς γέενναν ἀπέλθῃ.

31 Ἐρρέθη δέ, Ὃς ἂν ἀπολύσῃ τὴν γυναῖκα αὐτοῦ, δότω αὐτῇ ἀποστάσιον. 32 ἐγὼ δὲ λέγω ὑμῖν ὅτι πᾶς ὁ ἀπολύων τὴν γυναῖκα αὐτοῦ παρεκτὸς λόγου πορνείας ποιεῖ αὐτὴν μοιχευθῆναι, καὶ ὃς ἐὰν ἀπολελυμένην γαμήσῃ, μοιχᾶται.

33 Πάλιν ἠκούσατε ὅτι ἐρρέθη τοῖς ἀρχαίοις, **Οὐκ ἐπιορκήσεις, ἀποδώσεις** δὲ τῷ **κυρίῳ τοὺς** ὅρκους σου. 34 ἐγὼ δὲ λέγω ὑμῖν μὴ ὀμόσαι ὅλως· μήτε ἐν

a22 NIV/NRSV notes add εἰκῇ

---

certainly not enter the kingdom of heaven.

Murder

21"You have heard that it was said to the people long ago, 'Do not murder,a and anyone who murders will be subject to judgment.' 22But I tell you that anyone who is angry with his brotherb will be subject to judgment. Again, anyone who says to his brother, 'Raca,'c is answerable to the Sanhedrin. But anyone who says, 'You fool!' will be in danger of the fire of hell.

23"Therefore, if you are offering your gift at the altar and there remember that your brother has something against you, 24leave your gift there in front of the altar. First go and be reconciled to your brother; then come and offer your gift.

25"Settle matters quickly with your adversary who is taking you to court. Do it while you are still with him on the way, or he may hand you over to the judge, and the judge may hand you over to the officer, and you may be thrown into prison. 26I tell you the truth, you will not get out until you have paid the last penny.d

Adultery

27"You have heard that it was said, 'Do not commit adultery.'e 28But I tell you that anyone who looks at a woman lustfully has already committed adultery with her in his heart. 29If your right eye causes you to sin, gouge it out and throw it away. It is better for you to lose one part of your body than for your whole body to be thrown into hell. 30And if your right hand causes you to sin, cut it off and throw it away. It is better for you to lose one part of your body than for your whole body to go into hell.

Divorce

31"It has been said, 'Anyone who divorces his wife must give her a certificate of divorce.'f 32But I tell you that anyone who divorces his wife, except for marital unfaithfulness, causes her to become an adulteress, and anyone who marries the divorced woman commits adultery.

Oaths

33"Again, you have heard that it was said to the people long ago, 'Do not break your oath, but keep the oaths you have made to the Lord.' 34But I tell you, Do not swear at

a21 Exodus 20:13   b22 Some manuscripts brother without cause   c22 An Aramaic term of contempt   d26 Greek kodrantes   e27 Exodus 20:14   f31 Deut. 24:1

for it is the throne of God, 35or by the earth, for it is his footstool, or by Jerusalem, for it is the city of the great King. 36And do not swear by your head, for you cannot make one hair white or black. 37Let your word be 'Yes, Yes' or 'No, No'; anything more than this comes from the evil one.e

Concerning Retaliation

38 "You have heard that it was said, 'An eye for an eye and a tooth for a tooth.' 39But I say to you, Do not resist an evil-doer. But if anyone strikes you on the right cheek, turn the other also; 40and if anyone wants to sue you and take your coat, give your cloak as well; 41and if anyone forces you to go one mile, go also the second mile. 42Give to everyone who begs from you, and do not refuse anyone who wants to borrow from you.

Love for Enemies

43 "You have heard that it was said, 'You shall love your neighbor and hate your enemy.' 44But I say to you, Love your enemies and pray for those who persecute you, 45so that you may be children of your Father in heaven; for he makes his sun rise on the evil and on the good, and sends rain on the righteous and on the unrighteous. 46For if you love those who love you, what reward do you have? Do not even the tax collectors do the same? 47And if you greet only your brothers and sisters,f what more are you doing than others? Do not even the Gentiles do the same? 48Be perfect, therefore, as your heavenly Father is perfect.

Concerning Almsgiving

6 "Beware of practicing your piety before others in order to be seen by them; for then you have no reward from your Father in heaven.

2 "So whenever you give alms, do not sound a trumpet before you, as the hypocrites do in the synagogues and in the streets, so that they may be praised by others. Truly I tell you, they have received their reward. 3But when you give alms, do not let your left hand know what your right hand is doing, 4so that your alms may be done in secret; and your Father who sees in secret will reward you.g

τῷ οὐρανῷ, ὅτι θρόνος ἐστὶν τοῦ θεοῦ, 35 μήτε ἐν τῇ γῇ, ὅτι ὑποπόδιόν ἐστιν τῶν ποδῶν αὐτοῦ, μήτε εἰς Ἱεροσόλυμα, ὅτι πόλις ἐστὶν τοῦ μεγάλου βασιλέως, 36 μήτε ἐν τῇ κεφαλῇ σου ὀμόσῃς, ὅτι οὐ δύνασαι μίαν τρίχα λευκὴν ποιῆσαι ἢ μέλαιναν. 37 ἔστω δὲ ὁ λόγος ὑμῶν ναὶ ναί,b οὒ οὔ· τὸ δὲ περισσὸν τούτων ἐκ τοῦ πονηροῦ ἐστιν.

38 Ἠκούσατε ὅτι ἐρρέθη, Ὀφθαλμὸν ἀντὶ ὀφθαλμοῦ καὶ ὀδόντα ἀντὶ ὀδόντος. 39 ἐγὼ δὲ λέγω ὑμῖν μὴ ἀντιστῆναι τῷ πονηρῷ· ἀλλ' ὅστις σε ῥαπίζει εἰς τὴν δεξιὰν σιαγόνα [σου]c, στρέψον αὐτῷ καὶ τὴν ἄλλην· 40 καὶ τῷ θέλοντί σοι κριθῆναι καὶ τὸν χιτῶνά σου λαβεῖν, ἄφες αὐτῷ καὶ τὸ ἱμάτιον· 41 καὶ ὅστις σε ἀγγαρεύσει μίλιον ἕν, ὕπαγε μετ' αὐτοῦ δύο. 42 τῷ αἰτοῦντί σε δός, καὶ τὸν θέλοντα ἀπὸ σοῦ δανίσασθαι μὴ ἀποστραφῇς.

43 Ἠκούσατε ὅτι ἐρρέθη, Ἀγαπήσεις τὸν πλησίον σου καὶ μισήσεις τὸν ἐχθρόν σου. 44 ἐγὼ δὲ λέγω ὑμῖν, ἀγαπᾶτε τοὺς ἐχθροὺς ὑμῶν καὶ προσεύχεσθε ὑπὲρ τῶν διωκόντων ὑμᾶςd, 45 ὅπως γένησθε υἱοὶ τοῦ πατρὸς ὑμῶν τοῦ ἐν οὐρανοῖς, ὅτι τὸν ἥλιον αὐτοῦ ἀνατέλλει ἐπὶ πονηροὺς καὶ ἀγαθοὺς καὶ βρέχει ἐπὶ δικαίους καὶ ἀδίκους. 46 ἐὰν γὰρ ἀγαπήσητε τοὺς ἀγαπῶντας ὑμᾶς, τίνα μισθὸν ἔχετε; οὐχὶ καὶ οἱ τελῶναι τὸ αὐτὸ ποιοῦσιν; 47 καὶ ἐὰν ἀσπάσησθε τοὺς ἀδελφοὺς ὑμῶν μόνον, τί περισσὸν ποιεῖτε; οὐχὶ καὶ οἱ ἐθνικοὶ τὸ αὐτὸ ποιοῦσιν; 48 Ἔσεσθε οὖν ὑμεῖς τέλειοι ὡς ὁ πατὴρ ὑμῶν ὁ οὐράνιος τέλειός ἐστιν.

6 Προσέχετε [δὲ]a τὴν δικαιοσύνην ὑμῶν μὴ ποιεῖν ἔμπροσθεν τῶν ἀνθρώπων πρὸς τὸ θεαθῆναι αὐτοῖς· εἰ δὲ μή γε, μισθὸν οὐκ ἔχετε παρὰ τῷ πατρὶ ὑμῶν τῷ ἐν τοῖς οὐρανοῖς.

2 Ὅταν οὖν ποιῇς ἐλεημοσύνην, μὴ σαλπίσῃς ἔμπροσθέν σου, ὥσπερ οἱ ὑποκριταὶ ποιοῦσιν ἐν ταῖς συναγωγαῖς καὶ ἐν ταῖς ῥύμαις, ὅπως δοξασθῶσιν ὑπὸ τῶν ἀνθρώπων· ἀμὴν λέγω ὑμῖν, ἀπέχουσιν τὸν μισθὸν αὐτῶν. 3 σοῦ δὲ ποιοῦντος ἐλεημοσύνην μὴ γνώτω ἡ ἀριστερά σου τί ποιεῖ ἡ δεξιά σου, 4 ὅπως ᾖ σου ἡ ἐλεημοσύνη ἐν τῷ κρυπτῷ· καὶ ὁ πατήρ σου ὁ βλέπων ἐν τῷ κρυπτῷ ἀποδώσει σοιb.

all: either by heaven, for it is God's throne; 35or by the earth, for it is his footstool; or by Jerusalem, for it is the city of the Great King. 36And do not swear by your head, for you cannot make even one hair white or black. 37Simply let your 'Yes' be 'Yes,' and your 'No,' 'No'; anything beyond this comes from the evil one.

An Eye for an Eye

38"You have heard that it was said, 'Eye for eye, and tooth for tooth.'g 39But I tell you, Do not resist an evil person. If someone strikes you on the right cheek, turn to him the other also. 40And if someone wants to sue you and take your tunic, let him have your cloak as well. 41If someone forces you to go one mile, go with him two miles. 42Give to the one who asks you, and do not turn away from the one who wants to borrow from you.

Love for Enemies

43"You have heard that it was said, 'Love your neighborh and hate your enemy.' 44But I tell you: Love your enemiesi and pray for those who persecute you, 45that you may be sons of your Father in heaven. He causes his sun to rise on the evil and the good, and sends rain on the righteous and the unrighteous. 46If you love those who love you, what reward will you get? Are not even the tax collectors doing that? 47And if you greet only your brothers, what are you doing more than others? Do not even pagans do that? 48Be perfect, therefore, as your heavenly Father is perfect.

Giving to the Needy

6 "Be careful not to do your 'acts of righteousness' before men, to be seen by them. If you do, you will have no reward from your Father in heaven.

2"So when you give to the needy, do not announce it with trumpets, as the hypocrites do in the synagogues and on the streets, to be honored by men. I tell you the truth, they have received their reward in full. 3But when you give to the needy, do not let your left hand know what your right hand is doing, 4so that your giving may be in secret. Then your Father, who sees what is done in secret, will reward you.

---

eOr *evil*   fGk *your brothers*   gOther ancient authorities add *openly*

b37 NIV text adds καὶ †   c39 NIV text omits σου †
d44 NIV note adds εὐλογεῖτε τοὺς καταρωμένους ὑμᾶς, καλῶς ποιεῖτε τοῖς μισοῦσιν ὑμᾶς   a1 NIV text omits δὲ †   b4 NRSV note g adds ἐν τῷ φανερῷ

g38 Exodus 21:24; Lev. 24:20; Deut. 19:21   h43 Lev. 19:18
i44 Some late manuscripts *enemies, bless those who curse you, do good to those who hate you*

NRSV

Concerning Prayer

5 "And whenever you pray, do not be like the hypocrites; for they love to stand and pray in the synagogues and at the street corners, so that they may be seen by others. Truly I tell you, they have received their reward. ⁶But whenever you pray, go into your room and shut the door and pray to your Father who is in secret; and your Father who sees in secret will reward you.[g]

7 "When you are praying, do not heap up empty phrases as the Gentiles do; for they think that they will be heard because of their many words. ⁸Do not be like them, for your Father knows what you need before you ask him.

9 "Pray then in this way:
　Our Father in heaven,
　　hallowed be your name.
10　Your kingdom come.
　　Your will be done,
　　　on earth as it is in heaven.
11　Give us this day our daily bread.[h]
12　And forgive us our debts,
　　　as we also have forgiven our
　　　　debtors.
13　And do not bring us to the time of
　　　trial,[i]
　　　but rescue us from the evil one.[j]

¹⁴For if you forgive others their trespasses, your heavenly Father will also forgive you; ¹⁵but if you do not forgive others, neither will your Father forgive your trespasses.

Concerning Fasting

16 "And whenever you fast, do not look dismal, like the hypocrites, for they disfigure their faces so as to show others that they are fasting. Truly I tell you, they have received their reward. ¹⁷But when you fast, put oil on your head and wash your face, ¹⁸so that your fasting may be seen not by others but by your Father who is in secret; and your Father who sees in secret will reward you.[g]

Concerning Treasures

19 "Do not store up for yourselves treasures on earth, where moth and rust[k] consume and where thieves break in and steal; ²⁰but store up for yourselves treasures in

Greek

5 Καὶ ὅταν προσεύχησθε, οὐκ ἔσεσθε ὡς οἱ ὑποκριταί, ὅτι φιλοῦσιν ἐν ταῖς συναγωγαῖς καὶ ἐν ταῖς γωνίαις τῶν πλατειῶν ἑστῶτες προσεύχεσθαι, ὅπως φανῶσιν τοῖς ἀνθρώποις· ἀμὴν λέγω ὑμῖν, ἀπέχουσιν τὸν μισθὸν αὐτῶν. 6 σὺ δὲ ὅταν προσεύχῃ, εἴσελθε εἰς τὸ ταμεῖόν σου καὶ κλείσας τὴν θύραν σου πρόσευξαι τῷ πατρί σου τῷ ἐν τῷ κρυπτῷ· καὶ ὁ πατήρ σου ὁ βλέπων ἐν τῷ κρυπτῷ ἀποδώσει σοι.[b] 7 Προσευχόμενοι δὲ μὴ βατταλογήσητε ὥσπερ οἱ ἐθνικοί, δοκοῦσιν γὰρ ὅτι ἐν τῇ πολυλογίᾳ αὐτῶν εἰσακουσθήσονται. 8 μὴ οὖν ὁμοιωθῆτε αὐτοῖς· οἶδεν γὰρ ὁ πατὴρ ὑμῶν ὧν χρείαν ἔχετε πρὸ τοῦ ὑμᾶς αἰτῆσαι αὐτόν. 9 Οὕτως οὖν προσεύχεσθε ὑμεῖς·

Πάτερ ἡμῶν ὁ ἐν τοῖς οὐρανοῖς·
ἁγιασθήτω τὸ ὄνομά σου·
10　ἐλθέτω ἡ βασιλεία σου·
γενηθήτω τὸ θέλημά σου,
ὡς ἐν οὐρανῷ καὶ ἐπὶ γῆς·
11　Τὸν ἄρτον ἡμῶν τὸν ἐπιούσιον
δὸς ἡμῖν σήμερον·
12　καὶ ἄφες ἡμῖν τὰ ὀφειλήματα
ἡμῶν,
ὡς καὶ ἡμεῖς ἀφήκαμεν τοῖς
ὀφειλέταις ἡμῶν·
13　καὶ μὴ εἰσενέγκῃς ἡμᾶς εἰς
πειρασμόν,
ἀλλὰ ῥῦσαι ἡμᾶς ἀπὸ τοῦ
πονηροῦ.[c]

14 Ἐὰν γὰρ ἀφῆτε τοῖς ἀνθρώποις τὰ παραπτώματα αὐτῶν, ἀφήσει καὶ ὑμῖν ὁ πατὴρ ὑμῶν ὁ οὐράνιος· 15 ἐὰν δὲ μὴ ἀφῆτε τοῖς ἀνθρώποις,[d] οὐδὲ ὁ πατὴρ ὑμῶν ἀφήσει τὰ παραπτώματα ὑμῶν.

16 Ὅταν δὲ νηστεύητε, μὴ γίνεσθε ὡς οἱ ὑποκριταὶ σκυθρωποί, ἀφανίζουσιν γὰρ τὰ πρόσωπα αὐτῶν ὅπως φανῶσιν τοῖς ἀνθρώποις νηστεύοντες· ἀμὴν λέγω ὑμῖν, ἀπέχουσιν τὸν μισθὸν αὐτῶν. 17 σὺ δὲ νηστεύων ἄλειψαί σου τὴν κεφαλὴν καὶ τὸ πρόσωπόν σου νίψαι, 18 ὅπως μὴ φανῇς τοῖς ἀνθρώποις νηστεύων ἀλλὰ τῷ πατρί σου τῷ ἐν τῷ κρυφαίῳ· καὶ ὁ πατήρ σου ὁ βλέπων ἐν τῷ κρυφαίῳ ἀποδώσει σοι.[b]

19 Μὴ θησαυρίζετε ὑμῖν θησαυροὺς ἐπὶ τῆς γῆς, ὅπου σὴς καὶ βρῶσις ἀφανίζει καὶ ὅπου κλέπται διορύσσουσιν καὶ κλέπτουσιν· 20 θησαυρίζετε δὲ ὑμῖν θησαυροὺς ἐν οὐρανῷ, ὅπου οὔτε

NIV

Prayer

⁵"And when you pray, do not be like the hypocrites, for they love to pray standing in the synagogues and on the street corners to be seen by men. I tell you the truth, they have received their reward in full. ⁶But when you pray, go into your room, close the door and pray to your Father, who is unseen. Then your Father, who sees what is done in secret, will reward you. ⁷And when you pray, do not keep on babbling like pagans, for they think they will be heard because of their many words. ⁸Do not be like them, for your Father knows what you need before you ask him.

⁹"This, then, is how you should pray:

" 'Our Father in heaven,
　hallowed be your name,
¹⁰your kingdom come,
　your will be done
　　on earth as it is in heaven.
¹¹Give us today our daily bread.
¹²Forgive us our debts,
　as we also have forgiven our debtors.
¹³And lead us not into temptation,
　but deliver us from the evil one.[a']

¹⁴For if you forgive men when they sin against you, your heavenly Father will also forgive you. ¹⁵But if you do not forgive men their sins, your Father will not forgive your sins.

Fasting

¹⁶"When you fast, do not look somber as the hypocrites do, for they disfigure their faces to show men they are fasting. I tell you the truth, they have received their reward in full. ¹⁷But when you fast, put oil on your head and wash your face, ¹⁸so that it will not be obvious to men that you are fasting, but only to your Father, who is unseen; and your Father, who sees what is done in secret, will reward you.

Treasures in Heaven

¹⁹"Do not store up for yourselves treasures on earth, where moth and rust destroy, and where thieves break in and steal. ²⁰But store up for yourselves treasures in

---

NRSV

heaven, where neither moth nor rust[k] consumes and where thieves do not break in and steal. [21]For where your treasure is, there your heart will be also.

The Sound Eye

22 "The eye is the lamp of the body. So, if your eye is healthy, your whole body will be full of light; [23]but if your eye is unhealthy, your whole body will be full of darkness. If then the light in you is darkness, how great is the darkness!

Serving Two Masters

24 "No one can serve two masters; for a slave will either hate the one and love the other, or be devoted to the one and despise the other. You cannot serve God and wealth.[l]

Do Not Worry

25 "Therefore I tell you, do not worry about your life, what you will eat or what you will drink,[m] or about your body, what you will wear. Is not life more than food, and the body more than clothing? [26]Look at the birds of the air; they neither sow nor reap nor gather into barns, and yet your heavenly Father feeds them. Are you not of more value than they? [27]And can any of you by worrying add a single hour to your span of life?[n] [28]And why do you worry about clothing? Consider the lilies of the field, how they grow; they neither toil nor spin, [29]yet I tell you, even Solomon in all his glory was not clothed like one of these. [30]But if God so clothes the grass of the field, which is alive today and tomorrow is thrown into the oven, will he not much more clothe you—you of little faith? [31]Therefore do not worry, saying, 'What will we eat?' or 'What will we drink?' or 'What will we wear?' [32]For it is the Gentiles who strive for all these things; and indeed your heavenly Father knows that you need all these things. [33]But strive first for the kingdom of God[o] and his[p] righteousness, and all these things will be given to you as well.

34 "So do not worry about tomorrow, for tomorrow will bring worries of its own. Today's trouble is enough for today.

Judging Others

7 "Do not judge, so that you may not be judged. [2]For with the judgment you make you will be judged, and the

Greek

σὴς οὔτε βρῶσις ἀφανίζει καὶ ὅπου κλέπται οὐ διορύσσουσιν οὐδὲ κλέπτουσιν· 21 ὅπου γάρ ἐστιν ὁ θησαυρός σου, ἐκεῖ ἔσται καὶ ἡ καρδία σου.

22 Ὁ λύχνος τοῦ σώματός ἐστιν ὁ ὀφθαλμός. ἐὰν οὖν ᾖ ὁ ὀφθαλμός σου ἁπλοῦς, ὅλον τὸ σῶμά σου φωτεινὸν ἔσται· 23 ἐὰν δὲ ὁ ὀφθαλμός σου πονηρὸς ᾖ, ὅλον τὸ σῶμά σου σκοτεινὸν ἔσται. εἰ οὖν τὸ φῶς τὸ ἐν σοὶ σκότος ἐστίν, τὸ σκότος πόσον.

24 Οὐδεὶς δύναται δυσὶ κυρίοις δουλεύειν· ἢ γὰρ τὸν ἕνα μισήσει καὶ τὸν ἕτερον ἀγαπήσει, ἢ ἑνὸς ἀνθέξεται καὶ τοῦ ἑτέρου καταφρονήσει. οὐ δύνασθε θεῷ δουλεύειν καὶ μαμωνᾷ.

25 Διὰ τοῦτο λέγω ὑμῖν, μὴ μεριμνᾶτε τῇ ψυχῇ ὑμῶν τί φάγητε [ἢ τί πίητε], μηδὲ τῷ σώματι ὑμῶν τί ἐνδύσησθε. οὐχὶ ἡ ψυχὴ πλεῖόν ἐστιν τῆς τροφῆς καὶ τὸ σῶμα τοῦ ἐνδύματος; 26 ἐμβλέψατε εἰς τὰ πετεινὰ τοῦ οὐρανοῦ ὅτι οὐ σπείρουσιν οὐδὲ θερίζουσιν οὐδὲ συνάγουσιν εἰς ἀποθήκας, καὶ ὁ πατὴρ ὑμῶν ὁ οὐράνιος τρέφει αὐτά· οὐχ ὑμεῖς μᾶλλον διαφέρετε αὐτῶν; 27 τίς δὲ ἐξ ὑμῶν μεριμνῶν δύναται προσθεῖναι ἐπὶ τὴν ἡλικίαν αὐτοῦ πῆχυν ἕνα; 28 καὶ περὶ ἐνδύματος τί μεριμνᾶτε; καταμάθετε τὰ κρίνα τοῦ ἀγροῦ πῶς αὐξάνουσιν· οὐ κοπιῶσιν οὐδὲ νήθουσιν· 29 λέγω δὲ ὑμῖν ὅτι οὐδὲ Σολομὼν ἐν πάσῃ τῇ δόξῃ αὐτοῦ περιεβάλετο ὡς ἓν τούτων. 30 εἰ δὲ τὸν χόρτον τοῦ ἀγροῦ σήμερον ὄντα καὶ αὔριον εἰς κλίβανον βαλλόμενον ὁ θεὸς οὕτως ἀμφιέννυσιν, οὐ πολλῷ μᾶλλον ὑμᾶς, ὀλιγόπιστοι; 31 μὴ οὖν μεριμνήσητε λέγοντες, Τί φάγωμεν; ἤ, Τί πίωμεν; ἤ, Τί περιβαλώμεθα; 32 πάντα γὰρ ταῦτα τὰ ἔθνη ἐπιζητοῦσιν· οἶδεν γὰρ ὁ πατὴρ ὑμῶν ὁ οὐράνιος ὅτι χρῄζετε τούτων ἁπάντων. 33 ζητεῖτε δὲ πρῶτον τὴν βασιλείαν [τοῦ θεοῦ] καὶ τὴν δικαιοσύνην αὐτοῦ, καὶ ταῦτα πάντα προστεθήσεται ὑμῖν. 34 μὴ οὖν μεριμνήσητε εἰς τὴν αὔριον, ἡ γὰρ αὔριον μεριμνήσει ἑαυτῆς· ἀρκετὸν τῇ ἡμέρᾳ ἡ κακία αὐτῆς.

7 Μὴ κρίνετε, ἵνα μὴ κριθῆτε· 2 ἐν ᾧ γὰρ κρίματι κρίνετε κριθήσεσθε,

NIV

heaven, where moth and rust do not destroy, and where thieves do not break in and steal. [21]For where your treasure is, there your heart will be also.

22 "The eye is the lamp of the body. If your eyes are good, your whole body will be full of light. [23]But if your eyes are bad, your whole body will be full of darkness. If then the light within you is darkness, how great is that darkness!

24 "No one can serve two masters. Either he will hate the one and love the other, or he will be devoted to the one and despise the other. You cannot serve both God and Money.

Do Not Worry

25 "Therefore I tell you, do not worry about your life, what you will eat or drink; or about your body, what you will wear. Is not life more important than food, and the body more important than clothes? [26]Look at the birds of the air; they do not sow or reap or store away in barns, and yet your heavenly Father feeds them. Are you not much more valuable than they? [27]Who of you by worrying can add a single hour to his life[b]?

28 "And why do you worry about clothes? See how the lilies of the field grow. They do not labor or spin. [29]Yet I tell you that not even Solomon in all his splendor was dressed like one of these. [30]If that is how God clothes the grass of the field, which is here today and tomorrow is thrown into the fire, will he not much more clothe you, O you of little faith? [31]So do not worry, saying, 'What shall we eat?' or 'What shall we drink?' or 'What shall we wear?' [32]For the pagans run after all these things, and your heavenly Father knows that you need them. [33]But seek first his kingdom and his righteousness, and all these things will be given to you as well. [34]Therefore do not worry about tomorrow, for tomorrow will worry about itself. Each day has enough trouble of its own.

Judging Others

7 "Do not judge, or you too will be judged. [2]For in the same way you judge others, you will be judged, and with

---

k Gk eating l Gk mammon m Other ancient authorities lack or what you will drink n Or add one cubit to your height o Other ancient authorities lack of God p Or its

b27 Or single cubit to his height

measure you give will be the measure you get. ³Why do you see the speck in your neighbor's^q eye, but do not notice the log in your own eye? ⁴Or how can you say to your neighbor,^r 'Let me take the speck out of your eye,' while the log is in your own eye? ⁵You hypocrite, first take the log out of your own eye, and then you will see clearly to take the speck out of your neighbor's^q eye.

Profaning the Holy

6 "Do not give what is holy to dogs; and do not throw your pearls before swine, or they will trample them under foot and turn and maul you.

Ask, Search, Knock

7 "Ask, and it will be given you; search, and you will find; knock, and the door will be opened for you. ⁸For everyone who asks receives, and everyone who searches finds, and for everyone who knocks, the door will be opened. ⁹Is there anyone among you who, if your child asks for bread, will give a stone? ¹⁰Or if the child asks for a fish, will give a snake? ¹¹If you then, who are evil, know how to give good gifts to your children, how much more will your Father in heaven give good things to those who ask him!

The Golden Rule

12 "In everything do to others as you would have them do to you; for this is the law and the prophets.

The Narrow Gate

13 "Enter through the narrow gate; for the gate is wide and the road is easy^s that leads to destruction, and there are many who take it. ¹⁴For the gate is narrow and the road is hard that leads to life, and there are few who find it.

A Tree and Its Fruit

15 "Beware of false prophets, who come to you in sheep's clothing but inwardly are ravenous wolves. ¹⁶You will know them by their fruits. Are grapes gathered from thorns, or figs from thistles? ¹⁷In the same way, every good tree bears good fruit, but the bad tree bears bad fruit. ¹⁸A good tree cannot bear bad fruit, nor can a bad tree bear good fruit. ¹⁹Every tree that does not bear good fruit is cut down and thrown into the fire. ²⁰Thus you will know them by their fruits.

καὶ ἐν ᾧ μέτρῳ μετρεῖτε μετρηθήσεται ὑμῖν. 3 τί δὲ βλέπεις τὸ κάρφος τὸ ἐν τῷ ὀφθαλμῷ τοῦ ἀδελφοῦ σου, τὴν δὲ ἐν τῷ σῷ ὀφθαλμῷ δοκὸν οὐ κατανοεῖς; 4 ἢ πῶς ἐρεῖς τῷ ἀδελφῷ σου, Ἄφες ἐκβάλω τὸ κάρφος ἐκ τοῦ ὀφθαλμοῦ σου, καὶ ἰδοὺ ἡ δοκὸς ἐν τῷ ὀφθαλμῷ σοῦ; 5 ὑποκριτά, ἔκβαλε πρῶτον ἐκ τοῦ ὀφθαλμοῦ σοῦ τὴν δοκόν, καὶ τότε διαβλέψεις ἐκβαλεῖν τὸ κάρφος ἐκ τοῦ ὀφθαλμοῦ τοῦ ἀδελφοῦ σου. 6 Μὴ δῶτε τὸ ἅγιον τοῖς κυσὶν μηδὲ βάλητε τοὺς μαργαρίτας ὑμῶν ἔμπροσθεν τῶν χοίρων, μήποτε καταπατήσουσιν αὐτοὺς ἐν τοῖς ποσὶν αὐτῶν καὶ στραφέντες ῥήξωσιν ὑμᾶς.

7 Αἰτεῖτε καὶ δοθήσεται ὑμῖν, ζητεῖτε καὶ εὑρήσετε, κρούετε καὶ ἀνοιγήσεται ὑμῖν· 8 πᾶς γὰρ ὁ αἰτῶν λαμβάνει καὶ ὁ ζητῶν εὑρίσκει καὶ τῷ κρούοντι ἀνοιγήσεται. 9 ἢ τίς ἐστιν ἐξ ὑμῶν ἄνθρωπος, ὃν αἰτήσει^a ὁ υἱὸς αὐτοῦ ἄρτον, μὴ λίθον ἐπιδώσει αὐτῷ; 10 ἢ καὶ ἰχθὺν αἰτήσει, μὴ ὄφιν ἐπιδώσει αὐτῷ; 11 εἰ οὖν ὑμεῖς πονηροὶ ὄντες οἴδατε δόματα ἀγαθὰ διδόναι τοῖς τέκνοις ὑμῶν, πόσῳ μᾶλλον ὁ πατὴρ ὑμῶν ὁ ἐν τοῖς οὐρανοῖς δώσει ἀγαθὰ τοῖς αἰτοῦσιν αὐτόν. 12 Πάντα οὖν ὅσα ἐὰν θέλητε ἵνα ποιῶσιν ὑμῖν οἱ ἄνθρωποι, οὕτως καὶ ὑμεῖς ποιεῖτε αὐτοῖς· οὗτος γάρ ἐστιν ὁ νόμος καὶ οἱ προφῆται.

13 Εἰσέλθατε διὰ τῆς στενῆς πύλης· ὅτι πλατεῖα ἡ πύλη^b καὶ εὐρύχωρος ἡ ὁδὸς ἡ ἀπάγουσα εἰς τὴν ἀπώλειαν καὶ πολλοί εἰσιν οἱ εἰσερχόμενοι δι' αὐτῆς· 14 τί^c στενὴ ἡ πύλη καὶ τεθλιμμένη ἡ ὁδὸς ἡ ἀπάγουσα εἰς τὴν ζωὴν καὶ ὀλίγοι εἰσιν οἱ εὑρίσκοντες αὐτήν.

15 Προσέχετε ἀπὸ τῶν ψευδοπροφητῶν, οἵτινες ἔρχονται πρὸς ὑμᾶς ἐν ἐνδύμασιν προβάτων, ἔσωθεν δέ εἰσιν λύκοι ἅρπαγες. 16 ἀπὸ τῶν καρπῶν αὐτῶν ἐπιγνώσεσθε αὐτούς. μήτι συλλέγουσιν ἀπὸ ἀκανθῶν σταφυλὰς ἢ ἀπὸ τριβόλων σῦκα; 17 οὕτως πᾶν δένδρον ἀγαθὸν καρποὺς καλοὺς ποιεῖ, τὸ δὲ σαπρὸν δένδρον καρποὺς πονηροὺς ποιεῖ. 18 οὐ δύναται δένδρον ἀγαθὸν καρποὺς πονηροὺς ποιεῖν οὐδὲ δένδρον σαπρὸν καρποὺς καλοὺς ποιεῖν. 19 πᾶν δένδρον μὴ ποιοῦν καρπὸν καλὸν ἐκκόπτεται καὶ εἰς πῦρ βάλλεται. 20 ἄρα γε ἀπὸ τῶν καρπῶν αὐτῶν ἐπιγνώσεσθε αὐτούς.

---

the measure you use, it will be measured to you.

³"Why do you look at the speck of sawdust in your brother's eye and pay no attention to the plank in your own eye? ⁴How can you say to your brother, 'Let me take the speck out of your eye,' when all the time there is a plank in your own eye? ⁵You hypocrite, first take the plank out of your own eye, and then you will see clearly to remove the speck from your brother's eye.

⁶"Do not give dogs what is sacred; do not throw your pearls to pigs. If you do, they may trample them under their feet, and then turn and tear you to pieces.

Ask, Seek, Knock

⁷"Ask and it will be given to you; seek and you will find; knock and the door will be opened to you. ⁸For everyone who asks receives; he who seeks finds; and to him who knocks, the door will be opened.

⁹"Which of you, if his son asks for bread, will give him a stone? ¹⁰Or if he asks for a fish, will give him a snake? ¹¹If you, then, though you are evil, know how to give good gifts to your children, how much more will your Father in heaven give good gifts to those who ask him! ¹²So in everything, do to others what you would have them do to you, for this sums up the Law and the Prophets.

The Narrow and Wide Gates

¹³"Enter through the narrow gate. For wide is the gate and broad is the road that leads to destruction, and many enter through it. ¹⁴But small is the gate and narrow the road that leads to life, and only a few find it.

A Tree and Its Fruit

¹⁵"Watch out for false prophets. They come to you in sheep's clothing, but inwardly they are ferocious wolves. ¹⁶By their fruit you will recognize them. Do people pick grapes from thornbushes, or figs from thistles? ¹⁷Likewise every good tree bears good fruit, but a bad tree bears bad fruit. ¹⁸A good tree cannot bear bad fruit, and a bad tree cannot bear good fruit. ¹⁹Every tree that does not bear good fruit is cut down and thrown into the fire. ²⁰Thus, by their fruit you will recognize them.

---

^q Gk *brother's*   ^r Gk *brother*   ^s Other ancient authorities read *for the road is wide and easy*

^a9 NIV text ἐὰν αἰτήσῃ †   ^b13 NRSV note s omits ἡ πύλη   ^c14 NIV text ὅτι δὲ

NRSV

Concerning Self-Deception

21 "Not everyone who says to me, 'Lord, Lord,' will enter the kingdom of heaven, but only the one who does the will of my Father in heaven. 22On that day many will say to me, 'Lord, Lord, did we not prophesy in your name, and cast out demons in your name, and do many deeds of power in your name?' 23Then I will declare to them, 'I never knew you; go away from me, you evildoers.'

Hearers and Doers

24 "Everyone then who hears these words of mine and acts on them will be like a wise man who built his house on rock. 25The rain fell, the floods came, and the winds blew and beat on that house, but it did not fall, because it had been founded on rock. 26And everyone who hears these words of mine and does not act on them will be like a foolish man who built his house on sand. 27The rain fell, and the floods came, and the winds blew and beat against that house, and it fell—and great was its fall!"

28 Now when Jesus had finished saying these things, the crowds were astounded at his teaching, 29for he taught them as one having authority, and not as their scribes.

Jesus Cleanses a Leper

8 When Jesus[t] had come down from the mountain, great crowds followed him; 2and there was a leper[u] who came to him and knelt before him, saying, "Lord, if you choose, you can make me clean." 3He stretched out his hand and touched him, saying, "I do choose. Be made clean!" Immediately his leprosy[u] was cleansed. 4Then Jesus said to him, "See that you say nothing to anyone; but go, show yourself to the priest, and offer the gift that Moses commanded, as a testimony to them."

Jesus Heals a Centurion's Servant

5 When he entered Capernaum, a centurion came to him, appealing to him 6and saying, "Lord, my servant is lying at home paralyzed, in terrible distress." 7And he said to him, "I will come and cure him." 8The centurion answered, "Lord, I am not worthy to have you come under my roof; but only speak the word, and my servant will be healed. 9For I also am a man under authority, with soldiers under me; and I

---

21 Οὐ πᾶς ὁ λέγων μοι, Κύριε κύριε, εἰσελεύσεται εἰς τὴν βασιλείαν τῶν οὐρανῶν, ἀλλ᾽ ὁ ποιῶν τὸ θέλημα τοῦ πατρός μου τοῦ ἐν τοῖς οὐρανοῖς. 22 πολλοὶ ἐροῦσίν μοι ἐν ἐκείνῃ τῇ ἡμέρᾳ, Κύριε κύριε, οὐ τῷ σῷ ὀνόματι ἐπροφητεύσαμεν, καὶ τῷ σῷ ὀνόματι δαιμόνια ἐξεβάλομεν, καὶ τῷ σῷ ὀνόματι δυνάμεις πολλὰς ἐποιήσαμεν; 23 καὶ τότε ὁμολογήσω αὐτοῖς ὅτι Οὐδέποτε ἔγνων ὑμᾶς· ἀποχωρεῖτε ἀπ᾽ ἐμοῦ οἱ ἐργαζόμενοι τὴν ἀνομίαν.

24 Πᾶς οὖν ὅστις ἀκούει μου τοὺς λόγους τούτους καὶ ποιεῖ αὐτούς, ὁμοιωθήσεται ἀνδρὶ φρονίμῳ, ὅστις ᾠκοδόμησεν αὐτοῦ τὴν οἰκίαν ἐπὶ τὴν πέτραν· 25 καὶ κατέβη ἡ βροχὴ καὶ ἦλθον οἱ ποταμοὶ καὶ ἔπνευσαν οἱ ἄνεμοι καὶ προσέπεσαν τῇ οἰκίᾳ ἐκείνῃ, καὶ οὐκ ἔπεσεν, τεθεμελίωτο γὰρ ἐπὶ τὴν πέτραν. 26 καὶ πᾶς ὁ ἀκούων μου τοὺς λόγους τούτους καὶ μὴ ποιῶν αὐτοὺς ὁμοιωθήσεται ἀνδρὶ μωρῷ, ὅστις ᾠκοδόμησεν αὐτοῦ τὴν οἰκίαν ἐπὶ τὴν ἄμμον· 27 καὶ κατέβη ἡ βροχὴ καὶ ἦλθον οἱ ποταμοὶ καὶ ἔπνευσαν οἱ ἄνεμοι καὶ προσέκοψαν τῇ οἰκίᾳ ἐκείνῃ, καὶ ἔπεσεν καὶ ἦν ἡ πτῶσις αὐτῆς μεγάλη.

28 Καὶ ἐγένετο ὅτε ἐτέλεσεν ὁ Ἰησοῦς τοὺς λόγους τούτους, ἐξεπλήσσοντο οἱ ὄχλοι ἐπὶ τῇ διδαχῇ αὐτοῦ· 29 ἦν γὰρ διδάσκων αὐτοὺς ὡς ἐξουσίαν ἔχων καὶ οὐχ ὡς οἱ γραμματεῖς αὐτῶν.

8 Καταβάντος δὲ αὐτοῦ ἀπὸ τοῦ ὄρους ἠκολούθησαν αὐτῷ ὄχλοι πολλοί. 2 καὶ ἰδοὺ λεπρὸς προσελθὼν προσεκύνει αὐτῷ λέγων, Κύριε, ἐὰν θέλῃς δύνασαί με καθαρίσαι. 3 καὶ ἐκτείνας τὴν χεῖρα ἥψατο αὐτοῦ λέγων, Θέλω, καθαρίσθητι· καὶ εὐθέως ἐκαθαρίσθη αὐτοῦ ἡ λέπρα. 4 καὶ λέγει αὐτῷ ὁ Ἰησοῦς, Ὅρα μηδενὶ εἴπῃς, ἀλλὰ ὕπαγε σεαυτὸν δεῖξον τῷ ἱερεῖ καὶ προσένεγκον τὸ δῶρον ὃ προσέταξεν Μωϋσῆς, εἰς μαρτύριον αὐτοῖς.

5 Εἰσελθόντος δὲ αὐτοῦ εἰς Καφαρναοὺμ προσῆλθεν αὐτῷ ἑκατόνταρχος παρακαλῶν αὐτὸν 6 καὶ λέγων, Κύριε, ὁ παῖς μου βέβληται ἐν τῇ οἰκίᾳ παραλυτικός, δεινῶς βασανιζόμενος. 7 καὶ λέγει αὐτῷ, Ἐγὼ ἐλθὼν θεραπεύσω αὐτόν. 8 καὶ ἀποκριθεὶς ὁ ἑκατόνταρχος ἔφη, Κύριε, οὐκ εἰμὶ ἱκανὸς ἵνα μου ὑπὸ τὴν στέγην εἰσέλθῃς, ἀλλὰ μόνον εἰπὲ λόγῳ, καὶ ἰαθήσεται ὁ παῖς μου. 9 καὶ γὰρ ἐγὼ ἄνθρωπός εἰμι ὑπὸ ἐξουσίαν, ἔχων ὑπ᾽ ἐμαυτὸν

NIV

21"Not everyone who says to me, 'Lord, Lord,' will enter the kingdom of heaven, but only he who does the will of my Father who is in heaven. 22Many will say to me on that day, 'Lord, Lord, did we not prophesy in your name, and in your name drive out demons and perform many miracles?' 23Then I will tell them plainly, 'I never knew you. Away from me, you evildoers!'

The Wise and Foolish Builders

24"Therefore everyone who hears these words of mine and puts them into practice is like a wise man who built his house on the rock. 25The rain came down, the streams rose, and the winds blew and beat against that house; yet it did not fall, because it had its foundation on the rock. 26But everyone who hears these words of mine and does not put them into practice is like a foolish man who built his house on sand. 27The rain came down, the streams rose, and the winds blew and beat against that house, and it fell with a great crash."

28When Jesus had finished saying these things, the crowds were amazed at his teaching, 29because he taught as one who had authority, and not as their teachers of the law.

The Man With Leprosy

8 When he came down from the mountainside, large crowds followed him. 2A man with leprosy[a] came and knelt before him and said, "Lord, if you are willing, you can make me clean."

3Jesus reached out his hand and touched the man. "I am willing," he said. "Be clean!" Immediately he was cured[b] of his leprosy. 4Then Jesus said to him, "See that you don't tell anyone. But go, show yourself to the priest and offer the gift Moses commanded, as a testimony to them."

The Faith of the Centurion

5When Jesus had entered Capernaum, a centurion came to him, asking for help. 6"Lord," he said, "my servant lies at home paralyzed and in terrible suffering."

7Jesus said to him, "I will go and heal him."

8The centurion replied, "Lord, I do not deserve to have you come under my roof. But just say the word, and my servant will be healed. 9For I myself am a man under authority, with soldiers under me. I tell

---

[t]Gk he   [u]The terms *leper* and *leprosy* can refer to several diseases

[a]2 The Greek word was used for various diseases affecting the skin—not necessarily leprosy.   [b]3 Greek *made clean*

say to one, 'Go,' and he goes, and to another, 'Come,' and he comes, and to my slave, 'Do this,' and the slave does it." [10]When Jesus heard him, he was amazed and said to those who followed him, "Truly I tell you, in no one[v] in Israel have I found such faith. [11]I tell you, many will come from east and west and will eat with Abraham and Isaac and Jacob in the kingdom of heaven, [12]while the heirs of the kingdom will be thrown into the outer darkness, where there will be weeping and gnashing of teeth." [13]And to the centurion Jesus said, "Go; let it be done for you according to your faith." And the servant was healed in that hour.

Jesus Heals Many at Peter's House

14 When Jesus entered Peter's house, he saw his mother-in-law lying in bed with a fever; [15]he touched her hand, and the fever left her, and she got up and began to serve him. [16]That evening they brought to him many who were possessed with demons; and he cast out the spirits with a word, and cured all who were sick. [17]This was to fulfill what had been spoken through the prophet Isaiah, "He took our infirmities and bore our diseases."

Would-Be Followers of Jesus

18 Now when Jesus saw great crowds around him, he gave orders to go over to the other side. [19]A scribe then approached and said, "Teacher, I will follow you wherever you go." [20]And Jesus said to him, "Foxes have holes, and birds of the air have nests; but the Son of Man has nowhere to lay his head." [21]Another of his disciples said to him, "Lord, first let me go and bury my father." [22]But Jesus said to him, "Follow me, and let the dead bury their own dead."

Jesus Stills the Storm

23 And when he got into the boat, his disciples followed him. [24]A windstorm arose on the sea, so great that the boat was being swamped by the waves; but he was asleep. [25]And they went and woke him up, saying, "Lord, save us! We are perishing!" [26]And he said to them, "Why are you

στρατιώτας, καὶ λέγω τούτῳ, Πορεύθητι, καὶ πορεύεται, καὶ ἄλλῳ, Ἔρχου, καὶ ἔρχεται, καὶ τῷ δούλῳ μου, Ποίησον τοῦτο, καὶ ποιεῖ. **10** ἀκούσας δὲ ὁ Ἰησοῦς ἐθαύμασεν καὶ εἶπεν τοῖς ἀκολουθοῦσιν, Ἀμὴν λέγω ὑμῖν, παρ' οὐδενὶ τοσαύτην πίστιν ἐν τῷ Ἰσραὴλ εὗρον[a]. **11** λέγω δὲ ὑμῖν ὅτι πολλοὶ ἀπὸ ἀνατολῶν καὶ δυσμῶν ἥξουσιν καὶ ἀνακλιθήσονται μετὰ Ἀβραὰμ καὶ Ἰσαὰκ καὶ Ἰακὼβ ἐν τῇ βασιλείᾳ τῶν οὐρανῶν, **12** οἱ δὲ υἱοὶ τῆς βασιλείας ἐκβληθήσονται εἰς τὸ σκότος τὸ ἐξώτερον· ἐκεῖ ἔσται ὁ κλαυθμὸς καὶ ὁ βρυγμὸς τῶν ὀδόντων. **13** καὶ εἶπεν ὁ Ἰησοῦς τῷ ἑκατοντάρχῃ, Ὕπαγε, ὡς ἐπίστευσας γενηθήτω σοι. καὶ ἰάθη ὁ παῖς [αὐτοῦ] ἐν τῇ ὥρᾳ ἐκείνῃ.

14 Καὶ ἐλθὼν ὁ Ἰησοῦς εἰς τὴν οἰκίαν Πέτρου εἶδεν τὴν πενθερὰν αὐτοῦ βεβλημένην καὶ πυρέσσουσαν· **15** καὶ ἥψατο τῆς χειρὸς αὐτῆς, καὶ ἀφῆκεν αὐτὴν ὁ πυρετός, καὶ ἠγέρθη καὶ διηκόνει αὐτῷ. **16** Ὀψίας δὲ γενομένης προσήνεγκαν αὐτῷ δαιμονιζομένους πολλούς· καὶ ἐξέβαλεν τὰ πνεύματα λόγῳ καὶ πάντας τοὺς κακῶς ἔχοντας ἐθεράπευσεν, **17** ὅπως πληρωθῇ τὸ ῥηθὲν διὰ Ἠσαΐου τοῦ προφήτου λέγοντος,

Αὐτὸς τὰς ἀσθενείας ἡμῶν ἔλαβεν καὶ τὰς νόσους ἐβάστασεν.

18 Ἰδὼν δὲ ὁ Ἰησοῦς ὄχλον περὶ αὐτὸν ἐκέλευσεν ἀπελθεῖν εἰς τὸ πέραν. **19** καὶ προσελθὼν εἷς γραμματεὺς εἶπεν αὐτῷ, Διδάσκαλε, ἀκολουθήσω σοι ὅπου ἐὰν ἀπέρχῃ. **20** καὶ λέγει αὐτῷ ὁ Ἰησοῦς, Αἱ ἀλώπεκες φωλεοὺς ἔχουσιν καὶ τὰ πετεινὰ τοῦ οὐρανοῦ κατασκηνώσεις, ὁ δὲ υἱὸς τοῦ ἀνθρώπου οὐκ ἔχει ποῦ τὴν κεφαλὴν κλίνῃ. **21** ἕτερος δὲ τῶν μαθητῶν [αὐτοῦ] εἶπεν αὐτῷ, Κύριε, ἐπίτρεψόν μοι πρῶτον ἀπελθεῖν καὶ θάψαι τὸν πατέρα μου. **22** ὁ δὲ Ἰησοῦς λέγει αὐτῷ, Ἀκολούθει μοι καὶ ἄφες τοὺς νεκροὺς θάψαι τοὺς ἑαυτῶν νεκρούς.

23 Καὶ ἐμβάντι αὐτῷ εἰς τὸ πλοῖον ἠκολούθησαν αὐτῷ οἱ μαθηταὶ αὐτοῦ. **24** καὶ ἰδοὺ σεισμὸς μέγας ἐγένετο ἐν τῇ θαλάσσῃ, ὥστε τὸ πλοῖον καλύπτεσθαι ὑπὸ τῶν κυμάτων, αὐτὸς δὲ ἐκάθευδεν. **25** καὶ προσελθόντες ἤγειραν αὐτὸν λέγοντες, Κύριε, σῶσον[b], ἀπολλύμεθα. **26** καὶ λέγει αὐτοῖς, Τί δειλοί ἐστε, ὀλιγόπιστοι; τότε ἐγερθεὶς

this one, 'Go,' and he goes; and that one, 'Come,' and he comes. I say to my servant, 'Do this,' and he does it."

[10]When Jesus heard this, he was astonished and said to those following him, "I tell you the truth, I have not found anyone in Israel with such great faith. [11]I say to you that many will come from the east and the west, and will take their places at the feast with Abraham, Isaac and Jacob in the kingdom of heaven. [12]But the subjects of the kingdom will be thrown outside, into the darkness, where there will be weeping and gnashing of teeth."

[13]Then Jesus said to the centurion, "Go! It will be done just as you believed it would." And his servant was healed at that very hour.

Jesus Heals Many

[14]When Jesus came into Peter's house, he saw Peter's mother-in-law lying in bed with a fever. [15]He touched her hand and the fever left her, and she got up and began to wait on him.

[16]When evening came, many who were demon-possessed were brought to him, and he drove out the spirits with a word and healed all the sick. [17]This was to fulfill what was spoken through the prophet Isaiah:

"He took up our infirmities
  and carried our diseases."[c]

The Cost of Following Jesus

[18]When Jesus saw the crowd around him, he gave orders to cross to the other side of the lake. [19]Then a teacher of the law came to him and said, "Teacher, I will follow you wherever you go."

[20]Jesus replied, "Foxes have holes and birds of the air have nests, but the Son of Man has no place to lay his head."

[21]Another disciple said to him, "Lord, first let me go and bury my father."

[22]But Jesus told him, "Follow me, and let the dead bury their own dead."

Jesus Calms the Storm

[23]Then he got into the boat and his disciples followed him. [24]Without warning, a furious storm came up on the lake, so that the waves swept over the boat. But Jesus was sleeping. [25]The disciples went and woke him, saying, "Lord, save us! We're going to drown!"

[26]He replied, "You of little faith, why are

NRSV

afraid, you of little faith?" Then he got up and rebuked the winds and the sea; and there was a dead calm. [27]They were amazed, saying, "What sort of man is this, that even the winds and the sea obey him?"

Jesus Heals the Gadarene Demoniacs

28 When he came to the other side, to the country of the Gadarenes,[w] two demoniacs coming out of the tombs met him. They were so fierce that no one could pass that way. [29]Suddenly they shouted, "What have you to do with us, Son of God? Have you come here to torment us before the time?" [30]Now a large herd of swine was feeding at some distance from them. [31]The demons begged him, "If you cast us out, send us into the herd of swine." [32]And he said to them, "Go!" So they came out and entered the swine; and suddenly, the whole herd rushed down the steep bank into the sea and perished in the water. [33]The swineherds ran off, and on going into the town, they told the whole story about what had happened to the demoniacs. [34]Then the whole town came out to meet Jesus; and when they saw him, they begged him to

9 leave their neighborhood. [1]And after getting into a boat he crossed the sea and came to his own town.

Jesus Heals a Paralytic

2 And just then some people were carrying a paralyzed man lying on a bed. When Jesus saw their faith, he said to the paralytic, "Take heart, son; your sins are forgiven." [3]Then some of the scribes said to themselves, "This man is blaspheming." [4]But Jesus, perceiving their thoughts, said, "Why do you think evil in your hearts? [5]For which is easier, to say, 'Your sins are forgiven,' or to say, 'Stand up and walk'? [6]But so that you may know that the Son of Man has authority on earth to forgive sins"—he then said to the paralytic— "Stand up, take your bed and go to your home." [7]And he stood up and went to his home. [8]When the crowds saw it, they were filled with awe, and they glorified God, who had given such authority to human beings.

The Call of Matthew

9 As Jesus was walking along, he saw a man called Matthew sitting at the tax booth; and he said to him, "Follow me." And he

Greek

ἐπετίμησεν τοῖς ἀνέμοις καὶ τῇ θαλάσσῃ, καὶ ἐγένετο γαλήνη μεγάλη. 27 οἱ δὲ ἄνθρωποι ἐθαύμασαν λέγοντες, Ποταπός ἐστιν οὗτος ὅτι καὶ οἱ ἄνεμοι καὶ ἡ θάλασσα αὐτῷ ὑπακούουσιν;

28 Καὶ ἐλθόντος αὐτοῦ εἰς τὸ πέραν εἰς τὴν χώραν τῶν Γαδαρηνῶν[c] ὑπήντησαν αὐτῷ δύο δαιμονιζόμενοι ἐκ τῶν μνημείων ἐξερχόμενοι, χαλεποὶ λίαν, ὥστε μὴ ἰσχύειν τινὰ παρελθεῖν διὰ τῆς ὁδοῦ ἐκείνης. 29 καὶ ἰδοὺ ἔκραξαν λέγοντες, Τί ἡμῖν καὶ σοί, υἱὲ τοῦ θεοῦ; ἦλθες ὧδε πρὸ καιροῦ βασανίσαι ἡμᾶς; 30 ἦν δὲ μακρὰν ἀπ' αὐτῶν ἀγέλη χοίρων πολλῶν βοσκομένη. 31 οἱ δὲ δαίμονες παρεκάλουν αὐτὸν λέγοντες, Εἰ ἐκβάλλεις ἡμᾶς, ἀπόστειλον ἡμᾶς εἰς τὴν ἀγέλην τῶν χοίρων. 32 καὶ εἶπεν αὐτοῖς, Ὑπάγετε. οἱ δὲ ἐξελθόντες ἀπῆλθον εἰς τοὺς χοίρους· καὶ ἰδοὺ ὥρμησεν πᾶσα ἡ ἀγέλη κατὰ τοῦ κρημνοῦ εἰς τὴν θάλασσαν καὶ ἀπέθανον ἐν τοῖς ὕδασιν. 33 οἱ δὲ βόσκοντες ἔφυγον, καὶ ἀπελθόντες εἰς τὴν πόλιν ἀπήγγειλαν πάντα καὶ τὰ τῶν δαιμονιζομένων. 34 καὶ ἰδοὺ πᾶσα ἡ πόλις ἐξῆλθεν εἰς ὑπάντησιν τῷ Ἰησοῦ καὶ ἰδόντες αὐτὸν παρεκάλεσαν ὅπως μεταβῇ ἀπὸ τῶν ὁρίων αὐτῶν.

9 Καὶ ἐμβὰς[a] εἰς πλοῖον διεπέρασεν καὶ ἦλθεν εἰς τὴν ἰδίαν πόλιν. 2 καὶ ἰδοὺ προσέφερον αὐτῷ παραλυτικὸν ἐπὶ κλίνης βεβλημένον. καὶ ἰδὼν ὁ Ἰησοῦς τὴν πίστιν αὐτῶν εἶπεν τῷ παραλυτικῷ, Θάρσει, τέκνον, ἀφίενταί σου αἱ ἁμαρτίαι. 3 καὶ ἰδού τινες τῶν γραμματέων εἶπαν ἐν ἑαυτοῖς, Οὗτος βλασφημεῖ. 4 καὶ ἰδὼν[b] ὁ Ἰησοῦς τὰς ἐνθυμήσεις αὐτῶν εἶπεν, Ἱνατί ἐνθυμεῖσθε πονηρὰ ἐν ταῖς καρδίαις ὑμῶν; 5 τί γάρ ἐστιν εὐκοπώτερον, εἰπεῖν, Ἀφίενταί σου αἱ ἁμαρτίαι, ἢ εἰπεῖν, Ἔγειρε καὶ περιπάτει; 6 ἵνα δὲ εἰδῆτε ὅτι ἐξουσίαν ἔχει ὁ υἱὸς τοῦ ἀνθρώπου ἐπὶ τῆς γῆς ἀφιέναι ἁμαρτίας – τότε λέγει τῷ παραλυτικῷ, Ἐγερθεὶς ἆρόν σου τὴν κλίνην καὶ ὕπαγε εἰς τὸν οἶκόν σου. 7 καὶ ἐγερθεὶς ἀπῆλθεν εἰς τὸν οἶκον αὐτοῦ. 8 ἰδόντες δὲ οἱ ὄχλοι ἐφοβήθησαν καὶ ἐδόξασαν τὸν θεὸν τὸν δόντα ἐξουσίαν τοιαύτην τοῖς ἀνθρώποις.

9 Καὶ παράγων ὁ Ἰησοῦς ἐκεῖθεν εἶδεν ἄνθρωπον καθήμενον ἐπὶ τὸ τελώνιον, Μαθθαῖον λεγόμενον, καὶ λέγει αὐτῷ, Ἀκολούθει μοι. καὶ ἀναστὰς

NIV

you so afraid?" Then he got up and rebuked the winds and the waves, and it was completely calm.

[27]The men were amazed and asked, "What kind of man is this? Even the winds and the waves obey him!"

The Healing of Two Demon-possessed Men

[28]When he arrived at the other side in the region of the Gadarenes,[d] two demon-possessed men coming from the tombs met him. They were so violent that no one could pass that way. [29]"What do you want with us, Son of God?" they shouted. "Have you come here to torture us before the appointed time?"

[30]Some distance from them a large herd of pigs was feeding. [31]The demons begged Jesus, "If you drive us out, send us into the herd of pigs."

[32]He said to them, "Go!" So they came out and went into the pigs, and the whole herd rushed down the steep bank into the lake and died in the water. [33]Those tending the pigs ran off, went into the town and reported all this, including what had happened to the demon-possessed men. [34]Then the whole town went out to meet Jesus. And when they saw him, they pleaded with him to leave their region.

Jesus Heals a Paralytic

9 Jesus stepped into a boat, crossed over and came to his own town. [2]Some men brought to him a paralytic, lying on a mat. When Jesus saw their faith, he said to the paralytic, "Take heart, son; your sins are forgiven."

[3]At this, some of the teachers of the law said to themselves, "This fellow is blaspheming!"

[4]Knowing their thoughts, Jesus said, "Why do you entertain evil thoughts in your hearts? [5]Which is easier: to say, 'Your sins are forgiven,' or to say, 'Get up and walk'? [6]But so that you may know that the Son of Man has authority on earth to forgive sins. . . ." Then he said to the paralytic, "Get up, take your mat and go home." [7]And the man got up and went home. [8]When the crowd saw this, they were filled with awe; and they praised God, who had given such authority to men.

The Calling of Matthew

[9]As Jesus went on from there, he saw a man named Matthew sitting at the tax collector's booth. "Follow me," he told him,

---

[w] Other ancient authorities read *Gergesenes*; others, *Gerasenes*

[c]28 NIV/NRSV notes Γεργεσηνῶν or Γερασηνῶν
[a]1 NIV text adds ὁ Ἰησοῦς † [b]4 NIV text εἰδὼς

[d]28 Some manuscripts *Gergesenes*; others *Gerasenes*

NRSV

got up and followed him.

10 And as he sat at dinner[x] in the house, many tax collectors and sinners came and were sitting[y] with him and his disciples. [11]When the Pharisees saw this, they said to his disciples, "Why does your teacher eat with tax collectors and sinners?" [12]But when he heard this, he said, "Those who are well have no need of a physician, but those who are sick. [13]Go and learn what this means, 'I desire mercy, not sacrifice.' For I have come to call not the righteous but sinners."

The Question about Fasting

14 Then the disciples of John came to him, saying, "Why do we and the Pharisees fast often,[z] but your disciples do not fast?" [15]And Jesus said to them, "The wedding guests cannot mourn as long as the bridegroom is with them, can they? The days will come when the bridegroom is taken away from them, and then they will fast. [16]No one sews a piece of unshrunk cloth on an old cloak, for the patch pulls away from the cloak, and a worse tear is made. [17]Neither is new wine put into old wineskins; otherwise, the skins burst, and the wine is spilled, and the skins are destroyed; but new wine is put into fresh wineskins, and so both are preserved."

A Girl Restored to Life and a Woman Healed

18 While he was saying these things to them, suddenly a leader of the synagogue[a] came in and knelt before him, saying, "My daughter has just died; but come and lay your hand on her, and she will live." [19]And Jesus got up and followed him, with his disciples. [20]Then suddenly a woman who had been suffering from hemorrhages for twelve years came up behind him and touched the fringe of his cloak, [21]for she said to herself, "If I only touch his cloak, I will be made well." [22]Jesus turned, and seeing her he said, "Take heart, daughter; your faith has made you well." And instantly the woman was made well. [23]When Jesus came to the leader's house and saw the flute players and the crowd making a commotion, [24]he said, "Go away; for the girl is not dead but sleeping." And they laughed at him. [25]But when the crowd had been put outside, he went in and took her by the hand, and the girl got up. [26]And the report of this spread throughout that district.

Greek

ἠκολούθησεν αὐτῷ. **10** Καὶ ἐγένετο αὐτοῦ ἀνακειμένου ἐν τῇ οἰκίᾳ, καὶ[c] ἰδοὺ πολλοὶ τελῶναι καὶ ἁμαρτωλοὶ ἐλθόντες συνανέκειντο τῷ Ἰησοῦ καὶ τοῖς μαθηταῖς αὐτοῦ. **11** καὶ ἰδόντες οἱ Φαρισαῖοι ἔλεγον τοῖς μαθηταῖς αὐτοῦ, Διὰ τί μετὰ τῶν τελωνῶν καὶ ἁμαρτωλῶν ἐσθίει ὁ διδάσκαλος ὑμῶν; **12** ὁ δὲ ἀκούσας εἶπεν, Οὐ χρείαν ἔχουσιν οἱ ἰσχύοντες ἰατροῦ ἀλλ' οἱ κακῶς ἔχοντες. **13** πορευθέντες δὲ μάθετε τί ἐστιν, Ἔλεος θέλω καὶ οὐ θυσίαν· οὐ γὰρ ἦλθον καλέσαι δικαίους ἀλλὰ ἁμαρτωλούς.

14 Τότε προσέρχονται αὐτῷ οἱ μαθηταὶ Ἰωάννου λέγοντες, Διὰ τί ἡμεῖς καὶ οἱ Φαρισαῖοι νηστεύομεν [πολλά][d], οἱ δὲ μαθηταί σου οὐ νηστεύουσιν; **15** καὶ εἶπεν αὐτοῖς ὁ Ἰησοῦς, Μὴ δύνανται οἱ υἱοὶ τοῦ νυμφῶνος πενθεῖν ἐφ' ὅσον μετ' αὐτῶν ἐστιν ὁ νυμφίος; ἐλεύσονται δὲ ἡμέραι ὅταν ἀπαρθῇ ἀπ' αὐτῶν ὁ νυμφίος, καὶ τότε νηστεύσουσιν. **16** οὐδεὶς δὲ ἐπιβάλλει ἐπίβλημα ράκους ἀγνάφου ἐπὶ ἱματίῳ παλαιῷ· αἴρει γὰρ τὸ πλήρωμα αὐτοῦ ἀπὸ τοῦ ἱματίου καὶ χεῖρον σχίσμα γίνεται. **17** οὐδὲ βάλλουσιν οἶνον νέον εἰς ἀσκοὺς παλαιούς· εἰ δὲ μή γε, ῥήγνυνται οἱ ἀσκοὶ καὶ ὁ οἶνος ἐκχεῖται καὶ οἱ ἀσκοὶ ἀπόλλυνται· ἀλλὰ βάλλουσιν οἶνον νέον εἰς ἀσκοὺς καινούς, καὶ ἀμφότεροι συντηροῦνται.

18 Ταῦτα αὐτοῦ λαλοῦντος αὐτοῖς ἰδοὺ ἄρχων εἷς ἐλθὼν προσεκύνει αὐτῷ λέγων ὅτι Ἡ θυγάτηρ μου ἄρτι ἐτελεύτησεν· ἀλλὰ ἐλθὼν ἐπίθες τὴν χεῖρά σου ἐπ' αὐτήν, καὶ ζήσεται. **19** καὶ ἐγερθεὶς ὁ Ἰησοῦς ἠκολούθησεν αὐτῷ καὶ οἱ μαθηταὶ αὐτοῦ. **20** Καὶ ἰδοὺ γυνὴ αἱμορροοῦσα δώδεκα ἔτη προσελθοῦσα ὄπισθεν ἥψατο τοῦ κρασπέδου τοῦ ἱματίου αὐτοῦ· **21** ἔλεγεν γὰρ ἐν ἑαυτῇ, Ἐὰν μόνον ἅψωμαι τοῦ ἱματίου αὐτοῦ σωθήσομαι. **22** ὁ δὲ Ἰησοῦς στραφεὶς καὶ ἰδὼν αὐτὴν εἶπεν, Θάρσει, θύγατερ· ἡ πίστις σου σέσωκέν σε. καὶ ἐσώθη ἡ γυνὴ ἀπὸ τῆς ὥρας ἐκείνης. **23** Καὶ ἐλθὼν ὁ Ἰησοῦς εἰς τὴν οἰκίαν τοῦ ἄρχοντος καὶ ἰδὼν τοὺς αὐλητὰς καὶ τὸν ὄχλον θορυβούμενον **24** ἔλεγεν, Ἀναχωρεῖτε, οὐ γὰρ ἀπέθανεν τὸ κοράσιον ἀλλὰ καθεύδει. καὶ κατεγέλων αὐτοῦ. **25** ὅτε δὲ ἐξεβλήθη ὁ ὄχλος εἰσελθὼν ἐκράτησεν τῆς χειρὸς αὐτῆς, καὶ ἠγέρθη τὸ κοράσιον. **26** καὶ ἐξῆλθεν ἡ φήμη αὕτη

NIV

and Matthew got up and followed him.

[10]While Jesus was having dinner at Matthew's house, many tax collectors and "sinners" came and ate with him and his disciples. [11]When the Pharisees saw this, they asked his disciples, "Why does your teacher eat with tax collectors and 'sinners'?" [12]On hearing this, Jesus said, "It is not the healthy who need a doctor, but the sick. [13]But go and learn what this means: 'I desire mercy, not sacrifice.'[a] For I have not come to call the righteous, but sinners."

Jesus Questioned About Fasting

[14]Then John's disciples came and asked him, "How is it that we and the Pharisees fast, but your disciples do not fast?"

[15]Jesus answered, "How can the guests of the bridegroom mourn while he is with them? The time will come when the bridegroom will be taken from them; then they will fast.

[16]"No one sews a patch of unshrunk cloth on an old garment, for the patch will pull away from the garment, making the tear worse. [17]Neither do men pour new wine into old wineskins. If they do, the skins will burst, the wine will run out and the wineskins will be ruined. No, they pour new wine into new wineskins, and both are preserved."

A Dead Girl and a Sick Woman

[18]While he was saying this, a ruler came and knelt before him and said, "My daughter has just died. But come and put your hand on her, and she will live." [19]Jesus got up and went with him, and so did his disciples.

[20]Just then a woman who had been subject to bleeding for twelve years came up behind him and touched the edge of his cloak. [21]She said to herself, "If I only touch his cloak, I will be healed."

[22]Jesus turned and saw her. "Take heart, daughter," he said, "your faith has healed you." And the woman was healed from that moment.

[23]When Jesus entered the ruler's house and saw the flute players and the noisy crowd, [24]he said, "Go away. The girl is not dead but asleep." But they laughed at him. [25]After the crowd had been put outside, he went in and took the girl by the hand, and she got up. [26]News of this spread through all that region.

---

[x] Gk reclined [y] Gk were reclining [z] Other ancient authorities lack often [a] Gk lacks of the synagogue

[c]10 NIV text omits καὶ † [d]14 NIV text and NRSV note z omit πολλά

[a]13 Hosea 6:6

NRSV

Jesus Heals Two Blind Men

27 As Jesus went on from there, two blind men followed him, crying loudly, "Have mercy on us, Son of David!" 28When he entered the house, the blind men came to him; and Jesus said to them, "Do you believe that I am able to do this?" They said to him, "Yes, Lord." 29Then he touched their eyes and said, "According to your faith let it be done to you." 30And their eyes were opened. Then Jesus sternly ordered them, "See that no one knows of this." 31But they went away and spread the news about him throughout that district.

Jesus Heals One Who Was Mute

32 After they had gone away, a demoniac who was mute was brought to him. 33And when the demon had been cast out, the one who had been mute spoke; and the crowds were amazed and said, "Never has anything like this been seen in Israel." 34But the Pharisees said, "By the ruler of the demons he casts out the demons."b

The Harvest Is Great, the Laborers Few

35 Then Jesus went about all the cities and villages, teaching in their synagogues, and proclaiming the good news of the kingdom, and curing every disease and every sickness. 36When he saw the crowds, he had compassion for them, because they were harassed and helpless, like sheep without a shepherd. 37Then he said to his disciples, "The harvest is plentiful, but the laborers are few; 38therefore ask the Lord of the harvest to send out laborers into his harvest."

The Twelve Apostles

10 Then Jesusc summoned his twelve disciples and gave them authority over unclean spirits, to cast them out, and to cure every disease and every sickness. 2These are the names of the twelve apostles: first, Simon, also known as Peter, and his brother Andrew; James son of Zebedee, and his brother John; 3Philip and Bartholomew; Thomas and Matthew the tax collector; James son of Alphaeus, and Thaddaeus;d 4Simon the Cananaean, and Judas Iscariot, the one who betrayed him.

The Mission of the Twelve

5 These twelve Jesus sent out with the

εἰς ὅλην τὴν γῆν ἐκείνην.

27 Καὶ παράγοντι ἐκεῖθεν τῷ Ἰησοῦ ἠκολούθησαν [αὐτῷ] δύο τυφλοὶ κράζοντες καὶ λέγοντες, Ἐλέησον ἡμᾶς, υἱὸς Δαυίδ. 28 ἐλθόντι δὲ εἰς τὴν οἰκίαν προσῆλθον αὐτῷ οἱ τυφλοί, καὶ λέγει αὐτοῖς ὁ Ἰησοῦς, Πιστεύετε ὅτι δύναμαι τοῦτο ποιῆσαι; λέγουσιν αὐτῷ, Ναὶ κύριε. 29 τότε ἥψατο τῶν ὀφθαλμῶν αὐτῶν λέγων, Κατὰ τὴν πίστιν ὑμῶν γενηθήτω ὑμῖν. 30 καὶ ἠνεῴχθησαν αὐτῶν οἱ ὀφθαλμοί. καὶ ἐνεβριμήθη αὐτοῖς ὁ Ἰησοῦς λέγων, Ὁρᾶτε μηδεὶς γινωσκέτω. 31 οἱ δὲ ἐξελθόντες διεφήμισαν αὐτὸν ἐν ὅλῃ τῇ γῇ ἐκείνῃ.

32 Αὐτῶν δὲ ἐξερχομένων ἰδοὺ προσήνεγκαν αὐτῷ ἄνθρωπον κωφὸν δαιμονιζόμενον. 33 καὶ ἐκβληθέντος τοῦ δαιμονίου ἐλάλησεν ὁ κωφός. καὶ ἐθαύμασαν οἱ ὄχλοι λέγοντες, Οὐδέποτε ἐφάνη οὕτως ἐν τῷ Ἰσραήλ. 34 οἱ δὲ Φαρισαῖοι ἔλεγον, Ἐν τῷ ἄρχοντι τῶν δαιμονίων ἐκβάλλει τὰ δαιμόνια.

35 Καὶ περιῆγεν ὁ Ἰησοῦς τὰς πόλεις πάσας καὶ τὰς κώμας διδάσκων ἐν ταῖς συναγωγαῖς αὐτῶν καὶ κηρύσσων τὸ εὐαγγέλιον τῆς βασιλείας καὶ θεραπεύων πᾶσαν νόσον καὶ πᾶσαν μαλακίαν. 36 Ἰδὼν δὲ τοὺς ὄχλους ἐσπλαγχνίσθη περὶ αὐτῶν, ὅτι ἦσαν ἐσκυλμένοι καὶ ἐρριμμένοι ὡσεὶ πρόβατα μὴ ἔχοντα ποιμένα. 37 τότε λέγει τοῖς μαθηταῖς αὐτοῦ, Ὁ μὲν θερισμὸς πολύς, οἱ δὲ ἐργάται ὀλίγοι· 38 δεήθητε οὖν τοῦ κυρίου τοῦ θερισμοῦ ὅπως ἐκβάλῃ ἐργάτας εἰς τὸν θερισμὸν αὐτοῦ.

10 Καὶ προσκαλεσάμενος τοὺς δώδεκα μαθητὰς αὐτοῦ ἔδωκεν αὐτοῖς ἐξουσίαν πνευμάτων ἀκαθάρτων ὥστε ἐκβάλλειν αὐτὰ καὶ θεραπεύειν πᾶσαν νόσον καὶ πᾶσαν μαλακίαν. 2 Τῶν δὲ δώδεκα ἀποστόλων τὰ ὀνόματά ἐστιν ταῦτα· πρῶτος Σίμων ὁ λεγόμενος Πέτρος καὶ Ἀνδρέας ὁ ἀδελφὸς αὐτοῦ, καὶ Ἰάκωβος ὁ τοῦ Ζεβεδαίου καὶ Ἰωάννης ὁ ἀδελφὸς αὐτοῦ, 3 Φίλιππος καὶ Βαρθολομαῖος, Θωμᾶς καὶ Μαθθαῖος ὁ τελώνης, Ἰάκωβος ὁ τοῦ Ἀλφαίου καὶ Θαδδαῖοςa, 4 Σίμων ὁ Καναναῖος καὶ Ἰούδας ὁ Ἰσκαριώτης ὁ καὶ παραδοὺς αὐτόν.

5 Τούτους τοὺς δώδεκα ἀπέστειλεν ὁ Ἰησοῦς παραγγείλας αὐτοῖς λέγων,

NIV

Jesus Heals the Blind and Mute

27As Jesus went on from there, two blind men followed him, calling out, "Have mercy on us, Son of David!"

28When he had gone indoors, the blind men came to him, and he asked them, "Do you believe that I am able to do this?"

"Yes, Lord," they replied.

29Then he touched their eyes and said, "According to your faith will it be done to you"; 30and their sight was restored. Jesus warned them sternly, "See that no one knows about this." 31But they went out and spread the news about him all over that region.

32While they were going out, a man who was demon-possessed and could not talk was brought to Jesus. 33And when the demon was driven out, the man who had been mute spoke. The crowd was amazed and said, "Nothing like this has ever been seen in Israel."

34But the Pharisees said, "It is by the prince of demons that he drives out demons."

The Workers Are Few

35Jesus went through all the towns and villages, teaching in their synagogues, preaching the good news of the kingdom and healing every disease and sickness. 36When he saw the crowds, he had compassion on them, because they were harassed and helpless, like sheep without a shepherd. 37Then he said to his disciples, "The harvest is plentiful but the workers are few. 38Ask the Lord of the harvest, therefore, to send out workers into his harvest field."

Jesus Sends Out the Twelve

10 He called his twelve disciples to him and gave them authority to drive out evila spirits and to heal every disease and sickness.

2These are the names of the twelve apostles: first, Simon (who is called Peter) and his brother Andrew; James son of Zebedee, and his brother John; 3Philip and Bartholomew; Thomas and Matthew the tax collector; James son of Alphaeus, and Thaddaeus; 4Simon the Zealot and Judas Iscariot, who betrayed him.

5These twelve Jesus sent out with the

---

b Other ancient authorities lack this verse   c Gk he
d Other ancient authorities read Lebbaeus, or Lebbaeus called Thaddaeus

a3 NRSV note d Λεββαῖος or Λεββαῖος ὁ ἐπικληθεὶς Θαδδαῖος

a1 Greek unclean

following instructions: "Go nowhere among the Gentiles, and enter no town of the Samaritans, 6but go rather to the lost sheep of the house of Israel. 7As you go, proclaim the good news, 'The kingdom of heaven has come near.'e 8Cure the sick, raise the dead, cleanse the lepers,f cast out demons. You received without payment; give without payment. 9Take no gold, or silver, or copper in your belts, 10no bag for your journey, or two tunics, or sandals, or a staff; for laborers deserve their food. 11Whatever town or village you enter, find out who in it is worthy, and stay there until you leave. 12As you enter the house, greet it. 13If the house is worthy, let your peace come upon it; but if it is not worthy, let your peace return to you. 14If anyone will not welcome you or listen to your words, shake off the dust from your feet as you leave that house or town. 15Truly I tell you, it will be more tolerable for the land of Sodom and Gomorrah on the day of judgment than for that town.

Coming Persecutions

16 "See, I am sending you out like sheep into the midst of wolves; so be wise as serpents and innocent as doves. 17Beware of them, for they will hand you over to councils and flog you in their synagogues; 18and you will be dragged before governors and kings because of me, as a testimony to them and the Gentiles. 19When they hand you over, do not worry about how you are to speak or what you are to say; for what you are to say will be given to you at that time; 20for it is not you who speak, but the Spirit of your Father speaking through you. 21Brother will betray brother to death, and a father his child, and children will rise against parents and have them put to death; 22and you will be hated by all because of my name. But the one who endures to the end will be saved. 23When they persecute you in one town, flee to the next; for truly I tell you, you will not have gone through all the towns of Israel before the Son of Man comes.

24 "A disciple is not above the teacher, nor a slave above the master; 25it is enough

Εἰς ὁδὸν ἐθνῶν μὴ ἀπέλθητε καὶ εἰς πόλιν Σαμαριτῶν μὴ εἰσέλθητε· 6 πορεύεσθε δὲ μᾶλλον πρὸς τὰ πρόβατα τὰ ἀπολωλότα οἴκου Ἰσραήλ. 7 πορευόμενοι δὲ κηρύσσετε λέγοντες ὅτι Ἤγγικεν ἡ βασιλεία τῶν οὐρανῶν. 8 ἀσθενοῦντας θεραπεύετε, νεκροὺς ἐγείρετε, λεπροὺς καθαρίζετε, δαιμόνια ἐκβάλλετε· δωρεὰν ἐλάβετε, δωρεὰν δότε. 9 Μὴ κτήσησθε χρυσὸν μηδὲ ἄργυρον μηδὲ χαλκὸν εἰς τὰς ζώνας ὑμῶν, 10 μὴ πήραν εἰς ὁδὸν μηδὲ δύο χιτῶνας μηδὲ ὑποδήματα μηδὲ ῥάβδον· ἄξιος γὰρ ὁ ἐργάτης τῆς τροφῆς αὐτοῦ. 11 εἰς ἣν δ' ἂν πόλιν ἢ κώμην εἰσέλθητε, ἐξετάσατε τίς ἐν αὐτῇ ἄξιός ἐστιν· κἀκεῖ μείνατε ἕως ἂν ἐξέλθητε. 12 εἰσερχόμενοι δὲ εἰς τὴν οἰκίαν ἀσπάσασθε αὐτήν· 13 καὶ ἐὰν μὲν ᾖ ἡ οἰκία ἀξία, ἐλθάτω ἡ εἰρήνη ὑμῶν ἐπ' αὐτήν, ἐὰν δὲ μὴ ᾖ ἀξία, ἡ εἰρήνη ὑμῶν πρὸς ὑμᾶς ἐπιστραφήτω. 14 καὶ ὃς ἂν μὴ δέξηται ὑμᾶς μηδὲ ἀκούσῃ τοὺς λόγους ὑμῶν, ἐξερχόμενοι ἔξω τῆς οἰκίας ἢ τῆς πόλεως ἐκείνης ἐκτινάξατε τὸν κονιορτὸν τῶν ποδῶν ὑμῶν. 15 ἀμὴν λέγω ὑμῖν, ἀνεκτότερον ἔσται γῇ Σοδόμων καὶ Γομόρρων ἐν ἡμέρᾳ κρίσεως ἢ τῇ πόλει ἐκείνῃ.

16 Ἰδοὺ ἐγὼ ἀποστέλλω ὑμᾶς ὡς πρόβατα ἐν μέσῳ λύκων· γίνεσθε οὖν φρόνιμοι ὡς οἱ ὄφεις καὶ ἀκέραιοι ὡς αἱ περιστεραί. 17 προσέχετε δὲ ἀπὸ τῶν ἀνθρώπων· παραδώσουσιν γὰρ ὑμᾶς εἰς συνέδρια καὶ ἐν ταῖς συναγωγαῖς αὐτῶν μαστιγώσουσιν ὑμᾶς· 18 καὶ ἐπὶ ἡγεμόνας δὲ καὶ βασιλεῖς ἀχθήσεσθε ἕνεκεν ἐμοῦ εἰς μαρτύριον αὐτοῖς καὶ τοῖς ἔθνεσιν. 19 ὅταν δὲ παραδῶσιν ὑμᾶς, μὴ μεριμνήσητε πῶς ἢ τί λαλήσητε· δοθήσεται γὰρ ὑμῖν ἐν ἐκείνῃ τῇ ὥρᾳ τί λαλήσητε· 20 οὐ γὰρ ὑμεῖς ἐστε οἱ λαλοῦντες ἀλλὰ τὸ πνεῦμα τοῦ πατρὸς ὑμῶν τὸ λαλοῦν ἐν ὑμῖν. 21 παραδώσει δὲ ἀδελφὸς ἀδελφὸν εἰς θάνατον καὶ πατὴρ τέκνον, καὶ ἐπαναστήσονται τέκνα ἐπὶ γονεῖς καὶ θανατώσουσιν αὐτούς. 22 καὶ ἔσεσθε μισούμενοι ὑπὸ πάντων διὰ τὸ ὄνομά μου· ὁ δὲ ὑπομείνας εἰς τέλος οὗτος σωθήσεται. 23 ὅταν δὲ διώκωσιν ὑμᾶς ἐν τῇ πόλει ταύτῃ, φεύγετε εἰς τὴν ἑτέραν· ἀμὴν γὰρ λέγω ὑμῖν, οὐ μὴ τελέσητε τὰς πόλεις τοῦb Ἰσραὴλ ἕως ἂν ἔλθῃ ὁ υἱὸς τοῦ ἀνθρώπου.

24 Οὐκ ἔστιν μαθητὴς ὑπὲρ τὸν διδάσκαλον οὐδὲ δοῦλος ὑπὲρ τὸν κύριον

following instructions: "Do not go among the Gentiles or enter any town of the Samaritans. 6Go rather to the lost sheep of Israel. 7As you go, preach this message: 'The kingdom of heaven is near.' 8Heal the sick, raise the dead, cleanse those who have leprosy,b drive out demons. Freely you have received, freely give. 9Do not take along any gold or silver or copper in your belts; 10take no bag for the journey, or extra tunic, or sandals or a staff; for the worker is worth his keep.

11"Whatever town or village you enter, search for some worthy person there and stay at his house until you leave. 12As you enter the home, give it your greeting. 13If the home is deserving, let your peace rest on it; if it is not, let your peace return to you. 14If anyone will not welcome you or listen to your words, shake the dust off your feet when you leave that home or town. 15I tell you the truth, it will be more bearable for Sodom and Gomorrah on the day of judgment than for that town. 16I am sending you out like sheep among wolves. Therefore be as shrewd as snakes and as innocent as doves.

17"Be on your guard against men; they will hand you over to the local councils and flog you in their synagogues. 18On my account you will be brought before governors and kings as witnesses to them and to the Gentiles. 19But when they arrest you, do not worry about what to say or how to say it. At that time you will be given what to say, 20for it will not be you speaking, but the Spirit of your Father speaking through you.

21"Brother will betray brother to death, and a father his child; children will rebel against their parents and have them put to death. 22All men will hate you because of me, but he who stands firm to the end will be saved. 23When you are persecuted in one place, flee to another. I tell you the truth, you will not finish going through the cities of Israel before the Son of Man comes.

24"A student is not above his teacher, nor a servant above his master. 25It is enough

---

e Or *is at hand*   f The terms *leper* and *leprosy* can refer to several diseases

b23 NIV text omits τοῦ †

b8 The Greek word was used for various diseases affecting the skin—not necessarily leprosy.

for the disciple to be like the teacher, and the slave like the master. If they have called the master of the house Beelzebul, how much more will they malign those of his household!

Whom to Fear

26 "So have no fear of them; for nothing is covered up that will not be uncovered, and nothing secret that will not become known. 27What I say to you in the dark, tell in the light; and what you hear whispered, proclaim from the housetops. 28Do not fear those who kill the body but cannot kill the soul; rather fear him who can destroy both soul and body in hell.g 29Are not two sparrows sold for a penny? Yet not one of them will fall to the ground apart from your Father. 30And even the hairs of your head are all counted. 31So do not be afraid; you are of more value than many sparrows.

32 "Everyone therefore who acknowledges me before others, I also will acknowledge before my Father in heaven; 33but whoever denies me before others, I also will deny before my Father in heaven.

Not Peace, but a Sword

34 "Do not think that I have come to bring peace to the earth; I have not come to bring peace, but a sword.
35   For I have come to set a man against
     his father,
    and a daughter against her mother,
    and a daughter-in-law against her
      mother-in-law;
36   and one's foes will be members of
     one's own household.

37Whoever loves father or mother more than me is not worthy of me; and whoever loves son or daughter more than me is not worthy of me; 38and whoever does not take up the cross and follow me is not worthy of me. 39Those who find their life will lose it, and those who lose their life for my sake will find it.

Rewards

40 "Whoever welcomes you welcomes me, and whoever welcomes me welcomes the one who sent me. 41Whoever welcomes a prophet in the name of a prophet will receive a prophet's reward; and whoever welcomes a righteous person in the name of a righteous person will receive the

αὐτοῦ. **25** ἀρκετὸν τῷ μαθητῇ ἵνα γένηται ὡς ὁ διδάσκαλος αὐτοῦ καὶ ὁ δοῦλος ὡς ὁ κύριος αὐτοῦ. εἰ τὸν οἰκοδεσπότην Βεελζεβοὺλc ἐπεκάλεσαν, πόσῳ μᾶλλον τοὺς οἰκιακοὺς αὐτοῦ. **26** Μὴ οὖν φοβηθῆτε αὐτούς· οὐδὲν γάρ ἐστιν κεκαλυμμένον ὃ οὐκ ἀποκαλυφθήσεται καὶ κρυπτὸν ὃ οὐ γνωσθήσεται. **27** ὃ λέγω ὑμῖν ἐν τῇ σκοτίᾳ εἴπατε ἐν τῷ φωτί, καὶ ὃ εἰς τὸ οὖς ἀκούετε κηρύξατε ἐπὶ τῶν δωμάτων. **28** καὶ μὴ φοβεῖσθε ἀπὸ τῶν ἀποκτεννόντων τὸ σῶμα, τὴν δὲ ψυχὴν μὴ δυναμένων ἀποκτεῖναι· φοβεῖσθε δὲ μᾶλλον τὸν δυνάμενον καὶ ψυχὴν καὶ σῶμα ἀπολέσαι ἐν γεέννῃ. **29** οὐχὶ δύο στρουθία ἀσσαρίου πωλεῖται; καὶ ἓν ἐξ αὐτῶν οὐ πεσεῖται ἐπὶ τὴν γῆν ἄνευ τοῦ πατρὸς ὑμῶν. **30** ὑμῶν δὲ καὶ αἱ τρίχες τῆς κεφαλῆς πᾶσαι ἠριθμημέναι εἰσίν. **31** μὴ οὖν φοβεῖσθε· πολλῶν στρουθίων διαφέρετε ὑμεῖς.

32 Πᾶς οὖν ὅστις ὁμολογήσει ἐν ἐμοὶ ἔμπροσθεν τῶν ἀνθρώπων, ὁμολογήσω κἀγὼ ἐν αὐτῷ ἔμπροσθεν τοῦ πατρός μου τοῦ ἐν [τοῖς]d οὐρανοῖς· **33** ὅστις δ᾽ ἂν ἀρνήσηταί με ἔμπροσθεν τῶν ἀνθρώπων, ἀρνήσομαι κἀγὼ αὐτὸν ἔμπροσθεν τοῦ πατρός μου τοῦ ἐν [τοῖς]e οὐρανοῖς.

34 Μὴ νομίσητε ὅτι ἦλθον βαλεῖν εἰρήνην ἐπὶ τὴν γῆν· οὐκ ἦλθον βαλεῖν εἰρήνην ἀλλὰ μάχαιραν. **35** ἦλθον γὰρ διχάσαι
    ἄνθρωπον **κατὰ τοῦ πατρὸς αὐτοῦ**
    καὶ **θυγατέρα κατὰ τῆς μητρὸς**
      αὐτῆς
    καὶ *νύμφην* **κατὰ τῆς πενθερᾶς**
      αὐτῆς,
36 καὶ **ἐχθροὶ τοῦ ἀνθρώπου οἱ**
     οἰκιακοὶ αὐτοῦ.

37 Ὁ φιλῶν πατέρα ἢ μητέρα ὑπὲρ ἐμὲ οὐκ ἔστιν μου ἄξιος, καὶ ὁ φιλῶν υἱὸν ἢ θυγατέρα ὑπὲρ ἐμὲ οὐκ ἔστιν μου ἄξιος· **38** καὶ ὃς οὐ λαμβάνει τὸν σταυρὸν αὐτοῦ καὶ ἀκολουθεῖ ὀπίσω μου, οὐκ ἔστιν μου ἄξιος. **39** ὁ εὑρὼν τὴν ψυχὴν αὐτοῦ ἀπολέσει αὐτήν, καὶ ὁ ἀπολέσας τὴν ψυχὴν αὐτοῦ ἕνεκεν ἐμοῦ εὑρήσει αὐτήν.

40 Ὁ δεχόμενος ὑμᾶς ἐμὲ δέχεται, καὶ ὁ ἐμὲ δεχόμενος δέχεται τὸν ἀποστείλαντά με. **41** ὁ δεχόμενος προφήτην εἰς ὄνομα προφήτου μισθὸν προφήτου λήμψεται, καὶ ὁ δεχόμενος δίκαιον εἰς ὄνομα δικαίου μισθὸν

for the student to be like his teacher, and the servant like his master. If the head of the house has been called Beelzebub,c how much more the members of his household!

26"So do not be afraid of them. There is nothing concealed that will not be disclosed, or hidden that will not be made known. 27What I tell you in the dark, speak in the daylight; what is whispered in your ear, proclaim from the roofs. 28Do not be afraid of those who kill the body but cannot kill the soul. Rather, be afraid of the One who can destroy both soul and body in hell. 29Are not two sparrows sold for a penny? Yet not one of them will fall to the ground apart from the will of your Father. 30And even the very hairs of your head are all numbered. 31So don't be afraid; you are worth more than many sparrows.

32"Whoever acknowledges me before men, I will also acknowledge him before my Father in heaven. 33But whoever disowns me before men, I will disown him before my Father in heaven.

34"Do not suppose that I have come to bring peace to the earth. I did not come to bring peace, but a sword. 35For I have come to turn

" 'a man against his father,
    a daughter against her mother,
  a daughter-in-law against her mother-
     in-law—
36   a man's enemies will be the members
     of his own household.'e

37"Anyone who loves his father or mother more than me is not worthy of me; anyone who loves his son or daughter more than me is not worthy of me; 38and anyone who does not take his cross and follow me is not worthy of me. 39Whoever finds his life will lose it, and whoever loses his life for my sake will find it.

40"He who receives you receives me, and he who receives me receives the one who sent me. 41Anyone who receives a prophet because he is a prophet will receive a prophet's reward, and anyone who receives a righteous man because he is a righteous man will receive a righteous

---

g Gk *Gehenna*

c25 NIV note Βεελζεβοὺλ †   d32 NIV text omits τοῖς †
e33 NIV text omits τοῖς †

c25 Greek *Beezeboul* or *Beelzeboul*   d29 Greek *an assarion*
e36 Micah 7:6

reward of the righteous; ⁴²and whoever gives even a cup of cold water to one of these little ones in the name of a disciple— truly I tell you, none of these will lose their reward."

11 Now when Jesus had finished instructing his twelve disciples, he went on from there to teach and proclaim his message in their cities.

Messengers from John the Baptist

2 When John heard in prison what the Messiah[h] was doing, he sent word by his[i] disciples ³and said to him, "Are you the one who is to come, or are we to wait for another?" ⁴Jesus answered them, "Go and tell John what you hear and see: ⁵the blind receive their sight, the lame walk, the lepers[j] are cleansed, the deaf hear, the dead are raised, and the poor have good news brought to them. ⁶And blessed is anyone who takes no offense at me."

Jesus Praises John the Baptist

7 As they went away, Jesus began to speak to the crowds about John: "What did you go out into the wilderness to look at? A reed shaken by the wind? ⁸What then did you go out to see? Someone[k] dressed in soft robes? Look, those who wear soft robes are in royal palaces. ⁹What then did you go out to see? A prophet?[l] Yes, I tell you, and more than a prophet. ¹⁰This is the one about whom it is written,

'See, I am sending my messenger
      ahead of you,
   who will prepare your way before
      you.'

¹¹Truly I tell you, among those born of women no one has arisen greater than John the Baptist; yet the least in the kingdom of heaven is greater than he. ¹²From the days of John the Baptist until now the kingdom of heaven has suffered violence,[m] and the violent take it by force. ¹³For all the prophets and the law prophesied until John came; ¹⁴and if you are willing to accept it, he is Elijah who is to come. ¹⁵Let anyone with ears[n] listen!

16 "But to what will I compare this generation? It is like children sitting in the marketplaces and calling to one another,

17   'We played the flute for you, and you
         did not dance;

δικαίου λήμψεται. **42** καὶ ὃς ἂν ποτίσῃ ἕνα τῶν μικρῶν τούτων ποτήριον ψυχροῦ μόνον εἰς ὄνομα μαθητοῦ, ἀμὴν λέγω ὑμῖν, οὐ μὴ ἀπολέσῃ τὸν μισθὸν αὐτοῦ.

11 Καὶ ἐγένετο ὅτε ἐτέλεσεν ὁ Ἰησοῦς διατάσσων τοῖς δώδεκα μαθηταῖς αὐτοῦ, μετέβη ἐκεῖθεν τοῦ διδάσκειν καὶ κηρύσσειν ἐν ταῖς πόλεσιν αὐτῶν.

2 Ὁ δὲ Ἰωάννης ἀκούσας ἐν τῷ δεσμωτηρίῳ τὰ ἔργα τοῦ Χριστοῦ πέμψας διὰ[a] τῶν μαθητῶν αὐτοῦ **3** εἶπεν αὐτῷ, Σὺ εἶ ὁ ἐρχόμενος ἢ ἕτερον προσδοκῶμεν; **4** καὶ ἀποκριθεὶς ὁ Ἰησοῦς εἶπεν αὐτοῖς, Πορευθέντες ἀπαγγείλατε Ἰωάννῃ ἃ ἀκούετε καὶ βλέπετε· **5** τυφλοὶ ἀναβλέπουσιν καὶ χωλοὶ περιπατοῦσιν, λεπροὶ καθαρίζονται καὶ κωφοὶ ἀκούουσιν, καὶ νεκροὶ ἐγείρονται καὶ πτωχοὶ εὐαγγελίζονται· **6** καὶ μακάριός ἐστιν ὃς ἐὰν μὴ σκανδαλισθῇ ἐν ἐμοί. **7** Τούτων δὲ πορευομένων ἤρξατο ὁ Ἰησοῦς λέγειν τοῖς ὄχλοις περὶ Ἰωάννου, Τί ἐξήλθατε εἰς τὴν ἔρημον θεάσασθαι; κάλαμον ὑπὸ ἀνέμου σαλευόμενον; **8** ἀλλὰ τί ἐξήλθατε ἰδεῖν; ἄνθρωπον ἐν μαλακοῖς ἠμφιεσμένον; ἰδοὺ οἱ τὰ μαλακὰ φοροῦντες ἐν τοῖς οἴκοις τῶν βασιλέων εἰσίν. **9** ἀλλὰ τί ἐξήλθατε ἰδεῖν; προφήτην;[b] ναὶ λέγω ὑμῖν, καὶ περισσότερον προφήτου. **10** οὗτός ἐστιν περὶ οὗ γέγραπται,

Ἰδοὺ ἐγὼ ἀποστέλλω τὸν ἄγγελόν
   μου πρὸ προσώπου σου,
ὃς κατασκευάσει τὴν ὁδόν σου
   ἔμπροσθέν σου.

11 ἀμὴν λέγω ὑμῖν· οὐκ ἐγήγερται ἐν γεννητοῖς γυναικῶν μείζων Ἰωάννου τοῦ βαπτιστοῦ· ὁ δὲ μικρότερος ἐν τῇ βασιλείᾳ τῶν οὐρανῶν μείζων αὐτοῦ ἐστιν. **12** ἀπὸ δὲ τῶν ἡμερῶν Ἰωάννου τοῦ βαπτιστοῦ ἕως ἄρτι ἡ βασιλεία τῶν οὐρανῶν βιάζεται καὶ βιασταὶ ἁρπάζουσιν αὐτήν. **13** πάντες γὰρ οἱ προφῆται καὶ ὁ νόμος ἕως Ἰωάννου ἐπροφήτευσαν· **14** καὶ εἰ θέλετε δέξασθαι, αὐτός ἐστιν Ἡλίας ὁ μέλλων ἔρχεσθαι. **15** ὁ ἔχων ὦτα[c] ἀκουέτω.

16 Τίνι δὲ ὁμοιώσω τὴν γενεὰν ταύτην; ὁμοία ἐστὶν παιδίοις καθημένοις ἐν ταῖς ἀγοραῖς ἃ προσφωνοῦντα τοῖς ἑτέροις **17** λέγουσιν,

Ηὐλήσαμεν ὑμῖν καὶ οὐκ ὠρχήσασθε,

man's reward. ⁴²And if anyone gives even a cup of cold water to one of these little ones because he is my disciple, I tell you the truth, he will certainly not lose his reward."

Jesus and John the Baptist

11 After Jesus had finished instructing his twelve disciples, he went on from there to teach and preach in the towns of Galilee.[a]

²When John heard in prison what Christ was doing, he sent his disciples ³to ask him, "Are you the one who was to come, or should we expect someone else?"

⁴Jesus replied, "Go back and report to John what you hear and see: ⁵The blind receive sight, the lame walk, those who have leprosy[b] are cured, the deaf hear, the dead are raised, and the good news is preached to the poor. ⁶Blessed is the man who does not fall away on account of me."

⁷As John's disciples were leaving, Jesus began to speak to the crowd about John: "What did you go out into the desert to see? A reed swayed by the wind? ⁸If not, what did you go out to see? A man dressed in fine clothes? No, those who wear fine clothes are in kings' palaces. ⁹Then what did you go out to see? A prophet? Yes, I tell you, and more than a prophet. ¹⁰This is the one about whom it is written:

" 'I will send my messenger ahead of
      you,
   who will prepare your way before
      you.'[c]

¹¹I tell you the truth: Among those born of women there has not risen anyone greater than John the Baptist; yet he who is least in the kingdom of heaven is greater than he. ¹²From the days of John the Baptist until now, the kingdom of heaven has been forcefully advancing, and forceful men lay hold of it. ¹³For all the Prophets and the Law prophesied until John. ¹⁴And if you are willing to accept it, he is the Elijah who was to come. ¹⁵He who has ears, let him hear.

¹⁶"To what can I compare this generation? They are like children sitting in the marketplaces and calling out to others:

¹⁷" 'We played the flute for you,
      and you did not dance;

---

h Or the Christ   i Other ancient authorities read two of his   j The terms leper and leprosy can refer to several diseases   k Or Why then did you go out? To see someone   l Other ancient authorities read Why then did you go out? To see a prophet?   m Or has been coming violently   n Other ancient authorities add to hear

a2 NRSV note i δύο τῶν μαθητῶν   b9 NRSV note l ἐξήλθατε; προφήτην ἰδεῖν;   c15 NRSV note n adds ἀκούειν

a1 Greek in their towns   b5 The Greek word was used for various diseases affecting the skin—not necessarily leprosy.   c10 Mal. 3:1

we wailed, and you did not mourn.' ¹⁸For John came neither eating nor drinking, and they say, 'He has a demon'; ¹⁹the Son of Man came eating and drinking, and they say, 'Look, a glutton and a drunkard, a friend of tax collectors and sinners!' Yet wisdom is vindicated by her deeds."ᵒ

Woes to Unrepentant Cities

20 Then he began to reproach the cities in which most of his deeds of power had been done, because they did not repent. ²¹"Woe to you, Chorazin! Woe to you, Bethsaida! For if the deeds of power done in you had been done in Tyre and Sidon, they would have repented long ago in sackcloth and ashes. ²²But I tell you, on the day of judgment it will be more tolerable for Tyre and Sidon than for you. ²³And you, Capernaum,

will you be exalted to heaven?

No, you will be brought down to Hades.

For if the deeds of power done in you had been done in Sodom, it would have remained until this day. ²⁴But I tell you that on the day of judgment it will be more tolerable for the land of Sodom than for you."

Jesus Thanks His Father

25 At that time Jesus said, "I thankᴾ you, Father, Lord of heaven and earth, because you have hidden these things from the wise and the intelligent and have revealed them to infants; ²⁶yes, Father, for such was your gracious will.q ²⁷All things have been handed over to me by my Father; and no one knows the Son except the Father, and no one knows the Father except the Son and anyone to whom the Son chooses to reveal him.

28 "Come to me, all you that are weary and are carrying heavy burdens, and I will give you rest. ²⁹Take my yoke upon you, and learn from me; for I am gentle and humble in heart, and you will find rest for your souls. ³⁰For my yoke is easy, and my burden is light."

Plucking Grain on the Sabbath

12 At that time Jesus went through the grainfields on the sabbath; his disciples were hungry, and they began to pluck heads of grain and to eat. ²When the Pharisees saw it, they said to him, "Look, your disciples are doing what is not lawful

ἐθρηνήσαμεν καὶ οὐκ ἐκόψασθε. **18** ἦλθεν γὰρ Ἰωάννης μήτε ἐσθίων μήτε πίνων, καὶ λέγουσιν, Δαιμόνιον ἔχει. **19** ἦλθεν ὁ υἱὸς τοῦ ἀνθρώπου ἐσθίων καὶ πίνων, καὶ λέγουσιν, Ἰδοὺ ἄνθρωπος φάγος καὶ οἰνοπότης, τελωνῶν φίλος καὶ ἁμαρτωλῶν. καὶ ἐδικαιώθη ἡ σοφία ἀπὸ τῶν ἔργωνᵈ αὐτῆς.

20 Τότε ἤρξατοᵉ ὀνειδίζειν τὰς πόλεις ἐν αἷς ἐγένοντο αἱ πλεῖσται δυνάμεις αὐτοῦ, ὅτι οὐ μετενόησαν· **21** Οὐαί σοι, Χοραζίν, οὐαί σοι, Βηθσαϊδά· ὅτι εἰ ἐν Τύρῳ καὶ Σιδῶνι ἐγένοντο αἱ δυνάμεις αἱ γενόμεναι ἐν ὑμῖν, πάλαι ἂν ἐν σάκκῳ καὶ σποδῷ μετενόησαν. **22** πλὴν λέγω ὑμῖν, Τύρῳ καὶ Σιδῶνι ἀνεκτότερον ἔσται ἐν ἡμέρᾳ κρίσεως ἢ ὑμῖν. **23** καὶ σύ, Καφαρναούμ,

μὴ ἕως οὐρανοῦ ὑψωθήσῃ;

ἕως ᾅδου καταβήσῃ·

ὅτι εἰ ἐν Σοδόμοις ἐγενήθησαν αἱ δυνάμεις αἱ γενόμεναι ἐν σοί, ἔμεινεν ἂν μέχρι τῆς σήμερον. **24** πλὴν λέγω ὑμῖν ὅτι γῇ Σοδόμων ἀνεκτότερον ἔσται ἐν ἡμέρᾳ κρίσεως ἢ σοί.

25 Ἐν ἐκείνῳ τῷ καιρῷ ἀποκριθεὶς ὁ Ἰησοῦς εἶπεν, Ἐξομολογοῦμαί σοι, πάτερ, κύριε τοῦ οὐρανοῦ καὶ τῆς γῆς, ὅτι ἔκρυψας ταῦτα ἀπὸ σοφῶν καὶ συνετῶν καὶ ἀπεκάλυψας αὐτὰ νηπίοις· **26** ναὶ ὁ πατήρ, ὅτι οὕτως εὐδοκία ἐγένετο ἔμπροσθέν σου. **27** Πάντα μοι παρεδόθη ὑπὸ τοῦ πατρός μου, καὶ οὐδεὶς ἐπιγινώσκει τὸν υἱὸν εἰ μὴ ὁ πατήρ, οὐδὲ τὸν πατέρα τις ἐπιγινώσκει εἰ μὴ ὁ υἱὸς καὶ ᾧ ἐὰν βούληται ὁ υἱὸς ἀποκαλύψαι. **28** Δεῦτε πρός με πάντες οἱ κοπιῶντες καὶ πεφορτισμένοι, κἀγὼ ἀναπαύσω ὑμᾶς. **29** ἄρατε τὸν ζυγόν μου ἐφ' ὑμᾶς καὶ μάθετε ἀπ' ἐμοῦ, ὅτι πραΰς εἰμι καὶ ταπεινὸς τῇ καρδίᾳ, καὶ εὑρήσετε ἀνάπαυσιν ταῖς ψυχαῖς ὑμῶν· **30** ὁ γὰρ ζυγός μου χρηστὸς καὶ τὸ φορτίον μου ἐλαφρόν ἐστιν.

12 Ἐν ἐκείνῳ τῷ καιρῷ ἐπορεύθη ὁ Ἰησοῦς τοῖς σάββασιν διὰ τῶν σπορίμων· οἱ δὲ μαθηταὶ αὐτοῦ ἐπείνασαν καὶ ἤρξαντο τίλλειν στάχυας καὶ ἐσθίειν. **2** οἱ δὲ Φαρισαῖοι ἰδόντες εἶπαν αὐτῷ, Ἰδοὺ οἱ μαθηταί σου ποιοῦσιν ὃ οὐκ ἔξεστιν ποιεῖν ἐν

we sang a dirge,

and you did not mourn.'

¹⁸For John came neither eating nor drinking, and they say, 'He has a demon.' ¹⁹The Son of Man came eating and drinking, and they say, 'Here is a glutton and a drunkard, a friend of tax collectors and "sinners." ' But wisdom is proved right by her actions."

Woe on Unrepentant Cities

²⁰Then Jesus began to denounce the cities in which most of his miracles had been performed, because they did not repent. ²¹"Woe to you, Korazin! Woe to you, Bethsaida! If the miracles that were performed in you had been performed in Tyre and Sidon, they would have repented long ago in sackcloth and ashes. ²²But I tell you, it will be more bearable for Tyre and Sidon on the day of judgment than for you. ²³And you, Capernaum, will you be lifted up to the skies? No, you will go down to the depths.ᵈ If the miracles that were performed in you had been performed in Sodom, it would have remained to this day. ²⁴But I tell you that it will be more bearable for Sodom on the day of judgment than for you."

Rest for the Weary

²⁵At that time Jesus said, "I praise you, Father, Lord of heaven and earth, because you have hidden these things from the wise and learned, and revealed them to little children. ²⁶Yes, Father, for this was your good pleasure.

²⁷"All things have been committed to me by my Father. No one knows the Son except the Father, and no one knows the Father except the Son and those to whom the Son chooses to reveal him.

²⁸"Come to me, all you who are weary and burdened, and I will give you rest. ²⁹Take my yoke upon you and learn from me, for I am gentle and humble in heart, and you will find rest for your souls. ³⁰For my yoke is easy and my burden is light."

Lord of the Sabbath

12 At that time Jesus went through the grainfields on the Sabbath. His disciples were hungry and began to pick some heads of grain and eat them. ²When the Pharisees saw this, they said to him, "Look! Your disciples are doing what is

---

ᵒ Other ancient authorities read *children*   ᴾ Or *praise*
q Or *for so it was well-pleasing in your sight*   ᵈ19 NRSV note ᵒ τέκνων   ᵉ20 NIV text adds ὁ Ἰησοῦς   ᵈ23 Greek *Hades*

to do on the sabbath." [3]He said to them, "Have you not read what David did when he and his companions were hungry? [4]He entered the house of God and ate the bread of the Presence, which it was not lawful for him or his companions to eat, but only for the priests. [5]Or have you not read in the law that on the sabbath the priests in the temple break the sabbath and yet are guiltless? [6]I tell you, something greater than the temple is here. [7]But if you had known what this means, 'I desire mercy and not sacrifice,' you would not have condemned the guiltless. [8]For the Son of Man is lord of the sabbath."

The Man with a Withered Hand

9 He left that place and entered their synagogue; [10]a man was there with a withered hand, and they asked him, "Is it lawful to cure on the sabbath?" so that they might accuse him. [11]He said to them, "Suppose one of you has only one sheep and it falls into a pit on the sabbath; will you not lay hold of it and lift it out? [12]How much more valuable is a human being than a sheep! So it is lawful to do good on the sabbath." [13]Then he said to the man, "Stretch out your hand." He stretched it out, and it was restored, as sound as the other. [14]But the Pharisees went out and conspired against him, how to destroy him.

God's Chosen Servant

15 When Jesus became aware of this, he departed. Many crowds[r] followed him, and he cured all of them, [16]and he ordered them not to make him known. [17]This was to fulfill what had been spoken through the prophet Isaiah:

[18] "Here is my servant, whom I have
    chosen,
  my beloved, with whom my soul is
    well pleased.
  I will put my Spirit upon him,
    and he will proclaim justice to the
    Gentiles.
[19] He will not wrangle or cry aloud,
    nor will anyone hear his voice in the
    streets.
[20] He will not break a bruised reed
    or quench a smoldering wick
  until he brings justice to victory.
[21]   And in his name the Gentiles will
    hope."

σαββάτῳ. **3** ὁ δὲ εἶπεν αὐτοῖς, Οὐκ ἀνέγνωτε τί ἐποίησεν Δαυὶδ ὅτε ἐπείνασεν καὶ οἱ μετ' αὐτοῦ, **4** πῶς εἰσῆλθεν εἰς τὸν οἶκον τοῦ θεοῦ καὶ τοὺς ἄρτους τῆς προθέσεως ἔφαγον, ὃ οὐκ ἐξὸν ἦν αὐτῷ φαγεῖν οὐδὲ τοῖς μετ' αὐτοῦ εἰ μὴ τοῖς ἱερεῦσιν μόνοις; **5** ἢ οὐκ ἀνέγνωτε ἐν τῷ νόμῳ ὅτι τοῖς σάββασιν οἱ ἱερεῖς ἐν τῷ ἱερῷ τὸ σάββατον βεβηλοῦσιν καὶ ἀναίτιοί εἰσιν; **6** λέγω δὲ ὑμῖν ὅτι τοῦ ἱεροῦ μεῖζόν ἐστιν ὧδε. **7** εἰ δὲ ἐγνώκειτε τί ἐστιν, Ἔλεος θέλω καὶ οὐ θυσίαν, οὐκ ἂν κατεδικάσατε τοὺς ἀναιτίους. **8** κύριος γάρ ἐστιν τοῦ σαββάτου ὁ υἱὸς τοῦ ἀνθρώπου.

9 Καὶ μεταβὰς ἐκεῖθεν ἦλθεν εἰς τὴν συναγωγὴν αὐτῶν· **10** καὶ ἰδοὺ ἄνθρωπος χεῖρα ἔχων ξηράν. καὶ ἐπηρώτησαν αὐτὸν λέγοντες, Εἰ ἔξεστιν τοῖς σάββασιν θεραπεῦσαι; ἵνα κατηγορήσωσιν αὐτοῦ. **11** ὁ δὲ εἶπεν αὐτοῖς, Τίς ἔσται ἐξ ὑμῶν ἄνθρωπος ὃς ἕξει πρόβατον ἓν καὶ ἐὰν ἐμπέσῃ τοῦτο τοῖς σάββασιν εἰς βόθυνον, οὐχὶ κρατήσει αὐτὸ καὶ ἐγερεῖ; **12** πόσῳ οὖν διαφέρει ἄνθρωπος προβάτου. ὥστε ἔξεστιν τοῖς σάββασιν καλῶς ποιεῖν. **13** τότε λέγει τῷ ἀνθρώπῳ, Ἔκτεινόν σου τὴν χεῖρα. καὶ ἐξέτεινεν καὶ ἀπεκατεστάθη ὑγιὴς ὡς ἡ ἄλλη. **14** ἐξελθόντες δὲ οἱ Φαρισαῖοι συμβούλιον ἔλαβον κατ' αὐτοῦ ὅπως αὐτὸν ἀπολέσωσιν.

15 Ὁ δὲ Ἰησοῦς γνοὺς ἀνεχώρησεν ἐκεῖθεν. καὶ ἠκολούθησαν αὐτῷ [ὄχλοι][a] πολλοί, καὶ ἐθεράπευσεν αὐτοὺς πάντας **16** καὶ ἐπετίμησεν αὐτοῖς ἵνα μὴ φανερὸν αὐτὸν ποιήσωσιν, **17** ἵνα πληρωθῇ τὸ ῥηθὲν διὰ Ἠσαΐου τοῦ προφήτου λέγοντος,
18 Ἰδοὺ ὁ παῖς μου ὃν ᾑρέτισα,
  ὁ ἀγαπητός μου εἰς ὃν
    εὐδόκησεν ἡ ψυχή μου·
  θήσω τὸ πνεῦμά μου ἐπ' αὐτόν,
    καὶ κρίσιν τοῖς ἔθνεσιν ἀπαγγελεῖ.
19 οὐκ ἐρίσει οὐδὲ κραυγάσει,
  οὐδὲ ἀκούσει τις ἐν ταῖς
    πλατείαις τὴν φωνὴν αὐτοῦ.
20 κάλαμον συντετριμμένον οὐ
    κατεάξει
  καὶ λίνον τυφόμενον οὐ σβέσει,
    ἕως ἂν ἐκβάλῃ εἰς νῖκος τὴν κρίσιν.
21 καὶ τῷ ὀνόματι αὐτοῦ ἔθνη
    ἐλπιοῦσιν.

unlawful on the Sabbath."

[3]He answered, "Haven't you read what David did when he and his companions were hungry? [4]He entered the house of God, and he and his companions ate the consecrated bread—which was not lawful for them to do, but only for the priests. [5]Or haven't you read in the Law that on the Sabbath the priests in the temple desecrate the day and yet are innocent? [6]I tell you that one[a] greater than the temple is here. [7]If you had known what these words mean, 'I desire mercy, not sacrifice,'[b] you would not have condemned the innocent. [8]For the Son of Man is Lord of the Sabbath."

[9]Going on from that place, he went into their synagogue, [10]and a man with a shriveled hand was there. Looking for a reason to accuse Jesus, they asked him, "Is it lawful to heal on the Sabbath?"

[11]He said to them, "If any of you has a sheep and it falls into a pit on the Sabbath, will you not take hold of it and lift it out? [12]How much more valuable is a man than a sheep! Therefore it is lawful to do good on the Sabbath."

[13]Then he said to the man, "Stretch out your hand." So he stretched it out and it was completely restored, just as sound as the other. [14]But the Pharisees went out and plotted how they might kill Jesus.

God's Chosen Servant

[15]Aware of this, Jesus withdrew from that place. Many followed him, and he healed all their sick, [16]warning them not to tell who he was. [17]This was to fulfill what was spoken through the prophet Isaiah:

[18]"Here is my servant whom I have
    chosen,
  the one I love, in whom I delight;
  I will put my Spirit on him,
    and he will proclaim justice to the
    nations.
[19]He will not quarrel or cry out;
  no one will hear his voice in the
    streets.
[20]A bruised reed he will not break,
  and a smoldering wick he will not
    snuff out,
  till he leads justice to victory.
[21]   In his name the nations will put their
    hope."[c]

---

[r] Other ancient authorities lack *crowds*   [a]15 NIV text and NRSV note r omit ὄχλοι   [a]6 Or *something*; also in verses 41 and 42   [b]7 Hosea 6:6
[c]21 Isaiah 42:1-4

Jesus and Beelzebul

22 Then they brought to him a demoniac who was blind and mute; and he cured him, so that the one who had been mute could speak and see. 23All the crowds were amazed and said, "Can this be the Son of David?" 24But when the Pharisees heard it, they said, "It is only by Beelzebul, the ruler of the demons, that this fellow casts out the demons." 25He knew what they were thinking and said to them, "Every kingdom divided against itself is laid waste, and no city or house divided against itself will stand. 26If Satan casts out Satan, he is divided against himself; how then will his kingdom stand? 27If I cast out demons by Beelzebul, by whom do your own exorcists[s] cast them out? Therefore they will be your judges. 28But if it is by the Spirit of God that I cast out demons, then the kingdom of God has come to you. 29Or how can one enter a strong man's house and plunder his property, without first tying up the strong man? Then indeed the house can be plundered. 30Whoever is not with me is against me, and whoever does not gather with me scatters. 31Therefore I tell you, people will be forgiven for every sin and blasphemy, but blasphemy against the Spirit will not be forgiven. 32Whoever speaks a word against the Son of Man will be forgiven, but whoever speaks against the Holy Spirit will not be forgiven, either in this age or in the age to come.

A Tree and Its Fruit

33 "Either make the tree good, and its fruit good; or make the tree bad, and its fruit bad; for the tree is known by its fruit. 34You brood of vipers! How can you speak good things, when you are evil? For out of the abundance of the heart the mouth speaks. 35The good person brings good things out of a good treasure, and the evil person brings evil things out of an evil treasure. 36I tell you, on the day of judgment you will have to give an account for every careless word you utter; 37for by your words you will be justified, and by your words you will be condemned."

The Sign of Jonah

38 Then some of the scribes and Pharisees said to him, "Teacher, we wish to see

---

22 Τότε προσηνέχθη αὐτῷ δαιμονιζό-μενος τυφλὸς καὶ κωφός[b], καὶ ἐθεράπευ-σεν αὐτόν, ὥστε τὸν κωφὸν λαλεῖν καὶ βλέπειν. **23** καὶ ἐξίσταντο πάντες οἱ ὄχλοι καὶ ἔλεγον, Μήτι οὗτός ἐστιν ὁ υἱὸς Δαυίδ; **24** οἱ δὲ Φαρισαῖοι ἀκού-σαντες εἶπον, Οὗτος οὐκ ἐκβάλλει τὰ δαιμόνια εἰ μὴ ἐν τῷ Βεελζεβοὺλ[c] ἄρχοντι τῶν δαιμονίων. **25** εἰδὼς δὲ τὰς ἐνθυμήσεις αὐτῶν εἶπεν αὐτοῖς, Πᾶσα βασιλεία μερισθεῖσα καθ' ἑαυτῆς ἐρημοῦται καὶ πᾶσα πόλις ἢ οἰκία μερισθεῖσα καθ' ἑαυτῆς οὐ σταθήσεται. **26** καὶ εἰ ὁ Σατανᾶς τὸν Σατανᾶν ἐκβάλλει, ἐφ' ἑαυτὸν ἐμερίσθη· πῶς οὖν σταθήσεται ἡ βασιλεία αὐτοῦ; **27** καὶ εἰ ἐγὼ ἐν Βεελζεβοὺλ[c] ἐκβάλλω τὰ δαιμόνια, οἱ υἱοὶ ὑμῶν ἐν τίνι ἐκβάλλουσιν; διὰ τοῦτο αὐτοὶ κριταὶ ἔσονται ὑμῶν. **28** εἰ δὲ ἐν πνεύματι θεοῦ ἐγὼ ἐκβάλλω τὰ δαιμόνια, ἄρα ἔφθασεν ἐφ' ὑμᾶς ἡ βασιλεία τοῦ θεοῦ. **29** ἢ πῶς δύναταί τις εἰσελθεῖν εἰς τὴν οἰκίαν τοῦ ἰσχυροῦ καὶ τὰ σκεύη αὐτοῦ ἁρπάσαι, ἐὰν μὴ πρῶτον δήσῃ τὸν ἰσχυρόν; καὶ τότε τὴν οἰκίαν αὐτοῦ διαρπάσει[d]. **30** ὁ μὴ ὢν μετ' ἐμοῦ κατ' ἐμοῦ ἐστιν, καὶ ὁ μὴ συνάγων μετ' ἐμοῦ σκορπίζει. **31** Διὰ τοῦτο λέγω ὑμῖν, πᾶσα ἁμαρτία καὶ βλασφημία ἀφεθήσεται τοῖς ἀνθρώποις, ἡ δὲ τοῦ πνεύματος βλασφημία οὐκ ἀφεθήσεται. **32** καὶ ὃς ἐὰν εἴπῃ λόγον κατὰ τοῦ υἱοῦ τοῦ ἀνθρώπου, ἀφεθήσεται αὐτῷ· ὃς δ' ἂν εἴπῃ κατὰ τοῦ πνεύματος τοῦ ἁγίου, οὐκ ἀφεθήσεται αὐτῷ οὔτε ἐν τούτῳ τῷ αἰῶνι οὔτε ἐν τῷ μέλλοντι.

33 Ἢ ποιήσατε τὸ δένδρον καλὸν καὶ τὸν καρπὸν αὐτοῦ καλόν, ἢ ποιήσατε τὸ δένδρον σαπρὸν καὶ τὸν καρπὸν αὐτοῦ σαπρόν· ἐκ γὰρ τοῦ καρποῦ τὸ δένδρον γινώσκεται. **34** γεννήματα ἐχιδνῶν, πῶς δύνασθε ἀγαθὰ λαλεῖν πονηροὶ ὄντες; ἐκ γὰρ τοῦ περισσεύ-ματος τῆς καρδίας τὸ στόμα λαλεῖ. **35** ὁ ἀγαθὸς ἄνθρωπος ἐκ τοῦ ἀγαθοῦ θησαυροῦ ἐκβάλλει ἀγαθά, καὶ ὁ πονηρὸς ἄνθρωπος ἐκ τοῦ πονηροῦ θησαυροῦ ἐκβάλλει πονηρά. **36** λέγω δὲ ὑμῖν ὅτι πᾶν ῥῆμα ἀργὸν ὃ λαλήσουσιν οἱ ἄνθρωποι ἀποδώσουσιν περὶ αὐτοῦ λόγον ἐν ἡμέρα κρίσεως· **37** ἐκ γὰρ τῶν λόγων σου δικαιωθήσῃ, καὶ ἐκ τῶν λόγων σου καταδικασθήσῃ.

38 Τότε ἀπεκρίθησαν αὐτῷ τινες τῶν γραμματέων καὶ Φαρισαίων λέγοντες,

---

Jesus and Beelzebub

22Then they brought him a demon-pos-sessed man who was blind and mute, and Jesus healed him, so that he could both talk and see. 23All the people were aston-ished and said, "Could this be the Son of David?"

24But when the Pharisees heard this, they said, "It is only by Beelzebub,[d] the prince of demons, that this fellow drives out de-mons."

25Jesus knew their thoughts and said to them, "Every kingdom divided against it-self will be ruined, and every city or house-hold divided against itself will not stand. 26If Satan drives out Satan, he is divided against himself. How then can his king-dom stand? 27And if I drive out demons by Beelzebub, by whom do your people drive them out? So then, they will be your judges. 28But if I drive out demons by the Spirit of God, then the kingdom of God has come upon you.

29"Or again, how can anyone enter a strong man's house and carry off his pos-sessions unless he first ties up the strong man? Then he can rob his house.

30"He who is not with me is against me, and he who does not gather with me scat-ters. 31And so I tell you, every sin and blasphemy will be forgiven men, but the blasphemy against the Spirit will not be forgiven. 32Anyone who speaks a word against the Son of Man will be forgiven, but anyone who speaks against the Holy Spirit will not be forgiven, either in this age or in the age to come.

33"Make a tree good and its fruit will be good, or make a tree bad and its fruit will be bad, for a tree is recognized by its fruit. 34You brood of vipers, how can you who are evil say anything good? For out of the overflow of the heart the mouth speaks. 35The good man brings good things out of the good stored up in him, and the evil man brings evil things out of the evil stored up in him. 36But I tell you that men will have to give account on the day of judg-ment for every careless word they have spoken. 37For by your words you will be acquitted, and by your words you will be condemned."

The Sign of Jonah

38Then some of the Pharisees and teachers of the law said to him, "Teacher, we want

---

[b]22 NIV text προσήνεγκαν αὐτῷ δαιμονιζόμενον τυφλὸν καὶ κωφόν †   [c]24, 27 NIV note Βεεζεβοὺλ †
[d]29 NIV text διαρπάσῃ †

[s] Gk sons

[d]24 Greek Beezeboul or Beelzeboul; also in verse 27

a sign from you." 39But he answered them, "An evil and adulterous generation asks for a sign, but no sign will be given to it except the sign of the prophet Jonah. 40For just as Jonah was three days and three nights in the belly of the sea monster, so for three days and three nights the Son of Man will be in the heart of the earth. 41The people of Nineveh will rise up at the judgment with this generation and condemn it, because they repented at the proclamation of Jonah, and see, something greater than Jonah is here! 42The queen of the South will rise up at the judgment with this generation and condemn it, because she came from the ends of the earth to listen to the wisdom of Solomon, and see, something greater than Solomon is here!

The Return of the Unclean Spirit

43 "When the unclean spirit has gone out of a person, it wanders through waterless regions looking for a resting place, but it finds none. 44Then it says, 'I will return to my house from which I came.' When it comes, it finds it empty, swept, and put in order. 45Then it goes and brings along seven other spirits more evil than itself, and they enter and live there; and the last state of that person is worse than the first. So will it be also with this evil generation."

The True Kindred of Jesus

46 While he was still speaking to the crowds, his mother and his brothers were standing outside, wanting to speak to him. 47Someone told him, "Look, your mother and your brothers are standing outside, wanting to speak to you."t 48But to the one who had told him this, Jesusu replied, "Who is my mother, and who are my brothers?" 49And pointing to his disciples, he said, "Here are my mother and my brothers! 50For whoever does the will of my Father in heaven is my brother and sister and mother."

The Parable of the Sower

13 That same day Jesus went out of the house and sat beside the sea. 2Such great crowds gathered around him that he got into a boat and sat there, while the whole crowd stood on the beach. 3And he told them many things in parables, saying: "Listen! A sower went out to sow.

Διδάσκαλε, θέλομεν ἀπὸ σοῦ σημεῖον ἰδεῖν. 39 ὁ δὲ ἀποκριθεὶς εἶπεν αὐτοῖς, Γενεὰ πονηρὰ καὶ μοιχαλὶς σημεῖον ἐπιζητεῖ, καὶ σημεῖον οὐ δοθήσεται αὐτῇ εἰ μὴ τὸ σημεῖον Ἰωνᾶ τοῦ προφήτου. 40 ὥσπερ γὰρ ἦν Ἰωνᾶς ἐν τῇ κοιλίᾳ τοῦ κήτους τρεῖς ἡμέρας καὶ τρεῖς νύκτας, οὕτως ἔσται ὁ υἱὸς τοῦ ἀνθρώπου ἐν τῇ καρδίᾳ τῆς γῆς τρεῖς ἡμέρας καὶ τρεῖς νύκτας. 41 ἄνδρες Νινευῖται ἀναστήσονται ἐν τῇ κρίσει μετὰ τῆς γενεᾶς ταύτης καὶ κατακρινοῦσιν αὐτήν, ὅτι μετενόησαν εἰς τὸ κήρυγμα Ἰωνᾶ, καὶ ἰδοὺ πλεῖον Ἰωνᾶ ὧδε. 42 βασίλισσα νότου ἐγερθήσεται ἐν τῇ κρίσει μετὰ τῆς γενεᾶς ταύτης καὶ κατακρινεῖ αὐτήν, ὅτι ἦλθεν ἐκ τῶν περάτων τῆς γῆς ἀκοῦσαι τὴν σοφίαν Σολομῶνος, καὶ ἰδοὺ πλεῖον Σολομῶνος ὧδε.

43 Ὅταν δὲ τὸ ἀκάθαρτον πνεῦμα ἐξέλθῃ ἀπὸ τοῦ ἀνθρώπου, διέρχεται δι᾽ ἀνύδρων τόπων ζητοῦν ἀνάπαυσιν καὶ οὐχ εὑρίσκει. 44 τότε λέγει, Εἰς τὸν οἶκόν μου ἐπιστρέψω ὅθεν ἐξῆλθον· καὶ ἐλθὸν εὑρίσκειe σχολάζοντα σεσαρωμένον καὶ κεκοσμημένον. 45 τότε πορεύεται καὶ παραλαμβάνει μεθ᾽ ἑαυτοῦ ἑπτὰ ἕτερα πνεύματα πονηρότερα ἑαυτοῦ καὶ εἰσελθόντα κατοικεῖ ἐκεῖ· καὶ γίνεται τὰ ἔσχατα τοῦ ἀνθρώπου ἐκείνου χείρονα τῶν πρώτων. οὕτως ἔσται καὶ τῇ γενεᾷ ταύτῃ τῇ πονηρᾷ.

46 Ἔτι αὐτοῦ λαλοῦντος τοῖς ὄχλοις ἰδοὺ ἡ μήτηρ καὶ οἱ ἀδελφοὶ αὐτοῦ εἱστήκεισαν ἔξω ζητοῦντες αὐτῷ λαλῆσαι. [47 εἶπεν δέ τις αὐτῷ, Ἰδοὺ ἡ μήτηρ σου καὶ οἱ ἀδελφοί σου ἔξω ἑστήκασιν ζητοῦντές σοι λαλῆσαι.] 48 ὁ δὲ ἀποκριθεὶς εἶπεν τῷ λέγοντι αὐτῷ, Τίς ἐστιν ἡ μήτηρ μου καὶ τίνες εἰσὶν οἱ ἀδελφοί μου; 49 καὶ ἐκτείνας τὴν χεῖρα αὐτοῦ ἐπὶ τοὺς μαθητὰς αὐτοῦ εἶπεν, Ἰδοὺ ἡ μήτηρ μου καὶ οἱ ἀδελφοί μου. 50 ὅστις γὰρ ἂν ποιήσῃ τὸ θέλημα τοῦ πατρός μου τοῦ ἐν οὐρανοῖς αὐτός μου ἀδελφὸς καὶ ἀδελφὴ καὶ μήτηρ ἐστίν.

13 Ἐν τῇ ἡμέρᾳ ἐκείνῃ ἐξελθὼν ὁ Ἰησοῦς τῆς οἰκίας ἐκάθητο παρὰ τὴν θάλασσαν· 2 καὶ συνήχθησαν πρὸς αὐτὸν ὄχλοι πολλοί, ὥστε αὐτὸν εἰς πλοῖον ἐμβάντα καθῆσθαι, καὶ πᾶς ὁ ὄχλος ἐπὶ τὸν αἰγιαλὸν εἱστήκει. 3 καὶ ἐλάλησεν αὐτοῖς πολλὰ ἐν παραβολαῖς λέγων, Ἰδοὺ ἐξῆλθεν ὁ σπείρων τοῦ σπείρειν. 4 καὶ ἐν τῷ σπείρειν

to see a miraculous sign from you."

39He answered, "A wicked and adulterous generation asks for a miraculous sign! But none will be given it except the sign of the prophet Jonah. 40Foras Jonah was three days and three nights in the belly of a huge fish, so the Son of Man will be three days and three nights in the heart of the earth. 41The men of Nineveh will stand up at the judgment with this generation and condemn it; for they repented at the preaching of Jonah, and now onee greater than Jonah is here. 42The Queen of the South will rise at the judgment with this generation and condemn it; for she came from the ends of the earth to listen to Solomon's wisdom, and now one greater than Solomon is here.

43"When an evilf spirit comes out of a man, it goes through arid places seeking rest and does not find it. 44Then it says, 'I will return to the house I left.' When it arrives, it finds the house unoccupied, swept clean and put in order. 45Then it goes and takes with it seven other spirits more wicked than itself, and they go in and live there. And the final condition of that man is worse than the first. That is how it will be with this wicked generation."

Jesus' Mother and Brothers

46While Jesus was still talking to the crowd, his mother and brothers stood outside, wanting to speak to him. 47Someone told him, "Your mother and brothers are standing outside, wanting to speak to you."g

48He replied to him, "Who is my mother, and who are my brothers?" 49Pointing to his disciples, he said, "Here are my mother and my brothers. 50For whoever does the will of my Father in heaven is my brother and sister and mother."

The Parable of the Sower

13 That same day Jesus went out of the house and sat by the lake. 2Such large crowds gathered around him that he got into a boat and sat in it, while all the people stood on the shore. 3Then he told them many things in parables, saying: "A farmer went out to sow his seed. 4As he

---

t Other ancient authorities lack verse 47   u Gk he   e44 NIV text adds τὸν οἶκον †   e41 Or something; also in verse 42   f43 Greek unclean
g47 Some manuscripts do not have verse 47.

4And as he sowed, some seeds fell on the path, and the birds came and ate them up. 5Other seeds fell on rocky ground, where they did not have much soil, and they sprang up quickly, since they had no depth of soil. 6But when the sun rose, they were scorched; and since they had no root, they withered away. 7Other seeds fell among thorns, and the thorns grew up and choked them. 8Other seeds fell on good soil and brought forth grain, some a hundredfold, some sixty, some thirty. 9Let anyone with earsv listen!"

The Purpose of the Parables

10 Then the disciples came and asked him, "Why do you speak to them in parables?" 11He answered, "To you it has been given to know the secretsw of the kingdom of heaven, but to them it has not been given. 12For to those who have, more will be given, and they will have an abundance; but from those who have nothing, even what they have will be taken away. 13The reason I speak to them in parables is that 'seeing they do not perceive, and hearing they do not listen, nor do they understand.' 14With them indeed is fulfilled the prophecy of Isaiah that says:

'You will indeed listen, but never
    understand,
  and you will indeed look, but never
    perceive.
15 For this people's heart has grown dull,
  and their ears are hard of hearing,
    and they have shut their eyes;
    so that they might not look with
      their eyes,
  and listen with their ears,
  and understand with their heart and
    turn—
  and I would heal them.'

16But blessed are your eyes, for they see, and your ears, for they hear. 17Truly I tell you, many prophets and righteous people longed to see what you see, but did not see it, and to hear what you hear, but did not hear it.

The Parable of the Sower Explained

18 "Hear then the parable of the sower. 19When anyone hears the word of the kingdom and does not understand it, the evil one comes and snatches away what is sown in the heart; this is what was sown on the path. 20As for what was sown on rocky ground, this is the one who hears the word and immediately receives it with joy; 21yet

αὐτὸν ἃ μὲν ἔπεσεν παρὰ τὴν ὁδόν, καὶ ἐλθόντα τὰ πετεινὰ κατέφαγεν αὐτά. 5 ἄλλα δὲ ἔπεσεν ἐπὶ τὰ πετρώδη ὅπου οὐκ εἶχεν γῆν πολλήν, καὶ εὐθέως ἐξανέτειλεν διὰ τὸ μὴ ἔχειν βάθος γῆς· 6 ἡλίου δὲ ἀνατείλαντος ἐκαυματίσθη καὶ διὰ τὸ μὴ ἔχειν ῥίζαν ἐξηράνθη. 7 ἄλλα δὲ ἔπεσεν ἐπὶ τὰς ἀκάνθας, καὶ ἀνέβησαν αἱ ἄκανθαι καὶ ἔπνιξαν αὐτά. 8 ἄλλα δὲ ἔπεσεν ἐπὶ τὴν γῆν τὴν καλὴν καὶ ἐδίδου καρπόν, ὃ μὲν ἑκατόν, ὃ δὲ ἑξήκοντα, ὃ δὲ τριάκοντα. 9 ὁ ἔχων ὦταa ἀκουέτω.

10 Καὶ προσελθόντες οἱ μαθηταὶ εἶπαν αὐτῷ, Διὰ τί ἐν παραβολαῖς λαλεῖς αὐτοῖς; 11 ὁ δὲ ἀποκριθεὶς εἶπεν αὐτοῖςb, Ὅτι ὑμῖν δέδοται γνῶναι τὰ μυστήρια τῆς βασιλείας τῶν οὐρανῶν, ἐκείνοις δὲ οὐ δέδοται. 12 ὅστις γὰρ ἔχει, δοθήσεται αὐτῷ καὶ περισσευθήσεται· ὅστις δὲ οὐκ ἔχει, καὶ ὃ ἔχει ἀρθήσεται ἀπ' αὐτοῦ. 13 διὰ τοῦτο ἐν παραβολαῖς αὐτοῖς λαλῶ, ὅτι βλέποντες οὐ βλέπουσιν καὶ ἀκούοντες οὐκ ἀκούουσιν οὐδὲ συνίουσιν, 14 καὶ ἀναπληροῦται αὐτοῖς ἡ προφητεία Ἡσαΐου ἡ λέγουσα,

Ἀκοῇ ἀκούσετε καὶ οὐ μὴ συνῆτε,
  καὶ βλέποντες βλέψετε καὶ οὐ
    μὴ ἴδητε.
15 ἐπαχύνθη γὰρ ἡ καρδία τοῦ λαοῦ
    τούτου,
  καὶ τοῖς ὠσὶν βαρέως ἤκουσαν
  καὶ τοὺς ὀφθαλμοὺς αὐτῶν
    ἐκάμμυσαν,
  μήποτε ἴδωσιν τοῖς ὀφθαλμοῖς
  καὶ τοῖς ὠσὶν ἀκούσωσιν
  καὶ τῇ καρδίᾳ συνῶσιν καὶ
    ἐπιστρέψωσιν
  καὶ ἰάσομαι αὐτούς.
16 ὑμῶν δὲ μακάριοι οἱ ὀφθαλμοὶ ὅτι βλέπουσιν καὶ τὰ ὦτα ὑμῶν ὅτι ἀκούουσιν. 17 ἀμὴν γὰρ λέγω ὑμῖν ὅτι πολλοὶ προφῆται καὶ δίκαιοι ἐπεθύμησαν ἰδεῖν ἃ βλέπετε καὶ οὐκ εἶδαν, καὶ ἀκοῦσαι ἃ ἀκούετε καὶ οὐκ ἤκουσαν.

18 Ὑμεῖς οὖν ἀκούσατε τὴν παραβολὴν τοῦ σπείραντος. 19 παντὸς ἀκούοντος τὸν λόγον τῆς βασιλείας καὶ μὴ συνιέντος ἔρχεται ὁ πονηρὸς καὶ ἁρπάζει τὸ ἐσπαρμένον ἐν τῇ καρδίᾳ αὐτοῦ, οὗτός ἐστιν ὁ παρὰ τὴν ὁδὸν σπαρείς. 20 ὁ δὲ ἐπὶ τὰ πετρώδη σπαρείς, οὗτός ἐστιν ὁ τὸν λόγον ἀκούων καὶ εὐθὺς μετὰ χαρᾶς λαμβάνων

was scattering the seed, some fell along the path, and the birds came and ate it up. 5Some fell on rocky places, where it did not have much soil. It sprang up quickly, because the soil was shallow. 6But when the sun came up, the plants were scorched, and they withered because they had no root. 7Other seed fell among thorns, which grew up and choked the plants. 8Still other seed fell on good soil, where it produced a crop—a hundred, sixty or thirty times what was sown. 9He who has ears, let him hear."

10The disciples came to him and asked, "Why do you speak to the people in parables?"

11He replied, "The knowledge of the secrets of the kingdom of heaven has been given to you, but not to them. 12Whoever has will be given more, and he will have an abundance. Whoever does not have, even what he has will be taken from him. 13This is why I speak to them in parables:

"Though seeing, they do not see;
  though hearing, they do not hear or
    understand.

14In them is fulfilled the prophecy of Isaiah:

" 'You will be ever hearing but never
    understanding;
  you will be ever seeing but never
    perceiving.
15For this people's heart has become
    calloused;
  they hardly hear with their ears,
  and they have closed their eyes.
Otherwise they might see with their
    eyes,
  hear with their ears,
  understand with their hearts
  and turn, and I would heal them.'a

16But blessed are your eyes because they see, and your ears because they hear. 17For I tell you the truth, many prophets and righteous men longed to see what you see but did not see it, and to hear what you hear but did not hear it.

18"Listen then to what the parable of the sower means: 19When anyone hears the message about the kingdom and does not understand it, the evil one comes and snatches away what was sown in his heart. This is the seed sown along the path. 20The one who received the seed that fell on rocky places is the man who hears the word and at once receives it with joy. 21But since he

vOther ancient authorities add *to hear*   wOr *mysteries*

a9 NRSV note v adds ὦτα ἀκούειν   b11 NIV text omits αὐτοῖς †

a15 Isaiah 6:9,10

such a person has no root, but endures only for a while, and when trouble or persecution arises on account of the word, that person immediately falls away.ˣ ²²As for what was sown among thorns, this is the one who hears the word, but the cares of the world and the lure of wealth choke the word, and it yields nothing. ²³But as for what was sown on good soil, this is the one who hears the word and understands it, who indeed bears fruit and yields, in one case a hundredfold, in another sixty, and in another thirty."

The Parable of Weeds among the Wheat

24 He put before them another parable: "The kingdom of heaven may be compared to someone who sowed good seed in his field; ²⁵but while everybody was asleep, an enemy came and sowed weeds among the wheat, and then went away. ²⁶So when the plants came up and bore grain, then the weeds appeared as well. ²⁷And the slaves of the householder came and said to him, 'Master, did you not sow good seed in your field? Where, then, did these weeds come from?' ²⁸He answered, 'An enemy has done this.' The slaves said to him, 'Then do you want us to go and gather them?' ²⁹But he replied, 'No; for in gathering the weeds you would uproot the wheat along with them. ³⁰Let both of them grow together until the harvest; and at harvest time I will tell the reapers, Collect the weeds first and bind them in bundles to be burned, but gather the wheat into my barn.' "

The Parable of the Mustard Seed

31 He put before them another parable: "The kingdom of heaven is like a mustard seed that someone took and sowed in his field; ³²it is the smallest of all the seeds, but when it has grown it is the greatest of shrubs and becomes a tree, so that the birds of the air come and make nests in its branches."

The Parable of the Yeast

33 He told them another parable: "The kingdom of heaven is like yeast that a woman took and mixed in withʸ three measures of flour until all of it was leavened."

The Use of Parables

34 Jesus told the crowds all these things in parables; without a parable he told them

αὐτόν. 21 οὐκ ἔχει δὲ ῥίζαν ἐν ἑαυτῷ ἀλλὰ πρόσκαιρός ἐστιν, γενομένης δὲ θλίψεως ἢ διωγμοῦ διὰ τὸν λόγον εὐθὺς σκανδαλίζεται. 22 ὁ δὲ εἰς τὰς ἀκάνθας σπαρείς, οὗτός ἐστιν ὁ τὸν λόγον ἀκούων, καὶ ἡ μέριμνα τοῦ αἰῶνος καὶ ἡ ἀπάτη τοῦ πλούτου συμπνίγει τὸν λόγον καὶ ἄκαρπος γίνεται. 23 ὁ δὲ ἐπὶ τὴν καλὴν γῆν σπαρείς, οὗτός ἐστιν ὁ τὸν λόγον ἀκούων καὶ συνιείς, ὃς δὴ καρποφορεῖ καὶ ποιεῖ ὃ μὲν ἑκατόν, ὃ δὲ ἑξήκοντα, ὃ δὲ τριάκοντα. 24 Ἄλλην παραβολὴν παρέθηκεν αὐτοῖς λέγων, Ὡμοιώθη ἡ βασιλεία τῶν οὐρανῶν ἀνθρώπῳ σπείραντι καλὸν σπέρμα ἐν τῷ ἀγρῷ αὐτοῦ. 25 ἐν δὲ τῷ καθεύδειν τοὺς ἀνθρώπους ἦλθεν αὐτοῦ ὁ ἐχθρὸς καὶ ἐπέσπειρεν ζιζάνια ἀνὰ μέσον τοῦ σίτου καὶ ἀπῆλθεν. 26 ὅτε δὲ ἐβλάστησεν ὁ χόρτος καὶ καρπὸν ἐποίησεν, τότε ἐφάνη καὶ τὰ ζιζάνια. 27 προσελθόντες δὲ οἱ δοῦλοι τοῦ οἰκοδεσπότου εἶπον αὐτῷ, Κύριε, οὐχὶ καλὸν σπέρμα ἔσπειρας ἐν τῷ σῷ ἀγρῷ; πόθεν οὖν ἔχει ζιζάνια; 28 ὁ δὲ ἔφη αὐτοῖς, Ἐχθρὸς ἄνθρωπος τοῦτο ἐποίησεν. οἱ δὲ δοῦλοι λέγουσιν αὐτῷ, Θέλεις οὖν ἀπελθόντες συλλέξωμεν αὐτά; 29 ὁ δέ φησιν, Οὔ, μήποτε συλλέγοντες τὰ ζιζάνια ἐκριζώσητε ἅμα αὐτοῖς τὸν σῖτον. 30 ἄφετε συναυξάνεσθαι ἀμφότερα ἕως τοῦ θερισμοῦ, καὶ ἐν καιρῷ τοῦ θερισμοῦ ἐρῶ τοῖς θερισταῖς, Συλλέξατε πρῶτον τὰ ζιζάνια καὶ δήσατε αὐτὰ εἰς δέσμας πρὸς τὸ κατακαῦσαι αὐτά, τὸν δὲ σῖτον συναγάγετε εἰς τὴν ἀποθήκην μου. 31 Ἄλλην παραβολὴν παρέθηκεν αὐτοῖς λέγων, Ὁμοία ἐστὶν ἡ βασιλεία τῶν οὐρανῶν κόκκῳ σινάπεως, ὃν λαβὼν ἄνθρωπος ἔσπειρεν ἐν τῷ ἀγρῷ αὐτοῦ· 32 ὃ μικρότερον μέν ἐστιν πάντων τῶν σπερμάτων, ὅταν δὲ αὐξηθῇ μεῖζον τῶν λαχάνων ἐστὶν καὶ γίνεται δένδρον, ὥστε ἐλθεῖν τὰ πετεινὰ τοῦ οὐρανοῦ καὶ κατασκηνοῦν ἐν τοῖς κλάδοις αὐτοῦ. 33 Ἄλλην παραβολὴν ἐλάλησεν αὐτοῖς· Ὁμοία ἐστὶν ἡ βασιλεία τῶν οὐρανῶν ζύμῃ, ἣν λαβοῦσα γυνὴ ἐνέκρυψεν εἰς ἀλεύρου σάτα τρία ἕως οὗ ἐζυμώθη ὅλον. 34 Ταῦτα πάντα ἐλάλησεν ὁ Ἰησοῦς ἐν παραβολαῖς τοῖς ὄχλοις καὶ χωρὶς παραβολῆς οὐδὲν ἐλάλει αὐτοῖς, 35 ὅπως

has no root, he lasts only a short time. When trouble or persecution comes because of the word, he quickly falls away. ²²The one who received the seed that fell among the thorns is the man who hears the word, but the worries of this life and the deceitfulness of wealth choke it, making it unfruitful. ²³But the one who received the seed that fell on good soil is the man who hears the word and understands it. He produces a crop, yielding a hundred, sixty or thirty times what was sown."

The Parable of the Weeds

²⁴Jesus told them another parable: "The kingdom of heaven is like a man who sowed good seed in his field. ²⁵But while everyone was sleeping, his enemy came and sowed weeds among the wheat, and went away. ²⁶When the wheat sprouted and formed heads, then the weeds also appeared.

²⁷"The owner's servants came to him and said, 'Sir, didn't you sow good seed in your field? Where then did the weeds come from?'

²⁸" 'An enemy did this,' he replied.

"The servants asked him, 'Do you want us to go and pull them up?'

²⁹" 'No,' he answered, 'because while you are pulling the weeds, you may root up the wheat with them. ³⁰Let both grow together until the harvest. At that time I will tell the harvesters: First collect the weeds and tie them in bundles to be burned; then gather the wheat and bring it into my barn.' "

The Parables of the Mustard Seed and the Yeast

³¹He told them another parable: "The kingdom of heaven is like a mustard seed, which a man took and planted in his field. ³²Though it is the smallest of all your seeds, yet when it grows, it is the largest of garden plants and becomes a tree, so that the birds of the air come and perch in its branches."

³³He told them still another parable: "The kingdom of heaven is like yeast that a woman took and mixed into a large amountᵇ of flour until it worked all through the dough."

³⁴Jesus spoke all these things to the crowd in parables; he did not say anything to them without using a parable. ³⁵So was

---

ˣ Gk *stumbles* ʸ Gk *hid in*

nothing. 35This was to fulfill what had been spoken through the prophet:z

"I will open my mouth to speak in parables;
I will proclaim what has been hidden from the foundation of the world."a

Jesus Explains the Parable of the Weeds

36 Then he left the crowds and went into the house. And his disciples approached him, saying, "Explain to us the parable of the weeds of the field." 37He answered, "The one who sows the good seed is the Son of Man; 38the field is the world, and the good seed are the children of the kingdom; the weeds are the children of the evil one, 39and the enemy who sowed them is the devil; the harvest is the end of the age, and the reapers are angels. 40Just as the weeds are collected and burned up with fire, so will it be at the end of the age. 41The Son of Man will send his angels, and they will collect out of his kingdom all causes of sin and all evildoers, 42and they will throw them into the furnace of fire, where there will be weeping and gnashing of teeth. 43Then the righteous will shine like the sun in the kingdom of their Father. Let anyone with earsb listen!

Three Parables

44 "The kingdom of heaven is like treasure hidden in a field, which someone found and hid; then in his joy he goes and sells all that he has and buys that field.

45 "Again, the kingdom of heaven is like a merchant in search of fine pearls; 46on finding one pearl of great value, he went and sold all that he had and bought it.

47 "Again, the kingdom of heaven is like a net that was thrown into the sea and caught fish of every kind; 48when it was full, they drew it ashore, sat down, and put the good into baskets but threw out the bad. 49So it will be at the end of the age. The angels will come out and separate the evil from the righteous 50and throw them into the furnace of fire, where there will be weeping and gnashing of teeth.

πληρωθῇ τὸ ῥηθὲν διὰc τοῦ προφήτου λέγοντος,

Ἀνοίξω ἐν παραβολαῖς τὸ στόμα μου,
ἐρεύξομαι κεκρυμμένα ἀπὸ καταβολῆς [κόσμου].

36 Τότε ἀφεὶς τοὺς ὄχλους ἦλθεν εἰς τὴν οἰκίαν. καὶ προσῆλθον αὐτῷ οἱ μαθηταὶ αὐτοῦ λέγοντες, Διασάφησον ἡμῖν τὴν παραβολὴν τῶν ζιζανίων τοῦ ἀγροῦ. **37** ὁ δὲ ἀποκριθεὶς εἶπεν, Ὁ σπείρων τὸ καλὸν σπέρμα ἐστὶν ὁ υἱὸς τοῦ ἀνθρώπου, **38** ὁ δὲ ἀγρός ἐστιν ὁ κόσμος, τὸ δὲ καλὸν σπέρμα οὗτοί εἰσιν οἱ υἱοὶ τῆς βασιλείας· τὰ δὲ ζιζάνιά εἰσιν οἱ υἱοὶ τοῦ πονηροῦ, **39** ὁ δὲ ἐχθρὸς ὁ σπείρας αὐτά ἐστιν ὁ διάβολος, ὁ δὲ θερισμὸς συντέλεια αἰῶνός ἐστιν, οἱ δὲ θερισταὶ ἄγγελοί εἰσιν. **40** ὥσπερ οὖν συλλέγεται τὰ ζιζάνια καὶ πυρὶ [κατα]καίεται, οὕτως ἔσται ἐν τῇ συντελείᾳ τοῦ αἰῶνος· **41** ἀποστελεῖ ὁ υἱὸς τοῦ ἀνθρώπου τοὺς ἀγγέλους αὐτοῦ, καὶ συλλέξουσιν ἐκ τῆς βασιλείας αὐτοῦ πάντα τὰ σκάνδαλα καὶ τοὺς ποιοῦντας τὴν ἀνομίαν **42** καὶ βαλοῦσιν αὐτοὺς εἰς τὴν κάμινον τοῦ πυρός· ἐκεῖ ἔσται ὁ κλαυθμὸς καὶ ὁ βρυγμὸς τῶν ὀδόντων. **43** Τότε οἱ δίκαιοι ἐκλάμψουσιν ὡς ὁ ἥλιος ἐν τῇ βασιλείᾳ τοῦ πατρὸς αὐτῶν. ὁ ἔχων ὦταd ἀκουέτω.

44 Ὁμοία ἐστὶν ἡ βασιλεία τῶν οὐρανῶν θησαυρῷ κεκρυμμένῳ ἐν τῷ ἀγρῷ, ὃν εὑρὼν ἄνθρωπος ἔκρυψεν, καὶ ἀπὸ τῆς χαρᾶς αὐτοῦ ὑπάγει καὶ πωλεῖ πάντα ὅσα ἔχει καὶ ἀγοράζει τὸν ἀγρὸν ἐκεῖνον.

45 Πάλιν ὁμοία ἐστὶν ἡ βασιλεία τῶν οὐρανῶν ἀνθρώπῳ ἐμπόρῳ ζητοῦντι καλοὺς μαργαρίτας· **46** εὑρὼν δὲ ἕνα πολύτιμον μαργαρίτην ἀπελθὼν πέπρακεν πάντα ὅσα εἶχεν καὶ ἠγόρασεν αὐτόν.

47 Πάλιν ὁμοία ἐστὶν ἡ βασιλεία τῶν οὐρανῶν σαγήνῃ βληθείσῃ εἰς τὴν θάλασσαν καὶ ἐκ παντὸς γένους συναγαγούσῃ· **48** ἣν ὅτε ἐπληρώθη ἀναβιβάσαντες ἐπὶ τὸν αἰγιαλὸν καὶ καθίσαντες συνέλεξαν τὰ καλὰ εἰς ἄγγη, τὰ δὲ σαπρὰ ἔξω ἔβαλον. **49** οὕτως ἔσται ἐν τῇ συντελείᾳ τοῦ αἰῶνος· ἐξελεύσονται οἱ ἄγγελοι καὶ ἀφοριοῦσιν τοὺς πονηροὺς ἐκ μέσου τῶν δικαίων **50** καὶ βαλοῦσιν αὐτοὺς εἰς τὴν κάμινον τοῦ πυρός· ἐκεῖ ἔσται ὁ κλαυθμὸς καὶ ὁ βρυγμὸς τῶν ὀδόντων.

fulfilled what was spoken through the prophet:

"I will open my mouth in parables,
I will utter things hidden since the creation of the world."c

The Parable of the Weeds Explained

36Then he left the crowd and went into the house. His disciples came to him and said, "Explain to us the parable of the weeds in the field."

37He answered, "The one who sowed the good seed is the Son of Man. 38The field is the world, and the good seed stands for the sons of the kingdom. The weeds are the sons of the evil one, 39and the enemy who sows them is the devil. The harvest is the end of the age, and the harvesters are angels.

40"As the weeds are pulled up and burned in the fire, so it will be at the end of the age. 41The Son of Man will send out his angels, and they will weed out of his kingdom everything that causes sin and all who do evil. 42They will throw them into the fiery furnace, where there will be weeping and gnashing of teeth. 43Then the righteous will shine like the sun in the kingdom of their Father. He who has ears, let him hear.

The Parables of the Hidden Treasure and the Pearl

44"The kingdom of heaven is like treasure hidden in a field. When a man found it, he hid it again, and then in his joy went and sold all he had and bought that field.

45"Again, the kingdom of heaven is like a merchant looking for fine pearls. 46When he found one of great value, he went away and sold everything he had and bought it.

The Parable of the Net

47"Once again, the kingdom of heaven is like a net that was let down into the lake and caught all kinds of fish. 48When it was full, the fishermen pulled it up on the shore. Then they sat down and collected the good fish in baskets, but threw the bad away. 49This is how it will be at the end of the age. The angels will come and separate the wicked from the righteous 50and throw them into the fiery furnace, where there will be weeping and gnashing of teeth.

---

z Other ancient authorities read *the prophet Isaiah*
a Other ancient authorities lack *of the world*   b Other ancient authorities add *to hear*

c35 NRSV note z διὰ Ἠσαΐου   d43 NRSV note b adds ὦτα ἀκούειν

c35 Psalm 78:2

Treasures New and Old

51 "Have you understood all this?" They answered, "Yes." [52]And he said to them, "Therefore every scribe who has been trained for the kingdom of heaven is like the master of a household who brings out of his treasure what is new and what is old." [53]When Jesus had finished these parables, he left that place.

The Rejection of Jesus at Nazareth

54 He came to his hometown and began to teach the people[c] in their synagogue, so that they were astounded and said, "Where did this man get this wisdom and these deeds of power? [55]Is not this the carpenter's son? Is not his mother called Mary? And are not his brothers James and Joseph and Simon and Judas? [56]And are not all his sisters with us? Where then did this man get all this?" [57]And they took offense at him. But Jesus said to them, "Prophets are not without honor except in their own country and in their own house." [58]And he did not do many deeds of power there, because of their unbelief.

The Death of John the Baptist

14 At that time Herod the ruler[d] heard reports about Jesus; [2]and he said to his servants, "This is John the Baptist; he has been raised from the dead, and for this reason these powers are at work in him." [3]For Herod had arrested John, bound him, and put him in prison on account of Herodias, his brother Philip's wife,[e] [4]because John had been telling him, "It is not lawful for you to have her." [5]Though Herod[f] wanted to put him to death, he feared the crowd, because they regarded him as a prophet. [6]But when Herod's birthday came, the daughter of Herodias danced before the company, and she pleased Herod [7]so much that he promised on oath to grant her whatever she might ask. [8]Prompted by her mother, she said, "Give me the head of John the Baptist here on a platter." [9]The king was grieved, yet out of regard for his oaths and for the guests, he commanded it to be given; [10]he sent and had John beheaded in the prison. [11]The head was brought on a platter and given to the girl, who brought it to her mother. [12]His disciples came and took the body and buried it; then they went and told Jesus.

---

[c] Gk *them* [d] Gk *tetrarch* [e] Other ancient authorities read *his brother's wife* [f] Gk *he*

---

51 [c]Συνήκατε ταῦτα πάντα; λέγουσιν αὐτῷ, Ναί. 52 ὁ δὲ εἶπεν αὐτοῖς, Διὰ τοῦτο πᾶς γραμματεὺς μαθητευθεὶς τῇ βασιλείᾳ τῶν οὐρανῶν ὅμοιός ἐστιν ἀνθρώπῳ οἰκοδεσπότῃ, ὅστις ἐκβάλλει ἐκ τοῦ θησαυροῦ αὐτοῦ καινὰ καὶ παλαιά.

53 Καὶ ἐγένετο ὅτε ἐτέλεσεν ὁ Ἰησοῦς τὰς παραβολὰς ταύτας, μετῆρεν ἐκεῖθεν. 54 καὶ ἐλθὼν εἰς τὴν πατρίδα αὐτοῦ ἐδίδασκεν αὐτοὺς ἐν τῇ συναγωγῇ αὐτῶν, ὥστε ἐκπλήσσεσθαι αὐτοὺς καὶ λέγειν, Πόθεν τούτῳ ἡ σοφία αὕτη καὶ αἱ δυνάμεις; 55 οὐχ οὗτός ἐστιν ὁ τοῦ τέκτονος υἱός; οὐχ ἡ μήτηρ αὐτοῦ λέγεται Μαριὰμ καὶ οἱ ἀδελφοὶ αὐτοῦ Ἰάκωβος καὶ Ἰωσὴφ καὶ Σίμων καὶ Ἰούδας; 56 καὶ αἱ ἀδελφαὶ αὐτοῦ οὐχὶ πᾶσαι πρὸς ἡμᾶς εἰσιν; πόθεν οὖν τούτῳ ταῦτα πάντα; 57 καὶ ἐσκανδαλίζοντο ἐν αὐτῷ. ὁ δὲ Ἰησοῦς εἶπεν αὐτοῖς, Οὐκ ἔστιν προφήτης ἄτιμος εἰ μὴ ἐν τῇ πατρίδι καὶ ἐν τῇ οἰκίᾳ αὐτοῦ. 58 καὶ οὐκ ἐποίησεν ἐκεῖ δυνάμεις πολλὰς διὰ τὴν ἀπιστίαν αὐτῶν.

14 Ἐν ἐκείνῳ τῷ καιρῷ ἤκουσεν Ἡρῴδης ὁ τετραάρχης τὴν ἀκοὴν Ἰησοῦ, 2 καὶ εἶπεν τοῖς παισὶν αὐτοῦ, Οὗτός ἐστιν Ἰωάννης ὁ βαπτιστής· αὐτὸς ἠγέρθη ἀπὸ τῶν νεκρῶν καὶ διὰ τοῦτο αἱ δυνάμεις ἐνεργοῦσιν ἐν αὐτῷ. 3 Ὁ γὰρ Ἡρῴδης κρατήσας τὸν Ἰωάννην ἔδησεν [αὐτὸν] καὶ ἐν φυλακῇ ἀπέθετο διὰ Ἡρῳδιάδα τὴν γυναῖκα Φιλίππου[a] τοῦ ἀδελφοῦ αὐτοῦ· 4 ἔλεγεν γὰρ ὁ Ἰωάννης αὐτῷ, Οὐκ ἔξεστίν σοι ἔχειν αὐτήν. 5 καὶ θέλων αὐτὸν ἀποκτεῖναι ἐφοβήθη τὸν ὄχλον, ὅτι ὡς προφήτην αὐτὸν εἶχον. 6 γενεσίοις δὲ γενομένοις τοῦ Ἡρῴδου ὠρχήσατο ἡ θυγάτηρ τῆς Ἡρῳδιάδος ἐν τῷ μέσῳ καὶ ἤρεσεν τῷ Ἡρῴδῃ, 7 ὅθεν μεθ᾽ ὅρκου ὡμολόγησεν αὐτῇ δοῦναι ὃ ἐὰν αἰτήσηται. 8 ἡ δὲ προβιβασθεῖσα ὑπὸ τῆς μητρὸς αὐτῆς, Δός μοι, φησίν, ὧδε ἐπὶ πίνακι τὴν κεφαλὴν Ἰωάννου τοῦ βαπτιστοῦ. 9 καὶ λυπηθεὶς ὁ βασιλεὺς διὰ τοὺς ὅρκους καὶ τοὺς συνανακειμένους ἐκέλευσεν δοθῆναι, 10 καὶ πέμψας ἀπεκεφάλισεν [τὸν] Ἰωάννην ἐν τῇ φυλακῇ. 11 καὶ ἠνέχθη ἡ κεφαλὴ αὐτοῦ ἐπὶ πίνακι καὶ ἐδόθη τῷ κορασίῳ, καὶ ἤνεγκεν τῇ μητρὶ αὐτῆς. 12 καὶ προσελθόντες οἱ μαθηταὶ αὐτοῦ ἦραν τὸ πτῶμα καὶ ἔθαψαν αὐτό[ν][b], καὶ ἐλθόντες ἀπήγγειλαν τῷ Ἰησοῦ.

---

[e] 51 NIV text adds Λέγει αὐτοῖς ὁ Ἰησοῦς †
[a] 3 NRSV note e omits Φιλίππου [b] 12 NIV text αὐτό †

---

[51]"Have you understood all these things?" Jesus asked.

"Yes," they replied.

[52]He said to them, "Therefore every teacher of the law who has been instructed about the kingdom of heaven is like the owner of a house who brings out of his storeroom new treasures as well as old."

A Prophet Without Honor

[53]When Jesus had finished these parables, he moved on from there. [54]Coming to his hometown, he began teaching the people in their synagogue, and they were amazed. "Where did this man get this wisdom and these miraculous powers?" they asked. [55]"Isn't this the carpenter's son? Isn't his mother's name Mary, and aren't his brothers James, Joseph, Simon and Judas? [56]Aren't all his sisters with us? Where then did this man get all these things?" [57]And they took offense at him.

But Jesus said to them, "Only in his hometown and in his own house is a prophet without honor."

[58]And he did not do many miracles there because of their lack of faith.

John the Baptist Beheaded

14 At that time Herod the tetrarch heard the reports about Jesus, [2]and he said to his attendants, "This is John the Baptist; he has risen from the dead! That is why miraculous powers are at work in him."

[3]Now Herod had arrested John and bound him and put him in prison because of Herodias, his brother Philip's wife, [4]for John had been saying to him: "It is not lawful for you to have her." [5]Herod wanted to kill John, but he was afraid of the people, because they considered him a prophet.

[6]On Herod's birthday the daughter of Herodias danced for them and pleased Herod so much [7]that he promised with an oath to give her whatever she asked. [8]Prompted by her mother, she said, "Give me here on a platter the head of John the Baptist." [9]The king was distressed, but because of his oaths and his dinner guests, he ordered that her request be granted [10]and had John beheaded in the prison. [11]His head was brought in on a platter and given to the girl, who carried it to her mother. [12]John's disciples came and took his body and buried it. Then they went and told Jesus.

Feeding the Five Thousand

13 Now when Jesus heard this, he withdrew from there in a boat to a deserted place by himself. But when the crowds heard it, they followed him on foot from the towns. 14When he went ashore, he saw a great crowd; and he had compassion for them and cured their sick. 15When it was evening, the disciples came to him and said, "This is a deserted place, and the hour is now late; send the crowds away so that they may go into the villages and buy food for themselves." 16Jesus said to them, "They need not go away; you give them something to eat." 17They replied, "We have nothing here but five loaves and two fish." 18And he said, "Bring them here to me." 19Then he ordered the crowds to sit down on the grass. Taking the five loaves and the two fish, he looked up to heaven, and blessed and broke the loaves, and gave them to the disciples, and the disciples gave them to the crowds. 20And all ate and were filled; and they took up what was left over of the broken pieces, twelve baskets full. 21And those who ate were about five thousand men, besides women and children.

Jesus Walks on the Water

22 Immediately he made the disciples get into the boat and go on ahead to the other side, while he dismissed the crowds. 23And after he had dismissed the crowds, he went up the mountain by himself to pray. When evening came, he was there alone, 24but by this time the boat, battered by the waves, was far from the land,g for the wind was against them. 25And early in the morning he came walking toward them on the sea. 26But when the disciples saw him walking on the sea, they were terrified, saying, "It is a ghost!" And they cried out in fear. 27But immediately Jesus spoke to them and said, "Take heart, it is I; do not be afraid."

28 Peter answered him, "Lord, if it is you, command me to come to you on the water." 29He said, "Come." So Peter got out of the boat, started walking on the water, and came toward Jesus. 30But when he noticed the strong wind,h he became frightened, and beginning to sink, he cried out, "Lord, save me!" 31Jesus immediately reached out his hand and caught him,

---

13 Ἀκούσας δὲ ὁ Ἰησοῦς ἀνεχώρησεν ἐκεῖθεν ἐν πλοίῳ εἰς ἔρημον τόπον κατ' ἰδίαν· καὶ ἀκούσαντες οἱ ὄχλοι ἠκολούθησαν αὐτῷ πεζῇ ἀπὸ τῶν πόλεων. **14** καὶ ἐξελθὼν εἶδεν πολὺν ὄχλον καὶ ἐσπλαγχνίσθη ἐπ' αὐτοῖς καὶ ἐθεράπευσεν τοὺς ἀρρώστους αὐτῶν. **15** ὀψίας δὲ γενομένης προσῆλθον αὐτῷ οἱ μαθηταὶ λέγοντες, Ἔρημός ἐστιν ὁ τόπος καὶ ἡ ὥρα ἤδη παρῆλθεν· ἀπόλυσον τοὺς ὄχλους, ἵνα ἀπελθόντες εἰς τὰς κώμας ἀγοράσωσιν ἑαυτοῖς βρώματα. **16** ὁ δὲ [Ἰησοῦς] εἶπεν αὐτοῖς, Οὐ χρείαν ἔχουσιν ἀπελθεῖν, δότε αὐτοῖς ὑμεῖς φαγεῖν. **17** οἱ δὲ λέγουσιν αὐτῷ, Οὐκ ἔχομεν ὧδε εἰ μὴ πέντε ἄρτους καὶ δύο ἰχθύας. **18** ὁ δὲ εἶπεν, Φέρετέ μοι ὧδε αὐτούς. **19** καὶ κελεύσας τοὺς ὄχλους ἀνακλιθῆναι ἐπὶ τοῦ χόρτου, λαβὼν τοὺς πέντε ἄρτους καὶ τοὺς δύο ἰχθύας, ἀναβλέψας εἰς τὸν οὐρανὸν εὐλόγησεν καὶ κλάσας ἔδωκεν τοῖς μαθηταῖς τοὺς ἄρτους, οἱ δὲ μαθηταὶ τοῖς ὄχλοις. **20** καὶ ἔφαγον πάντες καὶ ἐχορτάσθησαν, καὶ ἦραν τὸ περισσεῦον τῶν κλασμάτων δώδεκα κοφίνους πλήρεις. **21** οἱ δὲ ἐσθίοντες ἦσαν ἄνδρες ὡσεὶ πεντακισχίλιοι χωρὶς γυναικῶν καὶ παιδίων.

22 Καὶ εὐθέως ἠνάγκασεν τοὺς μαθητὰς ἐμβῆναι εἰς τὸ πλοῖον καὶ προάγειν αὐτὸν εἰς τὸ πέραν, ἕως οὗ ἀπολύσῃ τοὺς ὄχλους. **23** καὶ ἀπολύσας τοὺς ὄχλους ἀνέβη εἰς τὸ ὄρος κατ' ἰδίαν προσεύξασθαι. ὀψίας δὲ γενομένης μόνος ἦν ἐκεῖ. **24** τὸ δὲ πλοῖον ἤδη σταδίους πολλοὺς ἀπὸ τῆς γῆς ἀπεῖχεν,c βασανιζόμενον ὑπὸ τῶν κυμάτων, ἦν γὰρ ἐναντίος ὁ ἄνεμος. **25** τετάρτῃ δὲ φυλακῇ τῆς νυκτὸς ἦλθεν d πρὸς αὐτοὺς περιπατῶν ἐπὶ τὴν θάλασσαν. **26** οἱ δὲ μαθηταὶ ἰδόντες αὐτὸν ἐπὶ τῆς θαλάσσης περιπατοῦντα ἐταράχθησαν λέγοντες ὅτι Φάντασμά ἐστιν, καὶ ἀπὸ τοῦ φόβου ἔκραξαν. **27** εὐθὺς δὲ ἐλάλησεν [ὁ Ἰησοῦς] αὐτοῖς λέγων, Θαρσεῖτε, ἐγώ εἰμι· μὴ φοβεῖσθε. **28** ἀποκριθεὶς δὲ αὐτῷ ὁ Πέτρος εἶπεν, Κύριε, εἰ σὺ εἶ, κέλευσόν με ἐλθεῖν πρὸς σὲ ἐπὶ τὰ ὕδατα. **29** ὁ δὲ εἶπεν, Ἐλθέ. καὶ καταβὰς ἀπὸ τοῦ πλοίου [ὁ] Πέτρος περιεπάτησεν ἐπὶ τὰ ὕδατα καὶ ἦλθεν πρὸς τὸν Ἰησοῦν. **30** βλέπων δὲ τὸν ἄνεμον [ἰσχυρὸν]e ἐφοβήθη, καὶ ἀρξάμενος καταποντίζεσθαι ἔκραξεν λέγων, Κύριε, σῶσόν με. **31** εὐθέως δὲ ὁ Ἰησοῦς ἐκτείνας τὴν χεῖρα ἐπελάβετο

Jesus Feeds the Five Thousand

13When Jesus heard what had happened, he withdrew by boat privately to a solitary place. Hearing of this, the crowds followed him on foot from the towns. 14When Jesus landed and saw a large crowd, he had compassion on them and healed their sick.

15As evening approached, the disciples came to him and said, "This is a remote place, and it's already getting late. Send the crowds away, so they can go to the villages and buy themselves some food."

16Jesus replied, "They do not need to go away. You give them something to eat."

17"We have here only five loaves of bread and two fish," they answered.

18"Bring them here to me," he said. 19And he directed the people to sit down on the grass. Taking the five loaves and the two fish and looking up to heaven, he gave thanks and broke the loaves. Then he gave them to the disciples, and the disciples gave them to the people. 20They all ate and were satisfied, and the disciples picked up twelve basketfuls of broken pieces that were left over. 21The number of those who ate was about five thousand men, besides women and children.

Jesus Walks on the Water

22Immediately Jesus made the disciples get into the boat and go on ahead of him to the other side, while he dismissed the crowd. 23After he had dismissed them, he went up on a mountainside by himself to pray. When evening came, he was there alone, 24but the boat was already a considerable distancea from land, buffeted by the waves because the wind was against it.

25During the fourth watch of the night Jesus went out to them, walking on the lake. 26When the disciples saw him walking on the lake, they were terrified. "It's a ghost," they said, and cried out in fear.

27But Jesus immediately said to them: "Take courage! It is I. Don't be afraid."

28"Lord, if it's you," Peter replied, "tell me to come to you on the water."

29"Come," he said.

Then Peter got down out of the boat, walked on the water and came toward Jesus. 30But when he saw the wind, he was afraid and, beginning to sink, cried out, "Lord, save me!"

31Immediately Jesus reached out his hand

---

g Other ancient authorities read *was out on the sea*
h Other ancient authorities read *the wind*

c24 NRSV note g μέσον τῆς θαλάσσης ἦν   d25 NIV text ἀπῆλθεν †   e30 NIV text and NRSV note h omit ἰσχυρὸν

a24 Greek *many stadia*

saying to him, "You of little faith, why did you doubt?" 32When they got into the boat, the wind ceased. 33And those in the boat worshiped him, saying, "Truly you are the Son of God."

Jesus Heals the Sick in Gennesaret

34 When they had crossed over, they came to land at Gennesaret. 35After the people of that place recognized him, they sent word throughout the region and brought all who were sick to him, 36and begged him that they might touch even the fringe of his cloak; and all who touched it were healed.

The Tradition of the Elders

15 Then Pharisees and scribes came to Jesus from Jerusalem and said, 2"Why do your disciples break the tradition of the elders? For they do not wash their hands before they eat." 3He answered them, "And why do you break the commandment of God for the sake of your tradition? 4For God said,[i] 'Honor your father and your mother,' and, 'Whoever speaks evil of father or mother must surely die.' 5But you say that whoever tells father or mother, 'Whatever support you might have had from me is given to God,'[j] then that person need not honor the father.[k] 6So, for the sake of your tradition, you make void the word[l] of God. 7You hypocrites! Isaiah prophesied rightly about you when he said:

8   'This people honors me with their lips,
      but their hearts are far from me;
9   in vain do they worship me,
      teaching human precepts as
      doctrines.' "

Things That Defile

10 Then he called the crowd to him and said to them, "Listen and understand: 11it is not what goes into the mouth that defiles a person, but it is what comes out of the mouth that defiles." 12Then the disciples approached and said to him, "Do you know that the Pharisees took offense when they heard what you said?" 13He answered, "Every plant that my heavenly Father has not planted will be uprooted. 14Let them alone; they are blind guides of the blind.[m] And if one blind person guides another, both will fall into a pit." 15But

αὐτοῦ καὶ λέγει αὐτῷ, Ὀλιγόπιστε, εἰς τί ἐδίστασας; 32 καὶ ἀναβάντων αὐτῶν εἰς τὸ πλοῖον ἐκόπασεν ὁ ἄνεμος. 33 οἱ δὲ ἐν τῷ πλοίῳ προσεκύνησαν αὐτῷ λέγοντες, Ἀληθῶς θεοῦ υἱὸς εἶ.

34 Καὶ διαπεράσαντες ἦλθον ἐπὶ τὴν γῆν εἰς Γεννησαρέτ. **35** καὶ ἐπιγνόντες αὐτὸν οἱ ἄνδρες τοῦ τόπου ἐκείνου ἀπέστειλαν εἰς ὅλην τὴν περίχωρον ἐκείνην καὶ προσήνεγκαν αὐτῷ πάντας τοὺς κακῶς ἔχοντας **36** καὶ παρεκάλουν αὐτὸν ἵνα μόνον ἅψωνται τοῦ κρασπέδου τοῦ ἱματίου αὐτοῦ· καὶ ὅσοι ἥψαντο διεσώθησαν.

15 Τότε προσέρχονται τῷ Ἰησοῦ ἀπὸ Ἱεροσολύμων Φαρισαῖοι καὶ γραμματεῖς λέγοντες, **2** Διὰ τί οἱ μαθηταί σου παραβαίνουσιν τὴν παράδοσιν τῶν πρεσβυτέρων; οὐ γὰρ νίπτονται τὰς χεῖρας [αὐτῶν] ὅταν ἄρτον ἐσθίωσιν. **3** ὁ δὲ ἀποκριθεὶς εἶπεν αὐτοῖς, Διὰ τί καὶ ὑμεῖς παραβαίνετε τὴν ἐντολὴν τοῦ θεοῦ διὰ τὴν παράδοσιν ὑμῶν; **4** ὁ γὰρ θεὸς εἶπεν[a], Τίμα τὸν πατέρα καὶ τὴν μητέρα, καί, Ὁ κακολογῶν πατέρα ἢ μητέρα θανάτω τελευτάτω. **5** ὑμεῖς δὲ λέγετε, Ὃς ἂν εἴπῃ τῷ πατρὶ ἢ τῇ μητρί, Δῶρον ὃ ἐὰν ἐξ ἐμοῦ ὠφεληθῇς, **6** οὐ μὴ τιμήσει τὸν πατέρα αὐτοῦ[b]· καὶ ἠκυρώσατε τὸν λόγον[c] τοῦ θεοῦ διὰ τὴν παράδοσιν ὑμῶν. **7** ὑποκριταί, καλῶς ἐπροφήτευσεν περὶ ὑμῶν Ἡσαΐας λέγων,

8 Ὁ λαὸς οὗτος τοῖς χείλεσίν με
     τιμᾷ,
   ἡ δὲ καρδία αὐτῶν πόρρω
     ἀπέχει ἀπ' ἐμοῦ·
9 μάτην δὲ σέβονταί με
     διδάσκοντες διδασκαλίας
     ἐντάλματα ἀνθρώπων.

10 Καὶ προσκαλεσάμενος τὸν ὄχλον εἶπεν αὐτοῖς, Ἀκούετε καὶ συνίετε· **11** οὐ τὸ εἰσερχόμενον εἰς τὸ στόμα κοινοῖ τὸν ἄνθρωπον, ἀλλὰ τὸ ἐκπορευόμενον ἐκ τοῦ στόματος τοῦτο κοινοῖ τὸν ἄνθρωπον. **12** Τότε προσελθόντες οἱ μαθηταὶ λέγουσιν αὐτῷ, Οἶδας ὅτι οἱ Φαρισαῖοι ἀκούσαντες τὸν λόγον ἐσκανδαλίσθησαν; **13** ὁ δὲ ἀποκριθεὶς εἶπεν, Πᾶσα φυτεία ἣν οὐκ ἐφύτευσεν ὁ πατήρ μου ὁ οὐράνιος ἐκριζωθήσεται. **14** ἄφετε αὐτούς· τυφλοί εἰσιν ὁδηγοὶ [τυφλῶν][d]· τυφλὸς δὲ τυφλὸν ἐὰν ὁδηγῇ, ἀμφότεροι εἰς βόθυνον πεσοῦνται.

and caught him. "You of little faith," he said, "why did you doubt?"

32And when they climbed into the boat, the wind died down. 33Then those who were in the boat worshiped him, saying, "Truly you are the Son of God."

34When they had crossed over, they landed at Gennesaret. 35And when the men of that place recognized Jesus, they sent word to all the surrounding country. People brought all their sick to him 36and begged him to let the sick just touch the edge of his cloak, and all who touched him were healed.

Clean and Unclean

15 Then some Pharisees and teachers of the law came to Jesus from Jerusalem and asked, 2"Why do your disciples break the tradition of the elders? They don't wash their hands before they eat!"

3Jesus replied, "And why do you break the command of God for the sake of your tradition? 4For God said, 'Honor your father and mother'[a] and 'Anyone who curses his father or mother must be put to death.'[b] 5But you say that if a man says to his father or mother, 'Whatever help you might otherwise have received from me is a gift devoted to God,' 6he is not to 'honor his father'[c] with it. Thus you nullify the word of God for the sake of your tradition. 7You hypocrites! Isaiah was right when he prophesied about you:

8" 'These people honor me with their
     lips,
   but their hearts are far from me.
9They worship me in vain;
   their teachings are but rules taught by
     men.'[d]

10Jesus called the crowd to him and said, "Listen and understand. 11What goes into a man's mouth does not make him 'unclean,' but what comes out of his mouth, that is what makes him 'unclean.' "

12Then the disciples came to him and asked, "Do you know that the Pharisees were offended when they heard this?"

13He replied, "Every plant that my heavenly Father has not planted will be pulled up by the roots. 14Leave them; they are blind guides.[e] If a blind man leads a blind man, both will fall into a pit."

---

[i]Other ancient authorities read *commanded, saying*   [j]Or *is an offering*   [k]Other ancient authorities add *or the mother*   [l]Other ancient authorities read *law*; others, *commandment*   [m]Other ancient authorities lack *of the blind*

[a]4 NRSV note i ἐνετείλατο λέγων   [b]6 NIV/NRSV notes add ἢ τὴν μητέρα (αὐτοῦ)   [c]6 NRSV note l τὸν νόμον or τὴν ἐντολήν   [d]14 NIV text and NRSV note m omit τυφλῶν

[a]4 Exodus 20:12; Deut. 5:16   [b]4 Exodus 21:17; Lev. 20:9   [c]6 Some manuscripts *father or his mother*   [d]9 Isaiah 29:13   [e]14 Some manuscripts *guides of the blind*

Peter said to him, "Explain this parable to us." [16]Then he said, "Are you also still without understanding? [17]Do you not see that whatever goes into the mouth enters the stomach, and goes out into the sewer? [18]But what comes out of the mouth proceeds from the heart, and this is what defiles. [19]For out of the heart come evil intentions, murder, adultery, fornication, theft, false witness, slander. [20]These are what defile a person, but to eat with unwashed hands does not defile."

The Canaanite Woman's Faith

21 Jesus left that place and went away to the district of Tyre and Sidon. [22]Just then a Canaanite woman from that region came out and started shouting, "Have mercy on me, Lord, Son of David; my daughter is tormented by a demon." [23]But he did not answer her at all. And his disciples came and urged him, saying, "Send her away, for she keeps shouting after us." [24]He answered, "I was sent only to the lost sheep of the house of Israel." [25]But she came and knelt before him, saying, "Lord, help me." [26]He answered, "It is not fair to take the children's food and throw it to the dogs." [27]She said, "Yes, Lord, yet even the dogs eat the crumbs that fall from their masters' table." [28]Then Jesus answered her, "Woman, great is your faith! Let it be done for you as you wish." And her daughter was healed instantly.

Jesus Cures Many People

29 After Jesus had left that place, he passed along the Sea of Galilee, and he went up the mountain, where he sat down. [30]Great crowds came to him, bringing with them the lame, the maimed, the blind, the mute, and many others. They put them at his feet, and he cured them, [31]so that the crowd was amazed when they saw the mute speaking, the maimed whole, the lame walking, and the blind seeing. And they praised the God of Israel.

Feeding the Four Thousand

32 Then Jesus called his disciples to him and said, "I have compassion for the crowd, because they have been with me now for three days and have nothing to eat; and I do not want to send them away hungry,

15 Ἀποκριθεὶς δὲ ὁ Πέτρος εἶπεν αὐτῷ, Φράσον ἡμῖν τὴν παραβολὴν [ταύτην]. 16 ὁ δὲ εἶπεν, Ἀκμὴν καὶ ὑμεῖς ἀσύνετοί ἐστε; 17 οὐ νοεῖτε ὅτι πᾶν τὸ εἰσπορευόμενον εἰς τὸ στόμα εἰς τὴν κοιλίαν χωρεῖ καὶ εἰς ἀφεδρῶνα ἐκβάλλεται; 18 τὰ δὲ ἐκπορευόμενα ἐκ τοῦ στόματος ἐκ τῆς καρδίας ἐξέρχεται, κἀκεῖνα κοινοῖ τὸν ἄνθρωπον. 19 ἐκ γὰρ τῆς καρδίας ἐξέρχονται διαλογισμοὶ πονηροί, φόνοι, μοιχεῖαι, πορνεῖαι, κλοπαί, ψευδομαρτυρίαι, βλασφημίαι. 20 ταῦτά ἐστιν τὰ κοινοῦντα τὸν ἄνθρωπον, τὸ δὲ ἀνίπτοις χερσὶν φαγεῖν οὐ κοινοῖ τὸν ἄνθρωπον.

21 Καὶ ἐξελθὼν ἐκεῖθεν ὁ Ἰησοῦς ἀνεχώρησεν εἰς τὰ μέρη Τύρου καὶ Σιδῶνος. 22 καὶ ἰδοὺ γυνὴ Χαναναία ἀπὸ τῶν ὁρίων ἐκείνων ἐξελθοῦσα ἔκραζεν λέγουσα, Ἐλέησόν με, κύριε υἱὸς Δαυίδ· ἡ θυγάτηρ μου κακῶς δαιμονίζεται. 23 ὁ δὲ οὐκ ἀπεκρίθη αὐτῇ λόγον. καὶ προσελθόντες οἱ μαθηταὶ αὐτοῦ ἠρώτουν αὐτὸν λέγοντες, Ἀπόλυσον αὐτήν, ὅτι κράζει ὄπισθεν ἡμῶν. 24 ὁ δὲ ἀποκριθεὶς εἶπεν, Οὐκ ἀπεστάλην εἰ μὴ εἰς τὰ πρόβατα τὰ ἀπολωλότα οἴκου Ἰσραήλ. 25 ἡ δὲ ἐλθοῦσα προσεκύνει αὐτῷ λέγουσα, Κύριε, βοήθει μοι. 26 ὁ δὲ ἀποκριθεὶς εἶπεν, Οὐκ ἔστιν καλὸν λαβεῖν τὸν ἄρτον τῶν τέκνων καὶ βαλεῖν τοῖς κυναρίοις. 27 ἡ δὲ εἶπεν, Ναὶ κύριε, καὶ γὰρ τὰ κυνάρια ἐσθίει ἀπὸ τῶν ψιχίων τῶν πιπτόντων ἀπὸ τῆς τραπέζης τῶν κυρίων αὐτῶν. 28 τότε ἀποκριθεὶς ὁ Ἰησοῦς εἶπεν αὐτῇ, Ὦ γύναι, μεγάλη σου ἡ πίστις· γενηθήτω σοι ὡς θέλεις. καὶ ἰάθη ἡ θυγάτηρ αὐτῆς ἀπὸ τῆς ὥρας ἐκείνης.

29 Καὶ μεταβὰς ἐκεῖθεν ὁ Ἰησοῦς ἦλθεν παρὰ τὴν θάλασσαν τῆς Γαλιλαίας, καὶ ἀναβὰς εἰς τὸ ὄρος ἐκάθητο ἐκεῖ. 30 καὶ προσῆλθον αὐτῷ ὄχλοι πολλοὶ ἔχοντες μεθ᾽ ἑαυτῶν χωλούς, τυφλούς, κυλλούς, κωφούς, καὶ ἑτέρους πολλοὺς καὶ ἔρριψαν αὐτοὺς παρὰ τοὺς πόδας αὐτοῦ, καὶ ἐθεράπευσεν αὐτούς· 31 ὥστε τὸν ὄχλον θαυμάσαι βλέποντας κωφοὺς λαλοῦντας, κυλλοὺς ὑγιεῖς καὶ χωλοὺς περιπατοῦντας καὶ τυφλοὺς βλέποντας· καὶ ἐδόξασαν τὸν θεὸν Ἰσραήλ.

32 Ὁ δὲ Ἰησοῦς προσκαλεσάμενος τοὺς μαθητὰς αὐτοῦ εἶπεν, Σπλαγχνίζομαι ἐπὶ τὸν ὄχλον, ὅτι ἤδη ἡμέραι τρεῖς προσμένουσίν μοι καὶ οὐκ ἔχουσιν τί φάγωσιν· καὶ ἀπολῦσαι αὐτοὺς

[15]Peter said, "Explain the parable to us." [16]"Are you still so dull?" Jesus asked them. [17]"Don't you see that whatever enters the mouth goes into the stomach and then out of the body? [18]But the things that come out of the mouth come from the heart, and these make a man 'unclean.' [19]For out of the heart come evil thoughts, murder, adultery, sexual immorality, theft, false testimony, slander. [20]These are what make a man 'unclean'; but eating with unwashed hands does not make him 'unclean.' "

The Faith of the Canaanite Woman

[21]Leaving that place, Jesus withdrew to the region of Tyre and Sidon. [22]A Canaanite woman from that vicinity came to him, crying out, "Lord, Son of David, have mercy on me! My daughter is suffering terribly from demon-possession."

[23]Jesus did not answer a word. So his disciples came to him and urged him, "Send her away, for she keeps crying out after us."

[24]He answered, "I was sent only to the lost sheep of Israel."

[25]The woman came and knelt before him. "Lord, help me!" she said.

[26]He replied, "It is not right to take the children's bread and toss it to their dogs."

[27]"Yes, Lord," she said, "but even the dogs eat the crumbs that fall from their masters' table."

[28]Then Jesus answered, "Woman, you have great faith! Your request is granted." And her daughter was healed from that very hour.

Jesus Feeds the Four Thousand

[29]Jesus left there and went along the Sea of Galilee. Then he went up on a mountainside and sat down. [30]Great crowds came to him, bringing the lame, the blind, the crippled, the mute and many others, and laid them at his feet; and he healed them. [31]The people were amazed when they saw the mute speaking, the crippled made well, the lame walking and the blind seeing. And they praised the God of Israel.

[32]Jesus called his disciples to him and said, "I have compassion for these people; they have already been with me three days and have nothing to eat. I do not want to send them away hungry, or they may

for they might faint on the way." [33]The disciples said to him, "Where are we to get enough bread in the desert to feed so great a crowd?" [34]Jesus asked them, "How many loaves have you?" They said, "Seven, and a few small fish." [35]Then ordering the crowd to sit down on the ground, [36]he took the seven loaves and the fish; and after giving thanks he broke them and gave them to the disciples, and the disciples gave them to the crowds. [37]And all of them ate and were filled; and they took up the broken pieces left over, seven baskets full. [38]Those who had eaten were four thousand men, besides women and children. [39]After sending away the crowds, he got into the boat and went to the region of Magadan.[n]

The Demand for a Sign

16 The Pharisees and Sadducees came, and to test Jesus[o] they asked him to show them a sign from heaven. [2]He answered them, "When it is evening, you say, 'It will be fair weather, for the sky is red.' [3]And in the morning, 'It will be stormy today, for the sky is red and threatening.' You know how to interpret the appearance of the sky, but you cannot interpret the signs of the times.[p] [4]An evil and adulterous generation asks for a sign, but no sign will be given to it except the sign of Jonah." Then he left them and went away.

The Yeast of the Pharisees and Sadducees

5 When the disciples reached the other side, they had forgotten to bring any bread. [6]Jesus said to them, "Watch out, and beware of the yeast of the Pharisees and Sadducees." [7]They said to one another, "It is because we have brought no bread." [8]And becoming aware of it, Jesus said, "You of little faith, why are you talking about having no bread? [9]Do you still not perceive? Do you not remember the five loaves for the five thousand, and how many baskets you gathered? [10]Or the seven loaves for the four thousand, and how many baskets you gathered? [11]How could

νήστεις οὐ θέλω, μήποτε ἐκλυθῶσιν ἐν τῇ ὁδῷ. **33** καὶ λέγουσιν αὐτῷ οἱ μαθηταί, Πόθεν ἡμῖν ἐν ἐρημίᾳ ἄρτοι τοσοῦτοι ὥστε χορτάσαι ὄχλον τοσοῦτον; **34** καὶ λέγει αὐτοῖς ὁ Ἰησοῦς, Πόσους ἄρτους ἔχετε; οἱ δὲ εἶπαν, Ἑπτὰ καὶ ὀλίγα ἰχθύδια. **35** καὶ παραγγείλας τῷ ὄχλῳ ἀναπεσεῖν ἐπὶ τὴν γῆν **36** ἔλαβεν τοὺς ἑπτὰ ἄρτους καὶ τοὺς ἰχθύας καὶ εὐχαριστήσας ἔκλασεν καὶ ἐδίδου τοῖς μαθηταῖς, οἱ δὲ μαθηταὶ τοῖς ὄχλοις. **37** καὶ ἔφαγον πάντες καὶ ἐχορτάσθησαν. καὶ τὸ περισσεῦον τῶν κλασμάτων ἦραν ἑπτὰ σπυρίδας πλήρεις. **38** οἱ δὲ ἐσθίοντες ἦσαν τετρακισχίλιοι ἄνδρες χωρὶς γυναικῶν καὶ παιδίων. **39** Καὶ ἀπολύσας τοὺς ὄχλους ἐνέβη εἰς τὸ πλοῖον καὶ ἦλθεν εἰς τὰ ὅρια Μαγαδάν.[e]

16 Καὶ προσελθόντες οἱ Φαρισαῖοι καὶ Σαδδουκαῖοι πειράζοντες ἐπηρώτησαν αὐτὸν σημεῖον ἐκ τοῦ οὐρανοῦ ἐπιδεῖξαι αὐτοῖς. **2** ὁ δὲ ἀποκριθεὶς εἶπεν αὐτοῖς, [Ὀψίας γενομένης λέγετε, Εὐδία, πυρράζει γὰρ ὁ οὐρανός· **3** καὶ πρωΐ, Σήμερον χειμών, πυρράζει γὰρ στυγνάζων ὁ οὐρανός. τὸ μὲν πρόσωπον τοῦ οὐρανοῦ γινώσκετε διακρίνειν, τὰ δὲ σημεῖα τῶν καιρῶν οὐ δύνασθε;] **4** Γενεὰ πονηρὰ καὶ μοιχαλὶς σημεῖον ἐπιζητεῖ, καὶ σημεῖον οὐ δοθήσεται αὐτῇ εἰ μὴ τὸ σημεῖον Ἰωνᾶ. καὶ καταλιπὼν αὐτοὺς ἀπῆλθεν.

5 Καὶ ἐλθόντες οἱ μαθηταὶ εἰς τὸ πέραν ἐπελάθοντο ἄρτους λαβεῖν. **6** ὁ δὲ Ἰησοῦς εἶπεν αὐτοῖς, Ὁρᾶτε καὶ προσέχετε ἀπὸ τῆς ζύμης τῶν Φαρισαίων καὶ Σαδδουκαίων. **7** οἱ δὲ διελογίζοντο ἐν ἑαυτοῖς λέγοντες ὅτι Ἄρτους οὐκ ἐλάβομεν. **8** γνοὺς δὲ ὁ Ἰησοῦς εἶπεν, Τί διαλογίζεσθε ἐν ἑαυτοῖς, ὀλιγόπιστοι, ὅτι ἄρτους οὐκ ἔχετε; **9** οὔπω νοεῖτε, οὐδὲ μνημονεύετε τοὺς πέντε ἄρτους τῶν πεντακισχιλίων καὶ πόσους κοφίνους ἐλάβετε; **10** οὐδὲ τοὺς ἑπτὰ ἄρτους τῶν τετρακισχιλίων καὶ πόσας σπυρίδας ἐλάβετε; **11** πῶς

collapse on the way."

[33]His disciples answered, "Where could we get enough bread in this remote place to feed such a crowd?"

[34]"How many loaves do you have?" Jesus asked.

"Seven," they replied, "and a few small fish."

[35]He told the crowd to sit down on the ground. [36]Then he took the seven loaves and the fish, and when he had given thanks, he broke them and gave them to the disciples, and they in turn to the people. [37]They all ate and were satisfied. Afterward the disciples picked up seven basketfuls of broken pieces that were left over. [38]The number of those who ate was four thousand, besides women and children. [39]After Jesus had sent the crowd away, he got into the boat and went to the vicinity of Magadan.

The Demand for a Sign

16 The Pharisees and Sadducees came to Jesus and tested him by asking him to show them a sign from heaven.

[2]He replied,[a] "When evening comes, you say, 'It will be fair weather, for the sky is red,' [3]and in the morning, 'Today it will be stormy, for the sky is red and overcast.' You know how to interpret the appearance of the sky, but you cannot interpret the signs of the times. [4]A wicked and adulterous generation looks for a miraculous sign, but none will be given it except the sign of Jonah." Jesus then left them and went away.

The Yeast of the Pharisees and Sadducees

[5]When they went across the lake, the disciples forgot to take bread. [6]"Be careful," Jesus said to them. "Be on your guard against the yeast of the Pharisees and Sadducees."

[7]They discussed this among themselves and said, "It is because we didn't bring any bread."

[8]Aware of their discussion, Jesus asked, "You of little faith, why are you talking among yourselves about having no bread? [9]Do you still not understand? Don't you remember the five loaves for the five thousand, and how many basketfuls you gathered? [10]Or the seven loaves for the four thousand, and how many basketfuls you gathered? [11]How is it you don't under-

n Other ancient authorities read *Magdala* or *Magdalan*
o Gk *him*   p Other ancient authorities lack [2]*When it is . . . of the times*

e39 NRSV note n Μαγδαλά or Μαγδαλάν

a2 Some early manuscripts do not have the rest of verse 2 and all of verse 3.

you fail to perceive that I was not speaking about bread? Beware of the yeast of the Pharisees and Sadducees!" [12]Then they understood that he had not told them to beware of the yeast of bread, but of the teaching of the Pharisees and Sadducees.

Peter's Declaration about Jesus

13 Now when Jesus came into the district of Caesarea Philippi, he asked his disciples, "Who do people say that the Son of Man is?" [14]And they said, "Some say John the Baptist, but others Elijah, and still others Jeremiah or one of the prophets." [15]He said to them, "But who do you say that I am?" [16]Simon Peter answered, "You are the Messiah,q the Son of the living God." [17]And Jesus answered him, "Blessed are you, Simon son of Jonah! For flesh and blood has not revealed this to you, but my Father in heaven. [18]And I tell you, you are Peter,r and on this rocks I will build my church, and the gates of Hades will not prevail against it. [19]I will give you the keys of the kingdom of heaven, and whatever you bind on earth will be bound in heaven, and whatever you loose on earth will be loosed in heaven." [20]Then he sternly ordered the disciples not to tell anyone that he wast the Messiah.q

Jesus Foretells His Death and Resurrection

21 From that time on, Jesus began to show his disciples that he must go to Jerusalem and undergo great suffering at the hands of the elders and chief priests and scribes, and be killed, and on the third day be raised. [22]And Peter took him aside and began to rebuke him, saying, "God forbid it, Lord! This must never happen to you." [23]But he turned and said to Peter, "Get behind me, Satan! You are a stumbling block to me; for you are setting your mind not on divine things but on human things."

The Cross and Self-Denial

24 Then Jesus told his disciples, "If any want to become my followers, let them deny themselves and take up their cross and follow me. [25]For those who want to save their life will lose it, and those who lose their life for my sake will find it. [26]For what will it profit them if they gain the whole world but forfeit their life? Or what will they give in return for their life?

οὐ νοεῖτε ὅτι οὐ περὶ ἄρτων εἶπον ὑμῖν; προσέχετε δὲ ἀπὸ τῆς ζύμης τῶν Φαρισαίων καὶ Σαδδουκαίων. **12** τότε συνῆκαν ὅτι οὐκ εἶπεν προσέχειν ἀπὸ τῆς ζύμης τῶν ἄρτων ἀλλὰ ἀπὸ τῆς διδαχῆς τῶν Φαρισαίων καὶ Σαδδουκαίων.

13 Ἐλθὼν δὲ ὁ Ἰησοῦς εἰς τὰ μέρη Καισαρείας τῆς Φιλίππου ἠρώτα τοὺς μαθητὰς αὐτοῦ λέγων, Τίνα λέγουσιν οἱ ἄνθρωποι εἶναι τὸν υἱὸν τοῦ ἀνθρώπου; **14** οἱ δὲ εἶπαν, Οἱ μὲν Ἰωάννην τὸν βαπτιστήν, ἄλλοι δὲ Ἠλίαν, ἕτεροι δὲ Ἰερεμίαν ἢ ἕνα τῶν προφητῶν. **15** λέγει αὐτοῖς, Ὑμεῖς δὲ τίνα με λέγετε εἶναι; **16** ἀποκριθεὶς δὲ Σίμων Πέτρος εἶπεν, Σὺ εἶ ὁ Χριστὸς ὁ υἱὸς τοῦ θεοῦ τοῦ ζῶντος. **17** ἀποκριθεὶς δὲ ὁ Ἰησοῦς εἶπεν αὐτῷ, Μακάριος εἶ, Σίμων Βαριωνᾶ, ὅτι σὰρξ καὶ αἷμα οὐκ ἀπεκάλυψέν σοι ἀλλ' ὁ πατήρ μου ὁ ἐν τοῖς οὐρανοῖς. **18** κἀγὼ δέ σοι λέγω ὅτι σὺ εἶ Πέτρος, καὶ ἐπὶ ταύτῃ τῇ πέτρᾳ οἰκοδομήσω μου τὴν ἐκκλησίαν καὶ πύλαι ᾅδου οὐ κατισχύσουσιν αὐτῆς. **19** δώσω σοι τὰς κλεῖδας τῆς βασιλείας τῶν οὐρανῶν, καὶ ὃ ἐὰν δήσῃς ἐπὶ τῆς γῆς ἔσται δεδεμένον ἐν τοῖς οὐρανοῖς, καὶ ὃ ἐὰν λύσῃς ἐπὶ τῆς γῆς ἔσται λελυμένον ἐν τοῖς οὐρανοῖς. **20** τότε διεστείλατοa τοῖς μαθηταῖςb ἵνα μηδενὶ εἴπωσιν ὅτι αὐτός ἐστινb ὁ Χριστός.

21 Ἀπὸ τότε ἤρξατο ὁ Ἰησοῦς δεικνύειν τοῖς μαθηταῖς αὐτοῦ ὅτι δεῖ αὐτὸν εἰς Ἱεροσόλυμα ἀπελθεῖν καὶ πολλὰ παθεῖν ἀπὸ τῶν πρεσβυτέρων καὶ ἀρχιερέων καὶ γραμματέων καὶ ἀποκτανθῆναι καὶ τῇ τρίτῃ ἡμέρᾳ ἐγερθῆναι. **22** καὶ προσλαβόμενος αὐτὸν ὁ Πέτρος ἤρξατο ἐπιτιμᾶν αὐτῷ λέγων, Ἵλεώς σοι, κύριε· οὐ μὴ ἔσται σοι τοῦτο. **23** ὁ δὲ στραφεὶς εἶπεν τῷ Πέτρῳ, Ὕπαγε ὀπίσω μου, Σατανᾶ· σκάνδαλον εἶ ἐμοῦ, ὅτι οὐ φρονεῖς τὰ τοῦ θεοῦ ἀλλὰ τὰ τῶν ἀνθρώπων. **24** Τότε ὁ Ἰησοῦς εἶπεν τοῖς μαθηταῖς αὐτοῦ, Εἴ τις θέλει ὀπίσω μου ἐλθεῖν, ἀπαρνησάσθω ἑαυτὸν καὶ ἀράτω τὸν σταυρὸν αὐτοῦ καὶ ἀκολουθείτω μοι. **25** ὃς γὰρ ἐὰν θέλῃ τὴν ψυχὴν αὐτοῦ σῶσαι ἀπολέσει αὐτήν· ὃς δ' ἂν ἀπολέσῃ τὴν ψυχὴν αὐτοῦ ἕνεκεν ἐμοῦ εὑρήσει αὐτήν. **26** τί γὰρ ὠφεληθήσεται ἄνθρωπος ἐὰν τὸν κόσμον ὅλον κερδήσῃ τὴν δὲ ψυχὴν αὐτοῦ ζημιωθῇ; ἢ τί δώσει ἄνθρωπος ἀντάλλαγμα τῆς ψυχῆς αὐτοῦ; **27** μέλλει

stand that I was not talking to you about bread? But be on your guard against the yeast of the Pharisees and Sadducees." [12]Then they understood that he was not telling them to guard against the yeast used in bread, but against the teaching of the Pharisees and Sadducees.

Peter's Confession of Christ

[13]When Jesus came to the region of Caesarea Philippi, he asked his disciples, "Who do people say the Son of Man is?" [14]They replied, "Some say John the Baptist; others say Elijah; and still others, Jeremiah or one of the prophets." [15]"But what about you?" he asked. "Who do you say I am?" [16]Simon Peter answered, "You are the Christ,b the Son of the living God." [17]Jesus replied, "Blessed are you, Simon son of Jonah, for this was not revealed to you by man, but by my Father in heaven. [18]And I tell you that you are Peter,c and on this rock I will build my church, and the gates of Hadesd will not overcome it.e [19]I will give you the keys of the kingdom of heaven; whatever you bind on earth will bef bound in heaven, and whatever you loose on earth will beg loosed in heaven." [20]Then he warned his disciples not to tell anyone that he was the Christ.

Jesus Predicts His Death

[21]From that time on Jesus began to explain to his disciples that he must go to Jerusalem and suffer many things at the hands of the elders, chief priests and teachers of the law, and that he must be killed and on the third day be raised to life.

[22]Peter took him aside and began to rebuke him. "Never, Lord!" he said. "This shall never happen to you!"

[23]Jesus turned and said to Peter, "Get behind me, Satan! You are a stumbling block to me; you do not have in mind the things of God, but the things of men."

[24]Then Jesus said to his disciples, "If anyone would come after me, he must deny himself and take up his cross and follow me. [25]For whoever wants to save his lifeh will lose it, but whoever loses his life for me will find it. [26]What good will it be for a man if he gains the whole world, yet forfeits his soul? Or what can a man give in exchange for his soul? [27]For the Son of

---

q Or the Christ   r Gk Petros   s Gk petra   t Other ancient authorities add Jesus

a20 NIV text ἐπετίμησεν †   b20 NRSV note t adds Ἰησοῦ

b16 Or Messiah; also in verse 20   c18 Peter means rock. d18 Or hell   e18 Or not prove stronger than it   f19 Or have been   g19 Or have been   h25 The Greek word means either life or soul; also in verse 26.

27 "For the Son of Man is to come with his angels in the glory of his Father, and then he will repay everyone for what has been done. 28Truly I tell you, there are some standing here who will not taste death before they see the Son of Man coming in his kingdom."

The Transfiguration

17 Six days later, Jesus took with him Peter and James and his brother John and led them up a high mountain, by themselves. 2And he was transfigured before them, and his face shone like the sun, and his clothes became dazzling white. 3Suddenly there appeared to them Moses and Elijah, talking with him. 4Then Peter said to Jesus, "Lord, it is good for us to be here; if you wish, Iᵘ will make three dwellingsᵛ here, one for you, one for Moses, and one for Elijah." 5While he was still speaking, suddenly a bright cloud overshadowed them, and from the cloud a voice said, "This is my Son, the Beloved;ʷ with him I am well pleased; listen to him!" 6When the disciples heard this, they fell to the ground and were overcome by fear. 7But Jesus came and touched them, saying, "Get up and do not be afraid." 8And when they looked up, they saw no one except Jesus himself alone.

9 As they were coming down the mountain, Jesus ordered them, "Tell no one about the vision until after the Son of Man has been raised from the dead." 10And the disciples asked him, "Why, then, do the scribes say that Elijah must come first?" 11He replied, "Elijah is indeed coming and will restore all things; 12but I tell you that Elijah has already come, and they did not recognize him, but they did to him whatever they pleased. So also the Son of Man is about to suffer at their hands." 13Then the disciples understood that he was speaking to them about John the Baptist.

Jesus Cures a Boy with a Demon

14 When they came to the crowd, a man came to him, knelt before him, 15and said, "Lord, have mercy on my son, for he is an epileptic and he suffers terribly; he often falls into the fire and often into the water.

γὰρ ὁ υἱὸς τοῦ ἀνθρώπου ἔρχεσθαι ἐν τῇ δόξῃ τοῦ πατρὸς αὐτοῦ μετὰ τῶν ἀγγέλων αὐτοῦ, καὶ τότε ἀποδώσει ἑκάστῳ κατὰ τὴν πρᾶξιν αὐτοῦ. **28** ἀμὴν λέγω ὑμῖν ὅτι εἰσίν τινες τῶν ὧδε ἑστώτων οἵτινες οὐ μὴ γεύσωνται θανάτου ἕως ἂν ἴδωσιν τὸν υἱὸν τοῦ ἀνθρώπου ἐρχόμενον ἐν τῇ βασιλείᾳ αὐτοῦ.

17 Καὶ μεθ' ἡμέρας ἓξ παραλαμβάνει ὁ Ἰησοῦς τὸν Πέτρον καὶ Ἰάκωβον καὶ Ἰωάννην τὸν ἀδελφὸν αὐτοῦ καὶ ἀναφέρει αὐτοὺς εἰς ὄρος ὑψηλὸν κατ' ἰδίαν. **2** καὶ μετεμορφώθη ἔμπροσθεν αὐτῶν, καὶ ἔλαμψεν τὸ πρόσωπον αὐτοῦ ὡς ὁ ἥλιος, τὰ δὲ ἱμάτια αὐτοῦ ἐγένετο λευκὰ ὡς τὸ φῶς. **3** καὶ ἰδοὺ ὤφθη αὐτοῖς Μωϋσῆς καὶ Ἡλίας συλλαλοῦντες μετ' αὐτοῦ. **4** ἀποκριθεὶς δὲ ὁ Πέτρος εἶπεν τῷ Ἰησοῦ, Κύριε, καλόν ἐστιν ἡμᾶς ὧδε εἶναι· εἰ θέλεις, ποιήσωᵃ ὧδε τρεῖς σκηνάς, σοὶ μίαν καὶ Μωϋσεῖ μίαν καὶ Ἡλίᾳ μίαν. **5** ἔτι αὐτοῦ λαλοῦντος ἰδοὺ νεφέλη φωτεινὴ ἐπεσκίασεν αὐτούς, καὶ ἰδοὺ φωνὴ ἐκ τῆς νεφέλης λέγουσα, Οὗτός ἐστιν ὁ υἱός μου ὁ ἀγαπητός, ἐν ᾧ εὐδόκησα· ἀκούετε αὐτοῦ. **6** καὶ ἀκούσαντες οἱ μαθηταὶ ἔπεσαν ἐπὶ πρόσωπον αὐτῶν καὶ ἐφοβήθησαν σφόδρα. **7** καὶ προσῆλθεν ὁ Ἰησοῦς καὶ ἁψάμενος αὐτῶν εἶπεν, Ἐγέρθητε καὶ μὴ φοβεῖσθε. **8** ἐπάραντες δὲ τοὺς ὀφθαλμοὺς αὐτῶν οὐδένα εἶδον εἰ μὴ αὐτὸν Ἰησοῦν μόνον.

9 Καὶ καταβαινόντων αὐτῶν ἐκ τοῦ ὄρους ἐνετείλατο αὐτοῖς ὁ Ἰησοῦς λέγων, Μηδενὶ εἴπητε τὸ ὅραμα ἕως οὗ ὁ υἱὸς τοῦ ἀνθρώπου ἐκ νεκρῶν ἐγερθῇ. **10** καὶ ἐπηρώτησαν αὐτὸν οἱ μαθηταὶ λέγοντες, Τί οὖν οἱ γραμματεῖς λέγουσιν ὅτι Ἡλίαν δεῖ ἐλθεῖν πρῶτον; **11** ὁ δὲ ἀποκριθεὶς εἶπεν, Ἡλίας μὲν ἔρχεται καὶ ἀποκαταστήσει πάντα· **12** λέγω δὲ ὑμῖν ὅτι Ἡλίας ἤδη ἦλθεν, καὶ οὐκ ἐπέγνωσαν αὐτὸν ἀλλὰ ἐποίησαν ἐν αὐτῷ ὅσα ἠθέλησαν· οὕτως καὶ ὁ υἱὸς τοῦ ἀνθρώπου μέλλει πάσχειν ὑπ' αὐτῶν. **13** τότε συνῆκαν οἱ μαθηταὶ ὅτι περὶ Ἰωάννου τοῦ βαπτιστοῦ εἶπεν αὐτοῖς.

14 Καὶ ἐλθόντων πρὸς τὸν ὄχλον προσῆλθεν αὐτῷ ἄνθρωπος γονυπετῶν αὐτὸν **15** καὶ λέγων, Κύριε, ἐλέησόν μου τὸν υἱόν, ὅτι σεληνιάζεται καὶ κακῶς πάσχει· πολλάκις γὰρ πίπτει εἰς τὸ πῦρ καὶ πολλάκις εἰς τὸ ὕδωρ.

Man is going to come in his Father's glory with his angels, and then he will reward each person according to what he has done. 28I tell you the truth, some who are standing here will not taste death before they see the Son of Man coming in his kingdom."

The Transfiguration

17 After six days Jesus took with him Peter, James and John the brother of James, and led them up a high mountain by themselves. 2There he was transfigured before them. His face shone like the sun, and his clothes became as white as the light. 3Just then there appeared before them Moses and Elijah, talking with Jesus.

4Peter said to Jesus, "Lord, it is good for us to be here. If you wish, I will put up three shelters—one for you, one for Moses and one for Elijah."

5While he was still speaking, a bright cloud enveloped them, and a voice from the cloud said, "This is my Son, whom I love; with him I am well pleased. Listen to him!"

6When the disciples heard this, they fell facedown to the ground, terrified. 7But Jesus came and touched them. "Get up," he said. "Don't be afraid." 8When they looked up, they saw no one except Jesus.

9As they were coming down the mountain, Jesus instructed them, "Don't tell anyone what you have seen, until the Son of Man has been raised from the dead."

10The disciples asked him, "Why then do the teachers of the law say that Elijah must come first?"

11Jesus replied, "To be sure, Elijah comes and will restore all things. 12But I tell you, Elijah has already come, and they did not recognize him, but have done to him everything they wished. In the same way the Son of Man is going to suffer at their hands." 13Then the disciples understood that he was talking to them about John the Baptist.

The Healing of a Boy With a Demon

14When they came to the crowd, a man approached Jesus and knelt before him. 15"Lord, have mercy on my son," he said. "He has seizures and is suffering greatly. He often falls into the fire or into the water.

NRSV

16And I brought him to your disciples, but they could not cure him." 17Jesus answered, "You faithless and perverse generation, how much longer must I be with you? How much longer must I put up with you? Bring him here to me." 18And Jesus rebuked the demon,x and ity came out of him, and the boy was cured instantly. 19Then the disciples came to Jesus privately and said, "Why could we not cast it out?" 20He said to them, "Because of your little faith. For truly I tell you, if you have faith the size of az mustard seed, you will say to this mountain, 'Move from here to there,' and it will move; and nothing will be impossible for you."a

Jesus Again Foretells His Death and Resurrection

22 As they were gatheringb in Galilee, Jesus said to them, "The Son of Man is going to be betrayed into human hands, 23and they will kill him, and on the third day he will be raised." And they were greatly distressed.

Jesus and the Temple Tax

24 When they reached Capernaum, the collectors of the temple taxc came to Peter and said, "Does your teacher not pay the temple tax?"c 25He said, "Yes, he does." And when he came home, Jesus spoke of it first, asking, "What do you think, Simon? From whom do kings of the earth take toll or tribute? From their children or from others?" 26When Peterd said, "From others," Jesus said to him, "Then the children are free. 27However, so that we do not give offense to them, go to the sea and cast a hook; take the first fish that comes up; and when you open its mouth, you will find a coin;e take that and give it to them for you and me."

True Greatness

18 At that time the disciples came to Jesus and asked, "Who is the greatest in the kingdom of heaven?" 2He called a child, whom he put among them, 3and said, "Truly I tell you, unless you change and become like children, you will never enter the kingdom of heaven. 4Whoever becomes humble like this child is the greatest in the kingdom of heaven. 5Whoever welcomes one such child in my name

[Greek]

16 καὶ προσήνεγκα αὐτὸν τοῖς μαθηταῖς σου, καὶ οὐκ ἠδυνήθησαν αὐτὸν θεραπεῦσαι. 17 ἀποκριθεὶς δὲ ὁ Ἰησοῦς εἶπεν, Ὦ γενεὰ ἄπιστος καὶ διεστραμμένη, ἕως πότε μεθ᾽ ὑμῶν ἔσομαι; ἕως πότε ἀνέξομαι ὑμῶν; φέρετέ μοι αὐτὸν ὧδε. 18 καὶ ἐπετίμησεν αὐτῷ ὁ Ἰησοῦς καὶ ἐξῆλθεν ἀπ᾽ αὐτοῦ τὸ δαιμόνιον καὶ ἐθεραπεύθη ὁ παῖς ἀπὸ τῆς ὥρας ἐκείνης. 19 Τότε προσελθόντες οἱ μαθηταὶ τῷ Ἰησοῦ κατ᾽ ἰδίαν εἶπον, Διὰ τί ἡμεῖς οὐκ ἠδυνήθημεν ἐκβαλεῖν αὐτό; 20 ὁ δὲ λέγει αὐτοῖς, Διὰ τὴν ὀλιγοπιστίαν ὑμῶν· ἀμὴν γὰρ λέγω ὑμῖν, ἐὰν ἔχητε πίστιν ὡς κόκκον σινάπεως, ἐρεῖτε τῷ ὄρει τούτῳ, Μετάβα ἔνθεν ἐκεῖ, καὶ μεταβήσεται· καὶ οὐδὲν ἀδυνατήσει ὑμῖν.b

22 Συστρεφομένωνc δὲ αὐτῶν ἐν τῇ Γαλιλαίᾳ εἶπεν αὐτοῖς ὁ Ἰησοῦς, Μέλλει ὁ υἱὸς τοῦ ἀνθρώπου παραδίδοσθαι εἰς χεῖρας ἀνθρώπων, 23 καὶ ἀποκτενοῦσιν αὐτόν, καὶ τῇ τρίτῃ ἡμέρᾳ ἐγερθήσεται. καὶ ἐλυπήθησαν σφόδρα.

24 Ἐλθόντων δὲ αὐτῶν εἰς Καφαρναοὺμ προσῆλθον οἱ τὰ δίδραχμα λαμβάνοντες τῷ Πέτρῳ καὶ εἶπαν, Ὁ διδάσκαλος ὑμῶν οὐ τελεῖ [τὰ] δίδραχμα; 25 λέγει, Ναί. καὶ ἐλθόντα εἰς τὴν οἰκίαν προέφθασεν αὐτὸν ὁ Ἰησοῦς λέγων, Τί σοι δοκεῖ, Σίμων; οἱ βασιλεῖς τῆς γῆς ἀπὸ τίνων λαμβάνουσιν τέλη ἢ κῆνσον; ἀπὸ τῶν υἱῶν αὐτῶν ἢ ἀπὸ τῶν ἀλλοτρίων; 26 εἰπόντος δέ, Ἀπὸ τῶν ἀλλοτρίων, ἔφη αὐτῷ ὁ Ἰησοῦς, Ἄρα γε ἐλεύθεροί εἰσιν οἱ υἱοί. 27 ἵνα δὲ μὴ σκανδαλίσωμεν αὐτούς, πορευθεὶς εἰςd θάλασσαν βάλε ἄγκιστρον καὶ τὸν ἀναβάντα πρῶτον ἰχθὺν ἆρον, καὶ ἀνοίξας τὸ στόμα αὐτοῦ εὑρήσεις στατῆρα· ἐκεῖνον λαβὼν δὸς αὐτοῖς ἀντὶ ἐμοῦ καὶ σοῦ.

18 Ἐν ἐκείνῃ τῇ ὥρᾳ προσῆλθον οἱ μαθηταὶ τῷ Ἰησοῦ λέγοντες, Τίς ἄρα μείζων ἐστὶν ἐν τῇ βασιλείᾳ τῶν οὐρανῶν; 2 καὶ προσκαλεσάμενος παιδίον ἔστησεν αὐτὸ ἐν μέσῳ αὐτῶν 3 καὶ εἶπεν, Ἀμὴν λέγω ὑμῖν, ἐὰν μὴ στραφῆτε καὶ γένησθε ὡς τὰ παιδία, οὐ μὴ εἰσέλθητε εἰς τὴν βασιλείαν τῶν οὐρανῶν. 4 ὅστις οὖν ταπεινώσει ἑαυτὸν ὡς τὸ παιδίον τοῦτο, οὗτός ἐστιν ὁ μείζων ἐν τῇ βασιλείᾳ τῶν οὐρανῶν. 5 καὶ ὃς ἐὰν δέξηται ἓν παιδίον τοιοῦτο ἐπὶ τῷ ὀνόματί μου,

NIV

16I brought him to your disciples, but they could not heal him."

17"O unbelieving and perverse generation," Jesus replied, "how long shall I stay with you? How long shall I put up with you? Bring the boy here to me." 18Jesus rebuked the demon, and it came out of the boy, and he was healed from that moment.

19Then the disciples came to Jesus in private and asked, "Why couldn't we drive it out?"

20He replied, "Because you have so little faith. I tell you the truth, if you have faith as small as a mustard seed, you can say to this mountain, 'Move from here to there' and it will move. Nothing will be impossible for you.a"

22When they came together in Galilee, he said to them, "The Son of Man is going to be betrayed into the hands of men. 23They will kill him, and on the third day he will be raised to life." And the disciples were filled with grief.

The Temple Tax

24After Jesus and his disciples arrived in Capernaum, the collectors of the two-drachma tax came to Peter and asked, "Doesn't your teacher pay the temple taxb?"

25"Yes, he does," he replied.

When Peter came into the house, Jesus was the first to speak. "What do you think, Simon?" he asked. "From whom do the kings of the earth collect duty and taxes—from their own sons or from others?"

26"From others," Peter answered.

"Then the sons are exempt," Jesus said to him. 27"But so that we may not offend them, go to the lake and throw out your line. Take the first fish you catch; open its mouth and you will find a four-drachma coin. Take it and give it to them for my tax and yours."

The Greatest in the Kingdom of Heaven

18 At that time the disciples came to Jesus and asked, "Who is the greatest in the kingdom of heaven?"

2He called a little child and had him stand among them. 3And he said: "I tell you the truth, unless you change and become like little children, you will never enter the kingdom of heaven. 4Therefore, whoever humbles himself like this child is the greatest in the kingdom of heaven.

5"And whoever welcomes a little child

---

x Gk it or him   y Gk the demon   z Gk faith as a grain of
a Other ancient authorities add verse 21, But this kind does not come out except by prayer and fasting   b Other ancient authorities read living   c Gk didrachma   d Gk he
e Gk stater; the stater was worth two didrachmas

b20 NIV/NRSV notes add 21 τοῦτο δὲ τὸ γένος οὐκ ἐκπορεύεται εἰ μὴ ἐν προσευχῇ καὶ νηστείᾳ.
c22 NRSV note b ἀναστρεφομένων
d27 NIV text adds τὴν †

a20 Some manuscripts you. 21But this kind does not go out except by prayer and fasting.   b24 Greek the two drachmas

welcomes me.

Temptations to Sin

6 "If any of you put a stumbling block before one of these little ones who believe in me, it would be better for you if a great millstone were fastened around your neck and you were drowned in the depth of the sea. [7]Woe to the world because of stumbling blocks! Occasions for stumbling are bound to come, but woe to the one by whom the stumbling block comes!

8 "If your hand or your foot causes you to stumble, cut it off and throw it away; it is better for you to enter life maimed or lame than to have two hands or two feet and to be thrown into the eternal fire. [9]And if your eye causes you to stumble, tear it out and throw it away; it is better for you to enter life with one eye than to have two eyes and to be thrown into the hell[f] of fire.

The Parable of the Lost Sheep

10 "Take care that you do not despise one of these little ones; for, I tell you, in heaven their angels continually see the face of my Father in heaven.[g] [12]What do you think? If a shepherd has a hundred sheep, and one of them has gone astray, does he not leave the ninety-nine on the mountains and go in search of the one that went astray? [13]And if he finds it, truly I tell you, he rejoices over it more than over the ninety-nine that never went astray. [14]So it is not the will of your[h] Father in heaven that one of these little ones should be lost.

Reproving Another Who Sins

15 "If another member of the church[i] sins against you,[j] go and point out the fault when the two of you are alone. If the member listens to you, you have regained that one.[k] [16]But if you are not listened to, take one or two others along with you, so that every word may be confirmed by the evidence of two or three witnesses. [17]If the member refuses to listen to them, tell it to the church; and if the offender refuses to listen even to the church, let such a one be to you as a Gentile and a tax collector. [18]Truly I tell you, whatever you bind on earth will be bound in heaven, and whatever you loose on earth will be loosed in heaven. [19]Again, truly I tell you, if two of you agree on earth about anything you ask, it will be done for you by my Father in

---

ἐμὲ δέχεται.

6 Ὃς δ' ἂν σκανδαλίσῃ ἕνα τῶν μικρῶν τούτων τῶν πιστευόντων εἰς ἐμέ, συμφέρει αὐτῷ ἵνα κρεμασθῇ μύλος ὀνικὸς περὶ τὸν τράχηλον αὐτοῦ καὶ καταποντισθῇ ἐν τῷ πελάγει τῆς θαλάσσης. 7 οὐαὶ τῷ κόσμῳ ἀπὸ τῶν σκανδάλων· ἀνάγκη γὰρ ἐλθεῖν τὰ σκάνδαλα, πλὴν οὐαὶ τῷ ἀνθρώπῳ δι᾽ οὗ τὸ σκάνδαλον ἔρχεται. 8 Εἰ δὲ ἡ χείρ σου ἢ ὁ πούς σου σκανδαλίζει σε, ἔκκοψον αὐτὸν καὶ βάλε ἀπὸ σοῦ· καλόν σοί ἐστιν εἰσελθεῖν εἰς τὴν ζωὴν κυλλὸν ἢ χωλὸν ἢ δύο χεῖρας ἢ δύο πόδας ἔχοντα βληθῆναι εἰς τὸ πῦρ τὸ αἰώνιον. 9 καὶ εἰ ὁ ὀφθαλμός σου σκανδαλίζει σε, ἔξελε αὐτὸν καὶ βάλε ἀπὸ σοῦ· καλόν σοί ἐστιν μονόφθαλμον εἰς τὴν ζωὴν εἰσελθεῖν ἢ δύο ὀφθαλμοὺς ἔχοντα βληθῆναι εἰς τὴν γέενναν τοῦ πυρός. 10 Ὁρᾶτε μὴ καταφρονήσητε ἑνὸς τῶν μικρῶν τούτων· λέγω γὰρ ὑμῖν ὅτι οἱ ἄγγελοι αὐτῶν ἐν οὐρανοῖς διὰ παντὸς βλέπουσι τὸ πρόσωπον τοῦ πατρός μου τοῦ ἐν οὐρανοῖς.[a] 12 Τί ὑμῖν δοκεῖ; ἐὰν γένηταί τινι ἀνθρώπῳ ἑκατὸν πρόβατα καὶ πλανηθῇ ἓν ἐξ αὐτῶν, οὐχὶ ἀφήσει τὰ ἐνενήκοντα ἐννέα ἐπὶ τὰ ὄρη καὶ πορευθεὶς ζητεῖ τὸ πλανώμενον; 13 καὶ ἐὰν γένηται εὑρεῖν αὐτό, ἀμὴν λέγω ὑμῖν ὅτι χαίρει ἐπ᾽ αὐτῷ μᾶλλον ἢ ἐπὶ τοῖς ἐνενήκοντα ἐννέα τοῖς μὴ πεπλανημένοις. 14 οὕτως οὐκ ἔστιν θέλημα ἔμπροσθεν[b] τοῦ πατρὸς ὑμῶν[c] τοῦ ἐν οὐρανοῖς ἵνα ἀπόληται ἓν τῶν μικρῶν τούτων.

15 Ἐὰν δὲ ἁμαρτήσῃ [εἰς σὲ] ὁ ἀδελφός σου, ὕπαγε ἔλεγξον αὐτὸν μεταξὺ σοῦ καὶ αὐτοῦ μόνου. ἐάν σου ἀκούσῃ, ἐκέρδησας τὸν ἀδελφόν σου· 16 ἐὰν δὲ μὴ ἀκούσῃ, παράλαβε μετὰ σοῦ ἔτι ἕνα ἢ δύο, ἵνα **ἐπὶ στόματος δύο μαρτύρων ἢ τριῶν σταθῇ πᾶν ῥῆμα**· 17 ἐὰν δὲ παρακούσῃ αὐτῶν, εἰπὲ τῇ ἐκκλησίᾳ· ἐὰν δὲ καὶ τῆς ἐκκλησίας παρακούσῃ, ἔστω σοι ὥσπερ ὁ ἐθνικὸς καὶ ὁ τελώνης. 18 Ἀμὴν λέγω ὑμῖν· ὅσα ἐὰν δήσητε ἐπὶ τῆς γῆς ἔσται δεδεμένα ἐν οὐρανῷ, καὶ ὅσα ἐὰν λύσητε ἐπὶ τῆς γῆς ἔσται λελυμένα ἐν οὐρανῷ. 19 Πάλιν [ἀμὴν] λέγω ὑμῖν ὅτι ἐὰν δύο συμφωνήσωσιν ἐξ ὑμῶν ἐπὶ τῆς γῆς περὶ παντὸς πράγματος οὗ ἐὰν αἰτήσωνται, γενήσεται αὐτοῖς παρὰ τοῦ πατρός μου

---

like this in my name welcomes me. [6]But if anyone causes one of these little ones who believe in me to sin, it would be better for him to have a large millstone hung around his neck and to be drowned in the depths of the sea.

[7]"Woe to the world because of the things that cause people to sin! Such things must come, but woe to the man through whom they come! [8]If your hand or your foot causes you to sin cut it off and throw it away. It is better for you to enter life maimed or crippled than to have two hands or two feet and be thrown into eternal fire. [9]And if your eye causes you to sin, gouge it out and throw it away. It is better for you to enter life with one eye than to have two eyes and be thrown into the fire of hell.

The Parable of the Lost Sheep

[10]"See that you do not look down on one of these little ones. For I tell you that their angels in heaven always see the face of my Father in heaven.[a]

[12]"What do you think? If a man owns a hundred sheep, and one of them wanders away, will he not leave the ninety-nine on the hills and go to look for the one that wandered off? [13]And if he finds it, I tell you the truth, he is happier about that one sheep than about the ninety-nine that did not wander off. [14]In the same way your Father in heaven is not willing that any of these little ones should be lost.

A Brother Who Sins Against You

[15]"If your brother sins against you,[b] go and show him his fault, just between the two of you. If he listens to you, you have won your brother over. [16]But if he will not listen, take one or two others along, so that 'every matter may be established by the testimony of two or three witnesses.'[c] [17]If he refuses to listen to them, tell it to the church; and if he refuses to listen even to the church, treat him as you would a pagan or a tax collector.

[18]"I tell you the truth, whatever you bind on earth will be[d] bound in heaven, and whatever you loose on earth will be[e] loosed in heaven.

[19]"Again, I tell you that if two of you on earth agree about anything you ask for, it will be done for you by my Father in

---

[f] Gk *Gehenna*   [g] Other ancient authorities add verse 11, *For the Son of Man came to save the lost*   [h] Other ancient authorities read *my*   [i] Gk *If your brother*   [j] Other ancient authorities lack *against you*   [k] Gk *the brother*

[a]10 NIV/NRSV notes add 11 ἦλθεν γὰρ ὁ υἱὸς τοῦ ἀνθρώπου σῶσαι τὸ ἀπολωλός.   [b]14 NIV text omits ἔμπροσθεν †   [c]14 NRSV note h μου

[a]10 Some manuscripts *heaven.* [11]*The Son of Man came to save what was lost.*   [b]15 Some manuscripts do not have *against you.*   [c]16 Deut. 19:15   [d]18 Or *have been*   [e]18 Or *have been*

heaven. [20]For where two or three are gathered in my name, I am there among them."

Forgiveness

21 Then Peter came and said to him, "Lord, if another member of the church[l] sins against me, how often should I forgive? As many as seven times?" [22]Jesus said to him, "Not seven times, but, I tell you, seventy-seven[m] times.

The Parable of the Unforgiving Servant

23 "For this reason the kingdom of heaven may be compared to a king who wished to settle accounts with his slaves. [24]When he began the reckoning, one who owed him ten thousand talents[n] was brought to him; [25]and, as he could not pay, his lord ordered him to be sold, together with his wife and children and all his possessions, and payment to be made. [26]So the slave fell on his knees before him, saying, 'Have patience with me, and I will pay you everything.' [27]And out of pity for him, the lord of that slave released him and forgave him the debt. [28]But that same slave, as he went out, came upon one of his fellow slaves who owed him a hundred denarii;[o] and seizing him by the throat, he said, 'Pay what you owe.' [29]Then his fellow slave fell down and pleaded with him, 'Have patience with me, and I will pay you.' [30]But he refused; then he went and threw him into prison until he would pay the debt. [31]When his fellow slaves saw what had happened, they were greatly distressed, and they went and reported to their lord all that had taken place. [32]Then his lord summoned him and said to him, 'You wicked slave! I forgave you all that debt because you pleaded with me. [33]Should you not have had mercy on your fellow slave, as I had mercy on you?' [34]And in anger his lord handed him over to be tortured until he would pay his entire debt. [35]So my heavenly Father will also do to every one of you, if you do not forgive your brother or sister[p] from your heart."

Teaching about Divorce

19 When Jesus had finished saying these things, he left Galilee and went to the region of Judea beyond the Jordan. [2]Large crowds followed him, and he cured them there.

τοῦ ἐν οὐρανοῖς. **20** οὗ γάρ εἰσιν δύο ἢ τρεῖς συνηγμένοι εἰς τὸ ἐμὸν ὄνομα, ἐκεῖ εἰμι ἐν μέσῳ αὐτῶν.

21 Τότε προσελθὼν ὁ Πέτρος εἶπεν αὐτῷ, Κύριε, ποσάκις ἁμαρτήσει εἰς ἐμὲ ὁ ἀδελφός μου καὶ ἀφήσω αὐτῷ; ἕως ἑπτάκις; **22** λέγει αὐτῷ ὁ Ἰησοῦς, Οὐ λέγω σοι ἕως ἑπτάκις ἀλλὰ ἕως ἑβδομηκοντάκις ἑπτά. **23** Διὰ τοῦτο ὡμοιώθη ἡ βασιλεία τῶν οὐρανῶν ἀνθρώπῳ βασιλεῖ, ὃς ἠθέλησεν συνᾶραι λόγον μετὰ τῶν δούλων αὐτοῦ. **24** ἀρξαμένου δὲ αὐτοῦ συναίρειν προσηνέχθη αὐτῷ εἷς ὀφειλέτης μυρίων ταλάντων. **25** μὴ ἔχοντος δὲ αὐτοῦ ἀποδοῦναι ἐκέλευσεν αὐτὸν ὁ κύριος πραθῆναι καὶ τὴν γυναῖκα καὶ τὰ τέκνα καὶ πάντα ὅσα ἔχει, καὶ ἀποδοθῆναι. **26** πεσὼν οὖν ὁ δοῦλος προσεκύνει αὐτῷ λέγων, Μακροθύμησον ἐπ᾽ ἐμοί, καὶ πάντα ἀποδώσω σοι. **27** σπλαγχνισθεὶς δὲ ὁ κύριος τοῦ δούλου ἐκείνου ἀπέλυσεν αὐτὸν καὶ τὸ δάνειον ἀφῆκεν αὐτῷ. **28** ἐξελθὼν δὲ ὁ δοῦλος ἐκεῖνος εὗρεν ἕνα τῶν συνδούλων αὐτοῦ, ὃς ὤφειλεν αὐτῷ ἑκατὸν δηνάρια, καὶ κρατήσας αὐτὸν ἔπνιγεν λέγων, Ἀπόδος εἴ τι ὀφείλεις. **29** πεσὼν οὖν ὁ σύνδουλος αὐτοῦ παρεκάλει αὐτὸν λέγων, Μακροθύμησον ἐπ᾽ ἐμοί, καὶ ἀποδώσω σοι. **30** ὁ δὲ οὐκ ἤθελεν ἀλλὰ ἀπελθὼν ἔβαλεν αὐτὸν εἰς φυλακὴν ἕως ἀποδῷ τὸ ὀφειλόμενον. **31** ἰδόντες οὖν οἱ σύνδουλοι αὐτοῦ τὰ γενόμενα ἐλυπήθησαν σφόδρα καὶ ἐλθόντες διεσάφησαν τῷ κυρίῳ ἑαυτῶν πάντα τὰ γενόμενα. **32** τότε προσκαλεσάμενος αὐτὸν ὁ κύριος αὐτοῦ λέγει αὐτῷ, Δοῦλε πονηρέ, πᾶσαν τὴν ὀφειλὴν ἐκείνην ἀφῆκά σοι, ἐπεὶ παρεκάλεσάς με· **33** οὐκ ἔδει καὶ σὲ ἐλεῆσαι τὸν σύνδουλόν σου, ὡς κἀγὼ σὲ ἠλέησα; **34** καὶ ὀργισθεὶς ὁ κύριος αὐτοῦ παρέδωκεν αὐτὸν τοῖς βασανισταῖς ἕως οὗ ἀποδῷ πᾶν τὸ ὀφειλόμενον. **35** Οὕτως καὶ ὁ πατήρ μου ὁ οὐράνιος ποιήσει ὑμῖν, ἐὰν μὴ ἀφῆτε ἕκαστος τῷ ἀδελφῷ αὐτοῦ ἀπὸ τῶν καρδιῶν ὑμῶν.

19 Καὶ ἐγένετο ὅτε ἐτέλεσεν ὁ Ἰησοῦς τοὺς λόγους τούτους, μετῆρεν ἀπὸ τῆς Γαλιλαίας καὶ ἦλθεν εἰς τὰ ὅρια τῆς Ἰουδαίας πέραν τοῦ Ἰορδάνου. **2** καὶ ἠκολούθησαν αὐτῷ ὄχλοι πολλοί, καὶ ἐθεράπευσεν αὐτοὺς ἐκεῖ.

---

heaven. [20]For where two or three come together in my name, there am I with them."

The Parable of the Unmerciful Servant

[21]Then Peter came to Jesus and asked, "Lord, how many times shall I forgive my brother when he sins against me? Up to seven times?"

[22]Jesus answered, "I tell you, not seven times, but seventy-seven times.[f]

[23]"Therefore, the kingdom of heaven is like a king who wanted to settle accounts with his servants. [24]As he began the settlement, a man who owed him ten thousand talents[g] was brought to him. [25]Since he was not able to pay, the master ordered that he and his wife and his children and all that he had be sold to repay the debt.

[26]"The servant fell on his knees before him. 'Be patient with me,' he begged, 'and I will pay back everything.' [27]The servant's master took pity on him, canceled the debt and let him go.

[28]"But when that servant went out, he found one of his fellow servants who owed him a hundred denarii.[h] He grabbed him and began to choke him. 'Pay back what you owe me!' he demanded.

[29]"His fellow servant fell to his knees and begged him, 'Be patient with me, and I will pay you back.'

[30]"But he refused. Instead, he went off and had the man thrown into prison until he could pay the debt. [31]When the other servants saw what had happened, they were greatly distressed and went and told their master everything that had happened.

[32]"Then the master called the servant in. 'You wicked servant,' he said, 'I canceled all that debt of yours because you begged me to. [33]Shouldn't you have had mercy on your fellow servant just as I had on you?' [34]In anger his master turned him over to the jailers to be tortured, until he should pay back all he owed.

[35]"This is how my heavenly Father will treat each of you unless you forgive your brother from your heart."

Divorce

19 When Jesus had finished saying these things, he left Galilee and went into the region of Judea to the other side of the Jordan. [2]Large crowds followed him, and he healed them there.

---

[l]Gk *if my brother*   [m]Or *seventy times seven*   [n]A talent was worth more than fifteen years' wages of a laborer   [o]The denarius was the usual day's wage for a laborer   [p]Gk *brother*

3 Some Pharisees came to him, and to test him they asked, "Is it lawful for a man to divorce his wife for any cause?" ⁴He answered, "Have you not read that the one who made them at the beginning 'made them male and female,' ⁵and said, 'For this reason a man shall leave his father and mother and be joined to his wife, and the two shall become one flesh'? ⁶So they are no longer two, but one flesh. Therefore what God has joined together, let no one separate." ⁷They said to him, "Why then did Moses command us to give a certificate of dismissal and to divorce her?" ⁸He said to them, "It was because you were so hard-hearted that Moses allowed you to divorce your wives, but from the beginning it was not so. ⁹And I say to you, whoever divorces his wife, except for unchastity, and marries another commits adultery."q

10 His disciples said to him, "If such is the case of a man with his wife, it is better not to marry." ¹¹But he said to them, "Not everyone can accept this teaching, but only those to whom it is given. ¹²For there are eunuchs who have been so from birth, and there are eunuchs who have been made eunuchs by others, and there are eunuchs who have made themselves eunuchs for the sake of the kingdom of heaven. Let anyone accept this who can."

Jesus Blesses Little Children

13 Then little children were being brought to him in order that he might lay his hands on them and pray. The disciples spoke sternly to those who brought them; ¹⁴but Jesus said, "Let the little children come to me, and do not stop them; for it is to such as these that the kingdom of heaven belongs." ¹⁵And he laid his hands on them and went on his way.

The Rich Young Man

16 Then someone came to him and said, "Teacher, what good deed must I do to have eternal life?" ¹⁷And he said to him, "Why do you ask me about what is good? There is only one who is good. If you wish to enter into life, keep the commandments." ¹⁸He said to him, "Which ones?" And Jesus said, "You shall not murder; You shall not commit adultery; You shall not steal; You shall not bear false witness; ¹⁹Honor your father and mother; also, You shall love

q Other ancient authorities read *except on the ground of unchastity, causes her to commit adultery*; others add at the end of the verse *and he who marries a divorced woman commits adultery*

3 Καὶ προσῆλθον αὐτῷ Φαρισαῖοι πειράζοντες αὐτὸν καὶ λέγοντες, Εἰ ἔξεστιν ἀνθρώπῳ ἀπολῦσαι τὴν γυναῖκα αὐτοῦ κατὰ πᾶσαν αἰτίαν; **4** ὁ δὲ ἀποκριθεὶς εἶπεν, Οὐκ ἀνέγνωτε ὅτι ὁ κτίσας ἀπ' ἀρχῆς **ἄρσεν καὶ θῆλυ ἐποίησεν αὐτούς;** 5 καὶ εἶπεν, **Ἕνεκα τούτου καταλείψει ἄνθρωπος τὸν πατέρα καὶ τὴν μητέρα καὶ κολληθήσεται τῇ γυναικὶ αὐτοῦ, καὶ ἔσονται οἱ δύο εἰς σάρκα μίαν.** 6 **ὥστε** οὐκέτι εἰσὶν δύο ἀλλὰ σὰρξ μία. ὃ οὖν ὁ θεὸς συνέζευξεν ἄνθρωπος μὴ χωριζέτω. 7 λέγουσιν αὐτῷ, Τί οὖν Μωϋσῆς ἐνετείλατο **δοῦναι βιβλίον ἀποστασίου καὶ ἀπολῦσαι** [αὐτήν]; 8 λέγει αὐτοῖς ὅτι Μωϋσῆς πρὸς τὴν σκληροκαρδίαν ὑμῶν ἐπέτρεψεν ὑμῖν ἀπολῦσαι τὰς γυναῖκας ὑμῶν, ἀπ' ἀρχῆς δὲ οὐ γέγονεν οὕτως. 9 λέγω δὲ ὑμῖν ὅτι ὃς ἂν ἀπολύσῃ τὴν γυναῖκα αὐτοῦ μὴ ἐπὶ πορνείᾳ καὶ γαμήσῃ ἄλλην μοιχᾶται.ᵃ 10 λέγουσιν αὐτῷ οἱ μαθηταὶ [αὐτοῦ]ᵇ, Εἰ οὕτως ἐστὶν ἡ αἰτία τοῦ ἀνθρώπου μετὰ τῆς γυναικός, οὐ συμφέρει γαμῆσαι. 11 ὁ δὲ εἶπεν αὐτοῖς, Οὐ πάντες χωροῦσιν τὸν λόγον [τοῦτον] ἀλλ' οἷς δέδοται. 12 εἰσὶν γὰρ εὐνοῦχοι οἵτινες ἐκ κοιλίας μητρὸς ἐγεννήθησαν οὕτως, καὶ εἰσὶν εὐνοῦχοι οἵτινες εὐνουχίσθησαν ὑπὸ τῶν ἀνθρώπων, καὶ εἰσὶν εὐνοῦχοι οἵτινες εὐνούχισαν ἑαυτοὺς διὰ τὴν βασιλείαν τῶν οὐρανῶν. ὁ δυνάμενος χωρεῖν χωρείτω.

13 Τότε προσηνέχθησαν αὐτῷ παιδία ἵνα τὰς χεῖρας ἐπιθῇ αὐτοῖς καὶ προσεύξηται· οἱ δὲ μαθηταὶ ἐπετίμησαν αὐτοῖς. 14 ὁ δὲ Ἰησοῦς εἶπεν, Ἄφετε τὰ παιδία καὶ μὴ κωλύετε αὐτὰ ἐλθεῖν πρός με, τῶν γὰρ τοιούτων ἐστὶν ἡ βασιλεία τῶν οὐρανῶν. 15 καὶ ἐπιθεὶς τὰς χεῖρας αὐτοῖς ἐπορεύθη ἐκεῖθεν.

16 Καὶ ἰδοὺ εἷς προσελθὼν αὐτῷ εἶπεν, Διδάσκαλε, τί ἀγαθὸν ποιήσω ἵνα σχῶ ζωὴν αἰώνιον; 17 ὁ δὲ εἶπεν αὐτῷ, Τί με ἐρωτᾷς περὶ τοῦ ἀγαθοῦ; εἷς ἐστιν ὁ ἀγαθός· εἰ δὲ θέλεις εἰς τὴν ζωὴν εἰσελθεῖν, τήρησον τὰς ἐντολάς. 18 λέγει αὐτῷ, Ποίας; ὁ δὲ Ἰησοῦς εἶπεν, Τὸ **Οὐ φονεύσεις, Οὐ μοιχεύσεις, Οὐ κλέψεις, Οὐ ψευδομαρτυρήσεις,** 19 **Τίμα τὸν πατέρα καὶ τὴν μητέρα,** καί, **Ἀγαπήσεις τὸν πλησίον σου ὡς**

ᵃ9 NRSV note q παρεκτὸς λόγου πορνείας ποιεῖ αὐτὴν μοιχευθῆναι and καὶ ὁ ἀπολελυμένην γαμῶν μοιχᾶται
ᵇ10 NIV text omits αὐτοῦ

³Some Pharisees came to him to test him. They asked, "Is it lawful for a man to divorce his wife for any and every reason?"

⁴"Haven't you read," he replied, "that at the beginning the Creator 'made them male and female,'ᵃ ⁵and said, 'For this reason a man will leave his father and mother and be united to his wife, and the two will become one flesh'ᵇ? ⁶So they are no longer two, but one. Therefore what God has joined together, let man not separate."

⁷"Why then," they asked, "did Moses command that a man give his wife a certificate of divorce and send her away?"

⁸Jesus replied, "Moses permitted you to divorce your wives because your hearts were hard. But it was not this way from the beginning. ⁹I tell you that anyone who divorces his wife, except for marital unfaithfulness, and marries another woman commits adultery."

¹⁰The disciples said to him, "If this is the situation between a husband and wife, it is better not to marry."

¹¹Jesus replied, "Not everyone can accept this word, but only those to whom it has been given. ¹²For some are eunuchs because they were born that way; others were made that way by men; and others have renounced marriageᶜ because of the kingdom of heaven. The one who can accept this should accept it."

The Little Children and Jesus

¹³Then little children were brought to Jesus for him to place his hands on them and pray for them. But the disciples rebuked those who brought them. ¹⁴Jesus said, "Let the little children come to me, and do not hinder them, for the kingdom of heaven belongs to such as these." ¹⁵When he had placed his hands on them, he went on from there.

The Rich Young Man

¹⁶Now a man came up to Jesus and asked, "Teacher, what good thing must I do to get eternal life?"

¹⁷"Why do you ask me about what is good?" Jesus replied. "There is only One who is good. If you want to enter life, obey the commandments."

¹⁸"Which ones?" the man inquired.

Jesus replied, " 'Do not murder, do not commit adultery, do not steal, do not give false testimony, ¹⁹honor your father and mother,'ᵈ and 'love your neighbor as

ᵃ4 Gen. 1:27   ᵇ5 Gen. 2:24   ᶜ12 Or *have made themselves eunuchs*   ᵈ19 Exodus 20:12-16; Deut. 5:16-20

your neighbor as yourself." [20]The young man said to him, "I have kept all these;[r] what do I still lack?" [21]Jesus said to him, "If you wish to be perfect, go, sell your possessions, and give the money[s] to the poor, and you will have treasure in heaven; then come, follow me." [22]When the young man heard this word, he went away grieving, for he had many possessions.

23 Then Jesus said to his disciples, "Truly I tell you, it will be hard for a rich person to enter the kingdom of heaven. [24]Again I tell you, it is easier for a camel to go through the eye of a needle than for someone who is rich to enter the kingdom of God." [25]When the disciples heard this, they were greatly astounded and said, "Then who can be saved?" [26]But Jesus looked at them and said, "For mortals it is impossible, but for God all things are possible."

27 Then Peter said in reply, "Look, we have left everything and followed you. What then will we have?" [28]Jesus said to them, "Truly I tell you, at the renewal of all things, when the Son of Man is seated on the throne of his glory, you who have followed me will also sit on twelve thrones, judging the twelve tribes of Israel. [29]And everyone who has left houses or brothers or sisters or father or mother or children or fields, for my name's sake, will receive a hundredfold,[t] and will inherit eternal life. [30]But many who are first will be last, and the last will be first.

The Laborers in the Vineyard

20 "For the kingdom of heaven is like a landowner who went out early in the morning to hire laborers for his vineyard. [2]After agreeing with the laborers for the usual daily wage,[u] he sent them into his vineyard. [3]When he went out about nine o'clock, he saw others standing idle in the marketplace; [4]and he said to them, 'You also go into the vineyard, and I will pay you whatever is right.' So they went. [5]When he went out again about noon and about three o'clock, he did the same. [6]And about five o'clock he went out and found others standing around; and he said to them, 'Why are you standing here idle all day?' [7]They said to him, 'Because no one

σεαυτόν. **20** λέγει αὐτῷ ὁ νεανίσκος, Πάντα ταῦτα ἐφύλαξα[c]· τί ἔτι ὑστερῶ; **21** ἔφη αὐτῷ ὁ Ἰησοῦς, Εἰ θέλεις τέλειος εἶναι, ὕπαγε πώλησόν σου τὰ ὑπάρχοντα καὶ δὸς [τοῖς] πτωχοῖς, καὶ ἕξεις θησαυρὸν ἐν οὐρανοῖς, καὶ δεῦρο ἀκολούθει μοι. **22** ἀκούσας δὲ ὁ νεανίσκος τὸν λόγον ἀπῆλθεν λυπούμενος· ἦν γὰρ ἔχων κτήματα πολλά.

23 Ὁ δὲ Ἰησοῦς εἶπεν τοῖς μαθηταῖς αὐτοῦ, Ἀμὴν λέγω ὑμῖν ὅτι πλούσιος δυσκόλως εἰσελεύσεται εἰς τὴν βασιλείαν τῶν οὐρανῶν. **24** πάλιν δὲ λέγω ὑμῖν, εὐκοπώτερόν ἐστιν κάμηλον διὰ τρυπήματος ῥαφίδος διελθεῖν ἢ πλούσιον εἰσελθεῖν εἰς τὴν βασιλείαν τοῦ θεοῦ. **25** ἀκούσαντες δὲ οἱ μαθηταὶ ἐξεπλήσσοντο σφόδρα λέγοντες, Τίς ἄρα δύναται σωθῆναι; **26** ἐμβλέψας δὲ ὁ Ἰησοῦς εἶπεν αὐτοῖς, Παρὰ ἀνθρώποις τοῦτο ἀδύνατόν ἐστιν, παρὰ δὲ θεῷ πάντα δυνατά. **27** Τότε ἀποκριθεὶς ὁ Πέτρος εἶπεν αὐτῷ, Ἰδοὺ ἡμεῖς ἀφήκαμεν πάντα καὶ ἠκολουθήσαμέν σοι· τί ἄρα ἔσται ἡμῖν; **28** ὁ δὲ Ἰησοῦς εἶπεν αὐτοῖς, Ἀμὴν λέγω ὑμῖν ὅτι ὑμεῖς οἱ ἀκολουθήσαντές μοι ἐν τῇ παλιγγενεσίᾳ, ὅταν καθίσῃ ὁ υἱὸς τοῦ ἀνθρώπου ἐπὶ θρόνου δόξης αὐτοῦ, καθήσεσθε καὶ ὑμεῖς ἐπὶ δώδεκα θρόνους κρίνοντες τὰς δώδεκα φυλὰς τοῦ Ἰσραήλ. **29** καὶ πᾶς ὅστις ἀφῆκεν οἰκίας ἢ ἀδελφοὺς ἢ ἀδελφὰς ἢ πατέρα ἢ μητέρα[d] ἢ τέκνα ἢ ἀγροὺς ἕνεκεν τοῦ ὀνόματός μου, ἑκατονταπλασίονα[e] λήμψεται καὶ ζωὴν αἰώνιον κληρονομήσει. **30** Πολλοὶ δὲ ἔσονται πρῶτοι ἔσχατοι καὶ ἔσχατοι πρῶτοι.

20 Ὁμοία γάρ ἐστιν ἡ βασιλεία τῶν οὐρανῶν ἀνθρώπῳ οἰκοδεσπότῃ, ὅστις ἐξῆλθεν ἅμα πρωῒ μισθώσασθαι ἐργάτας εἰς τὸν ἀμπελῶνα αὐτοῦ. **2** συμφωνήσας δὲ μετὰ τῶν ἐργατῶν ἐκ δηναρίου τὴν ἡμέραν ἀπέστειλεν αὐτοὺς εἰς τὸν ἀμπελῶνα αὐτοῦ. **3** καὶ ἐξελθὼν περὶ τρίτην ὥραν εἶδεν ἄλλους ἑστῶτας ἐν τῇ ἀγορᾷ ἀργοὺς **4** καὶ ἐκείνοις εἶπεν, Ὑπάγετε καὶ ὑμεῖς εἰς τὸν ἀμπελῶνα, καὶ ὃ ἐὰν ᾖ δίκαιον δώσω ὑμῖν. **5** οἱ δὲ ἀπῆλθον. πάλιν [δὲ][a] ἐξελθὼν περὶ ἕκτην καὶ ἐνάτην ὥραν ἐποίησεν ὡσαύτως. **6** περὶ δὲ τὴν ἑνδεκάτην ἐξελθὼν εὗρεν ἄλλους ἑστῶτας καὶ λέγει αὐτοῖς, Τί ὧδε ἑστήκατε ὅλην τὴν ἡμέραν ἀργοί; **7** λέγουσιν αὐτῷ, Ὅτι οὐδεὶς ἡμᾶς

yourself.'[e]"

[20]"All these I have kept," the young man said. "What do I still lack?"

[21]Jesus answered, "If you want to be perfect, go, sell your possessions and give to the poor, and you will have treasure in heaven. Then come, follow me."

[22]When the young man heard this, he went away sad, because he had great wealth.

[23]Then Jesus said to his disciples, "I tell you the truth, it is hard for a rich man to enter the kingdom of heaven. [24]Again I tell you, it is easier for a camel to go through the eye of a needle than for a rich man to enter the kingdom of God."

[25]When the disciples heard this, they were greatly astonished and asked, "Who then can be saved?"

[26]Jesus looked at them and said, "With man this is impossible, but with God all things are possible."

[27]Peter answered him, "We have left everything to follow you! What then will there be for us?"

[28]Jesus said to them, "I tell you the truth, at the renewal of all things, when the Son of Man sits on his glorious throne, you who have followed me will also sit on twelve thrones, judging the twelve tribes of Israel. [29]And everyone who has left houses or brothers or sisters or father or mother[f] or children or fields for my sake will receive a hundred times as much and will inherit eternal life. [30]But many who are first will be last, and many who are last will be first.

The Parable of the Workers in the Vineyard

20 "For the kingdom of heaven is like a landowner who went out early in the morning to hire men to work in his vineyard. [2]He agreed to pay them a denarius for the day and sent them into his vineyard.

[3]"About the third hour he went out and saw others standing in the marketplace doing nothing. [4]He told them, 'You also go and work in my vineyard, and I will pay you whatever is right.' [5]So they went.

"He went out again about the sixth hour and the ninth hour and did the same thing. [6]About the eleventh hour he went out and found still others standing around. He asked them, 'Why have you been standing here all day long doing nothing?'

[7]"'Because no one has hired us,' they answered.

---

[r] Other ancient authorities add *from my youth*　[s] Gk lacks *the money*　[t] Other ancient authorities read *manifold*　[u] Gk *a denarius*

[c]20 NRSV note r adds ἐκ νεότητός μου　[d]29 NIV note adds ἢ γυναῖκα　[e]29 NRSV note t πολλαπλασίονα　[a]5 NIV text omits δὲ †

[e]19 Lev. 19:18　[f]29 Some manuscripts *mother or wife*

has hired us.' He said to them, 'You also go into the vineyard.' 8When evening came, the owner of the vineyard said to his manager, 'Call the laborers and give them their pay, beginning with the last and then going to the first.' 9When those hired about five o'clock came, each of them received the usual daily wage.u 10Now when the first came, they thought they would receive more; but each of them also received the usual daily wage.u 11And when they received it, they grumbled against the landowner, 12saying, 'These last worked only one hour, and you have made them equal to us who have borne the burden of the day and the scorching heat.' 13But he replied to one of them, 'Friend, I am doing you no wrong; did you not agree with me for the usual daily wage?u 14Take what belongs to you and go; I choose to give to this last the same as I give to you. 15Am I not allowed to do what I choose with what belongs to me? Or are you envious because I am generous?'v 16So the last will be first, and the first will be last."w

A Third Time Jesus Foretells His Death and Resurrection

17 While Jesus was going up to Jerusalem, he took the twelve disciples aside by themselves, and said to them on the way, 18"See, we are going up to Jerusalem, and the Son of Man will be handed over to the chief priests and scribes, and they will condemn him to death; 19then they will hand him over to the Gentiles to be mocked and flogged and crucified; and on the third day he will be raised."

The Request of the Mother of James and John

20 Then the mother of the sons of Zebedee came to him with her sons, and kneeling before him, she asked a favor of him. 21And he said to her, "What do you want?" She said to him, "Declare that these two sons of mine will sit, one at your right hand and one at your left, in your kingdom." 22But Jesus answered, "You do not know what you are asking. Are you able to drink the cup that I am about to drink?"x They said to him, "We are able." 23He said to them, "You will indeed drink my cup, but to sit at my right hand and at my left, this is not mine to grant, but it is for those for whom it has been prepared by my Father."

24 When the ten heard it, they were angry

ἐμισθώσατο. λέγει αὐτοῖς, Ὑπάγετε καὶ ὑμεῖς εἰς τὸν ἀμπελῶνα. 8 ὀψίας δὲ γενομένης λέγει ὁ κύριος τοῦ ἀμπελῶνος τῷ ἐπιτρόπῳ αὐτοῦ, Κάλεσον τοὺς ἐργάτας καὶ ἀπόδος αὐτοῖς τὸν μισθὸν ἀρξάμενος ἀπὸ τῶν ἐσχάτων ἕως τῶν πρώτων. 9 καὶ ἐλθόντες οἱ περὶ τὴν ἑνδεκάτην ὥραν ἔλαβον ἀνὰ δηνάριον. 10 καὶ ἐλθόντες οἱ πρῶτοι ἐνόμισαν ὅτι πλεῖον λήμψονται· καὶ ἔλαβον [τὸ] ἀνὰ δηνάριον καὶ αὐτοί. 11 λαβόντες δὲ ἐγόγγυζον κατὰ τοῦ οἰκοδεσπότου 12 λέγοντες, Οὗτοι οἱ ἔσχατοι μίαν ὥραν ἐποίησαν, καὶ ἴσους ἡμῖν αὐτοὺς ἐποίησας τοῖς βαστάσασι τὸ βάρος τῆς ἡμέρας καὶ τὸν καύσωνα. 13 ὁ δὲ ἀποκριθεὶς ἑνὶ αὐτῶν εἶπεν, Ἑταῖρε, οὐκ ἀδικῶ σε· οὐχὶ δηναρίου συνεφώνησάς μοι; 14 ἆρον τὸ σὸν καὶ ὕπαγε. θέλω δὲ τούτῳ τῷ ἐσχάτῳ δοῦναι ὡς καὶ σοί· 15 [ἢ]b οὐκ ἔξεστίν μοι ὃ θέλω ποιῆσαι ἐν τοῖς ἐμοῖς; ἢ ὁ ὀφθαλμός σου πονηρός ἐστιν ὅτι ἐγὼ ἀγαθός εἰμι; 16 Οὕτως ἔσονται οἱ ἔσχατοι πρῶτοι καὶ οἱ πρῶτοι ἔσχατοι.c

17 Καὶ ἀναβαίνων ὁ Ἰησοῦς εἰς Ἰεροσόλυμα παρέλαβεν τοὺς δώδεκα [μαθητὰς] κατ' ἰδίαν καὶ ἐν τῇ ὁδῷd εἶπεν αὐτοῖς, 18 Ἰδοὺ ἀναβαίνομεν εἰς Ἰεροσόλυμα, καὶ ὁ υἱὸς τοῦ ἀνθρώπου παραδοθήσεται τοῖς ἀρχιερεῦσιν καὶ γραμματεῦσιν, καὶ κατακρινοῦσιν αὐτὸν θανάτῳ 19 καὶ παραδώσουσιν αὐτὸν τοῖς ἔθνεσιν εἰς τὸ ἐμπαῖξαι καὶ μαστιγῶσαι καὶ σταυρῶσαι, καὶ τῇ τρίτῃ ἡμέρᾳ ἐγερθήσεται.

20 Τότε προσῆλθεν αὐτῷ ἡ μήτηρ τῶν υἱῶν Ζεβεδαίου μετὰ τῶν υἱῶν αὐτῆς προσκυνοῦσα καὶ αἰτοῦσά τι ἀπ' αὐτοῦ. 21 ὁ δὲ εἶπεν αὐτῇ, Τί θέλεις; λέγει αὐτῷ, Εἰπὲ ἵνα καθίσωσιν οὗτοι οἱ δύο υἱοί μου εἷς ἐκ δεξιῶν σου καὶ εἷς ἐξ εὐωνύμων σου ἐν τῇ βασιλείᾳ σου. 22 ἀποκριθεὶς δὲ ὁ Ἰησοῦς εἶπεν, Οὐκ οἴδατε τί αἰτεῖσθε. δύνασθε πιεῖν τὸ ποτήριον ὃ ἐγὼ μέλλω πίνειν̣e; λέγουσιν αὐτῷ, Δυνάμεθα. 23 λέγει αὐτοῖς, Τὸ μὲν ποτήριόν μου πίεσθε, τὸ δὲ καθίσαι ἐκ δεξιῶν μου καὶ ἐξ εὐωνύμων οὐκ ἔστιν ἐμὸν [τοῦτο]f δοῦναι, ἀλλ' οἷς ἡτοίμασται ὑπὸ τοῦ πατρός μου. 24 Καὶ ἀκούσαντες οἱ δέκα ἠγανάκτησαν περὶ τῶν δύο

"He said to them, 'You also go and work in my vineyard.'

8"When evening came, the owner of the vineyard said to his foreman, 'Call the workers and pay them their wages, beginning with the last ones hired and going on to the first.'

9"The workers who were hired about the eleventh hour came and each received a denarius. 10So when those came who were hired first, they expected to receive more. But each one of them also received a denarius. 11When they received it, they began to grumble against the landowner. 12'These men who were hired last worked only one hour,' they said, 'and you have made them equal to us who have borne the burden of the work and the heat of the day.'

13"But he answered one of them, 'Friend, I am not being unfair to you. Didn't you agree to work for a denarius? 14Take your pay and go. I want to give the man who was hired last the same as I gave you. 15Don't I have the right to do what I want with my own money? Or are you envious because I am generous?'

16"So the last will be first, and the first will be last."

Jesus Again Predicts His Death

17Now as Jesus was going up to Jerusalem, he took the twelve disciples aside and said to them, 18"We are going up to Jerusalem, and the Son of Man will be betrayed to the chief priests and the teachers of the law. They will condemn him to death 19and will turn him over to the Gentiles to be mocked and flogged and crucified. On the third day he will be raised to life!"

A Mother's Request

20Then the mother of Zebedee's sons came to Jesus with her sons and, kneeling down, asked a favor of him.

21"What is it you want?" he asked.

She said, "Grant that one of these two sons of mine may sit at your right and the other at your left in your kingdom."

22"You don't know what you are asking," Jesus said to them. "Can you drink the cup I am going to drink?"

"We can," they answered.

23Jesus said to them, "You will indeed drink from my cup, but to sit at my right or left is not for me to grant. These places belong to those for whom they have been prepared by my Father."

24When the ten heard about this, they

---

u Gk *a denarius*   v Gk *is your eye evil because I am good?*   w Other ancient authorities add *for many are called but few are chosen*   x Other ancient authorities add *or to be baptized with the baptism that I am baptized with?*

b15 NIV text omits ἢ   c16 NRSV note w adds πολλοὶ γάρ εἰσιν κλητοί, ὀλίγοι δὲ ἐκλεκτοί.   d17 NIV text omits ἐν τῇ ὁδῷ †   e22 NRSV note x adds ἢ τὸ βάπτισμα ὃ ἐγὼ βαπτίζομαι βαπτισθῆναι;   f23 NIV text omits τοῦτο

NRSV

with the two brothers. ²⁵But Jesus called them to him and said, "You know that the rulers of the Gentiles lord it over them, and their great ones are tyrants over them. ²⁶It will not be so among you; but whoever wishes to be great among you must be your servant, ²⁷and whoever wishes to be first among you must be your slave; ²⁸just as the Son of Man came not to be served but to serve, and to give his life a ransom for many."

Jesus Heals Two Blind Men

29 As they were leaving Jericho, a large crowd followed him. ³⁰There were two blind men sitting by the roadside. When they heard that Jesus was passing by, they shouted, "Lord,^y have mercy on us, Son of David!" ³¹The crowd sternly ordered them to be quiet; but they shouted even more loudly, "Have mercy on us, Lord, Son of David!" ³²Jesus stood still and called them, saying, "What do you want me to do for you?" ³³They said to him, "Lord, let our eyes be opened." ³⁴Moved with compassion, Jesus touched their eyes. Immediately they regained their sight and followed him.

Jesus' Triumphal Entry into Jerusalem

21 When they had come near Jerusalem and had reached Bethphage, at the Mount of Olives, Jesus sent two disciples, ²saying to them, "Go into the village ahead of you, and immediately you will find a donkey tied, and a colt with her; untie them and bring them to me. ³If anyone says anything to you, just say this, 'The Lord needs them.' And he will send them immediately.^z" ⁴This took place to fulfill what had been spoken through the prophet, saying,

⁵ "Tell the daughter of Zion,
Look, your king is coming to you,
humble, and mounted on a donkey,
and on a colt, the foal of a donkey."

⁶The disciples went and did as Jesus had directed them; ⁷they brought the donkey and the colt, and put their cloaks on them, and he sat on them. ⁸A very large crowd^a spread their cloaks on the road, and others cut branches from the trees and spread them on the road. ⁹The crowds that went ahead of him and that followed were shouting,

"Hosanna to the Son of David!

NIV

were indignant with the two brothers. ²⁵Jesus called them together and said, "You know that the rulers of the Gentiles lord it over them, and their high officials exercise authority over them. ²⁶Not so with you. Instead, whoever wants to become great among you must be your servant, ²⁷and whoever wants to be first must be your slave— ²⁸just as the Son of Man did not come to be served, but to serve, and to give his life as a ransom for many."

Two Blind Men Receive Sight

²⁹As Jesus and his disciples were leaving Jericho, a large crowd followed him. ³⁰Two blind men were sitting by the roadside, and when they heard that Jesus was going by, they shouted, "Lord, Son of David, have mercy on us!"

³¹The crowd rebuked them and told them to be quiet, but they shouted all the louder, "Lord, Son of David, have mercy on us!"

³²Jesus stopped and called them. "What do you want me to do for you?" he asked.

³³"Lord," they answered, "we want our sight."

³⁴Jesus had compassion on them and touched their eyes. Immediately they received their sight and followed him.

The Triumphal Entry

21 As they approached Jerusalem and came to Bethphage on the Mount of Olives, Jesus sent two disciples, ²saying to them, "Go to the village ahead of you, and at once you will find a donkey tied there, with her colt by her. Untie them and bring them to me. ³If anyone says anything to you, tell him that the Lord needs them, and he will send them right away."

⁴This took place to fulfill what was spoken through the prophet:

⁵"Say to the Daughter of Zion,
'See, your king comes to you,
gentle and riding on a donkey,
on a colt, the foal of a donkey.' "^a

⁶The disciples went and did as Jesus had instructed them. ⁷They brought the donkey and the colt, placed their cloaks on them, and Jesus sat on them. ⁸A very large crowd spread their cloaks on the road, while others cut branches from the trees and spread them on the road. ⁹The crowds that went ahead of him and those that followed shouted,

"Hosanna^b to the Son of David!"

---

y Other ancient authorities lack *Lord* z Or *'The Lord needs them and will send them back immediately.'* a Or *Most of the crowd*

a5 Zech. 9:9 b9 A Hebrew expression meaning "Save!" which became an exclamation of praise; also in verse 15

Blessed is the one who comes in the
name of the Lord!
Hosanna in the highest heaven!"
[10]When he entered Jerusalem, the whole
city was in turmoil, asking, "Who is this?"
[11]The crowds were saying, "This is the
prophet Jesus from Nazareth in Galilee."

Jesus Cleanses the Temple

12 Then Jesus entered the temple[b] and
drove out all who were selling and buying
in the temple, and he overturned the tables
of the money changers and the seats of
those who sold doves. [13]He said to them,
"It is written,

'My house shall be called a house of
prayer';
but you are making it a den of
robbers."

14 The blind and the lame came to him in
the temple, and he cured them. [15]But when
the chief priests and the scribes saw the
amazing things that he did, and heard[c] the
children crying out in the temple, "Hosanna to the Son of David," they became
angry [16]and said to him, "Do you hear
what these are saying?" Jesus said to them,
"Yes; have you never read,

'Out of the mouths of infants and
nursing babies
you have prepared praise for
yourself'?"

[17]He left them, went out of the city to
Bethany, and spent the night there.

Jesus Curses the Fig Tree

18 In the morning, when he returned to
the city, he was hungry. [19]And seeing a fig
tree by the side of the road, he went to it
and found nothing at all on it but leaves.
Then he said to it, "May no fruit ever come
from you again!" And the fig tree withered at once. [20]When the disciples saw it,
they were amazed, saying, "How did the
fig tree wither at once?" [21]Jesus answered
them, "Truly I tell you, if you have faith
and do not doubt, not only will you do
what has been done to the fig tree, but
even if you say to this mountain, 'Be lifted
up and thrown into the sea,' it will be
done. [22]Whatever you ask for in prayer
with faith, you will receive."

The Authority of Jesus Questioned

23 When he entered the temple, the chief

Εὐλογημένος ὁ ἐρχόμενος ἐν
ὀνόματι κυρίου·
Ὡσαννὰ ἐν τοῖς ὑψίστοις.
10 καὶ εἰσελθόντος αὐτοῦ εἰς Ἱεροσόλυμα ἐσείσθη πᾶσα ἡ πόλις λέγουσα,
Τίς ἐστιν οὗτος; 11 οἱ δὲ ὄχλοι ἔλεγον,
Οὗτός ἐστιν ὁ προφήτης Ἰησοῦς ὁ
ἀπὸ Ναζαρὲθ τῆς Γαλιλαίας.
12 Καὶ εἰσῆλθεν Ἰησοῦς εἰς τὸ ἱερὸν[a]
καὶ ἐξέβαλεν πάντας τοὺς πωλοῦντας
καὶ ἀγοράζοντας ἐν τῷ ἱερῷ, καὶ τὰς
τραπέζας τῶν κολλυβιστῶν κατέστρεψεν καὶ τὰς καθέδρας τῶν πωλούντων τὰς περιστεράς, 13 καὶ λέγει
αὐτοῖς, Γέγραπται,

Ὁ οἶκός μου οἶκος προσευχῆς
κληθήσεται,
ὑμεῖς δὲ αὐτὸν ποιεῖτε σπήλαιον
λῃστῶν.

14 Καὶ προσῆλθον αὐτῷ τυφλοὶ καὶ
χωλοὶ ἐν τῷ ἱερῷ, καὶ ἐθεράπευσεν
αὐτούς. 15 ἰδόντες δὲ οἱ ἀρχιερεῖς καὶ
οἱ γραμματεῖς τὰ θαυμάσια ἃ ἐποίησεν
καὶ τοὺς παῖδας τοὺς κράζοντας ἐν
τῷ ἱερῷ καὶ λέγοντας, Ὡσαννὰ τῷ υἱῷ
Δαυίδ, ἠγανάκτησαν 16 καὶ εἶπαν αὐτῷ,
Ἀκούεις τί οὗτοι λέγουσιν; ὁ δὲ Ἰησοῦς
λέγει αὐτοῖς, Ναί. οὐδέποτε ἀνέγνωτε
ὅτι Ἐκ στόματος νηπίων καὶ θηλαζόν-
των κατηρτίσω αἶνον; 17 Καὶ καταλιπὼν αὐτοὺς ἐξῆλθεν ἔξω τῆς πόλεως
εἰς Βηθανίαν καὶ ηὐλίσθη ἐκεῖ.
18 Πρωὶ δὲ ἐπανάγων εἰς τὴν πόλιν
ἐπείνασεν. 19 καὶ ἰδὼν συκῆν μίαν ἐπὶ
τῆς ὁδοῦ ἦλθεν ἐπ' αὐτὴν καὶ οὐδὲν
εὗρεν ἐν αὐτῇ εἰ μὴ φύλλα μόνον, καὶ
λέγει αὐτῇ, Μηκέτι ἐκ σοῦ καρπὸς
γένηται εἰς τὸν αἰῶνα. καὶ ἐξηράνθη
παραχρῆμα ἡ συκῆ. 20 καὶ ἰδόντες οἱ
μαθηταὶ ἐθαύμασαν λέγοντες, Πῶς
παραχρῆμα ἐξηράνθη ἡ συκῆ; 21 ἀποκριθεὶς δὲ ὁ Ἰησοῦς εἶπεν αὐτοῖς,
Ἀμὴν λέγω ὑμῖν, ἐὰν ἔχητε πίστιν
καὶ μὴ διακριθῆτε, οὐ μόνον τὸ τῆς
συκῆς ποιήσετε, ἀλλὰ κἂν τῷ ὄρει
τούτῳ εἴπητε, Ἄρθητι καὶ βλήθητι εἰς
τὴν θάλασσαν, γενήσεται· 22 καὶ πάντα
ὅσα ἂν αἰτήσητε ἐν τῇ προσευχῇ
πιστεύοντες λήμψεσθε.
23 Καὶ ἐλθόντος αὐτοῦ εἰς τὸ ἱερὸν

"Blessed is he who comes in the name
of the Lord!"[c]

"Hosanna[d] in the highest!"

[10]When Jesus entered Jerusalem, the
whole city was stirred and asked, "Who is
this?"

[11]The crowds answered, "This is Jesus,
the prophet from Nazareth in Galilee."

Jesus at the Temple

[12]Jesus entered the temple area and drove
out all who were buying and selling there.
He overturned the tables of the money
changers and the benches of those selling
doves. [13]"It is written," he said to them,
" 'My house will be called a house of
prayer,'[e] but you are making it a 'den of
robbers.'[f]"

[14]The blind and the lame came to him at
the temple, and he healed them. [15]But when
the chief priests and the teachers of the
law saw the wonderful things he did and
the children shouting in the temple area,
"Hosanna to the Son of David," they were
indignant.

[16]"Do you hear what these children are
saying?" they asked him.

"Yes," replied Jesus, "have you never
read,

" 'From the lips of children and infants
you have ordained praise'[g]?"

[17]And he left them and went out of the
city to Bethany, where he spent the night.

The Fig Tree Withers

[18]Early in the morning, as he was on his
way back to the city, he was hungry. [19]See-
ing a fig tree by the road, he went up to it
but found nothing on it except leaves. Then
he said to it, "May you never bear fruit
again!" Immediately the tree withered.

[20]When the disciples saw this, they were
amazed. "How did the fig tree wither so
quickly?" they asked.

[21]Jesus replied, "I tell you the truth, if
you have faith and do not doubt, not only
can you do what was done to the fig tree,
but also you can say to this mountain, 'Go,
throw yourself into the sea,' and it will be
done. [22]If you believe, you will receive
whatever you ask for in prayer."

The Authority of Jesus Questioned

[23]Jesus entered the temple courts, and,

---

[b] Other ancient authorities add *of God*   [c] Gk lacks *heard*   [a] 12 NRSV note b adds τοῦ θεοῦ

[c] 9 Psalm 118:26   [d] 9 A Hebrew expression meaning
"Save!" which became an exclamation of praise; also in
verse 15   [e] 13 Isaiah 56:7   [f] 13 Jer. 7:11   [g] 16 Psalm 8:2

priests and the elders of the people came to him as he was teaching, and said, "By what authority are you doing these things, and who gave you this authority?" 24Jesus said to them, "I will also ask you one question; if you tell me the answer, then I will also tell you by what authority I do these things. 25Did the baptism of John come from heaven, or was it of human origin?" And they argued with one another, "If we say, 'From heaven,' he will say to us, 'Why then did you not believe him?' 26But if we say, 'Of human origin,' we are afraid of the crowd; for all regard John as a prophet." 27So they answered Jesus, "We do not know." And he said to them, "Neither will I tell you by what authority I am doing these things.

The Parable of the Two Sons

28 "What do you think? A man had two sons; he went to the first and said, 'Son, go and work in the vineyard today.' 29He answered, 'I will not'; but later he changed his mind and went. 30The father[d] went to the second and said the same; and he answered, 'I go, sir'; but he did not go. 31Which of the two did the will of his father?" They said, "The first." Jesus said to them, "Truly I tell you, the tax collectors and the prostitutes are going into the kingdom of God ahead of you. 32For John came to you in the way of righteousness and you did not believe him, but the tax collectors and the prostitutes believed him; and even after you saw it, you did not change your minds and believe him.

The Parable of the Wicked Tenants

33 "Listen to another parable. There was a landowner who planted a vineyard, put a fence around it, dug a wine press in it, and built a watchtower. Then he leased it to tenants and went to another country. 34When the harvest time had come, he sent his slaves to the tenants to collect his produce. 35But the tenants seized his slaves and beat one, killed another, and stoned another. 36Again he sent other slaves, more than the first; and they treated them in the same way. 37Finally he sent his son to them, saying, 'They will respect my son.' 38But

[d] Gk He

προσῆλθον αὐτῷ διδάσκοντι οἱ ἀρχιερεῖς καὶ οἱ πρεσβύτεροι τοῦ λαοῦ λέγοντες, Ἐν ποίᾳ ἐξουσίᾳ ταῦτα ποιεῖς; καὶ τίς σοι ἔδωκεν τὴν ἐξουσίαν ταύτην; **24** ἀποκριθεὶς δὲ ὁ Ἰησοῦς εἶπεν αὐτοῖς, Ἐρωτήσω ὑμᾶς κἀγὼ λόγον ἕνα, ὃν ἐὰν εἴπητέ μοι κἀγὼ ὑμῖν ἐρῶ ἐν ποίᾳ ἐξουσίᾳ ταῦτα ποιῶ· **25** τὸ βάπτισμα τὸ Ἰωάννου πόθεν ἦν; ἐξ οὐρανοῦ ἢ ἐξ ἀνθρώπων; οἱ δὲ διελογίζοντο ἐν ἑαυτοῖς λέγοντες, Ἐὰν εἴπωμεν, Ἐξ οὐρανοῦ, ἐρεῖ ἡμῖν, Διὰ τί οὖν οὐκ ἐπιστεύσατε αὐτῷ; **26** ἐὰν δὲ εἴπωμεν, Ἐξ ἀνθρώπων, φοβούμεθα τὸν ὄχλον, πάντες γὰρ ὡς προφήτην ἔχουσιν τὸν Ἰωάννην. **27** καὶ ἀποκριθέντες τῷ Ἰησοῦ εἶπαν, Οὐκ οἴδαμεν. ἔφη αὐτοῖς καὶ αὐτός, Οὐδὲ ἐγὼ λέγω ὑμῖν ἐν ποίᾳ ἐξουσίᾳ ταῦτα ποιῶ.

28 Τί δὲ ὑμῖν δοκεῖ; ἄνθρωπος εἶχεν τέκνα δύο. καὶ προσελθὼν τῷ πρώτῳ εἶπεν, Τέκνον, ὕπαγε σήμερον ἐργάζου ἐν τῷ ἀμπελῶνι. **29** ὁ δὲ ἀποκριθεὶς εἶπεν, Οὐ θέλω, ὕστερον δὲ μεταμεληθεὶς ἀπῆλθεν. **30** προσελθὼν δὲ τῷ ἑτέρῳ εἶπεν ὡσαύτως. ὁ δὲ ἀποκριθεὶς εἶπεν, Ἐγώ, κύριε, καὶ οὐκ ἀπῆλθεν. **31** τίς ἐκ τῶν δύο ἐποίησεν τὸ θέλημα τοῦ πατρός; λέγουσιν, Ὁ πρῶτος. λέγει αὐτοῖς ὁ Ἰησοῦς, Ἀμὴν λέγω ὑμῖν ὅτι οἱ τελῶναι καὶ αἱ πόρναι προάγουσιν ὑμᾶς εἰς τὴν βασιλείαν τοῦ θεοῦ. **32** ἦλθεν γὰρ Ἰωάννης πρὸς ὑμᾶς ἐν ὁδῷ δικαιοσύνης, καὶ οὐκ ἐπιστεύσατε αὐτῷ, οἱ δὲ τελῶναι καὶ αἱ πόρναι ἐπίστευσαν αὐτῷ· ὑμεῖς δὲ ἰδόντες οὐδὲ μετεμελήθητε ὕστερον τοῦ πιστεῦσαι αὐτῷ.

33 Ἄλλην παραβολὴν ἀκούσατε. Ἄνθρωπος ἦν οἰκοδεσπότης ὅστις ἐφύτευσεν ἀμπελῶνα καὶ φραγμὸν αὐτῷ περιέθηκεν καὶ ὤρυξεν ἐν αὐτῷ ληνὸν καὶ ᾠκοδόμησεν πύργον καὶ ἐξέδετο αὐτὸν γεωργοῖς καὶ ἀπεδήμησεν. **34** ὅτε δὲ ἤγγισεν ὁ καιρὸς τῶν καρπῶν, ἀπέστειλεν τοὺς δούλους αὐτοῦ πρὸς τοὺς γεωργοὺς λαβεῖν τοὺς καρποὺς αὐτοῦ. **35** καὶ λαβόντες οἱ γεωργοὶ τοὺς δούλους αὐτοῦ ὃν μὲν ἔδειραν, ὃν δὲ ἀπέκτειναν, ὃν δὲ ἐλιθοβόλησαν. **36** πάλιν ἀπέστειλεν ἄλλους δούλους πλείονας τῶν πρώτων, καὶ ἐποίησαν αὐτοῖς ὡσαύτως. **37** ὕστερον δὲ ἀπέστειλεν πρὸς αὐτοὺς τὸν υἱὸν αὐτοῦ λέγων, Ἐντραπήσονται τὸν υἱόν μου.

while he was teaching, the chief priests and the elders of the people came to him. "By what authority are you doing these things?" they asked. "And who gave you this authority?"

24Jesus replied, "I will also ask you one question. If you answer me, I will tell you by what authority I am doing these things. 25John's baptism—where did it come from? Was it from heaven, or from men?"

They discussed it among themselves and said, "If we say, 'From heaven,' he will ask, 'Then why didn't you believe him?' 26But if we say, 'From men'—we are afraid of the people, for they all hold that John was a prophet."

27So they answered Jesus, "We don't know."

Then he said, "Neither will I tell you by what authority I am doing these things.

The Parable of the Two Sons

28"What do you think? There was a man who had two sons. He went to the first and said, 'Son, go and work today in the vineyard.'

29" 'I will not,' he answered, but later he changed his mind and went.

30"Then the father went to the other son and said the same thing. He answered, 'I will, sir,' but he did not go.

31"Which of the two did what his father wanted?"

"The first," they answered.

Jesus said to them, "I tell you the truth, the tax collectors and the prostitutes are entering the kingdom of God ahead of you. 32For John came to you to show you the way of righteousness, and you did not believe him, but the tax collectors and the prostitutes did. And even after you saw this, you did not repent and believe him.

The Parable of the Tenants

33"Listen to another parable: There was a landowner who planted a vineyard. He put a wall around it, dug a winepress in it and built a watchtower. Then he rented the vineyard to some farmers and went away on a journey. 34When the harvest time approached, he sent his servants to the tenants to collect his fruit.

35"The tenants seized his servants; they beat one, killed another, and stoned a third. 36Then he sent other servants to them, more than the first time, and the tenants treated them the same way. 37Last of all, he sent his son to them. 'They will respect my son,' he said.

when the tenants saw the son, they said to themselves, 'This is the heir; come, let us kill him and get his inheritance.' 39So they seized him, threw him out of the vineyard, and killed him. 40Now when the owner of the vineyard comes, what will he do to those tenants?" 41They said to him, "He will put those wretches to a miserable death, and lease the vineyard to other tenants who will give him the produce at the harvest time."

42 Jesus said to them, "Have you never read in the scriptures:

'The stone that the builders rejected
    has become the cornerstone;e
this was the Lord's doing,
    and it is amazing in our eyes'?
43Therefore I tell you, the kingdom of God will be taken away from you and given to a people that produces the fruits of the kingdom.f 44The one who falls on this stone will be broken to pieces; and it will crush anyone on whom it falls."g

45 When the chief priests and the Pharisees heard his parables, they realized that he was speaking about them. 46They wanted to arrest him, but they feared the crowds, because they regarded him as a prophet.

The Parable of the Wedding Banquet

22 Once more Jesus spoke to them in parables, saying: 2"The kingdom of heaven may be compared to a king who gave a wedding banquet for his son. 3He sent his slaves to call those who had been invited to the wedding banquet, but they would not come. 4Again he sent other slaves, saying, 'Tell those who have been invited: Look, I have prepared my dinner, my oxen and my fat calves have been slaughtered, and everything is ready; come to the wedding banquet.' 5But they made light of it and went away, one to his farm, another to his business, 6while the rest seized his slaves, mistreated them, and killed them. 7The king was enraged. He sent his troops, destroyed those murderers, and burned their city. 8Then he said to his slaves, 'The wedding is ready, but those invited were not worthy. 9Go therefore into

38 οἱ δὲ γεωργοὶ ἰδόντες τὸν υἱὸν εἶπον ἐν ἑαυτοῖς, Οὗτός ἐστιν ὁ κληρονόμος· δεῦτε ἀποκτείνωμεν αὐτὸν καὶ σχῶμεν τὴν κληρονομίαν αὐτοῦ, **39** καὶ λαβόντες αὐτὸν ἐξέβαλον ἔξω τοῦ ἀμπελῶνος καὶ ἀπέκτειναν. **40** ὅταν οὖν ἔλθῃ ὁ κύριος τοῦ ἀμπελῶνος, τί ποιήσει τοῖς γεωργοῖς ἐκείνοις; **41** λέγουσιν αὐτῷ, Κακοὺς κακῶς ἀπολέσει αὐτοὺς καὶ τὸν ἀμπελῶνα ἐκδώσεται ἄλλοις γεωργοῖς, οἵτινες ἀποδώσουσιν αὐτῷ τοὺς καρποὺς ἐν τοῖς καιροῖς αὐτῶν. **42** λέγει αὐτοῖς ὁ Ἰησοῦς, Οὐδέποτε ἀνέγνωτε ἐν ταῖς γραφαῖς,

Λίθον ὃν ἀπεδοκίμασαν οἱ
    οἰκοδομοῦντες,
οὗτος ἐγενήθη εἰς κεφαλὴν
    γωνίας·
παρὰ κυρίου ἐγένετο αὕτη
    καὶ ἔστιν θαυμαστὴ ἐν ὀφθαλμοῖς
    ἡμῶν;
43 διὰ τοῦτο λέγω ὑμῖν ὅτι ἀρθήσεται ἀφ' ὑμῶν ἡ βασιλεία τοῦ θεοῦ καὶ δοθήσεται ἔθνει ποιοῦντι τοὺς καρποὺς αὐτῆς. [**44** Καὶ ὁ πεσὼν ἐπὶ τὸν λίθον τοῦτον συνθλασθήσεται· ἐφ' ὃν δ' ἂν πέσῃ λικμήσει αὐτόν.]

45 Καὶ ἀκούσαντες οἱ ἀρχιερεῖς καὶ οἱ Φαρισαῖοι τὰς παραβολὰς αὐτοῦ ἔγνωσαν ὅτι περὶ αὐτῶν λέγει· **46** καὶ ζητοῦντες αὐτὸν κρατῆσαι ἐφοβήθησαν τοὺς ὄχλους, ἐπεὶ εἰς προφήτην αὐτὸν εἶχον.

22 Καὶ ἀποκριθεὶς ὁ Ἰησοῦς πάλιν εἶπεν ἐν παραβολαῖς αὐτοῖς λέγων, **2** Ὡμοιώθη ἡ βασιλεία τῶν οὐρανῶν ἀνθρώπῳ βασιλεῖ, ὅστις ἐποίησεν γάμους τῷ υἱῷ αὐτοῦ. **3** καὶ ἀπέστειλεν τοὺς δούλους αὐτοῦ καλέσαι τοὺς κεκλημένους εἰς τοὺς γάμους, καὶ οὐκ ἤθελον ἐλθεῖν. **4** πάλιν ἀπέστειλεν ἄλλους δούλους λέγων, Εἴπατε τοῖς κεκλημένοις, Ἰδοὺ τὸ ἄριστόν μου ἡτοίμακα, οἱ ταῦροί μου καὶ τὰ σιτιστὰ τεθυμένα καὶ πάντα ἕτοιμα· δεῦτε εἰς τοὺς γάμους. **5** οἱ δὲ ἀμελήσαντες ἀπῆλθον, ὃς μὲν εἰς τὸν ἴδιον ἀγρόν, ὃς δὲ ἐπὶ τὴν ἐμπορίαν αὐτοῦ· **6** οἱ δὲ λοιποὶ κρατήσαντες τοὺς δούλους αὐτοῦ ὕβρισαν καὶ ἀπέκτειναν. **7** ὁ δὲ βασιλεὺς ὠργίσθη καὶ πέμψας τὰ στρατεύματα αὐτοῦ ἀπώλεσεν τοὺς φονεῖς ἐκείνους καὶ τὴν πόλιν αὐτῶν ἐνέπρησεν. **8** τότε λέγει τοῖς δούλοις αὐτοῦ, Ὁ μὲν γάμος ἕτοιμός ἐστιν, οἱ δὲ κεκλημένοι οὐκ ἦσαν ἄξιοι· **9** πορεύεσθε οὖν ἐπὶ τὰς

38"But when the tenants saw the son, they said to each other, 'This is the heir. Come, let's kill him and take his inheritance.' 39So they took him and threw him out of the vineyard and killed him.

40"Therefore, when the owner of the vineyard comes, what will he do to those tenants?"

41"He will bring those wretches to a wretched end," they replied, "and he will rent the vineyard to other tenants, who will give him his share of the crop at harvest time."

42Jesus said to them, "Have you never read in the Scriptures:

" 'The stone the builders rejected
    has become the capstone;h
the Lord has done this,
    and it is marvelous in our eyes'i?

43"Therefore I tell you that the kingdom of God will be taken away from you and given to a people who will produce its fruit. 44He who falls on this stone will be broken to pieces, but he on whom it falls will be crushed."j

45When the chief priests and the Pharisees heard Jesus' parables, they knew he was talking about them. 46They looked for a way to arrest him, but they were afraid of the crowd because the people held that he was a prophet.

The Parable of the Wedding Banquet

22 Jesus spoke to them again in parables, saying: 2"The kingdom of heaven is like a king who prepared a wedding banquet for his son. 3He sent his servants to those who had been invited to the banquet to tell them to come, but they refused to come.

4"Then he sent some more servants and said, 'Tell those who have been invited that I have prepared my dinner: My oxen and fattened cattle have been butchered, and everything is ready. Come to the wedding banquet.'

5"But they paid no attention and went off—one to his field, another to his business. 6The rest seized his servants, mistreated them and killed them. 7The king was enraged. He sent his army and destroyed those murderers and burned their city.

8"Then he said to his servants, 'The wedding banquet is ready, but those I invited did not deserve to come. 9Go to the street the main streets, and invite everyone you find to the wedding banquet.' [10]Those slaves went out into the streets and gathered all whom they found, both good and bad; so the wedding hall was filled with guests.

11 "But when the king came in to see the guests, he noticed a man there who was not wearing a wedding robe, [12]and he said to him, 'Friend, how did you get in here without a wedding robe?' And he was speechless. [13]Then the king said to the attendants, 'Bind him hand and foot, and throw him into the outer darkness, where there will be weeping and gnashing of teeth.' [14]For many are called, but few are chosen."

The Question about Paying Taxes

15 Then the Pharisees went and plotted to entrap him in what he said. [16]So they sent their disciples to him, along with the Herodians, saying, "Teacher, we know that you are sincere, and teach the way of God in accordance with truth, and show deference to no one; for you do not regard people with partiality. [17]Tell us, then, what you think. Is it lawful to pay taxes to the emperor, or not?" [18]But Jesus, aware of their malice, said, "Why are you putting me to the test, you hypocrites? [19]Show me the coin used for the tax." And they brought him a denarius. [20]Then he said to them, "Whose head is this, and whose title?" [21]They answered, "The emperor's." Then he said to them, "Give therefore to the emperor the things that are the emperor's, and to God the things that are God's." [22]When they heard this, they were amazed; and they left him and went away.

The Question about the Resurrection

23 The same day some Sadducees came to him, saying there is no resurrection;[h] and they asked him a question, saying, [24]"Teacher, Moses said, 'If a man dies childless, his brother shall marry the widow, and raise up children for his brother.' [25]Now there were seven brothers among us; the first married, and died childless, leaving the widow to his brother. [26]The second did the same, so also the third, down to the seventh. [27]Last of all, the woman herself died. [28]In the resurrection, then, whose wife of the seven will she be? For all of them had married her."

29 Jesus answered them, "You are wrong,

διεξόδους τῶν ὁδῶν καὶ ὅσους ἐὰν εὕρητε καλέσατε εἰς τοὺς γάμους. **10** καὶ ἐξελθόντες οἱ δοῦλοι ἐκεῖνοι εἰς τὰς ὁδοὺς συνήγαγον πάντας οὓς εὗρον, πονηρούς τε καὶ ἀγαθούς· καὶ ἐπλήσθη ὁ γάμος ἀνακειμένων. **11** εἰσελθὼν δὲ ὁ βασιλεὺς θεάσασθαι τοὺς ἀνακειμένους εἶδεν ἐκεῖ ἄνθρωπον οὐκ ἐνδεδυμένον ἔνδυμα γάμου, **12** καὶ λέγει αὐτῷ, Ἑταῖρε, πῶς εἰσῆλθες ὧδε μὴ ἔχων ἔνδυμα γάμου; ὁ δὲ ἐφιμώθη. **13** τότε ὁ βασιλεὺς εἶπεν τοῖς διακόνοις, Δήσαντες αὐτοῦ πόδας καὶ χεῖρας ἐκβάλετε αὐτὸν εἰς τὸ σκότος τὸ ἐξώτερον· ἐκεῖ ἔσται ὁ κλαυθμὸς καὶ ὁ βρυγμὸς τῶν ὀδόντων. **14** πολλοὶ γάρ εἰσιν κλητοί, ὀλίγοι δὲ ἐκλεκτοί.

15 Τότε πορευθέντες οἱ Φαρισαῖοι συμβούλιον ἔλαβον ὅπως αὐτὸν παγιδεύσωσιν ἐν λόγῳ. **16** καὶ ἀποστέλλουσιν αὐτῷ τοὺς μαθητὰς αὐτῶν μετὰ τῶν Ἡρῳδιανῶν λέγοντες, Διδάσκαλε, οἴδαμεν ὅτι ἀληθὴς εἶ καὶ τὴν ὁδὸν τοῦ θεοῦ ἐν ἀληθείᾳ διδάσκεις καὶ οὐ μέλει σοι περὶ οὐδενός· οὐ γὰρ βλέπεις εἰς πρόσωπον ἀνθρώπων. **17** εἰπὲ οὖν ἡμῖν τί σοι δοκεῖ· ἔξεστιν δοῦναι κῆνσον Καίσαρι ἢ οὔ; **18** γνοὺς δὲ ὁ Ἰησοῦς τὴν πονηρίαν αὐτῶν εἶπεν, Τί με πειράζετε, ὑποκριταί; **19** ἐπιδείξατέ μοι τὸ νόμισμα τοῦ κήνσου. οἱ δὲ προσήνεγκαν αὐτῷ δηνάριον. **20** καὶ λέγει αὐτοῖς, Τίνος ἡ εἰκὼν αὕτη καὶ ἡ ἐπιγραφή; **21** λέγουσιν αὐτῷ, Καίσαρος. τότε λέγει αὐτοῖς, Ἀπόδοτε οὖν τὰ Καίσαρος Καίσαρι καὶ τὰ τοῦ θεοῦ τῷ θεῷ. **22** καὶ ἀκούσαντες ἐθαύμασαν, καὶ ἀφέντες αὐτὸν ἀπῆλθαν.

23 Ἐν ἐκείνῃ τῇ ἡμέρᾳ προσῆλθον αὐτῷ Σαδδουκαῖοι, λέγοντες[a] μὴ εἶναι ἀνάστασιν, καὶ ἐπηρώτησαν αὐτὸν **24** λέγοντες, Διδάσκαλε, Μωϋσῆς εἶπεν, Ἐάν τις ἀποθάνῃ μὴ ἔχων τέκνα, ἐπιγαμβρεύσει ὁ ἀδελφὸς αὐτοῦ τὴν γυναῖκα αὐτοῦ καὶ ἀναστήσει σπέρμα τῷ ἀδελφῷ αὐτοῦ. **25** ἦσαν δὲ παρ' ἡμῖν ἑπτὰ ἀδελφοί· καὶ ὁ πρῶτος γήμας ἐτελεύτησεν, καὶ μὴ ἔχων σπέρμα ἀφῆκεν τὴν γυναῖκα αὐτοῦ τῷ ἀδελφῷ αὐτοῦ. **26** ὁμοίως καὶ ὁ δεύτερος καὶ ὁ τρίτος ἕως τῶν ἑπτά. **27** ὕστερον δὲ πάντων ἀπέθανεν ἡ γυνή. **28** ἐν τῇ ἀναστάσει οὖν τίνος τῶν ἑπτὰ ἔσται γυνή; πάντες γὰρ ἔσχον αὐτήν· **29** ἀποκριθεὶς δὲ ὁ Ἰησοῦς εἶπεν αὐτοῖς,

---

corners and invite to the banquet anyone you find.' [10]So the servants went out into the streets and gathered all the people they could find, both good and bad, and the wedding hall was filled with guests.

[11]"But when the king came in to see the guests, he noticed a man there who was not wearing wedding clothes. [12]'Friend,' he asked, 'how did you get in here without wedding clothes?' The man was speechless.

[13]"Then the king told the attendants, 'Tie him hand and foot, and throw him outside, into the darkness, where there will be weeping and gnashing of teeth.'

[14]"For many are invited, but few are chosen."

Paying Taxes to Caesar

[15]Then the Pharisees went out and laid plans to trap him in his words. [16]They sent their disciples to him along with the Herodians. "Teacher," they said, "we know you are a man of integrity and that you teach the way of God in accordance with the truth. You aren't swayed by men, because you pay no attention to who they are. [17]Tell us then, what is your opinion? Is it right to pay taxes to Caesar or not?"

[18]But Jesus, knowing their evil intent, said, "You hypocrites, why are you trying to trap me? [19]Show me the coin used for paying the tax." They brought him a denarius, [20]and he asked them, "Whose portrait is this? And whose inscription?"

[21]"Caesar's," they replied.

Then he said to them, "Give to Caesar what is Caesar's, and to God what is God's."

[22]When they heard this, they were amazed. So they left him and went away.

Marriage at the Resurrection

[23]That same day the Sadducees, who say there is no resurrection, came to him with a question. [24]"Teacher," they said, "Moses told us that if a man dies without having children, his brother must marry the widow and have children for him. [25]Now there were seven brothers among us. The first one married and died, and since he had no children, he left his wife to his brother. [26]The same thing happened to the second and third brother, right on down to the seventh. [27]Finally, the woman died. [28]Now then, at the resurrection, whose wife will she be of the seven, since all of them were married to her?"

[29]Jesus replied, "You are in error because

---

[h] Other ancient authorities read *who say that there is no resurrection*

[a]23 NRSV note h οἱ λέγοντες;

because you know neither the scriptures nor the power of God. [30]For in the resurrection they neither marry nor are given in marriage, but are like angels[i] in heaven. [31]And as for the resurrection of the dead, have you not read what was said to you by God, [32]'I am the God of Abraham, the God of Isaac, and the God of Jacob'? He is God not of the dead, but of the living." [33]And when the crowd heard it, they were astounded at his teaching.

The Greatest Commandment

34 When the Pharisees heard that he had silenced the Sadducees, they gathered together, [35]and one of them, a lawyer, asked him a question to test him. [36]"Teacher, which commandment in the law is the greatest?" [37]He said to him, " 'You shall love the Lord your God with all your heart, and with all your soul, and with all your mind.' [38]This is the greatest and first commandment. [39]And a second is like it: 'You shall love your neighbor as yourself.' [40]On these two commandments hang all the law and the prophets."

The Question about David's Son

41 Now while the Pharisees were gathered together, Jesus asked them this question: [42]"What do you think of the Messiah?[j] Whose son is he?" They said to him, "The son of David." [43]He said to them, "How is it then that David by the Spirit[k] calls him Lord, saying,

[44] 'The Lord said to my Lord,
    "Sit at my right hand,
        until I put your enemies under your
        feet" '?

[45]If David thus calls him Lord, how can he be his son?" [46]No one was able to give him an answer, nor from that day did anyone dare to ask him any more questions.

Jesus Denounces Scribes and Pharisees

23 Then Jesus said to the crowds and to his disciples, [2]"The scribes and the Pharisees sit on Moses' seat; [3]therefore, do whatever they teach you and follow it; but do not do as they do, for they do not practice what they teach. [4]They tie up heavy burdens, hard to bear,[l] and lay them on the shoulders of others; but they themselves are unwilling to lift a finger to move them. [5]They do all their deeds to be seen

---

Πλανᾶσθε μὴ εἰδότες τὰς γραφὰς μηδὲ τὴν δύναμιν τοῦ θεοῦ· **30** ἐν γὰρ τῇ ἀναστάσει οὔτε γαμοῦσιν οὔτε γαμίζονται, ἀλλ᾽ ὡς ἄγγελοι[b] ἐν τῷ οὐρανῷ εἰσιν. **31** περὶ δὲ τῆς ἀναστάσεως τῶν νεκρῶν οὐκ ἀνέγνωτε τὸ ῥηθὲν ὑμῖν ὑπὸ τοῦ θεοῦ λέγοντος, **32** Ἐγώ εἰμι ὁ θεὸς Ἀβραὰμ καὶ ὁ θεὸς Ἰσαὰκ καὶ ὁ θεὸς Ἰακώβ; οὐκ ἔστιν [ὁ] θεὸς νεκρῶν ἀλλὰ ζώντων. **33** καὶ ἀκούσαντες οἱ ὄχλοι ἐξεπλήσσοντο ἐπὶ τῇ διδαχῇ αὐτοῦ.

34 Οἱ δὲ Φαρισαῖοι ἀκούσαντες ὅτι ἐφίμωσεν τοὺς Σαδδουκαίους συνήχθησαν ἐπὶ τὸ αὐτό, **35** καὶ ἐπηρώτησεν εἷς ἐξ αὐτῶν [νομικὸς] πειράζων αὐτόν, **36** Διδάσκαλε, ποία ἐντολὴ μεγάλη ἐν τῷ νόμῳ; **37** ὁ δὲ ἔφη αὐτῷ, Ἀγαπήσεις κύριον τὸν θεόν σου ἐν ὅλῃ τῇ καρδίᾳ σου καὶ ἐν ὅλῃ τῇ ψυχῇ σου καὶ ἐν ὅλῃ τῇ διανοίᾳ σου· **38** αὕτη ἐστὶν ἡ μεγάλη καὶ πρώτη ἐντολή. **39** δευτέρα δὲ ὁμοία αὐτῇ, Ἀγαπήσεις τὸν πλησίον σου ὡς σεαυτόν. **40** ἐν ταύταις ταῖς δυσὶν ἐντολαῖς ὅλος ὁ νόμος κρέμαται καὶ οἱ προφῆται.

41 Συνηγμένων δὲ τῶν Φαρισαίων ἐπηρώτησεν αὐτοὺς ὁ Ἰησοῦς **42** λέγων, Τί ὑμῖν δοκεῖ περὶ τοῦ Χριστοῦ; τίνος υἱός ἐστιν; λέγουσιν αὐτῷ, Τοῦ Δαυίδ. **43** λέγει αὐτοῖς, Πῶς οὖν Δαυὶδ ἐν πνεύματι καλεῖ αὐτὸν κύριον λέγων,

44 Εἶπεν κύριος τῷ κυρίῳ μου,
  Κάθου ἐκ δεξιῶν μου,
    ἕως ἂν θῶ τοὺς ἐχθρούς σου
    ὑποκάτω τῶν ποδῶν σου;

45 εἰ οὖν Δαυὶδ καλεῖ αὐτὸν κύριον, πῶς υἱὸς αὐτοῦ ἐστιν; **46** καὶ οὐδεὶς ἐδύνατο ἀποκριθῆναι αὐτῷ λόγον οὐδὲ ἐτόλμησέν τις ἀπ᾽ ἐκείνης τῆς ἡμέρας ἐπερωτῆσαι αὐτὸν οὐκέτι.

23 Τότε ὁ Ἰησοῦς ἐλάλησεν τοῖς ὄχλοις καὶ τοῖς μαθηταῖς αὐτοῦ **2** λέγων, Ἐπὶ τῆς Μωϋσέως καθέδρας ἐκάθισαν οἱ γραμματεῖς καὶ οἱ Φαρισαῖοι. **3** πάντα οὖν ὅσα ἐὰν εἴπωσιν ὑμῖν ποιήσατε καὶ τηρεῖτε, κατὰ δὲ τὰ ἔργα αὐτῶν μὴ ποιεῖτε· λέγουσιν γὰρ καὶ οὐ ποιοῦσιν. **4** δεσμεύουσιν δὲ φορτία βαρέα [καὶ δυσβάστακτα][a] καὶ ἐπιτιθέασιν ἐπὶ τοὺς ὤμους τῶν ἀνθρώπων, αὐτοὶ δὲ τῷ δακτύλῳ αὐτῶν οὐ θέλουσιν κινῆσαι αὐτά. **5** πάντα δὲ τὰ ἔργα αὐτῶν ποιοῦσιν πρὸς τὸ

---

you do not know the Scriptures or the power of God. [30]At the resurrection people will neither marry nor be given in marriage; they will be like the angels in heaven. [31]But about the resurrection of the dead— have you not read what God said to you, [32]'I am the God of Abraham, the God of Isaac, and the God of Jacob'[a]? He is not the God of the dead but of the living."

[33]When the crowds heard this, they were astonished at his teaching.

The Greatest Commandment

[34]Hearing that Jesus had silenced the Sadducees, the Pharisees got together. [35]One of them, an expert in the law, tested him with this question: [36]"Teacher, which is the greatest commandment in the Law?"

[37]Jesus replied: " 'Love the Lord your God with all your heart and with all your soul and with all your mind.'[b] [38]This is the first and greatest commandment. [39]And the second is like it: 'Love your neighbor as yourself.'[c] [40]All the Law and the Prophets hang on these two commandments."

Whose Son Is the Christ?

[41]While the Pharisees were gathered together, Jesus asked them, [42]"What do you think about the Christ[d]? Whose son is he?"

"The son of David," they replied.

[43]He said to them, "How is it then that David, speaking by the Spirit, calls him 'Lord'? For he says,

[44]" 'The Lord said to my Lord:
  "Sit at my right hand
  until I put your enemies
    under your feet." '[e]

[45]If then David calls him 'Lord,' how can he be his son?" [46]No one could say a word in reply, and from that day on no one dared to ask him any more questions.

Seven Woes

23 Then Jesus said to the crowds and to his disciples: [2]"The teachers of the law and the Pharisees sit in Moses' seat. [3]So you must obey them and do everything they tell you. But do not do what they do, for they do not practice what they preach. [4]They tie up heavy loads and put them on men's shoulders, but they themselves are not willing to lift a finger to move them.

[5]"Everything they do is done for men to

---

[i]Other ancient authorities add *of God*   [j]Or *Christ*
[k]Gk *in spirit*   [l]Other ancient authorities lack *hard to bear*

[b]30 NRSV note i adds [τοῦ] θεοῦ   [a]4 NIV text and NRSV note l omit καὶ δυσβάστακτα

[a]32 Exodus 3:6   [b]37 Deut. 6:5   [c]39 Lev. 19:18
[d]42 Or *Messiah*   [e]44 Psalm 110:1

by others; for they make their phylacteries broad and their fringes long. ⁶They love to have the place of honor at banquets and the best seats in the synagogues, ⁷and to be greeted with respect in the marketplaces, and to have people call them rabbi. ⁸But you are not to be called rabbi, for you have one teacher, and you are all students.ᵐ ⁹And call no one your father on earth, for you have one Father—the one in heaven. ¹⁰Nor are you to be called instructors, for you have one instructor, the Messiah.ⁿ ¹¹The greatest among you will be your servant. ¹²All who exalt themselves will be humbled, and all who humble themselves will be exalted.

13 "But woe to you, scribes and Pharisees, hypocrites! For you lock people out of the kingdom of heaven. For you do not go in yourselves, and when others are going in, you stop them.ᵒ ¹⁵Woe to you, scribes and Pharisees, hypocrites! For you cross sea and land to make a single convert, and you make the new convert twice as much a child of hellᵖ as yourselves.

16 "Woe to you, blind guides, who say, 'Whoever swears by the sanctuary is bound by nothing, but whoever swears by the gold of the sanctuary is bound by the oath.' ¹⁷You blind fools! For which is greater, the gold or the sanctuary that has made the gold sacred? ¹⁸And you say, 'Whoever swears by the altar is bound by nothing, but whoever swears by the gift that is on the altar is bound by the oath.' ¹⁹How blind you are! For which is greater, the gift or the altar that makes the gift sacred? ²⁰So whoever swears by the altar, swears by it and by everything on it; ²¹and whoever swears by the sanctuary, swears by it and by the one who dwells in it; ²²and whoever swears by heaven, swears by the throne of God and by the one who is seated upon it.

23 "Woe to you, scribes and Pharisees, hypocrites! For you tithe mint, dill, and cummin, and have neglected the weightier matters of the law: justice and mercy and faith. It is these you ought to have practiced without neglecting the others. ²⁴You blind guides! You strain out a gnat but

θεαθῆναι τοῖς ἀνθρώποις· πλατύνουσιν γὰρ τὰ φυλακτήρια αὐτῶν καὶ μεγαλύνουσιν τὰ κράσπεδαᵇ, 6 φιλοῦσιν δὲ τὴν πρωτοκλισίαν ἐν τοῖς δείπνοις καὶ τὰς πρωτοκαθεδρίας ἐν ταῖς συναγωγαῖς 7 καὶ τοὺς ἀσπασμοὺς ἐν ταῖς ἀγοραῖς καὶ καλεῖσθαι ὑπὸ τῶν ἀνθρώπων, Ῥαββί. 8 ὑμεῖς δὲ μὴ κληθῆτε, Ῥαββί· εἷς γάρ ἐστιν ὑμῶν ὁ διδάσκαλος, πάντες δὲ ὑμεῖς ἀδελφοί ἐστε. 9 καὶ πατέρα μὴ καλέσητε ὑμῶν ἐπὶ τῆς γῆς, εἷς γάρ ἐστιν ὑμῶν ὁ πατὴρ ὁ οὐράνιος. 10 μηδὲ κληθῆτε καθηγηταί, ὅτι καθηγητὴς ὑμῶν ἐστιν εἷς ὁ Χριστός. 11 ὁ δὲ μείζων ὑμῶν ἔσται ὑμῶν διάκονος. 12 ὅστις δὲ ὑψώσει ἑαυτὸν ταπεινωθήσεται καὶ ὅστις ταπεινώσει ἑαυτὸν ὑψωθήσεται.

13 Οὐαὶ δὲ ὑμῖν, γραμματεῖς καὶ Φαρισαῖοι ὑποκριταί, ὅτι κλείετε τὴν βασιλείαν τῶν οὐρανῶν ἔμπροσθεν τῶν ἀνθρώπων· ὑμεῖς γὰρ οὐκ εἰσέρχεσθε οὐδὲ τοὺς εἰσερχομένους ἀφίετε εἰσελθεῖν.ᶜ

15 Οὐαὶ ὑμῖν, γραμματεῖς καὶ Φαρισαῖοι ὑποκριταί, ὅτι περιάγετε τὴν θάλασσαν καὶ τὴν ξηρὰν ποιῆσαι ἕνα προσήλυτον, καὶ ὅταν γένηται ποιεῖτε αὐτὸν υἱὸν γεέννης διπλότερον ὑμῶν.

16 Οὐαὶ ὑμῖν, ὁδηγοὶ τυφλοὶ οἱ λέγοντες, Ὃς ἂν ὀμόσῃ ἐν τῷ ναῷ, οὐδέν ἐστιν· ὃς δ' ἂν ὀμόσῃ ἐν τῷ χρυσῷ τοῦ ναοῦ, ὀφείλει. 17 μωροὶ καὶ τυφλοί, τίς γὰρ μείζων ἐστίν, ὁ χρυσὸς ἢ ὁ ναὸς ὁ ἁγιάσας τὸν χρυσόν; 18 καί, Ὃς ἂν ὀμόσῃ ἐν τῷ θυσιαστηρίῳ, οὐδέν ἐστιν· ὃς δ' ἂν ὀμόσῃ ἐν τῷ δώρῳ τῷ ἐπάνω αὐτοῦ, ὀφείλει. 19 τυφλοί, τί γὰρ μεῖζον, τὸ δῶρον ἢ τὸ θυσιαστήριον τὸ ἁγιάζον τὸ δῶρον; 20 ὁ οὖν ὀμόσας ἐν τῷ θυσιαστηρίῳ ὀμνύει ἐν αὐτῷ καὶ ἐν πᾶσι τοῖς ἐπάνω αὐτοῦ· 21 καὶ ὁ ὀμόσας ἐν τῷ ναῷ ὀμνύει ἐν αὐτῷ καὶ ἐν τῷ κατοικοῦντι αὐτόν, 22 καὶ ὁ ὀμόσας ἐν τῷ οὐρανῷ ὀμνύει ἐν τῷ θρόνῳ τοῦ θεοῦ καὶ ἐν τῷ καθημένῳ ἐπάνω αὐτοῦ.

23 Οὐαὶ ὑμῖν, γραμματεῖς καὶ Φαρισαῖοι ὑποκριταί, ὅτι ἀποδεκατοῦτε τὸ ἡδύοσμον καὶ τὸ ἄνηθον καὶ τὸ κύμινον καὶ ἀφήκατε τὰ βαρύτερα τοῦ νόμου, τὴν κρίσιν καὶ τὸ ἔλεος καὶ τὴν πίστιν· ταῦτα [δὲ]ᵈ ἔδει ποιῆσαι κἀκεῖνα μὴ ἀφιέναι. 24 ὁδηγοὶ τυφλοί, οἱ διϋλίζοντες τὸν κώνωπα, τὴν δὲ

see: They make their phylacteriesᵃ wide and the tassels on their garments long; ⁶they love the place of honor at banquets and the most important seats in the synagogues; ⁷they love to be greeted in the marketplaces and to have men call them 'Rabbi.'

⁸"But you are not to be called 'Rabbi,' for you have only one Master and you are all brothers. ⁹And do not call anyone on earth 'father,' for you have one Father, and he is in heaven. ¹⁰Nor are you to be called 'teacher,' for you have one Teacher, the Christ.ᵇ ¹¹The greatest among you will be your servant. ¹²For whoever exalts himself will be humbled, and whoever humbles himself will be exalted.

¹³"Woe to you, teachers of the law and Pharisees, you hypocrites! You shut the kingdom of heaven in men's faces. You yourselves do not enter, nor will you let those enter who are trying to.ᶜ

¹⁵"Woe to you, teachers of the law and Pharisees, you hypocrites! You travel over land and sea to win a single convert, and when he becomes one, you make him twice as much a son of hell as you are.

¹⁶"Woe to you, blind guides! You say, 'If anyone swears by the temple, it means nothing; but if anyone swears by the gold of the temple, he is bound by his oath.' ¹⁷You blind fools! Which is greater: the gold, or the temple that makes the gold sacred? ¹⁸You also say, 'If anyone swears by the altar, it means nothing; but if anyone swears by the gift on it, he is bound by his oath.' ¹⁹You blind men! Which is greater: the gift, or the altar that makes the gift sacred? ²⁰Therefore, he who swears by the altar swears by it and by everything on it. ²¹And he who swears by the temple swears by it and by the one who dwells in it. ²²And he who swears by heaven swears by God's throne and by the one who sits on it.

²³"Woe to you, teachers of the law and Pharisees, you hypocrites! You give a tenth of your spices—mint, dill and cummin. But you have neglected the more important matters of the law—justice, mercy and faithfulness. You should have practiced the latter, without neglecting the former. ²⁴You blind guides! You strain out a gnat but

---

ᵐ Gk *brothers*   ⁿ Or *the Christ*   ᵒ Other authorities add here (or after verse 12) verse 14, *Woe to you, scribes and Pharisees, hypocrites! For you devour widows' houses and for the sake of appearance you make long prayers; therefore you will receive the greater condemnation*   ᵖ Gk *Gehenna*

ᵇ5 NIV text adds τῶν ἱματίων αὐτῶν †   ᶜ13 NIV/NRSV notes 14 Οὐαὶ δὲ ὑμῖν, γραμματεῖς καὶ Φαρισαῖοι ὑποκριταί, ὅτι κατεσθίετε τὰς οἰκίας τῶν χηρῶν καὶ προφάσει μακρὰ προσευχόμενοι· διὰ τοῦτο λήμψεσθε περισσότερον κρίμα.   ᵈ23 NIV text omits δέ †

ᵃ5 That is, boxes containing Scripture verses, worn on forehead and arm   ᵇ10 Or *Messiah*   ᶜ13 Some manuscripts to. ¹⁴Woe to you, teachers of the law and Pharisees, you hypocrites! You devour widows' houses and for a show make lengthy prayers. Therefore you will be punished more severely.

swallow a camel!

25 "Woe to you, scribes and Pharisees, hypocrites! For you clean the outside of the cup and of the plate, but inside they are full of greed and self-indulgence. 26You blind Pharisee! First clean the inside of the cup,q so that the outside also may become clean.

27 "Woe to you, scribes and Pharisees, hypocrites! For you are like whitewashed tombs, which on the outside look beautiful, but inside they are full of the bones of the dead and of all kinds of filth. 28So you also on the outside look righteous to others, but inside you are full of hypocrisy and lawlessness.

29 "Woe to you, scribes and Pharisees, hypocrites! For you build the tombs of the prophets and decorate the graves of the righteous, 30and you say, 'If we had lived in the days of our ancestors, we would not have taken part with them in shedding the blood of the prophets.' 31Thus you testify against yourselves that you are descendants of those who murdered the prophets. 32Fill up, then, the measure of your ancestors. 33You snakes, you brood of vipers! How can you escape being sentenced to hell?r 34Therefore I send you prophets, sages, and scribes, some of whom you will kill and crucify, and some you will flog in your synagogues and pursue from town to town, 35so that upon you may come all the righteous blood shed on earth, from the blood of righteous Abel to the blood of Zechariah son of Barachiah, whom you murdered between the sanctuary and the altar. 36Truly I tell you, all this will come upon this generation.

The Lament over Jerusalem

37 "Jerusalem, Jerusalem, the city that kills the prophets and stones those who are sent to it! How often have I desired to gather your children together as a hen gathers her brood under her wings, and you were not willing! 38See, your house is left to you, desolate.s 39For I tell you, you will not see me again until you say, 'Blessed is the one who comes in the name of the Lord.' "

The Destruction of the Temple Foretold

24 As Jesus came out of the temple and was going away, his disciples came to point out to him the buildings of the temple. 2Then he asked them, "You see

---

κάμηλον καταπίνοντες.

25 Οὐαὶ ὑμῖν, γραμματεῖς καὶ Φαρισαῖοι ὑποκριταί, ὅτι καθαρίζετε τὸ ἔξωθεν τοῦ ποτηρίου καὶ τῆς παροψίδος, ἔσωθεν δὲ γέμουσιν ἐξ ἁρπαγῆς καὶ ἀκρασίας. 26 Φαρισαῖε τυφλέ, καθάρισον πρῶτον τὸ ἐντὸς τοῦ ποτηρίου e, ἵνα γένηται καὶ τὸ ἐκτὸς αὐτοῦ καθαρόν.

27 Οὐαὶ ὑμῖν, γραμματεῖς καὶ Φαρισαῖοι ὑποκριταί, ὅτι παρομοιάζετε τάφοις κεκονιαμένοις, οἵτινες ἔξωθεν μὲν φαίνονται ὡραῖοι, ἔσωθεν δὲ γέμουσιν ὀστέων νεκρῶν καὶ πάσης ἀκαθαρσίας. 28 οὕτως καὶ ὑμεῖς ἔξωθεν μὲν φαίνεσθε τοῖς ἀνθρώποις δίκαιοι, ἔσωθεν δέ ἐστε μεστοὶ ὑποκρίσεως καὶ ἀνομίας.

29 Οὐαὶ ὑμῖν, γραμματεῖς καὶ Φαρισαῖοι ὑποκριταί, ὅτι οἰκοδομεῖτε τοὺς τάφους τῶν προφητῶν καὶ κοσμεῖτε τὰ μνημεῖα τῶν δικαίων, 30 καὶ λέγετε, Εἰ ἤμεθα ἐν ταῖς ἡμέραις τῶν πατέρων ἡμῶν, οὐκ ἂν ἤμεθα αὐτῶν κοινωνοὶ ἐν τῷ αἵματι τῶν προφητῶν. 31 ὥστε μαρτυρεῖτε ἑαυτοῖς ὅτι υἱοί ἐστε τῶν φονευσάντων τοὺς προφήτας. 32 καὶ ὑμεῖς πληρώσατε τὸ μέτρον τῶν πατέρων ὑμῶν. 33 ὄφεις, γεννήματα ἐχιδνῶν, πῶς φύγητε ἀπὸ τῆς κρίσεως τῆς γεέννης; 34 διὰ τοῦτο ἰδοὺ ἐγὼ ἀποστέλλω πρὸς ὑμᾶς προφήτας καὶ σοφοὺς καὶ γραμματεῖς· ἐξ αὐτῶν ἀποκτενεῖτε καὶ σταυρώσετε καὶ ἐξ αὐτῶν μαστιγώσετε ἐν ταῖς συναγωγαῖς ὑμῶν καὶ διώξετε ἀπὸ πόλεως εἰς πόλιν· 35 ὅπως ἔλθῃ ἐφ' ὑμᾶς πᾶν αἷμα δίκαιον ἐκχυννόμενον ἐπὶ τῆς γῆς ἀπὸ τοῦ αἵματος Ἅβελ τοῦ δικαίου ἕως τοῦ αἵματος Ζαχαρίου υἱοῦ Βαραχίου, ὃν ἐφονεύσατε μεταξὺ τοῦ ναοῦ καὶ τοῦ θυσιαστηρίου. 36 ἀμὴν λέγω ὑμῖν, ἥξει ταῦτα πάντα ἐπὶ τὴν γενεὰν ταύτην.

37 Ἰερουσαλὴμ Ἰερουσαλήμ, ἡ ἀποκτείνουσα τοὺς προφήτας καὶ λιθοβολοῦσα τοὺς ἀπεσταλμένους πρὸς αὐτήν, ποσάκις ἠθέλησα ἐπισυναγαγεῖν τὰ τέκνα σου, ὃν τρόπον ὄρνις ἐπισυνάγει τὰ νοσσία αὐτῆς ὑπὸ τὰς πτέρυγας, καὶ οὐκ ἠθελήσατε. 38 ἰδοὺ ἀφίεται ὑμῖν ὁ οἶκος ὑμῶν ἔρημος. 39 λέγω γὰρ ὑμῖν, οὐ μή με ἴδητε ἀπ' ἄρτι ἕως ἂν εἴπητε, Εὐλογημένος ὁ ἐρχόμενος ἐν ὀνόματι κυρίου.

24 Καὶ ἐξελθὼν ὁ Ἰησοῦς ἀπὸ τοῦ ἱεροῦ ἐπορεύετο, καὶ προσῆλθον οἱ μαθηταὶ αὐτοῦ ἐπιδεῖξαι αὐτῷ τὰς οἰκοδομὰς τοῦ ἱεροῦ. 2 ὁ δὲ ἀποκριθεὶς

---

swallow a camel.

25"Woe to you, teachers of the law and Pharisees, you hypocrites! You clean the outside of the cup and dish, but inside they are full of greed and self-indulgence. 26Blind Pharisee! First clean the inside of the cup and dish, and then the outside also will be clean.

27"Woe to you, teachers of the law and Pharisees, you hypocrites! You are like whitewashed tombs, which look beautiful on the outside but on the inside are full of dead men's bones and everything unclean. 28In the same way, on the outside you appear to people as righteous but on the inside you are full of hypocrisy and wickedness.

29"Woe to you, teachers of the law and Pharisees, you hypocrites! You build tombs for the prophets and decorate the graves of the righteous. 30And you say, 'If we had lived in the days of our forefathers, we would not have taken part with them in shedding the blood of the prophets.' 31So you testify against yourselves that you are the descendants of those who murdered the prophets. 32Fill up, then, the measure of the sin of your forefathers!

33"You snakes! You brood of vipers! How will you escape being condemned to hell? 34Therefore I am sending you prophets and wise men and teachers. Some of them you will kill and crucify; others you will flog in your synagogues and pursue from town to town. 35And so upon you will come all the righteous blood that has been shed on earth, from the blood of righteous Abel to the blood of Zechariah son of Berekiah, whom you murdered between the temple and the altar. 36I tell you the truth, all this will come upon this generation.

37"O Jerusalem, Jerusalem, you who kill the prophets and stone those sent to you, how often I have longed to gather your children together, as a hen gathers her chicks under her wings, but you were not willing. 38Look, your house is left to you desolate. 39For I tell you, you will not see me again until you say, 'Blessed is he who comes in the name of the Lord.'d"

Signs of the End of the Age

24 Jesus left the temple and was walking away when his disciples came up to him to call his attention to its buildings. 2"Do you see all these things?"

---

all these, do you not? Truly I tell you, not one stone will be left here upon another; all will be thrown down."

Signs of the End of the Age

3 When he was sitting on the Mount of Olives, the disciples came to him privately, saying, "Tell us, when will this be, and what will be the sign of your coming and of the end of the age?" [4]Jesus answered them, "Beware that no one leads you astray. [5]For many will come in my name, saying, 'I am the Messiah!'[t] and they will lead many astray. [6]And you will hear of wars and rumors of wars; see that you are not alarmed; for this must take place, but the end is not yet. [7]For nation will rise against nation, and kingdom against kingdom, and there will be famines[u] and earthquakes in various places: [8]all this is but the beginning of the birth pangs.

Persecutions Foretold

9 "Then they will hand you over to be tortured and will put you to death, and you will be hated by all nations because of my name. [10]Then many will fall away,[v] and they will betray one another and hate one another. [11]And many false prophets will arise and lead many astray. [12]And because of the increase of lawlessness, the love of many will grow cold. [13]But the one who endures to the end will be saved. [14]And this good news[w] of the kingdom will be proclaimed throughout the world, as a testimony to all the nations; and then the end will come.

The Desolating Sacrilege

15 "So when you see the desolating sacrilege standing in the holy place, as was spoken of by the prophet Daniel (let the reader understand), [16]then those in Judea must flee to the mountains; [17]the one on the housetop must not go down to take what is in the house; [18]the one in the field must not turn back to get a coat. [19]Woe to those who are pregnant and to those who are nursing infants in those days! [20]Pray that your flight may not be in winter or on a sabbath. [21]For at that time there will be great suffering, such as has not been from the beginning of the world until now, no, and never will be. [22]And if those days had not been cut short, no one would be saved; but for the sake of the elect those days will be cut short. [23]Then if anyone says to you,

εἶπεν αὐτοῖς, Οὐ βλέπετε ταῦτα πάντα; ἀμὴν λέγω ὑμῖν, οὐ μὴ ἀφεθῇ ὧδε λίθος ἐπὶ λίθον ὃς οὐ καταλυθήσεται.

3 Καθημένου δὲ αὐτοῦ ἐπὶ τοῦ Ὄρους τῶν Ἐλαιῶν προσῆλθον αὐτῷ οἱ μαθηταὶ κατ᾽ ἰδίαν λέγοντες, Εἰπὲ ἡμῖν πότε ταῦτα ἔσται καὶ τί τὸ σημεῖον τῆς σῆς παρουσίας καὶ συντελείας τοῦ αἰῶνος; 4 καὶ ἀποκριθεὶς ὁ Ἰησοῦς εἶπεν αὐτοῖς, Βλέπετε μή τις ὑμᾶς πλανήσῃ· 5 πολλοὶ γὰρ ἐλεύσονται ἐπὶ τῷ ὀνόματί μου λέγοντες, Ἐγώ εἰμι ὁ Χριστός, καὶ πολλοὺς πλανήσουσιν. 6 μελλήσετε δὲ ἀκούειν πολέμους καὶ ἀκοὰς πολέμων· ὁρᾶτε μὴ θροεῖσθε· δεῖ γὰρ γενέσθαι, ἀλλ᾽ οὔπω ἐστὶν τὸ τέλος. 7 ἐγερθήσεται γὰρ ἔθνος ἐπὶ ἔθνος καὶ βασιλεία ἐπὶ βασιλείαν καὶ ἔσονται λιμοὶ[a] καὶ σεισμοὶ κατὰ τόπους· 8 πάντα δὲ ταῦτα ἀρχὴ ὠδίνων. 9 τότε παραδώσουσιν ὑμᾶς εἰς θλῖψιν καὶ ἀποκτενοῦσιν ὑμᾶς, καὶ ἔσεσθε μισούμενοι ὑπὸ πάντων τῶν ἐθνῶν διὰ τὸ ὄνομά μου. 10 καὶ τότε σκανδαλισθήσονται πολλοὶ καὶ ἀλλήλους παραδώσουσιν καὶ μισήσουσιν ἀλλήλους· 11 καὶ πολλοὶ ψευδοπροφῆται ἐγερθήσονται καὶ πλανήσουσιν πολλούς· 12 καὶ διὰ τὸ πληθυνθῆναι τὴν ἀνομίαν ψυγήσεται ἡ ἀγάπη τῶν πολλῶν. 13 ὁ δὲ ὑπομείνας εἰς τέλος οὗτος σωθήσεται. 14 καὶ κηρυχθήσεται τοῦτο τὸ εὐαγγέλιον τῆς βασιλείας ἐν ὅλῃ τῇ οἰκουμένῃ εἰς μαρτύριον πᾶσιν τοῖς ἔθνεσιν, καὶ τότε ἥξει τὸ τέλος.

15 Ὅταν οὖν ἴδητε τὸ βδέλυγμα τῆς ἐρημώσεως τὸ ῥηθὲν διὰ Δανιὴλ τοῦ προφήτου ἑστὸς ἐν τόπῳ ἁγίῳ, ὁ ἀναγινώσκων νοείτω, 16 τότε οἱ ἐν τῇ Ἰουδαίᾳ φευγέτωσαν εἰς τὰ ὄρη, 17 ὁ ἐπὶ τοῦ δώματος μὴ καταβάτω ἆραι τὰ ἐκ τῆς οἰκίας αὐτοῦ, 18 καὶ ὁ ἐν τῷ ἀγρῷ μὴ ἐπιστρεψάτω ὀπίσω ἆραι τὸ ἱμάτιον αὐτοῦ. 19 οὐαὶ δὲ ταῖς ἐν γαστρὶ ἐχούσαις καὶ ταῖς θηλαζούσαις ἐν ἐκείναις ταῖς ἡμέραις. 20 προσεύχεσθε δὲ ἵνα μὴ γένηται ἡ φυγὴ ὑμῶν χειμῶνος μηδὲ σαββάτῳ. 21 ἔσται γὰρ τότε θλῖψις μεγάλη οἵα οὐ γέγονεν ἀπ᾽ ἀρχῆς κόσμου ἕως τοῦ νῦν οὐδ᾽ οὐ μὴ γένηται. 22 καὶ εἰ μὴ ἐκολοβώθησαν αἱ ἡμέραι ἐκεῖναι, οὐκ ἂν ἐσώθη πᾶσα σάρξ· διὰ δὲ τοὺς ἐκλεκτοὺς κολοβωθήσονται αἱ ἡμέραι ἐκεῖναι. 23 τότε ἐάν τις ὑμῖν εἴπῃ, Ἰδοὺ ὧδε ὁ Χριστός, ἤ,

he asked. "I tell you the truth, not one stone here will be left on another; every one will be thrown down."

[3]As Jesus was sitting on the Mount of Olives, the disciples came to him privately. "Tell us," they said, "when will this happen, and what will be the sign of your coming and of the end of the age?"

[4]Jesus answered: "Watch out that no one deceives you. [5]For many will come in my name, claiming, 'I am the Christ,[a]' and will deceive many. [6]You will hear of wars and rumors of wars, but see to it that you are not alarmed. Such things must happen, but the end is still to come. [7]Nation will rise against nation, and kingdom against kingdom. There will be famines and earthquakes in various places. [8]All these are the beginning of birth pains.

[9]"Then you will be handed over to be persecuted and put to death, and you will be hated by all nations because of me. [10]At that time many will turn away from the faith and will betray and hate each other, [11]and many false prophets will appear and deceive many people. [12]Because of the increase of wickedness, the love of most will grow cold, [13]but he who stands firm to the end will be saved. [14]And this gospel of the kingdom will be preached in the whole world as a testimony to all nations, and then the end will come.

[15]"So when you see standing in the holy place 'the abomination that causes desolation,'[b] spoken of through the prophet Daniel—let the reader understand—[16]then let those who are in Judea flee to the mountains. [17]Let no one on the roof of his house go down to take anything out of the house. [18]Let no one in the field go back to get his cloak. [19]How dreadful it will be in those days for pregnant women and nursing mothers! [20]Pray that your flight will not take place in winter or on the Sabbath. [21]For then there will be great distress, unequaled from the beginning of the world until now—and never to be equaled again. [22]If those days had not been cut short, no one would survive, but for the sake of the elect those days will be shortened. [23]At that time if anyone says to you, 'Look,

---

[t] Or the Christ   [u] Other ancient authorities add and pestilences   [v] Or stumble   [w] Or gospel

[a]7 NRSV note u adds καὶ λοιμοί

[a]5 Or Messiah; also in verse 23   [b]15 Daniel 9:27; 11:31; 12:11

'Look! Here is the Messiah!'[x] or 'There he is!'—do not believe it. 24For false messiahs[y] and false prophets will appear and produce great signs and omens, to lead astray, if possible, even the elect. 25Take note, I have told you beforehand. 26So, if they say to you, 'Look! He is in the wilderness,' do not go out. If they say, 'Look! He is in the inner rooms,' do not believe it. 27For as the lightning comes from the east and flashes as far as the west, so will be the coming of the Son of Man. 28Wherever the corpse is, there the vultures will gather.

The Coming of the Son of Man

29 "Immediately after the suffering of those days

the sun will be darkened,
    and the moon will not give its light;
the stars will fall from heaven,
    and the powers of heaven will be shaken.

30Then the sign of the Son of Man will appear in heaven, and then all the tribes of the earth will mourn, and they will see 'the Son of Man coming on the clouds of heaven' with power and great glory. 31And he will send out his angels with a loud trumpet call, and they will gather his elect from the four winds, from one end of heaven to the other.

The Lesson of the Fig Tree

32 "From the fig tree learn its lesson: as soon as its branch becomes tender and puts forth its leaves, you know that summer is near. 33So also, when you see all these things, you know that he[z] is near, at the very gates. 34Truly I tell you, this generation will not pass away until all these things have taken place. 35Heaven and earth will pass away, but my words will not pass away.

The Necessity for Watchfulness

36 "But about that day and hour no one knows, neither the angels of heaven, nor the Son,[a] but only the Father. 37For as the days of Noah were, so will be the coming of the Son of Man. 38For as in those days before the flood they were eating and drinking, marrying and giving in marriage, until the day Noah entered the ark, 39and they knew nothing until the flood came and swept them all away, so too will be

Ὧδε, μὴ πιστεύσητε· 24 ἐγερθήσονται γὰρ ψευδόχριστοι καὶ ψευδοπροφῆται καὶ δώσουσιν σημεῖα μεγάλα καὶ τέρατα ὥστε πλανῆσαι, εἰ δυνατόν, καὶ τοὺς ἐκλεκτούς. 25 ἰδοὺ προείρηκα ὑμῖν. 26 ἐὰν οὖν εἴπωσιν ὑμῖν, Ἰδοὺ ἐν τῇ ἐρήμῳ ἐστίν, μὴ ἐξέλθητε· Ἰδοὺ ἐν τοῖς ταμείοις, μὴ πιστεύσητε· 27 ὥσπερ γὰρ ἡ ἀστραπὴ ἐξέρχεται ἀπὸ ἀνατολῶν καὶ φαίνεται ἕως δυσμῶν, οὕτως ἔσται ἡ παρουσία τοῦ υἱοῦ τοῦ ἀνθρώπου· 28 ὅπου ἐὰν ᾖ τὸ πτῶμα, ἐκεῖ συναχθήσονται οἱ ἀετοί.

29 Εὐθέως δὲ μετὰ τὴν θλῖψιν τῶν ἡμερῶν ἐκείνων

ὁ ἥλιος σκοτισθήσεται,
    καὶ ἡ σελήνη οὐ δώσει τὸ φέγγος αὐτῆς,
καὶ οἱ ἀστέρες πεσοῦνται ἀπὸ τοῦ οὐρανοῦ,
    καὶ αἱ δυνάμεις τῶν οὐρανῶν σαλευθήσονται.

30 καὶ τότε φανήσεται τὸ σημεῖον τοῦ υἱοῦ τοῦ ἀνθρώπου ἐν οὐρανῷ, καὶ τότε κόψονται πᾶσαι αἱ φυλαὶ τῆς γῆς καὶ ὄψονται **τὸν υἱὸν τοῦ ἀνθρώπου ἐρχόμενον ἐπὶ τῶν νεφελῶν τοῦ οὐρανοῦ** μετὰ δυνάμεως καὶ δόξης πολλῆς· 31 καὶ ἀποστελεῖ τοὺς ἀγγέλους αὐτοῦ μετὰ σάλπιγγος μεγάλης, καὶ ἐπισυνάξουσιν τοὺς ἐκλεκτοὺς αὐτοῦ ἐκ τῶν τεσσάρων ἀνέμων ἀπ' ἄκρων οὐρανῶν ἕως [τῶν] ἄκρων αὐτῶν.

32 Ἀπὸ δὲ τῆς συκῆς μάθετε τὴν παραβολήν· ὅταν ἤδη ὁ κλάδος αὐτῆς γένηται ἁπαλὸς καὶ τὰ φύλλα ἐκφύῃ, γινώσκετε ὅτι ἐγγὺς τὸ θέρος· 33 οὕτως καὶ ὑμεῖς, ὅταν ἴδητε πάντα ταῦτα γινώσκετε ὅτι ἐγγύς ἐστιν ἐπὶ θύραις. 34 ἀμὴν λέγω ὑμῖν ὅτι οὐ μὴ παρέλθῃ ἡ γενεὰ αὕτη ἕως ἂν πάντα ταῦτα γένηται. 35 ὁ οὐρανὸς καὶ ἡ γῆ παρελεύσεται, οἱ δὲ λόγοι μου οὐ μὴ παρέλθωσιν.

36 Περὶ δὲ τῆς ἡμέρας ἐκείνης καὶ ὥρας οὐδεὶς οἶδεν, οὐδὲ οἱ ἄγγελοι τῶν οὐρανῶν οὐδὲ ὁ υἱός, εἰ μὴ ὁ πατὴρ μόνος. 37 ὥσπερ γὰρ αἱ ἡμέραι τοῦ Νῶε, οὕτως ἔσται ἡ παρουσία τοῦ υἱοῦ τοῦ ἀνθρώπου. 38 ὡς γὰρ ἦσαν ἐν ταῖς ἡμέραις [ἐκείναις] ταῖς πρὸ τοῦ κατακλυσμοῦ τρώγοντες καὶ πίνοντες, γαμοῦντες καὶ γαμίζοντες, ἄχρι ἧς ἡμέρας εἰσῆλθεν Νῶε εἰς τὴν κιβωτόν, 39 καὶ οὐκ ἔγνωσαν ἕως ἦλθεν ὁ κατακλυσμὸς καὶ ἦρεν ἅπαντας, οὕτως ἔσται

here is the Christ!' or, 'There he is!' do not believe it. 24For false Christs and false prophets will appear and perform great signs and miracles to deceive even the elect—if that were possible. 25See, I have told you ahead of time.

26"So if anyone tells you, 'There he is, out in the desert,' do not go out; or, 'Here he is, in the inner rooms,' do not believe it. 27For as lightning that comes from the east is visible even in the west, so will be the coming of the Son of Man. 28Wherever there is a carcass, there the vultures will gather.

29"Immediately after the distress of those days

" 'the sun will be darkened,
    and the moon will not give its light;
the stars will fall from the sky,
    and the heavenly bodies will be shaken.'[c]

30"At that time the sign of the Son of Man will appear in the sky, and all the nations of the earth will mourn. They will see the Son of Man coming on the clouds of the sky, with power and great glory. 31And he will send his angels with a loud trumpet call, and they will gather his elect from the four winds, from one end of the heavens to the other.

32"Now learn this lesson from the fig tree: As soon as its twigs get tender and its leaves come out, you know that summer is near. 33Even so, when you see all these things, you know that it[d] is near, right at the door. 34I tell you the truth, this generation[e] will certainly not pass away until all these things have happened. 35Heaven and earth will pass away, but my words will never pass away.

The Day and Hour Unknown

36"No one knows about that day or hour, not even the angels in heaven, nor the Son,[f] but only the Father. 37As it was in the days of Noah, so it will be at the coming of the Son of Man. 38For in the days before the flood, people were eating and drinking, marrying and giving in marriage, up to the day Noah entered the ark; 39and they knew nothing about what would happen until the flood came and took them all

---

[x] Or *the Christ*   [y] Or *christs*   [z] Or *it*   [a] Other ancient authorities lack *nor the Son*

[c]29 Isaiah 13:10; 34:4   [d]33 Or *he*   [e]34 Or *race*   [f]36 Some manuscripts do not have *nor the Son*.

the coming of the Son of Man. 40Then two will be in the field; one will be taken and one will be left. 41Two women will be grinding meal together; one will be taken and one will be left. 42Keep awake therefore, for you do not know on what day[b] your Lord is coming. 43But understand this: if the owner of the house had known in what part of the night the thief was coming, he would have stayed awake and would not have let his house be broken into. 44Therefore you also must be ready, for the Son of Man is coming at an unexpected hour.

The Faithful or the Unfaithful Slave

45 "Who then is the faithful and wise slave, whom his master has put in charge of his household, to give the other slaves[c] their allowance of food at the proper time? 46Blessed is that slave whom his master will find at work when he arrives. 47Truly I tell you, he will put that one in charge of all his possessions. 48But if that wicked slave says to himself, 'My master is delayed,' 49and he begins to beat his fellow slaves, and eats and drinks with drunkards, 50the master of that slave will come on a day when he does not expect him and at an hour that he does not know. 51He will cut him in pieces[d] and put him with the hypocrites, where there will be weeping and gnashing of teeth.

The Parable of the Ten Bridesmaids

25 "Then the kingdom of heaven will be like this. Ten bridesmaids[e] took their lamps and went to meet the bridegroom.[f] 2Five of them were foolish, and five were wise. 3When the foolish took their lamps, they took no oil with them; 4but the wise took flasks of oil with their lamps. 5As the bridegroom was delayed, all of them became drowsy and slept. 6But at midnight there was a shout, 'Look! Here is the bridegroom! Come out to meet him.' 7Then all those bridesmaids[e] got up and trimmed their lamps. 8The foolish said to the wise, 'Give us some of your oil, for our lamps are going out.' 9But the wise replied, 'No! there will not be enough for you and for us; you had better go to the dealers and buy some for yourselves.' 10And while they went to buy it, the bridegroom came, and those who were ready

[καὶ]b ἡ παρουσία τοῦ υἱοῦ τοῦ ἀνθρώπου. **40** τότε δύο ἔσονται ἐν τῷ ἀγρῷ, εἷς παραλαμβάνεται καὶ εἷς ἀφίεται· **41** δύο ἀλήθουσαι ἐν τῷ μύλῳ, μία παραλαμβάνεται καὶ μία ἀφίεται. **42** γρηγορεῖτε οὖν, ὅτι οὐκ οἴδατε ποίᾳ ἡμέρᾳ[c] ὁ κύριος ὑμῶν ἔρχεται. **43** ἐκεῖνο δὲ γινώσκετε ὅτι εἰ ᾔδει ὁ οἰκοδεσπότης ποίᾳ φυλακῇ ὁ κλέπτης ἔρχεται, ἐγρηγόρησεν ἂν καὶ οὐκ ἂν εἴασεν διορυχθῆναι τὴν οἰκίαν αὐτοῦ. **44** διὰ τοῦτο καὶ ὑμεῖς γίνεσθε ἕτοιμοι, ὅτι ᾗ οὐ δοκεῖτε ὥρᾳ ὁ υἱὸς τοῦ ἀνθρώπου ἔρχεται.

45 Τίς ἄρα ἐστὶν ὁ πιστὸς δοῦλος καὶ φρόνιμος ὃν κατέστησεν ὁ κύριος ἐπὶ τῆς οἰκετείας αὐτοῦ τοῦ δοῦναι αὐτοῖς τὴν τροφὴν ἐν καιρῷ; **46** μακάριος ὁ δοῦλος ἐκεῖνος ὃν ἐλθὼν ὁ κύριος αὐτοῦ εὑρήσει οὕτως ποιοῦντα· **47** ἀμὴν λέγω ὑμῖν ὅτι ἐπὶ πᾶσιν τοῖς ὑπάρχουσιν αὐτοῦ καταστήσει αὐτόν. **48** ἐὰν δὲ εἴπῃ ὁ κακὸς δοῦλος ἐκεῖνος ἐν τῇ καρδίᾳ αὐτοῦ, Χρονίζει μου ὁ κύριος, **49** καὶ ἄρξηται τύπτειν τοὺς συνδούλους αὐτοῦ, ἐσθίῃ δὲ καὶ πίνῃ μετὰ τῶν μεθυόντων, **50** ἥξει ὁ κύριος τοῦ δούλου ἐκείνου ἐν ἡμέρᾳ ᾗ οὐ προσδοκᾷ καὶ ἐν ὥρᾳ ᾗ οὐ γινώσκει, **51** καὶ διχοτομήσει αὐτὸν καὶ τὸ μέρος αὐτοῦ μετὰ τῶν ὑποκριτῶν θήσει· ἐκεῖ ἔσται ὁ κλαυθμὸς καὶ ὁ βρυγμὸς τῶν ὀδόντων.

25 Τότε ὁμοιωθήσεται ἡ βασιλεία τῶν οὐρανῶν δέκα παρθένοις, αἵτινες λαβοῦσαι τὰς λαμπάδας ἑαυτῶν ἐξῆλθον εἰς ὑπάντησιν τοῦ νυμφίου[a]. **2** πέντε δὲ ἐξ αὐτῶν ἦσαν μωραὶ καὶ πέντε φρόνιμοι. **3** αἱ γὰρ μωραὶ λαβοῦσαι τὰς λαμπάδας αὐτῶν οὐκ ἔλαβον μεθ᾽ ἑαυτῶν ἔλαιον. **4** αἱ δὲ φρόνιμοι ἔλαβον ἔλαιον ἐν τοῖς ἀγγείοις μετὰ τῶν λαμπάδων ἑαυτῶν. **5** χρονίζοντος δὲ τοῦ νυμφίου ἐνύσταξαν πᾶσαι καὶ ἐκάθευδον. **6** μέσης δὲ νυκτὸς κραυγὴ γέγονεν, Ἰδοὺ ὁ νυμφίος, ἐξέρχεσθε εἰς ἀπάντησιν [αὐτοῦ]. **7** τότε ἠγέρθησαν πᾶσαι αἱ παρθένοι ἐκεῖναι καὶ ἐκόσμησαν τὰς λαμπάδας ἑαυτῶν. **8** αἱ δὲ μωραὶ ταῖς φρονίμοις εἶπαν, Δότε ἡμῖν ἐκ τοῦ ἐλαίου ὑμῶν, ὅτι αἱ λαμπάδες ἡμῶν σβέννυνται. **9** ἀπεκρίθησαν δὲ αἱ φρόνιμοι λέγουσαι, Μήποτε οὐ μὴ ἀρκέσῃ ἡμῖν καὶ ὑμῖν· πορεύεσθε μᾶλλον πρὸς τοὺς πωλοῦντας καὶ ἀγοράσατε ἑαυταῖς. **10** ἀπερχομένων δὲ αὐτῶν ἀγοράσαι ἦλθεν ὁ νυμφίος,

away. That is how it will be at the coming of the Son of Man. 40Two men will be in the field; one will be taken and the other left. 41Two women will be grinding with a hand mill; one will be taken and the other left.

42"Therefore keep watch, because you do not know on what day your Lord will come. 43But understand this: If the owner of the house had known at what time of night the thief was coming, he would have kept watch and would not have let his house be broken into. 44So you also must be ready, because the Son of Man will come at an hour when you do not expect him.

45"Who then is the faithful and wise servant, whom the master has put in charge of the servants in his household to give them their food at the proper time? 46It will be good for that servant whose master finds him doing so when he returns. 47I tell you the truth, he will put him in charge of all his possessions. 48But suppose that servant is wicked and says to himself, 'My master is staying away a long time,' 49and he then begins to beat his fellow servants and to eat and drink with drunkards. 50The master of that servant will come on a day when he does not expect him and at an hour he is not aware of. 51He will cut him to pieces and assign him a place with the hypocrites, where there will be weeping and gnashing of teeth.

The Parable of the Ten Virgins

25 "At that time the kingdom of heaven will be like ten virgins who took their lamps and went out to meet the bridegroom. 2Five of them were foolish and five were wise. 3The foolish ones took their lamps but did not take any oil with them. 4The wise, however, took oil in jars along with their lamps. 5The bridegroom was a long time in coming, and they all became drowsy and fell asleep.

6"At midnight the cry rang out: 'Here's the bridegroom! Come out to meet him!'

7"Then all the virgins woke up and trimmed their lamps. 8The foolish ones said to the wise, 'Give us some of your oil; our lamps are going out.'

9"'No,' they replied, 'there may not be enough for both us and you. Instead, go to those who sell oil and buy some for yourselves.'

10"But while they were on their way to buy the oil, the bridegroom arrived. The

---

b Other ancient authorities read *at what hour*   c Gk *to give them*   d *Or cut him off*   e Gk *virgins*   f Other ancient authorities add *and the bride*

b39 NIV text omits καὶ †   c42 NRSV note b ὥρᾳ   a1 NRSV note f adds καὶ τῆς νύμφης

went with him into the wedding banquet; and the door was shut. [11]Later the other bridesmaids[e] came also, saying, 'Lord, lord, open to us.' [12]But he replied, 'Truly I tell you, I do not know you.' [13]Keep awake therefore, for you know neither the day nor the hour.[g]

The Parable of the Talents

14 "For it is as if a man, going on a journey, summoned his slaves and entrusted his property to them; [15]to one he gave five talents,[h] to another two, to another one, to each according to his ability. Then he went away. [16]The one who had received the five talents went off at once and traded with them, and made five more talents. [17]In the same way, the one who had the two talents made two more talents. [18]But the one who had received the one talent went off and dug a hole in the ground and hid his master's money. [19]After a long time the master of those slaves came and settled accounts with them. [20]Then the one who had received the five talents came forward, bringing five more talents, saying, 'Master, you handed over to me five talents; see, I have made five more talents.' [21]His master said to him, 'Well done, good and trustworthy slave; you have been trustworthy in a few things, I will put you in charge of many things; enter into the joy of your master.' [22]And the one with the two talents also came forward, saying, 'Master, you handed over to me two talents; see, I have made two more talents.' [23]His master said to him, 'Well done, good and trustworthy slave; you have been trustworthy in a few things, I will put you in charge of many things; enter into the joy of your master.' [24]Then the one who had received the one talent also came forward, saying, 'Master, I knew that you were a harsh man, reaping where you did not sow, and gathering where you did not scatter seed; [25]so I was afraid, and I went and hid your talent in the ground. Here you have what is yours.' [26]But his master replied, 'You wicked and lazy slave! You knew, did you, that I reap where I did not sow, and gather where I did not scatter? [27]Then you ought to have invested my money with the bankers, and on my return I would have received what was my

καὶ αἱ ἕτοιμοι εἰσῆλθον μετ᾽ αὐτοῦ εἰς τοὺς γάμους καὶ ἐκλείσθη ἡ θύρα. 11 ὕστερον δὲ ἔρχονται καὶ αἱ λοιπαὶ παρθένοι λέγουσαι, Κύριε κύριε, ἄνοιξον ἡμῖν. 12 ὁ δὲ ἀποκριθεὶς εἶπεν, Ἀμὴν λέγω ὑμῖν, οὐκ οἶδα ὑμᾶς. 13 Γρηγορεῖτε οὖν, ὅτι οὐκ οἴδατε τὴν ἡμέραν οὐδὲ τὴν ὥραν[b].

14 Ὥσπερ γὰρ ἄνθρωπος ἀποδημῶν ἐκάλεσεν τοὺς ἰδίους δούλους καὶ παρέδωκεν αὐτοῖς τὰ ὑπάρχοντα αὐτοῦ, 15 καὶ ᾧ μὲν ἔδωκεν πέντε τάλαντα, ᾧ δὲ δύο, ᾧ δὲ ἕν, ἑκάστῳ κατὰ τὴν ἰδίαν δύναμιν, καὶ ἀπεδήμησεν. εὐθέως[c] 16 πορευθεὶς ὁ τὰ πέντε τάλαντα λαβὼν ἠργάσατο ἐν αὐτοῖς καὶ ἐκέρδησεν ἄλλα πέντε· 17 ὡσαύτως ὁ τὰ δύο ἐκέρδησεν ἄλλα δύο. 18 ὁ δὲ τὸ ἓν λαβὼν ἀπελθὼν ὤρυξεν γῆν καὶ ἔκρυψεν τὸ ἀργύριον τοῦ κυρίου αὐτοῦ. 19 μετὰ δὲ πολὺν χρόνον ἔρχεται ὁ κύριος τῶν δούλων ἐκείνων καὶ συναίρει λόγον μετ᾽ αὐτῶν. 20 καὶ προσελθὼν ὁ τὰ πέντε τάλαντα λαβὼν προσήνεγκεν ἄλλα πέντε τάλαντα λέγων, Κύριε, πέντε τάλαντά μοι παρέδωκας· ἴδε ἄλλα πέντε τάλαντα ἐκέρδησα. 21 ἔφη αὐτῷ ὁ κύριος αὐτοῦ, Εὖ, δοῦλε ἀγαθὲ καὶ πιστέ, ἐπὶ ὀλίγα ἦς πιστός, ἐπὶ πολλῶν σε καταστήσω· εἴσελθε εἰς τὴν χαρὰν τοῦ κυρίου σου. 22 προσελθὼν [δὲ] καὶ ὁ τὰ δύο τάλαντα εἶπεν, Κύριε, δύο τάλαντά μοι παρέδωκας· ἴδε ἄλλα δύο τάλαντα ἐκέρδησα. 23 ἔφη αὐτῷ ὁ κύριος αὐτοῦ, Εὖ, δοῦλε ἀγαθὲ καὶ πιστέ, ἐπὶ ὀλίγα ἦς πιστός, ἐπὶ πολλῶν σε καταστήσω· εἴσελθε εἰς τὴν χαρὰν τοῦ κυρίου σου. 24 προσελθὼν δὲ καὶ ὁ τὸ ἓν τάλαντον εἰληφὼς εἶπεν, Κύριε, ἔγνων σε ὅτι σκληρὸς εἶ ἄνθρωπος, θερίζων ὅπου οὐκ ἔσπειρας καὶ συνάγων ὅθεν οὐ διεσκόρπισας, 25 καὶ φοβηθεὶς ἀπελθὼν ἔκρυψα τὸ τάλαντόν σου ἐν τῇ γῇ· ἴδε ἔχεις τὸ σόν. 26 ἀποκριθεὶς δὲ ὁ κύριος αὐτοῦ εἶπεν αὐτῷ, Πονηρὲ δοῦλε καὶ ὀκνηρέ, ᾔδεις ὅτι θερίζω ὅπου οὐκ ἔσπειρα καὶ συνάγω ὅθεν οὐ διεσκόρπισα; 27 ἔδει σε οὖν βαλεῖν τὰ ἀργύριά μου τοῖς τραπεζίταις, καὶ ἐλθὼν ἐγὼ ἐκομισάμην

virgins who were ready went in with him to the wedding banquet. And the door was shut.

[11]"Later the others also came. 'Sir! Sir!' they said. 'Open the door for us!'

[12]"But he replied, 'I tell you the truth, I don't know you.'

[13]"Therefore keep watch, because you do not know the day or the hour.

The Parable of the Talents

[14]"Again, it will be like a man going on a journey, who called his servants and entrusted his property to them. [15]To the one he gave five talents[a] of money, to another two talents, and to another one talent, each according to his ability. Then he went on his journey. [16]The man who had received the five talents went at once and put his money to work and gained five more. [17]So also, the one with the two talents gained two more. [18]But the man who had received the one talent went off, dug a hole in the ground and hid his master's money.

[19]"After a long time the master of those servants returned and settled accounts with them. [20]The man who had received the five talents brought the other five. 'Master,' he said, 'you entrusted me with five talents. See, I have gained five more.'

[21]"His master replied, 'Well done, good and faithful servant! You have been faithful with a few things; I will put you in charge of many things. Come and share your master's happiness!'

[22]"The man with the two talents also came. 'Master,' he said, 'you entrusted me with two talents; see, I have gained two more.'

[23]"His master replied, 'Well done, good and faithful servant! You have been faithful with a few things; I will put you in charge of many things. Come and share your master's happiness!'

[24]"Then the man who had received the one talent came. 'Master,' he said, 'I knew that you are a hard man, harvesting where you have not sown and gathering where you have not scattered seed. [25]So I was afraid and went out and hid your talent in the ground. See, here is what belongs to you.'

[26]"His master replied, 'You wicked, lazy servant! So you knew that I harvest where I have not sown and gather where I have not scattered seed? [27]Well then, you should have put my money on deposit with the bankers, so that when I returned I would

---

[e] Gk virgins [g] Other ancient authorities add in which the Son of Man is coming [h] A talent was worth more than fifteen years' wages of a laborer

[b] 13 NRSV note g adds ἐν ᾗ ὁ υἱὸς τοῦ ἀνθρώπου ἔρχεται [c] 15 NIV/NRSV texts read εὐθέως in verse 16

[a] 15 A talent was worth more than a thousand dollars.

own with interest. 28So take the talent from him, and give it to the one with the ten talents. 29For to all those who have, more will be given, and they will have an abundance; but from those who have nothing, even what they have will be taken away. 30As for this worthless slave, throw him into the outer darkness, where there will be weeping and gnashing of teeth.'

The Judgment of the Nations

31 "When the Son of Man comes in his glory, and all the angels with him, then he will sit on the throne of his glory. 32All the nations will be gathered before him, and he will separate people one from another as a shepherd separates the sheep from the goats, 33and he will put the sheep at his right hand and the goats at the left. 34Then the king will say to those at his right hand, 'Come, you that are blessed by my Father, inherit the kingdom prepared for you from the foundation of the world; 35for I was hungry and you gave me food, I was thirsty and you gave me something to drink, I was a stranger and you welcomed me, 36I was naked and you gave me clothing, I was sick and you took care of me, I was in prison and you visited me.' 37Then the righteous will answer him, 'Lord, when was it that we saw you hungry and gave you food, or thirsty and gave you something to drink? 38And when was it that we saw you a stranger and welcomed you, or naked and gave you clothing? 39And when was it that we saw you sick or in prison and visited you?' 40And the king will answer them, 'Truly I tell you, just as you did it to one of the least of these who are members of my family,i you did it to me.' 41Then he will say to those at his left hand, 'You that are accursed, depart from me into the eternal fire prepared for the devil and his angels; 42for I was hungry and you gave me no food, I was thirsty and you gave me nothing to drink, 43I was a stranger and you did not welcome me, naked and you did not give me clothing, sick and in prison and you did not visit me.' 44Then they also will answer, 'Lord, when was it that we saw you hungry or thirsty or a stranger or naked or sick or in prison, and did not take care of you?' 45Then he will answer them, 'Truly I tell you, just as you did not do it to one of the least of these, you did not do it to me.' 46And these will go away into eternal punishment, but the righteous into eternal life."

i Gk these my brothers

ἂν τὸ ἐμὸν σὺν τόκῳ. **28** ἄρατε οὖν ἀπ᾽ αὐτοῦ τὸ τάλαντον καὶ δότε τῷ ἔχοντι τὰ δέκα τάλαντα· **29** τῷ γὰρ ἔχοντι παντὶ δοθήσεται καὶ περισσευθήσεται, τοῦ δὲ μὴ ἔχοντος καὶ ὃ ἔχει ἀρθήσεται ἀπ᾽ αὐτοῦ. **30** καὶ τὸν ἀχρεῖον δοῦλον ἐκβάλετε εἰς τὸ σκότος τὸ ἐξώτερον· ἐκεῖ ἔσται ὁ κλαυθμὸς καὶ ὁ βρυγμὸς τῶν ὀδόντων.

31 Ὅταν δὲ ἔλθῃ ὁ υἱὸς τοῦ ἀνθρώπου ἐν τῇ δόξῃ αὐτοῦ καὶ πάντες οἱ ἄγγελοι μετ᾽ αὐτοῦ, τότε καθίσει ἐπὶ θρόνου δόξης αὐτοῦ· **32** καὶ συναχθήσονται ἔμπροσθεν αὐτοῦ πάντα τὰ ἔθνη, καὶ ἀφορίσει αὐτοὺς ἀπ᾽ ἀλλήλων, ὥσπερ ὁ ποιμὴν ἀφορίζει τὰ πρόβατα ἀπὸ τῶν ἐρίφων, **33** καὶ στήσει τὰ μὲν πρόβατα ἐκ δεξιῶν αὐτοῦ, τὰ δὲ ἐρίφια ἐξ εὐωνύμων. **34** τότε ἐρεῖ ὁ βασιλεὺς τοῖς ἐκ δεξιῶν αὐτοῦ, Δεῦτε οἱ εὐλογημένοι τοῦ πατρός μου, κληρονομήσατε τὴν ἡτοιμασμένην ὑμῖν βασιλείαν ἀπὸ καταβολῆς κόσμου. **35** ἐπείνασα γὰρ καὶ ἐδώκατέ μοι φαγεῖν, ἐδίψησα καὶ ἐποτίσατέ με, ξένος ἤμην καὶ συνηγάγετέ με, **36** γυμνὸς καὶ περιεβάλετέ με, ἠσθένησα καὶ ἐπεσκέψασθέ με, ἐν φυλακῇ ἤμην καὶ ἤλθατε πρός με. **37** τότε ἀποκριθήσονται αὐτῷ οἱ δίκαιοι λέγοντες, Κύριε, πότε σε εἴδομεν πεινῶντα καὶ ἐθρέψαμεν, ἢ διψῶντα καὶ ἐποτίσαμεν; **38** πότε δέ σε εἴδομεν ξένον καὶ συνηγάγομεν, ἢ γυμνὸν καὶ περιεβάλομεν; **39** πότε δέ σε εἴδομεν ἀσθενοῦντα ἢ ἐν φυλακῇ καὶ ἤλθομεν πρός σε; **40** καὶ ἀποκριθεὶς ὁ βασιλεὺς ἐρεῖ αὐτοῖς, Ἀμὴν λέγω ὑμῖν, ἐφ᾽ ὅσον ἐποιήσατε ἑνὶ τούτων τῶν ἀδελφῶν μου τῶν ἐλαχίστων, ἐμοὶ ἐποιήσατε. **41** Τότε ἐρεῖ καὶ τοῖς ἐξ εὐωνύμων, Πορεύεσθε ἀπ᾽ ἐμοῦ [οἱ] κατηραμένοι εἰς τὸ πῦρ τὸ αἰώνιον τὸ ἡτοιμασμένον τῷ διαβόλῳ καὶ τοῖς ἀγγέλοις αὐτοῦ. **42** ἐπείνασα γὰρ καὶ οὐκ ἐδώκατέ μοι φαγεῖν, ἐδίψησα καὶ οὐκ ἐποτίσατέ με, **43** ξένος ἤμην καὶ οὐ συνηγάγετέ με, γυμνὸς καὶ οὐ περιεβάλετέ με, ἀσθενὴς καὶ ἐν φυλακῇ καὶ οὐκ ἐπεσκέψασθέ με. **44** τότε ἀποκριθήσονται καὶ αὐτοὶ λέγοντες, Κύριε, πότε σε εἴδομεν πεινῶντα ἢ διψῶντα ἢ ξένον ἢ γυμνὸν ἢ ἀσθενῆ ἢ ἐν φυλακῇ καὶ οὐ διηκονήσαμέν σοι; **45** τότε ἀποκριθήσεται αὐτοῖς λέγων, Ἀμὴν λέγω ὑμῖν, ἐφ᾽ ὅσον οὐκ ἐποιήσατε ἑνὶ τούτων τῶν ἐλαχίστων, οὐδὲ ἐμοὶ ἐποιήσατε. **46** καὶ ἀπελεύσονται οὗτοι εἰς κόλασιν αἰώνιον, οἱ δὲ δίκαιοι εἰς ζωὴν αἰώνιον.

have received it back with interest.

28" 'Take the talent from him and give it to the one who has the ten talents. 29For everyone who has will be given more, and he will have an abundance. Whoever does not have, even what he has will be taken from him. 30And throw that worthless servant outside, into the darkness, where there will be weeping and gnashing of teeth.'

The Sheep and the Goats

31"When the Son of Man comes in his glory, and all the angels with him, he will sit on his throne in heavenly glory. 32All the nations will be gathered before him, and he will separate the people one from another as a shepherd separates the sheep from the goats. 33He will put the sheep on his right and the goats on his left.

34"Then the King will say to those on his right, 'Come, you who are blessed by my Father; take your inheritance, the kingdom prepared for you since the creation of the world. 35For I was hungry and you gave me something to eat, I was thirsty and you gave me something to drink, I was a stranger and you invited me in, 36I needed clothes and you clothed me, I was sick and you looked after me, I was in prison and you came to visit me.'

37"Then the righteous will answer him, 'Lord, when did we see you hungry and feed you, or thirsty and give you something to drink? 38When did we see you a stranger and invite you in, or needing clothes and clothe you? 39When did we see you sick or in prison and go to visit you?'

40"The King will reply, 'I tell you the truth, whatever you did for one of the least of these brothers of mine, you did for me.'

41"Then he will say to those on his left, 'Depart from me, you who are cursed, into the eternal fire prepared for the devil and his angels. 42For I was hungry and you gave me nothing to eat, I was thirsty and you gave me nothing to drink, 43I was a stranger and you did not invite me in, I needed clothes and you did not clothe me, I was sick and in prison and you did not look after me.'

44"They also will answer, 'Lord, when did we see you hungry or thirsty or a stranger or needing clothes or sick or in prison, and did not help you?'

45"He will reply, 'I tell you the truth, whatever you did not do for one of the least of these, you did not do for me.'

46"Then they will go away to eternal punishment, but the righteous to eternal life."

NRSV

The Plot to Kill Jesus

26 When Jesus had finished saying all these things, he said to his disciples, 2"You know that after two days the Passover is coming, and the Son of Man will be handed over to be crucified."

3 Then the chief priests and the elders of the people gathered in the palace of the high priest, who was called Caiaphas, 4and they conspired to arrest Jesus by stealth and kill him. 5But they said, "Not during the festival, or there may be a riot among the people."

The Anointing at Bethany

6 Now while Jesus was at Bethany in the house of Simon the leper,ʲ 7a woman came to him with an alabaster jar of very costly ointment, and she poured it on his head as he sat at the table. 8But when the disciples saw it, they were angry and said, "Why this waste? 9For this ointment could have been sold for a large sum, and the money given to the poor." 10But Jesus, aware of this, said to them, "Why do you trouble the woman? She has performed a good service for me. 11For you always have the poor with you, but you will not always have me. 12By pouring this ointment on my body she has prepared me for burial. 13Truly I tell you, wherever this good newsᵏ is proclaimed in the whole world, what she has done will be told in remembrance of her."

Judas Agrees to Betray Jesus

14 Then one of the twelve, who was called Judas Iscariot, went to the chief priests 15and said, "What will you give me if I betray him to you?" They paid him thirty pieces of silver. 16And from that moment he began to look for an opportunity to betray him.

The Passover with the Disciples

17 On the first day of Unleavened Bread the disciples came to Jesus, saying, "Where do you want us to make the preparations for you to eat the Passover?" 18He said, "Go into the city to a certain man, and say to him, 'The Teacher says, My time is near; I will keep the Passover at your house with my disciples.' " 19So the disciples did as Jesus had directed them, and they prepared the Passover meal.

20 When it was evening, he took his place

Greek

26 Καὶ ἐγένετο ὅτε ἐτέλεσεν ὁ Ἰησοῦς πάντας τοὺς λόγους τούτους, εἶπεν τοῖς μαθηταῖς αὐτοῦ, 2 Οἴδατε ὅτι μετὰ δύο ἡμέρας τὸ πάσχα γίνεται, καὶ ὁ υἱὸς τοῦ ἀνθρώπου παραδίδοται εἰς τὸ σταυρωθῆναι. 3 Τότε συνήχθησαν οἱ ἀρχιερεῖς καὶ οἱ πρεσβύτεροι τοῦ λαοῦ εἰς τὴν αὐλὴν τοῦ ἀρχιερέως τοῦ λεγομένου Καϊάφα 4 καὶ συνεβουλεύσαντο ἵνα τὸν Ἰησοῦν δόλῳ κρατήσωσιν καὶ ἀποκτείνωσιν· 5 ἔλεγον δέ, Μὴ ἐν τῇ ἑορτῇ, ἵνα μὴ θόρυβος γένηται ἐν τῷ λαῷ.

6 Τοῦ δὲ Ἰησοῦ γενομένου ἐν Βηθανίᾳ ἐν οἰκίᾳ Σίμωνος τοῦ λεπροῦ, 7 προσῆλθεν αὐτῷ γυνὴ ἔχουσα ἀλάβαστρον μύρου βαρυτίμου καὶ κατέχεεν ἐπὶ τῆς κεφαλῆς αὐτοῦ ἀνακειμένου. 8 ἰδόντες δὲ οἱ μαθηταὶ ἠγανάκτησαν λέγοντες, Εἰς τί ἡ ἀπώλεια αὕτη; 9 ἐδύνατο γὰρ τοῦτοᵃ πραθῆναι πολλοῦ καὶ δοθῆναι πτωχοῖς. 10 γνοὺς δὲ ὁ Ἰησοῦς εἶπεν αὐτοῖς, Τί κόπους παρέχετε τῇ γυναικί; ἔργον γὰρ καλὸν ἠργάσατο εἰς ἐμέ· 11 πάντοτε γὰρ τοὺς πτωχοὺς ἔχετε μεθ᾽ ἑαυτῶν, ἐμὲ δὲ οὐ πάντοτε ἔχετε· 12 βαλοῦσα γὰρ αὕτη τὸ μύρον τοῦτο ἐπὶ τοῦ σώματός μου πρὸς τὸ ἐνταφιάσαι με ἐποίησεν. 13 ἀμὴν λέγω ὑμῖν, ὅπου ἐὰν κηρυχθῇ τὸ εὐαγγέλιον τοῦτο ἐν ὅλῳ τῷ κόσμῳ, λαληθήσεται καὶ ὃ ἐποίησεν αὕτη εἰς μνημόσυνον αὐτῆς.

14 Τότε πορευθεὶς εἷς τῶν δώδεκα, ὁ λεγόμενος Ἰούδας Ἰσκαριώτης, πρὸς τοὺς ἀρχιερεῖς 15 εἶπεν, Τί θέλετέ μοι δοῦναι, κἀγὼ ὑμῖν παραδώσω αὐτόν; οἱ δὲ ἔστησαν αὐτῷ τριάκοντα ἀργύρια. 16 καὶ ἀπὸ τότε ἐζήτει εὐκαιρίαν ἵνα αὐτὸν παραδῷ.

17 Τῇ δὲ πρώτῃ τῶν ἀζύμων προσῆλθον οἱ μαθηταὶ τῷ Ἰησοῦ λέγοντες, Ποῦ θέλεις ἑτοιμάσωμέν σοι φαγεῖν τὸ πάσχα; 18 ὁ δὲ εἶπεν, Ὑπάγετε εἰς τὴν πόλιν πρὸς τὸν δεῖνα καὶ εἴπατε αὐτῷ, Ὁ διδάσκαλος λέγει, Ὁ καιρός μου ἐγγύς ἐστιν, πρὸς σὲ ποιῶ τὸ πάσχα μετὰ τῶν μαθητῶν μου. 19 καὶ ἐποίησαν οἱ μαθηταὶ ὡς συνέταξεν αὐτοῖς ὁ Ἰησοῦς καὶ ἡτοίμασαν τὸ πάσχα. 20 Ὀψίας δὲ γενομένης

NIV

The Plot Against Jesus

26 When Jesus had finished saying all these things, he said to his disciples, 2"As you know, the Passover is two days away—and the Son of Man will be handed over to be crucified."

3Then the chief priests and the elders of the people assembled in the palace of the high priest, whose name was Caiaphas, 4and they plotted to arrest Jesus in some sly way and kill him. 5"But not during the Feast," they said, "or there may be a riot among the people."

Jesus Anointed at Bethany

6While Jesus was in Bethany in the home of a man known as Simon the Leper, 7a woman came to him with an alabaster jar of very expensive perfume, which she poured on his head as he was reclining at the table.

8When the disciples saw this, they were indignant. "Why this waste?" they asked. 9"This perfume could have been sold at a high price and the money given to the poor."

10Aware of this, Jesus said to them, "Why are you bothering this woman? She has done a beautiful thing to me. 11The poor you will always have with you, but you will not always have me. 12When she poured this perfume on my body, she did it to prepare me for burial. 13I tell you the truth, wherever this gospel is preached throughout the world, what she has done will also be told, in memory of her."

Judas Agrees to Betray Jesus

14Then one of the Twelve—the one called Judas Iscariot—went to the chief priests 15and asked, "What are you willing to give me if I hand him over to you?" So they counted out for him thirty silver coins. 16From then on Judas watched for an opportunity to hand him over.

The Lord's Supper

17On the first day of the Feast of Unleavened Bread, the disciples came to Jesus and asked, "Where do you want us to make preparations for you to eat the Passover?"

18He replied, "Go into the city to a certain man and tell him, 'The Teacher says: My appointed time is near. I am going to celebrate the Passover with my disciples at your house.' " 19So the disciples did as Jesus had directed them and prepared the Passover.

20When evening came, Jesus was reclin-

ʲ The terms *leper* and *leprosy* can refer to several diseases
ᵏ Or *gospel*

ᵃ9 NIV text adds τὸ μύρον †

with the twelve;[l] 21and while they were eating, he said, "Truly I tell you, one of you will betray me." 22And they became greatly distressed and began to say to him one after another, "Surely not I, Lord?" 23He answered, "The one who has dipped his hand into the bowl with me will betray me. 24The Son of Man goes as it is written of him, but woe to that one by whom the Son of Man is betrayed! It would have been better for that one not to have been born." 25Judas, who betrayed him, said, "Surely not I, Rabbi?" He replied, "You have said so."

The Institution of the Lord's Supper

26 While they were eating, Jesus took a loaf of bread, and after blessing it he broke it, gave it to the disciples, and said, "Take, eat; this is my body." 27Then he took a cup, and after giving thanks he gave it to them, saying, "Drink from it, all of you; 28for this is my blood of the[m] covenant, which is poured out for many for the forgiveness of sins. 29I tell you, I will never again drink of this fruit of the vine until that day when I drink it new with you in my Father's kingdom."

30 When they had sung the hymn, they went out to the Mount of Olives.

Peter's Denial Foretold

31 Then Jesus said to them, "You will all become deserters because of me this night; for it is written,

'I will strike the shepherd,
   and the sheep of the flock will be
     scattered.'

32But after I am raised up, I will go ahead of you to Galilee." 33Peter said to him, "Though all become deserters because of you, I will never desert you." 34Jesus said to him, "Truly I tell you, this very night, before the cock crows, you will deny me three times." 35Peter said to him, "Even though I must die with you, I will not deny you." And so said all the disciples.

Jesus Prays in Gethsemane

36 Then Jesus went with them to a place called Gethsemane; and he said to his disciples, "Sit here while I go over there and pray." 37He took with him Peter and the two sons of Zebedee, and began to be grieved and agitated. 38Then he said to them, "I am deeply grieved, even to death;

ἀνέκειτο μετὰ τῶν δώδεκα[b]. 21 καὶ ἐσθιόντων αὐτῶν εἶπεν, Ἀμὴν λέγω ὑμῖν ὅτι εἷς ἐξ ὑμῶν παραδώσει με. 22 καὶ λυπούμενοι σφόδρα ἤρξαντο λέγειν αὐτῷ εἷς ἕκαστος, Μήτι ἐγώ εἰμι, κύριε; 23 ὁ δὲ ἀποκριθεὶς εἶπεν, Ὁ ἐμβάψας μετ' ἐμοῦ τὴν χεῖρα ἐν τῷ τρυβλίῳ οὗτός με παραδώσει. 24 ὁ μὲν υἱὸς τοῦ ἀνθρώπου ὑπάγει καθὼς γέγραπται περὶ αὐτοῦ, οὐαὶ δὲ τῷ ἀνθρώπῳ ἐκείνῳ δι' οὗ ὁ υἱὸς τοῦ ἀνθρώπου παραδίδοται· καλὸν ἦν αὐτῷ εἰ οὐκ ἐγεννήθη ὁ ἄνθρωπος ἐκεῖνος. 25 ἀποκριθεὶς δὲ Ἰούδας ὁ παραδιδοὺς αὐτὸν εἶπεν, Μήτι ἐγώ εἰμι, ῥαββί; λέγει αὐτῷ, Σὺ εἶπας.

26 Ἐσθιόντων δὲ αὐτῶν λαβὼν ὁ Ἰησοῦς ἄρτον καὶ εὐλογήσας ἔκλασεν καὶ δοὺς τοῖς μαθηταῖς εἶπεν, Λάβετε φάγετε, τοῦτό ἐστιν τὸ σῶμά μου. 27 καὶ λαβὼν ποτήριον καὶ εὐχαριστήσας ἔδωκεν αὐτοῖς λέγων, Πίετε ἐξ αὐτοῦ πάντες, 28 τοῦτο γάρ ἐστιν τὸ αἷμά μου τῆς διαθήκης[c] τὸ περὶ πολλῶν ἐκχυννόμενον εἰς ἄφεσιν ἁμαρτιῶν. 29 λέγω δὲ ὑμῖν, οὐ μὴ πίω ἀπ' ἄρτι ἐκ τούτου τοῦ γενήματος τῆς ἀμπέλου ἕως τῆς ἡμέρας ἐκείνης ὅταν αὐτὸ πίνω μεθ' ὑμῶν καινὸν ἐν τῇ βασιλείᾳ τοῦ πατρός μου. 30 Καὶ ὑμνήσαντες ἐξῆλθον εἰς τὸ Ὄρος τῶν Ἐλαιῶν.

31 Τότε λέγει αὐτοῖς ὁ Ἰησοῦς, Πάντες ὑμεῖς σκανδαλισθήσεσθε ἐν ἐμοὶ ἐν τῇ νυκτὶ ταύτῃ, γέγραπται γάρ,

Πατάξω τὸν ποιμένα,
καὶ διασκορπισθήσονται τὰ
   πρόβατα τῆς ποίμνης.

32 μετὰ δὲ τὸ ἐγερθῆναί με προάξω ὑμᾶς εἰς τὴν Γαλιλαίαν. 33 ἀποκριθεὶς δὲ ὁ Πέτρος εἶπεν αὐτῷ, Εἰ πάντες σκανδαλισθήσονται ἐν σοί, ἐγὼ οὐδέποτε σκανδαλισθήσομαι. 34 ἔφη αὐτῷ ὁ Ἰησοῦς, Ἀμὴν λέγω σοι ὅτι ἐν ταύτῃ τῇ νυκτὶ πρὶν ἀλέκτορα φωνῆσαι τρὶς ἀπαρνήσῃ με. 35 λέγει αὐτῷ ὁ Πέτρος, Κἂν δέῃ με σὺν σοὶ ἀποθανεῖν, οὐ μή σε ἀπαρνήσομαι. ὁμοίως καὶ πάντες οἱ μαθηταὶ εἶπαν.

36 Τότε ἔρχεται μετ' αὐτῶν ὁ Ἰησοῦς εἰς χωρίον λεγόμενον Γεθσημανὶ καὶ λέγει τοῖς μαθηταῖς, Καθίσατε αὐτοῦ ἕως [οὗ] ἀπελθὼν ἐκεῖ προσεύξωμαι. 37 καὶ παραλαβὼν τὸν Πέτρον καὶ τοὺς δύο υἱοὺς Ζεβεδαίου ἤρξατο λυπεῖσθαι καὶ ἀδημονεῖν. 38 τότε λέγει αὐτοῖς, Περίλυπός ἐστιν ἡ ψυχή μου ἕως

ing at the table with the Twelve. 21And while they were eating, he said, "I tell you the truth, one of you will betray me."

22They were very sad and began to say to him one after the other, "Surely not I, Lord?"

23Jesus replied, "The one who has dipped his hand into the bowl with me will betray me. 24The Son of Man will go just as it is written about him. But woe to that man who betrays the Son of Man! It would be better for him if he had not been born."

25Then Judas, the one who would betray him, said, "Surely not I, Rabbi?"

Jesus answered, "Yes, it is you."[a]

26While they were eating, Jesus took bread, gave thanks and broke it, and gave it to his disciples, saying, "Take and eat; this is my body."

27Then he took the cup, gave thanks and offered it to them, saying, "Drink from it, all of you. 28This is my blood of the[b] covenant, which is poured out for many for the forgiveness of sins. 29I tell you, I will not drink of this fruit of the vine from now on until that day when I drink it anew with you in my Father's kingdom."

30When they had sung a hymn, they went out to the Mount of Olives.

Jesus Predicts Peter's Denial

31Then Jesus told them, "This very night you will all fall away on account of me, for it is written:

" 'I will strike the shepherd,
   and the sheep of the flock will be
     scattered.'[c]

32But after I have risen, I will go ahead of you into Galilee."

33Peter replied, "Even if all fall away on account of you, I never will."

34"I tell you the truth," Jesus answered, "this very night, before the rooster crows, you will disown me three times."

35But Peter declared, "Even if I have to die with you, I will never disown you." And all the other disciples said the same.

Gethsemane

36Then Jesus went with his disciples to a place called Gethsemane, and he said to them, "Sit here while I go over there and pray." 37He took Peter and the two sons of Zebedee along with him, and he began to be sorrowful and troubled. 38Then he said to them, "My soul is overwhelmed with

---

[l]Other ancient authorities add *disciples*   [m]Other ancient authorities add *new*

[b]20 NRSV note l adds μαθητῶν   [c]28 NIV/NRSV notes καινῆς διαθήκης

[a]25 Or *"You yourself have said it"*   [b]28 Some manuscripts *the new*   [c]31 Zech. 13:7

remain here, and stay awake with me." [39]And going a little farther, he threw himself on the ground and prayed, "My Father, if it is possible, let this cup pass from me; yet not what I want but what you want." [40]Then he came to the disciples and found them sleeping; and he said to Peter, "So, could you not stay awake with me one hour? [41]Stay awake and pray that you may not come into the time of trial;[n] the spirit indeed is willing, but the flesh is weak." [42]Again he went away for the second time and prayed, "My Father, if this cannot pass unless I drink it, your will be done." [43]Again he came and found them sleeping, for their eyes were heavy. [44]So leaving them again, he went away and prayed for the third time, saying the same words. [45]Then he came to the disciples and said to them, "Are you still sleeping and taking your rest? See, the hour is at hand, and the Son of Man is betrayed into the hands of sinners. [46]Get up, let us be going. See, my betrayer is at hand."

The Betrayal and Arrest of Jesus

[47] While he was still speaking, Judas, one of the twelve, arrived; with him was a large crowd with swords and clubs, from the chief priests and the elders of the people. [48]Now the betrayer had given them a sign, saying, "The one I will kiss is the man; arrest him." [49]At once he came up to Jesus and said, "Greetings, Rabbi!" and kissed him. [50]Jesus said to him, "Friend, do what you are here to do." Then they came and laid hands on Jesus and arrested him. [51]Suddenly, one of those with Jesus put his hand on his sword, drew it, and struck the slave of the high priest, cutting off his ear. [52]Then Jesus said to him, "Put your sword back into its place; for all who take the sword will perish by the sword. [53]Do you think that I cannot appeal to my Father, and he will at once send me more than twelve legions of angels? [54]But how then would the scriptures be fulfilled, which say it must happen in this way?" [55]At that hour Jesus said to the crowds, "Have you come out with swords and clubs to arrest me as though I were a bandit? Day after day I sat in the temple teaching,

θανάτου· μείνατε ὧδε καὶ γρηγορεῖτε μετ᾽ ἐμοῦ. 39 καὶ προελθὼν μικρὸν ἔπεσεν ἐπὶ πρόσωπον αὐτοῦ προσευχόμενος καὶ λέγων, Πάτερ μου, εἰ δυνατόν ἐστιν, παρελθάτω ἀπ᾽ ἐμοῦ τὸ ποτήριον τοῦτο· πλὴν οὐχ ὡς ἐγὼ θέλω ἀλλ᾽ ὡς σύ. 40 καὶ ἔρχεται πρὸς τοὺς μαθητὰς καὶ εὑρίσκει αὐτοὺς καθεύδοντας, καὶ λέγει τῷ Πέτρῳ, Οὕτως οὐκ ἰσχύσατε μίαν ὥραν γρηγορῆσαι μετ᾽ ἐμοῦ; 41 γρηγορεῖτε καὶ προσεύχεσθε, ἵνα μὴ εἰσέλθητε εἰς πειρασμόν· τὸ μὲν πνεῦμα πρόθυμον ἡ δὲ σὰρξ ἀσθενής. 42 πάλιν ἐκ δευτέρου ἀπελθὼν προσηύξατο λέγων, Πάτερ μου, εἰ οὐ δύναται τοῦτο παρελθεῖν ἐὰν μὴ αὐτὸ πίω, γενηθήτω τὸ θέλημά σου. 43 καὶ ἐλθὼν πάλιν εὗρεν αὐτοὺς καθεύδοντας, ἦσαν γὰρ αὐτῶν οἱ ὀφθαλμοὶ βεβαρημένοι. 44 καὶ ἀφεὶς αὐτοὺς πάλιν ἀπελθὼν προσηύξατο ἐκ τρίτου τὸν αὐτὸν λόγον εἰπὼν πάλιν. 45 τότε ἔρχεται πρὸς τοὺς μαθητὰς καὶ λέγει αὐτοῖς, Καθεύδετε [τὸ] λοιπὸν καὶ ἀναπαύεσθε· ἰδοὺ ἤγγικεν ἡ ὥρα καὶ ὁ υἱὸς τοῦ ἀνθρώπου παραδίδοται εἰς χεῖρας ἁμαρτωλῶν. 46 ἐγείρεσθε ἄγωμεν· ἰδοὺ ἤγγικεν ὁ παραδιδούς με.

47 Καὶ ἔτι αὐτοῦ λαλοῦντος ἰδοὺ Ἰούδας εἷς τῶν δώδεκα ἦλθεν καὶ μετ᾽ αὐτοῦ ὄχλος πολὺς μετὰ μαχαιρῶν καὶ ξύλων ἀπὸ τῶν ἀρχιερέων καὶ πρεσβυτέρων τοῦ λαοῦ. 48 ὁ δὲ παραδιδοὺς αὐτὸν ἔδωκεν αὐτοῖς σημεῖον λέγων, Ὃν ἂν φιλήσω αὐτός ἐστιν, κρατήσατε αὐτόν. 49 καὶ εὐθέως προσελθὼν τῷ Ἰησοῦ εἶπεν, Χαῖρε, ῥαββί, καὶ κατεφίλησεν αὐτόν. 50 ὁ δὲ Ἰησοῦς εἶπεν αὐτῷ, Ἑταῖρε, ἐφ᾽ ὃ πάρει. τότε προσελθόντες ἐπέβαλον τὰς χεῖρας ἐπὶ τὸν Ἰησοῦν καὶ ἐκράτησαν αὐτόν. 51 καὶ ἰδοὺ εἷς τῶν μετὰ Ἰησοῦ ἐκτείνας τὴν χεῖρα ἀπέσπασεν τὴν μάχαιραν αὐτοῦ καὶ πατάξας τὸν δοῦλον τοῦ ἀρχιερέως ἀφεῖλεν αὐτοῦ τὸ ὠτίον. 52 τότε λέγει αὐτῷ ὁ Ἰησοῦς, Ἀπόστρεψον τὴν μάχαιράν σου εἰς τὸν τόπον αὐτῆς· πάντες γὰρ οἱ λαβόντες μάχαιραν ἐν μαχαίρῃ ἀπολοῦνται. 53 ἢ δοκεῖς ὅτι οὐ δύναμαι παρακαλέσαι τὸν πατέρα μου, καὶ παραστήσει μοι ἄρτι πλείω δώδεκα λεγιῶνας ἀγγέλων; 54 πῶς οὖν πληρωθῶσιν αἱ γραφαὶ ὅτι οὕτως δεῖ γενέσθαι; 55 Ἐν ἐκείνῃ τῇ ὥρᾳ εἶπεν ὁ Ἰησοῦς τοῖς ὄχλοις, Ὡς ἐπὶ λῃστὴν ἐξήλθατε μετὰ μαχαιρῶν καὶ ξύλων συλλαβεῖν με; καθ᾽ ἡμέραν ἐν τῷ ἱερῷ

sorrow to the point of death. Stay here and keep watch with me."

[39]Going a little farther, he fell with his face to the ground and prayed, "My Father, if it is possible, may this cup be taken from me. Yet not as I will, but as you will." [40]Then he returned to his disciples and found them sleeping. "Could you men not keep watch with me for one hour?" he asked Peter. [41]"Watch and pray so that you will not fall into temptation. The spirit is willing, but the body is weak."

[42]He went away a second time and prayed, "My Father, if it is not possible for this cup to be taken away unless I drink it, may your will be done."

[43]When he came back, he again found them sleeping, because their eyes were heavy. [44]So he left them and went away once more and prayed the third time, saying the same thing.

[45]Then he returned to the disciples and said to them, "Are you still sleeping and resting? Look, the hour is near, and the Son of Man is betrayed into the hands of sinners. [46]Rise, let us go! Here comes my betrayer!"

Jesus Arrested

[47]While he was still speaking, Judas, one of the Twelve, arrived. With him was a large crowd armed with swords and clubs, sent from the chief priests and the elders of the people. [48]Now the betrayer had arranged a signal with them: "The one I kiss is the man; arrest him." [49]Going at once to Jesus, Judas said, "Greetings, Rabbi!" and kissed him.

[50]Jesus replied, "Friend, do what you came for."[d]

Then the men stepped forward, seized Jesus and arrested him. [51]With that, one of Jesus' companions reached for his sword, drew it out and struck the servant of the high priest, cutting off his ear.

[52]"Put your sword back in its place," Jesus said to him, "for all who draw the sword will die by the sword. [53]Do you think I cannot call on my Father, and he will at once put at my disposal more than twelve legions of angels? [54]But how then would the Scriptures be fulfilled that say it must happen in this way?"

[55]At that time Jesus said to the crowd, "Am I leading a rebellion, that you have come out with swords and clubs to capture me? Every day I sat in the temple

---

and you did not arrest me. 56But all this has taken place, so that the scriptures of the prophets may be fulfilled." Then all the disciples deserted him and fled.

Jesus before the High Priest

57 Those who had arrested Jesus took him to Caiaphas the high priest, in whose house the scribes and the elders had gathered. 58But Peter was following him at a distance, as far as the courtyard of the high priest; and going inside, he sat with the guards in order to see how this would end. 59Now the chief priests and the whole council were looking for false testimony against Jesus so that they might put him to death, 60but they found none, though many false witnesses came forward. At last two came forward 61and said, "This fellow said, 'I am able to destroy the temple of God and to build it in three days.' " 62The high priest stood up and said, "Have you no answer? What is it that they testify against you?" 63But Jesus was silent. Then the high priest said to him, "I put you under oath before the living God, tell us if you are the Messiah,o the Son of God." 64Jesus said to him, "You have said so. But I tell you,

From now on you will see the Son of Man

    seated at the right hand of Power

    and coming on the clouds of heaven."

65Then the high priest tore his clothes and said, "He has blasphemed! Why do we still need witnesses? You have now heard his blasphemy. 66What is your verdict?" They answered, "He deserves death." 67Then they spat in his face and struck him; and some slapped him, 68saying, "Prophesy to us, you Messiah!o Who is it that struck you?"

Peter's Denial of Jesus

69 Now Peter was sitting outside in the courtyard. A servant-girl came to him and said, "You also were with Jesus the Galilean." 70But he denied it before all of them, saying, "I do not know what you are talking about." 71When he went out to the porch, another servant-girl saw him, and she said to the bystanders, "This man was with Jesus of Nazareth."p 72Again he denied it with an oath, "I do not know the

---

ἐκαθεζόμην διδάσκων καὶ οὐκ ἐκρατήσατέ με. 56 τοῦτο δὲ ὅλον γέγονεν ἵνα πληρωθῶσιν αἱ γραφαὶ τῶν προφητῶν. Τότε οἱ μαθηταὶ πάντες ἀφέντες αὐτὸν ἔφυγον.

57 Οἱ δὲ κρατήσαντες τὸν Ἰησοῦν ἀπήγαγον πρὸς Καϊάφαν τὸν ἀρχιερέα, ὅπου οἱ γραμματεῖς καὶ οἱ πρεσβύτεροι συνήχθησαν. 58 ὁ δὲ Πέτρος ἠκολούθει αὐτῷ ἀπὸ μακρόθεν ἕως τῆς αὐλῆς τοῦ ἀρχιερέως καὶ εἰσελθὼν ἔσω ἐκάθητο μετὰ τῶν ὑπηρετῶν ἰδεῖν τὸ τέλος. 59 οἱ δὲ ἀρχιερεῖς καὶ τὸ συνέδριον ὅλον ἐζήτουν ψευδομαρτυρίαν κατὰ τοῦ Ἰησοῦ ὅπως αὐτὸν θανατώσωσιν, 60 καὶ οὐχ εὗρον πολλῶν προσελθόντων ψευδομαρτύρων. ὕστερον δὲ προσελθόντες δύο 61 εἶπαν, Οὗτος ἔφη, Δύναμαι καταλῦσαι τὸν ναὸν τοῦ θεοῦ καὶ διὰ τριῶν ἡμερῶν οἰκοδομῆσαι. 62 καὶ ἀναστὰς ὁ ἀρχιερεὺς εἶπεν αὐτῷ, Οὐδὲν ἀποκρίνῃ τί οὗτοί σου καταμαρτυροῦσιν; 63 ὁ δὲ Ἰησοῦς ἐσιώπα. καὶ ὁ ἀρχιερεὺς εἶπεν αὐτῷ, Ἐξορκίζω σε κατὰ τοῦ θεοῦ τοῦ ζῶντος ἵνα ἡμῖν εἴπῃς εἰ σὺ εἶ ὁ Χριστὸς ὁ υἱὸς τοῦ θεοῦ. 64 λέγει αὐτῷ ὁ Ἰησοῦς, Σὺ εἶπας· πλὴν λέγω ὑμῖν,

ἀπ' ἄρτι ὄψεσθε τὸν υἱὸν τοῦ ἀνθρώπου

    καθήμενον ἐκ δεξιῶν τῆς δυνάμεως

    καὶ ἐρχόμενον ἐπὶ τῶν νεφελῶν τοῦ οὐρανοῦ.

65 τότε ὁ ἀρχιερεὺς διέρρηξεν τὰ ἱμάτια αὐτοῦ λέγων, Ἐβλασφήμησεν· τί ἔτι χρείαν ἔχομεν μαρτύρων; ἴδε νῦν ἠκούσατε τὴν βλασφημίαν· 66 τί ὑμῖν δοκεῖ; οἱ δὲ ἀποκριθέντες εἶπαν, Ἔνοχος θανάτου ἐστίν. 67 Τότε ἐνέπτυσαν εἰς τὸ πρόσωπον αὐτοῦ καὶ ἐκολάφισαν αὐτόν, οἱ δὲ ἐράπισαν 68 λέγοντες, Προφήτευσον ἡμῖν, Χριστέ, τίς ἐστιν ὁ παίσας σε;

69 Ὁ δὲ Πέτρος ἐκάθητο ἔξω ἐν τῇ αὐλῇ· καὶ προσῆλθεν αὐτῷ μία παιδίσκη λέγουσα, Καὶ σὺ ἦσθα μετὰ Ἰησοῦ τοῦ Γαλιλαίου. 70 ὁ δὲ ἠρνήσατο ἔμπροσθεν πάντων λέγων, Οὐκ οἶδα τί λέγεις. 71 ἐξελθόντα δὲ εἰς τὸν πυλῶνα εἶδεν αὐτὸν ἄλλη καὶ λέγει τοῖς ἐκεῖ, Οὗτος ἦν μετὰ Ἰησοῦ τοῦ Ναζωραίου. 72 καὶ πάλιν ἠρνήσατο μετὰ ὅρκου ὅτι Οὐκ

---

courts teaching, and you did not arrest me. 56But this has all taken place that the writings of the prophets might be fulfilled." Then all the disciples deserted him and fled.

Before the Sanhedrin

57Those who had arrested Jesus took him to Caiaphas, the high priest, where the teachers of the law and the elders had assembled. 58But Peter followed him at a distance, right up to the courtyard of the high priest. He entered and sat down with the guards to see the outcome.

59The chief priests and the whole Sanhedrin were looking for false evidence against Jesus so that they could put him to death. 60But they did not find any, though many false witnesses came forward.

Finally two came forward 61and declared, "This fellow said, 'I am able to destroy the temple of God and rebuild it in three days.' "

62Then the high priest stood up and said to Jesus, "Are you not going to answer? What is this testimony that these men are bringing against you?" 63But Jesus remained silent.

The high priest said to him, "I charge you under oath by the living God: Tell us if you are the Christ,e the Son of God."

64"Yes, it is as you say," Jesus replied. "But I say to all of you: In the future you will see the Son of Man sitting at the right hand of the Mighty One and coming on the clouds of heaven."

65Then the high priest tore his clothes and said, "He has spoken blasphemy! Why do we need any more witnesses? Look, now you have heard the blasphemy. 66What do you think?"

"He is worthy of death," they answered.

67Then they spit in his face and struck him with their fists. Others slapped him 68and said, "Prophesy to us, Christ. Who hit you?"

Peter Disowns Jesus

69Now Peter was sitting out in the courtyard, and a servant girl came to him. "You also were with Jesus of Galilee," she said.

70But he denied it before them all. "I don't know what you're talking about," he said.

71Then he went out to the gateway, where another girl saw him and said to the people there, "This fellow was with Jesus of Nazareth."

72He denied it again, with an oath: "I

---

man." [73]After a little while the bystanders came up and said to Peter, "Certainly you are also one of them, for your accent betrays you." [74]Then he began to curse, and he swore an oath, "I do not know the man!" At that moment the cock crowed. [75]Then Peter remembered what Jesus had said: "Before the cock crows, you will deny me three times." And he went out and wept bitterly.

Jesus Brought before Pilate

27 When morning came, all the chief priests and the elders of the people conferred together against Jesus in order to bring about his death. [2]They bound him, led him away, and handed him over to Pilate the governor.

The Suicide of Judas

3 When Judas, his betrayer, saw that Jesus[q] was condemned, he repented and brought back the thirty pieces of silver to the chief priests and the elders. [4]He said, "I have sinned by betraying innocent[r] blood." But they said, "What is that to us? See to it yourself." [5]Throwing down the pieces of silver in the temple, he departed; and he went and hanged himself. [6]But the chief priests, taking the pieces of silver, said, "It is not lawful to put them into the treasury, since they are blood money." [7]After conferring together, they used them to buy the potter's field as a place to bury foreigners. [8]For this reason that field has been called the Field of Blood to this day. [9]Then was fulfilled what had been spoken through the prophet Jeremiah,[s] "And they took[t] the thirty pieces of silver, the price of the one on whom a price had been set,[u] on whom some of the people of Israel had set a price, [10]and they gave[v] them for the potter's field, as the Lord commanded me."

Pilate Questions Jesus

11 Now Jesus stood before the governor; and the governor asked him, "Are you the King of the Jews?" Jesus said, "You say so." [12]But when he was accused by the chief priests and elders, he did not answer. [13]Then Pilate said to him, "Do you not hear how many accusations they make against you?" [14]But he gave him no answer, not even to a single charge, so that the governor was greatly amazed.

οἶδα τὸν ἄνθρωπον. **73** μετὰ μικρὸν δὲ προσελθόντες οἱ ἑστῶτες εἶπον τῷ Πέτρῳ, Ἀληθῶς καὶ σὺ ἐξ αὐτῶν εἶ, καὶ γὰρ ἡ λαλιά σου δῆλόν σε ποιεῖ. **74** τότε ἤρξατο καταθεματίζειν καὶ ὀμνύειν ὅτι Οὐκ οἶδα τὸν ἄνθρωπον. καὶ εὐθέως ἀλέκτωρ ἐφώνησεν. **75** καὶ ἐμνήσθη ὁ Πέτρος τοῦ ῥήματος Ἰησοῦ εἰρηκότος ὅτι Πρὶν ἀλέκτορα φωνῆσαι τρὶς ἀπαρνήσῃ με· καὶ ἐξελθὼν ἔξω ἔκλαυσεν πικρῶς.

27 Πρωΐας δὲ γενομένης συμβού-λιον ἔλαβον πάντες οἱ ἀρχιερεῖς καὶ οἱ πρεσβύτεροι τοῦ λαοῦ κατὰ τοῦ Ἰησοῦ ὥστε θανατῶσαι αὐτόν· **2** καὶ δήσαντες αὐτὸν ἀπήγαγον καὶ παρέδω-καν Πιλάτῳ τῷ ἡγεμόνι.

3 Τότε ἰδὼν Ἰούδας ὁ παραδιδοὺς αὐτὸν ὅτι κατεκρίθη, μεταμεληθεὶς ἔστρεψεν τὰ τριάκοντα ἀργύρια τοῖς ἀρχιερεῦσιν καὶ πρεσβυτέροις **4** λέγων, Ἥμαρτον παραδοὺς αἷμα ἀθῷον[a]. οἱ δὲ εἶπαν, Τί πρὸς ἡμᾶς; σὺ ὄψῃ. **5** καὶ ῥίψας τὰ ἀργύρια εἰς τὸν ναὸν ἀνεχώρησεν, καὶ ἀπελθὼν ἀπήγξατο. **6** οἱ δὲ ἀρχιερεῖς λαβόντες τὰ ἀργύρια εἶπαν, Οὐκ ἔξεστιν βαλεῖν αὐτὰ εἰς τὸν κορβανᾶν, ἐπεὶ τιμὴ αἵματός ἐστιν. **7** συμβούλιον δὲ λαβόντες ἠγόρασαν ἐξ αὐτῶν τὸν Ἀγρὸν τοῦ Κεραμέως εἰς ταφὴν τοῖς ξένοις. **8** διὸ ἐκλήθη ὁ ἀγρὸς ἐκεῖνος Ἀγρὸς Αἵματος ἕως τῆς σήμερον. **9** τότε ἐπληρώθη τὸ ῥηθὲν διὰ Ἰερεμίου[b] τοῦ προφήτου λέγοντος, Καὶ ἔλαβον τὰ τριάκοντα ἀργύρια, τὴν τιμὴν τοῦ τετιμημένου ὃν ἐτιμή-σαντο ἀπὸ υἱῶν Ἰσραήλ, **10** καὶ ἔδωκαν[c] αὐτὰ εἰς τὸν ἀγρὸν τοῦ κεραμέως, καθὰ συνέταξέν μοι κύριος.

11 Ὁ δὲ Ἰησοῦς ἐστάθη ἔμπροσθεν τοῦ ἡγεμόνος· καὶ ἐπηρώτησεν αὐτὸν ὁ ἡγεμὼν λέγων, Σὺ εἶ ὁ βασιλεὺς τῶν Ἰουδαίων; ὁ δὲ Ἰησοῦς ἔφη, Σὺ λέγεις. **12** καὶ ἐν τῷ κατηγορεῖσθαι αὐτὸν ὑπὸ τῶν ἀρχιερέων καὶ πρεσβυτέρων οὐδὲν ἀπεκρίνατο. **13** τότε λέγει αὐτῷ ὁ Πιλᾶτος, Οὐκ ἀκούεις πόσα σου κατα-μαρτυροῦσιν; **14** καὶ οὐκ ἀπεκρίθη αὐτῷ πρὸς οὐδὲ ἓν ῥῆμα, ὥστε θαυμάζειν τὸν ἡγεμόνα λίαν.

don't know the man!"

[73]After a little while, those standing there went up to Peter and said, "Surely you are one of them, for your accent gives you away."

[74]Then he began to call down curses on himself and he swore to them, "I don't know the man!"

Immediately a rooster crowed. [75]Then Peter remembered the word Jesus had spoken: "Before the rooster crows, you will disown me three times." And he went outside and wept bitterly.

Judas Hangs Himself

27 Early in the morning, all the chief priests and the elders of the people came to the decision to put Jesus to death. [2]They bound him, led him away and handed him over to Pilate, the governor.

[3]When Judas, who had betrayed him, saw that Jesus was condemned, he was seized with remorse and returned the thirty silver coins to the chief priests and the elders. [4]"I have sinned," he said, "for I have betrayed innocent blood."

"What is that to us?" they replied. "That's your responsibility."

[5]So Judas threw the money into the temple and left. Then he went away and hanged himself.

[6]The chief priests picked up the coins and said, "It is against the law to put this into the treasury, since it is blood money." [7]So they decided to use the money to buy the potter's field as a burial place for foreigners. [8]That is why it has been called the Field of Blood to this day. [9]Then what was spoken by Jeremiah the prophet was fulfilled: "They took the thirty silver coins, the price set on him by the people of Israel, [10]and they used them to buy the potter's field, as the Lord commanded me."[a]

Jesus Before Pilate

[11]Meanwhile Jesus stood before the governor, and the governor asked him, "Are you the king of the Jews?"

"Yes, it is as you say," Jesus replied.

[12]When he was accused by the chief priests and the elders, he gave no answer. [13]Then Pilate asked him, "Don't you hear the testimony they are bringing against you?" [14]But Jesus made no reply, not even to a single charge—to the great amazement of the governor.

[q] Gk he   [r] Other ancient authorities read righteous
[s] Other ancient authorities read Zechariah or Isaiah
[t] Or I took   [u] Or the price of the precious One   [v] Other ancient authorities read I gave

[a]4 NRSV note r δίκαιον   [b]9 NRSV note s Ζαχαρίου or Ἰησαΐου   [c]10 NRSV note v ἔδωκα

[a]10 See Zech. 11:12,13; Jer. 19:1-13; 32:6-9.

Barabbas or Jesus?

15 Now at the festival the governor was accustomed to release a prisoner for the crowd, anyone whom they wanted. 16At that time they had a notorious prisoner, called Jesusʷ Barabbas. 17So after they had gathered, Pilate said to them, "Whom do you want me to release for you, Jesusʷ Barabbas or Jesus who is called the Messiah?"ˣ 18For he realized that it was out of jealousy that they had handed him over. 19While he was sitting on the judgment seat, his wife sent word to him, "Have nothing to do with that innocent man, for today I have suffered a great deal because of a dream about him." 20Now the chief priests and the elders persuaded the crowds to ask for Barabbas and to have Jesus killed. 21The governor again said to them, "Which of the two do you want me to release for you?" And they said, "Barabbas." 22Pilate said to them, "Then what should I do with Jesus who is called the Messiah?"ˣ All of them said, "Let him be crucified!" 23Then he asked, "Why, what evil has he done?" But they shouted all the more, "Let him be crucified!"

Pilate Hands Jesus over to Be Crucified

24 So when Pilate saw that he could do nothing, but rather that a riot was beginning, he took some water and washed his hands before the crowd, saying, "I am innocent of this man's blood;ʸ see to it yourselves." 25Then the people as a whole answered, "His blood be on us and on our children!" 26So he released Barabbas for them; and after flogging Jesus, he handed him over to be crucified.

The Soldiers Mock Jesus

27 Then the soldiers of the governor took Jesus into the governor's headquarters,ᶻ and they gathered the whole cohort around him. 28They stripped him and put a scarlet robe on him, 29and after twisting some thorns into a crown, they put it on his head. They put a reed in his right hand and knelt before him and mocked him, saying, "Hail, King of the Jews!" 30They spat on him, and took the reed and struck him on the head. 31After mocking him, they stripped him of the robe and put his own clothes on him. Then they led him away to crucify him.

---

15 Κατὰ δὲ ἑορτὴν εἰώθει ὁ ἡγεμὼν ἀπολύειν ἕνα τῷ ὄχλῳ δέσμιον ὃν ἤθελον. **16** εἶχον δὲ τότε δέσμιον ἐπίσημον λεγόμενον [Ἰησοῦν]ᵈ Βαραββᾶν. **17** συνηγμένων οὖν αὐτῶν εἶπεν αὐτοῖς ὁ Πιλᾶτος, Τίνα θέλετε ἀπολύσω ὑμῖν, [Ἰησοῦν τὸν]ᵉ Βαραββᾶν ἢ Ἰησοῦν τὸν λεγόμενον Χριστόν; **18** ᾔδει γὰρ ὅτι διὰ φθόνον παρέδωκαν αὐτόν. **19** Καθημένου δὲ αὐτοῦ ἐπὶ τοῦ βήματος ἀπέστειλεν πρὸς αὐτὸν ἡ γυνὴ αὐτοῦ λέγουσα, Μηδὲν σοὶ καὶ τῷ δικαίῳ ἐκείνῳ· πολλὰ γὰρ ἔπαθον σήμερον κατ᾽ ὄναρ δι᾽ αὐτόν. **20** Οἱ δὲ ἀρχιερεῖς καὶ οἱ πρεσβύτεροι ἔπεισαν τοὺς ὄχλους ἵνα αἰτήσωνται τὸν Βαραββᾶν, τὸν δὲ Ἰησοῦν ἀπολέσωσιν. **21** ἀποκριθεὶς δὲ ὁ ἡγεμὼν εἶπεν αὐτοῖς, Τίνα θέλετε ἀπὸ τῶν δύο ἀπολύσω ὑμῖν; οἱ δὲ εἶπαν, Τὸν Βαραββᾶν. **22** λέγει αὐτοῖς ὁ Πιλᾶτος, Τί οὖν ποιήσω Ἰησοῦν τὸν λεγόμενον Χριστόν; λέγουσιν πάντες, Σταυρωθήτω. **23** ὁ δὲ ἔφη, Τί γὰρ κακὸν ἐποίησεν; οἱ δὲ περισσῶς ἔκραζον λέγοντες, Σταυρωθήτω. **24** ἰδὼν δὲ ὁ Πιλᾶτος ὅτι οὐδὲν ὠφελεῖ ἀλλὰ μᾶλλον θόρυβος γίνεται, λαβὼν ὕδωρ ἀπενίψατο τὰς χεῖρας ἀπέναντι τοῦ ὄχλου λέγων, Ἀθῷός εἰμι ἀπὸ τοῦ αἵματος τούτουᶠ· ὑμεῖς ὄψεσθε. **25** καὶ ἀποκριθεὶς πᾶς ὁ λαὸς εἶπεν, Τὸ αἷμα αὐτοῦ ἐφ᾽ ἡμᾶς καὶ ἐπὶ τὰ τέκνα ἡμῶν. **26** τότε ἀπέλυσεν αὐτοῖς τὸν Βαραββᾶν, τὸν δὲ Ἰησοῦν φραγελλώσας παρέδωκεν ἵνα σταυρωθῇ.

27 Τότε οἱ στρατιῶται τοῦ ἡγεμόνος παραλαβόντες τὸν Ἰησοῦν εἰς τὸ πραιτώριον συνήγαγον ἐπ᾽ αὐτὸν ὅλην τὴν σπεῖραν. **28** καὶ ἐκδύσαντες αὐτὸν χλαμύδα κοκκίνην περιέθηκαν αὐτῷ, **29** καὶ πλέξαντες στέφανον ἐξ ἀκανθῶν ἐπέθηκαν ἐπὶ τῆς κεφαλῆς αὐτοῦ καὶ κάλαμον ἐν τῇ δεξιᾷ αὐτοῦ, καὶ γονυπετήσαντες ἔμπροσθεν αὐτοῦ ἐνέπαιξαν αὐτῷ λέγοντες, Χαῖρε, βασιλεῦ τῶν Ἰουδαίων, **30** καὶ ἐμπτύσαντες εἰς αὐτὸν ἔλαβον τὸν κάλαμον καὶ ἔτυπτον εἰς τὴν κεφαλὴν αὐτοῦ. **31** καὶ ὅτε ἐνέπαιξαν αὐτῷ, ἐξέδυσαν αὐτὸν τὴν χλαμύδα καὶ ἐνέδυσαν αὐτὸν τὰ ἱμάτια αὐτοῦ καὶ ἀπήγαγον αὐτὸν εἰς τὸ σταυρῶσαι.

15Now it was the governor's custom at the Feast to release a prisoner chosen by the crowd. 16At that time they had a notorious prisoner, called Barabbas. 17So when the crowd had gathered, Pilate asked them, "Which one do you want me to release to you: Barabbas, or Jesus who is called Christ?" 18For he knew it was out of envy that they had handed Jesus over to him.

19While Pilate was sitting on the judge's seat, his wife sent him this message: "Don't have anything to do with that innocent man, for I have suffered a great deal today in a dream because of him."

20But the chief priests and the elders persuaded the crowd to ask for Barabbas and to have Jesus executed.

21"Which of the two do you want me to release to you?" asked the governor.

"Barabbas," they answered.

22"What shall I do, then, with Jesus who is called Christ?" Pilate asked.

They all answered, "Crucify him!"

23"Why? What crime has he committed?" asked Pilate.

But they shouted all the louder, "Crucify him!"

24When Pilate saw that he was getting nowhere, but that instead an uproar was starting, he took water and washed his hands in front of the crowd. "I am innocent of this man's blood," he said. "It is your responsibility!"

25All the people answered, "Let his blood be on us and on our children!"

26Then he released Barabbas to them. But he had Jesus flogged, and handed him over to be crucified.

The Soldiers Mock Jesus

27Then the governor's soldiers took Jesus into the Praetorium and gathered the whole company of soldiers around him. 28They stripped him and put a scarlet robe on him, 29and then twisted together a crown of thorns and set it on his head. They put a staff in his right hand and knelt in front of him and mocked him. "Hail, king of the Jews!" they said. 30They spit on him, and took the staff and struck him on the head again and again. 31After they had mocked him, they took off the robe and put his own clothes on him. Then they led him away to crucify him.

ʷ Other ancient authorities lack *Jesus*   ˣ Or *the Christ*
ʸ Other ancient authorities read *this righteous blood,* or *this righteous man's blood*   ᶻ Gk *the praetorium*

ᵈ16 NIV text and NRSV note w omit Ἰησοῦν
ᵉ17 NIV text and NRSV note w omit Ἰησοῦν τὸν
ᶠ24 NRSV note y τοῦ δικαίου τούτου or τούτου τοῦ δικαίου

The Crucifixion of Jesus

32 As they went out, they came upon a man from Cyrene named Simon; they compelled this man to carry his cross. 33And when they came to a place called Golgotha (which means Place of a Skull), 34they offered him wine to drink, mixed with gall; but when he tasted it, he would not drink it. 35And when they had crucified him, they divided his clothes among themselves by casting lots;[a] 36then they sat down there and kept watch over him. 37Over his head they put the charge against him, which read, "This is Jesus, the King of the Jews."

38 Then two bandits were crucified with him, one on his right and one on his left. 39Those who passed by derided[b] him, shaking their heads 40and saying, "You who would destroy the temple and build it in three days, save yourself! If you are the Son of God, come down from the cross." 41In the same way the chief priests also, along with the scribes and elders, were mocking him, saying, 42"He saved others; he cannot save himself.[c] He is the King of Israel; let him come down from the cross now, and we will believe in him. 43He trusts in God; let God deliver him now, if he wants to; for he said, 'I am God's Son.' " 44The bandits who were crucified with him also taunted him in the same way.

The Death of Jesus

45 From noon on, darkness came over the whole land[d] until three in the afternoon. 46And about three o'clock Jesus cried with a loud voice, "Eli, Eli, lema sabachthani?" that is, "My God, my God, why have you forsaken me?" 47When some of the bystanders heard it, they said, "This man is calling for Elijah." 48At once one of them ran and got a sponge, filled it with sour wine, put it on a stick, and gave it to him to drink. 49But the others said, "Wait, let us see whether Elijah will come to save him."[e] 50Then Jesus cried again with a loud voice and breathed his last.[f] 51At that moment the curtain of the temple was torn in two, from top to bottom. The earth shook, and the rocks were split. 52The tombs also were opened, and many bodies of the saints who had fallen asleep were raised. 53After his resurrection they came out of the tombs

32 Ἐξερχόμενοι δὲ εὗρον ἄνθρωπον Κυρηναῖον ὀνόματι Σίμωνα, τοῦτον ἠγγάρευσαν ἵνα ἄρῃ τὸν σταυρὸν αὐτοῦ. 33 Καὶ ἐλθόντες εἰς τόπον λεγόμενον Γολγοθᾶ, ὅ ἐστιν Κρανίου Τόπος λεγόμενος, 34 ἔδωκαν αὐτῷ πιεῖν οἶνον μετὰ χολῆς μεμιγμένον· καὶ γευσάμενος οὐκ ἠθέλησεν πιεῖν. 35 σταυρώσαντες δὲ αὐτὸν διεμερίσαντο τὰ ἱμάτια αὐτοῦ βάλλοντες κλῆρον[g], 36 καὶ καθήμενοι ἐτήρουν αὐτὸν ἐκεῖ. 37 καὶ ἐπέθηκαν ἐπάνω τῆς κεφαλῆς αὐτοῦ τὴν αἰτίαν αὐτοῦ γεγραμμένην· Οὗτός ἐστιν Ἰησοῦς ὁ βασιλεὺς τῶν Ἰουδαίων. 38 Τότε σταυροῦνται σὺν αὐτῷ δύο λῃσταί, εἷς ἐκ δεξιῶν καὶ εἷς ἐξ εὐωνύμων. 39 Οἱ δὲ παραπορευόμενοι ἐβλασφήμουν αὐτὸν κινοῦντες τὰς κεφαλὰς αὐτῶν 40 καὶ λέγοντες, Ὁ καταλύων τὸν ναὸν καὶ ἐν τρισὶν ἡμέραις οἰκοδομῶν, σῶσον σεαυτόν, εἰ υἱὸς εἶ τοῦ θεοῦ, [καὶ][h] κατάβηθι ἀπὸ τοῦ σταυροῦ. 41 ὁμοίως καὶ οἱ ἀρχιερεῖς ἐμπαίζοντες μετὰ τῶν γραμματέων καὶ πρεσβυτέρων ἔλεγον, 42 Ἄλλους ἔσωσεν, ἑαυτὸν οὐ δύναται σῶσαι· βασιλεὺς Ἰσραήλ ἐστιν, καταβάτω νῦν ἀπὸ τοῦ σταυροῦ καὶ πιστεύσομεν ἐπ᾽ αὐτόν. 43 πέποιθεν ἐπὶ τὸν θεόν, ῥυσάσθω νῦν εἰ θέλει αὐτόν· εἶπεν γὰρ ὅτι Θεοῦ εἰμι υἱός. 44 τὸ δ᾽ αὐτὸ καὶ οἱ λῃσταὶ οἱ συσταυρωθέντες σὺν αὐτῷ ὠνείδιζον αὐτόν.

45 Ἀπὸ δὲ ἕκτης ὥρας σκότος ἐγένετο ἐπὶ πᾶσαν τὴν γῆν ἕως ὥρας ἐνάτης. 46 περὶ δὲ τὴν ἐνάτην ὥραν ἀνεβόησεν ὁ Ἰησοῦς φωνῇ μεγάλῃ λέγων, Ηλι ηλι[i] λεμα σαβαχθανι; τοῦτ᾽ ἔστιν, Θεέ μου θεέ μου, ἱνατί με ἐγκατέλιπες; 47 τινὲς δὲ τῶν ἐκεῖ ἑστηκότων ἀκούσαντες ἔλεγον ὅτι Ἠλίαν φωνεῖ οὗτος. 48 καὶ εὐθέως δραμὼν εἷς ἐξ αὐτῶν καὶ λαβὼν σπόγγον πλήσας τε ὄξους καὶ περιθεὶς καλάμῳ ἐπότιζεν αὐτόν. 49 οἱ δὲ λοιποὶ ἔλεγον, Ἄφες ἴδωμεν εἰ ἔρχεται Ἠλίας σώσων αὐτόν.[j] 50 ὁ δὲ Ἰησοῦς πάλιν κράξας φωνῇ μεγάλῃ ἀφῆκεν τὸ πνεῦμα. 51 Καὶ ἰδοὺ τὸ καταπέτασμα τοῦ ναοῦ ἐσχίσθη ἀπ᾽ ἄνωθεν ἕως κάτω εἰς δύο καὶ ἡ γῆ ἐσείσθη καὶ αἱ πέτραι ἐσχίσθησαν, 52 καὶ τὰ μνημεῖα ἀνεῴχθησαν καὶ πολλὰ σώματα τῶν κεκοιμημένων ἁγίων ἠγέρθησαν, 53 καὶ ἐξελθόντες ἐκ τῶν

The Crucifixion

32As they were going out, they met a man from Cyrene, named Simon, and they forced him to carry the cross. 33They came to a place called Golgotha (which means The Place of the Skull). 34There they offered Jesus wine to drink, mixed with gall; but after tasting it, he refused to drink it. 35When they had crucified him, they divided up his clothes by casting lots.[b] 36And sitting down, they kept watch over him there. 37Above his head they placed the written charge against him: THIS IS JESUS, THE KING OF THE JEWS. 38Two robbers were crucified with him, one on his right and one on his left. 39Those who passed by hurled insults at him, shaking their heads 40and saying, "You who are going to destroy the temple and build it in three days, save yourself! Come down from the cross, if you are the Son of God!" 41In the same way the chief priests, the teachers of the law and the elders mocked him. 42"He saved others," they said, "but he can't save himself! He's the King of Israel! Let him come down now from the cross, and we will believe in him. 43He trusts in God. Let God rescue him now if he wants him, for he said, 'I am the Son of God.' " 44In the same way the robbers who were crucified with him also heaped insults on him.

The Death of Jesus

45From the sixth hour until the ninth hour darkness came over all the land. 46About the ninth hour Jesus cried out in a loud voice, "Eloi, Eloi,[c] lama sabachthani?"—which means, "My God, my God, why have you forsaken me?"[d]

47When some of those standing there heard this, they said, "He's calling Elijah."

48Immediately one of them ran and got a sponge. He filled it with wine vinegar, put it on a stick, and offered it to Jesus to drink. 49The rest said, "Now leave him alone. Let's see if Elijah comes to save him."

50And when Jesus had cried out again in a loud voice, he gave up his spirit.

51At that moment the curtain of the temple was torn in two from top to bottom. The earth shook and the rocks split. 52The tombs broke open and the bodies of many holy people who had died were raised to life. 53They came out of the tombs,

a Other ancient authorities add in order that what had been spoken through the prophet might be fulfilled, "They divided my clothes among themselves, and for my clothing they cast lots."   b Or blasphemed   c Or is he unable to save himself?   d Or earth   e Other ancient authorities add And another took a spear and pierced his side, and out came water and blood   f Or gave up his spirit

g35 NIV/NRSV notes add ἵνα πληρωθῇ τὸ ῥηθὲν διὰ τοῦ προφήτου· διεμερίσαντο τὰ ἱμάτιά μου ἑαυτοῖς καὶ ἐπὶ τὸν ἱματισμόν μου ἔβαλον κλῆρον.   h40 NIV text omits καὶ   i46 NIV text ἐλωΐ, ἐλωΐ †   j49 NRSV note e adds ἄλλος δὲ λαβὼν λόγχην ἔνυξεν αὐτοῦ τὴν πλευράν, καὶ ἐξῆλθεν ὕδωρ καὶ αἷμα.

b35 A few late manuscripts lots that the word spoken by the prophet might be fulfilled: "They divided my garments among themselves and cast lots for my clothing" (Psalm 22:18)   c46 Some manuscripts Eli, Eli   d46 Psalm 22:1

and entered the holy city and appeared to many. [54]Now when the centurion and those with him, who were keeping watch over Jesus, saw the earthquake and what took place, they were terrified and said, "Truly this man was God's Son!"[g]

55 Many women were also there, looking on from a distance; they had followed Jesus from Galilee and had provided for him. [56]Among them were Mary Magdalene, and Mary the mother of James and Joseph, and the mother of the sons of Zebedee.

The Burial of Jesus

57 When it was evening, there came a rich man from Arimathea, named Joseph, who was also a disciple of Jesus. [58]He went to Pilate and asked for the body of Jesus; then Pilate ordered it to be given to him. [59]So Joseph took the body and wrapped it in a clean linen cloth [60]and laid it in his own new tomb, which he had hewn in the rock. He then rolled a great stone to the door of the tomb and went away. [61]Mary Magdalene and the other Mary were there, sitting opposite the tomb.

The Guard at the Tomb

62 The next day, that is, after the day of Preparation, the chief priests and the Pharisees gathered before Pilate [63]and said, "Sir, we remember what that impostor said while he was still alive, 'After three days I will rise again.' [64]Therefore command the tomb to be made secure until the third day; otherwise his disciples may go and steal him away, and tell the people, 'He has been raised from the dead,' and the last deception would be worse than the first." [65]Pilate said to them, "You have a guard[h] of soldiers; go, make it as secure as you can."[i] [66]So they went with the guard and made the tomb secure by sealing the stone.

The Resurrection of Jesus

28 After the sabbath, as the first day of the week was dawning, Mary Magdalene and the other Mary went to see the tomb. [2]And suddenly there was a great earthquake; for an angel of the Lord, descending from heaven, came and rolled back the stone and sat on it. [3]His appearance was like lightning, and his clothing white as snow. [4]For fear of him the guards shook and became like dead men. [5]But the

μνημείων μετὰ τὴν ἔγερσιν αὐτοῦ εἰσῆλθον εἰς τὴν ἁγίαν πόλιν καὶ ἐνεφανίσθησαν πολλοῖς. **54** Ὁ δὲ ἑκατόνταρχος καὶ οἱ μετ' αὐτοῦ τηροῦντες τὸν Ἰησοῦν ἰδόντες τὸν σεισμὸν καὶ τὰ γενόμενα ἐφοβήθησαν σφόδρα, λέγοντες, Ἀληθῶς θεοῦ υἱὸς ἦν οὗτος. **55** Ἦσαν δὲ ἐκεῖ γυναῖκες πολλαὶ ἀπὸ μακρόθεν θεωροῦσαι, αἵτινες ἠκολούθησαν τῷ Ἰησοῦ ἀπὸ τῆς Γαλιλαίας διακονοῦσαι αὐτῷ· **56** ἐν αἷς ἦν Μαρία ἡ Μαγδαληνὴ καὶ Μαρία ἡ τοῦ Ἰακώβου καὶ Ἰωσὴφ[k] μήτηρ καὶ ἡ μήτηρ τῶν υἱῶν Ζεβεδαίου.

57 Ὀψίας δὲ γενομένης ἦλθεν ἄνθρωπος πλούσιος ἀπὸ Ἀριμαθαίας, τοὔνομα Ἰωσήφ, ὃς καὶ αὐτὸς ἐμαθητεύθη τῷ Ἰησοῦ· **58** οὗτος προσελθὼν τῷ Πιλάτῳ ᾐτήσατο τὸ σῶμα τοῦ Ἰησοῦ. τότε ὁ Πιλᾶτος ἐκέλευσεν ἀποδοθῆναι. **59** καὶ λαβὼν τὸ σῶμα ὁ Ἰωσὴφ ἐνετύλιξεν αὐτὸ [ἐν] σινδόνι καθαρᾷ **60** καὶ ἔθηκεν αὐτὸ ἐν τῷ καινῷ αὐτοῦ μνημείῳ ὃ ἐλατόμησεν ἐν τῇ πέτρᾳ καὶ προσκυλίσας λίθον μέγαν τῇ θύρᾳ τοῦ μνημείου ἀπῆλθεν. **61** ἦν δὲ ἐκεῖ Μαριὰμ ἡ Μαγδαληνὴ καὶ ἡ ἄλλη Μαρία καθήμεναι ἀπέναντι τοῦ τάφου.

62 Τῇ δὲ ἐπαύριον, ἥτις ἐστὶν μετὰ τὴν παρασκευήν, συνήχθησαν οἱ ἀρχιερεῖς καὶ οἱ Φαρισαῖοι πρὸς Πιλᾶτον **63** λέγοντες, Κύριε, ἐμνήσθημεν ὅτι ἐκεῖνος ὁ πλάνος εἶπεν ἔτι ζῶν, Μετὰ τρεῖς ἡμέρας ἐγείρομαι. **64** κέλευσον οὖν ἀσφαλισθῆναι τὸν τάφον ἕως τῆς τρίτης ἡμέρας, μήποτε ἐλθόντες οἱ μαθηταὶ αὐτοῦ κλέψωσιν αὐτὸν καὶ εἴπωσιν τῷ λαῷ, Ἠγέρθη ἀπὸ τῶν νεκρῶν, καὶ ἔσται ἡ ἐσχάτη πλάνη χείρων τῆς πρώτης. **65** ἔφη αὐτοῖς ὁ Πιλᾶτος, Ἔχετε κουστωδίαν· ὑπάγετε ἀσφαλίσασθε ὡς οἴδατε. **66** οἱ δὲ πορευθέντες ἠσφαλίσαντο τὸν τάφον σφραγίσαντες τὸν λίθον μετὰ τῆς κουστωδίας.

28 Ὀψὲ δὲ σαββάτων, τῇ ἐπιφωσκούσῃ εἰς μίαν σαββάτων ἦλθεν Μαριὰμ ἡ Μαγδαληνὴ καὶ ἡ ἄλλη Μαρία θεωρῆσαι τὸν τάφον. **2** καὶ ἰδοὺ σεισμὸς ἐγένετο μέγας· ἄγγελος γὰρ κυρίου καταβὰς ἐξ οὐρανοῦ καὶ προσελθὼν ἀπεκύλισεν τὸν λίθον καὶ ἐκάθητο ἐπάνω αὐτοῦ. **3** ἦν δὲ ἡ εἰδέα αὐτοῦ ὡς ἀστραπὴ καὶ τὸ ἔνδυμα αὐτοῦ λευκὸν ὡς χιών. **4** ἀπὸ δὲ τοῦ φόβου αὐτοῦ ἐσείσθησαν οἱ τηροῦντες καὶ ἐγενήθησαν ὡς νεκροί. **5** ἀποκριθεὶς

and after Jesus' resurrection they went into the holy city and appeared to many people. [54]When the centurion and those with him who were guarding Jesus saw the earthquake and all that had happened, they were terrified, and exclaimed, "Surely he was the Son[e] of God!"

[55]Many women were there, watching from a distance. They had followed Jesus from Galilee to care for his needs. [56]Among them were Mary Magdalene, Mary the mother of James and Joses, and the mother of Zebedee's sons.

The Burial of Jesus

[57]As evening approached, there came a rich man from Arimathea, named Joseph, who had himself become a disciple of Jesus. [58]Going to Pilate, he asked for Jesus' body, and Pilate ordered that it be given to him. [59]Joseph took the body, wrapped it in a clean linen cloth, [60]and placed it in his own new tomb that he had cut out of the rock. He rolled a big stone in front of the entrance to the tomb and went away. [61]Mary Magdalene and the other Mary were sitting there opposite the tomb.

The Guard at the Tomb

[62]The next day, the one after Preparation Day, the chief priests and the Pharisees went to Pilate. [63]"Sir," they said, "we remember that while he was still alive that deceiver said, 'After three days I will rise again.' [64]So give the order for the tomb to be made secure until the third day. Otherwise, his disciples may come and steal the body and tell the people that he has been raised from the dead. This last deception will be worse than the first."

[65]"Take a guard," Pilate answered. "Go, make the tomb as secure as you know how." [66]So they went and made the tomb secure by putting a seal on the stone and posting the guard.

The Resurrection

28 After the Sabbath, at dawn on the first day of the week, Mary Magdalene and the other Mary went to look at the tomb.

[2]There was a violent earthquake, for an angel of the Lord came down from heaven and, going to the tomb, rolled back the stone and sat on it. [3]His appearance was like lightning, and his clothes were white as snow. [4]The guards were so afraid of him that they shook and became like dead men.

---

[g] Or *a son of God*   [h] Or *Take a guard*   [i] Gk *you know how*   [k]56 NIV text Ἰωσῆ †   [e]54 Or *a son*

angel said to the women, "Do not be afraid; I know that you are looking for Jesus who was crucified. [6]He is not here; for he has been raised, as he said. Come, see the place where he[j] lay. [7]Then go quickly and tell his disciples, 'He has been raised from the dead,[k] and indeed he is going ahead of you to Galilee; there you will see him.' This is my message for you." [8]So they left the tomb quickly with fear and great joy, and ran to tell his disciples. [9]Suddenly Jesus met them and said, "Greetings!" And they came to him, took hold of his feet, and worshiped him. [10]Then Jesus said to them, "Do not be afraid; go and tell my brothers to go to Galilee; there they will see me."

The Report of the Guard

11 While they were going, some of the guard went into the city and told the chief priests everything that had happened. [12]After the priests[l] had assembled with the elders, they devised a plan to give a large sum of money to the soldiers, [13]telling them, "You must say, 'His disciples came by night and stole him away while we were asleep.' [14]If this comes to the governor's ears, we will satisfy him and keep you out of trouble." [15]So they took the money and did as they were directed. And this story is still told among the Jews to this day.

The Commissioning of the Disciples

16 Now the eleven disciples went to Galilee, to the mountain to which Jesus had directed them. [17]When they saw him, they worshiped him; but some doubted. [18]And Jesus came and said to them, "All authority in heaven and on earth has been given to me. [19]Go therefore and make disciples of all nations, baptizing them in the name of the Father and of the Son and of the Holy Spirit, [20]and teaching them to obey everything that I have commanded you. And remember, I am with you always, to the end of the age."[m]

δὲ ὁ ἄγγελος εἶπεν ταῖς γυναιξίν, Μὴ φοβεῖσθε ὑμεῖς, οἶδα γὰρ ὅτι Ἰησοῦν τὸν ἐσταυρωμένον ζητεῖτε· **6** οὐκ ἔστιν ὧδε, ἠγέρθη γὰρ καθὼς εἶπεν· δεῦτε ἴδετε τὸν τόπον ὅπου ἔκειτο[a]. **7** καὶ ταχὺ πορευθεῖσαι εἴπατε τοῖς μαθηταῖς αὐτοῦ ὅτι Ἠγέρθη ἀπὸ τῶν νεκρῶν, καὶ ἰδοὺ προάγει ὑμᾶς εἰς τὴν Γαλιλαίαν, ἐκεῖ αὐτὸν ὄψεσθε· ἰδοὺ εἶπον ὑμῖν. **8** καὶ ἀπελθοῦσαι ταχὺ ἀπὸ τοῦ μνημείου μετὰ φόβου καὶ χαρᾶς μεγάλης ἔδραμον ἀπαγγεῖλαι τοῖς μαθηταῖς αὐτοῦ. **9** καὶ ἰδοὺ Ἰησοῦς ὑπήντησεν αὐταῖς λέγων, Χαίρετε. αἱ δὲ προσελθοῦσαι ἐκράτησαν αὐτοῦ τοὺς πόδας καὶ προσεκύνησαν αὐτῷ. **10** τότε λέγει αὐταῖς ὁ Ἰησοῦς, Μὴ φοβεῖσθε· ὑπάγετε ἀπαγγείλατε τοῖς ἀδελφοῖς μου ἵνα ἀπέλθωσιν εἰς τὴν Γαλιλαίαν, κἀκεῖ με ὄψονται.

11 Πορευομένων δὲ αὐτῶν ἰδού τινες τῆς κουστωδίας ἐλθόντες εἰς τὴν πόλιν ἀπήγγειλαν τοῖς ἀρχιερεῦσιν ἅπαντα τὰ γενόμενα. **12** καὶ συναχθέντες μετὰ τῶν πρεσβυτέρων συμβούλιόν τε λαβόντες ἀργύρια ἱκανὰ ἔδωκαν τοῖς στρατιώταις **13** λέγοντες, Εἴπατε ὅτι Οἱ μαθηταὶ αὐτοῦ νυκτὸς ἐλθόντες ἔκλεψαν αὐτὸν ἡμῶν κοιμωμένων. **14** καὶ ἐὰν ἀκουσθῇ τοῦτο ἐπὶ τοῦ ἡγεμόνος, ἡμεῖς πείσομεν [αὐτὸν] καὶ ὑμᾶς ἀμερίμνους ποιήσομεν. **15** οἱ δὲ λαβόντες τὰ ἀργύρια ἐποίησαν ὡς ἐδιδάχθησαν. Καὶ διεφημίσθη ὁ λόγος οὗτος παρὰ Ἰουδαίοις μέχρι τῆς σήμερον [ἡμέρας].

16 Οἱ δὲ ἕνδεκα μαθηταὶ ἐπορεύθησαν εἰς τὴν Γαλιλαίαν εἰς τὸ ὄρος οὗ ἐτάξατο αὐτοῖς ὁ Ἰησοῦς, **17** καὶ ἰδόντες αὐτὸν προσεκύνησαν, οἱ δὲ ἐδίστασαν. **18** καὶ προσελθὼν ὁ Ἰησοῦς ἐλάλησεν αὐτοῖς λέγων, Ἐδόθη μοι πᾶσα ἐξουσία ἐν οὐρανῷ καὶ ἐπὶ [τῆς] γῆς. **19** πορευθέντες οὖν μαθητεύσατε πάντα τὰ ἔθνη, βαπτίζοντες αὐτοὺς εἰς τὸ ὄνομα τοῦ πατρὸς καὶ τοῦ υἱοῦ καὶ τοῦ ἁγίου πνεύματος, **20** διδάσκοντες αὐτοὺς τηρεῖν πάντα ὅσα ἐνετειλάμην ὑμῖν· καὶ ἰδοὺ ἐγὼ μεθ᾽ ὑμῶν εἰμι πάσας τὰς ἡμέρας ἕως τῆς συντελείας τοῦ αἰῶνος.[b]

[5]The angel said to the women, "Do not be afraid, for I know that you are looking for Jesus, who was crucified. [6]He is not here; he has risen, just as he said. Come and see the place where he lay. [7]Then go quickly and tell his disciples: 'He has risen from the dead and is going ahead of you into Galilee. There you will see him.' Now I have told you."

[8]So the women hurried away from the tomb, afraid yet filled with joy, and ran to tell his disciples. [9]Suddenly Jesus met them. "Greetings," he said. They came to him, clasped his feet and worshiped him. [10]Then Jesus said to them, "Do not be afraid. Go and tell my brothers to go to Galilee; there they will see me."

The Guards' Report

[11]While the women were on their way, some of the guards went into the city and reported to the chief priests everything that had happened. [12]When the chief priests had met with the elders and devised a plan, they gave the soldiers a large sum of money, [13]telling them, "You are to say, 'His disciples came during the night and stole him away while we were asleep.' [14]If this report gets to the governor, we will satisfy him and keep you out of trouble." [15]So the soldiers took the money and did as they were instructed. And this story has been widely circulated among the Jews to this very day.

The Great Commission

[16]Then the eleven disciples went to Galilee, to the mountain where Jesus had told them to go. [17]When they saw him, they worshiped him; but some doubted. [18]Then Jesus came to them and said, "All authority in heaven and on earth has been given to me. [19]Therefore go and make disciples of all nations, baptizing them in[a] the name of the Father and of the Son and of the Holy Spirit, [20]and teaching them to obey everything I have commanded you. And surely I am with you always, to the very end of the age."

---

[j]Other ancient authorities read *the Lord*   [k]Other ancient authorities lack *from the dead*   [l]Gk *they*   [m]Other ancient authorities add *Amen*

[a]6 NRSV note j adds ὁ κύριος   [b]19 NRSV note m adds ἀμήν.

[a]19 Or *into*; see Acts 8:16; 19:5; Romans 6:3; 1 Cor. 1:13; 10:2 and Gal. 3:27.

NRSV

The Proclamation of John the Baptist

1 The beginning of the good news[a] of Jesus Christ, the Son of God.[b]

2 As it is written in the prophet Isaiah,[c]

"See, I am sending my messenger
     ahead of you,[d]
who will prepare your way;
3   the voice of one crying out in the
     wilderness:
'Prepare the way of the Lord,
     make his paths straight,' "

4 John the baptizer appeared[e] in the wilderness, proclaiming a baptism of repentance for the forgiveness of sins. 5 And people from the whole Judean countryside and all the people of Jerusalem were going out to him, and were baptized by him in the river Jordan, confessing their sins. 6 Now John was clothed with camel's hair, with a leather belt around his waist, and he ate locusts and wild honey. 7 He proclaimed, "The one who is more powerful than I is coming after me; I am not worthy to stoop down and untie the thong of his sandals. 8 I have baptized you with[f] water; but he will baptize you with[f] the Holy Spirit."

The Baptism of Jesus

9 In those days Jesus came from Nazareth of Galilee and was baptized by John in the Jordan. 10 And just as he was coming up out of the water, he saw the heavens torn apart and the Spirit descending like a dove on him. 11 And a voice came from heaven, "You are my Son, the Beloved;[g] with you I am well pleased."

The Temptation of Jesus

12 And the Spirit immediately drove him out into the wilderness. 13 He was in the wilderness forty days, tempted by Satan; and he was with the wild beasts; and the angels waited on him.

The Beginning of the Galilean Ministry

14 Now after John was arrested, Jesus came to Galilee, proclaiming the good news[h] of God,[i] 15 and saying, "The time is fulfilled, and the kingdom of God has come near;[j] repent, and believe in the good news."[h]

ΚΑΤΑ ΜΑΡΚΟΝ

1 Ἀρχὴ τοῦ εὐαγγελίου Ἰησοῦ Χριστοῦ [υἱοῦ θεοῦ].

2 Καθὼς γέγραπται ἐν τῷ Ἡσαΐᾳ τῷ προφήτῃ[a],

Ἰδοὺ ἀποστέλλω τὸν ἄγγελόν μου
     πρὸ προσώπου σου,
ὃς κατασκευάσει τὴν ὁδόν σου·
3 φωνὴ βοῶντος ἐν τῇ ἐρήμῳ,
Ἑτοιμάσατε τὴν ὁδὸν κυρίου,
εὐθείας ποιεῖτε τὰς τρίβους
     αὐτοῦ.

4 ἐγένετο Ἰωάννης [ὁ][b] βαπτίζων ἐν τῇ ἐρήμῳ καὶ κηρύσσων βάπτισμα μετανοίας εἰς ἄφεσιν ἁμαρτιῶν. 5 καὶ ἐξεπορεύετο πρὸς αὐτὸν πᾶσα ἡ Ἰουδαία χώρα καὶ οἱ Ἱεροσολυμῖται πάντες, καὶ ἐβαπτίζοντο ὑπ' αὐτοῦ ἐν τῷ Ἰορδάνῃ ποταμῷ ἐξομολογούμενοι τὰς ἁμαρτίας αὐτῶν. 6 καὶ ἦν ὁ Ἰωάννης ἐνδεδυμένος τρίχας καμήλου καὶ ζώνην δερματίνην περὶ τὴν ὀσφὺν αὐτοῦ καὶ ἐσθίων ἀκρίδας καὶ μέλι ἄγριον. 7 καὶ ἐκήρυσσεν λέγων, Ἔρχεται ὁ ἰσχυρότερός μου ὀπίσω μου, οὗ οὐκ εἰμὶ ἱκανὸς κύψας λῦσαι τὸν ἱμάντα τῶν ὑποδημάτων αὐτοῦ. 8 ἐγὼ ἐβάπτισα ὑμᾶς ὕδατι, αὐτὸς δὲ βαπτίσει ὑμᾶς ἐν πνεύματι ἁγίῳ.

9 Καὶ ἐγένετο ἐν ἐκείναις ταῖς ἡμέραις ἦλθεν Ἰησοῦς ἀπὸ Ναζαρὲτ τῆς Γαλιλαίας καὶ ἐβαπτίσθη εἰς τὸν Ἰορδάνην ὑπὸ Ἰωάννου. 10 καὶ εὐθὺς ἀναβαίνων ἐκ τοῦ ὕδατος εἶδεν σχιζομένους τοὺς οὐρανοὺς καὶ τὸ πνεῦμα ὡς περιστερὰν καταβαῖνον εἰς αὐτόν· 11 καὶ φωνὴ ἐγένετο ἐκ τῶν οὐρανῶν, Σὺ εἶ ὁ υἱός μου ὁ ἀγαπητός, ἐν σοὶ εὐδόκησα.

12 Καὶ εὐθὺς τὸ πνεῦμα αὐτὸν ἐκβάλλει εἰς τὴν ἔρημον. 13 καὶ ἦν ἐν τῇ ἐρήμῳ τεσσεράκοντα ἡμέρας πειραζόμενος ὑπὸ τοῦ Σατανᾶ, καὶ ἦν μετὰ τῶν θηρίων, καὶ οἱ ἄγγελοι διηκόνουν αὐτῷ.

14 Μετὰ δὲ τὸ παραδοθῆναι τὸν Ἰωάννην ἦλθεν ὁ Ἰησοῦς εἰς τὴν Γαλιλαίαν κηρύσσων τὸ εὐαγγέλιον τοῦ θεοῦ[c] 15 καὶ λέγων ὅτι Πεπλήρωται ὁ καιρὸς καὶ ἤγγικεν ἡ βασιλεία τοῦ θεοῦ· μετανοεῖτε καὶ πιστεύετε ἐν τῷ εὐαγγελίῳ.

NIV

John the Baptist Prepares the Way

1 The beginning of the gospel about Jesus Christ, the Son of God.[a]

2 It is written in Isaiah the prophet:

"I will send my messenger ahead of you,
     who will prepare your way"[b]—
3 "a voice of one calling in the desert,
'Prepare the way for the Lord,
     make straight paths for him.' "[c]

4 And so John came, baptizing in the desert region and preaching a baptism of repentance for the forgiveness of sins. 5 The whole Judean countryside and all the people of Jerusalem went out to him. Confessing their sins, they were baptized by him in the Jordan River. 6 John wore clothing made of camel's hair, with a leather belt around his waist, and he ate locusts and wild honey. 7 And this was his message: "After me will come one more powerful than I, the thongs of whose sandals I am not worthy to stoop down and untie. 8 I baptize you with[d] water, but he will baptize you with the Holy Spirit."

The Baptism and Temptation of Jesus

9 At that time Jesus came from Nazareth in Galilee and was baptized by John in the Jordan. 10 As Jesus was coming up out of the water, he saw heaven being torn open and the Spirit descending on him like a dove. 11 And a voice came from heaven: "You are my Son, whom I love; with you I am well pleased."

12 At once the Spirit sent him out into the desert, 13 and he was in the desert forty days, being tempted by Satan. He was with the wild animals, and angels attended him.

The Calling of the First Disciples

14 After John was put in prison, Jesus went into Galilee, proclaiming the good news of God. 15 "The time has come," he said. "The kingdom of God is near. Repent and believe the good news!"

---

a Or *gospel*   b Other ancient authorities lack *the Son of God*   c Other ancient authorities read *in the prophets* d Gk *before your face*   e Other ancient authorities read *John was baptizing*   f Or *in*   f Or *in*   g Or *my beloved Son* h Or *gospel*   i Other ancient authorities read *of the kingdom*   j Or *is at hand*

a2 NRSV note c ἐν τοῖς προφήταις   b4 NRSV note e omits ὁ   c14 NRSV note i τῆς βασιλείας

a1 Some manuscripts do not have *the Son of God*. b2 Mal. 3:1   c3 Isaiah 40:3   d8 Or *in*

Jesus Calls the First Disciples

16 As Jesus passed along the Sea of Galilee, he saw Simon and his brother Andrew casting a net into the sea—for they were fishermen. [17]And Jesus said to them, "Follow me and I will make you fish for people." [18]And immediately they left their nets and followed him. [19]As he went a little farther, he saw James son of Zebedee and his brother John, who were in their boat mending the nets. [20]Immediately he called them; and they left their father Zebedee in the boat with the hired men, and followed him.

The Man with an Unclean Spirit

21 They went to Capernaum; and when the sabbath came, he entered the synagogue and taught. [22]They were astounded at his teaching, for he taught them as one having authority, and not as the scribes. [23]Just then there was in their synagogue a man with an unclean spirit, [24]and he cried out, "What have you to do with us, Jesus of Nazareth? Have you come to destroy us? I know who you are, the Holy One of God." [25]But Jesus rebuked him, saying, "Be silent, and come out of him!" [26]And the unclean spirit, convulsing him and crying with a loud voice, came out of him. [27]They were all amazed, and they kept on asking one another, "What is this? A new teaching—with authority! He[k] commands even the unclean spirits, and they obey him." [28]At once his fame began to spread throughout the surrounding region of Galilee.

Jesus Heals Many at Simon's House

29 As soon as they[l] left the synagogue, they entered the house of Simon and Andrew, with James and John. [30]Now Simon's mother-in-law was in bed with a fever, and they told him about her at once. [31]He came and took her by the hand and lifted her up. Then the fever left her, and she began to serve them.

32 That evening, at sundown, they brought to him all who were sick or possessed with demons. [33]And the whole city was gathered around the door. [34]And he cured many who were sick with various diseases, and cast out many demons; and he would not permit the demons to speak, because they knew him.

16 Καὶ παράγων παρὰ τὴν θάλασσαν τῆς Γαλιλαίας εἶδεν Σίμωνα καὶ Ἀνδρέαν τὸν ἀδελφὸν Σίμωνος ἀμφιβάλλοντας ἐν τῇ θαλάσσῃ· ἦσαν γὰρ ἁλιεῖς. 17 καὶ εἶπεν αὐτοῖς ὁ Ἰησοῦς, Δεῦτε ὀπίσω μου, καὶ ποιήσω ὑμᾶς γενέσθαι ἁλιεῖς ἀνθρώπων. 18 καὶ εὐθὺς ἀφέντες τὰ δίκτυα ἠκολούθησαν αὐτῷ. 19 Καὶ προβὰς ὀλίγον εἶδεν Ἰάκωβον τὸν τοῦ Ζεβεδαίου καὶ Ἰωάννην τὸν ἀδελφὸν αὐτοῦ καὶ αὐτοὺς ἐν τῷ πλοίῳ καταρτίζοντας τὰ δίκτυα, 20 καὶ εὐθὺς ἐκάλεσεν αὐτούς. καὶ ἀφέντες τὸν πατέρα αὐτῶν Ζεβεδαῖον ἐν τῷ πλοίῳ μετὰ τῶν μισθωτῶν ἀπῆλθον ὀπίσω αὐτοῦ.

21 Καὶ εἰσπορεύονται εἰς Καφαρναούμ· καὶ εὐθὺς τοῖς σάββασιν εἰσελθὼν εἰς τὴν συναγωγὴν ἐδίδασκεν. 22 καὶ ἐξεπλήσσοντο ἐπὶ τῇ διδαχῇ αὐτοῦ· ἦν γὰρ διδάσκων αὐτοὺς ὡς ἐξουσίαν ἔχων καὶ οὐχ ὡς οἱ γραμματεῖς. 23 καὶ εὐθὺς ἦν ἐν τῇ συναγωγῇ αὐτῶν ἄνθρωπος ἐν πνεύματι ἀκαθάρτῳ καὶ ἀνέκραξεν 24 λέγων, Τί ἡμῖν καὶ σοί, Ἰησοῦ Ναζαρηνέ; ἦλθες ἀπολέσαι ἡμᾶς; οἶδά σε τίς εἶ, ὁ ἅγιος τοῦ θεοῦ. 25 καὶ ἐπετίμησεν αὐτῷ ὁ Ἰησοῦς λέγων, Φιμώθητι καὶ ἔξελθε ἐξ αὐτοῦ. 26 καὶ σπαράξαν αὐτὸν τὸ πνεῦμα τὸ ἀκάθαρτον καὶ φωνῆσαν φωνῇ μεγάλῃ ἐξῆλθεν ἐξ αὐτοῦ. 27 καὶ ἐθαμβήθησαν ἅπαντες ὥστε συζητεῖν πρὸς ἑαυτοὺς λέγοντας, Τί ἐστιν τοῦτο; διδαχὴ καινὴ κατ' ἐξουσίαν· καὶ τοῖς πνεύμασι τοῖς ἀκαθάρτοις ἐπιτάσσει, καὶ ὑπακούουσιν αὐτῷ. 28 καὶ ἐξῆλθεν ἡ ἀκοὴ αὐτοῦ εὐθὺς πανταχοῦ εἰς ὅλην τὴν περίχωρον τῆς Γαλιλαίας.

29 Καὶ εὐθὺς ἐκ τῆς συναγωγῆς ἐξελθόντες ἦλθον[d] εἰς τὴν οἰκίαν Σίμωνος καὶ Ἀνδρέου μετὰ Ἰακώβου καὶ Ἰωάννου. 30 ἡ δὲ πενθερὰ Σίμωνος κατέκειτο πυρέσσουσα, καὶ εὐθὺς λέγουσιν αὐτῷ περὶ αὐτῆς. 31 καὶ προσελθὼν ἤγειρεν αὐτὴν κρατήσας τῆς χειρός· καὶ ἀφῆκεν αὐτὴν ὁ πυρετός, καὶ διηκόνει αὐτοῖς. 32 Ὀψίας δὲ γενομένης, ὅτε ἔδυ ὁ ἥλιος, ἔφερον πρὸς αὐτὸν πάντας τοὺς κακῶς ἔχοντας καὶ τοὺς δαιμονιζομένους· 33 καὶ ἦν ὅλη ἡ πόλις ἐπισυνηγμένη πρὸς τὴν θύραν. 34 καὶ ἐθεράπευσεν πολλοὺς κακῶς ἔχοντας ποικίλαις νόσοις καὶ δαιμόνια πολλὰ ἐξέβαλεν καὶ οὐκ ἤφιεν λαλεῖν τὰ δαιμόνια, ὅτι ᾔδεισαν αὐτόν.

[16]As Jesus walked beside the Sea of Galilee, he saw Simon and his brother Andrew casting a net into the lake, for they were fishermen. [17]"Come, follow me," Jesus said, "and I will make you fishers of men." [18]At once they left their nets and followed him.

[19]When he had gone a little farther, he saw James son of Zebedee and his brother John in a boat, preparing their nets. [20]Without delay he called them, and they left their father Zebedee in the boat with the hired men and followed him.

Jesus Drives Out an Evil Spirit

[21]They went to Capernaum, and when the Sabbath came, Jesus went into the synagogue and began to teach. [22]The people were amazed at his teaching, because he taught them as one who had authority, not as the teachers of the law. [23]Just then a man in their synagogue who was possessed by an evil[e] spirit cried out, [24]"What do you want with us, Jesus of Nazareth? Have you come to destroy us? I know who you are—the Holy One of God!"

[25]"Be quiet!" said Jesus sternly. "Come out of him!" [26]The evil spirit shook the man violently and came out of him with a shriek.

[27]The people were all so amazed that they asked each other, "What is this? A new teaching—and with authority! He even gives orders to evil spirits and they obey him." [28]News about him spread quickly over the whole region of Galilee.

Jesus Heals Many

[29]As soon as they left the synagogue, they went with James and John to the home of Simon and Andrew. [30]Simon's mother-in-law was in bed with a fever, and they told Jesus about her. [31]So he went to her, took her hand and helped her up. The fever left her and she began to wait on them.

[32]That evening after sunset the people brought to Jesus all the sick and demon-possessed. [33]The whole town gathered at the door, [34]and Jesus healed many who had various diseases. He also drove out many demons, but he would not let the demons speak because they knew who he was.

---

k Or *A new teaching! With authority he*   l Other ancient authorities read *he*   d 29 NRSV note l ἐξελθὼν ἦλθεν   e 23 Greek *unclean*; also in verses 26 and 27

A Preaching Tour in Galilee

35 In the morning, while it was still very dark, he got up and went out to a deserted place, and there he prayed. 36And Simon and his companions hunted for him. 37When they found him, they said to him, "Everyone is searching for you." 38He answered, "Let us go on to the neighboring towns, so that I may proclaim the message there also; for that is what I came out to do." 39And he went throughout Galilee, proclaiming the message in their synagogues and casting out demons.

Jesus Cleanses a Leper

40 A leperᵐ came to him begging him, and kneelingⁿ he said to him, "If you choose, you can make me clean." 41Moved with pity,ᵒ Jesusᵖ stretched out his hand and touched him, and said to him, "I do choose. Be made clean!" 42Immediately the leprosyᵐ left him, and he was made clean. 43After sternly warning him he sent him away at once, 44saying to him, "See that you say nothing to anyone; but go, show yourself to the priest, and offer for your cleansing what Moses commanded, as a testimony to them." 45But he went out and began to proclaim it freely, and to spread the word, so that Jesusᵖ could no longer go into a town openly, but stayed out in the country; and people came to him from every quarter.

Jesus Heals a Paralytic

2 When he returned to Capernaum after some days, it was reported that he was at home. 2So many gathered around that there was no longer room for them, not even in front of the door; and he was speaking the word to them. 3Then some peopleq came, bringing to him a paralyzed man, carried by four of them. 4And when they could not bring him to Jesus because of the crowd, they removed the roof above him; and after having dug through it, they let down the mat on which the paralytic lay. 5When Jesus saw their faith, he said to the paralytic, "Son, your sins are forgiven." 6Now some of the scribes were sitting there, questioning in their hearts, 7"Why does this fellow speak in this way? It is blasphemy! Who can forgive sins but God alone?" 8At once Jesus perceived in his spirit that they were discussing these questions among themselves; and he said to

35 Καὶ πρωὶ ἔννυχα λίαν ἀναστὰς ἐξῆλθεν καὶ ἀπῆλθεν εἰς ἔρημον τόπον κἀκεῖ προσηύχετο. **36** καὶ κατεδίωξεν αὐτὸν Σίμων καὶ οἱ μετ' αὐτοῦ, **37** καὶ εὗρον αὐτὸν καὶ λέγουσιν αὐτῷ ὅτι Πάντες ζητοῦσίν σε. **38** καὶ λέγει αὐτοῖς, Ἄγωμεν ἀλλαχοῦ εἰς τὰς ἐχομένας κωμοπόλεις, ἵνα καὶ ἐκεῖ κηρύξω· εἰς τοῦτο γὰρ ἐξῆλθον. **39** καὶ ἦλθεν κηρύσσων εἰς τὰς συναγωγὰς αὐτῶν εἰς ὅλην τὴν Γαλιλαίαν καὶ τὰ δαιμόνια ἐκβάλλων.

40 Καὶ ἔρχεται πρὸς αὐτὸν λεπρὸς παρακαλῶν αὐτὸν [καὶ γονυπετῶν] καὶ λέγων αὐτῷ ὅτι Ἐὰν θέλῃς δύνασαί με καθαρίσαι. **41** καὶ σπλαγχνισθεὶςᵉ ἐκτείνας τὴν χεῖρα αὐτοῦ ἥψατο καὶ λέγει αὐτῷ, Θέλω, καθαρίσθητι· **42** καὶ εὐθὺς ἀπῆλθεν ἀπ' αὐτοῦ ἡ λέπρα, καὶ ἐκαθαρίσθη. **43** καὶ ἐμβριμησάμενος αὐτῷ εὐθὺς ἐξέβαλεν αὐτόν **44** καὶ λέγει αὐτῷ, Ὅρα μηδενὶ μηδὲν εἴπῃς, ἀλλὰ ὕπαγε σεαυτὸν δεῖξον τῷ ἱερεῖ καὶ προσένεγκε περὶ τοῦ καθαρισμοῦ σου ἃ προσέταξεν Μωϋσῆς, εἰς μαρτύριον αὐτοῖς. **45** ὁ δὲ ἐξελθὼν ἤρξατο κηρύσσειν πολλὰ καὶ διαφημίζειν τὸν λόγον, ὥστε μηκέτι αὐτὸν δύνασθαι φανερῶς εἰς πόλιν εἰσελθεῖν, ἀλλ' ἔξω ἐπ' ἐρήμοις τόποις ἦν· καὶ ἤρχοντο πρὸς αὐτὸν πάντοθεν.

2 Καὶ εἰσελθὼν πάλιν εἰς Καφαρναοὺμ δι' ἡμερῶν ἠκούσθη ὅτι ἐν οἴκῳ ἐστίν. **2** καὶ συνήχθησαν πολλοὶ ὥστε μηκέτι χωρεῖν μηδὲ τὰ πρὸς τὴν θύραν, καὶ ἐλάλει αὐτοῖς τὸν λόγον. **3** καὶ ἔρχονται φέροντες πρὸς αὐτὸν παραλυτικὸν αἰρόμενον ὑπὸ τεσσάρων. **4** καὶ μὴ δυνάμενοι προσενέγκαι αὐτῷ διὰ τὸν ὄχλον ἀπεστέγασαν τὴν στέγην ὅπου ἦν, καὶ ἐξορύξαντες χαλῶσι τὸν κράβαττον ὅπου ὁ παραλυτικὸς κατέκειτο. **5** καὶ ἰδὼν ὁ Ἰησοῦς τὴν πίστιν αὐτῶν λέγει τῷ παραλυτικῷ, Τέκνον, ἀφίενταί σου αἱ ἁμαρτίαι. **6** ἦσαν δέ τινες τῶν γραμματέων ἐκεῖ καθήμενοι καὶ διαλογιζόμενοι ἐν ταῖς καρδίαις αὐτῶν, **7** Τί οὗτος οὕτως λαλεῖ; βλασφημεῖ· τίς δύναται ἀφιέναι ἁμαρτίας εἰ μὴ εἷς ὁ θεός; **8** καὶ εὐθὺς ἐπιγνοὺς ὁ Ἰησοῦς τῷ πνεύματι αὐτοῦ ὅτι οὕτως διαλογίζονται ἐν ἑαυτοῖς

Jesus Prays in a Solitary Place

35Very early in the morning, while it was still dark, Jesus got up, left the house and went off to a solitary place, where he prayed. 36Simon and his companions went to look for him, 37and when they found him, they exclaimed: "Everyone is looking for you!"

38Jesus replied, "Let us go somewhere else—to the nearby villages—so I can preach there also. That is why I have come." 39So he traveled throughout Galilee, preaching in their synagogues and driving out demons.

A Man With Leprosy

40A man with leprosyᶠ came to him and begged him on his knees, "If you are willing, you can make me clean."

41Filled with compassion, Jesus reached out his hand and touched the man. "I am willing," he said. "Be clean!" 42Immediately the leprosy left him and he was cured. 43Jesus sent him away at once with a strong warning: 44"See that you don't tell this to anyone. But go, show yourself to the priest and offer the sacrifices that Moses commanded for your cleansing, as a testimony to them." 45Instead he went out and began to talk freely, spreading the news. As a result, Jesus could no longer enter a town openly but stayed outside in lonely places. Yet the people still came to him from everywhere.

Jesus Heals a Paralytic

2 A few days later, when Jesus again entered Capernaum, the people heard that he had come home. 2So many gathered that there was no room left, not even outside the door, and he preached the word to them. 3Some men came, bringing to him a paralytic, carried by four of them. 4Since they could not get him to Jesus because of the crowd, they made an opening in the roof above Jesus and, after digging through it, lowered the mat the paralyzed man was lying on. 5When Jesus saw their faith, he said to the paralytic, "Son, your sins are forgiven."

6Now some teachers of the law were sitting there, thinking to themselves, 7"Why does this fellow talk like that? He's blaspheming! Who can forgive sins but God alone?"

8Immediately Jesus knew in his spirit that this was what they were thinking in their

---

ᵐ The terms *leper* and *leprosy* can refer to several diseases
ⁿ Other ancient authorities lack *kneeling* ᵒ Other ancient authorities read *anger* ᵖ Gk *he* q Gk *they*

ᵉ41 NRSV note o ὀργισθείς

f40 The Greek word was used for various diseases affecting the skin—not necessarily leprosy.

them, "Why do you raise such questions in your hearts? [9]Which is easier, to say to the paralytic, 'Your sins are forgiven,' or to say, 'Stand up and take your mat and walk'? [10]But so that you may know that the Son of Man has authority on earth to forgive sins"—he said to the paralytic— [11]"I say to you, stand up, take your mat and go to your home." [12]And he stood up, and immediately took the mat and went out before all of them; so that they were all amazed and glorified God, saying, "We have never seen anything like this!"

Jesus Calls Levi

13 Jesus[r] went out again beside the sea; the whole crowd gathered around him, and he taught them. [14]As he was walking along, he saw Levi son of Alphaeus sitting at the tax booth, and he said to him, "Follow me." And he got up and followed him.

15 And as he sat at dinner[s] in Levi's[t] house, many tax collectors and sinners were also sitting[u] with Jesus and his disciples—for there were many who followed him. [16]When the scribes of[v] the Pharisees saw that he was eating with sinners and tax collectors, they said to his disciples, "Why does he eat[w] with tax collectors and sinners?" [17]When Jesus heard this, he said to them, "Those who are well have no need of a physician, but those who are sick; I have come to call not the righteous but sinners."

The Question about Fasting

18 Now John's disciples and the Pharisees were fasting; and people[q] came and said to him, "Why do John's disciples and the disciples of the Pharisees fast, but your disciples do not fast?" [19]Jesus said to them, "The wedding guests cannot fast while the bridegroom is with them, can they? As long as they have the bridegroom with them, they cannot fast. [20]The days will come when the bridegroom is taken away from them, and then they will fast on that day.

21 "No one sews a piece of unshrunk cloth on an old cloak; otherwise, the patch pulls away from it, the new from the old, and a worse tear is made. [22]And no one puts new wine into old wineskins; otherwise, the wine will burst the skins, and the wine is lost, and so are the skins; but one

λέγει αὐτοῖς, Τί ταῦτα διαλογίζεσθε ἐν ταῖς καρδίαις ὑμῶν; **9** τί ἐστιν εὐκοπώτερον, εἰπεῖν τῷ παραλυτικῷ, Ἀφίενταί σου αἱ ἁμαρτίαι, ἢ εἰπεῖν, Ἔγειρε καὶ ἆρον τὸν κράβαττόν σου καὶ περιπάτει; **10** ἵνα δὲ εἰδῆτε ὅτι ἐξουσίαν ἔχει ὁ υἱὸς τοῦ ἀνθρώπου ἀφιέναι ἁμαρτίας ἐπὶ τῆς γῆς – λέγει τῷ παραλυτικῷ, **11** Σοὶ λέγω, ἔγειρε ἆρον τὸν κράβαττόν σου καὶ ὕπαγε εἰς τὸν οἶκόν σου. **12** καὶ ἠγέρθη καὶ εὐθὺς ἄρας τὸν κράβαττον ἐξῆλθεν ἔμπροσθεν πάντων, ὥστε ἐξίστασθαι πάντας καὶ δοξάζειν τὸν θεὸν λέγοντας ὅτι Οὕτως οὐδέποτε εἴδομεν.

13 Καὶ ἐξῆλθεν πάλιν παρὰ τὴν θάλασσαν· καὶ πᾶς ὁ ὄχλος ἤρχετο πρὸς αὐτόν, καὶ ἐδίδασκεν αὐτούς. **14** καὶ παράγων εἶδεν Λευὶν τὸν τοῦ Ἀλφαίου καθήμενον ἐπὶ τὸ τελώνιον, καὶ λέγει αὐτῷ, Ἀκολούθει μοι. καὶ ἀναστὰς ἠκολούθησεν αὐτῷ. **15** Καὶ γίνεται κατακεῖσθαι αὐτὸν ἐν τῇ οἰκίᾳ αὐτοῦ, καὶ πολλοὶ τελῶναι καὶ ἁμαρτωλοὶ συνανέκειντο τῷ Ἰησοῦ καὶ τοῖς μαθηταῖς αὐτοῦ· ἦσαν γὰρ πολλοὶ καὶ ἠκολούθουν αὐτῷ. **16** καὶ οἱ γραμματεῖς τῶν Φαρισαίων[a] ἰδόντες ὅτι ἐσθίει μετὰ τῶν ἁμαρτωλῶν καὶ τελωνῶν ἔλεγον τοῖς μαθηταῖς αὐτοῦ, Ὅτι μετὰ τῶν τελωνῶν καὶ ἁμαρτωλῶν ἐσθίει[b]; **17** καὶ ἀκούσας ὁ Ἰησοῦς λέγει αὐτοῖς [ὅτι] Οὐ χρείαν ἔχουσιν οἱ ἰσχύοντες ἰατροῦ ἀλλ' οἱ κακῶς ἔχοντες· οὐκ ἦλθον καλέσαι δικαίους ἀλλὰ ἁμαρτωλούς.

18 Καὶ ἦσαν οἱ μαθηταὶ Ἰωάννου καὶ οἱ Φαρισαῖοι νηστεύοντες. καὶ ἔρχονται καὶ λέγουσιν αὐτῷ, Διὰ τί οἱ μαθηταὶ Ἰωάννου καὶ οἱ μαθηταὶ τῶν Φαρισαίων νηστεύουσιν, οἱ δὲ σοὶ μαθηταὶ οὐ νηστεύουσιν; **19** καὶ εἶπεν αὐτοῖς ὁ Ἰησοῦς, Μὴ δύνανται οἱ υἱοὶ τοῦ νυμφῶνος ἐν ᾧ ὁ νυμφίος μετ' αὐτῶν ἐστιν νηστεύειν; ὅσον χρόνον ἔχουσιν τὸν νυμφίον μετ' αὐτῶν οὐ δύνανται νηστεύειν. **20** ἐλεύσονται δὲ ἡμέραι ὅταν ἀπαρθῇ ἀπ' αὐτῶν ὁ νυμφίος, καὶ τότε νηστεύσουσιν ἐν ἐκείνῃ τῇ ἡμέρᾳ. **21** οὐδεὶς ἐπίβλημα ῥάκους ἀγνάφου ἐπιράπτει ἐπὶ ἱμάτιον παλαιόν· εἰ δὲ μή, αἴρει τὸ πλήρωμα ἀπ' αὐτοῦ τὸ καινὸν τοῦ παλαιοῦ καὶ χεῖρον σχίσμα γίνεται. **22** καὶ οὐδεὶς βάλλει οἶνον νέον εἰς ἀσκοὺς παλαιούς· εἰ δὲ μή, ῥήξει ὁ οἶνος τοὺς ἀσκοὺς καὶ ὁ οἶνος ἀπόλλυται καὶ οἱ ἀσκοί· ἀλλὰ οἶνον

hearts, and he said to them, "Why are you thinking these things? [9]Which is easier: to say to the paralytic, 'Your sins are forgiven,' or to say, 'Get up, take your mat and walk'? [10]But that you may know that the Son of Man has authority on earth to forgive sins . . . ." He said to the paralytic, [11]"I tell you, get up, take your mat and go home." [12]He got up, took his mat and walked out in full view of them all. This amazed everyone and they praised God, saying, "We have never seen anything like this!"

The Calling of Levi

[13]Once again Jesus went out beside the lake. A large crowd came to him, and he began to teach them. [14]As he walked along, he saw Levi son of Alphaeus sitting at the tax collector's booth. "Follow me," Jesus told him, and Levi got up and followed him.

[15]While Jesus was having dinner at Levi's house, many tax collectors and "sinners" were eating with him and his disciples, for there were many who followed him. [16]When the teachers of the law who were Pharisees saw him eating with the "sinners" and tax collectors, they asked his disciples: "Why does he eat with tax collectors and 'sinners'?"

[17]On hearing this, Jesus said to them, "It is not the healthy who need a doctor, but the sick. I have not come to call the righteous, but sinners."

Jesus Questioned About Fasting

[18]Now John's disciples and the Pharisees were fasting. Some people came and asked Jesus, "How is it that John's disciples and the disciples of the Pharisees are fasting, but yours are not?"

[19]Jesus answered, "How can the guests of the bridegroom fast while he is with them? They cannot, so long as they have him with them. [20]But the time will come when the bridegroom will be taken from them, and on that day they will fast.

[21]"No one sews a patch of unshrunk cloth on an old garment. If he does, the new piece will pull away from the old, making the tear worse. [22]And no one pours new wine into old wineskins. If he does, the wine will burst the skins, and both the wine and the wineskins will be ruined.

---

q Gk *they*   r Gk *He*   s Gk *reclined*   t Gk *his*
u Gk *reclining*   v Other ancient authorities read *and*
w Other ancient authorities add *and drink*

a 16 NRSV note v καὶ οἱ Φαρισαῖοι   b 16 NRSV note w adds καὶ πίνει

puts new wine into fresh wineskins."ˣ

Pronouncement about the Sabbath

23 One sabbath he was going through the grainfields; and as they made their way his disciples began to pluck heads of grain. ²⁴The Pharisees said to him, "Look, why are they doing what is not lawful on the sabbath?" ²⁵And he said to them, "Have you never read what David did when he and his companions were hungry and in need of food? ²⁶He entered the house of God, when Abiathar was high priest, and ate the bread of the Presence, which it is not lawful for any but the priests to eat, and he gave some to his companions." ²⁷Then he said to them, "The sabbath was made for humankind, and not humankind for the sabbath; ²⁸so the Son of Man is lord even of the sabbath."

The Man with a Withered Hand

3 Again he entered the synagogue, and a man was there who had a withered hand. ²They watched him to see whether he would cure him on the sabbath, so that they might accuse him. ³And he said to the man who had the withered hand, "Come forward." ⁴Then he said to them, "Is it lawful to do good or to do harm on the sabbath, to save life or to kill?" But they were silent. ⁵He looked around at them with anger; he was grieved at their hardness of heart and said to the man, "Stretch out your hand." He stretched it out, and his hand was restored. ⁶The Pharisees went out and immediately conspired with the Herodians against him, how to destroy him.

A Multitude at the Seaside

7 Jesus departed with his disciples to the sea, and a great multitude from Galilee followed him; ⁸hearing all that he was doing, they came to him in great numbers from Judea, Jerusalem, Idumea, beyond the Jordan, and the region around Tyre and Sidon. ⁹He told his disciples to have a boat ready for him because of the crowd, so that they would not crush him; ¹⁰for he had cured many, so that all who had diseases pressed upon him to touch him. ¹¹Whenever the unclean spirits saw him, they fell down before him and shouted, "You are the Son of God!" ¹²But he sternly

νέον εἰς ἀσκοὺς καινούς.

23 Καὶ ἐγένετο αὐτὸν ἐν τοῖς σάββασιν παραπορεύεσθαι διὰ τῶν σπορίμων, καὶ οἱ μαθηταὶ αὐτοῦ ἤρξαντο ὁδὸν ποιεῖν τίλλοντες τοὺς στάχυας. **24** καὶ οἱ Φαρισαῖοι ἔλεγον αὐτῷ, Ἴδε τί ποιοῦσιν τοῖς σάββασιν ὃ οὐκ ἔξεστιν; **25** καὶ λέγει αὐτοῖς, Οὐδέποτε ἀνέγνωτε τί ἐποίησεν Δαυὶδ ὅτε χρείαν ἔσχεν καὶ ἐπείνασεν αὐτὸς καὶ οἱ μετ' αὐτοῦ, **26** πῶςᶜ εἰσῆλθεν εἰς τὸν οἶκον τοῦ θεοῦ ἐπὶ Ἀβιαθὰρ ἀρχιερέως καὶ τοὺς ἄρτους τῆς προθέσεως ἔφαγεν, οὓς οὐκ ἔξεστιν φαγεῖν εἰ μὴ τοὺς ἱερεῖς, καὶ ἔδωκεν καὶ τοῖς σὺν αὐτῷ οὖσιν; **27** καὶ ἔλεγεν αὐτοῖς, Τὸ σάββατον διὰ τὸν ἄνθρωπον ἐγένετο καὶ οὐχ ὁ ἄνθρωπος διὰ τὸ σάββατον· **28** ὥστε κύριός ἐστιν ὁ υἱὸς τοῦ ἀνθρώπου καὶ τοῦ σαββάτου.

3 Καὶ εἰσῆλθεν πάλιν εἰς τὴν συναγωγήν. καὶ ἦν ἐκεῖ ἄνθρωπος ἐξηραμμένην ἔχων τὴν χεῖρα. **2** καὶ παρετήρουν αὐτὸν εἰ τοῖς σάββασιν θεραπεύσει αὐτόν, ἵνα κατηγορήσωσιν αὐτοῦ. **3** καὶ λέγει τῷ ἀνθρώπῳ τῷ τὴν ξηρὰν χεῖρα ἔχοντι, Ἔγειρε εἰς τὸ μέσον. **4** καὶ λέγει αὐτοῖς, Ἔξεστιν τοῖς σάββασιν ἀγαθὸν ποιῆσαι ἢ κακοποιῆσαι, ψυχὴν σῶσαι ἢ ἀποκτεῖναι; οἱ δὲ ἐσιώπων. **5** καὶ περιβλεψάμενος αὐτοὺς μετ' ὀργῆς, συλλυπούμενος ἐπὶ τῇ πωρώσει τῆς καρδίας αὐτῶν λέγει τῷ ἀνθρώπῳ, Ἔκτεινον τὴν χεῖρα. καὶ ἐξέτεινεν καὶ ἀπεκατεστάθη ἡ χεὶρ αὐτοῦ. **6** καὶ ἐξελθόντες οἱ Φαρισαῖοι εὐθὺς μετὰ τῶν Ἡρῳδιανῶν συμβούλιον ἐδίδουν κατ' αὐτοῦ ὅπως αὐτὸν ἀπολέσωσιν.

7 Καὶ ὁ Ἰησοῦς μετὰ τῶν μαθητῶν αὐτοῦ ἀνεχώρησεν πρὸς τὴν θάλασσαν, καὶ πολὺ πλῆθος ἀπὸ τῆς Γαλιλαίας [ἠκολούθησεν],ᵃ καὶ ἀπὸ τῆς Ἰουδαίας **8** καὶ ἀπὸ Ἱεροσολύμων καὶ ἀπὸ τῆς Ἰδουμαίας καὶ ᵇ πέραν τοῦ Ἰορδάνου καὶ περὶ Τύρον καὶ Σιδῶνα, πλῆθος πολὺ ἀκούοντες ὅσα ἐποίει ἦλθον πρὸς αὐτόν. **9** καὶ εἶπεν τοῖς μαθηταῖς αὐτοῦ ἵνα πλοιάριον προσκαρτερῇ αὐτῷ διὰ τὸν ὄχλον ἵνα μὴ θλίβωσιν αὐτόν· **10** πολλοὺς γὰρ ἐθεράπευσεν, ὥστε ἐπιπίπτειν αὐτῷ ἵνα αὐτοῦ ἅψωνται ὅσοι εἶχον μάστιγας. **11** καὶ τὰ πνεύματα τὰ ἀκάθαρτα, ὅταν αὐτὸν ἐθεώρουν, προσέπιπτον αὐτῷ καὶ ἔκραζον λέγοντες ὅτι Σὺ εἶ ὁ υἱὸς τοῦ θεοῦ. **12** καὶ πολλὰ ἐπετίμα αὐτοῖς ἵνα

No, he pours new wine into new wineskins."

Lord of the Sabbath

²³One Sabbath Jesus was going through the grainfields, and as his disciples walked along, they began to pick some heads of grain. ²⁴The Pharisees said to him, "Look, why are they doing what is unlawful on the Sabbath?"

²⁵He answered, "Have you never read what David did when he and his companions were hungry and in need? ²⁶In the days of Abiathar the high priest, he entered the house of God and ate the consecrated bread, which is lawful only for priests to eat. And he also gave some to his companions."

²⁷Then he said to them, "The Sabbath was made for man, not man for the Sabbath. ²⁸So the Son of Man is Lord even of the Sabbath."

3 Another time he went into the synagogue, and a man with a shriveled hand was there. ²Some of them were looking for a reason to accuse Jesus, so they watched him closely to see if he would heal him on the Sabbath. ³Jesus said to the man with the shriveled hand, "Stand up in front of everyone."

⁴Then Jesus asked them, "Which is lawful on the Sabbath: to do good or to do evil, to save life or to kill?" But they remained silent.

⁵He looked around at them in anger and, deeply distressed at their stubborn hearts, said to the man, "Stretch out your hand." He stretched it out, and his hand was completely restored. ⁶Then the Pharisees went out and began to plot with the Herodians how they might kill Jesus.

Crowds Follow Jesus

⁷Jesus withdrew with his disciples to the lake, and a large crowd from Galilee followed. ⁸When they heard all he was doing, many people came to him from Judea, Jerusalem, Idumea, and the regions across the Jordan and around Tyre and Sidon. ⁹Because of the crowd he told his disciples to have a small boat ready for him, to keep the people from crowding him. ¹⁰For he had healed many, so that those with diseases were pushing forward to touch him. ¹¹Whenever the evilᵃ spirits saw him, they fell down before him and cried out, "You are the Son of God." ¹²But he gave them

---

ˣ Other ancient authorities lack *but one puts new wine into fresh wineskins*

ᶜ26 NIV text omits πῶς † ᵃ8 NIV/NRSV texts begin verse 8 after [ἠκολούθησεν], ᵇ8 NIV text adds οἱ †

ᵃ11 Greek *unclean*; also in verse 30

ordered them not to make him known.

Jesus Appoints the Twelve

13 He went up the mountain and called to him those whom he wanted, and they came to him. [14]And he appointed twelve, whom he also named apostles,[y] to be with him, and to be sent out to proclaim the message, [15]and to have authority to cast out demons. [16]So he appointed the twelve:[z] Simon (to whom he gave the name Peter); [17]James son of Zebedee and John the brother of James (to whom he gave the name Boanerges, that is, Sons of Thunder); [18]and Andrew, and Philip, and Bartholomew, and Matthew, and Thomas, and James son of Alphaeus, and Thaddaeus, and Simon the Cananaean, [19]and Judas Iscariot, who betrayed him.

Jesus and Beelzebul

Then he went home; [20]and the crowd came together again, so that they could not even eat. [21]When his family heard it, they went out to restrain him, for people were saying, "He has gone out of his mind." [22]And the scribes who came down from Jerusalem said, "He has Beelzebul, and by the ruler of the demons he casts out demons." [23]And he called them to him, and spoke to them in parables, "How can Satan cast out Satan? [24]If a kingdom is divided against itself, that kingdom cannot stand. [25]And if a house is divided against itself, that house will not be able to stand. [26]And if Satan has risen up against himself and is divided, he cannot stand, but his end has come. [27]But no one can enter a strong man's house and plunder his property without first tying up the strong man; then indeed the house can be plundered.

28 "Truly I tell you, people will be forgiven for their sins and whatever blasphemies they utter; [29]but whoever blasphemes against the Holy Spirit can never have forgiveness, but is guilty of an eternal sin"— [30]for they had said, "He has an unclean spirit."

The True Kindred of Jesus

31 Then his mother and his brothers came; and standing outside, they sent to him and called him. [32]A crowd was sitting around him; and they said to him, "Your mother and your brothers and sisters[a] are outside, asking for you." [33]And he replied,

[y] Other ancient authorities lack *whom he also named apostles*   [z] Other ancient authorities lack *So he appointed the twelve*   [a] Other ancient authorities lack *and sisters*

μὴ αὐτὸν φανερὸν ποιήσωσιν.

13 Καὶ ἀναβαίνει εἰς τὸ ὄρος καὶ προσκαλεῖται οὓς ἤθελεν αὐτός, καὶ ἀπῆλθον πρὸς αὐτόν. 14 καὶ ἐποίησεν δώδεκα [οὓς καὶ ἀποστόλους ὠνόμασεν] ἵνα ὦσιν μετ' αὐτοῦ καὶ ἵνα ἀποστέλλῃ αὐτοὺς κηρύσσειν 15 καὶ ἔχειν ἐξουσίαν ἐκβάλλειν τὰ δαιμόνια· 16 [καὶ ἐποίησεν τοὺς δώδεκα,] καὶ ἐπέθηκεν ὄνομα τῷ Σίμωνι Πέτρον, 17 καὶ Ἰάκωβον τὸν τοῦ Ζεβεδαίου καὶ Ἰωάννην τὸν ἀδελφὸν τοῦ Ἰακώβου καὶ ἐπέθηκεν αὐτοῖς ὀνόμα[τα] Βοανηργές, ὅ ἐστιν Υἱοὶ Βροντῆς· 18 καὶ Ἀνδρέαν καὶ Φίλιππον καὶ Βαρθολομαῖον καὶ Μαθθαῖον καὶ Θωμᾶν καὶ Ἰάκωβον τὸν τοῦ Ἀλφαίου καὶ Θαδδαῖον καὶ Σίμωνα τὸν Καναναῖον 19 καὶ Ἰούδαν Ἰσκαριώθ, ὃς καὶ παρέδωκεν αὐτόν.

20 Καὶ ἔρχεται εἰς οἶκον· καὶ συνέρχεται πάλιν [ὁ] ὄχλος, ὥστε μὴ δύνασθαι αὐτοὺς μηδὲ ἄρτον φαγεῖν. 21 καὶ ἀκούσαντες οἱ παρ' αὐτοῦ ἐξῆλθον κρατῆσαι αὐτόν· ἔλεγον γὰρ ὅτι ἐξέστη. 22 καὶ οἱ γραμματεῖς οἱ ἀπὸ Ἱεροσολύμων καταβάντες ἔλεγον ὅτι Βεελζεβοὺλ[c] ἔχει καὶ ὅτι ἐν τῷ ἄρχοντι τῶν δαιμονίων ἐκβάλλει τὰ δαιμόνια. 23 καὶ προσκαλεσάμενος αὐτοὺς ἐν παραβολαῖς ἔλεγεν αὐτοῖς, Πῶς δύναται Σατανᾶς Σατανᾶν ἐκβάλλειν; 24 καὶ ἐὰν βασιλεία ἐφ' ἑαυτὴν μερισθῇ, οὐ δύναται σταθῆναι ἡ βασιλεία ἐκείνη. 25 καὶ ἐὰν οἰκία ἐφ' ἑαυτὴν μερισθῇ, οὐ δυνήσεται ἡ οἰκία ἐκείνη σταθῆναι. 26 καὶ εἰ ὁ Σατανᾶς ἀνέστη ἐφ' ἑαυτὸν καὶ ἐμερίσθη, οὐ δύναται στῆναι ἀλλὰ τέλος ἔχει. 27 ἀλλ' οὐ δύναται οὐδεὶς εἰς τὴν οἰκίαν τοῦ ἰσχυροῦ εἰσελθὼν τὰ σκεύη αὐτοῦ διαρπάσαι, ἐὰν μὴ πρῶτον τὸν ἰσχυρὸν δήσῃ, καὶ τότε τὴν οἰκίαν αὐτοῦ διαρπάσει. 28 Ἀμὴν λέγω ὑμῖν ὅτι πάντα ἀφεθήσεται τοῖς υἱοῖς τῶν ἀνθρώπων τὰ ἁμαρτήματα καὶ αἱ βλασφημίαι ὅσα ἐὰν βλασφημήσωσιν· 29 ὃς δ' ἂν βλασφημήσῃ εἰς τὸ πνεῦμα τὸ ἅγιον, οὐκ ἔχει ἄφεσιν εἰς τὸν αἰῶνα, ἀλλὰ ἔνοχός ἐστιν αἰωνίου ἁμαρτήματος. 30 ὅτι ἔλεγον, Πνεῦμα ἀκάθαρτον ἔχει.

31 Καὶ ἔρχεται ἡ μήτηρ αὐτοῦ καὶ οἱ ἀδελφοὶ αὐτοῦ καὶ ἔξω στήκοντες ἀπέστειλαν πρὸς αὐτὸν καλοῦντες αὐτόν. 32 καὶ ἐκάθητο περὶ αὐτὸν ὄχλος, καὶ λέγουσιν αὐτῷ, Ἰδοὺ ἡ μήτηρ σου καὶ οἱ ἀδελφοί σου [καὶ αἱ ἀδελφαί σου] ἔξω ζητοῦσίν σε. 33 καὶ ἀποκριθεὶς

[c]22 NIV note Βεεζεβοὺλ †

strict orders not to tell who he was.

The Appointing of the Twelve Apostles

[13]Jesus went up on a mountainside and called to him those he wanted, and they came to him. [14]He appointed twelve—designating them apostles[b]—that they might be with him and that he might send them out to preach [15]and to have authority to drive out demons. [16]These are the twelve he appointed: Simon (to whom he gave the name Peter); [17]James son of Zebedee and his brother John (to them he gave the name Boanerges, which means Sons of Thunder); [18]Andrew, Philip, Bartholomew, Matthew, Thomas, James son of Alphaeus, Thaddaeus, Simon the Zealot [19]and Judas Iscariot, who betrayed him.

Jesus and Beelzebub

[20]Then Jesus entered a house, and again a crowd gathered, so that he and his disciples were not even able to eat. [21]When his family heard about this, they went to take charge of him, for they said, "He is out of his mind."

[22]And the teachers of the law who came down from Jerusalem said, "He is possessed by Beelzebub[c]! By the prince of demons he is driving out demons."

[23]So Jesus called them and spoke to them in parables: "How can Satan drive out Satan? [24]If a kingdom is divided against itself, that kingdom cannot stand. [25]If a house is divided against itself, that house cannot stand. [26]And if Satan opposes himself and is divided, he cannot stand; his end has come. [27]In fact, no one can enter a strong man's house and carry off his possessions unless he first ties up the strong man. Then he can rob his house. [28]I tell you the truth, all the sins and blasphemies of men will be forgiven them. [29]But whoever blasphemes against the Holy Spirit will never be forgiven; he is guilty of an eternal sin."

[30]He said this because they were saying, "He has an evil spirit."

Jesus' Mother and Brothers

[31]Then Jesus' mother and brothers arrived. Standing outside, they sent someone in to call him. [32]A crowd was sitting around him, and they told him, "Your mother and brothers are outside looking for you."

[b]14 Some manuscripts do not have *designating them apostles*.   [c]22 Greek *Beezeboul* or *Beelzeboul*

"Who are my mother and my brothers?" 34And looking at those who sat around him, he said, "Here are my mother and my brothers! 35Whoever does the will of God is my brother and sister and mother."

The Parable of the Sower

4 Again he began to teach beside the sea. Such a very large crowd gathered around him that he got into a boat on the sea and sat there, while the whole crowd was beside the sea on the land. 2He began to teach them many things in parables, and in his teaching he said to them: 3"Listen! A sower went out to sow. 4And as he sowed, some seed fell on the path, and the birds came and ate it up. 5Other seed fell on rocky ground, where it did not have much soil, and it sprang up quickly, since it had no depth of soil. 6And when the sun rose, it was scorched; and since it had no root, it withered away. 7Other seed fell among thorns, and the thorns grew up and choked it, and it yielded no grain. 8Other seed fell into good soil and brought forth grain, growing up and increasing and yielding thirty and sixty and a hundredfold." 9And he said, "Let anyone with ears to hear listen!"

The Purpose of the Parables

10 When he was alone, those who were around him along with the twelve asked him about the parables. 11And he said to them, "To you has been given the secret[b] of the kingdom of God, but for those outside, everything comes in parables; 12in order that

   'they may indeed look, but not
      perceive,
   and may indeed listen, but not
      understand;
   so that they may not turn again and be
      forgiven.' "

13 And he said to them, "Do you not understand this parable? Then how will you understand all the parables? 14The sower sows the word. 15These are the ones on the path where the word is sown: when they hear, Satan immediately comes and takes away the word that is sown in them. 16And these are the ones sown on rocky ground: when they hear the word, they immediately receive it with joy. 17But they have no root, and endure only for a while;

αὐτοῖς λέγει, Τίς ἐστιν ἡ μήτηρ μου καὶ οἱ ἀδελφοί [μου]; 34 καὶ περιβλεψά- μενος τοὺς περὶ αὐτὸν κύκλῳ καθημέ- νους λέγει, Ἴδε ἡ μήτηρ μου καὶ οἱ ἀδελφοί μου. 35 ὃς [γὰρ] ἂν ποιήσῃ τὸ θέλημα τοῦ θεοῦ, οὗτος ἀδελφός μου καὶ ἀδελφὴ καὶ μήτηρ ἐστίν.

4 Καὶ πάλιν ἤρξατο διδάσκειν παρὰ τὴν θάλασσαν· καὶ συνάγεται πρὸς αὐτὸν ὄχλος πλεῖστος, ὥστε αὐτὸν εἰς πλοῖον ἐμβάντα καθῆσθαι ἐν τῇ θαλάσ- σῃ, καὶ πᾶς ὁ ὄχλος πρὸς τὴν θάλασσαν ἐπὶ τῆς γῆς ἦσαν. 2 καὶ ἐδίδασκεν αὐτοὺς ἐν παραβολαῖς πολλά καὶ ἔλεγεν αὐτοῖς ἐν τῇ διδαχῇ αὐτοῦ, 3 Ἀκούετε. ἰδοὺ ἐξῆλθεν ὁ σπείρων σπεῖραι. 4 καὶ ἐγένετο ἐν τῷ σπείρειν ὃ μὲν ἔπεσεν παρὰ τὴν ὁδόν, καὶ ἦλθεν τὰ πετεινὰ καὶ κατέφαγεν αὐτό. 5 καὶ ἄλλο ἔπεσεν ἐπὶ τὸ πετρῶδες ὅπου οὐκ εἶχεν γῆν πολλήν, καὶ εὐθὺς ἐξανέτειλεν διὰ τὸ μὴ ἔχειν βάθος γῆς· 6 καὶ ὅτε ἀνέτειλεν ὁ ἥλιος ἐκαυματίσθη[a] καὶ διὰ τὸ μὴ ἔχειν ῥίζαν ἐξηράνθη. 7 καὶ ἄλλο ἔπεσεν εἰς τὰς ἀκάνθας, καὶ ἀνέβησαν αἱ ἄκανθαι καὶ συνέπνιξαν αὐτό, καὶ καρ- πὸν οὐκ ἔδωκεν. 8 καὶ ἄλλα ἔπεσεν εἰς τὴν γῆν τὴν καλὴν καὶ ἐδίδου καρπὸν ἀναβαίνοντα καὶ αὐξανόμενα καὶ ἔφερεν ἐν τριάκοντα καὶ ἓν ἑξήκοντα καὶ ἐν ἑκατόν. 9 καὶ ἔλεγεν, Ὃς ἔχει ὦτα ἀκούειν ἀκουέτω.

10 Καὶ ὅτε ἐγένετο κατὰ μόνας, ἠρώτων αὐτὸν οἱ περὶ αὐτὸν σὺν τοῖς δώδεκα τὰς παραβολάς. 11 καὶ ἔλεγεν αὐτοῖς, Ὑμῖν τὸ μυστήριον δέδοται τῆς βασιλείας τοῦ θεοῦ· ἐκείνοις δὲ τοῖς ἔξω ἐν παραβολαῖς τὰ πάντα γίνεται, 12 ἵνα

βλέποντες βλέπωσιν καὶ μὴ ἴδωσιν, καὶ ἀκούοντες ἀκούσωσιν καὶ μὴ συνιῶσιν,
μήποτε ἐπιστρέψωσιν καὶ ἀφεθῇ αὐτοῖς.

13 Καὶ λέγει αὐτοῖς, Οὐκ οἴδατε τὴν παραβολὴν ταύτην, καὶ πῶς πάσας τὰς παραβολὰς γνώσεσθε; 14 ὁ σπείρων τὸν λόγον σπείρει. 15 οὗτοι δέ εἰσιν οἱ παρὰ τὴν ὁδόν· ὅπου σπείρεται ὁ λόγος καὶ ὅταν ἀκούσωσιν, εὐθὺς ἔρχεται ὁ Σατανᾶς καὶ αἴρει τὸν λόγον τὸν ἐσπαρμένον εἰς αὐτούς. 16 καὶ οὗτοί εἰσιν[b] οἱ ἐπὶ τὰ πετρώδη σπειρόμενοι, οἳ ὅταν ἀκούσωσιν τὸν λόγον εὐθὺς μετὰ χαρᾶς λαμβάνουσιν αὐτόν, 17 καὶ οὐκ ἔχουσιν ῥίζαν ἐν ἑαυτοῖς ἀλλὰ πρόσκαιροί εἰσιν, εἶτα

33"Who are my mother and my brothers?" he asked.

34Then he looked at those seated in a circle around him and said, "Here are my mother and my brothers! 35Whoever does God's will is my brother and sister and mother."

The Parable of the Sower

4 Again Jesus began to teach by the lake. The crowd that gathered around him was so large that he got into a boat and sat in it out on the lake, while all the people were along the shore at the water's edge. 2He taught them many things by parables, and in his teaching said: 3"Listen! A farmer went out to sow his seed. 4As he was scattering the seed, some fell along the path, and the birds came and ate it up. 5Some fell on rocky places, where it did not have much soil. It sprang up quickly, because the soil was shallow. 6But when the sun came up, the plants were scorched, and they withered because they had no root. 7Other seed fell among thorns, which grew up and choked the plants, so that they did not bear grain. 8Still other seed fell on good soil. It came up, grew and produced a crop, multiplying thirty, sixty, or even a hundred times."

9Then Jesus said, "He who has ears to hear, let him hear."

10When he was alone, the Twelve and the others around him asked him about the parables. 11He told them, "The secret of the kingdom of God has been given to you. But to those on the outside everything is said in parables 12so that,

" 'they may be ever seeing but never
      perceiving,
  and ever hearing but never under-
      standing;
otherwise they might turn and be
      forgiven!'[a]"

13Then Jesus said to them, "Don't you understand this parable? How then will you understand any parable? 14The farmer sows the word. 15Some people are like seed along the path, where the word is sown. As soon as they hear it, Satan comes and takes away the word that was sown in them. 16Others, like seed sown on rocky places, hear the word and at once receive it with joy. 17But since they have no root, they last only a short time. When trouble

b Or *mystery*

a6 NIV text ἐκαυματίσθησαν †   b16 NIV text adds ὁμοίως †

a12 Isaiah 6:9,10

then, when trouble or persecution arises on account of the word, immediately they fall away.c 18And others are those sown among the thorns: these are the ones who hear the word, 19but the cares of the world, and the lure of wealth, and the desire for other things come in and choke the word, and it yields nothing. 20And these are the ones sown on the good soil: they hear the word and accept it and bear fruit, thirty and sixty and a hundredfold."

A Lamp under a Bushel Basket

21 He said to them, "Is a lamp brought in to be put under the bushel basket, or under the bed, and not on the lampstand? 22For there is nothing hidden, except to be disclosed; nor is anything secret, except to come to light. 23Let anyone with ears to hear listen!" 24And he said to them, "Pay attention to what you hear; the measure you give will be the measure you get, and still more will be given you. 25For to those who have, more will be given; and from those who have nothing, even what they have will be taken away."

The Parable of the Growing Seed

26 He also said, "The kingdom of God is as if someone would scatter seed on the ground, 27and would sleep and rise night and day, and the seed would sprout and grow, he does not know how. 28The earth produces of itself, first the stalk, then the head, then the full grain in the head. 29But when the grain is ripe, at once he goes in with his sickle, because the harvest has come."

The Parable of the Mustard Seed

30 He also said, "With what can we compare the kingdom of God, or what parable will we use for it? 31It is like a mustard seed, which, when sown upon the ground, is the smallest of all the seeds on earth; 32yet when it is sown it grows up and becomes the greatest of all shrubs, and puts forth large branches, so that the birds of the air can make nests in its shade."

The Use of Parables

33 With many such parables he spoke the word to them, as they were able to hear it; 34he did not speak to them except in parables, but he explained everything in private to his disciples.

γενομένης θλίψεως ἢ διωγμοῦ διὰ τὸν λόγον εὐθὺς σκανδαλίζονται. 18 καὶ ἄλλοι εἰσὶν οἱ εἰς τὰς ἀκάνθας σπειρό-μενοι· οὗτοί εἰσιν οἱ τὸν λόγον ἀκούσαν-τες, 19 καὶ αἱ μέριμναι τοῦ αἰῶνοςc καὶ ἡ ἀπάτη τοῦ πλούτου καὶ αἱ περὶ τὰ λοιπὰ ἐπιθυμίαι εἰσπορευόμεναι συμπνίγουσιν τὸν λόγον καὶ ἄκαρπος γίνεται. 20 καὶ ἐκεῖνοί εἰσιν οἱ ἐπὶ τὴν γῆν τὴν καλὴν σπαρέντες, οἵτινες ἀκούουσιν τὸν λόγον καὶ παραδέχονται καὶ καρποφοροῦσιν ἓν τριάκοντα καὶ ἓν ἑξήκοντα καὶ ἓν ἑκατόν.

21 Καὶ ἔλεγεν αὐτοῖς, Μήτι ἔρχεται ὁ λύχνος ἵνα ὑπὸ τὸν μόδιον τεθῇ ἢ ὑπὸ τὴν κλίνην; οὐχ ἵνα ἐπὶ τὴν λυχνίαν τεθῇ; 22 οὐ γάρ ἐστιν κρυπτὸν ἐὰν μὴ ἵνα φανερωθῇ, οὐδὲ ἐγένετο ἀπόκρυφον ἀλλ᾽ ἵνα ἔλθῃ εἰς φανερόν. 23 εἴ τις ἔχει ὦτα ἀκούειν ἀκουέτω.

24 Καὶ ἔλεγεν αὐτοῖς, Βλέπετε τί ἀκούετε. ἐν ᾧ μέτρῳ μετρεῖτε μετρηθή-σεται ὑμῖν καὶ προστεθήσεται ὑμῖν. 25 ὃς γὰρ ἔχει, δοθήσεται αὐτῷ· καὶ ὃς οὐκ ἔχει, καὶ ὃ ἔχει ἀρθήσεται ἀπ᾽ αὐτοῦ.

26 Καὶ ἔλεγεν, Οὕτως ἐστὶν ἡ βασιλεία τοῦ θεοῦ ὡς ἄνθρωπος βάλῃ τὸν σπόρον ἐπὶ τῆς γῆς 27 καὶ καθεύδῃ καὶ ἐγείρη-ται νύκτα καὶ ἡμέραν, καὶ ὁ σπόρος βλαστᾷ καὶ μηκύνηται ὡς οὐκ οἶδεν αὐτός. 28 αὐτομάτη ἡ γῆ καρποφορεῖ, πρῶτον χόρτον εἶτα στάχυν εἶτα πλήρη[ς] σῖτον ἐν τῷ στάχυϊ. 29 ὅταν δὲ παραδοῖ ὁ καρπός, εὐθὺς ἀποστέλλει τὸ δρέπανον, ὅτι παρέστηκεν ὁ θερισμός.

30 Καὶ ἔλεγεν, Πῶς ὁμοιώσωμεν τὴν βασιλείαν τοῦ θεοῦ ἢ ἐν τίνι αὐτὴν παραβολῇ θῶμεν; 31 ὡς κόκκῳ σινάπεως, ὃς ὅταν σπαρῇ ἐπὶ τῆς γῆς, μικρότερον ὂν πάντων τῶν σπερμάτων τῶν ἐπὶ τῆς γῆς, 32 καὶ ὅταν σπαρῇ, ἀναβαίνει καὶ γίνεται μεῖζον πάντων τῶν λαχάνων καὶ ποιεῖ κλάδους μεγάλους, ὥστε δύνασθαι ὑπὸ τὴν σκιὰν αὐτοῦ τὰ πετεινὰ τοῦ οὐρανοῦ κατασκηνοῦν.

33 καὶ τοιαύταις παραβολαῖς πολλαῖς ἐλάλει αὐτοῖς τὸν λόγον καθὼς ἠδύναντο ἀκούειν· 34 χωρὶς δὲ παραβολῆς οὐκ ἐλάλει αὐτοῖς, κατ᾽ ἰδίαν δὲ τοῖς ἰδίοις μαθηταῖς ἐπέλυεν πάντα.

or persecution comes because of the word, they quickly fall away. 18Still others, like seed sown among thorns, hear the word; 19but the worries of this life, the deceitful-ness of wealth and the desires for other things come in and choke the word, mak-ing it unfruitful. 20Others, like seed sown on good soil, hear the word, accept it, and produce a crop—thirty, sixty or even a hundred times what was sown."

A Lamp on a Stand

21He said to them, "Do you bring in a lamp to put it under a bowl or a bed? Instead, don't you put it on its stand? 22For whatever is hidden is meant to be dis-closed, and whatever is concealed is meant to be brought out into the open. 23If any-one has ears to hear, let him hear."

24"Consider carefully what you hear," he continued. "With the measure you use, it will be measured to you—and even more. 25Whoever has will be given more; who-ever does not have, even what he has will be taken from him."

The Parable of the Growing Seed

26He also said, "This is what the king-dom of God is like. A man scatters seed on the ground. 27Night and day, whether he sleeps or gets up, the seed sprouts and grows, though he does not know how. 28All by itself the soil produces grain—first the stalk, then the head, then the full kernel in the head. 29As soon as the grain is ripe, he puts the sickle to it, because the harvest has come."

The Parable of the Mustard Seed

30Again he said, "What shall we say the kingdom of God is like, or what parable shall we use to describe it? 31It is like a mustard seed, which is the smallest seed you plant in the ground. 32Yet when planted, it grows and becomes the largest of all garden plants, with such big branches that the birds of the air can perch in its shade."

33With many similar parables Jesus spoke the word to them, as much as they could understand. 34He did not say anything to them without using a parable. But when he was alone with his own disciples, he explained everything.

---

c Or *stumble*   c19 NIV text βίου †

Jesus Stills a Storm

35 On that day, when evening had come, he said to them, "Let us go across to the other side." [36]And leaving the crowd behind, they took him with them in the boat, just as he was. Other boats were with him. [37]A great windstorm arose, and the waves beat into the boat, so that the boat was already being swamped. [38]But he was in the stern, asleep on the cushion; and they woke him up and said to him, "Teacher, do you not care that we are perishing?" [39]He woke up and rebuked the wind, and said to the sea, "Peace! Be still!" Then the wind ceased, and there was a dead calm. [40]He said to them, "Why are you afraid? Have you still no faith?" [41]And they were filled with great awe and said to one another, "Who then is this, that even the wind and the sea obey him?"

Jesus Heals the Gerasene Demoniac

5 They came to the other side of the sea, to the country of the Gerasenes.[d] [2]And when he had stepped out of the boat, immediately a man out of the tombs with an unclean spirit met him. [3]He lived among the tombs; and no one could restrain him any more, even with a chain; [4]for he had often been restrained with shackles and chains, but the chains he wrenched apart, and the shackles he broke in pieces; and no one had the strength to subdue him. [5]Night and day among the tombs and on the mountains he was always howling and bruising himself with stones. [6]When he saw Jesus from a distance, he ran and bowed down before him; [7]and he shouted at the top of his voice, "What have you to do with me, Jesus, Son of the Most High God? I adjure you by God, do not torment me." [8]For he had said to him, "Come out of the man, you unclean spirit!" [9]Then Jesus[e] asked him, "What is your name?" He replied, "My name is Legion; for we are many." [10]He begged him earnestly not to send them out of the country. [11]Now there on the hillside a great herd of swine was feeding; [12]and the unclean spirits[f] begged him, "Send us into the swine; let us enter them." [13]So he gave them permission. And the unclean spirits came out and entered the swine; and the herd, numbering about two thousand, rushed down the steep bank into the sea, and were drowned

35 Καὶ λέγει αὐτοῖς ἐν ἐκείνῃ τῇ ἡμέρᾳ ὀψίας γενομένης, Διέλθωμεν εἰς τὸ πέραν. 36 καὶ ἀφέντες τὸν ὄχλον παραλαμβάνουσιν αὐτὸν ὡς ἦν ἐν τῷ πλοίῳ, καὶ ἄλλα πλοῖα ἦν μετ᾽ αὐτοῦ. 37 καὶ γίνεται λαῖλαψ μεγάλη ἀνέμου καὶ τὰ κύματα ἐπέβαλλεν εἰς τὸ πλοῖον, ὥστε ἤδη γεμίζεσθαι τὸ πλοῖον. 38 καὶ αὐτὸς ἦν ἐν τῇ πρύμνῃ ἐπὶ τὸ προσκεφάλαιον καθεύδων. καὶ ἐγείρουσιν αὐτὸν καὶ λέγουσιν αὐτῷ, Διδάσκαλε, οὐ μέλει σοι ὅτι ἀπολλύμεθα; 39 καὶ διεγερθεὶς ἐπετίμησεν τῷ ἀνέμῳ καὶ εἶπεν τῇ θαλάσσῃ, Σιώπα, πεφίμωσο. καὶ ἐκόπασεν ὁ ἄνεμος καὶ ἐγένετο γαλήνη μεγάλη. 40 καὶ εἶπεν αὐτοῖς, Τί δειλοί ἐστε; οὔπω ἔχετε πίστιν; 41 καὶ ἐφοβήθησαν φόβον μέγαν καὶ ἔλεγον πρὸς ἀλλήλους, Τίς ἄρα οὗτός ἐστιν ὅτι καὶ ὁ ἄνεμος καὶ ἡ θάλασσα ὑπακούει αὐτῷ;

5 Καὶ ἦλθον εἰς τὸ πέραν τῆς θαλάσσης εἰς τὴν χώραν τῶν Γερασηνῶν[a]. 2 καὶ ἐξελθόντος αὐτοῦ ἐκ τοῦ πλοίου εὐθὺς ὑπήντησεν αὐτῷ ἐκ τῶν μνημείων ἄνθρωπος ἐν πνεύματι ἀκαθάρτῳ, 3 ὃς τὴν κατοίκησιν εἶχεν ἐν τοῖς μνήμασιν, καὶ οὐδὲ ἁλύσει οὐκέτι οὐδεὶς ἐδύνατο αὐτὸν δῆσαι 4 διὰ τὸ αὐτὸν πολλάκις πέδαις καὶ ἁλύσεσιν δεδέσθαι καὶ διεσπάσθαι ὑπ᾽ αὐτοῦ τὰς ἁλύσεις καὶ τὰς πέδας συντετρῖφθαι, καὶ οὐδεὶς ἴσχυεν αὐτὸν δαμάσαι· 5 καὶ διὰ παντὸς νυκτὸς καὶ ἡμέρας ἐν τοῖς μνήμασιν καὶ ἐν τοῖς ὄρεσιν ἦν κράζων καὶ κατακόπτων ἑαυτὸν λίθοις. 6 καὶ ἰδὼν τὸν Ἰησοῦν ἀπὸ μακρόθεν ἔδραμεν καὶ προσεκύνησεν αὐτῷ 7 καὶ κράξας φωνῇ μεγάλῃ λέγει, Τί ἐμοὶ καὶ σοί, Ἰησοῦ υἱὲ τοῦ θεοῦ τοῦ ὑψίστου; ὁρκίζω σε τὸν θεόν, μή με βασανίσῃς. 8 ἔλεγεν γὰρ αὐτῷ, Ἔξελθε τὸ πνεῦμα τὸ ἀκάθαρτον ἐκ τοῦ ἀνθρώπου. 9 καὶ ἐπηρώτα αὐτόν, Τί ὄνομά σοι; καὶ λέγει αὐτῷ, Λεγιὼν ὄνομά μοι, ὅτι πολλοί ἐσμεν. 10 καὶ παρεκάλει αὐτὸν πολλὰ ἵνα μὴ αὐτὰ ἀποστείλῃ ἔξω τῆς χώρας.

11 Ἦν δὲ ἐκεῖ πρὸς τῷ ὄρει ἀγέλη χοίρων μεγάλη βοσκομένη· 12 καὶ παρεκάλεσαν αὐτὸν λέγοντες, Πέμψον ἡμᾶς εἰς τοὺς χοίρους, ἵνα εἰς αὐτοὺς εἰσέλθωμεν. 13 καὶ ἐπέτρεψεν αὐτοῖς. καὶ ἐξελθόντα τὰ πνεύματα τὰ ἀκάθαρτα εἰσῆλθον εἰς τοὺς χοίρους, καὶ ὥρμησεν ἡ ἀγέλη κατὰ τοῦ κρημνοῦ εἰς τὴν θάλασσαν, ὡς δισχίλιοι, καὶ

Jesus Calms the Storm

[35]That day when evening came, he said to his disciples, "Let us go over to the other side." [36]Leaving the crowd behind, they took him along, just as he was, in the boat. There were also other boats with him. [37]A furious squall came up, and the waves broke over the boat, so that it was nearly swamped. [38]Jesus was in the stern, sleeping on a cushion. The disciples woke him and said to him, "Teacher, don't you care if we drown?"

[39]He got up, rebuked the wind and said to the waves, "Quiet! Be still!" Then the wind died down and it was completely calm.

[40]He said to his disciples, "Why are you so afraid? Do you still have no faith?"

[41]They were terrified and asked each other, "Who is this? Even the wind and the waves obey him!"

The Healing of a Demon-possessed Man

5 They went across the lake to the region of the Gerasenes.[a] [2]When Jesus got out of the boat, a man with an evil[b] spirit came from the tombs to meet him. [3]This man lived in the tombs, and no one could bind him any more, not even with a chain. [4]For he had often been chained hand and foot, but he tore the chains apart and broke the irons on his feet. No one was strong enough to subdue him. [5]Night and day among the tombs and in the hills he would cry out and cut himself with stones.

[6]When he saw Jesus from a distance, he ran and fell on his knees in front of him. [7]He shouted at the top of his voice, "What do you want with me, Jesus, Son of the Most High God? Swear to God that you won't torture me!" [8]For Jesus had said to him, "Come out of this man, you evil spirit!"

[9]Then Jesus asked him, "What is your name?"

"My name is Legion," he replied, "for we are many." [10]And he begged Jesus again and again not to send them out of the area.

[11]A large herd of pigs was feeding on the nearby hillside. [12]The demons begged Jesus, "Send us among the pigs; allow us to go into them." [13]He gave them permission, and the evil spirits came out and went into the pigs. The herd, about two thousand in number, rushed down the steep

NRSV

in the sea.

14 The swineherds ran off and told it in the city and in the country. Then people came to see what it was that had happened. [15]They came to Jesus and saw the demoniac sitting there, clothed and in his right mind, the very man who had had the legion; and they were afraid. [16]Those who had seen what had happened to the demoniac and to the swine reported it. [17]Then they began to beg Jesus[g] to leave their neighborhood. [18]As he was getting into the boat, the man who had been possessed by demons begged him that he might be with him. [19]But Jesus[e] refused, and said to him, "Go home to your friends, and tell them how much the Lord has done for you, and what mercy he has shown you." [20]And he went away and began to proclaim in the Decapolis how much Jesus had done for him; and everyone was amazed.

A Girl Restored to Life and a Woman Healed

21 When Jesus had crossed again in the boat[h] to the other side, a great crowd gathered around him; and he was by the sea. [22]Then one of the leaders of the synagogue named Jairus came and, when he saw him, fell at his feet [23]and begged him repeatedly, "My little daughter is at the point of death. Come and lay your hands on her, so that she may be made well, and live." [24]So he went with him.

And a large crowd followed him and pressed in on him. [25]Now there was a woman who had been suffering from hemorrhages for twelve years. [26]She had endured much under many physicians, and had spent all that she had; and she was no better, but rather grew worse. [27]She had heard about Jesus, and came up behind him in the crowd and touched his cloak, [28]for she said, "If I but touch his clothes, I will be made well." [29]Immediately her hemorrhage stopped; and she felt in her body that she was healed of her disease. [30]Immediately aware that power had gone forth from him, Jesus turned about in the crowd and said, "Who touched my clothes?" [31]And his disciples said to him, "You see the crowd pressing in on you; how can you say, 'Who touched me?' " [32]He looked all around to see who had

Greek

ἐπνίγοντο ἐν τῇ θαλάσσῃ. **14** καὶ οἱ βόσκοντες αὐτοὺς ἔφυγον καὶ ἀπήγγειλαν εἰς τὴν πόλιν καὶ εἰς τοὺς ἀγρούς· καὶ ἦλθον ἰδεῖν τί ἐστιν τὸ γεγονὸς **15** καὶ ἔρχονται πρὸς τὸν Ἰησοῦν καὶ θεωροῦσιν τὸν δαιμονιζόμενον καθήμενον ἱματισμένον καὶ σωφρονοῦντα, τὸν ἐσχηκότα τὸν λεγιῶνα, καὶ ἐφοβήθησαν. **16** καὶ διηγήσαντο αὐτοῖς οἱ ἰδόντες πῶς ἐγένετο τῷ δαιμονιζομένῳ καὶ περὶ τῶν χοίρων. **17** καὶ ἤρξαντο παρακαλεῖν αὐτὸν ἀπελθεῖν ἀπὸ τῶν ὁρίων αὐτῶν. **18** καὶ ἐμβαίνοντος αὐτοῦ εἰς τὸ πλοῖον παρεκάλει αὐτὸν ὁ δαιμονισθεὶς ἵνα μετ᾽ αὐτοῦ ᾖ. **19** καὶ οὐκ ἀφῆκεν αὐτόν, ἀλλὰ λέγει αὐτῷ, Ὕπαγε εἰς τὸν οἶκόν σου πρὸς τοὺς σοὺς καὶ ἀπάγγειλον αὐτοῖς ὅσα ὁ κύριός σοι πεποίηκεν καὶ ἠλέησέν σε. **20** καὶ ἀπῆλθεν καὶ ἤρξατο κηρύσσειν ἐν τῇ Δεκαπόλει ὅσα ἐποίησεν αὐτῷ ὁ Ἰησοῦς, καὶ πάντες ἐθαύμαζον.

21 Καὶ διαπεράσαντος τοῦ Ἰησοῦ [ἐν τῷ πλοίῳ] πάλιν εἰς τὸ πέραν συνήχθη ὄχλος πολὺς ἐπ᾽ αὐτόν, καὶ ἦν παρὰ τὴν θάλασσαν. **22** καὶ ἔρχεται εἷς τῶν ἀρχισυναγώγων, ὀνόματι Ἰάϊρος, καὶ ἰδὼν αὐτὸν πίπτει πρὸς τοὺς πόδας αὐτοῦ **23** καὶ παρακαλεῖ αὐτὸν πολλὰ λέγων ὅτι Τὸ θυγάτριόν μου ἐσχάτως ἔχει, ἵνα ἐλθὼν ἐπιθῇς τὰς χεῖρας αὐτῇ ἵνα σωθῇ καὶ ζήσῃ. **24** καὶ ἀπῆλθεν μετ᾽ αὐτοῦ.

Καὶ ἠκολούθει αὐτῷ ὄχλος πολὺς καὶ συνέθλιβον αὐτόν. **25** καὶ γυνὴ οὖσα ἐν ῥύσει αἵματος δώδεκα ἔτη **26** καὶ πολλὰ παθοῦσα ὑπὸ πολλῶν ἰατρῶν καὶ δαπανήσασα τὰ παρ᾽ αὐτῆς πάντα καὶ μηδὲν ὠφεληθεῖσα ἀλλὰ μᾶλλον εἰς τὸ χεῖρον ἐλθοῦσα, **27** ἀκούσασα περὶ τοῦ Ἰησοῦ, ἐλθοῦσα ἐν τῷ ὄχλῳ ὄπισθεν ἥψατο τοῦ ἱματίου αὐτοῦ· **28** ἔλεγεν γὰρ ὅτι Ἐὰν ἅψωμαι κἂν τῶν ἱματίων αὐτοῦ σωθήσομαι. **29** καὶ εὐθὺς ἐξηράνθη ἡ πηγὴ τοῦ αἵματος αὐτῆς καὶ ἔγνω τῷ σώματι ὅτι ἴαται ἀπὸ τῆς μάστιγος. **30** καὶ εὐθὺς ὁ Ἰησοῦς ἐπιγνοὺς ἐν ἑαυτῷ τὴν ἐξ αὐτοῦ δύναμιν ἐξελθοῦσαν ἐπιστραφεὶς ἐν τῷ ὄχλῳ ἔλεγεν, Τίς μου ἥψατο τῶν ἱματίων; **31** καὶ ἔλεγον αὐτῷ οἱ μαθηταὶ αὐτοῦ, Βλέπεις τὸν ὄχλον συνθλίβοντά σε καὶ λέγεις, Τίς μου ἥψατο; **32** καὶ περιεβλέπετο ἰδεῖν

NIV

bank into the lake and were drowned.

[14]Those tending the pigs ran off and reported this in the town and countryside, and the people went out to see what had happened. [15]When they came to Jesus, they saw the man who had been possessed by the legion of demons, sitting there, dressed and in his right mind; and they were afraid. [16]Those who had seen it told the people what had happened to the demon-possessed man—and told about the pigs as well. [17]Then the people began to plead with Jesus to leave their region.

[18]As Jesus was getting into the boat, the man who had been demon-possessed begged to go with him. [19]Jesus did not let him, but said, "Go home to your family and tell them how much the Lord has done for you, and how he has had mercy on you." [20]So the man went away and began to tell in the Decapolis[c] how much Jesus had done for him. And all the people were amazed.

A Dead Girl and a Sick Woman

[21]When Jesus had again crossed over by boat to the other side of the lake, a large crowd gathered around him while he was by the lake. [22]Then one of the synagogue rulers, named Jairus, came there. Seeing Jesus, he fell at his feet [23]and pleaded earnestly with him, "My little daughter is dying. Please come and put your hands on her so that she will be healed and live." [24]So Jesus went with him.

A large crowd followed and pressed around him. [25]And a woman was there who had been subject to bleeding for twelve years. [26]She had suffered a great deal under the care of many doctors and had spent all she had, yet instead of getting better she grew worse. [27]When she heard about Jesus, she came up behind him in the crowd and touched his cloak, [28]because she thought, "If I just touch his clothes, I will be healed." [29]Immediately her bleeding stopped and she felt in her body that she was freed from her suffering.

[30]At once Jesus realized that power had gone out from him. He turned around in the crowd and asked, "Who touched my clothes?"

[31]"You see the people crowding against you," his disciples answered, "and yet you can ask, 'Who touched me?' "

[32]But Jesus kept looking around to see

e Gk he   g Gk him   h Other ancient authorities lack in the boat

c20 That is, the Ten Cities

NRSV

done it. ³³But the woman, knowing what had happened to her, came in fear and trembling, fell down before him, and told him the whole truth. ³⁴He said to her, "Daughter, your faith has made you well; go in peace, and be healed of your disease."

35 While he was still speaking, some people came from the leader's house to say, "Your daughter is dead. Why trouble the teacher any further?" ³⁶But overhearingⁱ what they said, Jesus said to the leader of the synagogue, "Do not fear, only believe." ³⁷He allowed no one to follow him except Peter, James, and John, the brother of James. ³⁸When they came to the house of the leader of the synagogue, he saw a commotion, people weeping and wailing loudly. ³⁹When he had entered, he said to them, "Why do you make a commotion and weep? The child is not dead but sleeping." ⁴⁰And they laughed at him. Then he put them all outside, and took the child's father and mother and those who were with him, and went in where the child was. ⁴¹He took her by the hand and said to her, "Talitha cum," which means, "Little girl, get up!" ⁴²And immediately the girl got up and began to walk about (she was twelve years of age). At this they were overcome with amazement. ⁴³He strictly ordered them that no one should know this, and told them to give her something to eat.

The Rejection of Jesus at Nazareth

6 He left that place and came to his hometown, and his disciples followed him. ²On the sabbath he began to teach in the synagogue, and many who heard him were astounded. They said, "Where did this man get all this? What is this wisdom that has been given to him? What deeds of power are being done by his hands? ³Is not this the carpenter, the son of Maryʲ and brother of James and Joses and Judas and Simon, and are not his sisters here with us?" And they took offenseᵏ at him. ⁴Then Jesus said to them, "Prophets are not without honor, except in their hometown, and among their own kin, and in their own house." ⁵And he could do no deed of power there, except that he laid his hands on a

Greek

τὴν τοῦτο ποιήσασαν. **33** ἡ δὲ γυνὴ φοβηθεῖσα καὶ τρέμουσα, εἰδυῖα ὃ γέγονεν αὐτῇ, ἦλθεν καὶ προσέπεσεν αὐτῷ καὶ εἶπεν αὐτῷ πᾶσαν τὴν ἀλήθειαν. **34** ὁ δὲ εἶπεν αὐτῇ, Θυγάτηρ, ἡ πίστις σου σέσωκέν σε· ὕπαγε εἰς εἰρήνην καὶ ἴσθι ὑγιὴς ἀπὸ τῆς μάστιγός σου.

35 Ἔτι αὐτοῦ λαλοῦντος ἔρχονται ἀπὸ τοῦ ἀρχισυναγώγου λέγοντες ὅτι Ἡ θυγάτηρ σου ἀπέθανεν· τί ἔτι σκύλλεις τὸν διδάσκαλον; **36** ὁ δὲ Ἰησοῦς παρακούσαςᵇ τὸν λόγον λαλούμενον λέγει τῷ ἀρχισυναγώγῳ, Μὴ φοβοῦ, μόνον πίστευε. **37** καὶ οὐκ ἀφῆκεν οὐδένα μετ' αὐτοῦ συνακολουθῆσαι εἰ μὴ τὸν Πέτρον καὶ Ἰάκωβον καὶ Ἰωάννην τὸν ἀδελφὸν Ἰακώβου. **38** καὶ ἔρχονται εἰς τὸν οἶκον τοῦ ἀρχισυναγώγου, καὶ θεωρεῖ θόρυβον καὶ κλαίοντας καὶ ἀλαλάζοντας πολλά, **39** καὶ εἰσελθὼν λέγει αὐτοῖς, Τί θορυβεῖσθε καὶ κλαίετε; τὸ παιδίον οὐκ ἀπέθανεν ἀλλὰ καθεύδει. **40** καὶ κατεγέλων αὐτοῦ. αὐτὸς δὲ ἐκβαλὼν πάντας παραλαμβάνει τὸν πατέρα τοῦ παιδίου καὶ τὴν μητέρα καὶ τοὺς μετ' αὐτοῦ καὶ εἰσπορεύεται ὅπου ἦν τὸ παιδίον. **41** καὶ κρατήσας τῆς χειρὸς τοῦ παιδίου λέγει αὐτῇ, Ταλιθα κουμ, ὅ ἐστιν μεθερμηνευόμενον Τὸ κοράσιον, σοὶ λέγω, ἔγειρε. **42** καὶ εὐθὺς ἀνέστη τὸ κοράσιον καὶ περιεπάτει· ἦν γὰρ ἐτῶν δώδεκα. καὶ ἐξέστησαν [εὐθὺς] ἐκστάσει μεγάλῃ. **43** καὶ διεστείλατο αὐτοῖς πολλὰ ἵνα μηδεὶς γνοῖ τοῦτο, καὶ εἶπεν δοθῆναι αὐτῇ φαγεῖν.

6 Καὶ ἐξῆλθεν ἐκεῖθεν καὶ ἔρχεται εἰς τὴν πατρίδα αὐτοῦ, καὶ ἀκολουθοῦσιν αὐτῷ οἱ μαθηταὶ αὐτοῦ. **2** καὶ γενομένου σαββάτου ἤρξατο διδάσκειν ἐν τῇ συναγωγῇ, καὶ πολλοὶ ἀκούοντες ἐξεπλήσσοντο λέγοντες, Πόθεν τούτῳ ταῦτα, καὶ τίς ἡ σοφία ἡ δοθεῖσα τούτῳ, καὶ αἱ δυνάμεις τοιαῦται διὰ τῶν χειρῶν αὐτοῦ γινόμεναι; **3** οὐχ οὗτός ἐστιν ὁ τέκτων, ὁ υἱόςᵃ τῆς Μαρίας καὶ ἀδελφὸς Ἰακώβου καὶ Ἰωσῆτος καὶ Ἰούδα καὶ Σίμωνος; καὶ οὐκ εἰσὶν αἱ ἀδελφαὶ αὐτοῦ ὧδε πρὸς ἡμᾶς; καὶ ἐσκανδαλίζοντο ἐν αὐτῷ. **4** καὶ ἔλεγεν αὐτοῖς ὁ Ἰησοῦς ὅτι Οὐκ ἔστιν προφήτης ἄτιμος εἰ μὴ ἐν τῇ πατρίδι αὐτοῦ καὶ ἐν τοῖς συγγενεῦσιν αὐτοῦ καὶ ἐν τῇ οἰκίᾳ αὐτοῦ. **5** καὶ οὐκ ἐδύνατο ἐκεῖ ποιῆσαι οὐδεμίαν δύναμιν, εἰ μὴ ὀλίγοις ἀρρώστοις ἐπιθεὶς τὰς

NIV

who had done it. ³³Then the woman, knowing what had happened to her, came and fell at his feet and, trembling with fear, told him the whole truth. ³⁴He said to her, "Daughter, your faith has healed you. Go in peace and be freed from your suffering."

³⁵While Jesus was still speaking, some men came from the house of Jairus, the synagogue ruler. "Your daughter is dead," they said. "Why bother the teacher any more?"

³⁶Ignoring what they said, Jesus told the synagogue ruler, "Don't be afraid; just believe."

³⁷He did not let anyone follow him except Peter, James and John the brother of James. ³⁸When they came to the home of the synagogue ruler, Jesus saw a commotion, with people crying and wailing loudly. ³⁹He went in and said to them, "Why all this commotion and wailing? The child is not dead but asleep." ⁴⁰But they laughed at him.

After he put them all out, he took the child's father and mother and the disciples who were with him, and went in where the child was. ⁴¹He took her by the hand and said to her, "Talitha koum!" (which means, "Little girl, I say to you, get up!"). ⁴²Immediately the girl stood up and walked around (she was twelve years old). At this they were completely astonished. ⁴³He gave strict orders not to let anyone know about this, and told them to give her something to eat.

A Prophet Without Honor

6 Jesus left there and went to his hometown, accompanied by his disciples. ²When the Sabbath came, he began to teach in the synagogue, and many who heard him were amazed.

"Where did this man get these things?" they asked. "What's this wisdom that has been given him, that he even does miracles! ³Isn't this the carpenter? Isn't this Mary's son and the brother of James, Joseph,ᵃ Judas and Simon? Aren't his sisters here with us?" And they took offense at him.

⁴Jesus said to them, "Only in his hometown, among his relatives and in his own house is a prophet without honor." ⁵He could not do any miracles there, except lay his hands on a few sick people and heal

---

ⁱ Or *ignoring*; other ancient authorities read *hearing* ʲOther ancient authorities read *son of the carpenter and of Mary* ᵏOr *stumbled*

ᵇ36 NRSV note i *ἀκούσας* ᵃ3 NRSV note j *τοῦ τέκτονος υἱὸς καὶ*

ᵃ3 Greek *Joses*, a variant of *Joseph*

few sick people and cured them. [6]And he was amazed at their unbelief.

The Mission of the Twelve

Then he went about among the villages teaching. [7]He called the twelve and began to send them out two by two, and gave them authority over the unclean spirits. [8]He ordered them to take nothing for their journey except a staff; no bread, no bag, no money in their belts; [9]but to wear sandals and not to put on two tunics. [10]He said to them, "Wherever you enter a house, stay there until you leave the place. [11]If any place will not welcome you and they refuse to hear you, as you leave, shake off the dust that is on your feet as a testimony against them." [12]So they went out and proclaimed that all should repent. [13]They cast out many demons, and anointed with oil many who were sick and cured them.

The Death of John the Baptist

14 King Herod heard of it, for Jesus'[l] name had become known. Some were[m] saying, "John the baptizer has been raised from the dead; and for this reason these powers are at work in him." [15]But others said, "It is Elijah." And others said, "It is a prophet, like one of the prophets of old." [16]But when Herod heard of it, he said, "John, whom I beheaded, has been raised."

17 For Herod himself had sent men who arrested John, bound him, and put him in prison on account of Herodias, his brother Philip's wife, because Herod[n] had married her. [18]For John had been telling Herod, "It is not lawful for you to have your brother's wife." [19]And Herodias had a grudge against him, and wanted to kill him. But she could not, [20]for Herod feared John, knowing that he was a righteous and holy man, and he protected him. When he heard him, he was greatly perplexed;[o] and yet he liked to listen to him. [21]But an opportunity came when Herod on his birthday gave a banquet for his courtiers and officers and for the leaders of Galilee. [22]When his daughter Herodias[p] came in and danced, she pleased Herod and his guests; and the king said to the girl, "Ask me for whatever you wish, and I will give it." [23]And he solemnly swore to her, "Whatever you ask

---

χεῖρας ἐθεράπευσεν. **6** καὶ ἐθαύμαζεν διὰ τὴν ἀπιστίαν αὐτῶν.

Καὶ περιῆγεν τὰς κώμας κύκλῳ διδάσκων. **7** καὶ προσκαλεῖται τοὺς δώδεκα καὶ ἤρξατο αὐτοὺς ἀποστέλλειν δύο δύο καὶ ἐδίδου αὐτοῖς ἐξουσίαν τῶν πνευμάτων τῶν ἀκαθάρτων, **8** καὶ παρήγγειλεν αὐτοῖς ἵνα μηδὲν αἴρωσιν εἰς ὁδὸν εἰ μὴ ῥάβδον μόνον, μὴ ἄρτον, μὴ πήραν, μὴ εἰς τὴν ζώνην χαλκόν, **9** ἀλλὰ ὑποδεδεμένους σανδάλια, καὶ μὴ ἐνδύσησθε δύο χιτῶνας. **10** καὶ ἔλεγεν αὐτοῖς, Ὅπου ἐὰν εἰσέλθητε εἰς οἰκίαν, ἐκεῖ μένετε ἕως ἂν ἐξέλθητε ἐκεῖθεν. **11** καὶ ὃς ἂν τόπος μὴ δέξηται ὑμᾶς μηδὲ ἀκούσωσιν ὑμῶν, ἐκπορευόμενοι ἐκεῖθεν ἐκτινάξατε τὸν χοῦν τὸν ὑποκάτω τῶν ποδῶν ὑμῶν εἰς μαρτύριον αὐτοῖς. **12** Καὶ ἐξελθόντες ἐκήρυξαν ἵνα μετανοῶσιν, **13** καὶ δαιμόνια πολλὰ ἐξέβαλλον, καὶ ἤλειφον ἐλαίῳ πολλοὺς ἀρρώστους καὶ ἐθεράπευον.

14 Καὶ ἤκουσεν ὁ βασιλεὺς Ἡρῴδης, φανερὸν γὰρ ἐγένετο τὸ ὄνομα αὐτοῦ, καὶ ἔλεγον[b] ὅτι Ἰωάννης ὁ βαπτίζων ἐγήγερται ἐκ νεκρῶν καὶ διὰ τοῦτο ἐνεργοῦσιν αἱ δυνάμεις ἐν αὐτῷ. **15** ἄλλοι δὲ ἔλεγον ὅτι Ἠλίας ἐστίν· ἄλλοι δὲ ἔλεγον ὅτι προφήτης ὡς εἷς τῶν προφητῶν. **16** ἀκούσας δὲ ὁ Ἡρῴδης ἔλεγεν, Ὃν ἐγὼ ἀπεκεφάλισα Ἰωάννην, οὗτος[c] ἠγέρθη. **17** Αὐτὸς γὰρ ὁ Ἡρῴδης ἀποστείλας ἐκράτησεν τὸν Ἰωάννην καὶ ἔδησεν αὐτὸν ἐν φυλακῇ διὰ Ἡρῳδιάδα τὴν γυναῖκα Φιλίππου τοῦ ἀδελφοῦ αὐτοῦ, ὅτι αὐτὴν ἐγάμησεν· **18** ἔλεγεν γὰρ ὁ Ἰωάννης τῷ Ἡρῴδῃ ὅτι Οὐκ ἔξεστίν σοι ἔχειν τὴν γυναῖκα τοῦ ἀδελφοῦ σου. **19** ἡ δὲ Ἡρῳδιὰς ἐνεῖχεν αὐτῷ καὶ ἤθελεν αὐτὸν ἀποκτεῖναι, καὶ οὐκ ἠδύνατο· **20** ὁ γὰρ Ἡρῴδης ἐφοβεῖτο τὸν Ἰωάννην, εἰδὼς αὐτὸν ἄνδρα δίκαιον καὶ ἅγιον, καὶ συνετήρει αὐτόν, καὶ ἀκούσας αὐτοῦ πολλὰ ἠπόρει,[d] καὶ ἡδέως αὐτοῦ ἤκουεν. **21** Καὶ γενομένης ἡμέρας εὐκαίρου ὅτε Ἡρῴδης τοῖς γενεσίοις αὐτοῦ δεῖπνον ἐποίησεν τοῖς μεγιστᾶσιν αὐτοῦ καὶ τοῖς χιλιάρχοις καὶ τοῖς πρώτοις τῆς Γαλιλαίας, **22** καὶ εἰσελθούσης τῆς θυγατρὸς αὐτοῦ Ἡρῳδιάδος[e] καὶ ὀρχησαμένης ἤρεσεν τῷ Ἡρῴδῃ καὶ τοῖς συνανακειμένοις. εἶπεν ὁ βασιλεὺς τῷ κορασίῳ, Αἴτησόν με ὃ ἐὰν θέλῃς, καὶ δώσω σοι· **23** καὶ ὤμοσεν αὐτῇ [πολλά][f],

---

them. [6]And he was amazed at their lack of faith.

Jesus Sends Out the Twelve

Then Jesus went around teaching from village to village. [7]Calling the Twelve to him, he sent them out two by two and gave them authority over evil[b] spirits.

[8]These were his instructions: "Take nothing for the journey except a staff—no bread, no bag, no money in your belts; [9]Wear sandals but not an extra tunic. [10]Whenever you enter a house, stay there until you leave that town. [11]And if any place will not welcome you or listen to you, shake the dust off your feet when you leave, as a testimony against them."

[12]They went out and preached that people should repent. [13]They drove out many demons and anointed many sick people with oil and healed them.

John the Baptist Beheaded

[14]King Herod heard about this, for Jesus' name had become well known. Some were saying,[c] "John the Baptist has been raised from the dead, and that is why miraculous powers are at work in him."

[15]Others said, "He is Elijah."

And still others claimed, "He is a prophet, like one of the prophets of long ago."

[16]But when Herod heard this, he said, "John, the man I beheaded, has been raised from the dead!"

[17]For Herod himself had given orders to have John arrested, and he had him bound and put in prison. He did this because of Herodias, his brother Philip's wife, whom he had married. [18]For John had been saying to Herod, "It is not lawful for you to have your brother's wife." [19]So Herodias nursed a grudge against John and wanted to kill him. But she was not able to, [20]because Herod feared John and protected him, knowing him to be a righteous and holy man. When Herod heard John, he was greatly puzzled[d]; yet he liked to listen to him.

[21]Finally the opportune time came. On his birthday Herod gave a banquet for his high officials and military commanders and the leading men of Galilee. [22]When the daughter of Herodias came in and danced, she pleased Herod and his dinner guests.

The king said to the girl, "Ask me for anything you want, and I'll give it to you." [23]And he promised her with an oath,

---

[l] Gk *his*   [m] Other ancient authorities read *He was*
[n] Gk *he*   [o] Other ancient authorities read *he did many things*   [p] Other ancient authorities read *the daughter of Herodias herself*

[b]14 NIV/NRSV notes ἔλεγεν   [c]16 NIV text adds ἐκ νεκρῶν †   [d]20 NIV/NRSV notes πολλὰ ἐποίει.
[e]22 NRSV note p θυγατρὸς αὐτῆς τῆς Ἡρῳδιάδος
[f]23 NIV text omits πολλά

[b]7 Greek *unclean*   [c]14 Some early manuscripts *He was saying*   [d]20 Some early manuscripts *he did many things*

me, I will give you, even half of my kingdom." [24]She went out and said to her mother, "What should I ask for?" She replied, "The head of John the baptizer." [25]Immediately she rushed back to the king and requested, "I want you to give me at once the head of John the Baptist on a platter." [26]The king was deeply grieved; yet out of regard for his oaths and for the guests, he did not want to refuse her. [27]Immediately the king sent a soldier of the guard with orders to bring John's[q] head. He went and beheaded him in the prison, [28]brought his head on a platter, and gave it to the girl. Then the girl gave it to her mother. [29]When his disciples heard about it, they came and took his body, and laid it in a tomb.

Feeding the Five Thousand

30 The apostles gathered around Jesus, and told him all that they had done and taught. [31]He said to them, "Come away to a deserted place all by yourselves and rest a while." For many were coming and going, and they had no leisure even to eat. [32]And they went away in the boat to a deserted place by themselves. [33]Now many saw them going and recognized them, and they hurried there on foot from all the towns and arrived ahead of them. [34]As he went ashore, he saw a great crowd; and he had compassion for them, because they were like sheep without a shepherd; and he began to teach them many things. [35]When it grew late, his disciples came to him and said, "This is a deserted place, and the hour is now very late; [36]send them away so that they may go into the surrounding country and villages and buy something for themselves to eat." [37]But he answered them, "You give them something to eat." They said to him, "Are we to go and buy two hundred denarii[r] worth of bread, and give it to them to eat?" [38]And he said to them, "How many loaves have you? Go and see." When they had found out, they said, "Five, and two fish." [39]Then he ordered them to get all the people to sit down in groups on the green grass. [40]So

Ὅ τι ἐάν με αἰτήσῃς δώσω σοι ἕως ἡμίσους τῆς βασιλείας μου. 24 καὶ ἐξελθοῦσα εἶπεν τῇ μητρὶ αὐτῆς, Τί αἰτήσωμαι; ἡ δὲ εἶπεν, Τὴν κεφαλὴν Ἰωάννου τοῦ βαπτίζοντος. 25 καὶ εἰσελθοῦσα εὐθὺς μετὰ σπουδῆς πρὸς τὸν βασιλέα ᾐτήσατο λέγουσα, Θέλω ἵνα ἐξαυτῆς δῷς μοι ἐπὶ πίνακι τὴν κεφαλὴν Ἰωάννου τοῦ βαπτιστοῦ. 26 καὶ περίλυπος γενόμενος ὁ βασιλεὺς διὰ τοὺς ὅρκους καὶ τοὺς ἀνακειμένους οὐκ ἠθέλησεν ἀθετῆσαι αὐτήν· 27 καὶ εὐθὺς ἀποστείλας ὁ βασιλεὺς σπεκουλάτορα ἐπέταξεν ἐνέγκαι τὴν κεφαλὴν αὐτοῦ. καὶ ἀπελθὼν ἀπεκεφάλισεν αὐτὸν ἐν τῇ φυλακῇ 28 καὶ ἤνεγκεν τὴν κεφαλὴν αὐτοῦ ἐπὶ πίνακι καὶ ἔδωκεν αὐτὴν τῷ κορασίῳ, καὶ τὸ κοράσιον ἔδωκεν αὐτὴν τῇ μητρὶ αὐτῆς. 29 καὶ ἀκούσαντες οἱ μαθηταὶ αὐτοῦ ἦλθον καὶ ἦραν τὸ πτῶμα αὐτοῦ καὶ ἔθηκαν αὐτὸ ἐν μνημείῳ.

30 Καὶ συνάγονται οἱ ἀπόστολοι πρὸς τὸν Ἰησοῦν καὶ ἀπήγγειλαν αὐτῷ πάντα ὅσα ἐποίησαν καὶ ὅσα ἐδίδαξαν. 31 καὶ λέγει αὐτοῖς, Δεῦτε ὑμεῖς αὐτοὶ κατ᾽ ἰδίαν εἰς ἔρημον τόπον καὶ ἀναπαύσασθε ὀλίγον. ἦσαν γὰρ οἱ ἐρχόμενοι καὶ οἱ ὑπάγοντες πολλοί, καὶ οὐδὲ φαγεῖν εὐκαίρουν. 32 καὶ ἀπῆλθον ἐν τῷ πλοίῳ εἰς ἔρημον τόπον κατ᾽ ἰδίαν. 33 καὶ εἶδον αὐτοὺς ὑπάγοντας καὶ ἐπέγνωσαν πολλοὶ καὶ πεζῇ ἀπὸ πασῶν τῶν πόλεων συνέδραμον ἐκεῖ καὶ προῆλθον αὐτούς. 34 καὶ ἐξελθὼν εἶδεν πολὺν ὄχλον καὶ ἐσπλαγχνίσθη ἐπ᾽ αὐτούς, ὅτι ἦσαν ὡς πρόβατα μὴ ἔχοντα ποιμένα, καὶ ἤρξατο διδάσκειν αὐτοὺς πολλά. 35 Καὶ ἤδη ὥρας πολλῆς γενομένης προσελθόντες αὐτῷ οἱ μαθηταὶ αὐτοῦ ἔλεγον ὅτι Ἔρημός ἐστιν ὁ τόπος καὶ ἤδη ὥρα πολλή· 36 ἀπόλυσον αὐτούς, ἵνα ἀπελθόντες εἰς τοὺς κύκλῳ ἀγροὺς καὶ κώμας ἀγοράσωσιν ἑαυτοῖς τί φάγωσιν. 37 ὁ δὲ ἀποκριθεὶς εἶπεν αὐτοῖς, Δότε αὐτοῖς ὑμεῖς φαγεῖν. καὶ λέγουσιν αὐτῷ, Ἀπελθόντες ἀγοράσωμεν δηναρίων διακοσίων ἄρτους καὶ δώσομεν αὐτοῖς φαγεῖν; 38 ὁ δὲ λέγει αὐτοῖς, Πόσους ἄρτους ἔχετε; ὑπάγετε ἴδετε. καὶ γνόντες λέγουσιν, Πέντε, καὶ δύο ἰχθύας. 39 καὶ ἐπέταξεν αὐτοῖς ἀνακλῖναι πάντας συμπόσια συμπόσια ἐπὶ τῷ χλωρῷ χόρτῳ. 40 καὶ ἀνέπεσαν

"Whatever you ask I will give you, up to half my kingdom."

[24]She went out and said to her mother, "What shall I ask for?"

"The head of John the Baptist," she answered.

[25]At once the girl hurried in to the king with the request: "I want you to give me right now the head of John the Baptist on a platter."

[26]The king was greatly distressed, but because of his oaths and his dinner guests, he did not want to refuse her. [27]So he immediately sent an executioner with orders to bring John's head. The man went, beheaded John in the prison, [28]and brought back his head on a platter. He presented it to the girl, and she gave it to her mother. [29]On hearing of this, John's disciples came and took his body and laid it in a tomb.

Jesus Feeds the Five Thousand

[30]The apostles gathered around Jesus and reported to him all they had done and taught. [31]Then, because so many people were coming and going that they did not even have a chance to eat, he said to them, "Come with me by yourselves to a quiet place and get some rest."

[32]So they went away by themselves in a boat to a solitary place. [33]But many who saw them leaving recognized them and ran on foot from all the towns and got there ahead of them. [34]When Jesus landed and saw a large crowd, he had compassion on them, because they were like sheep without a shepherd. So he began teaching them many things.

[35]By this time it was late in the day, so his disciples came to him. "This is a remote place," they said, "and it's already very late. [36]Send the people away so they can go to the surrounding countryside and villages and buy themselves something to eat."

[37]But he answered, "You give them something to eat."

They said to him, "That would take eight months of a man's wages[e]! Are we to go and spend that much on bread and give it to them to eat?"

[38]"How many loaves do you have?" he asked. "Go and see."

When they found out, they said, "Five— and two fish."

[39]Then Jesus directed them to have all the people sit down in groups on the green

NRSV

they sat down in groups of hundreds and of fifties. 41Taking the five loaves and the two fish, he looked up to heaven, and blessed and broke the loaves, and gave them to his disciples to set before the people; and he divided the two fish among them all. 42And all ate and were filled; 43and they took up twelve baskets full of broken pieces and of the fish. 44Those who had eaten the loaves numbered five thousand men.

Jesus Walks on the Water

45 Immediately he made his disciples get into the boat and go on ahead to the other side, to Bethsaida, while he dismissed the crowd. 46After saying farewell to them, he went up on the mountain to pray.

47 When evening came, the boat was out on the sea, and he was alone on the land. 48When he saw that they were straining at the oars against an adverse wind, he came towards them early in the morning, walking on the sea. He intended to pass them by. 49But when they saw him walking on the sea, they thought it was a ghost and cried out; 50for they all saw him and were terrified. But immediately he spoke to them and said, "Take heart, it is I; do not be afraid." 51Then he got into the boat with them and the wind ceased. And they were utterly astounded, 52for they did not understand about the loaves, but their hearts were hardened.

Healing the Sick in Gennesaret

53 When they had crossed over, they came to land at Gennesaret and moored the boat. 54When they got out of the boat, people at once recognized him, 55and rushed about that whole region and began to bring the sick on mats to wherever they heard he was. 56And wherever he went, into villages or cities or farms, they laid the sick in the marketplaces, and begged him that they might touch even the fringe of his cloak; and all who touched it were healed.

The Tradition of the Elders

7 Now when the Pharisees and some of the scribes who had come from Jerusalem gathered around him, 2they noticed that some of his disciples were eating with defiled hands, that is, without washing them. 3(For the Pharisees, and all the Jews,

Greek

πρασιαὶ πρασιαὶ κατὰ ἑκατὸν καὶ κατὰ πεντήκοντα. 41 καὶ λαβὼν τοὺς πέντε ἄρτους καὶ τοὺς δύο ἰχθύας ἀναβλέψας εἰς τὸν οὐρανὸν εὐλόγησεν καὶ κατέκλασεν τοὺς ἄρτους καὶ ἐδίδου τοῖς μαθηταῖς [αὐτοῦ] ἵνα παρατιθῶσιν αὐτοῖς, καὶ τοὺς δύο ἰχθύας ἐμέρισεν πᾶσιν. 42 καὶ ἔφαγον πάντες καὶ ἐχορτάσθησαν, 43 καὶ ἦραν κλάσματα δώδεκα κοφίνων πληρώματα καὶ ἀπὸ τῶν ἰχθύων. 44 καὶ ἦσαν οἱ φαγόντες [τοὺς ἄρτους]g πεντακισχίλιοι ἄνδρες.

45 Καὶ εὐθὺς ἠνάγκασεν τοὺς μαθητὰς αὐτοῦ ἐμβῆναι εἰς τὸ πλοῖον καὶ προάγειν εἰς τὸ πέρανh πρὸς Βηθσαϊδάν, ἕως αὐτὸς ἀπολύει τὸν ὄχλον. 46 καὶ ἀποταξάμενος αὐτοῖς ἀπῆλθεν εἰς τὸ ὄρος προσεύξασθαι. 47 καὶ ὀψίας γενομένης ἦν τὸ πλοῖον ἐν μέσῳ τῆς θαλάσσης, καὶ αὐτὸς μόνος ἐπὶ τῆς γῆς. 48 καὶ ἰδὼν αὐτοὺς βασανιζομένους ἐν τῷ ἐλαύνειν, ἦν γὰρ ὁ ἄνεμος ἐναντίος αὐτοῖς, περὶ τετάρτην φυλακὴν τῆς νυκτὸς ἔρχεται πρὸς αὐτοὺς περιπατῶν ἐπὶ τῆς θαλάσσης καὶ ἤθελεν παρελθεῖν αὐτούς. 49 οἱ δὲ ἰδόντες αὐτὸν ἐπὶ τῆς θαλάσσης περιπατοῦντα ἔδοξαν ὅτι φάντασμά ἐστιν, καὶ ἀνέκραξαν· 50 πάντες γὰρ αὐτὸν εἶδον καὶ ἐταράχθησαν. ὁ δὲ εὐθὺς ἐλάλησεν μετ' αὐτῶν, καὶ λέγει αὐτοῖς, Θαρσεῖτε, ἐγώ εἰμι· μὴ φοβεῖσθε. 51 καὶ ἀνέβη πρὸς αὐτοὺς εἰς τὸ πλοῖον καὶ ἐκόπασεν ὁ ἄνεμος, καὶ λίαν [ἐκ περισσοῦ] ἐν ἑαυτοῖς ἐξίσταντο· 52 οὐ γὰρ συνῆκαν ἐπὶ τοῖς ἄρτοις, ἀλλ' ἦν αὐτῶν ἡ καρδία πεπωρωμένη.

53 Καὶ διαπεράσαντες ἐπὶ τὴν γῆν ἦλθον εἰς Γεννησαρὲτ καὶ προσωρμίσθησαν. 54 καὶ ἐξελθόντων αὐτῶν ἐκ τοῦ πλοίου εὐθὺς ἐπιγνόντες αὐτὸν 55 περιέδραμον ὅλην τὴν χώραν ἐκείνην καὶ ἤρξαντο ἐπὶ τοῖς κραβάττοις τοὺς κακῶς ἔχοντας περιφέρειν ὅπου ἤκουον ὅτι ἐστίν. 56 καὶ ὅπου ἂν εἰσεπορεύετο εἰς κώμας ἢ εἰς πόλεις ἢ εἰς ἀγρούς, ἐν ταῖς ἀγοραῖς ἐτίθεσαν τοὺς ἀσθενοῦντας καὶ παρεκάλουν αὐτὸν ἵνα κἂν τοῦ κρασπέδου τοῦ ἱματίου αὐτοῦ ἅψωνται· καὶ ὅσοι ἂν ἥψαντο αὐτοῦ ἐσῴζοντο.

7 Καὶ συνάγονται πρὸς αὐτὸν οἱ Φαρισαῖοι καί τινες τῶν γραμματέων ἐλθόντες ἀπὸ Ἱεροσολύμων. 2 καὶ ἰδόντες τινὰς τῶν μαθητῶν αὐτοῦ ὅτι κοιναῖς χερσίν, τοῦτ' ἔστιν ἀνίπτοις, ἐσθίουσιν τοὺς ἄρτους 3 — οἱ γὰρ

g44 NIV text omits τοὺς ἄρτους   h45 NIV text omits εἰς τὸ πέραν

NIV

grass. 40So they sat down in groups of hundreds and fifties. 41Taking the five loaves and the two fish and looking up to heaven, he gave thanks and broke the loaves. Then he gave them to his disciples to set before the people. He also divided the two fish among them all. 42They all ate and were satisfied, 43and the disciples picked up twelve basketfuls of broken pieces of bread and fish. 44The number of the men who had eaten was five thousand.

Jesus Walks on the Water

45Immediately Jesus made his disciples get into the boat and go on ahead of him to Bethsaida, while he dismissed the crowd. 46After leaving them, he went up on a mountainside to pray.

47When evening came, the boat was in the middle of the lake, and he was alone on land. 48He saw the disciples straining at the oars, because the wind was against them. About the fourth watch of the night he went out to them, walking on the lake. He was about to pass by them, 49but when they saw him walking on the lake, they thought he was a ghost. They cried out, 50because they all saw him and were terrified.

Immediately he spoke to them and said, "Take courage! It is I. Don't be afraid." 51Then he climbed into the boat with them, and the wind died down. They were completely amazed, 52for they had not understood about the loaves; their hearts were hardened.

53When they had crossed over, they landed at Gennesaret and anchored there. 54As soon as they got out of the boat, people recognized Jesus. 55They ran throughout that whole region and carried the sick on mats to wherever they heard he was. 56And wherever he went—into villages, towns or countryside—they placed the sick in the marketplaces. They begged him to let them touch even the edge of his cloak, and all who touched him were healed.

Clean and Unclean

7 The Pharisees and some of the teachers of the law who had come from Jerusalem gathered around Jesus and 2saw some of his disciples eating food with hands that were "unclean," that is, unwashed. 3(The Pharisees and all the Jews

NRSV

do not eat unless they thoroughly wash their hands,[s] thus observing the tradition of the elders; [4]and they do not eat anything from the market unless they wash it;[t] and there are also many other traditions that they observe, the washing of cups, pots, and bronze kettles.[u] [5]So the Pharisees and the scribes asked him, "Why do your disciples not live[v] according to the tradition of the elders, but eat with defiled hands?" [6]He said to them, "Isaiah prophesied rightly about you hypocrites, as it is written,

'This people honors me with their lips,
    but their hearts are far from me;
[7] in vain do they worship me,
    teaching human precepts as
        doctrines.'

[8]You abandon the commandment of God and hold to human tradition."

[9] Then he said to them, "You have a fine way of rejecting the commandment of God in order to keep your tradition! [10]For Moses said, 'Honor your father and your mother'; and, 'Whoever speaks evil of father or mother must surely die.' [11]But you say that if anyone tells father or mother, 'Whatever support you might have had from me is Corban' (that is, an offering to God[w])— [12]then you no longer permit doing anything for a father or mother, [13]thus making void the word of God through your tradition that you have handed on. And you do many things like this."

[14] Then he called the crowd again and said to them, "Listen to me, all of you, and understand: [15]there is nothing outside a person that by going in can defile, but the things that come out are what defile."[x]

[17] When he had left the crowd and entered the house, his disciples asked him about the parable. [18]He said to them, "Then do you also fail to understand? Do you not see that whatever goes into a person from outside cannot defile, [19]since it enters, not the heart but the stomach, and goes out

---

Greek

Φαρισαῖοι καὶ πάντες οἱ Ἰουδαῖοι ἐὰν μὴ πυγμῇ νίψωνται τὰς χεῖρας οὐκ ἐσθίουσιν, κρατοῦντες τὴν παράδοσιν τῶν πρεσβυτέρων, **4** καὶ ἀπ᾽ ἀγορᾶς[a] ἐὰν μὴ βαπτίσωνται οὐκ ἐσθίουσιν, καὶ ἄλλα πολλά ἐστιν ἃ παρέλαβον κρατεῖν, βαπτισμοὺς ποτηρίων καὶ ξεστῶν καὶ χαλκίων [καὶ κλινῶν][b] — **5** καὶ ἐπερωτῶσιν αὐτὸν οἱ Φαρισαῖοι καὶ οἱ γραμματεῖς, Διὰ τί οὐ περιπατοῦσιν οἱ μαθηταί σου κατὰ τὴν παράδοσιν τῶν πρεσβυτέρων, ἀλλὰ κοιναῖς χερσὶν ἐσθίουσιν τὸν ἄρτον; **6** ὁ δὲ εἶπεν αὐτοῖς, Καλῶς ἐπροφήτευσεν Ἠσαΐας περὶ ὑμῶν τῶν ὑποκριτῶν, ὡς γέγραπται [ὅτι]

Οὗτος ὁ λαὸς τοῖς χείλεσίν με
    τιμᾷ,
ἡ δὲ καρδία αὐτῶν πόρρω
    ἀπέχει ἀπ᾽ ἐμοῦ·
7 μάτην δὲ σέβονταί με
    διδάσκοντες διδασκαλίας
    ἐντάλματα ἀνθρώπων.

8 ἀφέντες τὴν ἐντολὴν τοῦ θεοῦ κρατεῖτε τὴν παράδοσιν τῶν ἀνθρώπων. **9** Καὶ ἔλεγεν αὐτοῖς, Καλῶς ἀθετεῖτε τὴν ἐντολὴν τοῦ θεοῦ, ἵνα τὴν παράδοσιν ὑμῶν στήσητε[c]. **10** Μωϋσῆς γὰρ εἶπεν, Τίμα τὸν πατέρα σου καὶ τὴν μητέρα σου, καί, Ὁ κακολογῶν πατέρα ἢ μητέρα θανάτῳ τελευτάτω. **11** ὑμεῖς δὲ λέγετε, Ἐὰν εἴπῃ ἄνθρωπος τῷ πατρὶ ἢ τῇ μητρί, Κορβᾶν, ὅ ἐστιν, Δῶρον, ὃ ἐὰν ἐξ ἐμοῦ ὠφεληθῇς, **12** οὐκέτι ἀφίετε αὐτὸν οὐδὲν ποιῆσαι τῷ πατρὶ ἢ τῇ μητρί, **13** ἀκυροῦντες τὸν λόγον τοῦ θεοῦ τῇ παραδόσει ὑμῶν ᾗ παρεδώκατε· καὶ παρόμοια τοιαῦτα πολλὰ ποιεῖτε.

14 Καὶ προσκαλεσάμενος πάλιν τὸν ὄχλον ἔλεγεν αὐτοῖς, Ἀκούσατέ μου πάντες καὶ σύνετε. **15** οὐδέν ἐστιν ἔξωθεν τοῦ ἀνθρώπου εἰσπορευόμενον εἰς αὐτὸν ὃ δύναται κοινῶσαι αὐτόν, ἀλλὰ τὰ ἐκ τοῦ ἀνθρώπου ἐκπορευόμενά ἐστιν τὰ κοινοῦντα τὸν ἄνθρωπον.[d] **17** Καὶ ὅτε εἰσῆλθεν εἰς[e] οἶκον ἀπὸ τοῦ ὄχλου, ἐπηρώτων αὐτὸν οἱ μαθηταὶ αὐτοῦ τὴν παραβολήν. **18** καὶ λέγει αὐτοῖς, Οὕτως καὶ ὑμεῖς ἀσύνετοί ἐστε; οὐ νοεῖτε ὅτι πᾶν τὸ ἔξωθεν εἰσπορευόμενον εἰς τὸν ἄνθρωπον οὐ δύναται αὐτὸν κοινῶσαι **19** ὅτι οὐκ εἰσπορεύεται αὐτοῦ εἰς τὴν καρδίαν ἀλλ᾽ εἰς τὴν κοιλίαν, καὶ εἰς τὸν

NIV

do not eat unless they give their hands a ceremonial washing, holding to the tradition of the elders. [4]When they come from the marketplace they do not eat unless they wash. And they observe many other traditions, such as the washing of cups, pitchers and kettles.[a])

[5]So the Pharisees and teachers of the law asked Jesus, "Why don't your disciples live according to the tradition of the elders instead of eating their food with 'unclean' hands?"

[6]He replied, "Isaiah was right when he prophesied about you hypocrites; as it is written:

" 'These people honor me with their lips,
    but their hearts are far from me.
[7]They worship me in vain;
    their teachings are but rules taught by
        men.'[b]

[8]You have let go of the commands of God and are holding on to the traditions of men."

[9]And he said to them: "You have a fine way of setting aside the commands of God in order to observe[c] your own traditions! [10]For Moses said, 'Honor your father and your mother,'[d] and, 'Anyone who curses his father or mother must be put to death.'[e] [11]But you say that if a man says to his father or mother: 'Whatever help you might otherwise have received from me is Corban' (that is, a gift devoted to God), [12]then you no longer let him do anything for his father or mother. [13]Thus you nullify the word of God by your tradition that you have handed down. And you do many things like that."

[14]Again Jesus called the crowd to him and said, "Listen to me, everyone, and understand this. [15]Nothing outside a man can make him 'unclean' by going into him. Rather, it is what comes out of a man that makes him 'unclean.'[f]

[17]After he had left the crowd and entered the house, his disciples asked him about this parable. [18]"Are you so dull?" he asked. "Don't you see that nothing that enters a man from the outside can make him 'unclean'? [19]For it doesn't go into his heart but into his stomach, and then out of

---

[s] Meaning of Gk uncertain   [t] Other ancient authorities read *and when they come from the marketplace, they do not eat unless they purify themselves*   [u] Other ancient authorities add *and beds*   [v] Gk *walk*   [w] Gk lacks *to God*   [x] Other ancient authorities add verse 16, *"Let anyone with ears to hear listen"*

[a]4 NIV text and NRSV note t add ὅταν ἔλθωσιν   [b]4 NIV/NRSV texts omit καὶ κλινῶν; NIV/NRSV notes as UBS   [c]9 NIV text τηρήσητε; NIV note as UBS   [d]15 NIV/NRSV notes add 16 εἴ τις ἔχει ὦτα ἀκούειν ἀκουέτω.   [e]17 NIV text adds τὸν †

[a]4 Some early manuscripts *pitchers, kettles and dining couches*   [b]6,7 Isaiah 29:13   [c]9 Some manuscripts *set up*   [d]10 Exodus 20:12; Deut. 5:16   [e]10 Exodus 21:17; Lev. 20:9   [f]15 Some early manuscripts *'unclean.'* [16]*If anyone has ears to hear, let him hear.*

into the sewer?" (Thus he declared all foods clean.) 20And he said, "It is what comes out of a person that defiles. 21For it is from within, from the human heart, that evil intentions come: fornication, theft, murder, 22adultery, avarice, wickedness, deceit, licentiousness, envy, slander, pride, folly. 23All these evil things come from within, and they defile a person."

The Syrophoenician Woman's Faith

24 From there he set out and went away to the region of Tyre.y He entered a house and did not want anyone to know he was there. Yet he could not escape notice, 25but a woman whose little daughter had an unclean spirit immediately heard about him, and she came and bowed down at his feet. 26Now the woman was a Gentile, of Syrophoenician origin. She begged him to cast the demon out of her daughter. 27He said to her, "Let the children be fed first, for it is not fair to take the children's food and throw it to the dogs." 28But she answered him, "Sir,z even the dogs under the table eat the children's crumbs." 29Then he said to her, "For saying that, you may go—the demon has left your daughter." 30So she went home, found the child lying on the bed, and the demon gone.

Jesus Cures a Deaf Man

31 Then he returned from the region of Tyre, and went by way of Sidon towards the Sea of Galilee, in the region of the Decapolis. 32They brought to him a deaf man who had an impediment in his speech; and they begged him to lay his hand on him. 33He took him aside in private, away from the crowd, and put his fingers into his ears, and he spat and touched his tongue. 34Then looking up to heaven, he sighed and said to him, "Ephphatha," that is, "Be opened." 35And immediately his ears were opened, his tongue was released, and he spoke plainly. 36Then Jesusa ordered them to tell no one; but the more he ordered them, the more zealously they proclaimed it. 37They were astounded beyond measure, saying, "He has done everything well; he even makes the deaf to hear and the mute to speak."

ἀφεδρῶνα ἐκπορεύεται, καθαρίζων πάντα τὰ βρώματα; 20 ἔλεγεν δὲ ὅτι Τὸ ἐκ τοῦ ἀνθρώπου ἐκπορευόμενον, ἐκεῖνο κοινοῖ τὸν ἄνθρωπον. 21 ἔσωθεν γὰρ ἐκ τῆς καρδίας τῶν ἀνθρώπων οἱ διαλογισμοὶ οἱ κακοὶ ἐκπορεύονται, πορνεῖαι, κλοπαί, φόνοι, 22 μοιχεῖαι, πλεονεξίαι, πονηρίαι, δόλος, ἀσέλγεια, ὀφθαλμὸς πονηρός, βλασφημία, ὑπερηφανία, ἀφροσύνη· 23 πάντα ταῦτα τὰ πονηρὰ ἔσωθεν ἐκπορεύεται καὶ κοινοῖ τὸν ἄνθρωπον.

24 Ἐκεῖθεν δὲ ἀναστὰς ἀπῆλθεν εἰς τὰ ὅρια Τύρουf. καὶ εἰσελθὼν εἰς οἰκίαν οὐδένα ἤθελεν γνῶναι, καὶ οὐκ ἠδυνήθη λαθεῖν· 25 ἀλλ' εὐθὺς ἀκούσασα γυνὴ περὶ αὐτοῦ, ἧς εἶχεν τὸ θυγάτριον αὐτῆς πνεῦμα ἀκάθαρτον, ἐλθοῦσα προσέπεσεν πρὸς τοὺς πόδας αὐτοῦ· 26 ἡ δὲ γυνὴ ἦν Ἑλληνίς, Συροφοινίκισσα τῷ γένει· καὶ ἠρώτα αὐτὸν ἵνα τὸ δαιμόνιον ἐκβάλῃ ἐκ τῆς θυγατρὸς αὐτῆς. 27 καὶ ἔλεγεν αὐτῇ, Ἄφες πρῶτον χορτασθῆναι τὰ τέκνα, οὐ γάρ ἐστιν καλὸν λαβεῖν τὸν ἄρτον τῶν τέκνων καὶ τοῖς κυναρίοις βαλεῖν. 28 ἡ δὲ ἀπεκρίθη καὶ λέγει αὐτῷ, Κύριε· καὶ g τὰ κυνάρια ὑποκάτω τῆς τραπέζης ἐσθίουσιν ἀπὸ τῶν ψιχίων τῶν παιδίων. 29 καὶ εἶπεν αὐτῇ, Διὰ τοῦτον τὸν λόγον ὕπαγε, ἐξελήλυθεν ἐκ τῆς θυγατρός σου τὸ δαιμόνιον. 30 καὶ ἀπελθοῦσα εἰς τὸν οἶκον αὐτῆς εὗρεν τὸ παιδίον βεβλημένον ἐπὶ τὴν κλίνην καὶ τὸ δαιμόνιον ἐξεληλυθός.

31 Καὶ πάλιν ἐξελθὼν ἐκ τῶν ὁρίων Τύρου ἦλθεν διὰ Σιδῶνος εἰς τὴν θάλασσαν τῆς Γαλιλαίας ἀνὰ μέσον τῶν ὁρίων Δεκαπόλεως. 32 καὶ φέρουσιν αὐτῷ κωφὸν καὶ μογιλάλον καὶ παρακαλοῦσιν αὐτὸν ἵνα ἐπιθῇ αὐτῷ τὴν χεῖρα. 33 καὶ ἀπολαβόμενος αὐτὸν ἀπὸ τοῦ ὄχλου κατ' ἰδίαν ἔβαλεν τοὺς δακτύλους αὐτοῦ εἰς τὰ ὦτα αὐτοῦ καὶ πτύσας ἥψατο τῆς γλώσσης αὐτοῦ, 34 καὶ ἀναβλέψας εἰς τὸν οὐρανὸν ἐστέναξεν καὶ λέγει αὐτῷ, Εφφαθα, ὅ ἐστιν, Διανοίχθητι. 35 καὶ [εὐθέως] ἠνοίγησαν αὐτοῦ αἱ ἀκοαί, καὶ ἐλύθη ὁ δεσμὸς τῆς γλώσσης αὐτοῦ καὶ ἐλάλει ὀρθῶς. 36 καὶ διεστείλατο αὐτοῖς ἵνα μηδενὶ λέγωσιν· ὅσον δὲ αὐτοῖς διεστέλλετο, αὐτοὶ μᾶλλον περισσότερον ἐκήρυσσον. 37 καὶ ὑπερπερισσῶς ἐξεπλήσσοντο λέγοντες, Καλῶς πάντα πεποίηκεν, καὶ τοὺς κωφοὺς ποιεῖ ἀκούειν καὶ [τοὺς] ἀλάλους λαλεῖν.

his body." (In saying this, Jesus declared all foods "clean.")

20He went on: "What comes out of a man is what makes him 'unclean.' 21For from within, out of men's hearts, come evil thoughts, sexual immorality, theft, murder, adultery, 22greed, malice, deceit, lewdness, envy, slander, arrogance and folly. 23All these evils come from inside and make a man 'unclean.' "

The Faith of a Syrophoenician Woman

24Jesus left that place and went to the vicinity of Tyre.g He entered a house and did not want anyone to know it; yet he could not keep his presence secret. 25In fact, as soon as she heard about him, a woman whose little daughter was possessed by an evilh spirit came and fell at his feet. 26The woman was a Greek, born in Syrian Phoenicia. She begged Jesus to drive the demon out of her daughter.

27"First let the children eat all they want," he told her, "for it is not right to take the children's bread and toss it to their dogs."

28"Yes, Lord," she replied, "but even the dogs under the table eat the children's crumbs."

29Then he told her, "For such a reply, you may go; the demon has left your daughter."

30She went home and found her child lying on the bed, and the demon gone.

The Healing of a Deaf and Mute Man

31Then Jesus left the vicinity of Tyre and went through Sidon, down to the Sea of Galilee and into the region of the Decapolis.i 32There some people brought to him a man who was deaf and could hardly talk, and they begged him to place his hand on the man.

33After he took him aside, away from the crowd, Jesus put his fingers into the man's ears. Then he spit and touched the man's tongue. 34He looked up to heaven and with a deep sigh said to him, "Ephphatha!" (which means, "Be opened!"). 35At this, the man's ears were opened, his tongue was loosened and he began to speak plainly.

36Jesus commanded them not to tell anyone. But the more he did so, the more they kept talking about it. 37People were overwhelmed with amazement. "He has done everything well," they said. "He even makes the deaf hear and the mute speak."

Feeding the Four Thousand

8 In those days when there was again a great crowd without anything to eat, he called his disciples and said to them, [2]"I have compassion for the crowd, because they have been with me now for three days and have nothing to eat. [3]If I send them away hungry to their homes, they will faint on the way—and some of them have come from a great distance." [4]His disciples replied, "How can one feed these people with bread here in the desert?" [5]He asked them, "How many loaves do you have?" They said, "Seven." [6]Then he ordered the crowd to sit down on the ground; and he took the seven loaves, and after giving thanks he broke them and gave them to his disciples to distribute; and they distributed them to the crowd. [7]They had also a few small fish; and after blessing them, he ordered that these too should be distributed. [8]They ate and were filled; and they took up the broken pieces left over, seven baskets full. [9]Now there were about four thousand people. And he sent them away. [10]And immediately he got into the boat with his disciples and went to the district of Dalmanutha.[b]

The Demand for a Sign

[11] The Pharisees came and began to argue with him, asking him for a sign from heaven, to test him. [12]And he sighed deeply in his spirit and said, "Why does this generation ask for a sign? Truly I tell you, no sign will be given to this generation." [13]And he left them, and getting into the boat again, he went across to the other side.

The Yeast of the Pharisees and of Herod

[14] Now the disciples[c] had forgotten to bring any bread; and they had only one loaf with them in the boat. [15]And he cautioned them, saying, "Watch out—beware of the yeast of the Pharisees and the yeast of Herod."[d] [16]They said to one another, "It is because we have no bread." [17]And becoming aware of it, Jesus said to them, "Why are you talking about having no bread? Do you still not perceive or understand? Are your hearts hardened? [18]Do you have eyes, and fail to see? Do you have ears, and fail to hear? And do you not remember? [19]When I broke the five loaves for the five thousand, how many baskets full of broken pieces did you collect?" They said to him, "Twelve." [20]"And the seven

[b] Other ancient authorities read *Mageda* or *Magdala*
[c] Gk *they*   [d] Other ancient authorities read *the Herodians*

8 Ἐν ἐκείναις ταῖς ἡμέραις πάλιν πολλοῦ ὄχλου ὄντος καὶ μὴ ἐχόντων τί φάγωσιν, προσκαλεσάμενος τοὺς μαθητὰς λέγει αὐτοῖς, **2** Σπλαγχνίζομαι ἐπὶ τὸν ὄχλον, ὅτι ἤδη ἡμέραι τρεῖς προσμένουσίν μοι καὶ οὐκ ἔχουσιν τί φάγωσιν· **3** καὶ ἐὰν ἀπολύσω αὐτοὺς νήστεις εἰς οἶκον αὐτῶν, ἐκλυθήσονται ἐν τῇ ὁδῷ· καί τινες αὐτῶν ἀπὸ μακρόθεν ἥκασιν. **4** καὶ ἀπεκρίθησαν αὐτῷ οἱ μαθηταὶ αὐτοῦ ὅτι Πόθεν τούτους δυνήσεταί τις ὧδε χορτάσαι ἄρτων ἐπ' ἐρημίας; **5** καὶ ἠρώτα αὐτούς, Πόσους ἔχετε ἄρτους; οἱ δὲ εἶπαν, Ἑπτά. **6** καὶ παραγγέλλει τῷ ὄχλῳ ἀναπεσεῖν ἐπὶ τῆς γῆς· καὶ λαβὼν τοὺς ἑπτὰ ἄρτους εὐχαριστήσας ἔκλασεν καὶ ἐδίδου τοῖς μαθηταῖς αὐτοῦ ἵνα παρατιθῶσιν, καὶ παρέθηκαν τῷ ὄχλῳ. **7** καὶ εἶχον ἰχθύδια ὀλίγα· καὶ εὐλογήσας αὐτὰ εἶπεν καὶ ταῦτα παρατιθέναι. **8** καὶ ἔφαγον καὶ ἐχορτάσθησαν, καὶ ἦραν περισσεύματα κλασμάτων ἑπτὰ σπυρίδας. **9** ἦσαν δὲ ὡς τετρακισχίλιοι. καὶ ἀπέλυσεν αὐτούς. **10** Καὶ εὐθὺς ἐμβὰς εἰς τὸ πλοῖον μετὰ τῶν μαθητῶν αὐτοῦ ἦλθεν εἰς τὰ μέρη Δαλμανουθά[a].

11 Καὶ ἐξῆλθον οἱ Φαρισαῖοι καὶ ἤρξαντο συζητεῖν αὐτῷ, ζητοῦντες παρ' αὐτοῦ σημεῖον ἀπὸ τοῦ οὐρανοῦ, πειράζοντες αὐτόν. **12** καὶ ἀναστενάξας τῷ πνεύματι αὐτοῦ λέγει, Τί ἡ γενεὰ αὕτη ζητεῖ σημεῖον; ἀμὴν λέγω ὑμῖν, εἰ δοθήσεται τῇ γενεᾷ ταύτῃ σημεῖον. **13** καὶ ἀφεὶς αὐτοὺς πάλιν ἐμβὰς[b] ἀπῆλθεν εἰς τὸ πέραν.

14 Καὶ ἐπελάθοντο λαβεῖν ἄρτους καὶ εἰ μὴ ἕνα ἄρτον οὐκ εἶχον μεθ' ἑαυτῶν ἐν τῷ πλοίῳ. **15** καὶ διεστέλλετο αὐτοῖς λέγων, Ὁρᾶτε, βλέπετε ἀπὸ τῆς ζύμης τῶν Φαρισαίων καὶ τῆς ζύμης Ἡρῴδου[c]. **16** καὶ διελογίζοντο πρὸς ἀλλήλους[d] ὅτι Ἄρτους οὐκ ἔχουσιν. **17** καὶ γνοὺς[e] λέγει αὐτοῖς, Τί διαλογίζεσθε ὅτι ἄρτους οὐκ ἔχετε; οὔπω νοεῖτε οὐδὲ συνίετε; πεπωρωμένην ἔχετε τὴν καρδίαν ὑμῶν; **18** ὀφθαλμοὺς ἔχοντες οὐ βλέπετε καὶ ὦτα ἔχοντες οὐκ ἀκούετε; καὶ οὐ μνημονεύετε, **19** ὅτε τοὺς πέντε ἄρτους ἔκλασα εἰς τοὺς πεντακισχιλίους, πόσους κοφίνους κλασμάτων πλήρεις ἤρατε; λέγουσιν αὐτῷ, Δώδεκα. **20** Ὅτε[f] τοὺς ἑπτὰ εἰς

[a]10 NRSV note b *Μαγεδά* or *Μαγδαλά* [b]13 NIV text *ἐμβὰς πάλιν εἰς τὸ πλοῖον* † [c]15 NRSV note d *τῶν Ἡρῳδιανῶν* [d]16 NIV text adds *λέγοντες* † [e]17 NIV text adds *ὁ Ἰησοῦς* † [f]20 NIV text add *καὶ* †

Jesus Feeds the Four Thousand

8 During those days another large crowd gathered. Since they had nothing to eat, Jesus called his disciples to him and said, [2]"I have compassion for these people; they have already been with me three days and have nothing to eat. [3]If I send them home hungry, they will collapse on the way, because some of them have come a long distance."

[4]His disciples answered, "But where in this remote place can anyone get enough bread to feed them?"

[5]"How many loaves do you have?" Jesus asked.

"Seven," they replied.

[6]He told the crowd to sit down on the ground. When he had taken the seven loaves and given thanks, he broke them and gave them to his disciples to set before the people, and they did so. [7]They had a few small fish as well; he gave thanks for them also and told the disciples to distribute them. [8]The people ate and were satisfied. Afterward the disciples picked up seven basketfuls of broken pieces that were left over. [9]About four thousand men were present. And having sent them away, [10]he got into the boat with his disciples and went to the region of Dalmanutha.

[11]The Pharisees came and began to question Jesus. To test him, they asked him for a sign from heaven. [12]He sighed deeply and said, "Why does this generation ask for a miraculous sign? I tell you the truth, no sign will be given to it." [13]Then he left them, got back into the boat and crossed to the other side.

The Yeast of the Pharisees and Herod

[14]The disciples had forgotten to bring bread, except for one loaf they had with them in the boat. [15]"Be careful," Jesus warned them. "Watch out for the yeast of the Pharisees and that of Herod."

[16]They discussed this with one another and said, "It is because we have no bread."

[17]Aware of their discussion, Jesus asked them: "Why are you talking about having no bread? Do you still not see or understand? Are your hearts hardened? [18]Do you have eyes but fail to see, and ears but fail to hear? And don't you remember? [19]When I broke the five loaves for the five thousand, how many basketfuls of pieces did you pick up?"

"Twelve," they replied.

[20]"And when I broke the seven loaves

for the four thousand, how many baskets full of broken pieces did you collect?" And they said to him, "Seven." [21]Then he said to them, "Do you not yet understand?"

Jesus Cures a Blind Man at Bethsaida

22 They came to Bethsaida. Some people[e] brought a blind man to him and begged him to touch him. [23]He took the blind man by the hand and led him out of the village; and when he had put saliva on his eyes and laid his hands on him, he asked him, "Can you see anything?" [24]And the man[f] looked up and said, "I can see people, but they look like trees, walking." [25]Then Jesus[f] laid his hands on his eyes again; and he looked intently and his sight was restored, and he saw everything clearly. [26]Then he sent him away to his home, saying, "Do not even go into the village."[g]

Peter's Declaration about Jesus

27 Jesus went on with his disciples to the villages of Caesarea Philippi; and on the way he asked his disciples, "Who do people say that I am?" [28]And they answered him, "John the Baptist; and others, Elijah; and still others, one of the prophets." [29]He asked them, "But who do you say that I am?" Peter answered him, "You are the Messiah."[h] [30]And he sternly ordered them not to tell anyone about him.

Jesus Foretells His Death and Resurrection

31 Then he began to teach them that the Son of Man must undergo great suffering, and be rejected by the elders, the chief priests, and the scribes, and be killed, and after three days rise again. [32]He said all this quite openly. And Peter took him aside and began to rebuke him. [33]But turning and looking at his disciples, he rebuked Peter and said, "Get behind me, Satan! For you are setting your mind not on divine things but on human things."

34 He called the crowd with his disciples, and said to them, "If any want to become my followers, let them deny themselves and take up their cross and follow me. [35]For those who want to save their life will lose it, and those who lose their life for my sake, and for the sake of the gospel,[i] will

τοὺς τετρακισχιλίους, πόσων σπυρίδων πληρώματα κλασμάτων ἤρατε; καὶ λέγουσιν [αὐτῷ], Ἑπτά. 21 καὶ ἔλεγεν αὐτοῖς, Οὔπω συνίετε;

22 Καὶ ἔρχονται εἰς Βηθσαϊδάν. καὶ φέρουσιν αὐτῷ τυφλὸν καὶ παρακαλοῦσιν αὐτὸν ἵνα αὐτοῦ ἅψηται. **23** καὶ ἐπιλαβόμενος τῆς χειρὸς τοῦ τυφλοῦ ἐξήνεγκεν αὐτὸν ἔξω τῆς κώμης καὶ πτύσας εἰς τὰ ὄμματα αὐτοῦ, ἐπιθεὶς τὰς χεῖρας αὐτῷ ἐπηρώτα αὐτόν, Εἴ τι βλέπεις; **24** καὶ ἀναβλέψας ἔλεγεν, Βλέπω τοὺς ἀνθρώπους ὅτι ὡς δένδρα ὁρῶ περιπατοῦντας. **25** εἶτα πάλιν ἐπέθηκεν τὰς χεῖρας ἐπὶ τοὺς ὀφθαλμοὺς αὐτοῦ, καὶ διέβλεψεν καὶ ἀπεκατέστη καὶ ἐνέβλεπεν τηλαυγῶς ἅπαντα. **26** καὶ ἀπέστειλεν αὐτὸν εἰς οἶκον αὐτοῦ λέγων, Μηδὲ εἰς τὴν κώμην εἰσέλθῃς[g].

27 Καὶ ἐξῆλθεν ὁ Ἰησοῦς καὶ οἱ μαθηταὶ αὐτοῦ εἰς τὰς κώμας Καισαρείας τῆς Φιλίππου· καὶ ἐν τῇ ὁδῷ ἐπηρώτα τοὺς μαθητὰς αὐτοῦ λέγων αὐτοῖς, Τίνα με λέγουσιν οἱ ἄνθρωποι εἶναι; **28** οἱ δὲ εἶπαν αὐτῷ λέγοντες [ὅτι] Ἰωάννην τὸν βαπτιστήν, καὶ ἄλλοι, Ἠλίαν, ἄλλοι δὲ ὅτι εἷς τῶν προφητῶν. **29** καὶ αὐτὸς ἐπηρώτα αὐτούς, Ὑμεῖς δὲ τίνα με λέγετε εἶναι; ἀποκριθεὶς ὁ Πέτρος λέγει αὐτῷ, Σὺ εἶ ὁ Χριστός. **30** καὶ ἐπετίμησεν αὐτοῖς ἵνα μηδενὶ λέγωσιν περὶ αὐτοῦ.

31 Καὶ ἤρξατο διδάσκειν αὐτοὺς ὅτι δεῖ τὸν υἱὸν τοῦ ἀνθρώπου πολλὰ παθεῖν καὶ ἀποδοκιμασθῆναι ὑπὸ τῶν πρεσβυτέρων καὶ τῶν ἀρχιερέων καὶ τῶν γραμματέων καὶ ἀποκτανθῆναι καὶ μετὰ τρεῖς ἡμέρας ἀναστῆναι· **32** καὶ παρρησίᾳ τὸν λόγον ἐλάλει. καὶ προσλαβόμενος ὁ Πέτρος αὐτὸν ἤρξατο ἐπιτιμᾶν αὐτῷ. **33** ὁ δὲ ἐπιστραφεὶς καὶ ἰδὼν τοὺς μαθητὰς αὐτοῦ ἐπετίμησεν Πέτρῳ καὶ λέγει, Ὕπαγε ὀπίσω μου, Σατανᾶ, ὅτι οὐ φρονεῖς τὰ τοῦ θεοῦ ἀλλὰ τὰ τῶν ἀνθρώπων. **34** Καὶ προσκαλεσάμενος τὸν ὄχλον σὺν τοῖς μαθηταῖς αὐτοῦ εἶπεν αὐτοῖς, Εἴ τις θέλει ὀπίσω μου ἀκολουθεῖν, ἀπαρνησάσθω ἑαυτὸν καὶ ἀράτω τὸν σταυρὸν αὐτοῦ καὶ ἀκολουθείτω μοι. **35** ὃς γὰρ ἐὰν θέλῃ τὴν ψυχὴν αὐτοῦ σῶσαι ἀπολέσει αὐτήν· ὃς δ' ἂν ἀπολέσει τὴν ψυχὴν αὐτοῦ ἕνεκεν ἐμοῦ καὶ[h] τοῦ εὐαγγελίου σώσει αὐτήν. **36** τί γὰρ

for the four thousand, how many basketfuls of pieces did you pick up?"

They answered, "Seven."

[21]He said to them, "Do you still not understand?"

The Healing of a Blind Man at Bethsaida

[22]They came to Bethsaida, and some people brought a blind man and begged Jesus to touch him. [23]He took the blind man by the hand and led him outside the village. When he had spit on the man's eyes and put his hands on him, Jesus asked, "Do you see anything?"

[24]He looked up and said, "I see people; they look like trees walking around."

[25]Once more Jesus put his hands on the man's eyes. Then his eyes were opened, his sight was restored, and he saw everything clearly. [26]Jesus sent him home, saying, "Don't go into the village.[a]"

Peter's Confession of Christ

[27]Jesus and his disciples went on to the villages around Caesarea Philippi. On the way he asked them, "Who do people say I am?"

[28]They replied, "Some say John the Baptist; others say Elijah; and still others, one of the prophets."

[29]"But what about you?" he asked. "Who do you say I am?"

Peter answered, "You are the Christ.[b]"

[30]Jesus warned them not to tell anyone about him.

Jesus Predicts His Death

[31]He then began to teach them that the Son of Man must suffer many things and be rejected by the elders, chief priests and teachers of the law, and that he must be killed and after three days rise again. [32]He spoke plainly about this, and Peter took him aside and began to rebuke him.

[33]But when Jesus turned and looked at his disciples, he rebuked Peter. "Get behind me, Satan!" he said. "You do not have in mind the things of God, but the things of men."

[34]Then he called the crowd to him along with his disciples and said: "If anyone would come after me, he must deny himself and take up his cross and follow me. [35]For whoever wants to save his life[c] will lose it, but whoever loses his life for me

---

NRSV

save it. [36]For what will it profit them to gain the whole world and forfeit their life? [37]Indeed, what can they give in return for their life? [38]Those who are ashamed of me and of my words[j] in this adulterous and sinful generation, of them the Son of Man will also be ashamed when he comes in the glory of his Father with the holy

9 angels." [1]And he said to them, "Truly I tell you, there are some standing here who will not taste death until they see that the kingdom of God has come with[k] power."

The Transfiguration

2 Six days later, Jesus took with him Peter and James and John, and led them up a high mountain apart, by themselves. And he was transfigured before them, [3]and his clothes became dazzling white, such as no one[l] on earth could bleach them. [4]And there appeared to them Elijah with Moses, who were talking with Jesus. [5]Then Peter said to Jesus, "Rabbi, it is good for us to be here; let us make three dwellings,[m] one for you, one for Moses, and one for Elijah." [6]He did not know what to say, for they were terrified. [7]Then a cloud overshadowed them, and from the cloud there came a voice, "This is my Son, the Beloved;[n] listen to him!" [8]Suddenly when they looked around, they saw no one with them any more, but only Jesus.

The Coming of Elijah

9 As they were coming down the mountain, he ordered them to tell no one about what they had seen, until after the Son of Man had risen from the dead. [10]So they kept the matter to themselves, questioning what this rising from the dead could mean. [11]Then they asked him, "Why do the scribes say that Elijah must come first?" [12]He said to them, "Elijah is indeed coming first to restore all things. How then is it written about the Son of Man, that he is to go through many sufferings and be treated with contempt? [13]But I tell you that Elijah has come, and they did to him whatever they pleased, as it is written about him."

The Healing of a Boy with a Spirit

14 When they came to the disciples, they saw a great crowd around them, and some scribes arguing with them. [15]When the whole crowd saw him, they were immediately overcome with awe, and they ran

[j]Other ancient authorities read *and of mine* [k]Or *in*
[l]Gk *no fuller* [m]Or *tents* [n]Or *my beloved Son*

Greek

ὠφελεῖ ἄνθρωπον κερδῆσαι τὸν κόσμον ὅλον καὶ ζημιωθῆναι τὴν ψυχὴν αὐτοῦ; **37** τί γὰρ δοῖ ἄνθρωπος ἀντάλλαγμα τῆς ψυχῆς αὐτοῦ; **38** ὃς γὰρ ἐὰν ἐπαισχυνθῇ με καὶ τοὺς ἐμοὺς λόγους[i] ἐν τῇ γενεᾷ ταύτῃ τῇ μοιχαλίδι καὶ ἁμαρτωλῷ, καὶ ὁ υἱὸς τοῦ ἀνθρώπου ἐπαισχυνθήσεται αὐτόν, ὅταν ἔλθῃ ἐν τῇ δόξῃ τοῦ πατρὸς αὐτοῦ μετὰ τῶν ἀγγέλων τῶν ἁγίων.

9 Καὶ ἔλεγεν αὐτοῖς, Ἀμὴν λέγω ὑμῖν ὅτι εἰσίν τινες ὧδε τῶν ἑστηκότων οἵτινες οὐ μὴ γεύσωνται θανάτου ἕως ἂν ἴδωσιν τὴν βασιλείαν τοῦ θεοῦ ἐληλυθυῖαν ἐν δυνάμει.

2 Καὶ μετὰ ἡμέρας ἓξ παραλαμβάνει ὁ Ἰησοῦς τὸν Πέτρον καὶ τὸν Ἰάκωβον καὶ τὸν Ἰωάννην καὶ ἀναφέρει αὐτοὺς εἰς ὄρος ὑψηλὸν κατ᾽ ἰδίαν μόνους. καὶ μετεμορφώθη ἔμπροσθεν αὐτῶν, **3** καὶ τὰ ἱμάτια αὐτοῦ ἐγένετο στίλβοντα λευκὰ λίαν, οἷα γναφεὺς ἐπὶ τῆς γῆς οὐ δύναται οὕτως λευκᾶναι. **4** καὶ ὤφθη αὐτοῖς Ἠλίας σὺν Μωϋσεῖ καὶ ἦσαν συλλαλοῦντες τῷ Ἰησοῦ. **5** καὶ ἀποκριθεὶς ὁ Πέτρος λέγει τῷ Ἰησοῦ, Ῥαββί, καλόν ἐστιν ἡμᾶς ὧδε εἶναι, καὶ ποιήσωμεν τρεῖς σκηνάς, σοὶ μίαν καὶ Μωϋσεῖ μίαν καὶ Ἠλίᾳ μίαν. **6** οὐ γὰρ ᾔδει τί ἀποκριθῇ, ἔκφοβοι γὰρ ἐγένοντο. **7** καὶ ἐγένετο νεφέλη ἐπισκιάζουσα αὐτοῖς, καὶ ἐγένετο φωνὴ ἐκ τῆς νεφέλης, Οὗτός ἐστιν ὁ υἱός μου ὁ ἀγαπητός, ἀκούετε αὐτοῦ. **8** καὶ ἐξάπινα περιβλεψάμενοι οὐκέτι οὐδένα εἶδον ἀλλὰ τὸν Ἰησοῦν μόνον μεθ᾽ ἑαυτῶν.

9 Καὶ καταβαινόντων αὐτῶν ἐκ τοῦ ὄρους διεστείλατο αὐτοῖς ἵνα μηδενὶ ἃ εἶδον διηγήσωνται, εἰ μὴ ὅταν ὁ υἱὸς τοῦ ἀνθρώπου ἐκ νεκρῶν ἀναστῇ. **10** καὶ τὸν λόγον ἐκράτησαν πρὸς ἑαυτοὺς συζητοῦντες τί ἐστιν τὸ ἐκ νεκρῶν ἀναστῆναι. **11** καὶ ἐπηρώτων αὐτὸν λέγοντες, Ὅτι λέγουσιν οἱ γραμματεῖς ὅτι Ἠλίαν δεῖ ἐλθεῖν πρῶτον; **12** ὁ δὲ ἔφη αὐτοῖς, Ἠλίας μὲν ἐλθὼν πρῶτον ἀποκαθιστάνει πάντα· καὶ πῶς γέγραπται ἐπὶ τὸν υἱὸν τοῦ ἀνθρώπου ἵνα πολλὰ πάθῃ καὶ ἐξουδενηθῇ; **13** ἀλλὰ λέγω ὑμῖν ὅτι καὶ Ἠλίας ἐλήλυθεν, καὶ ἐποίησαν αὐτῷ ὅσα ἤθελον, καθὼς γέγραπται ἐπ᾽ αὐτόν.

14 Καὶ ἐλθόντες πρὸς τοὺς μαθητὰς εἶδον ὄχλον πολὺν περὶ αὐτοὺς καὶ γραμματεῖς συζητοῦντας πρὸς αὐτούς. **15** καὶ εὐθὺς πᾶς ὁ ὄχλος ἰδόντες αὐτὸν ἐξεθαμβήθησαν καὶ προστρέχοντες ἠσπάζοντο αὐτόν. **16** καὶ

[i]38 NRSV note j omits λόγους

NIV

and for the gospel will save it. [36]What good is it for a man to gain the whole world, yet forfeit his soul? [37]Or what can a man give in exchange for his soul? [38]If anyone is ashamed of me and my words in this adulterous and sinful generation, the Son of Man will be ashamed of him when he comes in his Father's glory with the holy angels."

9 And he said to them, "I tell you the truth, some who are standing here will not taste death before they see the kingdom of God come with power."

The Transfiguration

[2]After six days Jesus took Peter, James and John with him and led them up a high mountain, where they were all alone. There he was transfigured before them. [3]His clothes became dazzling white, whiter than anyone in the world could bleach them. [4]And there appeared before them Elijah and Moses, who were talking with Jesus.

[5]Peter said to Jesus, "Rabbi, it is good for us to be here. Let us put up three shelters—one for you, one for Moses and one for Elijah." [6](He did not know what to say, they were so frightened.)

[7]Then a cloud appeared and enveloped them, and a voice came from the cloud: "This is my Son, whom I love. Listen to him!"

[8]Suddenly, when they looked around, they no longer saw anyone with them except Jesus.

[9]As they were coming down the mountain, Jesus gave them orders not to tell anyone what they had seen until the Son of Man had risen from the dead. [10]They kept the matter to themselves, discussing what "rising from the dead" meant.

[11]And they asked him, "Why do the teachers of the law say that Elijah must come first?"

[12]Jesus replied, "To be sure, Elijah does come first, and restores all things. Why then is it written that the Son of Man must suffer much and be rejected? [13]But I tell you, Elijah has come, and they have done to him everything they wished, just as it is written about him."

The Healing of a Boy With an Evil Spirit

[14]When they came to the other disciples, they saw a large crowd around them and the teachers of the law arguing with them. [15]As soon as all the people saw Jesus, they were overwhelmed with wonder and ran to greet him.

forward to greet him. [16]He asked them, "What are you arguing about with them?" [17]Someone from the crowd answered him, "Teacher, I brought you my son; he has a spirit that makes him unable to speak; [18]and whenever it seizes him, it dashes him down; and he foams and grinds his teeth and becomes rigid; and I asked your disciples to cast it out, but they could not do so." [19]He answered them, "You faithless generation, how much longer must I be among you? How much longer must I put up with you? Bring him to me." [20]And they brought the boy[o] to him. When the spirit saw him, immediately it convulsed the boy,[o] and he fell on the ground and rolled about, foaming at the mouth. [21]Jesus[p] asked the father, "How long has this been happening to him?" And he said, "From childhood. [22]It has often cast him into the fire and into the water, to destroy him; but if you are able to do anything, have pity on us and help us." [23]Jesus said to him, "If you are able!—All things can be done for the one who believes." [24]Immediately the father of the child cried out,[q] "I believe; help my unbelief!" [25]When Jesus saw that a crowd came running together, he rebuked the unclean spirit, saying to it, "You spirit that keeps this boy from speaking and hearing, I command you, come out of him, and never enter him again!" [26]After crying out and convulsing him terribly, it came out, and the boy was like a corpse, so that most of them said, "He is dead." [27]But Jesus took him by the hand and lifted him up, and he was able to stand. [28]When he had entered the house, his disciples asked him privately, "Why could we not cast it out?" [29]He said to them, "This kind can come out only through prayer."[r]

Jesus Again Foretells His Death and Resurrection

30 They went on from there and passed through Galilee. He did not want anyone to know it; [31]for he was teaching his disciples, saying to them, "The Son of Man is to be betrayed into human hands, and they will kill him, and three days after being killed, he will rise again." [32]But they did not understand what he was saying and were afraid to ask him.

Who Is the Greatest?

33 Then they came to Capernaum; and when he was in the house he asked them,

ἐπηρώτησεν αὐτούς, Τί συζητεῖτε πρὸς αὐτούς; 17 καὶ ἀπεκρίθη αὐτῷ εἷς ἐκ τοῦ ὄχλου, Διδάσκαλε, ἤνεγκα τὸν υἱόν μου πρὸς σέ, ἔχοντα πνεῦμα ἄλαλον· 18 καὶ ὅπου ἐὰν αὐτὸν καταλάβῃ ῥήσσει αὐτόν, καὶ ἀφρίζει καὶ τρίζει τοὺς ὀδόντας καὶ ξηραίνεται· καὶ εἶπα τοῖς μαθηταῖς σου ἵνα αὐτὸ ἐκβάλωσιν, καὶ οὐκ ἴσχυσαν. 19 ὁ δὲ ἀποκριθεὶς αὐτοῖς λέγει, Ὦ γενεὰ ἄπιστος, ἕως πότε πρὸς ὑμᾶς ἔσομαι; ἕως πότε ἀνέξομαι ὑμῶν; φέρετε αὐτὸν πρός με. 20 καὶ ἤνεγκαν αὐτὸν πρὸς αὐτόν. καὶ ἰδὼν αὐτὸν τὸ πνεῦμα εὐθὺς συνεσπάραξεν αὐτόν, καὶ πεσὼν ἐπὶ τῆς γῆς ἐκυλίετο ἀφρίζων. 21 καὶ ἐπηρώτησεν τὸν πατέρα αὐτοῦ, Πόσος χρόνος ἐστὶν ὡς τοῦτο γέγονεν αὐτῷ; ὁ δὲ εἶπεν, Ἐκ παιδιόθεν· 22 καὶ πολλάκις καὶ εἰς πῦρ αὐτὸν ἔβαλεν καὶ εἰς ὕδατα ἵνα ἀπολέσῃ αὐτόν· ἀλλ' εἴ τι δύνῃ, βοήθησον ἡμῖν σπλαγχνισθεὶς ἐφ' ἡμᾶς. 23 ὁ δὲ Ἰησοῦς εἶπεν αὐτῷ, Τὸ Εἰ δύνῃ, πάντα δυνατὰ τῷ πιστεύοντι. 24 εὐθὺς κράξας ὁ πατὴρ τοῦ παιδίου[a] ἔλεγεν, Πιστεύω· βοήθει μου τῇ ἀπιστίᾳ. 25 ἰδὼν δὲ ὁ Ἰησοῦς ὅτι ἐπισυντρέχει ὄχλος, ἐπετίμησεν τῷ πνεύματι τῷ ἀκαθάρτῳ λέγων αὐτῷ, Τὸ ἄλαλον καὶ κωφὸν πνεῦμα, ἐγὼ ἐπιτάσσω σοι, ἔξελθε ἐξ αὐτοῦ καὶ μηκέτι εἰσέλθῃς εἰς αὐτόν. 26 καὶ κράξας καὶ πολλὰ σπαράξας ἐξῆλθεν· καὶ ἐγένετο ὡσεὶ νεκρός, ὥστε τοὺς πολλοὺς λέγειν ὅτι ἀπέθανεν. 27 ὁ δὲ Ἰησοῦς κρατήσας τῆς χειρὸς αὐτοῦ ἤγειρεν αὐτόν, καὶ ἀνέστη. 28 καὶ εἰσελθόντος αὐτοῦ εἰς οἶκον οἱ μαθηταὶ αὐτοῦ κατ' ἰδίαν ἐπηρώτων αὐτόν, Ὅτι ἡμεῖς οὐκ ἠδυνήθημεν ἐκβαλεῖν αὐτό; 29 καὶ εἶπεν αὐτοῖς, Τοῦτο τὸ γένος ἐν οὐδενὶ δύναται ἐξελθεῖν εἰ μὴ ἐν προσευχῇ[b].

30 Κἀκεῖθεν ἐξελθόντες παρεπορεύοντο διὰ τῆς Γαλιλαίας, καὶ οὐκ ἤθελεν ἵνα τις γνοῖ· 31 ἐδίδασκεν γὰρ τοὺς μαθητὰς αὐτοῦ καὶ ἔλεγεν αὐτοῖς ὅτι Ὁ υἱὸς τοῦ ἀνθρώπου παραδίδοται εἰς χεῖρας ἀνθρώπων, καὶ ἀποκτενοῦσιν αὐτόν, καὶ ἀποκτανθεὶς μετὰ τρεῖς ἡμέρας ἀναστήσεται. 32 οἱ δὲ ἠγνόουν τὸ ῥῆμα, καὶ ἐφοβοῦντο αὐτὸν ἐπερωτῆσαι.

33 Καὶ ἦλθον εἰς Καφαρναούμ. καὶ ἐν τῇ οἰκίᾳ γενόμενος ἐπηρώτα αὐτούς,

[16]"What are you arguing with them about?" he asked.

[17]A man in the crowd answered, "Teacher, I brought you my son, who is possessed by a spirit that has robbed him of speech. [18]Whenever it seizes him, it throws him to the ground. He foams at the mouth, gnashes his teeth and becomes rigid. I asked your disciples to drive out the spirit, but they could not."

[19]"O unbelieving generation," Jesus replied, "how long shall I stay with you? How long shall I put up with you? Bring the boy to me."

[20]So they brought him. When the spirit saw Jesus, it immediately threw the boy into a convulsion. He fell to the ground and rolled around, foaming at the mouth.

[21]Jesus asked the boy's father, "How long has he been like this?"

"From childhood," he answered. [22]"It has often thrown him into fire or water to kill him. But if you can do anything, take pity on us and help us."

[23]"'If you can'?" said Jesus. "Everything is possible for him who believes."

[24]Immediately the boy's father exclaimed, "I do believe; help me overcome my unbelief!"

[25]When Jesus saw that a crowd was running to the scene, he rebuked the evil[a] spirit. "You deaf and mute spirit," he said, "I command you, come out of him and never enter him again."

[26]The spirit shrieked, convulsed him violently and came out. The boy looked so much like a corpse that many said, "He's dead." [27]But Jesus took him by the hand and lifted him to his feet, and he stood up.

[28]After Jesus had gone indoors, his disciples asked him privately, "Why couldn't we drive it out?"

[29]He replied, "This kind can come out only by prayer.[b]"

[30]They left that place and passed through Galilee. Jesus did not want anyone to know where they were, [31]because he was teaching his disciples. He said to them, "The Son of Man is going to be betrayed into the hands of men. They will kill him, and after three days he will rise." [32]But they did not understand what he meant and were afraid to ask him about it.

Who Is the Greatest?

[33]They came to Capernaum. When he was in the house, he asked them, "What

---

o Gk him   p Gk He   q Other ancient authorities add with tears   r Other ancient authorities add and fasting

a24 NRSV note q adds μετὰ δακρύων   b29 NIV/NRSV notes add καὶ νηστείᾳ

a25 Greek unclean   b29 Some manuscripts prayer and fasting

"What were you arguing about on the way?" 34But they were silent, for on the way they had argued with one another who was the greatest. 35He sat down, called the twelve, and said to them, "Whoever wants to be first must be last of all and servant of all." 36Then he took a little child and put it among them; and taking it in his arms, he said to them, 37"Whoever welcomes one such child in my name welcomes me, and whoever welcomes me welcomes not me but the one who sent me."

Another Exorcist

38 John said to him, "Teacher, we saw someone[s] casting out demons in your name, and we tried to stop him, because he was not following us." 39But Jesus said, "Do not stop him; for no one who does a deed of power in my name will be able soon afterward to speak evil of me. 40Whoever is not against us is for us. 41For truly I tell you, whoever gives you a cup of water to drink because you bear the name of Christ will by no means lose the reward.

Temptations to Sin

42 "If any of you put a stumbling block before one of these little ones who believe in me,[t] it would be better for you if a great millstone were hung around your neck and you were thrown into the sea. 43If your hand causes you to stumble, cut it off; it is better for you to enter life maimed than to have two hands and to go to hell,[u] to the unquenchable fire.[v] 45And if your foot causes you to stumble, cut it off; it is better for you to enter life lame than to have two feet and to be thrown into hell.[u,v] 47And if your eye causes you to stumble, tear it out; it is better for you to enter the kingdom of God with one eye than to have two eyes and to be thrown into hell,[u] 48where their worm never dies, and the fire is never quenched.

49 "For everyone will be salted with fire.[w] 50Salt is good; but if salt has lost its saltiness, how can you season it?[x] Have salt in yourselves, and be at peace with one another."

Teaching about Divorce

10 He left that place and went to the region of Judea and[y] beyond the

---

Τί ἐν τῇ ὁδῷ διελογίζεσθε; **34** οἱ δὲ ἐσιώπων· πρὸς ἀλλήλους γὰρ διελέχθησαν ἐν τῇ ὁδῷ τίς μείζων. **35** καὶ καθίσας ἐφώνησεν τοὺς δώδεκα καὶ λέγει αὐτοῖς, Εἴ τις θέλει πρῶτος εἶναι, ἔσται πάντων ἔσχατος καὶ πάντων διάκονος. **36** καὶ λαβὼν παιδίον ἔστησεν αὐτὸ ἐν μέσῳ αὐτῶν καὶ ἐναγκαλισάμενος αὐτὸ εἶπεν αὐτοῖς, **37** Ὃς ἂν ἓν τῶν τοιούτων παιδίων δέξηται ἐπὶ τῷ ὀνόματί μου, ἐμὲ δέχεται· καὶ ὃς ἂν ἐμὲ δέχηται, οὐκ ἐμὲ δέχεται ἀλλὰ τὸν ἀποστείλαντά με.

38 Ἔφη αὐτῷ ὁ Ἰωάννης, Διδάσκαλε, εἴδομέν τινα ἐν τῷ ὀνόματί σου ἐκβάλλοντα δαιμόνια[c] καὶ ἐκωλύομεν αὐτόν, ὅτι οὐκ ἠκολούθει ἡμῖν. **39** ὁ δὲ Ἰησοῦς εἶπεν, Μὴ κωλύετε αὐτόν. οὐδεὶς γάρ ἐστιν ὃς ποιήσει δύναμιν ἐπὶ τῷ ὀνόματί μου καὶ δυνήσεται ταχὺ κακολογῆσαί με· **40** ὃς γὰρ οὐκ ἔστιν καθ' ἡμῶν, ὑπὲρ ἡμῶν ἐστιν. **41** Ὃς γὰρ ἂν ποτίσῃ ὑμᾶς ποτήριον ὕδατος ἐν ὀνόματι ὅτι Χριστοῦ ἐστε, ἀμὴν λέγω ὑμῖν ὅτι οὐ μὴ ἀπολέσῃ τὸν μισθὸν αὐτοῦ.

42 Καὶ ὃς ἂν σκανδαλίσῃ ἕνα τῶν μικρῶν τούτων τῶν πιστευόντων [εἰς ἐμέ], καλόν ἐστιν αὐτῷ μᾶλλον εἰ περίκειται μύλος ὀνικὸς περὶ τὸν τράχηλον αὐτοῦ καὶ βέβληται εἰς τὴν θάλασσαν. **43** Καὶ ἐὰν σκανδαλίζῃ σε ἡ χείρ σου, ἀπόκοψον αὐτήν· καλόν ἐστίν σε κυλλὸν εἰσελθεῖν εἰς τὴν ζωὴν ἢ τὰς δύο χεῖρας ἔχοντα ἀπελθεῖν εἰς τὴν γέενναν, εἰς τὸ πῦρ τὸ ἄσβεστον.[d] **45** καὶ ἐὰν ὁ πούς σου σκανδαλίζῃ σε, ἀπόκοψον αὐτόν· καλόν ἐστίν σε εἰσελθεῖν εἰς τὴν ζωὴν χωλὸν ἢ τοὺς δύο πόδας ἔχοντα βληθῆναι εἰς τὴν γέενναν.[e] **47** καὶ ἐὰν ὁ ὀφθαλμός σου σκανδαλίζῃ σε, ἔκβαλε αὐτόν· καλόν σέ ἐστιν μονόφθαλμον εἰσελθεῖν εἰς τὴν βασιλείαν τοῦ θεοῦ ἢ δύο ὀφθαλμοὺς ἔχοντα βληθῆναι εἰς τὴν γέενναν, **48** ὅπου ὁ σκώληξ αὐτῶν οὐ τελευτᾷ καὶ τὸ πῦρ οὐ σβέννυται. **49** πᾶς γὰρ πυρὶ ἁλισθήσεται.[f] **50** Καλὸν τὸ ἅλας· ἐὰν δὲ τὸ ἅλας ἄναλον γένηται, ἐν τίνι αὐτὸ ἀρτύσετε; ἔχετε ἐν ἑαυτοῖς ἅλα καὶ εἰρηνεύετε ἐν ἀλλήλοις.

10 Καὶ ἐκεῖθεν ἀναστὰς ἔρχεται εἰς τὰ ὅρια τῆς Ἰουδαίας [καὶ]

---

were you arguing about on the road?" 34But they kept quiet because on the way they had argued about who was the greatest.

35Sitting down, Jesus called the Twelve and said, "If anyone wants to be first, he must be the very last, and the servant of all."

36He took a little child and had him stand among them. Taking him in his arms, he said to them, 37"Whoever welcomes one of these little children in my name welcomes me; and whoever welcomes me does not welcome me but the one who sent me."

Whoever Is Not Against Us Is for Us

38"Teacher," said John, "we saw a man driving out demons in your name and we told him to stop, because he was not one of us."

39"Do not stop him," Jesus said. "No one who does a miracle in my name can in the next moment say anything bad about me, 40for whoever is not against us is for us. 41I tell you the truth, anyone who gives you a cup of water in my name because you belong to Christ will certainly not lose his reward.

Causing to Sin

42"And if anyone causes one of these little ones who believe in me to sin, it would be better for him to be thrown into the sea with a large millstone tied around his neck. 43If your hand causes you to sin, cut it off. It is better for you to enter life maimed than with two hands to go into hell, where the fire never goes out.[c] 45And if your foot causes you to sin, cut it off. It is better for you to enter life crippled than to have two feet and be thrown into hell.[d] 47And if your eye causes you to sin, pluck it out. It is better for you to enter the kingdom of God with one eye than to have two eyes and be thrown into hell, 48where

" 'their worm does not die,
and the fire is not quenched.'[e]

49Everyone will be salted with fire.

50"Salt is good, but if it loses its saltiness, how can you make it salty again? Have salt in yourselves, and be at peace with each other."

Divorce

10 Jesus then left that place and went into the region of Judea and across

---

[s] Other ancient authorities add *who does not follow us*
[t] Other ancient authorities lack *in me*   [u] Gk *Gehenna*
[v] Verses 44 and 46 (which are identical with verse 48) are lacking in the best ancient authorities   [w] Other ancient authorities either add or substitute *and every sacrifice will be salted with salt*   [x] Or *how can you restore its saltiness?*   [y] Other ancient authorities lack *and*

[c]38 NRSV note s adds ὃς οὐκ ἀκολουθεῖ ἡμῖν
[d]43 NIV/NRSV notes add 44 ὅπου ὁ σκώληξ αὐτῶν οὐ τελευτᾷ καὶ τὸ πῦρ οὐ σβέννυται.   [e]45 NIV/NRSV notes add 46 ὅπου ὁ σκώληξ αὐτῶν οὐ τελευτᾷ καὶ τὸ πῦρ οὐ σβέννυται.   [f]49 NRSV note w καὶ πᾶσα θυσία ἁλὶ ἁλισθήσεται

[c]43 Some manuscripts *out,* 44 *where* / " 'their worm does not die, / and the fire is not quenched.'*   [d]45 Some manuscripts *hell,* 46 *where* / " 'their worm does not die, / and the fire is not quenched.'*   [e]48 Isaiah 66:24

Jordan. And crowds again gathered around him; and, as was his custom, he again taught them.

2 Some Pharisees came, and to test him they asked, "Is it lawful for a man to divorce his wife?" [3]He answered them, "What did Moses command you?" [4]They said, "Moses allowed a man to write a certificate of dismissal and to divorce her." [5]But Jesus said to them, "Because of your hardness of heart he wrote this commandment for you. [6]But from the beginning of creation, 'God made them male and female.' [7]For this reason a man shall leave his father and mother and be joined to his wife,[z] [8]and the two shall become one flesh.' So they are no longer two, but one flesh. [9]Therefore what God has joined together, let no one separate."

10 Then in the house the disciples asked him again about this matter. [11]He said to them, "Whoever divorces his wife and marries another commits adultery against her; [12]and if she divorces her husband and marries another, she commits adultery."

Jesus Blesses Little Children

13 People were bringing little children to him in order that he might touch them; and the disciples spoke sternly to them. [14]But when Jesus saw this, he was indignant and said to them, "Let the little children come to me; do not stop them; for it is to such as these that the kingdom of God belongs. [15]Truly I tell you, whoever does not receive the kingdom of God as a little child will never enter it." [16]And he took them up in his arms, laid his hands on them, and blessed them.

The Rich Man

17 As he was setting out on a journey, a man ran up and knelt before him, and asked him, "Good Teacher, what must I do to inherit eternal life?" [18]Jesus said to him, "Why do you call me good? No one is good but God alone. [19]You know the commandments: 'You shall not murder; You shall not commit adultery; You shall not steal; You shall not bear false witness; You shall not defraud; Honor your father and mother.'" [20]He said to him, "Teacher, I have kept all these since my youth." [21]Jesus,

πέραν τοῦ Ἰορδάνου, καὶ συμπορεύονται πάλιν ὄχλοι πρὸς αὐτόν, καὶ ὡς εἰώθει πάλιν ἐδίδασκεν αὐτούς. **2** καὶ προσελθόντες Φαρισαῖοι ἐπηρώτων αὐτὸν εἰ ἔξεστιν ἀνδρὶ γυναῖκα ἀπολῦσαι, πειράζοντες αὐτόν. **3** ὁ δὲ ἀποκριθεὶς εἶπεν αὐτοῖς, Τί ὑμῖν ἐνετείλατο Μωϊσῆς; **4** οἱ δὲ εἶπαν, Ἐπέτρεψεν Μωϊσῆς **βιβλίον ἀποστασίου γράψαι καὶ ἀπολῦσαι.** **5** ὁ δὲ Ἰησοῦς εἶπεν αὐτοῖς, Πρὸς τὴν σκληροκαρδίαν ὑμῶν ἔγραψεν ὑμῖν τὴν ἐντολὴν ταύτην. **6** ἀπὸ δὲ ἀρχῆς κτίσεως **ἄρσεν καὶ θῆλυ ἐποίησεν αὐτούς· 7** ἕνεκεν τούτου **καταλείψει ἄνθρωπος τὸν πατέρα αὐτοῦ καὶ τὴν μητέρα [καὶ προσκολληθήσεται πρὸς τὴν γυναῖκα αὐτοῦ], 8** καὶ ἔσονται οἱ δύο εἰς σάρκα μίαν·** ὥστε οὐκέτι εἰσὶν δύο ἀλλὰ μία σάρξ. **9** ὃ οὖν ὁ θεὸς συνέζευξεν ἄνθρωπος μὴ χωριζέτω. **10** Καὶ εἰς τὴν οἰκίαν πάλιν οἱ μαθηταὶ περὶ τούτου ἐπηρώτων αὐτόν. **11** καὶ λέγει αὐτοῖς, Ὃς ἂν ἀπολύσῃ τὴν γυναῖκα αὐτοῦ καὶ γαμήσῃ ἄλλην μοιχᾶται ἐπ᾽ αὐτήν· **12** καὶ ἐὰν αὐτὴ ἀπολύσασα τὸν ἄνδρα αὐτῆς γαμήσῃ ἄλλον μοιχᾶται.

13 Καὶ προσέφερον αὐτῷ παιδία ἵνα αὐτῶν ἅψηται· οἱ δὲ μαθηταὶ ἐπετίμησαν αὐτοῖς. **14** ἰδὼν δὲ ὁ Ἰησοῦς ἠγανάκτησεν καὶ εἶπεν αὐτοῖς, Ἄφετε τὰ παιδία ἔρχεσθαι πρός με, μὴ κωλύετε αὐτά, τῶν γὰρ τοιούτων ἐστὶν ἡ βασιλεία τοῦ θεοῦ. **15** ἀμὴν λέγω ὑμῖν, ὃς ἂν μὴ δέξηται τὴν βασιλείαν τοῦ θεοῦ ὡς παιδίον, οὐ μὴ εἰσέλθῃ εἰς αὐτήν. **16** καὶ ἐναγκαλισάμενος αὐτὰ κατευλόγει τιθεὶς τὰς χεῖρας ἐπ᾽ αὐτά.

17 Καὶ ἐκπορευομένου αὐτοῦ εἰς ὁδὸν προσδραμὼν εἷς καὶ γονυπετήσας αὐτὸν ἐπηρώτα αὐτόν, Διδάσκαλε ἀγαθέ, τί ποιήσω ἵνα ζωὴν αἰώνιον κληρονομήσω; **18** ὁ δὲ Ἰησοῦς εἶπεν αὐτῷ, Τί με λέγεις ἀγαθόν; οὐδεὶς ἀγαθὸς εἰ μὴ εἷς ὁ θεός. **19** τὰς ἐντολὰς οἶδας· **Μὴ φονεύσῃς, Μὴ μοιχεύσῃς, Μὴ κλέψῃς, Μὴ ψευδομαρτυρήσῃς,** Μὴ ἀποστερήσῃς, Τίμα τὸν πατέρα σου καὶ τὴν μητέρα. **20** ὁ δὲ ἔφη αὐτῷ, Διδάσκαλε, ταῦτα πάντα ἐφυλαξάμην ἐκ νεότητός

the Jordan. Again crowds of people came to him, and as was his custom, he taught them.

[2]Some Pharisees came and tested him by asking, "Is it lawful for a man to divorce his wife?"

[3]"What did Moses command you?" he replied.

[4]They said, "Moses permitted a man to write a certificate of divorce and send her away."

[5]"It was because your hearts were hard that Moses wrote you this law," Jesus replied. [6]"But at the beginning of creation God 'made them male and female.'[a] [7]For this reason a man will leave his father and mother and be united to his wife,[b] [8]and the two will become one flesh.'[c] So they are no longer two, but one. [9]Therefore what God has joined together, let man not separate."

[10]When they were in the house again, the disciples asked Jesus about this. [11]He answered, "Anyone who divorces his wife and marries another woman commits adultery against her. [12]And if she divorces her husband and marries another man, she commits adultery."

The Little Children and Jesus

[13]People were bringing little children to Jesus to have him touch them, but the disciples rebuked them. [14]When Jesus saw this, he was indignant. He said to them, "Let the little children come to me, and do not hinder them, for the kingdom of God belongs to such as these. [15]I tell you the truth, anyone who will not receive the kingdom of God like a little child will never enter it." [16]And he took the children in his arms, put his hands on them and blessed them.

The Rich Young Man

[17]As Jesus started on his way, a man ran up to him and fell on his knees before him. "Good teacher," he asked, "what must I do to inherit eternal life?"

[18]"Why do you call me good?" Jesus answered. "No one is good—except God alone. [19]You know the commandments: 'Do not murder, do not commit adultery, do not steal, do not give false testimony, do not defraud, honor your father and mother.'[d]"

[20]"Teacher," he declared, "all these I have kept since I was a boy."

---

[a]6 Gen. 1:27   [b]7 Some early manuscripts do not have *and be united to his wife.*   [c]8 Gen. 2:24   [d]19 Exodus 20:12-16; Deut. 5:16-20

---

[z]Other ancient authorities lack *and be joined to his wife*

looking at him, loved him and said, "You lack one thing; go, sell what you own, and give the money[a] to the poor, and you will have treasure in heaven; then come, follow me." 22When he heard this, he was shocked and went away grieving, for he had many possessions.

23 Then Jesus looked around and said to his disciples, "How hard it will be for those who have wealth to enter the kingdom of God!" 24And the disciples were perplexed at these words. But Jesus said to them again, "Children, how hard it is[b] to enter the kingdom of God! 25It is easier for a camel to go through the eye of a needle than for someone who is rich to enter the kingdom of God." 26They were greatly astounded and said to one another,[c] "Then who can be saved?" 27Jesus looked at them and said, "For mortals it is impossible, but not for God; for God all things are possible."

28 Peter began to say to him, "Look, we have left everything and followed you." 29Jesus said, "Truly I tell you, there is no one who has left house or brothers or sisters or mother or father or children or fields, for my sake and for the sake of the good news,[d] 30who will not receive a hundredfold now in this age—houses, brothers and sisters, mothers and children, and fields with persecutions—and in the age to come eternal life. 31But many who are first will be last, and the last will be first."

A Third Time Jesus Foretells His Death and Resurrection

32 They were on the road, going up to Jerusalem, and Jesus was walking ahead of them; they were amazed, and those who followed were afraid. He took the twelve aside again and began to tell them what was to happen to him, 33saying, "See, we are going up to Jerusalem, and the Son of Man will be handed over to the chief priests and the scribes, and they will condemn him to death; then they will hand him over to the Gentiles; 34they will mock him, and spit upon him, and flog him, and kill him; and after three days he will rise again."

The Request of James and John

35 James and John, the sons of Zebedee, came forward to him and said to him, "Teacher, we want you to do for us what-

μου. **21** ὁ δὲ Ἰησοῦς ἐμβλέψας αὐτῷ ἠγάπησεν αὐτὸν καὶ εἶπεν αὐτῷ, Ἕν σε ὑστερεῖ· ὕπαγε, ὅσα ἔχεις πώλησον καὶ δὸς [τοῖς] πτωχοῖς, καὶ ἕξεις θησαυρὸν ἐν οὐρανῷ, καὶ δεῦρο ἀκολούθει μοι. **22** ὁ δὲ στυγνάσας ἐπὶ τῷ λόγῳ ἀπῆλθεν λυπούμενος· ἦν γὰρ ἔχων κτήματα πολλά.

23 Καὶ περιβλεψάμενος ὁ Ἰησοῦς λέγει τοῖς μαθηταῖς αὐτοῦ, Πῶς δυσκόλως οἱ τὰ χρήματα ἔχοντες εἰς τὴν βασιλείαν τοῦ θεοῦ εἰσελεύσονται. **24** οἱ δὲ μαθηταὶ ἐθαμβοῦντο ἐπὶ τοῖς λόγοις αὐτοῦ. ὁ δὲ Ἰησοῦς πάλιν ἀποκριθεὶς λέγει αὐτοῖς, Τέκνα, πῶς δύσκολόν ἐστιν[a] εἰς τὴν βασιλείαν τοῦ θεοῦ εἰσελθεῖν· **25** εὐκοπώτερόν ἐστιν κάμηλον διὰ [τῆς] τρυμαλιᾶς [τῆς] ῥαφίδος διελθεῖν ἢ πλούσιον εἰς τὴν βασιλείαν τοῦ θεοῦ εἰσελθεῖν. **26** οἱ δὲ περισσῶς ἐξεπλήσσοντο λέγοντες πρὸς ἑαυτούς[b], Καὶ τίς δύναται σωθῆναι; **27** ἐμβλέψας αὐτοῖς ὁ Ἰησοῦς λέγει, Παρὰ ἀνθρώποις ἀδύνατον, ἀλλ᾽ οὐ παρὰ θεῷ· πάντα γὰρ δυνατὰ παρὰ τῷ θεῷ. **28** Ἤρξατο λέγειν ὁ Πέτρος αὐτῷ, Ἰδοὺ ἡμεῖς ἀφήκαμεν πάντα καὶ ἠκολουθήκαμέν σοι. **29** ἔφη ὁ Ἰησοῦς, Ἀμὴν λέγω ὑμῖν, οὐδείς ἐστιν ὃς ἀφῆκεν οἰκίαν ἢ ἀδελφοὺς ἢ ἀδελφὰς ἢ μητέρα ἢ πατέρα ἢ τέκνα ἢ ἀγροὺς ἕνεκεν ἐμοῦ καὶ ἕνεκεν τοῦ εὐαγγελίου, **30** ἐὰν μὴ λάβῃ ἑκατονταπλασίονα νῦν ἐν τῷ καιρῷ τούτῳ οἰκίας καὶ ἀδελφοὺς καὶ ἀδελφὰς καὶ μητέρας καὶ τέκνα καὶ ἀγροὺς μετὰ διωγμῶν, καὶ ἐν τῷ αἰῶνι τῷ ἐρχομένῳ ζωὴν αἰώνιον. **31** πολλοὶ δὲ ἔσονται πρῶτοι ἔσχατοι καὶ [οἱ] ἔσχατοι πρῶτοι.

32 Ἦσαν δὲ ἐν τῇ ὁδῷ ἀναβαίνοντες εἰς Ἱεροσόλυμα, καὶ ἦν προάγων αὐτοὺς ὁ Ἰησοῦς, καὶ ἐθαμβοῦντο, οἱ δὲ ἀκολουθοῦντες ἐφοβοῦντο. καὶ παραλαβὼν πάλιν τοὺς δώδεκα ἤρξατο αὐτοῖς λέγειν τὰ μέλλοντα αὐτῷ συμβαίνειν **33** ὅτι Ἰδοὺ ἀναβαίνομεν εἰς Ἱεροσόλυμα, καὶ ὁ υἱὸς τοῦ ἀνθρώπου παραδοθήσεται τοῖς ἀρχιερεῦσιν καὶ τοῖς γραμματεῦσιν, καὶ κατακρινοῦσιν αὐτὸν θανάτῳ καὶ παραδώσουσιν αὐτὸν τοῖς ἔθνεσιν **34** καὶ ἐμπαίξουσιν αὐτῷ καὶ ἐμπτύσουσιν αὐτῷ καὶ μαστιγώσουσιν αὐτὸν καὶ ἀποκτενοῦσιν, καὶ μετὰ τρεῖς ἡμέρας ἀναστήσεται.

35 Καὶ προσπορεύονται αὐτῷ Ἰάκωβος καὶ Ἰωάννης οἱ υἱοὶ Ζεβεδαίου λέγοντες αὐτῷ, Διδάσκαλε, θέλομεν ἵνα ὃ ἐὰν

21Jesus looked at him and loved him. "One thing you lack," he said. "Go, sell everything you have and give to the poor, and you will have treasure in heaven. Then come, follow me."

22At this the man's face fell. He went away sad, because he had great wealth.

23Jesus looked around and said to his disciples, "How hard it is for the rich to enter the kingdom of God!"

24The disciples were amazed at his words. But Jesus said again, "Children, how hard it is[e] to enter the kingdom of God! 25It is easier for a camel to go through the eye of a needle than for a rich man to enter the kingdom of God."

26The disciples were even more amazed, and said to each other, "Who then can be saved?"

27Jesus looked at them and said, "With man this is impossible, but not with God; all things are possible with God."

28Peter said to him, "We have left everything to follow you!"

29"I tell you the truth," Jesus replied, "no one who has left home or brothers or sisters or mother or father or children or fields for me and the gospel 30will fail to receive a hundred times as much in this present age (homes, brothers, sisters, mothers, children and fields—and with them, persecutions) and in the age to come, eternal life. 31But many who are first will be last, and the last first."

Jesus Again Predicts His Death

32They were on their way up to Jerusalem, with Jesus leading the way, and the disciples were astonished, while those who followed were afraid. Again he took the Twelve aside and told them what was going to happen to him. 33"We are going up to Jerusalem," he said, "and the Son of Man will be betrayed to the chief priests and teachers of the law. They will condemn him to death and will hand him over to the Gentiles, 34who will mock him and spit on him, flog him and kill him. Three days later he will rise."

The Request of James and John

35Then James and John, the sons of Zebedee, came to him. "Teacher," they said, "we want you to do for us whatever we ask."

---

a Gk lacks *the money*   b Other ancient authorities add *for those who trust in riches*   c Other ancient authorities read *to him*   d Or *gospel*

a24 NIV/NRSV notes add τοὺς πεποιθότας ἐπὶ (τοῖς) χρήμασιν   b26 NRSV note c αὐτόν

e24 Some manuscripts *is for those who trust in riches*

ever we ask of you." [36]And he said to them, "What is it you want me to do for you?" [37]And they said to him, "Grant us to sit, one at your right hand and one at your left, in your glory." [38]But Jesus said to them, "You do not know what you are asking. Are you able to drink the cup that I drink, or be baptized with the baptism that I am baptized with?" [39]They replied, "We are able." Then Jesus said to them, "The cup that I drink you will drink; and with the baptism with which I am baptized, you will be baptized; [40]but to sit at my right hand or at my left is not mine to grant, but it is for those for whom it has been prepared."

[41] When the ten heard this, they began to be angry with James and John. [42]So Jesus called them and said to them, "You know that among the Gentiles those whom they recognize as their rulers lord it over them, and their great ones are tyrants over them. [43]But it is not so among you; but whoever wishes to become great among you must be your servant, [44]and whoever wishes to be first among you must be slave of all. [45]For the Son of Man came not to be served but to serve, and to give his life a ransom for many."

The Healing of Blind Bartimaeus

[46] They came to Jericho. As he and his disciples and a large crowd were leaving Jericho, Bartimaeus son of Timaeus, a blind beggar, was sitting by the roadside. [47]When he heard that it was Jesus of Nazareth, he began to shout out and say, "Jesus, Son of David, have mercy on me!" [48]Many sternly ordered him to be quiet, but he cried out even more loudly, "Son of David, have mercy on me!" [49]Jesus stood still and said, "Call him here." And they called the blind man, saying to him, "Take heart; get up, he is calling you." [50]So throwing off his cloak, he sprang up and came to Jesus. [51]Then Jesus said to him, "What do you want me to do for you?" The blind man said to him, "My teacher,[e] let me see again." [52]Jesus said to him, "Go; your faith has made you well." Immediately he regained his sight and followed him on the way.

Jesus' Triumphal Entry into Jerusalem

11 When they were approaching Jerusalem, at Bethphage and Bethany, near the Mount of Olives, he sent

[e] Aramaic *Rabbouni*

αἰτήσωμέν σε ποιήσῃς ἡμῖν. **36** ὁ δὲ εἶπεν αὐτοῖς, Τί θέλετέ [με] ποιήσω ὑμῖν; **37** οἱ δὲ εἶπαν αὐτῷ, Δὸς ἡμῖν ἵνα εἷς σου ἐκ δεξιῶν καὶ εἷς ἐξ ἀριστερῶν καθίσωμεν ἐν τῇ δόξῃ σου. **38** ὁ δὲ Ἰησοῦς εἶπεν αὐτοῖς, Οὐκ οἴδατε τί αἰτεῖσθε. δύνασθε πιεῖν τὸ ποτήριον ὃ ἐγὼ πίνω ἢ τὸ βάπτισμα ὃ ἐγὼ βαπτίζομαι βαπτισθῆναι; **39** οἱ δὲ εἶπαν αὐτῷ, Δυνάμεθα. ὁ δὲ Ἰησοῦς εἶπεν αὐτοῖς, Τὸ ποτήριον ὃ ἐγὼ πίνω πίεσθε καὶ τὸ βάπτισμα ὃ ἐγὼ βαπτίζομαι βαπτισθήσεσθε, **40** τὸ δὲ καθίσαι ἐκ δεξιῶν μου ἢ ἐξ εὐωνύμων οὐκ ἔστιν ἐμὸν δοῦναι, ἀλλ' οἷς ἡτοίμασται. **41** Καὶ ἀκούσαντες οἱ δέκα ἤρξαντο ἀγανακτεῖν περὶ Ἰακώβου καὶ Ἰωάννου. **42** καὶ προσκαλεσάμενος αὐτοὺς ὁ Ἰησοῦς λέγει αὐτοῖς, Οἴδατε ὅτι οἱ δοκοῦντες ἄρχειν τῶν ἐθνῶν κατακυριεύουσιν αὐτῶν καὶ οἱ μεγάλοι αὐτῶν κατεξουσιάζουσιν αὐτῶν. **43** οὐχ οὕτως δέ ἐστιν ἐν ὑμῖν, ἀλλ' ὃς ἂν θέλῃ μέγας γενέσθαι ἐν ὑμῖν ἔσται ὑμῶν διάκονος, **44** καὶ ὃς ἂν θέλῃ ἐν ὑμῖν εἶναι πρῶτος ἔσται πάντων δοῦλος· **45** καὶ γὰρ ὁ υἱὸς τοῦ ἀνθρώπου οὐκ ἦλθεν διακονηθῆναι ἀλλὰ διακονῆσαι καὶ δοῦναι τὴν ψυχὴν αὐτοῦ λύτρον ἀντὶ πολλῶν.

46 Καὶ ἔρχονται εἰς Ἰεριχώ. καὶ ἐκπορευομένου αὐτοῦ ἀπὸ Ἰεριχὼ καὶ τῶν μαθητῶν αὐτοῦ καὶ ὄχλου ἱκανοῦ ὁ υἱὸς Τιμαίου Βαρτιμαῖος, τυφλὸς προσαίτης, ἐκάθητο παρὰ τὴν ὁδόν.[c] **47** καὶ ἀκούσας ὅτι Ἰησοῦς ὁ Ναζαρηνός ἐστιν ἤρξατο κράζειν καὶ λέγειν, Υἱὲ Δαυὶδ Ἰησοῦ, ἐλέησόν με. **48** καὶ ἐπετίμων αὐτῷ πολλοὶ ἵνα σιωπήσῃ· ὁ δὲ πολλῷ μᾶλλον ἔκραζεν, Υἱὲ Δαυίδ, ἐλέησόν με. **49** καὶ στὰς ὁ Ἰησοῦς εἶπεν, Φωνήσατε αὐτόν. καὶ φωνοῦσιν τὸν τυφλὸν λέγοντες αὐτῷ, Θάρσει, ἔγειρε, φωνεῖ σε. **50** ὁ δὲ ἀποβαλὼν τὸ ἱμάτιον αὐτοῦ ἀναπηδήσας ἦλθεν πρὸς τὸν Ἰησοῦν. **51** καὶ ἀποκριθεὶς αὐτῷ ὁ Ἰησοῦς εἶπεν, Τί σοι θέλεις ποιήσω; ὁ δὲ τυφλὸς εἶπεν αὐτῷ, Ραββουνι, ἵνα ἀναβλέψω. **52** καὶ ὁ Ἰησοῦς εἶπεν αὐτῷ, Ὕπαγε, ἡ πίστις σου σέσωκέν σε. καὶ εὐθὺς ἀνέβλεψεν καὶ ἠκολούθει αὐτῷ ἐν τῇ ὁδῷ.

11 Καὶ ὅτε ἐγγίζουσιν εἰς Ἰεροσόλυμα εἰς Βηθφαγὴ καὶ Βηθανίαν πρὸς τὸ Ὄρος τῶν Ἐλαιῶν, ἀποστέλλει δύο τῶν μαθητῶν αὐτοῦ

[c]46 NIV text τυφλός, ἐκάθητο παρὰ τὴν ὁδὸν προσαιτῶν. †

---

[36]"What do you want me to do for you?" he asked.

[37]They replied, "Let one of us sit at your right and the other at your left in your glory."

[38]"You don't know what you are asking," Jesus said. "Can you drink the cup I drink or be baptized with the baptism I am baptized with?"

[39]"We can," they answered.

Jesus said to them, "You will drink the cup I drink and be baptized with the baptism I am baptized with, [40]but to sit at my right or left is not for me to grant. These places belong to those for whom they have been prepared."

[41]When the ten heard about this, they became indignant with James and John. [42]Jesus called them together and said, "You know that those who are regarded as rulers of the Gentiles lord it over them, and their high officials exercise authority over them. [43]Not so with you. Instead, whoever wants to become great among you must be your servant, [44]and whoever wants to be first must be slave of all. [45]For even the Son of Man did not come to be served, but to serve, and to give his life as a ransom for many."

Blind Bartimaeus Receives His Sight

[46]Then they came to Jericho. As Jesus and his disciples, together with a large crowd, were leaving the city, a blind man, Bartimaeus (that is, the Son of Timaeus), was sitting by the roadside begging. [47]When he heard that it was Jesus of Nazareth, he began to shout, "Jesus, Son of David, have mercy on me!"

[48]Many rebuked him and told him to be quiet, but he shouted all the more, "Son of David, have mercy on me!"

[49]Jesus stopped and said, "Call him."

So they called to the blind man, "Cheer up! On your feet! He's calling you." [50]Throwing his cloak aside, he jumped to his feet and came to Jesus.

[51]"What do you want me to do for you?" Jesus asked him.

The blind man said, "Rabbi, I want to see."

[52]"Go," said Jesus, "your faith has healed you." Immediately he received his sight and followed Jesus along the road.

The Triumphal Entry

11 As they approached Jerusalem and came to Bethphage and Bethany at the Mount of Olives, Jesus sent two of his disciples ²and said to them, "Go into the village ahead of you, and immediately as you enter it, you will find tied there a colt that has never been ridden; untie it and bring it. ³If anyone says to you, 'Why are you doing this?' just say this, 'The Lord needs it and will send it back here immediately.' " ⁴They went away and found a colt tied near a door, outside in the street. As they were untying it, ⁵some of the bystanders said to them, "What are you doing, untying the colt?" ⁶They told them what Jesus had said; and they allowed them to take it. ⁷Then they brought the colt to Jesus and threw their cloaks on it; and he sat on it. ⁸Many people spread their cloaks on the road, and others spread leafy branches that they had cut in the fields. ⁹Then those who went ahead and those who followed were shouting,

"Hosanna!
   Blessed is the one who comes in the
      name of the Lord!
10   Blessed is the coming kingdom of
      our ancestor David!
   Hosanna in the highest heaven!"

11 Then he entered Jerusalem and went into the temple; and when he had looked around at everything, as it was already late, he went out to Bethany with the twelve.

Jesus Curses the Fig Tree

12 On the following day, when they came from Bethany, he was hungry. ¹³Seeing in the distance a fig tree in leaf, he went to see whether perhaps he would find anything on it. When he came to it, he found nothing but leaves, for it was not the season for figs. ¹⁴He said to it, "May no one ever eat fruit from you again." And his disciples heard it.

Jesus Cleanses the Temple

15 Then they came to Jerusalem. And he entered the temple and began to drive out those who were selling and those who were buying in the temple, and he overturned the tables of the money changers and the seats of those who sold doves; ¹⁶and he would not allow anyone to carry anything through the temple. ¹⁷He was teaching and saying, "Is it not written,
   'My house shall be called a house of
      prayer for all the nations'?
   But you have made it a den of
      robbers."

2 καὶ λέγει αὐτοῖς, Ὑπάγετε εἰς τὴν κώμην τὴν κατέναντι ὑμῶν, καὶ εὐθὺς εἰσπορευόμενοι εἰς αὐτὴν εὑρήσετε πῶλον δεδεμένον ἐφ' ὃν οὐδεὶς οὔπω ἀνθρώπων ἐκάθισεν· λύσατε αὐτὸν καὶ φέρετε. 3 καὶ ἐάν τις ὑμῖν εἴπῃ, Τί ποιεῖτε τοῦτο; εἴπατε, Ὁ κύριος αὐτοῦ χρείαν ἔχει, καὶ εὐθὺς αὐτὸν ἀποστέλλει πάλιν ὧδε. 4 καὶ ἀπῆλθον καὶ εὗρον πῶλον δεδεμένον πρὸς θύραν ἔξω ἐπὶ τοῦ ἀμφόδου καὶ λύουσιν αὐτόν. 5 καί τινες τῶν ἐκεῖ ἑστηκότων ἔλεγον αὐτοῖς, Τί ποιεῖτε λύοντες τὸν πῶλον; 6 οἱ δὲ εἶπαν αὐτοῖς καθὼς εἶπεν ὁ Ἰησοῦς, καὶ ἀφῆκαν αὐτούς. 7 καὶ φέρουσιν τὸν πῶλον πρὸς τὸν Ἰησοῦν καὶ ἐπιβάλλουσιν αὐτῷ τὰ ἱμάτια αὐτῶν, καὶ ἐκάθισεν ἐπ' αὐτόν. 8 καὶ πολλοὶ τὰ ἱμάτια αὐτῶν ἔστρωσαν εἰς τὴν ὁδόν, ἄλλοι δὲ στιβάδας κόψαντες ἐκ τῶν ἀγρῶν. 9 καὶ οἱ προάγοντες καὶ οἱ ἀκολουθοῦντες ἔκραζον,

Ὡσαννά·
   Εὐλογημένος ὁ ἐρχόμενος ἐν
      ὀνόματι κυρίου·
10 Εὐλογημένη ἡ ἐρχομένη βασιλεία
      τοῦ πατρὸς ἡμῶν Δαυίδ·
   Ὡσαννὰ ἐν τοῖς ὑψίστοις.

11 Καὶ εἰσῆλθεν εἰς Ἱεροσόλυμα εἰς τὸ ἱερὸν καὶ περιβλεψάμενος πάντα, ὀψίας ἤδη οὔσης τῆς ὥρας, ἐξῆλθεν εἰς Βηθανίαν μετὰ τῶν δώδεκα. 12 Καὶ τῇ ἐπαύριον ἐξελθόντων αὐτῶν ἀπὸ Βηθανίας ἐπείνασεν. 13 καὶ ἰδὼν συκῆν ἀπὸ μακρόθεν ἔχουσαν φύλλα ἦλθεν, εἰ ἄρα τι εὑρήσει ἐν αὐτῇ, καὶ ἐλθὼν ἐπ' αὐτὴν οὐδὲν εὗρεν εἰ μὴ φύλλα· ὁ γὰρ καιρὸς οὐκ ἦν σύκων. 14 καὶ ἀποκριθεὶς εἶπεν αὐτῇ, Μηκέτι εἰς τὸν αἰῶνα ἐκ σοῦ μηδεὶς καρπὸν φάγοι. καὶ ἤκουον οἱ μαθηταὶ αὐτοῦ. 15 Καὶ ἔρχονται εἰς Ἱεροσόλυμα. καὶ εἰσελθὼν εἰς τὸ ἱερὸν ἤρξατο ἐκβάλλειν τοὺς πωλοῦντας καὶ τοὺς ἀγοράζοντας ἐν τῷ ἱερῷ, καὶ τὰς τραπέζας τῶν κολλυβιστῶν καὶ τὰς καθέδρας τῶν πωλούντων τὰς περιστερὰς κατέστρεψεν, 16 καὶ οὐκ ἤφιεν ἵνα τις διενέγκῃ σκεῦος διὰ τοῦ ἱεροῦ. 17 καὶ ἐδίδασκεν καὶ ἔλεγεν αὐτοῖς, Οὐ γέγραπται ὅτι

Ὁ οἶκός μου οἶκος προσευχῆς
   κληθήσεται πᾶσιν τοῖς
   ἔθνεσιν;
   ὑμεῖς δὲ πεποιήκατε αὐτὸν
      σπήλαιον λῃστῶν.

two of his disciples, ²saying to them, "Go to the village ahead of you, and just as you enter it, you will find a colt tied there, which no one has ever ridden. Untie it and bring it here. ³If anyone asks you, 'Why are you doing this?' tell him, 'The Lord needs it and will send it back here shortly.' "

⁴They went and found a colt outside in the street, tied at a doorway. As they untied it, ⁵some people standing there asked, "What are you doing, untying that colt?" ⁶They answered as Jesus had told them to, and the people let them go. ⁷When they brought the colt to Jesus and threw their cloaks over it, he sat on it. ⁸Many people spread their cloaks on the road, while others spread branches they had cut in the fields. ⁹Those who went ahead and those who followed shouted,

"Hosanna!ᵃ"

"Blessed is he who comes in the name
   of the Lord!"ᵇ

10"Blessed is the coming kingdom of our
   father David!"

"Hosanna in the highest!"

¹¹Jesus entered Jerusalem and went to the temple. He looked around at everything, but since it was already late, he went out to Bethany with the Twelve.

Jesus Clears the Temple

¹²The next day as they were leaving Bethany, Jesus was hungry. ¹³Seeing in the distance a fig tree in leaf, he went to find out if it had any fruit. When he reached it, he found nothing but leaves, because it was not the season for figs. ¹⁴Then he said to the tree, "May no one ever eat fruit from you again." And his disciples heard him say it.

¹⁵On reaching Jerusalem, Jesus entered the temple area and began driving out those who were buying and selling there. He overturned the tables of the money changers and the benches of those selling doves, ¹⁶and would not allow anyone to carry merchandise through the temple courts. ¹⁷And as he taught them, he said, "Is it not written:

" 'My house will be called
   a house of prayer for all nations'ᶜ?

But you have made it 'a den of robbers.'ᵈ"

ᵃ9 A Hebrew expression meaning "Save!" which became an exclamation of praise; also in verse 10
ᵇ9 Psalm 118:25,26   ᶜ17 Isaiah 56:7   ᵈ17 Jer. 7:11

NRSV

18And when the chief priests and the scribes heard it, they kept looking for a way to kill him; for they were afraid of him, because the whole crowd was spellbound by his teaching. 19And when evening came, Jesus and his disciplesf went out of the city.

The Lesson from the Withered Fig Tree

20 In the morning as they passed by, they saw the fig tree withered away to its roots. 21Then Peter remembered and said to him, "Rabbi, look! The fig tree that you cursed has withered." 22Jesus answered them, "Haveg faith in God. 23Truly I tell you, if you say to this mountain, 'Be taken up and thrown into the sea,' and if you do not doubt in your heart, but believe that what you say will come to pass, it will be done for you. 24So I tell you, whatever you ask for in prayer, believe that you have receivedh it, and it will be yours.

25 "Whenever you stand praying, forgive, if you have anything against anyone; so that your Father in heaven may also forgive you your trespasses."i

Jesus' Authority Is Questioned

27 Again they came to Jerusalem. As he was walking in the temple, the chief priests, the scribes, and the elders came to him 28and said, "By what authority are you doing these things? Who gave you this authority to do them?" 29Jesus said to them, "I will ask you one question; answer me, and I will tell you by what authority I do these things. 30Did the baptism of John come from heaven, or was it of human origin? Answer me." 31They argued with one another, "If we say, 'From heaven,' he will say, 'Why then did you not believe him?' 32But shall we say, 'Of human origin'?"—they were afraid of the crowd, for all regarded John as truly a prophet. 33So they answered Jesus, "We do not know." And Jesus said to them, "Neither will I tell you by what authority I am doing these things."

The Parable of the Wicked Tenants

12 Then he began to speak to them in parables. "A man planted a vineyard, put a fence around it, dug a pit for the wine press, and built a watchtower;

Greek

18 καὶ ἤκουσαν οἱ ἀρχιερεῖς καὶ οἱ γραμματεῖς καὶ ἐζήτουν πῶς αὐτὸν ἀπολέσωσιν· ἐφοβοῦντο γὰρ αὐτόν, πᾶς γὰρ ὁ ὄχλος ἐξεπλήσσετο ἐπὶ τῇ διδαχῇ αὐτοῦ. 19 Καὶ ὅταν ὀψὲ ἐγένετο, ἐξεπορεύοντοa ἔξω τῆς πόλεως.

20 Καὶ παραπορευόμενοι πρωὶ εἶδον τὴν συκῆν ἐξηραμμένην ἐκ ῥιζῶν. 21 καὶ ἀναμνησθεὶς ὁ Πέτρος λέγει αὐτῷ, Ῥαββί, ἴδε ἡ συκῆ ἣν κατηράσω ἐξήρανται. 22 καὶ ἀποκριθεὶς ὁ Ἰησοῦς λέγει αὐτοῖς, Ἔχετεb πίστιν θεοῦ. 23 ἀμὴν λέγω ὑμῖν ὅτι ὃς ἂν εἴπῃ τῷ ὄρει τούτῳ, Ἄρθητι καὶ βλήθητι εἰς τὴν θάλασσαν, καὶ μὴ διακριθῇ ἐν τῇ καρδίᾳ αὐτοῦ ἀλλὰ πιστεύῃ ὅτι ὃ λαλεῖ γίνεται, ἔσται αὐτῷ. 24 διὰ τοῦτο λέγω ὑμῖν, πάντα ὅσα προσεύχεσθε καὶ αἰτεῖσθε, πιστεύετε ὅτι ἐλάβετεc, καὶ ἔσται ὑμῖν. 25 καὶ ὅταν στήκετε προσευχόμενοι, ἀφίετε εἴ τι ἔχετε κατά τινος, ἵνα καὶ ὁ πατὴρ ὑμῶν ὁ ἐν τοῖς οὐρανοῖς ἀφῇ ὑμῖν τὰ παραπτώματα ὑμῶν.d

27 Καὶ ἔρχονται πάλιν εἰς Ἱεροσόλυμα. καὶ ἐν τῷ ἱερῷ περιπατοῦντος αὐτοῦ ἔρχονται πρὸς αὐτὸν οἱ ἀρχιερεῖς καὶ οἱ γραμματεῖς καὶ οἱ πρεσβύτεροι 28 καὶ ἔλεγον αὐτῷ, Ἐν ποίᾳ ἐξουσίᾳ ταῦτα ποιεῖς; ἢ τίς σοι ἔδωκεν τὴν ἐξουσίαν ταύτην ἵνα ταῦτα ποιῇς; 29 ὁ δὲ Ἰησοῦς εἶπεν αὐτοῖς, Ἐπερωτήσω ὑμᾶς ἕνα λόγον, καὶ ἀποκρίθητέ μοι καὶ ἐρῶ ὑμῖν ἐν ποίᾳ ἐξουσίᾳ ταῦτα ποιῶ· 30 τὸ βάπτισμα τὸ Ἰωάννου ἐξ οὐρανοῦ ἦν ἢ ἐξ ἀνθρώπων; ἀποκρίθητέ μοι. 31 καὶ διελογίζοντο πρὸς ἑαυτοὺς λέγοντες, Ἐὰν εἴπωμεν, Ἐξ οὐρανοῦ, ἐρεῖ, Διὰ τί [οὖν] οὐκ ἐπιστεύσατε αὐτῷ; 32 ἀλλὰ εἴπωμεν, Ἐξ ἀνθρώπων; – ἐφοβοῦντο τὸν ὄχλον· ἅπαντες γὰρ εἶχον τὸν Ἰωάννην ὄντως ὅτι προφήτης ἦν. 33 καὶ ἀποκριθέντες τῷ Ἰησοῦ λέγουσιν, Οὐκ οἴδαμεν. καὶ ὁ Ἰησοῦς λέγει αὐτοῖς, Οὐδὲ ἐγὼ λέγω ὑμῖν ἐν ποίᾳ ἐξουσίᾳ ταῦτα ποιῶ.

12 Καὶ ἤρξατο αὐτοῖς ἐν παραβολαῖς λαλεῖν, Ἀμπελῶνα ἄνθρωπος ἐφύτευσεν καὶ περιέθηκεν φραγμὸν καὶ ὤρυξεν ὑπολήνιον καὶ ᾠκοδόμησεν πύργον καὶ ἐξέδετο αὐτὸν

NIV

18The chief priests and the teachers of the law heard this and began looking for a way to kill him, for they feared him, because the whole crowd was amazed at his teaching.

19When evening came, theye went out of the city.

The Withered Fig Tree

20In the morning, as they went along, they saw the fig tree withered from the roots. 21Peter remembered and said to Jesus, "Rabbi, look! The fig tree you cursed has withered!"

22"Havef faith in God," Jesus answered. 23"I tell you the truth, if anyone says to this mountain, 'Go, throw yourself into the sea,' and does not doubt in his heart but believes that what he says will happen, it will be done for him. 24Therefore I tell you, whatever you ask for in prayer, believe that you have received it, and it will be yours. 25And when you stand praying, if you hold anything against anyone, forgive him, so that your Father in heaven may forgive you your sins.g"

The Authority of Jesus Questioned

27They arrived again in Jerusalem, and while Jesus was walking in the temple courts, the chief priests, the teachers of the law and the elders came to him. 28"By what authority are you doing these things?" they asked. "And who gave you authority to do this?"

29Jesus replied, "I will ask you one question. Answer me, and I will tell you by what authority I am doing these things. 30John's baptism—was it from heaven, or from men? Tell me!"

31They discussed it among themselves and said, "If we say, 'From heaven,' he will ask, 'Then why didn't you believe him?' 32But if we say, 'From men' . . . ." (They feared the people, for everyone held that John really was a prophet.)

33So they answered Jesus, "We don't know."

Jesus said, "Neither will I tell you by what authority I am doing these things."

The Parable of the Tenants

12 He then began to speak to them in parables: "A man planted a vineyard. He put a wall around it, dug a pit for the winepress and built a watchtower. Then

---

fGk they: other ancient authorities read he gOther ancient authorities read "If you have hOther ancient authorities read are receiving iOther ancient authorities add verse 26, "But if you do not forgive, neither will your Father in heaven forgive your trespasses."

a19 NIV/NRSV notes ἐξεπορεύετο b22 NIV/NRSV notes Εἰ ἔχετε c24 NRSV note h λαμβάνετε d25 NIV/NRSV notes add 26 εἰ δὲ ὑμεῖς οὐκ ἀφίετε, οὐδὲ ὁ πατὴρ ὑμῶν ὁ ἐν τοῖς οὐρανοῖς ἀφήσει τὰ παραπτώματα ὑμῶν.

e19 Some early manuscripts he f22 Some early manuscripts If you have g25 Some manuscripts sins. 26But if you do not forgive, neither will your Father who is in heaven forgive your sins.

then he leased it to tenants and went to another country. ²When the season came, he sent a slave to the tenants to collect from them his share of the produce of the vineyard. ³But they seized him, and beat him, and sent him away empty-handed. ⁴And again he sent another slave to them; this one they beat over the head and insulted. ⁵Then he sent another, and that one they killed. And so it was with many others; some they beat, and others they killed. ⁶He had still one other, a beloved son. Finally he sent him to them, saying, 'They will respect my son.' ⁷But those tenants said to one another, 'This is the heir; come, let us kill him, and the inheritance will be ours.' ⁸So they seized him, killed him, and threw him out of the vineyard. ⁹What then will the owner of the vineyard do? He will come and destroy the tenants and give the vineyard to others. ¹⁰Have you not read this scripture:

'The stone that the builders rejected
  has become the cornerstone;ʲ
¹¹ this was the Lord's doing,
  and it is amazing in our eyes'?"

12 When they realized that he had told this parable against them, they wanted to arrest him, but they feared the crowd. So they left him and went away.

The Question about Paying Taxes

13 Then they sent to him some Pharisees and some Herodians to trap him in what he said. ¹⁴And they came and said to him, "Teacher, we know that you are sincere, and show deference to no one; for you do not regard people with partiality, but teach the way of God in accordance with truth. Is it lawful to pay taxes to the emperor, or not? ¹⁵Should we pay them, or should we not?" But knowing their hypocrisy, he said to them, "Why are you putting me to the test? Bring me a denarius and let me see it." ¹⁶And they brought one. Then he said to them, "Whose head is this, and whose title?" They answered, "The emperor's." ¹⁷Jesus said to them, "Give to the emperor the things that are the emperor's, and to God the things that are God's." And they were utterly amazed at him.

γεωργοῖς καὶ ἀπεδήμησεν. **2** καὶ ἀπέστειλεν πρὸς τοὺς γεωργοὺς τῷ καιρῷ δοῦλον ἵνα παρὰ τῶν γεωργῶν λάβῃ ἀπὸ τῶν καρπῶν τοῦ ἀμπελῶνος· **3** καὶ λαβόντες αὐτὸν ἔδειραν καὶ ἀπέστειλαν κενόν. **4** καὶ πάλιν ἀπέστειλεν πρὸς αὐτοὺς ἄλλον δοῦλον· κἀκεῖνον ἐκεφαλίωσαν καὶ ἠτίμασαν. **5** καὶ ἄλλον ἀπέστειλεν· κἀκεῖνον ἀπέκτειναν, καὶ πολλοὺς ἄλλους, οὓς μὲν δέροντες οὓς δὲ ἀποκτέννοντες. **6** ἔτι ἕνα εἶχεν υἱὸν ἀγαπητόν· ἀπέστειλεν αὐτὸν ἔσχατον πρὸς αὐτοὺς λέγων ὅτι Ἐντραπήσονται τὸν υἱόν μου. **7** ἐκεῖνοι δὲ οἱ γεωργοὶ πρὸς ἑαυτοὺς εἶπαν ὅτι Οὗτός ἐστιν ὁ κληρονόμος· δεῦτε ἀποκτείνωμεν αὐτόν, καὶ ἡμῶν ἔσται ἡ κληρονομία. **8** καὶ λαβόντες ἀπέκτειναν αὐτὸν καὶ ἐξέβαλον αὐτὸν ἔξω τοῦ ἀμπελῶνος. **9** τί [οὖν] ποιήσει ὁ κύριος τοῦ ἀμπελῶνος; ἐλεύσεται καὶ ἀπολέσει τοὺς γεωργοὺς καὶ δώσει τὸν ἀμπελῶνα ἄλλοις. **10** οὐδὲ τὴν γραφὴν ταύτην ἀνέγνωτε,

Λίθον ὃν ἀπεδοκίμασαν οἱ οἰκοδομοῦντες,
  οὗτος ἐγενήθη εἰς κεφαλὴν γωνίας·
11 παρὰ κυρίου ἐγένετο αὕτη καὶ ἔστιν θαυμαστὴ ἐν ὀφθαλμοῖς ἡμῶν;

12 Καὶ ἐζήτουν αὐτὸν κρατῆσαι, καὶ ἐφοβήθησαν τὸν ὄχλον, ἔγνωσαν γὰρ ὅτι πρὸς αὐτοὺς τὴν παραβολὴν εἶπεν. καὶ ἀφέντες αὐτὸν ἀπῆλθον.

13 Καὶ ἀποστέλλουσιν πρὸς αὐτόν τινας τῶν Φαρισαίων καὶ τῶν Ἡρῳδιανῶν ἵνα αὐτὸν ἀγρεύσωσιν λόγῳ. **14** καὶ ἐλθόντες λέγουσιν αὐτῷ, Διδάσκαλε, οἴδαμεν ὅτι ἀληθὴς εἶ καὶ οὐ μέλει σοι περὶ οὐδενός· οὐ γὰρ βλέπεις εἰς πρόσωπον ἀνθρώπων, ἀλλ᾽ ἐπ᾽ ἀληθείας τὴν ὁδὸν τοῦ θεοῦ διδάσκεις· ἔξεστιν δοῦναι κῆνσον Καίσαρι ἢ οὔ;ᵃ δῶμεν ἢ μὴ δῶμεν; **15** ὁ δὲ εἰδὼς αὐτῶν τὴν ὑπόκρισιν εἶπεν αὐτοῖς, Τί με πειράζετε; φέρετέ μοι δηνάριον ἵνα ἴδω. **16** οἱ δὲ ἤνεγκαν. καὶ λέγει αὐτοῖς, Τίνος ἡ εἰκὼν αὕτη καὶ ἡ ἐπιγραφή; οἱ δὲ εἶπαν αὐτῷ, Καίσαρος. **17** ὁ δὲ Ἰησοῦς εἶπεν αὐτοῖς, Τὰ Καίσαρος ἀπόδοτε Καίσαρι καὶ τὰ τοῦ θεοῦ τῷ θεῷ. καὶ ἐξεθαύμαζον ἐπ᾽ αὐτῷ.

he rented the vineyard to some farmers and went away on a journey. ²At harvest time he sent a servant to the tenants to collect from them some of the fruit of the vineyard. ³But they seized him, beat him and sent him away empty-handed. ⁴Then he sent another servant to them; they struck this man on the head and treated him shamefully. ⁵He sent still another, and that one they killed. He sent many others; some of them they beat, others they killed.

⁶"He had one left to send, a son, whom he loved. He sent him last of all, saying, 'They will respect my son.'

⁷"But the tenants said to one another, 'This is the heir. Come, let's kill him, and the inheritance will be ours.' ⁸So they took him and killed him, and threw him out of the vineyard.

⁹"What then will the owner of the vineyard do? He will come and kill those tenants and give the vineyard to others. ¹⁰Haven't you read this scripture:

" 'The stone the builders rejected
  has become the capstoneᵃ;
¹¹the Lord has done this,
  and it is marvelous in our eyes'ᵇ?"

¹²Then they looked for a way to arrest him because they knew he had spoken the parable against them. But they were afraid of the crowd; so they left him and went away.

Paying Taxes to Caesar

¹³Later they sent some of the Pharisees and Herodians to Jesus to catch him in his words. ¹⁴They came to him and said, "Teacher, we know you are a man of integrity. You aren't swayed by men, because you pay no attention to who they are; but you teach the way of God in accordance with the truth. Is it right to pay taxes to Caesar or not? ¹⁵Should we pay or shouldn't we?"

But Jesus knew their hypocrisy. "Why are you trying to trap me?" he asked. "Bring me a denarius and let me look at it." ¹⁶They brought the coin, and he asked them, "Whose portrait is this? And whose inscription?"

"Caesar's," they replied.

¹⁷Then Jesus said to them, "Give to Caesar what is Caesar's and to God what is God's."

And they were amazed at him.

ʲOr *keystone*   ᵃ14 NIV/NRSV texts begin verse 15 after οὔ;   ᵃ10 Or *cornerstone*   ᵇ11 Psalm 118:22,23

NRSV

The Question about the Resurrection

18 Some Sadducees, who say there is no resurrection, came to him and asked him a question, saying, 19"Teacher, Moses wrote for us that if a man's brother dies, leaving a wife but no child, the man^k shall marry the widow and raise up children for his brother. 20There were seven brothers; the first married and, when he died, left no children; 21and the second married her and died, leaving no children; and the third likewise; 22none of the seven left children. Last of all the woman herself died. 23In the resurrection^l whose wife will she be? For the seven had married her."

24 Jesus said to them, "Is not this the reason you are wrong, that you know neither the scriptures nor the power of God? 25For when they rise from the dead, they neither marry nor are given in marriage, but are like angels in heaven. 26And as for the dead being raised, have you not read in the book of Moses, in the story about the bush, how God said to him, 'I am the God of Abraham, the God of Isaac, and the God of Jacob'? 27He is God not of the dead, but of the living; you are quite wrong."

The First Commandment

28 One of the scribes came near and heard them disputing with one another, and seeing that he answered them well, he asked him, "Which commandment is the first of all?" 29Jesus answered, "The first is, 'Hear, O Israel: the Lord our God, the Lord is one; 30you shall love the Lord your God with all your heart, and with all your soul, and with all your mind, and with all your strength.' 31The second is this, 'You shall love your neighbor as yourself.' There is no other commandment greater than these." 32Then the scribe said to him, "You are right, Teacher; you have truly said that 'he is one, and besides him there is no other'; 33and 'to love him with all the heart, and with all the understanding, and with all the strength,' and 'to love one's neighbor as oneself,'—this is much more important than all whole burnt offerings and sacrifices." 34When Jesus saw that he answered wisely, he said to him, "You are not far from the kingdom of God." After that no one dared to ask him any question.

NIV

Marriage at the Resurrection

18Then the Sadducees, who say there is no resurrection, came to him with a question. 19"Teacher," they said, "Moses wrote for us that if a man's brother dies and leaves a wife but no children, the man must marry the widow and have children for his brother. 20Now there were seven brothers. The first one married and died without leaving any children. 21The second one married the widow, but he also died, leaving no child. It was the same with the third. 22In fact, none of the seven left any children. Last of all, the woman died too. 23At the resurrection^c whose wife will she be, since the seven were married to her?"

24Jesus replied, "Are you not in error because you do not know the Scriptures or the power of God? 25When the dead rise, they will neither marry nor be given in marriage; they will be like the angels in heaven. 26Now about the dead rising—have you not read in the book of Moses, in the account of the bush, how God said to him, 'I am the God of Abraham, the God of Isaac, and the God of Jacob'^d? 27He is not the God of the dead, but of the living. You are badly mistaken!"

The Greatest Commandment

28One of the teachers of the law came and heard them debating. Noticing that Jesus had given them a good answer, he asked him, "Of all the commandments, which is the most important?"

29"The most important one," answered Jesus, "is this: 'Hear, O Israel, the Lord our God, the Lord is one.^e 30Love the Lord your God with all your heart and with all your soul and with all your mind and with all your strength.'^f 31The second is this: 'Love your neighbor as yourself.'^g There is no commandment greater than these."

32"Well said, teacher," the man replied. "You are right in saying that God is one and there is no other but him. 33To love him with all your heart, with all your understanding and with all your strength, and to love your neighbor as yourself is more important than all burnt offerings and sacrifices."

34When Jesus saw that he had answered wisely, he said to him, "You are not far from the kingdom of God." And from then on no one dared ask him any more questions.

---

^k Gk *his brother* ^l Other ancient authorities add *when they rise*

^b23 NIV/NRSV texts omit ὅταν ἀναστῶσιν; NIV/NRSV notes as UBS ^c27 NIV text adds ὁ† ^d34 NIV text omits αὐτὸν

^c23 Some manuscripts *resurrection, when men rise from the dead,* ^d26 Exodus 3:6 ^e29 Or *the Lord our God is one Lord* ^f30 Deut. 6:4,5 ^g31 Lev. 19:18

The Question about David's Son

35 While Jesus was teaching in the temple, he said, "How can the scribes say that the Messiah[m] is the son of David? 36David himself, by the Holy Spirit, declared,

'The Lord said to my Lord,
"Sit at my right hand,
     until I put your enemies under your
       feet." '

37David himself calls him Lord; so how can he be his son?" And the large crowd was listening to him with delight.

Jesus Denounces the Scribes

38 As he taught, he said, "Beware of the scribes, who like to walk around in long robes, and to be greeted with respect in the marketplaces, 39and to have the best seats in the synagogues and places of honor at banquets! 40They devour widows' houses and for the sake of appearance say long prayers. They will receive the greater condemnation."

The Widow's Offering

41 He sat down opposite the treasury, and watched the crowd putting money into the treasury. Many rich people put in large sums. 42A poor widow came and put in two small copper coins, which are worth a penny. 43Then he called his disciples and said to them, "Truly I tell you, this poor widow has put in more than all those who are contributing to the treasury. 44For all of them have contributed out of their abundance; but she out of her poverty has put in everything she had, all she had to live on."

The Destruction of the Temple Foretold

13 As he came out of the temple, one of his disciples said to him, "Look, Teacher, what large stones and what large buildings!" 2Then Jesus asked him, "Do you see these great buildings? Not one stone will be left here upon another; all will be thrown down."

3 When he was sitting on the Mount of Olives opposite the temple, Peter, James, John, and Andrew asked him privately, 4"Tell us, when will this be, and what will be the sign that all these things are about to be accomplished?" 5Then Jesus began to say to them, "Beware that no one leads

---

35 Καὶ ἀποκριθεὶς ὁ Ἰησοῦς ἔλεγεν διδάσκων ἐν τῷ ἱερῷ, Πῶς λέγουσιν οἱ γραμματεῖς ὅτι ὁ Χριστὸς υἱός Δαυὶδ ἐστιν; 36 αὐτὸς Δαυὶδ εἶπεν ἐν τῷ πνεύματι τῷ ἁγίῳ,

Εἶπεν κύριος τῷ κυρίῳ μου,
Κάθου ἐκ δεξιῶν μου,
   ἕως ἂν θῶ τοὺς ἐχθρούς σου
     ὑποκάτω τῶν ποδῶν σου.

37 αὐτὸς Δαυὶδ λέγει αὐτὸν κύριον, καὶ πόθεν αὐτοῦ ἐστιν υἱός; καὶ [ὁ] πολὺς ὄχλος ἤκουεν αὐτοῦ ἡδέως.

38 Καὶ ἐν τῇ διδαχῇ αὐτοῦ ἔλεγεν, Βλέπετε ἀπὸ τῶν γραμματέων τῶν θελόντων ἐν στολαῖς περιπατεῖν καὶ ἀσπασμοὺς ἐν ταῖς ἀγοραῖς 39 καὶ πρωτοκαθεδρίας ἐν ταῖς συναγωγαῖς καὶ πρωτοκλισίας ἐν τοῖς δείπνοις, 40 οἱ κατεσθίοντες τὰς οἰκίας τῶν χηρῶν καὶ προφάσει μακρὰ προσευχόμενοι· οὗτοι λήμψονται περισσότερον κρίμα.

41 Καὶ καθίσας κατέναντι τοῦ γαζοφυλακίου ἐθεώρει πῶς ὁ ὄχλος βάλλει χαλκὸν εἰς τὸ γαζοφυλάκιον. καὶ πολλοὶ πλούσιοι ἔβαλλον πολλά· 42 καὶ ἐλθοῦσα μία χήρα πτωχὴ ἔβαλεν λεπτὰ δύο, ὅ ἐστιν κοδράντης. 43 καὶ προσκαλεσάμενος τοὺς μαθητὰς αὐτοῦ εἶπεν αὐτοῖς, Ἀμὴν λέγω ὑμῖν ὅτι ἡ χήρα αὕτη ἡ πτωχὴ πλεῖον πάντων ἔβαλεν τῶν βαλλόντων εἰς τὸ γαζοφυλάκιον· 44 πάντες γὰρ ἐκ τοῦ περισσεύοντος αὐτοῖς ἔβαλον, αὕτη δὲ ἐκ τῆς ὑστερήσεως αὐτῆς πάντα ὅσα εἶχεν ἔβαλεν ὅλον τὸν βίον αὐτῆς.

13 Καὶ ἐκπορευομένου αὐτοῦ ἐκ τοῦ ἱεροῦ λέγει αὐτῷ εἷς τῶν μαθητῶν αὐτοῦ, Διδάσκαλε, ἴδε ποταποὶ λίθοι καὶ ποταπαὶ οἰκοδομαί. 2 καὶ ὁ Ἰησοῦς εἶπεν αὐτῷ, Βλέπεις ταύτας τὰς μεγάλας οἰκοδομάς; οὐ μὴ ἀφεθῇ ὧδε λίθος ἐπὶ λίθον ὃς οὐ μὴ καταλυθῇ.

3 Καὶ καθημένου αὐτοῦ εἰς τὸ Ὄρος τῶν Ἐλαιῶν κατέναντι τοῦ ἱεροῦ ἐπηρώτα αὐτὸν κατ᾽ ἰδίαν Πέτρος καὶ Ἰάκωβος καὶ Ἰωάννης καὶ Ἀνδρέας, 4 Εἰπὸν ἡμῖν, πότε ταῦτα ἔσται καὶ τί τὸ σημεῖον ὅταν μέλλῃ ταῦτα συντελεῖσθαι πάντα; 5 ὁ δὲ Ἰησοῦς ἤρξατο λέγειν αὐτοῖς, Βλέπετε μή τις ὑμᾶς

Whose Son Is the Christ?

35While Jesus was teaching in the temple courts, he asked, "How is it that the teachers of the law say that the Christ[h] is the son of David? 36David himself, speaking by the Holy Spirit, declared:

" 'The Lord said to my Lord:
   "Sit at my right hand
   until I put your enemies
     under your feet." '[i]

37David himself calls him 'Lord.' How then can he be his son?"

The large crowd listened to him with delight.

38As he taught, Jesus said, "Watch out for the teachers of the law. They like to walk around in flowing robes and be greeted in the marketplaces, 39and have the most important seats in the synagogues and the places of honor at banquets. 40They devour widows' houses and for a show make lengthy prayers. Such men will be punished most severely."

The Widow's Offering

41Jesus sat down opposite the place where the offerings were put and watched the crowd putting their money into the temple treasury. Many rich people threw in large amounts. 42But a poor widow came and put in two very small copper coins,[j] worth only a fraction of a penny.[k]

43Calling his disciples to him, Jesus said, "I tell you the truth, this poor widow has put more into the treasury than all the others. 44They all gave out of their wealth; but she, out of her poverty, put in everything—all she had to live on."

Signs of the End of the Age

13 As he was leaving the temple, one of his disciples said to him, "Look, Teacher! What massive stones! What magnificent buildings!"

2"Do you see all these great buildings?" replied Jesus. "Not one stone here will be left on another; every one will be thrown down."

3As Jesus was sitting on the Mount of Olives opposite the temple, Peter, James, John and Andrew asked him privately, 4"Tell us, when will these things happen? And what will be the sign that they are all about to be fulfilled?"

5Jesus said to them: "Watch out that no

---

h35 Or Messiah   i36 Psalm 110:1   j42 Greek *two lepta*
k42 Greek *kodrantes*

you astray. 6Many will come in my name and say, 'I am he!'ⁿ and they will lead many astray. 7When you hear of wars and rumors of wars, do not be alarmed; this must take place, but the end is still to come. 8For nation will rise against nation, and kingdom against kingdom; there will be earthquakes in various places; there will be famines. This is but the beginning of the birth pangs.

Persecution Foretold

9 "As for yourselves, beware; for they will hand you over to councils; and you will be beaten in synagogues; and you will stand before governors and kings because of me, as a testimony to them. 10And the good newsᵒ must first be proclaimed to all nations. 11When they bring you to trial and hand you over, do not worry beforehand about what you are to say; but say whatever is given you at that time, for it is not you who speak, but the Holy Spirit. 12Brother will betray brother to death, and a father his child, and children will rise against parents and have them put to death; 13and you will be hated by all because of my name. But the one who endures to the end will be saved.

The Desolating Sacrilege

14 "But when you see the desolating sacrilege set up where it ought not to be (let the reader understand), then those in Judea must flee to the mountains; 15the one on the housetop must not go down or enter the house to take anything away; 16the one in the field must not turn back to get a coat. 17Woe to those who are pregnant and to those who are nursing infants in those days! 18Pray that it may not be in winter. 19For in those days there will be suffering, such as has not been from the beginning of the creation that God created until now, no, and never will be. 20And if the Lord had not cut short those days, no one would be saved; but for the sake of the elect, whom he chose, he has cut short those days. 21And if anyone says to you at that time, 'Look! Here is the Messiah!'ᵖ or 'Look! There he is!'—do not believe it. 22False messiahs�q and false prophets will appear and produce signs and omens, to lead astray, if possible, the elect. 23But be alert; I have already told you everything.

The Coming of the Son of Man

24 "But in those days, after that suffering,

πλανήσῃ· **6** πολλοὶ ἐλεύσονται ἐπὶ τῷ ὀνόματί μου λέγοντες ὅτι Ἐγώ εἰμι, καὶ πολλοὺς πλανήσουσιν. **7** ὅταν δὲ ἀκούσητε πολέμους καὶ ἀκοὰς πολέμων, μὴ θροεῖσθε· δεῖ γενέσθαι, ἀλλ' οὔπω τὸ τέλος. **8** ἐγερθήσεται γὰρ ἔθνος ἐπ' ἔθνος καὶ βασιλεία ἐπὶ βασιλείαν, ἔσονται σεισμοὶ κατὰ τόπους, ἔσονται λιμοί· ἀρχὴ ὠδίνων ταῦτα. **9** βλέπετε δὲ ὑμεῖς ἑαυτούς· παραδώσουσιν ὑμᾶς εἰς συνέδρια καὶ εἰς συναγωγὰς δαρήσεσθε καὶ ἐπὶ ἡγεμόνων καὶ βασιλέων σταθήσεσθε ἕνεκεν ἐμοῦ εἰς μαρτύριον αὐτοῖς. **10** καὶ εἰς πάντα τὰ ἔθνη πρῶτον δεῖ κηρυχθῆναι τὸ εὐαγγέλιον. **11** καὶ ὅταν ἄγωσιν ὑμᾶς παραδιδόντες, μὴ προμεριμνᾶτε τί λαλήσητε, ἀλλ' ὃ ἐὰν δοθῇ ὑμῖν ἐν ἐκείνῃ τῇ ὥρᾳ τοῦτο λαλεῖτε· οὐ γάρ ἐστε ὑμεῖς οἱ λαλοῦντες ἀλλὰ τὸ πνεῦμα τὸ ἅγιον. **12** καὶ παραδώσει ἀδελφὸς ἀδελφὸν εἰς θάνατον καὶ πατὴρ τέκνον, καὶ ἐπαναστήσονται τέκνα ἐπὶ γονεῖς καὶ θανατώσουσιν αὐτούς· **13** καὶ ἔσεσθε μισούμενοι ὑπὸ πάντων διὰ τὸ ὄνομά μου. ὁ δὲ ὑπομείνας εἰς τέλος οὗτος σωθήσεται.

14 Ὅταν δὲ ἴδητε τὸ βδέλυγμα τῆς ἐρημώσεως ἑστηκότα ὅπου οὐ δεῖ, ὁ ἀναγινώσκων νοείτω, τότε οἱ ἐν τῇ Ἰουδαίᾳ φευγέτωσαν εἰς τὰ ὄρη, **15** ὁ [δὲ]ᵃ ἐπὶ τοῦ δώματος μὴ καταβάτω μηδὲ εἰσελθάτω ἆραί τι ἐκ τῆς οἰκίας αὐτοῦ, **16** καὶ ὁ εἰς τὸν ἀγρὸν μὴ ἐπιστρεψάτω εἰς τὰ ὀπίσω ἆραι τὸ ἱμάτιον αὐτοῦ. **17** οὐαὶ δὲ ταῖς ἐν γαστρὶ ἐχούσαις καὶ ταῖς θηλαζούσαις ἐν ἐκείναις ταῖς ἡμέραις. **18** προσεύχεσθε δὲ ἵνα μὴ γένηται χειμῶνος· **19** ἔσονται γὰρ αἱ ἡμέραι ἐκεῖναι θλῖψις οἵα οὐ γέγονεν τοιαύτη ἀπ' ἀρχῆς κτίσεως ἣν ἔκτισεν ὁ θεὸς ἕως τοῦ νῦν καὶ οὐ μὴ γένηται. **20** καὶ εἰ μὴ ἐκολόβωσεν κύριος τὰς ἡμέρας, οὐκ ἂν ἐσώθη πᾶσα σάρξ· ἀλλὰ διὰ τοὺς ἐκλεκτοὺς οὓς ἐξελέξατο ἐκολόβωσεν τὰς ἡμέρας. **21** καὶ τότε ἐάν τις ὑμῖν εἴπῃ, Ἴδε ὧδε ὁ Χριστός, Ἴδε ἐκεῖ, μὴ πιστεύετε· **22** ἐγερθήσονται γὰρ ψευδόχριστοι καὶ ψευδοπροφῆται καὶ δώσουσιν σημεῖα καὶ τέρατα πρὸς τὸ ἀποπλανᾶν, εἰ δυνατόν, τοὺς ἐκλεκτούς. **23** ὑμεῖς δὲ βλέπετε· προείρηκα ὑμῖν πάντα.

24 Ἀλλὰ ἐν ἐκείναις ταῖς ἡμέραις μετὰ τὴν θλῖψιν ἐκείνην

one deceives you. 6Many will come in my name, claiming, 'I am he,' and will deceive many. 7When you hear of wars and rumors of wars, do not be alarmed. Such things must happen, but the end is still to come. 8Nation will rise against nation, and kingdom against kingdom. There will be earthquakes in various places, and famines. These are the beginning of birth pains.

9"You must be on your guard. You will be handed over to the local councils and flogged in the synagogues. On account of me you will stand before governors and kings as witnesses to them. 10And the gospel must first be preached to all nations. 11Whenever you are arrested and brought to trial, do not worry beforehand about what to say. Just say whatever is given you at the time, for it is not you speaking, but the Holy Spirit.

12"Brother will betray brother to death, and a father his child. Children will rebel against their parents and have them put to death. 13All men will hate you because of me, but he who stands firm to the end will be saved.

14"When you see 'the abomination that causes desolation'ᵃ standing where itᵇ does not belong—let the reader understand—then let those who are in Judea flee to the mountains. 15Let no one on the roof of his house go down or enter the house to take anything out. 16Let no one in the field go back to get his cloak. 17How dreadful it will be in those days for pregnant women and nursing mothers! 18Pray that this will not take place in winter, 19because those will be days of distress unequaled from the beginning, when God created the world, until now—and never to be equaled again. 20If the Lord had not cut short those days, no one would survive. But for the sake of the elect, whom he has chosen, he has shortened them. 21At that time if anyone says to you, 'Look, here is the Christᶜ!' or, 'Look, there he is!' do not believe it. 22For false Christs and false prophets will appear and perform signs and miracles to deceive the elect—if that were possible. 23So be on your guard; I have told you everything ahead of time.

24"But in those days, following that distress,

n Gk I am   o Or gospel   p Or the Christ   q Or christs

a15 NIV text omits δὲ †

a14 Daniel 9:27; 11:31; 12:11   b14 Or he; also in verse 29   c21 Or Messiah

NRSV

the sun will be darkened,
    and the moon will not give its light,
25 and the stars will be falling from heaven,
    and the powers in the heavens will
        be shaken.

26Then they will see 'the Son of Man coming in clouds' with great power and glory. 27Then he will send out the angels, and gather his elect from the four winds, from the ends of the earth to the ends of heaven.

The Lesson of the Fig Tree

28 "From the fig tree learn its lesson: as soon as its branch becomes tender and puts forth its leaves, you know that summer is near. 29So also, when you see these things taking place, you know that he[r] is near, at the very gates. 30Truly I tell you, this generation will not pass away until all these things have taken place. 31Heaven and earth will pass away, but my words will not pass away.

The Necessity for Watchfulness

32 "But about that day or hour no one knows, neither the angels in heaven, nor the Son, but only the Father. 33Beware, keep alert;[s] for you do not know when the time will come. 34It is like a man going on a journey, when he leaves home and puts his slaves in charge, each with his work, and commands the doorkeeper to be on the watch. 35Therefore, keep awake—for you do not know when the master of the house will come, in the evening, or at midnight, or at cockcrow, or at dawn, 36or else he may find you asleep when he comes suddenly. 37And what I say to you I say to all: Keep awake."

The Plot to Kill Jesus

14 It was two days before the Passover and the festival of Unleavened Bread. The chief priests and the scribes were looking for a way to arrest Jesus[t] by stealth and kill him; 2for they said, "Not during the festival, or there may be a riot among the people."

The Anointing at Bethany

3 While he was at Bethany in the house of Simon the leper,[u] as he sat at the table, a woman came with an alabaster jar of very costly ointment of nard, and she broke open the jar and poured the ointment on his head. 4But some were there who said to one another in anger, "Why was the

Greek

ὁ ἥλιος σκοτισθήσεται,
    καὶ ἡ σελήνη οὐ δώσει τὸ
        φέγγος αὐτῆς,
25 καὶ οἱ ἀστέρες ἔσονται ἐκ τοῦ
        οὐρανοῦ πίπτοντες,
    καὶ αἱ δυνάμεις αἱ ἐν τοῖς
        οὐρανοῖς σαλευθήσονται.

26 καὶ τότε ὄψονται τὸν υἱὸν τοῦ ἀνθρώπου ἐρχόμενον ἐν νεφέλαις μετὰ δυνάμεως πολλῆς καὶ δόξης. 27 καὶ τότε ἀποστελεῖ τοὺς ἀγγέλους καὶ ἐπισυνάξει τοὺς ἐκλεκτοὺς [αὐτοῦ] ἐκ τῶν τεσσάρων ἀνέμων ἀπ᾽ ἄκρου γῆς ἕως ἄκρου οὐρανοῦ.

28 Ἀπὸ δὲ τῆς συκῆς μάθετε τὴν παραβολήν· ὅταν ἤδη ὁ κλάδος αὐτῆς ἁπαλὸς γένηται καὶ ἐκφύῃ τὰ φύλλα, γινώσκετε ὅτι ἐγγὺς τὸ θέρος ἐστίν· 29 οὕτως καὶ ὑμεῖς, ὅταν ἴδητε ταῦτα γινόμενα, γινώσκετε ὅτι ἐγγύς ἐστιν ἐπὶ θύραις. 30 ἀμὴν λέγω ὑμῖν ὅτι οὐ μὴ παρέλθῃ ἡ γενεὰ αὕτη μέχρις οὗ ταῦτα πάντα γένηται. 31 ὁ οὐρανὸς καὶ ἡ γῆ παρελεύσονται, οἱ δὲ λόγοι μου οὐ μὴ παρελεύσονται.

32 Περὶ δὲ τῆς ἡμέρας ἐκείνης ἢ τῆς ὥρας οὐδεὶς οἶδεν, οὐδὲ οἱ ἄγγελοι ἐν οὐρανῷ οὐδὲ ὁ υἱός, εἰ μὴ ὁ πατήρ. 33 βλέπετε, ἀγρυπνεῖτε[b]· οὐκ οἴδατε γὰρ πότε ὁ καιρός ἐστιν. 34 ὡς ἄνθρωπος ἀπόδημος ἀφεὶς τὴν οἰκίαν αὐτοῦ καὶ δοὺς τοῖς δούλοις αὐτοῦ τὴν ἐξουσίαν ἑκάστῳ τὸ ἔργον αὐτοῦ καὶ τῷ θυρωρῷ ἐνετείλατο ἵνα γρηγορῇ. 35 γρηγορεῖτε οὖν· οὐκ οἴδατε γὰρ πότε ὁ κύριος τῆς οἰκίας ἔρχεται, ἢ ὀψὲ ἢ μεσονύκτιον ἢ ἀλεκτοροφωνίας ἢ πρωΐ, 36 μὴ ἐλθὼν ἐξαίφνης εὕρῃ ὑμᾶς καθεύδοντας. 37 ὃ δὲ ὑμῖν λέγω πᾶσιν λέγω, γρηγορεῖτε.

14 ⁱἮν δὲ τὸ πάσχα καὶ τὰ ἄζυμα μετὰ δύο ἡμέρας. καὶ ἐζήτουν οἱ ἀρχιερεῖς καὶ οἱ γραμματεῖς πῶς αὐτὸν ἐν δόλῳ κρατήσαντες ἀποκτείνωσιν· 2 ἔλεγον γάρ, Μὴ ἐν τῇ ἑορτῇ, μήποτε ἔσται θόρυβος τοῦ λαοῦ.

3 Καὶ ὄντος αὐτοῦ ἐν Βηθανίᾳ ἐν τῇ οἰκίᾳ Σίμωνος τοῦ λεπροῦ, κατακειμένου αὐτοῦ ἦλθεν γυνὴ ἔχουσα ἀλάβαστρον μύρου νάρδου πιστικῆς πολυτελοῦς, συντρίψασα τὴν ἀλάβαστρον κατέχεεν αὐτοῦ τῆς κεφαλῆς. 4 ἦσαν δέ τινες ἀγανακτοῦντες πρὸς ἑαυτούς, Εἰς τί

NIV

" 'the sun will be darkened,
    and the moon will not give its light;
25the stars will fall from the sky,
    and the heavenly bodies will be
        shaken.'[d]

26"At that time men will see the Son of Man coming in clouds with great power and glory. 27And he will send his angels and gather his elect from the four winds, from the ends of the earth to the ends of the heavens.

28"Now learn this lesson from the fig tree: As soon as its twigs get tender and its leaves come out, you know that summer is near. 29Even so, when you see these things happening, you know that it is near, right at the door. 30I tell you the truth, this generation[e] will certainly not pass away until all these things have happened. 31Heaven and earth will pass away, but my words will never pass away.

The Day and Hour Unknown

32"No one knows about that day or hour, not even the angels in heaven, nor the Son, but only the Father. 33Be on guard! Be alert[f]! You do not know when that time will come. 34It's like a man going away: He leaves his house and puts his servants in charge, each with his assigned task, and tells the one at the door to keep watch.

35"Therefore keep watch because you do not know when the owner of the house will come back—whether in the evening, or at midnight, or when the rooster crows, or at dawn. 36If he comes suddenly, do not let him find you sleeping. 37What I say to you, I say to everyone: 'Watch!' "

Jesus Anointed at Bethany

14 Now the Passover and the Feast of Unleavened Bread were only two days away, and the chief priests and the teachers of the law were looking for some sly way to arrest Jesus and kill him. 2"But not during the Feast," they said, "or the people may riot."

3While he was in Bethany, reclining at the table in the home of a man known as Simon the Leper, a woman came with an alabaster jar of very expensive perfume, made of pure nard. She broke the jar and poured the perfume on his head.

4Some of those present were saying indignantly to one another, "Why this waste

---

r Or it s Other ancient authorities add and pray t Gk him
u The terms leper and leprosy can refer to several diseases

b33 NIV/NRSV notes ἀγρυπνεῖτε καὶ προσεύχεσθε·

d25 Isaiah 13:10; 34:4 e30 Or race f33 Some manuscripts alert and pray

ointment wasted in this way? [5]For this ointment could have been sold for more than three hundred denarii,[v] and the money given to the poor." And they scolded her. [6]But Jesus said, "Let her alone; why do you trouble her? She has performed a good service for me. [7]For you always have the poor with you, and you can show kindness to them whenever you wish; but you will not always have me. [8]She has done what she could; she has anointed my body beforehand for its burial. [9]Truly I tell you, wherever the good news[w] is proclaimed in the whole world, what she has done will be told in remembrance of her."

Judas Agrees to Betray Jesus

10 Then Judas Iscariot, who was one of the twelve, went to the chief priests in order to betray him to them. [11]When they heard it, they were greatly pleased, and promised to give him money. So he began to look for an opportunity to betray him.

The Passover with the Disciples

12 On the first day of Unleavened Bread, when the Passover lamb is sacrificed, his disciples said to him, "Where do you want us to go and make the preparations for you to eat the Passover?" [13]So he sent two of his disciples, saying to them, "Go into the city, and a man carrying a jar of water will meet you; follow him, [14]and wherever he enters, say to the owner of the house, 'The Teacher asks, Where is my guest room where I may eat the Passover with my disciples?' [15]He will show you a large room upstairs, furnished and ready. Make preparations for us there." [16]So the disciples set out and went to the city, and found everything as he had told them; and they prepared the Passover meal.

17 When it was evening, he came with the twelve. [18]And when they had taken their places and were eating, Jesus said, "Truly I tell you, one of you will betray me, one who is eating with me." [19]They began to be distressed and to say to him one after another, "Surely, not I?" [20]He said to them, "It is one of the twelve, one who is dipping bread[x] into the bowl[y] with me. [21]For the Son of Man goes as it is written of him, but woe to that one by whom the Son of Man is betrayed! It would have been better for that one not to have been born."

ἡ ἀπώλεια αὕτη τοῦ μύρου γέγονεν; [5]ἠδύνατο γὰρ τοῦτο τὸ μύρον πραθῆναι ἐπάνω δηναρίων τριακοσίων καὶ δοθῆναι τοῖς πτωχοῖς· καὶ ἐνεβριμῶντο αὐτῇ. [6]ὁ δὲ Ἰησοῦς εἶπεν, Ἄφετε αὐτήν· τί αὐτῇ κόπους παρέχετε; καλὸν ἔργον ἠργάσατο ἐν ἐμοί. [7]πάντοτε γὰρ τοὺς πτωχοὺς ἔχετε μεθ' ἑαυτῶν καὶ ὅταν θέλητε δύνασθε αὐτοῖς εὖ ποιῆσαι, ἐμὲ δὲ οὐ πάντοτε ἔχετε. [8]ὃ ἔσχεν ἐποίησεν· προέλαβεν μυρίσαι τὸ σῶμά μου εἰς τὸν ἐνταφιασμόν. [9]ἀμὴν δὲ λέγω ὑμῖν, ὅπου ἐὰν κηρυχθῇ τὸ εὐαγγέλιον εἰς ὅλον τὸν κόσμον, καὶ ὃ ἐποίησεν αὕτη λαληθήσεται εἰς μνημόσυνον αὐτῆς.

[10]Καὶ Ἰούδας Ἰσκαριὼθ ὁ εἷς τῶν δώδεκα ἀπῆλθεν πρὸς τοὺς ἀρχιερεῖς ἵνα αὐτὸν παραδοῖ αὐτοῖς. [11]οἱ δὲ ἀκούσαντες ἐχάρησαν καὶ ἐπηγγείλαντο αὐτῷ ἀργύριον δοῦναι. καὶ ἐζήτει πῶς αὐτὸν εὐκαίρως παραδοῖ.

[12]Καὶ τῇ πρώτῃ ἡμέρᾳ τῶν ἀζύμων, ὅτε τὸ πάσχα ἔθυον, λέγουσιν αὐτῷ οἱ μαθηταὶ αὐτοῦ, Ποῦ θέλεις ἀπελθόντες ἑτοιμάσωμεν ἵνα φάγῃς τὸ πάσχα; [13]καὶ ἀποστέλλει δύο τῶν μαθητῶν αὐτοῦ καὶ λέγει αὐτοῖς, Ὑπάγετε εἰς τὴν πόλιν, καὶ ἀπαντήσει ὑμῖν ἄνθρωπος κεράμιον ὕδατος βαστάζων· ἀκολουθήσατε αὐτῷ [14]καὶ ὅπου ἐὰν εἰσέλθῃ εἴπατε τῷ οἰκοδεσπότῃ ὅτι Ὁ διδάσκαλος λέγει, Ποῦ ἐστιν τὸ κατάλυμά μου ὅπου τὸ πάσχα μετὰ τῶν μαθητῶν μου φάγω; [15]καὶ αὐτὸς ὑμῖν δείξει ἀνάγαιον μέγα ἐστρωμένον ἕτοιμον· καὶ ἐκεῖ ἑτοιμάσατε ἡμῖν. [16]καὶ ἐξῆλθον οἱ μαθηταὶ καὶ ἦλθον εἰς τὴν πόλιν καὶ εὗρον καθὼς εἶπεν αὐτοῖς καὶ ἡτοίμασαν τὸ πάσχα. [17]Καὶ ὀψίας γενομένης ἔρχεται μετὰ τῶν δώδεκα. [18]καὶ ἀνακειμένων αὐτῶν καὶ ἐσθιόντων ὁ Ἰησοῦς εἶπεν, Ἀμὴν λέγω ὑμῖν ὅτι εἷς ἐξ ὑμῶν παραδώσει με ὁ ἐσθίων μετ' ἐμοῦ. [19]ἤρξαντο λυπεῖσθαι καὶ λέγειν αὐτῷ εἷς κατὰ εἷς, Μήτι ἐγώ; [20]ὁ δὲ εἶπεν αὐτοῖς, Εἷς τῶν δώδεκα, ὁ ἐμβαπτόμενος μετ' ἐμοῦ εἰς τὸ[a] τρύβλιον. [21]ὅτι ὁ μὲν υἱὸς τοῦ ἀνθρώπου ὑπάγει καθὼς γέγραπται περὶ αὐτοῦ, οὐαὶ δὲ τῷ ἀνθρώπῳ ἐκείνῳ δι' οὗ ὁ υἱὸς τοῦ ἀνθρώπου παραδίδοται· καλὸν αὐτῷ εἰ οὐκ ἐγεννήθη ὁ ἄνθρωπος ἐκεῖνος.

of perfume? [5]It could have been sold for more than a year's wages[a] and the money given to the poor." And they rebuked her harshly.

[6]"Leave her alone," said Jesus. "Why are you bothering her? She has done a beautiful thing to me. [7]The poor you will always have with you, and you can help them any time you want. But you will not always have me. [8]She did what she could. She poured perfume on my body beforehand to prepare for my burial. [9]I tell you the truth, wherever the gospel is preached throughout the world, what she has done will also be told, in memory of her."

[10]Then Judas Iscariot, one of the Twelve, went to the chief priests to betray Jesus to them. [11]They were delighted to hear this and promised to give him money. So he watched for an opportunity to hand him over.

The Lord's Supper

[12]On the first day of the Feast of Unleavened Bread, when it was customary to sacrifice the Passover lamb, Jesus' disciples asked him, "Where do you want us to go and make preparations for you to eat the Passover?"

[13]So he sent two of his disciples, telling them, "Go into the city, and a man carrying a jar of water will meet you. Follow him. [14]Say to the owner of the house he enters, 'The Teacher asks: Where is my guest room, where I may eat the Passover with my disciples?' [15]He will show you a large upper room, furnished and ready. Make preparations for us there."

[16]The disciples left, went into the city and found things just as Jesus had told them. So they prepared the Passover.

[17]When evening came, Jesus arrived with the Twelve. [18]While they were reclining at the table eating, he said, "I tell you the truth, one of you will betray me—one who is eating with me."

[19]They were saddened, and one by one they said to him, "Surely not I?"

[20]"It is one of the Twelve," he replied, "one who dips bread into the bowl with me. [21]The Son of Man will go just as it is written about him. But woe to that man who betrays the Son of Man! It would be better for him if he had not been born."

[v] The denarius was the usual day's wage for a laborer [w] Or gospel [x] Gk lacks bread [y] Other ancient authorities read same bowl

[a]20 NRSV note y and adds ἐν †

[a]5 Greek than three hundred denarii

NRSV

The Institution of the Lord's Supper

22 While they were eating, he took a loaf of bread, and after blessing it he broke it, gave it to them, and said, "Take; this is my body." 23Then he took a cup, and after giving thanks he gave it to them, and all of them drank from it. 24He said to them, "This is my blood of thez covenant, which is poured out for many. 25Truly I tell you, I will never again drink of the fruit of the vine until that day when I drink it new in the kingdom of God."

Peter's Denial Foretold

26 When they had sung the hymn, they went out to the Mount of Olives. 27And Jesus said to them, "You will all become deserters; for it is written,

'I will strike the shepherd,
    and the sheep will be scattered.'
28But after I am raised up, I will go before you to Galilee." 29Peter said to him, "Even though all become deserters, I will not." 30Jesus said to him, "Truly I tell you, this day, this very night, before the cock crows twice, you will deny me three times." 31But he said vehemently, "Even though I must die with you, I will not deny you." And all of them said the same.

Jesus Prays in Gethsemane

32 They went to a place called Gethsemane; and he said to his disciples, "Sit here while I pray." 33He took with him Peter and James and John, and began to be distressed and agitated. 34And he said to them, "I am deeply grieved, even to death; remain here, and keep awake." 35And going a little farther, he threw himself on the ground and prayed that, if it were possible, the hour might pass from him. 36He said, "Abba,a Father, for you all things are possible; remove this cup from me; yet, not what I want, but what you want." 37He came and found them sleeping; and he said to Peter, "Simon, are you asleep? Could you not keep awake one hour? 38Keep awake and pray that you may not come into the time of trial;b the spirit indeed is willing, but the flesh is weak." 39And again he went away and prayed, saying the same words. 40And once more

Greek

22 Καὶ ἐσθιόντων αὐτῶνb λαβὼν ἄρτον εὐλογήσας ἔκλασεν καὶ ἔδωκεν αὐτοῖς καὶ εἶπεν, Λάβετε, τοῦτό ἐστιν τὸ σῶμά μου. 23 καὶ λαβὼν ποτήριον εὐχαριστήσας ἔδωκεν αὐτοῖς, καὶ ἔπιον ἐξ αὐτοῦ πάντες. 24 καὶ εἶπεν αὐτοῖς, Τοῦτό ἐστιν τὸ αἷμά μου τῆς διαθήκηςc τὸ ἐκχυννόμενον ὑπὲρ πολλῶν. 25 ἀμὴν λέγω ὑμῖν ὅτι οὐκέτι οὐ μὴ πίω ἐκ τοῦ γενήματος τῆς ἀμπέλου ἕως τῆς ἡμέρας ἐκείνης ὅταν αὐτὸ πίνω καινὸν ἐν τῇ βασιλείᾳ τοῦ θεοῦ. 26 Καὶ ὑμνήσαντες ἐξῆλθον εἰς τὸ Ὄρος τῶν Ἐλαιῶν.

27 Καὶ λέγει αὐτοῖς ὁ Ἰησοῦς ὅτι Πάντες σκανδαλισθήσεσθε, ὅτι γέγραπται,

Πατάξω τὸν ποιμένα,
    καὶ τὰ πρόβατα διασκορπισθήσονται.

28 ἀλλὰ μετὰ τὸ ἐγερθῆναί με προάξω ὑμᾶς εἰς τὴν Γαλιλαίαν. 29 ὁ δὲ Πέτρος ἔφη αὐτῷ, Εἰ καὶ πάντες σκανδαλισθήσονται, ἀλλ' οὐκ ἐγώ. 30 καὶ λέγει αὐτῷ ὁ Ἰησοῦς, Ἀμὴν λέγω σοι ὅτι σὺ σήμερον ταύτῃ τῇ νυκτὶ πρὶν ἢ δὶς ἀλέκτορα φωνῆσαι τρίς με ἀπαρνήσῃ. 31 ὁ δὲ ἐκπερισσῶς ἐλάλει, Ἐὰν δέῃ με συναποθανεῖν σοι, οὐ μή σε ἀπαρνήσομαι. ὡσαύτως δὲ καὶ πάντες ἔλεγον.

32 Καὶ ἔρχονται εἰς χωρίον οὗ τὸ ὄνομα Γεθσημανὶ καὶ λέγει τοῖς μαθηταῖς αὐτοῦ, Καθίσατε ὧδε ἕως προσεύξωμαι. 33 καὶ παραλαμβάνει τὸν Πέτρον καὶ [τὸν]d Ἰάκωβον καὶ [τὸν]d Ἰωάννην μετ' αὐτοῦ καὶ ἤρξατο ἐκθαμβεῖσθαι καὶ ἀδημονεῖν 34 καὶ λέγει αὐτοῖς, Περίλυπός ἐστιν ἡ ψυχή μου ἕως θανάτου· μείνατε ὧδε καὶ γρηγορεῖτε. 35 καὶ προελθὼν μικρὸν ἔπιπτεν ἐπὶ τῆς γῆς καὶ προσηύχετο ἵνα εἰ δυνατόν ἐστιν παρέλθῃ ἀπ' αὐτοῦ ἡ ὥρα, 36 καὶ ἔλεγεν, Αββα ὁ πατήρ, πάντα δυνατά σοι· παρένεγκε τὸ ποτήριον τοῦτο ἀπ' ἐμοῦ· ἀλλ' οὐ τί ἐγὼ θέλω ἀλλὰ τί σύ. 37 καὶ ἔρχεται καὶ εὑρίσκει αὐτοὺς καθεύδοντας, καὶ λέγει τῷ Πέτρῳ, Σίμων, καθεύδεις; οὐκ ἴσχυσας μίαν ὥραν γρηγορῆσαι; 38 γρηγορεῖτε καὶ προσεύχεσθε, ἵνα μὴ ἔλθητε εἰς πειρασμόν· τὸ μὲν πνεῦμα πρόθυμον ἡ δὲ σὰρξ ἀσθενής. 39 καὶ πάλιν ἀπελθὼν προσηύξατο τὸν αὐτὸν λόγον εἰπών. 40 καὶ πάλιν ἐλθὼν εὗρεν αὐτοὺς

NIV

22While they were eating, Jesus took bread, gave thanks and broke it, and gave it to his disciples, saying, "Take it; this is my body."

23Then he took the cup, gave thanks and offered it to them, and they all drank from it.

24"This is my blood of theb covenant, which is poured out for many," he said to them. 25"I tell you the truth, I will not drink again of the fruit of the vine until that day when I drink it anew in the kingdom of God."

26When they had sung a hymn, they went out to the Mount of Olives.

Jesus Predicts Peter's Denial

27"You will all fall away," Jesus told them, "for it is written:

" 'I will strike the shepherd,
    and the sheep will be scattered.'c

28But after I have risen, I will go ahead of you into Galilee."

29Peter declared, "Even if all fall away, I will not."

30"I tell you the truth," Jesus answered, "today—yes, tonight—before the rooster crows twiced you yourself will disown me three times."

31But Peter insisted emphatically, "Even if I have to die with you, I will never disown you." And all the others said the same.

Gethsemane

32They went to a place called Gethsemane, and Jesus said to his disciples, "Sit here while I pray." 33He took Peter, James and John along with him, and he began to be deeply distressed and troubled. 34"My soul is overwhelmed with sorrow to the point of death," he said to them. "Stay here and keep watch."

35Going a little farther, he fell to the ground and prayed that if possible the hour might pass from him. 36"Abba,e Father," he said, "everything is possible for you. Take this cup from me. Yet not what I will, but what you will."

37Then he returned to his disciples and found them sleeping. "Simon," he said to Peter, "are you asleep? Could you not keep watch for one hour? 38Watch and pray so that you will not fall into temptation. The spirit is willing, but the body is weak."

39Once more he went away and prayed the same thing. 40When he came back, he

z Other ancient authorities add *new*   a Aramaic for *Father*   b Or *into temptation*

b22 NIV text adds ὁ Ἰησοῦς †   c24 NIV/NRSV notes καινῆς διαθήκης   d33 NIV text omits τὸν †

b24 Some manuscripts *the new*   c27 Zech. 13:7   d30 Some early manuscripts do not have *twice*.   e36 Aramaic for *Father*

he came and found them sleeping, for their eyes were very heavy; and they did not know what to say to him. 41He came a third time and said to them, "Are you still sleeping and taking your rest? Enough! The hour has come; the Son of Man is betrayed into the hands of sinners. 42Get up, let us be going. See, my betrayer is at hand."

The Betrayal and Arrest of Jesus

43 Immediately, while he was still speaking, Judas, one of the twelve, arrived; and with him there was a crowd with swords and clubs, from the chief priests, the scribes, and the elders. 44Now the betrayer had given them a sign, saying, "The one I will kiss is the man; arrest him and lead him away under guard." 45So when he came, he went up to him at once and said, "Rabbi!" and kissed him. 46Then they laid hands on him and arrested him. 47But one of those who stood near drew his sword and struck the slave of the high priest, cutting off his ear. 48Then Jesus said to them, "Have you come out with swords and clubs to arrest me as though I were a bandit? 49Day after day I was with you in the temple teaching, and you did not arrest me. But let the scriptures be fulfilled." 50All of them deserted him and fled.

51 A certain young man was following him, wearing nothing but a linen cloth. They caught hold of him, 52but he left the linen cloth and ran off naked.

Jesus before the Council

53 They took Jesus to the high priest; and all the chief priests, the elders, and the scribes were assembled. 54Peter had followed him at a distance, right into the courtyard of the high priest; and he was sitting with the guards, warming himself at the fire. 55Now the chief priests and the whole council were looking for testimony against Jesus to put him to death; but they found none. 56For many gave false testimony against him, and their testimony did not agree. 57Some stood up and gave false testimony against him, saying, 58"We heard him say, 'I will destroy this temple that is made with hands, and in three days I will build another, not made with hands.' " 59But even on this point their testimony did not agree. 60Then the high priest stood up before them and asked Jesus, "Have

καθεύδοντας, ἦσαν γὰρ αὐτῶν οἱ ὀφθαλμοὶ καταβαρυνόμενοι, καὶ οὐκ ᾔδεισαν τί ἀποκριθῶσιν αὐτῷ. 41 καὶ ἔρχεται τὸ τρίτον καὶ λέγει αὐτοῖς, Καθεύδετε τὸ λοιπὸν καὶ ἀναπαύεσθε· ἀπέχει· ἦλθεν ἡ ὥρα, ἰδοὺ παραδίδοται ὁ υἱὸς τοῦ ἀνθρώπου εἰς τὰς χεῖρας τῶν ἁμαρτωλῶν. 42 ἐγείρεσθε ἄγωμεν· ἰδοὺ ὁ παραδιδούς με ἤγγικεν.

43 Καὶ εὐθὺς ἔτι αὐτοῦ λαλοῦντος παραγίνεται Ἰούδας εἷς τῶν δώδεκα καὶ μετ' αὐτοῦ ὄχλος μετὰ μαχαιρῶν καὶ ξύλων παρὰ τῶν ἀρχιερέων καὶ τῶν γραμματέων καὶ τῶν πρεσβυτέρων. 44 δεδώκει δὲ ὁ παραδιδοὺς αὐτὸν σύσσημον αὐτοῖς λέγων, Ὃν ἂν φιλήσω αὐτός ἐστιν, κρατήσατε αὐτὸν καὶ ἀπάγετε ἀσφαλῶς. 45 καὶ ἐλθὼν εὐθὺς προσελθὼν αὐτῷ λέγει, Ῥαββί, καὶ κατεφίλησεν αὐτόν· 46 οἱ δὲ ἐπέβαλον τὰς χεῖρας αὐτῷ καὶ ἐκράτησαν αὐτόν. 47 εἷς δέ [τις] τῶν παρεστηκότων σπασάμενος τὴν μάχαιραν ἔπαισεν τὸν δοῦλον τοῦ ἀρχιερέως καὶ ἀφεῖλεν αὐτοῦ τὸ ὠτάριον. 48 καὶ ἀποκριθεὶς ὁ Ἰησοῦς εἶπεν αὐτοῖς, Ὡς ἐπὶ λῃστὴν ἐξήλθατε μετὰ μαχαιρῶν καὶ ξύλων συλλαβεῖν με; 49 καθ' ἡμέραν ἤμην πρὸς ὑμᾶς ἐν τῷ ἱερῷ διδάσκων καὶ οὐκ ἐκρατήσατέ με· ἀλλ' ἵνα πληρωθῶσιν αἱ γραφαί. 50 καὶ ἀφέντες αὐτὸν ἔφυγον πάντες.

51 Καὶ νεανίσκος τις συνηκολούθει αὐτῷ περιβεβλημένος σινδόνα ἐπὶ γυμνοῦ, καὶ κρατοῦσιν αὐτόν· 52 ὁ δὲ καταλιπὼν τὴν σινδόνα γυμνὸς ἔφυγεν.

53 Καὶ ἀπήγαγον τὸν Ἰησοῦν πρὸς τὸν ἀρχιερέα, καὶ συνέρχονται πάντες οἱ ἀρχιερεῖς καὶ οἱ πρεσβύτεροι καὶ οἱ γραμματεῖς. 54 καὶ ὁ Πέτρος ἀπὸ μακρόθεν ἠκολούθησεν αὐτῷ ἕως ἔσω εἰς τὴν αὐλὴν τοῦ ἀρχιερέως καὶ ἦν συγκαθήμενος μετὰ τῶν ὑπηρετῶν καὶ θερμαινόμενος πρὸς τὸ φῶς. 55 οἱ δὲ ἀρχιερεῖς καὶ ὅλον τὸ συνέδριον ἐζήτουν κατὰ τοῦ Ἰησοῦ μαρτυρίαν εἰς τὸ θανατῶσαι αὐτόν, καὶ οὐχ ηὕρισκον· 56 πολλοὶ γὰρ ἐψευδομαρτύρουν κατ' αὐτοῦ, καὶ ἴσαι αἱ μαρτυρίαι οὐκ ἦσαν. 57 καί τινες ἀναστάντες ἐψευδομαρτύρουν κατ' αὐτοῦ λέγοντες 58 ὅτι Ἡμεῖς ἠκούσαμεν αὐτοῦ λέγοντος ὅτι Ἐγὼ καταλύσω τὸν ναὸν τοῦτον τὸν χειροποίητον καὶ διὰ τριῶν ἡμερῶν ἄλλον ἀχειροποίητον οἰκοδομήσω 59 καὶ οὐδὲ οὕτως ἴση ἦν ἡ μαρτυρία αὐτῶν. 60 καὶ ἀναστὰς ὁ ἀρχιερεὺς εἰς μέσον ἐπηρώτησεν τὸν Ἰησοῦν λέγων, Οὐκ

again found them sleeping, because their eyes were heavy. They did not know what to say to him. 41Returning the third time, he said to them, "Are you still sleeping and resting? Enough! The hour has come. Look, the Son of Man is betrayed into the hands of sinners. 42Rise! Let us go! Here comes my betrayer!"

Jesus Arrested

43Just as he was speaking, Judas, one of the Twelve, appeared. With him was a crowd armed with swords and clubs, sent from the chief priests, the teachers of the law, and the elders.

44Now the betrayer had arranged a signal with them: "The one I kiss is the man; arrest him and lead him away under guard." 45Going at once to Jesus, Judas said, "Rabbi!" and kissed him. 46The men seized Jesus and arrested him. 47Then one of those standing near drew his sword and struck the servant of the high priest, cutting off his ear.

48"Am I leading a rebellion," said Jesus, "that you have come out with swords and clubs to capture me? 49Every day I was with you, teaching in the temple courts, and you did not arrest me. But the Scriptures must be fulfilled." 50Then everyone deserted him and fled.

51A young man, wearing nothing but a linen garment, was following Jesus. When they seized him, 52he fled naked, leaving his garment behind.

Before the Sanhedrin

53They took Jesus to the high priest, and all the chief priests, elders and teachers of the law came together. 54Peter followed him at a distance, right into the courtyard of the high priest. There he sat with the guards and warmed himself at the fire.

55The chief priests and the whole Sanhedrin were looking for evidence against Jesus so that they could put him to death, but they did not find any. 56Many testified falsely against him, but their statements did not agree.

57Then some stood up and gave this false testimony against him: 58"We heard him say, 'I will destroy this man-made temple and in three days will build another, not made by man.' " 59Yet even then their testimony did not agree.

60Then the high priest stood up before them and asked Jesus, "Are you not going

you no answer? What is it that they testify against you?" 61But he was silent and did not answer. Again the high priest asked him, "Are you the Messiah,c the Son of the Blessed One?" 62Jesus said, "I am; and

'you will see the Son of Man
     seated at the right hand of the Power,'
and 'coming with the clouds of
     heaven.' "

63Then the high priest tore his clothes and said, "Why do we still need witnesses? 64You have heard his blasphemy! What is your decision?" All of them condemned him as deserving death. 65Some began to spit on him, to blindfold him, and to strike him, saying to him, "Prophesy!" The guards also took him over and beat him.

Peter Denies Jesus

66 While Peter was below in the court-yard, one of the servant-girls of the high priest came by. 67When she saw Peter warming himself, she stared at him and said, "You also were with Jesus, the man from Nazareth." 68But he denied it, say-ing, "I do not know or understand what you are talking about." And he went out into the forecourt.d Then the cock crowed.e 69And the servant-girl, on seeing him, be-gan again to say to the bystanders, "This man is one of them." 70But again he denied it. Then after a little while the bystanders again said to Peter, "Certainly you are one of them; for you are a Galilean." 71But he began to curse, and he swore an oath, "I do not know this man you are talking about." 72At that moment the cock crowed for the second time. Then Peter remem-bered that Jesus had said to him, "Before the cock crows twice, you will deny me three times." And he broke down and wept.

Jesus before Pilate

15 As soon as it was morning, the chief priests held a consultation with the elders and scribes and the whole council. They bound Jesus, led him away, and handed him over to Pilate. 2Pilate asked him, "Are you the King of the Jews?"

ἀποκρίνῃ οὐδὲν τί οὗτοί σου κατα-μαρτυροῦσιν; **61** ὁ δὲ ἐσιώπα καὶ οὐκ ἀπεκρίνατο οὐδέν. πάλιν ὁ ἀρχιερεὺς ἐπηρώτα αὐτὸν καὶ λέγει αὐτῷ, Σὺ εἶ ὁ Χριστὸς ὁ υἱὸς τοῦ εὐλογητοῦ; **62** ὁ δὲ Ἰησοῦς εἶπεν, Ἐγώ εἰμι,

καὶ **ὄψεσθε τὸν υἱὸν τοῦ ἀνθρώπου ἐκ δεξιῶν καθήμενον τῆς δυνάμεως**

καὶ **ἐρχόμενον μετὰ τῶν νεφελῶν τοῦ οὐρανοῦ.**

63 ὁ δὲ ἀρχιερεὺς διαρρήξας τοὺς χιτῶνας αὐτοῦ λέγει, Τί ἔτι χρείαν ἔχομεν μαρτύρων; **64** ἠκούσατε τῆς βλασφημίας· τί ὑμῖν φαίνεται; οἱ δὲ πάντες κατέκριναν αὐτὸν ἔνοχον εἶναι θανάτου. **65** Καὶ ἤρξαντό τινες ἐμπτύειν αὐτῷ καὶ περικαλύπτειν αὐτοῦ τὸ πρό-σωπον καὶ κολαφίζειν αὐτὸν καὶ λέγειν αὐτῷ, Προφήτευσον, καὶ οἱ ὑπηρέται ῥαπίσμασιν αὐτὸν ἔλαβον.

66 Καὶ ὄντος τοῦ Πέτρου κάτω ἐν τῇ αὐλῇ ἔρχεται μία τῶν παιδισκῶν τοῦ ἀρχιερέως **67** καὶ ἰδοῦσα τὸν Πέτρον θερμαινόμενον ἐμβλέψασα αὐτῷ λέγει, Καὶ σὺ μετὰ τοῦ Ναζαρηνοῦ ἦσθα τοῦ Ἰησοῦ. **68** ὁ δὲ ἠρνήσατο λέγων, Οὔτε οἶδα οὔτε ἐπίσταμαι σὺ τί λέγεις. καὶ ἐξῆλθεν ἔξω εἰς τὸ προαύλιον [καὶ ἀλέκτωρ ἐφώνησεν]e. **69** καὶ ἡ παιδίσκη ἰδοῦσα αὐτὸν ἤρξατο πάλιν λέγειν τοῖς παρεστῶσιν ὅτι Οὗτος ἐξ αὐτῶν ἐστιν. **70** ὁ δὲ πάλιν ἠρνεῖτο. καὶ μετὰ μικρὸν πάλιν οἱ παρεστῶτες ἔλεγον τῷ Πέτρῳ, Ἀληθῶς ἐξ αὐτῶν εἶ, καὶ γὰρ Γαλιλαῖος εἶ. **71** ὁ δὲ ἤρξατο ἀναθεματίζειν καὶ ὀμνύναι ὅτι Οὐκ οἶδα τὸν ἄνθρωπον τοῦτον ὃν λέγετε. **72** καὶ εὐθὺς ἐκ δευτέρου ἀλέκτωρ ἐφώνησεν. καὶ ἀνεμνήσθη ὁ Πέτρος τὸ ῥῆμα ὡς εἶπεν αὐτῷ ὁ Ἰησοῦς ὅτι Πρὶν ἀλέκτορα φωνῆσαι δὶς τρίς με ἀπαρνήσῃ· καὶ ἐπιβαλὼν ἔκλαιεν.

15 Καὶ εὐθὺς πρωῒ συμβούλιον ποιήσαντες οἱ ἀρχιερεῖς μετὰ τῶν πρεσβυτέρων καὶ γραμματέων καὶ ὅλον τὸ συνέδριον, δήσαντες τὸν Ἰησοῦν ἀπήνεγκαν καὶ παρέδωκαν Πιλάτῳ. **2** καὶ ἐπηρώτησεν αὐτὸν ὁ Πιλᾶτος, Σὺ εἶ ὁ βασιλεὺς τῶν Ἰουδαίων; ὁ δὲ ἀποκριθεὶς

---

to answer? What is this testimony that these men are bringing against you?" 61But Jesus remained silent and gave no answer.

Again the high priest asked him, "Are you the Christ,f the Son of the Blessed One?"

62"I am," said Jesus. "And you will see the Son of Man sitting at the right hand of the Mighty One and coming on the clouds of heaven."

63The high priest tore his clothes. "Why do we need any more witnesses?" he asked. 64"You have heard the blasphemy. What do you think?"

They all condemned him as worthy of death. 65Then some began to spit at him; they blindfolded him, struck him with their fists, and said, "Prophesy!" And the guards took him and beat him.

Peter Disowns Jesus

66While Peter was below in the court-yard, one of the servant girls of the high priest came by. 67When she saw Peter warming himself, she looked closely at him.

"You also were with that Nazarene, Jesus," she said.

68But he denied it. "I don't know or un-derstand what you're talking about," he said, and went out into the entryway.g

69When the servant girl saw him there, she said again to those standing around, "This fellow is one of them." 70Again he denied it.

After a little while, those standing near said to Peter, "Surely you are one of them, for you are a Galilean."

71He began to call down curses on him-self, and he swore to them, "I don't know this man you're talking about."

72Immediately the rooster crowed the sec-ond time.h Then Peter remembered the word Jesus had spoken to him: "Before the rooster crows twicei you will disown me three times." And he broke down and wept.

Jesus Before Pilate

15 Very early in the morning, the chief priests, with the elders, the teachers of the law and the whole San-hedrin, reached a decision. They bound Jesus, led him away and handed him over to Pilate.

2"Are you the king of the Jews?" asked Pilate.

---

c Or *the Christ*   d Or *gateway*   e Other ancient authorities lack *Then the cock crowed*

e68 NIV text and NRSV note e omit καὶ ἀλέκτωρ ἐφώνησεν; NIV note as UBS

f61 Or *Messiah*   g68 Some early manuscripts *entryway and the rooster crowed*   h72 Some early manuscripts do not have *the second time*.   i72 Some early manuscripts do not have *twice*.

He answered him, "You say so." ³Then the chief priests accused him of many things. ⁴Pilate asked him again, "Have you no answer? See how many charges they bring against you." ⁵But Jesus made no further reply, so that Pilate was amazed.

Pilate Hands Jesus over to Be Crucified

6 Now at the festival he used to release a prisoner for them, anyone for whom they asked. ⁷Now a man called Barabbas was in prison with the rebels who had committed murder during the insurrection. ⁸So the crowd came and began to ask Pilate to do for them according to his custom. ⁹Then he answered them, "Do you want me to release for you the King of the Jews?" ¹⁰For he realized that it was out of jealousy that the chief priests had handed him over. ¹¹But the chief priests stirred up the crowd to have him release Barabbas for them instead. ¹²Pilate spoke to them again, "Then what do you wish me to do^f with the man you call^g the King of the Jews?" ¹³They shouted back, "Crucify him!" ¹⁴Pilate asked them, "Why, what evil has he done?" But they shouted all the more, "Crucify him!" ¹⁵So Pilate, wishing to satisfy the crowd, released Barabbas for them; and after flogging Jesus, he handed him over to be crucified.

The Soldiers Mock Jesus

16 Then the soldiers led him into the courtyard of the palace (that is, the governor's headquarters^h); and they called together the whole cohort. ¹⁷And they clothed him in a purple cloak; and after twisting some thorns into a crown, they put it on him. ¹⁸And they began saluting him, "Hail, King of the Jews!" ¹⁹They struck his head with a reed, spat upon him, and knelt down in homage to him. ²⁰After mocking him, they stripped him of the purple cloak and put his own clothes on him. Then they led him out to crucify him.

The Crucifixion of Jesus

21 They compelled a passer-by, who was coming in from the country, to carry his cross; it was Simon of Cyrene, the father of Alexander and Rufus. ²²Then they brought Jesus^i to the place called Golgotha (which means the place of a skull). ²³And they offered him wine mixed with myrrh; but he did not take it. ²⁴And they crucified him, and divided his clothes among them,

f Other ancient authorities read *what should I do*
g Other ancient authorities lack *the man you call*
h Gk *the praetorium*   i Gk *him*

αὐτῷ λέγει, Σὺ λέγεις. 3 καὶ κατηγόρουν αὐτοῦ οἱ ἀρχιερεῖς πολλά. 4 ὁ δὲ Πιλᾶτος πάλιν ἐπηρώτα αὐτὸν λέγων, Οὐκ ἀποκρίνῃ οὐδέν; ἴδε πόσα σου κατηγοροῦσιν. 5 ὁ δὲ Ἰησοῦς οὐκέτι οὐδὲν ἀπεκρίθη, ὥστε θαυμάζειν τὸν Πιλᾶτον.

6 Κατὰ δὲ ἑορτὴν ἀπέλυεν αὐτοῖς ἕνα δέσμιον ὃν παρῃτοῦντο. 7 ἦν δὲ ὁ λεγόμενος Βαραββᾶς μετὰ τῶν στασιαστῶν δεδεμένος οἵτινες ἐν τῇ στάσει φόνον πεποιήκεισαν. 8 καὶ ἀναβὰς ὁ ὄχλος ἤρξατο αἰτεῖσθαι καθὼς ἐποίει αὐτοῖς. 9 ὁ δὲ Πιλᾶτος ἀπεκρίθη αὐτοῖς λέγων, Θέλετε ἀπολύσω ὑμῖν τὸν βασιλέα τῶν Ἰουδαίων; 10 ἐγίνωσκεν γὰρ ὅτι διὰ φθόνον παραδεδώκεισαν αὐτὸν οἱ ἀρχιερεῖς. 11 οἱ δὲ ἀρχιερεῖς ἀνέσεισαν τὸν ὄχλον ἵνα μᾶλλον τὸν Βαραββᾶν ἀπολύσῃ αὐτοῖς. 12 ὁ δὲ Πιλᾶτος πάλιν ἀποκριθεὶς ἔλεγεν αὐτοῖς, Τί οὖν [θέλετε]^a ποιήσω [ὃν λέγετε] τὸν βασιλέα τῶν Ἰουδαίων; 13 οἱ δὲ πάλιν ἔκραξαν, Σταύρωσον αὐτόν. 14 ὁ δὲ Πιλᾶτος ἔλεγεν αὐτοῖς, Τί γὰρ ἐποίησεν κακόν; οἱ δὲ περισσῶς ἔκραξαν, Σταύρωσον αὐτόν. 15 ὁ δὲ Πιλᾶτος βουλόμενος τῷ ὄχλῳ τὸ ἱκανὸν ποιῆσαι ἀπέλυσεν αὐτοῖς τὸν Βαραββᾶν, καὶ παρέδωκεν τὸν Ἰησοῦν φραγελλώσας ἵνα σταυρωθῇ.

16 Οἱ δὲ στρατιῶται ἀπήγαγον αὐτὸν ἔσω τῆς αὐλῆς, ὅ ἐστιν πραιτώριον, καὶ συγκαλοῦσιν ὅλην τὴν σπεῖραν. 17 καὶ ἐνδιδύσκουσιν αὐτὸν πορφύραν καὶ περιτιθέασιν αὐτῷ πλέξαντες ἀκάνθινον στέφανον· 18 καὶ ἤρξαντο ἀσπάζεσθαι αὐτόν, Χαῖρε, βασιλεῦ τῶν Ἰουδαίων· 19 καὶ ἔτυπτον αὐτοῦ τὴν κεφαλὴν καλάμῳ καὶ ἐνέπτυον αὐτῷ καὶ τιθέντες τὰ γόνατα προσεκύνουν αὐτῷ. 20 καὶ ὅτε ἐνέπαιξαν αὐτῷ, ἐξέδυσαν αὐτὸν τὴν πορφύραν καὶ ἐνέδυσαν αὐτὸν τὰ ἱμάτια αὐτοῦ. καὶ ἐξάγουσιν αὐτὸν ἵνα σταυρώσωσιν αὐτόν.

21 Καὶ ἀγγαρεύουσιν παράγοντά τινα Σίμωνα Κυρηναῖον ἐρχόμενον ἀπ' ἀγροῦ, τὸν πατέρα Ἀλεξάνδρου καὶ Ῥούφου, ἵνα ἄρῃ τὸν σταυρὸν αὐτοῦ. 22 καὶ φέρουσιν αὐτὸν ἐπὶ τὸν Γολγοθᾶν τόπον, ὅ ἐστιν μεθερμηνευόμενον Κρανίου Τόπος. 23 καὶ ἐδίδουν αὐτῷ ἐσμυρνισμένον οἶνον· ὃς δὲ οὐκ ἔλαβεν. 24 καὶ σταυροῦσιν αὐτὸν

καὶ διαμερίζονται τὰ ἱμάτια αὐτοῦ,

a 12 NIV text and NRSV note f omits θέλετε

"Yes, it is as you say," Jesus replied. ³The chief priests accused him of many things. ⁴So again Pilate asked him, "Aren't you going to answer? See how many things they are accusing you of." ⁵But Jesus still made no reply, and Pilate was amazed.

⁶Now it was the custom at the Feast to release a prisoner whom the people requested. ⁷A man called Barabbas was in prison with the insurrectionists who had committed murder in the uprising. ⁸The crowd came up and asked Pilate to do for them what he usually did.

⁹"Do you want me to release to you the king of the Jews?" asked Pilate, ¹⁰knowing it was out of envy that the chief priests had handed Jesus over to him. ¹¹But the chief priests stirred up the crowd to have Pilate release Barabbas instead.

¹²"What shall I do, then, with the one you call the king of the Jews?" Pilate asked them.

¹³"Crucify him!" they shouted.

¹⁴"Why? What crime has he committed?" asked Pilate.

But they shouted all the louder, "Crucify him!"

¹⁵Wanting to satisfy the crowd, Pilate released Barabbas to them. He had Jesus flogged, and handed him over to be crucified.

The Soldiers Mock Jesus

¹⁶The soldiers led Jesus away into the palace (that is, the Praetorium) and called together the whole company of soldiers. ¹⁷They put a purple robe on him, then twisted together a crown of thorns and set it on him. ¹⁸And they began to call out to him, "Hail, king of the Jews!" ¹⁹Again and again they struck him on the head with a staff and spit on him. Falling on their knees, they paid homage to him. ²⁰And when they had mocked him, they took off the purple robe and put his own clothes on him. Then they led him out to crucify him.

The Crucifixion

²¹A certain man from Cyrene, Simon, the father of Alexander and Rufus, was passing by on his way in from the country, and they forced him to carry the cross. ²²They brought Jesus to the place called Golgotha (which means The Place of the Skull). ²³Then they offered him wine mixed with myrrh, but he did not take it. ²⁴And they crucified him. Dividing up his clothes, they

NRSV

casting lots to decide what each should take.

25 It was nine o'clock in the morning when they crucified him. [26]The inscription of the charge against him read, "The King of the Jews." [27]And with him they crucified two bandits, one on his right and one on his left.[j] [29]Those who passed by derided[k] him, shaking their heads and saying, "Aha! You who would destroy the temple and build it in three days, [30]save yourself, and come down from the cross!" [31]In the same way the chief priests, along with the scribes, were also mocking him among themselves and saying, "He saved others; he cannot save himself. [32]Let the Messiah,[l] the King of Israel, come down from the cross now, so that we may see and believe." Those who were crucified with him also taunted him.

The Death of Jesus

33 When it was noon, darkness came over the whole land[m] until three in the afternoon. [34]At three o'clock Jesus cried out with a loud voice, "Eloi, Eloi, lema sabachthani?" which means, "My God, my God, why have you forsaken me?"[n] [35]When some of the bystanders heard it, they said, "Listen, he is calling for Elijah." [36]And someone ran, filled a sponge with sour wine, put it on a stick, and gave it to him to drink, saying, "Wait, let us see whether Elijah will come to take him down." [37]Then Jesus gave a loud cry and breathed his last. [38]And the curtain of the temple was torn in two, from top to bottom. [39]Now when the centurion, who stood facing him, saw that in this way he[o] breathed his last, he said, "Truly this man was God's Son!"[p]

40 There were also women looking on from a distance; among them were Mary Magdalene, and Mary the mother of James the younger and of Joses, and Salome. [41]These used to follow him and provided for him when he was in Galilee; and there were many other women who had come up with him to Jerusalem.

The Burial of Jesus

42 When evening had come, and since it was the day of Preparation, that is, the day before the sabbath, [43]Joseph of Arimathea,

[Greek]

βάλλοντες κλῆρον ἐπ' αὐτὰ τίς τί ἄρῃ.

25 ἦν δὲ ὥρα τρίτη καὶ ἐσταύρωσαν αὐτόν. 26 καὶ ἦν ἡ ἐπιγραφὴ τῆς αἰτίας αὐτοῦ ἐπιγεγραμμένη, Ὁ βασιλεὺς τῶν Ἰουδαίων. 27 Καὶ σὺν αὐτῷ σταυροῦσιν δύο λῃστάς, ἕνα ἐκ δεξιῶν καὶ ἕνα ἐξ εὐωνύμων αὐτοῦ.[b] 29 Καὶ οἱ παραπορευόμενοι ἐβλασφήμουν αὐτὸν κινοῦντες τὰς κεφαλὰς αὐτῶν καὶ λέγοντες, Οὐὰ ὁ καταλύων τὸν ναὸν καὶ οἰκοδομῶν ἐν τρισὶν ἡμέραις, 30 σῶσον σεαυτὸν καταβὰς ἀπὸ τοῦ σταυροῦ. 31 ὁμοίως καὶ οἱ ἀρχιερεῖς ἐμπαίζοντες πρὸς ἀλλήλους μετὰ τῶν γραμματέων ἔλεγον, Ἄλλους ἔσωσεν, ἑαυτὸν οὐ δύναται σῶσαι· 32 ὁ Χριστὸς ὁ βασιλεὺς Ἰσραὴλ καταβάτω νῦν ἀπὸ τοῦ σταυροῦ, ἵνα ἴδωμεν καὶ πιστεύσωμεν. καὶ οἱ συνεσταυρωμένοι σὺν αὐτῷ ὠνείδιζον αὐτόν.

33 Καὶ γενομένης ὥρας ἕκτης σκότος ἐγένετο ἐφ' ὅλην τὴν γῆν ἕως ὥρας ἐνάτης. 34 καὶ τῇ ἐνάτῃ ὥρᾳ ἐβόησεν ὁ Ἰησοῦς φωνῇ μεγάλῃ, Ελωι ελωι λεμα σαβαχθανι; ὅ ἐστιν μεθερμηνευόμενον Ὁ θεός μου ὁ θεός μου, εἰς τί ἐγκατέλιπές με[c]; 35 καί τινες τῶν παρεστηκότων ἀκούσαντες ἔλεγον, Ἴδε Ἠλίαν φωνεῖ. 36 δραμὼν δέ τις [καὶ] γεμίσας σπόγγον ὄξους περιθεὶς καλάμῳ ἐπότιζεν αὐτὸν λέγων, Ἄφετε ἴδωμεν εἰ ἔρχεται Ἠλίας καθελεῖν αὐτόν. 37 ὁ δὲ Ἰησοῦς ἀφεὶς φωνὴν μεγάλην ἐξέπνευσεν. 38 Καὶ τὸ καταπέτασμα τοῦ ναοῦ ἐσχίσθη εἰς δύο ἀπ' ἄνωθεν ἕως κάτω. 39 Ἰδὼν δὲ ὁ κεντυρίων ὁ παρεστηκὼς ἐξ ἐναντίας αὐτοῦ ὅτι οὕτως[d] ἐξέπνευσεν εἶπεν, Ἀληθῶς οὗτος ὁ ἄνθρωπος υἱὸς θεοῦ ἦν. 40 Ἦσαν δὲ καὶ γυναῖκες ἀπὸ μακρόθεν θεωροῦσαι, ἐν αἷς καὶ Μαρία ἡ Μαγδαληνὴ καὶ Μαρία ἡ Ἰακώβου τοῦ μικροῦ καὶ Ἰωσῆτος μήτηρ καὶ Σαλώμη, 41 αἳ ὅτε ἦν ἐν τῇ Γαλιλαίᾳ ἠκολούθουν αὐτῷ καὶ διηκόνουν αὐτῷ, καὶ ἄλλαι πολλαὶ αἱ συναναβᾶσαι αὐτῷ εἰς Ἱεροσόλυμα.

42 Καὶ ἤδη ὀψίας γενομένης, ἐπεὶ ἦν παρασκευὴ ὅ ἐστιν προσάββατον, 43 ἐλθὼν Ἰωσὴφ [ὁ] ἀπὸ Ἁριμαθαίας

NIV

cast lots to see what each would get.

[25]It was the third hour when they crucified him. [26]The written notice of the charge against him read: THE KING OF THE JEWS. [27]They crucified two robbers with him, one on his right and one on his left.[a] [29]Those who passed by hurled insults at him, shaking their heads and saying, "So! You who are going to destroy the temple and build it in three days, [30]come down from the cross and save yourself!" [31]In the same way the chief priests and the teachers of the law mocked him among themselves. "He saved others," they said, "but he can't save himself! [32]Let this Christ,[b] this King of Israel, come down now from the cross, that we may see and believe." Those crucified with him also heaped insults on him.

The Death of Jesus

[33]At the sixth hour darkness came over the whole land until the ninth hour. [34]And at the ninth hour Jesus cried out in a loud voice, "Eloi, Eloi, lama sabachthani?"—which means, "My God, my God, why have you forsaken me?"[c]

[35]When some of those standing near heard this, they said, "Listen, he's calling Elijah."

[36]One man ran, filled a sponge with wine vinegar, put it on a stick, and offered it to Jesus to drink. "Now leave him alone. Let's see if Elijah comes to take him down," he said.

[37]With a loud cry, Jesus breathed his last.

[38]The curtain of the temple was torn in two from top to bottom. [39]And when the centurion, who stood there in front of Jesus, heard his cry and[d] saw how he died, he said, "Surely this man was the Son[e] of God!"

[40]Some women were watching from a distance. Among them were Mary Magdalene, Mary the mother of James the younger and of Joses, and Salome. [41]In Galilee these women had followed him and cared for his needs. Many other women who had come up with him to Jerusalem were also there.

The Burial of Jesus

[42]It was Preparation Day (that is, the day before the Sabbath). So as evening approached, [43]Joseph of Arimathea, a

---

[j]Other ancient authorities add verse 28, *And the scripture was fulfilled that says, "And he was counted among the lawless."* [k]Or *blasphemed* [l]Or *the Christ* [m]Or *earth* [n]Other ancient authorities read *made me a reproach* [o]Other ancient authorities add *cried out and* [p]Or *a son of God*

[b]27 NIV/NRSV notes add 28 καὶ ἐπληρώθη ἡ γραφὴ ἡ λέγουσα, Καὶ μετὰ ἀνόμων ἐλογίσθη. [c]34 NRSV note n ὠνείδισάς με [d]39 NIV text and NRSV note o add κράξας

[a]27 Some manuscripts *left,* [28]*and the scripture was fulfilled which says, "He was counted with the lawless ones"* (Isaiah 53:12) [b]32 Or *Messiah* [c]34 Psalm 22:1 [d]39 Some manuscripts do not have *heard his cry and.* [e]39 Or *a son*

a respected member of the council, who was also himself waiting expectantly for the kingdom of God, went boldly to Pilate and asked for the body of Jesus. 44Then Pilate wondered if he were already dead; and summoning the centurion, he asked him whether he had been dead for some time. 45When he learned from the centurion that he was dead, he granted the body to Joseph. 46Then Joseph^q bought a linen cloth, and taking down the body,^r wrapped it in the linen cloth, and laid it in a tomb that had been hewn out of the rock. He then rolled a stone against the door of the tomb. 47Mary Magdalene and Mary the mother of Joses saw where the body^r was laid.

The Resurrection of Jesus

16 When the sabbath was over, Mary Magdalene, and Mary the mother of James, and Salome bought spices, so that they might go and anoint him. 2And very early on the first day of the week, when the sun had risen, they went to the tomb. 3They had been saying to one another, "Who will roll away the stone for us from the entrance to the tomb?" 4When they looked up, they saw that the stone, which was very large, had already been rolled back. 5As they entered the tomb, they saw a young man, dressed in a white robe, sitting on the right side; and they were alarmed. 6But he said to them, "Do not be alarmed; you are looking for Jesus of Nazareth, who was crucified. He has been raised; he is not here. Look, there is the place they laid him. 7But go, tell his disciples and Peter that he is going ahead of you to Galilee; there you will see him, just as he told you." 8So they went out and fled from the tomb, for terror and amazement had seized them; and they said nothing to anyone, for they were afraid.^s

THE SHORTER ENDING OF MARK

⟦And all that had been commanded them they told briefly to those around Peter. And afterward Jesus himself sent out through them, from east to west, the sacred and imperishable proclamation of eternal salvation.^t⟧

εὐσχήμων βουλευτής, ὃς καὶ αὐτὸς ἦν προσδεχόμενος τὴν βασιλείαν τοῦ θεοῦ, τολμήσας εἰσῆλθεν πρὸς τὸν Πιλᾶτον καὶ ᾐτήσατο τὸ σῶμα τοῦ Ἰησοῦ. 44 ὁ δὲ Πιλᾶτος ἐθαύμασεν εἰ ἤδη τέθνηκεν καὶ προσκαλεσάμενος τὸν κεντυρίωνα ἐπηρώτησεν αὐτὸν εἰ πάλαι ἀπέθανεν· 45 καὶ γνοὺς ἀπὸ τοῦ κεντυρίωνος ἐδωρήσατο τὸ πτῶμα τῷ Ἰωσήφ. 46 καὶ ἀγοράσας σινδόνα καθελὼν αὐτὸν ἐνείλησεν τῇ σινδόνι καὶ ἔθηκεν αὐτὸν ἐν μνημείῳ ὃ ἦν λελατομημένον ἐκ πέτρας καὶ προσεκύλισεν λίθον ἐπὶ τὴν θύραν τοῦ μνημείου. 47 ἡ δὲ Μαρία ἡ Μαγδαληνὴ καὶ Μαρία ἡ Ἰωσῆτος ἐθεώρουν ποῦ τέθειται.

16 Καὶ διαγενομένου τοῦ σαββάτου Μαρία ἡ Μαγδαληνὴ καὶ Μαρία ἡ [τοῦ] Ἰακώβου καὶ Σαλώμη ἠγόρασαν ἀρώματα ἵνα ἐλθοῦσαι ἀλείψωσιν αὐτόν. 2 καὶ λίαν πρωῒ τῇ μιᾷ τῶν σαββάτων ἔρχονται ἐπὶ τὸ μνημεῖον ἀνατείλαντος τοῦ ἡλίου. 3 καὶ ἔλεγον πρὸς ἑαυτάς, Τίς ἀποκυλίσει ἡμῖν τὸν λίθον ἐκ τῆς θύρας τοῦ μνημείου; 4 καὶ ἀναβλέψασαι θεωροῦσιν ὅτι ἀποκεκύλισται ὁ λίθος· ἦν γὰρ μέγας σφόδρα. 5 καὶ εἰσελθοῦσαι εἰς τὸ μνημεῖον εἶδον νεανίσκον καθήμενον ἐν τοῖς δεξιοῖς περιβεβλημένον στολὴν λευκήν, καὶ ἐξεθαμβήθησαν. 6 ὁ δὲ λέγει αὐταῖς, Μὴ ἐκθαμβεῖσθε· Ἰησοῦν ζητεῖτε τὸν Ναζαρηνὸν τὸν ἐσταυρωμένον· ἠγέρθη, οὐκ ἔστιν ὧδε· ἴδε ὁ τόπος ὅπου ἔθηκαν αὐτόν. 7 ἀλλὰ ὑπάγετε εἴπατε τοῖς μαθηταῖς αὐτοῦ καὶ τῷ Πέτρῳ ὅτι Προάγει ὑμᾶς εἰς τὴν Γαλιλαίαν· ἐκεῖ αὐτὸν ὄψεσθε, καθὼς εἶπεν ὑμῖν. 8 καὶ ἐξελθοῦσαι ἔφυγον ἀπὸ τοῦ μνημείου, εἶχεν γὰρ αὐτὰς τρόμος καὶ ἔκστασις· καὶ οὐδενὶ οὐδὲν εἶπαν· ἐφοβοῦντο γάρ.

⟦Πάντα δὲ τὰ παρηγγελμένα τοῖς περὶ τὸν Πέτρον συντόμως ἐξήγγειλαν. Μετὰ δὲ ταῦτα καὶ αὐτὸς ὁ Ἰησοῦς ἀπὸ ἀνατολῆς καὶ ἄχρι δύσεως ἐξαπέστειλεν δι᾽ αὐτῶν τὸ ἱερὸν καὶ ἄφθαρτον κήρυγμα τῆς αἰωνίου σωτηρίας. ἀμήν.^a⟧

The Resurrection

16 When the Sabbath was over, Mary Magdalene, Mary the mother of James, and Salome bought spices so that they might go to anoint Jesus' body. 2Very early on the first day of the week, just after sunrise, they were on their way to the tomb 3and they asked each other, "Who will roll the stone away from the entrance of the tomb?"

4But when they looked up, they saw that the stone, which was very large, had been rolled away. 5As they entered the tomb, they saw a young man dressed in a white robe sitting on the right side, and they were alarmed.

6"Don't be alarmed," he said. "You are looking for Jesus the Nazarene, who was crucified. He has risen! He is not here. See the place where they laid him. 7But go, tell his disciples and Peter, 'He is going ahead of you into Galilee. There you will see him, just as he told you.' "

8Trembling and bewildered, the women went out and fled from the tomb. They said nothing to anyone, because they were afraid.

prominent member of the Council, who was himself waiting for the kingdom of God, went boldly to Pilate and asked for Jesus' body. 44Pilate was surprised to hear that he was already dead. Summoning the centurion, he asked him if Jesus had already died. 45When he learned from the centurion that it was so, he gave the body to Joseph. 46So Joseph bought some linen cloth, took down the body, wrapped it in the linen, and placed it in a tomb cut out of rock. Then he rolled a stone against the entrance of the tomb. 47Mary Magdalene and Mary the mother of Joses saw where he was laid.

---

^q Gk *he*   ^r Gk *it*   ^s Some of the most ancient authorities bring the book to a close at the end of verse 8. One authority concludes the book with the shorter ending; others include the shorter ending and then continue with verses 9-20. In most authorities verses 9-20 follow immediately after verse 8, though in some of these authorities the passage is marked as being doubtful.
^t Other ancient authorities add *Amen*

^a8 NRSV text omits ἀμήν; NRSV note t as UBS.

THE LONGER ENDING OF MARK

Jesus Appears to Mary Magdalene

9 ⟦Now after he rose early on the first day of the week, he appeared first to Mary Magdalene, from whom he had cast out seven demons. 10She went out and told those who had been with him, while they were mourning and weeping. 11But when they heard that he was alive and had been seen by her, they would not believe it.

Jesus Appears to Two Disciples

12 After this he appeared in another form to two of them, as they were walking into the country. 13And they went back and told the rest, but they did not believe them.

Jesus Commissions the Disciples

14 Later he appeared to the eleven themselves as they were sitting at the table; and he upbraided them for their lack of faith and stubbornness, because they had not believed those who saw him after he had risen.u 15And he said to them, "Go into all the world and proclaim the good newsv to the whole creation. 16The one who believes and is baptized will be saved; but the one who does not believe will be condemned. 17And these signs will accompany those who believe: by using my name they will cast out demons; they will speak in new tongues; 18they will pick up snakes in their hands,w and if they drink any deadly thing, it will not hurt them; they will lay their hands on the sick, and they will recover."

The Ascension of Jesus

19 So then the Lord Jesus, after he had spoken to them, was taken up into heaven and sat down at the right hand of God. 20And they went out and proclaimed the good news everywhere, while the Lord worked with them and confirmed the message by the signs that accompanied it.x⟧

⟦9 Ἀναστὰς δὲ πρωὶ πρώτῃ σαββάτου ἐφάνη πρῶτον Μαρίᾳ τῇ Μαγδαληνῇ, παρ᾿ ἧς ἐκβεβλήκει ἑπτὰ δαιμόνια. 10 ἐκείνη πορευθεῖσα ἀπήγγειλεν τοῖς μετ᾿ αὐτοῦ γενομένοις πενθοῦσι καὶ κλαίουσιν· 11 κἀκεῖνοι ἀκούσαντες ὅτι ζῇ καὶ ἐθεάθη ὑπ᾿ αὐτῆς ἠπίστησαν.

12 Μετὰ δὲ ταῦτα δυσὶν ἐξ αὐτῶν περιπατοῦσιν ἐφανερώθη ἐν ἑτέρᾳ μορφῇ πορευομένοις εἰς ἀγρόν· 13 κἀκεῖνοι ἀπελθόντες ἀπήγγειλαν τοῖς λοιποῖς· οὐδὲ ἐκείνοις ἐπίστευσαν. 14 Ὕστερον [δὲ] ἀνακειμένοις αὐτοῖς τοῖς ἕνδεκα ἐφανερώθη καὶ ὠνείδισεν τὴν ἀπιστίαν αὐτῶν καὶ σκληροκαρδίαν ὅτι τοῖς θεασαμένοις αὐτὸν ἐγηγερμένον οὐκ ἐπίστευσαν.b 15 καὶ εἶπεν αὐτοῖς, Πορευθέντες εἰς τὸν κόσμον ἅπαντα κηρύξατε τὸ εὐαγγέλιον πάσῃ τῇ κτίσει. 16 ὁ πιστεύσας καὶ βαπτισθεὶς σωθήσεται, ὁ δὲ ἀπιστήσας κατακριθήσεται. 17 σημεῖα δὲ τοῖς πιστεύσασιν ταῦτα παρακολουθήσει· ἐν τῷ ὀνόματί μου δαιμόνια ἐκβαλοῦσιν, γλώσσαις λαλήσουσιν καιναῖς, 18 [καὶ ἐν ταῖς χερσὶν] ὄφεις ἀροῦσιν κἂν θανάσιμόν τι πίωσιν οὐ μὴ αὐτοὺς βλάψῃ, ἐπὶ ἀρρώστους χεῖρας ἐπιθήσουσιν καὶ καλῶς ἕξουσιν.

19 Ὁ μὲν οὖν κύριος Ἰησοῦς μετὰ τὸ λαλῆσαι αὐτοῖς ἀνελήμφθη εἰς τὸν οὐρανὸν καὶ ἐκάθισεν ἐκ δεξιῶν τοῦ θεοῦ. 20 ἐκεῖνοι δὲ ἐξελθόντες ἐκήρυξαν πανταχοῦ, τοῦ κυρίου συνεργοῦντος καὶ τὸν λόγον βεβαιοῦντος διὰ τῶν ἐπακολουθούντων σημείων.c⟧

[The earliest manuscripts and some other ancient witnesses do not have Mark 16:9-20.]

9When Jesus rose early on the first day of the week, he appeared first to Mary Magdalene, out of whom he had driven seven demons. 10She went and told those who had been with him and who were mourning and weeping. 11When they heard that Jesus was alive and that she had seen him, they did not believe it.

12Afterward Jesus appeared in a different form to two of them while they were walking in the country. 13These returned and reported it to the rest; but they did not believe them either.

14Later Jesus appeared to the Eleven as they were eating; he rebuked them for their lack of faith and their stubborn refusal to believe those who had seen him after he had risen.

15He said to them, "Go into all the world and preach the good news to all creation. 16Whoever believes and is baptized will be saved, but whoever does not believe will be condemned. 17And these signs will accompany those who believe: In my name they will drive out demons; they will speak in new tongues; 18they will pick up snakes with their hands; and when they drink deadly poison, it will not hurt them at all; they will place their hands on sick people, and they will get well."

19After the Lord Jesus had spoken to them, he was taken up into heaven and he sat at the right hand of God. 20Then the disciples went out and preached everywhere, and the Lord worked with them and confirmed his word by the signs that accompanied it.

---

u Other ancient authorities add, in whole or in part, *And they excused themselves, saying, "This age of lawlessness and unbelief is under Satan, who does not allow the truth and power of God to prevail over the unclean things of the spirits. Therefore reveal your righteousness now"—thus they spoke to Christ. And Christ replied to them, "The term of years of Satan's power has been fulfilled, but other terrible things draw near. And for those who have sinned I was handed over to death, that they may return to the truth and sin no more, that they may inherit the spiritual and imperishable glory of righteousness that is in heaven."*   v Or *gospel*   w Other ancient authorities lack *in their hands*   x Other ancient authorities add *Amen*

b14 NRSV note u adds κἀκεῖνοι ἀπελογοῦντο λέγοντες ὅτι ὁ αἰὼν οὗτος τῆς ἀνομίας καὶ τῆς ἀπιστίας ὑπὸ τὸν Σατανᾶν ἐστιν, ὁ μὴ ἐῶν τὰ ὑπὸ τῶν πνευμάτων ἀκάθαρτα τὴν ἀλήθειαν τοῦ θεοῦ καταλαβέσθαι δύναμιν· διὰ τοῦτο ἀποκάλυψον σοῦ τὴν δικαιοσύνην ἤδη. ἐκεῖνοι ἔλεγον τῷ Χριστῷ, καὶ ὁ Χριστὸς ἐκείνοις προσέλεγεν ὅτι πεπλήρωται ὁ ὅρος τῶν ἐτῶν τῆς ἐξουσίας τοῦ Σατανᾶ, ἀλλὰ ἐγγίζει ἄλλα δεινὰ καὶ ὑπὲρ ὧν ἐγὼ ἁμαρτησάντων παρεδόθην εἰς θάνατον ἵνα ὑποστρέψωσιν εἰς τὴν ἀλήθειαν καὶ μηκέτι ἁμαρτήσωσιν· ἵνα τὴν ἐν τῷ οὐρανῷ πνευματικὴν καὶ ἄφθαρτον τῆς δικαιοσύνης δόξαν κληρονομήσωσιν.

c20 NRSV note x adds ἀμήν.

NRSV

Dedication to Theophilus

1 Since many have undertaken to set down an orderly account of the events that have been fulfilled among us, [2]just as they were handed on to us by those who from the beginning were eyewitnesses and servants of the word, [3]I too decided, after investigating everything carefully from the very first,[a] to write an orderly account for you, most excellent Theophilus, [4]so that you may know the truth concerning the things about which you have been instructed.

The Birth of John the Baptist Foretold

5 In the days of King Herod of Judea, there was a priest named Zechariah, who belonged to the priestly order of Abijah. His wife was a descendant of Aaron, and her name was Elizabeth. [6]Both of them were righteous before God, living blamelessly according to all the commandments and regulations of the Lord. [7]But they had no children, because Elizabeth was barren, and both were getting on in years.

8 Once when he was serving as priest before God and his section was on duty, [9]he was chosen by lot, according to the custom of the priesthood, to enter the sanctuary of the Lord and offer incense. [10]Now at the time of the incense offering, the whole assembly of the people was praying outside. [11]Then there appeared to him an angel of the Lord, standing at the right side of the altar of incense. [12]When Zechariah saw him, he was terrified; and fear overwhelmed him. [13]But the angel said to him, "Do not be afraid, Zechariah, for your prayer has been heard. Your wife Elizabeth will bear you a son, and you will name him John. [14]You will have joy and gladness, and many will rejoice at his birth, [15]for he will be great in the sight of the Lord. He must never drink wine or strong drink; even before his birth he will be filled with the Holy Spirit. [16]He will turn many of the people of Israel to the Lord their God. [17]With the spirit and power of Elijah he will go before him, to turn the hearts of parents to their children, and the disobedient to the wisdom of the righteous, to make ready a people prepared for the Lord." [18]Zechariah said to the angel, "How will I know that this is so? For I am an old man, and my wife is getting on in years." [19]The

ΚΑΤΑ ΛΟΥΚΑΝ

1 Ἐπειδήπερ πολλοὶ ἐπεχείρησαν ἀνατάξασθαι διήγησιν περὶ τῶν πεπληροφορημένων ἐν ἡμῖν πραγμάτων, 2 καθὼς παρέδοσαν ἡμῖν οἱ ἀπ' ἀρχῆς αὐτόπται καὶ ὑπηρέται γενόμενοι τοῦ λόγου, 3 ἔδοξε κἀμοὶ παρηκολουθηκότι ἄνωθεν πᾶσιν ἀκριβῶς καθεξῆς σοι γράψαι, κράτιστε Θεόφιλε, 4 ἵνα ἐπιγνῷς περὶ ὧν κατηχήθης λόγων τὴν ἀσφάλειαν.

5 Ἐγένετο ἐν ταῖς ἡμέραις Ἡρῴδου βασιλέως τῆς Ἰουδαίας ἱερεύς τις ὀνόματι Ζαχαρίας ἐξ ἐφημερίας Ἀβιά, καὶ γυνὴ αὐτῷ ἐκ τῶν θυγατέρων Ἀαρὼν καὶ τὸ ὄνομα αὐτῆς Ἐλισάβετ. 6 ἦσαν δὲ δίκαιοι ἀμφότεροι ἐναντίον τοῦ θεοῦ, πορευόμενοι ἐν πάσαις ταῖς ἐντολαῖς καὶ δικαιώμασιν τοῦ κυρίου ἄμεμπτοι. 7 καὶ οὐκ ἦν αὐτοῖς τέκνον, καθότι ἦν ἡ Ἐλισάβετ στεῖρα, καὶ ἀμφότεροι προβεβηκότες ἐν ταῖς ἡμέραις αὐτῶν ἦσαν. 8 Ἐγένετο δὲ ἐν τῷ ἱερατεύειν αὐτὸν ἐν τῇ τάξει τῆς ἐφημερίας αὐτοῦ ἔναντι τοῦ θεοῦ, 9 κατὰ τὸ ἔθος τῆς ἱερατείας ἔλαχε τοῦ θυμιᾶσαι εἰσελθὼν εἰς τὸν ναὸν τοῦ κυρίου, 10 καὶ πᾶν τὸ πλῆθος ἦν τοῦ λαοῦ προσευχόμενον ἔξω τῇ ὥρᾳ τοῦ θυμιάματος. 11 ὤφθη δὲ αὐτῷ ἄγγελος κυρίου ἑστὼς ἐκ δεξιῶν τοῦ θυσιαστηρίου τοῦ θυμιάματος. 12 καὶ ἐταράχθη Ζαχαρίας ἰδὼν καὶ φόβος ἐπέπεσεν ἐπ' αὐτόν. 13 εἶπεν δὲ πρὸς αὐτὸν ὁ ἄγγελος, Μὴ φοβοῦ, Ζαχαρία, διότι εἰσηκούσθη ἡ δέησίς σου, καὶ ἡ γυνή σου Ἐλισάβετ γεννήσει υἱόν σοι καὶ καλέσεις τὸ ὄνομα αὐτοῦ Ἰωάννην. 14 καὶ ἔσται χαρά σοι καὶ ἀγαλλίασις καὶ πολλοὶ ἐπὶ τῇ γενέσει αὐτοῦ χαρήσονται. 15 ἔσται γὰρ μέγας ἐνώπιον [τοῦ] κυρίου, καὶ οἶνον καὶ σίκερα οὐ μὴ πίῃ, καὶ πνεύματος ἁγίου πλησθήσεται ἔτι ἐκ κοιλίας μητρὸς αὐτοῦ, 16 καὶ πολλοὺς τῶν υἱῶν Ἰσραὴλ ἐπιστρέψει ἐπὶ κύριον τὸν θεὸν αὐτῶν. 17 καὶ αὐτὸς προελεύσεται ἐνώπιον αὐτοῦ ἐν πνεύματι καὶ δυνάμει Ἠλίου, ἐπιστρέψαι καρδίας πατέρων ἐπὶ τέκνα καὶ ἀπειθεῖς ἐν φρονήσει δικαίων, ἑτοιμάσαι κυρίῳ λαὸν κατεσκευασμένον. 18 Καὶ εἶπεν Ζαχαρίας πρὸς τὸν ἄγγελον, Κατὰ τί γνώσομαι τοῦτο; ἐγὼ γάρ εἰμι πρεσβύτης καὶ ἡ γυνή μου προβεβηκυῖα ἐν ταῖς ἡμέραις αὐτῆς. 19 καὶ ἀποκριθεὶς ὁ

NIV

Introduction

1 Many have undertaken to draw up an account of the things that have been fulfilled[a] among us, [2]just as they were handed down to us by those who from the first were eyewitnesses and servants of the word. [3]Therefore, since I myself have carefully investigated everything from the beginning, it seemed good also to me to write an orderly account for you, most excellent Theophilus, [4]so that you may know the certainty of the things you have been taught.

The Birth of John the Baptist Foretold

[5]In the time of Herod king of Judea there was a priest named Zechariah, who belonged to the priestly division of Abijah; his wife Elizabeth was also a descendant of Aaron. [6]Both of them were upright in the sight of God, observing all the Lord's commandments and regulations blamelessly. [7]But they had no children, because Elizabeth was barren; and they were both well along in years.

[8]Once when Zechariah's division was on duty and he was serving as priest before God, [9]he was chosen by lot, according to the custom of the priesthood, to go into the temple of the Lord and burn incense. [10]And when the time for the burning of incense came, all the assembled worshipers were praying outside.

[11]Then an angel of the Lord appeared to him, standing at the right side of the altar of incense. [12]When Zechariah saw him, he was startled and was gripped with fear. [13]But the angel said to him: "Do not be afraid, Zechariah; your prayer has been heard. Your wife Elizabeth will bear you a son, and you are to give him the name John. [14]He will be a joy and delight to you, and many will rejoice because of his birth, [15]for he will be great in the sight of the Lord. He is never to take wine or other fermented drink, and he will be filled with the Holy Spirit even from birth.[b] [16]Many of the people of Israel will he bring back to the Lord their God. [17]And he will go on before the Lord, in the spirit and power of Elijah, to turn the hearts of the fathers to their children and the disobedient to the wisdom of the righteous—to make ready a people prepared for the Lord."

[18]Zechariah asked the angel, "How can I be sure of this? I am an old man and my wife is well along in years."

ᵃ Or *for a long time*

ᵃ1 Or *been surely believed*   ᵇ15 Or *from his mother's womb*

angel replied, "I am Gabriel. I stand in the presence of God, and I have been sent to speak to you and to bring you this good news. [20]But now, because you did not believe my words, which will be fulfilled in their time, you will become mute, unable to speak, until the day these things occur."

21 Meanwhile the people were waiting for Zechariah, and wondered at his delay in the sanctuary. [22]When he did come out, he could not speak to them, and they realized that he had seen a vision in the sanctuary. He kept motioning to them and remained unable to speak. [23]When his time of service was ended, he went to his home.

24 After those days his wife Elizabeth conceived, and for five months she remained in seclusion. She said, [25]"This is what the Lord has done for me when he looked favorably on me and took away the disgrace I have endured among my people."

The Birth of Jesus Foretold

26 In the sixth month the angel Gabriel was sent by God to a town in Galilee called Nazareth, [27]to a virgin engaged to a man whose name was Joseph, of the house of David. The virgin's name was Mary. [28]And he came to her and said, "Greetings, favored one! The Lord is with you."[b] [29]But she was much perplexed by his words and pondered what sort of greeting this might be. [30]The angel said to her, "Do not be afraid, Mary, for you have found favor with God. [31]And now, you will conceive in your womb and bear a son, and you will name him Jesus. [32]He will be great, and will be called the Son of the Most High, and the Lord God will give to him the throne of his ancestor David. [33]He will reign over the house of Jacob forever, and of his kingdom there will be no end." [34]Mary said to the angel, "How can this be, since I am a virgin?"[c] [35]The angel said to her, "The Holy Spirit will come upon you, and the power of the Most High will overshadow you; therefore the child to be born[d] will be holy; he will be called Son of God. [36]And now, your relative Elizabeth in her old age has also conceived a son; and this is the sixth month for her who was said to be barren. [37]For nothing will be impossible with God." [38]Then Mary

ἄγγελος εἶπεν αὐτῷ, Ἐγώ εἰμι Γαβριὴλ ὁ παρεστηκὼς ἐνώπιον τοῦ θεοῦ καὶ ἀπεστάλην λαλῆσαι πρὸς σὲ καὶ εὐαγγελίσασθαί σοι ταῦτα· **20** καὶ ἰδοὺ ἔσῃ σιωπῶν καὶ μὴ δυνάμενος λαλῆσαι ἄχρι ἧς ἡμέρας γένηται ταῦτα, ἀνθ' ὧν οὐκ ἐπίστευσας τοῖς λόγοις μου, οἵτινες πληρωθήσονται εἰς τὸν καιρὸν αὐτῶν.

21 Καὶ ἦν ὁ λαὸς προσδοκῶν τὸν Ζαχαρίαν καὶ ἐθαύμαζον ἐν τῷ χρονίζειν ἐν τῷ ναῷ αὐτόν. **22** ἐξελθὼν δὲ οὐκ ἐδύνατο λαλῆσαι αὐτοῖς, καὶ ἐπέγνωσαν ὅτι ὀπτασίαν ἑώρακεν ἐν τῷ ναῷ· καὶ αὐτὸς ἦν διανεύων αὐτοῖς καὶ διέμενεν κωφός. **23** καὶ ἐγένετο ὡς ἐπλήσθησαν αἱ ἡμέραι τῆς λειτουργίας αὐτοῦ, ἀπῆλθεν εἰς τὸν οἶκον αὐτοῦ. **24** Μετὰ δὲ ταύτας τὰς ἡμέρας συνέλαβεν Ἐλισάβετ ἡ γυνὴ αὐτοῦ καὶ περιέκρυβεν ἑαυτὴν μῆνας πέντε λέγουσα[a] **25** ὅτι Οὕτως μοι πεποίηκεν κύριος ἐν ἡμέραις αἷς ἐπεῖδεν ἀφελεῖν ὄνειδός μου ἐν ἀνθρώποις.

26 Ἐν δὲ τῷ μηνὶ τῷ ἕκτῳ ἀπεστάλη ὁ ἄγγελος Γαβριὴλ ἀπὸ τοῦ θεοῦ εἰς πόλιν τῆς Γαλιλαίας ᾗ ὄνομα Ναζαρὲθ **27** πρὸς παρθένον ἐμνηστευμένην ἀνδρὶ ᾧ ὄνομα Ἰωσὴφ ἐξ οἴκου Δαυὶδ καὶ τὸ ὄνομα τῆς παρθένου Μαριάμ. **28** καὶ εἰσελθὼν[b] πρὸς αὐτὴν εἶπεν, Χαῖρε, κεχαριτωμένη, ὁ κύριος μετὰ σοῦ.[c] **29** ἡ δὲ ἐπὶ τῷ λόγῳ διεταράχθη καὶ διελογίζετο ποταπὸς εἴη ὁ ἀσπασμὸς οὗτος. **30** καὶ εἶπεν ὁ ἄγγελος αὐτῇ, Μὴ φοβοῦ, Μαριάμ, εὗρες γὰρ χάριν παρὰ τῷ θεῷ. **31** καὶ ἰδοὺ συλλήμψῃ ἐν γαστρὶ καὶ τέξῃ υἱὸν καὶ καλέσεις τὸ ὄνομα αὐτοῦ Ἰησοῦν. **32** οὗτος ἔσται μέγας καὶ υἱὸς ὑψίστου κληθήσεται καὶ δώσει αὐτῷ κύριος ὁ θεὸς τὸν θρόνον Δαυὶδ τοῦ πατρὸς αὐτοῦ, **33** καὶ βασιλεύσει ἐπὶ τὸν οἶκον Ἰακὼβ εἰς τοὺς αἰῶνας καὶ τῆς βασιλείας αὐτοῦ οὐκ ἔσται τέλος. **34** εἶπεν δὲ Μαριὰμ πρὸς τὸν ἄγγελον, Πῶς ἔσται τοῦτο, ἐπεὶ ἄνδρα οὐ γινώσκω; **35** καὶ ἀποκριθεὶς ὁ ἄγγελος εἶπεν αὐτῇ, Πνεῦμα ἅγιον ἐπελεύσεται ἐπὶ σὲ καὶ δύναμις ὑψίστου ἐπισκιάσει σοι· διὸ καὶ τὸ γεννώμενον[d] ἅγιον κληθήσεται υἱὸς θεοῦ. **36** καὶ ἰδοὺ Ἐλισάβετ ἡ συγγενίς σου καὶ αὐτὴ συνείληφεν υἱὸν ἐν γήρει αὐτῆς καὶ οὗτος μὴν ἕκτος ἐστὶν αὐτῇ τῇ καλουμένῃ στείρᾳ· **37** ὅτι οὐκ ἀδυνατήσει παρὰ τοῦ θεοῦ πᾶν ῥῆμα.

[19]The angel answered, "I am Gabriel. I stand in the presence of God, and I have been sent to speak to you and to tell you this good news. [20]And now you will be silent and not able to speak until the day this happens, because you did not believe my words, which will come true at their proper time."

[21]Meanwhile, the people were waiting for Zechariah and wondering why he stayed so long in the temple. [22]When he came out, he could not speak to them. They realized he had seen a vision in the temple, for he kept making signs to them but remained unable to speak.

[23]When his time of service was completed, he returned home. [24]After this his wife Elizabeth became pregnant and for five months remained in seclusion. [25]"The Lord has done this for me," she said. "In these days he has shown his favor and taken away my disgrace among the people."

The Birth of Jesus Foretold

[26]In the sixth month, God sent the angel Gabriel to Nazareth, a town in Galilee, [27]to a virgin pledged to be married to a man named Joseph, a descendant of David. The virgin's name was Mary. [28]The angel went to her and said, "Greetings, you who are highly favored! The Lord is with you."

[29]Mary was greatly troubled at his words and wondered what kind of greeting this might be. [30]But the angel said to her, "Do not be afraid, Mary, you have found favor with God. [31]You will be with child and give birth to a son, and you are to give him the name Jesus. [32]He will be great and will be called the Son of the Most High. The Lord God will give him the throne of his father David, [33]and he will reign over the house of Jacob forever; his kingdom will never end."

[34]"How will this be," Mary asked the angel, "since I am a virgin?"

[35]The angel answered, "The Holy Spirit will come upon you, and the power of the Most High will overshadow you. So the holy one to be born will be called[c] the Son of God. [36]Even Elizabeth your relative is going to have a child in her old age, and she who was said to be barren is in her sixth month. [37]For nothing is impossible with God."

---

[b] Other ancient authorities add *Blessed are you among women*　[c] Gk *I do not know a man*　[d] Other ancient authorities add *of you*

[a]24 NIV reads λέγουσα in verse 25　[b]28 NIV text adds ὁ ἄγγελος †　[c]28 NRSV note b adds εὐλογημένη σὺ ἐν γυναιξίν.　[d]35 NRSV note d adds ἐκ σοῦ

[c]35 Or *So the child to be born will be called holy,*

said, "Here am I, the servant of the Lord; let it be with me according to your word." Then the angel departed from her.

Mary Visits Elizabeth

39 In those days Mary set out and went with haste to a Judean town in the hill country, 40where she entered the house of Zechariah and greeted Elizabeth. 41When Elizabeth heard Mary's greeting, the child leaped in her womb. And Elizabeth was filled with the Holy Spirit 42and exclaimed with a loud cry, "Blessed are you among women, and blessed is the fruit of your womb. 43And why has this happened to me, that the mother of my Lord comes to me? 44For as soon as I heard the sound of your greeting, the child in my womb leaped for joy. 45And blessed is she who believed that there would bee a fulfillment of what was spoken to her by the Lord."

Mary's Song of Praise

46 And Maryf said,
    "My soul magnifies the Lord,
47   and my spirit rejoices in God my
        Savior,
48 for he has looked with favor on the
        lowliness of his servant.
    Surely, from now on all generations
        will call me blessed;
49 for the Mighty One has done great
        things for me,
        and holy is his name.
50 His mercy is for those who fear him
        from generation to generation.
51 He has shown strength with his arm;
        he has scattered the proud in the
        thoughts of their hearts.
52 He has brought down the powerful
        from their thrones,
        and lifted up the lowly;
53 he has filled the hungry with good
        things,
        and sent the rich away empty.
54 He has helped his servant Israel,
        in remembrance of his mercy,
55 according to the promise he made to
        our ancestors,
        to Abraham and to his descendants
        forever."

56 And Mary remained with her about three months and then returned to her home.

The Birth of John the Baptist

57 Now the time came for Elizabeth to

---

38 εἶπεν δὲ Μαριάμ, Ἰδοὺ ἡ δούλη κυρίου· γένοιτό μοι κατὰ τὸ ῥῆμά σου. καὶ ἀπῆλθεν ἀπ᾽ αὐτῆς ὁ ἄγγελος.

39 Ἀναστᾶσα δὲ Μαριάμ ἐν ταῖς ἡμέραις ταύταις ἐπορεύθη εἰς τὴν ὀρεινὴν μετὰ σπουδῆς εἰς πόλιν Ἰούδα, **40** καὶ εἰσῆλθεν εἰς τὸν οἶκον Ζαχαρίου καὶ ἠσπάσατο τὴν Ἐλισάβετ. **41** καὶ ἐγένετο ὡς ἤκουσεν τὸν ἀσπασμὸν τῆς Μαρίας ἡ Ἐλισάβετ, ἐσκίρτησεν τὸ βρέφος ἐν τῇ κοιλίᾳ αὐτῆς, καὶ ἐπλήσθη πνεύματος ἁγίου ἡ Ἐλισάβετ, **42** καὶ ἀνεφώνησεν κραυγῇ μεγάλῃ καὶ εἶπεν, Εὐλογημένη σὺ ἐν γυναιξὶν καὶ εὐλογημένος ὁ καρπὸς τῆς κοιλίας σου. **43** καὶ πόθεν μοι τοῦτο ἵνα ἔλθῃ ἡ μήτηρ τοῦ κυρίου μου πρὸς ἐμέ; **44** ἰδοὺ γὰρ ὡς ἐγένετο ἡ φωνὴ τοῦ ἀσπασμοῦ σου εἰς τὰ ὦτά μου, ἐσκίρτησεν ἐν ἀγαλλιάσει τὸ βρέφος ἐν τῇ κοιλίᾳ μου. **45** καὶ μακαρία ἡ πιστεύσασα ὅτι ἔσται τελείωσις τοῖς λελαλημένοις αὐτῇ παρὰ κυρίου.

46 Καὶ εἶπεν Μαριάμe,
47 Μεγαλύνει ἡ ψυχή μου τὸν κύριον,
    καὶ ἠγαλλίασεν τὸ πνεῦμά μου
        ἐπὶ τῷ θεῷ τῷ σωτῆρί μου,
48 ὅτι ἐπέβλεψεν ἐπὶ τὴν ταπείνωσιν
        τῆς δούλης αὐτοῦ.
    ἰδοὺ γὰρ ἀπὸ τοῦ νῦν μακαρι-
        οῦσίν με πᾶσαι αἱ γενεαί,
49 ὅτι ἐποίησέν μοι μεγάλα ὁ
        δυνατός.
    καὶ ἅγιον τὸ ὄνομα αὐτοῦ,
50 καὶ τὸ ἔλεος αὐτοῦ εἰς γενεὰς καὶ
        γενεὰς
        τοῖς φοβουμένοις αὐτόν.
51 Ἐποίησεν κράτος ἐν βραχίονι
        αὐτοῦ,
    διεσκόρπισεν ὑπερηφάνους
        διανοίᾳ καρδίας αὐτῶν·
52 καθεῖλεν δυνάστας ἀπὸ θρόνων
        καὶ ὕψωσεν ταπεινούς,
53 πεινῶντας ἐνέπλησεν ἀγαθῶν
        καὶ πλουτοῦντας ἐξαπέστειλεν
        κενούς.
54 ἀντελάβετο Ἰσραὴλ παιδὸς αὐτοῦ,
        μνησθῆναι ἐλέους,
55 καθὼς ἐλάλησεν πρὸς τοὺς
        πατέρας ἡμῶν,
    τῷ Ἀβραὰμ καὶ τῷ σπέρματι
        αὐτοῦ εἰς τὸν αἰῶνα.

56 Ἔμεινεν δὲ Μαριὰμ σὺν αὐτῇ ὡς μῆνας τρεῖς, καὶ ὑπέστρεψεν εἰς τὸν οἶκον αὐτῆς.

57 Τῇ δὲ Ἐλισάβετ ἐπλήσθη ὁ χρόνος

38"I am the Lord's servant," Mary answered. "May it be to me as you have said." Then the angel left her.

Mary Visits Elizabeth

39At that time Mary got ready and hurried to a town in the hill country of Judea, 40where she entered Zechariah's home and greeted Elizabeth. 41When Elizabeth heard Mary's greeting, the baby leaped in her womb, and Elizabeth was filled with the Holy Spirit. 42In a loud voice she exclaimed: "Blessed are you among women, and blessed is the child you will bear! 43But why am I so favored, that the mother of my Lord should come to me? 44As soon as the sound of your greeting reached my ears, the baby in my womb leaped for joy. 45Blessed is she who has believed that what the Lord has said to her will be accomplished!"

Mary's Song

46And Mary said:

    "My soul glorifies the Lord
47   and my spirit rejoices in God my
        Savior,
48for he has been mindful
    of the humble state of his servant.
    From now on all generations will call
        me blessed,
49   for the Mighty One has done great
        things for me—
        holy is his name.
50His mercy extends to those who fear
        him,
    from generation to generation.
51He has performed mighty deeds with
        his arm;
    he has scattered those who are proud
        in their inmost thoughts.
52He has brought down rulers from their
        thrones
    but has lifted up the humble.
53He has filled the hungry with good
        things
    but has sent the rich away empty.
54He has helped his servant Israel,
    remembering to be merciful
55to Abraham and his descendants
        forever,
    even as he said to our fathers."

56Mary stayed with Elizabeth for about three months and then returned home.

The Birth of John the Baptist

57When it was time for Elizabeth to have

---

e Or believed, for there will be   f Other ancient authorities read Elizabeth

e46 NRSV note f Elisabeth (in Latin sources)

give birth, and she bore a son. [58]Her neighbors and relatives heard that the Lord had shown his great mercy to her, and they rejoiced with her.

59 On the eighth day they came to circumcise the child, and they were going to name him Zechariah after his father. [60]But his mother said, "No; he is to be called John." [61]They said to her, "None of your relatives has this name." [62]Then they began motioning to his father to find out what name he wanted to give him. [63]He asked for a writing tablet and wrote, "His name is John." And all of them were amazed. [64]Immediately his mouth was opened and his tongue freed, and he began to speak, praising God. [65]Fear came over all their neighbors, and all these things were talked about throughout the entire hill country of Judea. [66]All who heard them pondered them and said, "What then will this child become?" For, indeed, the hand of the Lord was with him.

Zechariah's Prophecy

67 Then his father Zechariah was filled with the Holy Spirit and spoke this prophecy:

[68] "Blessed be the Lord God of Israel,
　　for he has looked favorably on his
　　　people and redeemed them.
[69] He has raised up a mighty savior[g]
　　for us
　　in the house of his servant David,
[70] as he spoke through the mouth of his
　　　holy prophets from of old,
[71] that we would be saved from our
　　　enemies and from the hand of all
　　　who hate us.
[72] Thus he has shown the mercy
　　　promised to our ancestors,
　　and has remembered his holy
　　　covenant,
[73] the oath that he swore to our ancestor
　　　Abraham,
　　to grant us [74]that we, being rescued
　　from the hands of our enemies,
　　might serve him without fear, [75]in
　　holiness and righteousness
　　before him all our days.
[76] And you, child, will be called the
　　　prophet of the Most High;
　　for you will go before the Lord to
　　　prepare his ways,

τοῦ τεκεῖν αὐτὴν καὶ ἐγέννησεν υἱόν. **58** καὶ ἤκουσαν οἱ περίοικοι καὶ οἱ συγγενεῖς αὐτῆς ὅτι ἐμεγάλυνεν κύριος τὸ ἔλεος αὐτοῦ μετ' αὐτῆς καὶ συνέχαιρον αὐτῇ. **59** Καὶ ἐγένετο ἐν τῇ ἡμέρᾳ τῇ ὀγδόῃ ἦλθον περιτεμεῖν τὸ παιδίον καὶ ἐκάλουν αὐτὸ ἐπὶ τῷ ὀνόματι τοῦ πατρὸς αὐτοῦ Ζαχαρίαν. **60** καὶ ἀποκριθεῖσα ἡ μήτηρ αὐτοῦ εἶπεν, Οὐχί, ἀλλὰ κληθήσεται Ἰωάννης. **61** καὶ εἶπαν πρὸς αὐτὴν ὅτι Οὐδείς ἐστιν ἐκ τῆς συγγενείας σου ὃς καλεῖται τῷ ὀνόματι τούτῳ. **62** ἐνένευον δὲ τῷ πατρὶ αὐτοῦ τὸ τί ἂν θέλοι καλεῖσθαι αὐτό. **63** καὶ αἰτήσας πινακίδιον ἔγραψεν λέγων, Ἰωάννης ἐστὶν ὄνομα αὐτοῦ. καὶ ἐθαύμασαν πάντες. **64** ἀνεῴχθη δὲ τὸ στόμα αὐτοῦ παραχρῆμα καὶ ἡ γλῶσσα αὐτοῦ, καὶ ἐλάλει εὐλογῶν τὸν θεόν. **65** καὶ ἐγένετο ἐπὶ πάντας φόβος τοὺς περιοικοῦντας αὐτούς, καὶ ἐν ὅλῃ τῇ ὀρεινῇ τῆς Ἰουδαίας διελαλεῖτο πάντα τὰ ῥήματα ταῦτα, **66** καὶ ἔθεντο πάντες οἱ ἀκούσαντες ἐν τῇ καρδίᾳ αὐτῶν λέγοντες, Τί ἄρα τὸ παιδίον τοῦτο ἔσται; καὶ γὰρ χεὶρ κυρίου ἦν μετ' αὐτοῦ.

67 Καὶ Ζαχαρίας ὁ πατὴρ αὐτοῦ ἐπλήσθη πνεύματος ἁγίου καὶ ἐπροφήτευσεν λέγων, **68** Εὐλογητὸς κύριος ὁ θεὸς τοῦ Ἰσραήλ, ὅτι ἐπεσκέψατο καὶ ἐποίησεν λύτρωσιν τῷ λαῷ αὐτοῦ, **69** καὶ ἤγειρεν κέρας σωτηρίας ἡμῖν ἐν οἴκῳ Δαυὶδ παιδὸς αὐτοῦ, **70** καθὼς ἐλάλησεν διὰ στόματος τῶν ἁγίων ἀπ' αἰῶνος προφητῶν αὐτοῦ, **71** σωτηρίαν ἐξ ἐχθρῶν ἡμῶν καὶ ἐκ χειρὸς πάντων τῶν μισούντων ἡμᾶς, **72** ποιῆσαι ἔλεος μετὰ τῶν πατέρων ἡμῶν καὶ μνησθῆναι διαθήκης ἁγίας αὐτοῦ, **73** ὅρκον ὃν ὤμοσεν πρὸς Ἀβραὰμ τὸν πατέρα ἡμῶν, τοῦ δοῦναι ἡμῖν[f] **74** ἀφόβως ἐκ χειρὸς ἐχθρῶν ῥυσθέντας λατρεύειν αὐτῷ **75** ἐν ὁσιότητι καὶ δικαιοσύνῃ ἐνώπιον αὐτοῦ πάσαις ταῖς ἡμέραις ἡμῶν. **76** Καὶ σὺ δέ, παιδίον, προφήτης ὑψίστου κληθήσῃ· προπορεύσῃ γὰρ ἐνώπιον κυρίου ἑτοιμάσαι ὁδοὺς αὐτοῦ,

---

her baby, she gave birth to a son. [58]Her neighbors and relatives heard that the Lord had shown her great mercy, and they shared her joy.

[59]On the eighth day they came to circumcise the child, and they were going to name him after his father Zechariah, [60]but his mother spoke up and said, "No! He is to be called John."

[61]They said to her, "There is no one among your relatives who has that name."

[62]Then they made signs to his father, to find out what he would like to name the child. [63]He asked for a writing tablet, and to everyone's astonishment he wrote, "His name is John." [64]Immediately his mouth was opened and his tongue was loosed, and he began to speak, praising God. [65]The neighbors were all filled with awe, and throughout the hill country of Judea people were talking about all these things. [66]Everyone who heard this wondered about it, asking, "What then is this child going to be?" For the Lord's hand was with him.

Zechariah's Song

[67]His father Zechariah was filled with the Holy Spirit and prophesied:

[68]"Praise be to the Lord, the God of
　　Israel,
　　because he has come and has
　　redeemed his people.
[69]He has raised up a horn[d] of salvation
　　for us
　　in the house of his servant David
[70](as he said through his holy prophets of
　　long ago),
[71]salvation from our enemies
　　and from the hand of all who hate
　　us—
[72]to show mercy to our fathers
　　and to remember his holy covenant,
[73] the oath he swore to our father
　　Abraham:
[74]to rescue us from the hand of our
　　enemies,
　　and to enable us to serve him without
　　fear
[75] in holiness and righteousness before
　　him all our days.

[76]And you, my child, will be called a
　　prophet of the Most High;
　　for you will go on before the Lord to
　　prepare the way for him,

---

g Gk *a horn of salvation*   f 73 NIV includes τοῦ δοῦναι ἡμῖν in verse 74   d 69 *Horn* here symbolizes strength.

NRSV

77 to give knowledge of salvation to his
people
by the forgiveness of their sins.
78 By the tender mercy of our God,
the dawn from on high will break
upon[h] us,
79 to give light to those who sit in
darkness and in the shadow of
death,
to guide our feet into the way of
peace."

80 The child grew and became strong in
spirit, and he was in the wilderness until
the day he appeared publicly to Israel.

The Birth of Jesus

2 In those days a decree went out from
Emperor Augustus that all the world
should be registered. 2This was the first
registration and was taken while Quirinius
was governor of Syria. 3All went to their
own towns to be registered. 4Joseph also
went from the town of Nazareth in Galilee
to Judea, to the city of David called Bethlehem, because he was descended from
the house and family of David. 5He went
to be registered with Mary, to whom he
was engaged and who was expecting a
child. 6While they were there, the time
came for her to deliver her child. 7And she
gave birth to her firstborn son and wrapped
him in bands of cloth, and laid him in a
manger, because there was no place for
them in the inn.

The Shepherds and the Angels

8 In that region there were shepherds
living in the fields, keeping watch over
their flock by night. 9Then an angel of the
Lord stood before them, and the glory of
the Lord shone around them, and they
were terrified. 10But the angel said to them,
"Do not be afraid; for see—I am bringing
you good news of great joy for all the
people: 11to you is born this day in the city
of David a Savior, who is the Messiah,[i] the
Lord. 12This will be a sign for you: you will
find a child wrapped in bands of cloth and
lying in a manger." 13And suddenly there
was with the angel a multitude of the heavenly host,[j] praising God and saying,
14 "Glory to God in the highest heaven,
and on earth peace among those
whom he favors!"[k]

15 When the angels had left them and
gone into heaven, the shepherds said to

Greek

77 τοῦ δοῦναι γνῶσιν σωτηρίας τῷ
λαῷ αὐτοῦ
ἐν ἀφέσει ἁμαρτιῶν αὐτῶν,
78 διὰ σπλάγχνα ἐλέους θεοῦ ἡμῶν,
ἐν οἷς ἐπισκέψεται[g] ἡμᾶς
ἀνατολὴ ἐξ ὕψους,
79 ἐπιφᾶναι τοῖς ἐν σκότει καὶ σκιᾷ
θανάτου καθημένοις,
τοῦ κατευθῦναι τοὺς πόδας ἡμῶν
εἰς ὁδὸν εἰρήνης.

80 Τὸ δὲ παιδίον ηὔξανεν καὶ
ἐκραταιοῦτο πνεύματι, καὶ ἦν ἐν ταῖς
ἐρήμοις ἕως ἡμέρας ἀναδείξεως αὐτοῦ
πρὸς τὸν Ἰσραήλ.

2 Ἐγένετο δὲ ἐν ταῖς ἡμέραις
ἐκείναις ἐξῆλθεν δόγμα παρὰ
Καίσαρος Αὐγούστου ἀπογράφεσθαι
πᾶσαν τὴν οἰκουμένην. 2 αὕτη ἀπο-
γραφὴ πρώτη ἐγένετο ἡγεμονεύοντος
τῆς Συρίας Κυρηνίου. 3 καὶ ἐπορεύοντο
πάντες ἀπογράφεσθαι, ἕκαστος εἰς
τὴν ἑαυτοῦ πόλιν. 4 Ἀνέβη δὲ καὶ
Ἰωσὴφ ἀπὸ τῆς Γαλιλαίας ἐκ πόλεως
Ναζαρὲθ εἰς τὴν Ἰουδαίαν εἰς πόλιν
Δαυὶδ ἥτις καλεῖται Βηθλέεμ, διὰ τὸ
εἶναι αὐτὸν ἐξ οἴκου καὶ πατριᾶς
Δαυίδ, 5 ἀπογράψασθαι σὺν Μαριὰμ
τῇ ἐμνηστευμένῃ αὐτῷ, οὔσῃ ἐγκύῳ.
6 ἐγένετο δὲ ἐν τῷ εἶναι αὐτοὺς ἐκεῖ
ἐπλήσθησαν αἱ ἡμέραι τοῦ τεκεῖν αὐτήν,
7 καὶ ἔτεκεν τὸν υἱὸν αὐτῆς τὸν πρωτότοκον, καὶ ἐσπαργάνωσεν αὐτὸν καὶ
ἀνέκλινεν αὐτὸν ἐν φάτνῃ, διότι οὐκ
ἦν αὐτοῖς τόπος ἐν τῷ καταλύματι.

8 Καὶ ποιμένες ἦσαν ἐν τῇ χώρᾳ τῇ
αὐτῇ ἀγραυλοῦντες καὶ φυλάσσοντες
φυλακὰς τῆς νυκτὸς ἐπὶ τὴν ποίμνην
αὐτῶν. 9 καὶ ἄγγελος κυρίου ἐπέστη
αὐτοῖς καὶ δόξα κυρίου περιέλαμψεν
αὐτούς, καὶ ἐφοβήθησαν φόβον μέγαν.
10 καὶ εἶπεν αὐτοῖς ὁ ἄγγελος, Μὴ
φοβεῖσθε, ἰδοὺ γὰρ εὐαγγελίζομαι ὑμῖν
χαρὰν μεγάλην ἥτις ἔσται παντὶ τῷ
λαῷ, 11 ὅτι ἐτέχθη ὑμῖν σήμερον σωτὴρ
ὅς ἐστιν Χριστὸς κύριος ἐν πόλει
Δαυίδ. 12 καὶ τοῦτο ὑμῖν τὸ σημεῖον,
εὑρήσετε βρέφος ἐσπαργανωμένον καὶ
κείμενον ἐν φάτνῃ. 13 καὶ ἐξαίφνης
ἐγένετο σὺν τῷ ἀγγέλῳ πλῆθος
στρατιᾶς οὐρανίου αἰνούντων τὸν θεὸν
καὶ λεγόντων,
14 Δόξα ἐν ὑψίστοις θεῷ
καὶ ἐπὶ γῆς εἰρήνη ἐν ἀνθρώποις
εὐδοκίας[a].

15 Καὶ ἐγένετο ὡς ἀπῆλθον ἀπ' αὐτῶν
εἰς τὸν οὐρανὸν οἱ ἄγγελοι, οἱ ποιμένες

NIV

77to give his people the knowledge of
salvation
through the forgiveness of their sins,
78because of the tender mercy of our God,
by which the rising sun will come to
us from heaven
79to shine on those living in darkness
and in the shadow of death,
to guide our feet into the path of
peace."

80And the child grew and became strong
in spirit; and he lived in the desert until he
appeared publicly to Israel.

The Birth of Jesus

2 In those days Caesar Augustus issued
a decree that a census should be taken
of the entire Roman world. 2(This was the
first census that took place while Quirinius
was governor of Syria.) 3And everyone
went to his own town to register.

4So Joseph also went up from the town
of Nazareth in Galilee to Judea, to Bethlehem the town of David, because he belonged to the house and line of David. 5He
went there to register with Mary, who was
pledged to be married to him and was
expecting a child. 6While they were there,
the time came for the baby to be born, 7and
she gave birth to her firstborn, a son. She
wrapped him in cloths and placed him in a
manger, because there was no room for
them in the inn.

The Shepherds and the Angels

8And there were shepherds living out in
the fields nearby, keeping watch over their
flocks at night. 9An angel of the Lord appeared to them, and the glory of the Lord
shone around them, and they were terrified. 10But the angel said to them, "Do not
be afraid. I bring you good news of great
joy that will be for all the people. 11Today
in the town of David a Savior has been
born to you; he is Christ[a] the Lord. 12This
will be a sign to you: You will find a baby
wrapped in cloths and lying in a manger."

13Suddenly a great company of the heavenly host appeared with the angel, praising God and saying,

14"Glory to God in the highest,
and on earth peace to men on whom
his favor rests."

15When the angels had left them and gone
into heaven, the shepherds said to one

h Other ancient authorities read *has broken upon*
i Or *the Christ*   j Gk *army*   k Other ancient authorities
read *peace, goodwill among people*

g78 NRSV note h ἐπεσκέψατο   a14 NRSV note k εὐδοκία

a11 Or *Messiah*. "The Christ" (Greek) and "the Messiah"
(Hebrew) both mean "the Anointed One"; also in verse
26.

one another, "Let us go now to Bethlehem and see this thing that has taken place, which the Lord has made known to us." [16]So they went with haste and found Mary and Joseph, and the child lying in the manger. [17]When they saw this, they made known what had been told them about this child; [18]and all who heard it were amazed at what the shepherds told them. [19]But Mary treasured all these words and pondered them in her heart. [20]The shepherds returned, glorifying and praising God for all they had heard and seen, as it had been told them.

Jesus Is Named

21 After eight days had passed, it was time to circumcise the child; and he was called Jesus, the name given by the angel before he was conceived in the womb.

Jesus Is Presented in the Temple

22 When the time came for their purification according to the law of Moses, they brought him up to Jerusalem to present him to the Lord [23](as it is written in the law of the Lord, "Every firstborn male shall be designated as holy to the Lord"), [24]and they offered a sacrifice according to what is stated in the law of the Lord, "a pair of turtledoves or two young pigeons."

25 Now there was a man in Jerusalem whose name was Simeon;[l] this man was righteous and devout, looking forward to the consolation of Israel, and the Holy Spirit rested on him. [26]It had been revealed to him by the Holy Spirit that he would not see death before he had seen the Lord's Messiah.[m] [27]Guided by the Spirit, Simeon[n] came into the temple; and when the parents brought in the child Jesus, to do for him what was customary under the law, [28]Simeon[o] took him in his arms and praised God, saying,

29 "Master, now you are dismissing your
     servant[p] in peace,
     according to your word;
30 for my eyes have seen your salvation,
31   which you have prepared in the
     presence of all peoples,
32 a light for revelation to the Gentiles
     and for glory to your people Israel."

33 And the child's father and mother were amazed at what was being said about him.

ἐλάλουν πρὸς ἀλλήλους. Διέλθωμεν δὴ ἕως Βηθλέεμ καὶ ἴδωμεν τὸ ῥῆμα τοῦτο τὸ γεγονὸς ὃ ὁ κύριος ἐγνώρισεν ἡμῖν. **16** καὶ ἦλθαν σπεύσαντες καὶ ἀνεῦραν τήν τε Μαριὰμ καὶ τὸν Ἰωσὴφ καὶ τὸ βρέφος κείμενον ἐν τῇ φάτνῃ· **17** ἰδόντες δὲ ἐγνώρισαν περὶ τοῦ ῥήματος τοῦ λαληθέντος αὐτοῖς περὶ τοῦ παιδίου τούτου. **18** καὶ πάντες οἱ ἀκούσαντες ἐθαύμασαν περὶ τῶν λαληθέντων ὑπὸ τῶν ποιμένων πρὸς αὐτούς· **19** ἡ δὲ Μαριὰμ πάντα συνετήρει τὰ ῥήματα ταῦτα συμβάλλουσα ἐν τῇ καρδίᾳ αὐτῆς. **20** καὶ ὑπέστρεψαν οἱ ποιμένες δοξάζοντες καὶ αἰνοῦντες τὸν θεὸν ἐπὶ πᾶσιν οἷς ἤκουσαν καὶ εἶδον καθὼς ἐλαλήθη πρὸς αὐτούς.

21 Καὶ ὅτε ἐπλήσθησαν ἡμέραι ὀκτὼ τοῦ περιτεμεῖν αὐτὸν καὶ ἐκλήθη τὸ ὄνομα αὐτοῦ Ἰησοῦς, τὸ κληθὲν ὑπὸ τοῦ ἀγγέλου πρὸ τοῦ συλλημφθῆναι αὐτὸν ἐν τῇ κοιλίᾳ.

22 Καὶ ὅτε ἐπλήσθησαν αἱ ἡμέραι τοῦ καθαρισμοῦ αὐτῶν κατὰ τὸν νόμον Μωϋσέως, ἀνήγαγον αὐτὸν εἰς Ἱεροσόλυμα παραστῆσαι τῷ κυρίῳ, **23** καθὼς γέγραπται ἐν νόμῳ κυρίου ὅτι **Πᾶν ἄρσεν διανοῖγον μήτραν ἅγιον τῷ κυρίῳ κληθήσεται, 24** καὶ τοῦ δοῦναι θυσίαν κατὰ τὸ εἰρημένον ἐν τῷ νόμῳ κυρίου, **ζεῦγος τρυγόνων ἢ δύο νοσσοὺς περιστερῶν.**

25 Καὶ ἰδοὺ ἄνθρωπος ἦν ἐν Ἱερουσαλὴμ ᾧ ὄνομα Συμεὼν καὶ ὁ ἄνθρωπος οὗτος δίκαιος καὶ εὐλαβὴς προσδεχόμενος παράκλησιν τοῦ Ἰσραήλ, καὶ πνεῦμα ἦν ἅγιον ἐπ᾽ αὐτόν· **26** καὶ ἦν αὐτῷ κεχρηματισμένον ὑπὸ τοῦ πνεύματος τοῦ ἁγίου μὴ ἰδεῖν θάνατον πρὶν [ἢ] ἂν ἴδῃ τὸν Χριστὸν κυρίου. **27** καὶ ἦλθεν ἐν τῷ πνεύματι εἰς τὸ ἱερόν· καὶ ἐν τῷ εἰσαγαγεῖν τοὺς γονεῖς τὸ παιδίον Ἰησοῦν τοῦ ποιῆσαι αὐτοὺς κατὰ τὸ εἰθισμένον τοῦ νόμου περὶ αὐτοῦ **28** καὶ αὐτὸς ἐδέξατο αὐτὸ εἰς τὰς ἀγκάλας καὶ εὐλόγησεν τὸν θεὸν καὶ εἶπεν,

29 Νῦν ἀπολύεις τὸν δοῦλόν σου,
     δέσποτα,
     κατὰ τὸ ῥῆμά σου ἐν εἰρήνῃ·
30 ὅτι εἶδον οἱ ὀφθαλμοί μου τὸ
     σωτήριόν σου,
31 ὃ ἡτοίμασας κατὰ πρόσωπον
     πάντων τῶν λαῶν,
32 φῶς εἰς ἀποκάλυψιν ἐθνῶν
     καὶ δόξαν λαοῦ σου Ἰσραήλ.

33 καὶ ἦν ὁ πατὴρ αὐτοῦ καὶ ἡ μήτηρ θαυμάζοντες ἐπὶ τοῖς λαλουμένοις περὶ

another, "Let's go to Bethlehem and see this thing that has happened, which the Lord has told us about." [16]So they hurried off and found Mary and Joseph, and the baby, who was lying in the manger. [17]When they had seen him, they spread the word concerning what had been told them about this child, [18]and all who heard it were amazed at what the shepherds said to them. [19]But Mary treasured up all these things and pondered them in her heart. [20]The shepherds returned, glorifying and praising God for all the things they had heard and seen, which were just as they had been told.

Jesus Presented in the Temple

[21]On the eighth day, when it was time to circumcise him, he was named Jesus, the name the angel had given him before he had been conceived.

[22]When the time of their purification according to the Law of Moses had been completed, Joseph and Mary took him to Jerusalem to present him to the Lord [23](as it is written in the Law of the Lord, "Every firstborn male is to be consecrated to the Lord"[b]), [24]and to offer a sacrifice in keeping with what is said in the Law of the Lord: "a pair of doves or two young pigeons."[c]

[25]Now there was a man in Jerusalem called Simeon, who was righteous and devout. He was waiting for the consolation of Israel, and the Holy Spirit was upon him. [26]It had been revealed to him by the Holy Spirit that he would not die before he had seen the Lord's Christ. [27]Moved by the Spirit, he went into the temple courts. When the parents brought in the child Jesus to do for him what the custom of the Law required, [28]Simeon took him in his arms and praised God, saying:

[29]"Sovereign Lord, as you have promised,
     you now dismiss[d] your servant in
     peace.
[30]For my eyes have seen your salvation,
[31]   which you have prepared in the sight
     of all people,
[32]a light for revelation to the Gentiles
     and for glory to your people Israel."

[33]The child's father and mother marveled at what was said about him. [34]Then Simeon

[l]Gk *Symeon*   [m]Or *the Lord's Christ*   [n]Gk *In the Spirit,*
he   [o]Gk *he*   [p]Gk *slave*

[b]23 Exodus 13:2,12   [c]24 Lev. 12:8   [d]29 Or *promised, / now dismiss*

[34]Then Simeon[l] blessed them and said to his mother Mary, "This child is destined for the falling and the rising of many in Israel, and to be a sign that will be opposed [35]so that the inner thoughts of many will be revealed—and a sword will pierce your own soul too."

[36] There was also a prophet, Anna[q] the daughter of Phanuel, of the tribe of Asher. She was of a great age, having lived with her husband seven years after her marriage, [37]then as a widow to the age of eighty-four. She never left the temple but worshiped there with fasting and prayer night and day. [38]At that moment she came, and began to praise God and to speak about the child[r] to all who were looking for the redemption of Jerusalem.

The Return to Nazareth

[39] When they had finished everything required by the law of the Lord, they returned to Galilee, to their own town of Nazareth. [40]The child grew and became strong, filled with wisdom; and the favor of God was upon him.

The Boy Jesus in the Temple

[41] Now every year his parents went to Jerusalem for the festival of the Passover. [42]And when he was twelve years old, they went up as usual for the festival. [43]When the festival was ended and they started to return, the boy Jesus stayed behind in Jerusalem, but his parents did not know it. [44]Assuming that he was in the group of travelers, they went a day's journey. Then they started to look for him among their relatives and friends. [45]When they did not find him, they returned to Jerusalem to search for him. [46]After three days they found him in the temple, sitting among the teachers, listening to them and asking them questions. [47]And all who heard him were amazed at his understanding and his answers. [48]When his parents[s] saw him they were astonished; and his mother said to him, "Child, why have you treated us like this? Look, your father and I have been searching for you in great anxiety." [49]He said to them, "Why were you searching for me? Did you not know that I must be in my Father's house?"[t] [50]But they did not understand what he said to them. [51]Then he went down with them and came to Nazareth, and was obedient to them. His mother treasured all these things in her

[l] Gk *Symeon* [q] Gk *Hanna* [r] Gk *him* [s] Gk *they* [t] Or *be about my Father's interests?*

αὐτοῦ. **34** καὶ εὐλόγησεν αὐτοὺς Συμεὼν καὶ εἶπεν πρὸς Μαριὰμ τὴν μητέρα αὐτοῦ, Ἰδοὺ οὗτος κεῖται εἰς πτῶσιν καὶ ἀνάστασιν πολλῶν ἐν τῷ Ἰσραὴλ καὶ εἰς σημεῖον ἀντιλεγόμενον **35** – καὶ σοῦ [δὲ] αὐτῆς τὴν ψυχὴν διελεύσεται ῥομφαία –, ὅπως ἂν ἀποκαλυφθῶσιν ἐκ πολλῶν καρδιῶν διαλογισμοί.

36 Καὶ ἦν Ἅννα προφῆτις, θυγάτηρ Φανουήλ, ἐκ φυλῆς Ἀσήρ· αὕτη προβεβηκυῖα ἐν ἡμέραις πολλαῖς, ζήσασα μετὰ ἀνδρὸς ἔτη ἑπτὰ ἀπὸ τῆς παρθενίας αὐτῆς **37** καὶ αὐτὴ χήρα ἕως ἐτῶν ὀγδοήκοντα τεσσάρων, ἣ οὐκ ἀφίστατο τοῦ ἱεροῦ νηστείαις καὶ δεήσεσιν λατρεύουσα νύκτα καὶ ἡμέραν. **38** καὶ αὐτὴ τῇ ὥρᾳ ἐπιστᾶσα ἀνθωμολογεῖτο τῷ θεῷ καὶ ἐλάλει περὶ αὐτοῦ πᾶσιν τοῖς προσδεχομένοις λύτρωσιν Ἰερουσαλήμ.

39 Καὶ ὡς ἐτέλεσαν πάντα τὰ κατὰ τὸν νόμον κυρίου, ἐπέστρεψαν εἰς τὴν Γαλιλαίαν εἰς πόλιν ἑαυτῶν Ναζαρέθ. **40** Τὸ δὲ παιδίον ηὔξανεν καὶ ἐκραταιοῦτο πληρούμενον σοφίᾳ, καὶ χάρις θεοῦ ἦν ἐπ᾽ αὐτό.

41 Καὶ ἐπορεύοντο οἱ γονεῖς αὐτοῦ κατ᾽ ἔτος εἰς Ἰερουσαλὴμ τῇ ἑορτῇ τοῦ πάσχα. **42** καὶ ὅτε ἐγένετο ἐτῶν δώδεκα, ἀναβαινόντων αὐτῶν κατὰ τὸ ἔθος τῆς ἑορτῆς **43** καὶ τελειωσάντων τὰς ἡμέρας, ἐν τῷ ὑποστρέφειν αὐτοὺς ὑπέμεινεν Ἰησοῦς ὁ παῖς ἐν Ἰερουσαλήμ, καὶ οὐκ ἔγνωσαν οἱ γονεῖς αὐτοῦ. **44** νομίσαντες δὲ αὐτὸν εἶναι ἐν τῇ συνοδίᾳ ἦλθον ἡμέρας ὁδὸν καὶ ἀνεζήτουν αὐτὸν ἐν τοῖς συγγενεῦσιν καὶ τοῖς γνωστοῖς, **45** καὶ μὴ εὑρόντες ὑπέστρεψαν εἰς Ἰερουσαλὴμ ἀναζητοῦντες αὐτόν. **46** καὶ ἐγένετο μετὰ ἡμέρας τρεῖς εὗρον αὐτὸν ἐν τῷ ἱερῷ καθεζόμενον ἐν μέσῳ τῶν διδασκάλων καὶ ἀκούοντα αὐτῶν καὶ ἐπερωτῶντα αὐτούς· **47** ἐξίσταντο δὲ πάντες οἱ ἀκούοντες αὐτοῦ ἐπὶ τῇ συνέσει καὶ ταῖς ἀποκρίσεσιν αὐτοῦ. **48** καὶ ἰδόντες αὐτὸν ἐξεπλάγησαν, καὶ εἶπεν πρὸς αὐτὸν ἡ μήτηρ αὐτοῦ, Τέκνον, τί ἐποίησας ἡμῖν οὕτως; ἰδοὺ ὁ πατήρ σου κἀγὼ ὀδυνώμενοι ἐζητοῦμέν σε. **49** καὶ εἶπεν πρὸς αὐτούς, Τί ὅτι ἐζητεῖτέ με; οὐκ ᾔδειτε ὅτι ἐν τοῖς τοῦ πατρός μου δεῖ εἶναί με; **50** καὶ αὐτοὶ οὐ συνῆκαν τὸ ῥῆμα ὃ ἐλάλησεν αὐτοῖς. **51** καὶ κατέβη μετ᾽ αὐτῶν καὶ ἦλθεν εἰς Ναζαρέθ καὶ ἦν ὑποτασσόμενος αὐτοῖς. καὶ ἡ μήτηρ αὐτοῦ διετήρει πάντα τὰ ῥήματα ἐν τῇ καρδίᾳ

---

blessed them and said to Mary, his mother: "This child is destined to cause the falling and rising of many in Israel, and to be a sign that will be spoken against, [35]so that the thoughts of many hearts will be revealed. And a sword will pierce your own soul too."

[36]There was also a prophetess, Anna, the daughter of Phanuel, of the tribe of Asher. She was very old; she had lived with her husband seven years after her marriage, [37]and then was a widow until she was eighty-four.[e] She never left the temple but worshiped night and day, fasting and praying. [38]Coming up to them at that very moment, she gave thanks to God and spoke about the child to all who were looking forward to the redemption of Jerusalem.

[39]When Joseph and Mary had done everything required by the Law of the Lord, they returned to Galilee to their own town of Nazareth. [40]And the child grew and became strong; he was filled with wisdom, and the grace of God was upon him.

The Boy Jesus at the Temple

[41]Every year his parents went to Jerusalem for the Feast of the Passover. [42]When he was twelve years old, they went up to the Feast, according to the custom. [43]After the Feast was over, while his parents were returning home, the boy Jesus stayed behind in Jerusalem, but they were unaware of it. [44]Thinking he was in their company, they traveled on for a day. Then they began looking for him among their relatives and friends. [45]When they did not find him, they went back to Jerusalem to look for him. [46]After three days they found him in the temple courts, sitting among the teachers, listening to them and asking them questions. [47]Everyone who heard him was amazed at his understanding and his answers. [48]When his parents saw him, they were astonished. His mother said to him, "Son, why have you treated us like this? Your father and I have been anxiously searching for you."

[49]"Why were you searching for me?" he asked. "Didn't you know I had to be in my Father's house?" [50]But they did not understand what he was saying to them.

[51]Then he went down to Nazareth with them and was obedient to them. But his mother treasured all these things in her

[e] 37 Or *widow for eighty-four years*

heart.

52 And Jesus increased in wisdom and in years,[u] and in divine and human favor.

The Proclamation of John the Baptist

3 In the fifteenth year of the reign of Emperor Tiberius, when Pontius Pilate was governor of Judea, and Herod was ruler[v] of Galilee, and his brother Philip ruler[v] of the region of Ituraea and Trachonitis, and Lysanias ruler[v] of Abilene, [2]during the high priesthood of Annas and Caiaphas, the word of God came to John son of Zechariah in the wilderness. [3]He went into all the region around the Jordan, proclaiming a baptism of repentance for the forgiveness of sins, [4]as it is written in the book of the words of the prophet Isaiah,

"The voice of one crying out in the
     wilderness:
'Prepare the way of the Lord,
     make his paths straight.
[5] Every valley shall be filled,
     and every mountain and hill shall be
          made low,
     and the crooked shall be made
          straight,
     and the rough ways made smooth;
[6] and all flesh shall see the salvation of
          God.' "

7 John said to the crowds that came out to be baptized by him, "You brood of vipers! Who warned you to flee from the wrath to come? [8]Bear fruits worthy of repentance. Do not begin to say to yourselves, 'We have Abraham as our ancestor'; for I tell you, God is able from these stones to raise up children to Abraham. [9]Even now the ax is lying at the root of the trees; every tree therefore that does not bear good fruit is cut down and thrown into the fire."

10 And the crowds asked him, "What then should we do?" [11]In reply he said to them, "Whoever has two coats must share with anyone who has none; and whoever has food must do likewise." [12]Even tax collectors came to be baptized, and they asked him, "Teacher, what should we do?" [13]He said to them, "Collect no more than the amount prescribed for you." [14]Soldiers also asked him, "And we, what should we do?" He said to them, "Do not extort money from anyone by threats or false accusation, and be satisfied with your wages."

αὐτῆς. **52** Καὶ Ἰησοῦς προέκοπτεν [ἐν τῇ][b] σοφίᾳ καὶ ἡλικίᾳ καὶ χάριτι παρὰ θεῷ καὶ ἀνθρώποις.

3 Ἐν ἔτει δὲ πεντεκαιδεκάτῳ τῆς ἡγεμονίας Τιβερίου Καίσαρος, ἡγεμονεύοντος Ποντίου Πιλάτου τῆς Ἰουδαίας, καὶ τετρααρχοῦντος τῆς Γαλιλαίας Ἡρῴδου, Φιλίππου δὲ τοῦ ἀδελφοῦ αὐτοῦ τετρααρχοῦντος τῆς Ἰτουραίας καὶ Τραχωνίτιδος χώρας, καὶ Λυσανίου τῆς Ἀβιληνῆς τετρααρχοῦντος, **2** ἐπὶ ἀρχιερέως Ἅννα καὶ Καϊάφα, ἐγένετο ῥῆμα θεοῦ ἐπὶ Ἰωάννην τὸν Ζαχαρίου υἱὸν ἐν τῇ ἐρήμῳ. **3** καὶ ἦλθεν εἰς πᾶσαν [τὴν] περίχωρον τοῦ Ἰορδάνου κηρύσσων βάπτισμα μετανοίας εἰς ἄφεσιν ἁμαρτιῶν, **4** ὡς γέγραπται ἐν βίβλῳ λόγων Ἡσαΐου τοῦ προφήτου,

Φωνὴ βοῶντος ἐν τῇ ἐρήμῳ,
Ἑτοιμάσατε τὴν ὁδὸν κυρίου,
     εὐθείας ποιεῖτε τὰς τρίβους
          αὐτοῦ·
5 πᾶσα φάραγξ πληρωθήσεται
     καὶ πᾶν ὄρος καὶ βουνὸς
          ταπεινωθήσεται,
     καὶ ἔσται τὰ σκολιὰ εἰς εὐθείαν
     καὶ αἱ τραχεῖαι εἰς ὁδοὺς λείας·
6 καὶ ὄψεται πᾶσα σὰρξ τὸ
          σωτήριον τοῦ θεοῦ.

7 Ἔλεγεν οὖν τοῖς ἐκπορευομένοις ὄχλοις βαπτισθῆναι ὑπ᾽ αὐτοῦ, Γεννήματα ἐχιδνῶν, τίς ὑπέδειξεν ὑμῖν φυγεῖν ἀπὸ τῆς μελλούσης ὀργῆς; **8** ποιήσατε οὖν καρποὺς ἀξίους τῆς μετανοίας καὶ μὴ ἄρξησθε λέγειν ἐν ἑαυτοῖς, Πατέρα ἔχομεν τὸν Ἀβραάμ. λέγω γὰρ ὑμῖν ὅτι δύναται ὁ θεὸς ἐκ τῶν λίθων τούτων ἐγεῖραι τέκνα τῷ Ἀβραάμ. **9** ἤδη δὲ καὶ ἡ ἀξίνη πρὸς τὴν ῥίζαν τῶν δένδρων κεῖται· πᾶν οὖν δένδρον μὴ ποιοῦν καρπὸν καλὸν ἐκκόπτεται καὶ εἰς πῦρ βάλλεται. **10** Καὶ ἐπηρώτων αὐτὸν οἱ ὄχλοι λέγοντες, Τί οὖν ποιήσωμεν; **11** ἀποκριθεὶς δὲ ἔλεγεν αὐτοῖς, Ὁ ἔχων δύο χιτῶνας μεταδότω τῷ μὴ ἔχοντι, καὶ ὁ ἔχων βρώματα ὁμοίως ποιείτω. **12** ἦλθον δὲ καὶ τελῶναι βαπτισθῆναι καὶ εἶπαν πρὸς αὐτόν, Διδάσκαλε, τί ποιήσωμεν; **13** ὁ δὲ εἶπεν πρὸς αὐτούς, Μηδὲν πλέον παρὰ τὸ διατεταγμένον ὑμῖν πράσσετε. **14** ἐπηρώτων δὲ αὐτὸν καὶ στρατευόμενοι λέγοντες, Τί ποιήσωμεν καὶ ἡμεῖς; καὶ εἶπεν αὐτοῖς, Μηδένα διασείσητε μηδὲ συκοφαντήσητε καὶ ἀρκεῖσθε τοῖς ὀψωνίοις ὑμῶν.

heart. [52]And Jesus grew in wisdom and stature, and in favor with God and men.

John the Baptist Prepares the Way

3 In the fifteenth year of the reign of Tiberius Caesar—when Pontius Pilate was governor of Judea, Herod tetrarch of Galilee, his brother Philip tetrarch of Iturea and Traconitis, and Lysanias tetrarch of Abilene— [2]during the high priesthood of Annas and Caiaphas, the word of God came to John son of Zechariah in the desert. [3]He went into all the country around the Jordan, preaching a baptism of repentance for the forgiveness of sins. [4]As is written in the book of the words of Isaiah the prophet:

"A voice of one calling in the desert,
'Prepare the way for the Lord,
     make straight paths for him.
[5]Every valley shall be filled in,
     every mountain and hill made low.
The crooked roads shall become
          straight,
     the rough ways smooth.
[6]And all mankind will see God's
          salvation.' "[a]

[7]John said to the crowds coming out to be baptized by him, "You brood of vipers! Who warned you to flee from the coming wrath? [8]Produce fruit in keeping with repentance. And do not begin to say to yourselves, 'We have Abraham as our father.' For I tell you that out of these stones God can raise up children for Abraham. [9]The ax is already at the root of the trees, and every tree that does not produce good fruit will be cut down and thrown into the fire."

[10]"What should we do then?" the crowd asked.

[11]John answered, "The man with two tunics should share with him who has none, and the one who has food should do the same."

[12]Tax collectors also came to be baptized. "Teacher," they asked, "what should we do?"

[13]"Don't collect any more than you are required to," he told them.

[14]Then some soldiers asked him, "And what should we do?"

He replied, "Don't extort money and don't accuse people falsely—be content with your pay."

---

[u] Or *in stature*   [v] Gk *tetrarch*   [b]52 NIV text omits ἐν τῇ †   [a]6 Isaiah 40:3-5

15 As the people were filled with expectation, and all were questioning in their hearts concerning John, whether he might be the Messiah,[w] [16]John answered all of them by saying, "I baptize you with water; but one who is more powerful than I is coming; I am not worthy to untie the thong of his sandals. He will baptize you with[x] the Holy Spirit and fire. [17]His winnowing fork is in his hand, to clear his threshing floor and to gather the wheat into his granary; but the chaff he will burn with unquenchable fire."

18 So, with many other exhortations, he proclaimed the good news to the people. [19]But Herod the ruler,[v] who had been rebuked by him because of Herodias, his brother's wife, and because of all the evil things that Herod had done, [20]added to them all by shutting up John in prison.

The Baptism of Jesus

21 Now when all the people were baptized, and when Jesus also had been baptized and was praying, the heaven was opened, [22]and the Holy Spirit descended upon him in bodily form like a dove. And a voice came from heaven, "You are my Son, the Beloved;[y] with you I am well pleased."[z]

The Ancestors of Jesus

23 Jesus was about thirty years old when he began his work. He was the son (as was thought) of Joseph son of Heli, [24]son of Matthat, son of Levi, son of Melchi, son of Jannai, son of Joseph, [25]son of Mattathias, son of Amos, son of Nahum, son of Esli, son of Naggai, [26]son of Maath, son of Mattathias, son of Semein, son of Josech, son of Joda, [27]son of Joanan, son of Rhesa, son of Zerubbabel, son of Shealtiel,[a] son of Neri, [28]son of Melchi, son of Addi, son of Cosam, son of Elmadam, son of Er, [29]son of Joshua, son of Eliezer, son of Jorim, son of Matthat, son of Levi, [30]son of Simeon, son of Judah, son of Joseph, son of Jonam, son of Eliakim, [31]son of Melea, son of Menna, son of Mattatha, son of Nathan, son of David, [32]son of Jesse, son of Obed,

15 Προσδοκῶντος δὲ τοῦ λαοῦ καὶ διαλογιζομένων πάντων ἐν ταῖς καρδίαις αὐτῶν περὶ τοῦ Ἰωάννου, μήποτε αὐτὸς εἴη ὁ Χριστός, 16 ἀπεκρίνατο λέγων πᾶσιν ὁ Ἰωάννης, Ἐγὼ μὲν ὕδατι βαπτίζω ὑμᾶς· ἔρχεται δὲ ὁ ἰσχυρότερός μου, οὗ οὐκ εἰμὶ ἱκανὸς λῦσαι τὸν ἱμάντα τῶν ὑποδημάτων αὐτοῦ· αὐτὸς ὑμᾶς βαπτίσει ἐν πνεύματι ἁγίῳ καὶ πυρί· 17 οὗ τὸ πτύον ἐν τῇ χειρὶ αὐτοῦ διακαθᾶραι τὴν ἅλωνα αὐτοῦ καὶ συναγαγεῖν τὸν σῖτον εἰς τὴν ἀποθήκην αὐτοῦ, τὸ δὲ ἄχυρον κατακαύσει πυρὶ ἀσβέστῳ. 18 Πολλὰ μὲν οὖν καὶ ἕτερα παρακαλῶν εὐηγγελίζετο τὸν λαόν. 19 ὁ δὲ Ἡρῴδης ὁ τετραάρχης, ἐλεγχόμενος ὑπ᾽ αὐτοῦ περὶ Ἡρῳδιάδος τῆς γυναικὸς τοῦ ἀδελφοῦ αὐτοῦ καὶ περὶ πάντων ὧν ἐποίησεν πονηρῶν ὁ Ἡρῴδης, 20 προσέθηκεν καὶ τοῦτο ἐπὶ πᾶσιν [καὶ] κατέκλεισεν τὸν Ἰωάννην ἐν φυλακῇ.

21 Ἐγένετο δὲ ἐν τῷ βαπτισθῆναι ἅπαντα τὸν λαὸν καὶ Ἰησοῦ βαπτισθέντος καὶ προσευχομένου ἀνεῳχθῆναι τὸν οὐρανὸν 22 καὶ καταβῆναι τὸ πνεῦμα τὸ ἅγιον σωματικῷ εἴδει ὡς περιστερὰν ἐπ᾽ αὐτόν, καὶ φωνὴν ἐξ οὐρανοῦ γενέσθαι, Σὺ εἶ ὁ υἱός μου ὁ ἀγαπητός, ἐν σοὶ εὐδόκησα[c].

23 Καὶ αὐτὸς ἦν Ἰησοῦς ἀρχόμενος ὡσεὶ ἐτῶν τριάκοντα, ὢν υἱός, ὡς ἐνομίζετο, Ἰωσὴφ τοῦ Ἡλὶ 24 τοῦ Μαθθὰτ τοῦ Λευὶ τοῦ Μελχὶ τοῦ Ἰανναὶ τοῦ Ἰωσὴφ 25 τοῦ Ματταθίου τοῦ Ἀμὼς τοῦ Ναοὺμ τοῦ Ἐσλὶ τοῦ Ναγγαὶ 26 τοῦ Μάαθ τοῦ Ματταθίου τοῦ Σεμεῒν τοῦ Ἰωσὴχ τοῦ Ἰωδὰ 27 τοῦ Ἰωανὰν τοῦ Ῥησὰ τοῦ Ζοροβαβὲλ τοῦ Σαλαθιὴλ τοῦ Νηρὶ 28 τοῦ Μελχὶ τοῦ Ἀδδὶ τοῦ Κωσὰμ τοῦ Ἐλμαδὰμ τοῦ Ἢρ 29 τοῦ Ἰησοῦ τοῦ Ἐλιέζερ τοῦ Ἰωρὶμ τοῦ Μαθθὰτ τοῦ Λευὶ 30 τοῦ Συμεὼν τοῦ Ἰούδα τοῦ Ἰωσὴφ τοῦ Ἰωνὰμ τοῦ Ἐλιακὶμ 31 τοῦ Μελεὰ τοῦ Μεννὰ τοῦ Ματταθὰ τοῦ Ναθὰμ τοῦ Δαυὶδ 32 τοῦ Ἰεσσαὶ τοῦ Ἰωβὴδ τοῦ Βόος τοῦ

[15]The people were waiting expectantly and were all wondering in their hearts if John might possibly be the Christ.[b] [16]John answered them all, "I baptize you with[c] water. But one more powerful than I will come, the thongs of whose sandals I am not worthy to untie. He will baptize you with the Holy Spirit and with fire. [17]His winnowing fork is in his hand to clear his threshing floor and to gather the wheat into his barn, but he will burn up the chaff with unquenchable fire." [18]And with many other words John exhorted the people and preached the good news to them.

[19]But when John rebuked Herod the tetrarch because of Herodias, his brother's wife, and all the other evil things he had done, [20]Herod added this to them all: He locked John up in prison.

The Baptism and Genealogy of Jesus

[21]When all the people were being baptized, Jesus was baptized too. And as he was praying, heaven was opened [22]and the Holy Spirit descended on him in bodily form like a dove. And a voice came from heaven: "You are my Son, whom I love; with you I am well pleased."

[23]Now Jesus himself was about thirty years old when he began his ministry. He was the son, so it was thought, of Joseph,

the son of Heli, [24]the son of Matthat,
the son of Levi, the son of Melki,
the son of Jannai, the son of Joseph,
[25]the son of Mattathias, the son of Amos,
the son of Nahum, the son of Esli,
the son of Naggai, [26]the son of Maath,
the son of Mattathias, the son of Semein,
the son of Josech, the son of Joda,
[27]the son of Joanan, the son of Rhesa,
the son of Zerubbabel, the son of Shealtiel,
the son of Neri, [28]the son of Melki,
the son of Addi, the son of Cosam,
the son of Elmadam, the son of Er,
[29]the son of Joshua, the son of Eliezer,
the son of Jorim, the son of Matthat,
the son of Levi, [30]the son of Simeon,
the son of Judah, the son of Joseph,
the son of Jonam, the son of Eliakim,
[31]the son of Melea, the son of Menna,
the son of Mattatha, the son of Nathan,
the son of David, [32]the son of Jesse,
the son of Obed, the son of Boaz,

---

[v] Gk tetrarch   [w] Or the Christ   [x] Or in   [y] Or my beloved Son   [z] Other ancient authorities read You are my Son, today I have begotten you   [a] Gk Salathiel

[c]22 NRSV note z Υἱός μου εἶ σύ, ἐγὼ σήμερον γεγέννηκά σε.

[b]15 Or Messiah   [c]16 Or in

son of Boaz, son of Sala,[b] son of Nahshon, [33]son of Amminadab, son of Admin, son of Arni,[c] son of Hezron, son of Perez, son of Judah, [34]son of Jacob, son of Isaac, son of Abraham, son of Terah, son of Nahor, [35]son of Serug, son of Reu, son of Peleg, son of Eber, son of Shelah, [36]son of Cainan, son of Arphaxad, son of Shem, son of Noah, son of Lamech, [37]son of Methuselah, son of Enoch, son of Jared, son of Mahalaleel, son of Cainan, [38]son of Enos, son of Seth, son of Adam, son of God.

The Temptation of Jesus

4 Jesus, full of the Holy Spirit, returned from the Jordan and was led by the Spirit in the wilderness, [2]where for forty days he was tempted by the devil. He ate nothing at all during those days, and when they were over, he was famished. [3]The devil said to him, "If you are the Son of God, command this stone to become a loaf of bread." [4]Jesus answered him, "It is written, 'One does not live by bread alone.' "

5 Then the devil[d] led him up and showed him in an instant all the kingdoms of the world. [6]And the devil[d] said to him, "To you I will give their glory and all this authority; for it has been given over to me, and I give it to anyone I please. [7]If you, then, will worship me, it will all be yours." [8]Jesus answered him, "It is written,

'Worship the Lord your God,
and serve only him.' "

9 Then the devil[d] took him to Jerusalem, and placed him on the pinnacle of the temple, saying to him, "If you are the Son of God, throw yourself down from here, [10]for it is written,

'He will command his angels
concerning you,
to protect you,'

[11]and

'On their hands they will bear you up,
so that you will not dash your foot
against a stone.' "

[12]Jesus answered him, "It is said, 'Do not put the Lord your God to the test.' " [13]When the devil had finished every test,

---

Σαλὰ[d] τοῦ Ναασσὼν **33** τοῦ Ἀμιναδὰβ τοῦ Ἀδμὶν τοῦ Ἀρνὶ[e] τοῦ Ἐσρὼμ τοῦ Φάρες τοῦ Ἰούδα **34** τοῦ Ἰακὼβ τοῦ Ἰσαὰκ τοῦ Ἀβραὰμ τοῦ Θάρα τοῦ Ναχὼρ **35** τοῦ Σεροὺχ τοῦ Ῥαγαὺ τοῦ Φάλεκ τοῦ Ἔβερ τοῦ Σαλὰ **36** τοῦ Καϊνὰμ τοῦ Ἀρφαξὰδ τοῦ Σὴμ τοῦ Νῶε τοῦ Λάμεχ **37** τοῦ Μαθουσαλὰ τοῦ Ἑνὼχ τοῦ Ἰάρετ τοῦ Μαλελεὴλ τοῦ Καϊνὰμ **38** τοῦ Ἑνὼς τοῦ Σὴθ τοῦ Ἀδὰμ τοῦ θεοῦ.

4 Ἰησοῦς δὲ πλήρης πνεύματος ἁγίου ὑπέστρεψεν ἀπὸ τοῦ Ἰορδάνου καὶ ἤγετο ἐν τῷ πνεύματι ἐν τῇ ἐρήμῳ **2** ἡμέρας τεσσεράκοντα πειραζόμενος ὑπὸ τοῦ διαβόλου. καὶ οὐκ ἔφαγεν οὐδὲν ἐν ταῖς ἡμέραις ἐκείναις καὶ συντελεσθεισῶν αὐτῶν ἐπείνασεν. **3** Εἶπεν δὲ αὐτῷ ὁ διάβολος, Εἰ υἱὸς εἶ τοῦ θεοῦ, εἰπὲ τῷ λίθῳ τούτῳ ἵνα γένηται ἄρτος. **4** καὶ ἀπεκρίθη πρὸς αὐτὸν ὁ Ἰησοῦς, Γέγραπται ὅτι Οὐκ ἐπ᾽ ἄρτῳ μόνῳ **ζήσεται** ὁ **ἄνθρωπος**. **5** Καὶ ἀναγαγὼν αὐτὸν[a] ἔδειξεν αὐτῷ πάσας τὰς βασιλείας τῆς οἰκουμένης ἐν στιγμῇ χρόνου **6** καὶ εἶπεν αὐτῷ ὁ διάβολος, Σοί δώσω τὴν ἐξουσίαν ταύτην ἅπασαν καὶ τὴν δόξαν αὐτῶν, ὅτι ἐμοὶ παραδέδοται καὶ ᾧ ἐὰν θέλω δίδωμι αὐτήν· **7** σὺ οὖν ἐὰν προσκυνήσῃς ἐνώπιον ἐμοῦ, ἔσται σοῦ πᾶσα. **8** καὶ ἀποκριθεὶς ὁ Ἰησοῦς εἶπεν αὐτῷ, Γέγραπται,

Κύριον τὸν θεόν σου προσκυνήσεις καὶ αὐτῷ μόνῳ **λατρεύσεις.**

9 Ἤγαγεν δὲ αὐτὸν εἰς Ἰερουσαλὴμ καὶ ἔστησεν ἐπὶ τὸ πτερύγιον τοῦ ἱεροῦ καὶ εἶπεν αὐτῷ, Εἰ υἱὸς εἶ τοῦ θεοῦ, βάλε σεαυτὸν ἐντεῦθεν κάτω· **10** γέγραπται γὰρ ὅτι

Τοῖς ἀγγέλοις αὐτοῦ ἐντελεῖται περὶ σοῦ
τοῦ διαφυλάξαι σε,

11 καὶ ὅτι

Ἐπὶ χειρῶν ἀροῦσίν σε,
μήποτε προσκόψῃς πρὸς λίθον
τὸν πόδα σου.

12 καὶ ἀποκριθεὶς εἶπεν αὐτῷ ὁ Ἰησοῦς ὅτι Εἴρηται, **Οὐκ ἐκπειράσεις κύριον τὸν θεόν σου. 13** Καὶ συντελέσας πάντα

---

the son of Salmon,[d] the son of Nahshon,

[33]the son of Amminadab, the son of Ram,[e]

the son of Hezron, the son of Perez, the son of Judah, [34]the son of Jacob, the son of Isaac, the son of Abraham, the son of Terah, the son of Nahor, [35]the son of Serug, the son of Reu, the son of Peleg, the son of Eber, the son of Shelah, [36]the son of Cainan, the son of Arphaxad, the son of Shem, the son of Noah, the son of Lamech, [37]the son of Methuselah, the son of Enoch,

the son of Jared, the son of Mahalalel, the son of Kenan, [38]the son of Enosh, the son of Seth, the son of Adam, the son of God.

The Temptation of Jesus

4 Jesus, full of the Holy Spirit, returned from the Jordan and was led by the Spirit in the desert, [2]where for forty days he was tempted by the devil. He ate nothing during those days, and at the end of them he was hungry.

[3]The devil said to him, "If you are the Son of God, tell this stone to become bread."

[4]Jesus answered, "It is written: 'Man does not live on bread alone.'[a]"

[5]The devil led him up to a high place and showed him in an instant all the kingdoms of the world. [6]And he said to him, "I will give you all their authority and splendor, for it has been given to me, and I can give it to anyone I want to. [7]So if you worship me, it will all be yours."

[8]Jesus answered, "It is written: 'Worship the Lord your God and serve him only.'[b]"

[9]The devil led him to Jerusalem and had him stand on the highest point of the temple. "If you are the Son of God," he said, "throw yourself down from here. [10]For it is written:

" 'He will command his angels
concerning you
to guard you carefully;

[11]they will lift you up in their hands,
so that you will not strike your foot
against a stone.'[c]"

[12]Jesus answered, "It says: 'Do not put the Lord your God to the test.'[d]"

[13]When the devil had finished all this

---

[b] Other ancient authorities read *Salmon*   [c] Other ancient authorities read *Amminadab, son of Aram*; others vary widely   [d] Gk *he*

[d]32 NIV text and NRSV note b *Σαλμών*; NIV note and NRSV text as UBS   [e]33 NIV text and NRSV note c *τοῦ Ἀμιναδὰβ τοῦ Ἀράμ*; NIV note and NRSV text as UBS   [a]5 NIV text adds *ὁ διάβολος εἰς ὄρος ὑψηλὸν* †

[d]32 Some early manuscripts *Sala* [e]33 Some manuscripts *Amminadab, the son of Admin, the son of Arni*; other manuscripts vary widely.   [a]4 Deut. 8:3 [b]8 Deut. 6:13 [c]11 Psalm 91:11,12 [d]12 Deut. 6:16

he departed from him until an opportune time.

The Beginning of the Galilean Ministry

14 Then Jesus, filled with the power of the Spirit, returned to Galilee, and a report about him spread through all the surrounding country. [15]He began to teach in their synagogues and was praised by everyone.

The Rejection of Jesus at Nazareth

16 When he came to Nazareth, where he had been brought up, he went to the synagogue on the sabbath day, as was his custom. He stood up to read, [17]and the scroll of the prophet Isaiah was given to him. He unrolled the scroll and found the place where it was written:

[18] "The Spirit of the Lord is upon me,
　　because he has anointed me
　　　to bring good news to the poor.
　He has sent me to proclaim release to
　　　the captives
　　and recovery of sight to the blind,
　　　to let the oppressed go free,
[19]　to proclaim the year of the Lord's
　　　favor."

[20]And he rolled up the scroll, gave it back to the attendant, and sat down. The eyes of all in the synagogue were fixed on him. [21]Then he began to say to them, "Today this scripture has been fulfilled in your hearing." [22]All spoke well of him and were amazed at the gracious words that came from his mouth. They said, "Is not this Joseph's son?" [23]He said to them, "Doubtless you will quote to me this proverb, 'Doctor, cure yourself!' And you will say, 'Do here also in your hometown the things that we have heard you did at Capernaum.' " [24]And he said, "Truly I tell you, no prophet is accepted in the prophet's hometown. [25]But the truth is, there were many widows in Israel in the time of Elijah, when the heaven was shut up three years and six months, and there was a severe famine over all the land; [26]yet Elijah was sent to none of them except to a widow at Zarephath in Sidon. [27]There were also many lepers[e] in Israel in the time of the prophet Elisha, and none of them was cleansed except Naaman the Syrian." [28]When they heard this, all in the synagogue were filled with rage. [29]They got up, drove him out of the town, and led him to the brow of the hill on which their

---

πειρασμὸν ὁ διάβολος ἀπέστη ἀπ᾽ αὐτοῦ ἄχρι καιροῦ.

14 Καὶ ὑπέστρεψεν ὁ Ἰησοῦς ἐν τῇ δυνάμει τοῦ πνεύματος εἰς τὴν Γαλιλαίαν. καὶ φήμη ἐξῆλθεν καθ᾽ ὅλης τῆς περιχώρου περὶ αὐτοῦ. **15** καὶ αὐτὸς ἐδίδασκεν ἐν ταῖς συναγωγαῖς αὐτῶν δοξαζόμενος ὑπὸ πάντων.

16 Καὶ ἦλθεν εἰς Ναζαρά, οὗ ἦν τεθραμμένος, καὶ εἰσῆλθεν κατὰ τὸ εἰωθὸς αὐτῷ ἐν τῇ ἡμέρᾳ τῶν σαββάτων εἰς τὴν συναγωγὴν καὶ ἀνέστη ἀναγνῶναι. **17** καὶ ἐπεδόθη αὐτῷ βιβλίον τοῦ προφήτου Ἠσαΐου καὶ ἀναπτύξας τὸ βιβλίον εὗρεν τὸν τόπον οὗ ἦν γεγραμμένον,

18 Πνεῦμα κυρίου ἐπ᾽ ἐμὲ
　　οὗ εἵνεκεν ἔχρισέν με
　　εὐαγγελίσασθαι πτωχοῖς,
　ἀπέσταλκέν με, κηρύξαι αἰχμαλώ-
　　τοις ἄφεσιν
　καὶ τυφλοῖς ἀνάβλεψιν,
　　ἀποστεῖλαι τεθραυσμένους ἐν
　　ἀφέσει,
19 κηρύξαι ἐνιαυτὸν κυρίου δεκτόν.

20 καὶ πτύξας τὸ βιβλίον ἀποδοὺς τῷ ὑπηρέτῃ ἐκάθισεν· καὶ πάντων οἱ ὀφθαλμοὶ ἐν τῇ συναγωγῇ ἦσαν ἀτενίζοντες αὐτῷ. **21** ἤρξατο δὲ λέγειν πρὸς αὐτοὺς ὅτι Σήμερον πεπλήρωται ἡ γραφὴ αὕτη ἐν τοῖς ὠσὶν ὑμῶν. **22** Καὶ πάντες ἐμαρτύρουν αὐτῷ καὶ ἐθαύμαζον ἐπὶ τοῖς λόγοις τῆς χάριτος τοῖς ἐκπορευομένοις ἐκ τοῦ στόματος αὐτοῦ καὶ ἔλεγον, Οὐχὶ υἱός ἐστιν Ἰωσὴφ οὗτος; **23** καὶ εἶπεν πρὸς αὐτούς, Πάντως ἐρεῖτέ μοι τὴν παραβολὴν ταύτην· Ἰατρέ, θεράπευσον σεαυτόν· ὅσα ἠκούσαμεν γενόμενα εἰς τὴν Καφαρναοὺμ ποίησον καὶ ὧδε ἐν τῇ πατρίδι σου. **24** εἶπεν δέ, Ἀμὴν λέγω ὑμῖν ὅτι οὐδεὶς προφήτης δεκτός ἐστιν ἐν τῇ πατρίδι αὐτοῦ. **25** ἐπ᾽ ἀληθείας δὲ λέγω ὑμῖν, πολλαὶ χῆραι ἦσαν ἐν ταῖς ἡμέραις Ἠλίου ἐν τῷ Ἰσραήλ, ὅτε ἐκλείσθη ὁ οὐρανὸς ἐπὶ ἔτη τρία καὶ μῆνας ἕξ, ὡς ἐγένετο λιμὸς μέγας ἐπὶ πᾶσαν τὴν γῆν, **26** καὶ πρὸς οὐδεμίαν αὐτῶν ἐπέμφθη Ἠλίας εἰ μὴ εἰς Σάρεπτα τῆς Σιδωνίας πρὸς γυναῖκα χήραν. **27** καὶ πολλοὶ λεπροὶ ἦσαν ἐν τῷ Ἰσραὴλ ἐπὶ Ἐλισαίου τοῦ προφήτου, καὶ οὐδεὶς αὐτῶν ἐκαθαρίσθη εἰ μὴ Ναιμὰν ὁ Σύρος. **28** καὶ ἐπλήσθησαν πάντες θυμοῦ ἐν τῇ συναγωγῇ ἀκούοντες ταῦτα **29** καὶ ἀναστάντες ἐξέβαλον αὐτὸν ἔξω τῆς πόλεως καὶ ἤγαγον αὐτὸν ἕως ὀφρύος τοῦ ὄρους ἐφ᾽ οὗ ἡ

---

tempting, he left him until an opportune time.

Jesus Rejected at Nazareth

[14]Jesus returned to Galilee in the power of the Spirit, and news about him spread through the whole countryside. [15]He taught in their synagogues, and everyone praised him.

[16]He went to Nazareth, where he had been brought up, and on the Sabbath day he went into the synagogue, as was his custom. And he stood up to read. [17]The scroll of the prophet Isaiah was handed to him. Unrolling it, he found the place where it is written:

[18]"The Spirit of the Lord is on me,
　　because he has anointed me
　　　to preach good news to the poor.
　He has sent me to proclaim freedom for
　　　the prisoners
　　and recovery of sight for the blind,
　to release the oppressed,
[19]　to proclaim the year of the Lord's
　　　favor."[e]

[20]Then he rolled up the scroll, gave it back to the attendant and sat down. The eyes of everyone in the synagogue were fastened on him, [21]and he began by saying to them, "Today this scripture is fulfilled in your hearing."

[22]All spoke well of him and were amazed at the gracious words that came from his lips. "Isn't this Joseph's son?" they asked.

[23]Jesus said to them, "Surely you will quote this proverb to me: 'Physician, heal yourself! Do here in your hometown what we have heard that you did in Capernaum.' "

[24]"I tell you the truth," he continued, "no prophet is accepted in his hometown. [25]I assure you that there were many widows in Israel in Elijah's time, when the sky was shut for three and a half years and there was a severe famine throughout the land. [26]Yet Elijah was not sent to any of them, but to a widow in Zarephath in the region of Sidon. [27]And there were many in Israel with leprosy[f] in the time of Elisha the prophet, yet not one of them was cleansed —only Naaman the Syrian."

[28]All the people in the synagogue were furious when they heard this. [29]They got up, drove him out of the town, and took him to the brow of the hill on which the

---

e The terms leper and leprosy can refer to several diseases

e19 Isaiah 61:1,2   f27 The Greek word was used for various diseases affecting the skin—not necessarily leprosy.

town was built, so that they might hurl him off the cliff. ³⁰But he passed through the midst of them and went on his way.

The Man with an Unclean Spirit

31 He went down to Capernaum, a city in Galilee, and was teaching them on the sabbath. ³²They were astounded at his teaching, because he spoke with authority. ³³In the synagogue there was a man who had the spirit of an unclean demon, and he cried out with a loud voice, ³⁴"Let us alone! What have you to do with us, Jesus of Nazareth? Have you come to destroy us? I know who you are, the Holy One of God." ³⁵But Jesus rebuked him, saying, "Be silent, and come out of him!" When the demon had thrown him down before them, he came out of him without having done him any harm. ³⁶They were all amazed and kept saying to one another, "What kind of utterance is this? For with authority and power he commands the unclean spirits, and out they come!" ³⁷And a report about him began to reach every place in the region.

Healings at Simon's House

38 After leaving the synagogue he entered Simon's house. Now Simon's mother-in-law was suffering from a high fever, and they asked him about her. ³⁹Then he stood over her and rebuked the fever, and it left her. Immediately she got up and began to serve them.

40 As the sun was setting, all those who had any who were sick with various kinds of diseases brought them to him; and he laid his hands on each of them and cured them. ⁴¹Demons also came out of many, shouting, "You are the Son of God!" But he rebuked them and would not allow them to speak, because they knew that he was the Messiah.ᶠ

Jesus Preaches in the Synagogues

42 At daybreak he departed and went into a deserted place. And the crowds were looking for him; and when they reached him, they wanted to prevent him from leaving them. ⁴³But he said to them, "I must proclaim the good news of the kingdom of God to the other cities also; for I was sent for this purpose." ⁴⁴So he continued proclaiming the message in the synagogues of Judea.ᵍ

πόλις ᾠκοδόμητο αὐτῶν ὥστε κατακρημνίσαι αὐτόν· 30 αὐτὸς δὲ διελθὼν διὰ μέσου αὐτῶν ἐπορεύετο.

31 Καὶ κατῆλθεν εἰς Καφαρναοὺμ πόλιν τῆς Γαλιλαίας. καὶ ἦν διδάσκων αὐτοὺς ἐν τοῖς σάββασιν· 32 καὶ ἐξεπλήσσοντο ἐπὶ τῇ διδαχῇ αὐτοῦ, ὅτι ἐν ἐξουσίᾳ ἦν ὁ λόγος αὐτοῦ. 33 καὶ ἐν τῇ συναγωγῇ ἦν ἄνθρωπος ἔχων πνεῦμα δαιμονίου ἀκαθάρτου καὶ ἀνέκραξεν φωνῇ μεγάλῃ, 34 Ἔα, τί ἡμῖν καὶ σοί, Ἰησοῦ Ναζαρηνέ; ἦλθες ἀπολέσαι ἡμᾶς; οἶδά σε τίς εἶ, ὁ ἅγιος τοῦ θεοῦ. 35 καὶ ἐπετίμησεν αὐτῷ ὁ Ἰησοῦς λέγων, Φιμώθητι καὶ ἔξελθε ἀπ' αὐτοῦ. καὶ ῥίψαν αὐτὸν τὸ δαιμόνιον εἰς τὸ μέσον ἐξῆλθεν ἀπ' αὐτοῦ μηδὲν βλάψαν αὐτόν. 36 καὶ ἐγένετο θάμβος ἐπὶ πάντας καὶ συνελάλουν πρὸς ἀλλήλους λέγοντες, Τίς ὁ λόγος οὗτος ὅτι ἐν ἐξουσίᾳ καὶ δυνάμει ἐπιτάσσει τοῖς ἀκαθάρτοις πνεύμασιν καὶ ἐξέρχονται; 37 καὶ ἐξεπορεύετο ἦχος περὶ αὐτοῦ εἰς πάντα τόπον τῆς περιχώρου.

38 Ἀναστὰς δὲ ἀπὸ τῆς συναγωγῆς εἰσῆλθεν εἰς τὴν οἰκίαν Σίμωνος. πενθερὰ δὲ τοῦ Σίμωνος ἦν συνεχομένη πυρετῷ μεγάλῳ καὶ ἠρώτησαν αὐτὸν περὶ αὐτῆς. 39 καὶ ἐπιστὰς ἐπάνω αὐτῆς ἐπετίμησεν τῷ πυρετῷ καὶ ἀφῆκεν αὐτήν· παραχρῆμα δὲ ἀναστᾶσα διηκόνει αὐτοῖς. 40 Δύνοντος δὲ τοῦ ἡλίου ἅπαντες ὅσοι εἶχον ἀσθενοῦντας νόσοις ποικίλαις ἤγαγον αὐτοὺς πρὸς αὐτόν· ὁ δὲ ἑνὶ ἑκάστῳ αὐτῶν τὰς χεῖρας ἐπιτιθεὶς ἐθεράπευεν αὐτούς. 41 ἐξήρχετο δὲ καὶ δαιμόνια ἀπὸ πολλῶν κρ[αυγ]άζοντα καὶ λέγοντα ὅτι Σὺ εἶ ὁ υἱὸς τοῦ θεοῦ. καὶ ἐπιτιμῶν οὐκ εἴα αὐτὰ λαλεῖν, ὅτι ᾔδεισαν τὸν Χριστὸν αὐτὸν εἶναι.

42 Γενομένης δὲ ἡμέρας ἐξελθὼν ἐπορεύθη εἰς ἔρημον τόπον· καὶ οἱ ὄχλοι ἐπεζήτουν αὐτὸν καὶ ἦλθον ἕως αὐτοῦ καὶ κατεῖχον αὐτὸν τοῦ μὴ πορεύεσθαι ἀπ' αὐτῶν. 43 ὁ δὲ εἶπεν πρὸς αὐτοὺς ὅτι Καὶ ταῖς ἑτέραις πόλεσιν εὐαγγελίσασθαί με δεῖ τὴν βασιλείαν τοῦ θεοῦ, ὅτι ἐπὶ τοῦτο ἀπεστάλην. 44 καὶ ἦν κηρύσσων εἰς τὰς συναγωγὰς τῆς Ἰουδαίαςᵇ.

town was built, in order to throw him down the cliff. ³⁰But he walked right through the crowd and went on his way.

Jesus Drives Out an Evil Spirit

³¹Then he went down to Capernaum, a town in Galilee, and on the Sabbath began to teach the people. ³²They were amazed at his teaching, because his message had authority.

³³In the synagogue there was a man possessed by a demon, an evilᵍ spirit. He cried out at the top of his voice, ³⁴"Ha! What do you want with us, Jesus of Nazareth? Have you come to destroy us? I know who you are—the Holy One of God!"

³⁵"Be quiet!" Jesus said sternly. "Come out of him!" Then the demon threw the man down before them all and came out without injuring him.

³⁶All the people were amazed and said to each other, "What is this teaching? With authority and power he gives orders to evil spirits and they come out!" ³⁷And the news about him spread throughout the surrounding area.

Jesus Heals Many

³⁸Jesus left the synagogue and went to the home of Simon. Now Simon's mother-in-law was suffering from a high fever, and they asked Jesus to help her. ³⁹So he bent over her and rebuked the fever, and it left her. She got up at once and began to wait on them.

⁴⁰When the sun was setting, the people brought to Jesus all who had various kinds of sickness, and laying his hands on each one, he healed them. ⁴¹Moreover, demons came out of many people, shouting, "You are the Son of God!" But he rebuked them and would not allow them to speak, because they knew he was the Christ.ʰ

⁴²At daybreak Jesus went out to a solitary place. The people were looking for him and when they came to where he was, they tried to keep him from leaving them. ⁴³But he said, "I must preach the good news of the kingdom of God to the other towns also, because that is why I was sent." ⁴⁴And he kept on preaching in the synagogues of Judea.ⁱ

ᶠ Or the Christ ᵍ Other ancient authorities read *Galilee*   ᵇ44 NIV/NRSV notes τῆς Γαλιλαίας   ᵍ33 Greek *unclean*; also in verse 36   ʰ41 Or *Messiah*
ⁱ44 Or *the land of the Jews*; some manuscripts *Galilee*

NRSV

Jesus Calls the First Disciples

5 Once while Jesus[h] was standing beside the lake of Gennesaret, and the crowd was pressing in on him to hear the word of God, [2]he saw two boats there at the shore of the lake; the fishermen had gone out of them and were washing their nets. [3]He got into one of the boats, the one belonging to Simon, and asked him to put out a little way from the shore. Then he sat down and taught the crowds from the boat. [4]When he had finished speaking, he said to Simon, "Put out into the deep water and let down your nets for a catch." [5]Simon answered, "Master, we have worked all night long but have caught nothing. Yet if you say so, I will let down the nets." [6]When they had done this, they caught so many fish that their nets were beginning to break. [7]So they signaled their partners in the other boat to come and help them. And they came and filled both boats, so that they began to sink. [8]But when Simon Peter saw it, he fell down at Jesus' knees, saying, "Go away from me, Lord, for I am a sinful man!" [9]For he and all who were with him were amazed at the catch of fish that they had taken; [10]and so also were James and John, sons of Zebedee, who were partners with Simon. Then Jesus said to Simon, "Do not be afraid; from now on you will be catching people." [11]When they had brought their boats to shore, they left everything and followed him.

Jesus Cleanses a Leper

[12]Once, when he was in one of the cities, there was a man covered with leprosy.[i] When he saw Jesus, he bowed with his face to the ground and begged him, "Lord, if you choose, you can make me clean." [13]Then Jesus[h] stretched out his hand, touched him, and said, "I do choose. Be made clean." Immediately the leprosy[i] left him. [14]And he ordered him to tell no one. "Go," he said, "and show yourself to the priest, and, as Moses commanded, make an offering for your cleansing, for a testimony to them." [15]But now more than ever the word about Jesus[j] spread abroad; many crowds would gather to hear him and to be cured of their diseases. [16]But he would withdraw to deserted places and pray.

Greek

5 Ἐγένετο δὲ ἐν τῷ τὸν ὄχλον ἐπικεῖσθαι αὐτῷ καὶ ἀκούειν τὸν λόγον τοῦ θεοῦ καὶ αὐτὸς ἦν ἑστὼς παρὰ τὴν λίμνην Γεννησαρέτ **2** καὶ εἶδεν δύο πλοῖα ἑστῶτα παρὰ τὴν λίμνην· οἱ δὲ ἁλιεῖς ἀπ᾽ αὐτῶν ἀποβάντες ἔπλυνον τὰ δίκτυα. **3** ἐμβὰς δὲ εἰς ἓν τῶν πλοίων, ὃ ἦν Σίμωνος, ἠρώτησεν αὐτὸν ἀπὸ τῆς γῆς ἐπαναγαγεῖν ὀλίγον, καθίσας δὲ ἐκ τοῦ πλοίου ἐδίδασκεν τοὺς ὄχλους. **4** ὡς δὲ ἐπαύσατο λαλῶν, εἶπεν πρὸς τὸν Σίμωνα, Ἐπανάγαγε εἰς τὸ βάθος καὶ χαλάσατε τὰ δίκτυα ὑμῶν εἰς ἄγραν. **5** καὶ ἀποκριθεὶς Σίμων εἶπεν, Ἐπιστάτα, δι᾽ ὅλης νυκτὸς κοπιάσαντες οὐδὲν ἐλάβομεν· ἐπὶ δὲ τῷ ῥήματί σου χαλάσω τὰ δίκτυα. **6** καὶ τοῦτο ποιήσαντες συνέκλεισαν πλῆθος ἰχθύων πολύ, διερρήσσετο δὲ τὰ δίκτυα αὐτῶν. **7** καὶ κατένευσαν τοῖς μετόχοις ἐν τῷ ἑτέρῳ πλοίῳ τοῦ ἐλθόντας συλλαβέσθαι αὐτοῖς· καὶ ἦλθον καὶ ἔπλησαν ἀμφότερα τὰ πλοῖα ὥστε βυθίζεσθαι αὐτά. **8** ἰδὼν δὲ Σίμων Πέτρος προσέπεσεν τοῖς γόνασιν Ἰησοῦ λέγων, Ἔξελθε ἀπ᾽ ἐμοῦ, ὅτι ἀνὴρ ἁμαρτωλός εἰμι, κύριε. **9** θάμβος γὰρ περιέσχεν αὐτὸν καὶ πάντας τοὺς σὺν αὐτῷ ἐπὶ τῇ ἄγρᾳ τῶν ἰχθύων ὧν συνέλαβον, **10** ὁμοίως δὲ καὶ Ἰάκωβον καὶ Ἰωάννην υἱοὺς Ζεβεδαίου, οἳ ἦσαν κοινωνοὶ τῷ Σίμωνι. καὶ εἶπεν πρὸς τὸν Σίμωνα ὁ Ἰησοῦς, Μὴ φοβοῦ· ἀπὸ τοῦ νῦν ἀνθρώπους ἔσῃ ζωγρῶν. **11** καὶ καταγαγόντες τὰ πλοῖα ἐπὶ τὴν γῆν ἀφέντες πάντα ἠκολούθησαν αὐτῷ.

12 Καὶ ἐγένετο ἐν τῷ εἶναι αὐτὸν ἐν μιᾷ τῶν πόλεων καὶ ἰδοὺ ἀνὴρ πλήρης λέπρας· ἰδὼν δὲ τὸν Ἰησοῦν, πεσὼν ἐπὶ πρόσωπον ἐδεήθη αὐτοῦ λέγων, Κύριε, ἐὰν θέλῃς δύνασαί με καθαρίσαι. **13** καὶ ἐκτείνας τὴν χεῖρα ἥψατο αὐτοῦ λέγων, Θέλω, καθαρίσθητι· καὶ εὐθέως ἡ λέπρα ἀπῆλθεν ἀπ᾽ αὐτοῦ. **14** καὶ αὐτὸς παρήγγειλεν αὐτῷ μηδενὶ εἰπεῖν, ἀλλὰ ἀπελθὼν δεῖξον σεαυτὸν τῷ ἱερεῖ καὶ προσένεγκε περὶ τοῦ καθαρισμοῦ σου καθὼς προσέταξεν Μωϋσῆς, εἰς μαρτύριον αὐτοῖς. **15** διήρχετο δὲ μᾶλλον ὁ λόγος περὶ αὐτοῦ, καὶ συνήρχοντο ὄχλοι πολλοὶ ἀκούειν καὶ θεραπεύεσθαι ἀπὸ τῶν ἀσθενειῶν αὐτῶν· **16** αὐτὸς δὲ ἦν ὑποχωρῶν ἐν ταῖς ἐρήμοις καὶ προσευχόμενος.

NIV

The Calling of the First Disciples

5 One day as Jesus was standing by the Lake of Gennesaret,[a] with the people crowding around him and listening to the word of God, [2]he saw at the water's edge two boats, left there by the fishermen, who were washing their nets. [3]He got into one of the boats, the one belonging to Simon, and asked him to put out a little from shore. Then he sat down and taught the people from the boat.

[4]When he had finished speaking, he said to Simon, "Put out into deep water, and let down[b] the nets for a catch."

[5]Simon answered, "Master, we've worked hard all night and haven't caught anything. But because you say so, I will let down the nets."

[6]When they had done so, they caught such a large number of fish that their nets began to break. [7]So they signaled their partners in the other boat to come and help them, and they came and filled both boats so full that they began to sink.

[8]When Simon Peter saw this, he fell at Jesus' knees and said, "Go away from me, Lord; I am a sinful man!" [9]For he and all his companions were astonished at the catch of fish they had taken, [10]and so were James and John, the sons of Zebedee, Simon's partners.

Then Jesus said to Simon, "Don't be afraid; from now on you will catch men." [11]So they pulled their boats up on shore, left everything and followed him.

The Man With Leprosy

[12]While Jesus was in one of the towns, a man came along who was covered with leprosy.[c] When he saw Jesus, he fell with his face to the ground and begged him, "Lord, if you are willing, you can make me clean."

[13]Jesus reached out his hand and touched the man. "I am willing," he said. "Be clean!" And immediately the leprosy left him.

[14]Then Jesus ordered him, "Don't tell anyone, but go, show yourself to the priest and offer the sacrifices that Moses commanded for your cleansing, as a testimony to them."

[15]Yet the news about him spread all the more, so that crowds of people came to hear him and to be healed of their sicknesses. [16]But Jesus often withdrew to lonely places and prayed.

---

[h] Gk *he*   [i] The terms *leper* and *leprosy* can refer to several diseases   [j] Gk *him*

[a]1 That is, Sea of Galilee   [b]4 The Greek verb is plural.
[c]12 The Greek word was used for various diseases affecting the skin—not necessarily leprosy.

NRSV

Jesus Heals a Paralytic

17 One day, while he was teaching, Pharisees and teachers of the law were sitting near by (they had come from every village of Galilee and Judea and from Jerusalem); and the power of the Lord was with him to heal.[k] 18Just then some men came, carrying a paralyzed man on a bed. They were trying to bring him in and lay him before Jesus;[j] 19but finding no way to bring him in because of the crowd, they went up on the roof and let him down with his bed through the tiles into the middle of the crowd[l] in front of Jesus. 20When he saw their faith, he said, "Friend,[m] your sins are forgiven you." 21Then the scribes and the Pharisees began to question, "Who is this who is speaking blasphemies? Who can forgive sins but God alone?" 22When Jesus perceived their questionings, he answered them, "Why do you raise such questions in your hearts? 23Which is easier, to say, 'Your sins are forgiven you,' or to say, 'Stand up and walk'? 24But so that you may know that the Son of Man has authority on earth to forgive sins"—he said to the one who was paralyzed—"I say to you, stand up and take your bed and go to your home." 25Immediately he stood up before them, took what he had been lying on, and went to his home, glorifying God. 26Amazement seized all of them, and they glorified God and were filled with awe, saying, "We have seen strange things today."

Jesus Calls Levi

27 After this he went out and saw a tax collector named Levi, sitting at the tax booth; and he said to him, "Follow me." 28And he got up, left everything, and followed him.

29 Then Levi gave a great banquet for him in his house; and there was a large crowd of tax collectors and others sitting at the table[n] with them. 30The Pharisees and their scribes were complaining to his disciples, saying, "Why do you eat and drink with tax collectors and sinners?" 31Jesus answered, "Those who are well have no need of a physician, but those who are sick; 32I have come to call not the righteous but sinners to repentance."

[Greek column]

17 Καὶ ἐγένετο ἐν μιᾷ τῶν ἡμερῶν καὶ αὐτὸς ἦν διδάσκων, καὶ ἦσαν καθήμενοι Φαρισαῖοι καὶ νομοδιδάσκαλοι οἳ ἦσαν ἐληλυθότες ἐκ πάσης κώμης τῆς Γαλιλαίας καὶ Ἰουδαίας καὶ Ἰερουσαλήμ· καὶ δύναμις κυρίου ἦν εἰς τὸ ἰᾶσθαι αὐτόν.[a] 18 καὶ ἰδοὺ ἄνδρες φέροντες ἐπὶ κλίνης ἄνθρωπον ὃς ἦν παραλελυμένος καὶ ἐζήτουν αὐτὸν εἰσενεγκεῖν καὶ θεῖναι [αὐτὸν] ἐνώπιον αὐτοῦ. 19 καὶ μὴ εὑρόντες ποίας εἰσενέγκωσιν αὐτὸν διὰ τὸν ὄχλον, ἀναβάντες ἐπὶ τὸ δῶμα διὰ τῶν κεράμων καθῆκαν αὐτὸν σὺν τῷ κλινιδίῳ εἰς τὸ μέσον ἔμπροσθεν τοῦ Ἰησοῦ. 20 καὶ ἰδὼν τὴν πίστιν αὐτῶν εἶπεν, Ἄνθρωπε, ἀφέωνταί σοι αἱ ἁμαρτίαι σου. 21 καὶ ἤρξαντο διαλογίζεσθαι οἱ γραμματεῖς καὶ οἱ Φαρισαῖοι λέγοντες, Τίς ἐστιν οὗτος ὃς λαλεῖ βλασφημίας; τίς δύναται ἁμαρτίας ἀφεῖναι εἰ μὴ μόνος ὁ θεός; 22 ἐπιγνοὺς δὲ ὁ Ἰησοῦς τοὺς διαλογισμοὺς αὐτῶν ἀποκριθεὶς εἶπεν πρὸς αὐτούς, Τί διαλογίζεσθε ἐν ταῖς καρδίαις ὑμῶν; 23 τί ἐστιν εὐκοπώτερον, εἰπεῖν, Ἀφέωνταί σοι αἱ ἁμαρτίαι σου, ἢ εἰπεῖν, Ἔγειρε καὶ περιπάτει; 24 ἵνα δὲ εἰδῆτε ὅτι ὁ υἱὸς τοῦ ἀνθρώπου ἐξουσίαν ἔχει ἐπὶ τῆς γῆς ἀφιέναι ἁμαρτίας – εἶπεν τῷ παραλελυμένῳ, Σοὶ λέγω, ἔγειρε καὶ ἄρας τὸ κλινίδιόν σου πορεύου εἰς τὸν οἶκόν σου. 25 καὶ παραχρῆμα ἀναστὰς ἐνώπιον αὐτῶν, ἄρας ἐφ᾽ ὃ κατέκειτο, ἀπῆλθεν εἰς τὸν οἶκον αὐτοῦ δοξάζων τὸν θεόν. 26 καὶ ἔκστασις ἔλαβεν ἅπαντας καὶ ἐδόξαζον τὸν θεὸν καὶ ἐπλήσθησαν φόβου λέγοντες ὅτι Εἴδομεν παράδοξα σήμερον.

27 Καὶ μετὰ ταῦτα ἐξῆλθεν καὶ ἐθεάσατο τελώνην ὀνόματι Λευὶν καθήμενον ἐπὶ τὸ τελώνιον, καὶ εἶπεν αὐτῷ, Ἀκολούθει μοι. 28 καὶ καταλιπὼν πάντα ἀναστὰς ἠκολούθει αὐτῷ. 29 Καὶ ἐποίησεν δοχὴν μεγάλην Λευὶς αὐτῷ ἐν τῇ οἰκίᾳ αὐτοῦ, καὶ ἦν ὄχλος πολὺς τελωνῶν καὶ ἄλλων οἳ ἦσαν μετ᾽ αὐτῶν κατακείμενοι. 30 καὶ ἐγόγγυζον οἱ Φαρισαῖοι καὶ οἱ γραμματεῖς αὐτῶν πρὸς τοὺς μαθητὰς αὐτοῦ λέγοντες, Διὰ τί μετὰ τῶν τελωνῶν καὶ ἁμαρτωλῶν ἐσθίετε καὶ πίνετε; 31 καὶ ἀποκριθεὶς ὁ Ἰησοῦς εἶπεν πρὸς αὐτούς, Οὐ χρείαν ἔχουσιν οἱ ὑγιαίνοντες ἰατροῦ ἀλλὰ οἱ κακῶς ἔχοντες· 32 οὐκ ἐλήλυθα καλέσαι δικαίους ἀλλὰ ἁμαρτωλοὺς εἰς μετάνοιαν.

NIV

Jesus Heals a Paralytic

17One day as he was teaching, Pharisees and teachers of the law, who had come from every village of Galilee and from Judea and Jerusalem, were sitting there. And the power of the Lord was present for him to heal the sick. 18Some men came carrying a paralytic on a mat and tried to take him into the house to lay him before Jesus. 19When they could not find a way to do this because of the crowd, they went up on the roof and lowered him on his mat through the tiles into the middle of the crowd, right in front of Jesus.

20When Jesus saw their faith, he said, "Friend, your sins are forgiven."

21The Pharisees and the teachers of the law began thinking to themselves, "Who is this fellow who speaks blasphemy? Who can forgive sins but God alone?"

22Jesus knew what they were thinking and asked, "Why are you thinking these things in your hearts? 23Which is easier: to say, 'Your sins are forgiven,' or to say, 'Get up and walk'? 24But that you may know that the Son of Man has authority on earth to forgive sins. . . ." He said to the paralyzed man, "I tell you, get up, take your mat and go home." 25Immediately he stood up in front of them, took what he had been lying on and went home praising God. 26Everyone was amazed and gave praise to God. They were filled with awe and said, "We have seen remarkable things today."

The Calling of Levi

27After this, Jesus went out and saw a tax collector by the name of Levi sitting at his tax booth. "Follow me," Jesus said to him, 28and Levi got up, left everything and followed him.

29Then Levi held a great banquet for Jesus at his house, and a large crowd of tax collectors and others were eating with them. 30But the Pharisees and the teachers of the law who belonged to their sect complained to his disciples, "Why do you eat and drink with tax collectors and 'sinners'?"

31Jesus answered them, "It is not the healthy who need a doctor, but the sick. 32I have not come to call the righteous, but sinners to repentance."

---

[j] Gk him   [k] Other ancient authorities read *was present to heal them*   [l] Gk *into the midst*   [m] Gk *Man*   [n] Gk *reclining*

[a] 17 NRSV note k αὐτούς

The Question about Fasting

33 Then they said to him, "John's disciples, like the disciples of the Pharisees, frequently fast and pray, but your disciples eat and drink. 34 Jesus said to them, "You cannot make wedding guests fast while the bridegroom is with them, can you? 35 The days will come when the bridegroom will be taken away from them, and then they will fast in those days." 36 He also told them a parable: "No one tears a piece from a new garment and sews it on an old garment; otherwise the new will be torn, and the piece from the new will not match the old. 37 And no one puts new wine into old wineskins; otherwise the new wine will burst the skins and will be spilled, and the skins will be destroyed. 38 But new wine must be put into fresh wineskins. 39 And no one after drinking old wine desires new wine, but says, 'The old is good.' "[o]

The Question about the Sabbath

6 One sabbath[p] while Jesus[q] was going through the grainfields, his disciples plucked some heads of grain, rubbed them in their hands, and ate them. 2 But some of the Pharisees said, "Why are you doing what is not lawful[r] on the sabbath?" 3 Jesus answered, "Have you not read what David did when he and his companions were hungry? 4 He entered the house of God and took and ate the bread of the Presence, which it is not lawful for any but the priests to eat, and gave some to his companions?" 5 Then he said to them, "The Son of Man is lord of the sabbath."

The Man with a Withered Hand

6 On another sabbath he entered the synagogue and taught, and there was a man there whose right hand was withered. 7 The scribes and the Pharisees watched him to see whether he would cure on the sabbath, so that they might find an accusation against him. 8 Even though he knew what they were thinking, he said to the man who had the withered hand, "Come and stand here." He got up and stood there. 9 Then Jesus said to them, "I ask you, is it lawful to do good or to do harm on the sabbath, to save life or to destroy it?"

[o] Other ancient authorities read *better;* others lack verse 39 [p] Other ancient authorities read *On the second first sabbath* [q] Gk *he* [r] Other ancient authorities add *to do*

33 *Οἱ δὲ εἶπαν πρὸς αὐτόν, Οἱ μαθηταὶ Ἰωάννου νηστεύουσιν πυκνὰ καὶ δεήσεις ποιοῦνται ὁμοίως καὶ οἱ τῶν Φαρισαίων, οἱ δὲ σοὶ ἐσθίουσιν καὶ πίνουσιν.* **34** *ὁ δὲ Ἰησοῦς εἶπεν πρὸς αὐτούς, Μὴ δύνασθε τοὺς υἱοὺς τοῦ νυμφῶνος ἐν ᾧ ὁ νυμφίος μετ' αὐτῶν ἐστιν ποιῆσαι νηστεῦσαι;* **35** *ἐλεύσονται δὲ ἡμέραι, καὶ ὅταν ἀπαρθῇ ἀπ' αὐτῶν ὁ νυμφίος, τότε νηστεύσουσιν ἐν ἐκείναις ταῖς ἡμέραις.* **36** *Ἔλεγεν δὲ καὶ παραβολὴν πρὸς αὐτοὺς ὅτι Οὐδεὶς ἐπίβλημα ἀπὸ ἱματίου καινοῦ σχίσας ἐπιβάλλει ἐπὶ ἱμάτιον παλαιόν· εἰ δὲ μή γε, καὶ τὸ καινὸν σχίσει καὶ τῷ παλαιῷ οὐ συμφωνήσει τὸ ἐπίβλημα τὸ ἀπὸ τοῦ καινοῦ.* **37** *καὶ οὐδεὶς βάλλει οἶνον νέον εἰς ἀσκοὺς παλαιούς· εἰ δὲ μή γε, ῥήξει ὁ οἶνος ὁ νέος τοὺς ἀσκοὺς καὶ αὐτὸς ἐκχυθήσεται καὶ οἱ ἀσκοὶ ἀπολοῦνται·* **38** *ἀλλὰ οἶνον νέον εἰς ἀσκοὺς καινοὺς βλητέον.* **39** *[καὶ] οὐδεὶς πιὼν παλαιὸν θέλει νέον· λέγει γάρ, Ὁ παλαιὸς χρηστός*[b] *ἐστιν.*

6 *Ἐγένετο δὲ ἐν σαββάτῳ*[a] *διαπορεύεσθαι αὐτὸν διὰ σπορίμων, καὶ ἔτιλλον οἱ μαθηταὶ αὐτοῦ καὶ ἤσθιον τοὺς στάχυας ψώχοντες ταῖς χερσίν.* **2** *τινὲς δὲ τῶν Φαρισαίων εἶπαν, Τί ποιεῖτε ὃ οὐκ ἔξεστιν τοῖς σάββασιν*[b]*;* **3** *καὶ ἀποκριθεὶς πρὸς αὐτοὺς εἶπεν ὁ Ἰησοῦς, Οὐδὲ τοῦτο ἀνέγνωτε ὃ ἐποίησεν Δαυὶδ ὅτε ἐπείνασεν αὐτὸς καὶ οἱ μετ' αὐτοῦ [ὄντες],* **4** *[ὡς]*[c] *εἰσῆλθεν εἰς τὸν οἶκον τοῦ θεοῦ καὶ τοὺς ἄρτους τῆς προθέσεως λαβὼν ἔφαγεν καὶ ἔδωκεν τοῖς μετ' αὐτοῦ, οὓς οὐκ ἔξεστιν φαγεῖν εἰ μὴ μόνους τοὺς ἱερεῖς;* **5** *καὶ ἔλεγεν αὐτοῖς, Κύριός ἐστιν τοῦ σαββάτου ὁ υἱὸς τοῦ ἀνθρώπου.*

6 *Ἐγένετο δὲ ἐν ἑτέρῳ σαββάτῳ εἰσελθεῖν αὐτὸν εἰς τὴν συναγωγὴν καὶ διδάσκειν. καὶ ἦν ἄνθρωπος ἐκεῖ καὶ ἡ χεὶρ αὐτοῦ ἡ δεξιὰ ἦν ξηρά.* **7** *παρετηροῦντο δὲ αὐτὸν οἱ γραμματεῖς καὶ οἱ Φαρισαῖοι εἰ ἐν τῷ σαββάτῳ θεραπεύει, ἵνα εὕρωσιν κατηγορεῖν αὐτοῦ.* **8** *αὐτὸς δὲ ᾔδει τοὺς διαλογισμοὺς αὐτῶν, εἶπεν δὲ τῷ ἀνδρὶ τῷ ξηρὰν ἔχοντι τὴν χεῖρα, Ἔγειρε καὶ στῆθι εἰς τὸ μέσον· καὶ ἀναστὰς ἔστη.* **9** *εἶπεν δὲ ὁ Ἰησοῦς πρὸς αὐτούς, Ἐπερωτῶ ὑμᾶς εἰ ἔξεστιν τῷ σαββάτῳ ἀγαθοποιῆσαι ἢ κακοποιῆσαι, ψυχὴν σῶσαι ἢ ἀπολέσαι;* **10** *καὶ περιβλεψά-*

[b] 39 NIV text and NRSV note o *χρηστότερος*
[a] 1 NRSV note p adds *δευτεροπρώτῳ* [b] 2 NRSV note r adds *ποιεῖν* † [c] 4 NIV text omits *ὡς* †

Jesus Questioned About Fasting

33 They said to him, "John's disciples often fast and pray, and so do the disciples of the Pharisees, but yours go on eating and drinking."

34 Jesus answered, "Can you make the guests of the bridegroom fast while he is with them? 35 But the time will come when the bridegroom will be taken from them; in those days they will fast."

36 He told them this parable: "No one tears a patch from a new garment and sews it on an old one. If he does, he will have torn the new garment, and the patch from the new will not match the old. 37 And no one pours new wine into old wineskins. If he does, the new wine will burst the skins, the wine will run out and the wineskins will be ruined. 38 No, new wine must be poured into new wineskins. 39 And no one after drinking old wine wants the new, for he says, 'The old is better.' "

Lord of the Sabbath

6 One Sabbath Jesus was going through the grainfields, and his disciples began to pick some heads of grain, rub them in their hands and eat the kernels. 2 Some of the Pharisees asked, "Why are you doing what is unlawful on the Sabbath?"

3 Jesus answered them, "Have you never read what David did when he and his companions were hungry? 4 He entered the house of God, and taking the consecrated bread, he ate what is lawful only for priests to eat. And he also gave some to his companions." 5 Then Jesus said to them, "The Son of Man is Lord of the Sabbath."

6 On another Sabbath he went into the synagogue and was teaching, and a man was there whose right hand was shriveled. 7 The Pharisees and the teachers of the law were looking for a reason to accuse Jesus, so they watched him closely to see if he would heal on the Sabbath. 8 But Jesus knew what they were thinking and said to the man with the shriveled hand, "Get up and stand in front of everyone." So he got up and stood there.

9 Then Jesus said to them, "I ask you, which is lawful on the Sabbath: to do good or to do evil, to save life or to destroy it?"

[NRSV]

[10]After looking around at all of them, he said to him, "Stretch out your hand." He did so, and his hand was restored. [11]But they were filled with fury and discussed with one another what they might do to Jesus.

Jesus Chooses the Twelve Apostles

12 Now during those days he went out to the mountain to pray; and he spent the night in prayer to God. [13]And when day came, he called his disciples and chose twelve of them, whom he also named apostles: [14]Simon, whom he named Peter, and his brother Andrew, and James, and John, and Philip, and Bartholomew, [15]and Matthew, and Thomas, and James son of Alphaeus, and Simon, who was called the Zealot, [16]and Judas son of James, and Judas Iscariot, who became a traitor.

Jesus Teaches and Heals

17 He came down with them and stood on a level place, with a great crowd of his disciples and a great multitude of people from all Judea, Jerusalem, and the coast of Tyre and Sidon. [18]They had come to hear him and to be healed of their diseases; and those who were troubled with unclean spirits were cured. [19]And all in the crowd were trying to touch him, for power came out from him and healed all of them.

Blessings and Woes

20 Then he looked up at his disciples and said:
  "Blessed are you who are poor,
    for yours is the kingdom of God.
[21] "Blessed are you who are hungry now,
    for you will be filled.
  "Blessed are you who weep now,
    for you will laugh.
22 "Blessed are you when people hate you, and when they exclude you, revile you, and defame you[s] on account of the Son of Man. [23]Rejoice in that day and leap for joy, for surely your reward is great in heaven; for that is what their ancestors did to the prophets.
[24] "But woe to you who are rich,
    for you have received your
      consolation.
[25] "Woe to you who are full now,
    for you will be hungry.
  "Woe to you who are laughing now,
    for you will mourn and weep.
26 "Woe to you when all speak well of

[s] Gk cast out your name as evil

[Greek]

μενος πάντας αὐτοὺς εἶπεν αὐτῷ, Ἔκτεινον τὴν χεῖρά σου. ὁ δὲ ἐποίησεν καὶ ἀπεκατεστάθη ἡ χεὶρ αὐτοῦ. 11 αὐτοὶ δὲ ἐπλήσθησαν ἀνοίας καὶ διελάλουν πρὸς ἀλλήλους τί ἂν ποιήσαιεν τῷ Ἰησοῦ.

12 Ἐγένετο δὲ ἐν ταῖς ἡμέραις ταύταις ἐξελθεῖν αὐτὸν εἰς τὸ ὄρος προσεύξασθαι, καὶ ἦν διανυκτερεύων ἐν τῇ προσευχῇ τοῦ θεοῦ. 13 καὶ ὅτε ἐγένετο ἡμέρα, προσεφώνησεν τοὺς μαθητὰς αὐτοῦ, καὶ ἐκλεξάμενος ἀπ᾽ αὐτῶν δώδεκα, οὓς καὶ ἀποστόλους ὠνόμασεν, 14 Σίμωνα ὃν καὶ ὠνόμασεν Πέτρον, καὶ Ἀνδρέαν τὸν ἀδελφὸν αὐτοῦ, καὶ Ἰάκωβον καὶ Ἰωάννην καὶ Φίλιππον καὶ Βαρθολομαῖον 15 καὶ Μαθθαῖον καὶ Θωμᾶν καὶ Ἰάκωβον Ἀλφαίου καὶ Σίμωνα τὸν καλούμενον Ζηλωτὴν 16 καὶ Ἰούδαν Ἰακώβου καὶ Ἰούδαν Ἰσκαριώθ, ὃς ἐγένετο προδότης.

17 Καὶ καταβὰς μετ᾽ αὐτῶν ἔστη ἐπὶ τόπου πεδινοῦ, καὶ ὄχλος πολὺς μαθητῶν αὐτοῦ, καὶ πλῆθος πολὺ τοῦ λαοῦ ἀπὸ πάσης τῆς Ἰουδαίας καὶ Ἰερουσαλὴμ καὶ τῆς παραλίου Τύρου καὶ Σιδῶνος, 18 οἳ ἦλθον ἀκοῦσαι αὐτοῦ καὶ ἰαθῆναι ἀπὸ τῶν νόσων αὐτῶν· καὶ οἱ ἐνοχλούμενοι ἀπὸ πνευμάτων ἀκαθάρτων ἐθεραπεύοντο, 19 καὶ πᾶς ὁ ὄχλος ἐζήτουν ἅπτεσθαι αὐτοῦ, ὅτι δύναμις παρ᾽ αὐτοῦ ἐξήρχετο καὶ ἰᾶτο πάντας.

20 Καὶ αὐτὸς ἐπάρας τοὺς ὀφθαλμοὺς αὐτοῦ εἰς τοὺς μαθητὰς αὐτοῦ ἔλεγεν,
  Μακάριοι οἱ πτωχοί,
    ὅτι ὑμετέρα ἐστὶν ἡ βασιλεία
      τοῦ θεοῦ.
21 μακάριοι οἱ πεινῶντες νῦν,
    ὅτι χορτασθήσεσθε.
  μακάριοι οἱ κλαίοντες νῦν,
    ὅτι γελάσετε.
22 μακάριοί ἐστε ὅταν μισήσωσιν ὑμᾶς οἱ ἄνθρωποι καὶ ὅταν ἀφορίσωσιν ὑμᾶς καὶ ὀνειδίσωσιν καὶ ἐκβάλωσιν τὸ ὄνομα ὑμῶν ὡς πονηρὸν ἕνεκα τοῦ υἱοῦ τοῦ ἀνθρώπου· 23 χάρητε ἐν ἐκείνῃ τῇ ἡμέρᾳ καὶ σκιρτήσατε, ἰδοὺ γὰρ ὁ μισθὸς ὑμῶν πολὺς ἐν τῷ οὐρανῷ· κατὰ τὰ αὐτὰ γὰρ ἐποίουν τοῖς προφήταις οἱ πατέρες αὐτῶν.
24 Πλὴν οὐαὶ ὑμῖν τοῖς πλουσίοις,
    ὅτι ἀπέχετε τὴν παράκλησιν ὑμῶν.
25 οὐαὶ ὑμῖν, οἱ ἐμπεπλησμένοι νῦν,
    ὅτι πεινάσετε.
  οὐαί, οἱ γελῶντες νῦν,
    ὅτι πενθήσετε καὶ κλαύσετε.
26 οὐαὶ ὅταν ὑμᾶς καλῶς εἴπωσιν πάντες οἱ ἄνθρωποι· κατὰ τὰ αὐτὰ

[NIV]

[10]He looked around at them all, and then said to the man, "Stretch out your hand." He did so, and his hand was completely restored. [11]But they were furious and began to discuss with one another what they might do to Jesus.

The Twelve Apostles

[12]One of those days Jesus went out to a mountainside to pray, and spent the night praying to God. [13]When morning came, he called his disciples to him and chose twelve of them, whom he also designated apostles: [14]Simon (whom he named Peter), his brother Andrew, James, John, Philip, Bartholomew, [15]Matthew, Thomas, James son of Alphaeus, Simon who was called the Zealot, [16]Judas son of James, and Judas Iscariot, who became a traitor.

Blessings and Woes

[17]He went down with them and stood on a level place. A large crowd of his disciples was there and a great number of people from all over Judea, from Jerusalem, and from the coast of Tyre and Sidon, [18]who had come to hear him and to be healed of their diseases. Those troubled by evil[a] spirits were cured, [19]and the people all tried to touch him, because power was coming from him and healing them all.

[20]Looking at his disciples, he said:

  "Blessed are you who are poor,
    for yours is the kingdom of God.
[21]Blessed are you who hunger now,
    for you will be satisfied.
  Blessed are you who weep now,
    for you will laugh.
[22]Blessed are you when men hate you,
    when they exclude you and insult
      you
    and reject your name as evil,
      because of the Son of Man.

[23]"Rejoice in that day and leap for joy, because great is your reward in heaven. For that is how their fathers treated the prophets.

[24]"But woe to you who are rich,
    for you have already received your
      comfort.
[25]Woe to you who are well fed now,
    for you will go hungry.
  Woe to you who laugh now,
    for you will mourn and weep.
[26]Woe to you when all men speak well of
      you,

[a]18 Greek unclean

you, for that is what their ancestors did to the false prophets.

Love for Enemies

27 "But I say to you that listen, Love your enemies, do good to those who hate you, 28bless those who curse you, pray for those who abuse you. 29If anyone strikes you on the cheek, offer the other also; and from anyone who takes away your coat do not withhold even your shirt. 30Give to everyone who begs from you; and if anyone takes away your goods, do not ask for them again. 31Do to others as you would have them do to you.

32 "If you love those who love you, what credit is that to you? For even sinners love those who love them. 33If you do good to those who do good to you, what credit is that to you? For even sinners do the same. 34If you lend to those from whom you hope to receive, what credit is that to you? Even sinners lend to sinners, to receive as much again. 35But love your enemies, do good, and lend, expecting nothing in return.t Your reward will be great, and you will be children of the Most High; for he is kind to the ungrateful and the wicked. 36Be merciful, just as your Father is merciful.

Judging Others

37 "Do not judge, and you will not be judged; do not condemn, and you will not be condemned. Forgive, and you will be forgiven; 38give, and it will be given to you. A good measure, pressed down, shaken together, running over, will be put into your lap; for the measure you give will be the measure you get back."

39 He also told them a parable: "Can a blind person guide a blind person? Will not both fall into a pit? 40A disciple is not above the teacher, but everyone who is fully qualified will be like the teacher. 41Why do you see the speck in your neighbor'su eye, but do not notice the log in your own eye? 42Or how can you say to your neighbor,v 'Friend,v let me take out the speck in your eye,' when you yourself do not see the log in your own eye? You hypocrite, first take the log out of your own eye, and then you will see clearly to take the speck out of your neighbor'su eye.

γὰρ ἐποίουν τοῖς ψευδοπροφήταις οἱ πατέρες αὐτῶν.

27 Ἀλλὰ ὑμῖν λέγω τοῖς ἀκούουσιν, ἀγαπᾶτε τοὺς ἐχθροὺς ὑμῶν, καλῶς ποιεῖτε τοῖς μισοῦσιν ὑμᾶς, 28 εὐλογεῖτε τοὺς καταρωμένους ὑμᾶς, προσεύχεσθε περὶ τῶν ἐπηρεαζόντων ὑμᾶς. 29 τῷ τύπτοντί σε ἐπὶ τὴν σιαγόνα πάρεχε καὶ τὴν ἄλλην, καὶ ἀπὸ τοῦ αἴροντός σου τὸ ἱμάτιον καὶ τὸν χιτῶνα μὴ κωλύσῃς. 30 παντὶ αἰτοῦντί σε δίδου, καὶ ἀπὸ τοῦ αἴροντος τὰ σὰ μὴ ἀπαίτει. 31 καὶ καθὼς θέλετε ἵνα ποιῶσιν ὑμῖν οἱ ἄνθρωποι ποιεῖτε αὐτοῖς ὁμοίως. 32 καὶ εἰ ἀγαπᾶτε τοὺς ἀγαπῶντας ὑμᾶς, ποία ὑμῖν χάρις ἐστίν; καὶ γὰρ οἱ ἁμαρτωλοὶ τοὺς ἀγαπῶντας αὐτοὺς ἀγαπῶσιν. 33 καὶ [γὰρ]d ἐὰν ἀγαθοποιῆτε τοὺς ἀγαθοποιοῦντας ὑμᾶς, ποία ὑμῖν χάρις ἐστίν; καὶ οἱ ἁμαρτωλοὶ τὸ αὐτὸ ποιοῦσιν. 34 καὶ ἐὰν δανίσητε παρ᾽ ὧν ἐλπίζετε λαβεῖν, ποία ὑμῖν χάρις [ἐστίν]; καὶ ἁμαρτωλοὶ ἁμαρτωλοῖς δανίζουσιν ἵνα ἀπολάβωσιν τὰ ἴσα. 35 πλὴν ἀγαπᾶτε τοὺς ἐχθροὺς ὑμῶν καὶ ἀγαθοποιεῖτε καὶ δανίζετε μηδένe ἀπελπίζοντες· καὶ ἔσται ὁ μισθὸς ὑμῶν πολύς, καὶ ἔσεσθε υἱοὶ ὑψίστου, ὅτι αὐτὸς χρηστός ἐστιν ἐπὶ τοὺς ἀχαρίστους καὶ πονηρούς. 36 Γίνεσθε οἰκτίρμονες καθὼς [καὶ]f ὁ πατὴρ ὑμῶν οἰκτίρμων ἐστίν.

37 Καὶ μὴ κρίνετε, καὶ οὐ μὴ κριθῆτε· καὶ μὴ καταδικάζετε, καὶ οὐ μὴ καταδικασθῆτε. ἀπολύετε, καὶ ἀπολυθήσεσθε· 38 δίδοτε, καὶ δοθήσεται ὑμῖν· μέτρον καλὸν πεπιεσμένον σεσαλευμένον ὑπερεκχυννόμενον δώσουσιν εἰς τὸν κόλπον ὑμῶν· ᾧ γὰρ μέτρῳ μετρεῖτε ἀντιμετρηθήσεται ὑμῖν. 39 Εἶπεν δὲ καὶ παραβολὴν αὐτοῖς· Μήτι δύναται τυφλὸς τυφλὸν ὁδηγεῖν; οὐχὶ ἀμφότεροι εἰς βόθυνον ἐμπεσοῦνται; 40 οὐκ ἔστιν μαθητὴς ὑπὲρ τὸν διδάσκαλον· κατηρτισμένος δὲ πᾶς ἔσται ὡς ὁ διδάσκαλος αὐτοῦ. 41 Τί δὲ βλέπεις τὸ κάρφος τὸ ἐν τῷ ὀφθαλμῷ τοῦ ἀδελφοῦ σου, τὴν δὲ δοκὸν τὴν ἐν τῷ ἰδίῳ ὀφθαλμῷ οὐ κατανοεῖς; 42 πῶς δύνασαι λέγειν τῷ ἀδελφῷ σου, Ἀδελφέ, ἄφες ἐκβάλω τὸ κάρφος τὸ ἐν τῷ ὀφθαλμῷ σου, αὐτὸς τὴν ἐν τῷ ὀφθαλμῷ σοῦ δοκὸν οὐ βλέπων; ὑποκριτά, ἔκβαλε πρῶτον τὴν δοκὸν ἐκ τοῦ ὀφθαλμοῦ σοῦ, καὶ τότε διαβλέψεις τὸ κάρφος τὸ ἐν τῷ ὀφθαλμῷ τοῦ ἀδελφοῦ σου ἐκβαλεῖν.

for that is how their fathers treated the false prophets.

Love for Enemies

27"But I tell you who hear me: Love your enemies, do good to those who hate you, 28bless those who curse you, pray for those who mistreat you. 29If someone strikes you on one cheek, turn to him the other also. If someone takes your cloak, do not stop him from taking your tunic. 30Give to everyone who asks you, and if anyone takes what belongs to you, do not demand it back. 31Do to others as you would have them do to you.

32"If you love those who love you, what credit is that to you? Even 'sinners' love those who love them. 33And if you do good to those who are good to you, what credit is that to you? Even 'sinners' do that. 34And if you lend to those from whom you expect repayment, what credit is that to you? Even 'sinners' lend to 'sinners,' expecting to be repaid in full. 35But love your enemies, do good to them, and lend to them without expecting to get anything back. Then your reward will be great, and you will be sons of the Most High, because he is kind to the ungrateful and wicked. 36Be merciful, just as your Father is merciful.

Judging Others

37"Do not judge, and you will not be judged. Do not condemn, and you will not be condemned. Forgive, and you will be forgiven. 38Give, and it will be given to you. A good measure, pressed down, shaken together and running over, will be poured into your lap. For with the measure you use, it will be measured to you."

39He also told them this parable: "Can a blind man lead a blind man? Will they not both fall into a pit? 40 A student is not above his teacher, but everyone who is fully trained will be like his teacher.

41"Why do you look at the speck of sawdust in your brother's eye and pay no attention to the plank in your own eye? 42How can you say to your brother, 'Brother, let me take the speck out of your eye,' when you yourself fail to see the plank in your own eye? You hypocrite, first take the plank out of your eye, and then you will see clearly to remove the speck from your brother's eye.

---

t Other ancient authorities read despairing of no one
u Gk brother's v Gk brother

d 33 NIV text omits γὰρ † e 35 NRSV note t μηδένα
f 36 NIV text omits καὶ †

NRSV

A Tree and Its Fruit

43 "No good tree bears bad fruit, nor again does a bad tree bear good fruit; 44for each tree is known by its own fruit. Figs are not gathered from thorns, nor are grapes picked from a bramble bush. 45The good person out of the good treasure of the heart produces good, and the evil person out of evil treasure produces evil; for it is out of the abundance of the heart that the mouth speaks.

The Two Foundations

46 "Why do you call me 'Lord, Lord,' and do not do what I tell you? 47I will show you what someone is like who comes to me, hears my words, and acts on them. 48That one is like a man building a house, who dug deeply and laid the foundation on rock; when a flood arose, the river burst against that house but could not shake it, because it had been well built.x 49But the one who hears and does not act is like a man who built a house on the ground without a foundation. When the river burst against it, immediately it fell, and great was the ruin of that house."

Jesus Heals a Centurion's Servant

7 After Jesusy had finished all his sayings in the hearing of the people, he entered Capernaum. 2A centurion there had a slave whom he valued highly, and who was ill and close to death. 3When he heard about Jesus, he sent some Jewish elders to him, asking him to come and heal his slave. 4When they came to Jesus, they appealed to him earnestly, saying, "He is worthy of having you do this for him, 5for he loves our people, and it is he who built our synagogue for us." 6And Jesus went with them, but when he was not far from the house, the centurion sent friends to say to him, "Lord, do not trouble yourself, for I am not worthy to have you come under my roof; 7therefore I did not presume to come to you. But only speak the word, and let my servant be healed. 8For I also am a man set under authority, with soldiers under me; and I say to one, 'Go,' and he goes, and to another, 'Come,' and he comes, and to my slave, 'Do this,' and the slave does it." 9When Jesus heard this he was amazed

Greek

43 Οὐ γάρ ἐστιν δένδρον καλὸν ποιοῦν καρπὸν σαπρόν, οὐδὲ πάλιν δένδρον σαπρὸν ποιοῦν καρπὸν καλόν. 44 ἕκαστον γὰρ δένδρον ἐκ τοῦ ἰδίου καρποῦ γινώσκεται· οὐ γὰρ ἐξ ἀκανθῶν συλλέγουσιν σῦκα οὐδὲ ἐκ βάτου σταφυλὴν τρυγῶσιν. 45 ὁ ἀγαθὸς ἄνθρωπος ἐκ τοῦ ἀγαθοῦ θησαυροῦ τῆς καρδίας προφέρει τὸ ἀγαθόν, καὶ ὁ πονηρὸς ἐκ τοῦ πονηροῦg προφέρει τὸ πονηρόν· ἐκ γὰρ περισσεύματος καρδίας λαλεῖ τὸ στόμα αὐτοῦ.

46 Τί δέ με καλεῖτε, Κύριε κύριε, καὶ οὐ ποιεῖτε ἃ λέγω; 47 πᾶς ὁ ἐρχόμενος πρός με καὶ ἀκούων μου τῶν λόγων καὶ ποιῶν αὐτούς, ὑποδείξω ὑμῖν τίνι ἐστὶν ὅμοιος· 48 ὅμοιός ἐστιν ἀνθρώπῳ οἰκοδομοῦντι οἰκίαν ὃς ἔσκαψεν καὶ ἐβάθυνεν καὶ ἔθηκεν θεμέλιον ἐπὶ τὴν πέτραν· πλημμύρης δὲ γενομένης προσέρηξεν ὁ ποταμὸς τῇ οἰκίᾳ ἐκείνῃ, καὶ οὐκ ἴσχυσεν σαλεῦσαι αὐτὴν διὰ τὸ καλῶς οἰκοδομῆσθαι αὐτήν.h 49 ὁ δὲ ἀκούσας καὶ μὴ ποιήσας ὅμοιός ἐστιν ἀνθρώπῳ οἰκοδομήσαντι οἰκίαν ἐπὶ τὴν γῆν χωρὶς θεμελίου, ᾗ προσέρηξεν ὁ ποταμός, καὶ εὐθὺς συνέπεσεν καὶ ἐγένετο τὸ ῥῆγμα τῆς οἰκίας ἐκείνης μέγα.

7 Ἐπειδὴ ἐπλήρωσεν πάντα τὰ ῥήματα αὐτοῦ εἰς τὰς ἀκοὰς τοῦ λαοῦ, εἰσῆλθεν εἰς Καφαρναούμ. 2 Ἑκατοντάρχου δέ τινος δοῦλος κακῶς ἔχων ἤμελλεν τελευτᾶν, ὃς ἦν αὐτῷ ἔντιμος. 3 ἀκούσας δὲ περὶ τοῦ Ἰησοῦ ἀπέστειλεν πρὸς αὐτὸν πρεσβυτέρους τῶν Ἰουδαίων ἐρωτῶν αὐτὸν ὅπως ἐλθὼν διασώσῃ τὸν δοῦλον αὐτοῦ. 4 οἱ δὲ παραγενόμενοι πρὸς τὸν Ἰησοῦν παρεκάλουν αὐτὸν σπουδαίως λέγοντες ὅτι "Ἄξιός ἐστιν ᾧ παρέξῃ τοῦτο· 5 ἀγαπᾷ γὰρ τὸ ἔθνος ἡμῶν καὶ τὴν συναγωγὴν αὐτὸς ᾠκοδόμησεν ἡμῖν. 6 ὁ δὲ Ἰησοῦς ἐπορεύετο σὺν αὐτοῖς. ἤδη δὲ αὐτοῦ οὐ μακρὰν ἀπέχοντος ἀπὸ τῆς οἰκίας ἔπεμψεν φίλους ὁ ἑκατοντάρχης λέγων αὐτῷ, Κύριε, μὴ σκύλλου, οὐ γὰρ ἱκανός εἰμι ἵνα ὑπὸ τὴν στέγην μου εἰσέλθῃς· 7 διὸ οὐδὲ ἐμαυτὸν ἠξίωσα πρὸς σὲ ἐλθεῖν· ἀλλὰ εἰπὲ λόγῳ, καὶ ἰαθήτω ὁ παῖς μου. 8 καὶ γὰρ ἐγὼ ἄνθρωπός εἰμι ὑπὸ ἐξουσίαν τασσόμενος ἔχων ὑπ᾽ ἐμαυτὸν στρατιώτας, καὶ λέγω τούτῳ, Πορεύθητι, καὶ πορεύεται, καὶ ἄλλῳ, Ἔρχου, καὶ ἔρχεται, καὶ τῷ δούλῳ μου, Ποίησον τοῦτο, καὶ ποιεῖ. 9 ἀκούσας δὲ ταῦτα

NIV

A Tree and Its Fruit

43"No good tree bears bad fruit, nor does a bad tree bear good fruit. 44Each tree is recognized by its own fruit. People do not pick figs from thornbushes, or grapes from briers. 45The good man brings good things out of the good stored up in his heart, and the evil man brings evil things out of the evil stored up in his heart. For out of the overflow of his heart his mouth speaks.

The Wise and Foolish Builders

46"Why do you call me, 'Lord, Lord,' and do not do what I say? 47I will show you what he is like who comes to me and hears my words and puts them into practice. 48He is like a man building a house, who dug down deep and laid the foundation on rock. When a flood came, the torrent struck that house but could not shake it, because it was well built. 49But the one who hears my words and does not put them into practice is like a man who built a house on the ground without a foundation. The moment the torrent struck that house, it collapsed and its destruction was complete."

The Faith of the Centurion

7 When Jesus had finished saying all this in the hearing of the people, he entered Capernaum. 2There a centurion's servant, whom his master valued highly, was sick and about to die. 3The centurion heard of Jesus and sent some elders of the Jews to him, asking him to come and heal his servant. 4When they came to Jesus, they pleaded earnestly with him, "This man deserves to have you do this, 5because he loves our nation and has built our synagogue." 6So Jesus went with them.

He was not far from the house when the centurion sent friends to say to him: "Lord, don't trouble yourself, for I do not deserve to have you come under my roof. 7That is why I did not even consider myself worthy to come to you. But say the word, and my servant will be healed. 8For I myself am a man under authority, with soldiers under me. I tell this one, 'Go,' and he goes; and that one, 'Come,' and he comes. I say to my servant, 'Do this,' and he does it."

9When Jesus heard this, he was amazed

---

x Other ancient authorities read founded upon the rock
y Gk he

g45 NIV text adds θησαυροῦ τῆς καρδίας αὐτοῦ †
h48 NRSV note x τεθεμελίωτο γὰρ ἐπὶ τὴν πέτραν

at him, and turning to the crowd that followed him, he said, "I tell you, not even in Israel have I found such faith." [10]When those who had been sent returned to the house, they found the slave in good health.

Jesus Raises the Widow's Son at Nain

11 Soon afterwards[z] he went to a town called Nain, and his disciples and a large crowd went with him. [12]As he approached the gate of the town, a man who had died was being carried out. He was his mother's only son, and she was a widow; and with her was a large crowd from the town. [13]When the Lord saw her, he had compassion for her and said to her, "Do not weep." [14]Then he came forward and touched the bier, and the bearers stood still. And he said, "Young man, I say to you, rise!" [15]The dead man sat up and began to speak, and Jesus[a] gave him to his mother. [16]Fear seized all of them; and they glorified God, saying, "A great prophet has risen among us!" and "God has looked favorably on his people!" [17]This word about him spread throughout Judea and all the surrounding country.

Messengers from John the Baptist

18 The disciples of John reported all these things to him. So John summoned two of his disciples [19]and sent them to the Lord to ask, "Are you the one who is to come, or are we to wait for another?" [20]When the men had come to him, they said, "John the Baptist has sent us to you to ask, 'Are you the one who is to come, or are we to wait for another?'" [21]Jesus[b] had just then cured many people of diseases, plagues, and evil spirits, and had given sight to many who were blind. [22]And he answered them, "Go and tell John what you have seen and heard: the blind receive their sight, the lame walk, the lepers[c] are cleansed, the deaf hear, the dead are raised, the poor have good news brought to them. [23]And blessed is anyone who takes no offense at me."

24 When John's messengers had gone, Jesus[a] began to speak to the crowds about John:[d] "What did you go out into the wilderness to look at? A reed shaken by the wind? [25]What then did you go out to see? Someone[e] dressed in soft robes? Look, those who put on fine clothing and live in luxury are in royal palaces. [26]What then

---

ὁ Ἰησοῦς ἐθαύμασεν αὐτὸν καὶ στραφεὶς τῷ ἀκολουθοῦντι αὐτῷ ὄχλῳ εἶπεν, Λέγω ὑμῖν, οὐδὲ ἐν τῷ Ἰσραὴλ τοσαύτην πίστιν εὗρον. **10** καὶ ὑποστρέψαντες εἰς τὸν οἶκον οἱ πεμφθέντες εὗρον τὸν δοῦλον ὑγιαίνοντα.

11 Καὶ ἐγένετο ἐν τῷ ἑξῆς[a] ἐπορεύθη εἰς πόλιν καλουμένην Ναΐν καὶ συνεπορεύοντο αὐτῷ οἱ μαθηταὶ αὐτοῦ καὶ ὄχλος πολύς. **12** ὡς δὲ ἤγγισεν τῇ πύλῃ τῆς πόλεως, καὶ ἰδοὺ ἐξεκομίζετο τεθνηκὼς μονογενὴς υἱὸς τῇ μητρὶ αὐτοῦ καὶ αὐτὴ ἦν χήρα, καὶ ὄχλος τῆς πόλεως ἱκανὸς ἦν σὺν αὐτῇ. **13** καὶ ἰδὼν αὐτὴν ὁ κύριος ἐσπλαγχνίσθη ἐπ' αὐτῇ καὶ εἶπεν αὐτῇ, Μὴ κλαῖε. **14** καὶ προσελθὼν ἥψατο τῆς σοροῦ, οἱ δὲ βαστάζοντες ἔστησαν, καὶ εἶπεν, Νεανίσκε, σοὶ λέγω, ἐγέρθητι. **15** καὶ ἀνεκάθισεν ὁ νεκρὸς καὶ ἤρξατο λαλεῖν, καὶ ἔδωκεν αὐτὸν τῇ μητρὶ αὐτοῦ. **16** ἔλαβεν δὲ φόβος πάντας καὶ ἐδόξαζον τὸν θεὸν λέγοντες ὅτι Προφήτης μέγας ἠγέρθη ἐν ἡμῖν καὶ ὅτι Ἐπεσκέψατο ὁ θεὸς τὸν λαὸν αὐτοῦ. **17** καὶ ἐξῆλθεν ὁ λόγος οὗτος ἐν ὅλῃ τῇ Ἰουδαίᾳ περὶ αὐτοῦ καὶ πάσῃ τῇ περιχώρῳ.

18 Καὶ ἀπήγγειλαν Ἰωάννῃ οἱ μαθηταὶ αὐτοῦ περὶ πάντων τούτων. καὶ προσκαλεσάμενος δύο τινὰς τῶν μαθητῶν αὐτοῦ ὁ Ἰωάννης **19** ἔπεμψεν πρὸς τὸν κύριον λέγων, Σὺ εἶ ὁ ἐρχόμενος ἢ ἄλλον προσδοκῶμεν; **20** παραγενόμενοι δὲ πρὸς αὐτὸν οἱ ἄνδρες εἶπαν, Ἰωάννης ὁ βαπτιστὴς ἀπέστειλεν ἡμᾶς πρὸς σὲ λέγων, Σὺ εἶ ὁ ἐρχόμενος ἢ ἄλλον προσδοκῶμεν; **21** ἐν ἐκείνῃ τῇ ὥρᾳ ἐθεράπευσεν πολλοὺς ἀπὸ νόσων καὶ μαστίγων καὶ πνευμάτων πονηρῶν καὶ τυφλοῖς πολλοῖς ἐχαρίσατο βλέπειν. **22** καὶ ἀποκριθεὶς εἶπεν αὐτοῖς, Πορευθέντες ἀπαγγείλατε Ἰωάννῃ ἃ εἴδετε καὶ ἠκούσατε· τυφλοὶ ἀναβλέπουσιν, χωλοὶ περιπατοῦσιν, λεπροὶ καθαρίζονται καὶ κωφοὶ ἀκούουσιν, νεκροὶ ἐγείρονται, πτωχοὶ εὐαγγελίζονται· **23** καὶ μακάριός ἐστιν ὃς ἐὰν μὴ σκανδαλισθῇ ἐν ἐμοί. **24** Ἀπελθόντων δὲ τῶν ἀγγέλων Ἰωάννου ἤρξατο λέγειν πρὸς τοὺς ὄχλους περὶ Ἰωάννου. Τί ἐξήλθατε εἰς τὴν ἔρημον θεάσασθαι; κάλαμον ὑπὸ ἀνέμου σαλευόμενον; **25** ἀλλὰ τί ἐξήλθατε ἰδεῖν; ἄνθρωπον ἐν μαλακοῖς ἱματίοις ἠμφιεσμένον; ἰδοὺ οἱ ἐν ἱματισμῷ ἐνδόξῳ καὶ τρυφῇ ὑπάρχοντες ἐν τοῖς βασιλείοις εἰσίν.

---

at him, and turning to the crowd following him, he said, "I tell you, I have not found such great faith even in Israel." [10]Then the men who had been sent returned to the house and found the servant well.

Jesus Raises a Widow's Son

[11]Soon afterward, Jesus went to a town called Nain, and his disciples and a large crowd went along with him. [12]As he approached the town gate, a dead person was being carried out—the only son of his mother, and she was a widow. And a large crowd from the town was with her. [13]When the Lord saw her, his heart went out to her and he said, "Don't cry."

[14]Then he went up and touched the coffin, and those carrying it stood still. He said, "Young man, I say to you, get up!" [15]The dead man sat up and began to talk, and Jesus gave him back to his mother.

[16]They were all filled with awe and praised God. "A great prophet has appeared among us," they said. "God has come to help his people." [17]This news about Jesus spread throughout Judea[a] and the surrounding country.

Jesus and John the Baptist

[18]John's disciples told him about all these things. Calling two of them, [19]he sent them to the Lord to ask, "Are you the one who was to come, or should we expect someone else?"

[20]When the men came to Jesus, they said, "John the Baptist sent us to you to ask, 'Are you the one who was to come, or should we expect someone else?'"

[21]At that very time Jesus cured many who had diseases, sicknesses and evil spirits, and gave sight to many who were blind. [22]So he replied to the messengers, "Go back and report to John what you have seen and heard: The blind receive sight, the lame walk, those who have leprosy[b] are cured, the deaf hear, the dead are raised, and the good news is preached to the poor. [23]Blessed is the man who does not fall away on account of me."

[24]After John's messengers left, Jesus began to speak to the crowd about John: "What did you go out into the desert to see? A reed swayed by the wind? [25]If not, what did you go out to see? A man dressed in fine clothes? No, those who wear expensive clothes and indulge in luxury are

---

did you go out to see? A prophet? Yes, I tell you, and more than a prophet. 27This is the one about whom it is written,

'See, I am sending my messenger
   ahead of you,
who will prepare your way before
   you.'

28I tell you, among those born of women no one is greater than John; yet the least in the kingdom of God is greater than he." 29(And all the people who heard this, including the tax collectors, acknowledged the justice of God,f because they had been baptized with John's baptism. 30But by refusing to be baptized by him, the Pharisees and the lawyers rejected God's purpose for themselves.)

31 "To what then will I compare the people of this generation, and what are they like? 32They are like children sitting in the marketplace and calling to one another,

'We played the flute for you, and you
   did not dance;
we wailed, and you did not weep.'

33For John the Baptist has come eating no bread and drinking no wine, and you say, 'He has a demon'; 34the Son of Man has come eating and drinking, and you say, 'Look, a glutton and a drunkard, a friend of tax collectors and sinners!' 35Nevertheless, wisdom is vindicated by all her children."

A Sinful Woman Forgiven

36 One of the Pharisees asked Jesusd to eat with him, and he went into the Pharisee's house and took his place at the table. 37And a woman in the city, who was a sinner, having learned that he was eating in the Pharisee's house, brought an alabaster jar of ointment. 38She stood behind him at his feet, weeping, and began to bathe his feet with her tears and to dry them with her hair. Then she continued kissing his feet and anointing them with the ointment. 39Now when the Pharisee who had invited him saw it, he said to himself, "If this man were a prophet, he would have known who and what kind of woman this is who is touching him—that she is a sinner." 40Jesus spoke up and said to him, "Simon, I have something to say to you." "Teacher," he replied, "Speak." 41"A certain creditor

---

26 ἀλλὰ τί ἐξήλθατε ἰδεῖν; προφήτην; ναὶ λέγω ὑμῖν, καὶ περισσότερον προφήτου. 27 οὗτός ἐστιν περὶ οὗ γέγραπται,
Ἰδοὺ ἀποστέλλω τὸν ἄγγελόν μου
   πρὸ προσώπου σου,
ὃς κατασκευάσει τὴν ὁδόν σου
   ἔμπροσθέν σου.
28 λέγω ὑμῖν, μείζων ἐν γεννητοῖς γυναικῶν Ἰωάννου οὐδείς ἐστιν· ὁ δὲ μικρότερος ἐν τῇ βασιλείᾳ τοῦ θεοῦ μείζων αὐτοῦ ἐστιν. 29 Καὶ πᾶς ὁ λαὸς ἀκούσας καὶ οἱ τελῶναι ἐδικαίωσαν τὸν θεὸν βαπτισθέντες τὸ βάπτισμα Ἰωάννου· 30 οἱ δὲ Φαρισαῖοι καὶ οἱ νομικοὶ τὴν βουλὴν τοῦ θεοῦ ἠθέτησαν εἰς ἑαυτοὺς μὴ βαπτισθέντες ὑπ' αὐτοῦ. 31 Τίνι οὖν ὁμοιώσω τοὺς ἀνθρώπους τῆς γενεᾶς ταύτης καὶ τίνι εἰσὶν ὅμοιοι; 32 ὅμοιοί εἰσιν παιδίοις τοῖς ἐν ἀγορᾷ καθημένοις καὶ προσφωνοῦσιν ἀλλήλοις ἃ λέγει,
Ηὐλήσαμεν ὑμῖν καὶ οὐκ ὠρχήσασθε,
ἐθρηνήσαμεν καὶ οὐκ ἐκλαύσατε.
33 ἐλήλυθεν γὰρ Ἰωάννης ὁ βαπτιστὴς μὴ ἐσθίων ἄρτον μήτε πίνων οἶνον, καὶ λέγετε, Δαιμόνιον ἔχει. 34 ἐλήλυθεν ὁ υἱὸς τοῦ ἀνθρώπου ἐσθίων καὶ πίνων, καὶ λέγετε, Ἰδοὺ ἄνθρωπος φάγος καὶ οἰνοπότης, φίλος τελωνῶν καὶ ἁμαρτωλῶν. 35 καὶ ἐδικαιώθη ἡ σοφία ἀπὸ πάντων τῶν τέκνων αὐτῆς.
36 Ἠρώτα δέ τις αὐτὸν τῶν Φαρισαίων ἵνα φάγῃ μετ' αὐτοῦ, καὶ εἰσελθὼν εἰς τὸν οἶκον τοῦ Φαρισαίου κατεκλίθη. 37 καὶ ἰδοὺ γυνὴ ἥτις ἦν ἐν τῇ πόλει ἁμαρτωλός, καὶ ἐπιγνοῦσα ὅτι κατάκειται ἐν τῇ οἰκίᾳ τοῦ Φαρισαίου, κομίσασα ἀλάβαστρον μύρου 38 καὶ στᾶσα ὀπίσω παρὰ τοὺς πόδας αὐτοῦ κλαίουσα τοῖς δάκρυσιν ἤρξατο βρέχειν τοὺς πόδας αὐτοῦ καὶ ταῖς θριξὶν τῆς κεφαλῆς αὐτῆς ἐξέμασσεν καὶ κατεφίλει τοὺς πόδας αὐτοῦ καὶ ἤλειφεν τῷ μύρῳ. 39 ἰδὼν δὲ ὁ Φαρισαῖος ὁ καλέσας αὐτὸν εἶπεν ἐν ἑαυτῷ λέγων, Οὗτος εἰ ἦν προφήτης, ἐγίνωσκεν ἂν τίς καὶ ποταπὴ ἡ γυνὴ ἥτις ἅπτεται αὐτοῦ, ὅτι ἁμαρτωλός ἐστιν. 40 καὶ ἀποκριθεὶς ὁ Ἰησοῦς εἶπεν πρὸς αὐτόν, Σίμων, ἔχω σοί τι εἰπεῖν. ὁ δέ, Διδάσκαλε, εἰπέ, φησίν. 41 δύο χρεοφειλέται ἦσαν δανιστῇ τινι· ὁ εἷς

---

in palaces. 26But what did you go out to see? A prophet? Yes, I tell you, and more than a prophet. 27This is the one about whom it is written:

" 'I will send my messenger ahead of
   you,
who will prepare your way before
   you.'c

28I tell you, among those born of women there is no one greater than John; yet the one who is least in the kingdom of God is greater than he."

29(All the people, even the tax collectors, when they heard Jesus' words, acknowledged that God's way was right, because they had been baptized by John. 30But the Pharisees and experts in the law rejected God's purpose for themselves, because they had not been baptized by John.)

31"To what, then, can I compare the people of this generation? What are they like? 32They are like children sitting in the marketplace and calling out to each other:

" 'We played the flute for you,
   and you did not dance;
we sang a dirge,
   and you did not cry.'

33For John the Baptist came neither eating bread nor drinking wine, and you say, 'He has a demon.' 34The Son of Man came eating and drinking, and you say, 'Here is a glutton and a drunkard, a friend of tax collectors and "sinners." ' 35But wisdom is proved right by all her children."

Jesus Anointed by a Sinful Woman

36Now one of the Pharisees invited Jesus to have dinner with him, so he went to the Pharisee's house and reclined at the table. 37When a woman who had lived a sinful life in that town learned that Jesus was eating at the Pharisee's house, she brought an alabaster jar of perfume, 38and as she stood behind him at his feet weeping, she began to wet his feet with her tears. Then she wiped them with her hair, kissed them and poured perfume on them.

39When the Pharisee who had invited him saw this, he said to himself, "If this man were a prophet, he would know who is touching him and what kind of woman she is—that she is a sinner."

40Jesus answered him, "Simon, I have something to tell you."

"Tell me, teacher," he said.

41"Two men owed money to a certain

---

d Gk *him*   f Or *praised God*   c27 Mal. 3:1

had two debtors; one owed five hundred denarii,[g] and the other fifty. [42]When they could not pay, he canceled the debts for both of them. Now which of them will love him more?" [43]Simon answered, "I suppose the one for whom he canceled the greater debt." And Jesus[c] said to him, "You have judged rightly." [44]Then turning toward the woman, he said to Simon, "Do you see this woman? I entered your house; you gave me no water for my feet, but she has bathed my feet with her tears and dried them with her hair. [45]You gave me no kiss, but from the time I came in she has not stopped kissing my feet. [46]You did not anoint my head with oil, but she has anointed my feet with ointment. [47]Therefore, I tell you, her sins, which were many, have been forgiven; hence she has shown great love. But the one to whom little is forgiven, loves little." [48]Then he said to her, "Your sins are forgiven." [49]But those who were at the table with him began to say among themselves, "Who is this who even forgives sins?" [50]And he said to the woman, "Your faith has saved you; go in peace."

Some Women Accompany Jesus

8 Soon afterwards he went on through cities and villages, proclaiming and bringing the good news of the kingdom of God. The twelve were with him, [2]as well as some women who had been cured of evil spirits and infirmities: Mary, called Magdalene, from whom seven demons had gone out, [3]and Joanna, the wife of Herod's steward Chuza, and Susanna, and many others, who provided for them[h] out of their resources.

The Parable of the Sower

4 When a great crowd gathered and people from town after town came to him, he said in a parable: [5]"A sower went out to sow his seed; and as he sowed, some fell on the path and was trampled on, and the birds of the air ate it up. [6]Some fell on the rock; and as it grew up, it withered for lack of moisture. [7]Some fell among thorns, and the thorns grew with it and choked it. [8]Some fell into good soil, and when it grew, it produced a hundredfold." As he said this, he called out, "Let anyone with ears to hear listen!"

ὤφειλεν δηνάρια πεντακόσια, ὁ δὲ ἕτερος πεντήκοντα. **42** μὴ ἐχόντων αὐτῶν ἀποδοῦναι ἀμφοτέροις ἐχαρίσατο. τίς οὖν αὐτῶν πλεῖον ἀγαπήσει αὐτόν; **43** ἀποκριθεὶς Σίμων εἶπεν, Ὑπολαμβάνω ὅτι ᾧ τὸ πλεῖον ἐχαρίσατο. ὁ δὲ εἶπεν αὐτῷ, Ὀρθῶς ἔκρινας. **44** καὶ στραφεὶς πρὸς τὴν γυναῖκα τῷ Σίμωνι ἔφη, Βλέπεις ταύτην τὴν γυναῖκα; εἰσῆλθόν σου εἰς τὴν οἰκίαν, ὕδωρ μοι ἐπὶ πόδας οὐκ ἔδωκας· αὕτη δὲ τοῖς δάκρυσιν ἔβρεξέν μου τοὺς πόδας καὶ ταῖς θριξὶν αὐτῆς ἐξέμαξεν. **45** φίλημά μοι οὐκ ἔδωκας· αὕτη δὲ ἀφ᾽ ἧς εἰσῆλθον οὐ διέλιπεν καταφιλοῦσά μου τοὺς πόδας. **46** ἐλαίῳ τὴν κεφαλήν μου οὐκ ἤλειψας· αὕτη δὲ μύρῳ ἤλειψεν τοὺς πόδας μου. **47** οὗ χάριν λέγω σοι, ἀφέωνται αἱ ἁμαρτίαι αὐτῆς αἱ πολλαί, ὅτι ἠγάπησεν πολύ· ᾧ δὲ ὀλίγον ἀφίεται, ὀλίγον ἀγαπᾷ. **48** εἶπεν δὲ αὐτῇ, Ἀφέωνταί σου αἱ ἁμαρτίαι. **49** καὶ ἤρξαντο οἱ συνανακείμενοι λέγειν ἐν ἑαυτοῖς, Τίς οὗτός ἐστιν ὃς καὶ ἁμαρτίας ἀφίησιν; **50** εἶπεν δὲ πρὸς τὴν γυναῖκα, Ἡ πίστις σου σέσωκέν σε· πορεύου εἰς εἰρήνην.

8 Καὶ ἐγένετο ἐν τῷ καθεξῆς καὶ αὐτὸς διώδευεν κατὰ πόλιν καὶ κώμην κηρύσσων καὶ εὐαγγελιζόμενος τὴν βασιλείαν τοῦ θεοῦ καὶ οἱ δώδεκα σὺν αὐτῷ, **2** καὶ γυναῖκές τινες αἳ ἦσαν τεθεραπευμέναι ἀπὸ πνευμάτων πονηρῶν καὶ ἀσθενειῶν, Μαρία ἡ καλουμένη Μαγδαληνή, ἀφ᾽ ἧς δαιμόνια ἑπτὰ ἐξεληλύθει, **3** καὶ Ἰωάννα γυνὴ Χουζᾶ ἐπιτρόπου Ἡρῴδου καὶ Σουσάννα καὶ ἕτεραι πολλαί, αἵτινες διηκόνουν αὐτοῖς[a] ἐκ τῶν ὑπαρχόντων αὐταῖς.

4 Συνιόντος δὲ ὄχλου πολλοῦ καὶ τῶν κατὰ πόλιν ἐπιπορευομένων πρὸς αὐτὸν εἶπεν διὰ παραβολῆς, **5** Ἐξῆλθεν ὁ σπείρων τοῦ σπεῖραι τὸν σπόρον αὐτοῦ. καὶ ἐν τῷ σπείρειν αὐτὸν ὃ μὲν ἔπεσεν παρὰ τὴν ὁδὸν καὶ κατεπατήθη, καὶ τὰ πετεινὰ τοῦ οὐρανοῦ κατέφαγεν αὐτό. **6** καὶ ἕτερον κατέπεσεν ἐπὶ τὴν πέτραν, καὶ φυὲν ἐξηράνθη διὰ τὸ μὴ ἔχειν ἰκμάδα. **7** καὶ ἕτερον ἔπεσεν ἐν μέσῳ τῶν ἀκανθῶν, καὶ συμφυεῖσαι αἱ ἄκανθαι ἀπέπνιξαν αὐτό. **8** καὶ ἕτερον ἔπεσεν εἰς τὴν γῆν τὴν ἀγαθὴν καὶ φυὲν ἐποίησεν καρπὸν ἑκατονταπλασίονα. ταῦτα λέγων ἐφώνει, Ὁ ἔχων ὦτα ἀκούειν ἀκουέτω.

moneylender. One owed him five hundred denarii,[d] and the other fifty. [42]Neither of them had the money to pay him back, so he canceled the debts of both. Now which of them will love him more?"

[43]Simon replied, "I suppose the one who had the bigger debt canceled."

"You have judged correctly," Jesus said. [44]Then he turned toward the woman and said to Simon, "Do you see this woman? I came into your house. You did not give me any water for my feet, but she wet my feet with her tears and wiped them with her hair. [45]You did not give me a kiss, but this woman, from the time I entered, has not stopped kissing my feet. [46]You did not put oil on my head, but she has poured perfume on my feet. [47]Therefore, I tell you, her many sins have been forgiven—for she loved much. But he who has been forgiven little loves little."

[48]Then Jesus said to her, "Your sins are forgiven."

[49]The other guests began to say among themselves, "Who is this who even forgives sins?"

[50]Jesus said to the woman, "Your faith has saved you; go in peace."

The Parable of the Sower

8 After this, Jesus traveled about from one town and village to another, proclaiming the good news of the kingdom of God. The Twelve were with him, [2]and also some women who had been cured of evil spirits and diseases: Mary (called Magdalene) from whom seven demons had come out; [3]Joanna the wife of Cuza, the manager of Herod's household; Susanna; and many others. These women were helping to support them out of their own means.

[4]While a large crowd was gathering and people were coming to Jesus from town after town, he told this parable: [5]"A farmer went out to sow his seed. As he was scattering the seed, some fell along the path; it was trampled on, and the birds of the air ate it up. [6]Some fell on rock, and when it came up, the plants withered because they had no moisture. [7]Other seed fell among thorns, which grew up with it and choked the plants. [8]Still other seed fell on good soil. It came up and yielded a crop, a hundred times more than was sown."

When he said this, he called out, "He who has ears to hear, let him hear."

---

[c] Gk *he*   [g] The denarius was the usual day's wage for a laborer   [h] Other ancient authorities read *him*   [a]3 NRSV note h αὐτῷ   [d]41 A denarius was a coin worth about a day's wages.

NRSV

The Purpose of the Parables

9 Then his disciples asked him what this parable meant. [10]He said, "To you it has been given to know the secrets[i] of the kingdom of God; but to others I speak[j] in parables, so that

'looking they may not perceive,
    and listening they may not
    understand.'

The Parable of the Sower Explained

11 "Now the parable is this: The seed is the word of God. [12]The ones on the path are those who have heard; then the devil comes and takes away the word from their hearts, so that they may not believe and be saved. [13]The ones on the rock are those who, when they hear the word, receive it with joy. But these have no root; they believe only for a while and in a time of testing fall away. [14]As for what fell among the thorns, these are the ones who hear; but as they go on their way, they are choked by the cares and riches and pleasures of life, and their fruit does not mature. [15]But as for that in the good soil, these are the ones who, when they hear the word, hold it fast in an honest and good heart, and bear fruit with patient endurance.

A Lamp under a Jar

16 "No one after lighting a lamp hides it under a jar, or puts it under a bed, but puts it on a lampstand, so that those who enter may see the light. [17]For nothing is hidden that will not be disclosed, nor is anything secret that will not become known and come to light. [18]Then pay attention to how you listen; for to those who have, more will be given; and from those who do not have, even what they seem to have will be taken away."

The True Kindred of Jesus

19 Then his mother and his brothers came to him, but they could not reach him because of the crowd. [20]And he was told, "Your mother and your brothers are standing outside, wanting to see you." [21]But he said to them, "My mother and my brothers are those who hear the word of God and do it."

Jesus Calms a Storm

22 One day he got into a boat with his disciples, and he said to them, "Let us go across to the other side of the lake." So they put out, [23]and while they were sailing

Greek

9 Ἐπηρώτων δὲ αὐτὸν οἱ μαθηταὶ αὐτοῦ τίς αὕτη εἴη ἡ παραβολή. **10** ὁ δὲ εἶπεν, Ὑμῖν δέδοται γνῶναι τὰ μυστήρια τῆς βασιλείας τοῦ θεοῦ, τοῖς δὲ λοιποῖς ἐν παραβολαῖς, ἵνα

βλέποντες μὴ βλέπωσιν
καὶ ἀκούοντες μὴ συνιῶσιν.

11 Ἔστιν δὲ αὕτη ἡ παραβολή· Ὁ σπόρος ἐστὶν ὁ λόγος τοῦ θεοῦ. **12** οἱ δὲ παρὰ τὴν ὁδόν εἰσιν οἱ ἀκούσαντες, εἶτα ἔρχεται ὁ διάβολος καὶ αἴρει τὸν λόγον ἀπὸ τῆς καρδίας αὐτῶν, ἵνα μὴ πιστεύσαντες σωθῶσιν. **13** οἱ δὲ ἐπὶ τῆς πέτρας οἳ ὅταν ἀκούσωσιν μετὰ χαρᾶς δέχονται τὸν λόγον, καὶ οὗτοι ῥίζαν οὐκ ἔχουσιν, οἳ πρὸς καιρὸν πιστεύουσιν καὶ ἐν καιρῷ πειρασμοῦ ἀφίστανται. **14** τὸ δὲ εἰς τὰς ἀκάνθας πεσόν, οὗτοί εἰσιν οἱ ἀκούσαντες, καὶ ὑπὸ μεριμνῶν καὶ πλούτου καὶ ἡδονῶν τοῦ βίου πορευόμενοι συμπνίγονται καὶ οὐ τελεσφοροῦσιν. **15** τὸ δὲ ἐν τῇ καλῇ γῇ, οὗτοί εἰσιν οἵτινες ἐν καρδίᾳ καλῇ καὶ ἀγαθῇ ἀκούσαντες τὸν λόγον κατέχουσιν καὶ καρποφοροῦσιν ἐν ὑπομονῇ.

16 Οὐδεὶς δὲ λύχνον ἅψας καλύπτει αὐτὸν σκεύει ἢ ὑποκάτω κλίνης τίθησιν, ἀλλ' ἐπὶ λυχνίας τίθησιν, ἵνα οἱ εἰσπορευόμενοι βλέπωσιν τὸ φῶς. **17** οὐ γάρ ἐστιν κρυπτὸν ὃ οὐ φανερὸν γενήσεται οὐδὲ ἀπόκρυφον ὃ οὐ μὴ γνωσθῇ καὶ εἰς φανερὸν ἔλθῃ. **18** βλέπετε οὖν πῶς ἀκούετε· ὃς ἂν γὰρ ἔχῃ, δοθήσεται αὐτῷ· καὶ ὃς ἂν μὴ ἔχῃ, καὶ ὃ δοκεῖ ἔχειν ἀρθήσεται ἀπ' αὐτοῦ.

19 Παρεγένετο δὲ πρὸς αὐτὸν ἡ μήτηρ καὶ οἱ ἀδελφοὶ αὐτοῦ καὶ οὐκ ἠδύναντο συντυχεῖν αὐτῷ διὰ τὸν ὄχλον. **20** ἀπηγγέλη δὲ αὐτῷ, Ἡ μήτηρ σου καὶ οἱ ἀδελφοί σου ἑστήκασιν ἔξω ἰδεῖν θέλοντές σε. **21** ὁ δὲ ἀποκριθεὶς εἶπεν πρὸς αὐτούς, Μήτηρ μου καὶ ἀδελφοί μου οὗτοί εἰσιν οἱ τὸν λόγον τοῦ θεοῦ ἀκούοντες καὶ ποιοῦντες.

22 Ἐγένετο δὲ ἐν μιᾷ τῶν ἡμερῶν καὶ αὐτὸς ἐνέβη εἰς πλοῖον καὶ οἱ μαθηταὶ αὐτοῦ καὶ εἶπεν πρὸς αὐτούς, Διέλθωμεν εἰς τὸ πέραν τῆς λίμνης, καὶ ἀνήχθησαν. **23** πλεόντων δὲ αὐτῶν

NIV

[9]His disciples asked him what this parable meant. [10]He said, "The knowledge of the secrets of the kingdom of God has been given to you, but to others I speak in parables, so that,

" 'though seeing, they may not see;
    though hearing, they may not
    understand.'[a]

[11]"This is the meaning of the parable: The seed is the word of God. [12]Those along the path are the ones who hear, and then the devil comes and takes away the word from their hearts, so that they may not believe and be saved. [13]Those on the rock are the ones who receive the word with joy when they hear it, but they have no root. They believe for a while, but in the time of testing they fall away. [14]The seed that fell among thorns stands for those who hear, but as they go on their way they are choked by life's worries, riches and pleasures, and they do not mature. [15]But the seed on good soil stands for those with a noble and good heart, who hear the word, retain it, and by persevering produce a crop.

A Lamp on a Stand

[16]"No one lights a lamp and hides it in a jar or puts it under a bed. Instead, he puts it on a stand, so that those who come in can see the light. [17]For there is nothing hidden that will not be disclosed, and nothing concealed that will not be known or brought out into the open. [18]Therefore consider carefully how you listen. Whoever has will be given more; whoever does not have, even what he thinks he has will be taken from him."

Jesus' Mother and Brothers

[19]Now Jesus' mother and brothers came to see him, but they were not able to get near him because of the crowd. [20]Someone told him, "Your mother and brothers are standing outside, wanting to see you."

[21]He replied, "My mother and brothers are those who hear God's word and put it into practice."

Jesus Calms the Storm

[22]One day Jesus said to his disciples, "Let's go over to the other side of the lake." So they got into a boat and set out. [23]As

---

[i] Or *mysteries*   [j] Gk lacks *I speak*   [a]10 Isaiah 6:9

he fell asleep. A windstorm swept down on the lake, and the boat was filling with water, and they were in danger. 24They went to him and woke him up, shouting, "Master, Master, we are perishing!" And he woke up and rebuked the wind and the raging waves; they ceased, and there was a calm. 25He said to them, "Where is your faith?" They were afraid and amazed, and said to one another, "Who then is this, that he commands even the winds and the water, and they obey him?"

Jesus Heals the Gerasene Demoniac

26 Then they arrived at the country of the Gerasenes,k which is opposite Galilee. 27As he stepped out on land, a man of the city who had demons met him. For a long time he had wornl no clothes, and he did not live in a house but in the tombs. 28When he saw Jesus, he fell down before him and shouted at the top of his voice, "What have you to do with me, Jesus, Son of the Most High God? I beg you, do not torment me"— 29for Jesusm had commanded the unclean spirit to come out of the man. (For many times it had seized him; he was kept under guard and bound with chains and shackles, but he would break the bonds and be driven by the demon into the wilds.) 30Jesus then asked him, "What is your name?" He said, "Legion"; for many demons had entered him. 31They begged him not to order them to go back into the abyss.

32 Now there on the hillside a large herd of swine was feeding; and the demonsn begged Jesuso to let them enter these. So he gave them permission. 33Then the demons came out of the man and entered the swine, and the herd rushed down the steep bank into the lake and was drowned.

34 When the swineherds saw what had happened, they ran off and told it in the city and in the country. 35Then people came out to see what had happened, and when they came to Jesus, they found the man from whom the demons had gone sitting at the feet of Jesus, clothed and in his right mind. And they were afraid. 36Those who had seen it told them how the one who had been possessed by demons had been healed. 37Then all the people of the surrounding country of the Gerasenesk asked Jesuso to leave them; for they were seized

ἀφύπνωσεν. καὶ κατέβη λαῖλαψ ἀνέμου εἰς τὴν λίμνην καὶ συνεπληροῦντο καὶ ἐκινδύνευον. **24** προσελθόντες δὲ διήγειραν αὐτὸν λέγοντες, Ἐπιστάτα ἐπιστάτα, ἀπολλύμεθα. ὁ δὲ διεγερθεὶς ἐπετίμησεν τῷ ἀνέμῳ καὶ τῷ κλύδωνι τοῦ ὕδατος· καὶ ἐπαύσαντο καὶ ἐγένετο γαλήνη. **25** εἶπεν δὲ αὐτοῖς, Ποῦ ἡ πίστις ὑμῶν; φοβηθέντες δὲ ἐθαύμασαν λέγοντες πρὸς ἀλλήλους, Τίς ἄρα οὗτός ἐστιν ὅτι καὶ τοῖς ἀνέμοις ἐπιτάσσει καὶ τῷ ὕδατι, καὶ ὑπακούουσιν αὐτῷ;

26 Καὶ κατέπλευσαν εἰς τὴν χώραν τῶν Γερασηνῶνb, ἥτις ἐστὶν ἀντιπέρα τῆς Γαλιλαίας. **27** ἐξελθόντι δὲ αὐτῷ ἐπὶ τὴν γῆν ὑπήντησεν ἀνήρ τις ἐκ τῆς πόλεως ἔχων δαιμόνια καὶ χρόνῳ ἱκανῷc οὐκ ἐνεδύσατο ἱμάτιον καὶ ἐν οἰκίᾳ οὐκ ἔμενεν ἀλλ᾽ ἐν τοῖς μνήμασιν. **28** ἰδὼν δὲ τὸν Ἰησοῦν ἀνακράξας προσέπεσεν αὐτῷ καὶ φωνῇ μεγάλῃ εἶπεν, Τί ἐμοὶ καὶ σοί, Ἰησοῦ υἱὲ τοῦ θεοῦ τοῦ ὑψίστου; δέομαί σου, μή με βασανίσῃς. **29** παρήγγειλεν γὰρ τῷ πνεύματι τῷ ἀκαθάρτῳ ἐξελθεῖν ἀπὸ τοῦ ἀνθρώπου. πολλοῖς γὰρ χρόνοις συνηρπάκει αὐτὸν καὶ ἐδεσμεύετο ἁλύσεσιν καὶ πέδαις φυλασσόμενος καὶ διαρρήσσων τὰ δεσμὰ ἠλαύνετο ὑπὸ τοῦ δαιμονίου εἰς τὰς ἐρήμους. **30** ἐπηρώτησεν δὲ αὐτὸν ὁ Ἰησοῦς, Τί σοι ὄνομά ἐστιν; ὁ δὲ εἶπεν, Λεγιών, ὅτι εἰσῆλθεν δαιμόνια πολλὰ εἰς αὐτόν. **31** καὶ παρεκάλουν αὐτὸν ἵνα μὴ ἐπιτάξῃ αὐτοῖς εἰς τὴν ἄβυσσον ἀπελθεῖν.

32 Ἦν δὲ ἐκεῖ ἀγέλη χοίρων ἱκανῶν βοσκομένη ἐν τῷ ὄρει· καὶ παρεκάλεσαν αὐτὸν ἵνα ἐπιτρέψῃ αὐτοῖς εἰς ἐκείνους εἰσελθεῖν· καὶ ἐπέτρεψεν αὐτοῖς. **33** ἐξελθόντα δὲ τὰ δαιμόνια ἀπὸ τοῦ ἀνθρώπου εἰσῆλθον εἰς τοὺς χοίρους, καὶ ὥρμησεν ἡ ἀγέλη κατὰ τοῦ κρημνοῦ εἰς τὴν λίμνην καὶ ἀπεπνίγη. **34** ἰδόντες δὲ οἱ βόσκοντες τὸ γεγονὸς ἔφυγον καὶ ἀπήγγειλαν εἰς τὴν πόλιν καὶ εἰς τοὺς ἀγρούς. **35** ἐξῆλθον δὲ ἰδεῖν τὸ γεγονὸς καὶ ἦλθον πρὸς τὸν Ἰησοῦν καὶ εὗρον καθήμενον τὸν ἄνθρωπον ἀφ᾽ οὗ τὰ δαιμόνια ἐξῆλθεν ἱματισμένον καὶ σωφρονοῦντα παρὰ τοὺς πόδας τοῦ Ἰησοῦ, καὶ ἐφοβήθησαν. **36** ἀπήγγειλαν δὲ αὐτοῖς οἱ ἰδόντες πῶς ἐσώθη ὁ δαιμονισθείς. **37** καὶ ἠρώτησεν αὐτὸν ἅπαν τὸ πλῆθος τῆς περιχώρου τῶν Γερασηνῶνb ἀπελθεῖν ἀπ᾽ αὐτῶν, ὅτι

they sailed, he fell asleep. A squall came down on the lake, so that the boat was being swamped, and they were in great danger.

24The disciples went and woke him, saying, "Master, Master, we're going to drown!"

He got up and rebuked the wind and the raging waters; the storm subsided, and all was calm. 25"Where is your faith?" he asked his disciples.

In fear and amazement they asked one another, "Who is this? He commands even the winds and the water, and they obey him."

The Healing of a Demon-possessed Man

26They sailed to the region of the Gerasenes,b which is across the lake from Galilee. 27When Jesus stepped ashore, he was met by a demon-possessed man from the town. For a long time this man had not worn clothes or lived in a house, but had lived in the tombs. 28When he saw Jesus, he cried out and fell at his feet, shouting at the top of his voice, "What do you want with me, Jesus, Son of the Most High God? I beg you, don't torture me!" 29For Jesus had commanded the evilc spirit to come out of the man. Many times it had seized him, and though he was chained hand and foot and kept under guard, he had broken his chains and had been driven by the demon into solitary places.

30Jesus asked him, "What is your name?"

"Legion," he replied, because many demons had gone into him. 31And they begged him repeatedly not to order them to go into the Abyss.

32A large herd of pigs was feeding there on the hillside. The demons begged Jesus to let them go into them, and he gave them permission. 33When the demons came out of the man, they went into the pigs, and the herd rushed down the steep bank into the lake and was drowned.

34When those tending the pigs saw what had happened, they ran off and reported this in the town and countryside, 35and the people went out to see what had happened. When they came to Jesus, they found the man from whom the demons had gone out, sitting at Jesus' feet, dressed and in his right mind; and they were afraid. 36Those who had seen it told the people how the demon-possessed man had been cured. 37Then all the people of the region of the

---

k Other ancient authorities read *Gadarenes*; others, *Gergesenes* l Other ancient authorities read *a man of the city who had had demons for a long time met him. He wore* m Gk *he* n Gk *they* o Gk *him*

b26,37 NIV/NRSV notes Γαδαρηνῶν or Γεργεσηνῶν c27 NRSV note l ἐκ χρόνων ἱκανῶν καὶ †

b26 Some manuscripts *Gadarenes*; other manuscripts *Gergesenes*; also in verse 37 c29 Greek *unclean*

NRSV

with great fear. So he got into the boat and returned. [38]The man from whom the demons had gone begged that he might be with him; but Jesus[m] sent him away, saying, [39]"Return to your home, and declare how much God has done for you." So he went away, proclaiming throughout the city how much Jesus had done for him.

A Girl Restored to Life and a Woman Healed

[40] Now when Jesus returned, the crowd welcomed him, for they were all waiting for him. [41]Just then there came a man named Jairus, a leader of the synagogue. He fell at Jesus' feet and begged him to come to his house, [42]for he had an only daughter, about twelve years old, who was dying.

As he went, the crowds pressed in on him. [43]Now there was a woman who had been suffering from hemorrhages for twelve years; and though she had spent all she had on physicians,[p] no one could cure her. [44]She came up behind him and touched the fringe of his clothes, and immediately her hemorrhage stopped. [45]Then Jesus asked, "Who touched me?" When all denied it, Peter[q] said, "Master, the crowds surround you and press in on you." [46]But Jesus said, "Someone touched me; for I noticed that power had gone out from me." [47]When the woman saw that she could not remain hidden, she came trembling; and falling down before him, she declared in the presence of all the people why she had touched him, and how she had been immediately healed. [48]He said to her, "Daughter, your faith has made you well; go in peace."

[49] While he was still speaking, someone came from the leader's house to say, "Your daughter is dead; do not trouble the teacher any longer." [50]When Jesus heard this, he replied, "Do not fear. Only believe, and she will be saved." [51]When he came to the house, he did not allow anyone to enter with him, except Peter, John, and James, and the child's father and mother. [52]They were all weeping and wailing for her; but he said, "Do not weep; for she is not dead but sleeping." [53]And they laughed at him, knowing that she was dead. [54]But he took her by the hand and called out, "Child, get

Greek

φόβῳ μεγάλῳ συνείχοντο· αὐτὸς δὲ ἐμβὰς εἰς πλοῖον ὑπέστρεψεν. 38 ἐδεῖτο δὲ αὐτοῦ ὁ ἀνὴρ ἀφ' οὗ ἐξεληλύθει τὰ δαιμόνια εἶναι σὺν αὐτῷ· ἀπέλυσεν δὲ αὐτὸν λέγων, 39 Ὑπόστρεφε εἰς τὸν οἶκόν σου καὶ διηγοῦ ὅσα σοι ἐποίησεν ὁ θεός. καὶ ἀπῆλθεν καθ' ὅλην τὴν πόλιν κηρύσσων ὅσα ἐποίησεν αὐτῷ ὁ Ἰησοῦς.

40 Ἐν δὲ τῷ ὑποστρέφειν τὸν Ἰησοῦν ἀπεδέξατο αὐτὸν ὁ ὄχλος· ἦσαν γὰρ πάντες προσδοκῶντες αὐτόν. 41 καὶ ἰδοὺ ἦλθεν ἀνὴρ ᾧ ὄνομα Ἰάϊρος καὶ οὗτος ἄρχων τῆς συναγωγῆς ὑπῆρχεν, καὶ πεσὼν παρὰ τοὺς πόδας [τοῦ] Ἰησοῦ παρεκάλει αὐτὸν εἰσελθεῖν εἰς τὸν οἶκον αὐτοῦ, 42 ὅτι θυγάτηρ μονογενὴς ἦν αὐτῷ ὡς ἐτῶν δώδεκα καὶ αὐτὴ ἀπέθνησκεν.

Ἐν δὲ τῷ ὑπάγειν αὐτὸν οἱ ὄχλοι συνέπνιγον αὐτόν. 43 καὶ γυνὴ οὖσα ἐν ῥύσει αἵματος ἀπὸ ἐτῶν δώδεκα, ἥτις [ἰατροῖς προσαναλώσασα ὅλον τὸν βίον][d] οὐκ ἴσχυσεν ἀπ' οὐδενὸς θεραπευθῆναι, 44 προσελθοῦσα ὄπισθεν ἥψατο τοῦ κρασπέδου τοῦ ἱματίου αὐτοῦ καὶ παραχρῆμα ἔστη ἡ ῥύσις τοῦ αἵματος αὐτῆς. 45 καὶ εἶπεν ὁ Ἰησοῦς, Τίς ὁ ἁψάμενός μου; ἀρνουμένων δὲ πάντων εἶπεν ὁ Πέτρος[e], Ἐπιστάτα, οἱ ὄχλοι συνέχουσίν σε καὶ ἀποθλίβουσιν. 46 ὁ δὲ Ἰησοῦς εἶπεν, Ἥψατό μού τις, ἐγὼ γὰρ ἔγνων δύναμιν ἐξεληλυθυῖαν ἀπ' ἐμοῦ. 47 ἰδοῦσα δὲ ἡ γυνὴ ὅτι οὐκ ἔλαθεν, τρέμουσα ἦλθεν καὶ προσπεσοῦσα αὐτῷ δι' ἣν αἰτίαν ἥψατο αὐτοῦ ἀπήγγειλεν ἐνώπιον παντὸς τοῦ λαοῦ καὶ ὡς ἰάθη παραχρῆμα. 48 ὁ δὲ εἶπεν αὐτῇ, Θυγάτηρ, ἡ πίστις σου σέσωκέν σε· πορεύου εἰς εἰρήνην.

49 Ἔτι αὐτοῦ λαλοῦντος ἔρχεταί τις παρὰ τοῦ ἀρχισυναγώγου λέγων ὅτι Τέθνηκεν ἡ θυγάτηρ σου· μηκέτι σκύλλε τὸν διδάσκαλον. 50 ὁ δὲ Ἰησοῦς ἀκούσας ἀπεκρίθη αὐτῷ, Μὴ φοβοῦ, μόνον πίστευσον, καὶ σωθήσεται. 51 ἐλθὼν δὲ εἰς τὴν οἰκίαν οὐκ ἀφῆκεν εἰσελθεῖν τινα σὺν αὐτῷ εἰ μὴ Πέτρον καὶ Ἰωάννην καὶ Ἰάκωβον καὶ τὸν πατέρα τῆς παιδὸς καὶ τὴν μητέρα. 52 ἔκλαιον δὲ πάντες καὶ ἐκόπτοντο αὐτήν. ὁ δὲ εἶπεν, Μὴ κλαίετε, οὐ γὰρ ἀπέθανεν ἀλλὰ καθεύδει. 53 καὶ κατεγέλων αὐτοῦ εἰδότες ὅτι ἀπέθανεν. 54 αὐτὸς δὲ κρατήσας τῆς χειρὸς αὐτῆς ἐφώνησεν

NIV

Gerasenes asked Jesus to leave them, because they were overcome with fear. So he got into the boat and left.

[38]The man from whom the demons had gone out begged to go with him, but Jesus sent him away, saying, [39]"Return home and tell how much God has done for you." So the man went away and told all over town how much Jesus had done for him.

A Dead Girl and a Sick Woman

[40]Now when Jesus returned, a crowd welcomed him, for they were all expecting him. [41]Then a man named Jairus, a ruler of the synagogue, came and fell at Jesus' feet, pleading with him to come to his house [42]because his only daughter, a girl of about twelve, was dying.

As Jesus was on his way, the crowds almost crushed him. [43]And a woman was there who had been subject to bleeding for twelve years,[d] but no one could heal her. [44]She came up behind him and touched the edge of his cloak, and immediately her bleeding stopped.

[45]"Who touched me?" Jesus asked.

When they all denied it, Peter said, "Master, the people are crowding and pressing against you."

[46]But Jesus said, "Someone touched me; I know that power has gone out from me."

[47]Then the woman, seeing that she could not go unnoticed, came trembling and fell at his feet. In the presence of all the people, she told why she had touched him and how she had been instantly healed. [48]Then he said to her, "Daughter, your faith has healed you. Go in peace."

[49]While Jesus was still speaking, someone came from the house of Jairus, the synagogue ruler. "Your daughter is dead," he said. "Don't bother the teacher any more."

[50]Hearing this, Jesus said to Jairus, "Don't be afraid; just believe, and she will be healed."

[51]When he arrived at the house of Jairus, he did not let anyone go in with him except Peter, John and James, and the child's father and mother. [52]Meanwhile, all the people were wailing and mourning for her. "Stop wailing," Jesus said. "She is not dead but asleep."

[53]They laughed at him, knowing that she was dead. [54]But he took her by the hand

---

m Gk *he*   p Other ancient authorities lack *and had spent all she had on physicians*   q Other ancient authorities add *and those who were with him*

d43 NIV text and NRSV note p omit ἰατροῖς προσαναλώσασα ὅλον τὸν βίον; NIV note and NRSV text as UBS
e45 NRSV note q καὶ οἱ σὺν αὐτῷ

d43 Many manuscripts *years, and she had spent all she had on doctors*

up!" ⁵⁵Her spirit returned, and she got up at once. Then he directed them to give her something to eat. ⁵⁶Her parents were astounded; but he ordered them to tell no one what had happened.

The Mission of the Twelve

9 Then Jesusʳ called the twelve together and gave them power and authority over all demons and to cure diseases, ²and he sent them out to proclaim the kingdom of God and to heal. ³He said to them, "Take nothing for your journey, no staff, nor bag, nor bread, nor money—not even an extra tunic. ⁴Whatever house you enter, stay there, and leave from there. ⁵Wherever they do not welcome you, as you are leaving that town shake the dust off your feet as a testimony against them." ⁶They departed and went through the villages, bringing the good news and curing diseases everywhere.

Herod's Perplexity

7 Now Herod the rulerˢ heard about all that had taken place, and he was perplexed, because it was said by some that John had been raised from the dead, ⁸by some that Elijah had appeared, and by others that one of the ancient prophets had arisen. ⁹Herod said, "John I beheaded; but who is this about whom I hear such things?" And he tried to see him.

Feeding the Five Thousand

10 On their return the apostles told Jesusᵗ all they had done. He took them with him and withdrew privately to a city called Bethsaida. ¹¹When the crowds found out about it, they followed him; and he welcomed them, and spoke to them about the kingdom of God, and healed those who needed to be cured.

12 The day was drawing to a close, and the twelve came to him and said, "Send the crowd away, so that they may go into the surrounding villages and countryside, to lodge and get provisions; for we are here in a deserted place." ¹³But he said to them, "You give them something to eat." They said, "We have no more than five loaves and two fish—unless we are to go and buy food for all these people." ¹⁴For there were about five thousand men. And he said to his disciples, "Make them sit down in groups of about fifty each." ¹⁵They did so and made them all sit down. ¹⁶And taking the five loaves and the two fish, he

λέγων, Ἡ παῖς, ἔγειρε. 55 καὶ ἐπέστρεψεν τὸ πνεῦμα αὐτῆς καὶ ἀνέστη παραχρῆμα καὶ διέταξεν αὐτῇ δοθῆναι φαγεῖν. 56 καὶ ἐξέστησαν οἱ γονεῖς αὐτῆς· ὁ δὲ παρήγγειλεν αὐτοῖς μηδενὶ εἰπεῖν τὸ γεγονός.

9 Συγκαλεσάμενος δὲ τοὺς δώδεκα ἔδωκεν αὐτοῖς δύναμιν καὶ ἐξουσίαν ἐπὶ πάντα τὰ δαιμόνια καὶ νόσους θεραπεύειν 2 καὶ ἀπέστειλεν αὐτοὺς κηρύσσειν τὴν βασιλείαν τοῦ θεοῦ καὶ ἰᾶσθαι [τοὺς ἀσθενεῖς], 3 καὶ εἶπεν πρὸς αὐτούς, Μηδὲν αἴρετε εἰς τὴν ὁδόν, μήτε ῥάβδον μήτε πήραν μήτε ἄρτον μήτε ἀργύριον μήτε [ἀνὰ] δύο χιτῶνας ἔχειν. 4 καὶ εἰς ἣν ἂν οἰκίαν εἰσέλθητε, ἐκεῖ μένετε καὶ ἐκεῖθεν ἐξέρχεσθε. 5 καὶ ὅσοι ἂν μὴ δέχωνται ὑμᾶς, ἐξερχόμενοι ἀπὸ τῆς πόλεως ἐκείνης τὸν κονιορτὸν ἀπὸ τῶν ποδῶν ὑμῶν ἀποτινάσσετε εἰς μαρτύριον ἐπ' αὐτούς. 6 ἐξερχόμενοι δὲ διήρχοντο κατὰ τὰς κώμας εὐαγγελιζόμενοι καὶ θεραπεύοντες πανταχοῦ.

7 Ἤκουσεν δὲ Ἡρῴδης ὁ τετραάρχης τὰ γινόμενα πάντα καὶ διηπόρει διὰ τὸ λέγεσθαι ὑπό τινων ὅτι Ἰωάννης ἠγέρθη ἐκ νεκρῶν, 8 ὑπό τινων δὲ ὅτι Ἠλίας ἐφάνη, ἄλλων δὲ ὅτι προφήτης τις τῶν ἀρχαίων ἀνέστη. 9 εἶπεν δὲ Ἡρῴδης, Ἰωάννην ἐγὼ ἀπεκεφάλισα· τίς δέ ἐστιν οὗτος περὶ οὗ ἀκούω τοιαῦτα; καὶ ἐζήτει ἰδεῖν αὐτόν.

10 Καὶ ὑποστρέψαντες οἱ ἀπόστολοι διηγήσαντο αὐτῷ ὅσα ἐποίησαν. καὶ παραλαβὼν αὐτοὺς ὑπεχώρησεν κατ' ἰδίαν εἰς πόλιν καλουμένην Βηθσαϊδά. 11 οἱ δὲ ὄχλοι γνόντες ἠκολούθησαν αὐτῷ· καὶ ἀποδεξάμενος αὐτοὺς ἐλάλει αὐτοῖς περὶ τῆς βασιλείας τοῦ θεοῦ, καὶ τοὺς χρείαν ἔχοντας θεραπείας ἰᾶτο. 12 Ἡ δὲ ἡμέρα ἤρξατο κλίνειν· προσελθόντες δὲ οἱ δώδεκα εἶπαν αὐτῷ, Ἀπόλυσον τὸν ὄχλον, ἵνα πορευθέντες εἰς τὰς κύκλῳ κώμας καὶ ἀγροὺς καταλύσωσιν καὶ εὕρωσιν ἐπισιτισμόν, ὅτι ὧδε ἐν ἐρήμῳ τόπῳ ἐσμέν. 13 εἶπεν δὲ πρὸς αὐτούς, Δότε αὐτοῖς ὑμεῖς φαγεῖν. οἱ δὲ εἶπαν, Οὐκ εἰσὶν ἡμῖν πλεῖον ἢ ἄρτοι πέντε καὶ ἰχθύες δύο, εἰ μήτι πορευθέντες ἡμεῖς ἀγοράσωμεν εἰς πάντα τὸν λαὸν τοῦτον βρώματα. 14 ἦσαν γὰρ ὡσεὶ ἄνδρες πεντακισχίλιοι. εἶπεν δὲ πρὸς τοὺς μαθητὰς αὐτοῦ, Κατακλίνατε αὐτοὺς κλισίας [ὡσεὶ] ἀνὰ πεντήκοντα. 15 καὶ ἐποίησαν οὕτως καὶ κατέκλιναν ἅπαντας. 16 λαβὼν δὲ τοὺς πέντε ἄρτους καὶ τοὺς

and said, "My child, get up!" ⁵⁵Her spirit returned, and at once she stood up. Then Jesus told them to give her something to eat. ⁵⁶Her parents were astonished, but he ordered them not to tell anyone what had happened.

Jesus Sends Out the Twelve

9 When Jesus had called the Twelve together, he gave them power and authority to drive out all demons and to cure diseases, ²and he sent them out to preach the kingdom of God and to heal the sick. ³He told them: "Take nothing for the journey—no staff, no bag, no bread, no money, no extra tunic. ⁴Whatever house you enter, stay there until you leave that town. ⁵If people do not welcome you, shake the dust off your feet when you leave their town, as a testimony against them." ⁶So they set out and went from village to village, preaching the gospel and healing people everywhere.

⁷Now Herod the tetrarch heard about all that was going on. And he was perplexed, because some were saying that John had been raised from the dead, ⁸others that Elijah had appeared, and still others that one of the prophets of long ago had come back to life. ⁹But Herod said, "I beheaded John. Who, then, is this I hear such things about?" And he tried to see him.

Jesus Feeds the Five Thousand

¹⁰When the apostles returned, they reported to Jesus what they had done. Then he took them with him and they withdrew by themselves to a town called Bethsaida, ¹¹but the crowds learned about it and followed him. He welcomed them and spoke to them about the kingdom of God, and healed those who needed healing.

¹²Late in the afternoon the Twelve came to him and said, "Send the crowd away so they can go to the surrounding villages and countryside and find food and lodging, because we are in a remote place here."

¹³He replied, "You give them something to eat."

They answered, "We have only five loaves of bread and two fish—unless we go and buy food for all this crowd." ¹⁴(About five thousand men were there.)

But he said to his disciples, "Have them sit down in groups of about fifty each." ¹⁵The disciples did so, and everybody sat down. ¹⁶Taking the five loaves and the

---

ʳ Gk he ˢ Gk tetrarch ᵗ Gk him

NRSV

looked up to heaven, and blessed and broke them, and gave them to the disciples to set before the crowd. [17]And all ate and were filled. What was left over was gathered up, twelve baskets of broken pieces.

Peter's Declaration about Jesus

18 Once when Jesus[u] was praying alone, with only the disciples near him, he asked them, "Who do the crowds say that I am?" [19]They answered, "John the Baptist; but others, Elijah; and still others, that one of the ancient prophets has arisen." [20]He said to them, "But who do you say that I am?" Peter answered, "The Messiah[v] of God."

Jesus Foretells His Death and Resurrection

21 He sternly ordered and commanded them not to tell anyone, [22]saying, "The Son of Man must undergo great suffering, and be rejected by the elders, chief priests, and scribes, and be killed, and on the third day be raised."

23 Then he said to them all, "If any want to become my followers, let them deny themselves and take up their cross daily and follow me. [24]For those who want to save their life will lose it, and those who lose their life for my sake will save it. [25]What does it profit them if they gain the whole world, but lose or forfeit themselves? [26]Those who are ashamed of me and of my words, of them the Son of Man will be ashamed when he comes in his glory and the glory of the Father and of the holy angels. [27]But truly I tell you, there are some standing here who will not taste death before they see the kingdom of God."

The Transfiguration

28 Now about eight days after these sayings Jesus[u] took with him Peter and John and James, and went up on the mountain to pray. [29]And while he was praying, the appearance of his face changed, and his clothes became dazzling white. [30]Suddenly they saw two men, Moses and Elijah, talking to him. [31]They appeared in glory and were speaking of his departure, which he was about to accomplish at Jerusalem. [32]Now Peter and his companions were weighed down with sleep; but since they had stayed awake,[w] they saw his glory and the two men who stood with him. [33]Just as they were leaving him, Peter said

[u] Gk he   [v] Or The Christ   [w] Or but when they were fully awake

Greek

δύο ἰχθύας ἀναβλέψας εἰς τὸν οὐρανὸν εὐλόγησεν αὐτοὺς καὶ κατέκλασεν καὶ ἐδίδου τοῖς μαθηταῖς παραθεῖναι τῷ ὄχλῳ. 17 καὶ ἔφαγον καὶ ἐχορτάσθησαν πάντες, καὶ ἤρθη τὸ περισσεῦσαν αὐτοῖς κλασμάτων κόφινοι δώδεκα.

18 Καὶ ἐγένετο ἐν τῷ εἶναι αὐτὸν προσευχόμενον κατὰ μόνας συνῆσαν αὐτῷ οἱ μαθηταί, καὶ ἐπηρώτησεν αὐτοὺς λέγων, Τίνα με λέγουσιν οἱ ὄχλοι εἶναι; 19 οἱ δὲ ἀποκριθέντες εἶπαν, Ἰωάννην τὸν βαπτιστήν, ἄλλοι δὲ Ἡλίαν, ἄλλοι δὲ ὅτι προφήτης τις τῶν ἀρχαίων ἀνέστη. 20 εἶπεν δὲ αὐτοῖς, Ὑμεῖς δὲ τίνα με λέγετε εἶναι; Πέτρος δὲ ἀποκριθεὶς εἶπεν, Τὸν Χριστὸν τοῦ θεοῦ.

21 Ὁ δὲ ἐπιτιμήσας αὐτοῖς παρήγγειλεν μηδενὶ λέγειν τοῦτο 22 εἰπὼν ὅτι Δεῖ τὸν υἱὸν τοῦ ἀνθρώπου πολλὰ παθεῖν καὶ ἀποδοκιμασθῆναι ἀπὸ τῶν πρεσβυτέρων καὶ ἀρχιερέων καὶ γραμματέων καὶ ἀποκτανθῆναι καὶ τῇ τρίτῃ ἡμέρᾳ ἐγερθῆναι. 23 Ἔλεγεν δὲ πρὸς πάντας, Εἴ τις θέλει ὀπίσω μου ἔρχεσθαι, ἀρνησάσθω ἑαυτὸν καὶ ἀράτω τὸν σταυρὸν αὐτοῦ καθ᾽ ἡμέραν καὶ ἀκολουθείτω μοι. 24 ὃς γὰρ ἂν θέλῃ τὴν ψυχὴν αὐτοῦ σῶσαι ἀπολέσει αὐτήν· ὃς δ᾽ ἂν ἀπολέσῃ τὴν ψυχὴν αὐτοῦ ἕνεκεν ἐμοῦ οὗτος σώσει αὐτήν. 25 τί γὰρ ὠφελεῖται ἄνθρωπος κερδήσας τὸν κόσμον ὅλον ἑαυτὸν δὲ ἀπολέσας ἢ ζημιωθείς; 26 ὃς γὰρ ἂν ἐπαισχυνθῇ με καὶ τοὺς ἐμοὺς λόγους, τοῦτον ὁ υἱὸς τοῦ ἀνθρώπου ἐπαισχυνθήσεται, ὅταν ἔλθῃ ἐν τῇ δόξῃ αὐτοῦ καὶ τοῦ πατρὸς καὶ τῶν ἁγίων ἀγγέλων. 27 λέγω δὲ ὑμῖν ἀληθῶς, εἰσίν τινες τῶν αὐτοῦ ἑστηκότων οἳ οὐ μὴ γεύσωνται θανάτου ἕως ἂν ἴδωσιν τὴν βασιλείαν τοῦ θεοῦ.

28 Ἐγένετο δὲ μετὰ τοὺς λόγους τούτους ὡσεὶ ἡμέραι ὀκτὼ [καὶ] παραλαβὼν Πέτρον καὶ Ἰωάννην καὶ Ἰάκωβον ἀνέβη εἰς τὸ ὄρος προσεύξασθαι. 29 καὶ ἐγένετο ἐν τῷ προσεύχεσθαι αὐτὸν τὸ εἶδος τοῦ προσώπου αὐτοῦ ἕτερον καὶ ὁ ἱματισμὸς αὐτοῦ λευκὸς ἐξαστράπτων. 30 καὶ ἰδοὺ ἄνδρες δύο συνελάλουν αὐτῷ, οἵτινες ἦσαν Μωϋσῆς καὶ Ἡλίας, 31 οἳ ὀφθέντες ἐν δόξῃ ἔλεγον τὴν ἔξοδον αὐτοῦ, ἣν ἤμελλεν πληροῦν ἐν Ἰερουσαλήμ. 32 ὁ δὲ Πέτρος καὶ οἱ σὺν αὐτῷ ἦσαν βεβαρημένοι ὕπνῳ· διαγρηγορήσαντες δὲ εἶδον τὴν δόξαν αὐτοῦ καὶ τοὺς δύο ἄνδρας τοὺς συνεστῶτας αὐτῷ. 33 καὶ ἐγένετο ἐν τῷ διαχωρίζεσθαι αὐτοὺς ἀπ᾽ αὐτοῦ

NIV

two fish and looking up to heaven, he gave thanks and broke them. Then he gave them to the disciples to set before the people. [17]They all ate and were satisfied, and the disciples picked up twelve basketfuls of broken pieces that were left over.

Peter's Confession of Christ

[18]Once when Jesus was praying in private and his disciples were with him, he asked them, "Who do the crowds say I am?"

[19]They replied, "Some say John the Baptist; others say Elijah; and still others, that one of the prophets of long ago has come back to life."

[20]"But what about you?" he asked. "Who do you say I am?"

Peter answered, "The Christ[a] of God."

[21]Jesus strictly warned them not to tell this to anyone. [22]And he said, "The Son of Man must suffer many things and be rejected by the elders, chief priests and teachers of the law, and he must be killed and on the third day be raised to life."

[23]Then he said to them all: "If anyone would come after me, he must deny himself and take up his cross daily and follow me. [24]For whoever wants to save his life will lose it, but whoever loses his life for me will save it. [25]What good is it for a man to gain the whole world, and yet lose or forfeit his very self? [26]If anyone is ashamed of me and my words, the Son of Man will be ashamed of him when he comes in his glory and in the glory of the Father and of the holy angels. [27]I tell you the truth, some who are standing here will not taste death before they see the kingdom of God."

The Transfiguration

[28]About eight days after Jesus said this, he took Peter, John and James with him and went up onto a mountain to pray. [29]As he was praying, the appearance of his face changed, and his clothes became as bright as a flash of lightning. [30]Two men, Moses and Elijah, [31]appeared in glorious splendor, talking with Jesus. They spoke about his departure, which he was about to bring to fulfillment at Jerusalem. [32]Peter and his companions were very sleepy, but when they became fully awake, they saw his glory and the two men standing with him. [33]As the men were leaving Jesus, Peter

[a]20 Or Messiah

to Jesus, "Master, it is good for us to be here; let us make three dwellings,ˣ one for you, one for Moses, and one for Elijah"—not knowing what he said. 34While he was saying this, a cloud came and overshadowed them; and they were terrified as they entered the cloud. 35Then from the cloud came a voice that said, "This is my Son, my Chosen;ʸ listen to him!" 36When the voice had spoken, Jesus was found alone. And they kept silent and in those days told no one any of the things they had seen.

Jesus Heals a Boy with a Demon

37 On the next day, when they had come down from the mountain, a great crowd met him. 38Just then a man from the crowd shouted, "Teacher, I beg you to look at my son; he is my only child. 39Suddenly a spirit seizes him, and all at once heᶻ shrieks. It convulses him until he foams at the mouth; it mauls him and will scarcely leave him. 40I begged your disciples to cast it out, but they could not." 41Jesus answered, "You faithless and perverse generation, how much longer must I be with you and bear with you? Bring your son here." 42While he was coming, the demon dashed him to the ground in convulsions. But Jesus rebuked the unclean spirit, healed the boy, and gave him back to his father. 43And all were astounded at the greatness of God.

Jesus Again Foretells His Death

While everyone was amazed at all that he was doing, he said to his disciples, 44"Let these words sink into your ears: The Son of Man is going to be betrayed into human hands." 45But they did not understand this saying; its meaning was concealed from them, so that they could not perceive it. And they were afraid to ask him about this saying.

True Greatness

46 An argument arose among them as to which one of them was the greatest. 47But Jesus, aware of their inner thoughts, took a little child and put it by his side, 48and said to them, "Whoever welcomes this child in my name welcomes me, and whoever welcomes me welcomes the one who sent me;

εἶπεν ὁ Πέτρος πρὸς τὸν Ἰησοῦν, Ἐπιστάτα, καλόν ἐστιν ἡμᾶς ὧδε εἶναι, καὶ ποιήσωμεν σκηνὰς τρεῖς, μίαν σοὶ καὶ μίαν Μωϋσεῖ καὶ μίαν Ἠλίᾳ, μὴ εἰδὼς ὃ λέγει. 34 ταῦτα δὲ αὐτοῦ λέγοντος ἐγένετο νεφέλη καὶ ἐπεσκίαζεν αὐτούς· ἐφοβήθησαν δὲ ἐν τῷ εἰσελθεῖν αὐτοὺς εἰς τὴν νεφέλην. 35 καὶ φωνὴ ἐγένετο ἐκ τῆς νεφέλης λέγουσα, Οὗτός ἐστιν ὁ υἱός μου ὁ ἐκλελεγμένοςᵃ, αὐτοῦ ἀκούετε. 36 καὶ ἐν τῷ γενέσθαι τὴν φωνὴν εὑρέθη Ἰησοῦς μόνος. καὶ αὐτοὶ ἐσίγησαν καὶ οὐδενὶ ἀπήγγειλαν ἐν ἐκείναις ταῖς ἡμέραις οὐδὲν ὧν ἑώρακαν.

37 Ἐγένετο δὲ τῇ ἑξῆς ἡμέρᾳ κατελθόντων αὐτῶν ἀπὸ τοῦ ὄρους συνήντησεν αὐτῷ ὄχλος πολύς. 38 καὶ ἰδοὺ ἀνὴρ ἀπὸ τοῦ ὄχλου ἐβόησεν λέγων, Διδάσκαλε, δέομαί σου ἐπιβλέψαι ἐπὶ τὸν υἱόν μου, ὅτι μονογενής μοί ἐστιν, 39 καὶ ἰδοὺ πνεῦμα λαμβάνει αὐτὸν καὶ ἐξαίφνης κράζει καὶ σπαράσσει αὐτὸν μετὰ ἀφροῦ καὶ μόγις ἀποχωρεῖ ἀπ᾽ αὐτοῦ συντρῖβον αὐτόν· 40 καὶ ἐδεήθην τῶν μαθητῶν σου ἵνα ἐκβάλωσιν αὐτό, καὶ οὐκ ἠδυνήθησαν. 41 ἀποκριθεὶς δὲ ὁ Ἰησοῦς εἶπεν, Ὦ γενεὰ ἄπιστος καὶ διεστραμμένη, ἕως πότε ἔσομαι πρὸς ὑμᾶς καὶ ἀνέξομαι ὑμῶν; προσάγαγε ὧδε τὸν υἱόν σου. 42 ἔτι δὲ προσερχομένου αὐτοῦ ἔρρηξεν αὐτὸν τὸ δαιμόνιον καὶ συνεσπάραξεν· ἐπετίμησεν δὲ ὁ Ἰησοῦς τῷ πνεύματι τῷ ἀκαθάρτῳ καὶ ἰάσατο τὸν παῖδα καὶ ἀπέδωκεν αὐτὸν τῷ πατρὶ αὐτοῦ. 43 ἐξεπλήσσοντο δὲ πάντες ἐπὶ τῇ μεγαλειότητι τοῦ θεοῦ.

Πάντων δὲ θαυμαζόντων ἐπὶ πᾶσιν οἷς ἐποίει εἶπεν πρὸς τοὺς μαθητὰς αὐτοῦ, 44 Θέσθε ὑμεῖς εἰς τὰ ὦτα ὑμῶν τοὺς λόγους τούτους· ὁ γὰρ υἱὸς τοῦ ἀνθρώπου μέλλει παραδίδοσθαι εἰς χεῖρας ἀνθρώπων. 45 οἱ δὲ ἠγνόουν τὸ ῥῆμα τοῦτο καὶ ἦν παρακεκαλυμμένον ἀπ᾽ αὐτῶν ἵνα μὴ αἴσθωνται αὐτό, καὶ ἐφοβοῦντο ἐρωτῆσαι αὐτὸν περὶ τοῦ ῥήματος τούτου.

46 Εἰσῆλθεν δὲ διαλογισμὸς ἐν αὐτοῖς, τὸ τίς ἂν εἴη μείζων αὐτῶν. 47 ὁ δὲ Ἰησοῦς εἰδὼς τὸν διαλογισμὸν τῆς καρδίας αὐτῶν, ἐπιλαβόμενος παιδίον ἔστησεν αὐτὸ παρ᾽ ἑαυτῷ 48 καὶ εἶπεν αὐτοῖς, Ὃς ἐὰν δέξηται τοῦτο τὸ παιδίον ἐπὶ τῷ ὀνόματί μου, ἐμὲ δέχεται· καὶ ὃς ἂν ἐμὲ δέξηται, δέχεται τὸν ἀποστείλαντά με· ὁ γὰρ μικρότερος

said to him, "Master, it is good for us to be here. Let us put up three shelters—one for you, one for Moses and one for Elijah." (He did not know what he was saying.) 34While he was speaking, a cloud appeared and enveloped them, and they were afraid as they entered the cloud. 35A voice came from the cloud, saying, "This is my Son, whom I have chosen; listen to him." 36When the voice had spoken, they found that Jesus was alone. The disciples kept this to themselves, and told no one at that time what they had seen.

The Healing of a Boy With an Evil Spirit

37The next day, when they came down from the mountain, a large crowd met him. 38A man in the crowd called out, "Teacher, I beg you to look at my son, for he is my only child. 39A spirit seizes him and he suddenly screams; it throws him into convulsions so that he foams at the mouth. It scarcely ever leaves him and is destroying him. 40I begged your disciples to drive it out, but they could not."

41"O unbelieving and perverse generation," Jesus replied, "how long shall I stay with you and put up with you? Bring your son here."

42Even while the boy was coming, the demon threw him to the ground in a convulsion. But Jesus rebuked the evilᵇ spirit, healed the boy and gave him back to his father. 43And they were all amazed at the greatness of God.

While everyone was marveling at all that Jesus did, he said to his disciples, 44"Listen carefully to what I am about to tell you: The Son of Man is going to be betrayed into the hands of men." 45But they did not understand what this meant. It was hidden from them, so that they did not grasp it, and they were afraid to ask him about it.

Who Will Be the Greatest?

46An argument started among the disciples as to which of them would be the greatest. 47Jesus, knowing their thoughts, took a little child and had him stand beside him. 48Then he said to them, "Whoever welcomes this little child in my name welcomes me; and whoever welcomes me welcomes the one who sent me. For he

---

ˣ Or tents ʸ Other ancient authorities read my Beloved
ᶻ Or it

ᵃ35 NRSV note y ἀγαπητός

ᵇ42 Greek unclean

NRSV

for the least among all of you is the greatest."

Another Exorcist

49 John answered, "Master, we saw someone casting out demons in your name, and we tried to stop him, because he does not follow with us." 50But Jesus said to him, "Do not stop him; for whoever is not against you is for you."

A Samaritan Village Refuses to Receive Jesus

51 When the days drew near for him to be taken up, he set his face to go to Jerusalem. 52And he sent messengers ahead of him. On their way they entered a village of the Samaritans to make ready for him; 53but they did not receive him, because his face was set toward Jerusalem. 54When his disciples James and John saw it, they said, "Lord, do you want us to command fire to come down from heaven and consume them?"a 55But he turned and rebuked them. 56Thenb they went on to another village.

Would-Be Followers of Jesus

57 As they were going along the road, someone said to him, "I will follow you wherever you go." 58And Jesus said to him, "Foxes have holes, and birds of the air have nests; but the Son of Man has nowhere to lay his head." 59To another he said, "Follow me." But he said, "Lord, first let me go and bury my father." 60But Jesusc said to him, "Let the dead bury their own dead; but as for you, go and proclaim the kingdom of God." 61Another said, "I will follow you, Lord; but let me first say farewell to those at my home." 62Jesus said to him, "No one who puts a hand to the plow and looks back is fit for the kingdom of God."

The Mission of the Seventy

10 After this the Lord appointed seventyd others and sent them on ahead of him in pairs to every town and place where he himself intended to go. 2He said to them, "The harvest is plentiful, but the laborers are few; therefore ask the Lord of the harvest to send out laborers

(Greek)

ἐν πᾶσιν ὑμῖν ὑπάρχων οὗτός ἐστιν μέγας.

49 Ἀποκριθεὶς δὲ Ἰωάννης εἶπεν, Ἐπιστάτα, εἴδομέν τινα ἐν τῷ ὀνόματί σου ἐκβάλλοντα δαιμόνια καὶ ἐκωλύομεν αὐτόν, ὅτι οὐκ ἀκολουθεῖ μεθ' ἡμῶν. **50** εἶπεν δὲ πρὸς αὐτὸν ὁ Ἰησοῦς, Μὴ κωλύετε· ὃς γὰρ οὐκ ἔστιν καθ' ὑμῶν, ὑπὲρ ὑμῶν ἐστιν.

51 Ἐγένετο δὲ ἐν τῷ συμπληροῦσθαι τὰς ἡμέρας τῆς ἀναλήμψεως αὐτοῦ καὶ αὐτὸς τὸ πρόσωπον ἐστήρισεν τοῦ πορεύεσθαι εἰς Ἰερουσαλήμ. **52** καὶ ἀπέστειλεν ἀγγέλους πρὸ προσώπου αὐτοῦ. καὶ πορευθέντες εἰσῆλθον εἰς κώμην Σαμαριτῶν ὡς ἑτοιμάσαι αὐτῷ· **53** καὶ οὐκ ἐδέξαντο αὐτόν, ὅτι τὸ πρόσωπον αὐτοῦ ἦν πορευόμενον εἰς Ἰερουσαλήμ. **54** ἰδόντες δὲ οἱ μαθηταὶ Ἰάκωβος καὶ Ἰωάννης εἶπαν, Κύριε, θέλεις εἴπωμεν πῦρ καταβῆναι ἀπὸ τοῦ οὐρανοῦ καὶ ἀναλῶσαι αὐτούςb; **55** στραφεὶς δὲ ἐπετίμησεν αὐτοῖς.c **56** καὶ ἐπορεύθησαν εἰς ἑτέραν κώμην.

57 Καὶ πορευομένων αὐτῶν ἐν τῇ ὁδῷ εἶπέν τις πρὸς αὐτόν, Ἀκολουθήσω σοι ὅπου ἐὰν ἀπέρχῃ. **58** καὶ εἶπεν αὐτῷ ὁ Ἰησοῦς, Αἱ ἀλώπεκες φωλεοὺς ἔχουσιν καὶ τὰ πετεινὰ τοῦ οὐρανοῦ κατασκηνώσεις, ὁ δὲ υἱὸς τοῦ ἀνθρώπου οὐκ ἔχει ποῦ τὴν κεφαλὴν κλίνῃ. **59** Εἶπεν δὲ πρὸς ἕτερον, Ἀκολούθει μοι. ὁ δὲ εἶπεν, [Κύριε,] ἐπίτρεψόν μοι ἀπελθόντι πρῶτον θάψαι τὸν πατέρα μου. **60** εἶπεν δὲ αὐτῷ, Ἄφες τοὺς νεκροὺς θάψαι τοὺς ἑαυτῶν νεκρούς, σὺ δὲ ἀπελθὼν διάγγελλε τὴν βασιλείαν τοῦ θεοῦ. **61** Εἶπεν δὲ καὶ ἕτερος, Ἀκολουθήσω σοι, κύριε· πρῶτον δὲ ἐπίτρεψόν μοι ἀποτάξασθαι τοῖς εἰς τὸν οἶκόν μου. **62** εἶπεν δὲ [πρὸς αὐτὸν]d ὁ Ἰησοῦς, Οὐδεὶς ἐπιβαλὼν τὴν χεῖρα ἐπ' ἄροτρον καὶ βλέπων εἰς τὰ ὀπίσω εὐθετός ἐστιν τῇ βασιλείᾳ τοῦ θεοῦ.

10 Μετὰ δὲ ταῦτα ἀνέδειξεν ὁ κύριος ἑτέρους ἑβδομήκοντα [δύο]a, καὶ ἀπέστειλεν αὐτοὺς ἀνὰ δύο [δύο] πρὸ προσώπου αὐτοῦ εἰς πᾶσαν πόλιν καὶ τόπον οὗ ἤμελλεν αὐτὸς ἔρχεσθαι. **2** ἔλεγεν δὲ πρὸς αὐτούς, Ὁ μὲν θερισμὸς πολύς, οἱ δὲ ἐργάται ὀλίγοι· δεήθητε οὖν τοῦ κυρίου τοῦ θερισμοῦ ὅπως ἐργάτας ἐκβάλῃ

NIV

who is least among you all—he is the greatest."

49"Master," said John, "we saw a man driving out demons in your name and we tried to stop him, because he is not one of us."

50"Do not stop him," Jesus said, "for whoever is not against you is for you."

Samaritan Opposition

51As the time approached for him to be taken up to heaven, Jesus resolutely set out for Jerusalem. 52And he sent messengers on ahead, who went into a Samaritan village to get things ready for him; 53but the people there did not welcome him, because he was heading for Jerusalem. 54When the disciples James and John saw this, they asked, "Lord, do you want us to call fire down from heaven to destroy themc?" 55But Jesus turned and rebuked them, 56andd they went to another village.

The Cost of Following Jesus

57As they were walking along the road, a man said to him, "I will follow you wherever you go."

58Jesus replied, "Foxes have holes and birds of the air have nests, but the Son of Man has no place to lay his head."

59He said to another man, "Follow me."

But the man replied, "Lord, first let me go and bury my father."

60Jesus said to him, "Let the dead bury their own dead, but you go and proclaim the kingdom of God."

61Still another said, "I will follow you, Lord; but first let me go back and say goodby to my family."

62Jesus replied, "No one who puts his hand to the plow and looks back is fit for service in the kingdom of God."

Jesus Sends Out the Seventy-two

10 After this the Lord appointed seventy-twoa others and sent them two by two ahead of him to every town and place where he was about to go. 2He told them, "The harvest is plentiful, but the workers are few. Ask the Lord of the harvest, therefore, to send out workers into

---

a Other ancient authorities add as Elijah did   b Other ancient authorities read rebuked them, and said, "You do not know what spirit you are of, 56for the Son of Man has not come to destroy the lives of human beings but to save them." Then   c Gk he   d Other ancient authorities read seventy-two

b54 NIV/NRSV notes add ὡς καὶ Ἡλίας ἐποίησεν
c55 NIV/NRSV notes add καὶ εἶπεν, Οὐκ οἴδατε οἵου πνεύματός ἐστε ὑμεῖς. 56 ὁ γὰρ υἱὸς τοῦ ἀνθρώπου οὐκ ἦλθεν ψυχὰς ἀνθρώπων ἀπολέσαι ἀλλὰ σῶσαι. The NIV note locates the entire addition in verse 55.   d62 NIV text omits πρὸς αὐτόν   a1 NIV note and NRSV text omit δύο; NIV text and NRSV note d as UBS

c54 Some manuscripts them, even as Elijah did   d55,56 Some manuscripts them. And he said, "You do not know what kind of spirit you are of, for the Son of Man did not come to destroy men's lives, but to save them." 56And   a1 Some manuscripts seventy; also in verse 17

into his harvest. 3Go on your way. See, I am sending you out like lambs into the midst of wolves. 4Carry no purse, no bag, no sandals; and greet no one on the road. 5Whatever house you enter, first say, 'Peace to this house!' 6And if anyone is there who shares in peace, your peace will rest on that person; but if not, it will return to you. 7Remain in the same house, eating and drinking whatever they provide, for the laborer deserves to be paid. Do not move about from house to house. 8Whenever you enter a town and its people welcome you, eat what is set before you; 9cure the sick who are there, and say to them, 'The kingdom of God has come near to you.'e 10But whenever you enter a town and they do not welcome you, go out into its streets and say, 11'Even the dust of your town that clings to our feet, we wipe off in protest against you. Yet know this: the kingdom of God has come near.'f 12I tell you, on that day it will be more tolerable for Sodom than for that town.

Woes to Unrepentant Cities

13 "Woe to you, Chorazin! Woe to you, Bethsaida! For if the deeds of power done in you had been done in Tyre and Sidon, they would have repented long ago, sitting in sackcloth and ashes. 14But at the judgment it will be more tolerable for Tyre and Sidon than for you. 15And you, Capernaum,

will you be exalted to heaven?
No, you will be brought down to Hades.

16 "Whoever listens to you listens to me, and whoever rejects you rejects me, and whoever rejects me rejects the one who sent me."

The Return of the Seventy

17 The seventyg returned with joy, saying, "Lord, in your name even the demons submit to us!" 18He said to them, "I watched Satan fall from heaven like a flash of lightning. 19See, I have given you authority to tread on snakes and scorpions, and over all the power of the enemy; and nothing will hurt you. 20Nevertheless, do not rejoice at this, that the spirits submit to you, but rejoice that your names are written in heaven."

Jesus Rejoices

21 At that same hour Jesush rejoiced in

εἰς τὸν θερισμὸν αὐτοῦ. 3 ὑπάγετε· ἰδοὺ ἀποστέλλω ὑμᾶς ὡς ἄρνας ἐν μέσῳ λύκων. 4 μὴ βαστάζετε βαλλάντιον, μὴ πήραν, μὴ ὑποδήματα, καὶ μηδένα κατὰ τὴν ὁδὸν ἀσπάσησθε. 5 εἰς ἣν δ᾿ ἂν εἰσέλθητε οἰκίαν, πρῶτον λέγετε, Εἰρήνη τῷ οἴκῳ τούτῳ. 6 καὶ ἐὰν ἐκεῖ ᾖ υἱὸς εἰρήνης, ἐπαναπαήσεται ἐπ᾿ αὐτὸν ἡ εἰρήνη ὑμῶν· εἰ δὲ μή γε, ἐφ᾿ ὑμᾶς ἀνακάμψει. 7 ἐν αὐτῇ δὲ τῇ οἰκίᾳ μένετε ἐσθίοντες καὶ πίνοντες τὰ παρ᾿ αὐτῶν· ἄξιος γὰρ ὁ ἐργάτης τοῦ μισθοῦ αὐτοῦ. μὴ μεταβαίνετε ἐξ οἰκίας εἰς οἰκίαν. 8 καὶ εἰς ἣν ἂν πόλιν εἰσέρχησθε καὶ δέχωνται ὑμᾶς, ἐσθίετε τὰ παρατιθέμενα ὑμῖν 9 καὶ θεραπεύετε τοὺς ἐν αὐτῇ ἀσθενεῖς καὶ λέγετε αὐτοῖς, Ἤγγικεν ἐφ᾿ ὑμᾶς ἡ βασιλεία τοῦ θεοῦ. 10 εἰς ἣν δ᾿ ἂν πόλιν εἰσέλθητε καὶ μὴ δέχωνται ὑμᾶς, ἐξελθόντες εἰς τὰς πλατείας αὐτῆς εἴπατε, 11 Καὶ τὸν κονιορτὸν τὸν κολληθέντα ἡμῖν ἐκ τῆς πόλεως ὑμῶν εἰς τοὺς πόδας ἀπομασσόμεθα ὑμῖν· πλὴν τοῦτο γινώσκετε ὅτι ἤγγικεν ἡ βασιλεία τοῦ θεοῦ. 12 λέγω ὑμῖν ὅτι Σοδόμοις ἐν τῇ ἡμέρᾳ ἐκείνῃ ἀνεκτότερον ἔσται ἢ τῇ πόλει ἐκείνῃ.

13 Οὐαί σοι, Χοραζίν, οὐαί σοι, Βηθσαϊδά· ὅτι εἰ ἐν Τύρῳ καὶ Σιδῶνι ἐγενήθησαν αἱ δυνάμεις αἱ γενόμεναι ἐν ὑμῖν, πάλαι ἂν ἐν σάκκῳ καὶ σποδῷ καθήμενοι μετενόησαν. 14 πλὴν Τύρῳ καὶ Σιδῶνι ἀνεκτότερον ἔσται ἐν τῇ κρίσει ἢ ὑμῖν. 15 καὶ σύ, Καφαρναούμ, μὴ ἕως οὐρανοῦ ὑψωθήσῃ;
ἕως τοῦ ᾅδου καταβήσῃ.

16 Ὁ ἀκούων ὑμῶν ἐμοῦ ἀκούει, καὶ ὁ ἀθετῶν ὑμᾶς ἐμὲ ἀθετεῖ· ὁ δὲ ἐμὲ ἀθετῶν ἀθετεῖ τὸν ἀποστείλαντά με.

17 Ὑπέστρεψαν δὲ οἱ ἑβδομήκοντα [δύο]a μετὰ χαρᾶς λέγοντες, Κύριε, καὶ τὰ δαιμόνια ὑποτάσσεται ἡμῖν ἐν τῷ ὀνόματί σου. 18 εἶπεν δὲ αὐτοῖς, Ἐθεώρουν τὸν Σατανᾶν ὡς ἀστραπὴν ἐκ τοῦ οὐρανοῦ πεσόντα. 19 ἰδοὺ δέδωκα ὑμῖν τὴν ἐξουσίαν τοῦ πατεῖν ἐπάνω ὄφεων καὶ σκορπίων, καὶ ἐπὶ πᾶσαν τὴν δύναμιν τοῦ ἐχθροῦ, καὶ οὐδὲν ὑμᾶς οὐ μὴ ἀδικήσῃ. 20 πλὴν ἐν τούτῳ μὴ χαίρετε ὅτι τὰ πνεύματα ὑμῖν ὑποτάσσεται, χαίρετε δὲ ὅτι τὰ ὀνόματα ὑμῶν ἐγγέγραπται ἐν τοῖς οὐρανοῖς.

21 Ἐν αὐτῇ τῇ ὥρᾳ ἠγαλλιάσατο

his harvest field. 3Go! I am sending you out like lambs among wolves. 4 Do not take a purse or bag or sandals; and do not greet anyone on the road.

5"When you enter a house, first say, 'Peace to this house.' 6If a man of peace is there, your peace will rest on him; if not, it will return to you. 7Stay in that house, eating and drinking whatever they give you, for the worker deserves his wages. Do not move around from house to house.

8"When you enter a town and are welcomed, eat what is set before you. 9Heal the sick who are there and tell them, 'The kingdom of God is near you.' 10But when you enter a town and are not welcomed, go into its streets and say, 11'Even the dust of your town that sticks to our feet we wipe off against you. Yet be sure of this: The kingdom of God is near.' 12I tell you, it will be more bearable on that day for Sodom than for that town.

13"Woe to you, Korazin! Woe to you, Bethsaida! For if the miracles that were performed in you had been performed in Tyre and Sidon, they would have repented long ago, sitting in sackcloth and ashes. 14But it will be more bearable for Tyre and Sidon at the judgment than for you. 15And you, Capernaum, will you be lifted up to the skies? No, you will go down to the depths.b

16"He who listens to you listens to me; he who rejects you rejects me; but he who rejects me rejects him who sent me."

17The seventy-two returned with joy and said, "Lord, even the demons submit to us in your name."

18He replied, "I saw Satan fall like lightning from heaven. 19I have given you authority to trample on snakes and scorpions and to overcome all the power of the enemy; nothing will harm you. 20However, do not rejoice that the spirits submit to you, but rejoice that your names are written in heaven."

21At that time Jesus, full of joy through

---

e Or *is at hand for you* f Or *is at hand* g Other ancient authorities read *seventy-two* h Gk *he*

a17 NIV note (#1) and NRSV text omit δύο; NIV text and NRSV note g as UBS

b15 Greek *Hades*

NRSV

the Holy Spirit[i] and said, "I thank[j] you, Father, Lord of heaven and earth, because you have hidden these things from the wise and the intelligent and have revealed them to infants; yes, Father, for such was your gracious will.[k] 22All things have been handed over to me by my Father; and no one knows who the Son is except the Father, or who the Father is except the Son and anyone to whom the Son chooses to reveal him."

23 Then turning to the disciples, Jesus[h] said to them privately, "Blessed are the eyes that see what you see! 24For I tell you that many prophets and kings desired to see what you see, but did not see it, and to hear what you hear, but did not hear it."

The Parable of the Good Samaritan

25 Just then a lawyer stood up to test Jesus.[l] "Teacher," he said, "what must I do to inherit eternal life?" 26He said to him, "What is written in the law? What do you read there?" 27He answered, "You shall love the Lord your God with all your heart, and with all your soul, and with all your strength, and with all your mind; and your neighbor as yourself." 28And he said to him, "You have given the right answer; do this, and you will live."

29 But wanting to justify himself, he asked Jesus, "And who is my neighbor?" 30Jesus replied, "A man was going down from Jerusalem to Jericho, and fell into the hands of robbers, who stripped him, beat him, and went away, leaving him half dead. 31Now by chance a priest was going down that road; and when he saw him, he passed by on the other side. 32So likewise a Levite, when he came to the place and saw him, passed by on the other side. 33But a Samaritan while traveling came near him; and when he saw him, he was moved with pity. 34He went to him and bandaged his wounds, having poured oil and wine on them. Then he put him on his own animal, brought him to an inn, and took care of him. 35The next day he took out two denarii,[m] gave them to the innkeeper, and said, 'Take care of him; and when I come back, I will repay you whatever more you spend.' 36Which of these three, do you think, was a neighbor to the man who fell into the hands of the robbers?" 37He said, "The one who showed him mercy." Jesus

Greek

[ἐν] τῷ πνεύματι τῷ ἁγίῳ[b] καὶ εἶπεν, Ἐξομολογοῦμαί σοι, πάτερ, κύριε τοῦ οὐρανοῦ καὶ τῆς γῆς, ὅτι ἀπέκρυψας ταῦτα ἀπὸ σοφῶν καὶ συνετῶν καὶ ἀπεκάλυψας αὐτὰ νηπίοις· ναὶ ὁ πατήρ, ὅτι οὕτως εὐδοκία ἐγένετο ἔμπροσθέν σου. 22 Πάντα μοι παρεδόθη ὑπὸ τοῦ πατρός μου, καὶ οὐδεὶς γινώσκει τίς ἐστιν ὁ υἱὸς εἰ μὴ ὁ πατήρ, καὶ τίς ἐστιν ὁ πατὴρ εἰ μὴ ὁ υἱὸς καὶ ᾧ ἐὰν βούληται ὁ υἱὸς ἀποκαλύψαι. 23 Καὶ στραφεὶς πρὸς τοὺς μαθητὰς κατ᾽ ἰδίαν εἶπεν, Μακάριοι οἱ ὀφθαλμοὶ οἱ βλέποντες ἃ βλέπετε. 24 λέγω γὰρ ὑμῖν ὅτι πολλοὶ προφῆται καὶ βασιλεῖς ἠθέλησαν ἰδεῖν ἃ ὑμεῖς βλέπετε καὶ οὐκ εἶδαν, καὶ ἀκοῦσαι ἃ ἀκούετε καὶ οὐκ ἤκουσαν.

25 Καὶ ἰδοὺ νομικός τις ἀνέστη ἐκπειράζων αὐτὸν λέγων, Διδάσκαλε, τί ποιήσας ζωὴν αἰώνιον κληρονομήσω; 26 ὁ δὲ εἶπεν πρὸς αὐτόν, Ἐν τῷ νόμῳ τί γέγραπται; πῶς ἀναγινώσκεις; 27 ὁ δὲ ἀποκριθεὶς εἶπεν, Ἀγαπήσεις κύριον τὸν θεόν σου ἐξ ὅλης [τῆς] καρδίας σου καὶ ἐν ὅλη τῇ ψυχῇ σου καὶ ἐν ὅλῃ τῇ ἰσχύϊ σου καὶ ἐν ὅλῃ τῇ διανοίᾳ σου, καὶ τὸν πλησίον σου ὡς σεαυτόν. 28 εἶπεν δὲ αὐτῷ, Ὀρθῶς ἀπεκρίθης· τοῦτο ποίει καὶ ζήσῃ. 29 ὁ δὲ θέλων δικαιῶσαι ἑαυτὸν εἶπεν πρὸς τὸν Ἰησοῦν, Καὶ τίς ἐστίν μου πλησίον; 30 ὑπολαβὼν ὁ Ἰησοῦς εἶπεν, Ἄνθρωπός τις κατέβαινεν ἀπὸ Ἰερουσαλὴμ εἰς Ἰεριχὼ καὶ λῃσταῖς περιέπεσεν, οἳ καὶ ἐκδύσαντες αὐτὸν καὶ πληγὰς ἐπιθέντες ἀπῆλθον ἀφέντες ἡμιθανῆ. 31 κατὰ συγκυρίαν δὲ ἱερεύς τις κατέβαινεν ἐν τῇ ὁδῷ ἐκείνῃ καὶ ἰδὼν αὐτὸν ἀντιπαρῆλθεν· 32 ὁμοίως δὲ καὶ Λευίτης [γενόμενος] κατὰ τὸν τόπον ἐλθὼν καὶ ἰδὼν ἀντιπαρῆλθεν. 33 Σαμαρίτης δέ τις ὁδεύων ἦλθεν κατ᾽ αὐτὸν καὶ ἰδὼν ἐσπλαγχνίσθη, 34 καὶ προσελθὼν κατέδησεν τὰ τραύματα αὐτοῦ ἐπιχέων ἔλαιον καὶ οἶνον, ἐπιβιβάσας δὲ αὐτὸν ἐπὶ τὸ ἴδιον κτῆνος ἤγαγεν αὐτὸν εἰς πανδοχεῖον καὶ ἐπεμελήθη αὐτοῦ. 35 καὶ ἐπὶ τὴν αὔριον ἐκβαλὼν ἔδωκεν δύο δηνάρια τῷ πανδοχεῖ καὶ εἶπεν, Ἐπιμελήθητι αὐτοῦ, καὶ ὅ τι ἂν προσδαπανήσῃς ἐγὼ ἐν τῷ ἐπανέρχεσθαί με ἀποδώσω σοι. 36 τίς τούτων τῶν τριῶν πλησίον δοκεῖ σοι γεγονέναι τοῦ ἐμπεσόντος εἰς τοὺς λῃστάς; 37 ὁ δὲ εἶπεν, Ὁ ποιήσας τὸ ἔλεος μετ᾽

NIV

the Holy Spirit, said, "I praise you, Father, Lord of heaven and earth, because you have hidden these things from the wise and learned, and revealed them to little children. Yes, Father, for this was your good pleasure.

22"All things have been committed to me by my Father. No one knows who the Son is except the Father, and no one knows who the Father is except the Son and those to whom the Son chooses to reveal him."

23Then he turned to his disciples and said privately, "Blessed are the eyes that see what you see. 24For I tell you that many prophets and kings wanted to see what you see but did not see it, and to hear what you hear but did not hear it."

The Parable of the Good Samaritan

25On one occasion an expert in the law stood up to test Jesus. "Teacher," he asked, "what must I do to inherit eternal life?"

26"What is written in the Law?" he replied. "How do you read it?"

27He answered: " 'Love the Lord your God with all your heart and with all your soul and with all your strength and with all your mind'[c]; and, 'Love your neighbor as yourself.'[d]"

28"You have answered correctly," Jesus replied. "Do this and you will live."

29But he wanted to justify himself, so he asked Jesus, "And who is my neighbor?"

30In reply Jesus said: "A man was going down from Jerusalem to Jericho, when he fell into the hands of robbers. They stripped him of his clothes, beat him and went away, leaving him half dead. 31A priest happened to be going down the same road, and when he saw the man, he passed by on the other side. 32So too, a Levite, when he came to the place and saw him, passed by on the other side. 33But a Samaritan, as he traveled, came where the man was; and when he saw him, he took pity on him. 34He went to him and bandaged his wounds, pouring on oil and wine. Then he put the man on his own donkey, took him to an inn and took care of him. 35The next day he took out two silver coins[e] and gave them to the innkeeper. 'Look after him,' he said, 'and when I return, I will reimburse you for any extra expense you may have.'

36"Which of these three do you think was a neighbor to the man who fell into the hands of robbers?"

37The expert in the law replied, "The one who had mercy on him."

---

h Gk he   i Other authorities read in the spirit   j Or praise   k Or for so it was well-pleasing in your sight   l Gk him   m The denarius was the usual day's wage for a laborer

b21 NRSV note i omits τῷ ἁγίῳ

c27 Deut. 6:5   d27 Lev. 19:18   e35 Greek two denarii

said to him, "Go and do likewise."

Jesus Visits Martha and Mary

38 Now as they went on their way, he entered a certain village, where a woman named Martha welcomed him into her home. 39She had a sister named Mary, who sat at the Lord's feet and listened to what he was saying. 40But Martha was distracted by her many tasks; so she came to him and asked, "Lord, do you not care that my sister has left me to do all the work by myself? Tell her then to help me." 41But the Lord answered her, "Martha, Martha, you are worried and distracted by many things; 42there is need of only one thing.[n] Mary has chosen the better part, which will not be taken away from her."

The Lord's Prayer

11 He was praying in a certain place, and after he had finished, one of his disciples said to him, "Lord, teach us to pray, as John taught his disciples." 2He said to them, "When you pray, say:

Father,[o] hallowed be your name.
    Your kingdom come.[p]
3   Give us each day our daily bread.[q]
4   And forgive us our sins,
        for we ourselves forgive everyone
            indebted to us.
        And do not bring us to the time of
            trial."[r]

Perseverance in Prayer

5 And he said to them, "Suppose one of you has a friend, and you go to him at midnight and say to him, 'Friend, lend me three loaves of bread; 6for a friend of mine has arrived, and I have nothing to set before him.' 7And he answers from within, 'Do not bother me; the door has already been locked, and my children are with me in bed; I cannot get up and give you anything.' 8I tell you, even though he will not get up and give him anything because he is his friend, at least because of his persistence he will get up and give him whatever he needs.

9 "So I say to you, Ask, and it will be given you; search, and you will find; knock, and the door will be opened for you. 10For everyone who asks receives, and everyone

αὐτοῦ. εἶπεν δὲ αὐτῷ ὁ Ἰησοῦς, Πορεύου καὶ σὺ ποίει ὁμοίως.

38 Ἐν δὲ τῷ πορεύεσθαι αὐτοὺς αὐτὸς εἰσῆλθεν εἰς κώμην τινά· γυνὴ δέ τις ὀνόματι Μάρθα ὑπεδέξατο αὐτόν. **39** καὶ τῇδε ἦν ἀδελφὴ καλουμένη Μαριάμ, [ἣ] καὶ παρακαθεσθεῖσα πρὸς τοὺς πόδας τοῦ κυρίου ἤκουεν τὸν λόγον αὐτοῦ. **40** ἡ δὲ Μάρθα περιεσπᾶτο περὶ πολλὴν διακονίαν· ἐπιστᾶσα δὲ εἶπεν, Κύριε, οὐ μέλει σοι ὅτι ἡ ἀδελφή μου μόνην με κατέλιπεν διακονεῖν; εἰπὲ οὖν αὐτῇ ἵνα μοι συναντιλάβηται. **41** ἀποκριθεὶς δὲ εἶπεν αὐτῇ ὁ κύριος, Μάρθα Μάρθα, μεριμνᾷς καὶ θορυβάζῃ περὶ πολλά, **42** ἑνὸς δέ ἐστιν χρεία·[c] Μαριὰμ γὰρ τὴν ἀγαθὴν μερίδα ἐξελέξατο ἥτις οὐκ ἀφαιρεθήσεται αὐτῆς.

11 Καὶ ἐγένετο ἐν τῷ εἶναι αὐτὸν ἐν τόπῳ τινὶ προσευχόμενον, ὡς ἐπαύσατο, εἶπέν τις τῶν μαθητῶν αὐτοῦ πρὸς αὐτόν, Κύριε, δίδαξον ἡμᾶς προσεύχεσθαι, καθὼς καὶ Ἰωάννης ἐδίδαξεν τοὺς μαθητὰς αὐτοῦ. **2** εἶπεν δὲ αὐτοῖς, Ὅταν προσεύχησθε λέγετε, Πάτερ,[a] ἁγιασθήτω τὸ ὄνομά σου· ἐλθέτω ἡ βασιλεία σου·[b]
3   τὸν ἄρτον ἡμῶν τὸν ἐπιούσιον
            δίδου ἡμῖν τὸ καθ' ἡμέραν·
4   καὶ ἄφες ἡμῖν τὰς ἁμαρτίας ἡμῶν,
            καὶ γὰρ αὐτοὶ ἀφίομεν παντὶ
                ὀφείλοντι ἡμῖν·
            καὶ μὴ εἰσενέγκῃς ἡμᾶς εἰς
                πειρασμόν.[c]

5 Καὶ εἶπεν πρὸς αὐτούς, Τίς ἐξ ὑμῶν ἕξει φίλον καὶ πορεύσεται πρὸς αὐτὸν μεσονυκτίου καὶ εἴπῃ αὐτῷ, Φίλε, χρῆσόν μοι τρεῖς ἄρτους, **6** ἐπειδὴ φίλος μου παρεγένετο ἐξ ὁδοῦ πρός με καὶ οὐκ ἔχω ὃ παραθήσω αὐτῷ· **7** κἀκεῖνος ἔσωθεν ἀποκριθεὶς εἴπῃ, Μή μοι κόπους πάρεχε· ἤδη ἡ θύρα κέκλεισται καὶ τὰ παιδία μου μετ' ἐμοῦ εἰς τὴν κοίτην εἰσίν· οὐ δύναμαι ἀναστὰς δοῦναί σοι. **8** λέγω ὑμῖν, εἰ καὶ οὐ δώσει αὐτῷ ἀναστὰς διὰ τὸ εἶναι φίλον αὐτοῦ, διά γε τὴν ἀναίδειαν αὐτοῦ ἐγερθεὶς δώσει αὐτῷ ὅσων χρῄζει. **9** κἀγὼ ὑμῖν λέγω, αἰτεῖτε καὶ δοθήσεται ὑμῖν, ζητεῖτε καὶ εὑρήσετε, κρούετε καὶ ἀνοιγήσεται ὑμῖν· **10** πᾶς γὰρ ὁ αἰτῶν λαμβάνει καὶ ὁ ζητῶν εὑρίσκει

Jesus told him, "Go and do likewise."

At the Home of Martha and Mary

38As Jesus and his disciples were on their way, he came to a village where a woman named Martha opened her home to him. 39She had a sister called Mary, who sat at the Lord's feet listening to what he said. 40But Martha was distracted by all the preparations that had to be made. She came to him and asked, "Lord, don't you care that my sister has left me to do the work by myself? Tell her to help me!"

41"Martha, Martha," the Lord answered, "you are worried and upset about many things, 42but only one thing is needed.[f] Mary has chosen what is better, and it will not be taken away from her."

Jesus' Teaching on Prayer

11 One day Jesus was praying in a certain place. When he finished, one of his disciples said to him, "Lord, teach us to pray, just as John taught his disciples."

2He said to them, "When you pray, say:

" 'Father,[a]
hallowed be your name,
your kingdom come.[b]
3Give us each day our daily bread.
4Forgive us our sins,
    for we also forgive everyone who sins
        against us.[c]
And lead us not into temptation.[d]' "

5Then he said to them, "Suppose one of you has a friend, and he goes to him at midnight and says, 'Friend, lend me three loaves of bread, 6because a friend of mine on a journey has come to me, and I have nothing to set before him.'

7"Then the one inside answers, 'Don't bother me. The door is already locked, and my children are with me in bed. I can't get up and give you anything.' 8I tell you, though he will not get up and give him the bread because he is his friend, yet because of the man's boldness[e] he will get up and give him as much as he needs.

9"So I say to you: Ask and it will be given to you; seek and you will find; knock and the door will be opened to you. 10For everyone who asks receives; he who seeks finds;

---

[n] Other ancient authorities read *few things are necessary, or only one*   [o] Other ancient authorities read *Our Father in heaven*   [p] A few ancient authorities read *Your Holy Spirit come upon us and cleanse us.* Other ancient authorities add *Your will be done, on earth as in heaven*   [q] Or *our bread for tomorrow*   [r] Or *us into temptation.* Other ancient authorities add *but rescue us from the evil one (or from evil)*

[c]42 NIV/NRSV notes ὀλίγων δέ ἐστιν χρεία ἢ ἑνός   [a]2 NIV/NRSV notes add ἡμῶν ὁ ἐν τοῖς οὐρανοῖς   [b]2 NRSV note p adds ἐλθέτω τὸ πνεῦμά σου τὸ ἅγιον ἐφ' ἡμᾶς καὶ καθαρισάτω ἡμᾶς; NIV/NRSV notes add γενηθήτω τὸ θέλημά σου ὡς ἐν οὐρανῷ καὶ ἐπὶ [τῆς] γῆς   [c]4 NIV/NRSV notes add ἀλλὰ ῥῦσαι ἡμᾶς ἀπὸ τοῦ πονηροῦ

[f]42 Some manuscripts *but few things are needed—or only one*   [a]2 Some manuscripts *Our Father in heaven*   [b]2 Some manuscripts *come. May your will be done on earth as it is in heaven.*   [c]4 Greek *everyone who is indebted to us*   [d]4 Some manuscripts *temptation but deliver us from the evil one*   [e]8 Or *persistence*

who searches finds, and for everyone who knocks, the door will be opened. [11]Is there anyone among you who, if your child asks for[s] a fish, will give a snake instead of a fish? [12]Or if the child asks for an egg, will give a scorpion? [13]If you then, who are evil, know how to give good gifts to your children, how much more will the heavenly Father give the Holy Spirit[t] to those who ask him!"

Jesus and Beelzebul

14 Now he was casting out a demon that was mute; when the demon had gone out, the one who had been mute spoke, and the crowds were amazed. [15]But some of them said, "He casts out demons by Beelzebul, the ruler of the demons." [16]Others, to test him, kept demanding from him a sign from heaven. [17]But he knew what they were thinking and said to them, "Every kingdom divided against itself becomes a desert, and house falls on house. [18]If Satan also is divided against himself, how will his kingdom stand? —for you say that I cast out the demons by Beelzebul. [19]Now if I cast out the demons by Beelzebul, by whom do your exorcists[u] cast them out? Therefore they will be your judges. [20]But if it is by the finger of God that I cast out the demons, then the kingdom of God has come to you. [21]When a strong man, fully armed, guards his castle, his property is safe. [22]But when one stronger than he attacks him and overpowers him, he takes away his armor in which he trusted and divides his plunder. [23]Whoever is not with me is against me, and whoever does not gather with me scatters.

The Return of the Unclean Spirit

24 "When the unclean spirit has gone out of a person, it wanders through waterless regions looking for a resting place, but not finding any, it says, 'I will return to my house from which I came.' [25]When it comes, it finds it swept and put in order. [26]Then it goes and brings seven other spirits more evil than itself, and they enter and live there; and the last state of that person is worse than the first."

True Blessedness

27 While he was saying this, a woman in the crowd raised her voice and said to him, "Blessed is the womb that bore you and the breasts that nursed you!" [28]But he

καὶ τῷ κρούοντι ἀνοιγ[ήσ]εται. **11** τίνα δὲ ἐξ ὑμῶν τὸν πατέρα αἰτήσει ὁ υἱός[d] ἰχθύν, καὶ ἀντὶ ἰχθύος ὄφιν αὐτῷ ἐπιδώσει; **12** ἢ καὶ αἰτήσει ᾠόν, ἐπιδώσει αὐτῷ σκορπίον; **13** εἰ οὖν ὑμεῖς πονηροὶ ὑπάρχοντες οἴδατε δόματα ἀγαθὰ διδόναι τοῖς τέκνοις ὑμῶν, πόσῳ μᾶλλον ὁ πατὴρ [ὁ][e] ἐξ οὐρανοῦ δώσει πνεῦμα ἅγιον τοῖς αἰτοῦσιν αὐτόν.

14 Καὶ ἦν ἐκβάλλων δαιμόνιον [καὶ αὐτὸ ἦν] κωφόν· ἐγένετο δὲ τοῦ δαιμονίου ἐξελθόντος ἐλάλησεν ὁ κωφὸς καὶ ἐθαύμασαν οἱ ὄχλοι. **15** τινὲς δὲ ἐξ αὐτῶν εἶπον, Ἐν Βεελζεβοὺλ τῷ ἄρχοντι τῶν δαιμονίων ἐκβάλλει τὰ δαιμόνια· **16** ἕτεροι δὲ πειράζοντες σημεῖον ἐξ οὐρανοῦ ἐζήτουν παρ᾽ αὐτοῦ. **17** αὐτὸς δὲ εἰδὼς αὐτῶν τὰ διανοήματα εἶπεν αὐτοῖς, Πᾶσα βασιλεία ἐφ᾽ ἑαυτὴν διαμερισθεῖσα ἐρημοῦται καὶ οἶκος ἐπὶ οἶκον πίπτει. **18** εἰ δὲ καὶ ὁ Σατανᾶς ἐφ᾽ ἑαυτὸν διεμερίσθη, πῶς σταθήσεται ἡ βασιλεία αὐτοῦ; ὅτι λέγετε ἐν Βεελζεβοὺλ[f] ἐκβάλλειν με τὰ δαιμόνια. **19** εἰ δὲ ἐγὼ ἐν Βεελζεβοὺλ[f] ἐκβάλλω τὰ δαιμόνια, οἱ υἱοὶ ὑμῶν ἐν τίνι ἐκβάλλουσιν; διὰ τοῦτο αὐτοὶ ὑμῶν κριταὶ ἔσονται. **20** εἰ δὲ ἐν δακτύλῳ θεοῦ [ἐγὼ] ἐκβάλλω τὰ δαιμόνια, ἄρα ἔφθασεν ἐφ᾽ ὑμᾶς ἡ βασιλεία τοῦ θεοῦ. **21** ὅταν ὁ ἰσχυρὸς καθωπλισμένος φυλάσσῃ τὴν ἑαυτοῦ αὐλήν, ἐν εἰρήνῃ ἐστὶν τὰ ὑπάρχοντα αὐτοῦ· **22** ἐπὰν δὲ ἰσχυρότερος αὐτοῦ[g] ἐπελθὼν νικήσῃ αὐτόν, τὴν πανοπλίαν αὐτοῦ αἴρει ἐφ᾽ ᾗ ἐπεποίθει καὶ τὰ σκῦλα αὐτοῦ διαδίδωσιν. **23** ὁ μὴ ὢν μετ᾽ ἐμοῦ κατ᾽ ἐμοῦ ἐστιν, καὶ ὁ μὴ συνάγων μετ᾽ ἐμοῦ σκορπίζει.

24 Ὅταν τὸ ἀκάθαρτον πνεῦμα ἐξέλθῃ ἀπὸ τοῦ ἀνθρώπου, διέρχεται δι᾽ ἀνύδρων τόπων ζητοῦν ἀνάπαυσιν καὶ μὴ εὑρίσκον [τότε] λέγει, Ὑποστρέψω εἰς τὸν οἶκόν μου ὅθεν ἐξῆλθον· **25** καὶ ἐλθὸν εὑρίσκει σεσαρωμένον καὶ κεκοσμημένον. **26** τότε πορεύεται καὶ παραλαμβάνει ἕτερα πνεύματα πονηρότερα ἑαυτοῦ ἑπτὰ καὶ εἰσελθόντα κατοικεῖ ἐκεῖ· καὶ γίνεται τὰ ἔσχατα τοῦ ἀνθρώπου ἐκείνου χείρονα τῶν πρώτων. **27** Ἐγένετο δὲ ἐν τῷ λέγειν αὐτὸν ταῦτα ἐπάρασά τις φωνὴν γυνὴ ἐκ τοῦ ὄχλου εἶπεν αὐτῷ, Μακαρία ἡ κοιλία ἡ βαστάσασά σε καὶ μαστοὶ οὓς ἐθήλασας. **28** αὐτὸς δὲ εἶπεν, Μενοῦν

and to him who knocks, the door will be opened.

[11]"Which of you fathers, if your son asks for[f] a fish, will give him a snake instead? [12]Or if he asks for an egg, will give him a scorpion? [13]If you then, though you are evil, know how to give good gifts to your children, how much more will your Father in heaven give the Holy Spirit to those who ask him!"

Jesus and Beelzebub

[14]Jesus was driving out a demon that was mute. When the demon left, the man who had been mute spoke, and the crowd was amazed. [15]But some of them said, "By Beelzebub,[g] the prince of demons, he is driving out demons." [16]Others tested him by asking for a sign from heaven.

[17]Jesus knew their thoughts and said to them: "Any kingdom divided against itself will be ruined, and a house divided against itself will fall. [18]If Satan is divided against himself, how can his kingdom stand? I say this because you claim that I drive out demons by Beelzebub. [19]Now if I drive out demons by Beelzebub, by whom do your followers drive them out? So then, they will be your judges. [20]But if I drive out demons by the finger of God, then the kingdom of God has come to you.

[21]"When a strong man, fully armed, guards his own house, his possessions are safe. [22]But when someone stronger attacks and overpowers him, he takes away the armor in which the man trusted and divides up the spoils.

[23]"He who is not with me is against me, and he who does not gather with me, scatters.

[24]"When an evil[h] spirit comes out of a man, it goes through arid places seeking rest and does not find it. Then it says, 'I will return to the house I left.' [25]When it arrives, it finds the house swept clean and put in order. [26]Then it goes and takes seven other spirits more wicked than itself, and they go in and live there. And the final condition of that man is worse than the first."

[27]As Jesus was saying these things, a woman in the crowd called out, "Blessed is the mother who gave you birth and nursed you."

[28]He replied, "Blessed rather are those

---

[s] Other ancient authorities add *bread, will give a stone; or if your child asks for*   [t] Other ancient authorities read *the Father give the Holy Spirit from heaven*   [u] Gk *sons*

[d] 11 NIV/NRSV notes add ἄρτον μὴ λίθον ἐπιδώσει αὐτῷ; ἢ καὶ   [e] 13 NRSV note t omits ὁ   [f] 15,18,19 NIV note Βεεζεβούλ †   [g] 22 NIV text omits αὐτοῦ †

[f] 11 Some manuscripts *for bread, will give him a stone; or if he asks for*   [g] 15 Greek *Beezeboul* or *Beelzeboul*; also in verses 18 and 19   [h] 24 Greek *unclean*

said, "Blessed rather are those who hear the word of God and obey it!"

The Sign of Jonah

29 When the crowds were increasing, he began to say, "This generation is an evil generation; it asks for a sign, but no sign will be given to it except the sign of Jonah. [30]For just as Jonah became a sign to the people of Nineveh, so the Son of Man will be to this generation. [31]The queen of the South will rise at the judgment with the people of this generation and condemn them, because she came from the ends of the earth to listen to the wisdom of Solomon, and see, something greater than Solomon is here! [32]The people of Nineveh will rise up at the judgment with this generation and condemn it, because they repented at the proclamation of Jonah, and see, something greater than Jonah is here!

The Light of the Body

33 "No one after lighting a lamp puts it in a cellar,[v] but on the lampstand so that those who enter may see the light. [34]Your eye is the lamp of your body. If your eye is healthy, your whole body is full of light; but if it is not healthy, your body is full of darkness. [35]Therefore consider whether the light in you is not darkness. [36]If then your whole body is full of light, with no part of it in darkness, it will be as full of light as when a lamp gives you light with its rays."

Jesus Denounces Pharisees and Lawyers

37 While he was speaking, a Pharisee invited him to dine with him; so he went in and took his place at the table. [38]The Pharisee was amazed to see that he did not first wash before dinner. [39]Then the Lord said to him, "Now you Pharisees clean the outside of the cup and of the dish, but inside you are full of greed and wickedness. [40]You fools! Did not the one who made the outside make the inside also? [41]So give for alms those things that are within; and see, everything will be clean for you.

42 "But woe to you Pharisees! For you tithe mint and rue and herbs of all kinds, and neglect justice and the love of God; it is these you ought to have practiced, without neglecting the others. [43]Woe to you Pharisees! For you love to have the seat of honor in the synagogues and to be greeted with respect in the marketplaces. [44]Woe to

---

μακάριοι οἱ ἀκούοντες τὸν λόγον τοῦ θεοῦ καὶ φυλάσσοντες.

29 Τῶν δὲ ὄχλων ἐπαθροιζομένων ἤρξατο λέγειν, Ἡ γενεὰ αὕτη γενεὰ πονηρά ἐστιν· σημεῖον ζητεῖ, καὶ σημεῖον οὐ δοθήσεται αὐτῇ εἰ μὴ τὸ σημεῖον Ἰωνᾶ. **30** καθὼς γὰρ ἐγένετο Ἰωνᾶς τοῖς Νινευίταις σημεῖον, οὕτως ἔσται καὶ ὁ υἱὸς τοῦ ἀνθρώπου τῇ γενεᾷ ταύτῃ. **31** βασίλισσα νότου ἐγερθήσεται ἐν τῇ κρίσει μετὰ τῶν ἀνδρῶν τῆς γενεᾶς ταύτης καὶ κατακρινεῖ αὐτούς, ὅτι ἦλθεν ἐκ τῶν περάτων τῆς γῆς ἀκοῦσαι τὴν σοφίαν Σολομῶνος, καὶ ἰδοὺ πλεῖον Σολομῶνος ὧδε. **32** ἄνδρες Νινευῖται ἀναστήσονται ἐν τῇ κρίσει μετὰ τῆς γενεᾶς ταύτης καὶ κατακρινοῦσιν αὐτήν· ὅτι μετενόησαν εἰς τὸ κήρυγμα Ἰωνᾶ, καὶ ἰδοὺ πλεῖον Ἰωνᾶ ὧδε.

33 Οὐδεὶς λύχνον ἅψας εἰς κρύπτην τίθησιν [οὐδὲ ὑπὸ τὸν μόδιον][h] ἀλλ᾽ ἐπὶ τὴν λυχνίαν, ἵνα οἱ εἰσπορευόμενοι τὸ φῶς βλέπωσιν. **34** ὁ λύχνος τοῦ σώματός ἐστιν ὁ ὀφθαλμός σου. ὅταν ὁ ὀφθαλμός σου ἁπλοῦς ᾖ, καὶ ὅλον τὸ σῶμά σου φωτεινόν ἐστιν· ἐπὰν δὲ πονηρὸς ᾖ, καὶ τὸ σῶμά σου σκοτεινόν. **35** σκόπει οὖν μὴ τὸ φῶς τὸ ἐν σοὶ σκότος ἐστίν. **36** εἰ οὖν τὸ σῶμά σου ὅλον φωτεινόν, μὴ ἔχον μέρος τι σκοτεινόν, ἔσται φωτεινὸν ὅλον ὡς ὅταν ὁ λύχνος τῇ ἀστραπῇ φωτίζῃ σε.

37 Ἐν δὲ τῷ λαλῆσαι ἐρωτᾷ αὐτὸν Φαρισαῖος ὅπως ἀριστήσῃ παρ᾽ αὐτῷ· εἰσελθὼν δὲ ἀνέπεσεν. **38** ὁ δὲ Φαρισαῖος ἰδὼν ἐθαύμασεν ὅτι οὐ πρῶτον ἐβαπτίσθη πρὸ τοῦ ἀρίστου. **39** εἶπεν δὲ ὁ κύριος πρὸς αὐτόν, Νῦν ὑμεῖς οἱ Φαρισαῖοι τὸ ἔξωθεν τοῦ ποτηρίου καὶ τοῦ πίνακος καθαρίζετε, τὸ δὲ ἔσωθεν ὑμῶν γέμει ἁρπαγῆς καὶ πονηρίας. **40** ἄφρονες, οὐχ ὁ ποιήσας τὸ ἔξωθεν καὶ τὸ ἔσωθεν ἐποίησεν; **41** πλὴν τὰ ἐνόντα δότε ἐλεημοσύνην, καὶ ἰδοὺ πάντα καθαρὰ ὑμῖν ἐστιν. **42** ἀλλὰ οὐαὶ ὑμῖν τοῖς Φαρισαίοις, ὅτι ἀποδεκατοῦτε τὸ ἡδύοσμον καὶ τὸ πήγανον καὶ πᾶν λάχανον καὶ παρέρχεσθε τὴν κρίσιν καὶ τὴν ἀγάπην τοῦ θεοῦ· ταῦτα δὲ ἔδει ποιῆσαι κἀκεῖνα μὴ παρεῖναι. **43** οὐαὶ ὑμῖν τοῖς Φαρισαίοις, ὅτι ἀγαπᾶτε τὴν πρωτοκαθεδρίαν ἐν ταῖς συναγωγαῖς καὶ τοὺς ἀσπασμοὺς ἐν ταῖς ἀγοραῖς. **44** οὐαὶ ὑμῖν, ὅτι ἐστὲ

---

who hear the word of God and obey it."

The Sign of Jonah

[29]As the crowds increased, Jesus said, "This is a wicked generation. It asks for a miraculous sign, but none will be given it except the sign of Jonah. [30]For as Jonah was a sign to the Ninevites, so also will the Son of Man be to this generation. [31]The Queen of the South will rise at the judgment with the men of this generation and condemn them; for she came from the ends of the earth to listen to Solomon's wisdom, and now one[i] greater than Solomon is here. [32]The men of Nineveh will stand up at the judgment with this generation and condemn it; for they repented at the preaching of Jonah, and now one greater than Jonah is here.

The Lamp of the Body

[33]"No one lights a lamp and puts it in a place where it will be hidden, or under a bowl. Instead he puts it on its stand, so that those who come in may see the light. [34]Your eye is the lamp of your body. When your eyes are good, your whole body also is full of light. But when they are bad, your body also is full of darkness. [35]See to it, then, that the light within you is not darkness. [36]Therefore, if your whole body is full of light, and no part of it dark, it will be completely lighted, as when the light of a lamp shines on you."

Six Woes

[37]When Jesus had finished speaking, a Pharisee invited him to eat with him; so he went in and reclined at the table. [38]But the Pharisee, noticing that Jesus did not first wash before the meal, was surprised. [39]Then the Lord said to him, "Now then, you Pharisees clean the outside of the cup and dish, but inside you are full of greed and wickedness. [40]You foolish people! Did not the one who made the outside make the inside also? [41]But give what is inside the dish[j] to the poor, and everything will be clean for you.

[42]"Woe to you Pharisees, because you give God a tenth of your mint, rue and all other kinds of garden herbs, but you neglect justice and the love of God. You should have practiced the latter without leaving the former undone.

[43]"Woe to you Pharisees, because you love the most important seats in the synagogues and greetings in the marketplaces.

---

[h]33 NRSV text omits οὐδὲ ὑπὸ τὸν μόδιον; NIV text and NRSV note v as UBS

[i]31 Or *something*; also in verse 32   [j]41 Or *what you have*

you! For you are like unmarked graves, and people walk over them without realizing it."

45 One of the lawyers answered him, "Teacher, when you say these things, you insult us too." 46And he said, "Woe also to you lawyers! For you load people with burdens hard to bear, and you yourselves do not lift a finger to ease them. 47Woe to you! For you build the tombs of the prophets whom your ancestors killed. 48So you are witnesses and approve of the deeds of your ancestors; for they killed them, and you build their tombs. 49Therefore also the Wisdom of God said, 'I will send them prophets and apostles, some of whom they will kill and persecute,' 50so that this generation may be charged with the blood of all the prophets shed since the foundation of the world, 51from the blood of Abel to the blood of Zechariah, who perished between the altar and the sanctuary. Yes, I tell you, it will be charged against this generation. 52Woe to you lawyers! For you have taken away the key of knowledge; you did not enter yourselves, and you hindered those who were entering."

53 When he went outside, the scribes and the Pharisees began to be very hostile toward him and to cross-examine him about many things, 54lying in wait for him, to catch him in something he might say.

A Warning against Hypocrisy

12 Meanwhile, when the crowd gathered by the thousands, so that they trampled on one another, he began to speak first to his disciples, "Beware of the yeast of the Pharisees, that is, their hypocrisy. 2Nothing is covered up that will not be uncovered, and nothing secret that will not become known. 3Therefore whatever you have said in the dark will be heard in the light, and what you have whispered behind closed doors will be proclaimed from the housetops.

Exhortation to Fearless Confession

4 "I tell you, my friends, do not fear those who kill the body, and after that can do nothing more. 5But I will warn you whom to fear: fear him who, after he has killed, has authority[w] to cast into hell.[x] Yes, I tell you, fear him! 6Are not five

ὡς τὰ μνημεῖα τὰ ἄδηλα, καὶ οἱ ἄνθρωποι [οἱ] περιπατοῦντες ἐπάνω οὐκ οἴδασιν.

45 Ἀποκριθεὶς δέ τις τῶν νομικῶν λέγει αὐτῷ, Διδάσκαλε, ταῦτα λέγων καὶ ἡμᾶς ὑβρίζεις. 46 ὁ δὲ εἶπεν, Καὶ ὑμῖν τοῖς νομικοῖς οὐαί, ὅτι φορτίζετε τοὺς ἀνθρώπους φορτία δυσβάστακτα, καὶ αὐτοὶ ἑνὶ τῶν δακτύλων ὑμῶν οὐ προσψαύετε τοῖς φορτίοις. 47 οὐαὶ ὑμῖν, ὅτι οἰκοδομεῖτε τὰ μνημεῖα τῶν προφητῶν, οἱ δὲ πατέρες ὑμῶν ἀπέκτειναν αὐτούς. 48 ἄρα μάρτυρές ἐστε καὶ συνευδοκεῖτε τοῖς ἔργοις τῶν πατέρων ὑμῶν, ὅτι αὐτοὶ μὲν ἀπέκτειναν αὐτούς, ὑμεῖς δὲ οἰκοδομεῖτε. 49 διὰ τοῦτο καὶ ἡ σοφία τοῦ θεοῦ εἶπεν, Ἀποστελῶ εἰς αὐτοὺς προφήτας καὶ ἀποστόλους, καὶ ἐξ αὐτῶν ἀποκτενοῦσιν καὶ διώξουσιν, 50 ἵνα ἐκζητηθῇ τὸ αἷμα πάντων τῶν προφητῶν τὸ ἐκκεχυμένον ἀπὸ καταβολῆς κόσμου ἀπὸ τῆς γενεᾶς ταύτης, 51 ἀπὸ[i] αἵματος Ἅβελ ἕως[i] αἵματος Ζαχαρίου τοῦ ἀπολομένου μεταξὺ τοῦ θυσιαστηρίου καὶ τοῦ οἴκου· ναὶ λέγω ὑμῖν, ἐκζητηθήσεται ἀπὸ τῆς γενεᾶς ταύτης. 52 οὐαὶ ὑμῖν τοῖς νομικοῖς, ὅτι ἤρατε τὴν κλεῖδα τῆς γνώσεως· αὐτοὶ οὐκ εἰσήλθατε καὶ τοὺς εἰσερχομένους ἐκωλύσατε. 53 Κἀκεῖθεν ἐξελθόντος αὐτοῦ ἤρξαντο οἱ γραμματεῖς καὶ οἱ Φαρισαῖοι δεινῶς ἐνέχειν καὶ ἀποστοματίζειν αὐτὸν περὶ πλειόνων, 54 ἐνεδρεύοντες αὐτὸν θηρεῦσαί τι ἐκ τοῦ στόματος αὐτοῦ.

12 Ἐν οἷς ἐπισυναχθεισῶν τῶν μυριάδων τοῦ ὄχλου, ὥστε καταπατεῖν ἀλλήλους, ἤρξατο λέγειν πρὸς τοὺς μαθητὰς αὐτοῦ πρῶτον, Προσέχετε ἑαυτοῖς ἀπὸ τῆς ζύμης, ἥτις ἐστὶν ὑπόκρισις, τῶν Φαρισαίων. 2 οὐδὲν δὲ συγκεκαλυμμένον ἐστὶν ὃ οὐκ ἀποκαλυφθήσεται καὶ κρυπτὸν ὃ οὐ γνωσθήσεται. 3 ἀνθ' ὧν ὅσα ἐν τῇ σκοτίᾳ εἴπατε ἐν τῷ φωτὶ ἀκουσθήσεται, καὶ ὃ πρὸς τὸ οὖς ἐλαλήσατε ἐν τοῖς ταμείοις κηρυχθήσεται ἐπὶ τῶν δωμάτων.

4 Λέγω δὲ ὑμῖν τοῖς φίλοις μου, μὴ φοβηθῆτε ἀπὸ τῶν ἀποκτεινόντων τὸ σῶμα καὶ μετὰ ταῦτα μὴ ἐχόντων περισσότερόν τι ποιῆσαι. 5 ὑποδείξω δὲ ὑμῖν τίνα φοβηθῆτε· φοβήθητε τὸν μετὰ τὸ ἀποκτεῖναι ἔχοντα ἐξουσίαν ἐμβαλεῖν εἰς τὴν γέενναν. ναὶ λέγω ὑμῖν, τοῦτον φοβήθητε. 6 οὐχὶ πέντε

44"Woe to you, because you are like unmarked graves, which men walk over without knowing it."

45One of the experts in the law answered him, "Teacher, when you say these things, you insult us also."

46Jesus replied, "And you experts in the law, woe to you, because you load people down with burdens they can hardly carry, and you yourselves will not lift one finger to help them.

47"Woe to you, because you build tombs for the prophets, and it was your forefathers who killed them. 48So you testify that you approve of what your forefathers did; they killed the prophets, and you build their tombs. 49Because of this, God in his wisdom said, 'I will send them prophets and apostles, some of whom they will kill and others they will persecute.' 50Therefore this generation will be held responsible for the blood of all the prophets that has been shed since the beginning of the world, 51from the blood of Abel to the blood of Zechariah, who was killed between the altar and the sanctuary. Yes, I tell you, this generation will be held responsible for it all.

52"Woe to you experts in the law, because you have taken away the key to knowledge. You yourselves have not entered, and you have hindered those who were entering."

53When Jesus left there, the Pharisees and the teachers of the law began to oppose him fiercely and to besiege him with questions, 54waiting to catch him in something he might say.

Warnings and Encouragements

12 Meanwhile, when a crowd of many thousands had gathered, so that they were trampling on one another, Jesus began to speak first to his disciples, saying: "Be on your guard against the yeast of the Pharisees, which is hypocrisy. 2There is nothing concealed that will not be disclosed, or hidden that will not be made known. 3What you have said in the dark will be heard in the daylight, and what you have whispered in the ear in the inner rooms will be proclaimed from the roofs.

4"I tell you, my friends, do not be afraid of those who kill the body and after that can do no more. 5But I will show you whom you should fear: Fear him who, after the killing of the body, has power to throw you into hell. Yes, I tell you, fear him. 6Are

---

sparrows sold for two pennies? Yet not one of them is forgotten in God's sight. 7But even the hairs of your head are all counted. Do not be afraid; you are of more value than many sparrows.

8 "And I tell you, everyone who acknowledges me before others, the Son of Man also will acknowledge before the angels of God; 9but whoever denies me before others will be denied before the angels of God. 10And everyone who speaks a word against the Son of Man will be forgiven; but whoever blasphemes against the Holy Spirit will not be forgiven. 11When they bring you before the synagogues, the rulers, and the authorities, do not worry about howʸ you are to defend yourselves or what you are to say; 12for the Holy Spirit will teach you at that very hour what you ought to say."

The Parable of the Rich Fool

13 Someone in the crowd said to him, "Teacher, tell my brother to divide the family inheritance with me." 14But he said to him, "Friend, who set me to be a judge or arbitrator over you?" 15And he said to them, "Take care! Be on your guard against all kinds of greed; for one's life does not consist in the abundance of possessions." 16Then he told them a parable: "The land of a rich man produced abundantly. 17And he thought to himself, 'What should I do, for I have no place to store my crops?' 18Then he said, 'I will do this: I will pull down my barns and build larger ones, and there I will store all my grain and my goods. 19And I will say to my soul, 'Soul, you have ample goods laid up for many years; relax, eat, drink, be merry.' 20But God said to him, 'You fool! This very night your life is being demanded of you. And the things you have prepared, whose will they be?' 21So it is with those who store up treasures for themselves but are not rich toward God."

Do Not Worry

22 He said to his disciples, "Therefore I tell you, do not worry about your life, what you will eat, or about your body, what you will wear. 23For life is more than food, and the body more than clothing. 24Consider the ravens: they neither sow nor reap,

στρουθία πωλοῦνται ἀσσαρίων δύο; καὶ ἓν ἐξ αὐτῶν οὐκ ἔστιν ἐπιλελησμένον ἐνώπιον τοῦ θεοῦ. 7 ἀλλὰ καὶ αἱ τρίχες τῆς κεφαλῆς ὑμῶν πᾶσαι ἠρίθμηνται. μὴ φοβεῖσθε· πολλῶν στρουθίων διαφέρετε.

8 Λέγω δὲ ὑμῖν, πᾶς ὃς ἂν ὁμολογήσῃ ἐν ἐμοὶ ἔμπροσθεν τῶν ἀνθρώπων, καὶ ὁ υἱὸς τοῦ ἀνθρώπου ὁμολογήσει ἐν αὐτῷ ἔμπροσθεν τῶν ἀγγέλων τοῦ θεοῦ· 9 ὁ δὲ ἀρνησάμενός με ἐνώπιον τῶν ἀνθρώπων ἀπαρνηθήσεται ἐνώπιον τῶν ἀγγέλων τοῦ θεοῦ. 10 καὶ πᾶς ὃς ἐρεῖ λόγον εἰς τὸν υἱὸν τοῦ ἀνθρώπου, ἀφεθήσεται αὐτῷ· τῷ δὲ εἰς τὸ ἅγιον πνεῦμα βλασφημήσαντι οὐκ ἀφεθήσεται. 11 ὅταν δὲ εἰσφέρωσιν ὑμᾶς ἐπὶ τὰς συναγωγὰς καὶ τὰς ἀρχὰς καὶ τὰς ἐξουσίας, μὴ μεριμνήσητε πῶς ἢ τίᵃ ἀπολογήσησθε ἢ τί εἴπητε· 12 τὸ γὰρ ἅγιον πνεῦμα διδάξει ὑμᾶς ἐν αὐτῇ τῇ ὥρᾳ ἃ δεῖ εἰπεῖν.

13 Εἶπεν δέ τις ἐκ τοῦ ὄχλου αὐτῷ, Διδάσκαλε, εἰπὲ τῷ ἀδελφῷ μου μερίσασθαι μετ᾽ ἐμοῦ τὴν κληρονομίαν. 14 ὁ δὲ εἶπεν αὐτῷ, Ἄνθρωπε, τίς με κατέστησεν κριτὴν ἢ μεριστὴν ἐφ᾽ ὑμᾶς; 15 εἶπεν δὲ πρὸς αὐτούς, Ὁρᾶτε καὶ φυλάσσεσθε ἀπὸ πάσης πλεονεξίας, ὅτι οὐκ ἐν τῷ περισσεύειν τινὶ ἡ ζωὴ αὐτοῦ ἐστιν ἐκ τῶν ὑπαρχόντων αὐτῷ. 16 Εἶπεν δὲ παραβολὴν πρὸς αὐτοὺς λέγων, Ἀνθρώπου τινὸς πλουσίου εὐφόρησεν ἡ χώρα. 17 καὶ διελογίζετο ἐν ἑαυτῷ λέγων, Τί ποιήσω, ὅτι οὐκ ἔχω ποῦ συνάξω τοὺς καρπούς μου; 18 καὶ εἶπεν, Τοῦτο ποιήσω, καθελῶ μου τὰς ἀποθήκας καὶ μείζονας οἰκοδομήσω καὶ συνάξω ἐκεῖ πάντα τὸν σῖτον καὶ τὰ ἀγαθά μου 19 καὶ ἐρῶ τῇ ψυχῇ μου, Ψυχή, ἔχεις πολλὰ ἀγαθὰ κείμενα εἰς ἔτη πολλά· ἀναπαύου, φάγε, πίε, εὐφραίνου. 20 εἶπεν δὲ αὐτῷ ὁ θεός, Ἄφρων, ταύτῃ τῇ νυκτὶ τὴν ψυχήν σου ἀπαιτοῦσιν ἀπὸ σοῦ· ἃ δὲ ἡτοίμασας, τίνι ἔσται; 21 οὕτως ὁ θησαυρίζων ἑαυτῷ καὶ μὴ εἰς θεὸν πλουτῶν.

22 Εἶπεν δὲ πρὸς τοὺς μαθητάς [αὐτοῦ], Διὰ τοῦτο λέγω ὑμῖν· μὴ μεριμνᾶτε τῇ ψυχῇ τί φάγητε, μηδὲ τῷ σώματι τί ἐνδύσησθε. 23 ἡ γὰρ ψυχὴ πλεῖόν ἐστιν τῆς τροφῆς καὶ τὸ σῶμα τοῦ ἐνδύματος. 24 κατανοήσατε τοὺς κόρακας ὅτι οὐ σπείρουσιν οὐδὲ

not five sparrows sold for two penniesᵃ? Yet not one of them is forgotten by God. 7Indeed, the very hairs of your head are all numbered. Don't be afraid; you are worth more than many sparrows.

8"I tell you, whoever acknowledges me before men, the Son of Man will also acknowledge him before the angels of God. 9But he who disowns me before men will be disowned before the angels of God. 10And everyone who speaks a word against the Son of Man will be forgiven, but anyone who blasphemes against the Holy Spirit will not be forgiven.

11"When you are brought before synagogues, rulers and authorities, do not worry about how you will defend yourselves or what you will say, 12for the Holy Spirit will teach you at that time what you should say."

The Parable of the Rich Fool

13Someone in the crowd said to him, "Teacher, tell my brother to divide the inheritance with me."

14Jesus replied, "Man, who appointed me a judge or an arbiter between you?" 15Then he said to them, "Watch out! Be on your guard against all kinds of greed; a man's life does not consist in the abundance of his possessions."

16And he told them this parable: "The ground of a certain rich man produced a good crop. 17He thought to himself, 'What shall I do? I have no place to store my crops.'

18"Then he said, 'This is what I'll do. I will tear down my barns and build bigger ones, and there I will store all my grain and my goods. 19And I'll say to myself, "You have plenty of good things laid up for many years. Take life easy; eat, drink and be merry." '

20"But God said to him, 'You fool! This very night your life will be demanded from you. Then who will get what you have prepared for yourself?'

21"This is how it will be with anyone who stores up things for himself but is not rich toward God."

Do Not Worry

22Then Jesus said to his disciples: "Therefore I tell you, do not worry about your life, what you will eat; or about your body, what you will wear. 23Life is more than food, and the body more than clothes. 24Consider the ravens: They do not sow or

---

they have neither storehouse nor barn, and yet God feeds them. Of how much more value are you than the birds! 25And can any of you by worrying add a single hour to your span of life?z 26If then you are not able to do so small a thing as that, why do you worry about the rest? 27Consider the lilies, how they grow: they neither toil nor spin;a yet I tell you, even Solomon in all his glory was not clothed like one of these. 28But if God so clothes the grass of the field, which is alive today and tomorrow is thrown into the oven, how much more will he clothe you—you of little faith! 29And do not keep striving for what you are to eat and what you are to drink, and do not keep worrying. 30For it is the nations of the world that strive after all these things, and your Father knows that you need them. 31Instead, strive for hisb kingdom, and these things will be given to you as well.

32 "Do not be afraid, little flock, for it is your Father's good pleasure to give you the kingdom. 33Sell your possessions, and give alms. Make purses for yourselves that do not wear out, an unfailing treasure in heaven, where no thief comes near and no moth destroys. 34For where your treasure is, there your heart will be also.

Watchful Slaves

35 "Be dressed for action and have your lamps lit; 36be like those who are waiting for their master to return from the wedding banquet, so that they may open the door for him as soon as he comes and knocks. 37Blessed are those slaves whom the master finds alert when he comes; truly I tell you, he will fasten his belt and have them sit down to eat, and he will come and serve them. 38If he comes during the middle of the night, or near dawn, and finds them so, blessed are those slaves.

39 "But know this: if the owner of the house had known at what hour the thief was coming, hec would not have let his house be broken into. 40You also must be ready, for the Son of Man is coming at an unexpected hour."

The Faithful or the Unfaithful Slave

41 Peter said, "Lord, are you telling this parable for us or for everyone?" 42And the Lord said, "Who then is the faithful and prudent manager whom his master will

---

θερίζουσιν, οἷς οὐκ ἔστιν ταμεῖον οὐδὲ ἀποθήκη, καὶ ὁ θεὸς τρέφει αὐτούς· πόσῳ μᾶλλον ὑμεῖς διαφέρετε τῶν πετεινῶν. 25 τίς δὲ ἐξ ὑμῶν μεριμνῶν δύναται ἐπὶ τὴν ἡλικίαν αὐτοῦ προσθεῖναι πῆχυνb; 26 εἰ οὖν οὐδὲ ἐλάχιστον δύνασθε, τί περὶ τῶν λοιπῶν μεριμνᾶτε; 27 κατανοήσατε τὰ κρίνα πῶς αὐξάνει· οὐ κοπιᾷ οὐδὲ νήθειc· λέγω δὲ ὑμῖν, οὐδὲ Σολομῶν ἐν πάσῃ τῇ δόξῃ αὐτοῦ περιεβάλετο ὡς ἓν τούτων. 28 εἰ δὲ ἐν ἀγρῷ τὸν χόρτον ὄντα σήμερον καὶ αὔριον εἰς κλίβανον βαλλόμενον ὁ θεὸς οὕτως ἀμφιέζει, πόσῳ μᾶλλον ὑμᾶς, ὀλιγόπιστοι. 29 καὶ ὑμεῖς μὴ ζητεῖτε τί φάγητε καὶ τί πίητε καὶ μὴ μετεωρίζεσθε· 30 ταῦτα γὰρ πάντα τὰ ἔθνη τοῦ κόσμου ἐπιζητοῦσιν, ὑμῶν δὲ ὁ πατὴρ οἶδεν ὅτι χρῄζετε τούτων. 31 πλὴν ζητεῖτε τὴν βασιλείαν αὐτοῦd, καὶ ταῦτα προστεθήσεται ὑμῖν. 32 Μὴ φοβοῦ, τὸ μικρὸν ποίμνιον, ὅτι εὐδόκησεν ὁ πατὴρ ὑμῶν δοῦναι ὑμῖν τὴν βασιλείαν. 33 Πωλήσατε τὰ ὑπάρχοντα ὑμῶν καὶ δότε ἐλεημοσύνην· ποιήσατε ἑαυτοῖς βαλλάντια μὴ παλαιούμενα, θησαυρὸν ἀνέκλειπτον ἐν τοῖς οὐρανοῖς, ὅπου κλέπτης οὐκ ἐγγίζει οὐδὲ σὴς διαφθείρει· 34 ὅπου γάρ ἐστιν ὁ θησαυρὸς ὑμῶν, ἐκεῖ καὶ ἡ καρδία ὑμῶν ἔσται. 35 Ἔστωσαν ὑμῶν αἱ ὀσφύες περιεζωσμέναι καὶ οἱ λύχνοι καιόμενοι· 36 καὶ ὑμεῖς ὅμοιοι ἀνθρώποις προσδεχομένοις τὸν κύριον ἑαυτῶν πότε ἀναλύσῃ ἐκ τῶν γάμων, ἵνα ἐλθόντος καὶ κρούσαντος εὐθέως ἀνοίξωσιν αὐτῷ. 37 μακάριοι οἱ δοῦλοι ἐκεῖνοι, οὓς ἐλθὼν ὁ κύριος εὑρήσει γρηγοροῦντας· ἀμὴν λέγω ὑμῖν ὅτι περιζώσεται καὶ ἀνακλινεῖ αὐτοὺς καὶ παρελθὼν διακονήσει αὐτοῖς. 38 κἂν ἐν τῇ δευτέρᾳ κἂν ἐν τῇ τρίτῃ φυλακῇ ἔλθῃ καὶ εὕρῃ οὕτως, μακάριοί εἰσιν ἐκεῖνοι. 39 τοῦτο δὲ γινώσκετε ὅτι εἰ ᾔδει ὁ οἰκοδεσπότης ποίᾳ ὥρᾳ ὁ κλέπτης ἔρχεται,e οὐκ ἂν ἀφῆκεν διορυχθῆναι τὸν οἶκον αὐτοῦ. 40 καὶ ὑμεῖς γίνεσθε ἕτοιμοι, ὅτι ᾗ ὥρᾳ οὐ δοκεῖτε ὁ υἱὸς τοῦ ἀνθρώπου ἔρχεται. 41 Εἶπεν δὲ ὁ Πέτρος, Κύριε, πρὸς ἡμᾶς τὴν παραβολὴν ταύτην λέγεις ἢ καὶ πρὸς πάντας; 42 καὶ εἶπεν ὁ κύριος, Τίς ἄρα ἐστὶν ὁ πιστὸς οἰκονόμος ὁ φρόνιμος, ὃν καταστήσει ὁ κύριος ἐπὶ

---

reap, they have no storeroom or barn; yet God feeds them. And how much more valuable you are than birds! 25Who of you by worrying can add a single hour to his life?b 26Since you cannot do this very little thing, why do you worry about the rest?

27"Consider how the lilies grow. They do not labor or spin. Yet I tell you, not even Solomon in all his splendor was dressed like one of these. 28If that is how God clothes the grass of the field, which is here today, and tomorrow is thrown into the fire, how much more will he clothe you, O you of little faith! 29And do not set your heart on what you will eat or drink; do not worry about it. 30For the pagan world runs after all such things, and your Father knows that you need them. 31But seek his kingdom, and these things will be given to you as well.

32"Do not be afraid, little flock, for your Father has been pleased to give you the kingdom. 33Sell your possessions and give to the poor. Provide purses for yourselves that will not wear out, a treasure in heaven that will not be exhausted, where no thief comes near and no moth destroys. 34For where your treasure is, there your heart will be also.

Watchfulness

35"Be dressed ready for service and keep your lamps burning, 36like men waiting for their master to return from a wedding banquet, so that when he comes and knocks they can immediately open the door for him. 37It will be good for those servants whose master finds them watching when he comes. I tell you the truth, he will dress himself to serve, will have them recline at the table and will come and wait on them. 38It will be good for those servants whose master finds them ready, even if he comes in the second or third watch of the night. 39But understand this: If the owner of the house had known at what hour the thief was coming, he would not have let his house be broken into. 40You also must be ready, because the Son of Man will come at an hour when you do not expect him."

41Peter asked, "Lord, are you telling this parable to us, or to everyone?"

42The Lord answered, "Who then is the faithful and wise manager, whom the master puts in charge of his servants to

---

z Or *add a cubit to your stature*   a Other ancient authorities read *Consider the lilies; they neither spin nor weave*   b Other ancient authorities read *God's*   c Other ancient authorities add *would have watched and*

b25 NIV text adds ἕνα †   c27 NRSV note a πῶς οὔτε νήθει οὔτε ὑφαίνει   d31 NRSV note b τοῦ θεοῦ   e39 NRSV note c adds ἐγρηγόρησεν ἂν καὶ

b25 Or *single cubit to his height*

put in charge of his slaves, to give them their allowance of food at the proper time? 43Blessed is that slave whom his master will find at work when he arrives. 44Truly I tell you, he will put that one in charge of all his possessions. 45But if that slave says to himself, 'My master is delayed in coming,' and if he begins to beat the other slaves, men and women, and to eat and drink and get drunk, 46the master of that slave will come on a day when he does not expect him and at an hour that he does not know, and will cut him in pieces,d and put him with the unfaithful. 47That slave who knew what his master wanted, but did not prepare himself or do what was wanted, will receive a severe beating. 48But the one who did not know and did what deserved a beating will receive a light beating. From everyone to whom much has been given, much will be required; and from the one to whom much has been entrusted, even more will be demanded.

Jesus the Cause of Division

49 "I came to bring fire to the earth, and how I wish it were already kindled! 50I have a baptism with which to be baptized, and what stress I am under until it is completed! 51Do you think that I have come to bring peace to the earth? No, I tell you, but rather division! 52From now on five in one household will be divided, three against two and two against three; 53they will be divided:

father against son
  and son against father,
mother against daughter
  and daughter against mother,
mother-in-law against her daughter-
    in-law
  and daughter-in-law against
    mother-in-law."

Interpreting the Time

54 He also said to the crowds, "When you see a cloud rising in the west, you immediately say, 'It is going to rain'; and so it happens. 55And when you see the south wind blowing, you say, 'There will be scorching heat'; and it happens. 56You hypocrites! You know how to interpret the appearance of earth and sky, but why do you not know how to interpret the present time?

Settling with Your Opponent

57 "And why do you not judge for your-

d Or *cut him off*

τῆς θεραπείας αὐτοῦ τοῦ διδόναι ἐν καιρῷ [τὸ] σιτομέτριον; 43 μακάριος ὁ δοῦλος ἐκεῖνος, ὃν ἐλθὼν ὁ κύριος αὐτοῦ εὑρήσει ποιοῦντα οὕτως. 44 ἀληθῶς λέγω ὑμῖν ὅτι ἐπὶ πᾶσιν τοῖς ὑπάρχουσιν αὐτοῦ καταστήσει αὐτόν. 45 ἐὰν δὲ εἴπῃ ὁ δοῦλος ἐκεῖνος ἐν τῇ καρδίᾳ αὐτοῦ, Χρονίζει ὁ κύριός μου ἔρχεσθαι, καὶ ἄρξηται τύπτειν τοὺς παῖδας καὶ τὰς παιδίσκας, ἐσθίειν τε καὶ πίνειν καὶ μεθύσκεσθαι, 46 ἥξει ὁ κύριος τοῦ δούλου ἐκείνου ἐν ἡμέρᾳ ᾗ οὐ προσδοκᾷ καὶ ἐν ὥρᾳ ᾗ οὐ γινώσκει, καὶ διχοτομήσει αὐτὸν καὶ τὸ μέρος αὐτοῦ μετὰ τῶν ἀπίστων θήσει. 47 ἐκεῖνος δὲ ὁ δοῦλος ὁ γνοὺς τὸ θέλημα τοῦ κυρίου αὐτοῦ καὶ μὴ ἑτοιμάσας ἢ ποιήσας πρὸς τὸ θέλημα αὐτοῦ δαρήσεται πολλάς· 48 ὁ δὲ μὴ γνούς, ποιήσας δὲ ἄξια πληγῶν δαρήσεται ὀλίγας. παντὶ δὲ ᾧ ἐδόθη πολύ, πολὺ ζητηθήσεται παρ' αὐτοῦ, καὶ ᾧ παρέθεντο πολύ, περισσότερον αἰτήσουσιν αὐτόν.

49 Πῦρ ἦλθον βαλεῖν ἐπὶ τὴν γῆν, καὶ τί θέλω εἰ ἤδη ἀνήφθη. 50 βάπτισμα δὲ ἔχω βαπτισθῆναι, καὶ πῶς συνέχομαι ἕως ὅτου τελεσθῇ. 51 δοκεῖτε ὅτι εἰρήνην παρεγενόμην δοῦναι ἐν τῇ γῇ; οὐχί, λέγω ὑμῖν, ἀλλ' ἢ διαμερισμόν. 52 ἔσονται γὰρ ἀπὸ τοῦ νῦν πέντε ἐν ἑνὶ οἴκῳ διαμεμερισμένοι, τρεῖς ἐπὶ δυσὶν καὶ δύο ἐπὶ τρισίν, 53 διαμερισθήσονται πατὴρ ἐπὶ υἱῷ
  καὶ υἱὸς ἐπὶ πατρί,
μήτηρ ἐπὶ τὴν θυγατέρα
  καὶ θυγάτηρ ἐπὶ τὴν μητέρα,
πενθερὰ ἐπὶ τὴν νύμφην αὐτῆς
  καὶ νύμφη ἐπὶ τὴν πενθεράν.

54 Ἔλεγεν δὲ καὶ τοῖς ὄχλοις, Ὅταν ἴδητε [τὴν] νεφέλην ἀνατέλλουσαν ἐπὶ δυσμῶν, εὐθέως λέγετε ὅτι Ὄμβρος ἔρχεται, καὶ γίνεται οὕτως· 55 καὶ ὅταν νότον πνέοντα, λέγετε ὅτι Καύσων ἔσται, καὶ γίνεται. 56 ὑποκριταί, τὸ πρόσωπον τῆς γῆς καὶ τοῦ οὐρανοῦ οἴδατε δοκιμάζειν, τὸν καιρὸν δὲ τοῦτον πῶς οὐκ οἴδατε δοκιμάζειν;

57 Τί δὲ καὶ ἀφ' ἑαυτῶν οὐ κρίνετε

give them their food allowance at the proper time? 43It will be good for that servant whom the master finds doing so when he returns. 44I tell you the truth, he will put him in charge of all his possessions. 45But suppose the servant says to himself, 'My master is taking a long time in coming,' and he then begins to beat the menservants and maidservants and to eat and drink and get drunk. 46The master of that servant will come on a day when he does not expect him and at an hour he is not aware of. He will cut him to pieces and assign him a place with the unbelievers.

47"That servant who knows his master's will and does not get ready or does not do what his master wants will be beaten with many blows. 48But the one who does not know and does things deserving punishment will be beaten with few blows. From everyone who has been given much, much will be demanded; and from the one who has been entrusted with much, much more will be asked.

Not Peace but Division

49"I have come to bring fire on the earth, and how I wish it were already kindled! 50But I have a baptism to undergo, and how distressed I am until it is completed! 51Do you think I came to bring peace on earth? No, I tell you, but division. 52From now on there will be five in one family divided against each other, three against two and two against three. 53They will be divided, father against son and son against father, mother against daughter and daughter against mother, mother-in-law against daughter-in-law and daughter-in-law against mother-in-law."

Interpreting the Times

54He said to the crowd: "When you see a cloud rising in the west, immediately you say, 'It's going to rain,' and it does. 55And when the south wind blows, you say, 'It's going to be hot,' and it is. 56Hypocrites! You know how to interpret the appearance of the earth and the sky. How is it that you don't know how to interpret this present time?

57"Why don't you judge for yourselves

selves what is right? [58]Thus, when you go with your accuser before a magistrate, on the way make an effort to settle the case,[e] or you may be dragged before the judge, and the judge hand you over to the officer, and the officer throw you in prison. [59]I tell you, you will never get out until you have paid the very last penny."

Repent or Perish

13 At that very time there were some present who told him about the Galileans whose blood Pilate had mingled with their sacrifices. [2]He asked them, "Do you think that because these Galileans suffered in this way they were worse sinners than all other Galileans? [3]No, I tell you; but unless you repent, you will all perish as they did. [4]Or those eighteen who were killed when the tower of Siloam fell on them—do you think that they were worse offenders than all the others living in Jerusalem? [5]No, I tell you; but unless you repent, you will all perish just as they did."

The Parable of the Barren Fig Tree

6 Then he told this parable: "A man had a fig tree planted in his vineyard; and he came looking for fruit on it and found none. [7]So he said to the gardener, 'See here! For three years I have come looking for fruit on this fig tree, and still I find none. Cut it down! Why should it be wasting the soil?' [8]He replied, 'Sir, let it alone for one more year, until I dig around it and put manure on it. [9]If it bears fruit next year, well and good; but if not, you can cut it down.' "

Jesus Heals a Crippled Woman

10 Now he was teaching in one of the synagogues on the sabbath. [11]And just then there appeared a woman with a spirit that had crippled her for eighteen years. She was bent over and was quite unable to stand up straight. [12]When Jesus saw her, he called her over and said, "Woman, you are set free from your ailment." [13]When he laid his hands on her, immediately she stood up straight and began praising God. [14]But the leader of the synagogue, indignant because Jesus had cured on the sabbath, kept saying to the crowd, "There are six days on which work ought to be done; come on those days and be cured, and not on the sabbath day." [15]But the Lord answered him and said, "You hypocrites! Does not each of you on the sabbath untie

τὸ δίκαιον; **58** ὡς γὰρ ὑπάγεις μετὰ τοῦ ἀντιδίκου σου ἐπ᾽ ἄρχοντα, ἐν τῇ ὁδῷ δὸς ἐργασίαν ἀπηλλάχθαι ἀπ᾽ αὐτοῦ, μήποτε κατασύρῃ σε πρὸς τὸν κριτήν, καὶ ὁ κριτής σε παραδώσει τῷ πράκτορι, καὶ ὁ πράκτωρ σε βαλεῖ εἰς φυλακήν. **59** λέγω σοι, οὐ μὴ ἐξέλθῃς ἐκεῖθεν, ἕως καὶ τὸ ἔσχατον λεπτὸν ἀποδῷς.

13 Παρῆσαν δέ τινες ἐν αὐτῷ τῷ καιρῷ ἀπαγγέλλοντες αὐτῷ περὶ τῶν Γαλιλαίων ὧν τὸ αἷμα Πιλᾶτος ἔμιξεν μετὰ τῶν θυσιῶν αὐτῶν. **2** καὶ ἀποκριθεὶς εἶπεν αὐτοῖς, Δοκεῖτε ὅτι οἱ Γαλιλαῖοι οὗτοι ἁμαρτωλοὶ παρὰ πάντας τοὺς Γαλιλαίους ἐγένοντο, ὅτι ταῦτα πεπόνθασιν; **3** οὐχί, λέγω ὑμῖν, ἀλλ᾽ ἐὰν μὴ μετανοῆτε πάντες ὁμοίως ἀπολεῖσθε. **4** ἢ ἐκεῖνοι οἱ δεκαοκτὼ ἐφ᾽ οὓς ἔπεσεν ὁ πύργος ἐν τῷ Σιλωὰμ καὶ ἀπέκτεινεν αὐτούς, δοκεῖτε ὅτι αὐτοὶ ὀφειλέται ἐγένοντο παρὰ πάντας τοὺς ἀνθρώπους τοὺς κατοικοῦντας Ἰερουσαλήμ; **5** οὐχί, λέγω ὑμῖν, ἀλλ᾽ ἐὰν μὴ μετανοῆτε πάντες ὡσαύτως ἀπολεῖσθε.

6 Ἔλεγεν δὲ ταύτην τὴν παραβολήν· Συκῆν εἶχέν τις πεφυτευμένην ἐν τῷ ἀμπελῶνι αὐτοῦ, καὶ ἦλθεν ζητῶν καρπὸν ἐν αὐτῇ καὶ οὐχ εὗρεν. **7** εἶπεν δὲ πρὸς τὸν ἀμπελουργόν, Ἰδοὺ τρία ἔτη ἀφ᾽ οὗ ἔρχομαι ζητῶν καρπὸν ἐν τῇ συκῇ ταύτῃ καὶ οὐχ εὑρίσκω· ἔκκοψον [οὖν][a] αὐτήν, ἱνατί καὶ τὴν γῆν καταργεῖ; **8** ὁ δὲ ἀποκριθεὶς λέγει αὐτῷ, Κύριε, ἄφες αὐτὴν καὶ τοῦτο τὸ ἔτος, ἕως ὅτου σκάψω περὶ αὐτὴν καὶ βάλω κόπρια, **9** κἂν μὲν ποιήσῃ καρπὸν εἰς τὸ μέλλον· εἰ δὲ μή γε, ἐκκόψεις αὐτήν.

10 Ἦν δὲ διδάσκων ἐν μιᾷ τῶν συναγωγῶν ἐν τοῖς σάββασιν. **11** καὶ ἰδοὺ γυνὴ πνεῦμα ἔχουσα ἀσθενείας ἔτη δεκαοκτὼ καὶ ἦν συγκύπτουσα καὶ μὴ δυναμένη ἀνακύψαι εἰς τὸ παντελές. **12** ἰδὼν δὲ αὐτὴν ὁ Ἰησοῦς προσεφώνησεν καὶ εἶπεν αὐτῇ, Γύναι, ἀπολέλυσαι τῆς ἀσθενείας σου, **13** καὶ ἐπέθηκεν αὐτῇ τὰς χεῖρας· καὶ παραχρῆμα ἀνωρθώθη καὶ ἐδόξαζεν τὸν θεόν. **14** ἀποκριθεὶς δὲ ὁ ἀρχισυνάγωγος, ἀγανακτῶν ὅτι τῷ σαββάτῳ ἐθεράπευσεν ὁ Ἰησοῦς, ἔλεγεν τῷ ὄχλῳ ὅτι Ἓξ ἡμέραι εἰσὶν ἐν αἷς δεῖ ἐργάζεσθαι· ἐν αὐταῖς οὖν ἐρχόμενοι θεραπεύεσθε καὶ μὴ τῇ ἡμέρᾳ τοῦ σαββάτου. **15** ἀπεκρίθη δὲ αὐτῷ ὁ κύριος καὶ εἶπεν, Ὑποκριταί, ἕκαστος ὑμῶν

what is right? [58]As you are going with your adversary to the magistrate, try hard to be reconciled to him on the way, or he may drag you off to the judge, and the judge turn you over to the officer, and the officer throw you into prison. [59]I tell you, you will not get out until you have paid the last penny.[c]"

Repent or Perish

13 Now there were some present at that time who told Jesus about the Galileans whose blood Pilate had mixed with their sacrifices. [2]Jesus answered, "Do you think that these Galileans were worse sinners than all the other Galileans because they suffered this way? [3]I tell you, no! But unless you repent, you too will all perish. [4]Or those eighteen who died when the tower in Siloam fell on them—do you think they were more guilty than all the others living in Jerusalem? [5]I tell you, no! But unless you repent, you too will all perish."

[6]Then he told this parable: "A man had a fig tree, planted in his vineyard, and he went to look for fruit on it, but did not find any. [7]So he said to the man who took care of the vineyard, 'For three years now I've been coming to look for fruit on this fig tree and haven't found any. Cut it down! Why should it use up the soil?'

[8]" 'Sir,' the man replied, 'leave it alone for one more year, and I'll dig around it and fertilize it. [9]If it bears fruit next year, fine! If not, then cut it down.' "

A Crippled Woman Healed on the Sabbath

[10]On a Sabbath Jesus was teaching in one of the synagogues, [11]and a woman was there who had been crippled by a spirit for eighteen years. She was bent over and could not straighten up at all. [12]When Jesus saw her, he called her forward and said to her, "Woman, you are set free from your infirmity." [13]Then he put his hands on her, and immediately she straightened up and praised God.

[14]Indignant because Jesus had healed on the Sabbath, the synagogue ruler said to the people, "There are six days for work. So come and be healed on those days, not on the Sabbath."

[15]The Lord answered him, "You hypocrites! Doesn't each of you on the Sabbath

---

[e] Gk *settle with him*   [a]7 NIV text omits οὖν   [c]59 Greek *lepton*

his ox or his donkey from the manger, and lead it away to give it water? 16And ought not this woman, a daughter of Abraham whom Satan bound for eighteen long years, be set free from this bondage on the sabbath day?" 17When he said this, all his opponents were put to shame; and the entire crowd was rejoicing at all the wonderful things that he was doing.

The Parable of the Mustard Seed

18 He said therefore, "What is the kingdom of God like? And to what should I compare it? 19It is like a mustard seed that someone took and sowed in the garden; it grew and became a tree, and the birds of the air made nests in its branches."

The Parable of the Yeast

20 And again he said, "To what should I compare the kingdom of God? 21It is like yeast that a woman took and mixed in with^f three measures of flour until all of it was leavened."

The Narrow Door

22 Jesus^g went through one town and village after another, teaching as he made his way to Jerusalem. 23Someone asked him, "Lord, will only a few be saved?" He said to them, 24"Strive to enter through the narrow door; for many, I tell you, will try to enter and will not be able. 25When once the owner of the house has got up and shut the door, and you begin to stand outside and to knock at the door, saying, 'Lord, open to us,' then in reply he will say to you, 'I do not know where you come from.' 26Then you will begin to say, 'We ate and drank with you, and you taught in our streets.' 27But he will say, 'I do not know where you come from; go away from me, all you evildoers!' 28There will be weeping and gnashing of teeth when you see Abraham and Isaac and Jacob and all the prophets in the kingdom of God, and you yourselves thrown out. 29Then people will come from east and west, from north and south, and will eat in the kingdom of God. 30Indeed, some are last who will be first, and some are first who will be last."

The Lament over Jerusalem

31 At that very hour some Pharisees came and said to him, "Get away from here, for

τῷ σαββάτῳ οὐ λύει τὸν βοῦν αὐτοῦ ἢ τὸν ὄνον ἀπὸ τῆς φάτνης καὶ ἀπαγαγὼν ποτίζει; 16 ταύτην δὲ θυγατέρα Ἀβραὰμ οὖσαν, ἣν ἔδησεν ὁ Σατανᾶς ἰδοὺ δέκα καὶ ὀκτὼ ἔτη, οὐκ ἔδει λυθῆναι ἀπὸ τοῦ δεσμοῦ τούτου τῇ ἡμέρᾳ τοῦ σαββάτου; 17 καὶ ταῦτα λέγοντος αὐτοῦ κατῃσχύνοντο πάντες οἱ ἀντικείμενοι αὐτῷ, καὶ πᾶς ὁ ὄχλος ἔχαιρεν ἐπὶ πᾶσιν τοῖς ἐνδόξοις τοῖς γινομένοις ὑπ' αὐτοῦ.

18 Ἔλεγεν οὖν, Τίνι ὁμοία ἐστὶν ἡ βασιλεία τοῦ θεοῦ καὶ τίνι ὁμοιώσω αὐτήν; 19 ὁμοία ἐστὶν κόκκῳ σινάπεως, ὃν λαβὼν ἄνθρωπος ἔβαλεν εἰς κῆπον ἑαυτοῦ, καὶ ηὔξησεν καὶ ἐγένετο εἰς δένδρον, καὶ τὰ πετεινὰ τοῦ οὐρανοῦ κατεσκήνωσεν ἐν τοῖς κλάδοις αὐτοῦ. 20 Καὶ πάλιν εἶπεν, Τίνι ὁμοιώσω τὴν βασιλείαν τοῦ θεοῦ; 21 ὁμοία ἐστὶν ζύμῃ, ἣν λαβοῦσα γυνὴ [ἐν]έκρυψεν εἰς ἀλεύρου σάτα τρία ἕως οὗ ἐζυμώθη ὅλον.

22 Καὶ διεπορεύετο κατὰ πόλεις καὶ κώμας διδάσκων καὶ πορείαν ποιούμενος εἰς Ἱεροσόλυμα. 23 εἶπεν δέ τις αὐτῷ, Κύριε, εἰ ὀλίγοι οἱ σῳζόμενοι; ὁ δὲ εἶπεν πρὸς αὐτούς, 24 Ἀγωνίζεσθε εἰσελθεῖν διὰ τῆς στενῆς θύρας, ὅτι πολλοί, λέγω ὑμῖν, ζητήσουσιν εἰσελθεῖν καὶ οὐκ ἰσχύσουσιν. 25 ἀφ' οὗ ἂν ἐγερθῇ ὁ οἰκοδεσπότης καὶ ἀποκλείσῃ τὴν θύραν καὶ ἄρξησθε ἔξω ἑστάναι καὶ κρούειν τὴν θύραν λέγοντες, Κύριε, ἄνοιξον ἡμῖν, καὶ ἀποκριθεὶς ἐρεῖ ὑμῖν, Οὐκ οἶδα ὑμᾶς πόθεν ἐστέ. 26 τότε ἄρξεσθε λέγειν, Ἐφάγομεν ἐνώπιόν σου καὶ ἐπίομεν καὶ ἐν ταῖς πλατείαις ἡμῶν ἐδίδαξας· 27 καὶ ἐρεῖ λέγων ὑμῖν, Οὐκ οἶδα [ὑμᾶς] πόθεν ἐστέ· ἀπόστητε ἀπ' ἐμοῦ πάντες ἐργάται ἀδικίας. 28 ἐκεῖ ἔσται ὁ κλαυθμὸς καὶ ὁ βρυγμὸς τῶν ὀδόντων, ὅταν ὄψεσθε Ἀβραὰμ καὶ Ἰσαὰκ καὶ Ἰακὼβ καὶ πάντας τοὺς προφήτας ἐν τῇ βασιλείᾳ τοῦ θεοῦ, ὑμᾶς δὲ ἐκβαλλομένους ἔξω. 29 καὶ ἥξουσιν ἀπὸ ἀνατολῶν καὶ δυσμῶν καὶ ἀπὸ βορρᾶ καὶ νότου καὶ ἀνακλιθήσονται ἐν τῇ βασιλείᾳ τοῦ θεοῦ. 30 καὶ ἰδοὺ εἰσὶν ἔσχατοι οἳ ἔσονται πρῶτοι καὶ εἰσὶν πρῶτοι οἳ ἔσονται ἔσχατοι.

31 Ἐν αὐτῇ τῇ ὥρᾳ προσῆλθάν τινες Φαρισαῖοι λέγοντες αὐτῷ, Ἔξελθε καὶ

untie his ox or donkey from the stall and lead it out to give it water? 16Then should not this woman, a daughter of Abraham, whom Satan has kept bound for eighteen long years, be set free on the Sabbath day from what bound her?"

17When he said this, all his opponents were humiliated, but the people were delighted with all the wonderful things he was doing.

The Parables of the Mustard Seed and the Yeast

18Then Jesus asked, "What is the kingdom of God like? What shall I compare it to? 19It is like a mustard seed, which a man took and planted in his garden. It grew and became a tree, and the birds of the air perched in its branches."

20Again he asked, "What shall I compare the kingdom of God to? 21It is like yeast that a woman took and mixed into a large amount^a of flour until it worked all through the dough."

The Narrow Door

22Then Jesus went through the towns and villages, teaching as he made his way to Jerusalem. 23Someone asked him, "Lord, are only a few people going to be saved?"

He said to them, 24"Make every effort to enter through the narrow door, because many, I tell you, will try to enter and will not be able to. 25Once the owner of the house gets up and closes the door, you will stand outside knocking and pleading, 'Sir, open the door for us.'

"But he will answer, 'I don't know you or where you come from.'

26"Then you will say, 'We ate and drank with you, and you taught in our streets.'

27"But he will reply, 'I don't know you or where you come from. Away from me, all you evildoers!'

28"There will be weeping there, and gnashing of teeth, when you see Abraham, Isaac and Jacob and all the prophets in the kingdom of God, but you yourselves thrown out. 29People will come from east and west and north and south, and will take their places at the feast in the kingdom of God. 30Indeed there are those who are last who will be first, and first who will be last."

Jesus' Sorrow for Jerusalem

31At that time some Pharisees came to Jesus and said to him, "Leave this place

Herod wants to kill you." [32]He said to them, "Go and tell that fox for me,[h] 'Listen, I am casting out demons and performing cures today and tomorrow, and on the third day I finish my work. [33]Yet today, tomorrow, and the next day I must be on my way, because it is impossible for a prophet to be killed outside of Jerusalem.' [34]Jerusalem, Jerusalem, the city that kills the prophets and stones those who are sent to it! How often have I desired to gather your children together as a hen gathers her brood under her wings, and you were not willing! [35]See, your house is left to you. And I tell you, you will not see me until the time comes when[i] you say, 'Blessed is the one who comes in the name of the Lord.' "

Jesus Heals the Man with Dropsy

14 On one occasion when Jesus[j] was going to the house of a leader of the Pharisees to eat a meal on the sabbath, they were watching him closely. [2]Just then, in front of him, there was a man who had dropsy. [3]And Jesus asked the lawyers and Pharisees, "Is it lawful to cure people on the sabbath, or not?" [4]But they were silent. So Jesus[j] took him and healed him, and sent him away. [5]Then he said to them, "If one of you has a child[k] or an ox that has fallen into a well, will you not immediately pull it out on a sabbath day?" [6]And they could not reply to this.

Humility and Hospitality

7 When he noticed how the guests chose the places of honor, he told them a parable. [8]"When you are invited by someone to a wedding banquet, do not sit down at the place of honor, in case someone more distinguished than you has been invited by your host; [9]and the host who invited both of you may come and say to you, 'Give this person your place,' and then in disgrace you would start to take the lowest place. [10]But when you are invited, go and sit down at the lowest place, so that when your host comes, he may say to you, 'Friend, move up higher'; then you will be honored in the presence of all who sit at the table with you. [11]For all who exalt themselves will be humbled, and those who humble themselves will be exalted."

12 He said also to the one who had invited him, "When you give a luncheon or

πορεύου ἐντεῦθεν, ὅτι Ἡρῴδης θέλει σε ἀποκτεῖναι. **32** καὶ εἶπεν αὐτοῖς, Πορευθέντες εἴπατε τῇ ἀλώπεκι ταύτῃ, Ἰδοὺ ἐκβάλλω δαιμόνια καὶ ἰάσεις ἀποτελῶ σήμερον καὶ αὔριον καὶ τῇ τρίτῃ τελειοῦμαι. **33** πλὴν δεῖ με σήμερον καὶ αὔριον καὶ τῇ ἐχομένῃ πορεύεσθαι, ὅτι οὐκ ἐνδέχεται προφή-την ἀπολέσθαι ἔξω Ἰερουσαλήμ. **34** Ἰερουσαλὴμ Ἰερουσαλήμ, ἡ ἀποκτεί-νουσα τοὺς προφήτας καὶ λιθοβολοῦσα τοὺς ἀπεσταλμένους πρὸς αὐτήν, ποσάκις ἠθέλησα ἐπισυνάξαι τὰ τέκνα σου ὃν τρόπον ὄρνις τὴν ἑαυτῆς νοσσιὰν ὑπὸ τὰς πτέρυγας, καὶ οὐκ ἠθελήσατε. **35** ἰδοὺ ἀφίεται ὑμῖν ὁ οἶκος ὑμῶν[b]. λέγω [δὲ][c] ὑμῖν, οὐ μὴ ἴδητέ με ἕως [ἥξει ὅτε][d] εἴπητε, **Εὐλογημένος ὁ ἐρχόμενος ἐν ὀνόματι κυρίου.**

14 Καὶ ἐγένετο ἐν τῷ ἐλθεῖν αὐτὸν εἰς οἶκόν τινος τῶν ἀρχόντων [τῶν] Φαρισαίων σαββάτῳ φαγεῖν ἄρτον καὶ αὐτοὶ ἦσαν παρατηρούμενοι αὐτόν. **2** καὶ ἰδοὺ ἄνθρωπός τις ἦν ὑδρωπικὸς ἔμπροσθεν αὐτοῦ. **3** καὶ ἀποκριθεὶς ὁ Ἰησοῦς εἶπεν πρὸς τοὺς νομικοὺς καὶ Φαρισαίους λέγων, Ἔξεστιν τῷ σαββά-τῳ θεραπεῦσαι ἢ οὔ; **4** οἱ δὲ ἡσύχασαν. καὶ ἐπιλαβόμενος ἰάσατο αὐτὸν καὶ ἀπέλυσεν. **5** καὶ πρὸς αὐτοὺς εἶπεν, Τίνος ὑμῶν υἱὸς[a] ἢ βοῦς εἰς φρέαρ πεσεῖται, καὶ οὐκ εὐθέως ἀνασπάσει αὐτὸν ἐν ἡμέρᾳ τοῦ σαββάτου; **6** καὶ οὐκ ἴσχυσαν ἀνταποκριθῆναι πρὸς ταῦτα.

7 Ἔλεγεν δὲ πρὸς τοὺς κεκλημένους παραβολήν, ἐπέχων πῶς τὰς πρωτο-κλισίας ἐξελέγοντο, λέγων πρὸς αὐτούς, **8** Ὅταν κληθῇς ὑπό τινος εἰς γάμους, μὴ κατακλιθῇς εἰς τὴν πρωτοκλισίαν, μήποτε ἐντιμότερός σου ᾖ κεκλημένος ὑπ' αὐτοῦ, **9** καὶ ἐλθὼν ὁ σὲ καὶ αὐτὸν καλέσας ἐρεῖ σοι, Δὸς τούτῳ τόπον, καὶ τότε ἄρξῃ μετὰ αἰσχύνης τὸν ἔσχατον τόπον κατέχειν. **10** ἀλλ' ὅταν κληθῇς, πορευθεὶς ἀνάπεσε εἰς τὸν ἔσχατον τόπον, ἵνα ὅταν ἔλθῃ ὁ κεκληκώς σε ἐρεῖ σοι, Φίλε, προσανά-βηθι ἀνώτερον· τότε ἔσται σοι δόξα ἐνώπιον πάντων τῶν συνανακειμένων σοι. **11** ὅτι πᾶς ὁ ὑψῶν ἑαυτὸν ταπεινω-θήσεται, καὶ ὁ ταπεινῶν ἑαυτὸν ὑψωθή-σεται. **12** Ἔλεγεν δὲ καὶ τῷ κεκληκότι αὐτόν, Ὅταν ποιῇς ἄριστον ἢ δεῖπνον,

and go somewhere else. Herod wants to kill you."

[32]He replied, "Go tell that fox, 'I will drive out demons and heal people today and tomorrow, and on the third day I will reach my goal.' [33]In any case, I must keep going today and tomorrow and the next day—for surely no prophet can die outside Jerusalem!

[34]"O Jerusalem, Jerusalem, you who kill the prophets and stone those sent to you, how often I have longed to gather your children together, as a hen gathers her chicks under her wings, but you were not willing! [35]Look, your house is left to you desolate. I tell you, you will not see me again until you say, 'Blessed is he who comes in the name of the Lord.'[b]"

Jesus at a Pharisee's House

14 One Sabbath, when Jesus went to eat in the house of a prominent Pharisee, he was being carefully watched. [2]There in front of him was a man suffering from dropsy. [3]Jesus asked the Pharisees and experts in the law, "Is it lawful to heal on the Sabbath or not?" [4]But they remained silent. So taking hold of the man, he healed him and sent him away.

[5]Then he asked them, "If one of you has a son[a] or an ox that falls into a well on the Sabbath day, will you not immediately pull him out?" [6]And they had nothing to say.

[7]When he noticed how the guests picked the places of honor at the table, he told them this parable: [8]"When someone invites you to a wedding feast, do not take the place of honor, for a person more distinguished than you may have been invited. [9]If so, the host who invited both of you will come and say to you, 'Give this man your seat.' Then, humiliated, you will have to take the least important place. [10]But when you are invited, take the lowest place, so that when your host comes, he will say to you, 'Friend, move up to a better place.' Then you will be honored in the presence of all your fellow guests. [11]For everyone who exalts himself will be humbled, and he who humbles himself will be exalted."

[12]Then Jesus said to his host, "When you give a luncheon or dinner, do not invite

---

[h] Gk lacks *for me* [i] Other ancient authorities lack *the time comes when* [j] Gk *he* [k] Other ancient authorities read *a donkey*

[b]35 NIV text adds ἔρημος [c]35 NIV text omits δὲ †
[d]35 NIV text and NRSV note i omit ἥξει ὅτε
[a]5 NIV/NRSV notes ὄνος

[b]35 Psalm 118:26 [a]5 Some manuscripts *donkey*

a dinner, do not invite your friends or your brothers or your relatives or rich neighbors, in case they may invite you in return, and you would be repaid. [13]But when you give a banquet, invite the poor, the crippled, the lame, and the blind. [14]And you will be blessed, because they cannot repay you, for you will be repaid at the resurrection of the righteous."

The Parable of the Great Dinner

15 One of the dinner guests, on hearing this, said to him, "Blessed is anyone who will eat bread in the kingdom of God!" [16]Then Jesus[l] said to him, "Someone gave a great dinner and invited many. [17]At the time for the dinner he sent his slave to say to those who had been invited, 'Come; for everything is ready now.' [18]But they all alike began to make excuses. The first said to him, 'I have bought a piece of land, and I must go out and see it; please accept my regrets.' [19]Another said, 'I have bought five yoke of oxen, and I am going to try them out; please accept my regrets.' [20]Another said, 'I have just been married, and therefore I cannot come.' [21]So the slave returned and reported this to his master. Then the owner of the house became angry and said to his slave, 'Go out at once into the streets and lanes of the town and bring in the poor, the crippled, the blind, and the lame.' [22]And the slave said, 'Sir, what you ordered has been done, and there is still room.' [23]Then the master said to the slave, 'Go out into the roads and lanes, and compel people to come in, so that my house may be filled. [24]For I tell you,[m] none of those who were invited will taste my dinner.' "

The Cost of Discipleship

25 Now large crowds were traveling with him; and he turned and said to them, [26]"Whoever comes to me and does not hate father and mother, wife and children, brothers and sisters, yes, and even life itself, cannot be my disciple. [27]Whoever does not carry the cross and follow me cannot be my disciple. [28]For which of you, intending to build a tower, does not first sit down and estimate the cost, to see whether he has enough to complete it? [29]Otherwise, when he has laid a foundation and is not

μὴ φώνει τοὺς φίλους σου μηδὲ τοὺς ἀδελφούς σου μηδὲ τοὺς συγγενεῖς σου μηδὲ γείτονας πλουσίους, μήποτε καὶ αὐτοὶ ἀντικαλέσωσίν σε καὶ γένηται ἀνταπόδομά σοι. **13** ἀλλ' ὅταν δοχὴν ποιῇς, κάλει πτωχούς, ἀναπείρους, χωλούς, τυφλούς· **14** καὶ μακάριος ἔσῃ, ὅτι οὐκ ἔχουσιν ἀνταποδοῦναί σοι, ἀνταποδοθήσεται γάρ σοι ἐν τῇ ἀναστάσει τῶν δικαίων.

15 Ἀκούσας δέ τις τῶν συνανακειμένων ταῦτα εἶπεν αὐτῷ, Μακάριος ὅστις φάγεται ἄρτον[b] ἐν τῇ βασιλείᾳ τοῦ θεοῦ. **16** ὁ δὲ εἶπεν αὐτῷ, Ἄνθρωπός τις ἐποίει δεῖπνον μέγα, καὶ ἐκάλεσεν πολλοὺς **17** καὶ ἀπέστειλεν τὸν δοῦλον αὐτοῦ τῇ ὥρᾳ τοῦ δείπνου εἰπεῖν τοῖς κεκλημένοις, Ἔρχεσθε, ὅτι ἤδη ἕτοιμά ἐστιν. **18** καὶ ἤρξαντο ἀπὸ μιᾶς πάντες παραιτεῖσθαι. ὁ πρῶτος εἶπεν αὐτῷ, Ἀγρὸν ἠγόρασα καὶ ἔχω ἀνάγκην ἐξελθὼν ἰδεῖν αὐτόν· ἐρωτῶ σε, ἔχε με παρῃτημένον. **19** καὶ ἕτερος εἶπεν, Ζεύγη βοῶν ἠγόρασα πέντε καὶ πορεύομαι δοκιμάσαι αὐτά· ἐρωτῶ σε, ἔχε με παρῃτημένον. **20** καὶ ἕτερος εἶπεν, Γυναῖκα ἔγημα καὶ διὰ τοῦτο οὐ δύναμαι ἐλθεῖν. **21** καὶ παραγενόμενος ὁ δοῦλος ἀπήγγειλεν τῷ κυρίῳ αὐτοῦ ταῦτα. τότε ὀργισθεὶς ὁ οἰκοδεσπότης εἶπεν τῷ δούλῳ αὐτοῦ, Ἔξελθε ταχέως εἰς τὰς πλατείας καὶ ῥύμας τῆς πόλεως καὶ τοὺς πτωχοὺς καὶ ἀναπείρους καὶ τυφλοὺς καὶ χωλοὺς εἰσάγαγε ὧδε. **22** καὶ εἶπεν ὁ δοῦλος, Κύριε, γέγονεν ὃ ἐπέταξας, καὶ ἔτι τόπος ἐστίν. **23** καὶ εἶπεν ὁ κύριος πρὸς τὸν δοῦλον, Ἔξελθε εἰς τὰς ὁδοὺς καὶ φραγμοὺς καὶ ἀνάγκασον εἰσελθεῖν, ἵνα γεμισθῇ μου ὁ οἶκος· **24** λέγω γὰρ ὑμῖν ὅτι οὐδεὶς τῶν ἀνδρῶν ἐκείνων τῶν κεκλημένων γεύσεταί μου τοῦ δείπνου.

25 Συνεπορεύοντο δὲ αὐτῷ ὄχλοι πολλοί, καὶ στραφεὶς εἶπεν πρὸς αὐτούς, **26** Εἴ τις ἔρχεται πρός με καὶ οὐ μισεῖ τὸν πατέρα ἑαυτοῦ καὶ τὴν μητέρα καὶ τὴν γυναῖκα καὶ τὰ τέκνα καὶ τοὺς ἀδελφοὺς καὶ τὰς ἀδελφὰς ἔτι τε καὶ τὴν ψυχὴν ἑαυτοῦ, οὐ δύναται εἶναί μου μαθητής. **27** ὅστις[c] οὐ βαστάζει τὸν σταυρὸν ἑαυτοῦ καὶ ἔρχεται ὀπίσω μου, οὐ δύναται εἶναί μου μαθητής. **28** τίς γὰρ ἐξ ὑμῶν θέλων πύργον οἰκοδομῆσαι οὐχὶ πρῶτον καθίσας ψηφίζει τὴν δαπάνην, εἰ ἔχει εἰς ἀπαρτισμόν; **29** ἵνα μήποτε θέντος αὐτοῦ θεμέλιον καὶ μὴ ἰσχύοντος

your friends, your brothers or relatives, or your rich neighbors; if you do, they may invite you back and so you will be repaid. [13]But when you give a banquet, invite the poor, the crippled, the lame, the blind, [14]and you will be blessed. Although they cannot repay you, you will be repaid at the resurrection of the righteous."

The Parable of the Great Banquet

[15]When one of those at the table with him heard this, he said to Jesus, "Blessed is the man who will eat at the feast in the kingdom of God."

[16]Jesus replied: "A certain man was preparing a great banquet and invited many guests. [17]At the time of the banquet he sent his servant to tell those who had been invited, 'Come, for everything is now ready.'

[18]"But they all alike began to make excuses. The first said, 'I have just bought a field, and I must go and see it. Please excuse me.'

[19]"Another said, 'I have just bought five yoke of oxen, and I'm on my way to try them out. Please excuse me.'

[20]"Still another said, 'I just got married, so I can't come.'

[21]"The servant came back and reported this to his master. Then the owner of the house became angry and ordered his servant, 'Go out quickly into the streets and alleys of the town and bring in the poor, the crippled, the blind and the lame.'

[22]" 'Sir,' the servant said, 'what you ordered has been done, but there is still room.'

[23]"Then the master told his servant, 'Go out to the roads and country lanes and make them come in, so that my house will be full. [24]I tell you, not one of those men who were invited will get a taste of my banquet.' "

The Cost of Being a Disciple

[25]Large crowds were traveling with Jesus, and turning to them he said: [26]"If anyone comes to me and does not hate his father and mother, his wife and children, his brothers and sisters—yes, even his own life—he cannot be my disciple. [27]And anyone who does not carry his cross and follow me cannot be my disciple.

[28]"Suppose one of you wants to build a tower. Will he not first sit down and estimate the cost to see if he has enough money to complete it? [29]For if he lays the foundation and is not able to finish it, everyone

---

[l]Gk *he*   [m]The Greek word for *you* here is plural

[b]15 NIV text ἄριστον †   [c]27 NIV text καὶ ὅστις †

able to finish, all who see it will begin to ridicule him, 30saying, 'This fellow began to build and was not able to finish.' 31Or what king, going out to wage war against another king, will not sit down first and consider whether he is able with ten thousand to oppose the one who comes against him with twenty thousand? 32If he cannot, then, while the other is still far away, he sends a delegation and asks for the terms of peace. 33So therefore, none of you can become my disciple if you do not give up all your possessions.

About Salt

34 "Salt is good; but if salt has lost its taste, how can its saltiness be restored?[n] 35It is fit neither for the soil nor for the manure pile; they throw it away. Let anyone with ears to hear listen!"

The Parable of the Lost Sheep

15 Now all the tax collectors and sinners were coming near to listen to him. 2And the Pharisees and the scribes were grumbling and saying, "This fellow welcomes sinners and eats with them."

3 So he told them this parable: 4"Which one of you, having a hundred sheep and losing one of them, does not leave the ninety-nine in the wilderness and go after the one that is lost until he finds it? 5When he has found it, he lays it on his shoulders and rejoices. 6And when he comes home, he calls together his friends and neighbors, saying to them, 'Rejoice with me, for I have found my sheep that was lost.' 7Just so, I tell you, there will be more joy in heaven over one sinner who repents than over ninety-nine righteous persons who need no repentance.

The Parable of the Lost Coin

8 "Or what woman having ten silver coins,[o] if she loses one of them, does not light a lamp, sweep the house, and search carefully until she finds it? 9When she has found it, she calls together her friends and neighbors, saying, 'Rejoice with me, for I have found the coin that I had lost.' 10Just so, I tell you, there is joy in the presence of the angels of God over one sinner who repents."

The Parable of the Prodigal and His Brother

11 Then Jesus[p] said, "There was a man who had two sons. 12The younger of them said to his father, 'Father, give me the share

ἐκτελέσαι πάντες οἱ θεωροῦντες ἄρξωνται αὐτῷ ἐμπαίζειν 30 λέγοντες ὅτι Οὗτος ὁ ἄνθρωπος ἤρξατο οἰκοδομεῖν καὶ οὐκ ἴσχυσεν ἐκτελέσαι. 31 ἢ τίς βασιλεὺς πορευόμενος ἑτέρῳ βασιλεῖ συμβαλεῖν εἰς πόλεμον οὐχὶ καθίσας πρῶτον βουλεύσεται εἰ δυνατός ἐστιν ἐν δέκα χιλιάσιν ὑπαντῆσαι τῷ μετὰ εἴκοσι χιλιάδων ἐρχομένῳ ἐπ' αὐτόν; 32 εἰ δὲ μή γε, ἔτι αὐτοῦ πόρρω ὄντος πρεσβείαν ἀποστείλας ἐρωτᾷ τὰ πρὸς εἰρήνην. 33 οὕτως οὖν πᾶς ἐξ ὑμῶν ὃς οὐκ ἀποτάσσεται πᾶσιν τοῖς ἑαυτοῦ ὑπάρχουσιν οὐ δύναται εἶναί μου μαθητής.

34 Καλὸν οὖν τὸ ἅλας· ἐὰν δὲ καὶ τὸ ἅλας μωρανθῇ, ἐν τίνι ἀρτυθήσεται; 35 οὔτε εἰς γῆν οὔτε εἰς κοπρίαν εὔθετόν ἐστιν, ἔξω βάλλουσιν αὐτό. ὁ ἔχων ὦτα ἀκούειν ἀκουέτω.

15 Ἦσαν δὲ αὐτῷ ἐγγίζοντες πάντες οἱ τελῶναι καὶ οἱ ἁμαρτωλοὶ ἀκούειν αὐτοῦ. 2 καὶ διεγόγγυζον οἵ τε Φαρισαῖοι καὶ οἱ γραμματεῖς λέγοντες ὅτι Οὗτος ἁμαρτωλοὺς προσδέχεται καὶ συνεσθίει αὐτοῖς. 3 εἶπεν δὲ πρὸς αὐτοὺς τὴν παραβολὴν ταύτην λέγων, 4 Τίς ἄνθρωπος ἐξ ὑμῶν ἔχων ἑκατὸν πρόβατα καὶ ἀπολέσας ἐξ αὐτῶν ἓν οὐ καταλείπει τὰ ἐνενήκοντα ἐννέα ἐν τῇ ἐρήμῳ καὶ πορεύεται ἐπὶ τὸ ἀπολωλὸς ἕως εὕρη αὐτό; 5 καὶ εὑρὼν ἐπιτίθησιν ἐπὶ τοὺς ὤμους αὐτοῦ χαίρων 6 καὶ ἐλθὼν εἰς τὸν οἶκον συγκαλεῖ τοὺς φίλους καὶ τοὺς γείτονας λέγων αὐτοῖς, Συγχάρητέ μοι, ὅτι εὗρον τὸ πρόβατόν μου τὸ ἀπολωλός. 7 λέγω ὑμῖν ὅτι οὕτως χαρὰ ἐν τῷ οὐρανῷ ἔσται ἐπὶ ἑνὶ ἁμαρτωλῷ μετανοοῦντι ἢ ἐπὶ ἐνενήκοντα ἐννέα δικαίοις οἵτινες οὐ χρείαν ἔχουσιν μετανοίας.

8 Ἢ τίς γυνὴ δραχμὰς ἔχουσα δέκα ἐὰν ἀπολέσῃ δραχμὴν μίαν, οὐχὶ ἅπτει λύχνον καὶ σαροῖ τὴν οἰκίαν καὶ ζητεῖ ἐπιμελῶς ἕως οὗ εὕρῃ; 9 καὶ εὑροῦσα συγκαλεῖ τὰς φίλας καὶ γείτονας λέγουσα, Συγχάρητέ μοι, ὅτι εὗρον τὴν δραχμὴν ἣν ἀπώλεσα. 10 οὕτως, λέγω ὑμῖν, γίνεται χαρὰ ἐνώπιον τῶν ἀγγέλων τοῦ θεοῦ ἐπὶ ἑνὶ ἁμαρτωλῷ μετανοοῦντι.

11 Εἶπεν δέ, Ἄνθρωπός τις εἶχεν δύο υἱούς. 12 καὶ εἶπεν ὁ νεώτερος αὐτῶν τῷ πατρί, Πάτερ, δός μοι τὸ ἐπιβάλλον μέρος τῆς οὐσίας. ὁ δὲ

who sees it will ridicule him, 30saying, 'This fellow began to build and was not able to finish.'

31"Or suppose a king is about to go to war against another king. Will he not first sit down and consider whether he is able with ten thousand men to oppose the one coming against him with twenty thousand? 32If he is not able, he will send a delegation while the other is still a long way off and will ask for terms of peace. 33In the same way, any of you who does not give up everything he has cannot be my disciple.

34"Salt is good, but if it loses its saltiness, how can it be made salty again? 35It is fit neither for the soil nor for the manure pile; it is thrown out.

"He who has ears to hear, let him hear."

The Parable of the Lost Sheep

15 Now the tax collectors and "sinners" were all gathering around to hear him. 2But the Pharisees and the teachers of the law muttered, "This man welcomes sinners and eats with them."

3Then Jesus told them this parable: 4"Suppose one of you has a hundred sheep and loses one of them. Does he not leave the ninety-nine in the open country and go after the lost sheep until he finds it? 5And when he finds it, he joyfully puts it on his shoulders 6and goes home. Then he calls his friends and neighbors together and says, 'Rejoice with me; I have found my lost sheep.' 7I tell you that in the same way there will be more rejoicing in heaven over one sinner who repents than over ninety-nine righteous persons who do not need to repent.

The Parable of the Lost Coin

8"Or suppose a woman has ten silver coins[a] and loses one. Does she not light a lamp, sweep the house and search carefully until she finds it? 9And when she finds it, she calls her friends and neighbors together and says, 'Rejoice with me; I have found my lost coin.' 10In the same way, I tell you, there is rejoicing in the presence of the angels of God over one sinner who repents."

The Parable of the Lost Son

11Jesus continued: "There was a man who had two sons. 12The younger one said to his father, 'Father, give me my share of the

n Or how can it be used for seasoning?   o Gk drachmas, each worth about a day's wage for a laborer   p Gk he

[n]8 Greek ten drachmas, each worth about a day's wages

of the property that will belong to me.' So he divided his property between them. 13A few days later the younger son gathered all he had and traveled to a distant country, and there he squandered his property in dissolute living. 14When he had spent everything, a severe famine took place throughout that country, and he began to be in need. 15So he went and hired himself out to one of the citizens of that country, who sent him to his fields to feed the pigs. 16He would gladly have filled himself withq the pods that the pigs were eating; and no one gave him anything. 17But when he came to himself he said, 'How many of my father's hired hands have bread enough and to spare, but here I am dying of hunger! 18I will get up and go to my father, and I will say to him, "Father, I have sinned against heaven and before you; 19I am no longer worthy to be called your son; treat me like one of your hired hands."' 20So he set off and went to his father. But while he was still far off, his father saw him and was filled with compassion; he ran and put his arms around him and kissed him. 21Then the son said to him, 'Father, I have sinned against heaven and before you; I am no longer worthy to be called your son.'r 22But the father said to his slaves, 'Quickly, bring out a robe—the best one— and put it on him; put a ring on his finger and sandals on his feet. 23And get the fatted calf and kill it, and let us eat and celebrate; 24for this son of mine was dead and is alive again; he was lost and is found!' And they began to celebrate.

25 "Now his elder son was in the field; and when he came and approached the house, he heard music and dancing. 26He called one of the slaves and asked what was going on. 27He replied, 'Your brother has come, and your father has killed the fatted calf, because he has got him back safe and sound.' 28Then he became angry and refused to go in. His father came out and began to plead with him. 29But he answered his father, 'Listen! For all these years I have been working like a slave for you, and I have never disobeyed your command; yet you have never given me even a young goat so that I might celebrate with my friends. 30But when this son of yours

διεῖλεν αὐτοῖς τὸν βίον. **13** καὶ μετ᾽ οὐ πολλὰς ἡμέρας συναγαγὼν πάντα ὁ νεώτερος υἱὸς ἀπεδήμησεν εἰς χώραν μακρὰν καὶ ἐκεῖ διεσκόρπισεν τὴν οὐσίαν αὐτοῦ ζῶν ἀσώτως. **14** δαπανήσαντος δὲ αὐτοῦ πάντα ἐγένετο λιμὸς ἰσχυρὰ κατὰ τὴν χώραν ἐκείνην, καὶ αὐτὸς ἤρξατο ὑστερεῖσθαι. **15** καὶ πορευθεὶς ἐκολλήθη ἑνὶ τῶν πολιτῶν τῆς χώρας ἐκείνης, καὶ ἔπεμψεν αὐτὸν εἰς τοὺς ἀγροὺς αὐτοῦ βόσκειν χοίρους, **16** καὶ ἐπεθύμει χορτασθῆναι ἐκa τῶν κερατίων ὧν ἤσθιον οἱ χοῖροι, καὶ οὐδεὶς ἐδίδου αὐτῷ. **17** εἰς ἑαυτὸν δὲ ἐλθὼν ἔφη, Πόσοι μίσθιοι τοῦ πατρός μου περισσεύονται ἄρτων, ἐγὼ δὲ λιμῷ ὧδε ἀπόλλυμαι. **18** ἀναστὰς πορεύσομαι πρὸς τὸν πατέρα μου καὶ ἐρῶ αὐτῷ, Πάτερ, ἥμαρτον εἰς τὸν οὐρανὸν καὶ ἐνώπιόν σου, **19** οὐκέτι εἰμὶ ἄξιος κληθῆναι υἱός σου· ποίησόν με ὡς ἕνα τῶν μισθίων σου. **20** καὶ ἀναστὰς ἦλθεν πρὸς τὸν πατέρα ἑαυτοῦ. ἔτι δὲ αὐτοῦ μακρὰν ἀπέχοντος εἶδεν αὐτὸν ὁ πατὴρ αὐτοῦ καὶ ἐσπλαγχνίσθη καὶ δραμὼν ἐπέπεσεν ἐπὶ τὸν τράχηλον αὐτοῦ καὶ κατεφίλησεν αὐτόν. **21** εἶπεν δὲ ὁ υἱὸς αὐτῷ, Πάτερ, ἥμαρτον εἰς τὸν οὐρανὸν καὶ ἐνώπιόν σου, οὐκέτι εἰμὶ ἄξιος κληθῆναι υἱός σου.b **22** εἶπεν δὲ ὁ πατὴρ πρὸς τοὺς δούλους αὐτοῦ, Ταχὺ ἐξενέγκατε στολὴν τὴν πρώτην καὶ ἐνδύσατε αὐτόν, καὶ δότε δακτύλιον εἰς τὴν χεῖρα αὐτοῦ καὶ ὑποδήματα εἰς τοὺς πόδας, **23** καὶ φέρετε τὸν μόσχον τὸν σιτευτόν, θύσατε, καὶ φαγόντες εὐφρανθῶμεν, **24** ὅτι οὗτος ὁ υἱός μου νεκρὸς ἦν καὶ ἀνέζησεν, ἦν ἀπολωλὼς καὶ εὑρέθη. καὶ ἤρξαντο εὐφραίνεσθαι.

25 Ἦν δὲ ὁ υἱὸς αὐτοῦ ὁ πρεσβύτερος ἐν ἀγρῷ· καὶ ὡς ἐρχόμενος ἤγγισεν τῇ οἰκίᾳ, ἤκουσεν συμφωνίας καὶ χορῶν, **26** καὶ προσκαλεσάμενος ἕνα τῶν παίδων ἐπυνθάνετο τί ἂν εἴη ταῦτα. **27** ὁ δὲ εἶπεν αὐτῷ ὅτι Ὁ ἀδελφός σου ἥκει, καὶ ἔθυσεν ὁ πατήρ σου τὸν μόσχον τὸν σιτευτόν, ὅτι ὑγιαίνοντα αὐτὸν ἀπέλαβεν. **28** ὠργίσθη δὲ καὶ οὐκ ἤθελεν εἰσελθεῖν, ὁ δὲ πατὴρ αὐτοῦ ἐξελθὼν παρεκάλει αὐτόν. **29** ὁ δὲ ἀποκριθεὶς εἶπεν τῷ πατρὶ αὐτοῦ, Ἰδοὺ τοσαῦτα ἔτη δουλεύω σοι καὶ οὐδέποτε ἐντολήν σου παρῆλθον, καὶ ἐμοὶ οὐδέποτε ἔδωκας ἔριφον ἵνα μετὰ τῶν φίλων μου εὐφρανθῶ· **30** ὅτε δὲ ὁ

estate.' So he divided his property between them.

13"Not long after that, the younger son got together all he had, set off for a distant country and there squandered his wealth in wild living. 14After he had spent everything, there was a severe famine in that whole country, and he began to be in need. 15So he went and hired himself out to a citizen of that country, who sent him to his fields to feed pigs. 16He longed to fill his stomach with the pods that the pigs were eating, but no one gave him anything.

17"When he came to his senses, he said, 'How many of my father's hired men have food to spare, and here I am starving to death! 18I will set out and go back to my father and say to him: Father, I have sinned against heaven and against you. 19I am no longer worthy to be called your son; make me like one of your hired men.' 20So he got up and went to his father.

"But while he was still a long way off, his father saw him and was filled with compassion for him; he ran to his son, threw his arms around him and kissed him.

21"The son said to him, 'Father, I have sinned against heaven and against you. I am no longer worthy to be called your son.'b'

22"But the father said to his servants, 'Quick! Bring the best robe and put it on him. Put a ring on his finger and sandals on his feet. 23Bring the fattened calf and kill it. Let's have a feast and celebrate. 24For this son of mine was dead and is alive again; he was lost and is found.' So they began to celebrate.

25"Meanwhile, the older son was in the field. When he came near the house, he heard music and dancing. 26So he called one of the servants and asked him what was going on. 27'Your brother has come,' he replied, 'and your father has killed the fattened calf because he has him back safe and sound.'

28"The older brother became angry and refused to go in. So his father went out and pleaded with him. 29But he answered his father, 'Look! All these years I've been slaving for you and never disobeyed your orders. Yet you never gave me even a young goat so I could celebrate with my friends. 30But when this son of yours who has

---

q Other ancient authorities read *filled his stomach with*
r Other ancient authorities add *treat me as one of your hired servants*

a16 NIV text and NRSV note q *γεμίσαι τὴν κοιλίαν αὐτοῦ ἀπὸ* b21 NIV/NRSV notes add *ποίησόν με ὡς ἕνα τῶν μισθίων σου.*

b21 Some early manuscripts *son. Make me like one of your hired men.*

came back, who has devoured your property with prostitutes, you killed the fatted calf for him!' [31]Then the father[p] said to him, 'Son, you are always with me, and all that is mine is yours. [32]But we had to celebrate and rejoice, because this brother of yours was dead and has come to life; he was lost and has been found.' "

The Parable of the Dishonest Manager

16 Then Jesus[p] said to the disciples, "There was a rich man who had a manager, and charges were brought to him that this man was squandering his property. [2]So he summoned him and said to him, 'What is this that I hear about you? Give me an accounting of your management, because you cannot be my manager any longer.' [3]Then the manager said to himself, 'What will I do, now that my master is taking the position away from me? I am not strong enough to dig, and I am ashamed to beg. [4]I have decided what to do so that, when I am dismissed as manager, people may welcome me into their homes.' [5]So, summoning his master's debtors one by one, he asked the first, 'How much do you owe my master?' [6]He answered, 'A hundred jugs of olive oil.' He said to him, 'Take your bill, sit down quickly, and make it fifty.' [7]Then he asked another, 'And how much do you owe?' He replied, 'A hundred containers of wheat.' He said to him, 'Take your bill and make it eighty.' [8]And his master commended the dishonest manager because he had acted shrewdly; for the children of this age are more shrewd in dealing with their own generation than are the children of light. [9]And I tell you, make friends for yourselves by means of dishonest wealth[s] so that when it is gone, they may welcome you into the eternal homes.[t]

10 "Whoever is faithful in a very little is faithful also in much; and whoever is dishonest in a very little is dishonest also in much. [11]If then you have not been faithful with the dishonest wealth,[s] who will entrust to you the true riches? [12]And if you have not been faithful with what belongs to another, who will give you what is your own? [13]No slave can serve two masters; for a slave will either hate the one and love the other, or be devoted to the one and

υἱός σου οὗτος ὁ καταφαγών σου τὸν βίον μετὰ πορνῶν ἦλθεν, ἔθυσας αὐτῷ τὸν σιτευτὸν μόσχον. **31** ὁ δὲ εἶπεν αὐτῷ, Τέκνον, σὺ πάντοτε μετ᾽ ἐμοῦ εἶ, καὶ πάντα τὰ ἐμὰ σά ἐστιν· **32** εὐφρανθῆναι δὲ καὶ χαρῆναι ἔδει, ὅτι ὁ ἀδελφός σου οὗτος νεκρὸς ἦν καὶ ἔζησεν[c], καὶ ἀπολωλὼς καὶ εὑρέθη.

16 Ἔλεγεν δὲ καὶ πρὸς τοὺς μαθητάς, Ἄνθρωπός τις ἦν πλούσιος ὃς εἶχεν οἰκονόμον, καὶ οὗτος διεβλήθη αὐτῷ ὡς διασκορπίζων τὰ ὑπάρχοντα αὐτοῦ. **2** καὶ φωνήσας αὐτὸν εἶπεν αὐτῷ, Τί τοῦτο ἀκούω περὶ σοῦ; ἀπόδος τὸν λόγον τῆς οἰκονομίας σου, οὐ γὰρ δύνῃ ἔτι οἰκονομεῖν. **3** εἶπεν δὲ ἐν ἑαυτῷ ὁ οἰκονόμος, Τί ποιήσω, ὅτι ὁ κύριός μου ἀφαιρεῖται τὴν οἰκονομίαν ἀπ᾽ ἐμοῦ; σκάπτειν οὐκ ἰσχύω, ἐπαιτεῖν αἰσχύνομαι. **4** ἔγνων τί ποιήσω, ἵνα ὅταν μετασταθῶ ἐκ τῆς οἰκονομίας δέξωνταί με εἰς τοὺς οἴκους αὐτῶν. **5** καὶ προσκαλεσάμενος ἕνα ἕκαστον τῶν χρεοφειλετῶν τοῦ κυρίου ἑαυτοῦ ἔλεγεν τῷ πρώτῳ, Πόσον ὀφείλεις τῷ κυρίῳ μου; **6** ὁ δὲ εἶπεν, Ἑκατὸν βάτους ἐλαίου. ὁ δὲ εἶπεν αὐτῷ, Δέξαι σου τὰ γράμματα καὶ καθίσας ταχέως γράψον πεντήκοντα. **7** ἔπειτα ἑτέρῳ εἶπεν, Σὺ δὲ πόσον ὀφείλεις; ὁ δὲ εἶπεν, Ἑκατὸν κόρους σίτου. λέγει αὐτῷ, Δέξαι σου τὰ γράμματα καὶ γράψον ὀγδοήκοντα. **8** καὶ ἐπῄνεσεν ὁ κύριος τὸν οἰκονόμον τῆς ἀδικίας ὅτι φρονίμως ἐποίησεν· ὅτι οἱ υἱοὶ τοῦ αἰῶνος τούτου φρονιμώτεροι ὑπὲρ τοὺς υἱοὺς τοῦ φωτὸς εἰς τὴν γενεὰν τὴν ἑαυτῶν εἰσιν. **9** Καὶ ἐγὼ ὑμῖν λέγω, ἑαυτοῖς ποιήσατε φίλους ἐκ τοῦ μαμωνᾶ τῆς ἀδικίας, ἵνα ὅταν ἐκλίπῃ δέξωνται ὑμᾶς εἰς τὰς αἰωνίους σκηνάς. **10** ὁ πιστὸς ἐν ἐλαχίστῳ καὶ ἐν πολλῷ πιστός ἐστιν, καὶ ὁ ἐν ἐλαχίστῳ ἄδικος καὶ ἐν πολλῷ ἄδικός ἐστιν. **11** εἰ οὖν ἐν τῷ ἀδίκῳ μαμωνᾷ πιστοὶ οὐκ ἐγένεσθε, τὸ ἀληθινὸν τίς ὑμῖν πιστεύσει; **12** καὶ εἰ ἐν τῷ ἀλλοτρίῳ πιστοὶ οὐκ ἐγένεσθε, τὸ ὑμέτερον τίς ὑμῖν δώσει; **13** Οὐδεὶς οἰκέτης δύναται δυσὶ κυρίοις δουλεύειν· ἢ γὰρ τὸν ἕνα μισήσει καὶ τὸν ἕτερον ἀγαπήσει, ἢ ἑνὸς ἀνθέξεται

squandered your property with prostitutes comes home, you kill the fattened calf for him!'

[31]" 'My son,' the father said, 'you are always with me, and everything I have is yours. [32]But we had to celebrate and be glad, because this brother of yours was dead and is alive again; he was lost and is found.' "

The Parable of the Shrewd Manager

16 Jesus told his disciples: "There was a rich man whose manager was accused of wasting his possessions. [2]So he called him in and asked him, 'What is this I hear about you? Give an account of your management, because you cannot be manager any longer.'

[3]"The manager said to himself, 'What shall I do now? My master is taking away my job. I'm not strong enough to dig, and I'm ashamed to beg— [4]I know what I'll do so that, when I lose my job here, people will welcome me into their houses.'

[5]"So he called in each one of his master's debtors. He asked the first, 'How much do you owe my master?'

[6]" 'Eight hundred gallons[a] of olive oil,' he replied.

"The manager told him, 'Take your bill, sit down quickly, and make it four hundred.'

[7]"Then he asked the second, 'And how much do you owe?'

" 'A thousand bushels[b] of wheat,' he replied.

"He told him, 'Take your bill and make it eight hundred.'

[8]"The master commended the dishonest manager because he had acted shrewdly. For the people of this world are more shrewd in dealing with their own kind than are the people of the light. [9]I tell you, use worldly wealth to gain friends for yourselves, so that when it is gone, you will be welcomed into eternal dwellings.

[10]"Whoever can be trusted with very little can also be trusted with much, and whoever is dishonest with very little will also be dishonest with much. [11]So if you have not been trustworthy in handling worldly wealth, who will trust you with true riches? [12]And if you have not been trustworthy with someone else's property, who will give you property of your own?

[13]"No servant can serve two masters. Either he will hate the one and love the other,

[p]Gk *he* [s]Gk *mammon* [t]Gk *tents*

[c]32 NIV text ἀνέζησεν †

[a]6 Greek *one hundred batous* (probably about 3 kiloliters)
[b]7 Greek *one hundred korous* (probably about 35 kiloliters)

despise the other. You cannot serve God and wealth."ˢ

The Law and the Kingdom of God

14 The Pharisees, who were lovers of money, heard all this, and they ridiculed him. ¹⁵So he said to them, "You are those who justify yourselves in the sight of others; but God knows your hearts; for what is prized by human beings is an abomination in the sight of God.

16 "The law and the prophets were in effect until John came; since then the good news of the kingdom of God is proclaimed, and everyone tries to enter it by force.ᵘ ¹⁷But it is easier for heaven and earth to pass away, than for one stroke of a letter in the law to be dropped.

18 "Anyone who divorces his wife and marries another commits adultery, and whoever marries a woman divorced from her husband commits adultery.

The Rich Man and Lazarus

19 "There was a rich man who was dressed in purple and fine linen and who feasted sumptuously every day. ²⁰And at his gate lay a poor man named Lazarus, covered with sores, ²¹who longed to satisfy his hunger with what fell from the rich man's table; even the dogs would come and lick his sores. ²²The poor man died and was carried away by the angels to be with Abraham.ᵛ The rich man also died and was buried. ²³In Hades, where he was being tormented, he looked up and saw Abraham far away with Lazarus by his side.ʷ ²⁴He called out, 'Father Abraham, have mercy on me, and send Lazarus to dip the tip of his finger in water and cool my tongue; for I am in agony in these flames.' ²⁵But Abraham said, 'Child, remember that during your lifetime you received your good things, and Lazarus in like manner evil things; but now he is comforted here, and you are in agony. ²⁶Besides all this, between you and us a great chasm has been fixed, so that those who might want to pass from here to you cannot do so, and no one can cross from there to us.' ²⁷He said, 'Then, father, I beg you to send him to my father's house— ²⁸for I have five brothers—that he may warn them, so that they will not also come into this place of torment.' ²⁹Abraham replied, 'They have Moses and the prophets; they should listen to them.' ³⁰He said, 'No, father

ˢ Gk mammon   ᵘ Or everyone is strongly urged to enter it
ᵛ Gk to Abraham's bosom   ʷ Gk in his bosom

καὶ τοῦ ἑτέρου καταφρονήσει. οὐ δύνασθε θεῷ δουλεύειν καὶ μαμωνᾷ.

14 Ἤκουον δὲ ταῦτα πάντα οἱ Φαρισαῖοι φιλάργυροι ὑπάρχοντες καὶ ἐξεμυκτήριζον αὐτόν. 15 καὶ εἶπεν αὐτοῖς, Ὑμεῖς ἐστε οἱ δικαιοῦντες ἑαυτοὺς ἐνώπιον τῶν ἀνθρώπων, ὁ δὲ θεὸς γινώσκει τὰς καρδίας ὑμῶν· ὅτι τὸ ἐν ἀνθρώποις ὑψηλὸν βδέλυγμα ἐνώπιον τοῦ θεοῦ. 16 Ὁ νόμος καὶ οἱ προφῆται μέχρι Ἰωάννου· ἀπὸ τότε ἡ βασιλεία τοῦ θεοῦ εὐαγγελίζεται καὶ πᾶς εἰς αὐτὴν βιάζεται. 17 Εὐκοπώτερον δέ ἐστιν τὸν οὐρανὸν καὶ τὴν γῆν παρελθεῖν ἢ τοῦ νόμου μίαν κεραίαν πεσεῖν. 18 Πᾶς ὁ ἀπολύων τὴν γυναῖκα αὐτοῦ καὶ γαμῶν ἑτέραν μοιχεύει, καὶ ὁ ἀπολελυμένην ἀπὸ ἀνδρὸς γαμῶν μοιχεύει.

19 Ἄνθρωπος δέ τις ἦν πλούσιος, καὶ ἐνεδιδύσκετο πορφύραν καὶ βύσσον εὐφραινόμενος καθ᾽ ἡμέραν λαμπρῶς. 20 πτωχὸς δέ τις ὀνόματι Λάζαρος ἐβέβλητο πρὸς τὸν πυλῶνα αὐτοῦ εἱλκωμένος 21 καὶ ἐπιθυμῶν χορτασθῆναι ἀπὸ τῶν πιπτόντων ἀπὸ τῆς τραπέζης τοῦ πλουσίου· ἀλλὰ καὶ οἱ κύνες ἐρχόμενοι ἐπέλειχον τὰ ἕλκη αὐτοῦ. 22 ἐγένετο δὲ ἀποθανεῖν τὸν πτωχὸν καὶ ἀπενεχθῆναι αὐτὸν ὑπὸ τῶν ἀγγέλων εἰς τὸν κόλπον Ἀβραάμ· ἀπέθανεν δὲ καὶ ὁ πλούσιος καὶ ἐτάφη. 23 καὶ ἐν τῷ ᾅδῃ ἐπάρας τοὺς ὀφθαλμοὺς αὐτοῦ, ὑπάρχων ἐν βασάνοις, ὁρᾷ Ἀβραὰμ ἀπὸ μακρόθεν καὶ Λάζαρον ἐν τοῖς κόλποις αὐτοῦ. 24 καὶ αὐτὸς φωνήσας εἶπεν, Πάτερ Ἀβραάμ, ἐλέησόν με καὶ πέμψον Λάζαρον ἵνα βάψῃ τὸ ἄκρον τοῦ δακτύλου αὐτοῦ ὕδατος καὶ καταψύξῃ τὴν γλῶσσάν μου, ὅτι ὀδυνῶμαι ἐν τῇ φλογὶ ταύτῃ. 25 εἶπεν δὲ Ἀβραάμ, Τέκνον, μνήσθητι ὅτι ἀπέλαβες τὰ ἀγαθά σου ἐν τῇ ζωῇ σου, καὶ Λάζαρος ὁμοίως τὰ κακά· νῦν δὲ ὧδε παρακαλεῖται, σὺ δὲ ὀδυνᾶσαι. 26 καὶ ἐν πᾶσι τούτοις μεταξὺ ἡμῶν καὶ ὑμῶν χάσμα μέγα ἐστήρικται, ὅπως οἱ θέλοντες διαβῆναι ἔνθεν πρὸς ὑμᾶς μὴ δύνωνται, μηδὲ ἐκεῖθεν πρὸς ἡμᾶς διαπερῶσιν. 27 εἶπεν δέ, Ἐρωτῶ σε οὖν, πάτερ, ἵνα πέμψῃς αὐτὸν εἰς τὸν οἶκον τοῦ πατρός μου, 28 ἔχω γὰρ πέντε ἀδελφούς, ὅπως διαμαρτύρηται αὐτοῖς, ἵνα μὴ καὶ αὐτοὶ ἔλθωσιν εἰς τὸν τόπον τοῦτον τῆς βασάνου. 29 λέγει δὲ Ἀβραάμ, Ἔχουσι Μωϋσέα καὶ τοὺς προφήτας· ἀκουσάτωσαν αὐτῶν. 30 ὁ δὲ εἶπεν, Οὐχί, πάτερ Ἀβραάμ, ἀλλ᾽

or he will be devoted to the one and despise the other. You cannot serve both God and Money."

¹⁴The Pharisees, who loved money, heard all this and were sneering at Jesus. ¹⁵He said to them, "You are the ones who justify yourselves in the eyes of men, but God knows your hearts. What is highly valued among men is detestable in God's sight.

Additional Teachings

¹⁶"The Law and the Prophets were proclaimed until John. Since that time, the good news of the kingdom of God is being preached, and everyone is forcing his way into it. ¹⁷It is easier for heaven and earth to disappear than for the least stroke of a pen to drop out of the Law.

¹⁸"Anyone who divorces his wife and marries another woman commits adultery, and the man who marries a divorced woman commits adultery.

The Rich Man and Lazarus

¹⁹"There was a rich man who was dressed in purple and fine linen and lived in luxury every day. ²⁰At his gate was laid a beggar named Lazarus, covered with sores ²¹and longing to eat what fell from the rich man's table. Even the dogs came and licked his sores.

²²"The time came when the beggar died and the angels carried him to Abraham's side. The rich man also died and was buried. ²³In hell,ᶜ where he was in torment, he looked up and saw Abraham far away, with Lazarus by his side. ²⁴So he called to him, 'Father Abraham, have pity on me and send Lazarus to dip the tip of his finger in water and cool my tongue, because I am in agony in this fire.'

²⁵"But Abraham replied, 'Son, remember that in your lifetime you received your good things, while Lazarus received bad things, but now he is comforted here and you are in agony. ²⁶And besides all this, between us and you a great chasm has been fixed, so that those who want to go from here to you cannot, nor can anyone cross over from there to us.'

²⁷"He answered, 'Then I beg you, father, send Lazarus to my father's house, ²⁸for I have five brothers. Let him warn them, so that they will not also come to this place of torment.'

²⁹"Abraham replied, 'They have Moses and the Prophets; let them listen to them.'

³⁰" 'No, father Abraham,' he said, 'but if

ᶜ23 Greek Hades

Abraham; but if someone goes to them from the dead, they will repent.' [31]He said to him, 'If they do not listen to Moses and the prophets, neither will they be convinced even if someone rises from the dead.' "

Some Sayings of Jesus

17 Jesus[x] said to his disciples, "Occasions for stumbling are bound to come, but woe to anyone by whom they come! [2]It would be better for you if a millstone were hung around your neck and you were thrown into the sea than for you to cause one of these little ones to stumble. [3]Be on your guard! If another disciple[y] sins, you must rebuke the offender, and if there is repentance, you must forgive. [4]And if the same person sins against you seven times a day, and turns back to you seven times and says, 'I repent,' you must forgive."

5 The apostles said to the Lord, "Increase our faith!" [6]The Lord replied, "If you had faith the size of a[z] mustard seed, you could say to this mulberry tree, 'Be uprooted and planted in the sea,' and it would obey you.

7 "Who among you would say to your slave who has just come in from plowing or tending sheep in the field, 'Come here at once and take your place at the table'? [8]Would you not rather say to him, 'Prepare supper for me, put on your apron and serve me while I eat and drink; later you may eat and drink'? [9]Do you thank the slave for doing what was commanded? [10]So you also, when you have done all that you were ordered to do, say, 'We are worthless slaves; we have done only what we ought to have done!' "

Jesus Cleanses Ten Lepers

11 On the way to Jerusalem Jesus[a] was going through the region between Samaria and Galilee. [12]As he entered a village, ten lepers[b] approached him. Keeping their distance, [13]they called out, saying, "Jesus, Master, have mercy on us!" [14]When he saw them, he said to them, "Go and show yourselves to the priests." And as they went, they were made clean. [15]Then one of them, when he saw that he was healed, turned back, praising God with a loud voice. [16]He prostrated himself at Jesus'[c] feet and thanked him. And he was a Samaritan. [17]Then Jesus asked, "Were not

[x] Gk *He*   [y] Gk *your brother*   [z] Gk *faith as a grain of*
he   [b] The terms *leper* and *leprosy* can refer to several diseases   [c] Gk *his*

ἐάν τις ἀπὸ νεκρῶν πορευθῇ πρὸς αὐτοὺς μετανοήσουσιν. **31** εἶπεν δὲ αὐτῷ, Εἰ Μωϋσέως καὶ τῶν προφητῶν οὐκ ἀκούουσιν, οὐδ' ἐάν τις ἐκ νεκρῶν ἀναστῇ πεισθήσονται.

17 Εἶπεν δὲ πρὸς τοὺς μαθητὰς αὐτοῦ, Ἀνένδεκτόν ἐστιν τοῦ τὰ σκάνδαλα μὴ ἐλθεῖν, πλὴν οὐαὶ δι' οὗ ἔρχεται· **2** λυσιτελεῖ αὐτῷ εἰ λίθος μυλικὸς περίκειται περὶ τὸν τράχηλον αὐτοῦ καὶ ἔρριπται εἰς τὴν θάλασσαν ἢ ἵνα σκανδαλίσῃ τῶν μικρῶν τούτων ἕνα. **3** προσέχετε ἑαυτοῖς. ἐὰν ἁμάρτῃ ὁ ἀδελφός σου ἐπιτίμησον αὐτῷ, καὶ ἐὰν μετανοήσῃ ἄφες αὐτῷ. **4** καὶ ἐὰν ἑπτάκις τῆς ἡμέρας ἁμαρτήσῃ εἰς σὲ καὶ ἑπτάκις ἐπιστρέψῃ πρὸς σὲ λέγων, Μετανοῶ, ἀφήσεις αὐτῷ.

5 Καὶ εἶπαν οἱ ἀπόστολοι τῷ κυρίῳ, Πρόσθες ἡμῖν πίστιν. **6** εἶπεν δὲ ὁ κύριος, Εἰ ἔχετε πίστιν ὡς κόκκον σινάπεως, ἐλέγετε ἂν τῇ συκαμίνῳ [ταύτῃ], Ἐκριζώθητι καὶ φυτεύθητι ἐν τῇ θαλάσσῃ· καὶ ὑπήκουσεν ἂν ὑμῖν.

7 Τίς δὲ ἐξ ὑμῶν δοῦλον ἔχων ἀροτριῶντα ἢ ποιμαίνοντα, ὃς εἰσελθόντι ἐκ τοῦ ἀγροῦ ἐρεῖ αὐτῷ, Εὐθέως παρελθὼν ἀνάπεσε, **8** ἀλλ' οὐχὶ ἐρεῖ αὐτῷ, Ἑτοίμασον τί δειπνήσω καὶ περιζωσάμενος διακόνει μοι ἕως φάγω καὶ πίω, καὶ μετὰ ταῦτα φάγεσαι καὶ πίεσαι σύ; **9** μὴ ἔχει χάριν τῷ δούλῳ ὅτι ἐποίησεν τὰ διαταχθέντα; **10** οὕτως καὶ ὑμεῖς, ὅταν ποιήσητε πάντα τὰ διαταχθέντα ὑμῖν, λέγετε ὅτι Δοῦλοι ἀχρεῖοί ἐσμεν, ὃ ὠφείλομεν ποιῆσαι πεποιήκαμεν.

11 Καὶ ἐγένετο ἐν τῷ πορεύεσθαι εἰς Ἰερουσαλὴμ καὶ αὐτὸς διήρχετο διὰ μέσον Σαμαρείας καὶ Γαλιλαίας. **12** καὶ εἰσερχομένου αὐτοῦ εἴς τινα κώμην ἀπήντησαν [αὐτῷ] δέκα λεπροὶ ἄνδρες, οἳ ἔστησαν πόρρωθεν **13** καὶ αὐτοὶ ἦραν φωνὴν λέγοντες, Ἰησοῦ ἐπιστάτα, ἐλέησον ἡμᾶς. **14** καὶ ἰδὼν εἶπεν αὐτοῖς, Πορευθέντες ἐπιδείξατε ἑαυτοὺς τοῖς ἱερεῦσιν. καὶ ἐγένετο ἐν τῷ ὑπάγειν αὐτοὺς ἐκαθαρίσθησαν. **15** εἷς δὲ ἐξ αὐτῶν, ἰδὼν ὅτι ἰάθη, ὑπέστρεψεν μετὰ φωνῆς μεγάλης δοξάζων τὸν θεόν, **16** καὶ ἔπεσεν ἐπὶ πρόσωπον παρὰ τοὺς πόδας αὐτοῦ εὐχαριστῶν αὐτῷ· καὶ αὐτὸς ἦν Σαμαρίτης. **17** ἀποκριθεὶς δὲ ὁ Ἰησοῦς εἶπεν, Οὐχὶ οἱ δέκα

someone from the dead goes to them, they will repent.'

[31]"He said to him, 'If they do not listen to Moses and the Prophets, they will not be convinced even if someone rises from the dead.' "

Sin, Faith, Duty

17 Jesus said to his disciples: "Things that cause people to sin are bound to come, but woe to that person through whom they come. [2]It would be better for him to be thrown into the sea with a millstone tied around his neck than for him to cause one of these little ones to sin. [3]So watch yourselves.

"If your brother sins, rebuke him, and if he repents, forgive him. [4]If he sins against you seven times in a day, and seven times comes back to you and says, 'I repent,' forgive him."

[5]The apostles said to the Lord, "Increase our faith!"

[6]He replied, "If you have faith as small as a mustard seed, you can say to this mulberry tree, 'Be uprooted and planted in the sea,' and it will obey you.

[7]"Suppose one of you had a servant plowing or looking after the sheep. Would he say to the servant when he comes in from the field, 'Come along now and sit down to eat'? [8]Would he not rather say, 'Prepare my supper, get yourself ready and wait on me while I eat and drink; after that you may eat and drink'? [9]Would he thank the servant because he did what he was told to do? [10]So you also, when you have done everything you were told to do, should say, 'We are unworthy servants; we have only done our duty.' "

Ten Healed of Leprosy

[11]Now on his way to Jerusalem, Jesus traveled along the border between Samaria and Galilee. [12]As he was going into a village, ten men who had leprosy[a] met him. They stood at a distance [13]and called out in a loud voice, "Jesus, Master, have pity on us!"

[14]When he saw them, he said, "Go, show yourselves to the priests." And as they went, they were cleansed.

[15]One of them, when he saw he was healed, came back, praising God in a loud voice. [16]He threw himself at Jesus' feet and thanked him—and he was a Samaritan.

[17]Jesus asked, "Were not all ten cleansed?

[a] 12 The Greek word was used for various diseases affecting the skin—not necessarily leprosy.

ten made clean? But the other nine, where are they? [18]Was none of them found to return and give praise to God except this foreigner?" [19]Then he said to him, "Get up and go on your way; your faith has made you well."

The Coming of the Kingdom

20 Once Jesus[a] was asked by the Pharisees when the kingdom of God was coming, and he answered, "The kingdom of God is not coming with things that can be observed; [21]nor will they say, 'Look, here it is!' or 'There it is!' For, in fact, the kingdom of God is among[d] you."

22 Then he said to the disciples, "The days are coming when you will long to see one of the days of the Son of Man, and you will not see it. [23]They will say to you, 'Look there!' or 'Look here!' Do not go, do not set off in pursuit. [24]For as the lightning flashes and lights up the sky from one side to the other, so will the Son of Man be in his day.[e] [25]But first he must endure much suffering and be rejected by this generation. [26]Just as it was in the days of Noah, so too it will be in the days of the Son of Man. [27]They were eating and drinking, and marrying and being given in marriage, until the day Noah entered the ark, and the flood came and destroyed all of them. [28]Likewise, just as it was in the days of Lot: they were eating and drinking, buying and selling, planting and building, [29]but on the day that Lot left Sodom, it rained fire and sulfur from heaven and destroyed all of them [30]—it will be like that on the day that the Son of Man is revealed. [31]On that day, anyone on the housetop who has belongings in the house must not come down to take them away; and likewise anyone in the field must not turn back. [32]Remember Lot's wife. [33]Those who try to make their life secure will lose it, but those who lose their life will keep it. [34]I tell you, on that night there will be two in one bed; one will be taken and the other left. [35]There will be two women grinding meal together; one will be taken and the other left."[f] [37]Then they asked him, "Where, Lord?" He said to them, "Where the corpse is, there the vultures will gather."

The Parable of the Widow and the Unjust Judge

18 Then Jesus[a] told them a parable about their need to pray always

---

ἐκαθαρίσθησαν· οἱ δὲ ἐννέα ποῦ; [18]οὐχ εὑρέθησαν ὑποστρέψαντες δοῦναι δόξαν τῷ θεῷ εἰ μὴ ὁ ἀλλογενὴς οὗτος; [19]καὶ εἶπεν αὐτῷ, Ἀναστὰς πορεύου· ἡ πίστις σου σέσωκέν σε.

[20]Ἐπερωτηθεὶς δὲ ὑπὸ τῶν Φαρισαίων πότε ἔρχεται ἡ βασιλεία τοῦ θεοῦ ἀπεκρίθη αὐτοῖς καὶ εἶπεν, Οὐκ ἔρχεται ἡ βασιλεία τοῦ θεοῦ μετὰ παρατηρήσεως, [21]οὐδὲ ἐροῦσιν, Ἰδοὺ ὧδε ἤ, Ἐκεῖ, ἰδοὺ γὰρ ἡ βασιλεία τοῦ θεοῦ ἐντὸς ὑμῶν ἐστιν. [22]Εἶπεν δὲ πρὸς τοὺς μαθητάς, Ἐλεύσονται ἡμέραι ὅτε ἐπιθυμήσετε μίαν τῶν ἡμερῶν τοῦ υἱοῦ τοῦ ἀνθρώπου ἰδεῖν καὶ οὐκ ὄψεσθε. [23]καὶ ἐροῦσιν ὑμῖν, Ἰδοὺ ἐκεῖ, [ἤ,] Ἰδοὺ ὧδε· μὴ ἀπέλθητε μηδὲ διώξητε. [24]ὥσπερ γὰρ ἡ ἀστραπὴ ἀστράπτουσα ἐκ τῆς ὑπὸ τὸν οὐρανὸν εἰς τὴν ὑπ' οὐρανὸν λάμπει, οὕτως ἔσται ὁ υἱὸς τοῦ ἀνθρώπου [ἐν τῇ ἡμέρᾳ αὐτοῦ]. [25]πρῶτον δὲ δεῖ αὐτὸν πολλὰ παθεῖν καὶ ἀποδοκιμασθῆναι ἀπὸ τῆς γενεᾶς ταύτης. [26]καὶ καθὼς ἐγένετο ἐν ταῖς ἡμέραις Νῶε, οὕτως ἔσται καὶ ἐν ταῖς ἡμέραις τοῦ υἱοῦ τοῦ ἀνθρώπου· [27]ἤσθιον, ἔπινον, ἐγάμουν, ἐγαμίζοντο, ἄχρι ἧς ἡμέρας εἰσῆλθεν Νῶε εἰς τὴν κιβωτὸν καὶ ἦλθεν ὁ κατακλυσμὸς καὶ ἀπώλεσεν πάντας. [28]ὁμοίως καθὼς ἐγένετο ἐν ταῖς ἡμέραις Λώτ· ἤσθιον, ἔπινον, ἠγόραζον, ἐπώλουν, ἐφύτευον, ᾠκοδόμουν· [29]ᾗ δὲ ἡμέρᾳ ἐξῆλθεν Λὼτ ἀπὸ Σοδόμων, ἔβρεξεν πῦρ καὶ θεῖον ἀπ' οὐρανοῦ καὶ ἀπώλεσεν πάντας. [30]κατὰ τὰ αὐτὰ ἔσται ᾗ ἡμέρᾳ ὁ υἱὸς τοῦ ἀνθρώπου ἀποκαλύπτεται. [31]ἐν ἐκείνῃ τῇ ἡμέρᾳ ὃς ἔσται ἐπὶ τοῦ δώματος καὶ τὰ σκεύη αὐτοῦ ἐν τῇ οἰκίᾳ, μὴ καταβάτω ἆραι αὐτά, καὶ ὁ ἐν ἀγρῷ ὁμοίως μὴ ἐπιστρεψάτω εἰς τὰ ὀπίσω. [32]μνημονεύετε τῆς γυναικὸς Λώτ. [33]ὃς ἐὰν ζητήσῃ τὴν ψυχὴν αὐτοῦ περιποιήσασθαι ἀπολέσει αὐτήν, ὃς δ' ἂν ἀπολέσῃ ζῳογονήσει αὐτήν. [34]λέγω ὑμῖν, ταύτῃ τῇ νυκτὶ ἔσονται δύο ἐπὶ κλίνης μιᾶς, ὁ εἷς παραλημφθήσεται καὶ ὁ ἕτερος ἀφεθήσεται· [35]ἔσονται δύο ἀλήθουσαι ἐπὶ τὸ αὐτό, ἡ μία παραλημφθήσεται, ἡ δὲ ἑτέρα ἀφεθήσεται.[a] [37]καὶ ἀποκριθέντες λέγουσιν αὐτῷ, Ποῦ, κύριε; ὁ δὲ εἶπεν αὐτοῖς, Ὅπου τὸ σῶμα, ἐκεῖ καὶ οἱ ἀετοὶ ἐπισυναχθήσονται.

18 Ἔλεγεν δὲ παραβολὴν αὐτοῖς πρὸς τὸ δεῖν πάντοτε προσ-

Where are the other nine? [18]Was no one found to return and give praise to God except this foreigner?" [19]Then he said to him, "Rise and go; your faith has made you well."

The Coming of the Kingdom of God

[20]Once, having been asked by the Pharisees when the kingdom of God would come, Jesus replied, "The kingdom of God does not come with your careful observation, [21]nor will people say, 'Here it is,' or 'There it is,' because the kingdom of God is within[b] you."

[22]Then he said to his disciples, "The time is coming when you will long to see one of the days of the Son of Man, but you will not see it. [23]Men will tell you, 'There he is!' or 'Here he is!' Do not go running off after them. [24]For the Son of Man in his day[c] will be like the lightning, which flashes and lights up the sky from one end to the other. [25]But first he must suffer many things and be rejected by this generation.

[26]"Just as it was in the days of Noah, so also will it be in the days of the Son of Man. [27]People were eating, drinking, marrying and being given in marriage up to the day Noah entered the ark. Then the flood came and destroyed them all.

[28]"It was the same in the days of Lot. People were eating and drinking, buying and selling, planting and building. [29]But the day Lot left Sodom, fire and sulfur rained down from heaven and destroyed them all.

[30]"It will be just like this on the day the Son of Man is revealed. [31]On that day no one who is on the roof of his house, with his goods inside, should go down to get them. Likewise, no one in the field should go back for anything. [32]Remember Lot's wife! [33]Whoever tries to keep his life will lose it, and whoever loses his life will preserve it. [34]I tell you, on that night two people will be in one bed; one will be taken and the other left. [35]Two women will be grinding grain together; one will be taken and the other left.[d]"

[37]"Where, Lord?" they asked.

He replied, "Where there is a dead body, there the vultures will gather."

The Parable of the Persistent Widow

18 Then Jesus told his disciples a parable to show them that they should

---

[a] Gk *he*   [d] Or *within*   [e] Other ancient authorities lack *in his day*   [f] Other ancient authorities add verse 36, *"Two will be in the field; one will be taken and the other left."*

[a]35 NIV/NRSV notes add 36 δύο ἔσονται ἐν τῷ ἀγρῷ· εἷς παραλημφθήσεται καὶ ὁ ἕτερος ἀφεθήσεται.

[b]21 Or *among*   [c]24 Some manuscripts do not have *in his day.*   [d]35 Some manuscripts *left.* 36*Two men will be in the field; one will be taken and the other left.*

and not to lose heart. 2He said, "In a certain city there was a judge who neither feared God nor had respect for people. 3In that city there was a widow who kept coming to him and saying, 'Grant me justice against my opponent.' 4For a while he refused; but later he said to himself, 'Though I have no fear of God and no respect for anyone, 5yet because this widow keeps bothering me, I will grant her justice, so that she may not wear me out by continually coming.' "h 6And the Lord said, "Listen to what the unjust judge says. 7And will not God grant justice to his chosen ones who cry to him day and night? Will he delay long in helping them? 8I tell you, he will quickly grant justice to them. And yet, when the Son of Man comes, will he find faith on earth?"

The Parable of the Pharisee and the Tax Collector

9 He also told this parable to some who trusted in themselves that they were righteous and regarded others with contempt: 10"Two men went up to the temple to pray, one a Pharisee and the other a tax collector. 11The Pharisee, standing by himself, was praying thus, 'God, I thank you that I am not like other people: thieves, rogues, adulterers, or even like this tax collector. 12I fast twice a week; I give a tenth of all my income.' 13But the tax collector, standing far off, would not even look up to heaven, but was beating his breast and saying, 'God, be merciful to me, a sinner!' 14I tell you, this man went down to his home justified rather than the other; for all who exalt themselves will be humbled, but all who humble themselves will be exalted."

Jesus Blesses Little Children

15 People were bringing even infants to him that he might touch them; and when the disciples saw it, they sternly ordered them not to do it. 16But Jesus called for them and said, "Let the little children come to me, and do not stop them; for it is to such as these that the kingdom of God belongs. 17Truly I tell you, whoever does not receive the kingdom of God as a little child will never enter it."

The Rich Ruler

18 A certain ruler asked him, "Good

εὔχεσθαι αὐτοὺς καὶ μὴ ἐγκακεῖν, 2 λέγων, Κριτής τις ἦν ἔν τινι πόλει τὸν θεὸν μὴ φοβούμενος καὶ ἄνθρωπον μὴ ἐντρεπόμενος. 3 χήρα δὲ ἦν ἐν τῇ πόλει ἐκείνῃ καὶ ἤρχετο πρὸς αὐτὸν λέγουσα, Ἐκδίκησόν με ἀπὸ τοῦ ἀντιδίκου μου. 4 καὶ οὐκ ἤθελεν ἐπὶ χρόνον. μετὰ δὲ ταῦτα εἶπεν ἐν ἑαυτῷ, Εἰ καὶ τὸν θεὸν οὐ φοβοῦμαι οὐδὲ ἄνθρωπον ἐντρέπομαι, 5 διά γε τὸ παρέχειν μοι κόπον τὴν χήραν ταύτην ἐκδικήσω αὐτήν, ἵνα μὴ εἰς τέλος ἐρχομένη ὑπωπιάζῃ με. 6 Εἶπεν δὲ ὁ κύριος, Ἀκούσατε τί ὁ κριτὴς τῆς ἀδικίας λέγει· 7 ὁ δὲ θεὸς οὐ μὴ ποιήσῃ τὴν ἐκδίκησιν τῶν ἐκλεκτῶν αὐτοῦ τῶν βοώντων αὐτῷ ἡμέρας καὶ νυκτός, καὶ μακροθυμεῖ ἐπ' αὐτοῖς; 8 λέγω ὑμῖν ὅτι ποιήσει τὴν ἐκδίκησιν αὐτῶν ἐν τάχει. πλὴν ὁ υἱὸς τοῦ ἀνθρώπου ἐλθὼν ἆρα εὑρήσει τὴν πίστιν ἐπὶ τῆς γῆς;

9 Εἶπεν δὲ καὶ πρός τινας τοὺς πεποιθότας ἐφ' ἑαυτοῖς ὅτι εἰσὶν δίκαιοι καὶ ἐξουθενοῦντας τοὺς λοιποὺς τὴν παραβολὴν ταύτην· 10 Ἄνθρωποι δύο ἀνέβησαν εἰς τὸ ἱερὸν προσεύξασθαι, ὁ εἷς Φαρισαῖος καὶ ὁ ἕτερος τελώνης. 11 ὁ Φαρισαῖος σταθεὶς πρὸς ἑαυτὸν ταῦτα προσηύχετο, Ὁ θεός, εὐχαριστῶ σοι ὅτι οὐκ εἰμὶ ὥσπερ οἱ λοιποὶ τῶν ἀνθρώπων, ἅρπαγες, ἄδικοι, μοιχοί, ἢ καὶ ὡς οὗτος ὁ τελώνης· 12 νηστεύω δὶς τοῦ σαββάτου, ἀποδεκατῶ πάντα ὅσα κτῶμαι. 13 ὁ δὲ τελώνης μακρόθεν ἑστὼς οὐκ ἤθελεν οὐδὲ τοὺς ὀφθαλμοὺς ἐπᾶραι εἰς τὸν οὐρανόν, ἀλλ' ἔτυπτεν τὸ στῆθος αὐτοῦ λέγων, Ὁ θεός, ἱλάσθητί μοι τῷ ἁμαρτωλῷ. 14 λέγω ὑμῖν, κατέβη οὗτος δεδικαιωμένος εἰς τὸν οἶκον αὐτοῦ παρ' ἐκεῖνον· ὅτι πᾶς ὁ ὑψῶν ἑαυτὸν ταπεινωθήσεται, ὁ δὲ ταπεινῶν ἑαυτὸν ὑψωθήσεται.

15 Προσέφερον δὲ αὐτῷ καὶ τὰ βρέφη ἵνα αὐτῶν ἅπτηται· ἰδόντες δὲ οἱ μαθηταὶ ἐπετίμων αὐτοῖς. 16 ὁ δὲ Ἰησοῦς προσεκαλέσατο αὐτὰ λέγων, Ἄφετε τὰ παιδία ἔρχεσθαι πρός με καὶ μὴ κωλύετε αὐτά, τῶν γὰρ τοιούτων ἐστὶν ἡ βασιλεία τοῦ θεοῦ. 17 ἀμὴν λέγω ὑμῖν, ὃς ἂν μὴ δέξηται τὴν βασιλείαν τοῦ θεοῦ ὡς παιδίον, οὐ μὴ εἰσέλθῃ εἰς αὐτήν.

18 Καὶ ἐπηρώτησέν τις αὐτὸν ἄρχων

always pray and not give up. 2He said: "In a certain town there was a judge who neither feared God nor cared about men. 3And there was a widow in that town who kept coming to him with the plea, 'Grant me justice against my adversary.'

4"For some time he refused. But finally he said to himself, 'Even though I don't fear God or care about men, 5yet because this widow keeps bothering me, I will see that she gets justice, so that she won't eventually wear me out with her coming!' "

6And the Lord said, "Listen to what the unjust judge says. 7And will not God bring about justice for his chosen ones, who cry out to him day and night? Will he keep putting them off? 8I tell you, he will see that they get justice, and quickly. However, when the Son of Man comes, will he find faith on the earth?"

The Parable of the Pharisee and the Tax Collector

9To some who were confident of their own righteousness and looked down on everybody else, Jesus told this parable: 10"Two men went up to the temple to pray, one a Pharisee and the other a tax collector. 11The Pharisee stood up and prayed about a himself: 'God, I thank you that I am not like other men—robbers, evildoers, adulterers—or even like this tax collector. 12I fast twice a week and give a tenth of all I get.'

13"But the tax collector stood at a distance. He would not even look up to heaven, but beat his breast and said, 'God, have mercy on me, a sinner.'

14"I tell you that this man, rather than the other, went home justified before God. For everyone who exalts himself will be humbled, and he who humbles himself will be exalted."

The Little Children and Jesus

15People were also bringing babies to Jesus to have him touch them. When the disciples saw this, they rebuked them. 16But Jesus called the children to him and said, "Let the little children come to me, and do not hinder them, for the kingdom of God belongs to such as these. 17I tell you the truth, anyone who will not receive the kingdom of God like a little child will never enter it."

The Rich Ruler

18A certain ruler asked him, "Good

---

h *Or so that she may not finally come and slap me in the face*   a*11 Or to*

Teacher, what must I do to inherit eternal life?" ¹⁹Jesus said to him, "Why do you call me good? No one is good but God alone. ²⁰You know the commandments: 'You shall not commit adultery; You shall not murder; You shall not steal; You shall not bear false witness; Honor your father and mother.' " ²¹He replied, "I have kept all these since my youth." ²²When Jesus heard this, he said to him, "There is still one thing lacking. Sell all that you own and distribute the money[i] to the poor, and you will have treasure in heaven; then come, follow me." ²³But when he heard this, he became sad; for he was very rich. ²⁴Jesus looked at him and said, "How hard it is for those who have wealth to enter the kingdom of God! ²⁵Indeed, it is easier for a camel to go through the eye of a needle than for someone who is rich to enter the kingdom of God."

26 Those who heard it said, "Then who can be saved?" ²⁷He replied, "What is impossible for mortals is possible for God."

28 Then Peter said, "Look, we have left our homes and followed you." ²⁹And he said to them, "Truly I tell you, there is no one who has left house or wife or brothers or parents or children, for the sake of the kingdom of God, ³⁰who will not get back very much more in this age, and in the age to come eternal life."

A Third Time Jesus Foretells His Death and Resurrection

31 Then he took the twelve aside and said to them, "See, we are going up to Jerusalem, and everything that is written about the Son of Man by the prophets will be accomplished. ³²For he will be handed over to the Gentiles; and he will be mocked and insulted and spat upon. ³³After they have flogged him, they will kill him, and on the third day he will rise again." ³⁴But they understood nothing about all these things; in fact, what he said was hidden from them, and they did not grasp what was said.

Jesus Heals a Blind Beggar Near Jericho

35 As he approached Jericho, a blind man was sitting by the roadside begging. ³⁶When he heard a crowd going by, he asked what was happening. ³⁷They told him, "Jesus of Nazareth[j] is passing by." ³⁸Then he shouted, "Jesus, Son of David, have mercy on me!" ³⁹Those who were in front sternly ordered him to be quiet; but

λέγων, Διδάσκαλε ἀγαθέ, τί ποιήσας ζωὴν αἰώνιον κληρονομήσω; **19** εἶπεν δὲ αὐτῷ ὁ Ἰησοῦς, Τί με λέγεις ἀγαθόν; οὐδεὶς ἀγαθὸς εἰ μὴ εἷς ὁ θεός. **20** τὰς ἐντολὰς οἶδας· **Μὴ μοιχεύσῃς, Μὴ φονεύσῃς, Μὴ κλέψῃς, Μὴ ψευδομαρτυρήσῃς, Τίμα τὸν πατέρα σου καὶ τὴν μητέρα. 21** ὁ δὲ εἶπεν, Ταῦτα πάντα ἐφύλαξα ἐκ νεότητος. **22** ἀκούσας δὲ ὁ Ἰησοῦς εἶπεν αὐτῷ, Ἔτι ἕν σοι λείπει· πάντα ὅσα ἔχεις πώλησον καὶ διάδος πτωχοῖς, καὶ ἕξεις θησαυρὸν ἐν [τοῖς] οὐρανοῖς, καὶ δεῦρο ἀκολούθει μοι. **23** ὁ δὲ ἀκούσας ταῦτα περίλυπος ἐγενήθη· ἦν γὰρ πλούσιος σφόδρα.

24 Ἰδὼν δὲ αὐτὸν ὁ Ἰησοῦς [περίλυπον γενόμενον][a] εἶπεν, Πῶς δυσκόλως οἱ τὰ χρήματα ἔχοντες εἰς τὴν βασιλείαν τοῦ θεοῦ εἰσπορεύονται· **25** εὐκοπώτερον γάρ ἐστιν κάμηλον διὰ τρήματος βελόνης εἰσελθεῖν ἢ πλούσιον εἰς τὴν βασιλείαν τοῦ θεοῦ εἰσελθεῖν. **26** εἶπαν δὲ οἱ ἀκούσαντες, Καὶ τίς δύναται σωθῆναι; **27** ὁ δὲ εἶπεν, Τὰ ἀδύνατα παρὰ ἀνθρώποις δυνατὰ παρὰ τῷ θεῷ ἐστιν. **28** Εἶπεν δὲ ὁ Πέτρος, Ἰδοὺ ἡμεῖς ἀφέντες τὰ ἴδια ἠκολουθήσαμέν σοι. **29** ὁ δὲ εἶπεν αὐτοῖς, Ἀμὴν λέγω ὑμῖν ὅτι οὐδείς ἐστιν ὃς ἀφῆκεν οἰκίαν ἢ γυναῖκα ἢ ἀδελφοὺς ἢ γονεῖς ἢ τέκνα ἕνεκεν τῆς βασιλείας τοῦ θεοῦ, **30** ὃς οὐχὶ μὴ [ἀπο]λάβῃ πολλαπλασίονα ἐν τῷ καιρῷ τούτῳ καὶ ἐν τῷ αἰῶνι τῷ ἐρχομένῳ ζωὴν αἰώνιον.

31 Παραλαβὼν δὲ τοὺς δώδεκα εἶπεν πρὸς αὐτούς, Ἰδοὺ ἀναβαίνομεν εἰς Ἰερουσαλήμ, καὶ τελεσθήσεται πάντα τὰ γεγραμμένα διὰ τῶν προφητῶν τῷ υἱῷ τοῦ ἀνθρώπου· **32** παραδοθήσεται γὰρ τοῖς ἔθνεσιν καὶ ἐμπαιχθήσεται καὶ ὑβρισθήσεται καὶ ἐμπτυσθήσεται **33** καὶ μαστιγώσαντες ἀποκτενοῦσιν αὐτόν,[b] καὶ τῇ ἡμέρᾳ τῇ τρίτῃ ἀναστήσεται. **34** καὶ αὐτοὶ οὐδὲν τούτων συνῆκαν καὶ ἦν τὸ ῥῆμα τοῦτο κεκρυμμένον ἀπ' αὐτῶν καὶ οὐκ ἐγίνωσκον τὰ λεγόμενα.

35 Ἐγένετο δὲ ἐν τῷ ἐγγίζειν αὐτὸν εἰς Ἰεριχὼ τυφλός τις ἐκάθητο παρὰ τὴν ὁδὸν ἐπαιτῶν. **36** ἀκούσας δὲ ὄχλου διαπορευομένου ἐπυνθάνετο τί εἴη τοῦτο. **37** ἀπήγγειλαν δὲ αὐτῷ ὅτι Ἰησοῦς ὁ Ναζωραῖος παρέρχεται. **38** καὶ ἐβόησεν λέγων, Ἰησοῦ υἱὲ Δαυίδ, ἐλέησόν με. **39** καὶ οἱ προάγοντες ἐπετίμων

teacher, what must I do to inherit eternal life?"

¹⁹"Why do you call me good?" Jesus answered. "No one is good—except God alone. ²⁰You know the commandments: 'Do not commit adultery, do not murder, do not steal, do not give false testimony, honor your father and mother.'[b]"

²¹"All these I have kept since I was a boy," he said.

²²When Jesus heard this, he said to him, "You still lack one thing. Sell everything you have and give to the poor, and you will have treasure in heaven. Then come, follow me."

²³When he heard this, he became very sad, because he was a man of great wealth. ²⁴Jesus looked at him and said, "How hard it is for the rich to enter the kingdom of God! ²⁵Indeed, it is easier for a camel to go through the eye of a needle than for a rich man to enter the kingdom of God."

²⁶Those who heard this asked, "Who then can be saved?"

²⁷Jesus replied, "What is impossible with men is possible with God."

²⁸Peter said to him, "We have left all we had to follow you!"

²⁹"I tell you the truth," Jesus said to them, "no one who has left home or wife or brothers or parents or children for the sake of the kingdom of God ³⁰will fail to receive many times as much in this age and, in the age to come, eternal life."

Jesus Again Predicts His Death

³¹Jesus took the Twelve aside and told them, "We are going up to Jerusalem, and everything that is written by the prophets about the Son of Man will be fulfilled. ³²He will be handed over to the Gentiles. They will mock him, insult him, spit on him, flog him and kill him. ³³On the third day he will rise again."

³⁴The disciples did not understand any of this. Its meaning was hidden from them, and they did not know what he was talking about.

A Blind Beggar Receives His Sight

³⁵As Jesus approached Jericho, a blind man was sitting by the roadside begging. ³⁶When he heard the crowd going by, he asked what was happening. ³⁷They told him, "Jesus of Nazareth is passing by."

³⁸He called out, "Jesus, Son of David, have mercy on me!"

³⁹Those who led the way rebuked him

---

[i] Gk lacks *the money*   [j] Gk *the Nazorean*

[a]24 NIV/NRSV texts omit περίλυπον γενόμενον
[b]33 NIV begins verse 33 after αὐτόν.

[b]20 Exodus 20:12-16; Deut. 5:16-20

he shouted even more loudly, "Son of David, have mercy on me!" [40]Jesus stood still and ordered the man to be brought to him; and when he came near, he asked him, [41]"What do you want me to do for you?" He said, "Lord, let me see again." [42]Jesus said to him, "Receive your sight; your faith has saved you." [43]Immediately he regained his sight and followed him, glorifying God; and all the people, when they saw it, praised God.

Jesus and Zacchaeus

19 He entered Jericho and was passing through it. [2]A man was there named Zacchaeus; he was a chief tax collector and was rich. [3]He was trying to see who Jesus was, but on account of the crowd he could not, because he was short in stature. [4]So he ran ahead and climbed a sycamore tree to see him, because he was going to pass that way. [5]When Jesus came to the place, he looked up and said to him, "Zacchaeus, hurry and come down; for I must stay at your house today." [6]So he hurried down and was happy to welcome him. [7]All who saw it began to grumble and said, "He has gone to be the guest of one who is a sinner." [8]Zacchaeus stood there and said to the Lord, "Look, half of my possessions, Lord, I will give to the poor; and if I have defrauded anyone of anything, I will pay back four times as much." [9]Then Jesus said to him, "Today salvation has come to this house, because he too is a son of Abraham. [10]For the Son of Man came to seek out and to save the lost."

The Parable of the Ten Pounds

11 As they were listening to this, he went on to tell a parable, because he was near Jerusalem, and because they supposed that the kingdom of God was to appear immediately. [12]So he said, "A nobleman went to a distant country to get royal power for himself and then return. [13]He summoned ten of his slaves, and gave them ten pounds,[k] and said to them, 'Do business with these until I come back.' [14]But the citizens of his country hated him and sent a delegation after him, saying, 'We do not want this man to rule over us.' [15]When he returned, having received royal power, he ordered these slaves, to whom he had given

αὐτῷ ἵνα σιγήσῃ, αὐτὸς δὲ πολλῷ μᾶλλον ἔκραζεν, Υἱὲ Δαυίδ, ἐλέησόν με. **40** σταθεὶς δὲ ὁ Ἰησοῦς ἐκέλευσεν αὐτὸν ἀχθῆναι πρὸς αὐτόν. ἐγγίσαντος δὲ αὐτοῦ ἐπηρώτησεν αὐτόν, **41** Τί σοι θέλεις ποιήσω; ὁ δὲ εἶπεν, Κύριε, ἵνα ἀναβλέψω. **42** καὶ ὁ Ἰησοῦς εἶπεν αὐτῷ, Ἀνάβλεψον· ἡ πίστις σου σέσωκέν σε. **43** καὶ παραχρῆμα ἀνέβλεψεν καὶ ἠκολούθει αὐτῷ δοξάζων τὸν θεόν. καὶ πᾶς ὁ λαὸς ἰδὼν ἔδωκεν αἶνον τῷ θεῷ.

19 Καὶ εἰσελθὼν διήρχετο τὴν Ἰεριχώ. **2** καὶ ἰδοὺ ἀνὴρ ὀνόματι καλούμενος[a] Ζακχαῖος, καὶ αὐτὸς ἦν ἀρχιτελώνης καὶ αὐτὸς πλούσιος· **3** καὶ ἐζήτει ἰδεῖν τὸν Ἰησοῦν τίς ἐστιν καὶ οὐκ ἠδύνατο ἀπὸ τοῦ ὄχλου, ὅτι τῇ ἡλικίᾳ μικρὸς ἦν. **4** καὶ προδραμὼν εἰς τὸ ἔμπροσθεν ἀνέβη ἐπὶ συκομορέαν ἵνα ἴδῃ αὐτόν ὅτι ἐκείνης ἤμελλεν διέρχεσθαι. **5** καὶ ὡς ἦλθεν ἐπὶ τὸν τόπον, ἀναβλέψας ὁ Ἰησοῦς εἶπεν πρὸς αὐτόν, Ζακχαῖε, σπεύσας κατάβηθι, σήμερον γὰρ ἐν τῷ οἴκῳ σου δεῖ με μεῖναι. **6** καὶ σπεύσας κατέβη καὶ ὑπεδέξατο αὐτὸν χαίρων. **7** καὶ ἰδόντες πάντες διεγόγγυζον λέγοντες ὅτι Παρὰ ἁμαρτωλῷ ἀνδρὶ εἰσῆλθεν καταλῦσαι. **8** σταθεὶς δὲ Ζακχαῖος εἶπεν πρὸς τὸν κύριον, Ἰδοὺ τὰ ἡμίσιά μου τῶν ὑπαρχόντων, κύριε, τοῖς πτωχοῖς δίδωμι, καὶ εἴ τινός τι ἐσυκοφάντησα ἀποδίδωμι τετραπλοῦν. **9** εἶπεν δὲ πρὸς αὐτὸν ὁ Ἰησοῦς ὅτι Σήμερον σωτηρία τῷ οἴκῳ τούτῳ ἐγένετο, καθότι καὶ αὐτὸς υἱὸς Ἀβραάμ ἐστιν· **10** ἦλθεν γὰρ ὁ υἱὸς τοῦ ἀνθρώπου ζητῆσαι καὶ σῶσαι τὸ ἀπολωλός.

11 Ἀκουόντων δὲ αὐτῶν ταῦτα προσθεὶς εἶπεν παραβολὴν διὰ τὸ ἐγγὺς εἶναι Ἰερουσαλὴμ αὐτὸν καὶ δοκεῖν αὐτοὺς ὅτι παραχρῆμα μέλλει ἡ βασιλεία τοῦ θεοῦ ἀναφαίνεσθαι. **12** εἶπεν οὖν, Ἄνθρωπός τις εὐγενὴς ἐπορεύθη εἰς χώραν μακρὰν λαβεῖν ἑαυτῷ βασιλείαν καὶ ὑποστρέψαι. **13** καλέσας δὲ δέκα δούλους ἑαυτοῦ ἔδωκεν αὐτοῖς δέκα μνᾶς καὶ εἶπεν πρὸς αὐτούς, Πραγματεύσασθε ἐν ᾧ ἔρχομαι. **14** οἱ δὲ πολῖται αὐτοῦ ἐμίσουν αὐτὸν καὶ ἀπέστειλαν πρεσβείαν ὀπίσω αὐτοῦ λέγοντες, Οὐ θέλομεν τοῦτον βασιλεῦσαι ἐφ' ἡμᾶς. **15** Καὶ ἐγένετο ἐν τῷ ἐπανελθεῖν αὐτὸν λαβόντα τὴν βασιλείαν καὶ εἶπεν φωνηθῆναι αὐτῷ τοὺς

and told him to be quiet, but he shouted all the more, "Son of David, have mercy on me!"

[40]Jesus stopped and ordered the man to be brought to him. When he came near, Jesus asked him, [41]"What do you want me to do for you?"

"Lord, I want to see," he replied.

[42]Jesus said to him, "Receive your sight; your faith has healed you." [43]Immediately he received his sight and followed Jesus, praising God. When all the people saw it, they also praised God.

Zacchaeus the Tax Collector

19 Jesus entered Jericho and was passing through. [2]A man was there by the name of Zacchaeus; he was a chief tax collector and was wealthy. [3]He wanted to see who Jesus was, but being a short man he could not, because of the crowd. [4]So he ran ahead and climbed a sycamore-fig tree to see him, since Jesus was coming that way.

[5]When Jesus reached the spot, he looked up and said to him, "Zacchaeus, come down immediately. I must stay at your house today." [6]So he came down at once and welcomed him gladly.

[7]All the people saw this and began to mutter, "He has gone to be the guest of a 'sinner.' "

[8]But Zacchaeus stood up and said to the Lord, "Look, Lord! Here and now I give half of my possessions to the poor, and if I have cheated anybody out of anything, I will pay back four times the amount."

[9]Jesus said to him, "Today salvation has come to this house, because this man, too, is a son of Abraham. [10]For the Son of Man came to seek and to save what was lost."

The Parable of the Ten Minas

[11]While they were listening to this, he went on to tell them a parable, because he was near Jerusalem and the people thought that the kingdom of God was going to appear at once. [12]He said: "A man of noble birth went to a distant country to have himself appointed king and then to return. [13]So he called ten of his servants and gave them ten minas.[a] 'Put this money to work,' he said, 'until I come back.'

[14]"But his subjects hated him and sent a delegation after him to say, 'We don't want this man to be our king.'

[15]"He was made king, however, and returned home. Then he sent for the servants

---

[k] The mina, rendered here by *pound,* was about three months' wages for a laborer

[a]2 NIV text omits καλούμενος †

[a]13 A mina was about three months' wages.

the money, to be summoned so that he might find out what they had gained by trading. ¹⁶The first came forward and said, 'Lord, your pound has made ten more pounds.' ¹⁷He said to him, 'Well done, good slave! Because you have been trustworthy in a very small thing, take charge of ten cities.' ¹⁸Then the second came, saying, 'Lord, your pound has made five pounds.' ¹⁹He said to him, 'And you, rule over five cities.' ²⁰Then the other came, saying, 'Lord, here is your pound. I wrapped it up in a piece of cloth, ²¹for I was afraid of you, because you are a harsh man; you take what you did not deposit, and reap what you did not sow.' ²²He said to him, 'I will judge you by your own words, you wicked slave! You knew, did you, that I was a harsh man, taking what I did not deposit and reaping what I did not sow? ²³Why then did you not put my money into the bank? Then when I returned, I could have collected it with interest.' ²⁴He said to the bystanders, 'Take the pound from him and give it to the one who has ten pounds.' ²⁵(And they said to him, 'Lord, he has ten pounds!') ²⁶'I tell you, to all those who have, more will be given; but from those who have nothing, even what they have will be taken away. ²⁷But as for these enemies of mine who did not want me to be king over them—bring them here and slaughter them in my presence.' "

Jesus' Triumphal Entry into Jerusalem

28 After he had said this, he went on ahead, going up to Jerusalem.

29 When he had come near Bethphage and Bethany, at the place called the Mount of Olives, he sent two of the disciples, ³⁰saying, "Go into the village ahead of you, and as you enter it you will find tied there a colt that has never been ridden. Untie it and bring it here. ³¹If anyone asks you, 'Why are you untying it?' just say this, 'The Lord needs it.' " ³²So those who were sent departed and found it as he had told them. ³³As they were untying the colt, its owners asked them, "Why are you untying the colt?" ³⁴They said, "The Lord needs it." ³⁵Then they brought it to Jesus; and after throwing their cloaks on the colt, they set Jesus on it. ³⁶As he rode along, people kept spreading their cloaks on the road. ³⁷As he was now approaching the path

δούλους τούτους οἷς δεδώκει τὸ ἀργύριον, ἵνα γνοῖ τί διεπραγματεύσαντο. 16 παρεγένετο δὲ ὁ πρῶτος λέγων, Κύριε, ἡ μνᾶ σου δέκα προσηργάσατο μνᾶς. 17 καὶ εἶπεν αὐτῷ, Εὖγε, ἀγαθὲ δοῦλε, ὅτι ἐν ἐλαχίστῳ πιστὸς ἐγένου, ἴσθι ἐξουσίαν ἔχων ἐπάνω δέκα πόλεων. 18 καὶ ἦλθεν ὁ δεύτερος λέγων, Ἡ μνᾶ σου, κύριε, ἐποίησεν πέντε μνᾶς. 19 εἶπεν δὲ καὶ τούτῳ, Καὶ σὺ ἐπάνω γίνου πέντε πόλεων. 20 καὶ ὁ ἕτερος ἦλθεν λέγων, Κύριε, ἰδοὺ ἡ μνᾶ σου ἣν εἶχον ἀποκειμένην ἐν σουδαρίῳ· 21 ἐφοβούμην γάρ σε, ὅτι ἄνθρωπος αὐστηρὸς εἶ, αἴρεις ὃ οὐκ ἔθηκας καὶ θερίζεις ὃ οὐκ ἔσπειρας. 22 λέγει αὐτῷ, Ἐκ τοῦ στόματός σου κρίνω σε, πονηρὲ δοῦλε. ἤδεις ὅτι ἐγὼ ἄνθρωπος αὐστηρός εἰμι, αἴρων ὃ οὐκ ἔθηκα καὶ θερίζων ὃ οὐκ ἔσπειρα; 23 καὶ διὰ τί οὐκ ἔδωκάς μου τὸ ἀργύριον ἐπὶ τράπεζαν; κἀγὼ ἐλθὼν σὺν τόκῳ ἂν αὐτὸ ἔπραξα. 24 καὶ τοῖς παρεστῶσιν εἶπεν, Ἄρατε ἀπ' αὐτοῦ τὴν μνᾶν καὶ δότε τῷ τὰς δέκα μνᾶς ἔχοντι 25 — καὶ εἶπαν αὐτῷ, Κύριε, ἔχει δέκα μνᾶς — 26 λέγω ὑμῖν ὅτι παντὶ τῷ ἔχοντι δοθήσεται, ἀπὸ δὲ τοῦ μὴ ἔχοντος καὶ ὃ ἔχει ἀρθήσεται. 27 πλὴν τοὺς ἐχθρούς μου τούτους τοὺς μὴ θελήσαντάς με βασιλεῦσαι ἐπ' αὐτοὺς ἀγάγετε ὧδε καὶ κατασφάξατε αὐτοὺς ἔμπροσθέν μου.

28 Καὶ εἰπὼν ταῦτα ἐπορεύετο ἔμπροσθεν ἀναβαίνων εἰς Ἱεροσόλυμα. 29 Καὶ ἐγένετο ὡς ἤγγισεν εἰς Βηθφαγὴ καὶ Βηθανία[ν] πρὸς τὸ ὄρος τὸ καλούμενον Ἐλαιῶν, ἀπέστειλεν δύο τῶν μαθητῶν 30 λέγων,ᵇ Ὑπάγετε εἰς τὴν κατέναντι κώμην, ἐν ᾗ εἰσπορευόμενοι εὑρήσετε πῶλον δεδεμένον, ἐφ' ὃν οὐδεὶς πώποτε ἀνθρώπων ἐκάθισεν, καὶ λύσαντες αὐτὸν ἀγάγετε. 31 καὶ ἐάν τις ὑμᾶς ἐρωτᾷ, Διὰ τί λύετε; οὕτως ἐρεῖτε ὅτι Ὁ κύριος αὐτοῦ χρείαν ἔχει. 32 ἀπελθόντες δὲ οἱ ἀπεσταλμένοι εὗρον καθὼς εἶπεν αὐτοῖς. 33 λυόντων δὲ αὐτῶν τὸν πῶλον εἶπαν οἱ κύριοι αὐτοῦ πρὸς αὐτούς, Τί λύετε τὸν πῶλον; 34 οἱ δὲ εἶπαν ὅτι Ὁ κύριος αὐτοῦ χρείαν ἔχει. 35 καὶ ἤγαγον αὐτὸν πρὸς τὸν Ἰησοῦν καὶ ἐπιρίψαντες αὐτῶν τὰ ἱμάτια ἐπὶ τὸν πῶλον ἐπεβίβασαν τὸν Ἰησοῦν. 36 πορευομένου δὲ αὐτοῦ ὑπεστρώννυον τὰ ἱμάτια αὐτῶν ἐν τῇ ὁδῷ.

37 Ἐγγίζοντος δὲ αὐτοῦ ἤδη πρὸς

ᵇ30 NIV text reads λέγων, in verse 29

to whom he had given the money, in order to find out what they had gained with it.

¹⁶"The first one came and said, 'Sir, your mina has earned ten more.'

¹⁷" 'Well done, my good servant!' his master replied. 'Because you have been trustworthy in a very small matter, take charge of ten cities.'

¹⁸"The second came and said, 'Sir, your mina has earned five more.'

¹⁹"His master answered, 'You take charge of five cities.'

²⁰"Then another servant came and said, 'Sir, here is your mina; I have kept it laid away in a piece of cloth. ²¹I was afraid of you, because you are a hard man. You take out what you did not put in and reap what you did not sow.'

²²"His master replied, 'I will judge you by your own words, you wicked servant! You knew, did you, that I am a hard man, taking out what I did not put in, and reaping what I did not sow? ²³Why then didn't you put my money on deposit, so that when I came back, I could have collected it with interest?'

²⁴"Then he said to those standing by, 'Take his mina away from him and give it to the one who has ten minas.'

²⁵" 'Sir,' they said, 'he already has ten!'

²⁶"He replied, 'I tell you that to everyone who has, more will be given, but as for the one who has nothing, even what he has will be taken away. ²⁷But those enemies of mine who did not want me to be king over them—bring them here and kill them in front of me.' "

The Triumphal Entry

²⁸After Jesus had said this, he went on ahead, going up to Jerusalem. ²⁹As he approached Bethphage and Bethany at the hill called the Mount of Olives, he sent two of his disciples, saying to them, ³⁰"Go to the village ahead of you, and as you enter it, you will find a colt tied there, which no one has ever ridden. Untie it and bring it here. ³¹If anyone asks you, 'Why are you untying it?' tell him, 'The Lord needs it.' "

³²Those who were sent ahead went and found it just as he had told them. ³³As they were untying the colt, its owners asked them, "Why are you untying the colt?"

³⁴They replied, "The Lord needs it."

³⁵They brought it to Jesus, threw their cloaks on the colt and put Jesus on it. ³⁶As he went along, people spread their cloaks on the road.

³⁷When he came near the place where

down from the Mount of Olives, the whole multitude of the disciples began to praise God joyfully with a loud voice for all the deeds of power that they had seen, [38]saying,

"Blessed is the king
who comes in the name of the Lord!
Peace in heaven,
and glory in the highest heaven!"

[39]Some of the Pharisees in the crowd said to him, "Teacher, order your disciples to stop." [40]He answered, "I tell you, if these were silent, the stones would shout out."

Jesus Weeps over Jerusalem

41 As he came near and saw the city, he wept over it, [42]saying, "If you, even you, had only recognized on this day the things that make for peace! But now they are hidden from your eyes. [43]Indeed, the days will come upon you, when your enemies will set up ramparts around you and surround you, and hem you in on every side. [44]They will crush you to the ground, you and your children within you, and they will not leave within you one stone upon another; because you did not recognize the time of your visitation from God."[1]

Jesus Cleanses the Temple

45 Then he entered the temple and began to drive out those who were selling things there; [46]and he said, "It is written,

'My house shall be a house of prayer';
but you have made it a den of
robbers."

47 Every day he was teaching in the temple. The chief priests, the scribes, and the leaders of the people kept looking for a way to kill him; [48]but they did not find anything they could do, for all the people were spellbound by what they heard.

The Authority of Jesus Questioned

20 One day, as he was teaching the people in the temple and telling the good news, the chief priests and the scribes came with the elders [2]and said to him, "Tell us, by what authority are you doing these things? Who is it who gave you this authority?" [3]He answered them, "I will also ask you a question, and you tell me: [4]Did the baptism of John come from heaven, or was it of human origin?" [5]They discussed it with one another, saying, "If we say, 'From heaven,' he will say, 'Why did you not believe him?' [6]But if we say, 'Of human origin,' all the people will

the road goes down the Mount of Olives, the whole crowd of disciples began joyfully to praise God in loud voices for all the miracles they had seen:

[38]"Blessed is the king who comes in the name of the Lord!"[b]

"Peace in heaven and glory in the highest!"

[39]Some of the Pharisees in the crowd said to Jesus, "Teacher, rebuke your disciples!" [40]"I tell you," he replied, "if they keep quiet, the stones will cry out."

[41]As he approached Jerusalem and saw the city, he wept over it [42]and said, "If you, even you, had only known on this day what would bring you peace—but now it is hidden from your eyes. [43]The days will come upon you when your enemies will build an embankment against you and encircle you and hem you in on every side. [44]They will dash you to the ground, you and the children within your walls. They will not leave one stone on another, because you did not recognize the time of God's coming to you."

Jesus at the Temple

[45]Then he entered the temple area and began driving out those who were selling. [46]"It is written," he said to them, " 'My house will be a house of prayer'[c]; but you have made it 'a den of robbers.'[d]"

[47]Every day he was teaching at the temple. But the chief priests, the teachers of the law and the leaders among the people were trying to kill him. [48]Yet they could not find any way to do it, because all the people hung on his words.

The Authority of Jesus Questioned

20 One day as he was teaching the people in the temple courts and preaching the gospel, the chief priests and the teachers of the law, together with the elders, came up to him. [2]"Tell us by what authority you are doing these things," they said. "Who gave you this authority?" [3]He replied, "I will also ask you a question. Tell me, [4]John's baptism—was it from heaven, or from men?" [5]They discussed it among themselves and said, "If we say, 'From heaven,' he will ask, 'Why didn't you believe him?' [6]But if we say, 'From men,' all the people will stone us; for they are convinced that John was a prophet." [7]So they answered that they did not know where it came from. [8]Then Jesus said to them, "Neither will I tell you by what authority I am doing these things."

The Parable of the Wicked Tenants

9 He began to tell the people this parable: "A man planted a vineyard, and leased it to tenants, and went to another country for a long time. [10]When the season came, he sent a slave to the tenants in order that they might give him his share of the produce of the vineyard; but the tenants beat him and sent him away empty-handed. [11]Next he sent another slave; that one also they beat and insulted and sent away empty-handed. [12]And he sent still a third; this one also they wounded and threw out. [13]Then the owner of the vineyard said, 'What shall I do? I will send my beloved son; perhaps they will respect him.' [14]But when the tenants saw him, they discussed it among themselves and said, 'This is the heir; let us kill him so that the inheritance may be ours.' [15]So they threw him out of the vineyard and killed him. What then will the owner of the vineyard do to them? [16]He will come and destroy those tenants and give the vineyard to others." When they heard this, they said, "Heaven forbid!" [17]But he looked at them and said, "What then does this text mean:

'The stone that the builders rejected
    has become the cornerstone'?[m]

[18]Everyone who falls on that stone will be broken to pieces; and it will crush anyone on whom it falls." [19]When the scribes and chief priests realized that he had told this parable against them, they wanted to lay hands on him at that very hour, but they feared the people.

The Question about Paying Taxes

20 So they watched him and sent spies who pretended to be honest, in order to trap him by what he said, so as to hand him over to the jurisdiction and authority of the governor. [21]So they asked him, "Teacher, we know that you are right in what you say and teach, and you show deference to no one, but teach the way of

ἡμᾶς, πεπεισμένος γάρ ἐστιν Ἰωάννην προφήτην εἶναι. **7** καὶ ἀπεκρίθησαν μὴ εἰδέναι πόθεν. **8** καὶ ὁ Ἰησοῦς εἶπεν αὐτοῖς, Οὐδὲ ἐγὼ λέγω ὑμῖν ἐν ποίᾳ ἐξουσίᾳ ταῦτα ποιῶ.

9 Ἤρξατο δὲ πρὸς τὸν λαὸν λέγειν τὴν παραβολὴν ταύτην· Ἄνθρωπός [τις] ἐφύτευσεν ἀμπελῶνα καὶ ἐξέδετο αὐτὸν γεωργοῖς καὶ ἀπεδήμησεν χρόνους ἱκανούς. **10** καὶ καιρῷ ἀπέστειλεν πρὸς τοὺς γεωργοὺς δοῦλον ἵνα ἀπὸ τοῦ καρποῦ τοῦ ἀμπελῶνος δώσουσιν αὐτῷ· οἱ δὲ γεωργοὶ ἐξαπέστειλαν αὐτὸν δείραντες κενόν. **11** καὶ προσέθετο ἕτερον πέμψαι δοῦλον· οἱ δὲ κἀκεῖνον δείραντες καὶ ἀτιμάσαντες ἐξαπέστειλαν κενόν. **12** καὶ προσέθετο τρίτον πέμψαι· οἱ δὲ καὶ τοῦτον τραυματίσαντες ἐξέβαλον. **13** εἶπεν δὲ ὁ κύριος τοῦ ἀμπελῶνος, Τί ποιήσω; πέμψω τὸν υἱόν μου τὸν ἀγαπητόν· ἴσως τοῦτον ἐντραπήσονται. **14** ἰδόντες δὲ αὐτὸν οἱ γεωργοὶ διελογίζοντο πρὸς ἀλλήλους λέγοντες, Οὗτός ἐστιν ὁ κληρονόμος· ἀποκτείνωμεν αὐτόν, ἵνα ἡμῶν γένηται ἡ κληρονομία. **15** καὶ ἐκβαλόντες αὐτὸν ἔξω τοῦ ἀμπελῶνος ἀπέκτειναν. τί οὖν ποιήσει αὐτοῖς ὁ κύριος τοῦ ἀμπελῶνος; **16** ἐλεύσεται καὶ ἀπολέσει τοὺς γεωργοὺς τούτους καὶ δώσει τὸν ἀμπελῶνα ἄλλοις. ἀκούσαντες δὲ εἶπαν, Μὴ γένοιτο. **17** ὁ δὲ ἐμβλέψας αὐτοῖς εἶπεν, Τί οὖν ἐστιν τὸ γεγραμμένον τοῦτο·

Λίθον ὃν ἀπεδοκίμασαν οἱ
    οἰκοδομοῦντες,
οὗτος ἐγενήθη εἰς κεφαλὴν
    γωνίας;

18 πᾶς ὁ πεσὼν ἐπ᾽ ἐκεῖνον τὸν λίθον συνθλασθήσεται· ἐφ᾽ ὃν δ᾽ ἂν πέσῃ, λικμήσει αὐτόν. **19** Καὶ ἐζήτησαν οἱ γραμματεῖς καὶ οἱ ἀρχιερεῖς ἐπιβαλεῖν ἐπ᾽ αὐτὸν τὰς χεῖρας ἐν αὐτῇ τῇ ὥρᾳ, καὶ ἐφοβήθησαν τὸν λαόν, ἔγνωσαν γὰρ ὅτι πρὸς αὐτοὺς εἶπεν τὴν παραβολὴν ταύτην. **20** Καὶ παρατηρήσαντες ἀπέστειλαν ἐγκαθέτους ὑποκρινομένους ἑαυτοὺς δικαίους εἶναι, ἵνα ἐπιλάβωνται αὐτοῦ λόγου, ὥστε παραδοῦναι αὐτὸν τῇ ἀρχῇ καὶ τῇ ἐξουσίᾳ τοῦ ἡγεμόνος. **21** καὶ ἐπηρώτησαν αὐτὸν λέγοντες, Διδάσκαλε, οἴδαμεν ὅτι ὀρθῶς λέγεις καὶ διδάσκεις καὶ οὐ λαμβάνεις πρόσωπον,

stone us, because they are persuaded that John was a prophet."

[7]So they answered, "We don't know where it was from."

[8]Jesus said, "Neither will I tell you by what authority I am doing these things."

The Parable of the Tenants

[9]He went on to tell the people this parable: "A man planted a vineyard, rented it to some farmers and went away for a long time. [10]At harvest time he sent a servant to the tenants so they would give him some of the fruit of the vineyard. But the tenants beat him and sent him away empty-handed. [11]He sent another servant, but that one also they beat and treated shamefully and sent away empty-handed. [12]He sent still a third, and they wounded him and threw him out.

[13]"Then the owner of the vineyard said, 'What shall I do? I will send my son, whom I love; perhaps they will respect him.'

[14]"But when the tenants saw him, they talked the matter over. 'This is the heir,' they said. 'Let's kill him, and the inheritance will be ours.' [15]So they threw him out of the vineyard and killed him.

"What then will the owner of the vineyard do to them? [16]He will come and kill those tenants and give the vineyard to others."

When the people heard this, they said, "May this never be!"

[17]Jesus looked directly at them and asked, "Then what is the meaning of that which is written:

" 'The stone the builders rejected
    has become the capstone[a][b]?

[18]Everyone who falls on that stone will be broken to pieces, but he on whom it falls will be crushed."

[19]The teachers of the law and the chief priests looked for a way to arrest him immediately, because they knew he had spoken this parable against them. But they were afraid of the people.

Paying Taxes to Caesar

[20]Keeping a close watch on him, they sent spies, who pretended to be honest. They hoped to catch Jesus in something he said so that they might hand him over to the power and authority of the governor. [21]So the spies questioned him: "Teacher, we know that you speak and teach what is right, and that you do not show partiality

---

m Or *keystone*   a 17 Or *cornerstone*   b 17 Psalm 118:22

God in accordance with truth. 22Is it lawful for us to pay taxes to the emperor, or not?" 23But he perceived their craftiness and said to them, 24"Show me a denarius. Whose head and whose title does it bear?" They said, "The emperor's." 25He said to them, "Then give to the emperor the things that are the emperor's, and to God the things that are God's." 26And they were not able in the presence of the people to trap him by what he said; and being amazed by his answer, they became silent.

The Question about the Resurrection

27 Some Sadducees, those who say there is no resurrection, came to him 28and asked him a question, "Teacher, Moses wrote for us that if a man's brother dies, leaving a wife but no children, the man[n] shall marry the widow and raise up children for his brother. 29Now there were seven brothers; the first married, and died childless; 30then the second 31and the third married her, and so in the same way all seven died childless. 32Finally the woman also died. 33In the resurrection, therefore, whose wife will the woman be? For the seven had married her."

34 Jesus said to them, "Those who belong to this age marry and are given in marriage; 35but those who are considered worthy of a place in that age and in the resurrection from the dead neither marry nor are given in marriage. 36Indeed they cannot die anymore, because they are like angels and are children of God, being children of the resurrection. 37And the fact that the dead are raised Moses himself showed, in the story about the bush, where he speaks of the Lord as the God of Abraham, the God of Isaac, and the God of Jacob. 38Now he is God not of the dead, but of the living; for to him all of them are alive." 39Then some of the scribes answered, "Teacher, you have spoken well." 40For they no longer dared to ask him another question.

The Question about David's Son

41 Then he said to them, "How can they say that the Messiah[o] is David's son? 42For David himself says in the book of Psalms,

'The Lord said to my Lord,
 "Sit at my right hand,
43   until I make your enemies your
       footstool." '

ἀλλ' ἐπ' ἀληθείας τὴν ὁδὸν τοῦ θεοῦ διδάσκεις· 22 ἔξεστιν ἡμᾶς Καίσαρι φόρον δοῦναι ἢ οὔ; 23 κατανοήσας δὲ αὐτῶν τὴν πανουργίαν εἶπεν πρὸς αὐτούς, 24 Δείξατέ μοι δηνάριον· τίνος ἔχει εἰκόνα καὶ ἐπιγραφήν;[a] οἱ δὲ εἶπαν, Καίσαρος. 25 ὁ δὲ εἶπεν πρὸς αὐτούς, Τοίνυν ἀπόδοτε τὰ Καίσαρος Καίσαρι καὶ τὰ τοῦ θεοῦ τῷ θεῷ. 26 καὶ οὐκ ἴσχυσαν ἐπιλαβέσθαι αὐτοῦ ῥήματος ἐναντίον τοῦ λαοῦ καὶ θαυμάσαντες ἐπὶ τῇ ἀποκρίσει αὐτοῦ ἐσίγησαν.

27 Προσελθόντες δέ τινες τῶν Σαδδουκαίων, οἱ [ἀντι]λέγοντες ἀνάστασιν μὴ εἶναι, ἐπηρώτησαν αὐτὸν 28 λέγοντες, Διδάσκαλε, Μωϋσῆς ἔγραψεν ἡμῖν, **ἐάν τινος ἀδελφὸς ἀποθάνῃ** ἔχων γυναῖκα, **καὶ οὗτος ἄτεκνος ᾖ**, ἵνα **λάβῃ ὁ ἀδελφὸς αὐτοῦ τὴν γυναῖκα καὶ ἐξαναστήσῃ σπέρμα τῷ ἀδελφῷ αὐτοῦ.** 29 ἑπτὰ οὖν ἀδελφοὶ ἦσαν· καὶ ὁ πρῶτος λαβὼν γυναῖκα ἀπέθανεν ἄτεκνος· 30 καὶ ὁ δεύτερος 31 καὶ ὁ τρίτος ἔλαβεν αὐτήν, ὡσαύτως δὲ καὶ οἱ ἑπτὰ οὐ κατέλιπον τέκνα καὶ ἀπέθανον. 32 ὕστερον καὶ ἡ γυνὴ ἀπέθανεν. 33 ἡ γυνὴ οὖν ἐν τῇ ἀναστάσει τίνος αὐτῶν γίνεται γυνή; οἱ γὰρ ἑπτὰ ἔσχον αὐτὴν γυναῖκα. 34 καὶ εἶπεν αὐτοῖς ὁ Ἰησοῦς, Οἱ υἱοὶ τοῦ αἰῶνος τούτου γαμοῦσιν καὶ γαμίσκονται, 35 οἱ δὲ καταξιωθέντες τοῦ αἰῶνος ἐκείνου τυχεῖν καὶ τῆς ἀναστάσεως τῆς ἐκ νεκρῶν οὔτε γαμοῦσιν οὔτε γαμίζονται· 36 οὐδὲ γὰρ ἀποθανεῖν ἔτι δύνανται, ἰσάγγελοι γάρ εἰσιν καὶ υἱοί εἰσιν θεοῦ τῆς ἀναστάσεως υἱοὶ ὄντες. 37 ὅτι δὲ ἐγείρονται οἱ νεκροί, καὶ Μωϋσῆς ἐμήνυσεν ἐπὶ τῆς βάτου, ὡς λέγει **κύριον τὸν θεὸν Ἀβραὰμ καὶ θεὸν Ἰσαὰκ καὶ θεὸν Ἰακώβ**. 38 θεὸς δὲ οὐκ ἔστιν νεκρῶν ἀλλὰ ζώντων, πάντες γὰρ αὐτῷ ζῶσιν. 39 ἀποκριθέντες δέ τινες τῶν γραμματέων εἶπαν, Διδάσκαλε, καλῶς εἶπας. 40 οὐκέτι γὰρ ἐτόλμων ἐπερωτᾶν αὐτὸν οὐδέν.

41 Εἶπεν δὲ πρὸς αὐτούς, Πῶς λέγουσιν τὸν Χριστὸν εἶναι Δαυὶδ υἱόν; 42 αὐτὸς γὰρ Δαυὶδ λέγει ἐν βίβλῳ ψαλμῶν,

Εἶπεν κύριος τῷ κυρίῳ μου,
  Κάθου ἐκ δεξιῶν μου,
43 ἕως ἂν θῶ τοὺς ἐχθρούς σου
     ὑποπόδιον τῶν ποδῶν σου.

---

but teach the way of God in accordance with the truth. 22Is it right for us to pay taxes to Caesar or not?"

23He saw through their duplicity and said to them, 24"Show me a denarius. Whose portrait and inscription are on it?"

25"Caesar's," they replied.

He said to them, "Then give to Caesar what is Caesar's, and to God what is God's."

26They were unable to trap him in what he had said there in public. And astonished by his answer, they became silent.

The Resurrection and Marriage

27Some of the Sadducees, who say there is no resurrection, came to Jesus with a question. 28"Teacher," they said, "Moses wrote for us that if a man's brother dies and leaves a wife but no children, the man must marry the widow and have children for his brother. 29Now there were seven brothers. The first one married a woman and died childless. 30The second 31and then the third married her, and in the same way the seven died, leaving no children. 32Finally, the woman died too. 33Now then, at the resurrection whose wife will she be, since the seven were married to her?"

34Jesus replied, "The people of this age marry and are given in marriage. 35But those who are considered worthy of taking part in that age and in the resurrection from the dead will neither marry nor be given in marriage, 36and they can no longer die; for they are like the angels. They are God's children, since they are children of the resurrection. 37But in the account of the bush, even Moses showed that the dead rise, for he calls the Lord 'the God of Abraham, and the God of Isaac, and the God of Jacob.'[c] 38He is not the God of the dead, but of the living, for to him all are alive."

39Some of the teachers of the law responded, "Well said, teacher!" 40And no one dared to ask him any more questions.

Whose Son Is the Christ?

41Then Jesus said to them, "How is it that they say the Christ[d] is the Son of David? 42David himself declares in the Book of Psalms:

" 'The Lord said to my Lord:
   "Sit at my right hand
43until I make your enemies
   a footstool for your feet." '[e]

---

[n] Gk *his brother*   [o] Or *the Christ*   [a]24 NIV text begins verse 25 after ἐπιγραφήν;   [c]37 Exodus 3:6   [d]41 Or *Messiah*   [e]43 Psalm 110:1

⁴⁴David thus calls him Lord; so how can he be his son?"

Jesus Denounces the Scribes

45 In the hearing of all the people he said to the^p disciples, ⁴⁶"Beware of the scribes, who like to walk around in long robes, and love to be greeted with respect in the marketplaces, and to have the best seats in the synagogues and places of honor at banquets. ⁴⁷They devour widows' houses and for the sake of appearance say long prayers. They will receive the greater condemnation."

The Widow's Offering

21 He looked up and saw rich people putting their gifts into the treasury; ²he also saw a poor widow put in two small copper coins. ³He said, "Truly I tell you, this poor widow has put in more than all of them; ⁴for all of them have contributed out of their abundance, but she out of her poverty has put in all she had to live on."

The Destruction of the Temple Foretold

5 When some were speaking about the temple, how it was adorned with beautiful stones and gifts dedicated to God, he said, ⁶"As for these things that you see, the days will come when not one stone will be left upon another; all will be thrown down."

Signs and Persecutions

7 They asked him, "Teacher, when will this be, and what will be the sign that this is about to take place?" ⁸And he said, "Beware that you are not led astray; for many will come in my name and say, 'I am he!'^q and, 'The time is near!'^r Do not go after them.

9 "When you hear of wars and insurrections, do not be terrified; for these things must take place first, but the end will not follow immediately." ¹⁰Then he said to them, "Nation will rise against nation, and kingdom against kingdom; ¹¹there will be great earthquakes, and in various places famines and plagues; and there will be dreadful portents and great signs from heaven.

12 "But before all this occurs, they will arrest you and persecute you; they will hand you over to synagogues and prisons, and you will be brought before kings and governors because of my name. ¹³This will give you an opportunity to testify. ¹⁴So

44 Δαυὶδ οὖν κύριον αὐτὸν καλεῖ, καὶ πῶς αὐτοῦ υἱός ἐστιν;

45 Ἀκούοντος δὲ παντὸς τοῦ λαοῦ εἶπεν τοῖς μαθηταῖς [αὐτοῦ]^b, *46* Προσέχετε ἀπὸ τῶν γραμματέων τῶν θελόντων περιπατεῖν ἐν στολαῖς καὶ φιλούντων ἀσπασμοὺς ἐν ταῖς ἀγοραῖς καὶ πρωτοκαθεδρίας ἐν ταῖς συναγωγαῖς καὶ πρωτοκλισίας ἐν τοῖς δείπνοις, *47* οἳ κατεσθίουσιν τὰς οἰκίας τῶν χηρῶν καὶ προφάσει μακρὰ προσεύχονται· οὗτοι λήμψονται περισσότερον κρίμα.

21 Ἀναβλέψας δὲ εἶδεν τοὺς βάλλοντας εἰς τὸ γαζοφυλάκιον τὰ δῶρα αὐτῶν πλουσίους. *2* εἶδεν δέ τινα χήραν πενιχρὰν βάλλουσαν ἐκεῖ λεπτὰ δύο, *3* καὶ εἶπεν, Ἀληθῶς λέγω ὑμῖν ὅτι ἡ χήρα αὕτη ἡ πτωχὴ πλεῖον πάντων ἔβαλεν· *4* πάντες γὰρ οὗτοι ἐκ τοῦ περισσεύοντος αὐτοῖς ἔβαλον εἰς τὰ δῶρα, αὕτη δὲ ἐκ τοῦ ὑστερήματος αὐτῆς πάντα τὸν βίον ὃν εἶχεν ἔβαλεν.

5 Καί τινων λεγόντων περὶ τοῦ ἱεροῦ ὅτι λίθοις καλοῖς καὶ ἀναθήμασιν κεκόσμηται εἶπεν, *6* Ταῦτα ἃ θεωρεῖτε, ἐλεύσονται ἡμέραι ἐν αἷς οὐκ ἀφεθήσεται λίθος ἐπὶ λίθῳ ὃς οὐ καταλυθήσεται.

7 Ἐπηρώτησαν δὲ αὐτὸν λέγοντες, Διδάσκαλε, πότε οὖν ταῦτα ἔσται καὶ τί τὸ σημεῖον ὅταν μέλλῃ ταῦτα γίνεσθαι; *8* ὁ δὲ εἶπεν, Βλέπετε μὴ πλανηθῆτε· πολλοὶ γὰρ ἐλεύσονται ἐπὶ τῷ ὀνόματί μου λέγοντες, Ἐγώ εἰμι, καί, Ὁ καιρὸς ἤγγικεν. μὴ πορευθῆτε ὀπίσω αὐτῶν. *9* ὅταν δὲ ἀκούσητε πολέμους καὶ ἀκαταστασίας, μὴ πτοηθῆτε· δεῖ γὰρ ταῦτα γενέσθαι πρῶτον, ἀλλ' οὐκ εὐθέως τὸ τέλος. *10* Τότε ἔλεγεν αὐτοῖς, Ἐγερθήσεται ἔθνος ἐπ' ἔθνος καὶ βασιλεία ἐπὶ βασιλείαν, *11* σεισμοί τε μεγάλοι καὶ κατὰ τόπους λιμοὶ καὶ λοιμοὶ ἔσονται, φόβητρά τε καὶ ἀπ' οὐρανοῦ σημεῖα μεγάλα ἔσται. *12* πρὸ δὲ τούτων πάντων ἐπιβαλοῦσιν ἐφ' ὑμᾶς τὰς χεῖρας αὐτῶν καὶ διώξουσιν, παραδιδόντες εἰς τὰς συναγωγὰς καὶ φυλακάς, ἀπαγομένους ἐπὶ βασιλεῖς καὶ ἡγεμόνας ἕνεκεν τοῦ ὀνόματός μου· *13* ἀποβήσεται ὑμῖν εἰς μαρτύριον.

⁴⁴David calls him 'Lord.' How then can he be his son?"

⁴⁵While all the people were listening, Jesus said to his disciples, ⁴⁶"Beware of the teachers of the law. They like to walk around in flowing robes and love to be greeted in the marketplaces and have the most important seats in the synagogues and the places of honor at banquets. ⁴⁷They devour widows' houses and for a show make lengthy prayers. Such men will be punished most severely."

The Widow's Offering

21 As he looked up, Jesus saw the rich putting their gifts into the temple treasury. ²He also saw a poor widow put in two very small copper coins.^a ³"I tell you the truth," he said, "this poor widow has put in more than all the others. ⁴All these people gave their gifts out of their wealth; but she out of her poverty put in all she had to live on."

Signs of the End of the Age

⁵Some of his disciples were remarking about how the temple was adorned with beautiful stones and with gifts dedicated to God. But Jesus said, ⁶"As for what you see here, the time will come when not one stone will be left on another; every one of them will be thrown down."

⁷"Teacher," they asked, "when will these things happen? And what will be the sign that they are about to take place?"

⁸He replied: "Watch out that you are not deceived. For many will come in my name, claiming, 'I am he,' and, 'The time is near.' Do not follow them. ⁹When you hear of wars and revolutions, do not be frightened. These things must happen first, but the end will not come right away."

¹⁰Then he said to them: "Nation will rise against nation, and kingdom against kingdom. ¹¹There will be great earthquakes, famines and pestilences in various places, and fearful events and great signs from heaven.

¹²"But before all this, they will lay hands on you and persecute you. They will deliver you to synagogues and prisons, and you will be brought before kings and governors, and all on account of my name. ¹³This will result in your being witnesses

make up your minds not to prepare your defense in advance; [15]for I will give you words[s] and a wisdom that none of your opponents will be able to withstand or contradict. [16]You will be betrayed even by parents and brothers, by relatives and friends; and they will put some of you to death. [17]You will be hated by all because of my name. [18]But not a hair of your head will perish. [19]By your endurance you will gain your souls.

The Destruction of Jerusalem Foretold

20 "When you see Jerusalem surrounded by armies, then know that its desolation has come near.[t] [21]Then those in Judea must flee to the mountains, and those inside the city must leave it, and those out in the country must not enter it; [22]for these are days of vengeance, as a fulfillment of all that is written. [23]Woe to those who are pregnant and to those who are nursing infants in those days! For there will be great distress on the earth and wrath against this people; [24]they will fall by the edge of the sword and be taken away as captives among all nations; and Jerusalem will be trampled on by the Gentiles, until the times of the Gentiles are fulfilled.

The Coming of the Son of Man

25 "There will be signs in the sun, the moon, and the stars, and on the earth distress among nations confused by the roaring of the sea and the waves. [26]People will faint from fear and foreboding of what is coming upon the world, for the powers of the heavens will be shaken. [27]Then they will see 'the Son of Man coming in a cloud' with power and great glory. [28]Now when these things begin to take place, stand up and raise your heads, because your redemption is drawing near."

The Lesson of the Fig Tree

29 Then he told them a parable: "Look at the fig tree and all the trees; [30]as soon as they sprout leaves you can see for yourselves and know that summer is already near. [31]So also, when you see these things taking place, you know that the kingdom of God is near. [32]Truly I tell you, this generation will not pass away until all things have taken place. [33]Heaven and earth will pass away, but my words will not pass away.

[14] θέτε οὖν ἐν ταῖς καρδίαις ὑμῶν μὴ προμελετᾶν ἀπολογηθῆναι· [15] ἐγὼ γὰρ δώσω ὑμῖν στόμα καὶ σοφίαν ᾗ οὐ δυνήσονται ἀντιστῆναι ἢ ἀντειπεῖν ἅπαντες οἱ ἀντικείμενοι ὑμῖν. [16] παραδοθήσεσθε δὲ καὶ ὑπὸ γονέων καὶ ἀδελφῶν καὶ συγγενῶν καὶ φίλων, καὶ θανατώσουσιν ἐξ ὑμῶν, [17] καὶ ἔσεσθε μισούμενοι ὑπὸ πάντων διὰ τὸ ὄνομά μου. [18] καὶ θρὶξ ἐκ τῆς κεφαλῆς ὑμῶν οὐ μὴ ἀπόληται. [19] ἐν τῇ ὑπομονῇ ὑμῶν κτήσασθε τὰς ψυχὰς ὑμῶν.

[20] Ὅταν δὲ ἴδητε κυκλουμένην ὑπὸ στρατοπέδων Ἰερουσαλήμ, τότε γνῶτε ὅτι ἤγγικεν ἡ ἐρήμωσις αὐτῆς. [21] τότε οἱ ἐν τῇ Ἰουδαίᾳ φευγέτωσαν εἰς τὰ ὄρη καὶ οἱ ἐν μέσῳ αὐτῆς ἐκχωρείτωσαν καὶ οἱ ἐν ταῖς χώραις μὴ εἰσερχέσθωσαν εἰς αὐτήν, [22] ὅτι ἡμέραι ἐκδικήσεως αὗταί εἰσιν τοῦ πλησθῆναι πάντα τὰ γεγραμμένα. [23] οὐαὶ ταῖς ἐν γαστρὶ ἐχούσαις καὶ ταῖς θηλαζούσαις ἐν ἐκείναις ταῖς ἡμέραις· ἔσται γὰρ ἀνάγκη μεγάλη ἐπὶ τῆς γῆς καὶ ὀργὴ τῷ λαῷ τούτῳ, [24] καὶ πεσοῦνται στόματι μαχαίρης καὶ αἰχμαλωτισθήσονται εἰς τὰ ἔθνη πάντα, καὶ Ἰερουσαλὴμ ἔσται πατουμένη ὑπὸ ἐθνῶν, ἄχρι οὗ πληρωθῶσιν καιροὶ ἐθνῶν.

[25] Καὶ ἔσονται σημεῖα ἐν ἡλίῳ καὶ σελήνῃ καὶ ἄστροις, καὶ ἐπὶ τῆς γῆς συνοχὴ ἐθνῶν ἐν ἀπορίᾳ ἤχους θαλάσσης καὶ σάλου, [26] ἀποψυχόντων ἀνθρώπων ἀπὸ φόβου καὶ προσδοκίας τῶν ἐπερχομένων τῇ οἰκουμένῃ, αἱ γὰρ δυνάμεις τῶν οὐρανῶν σαλευθήσονται. [27] καὶ τότε ὄψονται τὸν υἱὸν τοῦ ἀνθρώπου ἐρχόμενον ἐν νεφέλῃ μετὰ δυνάμεως καὶ δόξης πολλῆς. [28] ἀρχομένων δὲ τούτων γίνεσθαι ἀνακύψατε καὶ ἐπάρατε τὰς κεφαλὰς ὑμῶν, διότι ἐγγίζει ἡ ἀπολύτρωσις ὑμῶν.

[29] Καὶ εἶπεν παραβολὴν αὐτοῖς· Ἴδετε τὴν συκῆν καὶ πάντα τὰ δένδρα· [30] ὅταν προβάλωσιν ἤδη, βλέποντες ἀφ᾽ ἑαυτῶν γινώσκετε ὅτι ἤδη ἐγγὺς τὸ θέρος ἐστίν· [31] οὕτως καὶ ὑμεῖς, ὅταν ἴδητε ταῦτα γινόμενα, γινώσκετε ὅτι ἐγγύς ἐστιν ἡ βασιλεία τοῦ θεοῦ. [32] ἀμὴν λέγω ὑμῖν ὅτι οὐ μὴ παρέλθῃ ἡ γενεὰ αὕτη ἕως ἂν πάντα γένηται. [33] ὁ οὐρανὸς καὶ ἡ γῆ παρελεύσονται, οἱ δὲ λόγοι μου οὐ μὴ παρελεύσονται.

to them. [14]But make up your mind not to worry beforehand how you will defend yourselves. [15]For I will give you words and wisdom that none of your adversaries will be able to resist or contradict. [16]You will be betrayed even by parents, brothers, relatives and friends, and they will put some of you to death. [17]All men will hate you because of me. [18]But not a hair of your head will perish. [19]By standing firm you will gain life.

[20]"When you see Jerusalem being surrounded by armies, you will know that its desolation is near. [21]Then let those who are in Judea flee to the mountains, let those in the city get out, and let those in the country not enter the city. [22]For this is the time of punishment in fulfillment of all that has been written. [23]How dreadful it will be in those days for pregnant women and nursing mothers! There will be great distress in the land and wrath against this people. [24]They will fall by the sword and will be taken as prisoners to all the nations. Jerusalem will be trampled on by the Gentiles until the times of the Gentiles are fulfilled.

[25]"There will be signs in the sun, moon and stars. On the earth, nations will be in anguish and perplexity at the roaring and tossing of the sea. [26]Men will faint from terror, apprehensive of what is coming on the world, for the heavenly bodies will be shaken. [27]At that time they will see the Son of Man coming in a cloud with power and great glory. [28]When these things begin to take place, stand up and lift up your heads, because your redemption is drawing near."

[29]He told them this parable: "Look at the fig tree and all the trees. [30]When they sprout leaves, you can see for yourselves and know that summer is near. [31]Even so, when you see these things happening, you know that the kingdom of God is near.

[32]"I tell you the truth, this generation[b] will certainly not pass away until all these things have happened. [33]Heaven and earth will pass away, but my words will never pass away.

Exhortation to Watch

34 "Be on guard so that your hearts are not weighed down with dissipation and drunkenness and the worries of this life, and that day catch you unexpectedly, 35like a trap. For it will come upon all who live on the face of the whole earth. 36Be alert at all times, praying that you may have the strength to escape all these things that will take place, and to stand before the Son of Man."

37 Every day he was teaching in the temple, and at night he would go out and spend the night on the Mount of Olives, as it was called. 38And all the people would get up early in the morning to listen to him in the temple.

The Plot to Kill Jesus

22 Now the festival of Unleavened Bread, which is called the Passover, was near. 2The chief priests and the scribes were looking for a way to put Jesusu to death, for they were afraid of the people.

3 Then Satan entered into Judas called Iscariot, who was one of the twelve; 4he went away and conferred with the chief priests and officers of the temple police about how he might betray him to them. 5They were greatly pleased and agreed to give him money. 6So he consented and began to look for an opportunity to betray him to them when no crowd was present.

The Preparation of the Passover

7 Then came the day of Unleavened Bread, on which the Passover lamb had to be sacrificed. 8So Jesusv sent Peter and John, saying, "Go and prepare the Passover meal for us that we may eat it." 9They asked him, "Where do you want us to make preparations for it?" 10"Listen," he said to them, "when you have entered the city, a man carrying a jar of water will meet you; follow him into the house he enters 11and say to the owner of the house, 'The teacher asks you, "Where is the guest room, where I may eat the Passover with my disciples?"' 12He will show you a large room upstairs, already furnished. Make preparations for us there." 13So they went and found everything as he had told them; and they prepared the Passover meal.

The Institution of the Lord's Supper

14 When the hour came, he took his place at the table, and the apostles with him. 15He said to them, "I have eagerly desired

u Gk *him*   v Gk *he*

34 Προσέχετε δὲ ἑαυτοῖς μήποτε βαρηθῶσιν ὑμῶν αἱ καρδίαι ἐν κραιπάλῃ καὶ μέθῃ καὶ μερίμναις βιωτικαῖς καὶ ἐπιστῇ ἐφ᾽ ὑμᾶς αἰφνίδιος ἡ ἡμέρα ἐκείνη **35** ὡς παγίς·ᵃ ἐπεισελεύσεται γὰρ ἐπὶ πάντας τοὺς καθημένους ἐπὶ πρόσωπον πάσης τῆς γῆς. **36** ἀγρυπνεῖτε δὲ ἐν παντὶ καιρῷ δεόμενοι ἵνα κατισχύσητε ἐκφυγεῖν ταῦτα πάντα τὰ μέλλοντα γίνεσθαι καὶ σταθῆναι ἔμπροσθεν τοῦ υἱοῦ τοῦ ἀνθρώπου.

37 Ἦν δὲ τὰς ἡμέρας ἐν τῷ ἱερῷ διδάσκων, τὰς δὲ νύκτας ἐξερχόμενος ηὐλίζετο εἰς τὸ ὄρος τὸ καλούμενον Ἐλαιῶν· **38** καὶ πᾶς ὁ λαὸς ὤρθριζεν πρὸς αὐτὸν ἐν τῷ ἱερῷ ἀκούειν αὐτοῦ.

22 Ἤγγιζεν δὲ ἡ ἑορτὴ τῶν ἀζύμων ἡ λεγομένη πάσχα. **2** καὶ ἐζήτουν οἱ ἀρχιερεῖς καὶ οἱ γραμματεῖς τὸ πῶς ἀνέλωσιν αὐτόν, ἐφοβοῦντο γὰρ τὸν λαόν. **3** Εἰσῆλθεν δὲ Σατανᾶς εἰς Ἰούδαν τὸν καλούμενον Ἰσκαριώτην, ὄντα ἐκ τοῦ ἀριθμοῦ τῶν δώδεκα· **4** καὶ ἀπελθὼν συνελάλησεν τοῖς ἀρχιερεῦσιν καὶ στρατηγοῖς τὸ πῶς αὐτοῖς παραδῷ αὐτόν. **5** καὶ ἐχάρησαν καὶ συνέθεντο αὐτῷ ἀργύριον δοῦναι. **6** καὶ ἐξωμολόγησεν, καὶ ἐζήτει εὐκαιρίαν τοῦ παραδοῦναι αὐτὸν ἄτερ ὄχλου αὐτοῖς.

7 Ἦλθεν δὲ ἡ ἡμέρα τῶν ἀζύμων, [ἐν] ᾗ ἔδει θύεσθαι τὸ πάσχα· **8** καὶ ἀπέστειλεν Πέτρον καὶ Ἰωάννην εἰπών, Πορευθέντες ἑτοιμάσατε ἡμῖν τὸ πάσχα ἵνα φάγωμεν. **9** οἱ δὲ εἶπαν αὐτῷ, Ποῦ θέλεις ἑτοιμάσωμεν; **10** ὁ δὲ εἶπεν αὐτοῖς, Ἰδοὺ εἰσελθόντων ὑμῶν εἰς τὴν πόλιν συναντήσει ὑμῖν ἄνθρωπος κεράμιον ὕδατος βαστάζων· ἀκολουθήσατε αὐτῷ εἰς τὴν οἰκίαν εἰς ἣν εἰσπορεύεται **11** καὶ ἐρεῖτε τῷ οἰκοδεσπότῃ τῆς οἰκίας, Λέγει σοι ὁ διδάσκαλος, Ποῦ ἐστιν τὸ κατάλυμα ὅπου τὸ πάσχα μετὰ τῶν μαθητῶν μου φάγω; **12** κἀκεῖνος ὑμῖν δείξει ἀνάγαιον μέγα ἐστρωμένον· ἐκεῖ ἑτοιμάσατε. **13** ἀπελθόντες δὲ εὗρον καθὼς εἰρήκει αὐτοῖς καὶ ἡτοίμασαν τὸ πάσχα.

14 Καὶ ὅτε ἐγένετο ἡ ὥρα, ἀνέπεσεν καὶ οἱ ἀπόστολοι σὺν αὐτῷ. **15** καὶ εἶπεν πρὸς αὐτούς, Ἐπιθυμίᾳ ἐπεθύ-

ᵃ35 NIV text includes ὡς παγὶς. in verse 34

34"Be careful, or your hearts will be weighed down with dissipation, drunkenness and the anxieties of life, and that day will close on you unexpectedly like a trap. 35For it will come upon all those who live on the face of the whole earth. 36Be always on the watch, and pray that you may be able to escape all that is about to happen, and that you may be able to stand before the Son of Man."

37Each day Jesus was teaching at the temple, and each evening he went out to spend the night on the hill called the Mount of Olives, 38and all the people came early in the morning to hear him at the temple.

Judas Agrees to Betray Jesus

22 Now the Feast of Unleavened Bread, called the Passover, was approaching, 2and the chief priests and the teachers of the law were looking for some way to get rid of Jesus, for they were afraid of the people. 3Then Satan entered Judas, called Iscariot, one of the Twelve. 4And Judas went to the chief priests and the officers of the temple guard and discussed with them how he might betray Jesus. 5They were delighted and agreed to give him money. 6He consented, and watched for an opportunity to hand Jesus over to them when no crowd was present.

The Last Supper

7Then came the day of Unleavened Bread on which the Passover lamb had to be sacrificed. 8Jesus sent Peter and John, saying, "Go and make preparations for us to eat the Passover."

9"Where do you want us to prepare for it?" they asked.

10He replied, "As you enter the city, a man carrying a jar of water will meet you. Follow him to the house that he enters, 11and say to the owner of the house, 'The Teacher asks: Where is the guest room, where I may eat the Passover with my disciples?' 12He will show you a large upper room, all furnished. Make preparations there."

13They left and found things just as Jesus had told them. So they prepared the Passover.

14When the hour came, Jesus and his apostles reclined at the table. 15And he said to them, "I have eagerly desired to eat

to eat this Passover with you before I suffer; [16]for I tell you, I will not eat it[w] until it is fulfilled in the kingdom of God." [17]Then he took a cup, and after giving thanks he said, "Take this and divide it among yourselves; [18]for I tell you that from now on I will not drink of the fruit of the vine until the kingdom of God comes." [19]Then he took a loaf of bread, and when he had given thanks, he broke it and gave it to them, saying, "This is my body, which is given for you. Do this in remembrance of me." [20]And he did the same with the cup after supper, saying, "This cup that is poured out for you is the new covenant in my blood.[x] [21]But see, the one who betrays me is with me, and his hand is on the table. [22]For the Son of Man is going as it has been determined, but woe to that one by whom he is betrayed!" [23]Then they began to ask one another, which one of them it could be who would do this.

The Dispute about Greatness

24 A dispute also arose among them as to which one of them was to be regarded as the greatest. [25]But he said to them, "The kings of the Gentiles lord it over them; and those in authority over them are called benefactors. [26]But not so with you; rather the greatest among you must become like the youngest, and the leader like one who serves. [27]For who is greater, the one who is at the table or the one who serves? Is it not the one at the table? But I am among you as one who serves.

28 "You are those who have stood by me in my trials; [29]and I confer on you, just as my Father has conferred on me, a kingdom, [30]so that you may eat and drink at my table in my kingdom, and you will sit on thrones judging the twelve tribes of Israel.

Jesus Predicts Peter's Denial

31 "Simon, Simon, listen! Satan has demanded[y] to sift all of you like wheat, [32]but I have prayed for you that your own faith may not fail; and you, when once you have turned back, strengthen your brothers." [33]And he said to him, "Lord, I am ready to go with you to prison and to death!" [34]Jesus[z] said, "I tell you, Peter, the cock will not crow this day, until you have denied three times that you know me."

μησα τοῦτο τὸ πάσχα φαγεῖν μεθ' ὑμῶν πρὸ τοῦ με παθεῖν· 16 λέγω γὰρ ὑμῖν ὅτι[a] οὐ μὴ φάγω αὐτὸ ἕως ὅτου πληρωθῇ ἐν τῇ βασιλείᾳ τοῦ θεοῦ. 17 καὶ δεξάμενος ποτήριον εὐχαριστήσας εἶπεν, Λάβετε τοῦτο καὶ διαμερίσατε εἰς ἑαυτούς· 18 λέγω γὰρ ὑμῖν, [ὅτι] οὐ μὴ πίω ἀπὸ τοῦ νῦν ἀπὸ τοῦ γενήματος τῆς ἀμπέλου ἕως οὗ ἡ βασιλεία τοῦ θεοῦ ἔλθῃ. 19 καὶ λαβὼν ἄρτον εὐχαριστήσας ἔκλασεν καὶ ἔδωκεν αὐτοῖς λέγων, Τοῦτό ἐστιν τὸ σῶμά μου τὸ ὑπὲρ ὑμῶν διδόμενον· τοῦτο ποιεῖτε εἰς τὴν ἐμὴν ἀνάμνησιν. 20 καὶ τὸ ποτήριον ὡσαύτως μετὰ τὸ δειπνῆσαι, λέγων, Τοῦτο τὸ ποτήριον ἡ καινὴ διαθήκη ἐν τῷ αἵματί μου τὸ ὑπὲρ ὑμῶν ἐκχυννόμενον. 21 πλὴν ἰδοὺ ἡ χεὶρ τοῦ παραδιδόντος με μετ' ἐμοῦ ἐπὶ τῆς τραπέζης. 22 ὅτι ὁ υἱὸς μὲν τοῦ ἀνθρώπου κατὰ τὸ ὡρισμένον πορεύεται, πλὴν οὐαὶ τῷ ἀνθρώπῳ ἐκείνῳ δι' οὗ παραδίδοται. 23 καὶ αὐτοὶ ἤρξαντο συζητεῖν πρὸς ἑαυτοὺς τὸ τίς ἄρα εἴη ἐξ αὐτῶν ὁ τοῦτο μέλλων πράσσειν.

24 Ἐγένετο δὲ καὶ φιλονεικία ἐν αὐτοῖς, τὸ τίς αὐτῶν δοκεῖ εἶναι μείζων. 25 ὁ δὲ εἶπεν αὐτοῖς, Οἱ βασιλεῖς τῶν ἐθνῶν κυριεύουσιν αὐτῶν καὶ οἱ ἐξουσιάζοντες αὐτῶν εὐεργέται καλοῦνται. 26 ὑμεῖς δὲ οὐχ οὕτως, ἀλλ' ὁ μείζων ἐν ὑμῖν γινέσθω ὡς ὁ νεώτερος καὶ ὁ ἡγούμενος ὡς ὁ διακονῶν. 27 τίς γὰρ μείζων, ὁ ἀνακείμενος ἢ ὁ διακονῶν; οὐχὶ ὁ ἀνακείμενος; ἐγὼ δὲ ἐν μέσῳ ὑμῶν εἰμι ὡς ὁ διακονῶν. 28 ὑμεῖς δέ ἐστε οἱ διαμεμενηκότες μετ' ἐμοῦ ἐν τοῖς πειρασμοῖς μου· 29 κἀγὼ διατίθεμαι ὑμῖν καθὼς διέθετό μοι ὁ πατήρ μου βασιλείαν, 30 ἵνα ἔσθητε καὶ πίνητε ἐπὶ τῆς τραπέζης μου ἐν τῇ βασιλείᾳ μου, καὶ καθήσεσθε ἐπὶ θρόνων τὰς δώδεκα φυλὰς κρίνοντες τοῦ Ἰσραήλ.

31 Σίμων Σίμων, ἰδοὺ ὁ Σατανᾶς ἐξῃτήσατο ὑμᾶς τοῦ σινιάσαι ὡς τὸν σῖτον· 32 ἐγὼ δὲ ἐδεήθην περὶ σοῦ ἵνα μὴ ἐκλίπῃ ἡ πίστις σου· καὶ σύ ποτε ἐπιστρέψας στήρισον τοὺς ἀδελφούς σου. 33 ὁ δὲ εἶπεν αὐτῷ, Κύριε, μετὰ σοῦ ἕτοιμός εἰμι καὶ εἰς φυλακὴν καὶ εἰς θάνατον πορεύεσθαι. 34 ὁ δὲ εἶπεν, Λέγω σοι, Πέτρε, οὐ φωνήσει σήμερον ἀλέκτωρ ἕως τρίς με ἀπαρνήσῃ εἰδέναι.

this Passover with you before I suffer. [16]For I tell you, I will not eat it again until it finds fulfillment in the kingdom of God."

[17]After taking the cup, he gave thanks and said, "Take this and divide it among you. [18]For I tell you I will not drink again of the fruit of the vine until the kingdom of God comes."

[19]And he took bread, gave thanks and broke it, and gave it to them, saying, "This is my body given for you; do this in remembrance of me."

[20]In the same way, after the supper he took the cup, saying, "This cup is the new covenant in my blood, which is poured out for you. [21]But the hand of him who is going to betray me is with mine on the table. [22]The Son of Man will go as it has been decreed, but woe to that man who betrays him." [23]They began to question among themselves which of them it might be who would do this.

[24]Also a dispute arose among them as to which of them was considered to be greatest. [25]Jesus said to them, "The kings of the Gentiles lord it over them; and those who exercise authority over them call themselves Benefactors. [26]But you are not to be like that. Instead, the greatest among you should be like the youngest, and the one who rules like the one who serves. [27]For who is greater, the one who is at the table or the one who serves? Is it not the one who is at the table? But I am among you as one who serves. [28]You are those who have stood by me in my trials. [29]And I confer on you a kingdom, just as my Father conferred one on me, [30]so that you may eat and drink at my table in my kingdom and sit on thrones, judging the twelve tribes of Israel.

[31]"Simon, Simon, Satan has asked to sift you[a] as wheat. [32]But I have prayed for you, Simon, that your faith may not fail. And when you have turned back, strengthen your brothers."

[33]But he replied, "Lord, I am ready to go with you to prison and to death."

[34]Jesus answered, "I tell you, Peter, before the rooster crows today, you will deny three times that you know me."

[w] Other ancient authorities read *never eat it again*
[x] Other ancient authorities lack, in whole or in part, verses 19b-20 (*which is given . . . in my blood*)   [y] Or *has obtained permission*   [z] Gk *He*

[a]16 NRSV note w adds οὐκέτι

[a]31 The Greek is plural.

NRSV

Purse, Bag, and Sword

35 He said to them, "When I sent you out without a purse, bag, or sandals, did you lack anything?" They said, "No, not a thing." 36He said to them, "But now, the one who has a purse must take it, and likewise a bag. And the one who has no sword must sell his cloak and buy one. 37For I tell you, this scripture must be fulfilled in me, 'And he was counted among the lawless'; and indeed what is written about me is being fulfilled." 38They said, "Lord, look, here are two swords." He replied, "It is enough."

Jesus Prays on the Mount of Olives

39 He came out and went, as was his custom, to the Mount of Olives; and the disciples followed him. 40When he reached the place, he said to them, "Pray that you may not come into the time of trial."a 41Then he withdrew from them about a stone's throw, knelt down, and prayed, 42"Father, if you are willing, remove this cup from me; yet, not my will but yours be done." ⟦43Then an angel from heaven appeared to him and gave him strength. 44In his anguish he prayed more earnestly, and his sweat became like great drops of blood falling down on the ground.⟧b 45When he got up from prayer, he came to the disciples and found them sleeping because of grief, 46and he said to them, "Why are you sleeping? Get up and pray that you may not come into the time of trial."a

The Betrayal and Arrest of Jesus

47 While he was still speaking, suddenly a crowd came, and the one called Judas, one of the twelve, was leading them. He approached Jesus to kiss him; 48but Jesus said to him, "Judas, is it with a kiss that you are betraying the Son of Man?" 49When those who were around him saw what was coming, they asked, "Lord, should we strike with the sword?" 50Then one of them struck the slave of the high priest and cut off his right ear. 51But Jesus said, "No more of this!" And he touched his ear and healed him. 52Then Jesus said to the chief priests, the officers of the temple police, and the elders who had come for him, "Have you come out with swords and clubs as if I were a bandit? 53When I was with you day

Greek

35 Καὶ εἶπεν αὐτοῖς, Ὅτε ἀπέστειλα ὑμᾶς ἄτερ βαλλαντίου καὶ πήρας καὶ ὑποδημάτων, μή τινος ὑστερήσατε; οἱ δὲ εἶπαν, Οὐθενός. 36 εἶπεν δὲ αὐτοῖς, Ἀλλὰ νῦν ὁ ἔχων βαλλάντιον ἀράτω, ὁμοίως καὶ πήραν, καὶ ὁ μὴ ἔχων πωλησάτω τὸ ἱμάτιον αὐτοῦ καὶ ἀγορασάτω μάχαιραν. 37 λέγω γὰρ ὑμῖν ὅτι τοῦτο τὸ γεγραμμένον δεῖ τελεσθῆναι ἐν ἐμοί, τὸ Καὶ μετὰ ἀνόμων ἐλογίσθη· καὶ γὰρ τὸ περὶ ἐμοῦ τέλος ἔχει. 38 οἱ δὲ εἶπαν, Κύριε, ἰδοὺ μάχαιραι ὧδε δύο. ὁ δὲ εἶπεν αὐτοῖς, Ἱκανόν ἐστιν.

39 Καὶ ἐξελθὼν ἐπορεύθη κατὰ τὸ ἔθος εἰς τὸ Ὄρος τῶν Ἐλαιῶν, ἠκολούθησαν δὲ αὐτῷ καὶ οἱ μαθηταί. 40 γενόμενος δὲ ἐπὶ τοῦ τόπου εἶπεν αὐτοῖς, Προσεύχεσθε μὴ εἰσελθεῖν εἰς πειρασμόν. 41 καὶ αὐτὸς ἀπεσπάσθη ἀπ' αὐτῶν ὡσεὶ λίθου βολὴν καὶ θεὶς τὰ γόνατα προσηύχετο 42 λέγων, Πάτερ, εἰ βούλει παρένεγκε τοῦτο τὸ ποτήριον ἀπ' ἐμοῦ· πλὴν μὴ τὸ θέλημά μου ἀλλὰ τὸ σὸν γινέσθω. ⟦43 ὤφθη δὲ αὐτῷ ἄγγελος ἀπ' οὐρανοῦ ἐνισχύων αὐτόν. 44 καὶ γενόμενος ἐν ἀγωνίᾳ ἐκτενέστερον προσηύχετο· καὶ ἐγένετο ὁ ἱδρὼς αὐτοῦ ὡσεὶ θρόμβοι αἵματος καταβαίνοντος ἐπὶ τὴν γῆν.⟧ 45 καὶ ἀναστὰς ἀπὸ τῆς προσευχῆς ἐλθὼν πρὸς τοὺς μαθητὰς εὗρεν κοιμωμένους αὐτοὺς ἀπὸ τῆς λύπης, 46 καὶ εἶπεν αὐτοῖς, Τί καθεύδετε; ἀναστάντες προσεύχεσθε, ἵνα μὴ εἰσέλθητε εἰς πειρασμόν.

47 Ἔτι αὐτοῦ λαλοῦντος ἰδοὺ ὄχλος, καὶ ὁ λεγόμενος Ἰούδας εἷς τῶν δώδεκα προήρχετο αὐτούς καὶ ἤγγισεν τῷ Ἰησοῦ φιλῆσαι αὐτόν. 48 Ἰησοῦς δὲ εἶπεν αὐτῷ, Ἰούδα, φιλήματι τὸν υἱὸν τοῦ ἀνθρώπου παραδίδως; 49 ἰδόντες δὲ οἱ περὶ αὐτὸν τὸ ἐσόμενον εἶπαν, Κύριε, εἰ πατάξομεν ἐν μαχαίρῃ; 50 καὶ ἐπάταξεν εἷς τις ἐξ αὐτῶν τοῦ ἀρχιερέως τὸν δοῦλον καὶ ἀφεῖλεν τὸ οὖς αὐτοῦ τὸ δεξιόν. 51 ἀποκριθεὶς δὲ ὁ Ἰησοῦς εἶπεν, Ἐᾶτε ἕως τούτου· καὶ ἁψάμενος τοῦ ὠτίου ἰάσατο αὐτόν. 52 εἶπεν δὲ Ἰησοῦς πρὸς τοὺς παραγενομένους ἐπ' αὐτὸν ἀρχιερεῖς καὶ στρατηγοὺς τοῦ ἱεροῦ καὶ πρεσβυτέρους, Ὡς ἐπὶ λῃστὴν ἐξήλθατε μετὰ μαχαιρῶν καὶ ξύλων; 53 καθ' ἡμέραν ὄντος μου μεθ' ὑμῶν ἐν τῷ ἱερῷ οὐκ

NIV

35Then Jesus asked them, "When I sent you without purse, bag or sandals, did you lack anything?"

"Nothing," they answered.

36He said to them, "But now if you have a purse, take it, and also a bag; and if you don't have a sword, sell your cloak and buy one. 37It is written: 'And he was numbered with the transgressors'b; and I tell you that this must be fulfilled in me. Yes, what is written about me is reaching its fulfillment."

38The disciples said, "See, Lord, here are two swords."

"That is enough," he replied.

Jesus Prays on the Mount of Olives

39Jesus went out as usual to the Mount of Olives, and his disciples followed him. 40On reaching the place, he said to them, "Pray that you will not fall into temptation." 41He withdrew about a stone's throw beyond them, knelt down and prayed, 42"Father, if you are willing, take this cup from me; yet not my will, but yours be done." 43An angel from heaven appeared to him and strengthened him. 44And being in anguish, he prayed more earnestly, and his sweat was like drops of blood falling to the ground.c

45When he rose from prayer and went back to the disciples, he found them asleep, exhausted from sorrow. 46"Why are you sleeping?" he asked them. "Get up and pray so that you will not fall into temptation."

Jesus Arrested

47While he was still speaking a crowd came up, and the man who was called Judas, one of the Twelve, was leading them. He approached Jesus to kiss him, 48but Jesus asked him, "Judas, are you betraying the Son of Man with a kiss?"

49When Jesus' followers saw what was going to happen, they said, "Lord, should we strike with our swords?" 50And one of them struck the servant of the high priest, cutting off his right ear.

51But Jesus answered, "No more of this!" And he touched the man's ear and healed him.

52Then Jesus said to the chief priests, the officers of the temple guard, and the elders, who had come for him, "Am I leading a rebellion, that you have come with swords and clubs? 53Every day I was with

a Or into temptation b Other ancient authorities lack verses 43 and 44

b37 Isaiah 53:12 c44 Some early manuscripts do not have verses 43 and 44.

after day in the temple, you did not lay hands on me. But this is your hour, and the power of darkness!"

Peter Denies Jesus

54 Then they seized him and led him away, bringing him into the high priest's house. But Peter was following at a distance. 55When they had kindled a fire in the middle of the courtyard and sat down together, Peter sat among them. 56Then a servant-girl, seeing him in the firelight, stared at him and said, "This man also was with him." 57But he denied it, saying, "Woman, I do not know him." 58A little later someone else, on seeing him, said, "You also are one of them." But Peter said, "Man, I am not!" 59Then about an hour later still another kept insisting, "Surely this man also was with him; for he is a Galilean." 60But Peter said, "Man, I do not know what you are talking about!" At that moment, while he was still speaking, the cock crowed. 61The Lord turned and looked at Peter. Then Peter remembered the word of the Lord, how he had said to him, "Before the cock crows today, you will deny me three times." 62And he went out and wept bitterly.

The Mocking and Beating of Jesus

63 Now the men who were holding Jesus began to mock him and beat him; 64they also blindfolded him and kept asking him, "Prophesy! Who is it that struck you?" 65They kept heaping many other insults on him.

Jesus before the Council

66 When day came, the assembly of the elders of the people, both chief priests and scribes, gathered together, and they brought him to their council. 67They said, "If you are the Messiah,c tell us." He replied, "If I tell you, you will not believe; 68and if I question you, you will not answer. 69But from now on the Son of Man will be seated at the right hand of the power of God." 70All of them asked, "Are you, then, the Son of God?" He said to them, "You say that I am." 71Then they said, "What further testimony do we need? We have heard it ourselves from his own lips!"

Jesus before Pilate

23 Then the assembly rose as a body and brought Jesusd before Pilate. 2They began to accuse him, saying, "We

ἐξετείνατε τὰς χεῖρας ἐπ' ἐμέ, ἀλλ' αὕτη ἐστὶν ὑμῶν ἡ ὥρα καὶ ἡ ἐξουσία τοῦ σκότους.

54 Συλλαβόντες δὲ αὐτὸν ἤγαγον καὶ εἰσήγαγον εἰς τὴν οἰκίαν τοῦ ἀρχιερέως· ὁ δὲ Πέτρος ἠκολούθει μακρόθεν. **55** περιαψάντων δὲ πῦρ ἐν μέσῳ τῆς αὐλῆς καὶ συγκαθισάντων ἐκάθητο ὁ Πέτρος μέσος αὐτῶν. **56** ἰδοῦσα δὲ αὐτὸν παιδίσκη τις καθημένον πρὸς τὸ φῶς καὶ ἀτενίσασα αὐτῷ εἶπεν, Καὶ οὗτος σὺν αὐτῷ ἦν. **57** ὁ δὲ ἠρνήσατο λέγων, Οὐκ οἶδα αὐτόν, γύναι. **58** καὶ μετὰ βραχὺ ἕτερος ἰδὼν αὐτὸν ἔφη, Καὶ σὺ ἐξ αὐτῶν εἶ. ὁ δὲ Πέτρος ἔφη, Ἄνθρωπε, οὐκ εἰμί. **59** καὶ διαστάσης ὡσεὶ ὥρας μιᾶς ἄλλος τις διϊσχυρίζετο λέγων, Ἐπ' ἀληθείας καὶ οὗτος μετ' αὐτοῦ ἦν, καὶ γὰρ Γαλιλαῖός ἐστιν. **60** εἶπεν δὲ ὁ Πέτρος, Ἄνθρωπε, οὐκ οἶδα ὃ λέγεις. καὶ παραχρῆμα ἔτι λαλοῦντος αὐτοῦ ἐφώνησεν ἀλέκτωρ. **61** καὶ στραφεὶς ὁ κύριος ἐνέβλεψεν τῷ Πέτρῳ, καὶ ὑπεμνήσθη ὁ Πέτρος τοῦ ῥήματος τοῦ κυρίου ὡς εἶπεν αὐτῷ ὅτι Πρὶν ἀλέκτορα φωνῆσαι σήμερον ἀπαρνήσῃ με τρίς. **62** καὶ ἐξελθὼν ἔξω ἔκλαυσεν πικρῶς.

63 Καὶ οἱ ἄνδρες οἱ συνέχοντες αὐτὸν ἐνέπαιζον αὐτῷ δέροντες, **64** καὶ περικαλύψαντες αὐτὸν ἐπηρώτων λέγοντες, Προφήτευσον, τίς ἐστιν ὁ παίσας σε; **65** καὶ ἕτερα πολλὰ βλασφημοῦντες ἔλεγον εἰς αὐτόν.

66 Καὶ ὡς ἐγένετο ἡμέρα, συνήχθη τὸ πρεσβυτέριον τοῦ λαοῦ, ἀρχιερεῖς τε καὶ γραμματεῖς, καὶ ἀπήγαγον αὐτὸν εἰς τὸ συνέδριον αὐτῶν **67** λέγοντες, Εἰ σὺ εἶ ὁ Χριστός, εἰπὸν ἡμῖν. εἶπεν δὲ αὐτοῖς, Ἐὰν ὑμῖν εἴπω, οὐ μὴ πιστεύσητε· **68** ἐὰν δὲ ἐρωτήσω, οὐ μὴ ἀποκριθῆτε. **69** ἀπὸ τοῦ νῦν δὲ ἔσται ὁ υἱὸς τοῦ ἀνθρώπου καθήμενος ἐκ δεξιῶν τῆς δυνάμεως τοῦ θεοῦ. **70** εἶπαν δὲ πάντες, Σὺ οὖν εἶ ὁ υἱὸς τοῦ θεοῦ; ὁ δὲ πρὸς αὐτοὺς ἔφη, Ὑμεῖς λέγετε ὅτι ἐγώ εἰμι. **71** οἱ δὲ εἶπαν, Τί ἔτι ἔχομεν μαρτυρίας χρείαν; αὐτοὶ γὰρ ἠκούσαμεν ἀπὸ τοῦ στόματος αὐτοῦ.

23 Καὶ ἀναστὰν ἅπαν τὸ πλῆθος αὐτῶν ἤγαγον αὐτὸν ἐπὶ τὸν Πιλᾶτον. **2** ἤρξαντο δὲ κατηγορεῖν

you in the temple courts, and you did not lay a hand on me. But this is your hour—when darkness reigns."

Peter Disowns Jesus

54Then seizing him, they led him away and took him into the house of the high priest. Peter followed at a distance. 55But when they had kindled a fire in the middle of the courtyard and had sat down together, Peter sat down with them. 56A servant girl saw him seated there in the firelight. She looked closely at him and said, "This man was with him."

57But he denied it. "Woman, I don't know him," he said.

58A little later someone else saw him and said, "You also are one of them."

"Man, I am not!" Peter replied.

59About an hour later another asserted, "Certainly this fellow was with him, for he is a Galilean."

60Peter replied, "Man, I don't know what you're talking about!" Just as he was speaking, the rooster crowed. 61The Lord turned and looked straight at Peter. Then Peter remembered the word the Lord had spoken to him: "Before the rooster crows today, you will disown me three times." 62And he went outside and wept bitterly.

The Guards Mock Jesus

63The men who were guarding Jesus began mocking and beating him. 64They blindfolded him and demanded, "Prophesy! Who hit you?" 65And they said many other insulting things to him.

Jesus Before Pilate and Herod

66At daybreak the council of the elders of the people, both the chief priests and teachers of the law, met together, and Jesus was led before them. 67"If you are the Christ,d they said, "tell us."

Jesus answered, "If I tell you, you will not believe me, 68and if I asked you, you would not answer. 69But from now on, the Son of Man will be seated at the right hand of the mighty God."

70They all asked, "Are you then the Son of God?"

He replied, "You are right in saying I am."

71Then they said, "Why do we need any more testimony? We have heard it from his own lips."

23 Then the whole assembly rose and led him off to Pilate. 2And they

---

c Or the Christ　d Gk him

d67 Or Messiah

found this man perverting our nation, forbidding us to pay taxes to the emperor, and saying that he himself is the Messiah, a king."[e] [3]Then Pilate asked him, "Are you the king of the Jews?" He answered, "You say so." [4]Then Pilate said to the chief priests and the crowds, "I find no basis for an accusation against this man." [5]But they were insistent and said, "He stirs up the people by teaching throughout all Judea, from Galilee where he began even to this place."

Jesus before Herod

[6] When Pilate heard this, he asked whether the man was a Galilean. [7]And when he learned that he was under Herod's jurisdiction, he sent him off to Herod, who was himself in Jerusalem at that time. [8]When Herod saw Jesus, he was very glad, for he had been wanting to see him for a long time, because he had heard about him and was hoping to see him perform some sign. [9]He questioned him at some length, but Jesus[f] gave him no answer. [10]The chief priests and the scribes stood by, vehemently accusing him. [11]Even Herod with his soldiers treated him with contempt and mocked him; then he put an elegant robe on him, and sent him back to Pilate. [12]That same day Herod and Pilate became friends with each other; before this they had been enemies.

Jesus Sentenced to Death

[13] Pilate then called together the chief priests, the leaders, and the people, [14]and said to them, "You brought me this man as one who was perverting the people; and here I have examined him in your presence and have not found this man guilty of any of your charges against him. [15]Neither has Herod, for he sent him back to us. Indeed, he has done nothing to deserve death. [16]I will therefore have him flogged and release him."[g]

[18] Then they all shouted out together, "Away with this fellow! Release Barabbas for us!" [19](This was a man who had been put in prison for an insurrection that had taken place in the city, and for murder.) [20]Pilate, wanting to release Jesus, addressed them again; [21]but they kept shouting, "Crucify, crucify him!" [22]A third time he said to them, "Why, what evil has he done? I have

αὐτοῦ λέγοντες, Τοῦτον εὕραμεν διαστρέφοντα τὸ ἔθνος ἡμῶν καὶ κωλύοντα φόρους Καίσαρι διδόναι καὶ λέγοντα ἑαυτὸν Χριστὸν βασιλέα εἶναι. [3] ὁ δὲ Πιλᾶτος ἠρώτησεν αὐτὸν λέγων, Σὺ εἶ ὁ βασιλεὺς τῶν Ἰουδαίων; ὁ δὲ ἀποκριθεὶς αὐτῷ ἔφη, Σὺ λέγεις. [4] ὁ δὲ Πιλᾶτος εἶπεν πρὸς τοὺς ἀρχιερεῖς καὶ τοὺς ὄχλους, Οὐδὲν εὑρίσκω αἴτιον ἐν τῷ ἀνθρώπῳ τούτῳ. [5] οἱ δὲ ἐπίσχυον λέγοντες ὅτι Ἀνασείει τὸν λαὸν διδάσκων καθ' ὅλης τῆς Ἰουδαίας, καὶ ἀρξάμενος ἀπὸ τῆς Γαλιλαίας ἕως ὧδε.

[6] Πιλᾶτος δὲ ἀκούσας ἐπηρώτησεν εἰ ὁ ἄνθρωπος Γαλιλαῖός ἐστιν, [7] καὶ ἐπιγνοὺς ὅτι ἐκ τῆς ἐξουσίας Ἡρῴδου ἐστὶν ἀνέπεμψεν αὐτὸν πρὸς Ἡρῴδην, ὄντα καὶ αὐτὸν ἐν Ἱεροσολύμοις ἐν ταύταις ταῖς ἡμέραις. [8] ὁ δὲ Ἡρῴδης ἰδὼν τὸν Ἰησοῦν ἐχάρη λίαν, ἦν γὰρ ἐξ ἱκανῶν χρόνων θέλων ἰδεῖν αὐτὸν διὰ τὸ ἀκούειν περὶ αὐτοῦ καὶ ἤλπιζέν τι σημεῖον ἰδεῖν ὑπ' αὐτοῦ γινόμενον. [9] ἐπηρώτα δὲ αὐτὸν ἐν λόγοις ἱκανοῖς, αὐτὸς δὲ οὐδὲν ἀπεκρίνατο αὐτῷ. [10] εἱστήκεισαν δὲ οἱ ἀρχιερεῖς καὶ οἱ γραμματεῖς εὐτόνως κατηγοροῦντες αὐτοῦ. [11] ἐξουθενήσας δὲ αὐτὸν [καὶ] ὁ Ἡρῴδης σὺν τοῖς στρατεύμασιν αὐτοῦ καὶ ἐμπαίξας περιβαλὼν ἐσθῆτα λαμπρὰν ἀνέπεμψεν αὐτὸν τῷ Πιλάτῳ. [12] ἐγένοντο δὲ φίλοι ὅ τε Ἡρῴδης καὶ ὁ Πιλᾶτος ἐν αὐτῇ τῇ ἡμέρᾳ μετ' ἀλλήλων· προϋπῆρχον γὰρ ἐν ἔχθρᾳ ὄντες πρὸς αὐτούς.

[13] Πιλᾶτος δὲ συγκαλεσάμενος τοὺς ἀρχιερεῖς καὶ τοὺς ἄρχοντας καὶ τὸν λαὸν [14] εἶπεν πρὸς αὐτούς, Προσηνέγκατέ μοι τὸν ἄνθρωπον τοῦτον ὡς ἀποστρέφοντα τὸν λαόν, καὶ ἰδοὺ ἐγὼ ἐνώπιον ὑμῶν ἀνακρίνας οὐθὲν εὗρον ἐν τῷ ἀνθρώπῳ τούτῳ αἴτιον ὧν κατηγορεῖτε κατ' αὐτοῦ. [15] ἀλλ' οὐδὲ Ἡρῴδης, ἀνέπεμψεν γὰρ αὐτὸν πρὸς ἡμᾶς, καὶ ἰδοὺ οὐδὲν ἄξιον θανάτου ἐστὶν πεπραγμένον αὐτῷ· [16] παιδεύσας οὖν αὐτὸν ἀπολύσω.[a] [18] ἀνέκραγον δὲ παμπληθεὶ λέγοντες, Αἶρε τοῦτον, ἀπόλυσον δὲ ἡμῖν τὸν Βαραββᾶν· [19] ὅστις ἦν διὰ στάσιν τινὰ γενομένην ἐν τῇ πόλει καὶ φόνον βληθεὶς ἐν τῇ φυλακῇ. [20] πάλιν δὲ ὁ Πιλᾶτος προσεφώνησεν αὐτοῖς θέλων ἀπολῦσαι τὸν Ἰησοῦν. [21] οἱ δὲ ἐπεφώνουν λέγοντες, Σταύρου σταύρου αὐτόν. [22] ὁ δὲ τρίτον εἶπεν πρὸς αὐτούς, Τί γὰρ κακὸν

began to accuse him, saying, "We have found this man subverting our nation. He opposes payment of taxes to Caesar and claims to be Christ,[a] a king."

[3]So Pilate asked Jesus, "Are you the king of the Jews?"

"Yes, it is as you say," Jesus replied.

[4]Then Pilate announced to the chief priests and the crowd, "I find no basis for a charge against this man."

[5]But they insisted, "He stirs up the people all over Judea[b] by his teaching. He started in Galilee and has come all the way here."

[6]On hearing this, Pilate asked if the man was a Galilean. [7]When he learned that Jesus was under Herod's jurisdiction, he sent him to Herod, who was also in Jerusalem at that time.

[8]When Herod saw Jesus, he was greatly pleased, because for a long time he had been wanting to see him. From what he had heard about him, he hoped to see him perform some miracle. [9]He plied him with many questions, but Jesus gave him no answer. [10]The chief priests and the teachers of the law were standing there, vehemently accusing him. [11]Then Herod and his soldiers ridiculed and mocked him. Dressing him in an elegant robe, they sent him back to Pilate. [12]That day Herod and Pilate became friends—before this they had been enemies.

[13]Pilate called together the chief priests, the rulers and the people, [14]and said to them, "You brought me this man as one who was inciting the people to rebellion. I have examined him in your presence and have found no basis for your charges against him. [15]Neither has Herod, for he sent him back to us; as you can see, he has done nothing to deserve death. [16]Therefore, I will punish him and then release him.[c]"

[18]With one voice they cried out, "Away with this man! Release Barabbas to us!" [19](Barabbas had been thrown into prison for an insurrection in the city, and for murder.)

[20]Wanting to release Jesus, Pilate appealed to them again. [21]But they kept shouting, "Crucify him! Crucify him!"

[22]For the third time he spoke to them: "Why? What crime has this man commit-

---

[e] Or *is an anointed king* [f] Gk *he* [g] Here, or after verse 19, other ancient authorities add verse 17, *Now he was obliged to release someone for them at the festival*

[a]16 NIV/NRSV notes add 17 ἀνάγκην δὲ εἶχεν ἀπολύειν αὐτοῖς κατὰ ἑορτὴν ἕνα.

[a]2 Or *Messiah*; also in verses 35 and 39 [b]5 Or *over the land of the Jews* [c]16 Some manuscripts *him.*" [17]*Now he was obliged to release one man to them at the Feast.*

found in him no ground for the sentence of death; I will therefore have him flogged and then release him." [23]But they kept urgently demanding with loud shouts that he should be crucified; and their voices prevailed. [24]So Pilate gave his verdict that their demand should be granted. [25]He released the man they asked for, the one who had been put in prison for insurrection and murder, and he handed Jesus over as they wished.

The Crucifixion of Jesus

26 As they led him away, they seized a man, Simon of Cyrene, who was coming from the country, and they laid the cross on him, and made him carry it behind Jesus. [27]A great number of the people followed him, and among them were women who were beating their breasts and wailing for him. [28]But Jesus turned to them and said, "Daughters of Jerusalem, do not weep for me, but weep for yourselves and for your children. [29]For the days are surely coming when they will say, 'Blessed are the barren, and the wombs that never bore, and the breasts that never nursed.' [30]Then they will begin to say to the mountains, 'Fall on us'; and to the hills, 'Cover us.' [31]For if they do this when the wood is green, what will happen when it is dry?"

32 Two others also, who were criminals, were led away to be put to death with him. [33]When they came to the place that is called The Skull, they crucified Jesus[h] there with the criminals, one on his right and one on his left. ⟦[34]Then Jesus said, "Father, forgive them; for they do not know what they are doing."⟧[i] And they cast lots to divide his clothing. [35]And the people stood by, watching; but the leaders scoffed at him, saying, "He saved others; let him save himself if he is the Messiah[j] of God, his chosen one!" [36]The soldiers also mocked him, coming up and offering him sour wine, [37]and saying, "If you are the King of the Jews, save yourself!" [38]There was also an inscription over him,[k] "This is the King of the Jews."

39 One of the criminals who were hanged there kept deriding[l] him and saying, "Are you not the Messiah?[j] Save yourself and us!" [40]But the other rebuked him, saying, "Do you not fear God, since you are under the same sentence of condemnation? [41]And

---

ἐποίησεν οὗτος; οὐδὲν αἴτιον θανάτου εὗρον ἐν αὐτῷ· παιδεύσας οὖν αὐτὸν ἀπολύσω. **23** οἱ δὲ ἐπέκειντο φωναῖς μεγάλαις αἰτούμενοι αὐτὸν σταυρωθῆναι, καὶ κατίσχυον αἱ φωναὶ αὐτῶν. **24** καὶ Πιλᾶτος ἐπέκρινεν γενέσθαι τὸ αἴτημα αὐτῶν· **25** ἀπέλυσεν δὲ τὸν διὰ στάσιν καὶ φόνον βεβλημένον εἰς φυλακὴν ὃν ᾐτοῦντο, τὸν δὲ Ἰησοῦν παρέδωκεν τῷ θελήματι αὐτῶν.

26 Καὶ ὡς ἀπήγαγον αὐτόν, ἐπιλαβόμενοι Σίμωνά τινα Κυρηναῖον ἐρχόμενον ἀπ᾽ ἀγροῦ ἐπέθηκαν αὐτῷ τὸν σταυρὸν φέρειν ὄπισθεν τοῦ Ἰησοῦ. **27** Ἠκολούθει δὲ αὐτῷ πολὺ πλῆθος τοῦ λαοῦ καὶ γυναικῶν αἳ ἐκόπτοντο καὶ ἐθρήνουν αὐτόν. **28** στραφεὶς δὲ πρὸς αὐτὰς [ὁ] Ἰησοῦς εἶπεν, Θυγατέρες Ἰερουσαλήμ, μὴ κλαίετε ἐπ᾽ ἐμέ· πλὴν ἐφ᾽ ἑαυτὰς κλαίετε καὶ ἐπὶ τὰ τέκνα ὑμῶν, **29** ὅτι ἰδοὺ ἔρχονται ἡμέραι ἐν αἷς ἐροῦσιν, Μακάριαι αἱ στεῖραι καὶ αἱ κοιλίαι αἳ οὐκ ἐγέννησαν καὶ μαστοὶ οἳ οὐκ ἔθρεψαν. **30** τότε ἄρξονται λέγειν τοῖς ὄρεσιν,

Πέσετε ἐφ᾽ ἡμᾶς,

καὶ τοῖς βουνοῖς,

Καλύψατε ἡμᾶς·

31 ὅτι εἰ ἐν τῷ ὑγρῷ ξύλῳ ταῦτα ποιοῦσιν, ἐν τῷ ξηρῷ τί γένηται;

32 Ἤγοντο δὲ καὶ ἕτεροι κακοῦργοι δύο σὺν αὐτῷ ἀναιρεθῆναι. **33** καὶ ὅτε ἦλθον ἐπὶ τὸν τόπον τὸν καλούμενον Κρανίον, ἐκεῖ ἐσταύρωσαν αὐτὸν καὶ τοὺς κακούργους, ὃν μὲν ἐκ δεξιῶν ὃν δὲ ἐξ ἀριστερῶν. **34** ⟦ὁ δὲ Ἰησοῦς ἔλεγεν, Πάτερ, ἄφες αὐτοῖς, οὐ γὰρ οἴδασιν τί ποιοῦσιν.⟧ διαμεριζόμενοι δὲ τὰ ἱμάτια αὐτοῦ ἔβαλον κλήρους. **35** καὶ εἱστήκει ὁ λαὸς θεωρῶν. ἐξεμυκτήριζον δὲ καὶ οἱ ἄρχοντες λέγοντες, Ἄλλους ἔσωσεν, σωσάτω ἑαυτόν, εἰ οὗτός ἐστιν ὁ Χριστὸς τοῦ θεοῦ ὁ ἐκλεκτός. **36** ἐνέπαιξαν δὲ αὐτῷ καὶ οἱ στρατιῶται προσερχόμενοι, ὄξος προσφέροντες αὐτῷ **37** καὶ λέγοντες, Εἰ σὺ εἶ ὁ βασιλεὺς τῶν Ἰουδαίων, σῶσον σεαυτόν. **38** ἦν δὲ καὶ ἐπιγραφὴ ἐπ᾽ αὐτῷ[b], Ὁ βασιλεὺς τῶν Ἰουδαίων οὗτος.

39 Εἷς δὲ τῶν κρεμασθέντων κακούργων ἐβλασφήμει αὐτὸν λέγων, Οὐχὶ σὺ εἶ ὁ Χριστός; σῶσον σεαυτὸν καὶ ἡμᾶς. **40** ἀποκριθεὶς δὲ ὁ ἕτερος ἐπιτιμῶν αὐτῷ ἔφη, Οὐδὲ φοβῇ σὺ τὸν θεόν, ὅτι ἐν τῷ αὐτῷ κρίματι εἶ;

---

ted? I have found in him no grounds for the death penalty. Therefore I will have him punished and then release him."

[23]But with loud shouts they insistently demanded that he be crucified, and their shouts prevailed. [24]So Pilate decided to grant their demand. [25]He released the man who had been thrown into prison for insurrection and murder, the one they asked for, and surrendered Jesus to their will.

The Crucifixion

[26]As they led him away, they seized Simon from Cyrene, who was on his way in from the country, and put the cross on him and made him carry it behind Jesus. [27]A large number of people followed him, including women who mourned and wailed for him. [28]Jesus turned and said to them, "Daughters of Jerusalem, do not weep for me; weep for yourselves and for your children. [29]For the time will come when you will say, 'Blessed are the barren women, the wombs that never bore and the breasts that never nursed!' [30]Then

" 'they will say to the mountains, "Fall on us!"
and to the hills, "Cover us!" '[d]

[31]For if men do these things when the tree is green, what will happen when it is dry?"

[32]Two other men, both criminals, were also led out with him to be executed. [33]When they came to the place called the Skull, there they crucified him, along with the criminals—one on his right, the other on his left. [34]Jesus said, "Father, forgive them, for they do not know what they are doing."[e] And they divided up his clothes by casting lots.

[35]The people stood watching, and the rulers even sneered at him. They said, "He saved others; let him save himself if he is the Christ of God, the Chosen One."

[36]The soldiers also came up and mocked him. They offered him wine vinegar [37]and said, "If you are the king of the Jews, save yourself."

[38]There was a written notice above him, which read: THIS IS THE KING OF THE JEWS.

[39]One of the criminals who hung there hurled insults at him: "Aren't you the Christ? Save yourself and us!"

[40]But the other criminal rebuked him. "Don't you fear God," he said, "since you are under the same sentence? [41]We are

---

[h] Gk him   [i] Other ancient authorities lack the sentence Then Jesus . . . what they are doing   [j] Or the Christ   [k] Other ancient authorities add written in Greek and Latin and Hebrew (that is, Aramaic)   [l] Or blaspheming

[b]38 NRSV note k adds [ἐπι]γεγραμμένη [ἐπ᾽ αὐτῷ] γράμμασιν Ἑλληνικοῖς καὶ Ῥωμαϊκοῖς καὶ Ἑβραϊκοῖς

[d]30 Hosea 10:8   [e]34 Some early manuscripts do not have this sentence.

we indeed have been condemned justly, for we are getting what we deserve for our deeds, but this man has done nothing wrong." [42]Then he said, "Jesus, remember me when you come into[m] your kingdom." [43]He replied, "Truly I tell you, today you will be with me in Paradise."

The Death of Jesus

44 It was now about noon, and darkness came over the whole land[n] until three in the afternoon, [45]while the sun's light failed;[o] and the curtain of the temple was torn in two. [46]Then Jesus, crying with a loud voice, said, "Father, into your hands I commend my spirit." Having said this, he breathed his last. [47]When the centurion saw what had taken place, he praised God and said, "Certainly this man was innocent."[p] [48]And when all the crowds who had gathered there for this spectacle saw what had taken place, they returned home, beating their breasts. [49]But all his acquaintances, including the women who had followed him from Galilee, stood at a distance, watching these things.

The Burial of Jesus

50 Now there was a good and righteous man named Joseph, who, though a member of the council, [51]had not agreed to their plan and action. He came from the Jewish town of Arimathea, and he was waiting expectantly for the kingdom of God. [52]This man went to Pilate and asked for the body of Jesus. [53]Then he took it down, wrapped it in a linen cloth, and laid it in a rock-hewn tomb where no one had ever been laid. [54]It was the day of Preparation, and the sabbath was beginning.[q] [55]The women who had come with him from Galilee followed, and they saw the tomb and how his body was laid. [56]Then they returned, and prepared spices and ointments.

On the sabbath they rested according to the commandment.

The Resurrection of Jesus

24 But on the first day of the week, at early dawn, they came to the tomb, taking the spices that they had prepared. [2]They found the stone rolled away from the tomb, [3]but when they went in, they did not find the body.[r] [4]While they were perplexed about this, suddenly two men in

[41] καὶ ἡμεῖς μὲν δικαίως, ἄξια γὰρ ὧν ἐπράξαμεν ἀπολαμβάνομεν· οὗτος δὲ οὐδὲν ἄτοπον ἔπραξεν. [42] καὶ ἔλεγεν, Ἰησοῦ, μνήσθητί μου ὅταν ἔλθῃς εἰς τὴν βασιλείαν[c] σου. [43] καὶ εἶπεν αὐτῷ, Ἀμήν σοι λέγω, σήμερον μετ' ἐμοῦ ἔσῃ ἐν τῷ παραδείσῳ.

[44] Καὶ ἦν ἤδη ὡσεὶ ὥρα ἕκτη καὶ σκότος ἐγένετο ἐφ' ὅλην τὴν γῆν ἕως ὥρας ἐνάτης [45] τοῦ ἡλίου ἐκλιπόντος[d], ἐσχίσθη δὲ τὸ καταπέτασμα τοῦ ναοῦ μέσον. [46] καὶ φωνήσας φωνῇ μεγάλῃ ὁ Ἰησοῦς εἶπεν, Πάτερ, εἰς χεῖράς σου παρατίθεμαι τὸ πνεῦμά μου. τοῦτο δὲ εἰπὼν ἐξέπνευσεν. [47] Ἰδὼν δὲ ὁ ἑκατοντάρχης τὸ γενόμενον ἐδόξαζεν τὸν θεὸν λέγων, Ὄντως ὁ ἄνθρωπος οὗτος δίκαιος ἦν. [48] καὶ πάντες οἱ συμπαραγενόμενοι ὄχλοι ἐπὶ τὴν θεωρίαν ταύτην, θεωρήσαντες τὰ γενόμενα, τύπτοντες τὰ στήθη ὑπέστρεφον. [49] εἱστήκεισαν δὲ πάντες οἱ γνωστοὶ αὐτῷ ἀπὸ μακρόθεν καὶ γυναῖκες αἱ συνακολουθοῦσαι αὐτῷ ἀπὸ τῆς Γαλιλαίας ὁρῶσαι ταῦτα.

[50] Καὶ ἰδοὺ ἀνὴρ ὀνόματι Ἰωσὴφ βουλευτὴς ὑπάρχων [καὶ] ἀνὴρ ἀγαθὸς καὶ δίκαιος [51] – οὗτος οὐκ ἦν συγκατατεθειμένος τῇ βουλῇ καὶ τῇ πράξει αὐτῶν – ἀπὸ Ἁριμαθαίας πόλεως τῶν Ἰουδαίων, ὃς προσεδέχετο τὴν βασιλείαν τοῦ θεοῦ, [52] οὗτος προσελθὼν τῷ Πιλάτῳ ᾐτήσατο τὸ σῶμα τοῦ Ἰησοῦ [53] καὶ καθελὼν ἐνετύλιξεν αὐτὸ σινδόνι καὶ ἔθηκεν αὐτὸν[e] ἐν μνήματι λαξευτῷ οὗ οὐκ ἦν οὐδεὶς οὔπω κείμενος. [54] καὶ ἡμέρα ἦν παρασκευῆς καὶ σάββατον ἐπέφωσκεν. [55] Κατακολουθήσασαι δὲ αἱ γυναῖκες, αἵτινες ἦσαν συνεληλυθυῖαι ἐκ τῆς Γαλιλαίας αὐτῷ, ἐθεάσαντο τὸ μνημεῖον καὶ ὡς ἐτέθη τὸ σῶμα αὐτοῦ, [56] ὑποστρέψασαι δὲ ἡτοίμασαν ἀρώματα καὶ μύρα.

Καὶ τὸ μὲν σάββατον ἡσύχασαν κατὰ τὴν ἐντολήν. 24 [1] τῇ δὲ μιᾷ τῶν σαββάτων ὄρθρου βαθέως ἐπὶ τὸ μνῆμα ἦλθον φέρουσαι ἃ ἡτοίμασαν ἀρώματα. [2] εὗρον δὲ τὸν λίθον ἀποκεκυλισμένον ἀπὸ τοῦ μνημείου, [3] εἰσελθοῦσαι δὲ οὐχ εὗρον τὸ σῶμα τοῦ κυρίου Ἰησοῦ[a]. [4] καὶ ἐγένετο ἐν τῷ ἀπορεῖσθαι αὐτὰς περὶ τούτου καὶ ἰδοὺ ἄνδρες δύο ἐπέστησαν αὐταῖς ἐν

punished justly, for we are getting what our deeds deserve. But this man has done nothing wrong."

[42]Then he said, "Jesus, remember me when you come into your kingdom.[f]"

[43]Jesus answered him, "I tell you the truth, today you will be with me in paradise."

Jesus' Death

[44]It was now about the sixth hour, and darkness came over the whole land until the ninth hour, [45]for the sun stopped shining. And the curtain of the temple was torn in two. [46]Jesus called out with a loud voice, "Father, into your hands I commit my spirit." When he had said this, he breathed his last.

[47]The centurion, seeing what had happened, praised God and said, "Surely this was a righteous man." [48]When all the people who had gathered to witness this sight saw what took place, they beat their breasts and went away. [49]But all those who knew him, including the women who had followed him from Galilee, stood at a distance, watching these things.

Jesus' Burial

[50]Now there was a man named Joseph, a member of the Council, a good and upright man, [51]who had not consented to their decision and action. He came from the Judean town of Arimathea and he was waiting for the kingdom of God. [52]Going to Pilate, he asked for Jesus' body. [53]Then he took it down, wrapped it in linen cloth and placed it in a tomb cut in the rock, one in which no one had yet been laid. [54]It was Preparation Day, and the Sabbath was about to begin.

[55]The women who had come with Jesus from Galilee followed Joseph and saw the tomb and how his body was laid in it. [56]Then they went home and prepared spices and perfumes. But they rested on the Sabbath in obedience to the commandment.

The Resurrection

24 On the first day of the week, very early in the morning, the women took the spices they had prepared and went to the tomb. [2]They found the stone rolled away from the tomb, [3]but when they entered, they did not find the body of the Lord Jesus. [4]While they were wondering about this, suddenly two men in clothes

l Or *the Christ*   *m* Other ancient authorities read *in*
n Or *earth*   *o* Or *the sun was eclipsed*. Other ancient authorities read *the sun was darkened*   *p* Or *righteous*
q Gk *was dawning*   *r* Other ancient authorities add *of the Lord Jesus*

*c*42 NIV/NRSV notes ἐν τῇ βασιλείᾳ   *d*45 NRSV note o καὶ ἐσκοτίσθη ὁ ἥλιος   *e*53 NIV/NRSV texts αὐτὸ †   *a*3 NRSV text omits τοῦ κυρίου Ἰησοῦ; NIV text and NRSV note r as UBS

*f*42 Some manuscripts *come with your kingly power*

NRSV

dazzling clothes stood beside them. 5The women[s] were terrified and bowed their faces to the ground, but the men[t] said to them, "Why do you look for the living among the dead? He is not here, but has risen.[u] 6Remember how he told you, while he was still in Galilee, 7that the Son of Man must be handed over to sinners, and be crucified, and on the third day rise again." 8Then they remembered his words, 9and returning from the tomb, they told all this to the eleven and to all the rest. 10Now it was Mary Magdalene, Joanna, Mary the mother of James, and the other women with them who told this to the apostles. 11But these words seemed to them an idle tale, and they did not believe them. 12But Peter got up and ran to the tomb; stooping and looking in, he saw the linen cloths by themselves; then he went home, amazed at what had happened.[v]

The Walk to Emmaus

13 Now on that same day two of them were going to a village called Emmaus, about seven miles[w] from Jerusalem, 14and talking with each other about all these things that had happened. 15While they were talking and discussing, Jesus himself came near and went with them, 16but their eyes were kept from recognizing him. 17And he said to them, "What are you discussing with each other while you walk along?" They stood still, looking sad.[x] 18Then one of them, whose name was Cleopas, answered him, "Are you the only stranger in Jerusalem who does not know the things that have taken place there in these days?" 19He asked them, "What things?" They replied, "The things about Jesus of Nazareth,[y] who was a prophet mighty in deed and word before God and all the people, 20and how our chief priests and leaders handed him over to be condemned to death and crucified him. 21But we had hoped that he was the one to redeem Israel.[z] Yes, and besides all this, it is now the third day since these things took place. 22Moreover, some women of our group astounded us. They were at the tomb

Greek

ἐσθῆτι ἀστραπτούσῃ. 5 ἐμφόβων δὲ γενομένων αὐτῶν καὶ κλινουσῶν τὰ πρόσωπα εἰς τὴν γῆν εἶπαν πρὸς αὐτάς, Τί ζητεῖτε τὸν ζῶντα μετὰ τῶν νεκρῶν· 6 οὐκ ἔστιν ὧδε, ἀλλὰ ἠγέρθη. μνήσθητε ὡς ἐλάλησεν ὑμῖν ἔτι ὢν ἐν τῇ Γαλιλαίᾳ 7 λέγων τὸν υἱὸν τοῦ ἀνθρώπου ὅτι δεῖ παραδοθῆναι εἰς χεῖρας ἀνθρώπων ἁμαρτωλῶν καὶ σταυρωθῆναι καὶ τῇ τρίτῃ ἡμέρᾳ ἀναστῆναι. 8 καὶ ἐμνήσθησαν τῶν ῥημάτων αὐτοῦ. 9 καὶ ὑποστρέψασαι ἀπὸ τοῦ μνημείου ἀπήγγειλαν ταῦτα πάντα τοῖς ἕνδεκα καὶ πᾶσιν τοῖς λοιποῖς. 10 ἦσαν δὲ ἡ Μαγδαληνὴ Μαρία καὶ Ἰωάννα καὶ Μαρία ἡ Ἰακώβου καὶ αἱ λοιπαὶ σὺν αὐταῖς. ἔλεγον πρὸς τοὺς ἀποστόλους ταῦτα, 11 καὶ ἐφάνησαν ἐνώπιον αὐτῶν ὡσεὶ λῆρος τὰ ῥήματα ταῦτα, καὶ ἠπίστουν αὐταῖς. 12 Ὁ δὲ Πέτρος ἀναστὰς ἔδραμεν ἐπὶ τὸ μνημεῖον καὶ παρακύψας βλέπει τὰ ὀθόνια μόνα, καὶ ἀπῆλθεν πρὸς ἑαυτὸν θαυμάζων τὸ γεγονός.

13 Καὶ ἰδοὺ δύο ἐξ αὐτῶν ἐν αὐτῇ τῇ ἡμέρᾳ ἦσαν πορευόμενοι εἰς κώμην ἀπέχουσαν σταδίους[b] ἑξήκοντα ἀπὸ Ἰερουσαλήμ, ᾗ ὄνομα Ἐμμαοῦς, 14 καὶ αὐτοὶ ὡμίλουν πρὸς ἀλλήλους περὶ πάντων τῶν συμβεβηκότων τούτων. 15 καὶ ἐγένετο ἐν τῷ ὁμιλεῖν αὐτοὺς καὶ συζητεῖν καὶ αὐτὸς Ἰησοῦς ἐγγίσας συνεπορεύετο αὐτοῖς, 16 οἱ δὲ ὀφθαλμοὶ αὐτῶν ἐκρατοῦντο τοῦ μὴ ἐπιγνῶναι αὐτόν. 17 εἶπεν δὲ πρὸς αὐτούς, Τίνες οἱ λόγοι οὗτοι οὓς ἀντιβάλλετε πρὸς ἀλλήλους περιπατοῦντες; καὶ ἐστάθησαν[c] σκυθρωποί. 18 ἀποκριθεὶς δὲ εἷς[d] ὀνόματι Κλεοπᾶς εἶπεν πρὸς αὐτόν, Σὺ μόνος παροικεῖς Ἰερουσαλὴμ καὶ οὐκ ἔγνως τὰ γενόμενα ἐν αὐτῇ ἐν ταῖς ἡμέραις ταύταις; 19 καὶ εἶπεν αὐτοῖς, Ποῖα; οἱ δὲ εἶπαν αὐτῷ, Τὰ περὶ Ἰησοῦ τοῦ Ναζαρηνοῦ[e], ὃς ἐγένετο ἀνὴρ προφήτης δυνατὸς ἐν ἔργῳ καὶ λόγῳ ἐναντίον τοῦ θεοῦ καὶ παντὸς τοῦ λαοῦ, 20 ὅπως τε παρέδωκαν αὐτὸν οἱ ἀρχιερεῖς καὶ οἱ ἄρχοντες ἡμῶν εἰς κρίμα θανάτου καὶ ἐσταύρωσαν αὐτόν. 21 ἡμεῖς δὲ ἠλπίζομεν ὅτι αὐτός ἐστιν ὁ μέλλων λυτροῦσθαι τὸν Ἰσραήλ· ἀλλά γε καὶ σὺν πᾶσιν τούτοις τρίτην ταύτην ἡμέραν ἄγει ἀφ' οὗ ταῦτα ἐγένετο. 22 ἀλλὰ καὶ γυναῖκές τινες ἐξ ἡμῶν ἐξέστησαν ἡμᾶς, γενόμεναι ὀρθριναὶ

NIV

that gleamed like lightning stood beside them. 5In their fright the women bowed down with their faces to the ground, but the men said to them, "Why do you look for the living among the dead? 6He is not here; he has risen! Remember how he told you, while he was still with you in Galilee: 7'The Son of Man must be delivered into the hands of sinful men, be crucified and on the third day be raised again.' " 8Then they remembered his words.

9When they came back from the tomb, they told all these things to the Eleven and to all the others. 10It was Mary Magdalene, Joanna, Mary the mother of James, and the others with them who told this to the apostles. 11But they did not believe the women, because their words seemed to them like nonsense. 12Peter, however, got up and ran to the tomb. Bending over, he saw the strips of linen lying by themselves, and he went away, wondering to himself what had happened.

On the Road to Emmaus

13Now that same day two of them were going to a village called Emmaus, about seven miles[a] from Jerusalem. 14They were talking with each other about everything that had happened. 15As they talked and discussed these things with each other, Jesus himself came up and walked along with them; 16but they were kept from recognizing him.

17He asked them, "What are you discussing together as you walk along?"

They stood still, their faces downcast. 18One of them, named Cleopas, asked him, "Are you only a visitor to Jerusalem and do not know the things that have happened there in these days?"

19"What things?" he asked.

"About Jesus of Nazareth," they replied. "He was a prophet, powerful in word and deed before God and all the people. 20The chief priests and our rulers handed him over to be sentenced to death, and they crucified him; 21but we had hoped that he was the one who was going to redeem Israel. And what is more, it is the third day since all this took place. 22In addition, some of our women amazed us. They went to

---

s Gk They   t Gk but they   u Other ancient authorities lack He is not here, but has risen   v Other ancient authorities lack verse 12   w Gk sixty stadia; other ancient authorities read a hundred sixty stadia   x Other ancient authorities read walk along, looking sad?"   y Other ancient authorities read Jesus the Nazorean   z Or to set Israel free

b 13 NRSV note w adds ἑκατὸν   c 17 NRSV note x omits καὶ ἐστάθησαν   d 18 NIV text adds ἐξ αὐτῶν †   e 19 NRSV note y Ναζωραίου

a 13 Greek sixty stadia (about 11 kilometers)

early this morning, 23and when they did not find his body there, they came back and told us that they had indeed seen a vision of angels who said that he was alive. 24Some of those who were with us went to the tomb and found it just as the women had said; but they did not see him." 25Then he said to them, "Oh, how foolish you are, and how slow of heart to believe all that the prophets have declared! 26Was it not necessary that the Messiaha should suffer these things and then enter into his glory?" 27Then beginning with Moses and all the prophets, he interpreted to them the things about himself in all the scriptures.

28 As they came near the village to which they were going, he walked ahead as if he were going on. 29But they urged him strongly, saying, "Stay with us, because it is almost evening and the day is now nearly over." So he went in to stay with them. 30When he was at the table with them, he took bread, blessed and broke it, and gave it to them. 31Then their eyes were opened, and they recognized him; and he vanished from their sight. 32They said to each other, "Were not our hearts burning within usb while he was talking to us on the road, while he was opening the scriptures to us?" 33That same hour they got up and returned to Jerusalem; and they found the eleven and their companions gathered together. 34They were saying, "The Lord has risen indeed, and he has appeared to Simon!" 35Then they told what had happened on the road, and how he had been made known to them in the breaking of the bread.

Jesus Appears to His Disciples

36 While they were talking about this, Jesus himself stood among them and said to them, "Peace be with you."c 37They were startled and terrified, and thought that they were seeing a ghost. 38He said to them, "Why are you frightened, and why do doubts arise in your hearts? 39Look at my hands and my feet; see that it is I myself. Touch me and see; for a ghost does not have flesh and bones as you see that I have." 40And when he had said this, he showed them his hands and his feet.d 41While in their joy they were disbelieving and still wondering, he said to them, "Have you anything here to eat?" 42They gave

ἐπὶ τὸ μνημεῖον, 23 καὶ μὴ εὑροῦσαι τὸ σῶμα αὐτοῦ ἦλθον λέγουσαι καὶ ὀπτασίαν ἀγγέλων ἑωρακέναι, οἳ λέγουσιν αὐτὸν ζῆν. 24 καὶ ἀπῆλθόν τινες τῶν σὺν ἡμῖν ἐπὶ τὸ μνημεῖον καὶ εὗρον οὕτως καθὼς καὶ αἱ γυναῖκες εἶπον, αὐτὸν δὲ οὐκ εἶδον. 25 καὶ αὐτὸς εἶπεν πρὸς αὐτούς, Ὦ ἀνόητοι καὶ βραδεῖς τῇ καρδίᾳ τοῦ πιστεύειν ἐπὶ πᾶσιν οἷς ἐλάλησαν οἱ προφῆται· 26 οὐχὶ ταῦτα ἔδει παθεῖν τὸν Χριστὸν καὶ εἰσελθεῖν εἰς τὴν δόξαν αὐτοῦ; 27 καὶ ἀρξάμενος ἀπὸ Μωϋσέως καὶ ἀπὸ πάντων τῶν προφητῶν διερμήνευσεν αὐτοῖς ἐν πάσαις ταῖς γραφαῖς τὰ περὶ ἑαυτοῦ.

28 Καὶ ἤγγισαν εἰς τὴν κώμην οὗ ἐπορεύοντο, καὶ αὐτὸς προσεποιήσατο πορρώτερον πορεύεσθαι. 29 καὶ παρεβιάσαντο αὐτὸν λέγοντες, Μεῖνον μεθ' ἡμῶν, ὅτι πρὸς ἑσπέραν ἐστὶν καὶ κέκλικεν ἤδη ἡ ἡμέρα. καὶ εἰσῆλθεν τοῦ μεῖναι σὺν αὐτοῖς. 30 καὶ ἐγένετο ἐν τῷ κατακλιθῆναι αὐτὸν μετ' αὐτῶν λαβὼν τὸν ἄρτον εὐλόγησεν καὶ κλάσας ἐπεδίδου αὐτοῖς, 31 αὐτῶν δὲ διηνοίχθησαν οἱ ὀφθαλμοὶ καὶ ἐπέγνωσαν αὐτόν· καὶ αὐτὸς ἄφαντος ἐγένετο ἀπ' αὐτῶν. 32 καὶ εἶπαν πρὸς ἀλλήλους, Οὐχὶ ἡ καρδία ἡμῶν καιομένη ἦν [ἐν ἡμῖν] ὡς ἐλάλει ἡμῖν ἐν τῇ ὁδῷ, ὡς διήνοιγεν ἡμῖν τὰς γραφάς; 33 καὶ ἀναστάντες αὐτῇ τῇ ὥρᾳ ὑπέστρεψαν εἰς Ἰερουσαλὴμ καὶ εὗρον ἠθροισμένους τοὺς ἕνδεκα καὶ τοὺς σὺν αὐτοῖς, 34 λέγοντας ὅτι ὄντως ἠγέρθη ὁ κύριος καὶ ὤφθη Σίμωνι. 35 καὶ αὐτοὶ ἐξηγοῦντο τὰ ἐν τῇ ὁδῷ καὶ ὡς ἐγνώσθη αὐτοῖς ἐν τῇ κλάσει τοῦ ἄρτου.

36 Ταῦτα δὲ αὐτῶν λαλούντων αὐτὸς ἔστη ἐν μέσῳ αὐτῶν καὶ λέγει αὐτοῖς, Εἰρήνη ὑμῖν. 37 πτοηθέντες δὲ καὶ ἔμφοβοι γενόμενοι ἐδόκουν πνεῦμα θεωρεῖν. 38 καὶ εἶπεν αὐτοῖς, Τί τεταραγμένοι ἐστὲ καὶ διὰ τί διαλογισμοὶ ἀναβαίνουσιν ἐν τῇ καρδίᾳ ὑμῶν; 39 ἴδετε τὰς χεῖράς μου καὶ τοὺς πόδας μου ὅτι ἐγώ εἰμι αὐτός· ψηλαφήσατέ με καὶ ἴδετε, ὅτι πνεῦμα σάρκα καὶ ὀστέα οὐκ ἔχει καθὼς ἐμὲ θεωρεῖτε ἔχοντα. 40 καὶ τοῦτο εἰπὼν ἔδειξεν αὐτοῖς τὰς χεῖρας καὶ τοὺς πόδας. 41 ἔτι δὲ ἀπιστούντων αὐτῶν ἀπὸ τῆς χαρᾶς καὶ θαυμαζόντων εἶπεν αὐτοῖς, Ἔχετέ τι βρώσιμον ἐνθάδε; 42 οἱ δὲ

the tomb early this morning 23but didn't find his body. They came and told us that they had seen a vision of angels, who said he was alive. 24Then some of our companions went to the tomb and found it just as the women had said, but him they did not see."

25He said to them, "How foolish you are, and how slow of heart to believe all that the prophets have spoken! 26Did not the Christb have to suffer these things and then enter his glory?" 27And beginning with Moses and all the Prophets, he explained to them what was said in all the Scriptures concerning himself.

28As they approached the village to which they were going, Jesus acted as if he were going farther. 29But they urged him strongly, "Stay with us, for it is nearly evening; the day is almost over." So he went in to stay with them.

30When he was at the table with them, he took bread, gave thanks, broke it and began to give it to them. 31Then their eyes were opened and they recognized him, and he disappeared from their sight. 32They asked each other, "Were not our hearts burning within us while he talked with us on the road and opened the Scriptures to us?"

33They got up and returned at once to Jerusalem. There they found the Eleven and those with them, assembled together 34and saying, "It is true! The Lord has risen and has appeared to Simon." 35Then the two told what had happened on the way, and how Jesus was recognized by them when he broke the bread.

Jesus Appears to the Disciples

36While they were still talking about this, Jesus himself stood among them and said to them, "Peace be with you."

37They were startled and frightened, thinking they saw a ghost. 38He said to them, "Why are you troubled, and why do doubts rise in your minds? 39Look at my hands and my feet. It is I myself! Touch me and see; a ghost does not have flesh and bones, as you see I have."

40When he had said this, he showed them his hands and feet. 41And while they still did not believe it because of joy and amazement, he asked them, "Do you have anything here to eat?" 42They gave him a piece

a Or *the Christ*   b Other ancient authorities lack *within us*   c Other ancient authorities lack *and said to them, "Peace be with you."*   d Other ancient authorities lack verse 40

b26 Or *Messiah*; also in verse 46

him a piece of broiled fish, 43and he took it and ate in their presence.

44 Then he said to them, "These are my words that I spoke to you while I was still with you—that everything written about me in the law of Moses, the prophets, and the psalms must be fulfilled." 45Then he opened their minds to understand the scriptures, 46and he said to them, "Thus it is written, that the Messiah[e] is to suffer and to rise from the dead on the third day, 47and that repentance and forgiveness of sins is to be proclaimed in his name to all nations,[f] beginning from Jerusalem. 48You are witnesses of these things. 49And see, I am sending upon you what my Father promised; so stay here in the city until you have been clothed with power from on high."

The Ascension of Jesus

50 Then he led them out as far as Bethany, and, lifting up his hands, he blessed them. 51While he was blessing them, he withdrew from them and was carried up into heaven.[g] 52And they worshiped him, and[h] returned to Jerusalem with great joy; 53and they were continually in the temple blessing God.[i]

ἐπέδωκαν αὐτῷ ἰχθύος ὀπτοῦ μέρος· 43 καὶ λαβὼν ἐνώπιον αὐτῶν ἔφαγεν.

44 Εἶπεν δὲ πρὸς αὐτούς, Οὗτοι οἱ λόγοι μου οὓς ἐλάλησα πρὸς ὑμᾶς ἔτι ὢν σὺν ὑμῖν, ὅτι δεῖ πληρωθῆναι πάντα τὰ γεγραμμένα ἐν τῷ νόμῳ Μωϋσέως καὶ τοῖς προφήταις καὶ ψαλμοῖς περὶ ἐμοῦ. 45 τότε διήνοιξεν αὐτῶν τὸν νοῦν τοῦ συνιέναι τὰς γραφάς· 46 καὶ εἶπεν αὐτοῖς ὅτι Οὕτως γέγραπται παθεῖν τὸν Χριστὸν καὶ ἀναστῆναι ἐκ νεκρῶν τῇ τρίτῃ ἡμέρᾳ, 47 καὶ κηρυχθῆναι ἐπὶ τῷ ὀνόματι αὐτοῦ μετάνοιαν εἰς[f] ἄφεσιν ἁμαρτιῶν εἰς πάντα τὰ ἔθνη. ἀρξάμενοι ἀπὸ Ἰερουσαλὴμ 48 ὑμεῖς μάρτυρες τούτων. 49 καὶ [ἰδοὺ] ἐγὼ ἀποστέλλω τὴν ἐπαγγελίαν τοῦ πατρός μου ἐφ' ὑμᾶς· ὑμεῖς δὲ καθίσατε ἐν τῇ πόλει ἕως οὗ ἐνδύσησθε ἐξ ὕψους δύναμιν.

50 Ἐξήγαγεν δὲ αὐτοὺς [ἔξω][g] ἕως πρὸς Βηθανίαν, καὶ ἐπάρας τὰς χεῖρας αὐτοῦ εὐλόγησεν αὐτούς. 51 καὶ ἐγένετο ἐν τῷ εὐλογεῖν αὐτὸν αὐτοὺς διέστη ἀπ' αὐτῶν καὶ ἀνεφέρετο εἰς τὸν οὐρανόν. 52 καὶ αὐτοὶ προσκυνήσαντες αὐτὸν ὑπέστρεψαν εἰς Ἰερουσαλὴμ μετὰ χαρᾶς μεγάλης 53 καὶ ἦσαν διὰ παντὸς ἐν τῷ ἱερῷ εὐλογοῦντες τὸν θεόν.[h]

of broiled fish, 43and he took it and ate it in their presence.

44He said to them, "This is what I told you while I was still with you: Everything must be fulfilled that is written about me in the Law of Moses, the Prophets and the Psalms."

45Then he opened their minds so they could understand the Scriptures. 46He told them, "This is what is written: The Christ will suffer and rise from the dead on the third day, 47and repentance and forgiveness of sins will be preached in his name to all nations, beginning at Jerusalem. 48You are witnesses of these things. 49I am going to send you what my Father has promised; but stay in the city until you have been clothed with power from on high."

The Ascension

50When he had led them out to the vicinity of Bethany, he lifted up his hands and blessed them. 51While he was blessing them, he left them and was taken up into heaven. 52Then they worshiped him and returned to Jerusalem with great joy. 53And they stayed continually at the temple, praising God.

---

e Or *the Christ*   f Or *nations. Beginning from Jerusalem you are witnesses*   g Other ancient authorities lack *and was carried up into heaven*   h Other ancient authorities lack *worshiped him, and*   i Other ancient authorities add *Amen*

f47 NIV/NRSV texts καί   g50 NIV text omits ἔξω †
h53 NRSV note i adds ἀμήν.

The Word Became Flesh

1 In the beginning was the Word, and the Word was with God, and the Word was God. ²He was in the beginning with God. ³All things came into being through him, and without him not one thing came into being. What has come into being ⁴in him was life,ª and the life was the light of all people. ⁵The light shines in the darkness, and the darkness did not overcome it.

6 There was a man sent from God, whose name was John. ⁷He came as a witness to testify to the light, so that all might believe through him. ⁸He himself was not the light, but he came to testify to the light. ⁹The true light, which enlightens everyone, was coming into the world.ᵇ

10 He was in the world, and the world came into being through him; yet the world did not know him. ¹¹He came to what was his own,ᶜ and his own people did not accept him. ¹²But to all who received him, who believed in his name, he gave power to become children of God, ¹³who were born, not of blood or of the will of the flesh or of the will of man, but of God.

14 And the Word became flesh and lived among us, and we have seen his glory, the glory as of a father's only son,ᵈ full of grace and truth. ¹⁵(John testified to him and cried out, "This was he of whom I said, 'He who comes after me ranks ahead of me because he was before me.' ")¹⁶From his fullness we have all received, grace upon grace. ¹⁷The law indeed was given through Moses; grace and truth came through Jesus Christ. ¹⁸No one has ever seen God. It is God the only Son,ᵉ who is close to the Father's heart,ᶠ who has made him known.

The Testimony of John the Baptist

19 This is the testimony given by John when the Jews sent priests and Levites from Jerusalem to ask him, "Who are you?" ²⁰He confessed and did not deny it, but confessed, "I am not the Messiah."ᵍ ²¹And they asked him, "What then? Are you

ΚΑΤΑ ΙΩΑΝΝΗΝ

1 Ἐν ἀρχῇ ἦν ὁ λόγος, καὶ ὁ λόγος ἦν πρὸς τὸν θεόν, καὶ θεὸς ἦν ὁ λόγος. **2** οὗτος ἦν ἐν ἀρχῇ πρὸς τὸν θεόν. **3** πάντα δι᾽ αὐτοῦ ἐγένετο, καὶ χωρὶς αὐτοῦ ἐγένετο οὐδὲ ἕν. ὃ γέγονεν **4** ἐν αὐτῷ ζωὴ ἦν, καὶ ἡ ζωὴ ἦν τὸ φῶς τῶν ἀνθρώπων· **5** καὶ τὸ φῶς ἐν τῇ σκοτίᾳ φαίνει, καὶ ἡ σκοτία αὐτὸ οὐ κατέλαβεν.

6 Ἐγένετο ἄνθρωπος, ἀπεσταλμένος παρὰ θεοῦ, ὄνομα αὐτῷ Ἰωάννης· **7** οὗτος ἦλθεν εἰς μαρτυρίαν ἵνα μαρτυρήσῃ περὶ τοῦ φωτός, ἵνα πάντες πιστεύσωσιν δι᾽ αὐτοῦ. **8** οὐκ ἦν ἐκεῖνος τὸ φῶς, ἀλλ᾽ ἵνα μαρτυρήσῃ περὶ τοῦ φωτός. **9** Ἦν τὸ φῶς τὸ ἀληθινόν, ὃ φωτίζει πάντα ἄνθρωπον, ἐρχόμενον εἰς τὸν κόσμον. **10** ἐν τῷ κόσμῳ ἦν, καὶ ὁ κόσμος δι᾽ αὐτοῦ ἐγένετο, καὶ ὁ κόσμος αὐτὸν οὐκ ἔγνω. **11** εἰς τὰ ἴδια ἦλθεν, καὶ οἱ ἴδιοι αὐτὸν οὐ παρέλαβον. **12** ὅσοι δὲ ἔλαβον αὐτόν, ἔδωκεν αὐτοῖς ἐξουσίαν τέκνα θεοῦ γενέσθαι, τοῖς πιστεύουσιν εἰς τὸ ὄνομα αὐτοῦ, **13** οἳ οὐκ ἐξ αἱμάτων οὐδὲ ἐκ θελήματος σαρκὸς οὐδὲ ἐκ θελήματος ἀνδρὸς ἀλλ᾽ ἐκ θεοῦ ἐγεννήθησαν.

14 Καὶ ὁ λόγος σὰρξ ἐγένετο καὶ ἐσκήνωσεν ἐν ἡμῖν, καὶ ἐθεασάμεθα τὴν δόξαν αὐτοῦ, δόξαν ὡς μονογενοῦς παρὰ πατρός, πλήρης χάριτος καὶ ἀληθείας. **15** Ἰωάννης μαρτυρεῖ περὶ αὐτοῦ καὶ κέκραγεν λέγων, Οὗτος ἦν ὃν εἶπον, Ὁ ὀπίσω μου ἐρχόμενος ἔμπροσθέν μου γέγονεν, ὅτι πρῶτός μου ἦν. **16** ὅτι ἐκ τοῦ πληρώματος αὐτοῦ ἡμεῖς πάντες ἐλάβομεν καὶ χάριν ἀντὶ χάριτος· **17** ὅτι ὁ νόμος διὰ Μωϋσέως ἐδόθη, ἡ χάρις καὶ ἡ ἀλήθεια διὰ Ἰησοῦ Χριστοῦ ἐγένετο. **18** θεὸν οὐδεὶς ἑώρακεν πώποτε· μονογενὴς θεὸςª ὁ ὢν εἰς τὸν κόλπον τοῦ πατρὸς ἐκεῖνος ἐξηγήσατο.

19 Καὶ αὕτη ἐστὶν ἡ μαρτυρία τοῦ Ἰωάννου, ὅτε ἀπέστειλαν [πρὸς αὐτόν]ᵇ οἱ Ἰουδαῖοι ἐξ Ἱεροσολύμων ἱερεῖς καὶ Λευίτας ἵνα ἐρωτήσωσιν αὐτόν, Σὺ τίς εἶ; **20** καὶ ὡμολόγησεν καὶ οὐκ ἠρνήσατο, καὶ ὡμολόγησεν ὅτι Ἐγὼ οὐκ εἰμὶ ὁ Χριστός. **21** καὶ ἠρώτησαν αὐτόν, Τί οὖν; Σὺ Ἠλίας εἶ; καὶ λέγει,

The Word Became Flesh

1 In the beginning was the Word, and the Word was with God, and the Word was God. ²He was with God in the beginning.

³Through him all things were made; without him nothing was made that has been made. ⁴In him was life, and that life was the light of men. ⁵The light shines in darkness, but the darkness has not understoodª it.

⁶There came a man who was sent from God; his name was John. ⁷He came as a witness to testify concerning that light, so that through him all men might believe. ⁸He himself was not the light; he came only as a witness to the light. ⁹The true light that gives light to every man was coming into the world.ᵇ

¹⁰He was in the world, and though the world was made through him, the world did not recognize him. ¹¹He came to that which was his own, but his own did not receive him. ¹²Yet to all who received him, to those who believed in his name, he gave the right to become children of God— ¹³children born not of natural descent,ᶜ nor of human decision or a husband's will, but born of God.

¹⁴The Word became flesh and made his dwelling among us. We have seen his glory, the glory of the One and Only,ᵈ who came from the Father, full of grace and truth.

¹⁵John testifies concerning him. He cries out, saying, "This was he of whom I said, 'He who comes after me has surpassed me because he was before me.' " ¹⁶From the fullness of his grace we have all received one blessing after another. ¹⁷For the law was given through Moses; grace and truth came through Jesus Christ. ¹⁸No one has ever seen God, but God the One and Only,ᵉᶠ who is at the Father's side, has made him known.

John the Baptist Denies Being the Christ

¹⁹Now this was John's testimony when the Jews of Jerusalem sent priests and Levites to ask him who he was. ²⁰He did not fail to confess, but confessed freely, "I am not the Christ.ᵍ"

²¹They asked him, "Then who are you? Are you Elijah?"

ª ³through him. And without him not one thing came into being that has come into being. ⁴In him was life   ᵇ Or He was the true light that enlightens everyone coming into the world   ᶜ Or to his own home   ᵈ Or the Father's only Son   ᵉ Other ancient authorities read It is an only Son, God, or It is the only Son   ᶠ Gk bosom   ᵍ Or the Christ

ª18 NIV/NRSV notes [ὁ] μονογενὴς υἱός   ᵇ19 NIV text omits πρὸς αὐτόν

ª5 Or darkness, and the darkness has not overcome   ᵇ9 Or This was the true light that gives light to every man who comes into the world   ᶜ13 Greek of bloods   ᵈ14 Or the Only Begotten   ᵉ18 Or the Only Begotten   ᶠ18 Some manuscripts but the only (or only begotten) Son   ᵍ20 Or Messiah. "The Christ" (Greek) and "the Messiah" (Hebrew) both mean "the Anointed One"; also in verse 25.

Elijah?" He said, "I am not." "Are you the prophet?" He answered, "No." 22Then they said to him, "Who are you? Let us have an answer for those who sent us. What do you say about yourself?" 23He said,

"I am the voice of one crying out in
the wilderness,
'Make straight the way of the Lord,' "
as the prophet Isaiah said.

24 Now they had been sent from the Pharisees. 25They asked him, "Why then are you baptizing if you are neither the Messiah,g nor Elijah, nor the prophet?" 26John answered them, "I baptize with water. Among you stands one whom you do not know, 27the one who is coming after me; I am not worthy to untie the thong of his sandal." 28This took place in Bethany across the Jordan where John was baptizing.

The Lamb of God

29 The next day he saw Jesus coming toward him and declared, "Here is the Lamb of God who takes away the sin of the world! 30This is he of whom I said, 'After me comes a man who ranks ahead of me because he was before me.' 31I myself did not know him; but I came baptizing with water for this reason, that he might be revealed to Israel." 32And John testified, "I saw the Spirit descending from heaven like a dove, and it remained on him. 33I myself did not know him, but the one who sent me to baptize with water said to me, 'He on whom you see the Spirit descend and remain is the one who baptizes with the Holy Spirit.' 34And I myself have seen and have testified that this is the Son of God."h

The First Disciples of Jesus

35 The next day John again was standing with two of his disciples, 36and as he watched Jesus walk by, he exclaimed, "Look, here is the Lamb of God!" 37The two disciples heard him say this, and they followed Jesus. 38When Jesus turned and saw them following, he said to them, "What are you looking for?" They said to him, "Rabbi" (which translated means Teacher), "where are you staying?" 39He said to them, "Come and see." They came and saw where he was staying, and they remained with him that day. It was about four o'clock in the afternoon. 40One of the

---

Οὐκ εἰμί. Ὁ προφήτης εἶ σύ; καὶ ἀπεκρίθη, Οὔ. 22 εἶπαν οὖν αὐτῷ, Τίς εἶ; ἵνα ἀπόκρισιν δῶμεν τοῖς πέμψασιν ἡμᾶς· τί λέγεις περὶ σεαυτοῦ; 23 ἔφη,

Ἐγὼ φωνὴ βοῶντος ἐν τῇ ἐρήμῳ,
Εὐθύνατε τὴν ὁδὸν κυρίου,

καθὼς εἶπεν Ἡσαΐας ὁ προφήτης. 24 Καὶ ἀπεσταλμένοι ἦσαν ἐκ τῶν Φαρισαίων. 25 καὶ ἠρώτησαν αὐτὸν καὶ εἶπαν αὐτῷ, Τί οὖν βαπτίζεις εἰ σὺ οὐκ εἶ ὁ Χριστὸς οὐδὲ Ἠλίας οὐδὲ ὁ προφήτης; 26 ἀπεκρίθη αὐτοῖς ὁ Ἰωάννης λέγων, Ἐγὼ βαπτίζω ἐν ὕδατι· μέσοςc ὑμῶν ἕστηκεν ὃν ὑμεῖς οὐκ οἴδατε, 27 ὁ ὀπίσω μου ἐρχόμενος, οὗ οὐκ εἰμὶ [ἐγὼ] ἄξιος ἵνα λύσω αὐτοῦ τὸν ἱμάντα τοῦ ὑποδήματος. 28 Ταῦτα ἐν Βηθανίᾳ ἐγένετο πέραν τοῦ Ἰορδάνου, ὅπου ἦν ὁ Ἰωάννης βαπτίζων.

29 Τῇ ἐπαύριον βλέπει τὸν Ἰησοῦν ἐρχόμενον πρὸς αὐτὸν καὶ λέγει, Ἴδε ὁ ἀμνὸς τοῦ θεοῦ ὁ αἴρων τὴν ἁμαρτίαν τοῦ κόσμου. 30 οὗτός ἐστιν ὑπὲρ οὗ ἐγὼ εἶπον, Ὀπίσω μου ἔρχεται ἀνὴρ ὃς ἔμπροσθέν μου γέγονεν, ὅτι πρῶτός μου ἦν. 31 κἀγὼ οὐκ ᾔδειν αὐτόν, ἀλλ᾽ ἵνα φανερωθῇ τῷ Ἰσραὴλ διὰ τοῦτο ἦλθον ἐγὼ ἐν ὕδατι βαπτίζων. 32 Καὶ ἐμαρτύρησεν Ἰωάννης λέγων ὅτι Τεθέαμαι τὸ πνεῦμα καταβαῖνον ὡς περιστερὰν ἐξ οὐρανοῦ καὶ ἔμεινεν ἐπ᾽ αὐτόν. 33 κἀγὼ οὐκ ᾔδειν αὐτόν, ἀλλ᾽ ὁ πέμψας με βαπτίζειν ἐν ὕδατι ἐκεῖνός μοι εἶπεν, Ἐφ᾽ ὃν ἂν ἴδῃς τὸ πνεῦμα καταβαῖνον καὶ μένον ἐπ᾽ αὐτόν, οὗτός ἐστιν ὁ βαπτίζων ἐν πνεύματι ἁγίῳ. 34 κἀγὼ ἑώρακα καὶ μεμαρτύρηκα ὅτι οὗτός ἐστιν ὁ υἱὸςd τοῦ θεοῦ.

35 Τῇ ἐπαύριον πάλιν εἱστήκει ὁ Ἰωάννης καὶ ἐκ τῶν μαθητῶν αὐτοῦ δύο 36 καὶ ἐμβλέψας τῷ Ἰησοῦ περιπατοῦντι λέγει, Ἴδε ὁ ἀμνὸς τοῦ θεοῦ. 37 καὶ ἤκουσαν οἱ δύο μαθηταὶ αὐτοῦ λαλοῦντος καὶ ἠκολούθησαν τῷ Ἰησοῦ. 38 στραφεὶς δὲ ὁ Ἰησοῦς καὶ θεασάμενος αὐτοὺς ἀκολουθοῦντας λέγει αὐτοῖς, Τί ζητεῖτε; οἱ δὲ εἶπαν αὐτῷ, Ῥαββί, ὃ λέγεται μεθερμηνευόμενον Διδάσκαλε, ποῦ μένεις; 39 λέγει αὐτοῖς, Ἔρχεσθε καὶ ὄψεσθε. ἦλθαν οὖν καὶ εἶδαν ποῦ μένει καὶ παρ᾽ αὐτῷ ἔμειναν τὴν ἡμέραν ἐκείνην· ὥρα ἦν ὡς δεκάτη.

He said, "I am not."

"Are you the Prophet?"

He answered, "No."

22Finally they said, "Who are you? Give us an answer to take back to those who sent us. What do you say about yourself?"

23John replied in the words of Isaiah the prophet, "I am the voice of one calling in the desert, 'Make straight the way for the Lord.' "h

24Now some Pharisees who had been sent 25questioned him, "Why then do you baptize if you are not the Christ, nor Elijah, nor the Prophet?"

26"I baptize withi water," John replied, "but among you stands one you do not know. 27He is the one who comes after me, the thongs of whose sandals I am not worthy to untie."

28This all happened at Bethany on the other side of the Jordan, where John was baptizing.

Jesus the Lamb of God

29The next day John saw Jesus coming toward him and said, "Look, the Lamb of God, who takes away the sin of the world! 30This is the one I meant when I said, 'A man who comes after me has surpassed me because he was before me.' 31I myself did not know him, but the reason I came baptizing with water was that he might be revealed to Israel."

32Then John gave this testimony: "I saw the Spirit come down from heaven as a dove and remain on him. 33I would not have known him, except that the one who sent me to baptize with water told me, 'The man on whom you see the Spirit come down and remain is he who will baptize with the Holy Spirit.' 34I have seen and I testify that this is the Son of God."

Jesus' First Disciples

35The next day John was there again with two of his disciples. 36When he saw Jesus passing by, he said, "Look, the Lamb of God!"

37When the two disciples heard him say this, they followed Jesus. 38Turning around, Jesus saw them following and asked, "What do you want?"

They said, "Rabbi" (which means Teacher), "where are you staying?"

39"Come," he replied, "and you will see."

So they went and saw where he was staying, and spent that day with him. It was about the tenth hour.

---

g Or *the Christ*   h Other ancient authorities read *is God's chosen one*   c26 NIV text adds δέ †   d34 NRSV note h ἐκλεκτός   h23 Isaiah 40:3   i26 Or *in*; also in verses 31 and 33

two who heard John speak and followed him was Andrew, Simon Peter's brother. 41He first found his brother Simon and said to him, "We have found the Messiah" (which is translated Anointed[i]). 42He brought Simon[j] to Jesus, who looked at him and said, "You are Simon son of John. You are to be called Cephas" (which is translated Peter[k]).

Jesus Calls Philip and Nathanael

43 The next day Jesus decided to go to Galilee. He found Philip and said to him, "Follow me." 44Now Philip was from Bethsaida, the city of Andrew and Peter. 45Philip found Nathanael and said to him, "We have found him about whom Moses in the law and also the prophets wrote, Jesus son of Joseph from Nazareth." 46Nathanael said to him, "Can anything good come out of Nazareth?" Philip said to him, "Come and see." 47When Jesus saw Nathanael coming toward him, he said of him, "Here is truly an Israelite in whom there is no deceit!" 48Nathanael asked him, "Where did you get to know me?" Jesus answered, "I saw you under the fig tree before Philip called you." 49Nathanael replied, "Rabbi, you are the Son of God! You are the King of Israel!" 50Jesus answered, "Do you believe because I told you that I saw you under the fig tree? You will see greater things than these." 51And he said to him, "Very truly, I tell you,[l] you will see heaven opened and the angels of God ascending and descending upon the Son of Man."

The Wedding at Cana

2 On the third day there was a wedding in Cana of Galilee, and the mother of Jesus was there. 2Jesus and his disciples had also been invited to the wedding. 3When the wine gave out, the mother of Jesus said to him, "They have no wine." 4And Jesus said to her, "Woman, what concern is that to you and to me? My hour has not yet come." 5His mother said to the servants, "Do whatever he tells you." 6Now standing there were six stone water jars for the Jewish rites of purification, each

---

40 Ἦν Ἀνδρέας ὁ ἀδελφὸς Σίμωνος Πέτρου εἷς ἐκ τῶν δύο τῶν ἀκουσάντων παρὰ Ἰωάννου καὶ ἀκολουθησάντων αὐτῷ· **41** εὑρίσκει οὗτος πρῶτον τὸν ἀδελφὸν τὸν ἴδιον Σίμωνα καὶ λέγει αὐτῷ, Εὑρήκαμεν τὸν Μεσσίαν, ὅ ἐστιν μεθερμηνευόμενον Χριστός· **42** ἤγαγεν αὐτὸν πρὸς τὸν Ἰησοῦν. ἐμβλέψας αὐτῷ ὁ Ἰησοῦς εἶπεν, Σὺ εἶ Σίμων ὁ υἱὸς Ἰωάννου, σὺ κληθήσῃ Κηφᾶς, ὃ ἑρμηνεύεται Πέτρος.

43 Τῇ ἐπαύριον ἠθέλησεν ἐξελθεῖν εἰς τὴν Γαλιλαίαν καὶ εὑρίσκει Φίλιππον. καὶ λέγει αὐτῷ ὁ Ἰησοῦς, Ἀκολούθει μοι. **44** ἦν δὲ ὁ Φίλιππος ἀπὸ Βηθσαϊδά, ἐκ τῆς πόλεως Ἀνδρέου καὶ Πέτρου. **45** εὑρίσκει Φίλιππος τὸν Ναθαναὴλ καὶ λέγει αὐτῷ, Ὃν ἔγραψεν Μωϋσῆς ἐν τῷ νόμῳ καὶ οἱ προφῆται εὑρήκαμεν, Ἰησοῦν υἱὸν τοῦ Ἰωσὴφ τὸν ἀπὸ Ναζαρέτ. **46** καὶ εἶπεν αὐτῷ Ναθαναήλ, Ἐκ Ναζαρὲτ δύναταί τι ἀγαθὸν εἶναι; λέγει αὐτῷ [ὁ] Φίλιππος, Ἔρχου καὶ ἴδε. **47** εἶδεν ὁ Ἰησοῦς τὸν Ναθαναὴλ ἐρχόμενον πρὸς αὐτὸν καὶ λέγει περὶ αὐτοῦ, Ἴδε ἀληθῶς Ἰσραηλίτης ἐν ᾧ δόλος οὐκ ἔστιν. **48** λέγει αὐτῷ Ναθαναήλ, Πόθεν με γινώσκεις; ἀπεκρίθη Ἰησοῦς καὶ εἶπεν αὐτῷ, Πρὸ τοῦ σε Φίλιππον φωνῆσαι ὄντα ὑπὸ τὴν συκῆν εἶδόν σε. **49** ἀπεκρίθη αὐτῷ Ναθαναήλ, Ῥαββί, σὺ εἶ ὁ υἱὸς τοῦ θεοῦ, σὺ βασιλεὺς εἶ τοῦ Ἰσραήλ. **50** ἀπεκρίθη Ἰησοῦς καὶ εἶπεν αὐτῷ, Ὅτι εἶπόν σοι ὅτι εἶδόν σε ὑποκάτω τῆς συκῆς, πιστεύεις; μείζω τούτων ὄψῃ. **51** καὶ λέγει αὐτῷ, Ἀμὴν ἀμὴν λέγω ὑμῖν, ὄψεσθε τὸν οὐρανὸν ἀνεῳγότα καὶ τοὺς ἀγγέλους τοῦ θεοῦ ἀναβαίνοντας καὶ καταβαίνοντας ἐπὶ τὸν υἱὸν τοῦ ἀνθρώπου.

2 Καὶ τῇ ἡμέρᾳ τῇ τρίτῃ γάμος ἐγένετο ἐν Κανὰ τῆς Γαλιλαίας, καὶ ἦν ἡ μήτηρ τοῦ Ἰησοῦ ἐκεῖ· **2** ἐκλήθη δὲ καὶ ὁ Ἰησοῦς καὶ οἱ μαθηταὶ αὐτοῦ εἰς τὸν γάμον. **3** καὶ ὑστερήσαντος οἴνου λέγει ἡ μήτηρ τοῦ Ἰησοῦ πρὸς αὐτόν, Οἶνον οὐκ ἔχουσιν. **4** [καὶ] λέγει αὐτῇ ὁ Ἰησοῦς, Τί ἐμοὶ καὶ σοί, γύναι; οὔπω ἥκει ἡ ὥρα μου. **5** λέγει ἡ μήτηρ αὐτοῦ τοῖς διακόνοις, Ὅ τι ἂν λέγῃ ὑμῖν ποιήσατε. **6** ἦσαν δὲ ἐκεῖ λίθιναι ὑδρίαι ἓξ κατὰ τὸν καθαρισμὸν τῶν Ἰουδαίων κείμεναι, χωροῦσαι ἀνὰ

40Andrew, Simon Peter's brother, was one of the two who heard what John had said and who had followed Jesus. 41The first thing Andrew did was to find his brother Simon and tell him, "We have found the Messiah" (that is, the Christ). 42And he brought him to Jesus.

Jesus looked at him and said, "You are Simon son of John. You will be called Cephas" (which, when translated, is Peter[j]).

Jesus Calls Philip and Nathanael

43The next day Jesus decided to leave for Galilee. Finding Philip, he said to him, "Follow me."

44Philip, like Andrew and Peter, was from the town of Bethsaida. 45Philip found Nathanael and told him, "We have found the one Moses wrote about in the Law, and about whom the prophets also wrote—Jesus of Nazareth, the son of Joseph."

46"Nazareth! Can anything good come from there?" Nathanael asked.

"Come and see," said Philip.

47When Jesus saw Nathanael approaching, he said of him, "Here is a true Israelite, in whom there is nothing false."

48"How do you know me?" Nathanael asked.

Jesus answered, "I saw you while you were still under the fig tree before Philip called you."

49Then Nathanael declared, "Rabbi, you are the Son of God; you are the King of Israel."

50Jesus said, "You believe[k] because I told you I saw you under the fig tree. You shall see greater things than that." 51He then added, "I tell you[l] the truth, you[m] shall see heaven open, and the angels of God ascending and descending on the Son of Man."

Jesus Changes Water to Wine

2 On the third day a wedding took place at Cana in Galilee. Jesus' mother was there, 2and Jesus and his disciples had also been invited to the wedding. 3When the wine was gone, Jesus' mother said to him, "They have no more wine."

4"Dear woman, why do you involve me?" Jesus replied. "My time has not yet come."

5His mother said to the servants, "Do whatever he tells you."

6Nearby stood six stone water jars, the kind used by the Jews for ceremonial

---

i Or Christ   j Gk him   k From the word for rock in Aramaic (kepha) and Greek (petra), respectively
l Both instances of the Greek word for you in this verse are plural

j42 Both Cephas (Aramaic) and Peter (Greek) mean rock.
k50 Or Do you believe . . . ?   l51 The Greek is plural.
m51 The Greek is plural.

holding twenty or thirty gallons. 7Jesus said to them, "Fill the jars with water." And they filled them up to the brim. 8He said to them, "Now draw some out, and take it to the chief steward." So they took it. 9When the steward tasted the water that had become wine, and did not know where it came from (though the servants who had drawn the water knew), the steward called the bridegroom 10and said to him, "Everyone serves the good wine first, and then the inferior wine after the guests have become drunk. But you have kept the good wine until now." 11Jesus did this, the first of his signs, in Cana of Galilee, and revealed his glory; and his disciples believed in him.

12 After this he went down to Capernaum with his mother, his brothers, and his disciples; and they remained there a few days.

Jesus Cleanses the Temple

13 The Passover of the Jews was near, and Jesus went up to Jerusalem. 14In the temple he found people selling cattle, sheep, and doves, and the money changers seated at their tables. 15Making a whip of cords, he drove all of them out of the temple, both the sheep and the cattle. He also poured out the coins of the money changers and overturned their tables. 16He told those who were selling the doves, "Take these things out of here! Stop making my Father's house a marketplace!" 17His disciples remembered that it was written, "Zeal for your house will consume me." 18The Jews then said to him, "What sign can you show us for doing this?" 19Jesus answered them, "Destroy this temple, and in three days I will raise it up." 20The Jews then said, "This temple has been under construction for forty-six years, and will you raise it up in three days?" 21But he was speaking of the temple of his body. 22After he was raised from the dead, his disciples remembered that he had said this; and they believed the scripture and the word that Jesus had spoken.

23 When he was in Jerusalem during the

μετρητὰς δύο ἢ τρεῖς. **7** λέγει αὐτοῖς ὁ Ἰησοῦς, Γεμίσατε τὰς ὑδρίας ὕδατος. καὶ ἐγέμισαν αὐτὰς ἕως ἄνω. **8** καὶ λέγει αὐτοῖς, Ἀντλήσατε νῦν καὶ φέρετε τῷ ἀρχιτρικλίνῳ· οἱ δὲ ἤνεγκαν. **9** ὡς δὲ ἐγεύσατο ὁ ἀρχιτρίκλινος τὸ ὕδωρ οἶνον γεγενημένον καὶ οὐκ ᾔδει πόθεν ἐστίν, οἱ δὲ διάκονοι ᾔδεισαν οἱ ἠντληκότες τὸ ὕδωρ, φωνεῖ τὸν νυμφίον ὁ ἀρχιτρίκλινος **10** καὶ λέγει αὐτῷ, Πᾶς ἄνθρωπος πρῶτον τὸν καλὸν οἶνον τίθησιν καὶ ὅταν μεθυσθῶσιν τὸν ἐλάσσω· σὺ τετήρηκας τὸν καλὸν οἶνον ἕως ἄρτι. **11** Ταύτην ἐποίησεν ἀρχὴν τῶν σημείων ὁ Ἰησοῦς ἐν Κανὰ τῆς Γαλιλαίας καὶ ἐφανέρωσεν τὴν δόξαν αὐτοῦ, καὶ ἐπίστευσαν εἰς αὐτὸν οἱ μαθηταὶ αὐτοῦ.

12 Μετὰ τοῦτο κατέβη εἰς Καφαρναοὺμ αὐτὸς καὶ ἡ μήτηρ αὐτοῦ καὶ οἱ ἀδελφοὶ [αὐτοῦ] καὶ οἱ μαθηταὶ αὐτοῦ καὶ ἐκεῖ ἔμειναν οὐ πολλὰς ἡμέρας.

13 Καὶ ἐγγὺς ἦν τὸ πάσχα τῶν Ἰουδαίων, καὶ ἀνέβη εἰς Ἱεροσόλυμα ὁ Ἰησοῦς. **14** καὶ εὗρεν ἐν τῷ ἱερῷ τοὺς πωλοῦντας βόας καὶ πρόβατα καὶ περιστερὰς καὶ τοὺς κερματιστὰς καθημένους, **15** καὶ ποιήσας φραγέλλιον ἐκ σχοινίων πάντας ἐξέβαλεν ἐκ τοῦ ἱεροῦ τά τε πρόβατα καὶ τοὺς βόας, καὶ τῶν κολλυβιστῶν ἐξέχεεν τὸ κέρμα καὶ τὰς τραπέζας ἀνέτρεψεν, **16** καὶ τοῖς τὰς περιστερὰς πωλοῦσιν εἶπεν, Ἄρατε ταῦτα ἐντεῦθεν, μὴ ποιεῖτε τὸν οἶκον τοῦ πατρός μου οἶκον ἐμπορίου. **17** Ἐμνήσθησαν οἱ μαθηταὶ αὐτοῦ ὅτι γεγραμμένον ἐστίν, Ὁ ζῆλος τοῦ οἴκου σου καταφάγεταί με. **18** ἀπεκρίθησαν οὖν οἱ Ἰουδαῖοι καὶ εἶπαν αὐτῷ, Τί σημεῖον δεικνύεις ἡμῖν ὅτι ταῦτα ποιεῖς; **19** ἀπεκρίθη Ἰησοῦς καὶ εἶπεν αὐτοῖς, Λύσατε τὸν ναὸν τοῦτον καὶ ἐν τρισὶν ἡμέραις ἐγερῶ αὐτόν. **20** εἶπαν οὖν οἱ Ἰουδαῖοι, Τεσσεράκοντα καὶ ἓξ ἔτεσιν οἰκοδομήθη ὁ ναὸς οὗτος, καὶ σὺ ἐν τρισὶν ἡμέραις ἐγερεῖς αὐτόν; **21** ἐκεῖνος δὲ ἔλεγεν περὶ τοῦ ναοῦ τοῦ σώματος αὐτοῦ. **22** ὅτε οὖν ἠγέρθη ἐκ νεκρῶν, ἐμνήσθησαν οἱ μαθηταὶ αὐτοῦ ὅτι τοῦτο ἔλεγεν, καὶ ἐπίστευσαν τῇ γραφῇ καὶ τῷ λόγῳ ὃν εἶπεν ὁ Ἰησοῦς.

23 Ὡς δὲ ἦν ἐν τοῖς Ἱεροσολύμοις

washing, each holding from twenty to thirty gallons.[a]

7Jesus said to the servants, "Fill the jars with water"; so they filled them to the brim.

8Then he told them, "Now draw some out and take it to the master of the banquet."

They did so, 9and the master of the banquet tasted the water that had been turned into wine. He did not realize where it had come from, though the servants who had drawn the water knew. Then he called the bridegroom aside 10and said, "Everyone brings out the choice wine first and then the cheaper wine after the guests have had too much to drink; but you have saved the best till now."

11This, the first of his miraculous signs, Jesus performed at Cana in Galilee. He thus revealed his glory, and his disciples put their faith in him.

Jesus Clears the Temple

12After this he went down to Capernaum with his mother and brothers and his disciples. There they stayed for a few days.

13When it was almost time for the Jewish Passover, Jesus went up to Jerusalem. 14In the temple courts he found men selling cattle, sheep and doves, and others sitting at tables exchanging money. 15So he made a whip out of cords, and drove all from the temple area, both sheep and cattle; he scattered the coins of the money changers and overturned their tables. 16To those who sold doves he said, "Get these out of here! How dare you turn my Father's house into a market!"

17His disciples remembered that it is written: "Zeal for your house will consume me."[b]

18Then the Jews demanded of him, "What miraculous sign can you show us to prove your authority to do all this?"

19Jesus answered them, "Destroy this temple, and I will raise it again in three days."

20The Jews replied, "It has taken forty-six years to build this temple, and you are going to raise it in three days?" 21But the temple he had spoken of was his body. 22After he was raised from the dead, his disciples recalled what he had said. Then they believed the Scripture and the words that Jesus had spoken.

23Now while he was in Jerusalem at the

*a*6 Greek *two to three metretes* (probably about 75 to 115 liters)   *b*17 Psalm 69:9

Passover festival, many believed in his name because they saw the signs that he was doing. 24But Jesus on his part would not entrust himself to them, because he knew all people 25and needed no one to testify about anyone; for he himself knew what was in everyone.

Nicodemus Visits Jesus

3 Now there was a Pharisee named Nicodemus, a leader of the Jews. 2He came to Jesus[m] by night and said to him, "Rabbi, we know that you are a teacher who has come from God; for no one can do these signs that you do apart from the presence of God." 3Jesus answered him, "Very truly, I tell you, no one can see the kingdom of God without being born from above."[n] 4Nicodemus said to him, "How can anyone be born after having grown old? Can one enter a second time into the mother's womb and be born?" 5Jesus answered, "Very truly, I tell you, no one can enter the kingdom of God without being born of water and Spirit. 6What is born of the flesh is flesh, and what is born of the Spirit is spirit.[o] 7Do not be astonished that I said to you, 'You[p] must be born from above.'[q] 8The wind[o] blows where it chooses, and you hear the sound of it, but you do not know where it comes from or where it goes. So it is with everyone who is born of the Spirit." 9Nicodemus said to him, "How can these things be?" 10Jesus answered him, "Are you a teacher of Israel, and yet you do not understand these things?

11 "Very truly, I tell you, we speak of what we know and testify to what we have seen; yet you[r] do not receive our testimony. 12If I have told you about earthly things and you do not believe, how can you believe if I tell you about heavenly things? 13No one has ascended into heaven except the one who descended from heaven, the Son of Man.[s] 14And just as Moses lifted up the serpent in the wilderness, so must the Son of Man be lifted up, 15that whoever believes in him may have eternal life.[t]

16 "For God so loved the world that he gave his only Son, so that everyone who believes in him may not perish but may have eternal life.

ἐν τῷ πάσχα ἐν τῇ ἑορτῇ, πολλοὶ ἐπίστευσαν εἰς τὸ ὄνομα αὐτοῦ θεωροῦντες αὐτοῦ τὰ σημεῖα ἃ ἐποίει· 24 αὐτὸς δὲ Ἰησοῦς οὐκ ἐπίστευεν αὐτὸν αὐτοῖς διὰ τὸ αὐτὸν γινώσκειν πάντας 25 καὶ ὅτι οὐ χρείαν εἶχεν ἵνα τις μαρτυρήσῃ περὶ τοῦ ἀνθρώπου· αὐτὸς γὰρ ἐγίνωσκεν τί ἦν ἐν τῷ ἀνθρώπῳ.

3 ⁷Ἦν δὲ ἄνθρωπος ἐκ τῶν Φαρισαίων, Νικόδημος ὄνομα αὐτῷ, ἄρχων τῶν Ἰουδαίων· 2 οὗτος ἦλθεν πρὸς αὐτὸν νυκτὸς καὶ εἶπεν αὐτῷ, Ῥαββί, οἴδαμεν ὅτι ἀπὸ θεοῦ ἐλήλυθας διδάσκαλος· οὐδεὶς γὰρ δύναται ταῦτα τὰ σημεῖα ποιεῖν ἃ σὺ ποιεῖς, ἐὰν μὴ ᾖ ὁ θεὸς μετ' αὐτοῦ. 3 ἀπεκρίθη Ἰησοῦς καὶ εἶπεν αὐτῷ, Ἀμὴν ἀμὴν λέγω σοι, ἐὰν μή τις γεννηθῇ ἄνωθεν, οὐ δύναται ἰδεῖν τὴν βασιλείαν τοῦ θεοῦ. 4 λέγει πρὸς αὐτὸν [ὁ] Νικόδημος, Πῶς δύναται ἄνθρωπος γεννηθῆναι γέρων ὤν; μὴ δύναται εἰς τὴν κοιλίαν τῆς μητρὸς αὐτοῦ δεύτερον εἰσελθεῖν καὶ γεννηθῆναι; 5 ἀπεκρίθη Ἰησοῦς, Ἀμὴν ἀμὴν λέγω σοι, ἐὰν μή τις γεννηθῇ ἐξ ὕδατος καὶ πνεύματος, οὐ δύναται εἰσελθεῖν εἰς τὴν βασιλείαν τοῦ θεοῦ. 6 τὸ γεγεννημένον ἐκ τῆς σαρκὸς σάρξ ἐστιν, καὶ τὸ γεγεννημένον ἐκ τοῦ πνεύματος πνεῦμά ἐστιν. 7 μὴ θαυμάσῃς ὅτι εἶπόν σοι, Δεῖ ὑμᾶς γεννηθῆναι ἄνωθεν. 8 τὸ πνεῦμα ὅπου θέλει πνεῖ καὶ τὴν φωνὴν αὐτοῦ ἀκούεις, ἀλλ' οὐκ οἶδας πόθεν ἔρχεται καὶ ποῦ ὑπάγει· οὕτως ἐστὶν πᾶς ὁ γεγεννημένος ἐκ τοῦ πνεύματος. 9 ἀπεκρίθη Νικόδημος καὶ εἶπεν αὐτῷ, Πῶς δύναται ταῦτα γενέσθαι; 10 ἀπεκρίθη Ἰησοῦς καὶ εἶπεν αὐτῷ, Σὺ εἶ ὁ διδάσκαλος τοῦ Ἰσραὴλ καὶ ταῦτα οὐ γινώσκεις; 11 ἀμὴν ἀμὴν λέγω σοι ὅτι ὃ οἴδαμεν λαλοῦμεν καὶ ὃ ἑωράκαμεν μαρτυροῦμεν, καὶ τὴν μαρτυρίαν ἡμῶν οὐ λαμβάνετε. 12 εἰ τὰ ἐπίγεια εἶπον ὑμῖν καὶ οὐ πιστεύετε, πῶς ἐὰν εἴπω ὑμῖν τὰ ἐπουράνια πιστεύσετε; 13 καὶ οὐδεὶς ἀναβέβηκεν εἰς τὸν οὐρανὸν εἰ μὴ ὁ ἐκ τοῦ οὐρανοῦ καταβάς, ὁ υἱὸς τοῦ ἀνθρώπου[a]. 14 καὶ καθὼς Μωϋσῆς ὕψωσεν τὸν ὄφιν ἐν τῇ ἐρήμῳ, οὕτως ὑψωθῆναι δεῖ τὸν υἱὸν τοῦ ἀνθρώπου, 15 ἵνα πᾶς ὁ πιστεύων ἐν αὐτῷ ἔχῃ ζωὴν αἰώνιον.

16 Οὕτως γὰρ ἠγάπησεν ὁ θεὸς τὸν κόσμον, ὥστε τὸν υἱὸν τὸν μονογενῆ ἔδωκεν, ἵνα πᾶς ὁ πιστεύων εἰς αὐτὸν μὴ ἀπόληται ἀλλ' ἔχῃ ζωὴν αἰώνιον.

Passover Feast, many people saw the miraculous signs he was doing and believed in his name.[c] 24But Jesus would not entrust himself to them, for he knew all men. 25He did not need man's testimony about man, for he knew what was in a man.

Jesus Teaches Nicodemus

3 Now there was a man of the Pharisees named Nicodemus, a member of the Jewish ruling council. 2He came to Jesus at night and said, "Rabbi, we know you are a teacher who has come from God. For no one could perform the miraculous signs you are doing if God were not with him." 3In reply Jesus declared, "I tell you the truth, no one can see the kingdom of God unless he is born again.[a]"

4"How can a man be born when he is old?" Nicodemus asked. "Surely he cannot enter a second time into his mother's womb to be born!"

5Jesus answered, "I tell you the truth, no one can enter the kingdom of God unless he is born of water and the Spirit. 6Flesh gives birth to flesh, but the Spirit[b] gives birth to spirit. 7You should not be surprised at my saying, 'You[c] must be born again.' 8The wind blows wherever it pleases. You hear its sound, but you cannot tell where it comes from or where it is going. So it is with everyone born of the Spirit."

9"How can this be?" Nicodemus asked.

10"You are Israel's teacher," said Jesus, "and do you not understand these things? 11I tell you the truth, we speak of what we know, and we testify to what we have seen, but still you people do not accept our testimony. 12I have spoken to you of earthly things and you do not believe; how then will you believe if I speak of heavenly things? 13No one has ever gone into heaven except the one who came from heaven—the Son of Man.[d] 14Just as Moses lifted up the snake in the desert, so the Son of Man must be lifted up, 15that everyone who believes in him may have eternal life.[e]

16"For God so loved the world that he gave his one and only Son,[f] that whoever believes in him shall not perish but have

---

m Gk *him*   n Or *born anew*   o The same Greek word means both *wind* and *spirit*   p The Greek word for *you* here is plural   q Or *anew*   r The Greek word for *you* here and in verse 12 is plural   s Other ancient authorities add *who is in heaven*   t Some interpreters hold that the quotation concludes with verse 15

ª13 NIV/NRSV notes add ὁ ὢν ἐν τῷ οὐρανῷ

c23 Or *and believed in him*   a3 Or *born from above*; also in verse 7   b6 Or *but spirit*   c7 The Greek is plural.   d13 Some manuscripts *Man, who is in heaven*   e15 Or *believes may have eternal life in him*   f16 Or *his only begotten Son*

NRSV

17 "Indeed, God did not send the Son into the world to condemn the world, but in order that the world might be saved through him. 18Those who believe in him are not condemned; but those who do not believe are condemned already, because they have not believed in the name of the only Son of God. 19And this is the judgment, that the light has come into the world, and people loved darkness rather than light because their deeds were evil. 20For all who do evil hate the light and do not come to the light, so that their deeds may not be exposed. 21But those who do what is true come to the light, so that it may be clearly seen that their deeds have been done in God."t

Jesus and John the Baptist

22 After this Jesus and his disciples went into the Judean countryside, and he spent some time there with them and baptized. 23John also was baptizing at Aenon near Salim because water was abundant there; and people kept coming and were being baptized 24—John, of course, had not yet been thrown into prison.

25 Now a discussion about purification arose between John's disciples and a Jew.u 26They came to John and said to him, "Rabbi, the one who was with you across the Jordan, to whom you testified, here he is baptizing, and all are going to him." 27John answered, "No one can receive anything except what has been given from heaven. 28You yourselves are my witnesses that I said, 'I am not the Messiah,v but I have been sent ahead of him.' 29He who has the bride is the bridegroom. The friend of the bridegroom, who stands and hears him, rejoices greatly at the bridegroom's voice. For this reason my joy has been fulfilled. 30He must increase, but I must decrease."w

The One Who Comes from Heaven

31 The one who comes from above is above all; the one who is of the earth belongs to the earth and speaks about earthly things. The one who comes from heaven is above all. 32He testifies to what he has seen and heard, yet no one accepts his testimony. 33Whoever has accepted his testimony has certifiedx this, that God is true. 34He whom God has sent speaks the words of God, for he gives the Spirit without

John 3:17-35 (Greek)

17 οὐ γὰρ ἀπέστειλεν ὁ θεὸς τὸν υἱὸν εἰς τὸν κόσμον ἵνα κρίνῃ τὸν κόσμον, ἀλλ᾽ ἵνα σωθῇ ὁ κόσμος δι᾽ αὐτοῦ. 18 ὁ πιστεύων εἰς αὐτὸν οὐ κρίνεται· ὁ δὲ μὴ πιστεύων ἤδη κέκριται, ὅτι μὴ πεπίστευκεν εἰς τὸ ὄνομα τοῦ μονογενοῦς υἱοῦ τοῦ θεοῦ. 19 αὕτη δέ ἐστιν ἡ κρίσις ὅτι τὸ φῶς ἐλήλυθεν εἰς τὸν κόσμον καὶ ἠγάπησαν οἱ ἄνθρωποι μᾶλλον τὸ σκότος ἢ τὸ φῶς· ἦν γὰρ αὐτῶν πονηρὰ τὰ ἔργα. 20 πᾶς γὰρ ὁ φαῦλα πράσσων μισεῖ τὸ φῶς καὶ οὐκ ἔρχεται πρὸς τὸ φῶς, ἵνα μὴ ἐλεγχθῇ τὰ ἔργα αὐτοῦ· 21 ὁ δὲ ποιῶν τὴν ἀλήθειαν ἔρχεται πρὸς τὸ φῶς, ἵνα φανερωθῇ αὐτοῦ τὰ ἔργα ὅτι ἐν θεῷ ἐστιν εἰργασμένα.

22 Μετὰ ταῦτα ἦλθεν ὁ Ἰησοῦς καὶ οἱ μαθηταὶ αὐτοῦ εἰς τὴν Ἰουδαίαν γῆν καὶ ἐκεῖ διέτριβεν μετ᾽ αὐτῶν καὶ ἐβάπτιζεν. 23 ἦν δὲ καὶ ὁ Ἰωάννης βαπτίζων ἐν Αἰνὼν ἐγγὺς τοῦ Σαλείμ, ὅτι ὕδατα πολλὰ ἦν ἐκεῖ, καὶ παρεγίνοντο καὶ ἐβαπτίζοντο· 24 οὔπω γὰρ ἦν βεβλημένος εἰς τὴν φυλακὴν ὁ Ἰωάννης. 25 Ἐγένετο οὖν ζήτησις ἐκ τῶν μαθητῶν Ἰωάννου μετὰ Ἰουδαίουb περὶ καθαρισμοῦ. 26 καὶ ἦλθον πρὸς τὸν Ἰωάννην καὶ εἶπαν αὐτῷ, Ῥαββί, ὃς ἦν μετὰ σοῦ πέραν τοῦ Ἰορδάνου, ᾧ σὺ μεμαρτύρηκας, ἴδε οὗτος βαπτίζει καὶ πάντες ἔρχονται πρὸς αὐτόν. 27 ἀπεκρίθη Ἰωάννης καὶ εἶπεν, Οὐ δύναται ἄνθρωπος λαμβάνειν οὐδὲ ἓν ἐὰν μὴ ᾖ δεδομένον αὐτῷ ἐκ τοῦ οὐρανοῦ. 28 αὐτοὶ ὑμεῖς μοι μαρτυρεῖτε ὅτι εἶπον [ὅτι] Οὐκ εἰμὶ ἐγὼ ὁ Χριστός, ἀλλ᾽ ὅτι Ἀπεσταλμένος εἰμὶ ἔμπροσθεν ἐκείνου. 29 ὁ ἔχων τὴν νύμφην νυμφίος ἐστίν· ὁ δὲ φίλος τοῦ νυμφίου ὁ ἑστηκὼς καὶ ἀκούων αὐτοῦ χαρᾷ χαίρει διὰ τὴν φωνὴν τοῦ νυμφίου. αὕτη οὖν ἡ χαρὰ ἡ ἐμὴ πεπλήρωται. 30 ἐκεῖνον δεῖ αὐξάνειν, ἐμὲ δὲ ἐλαττοῦσθαι.

31 Ὁ ἄνωθεν ἐρχόμενος ἐπάνω πάντων ἐστίν· ὁ ὢν ἐκ τῆς γῆς ἐκ τῆς γῆς ἐστιν καὶ ἐκ τῆς γῆς λαλεῖ. ὁ ἐκ τοῦ οὐρανοῦ ἐρχόμενος [ἐπάνω πάντων ἐστίν·] 32 ὃ ἑώρακεν καὶ ἤκουσεν τοῦτο μαρτυρεῖ, καὶ τὴν μαρτυρίαν αὐτοῦ οὐδεὶς λαμβάνει. 33 ὁ λαβὼν αὐτοῦ τὴν μαρτυρίαν ἐσφράγισεν ὅτι ὁ θεὸς ἀληθής ἐστιν. 34 ὃν γὰρ ἀπέστειλεν ὁ θεὸς τὰ ῥήματα τοῦ θεοῦ λαλεῖ, οὐ γὰρ ἐκ μέτρου δίδωσιν τὸ πνεῦμα. 35 ὁ

NIV

eternal life. 17For God did not send his Son into the world to condemn the world, but to save the world through him. 18Whoever believes in him is not condemned, but whoever does not believe stands condemned already because he has not believed in the name of God's one and only Son.g 19This is the verdict: Light has come into the world, but men loved darkness instead of light because their deeds were evil. 20Everyone who does evil hates the light, and will not come into the light for fear that his deeds will be exposed. 21But whoever lives by the truth comes into the light, so that it may be seen plainly that what he has done has been done through God."h

John the Baptist's Testimony About Jesus

22After this, Jesus and his disciples went out into the Judean countryside, where he spent some time with them, and baptized. 23Now John also was baptizing at Aenon near Salim, because there was plenty of water, and people were constantly coming to be baptized. 24(This was before John was put in prison.) 25An argument developed between some of John's disciples and a certain Jewi over the matter of ceremonial washing. 26They came to John and said to him, "Rabbi, that man who was with you on the other side of the Jordan—the one you testified about—well, he is baptizing, and everyone is going to him."

27To this John replied, "A man can receive only what is given him from heaven. 28You yourselves can testify that I said, 'I am not the Christj but am sent ahead of him.' 29The bride belongs to the bridegroom. The friend who attends the bridegroom waits and listens for him, and is full of joy when he hears the bridegroom's voice. That joy is mine, and it is now complete. 30He must become greater; I must become less.

31"The one who comes from above is above all; the one who is from the earth belongs to the earth, and speaks as one from the earth. The one who comes from heaven is above all. 32He testifies to what he has seen and heard, but no one accepts his testimony. 33The man who has accepted it has certified that God is truthful. 34For the one whom God has sent speaks the words of God, for Godk gives the Spirit

---

t Some interpreters hold that the quotation concludes with verse 15   u Other ancient authorities read *the Jews*   v Or *the Christ*   w Some interpreters hold that the quotation continues through verse 36   x Gk *set a seal to*

b25 NIV/NRSV notes Ἰουδαίων

g18 Or *God's only begotten Son*   h21 Some interpreters end the quotation after verse 15.   i25 Some manuscripts *and certain Jews*   j28 Or *Messiah*   k34 Greek *he*

measure. [35]The Father loves the Son and has placed all things in his hands. [36]Whoever believes in the Son has eternal life; whoever disobeys the Son will not see life, but must endure God's wrath.

Jesus and the Woman of Samaria

4 Now when Jesus[y] learned that the Pharisees had heard, "Jesus is making and baptizing more disciples than John" [2]— although it was not Jesus himself but his disciples who baptized— [3]he left Judea and started back to Galilee. [4]But he had to go through Samaria. [5]So he came to a Samaritan city called Sychar, near the plot of ground that Jacob had given to his son Joseph. [6]Jacob's well was there, and Jesus, tired out by his journey, was sitting by the well. It was about noon.

[7] A Samaritan woman came to draw water, and Jesus said to her, "Give me a drink." [8](His disciples had gone to the city to buy food.) [9]The Samaritan woman said to him, "How is it that you, a Jew, ask a drink of me, a woman of Samaria?" (Jews do not share things in common with Samaritans.)[z] [10]Jesus answered her, "If you knew the gift of God, and who it is that is saying to you, 'Give me a drink,' you would have asked him, and he would have given you living water." [11]The woman said to him, "Sir, you have no bucket, and the well is deep. Where do you get that living water? [12]Are you greater than our ancestor Jacob, who gave us the well, and with his sons and his flocks drank from it?" [13]Jesus said to her, "Everyone who drinks of this water will be thirsty again, [14]but those who drink of the water that I will give them will never be thirsty. The water that I will give will become in them a spring of water gushing up to eternal life." [15]The woman said to him, "Sir, give me this water, so that I may never be thirsty or have to keep coming here to draw water."

[16] Jesus said to her, "Go, call your husband, and come back." [17]The woman answered him, "I have no husband." Jesus said to her, "You are right in saying, 'I have no husband'; [18]for you have had five

πατὴρ ἀγαπᾷ τὸν υἱὸν καὶ πάντα δέδωκεν ἐν τῇ χειρὶ αὐτοῦ. **36** ὁ πιστεύων εἰς τὸν υἱὸν ἔχει ζωὴν αἰώνιον· ὁ δὲ ἀπειθῶν τῷ υἱῷ οὐκ ὄψεται ζωήν, ἀλλ' ἡ ὀργὴ τοῦ θεοῦ μένει ἐπ' αὐτόν.

4 Ὡς οὖν ἔγνω ὁ Ἰησοῦς ὅτι[a] ἤκουσαν οἱ φαρισαῖοι ὅτι Ἰησοῦς πλείονας μαθητὰς ποιεῖ καὶ βαπτίζει ἢ Ἰωάννης **2** – καίτοιγε Ἰησοῦς αὐτὸς οὐκ ἐβάπτιζεν ἀλλ' οἱ μαθηταὶ αὐτοῦ – **3** ἀφῆκεν τὴν Ἰουδαίαν καὶ ἀπῆλθεν πάλιν εἰς τὴν Γαλιλαίαν. **4** ἔδει δὲ αὐτὸν διέρχεσθαι διὰ τῆς Σαμαρείας. **5** ἔρχεται οὖν εἰς πόλιν τῆς Σαμαρείας λεγομένην Συχὰρ πλησίον τοῦ χωρίου ὃ ἔδωκεν Ἰακὼβ [τῷ] Ἰωσὴφ τῷ υἱῷ αὐτοῦ· **6** ἦν δὲ ἐκεῖ πηγὴ τοῦ Ἰακώβ. ὁ οὖν Ἰησοῦς κεκοπιακὼς ἐκ τῆς ὁδοιπορίας ἐκαθέζετο οὕτως ἐπὶ τῇ πηγῇ· ὥρα ἦν ὡς ἕκτη.

7 Ἔρχεται γυνὴ ἐκ τῆς Σαμαρείας ἀντλῆσαι ὕδωρ. λέγει αὐτῇ ὁ Ἰησοῦς, Δός μοι πεῖν· **8** οἱ γὰρ μαθηταὶ αὐτοῦ ἀπεληλύθεισαν εἰς τὴν πόλιν ἵνα τροφὰς ἀγοράσωσιν. **9** λέγει οὖν αὐτῷ ἡ γυνὴ ἡ Σαμαρῖτις, Πῶς σὺ Ἰουδαῖος ὢν παρ' ἐμοῦ πεῖν αἰτεῖς γυναικὸς Σαμαρίτιδος οὔσης; οὐ γὰρ συγχρῶνται Ἰουδαῖοι Σαμαρίταις. **10** ἀπεκρίθη Ἰησοῦς καὶ εἶπεν αὐτῇ, Εἰ ᾔδεις τὴν δωρεὰν τοῦ θεοῦ καὶ τίς ἐστιν ὁ λέγων σοι, Δός μοι πεῖν, σὺ ἂν ᾔτησας αὐτὸν καὶ ἔδωκεν ἄν σοι ὕδωρ ζῶν. **11** λέγει αὐτῷ [ἡ γυνή], Κύριε, οὔτε ἄντλημα ἔχεις καὶ τὸ φρέαρ ἐστὶν βαθύ· πόθεν οὖν ἔχεις τὸ ὕδωρ τὸ ζῶν; **12** μὴ σὺ μείζων εἶ τοῦ πατρὸς ἡμῶν Ἰακώβ, ὃς ἔδωκεν ἡμῖν τὸ φρέαρ καὶ αὐτὸς ἐξ αὐτοῦ ἔπιεν καὶ οἱ υἱοὶ αὐτοῦ καὶ τὰ θρέμματα αὐτοῦ; **13** ἀπεκρίθη Ἰησοῦς καὶ εἶπεν αὐτῇ, Πᾶς ὁ πίνων ἐκ τοῦ ὕδατος τούτου διψήσει πάλιν· **14** ὃς δ' ἂν πίῃ ἐκ τοῦ ὕδατος οὗ ἐγὼ δώσω αὐτῷ, οὐ μὴ διψήσει εἰς τὸν αἰῶνα, ἀλλὰ τὸ ὕδωρ ὃ δώσω αὐτῷ γενήσεται ἐν αὐτῷ πηγὴ ὕδατος ἁλλομένου εἰς ζωὴν αἰώνιον. **15** λέγει πρὸς αὐτὸν ἡ γυνή, Κύριε, δός μοι τοῦτο τὸ ὕδωρ, ἵνα μὴ διψῶ μηδὲ διέρχωμαι ἐνθάδε ἀντλεῖν.

16 Λέγει αὐτῇ, Ὕπαγε φώνησον τὸν ἄνδρα σου καὶ ἐλθὲ ἐνθάδε. **17** ἀπεκρίθη ἡ γυνὴ καὶ εἶπεν αὐτῷ, Οὐκ ἔχω ἄνδρα. λέγει αὐτῇ ὁ Ἰησοῦς, Καλῶς εἶπας ὅτι Ἄνδρα οὐκ ἔχω· **18** πέντε

without limit. [35]The Father loves the Son and has placed everything in his hands. [36]Whoever believes in the Son has eternal life, but whoever rejects the Son will not see life, for God's wrath remains on him."[l]

Jesus Talks With a Samaritan Woman

4 The Pharisees heard that Jesus was gaining and baptizing more disciples than John, [2]although in fact it was not Jesus who baptized, but his disciples. [3]When the Lord learned of this, he left Judea and went back once more to Galilee.

[4]Now he had to go through Samaria. [5]So he came to a town in Samaria called Sychar, near the plot of ground Jacob had given to his son Joseph. [6]Jacob's well was there, and Jesus, tired as he was from the journey, sat down by the well. It was about the sixth hour.

[7]When a Samaritan woman came to draw water, Jesus said to her, "Will you give me a drink?" [8](His disciples had gone into the town to buy food.)

[9]The Samaritan woman said to him, "You are a Jew and I am a Samaritan woman. How can you ask me for a drink?" (For Jews do not associate with Samaritans.[a])

[10]Jesus answered her, "If you knew the gift of God and who it is that asks you for a drink, you would have asked him and he would have given you living water."

[11]"Sir," the woman said, "you have nothing to draw with and the well is deep. Where can you get this living water? [12]Are you greater than our father Jacob, who gave us the well and drank from it himself, as did also his sons and his flocks and herds?"

[13]Jesus answered, "Everyone who drinks this water will be thirsty again, [14]but whoever drinks the water I give him will never thirst. Indeed, the water I give him will become in him a spring of water welling up to eternal life."

[15]The woman said to him, "Sir, give me this water so that I won't get thirsty and have to keep coming here to draw water."

[16]He told her, "Go, call your husband and come back."

[17]"I have no husband," she replied.

Jesus said to her, "You are right when you say you have no husband. [18]The fact

---

[y] Other ancient authorities read *the Lord*   [z] Other ancient authorities lack this sentence

[a]1 NIV text translates the phrase Ὡς οὖν ἔγνω ὁ Ἰησοῦς ὅτι in verse 3; NIV text and NRSV note y read κύριος for Ἰησοῦς

[l]36 Some interpreters end the quotation after verse 30.   [a]9 Or *do not use dishes Samaritans have used*

husbands, and the one you have now is not your husband. What you have said is true!" [19]The woman said to him, "Sir, I see that you are a prophet. [20]Our ancestors worshiped on this mountain, but you[a] say that the place where people must worship is in Jerusalem." [21]Jesus said to her, "Woman, believe me, the hour is coming when you will worship the Father neither on this mountain nor in Jerusalem. [22]You worship what you do not know; we worship what we know, for salvation is from the Jews. [23]But the hour is coming, and is now here, when the true worshipers will worship the Father in spirit and truth, for the Father seeks such as these to worship him. [24]God is spirit, and those who worship him must worship in spirit and truth." [25]The woman said to him, "I know that Messiah is coming" (who is called Christ). "When he comes, he will proclaim all things to us." [26]Jesus said to her, "I am he,[b] the one who is speaking to you."

[27] Just then his disciples came. They were astonished that he was speaking with a woman, but no one said, "What do you want?" or, "Why are you speaking with her?" [28]Then the woman left her water jar and went back to the city. She said to the people, [29]"Come and see a man who told me everything I have ever done! He cannot be the Messiah,[c] can he?" [30]They left the city and were on their way to him.

[31] Meanwhile the disciples were urging him, "Rabbi, eat something." [32]But he said to them, "I have food to eat that you do not know about." [33]So the disciples said to one another, "Surely no one has brought him something to eat?" [34]Jesus said to them, "My food is to do the will of him who sent me and to complete his work. [35]Do you not say, 'Four months more, then comes the harvest'? But I tell you, look around you, and see how the fields are ripe for harvesting. [36]The reaper is already receiving[d] wages and is gathering fruit for eternal life, so that sower and reaper may rejoice together. [37]For here the saying holds true, 'One sows and another reaps.' [38]I sent you to reap that for which you did not labor. Others have labored, and you have entered into their labor."

γὰρ ἄνδρας ἔσχες καὶ νῦν ὃν ἔχεις οὐκ ἔστιν σου ἀνήρ· τοῦτο ἀληθὲς εἴρηκας. 19 λέγει αὐτῷ ἡ γυνή, Κύριε, θεωρῶ ὅτι προφήτης εἶ σύ. 20 οἱ πατέρες ἡμῶν ἐν τῷ ὄρει τούτῳ προσεκύνησαν· καὶ ὑμεῖς λέγετε ὅτι ἐν Ἱεροσολύμοις ἐστὶν ὁ τόπος ὅπου προσκυνεῖν δεῖ. 21 λέγει αὐτῇ ὁ Ἰησοῦς, Πίστευέ μοι, γύναι, ὅτι ἔρχεται ὥρα ὅτε οὔτε ἐν τῷ ὄρει τούτῳ οὔτε ἐν Ἱεροσολύμοις προσκυνήσετε τῷ πατρί. 22 ὑμεῖς προσκυνεῖτε ὃ οὐκ οἴδατε· ἡμεῖς προσκυνοῦμεν ὃ οἴδαμεν, ὅτι ἡ σωτηρία ἐκ τῶν Ἰουδαίων ἐστίν. 23 ἀλλὰ ἔρχεται ὥρα καὶ νῦν ἐστιν, ὅτε οἱ ἀληθινοὶ προσκυνηταὶ προσκυνήσουσιν τῷ πατρὶ ἐν πνεύματι καὶ ἀληθείᾳ· καὶ γὰρ ὁ πατὴρ τοιούτους ζητεῖ τοὺς προσκυνοῦντας αὐτόν. 24 πνεῦμα ὁ θεός, καὶ τοὺς προσκυνοῦντας αὐτὸν ἐν πνεύματι καὶ ἀληθείᾳ δεῖ προσκυνεῖν. 25 λέγει αὐτῷ ἡ γυνή, Οἶδα ὅτι Μεσσίας ἔρχεται ὁ λεγόμενος Χριστός· ὅταν ἔλθῃ ἐκεῖνος, ἀναγγελεῖ ἡμῖν ἅπαντα. 26 λέγει αὐτῇ ὁ Ἰησοῦς, Ἐγώ εἰμι, ὁ λαλῶν σοι.

27 Καὶ ἐπὶ τούτῳ ἦλθαν οἱ μαθηταὶ αὐτοῦ καὶ ἐθαύμαζον ὅτι μετὰ γυναικὸς ἐλάλει· οὐδεὶς μέντοι εἶπεν, Τί ζητεῖς ἢ Τί λαλεῖς μετ' αὐτῆς; 28 ἀφῆκεν οὖν τὴν ὑδρίαν αὐτῆς ἡ γυνὴ καὶ ἀπῆλθεν εἰς τὴν πόλιν καὶ λέγει τοῖς ἀνθρώποις, 29 Δεῦτε ἴδετε ἄνθρωπον ὃς εἶπέν μοι πάντα ὅσα ἐποίησα, μήτι οὗτός ἐστιν ὁ Χριστός; 30 ἐξῆλθον ἐκ τῆς πόλεως καὶ ἤρχοντο πρὸς αὐτόν.

31 Ἐν τῷ μεταξὺ ἠρώτων αὐτὸν οἱ μαθηταὶ λέγοντες, Ῥαββί, φάγε. 32 ὁ δὲ εἶπεν αὐτοῖς, Ἐγὼ βρῶσιν ἔχω φαγεῖν ἣν ὑμεῖς οὐκ οἴδατε. 33 ἔλεγον οὖν οἱ μαθηταὶ πρὸς ἀλλήλους, Μή τις ἤνεγκεν αὐτῷ φαγεῖν; 34 λέγει αὐτοῖς ὁ Ἰησοῦς, Ἐμὸν βρῶμά ἐστιν ἵνα ποιήσω τὸ θέλημα τοῦ πέμψαντός με καὶ τελειώσω αὐτοῦ τὸ ἔργον. 35 οὐχ ὑμεῖς λέγετε ὅτι Ἔτι τετράμηνός ἐστιν καὶ ὁ θερισμὸς ἔρχεται; ἰδοὺ λέγω ὑμῖν, ἐπάρατε τοὺς ὀφθαλμοὺς ὑμῶν καὶ θεάσασθε τὰς χώρας ὅτι λευκαί εἰσιν πρὸς θερισμόν. ἤδη[b] 36 ὁ θερίζων μισθὸν λαμβάνει καὶ συνάγει καρπὸν εἰς ζωὴν αἰώνιον, ἵνα ὁ σπείρων ὁμοῦ χαίρῃ καὶ ὁ θερίζων. 37 ἐν γὰρ τούτῳ ὁ λόγος ἐστὶν ἀληθινὸς ὅτι Ἄλλος ἐστὶν ὁ σπείρων καὶ ἄλλος ὁ θερίζων. 38 ἐγὼ ἀπέστειλα ὑμᾶς θερίζειν ὃ οὐχ ὑμεῖς κεκοπιάκατε· ἄλλοι κεκοπιάκασιν καὶ ὑμεῖς εἰς τὸν κόπον αὐτῶν εἰσεληλύθατε.

is, you have had five husbands, and the man you now have is not your husband. What you have just said is quite true."

[19]"Sir," the woman said, "I can see that you are a prophet. [20]Our fathers worshiped on this mountain, but you Jews claim that the place where we must worship is in Jerusalem."

[21]Jesus declared, "Believe me, woman, a time is coming when you will worship the Father neither on this mountain nor in Jerusalem. [22]You Samaritans worship what you do not know; we worship what we do know, for salvation is from the Jews. [23]Yet a time is coming and has now come when the true worshipers will worship the Father in spirit and truth, for they are the kind of worshipers the Father seeks. [24]God is spirit, and his worshipers must worship in spirit and in truth."

[25]The woman said, "I know that Messiah" (called Christ) "is coming. When he comes, he will explain everything to us."

[26]Then Jesus declared, "I who speak to you am he."

The Disciples Rejoin Jesus

[27]Just then his disciples returned and were surprised to find him talking with a woman. But no one asked, "What do you want?" or "Why are you talking with her?"

[28]Then, leaving her water jar, the woman went back to the town and said to the people, [29]"Come, see a man who told me everything I ever did. Could this be the Christ[b]?" [30]They came out of the town and made their way toward him.

[31]Meanwhile his disciples urged him, "Rabbi, eat something."

[32]But he said to them, "I have food to eat that you know nothing about."

[33]Then his disciples said to each other, "Could someone have brought him food?"

[34]"My food," said Jesus, "is to do the will of him who sent me and to finish his work. [35]Do you not say, 'Four months more and then the harvest'? I tell you, open your eyes and look at the fields! They are ripe for harvest. [36]Even now the reaper draws his wages, even now he harvests the crop for eternal life, so that the sower and the reaper may be glad together. [37]Thus the saying 'One sows and another reaps' is true. [38]I sent you to reap what you have not worked for. Others have done the hard work, and you have reaped the benefits of their labor."

39 Many Samaritans from that city believed in him because of the woman's testimony, "He told me everything I have ever done." 40So when the Samaritans came to him, they asked him to stay with them; and he stayed there two days. 41And many more believed because of his word. 42They said to the woman, "It is no longer because of what you said that we believe, for we have heard for ourselves, and we know that this is truly the Savior of the world."

Jesus Returns to Galilee

43 When the two days were over, he went from that place to Galilee 44(for Jesus himself had testified that a prophet has no honor in the prophet's own country). 45When he came to Galilee, the Galileans welcomed him, since they had seen all that he had done in Jerusalem at the festival; for they too had gone to the festival.

Jesus Heals an Official's Son

46 Then he came again to Cana in Galilee where he had changed the water into wine. Now there was a royal official whose son lay ill in Capernaum. 47When he heard that Jesus had come from Judea to Galilee, he went and begged him to come down and heal his son, for he was at the point of death. 48Then Jesus said to him, "Unless you[e] see signs and wonders you will not believe." 49The official said to him, "Sir, come down before my little boy dies." 50Jesus said to him, "Go; your son will live." The man believed the word that Jesus spoke to him and started on his way. 51As he was going down, his slaves met him and told him that his child was alive. 52So he asked them the hour when he began to recover, and they said to him, "Yesterday at one in the afternoon the fever left him." 53The father realized that this was the hour when Jesus had said to him, "Your son will live." So he himself believed, along with his whole household. 54Now this was the second sign that Jesus did after coming from Judea to Galilee.

Jesus Heals on the Sabbath

5 After this there was a festival of the Jews, and Jesus went up to Jerusalem. 2 Now in Jerusalem by the Sheep Gate there is a pool, called in Hebrew[f] Beth-zatha,[g] which has five porticoes. 3In these

---

39 Ἐκ δὲ τῆς πόλεως ἐκείνης πολλοὶ ἐπίστευσαν εἰς αὐτὸν τῶν Σαμαριτῶν διὰ τὸν λόγον τῆς γυναικὸς μαρτυρούσης ὅτι Εἶπέν μοι πάντα ἃ ἐποίησα **40** ὡς οὖν ἦλθον πρὸς αὐτὸν οἱ Σαμαρῖται, ἠρώτων αὐτὸν μεῖναι παρ᾽ αὐτοῖς· καὶ ἔμεινεν ἐκεῖ δύο ἡμέρας. **41** καὶ πολλῷ πλείους ἐπίστευσαν διὰ τὸν λόγον αὐτοῦ, **42** τῇ τε γυναικὶ ἔλεγον ὅτι Οὐκέτι διὰ τὴν σὴν λαλιὰν πιστεύομεν, αὐτοὶ γὰρ ἀκηκόαμεν καὶ οἴδαμεν ὅτι οὗτός ἐστιν ἀληθῶς ὁ σωτὴρ τοῦ κόσμου.

43 Μετὰ δὲ τὰς δύο ἡμέρας ἐξῆλθεν ἐκεῖθεν εἰς τὴν Γαλιλαίαν· **44** αὐτὸς γὰρ Ἰησοῦς ἐμαρτύρησεν ὅτι προφήτης ἐν τῇ ἰδίᾳ πατρίδι τιμὴν οὐκ ἔχει. **45** ὅτε οὖν ἦλθεν εἰς τὴν Γαλιλαίαν, ἐδέξαντο αὐτὸν οἱ Γαλιλαῖοι πάντα ἑωρακότες ὅσα ἐποίησεν ἐν Ἱεροσολύμοις ἐν τῇ ἑορτῇ, καὶ αὐτοὶ γὰρ ἦλθον εἰς τὴν ἑορτήν.

46 Ἦλθεν οὖν πάλιν εἰς τὴν Κανὰ τῆς Γαλιλαίας, ὅπου ἐποίησεν τὸ ὕδωρ οἶνον. καὶ ἦν τις βασιλικὸς οὗ ὁ υἱὸς ἠσθένει ἐν Καφαρναούμ. **47** οὗτος ἀκούσας ὅτι Ἰησοῦς ἥκει ἐκ τῆς Ἰουδαίας εἰς τὴν Γαλιλαίαν ἀπῆλθεν πρὸς αὐτὸν καὶ ἠρώτα ἵνα καταβῇ καὶ ἰάσηται αὐτοῦ τὸν υἱόν, ἤμελλεν γὰρ ἀποθνήσκειν. **48** εἶπεν οὖν ὁ Ἰησοῦς πρὸς αὐτόν, Ἐὰν μὴ σημεῖα καὶ τέρατα ἴδητε, οὐ μὴ πιστεύσητε. **49** λέγει πρὸς αὐτὸν ὁ βασιλικός, Κύριε, κατάβηθι πρὶν ἀποθανεῖν τὸ παιδίον μου. **50** λέγει αὐτῷ ὁ Ἰησοῦς, Πορεύου, ὁ υἱός σου ζῇ. ἐπίστευσεν ὁ ἄνθρωπος τῷ λόγῳ ὃν εἶπεν αὐτῷ ὁ Ἰησοῦς καὶ ἐπορεύετο. **51** ἤδη δὲ αὐτοῦ καταβαίνοντος οἱ δοῦλοι αὐτοῦ ὑπήντησαν αὐτῷ λέγοντες ὅτι ὁ παῖς αὐτοῦ ζῇ. **52** ἐπύθετο οὖν τὴν ὥραν παρ᾽ αὐτῶν ἐν ᾗ κομψότερον ἔσχεν· εἶπαν οὖν αὐτῷ ὅτι Ἐχθὲς ὥραν ἑβδόμην ἀφῆκεν αὐτὸν ὁ πυρετός. **53** ἔγνω οὖν ὁ πατὴρ ὅτι [ἐν] ἐκείνῃ τῇ ὥρᾳ ἐν ᾗ εἶπεν αὐτῷ ὁ Ἰησοῦς, Ὁ υἱός σου ζῇ, καὶ ἐπίστευσεν αὐτὸς καὶ ἡ οἰκία αὐτοῦ ὅλη. **54** Τοῦτο [δὲ] πάλιν δεύτερον σημεῖον ἐποίησεν ὁ Ἰησοῦς ἐλθὼν ἐκ τῆς Ἰουδαίας εἰς τὴν Γαλιλαίαν.

5 Μετὰ ταῦτα ἦν ἑορτὴ τῶν Ἰουδαίων καὶ ἀνέβη Ἰησοῦς εἰς Ἱεροσόλυμα. **2** ἔστιν δὲ ἐν τοῖς Ἱεροσολύμοις ἐπὶ τῇ προβατικῇ κολυμβήθρα ἡ ἐπιλεγομένη Ἑβραϊστὶ Βηθζαθὰ[a]

Many Samaritans Believe

39Many of the Samaritans from that town believed in him because of the woman's testimony, "He told me everything I ever did." 40So when the Samaritans came to him, they urged him to stay with them, and he stayed two days. 41And because of his words many more became believers.

42They said to the woman, "We no longer believe just because of what you said; now we have heard for ourselves, and we know that this man really is the Savior of the world."

Jesus Heals the Official's Son

43After the two days he left for Galilee. 44(Now Jesus himself had pointed out that a prophet has no honor in his own country.) 45When he arrived in Galilee, the Galileans welcomed him. They had seen all that he had done in Jerusalem at the Passover Feast, for they also had been there.

46Once more he visited Cana in Galilee, where he had turned the water into wine. And there was a certain royal official whose son lay sick at Capernaum. 47When this man heard that Jesus had arrived in Galilee from Judea, he went to him and begged him to come and heal his son, who was close to death.

48"Unless you people see miraculous signs and wonders," Jesus told him, "you will never believe."

49The royal official said, "Sir, come down before my child dies."

50Jesus replied, "You may go. Your son will live."

The man took Jesus at his word and departed. 51While he was still on the way, his servants met him with the news that his boy was living. 52When he inquired as to the time when his son got better, they said to him, "The fever left him yesterday at the seventh hour."

53Then the father realized that this was the exact time at which Jesus had said to him, "Your son will live." So he and all his household believed.

54This was the second miraculous sign that Jesus performed, having come from Judea to Galilee.

The Healing at the Pool

5 Some time later, Jesus went up to Jerusalem for a feast of the Jews. 2Now there is in Jerusalem near the Sheep Gate a pool, which in Aramaic is called Bethesda[d]

---

e Both instances of the Greek word for *you* in this verse are plural   f That is, *Aramaic*   g Other ancient authorities read *Bethesda*, others *Bethsaida*

a2 NIV text Βηθεσδά; NIV note Βηθζαθά or Βηθσαϊδά; NRSV note Βηθεσδά or Βηθσαϊδά

a2 Some manuscripts *Bethzatha*; other manuscripts *Bethsaida*

lay many invalids—blind, lame, and paralyzed.[h] [5]One man was there who had been ill for thirty-eight years. [6]When Jesus saw him lying there and knew that he had been there a long time, he said to him, "Do you want to be made well?" [7]The sick man answered him, "Sir, I have no one to put me into the pool when the water is stirred up; and while I am making my way, someone else steps down ahead of me." [8]Jesus said to him, "Stand up, take your mat and walk." [9]At once the man was made well, and he took up his mat and began to walk.

Now that day was a sabbath. [10]So the Jews said to the man who had been cured, "It is the sabbath; it is not lawful for you to carry your mat." [11]But he answered them, "The man who made me well said to me, 'Take up your mat and walk.' " [12]They asked him, "Who is the man who said to you, 'Take it up and walk'?" [13]Now the man who had been healed did not know who it was, for Jesus had disappeared in[i] the crowd that was there. [14]Later Jesus found him in the temple and said to him, "See, you have been made well! Do not sin any more, so that nothing worse happens to you." [15]The man went away and told the Jews that it was Jesus who had made him well. [16]Therefore the Jews started persecuting Jesus, because he was doing such things on the sabbath. [17]But Jesus answered them, "My Father is still working, and I also am working." [18]For this reason the Jews were seeking all the more to kill him, because he was not only breaking the sabbath, but was also calling God his own Father, thereby making himself equal to God.

The Authority of the Son

19 Jesus said to them, "Very truly, I tell you, the Son can do nothing on his own, but only what he sees the Father doing; for whatever the Father[j] does, the Son does likewise. [20]The Father loves the Son and shows him all that he himself is doing; and he will show him greater works than these, so that you will be astonished. [21]Indeed, just as the Father raises the dead and gives

πέντε στοὰς ἔχουσα. **3** ἐν ταύταις κατέκειτο πλῆθος τῶν ἀσθενούντων, τυφλῶν, χωλῶν, ξηρῶν[b]. **5** ἦν δέ τις ἄνθρωπος ἐκεῖ τριάκοντα [καὶ] ὀκτὼ ἔτη ἔχων ἐν τῇ ἀσθενείᾳ αὐτοῦ· **6** τοῦτον ἰδὼν ὁ Ἰησοῦς κατακείμενον καὶ γνοὺς ὅτι πολὺν ἤδη χρόνον ἔχει, λέγει αὐτῷ, Θέλεις ὑγιὴς γενέσθαι; **7** ἀπεκρίθη αὐτῷ ὁ ἀσθενῶν, Κύριε, ἄνθρωπον οὐκ ἔχω ἵνα ὅταν ταραχθῇ τὸ ὕδωρ βάλῃ με εἰς τὴν κολυμβήθραν· ἐν ᾧ δὲ ἔρχομαι ἐγώ, ἄλλος πρὸ ἐμοῦ καταβαίνει. **8** λέγει αὐτῷ ὁ Ἰησοῦς, Ἔγειρε ἆρον τὸν κράβαττόν σου καὶ περιπάτει. **9** καὶ εὐθέως ἐγένετο ὑγιὴς ὁ ἄνθρωπος καὶ ἦρεν τὸν κράβαττον αὐτοῦ καὶ περιεπάτει.

Ἦν δὲ σάββατον ἐν ἐκείνῃ τῇ ἡμέρᾳ. **10** ἔλεγον οὖν οἱ Ἰουδαῖοι τῷ τεθεραπευμένῳ, Σάββατόν ἐστι, καὶ οὐκ ἔξεστίν σοι ἆραι τὸν κράβαττόν σου. **11** ὁ δὲ ἀπεκρίθη αὐτοῖς, Ὁ ποιήσας με ὑγιῆ ἐκεῖνός μοι εἶπεν, Ἆρον τὸν κράβαττόν σου καὶ περιπάτει. **12** ἠρώτησαν αὐτόν, Τίς ἐστιν ὁ ἄνθρωπος ὁ εἰπών σοι, Ἆρον καὶ περιπάτει; **13** ὁ δὲ ἰαθεὶς οὐκ ᾔδει τίς ἐστιν, ὁ γὰρ Ἰησοῦς ἐξένευσεν ὄχλου ὄντος ἐν τῷ τόπῳ. **14** μετὰ ταῦτα εὑρίσκει αὐτὸν ὁ Ἰησοῦς ἐν τῷ ἱερῷ καὶ εἶπεν αὐτῷ, Ἴδε ὑγιὴς γέγονας, μηκέτι ἁμάρτανε, ἵνα μὴ χεῖρόν σοί τι γένηται. **15** ἀπῆλθεν ὁ ἄνθρωπος καὶ ἀνήγγειλεν τοῖς Ἰουδαίοις ὅτι Ἰησοῦς ἐστιν ὁ ποιήσας αὐτὸν ὑγιῆ. **16** καὶ διὰ τοῦτο ἐδίωκον οἱ Ἰουδαῖοι τὸν Ἰησοῦν, ὅτι ταῦτα ἐποίει ἐν σαββάτῳ. **17** ὁ δὲ [Ἰησοῦς] ἀπεκρίνατο αὐτοῖς, Ὁ πατήρ μου ἕως ἄρτι ἐργάζεται κἀγὼ ἐργάζομαι · **18** διὰ τοῦτο οὖν μᾶλλον ἐζήτουν αὐτὸν οἱ Ἰουδαῖοι ἀποκτεῖναι, ὅτι οὐ μόνον ἔλυεν τὸ σάββατον, ἀλλὰ καὶ πατέρα ἴδιον ἔλεγεν τὸν θεὸν ἴσον ἑαυτὸν ποιῶν τῷ θεῷ.

19 Ἀπεκρίνατο οὖν ὁ Ἰησοῦς καὶ ἔλεγεν αὐτοῖς, Ἀμὴν ἀμὴν λέγω ὑμῖν, οὐ δύναται ὁ υἱὸς ποιεῖν ἀφ᾽ ἑαυτοῦ οὐδὲν ἐὰν μή τι βλέπῃ τὸν πατέρα ποιοῦντα· ἃ γὰρ ἂν ἐκεῖνος ποιῇ, ταῦτα καὶ ὁ υἱὸς ὁμοίως ποιεῖ. **20** ὁ γὰρ πατὴρ φιλεῖ τὸν υἱὸν καὶ πάντα δείκνυσιν αὐτῷ ἃ αὐτὸς ποιεῖ, καὶ μείζονα τούτων δείξει αὐτῷ ἔργα, ἵνα ὑμεῖς θαυμάζητε. **21** ὥσπερ γὰρ ὁ πατὴρ ἐγείρει τοὺς νεκροὺς καὶ ζῳοποιεῖ,

and which is surrounded by five covered colonnades. [3]Here a great number of disabled people used to lie—the blind, the lame, the paralyzed.[b] [5]One who was there had been an invalid for thirty-eight years. [6]When Jesus saw him lying there and learned that he had been in this condition for a long time, he asked him, "Do you want to get well?"

[7]"Sir," the invalid replied, "I have no one to help me into the pool when the water is stirred. While I am trying to get in, someone else goes down ahead of me." [8]Then Jesus said to him, "Get up! Pick up your mat and walk." [9]At once the man was cured; he picked up his mat and walked.

The day on which this took place was a Sabbath, [10]and so the Jews said to the man who had been healed, "It is the Sabbath; the law forbids you to carry your mat."

[11]But he replied, "The man who made me well said to me, 'Pick up your mat and walk.' "

[12]So they asked him, "Who is this fellow who told you to pick it up and walk?"

[13]The man who was healed had no idea who it was, for Jesus had slipped away into the crowd that was there.

[14]Later Jesus found him at the temple and said to him, "See, you are well again. Stop sinning or something worse may happen to you." [15]The man went away and told the Jews that it was Jesus who had made him well.

Life Through the Son

[16]So, because Jesus was doing these things on the Sabbath, the Jews persecuted him. [17]Jesus said to them, "My Father is always at his work to this very day, and I, too, am working." [18]For this reason the Jews tried all the harder to kill him; not only was he breaking the Sabbath, but he was even calling God his own Father, making himself equal with God.

[19]Jesus gave them this answer: "I tell you the truth, the Son can do nothing by himself; he can do only what he sees his Father doing, because whatever the Father does the Son also does. [20]For the Father loves the Son and shows him all he does. Yes, to your amazement he will show him even greater things than these. [21]For just as the Father raises the dead and gives them life,

---

[h] Other ancient authorities add, wholly or in part, *waiting for the stirring of the water;* [4]*for an angel of the Lord went down at certain seasons into the pool, and stirred up the water; whoever stepped in first after the stirring of the water was made well from whatever disease that person had.*
[i] *Or had left because of*   [j] *Gk that one*

[b]3 NIV/NRSV notes add ἐκδεχομένων τὴν τοῦ ὕδατος κίνησιν. 4 ἄγγελος γὰρ κυρίου κατὰ καιρὸν ἐλούετο ἐν τῇ κολυμβήθρᾳ καὶ ἐτάρασσε τὸ ὕδωρ· ὁ οὖν πρῶτος ἐμβὰς μετὰ τὴν ταραχὴν τοῦ ὕδατος ὑγιὴς ἐγίνετο οἵῳ δήποτ᾽ οὖν κατείχετο νοσήματι

[b]3 Some less important manuscripts *paralyzed—and they waited for the moving of the waters.* [4]*From time to time an angel of the Lord would come down and stir up the waters. The first one into the pool after each such disturbance would be cured of whatever disease he had.*

them life, so also the Son gives life to whomever he wishes. 22The Father judges no one but has given all judgment to the Son, 23so that all may honor the Son just as they honor the Father. Anyone who does not honor the Son does not honor the Father who sent him. 24Very truly, I tell you, anyone who hears my word and believes him who sent me has eternal life, and does not come under judgment, but has passed from death to life.

25 "Very truly, I tell you, the hour is coming, and is now here, when the dead will hear the voice of the Son of God, and those who hear will live. 26For just as the Father has life in himself, so he has granted the Son also to have life in himself; 27and he has given him authority to execute judgment, because he is the Son of Man. 28Do not be astonished at this; for the hour is coming when all who are in their graves will hear his voice 29and will come out— those who have done good, to the resurrection of life, and those who have done evil, to the resurrection of condemnation.

Witnesses to Jesus

30 "I can do nothing on my own. As I hear, I judge; and my judgment is just, because I seek to do not my own will but the will of him who sent me.

31 "If I testify about myself, my testimony is not true. 32There is another who testifies on my behalf, and I know that his testimony to me is true. 33You sent messengers to John, and he testified to the truth. 34Not that I accept such human testimony, but I say these things so that you may be saved. 35He was a burning and shining lamp, and you were willing to rejoice for a while in his light. 36But I have a testimony greater than John's. The works that the Father has given me to complete, the very works that I am doing, testify on my behalf that the Father has sent me. 37And the Father who sent me has himself testified on my behalf. You have never heard his voice or seen his form, 38and you do not have his word abiding in you, because you do not believe him whom he has sent.

39 "You search the scriptures because you think that in them you have eternal life; and it is they that testify on my behalf. 40Yet you refuse to come to me to have life.

οὕτως καὶ ὁ υἱὸς οὓς θέλει ζῳοποιεῖ. 22 οὐδὲ γὰρ ὁ πατὴρ κρίνει οὐδένα, ἀλλὰ τὴν κρίσιν πᾶσαν δέδωκεν τῷ υἱῷ, 23 ἵνα πάντες τιμῶσι τὸν υἱὸν καθὼς τιμῶσι τὸν πατέρα. ὁ μὴ τιμῶν τὸν υἱὸν οὐ τιμᾷ τὸν πατέρα τὸν πέμψαντα αὐτόν. 24 Ἀμὴν ἀμὴν λέγω ὑμῖν ὅτι ὁ τὸν λόγον μου ἀκούων καὶ πιστεύων τῷ πέμψαντί με ἔχει ζωὴν αἰώνιον καὶ εἰς κρίσιν οὐκ ἔρχεται, ἀλλὰ μεταβέβηκεν ἐκ τοῦ θανάτου εἰς τὴν ζωήν. 25 ἀμὴν ἀμὴν λέγω ὑμῖν ὅτι ἔρχεται ὥρα καὶ νῦν ἐστιν ὅτε οἱ νεκροὶ ἀκούσουσιν τῆς φωνῆς τοῦ υἱοῦ τοῦ θεοῦ καὶ οἱ ἀκούσαντες ζήσουσιν. 26 ὥσπερ γὰρ ὁ πατὴρ ἔχει ζωὴν ἐν ἑαυτῷ, οὕτως καὶ τῷ υἱῷ ἔδωκεν ζωὴν ἔχειν ἐν ἑαυτῷ. 27 καὶ ἐξουσίαν ἔδωκεν αὐτῷ κρίσιν ποιεῖν, ὅτι υἱὸς ἀνθρώπου ἐστίν. 28 μὴ θαυμάζετε τοῦτο, ὅτι ἔρχεται ὥρα ἐν ᾗ πάντες οἱ ἐν τοῖς μνημείοις ἀκούσουσιν τῆς φωνῆς αὐτοῦ 29 καὶ ἐκπορεύσονται οἱ τὰ ἀγαθὰ ποιήσαντες εἰς ἀνάστασιν ζωῆς, οἱ δὲ τὰ φαῦλα πράξαντες εἰς ἀνάστασιν κρίσεως.

30 Οὐ δύναμαι ἐγὼ ποιεῖν ἀπ᾽ ἐμαυτοῦ οὐδέν· καθὼς ἀκούω κρίνω, καὶ ἡ κρίσις ἡ ἐμὴ δικαία ἐστίν, ὅτι οὐ ζητῶ τὸ θέλημα τὸ ἐμὸν ἀλλὰ τὸ θέλημα τοῦ πέμψαντός με.

31 ἐὰν ἐγὼ μαρτυρῶ περὶ ἐμαυτοῦ, ἡ μαρτυρία μου οὐκ ἔστιν ἀληθής· 32 ἄλλος ἐστὶν ὁ μαρτυρῶν περὶ ἐμοῦ, καὶ οἶδα ὅτι ἀληθής ἐστιν ἡ μαρτυρία ἣν μαρτυρεῖ περὶ ἐμοῦ. 33 ὑμεῖς ἀπεστάλκατε πρὸς Ἰωάννην, καὶ μεμαρτύρηκεν τῇ ἀληθείᾳ· 34 ἐγὼ δὲ οὐ παρὰ ἀνθρώπου τὴν μαρτυρίαν λαμβάνω, ἀλλὰ ταῦτα λέγω ἵνα ὑμεῖς σωθῆτε. 35 ἐκεῖνος ἦν ὁ λύχνος ὁ καιόμενος καὶ φαίνων, ὑμεῖς δὲ ἠθελήσατε ἀγαλλιαθῆναι πρὸς ὥραν ἐν τῷ φωτὶ αὐτοῦ. 36 ἐγὼ δὲ ἔχω τὴν μαρτυρίαν μείζω τοῦ Ἰωάννου· τὰ γὰρ ἔργα ἃ δέδωκέν μοι ὁ πατὴρ ἵνα τελειώσω αὐτά, αὐτὰ τὰ ἔργα ἃ ποιῶ μαρτυρεῖ περὶ ἐμοῦ ὅτι ὁ πατήρ με ἀπέσταλκεν. 37 καὶ ὁ πέμψας με πατὴρ ἐκεῖνος μεμαρτύρηκεν περὶ ἐμοῦ. οὔτε φωνὴν αὐτοῦ πώποτε ἀκηκόατε οὔτε εἶδος αὐτοῦ ἑωράκατε, 38 καὶ τὸν λόγον αὐτοῦ οὐκ ἔχετε ἐν ὑμῖν μένοντα, ὅτι ὃν ἀπέστειλεν ἐκεῖνος, τούτῳ ὑμεῖς οὐ πιστεύετε. 39 ἐραυνᾶτε τὰς γραφάς, ὅτι ὑμεῖς δοκεῖτε ἐν αὐταῖς ζωὴν αἰώνιον ἔχειν· καὶ ἐκεῖναί εἰσιν αἱ μαρτυροῦσαι περὶ ἐμοῦ· 40 καὶ οὐ θέλετε ἐλθεῖν πρός με ἵνα ζωὴν ἔχητε.

even so the Son gives life to whom he is pleased to give it. 22Moreover, the Father judges no one, but has entrusted all judgment to the Son, 23that all may honor the Son just as they honor the Father. He who does not honor the Son does not honor the Father, who sent him.

24"I tell you the truth, whoever hears my word and believes him who sent me has eternal life and will not be condemned; he has crossed over from death to life. 25I tell you the truth, a time is coming and has now come when the dead will hear the voice of the Son of God and those who hear will live. 26For as the Father has life in himself, so he has granted the Son to have life in himself. 27And he has given him authority to judge because he is the Son of Man.

28"Do not be amazed at this, for a time is coming when all who are in their graves will hear his voice 29and come out—those who have done good will rise to live, and those who have done evil will rise to be condemned. 30By myself I can do nothing; I judge only as I hear, and my judgment is just, for I seek not to please myself but him who sent me.

Testimonies About Jesus

31"If I testify about myself, my testimony is not valid. 32There is another who testifies in my favor, and I know that his testimony about me is valid.

33"You have sent to John and he has testified to the truth. 34Not that I accept human testimony; but I mention it that you may be saved. 35John was a lamp that burned and gave light, and you chose for a time to enjoy his light.

36"I have testimony weightier than that of John. For the very work that the Father has given me to finish, and which I am doing, testifies that the Father has sent me. 37And the Father who sent me has himself testified concerning me. You have never heard his voice nor seen his form, 38nor does his word dwell in you, for you do not believe the one he sent. 39You diligently study[c] the Scriptures because you think that by them you possess eternal life. These are the Scriptures that testify about me, 40yet you refuse to come to me to have life.

---

c39 Or Study diligently (the imperative)

41I do not accept glory from human beings. 42But I know that you do not have the love of God ink you. 43I have come in my Father's name, and you do not accept me; if another comes in his own name, you will accept him. 44How can you believe when you accept glory from one another and do not seek the glory that comes from the one who alone is God? 45Do not think that I will accuse you before the Father; your accuser is Moses, on whom you have set your hope. 46If you believed Moses, you would believe me, for he wrote about me. 47But if you do not believe what he wrote, how will you believe what I say?"

Feeding the Five Thousand

6 After this Jesus went to the other side of the Sea of Galilee, also called the Sea of Tiberias.l) 2A large crowd kept following him, because they saw the signs that he was doing for the sick. 3Jesus went up the mountain and sat down there with his disciples. 4Now the Passover, the festival of the Jews, was near. 5When he looked up and saw a large crowd coming toward him, Jesus said to Philip, "Where are we to buy bread for these people to eat?" 6He said this to test him, for he himself knew what he was going to do. 7Philip answered him, "Six months' wagesm would not buy enough bread for each of them to get a little." 8One of his disciples, Andrew, Simon Peter's brother, said to him, 9"There is a boy here who has five barley loaves and two fish. But what are they among so many people?" 10Jesus said, "Make the people sit down." Now there was a great deal of grass in the place; so theyn sat down, about five thousand in all. 11Then Jesus took the loaves, and when he had given thanks, he distributed them to those who were seated; so also the fish, as much as they wanted. 12When they were satisfied, he told his disciples, "Gather up the fragments left over, so that nothing may be lost." 13So they gathered them up, and from the fragments of the five barley loaves, left by those who had eaten, they filled twelve baskets. 14When the people saw the sign that he had done, they began to say, "This is indeed the prophet who is to come into

41"I do not accept praise from men, 42but I know you. I know that you do not have the love of God in your hearts. 43I have come in my Father's name, and you do not accept me; but if someone else comes in his own name, you will accept him. 44How can you believe if you accept praise from one another, yet make no effort to obtain the praise that comes from the only Godd?

45"But do not think I will accuse you before the Father. Your accuser is Moses, on whom your hopes are set. 46If you believed Moses, you would believe me, for he wrote about me. 47But since you do not believe what he wrote, how are you going to believe what I say?"

Jesus Feeds the Five Thousand

6 Some time after this, Jesus crossed to the far shore of the Sea of Galilee (that is, the Sea of Tiberias), 2and a great crowd of people followed him because they saw the miraculous signs he had performed on the sick. 3Then Jesus went up on a mountainside and sat down with his disciples. 4The Jewish Passover Feast was near.

5When Jesus looked up and saw a great crowd coming toward him, he said to Philip, "Where shall we buy bread for these people to eat?" 6He asked this only to test him, for he already had in mind what he was going to do.

7Philip answered him, "Eight months' wagesa would not buy enough bread for each one to have a bite!"

8Another of his disciples, Andrew, Simon Peter's brother, spoke up, 9"Here is a boy with five small barley loaves and two small fish, but how far will they go among so many?"

10Jesus said, "Have the people sit down." There was plenty of grass in that place, and the men sat down, about five thousand of them. 11Jesus then took the loaves, gave thanks, and distributed to those who were seated as much as they wanted. He did the same with the fish.

12When they had all had enough to eat, he said to his disciples, "Gather the pieces that are left over. Let nothing be wasted." 13So they gathered them and filled twelve baskets with the pieces of the five barley loaves left over by those who had eaten.

14After the people saw the miraculous sign that Jesus did, they began to say, "Surely this is the Prophet who is to come

k Or among   l Gk of Galilee of Tiberias   m Gk Two hundred denarii; the denarius was the usual day's wage for a laborer   n Gk the men

c44 NIV note omits θεοῦ

d44 Some early manuscripts the Only One   a7 Greek two hundred denarii

the world."

15 When Jesus realized that they were about to come and take him by force to make him king, he withdrew again to the mountain by himself.

Jesus Walks on the Water

16 When evening came, his disciples went down to the sea, 17 got into a boat, and started across the sea to Capernaum. It was now dark, and Jesus had not yet come to them. 18 The sea became rough because a strong wind was blowing. 19 When they had rowed about three or four miles,[o] they saw Jesus walking on the sea and coming near the boat, and they were terrified. 20 But he said to them, "It is I;[p] do not be afraid." 21 Then they wanted to take him into the boat, and immediately the boat reached the land toward which they were going.

The Bread from Heaven

22 The next day the crowd that had stayed on the other side of the sea saw that there had been only one boat there. They also saw that Jesus had not got into the boat with his disciples, but that his disciples had gone away alone. 23 Then some boats from Tiberias came near the place where they had eaten the bread after the Lord had given thanks.[q] 24 So when the crowd saw that neither Jesus nor his disciples were there, they themselves got into the boats and went to Capernaum looking for Jesus.

25 When they found him on the other side of the sea, they said to him, "Rabbi, when did you come here?" 26 Jesus answered them, "Very truly, I tell you, you are looking for me, not because you saw signs, but because you ate your fill of the loaves. 27 Do not work for the food that perishes, but for the food that endures for eternal life, which the Son of Man will give you. For it is on him that God the Father has set his seal." 28 Then they said to him, "What must we do to perform the works of God?" 29 Jesus answered them, "This is the work of God, that you believe in him whom he has sent." 30 So they said to him, "What sign are you going to give us then, so that we may see it and believe you? What work are you performing? 31 Our ancestors ate the manna in the wilderness; as it is written, 'He gave them bread from heaven to eat.' " 32 Then Jesus said to them, "Very truly, I tell you, it was not Moses

[o] Gk *about twenty-five or thirty stadia* [p] Gk *I am* [q] Other ancient authorities lack *after the Lord had given thanks*

ἐρχόμενος εἰς τὸν κόσμον. **15** *Ἰησοῦς οὖν γνοὺς ὅτι μέλλουσιν ἔρχεσθαι καὶ ἁρπάζειν αὐτὸν ἵνα ποιήσωσιν βασιλέα, ἀνεχώρησεν πάλιν εἰς τὸ ὄρος αὐτὸς μόνος.*

16 *Ὡς δὲ ὀψία ἐγένετο κατέβησαν οἱ μαθηταὶ αὐτοῦ ἐπὶ τὴν θάλασσαν* **17** *καὶ ἐμβάντες εἰς πλοῖον ἤρχοντο πέραν τῆς θαλάσσης εἰς Καφαρναούμ. καὶ σκοτία ἤδη ἐγεγόνει καὶ οὔπω ἐληλύθει πρὸς αὐτοὺς ὁ Ἰησοῦς,* **18** *ἥ τε θάλασσα ἀνέμου μεγάλου πνέοντος διεγείρετο.* **19** *ἐληλακότες οὖν ὡς σταδίους εἴκοσι πέντε ἢ τριάκοντα θεωροῦσιν τὸν Ἰησοῦν περιπατοῦντα ἐπὶ τῆς θαλάσσης καὶ ἐγγὺς τοῦ πλοίου γινόμενον, καὶ ἐφοβήθησαν.* **20** *ὁ δὲ λέγει αὐτοῖς, Ἐγώ εἰμι· μὴ φοβεῖσθε.* **21** *ἤθελον οὖν λαβεῖν αὐτὸν εἰς τὸ πλοῖον, καὶ εὐθέως ἐγένετο τὸ πλοῖον ἐπὶ τῆς γῆς εἰς ἣν ὑπῆγον.*

22 *Τῇ ἐπαύριον ὁ ὄχλος ὁ ἑστηκὼς πέραν τῆς θαλάσσης εἶδον ὅτι πλοιάριον ἄλλο οὐκ ἦν ἐκεῖ εἰ μὴ ἓν καὶ ὅτι οὐ συνεισῆλθεν τοῖς μαθηταῖς αὐτοῦ ὁ Ἰησοῦς εἰς τὸ πλοῖον ἀλλὰ μόνοι οἱ μαθηταὶ αὐτοῦ ἀπῆλθον·* **23** *ἄλλα ἦλθεν πλοιά[ρια] ἐκ Τιβεριάδος ἐγγὺς τοῦ τόπου ὅπου ἔφαγον τὸν ἄρτον εὐχαριστήσαντος τοῦ κυρίου.* **24** *ὅτε οὖν εἶδεν ὁ ὄχλος ὅτι Ἰησοῦς οὐκ ἔστιν ἐκεῖ οὐδὲ οἱ μαθηταὶ αὐτοῦ, ἐνέβησαν αὐτοὶ εἰς τὰ πλοιάρια καὶ ἦλθον εἰς Καφαρναοὺμ ζητοῦντες τὸν Ἰησοῦν.* **25** *καὶ εὑρόντες αὐτὸν πέραν τῆς θαλάσσης εἶπον αὐτῷ, Ῥαββί, πότε ὧδε γέγονας;* **26** *ἀπεκρίθη αὐτοῖς ὁ Ἰησοῦς καὶ εἶπεν, Ἀμὴν ἀμὴν λέγω ὑμῖν, ζητεῖτέ με οὐχ ὅτι εἴδετε σημεῖα, ἀλλ᾽ ὅτι ἐφάγετε ἐκ τῶν ἄρτων καὶ ἐχορτάσθητε.* **27** *ἐργάζεσθε μὴ τὴν βρῶσιν τὴν ἀπολλυμένην ἀλλὰ τὴν βρῶσιν τὴν μένουσαν εἰς ζωὴν αἰώνιον, ἣν ὁ υἱὸς τοῦ ἀνθρώπου ὑμῖν δώσει· τοῦτον γὰρ ὁ πατὴρ ἐσφράγισεν ὁ θεός.* **28** *εἶπον οὖν πρὸς αὐτόν, Τί ποιῶμεν ἵνα ἐργαζώμεθα τὰ ἔργα τοῦ θεοῦ;* **29** *ἀπεκρίθη [ὁ] Ἰησοῦς καὶ εἶπεν αὐτοῖς, Τοῦτό ἐστιν τὸ ἔργον τοῦ θεοῦ, ἵνα πιστεύητε εἰς ὃν ἀπέστειλεν ἐκεῖνος.* **30** *εἶπον οὖν αὐτῷ, Τί οὖν ποιεῖς σὺ σημεῖον, ἵνα ἴδωμεν καὶ πιστεύσωμέν σοι; τί ἐργάζῃ;* **31** *οἱ πατέρες ἡμῶν τὸ μάννα ἔφαγον ἐν τῇ ἐρήμῳ, καθώς ἐστιν γεγραμμένον,* **Ἄρτον ἐκ τοῦ οὐρανοῦ ἔδωκεν αὐτοῖς φαγεῖν.** **32** *εἶπεν οὖν αὐτοῖς ὁ Ἰησοῦς, Ἀμὴν ἀμὴν λέγω ὑμῖν, οὐ Μωϋσῆς*

into the world." 15 Jesus, knowing that they intended to come and make him king by force, withdrew again to a mountain by himself.

Jesus Walks on the Water

16 When evening came, his disciples went down to the lake, 17 where they got into a boat and set off across the lake for Capernaum. By now it was dark, and Jesus had not yet joined them. 18 A strong wind was blowing and the waters grew rough. 19 When they had rowed three or three and a half miles,[b] they saw Jesus approaching the boat, walking on the water; and they were terrified. 20 But he said to them, "It is I; don't be afraid." 21 Then they were willing to take him into the boat, and immediately the boat reached the shore where they were heading.

22 The next day the crowd that had stayed on the opposite shore of the lake realized that only one boat had been there, and that Jesus had not entered it with his disciples, but that they had gone away alone. 23 Then some boats from Tiberias landed near the place where the people had eaten the bread after the Lord had given thanks. 24 Once the crowd realized that neither Jesus nor his disciples were there, they got into the boats and went to Capernaum in search of Jesus.

Jesus the Bread of Life

25 When they found him on the other side of the lake, they asked him, "Rabbi, when did you get here?"

26 Jesus answered, "I tell you the truth, you are looking for me, not because you saw miraculous signs but because you ate the loaves and had your fill. 27 Do not work for food that spoils, but for food that endures to eternal life, which the Son of Man will give you. On him God the Father has placed his seal of approval."

28 Then they asked him, "What must we do to do the works God requires?"

29 Jesus answered, "The work of God is this: to believe in the one he has sent."

30 So they asked him, "What miraculous sign then will you give that we may see it and believe you? What will you do? 31 Our forefathers ate the manna in the desert; as it is written: 'He gave them bread from heaven to eat.'[c]"

32 Jesus said to them, "I tell you the truth, it is not Moses who has given you the

[b] *19* Greek *rowed twenty-five or thirty stadia* (about 5 or 6 kilometers) [c] *31* Exodus 16:4; Neh. 9:15; Psalm 78:24,25

who gave you the bread from heaven, but it is my Father who gives you the true bread from heaven. 33For the bread of God is that which[r] comes down from heaven and gives life to the world." 34They said to him, "Sir, give us this bread always."

35 Jesus said to them, "I am the bread of life. Whoever comes to me will never be hungry, and whoever believes in me will never be thirsty. 36But I said to you that you have seen me and yet do not believe. 37Everything that the Father gives me will come to me, and anyone who comes to me I will never drive away; 38for I have come down from heaven, not to do my own will, but the will of him who sent me. 39And this is the will of him who sent me, that I should lose nothing of all that he has given me, but raise it up on the last day. 40This is indeed the will of my Father, that all who see the Son and believe in him may have eternal life; and I will raise them up on the last day."

41 Then the Jews began to complain about him because he said, "I am the bread that came down from heaven." 42They were saying, "Is not this Jesus, the son of Joseph, whose father and mother we know? How can he now say, 'I have come down from heaven'?" 43Jesus answered them, "Do not complain among yourselves. 44No one can come to me unless drawn by the Father who sent me; and I will raise that person up on the last day. 45It is written in the prophets, 'And they shall all be taught by God.' Everyone who has heard and learned from the Father comes to me. 46Not that anyone has seen the Father except the one who is from God; he has seen the Father. 47Very truly, I tell you, whoever believes has eternal life. 48I am the bread of life. 49Your ancestors ate the manna in the wilderness, and they died. 50This is the bread that comes down from heaven, so that one may eat of it and not die. 51I am the living bread that came down from heaven. Whoever eats of this bread will live forever; and the bread that I will give for the life of the world is my flesh."

δέδωκεν ὑμῖν τὸν ἄρτον ἐκ τοῦ οὐρανοῦ, ἀλλ' ὁ πατήρ μου δίδωσιν ὑμῖν τὸν ἄρτον ἐκ τοῦ οὐρανοῦ τὸν ἀληθινόν· 33 ὁ γὰρ ἄρτος τοῦ θεοῦ ἐστιν ὁ καταβαίνων ἐκ τοῦ οὐρανοῦ καὶ ζωὴν διδοὺς τῷ κόσμῳ.

34 Εἶπον οὖν πρὸς αὐτόν, Κύριε, πάντοτε δὸς ἡμῖν τὸν ἄρτον τοῦτον. 35 εἶπεν[a] αὐτοῖς ὁ Ἰησοῦς, Ἐγώ εἰμι ὁ ἄρτος τῆς ζωῆς· ὁ ἐρχόμενος πρὸς ἐμὲ οὐ μὴ πεινάσῃ, καὶ ὁ πιστεύων εἰς ἐμὲ οὐ μὴ διψήσει πώποτε. 36 ἀλλ' εἶπον ὑμῖν ὅτι καὶ ἑωράκατέ [με] καὶ οὐ πιστεύετε. 37 Πᾶν ὃ δίδωσίν μοι ὁ πατὴρ πρὸς ἐμὲ ἥξει, καὶ τὸν ἐρχόμενον πρὸς ἐμὲ οὐ μὴ ἐκβάλω ἔξω, 38 ὅτι καταβέβηκα ἀπὸ τοῦ οὐρανοῦ οὐχ ἵνα ποιῶ τὸ θέλημα τὸ ἐμὸν ἀλλὰ τὸ θέλημα τοῦ πέμψαντός με. 39 τοῦτο δέ ἐστιν τὸ θέλημα τοῦ πέμψαντός με, ἵνα πᾶν ὃ δέδωκέν μοι μὴ ἀπολέσω ἐξ αὐτοῦ, ἀλλὰ ἀναστήσω αὐτὸ [ἐν] τῇ ἐσχάτῃ ἡμέρᾳ. 40 τοῦτο γάρ ἐστιν τὸ θέλημα τοῦ πατρός μου, ἵνα πᾶς ὁ θεωρῶν τὸν υἱὸν καὶ πιστεύων εἰς αὐτὸν ἔχῃ ζωὴν αἰώνιον, καὶ ἀναστήσω αὐτὸν ἐγὼ [ἐν] τῇ ἐσχάτῃ ἡμέρᾳ.

41 Ἐγόγγυζον οὖν οἱ Ἰουδαῖοι περὶ αὐτοῦ ὅτι εἶπεν, Ἐγώ εἰμι ὁ ἄρτος ὁ καταβὰς ἐκ τοῦ οὐρανοῦ, 42 καὶ ἔλεγον, Οὐχ οὗτός ἐστιν Ἰησοῦς ὁ υἱὸς Ἰωσήφ, οὗ ἡμεῖς οἴδαμεν τὸν πατέρα καὶ τὴν μητέρα; πῶς νῦν λέγει ὅτι Ἐκ τοῦ οὐρανοῦ καταβέβηκα; 43 ἀπεκρίθη Ἰησοῦς καὶ εἶπεν αὐτοῖς, Μὴ γογγύζετε μετ' ἀλλήλων. 44 οὐδεὶς δύναται ἐλθεῖν πρός με ἐὰν μὴ ὁ πατὴρ ὁ πέμψας με ἑλκύσῃ αὐτόν, κἀγὼ ἀναστήσω αὐτὸν ἐν τῇ ἐσχάτῃ ἡμέρᾳ. 45 ἔστιν γεγραμμένον ἐν τοῖς προφήταις, Καὶ ἔσονται πάντες διδακτοὶ θεοῦ· πᾶς ὁ ἀκούσας παρὰ τοῦ πατρὸς καὶ μαθὼν ἔρχεται πρὸς ἐμέ. 46 οὐχ ὅτι τὸν πατέρα ἑώρακέν τις εἰ μὴ ὁ ὢν παρὰ τοῦ θεοῦ, οὗτος ἑώρακεν τὸν πατέρα. 47 ἀμὴν ἀμὴν λέγω ὑμῖν, ὁ πιστεύων ἔχει ζωὴν αἰώνιον. 48 ἐγώ εἰμι ὁ ἄρτος τῆς ζωῆς. 49 οἱ πατέρες ὑμῶν ἔφαγον ἐν τῇ ἐρήμῳ τὸ μάννα καὶ ἀπέθανον· 50 οὗτός ἐστιν ὁ ἄρτος ὁ ἐκ τοῦ οὐρανοῦ καταβαίνων, ἵνα τις ἐξ αὐτοῦ φάγῃ καὶ μὴ ἀποθάνῃ. 51 ἐγώ εἰμι ὁ ἄρτος ὁ ζῶν ὁ ἐκ τοῦ οὐρανοῦ καταβάς· ἐάν τις φάγῃ ἐκ τούτου τοῦ ἄρτου ζήσει εἰς τὸν αἰῶνα, καὶ ὁ ἄρτος δὲ ὃν ἐγὼ δώσω ἡ σάρξ μού ἐστιν ὑπὲρ τῆς τοῦ κόσμου ζωῆς.

bread from heaven, but it is my Father who gives you the true bread from heaven. 33For the bread of God is he who comes down from heaven and gives life to the world."

34"Sir," they said, "from now on give us this bread."

35Then Jesus declared, "I am the bread of life. He who comes to me will never go hungry, and he who believes in me will never be thirsty. 36But as I told you, you have seen me and still you do not believe. 37All that the Father gives me will come to me, and whoever comes to me I will never drive away. 38For I have come down from heaven not to do my will but to do the will of him who sent me. 39And this is the will of him who sent me, that I shall lose none of all that he has given me, but raise them up at the last day. 40For my Father's will is that everyone who looks to the Son and believes in him shall have eternal life, and I will raise him up at the last day."

41At this the Jews began to grumble about him because he said, "I am the bread that came down from heaven." 42They said, "Is this not Jesus, the son of Joseph, whose father and mother we know? How can he now say, 'I came down from heaven'?"

43"Stop grumbling among yourselves," Jesus answered. 44"No one can come to me unless the Father who sent me draws him, and I will raise him up at the last day. 45It is written in the Prophets: 'They will all be taught by God.'[d] Everyone who listens to the Father and learns from him comes to me. 46No one has seen the Father except the one who is from God; only he has seen the Father. 47I tell you the truth, he who believes has everlasting life. 48I am the bread of life. 49Your forefathers ate the manna in the desert, yet they died. 50But here is the bread that comes down from heaven, which a man may eat and not die. 51I am the living bread that came down from heaven. If anyone eats of this bread, he will live forever. This bread is my flesh, which I will give for the life of the world."

---

[r] Or he who

[a]35 NIV text adds οὖν †

[d]45 Isaiah 54:13

52 The Jews then disputed among themselves, saying, "How can this man give us his flesh to eat?" ⁵³So Jesus said to them, "Very truly, I tell you, unless you eat the flesh of the Son of Man and drink his blood, you have no life in you. ⁵⁴Those who eat my flesh and drink my blood have eternal life, and I will raise them up on the last day; ⁵⁵for my flesh is true food and my blood is true drink. ⁵⁶Those who eat my flesh and drink my blood abide in me, and I in them. ⁵⁷Just as the living Father sent me, and I live because of the Father, so whoever eats me will live because of me. ⁵⁸This is the bread that came down from heaven, not like that which your ancestors ate, and they died. But the one who eats this bread will live forever." ⁵⁹He said these things while he was teaching in the synagogue at Capernaum.

The Words of Eternal Life

60 When many of his disciples heard it, they said, "This teaching is difficult; who can accept it?" ⁶¹But Jesus, being aware that his disciples were complaining about it, said to them, "Does this offend you? ⁶²Then what if you were to see the Son of Man ascending to where he was before? ⁶³It is the spirit that gives life; the flesh is useless. The words that I have spoken to you are spirit and life. ⁶⁴But among you there are some who do not believe." For Jesus knew from the first who were the ones that did not believe, and who was the one that would betray him. ⁶⁵And he said, "For this reason I have told you that no one can come to me unless it is granted by the Father."

66 Because of this many of his disciples turned back and no longer went about with him. ⁶⁷So Jesus asked the twelve, "Do you also wish to go away?" ⁶⁸Simon Peter answered him, "Lord, to whom can we go? You have the words of eternal life. ⁶⁹We have come to believe and know that you are the Holy One of God."^s ⁷⁰Jesus answered them, "Did I not choose you, the twelve? Yet one of you is a devil." ⁷¹He was speaking of Judas son of Simon Iscariot,^t for he, though one of the twelve, was going to betray him.

52 Ἐμάχοντο οὖν πρὸς ἀλλήλους οἱ Ἰουδαῖοι λέγοντες, Πῶς δύναται οὗτος ἡμῖν δοῦναι τὴν σάρκα [αὐτοῦ] φαγεῖν; **53** εἶπεν οὖν αὐτοῖς ὁ Ἰησοῦς, Ἀμὴν ἀμὴν λέγω ὑμῖν, ἐὰν μὴ φάγητε τὴν σάρκα τοῦ υἱοῦ τοῦ ἀνθρώπου καὶ πίητε αὐτοῦ τὸ αἷμα, οὐκ ἔχετε ζωὴν ἐν ἑαυτοῖς. **54** ὁ τρώγων μου τὴν σάρκα καὶ πίνων μου τὸ αἷμα ἔχει ζωὴν αἰώνιον, κἀγὼ ἀναστήσω αὐτὸν τῇ ἐσχάτῃ ἡμέρᾳ. **55** ἡ γὰρ σάρξ μου ἀληθής ἐστιν βρῶσις, καὶ τὸ αἷμά μου ἀληθής ἐστιν πόσις. **56** ὁ τρώγων μου τὴν σάρκα καὶ πίνων μου τὸ αἷμα ἐν ἐμοὶ μένει κἀγὼ ἐν αὐτῷ. **57** καθὼς ἀπέστειλέν με ὁ ζῶν πατὴρ κἀγὼ ζῶ διὰ τὸν πατέρα, καὶ ὁ τρώγων με κἀκεῖνος ζήσει δι' ἐμέ. **58** οὗτός ἐστιν ὁ ἄρτος ὁ ἐξ οὐρανοῦ καταβάς, οὐ καθὼς ἔφαγον οἱ πατέρες^b καὶ ἀπέθανον· ὁ τρώγων τοῦτον τὸν ἄρτον ζήσει εἰς τὸν αἰῶνα. **59** Ταῦτα εἶπεν ἐν συναγωγῇ διδάσκων ἐν Καφαρναούμ.

60 Πολλοὶ οὖν ἀκούσαντες ἐκ τῶν μαθητῶν αὐτοῦ εἶπαν, Σκληρός ἐστιν ὁ λόγος οὗτος· τίς δύναται αὐτοῦ ἀκούειν; **61** εἰδὼς δὲ ὁ Ἰησοῦς ἐν ἑαυτῷ ὅτι γογγύζουσιν περὶ τούτου οἱ μαθηταὶ αὐτοῦ εἶπεν αὐτοῖς, Τοῦτο ὑμᾶς σκανδαλίζει; **62** ἐὰν οὖν θεωρῆτε τὸν υἱὸν τοῦ ἀνθρώπου ἀναβαίνοντα ὅπου ἦν τὸ πρότερον; **63** τὸ πνεῦμά ἐστιν τὸ ζῳοποιοῦν, ἡ σὰρξ οὐκ ὠφελεῖ οὐδέν· τὰ ῥήματα ἃ ἐγὼ λελάληκα ὑμῖν πνεῦμά ἐστιν καὶ ζωή ἐστιν. **64** ἀλλ' εἰσὶν ἐξ ὑμῶν τινες οἳ οὐ πιστεύουσιν. ᾔδει γὰρ ἐξ ἀρχῆς ὁ Ἰησοῦς τίνες εἰσὶν οἱ μὴ πιστεύοντες καὶ τίς ἐστιν ὁ παραδώσων αὐτόν. **65** καὶ ἔλεγεν, Διὰ τοῦτο εἴρηκα ὑμῖν ὅτι οὐδεὶς δύναται ἐλθεῖν πρός με ἐὰν μὴ ᾖ δεδομένον αὐτῷ ἐκ τοῦ πατρός.

66 Ἐκ τούτου πολλοὶ [ἐκ] τῶν μαθητῶν αὐτοῦ ἀπῆλθον εἰς τὰ ὀπίσω καὶ οὐκέτι μετ' αὐτοῦ περιεπάτουν. **67** εἶπεν οὖν ὁ Ἰησοῦς τοῖς δώδεκα, Μὴ καὶ ὑμεῖς θέλετε ὑπάγειν; **68** ἀπεκρίθη αὐτῷ Σίμων Πέτρος, Κύριε, πρὸς τίνα ἀπελευσόμεθα; ῥήματα ζωῆς αἰωνίου ἔχεις, **69** καὶ ἡμεῖς πεπιστεύκαμεν καὶ ἐγνώκαμεν ὅτι σὺ εἶ ὁ ἅγιος τοῦ θεοῦ^c. **70** ἀπεκρίθη αὐτοῖς ὁ Ἰησοῦς, Οὐκ ἐγὼ ὑμᾶς τοὺς δώδεκα ἐξελεξάμην; καὶ ἐξ ὑμῶν εἷς διάβολός ἐστιν. **71** ἔλεγεν δὲ τὸν Ἰούδαν Σίμωνος Ἰσκαριώτου^d· οὗτος γὰρ ἔμελλεν παραδιδόναι αὐτόν,

⁵²Then the Jews began to argue sharply among themselves, "How can this man give us his flesh to eat?"

⁵³Jesus said to them, "I tell you the truth, unless you eat the flesh of the Son of Man and drink his blood, you have no life in you. ⁵⁴Whoever eats my flesh and drinks my blood has eternal life, and I will raise him up at the last day. ⁵⁵For my flesh is real food and my blood is real drink. ⁵⁶Whoever eats my flesh and drinks my blood remains in me, and I in him. ⁵⁷Just as the living Father sent me and I live because of the Father, so the one who feeds on me will live because of me. ⁵⁸This is the bread that came down from heaven. Your forefathers ate manna and died, but he who feeds on this bread will live forever." ⁵⁹He said this while teaching in the synagogue in Capernaum.

Many Disciples Desert Jesus

⁶⁰On hearing it, many of his disciples said, "This is a hard teaching. Who can accept it?"

⁶¹Aware that his disciples were grumbling about this, Jesus said to them, "Does this offend you? ⁶²What if you see the Son of Man ascend to where he was before! ⁶³The Spirit gives life; the flesh counts for nothing. The words I have spoken to you are spirit^e and they are life. ⁶⁴Yet there are some of you who do not believe." For Jesus had known from the beginning which of them did not believe and who would betray him. ⁶⁵He went on to say, "This is why I told you that no one can come to me unless the Father has enabled him."

⁶⁶From this time many of his disciples turned back and no longer followed him.

⁶⁷"You do not want to leave too, do you?" Jesus asked the Twelve.

⁶⁸Simon Peter answered him, "Lord, to whom shall we go? You have the words of eternal life. ⁶⁹We believe and know that you are the Holy One of God."

⁷⁰Then Jesus replied, "Have I not chosen you, the Twelve? Yet one of you is a devil!" ⁷¹(He meant Judas, the son of Simon Iscariot, who, though one of the Twelve, was later to betray him.)

---

^sOther ancient authorities read *the Christ, the Son of the living God*   ^tOther ancient authorities read *Judas Iscariot son of Simon*; others, *Judas son of Simon from Karyot* (Kerioth)

^b58 NIV text adds ὑμῖν τὸ μάννα   ^c69 NRSV note s ὁ Χριστὸς ὁ υἱὸς τοῦ θεοῦ τοῦ ζῶντος.   ^d71 NRSV note t Ἰούδαν Σίμωνος Ἰσκαριώτην or Ἰούδαν Σίμωνος ἀπὸ Καριώτου †

^e63 Or *Spirit*

NRSV

The Unbelief of Jesus' Brothers

7 After this Jesus went about in Galilee. He did not wish[u] to go about in Judea because the Jews were looking for an opportunity to kill him. 2Now the Jewish festival of Booths[v] was near. 3So his brothers said to him, "Leave here and go to Judea so that your disciples also may see the works you are doing; 4for no one who wants[w] to be widely known acts in secret. If you do these things, show yourself to the world." 5(For not even his brothers believed in him.) 6Jesus said to them, "My time has not yet come, but your time is always here. 7The world cannot hate you, but it hates me because I testify against it that its works are evil. 8Go to the festival yourselves. I am not[x] going to this festival, for my time has not yet fully come." 9After saying this, he remained in Galilee.

Jesus at the Festival of Booths

10 But after his brothers had gone to the festival, then he also went, not publicly but as it were[y] in secret. 11The Jews were looking for him at the festival and saying, "Where is he?" 12And there was considerable complaining about him among the crowds. While some were saying, "He is a good man," others were saying, "No, he is deceiving the crowd." 13Yet no one would speak openly about him for fear of the Jews.

14 About the middle of the festival Jesus went up into the temple and began to teach. 15The Jews were astonished at it, saying, "How does this man have such learning,[z] when he has never been taught?" 16Then Jesus answered them, "My teaching is not mine but his who sent me. 17Anyone who resolves to do the will of God will know whether the teaching is from God or whether I am speaking on my own. 18Those who speak on their own seek their own glory; but the one who seeks the glory of him who sent him is true, and there is nothing false in him.

19 "Did not Moses give you the law? Yet none of you keeps the law. Why are you looking for an opportunity to kill me?" 20The crowd answered, "You have a

Greek

εἷς[e] ἐκ τῶν δώδεκα.

7 Καὶ μετὰ ταῦτα περιεπάτει ὁ Ἰησοῦς ἐν τῇ Γαλιλαίᾳ· οὐ γὰρ ἤθελεν[a] ἐν τῇ Ἰουδαίᾳ περιπατεῖν, ὅτι ἐζήτουν αὐτὸν οἱ Ἰουδαῖοι ἀποκτεῖναι. 2 ἦν δὲ ἐγγὺς ἡ ἑορτὴ τῶν Ἰουδαίων ἡ σκηνοπηγία. 3 εἶπον οὖν πρὸς αὐτὸν οἱ ἀδελφοὶ αὐτοῦ, Μετάβηθι ἐντεῦθεν καὶ ὕπαγε εἰς τὴν Ἰουδαίαν, ἵνα καὶ οἱ μαθηταί σου θεωρήσουσιν σοῦ[b] τὰ ἔργα ἃ ποιεῖς· 4 οὐδεὶς γάρ τι ἐν κρυπτῷ ποιεῖ καὶ ζητεῖ αὐτὸς[c] ἐν παρρησίᾳ εἶναι. εἰ ταῦτα ποιεῖς, φανέρωσον σεαυτὸν τῷ κόσμῳ. 5 οὐδὲ γὰρ οἱ ἀδελφοὶ αὐτοῦ ἐπίστευον εἰς αὐτόν. 6 λέγει οὖν αὐτοῖς ὁ Ἰησοῦς, Ὁ καιρὸς ὁ ἐμὸς οὔπω πάρεστιν, ὁ δὲ καιρὸς ὁ ὑμέτερος πάντοτέ ἐστιν ἕτοιμος. 7 οὐ δύναται ὁ κόσμος μισεῖν ὑμᾶς, ἐμὲ δὲ μισεῖ, ὅτι ἐγὼ μαρτυρῶ περὶ αὐτοῦ ὅτι τὰ ἔργα αὐτοῦ πονηρά ἐστιν. 8 ὑμεῖς ἀνάβητε εἰς τὴν ἑορτήν· ἐγὼ οὐκ[d] ἀναβαίνω εἰς τὴν ἑορτὴν ταύτην, ὅτι ὁ ἐμὸς καιρὸς οὔπω πεπλήρωται. 9 ταῦτα δὲ εἰπὼν αὐτὸς ἔμεινεν ἐν τῇ Γαλιλαίᾳ.

10 Ὡς δὲ ἀνέβησαν οἱ ἀδελφοὶ αὐτοῦ εἰς τὴν ἑορτήν, τότε καὶ αὐτὸς ἀνέβη οὐ φανερῶς ἀλλὰ [ὡς] ἐν κρυπτῷ. 11 οἱ οὖν Ἰουδαῖοι ἐζήτουν αὐτὸν ἐν τῇ ἑορτῇ καὶ ἔλεγον, Ποῦ ἐστιν ἐκεῖνος; 12 καὶ γογγυσμὸς περὶ αὐτοῦ ἦν πολὺς ἐν τοῖς ὄχλοις· οἱ μὲν ἔλεγον ὅτι Ἀγαθός ἐστιν, ἄλλοι [δὲ] ἔλεγον, Οὔ, ἀλλὰ πλανᾷ τὸν ὄχλον. 13 οὐδεὶς μέντοι παρρησίᾳ ἐλάλει περὶ αὐτοῦ διὰ τὸν φόβον τῶν Ἰουδαίων.

14 Ἤδη δὲ τῆς ἑορτῆς μεσούσης ἀνέβη Ἰησοῦς εἰς τὸ ἱερὸν καὶ ἐδίδασκεν. 15 ἐθαύμαζον οὖν οἱ Ἰουδαῖοι λέγοντες, Πῶς οὗτος γράμματα οἶδεν μὴ μεμαθηκώς; 16 ἀπεκρίθη οὖν αὐτοῖς [ὁ] Ἰησοῦς καὶ εἶπεν, Ἡ ἐμὴ διδαχὴ οὐκ ἔστιν ἐμὴ ἀλλὰ τοῦ πέμψαντός με· 17 ἐάν τις θέλῃ τὸ θέλημα αὐτοῦ ποιεῖν, γνώσεται περὶ τῆς διδαχῆς πότερον ἐκ τοῦ θεοῦ ἐστιν ἢ ἐγὼ ἀπ' ἐμαυτοῦ λαλῶ. 18 ὁ ἀφ' ἑαυτοῦ λαλῶν τὴν δόξαν τὴν ἰδίαν ζητεῖ· ὁ δὲ ζητῶν τὴν δόξαν τοῦ πέμψαντος αὐτὸν οὗτος ἀληθής ἐστιν καὶ ἀδικία ἐν αὐτῷ οὐκ ἔστιν. 19 οὐ Μωϋσῆς δέδωκεν ὑμῖν τὸν νόμον; καὶ οὐδεὶς ἐξ ὑμῶν ποιεῖ τὸν νόμον. τί με ζητεῖτε ἀποκτεῖναι; 20 ἀπεκρίθη ὁ ὄχλος, Δαιμόνιον ἔχεις·

NIV

Jesus Goes to the Feast of Tabernacles

7 After this, Jesus went around in Galilee, purposely staying away from Judea because the Jews there were waiting to take his life. 2But when the Jewish Feast of Tabernacles was near, 3Jesus' brothers said to him, "You ought to leave here and go to Judea, so that your disciples may see the miracles you do. 4No one who wants to become a public figure acts in secret. Since you are doing these things, show yourself to the world." 5For even his own brothers did not believe in him.

6Therefore Jesus told them, "The right time for me has not yet come; for you any time is right. 7The world cannot hate you, but it hates me because I testify that what it does is evil. 8You go to the Feast. I am not yet[a] going up to this Feast, because for me the right time has not yet come." 9Having said this, he stayed in Galilee.

10However, after his brothers had left for the Feast, he went also, not publicly, but in secret. 11Now at the Feast the Jews were watching for him and asking, "Where is that man?"

12Among the crowds there was widespread whispering about him. Some said, "He is a good man."

Others replied, "No, he deceives the people." 13But no one would say anything publicly about him for fear of the Jews.

Jesus Teaches at the Feast

14Not until halfway through the Feast did Jesus go up to the temple courts and begin to teach. 15The Jews were amazed and asked, "How did this man get such learning without having studied?"

16Jesus answered, "My teaching is not my own. It comes from him who sent me. 17If anyone chooses to do God's will, he will find out whether my teaching comes from God or whether I speak on my own. 18He who speaks on his own does so to gain honor for himself, but he who works for the honor of the one who sent him is a man of truth; there is nothing false about him. 19Has not Moses given you the law? Yet not one of you keeps the law. Why are you trying to kill me?"

20"You are demon-possessed," the crowd

---

u Other ancient authorities read *was not at liberty*
v Or *Tabernacles*   w Other ancient authorities read *wants it*   x Other ancient authorities add *yet*   y Other ancient authorities lack *as it were*   z Or *this man know his letters*

e71 NIV text adds ὢν †   a1 NRSV note u εἶχεν ἐξουσίαν
b3 NIV text omits σοῦ †   c4 NRSV note w αὐτὸ †
d8 NIV text and NRSV note x οὔπω; NIV note and NRSV text as UBS

a8 Some early manuscripts do not have *yet.*

demon! Who is trying to kill you?" 21Jesus answered them, "I performed one work, and all of you are astonished. 22Moses gave you circumcision (it is, of course, not from Moses, but from the patriarchs), and you circumcise a man on the sabbath. 23If a man receives circumcision on the sabbath in order that the law of Moses may not be broken, are you angry with me because I healed a man's whole body on the sabbath? 24Do not judge by appearances, but judge with right judgment."

Is This the Christ?

25 Now some of the people of Jerusalem were saying, "Is not this the man whom they are trying to kill? 26And here he is, speaking openly, but they say nothing to him! Can it be that the authorities really know that this is the Messiah?a 27Yet we know where this man is from; but when the Messiaha comes, no one will know where he is from." 28Then Jesus cried out as he was teaching in the temple, "You know me, and you know where I am from. I have not come on my own. But the one who sent me is true, and you do not know him. 29I know him, because I am from him, and he sent me." 30Then they tried to arrest him, but no one laid hands on him, because his hour had not yet come. 31Yet many in the crowd believed in him and were saying, "When the Messiaha comes, will he do more signs than this man has done?"b

Officers Are Sent to Arrest Jesus

32 The Pharisees heard the crowd muttering such things about him, and the chief priests and Pharisees sent temple police to arrest him. 33Jesus then said, "I will be with you a little while longer, and then I am going to him who sent me. 34You will search for me, but you will not find me; and where I am, you cannot come." 35The Jews said to one another, "Where does this man intend to go that we will not find him? Does he intend to go to the Dispersion among the Greeks and teach the Greeks? 36What does he mean by saying, 'You will search for me and you will not find me' and 'Where I am, you cannot come'?"

Rivers of Living Water

37 On the last day of the festival, the great day, while Jesus was standing there, he cried out, "Let anyone who is thirsty

---

τίς σε ζητεῖ ἀποκτεῖναι; 21 ἀπεκρίθη Ἰησοῦς καὶ εἶπεν αὐτοῖς, Ἓν ἔργον ἐποίησα καὶ πάντες θαυμάζετε. 22 διὰ τοῦτο Μωϋσῆς δέδωκεν ὑμῖν τὴν περιτομήν – οὐχ ὅτι ἐκ τοῦ Μωϋσέως ἐστὶν ἀλλ' ἐκ τῶν πατέρων – καὶ ἐν σαββάτῳ περιτέμνετε ἄνθρωπον. 23 εἰ περιτομὴν λαμβάνει ἄνθρωπος ἐν σαββάτῳ ἵνα μὴ λυθῇ ὁ νόμος Μωϋσέως, ἐμοὶ χολᾶτε ὅτι ὅλον ἄνθρωπον ὑγιῆ ἐποίησα ἐν σαββάτῳ; 24 μὴ κρίνετε κατ' ὄψιν, ἀλλὰ τὴν δικαίαν κρίσιν κρίνετε.

25 Ἔλεγον οὖν τινες ἐκ τῶν Ἱεροσολυμιτῶν, Οὐχ οὗτός ἐστιν ὃν ζητοῦσιν ἀποκτεῖναι; 26 καὶ ἴδε παρρησίᾳ λαλεῖ καὶ οὐδὲν αὐτῷ λέγουσιν. μήποτε ἀληθῶς ἔγνωσαν οἱ ἄρχοντες ὅτι οὗτός ἐστιν ὁ Χριστός; 27 ἀλλὰ τοῦτον οἴδαμεν πόθεν ἐστίν· ὁ δὲ Χριστὸς ὅταν ἔρχηται οὐδεὶς γινώσκει πόθεν ἐστίν. 28 ἔκραξεν οὖν ἐν τῷ ἱερῷ διδάσκων ὁ Ἰησοῦς καὶ λέγων, Κἀμὲ οἴδατε καὶ οἴδατε πόθεν εἰμί· καὶ ἀπ' ἐμαυτοῦ οὐκ ἐλήλυθα, ἀλλ' ἔστιν ἀληθινὸς ὁ πέμψας με, ὃν ὑμεῖς οὐκ οἴδατε· 29 ἐγὼ οἶδα αὐτόν, ὅτι παρ' αὐτοῦ εἰμι κἀκεῖνός με ἀπέστειλεν. 30 Ἐζήτουν οὖν αὐτὸν πιάσαι, καὶ οὐδεὶς ἐπέβαλεν ἐπ' αὐτὸν τὴν χεῖρα, ὅτι οὔπω ἐληλύθει ἡ ὥρα αὐτοῦ. 31 Ἐκ τοῦ ὄχλου δὲ πολλοὶ ἐπίστευσαν εἰς αὐτὸν καὶ ἔλεγον, Ὁ Χριστὸς ὅταν ἔλθῃ μὴ πλείονα σημεῖα ποιήσει ὧν οὗτος ἐποίησενe;

32 Ἤκουσαν οἱ Φαρισαῖοι τοῦ ὄχλου γογγύζοντος περὶ αὐτοῦ ταῦτα, καὶ ἀπέστειλαν οἱ ἀρχιερεῖς καὶ οἱ Φαρισαῖοι ὑπηρέτας ἵνα πιάσωσιν αὐτόν. 33 εἶπεν οὖν ὁ Ἰησοῦς, Ἔτι χρόνον μικρὸν μεθ' ὑμῶν εἰμι καὶ ὑπάγω πρὸς τὸν πέμψαντά με. 34 ζητήσετέ με καὶ οὐχ εὑρήσετέ [με], καὶ ὅπου εἰμὶ ἐγὼ ὑμεῖς οὐ δύνασθε ἐλθεῖν. 35 εἶπον οὖν οἱ Ἰουδαῖοι πρὸς ἑαυτούς, Ποῦ οὗτος μέλλει πορεύεσθαι ὅτι ἡμεῖς οὐχ εὑρήσομεν αὐτόν; μὴ εἰς τὴν διασπορὰν τῶν Ἑλλήνων μέλλει πορεύεσθαι καὶ διδάσκειν τοὺς Ἕλληνας; 36 τίς ἐστιν ὁ λόγος οὗτος ὃν εἶπεν, Ζητήσετέ με καὶ οὐχ εὑρήσετέ [με], καὶ ὅπου εἰμὶ ἐγὼ ὑμεῖς οὐ δύνασθε ἐλθεῖν;

37 Ἐν δὲ τῇ ἐσχάτῃ ἡμέρᾳ τῇ μεγάλῃ τῆς ἑορτῆς εἱστήκει ὁ Ἰησοῦς καὶ ἔκραξεν λέγων, Ἐάν τις διψᾷ ἐρχέσθω

---

answered. "Who is trying to kill you?"

21Jesus said to them, "I did one miracle, and you are all astonished. 22Yet, because Moses gave you circumcision (though actually it did not come from Moses, but from the patriarchs), you circumcise a child on the Sabbath. 23Now if a child can be circumcised on the Sabbath so that the law of Moses may not be broken, why are you angry with me for healing the whole man on the Sabbath? 24Stop judging by mere appearances, and make a right judgment."

Is Jesus the Christ?

25At that point some of the people of Jerusalem began to ask, "Isn't this the man they are trying to kill? 26Here he is, speaking publicly, and they are not saying a word to him. Have the authorities really concluded that he is the Christb? 27But we know where this man is from; when the Christ comes, no one will know where he is from."

28Then Jesus, still teaching in the temple courts, cried out, "Yes, you know me, and you know where I am from. I am not here on my own, but he who sent me is true. You do not know him, 29but I know him because I am from him and he sent me."

30At this they tried to seize him, but no one laid a hand on him, because his time had not yet come. 31Still, many in the crowd put their faith in him. They said, "When the Christ comes, will he do more miraculous signs than this man?"

32The Pharisees heard the crowd whispering such things about him. Then the chief priests and the Pharisees sent temple guards to arrest him.

33Jesus said, "I am with you for only a short time, and then I go to the one who sent me. 34You will look for me, but you will not find me; and where I am, you cannot come."

35The Jews said to one another, "Where does this man intend to go that we cannot find him? Will he go where our people live scattered among the Greeks, and teach the Greeks? 36What did he mean when he said, 'You will look for me, but you will not find me,' and 'Where I am, you cannot come'?"

37On the last and greatest day of the Feast, Jesus stood and said in a loud voice, "If anyone is thirsty, let him come to me and

---

a Or the Christ   b Other ancient authorities read is doing   e31 NRSV note b ποιεῖ   b26 Or Messiah; also in verses 27, 31, 41 and 42

NRSV

come to me, [38]and let the one who believes in me drink. As[c] the scripture has said, 'Out of the believer's heart[d] shall flow rivers of living water.' " [39]Now he said this about the Spirit, which believers in him were to receive; for as yet there was no Spirit,[e] because Jesus was not yet glorified.

Division among the People

[40] When they heard these words, some in the crowd said, "This is really the prophet." [41]Others said, "This is the Messiah."[a] But some asked, "Surely the Messiah[a] does not come from Galilee, does he? [42]Has not the scripture said that the Messiah[a] is descended from David and comes from Bethlehem, the village where David lived?" [43]So there was a division in the crowd because of him. [44]Some of them wanted to arrest him, but no one laid hands on him.

The Unbelief of Those in Authority

[45] Then the temple police went back to the chief priests and Pharisees, who asked them, "Why did you not arrest him?" [46]The police answered, "Never has anyone spoken like this!" [47]Then the Pharisees replied, "Surely you have not been deceived too, have you? [48]Has any one of the authorities or of the Pharisees believed in him? [49]But this crowd, which does not know the law—they are accursed." [50]Nicodemus, who had gone to Jesus[f] before, and who was one of them, asked, [51]"Our law does not judge people without first giving them a hearing to find out what they are doing, does it?" [52]They replied, "Surely you are not also from Galilee, are you? Search and you will see that no prophet is to arise from Galilee."

The Woman Caught in Adultery

8 [[53]Then each of them went home, [1]while Jesus went to the Mount of Olives. [2]Early in the morning he came again to the temple. All the people came to him and he sat down and began to teach them. [3]The scribes and the Pharisees brought a woman who had been caught in adultery; and making her stand before all of them, [4]they said to him, "Teacher, this woman was caught in the very act of committing adultery. [5]Now in the law Moses commanded us to stone such women. Now

NIV

drink. [38]Whoever believes in me, as[c] the Scripture has said, streams of living water will flow from within him." [39]By this he meant the Spirit, whom those who believed in him were later to receive. Up to that time the Spirit had not been given, since Jesus had not yet been glorified.

[40]On hearing his words, some of the people said, "Surely this man is the Prophet."

[41]Others said, "He is the Christ."

Still others asked, "How can the Christ come from Galilee? [42]Does not the Scripture say that the Christ will come from David's family[d] and from Bethlehem, the town where David lived?" [43]Thus the people were divided because of Jesus. [44]Some wanted to seize him, but no one laid a hand on him.

Unbelief of the Jewish Leaders

[45]Finally the temple guards went back to the chief priests and Pharisees, who asked them, "Why didn't you bring him in?"

[46]"No one ever spoke the way this man does," the guards declared.

[47]"You mean he has deceived you also?" the Pharisees retorted. [48]"Has any of the rulers or of the Pharisees believed in him? [49]No! But this mob that knows nothing of the law—there is a curse on them."

[50]Nicodemus, who had gone to Jesus earlier and who was one of their own number, asked, [51]"Does our law condemn anyone without first hearing him to find out what he is doing?"

[52]They replied, "Are you from Galilee, too? Look into it, and you will find that a prophet[e] does not come out of Galilee."

[The earliest manuscripts and many other ancient witnesses do not have John 7:53-8:11.]

[53]Then each went to his own home.

8 But Jesus went to the Mount of Olives. [2]At dawn he appeared again in the temple courts, where all the people gathered around him, and he sat down to teach them. [3]The teachers of the law and the Pharisees brought in a woman caught in adultery. They made her stand before the group [4]and said to Jesus, "Teacher, this woman was caught in the act of adultery. [5]In the Law Moses commanded us to stone such women. Now what do you say?"

---

[a] Or *the Christ* [c] Or *come to me and drink.* [38]*The one who believes in me, as* [d] Gk *out of his belly* [e] Other ancient authorities read *for as yet the Spirit* (others, *Holy Spirit*) *had not been given* [f] Gk *him*

[f]39 NRSV note e adds *[ἅγιον] δεδομένον* [g]52 NIV note adds *ὁ*

[c]37,38 Or */ If anyone is thirsty, let him come to me. / And let him drink,* [38]*who believes in me. / As* [d]42 Greek *seed* [e]52 Two early manuscripts *the Prophet*

NRSV

what do you say?" 6They said this to test him, so that they might have some charge to bring against him. Jesus bent down and wrote with his finger on the ground. 7When they kept on questioning him, he straightened up and said to them, "Let anyone among you who is without sin be the first to throw a stone at her." 8And once again he bent down and wrote on the ground.g 9When they heard it, they went away, one by one, beginning with the elders; and Jesus was left alone with the woman standing before him. 10Jesus straightened up and said to her, "Woman, where are they? Has no one condemned you?" 11She said, "No one, sir."h And Jesus said, "Neither do I condemn you. Go your way, and from now on do not sin again."]i

Jesus the Light of the World

12 Again Jesus spoke to them, saying, "I am the light of the world. Whoever follows me will never walk in darkness but will have the light of life." 13Then the Pharisees said to him, "You are testifying on your own behalf; your testimony is not valid." 14Jesus answered, "Even if I testify on my own behalf, my testimony is valid because I know where I have come from and where I am going, but you do not know where I come from or where I am going. 15You judge by human standards;j I judge no one. 16Yet even if I do judge, my judgment is valid; for it is not I alone who judge, but I and the Fatherk who sent me. 17In your law it is written that the testimony of two witnesses is valid. 18I testify on my own behalf, and the Father who sent me testifies on my behalf." 19Then they said to him, "Where is your Father?" Jesus answered, "You know neither me nor my Father. If you knew me, you would know my Father also." 20He spoke these words while he was teaching in the treasury of the temple, but no one arrested him, because his hour had not yet come.

Jesus Foretells His Death

21 Again he said to them, "I am going away, and you will search for me, but you will die in your sin. Where I am going, you cannot come." 22Then the Jews said, "Is he going to kill himself? Is that what he means by saying, 'Where I am going, you cannot

Greek

οὖν τί λέγεις; 6 τοῦτο δὲ ἔλεγον πειράζοντες αὐτόν, ἵνα ἔχωσιν κατηγορεῖν αὐτοῦ. ὁ δὲ Ἰησοῦς κάτω κύψας τῷ δακτύλῳ κατέγραφεν εἰς τὴν γῆν. 7 ὡς δὲ ἐπέμενον ἐρωτῶντες αὐτόν, ἀνέκυψεν καὶ εἶπεν αὐτοῖς, Ὁ ἀναμάρτητος ὑμῶν πρῶτος ἐπ᾽ αὐτὴν βαλέτω λίθον. 8 καὶ πάλιν κατακύψας ἔγραφεν εἰς τὴν γῆνa. 9 οἱ δὲ ἀκούσαντες ἐξήρχοντο εἷς καθ᾽ εἷς ἀρξάμενοι ἀπὸ τῶν πρεσβυτέρων καὶ κατελείφθη μόνος καὶ ἡ γυνὴ ἐν μέσῳ οὖσα. 10 ἀνακύψας δὲ ὁ Ἰησοῦς εἶπεν αὐτῇ, Γύναι, ποῦ εἰσιν; οὐδείς σε κατέκρινεν; 11 ἡ δὲ εἶπεν, Οὐδείς, κύριε. εἶπεν δὲ ὁ Ἰησοῦς, Οὐδὲ ἐγώ σε κατακρίνω· πορεύου, [καὶ] ἀπὸ τοῦ νῦν μηκέτι ἁμάρτανε.]]

12 Πάλιν οὖν αὐτοῖς ἐλάλησεν ὁ Ἰησοῦς λέγων, Ἐγώ εἰμι τὸ φῶς τοῦ κόσμου· ὁ ἀκολουθῶν ἐμοὶ οὐ μὴ περιπατήσῃ ἐν τῇ σκοτίᾳ, ἀλλ᾽ ἕξει τὸ φῶς τῆς ζωῆς. 13 εἶπον οὖν αὐτῷ οἱ Φαρισαῖοι, Σὺ περὶ σεαυτοῦ μαρτυρεῖς· ἡ μαρτυρία σου οὐκ ἔστιν ἀληθής. 14 ἀπεκρίθη Ἰησοῦς καὶ εἶπεν αὐτοῖς, Κἂν ἐγὼ μαρτυρῶ περὶ ἐμαυτοῦ, ἀληθής ἐστιν ἡ μαρτυρία μου, ὅτι οἶδα πόθεν ἦλθον καὶ ποῦ ὑπάγω· ὑμεῖς δὲ οὐκ οἴδατε πόθεν ἔρχομαι ἢ ποῦ ὑπάγω. 15 ὑμεῖς κατὰ τὴν σάρκα κρίνετε, ἐγὼ οὐ κρίνω οὐδένα. 16 καὶ ἐὰν κρίνω δὲ ἐγώ, ἡ κρίσις ἡ ἐμὴ ἀληθινή ἐστιν, ὅτι μόνος οὐκ εἰμί, ἀλλ᾽ ἐγὼ καὶ ὁ πέμψας με πατήρb. 17 καὶ ἐν τῷ νόμῳ δὲ τῷ ὑμετέρῳ γέγραπται ὅτι δύο ἀνθρώπων ἡ μαρτυρία ἀληθής ἐστιν. 18 ἐγώ εἰμι ὁ μαρτυρῶν περὶ ἐμαυτοῦ καὶ μαρτυρεῖ περὶ ἐμοῦ ὁ πέμψας με πατήρ. 19 ἔλεγον οὖν αὐτῷ, Ποῦ ἐστιν ὁ πατήρ σου; ἀπεκρίθη Ἰησοῦς, Οὔτε ἐμὲ οἴδατε οὔτε τὸν πατέρα μου· εἰ ἐμὲ ᾔδειτε, καὶ τὸν πατέρα μου ἂν ᾔδειτε. 20 Ταῦτα τὰ ῥήματα ἐλάλησεν ἐν τῷ γαζοφυλακίῳ διδάσκων ἐν τῷ ἱερῷ· καὶ οὐδεὶς ἐπίασεν αὐτόν, ὅτι οὔπω ἐληλύθει ἡ ὥρα αὐτοῦ.

21 Εἶπεν οὖν πάλιν αὐτοῖς, Ἐγὼ ὑπάγω καὶ ζητήσετέ με, καὶ ἐν τῇ ἁμαρτίᾳ ὑμῶν ἀποθανεῖσθε· ὅπου ἐγὼ ὑπάγω ὑμεῖς οὐ δύνασθε ἐλθεῖν. 22 ἔλεγον οὖν οἱ Ἰουδαῖοι, Μήτι ἀποκτενεῖ ἑαυτόν, ὅτι λέγει, Ὅπου ἐγὼ ὑπάγω ὑμεῖς οὐ δύνασθε ἐλθεῖν;

NIV

6They were using this question as a trap, in order to have a basis for accusing him.

But Jesus bent down and started to write on the ground with his finger. 7When they kept on questioning him, he straightened up and said to them, "If any one of you is without sin, let him be the first to throw a stone at her." 8Again he stooped down and wrote on the ground.

9At this, those who heard began to go away one at a time, the older ones first, until only Jesus was left, with the woman still standing there. 10Jesus straightened up and asked her, "Woman, where are they? Has no one condemned you?"

11"No one, sir," she said.

"Then neither do I condemn you," Jesus declared. "Go now and leave your life of sin."

The Validity of Jesus' Testimony

12When Jesus spoke again to the people, he said, "I am the light of the world. Whoever follows me will never walk in darkness, but will have the light of life."

13The Pharisees challenged him, "Here you are, appearing as your own witness; your testimony is not valid."

14Jesus answered, "Even if I testify on my own behalf, my testimony is valid, for I know where I came from and where I am going. But you have no idea where I come from or where I am going. 15You judge by human standards; I pass judgment on no one. 16But if I do judge, my decisions are right, because I am not alone. I stand with the Father, who sent me. 17In your own Law it is written that the testimony of two men is valid. 18I am one who testifies for myself; my other witness is the Father, who sent me."

19Then they asked him, "Where is your father?"

"You do not know me or my Father," Jesus replied. "If you knew me, you would know my Father also." 20He spoke these words while teaching in the temple area near the place where the offerings were put. Yet no one seized him, because his time had not yet come.

21Once more Jesus said to them, "I am going away, and you will look for me, and you will die in your sin. Where I go, you cannot come."

22This made the Jews ask, "Will he kill himself? Is that why he says, 'Where I go, you cannot come'?"

---

g Other ancient authorities add *the sins of each of them* h Or *Lord* i The most ancient authorities lack 7.53-8.11; other authorities add the passage here or after 7.36 or after 21.25 or after Luke 21.38, with variations of text; some mark the passage as doubtful. j Gk *according to the flesh* k Other ancient authorities read *he*

a8 NRSV note g adds ἑνὸς ἑκάστου αὐτῶν τὰς ἁμαρτίας † b16 NRSV note k omits πατήρ

NRSV

come'?" [23]He said to them, "You are from below, I am from above; you are of this world, I am not of this world. [24]I told you that you would die in your sins, for you will die in your sins unless you believe that I am he."[l] [25]They said to him, "Who are you?" Jesus said to them, "Why do I speak to you at all?[m] [26]I have much to say about you and much to condemn; but the one who sent me is true, and I declare to the world what I have heard from him." [27]They did not understand that he was speaking to them about the Father. [28]So Jesus said, "When you have lifted up the Son of Man, then you will realize that I am he,[l] and that I do nothing on my own, but I speak these things as the Father instructed me. [29]And the one who sent me is with me; he has not left me alone, for I always do what is pleasing to him." [30]As he was saying these things, many believed in him.

True Disciples

31 Then Jesus said to the Jews who had believed in him, "If you continue in my word, you are truly my disciples; [32]and you will know the truth, and the truth will make you free." [33]They answered him, "We are descendants of Abraham and have never been slaves to anyone. What do you mean by saying, 'You will be made free'?"

34 Jesus answered them, "Very truly, I tell you, everyone who commits sin is a slave to sin. [35]The slave does not have a permanent place in the household; the son has a place there forever. [36]So if the Son makes you free, you will be free indeed. [37]I know that you are descendants of Abraham; yet you look for an opportunity to kill me, because there is no place in you for my word. [38]I declare what I have seen in the Father's presence; as for you, you should do what you have heard from the Father."[n]

Jesus and Abraham

39 They answered him, "Abraham is our father." Jesus said to them, "If you were Abraham's children, you would be doing[o] what Abraham did, [40]but now you are trying to kill me, a man who has told you the truth that I heard from God. This is not what Abraham did. [41]You are indeed doing what your father does." They said to

Greek

23 καὶ ἔλεγεν αὐτοῖς, Ὑμεῖς ἐκ τῶν κάτω ἐστέ, ἐγὼ ἐκ τῶν ἄνω εἰμί· ὑμεῖς ἐκ τούτου τοῦ κόσμου ἐστέ, ἐγὼ οὐκ εἰμὶ ἐκ τοῦ κόσμου τούτου. **24** εἶπον οὖν ὑμῖν ὅτι ἀποθανεῖσθε ἐν ταῖς ἁμαρτίαις ὑμῶν· ἐὰν γὰρ μὴ πιστεύσητε ὅτι ἐγώ εἰμι, ἀποθανεῖσθε ἐν ταῖς ἁμαρτίαις ὑμῶν. **25** ἔλεγον οὖν αὐτῷ, Σὺ τίς εἶ; εἶπεν αὐτοῖς ὁ Ἰησοῦς, Τὴν ἀρχὴν ὅ τι καὶ λαλῶ ὑμῖν; **26** πολλὰ ἔχω περὶ ὑμῶν λαλεῖν καὶ κρίνειν, ἀλλ' ὁ πέμψας με ἀληθής ἐστιν, κἀγὼ ἃ ἤκουσα παρ' αὐτοῦ ταῦτα λαλῶ εἰς τὸν κόσμον. **27** οὐκ ἔγνωσαν ὅτι τὸν πατέρα αὐτοῖς ἔλεγεν. **28** εἶπεν οὖν [αὐτοῖς][c] ὁ Ἰησοῦς, Ὅταν ὑψώσητε τὸν υἱὸν τοῦ ἀνθρώπου, τότε γνώσεσθε ὅτι ἐγώ εἰμι, καὶ ἀπ' ἐμαυτοῦ ποιῶ οὐδέν, ἀλλὰ καθὼς ἐδίδαξέν με ὁ πατὴρ ταῦτα λαλῶ. **29** καὶ ὁ πέμψας με μετ' ἐμοῦ ἐστιν· οὐκ ἀφῆκέν με μόνον, ὅτι ἐγὼ τὰ ἀρεστὰ αὐτῷ ποιῶ πάντοτε. **30** Ταῦτα αὐτοῦ λαλοῦντος πολλοὶ ἐπίστευσαν εἰς αὐτόν.

31 Ἔλεγεν οὖν ὁ Ἰησοῦς πρὸς τοὺς πεπιστευκότας αὐτῷ Ἰουδαίους, Ἐὰν ὑμεῖς μείνητε ἐν τῷ λόγῳ τῷ ἐμῷ, ἀληθῶς μαθηταί μού ἐστε **32** καὶ γνώσεσθε τὴν ἀλήθειαν, καὶ ἡ ἀλήθεια ἐλευθερώσει ὑμᾶς. **33** ἀπεκρίθησαν πρὸς αὐτόν, Σπέρμα Ἀβραάμ ἐσμεν καὶ οὐδενὶ δεδουλεύκαμεν πώποτε· πῶς σὺ λέγεις ὅτι Ἐλεύθεροι γενήσεσθε; **34** ἀπεκρίθη αὐτοῖς ὁ Ἰησοῦς, Ἀμὴν ἀμὴν λέγω ὑμῖν ὅτι πᾶς ὁ ποιῶν τὴν ἁμαρτίαν δοῦλός ἐστιν τῆς ἁμαρτίας. **35** ὁ δὲ δοῦλος οὐ μένει ἐν τῇ οἰκίᾳ εἰς τὸν αἰῶνα, ὁ[d] υἱὸς μένει εἰς τὸν αἰῶνα. **36** ἐὰν οὖν ὁ υἱὸς ὑμᾶς ἐλευθερώσῃ, ὄντως ἐλεύθεροι ἔσεσθε. **37** οἶδα ὅτι σπέρμα Ἀβραάμ ἐστε· ἀλλὰ ζητεῖτέ με ἀποκτεῖναι, ὅτι ὁ λόγος ὁ ἐμὸς οὐ χωρεῖ ἐν ὑμῖν. **38** ἃ ἐγὼ ἑώρακα παρὰ τῷ πατρὶ λαλῶ· καὶ ὑμεῖς οὖν ἃ ἠκούσατε παρὰ τοῦ πατρὸς[e] ποιεῖτε.

39 Ἀπεκρίθησαν καὶ εἶπαν αὐτῷ, Ὁ πατὴρ ἡμῶν Ἀβραάμ ἐστιν. λέγει αὐτοῖς ὁ Ἰησοῦς, Εἰ τέκνα τοῦ Ἀβραάμ ἐστε[f], τὰ ἔργα τοῦ Ἀβραὰμ ἐποιεῖτε[g]· **40** νῦν δὲ ζητεῖτέ με ἀποκτεῖναι ἄνθρωπον ὃς τὴν ἀλήθειαν ὑμῖν λελάληκα ἣν ἤκουσα παρὰ τοῦ θεοῦ· τοῦτο Ἀβραὰμ οὐκ ἐποίησεν. **41** ὑμεῖς ποιεῖτε τὰ ἔργα τοῦ πατρὸς ὑμῶν.

NIV

[23]But he continued, "You are from below; I am from above. You are of this world; I am not of this world. [24]I told you that you would die in your sins; if you do not believe that I am [the one I claim to be,][a] you will indeed die in your sins."

[25]"Who are you?" they asked.

"Just what I have been claiming all along," Jesus replied. [26]"I have much to say in judgment of you. But he who sent me is reliable, and what I have heard from him I tell the world."

[27]They did not understand that he was telling them about his Father. [28]So Jesus said, "When you have lifted up the Son of Man, then you will know that I am [the one I claim to be] and that I do nothing on my own but speak just what the Father has taught me. [29]The one who sent me is with me; he has not left me alone, for I always do what pleases him." [30]Even as he spoke, many put their faith in him.

The Children of Abraham

[31]To the Jews who had believed him, Jesus said, "If you hold to my teaching, you are really my disciples. [32]Then you will know the truth, and the truth will set you free."

[33]They answered him, "We are Abraham's descendants[b] and have never been slaves of anyone. How can you say that we shall be set free?"

[34]Jesus replied, "I tell you the truth, everyone who sins is a slave to sin. [35]Now a slave has no permanent place in the family, but a son belongs to it forever. [36]So if the Son sets you free, you will be free indeed. [37]I know you are Abraham's descendants. Yet you are ready to kill me, because you have no room for my word. [38]I am telling you what I have seen in the Father's presence, and you do what you have heard from your father.[c]"

[39]"Abraham is our father," they answered.

"If you were Abraham's children," said Jesus, "then you would[d] do the things Abraham did. [40]As it is, you are determined to kill me, a man who has told you the truth that I heard from God. Abraham did not do such things. [41]You are doing the things your own father does."

---

[l]Gk *I am*   [m]Or *What I have told you from the beginning*   [n]Other ancient authorities read *you do what you have heard from your father*   [o]Other ancient authorities read *If you are Abraham's children, then do*

[c]28 NIV text omits αὐτοῖς †   [d]35 NIV text adds δὲ †   [e]38 NIV text and NRSV note n add ὑμῶν; NIV note and NRSV text as UBS   [f]39 NIV/NRSV text ἦτε; NIV/NRSV notes as UBS †   [g]39 NRSV note ο ποιεῖτε

[a]24 Or *I am he*; also in verse 28   [b]33 Greek *seed*; also in verse 37   [c]38 Or *presence. Therefore do what you have heard from the Father.*   [d]39 Some early manuscripts "If you are Abraham's children," said Jesus, "then

him, "We are not illegitimate children; we have one father, God himself." [42]Jesus said to them, "If God were your Father, you would love me, for I came from God and now I am here. I did not come on my own, but he sent me. [43]Why do you not understand what I say? It is because you cannot accept my word. [44]You are from your father the devil, and you choose to do your father's desires. He was a murderer from the beginning and does not stand in the truth, because there is no truth in him. When he lies, he speaks according to his own nature, for he is a liar and the father of lies. [45]But because I tell the truth, you do not believe me. [46]Which of you convicts me of sin? If I tell the truth, why do you not believe me? [47]Whoever is from God hears the words of God. The reason you do not hear them is that you are not from God."

48 The Jews answered him, "Are we not right in saying that you are a Samaritan and have a demon?" [49]Jesus answered, "I do not have a demon; but I honor my Father, and you dishonor me. [50]Yet I do not seek my own glory; there is one who seeks it and he is the judge. [51]Very truly, I tell you, whoever keeps my word will never see death." [52]The Jews said to him, "Now we know that you have a demon. Abraham died, and so did the prophets; yet you say, 'Whoever keeps my word will never taste death.' [53]Are you greater than our father Abraham, who died? The prophets also died. Who do you claim to be?" [54]Jesus answered, "If I glorify myself, my glory is nothing. It is my Father who glorifies me, he of whom you say, 'He is our God,' [55]though you do not know him. But I know him; if I would say that I do not know him, I would be a liar like you. But I do know him and I keep his word. [56]Your ancestor Abraham rejoiced that he would see my day; he saw it and was glad." [57]Then the Jews said to him, "You are not yet fifty years old, and have you seen Abraham?"[P] [58]Jesus said to them, "Very truly, I tell you,

εἶπαν [οὖν][h] αὐτῷ, Ἡμεῖς ἐκ πορνείας οὐ γεγεννήμεθα· ἕνα πατέρα ἔχομεν τὸν θεόν. **42** εἶπεν αὐτοῖς ὁ Ἰησοῦς, Εἰ ὁ θεὸς πατὴρ ὑμῶν ἦν ἠγαπᾶτε ἂν ἐμέ, ἐγὼ γὰρ ἐκ τοῦ θεοῦ ἐξῆλθον καὶ ἥκω· οὐδὲ γὰρ ἀπ᾽ ἐμαυτοῦ ἐλήλυθα, ἀλλ᾽ ἐκεῖνός με ἀπέστειλεν. **43** διὰ τί τὴν λαλιὰν τὴν ἐμὴν οὐ γινώσκετε; ὅτι οὐ δύνασθε ἀκούειν τὸν λόγον τὸν ἐμόν. **44** ὑμεῖς ἐκ τοῦ πατρὸς τοῦ διαβόλου ἐστὲ καὶ τὰς ἐπιθυμίας τοῦ πατρὸς ὑμῶν θέλετε ποιεῖν. ἐκεῖνος ἀνθρωποκτόνος ἦν ἀπ᾽ ἀρχῆς καὶ ἐν τῇ ἀληθείᾳ οὐκ ἔστηκεν, ὅτι οὐκ ἔστιν ἀλήθεια ἐν αὐτῷ. ὅταν λαλῇ τὸ ψεῦδος, ἐκ τῶν ἰδίων λαλεῖ, ὅτι ψεύστης ἐστὶν καὶ ὁ πατὴρ αὐτοῦ. **45** ἐγὼ δὲ ὅτι τὴν ἀλήθειαν λέγω, οὐ πιστεύετέ μοι. **46** τίς ἐξ ὑμῶν ἐλέγχει με περὶ ἁμαρτίας; εἰ ἀλήθειαν λέγω, διὰ τί ὑμεῖς οὐ πιστεύετέ μοι; **47** ὁ ὢν ἐκ τοῦ θεοῦ τὰ ῥήματα τοῦ θεοῦ ἀκούει· διὰ τοῦτο ὑμεῖς οὐκ ἀκούετε, ὅτι ἐκ τοῦ θεοῦ οὐκ ἐστέ.

48 Ἀπεκρίθησαν οἱ Ἰουδαῖοι καὶ εἶπαν αὐτῷ, Οὐ καλῶς λέγομεν ἡμεῖς ὅτι Σαμαρίτης εἶ σὺ καὶ δαιμόνιον ἔχεις; **49** ἀπεκρίθη Ἰησοῦς, Ἐγὼ δαιμόνιον οὐκ ἔχω, ἀλλὰ τιμῶ τὸν πατέρα μου, καὶ ὑμεῖς ἀτιμάζετέ με. **50** ἐγὼ δὲ οὐ ζητῶ τὴν δόξαν μου· ἔστιν ὁ ζητῶν καὶ κρίνων. **51** ἀμὴν ἀμὴν λέγω ὑμῖν, ἐάν τις τὸν ἐμὸν λόγον τηρήσῃ, θάνατον οὐ μὴ θεωρήσῃ εἰς τὸν αἰῶνα. **52** εἶπον [οὖν] αὐτῷ οἱ Ἰουδαῖοι, Νῦν ἐγνώκαμεν ὅτι δαιμόνιον ἔχεις. Ἀβραὰμ ἀπέθανεν καὶ οἱ προφῆται, καὶ σὺ λέγεις, Ἐάν τις τὸν λόγον μου τηρήσῃ, οὐ μὴ γεύσηται θανάτου εἰς τὸν αἰῶνα. **53** μὴ σὺ μείζων εἶ τοῦ πατρὸς ἡμῶν Ἀβραάμ, ὅστις ἀπέθανεν; καὶ οἱ προφῆται ἀπέθανον. τίνα σεαυτὸν ποιεῖς; **54** ἀπεκρίθη Ἰησοῦς, Ἐὰν ἐγὼ δοξάσω ἐμαυτόν, ἡ δόξα μου οὐδέν ἐστιν· ἔστιν ὁ πατήρ μου ὁ δοξάζων με, ὃν ὑμεῖς λέγετε ὅτι θεὸς ἡμῶν ἐστιν, **55** καὶ οὐκ ἐγνώκατε αὐτόν, ἐγὼ δὲ οἶδα αὐτόν. κἂν εἴπω ὅτι οὐκ οἶδα αὐτόν, ἔσομαι ὅμοιος ὑμῖν ψεύστης· ἀλλὰ οἶδα αὐτὸν καὶ τὸν λόγον αὐτοῦ τηρῶ. **56** Ἀβραὰμ ὁ πατὴρ ὑμῶν ἠγαλλιάσατο ἵνα ἴδῃ τὴν ἡμέραν τὴν ἐμήν, καὶ εἶδεν καὶ ἐχάρη. **57** εἶπον οὖν οἱ Ἰουδαῖοι πρὸς αὐτόν, Πεντήκοντα ἔτη οὔπω ἔχεις καὶ Ἀβραὰμ ἑώρακας[i]; **58** εἶπεν αὐτοῖς Ἰησοῦς, Ἀμὴν ἀμὴν λέγω ὑμῖν, πρὶν Ἀβραὰμ γενέσθαι

"We are not illegitimate children," they protested. "The only Father we have is God himself."

The Children of the Devil

[42]Jesus said to them, "If God were your Father, you would love me, for I came from God and now am here. I have not come on my own; but he sent me. [43]Why is my language not clear to you? Because you are unable to hear what I say. [44]You belong to your father, the devil, and you want to carry out your father's desire. He was a murderer from the beginning, not holding to the truth, for there is no truth in him. When he lies, he speaks his native language, for he is a liar and the father of lies. [45]Yet because I tell the truth, you do not believe me! [46]Can any of you prove me guilty of sin? If I am telling the truth, why don't you believe me? [47]He who belongs to God hears what God says. The reason you do not hear is that you do not belong to God."

The Claims of Jesus About Himself

[48]The Jews answered him, "Aren't we right in saying that you are a Samaritan and demon-possessed?"

[49]"I am not possessed by a demon," said Jesus, "but I honor my Father and you dishonor me. [50]I am not seeking glory for myself; but there is one who seeks it, and he is the judge. [51]I tell you the truth, if anyone keeps my word, he will never see death."

[52]At this the Jews exclaimed, "Now we know that you are demon-possessed! Abraham died and so did the prophets, yet you say that if anyone keeps your word, he will never taste death. [53]Are you greater than our father Abraham? He died, and so did the prophets. Who do you think you are?"

[54]Jesus replied, "If I glorify myself, my glory means nothing. My Father, whom you claim as your God, is the one who glorifies me. [55]Though you do not know him, I know him. If I said I did not, I would be a liar like you, but I do know him and keep his word. [56]Your father Abraham rejoiced at the thought of seeing my day; he saw it and was glad."

[57]"You are not yet fifty years old," the Jews said to him, "and you have seen Abraham!"

[58]"I tell you the truth," Jesus answered,

P Other ancient authorities read *has Abraham seen you?*   [h]41 NIV text omits οὖν †   [i]57 NRSV note p ἑώρακέν σε

NRSV
before Abraham was, I am." 59So they picked up stones to throw at him, but Jesus hid himself and went out of the temple.

A Man Born Blind Receives Sight

9 As he walked along, he saw a man blind from birth. 2His disciples asked him, "Rabbi, who sinned, this man or his parents, that he was born blind?" 3Jesus answered, "Neither this man nor his parents sinned; he was born blind so that God's works might be revealed in him. 4Weq must work the works of him who sent mer while it is day; night is coming when no one can work. 5As long as I am in the world, I am the light of the world." 6When he had said this, he spat on the ground and made mud with the saliva and spread the mud on the man's eyes, 7saying to him, "Go, wash in the pool of Siloam" (which means Sent). Then he went and washed and came back able to see. 8The neighbors and those who had seen him before as a beggar began to ask, "Is this not the man who used to sit and beg?" 9Some were saying, "It is he." Others were saying, "No, but it is someone like him." He kept saying, "I am the man." 10But they kept asking him, "Then how were your eyes opened?" 11He answered, "The man called Jesus made mud, spread it on my eyes, and said to me, 'Go to Siloam and wash.' Then I went and washed and received my sight." 12They said to him, "Where is he?" He said, "I do not know."

The Pharisees Investigate the Healing

13 They brought to the Pharisees the man who had formerly been blind. 14Now it was a sabbath day when Jesus made the mud and opened his eyes. 15Then the Pharisees also began to ask him how he had received his sight. He said to them, "He put mud on my eyes. Then I washed, and now I see." 16Some of the Pharisees said, "This man is not from God, for he does not observe the sabbath." But others said, "How can a man who is a sinner perform such signs?" And they were divided. 17So they said again to the blind man, "What do you say about him? It was your eyes he opened." He said, "He is a prophet."

18 The Jews did not believe that he had

ἐγὼ εἰμί. 59 ἦραν οὖν λίθους ἵνα βάλωσιν ἐπ' αὐτόν. Ἰησοῦς δὲ ἐκρύβη καὶ ἐξῆλθεν ἐκ τοῦ ἱεροῦ.

9 Καὶ παράγων εἶδεν ἄνθρωπον τυφλὸν ἐκ γενετῆς. 2 καὶ ἠρώτησαν αὐτὸν οἱ μαθηταὶ αὐτοῦ λέγοντες, Ῥαββί, τίς ἥμαρτεν, οὗτος ἢ οἱ γονεῖς αὐτοῦ, ἵνα τυφλὸς γεννηθῇ; 3 ἀπεκρίθη Ἰησοῦς, Οὔτε οὗτος ἥμαρτεν οὔτε οἱ γονεῖς αὐτοῦ, ἀλλ' ἵνα φανερωθῇ τὰ ἔργα τοῦ θεοῦ ἐν αὐτῷ. 4 ἡμᾶςa δεῖ ἐργάζεσθαι τὰ ἔργα τοῦ πέμψαντός μεb ἕως ἡμέρα ἐστίν· ἔρχεται νὺξ ὅτε οὐδεὶς δύναται ἐργάζεσθαι. 5 ὅταν ἐν τῷ κόσμῳ ὦ, φῶς εἰμι τοῦ κόσμου. 6 ταῦτα εἰπὼν ἔπτυσεν χαμαὶ καὶ ἐποίησεν πηλὸν ἐκ τοῦ πτύσματος καὶ ἐπέχρισεν αὐτοῦ τὸν πηλὸν ἐπὶ τοὺς ὀφθαλμοὺς 7 καὶ εἶπεν αὐτῷ, Ὕπαγε νίψαι εἰς τὴν κολυμβήθραν τοῦ Σιλωάμ (ὃ ἑρμηνεύεται Ἀπεσταλμένος). ἀπῆλθεν οὖν καὶ ἐνίψατο καὶ ἦλθεν βλέπων. 8 Οἱ οὖν γείτονες καὶ οἱ θεωροῦντες αὐτὸν τὸ πρότερον ὅτι προσαίτης ἦν ἔλεγον, Οὐχ οὗτός ἐστιν ὁ καθήμενος καὶ προσαιτῶν; 9 ἄλλοι ἔλεγον ὅτι Οὗτός ἐστιν, ἄλλοι ἔλεγον, Οὐχί, ἀλλὰ ὅμοιος αὐτῷ ἐστιν. ἐκεῖνος ἔλεγεν ὅτι Ἐγώ εἰμι. 10 ἔλεγον οὖν αὐτῷ, Πῶς [οὖν] ἠνεῴχθησάν σου οἱ ὀφθαλμοί; 11 ἀπεκρίθη ἐκεῖνος, Ὁ ἄνθρωπος ὁ λεγόμενος Ἰησοῦς πηλὸν ἐποίησεν καὶ ἐπέχρισέν μου τοὺς ὀφθαλμοὺς καὶ εἶπέν μοι ὅτι Ὕπαγε εἰς τὸν Σιλωὰμ καὶ νίψαι· ἀπελθὼν οὖν καὶ νιψάμενος ἀνέβλεψα. 12 καὶ εἶπαν αὐτῷ, Ποῦ ἐστιν ἐκεῖνος; λέγει, Οὐκ οἶδα.

13 Ἄγουσιν αὐτὸν πρὸς τοὺς Φαρισαίους τόν ποτε τυφλόν. 14 ἦν δὲ σάββατον ἐν ᾗ ἡμέρα τὸν πηλὸν ἐποίησεν ὁ Ἰησοῦς καὶ ἀνέῳξεν αὐτοῦ τοὺς ὀφθαλμούς. 15 πάλιν οὖν ἠρώτων αὐτὸν καὶ οἱ Φαρισαῖοι πῶς ἀνέβλεψεν. ὁ δὲ εἶπεν αὐτοῖς, Πηλὸν ἐπέθηκέν μου ἐπὶ τοὺς ὀφθαλμούς, καὶ ἐνιψάμην καὶ βλέπω. 16 ἔλεγον οὖν ἐκ τῶν Φαρισαίων τινές, Οὐκ ἔστιν οὗτος παρὰ θεοῦ ὁ ἄνθρωπος, ὅτι τὸ σάββατον οὐ τηρεῖ. ἄλλοι [δὲ] ἔλεγον, Πῶς δύναται ἄνθρωπος ἁμαρτωλὸς τοιαῦτα σημεῖα ποιεῖν; καὶ σχίσμα ἦν ἐν αὐτοῖς. 17 λέγουσιν οὖν τῷ τυφλῷ πάλιν, Τί σὺ λέγεις περὶ αὐτοῦ, ὅτι ἠνέῳξέν σου τοὺς ὀφθαλμούς; ὁ δὲ εἶπεν ὅτι Προφήτης ἐστίν. 18 Οὐκ ἐπίστευσαν οὖν οἱ Ἰουδαῖοι περὶ αὐτοῦ ὅτι ἦν

NIV
"before Abraham was born, I am!" 59At this, they picked up stones to stone him, but Jesus hid himself, slipping away from the temple grounds.

Jesus Heals a Man Born Blind

9 As he went along, he saw a man blind from birth. 2His disciples asked him, "Rabbi, who sinned, this man or his parents, that he was born blind?"

3"Neither this man nor his parents sinned," said Jesus, "but this happened so that the work of God might be displayed in his life. 4As long as it is day, we must do the work of him who sent me. Night is coming, when no one can work. 5While I am in the world, I am the light of the world."

6Having said this, he spit on the ground, made some mud with the saliva, and put it on the man's eyes. 7"Go," he told him, "wash in the Pool of Siloam" (this word means Sent). So the man went and washed, and came home seeing.

8His neighbors and those who had formerly seen him begging asked, "Isn't this the same man who used to sit and beg?" 9Some claimed that he was.

Others said, "No, he only looks like him." But he himself insisted, "I am the man."

10"How then were your eyes opened?" they demanded.

11He replied, "The man they call Jesus made some mud and put it on my eyes. He told me to go to Siloam and wash. So I went and washed, and then I could see."

12"Where is this man?" they asked him.
"I don't know," he said.

The Pharisees Investigate the Healing

13They brought to the Pharisees the man who had been blind. 14Now the day on which Jesus had made the mud and opened the man's eyes was a Sabbath. 15Therefore the Pharisees also asked him how he had received his sight. "He put mud on my eyes," the man replied, "and I washed, and now I see."

16Some of the Pharisees said, "This man is not from God, for he does not keep the Sabbath."

But others asked, "How can a sinner do such miraculous signs?" So they were divided.

17Finally they turned again to the blind man, "What have you to say about him? It was your eyes he opened."

The man replied, "He is a prophet."

18The Jews still did not believe that he

q Other ancient authorities read *I*   r Other ancient authorities read *us*

a4 NRSV note q ἐμέ   b4 NRSV note r ἡμᾶς

been blind and had received his sight until they called the parents of the man who had received his sight [19]and asked them, "Is this your son, who you say was born blind? How then does he now see?" [20]His parents answered, "We know that this is our son, and that he was born blind; [21]but we do not know how it is that now he sees, nor do we know who opened his eyes. Ask him; he is of age. He will speak for himself." [22]His parents said this because they were afraid of the Jews; for the Jews had already agreed that anyone who confessed Jesus[s] to be the Messiah[t] would be put out of the synagogue. [23]Therefore his parents said, "He is of age; ask him."

24 So for the second time they called the man who had been blind, and they said to him, "Give glory to God! We know that this man is a sinner." [25]He answered, "I do not know whether he is a sinner. One thing I do know, that though I was blind, now I see." [26]They said to him, "What did he do to you? How did he open your eyes?" [27]He answered them, "I have told you already, and you would not listen. Why do you want to hear it again? Do you also want to become his disciples?" [28]Then they reviled him, saying, "You are his disciple, but we are disciples of Moses. [29]We know that God has spoken to Moses, but as for this man, we do not know where he comes from." [30]The man answered, "Here is an astonishing thing! You do not know where he comes from, and yet he opened my eyes. [31]We know that God does not listen to sinners, but he does listen to one who worships him and obeys his will. [32]Never since the world began has it been heard that anyone opened the eyes of a person born blind. [33]If this man were not from God, he could do nothing." [34]They answered him, "You were born entirely in sins, and are you trying to teach us?" And they drove him out.

Spiritual Blindness

35 Jesus heard that they had driven him out, and when he found him, he said, "Do you believe in the Son of Man?"[u] [36]He answered, "And who is he, sir?[v] Tell me, so that I may believe in him." [37]Jesus said to him, "You have seen him, and the one speaking with you is he." [38]He said, "Lord,[v]

τυφλὸς καὶ ἀνέβλεψεν ἕως ὅτου ἐφώνησαν τοὺς γονεῖς αὐτοῦ τοῦ ἀναβλέψαντος[c] 19 καὶ ἠρώτησαν αὐτοὺς λέγοντες, Οὗτός ἐστιν ὁ υἱὸς ὑμῶν, ὃν ὑμεῖς λέγετε ὅτι τυφλὸς ἐγεννήθη; πῶς οὖν βλέπει ἄρτι; 20 ἀπεκρίθησαν οὖν οἱ γονεῖς αὐτοῦ καὶ εἶπαν, Οἴδαμεν ὅτι οὗτός ἐστιν ὁ υἱὸς ἡμῶν καὶ ὅτι τυφλὸς ἐγεννήθη· 21 πῶς δὲ νῦν βλέπει οὐκ οἴδαμεν, ἢ τίς ἤνοιξεν αὐτοῦ τοὺς ὀφθαλμοὺς ἡμεῖς οὐκ οἴδαμεν· αὐτὸν ἐρωτήσατε, ἡλικίαν ἔχει, αὐτὸς περὶ ἑαυτοῦ λαλήσει. 22 ταῦτα εἶπαν οἱ γονεῖς αὐτοῦ ὅτι ἐφοβοῦντο τοὺς Ἰουδαίους· ἤδη γὰρ συνετέθειντο οἱ Ἰουδαῖοι ἵνα ἐάν τις αὐτὸν ὁμολογήσῃ Χριστόν, ἀποσυνάγωγος γένηται. 23 διὰ τοῦτο οἱ γονεῖς αὐτοῦ εἶπαν ὅτι Ἡλικίαν ἔχει, αὐτὸν ἐπερωτήσατε.

24 Ἐφώνησαν οὖν τὸν ἄνθρωπον ἐκ δευτέρου ὃς ἦν τυφλὸς καὶ εἶπαν αὐτῷ, Δὸς δόξαν τῷ θεῷ· ἡμεῖς οἴδαμεν ὅτι οὗτος ὁ ἄνθρωπος ἁμαρτωλός ἐστιν. 25 ἀπεκρίθη οὖν ἐκεῖνος, Εἰ ἁμαρτωλός ἐστιν οὐκ οἶδα· ἓν οἶδα ὅτι τυφλὸς ὢν ἄρτι βλέπω. 26 εἶπον οὖν αὐτῷ, Τί ἐποίησέν σοι; πῶς ἤνοιξέν σου τοὺς ὀφθαλμούς; 27 ἀπεκρίθη αὐτοῖς, Εἶπον ὑμῖν ἤδη καὶ οὐκ ἠκούσατε· τί πάλιν θέλετε ἀκούειν; μὴ καὶ ὑμεῖς θέλετε αὐτοῦ μαθηταὶ γενέσθαι; 28 καὶ ἐλοιδόρησαν αὐτὸν καὶ εἶπον, Σὺ μαθητὴς εἶ ἐκείνου, ἡμεῖς δὲ τοῦ Μωϋσέως ἐσμὲν μαθηταί· 29 ἡμεῖς οἴδαμεν ὅτι Μωϋσεῖ λελάληκεν ὁ θεός, τοῦτον δὲ οὐκ οἴδαμεν πόθεν ἐστίν. 30 ἀπεκρίθη ὁ ἄνθρωπος καὶ εἶπεν αὐτοῖς, Ἐν τούτῳ γὰρ τὸ θαυμαστόν ἐστιν, ὅτι ὑμεῖς οὐκ οἴδατε πόθεν ἐστίν, καὶ ἤνοιξέν μου τοὺς ὀφθαλμούς. 31 οἴδαμεν ὅτι ἁμαρτωλῶν ὁ θεὸς οὐκ ἀκούει, ἀλλ' ἐάν τις θεοσεβὴς ᾖ καὶ τὸ θέλημα αὐτοῦ ποιῇ τούτου ἀκούει. 32 ἐκ τοῦ αἰῶνος οὐκ ἠκούσθη ὅτι ἠνέῳξέν τις ὀφθαλμοὺς τυφλοῦ γεγεννημένου· 33 εἰ μὴ ἦν οὗτος παρὰ θεοῦ, οὐκ ἠδύνατο ποιεῖν οὐδέν. 34 ἀπεκρίθησαν καὶ εἶπαν αὐτῷ, Ἐν ἁμαρτίαις σὺ ἐγεννήθης ὅλος καὶ σὺ διδάσκεις ἡμᾶς; καὶ ἐξέβαλον αὐτὸν ἔξω.

35 Ἤκουσεν Ἰησοῦς ὅτι ἐξέβαλον αὐτὸν ἔξω καὶ εὑρὼν αὐτὸν εἶπεν, Σὺ πιστεύεις εἰς τὸν υἱὸν τοῦ ἀνθρώπου[d]; 36 ἀπεκρίθη ἐκεῖνος καὶ εἶπεν, Καὶ τίς ἐστιν, κύριε, ἵνα πιστεύσω εἰς αὐτόν; 37 εἶπεν αὐτῷ ὁ Ἰησοῦς, Καὶ ἑώρακας αὐτὸν καὶ ὁ λαλῶν μετὰ σοῦ ἐκεῖνός ἐστιν. 38 ὁ δὲ ἔφη, Πιστεύω,

had been blind and had received his sight until they sent for the man's parents. [19]"Is this your son?" they asked. "Is this the one you say was born blind? How is it that now he can see?"

[20]"We know he is our son," the parents answered, "and we know he was born blind. [21]But how he can see now, or who opened his eyes, we don't know. Ask him. He is of age; he will speak for himself." [22]His parents said this because they were afraid of the Jews, for already the Jews had decided that anyone who acknowledged that Jesus was the Christ[a] would be put out of the synagogue. [23]That was why his parents said, "He is of age; ask him."

[24]A second time they summoned the man who had been blind. "Give glory to God,[b]" they said. "We know this man is a sinner."

[25]He replied, "Whether he is a sinner or not, I don't know. One thing I do know. I was blind but now I see!"

[26]Then they asked him, "What did he do to you? How did he open your eyes?"

[27]He answered, "I have told you already and you did not listen. Why do you want to hear it again? Do you want to become his disciples, too?"

[28]Then they hurled insults at him and said, "You are this fellow's disciple! We are disciples of Moses! [29]We know that God spoke to Moses, but as for this fellow, we don't even know where he comes from."

[30]The man answered, "Now that is remarkable! You don't know where he comes from, yet he opened my eyes. [31]We know that God does not listen to sinners. He listens to the godly man who does his will. [32]Nobody has ever heard of opening the eyes of a man born blind. [33]If this man were not from God, he could do nothing."

[34]To this they replied, "You were steeped in sin at birth; how dare you lecture us!" And they threw him out.

Spiritual Blindness

[35]Jesus heard that they had thrown him out, and when he found him, he said, "Do you believe in the Son of Man?"

[36]"Who is he, sir?" the man asked. "Tell me so that I may believe in him."

[37]Jesus said, "You have now seen him; in fact, he is the one speaking with you."

[38]Then the man said, "Lord, I believe,"

---

[s] Gk *him*   [t] Or *the Christ*   [u] Other ancient authorities read *the Son of God*   [v] *Sir* and *Lord* translate the same Greek word

[c]18 NIV text omits τοῦ ἀναβλέψαντος †
[d]35 NRSV note u θεοῦ

[a]22 Or *Messiah*   [b]24 A solemn charge to tell the truth (see Joshua 7:19)

I believe." And he worshiped him. [39]Jesus said, "I came into this world for judgment so that those who do not see may see, and those who do see may become blind." [40]Some of the Pharisees near him heard this and said to him, "Surely we are not blind, are we?" [41]Jesus said to them, "If you were blind, you would not have sin. But now that you say, 'We see,' your sin remains.

Jesus the Good Shepherd

10 "Very truly, I tell you, anyone who does not enter the sheepfold by the gate but climbs in by another way is a thief and a bandit. [2]The one who enters by the gate is the shepherd of the sheep. [3]The gatekeeper opens the gate for him, and the sheep hear his voice. He calls his own sheep by name and leads them out. [4]When he has brought out all his own, he goes ahead of them, and the sheep follow him because they know his voice. [5]They will not follow a stranger, but they will run from him because they do not know the voice of strangers." [6]Jesus used this figure of speech with them, but they did not understand what he was saying to them.

7 So again Jesus said to them, "Very truly, I tell you, I am the gate for the sheep. [8]All who came before me are thieves and bandits; but the sheep did not listen to them. [9]I am the gate. Whoever enters by me will be saved, and will come in and go out and find pasture. [10]The thief comes only to steal and kill and destroy. I came that they may have life, and have it abundantly.

11 "I am the good shepherd. The good shepherd lays down his life for the sheep. [12]The hired hand, who is not the shepherd and does not own the sheep, sees the wolf coming and leaves the sheep and runs away—and the wolf snatches them and scatters them. [13]The hired hand runs away because a hired hand does not care for the sheep. [14]I am the good shepherd. I know my own and my own know me, [15]just as the Father knows me and I know the Father. And I lay down my life for the sheep. [16]I have other sheep that do not belong to this fold. I must bring them also, and they

κύριε· καὶ προσεκύνησεν αὐτῷ. **39** καὶ εἶπεν ὁ Ἰησοῦς, Εἰς κρίμα ἐγὼ εἰς τὸν κόσμον τοῦτον ἦλθον, ἵνα οἱ μὴ βλέποντες βλέπωσιν καὶ οἱ βλέποντες τυφλοὶ γένωνται.

40 Ἤκουσαν ἐκ τῶν Φαρισαίων ταῦτα οἱ μετ' αὐτοῦ ὄντες καὶ εἶπον αὐτῷ, Μὴ καὶ ἡμεῖς τυφλοί ἐσμεν; **41** εἶπεν αὐτοῖς ὁ Ἰησοῦς, Εἰ τυφλοὶ ἦτε, οὐκ ἂν εἴχετε ἁμαρτίαν· νῦν δὲ λέγετε ὅτι Βλέπομεν, ἡ ἁμαρτία ὑμῶν μένει.

10 Ἀμὴν ἀμὴν λέγω ὑμῖν, ὁ μὴ εἰσερχόμενος διὰ τῆς θύρας εἰς τὴν αὐλὴν τῶν προβάτων ἀλλὰ ἀναβαίνων ἀλλαχόθεν ἐκεῖνος κλέπτης ἐστὶν καὶ λῃστής· **2** ὁ δὲ εἰσερχόμενος διὰ τῆς θύρας ποιμήν ἐστιν τῶν προβάτων. **3** τούτῳ ὁ θυρωρὸς ἀνοίγει, καὶ τὰ πρόβατα τῆς φωνῆς αὐτοῦ ἀκούει καὶ τὰ ἴδια πρόβατα φωνεῖ κατ' ὄνομα καὶ ἐξάγει αὐτά. **4** ὅταν τὰ ἴδια πάντα ἐκβάλῃ, ἔμπροσθεν αὐτῶν πορεύεται, καὶ τὰ πρόβατα αὐτῷ ἀκολουθεῖ, ὅτι οἴδασιν τὴν φωνὴν αὐτοῦ· **5** ἀλλοτρίῳ δὲ οὐ μὴ ἀκολουθήσουσιν, ἀλλὰ φεύξονται ἀπ' αὐτοῦ, ὅτι οὐκ οἴδασιν τῶν ἀλλοτρίων τὴν φωνήν. **6** Ταύτην τὴν παροιμίαν εἶπεν αὐτοῖς ὁ Ἰησοῦς, ἐκεῖνοι δὲ οὐκ ἔγνωσαν τίνα ἦν ἃ ἐλάλει αὐτοῖς.

7 Εἶπεν οὖν πάλιν ὁ Ἰησοῦς, Ἀμὴν ἀμὴν λέγω ὑμῖν ὅτι ἐγώ εἰμι ἡ θύρα τῶν προβάτων. **8** πάντες ὅσοι ἦλθον [πρὸ ἐμοῦ] κλέπται εἰσὶν καὶ λῃσταί, ἀλλ' οὐκ ἤκουσαν αὐτῶν τὰ πρόβατα. **9** ἐγώ εἰμι ἡ θύρα· δι' ἐμοῦ ἐάν τις εἰσέλθῃ σωθήσεται καὶ εἰσελεύσεται καὶ ἐξελεύσεται καὶ νομὴν εὑρήσει. **10** ὁ κλέπτης οὐκ ἔρχεται εἰ μὴ ἵνα κλέψῃ καὶ θύσῃ καὶ ἀπολέσῃ· ἐγὼ ἦλθον ἵνα ζωὴν ἔχωσιν καὶ περισσὸν ἔχωσιν. **11** Ἐγώ εἰμι ὁ ποιμὴν ὁ καλός. ὁ ποιμὴν ὁ καλὸς τὴν ψυχὴν αὐτοῦ τίθησιν ὑπὲρ τῶν προβάτων· **12** ὁ μισθωτὸς καὶ οὐκ ὢν ποιμήν, οὗ οὐκ ἔστιν τὰ πρόβατα ἴδια, θεωρεῖ τὸν λύκον ἐρχόμενον καὶ ἀφίησιν τὰ πρόβατα καὶ φεύγει – καὶ ὁ λύκος ἁρπάζει αὐτὰ καὶ σκορπίζει – **13** ὅτι μισθωτός ἐστιν καὶ οὐ μέλει αὐτῷ περὶ τῶν προβάτων. **14** Ἐγώ εἰμι ὁ ποιμὴν ὁ καλὸς καὶ γινώσκω τὰ ἐμὰ καὶ γινώσκουσί με τὰ ἐμά, **15** καθὼς γινώσκει με ὁ πατὴρ κἀγὼ γινώσκω τὸν πατέρα, καὶ τὴν ψυχήν μου τίθημι ὑπὲρ τῶν προβάτων. **16** καὶ ἄλλα πρόβατα ἔχω ἃ οὐκ ἔστιν ἐκ τῆς αὐλῆς ταύτης· κἀκεῖνα δεῖ με ἀγαγεῖν

and he worshiped him.

[39]Jesus said, "For judgment I have come into this world, so that the blind will see and those who see will become blind."

[40]Some Pharisees who were with him heard him say this and asked, "What? Are we blind too?"

[41]Jesus said, "If you were blind, you would not be guilty of sin; but now that you claim you can see, your guilt remains.

The Shepherd and His Flock

10 "I tell you the truth, the man who does not enter the sheep pen by the gate, but climbs in by some other way, is a thief and a robber. [2]The man who enters by the gate is the shepherd of his sheep. [3]The watchman opens the gate for him, and the sheep listen to his voice. He calls his own sheep by name and leads them out. [4]When he has brought out all his own, he goes on ahead of them, and his sheep follow him because they know his voice. [5]But they will never follow a stranger; in fact, they will run away from him because they do not recognize a stranger's voice." [6]Jesus used this figure of speech, but they did not understand what he was telling them.

[7]Therefore Jesus said again, "I tell you the truth, I am the gate for the sheep. [8]All who ever came before me were thieves and robbers, but the sheep did not listen to them. [9]I am the gate; whoever enters through me will be saved.[a] He will come in and go out, and find pasture. [10]The thief comes only to steal and kill and destroy; I have come that they may have life, and have it to the full.

[11]"I am the good shepherd. The good shepherd lays down his life for the sheep. [12]The hired hand is not the shepherd who owns the sheep. So when he sees the wolf coming, he abandons the sheep and runs away. Then the wolf attacks the flock and scatters it. [13]The man runs away because he is a hired hand and cares nothing for the sheep.

[14]"I am the good shepherd; I know my sheep and my sheep know me— [15]just as the Father knows me and I know the Father—and I lay down my life for the sheep. [16]I have other sheep that are not of this sheep pen. I must bring them also. They

---

a9 Or kept safe

will listen to my voice. So there will be one flock, one shepherd. [17]For this reason the Father loves me, because I lay down my life in order to take it up again. [18]No one takes[w] it from me, but I lay it down of my own accord. I have power to lay it down, and I have power to take it up again. I have received this command from my Father."

19 Again the Jews were divided because of these words. [20]Many of them were saying, "He has a demon and is out of his mind. Why listen to him?" [21]Others were saying, "These are not the words of one who has a demon. Can a demon open the eyes of the blind?"

Jesus Is Rejected by the Jews

22 At that time the festival of the Dedication took place in Jerusalem. It was winter, [23]and Jesus was walking in the temple, in the portico of Solomon. [24]So the Jews gathered around him and said to him, "How long will you keep us in suspense? If you are the Messiah,[x] tell us plainly." [25]Jesus answered, "I have told you, and you do not believe. The works that I do in my Father's name testify to me; [26]but you do not believe, because you do not belong to my sheep. [27]My sheep hear my voice. I know them, and they follow me. [28]I give them eternal life, and they will never perish. No one will snatch them out of my hand. [29]What my Father has given me is greater than all else, and no one can snatch it out of the Father's hand.[y] [30]The Father and I are one."

31 The Jews took up stones again to stone him. [32]Jesus replied, "I have shown you many good works from the Father. For which of these are you going to stone me?" [33]The Jews answered, "It is not for a good work that we are going to stone you, but for blasphemy, because you, though only a human being, are making yourself God." [34]Jesus answered, "Is it not written in your law,[z] 'I said, you are gods'? [35]If those to whom the word of God came were called 'gods'—and the scripture cannot be

καὶ τῆς φωνῆς μου ἀκούσουσιν, καὶ γενήσονται μία ποίμνη, εἷς ποιμήν. **17** διὰ τοῦτό με ὁ πατὴρ ἀγαπᾷ ὅτι ἐγὼ τίθημι τὴν ψυχήν μου, ἵνα πάλιν λάβω αὐτήν. **18** οὐδεὶς αἴρει[a] αὐτὴν ἀπ᾽ ἐμοῦ, ἀλλ᾽ ἐγὼ τίθημι αὐτὴν ἀπ᾽ ἐμαυτοῦ. ἐξουσίαν ἔχω θεῖναι αὐτήν, καὶ ἐξουσίαν ἔχω πάλιν λαβεῖν αὐτήν· ταύτην τὴν ἐντολὴν ἔλαβον παρὰ τοῦ πατρός μου.

19 Σχίσμα πάλιν ἐγένετο ἐν τοῖς Ἰουδαίοις διὰ τοὺς λόγους τούτους. **20** ἔλεγον δὲ πολλοὶ ἐξ αὐτῶν, Δαιμόνιον ἔχει καὶ μαίνεται· τί αὐτοῦ ἀκούετε; **21** ἄλλοι[b] ἔλεγον, Ταῦτα τὰ ῥήματα οὐκ ἔστιν δαιμονιζομένου· μὴ δαιμόνιον δύναται τυφλῶν ὀφθαλμοὺς ἀνοῖξαι;

22 Ἐγένετο τότε τὰ ἐγκαίνια ἐν τοῖς Ἱεροσολύμοις, χειμὼν ἦν, **23** καὶ περιεπάτει ὁ Ἰησοῦς ἐν τῷ ἱερῷ ἐν τῇ στοᾷ τοῦ Σολομῶνος. **24** ἐκύκλωσαν οὖν αὐτὸν οἱ Ἰουδαῖοι καὶ ἔλεγον αὐτῷ, Ἕως πότε τὴν ψυχὴν ἡμῶν αἴρεις; εἰ σὺ εἶ ὁ Χριστός, εἰπὲ ἡμῖν παρρησίᾳ. **25** ἀπεκρίθη αὐτοῖς ὁ Ἰησοῦς, Εἶπον ὑμῖν καὶ οὐ πιστεύετε· τὰ ἔργα ἃ ἐγὼ ποιῶ ἐν τῷ ὀνόματι τοῦ πατρός μου ταῦτα μαρτυρεῖ περὶ ἐμοῦ· **26** ἀλλὰ ὑμεῖς οὐ πιστεύετε, ὅτι οὐκ ἐστὲ ἐκ τῶν προβάτων τῶν ἐμῶν. **27** τὰ πρόβατα τὰ ἐμὰ τῆς φωνῆς μου ἀκούουσιν, κἀγὼ γινώσκω αὐτὰ καὶ ἀκολουθοῦσίν μοι, **28** κἀγὼ δίδωμι αὐτοῖς ζωὴν αἰώνιον καὶ οὐ μὴ ἀπόλωνται εἰς τὸν αἰῶνα καὶ οὐχ ἁρπάσει τις αὐτὰ ἐκ τῆς χειρός μου. **29** ὁ πατήρ μου ὃ δέδωκέν μοι πάντων μεῖζόν ἐστιν[c], καὶ οὐδεὶς δύναται ἁρπάζειν ἐκ τῆς χειρὸς τοῦ πατρός. **30** ἐγὼ καὶ ὁ πατὴρ ἕν ἐσμεν.

31 Ἐβάστασαν πάλιν λίθους οἱ Ἰουδαῖοι ἵνα λιθάσωσιν αὐτόν. **32** ἀπεκρίθη αὐτοῖς ὁ Ἰησοῦς, Πολλὰ ἔργα καλὰ ἔδειξα ὑμῖν ἐκ τοῦ πατρός· διὰ ποῖον αὐτῶν ἔργον ἐμὲ λιθάζετε; **33** ἀπεκρίθησαν αὐτῷ οἱ Ἰουδαῖοι, Περὶ καλοῦ ἔργου οὐ λιθάζομέν σε ἀλλὰ περὶ βλασφημίας, καὶ ὅτι σὺ ἄνθρωπος ὢν ποιεῖς σεαυτὸν θεόν. **34** ἀπεκρίθη αὐτοῖς [ὁ] Ἰησοῦς, Οὐκ ἔστιν γεγραμμένον ἐν τῷ νόμῳ ὑμῶν[d] ὅτι Ἐγὼ εἶπα, Θεοί ἐστε; **35** εἰ ἐκείνους εἶπεν θεοὺς πρὸς οὓς ὁ λόγος τοῦ θεοῦ ἐγένετο, καὶ οὐ δύναται λυθῆναι ἡ

too will listen to my voice, and there shall be one flock and one shepherd. [17]The reason my Father loves me is that I lay down my life—only to take it up again. [18]No one takes it from me, but I lay it down of my own accord. I have authority to lay it down and authority to take it up again. This command I received from my Father."

[19]At these words the Jews were again divided. [20]Many of them said, "He is demon-possessed and raving mad. Why listen to him?"

[21]But others said, "These are not the sayings of a man possessed by a demon. Can a demon open the eyes of the blind?"

The Unbelief of the Jews

[22]Then came the Feast of Dedication[b] at Jerusalem. It was winter, [23]and Jesus was in the temple area walking in Solomon's Colonnade. [24]The Jews gathered around him, saying, "How long will you keep us in suspense? If you are the Christ,[c] tell us plainly."

[25]Jesus answered, "I did tell you, but you do not believe. The miracles I do in my Father's name speak for me, [26]but you do not believe because you are not my sheep. [27]My sheep listen to my voice; I know them, and they follow me. [28]I give them eternal life, and they shall never perish; no one can snatch them out of my hand. [29]My Father, who has given them to me, is greater than all[d]; no one can snatch them out of my Father's hand. [30]I and the Father are one."

[31]Again the Jews picked up stones to stone him, [32]but Jesus said to them, "I have shown you many great miracles from the Father. For which of these do you stone me?"

[33]"We are not stoning you for any of these," replied the Jews, "but for blasphemy, because you, a mere man, claim to be God."

[34]Jesus answered them, "Is it not written in your Law, 'I have said you are gods'[e]? [35]If he called them 'gods,' to whom the word of God came—and the Scripture

[w] Other ancient authorities read *has taken*   [x] Or *the Christ*   [y] Other ancient authorities read *My Father who has given them to me is greater than all, and no one can snatch them out of the Father's hand*   [z] Other ancient authorities read *in the law*

[a]18 NRSV note w *ἦρεν*   [b]21 NIV text adds *δὲ* †   [c]29 NIV text and NRSV note y *ὃς δέδωκέν μοι αὐτὰ μείζων πάντων ἐστίν;* NIV note and NRSV text as UBS   [d]34 NRSV note z omits *ὑμῶν* †

[b]22 That is, Hanukkah   [c]24 Or *Messiah*   [d]29 Many early manuscripts *What my Father has given me is greater than all*   [e]34 Psalm 82:6

annulled— ³⁶can you say that the one whom the Father has sanctified and sent into the world is blaspheming because I said, 'I am God's Son'? ³⁷If I am not doing the works of my Father, then do not believe me. ³⁸But if I do them, even though you do not believe me, believe the works, so that you may know and understand[a] that the Father is in me and I am in the Father." ³⁹Then they tried to arrest him again, but he escaped from their hands.

40 He went away again across the Jordan to the place where John had been baptizing earlier, and he remained there. ⁴¹Many came to him, and they were saying, "John performed no sign, but everything that John said about this man was true." ⁴²And many believed in him there.

The Death of Lazarus

11 Now a certain man was ill, Lazarus of Bethany, the village of Mary and her sister Martha. ²Mary was the one who anointed the Lord with perfume and wiped his feet with her hair; her brother Lazarus was ill. ³So the sisters sent a message to Jesus,[b] "Lord, he whom you love is ill." ⁴But when Jesus heard it, he said, "This illness does not lead to death; rather it is for God's glory, so that the Son of God may be glorified through it." ⁵Accordingly, though Jesus loved Martha and her sister and Lazarus, ⁶after having heard that Lazarus[c] was ill, he stayed two days longer in the place where he was.

7 Then after this he said to the disciples, "Let us go to Judea again." ⁸The disciples said to him, "Rabbi, the Jews were just now trying to stone you, and are you going there again?" ⁹Jesus answered, "Are there not twelve hours of daylight? Those who walk during the day do not stumble, because they see the light of this world. ¹⁰But those who walk at night stumble, because the light is not in them." ¹¹After saying this, he told them, "Our friend Lazarus has fallen asleep, but I am going there to awaken him." ¹²The disciples said to him, "Lord, if he has fallen asleep, he will be all right." ¹³Jesus, however, had been speaking about his death, but they thought that he was referring merely to sleep. ¹⁴Then Jesus told them plainly,

γραφή, **36** ὃν ὁ πατὴρ ἡγίασεν καὶ ἀπέστειλεν εἰς τὸν κόσμον ὑμεῖς λέγετε ὅτι Βλασφημεῖς, ὅτι εἶπον, Υἱὸς τοῦ θεοῦ εἰμι; **37** εἰ οὐ ποιῶ τὰ ἔργα τοῦ πατρός μου, μὴ πιστεύετέ μοι· **38** εἰ δὲ ποιῶ, κἂν ἐμοὶ μὴ πιστεύητε, τοῖς ἔργοις πιστεύετε, ἵνα γνῶτε καὶ γινώσκητε[e] ὅτι ἐν ἐμοὶ ὁ πατὴρ κἀγὼ ἐν τῷ πατρί. **39** Ἐζήτουν [οὖν] αὐτὸν πάλιν πιάσαι, καὶ ἐξῆλθεν ἐκ τῆς χειρὸς αὐτῶν.

40 Καὶ ἀπῆλθεν πάλιν πέραν τοῦ Ἰορδάνου εἰς τὸν τόπον ὅπου ἦν Ἰωάννης τὸ πρῶτον βαπτίζων καὶ ἔμεινεν ἐκεῖ. **41** καὶ πολλοὶ ἦλθον πρὸς αὐτὸν καὶ ἔλεγον ὅτι Ἰωάννης μὲν σημεῖον ἐποίησεν οὐδέν, πάντα δὲ ὅσα εἶπεν Ἰωάννης περὶ τούτου ἀληθῆ ἦν. **42** καὶ πολλοὶ ἐπίστευσαν εἰς αὐτὸν ἐκεῖ.

11 Ἦν δέ τις ἀσθενῶν, Λάζαρος ἀπὸ Βηθανίας, ἐκ τῆς κώμης Μαρίας καὶ Μάρθας τῆς ἀδελφῆς αὐτῆς. **2** ἦν δὲ Μαριὰμ ἡ ἀλείψασα τὸν κύριον μύρῳ καὶ ἐκμάξασα τοὺς πόδας αὐτοῦ ταῖς θριξὶν αὐτῆς, ἧς ὁ ἀδελφὸς Λάζαρος ἠσθένει. **3** ἀπέστειλαν οὖν αἱ ἀδελφαὶ πρὸς αὐτὸν λέγουσαι, Κύριε, ἴδε ὃν φιλεῖς ἀσθενεῖ. **4** ἀκούσας δὲ ὁ Ἰησοῦς εἶπεν, Αὕτη ἡ ἀσθένεια οὐκ ἔστιν πρὸς θάνατον ἀλλ' ὑπὲρ τῆς δόξης τοῦ θεοῦ, ἵνα δοξασθῇ ὁ υἱὸς τοῦ θεοῦ δι' αὐτῆς. **5** ἠγάπα δὲ ὁ Ἰησοῦς τὴν Μάρθαν καὶ τὴν ἀδελφὴν αὐτῆς καὶ τὸν Λάζαρον. **6** ὡς οὖν ἤκουσεν ὅτι ἀσθενεῖ, τότε μὲν ἔμεινεν ἐν ᾧ ἦν τόπῳ δύο ἡμέρας, **7** ἔπειτα μετὰ τοῦτο λέγει τοῖς μαθηταῖς, Ἄγωμεν εἰς τὴν Ἰουδαίαν πάλιν. **8** λέγουσιν αὐτῷ οἱ μαθηταί, Ῥαββί, νῦν ἐζήτουν σε λιθάσαι οἱ Ἰουδαῖοι, καὶ πάλιν ὑπάγεις ἐκεῖ; **9** ἀπεκρίθη Ἰησοῦς, Οὐχὶ δώδεκα ὧραί εἰσιν τῆς ἡμέρας; ἐάν τις περιπατῇ ἐν τῇ ἡμέρᾳ, οὐ προσκόπτει, ὅτι τὸ φῶς τοῦ κόσμου τούτου βλέπει· **10** ἐὰν δέ τις περιπατῇ ἐν τῇ νυκτί, προσκόπτει, ὅτι τὸ φῶς οὐκ ἔστιν ἐν αὐτῷ. **11** ταῦτα εἶπεν, καὶ μετὰ τοῦτο λέγει αὐτοῖς, Λάζαρος ὁ φίλος ἡμῶν κεκοίμηται· ἀλλὰ πορεύομαι ἵνα ἐξυπνίσω αὐτόν. **12** εἶπαν οὖν οἱ μαθηταὶ αὐτῷ, Κύριε, εἰ κεκοίμηται σωθήσεται. **13** εἰρήκει δὲ ὁ Ἰησοῦς περὶ τοῦ θανάτου αὐτοῦ, ἐκεῖνοι δὲ ἔδοξαν ὅτι περὶ τῆς κοιμήσεως τοῦ ὕπνου λέγει. **14** τότε οὖν εἶπεν αὐτοῖς ὁ Ἰησοῦς παρρησίᾳ, Λάζαρος ἀπέθανεν,

cannot be broken— ³⁶what about the one whom the Father set apart as his very own and sent into the world? Why then do you accuse me of blasphemy because I said, 'I am God's Son'? ³⁷Do not believe me unless I do what my Father does. ³⁸But if I do it, even though you do not believe me, believe the miracles, that you may know and understand that the Father is in me, and I in the Father." ³⁹Again they tried to seize him, but he escaped their grasp.

⁴⁰Then Jesus went back across the Jordan to the place where John had been baptizing in the early days. Here he stayed ⁴¹and many people came to him. They said, "Though John never performed a miraculous sign, all that John said about this man was true." ⁴²And in that place many believed in Jesus.

The Death of Lazarus

11 Now a man named Lazarus was sick. He was from Bethany, the village of Mary and her sister Martha. ²This Mary, whose brother Lazarus now lay sick, was the same one who poured perfume on the Lord and wiped his feet with her hair. ³So the sisters sent word to Jesus, "Lord, the one you love is sick."

⁴When he heard this, Jesus said, "This sickness will not end in death. No, it is for God's glory so that God's Son may be glorified through it." ⁵Jesus loved Martha and her sister and Lazarus. ⁶Yet when he heard that Lazarus was sick, he stayed where he was two more days.

⁷Then he said to his disciples, "Let us go back to Judea."

⁸"But Rabbi," they said, "a short while ago the Jews tried to stone you, and yet you are going back there?"

⁹Jesus answered, "Are there not twelve hours of daylight? A man who walks by day will not stumble, for he sees by this world's light. ¹⁰It is when he walks by night that he stumbles, for he has no light."

¹¹After he had said this, he went on to tell them, "Our friend Lazarus has fallen asleep; but I am going there to wake him up."

¹²His disciples replied, "Lord, if he sleeps, he will get better." ¹³Jesus had been speaking of his death, but his disciples thought he meant natural sleep.

¹⁴So then he told them plainly, "Lazarus

---

[a] Other ancient authorities lack *and understand*; others read *and believe*   [b] Gk *him*   [c] Gk *he*

[e]38 NRSV note a omits καὶ γινώσκητε or reads καὶ πιστεύητε

"Lazarus is dead. ¹⁵For your sake I am glad I was not there, so that you may believe. But let us go to him." ¹⁶Thomas, who was called the Twin,ᵈ said to his fellow disciples, "Let us also go, that we may die with him."

Jesus the Resurrection and the Life

17 When Jesus arrived, he found that Lazarusᵉ had already been in the tomb four days. ¹⁸Now Bethany was near Jerusalem, some two milesᶠ away, ¹⁹and many of the Jews had come to Martha and Mary to console them about their brother. ²⁰When Martha heard that Jesus was coming, she went and met him, while Mary stayed at home. ²¹Martha said to Jesus, "Lord, if you had been here, my brother would not have died. ²²But even now I know that God will give you whatever you ask of him." ²³Jesus said to her, "Your brother will rise again." ²⁴Martha said to him, "I know that he will rise again in the resurrection on the last day." ²⁵Jesus said to her, "I am the resurrection and the life.ᵍ Those who believe in me, even though they die, will live, ²⁶and everyone who lives and believes in me will never die. Do you believe this?" ²⁷She said to him, "Yes, Lord, I believe that you are the Messiah,ʰ the Son of God, the one coming into the world."

Jesus Weeps

28 When she had said this, she went back and called her sister Mary, and told her privately, "The Teacher is here and is calling for you." ²⁹And when she heard it, she got up quickly and went to him. ³⁰Now Jesus had not yet come to the village, but was still at the place where Martha had met him. ³¹The Jews who were with her in the house, consoling her, saw Mary get up quickly and go out. They followed her because they thought that she was going to the tomb to weep there. ³²When Mary came where Jesus was and saw him, she knelt at his feet and said to him, "Lord, if you had been here, my brother would not have died." ³³When Jesus saw her weeping, and the Jews who came with her also weeping, he was greatly disturbed in spirit and deeply moved. ³⁴He said, "Where have you laid him?" They said to him, "Lord, come and see." ³⁵Jesus began to weep. ³⁶So the Jews said, "See how he loved him!" ³⁷But some of them said, "Could not he who opened the eyes of the blind man

ᵈ Gk *Didymus* ᵉ Gk *he* ᶠ Gk *fifteen stadia* ᵍ Other ancient authorities lack *and the life* ʰ Or *the Christ*

15 καὶ χαίρω δι᾽ ὑμᾶς ἵνα πιστεύσητε, ὅτι οὐκ ἤμην ἐκεῖ· ἀλλὰ ἄγωμεν πρὸς αὐτόν. 16 εἶπεν οὖν Θωμᾶς ὁ λεγόμενος Δίδυμος τοῖς συμμαθηταῖς, Ἄγωμεν καὶ ἡμεῖς ἵνα ἀποθάνωμεν μετ᾽ αὐτοῦ.

17 Ἐλθὼν οὖν ὁ Ἰησοῦς εὗρεν αὐτὸν τέσσαρας ἤδη ἡμέρας ἔχοντα ἐν τῷ μνημείῳ. 18 ἦν δὲ ἡ Βηθανία ἐγγὺς τῶν Ἱεροσολύμων ὡς ἀπὸ σταδίων δεκαπέντε. 19 πολλοὶ δὲ ἐκ τῶν Ἰουδαίων ἐληλύθεισαν πρὸς τὴν Μάρθαν καὶ Μαριὰμ ἵνα παραμυθήσωνται αὐτὰς περὶ τοῦ ἀδελφοῦ. 20 ἡ οὖν Μάρθα ὡς ἤκουσεν ὅτι Ἰησοῦς ἔρχεται ὑπήντησεν αὐτῷ· Μαριὰμ δὲ ἐν τῷ οἴκῳ ἐκαθέζετο. 21 εἶπεν οὖν ἡ Μάρθα πρὸς τὸν Ἰησοῦν, Κύριε, εἰ ἦς ὧδε οὐκ ἂν ἀπέθανεν ὁ ἀδελφός μου· 22 [ἀλλὰ] καὶ νῦν οἶδα ὅτι ὅσα ἂν αἰτήσῃ τὸν θεὸν δώσει σοι ὁ θεός. 23 λέγει αὐτῇ ὁ Ἰησοῦς, Ἀναστήσεται ὁ ἀδελφός σου. 24 λέγει αὐτῷ ἡ Μάρθα, Οἶδα ὅτι ἀναστήσεται ἐν τῇ ἀναστάσει ἐν τῇ ἐσχάτῃ ἡμέρᾳ. 25 εἶπεν αὐτῇ ὁ Ἰησοῦς, Ἐγώ εἰμι ἡ ἀνάστασις καὶ ἡ ζωή· ὁ πιστεύων εἰς ἐμὲ κἂν ἀποθάνῃ ζήσεται, 26 καὶ πᾶς ὁ ζῶν καὶ πιστεύων εἰς ἐμὲ οὐ μὴ ἀποθάνῃ εἰς τὸν αἰῶνα. πιστεύεις τοῦτο; 27 λέγει αὐτῷ, Ναὶ κύριε, ἐγὼ πεπίστευκα ὅτι σὺ εἶ ὁ Χριστὸς ὁ υἱὸς τοῦ θεοῦ ὁ εἰς τὸν κόσμον ἐρχόμενος.

28 Καὶ τοῦτο εἰποῦσα ἀπῆλθεν καὶ ἐφώνησεν Μαριὰμ τὴν ἀδελφὴν αὐτῆς λάθρα εἰποῦσα, Ὁ διδάσκαλος πάρεστιν καὶ φωνεῖ σε. 29 ἐκείνη δὲ ὡς ἤκουσεν ἠγέρθη ταχὺ καὶ ἤρχετο πρὸς αὐτόν. 30 οὔπω δὲ ἐληλύθει ὁ Ἰησοῦς εἰς τὴν κώμην, ἀλλ᾽ ἦν ἔτι ἐν τῷ τόπῳ ὅπου ὑπήντησεν αὐτῷ ἡ Μάρθα. 31 οἱ οὖν Ἰουδαῖοι οἱ ὄντες μετ᾽ αὐτῆς ἐν τῇ οἰκίᾳ καὶ παραμυθούμενοι αὐτήν, ἰδόντες τὴν Μαριὰμ ὅτι ταχέως ἀνέστη καὶ ἐξῆλθεν, ἠκολούθησαν αὐτῇ δόξαντες ὅτι ὑπάγει εἰς τὸ μνημεῖον ἵνα κλαύσῃ ἐκεῖ. 32 ἡ οὖν Μαριὰμ ὡς ἦλθεν ὅπου ἦν Ἰησοῦς ἰδοῦσα αὐτὸν ἔπεσεν αὐτοῦ πρὸς τοὺς πόδας λέγουσα αὐτῷ, Κύριε, εἰ ἦς ὧδε οὐκ ἄν μου ἀπέθανεν ὁ ἀδελφός. 33 Ἰησοῦς οὖν ὡς εἶδεν αὐτὴν κλαίουσαν καὶ τοὺς συνελθόντας αὐτῇ Ἰουδαίους κλαίοντας, ἐνεβριμήσατο τῷ πνεύματι καὶ ἐτάραξεν ἑαυτὸν 34 καὶ εἶπεν, Ποῦ τεθείκατε αὐτόν; λέγουσιν αὐτῷ, Κύριε, ἔρχου καὶ ἴδε. 35 ἐδάκρυσεν ὁ Ἰησοῦς. 36 ἔλεγον οὖν οἱ Ἰουδαῖοι, Ἴδε πῶς ἐφίλει αὐτόν. 37 τινὲς δὲ ἐξ αὐτῶν εἶπαν, Οὐκ ἐδύνατο οὗτος ὁ ἀνοίξας

is dead, ¹⁵and for your sake I am glad I was not there, so that you may believe. But let us go to him."

¹⁶Then Thomas (called Didymus) said to the rest of the disciples, "Let us also go, that we may die with him."

Jesus Comforts the Sisters

¹⁷On his arrival, Jesus found that Lazarus had already been in the tomb for four days. ¹⁸Bethany was less than two milesᵃ from Jerusalem, ¹⁹and many Jews had come to Martha and Mary to comfort them in the loss of their brother. ²⁰When Martha heard that Jesus was coming, she went out to meet him, but Mary stayed at home.

²¹"Lord," Martha said to Jesus, "if you had been here, my brother would not have died. ²²But I know that even now God will give you whatever you ask."

²³Jesus said to her, "Your brother will rise again."

²⁴Martha answered, "I know he will rise again in the resurrection at the last day."

²⁵Jesus said to her, "I am the resurrection and the life. He who believes in me will live, even though he dies; ²⁶and whoever lives and believes in me will never die. Do you believe this?"

²⁷"Yes, Lord," she told him, "I believe that you are the Christ,ᵇ the Son of God, who was to come into the world."

²⁸And after she had said this, she went back and called her sister Mary aside. "The Teacher is here," she said, "and is asking for you." ²⁹When Mary heard this, she got up quickly and went to him. ³⁰Now Jesus had not yet entered the village, but was still at the place where Martha had met him. ³¹When the Jews who had been with Mary in the house, comforting her, noticed how quickly she got up and went out, they followed her, supposing she was going to the tomb to mourn there.

³²When Mary reached the place where Jesus was and saw him, she fell at his feet and said, "Lord, if you had been here, my brother would not have died."

³³When Jesus saw her weeping, and the Jews who had come along with her also weeping, he was deeply moved in spirit and troubled. ³⁴"Where have you laid him?" he asked.

"Come and see, Lord," they replied.

³⁵Jesus wept.

³⁶Then the Jews said, "See how he loved him!"

³⁷But some of them said, "Could not he

ᵃ18 Greek *fifteen stadia* (about 3 kilometers) ᵇ27 Or *Messiah* have kept this man from dying?"

Jesus Raises Lazarus to Life

38 Then Jesus, again greatly disturbed, came to the tomb. It was a cave, and a stone was lying against it. 39Jesus said, "Take away the stone." Martha, the sister of the dead man, said to him, "Lord, already there is a stench because he has been dead four days." 40Jesus said to her, "Did I not tell you that if you believed, you would see the glory of God?" 41So they took away the stone. And Jesus looked upward and said, "Father, I thank you for having heard me. 42I knew that you always hear me, but I have said this for the sake of the crowd standing here, so that they may believe that you sent me." 43When he had said this, he cried with a loud voice, "Lazarus, come out!" 44The dead man came out, his hands and feet bound with strips of cloth, and his face wrapped in a cloth. Jesus said to them, "Unbind him, and let him go."

The Plot to Kill Jesus

45 Many of the Jews therefore, who had come with Mary and had seen what Jesus did, believed in him. 46But some of them went to the Pharisees and told them what he had done. 47So the chief priests and the Pharisees called a meeting of the council, and said, "What are we to do? This man is performing many signs. 48If we let him go on like this, everyone will believe in him, and the Romans will come and destroy both our holy placeⁱ and our nation." 49But one of them, Caiaphas, who was high priest that year, said to them, "You know nothing at all! 50You do not understand that it is better for you to have one man die for the people than to have the whole nation destroyed." 51He did not say this on his own, but being high priest that year he prophesied that Jesus was about to die for the nation, 52and not for the nation only, but to gather into one the dispersed children of God. 53So from that day on they planned to put him to death.

54 Jesus therefore no longer walked about openly among the Jews, but went from there to a town called Ephraim in the region

τοὺς ὀφθαλμοὺς τοῦ τυφλοῦ ποιῆσαι ἵνα καὶ οὗτος μὴ ἀποθάνῃ;

38 Ἰησοῦς οὖν πάλιν ἐμβριμώμενος ἐν ἑαυτῷ ἔρχεται εἰς τὸ μνημεῖον· ἦν δὲ σπήλαιον καὶ λίθος ἐπέκειτο ἐπ' αὐτῷ. **39** λέγει ὁ Ἰησοῦς, "Ἄρατε τὸν λίθον. λέγει αὐτῷ ἡ ἀδελφὴ τοῦ τετελευτηκότος Μάρθα, Κύριε, ἤδη ὄζει, τεταρταῖος γάρ ἐστιν. **40** λέγει αὐτῇ ὁ Ἰησοῦς, Οὐκ εἶπόν σοι ὅτι ἐὰν πιστεύσῃς ὄψῃ τὴν δόξαν τοῦ θεοῦ; **41** ἦραν οὖν τὸν λίθον. ὁ δὲ Ἰησοῦς ἦρεν τοὺς ὀφθαλμοὺς ἄνω καὶ εἶπεν, Πάτερ, εὐχαριστῶ σοι ὅτι ἤκουσάς μου. **42** ἐγὼ δὲ ᾔδειν ὅτι πάντοτέ μου ἀκούεις, ἀλλὰ διὰ τὸν ὄχλον τὸν περιεστῶτα εἶπον, ἵνα πιστεύσωσιν ὅτι σύ με ἀπέστειλας. **43** καὶ ταῦτα εἰπὼν φωνῇ μεγάλῃ ἐκραύγασεν, Λάζαρε, δεῦρο ἔξω. **44** ἐξῆλθεν ὁ τεθνηκὼς δεδεμένος τοὺς πόδας καὶ τὰς χεῖρας κειρίαις καὶ ἡ ὄψις αὐτοῦ σουδαρίῳ περιεδέδετο. λέγει αὐτοῖς ὁ Ἰησοῦς, Λύσατε αὐτὸν καὶ ἄφετε αὐτὸν ὑπάγειν.

45 Πολλοὶ οὖν ἐκ τῶν Ἰουδαίων οἱ ἐλθόντες πρὸς τὴν Μαριὰμ καὶ θεασάμενοι ἃ ἐποίησεν ἐπίστευσαν εἰς αὐτόν· **46** τινὲς δὲ ἐξ αὐτῶν ἀπῆλθον πρὸς τοὺς Φαρισαίους καὶ εἶπαν αὐτοῖς ἃ ἐποίησεν Ἰησοῦς. **47** συνήγαγον οὖν οἱ ἀρχιερεῖς καὶ οἱ Φαρισαῖοι συνέδριον καὶ ἔλεγον, Τί ποιοῦμεν ὅτι οὗτος ὁ ἄνθρωπος πολλὰ ποιεῖ σημεῖα; **48** ἐὰν ἀφῶμεν αὐτὸν οὕτως, πάντες πιστεύσουσιν εἰς αὐτόν, καὶ ἐλεύσονται οἱ Ῥωμαῖοι καὶ ἀροῦσιν ἡμῶν καὶ τὸν τόπον καὶ τὸ ἔθνος. **49** εἷς δέ τις ἐξ αὐτῶν Καϊάφας, ἀρχιερεὺς ὢν τοῦ ἐνιαυτοῦ ἐκείνου, εἶπεν αὐτοῖς, Ὑμεῖς οὐκ οἴδατε οὐδέν, **50** οὐδὲ λογίζεσθε ὅτι συμφέρει ὑμῖν ἵνα εἷς ἄνθρωπος ἀποθάνῃ ὑπὲρ τοῦ λαοῦ καὶ μὴ ὅλον τὸ ἔθνος ἀπόληται. **51** τοῦτο δὲ ἀφ' ἑαυτοῦ οὐκ εἶπεν, ἀλλὰ ἀρχιερεὺς ὢν τοῦ ἐνιαυτοῦ ἐκείνου ἐπροφήτευσεν ὅτι ἔμελλεν Ἰησοῦς ἀποθνῄσκειν ὑπὲρ τοῦ ἔθνους, **52** καὶ οὐχ ὑπὲρ τοῦ ἔθνους μόνον ἀλλ' ἵνα καὶ τὰ τέκνα τοῦ θεοῦ τὰ διεσκορπισμένα συναγάγῃ εἰς ἕν. **53** ἀπ' ἐκείνης οὖν τῆς ἡμέρας ἐβουλεύσαντο ἵνα ἀποκτείνωσιν αὐτόν.

54 Ὁ οὖν Ἰησοῦς οὐκέτι παρρησίᾳ περιεπάτει ἐν τοῖς Ἰουδαίοις, ἀλλὰ ἀπῆλθεν ἐκεῖθεν εἰς τὴν χώραν ἐγγὺς τῆς ἐρήμου, εἰς Ἐφραὶμ λεγομένην

who opened the eyes of the blind man have kept this man from dying?"

Jesus Raises Lazarus From the Dead

38Jesus, once more deeply moved, came to the tomb. It was a cave with a stone laid across the entrance. 39"Take away the stone," he said.

"But, Lord," said Martha, the sister of the dead man, "by this time there is a bad odor, for he has been there four days."

40Then Jesus said, "Did I not tell you that if you believed, you would see the glory of God?"

41So they took away the stone. Then Jesus looked up and said, "Father, I thank you that you have heard me. 42I knew that you always hear me, but I said this for the benefit of the people standing here, that they may believe that you sent me."

43When he had said this, Jesus called in a loud voice, "Lazarus, come out!" 44The dead man came out, his hands and feet wrapped with strips of linen, and a cloth around his face.

Jesus said to them, "Take off the grave clothes and let him go."

The Plot to Kill Jesus

45Therefore many of the Jews who had come to visit Mary, and had seen what Jesus did, put their faith in him. 46But some of them went to the Pharisees and told them what Jesus had done. 47Then the chief priests and the Pharisees called a meeting of the Sanhedrin.

"What are we accomplishing?" they asked. "Here is this man performing many miraculous signs. 48If we let him go on like this, everyone will believe in him, and then the Romans will come and take away both our placeᶜ and our nation."

49Then one of them, named Caiaphas, who was high priest that year, spoke up, "You know nothing at all! 50You do not realize that it is better for you that one man die for the people than that the whole nation perish."

51He did not say this on his own, but as high priest that year he prophesied that Jesus would die for the Jewish nation, 52and not only for that nation but also for the scattered children of God, to bring them together and make them one. 53So from that day on they plotted to take his life.

54Therefore Jesus no longer moved about publicly among the Jews. Instead he withdrew to a region near the desert, to a village

---

ⁱ Or *our temple*; Greek *our place*

ᶜ48 Or *temple*

near the wilderness; and he remained there with the disciples.

55 Now the Passover of the Jews was near, and many went up from the country to Jerusalem before the Passover to purify themselves. 56They were looking for Jesus and were asking one another as they stood in the temple, "What do you think? Surely he will not come to the festival, will he?" 57Now the chief priests and the Pharisees had given orders that anyone who knew where Jesusʲ was should let them know, so that they might arrest him.

Mary Anoints Jesus

12 Six days before the Passover Jesus came to Bethany, the home of Lazarus, whom he had raised from the dead. 2There they gave a dinner for him. Martha served, and Lazarus was one of those at the table with him. 3Mary took a pound of costly perfume made of pure nard, anointed Jesus' feet, and wiped themᵏ with her hair. The house was filled with the fragrance of the perfume. 4But Judas Iscariot, one of his disciples (the one who was about to betray him), said, 5"Why was this perfume not sold for three hundred denariiˡ and the money given to the poor?" 6(He said this not because he cared about the poor, but because he was a thief; he kept the common purse and used to steal what was put into it.) 7Jesus said, "Leave her alone. She bought itᵐ so that she might keep it for the day of my burial. 8You always have the poor with you, but you do not always have me."

The Plot to Kill Lazarus

9 When the great crowd of the Jews learned that he was there, they came not only because of Jesus but also to see Lazarus, whom he had raised from the dead. 10So the chief priests planned to put Lazarus to death as well, 11since it was on account of him that many of the Jews were deserting and were believing in Jesus.

Jesus' Triumphal Entry into Jerusalem

12 The next day the great crowd that had come to the festival heard that Jesus was coming to Jerusalem. 13So they took branches of palm trees and went out to meet him, shouting,

"Hosanna!

πόλιν, κἀκεῖ ἔμεινεν μετὰ τῶν μαθητῶν.

55 Ἦν δὲ ἐγγὺς τὸ πάσχα τῶν Ἰουδαίων, καὶ ἀνέβησαν πολλοὶ εἰς Ἱεροσόλυμα ἐκ τῆς χώρας πρὸ τοῦ πάσχα ἵνα ἁγνίσωσιν ἑαυτούς. **56** ἐζήτουν οὖν τὸν Ἰησοῦν καὶ ἔλεγον μετ᾽ ἀλλήλων ἐν τῷ ἱερῷ ἑστηκότες, Τί δοκεῖ ὑμῖν; ὅτι οὐ μὴ ἔλθῃ εἰς τὴν ἑορτήν; **57** δεδώκεισαν δὲ οἱ ἀρχιερεῖς καὶ οἱ Φαρισαῖοι ἐντολὰς ἵνα ἐάν τις γνῷ ποῦ ἐστιν μηνύσῃ, ὅπως πιάσωσιν αὐτόν.

12 Ὁ οὖν Ἰησοῦς πρὸ ἓξ ἡμερῶν τοῦ πάσχα ἦλθεν εἰς Βηθανίαν, ὅπου ἦν Λάζαρος, ὃν ἤγειρεν ἐκ νεκρῶν Ἰησοῦς. **2** ἐποίησαν οὖν αὐτῷ δεῖπνον ἐκεῖ, καὶ ἡ Μάρθα διηκόνει, ὁ δὲ Λάζαρος εἷς ἦν ἐκ τῶν ἀνακειμένων σὺν αὐτῷ. **3** ἡ οὖν Μαριὰμ λαβοῦσα λίτραν μύρου νάρδου πιστικῆς πολυτίμου ἤλειψεν τοὺς πόδας τοῦ Ἰησοῦ καὶ ἐξέμαξεν ταῖς θριξὶν αὐτῆς τοὺς πόδας αὐτοῦ· ἡ δὲ οἰκία ἐπληρώθη ἐκ τῆς ὀσμῆς τοῦ μύρου. **4** λέγει δὲ Ἰούδας ὁ Ἰσκαριώτης εἷς [ἐκ] τῶν μαθητῶν αὐτοῦ, ὁ μέλλων αὐτὸν παραδιδόναι, **5** Διὰ τί τοῦτο τὸ μύρον οὐκ ἐπράθη τριακοσίων δηναρίων καὶ ἐδόθη πτωχοῖς; **6** εἶπεν δὲ τοῦτο οὐχ ὅτι περὶ τῶν πτωχῶν ἔμελεν αὐτῷ, ἀλλ᾽ ὅτι κλέπτης ἦν καὶ τὸ γλωσσόκομον ἔχων τὰ βαλλόμενα ἐβάσταζεν. **7** εἶπεν οὖν ὁ Ἰησοῦς, Ἄφες αὐτήν, ἵνα εἰς τὴν ἡμέραν τοῦ ἐνταφιασμοῦ μου τηρήσῃ αὐτό· **8** τοὺς πτωχοὺς γὰρ πάντοτε ἔχετε μεθ᾽ ἑαυτῶν, ἐμὲ δὲ οὐ πάντοτε ἔχετε.

9 Ἔγνω οὖν [ὁ] ὄχλος πολὺς ἐκ τῶν Ἰουδαίων ὅτι ἐκεῖ ἐστιν καὶ ἦλθον οὐ διὰ τὸν Ἰησοῦν μόνον, ἀλλ᾽ ἵνα καὶ τὸν Λάζαρον ἴδωσιν ὃν ἤγειρεν ἐκ νεκρῶν. **10** ἐβουλεύσαντο δὲ οἱ ἀρχιερεῖς ἵνα καὶ τὸν Λάζαρον ἀποκτείνωσιν, **11** ὅτι πολλοὶ δι᾽ αὐτὸν ὑπῆγον τῶν Ἰουδαίων καὶ ἐπίστευον εἰς τὸν Ἰησοῦν.

12 Τῇ ἐπαύριον ὁ ὄχλος πολὺς ὁ ἐλθὼν εἰς τὴν ἑορτήν, ἀκούσαντες ὅτι ἔρχεται ὁ Ἰησοῦς εἰς Ἱεροσόλυμα **13** ἔλαβον τὰ βαΐα τῶν φοινίκων καὶ ἐξῆλθον εἰς ὑπάντησιν αὐτῷ καὶ ἐκραύγαζον·

Ὡσαννά·

---

called Ephraim, where he stayed with his disciples.

55When it was almost time for the Jewish Passover, many went up from the country to Jerusalem for their ceremonial cleansing before the Passover. 56They kept looking for Jesus, and as they stood in the temple area they asked one another, "What do you think? Isn't he coming to the Feast at all?" 57But the chief priests and Pharisees had given orders that if anyone found out where Jesus was, he should report it so that they might arrest him.

Jesus Anointed at Bethany

12 Six days before the Passover, Jesus arrived at Bethany, where Lazarus lived, whom Jesus had raised from the dead. 2Here a dinner was given in Jesus' honor. Martha served, while Lazarus was among those reclining at the table with him. 3Then Mary took about a pintᵃ of pure nard, an expensive perfume; she poured it on Jesus' feet and wiped his feet with her hair. And the house was filled with the fragrance of the perfume.

4But one of his disciples, Judas Iscariot, who was later to betray him, objected, 5"Why wasn't this perfume sold and the money given to the poor? It was worth a year's wages.ᵇ" 6He did not say this because he cared about the poor but because he was a thief; as keeper of the money bag, he used to help himself to what was put into it.

7"Leave her alone," Jesus replied. "⌞It was intended⌟ that she should save this perfume for the day of my burial. 8You will always have the poor among you, but you will not always have me."

9Meanwhile a large crowd of Jews found out that Jesus was there and came, not only because of him but also to see Lazarus, whom he had raised from the dead. 10So the chief priests made plans to kill Lazarus as well, 11for on account of him many of the Jews were going over to Jesus and putting their faith in him.

The Triumphal Entry

12The next day the great crowd that had come for the Feast heard that Jesus was on his way to Jerusalem. 13They took palm branches and went out to meet him, shouting,

"Hosanna!ᶜ"

ʲGk he   ᵏGk his feet   ˡThree hundred denarii would be nearly a year's wages for a laborer   ᵐGk lacks She bought it

ᵃ3 Greek a litra (probably about 0.5 liter)   ᵇ5 Greek three hundred denarii   ᶜ13 A Hebrew expression meaning "Save!" which became an exclamation of praise

Blessed is the one who comes in the
name of the Lord—
the King of Israel!"

[14]Jesus found a young donkey and sat on
it; as it is written:

[15] "Do not be afraid, daughter of Zion.
Look, your king is coming,
sitting on a donkey's colt!"

[16]His disciples did not understand these
things at first; but when Jesus was glorified, then they remembered that these
things had been written of him and had
been done to him. [17]So the crowd that had
been with him when he called Lazarus out
of the tomb and raised him from the dead
continued to testify.[n] [18]It was also because
they heard that he had performed this sign
that the crowd went to meet him. [19]The
Pharisees then said to one another, "You
see, you can do nothing. Look, the world
has gone after him!"

Some Greeks Wish to See Jesus

20 Now among those who went up to
worship at the festival were some Greeks.
[21]They came to Philip, who was from
Bethsaida in Galilee, and said to him, "Sir,
we wish to see Jesus." [22]Philip went and
told Andrew; then Andrew and Philip went
and told Jesus. [23]Jesus answered them,
"The hour has come for the Son of Man to
be glorified. [24]Very truly, I tell you, unless
a grain of wheat falls into the earth and
dies, it remains just a single grain; but if it
dies, it bears much fruit. [25]Those who love
their life lose it, and those who hate their
life in this world will keep it for eternal
life. [26]Whoever serves me must follow me,
and where I am, there will my servant be
also. Whoever serves me, the Father will
honor.

Jesus Speaks about His Death

27 "Now my soul is troubled. And what
should I say—'Father, save me from this
hour'? No, it is for this reason that I have
come to this hour. [28]Father, glorify your
name." Then a voice came from heaven, "I
have glorified it, and I will glorify it again."
[29]The crowd standing there heard it and
said that it was thunder. Others said, "An
angel has spoken to him." [30]Jesus answered, "This voice has come for your sake,
not for mine. [31]Now is the judgment of
this world; now the ruler of this world will

εὐλογημένος ὁ ἐρχόμενος ἐν
ὀνόματι κυρίου,
[καὶ] ὁ βασιλεὺς τοῦ Ἰσραήλ.
14 εὑρὼν δὲ ὁ Ἰησοῦς ὀνάριον ἐκάθισεν
ἐπ' αὐτό, καθώς ἐστιν γεγραμμένον,
15 Μὴ φοβοῦ, θυγάτηρ Σιών·
ἰδοὺ ὁ βασιλεύς σου ἔρχεται,
καθήμενος ἐπὶ πῶλον ὄνου.
16 ταῦτα οὐκ ἔγνωσαν αὐτοῦ οἱ μαθηταὶ
τὸ πρῶτον, ἀλλ' ὅτε ἐδοξάσθη Ἰησοῦς
τότε ἐμνήσθησαν ὅτι ταῦτα ἦν ἐπ'
αὐτῷ γεγραμμένα καὶ ταῦτα ἐποίησαν
αὐτῷ. **17** ἐμαρτύρει οὖν ὁ ὄχλος ὁ ὢν
μετ' αὐτοῦ ὅτε[a] τὸν Λάζαρον ἐφώνησεν
ἐκ τοῦ μνημείου καὶ ἤγειρεν αὐτὸν ἐκ
νεκρῶν. **18** διὰ τοῦτο [καὶ][b] ὑπήντησεν
αὐτῷ ὁ ὄχλος, ὅτι ἤκουσαν τοῦτο
αὐτὸν πεποιηκέναι τὸ σημεῖον. **19** οἱ
οὖν Φαρισαῖοι εἶπαν πρὸς ἑαυτούς,
Θεωρεῖτε ὅτι οὐκ ὠφελεῖτε οὐδέν· ἴδε
ὁ κόσμος[c] ὀπίσω αὐτοῦ ἀπῆλθεν.

20 Ἦσαν δὲ Ἕλληνές τινες ἐκ τῶν
ἀναβαινόντων ἵνα προσκυνήσωσιν ἐν
τῇ ἑορτῇ· **21** οὗτοι οὖν προσῆλθον
Φιλίππῳ τῷ ἀπὸ Βηθσαϊδὰ τῆς Γαλιλαίας καὶ ἠρώτων αὐτὸν λέγοντες,
Κύριε, θέλομεν τὸν Ἰησοῦν ἰδεῖν.
22 ἔρχεται ὁ Φίλιππος καὶ λέγει τῷ
Ἀνδρέᾳ, ἔρχεται Ἀνδρέας καὶ Φίλιππος καὶ λέγουσιν τῷ Ἰησοῦ. **23** ὁ δὲ
Ἰησοῦς ἀποκρίνεται αὐτοῖς λέγων,
Ἐλήλυθεν ἡ ὥρα ἵνα δοξασθῇ ὁ υἱὸς
τοῦ ἀνθρώπου. **24** ἀμὴν ἀμὴν λέγω ὑμῖν,
ἐὰν μὴ ὁ κόκκος τοῦ σίτου πεσὼν εἰς
τὴν γῆν ἀποθάνῃ, αὐτὸς μόνος μένει·
ἐὰν δὲ ἀποθάνῃ, πολὺν καρπὸν φέρει.
25 ὁ φιλῶν τὴν ψυχὴν αὐτοῦ ἀπολλύει
αὐτήν, καὶ ὁ μισῶν τὴν ψυχὴν αὐτοῦ
ἐν τῷ κόσμῳ τούτῳ εἰς ζωὴν αἰώνιον
φυλάξει αὐτήν. **26** ἐὰν ἐμοί τις διακονῇ,
ἐμοὶ ἀκολουθείτω, καὶ ὅπου εἰμὶ ἐγὼ
ἐκεῖ καὶ ὁ διάκονος ὁ ἐμὸς ἔσται· ἐάν
τις ἐμοὶ διακονῇ τιμήσει αὐτὸν ὁ
πατήρ.

27 Νῦν ἡ ψυχή μου τετάρακται, καὶ
τί εἴπω; Πάτερ, σῶσόν με ἐκ τῆς ὥρας
ταύτης; ἀλλὰ διὰ τοῦτο ἦλθον εἰς τὴν
ὥραν ταύτην. **28** πάτερ, δόξασόν σου
τὸ ὄνομα. ἦλθεν οὖν φωνὴ ἐκ τοῦ
οὐρανοῦ, Καὶ ἐδόξασα καὶ πάλιν δοξάσω.
29 ὁ οὖν ὄχλος ὁ ἑστὼς καὶ ἀκούσας
ἔλεγεν βροντὴν γεγονέναι, ἄλλοι
ἔλεγον, Ἄγγελος αὐτῷ λελάληκεν.
30 ἀπεκρίθη Ἰησοῦς καὶ εἶπεν, Οὐ δι'
ἐμὲ ἡ φωνὴ αὕτη γέγονεν ἀλλὰ δι'
ὑμᾶς. **31** νῦν κρίσις ἐστὶν τοῦ κόσμου
τούτου, νῦν ὁ ἄρχων τοῦ κόσμου τούτου

"Blessed is he who comes in the name
of the Lord!"[d]

"Blessed is the King of Israel!"

[14]Jesus found a young donkey and sat upon
it, as it is written,

[15]"Do not be afraid, O Daughter of Zion;
see, your king is coming,
seated on a donkey's colt."[e]

[16]At first his disciples did not understand
all this. Only after Jesus was glorified did
they realize that these things had been written about him and that they had done these
things to him. [17]Now the crowd that was with him when
he called Lazarus from the tomb and raised
him from the dead continued to spread the
word. [18]Many people, because they had
heard that he had given this miraculous
sign, went out to meet him. [19]So the Pharisees said to one another, "See, this is getting us nowhere. Look how the whole
world has gone after him!"

Jesus Predicts His Death

[20]Now there were some Greeks among
those who went up to worship at the Feast.
[21]They came to Philip, who was from
Bethsaida in Galilee, with a request. "Sir,"
they said, "we would like to see Jesus."
[22]Philip went to tell Andrew; Andrew and
Philip in turn told Jesus.

[23]Jesus replied, "The hour has come for
the Son of Man to be glorified. [24]I tell you
the truth, unless a kernel of wheat falls to
the ground and dies, it remains only a
single seed. But if it dies, it produces many
seeds. [25]The man who loves his life will
lose it, while the man who hates his life in
this world will keep it for eternal life.
[26]Whoever serves me must follow me; and
where I am, my servant also will be. My
Father will honor the one who serves me.

[27]"Now my heart is troubled, and what
shall I say? 'Father, save me from this
hour'? No, it was for this very reason I
came to this hour. [28]Father, glorify your
name!"

Then a voice came from heaven, "I have
glorified it, and will glorify it again." [29]The
crowd that was there and heard it said it
had thundered; others said an angel had
spoken to him.

[30]Jesus said, "This voice was for your
benefit, not mine. [31]Now is the time for
judgment on this world; now the prince of

---

[n] Other ancient authorities read *with him began to testify
that he had called. . .from the dead*

[a]17 NRSV note n ὅτι   [b]18 NIV text omits καὶ †
[c]19 NIV text adds ὅλος †

[d]13 Psalm 118:25, 26   [e]15 Zech. 9:9

be driven out. 32And I, when I am lifted up from the earth, will draw all people[o] to myself." 33He said this to indicate the kind of death he was to die. 34The crowd answered him, "We have heard from the law that the Messiah[p] remains forever. How can you say that the Son of Man must be lifted up? Who is this Son of Man?" 35Jesus said to them, "The light is with you for a little longer. Walk while you have the light, so that the darkness may not overtake you. If you walk in the darkness, you do not know where you are going. 36While you have the light, believe in the light, so that you may become children of light."

The Unbelief of the People

After Jesus had said this, he departed and hid from them. 37Although he had performed so many signs in their presence, they did not believe in him. 38This was to fulfill the word spoken by the prophet Isaiah:

"Lord, who has believed our message,
and to whom has the arm of the
Lord been revealed?"

39And so they could not believe, because Isaiah also said,

40 "He has blinded their eyes
and hardened their heart,
so that they might not look with their
eyes,
and understand with their heart and
turn—
and I would heal them."

41Isaiah said this because[q] he saw his glory and spoke about him. 42Nevertheless many, even of the authorities, believed in him. But because of the Pharisees they did not confess it, for fear that they would be put out of the synagogue; 43for they loved human glory more than the glory that comes from God.

Summary of Jesus' Teaching

44 Then Jesus cried aloud: "Whoever believes in me believes not in me but in him who sent me. 45And whoever sees me sees him who sent me. 46I have come as light into the world, so that everyone who believes in me should not remain in the darkness. 47I do not judge anyone who hears my words and does not keep them, for I came not to judge the world, but to save the world. 48The one who rejects me and does not receive my word has a judge; on

ἐκβληθήσεται ἔξω· **32** κἀγὼ ἐὰν ὑψωθῶ ἐκ τῆς γῆς, πάντας[d] ἑλκύσω πρὸς ἐμαυτόν. **33** τοῦτο δὲ ἔλεγεν σημαίνων ποίῳ θανάτῳ ἤμελλεν ἀποθνῄσκειν. **34** ἀπεκρίθη οὖν αὐτῷ ὁ ὄχλος, Ἡμεῖς ἠκούσαμεν ἐκ τοῦ νόμου ὅτι ὁ Χριστὸς μένει εἰς τὸν αἰῶνα, καὶ πῶς λέγεις σὺ ὅτι δεῖ ὑψωθῆναι τὸν υἱὸν τοῦ ἀνθρώπου; τίς ἐστιν οὗτος ὁ υἱὸς τοῦ ἀνθρώπου; **35** εἶπεν οὖν αὐτοῖς ὁ Ἰησοῦς, Ἔτι μικρὸν χρόνον τὸ φῶς ἐν ὑμῖν ἐστιν. περιπατεῖτε ὡς τὸ φῶς ἔχετε, ἵνα μὴ σκοτία ὑμᾶς καταλάβῃ· καὶ ὁ περιπατῶν ἐν τῇ σκοτίᾳ οὐκ οἶδεν ποῦ ὑπάγει. **36** ὡς τὸ φῶς ἔχετε, πιστεύετε εἰς τὸ φῶς, ἵνα υἱοὶ φωτὸς γένησθε.

Ταῦτα ἐλάλησεν Ἰησοῦς, καὶ ἀπελθὼν ἐκρύβη ἀπ᾽ αὐτῶν. **37** Τοσαῦτα δὲ αὐτοῦ σημεῖα πεποιηκότος ἔμπροσθεν αὐτῶν οὐκ ἐπίστευον εἰς αὐτόν, **38** ἵνα ὁ λόγος Ἡσαΐου τοῦ προφήτου πληρωθῇ ὃν εἶπεν,

Κύριε, τίς ἐπίστευσεν τῇ ἀκοῇ
ἡμῶν;
καὶ ὁ βραχίων κυρίου τίνι
ἀπεκαλύφθη;

39 διὰ τοῦτο οὐκ ἠδύναντο πιστεύειν, ὅτι πάλιν εἶπεν Ἡσαΐας, **40** Τετύφλωκεν αὐτῶν τοὺς ὀφθαλμοὺς καὶ ἐπώρωσεν αὐτῶν τὴν καρδίαν,
ἵνα μὴ ἴδωσιν τοῖς ὀφθαλμοῖς
καὶ νοήσωσιν τῇ καρδίᾳ καὶ
στραφῶσιν,
καὶ ἰάσομαι αὐτούς.

41 ταῦτα εἶπεν Ἡσαΐας ὅτι[e] εἶδεν τὴν δόξαν αὐτοῦ, καὶ ἐλάλησεν περὶ αὐτοῦ. **42** ὅμως μέντοι καὶ ἐκ τῶν ἀρχόντων πολλοὶ ἐπίστευσαν εἰς αὐτόν, ἀλλὰ διὰ τοὺς Φαρισαίους οὐχ ὡμολόγουν ἵνα μὴ ἀποσυνάγωγοι γένωνται· **43** ἠγάπησαν γὰρ τὴν δόξαν τῶν ἀνθρώπων μᾶλλον ἤπερ τὴν δόξαν τοῦ θεοῦ. **44** Ἰησοῦς δὲ ἔκραξεν καὶ εἶπεν, Ὁ πιστεύων εἰς ἐμὲ οὐ πιστεύει εἰς ἐμὲ ἀλλὰ εἰς τὸν πέμψαντά με, **45** καὶ ὁ θεωρῶν ἐμὲ θεωρεῖ τὸν πέμψαντά με. **46** ἐγὼ φῶς εἰς τὸν κόσμον ἐλήλυθα, ἵνα πᾶς ὁ πιστεύων εἰς ἐμὲ ἐν τῇ σκοτίᾳ μὴ μείνῃ. **47** καὶ ἐάν τίς μου ἀκούσῃ τῶν ῥημάτων καὶ μὴ φυλάξῃ, ἐγὼ οὐ κρίνω αὐτόν· οὐ γὰρ ἦλθον ἵνα κρίνω τὸν κόσμον, ἀλλ᾽ ἵνα σώσω τὸν κόσμον. **48** ὁ ἀθετῶν ἐμὲ καὶ μὴ λαμβάνων τὰ ῥήματά μου ἔχει τὸν

this world will be driven out. 32But I, when I am lifted up from the earth, will draw all men to myself." 33He said this to show the kind of death he was going to die.

34The crowd spoke up, "We have heard from the Law that the Christ[f] will remain forever, so how can you say, 'The Son of Man must be lifted up'? Who is this 'Son of Man'?"

35Then Jesus told them, "You are going to have the light just a little while longer. Walk while you have the light, before darkness overtakes you. The man who walks in the dark does not know where he is going. 36Put your trust in the light while you have it, so that you may become sons of light." When he had finished speaking, Jesus left and hid himself from them.

The Jews Continue in Their Unbelief

37Even after Jesus had done all these miraculous signs in their presence, they still would not believe in him. 38This was to fulfill the word of Isaiah the prophet:

"Lord, who has believed our message
and to whom has the arm of the Lord
been revealed?"[g]

39For this reason they could not believe, because, as Isaiah says elsewhere:

40"He has blinded their eyes
and deadened their hearts,
so they can neither see with their eyes,
nor understand with their hearts,
nor turn—and I would heal them."[h]

41Isaiah said this because he saw Jesus' glory and spoke about him.

42Yet at the same time many even among the leaders believed in him. But because of the Pharisees they would not confess their faith for fear they would be put out of the synagogue; 43for they loved praise from men more than praise from God.

44Then Jesus cried out, "When a man believes in me, he does not believe in me only, but in the one who sent me. 45When he looks at me, he sees the one who sent me. 46I have come into the world as a light, so that no one who believes in me should stay in darkness.

47"As for the person who hears my words but does not keep them, I do not judge him. For I did not come to judge the world, but to save it. 48There is a judge for the one who rejects me and does not accept my

---

[o] Other ancient authorities read *all things*   [p] Or *the Christ*   [q] Other ancient witnesses read *when*

[d]32 NRSV note o πάντα   [e]41 NRSV note q ὅτε

[f]34 Or *Messiah*   [g]38 Isaiah 53:1   [h]40 Isaiah 6:10

the last day the word that I have spoken will serve as judge, 49for I have not spoken on my own, but the Father who sent me has himself given me a commandment about what to say and what to speak. 50And I know that his commandment is eternal life. What I speak, therefore, I speak just as the Father has told me."

Jesus Washes the Disciples' Feet

13 Now before the festival of the Passover, Jesus knew that his hour had come to depart from this world and go to the Father. Having loved his own who were in the world, he loved them to the end. 2The devil had already put it into the heart of Judas son of Simon Iscariot to betray him. And during supper 3Jesus, knowing that the Father had given all things into his hands, and that he had come from God and was going to God, 4got up from the table,r took off his outer robe, and tied a towel around himself. 5Then he poured water into a basin and began to wash the disciples' feet and to wipe them with the towel that was tied around him. 6He came to Simon Peter, who said to him, "Lord, are you going to wash my feet?" 7Jesus answered, "You do not know now what I am doing, but later you will understand." 8Peter said to him, "You will never wash my feet." Jesus answered, "Unless I wash you, you have no share with me." 9Simon Peter said to him, "Lord, not my feet only but also my hands and my head!" 10Jesus said to him, "One who has bathed does not need to wash, except for the feet,s but is entirely clean. And yout are clean, though not all of you." 11For he knew who was to betray him; for this reason he said, "Not all of you are clean."

12 After he had washed their feet, had put on his robe, and had returned to the table, he said to them, "Do you know what I have done to you? 13You call me Teacher and Lord—and you are right, for that is what I am. 14So if I, your Lord and Teacher, have washed your feet, you also ought to wash one another's feet. 15For I have set you an example, that you also should do as I have done to you. 16Very truly, I tell

κρίνοντα αὐτόν· ὁ λόγος ὃν ἐλάλησα ἐκεῖνος κρινεῖ αὐτὸν ἐν τῇ ἐσχάτῃ ἡμέρᾳ. **49** ὅτι ἐγὼ ἐξ ἐμαυτοῦ οὐκ ἐλάλησα, ἀλλ᾽ ὁ πέμψας με πατὴρ αὐτός μοι ἐντολὴν δέδωκεν τί εἴπω καὶ τί λαλήσω. **50** καὶ οἶδα ὅτι ἡ ἐντολὴ αὐτοῦ ζωὴ αἰώνιός ἐστιν. ἃ οὖν ἐγὼ λαλῶ, καθὼς εἴρηκέν μοι ὁ πατήρ, οὕτως λαλῶ.

13 Πρὸ δὲ τῆς ἑορτῆς τοῦ πάσχα εἰδὼς ὁ Ἰησοῦς ὅτι ἦλθεν αὐτοῦ ἡ ὥρα ἵνα μεταβῇ ἐκ τοῦ κόσμου τούτου πρὸς τὸν πατέρα, ἀγαπήσας τοὺς ἰδίους τοὺς ἐν τῷ κόσμῳ εἰς τέλος ἠγάπησεν αὐτούς. **2** καὶ δείπνου γινομένου, τοῦ διαβόλου ἤδη βεβληκότος εἰς τὴν καρδίαν ἵνα παραδοῖ αὐτὸν Ἰούδας Σίμωνος Ἰσκαριώτου, **3** εἰδὼς ὅτι πάντα ἔδωκεν αὐτῷ ὁ πατὴρ εἰς τὰς χεῖρας καὶ ὅτι ἀπὸ θεοῦ ἐξῆλθεν καὶ πρὸς τὸν θεὸν ὑπάγει, **4** ἐγείρεται ἐκ τοῦ δείπνου καὶ τίθησιν τὰ ἱμάτια καὶ λαβὼν λέντιον διέζωσεν ἑαυτόν· **5** εἶτα βάλλει ὕδωρ εἰς τὸν νιπτῆρα καὶ ἤρξατο νίπτειν τοὺς πόδας τῶν μαθητῶν καὶ ἐκμάσσειν τῷ λεντίῳ ᾧ ἦν διεζωσμένος. **6** ἔρχεται οὖν πρὸς Σίμωνα Πέτρον· λέγει αὐτῷ, Κύριε, σύ μου νίπτεις τοὺς πόδας; **7** ἀπεκρίθη Ἰησοῦς καὶ εἶπεν αὐτῷ, Ὃ ἐγὼ ποιῶ σὺ οὐκ οἶδας ἄρτι, γνώσῃ δὲ μετὰ ταῦτα. **8** λέγει αὐτῷ Πέτρος, Οὐ μὴ νίψῃς μου τοὺς πόδας εἰς τὸν αἰῶνα. ἀπεκρίθη Ἰησοῦς αὐτῷ, Ἐὰν μὴ νίψω σε, οὐκ ἔχεις μέρος μετ᾽ ἐμοῦ. **9** λέγει αὐτῷ Σίμων Πέτρος, Κύριε, μὴ τοὺς πόδας μου μόνον ἀλλὰ καὶ τὰς χεῖρας καὶ τὴν κεφαλήν. **10** λέγει αὐτῷ ὁ Ἰησοῦς, Ὁ λελουμένος οὐκ ἔχει χρείαν εἰ μὴ τοὺς πόδας νίψασθαι, ἀλλ᾽ ἔστιν καθαρὸς ὅλος· καὶ ὑμεῖς καθαροί ἐστε, ἀλλ᾽ οὐχὶ πάντες. **11** ᾔδει γὰρ τὸν παραδιδόντα αὐτόν· διὰ τοῦτο εἶπεν ὅτι Οὐχὶ πάντες καθαροί ἐστε.

12 Ὅτε οὖν ἔνιψεν τοὺς πόδας αὐτῶν [καὶ]a ἔλαβεν τὰ ἱμάτια αὐτοῦ καὶ ἀνέπεσεν πάλιν, εἶπεν αὐτοῖς, Γινώσκετε τί πεποίηκα ὑμῖν; **13** ὑμεῖς φωνεῖτέ με Ὁ διδάσκαλος καὶ Ὁ κύριος, καὶ καλῶς λέγετε, εἰμὶ γάρ. **14** εἰ οὖν ἐγὼ ἔνιψα ὑμῶν τοὺς πόδας ὁ κύριος καὶ ὁ διδάσκαλος, καὶ ὑμεῖς ὀφείλετε ἀλλήλων νίπτειν τοὺς πόδας· **15** ὑπόδειγμα γὰρ ἔδωκα ὑμῖν ἵνα καθὼς ἐγὼ ἐποίησα ὑμῖν καὶ ὑμεῖς ποιῆτε. **16** ἀμὴν

words; that very word which I spoke will condemn him at the last day. 49For I did not speak of my own accord, but the Father who sent me commanded me what to say and how to say it. 50I know that his command leads to eternal life. So whatever I say is just what the Father has told me to say."

Jesus Washes His Disciples' Feet

13 It was just before the Passover Feast. Jesus knew that the time had come for him to leave this world and go to the Father. Having loved his own who were in the world, he now showed them the full extent of his love.a

2The evening meal was being served, and the devil had already prompted Judas Iscariot, son of Simon, to betray Jesus. 3Jesus knew that the Father had put all things under his power, and that he had come from God and was returning to God; 4so he got up from the meal, took off his outer clothing, and wrapped a towel around his waist. 5After that, he poured water into a basin and began to wash his disciples' feet, drying them with the towel that was wrapped around him.

6He came to Simon Peter, who said to him, "Lord, are you going to wash my feet?"

7Jesus replied, "You do not realize now what I am doing, but later you will understand."

8"No," said Peter, "you shall never wash my feet."

Jesus answered, "Unless I wash you, you have no part with me."

9"Then, Lord," Simon Peter replied, "not just my feet but my hands and my head as well!"

10Jesus answered, "A person who has had a bath needs only to wash his feet; his whole body is clean. And you are clean, though not every one of you." 11For he knew who was going to betray him, and that was why he said not every one was clean.

12When he had finished washing their feet, he put on his clothes and returned to his place. "Do you understand what I have done for you?" he asked them. 13"You call me 'Teacher' and 'Lord,' and rightly so, for that is what I am. 14Now that I, your Lord and Teacher, have washed your feet, you also should wash one another's feet. 15I have set you an example that you should do as I have done for you. 16I tell you the

---

r Gk *from supper* s Other ancient authorities lack *except for the feet* t The Greek word for *you* here is plural

a12 NIV text omits καί †

a1 Or *he loved them to the last*

you, servants[u] are not greater than their master, nor are messengers greater than the one who sent them. [17]If you know these things, you are blessed if you do them. [18]I am not speaking of all of you; I know whom I have chosen. But it is to fulfill the scripture, 'The one who ate my bread[v] has lifted his heel against me.' [19]I tell you this now, before it occurs, so that when it does occur, you may believe that I am he.[w] [20]Very truly, I tell you, whoever receives one whom I send receives me; and whoever receives me receives him who sent me."

Jesus Foretells His Betrayal

21 After saying this Jesus was troubled in spirit, and declared, "Very truly, I tell you, one of you will betray me." [22]The disciples looked at one another, uncertain of whom he was speaking. [23]One of his disciples—the one whom Jesus loved—was reclining next to him; [24]Simon Peter therefore motioned to him to ask Jesus of whom he was speaking. [25]So while reclining next to Jesus, he asked him, "Lord, who is it?" [26]Jesus answered, "It is the one to whom I give this piece of bread when I have dipped it in the dish."[x] So when he had dipped the piece of bread, he gave it to Judas son of Simon Iscariot.[y] [27]After he received the piece of bread,[z] Satan entered into him. Jesus said to him, "Do quickly what you are going to do." [28]Now no one at the table knew why he said this to him. [29]Some thought that, because Judas had the common purse, Jesus was telling him, "Buy what we need for the festival"; or, that he should give something to the poor. [30]So, after receiving the piece of bread, he immediately went out. And it was night.

The New Commandment

31 When he had gone out, Jesus said, "Now the Son of Man has been glorified, and God has been glorified in him. [32]If God has been glorified in him,[a] God will also glorify him in himself and will glorify him at once. [33]Little children, I am with you only a little longer. You will look for me; and as I said to the Jews so now I say to you, 'Where I am going, you cannot come.' [34]I give you a new commandment, that you love one another. Just as I have loved you, you also should love one

---

ἀμὴν λέγω ὑμῖν, οὐκ ἔστιν δοῦλος μείζων τοῦ κυρίου αὐτοῦ οὐδὲ ἀπόστολος μείζων τοῦ πέμψαντος αὐτόν. **17** εἰ ταῦτα οἴδατε, μακάριοί ἐστε ἐὰν ποιῆτε αὐτά. **18** οὐ περὶ πάντων ὑμῶν λέγω· ἐγὼ οἶδα τίνας ἐξελεξάμην· ἀλλ' ἵνα ἡ γραφὴ πληρωθῇ, Ὁ τρώγων μου[b] τὸν ἄρτον ἐπῆρεν ἐπ' ἐμὲ τὴν πτέρναν αὐτοῦ. **19** ἀπ' ἄρτι λέγω ὑμῖν πρὸ τοῦ γενέσθαι, ἵνα πιστεύσητε ὅταν γένηται ὅτι ἐγώ εἰμι. **20** ἀμὴν ἀμὴν λέγω ὑμῖν, ὁ λαμβάνων ἄν τινα πέμψω ἐμὲ λαμβάνει, ὁ δὲ ἐμὲ λαμβάνων λαμβάνει τὸν πέμψαντά με.

21 Ταῦτα εἰπὼν [ὁ] Ἰησοῦς ἐταράχθη τῷ πνεύματι καὶ ἐμαρτύρησεν καὶ εἶπεν, Ἀμὴν ἀμὴν λέγω ὑμῖν ὅτι εἷς ἐξ ὑμῶν παραδώσει με. **22** ἔβλεπον εἰς ἀλλήλους οἱ μαθηταὶ ἀπορούμενοι περὶ τίνος λέγει. **23** ἦν ἀνακείμενος εἷς ἐκ τῶν μαθητῶν αὐτοῦ ἐν τῷ κόλπῳ τοῦ Ἰησοῦ, ὃν ἠγάπα ὁ Ἰησοῦς. **24** νεύει οὖν τούτῳ Σίμων Πέτρος πυθέσθαι τίς ἂν εἴη περὶ οὗ λέγει. **25** ἀναπεσὼν οὖν ἐκεῖνος οὕτως ἐπὶ τὸ στῆθος τοῦ Ἰησοῦ λέγει αὐτῷ, Κύριε, τίς ἐστιν; **26** ἀποκρίνεται [ὁ] Ἰησοῦς, Ἐκεῖνός ἐστιν ᾧ ἐγὼ βάψω τὸ ψωμίον καὶ δώσω αὐτῷ. βάψας οὖν τὸ ψωμίον [λαμβάνει καὶ][c] δίδωσιν Ἰούδα Σίμωνος Ἰσκαριώτου[d]. **27** καὶ μετὰ τὸ ψωμίον τότε εἰσῆλθεν εἰς ἐκεῖνον ὁ Σατανᾶς. λέγει οὖν αὐτῷ ὁ Ἰησοῦς, Ὃ ποιεῖς ποίησον τάχιον. **28** τοῦτο [δὲ] οὐδεὶς ἔγνω τῶν ἀνακειμένων πρὸς τί εἶπεν αὐτῷ· **29** τινὲς γὰρ ἐδόκουν, ἐπεὶ τὸ γλωσσόκομον εἶχεν Ἰούδας, ὅτι λέγει αὐτῷ [ὁ] Ἰησοῦς, Ἀγόρασον ὧν χρείαν ἔχομεν εἰς τὴν ἑορτήν, ἢ τοῖς πτωχοῖς ἵνα τι δῷ. **30** λαβὼν οὖν τὸ ψωμίον ἐκεῖνος ἐξῆλθεν εὐθύς. ἦν δὲ νύξ.

31 Ὅτε οὖν ἐξῆλθεν, λέγει Ἰησοῦς, Νῦν ἐδοξάσθη ὁ υἱὸς τοῦ ἀνθρώπου, καὶ ὁ θεὸς ἐδοξάσθη ἐν αὐτῷ· **32** [εἰ ὁ θεὸς ἐδοξάσθη ἐν αὐτῷ,] καὶ ὁ θεὸς δοξάσει αὐτὸν ἐν αὐτῷ, καὶ εὐθὺς δοξάσει αὐτόν. **33** τεκνία, ἔτι μικρὸν μεθ' ὑμῶν εἰμι· ζητήσετέ με, καὶ καθὼς εἶπον τοῖς Ἰουδαίοις ὅτι Ὅπου ἐγὼ ὑπάγω ὑμεῖς οὐ δύνασθε ἐλθεῖν, καὶ ὑμῖν λέγω ἄρτι. **34** ἐντολὴν καινὴν δίδωμι ὑμῖν, ἵνα ἀγαπᾶτε ἀλλήλους, καθὼς ἠγάπησα ὑμᾶς ἵνα καὶ ὑμεῖς

---

truth, no servant is greater than his master, nor is a messenger greater than the one who sent him. [17]Now that you know these things, you will be blessed if you do them.

Jesus Predicts His Betrayal

[18]"I am not referring to all of you; I know those I have chosen. But this is to fulfill the scripture: 'He who shares my bread has lifted up his heel against me.'[b]

[19]"I am telling you now before it happens, so that when it does happen you will believe that I am He. [20]I tell you the truth, whoever accepts anyone I send accepts me; and whoever accepts me accepts the one who sent me."

[21]After he had said this, Jesus was troubled in spirit and testified, "I tell you the truth, one of you is going to betray me."

[22]His disciples stared at one another, at a loss to know which of them he meant. [23]One of them, the disciple whom Jesus loved, was reclining next to him. [24]Simon Peter motioned to this disciple and said, "Ask him which one he means."

[25]Leaning back against Jesus, he asked him, "Lord, who is it?"

[26]Jesus answered, "It is the one to whom I will give this piece of bread when I have dipped it in the dish." Then, dipping the piece of bread, he gave it to Judas Iscariot, son of Simon. [27]As soon as Judas took the bread, Satan entered into him.

"What you are about to do, do quickly," Jesus told him, [28]but no one at the meal understood why Jesus said this to him. [29]Since Judas had charge of the money, some thought Jesus was telling him to buy what was needed for the Feast, or to give something to the poor. [30]As soon as Judas had taken the bread, he went out. And it was night.

Jesus Predicts Peter's Denial

[31]When he was gone, Jesus said, "Now is the Son of Man glorified and God is glorified in him. [32]If God is glorified in him,[c] God will glorify the Son in himself, and will glorify him at once.

[33]"My children, I will be with you only a little longer. You will look for me, and just as I told the Jews, so I tell you now: Where I am going, you cannot come.

[34]"A new command I give you: Love one another. As I have loved you, so you must

---

[u] Gk *slaves*   [v] *Other ancient authorities read* ate bread with me   [w] Gk *I am*   [x] Gk *dipped it*   [y] *Other ancient authorities read* Judas Iscariot son of Simon; *others,* Judas son of Simon from Karyot (Kerioth)   [z] Gk *After the piece of bread*   [a] *Other ancient authorities lack* If God has been glorified in him

[b]18 NRSV note v μετ' ἐμοῦ   [c]26 NIV text omits λαμβάνει καὶ   [d]26 NRSV note y Ἰούδα Σίμωνος Ἰσκαριώτη or Ἰούδα Σίμωνος ἀπὸ Καρυώτου †

[b]18 Psalm 41:9   [c]32 Many early manuscripts do not have If God is glorified in him.

another. 35By this everyone will know that you are my disciples, if you have love for one another."

Jesus Foretells Peter's Denial

36 Simon Peter said to him, "Lord, where are you going?" Jesus answered, "Where I am going, you cannot follow me now; but you will follow afterward." 37Peter said to him, "Lord, why can I not follow you now? I will lay down my life for you." 38Jesus answered, "Will you lay down your life for me? Very truly, I tell you, before the cock crows, you will have denied me three times.

Jesus the Way to the Father

14 "Do not let your hearts be troubled. Believeb in God, believe also in me. 2In my Father's house there are many dwelling places. If it were not so, would I have told you that I go to prepare a place for you?c 3And if I go and prepare a place for you, I will come again and will take you to myself, so that where I am, there you may be also. 4And you know the way to the place where I am going."d 5Thomas said to him, "Lord, we do not know where you are going. How can we know the way?" 6Jesus said to him, "I am the way, and the truth, and the life. No one comes to the Father except through me. 7If you know me, you will knowe my Father also. From now on you do know him and have seen him."

8 Philip said to him, "Lord, show us the Father, and we will be satisfied." 9Jesus said to him, "Have I been with you all this time, Philip, and you still do not know me? Whoever has seen me has seen the Father. How can you say, 'Show us the Father'? 10Do you not believe that I am in the Father and the Father is in me? The words that I say to you I do not speak on my own; but the Father who dwells in me does his works. 11Believe me that I am in the Father and the Father is in me; but if you do not, then believe me because of the works themselves. 12Very truly, I tell you, the one who believes in me will also do the works that I do and, in fact, will do greater works than these, because I am going to the Father. 13I will do whatever you ask in my name, so that the Father may be glorified in the Son. 14If in my name you ask

ἀγαπᾶτε ἀλλήλους. 35 ἐν τούτῳ γνώσονται πάντες ὅτι ἐμοὶ μαθηταί ἐστε, ἐὰν ἀγάπην ἔχητε ἐν ἀλλήλοις.

36 Λέγει αὐτῷ Σίμων Πέτρος, Κύριε, ποῦ ὑπάγεις; ἀπεκρίθη [αὐτῷ]e Ἰησοῦς, Ὅπου ὑπάγω οὐ δύνασαί μοι νῦν ἀκολουθῆσαι, ἀκολουθήσεις δὲ ὕστερον. 37 λέγει αὐτῷ ὁ Πέτρος, Κύριε, διὰ τί οὐ δύναμαί σοι ἀκολουθῆσαι ἄρτι; τὴν ψυχήν μου ὑπὲρ σοῦ θήσω. 38 ἀποκρίνεται Ἰησοῦς, Τὴν ψυχήν σου ὑπὲρ ἐμοῦ θήσεις; ἀμὴν ἀμὴν λέγω σοι, οὐ μὴ ἀλέκτωρ φωνήσῃ ἕως οὗ ἀρνήσῃ με τρίς.

14 Μὴ ταρασσέσθω ὑμῶν ἡ καρδία· πιστεύετε εἰς τὸν θεὸν καὶ εἰς ἐμὲ πιστεύετε. 2 ἐν τῇ οἰκίᾳ τοῦ πατρός μου μοναὶ πολλαί εἰσιν· εἰ δὲ μή, εἶπον ἂν ὑμῖν ὅτι πορεύομαι ἑτοιμάσαι τόπον ὑμῖν; 3 καὶ ἐὰν πορευθῶ καὶ ἑτοιμάσω τόπον ὑμῖν, πάλιν ἔρχομαι καὶ παραλήμψομαι ὑμᾶς πρὸς ἐμαυτόν, ἵνα ὅπου εἰμὶ ἐγὼ καὶ ὑμεῖς ἦτε. 4 καὶ ὅπου [ἐγὼ] ὑπάγω οἴδατε τὴν ὁδόνa. 5 Λέγει αὐτῷ Θωμᾶς, Κύριε, οὐκ οἴδαμεν ποῦ ὑπάγεις· πῶς δυνάμεθα τὴν ὁδὸν εἰδέναι; 6 λέγει αὐτῷ [ὁ] Ἰησοῦς, Ἐγώ εἰμι ἡ ὁδὸς καὶ ἡ ἀλήθεια καὶ ἡ ζωή· οὐδεὶς ἔρχεται πρὸς τὸν πατέρα εἰ μὴ δι' ἐμοῦ. 7 εἰ ἐγνώκατέ με, καὶ τὸν πατέρα μου γνώσεσθεb. καὶ ἀπ' ἄρτι γινώσκετε αὐτὸν καὶ ἑωράκατε αὐτόν. 8 λέγει αὐτῷ Φίλιππος, Κύριε, δεῖξον ἡμῖν τὸν πατέρα, καὶ ἀρκεῖ ἡμῖν. 9 λέγει αὐτῷ ὁ Ἰησοῦς, Τοσούτῳ χρόνῳ μεθ' ὑμῶν εἰμι καὶ οὐκ ἔγνωκάς με, Φίλιππε; ὁ ἑωρακὼς ἐμὲ ἑώρακεν τὸν πατέρα· πῶς σὺ λέγεις, Δεῖξον ἡμῖν τὸν πατέρα; 10 οὐ πιστεύεις ὅτι ἐγὼ ἐν τῷ πατρὶ καὶ ὁ πατὴρ ἐν ἐμοί ἐστιν; τὰ ῥήματα ἃ ἐγὼ λέγω ὑμῖν ἀπ' ἐμαυτοῦ οὐ λαλῶ, ὁ δὲ πατὴρ ἐν ἐμοὶ μένων ποιεῖ τὰ ἔργα αὐτοῦ. 11 πιστεύετέ μοι ὅτι ἐγὼ ἐν τῷ πατρὶ καὶ ὁ πατὴρ ἐν ἐμοί· εἰ δὲ μή, διὰ τὰ ἔργα αὐτὰ πιστεύετε. 12 ἀμὴν ἀμὴν λέγω ὑμῖν, ὁ πιστεύων εἰς ἐμὲ τὰ ἔργα ἃ ἐγὼ ποιῶ κἀκεῖνος ποιήσει καὶ μείζονα τούτων ποιήσει, ὅτι ἐγὼ πρὸς τὸν πατέρα πορεύομαι· 13 καὶ ὅ τι ἂν αἰτήσητε ἐν τῷ ὀνόματί μου τοῦτο ποιήσω, ἵνα δοξασθῇ ὁ πατὴρ ἐν τῷ υἱῷ· 14 ἐάν τι αἰτήσητέ

love one another. 35By this all men will know that you are my disciples, if you love one another."

36Simon Peter asked him, "Lord, where are you going?"

Jesus replied, "Where I am going, you cannot follow now, but you will follow later."

37Peter asked, "Lord, why can't I follow you now? I will lay down my life for you."

38Then Jesus answered, "Will you really lay down your life for me? I tell you the truth, before the rooster crows, you will disown me three times!

Jesus Comforts His Disciples

14 "Do not let your hearts be troubled. Trust in Goda; trust also in me. 2In my Father's house are many rooms; if it were not so, I would have told you. I am going there to prepare a place for you. 3And if I go and prepare a place for you, I will come back and take you to be with me that you also may be where I am. 4You know the way to the place where I am going."

Jesus the Way to the Father

5Thomas said to him, "Lord, we don't know where you are going, so how can we know the way?"

6Jesus answered, "I am the way and the truth and the life. No one comes to the Father except through me. 7If you really knew me, you would knowb my Father as well. From now on, you do know him and have seen him."

8Philip said, "Lord, show us the Father and that will be enough for us."

9Jesus answered: "Don't you know me, Philip, even after I have been among you such a long time? Anyone who has seen me has seen the Father. How can you say, 'Show us the Father'? 10Don't you believe that I am in the Father, and that the Father is in me? The words I say to you are not just my own. Rather, it is the Father, living in me, who is doing his work. 11Believe me when I say that I am in the Father and the Father is in me; or at least believe on the evidence of the miracles themselves. 12I tell you the truth, anyone who has faith in me will do what I have been doing. He will do even greater things than these, because I am going to the Father. 13And I will do whatever you ask in my name, so that the Son may bring glory to the Father.

---

b Or You believe   c Or If it were not so, I would have told you; for I go to prepare a place for you   d Other ancient authorities read Where I am going you know, and the way you know   e Other ancient authorities read If you had known me, you would have known

e36 NIV text omits αὐτῷ †   a4 NRSV note d καὶ τὴν ὁδὸν οἴδατε   b7 NIV text and NRSV note e ἐγνώκειτέ με, καὶ τὸν πατέρα μου ἂν ᾔδειτε; NIV note and NRSV text as UBS

a1 Or You trust in God   b7 Some early manuscripts If you really have known me, you will know

me^f for anything, I will do it.

The Promise of the Holy Spirit

15 "If you love me, you will keep^g my commandments. 16And I will ask the Father, and he will give you another Advocate,^h to be with you forever. 17This is the Spirit of truth, whom the world cannot receive, because it neither sees him nor knows him. You know him, because he abides with you, and he will be in^i you.

18 "I will not leave you orphaned; I am coming to you. 19In a little while the world will no longer see me, but you will see me; because I live, you also will live. 20On that day you will know that I am in my Father, and you in me, and I in you. 21They who have my commandments and keep them are those who love me; and those who love me will be loved by my Father, and I will love them and reveal myself to them." 22Judas (not Iscariot) said to him, "Lord, how is it that you will reveal yourself to us, and not to the world?" 23Jesus answered him, "Those who love me will keep my word, and my Father will love them, and we will come to them and make our home with them. 24Whoever does not love me does not keep my words; and the word that you hear is not mine, but is from the Father who sent me.

25 "I have said these things to you while I am still with you. 26But the Advocate,^h the Holy Spirit, whom the Father will send in my name, will teach you everything, and remind you of all that I have said to you. 27Peace I leave with you; my peace I give to you. I do not give to you as the world gives. Do not let your hearts be troubled, and do not let them be afraid. 28You heard me say to you, 'I am going away, and I am coming to you.' If you loved me, you would rejoice that I am going to the Father, because the Father is greater than I. 29And now I have told you this before it occurs, so that when it does occur, you may believe. 30I will no longer talk much with you, for the ruler of this world is coming. He has no power over me; 31but I do as the Father has commanded me, so that the world may know that I love the Father. Rise, let us be on our way.

Jesus the True Vine

15 "I am the true vine, and my Father is the vinegrower. 2He removes

---

με ἐν τῷ ὀνόματί μου ἐγὼ ποιήσω.

15 Ἐὰν ἀγαπᾶτέ με, τὰς ἐντολὰς τὰς ἐμὰς τηρήσετε^c· 16 κἀγὼ ἐρωτήσω τὸν πατέρα καὶ ἄλλον παράκλητον δώσει ὑμῖν, ἵνα μεθ᾽ ὑμῶν εἰς τὸν αἰῶνα ᾖ, 17 τὸ πνεῦμα τῆς ἀληθείας, ὃ ὁ κόσμος οὐ δύναται λαβεῖν, ὅτι οὐ θεωρεῖ αὐτὸ οὐδὲ γινώσκει· ὑμεῖς γινώσκετε αὐτό, ὅτι παρ᾽ ὑμῖν μένει καὶ ἐν ὑμῖν ἔσται^d. 18 Οὐκ ἀφήσω ὑμᾶς ὀρφανούς, ἔρχομαι πρὸς ὑμᾶς. 19 ἔτι μικρὸν καὶ ὁ κόσμος με οὐκέτι θεωρεῖ, ὑμεῖς δὲ θεωρεῖτέ με, ὅτι ἐγὼ ζῶ καὶ ὑμεῖς ζήσετε. 20 ἐν ἐκείνῃ τῇ ἡμέρᾳ γνώσεσθε ὑμεῖς ὅτι ἐγὼ ἐν τῷ πατρί μου καὶ ὑμεῖς ἐν ἐμοὶ κἀγὼ ἐν ὑμῖν. 21 ὁ ἔχων τὰς ἐντολάς μου καὶ τηρῶν αὐτὰς ἐκεῖνός ἐστιν ὁ ἀγαπῶν με· ὁ δὲ ἀγαπῶν με ἀγαπηθήσεται ὑπὸ τοῦ πατρός μου, κἀγὼ ἀγαπήσω αὐτὸν καὶ ἐμφανίσω αὐτῷ ἐμαυτόν. 22 Λέγει αὐτῷ Ἰούδας, οὐχ ὁ Ἰσκαριώτης, Κύριε, [καὶ] τί γέγονεν ὅτι ἡμῖν μέλλεις ἐμφανίζειν σεαυτὸν καὶ οὐχὶ τῷ κόσμῳ; 23 ἀπεκρίθη Ἰησοῦς καὶ εἶπεν αὐτῷ, Ἐάν τις ἀγαπᾷ με τὸν λόγον μου τηρήσει, καὶ ὁ πατήρ μου ἀγαπήσει αὐτὸν καὶ πρὸς αὐτὸν ἐλευσόμεθα καὶ μονὴν παρ᾽ αὐτῷ ποιησόμεθα. 24 ὁ μὴ ἀγαπῶν με τοὺς λόγους μου οὐ τηρεῖ· καὶ ὁ λόγος ὃν ἀκούετε οὐκ ἔστιν ἐμὸς ἀλλὰ τοῦ πέμψαντός με πατρός.

25 Ταῦτα λελάληκα ὑμῖν παρ᾽ ὑμῖν μένων· 26 ὁ δὲ παράκλητος, τὸ πνεῦμα τὸ ἅγιον, ὃ πέμψει ὁ πατὴρ ἐν τῷ ὀνόματί μου, ἐκεῖνος ὑμᾶς διδάξει πάντα καὶ ὑπομνήσει ὑμᾶς πάντα ἃ εἶπον ὑμῖν [ἐγώ]. 27 Εἰρήνην ἀφίημι ὑμῖν, εἰρήνην τὴν ἐμὴν δίδωμι ὑμῖν· οὐ καθὼς ὁ κόσμος δίδωσιν ἐγὼ δίδωμι ὑμῖν. μὴ ταρασσέσθω ὑμῶν ἡ καρδία μηδὲ δειλιάτω. 28 ἠκούσατε ὅτι ἐγὼ εἶπον ὑμῖν, Ὑπάγω καὶ ἔρχομαι πρὸς ὑμᾶς. εἰ ἠγαπᾶτέ με ἐχάρητε ἂν ὅτι πορεύομαι πρὸς τὸν πατέρα, ὅτι ὁ πατὴρ μείζων μού ἐστιν. 29 καὶ νῦν εἴρηκα ὑμῖν πρὶν γενέσθαι, ἵνα ὅταν γένηται πιστεύσητε. 30 οὐκέτι πολλὰ λαλήσω μεθ᾽ ὑμῶν, ἔρχεται γὰρ ὁ τοῦ κόσμου ἄρχων· καὶ ἐν ἐμοὶ οὐκ ἔχει οὐδέν, 31 ἀλλ᾽ ἵνα γνῷ ὁ κόσμος ὅτι ἀγαπῶ τὸν πατέρα, καὶ καθὼς ἐνετείλατο μοι ὁ πατήρ, οὕτως ποιῶ. Ἐγείρεσθε, ἄγωμεν ἐντεῦθεν.

15 Ἐγώ εἰμι ἡ ἄμπελος ἡ ἀληθινὴ καὶ ὁ πατήρ μου ὁ γεωργός ἐστιν. 2 πᾶν κλῆμα ἐν ἐμοὶ μὴ φέρον

14You may ask me for anything in my name, and I will do it.

Jesus Promises the Holy Spirit

15"If you love me, you will obey what I command. 16And I will ask the Father, and he will give you another Counselor to be with you forever— 17the Spirit of truth. The world cannot accept him, because it neither sees him nor knows him. But you know him, for he lives with you and will be^c in you. 18I will not leave you as orphans; I will come to you. 19Before long, the world will not see me anymore, but you will see me. Because I live, you also will live. 20On that day you will realize that I am in my Father, and you are in me, and I am in you. 21Whoever has my commands and obeys them, he is the one who loves me. He who loves me will be loved by my Father, and I too will love him and show myself to him."

22Then Judas (not Judas Iscariot) said, "But, Lord, why do you intend to show yourself to us and not to the world?"

23Jesus replied, "If anyone loves me, he will obey my teaching. My Father will love him, and we will come to him and make our home with him. 24He who does not love me will not obey my teaching. These words you hear are not my own; they belong to the Father who sent me.

25"All this I have spoken while still with you. 26But the Counselor, the Holy Spirit, whom the Father will send in my name, will teach you all things and will remind you of everything I have said to you. 27Peace I leave with you; my peace I give you. I do not give to you as the world gives. Do not let your hearts be troubled and do not be afraid. 28"You heard me say, 'I am going away and I am coming back to you.' If you loved me, you would be glad that I am going to the Father, for the Father is greater than I. 29I have told you now before it happens, so that when it does happen you will believe. 30I will not speak with you much longer, for the prince of this world is coming. He has no hold on me, 31but the world must learn that I love the Father and that I do exactly what my Father has commanded me.

"Come now; let us leave.

The Vine and the Branches

15 "I am the true vine, and my Father is the gardener. 2He cuts off every

---

^f Other ancient authorities lack *me*   ^g Other ancient authorities read *me, keep*   ^h Or *Helper*   ^i Or *among*

^c15 NRSV note g τηρήσατε   ^d17 NIV note ἐστιν

^c17 Some early manuscripts *and is*

every branch in me that bears no fruit. Every branch that bears fruit he prunes[k] to make it bear more fruit. [3]You have already been cleansed[k] by the word that I have spoken to you. [4]Abide in me as I abide in you. Just as the branch cannot bear fruit by itself unless it abides in the vine, neither can you unless you abide in me. [5]I am the vine, you are the branches. Those who abide in me and I in them bear much fruit, because apart from me you can do nothing. [6]Whoever does not abide in me is thrown away like a branch and withers; such branches are gathered, thrown into the fire, and burned. [7]If you abide in me, and my words abide in you, ask for whatever you wish, and it will be done for you. [8]My Father is glorified by this, that you bear much fruit and become[l] my disciples. [9]As the Father has loved me, so I have loved you; abide in my love. [10]If you keep my commandments, you will abide in my love, just as I have kept my Father's commandments and abide in his love. [11]I have said these things to you so that my joy may be in you, and that your joy may be complete.

12 "This is my commandment, that you love one another as I have loved you. [13]No one has greater love than this, to lay down one's life for one's friends. [14]You are my friends if you do what I command you. [15]I do not call you servants[m] any longer, because the servant[n] does not know what the master is doing; but I have called you friends, because I have made known to you everything that I have heard from my Father. [16]You did not choose me but I chose you. And I appointed you to go and bear fruit, fruit that will last, so that the Father will give you whatever you ask him in my name. [17]I am giving you these commands so that you may love one another.

The World's Hatred

18 "If the world hates you, be aware that it hated me before it hated you. [19]If you belonged to the world,[o] the world would love you as its own. Because you do not belong to the world, but I have chosen you out of the world—therefore the world hates you. [20]Remember the word that I said to you, 'Servants[p] are not greater than their master.' If they persecuted me, they will persecute you; if they kept my word, they will keep yours also. [21]But they will do all

καρπὸν αἴρει αὐτό, καὶ πᾶν τὸ καρπὸν φέρον καθαίρει αὐτὸ ἵνα καρπὸν πλείονα φέρῃ. 3 ἤδη ὑμεῖς καθαροί ἐστε διὰ τὸν λόγον ὃν λελάληκα ὑμῖν· 4 μείνατε ἐν ἐμοί, κἀγὼ ἐν ὑμῖν. καθὼς τὸ κλῆμα οὐ δύναται καρπὸν φέρειν ἀφ᾽ ἑαυτοῦ ἐὰν μὴ μένῃ ἐν τῇ ἀμπέλῳ, οὕτως οὐδὲ ὑμεῖς ἐὰν μὴ ἐν ἐμοὶ μένητε. 5 ἐγώ εἰμι ἡ ἄμπελος, ὑμεῖς τὰ κλήματα. ὁ μένων ἐν ἐμοὶ κἀγὼ ἐν αὐτῷ οὗτος φέρει καρπὸν πολύν, ὅτι χωρὶς ἐμοῦ οὐ δύνασθε ποιεῖν οὐδέν. 6 ἐὰν μή τις μένῃ ἐν ἐμοί, ἐβλήθη ἔξω ὡς τὸ κλῆμα καὶ ἐξηράνθη καὶ συνάγουσιν αὐτὰ καὶ εἰς τὸ πῦρ βάλλουσιν καὶ καίεται. 7 ἐὰν μείνητε ἐν ἐμοὶ καὶ τὰ ῥήματά μου ἐν ὑμῖν μείνῃ, ὃ ἐὰν θέλητε αἰτήσασθε, καὶ γενήσεται ὑμῖν. 8 ἐν τούτῳ ἐδοξάσθη ὁ πατήρ μου, ἵνα καρπὸν πολὺν φέρητε καὶ γένησθε ἐμοὶ μαθηταί. 9 καθὼς ἠγάπησέν με ὁ πατήρ, κἀγὼ ὑμᾶς ἠγάπησα· μείνατε ἐν τῇ ἀγάπῃ τῇ ἐμῇ. 10 ἐὰν τὰς ἐντολάς μου τηρήσητε, μενεῖτε ἐν τῇ ἀγάπῃ μου, καθὼς ἐγὼ τὰς ἐντολὰς τοῦ πατρός μου τετήρηκα καὶ μένω αὐτοῦ ἐν τῇ ἀγάπῃ.

11 Ταῦτα λελάληκα ὑμῖν ἵνα ἡ χαρὰ ἡ ἐμὴ ἐν ὑμῖν ᾖ καὶ ἡ χαρὰ ὑμῶν πληρωθῇ. 12 αὕτη ἐστὶν ἡ ἐντολὴ ἡ ἐμή, ἵνα ἀγαπᾶτε ἀλλήλους καθὼς ἠγάπησα ὑμᾶς. 13 μείζονα ταύτης ἀγάπην οὐδεὶς ἔχει, ἵνα τις τὴν ψυχὴν αὐτοῦ θῇ ὑπὲρ τῶν φίλων αὐτοῦ. 14 ὑμεῖς φίλοι μού ἐστε ἐὰν ποιῆτε ἃ ἐγὼ ἐντέλλομαι ὑμῖν. 15 οὐκέτι λέγω ὑμᾶς δούλους, ὅτι ὁ δοῦλος οὐκ οἶδεν τί ποιεῖ αὐτοῦ ὁ κύριος· ὑμᾶς δὲ εἴρηκα φίλους, ὅτι πάντα ἃ ἤκουσα παρὰ τοῦ πατρός μου ἐγνώρισα ὑμῖν. 16 οὐχ ὑμεῖς με ἐξελέξασθε, ἀλλ᾽ ἐγὼ ἐξελεξάμην ὑμᾶς καὶ ἔθηκα ὑμᾶς ἵνα ὑμεῖς ὑπάγητε καὶ καρπὸν φέρητε καὶ ὁ καρπὸς ὑμῶν μένῃ, ἵνα ὅ τι ἂν αἰτήσητε τὸν πατέρα ἐν τῷ ὀνόματί μου δῷ ὑμῖν. 17 ταῦτα ἐντέλλομαι ὑμῖν, ἵνα ἀγαπᾶτε ἀλλήλους.

18 Εἰ ὁ κόσμος ὑμᾶς μισεῖ, γινώσκετε ὅτι ἐμὲ πρῶτον ὑμῶν[a] μεμίσηκεν. 19 εἰ ἐκ τοῦ κόσμου ἦτε, ὁ κόσμος ἂν τὸ ἴδιον ἐφίλει· ὅτι δὲ ἐκ τοῦ κόσμου οὐκ ἐστέ, ἀλλ᾽ ἐγὼ ἐξελεξάμην ὑμᾶς ἐκ τοῦ κόσμου, διὰ τοῦτο μισεῖ ὑμᾶς ὁ κόσμος. 20 μνημονεύετε τοῦ λόγου οὗ ἐγὼ εἶπον ὑμῖν, Οὐκ ἔστιν δοῦλος μείζων τοῦ κυρίου αὐτοῦ. εἰ ἐμὲ ἐδίωξαν, καὶ ὑμᾶς διώξουσιν· εἰ τὸν λόγον μου ἐτήρησαν, καὶ τὸν ὑμέτερον τηρήσουσιν.

branch in me that bears no fruit, while every branch that does bear fruit he prunes[a] so that it will be even more fruitful. [3]You are already clean because of the word I have spoken to you. [4]Remain in me, and I will remain in you. No branch can bear fruit by itself; it must remain in the vine. Neither can you bear fruit unless you remain in me.

[5]"I am the vine; you are the branches. If a man remains in me and I in him, he will bear much fruit; apart from me you can do nothing. [6]If anyone does not remain in me, he is like a branch that is thrown away and withers; such branches are picked up, thrown into the fire and burned. [7]If you remain in me and my words remain in you, ask whatever you wish, and it will be given you. [8]This is to my Father's glory, that you bear much fruit, showing yourselves to be my disciples.

[9]"As the Father has loved me, so have I loved you. Now remain in my love. [10]If you obey my commands, you will remain in my love, just as I have obeyed my Father's commands and remain in his love. [11]I have told you this so that my joy may be in you and that your joy may be complete. [12]My command is this: Love each other as I have loved you. [13]Greater love has no one than this, that he lay down his life for his friends. [14]You are my friends if you do what I command. [15]I no longer call you servants, because a servant does not know his master's business. Instead, I have called you friends, for everything that I learned from my Father I have made known to you. [16]You did not choose me, but I chose you and appointed you to go and bear fruit—fruit that will last. Then the Father will give you whatever you ask in my name. [17]This is my command: Love each other.

The World Hates the Disciples

[18]"If the world hates you, keep in mind that it hated me first. [19]If you belonged to the world, it would love you as its own. As it is, you do not belong to the world, but I have chosen you out of the world. That is why the world hates you. [20]Remember the words I spoke to you: 'No servant is greater than his master.'[b] If they persecuted me, they will persecute you also. If they obeyed my teaching, they will obey yours also.

---

k The same Greek root refers to pruning and cleansing
l Or be   m Gk slaves   n Gk slave   o Gk were of the world
p Gk Slaves

a18 NIV text omits ὑμῶν †

a2 The Greek for prunes also means cleans.
b20 John 13:16

these things to you on account of my name, because they do not know him who sent me. 22If I had not come and spoken to them, they would not have sin; but now they have no excuse for their sin. 23Whoever hates me hates my Father also. 24If I had not done among them the works that no one else did, they would not have sin. But now they have seen and hated both me and my Father. 25It was to fulfill the word that is written in their law, 'They hated me without a cause.'

26 "When the Advocate[q] comes, whom I will send to you from the Father, the Spirit of truth who comes from the Father, he will testify on my behalf. 27You also are to testify because you have been with me from the beginning.

16 "I have said these things to you to keep you from stumbling. 2They will put you out of the synagogues. Indeed, an hour is coming when those who kill you will think that by doing so they are offering worship to God. 3And they will do this because they have not known the Father or me. 4But I have said these things to you so that when their hour comes you may remember that I told you about them.

The Work of the Spirit

"I did not say these things to you from the beginning, because I was with you. 5But now I am going to him who sent me; yet none of you asks me, 'Where are you going?' 6But because I have said these things to you, sorrow has filled your hearts. 7Nevertheless I tell you the truth: it is to your advantage that I go away, for if I do not go away, the Advocate[q] will not come to you; but if I go, I will send him to you. 8And when he comes, he will prove the world wrong about[r] sin and righteousness and judgment: 9about sin, because they do not believe in me; 10about righteousness, because I am going to the Father and you will see me no longer; 11about judgment, because the ruler of this world has been condemned.

12 "I still have many things to say to you, but you cannot bear them now. 13When the Spirit of truth comes, he will guide you into all the truth; for he will not speak on his own, but will speak whatever he hears, and he will declare to you the things that are to come. 14He will glorify me, because he will take what is mine and declare it to you. 15All that the Father has is mine. For

21 ἀλλὰ ταῦτα πάντα ποιήσουσιν εἰς ὑμᾶς διὰ τὸ ὄνομά μου, ὅτι οὐκ οἴδασιν τὸν πέμψαντά με. 22 εἰ μὴ ἦλθον καὶ ἐλάλησα αὐτοῖς, ἁμαρτίαν οὐκ εἴχοσαν· νῦν δὲ πρόφασιν οὐκ ἔχουσιν περὶ τῆς ἁμαρτίας αὐτῶν. 23 ὁ ἐμὲ μισῶν καὶ τὸν πατέρα μου μισεῖ. 24 εἰ τὰ ἔργα μὴ ἐποίησα ἐν αὐτοῖς ἃ οὐδεὶς ἄλλος ἐποίησεν, ἁμαρτίαν οὐκ εἴχοσαν· νῦν δὲ καὶ ἑωράκασιν καὶ μεμισήκασιν καὶ ἐμὲ καὶ τὸν πατέρα μου. 25 ἀλλ' ἵνα πληρωθῇ ὁ λόγος ὁ ἐν τῷ νόμῳ αὐτῶν γεγραμμένος ὅτι Ἐμίσησάν με δωρεάν. 26 Ὅταν ἔλθῃ ὁ παράκλητος ὃν ἐγὼ πέμψω ὑμῖν παρὰ τοῦ πατρός, τὸ πνεῦμα τῆς ἀληθείας ὃ παρὰ τοῦ πατρὸς ἐκπορεύεται, ἐκεῖνος μαρτυρήσει περὶ ἐμοῦ· 27 καὶ ὑμεῖς δὲ μαρτυρεῖτε, ὅτι ἀπ' ἀρχῆς μετ' ἐμοῦ ἐστε.

16 Ταῦτα λελάληκα ὑμῖν ἵνα μὴ σκανδαλισθῆτε. 2 ἀποσυναγώγους ποιήσουσιν ὑμᾶς· ἀλλ' ἔρχεται ὥρα ἵνα πᾶς ὁ ἀποκτείνας ὑμᾶς δόξῃ λατρείαν προσφέρειν τῷ θεῷ. 3 καὶ ταῦτα ποιήσουσιν ὅτι οὐκ ἔγνωσαν τὸν πατέρα οὐδὲ ἐμέ. 4 ἀλλὰ ταῦτα λελάληκα ὑμῖν ἵνα ὅταν ἔλθῃ ἡ ὥρα αὐτῶν[a] μνημονεύητε αὐτῶν[a] ὅτι ἐγὼ εἶπον ὑμῖν.

Ταῦτα δὲ ὑμῖν ἐξ ἀρχῆς οὐκ εἶπον, ὅτι μεθ' ὑμῶν ἤμην. 5 νῦν δὲ ὑπάγω πρὸς τὸν πέμψαντά με, καὶ οὐδεὶς ἐξ ὑμῶν ἐρωτᾷ με, Ποῦ ὑπάγεις; 6 ἀλλ' ὅτι ταῦτα λελάληκα ὑμῖν ἡ λύπη πεπλήρωκεν ὑμῶν τὴν καρδίαν. 7 ἀλλ' ἐγὼ τὴν ἀλήθειαν λέγω ὑμῖν, συμφέρει ὑμῖν ἵνα ἐγὼ ἀπέλθω. ἐὰν γὰρ μὴ ἀπέλθω, ὁ παράκλητος οὐκ ἐλεύσεται πρὸς ὑμᾶς· ἐὰν δὲ πορευθῶ, πέμψω αὐτὸν πρὸς ὑμᾶς. 8 καὶ ἐλθὼν ἐκεῖνος ἐλέγξει τὸν κόσμον περὶ ἁμαρτίας καὶ περὶ δικαιοσύνης καὶ περὶ κρίσεως· 9 περὶ ἁμαρτίας μέν, ὅτι οὐ πιστεύουσιν εἰς ἐμέ· 10 περὶ δικαιοσύνης δέ, ὅτι πρὸς τὸν πατέρα ὑπάγω καὶ οὐκέτι θεωρεῖτέ με· 11 περὶ δὲ κρίσεως, ὅτι ὁ ἄρχων τοῦ κόσμου τούτου κέκριται.

12 Ἔτι πολλὰ ἔχω ὑμῖν λέγειν, ἀλλ' οὐ δύνασθε βαστάζειν ἄρτι· 13 ὅταν δὲ ἔλθῃ ἐκεῖνος, τὸ πνεῦμα τῆς ἀληθείας, ὁδηγήσει ὑμᾶς ἐν τῇ ἀληθείᾳ πάσῃ· οὐ γὰρ λαλήσει ἀφ' ἑαυτοῦ, ἀλλ' ὅσα ἀκούσει λαλήσει καὶ τὰ ἐρχόμενα ἀναγγελεῖ ὑμῖν. 14 ἐκεῖνος ἐμὲ δοξάσει, ὅτι ἐκ τοῦ ἐμοῦ λήμψεται καὶ ἀναγγελεῖ ὑμῖν. 15 πάντα ὅσα ἔχει ὁ πατὴρ ἐμά

21They will treat you this way because of my name, for they do not know the One who sent me. 22If I had not come and spoken to them, they would not be guilty of sin. Now, however, they have no excuse for their sin. 23He who hates me hates my Father as well. 24If I had not done among them what no one else did, they would not be guilty of sin. But now they have seen these miracles, and yet they have hated both me and my Father. 25But this is to fulfill what is written in their Law: 'They hated me without reason.'[c]

26"When the Counselor comes, whom I will send to you from the Father, the Spirit of truth who goes out from the Father, he will testify about me. 27And you also must testify, for you have been with me from the beginning.

16 "All this I have told you so that you will not go astray. 2They will put you out of the synagogue; in fact, a time is coming when anyone who kills you will think he is offering a service to God. 3They will do such things because they have not known the Father or me. 4I have told you this, so that when the time comes you will remember that I warned you. I did not tell you this at first because I was with you.

The Work of the Holy Spirit

5"Now I am going to him who sent me, yet none of you asks me, 'Where are you going?' 6Because I have said these things, you are filled with grief. 7But I tell you the truth: It is for your good that I am going away. Unless I go away, the Counselor will not come to you; but if I go, I will send him to you. 8When he comes, he will convict the world of guilt[d] in regard to sin and righteousness and judgment: 9in regard to sin, because men do not believe in me; 10in regard to righteousness, because I am going to the Father, where you can see me no longer; 11and in regard to judgment, because the prince of this world now stands condemned.

12"I have much more to say to you, more than you can now bear. 13But when he, the Spirit of truth, comes, he will guide you into all truth. He will not speak on his own; he will speak only what he hears, and he will tell you what is yet to come. 14He will bring glory to me by taking from what is mine and making it known to you. 15All that belongs to the Father is mine.

q Or *Helper*   r Or *convict the world of*

a4 NIV text twice omits αὐτῶν

c25 Psalms 35:19; 69:4   d8 Or *will expose the guilt of the world*

NRSV

this reason I said that he will take what is mine and declare it to you.

Sorrow Will Turn into Joy

16 "A little while, and you will no longer see me, and again a little while, and you will see me." [17]Then some of his disciples said to one another, "What does he mean by saying to us, 'A little while, and you will no longer see me, and again a little while, and you will see me'; and 'Because I am going to the Father'?" [18]They said, "What does he mean by this 'a little while'? We do not know what he is talking about." [19]Jesus knew that they wanted to ask him, so he said to them, "Are you discussing among yourselves what I meant when I said, 'A little while, and you will no longer see me, and again a little while, and you will see me'? [20]Very truly, I tell you, you will weep and mourn, but the world will rejoice; you will have pain, but your pain will turn into joy. [21]When a woman is in labor, she has pain, because her hour has come. But when her child is born, she no longer remembers the anguish because of the joy of having brought a human being into the world. [22]So you have pain now; but I will see you again, and your hearts will rejoice, and no one will take your joy from you. [23]On that day you will ask nothing of me.[s] Very truly, I tell you, if you ask anything of the Father in my name, he will give it to you.[t] [24]Until now you have not asked for anything in my name. Ask and you will receive, so that your joy may be complete.

Peace for the Disciples

25 "I have said these things to you in figures of speech. The hour is coming when I will no longer speak to you in figures, but will tell you plainly of the Father. [26]On that day you will ask in my name. I do not say to you that I will ask the Father on your behalf; [27]for the Father himself loves you, because you have loved me and have believed that I came from God.[u] [28]I came from the Father and have come into the world; again, I am leaving the world and am going to the Father."

29 His disciples said, "Yes, now you are speaking plainly, not in any figure of speech! [30]Now we know that you know all things, and do not need to have anyone question you; by this we believe that you came from God." [31]Jesus answered them,

John 16:16-31 (Greek)

ἐστιν· διὰ τοῦτο εἶπον ὅτι ἐκ τοῦ ἐμοῦ λαμβάνει καὶ ἀναγγελεῖ ὑμῖν.

16 Μικρὸν καὶ οὐκέτι θεωρεῖτέ με, καὶ πάλιν μικρὸν καὶ ὄψεσθέ με. **17** εἶπαν οὖν ἐκ τῶν μαθητῶν αὐτοῦ πρὸς ἀλλήλους, Τί ἐστιν τοῦτο ὃ λέγει ἡμῖν, Μικρὸν καὶ οὐ θεωρεῖτέ με, καὶ πάλιν μικρὸν καὶ ὄψεσθέ με; καί, Ὅτι ὑπάγω πρὸς τὸν πατέρα; **18** ἔλεγον οὖν, Τί ἐστιν τοῦτο [ὃ λέγει], τὸ μικρόν; οὐκ οἴδαμεν τί λαλεῖ. **19** ἔγνω [ὁ] Ἰησοῦς ὅτι ἤθελον αὐτὸν ἐρωτᾶν, καὶ εἶπεν αὐτοῖς, Περὶ τούτου ζητεῖτε μετ᾽ ἀλλήλων ὅτι εἶπον, Μικρὸν καὶ οὐ θεωρεῖτέ με, καὶ πάλιν μικρὸν καὶ ὄψεσθέ με; **20** ἀμὴν ἀμὴν λέγω ὑμῖν ὅτι κλαύσετε καὶ θρηνήσετε ὑμεῖς, ὁ δὲ κόσμος χαρήσεται· ὑμεῖς λυπηθήσεσθε, ἀλλ᾽ ἡ λύπη ὑμῶν εἰς χαρὰν γενήσεται. **21** ἡ γυνὴ ὅταν τίκτῃ λύπην ἔχει, ὅτι ἦλθεν ἡ ὥρα αὐτῆς· ὅταν δὲ γεννήσῃ τὸ παιδίον, οὐκέτι μνημονεύει τῆς θλίψεως διὰ τὴν χαρὰν ὅτι ἐγεννήθη ἄνθρωπος εἰς τὸν κόσμον. **22** καὶ ὑμεῖς οὖν νῦν μὲν λύπην ἔχετε· πάλιν δὲ ὄψομαι ὑμᾶς, καὶ χαρήσεται ὑμῶν ἡ καρδία, καὶ τὴν χαρὰν ὑμῶν οὐδεὶς αἴρει ἀφ᾽ ὑμῶν. **23** καὶ ἐν ἐκείνῃ τῇ ἡμέρᾳ ἐμὲ οὐκ ἐρωτήσετε οὐδέν. ἀμὴν ἀμὴν λέγω ὑμῖν, ἄν τι αἰτήσητε τὸν πατέρα ἐν τῷ ὀνόματί μου δώσει ὑμῖν.[b] **24** ἕως ἄρτι οὐκ ᾐτήσατε οὐδὲν ἐν τῷ ὀνόματί μου· αἰτεῖτε καὶ λήμψεσθε, ἵνα ἡ χαρὰ ὑμῶν ᾖ πεπληρωμένη.

25 Ταῦτα ἐν παροιμίαις λελάληκα ὑμῖν· ἔρχεται ὥρα ὅτε οὐκέτι ἐν παροιμίαις λαλήσω ὑμῖν, ἀλλὰ παρρησίᾳ περὶ τοῦ πατρὸς ἀπαγγελῶ ὑμῖν. **26** ἐν ἐκείνῃ τῇ ἡμέρᾳ ἐν τῷ ὀνόματί μου αἰτήσεσθε, καὶ οὐ λέγω ὑμῖν ὅτι ἐγὼ ἐρωτήσω τὸν πατέρα περὶ ὑμῶν· **27** αὐτὸς γὰρ ὁ πατὴρ φιλεῖ ὑμᾶς, ὅτι ὑμεῖς ἐμὲ πεφιλήκατε καὶ πεπιστεύκατε[c] ὅτι ἐγὼ παρὰ [τοῦ] θεοῦ ἐξῆλθον. **28** ἐξῆλθον παρὰ τοῦ πατρὸς καὶ ἐλήλυθα εἰς τὸν κόσμον· πάλιν ἀφίημι τὸν κόσμον καὶ πορεύομαι πρὸς τὸν πατέρα. **29** Λέγουσιν οἱ μαθηταὶ αὐτοῦ, Ἴδε νῦν ἐν παρρησίᾳ λαλεῖς καὶ παροιμίαν οὐδεμίαν λέγεις. **30** νῦν οἴδαμεν ὅτι οἶδας πάντα καὶ οὐ χρείαν ἔχεις ἵνα τίς σε ἐρωτᾷ· ἐν τούτῳ πιστεύομεν ὅτι ἀπὸ θεοῦ ἐξῆλθες. **31** ἀπεκρίθη αὐτοῖς Ἰησοῦς, Ἄρτι πιστεύετε;

NIV

That is why I said the Spirit will take from what is mine and make it known to you.

[16]"In a little while you will see me no more, and then after a little while you will see me."

The Disciples' Grief Will Turn to Joy

[17]Some of his disciples said to one another, "What does he mean by saying, 'In a little while you will see me no more, and then after a little while you will see me,' and 'Because I am going to the Father'?" [18]They kept asking, "What does he mean by 'a little while'? We don't understand what he is saying."

[19]Jesus saw that they wanted to ask him about this, so he said to them, "Are you asking one another what I meant when I said, 'In a little while you will see me no more, and then after a little while you will see me'? [20]I tell you the truth, you will weep and mourn while the world rejoices. You will grieve, but your grief will turn to joy. [21]A woman giving birth to a child has pain because her time has come; but when her baby is born she forgets the anguish because of her joy that a child is born into the world. [22]So with you: Now is your time of grief, but I will see you again and you will rejoice, and no one will take away your joy. [23]In that day you will no longer ask me anything. I tell you the truth, my Father will give you whatever you ask in my name. [24]Until now you have not asked for anything in my name. Ask and you will receive, and your joy will be complete.

[25]"Though I have been speaking figuratively, a time is coming when I will no longer use this kind of language but will tell you plainly about my Father. [26]In that day you will ask in my name. I am not saying that I will ask the Father on your behalf. [27]No, the Father himself loves you because you have loved me and have believed that I came from God. [28]I came from the Father and entered the world; now I am leaving the world and going back to the Father."

[29]Then Jesus' disciples said, "Now you are speaking clearly and without figures of speech. [30]Now we can see that you know all things and that you do not even need to have anyone ask you questions. This makes us believe that you came from God."

[31]"You believe at last!"[b] Jesus answered.

---

[s] Or *will ask me no question*   [t] Other ancient authorities read *Father, he will give it to you in my name*   [u] Other ancient authorities read *the Father*

[b]23 NRSV note t reads ἐν τῷ ὀνόματί μου after ὑμῖν
[c]27 NRSV note u πατρός

[b]31 Or *"Do you now believe?"*

"Do you now believe? 32The hour is coming, indeed it has come, when you will be scattered, each one to his home, and you will leave me alone. Yet I am not alone because the Father is with me. 33I have said this to you, so that in me you may have peace. In the world you face persecution. But take courage; I have conquered the world!"

Jesus Prays for His Disciples

17 After Jesus had spoken these words, he looked up to heaven and said, "Father, the hour has come; glorify your Son so that the Son may glorify you, 2since you have given him authority over all people,ᵛ to give eternal life to all whom you have given him. 3And this is eternal life, that they may know you, the only true God, and Jesus Christ whom you have sent. 4I glorified you on earth by finishing the work that you gave me to do. 5So now, Father, glorify me in your own presence with the glory that I had in your presence before the world existed.

6 "I have made your name known to those whom you gave me from the world. They were yours, and you gave them to me, and they have kept your word. 7Now they know that everything you have given me is from you; 8for the words that you gave to me I have given to them, and they have received them and know in truth that I came from you; and they have believed that you sent me. 9I am asking on their behalf; I am not asking on behalf of the world, but on behalf of those whom you gave me, because they are yours. 10All mine are yours, and yours are mine; and I have been glorified in them. 11And now I am no longer in the world, but they are in the world, and I am coming to you. Holy Father, protect them in your name that you have given me, so that they may be one, as we are one. 12While I was with them, I protected them in your name thatʷ you have given me. I guarded them, and not one of them was lost except the one destined to be lost,ˣ so that the scripture might be fulfilled. 13But now I am coming to you, and I speak these things in the world so that they may have my joy made complete in themselves.ʸ 14I have given them your word, and the world has hated them

---

32 ἰδοὺ ἔρχεται ὥρα καὶ ἐλήλυθεν ἵνα σκορπισθῆτε ἕκαστος εἰς τὰ ἴδια κἀμὲ μόνον ἀφῆτε· καὶ οὐκ εἰμὶ μόνος, ὅτι ὁ πατὴρ μετ᾽ ἐμοῦ ἐστιν. **33** ταῦτα λελάληκα ὑμῖν ἵνα ἐν ἐμοὶ εἰρήνην ἔχητε· ἐν τῷ κόσμῳ θλῖψιν ἔχετε· ἀλλὰ θαρσεῖτε, ἐγὼ νενίκηκα τὸν κόσμον.

17 Ταῦτα ἐλάλησεν Ἰησοῦς καὶ ἐπάρας τοὺς ὀφθαλμοὺς αὐτοῦ εἰς τὸν οὐρανὸν εἶπεν, Πάτερ, ἐλήλυθεν ἡ ὥρα· δόξασόν σου τὸν υἱόν, ἵνα ὁ υἱὸς δοξάσῃ σέ, **2** καθὼς ἔδωκας αὐτῷ ἐξουσίαν πάσης σαρκός, ἵνα πᾶν ὃ δέδωκας αὐτῷ δώσῃ αὐτοῖς ζωὴν αἰώνιον. **3** αὕτη δέ ἐστιν ἡ αἰώνιος ζωὴ ἵνα γινώσκωσιν σὲ τὸν μόνον ἀληθινὸν θεὸν καὶ ὃν ἀπέστειλας Ἰησοῦν Χριστόν. **4** ἐγώ σε ἐδόξασα ἐπὶ τῆς γῆς τὸ ἔργον τελειώσας ὃ δέδωκάς μοι ἵνα ποιήσω· **5** καὶ νῦν δόξασόν με σύ, πάτερ, παρὰ σεαυτῷ τῇ δόξῃ ᾗ εἶχον πρὸ τοῦ τὸν κόσμον εἶναι παρὰ σοί. **6** Ἐφανέρωσά σου τὸ ὄνομα τοῖς ἀνθρώποις οὓς ἔδωκάς μοι ἐκ τοῦ κόσμου. σοὶ ἦσαν κἀμοὶ αὐτοὺς ἔδωκας καὶ τὸν λόγον σου τετήρηκαν. **7** νῦν ἔγνωκαν ὅτι πάντα ὅσα δέδωκάς μοι παρὰ σοῦ εἰσιν· **8** ὅτι τὰ ῥήματα ἃ ἔδωκάς μοι δέδωκα αὐτοῖς, καὶ αὐτοὶ ἔλαβον καὶ ἔγνωσαν ἀληθῶς ὅτι παρὰ σοῦ ἐξῆλθον, καὶ ἐπίστευσαν ὅτι σύ με ἀπέστειλας. **9** ἐγὼ περὶ αὐτῶν ἐρωτῶ, οὐ περὶ τοῦ κόσμου ἐρωτῶ ἀλλὰ περὶ ὧν δέδωκάς μοι, ὅτι σοί εἰσιν, **10** καὶ τὰ ἐμὰ πάντα σά ἐστιν καὶ τὰ σὰ ἐμά, καὶ δεδόξασμαι ἐν αὐτοῖς. **11** καὶ οὐκέτι εἰμὶ ἐν τῷ κόσμῳ, καὶ αὐτοὶ ἐν τῷ κόσμῳ εἰσίν, κἀγὼ πρὸς σὲ ἔρχομαι. Πάτερ ἅγιε, τήρησον αὐτοὺς ἐν τῷ ὀνόματί σου ᾧ δέδωκάς μοι, ἵνα ὦσιν ἓν καθὼς ἡμεῖς. **12** ὅτε ἤμην μετ᾽ αὐτῶν ἐγὼ ἐτήρουν αὐτοὺς ἐν τῷ ὀνόματί σου ᾧᵃ δέδωκάς μοι, καὶ ἐφύλαξα, καὶ οὐδεὶς ἐξ αὐτῶν ἀπώλετο εἰ μὴ ὁ υἱὸς τῆς ἀπωλείας, ἵνα ἡ γραφὴ πληρωθῇ. **13** νῦν δὲ πρὸς σὲ ἔρχομαι καὶ ταῦτα λαλῶ ἐν τῷ κόσμῳ ἵνα ἔχωσιν τὴν χαρὰν τὴν ἐμὴν πεπληρωμένην ἐν ἑαυτοῖς. **14** ἐγὼ δέδωκα αὐτοῖς τὸν λόγον σου καὶ ὁ κόσμος

32"But a time is coming, and has come, when you will be scattered, each to his own home. You will leave me all alone. Yet I am not alone, for my Father is with me.

33"I have told you these things, so that in me you may have peace. In this world you will have trouble. But take heart! I have overcome the world."

Jesus Prays for Himself

17 After Jesus said this, he looked toward heaven and prayed:

"Father, the time has come. Glorify your Son, that your Son may glorify you. 2For you granted him authority over all people that he might give eternal life to all those you have given him. 3Now this is eternal life: that they may know you, the only true God, and Jesus Christ, whom you have sent. 4I have brought you glory on earth by completing the work you gave me to do. 5And now, Father, glorify me in your presence with the glory I had with you before the world began.

Jesus Prays for His Disciples

6"I have revealed youᵃ to those whom you gave me out of the world. They were yours; you gave them to me and they have obeyed your word. 7Now they know that everything you have given me comes from you. 8For I gave them the words you gave me and they accepted them. They knew with certainty that I came from you, and they believed that you sent me. 9I pray for them. I am not praying for the world, but for those you have given me, for they are yours. 10All I have is yours, and all you have is mine. And glory has come to me through them. 11I will remain in the world no longer, but they are still in the world, and I am coming to you. Holy Father, protect them by the power of your name—the name you gave me—so that they may be one as we are one. 12While I was with them, I protected them and kept them safe by that name you gave me. None has been lost except the one doomed to destruction so that Scripture would be fulfilled.

13"I am coming to you now, but I say these things while I am still in the world, so that they may have the full measure of my joy within them. 14I have given them your word and the world has

---

ᵛ Gk *flesh*   ʷ Other ancient authorities read *protected in your name those whom*   ˣ Gk *except the son of destruction*
ʸ Or *among themselves*

ᵃ12 NRSV note w οὕς

ᵃ6 Greek *your name*; also in verse 26

because they do not belong to the world, just as I do not belong to the world. [15]I am not asking you to take them out of the world, but I ask you to protect them from the evil one.[z] [16]They do not belong to the world, just as I do not belong to the world. [17]Sanctify them in the truth; your word is truth. [18]As you have sent me into the world, so I have sent them into the world. [19]And for their sakes I sanctify myself, so that they also may be sanctified in truth.

20 "I ask not only on behalf of these, but also on behalf of those who will believe in me through their word, [21]that they may all be one. As you, Father, are in me and I am in you, may they also be in us,[a] so that the world may believe that you have sent me. [22]The glory that you have given me I have given them, so that they may be one, as we are one, [23]I in them and you in me, that they may become completely one, so that the world may know that you have sent me and have loved them even as you have loved me. [24]Father, I desire that those also, whom you have given me, may be with me where I am, to see my glory, which you have given me because you loved me before the foundation of the world.

25 "Righteous Father, the world does not know you, but I know you; and these know that you have sent me. [26]I made your name known to them, and I will make it known, so that the love with which you have loved me may be in them, and I in them."

The Betrayal and Arrest of Jesus

18 After Jesus had spoken these words, he went out with his disciples across the Kidron valley to a place where there was a garden, which he and his disciples entered. [2]Now Judas, who betrayed him, also knew the place, because Jesus often met there with his disciples. [3]So Judas brought a detachment of soldiers together with police from the chief priests and the Pharisees, and they came there with lanterns and torches and weapons. [4]Then Jesus, knowing all that was to happen to him, came forward and asked them, "Whom are you looking for?" [5]They

ἐμίσησεν αὐτούς, ὅτι οὐκ εἰσὶν ἐκ τοῦ κόσμου καθὼς ἐγὼ οὐκ εἰμὶ ἐκ τοῦ κόσμου. **15** οὐκ ἐρωτῶ ἵνα ἄρῃς αὐτοὺς ἐκ τοῦ κόσμου, ἀλλ' ἵνα τηρήσῃς αὐτοὺς ἐκ τοῦ πονηροῦ. **16** ἐκ τοῦ κόσμου οὐκ εἰσὶν καθὼς ἐγὼ οὐκ εἰμὶ ἐκ τοῦ κόσμου. **17** ἁγίασον αὐτοὺς ἐν τῇ ἀληθείᾳ· ὁ λόγος ὁ σὸς ἀλήθειά ἐστιν. **18** καθὼς ἐμὲ ἀπέστειλας εἰς τὸν κόσμον, κἀγὼ ἀπέστειλα αὐτοὺς εἰς τὸν κόσμον· **19** καὶ ὑπὲρ αὐτῶν ἐγὼ ἁγιάζω ἐμαυτόν, ἵνα ὦσιν καὶ αὐτοὶ ἡγιασμένοι ἐν ἀληθείᾳ.

20 Οὐ περὶ τούτων δὲ ἐρωτῶ μόνον, ἀλλὰ καὶ περὶ τῶν πιστευόντων διὰ τοῦ λόγου αὐτῶν εἰς ἐμέ, **21** ἵνα πάντες ἓν ὦσιν, καθὼς σύ, πάτερ, ἐν ἐμοὶ κἀγὼ ἐν σοί, ἵνα καὶ αὐτοὶ ἐν ἡμῖν[b] ὦσιν, ἵνα ὁ κόσμος πιστεύῃ ὅτι σύ με ἀπέστειλας. **22** κἀγὼ τὴν δόξαν ἣν δέδωκάς μοι δέδωκα αὐτοῖς, ἵνα ὦσιν ἓν καθὼς ἡμεῖς ἕν· **23** ἐγὼ ἐν αὐτοῖς καὶ σὺ ἐν ἐμοί, ἵνα ὦσιν τετελειωμένοι εἰς ἕν, ἵνα γινώσκῃ ὁ κόσμος ὅτι σύ με ἀπέστειλας καὶ ἠγάπησας αὐτοὺς καθὼς ἐμὲ ἠγάπησας. **24** Πάτερ, ὃ δέδωκάς μοι, θέλω ἵνα ὅπου εἰμὶ ἐγὼ κἀκεῖνοι ὦσιν μετ' ἐμοῦ, ἵνα θεωρῶσιν τὴν δόξαν τὴν ἐμήν, ἣν δέδωκάς μοι ὅτι ἠγάπησάς με πρὸ καταβολῆς κόσμου. **25** πάτερ δίκαιε, καὶ ὁ κόσμος σε οὐκ ἔγνω, ἐγὼ δέ σε ἔγνων, καὶ οὗτοι ἔγνωσαν ὅτι σύ με ἀπέστειλας· **26** καὶ ἐγνώρισα αὐτοῖς τὸ ὄνομά σου καὶ γνωρίσω, ἵνα ἡ ἀγάπη ἣν ἠγάπησάς με ἐν αὐτοῖς ᾖ κἀγὼ ἐν αὐτοῖς.

18 Ταῦτα εἰπὼν Ἰησοῦς ἐξῆλθεν σὺν τοῖς μαθηταῖς αὐτοῦ πέραν τοῦ χειμάρρου τοῦ Κεδρὼν ὅπου ἦν κῆπος, εἰς ὃν εἰσῆλθεν αὐτὸς καὶ οἱ μαθηταὶ αὐτοῦ. **2** ᾔδει δὲ καὶ Ἰούδας ὁ παραδιδοὺς αὐτὸν τὸν τόπον, ὅτι πολλάκις συνήχθη Ἰησοῦς ἐκεῖ μετὰ τῶν μαθητῶν αὐτοῦ. **3** ὁ οὖν Ἰούδας λαβὼν τὴν σπεῖραν καὶ ἐκ τῶν ἀρχιερέων καὶ ἐκ τῶν Φαρισαίων ὑπηρέτας ἔρχεται ἐκεῖ μετὰ φανῶν καὶ λαμπάδων καὶ ὅπλων. **4** Ἰησοῦς οὖν εἰδὼς πάντα τὰ ἐρχόμενα ἐπ' αὐτὸν ἐξῆλθεν καὶ λέγει αὐτοῖς, Τίνα

hated them, for they are not of the world any more than I am of the world. [15]My prayer is not that you take them out of the world but that you protect them from the evil one. [16]They are not of the world, even as I am not of it. [17]Sanctify[b] them by the truth; your word is truth. [18]As you sent me into the world, I have sent them into the world. [19]For them I sanctify myself, that they too may be truly sanctified.

Jesus Prays for All Believers

[20]"My prayer is not for them alone. I pray also for those who will believe in me through their message, [21]that all of them may be one, Father, just as you are in me and I am in you. May they also be in us so that the world may believe that you have sent me. [22]I have given them the glory that you gave me, that they may be one as we are one: [23]I in them and you in me. May they be brought to complete unity to let the world know that you sent me and have loved them even as you have loved me.

[24]"Father, I want those you have given me to be with me where I am, and to see my glory, the glory you have given me because you loved me before the creation of the world.

[25]"Righteous Father, though the world does not know you, I know you, and they know that you have sent me. [26]I have made you known to them, and will continue to make you known in order that the love you have for me may be in them and that I myself may be in them."

Jesus Arrested

18 When he had finished praying, Jesus left with his disciples and crossed the Kidron Valley. On the other side there was an olive grove, and he and his disciples went into it.

[2]Now Judas, who betrayed him, knew the place, because Jesus had often met there with his disciples. [3]So Judas came to the grove, guiding a detachment of soldiers and some officials from the chief priests and Pharisees. They were carrying torches, lanterns and weapons.

[4]Jesus, knowing all that was going to happen to him, went out and asked them, "Who is it you want?"

---

z Or *from evil*   a Other ancient authorities read *be one in us*

b21 NRSV note a adds ἕν

b17 Greek *hagiazo* (set apart for sacred use or *make holy*); also in verse 19

NRSV

answered, "Jesus of Nazareth."[b] Jesus replied, "I am he."[c] Judas, who betrayed him, was standing with them. [6]When Jesus[d] said to them, "I am he," they stepped back and fell to the ground. [7]Again he asked them, "Whom are you looking for?" And they said, "Jesus of Nazareth."[b] [8]Jesus answered, "I told you that I am he.[c] So if you are looking for me, let these men go." [9]This was to fulfill the word that he had spoken, "I did not lose a single one of those whom you gave me." [10]Then Simon Peter, who had a sword, drew it, struck the high priest's slave, and cut off his right ear. The slave's name was Malchus. [11]Jesus said to Peter, "Put your sword back into its sheath. Am I not to drink the cup that the Father has given me?"

Jesus before the High Priest

12 So the soldiers, their officer, and the Jewish police arrested Jesus and bound him. [13]First they took him to Annas, who was the father-in-law of Caiaphas, the high priest that year. [14]Caiaphas was the one who had advised the Jews that it was better to have one person die for the people.

Peter Denies Jesus

15 Simon Peter and another disciple followed Jesus. Since that disciple was known to the high priest, he went with Jesus into the courtyard of the high priest, [16]but Peter was standing outside at the gate. So the other disciple, who was known to the high priest, went out, spoke to the woman who guarded the gate, and brought Peter in. [17]The woman said to Peter, "You are not also one of this man's disciples, are you?" He said, "I am not." [18]Now the slaves and the police had made a charcoal fire because it was cold, and they were standing around it and warming themselves. Peter also was standing with them and warming himself.

The High Priest Questions Jesus

19 Then the high priest questioned Jesus about his disciples and about his teaching. [20]Jesus answered, "I have spoken openly to the world; I have always taught in synagogues and in the temple, where all the Jews come together. I have said nothing in secret. [21]Why do you ask me? Ask those who heard what I said to them; they know what I said." [22]When he had said this, one

Greek

ζητεῖτε; **5** ἀπεκρίθησαν αὐτῷ, Ἰησοῦν τὸν Ναζωραῖον. λέγει αὐτοῖς, Ἐγώ εἰμι. εἱστήκει δὲ καὶ Ἰούδας ὁ παραδιδοὺς αὐτὸν μετ᾽ αὐτῶν. **6** ὡς οὖν εἶπεν αὐτοῖς, Ἐγώ εἰμι, ἀπῆλθον εἰς τὰ ὀπίσω καὶ ἔπεσαν χαμαί. **7** πάλιν οὖν ἐπηρώτησεν αὐτούς, Τίνα ζητεῖτε; οἱ δὲ εἶπαν, Ἰησοῦν τὸν Ναζωραῖον. **8** ἀπεκρίθη Ἰησοῦς, Εἶπον ὑμῖν ὅτι ἐγώ εἰμι. εἰ οὖν ἐμὲ ζητεῖτε, ἄφετε τούτους ὑπάγειν· **9** ἵνα πληρωθῇ ὁ λόγος ὃν εἶπεν ὅτι Οὓς δέδωκάς μοι οὐκ ἀπώλεσα ἐξ αὐτῶν οὐδένα. **10** Σίμων οὖν Πέτρος ἔχων μάχαιραν εἵλκυσεν αὐτὴν καὶ ἔπαισεν τὸν τοῦ ἀρχιερέως δοῦλον καὶ ἀπέκοψεν αὐτοῦ τὸ ὠτάριον τὸ δεξιόν· ἦν δὲ ὄνομα τῷ δούλῳ Μάλχος. **11** εἶπεν οὖν ὁ Ἰησοῦς τῷ Πέτρῳ, Βάλε τὴν μάχαιραν εἰς τὴν θήκην· τὸ ποτήριον ὃ δέδωκέν μοι ὁ πατὴρ οὐ μὴ πίω αὐτό;

12 Ἡ οὖν σπεῖρα καὶ ὁ χιλίαρχος καὶ οἱ ὑπηρέται τῶν Ἰουδαίων συνέλαβον τὸν Ἰησοῦν καὶ ἔδησαν αὐτὸν **13** καὶ ἤγαγον πρὸς Ἅνναν πρῶτον· ἦν γὰρ πενθερὸς τοῦ Καϊάφα, ὃς ἦν ἀρχιερεὺς τοῦ ἐνιαυτοῦ ἐκείνου· **14** ἦν δὲ Καϊάφας ὁ συμβουλεύσας τοῖς Ἰουδαίοις ὅτι συμφέρει ἕνα ἄνθρωπον ἀποθανεῖν ὑπὲρ τοῦ λαοῦ.

15 Ἠκολούθει δὲ τῷ Ἰησοῦ Σίμων Πέτρος καὶ ἄλλος μαθητής. ὁ δὲ μαθητὴς ἐκεῖνος ἦν γνωστὸς τῷ ἀρχιερεῖ καὶ συνεισῆλθεν τῷ Ἰησοῦ εἰς τὴν αὐλὴν τοῦ ἀρχιερέως, **16** ὁ δὲ Πέτρος εἱστήκει πρὸς τῇ θύρᾳ ἔξω. ἐξῆλθεν οὖν ὁ μαθητὴς ὁ ἄλλος ὁ γνωστὸς τοῦ ἀρχιερέως καὶ εἶπεν τῇ θυρωρῷ καὶ εἰσήγαγεν τὸν Πέτρον. **17** λέγει οὖν τῷ Πέτρῳ ἡ παιδίσκη ἡ θυρωρός, Μὴ καὶ σὺ ἐκ τῶν μαθητῶν εἶ τοῦ ἀνθρώπου τούτου; λέγει ἐκεῖνος, Οὐκ εἰμί. **18** εἱστήκεισαν δὲ οἱ δοῦλοι καὶ οἱ ὑπηρέται ἀνθρακιὰν πεποιηκότες, ὅτι ψῦχος ἦν, καὶ ἐθερμαίνοντο· ἦν δὲ καὶ ὁ Πέτρος μετ᾽ αὐτῶν ἑστὼς καὶ θερμαινόμενος.

19 Ὁ οὖν ἀρχιερεὺς ἠρώτησεν τὸν Ἰησοῦν περὶ τῶν μαθητῶν αὐτοῦ καὶ περὶ τῆς διδαχῆς αὐτοῦ. **20** ἀπεκρίθη αὐτῷ Ἰησοῦς, Ἐγὼ παρρησίᾳ λελάληκα τῷ κόσμῳ, ἐγὼ πάντοτε ἐδίδαξα ἐν συναγωγῇ καὶ ἐν τῷ ἱερῷ, ὅπου πάντες οἱ Ἰουδαῖοι συνέρχονται, καὶ ἐν κρυπτῷ ἐλάλησα οὐδέν. **21** τί με ἐρωτᾷς; ἐρώτησον τοὺς ἀκηκοότας τί ἐλάλησα αὐτοῖς· ἴδε οὗτοι οἴδασιν ἃ εἶπον ἐγώ. **22** ταῦτα δὲ αὐτοῦ εἰπόντος εἷς

NIV

[5]"Jesus of Nazareth," they replied.

"I am he," Jesus said. (And Judas the traitor was standing there with them.) [6]When Jesus said, "I am he," they drew back and fell to the ground.

[7]Again he asked them, "Who is it you want?"

And they said, "Jesus of Nazareth."

[8]"I told you that I am he," Jesus answered. "If you are looking for me, then let these men go." [9]This happened so that the words he had spoken would be fulfilled: "I have not lost one of those you gave me."[a]

[10]Then Simon Peter, who had a sword, drew it and struck the high priest's servant, cutting off his right ear. (The servant's name was Malchus.)

[11]Jesus commanded Peter, "Put your sword away! Shall I not drink the cup the Father has given me?"

Jesus Taken to Annas

[12]Then the detachment of soldiers with its commander and the Jewish officials arrested Jesus. They bound him [13]and brought him first to Annas, who was the father-in-law of Caiaphas, the high priest that year. [14]Caiaphas was the one who had advised the Jews that it would be good if one man died for the people.

Peter's First Denial

[15]Simon Peter and another disciple were following Jesus. Because this disciple was known to the high priest, he went with Jesus into the high priest's courtyard, [16]but Peter had to wait outside at the door. The other disciple, who was known to the high priest, came back, spoke to the girl on duty there and brought Peter in.

[17]"You are not one of his disciples, are you?" the girl at the door asked Peter.

He replied, "I am not."

[18]It was cold, and the servants and officials stood around a fire they had made to keep warm. Peter also was standing with them, warming himself.

The High Priest Questions Jesus

[19]Meanwhile, the high priest questioned Jesus about his disciples and his teaching.

[20]"I have spoken openly to the world," Jesus replied. "I always taught in synagogues or at the temple, where all the Jews come together. I said nothing in secret. [21]Why question me? Ask those who heard me. Surely they know what I said."

[22]When Jesus said this, one of the officials

[b] Gk the Nazorean   [c] Gk I am   [d] Gk he   [a]9 John 6:39

of the police standing nearby struck Jesus on the face, saying, "Is that how you answer the high priest?" 23Jesus answered, "If I have spoken wrongly, testify to the wrong. But if I have spoken rightly, why do you strike me?" 24Then Annas sent him bound to Caiaphas the high priest.

Peter Denies Jesus Again

25 Now Simon Peter was standing and warming himself. They asked him, "You are not also one of his disciples, are you?" He denied it and said, "I am not." 26One of the slaves of the high priest, a relative of the man whose ear Peter had cut off, asked, "Did I not see you in the garden with him?" 27Again Peter denied it, and at that moment the cock crowed.

Jesus before Pilate

28 Then they took Jesus from Caiaphas to Pilate's headquarters.e It was early in the morning. They themselves did not enter the headquarters,e so as to avoid ritual defilement and to be able to eat the Passover. 29So Pilate went out to them and said, "What accusation do you bring against this man?" 30They answered, "If this man were not a criminal, we would not have handed him over to you." 31Pilate said to them, "Take him yourselves and judge him according to your law." The Jews replied, "We are not permitted to put anyone to death." 32(This was to fulfill what Jesus had said when he indicated the kind of death he was to die.)

33 Then Pilate entered the headquarterse again, summoned Jesus, and asked him, "Are you the King of the Jews?" 34Jesus answered, "Do you ask this on your own, or did others tell you about me?" 35Pilate replied, "I am not a Jew, am I? Your own nation and the chief priests have handed you over to me. What have you done?" 36Jesus answered, "My kingdom is not from this world. If my kingdom were from this world, my followers would be fighting to keep me from being handed over to the Jews. But as it is, my kingdom is not from here." 37Pilate asked him, "So you are a king?" Jesus answered, "You say that I am a king. For this I was born, and for this I came into the world, to testify to the truth.

παρεστηκὼς τῶν ὑπηρετῶν ἔδωκεν ῥάπισμα τῷ Ἰησοῦ εἰπών, Οὕτως ἀποκρίνῃ τῷ ἀρχιερεῖ; **23** ἀπεκρίθη αὐτῷ Ἰησοῦς, Εἰ κακῶς ἐλάλησα, μαρτύρησον περὶ τοῦ κακοῦ· εἰ δὲ καλῶς, τί με δέρεις; **24** ἀπέστειλεν οὖν αὐτὸν ὁ Ἅννας δεδεμένον πρὸς Καϊάφαν τὸν ἀρχιερέα.

25 Ἦν δὲ Σίμων Πέτρος ἑστὼς καὶ θερμαινόμενος. εἶπον οὖν αὐτῷ, Μὴ καὶ σὺ ἐκ τῶν μαθητῶν αὐτοῦ εἶ; ἠρνήσατο ἐκεῖνος καὶ εἶπεν, Οὐκ εἰμί. **26** λέγει εἷς ἐκ τῶν δούλων τοῦ ἀρχιερέως, συγγενὴς ὢν οὗ ἀπέκοψεν Πέτρος τὸ ὠτίον, Οὐκ ἐγώ σε εἶδον ἐν τῷ κήπῳ μετ' αὐτοῦ; **27** πάλιν οὖν ἠρνήσατο Πέτρος, καὶ εὐθέως ἀλέκτωρ ἐφώνησεν.

28 Ἄγουσιν οὖν τὸν Ἰησοῦν ἀπὸ τοῦ Καϊάφα εἰς τὸ πραιτώριον· ἦν δὲ πρωΐ· καὶ αὐτοὶ οὐκ εἰσῆλθον εἰς τὸ πραιτώριον, ἵνα μὴ μιανθῶσιν ἀλλὰ φάγωσιν τὸ πάσχα. **29** ἐξῆλθεν οὖν ὁ Πιλᾶτος ἔξω πρὸς αὐτοὺς καὶ φησίν, Τίνα κατηγορίαν φέρετε [κατὰ] τοῦ ἀνθρώπου τούτου; **30** ἀπεκρίθησαν καὶ εἶπαν αὐτῷ, Εἰ μὴ ἦν οὗτος κακὸν ποιῶν, οὐκ ἄν σοι παρεδώκαμεν αὐτόν. **31** εἶπεν οὖν αὐτοῖς ὁ Πιλᾶτος, Λάβετε αὐτὸν ὑμεῖς καὶ κατὰ τὸν νόμον ὑμῶν κρίνατε αὐτόν. εἶπον αὐτῷ οἱ Ἰουδαῖοι, Ἡμῖν οὐκ ἔξεστιν ἀποκτεῖναι οὐδένα· **32** ἵνα ὁ λόγος τοῦ Ἰησοῦ πληρωθῇ ὃν εἶπεν σημαίνων ποίῳ θανάτῳ ἤμελλεν ἀποθνήσκειν. **33** Εἰσῆλθεν οὖν πάλιν εἰς τὸ πραιτώριον ὁ Πιλᾶτος καὶ ἐφώνησεν τὸν Ἰησοῦν καὶ εἶπεν αὐτῷ, Σὺ εἶ ὁ βασιλεὺς τῶν Ἰουδαίων; **34** ἀπεκρίθη Ἰησοῦς, Ἀπὸ σεαυτοῦ σὺ τοῦτο λέγεις ἢ ἄλλοι εἶπόν σοι περὶ ἐμοῦ; **35** ἀπεκρίθη ὁ Πιλᾶτος, Μήτι ἐγὼ Ἰουδαῖός εἰμι; τὸ ἔθνος τὸ σὸν καὶ οἱ ἀρχιερεῖς παρέδωκάν σε ἐμοί· τί ἐποίησας; **36** ἀπεκρίθη Ἰησοῦς, Ἡ βασιλεία ἡ ἐμὴ οὐκ ἔστιν ἐκ τοῦ κόσμου τούτου· εἰ ἐκ τοῦ κόσμου τούτου ἦν ἡ βασιλεία ἡ ἐμή, οἱ ὑπηρέται οἱ ἐμοὶ ἠγωνίζοντο [ἄν] ἵνα μὴ παραδοθῶ τοῖς Ἰουδαίοις· νῦν δὲ ἡ βασιλεία ἡ ἐμὴ οὐκ ἔστιν ἐντεῦθεν. **37** εἶπεν οὖν αὐτῷ ὁ Πιλᾶτος, Οὐκοῦν βασιλεὺς εἶ σύ; ἀπεκρίθη ὁ Ἰησοῦς, Σὺ λέγεις ὅτι βασιλεύς εἰμι. ἐγὼ εἰς τοῦτο γεγέννημαι καὶ εἰς τοῦτο ἐλήλυθα εἰς τὸν κόσμον, ἵνα μαρτυρήσω τῇ ἀληθείᾳ·

nearby struck him in the face. "Is this the way you answer the high priest?" he demanded.

23"If I said something wrong," Jesus replied, "testify as to what is wrong. But if I spoke the truth, why did you strike me?" 24Then Annas sent him, still bound, to Caiaphas the high priest.b

Peter's Second and Third Denials

25As Simon Peter stood warming himself, he was asked, "You are not one of his disciples, are you?"

He denied it, saying, "I am not."

26One of the high priest's servants, a relative of the man whose ear Peter had cut off, challenged him, "Didn't I see you with him in the olive grove?" 27Again Peter denied it, and at that moment a rooster began to crow.

Jesus Before Pilate

28Then the Jews led Jesus from Caiaphas to the palace of the Roman governor. By now it was early morning, and to avoid ceremonial uncleanness the Jews did not enter the palace; they wanted to be able to eat the Passover. 29So Pilate came out to them and asked, "What charges are you bringing against this man?"

30"If he were not a criminal," they replied, "we would not have handed him over to you."

31Pilate said, "Take him yourselves and judge him by your own law."

"But we have no right to execute anyone," the Jews objected. 32This happened so that the words Jesus had spoken indicating the kind of death he was going to die would be fulfilled.

33Pilate then went back inside the palace, summoned Jesus and asked him, "Are you the king of the Jews?"

34"Is that your own idea," Jesus asked, "or did others talk to you about me?"

35"Am I a Jew?" Pilate replied. "It was your people and your chief priests who handed you over to me. What is it you have done?"

36Jesus said, "My kingdom is not of this world. If it were, my servants would fight to prevent my arrest by the Jews. But now my kingdom is from another place."

37"You are a king, then!" said Pilate.

Jesus answered, "You are right in saying I am a king. In fact, for this reason I was born, and for this I came into the world, to

e Gk *the praetorium*

b24 Or *(Now Annas had sent him, still bound, to Caiaphas the high priest.)*

Everyone who belongs to the truth listens to my voice." 38Pilate asked him, "What is truth?"

Jesus Sentenced to Death

After he had said this, he went out to the Jews again and told them, "I find no case against him. 39But you have a custom that I release someone for you at the Passover. Do you want me to release for you the King of the Jews?" 40They shouted in reply, "Not this man, but Barabbas!" Now Barabbas was a bandit.

19 Then Pilate took Jesus and had him flogged. 2And the soldiers wove a crown of thorns and put it on his head, and they dressed him in a purple robe. 3They kept coming up to him, saying, "Hail, King of the Jews!" and striking him on the face. 4Pilate went out again and said to them, "Look, I am bringing him out to you to let you know that I find no case against him." 5So Jesus came out, wearing the crown of thorns and the purple robe. Pilate said to them, "Here is the man!" 6When the chief priests and the police saw him, they shouted, "Crucify him! Crucify him!" Pilate said to them, "Take him yourselves and crucify him; I find no case against him." 7The Jews answered him, "We have a law, and according to that law he ought to die because he has claimed to be the Son of God."

8 Now when Pilate heard this, he was more afraid than ever. 9He entered his headquarters[f] again and asked Jesus, "Where are you from?" But Jesus gave him no answer. 10Pilate therefore said to him, "Do you refuse to speak to me? Do you not know that I have power to release you, and power to crucify you?" 11Jesus answered him, "You would have no power over me unless it had been given you from above; therefore the one who handed me over to you is guilty of a greater sin." 12From then on Pilate tried to release him, but the Jews cried out, "If you release this man, you are no friend of the emperor. Everyone who claims to be a king sets himself against the emperor."

13 When Pilate heard these words, he brought Jesus outside and sat[g] on the judge's bench at a place called The Stone Pavement, or in Hebrew[h] Gabbatha. 14Now

πᾶς ὁ ὢν ἐκ τῆς ἀληθείας ἀκούει μου τῆς φωνῆς. 38 λέγει αὐτῷ ὁ Πιλᾶτος, Τί ἐστιν ἀλήθεια;

Καὶ τοῦτο εἰπὼν πάλιν ἐξῆλθεν πρὸς τοὺς Ἰουδαίους καὶ λέγει αὐτοῖς, Ἐγὼ οὐδεμίαν εὑρίσκω ἐν αὐτῷ αἰτίαν. 39 ἔστιν δὲ συνήθεια ὑμῖν ἵνα ἕνα ἀπολύσω ὑμῖν ἐν τῷ πάσχα· βούλεσθε οὖν ἀπολύσω ὑμῖν τὸν βασιλέα τῶν Ἰουδαίων; 40 ἐκραύγασαν οὖν πάλιν λέγοντες, Μὴ τοῦτον ἀλλὰ τὸν Βαραββᾶν. ἦν δὲ ὁ Βαραββᾶς λῃστής.

19 Τότε οὖν ἔλαβεν ὁ Πιλᾶτος τὸν Ἰησοῦν καὶ ἐμαστίγωσεν. 2 καὶ οἱ στρατιῶται πλέξαντες στέφανον ἐξ ἀκανθῶν ἐπέθηκαν αὐτοῦ τῇ κεφαλῇ καὶ ἱμάτιον πορφυροῦν περιέβαλον αὐτὸν 3 καὶ ἤρχοντο πρὸς αὐτὸν καὶ ἔλεγον, Χαῖρε ὁ βασιλεὺς τῶν Ἰουδαίων· καὶ ἐδίδοσαν αὐτῷ ῥαπίσματα. 4 Καὶ ἐξῆλθεν πάλιν ἔξω ὁ Πιλᾶτος καὶ λέγει αὐτοῖς, Ἴδε ἄγω ὑμῖν αὐτὸν ἔξω, ἵνα γνῶτε ὅτι οὐδεμίαν αἰτίαν εὑρίσκω ἐν αὐτῷ. 5 ἐξῆλθεν οὖν ὁ Ἰησοῦς ἔξω, φορῶν τὸν ἀκάνθινον στέφανον καὶ τὸ πορφυροῦν ἱμάτιον. καὶ λέγει αὐτοῖς, Ἰδοὺ ὁ ἄνθρωπος. 6 ὅτε οὖν εἶδον αὐτὸν οἱ ἀρχιερεῖς καὶ οἱ ὑπηρέται ἐκραύγασαν λέγοντες, Σταύρωσον σταύρωσον. λέγει αὐτοῖς ὁ Πιλᾶτος, Λάβετε αὐτὸν ὑμεῖς καὶ σταυρώσατε· ἐγὼ γὰρ οὐχ εὑρίσκω ἐν αὐτῷ αἰτίαν. 7 ἀπεκρίθησαν αὐτῷ οἱ Ἰουδαῖοι, Ἡμεῖς νόμον ἔχομεν καὶ κατὰ τὸν νόμον ὀφείλει ἀποθανεῖν, ὅτι υἱὸν θεοῦ ἑαυτὸν ἐποίησεν.

8 Ὅτε οὖν ἤκουσεν ὁ Πιλᾶτος τοῦτον τὸν λόγον, μᾶλλον ἐφοβήθη, 9 καὶ εἰσῆλθεν εἰς τὸ πραιτώριον πάλιν καὶ λέγει τῷ Ἰησοῦ, Πόθεν εἶ σύ; ὁ δὲ Ἰησοῦς ἀπόκρισιν οὐκ ἔδωκεν αὐτῷ. 10 λέγει οὖν αὐτῷ ὁ Πιλᾶτος, Ἐμοὶ οὐ λαλεῖς; οὐκ οἶδας ὅτι ἐξουσίαν ἔχω ἀπολῦσαί σε καὶ ἐξουσίαν ἔχω σταυρῶσαί σε; 11 ἀπεκρίθη [αὐτῷ] Ἰησοῦς, Οὐκ εἶχες ἐξουσίαν κατ' ἐμοῦ οὐδεμίαν εἰ μὴ ἦν δεδομένον σοι ἄνωθεν· διὰ τοῦτο ὁ παραδούς μέ σοι μείζονα ἁμαρτίαν ἔχει. 12 ἐκ τούτου ὁ Πιλᾶτος ἐζήτει ἀπολῦσαι αὐτόν· οἱ δὲ Ἰουδαῖοι ἐκραύγασαν λέγοντες, Ἐὰν τοῦτον ἀπολύσῃς, οὐκ εἶ φίλος τοῦ Καίσαρος· πᾶς ὁ βασιλέα ἑαυτὸν ποιῶν ἀντιλέγει τῷ Καίσαρι.

13 Ὁ οὖν Πιλᾶτος ἀκούσας τῶν λόγων τούτων ἤγαγεν ἔξω τὸν Ἰησοῦν καὶ ἐκάθισεν ἐπὶ βήματος εἰς τόπον λεγόμενον Λιθόστρωτον, Ἑβραϊστὶ δὲ

testify to the truth. Everyone on the side of truth listens to me."

38"What is truth?" Pilate asked. With this he went out again to the Jews and said, "I find no basis for a charge against him. 39But it is your custom for me to release to you one prisoner at the time of the Passover. Do you want me to release 'the king of the Jews'?"

40They shouted back, "No, not him! Give us Barabbas!" Now Barabbas had taken part in a rebellion.

Jesus Sentenced to be Crucified

19 Then Pilate took Jesus and had him flogged. 2The soldiers twisted together a crown of thorns and put it on his head. They clothed him in a purple robe 3and went up to him again and again, saying, "Hail, king of the Jews!" And they struck him in the face.

4Once more Pilate came out and said to the Jews, "Look, I am bringing him out to you to let you know that I find no basis for a charge against him." 5When Jesus came out wearing the crown of thorns and the purple robe, Pilate said to them, "Here is the man!"

6As soon as the chief priests and their officials saw him, they shouted, "Crucify! Crucify!"

But Pilate answered, "You take him and crucify him. As for me, I find no basis for a charge against him."

7The Jews insisted, "We have a law, and according to that law he must die, because he claimed to be the Son of God."

8When Pilate heard this, he was even more afraid, 9and he went back inside the palace. "Where do you come from?" he asked Jesus, but Jesus gave him no answer. 10"Do you refuse to speak to me?" Pilate said. "Don't you realize I have power either to free you or to crucify you?"

11Jesus answered, "You would have no power over me if it were not given to you from above. Therefore the one who handed me over to you is guilty of a greater sin."

12From then on, Pilate tried to set Jesus free, but the Jews kept shouting, "If you let this man go, you are no friend of Caesar. Anyone who claims to be a king opposes Caesar."

13When Pilate heard this, he brought Jesus out and sat down on the judge's seat at a place known as the Stone Pavement (which in Aramaic is Gabbatha). 14It was

---

[f] Gk *the praetorium*   [g] Or *seated him*   [h] That is, *Aramaic*

NRSV

it was the day of Preparation for the Passover; and it was about noon. He said to the Jews, "Here is your King!" [15]They cried out, "Away with him! Away with him! Crucify him!" Pilate asked them, "Shall I crucify your King?" The chief priests answered, "We have no king but the emperor." [16]Then he handed him over to them to be crucified.

The Crucifixion of Jesus

So they took Jesus; [17]and carrying the cross by himself, he went out to what is called The Place of the Skull, which in Hebrew[h] is called Golgotha. [18]There they crucified him, and with him two others, one on either side, with Jesus between them. [19]Pilate also had an inscription written and put on the cross. It read, "Jesus of Nazareth,[i] the King of the Jews." [20]Many of the Jews read this inscription, because the place where Jesus was crucified was near the city; and it was written in Hebrew,[h] in Latin, and in Greek. [21]Then the chief priests of the Jews said to Pilate, "Do not write, 'The King of the Jews,' but, 'This man said, I am King of the Jews.'" [22]Pilate answered, "What I have written I have written." [23]When the soldiers had crucified Jesus, they took his clothes and divided them into four parts, one for each soldier. They also took his tunic; now the tunic was seamless, woven in one piece from the top. [24]So they said to one another, "Let us not tear it, but cast lots for it to see who will get it." This was to fulfill what the scripture says,

"They divided my clothes among
    themselves,
and for my clothing they cast lots."

[25]And that is what the soldiers did.
Meanwhile, standing near the cross of Jesus were his mother, and his mother's sister, Mary the wife of Clopas, and Mary Magdalene. [26]When Jesus saw his mother and the disciple whom he loved standing beside her, he said to his mother, "Woman, here is your son." [27]Then he said to the disciple, "Here is your mother." And from that hour the disciple took her into his own home.

28 After this, when Jesus knew that all

Greek

Γαββαθα. **14** ἦν δὲ παρασκευὴ τοῦ πάσχα, ὥρα ἦν ὡς ἕκτη. καὶ λέγει τοῖς Ἰουδαίοις, Ἴδε ὁ βασιλεὺς ὑμῶν. **15** ἐκραύγασαν οὖν ἐκεῖνοι, Ἆρον ἆρον, σταύρωσον αὐτόν. λέγει αὐτοῖς ὁ Πιλᾶτος, Τὸν βασιλέα ὑμῶν σταυρώσω; ἀπεκρίθησαν οἱ ἀρχιερεῖς, Οὐκ ἔχομεν βασιλέα εἰ μὴ Καίσαρα. **16** τότε οὖν παρέδωκεν αὐτὸν αὐτοῖς ἵνα σταυρωθῇ.

Παρέλαβον οὖν τὸν Ἰησοῦν, **17** καὶ βαστάζων ἑαυτῷ τὸν σταυρὸν ἐξῆλθεν εἰς τὸν λεγόμενον Κρανίου Τόπον, ὃ λέγεται Ἑβραϊστὶ Γολγοθα, **18** ὅπου αὐτὸν ἐσταύρωσαν, καὶ μετ' αὐτοῦ ἄλλους δύο ἐντεῦθεν καὶ ἐντεῦθεν, μέσον δὲ τὸν Ἰησοῦν. **19** ἔγραψεν δὲ καὶ τίτλον ὁ Πιλᾶτος καὶ ἔθηκεν ἐπὶ τοῦ σταυροῦ· ἦν δὲ γεγραμμένον, Ἰησοῦς ὁ Ναζωραῖος ὁ βασιλεὺς τῶν Ἰουδαίων. **20** τοῦτον οὖν τὸν τίτλον πολλοὶ ἀνέγνωσαν τῶν Ἰουδαίων, ὅτι ἐγγὺς ἦν ὁ τόπος τῆς πόλεως ὅπου ἐσταυρώθη ὁ Ἰησοῦς· καὶ ἦν γεγραμμένον Ἑβραϊστί, Ῥωμαϊστί, Ἑλληνιστί. **21** ἔλεγον οὖν τῷ Πιλάτῳ οἱ ἀρχιερεῖς τῶν Ἰουδαίων, Μὴ γράφε, Ὁ βασιλεὺς τῶν Ἰουδαίων, ἀλλ' ὅτι ἐκεῖνος εἶπεν, Βασιλεύς εἰμι τῶν Ἰουδαίων. **22** ἀπεκρίθη ὁ Πιλᾶτος, Ὃ γέγραφα, γέγραφα.

23 Οἱ οὖν στρατιῶται, ὅτε ἐσταύρωσαν τὸν Ἰησοῦν, ἔλαβον τὰ ἱμάτια αὐτοῦ καὶ ἐποίησαν τέσσαρα μέρη, ἑκάστῳ στρατιώτῃ μέρος, καὶ τὸν χιτῶνα. ἦν δὲ ὁ χιτὼν ἄραφος, ἐκ τῶν ἄνωθεν ὑφαντὸς δι' ὅλου. **24** εἶπαν οὖν πρὸς ἀλλήλους, Μὴ σχίσωμεν αὐτόν, ἀλλὰ λάχωμεν περὶ αὐτοῦ τίνος ἔσται· ἵνα ἡ γραφὴ πληρωθῇ [ἡ λέγουσα],

Διεμερίσαντο τὰ ἱμάτιά μου
    ἑαυτοῖς
καὶ ἐπὶ τὸν ἱματισμόν μου
    ἔβαλον κλῆρον.

Οἱ μὲν οὖν στρατιῶται ταῦτα ἐποίησαν. **25** εἱστήκεισαν δὲ παρὰ τῷ σταυρῷ τοῦ Ἰησοῦ ἡ μήτηρ αὐτοῦ καὶ ἡ ἀδελφὴ τῆς μητρὸς αὐτοῦ, Μαρία ἡ τοῦ Κλωπᾶ καὶ Μαρία ἡ Μαγδαληνή. **26** Ἰησοῦς οὖν ἰδὼν τὴν μητέρα καὶ τὸν μαθητὴν παρεστῶτα ὃν ἠγάπα, λέγει τῇ μητρί, Γύναι, ἴδε ὁ υἱός σου. **27** εἶτα λέγει τῷ μαθητῇ, Ἴδε ἡ μήτηρ σου. καὶ ἀπ' ἐκείνης τῆς ὥρας ἔλαβεν ὁ μαθητὴς αὐτὴν εἰς τὰ ἴδια.

28 Μετὰ τοῦτο εἰδὼς ὁ Ἰησοῦς ὅτι

NIV

the day of Preparation of Passover Week, about the sixth hour.
"Here is your king," Pilate said to the Jews.
[15]But they shouted, "Take him away! Take him away! Crucify him!"
"Shall I crucify your king?" Pilate asked.
"We have no king but Caesar," the chief priests answered.
[16]Finally Pilate handed him over to them to be crucified.

The Crucifixion

So the soldiers took charge of Jesus. [17]Carrying his own cross, he went out to the place of the Skull (which in Aramaic is called Golgotha). [18]Here they crucified him, and with him two others—one on each side and Jesus in the middle.
[19]Pilate had a notice prepared and fastened to the cross. It read: JESUS OF NAZARETH, THE KING OF THE JEWS. [20]Many of the Jews read this sign, for the place where Jesus was crucified was near the city, and the sign was written in Aramaic, Latin and Greek. [21]The chief priests of the Jews protested to Pilate, "Do not write 'The King of the Jews,' but that this man claimed to be king of the Jews."
[22]Pilate answered, "What I have written, I have written."
[23]When the soldiers crucified Jesus, they took his clothes, dividing them into four shares, one for each of them, with the undergarment remaining. This garment was seamless, woven in one piece from top to bottom.
[24]"Let's not tear it," they said to one another. "Let's decide by lot who will get it."
This happened that the scripture might be fulfilled which said,

"They divided my garments among
    them
and cast lots for my clothing."[a]

So this is what the soldiers did.
[25]Near the cross of Jesus stood his mother, his mother's sister, Mary the wife of Clopas, and Mary Magdalene. [26]When Jesus saw his mother there, and the disciple whom he loved standing nearby, he said to his mother, "Dear woman, here is your son," [27]and to the disciple, "Here is your mother." From that time on, this disciple took her into his home.

The Death of Jesus

[28]Later, knowing that all was now

---

[h] That is, *Aramaic*   [i] Gk *the Nazorean*   [a]24 Psalm 22:18

was now finished, he said (in order to fulfill the scripture), "I am thirsty." 29A jar full of sour wine was standing there. So they put a sponge full of the wine on a branch of hyssop and held it to his mouth. 30When Jesus had received the wine, he said, "It is finished." Then he bowed his head and gave up his spirit.

Jesus' Side Is Pierced

31 Since it was the day of Preparation, the Jews did not want the bodies left on the cross during the sabbath, especially because that sabbath was a day of great solemnity. So they asked Pilate to have the legs of the crucified men broken and the bodies removed. 32Then the soldiers came and broke the legs of the first and of the other who had been crucified with him. 33But when they came to Jesus and saw that he was already dead, they did not break his legs. 34Instead, one of the soldiers pierced his side with a spear, and at once blood and water came out.35(He who saw this has testified so that you also may believe. His testimony is true, and he knowsj that he tells the truth.) 36These things occurred so that the scripture might be fulfilled, "None of his bones shall be broken." 37And again another passage of scripture says, "They will look on the one whom they have pierced."

The Burial of Jesus

38 After these things, Joseph of Arimathea, who was a disciple of Jesus, though a secret one because of his fear of the Jews, asked Pilate to let him take away the body of Jesus. Pilate gave him permission; so he came and removed his body. 39Nicodemus, who had at first come to Jesus by night, also came, bringing a mixture of myrrh and aloes, weighing about a hundred pounds. 40They took the body of Jesus and wrapped it with the spices in linen cloths, according to the burial custom of the Jews. 41Now there was a garden in the place where he was crucified, and in the garden there was a new tomb in which no one had ever been laid. 42And so, because it was the Jewish day of Preparation, and the tomb was nearby, they laid Jesus there.

The Resurrection of Jesus

20 Early on the first day of the week, while it was still dark, Mary Magdalene came to the tomb and saw that the stone had been removed from the tomb.

j Or *there is one who knows*

ἤδη πάντα τετέλεσται, ἵνα τελειωθῇ ἡ γραφή, λέγει, Διψῶ. 29 σκεῦος ἔκειτο ὄξους μεστόν· σπόγγον οὖν μεστὸν τοῦ ὄξους ὑσσώπῳ περιθέντες προσήνεγκαν αὐτοῦ τῷ στόματι. 30 ὅτε οὖν ἔλαβεν τὸ ὄξος [ὁ] Ἰησοῦς εἶπεν, Τετέλεσται, καὶ κλίνας τὴν κεφαλὴν παρέδωκεν τὸ πνεῦμα.

31 Οἱ οὖν Ἰουδαῖοι, ἐπεὶ παρασκευὴ ἦν, ἵνα μὴ μείνῃ ἐπὶ τοῦ σταυροῦ τὰ σώματα ἐν τῷ σαββάτῳ, ἦν γὰρ μεγάλη ἡ ἡμέρα ἐκείνου τοῦ σαββάτου, ἠρώτησαν τὸν Πιλᾶτον ἵνα κατεαγῶσιν αὐτῶν τὰ σκέλη καὶ ἀρθῶσιν. 32 ἦλθον οὖν οἱ στρατιῶται καὶ τοῦ μὲν πρώτου κατέαξαν τὰ σκέλη καὶ τοῦ ἄλλου τοῦ συσταυρωθέντος αὐτῷ· 33 ἐπὶ δὲ τὸν Ἰησοῦν ἐλθόντες, ὡς εἶδον ἤδη αὐτὸν τεθνηκότα, οὐ κατέαξαν αὐτοῦ τὰ σκέλη, 34 ἀλλ' εἷς τῶν στρατιωτῶν λόγχῃ αὐτοῦ τὴν πλευρὰν ἔνυξεν, καὶ ἐξῆλθεν εὐθὺς αἷμα καὶ ὕδωρ. 35 καὶ ὁ ἑωρακὼς μεμαρτύρηκεν, καὶ ἀληθινὴ αὐτοῦ ἐστιν ἡ μαρτυρία, καὶ ἐκεῖνος οἶδεν ὅτι ἀληθῆ λέγει, ἵνα καὶ ὑμεῖς πιστεύ[σ]ητε. 36 ἐγένετο γὰρ ταῦτα ἵνα ἡ γραφὴ πληρωθῇ, Ὀστοῦν οὐ συντριβήσεται αὐτοῦ. 37 καὶ πάλιν ἑτέρα γραφὴ λέγει, Ὄψονται εἰς ὃν ἐξεκέντησαν.

38 Μετὰ δὲ ταῦτα ἠρώτησεν τὸν Πιλᾶτον Ἰωσὴφ [ὁ] ἀπὸ Ἀριμαθαίας, ὢν μαθητὴς τοῦ Ἰησοῦ κεκρυμμένος δὲ διὰ τὸν φόβον τῶν Ἰουδαίων, ἵνα ἄρῃ τὸ σῶμα τοῦ Ἰησοῦ· καὶ ἐπέτρεψεν ὁ Πιλᾶτος. ἦλθεν οὖν καὶ ἦρεν τὸ σῶμα αὐτοῦ. 39 ἦλθεν δὲ καὶ Νικόδημος, ὁ ἐλθὼν πρὸς αὐτὸν νυκτὸς τὸ πρῶτον, φέρων μίγμα σμύρνης καὶ ἀλόης ὡς λίτρας ἑκατόν. 40 ἔλαβον οὖν τὸ σῶμα τοῦ Ἰησοῦ καὶ ἔδησαν αὐτὸ ὀθονίοις μετὰ τῶν ἀρωμάτων, καθὼς ἔθος ἐστὶν τοῖς Ἰουδαίοις ἐνταφιάζειν. 41 ἦν δὲ ἐν τῷ τόπῳ ὅπου ἐσταυρώθη κῆπος, καὶ ἐν τῷ κήπῳ μνημεῖον καινὸν ἐν ᾧ οὐδέπω οὐδεὶς ἦν τεθειμένος· 42 ἐκεῖ οὖν διὰ τὴν παρασκευὴν τῶν Ἰουδαίων, ὅτι ἐγγὺς ἦν τὸ μνημεῖον, ἔθηκαν τὸν Ἰησοῦν.

20 Τῇ δὲ μιᾷ τῶν σαββάτων Μαρία ἡ Μαγδαληνὴ ἔρχεται πρωῒ σκοτίας ἔτι οὔσης εἰς τὸ μνημεῖον καὶ βλέπει τὸν λίθον ἠρμένον ἐκ τοῦ

completed, and so that the Scripture would be fulfilled, Jesus said, "I am thirsty." 29A jar of wine vinegar was there, so they soaked a sponge in it, put the sponge on a stalk of the hyssop plant, and lifted it to Jesus' lips. 30When he had received the drink, Jesus said, "It is finished." With that, he bowed his head and gave up his spirit.

31Now it was the day of Preparation, and the next day was to be a special Sabbath. Because the Jews did not want the bodies left on the crosses during the Sabbath, they asked Pilate to have the legs broken and the bodies taken down. 32The soldiers therefore came and broke the legs of the first man who had been crucified with Jesus, and then those of the other. 33But when they came to Jesus and found that he was already dead, they did not break his legs. 34Instead, one of the soldiers pierced Jesus' side with a spear, bringing a sudden flow of blood and water. 35The man who saw it has given testimony, and his testimony is true. He knows that he tells the truth, and he testifies so that you also may believe. 36These things happened so that the scripture would be fulfilled: "Not one of his bones will be broken,"b 37and, as another scripture says, "They will look on the one they have pierced."c

The Burial of Jesus

38Later, Joseph of Arimathea asked Pilate for the body of Jesus. Now Joseph was a disciple of Jesus, but secretly because he feared the Jews. With Pilate's permission, he came and took the body away. 39He was accompanied by Nicodemus, the man who earlier had visited Jesus at night. Nicodemus brought a mixture of myrrh and aloes, about seventy-five pounds.d 40Taking Jesus' body, the two of them wrapped it, with the spices, in strips of linen. This was in accordance with Jewish burial customs. 41At the place where Jesus was crucified, there was a garden, and in the garden a new tomb, in which no one had ever been laid. 42Because it was the Jewish day of Preparation and since the tomb was nearby, they laid Jesus there.

The Empty Tomb

20 Early on the first day of the week, while it was still dark, Mary Magdalene went to the tomb and saw that the stone had been removed from the entrance.

b36 Exodus 12:46; Num. 9:12; Psalm 34:20   c37 Zech. 12:10   d39 Greek *a hundred litrai* (about 34 kilograms)

2So she ran and went to Simon Peter and the other disciple, the one whom Jesus loved, and said to them, "They have taken the Lord out of the tomb, and we do not know where they have laid him." 3Then Peter and the other disciple set out and went toward the tomb. 4The two were running together, but the other disciple outran Peter and reached the tomb first. 5He bent down to look in and saw the linen wrappings lying there, but he did not go in. 6Then Simon Peter came, following him, and went into the tomb. He saw the linen wrappings lying there, 7and the cloth that had been on Jesus' head, not lying with the linen wrappings but rolled up in a place by itself. 8Then the other disciple, who reached the tomb first, also went in, and he saw and believed; 9for as yet they did not understand the scripture, that he must rise from the dead. 10Then the disciples returned to their homes.

Jesus Appears to Mary Magdalene

11 But Mary stood weeping outside the tomb. As she wept, she bent over to look[k] into the tomb; 12and she saw two angels in white, sitting where the body of Jesus had been lying, one at the head and the other at the feet. 13They said to her, "Woman, why are you weeping?" She said to them, "They have taken away my Lord, and I do not know where they have laid him." 14When she had said this, she turned around and saw Jesus standing there, but she did not know that it was Jesus. 15Jesus said to her, "Woman, why are you weeping? Whom are you looking for?" Supposing him to be the gardener, she said to him, "Sir, if you have carried him away, tell me where you have laid him, and I will take him away." 16Jesus said to her, "Mary!" She turned and said to him in Hebrew,[l] "Rabbouni!" (which means Teacher). 17Jesus said to her, "Do not hold on to me, because I have not yet ascended to the Father. But go to my brothers and say to them, 'I am ascending to my Father and your Father, to my God and your God.' " 18Mary Magdalene went and announced to the disciples, "I have seen the Lord"; and she told them that he had said these things to her.

Jesus Appears to the Disciples

19 When it was evening on that day, the first day of the week, and the doors of the

μνημείου. 2 τρέχει οὖν καὶ ἔρχεται πρὸς Σίμωνα Πέτρον καὶ πρὸς τὸν ἄλλον μαθητὴν ὃν ἐφίλει ὁ Ἰησοῦς καὶ λέγει αὐτοῖς, Ἦραν τὸν κύριον ἐκ τοῦ μνημείου καὶ οὐκ οἴδαμεν ποῦ ἔθηκαν αὐτόν. 3 Ἐξῆλθεν οὖν ὁ Πέτρος καὶ ὁ ἄλλος μαθητής καὶ ἤρχοντο εἰς τὸ μνημεῖον. 4 ἔτρεχον δὲ οἱ δύο ὁμοῦ· καὶ ὁ ἄλλος μαθητὴς προέδραμεν τάχιον τοῦ Πέτρου καὶ ἦλθεν πρῶτος εἰς τὸ μνημεῖον, 5 καὶ παρακύψας βλέπει κείμενα τὰ ὀθόνια, οὐ μέντοι εἰσῆλθεν. 6 ἔρχεται οὖν καὶ Σίμων Πέτρος ἀκολουθῶν αὐτῷ καὶ εἰσῆλθεν εἰς τὸ μνημεῖον, καὶ θεωρεῖ τὰ ὀθόνια κείμενα, 7 καὶ τὸ σουδάριον, ὃ ἦν ἐπὶ τῆς κεφαλῆς αὐτοῦ, οὐ μετὰ τῶν ὀθονίων κείμενον ἀλλὰ χωρὶς ἐντετυλιγμένον εἰς ἕνα τόπον. 8 τότε οὖν εἰσῆλθεν καὶ ὁ ἄλλος μαθητὴς ὁ ἐλθὼν πρῶτος εἰς τὸ μνημεῖον καὶ εἶδεν καὶ ἐπίστευσεν· 9 οὐδέπω γὰρ ᾔδεισαν τὴν γραφὴν ὅτι δεῖ αὐτὸν ἐκ νεκρῶν ἀναστῆναι. 10 ἀπῆλθον οὖν πάλιν πρὸς αὐτοὺς οἱ μαθηταί.

11 Μαρία δὲ εἱστήκει πρὸς τῷ μνημείῳ ἔξω κλαίουσα. ὡς οὖν ἔκλαιεν, παρέκυψεν εἰς τὸ μνημεῖον 12 καὶ θεωρεῖ δύο ἀγγέλους ἐν λευκοῖς καθεζομένους, ἕνα πρὸς τῇ κεφαλῇ καὶ ἕνα πρὸς τοῖς ποσίν, ὅπου ἔκειτο τὸ σῶμα τοῦ Ἰησοῦ. 13 καὶ λέγουσιν αὐτῇ ἐκεῖνοι, Γύναι, τί κλαίεις; λέγει αὐτοῖς ὅτι Ἦραν τὸν κύριόν μου, καὶ οὐκ οἶδα ποῦ ἔθηκαν αὐτόν. 14 ταῦτα εἰποῦσα ἐστράφη εἰς τὰ ὀπίσω καὶ θεωρεῖ τὸν Ἰησοῦν ἑστῶτα καὶ οὐκ ᾔδει ὅτι Ἰησοῦς ἐστιν. 15 λέγει αὐτῇ Ἰησοῦς, Γύναι, τί κλαίεις; τίνα ζητεῖς; ἐκείνη δοκοῦσα ὅτι ὁ κηπουρός ἐστιν λέγει αὐτῷ, Κύριε, εἰ σὺ ἐβάστασας αὐτόν, εἰπέ μοι ποῦ ἔθηκας αὐτόν, κἀγὼ αὐτὸν ἀρῶ. 16 λέγει αὐτῇ Ἰησοῦς, Μαριάμ. στραφεῖσα ἐκείνη λέγει αὐτῷ Ἑβραϊστί, Ραββουνι (ὃ λέγεται Διδάσκαλε). 17 λέγει αὐτῇ Ἰησοῦς, Μή μου ἅπτου, οὔπω γὰρ ἀναβέβηκα πρὸς τὸν πατέρα· πορεύου δὲ πρὸς τοὺς ἀδελφούς μου καὶ εἰπὲ αὐτοῖς, Ἀναβαίνω πρὸς τὸν πατέρα μου καὶ πατέρα ὑμῶν καὶ θεόν μου καὶ θεὸν ὑμῶν. 18 ἔρχεται Μαριὰμ ἡ Μαγδαληνὴ ἀγγέλλουσα τοῖς μαθηταῖς ὅτι Ἑώρακα τὸν κύριον, καὶ ταῦτα εἶπεν αὐτῇ.

19 Οὔσης οὖν ὀψίας τῇ ἡμέρᾳ ἐκείνῃ τῇ μιᾷ σαββάτων καὶ τῶν θυρῶν

2So she came running to Simon Peter and the other disciple, the one Jesus loved, and said, "They have taken the Lord out of the tomb, and we don't know where they have put him!"

3So Peter and the other disciple started for the tomb. 4Both were running, but the other disciple outran Peter and reached the tomb first. 5He bent over and looked in at the strips of linen lying there but did not go in. 6Then Simon Peter, who was behind him, arrived and went into the tomb. He saw the strips of linen lying there, 7as well as the burial cloth that had been around Jesus' head. The cloth was folded up by itself, separate from the linen. 8Finally the other disciple, who had reached the tomb first, also went inside. He saw and believed. 9(They still did not understand from Scripture that Jesus had to rise from the dead.)

Jesus Appears to Mary Magdalene

10Then the disciples went back to their homes, 11but Mary stood outside the tomb crying. As she wept, she bent over to look into the tomb 12and saw two angels in white, seated where Jesus' body had been, one at the head and the other at the foot.

13They asked her, "Woman, why are you crying?"

"They have taken my Lord away," she said, "and I don't know where they have put him." 14At this, she turned around and saw Jesus standing there, but she did not realize that it was Jesus.

15"Woman," he said, "why are you crying? Who is it you are looking for?"

Thinking he was the gardener, she said, "Sir, if you have carried him away, tell me where you have put him, and I will get him."

16Jesus said to her, "Mary."

She turned toward him and cried out in Aramaic, "Rabboni!" (which means Teacher).

17Jesus said, "Do not hold on to me, for I have not yet returned to the Father. Go instead to my brothers and tell them, 'I am returning to my Father and your Father, to my God and your God.' "

18Mary Magdalene went to the disciples with the news: "I have seen the Lord!" And she told them that he had said these things to her.

Jesus Appears to His Disciples

19On the evening of that first day of the week, when the disciples were together,

---

[k] Gk lacks *to look*   [l] That is, *Aramaic*

house where the disciples had met were locked for fear of the Jews, Jesus came and stood among them and said, "Peace be with you." 20After he said this, he showed them his hands and his side. Then the disciples rejoiced when they saw the Lord. 21Jesus said to them again, "Peace be with you. As the Father has sent me, so I send you." 22When he had said this, he breathed on them and said to them, "Receive the Holy Spirit. 23If you forgive the sins of any, they are forgiven them; if you retain the sins of any, they are retained."

Jesus and Thomas

24 But Thomas (who was called the Twinm), one of the twelve, was not with them when Jesus came. 25So the other disciples told him, "We have seen the Lord." But he said to them, "Unless I see the mark of the nails in his hands, and put my finger in the mark of the nails and my hand in his side, I will not believe."

26 A week later his disciples were again in the house, and Thomas was with them. Although the doors were shut, Jesus came and stood among them and said, "Peace be with you." 27Then he said to Thomas, "Put your finger here and see my hands. Reach out your hand and put it in my side. Do not doubt but believe." 28Thomas answered him, "My Lord and my God!" 29Jesus said to him, "Have you believed because you have seen me? Blessed are those who have not seen and yet have come to believe."

The Purpose of This Book

30 Now Jesus did many other signs in the presence of his disciples, which are not written in this book. 31But these are written so that you may come to believen that Jesus is the Messiah,o the Son of God, and that through believing you may have life in his name.

Jesus Appears to Seven Disciples

21 After these things Jesus showed himself again to the disciples by the Sea of Tiberias; and he showed himself in this way. 2Gathered there together were Simon Peter, Thomas called the Twin,m Nathanael of Cana in Galilee, the sons of Zebedee, and two others of his disciples. 3Simon Peter said to them, "I am going fishing." They said to him, "We will go with you." They went out and got into the

---

κεκλεισμένων ὅπου ἦσαν οἱ μαθηταὶ διὰ τὸν φόβον τῶν Ἰουδαίων, ἦλθεν ὁ Ἰησοῦς καὶ ἔστη εἰς τὸ μέσον καὶ λέγει αὐτοῖς, Εἰρήνη ὑμῖν. **20** καὶ τοῦτο εἰπὼν ἔδειξεν τὰς χεῖρας καὶ τὴν πλευρὰν αὐτοῖς. ἐχάρησαν οὖν οἱ μαθηταὶ ἰδόντες τὸν κύριον. **21** εἶπεν οὖν αὐτοῖς [ὁ Ἰησοῦς] πάλιν, Εἰρήνη ὑμῖν· καθὼς ἀπέσταλκέν με ὁ πατήρ, κἀγὼ πέμπω ὑμᾶς. **22** καὶ τοῦτο εἰπὼν ἐνεφύσησεν καὶ λέγει αὐτοῖς, Λάβετε πνεῦμα ἅγιον· **23** ἄν τινων ἀφῆτε τὰς ἁμαρτίας ἀφέωνται αὐτοῖς, ἄν τινων κρατῆτε κεκράτηνται.

24 Θωμᾶς δὲ εἷς ἐκ τῶν δώδεκα, ὁ λεγόμενος Δίδυμος, οὐκ ἦν μετ' αὐτῶν ὅτε ἦλθεν Ἰησοῦς. **25** ἔλεγον οὖν αὐτῷ οἱ ἄλλοι μαθηταί, Ἑωράκαμεν τὸν κύριον. ὁ δὲ εἶπεν αὐτοῖς, Ἐὰν μὴ ἴδω ἐν ταῖς χερσὶν αὐτοῦ τὸν τύπον τῶν ἥλων καὶ βάλω τὸν δάκτυλόν μου εἰς τὸν τύπον τῶν ἥλων καὶ βάλω μου τὴν χεῖρα εἰς τὴν πλευρὰν αὐτοῦ, οὐ μὴ πιστεύσω. **26** Καὶ μεθ' ἡμέρας ὀκτὼ πάλιν ἦσαν ἔσω οἱ μαθηταὶ αὐτοῦ καὶ Θωμᾶς μετ' αὐτῶν. ἔρχεται ὁ Ἰησοῦς τῶν θυρῶν κεκλεισμένων καὶ ἔστη εἰς τὸ μέσον καὶ εἶπεν, Εἰρήνη ὑμῖν. **27** εἶτα λέγει τῷ Θωμᾷ, Φέρε τὸν δάκτυλόν σου ὧδε καὶ ἴδε τὰς χεῖράς μου καὶ φέρε τὴν χεῖρά σου καὶ βάλε εἰς τὴν πλευράν μου, καὶ μὴ γίνου ἄπιστος ἀλλὰ πιστός. **28** ἀπεκρίθη Θωμᾶς καὶ εἶπεν αὐτῷ, Ὁ κύριός μου καὶ ὁ θεός μου. **29** λέγει αὐτῷ ὁ Ἰησοῦς, Ὅτι ἑώρακάς με πεπίστευκας; μακάριοι οἱ μὴ ἰδόντες καὶ πιστεύσαντες.

30 Πολλὰ μὲν οὖν καὶ ἄλλα σημεῖα ἐποίησεν ὁ Ἰησοῦς ἐνώπιον τῶν μαθητῶν [αὐτοῦ], ἃ οὐκ ἔστιν γεγραμμένα ἐν τῷ βιβλίῳ τούτῳ· **31** ταῦτα δὲ γέγραπται ἵνα πιστεύ[σ]ητεa ὅτι Ἰησοῦς ἐστιν ὁ Χριστὸς ὁ υἱὸς τοῦ θεοῦ, καὶ ἵνα πιστεύοντες ζωὴν ἔχητε ἐν τῷ ὀνόματι αὐτοῦ.

21 Μετὰ ταῦτα ἐφανέρωσεν ἑαυτὸν πάλιν ὁ Ἰησοῦς τοῖς μαθηταῖς ἐπὶ τῆς θαλάσσης τῆς Τιβεριάδος· ἐφανέρωσεν δὲ οὕτως. **2** ἦσαν ὁμοῦ Σίμων Πέτρος καὶ Θωμᾶς ὁ λεγόμενος Δίδυμος καὶ Ναθαναὴλ ὁ ἀπὸ Κανὰ τῆς Γαλιλαίας καὶ οἱ τοῦ Ζεβεδαίου καὶ ἄλλοι ἐκ τῶν μαθητῶν αὐτοῦ δύο. **3** λέγει αὐτοῖς Σίμων Πέτρος, Ὑπάγω ἁλιεύειν. λέγουσιν αὐτῷ, Ἐρχόμεθα καὶ ἡμεῖς σὺν σοί. ἐξῆλθον καὶ ἐνέβησαν εἰς τὸ πλοῖον,

---

with the doors locked for fear of the Jews, Jesus came and stood among them and said, "Peace be with you!" 20After he said this, he showed them his hands and side. The disciples were overjoyed when they saw the Lord.

21Again Jesus said, "Peace be with you! As the Father has sent me, I am sending you." 22And with that he breathed on them and said, "Receive the Holy Spirit. 23If you forgive anyone his sins, they are forgiven; if you do not forgive them, they are not forgiven."

Jesus Appears to Thomas

24Now Thomas (called Didymus), one of the Twelve, was not with the disciples when Jesus came. 25So the other disciples told him, "We have seen the Lord!"

But he said to them, "Unless I see the nail marks in his hands and put my finger where the nails were, and put my hand into his side, I will not believe it."

26A week later his disciples were in the house again, and Thomas was with them. Though the doors were locked, Jesus came and stood among them and said, "Peace be with you!" 27Then he said to Thomas, "Put your finger here; see my hands. Reach out your hand and put it into my side. Stop doubting and believe."

28Thomas said to him, "My Lord and my God!"

29Then Jesus told him, "Because you have seen me, you have believed; blessed are those who have not seen and yet have believed."

30Jesus did many other miraculous signs in the presence of his disciples, which are not recorded in this book. 31But these are written that you maya believe that Jesus is the Christ, the Son of God, and that by believing you may have life in his name.

Jesus and the Miraculous Catch of Fish

21 Afterward Jesus appeared again to his disciples, by the Sea of Tiberias.a It happened this way: 2Simon Peter, Thomas (called Didymus), Nathanael from Cana in Galilee, the sons of Zebedee, and two other disciples were together. 3"I'm going out to fish," Simon Peter told them, and they said, "We'll go with you." So they went out and got into

---

m Gk Didymus   n Other ancient authorities read may continue to believe   o Or the Christ

a31 NIV/NRSV notes πιστεύητε

a31 Some manuscripts may continue to   a1 That is, Sea of Galilee

boat, but that night they caught nothing.

4 Just after daybreak, Jesus stood on the beach; but the disciples did not know that it was Jesus. [5]Jesus said to them, "Children, you have no fish, have you?" They answered him, "No." [6]He said to them, "Cast the net to the right side of the boat, and you will find some." So they cast it, and now they were not able to haul it in because there were so many fish. [7]That disciple whom Jesus loved said to Peter, "It is the Lord!" When Simon Peter heard that it was the Lord, he put on some clothes, for he was naked, and jumped into the sea. [8]But the other disciples came in the boat, dragging the net full of fish, for they were not far from the land, only about a hundred yards[p] off.

9 When they had gone ashore, they saw a charcoal fire there, with fish on it, and bread. [10]Jesus said to them, "Bring some of the fish that you have just caught." [11]So Simon Peter went aboard and hauled the net ashore, full of large fish, a hundred fifty-three of them; and though there were so many, the net was not torn. [12]Jesus said to them, "Come and have breakfast." Now none of the disciples dared to ask him, "Who are you?" because they knew it was the Lord. [13]Jesus came and took the bread and gave it to them, and did the same with the fish. [14]This was now the third time that Jesus appeared to the disciples after he was raised from the dead.

Jesus and Peter

15 When they had finished breakfast, Jesus said to Simon Peter, "Simon son of John, do you love me more than these?" He said to him, "Yes, Lord; you know that I love you." Jesus said to him, "Feed my lambs." [16]A second time he said to him, "Simon son of John, do you love me?" He said to him, "Yes, Lord; you know that I love you." Jesus said to him, "Tend my sheep." [17]He said to him the third time, "Simon son of John, do you love me?" Peter felt hurt because he said to him the third time, "Do you love me?" And he said to him, "Lord, you know everything; you know that I love you." Jesus said to him, "Feed my sheep. [18]Very truly, I tell you,

καὶ ἐν ἐκείνῃ τῇ νυκτὶ ἐπίασαν οὐδέν. **4** πρωΐας δὲ ἤδη γενομένης ἔστη Ἰησοῦς εἰς τὸν αἰγιαλόν, οὐ μέντοι ᾔδεισαν οἱ μαθηταὶ ὅτι Ἰησοῦς ἐστιν. **5** λέγει οὖν αὐτοῖς [ὁ] Ἰησοῦς, Παιδία, μή τι προσφάγιον ἔχετε; ἀπεκρίθησαν αὐτῷ, Οὔ. **6** ὁ δὲ εἶπεν αὐτοῖς, Βάλετε εἰς τὰ δεξιὰ μέρη τοῦ πλοίου τὸ δίκτυον, καὶ εὑρήσετε. ἔβαλον οὖν, καὶ οὐκέτι αὐτὸ ἑλκύσαι ἴσχυον ἀπὸ τοῦ πλήθους τῶν ἰχθύων. **7** λέγει οὖν ὁ μαθητὴς ἐκεῖνος ὃν ἠγάπα ὁ Ἰησοῦς τῷ Πέτρῳ, Ὁ κύριός ἐστιν. Σίμων οὖν Πέτρος ἀκούσας ὅτι ὁ κύριός ἐστιν τὸν ἐπενδύτην διεζώσατο, ἦν γὰρ γυμνός, καὶ ἔβαλεν ἑαυτὸν εἰς τὴν θάλασσαν, **8** οἱ δὲ ἄλλοι μαθηταὶ τῷ πλοιαρίῳ ἦλθον, οὐ γὰρ ἦσαν μακρὰν ἀπὸ τῆς γῆς ἀλλὰ ὡς ἀπὸ πηχῶν διακοσίων, σύροντες τὸ δίκτυον τῶν ἰχθύων. **9** ὡς οὖν ἀπέβησαν εἰς τὴν γῆν βλέπουσιν ἀνθρακιὰν κειμένην καὶ ὀψάριον ἐπικείμενον καὶ ἄρτον. **10** λέγει αὐτοῖς ὁ Ἰησοῦς, Ἐνέγκατε ἀπὸ τῶν ὀψαρίων ὧν ἐπιάσατε νῦν. **11** ἀνέβη οὖν Σίμων Πέτρος καὶ εἵλκυσεν τὸ δίκτυον εἰς τὴν γῆν μεστὸν ἰχθύων μεγάλων ἑκατὸν πεντήκοντα τριῶν· καὶ τοσούτων ὄντων οὐκ ἐσχίσθη τὸ δίκτυον. **12** λέγει αὐτοῖς ὁ Ἰησοῦς, Δεῦτε ἀριστήσατε. οὐδεὶς δὲ ἐτόλμα τῶν μαθητῶν ἐξετάσαι αὐτόν, Σὺ τίς εἶ; εἰδότες ὅτι ὁ κύριός ἐστιν. **13** ἔρχεται Ἰησοῦς καὶ λαμβάνει τὸν ἄρτον καὶ δίδωσιν αὐτοῖς, καὶ τὸ ὀψάριον ὁμοίως. **14** τοῦτο ἤδη τρίτον ἐφανερώθη Ἰησοῦς τοῖς μαθηταῖς ἐγερθεὶς ἐκ νεκρῶν.

15 Ὅτε οὖν ἠρίστησαν λέγει τῷ Σίμωνι Πέτρῳ ὁ Ἰησοῦς, Σίμων Ἰωάννου, ἀγαπᾷς με πλέον τούτων; λέγει αὐτῷ, Ναὶ κύριε, σὺ οἶδας ὅτι φιλῶ σε. λέγει αὐτῷ, Βόσκε τὰ ἀρνία μου. **16** λέγει αὐτῷ πάλιν δεύτερον, Σίμων Ἰωάννου, ἀγαπᾷς με; λέγει αὐτῷ, Ναὶ κύριε, σὺ οἶδας ὅτι φιλῶ σε. λέγει αὐτῷ, Ποίμαινε τὰ πρόβατά μου. **17** λέγει αὐτῷ τὸ τρίτον, Σίμων Ἰωάννου, φιλεῖς με; ἐλυπήθη ὁ Πέτρος ὅτι εἶπεν αὐτῷ τὸ τρίτον, Φιλεῖς με; καὶ λέγει αὐτῷ, Κύριε, πάντα σὺ οἶδας, σὺ γινώσκεις ὅτι φιλῶ σε. λέγει αὐτῷ [ὁ Ἰησοῦς], Βόσκε τὰ πρόβατά μου. **18** ἀμὴν ἀμὴν λέγω σοι, ὅτε ἦς

the boat, but that night they caught nothing.

[4]Early in the morning, Jesus stood on the shore, but the disciples did not realize that it was Jesus.

[5]He called out to them, "Friends, haven't you any fish?"

"No," they answered.

[6]He said, "Throw your net on the right side of the boat and you will find some." When they did, they were unable to haul the net in because of the large number of fish.

[7]Then the disciple whom Jesus loved said to Peter, "It is the Lord!" As soon as Simon Peter heard him say, "It is the Lord," he wrapped his outer garment around him (for he had taken it off) and jumped into the water. [8]The other disciples followed in the boat, towing the net full of fish, for they were not far from shore, about a hundred yards.[b] [9]When they landed, they saw a fire of burning coals there with fish on it, and some bread.

[10]Jesus said to them, "Bring some of the fish you have just caught."

[11]Simon Peter climbed aboard and dragged the net ashore. It was full of large fish, 153, but even with so many the net was not torn. [12]Jesus said to them, "Come and have breakfast." None of the disciples dared ask him, "Who are you?" They knew it was the Lord. [13]Jesus came, took the bread and gave it to them, and did the same with the fish. [14]This was now the third time Jesus appeared to his disciples after he was raised from the dead.

Jesus Reinstates Peter

[15]When they had finished eating, Jesus said to Simon Peter, "Simon son of John, do you truly love me more than these?"

"Yes, Lord," he said, "you know that I love you."

Jesus said, "Feed my lambs."

[16]Again Jesus said, "Simon son of John, do you truly love me?"

He answered, "Yes, Lord, you know that I love you."

Jesus said, "Take care of my sheep."

[17]The third time he said to him, "Simon son of John, do you love me?"

Peter was hurt because Jesus asked him the third time, "Do you love me?" He said, "Lord, you know all things; you know that I love you."

Jesus said, "Feed my sheep. [18]I tell you

when you were younger, you used to fasten your own belt and to go wherever you wished. But when you grow old, you will stretch out your hands, and someone else will fasten a belt around you and take you where you do not wish to go." ¹⁹(He said this to indicate the kind of death by which he would glorify God.) After this he said to him, "Follow me."

Jesus and the Beloved Disciple

20 Peter turned and saw the disciple whom Jesus loved following them; he was the one who had reclined next to Jesus at the supper and had said, "Lord, who is it that is going to betray you?" ²¹When Peter saw him, he said to Jesus, "Lord, what about him?" ²²Jesus said to him, "If it is my will that he remain until I come, what is that to you? Follow me!" ²³So the rumor spread in the communityq that this disciple would not die. Yet Jesus did not say to him that he would not die, but, "If it is my will that he remain until I come, what is that to you?"r

24 This is the disciple who is testifying to these things and has written them, and we know that his testimony is true. ²⁵But there are also many other things that Jesus did; if every one of them were written down, I suppose that the world itself could not contain the books that would be written.

νεώτερος, ἐζώννυες σεαυτὸν καὶ περιεπάτεις ὅπου ἤθελες· ὅταν δὲ γηράσῃς, ἐκτενεῖς τὰς χεῖράς σου, καὶ ἄλλος σε ζώσει καὶ οἴσει ὅπου οὐ θέλεις. 19 τοῦτο δὲ εἶπεν σημαίνων ποίῳ θανάτῳ δοξάσει τὸν θεόν. καὶ τοῦτο εἰπὼν λέγει αὐτῷ, Ἀκολούθει μοι.

20 Ἐπιστραφεὶς ὁ Πέτρος βλέπει τὸν μαθητὴν ὃν ἠγάπα ὁ Ἰησοῦς ἀκολουθοῦντα, ὃς καὶ ἀνέπεσεν ἐν τῷ δείπνῳ ἐπὶ τὸ στῆθος αὐτοῦ καὶ εἶπεν, Κύριε, τίς ἐστιν ὁ παραδιδούς σε; 21 τοῦτον οὖν ἰδὼν ὁ Πέτρος λέγει τῷ Ἰησοῦ, Κύριε, οὗτος δὲ τί; 22 λέγει αὐτῷ ὁ Ἰησοῦς, Ἐὰν αὐτὸν θέλω μένειν ἕως ἔρχομαι, τί πρὸς σέ; σύ μοι ἀκολούθει. 23 ἐξῆλθεν οὖν οὗτος ὁ λόγος εἰς τοὺς ἀδελφοὺς ὅτι ὁ μαθητὴς ἐκεῖνος οὐκ ἀποθνῄσκει· οὐκ εἶπεν δὲ αὐτῷ ὁ Ἰησοῦς ὅτι οὐκ ἀποθνῄσκει ἀλλ', Ἐὰν αὐτὸν θέλω μένειν ἕως ἔρχομαι[, τί πρὸς σέ];

24 Οὗτός ἐστιν ὁ μαθητὴς ὁ μαρτυρῶν περὶ τούτων καὶ ὁ γράψας ταῦτα, καὶ οἴδαμεν ὅτι ἀληθὴς αὐτοῦ ἡ μαρτυρία ἐστίν.

25 Ἔστιν δὲ καὶ ἄλλα πολλὰ ἃ ἐποίησεν ὁ Ἰησοῦς, ἅτινα ἐὰν γράφηται καθ' ἕν, οὐδ' αὐτὸν οἶμαι τὸν κόσμον χωρῆσαι τὰ γραφόμενα βιβλία.

the truth, when you were younger you dressed yourself and went where you wanted; but when you are old you will stretch out your hands, and someone else will dress you and lead you where you do not want to go." ¹⁹Jesus said this to indicate the kind of death by which Peter would glorify God. Then he said to him, "Follow me!"

²⁰Peter turned and saw that the disciple whom Jesus loved was following them. (This was the one who had leaned back against Jesus at the supper and had said, "Lord, who is going to betray you?") ²¹When Peter saw him, he asked, "Lord, what about him?"

²²Jesus answered, "If I want him to remain alive until I return, what is that to you? You must follow me." ²³Because of this, the rumor spread among the brothers that this disciple would not die. But Jesus did not say that he would not die; he only said, "If I want him to remain alive until I return, what is that to you?"

²⁴This is the disciple who testifies to these things and who wrote them down. We know that his testimony is true.

²⁵Jesus did many other things as well. If every one of them were written down, I suppose that even the whole world would not have room for the books that would be written.

NRSV

The Promise of the Holy Spirit

1 In the first book, Theophilus, I wrote about all that Jesus did and taught from the beginning [2]until the day when he was taken up to heaven, after giving instructions through the Holy Spirit to the apostles whom he had chosen. [3]After his suffering he presented himself alive to them by many convincing proofs, appearing to them during forty days and speaking about the kingdom of God. [4]While staying[a] with them, he ordered them not to leave Jerusalem, but to wait there for the promise of the Father. "This," he said, "is what you have heard from me; [5]for John baptized with water, but you will be baptized with[b] the Holy Spirit not many days from now."

The Ascension of Jesus

6 So when they had come together, they asked him, "Lord, is this the time when you will restore the kingdom to Israel?" [7]He replied, "It is not for you to know the times or periods that the Father has set by his own authority. [8]But you will receive power when the Holy Spirit has come upon you; and you will be my witnesses in Jerusalem, in all Judea and Samaria, and to the ends of the earth." [9]When he had said this, as they were watching, he was lifted up, and a cloud took him out of their sight. [10]While he was going and they were gazing up toward heaven, suddenly two men in white robes stood by them. [11]They said, "Men of Galilee, why do you stand looking up toward heaven? This Jesus, who has been taken up from you into heaven, will come in the same way as you saw him go into heaven."

Matthias Chosen to Replace Judas

12 Then they returned to Jerusalem from the mount called Olivet, which is near Jerusalem, a sabbath day's journey away. [13]When they had entered the city, they went to the room upstairs where they were staying, Peter, and John, and James, and Andrew, Philip and Thomas, Bartholomew and Matthew, James son of Alphaeus, and Simon the Zealot, and Judas son of[c] James. [14]All these were constantly devoting themselves to prayer, together with certain women, including Mary the mother of Jesus, as well as his brothers.

15 In those days Peter stood up among the believers[d] (together the crowd numbered about one hundred twenty persons)

ΠΡΑΞΕΙΣ ΑΠΟΣΤΟΛΩΝ

1 Τὸν μὲν πρῶτον λόγον ἐποιησάμην περὶ πάντων, ὦ Θεόφιλε, ὧν ἤρξατο ὁ Ἰησοῦς ποιεῖν τε καὶ διδάσκειν, **2** ἄχρι ἧς ἡμέρας ἐντειλάμενος τοῖς ἀποστόλοις διὰ πνεύματος ἁγίου οὓς ἐξελέξατο ἀνελήμφθη· **3** οἷς καὶ παρέστησεν ἑαυτὸν ζῶντα μετὰ τὸ παθεῖν αὐτὸν ἐν πολλοῖς τεκμηρίοις, δι' ἡμερῶν τεσσεράκοντα ὀπτανόμενος αὐτοῖς καὶ λέγων τὰ περὶ τῆς βασιλείας τοῦ θεοῦ· **4** καὶ συναλιζόμενος παρήγγειλεν αὐτοῖς ἀπὸ Ἰεροσολύμων μὴ χωρίζεσθαι ἀλλὰ περιμένειν τὴν ἐπαγγελίαν τοῦ πατρὸς ἣν ἠκούσατέ μου, **5** ὅτι Ἰωάννης μὲν ἐβάπτισεν ὕδατι, ὑμεῖς δὲ ἐν πνεύματι βαπτισθήσεσθε ἁγίῳ οὐ μετὰ πολλὰς ταύτας ἡμέρας.

6 Οἱ μὲν οὖν συνελθόντες ἠρώτων αὐτὸν λέγοντες, Κύριε, εἰ ἐν τῷ χρόνῳ τούτῳ ἀποκαθιστάνεις τὴν βασιλείαν τῷ Ἰσραήλ; **7** εἶπεν δὲ πρὸς αὐτούς, Οὐχ ὑμῶν ἐστιν γνῶναι χρόνους ἢ καιροὺς οὓς ὁ πατὴρ ἔθετο ἐν τῇ ἰδίᾳ ἐξουσίᾳ, **8** ἀλλὰ λήμψεσθε δύναμιν ἐπελθόντος τοῦ ἁγίου πνεύματος ἐφ' ὑμᾶς καὶ ἔσεσθέ μου μάρτυρες ἔν τε Ἰερουσαλὴμ καὶ [ἐν] πάσῃ τῇ Ἰουδαίᾳ καὶ Σαμαρείᾳ καὶ ἕως ἐσχάτου τῆς γῆς. **9** καὶ ταῦτα εἰπὼν βλεπόντων αὐτῶν ἐπήρθη καὶ νεφέλη ὑπέλαβεν αὐτὸν ἀπὸ τῶν ὀφθαλμῶν αὐτῶν. **10** καὶ ὡς ἀτενίζοντες ἦσαν εἰς τὸν οὐρανὸν πορευομένου αὐτοῦ, καὶ ἰδοὺ ἄνδρες δύο παρειστήκεισαν αὐτοῖς ἐν ἐσθήσεσι λευκαῖς, **11** οἳ καὶ εἶπαν, Ἄνδρες Γαλιλαῖοι, τί ἑστήκατε [ἐμ]βλέποντες εἰς τὸν οὐρανόν; οὗτος ὁ Ἰησοῦς ὁ ἀναλημφθεὶς ἀφ' ὑμῶν εἰς τὸν οὐρανὸν οὕτως ἐλεύσεται ὃν τρόπον ἐθεάσασθε αὐτὸν πορευόμενον εἰς τὸν οὐρανόν.

12 Τότε ὑπέστρεψαν εἰς Ἰερουσαλὴμ ἀπὸ ὄρους τοῦ καλουμένου Ἐλαιῶνος, ὅ ἐστιν ἐγγὺς Ἰερουσαλὴμ σαββάτου ἔχον ὁδόν. **13** καὶ ὅτε εἰσῆλθον, εἰς τὸ ὑπερῷον ἀνέβησαν οὗ ἦσαν καταμένοντες, ὅ τε Πέτρος καὶ Ἰωάννης καὶ Ἰάκωβος καὶ Ἀνδρέας, Φίλιππος καὶ Θωμᾶς, Βαρθολομαῖος καὶ Μαθθαῖος, Ἰάκωβος Ἀλφαίου καὶ Σίμων ὁ ζηλωτὴς καὶ Ἰούδας Ἰακώβου. **14** οὗτοι πάντες ἦσαν προσκαρτεροῦντες ὁμοθυμαδὸν τῇ προσευχῇ σὺν γυναιξὶν καὶ Μαριὰμ τῇ μητρὶ τοῦ Ἰησοῦ καὶ τοῖς ἀδελφοῖς αὐτοῦ.

15 Καὶ ἐν ταῖς ἡμέραις ταύταις ἀναστὰς Πέτρος ἐν μέσῳ τῶν ἀδελφῶν εἶπεν· ἦν τε ὄχλος ὀνομάτων ἐπὶ τὸ αὐτὸ ὡσεὶ ἑκατὸν εἴκοσι· **16** Ἄνδρες

NIV

Jesus Taken Up Into Heaven

1 In my former book, Theophilus, I wrote about all that Jesus began to do and to teach [2]until the day he was taken up to heaven, after giving instructions through the Holy Spirit to the apostles he had chosen. [3]After his suffering, he showed himself to these men and gave many convincing proofs that he was alive. He appeared to them over a period of forty days and spoke about the kingdom of God. [4]On one occasion, while he was eating with them, he gave them this command: "Do not leave Jerusalem, but wait for the gift my Father promised, which you have heard me speak about. [5]For John baptized with[a] water, but in a few days you will be baptized with the Holy Spirit."

[6]So when they met together, they asked him, "Lord, are you at this time going to restore the kingdom to Israel?"

[7]He said to them: "It is not for you to know the times or dates the Father has set by his own authority. [8]But you will receive power when the Holy Spirit comes on you; and you will be my witnesses in Jerusalem, and in all Judea and Samaria, and to the ends of the earth."

[9]After he said this, he was taken up before their very eyes, and a cloud hid him from their sight.

[10]They were looking intently up into the sky as he was going, when suddenly two men dressed in white stood beside them. [11]"Men of Galilee," they said, "why do you stand here looking into the sky? This same Jesus, who has been taken from you into heaven, will come back in the same way you have seen him go into heaven."

Matthias Chosen to Replace Judas

[12]Then they returned to Jerusalem from the hill called the Mount of Olives, a Sabbath day's walk[b] from the city. [13]When they arrived, they went upstairs to the room where they were staying. Those present were Peter, John, James and Andrew; Philip and Thomas, Bartholomew and Matthew; James son of Alphaeus and Simon the Zealot, and Judas son of James. [14]They all joined together constantly in prayer, along with the women and Mary the mother of Jesus, and with his brothers.

[15]In those days Peter stood up among the believers[c] (a group numbering about a hundred and twenty) [16]and said, "Brothers,

---

a Or eating   *b Or by*   *c Or the brother of*   *d Gk brothers*

a5 Or in   *b12 That is, about 3/4 mile (about 1,100 meters)*   *c15 Greek brothers*

and said, [16]"Friends,[e] the scripture had to be fulfilled, which the Holy Spirit through David foretold concerning Judas, who became a guide for those who arrested Jesus— [17]for he was numbered among us and was allotted his share in this ministry." [18](Now this man acquired a field with the reward of his wickedness; and falling headlong,[f] he burst open in the middle and all his bowels gushed out. [19]This became known to all the residents of Jerusalem, so that the field was called in their language Hakeldama, that is, Field of Blood.) [20]"For it is written in the book of Psalms,

'Let his homestead become desolate,
    and let there be no one to live in it';
and

'Let another take his position of
    overseer.'

[21]So one of the men who have accompanied us during all the time that the Lord Jesus went in and out among us, [22]beginning from the baptism of John until the day when he was taken up from us—one of these must become a witness with us to his resurrection." [23]So they proposed two, Joseph called Barsabbas, who was also known as Justus, and Matthias. [24]Then they prayed and said, "Lord, you know everyone's heart. Show us which one of these two you have chosen [25]to take the place[g] in this ministry and apostleship from which Judas turned aside to go to his own place." [26]And they cast lots for them, and the lot fell on Matthias; and he was added to the eleven apostles.

The Coming of the Holy Spirit

2 When the day of Pentecost had come, they were all together in one place. [2]And suddenly from heaven there came a sound like the rush of a violent wind, and it filled the entire house where they were sitting. [3]Divided tongues, as of fire, appeared among them, and a tongue rested on each of them. [4]All of them were filled with the Holy Spirit and began to speak in other languages, as the Spirit gave them ability.

[5] Now there were devout Jews from every nation under heaven living in Jerusalem. [6]And at this sound the crowd gathered and was bewildered, because each

---

ἀδελφοί, ἔδει πληρωθῆναι τὴν γραφὴν ἣν προεῖπεν τὸ πνεῦμα τὸ ἅγιον διὰ στόματος Δαυὶδ περὶ Ἰούδα τοῦ γενομένου ὁδηγοῦ τοῖς συλλαβοῦσιν Ἰησοῦν, 17 ὅτι κατηριθμημένος ἦν ἐν ἡμῖν καὶ ἔλαχεν τὸν κλῆρον τῆς διακονίας ταύτης. 18 Οὗτος μὲν οὖν ἐκτήσατο χωρίον ἐκ μισθοῦ τῆς ἀδικίας καὶ πρηνὴς γενόμενος ἐλάκησεν μέσος καὶ ἐξεχύθη πάντα τὰ σπλάγχνα αὐτοῦ· 19 καὶ γνωστὸν ἐγένετο πᾶσι τοῖς κατοικοῦσιν Ἰερουσαλήμ, ὥστε κληθῆναι τὸ χωρίον ἐκεῖνο τῇ ἰδίᾳ[a] διαλέκτῳ αὐτῶν Ἀκελδαμάχ, τοῦτ' ἔστιν Χωρίον Αἵματος. 20 Γέγραπται γὰρ ἐν βίβλῳ ψαλμῶν,

Γενηθήτω ἡ ἔπαυλις αὐτοῦ ἔρημος
    καὶ μὴ ἔστω ὁ κατοικῶν ἐν αὐτῇ,
καί,

Τὴν ἐπισκοπὴν αὐτοῦ λαβέτω
    ἕτερος.

21 δεῖ οὖν τῶν συνελθόντων ἡμῖν ἀνδρῶν ἐν παντὶ χρόνῳ ᾧ εἰσῆλθεν καὶ ἐξῆλθεν ἐφ' ἡμᾶς ὁ κύριος Ἰησοῦς, 22 ἀρξάμενος ἀπὸ τοῦ βαπτίσματος Ἰωάννου ἕως τῆς ἡμέρας ἧς ἀνελήμφθη ἀφ' ἡμῶν, μάρτυρα τῆς ἀναστάσεως αὐτοῦ σὺν ἡμῖν γενέσθαι ἕνα τούτων. 23 καὶ ἔστησαν δύο, Ἰωσὴφ τὸν καλούμενον Βαρσαββᾶν ὃς ἐπεκλήθη Ἰοῦστος, καὶ Μαθθίαν. 24 καὶ προσευξάμενοι εἶπαν, Σὺ κύριε καρδιογνῶστα πάντων, ἀνάδειξον ὃν ἐξελέξω ἐκ τούτων τῶν δύο ἕνα 25 λαβεῖν τὸν τόπον τῆς διακονίας ταύτης καὶ ἀποστολῆς ἀφ' ἧς παρέβη Ἰούδας πορευθῆναι εἰς τὸν τόπον[b] τὸν ἴδιον. 26 καὶ ἔδωκαν κλήρους αὐτοῖς καὶ ἔπεσεν ὁ κλῆρος ἐπὶ Μαθθίαν καὶ συγκατεψηφίσθη μετὰ τῶν ἕνδεκα ἀποστόλων.

2 Καὶ ἐν τῷ συμπληροῦσθαι τὴν ἡμέραν τῆς πεντηκοστῆς ἦσαν πάντες ὁμοῦ ἐπὶ τὸ αὐτό. 2 καὶ ἐγένετο ἄφνω ἐκ τοῦ οὐρανοῦ ἦχος ὥσπερ φερομένης πνοῆς βιαίας καὶ ἐπλήρωσεν ὅλον τὸν οἶκον οὗ ἦσαν καθήμενοι 3 καὶ ὤφθησαν αὐτοῖς διαμεριζόμεναι γλῶσσαι ὡσεὶ πυρὸς καὶ ἐκάθισεν ἐφ' ἕνα ἕκαστον αὐτῶν, 4 καὶ ἐπλήσθησαν πάντες πνεύματος ἁγίου καὶ ἤρξαντο λαλεῖν ἑτέραις γλώσσαις καθὼς τὸ πνεῦμα ἐδίδου ἀποφθέγγεσθαι αὐτοῖς.

5 Ἦσαν δὲ εἰς Ἰερουσαλὴμ κατοικοῦντες Ἰουδαῖοι, ἄνδρες εὐλαβεῖς ἀπὸ παντὸς ἔθνους τῶν ὑπὸ τὸν οὐρανόν. 6 γενομένης δὲ τῆς φωνῆς ταύτης συνῆλθεν τὸ πλῆθος καὶ συνεχύθη, ὅτι

---

the Scripture had to be fulfilled which the Holy Spirit spoke long ago through the mouth of David concerning Judas, who served as guide for those who arrested Jesus— [17]he was one of our number and shared in this ministry."

[18](With the reward he got for his wickedness, Judas bought a field; there he fell headlong, his body burst open and all his intestines spilled out. [19]Everyone in Jerusalem heard about this, so they called that field in their language Akeldama, that is, Field of Blood.)

[20]"For," said Peter, "it is written in the book of Psalms,

" 'May his place be deserted;
    let there be no one to dwell in it,'[d]

and,

" 'May another take his place of
    leadership.'[e]

[21]Therefore it is necessary to choose one of the men who have been with us the whole time the Lord Jesus went in and out among us, [22]beginning from John's baptism to the time when Jesus was taken up from us. For one of these must become a witness with us of his resurrection."

[23]So they proposed two men: Joseph called Barsabbas (also known as Justus) and Matthias. [24]Then they prayed, "Lord, you know everyone's heart. Show us which of these two you have chosen [25]to take over this apostolic ministry, which Judas left to go where he belongs." [26]Then they cast lots, and the lot fell to Matthias; so he was added to the eleven apostles.

The Holy Spirit Comes at Pentecost

2 When the day of Pentecost came, they were all together in one place. [2]Suddenly a sound like the blowing of a violent wind came from heaven and filled the whole house where they were sitting. [3]They saw what seemed to be tongues of fire that separated and came to rest on each of them. [4]All of them were filled with the Holy Spirit and began to speak in other tongues[a] as the Spirit enabled them.

[5]Now there were staying in Jerusalem God-fearing Jews from every nation under heaven. [6]When they heard this sound, a crowd came together in bewilderment,

---

one heard them speaking in the native language of each. 7Amazed and astonished, they asked, "Are not all these who are speaking Galileans? 8And how is it that we hear, each of us, in our own native language? 9Parthians, Medes, Elamites, and residents of Mesopotamia, Judea and Cappadocia, Pontus and Asia, 10Phrygia and Pamphylia, Egypt and the parts of Libya belonging to Cyrene, and visitors from Rome, both Jews and proselytes, 11Cretans and Arabs—in our own languages we hear them speaking about God's deeds of power." 12All were amazed and perplexed, saying to one another, "What does this mean?" 13But others sneered and said, "They are filled with new wine."

Peter Addresses the Crowd

14 But Peter, standing with the eleven, raised his voice and addressed them, "Men of Judea and all who live in Jerusalem, let this be known to you, and listen to what I say. 15Indeed, these are not drunk, as you suppose, for it is only nine o'clock in the morning. 16No, this is what was spoken through the prophet Joel:

17 'In the last days it will be, God declares,
  that I will pour out my Spirit upon all flesh,
    and your sons and your daughters shall prophesy,
    and your young men shall see visions,
    and your old men shall dream dreams.
18 Even upon my slaves, both men and women,
    in those days I will pour out my Spirit;
    and they shall prophesy.
19 And I will show portents in the heaven above
    and signs on the earth below,
    blood, and fire, and smoky mist.
20 The sun shall be turned to darkness
    and the moon to blood,
    before the coming of the Lord's great and glorious day.
21 Then everyone who calls on the name of the Lord shall be saved.'

ἤκουον εἷς ἕκαστος τῇ ἰδίᾳ διαλέκτῳ λαλούντων αὐτῶν. 7 ἐξίσταντο δὲ καὶ ἐθαύμαζον λέγοντες, Οὐχ ἰδοὺ ἅπαντες οὗτοί εἰσιν οἱ λαλοῦντες Γαλιλαῖοι; 8 καὶ πῶς ἡμεῖς ἀκούομεν ἕκαστος τῇ ἰδίᾳ διαλέκτῳ ἡμῶν ἐν ᾗ ἐγεννήθημεν; 9 Πάρθοι καὶ Μῆδοι καὶ Ἐλαμῖται καὶ οἱ κατοικοῦντες τὴν Μεσοποταμίαν, Ἰουδαίαν τε καὶ Καππαδοκίαν, Πόντον καὶ τὴν Ἀσίαν, 10 Φρυγίαν τε καὶ Παμφυλίαν, Αἴγυπτον καὶ τὰ μέρη τῆς Λιβύης τῆς κατὰ Κυρήνην, καὶ οἱ ἐπιδημοῦντες Ῥωμαῖοι, 11 Ἰουδαῖοί τε καὶ προσήλυτοι, Κρῆτες καὶ Ἄραβες, ἀκούομεν λαλούντων αὐτῶν ταῖς ἡμετέραις γλώσσαις τὰ μεγαλεῖα τοῦ θεοῦ. 12 ἐξίσταντο δὲ πάντες καὶ διηπόρουν, ἄλλος πρὸς ἄλλον λέγοντες, Τί θέλει τοῦτο εἶναι; 13 ἕτεροι δὲ διαχλευάζοντες ἔλεγον ὅτι Γλεύκους μεμεστωμένοι εἰσίν.

14 Σταθεὶς δὲ ὁ Πέτρος σὺν τοῖς ἕνδεκα ἐπῆρεν τὴν φωνὴν αὐτοῦ καὶ ἀπεφθέγξατο αὐτοῖς, Ἄνδρες Ἰουδαῖοι καὶ οἱ κατοικοῦντες Ἰερουσαλὴμ πάντες, τοῦτο ὑμῖν γνωστὸν ἔστω καὶ ἐνωτίσασθε τὰ ῥήματά μου. 15 οὐ γὰρ ὡς ὑμεῖς ὑπολαμβάνετε οὗτοι μεθύουσιν, ἔστιν γὰρ ὥρα τρίτη τῆς ἡμέρας, 16 ἀλλὰ τοῦτό ἐστιν τὸ εἰρημένον διὰ τοῦ προφήτου Ἰωήλ·
17 Καὶ ἔσται ἐν ταῖς ἐσχάταις ἡμέραις, λέγει ὁ θεός,
  ἐκχεῶ ἀπὸ τοῦ πνεύματός μου
    ἐπὶ πᾶσαν σάρκα,
    καὶ προφητεύσουσιν οἱ υἱοὶ ὑμῶν
    καὶ αἱ θυγατέρες ὑμῶν
  καὶ οἱ νεανίσκοι ὑμῶν ὁράσεις ὄψονται
  καὶ οἱ πρεσβύτεροι ὑμῶν ἐνυπνίοις ἐνυπνιασθήσονται·
18 καί γε ἐπὶ τοὺς δούλους μου καὶ ἐπὶ τὰς δούλας μου
  ἐν ταῖς ἡμέραις ἐκείναις ἐκχεῶ ἀπὸ τοῦ πνεύματός μου,
  καὶ προφητεύσουσιν.
19 καὶ δώσω τέρατα ἐν τῷ οὐρανῷ ἄνω
  καὶ σημεῖα ἐπὶ τῆς γῆς κάτω,
  αἷμα καὶ πῦρ καὶ ἀτμίδα καπνοῦ·
20 ὁ ἥλιος μεταστραφήσεται εἰς σκότος
  καὶ ἡ σελήνη εἰς αἷμα,
  πρὶν ἐλθεῖν ἡμέραν κυρίου τὴν μεγάλην καὶ ἐπιφανῆ.
21 καὶ ἔσται πᾶς ὃς ἂν ἐπικαλέσηται τὸ ὄνομα κυρίου σωθήσεται.

because each one heard them speaking in his own language. 7Utterly amazed, they asked: "Are not all these men who are speaking Galileans? 8Then how is it that each of us hears them in his own native language? 9Parthians, Medes and Elamites; residents of Mesopotamia, Judea and Cappadocia, Pontus and Asia, 10Phrygia and Pamphylia, Egypt and the parts of Libya near Cyrene; visitors from Rome 11(both Jews and converts to Judaism); Cretans and Arabs—we hear them declaring the wonders of God in our own tongues!" 12Amazed and perplexed, they asked one another, "What does this mean?"

13Some, however, made fun of them and said, "They have had too much wine.b"

Peter Addresses the Crowd

14Then Peter stood up with the Eleven, raised his voice and addressed the crowd: "Fellow Jews and all of you who live in Jerusalem, let me explain this to you; listen carefully to what I say. 15These men are not drunk, as you suppose. It's only nine in the morning! 16No, this is what was spoken by the prophet Joel:

17" 'In the last days, God says,
  I will pour out my Spirit on all people.
  Your sons and daughters will prophesy,
    your young men will see visions,
    your old men will dream dreams.
18Even on my servants, both men and women,
  I will pour out my Spirit in those days,
  and they will prophesy.
19I will show wonders in the heaven above
  and signs on the earth below,
  blood and fire and billows of smoke.
20The sun will be turned to darkness
  and the moon to blood
  before the coming of the great and glorious day of the Lord.
21And everyone who calls
  on the name of the Lord will be saved.'c

b13 Or *sweet wine* c21 Joel 2:28-32

22 "You that are Israelites,[h] listen to what I have to say: Jesus of Nazareth,[i] a man attested to you by God with deeds of power, wonders, and signs that God did through him among you, as you yourselves know— 23this man, handed over to you according to the definite plan and foreknowledge of God, you crucified and killed by the hands of those outside the law. 24But God raised him up, having freed him from death,[j] because it was impossible for him to be held in its power. 25For David says concerning him,

'I saw the Lord always before me,
    for he is at my right hand so that I
        will not be shaken;
26 therefore my heart was glad, and my
        tongue rejoiced;
    moreover my flesh will live in hope.
27 For you will not abandon my soul to
        Hades,
    or let your Holy One experience
        corruption.
28 You have made known to me the
        ways of life;
    you will make me full of gladness
        with your presence.'

29 "Fellow Israelites,[k] I may say to you confidently of our ancestor David that he both died and was buried, and his tomb is with us to this day. 30Since he was a prophet, he knew that God had sworn with an oath to him that he would put one of his descendants on his throne. 31Foreseeing this, David[l] spoke of the resurrection of the Messiah,[m] saying,

'He was not abandoned to Hades,
    nor did his flesh experience
        corruption.'

32This Jesus God raised up, and of that all of us are witnesses. 33Being therefore exalted at[n] the right hand of God, and having received from the Father the promise of the Holy Spirit, he has poured out this that you both see and hear. 34For David did not ascend into the heavens, but he himself says,

'The Lord said to my Lord,
    "Sit at my right hand,
35   until I make your enemies your
            footstool." '

36Therefore let the entire house of Israel know with certainty that God has made him both Lord and Messiah,[o] this Jesus whom you crucified."

---

22 Ἄνδρες Ἰσραηλῖται, ἀκούσατε τοὺς λόγους τούτους· Ἰησοῦν τὸν Ναζωραῖον, ἄνδρα ἀποδεδειγμένον ἀπὸ τοῦ θεοῦ εἰς ὑμᾶς δυνάμεσι καὶ τέρασι καὶ σημείοις οἷς ἐποίησεν δι' αὐτοῦ ὁ θεὸς ἐν μέσῳ ὑμῶν καθὼς αὐτοὶ οἴδατε, 23 τοῦτον τῇ ὡρισμένῃ βουλῇ καὶ προγνώσει τοῦ θεοῦ ἔκδοτον διὰ χειρὸς ἀνόμων προσπήξαντες ἀνείλατε, 24 ὃν ὁ θεὸς ἀνέστησεν λύσας τὰς ὠδῖνας τοῦ θανάτου, καθότι οὐκ ἦν δυνατὸν κρατεῖσθαι αὐτὸν ὑπ' αὐτοῦ. 25 Δαυὶδ γὰρ λέγει εἰς αὐτόν,

Προορώμην τὸν κύριον ἐνώπιόν
    μου διὰ παντός,
    ὅτι ἐκ δεξιῶν μού ἐστιν ἵνα μὴ
        σαλευθῶ.
26 διὰ τοῦτο ηὐφράνθη ἡ καρδία μου
    καὶ ἠγαλλιάσατο ἡ γλῶσσά μου,
    ἔτι δὲ καὶ ἡ σάρξ μου
        κατασκηνώσει ἐπ' ἐλπίδι,
27 ὅτι οὐκ ἐγκαταλείψεις τὴν ψυχήν
    μου εἰς ᾅδην
    οὐδὲ δώσεις τὸν ὅσιόν σου ἰδεῖν
        διαφθοράν.
28 ἐγνώρισάς μοι ὁδοὺς ζωῆς,
    πληρώσεις με εὐφροσύνης μετὰ
        τοῦ προσώπου σου.

29 Ἄνδρες ἀδελφοί, ἐξὸν εἰπεῖν μετὰ παρρησίας πρὸς ὑμᾶς περὶ τοῦ πατριάρχου Δαυὶδ ὅτι καὶ ἐτελεύτησεν καὶ ἐτάφη, καὶ τὸ μνῆμα αὐτοῦ ἔστιν ἐν ἡμῖν ἄχρι τῆς ἡμέρας ταύτης. 30 προφήτης οὖν ὑπάρχων, καὶ εἰδὼς ὅτι ὅρκῳ ὤμοσεν αὐτῷ ὁ θεὸς ἐκ καρποῦ τῆς ὀσφύος αὐτοῦ καθίσαι ἐπὶ τὸν θρόνον αὐτοῦ, 31 προϊδὼν ἐλάλησεν περὶ τῆς ἀναστάσεως τοῦ Χριστοῦ ὅτι

οὔτε ἐγκατελείφθη εἰς ᾅδην
    οὔτε ἡ σὰρξ αὐτοῦ εἶδεν
        διαφθοράν.

32 τοῦτον τὸν Ἰησοῦν ἀνέστησεν ὁ θεός, οὗ πάντες ἡμεῖς ἐσμεν μάρτυρες· 33 τῇ δεξιᾷ οὖν τοῦ θεοῦ ὑψωθείς, τήν τε ἐπαγγελίαν τοῦ πνεύματος τοῦ ἁγίου λαβὼν παρὰ τοῦ πατρός, ἐξέχεεν τοῦτο ὃ ὑμεῖς [καὶ][a] βλέπετε καὶ ἀκούετε. 34 οὐ γὰρ Δαυὶδ ἀνέβη εἰς τοὺς οὐρανούς, λέγει δὲ αὐτός,

Εἶπεν [ὁ] κύριος τῷ κυρίῳ μου,
Κάθου ἐκ δεξιῶν μου,
35 ἕως ἂν θῶ τοὺς ἐχθρούς σου
        ὑποπόδιον τῶν ποδῶν σου.

36 ἀσφαλῶς οὖν γινωσκέτω πᾶς οἶκος Ἰσραὴλ ὅτι καὶ κύριον αὐτὸν καὶ Χριστὸν ἐποίησεν ὁ θεός, τοῦτον τὸν Ἰησοῦν ὃν ὑμεῖς ἐσταυρώσατε.

22"Men of Israel, listen to this: Jesus of Nazareth was a man accredited by God to you by miracles, wonders and signs, which God did among you through him, as you yourselves know. 23This man was handed over to you by God's set purpose and foreknowledge; and you, with the help of wicked men,[d] put him to death by nailing him to the cross. 24But God raised him from the dead, freeing him from the agony of death, because it was impossible for death to keep its hold on him. 25David said about him:

" 'I saw the Lord always before me.
    Because he is at my right hand,
    I will not be shaken.
26Therefore my heart is glad and my
        tongue rejoices;
    my body also will live in hope,
27because you will not abandon me to the
        grave,
    nor will you let your Holy One see
        decay.
28You have made known to me the paths
        of life;
    you will fill me with joy in your
        presence.'[e]

29"Brothers, I can tell you confidently that the patriarch David died and was buried, and his tomb is here to this day. 30But he was a prophet and knew that God had promised him on oath that he would place one of his descendants on his throne. 31Seeing what was ahead, he spoke of the resurrection of the Christ,[f] that he was not abandoned to the grave, nor did his body see decay. 32God has raised this Jesus to life, and we are all witnesses of the fact. 33Exalted to the right hand of God, he has received from the Father the promised Holy Spirit and has poured out what you now see and hear. 34For David did not ascend to heaven, and yet he said,

" 'The Lord said to my Lord:
    "Sit at my right hand
35until I make your enemies
    a footstool for your feet." '[g]

36"Therefore let all Israel be assured of this: God has made this Jesus, whom you crucified, both Lord and Christ."

---

[h] Gk Men, Israelites [i] Gk the Nazorean [j] Gk the pains of death [k] Gk Men, brothers [l] Gk he [m] Or the Christ
[n] Or by [o] Or Christ

[a] 33 NIV text omits καί †

[d] 23 Or of those not having the law (that is, Gentiles)
[e] 28 Psalm 16:8-11 [f] 31 Or Messiah. "The Christ" (Greek) and "the Messiah" (Hebrew) both mean "the Anointed One"; also in verse 36. [g] 35 Psalm 110:1

NRSV

The First Converts

37 Now when they heard this, they were cut to the heart and said to Peter and to the other apostles, "Brothers,[p] what should we do?" 38Peter said to them, "Repent, and be baptized every one of you in the name of Jesus Christ so that your sins may be forgiven; and you will receive the gift of the Holy Spirit. 39For the promise is for you, for your children, and for all who are far away, everyone whom the Lord our God calls to him." 40And he testified with many other arguments and exhorted them, saying, "Save yourselves from this corrupt generation." 41So those who welcomed his message were baptized, and that day about three thousand persons were added. 42They devoted themselves to the apostles' teaching and fellowship, to the breaking of bread and the prayers.

Life among the Believers

43 Awe came upon everyone, because many wonders and signs were being done by the apostles. 44All who believed were together and had all things in common; 45they would sell their possessions and goods and distribute the proceeds[q] to all, as any had need. 46Day by day, as they spent much time together in the temple, they broke bread at home[r] and ate their food with glad and generous[s] hearts, 47praising God and having the goodwill of all the people. And day by day the Lord added to their number those who were being saved.

Peter Heals a Crippled Beggar

3 One day Peter and John were going up to the temple at the hour of prayer, at three o'clock in the afternoon. 2And a man lame from birth was being carried in. People would lay him daily at the gate of the temple called the Beautiful Gate so that he could ask for alms from those entering the temple. 3When he saw Peter and John about to go into the temple, he asked them for alms. 4Peter looked intently at him, as did John, and said, "Look at us." 5And he fixed his attention on them, expecting to receive something from them. 6But Peter said, "I have no silver or gold, but what I have I give you; in the name of Jesus Christ of Nazareth,[t] stand up and walk." 7And he took him by the right hand and raised him up; and immediately his

Greek

37 Ἀκούσαντες δὲ κατενύγησαν τὴν καρδίαν εἶπόν τε πρὸς τὸν Πέτρον καὶ τοὺς λοιποὺς ἀποστόλους, Τί ποιήσωμεν, ἄνδρες ἀδελφοί; 38 Πέτρος δὲ πρὸς αὐτούς, Μετανοήσατε, [φησίν,] καὶ βαπτισθήτω ἕκαστος ὑμῶν ἐπὶ τῷ ὀνόματι Ἰησοῦ Χριστοῦ εἰς ἄφεσιν τῶν ἁμαρτιῶν ὑμῶν καὶ λήμψεσθε τὴν δωρεὰν τοῦ ἁγίου πνεύματος. 39 ὑμῖν γάρ ἐστιν ἡ ἐπαγγελία καὶ τοῖς τέκνοις ὑμῶν καὶ πᾶσιν τοῖς εἰς μακράν, ὅσους ἂν προσκαλέσηται κύριος ὁ θεὸς ἡμῶν. 40 ἑτέροις τε λόγοις πλείοσιν διεμαρτύρατο καὶ παρεκάλει αὐτοὺς λέγων, Σώθητε ἀπὸ τῆς γενεᾶς τῆς σκολιᾶς ταύτης. 41 οἱ μὲν οὖν ἀποδεξάμενοι τὸν λόγον αὐτοῦ ἐβαπτίσθησαν καὶ προσετέθησαν ἐν τῇ ἡμέρᾳ ἐκείνῃ ψυχαὶ ὡσεὶ τρισχίλιαι. 42 ἦσαν δὲ προσκαρτεροῦντες τῇ διδαχῇ τῶν ἀποστόλων καὶ τῇ κοινωνίᾳ, τῇ κλάσει τοῦ ἄρτου καὶ ταῖς προσευχαῖς.

43 Ἐγίνετο δὲ πάσῃ ψυχῇ φόβος, πολλά τε τέρατα καὶ σημεῖα διὰ τῶν ἀποστόλων ἐγίνετο. 44 πάντες δὲ οἱ πιστεύοντες ἦσαν ἐπὶ τὸ αὐτὸ καὶ εἶχον ἅπαντα κοινὰ 45 καὶ τὰ κτήματα καὶ τὰς ὑπάρξεις ἐπίπρασκον καὶ διεμέριζον αὐτὰ πᾶσιν καθότι ἄν τις χρείαν εἶχεν· 46 καθ' ἡμέραν τε προσκαρτεροῦντες ὁμοθυμαδὸν ἐν τῷ ἱερῷ, κλῶντές τε κατ' οἶκον ἄρτον, μετελάμβανον τροφῆς ἐν ἀγαλλιάσει καὶ ἀφελότητι καρδίας 47 αἰνοῦντες τὸν θεὸν καὶ ἔχοντες χάριν πρὸς ὅλον τὸν λαόν. ὁ δὲ κύριος προσετίθει τοὺς σῳζομένους καθ' ἡμέραν ἐπὶ τὸ αὐτό.

3 Πέτρος δὲ καὶ Ἰωάννης ἀνέβαινον εἰς τὸ ἱερὸν ἐπὶ τὴν ὥραν τῆς προσευχῆς τὴν ἐνάτην. 2 καί τις ἀνὴρ χωλὸς ἐκ κοιλίας μητρὸς αὐτοῦ ὑπάρχων ἐβαστάζετο, ὃν ἐτίθουν καθ' ἡμέραν πρὸς τὴν θύραν τοῦ ἱεροῦ τὴν λεγομένην Ὡραίαν τοῦ αἰτεῖν ἐλεημοσύνην παρὰ τῶν εἰσπορευομένων εἰς τὸ ἱερόν· 3 ὃς ἰδὼν Πέτρον καὶ Ἰωάννην μέλλοντας εἰσιέναι εἰς τὸ ἱερόν, ἠρώτα ἐλεημοσύνην λαβεῖν. 4 ἀτενίσας δὲ Πέτρος εἰς αὐτὸν σὺν τῷ Ἰωάννῃ εἶπεν, Βλέψον εἰς ἡμᾶς. 5 ὁ δὲ ἐπεῖχεν αὐτοῖς προσδοκῶν τι παρ' αὐτῶν λαβεῖν. 6 εἶπεν δὲ Πέτρος, Ἀργύριον καὶ χρυσίον οὐχ ὑπάρχει μοι, ὃ δὲ ἔχω τοῦτό σοι δίδωμι· ἐν τῷ ὀνόματι Ἰησοῦ Χριστοῦ τοῦ Ναζωραίου [ἔγειρε καὶ][a] περιπάτει. 7 καὶ πιάσας αὐτὸν τῆς δεξιᾶς χειρὸς ἤγειρεν αὐτόν· παραχρῆμα δὲ ἐστερεώ-

NIV

37When the people heard this, they were cut to the heart and said to Peter and the other apostles, "Brothers, what shall we do?"

38Peter replied, "Repent and be baptized, every one of you, in the name of Jesus Christ for the forgiveness of your sins. And you will receive the gift of the Holy Spirit. 39The promise is for you and your children and for all who are far off—for all whom the Lord our God will call."

40With many other words he warned them; and he pleaded with them, "Save yourselves from this corrupt generation." 41Those who accepted his message were baptized, and about three thousand were added to their number that day.

The Fellowship of the Believers

42They devoted themselves to the apostles' teaching and to the fellowship, to the breaking of bread and to prayer. 43Everyone was filled with awe, and many wonders and miraculous signs were done by the apostles. 44All the believers were together and had everything in common. 45Selling their possessions and goods, they gave to anyone as he had need. 46Every day they continued to meet together in the temple courts. They broke bread in their homes and ate together with glad and sincere hearts, 47praising God and enjoying the favor of all the people. And the Lord added to their number daily those who were being saved.

Peter Heals the Crippled Beggar

3 One day Peter and John were going up to the temple at the time of prayer—at three in the afternoon. 2Now a man crippled from birth was being carried to the temple gate called Beautiful, where he was put every day to beg from those going into the temple courts. 3When he saw Peter and John about to enter, he asked them for money. 4Peter looked straight at him, as did John. Then Peter said, "Look at us!" 5So the man gave them his attention, expecting to get something from them.

6Then Peter said, "Silver or gold I do not have, but what I have I give you. In the name of Jesus Christ of Nazareth, walk." 7Taking him by the right hand, he helped him up, and instantly the man's feet and feet and ankles were made strong. ⁸Jumping up, he stood and began to walk, and he entered the temple with them, walking and leaping and praising God. ⁹All the people saw him walking and praising God, ¹⁰and they recognized him as the one who used to sit and ask for alms at the Beautiful Gate of the temple; and they were filled with wonder and amazement at what had happened to him.

Peter Speaks in Solomon's Portico

11 While he clung to Peter and John, all the people ran together to them in the portico called Solomon's Portico, utterly astonished. ¹²When Peter saw it, he addressed the people, "You Israelites,ᵘ why do you wonder at this, or why do you stare at us, as though by our own power or piety we had made him walk? ¹³The God of Abraham, the God of Isaac, and the God of Jacob, the God of our ancestors has glorified his servantᵛ Jesus, whom you handed over and rejected in the presence of Pilate, though he had decided to release him. ¹⁴But you rejected the Holy and Righteous One and asked to have a murderer given to you, ¹⁵and you killed the Author of life, whom God raised from the dead. To this we are witnesses. ¹⁶And by faith in his name, his name itself has made this man strong, whom you see and know; and the faith that is through Jesusʷ has given him this perfect health in the presence of all of you.

17 "And now, friends,ˣ I know that you acted in ignorance, as did also your rulers. ¹⁸In this way God fulfilled what he had foretold through all the prophets, that his Messiahʸ would suffer. ¹⁹Repent therefore, and turn to God so that your sins may be wiped out, ²⁰so that times of refreshing may come from the presence of the Lord, and that he may send the Messiahᶻ appointed for you, that is, Jesus, ²¹who must remain in heaven until the time of universal restoration that God announced long ago through his holy prophets. ²²Moses said, 'The Lord your God will raise up for you from your own peopleˣ a prophet like me. You must listen to whatever he tells you. ²³And it will be that everyone who does not listen to that prophet will be

θησαν αἱ βάσεις αὐτοῦ καὶ τὰ σφυδρά, 8 καὶ ἐξαλλόμενος ἔστη καὶ περιεπάτει καὶ εἰσῆλθεν σὺν αὐτοῖς εἰς τὸ ἱερὸν περιπατῶν καὶ ἁλλόμενος καὶ αἰνῶν τὸν θεόν. 9 καὶ εἶδεν πᾶς ὁ λαὸς αὐτὸν περιπατοῦντα καὶ αἰνοῦντα τὸν θεόν· 10 ἐπεγίνωσκον δὲ αὐτὸν ὅτι αὐτὸς ἦν ὁ πρὸς τὴν ἐλεημοσύνην καθήμενος ἐπὶ τῇ Ὡραίᾳ Πύλῃ τοῦ ἱεροῦ καὶ ἐπλήσθησαν θάμβους καὶ ἐκστάσεως ἐπὶ τῷ συμβεβηκότι αὐτῷ.

11 Κρατοῦντος δὲ αὐτοῦ τὸν Πέτρον καὶ τὸν Ἰωάννην συνέδραμεν πᾶς ὁ λαὸς πρὸς αὐτοὺς ἐπὶ τῇ στοᾷ τῇ καλουμένῃ Σολομῶντος ἔκθαμβοι. 12 ἰδὼν δὲ ὁ Πέτρος ἀπεκρίνατο πρὸς τὸν λαόν, Ἄνδρες Ἰσραηλῖται, τί θαυμάζετε ἐπὶ τούτῳ ἢ ἡμῖν τί ἀτενίζετε ὡς ἰδίᾳ δυνάμει ἢ εὐσεβείᾳ πεποιηκόσιν τοῦ περιπατεῖν αὐτόν; 13 ὁ θεὸς Ἀβραὰμ καὶ [ὁ θεὸς]ᵇ Ἰσαὰκ καὶ [ὁ θεὸς]ᵇ Ἰακώβ, ὁ θεὸς τῶν πατέρων ἡμῶν, ἐδόξασεν τὸν παῖδα αὐτοῦ Ἰησοῦν ὃν ὑμεῖς μὲνᶜ παρεδώκατε καὶ ἠρνήσασθε κατὰ πρόσωπον Πιλάτου, κρίναντος ἐκείνου ἀπολύειν· 14 ὑμεῖς δὲ τὸν ἅγιον καὶ δίκαιον ἠρνήσασθε καὶ ᾐτήσασθε ἄνδρα φονέα χαρισθῆναι ὑμῖν, 15 τὸν δὲ ἀρχηγὸν τῆς ζωῆς ἀπεκτείνατε ὃν ὁ θεὸς ἤγειρεν ἐκ νεκρῶν, οὗ ἡμεῖς μάρτυρές ἐσμεν. 16 καὶ ἐπὶ τῇ πίστει τοῦ ὀνόματος αὐτοῦ τοῦτον ὃν θεωρεῖτε καὶ οἴδατε, ἐστερέωσεν τὸ ὄνομα αὐτοῦ, καὶ ἡ πίστις ἡ δι' αὐτοῦ ἔδωκεν αὐτῷ τὴν ὁλοκληρίαν ταύτην ἀπέναντι πάντων ὑμῶν. 17 καὶ νῦν, ἀδελφοί, οἶδα ὅτι κατὰ ἄγνοιαν ἐπράξατε ὥσπερ καὶ οἱ ἄρχοντες ὑμῶν· 18 ὁ δὲ θεός, ἃ προκατήγγειλεν διὰ στόματος πάντων τῶν προφητῶν παθεῖν τὸν Χριστὸν αὐτοῦ, ἐπλήρωσεν οὕτως. 19 μετανοήσατε οὖν καὶ ἐπιστρέψατε εἰς τὸ ἐξαλειφθῆναι ὑμῶν τὰς ἁμαρτίας, 20 ὅπως ἂν ἔλθωσιν καιροὶ ἀναψύξεως ἀπὸ προσώπου τοῦ κυρίουᵈ καὶ ἀποστείλῃ τὸν προκεχειρισμένον ὑμῖν Χριστόν Ἰησοῦν, 21 ὃν δεῖ οὐρανὸν μὲν δέξασθαι ἄχρι χρόνων ἀποκαταστάσεως πάντων ὧν ἐλάλησεν ὁ θεὸς διὰ στόματος τῶν ἁγίων ἀπ' αἰῶνος αὐτοῦ προφητῶν. 22 Μωϋσῆς μὲν εἶπεν ὅτι Προφήτην ὑμῖν ἀναστήσει κύριος ὁ θεὸς ὑμῶν ἐκ τῶν ἀδελφῶν ὑμῶν ὡς ἐμέ· αὐτοῦ ἀκούσεσθε κατὰ πάντα ὅσα ἂν λαλήσῃ πρὸς ὑμᾶς. 23 ἔσται δὲ πᾶσα ψυχὴ ἥτις ἐὰν μὴ ἀκούσῃ

ankles became strong. ⁸He jumped to his feet and began to walk. Then he went with them into the temple courts, walking and jumping, and praising God. ⁹When all the people saw him walking and praising God, ¹⁰they recognized him as the same man who used to sit begging at the temple gate called Beautiful, and they were filled with wonder and amazement at what had happened to him.

Peter Speaks to the Onlookers

11While the beggar held on to Peter and John, all the people were astonished and came running to them in the place called Solomon's Colonnade. ¹²When Peter saw this, he said to them: "Men of Israel, why does this surprise you? Why do you stare at us as if by our own power or godliness we had made this man walk? ¹³The God of Abraham, Isaac and Jacob, the God of our fathers, has glorified his servant Jesus. You handed him over to be killed, and you disowned him before Pilate, though he had decided to let him go. ¹⁴You disowned the Holy and Righteous One and asked that a murderer be released to you. ¹⁵You killed the author of life, but God raised him from the dead. We are witnesses of this. ¹⁶By faith in the name of Jesus, this man whom you see and know was made strong. It is Jesus' name and the faith that comes through him that has given this complete healing to him, as you can all see.

17"Now, brothers, I know that you acted in ignorance, as did your leaders. ¹⁸But this is how God fulfilled what he had foretold through all the prophets, saying that his Christᵃ would suffer. ¹⁹Repent, then, and turn to God, so that your sins may be wiped out, that times of refreshing may come from the Lord, ²⁰and that he may send the Christ, who has been appointed for you—even Jesus. ²¹He must remain in heaven until the time comes for God to restore everything, as he promised long ago through his holy prophets. ²²For Moses said, 'The Lord your God will raise up for you a prophet like me from among your own people; you must listen to everything he tells you. ²³Anyone who does not listen

---

ᵘ Gk *Men, Israelites*   ᵛ Or *child*   ʷ Gk *him*   ˣ Gk *brothers*   ʸ Or *his Christ*   ᶻ Or *the Christ*

ᵇ13 NIV text twice omits ὁ θεὸς †   ᶜ13 NIV text omits μὲν †   ᵈ20 NIV begins verse 20 after κυρίου

ᵃ18 Or *Messiah*; also in verse 20

utterly rooted out of the people.' 24And all the prophets, as many as have spoken, from Samuel and those after him, also predicted these days. 25You are the descendants of the prophets and of the covenant that God gave to your ancestors, saying to Abraham, 'And in your descendants all the families of the earth shall be blessed.' 26When God raised up his servant,v he sent him first to you, to bless you by turning each of you from your wicked ways."

Peter and John before the Council

4 While Peter and Johna were speaking to the people, the priests, the captain of the temple, and the Sadducees came to them, 2much annoyed because they were teaching the people and proclaiming that in Jesus there is the resurrection of the dead. 3So they arrested them and put them in custody until the next day, for it was already evening. 4But many of those who heard the word believed; and they numbered about five thousand.

5 The next day their rulers, elders, and scribes assembled in Jerusalem, 6with Annas the high priest, Caiaphas, John,b and Alexander, and all who were of the high-priestly family. 7When they had made the prisonersc stand in their midst, they inquired, "By what power or by what name did you do this?" 8Then Peter, filled with the Holy Spirit, said to them, "Rulers of the people and elders, 9if we are questioned today because of a good deed done to someone who was sick and are asked how this man has been healed, 10let it be known to all of you, and to all the people of Israel, that this man is standing before you in good health by the name of Jesus Christ of Nazareth,d whom you crucified, whom God raised from the dead. 11This Jesuse is

'the stone that was rejected by you,
    the builders;
    it has become the cornerstone.'f

12There is salvation in no one else, for there is no other name under heaven given among mortals by which we must be saved."

13 Now when they saw the boldness of Peter and John and realized that they were uneducated and ordinary men, they were amazed and recognized them as

τοῦ προφήτου ἐκείνου ἐξολεθρευθήσε-
ται ἐκ τοῦ λαοῦ. 24 καὶ πάντες δὲ οἱ
προφῆται ἀπὸ Σαμουὴλ καὶ τῶν καθεξῆς
ὅσοι ἐλάλησαν καὶ κατήγγειλαν τὰς
ἡμέρας ταύτας. 25 ὑμεῖς ἐστε οἱ υἱοὶ
τῶν προφητῶν καὶ τῆς διαθήκης ἧς
διέθετο ὁ θεὸς πρὸς τοὺς πατέρας
ὑμῶν λέγων πρὸς Ἀβραάμ, Καὶ ἐν τῷ
σπέρματί σου [ἐν]ευλογηθήσονται
πᾶσαι αἱ πατριαὶ τῆς γῆς. 26 ὑμῖν
πρῶτον ἀναστήσας ὁ θεὸς τὸν παῖδα
αὐτοῦ ἀπέστειλεν αὐτὸν εὐλογοῦντα
ὑμᾶς ἐν τῷ ἀποστρέφειν ἕκαστον ἀπὸ
τῶν πονηριῶν ὑμῶν.

4 Λαλούντων δὲ αὐτῶν πρὸς τὸν
λαὸν ἐπέστησαν αὐτοῖς οἱ ἱερεῖς
καὶ ὁ στρατηγὸς τοῦ ἱεροῦ καὶ οἱ
Σαδδουκαῖοι, 2 διαπονούμενοι διὰ τὸ
διδάσκειν αὐτοὺς τὸν λαὸν καὶ καταγγέλλειν ἐν τῷ Ἰησοῦ τὴν ἀνάστασιν
τὴν ἐκ νεκρῶν, 3 καὶ ἐπέβαλον αὐτοῖς
τὰς χεῖρας καὶ ἔθεντο εἰς τήρησιν εἰς
τὴν αὔριον· ἦν γὰρ ἑσπέρα ἤδη 4 πολλοὶ
δὲ τῶν ἀκουσάντων τὸν λόγον ἐπίστευσαν, καὶ ἐγενήθη [ὁ] ἀριθμὸς τῶν
ἀνδρῶν [ὡς] χιλιάδες πέντε.

5 Ἐγένετο δὲ ἐπὶ τὴν αὔριον συναχθῆναι αὐτῶν τοὺς ἄρχοντας καὶ τοὺς
πρεσβυτέρους καὶ τοὺς γραμματεῖς ἐν
Ἰερουσαλήμ, 6 καὶ Ἅννας ὁ ἀρχιερεὺς
καὶ Καϊάφας καὶ Ἰωάννηςa καὶ Ἀλέξανδρος καὶ ὅσοι ἦσαν ἐκ γένους ἀρχ-
ιερατικοῦ, 7 καὶ στήσαντες αὐτοὺς ἐν
τῷ μέσῳ ἐπυνθάνοντο, Ἐν ποίᾳ δυνάμει
ἢ ἐν ποίῳ ὀνόματι ἐποιήσατε τοῦτο
ὑμεῖς; 8 τότε Πέτρος πλησθεὶς πνεύματος ἁγίου εἶπεν πρὸς αὐτούς,
Ἄρχοντες τοῦ λαοῦ καὶ πρεσβύτεροι,
9 εἰ ἡμεῖς σήμερον ἀνακρινόμεθα ἐπὶ
εὐεργεσίᾳ ἀνθρώπου ἀσθενοῦς ἐν τίνι
οὗτος σέσωται, 10 γνωστὸν ἔστω πᾶσιν
ὑμῖν καὶ παντὶ τῷ λαῷ Ἰσραὴλ ὅτι ἐν
τῷ ὀνόματι Ἰησοῦ Χριστοῦ τοῦ
Ναζωραίου ὃν ὑμεῖς ἐσταυρώσατε, ὃν
ὁ θεὸς ἤγειρεν ἐκ νεκρῶν, ἐν τούτῳ
οὗτος παρέστηκεν ἐνώπιον ὑμῶν ὑγιής.
11 οὗτός ἐστιν

ὁ λίθος, ὁ ἐξουθενηθεὶς ὑφ' ὑμῶν
    τῶν οἰκοδόμων,
ὁ γενόμενος εἰς κεφαλὴν γωνίας.

12 καὶ οὐκ ἔστιν ἐν ἄλλῳ οὐδενὶ ἡ
σωτηρία, οὐδὲ γὰρ ὄνομά ἐστιν ἕτερον
ὑπὸ τὸν οὐρανὸν τὸ δεδομένον ἐν
ἀνθρώποις ἐν ᾧ δεῖ σωθῆναι ἡμᾶς.
13 Θεωροῦντες δὲ τὴν τοῦ Πέτρου
παρρησίαν καὶ Ἰωάννου καὶ καταλαβό-
μενοι ὅτι ἄνθρωποι ἀγράμματοί εἰσιν
καὶ ἰδιῶται, ἐθαύμαζον ἐπεγίνωσκόν

to him will be completely cut off from among his people.'b

24"Indeed, all the prophets from Samuel on, as many as have spoken, have foretold these days. 25And you are heirs of the prophets and of the covenant God made with your fathers. He said to Abraham, 'Through your offspring all peoples on earth will be blessed.'c 26When God raised up his servant, he sent him first to you to bless you by turning each of you from your wicked ways."

Peter and John Before the Sanhedrin

4 The priests and the captain of the temple guard and the Sadducees came up to Peter and John while they were speaking to the people. 2They were greatly disturbed because the apostles were teaching the people and proclaiming in Jesus the resurrection of the dead. 3They seized Peter and John, and because it was evening, they put them in jail until the next day. 4But many who heard the message believed, and the number of men grew to about five thousand.

5The next day the rulers, elders and teachers of the law met in Jerusalem. 6Annas the high priest was there, and so were Caiaphas, John, Alexander and the other men of the high priest's family. 7They had Peter and John brought before them and began to question them: "By what power or what name did you do this?"

8Then Peter, filled with the Holy Spirit, said to them: "Rulers and elders of the people! 9If we are being called to account today for an act of kindness shown to a cripple and are asked how he was healed, 10then know this, you and all the people of Israel: It is by the name of Jesus Christ of Nazareth, whom you crucified but whom God raised from the dead, that this man stands before you healed. 11He is

" 'the stone you builders rejected,
    which has become the capstone.'a'b

12Salvation is found in no one else, for there is no other name under heaven given to men by which we must be saved."

13When they saw the courage of Peter and John and realized that they were unschooled, ordinary men, they were astonished and they took note that these men

---

v Or *child*   a Gk *While they*   b Other ancient authorities read *Jonathan*   c Gk *them*   d Gk *the Nazorean*   e Gk *This*
f Or *keystone*

a6 NRSV note b *Ἰωνάθας*

b23 Deut. 18:15,18,19   c25 Gen. 22:18; 26:4
a11 Or *cornerstone*   b11 Psalm 118:22

companions of Jesus. [14]When they saw the man who had been cured standing beside them, they had nothing to say in opposition. [15]So they ordered them to leave the council while they discussed the matter with one another. [16]They said, "What will we do with them? For it is obvious to all who live in Jerusalem that a notable sign has been done through them; we cannot deny it. [17]But to keep it from spreading further among the people, let us warn them to speak no more to anyone in this name." [18]So they called them and ordered them not to speak or teach at all in the name of Jesus. [19]But Peter and John answered them, "Whether it is right in God's sight to listen to you rather than to God, you must judge; [20]for we cannot keep from speaking about what we have seen and heard." [21]After threatening them again, they let them go, finding no way to punish them because of the people, for all of them praised God for what had happened. [22]For the man on whom this sign of healing had been performed was more than forty years old.

The Believers Pray for Boldness

23 After they were released, they went to their friends[g] and reported what the chief priests and the elders had said to them. [24]When they heard it, they raised their voices together to God and said, "Sovereign Lord, who made the heaven and the earth, the sea, and everything in them, [25]it is you who said by the Holy Spirit through our ancestor David, your servant:[h]

'Why did the Gentiles rage,
    and the peoples imagine vain
        things?
[26] The kings of the earth took their stand,
    and the rulers have gathered
        together
    against the Lord and against his
        Messiah.'[i]

[27]For in this city, in fact, both Herod and Pontius Pilate, with the Gentiles and the peoples of Israel, gathered together against your holy servant[h] Jesus, whom you anointed, [28]to do whatever your hand and your plan had predestined to take place. [29]And now, Lord, look at their threats, and grant to your servants[j] to speak your word with all boldness, [30]while you stretch out your hand to heal, and signs and wonders are performed through the name of your

τε αὐτοὺς ὅτι σὺν τῷ Ἰησοῦ ἦσαν, **14** τόν τε ἄνθρωπον βλέποντες σὺν αὐτοῖς ἑστῶτα τὸν τεθεραπευμένον οὐδὲν εἶχον ἀντειπεῖν. **15** κελεύσαντες δὲ αὐτοὺς ἔξω τοῦ συνεδρίου ἀπελθεῖν συνέβαλλον πρὸς ἀλλήλους **16** λέγοντες, Τί ποιήσωμεν τοῖς ἀνθρώποις τούτοις; ὅτι μὲν γὰρ γνωστὸν σημεῖον γέγονεν δι᾿ αὐτῶν πᾶσιν τοῖς κατοικοῦσιν Ἰερουσαλὴμ φανερὸν καὶ οὐ δυνάμεθα ἀρνεῖσθαι· **17** ἀλλ᾿ ἵνα μὴ ἐπὶ πλεῖον διανεμηθῇ εἰς τὸν λαὸν ἀπειλησώμεθα αὐτοῖς μηκέτι λαλεῖν ἐπὶ τῷ ὀνόματι τούτῳ μηδενὶ ἀνθρώπων. **18** καὶ καλέσαντες αὐτοὺς παρήγγειλαν τὸ καθόλου μὴ φθέγγεσθαι μηδὲ διδάσκειν ἐπὶ τῷ ὀνόματι τοῦ Ἰησοῦ. **19** ὁ δὲ Πέτρος καὶ Ἰωάννης ἀποκριθέντες εἶπον πρὸς αὐτούς, Εἰ δίκαιόν ἐστιν ἐνώπιον τοῦ θεοῦ ὑμῶν ἀκούειν μᾶλλον ἢ τοῦ θεοῦ, κρίνατε· **20** οὐ δυνάμεθα γὰρ ἡμεῖς ἃ εἴδαμεν καὶ ἠκούσαμεν μὴ λαλεῖν. **21** οἱ δὲ προσαπειλησάμενοι ἀπέλυσαν αὐτούς, μηδὲν εὑρίσκοντες τὸ πῶς κολάσωνται αὐτούς, διὰ τὸν λαόν, ὅτι πάντες ἐδόξαζον τὸν θεὸν ἐπὶ τῷ γεγονότι. **22** ἐτῶν γὰρ ἦν πλειόνων τεσσεράκοντα ὁ ἄνθρωπος ἐφ᾿ ὃν γεγόνει τὸ σημεῖον τοῦτο τῆς ἰάσεως.

23 Ἀπολυθέντες δὲ ἦλθον πρὸς τοὺς ἰδίους καὶ ἀπήγγειλαν ὅσα πρὸς αὐτοὺς οἱ ἀρχιερεῖς καὶ οἱ πρεσβύτεροι εἶπαν. **24** οἱ δὲ ἀκούσαντες ὁμοθυμαδὸν ἦραν φωνὴν πρὸς τὸν θεὸν καὶ εἶπαν, Δέσποτα, σὺ ὁ ποιήσας τὸν οὐρανὸν καὶ τὴν γῆν καὶ τὴν θάλασσαν καὶ πάντα τὰ ἐν αὐτοῖς, **25** ὁ τοῦ πατρὸς ἡμῶν διὰ πνεύματος ἁγίου στόματος Δαυὶδ παιδός σου εἰπών,

Ἱνατί ἐφρύαξαν ἔθνη
    καὶ λαοὶ ἐμελέτησαν κενά;
26 παρέστησαν οἱ βασιλεῖς τῆς γῆς
    καὶ οἱ ἄρχοντες συνήχθησαν ἐπὶ
        τὸ αὐτὸ
    κατὰ τοῦ κυρίου καὶ κατὰ τοῦ
        Χριστοῦ αὐτοῦ.

27 συνήχθησαν γὰρ ἐπ᾿ ἀληθείας ἐν τῇ πόλει ταύτῃ ἐπὶ τὸν ἅγιον παῖδά σου Ἰησοῦν ὃν ἔχρισας, Ἡρῴδης τε καὶ Πόντιος Πιλᾶτος σὺν ἔθνεσιν καὶ λαοῖς Ἰσραήλ, **28** ποιῆσαι ὅσα ἡ χείρ σου καὶ ἡ βουλή [σου] προώρισεν γενέσθαι. **29** καὶ τὰ νῦν, κύριε, ἔπιδε ἐπὶ τὰς ἀπειλὰς αὐτῶν καὶ δὸς τοῖς δούλοις σου μετὰ παρρησίας πάσης λαλεῖν τὸν λόγον σου, **30** ἐν τῷ τὴν χεῖρά [σου] ἐκτείνειν σε εἰς ἴασιν καὶ σημεῖα καὶ τέρατα γίνεσθαι διὰ τοῦ ὀνόματος τοῦ

had been with Jesus. [14]But since they could see the man who had been healed standing there with them, there was nothing they could say. [15]So they ordered them to withdraw from the Sanhedrin and then conferred together. [16]"What are we going to do with these men?" they asked. "Everybody living in Jerusalem knows they have done an outstanding miracle, and we cannot deny it. [17]But to stop this thing from spreading any further among the people, we must warn these men to speak no longer to anyone in this name."

[18]Then they called them in again and commanded them not to speak or teach at all in the name of Jesus. [19]But Peter and John replied, "Judge for yourselves whether it is right in God's sight to obey you rather than God. [20]For we cannot help speaking about what we have seen and heard."

[21]After further threats they let them go. They could not decide how to punish them, because all the people were praising God for what had happened. [22]For the man who was miraculously healed was over forty years old.

The Believers' Prayer

[23]On their release, Peter and John went back to their own people and reported all that the chief priests and elders had said to them. [24]When they heard this, they raised their voices together in prayer to God. "Sovereign Lord," they said, "you made the heaven and the earth and the sea, and everything in them. [25]You spoke by the Holy Spirit through the mouth of your servant, our father David:

" 'Why do the nations rage
    and the peoples plot in vain?
[26]The kings of the earth take their stand
    and the rulers gather together
    against the Lord
    and against his Anointed One.'[c][d]

[27]Indeed Herod and Pontius Pilate met together with the Gentiles and the people[e] of Israel in this city to conspire against your holy servant Jesus, whom you anointed. [28]They did what your power and will had decided beforehand should happen. [29]Now, Lord, consider their threats and enable your servants to speak your word with great boldness. [30]Stretch out your hand to heal and perform miraculous signs and wonders through the name of your

g Gk *their own*   h Or *child*   i Or *his Christ*   j Gk *slaves*

c26 That is, Christ or Messiah   d26 Psalm 2:1,2
e27 The Greek is plural.

holy servant[h] Jesus." [31]When they had prayed, the place in which they were gathered together was shaken; and they were all filled with the Holy Spirit and spoke the word of God with boldness.

The Believers Share Their Possessions

32 Now the whole group of those who believed were of one heart and soul, and no one claimed private ownership of any possessions, but everything they owned was held in common. [33]With great power the apostles gave their testimony to the resurrection of the Lord Jesus, and great grace was upon them all. [34]There was not a needy person among them, for as many as owned lands or houses sold them and brought the proceeds of what was sold. [35]They laid it at the apostles' feet, and it was distributed to each as any had need. [36]There was a Levite, a native of Cyprus, Joseph, to whom the apostles gave the name Barnabas (which means "son of encouragement"). [37]He sold a field that belonged to him, then brought the money, and laid it at the apostles' feet.

Ananias and Sapphira

5 But a man named Ananias, with the consent of his wife Sapphira, sold a piece of property; [2]with his wife's knowledge, he kept back some of the proceeds, and brought only a part and laid it at the apostles' feet. [3]"Ananias," Peter asked, "why has Satan filled your heart to lie to the Holy Spirit and to keep back part of the proceeds of the land? [4]While it remained unsold, did it not remain your own? And after it was sold, were not the proceeds at your disposal? How is it that you have contrived this deed in your heart? You did not lie to us[k] but to God!" [5]Now when Ananias heard these words, he fell down and died. And great fear seized all who heard of it. [6]The young men came and wrapped up his body,[l] then carried him out and buried him.

7 After an interval of about three hours his wife came in, not knowing what had happened. [8]Peter said to her, "Tell me whether you and your husband sold the land for such and such a price." And she said, "Yes, that was the price." [9]Then Peter said to her, "How is it that you have agreed together to put the Spirit of the Lord to the test? Look, the feet of those who have buried your husband are at the door, and they will carry you out." [10]Immediately she fell

ἁγίου παιδός σου Ἰησοῦ. **31** καὶ δεηθέντων αὐτῶν ἐσαλεύθη ὁ τόπος ἐν ᾧ ἦσαν συνηγμένοι, καὶ ἐπλήσθησαν ἅπαντες τοῦ ἁγίου πνεύματος καὶ ἐλάλουν τὸν λόγον τοῦ θεοῦ μετὰ παρρησίας. **32** Τοῦ δὲ πλήθους τῶν πιστευσάντων ἦν καρδία καὶ ψυχὴ μία, καὶ οὐδὲ εἷς τι τῶν ὑπαρχόντων αὐτῷ ἔλεγεν ἴδιον εἶναι ἀλλ' ἦν αὐτοῖς ἅπαντα κοινά. **33** καὶ δυνάμει μεγάλῃ ἀπεδίδουν τὸ μαρτύριον οἱ ἀπόστολοι τῆς ἀναστάσεως τοῦ κυρίου Ἰησοῦ, χάρις τε μεγάλη ἦν ἐπὶ πάντας αὐτούς. **34** οὐδὲ γὰρ ἐνδεής τις ἦν ἐν αὐτοῖς· ὅσοι γὰρ κτήτορες χωρίων ἢ οἰκιῶν ὑπῆρχον, πωλοῦντες ἔφερον τὰς τιμὰς τῶν πιπρασκομένων **35** καὶ ἐτίθουν παρὰ τοὺς πόδας τῶν ἀποστόλων, διεδίδετο δὲ ἑκάστῳ καθότι ἄν τις χρείαν εἶχεν. **36** Ἰωσὴφ δὲ ὁ ἐπικληθεὶς Βαρναβᾶς ἀπὸ τῶν ἀποστόλων, ὅ ἐστιν μεθερμηνευόμενον υἱὸς παρακλήσεως, Λευίτης, Κύπριος τῷ γένει, **37** ὑπάρχοντος αὐτῷ ἀγροῦ πωλήσας ἤνεγκεν τὸ χρῆμα καὶ ἔθηκεν πρὸς τοὺς πόδας τῶν ἀποστόλων.

5 Ἀνὴρ δέ τις Ἁνανίας ὀνόματι σὺν Σαπφίρῃ τῇ γυναικὶ αὐτοῦ ἐπώλησεν κτῆμα **2** καὶ ἐνοσφίσατο ἀπὸ τῆς τιμῆς, συνειδυίης καὶ τῆς γυναικός, καὶ ἐνέγκας μέρος τι παρὰ τοὺς πόδας τῶν ἀποστόλων ἔθηκεν. **3** εἶπεν δὲ ὁ Πέτρος, Ἁνανία, διὰ τί ἐπλήρωσεν ὁ Σατανᾶς τὴν καρδίαν σου, ψεύσασθαί σε τὸ πνεῦμα τὸ ἅγιον καὶ νοσφίσασθαι ἀπὸ τῆς τιμῆς τοῦ χωρίου; **4** οὐχὶ μένον σοὶ ἔμενεν καὶ πραθὲν ἐν τῇ σῇ ἐξουσίᾳ ὑπῆρχεν; τί ὅτι ἔθου ἐν τῇ καρδίᾳ σου τὸ πρᾶγμα τοῦτο; οὐκ ἐψεύσω ἀνθρώποις ἀλλὰ τῷ θεῷ. **5** ἀκούων δὲ ὁ Ἁνανίας τοὺς λόγους τούτους πεσὼν ἐξέψυξεν, καὶ ἐγένετο φόβος μέγας ἐπὶ πάντας τοὺς ἀκούοντας. **6** ἀναστάντες δὲ οἱ νεώτεροι συνέστειλαν αὐτὸν καὶ ἐξενέγκαντες ἔθαψαν.

7 Ἐγένετο δὲ ὡς ὡρῶν τριῶν διάστημα καὶ ἡ γυνὴ αὐτοῦ μὴ εἰδυῖα τὸ γεγονὸς εἰσῆλθεν. **8** ἀπεκρίθη δὲ πρὸς αὐτὴν Πέτρος, Εἰπέ μοι, εἰ τοσούτου τὸ χωρίον ἀπέδοσθε; ἡ δὲ εἶπεν, Ναί, τοσούτου. **9** ὁ δὲ Πέτρος πρὸς αὐτήν, Τί ὅτι συνεφωνήθη ὑμῖν πειράσαι τὸ πνεῦμα κυρίου; ἰδοὺ οἱ πόδες τῶν θαψάντων τὸν ἄνδρα σου ἐπὶ τῇ θύρᾳ καὶ ἐξοίσουσίν σε. **10** ἔπεσεν δὲ παραχρῆμα πρὸς τοὺς πόδας αὐτοῦ καὶ

holy servant Jesus."

[31]After they prayed, the place where they were meeting was shaken. And they were all filled with the Holy Spirit and spoke the word of God boldly.

The Believers Share Their Possessions

[32]All the believers were one in heart and mind. No one claimed that any of his possessions was his own, but they shared everything they had. [33]With great power the apostles continued to testify to the resurrection of the Lord Jesus, and much grace was upon them all. [34]There were no needy persons among them. For from time to time those who owned lands or houses sold them, brought the money from the sales [35]and put it at the apostles' feet, and it was distributed to anyone as he had need.

[36]Joseph, a Levite from Cyprus, whom the apostles called Barnabas (which means Son of Encouragement), [37]sold a field he owned and brought the money and put it at the apostles' feet.

Ananias and Sapphira

5 Now a man named Ananias, together with his wife Sapphira, also sold a piece of property. [2]With his wife's full knowledge he kept back part of the money for himself, but brought the rest and put it at the apostles' feet.

[3]Then Peter said, "Ananias, how is it that Satan has so filled your heart that you have lied to the Holy Spirit and have kept for yourself some of the money you received for the land? [4]Didn't it belong to you before it was sold? And after it was sold, wasn't the money at your disposal? What made you think of doing such a thing? You have not lied to men but to God."

[5]When Ananias heard this, he fell down and died. And great fear seized all who heard what had happened. [6]Then the young men came forward, wrapped up his body, and carried him out and buried him.

[7]About three hours later his wife came in, not knowing what had happened. [8]Peter asked her, "Tell me, is this the price you and Ananias got for the land?"

"Yes," she said, "that is the price."

[9]Peter said to her, "How could you agree to test the Spirit of the Lord? Look! The feet of the men who buried your husband are at the door, and they will carry you out also."

[10]At that moment she fell down at his

---

[h] Or child   [k] Gk to men   [l] Meaning of Gk uncertain

down at his feet and died. When the young men came in they found her dead, so they carried her out and buried her beside her husband. [11]And great fear seized the whole church and all who heard of these things.

The Apostles Heal Many

12 Now many signs and wonders were done among the people through the apostles. And they were all together in Solomon's Portico. [13]None of the rest dared to join them, but the people held them in high esteem. [14]Yet more than ever believers were added to the Lord, great numbers of both men and women, [15]so that they even carried out the sick into the streets, and laid them on cots and mats, in order that Peter's shadow might fall on some of them as he came by. [16]A great number of people would also gather from the towns around Jerusalem, bringing the sick and those tormented by unclean spirits, and they were all cured.

The Apostles Are Persecuted

17 Then the high priest took action; he and all who were with him (that is, the sect of the Sadducees), being filled with jealousy, [18]arrested the apostles and put them in the public prison. [19]But during the night an angel of the Lord opened the prison doors, brought them out, and said, [20]"Go, stand in the temple and tell the people the whole message about this life." [21]When they heard this, they entered the temple at daybreak and went on with their teaching.

When the high priest and those with him arrived, they called together the council and the whole body of the elders of Israel, and sent to the prison to have them brought. [22]But when the temple police went there, they did not find them in the prison; so they returned and reported, [23]"We found the prison securely locked and the guards standing at the doors, but when we opened them, we found no one inside." [24]Now when the captain of the temple and the chief priests heard these words, they were perplexed about them, wondering what might be going on. [25]Then someone arrived and announced, "Look, the men whom you put in prison are standing in the temple and teaching the people!" [26]Then the captain went with the temple police and brought them, but without violence, for they were afraid of being stoned by the people.

ἐξέψυξεν· εἰσελθόντες δὲ οἱ νεανίσκοι εὗρον αὐτὴν νεκρὰν καὶ ἐξενέγκαντες ἔθαψαν πρὸς τὸν ἄνδρα αὐτῆς, 11 καὶ ἐγένετο φόβος μέγας ἐφ᾽ ὅλην τὴν ἐκκλησίαν καὶ ἐπὶ πάντας τοὺς ἀκούοντας ταῦτα.

12 Διὰ δὲ τῶν χειρῶν τῶν ἀποστόλων ἐγίνετο σημεῖα καὶ τέρατα πολλὰ ἐν τῷ λαῷ. καὶ ἦσαν ὁμοθυμαδὸν ἅπαντες ἐν τῇ Στοᾷ Σολομῶντος, 13 τῶν δὲ λοιπῶν οὐδεὶς ἐτόλμα κολλᾶσθαι αὐτοῖς, ἀλλ᾽ ἐμεγάλυνεν αὐτοὺς ὁ λαός. 14 μᾶλλον δὲ προσετίθεντο πιστεύοντες τῷ κυρίῳ, πλήθη ἀνδρῶν τε καὶ γυναικῶν, 15 ὥστε καὶ εἰς τὰς πλατείας ἐκφέρειν τοὺς ἀσθενεῖς καὶ τιθέναι ἐπὶ κλιναρίων καὶ κραβάττων, ἵνα ἐρχομένου Πέτρου κἂν ἡ σκιὰ ἐπισκιάσῃ τινὶ αὐτῶν. 16 συνήρχετο δὲ καὶ τὸ πλῆθος τῶν πέριξ πόλεων Ἰερουσαλὴμ φέροντες ἀσθενεῖς καὶ ὀχλουμένους ὑπὸ πνευμάτων ἀκαθάρτων, οἵτινες ἐθεραπεύοντο ἅπαντες.

17 Ἀναστὰς δὲ ὁ ἀρχιερεὺς καὶ πάντες οἱ σὺν αὐτῷ, ἡ οὖσα αἵρεσις τῶν Σαδδουκαίων, ἐπλήσθησαν ζήλου 18 καὶ ἐπέβαλον τὰς χεῖρας ἐπὶ τοὺς ἀποστόλους καὶ ἔθεντο αὐτοὺς ἐν τηρήσει δημοσίᾳ. 19 ἄγγελος δὲ κυρίου διὰ νυκτὸς ἀνοίξας τὰς θύρας τῆς φυλακῆς ἐξαγαγών τε αὐτοὺς εἶπεν,ᵃ 20 Πορεύεσθε καὶ σταθέντες λαλεῖτε ἐν τῷ ἱερῷ τῷ λαῷ πάντα τὰ ῥήματα τῆς ζωῆς ταύτης. 21 ἀκούσαντες δὲ εἰσῆλθον ὑπὸ τὸν ὄρθρον εἰς τὸ ἱερὸν καὶ ἐδίδασκον. Παραγενόμενος δὲ ὁ ἀρχιερεὺς καὶ οἱ σὺν αὐτῷ συνεκάλεσαν τὸ συνέδριον καὶ πᾶσαν τὴν γερουσίαν τῶν υἱῶν Ἰσραὴλ καὶ ἀπέστειλαν εἰς τὸ δεσμωτήριον ἀχθῆναι αὐτούς. 22 οἱ δὲ παραγενόμενοι ὑπηρέται οὐχ εὗρον αὐτοὺς ἐν τῇ φυλακῇ· ἀναστρέψαντες δὲ ἀπήγγειλαν 23 λέγοντες ὅτι Τὸ δεσμωτήριον εὕρομεν κεκλεισμένον ἐν πάσῃ ἀσφαλείᾳ καὶ τοὺς φύλακας ἑστῶτας ἐπὶ τῶν θυρῶν, ἀνοίξαντες δὲ ἔσω οὐδένα εὕρομεν. 24 ὡς δὲ ἤκουσαν τοὺς λόγους τούτους ὅ τε στρατηγὸς τοῦ ἱεροῦ καὶ οἱ ἀρχιερεῖς, διηπόρουν περὶ αὐτῶν τί ἂν γένοιτο τοῦτο. 25 παραγενόμενος δέ τις ἀπήγγειλεν αὐτοῖς ὅτι Ἰδοὺ οἱ ἄνδρες οὓς ἔθεσθε ἐν τῇ φυλακῇ εἰσὶν ἐν τῷ ἱερῷ ἑστῶτες καὶ διδάσκοντες τὸν λαόν. 26 τότε ἀπελθὼν ὁ στρατηγὸς σὺν τοῖς ὑπηρέταις ἦγεν αὐτοὺς οὐ μετὰ βίας, ἐφοβοῦντο γὰρ τὸν λαὸν μὴ λιθασθῶσιν.

feet and died. Then the young men came in and, finding her dead, carried her out and buried her beside her husband. [11]Great fear seized the whole church and all who heard about these events.

The Apostles Heal Many

[12]The apostles performed many miraculous signs and wonders among the people. And all the believers used to meet together in Solomon's Colonnade. [13]No one else dared join them, even though they were highly regarded by the people. [14]Nevertheless, more and more men and women believed in the Lord and were added to their number. [15]As a result, people brought the sick into the streets and laid them on beds and mats so that at least Peter's shadow might fall on some of them as he passed by. [16]Crowds gathered also from the towns around Jerusalem, bringing their sick and those tormented by evilᵃ spirits, and all of them were healed.

The Apostles Persecuted

[17]Then the high priest and all his associates, who were members of the party of the Sadducees, were filled with jealousy. [18]They arrested the apostles and put them in the public jail. [19]But during the night an angel of the Lord opened the doors of the jail and brought them out. [20]"Go, stand in the temple courts," he said, "and tell the people the full message of this new life."

[21]At daybreak they entered the temple courts, as they had been told, and began to teach the people.

When the high priest and his associates arrived, they called together the Sanhedrin—the full assembly of the elders of Israel—and sent to the jail for the apostles. [22]But on arriving at the jail, the officers did not find them there. So they went back and reported, [23]"We found the jail securely locked, with the guards standing at the doors; but when we opened them, we found no one inside." [24]On hearing this report, the captain of the temple guard and the chief priests were puzzled, wondering what would come of this.

[25]Then someone came and said, "Look! The men you put in jail are standing in the temple courts teaching the people." [26]At that, the captain went with his officers and brought the apostles. They did not use force, because they feared that the people would stone them.

ᵃ19 NIV translates εἶπεν in verse 20   ᵃ16 Greek unclean

NRSV

27 When they had brought them, they had them stand before the council. The high priest questioned them, 28saying, "We gave you strict orders not to teach in this name,m yet here you have filled Jerusalem with your teaching and you are determined to bring this man's blood on us." 29But Peter and the apostles answered, "We must obey God rather than any human authority.n 30The God of our ancestors raised up Jesus, whom you had killed by hanging him on a tree. 31God exalted him at his right hand as Leader and Savior that he might give repentance to Israel and forgiveness of sins. 32And we are witnesses to these things, and so is the Holy Spirit whom God has given to those who obey him."

33 When they heard this, they were enraged and wanted to kill them. 34But a Pharisee in the council named Gamaliel, a teacher of the law, respected by all the people, stood up and ordered the men to be put outside for a short time. 35Then he said to them, "Fellow Israelites,o consider carefully what you propose to do to these men. 36For some time ago Theudas rose up, claiming to be somebody, and a number of men, about four hundred, joined him; but he was killed, and all who followed him were dispersed and disappeared. 37After him Judas the Galilean rose up at the time of the census and got people to follow him; he also perished, and all who followed him were scattered. 38So in the present case, I tell you, keep away from these men and let them alone; because if this plan or this undertaking is of human origin, it will fail; 39but if it is of God, you will not be able to overthrow them—in that case you may even be found fighting against God!"

They were convinced by him, 40and when they had called in the apostles, they had them flogged. Then they ordered them not to speak in the name of Jesus, and let them go. 41As they left the council, they rejoiced that they were considered worthy to suffer dishonor for the sake of the name. 42And every day in the temple and at homep they did not cease to teach and proclaim Jesus as the Messiah.q

27 Ἀγαγόντες δὲ αὐτοὺς ἔστησαν ἐν τῷ συνεδρίῳ. καὶ ἐπηρώτησεν αὐτοὺς ὁ ἀρχιερεὺς 28 λέγων, [Οὐ]b παραγγελίᾳ παρηγγείλαμεν ὑμῖν μὴ διδάσκειν ἐπὶ τῷ ὀνόματι τούτῳ, καὶ ἰδοὺ πεπληρώκατε τὴν Ἰερουσαλὴμ τῆς διδαχῆς ὑμῶν καὶ βούλεσθε ἐπαγαγεῖν ἐφ' ἡμᾶς τὸ αἷμα τοῦ ἀνθρώπου τούτου. 29 ἀποκριθεὶς δὲ Πέτρος καὶ οἱ ἀπόστολοι εἶπαν, Πειθαρχεῖν δεῖ θεῷ μᾶλλον ἢ ἀνθρώποις. 30 ὁ θεὸς τῶν πατέρων ἡμῶν ἤγειρεν Ἰησοῦν ὃν ὑμεῖς διεχειρίσασθε κρεμάσαντες ἐπὶ ξύλου· 31 τοῦτον ὁ θεὸς ἀρχηγὸν καὶ σωτῆρα ὕψωσεν τῇ δεξιᾷ αὐτοῦ [τοῦ] δοῦναι μετάνοιαν τῷ Ἰσραὴλ καὶ ἄφεσιν ἁμαρτιῶν. 32 καὶ ἡμεῖς ἐσμεν μάρτυρες τῶν ῥημάτων τούτων καὶ τὸ πνεῦμα τὸ ἅγιον ὃ ἔδωκεν ὁ θεὸς τοῖς πειθαρχοῦσιν αὐτῷ.

33 Οἱ δὲ ἀκούσαντες διεπρίοντο καὶ ἐβούλοντο ἀνελεῖν αὐτούς. 34 ἀναστὰς δέ τις ἐν τῷ συνεδρίῳ Φαρισαῖος ὀνόματι Γαμαλιήλ, νομοδιδάσκαλος τίμιος παντὶ τῷ λαῷ, ἐκέλευσεν ἔξω βραχὺ τοὺς ἀνθρώπους ποιῆσαι 35 εἶπέν τε πρὸς αὐτούς, Ἄνδρες Ἰσραηλῖται, προσέχετε ἑαυτοῖς ἐπὶ τοῖς ἀνθρώποις τούτοις τί μέλλετε πράσσειν. 36 πρὸ γὰρ τούτων τῶν ἡμερῶν ἀνέστη Θευδᾶς λέγων εἶναί τινα ἑαυτόν, ᾧ προσεκλίθη ἀνδρῶν ἀριθμὸς ὡς τετρακοσίων· ὃς ἀνῃρέθη, καὶ πάντες ὅσοι ἐπείθοντο αὐτῷ διελύθησαν καὶ ἐγένοντο εἰς οὐδέν. 37 μετὰ τοῦτον ἀνέστη Ἰούδας ὁ Γαλιλαῖος ἐν ταῖς ἡμέραις τῆς ἀπογραφῆς καὶ ἀπέστησεν λαὸν ὀπίσω αὐτοῦ· κἀκεῖνος ἀπώλετο καὶ πάντες ὅσοι ἐπείθοντο αὐτῷ διεσκορπίσθησαν. 38 καὶ τὰ νῦν λέγω ὑμῖν, ἀπόστητε ἀπὸ τῶν ἀνθρώπων τούτων καὶ ἄφετε αὐτούς· ὅτι ἐὰν ᾖ ἐξ ἀνθρώπων ἡ βουλὴ αὕτη ἢ τὸ ἔργον τοῦτο, καταλυθήσεται, 39 εἰ δὲ ἐκ θεοῦ ἐστιν, οὐ δυνήσεσθε καταλῦσαι αὐτούς, μήποτε καὶ θεομάχοι εὑρεθῆτε.c ἐπείσθησαν δὲ αὐτῷ 40 καὶ προσκαλεσάμενοι τοὺς ἀποστόλους δείραντες παρήγγειλαν μὴ λαλεῖν ἐπὶ τῷ ὀνόματι τοῦ Ἰησοῦ καὶ ἀπέλυσαν. 41 Οἱ μὲν οὖν ἐπορεύοντο χαίροντες ἀπὸ προσώπου τοῦ συνεδρίου, ὅτι κατηξιώθησαν ὑπὲρ τοῦ ὀνόματος ἀτιμασθῆναι, 42 πᾶσάν τε ἡμέραν ἐν τῷ ἱερῷ καὶ κατ' οἶκον οὐκ ἐπαύοντο διδάσκοντες καὶ εὐαγγελιζόμενοι τὸν Χριστὸν Ἰησοῦν.

NIV

27Having brought the apostles, they made them appear before the Sanhedrin to be questioned by the high priest. 28"We gave you strict orders not to teach in this name," he said. "Yet you have filled Jerusalem with your teaching and are determined to make us guilty of this man's blood."

29Peter and the other apostles replied: "We must obey God rather than men! 30The God of our fathers raised Jesus from the dead—whom you had killed by hanging him on a tree. 31God exalted him to his own right hand as Prince and Savior that he might give repentance and forgiveness of sins to Israel. 32We are witnesses of these things, and so is the Holy Spirit, whom God has given to those who obey him."

33When they heard this, they were furious and wanted to put them to death. 34But a Pharisee named Gamaliel, a teacher of the law, who was honored by all the people, stood up in the Sanhedrin and ordered that the men be put outside for a little while. 35Then he addressed them: "Men of Israel, consider carefully what you intend to do to these men. 36Some time ago Theudas appeared, claiming to be somebody, and about four hundred men rallied to him. He was killed, all his followers were dispersed, and it all came to nothing. 37After him, Judas the Galilean appeared in the days of the census and led a band of people in revolt. He too was killed, and all his followers were scattered. 38Therefore, in the present case I advise you: Leave these men alone! Let them go! For if their purpose or activity is of human origin, it will fail. 39But if it is from God, you will not be able to stop these men; you will only find yourselves fighting against God."

40His speech persuaded them. They called the apostles in and had them flogged. Then they ordered them not to speak in the name of Jesus, and let them go.

41The apostles left the Sanhedrin, rejoicing because they had been counted worthy of suffering disgrace for the Name. 42Day after day, in the temple courts and from house to house, they never stopped teaching and proclaiming the good news that Jesus is the Christ.b

---

m Other ancient authorities read *Did we not give you strict orders not to teach in this name?* n Gk *than men* o Gk *Men, Israelites* p Or *from house to house* q Or *the Christ*

b28 NIV/NRSV texts omit Οὐ; NRSV note m as UBS.
c39 NIV begins verse 40 after εὑρεθῆτε.

b42 Or *Messiah*

NRSV

Seven Chosen to Serve

6 Now during those days, when the disciples were increasing in number, the Hellenists complained against the Hebrews because their widows were being neglected in the daily distribution of food. [2]And the twelve called together the whole community of the disciples and said, "It is not right that we should neglect the word of God in order to wait on tables.[r] [3]Therefore, friends,[s] select from among yourselves seven men of good standing, full of the Spirit and of wisdom, whom we may appoint to this task, [4]while we, for our part, will devote ourselves to prayer and to serving the word." [5]What they said pleased the whole community, and they chose Stephen, a man full of faith and the Holy Spirit, together with Philip, Prochorus, Nicanor, Timon, Parmenas, and Nicolaus, a proselyte of Antioch. [6]They had these men stand before the apostles, who prayed and laid their hands on them.

[7] The word of God continued to spread; the number of the disciples increased greatly in Jerusalem, and a great many of the priests became obedient to the faith.

The Arrest of Stephen

[8] Stephen, full of grace and power, did great wonders and signs among the people. [9]Then some of those who belonged to the synagogue of the Freedmen (as it was called), Cyrenians, Alexandrians, and others of those from Cilicia and Asia, stood up and argued with Stephen. [10]But they could not withstand the wisdom and the Spirit[t] with which he spoke. [11]Then they secretly instigated some men to say, "We have heard him speak blasphemous words against Moses and God." [12]They stirred up the people as well as the elders and the scribes; then they suddenly confronted him, seized him, and brought him before the council. [13]They set up false witnesses who said, "This man never stops saying things against this holy place and the law; [14]for we have heard him say that this Jesus of Nazareth[u] will destroy this place and will change the customs that Moses handed on to us." [15]And all who sat in the council looked intently at him, and they saw that his face was like the face of an angel.

Greek

6 Ἐν δὲ ταῖς ἡμέραις ταύταις πληθυνόντων τῶν μαθητῶν ἐγένετο γογγυσμὸς τῶν Ἑλληνιστῶν πρὸς τοὺς Ἑβραίους, ὅτι παρεθεωροῦντο ἐν τῇ διακονίᾳ τῇ καθημερινῇ αἱ χῆραι αὐτῶν. **2** προσκαλεσάμενοι δὲ οἱ δώδεκα τὸ πλῆθος τῶν μαθητῶν εἶπαν, Οὐκ ἀρεστόν ἐστιν ἡμᾶς καταλείψαντας τὸν λόγον τοῦ θεοῦ διακονεῖν τραπέζαις. **3** ἐπισκέψασθε δέ, ἀδελφοί, ἄνδρας ἐξ ὑμῶν μαρτυρουμένους ἑπτά, πλήρεις πνεύματος καὶ σοφίας, οὓς καταστήσομεν ἐπὶ τῆς χρείας ταύτης, **4** ἡμεῖς δὲ τῇ προσευχῇ καὶ τῇ διακονίᾳ τοῦ λόγου προσκαρτερήσομεν. **5** καὶ ἤρεσεν ὁ λόγος ἐνώπιον παντὸς τοῦ πλήθους καὶ ἐξελέξαντο Στέφανον, ἄνδρα πλήρης πίστεως καὶ πνεύματος ἁγίου, καὶ Φίλιππον καὶ Πρόχορον καὶ Νικάνορα καὶ Τίμωνα καὶ Παρμενᾶν καὶ Νικόλαον προσήλυτον Ἀντιοχέα, **6** οὓς ἔστησαν ἐνώπιον τῶν ἀποστόλων, καὶ προσευξάμενοι ἐπέθηκαν αὐτοῖς τὰς χεῖρας.

7 Καὶ ὁ λόγος τοῦ θεοῦ ηὔξανεν καὶ ἐπληθύνετο ὁ ἀριθμὸς τῶν μαθητῶν ἐν Ἰερουσαλὴμ σφόδρα, πολύς τε ὄχλος τῶν ἱερέων ὑπήκουον τῇ πίστει.

8 Στέφανος δὲ πλήρης χάριτος καὶ δυνάμεως ἐποίει τέρατα καὶ σημεῖα μεγάλα ἐν τῷ λαῷ. **9** ἀνέστησαν δέ τινες τῶν ἐκ τῆς συναγωγῆς τῆς λεγομένης Λιβερτίνων καὶ Κυρηναίων καὶ Ἀλεξανδρέων καὶ τῶν ἀπὸ Κιλικίας καὶ Ἀσίας συζητοῦντες τῷ Στεφάνῳ, **10** καὶ οὐκ ἴσχυον ἀντιστῆναι τῇ σοφίᾳ καὶ τῷ πνεύματι ᾧ ἐλάλει. **11** τότε ὑπέβαλον ἄνδρας λέγοντας ὅτι Ἀκηκόαμεν αὐτοῦ λαλοῦντος ῥήματα βλάσφημα εἰς Μωϋσῆν καὶ τὸν θεόν· **12** συνεκίνησάν τε τὸν λαὸν καὶ τοὺς πρεσβυτέρους καὶ τοὺς γραμματεῖς καὶ ἐπιστάντες συνήρπασαν αὐτὸν καὶ ἤγαγον εἰς τὸ συνέδριον, **13** ἔστησάν τε μάρτυρας ψευδεῖς λέγοντας, Ὁ ἄνθρωπος οὗτος οὐ παύεται λαλῶν ῥήματα κατὰ τοῦ τόπου τοῦ ἁγίου [τούτου] καὶ τοῦ νόμου· **14** ἀκηκόαμεν γὰρ αὐτοῦ λέγοντος ὅτι Ἰησοῦς ὁ Ναζωραῖος οὗτος καταλύσει τὸν τόπον τοῦτον καὶ ἀλλάξει τὰ ἔθη ἃ παρέδωκεν ἡμῖν Μωϋσῆς. **15** καὶ ἀτενίσαντες εἰς αὐτὸν πάντες οἱ καθεζόμενοι ἐν τῷ συνεδρίῳ εἶδον τὸ πρόσωπον αὐτοῦ ὡσεὶ πρόσωπον ἀγγέλου.

NIV

The Choosing of the Seven

6 In those days when the number of disciples was increasing, the Grecian Jews among them complained against the Hebraic Jews because their widows were being overlooked in the daily distribution of food. [2]So the Twelve gathered all the disciples together and said, "It would not be right for us to neglect the ministry of the word of God in order to wait on tables. [3]Brothers, choose seven men from among you who are known to be full of the Spirit and wisdom. We will turn this responsibility over to them [4]and will give our attention to prayer and the ministry of the word."

[5]This proposal pleased the whole group. They chose Stephen, a man full of faith and of the Holy Spirit; also Philip, Procorus, Nicanor, Timon, Parmenas, and Nicolas from Antioch, a convert to Judaism. [6]They presented these men to the apostles, who prayed and laid their hands on them.

[7]So the word of God spread. The number of disciples in Jerusalem increased rapidly, and a large number of priests became obedient to the faith.

Stephen Seized

[8]Now Stephen, a man full of God's grace and power, did great wonders and miraculous signs among the people. [9]Opposition arose, however, from members of the Synagogue of the Freedmen (as it was called)—Jews of Cyrene and Alexandria as well as the provinces of Cilicia and Asia. These men began to argue with Stephen, [10]but they could not stand up against his wisdom or the Spirit by whom he spoke.

[11]Then they secretly persuaded some men to say, "We have heard Stephen speak words of blasphemy against Moses and against God."

[12]So they stirred up the people and the elders and the teachers of the law. They seized Stephen and brought him before the Sanhedrin. [13]They produced false witnesses, who testified, "This fellow never stops speaking against this holy place and against the law. [14]For we have heard him say that this Jesus of Nazareth will destroy this place and change the customs Moses handed down to us."

[15]All who were sitting in the Sanhedrin looked intently at Stephen, and they saw that his face was like the face of an angel.

---

[r] Or keep accounts   [s] Gk brothers   [t] Or spirit   [u] Gk the Nazorean

Stephen's Speech to the Council

7 Then the high priest asked him, "Are these things so?" [2]And Stephen replied:

"Brothers[v] and fathers, listen to me. The God of glory appeared to our ancestor Abraham when he was in Mesopotamia, before he lived in Haran, [3]and said to him, 'Leave your country and your relatives and go to the land that I will show you.' [4]Then he left the country of the Chaldeans and settled in Haran. After his father died, God had him move from there to this country in which you are now living. [5]He did not give him any of it as a heritage, not even a foot's length, but promised to give it to him as his possession and to his descendants after him, even though he had no child. [6]And God spoke in these terms, that his descendants would be resident aliens in a country belonging to others, who would enslave them and mistreat them during four hundred years. [7]'But I will judge the nation that they serve,' said God, 'and after that they shall come out and worship me in this place.' [8]Then he gave him the covenant of circumcision. And so Abraham[w] became the father of Isaac and circumcised him on the eighth day; and Isaac became the father of Jacob, and Jacob of the twelve patriarchs.

9 "The patriarchs, jealous of Joseph, sold him into Egypt; but God was with him, [10]and rescued him from all his afflictions, and enabled him to win favor and to show wisdom when he stood before Pharaoh, king of Egypt, who appointed him ruler over Egypt and over all his household. [11]Now there came a famine throughout Egypt and Canaan, and great suffering, and our ancestors could find no food. [12]But when Jacob heard that there was grain in Egypt, he sent our ancestors there on their first visit. [13]On the second visit Joseph made himself known to his brothers, and Joseph's family became known to Pharaoh. [14]Then Joseph sent and invited his father Jacob and all his relatives to come to him, seventy-five in all; [15]so Jacob went down to Egypt. He himself died there as well as our ancestors, [16]and their bodies[x] were brought back to Shechem and laid in the tomb that Abraham had bought for a sum of silver from the sons of Hamor in Shechem.

---

7 Εἶπεν δὲ ὁ ἀρχιερεύς, Εἰ ταῦτα οὕτως ἔχει; **2** ὁ δὲ ἔφη, Ἄνδρες ἀδελφοὶ καὶ πατέρες, ἀκούσατε. Ὁ θεὸς τῆς δόξης ὤφθη τῷ πατρὶ ἡμῶν Ἀβραὰμ ὄντι ἐν τῇ Μεσοποταμίᾳ πρὶν ἢ κατοικῆσαι αὐτὸν ἐν Χαρρὰν **3** καὶ εἶπεν πρὸς αὐτόν, Ἔξελθε ἐκ τῆς γῆς σου καὶ [ἐκ] τῆς συγγενείας σου, καὶ δεῦρο εἰς τὴν γῆν ἣν ἄν σοι δείξω. **4** τότε ἐξελθὼν ἐκ γῆς Χαλδαίων κατῴκησεν ἐν Χαρράν. κἀκεῖθεν μετὰ τὸ ἀποθανεῖν τὸν πατέρα αὐτοῦ μετῴκισεν αὐτὸν εἰς τὴν γῆν ταύτην εἰς ἣν ὑμεῖς νῦν κατοικεῖτε, **5** καὶ οὐκ ἔδωκεν αὐτῷ κληρονομίαν ἐν αὐτῇ οὐδὲ βῆμα ποδός καὶ ἐπηγγείλατο **δοῦναι αὐτῷ εἰς κατάσχεσιν αὐτὴν καὶ τῷ σπέρματι αὐτοῦ μετ᾽ αὐτόν,** οὐκ ὄντος αὐτῷ τέκνου. **6** ἐλάλησεν δὲ[a] οὕτως ὁ θεὸς ὅτι **ἔσται τὸ σπέρμα αὐτοῦ πάροικον ἐν γῇ ἀλλοτρίᾳ καὶ δουλώσουσιν αὐτὸ καὶ κακώσουσιν ἔτη τετρακόσια· 7 καὶ τὸ ἔθνος ᾧ ἐὰν δουλεύσουσιν κρινῶ ἐγώ,** ὁ θεὸς εἶπεν, **καὶ μετὰ ταῦτα ἐξελεύσονται καὶ λατρεύσουσίν μοι ἐν τῷ τόπῳ τούτῳ.** **8** καὶ ἔδωκεν αὐτῷ διαθήκην περιτομῆς· καὶ οὕτως ἐγέννησεν τὸν Ἰσαὰκ καὶ περιέτεμεν αὐτὸν τῇ ἡμέρᾳ τῇ ὀγδόῃ, καὶ Ἰσαὰκ τὸν Ἰακώβ, καὶ Ἰακὼβ τοὺς δώδεκα πατριάρχας.

9 Καὶ οἱ πατριάρχαι ζηλώσαντες τὸν Ἰωσὴφ ἀπέδοντο εἰς Αἴγυπτον. καὶ ἦν ὁ θεὸς μετ᾽ αὐτοῦ **10** καὶ ἐξείλατο αὐτὸν ἐκ πασῶν τῶν θλίψεων αὐτοῦ καὶ ἔδωκεν αὐτῷ χάριν καὶ σοφίαν ἐναντίον Φαραὼ βασιλέως Αἰγύπτου καὶ κατέστησεν αὐτὸν ἡγούμενον ἐπ᾽ Αἴγυπτον καὶ [ἐφ᾽][b] ὅλον τὸν οἶκον αὐτοῦ. **11** ἦλθεν δὲ λιμὸς ἐφ᾽ ὅλην τὴν Αἴγυπτον καὶ Χανάαν καὶ θλῖψις μεγάλη, καὶ οὐχ ηὕρισκον χορτάσματα οἱ πατέρες ἡμῶν. **12** ἀκούσας δὲ Ἰακὼβ ὄντα σιτία εἰς Αἴγυπτον ἐξαπέστειλεν τοὺς πατέρας ἡμῶν πρῶτον. **13** καὶ ἐν τῷ δευτέρῳ ἀνεγνωρίσθη Ἰωσὴφ τοῖς ἀδελφοῖς αὐτοῦ καὶ φανερὸν ἐγένετο τῷ Φαραὼ τὸ γένος [τοῦ] Ἰωσήφ. **14** ἀποστείλας δὲ Ἰωσὴφ μετεκαλέσατο Ἰακὼβ τὸν πατέρα αὐτοῦ καὶ πᾶσαν τὴν συγγένειαν ἐν ψυχαῖς ἑβδομήκοντα πέντε. **15** καὶ κατέβη Ἰακὼβ εἰς Αἴγυπτον καὶ ἐτελεύτησεν αὐτὸς καὶ οἱ πατέρες ἡμῶν, **16** καὶ μετετέθησαν εἰς Συχὲμ καὶ ἐτέθησαν ἐν τῷ μνήματι ᾧ ὠνήσατο Ἀβραὰμ τιμῆς ἀργυρίου παρὰ τῶν υἱῶν Ἑμμὼρ ἐν Συχέμ.

Stephen's Speech to the Sanhedrin

7 Then the high priest asked him, "Are these charges true?"

[2]To this he replied: "Brothers and fathers, listen to me! The God of glory appeared to our father Abraham while he was still in Mesopotamia, before he lived in Haran. [3]'Leave your country and your people,' God said, 'and go to the land I will show you.'[a]

[4]"So he left the land of the Chaldeans and settled in Haran. After the death of his father, God sent him to this land where you are now living. [5]He gave him no inheritance here, not even a foot of ground. But God promised him that he and his descendants after him would possess the land, even though at that time Abraham had no child. [6]God spoke to him in this way: 'Your descendants will be strangers in a country not their own, and they will be enslaved and mistreated four hundred years. [7]But I will punish the nation they serve as slaves,' God said, 'and afterward they will come out of that country and worship me in this place.'[b] [8]Then he gave Abraham the covenant of circumcision. And Abraham became the father of Isaac and circumcised him eight days after his birth. Later Isaac became the father of Jacob, and Jacob became the father of the twelve patriarchs.

9 "Because the patriarchs were jealous of Joseph, they sold him as a slave into Egypt. But God was with him [10]and rescued him from all his troubles. He gave Joseph wisdom and enabled him to gain the goodwill of Pharaoh king of Egypt; so he made him ruler over Egypt and all his palace.

[11]"Then a famine struck all Egypt and Canaan, bringing great suffering, and our fathers could not find food. [12]When Jacob heard that there was grain in Egypt, he sent our fathers on their first visit. [13]On their second visit, Joseph told his brothers who he was, and Pharaoh learned about Joseph's family. [14]After this, Joseph sent for his father Jacob and his whole family, seventy-five in all. [15]Then Jacob went down to Egypt, where he and our fathers died. [16]Their bodies were brought back to Shechem and placed in the tomb that Abraham had bought from the sons of Hamor at Shechem for a certain sum of money.

---

v Gk Men, brothers   w Gk he   x Gk they   a6 NIV text adds αὐτῷ †   b10 NIV text omits ἐφ᾽ †   a3 Gen. 12:1   b7 Gen. 15:13,14

17 "But as the time drew near for the fulfillment of the promise that God had made to Abraham, our people in Egypt increased and multiplied 18until another king who had not known Joseph ruled over Egypt. 19He dealt craftily with our race and forced our ancestors to abandon their infants so that they would die. 20At this time Moses was born, and he was beautiful before God. For three months he was brought up in his father's house; 21and when he was abandoned, Pharaoh's daughter adopted him and brought him up as her own son. 22So Moses was instructed in all the wisdom of the Egyptians and was powerful in his words and deeds.

23 "When he was forty years old, it came into his heart to visit his relatives, the Israelites.y 24When he saw one of them being wronged, he defended the oppressed man and avenged him by striking down the Egyptian. 25He supposed that his kinsfolk would understand that God through him was rescuing them, but they did not understand. 26The next day he came to some of them as they were quarreling and tried to reconcile them, saying, 'Men, you are brothers; why do you wrong each other?' 27But the man who was wronging his neighbor pushed Mosesz aside, saying, 'Who made you a ruler and a judge over us? 28Do you want to kill me as you killed the Egyptian yesterday?' 29When he heard this, Moses fled and became a resident alien in the land of Midian. There he became the father of two sons.

30 "Now when forty years had passed, an angel appeared to him in the wilderness of Mount Sinai, in the flame of a burning bush. 31When Moses saw it, he was amazed at the sight; and as he approached to look, there came the voice of the Lord: 32'I am the God of your ancestors, the God of Abraham, Isaac, and Jacob.' Moses began to tremble and did not dare to look. 33Then the Lord said to him, 'Take off the sandals from your feet, for the place where you are standing is holy ground. 34I have surely seen the mistreatment of my people who are in Egypt and have heard their groaning, and I have come down to rescue them. Come now, I will send you to Egypt.'

35 "It was this Moses whom they rejected

17 Καθὼς δὲ ἤγγιζεν ὁ χρόνος τῆς ἐπαγγελίας ἧς ὡμολόγησεν ὁ θεὸς τῷ Ἀβραάμ, ηὔξησεν ὁ λαὸς καὶ ἐπληθύνθη ἐν Αἰγύπτῳ 18 ἄχρι οὗ ἀνέστη βασιλεὺς ἕτερος [ἐπ᾽ Αἴγυπτον] ὃς οὐκ ᾔδει τὸν Ἰωσήφ. 19 οὗτος κατασοφισάμενος τὸ γένος ἡμῶν ἐκάκωσεν τοὺς πατέρας [ἡμῶν] τοῦ ποιεῖν τὰ βρέφη ἔκθετα αὐτῶν εἰς τὸ μὴ ζῳογονεῖσθαι. 20 ἐν ᾧ καιρῷ ἐγεννήθη Μωϋσῆς καὶ ἦν ἀστεῖος τῷ θεῷ· ὃς ἀνετράφη μῆνας τρεῖς ἐν τῷ οἴκῳ τοῦ πατρός, 21 ἐκτεθέντος δὲ αὐτοῦ ἀνείλατο αὐτὸν ἡ θυγάτηρ Φαραὼ καὶ ἀνεθρέψατο αὐτὸν ἑαυτῇ εἰς υἱόν. 22 καὶ ἐπαιδεύθη Μωϋσῆς [ἐν] πάσῃ σοφίᾳ Αἰγυπτίων, ἦν δὲ δυνατὸς ἐν λόγοις καὶ ἔργοις αὐτοῦ.

23 Ὡς δὲ ἐπληροῦτο αὐτῷ τεσσερακονταετὴς χρόνος, ἀνέβη ἐπὶ τὴν καρδίαν αὐτοῦ ἐπισκέψασθαι τοὺς ἀδελφοὺς αὐτοῦ τοὺς υἱοὺς Ἰσραήλ. 24 καὶ ἰδών τινα ἀδικούμενον ἠμύνατο καὶ ἐποίησεν ἐκδίκησιν τῷ καταπονουμένῳ πατάξας τὸν Αἰγύπτιον. 25 ἐνόμιζεν δὲ συνιέναι τοὺς ἀδελφοὺς [αὐτοῦ] ὅτι ὁ θεὸς διὰ χειρὸς αὐτοῦ δίδωσιν σωτηρίαν αὐτοῖς· οἱ δὲ οὐ συνῆκαν. 26 τῇ τε ἐπιούσῃ ἡμέρᾳ ὤφθη αὐτοῖς μαχομένοις καὶ συνήλλασσεν αὐτοὺς εἰς εἰρήνην εἰπών, Ἄνδρες, ἀδελφοί ἐστε· ἱνατί ἀδικεῖτε ἀλλήλους; 27 ὁ δὲ ἀδικῶν τὸν πλησίον ἀπώσατο αὐτὸν εἰπών, Τίς σε κατέστησεν ἄρχοντα καὶ δικαστὴν ἐφ᾽ ἡμῶν; 28 μὴ ἀνελεῖν με σὺ θέλεις ὃν τρόπον ἀνεῖλες ἐχθὲς τὸν Αἰγύπτιον; 29 ἔφυγεν δὲ Μωϋσῆς ἐν τῷ λόγῳ τούτῳ καὶ ἐγένετο πάροικος ἐν γῇ Μαδιάμ, οὗ ἐγέννησεν υἱοὺς δύο.

30 Καὶ πληρωθέντων ἐτῶν τεσσεράκοντα ὤφθη αὐτῷ ἐν τῇ ἐρήμῳ τοῦ ὄρους Σινᾶ ἄγγελος ἐν φλογὶ πυρὸς βάτου. 31 ὁ δὲ Μωϋσῆς ἰδὼν ἐθαύμαζεν τὸ ὅραμα, προσερχομένου δὲ αὐτοῦ κατανοῆσαι ἐγένετο φωνὴ κυρίου, 32 Ἐγὼ ὁ θεὸς τῶν πατέρων σου, ὁ θεὸς Ἀβραὰμ καὶ Ἰσαὰκ καὶ Ἰακώβ. ἔντρομος δὲ γενόμενος Μωϋσῆς οὐκ ἐτόλμα κατανοῆσαι. 33 εἶπεν δὲ αὐτῷ ὁ κύριος, Λῦσον τὸ ὑπόδημα τῶν ποδῶν σου, ὁ γὰρ τόπος ἐφ᾽ ᾧ ἕστηκας γῆ ἁγία ἐστίν. 34 ἰδὼν εἶδον τὴν κάκωσιν τοῦ λαοῦ μου τοῦ ἐν Αἰγύπτῳ καὶ τοῦ στεναγμοῦ αὐτῶν ἤκουσα, καὶ κατέβην ἐξελέσθαι αὐτούς· καὶ νῦν δεῦρο ἀποστείλω σε εἰς Αἴγυπτον. 35 Τοῦτον τὸν Μωϋσῆν, ὃν ἠρνήσαντο

17"As the time drew near for God to fulfill his promise to Abraham, the number of our people in Egypt greatly increased. 18Then another king, who knew nothing about Joseph, became ruler of Egypt. 19He dealt treacherously with our people and oppressed our forefathers by forcing them to throw out their newborn babies so that they would die. 20"At that time Moses was born, and he was no ordinary child.c For three months he was cared for in his father's house. 21When he was placed outside, Pharaoh's daughter took him and brought him up as her own son. 22Moses was educated in all the wisdom of the Egyptians and was powerful in speech and action.

23"When Moses was forty years old, he decided to visit his fellow Israelites. 24He saw one of them being mistreated by an Egyptian, so he went to his defense and avenged him by killing the Egyptian. 25Moses thought that his own people would realize that God was using him to rescue them, but they did not. 26The next day Moses came upon two Israelites who were fighting. He tried to reconcile them by saying, 'Men, you are brothers; why do you want to hurt each other?'

27"But the man who was mistreating the other pushed Moses aside and said, 'Who made you ruler and judge over us? 28Do you want to kill me as you killed the Egyptian yesterday?'d 29When Moses heard this, he fled to Midian, where he settled as a foreigner and had two sons.

30"After forty years had passed, an angel appeared to Moses in the flames of a burning bush in the desert near Mount Sinai. 31When he saw this, he was amazed at the sight. As he went over to look more closely, he heard the Lord's voice: 32'I am the God of your fathers, the God of Abraham, Isaac and Jacob.'e Moses trembled with fear and did not dare to look.

33"Then the Lord said to him, 'Take off your sandals; the place where you are standing is holy ground. 34I have indeed seen the oppression of my people in Egypt. I have heard their groaning and have come down to set them free. Now come, I will send you back to Egypt.'f

35"This is the same Moses whom they

---

y Gk his brothers, the sons of Israel   z Gk him

c20 Or was fair in the sight of God   d28 Exodus 2:14
e32 Exodus 3:6   f34 Exodus 3:5,7,8,10

when they said, 'Who made you a ruler and a judge?' and whom God now sent as both ruler and liberator through the angel who appeared to him in the bush. [36]He led them out, having performed wonders and signs in Egypt, at the Red Sea, and in the wilderness for forty years. [37]This is the Moses who said to the Israelites, 'God will raise up a prophet for you from your own people[a] as he raised me up.' [38]He is the one who was in the congregation in the wilderness with the angel who spoke to him at Mount Sinai, and with our ancestors; and he received living oracles to give to us. [39]Our ancestors were unwilling to obey him; instead, they pushed him aside, and in their hearts they turned back to Egypt, [40]saying to Aaron, 'Make gods for us who will lead the way for us; as for this Moses who led us out from the land of Egypt, we do not know what has happened to him.' [41]At that time they made a calf, offered a sacrifice to the idol, and reveled in the works of their hands. [42]But God turned away from them and handed them over to worship the host of heaven, as it is written in the book of the prophets:

'Did you offer to me slain victims and
    sacrifices
    forty years in the wilderness, O
    house of Israel?
[43] No; you took along the tent of Moloch,
    and the star of your god Rephan,
    the images that you made to
    worship;
so I will remove you beyond Babylon.'
[44] "Our ancestors had the tent of testimony in the wilderness, as God[b] directed when he spoke to Moses, ordering him to make it according to the pattern he had seen. [45]Our ancestors in turn brought it in with Joshua when they dispossessed the nations that God drove out before our ancestors. And it was there until the time of David, [46]who found favor with God and asked that he might find a dwelling place for the house of Jacob.[c] [47]But it was Solomon who built a house for him. [48]Yet

εἰπόντες, Τίς σε κατέστησεν ἄρχοντα καὶ δικαστήν; τοῦτον ὁ θεὸς [καὶ]ᶜ ἄρχοντα καὶ λυτρωτὴν ἀπέσταλκεν σὺν χειρὶ ἀγγέλου τοῦ ὀφθέντος αὐτῷ ἐν τῇ βάτῳ. **36** οὗτος ἐξήγαγεν αὐτοὺς ποιήσας τέρατα καὶ σημεῖα ἐν γῇ Αἰγύπτῳ καὶ ἐν Ἐρυθρᾷ Θαλάσσῃ καὶ ἐν τῇ ἐρήμῳ ἔτη τεσσεράκοντα. **37** οὗτός ἐστιν ὁ Μωϋσῆς ὁ εἴπας τοῖς υἱοῖς Ἰσραήλ, Προφήτην ὑμῖν ἀναστήσει ὁ θεὸς ἐκ τῶν ἀδελφῶν ὑμῶν ὡς ἐμέ. **38** οὗτός ἐστιν ὁ γενόμενος ἐν τῇ ἐκκλησίᾳ ἐν τῇ ἐρήμῳ μετὰ τοῦ ἀγγέλου τοῦ λαλοῦντος αὐτῷ ἐν τῷ ὄρει Σινᾶ καὶ τῶν πατέρων ἡμῶν, ὃς ἐδέξατο λόγια ζῶντα δοῦναι ἡμῖν, **39** ᾧ οὐκ ἠθέλησαν ὑπήκοοι γενέσθαι οἱ πατέρες ἡμῶν, ἀλλὰ ἀπώσαντο καὶ ἐστράφησαν ἐν ταῖς καρδίαις αὐτῶν εἰς Αἴγυπτον **40** εἰπόντες τῷ Ἀαρών, Ποίησον ἡμῖν θεοὺς οἳ προπορεύσονται ἡμῶν· ὁ γὰρ Μωϋσῆς οὗτος, ὃς ἐξήγαγεν ἡμᾶς ἐκ γῆς Αἰγύπτου, οὐκ οἴδαμεν τί ἐγένετο αὐτῷ. **41** καὶ ἐμοσχοποίησαν ἐν ταῖς ἡμέραις ἐκείναις καὶ ἀνήγαγον θυσίαν τῷ εἰδώλῳ καὶ εὐφραίνοντο ἐν τοῖς ἔργοις τῶν χειρῶν αὐτῶν. **42** ἔστρεψεν δὲ ὁ θεὸς καὶ παρέδωκεν αὐτοὺς λατρεύειν τῇ στρατιᾷ τοῦ οὐρανοῦ καθὼς γέγραπται ἐν βίβλῳ τῶν προφητῶν,

Μὴ σφάγια καὶ θυσίας
    προσηνέγκατέ μοι
    ἔτη τεσσεράκοντα ἐν τῇ ἐρήμῳ,
    οἶκος Ἰσραήλ;
43 καὶ ἀνελάβετε τὴν σκηνὴν τοῦ
    Μολὸχ
    καὶ τὸ ἄστρον τοῦ θεοῦ [ὑμῶν]
    Ῥαιφάν,
    τοὺς τύπους οὓς ἐποιήσατε
    προσκυνεῖν αὐτοῖς,
καὶ μετοικιῶ ὑμᾶς ἐπέκεινα
    Βαβυλῶνος.

44 Ἡ σκηνὴ τοῦ μαρτυρίου ἦν τοῖς πατράσιν ἡμῶν ἐν τῇ ἐρήμῳ καθὼς διετάξατο ὁ λαλῶν τῷ Μωϋσῇ ποιῆσαι αὐτὴν κατὰ τὸν τύπον ὃν ἑωράκει· **45** ἣν καὶ εἰσήγαγον διαδεξάμενοι οἱ πατέρες ἡμῶν μετὰ Ἰησοῦ ἐν τῇ κατασχέσει τῶν ἐθνῶν, ὧν ἐξῶσεν ὁ θεὸς ἀπὸ προσώπου τῶν πατέρων ἡμῶν ἕως τῶν ἡμερῶν Δαυίδ, **46** ὃς εὗρεν χάριν ἐνώπιον τοῦ θεοῦ καὶ ᾐτήσατο εὑρεῖν σκήνωμα τῷ οἴκῳᵈ Ἰακώβ. **47** Σολομῶν δὲ οἰκοδόμησεν αὐτῷ οἶκον.

had rejected with the words, 'Who made you ruler and judge?' He was sent to be their ruler and deliverer by God himself, through the angel who appeared to him in the bush. [36]He led them out of Egypt and did wonders and miraculous signs in Egypt, at the Red Sea[g] and for forty years in the desert.

[37]"This is that Moses who told the Israelites, 'God will send you a prophet like me from your own people.'[h] [38]He was in the assembly in the desert, with the angel who spoke to him on Mount Sinai, and with our fathers; and he received living words to pass on to us.

[39]"But our fathers refused to obey him. Instead, they rejected him and in their hearts turned back to Egypt. [40]They told Aaron, 'Make us gods who will go before us. As for this fellow Moses who led us out of Egypt—we don't know what has happened to him!'[i] [41]That was the time they made an idol in the form of a calf. They brought sacrifices to it and held a celebration in honor of what their hands had made. [42]But God turned away and gave them over to the worship of the heavenly bodies. This agrees with what is written in the book of the prophets:

" 'Did you bring me sacrifices and
    offerings
    forty years in the desert, O house of
    Israel?
[43]You have lifted up the shrine of Molech
    and the star of your god Rephan,
    the idols you made to worship.
Therefore I will send you into exile'[j]
    beyond Babylon.

[44]"Our forefathers had the tabernacle of the Testimony with them in the desert. It had been made as God directed Moses, according to the pattern he had seen. [45]Having received the tabernacle, our fathers under Joshua brought it with them when they took the land from the nations God drove out before them. It remained in the land until the time of David, [46]who enjoyed God's favor and asked that he might provide a dwelling place for the God of Jacob.[k] [47]But it was Solomon who built the house for him.

---

a Gk your brothers   b Gk he   c Other ancient authorities read for the God of Jacob

c35 NIV text omits καὶ †   d46 NIV text and NRSV note c θεῷ; NIV note and NRSV text as UBS

g36 That is, Sea of Reeds   h37 Deut. 18:15   i40 Exodus 32:1   j43 Amos 5:25-27   k46 Some early manuscripts the house of Jacob

the Most High does not dwell in houses made with human hands;[d] as the prophet says,

49 'Heaven is my throne,
 and the earth is my footstool.
What kind of house will you build for
 me, says the Lord,
 or what is the place of my rest?
50 Did not my hand make all these
 things?'

51 "You stiff-necked people, uncircumcised in heart and ears, you are forever opposing the Holy Spirit, just as your ancestors used to do. 52Which of the prophets did your ancestors not persecute? They killed those who foretold the coming of the Righteous One, and now you have become his betrayers and murderers. 53You are the ones that received the law as ordained by angels, and yet you have not kept it."

The Stoning of Stephen

54 When they heard these things, they became enraged and ground their teeth at Stephen.[e] 55But filled with the Holy Spirit, he gazed into heaven and saw the glory of God and Jesus standing at the right hand of God. 56"Look," he said, "I see the heavens opened and the Son of Man standing at the right hand of God!" 57But they covered their ears, and with a loud shout all rushed together against him. 58Then they dragged him out of the city and began to stone him; and the witnesses laid their coats at the feet of a young man named Saul. 59While they were stoning Stephen, he prayed, "Lord Jesus, receive my spirit." 60Then he knelt down and cried out in a loud voice, "Lord, do not hold this sin against them." When he had said this, he

8 died.[f] 1And Saul approved of their killing him.

Saul Persecutes the Church

That day a severe persecution began against the church in Jerusalem, and all except the apostles were scattered throughout the countryside of Judea and Samaria. 2Devout men buried Stephen and made loud lamentation over him. 3But Saul was ravaging the church by entering house after house; dragging off both men and women, he committed them to prison.

---

48 ἀλλ᾿ οὐχ ὁ ὕψιστος ἐν χειροποιήτοις κατοικεῖ, καθὼς ὁ προφήτης λέγει,
49 Ὁ οὐρανός μοι θρόνος,
 ἡ δὲ γῆ ὑποπόδιον τῶν ποδῶν
  μου·
 ποῖον οἶκον οἰκοδομήσετέ μοι,
  λέγει κύριος,
 ἢ τίς τόπος τῆς καταπαύσεώς
  μου;
50 οὐχὶ ἡ χείρ μου ἐποίησεν ταῦτα
 πάντα,

51 Σκληροτράχηλοι καὶ ἀπερίτμητοι καρδίαις καὶ τοῖς ὠσίν, ὑμεῖς ἀεὶ τῷ πνεύματι τῷ ἁγίῳ ἀντιπίπτετε ὡς οἱ πατέρες ὑμῶν καὶ ὑμεῖς. 52 τίνα τῶν προφητῶν οὐκ ἐδίωξαν οἱ πατέρες ὑμῶν; καὶ ἀπέκτειναν τοὺς προκαταγγείλαντας περὶ τῆς ἐλεύσεως τοῦ δικαίου, οὗ νῦν ὑμεῖς προδόται καὶ φονεῖς ἐγένεσθε, 53 οἵτινες ἐλάβετε τὸν νόμον εἰς διαταγὰς ἀγγέλων καὶ οὐκ ἐφυλάξατε.

54 Ἀκούοντες δὲ ταῦτα διεπρίοντο ταῖς καρδίαις αὐτῶν καὶ ἔβρυχον τοὺς ὀδόντας ἐπ᾿ αὐτόν. 55 ὑπάρχων δὲ πλήρης πνεύματος ἁγίου ἀτενίσας εἰς τὸν οὐρανὸν εἶδεν δόξαν θεοῦ καὶ Ἰησοῦν ἑστῶτα ἐκ δεξιῶν τοῦ θεοῦ 56 καὶ εἶπεν, Ἰδοὺ θεωρῶ τοὺς οὐρανοὺς διηνοιγμένους καὶ τὸν υἱὸν τοῦ ἀνθρώπου ἐκ δεξιῶν ἑστῶτα τοῦ θεοῦ. 57 κράξαντες δὲ φωνῇ μεγάλῃ συνέσχον τὰ ὦτα αὐτῶν καὶ ὥρμησαν ὁμοθυμαδὸν ἐπ᾿ αὐτὸν 58 καὶ ἐκβαλόντες ἔξω τῆς πόλεως ἐλιθοβόλουν. καὶ οἱ μάρτυρες ἀπέθεντο τὰ ἱμάτια αὐτῶν παρὰ τοὺς πόδας νεανίου καλουμένου Σαύλου. 59 καὶ ἐλιθοβόλουν τὸν Στέφανον ἐπικαλούμενον καὶ λέγοντα, Κύριε Ἰησοῦ, δέξαι τὸ πνεῦμά μου. 60 θεὶς δὲ τὰ γόνατα ἔκραξεν φωνῇ μεγάλῃ, Κύριε, μὴ στήσῃς αὐτοῖς ταύτην τὴν ἁμαρτίαν. καὶ τοῦτο εἰπὼν ἐκοιμήθη.

8 Σαῦλος δὲ ἦν συνευδοκῶν τῇ ἀναιρέσει αὐτοῦ.

Ἐγένετο δὲ ἐν ἐκείνῃ τῇ ἡμέρᾳ διωγμὸς μέγας ἐπὶ τὴν ἐκκλησίαν τὴν ἐν Ἱεροσολύμοις, πάντες δὲ διεσπάρησαν κατὰ τὰς χώρας τῆς Ἰουδαίας καὶ Σαμαρείας πλὴν τῶν ἀποστόλων. 2 συνεκόμισαν δὲ τὸν Στέφανον ἄνδρες εὐλαβεῖς καὶ ἐποίησαν κοπετὸν μέγαν ἐπ᾿ αὐτῷ. 3 Σαῦλος δὲ ἐλυμαίνετο τὴν ἐκκλησίαν κατὰ τοὺς οἴκους εἰσπορευόμενος, σύρων τε ἄνδρας καὶ γυναῖκας παρεδίδου εἰς φυλακήν.

48"However, the Most High does not live in houses made by men. As the prophet says:

49" 'Heaven is my throne,
 and the earth is my footstool.
What kind of house will you build for
 me?
    says the Lord.
Or where will my resting place be?
50Has not my hand made all these things?'[l]

51"You stiff-necked people, with uncircumcised hearts and ears! You are just like your fathers: You always resist the Holy Spirit! 52Was there ever a prophet your fathers did not persecute? They even killed those who predicted the coming of the Righteous One. And now you have betrayed and murdered him— 53you who have received the law that was put into effect through angels but have not obeyed it."

The Stoning of Stephen

54When they heard this, they were furious and gnashed their teeth at him. 55But Stephen, full of the Holy Spirit, looked up to heaven and saw the glory of God, and Jesus standing at the right hand of God. 56"Look," he said, "I see heaven open and the Son of Man standing at the right hand of God."

57At this they covered their ears and, yelling at the top of their voices, they all rushed at him, 58dragged him out of the city and began to stone him. Meanwhile, the witnesses laid their clothes at the feet of a young man named Saul.

59While they were stoning him, Stephen prayed, "Lord Jesus, receive my spirit." 60Then he fell on his knees and cried out, "Lord, do not hold this sin against them." When he had said this, he fell asleep.

8 And Saul was there, giving approval to his death.

The Church Persecuted and Scattered

On that day a great persecution broke out against the church at Jerusalem, and all except the apostles were scattered throughout Judea and Samaria. 2Godly men buried Stephen and mourned deeply for him. 3But Saul began to destroy the church. Going from house to house, he dragged off men and women and put them in prison.

---

[d] Gk *with hands* [e] Gk *him* [f] Gk *fell asleep*   [l]50 Isaiah 66:1,2

Philip Preaches in Samaria

4 Now those who were scattered went from place to place, proclaiming the word. [5]Philip went down to the city[g] of Samaria and proclaimed the Messiah[h] to them. [6]The crowds with one accord listened eagerly to what was said by Philip, hearing and seeing the signs that he did, [7]for unclean spirits, crying with loud shrieks, came out of many who were possessed; and many others who were paralyzed or lame were cured. [8]So there was great joy in that city.

9 Now a certain man named Simon had previously practiced magic in the city and amazed the people of Samaria, saying that he was someone great. [10]All of them, from the least to the greatest, listened to him eagerly, saying, "This man is the power of God that is called Great." [11]And they listened eagerly to him because for a long time he had amazed them with his magic. [12]But when they believed Philip, who was proclaiming the good news about the kingdom of God and the name of Jesus Christ, they were baptized, both men and women. [13]Even Simon himself believed. After being baptized, he stayed constantly with Philip and was amazed when he saw the signs and great miracles that took place.

14 Now when the apostles at Jerusalem heard that Samaria had accepted the word of God, they sent Peter and John to them. [15]The two went down and prayed for them that they might receive the Holy Spirit [16](for as yet the Spirit had not come[i] upon any of them; they had only been baptized in the name of the Lord Jesus). [17]Then Peter and John[j] laid their hands on them, and they received the Holy Spirit. [18]Now when Simon saw that the Spirit was given through the laying on of the apostles' hands, he offered them money, [19]saying, "Give me also this power so that anyone on whom I lay my hands may receive the Holy Spirit." [20]But Peter said to him, "May your silver perish with you, because you thought you could obtain God's gift with money! [21]You have no part or share in this, for your heart is not right before God. [22]Repent therefore of this wickedness of yours, and pray to the Lord that, if possible, the intent of your heart may be

---

4 Οἱ μὲν οὖν διασπαρέντες διῆλθον εὐαγγελιζόμενοι τὸν λόγον. **5** Φίλιππος δὲ κατελθὼν εἰς [τὴν][a] πόλιν τῆς Σαμαρείας ἐκήρυσσεν αὐτοῖς τὸν Χριστόν. **6** προσεῖχον δὲ οἱ ὄχλοι τοῖς λεγομένοις ὑπὸ τοῦ Φιλίππου ὁμοθυμαδὸν ἐν τῷ ἀκούειν αὐτοὺς καὶ βλέπειν τὰ σημεῖα ἃ ἐποίει. **7** πολλοὶ γὰρ τῶν ἐχόντων πνεύματα ἀκάθαρτα βοῶντα φωνῇ μεγάλῃ ἐξήρχοντο, πολλοὶ δὲ παραλελυμένοι καὶ χωλοὶ ἐθεραπεύθησαν· **8** ἐγένετο δὲ πολλὴ χαρὰ ἐν τῇ πόλει ἐκείνῃ.

9 Ἀνὴρ δέ τις ὀνόματι Σίμων προϋπῆρχεν ἐν τῇ πόλει μαγεύων καὶ ἐξιστάνων τὸ ἔθνος τῆς Σαμαρείας, λέγων εἶναί τινα ἑαυτὸν μέγαν, **10** ᾧ προσεῖχον πάντες ἀπὸ μικροῦ ἕως μεγάλου λέγοντες, Οὗτός ἐστιν ἡ δύναμις τοῦ θεοῦ ἡ καλουμένη Μεγάλη. **11** προσεῖχον δὲ αὐτῷ διὰ τὸ ἱκανῷ χρόνῳ ταῖς μαγείαις ἐξεστακέναι αὐτούς. **12** ὅτε δὲ ἐπίστευσαν τῷ Φιλίππῳ εὐαγγελιζομένῳ περὶ τῆς βασιλείας τοῦ θεοῦ καὶ τοῦ ὀνόματος Ἰησοῦ Χριστοῦ, ἐβαπτίζοντο ἄνδρες τε καὶ γυναῖκες. **13** ὁ δὲ Σίμων καὶ αὐτὸς ἐπίστευσεν καὶ βαπτισθεὶς ἦν προσκαρτερῶν τῷ Φιλίππῳ, θεωρῶν τε σημεῖα καὶ δυνάμεις μεγάλας γινομένας ἐξίστατο.

14 Ἀκούσαντες δὲ οἱ ἐν Ἱεροσολύμοις ἀπόστολοι ὅτι δέδεκται ἡ Σαμάρεια τὸν λόγον τοῦ θεοῦ, ἀπέστειλαν πρὸς αὐτοὺς Πέτρον καὶ Ἰωάννην, **15** οἵτινες καταβάντες προσηύξαντο περὶ αὐτῶν ὅπως λάβωσιν πνεῦμα ἅγιον· **16** οὐδέπω γὰρ ἦν ἐπ' οὐδενὶ αὐτῶν ἐπιπεπτωκός, μόνον δὲ βεβαπτισμένοι ὑπῆρχον εἰς τὸ ὄνομα τοῦ κυρίου Ἰησοῦ. **17** τότε ἐπετίθεσαν τὰς χεῖρας ἐπ' αὐτοὺς καὶ ἐλάμβανον πνεῦμα ἅγιον. **18** ἰδὼν δὲ ὁ Σίμων ὅτι διὰ τῆς ἐπιθέσεως τῶν χειρῶν τῶν ἀποστόλων δίδοται τὸ πνεῦμα, προσήνεγκεν αὐτοῖς χρήματα **19** λέγων, Δότε κἀμοὶ τὴν ἐξουσίαν ταύτην ἵνα ᾧ ἐὰν ἐπιθῶ τὰς χεῖρας λαμβάνῃ πνεῦμα ἅγιον. **20** Πέτρος δὲ εἶπεν πρὸς αὐτόν, Τὸ ἀργύριόν σου σὺν σοὶ εἴη εἰς ἀπώλειαν ὅτι τὴν δωρεὰν τοῦ θεοῦ ἐνόμισας διὰ χρημάτων κτᾶσθαι. **21** οὐκ ἔστιν σοι μερὶς οὐδὲ κλῆρος ἐν τῷ λόγῳ τούτῳ, ἡ γὰρ καρδία σου οὐκ ἔστιν εὐθεῖα ἔναντι τοῦ θεοῦ. **22** μετανόησον οὖν ἀπὸ τῆς κακίας σου ταύτης καὶ δεήθητι τοῦ κυρίου, εἰ ἄρα ἀφεθήσεταί σοι ἡ ἐπίνοια

Philip in Samaria

[4]Those who had been scattered preached the word wherever they went. [5]Philip went down to a city in Samaria and proclaimed the Christ[a] there. [6]When the crowds heard Philip and saw the miraculous signs he did, they all paid close attention to what he said. [7]With shrieks, evil[b] spirits came out of many, and many paralytics and cripples were healed. [8]So there was great joy in that city.

Simon the Sorcerer

[9]Now for some time a man named Simon had practiced sorcery in the city and amazed all the people of Samaria. He boasted that he was someone great, [10]and all the people, both high and low, gave him their attention and exclaimed, "This man is the divine power known as the Great Power." [11]They followed him because he had amazed them for a long time with his magic. [12]But when they believed Philip as he preached the good news of the kingdom of God and the name of Jesus Christ, they were baptized, both men and women. [13]Simon himself believed and was baptized. And he followed Philip everywhere, astonished by the great signs and miracles he saw.

[14]When the apostles in Jerusalem heard that Samaria had accepted the word of God, they sent Peter and John to them. [15]When they arrived, they prayed for them that they might receive the Holy Spirit, [16]because the Holy Spirit had not yet come upon any of them; they had simply been baptized into[c] the name of the Lord Jesus. [17]Then Peter and John placed their hands on them, and they received the Holy Spirit.

[18]When Simon saw that the Spirit was given at the laying on of the apostles' hands, he offered them money [19]and said, "Give me also this ability so that everyone on whom I lay my hands may receive the Holy Spirit."

[20]Peter answered: "May your money perish with you, because you thought you could buy the gift of God with money! [21]You have no part or share in this ministry, because your heart is not right before God. [22]Repent of this wickedness and pray to the Lord. Perhaps he will forgive you for having such a thought in your heart.

---

g Other ancient authorities read *a city*   h Or *the Christ*
i Gk *fallen*   j Gk *they*

a5 NRSV note g omits τὴν

a5 Or *Messiah*   b7 Greek *unclean*   c16 Or *in*

forgiven you. 23For I see that you are in the gall of bitterness and the chains of wickedness." 24Simon answered, "Pray for me to the Lord, that nothing of what you[k] have said may happen to me."

25 Now after Peter and John[l] had testified and spoken the word of the Lord, they returned to Jerusalem, proclaiming the good news to many villages of the Samaritans.

Philip and the Ethiopian Eunuch

26 Then an angel of the Lord said to Philip, "Get up and go toward the south[m] to the road that goes down from Jerusalem to Gaza." (This is a wilderness road.) 27So he got up and went. Now there was an Ethiopian eunuch, a court official of the Candace, queen of the Ethiopians, in charge of her entire treasury. He had come to Jerusalem to worship 28and was returning home; seated in his chariot, he was reading the prophet Isaiah. 29Then the Spirit said to Philip, "Go over to this chariot and join it." 30So Philip ran up to it and heard him reading the prophet Isaiah. He asked, "Do you understand what you are reading?" 31He replied, "How can I, unless someone guides me?" And he invited Philip to get in and sit beside him. 32Now the passage of the scripture that he was reading was this:

"Like a sheep he was led to the
  slaughter,
  and like a lamb silent before its
    shearer,
  so he does not open his mouth.
33 In his humiliation justice was denied
    him.
  Who can describe his generation?
    For his life is taken away from the
      earth."

34The eunuch asked Philip, "About whom, may I ask you, does the prophet say this, about himself or about someone else?" 35Then Philip began to speak, and starting with this scripture, he proclaimed to him the good news about Jesus. 36As they were going along the road, they came to some water; and the eunuch said, "Look, here is water! What is to prevent me from being baptized?"[n] 38He commanded the chariot to stop, and both of them, Philip and the eunuch, went down into the water, and

τῆς καρδίας σου. 23 εἰς γὰρ χολὴν πικρίας καὶ σύνδεσμον ἀδικίας ὁρῶ σε ὄντα. 24 ἀποκριθεὶς δὲ ὁ Σίμων εἶπεν, Δεήθητε ὑμεῖς ὑπὲρ ἐμοῦ πρὸς τὸν κύριον ὅπως μηδὲν ἐπέλθῃ ἐπ' ἐμὲ ὧν εἰρήκατε. 25 Οἱ μὲν οὖν διαμαρτυράμενοι καὶ λαλήσαντες τὸν λόγον τοῦ κυρίου ὑπέστρεφον εἰς Ἱεροσόλυμα, πολλάς τε κώμας τῶν Σαμαριτῶν εὐηγγελίζοντο. 26 Ἄγγελος δὲ κυρίου ἐλάλησεν πρὸς Φίλιππον λέγων, Ἀνάστηθι καὶ πορεύου κατὰ μεσημβρίαν ἐπὶ τὴν ὁδὸν τὴν καταβαίνουσαν ἀπὸ Ἰερουσαλὴμ εἰς Γάζαν, αὕτη ἐστὶν ἔρημος. 27 καὶ ἀναστὰς ἐπορεύθη. καὶ ἰδοὺ ἀνὴρ Αἰθίοψ εὐνοῦχος δυνάστης Κανδάκης βασιλίσσης Αἰθιόπων, ὃς ἦν ἐπὶ πάσης τῆς γάζης αὐτῆς, ὃς ἐληλύθει προσκυνήσων εἰς Ἱερουσαλήμ, 28 ἦν τε ὑποστρέφων καὶ καθήμενος ἐπὶ τοῦ ἅρματος αὐτοῦ καὶ ἀνεγίνωσκεν τὸν προφήτην Ἡσαΐαν. 29 εἶπεν δὲ τὸ πνεῦμα τῷ Φιλίππῳ, Πρόσελθε καὶ κολλήθητι τῷ ἅρματι τούτῳ. 30 προσδραμὼν δὲ ὁ Φίλιππος ἤκουσεν αὐτοῦ ἀναγινώσκοντος Ἡσαΐαν τὸν προφήτην καὶ εἶπεν, Ἆρά γε γινώσκεις ἃ ἀναγινώσκεις; 31 ὁ δὲ εἶπεν, Πῶς γὰρ ἂν δυναίμην ἐὰν μή τις ὁδηγήσει με; παρεκάλεσέν τε τὸν Φίλιππον ἀναβάντα καθίσαι σὺν αὐτῷ. 32 ἡ δὲ περιοχὴ τῆς γραφῆς ἣν ἀνεγίνωσκεν ἦν αὕτη·

Ὡς πρόβατον ἐπὶ σφαγὴν ἤχθη
  καὶ ὡς ἀμνὸς ἐναντίον τοῦ
    κείραντος αὐτὸν ἄφωνος,
  οὕτως οὐκ ἀνοίγει τὸ στόμα
    αὐτοῦ.
33 Ἐν τῇ ταπεινώσει [αὐτοῦ] ἡ
    κρίσις αὐτοῦ ἤρθη·
  τὴν γενεὰν αὐτοῦ τίς διηγήσεται;
    ὅτι αἴρεται ἀπὸ τῆς γῆς ἡ
      ζωὴ αὐτοῦ.

34 Ἀποκριθεὶς δὲ ὁ εὐνοῦχος τῷ Φιλίππῳ εἶπεν, Δέομαί σου, περὶ τίνος ὁ προφήτης λέγει τοῦτο[b]; περὶ ἑαυτοῦ ἢ περὶ ἑτέρου τινός; 35 ἀνοίξας δὲ ὁ Φίλιππος τὸ στόμα αὐτοῦ καὶ ἀρξάμενος ἀπὸ τῆς γραφῆς ταύτης εὐηγγελίσατο αὐτῷ τὸν Ἰησοῦν. 36 ὡς δὲ ἐπορεύοντο κατὰ τὴν ὁδόν, ἦλθον ἐπί τι ὕδωρ, καί φησιν ὁ εὐνοῦχος, Ἰδοὺ ὕδωρ, τί κωλύει με βαπτισθῆναι;[c] 38 καὶ ἐκέλευσεν στῆναι τὸ ἅρμα καὶ κατέβησαν ἀμφότεροι εἰς τὸ ὕδωρ, ὅ τε Φίλιππος καὶ ὁ

23"For I see that you are full of bitterness and captive to sin."

24Then Simon answered, "Pray to the Lord for me so that nothing you have said may happen to me."

25When they had testified and proclaimed the word of the Lord, Peter and John returned to Jerusalem, preaching the gospel in many Samaritan villages.

Philip and the Ethiopian

26Now an angel of the Lord said to Philip, "Go south to the road—the desert road—that goes down from Jerusalem to Gaza." 27So he started out, and on his way he met an Ethiopian[d] eunuch, an important official in charge of all the treasury of Candace, queen of the Ethiopians. This man had gone to Jerusalem to worship, 28and on his way home was sitting in his chariot reading the book of Isaiah the prophet. 29The Spirit told Philip, "Go to that chariot and stay near it."

30Then Philip ran up to the chariot and heard the man reading Isaiah the prophet. "Do you understand what you are reading?" Philip asked.

31"How can I," he said, "unless someone explains it to me?" So he invited Philip to come up and sit with him.

32The eunuch was reading this passage of Scripture:

"He was led like a sheep to the
  slaughter,
  and as a lamb before the shearer is
    silent,
  so he did not open his mouth.
33In his humiliation he was deprived of
    justice.
  Who can speak of his descendants?
  For his life was taken from the
    earth."[e]

34The eunuch asked Philip, "Tell me, please, who is the prophet talking about, himself or someone else?" 35Then Philip began with that very passage of Scripture and told him the good news about Jesus.

36As they traveled along the road, they came to some water and the eunuch said, "Look, here is water. Why shouldn't I be baptized?"[f] 38And he gave orders to stop the chariot. Then both Philip and the eunuch went down into the water and

---

k The Greek word for *you* and the verb *pray* are plural
l Gk *after they*   m Or *go at noon*   n Other ancient authorities add all or most of verse 37, *And Philip said, "If you believe with all your heart, you may." And he replied, "I believe that Jesus Christ is the Son of God."*

b34 NIV text omits τοῦτο †   c36 NIV/NRSV notes add 37 εἶπε δὲ αὐτῷ, Εἰ πιστεύεις ἐξ ὅλης καρδίας σου, ἔξεστιν· ἀποκριθεὶς δὲ εἶπε, Πιστεύω τὸν υἱὸν τοῦ θεοῦ εἶναι Ἰησοῦν Χριστόν

d27 That is, from the upper Nile region   e33 Isaiah 53:7,8   f36 Some late manuscripts *baptized?"* 37*Philip said, "If you believe with all your heart, you may." The eunuch answered, "I believe that Jesus Christ is the Son of God."*

Philip[o] baptized him. 39When they came up out of the water, the Spirit of the Lord snatched Philip away; the eunuch saw him no more, and went on his way rejoicing. 40But Philip found himself at Azotus, and as he was passing through the region, he proclaimed the good news to all the towns until he came to Caesarea.

The Conversion of Saul

9 Meanwhile Saul, still breathing threats and murder against the disciples of the Lord, went to the high priest 2and asked him for letters to the synagogues at Damascus, so that if he found any who belonged to the Way, men or women, he might bring them bound to Jerusalem. 3Now as he was going along and approaching Damascus, suddenly a light from heaven flashed around him. 4He fell to the ground and heard a voice saying to him, "Saul, Saul, why do you persecute me?" 5He asked, "Who are you, Lord?" The reply came, "I am Jesus, whom you are persecuting. 6But get up and enter the city, and you will be told what you are to do." 7The men who were traveling with him stood speechless because they heard the voice but saw no one. 8Saul got up from the ground, and though his eyes were open, he could see nothing; so they led him by the hand and brought him into Damascus. 9For three days he was without sight, and neither ate nor drank.

10 Now there was a disciple in Damascus named Ananias. The Lord said to him in a vision, "Ananias." He answered, "Here I am, Lord." 11The Lord said to him, "Get up and go to the street called Straight, and at the house of Judas look for a man of Tarsus named Saul. At this moment he is praying, 12and he has seen in a vision[p] a man named Ananias come in and lay his hands on him so that he might regain his sight." 13But Ananias answered, "Lord, I have heard from many about this man, how much evil he has done to your saints in Jerusalem; 14and here he has authority from the chief priests to bind all who invoke your name." 15But the Lord said to him, "Go, for he is an instrument whom I have chosen to bring my name before Gentiles and kings and before the people of Israel; 16I myself will show him how much he must suffer for the sake of my name."

εὐνοῦχος, καὶ ἐβάπτισεν αὐτόν. 39 ὅτε δὲ ἀνέβησαν ἐκ τοῦ ὕδατος, πνεῦμα κυρίου ἥρπασεν τὸν Φίλιππον καὶ οὐκ εἶδεν αὐτὸν οὐκέτι ὁ εὐνοῦχος, ἐπορεύετο γὰρ τὴν ὁδὸν αὐτοῦ χαίρων. 40 Φίλιππος δὲ εὑρέθη εἰς Ἄζωτον· καὶ διερχόμενος εὐηγγελίζετο τὰς πόλεις πάσας ἕως τοῦ ἐλθεῖν αὐτὸν εἰς Καισάρειαν.

9 Ὁ δὲ Σαῦλος ἔτι ἐμπνέων ἀπειλῆς καὶ φόνου εἰς τοὺς μαθητὰς τοῦ κυρίου, προσελθὼν τῷ ἀρχιερεῖ 2 ᾐτήσατο παρ' αὐτοῦ ἐπιστολὰς εἰς Δαμασκὸν πρὸς τὰς συναγωγάς, ὅπως ἐάν τινας εὕρῃ τῆς ὁδοῦ ὄντας, ἄνδρας τε καὶ γυναῖκας, δεδεμένους ἀγάγῃ εἰς Ἰερουσαλήμ. 3 ἐν δὲ τῷ πορεύεσθαι ἐγένετο αὐτὸν ἐγγίζειν τῇ Δαμασκῷ, ἐξαίφνης τε αὐτὸν περιήστραψεν φῶς ἐκ τοῦ οὐρανοῦ 4 καὶ πεσὼν ἐπὶ τὴν γῆν ἤκουσεν φωνὴν λέγουσαν αὐτῷ, Σαοὺλ Σαούλ, τί με διώκεις; 5 εἶπεν δέ, Τίς εἶ, κύριε; ὁ δέ, Ἐγώ εἰμι Ἰησοῦς ὃν σὺ διώκεις· 6 ἀλλὰ ἀνάστηθι καὶ εἴσελθε εἰς τὴν πόλιν καὶ λαληθήσεταί σοι ὅ τί σε δεῖ ποιεῖν. 7 οἱ δὲ ἄνδρες οἱ συνοδεύοντες αὐτῷ εἱστήκεισαν ἐνεοί, ἀκούοντες μὲν τῆς φωνῆς μηδένα δὲ θεωροῦντες. 8 ἠγέρθη δὲ Σαῦλος ἀπὸ τῆς γῆς, ἀνεῳγμένων δὲ τῶν ὀφθαλμῶν αὐτοῦ οὐδὲν ἔβλεπεν· χειραγωγοῦντες δὲ αὐτὸν εἰσήγαγον εἰς Δαμασκόν. 9 καὶ ἦν ἡμέρας τρεῖς μὴ βλέπων καὶ οὐκ ἔφαγεν οὐδὲ ἔπιεν.

10 Ἦν δέ τις μαθητὴς ἐν Δαμασκῷ ὀνόματι Ἀνανίας, καὶ εἶπεν πρὸς αὐτὸν ἐν ὁράματι ὁ κύριος, Ἀνανία. ὁ δὲ εἶπεν, Ἰδοὺ ἐγώ, κύριε. 11 ὁ δὲ κύριος πρὸς αὐτόν, Ἀναστὰς πορεύθητι ἐπὶ τὴν ῥύμην τὴν καλουμένην Εὐθεῖαν καὶ ζήτησον ἐν οἰκίᾳ Ἰούδα Σαῦλον ὀνόματι Ταρσέα· ἰδοὺ γὰρ προσεύχεται 12 καὶ εἶδεν ἄνδρα [ἐν ὁράματι] Ἀνανίαν ὀνόματι εἰσελθόντα καὶ ἐπιθέντα αὐτῷ [τὰς] χεῖρας ὅπως ἀναβλέψῃ. 13 ἀπεκρίθη δὲ Ἀνανίας, Κύριε, ἤκουσα ἀπὸ πολλῶν περὶ τοῦ ἀνδρὸς τούτου ὅσα κακὰ τοῖς ἁγίοις σου ἐποίησεν ἐν Ἰερουσαλήμ· 14 καὶ ὧδε ἔχει ἐξουσίαν παρὰ τῶν ἀρχιερέων δῆσαι πάντας τοὺς ἐπικαλουμένους τὸ ὄνομά σου. 15 εἶπεν δὲ πρὸς αὐτὸν ὁ κύριος, Πορεύου, ὅτι σκεῦος ἐκλογῆς ἐστίν μοι οὗτος τοῦ βαστάσαι τὸ ὄνομά μου ἐνώπιον ἐθνῶν τε καὶ βασιλέων υἱῶν τε Ἰσραήλ· 16 ἐγὼ γὰρ ὑποδείξω αὐτῷ ὅσα δεῖ αὐτὸν ὑπὲρ τοῦ ὀνόματός μου παθεῖν. 17 Ἀπῆλθεν

Saul's Conversion

Philip baptized him. 39When they came up out of the water, the Spirit of the Lord suddenly took Philip away, and the eunuch did not see him again, but went on his way rejoicing. 40Philip, however, appeared at Azotus and traveled about, preaching the gospel in all the towns until he reached Caesarea.

9 Meanwhile, Saul was still breathing out murderous threats against the Lord's disciples. He went to the high priest 2and asked him for letters to the synagogues in Damascus, so that if he found any there who belonged to the Way, whether men or women, he might take them as prisoners to Jerusalem. 3As he neared Damascus on his journey, suddenly a light from heaven flashed around him. 4He fell to the ground and heard a voice say to him, "Saul, Saul, why do you persecute me?"

5"Who are you, Lord?" Saul asked.

"I am Jesus, whom you are persecuting," he replied. 6"Now get up and go into the city, and you will be told what you must do."

7The men traveling with Saul stood there speechless; they heard the sound but did not see anyone. 8Saul got up from the ground, but when he opened his eyes he could see nothing. So they led him by the hand into Damascus. 9For three days he was blind, and did not eat or drink anything.

10In Damascus there was a disciple named Ananias. The Lord called to him in a vision, "Ananias!"

"Yes, Lord," he answered.

11The Lord told him, "Go to the house of Judas on Straight Street and ask for a man from Tarsus named Saul, for he is praying. 12In a vision he has seen a man named Ananias come and place his hands on him to restore his sight."

13"Lord," Ananias answered, "I have heard many reports about this man and all the harm he has done to your saints in Jerusalem. 14And he has come here with authority from the chief priests to arrest all who call on your name."

15But the Lord said to Ananias, "Go! This man is my chosen instrument to carry my name before the Gentiles and their kings and before the people of Israel. 16I will show him how much he must suffer for my name."

°Gk *he* ᵖOther ancient authorities lack *in a vision*

[17]So Ananias went and entered the house. He laid his hands on Saul[q] and said, "Brother Saul, the Lord Jesus, who appeared to you on your way here, has sent me so that you may regain your sight and be filled with the Holy Spirit." [18]And immediately something like scales fell from his eyes, and his sight was restored. Then he got up and was baptized, [19]and after taking some food, he regained his strength.

Saul Preaches in Damascus

For several days he was with the disciples in Damascus, [20]and immediately he began to proclaim Jesus in the synagogues, saying, "He is the Son of God." [21]All who heard him were amazed and said, "Is not this the man who made havoc in Jerusalem among those who invoked this name? And has he not come here for the purpose of bringing them bound before the chief priests?" [22]Saul became increasingly more powerful and confounded the Jews who lived in Damascus by proving that Jesus[r] was the Messiah.[s]

Saul Escapes from the Jews

[23]After some time had passed, the Jews plotted to kill him, [24]but their plot became known to Saul. They were watching the gates day and night so that they might kill him; [25]but his disciples took him by night and let him down through an opening in the wall,[t] lowering him in a basket.

Saul in Jerusalem

[26]When he had come to Jerusalem, he attempted to join the disciples; and they were all afraid of him, for they did not believe that he was a disciple. [27]But Barnabas took him, brought him to the apostles, and described for them how on the road he had seen the Lord, who had spoken to him, and how in Damascus he had spoken boldly in the name of Jesus. [28]So he went in and out among them in Jerusalem, speaking boldly in the name of the Lord. [29]He spoke and argued with the Hellenists; but they were attempting to kill him. [30]When the believers[u] learned of it, they brought him down to Caesarea and sent him off to Tarsus.

[31]Meanwhile the church throughout Judea, Galilee, and Samaria had peace and was built up. Living in the fear of the Lord and in the comfort of the Holy Spirit, it increased in numbers.

δὲ Ἀνανίας καὶ εἰσῆλθεν εἰς τὴν οἰκίαν καὶ ἐπιθεὶς ἐπ' αὐτὸν τὰς χεῖρας εἶπεν, Σαοὺλ ἀδελφέ, ὁ κύριος ἀπέσταλκέν με, Ἰησοῦς ὁ ὀφθείς σοι ἐν τῇ ὁδῷ ᾗ ἤρχου, ὅπως ἀναβλέψῃς καὶ πλησθῇς πνεύματος ἁγίου. 18 καὶ εὐθέως ἀπέπεσαν αὐτοῦ ἀπὸ τῶν ὀφθαλμῶν ὡς λεπίδες, ἀνέβλεψέν τε καὶ ἀναστὰς ἐβαπτίσθη 19 καὶ λαβὼν τροφὴν ἐνίσχυσεν.

Ἐγένετο δὲ μετὰ τῶν ἐν Δαμασκῷ μαθητῶν ἡμέρας τινάς 20 καὶ εὐθέως ἐν ταῖς συναγωγαῖς ἐκήρυσσεν τὸν Ἰησοῦν ὅτι οὗτός ἐστιν ὁ υἱὸς τοῦ θεοῦ. 21 ἐξίσταντο δὲ πάντες οἱ ἀκούοντες καὶ ἔλεγον, Οὐχ οὗτός ἐστιν ὁ πορθήσας εἰς Ἰερουσαλὴμ τοὺς ἐπικαλουμένους τὸ ὄνομα τοῦτο, καὶ ὧδε εἰς τοῦτο ἐληλύθει ἵνα δεδεμένους αὐτοὺς ἀγάγῃ ἐπὶ τοὺς ἀρχιερεῖς; 22 Σαῦλος δὲ μᾶλλον ἐνεδυναμοῦτο καὶ συνέχυννεν [τοὺς] Ἰουδαίους τοὺς κατοικοῦντας ἐν Δαμασκῷ συμβιβάζων ὅτι οὗτός ἐστιν ὁ Χριστός.

23 Ὡς δὲ ἐπληροῦντο ἡμέραι ἱκαναί, συνεβουλεύσαντο οἱ Ἰουδαῖοι ἀνελεῖν αὐτόν· 24 ἐγνώσθη δὲ τῷ Σαύλῳ ἡ ἐπιβουλὴ αὐτῶν. παρετηροῦντο δὲ καὶ τὰς πύλας ἡμέρας τε καὶ νυκτὸς ὅπως αὐτὸν ἀνέλωσιν· 25 λαβόντες δὲ οἱ μαθηταὶ αὐτοῦ νυκτὸς διὰ τοῦ τείχους καθῆκαν αὐτὸν χαλάσαντες ἐν σπυρίδι.

26 Παραγενόμενος δὲ εἰς Ἰερουσαλὴμ ἐπείραζεν κολλᾶσθαι τοῖς μαθηταῖς, καὶ πάντες ἐφοβοῦντο αὐτὸν μὴ πιστεύοντες ὅτι ἐστὶν μαθητής. 27 Βαρναβᾶς δὲ ἐπιλαβόμενος αὐτὸν ἤγαγεν πρὸς τοὺς ἀποστόλους καὶ διηγήσατο αὐτοῖς πῶς ἐν τῇ ὁδῷ εἶδεν τὸν κύριον καὶ ὅτι ἐλάλησεν αὐτῷ καὶ πῶς ἐν Δαμασκῷ ἐπαρρησιάσατο ἐν τῷ ὀνόματι τοῦ Ἰησοῦ. 28 καὶ ἦν μετ' αὐτῶν εἰσπορευόμενος καὶ ἐκπορευόμενος εἰς Ἰερουσαλήμ, παρρησιαζόμενος ἐν τῷ ὀνόματι τοῦ κυρίου, 29 ἐλάλει τε καὶ συνεζήτει πρὸς τοὺς Ἑλληνιστάς, οἱ δὲ ἐπεχείρουν ἀνελεῖν αὐτόν. 30 ἐπιγνόντες δὲ οἱ ἀδελφοὶ κατήγαγον αὐτὸν εἰς Καισάρειαν καὶ ἐξαπέστειλαν αὐτὸν εἰς Ταρσόν.

31 Ἡ μὲν οὖν ἐκκλησία καθ' ὅλης τῆς Ἰουδαίας καὶ Γαλιλαίας καὶ Σαμαρείας εἶχεν εἰρήνην οἰκοδομουμένη καὶ πορευομένη τῷ φόβῳ τοῦ κυρίου καὶ τῇ παρακλήσει τοῦ ἁγίου πνεύματος ἐπληθύνετο.

[17]Then Ananias went to the house and entered it. Placing his hands on Saul, he said, "Brother Saul, the Lord—Jesus, who appeared to you on the road as you were coming here—has sent me so that you may see again and be filled with the Holy Spirit." [18]Immediately, something like scales fell from Saul's eyes, and he could see again. He got up and was baptized, [19]and after taking some food, he regained his strength.

Saul in Damascus and Jerusalem

Saul spent several days with the disciples in Damascus. [20]At once he began to preach in the synagogues that Jesus is the Son of God. [21]All those who heard him were astonished and asked, "Isn't he the man who raised havoc in Jerusalem among those who call on this name? And hasn't he come here to take them as prisoners to the chief priests?" [22]Yet Saul grew more and more powerful and baffled the Jews living in Damascus by proving that Jesus is the Christ.[a]

[23]After many days had gone by, the Jews conspired to kill him, [24]but Saul learned of their plan. Day and night they kept close watch on the city gates in order to kill him. [25]But his followers took him by night and lowered him in a basket through an opening in the wall.

[26]When he came to Jerusalem, he tried to join the disciples, but they were all afraid of him, not believing that he really was a disciple. [27]But Barnabas took him and brought him to the apostles. He told them how Saul on his journey had seen the Lord and that the Lord had spoken to him, and how in Damascus he had preached fearlessly in the name of Jesus. [28]So Saul stayed with them and moved about freely in Jerusalem, speaking boldly in the name of the Lord. [29]He talked and debated with the Grecian Jews, but they tried to kill him. [30]When the brothers learned of this, they took him down to Caesarea and sent him off to Tarsus.

[31]Then the church throughout Judea, Galilee and Samaria enjoyed a time of peace. It was strengthened; and encouraged by the Holy Spirit, it grew in numbers, living in the fear of the Lord.

---

[q]Gk him [r]Gk that this [s]Or the Christ [t]Gk through the wall [u]Gk brothers

[a]22 Or Messiah

The Healing of Aeneas

32 Now as Peter went here and there among all the believers,[v] he came down also to the saints living in Lydda. 33There he found a man named Aeneas, who had been bedridden for eight years, for he was paralyzed. 34Peter said to him, "Aeneas, Jesus Christ heals you; get up and make your bed!" And immediately he got up. 35And all the residents of Lydda and Sharon saw him and turned to the Lord.

Peter in Lydda and Joppa

36 Now in Joppa there was a disciple whose name was Tabitha, which in Greek is Dorcas.[w] She was devoted to good works and acts of charity. 37At that time she became ill and died. When they had washed her, they laid her in a room upstairs. 38Since Lydda was near Joppa, the disciples, who heard that Peter was there, sent two men to him with the request, "Please come to us without delay." 39So Peter got up and went with them; and when he arrived, they took him to the room upstairs. All the widows stood beside him, weeping and showing tunics and other clothing that Dorcas had made while she was with them. 40Peter put all of them outside, and then he knelt down and prayed. He turned to the body and said, "Tabitha, get up." Then she opened her eyes, and seeing Peter, she sat up. 41He gave her his hand and helped her up. Then calling the saints and widows, he showed her to be alive. 42This became known throughout Joppa, and many believed in the Lord. 43Meanwhile he stayed in Joppa for some time with a certain Simon, a tanner.

Peter and Cornelius

10 In Caesarea there was a man named Cornelius, a centurion of the Italian Cohort, as it was called. 2He was a devout man who feared God with all his household; he gave alms generously to the people and prayed constantly to God. 3One afternoon at about three o'clock he had a vision in which he clearly saw an angel of God coming in and saying to him, "Cornelius." 4He stared at him in terror and said, "What is it, Lord?" He answered, "Your prayers and your alms have ascended as a memorial before God. 5Now send men to Joppa for a certain Simon

Aeneas and Dorcas

32As Peter traveled about the country, he went to visit the saints in Lydda. 33There he found a man named Aeneas, a paralytic who had been bedridden for eight years. 34"Aeneas," Peter said to him, "Jesus Christ heals you. Get up and take care of your mat." Immediately Aeneas got up. 35All those who lived in Lydda and Sharon saw him and turned to the Lord.

36In Joppa there was a disciple named Tabitha (which, when translated, is Dorcas[b]), who was always doing good and helping the poor. 37About that time she became sick and died, and her body was washed and placed in an upstairs room. 38Lydda was near Joppa; so when the disciples heard that Peter was in Lydda, they sent two men to him and urged him, "Please come at once!"

39Peter went with them, and when he arrived he was taken upstairs to the room. All the widows stood around him, crying and showing him the robes and other clothing that Dorcas had made while she was still with them.

40Peter sent them all out of the room; then he got down on his knees and prayed. Turning toward the dead woman, he said, "Tabitha, get up." She opened her eyes, and seeing Peter she sat up. 41He took her by the hand and helped her to her feet. Then he called the believers and the widows and presented her to them alive. 42This became known all over Joppa, and many people believed in the Lord. 43Peter stayed in Joppa for some time with a tanner named Simon.

Cornelius Calls for Peter

10 At Caesarea there was a man named Cornelius, a centurion in what was known as the Italian Regiment. 2He and all his family were devout and God-fearing; he gave generously to those in need and prayed to God regularly. 3One day at about three in the afternoon he had a vision. He distinctly saw an angel of God, who came to him and said, "Cornelius!"

4Cornelius stared at him in fear. "What is it, Lord?" he asked.

The angel answered, "Your prayers and gifts to the poor have come up as a memorial offering before God. 5Now send men to Joppa to bring back a man named Simon

v Gk all of them   w The name Tabitha in Aramaic and the name Dorcas in Greek mean a gazelle

b36 Both Tabitha (Aramaic) and Dorcas (Greek) mean gazelle.

who is called Peter; ⁶he is lodging with Simon, a tanner, whose house is by the seaside." ⁷When the angel who spoke to him had left, he called two of his slaves and a devout soldier from the ranks of those who served him, ⁸and after telling them everything, he sent them to Joppa.

9 About noon the next day, as they were on their journey and approaching the city, Peter went up on the roof to pray. ¹⁰He became hungry and wanted something to eat; and while it was being prepared, he fell into a trance. ¹¹He saw the heaven opened and something like a large sheet coming down, being lowered to the ground by its four corners. ¹²In it were all kinds of four-footed creatures and reptiles and birds of the air. ¹³Then he heard a voice saying, "Get up, Peter; kill and eat." ¹⁴But Peter said, "By no means, Lord; for I have never eaten anything that is profane or unclean." ¹⁵The voice said to him again, a second time, "What God has made clean, you must not call profane." ¹⁶This happened three times, and the thing was suddenly taken up to heaven.

17 Now while Peter was greatly puzzled about what to make of the vision that he had seen, suddenly the men sent by Cornelius appeared. They were asking for Simon's house and were standing by the gate. ¹⁸They called out to ask whether Simon, who was called Peter, was staying there. ¹⁹While Peter was still thinking about the vision, the Spirit said to him, "Look, threeˣ men are searching for you. ²⁰Now get up, go down, and go with them without hesitation; for I have sent them." ²¹So Peter went down to the men and said, "I am the one you are looking for; what is the reason for your coming?" ²²They answered, "Cornelius, a centurion, an upright and God-fearing man, who is well spoken of by the whole Jewish nation, was directed by a holy angel to send for you to come to his house and to hear what you have to say." ²³So Peterʸ invited them in and gave them lodging.

The next day he got up and went with them, and some of the believersᶻ from Joppa accompanied him. ²⁴The following day they came to Caesarea. Cornelius was

ἐπικαλεῖται Πέτρος· 6 οὗτος ξενίζεται παρά τινι Σίμωνι βυρσεῖ, ᾧ ἐστιν οἰκία παρὰ θάλασσαν. 7 ὡς δὲ ἀπῆλθεν ὁ ἄγγελος ὁ λαλῶν αὐτῷ, φωνήσας δύο τῶν οἰκετῶν καὶ στρατιώτην εὐσεβῆ τῶν προσκαρτερούντων αὐτῷ 8 καὶ ἐξηγησάμενος ἅπαντα αὐτοῖς ἀπέστειλεν αὐτοὺς εἰς τὴν Ἰόππην.

9 Τῇ δὲ ἐπαύριον, ὁδοιπορούντων ἐκείνων καὶ τῇ πόλει ἐγγιζόντων, ἀνέβη Πέτρος ἐπὶ τὸ δῶμα προσεύξασθαι περὶ ὥραν ἕκτην. 10 ἐγένετο δὲ πρόσπεινος καὶ ἤθελεν γεύσασθαι. παρασκευαζόντων δὲ αὐτῶν ἐγένετο ἐπ᾽ αὐτὸν ἔκστασις 11 καὶ θεωρεῖ τὸν οὐρανὸν ἀνεῳγμένον καὶ καταβαῖνον σκεῦός τι ὡς ὀθόνην μεγάλην τέσσαρσιν ἀρχαῖς καθιέμενον ἐπὶ τῆς γῆς, 12 ἐν ᾧ ὑπῆρχεν πάντα τὰ τετράποδα καὶ ἑρπετὰ τῆς γῆς καὶ πετεινὰ τοῦ οὐρανοῦ. 13 καὶ ἐγένετο φωνὴ πρὸς αὐτόν, Ἀναστάς, Πέτρε, θῦσον καὶ φάγε. 14 ὁ δὲ Πέτρος εἶπεν, Μηδαμῶς, κύριε, ὅτι οὐδέποτε ἔφαγον πᾶν κοινὸν καὶ ἀκάθαρτον. 15 καὶ φωνὴ πάλιν ἐκ δευτέρου πρὸς αὐτόν, Ἅ ὁ θεὸς ἐκαθάρισεν, σὺ μὴ κοίνου. 16 τοῦτο δὲ ἐγένετο ἐπὶ τρὶς καὶ εὐθὺς ἀνελήμφθη τὸ σκεῦος εἰς τὸν οὐρανόν.

17 Ὡς δὲ ἐν ἑαυτῷ διηπόρει ὁ Πέτρος τί ἂν εἴη τὸ ὅραμα ὃ εἶδεν, ἰδοὺ οἱ ἄνδρες οἱ ἀπεσταλμένοι ὑπὸ τοῦ Κορνηλίου διερωτήσαντες τὴν οἰκίαν τοῦ Σίμωνος ἐπέστησαν ἐπὶ τὸν πυλῶνα, 18 καὶ φωνήσαντες ἐπυνθάνοντο εἰ Σίμων ὁ ἐπικαλούμενος Πέτρος ἐνθάδε ξενίζεται. 19 τοῦ δὲ Πέτρου διενθυμουμένου περὶ τοῦ ὁράματος εἶπεν [αὐτῷ] τὸ πνεῦμα, Ἰδοὺ ἄνδρες τρεῖςᵃ ζητοῦντές σε, 20 ἀλλὰ ἀναστὰς κατάβηθι καὶ πορεύου σὺν αὐτοῖς μηδὲν διακρινόμενος ὅτι ἐγὼ ἀπέσταλκα αὐτούς. 21 καταβὰς δὲ Πέτρος πρὸς τοὺς ἄνδρας εἶπεν, Ἰδοὺ ἐγώ εἰμι ὃν ζητεῖτε· τίς ἡ αἰτία δι᾽ ἣν πάρεστε; 22 οἱ δὲ εἶπαν, Κορνήλιος ἑκατοντάρχης, ἀνὴρ δίκαιος καὶ φοβούμενος τὸν θεόν, μαρτυρούμενός τε ὑπὸ ὅλου τοῦ ἔθνους τῶν Ἰουδαίων, ἐχρηματίσθη ὑπὸ ἀγγέλου ἁγίου μεταπέμψασθαί σε εἰς τὸν οἶκον αὐτοῦ καὶ ἀκοῦσαι ῥήματα παρὰ σοῦ. 23 εἰσκαλεσάμενος οὖν αὐτοὺς ἐξένισεν.

Τῇ δὲ ἐπαύριον ἀναστὰς ἐξῆλθεν σὺν αὐτοῖς καί τινες τῶν ἀδελφῶν τῶν ἀπὸ Ἰόππης συνῆλθον αὐτῷ. 24 τῇ δὲ ἐπαύριον εἰσῆλθεν εἰς τὴν Καισάρειαν. ὁ δὲ Κορνήλιος ἦν προσδοκῶν αὐτοὺς

who is called Peter. ⁶He is staying with Simon the tanner, whose house is by the sea."

⁷When the angel who spoke to him had gone, Cornelius called two of his servants and a devout soldier who was one of his attendants. ⁸He told them everything that had happened and sent them to Joppa.

Peter's Vision

⁹About noon the following day as they were on their journey and approaching the city, Peter went up on the roof to pray. ¹⁰He became hungry and wanted something to eat, and while the meal was being prepared, he fell into a trance. ¹¹He saw heaven opened and something like a large sheet being let down to earth by its four corners. ¹²It contained all kinds of four-footed animals, as well as reptiles of the earth and birds of the air. ¹³Then a voice told him, "Get up, Peter. Kill and eat."

¹⁴"Surely not, Lord!" Peter replied. "I have never eaten anything impure or unclean."

¹⁵The voice spoke to him a second time, "Do not call anything impure that God has made clean."

¹⁶This happened three times, and immediately the sheet was taken back to heaven.

¹⁷While Peter was wondering about the meaning of the vision, the men sent by Cornelius found out where Simon's house was and stopped at the gate. ¹⁸They called out, asking if Simon who was known as Peter was staying there.

¹⁹While Peter was still thinking about the vision, the Spirit said to him, "Simon, threeᵃ men are looking for you. ²⁰So get up and go downstairs. Do not hesitate to go with them, for I have sent them."

²¹Peter went down and said to the men, "I'm the one you're looking for. Why have you come?"

²²The men replied, "We have come from Cornelius the centurion. He is a righteous and God-fearing man, who is respected by all the Jewish people. A holy angel told him to have you come to his house so that he could hear what you have to say." ²³Then Peter invited the men into the house to be his guests.

Peter at Cornelius' House

The next day Peter started out with them, and some of the brothers from Joppa went along. ²⁴The following day he arrived in

---

ˣ One ancient authority reads *two*; others lack the word   ʸ Gk *he*   ᶻ Gk *brothers*

ᵃ19 NIV/NRSV notes δύο or omit τρεῖς

ᵃ19 One early manuscript *two*; other manuscripts do not have the number.

expecting them and had called together his relatives and close friends. 25On Peter's arrival Cornelius met him, and falling at his feet, worshiped him. 26But Peter made him get up, saying, "Stand up; I am only a mortal." 27And as he talked with him, he went in and found that many had assembled; 28and he said to them, "You yourselves know that it is unlawful for a Jew to associate with or to visit a Gentile; but God has shown me that I should not call anyone profane or unclean. 29So when I was sent for, I came without objection. Now may I ask why you sent for me?"

30 Cornelius replied, "Four days ago at this very hour, at three o'clock, I was praying in my house when suddenly a man in dazzling clothes stood before me. 31He said, 'Cornelius, your prayer has been heard and your alms have been remembered before God. 32Send therefore to Joppa and ask for Simon, who is called Peter; he is staying in the home of Simon, a tanner, by the sea.' 33Therefore I sent for you immediately, and you have been kind enough to come. So now all of us are here in the presence of God to listen to all that the Lord has commanded you to say."

Gentiles Hear the Good News

34 Then Peter began to speak to them: "I truly understand that God shows no partiality, 35but in every nation anyone who fears him and does what is right is acceptable to him. 36You know the message he sent to the people of Israel, preaching peace by Jesus Christ—he is Lord of all. 37That message spread throughout Judea, beginning in Galilee after the baptism that John announced: 38how God anointed Jesus of Nazareth with the Holy Spirit and with power; how he went about doing good and healing all who were oppressed by the devil, for God was with him. 39We are witnesses to all that he did both in Judea and in Jerusalem. They put him to death by hanging him on a tree; 40but God raised him on the third day and allowed him to appear, 41not to all the people but to us who were chosen by God as witnesses,

συγκαλεσάμενος τοὺς συγγενεῖς αὐτοῦ καὶ τοὺς ἀναγκαίους φίλους. 25 ὡς δὲ ἐγένετο τοῦ εἰσελθεῖν τὸν Πέτρον, συναντήσας αὐτῷ ὁ Κορνήλιος πεσὼν ἐπὶ τοὺς πόδας προσεκύνησεν. 26 ὁ δὲ Πέτρος ἤγειρεν αὐτὸν λέγων, Ἀνάστηθι· καὶ ἐγὼ αὐτὸς ἄνθρωπός εἰμι. 27 καὶ συνομιλῶν αὐτῷ εἰσῆλθεν καὶ εὑρίσκει συνεληλυθότας πολλούς, 28 ἔφη τε πρὸς αὐτούς, Ὑμεῖς ἐπίστασθε ὡς ἀθέμιτόν ἐστιν ἀνδρὶ Ἰουδαίῳ κολλᾶσθαι ἢ προσέρχεσθαι ἀλλοφύλῳ· κἀμοὶ ὁ θεὸς ἔδειξεν μηδένα κοινὸν ἢ ἀκάθαρτον λέγειν ἄνθρωπον· 29 διὸ καὶ ἀναντιρρήτως ἦλθον μεταπεμφθείς. πυνθάνομαι οὖν τίνι λόγῳ μετεπέμψασθέ με; 30 καὶ ὁ Κορνήλιος ἔφη, Ἀπὸ τετάρτης ἡμέρας μέχρι ταύτης τῆς ὥρας ἤμην τὴν ἐνάτην προσευχόμενος ἐν τῷ οἴκῳ μου, καὶ ἰδοὺ ἀνὴρ ἔστη ἐνώπιόν μου ἐν ἐσθῆτι λαμπρᾷ 31 καὶ φησίν, Κορνήλιε, εἰσηκούσθη σου ἡ προσευχὴ καὶ αἱ ἐλεημοσύναι σου ἐμνήσθησαν ἐνώπιον τοῦ θεοῦ. 32 πέμψον οὖν εἰς Ἰόππην καὶ μετακάλεσαι Σίμωνα ὃς ἐπικαλεῖται Πέτρος, οὗτος ξενίζεται ἐν οἰκίᾳ Σίμωνος βυρσέως παρὰ θάλασσαν. 33 ἐξαυτῆς οὖν ἔπεμψα πρὸς σέ, σύ τε καλῶς ἐποίησας παραγενόμενος. νῦν οὖν πάντες ἡμεῖς ἐνώπιον τοῦ θεοῦ πάρεσμεν ἀκοῦσαι πάντα τὰ προστεταγμένα σοι ὑπὸ τοῦ κυρίου.

34 Ἀνοίξας δὲ Πέτρος τὸ στόμα εἶπεν, Ἐπ' ἀληθείας καταλαμβάνομαι ὅτι οὐκ ἔστιν προσωπολήμπτης ὁ θεός, 35 ἀλλ' ἐν παντὶ ἔθνει ὁ φοβούμενος αὐτὸν καὶ ἐργαζόμενος δικαιοσύνην δεκτὸς αὐτῷ ἐστιν. 36 τὸν λόγον [ὃν] ἀπέστειλεν τοῖς υἱοῖς Ἰσραὴλ εὐαγγελιζόμενος εἰρήνην διὰ Ἰησοῦ Χριστοῦ, οὗτός ἐστιν πάντων κύριος, 37 ὑμεῖς οἴδατε τὸ γενόμενον ῥῆμα καθ' ὅλης τῆς Ἰουδαίας, ἀρξάμενος ἀπὸ τῆς Γαλιλαίας μετὰ τὸ βάπτισμα ὃ ἐκήρυξεν Ἰωάννης, 38 Ἰησοῦν τὸν ἀπὸ Ναζαρέθ, ὡς ἔχρισεν αὐτὸν ὁ θεὸς πνεύματι ἁγίῳ καὶ δυνάμει, ὃς διῆλθεν εὐεργετῶν καὶ ἰώμενος πάντας τοὺς καταδυναστευομένους ὑπὸ τοῦ διαβόλου, ὅτι ὁ θεὸς ἦν μετ' αὐτοῦ. 39 καὶ ἡμεῖς μάρτυρες πάντων ὧν ἐποίησεν ἔν τε τῇ χώρᾳ τῶν Ἰουδαίων καὶ [ἐν] Ἰερουσαλήμ. ὃν καὶ ἀνεῖλαν κρεμάσαντες ἐπὶ ξύλου, 40 τοῦτον ὁ θεὸς ἤγειρεν [ἐν] τῇ τρίτῃ ἡμέρᾳ καὶ ἔδωκεν αὐτὸν ἐμφανῆ γενέσθαι, 41 οὐ παντὶ τῷ λαῷ ἀλλὰ μάρτυσιν τοῖς προκεχειροτονημένοις ὑπὸ τοῦ θεοῦ, ἡμῖν, οἵτινες

Caesarea. Cornelius was expecting them and had called together his relatives and close friends. 25As Peter entered the house, Cornelius met him and fell at his feet in reverence. 26But Peter made him get up. "Stand up," he said, "I am only a man myself."

27Talking with him, Peter went inside and found a large gathering of people. 28He said to them: "You are well aware that it is against our law for a Jew to associate with a Gentile or visit him. But God has shown me that I should not call any man impure or unclean. 29So when I was sent for, I came without raising any objection. May I ask why you sent for me?"

30Cornelius answered: "Four days ago I was in my house praying at this hour, at three in the afternoon. Suddenly a man in shining clothes stood before me 31and said, 'Cornelius, God has heard your prayer and remembered your gifts to the poor. 32Send to Joppa for Simon who is called Peter. He is a guest in the home of Simon the tanner, who lives by the sea.' 33So I sent for you immediately, and it was good of you to come. Now we are all here in the presence of God to listen to everything the Lord has commanded you to tell us."

34Then Peter began to speak: "I now realize how true it is that God does not show favoritism 35but accepts men from every nation who fear him and do what is right. 36You know the message God sent to the people of Israel, telling the good news of peace through Jesus Christ, who is Lord of all. 37You know what has happened throughout Judea, beginning in Galilee after the baptism that John preached—38how God anointed Jesus of Nazareth with the Holy Spirit and power, and how he went around doing good and healing all who were under the power of the devil, because God was with him.

39"We are witnesses of everything he did in the country of the Jews and in Jerusalem. They killed him by hanging him on a tree, 40but God raised him from the dead on the third day and caused him to be seen. 41He was not seen by all the people, but by witnesses whom God had already

and who ate and drank with him after he rose from the dead. ⁴²He commanded us to preach to the people and to testify that he is the one ordained by God as judge of the living and the dead. ⁴³All the prophets testify about him that everyone who believes in him receives forgiveness of sins through his name."

Gentiles Receive the Holy Spirit

44 While Peter was still speaking, the Holy Spirit fell upon all who heard the word. ⁴⁵The circumcised believers who had come with Peter were astounded that the gift of the Holy Spirit had been poured out even on the Gentiles, ⁴⁶for they heard them speaking in tongues and extolling God. Then Peter said, ⁴⁷"Can anyone withhold the water for baptizing these people who have received the Holy Spirit just as we have?" ⁴⁸So he ordered them to be baptized in the name of Jesus Christ. Then they invited him to stay for several days.

Peter's Report to the Church at Jerusalem

11 Now the apostles and the believersᵃ who were in Judea heard that the Gentiles had also accepted the word of God. ²So when Peter went up to Jerusalem, the circumcised believersᵇ criticized him, ³saying, "Why did you go to uncircumcised men and eat with them?" ⁴Then Peter began to explain it to them, step by step, saying, ⁵"I was in the city of Joppa praying, and in a trance I saw a vision. There was something like a large sheet coming down from heaven, being lowered by its four corners; and it came close to me. ⁶As I looked at it closely I saw four-footed animals, beasts of prey, reptiles, and birds of the air. ⁷I also heard a voice saying to me, 'Get up, Peter; kill and eat.' ⁸But I replied, 'By no means, Lord; for nothing profane or unclean has ever entered my mouth.' ⁹But a second time the voice answered from heaven, 'What God has made clean, you must not call profane.' ¹⁰This happened three times; then everything was pulled up again to heaven. ¹¹At that very moment three men, sent to me from Caesarea, arrived at the house where we were. ¹²The Spirit told me to go with them and not to make a distinction between us and them.ᶜ These six brothers

chosen—by us who ate and drank with him after he rose from the dead. ⁴²He commanded us to preach to the people and to testify that he is the one whom God appointed as judge of the living and the dead. ⁴³All the prophets testify about him that everyone who believes in him receives forgiveness of sins through his name."

⁴⁴While Peter was still speaking these words, the Holy Spirit came on all who heard the message. ⁴⁵The circumcised believers who had come with Peter were astonished that the gift of the Holy Spirit had been poured out even on the Gentiles. ⁴⁶For they heard them speaking in tonguesᵇ and praising God.

Then Peter said, ⁴⁷"Can anyone keep these people from being baptized with water? They have received the Holy Spirit just as we have." ⁴⁸So he ordered that they be baptized in the name of Jesus Christ. Then they asked Peter to stay with them for a few days.

Peter Explains His Actions

11 The apostles and the brothers throughout Judea heard that the Gentiles also had received the word of God. ²So when Peter went up to Jerusalem, the circumcised believers criticized him ³and said, "You went into the house of uncircumcised men and ate with them."

⁴Peter began and explained everything to them precisely as it had happened: ⁵"I was in the city of Joppa praying, and in a trance I saw a vision. I saw something like a large sheet being let down from heaven by its four corners, and it came down to where I was. ⁶I looked into it and saw four-footed animals of the earth, wild beasts, reptiles, and birds of the air. ⁷Then I heard a voice telling me, 'Get up, Peter. Kill and eat.'

⁸"I replied, 'Surely not, Lord! Nothing impure or unclean has ever entered my mouth.'

⁹"The voice spoke from heaven a second time, 'Do not call anything impure that God has made clean.' ¹⁰This happened three times, and then it was all pulled up to heaven again.

¹¹"Right then three men who had been sent to me from Caesarea stopped at the house where I was staying. ¹²The Spirit told me to have no hesitation about going with them. These six brothers also went

also accompanied me, and we entered the man's house. [13]He told us how he had seen the angel standing in his house and saying, 'Send to Joppa and bring Simon, who is called Peter; [14]he will give you a message by which you and your entire household will be saved.' [15]And as I began to speak, the Holy Spirit fell upon them just as it had upon us at the beginning. [16]And I remembered the word of the Lord, how he had said, 'John baptized with water, but you will be baptized with the Holy Spirit.' [17]If then God gave them the same gift that he gave us when we believed in the Lord Jesus Christ, who was I that I could hinder God?" [18]When they heard this, they were silenced. And they praised God, saying, "Then God has given even to the Gentiles the repentance that leads to life."

The Church in Antioch

19 Now those who were scattered because of the persecution that took place over Stephen traveled as far as Phoenicia, Cyprus, and Antioch, and they spoke the word to no one except Jews. [20]But among them were some men of Cyprus and Cyrene who, on coming to Antioch, spoke to the Hellenists[d] also, proclaiming the Lord Jesus. [21]The hand of the Lord was with them, and a great number became believers and turned to the Lord. [22]News of this came to the ears of the church in Jerusalem, and they sent Barnabas to Antioch. [23]When he came and saw the grace of God, he rejoiced, and he exhorted them all to remain faithful to the Lord with steadfast devotion; [24]for he was a good man, full of the Holy Spirit and of faith. And a great many people were brought to the Lord. [25]Then Barnabas went to Tarsus to look for Saul, [26]and when he had found him, he brought him to Antioch. So it was that for an entire year they met with[e] the church and taught a great many people, and it was in Antioch that the disciples were first called "Christians."

27 At that time prophets came down from Jerusalem to Antioch. [28]One of them named Agabus stood up and predicted by the Spirit that there would be a severe famine over all the world; and this took place

οὗτοι καὶ εἰσήλθομεν εἰς τὸν οἶκον τοῦ ἀνδρός. **13** ἀπήγγειλεν δὲ ἡμῖν πῶς εἶδεν [τὸν] ἄγγελον ἐν τῷ οἴκῳ αὐτοῦ σταθέντα καὶ εἰπόντα, Ἀπόστειλον εἰς Ἰόππην καὶ μετάπεμψαι Σίμωνα τὸν ἐπικαλούμενον Πέτρον, **14** ὃς λαλήσει ῥήματα πρὸς σὲ ἐν οἷς σωθήσῃ σὺ καὶ πᾶς ὁ οἶκός σου. **15** ἐν δὲ τῷ ἄρξασθαί με λαλεῖν ἐπέπεσεν τὸ πνεῦμα τὸ ἅγιον ἐπ' αὐτοὺς ὥσπερ καὶ ἐφ' ἡμᾶς ἐν ἀρχῇ. **16** ἐμνήσθην δὲ τοῦ ῥήματος τοῦ κυρίου ὡς ἔλεγεν, Ἰωάννης μὲν ἐβάπτισεν ὕδατι, ὑμεῖς δὲ βαπτισθήσεσθε ἐν πνεύματι ἁγίῳ. **17** εἰ οὖν τὴν ἴσην δωρεὰν ἔδωκεν αὐτοῖς ὁ θεὸς ὡς καὶ ἡμῖν πιστεύσασιν ἐπὶ τὸν κύριον Ἰησοῦν Χριστόν, ἐγὼ τίς ἤμην δυνατὸς κωλῦσαι τὸν θεόν; **18** ἀκούσαντες δὲ ταῦτα ἡσύχασαν καὶ ἐδόξασαν τὸν θεὸν λέγοντες, Ἄρα καὶ τοῖς ἔθνεσιν ὁ θεὸς τὴν μετάνοιαν εἰς ζωὴν ἔδωκεν.

19 Οἱ μὲν οὖν διασπαρέντες ἀπὸ τῆς θλίψεως τῆς γενομένης ἐπὶ Στεφάνῳ διῆλθον ἕως Φοινίκης καὶ Κύπρου καὶ Ἀντιοχείας μηδενὶ λαλοῦντες τὸν λόγον εἰ μὴ μόνον Ἰουδαίοις. **20** ἦσαν δέ τινες ἐξ αὐτῶν ἄνδρες Κύπριοι καὶ Κυρηναῖοι, οἵτινες ἐλθόντες εἰς Ἀντιόχειαν ἐλάλουν καὶ πρὸς τοὺς Ἑλληνιστὰς[b] εὐαγγελιζόμενοι τὸν κύριον Ἰησοῦν. **21** καὶ ἦν χεὶρ κυρίου μετ' αὐτῶν, πολύς τε ἀριθμὸς ὁ πιστεύσας ἐπέστρεψεν ἐπὶ τὸν κύριον. **22** ἠκούσθη δὲ ὁ λόγος εἰς τὰ ὦτα τῆς ἐκκλησίας τῆς οὔσης ἐν Ἰερουσαλὴμ περὶ αὐτῶν καὶ ἐξαπέστειλαν Βαρναβᾶν [διελθεῖν][c] ἕως Ἀντιοχείας. **23** ὃς παραγενόμενος καὶ ἰδὼν τὴν χάριν [τὴν] τοῦ θεοῦ, ἐχάρη καὶ παρεκάλει πάντας τῇ προθέσει τῆς καρδίας προσμένειν τῷ κυρίῳ, **24** ὅτι ἦν ἀνὴρ ἀγαθὸς καὶ πλήρης πνεύματος ἁγίου καὶ πίστεως. καὶ προσετέθη ὄχλος ἱκανὸς τῷ κυρίῳ. **25** ἐξῆλθεν δὲ εἰς Ταρσὸν ἀναζητῆσαι Σαῦλον, **26** καὶ εὑρὼν ἤγαγεν εἰς Ἀντιόχειαν. ἐγένετο δὲ αὐτοῖς καὶ ἐνιαυτὸν ὅλον συναχθῆναι ἐν τῇ ἐκκλησίᾳ καὶ διδάξαι ὄχλον ἱκανόν, χρηματίσαι τε πρώτως ἐν Ἀντιοχείᾳ τοὺς μαθητὰς Χριστιανούς.

27 Ἐν ταύταις δὲ ταῖς ἡμέραις κατῆλθον ἀπὸ Ἱεροσολύμων προφῆται εἰς Ἀντιόχειαν. **28** ἀναστὰς δὲ εἷς ἐξ αὐτῶν ὀνόματι Ἄγαβος ἐσήμανεν διὰ τοῦ πνεύματος λιμὸν μεγάλην μέλλειν ἔσεσθαι ἐφ' ὅλην τὴν οἰκουμένην, ἥτις

with me, and we entered the man's house. [13]He told us how he had seen an angel appear in his house and say, 'Send to Joppa for Simon who is called Peter. [14]He will bring you a message through which you and all your household will be saved.'

[15]"As I began to speak, the Holy Spirit came on them as he had come on us at the beginning. [16]Then I remembered what the Lord had said: 'John baptized with[a] water, but you will be baptized with the Holy Spirit.' [17]So if God gave them the same gift as he gave us, who believed in the Lord Jesus Christ, who was I to think that I could oppose God?"

[18]When they heard this, they had no further objections and praised God, saying, "So then, God has granted even to the Gentiles repentance unto life."

The Church in Antioch

[19]Now those who had been scattered by the persecution in connection with Stephen traveled as far as Phoenicia, Cyprus and Antioch, telling the message only to Jews. [20]Some of them, however, men from Cyprus and Cyrene, went to Antioch and began to speak to Greeks also, telling them the good news about the Lord Jesus. [21]The Lord's hand was with them, and a great number of people believed and turned to the Lord.

[22]News of this reached the ears of the church at Jerusalem, and they sent Barnabas to Antioch. [23]When he arrived and saw the evidence of the grace of God, he was glad and encouraged them all to remain true to the Lord with all their hearts. [24]He was a good man, full of the Holy Spirit and faith, and a great number of people were brought to the Lord.

[25]Then Barnabas went to Tarsus to look for Saul, [26]and when he found him, he brought him to Antioch. So for a whole year Barnabas and Saul met with the church and taught great numbers of people. The disciples were called Christians first at Antioch.

[27]During this time some prophets came down from Jerusalem to Antioch. [28]One of them, named Agabus, stood up and through the Spirit predicted that a severe famine would spread over the entire Roman world. (This happened during the

---

[d] Other ancient authorities read *Greeks*
[e] Or *were guests of*

[b]20 NIV text and NRSV note d Ἕλληνας   [c]22 NIV text omits διελθεῖν

[a]16 Or *in*

during the reign of Claudius. ²⁹The disciples determined that according to their ability, each would send relief to the believersᶠ living in Judea; ³⁰this they did, sending it to the elders by Barnabas and Saul.

James Killed and Peter Imprisoned

12 About that time King Herod laid violent hands upon some who belonged to the church. ²He had James, the brother of John, killed with the sword. ³After he saw that it pleased the Jews, he proceeded to arrest Peter also. (This was during the festival of Unleavened Bread.) ⁴When he had seized him, he put him in prison and handed him over to four squads of soldiers to guard him, intending to bring him out to the people after the Passover. ⁵While Peter was kept in prison, the church prayed fervently to God for him.

Peter Delivered from Prison

6 The very night before Herod was going to bring him out, Peter, bound with two chains, was sleeping between two soldiers, while guards in front of the door were keeping watch over the prison. ⁷Suddenly an angel of the Lord appeared and a light shone in the cell. He tapped Peter on the side and woke him, saying, "Get up quickly." And the chains fell off his wrists. ⁸The angel said to him, "Fasten your belt and put on your sandals." He did so. Then he said to him, "Wrap your cloak around you and follow me." ⁹Peterᵍ went out and followed him; he did not realize that what was happening with the angel's help was real; he thought he was seeing a vision. ¹⁰After they had passed the first and the second guard, they came before the iron gate leading into the city. It opened for them of its own accord, and they went outside and walked along a lane, when suddenly the angel left him. ¹¹Then Peter came to himself and said, "Now I am sure that the Lord has sent his angel and rescued me from the hands of Herod and from all that the Jewish people were expecting."

12 As soon as he realized this, he went to the house of Mary, the mother of John whose other name was Mark, where many had gathered and were praying. ¹³When he knocked at the outer gate, a maid named

ἐγένετο ἐπὶ Κλαυδίου. **29** τῶν δὲ μαθητῶν, καθὼς εὐπορεῖτό τις ὥρισαν ἕκαστος αὐτῶν εἰς διακονίαν πέμψαι τοῖς κατοικοῦσιν ἐν τῇ Ἰουδαίᾳ ἀδελφοῖς· **30** ὃ καὶ ἐποίησαν ἀποστείλαντες πρὸς τοὺς πρεσβυτέρους διὰ χειρὸς Βαρναβᾶ καὶ Σαύλου.

12 Κατ' ἐκεῖνον δὲ τὸν καιρὸν ἐπέβαλεν Ἡρῴδης ὁ βασιλεὺς τὰς χεῖρας κακῶσαί τινας τῶν ἀπὸ τῆς ἐκκλησίας. **2** ἀνεῖλεν δὲ Ἰάκωβον τὸν ἀδελφὸν Ἰωάννου μαχαίρῃ. **3** ἰδὼν δὲ ὅτι ἀρεστόν ἐστιν τοῖς Ἰουδαίοις προσέθετο συλλαβεῖν καὶ Πέτρον, – ἦσαν δὲ [αἱ] ἡμέραι τῶν ἀζύμων – **4** ὃν καὶ πιάσας ἔθετο εἰς φυλακὴν παραδοὺς τέσσαρσιν τετραδίοις στρατιωτῶν φυλάσσειν αὐτόν, βουλόμενος μετὰ τὸ πάσχα ἀναγαγεῖν αὐτὸν τῷ λαῷ. **5** ὁ μὲν οὖν Πέτρος ἐτηρεῖτο ἐν τῇ φυλακῇ· προσευχὴ δὲ ἦν ἐκτενῶς γινομένη ὑπὸ τῆς ἐκκλησίας πρὸς τὸν θεὸν περὶ αὐτοῦ.

6 Ὅτε δὲ ἤμελλεν προαγαγεῖν αὐτὸν ὁ Ἡρῴδης, τῇ νυκτὶ ἐκείνῃ ἦν ὁ Πέτρος κοιμώμενος μεταξὺ δύο στρατιωτῶν δεδεμένος ἁλύσεσιν δυσὶν φύλακές τε πρὸ τῆς θύρας ἐτήρουν τὴν φυλακήν. **7** καὶ ἰδοὺ ἄγγελος κυρίου ἐπέστη καὶ φῶς ἔλαμψεν ἐν τῷ οἰκήματι· πατάξας δὲ τὴν πλευρὰν τοῦ Πέτρου ἤγειρεν αὐτὸν λέγων, Ἀνάστα ἐν τάχει. καὶ ἐξέπεσαν αὐτοῦ αἱ ἁλύσεις ἐκ τῶν χειρῶν. **8** εἶπεν δὲ ὁ ἄγγελος πρὸς αὐτόν, Ζῶσαι καὶ ὑπόδησαι τὰ σανδάλιά σου. ἐποίησεν δὲ οὕτως. καὶ λέγει αὐτῷ, Περιβαλοῦ τὸ ἱμάτιόν σου καὶ ἀκολούθει μοι. **9** καὶ ἐξελθὼν ἠκολούθει καὶ οὐκ ᾔδει ὅτι ἀληθές ἐστιν τὸ γινόμενον διὰ τοῦ ἀγγέλου· ἐδόκει δὲ ὅραμα βλέπειν. **10** διελθόντες δὲ πρώτην φυλακὴν καὶ δευτέραν ἦλθαν ἐπὶ τὴν πύλην τὴν σιδηρᾶν τὴν φέρουσαν εἰς τὴν πόλιν, ἥτις αὐτομάτη ἠνοίγη αὐτοῖς καὶ ἐξελθόντες προῆλθον ῥύμην μίαν, καὶ εὐθέως ἀπέστη ὁ ἄγγελος ἀπ' αὐτοῦ. **11** καὶ ὁ Πέτρος ἐν ἑαυτῷ γενόμενος εἶπεν, Νῦν οἶδα ἀληθῶς ὅτι ἐξαπέστειλεν [ὁ] κύριος τὸν ἄγγελον αὐτοῦ καὶ ἐξείλατό με ἐκ χειρὸς Ἡρῴδου καὶ πάσης τῆς προσδοκίας τοῦ λαοῦ τῶν Ἰουδαίων. **12** συνιδών τε ἦλθεν ἐπὶ τὴν οἰκίαν τῆς Μαρίας τῆς μητρὸς Ἰωάννου τοῦ ἐπικαλουμένου Μάρκου, οὗ ἦσαν ἱκανοὶ συνηθροισμένοι καὶ προσευχόμενοι. **13** κρούσαντος δὲ αὐτοῦ τὴν θύραν τοῦ πυλῶνος προσῆλθεν

reign of Claudius.) ²⁹The disciples, each according to his ability, decided to provide help for the brothers living in Judea. ³⁰This they did, sending their gift to the elders by Barnabas and Saul.

Peter's Miraculous Escape From Prison

12 It was about this time that King Herod arrested some who belonged to the church, intending to persecute them. ²He had James, the brother of John, put to death with the sword. ³When he saw that this pleased the Jews, he proceeded to seize Peter also. This happened during the Feast of Unleavened Bread. ⁴After arresting him, he put him in prison, handing him over to be guarded by four squads of four soldiers each. Herod intended to bring him out for public trial after the Passover.

⁵So Peter was kept in prison, but the church was earnestly praying to God for him.

⁶The night before Herod was to bring him to trial, Peter was sleeping between two soldiers, bound with two chains, and sentries stood guard at the entrance. ⁷Suddenly an angel of the Lord appeared and a light shone in the cell. He struck Peter on the side and woke him up. "Quick, get up!" he said, and the chains fell off Peter's wrists.

⁸Then the angel said to him, "Put on your clothes and sandals." And Peter did so. "Wrap your cloak around you and follow me," the angel told him. ⁹Peter followed him out of the prison, but he had no idea that what the angel was doing was really happening; he thought he was seeing a vision. ¹⁰They passed the first and second guards and came to the iron gate leading to the city. It opened for them by itself, and they went through it. When they had walked the length of one street, suddenly the angel left him.

¹¹Then Peter came to himself and said, "Now I know without a doubt that the Lord sent his angel and rescued me from Herod's clutches and from everything the Jewish people were anticipating."

¹²When this had dawned on him, he went to the house of Mary the mother of John, also called Mark, where many people had gathered and were praying. ¹³Peter knocked at the outer entrance, and a

Rhoda came to answer. [14]On recognizing Peter's voice, she was so overjoyed that, instead of opening the gate, she ran in and announced that Peter was standing at the gate. [15]They said to her, "You are out of your mind!" But she insisted that it was so. They said, "It is his angel." [16]Meanwhile Peter continued knocking; and when they opened the gate, they saw him and were amazed. [17]He motioned to them with his hand to be silent, and described for them how the Lord had brought him out of the prison. And he added, "Tell this to James and to the believers."[h] Then he left and went to another place.

18 When morning came, there was no small commotion among the soldiers over what had become of Peter. [19]When Herod had searched for him and could not find him, he examined the guards and ordered them to be put to death. Then he went down from Judea to Caesarea and stayed there.

The Death of Herod

20 Now Herod[i] was angry with the people of Tyre and Sidon. So they came to him in a body; and after winning over Blastus, the king's chamberlain, they asked for a reconciliation, because their country depended on the king's country for food. [21]On an appointed day Herod put on his royal robes, took his seat on the platform, and delivered a public address to them. [22]The people kept shouting, "The voice of a god, and not of a mortal!" [23]And immediately, because he had not given the glory to God, an angel of the Lord struck him down, and he was eaten by worms and died.

24 But the word of God continued to advance and gain adherents. [25]Then after completing their mission Barnabas and Saul returned to[j] Jerusalem and brought with them John, whose other name was Mark.

Barnabas and Saul Commissioned

13 Now in the church at Antioch there were prophets and teachers: Barnabas, Simeon who was called Niger, Lucius of Cyrene, Manaen a member of the court of Herod the ruler,[k] and Saul. [2]While they were worshiping the Lord and fasting, the Holy Spirit said, "Set apart for me Barnabas and Saul for the work to which I have called them." [3]Then after

παιδίσκη ὑπακοῦσαι ὀνόματι Ῥόδη. **14** καὶ ἐπιγνοῦσα τὴν φωνὴν τοῦ Πέτρου ἀπὸ τῆς χαρᾶς οὐκ ἤνοιξεν τὸν πυλῶνα, εἰσδραμοῦσα δὲ ἀπήγγειλεν ἑστάναι τὸν Πέτρον πρὸ τοῦ πυλῶνος. **15** οἱ δὲ πρὸς αὐτὴν εἶπαν, Μαίνῃ. ἡ δὲ διϊσχυρίζετο οὕτως ἔχειν. οἱ δὲ ἔλεγον, Ὁ ἄγγελός ἐστιν αὐτοῦ. **16** ὁ δὲ Πέτρος ἐπέμενεν κρούων· ἀνοίξαντες δὲ εἶδαν αὐτὸν καὶ ἐξέστησαν. **17** κατασείσας δὲ αὐτοῖς τῇ χειρὶ σιγᾶν διηγήσατο [αὐτοῖς] πῶς ὁ κύριος αὐτὸν ἐξήγαγεν ἐκ τῆς φυλακῆς εἶπέν τε, Ἀπαγγείλατε Ἰακώβῳ καὶ τοῖς ἀδελφοῖς ταῦτα. καὶ ἐξελθὼν ἐπορεύθη εἰς ἕτερον τόπον.

18 Γενομένης δὲ ἡμέρας ἦν τάραχος οὐκ ὀλίγος ἐν τοῖς στρατιώταις τί ἄρα ὁ Πέτρος ἐγένετο. **19** Ἡρῴδης δὲ ἐπιζητήσας αὐτὸν καὶ μὴ εὑρών, ἀνακρίνας τοὺς φύλακας ἐκέλευσεν ἀπαχθῆναι, καὶ κατελθὼν ἀπὸ τῆς Ἰουδαίας εἰς Καισάρειαν διέτριβεν.

20 Ἦν δὲ θυμομαχῶν Τυρίοις καὶ Σιδωνίοις· ὁμοθυμαδὸν δὲ παρῆσαν πρὸς αὐτὸν καὶ πείσαντες Βλάστον, τὸν ἐπὶ τοῦ κοιτῶνος τοῦ βασιλέως, ἠτοῦντο εἰρήνην διὰ τὸ τρέφεσθαι αὐτῶν τὴν χώραν ἀπὸ τῆς βασιλικῆς. **21** τακτῇ δὲ ἡμέρᾳ ὁ Ἡρῴδης ἐνδυσάμενος ἐσθῆτα βασιλικὴν [καὶ] καθίσας ἐπὶ τοῦ βήματος ἐδημηγόρει πρὸς αὐτούς, **22** ὁ δὲ δῆμος ἐπεφώνει, Θεοῦ φωνὴ καὶ οὐκ ἀνθρώπου. **23** παραχρῆμα δὲ ἐπάταξεν αὐτὸν ἄγγελος κυρίου ἀνθ᾽ ὧν οὐκ ἔδωκεν τὴν δόξαν τῷ θεῷ, καὶ γενόμενος σκωληκόβρωτος ἐξέψυξεν.

24 Ὁ δὲ λόγος τοῦ θεοῦ ηὔξανεν καὶ ἐπληθύνετο. **25** Βαρναβᾶς δὲ καὶ Σαῦλος ὑπέστρεψαν εἰς[a] Ἰερουσαλὴμ πληρώσαντες τὴν διακονίαν, συμπαραλαβόντες Ἰωάννην τὸν ἐπικληθέντα Μᾶρκον.

13 Ἦσαν δὲ ἐν Ἀντιοχείᾳ κατὰ τὴν οὖσαν ἐκκλησίαν προφῆται καὶ διδάσκαλοι ὅ τε Βαρναβᾶς καὶ Συμεὼν ὁ καλούμενος Νίγερ καὶ Λούκιος ὁ Κυρηναῖος, Μαναήν τε Ἡρῴδου τοῦ τετραάρχου σύντροφος καὶ Σαῦλος. **2** λειτουργούντων δὲ αὐτῶν τῷ κυρίῳ καὶ νηστευόντων εἶπεν τὸ πνεῦμα τὸ ἅγιον, Ἀφορίσατε δή μοι τὸν Βαρναβᾶν καὶ Σαῦλον εἰς τὸ ἔργον ὃ προσκέκλημαι αὐτούς. **3** τότε

servant girl named Rhoda came to answer the door. [14]When she recognized Peter's voice, she was so overjoyed she ran back without opening it and exclaimed, "Peter is at the door!"

[15]"You're out of your mind," they told her. When she kept insisting that it was so, they said, "It must be his angel."

[16]But Peter kept on knocking, and when they opened the door and saw him, they were astonished. [17]Peter motioned with his hand for them to be quiet and described how the Lord had brought him out of prison. "Tell James and the brothers about this," he said, and then he left for another place.

[18]In the morning, there was no small commotion among the soldiers as to what had become of Peter. [19]After Herod had a thorough search made for him and did not find him, he cross-examined the guards and ordered that they be executed.

Herod's Death

Then Herod went from Judea to Caesarea and stayed there a while. [20]He had been quarreling with the people of Tyre and Sidon; they now joined together and sought an audience with him. Having secured the support of Blastus, a trusted personal servant of the king, they asked for peace, because they depended on the king's country for their food supply.

[21]On the appointed day Herod, wearing his royal robes, sat on his throne and delivered a public address to the people. [22]They shouted, "This is the voice of a god, not of a man." [23]Immediately, because Herod did not give praise to God, an angel of the Lord struck him down, and he was eaten by worms and died.

[24]But the word of God continued to increase and spread.

[25]When Barnabas and Saul had finished their mission, they returned from[a] Jerusalem, taking with them John, also called Mark.

Barnabas and Saul Sent Off

13 In the church at Antioch there were prophets and teachers: Barnabas, Simeon called Niger, Lucius of Cyrene, Manaen (who had been brought up with Herod the tetrarch) and Saul. [2]While they were worshiping the Lord and fasting, the Holy Spirit said, "Set apart for me Barnabas and Saul for the work to which I have called them." [3]So after they

---

[h] Gk *brothers*   [i] Gk *he*   [j] Other ancient authorities read *from*   [k] Gk *tetrarch*

[a] 25 NIV text and NRSV note j ἀπὸ; NIV note and NRSV text as UBS

[a] 25 Some manuscripts *to*

fasting and praying they laid their hands on them and sent them off.

The Apostles Preach in Cyprus

4 So, being sent out by the Holy Spirit, they went down to Seleucia; and from there they sailed to Cyprus. 5When they arrived at Salamis, they proclaimed the word of God in the synagogues of the Jews. And they had John also to assist them. 6When they had gone through the whole island as far as Paphos, they met a certain magician, a Jewish false prophet, named Bar-Jesus. 7He was with the proconsul, Sergius Paulus, an intelligent man, who summoned Barnabas and Saul and wanted to hear the word of God. 8But the magician Elymas (for that is the translation of his name) opposed them and tried to turn the proconsul away from the faith. 9But Saul, also known as Paul, filled with the Holy Spirit, looked intently at him 10and said, "You son of the devil, you enemy of all righteousness, full of all deceit and villainy, will you not stop making crooked the straight paths of the Lord? 11And now listen—the hand of the Lord is against you, and you will be blind for a while, unable to see the sun." Immediately mist and darkness came over him, and he went about groping for someone to lead him by the hand. 12When the proconsul saw what had happened, he believed, for he was astonished at the teaching about the Lord.

Paul and Barnabas in Antioch of Pisidia

13 Then Paul and his companions set sail from Paphos and came to Perga in Pamphylia. John, however, left them and returned to Jerusalem; 14but they went on from Perga and came to Antioch in Pisidia. And on the sabbath day they went into the synagogue and sat down. 15After the reading of the law and the prophets, the officials of the synagogue sent them a message, saying, "Brothers, if you have any word of exhortation for the people, give it." 16So Paul stood up and with a gesture began to speak:

"You Israelites,[l] and others who fear God, listen. 17The God of this people Israel chose our ancestors and made the people great during their stay in the land of Egypt, and with uplifted arm he led them out of it. 18For about forty years he put up with[m]

νηστεύσαντες καὶ προσευξάμενοι καὶ ἐπιθέντες τὰς χεῖρας αὐτοῖς ἀπέλυσαν.

4 Αὐτοὶ μὲν οὖν ἐκπεμφθέντες ὑπὸ τοῦ ἁγίου πνεύματος κατῆλθον εἰς Σελεύκειαν, ἐκεῖθέν τε ἀπέπλευσαν εἰς Κύπρον 5 καὶ γενόμενοι ἐν Σαλαμῖνι κατήγγελλον τὸν λόγον τοῦ θεοῦ ἐν ταῖς συναγωγαῖς τῶν Ἰουδαίων. εἶχον δὲ καὶ Ἰωάννην ὑπηρέτην. 6 διελθόντες δὲ ὅλην τὴν νῆσον ἄχρι Πάφου εὗρον ἄνδρα τινὰ μάγον ψευδοπροφήτην Ἰουδαῖον ᾧ ὄνομα Βαριησοῦ 7 ὃς ἦν σὺν τῷ ἀνθυπάτῳ Σεργίῳ Παύλῳ, ἀνδρὶ συνετῷ. οὗτος προσκαλεσάμενος Βαρναβᾶν καὶ Σαῦλον ἐπεζήτησεν ἀκοῦσαι τὸν λόγον τοῦ θεοῦ. 8 ἀνθίστατο δὲ αὐτοῖς Ἐλύμας ὁ μάγος, οὕτως γὰρ μεθερμηνεύεται τὸ ὄνομα αὐτοῦ, ζητῶν διαστρέψαι τὸν ἀνθύπατον ἀπὸ τῆς πίστεως. 9 Σαῦλος δέ, ὁ καὶ Παῦλος, πλησθεὶς πνεύματος ἁγίου ἀτενίσας εἰς αὐτὸν 10 εἶπεν,[a] Ὦ πλήρης παντὸς δόλου καὶ πάσης ῥᾳδιουργίας, υἱὲ διαβόλου, ἐχθρὲ πάσης δικαιοσύνης, οὐ παύσῃ διαστρέφων τὰς ὁδοὺς [τοῦ] κυρίου τὰς εὐθείας; 11 καὶ νῦν ἰδοὺ χεὶρ κυρίου ἐπὶ σὲ καὶ ἔσῃ τυφλὸς μὴ βλέπων τὸν ἥλιον ἄχρι καιροῦ. παραχρῆμά τε ἔπεσεν ἐπ᾽ αὐτὸν ἀχλὺς καὶ σκότος καὶ περιάγων ἐζήτει χειραγωγούς. 12 τότε ἰδὼν ὁ ἀνθύπατος τὸ γεγονὸς ἐπίστευσεν ἐκπλησσόμενος ἐπὶ τῇ διδαχῇ τοῦ κυρίου.

13 Ἀναχθέντες δὲ ἀπὸ τῆς Πάφου οἱ περὶ Παῦλον ἦλθον εἰς Πέργην τῆς Παμφυλίας, Ἰωάννης δὲ ἀποχωρήσας ἀπ᾽ αὐτῶν ὑπέστρεψεν εἰς Ἱεροσόλυμα. 14 αὐτοὶ δὲ διελθόντες ἀπὸ τῆς Πέργης παρεγένοντο εἰς Ἀντιόχειαν τὴν Πισιδίαν, καὶ [εἰσ]ελθόντες εἰς τὴν συναγωγὴν τῇ ἡμέρᾳ τῶν σαββάτων ἐκάθισαν. 15 μετὰ δὲ τὴν ἀνάγνωσιν τοῦ νόμου καὶ τῶν προφητῶν ἀπέστειλαν οἱ ἀρχισυνάγωγοι πρὸς αὐτοὺς λέγοντες,

Ἄνδρες ἀδελφοί, εἴ τίς ἐστιν ἐν ὑμῖν λόγος παρακλήσεως πρὸς τὸν λαόν, λέγετε. 16 ἀναστὰς δὲ Παῦλος καὶ κατασείσας τῇ χειρὶ εἶπεν· Ἄνδρες Ἰσραηλῖται καὶ οἱ φοβούμενοι τὸν θεόν, ἀκούσατε. 17 ὁ θεὸς τοῦ λαοῦ τούτου Ἰσραὴλ ἐξελέξατο τοὺς πατέρας ἡμῶν καὶ τὸν λαὸν ὕψωσεν ἐν τῇ παροικίᾳ ἐν γῇ Αἰγύπτου καὶ μετὰ βραχίονος ὑψηλοῦ ἐξήγαγεν αὐτοὺς ἐξ αὐτῆς, 18 καὶ ὡς τεσσερακονταετῆ χρόνον ἐτροποφόρησεν[b] αὐτοὺς ἐν τῇ ἐρήμῳ

had fasted and prayed, they placed their hands on them and sent them off.

On Cyprus

4The two of them, sent on their way by the Holy Spirit, went down to Seleucia and sailed from there to Cyprus. 5When they arrived at Salamis, they proclaimed the word of God in the Jewish synagogues. John was with them as their helper.

6They traveled through the whole island until they came to Paphos. There they met a Jewish sorcerer and false prophet named Bar-Jesus, 7who was an attendant of the proconsul, Sergius Paulus. The proconsul, an intelligent man, sent for Barnabas and Saul because he wanted to hear the word of God. 8But Elymas the sorcerer (for that is what his name means) opposed them and tried to turn the proconsul from the faith. 9Then Saul, who was also called Paul, filled with the Holy Spirit, looked straight at Elymas and said, 10"You are a child of the devil and an enemy of everything that is right! You are full of all kinds of deceit and trickery. Will you never stop perverting the right ways of the Lord? 11Now the hand of the Lord is against you. You are going to be blind, and for a time you will be unable to see the light of the sun."

Immediately mist and darkness came over him, and he groped about, seeking someone to lead him by the hand. 12When the proconsul saw what had happened, he believed, for he was amazed at the teaching about the Lord.

In Pisidian Antioch

13From Paphos, Paul and his companions sailed to Perga in Pamphylia, where John left them to return to Jerusalem. 14From Perga they went on to Pisidian Antioch. On the Sabbath they entered the synagogue and sat down. 15After the reading from the Law and the Prophets, the synagogue rulers sent word to them, saying, "Brothers, if you have a message of encouragement for the people, please speak."

16Standing up, Paul motioned with his hand and said: "Men of Israel and you Gentiles who worship God, listen to me! 17The God of the people of Israel chose our fathers; he made the people prosper during their stay in Egypt, with mighty power he led them out of that country, 18he endured their conduct[a] for about forty years in the

---

l Gk Men, Israelites   m Other ancient authorities read cared for

a10 NIV reads εἶπεν in verse 9   b18 NIV/NRSV notes ἐτροφοφόρησεν

a18 Some manuscripts and cared for them

them in the wilderness. [19]After he had destroyed seven nations in the land of Canaan, he gave them their land as an inheritance [20]for about four hundred fifty years. After that he gave them judges until the time of the prophet Samuel. [21]Then they asked for a king; and God gave them Saul son of Kish, a man of the tribe of Benjamin, who reigned for forty years. [22]When he had removed him, he made David their king. In his testimony about him he said, 'I have found David, son of Jesse, to be a man after my heart, who will carry out all my wishes.' [23]Of this man's posterity God has brought to Israel a Savior, Jesus, as he promised;[24]before his coming John had already proclaimed a baptism of repentance to all the people of Israel. [25]And as John was finishing his work, he said, 'What do you suppose that I am? I am not he. No, but one is coming after me; I am not worthy to untie the thong of the sandals[n] on his feet.'

26 "My brothers, you descendants of Abraham's family, and others who fear God, to us[o] the message of this salvation has been sent. [27]Because the residents of Jerusalem and their leaders did not recognize him or understand the words of the prophets that are read every sabbath, they fulfilled those words by condemning him. [28]Even though they found no cause for a sentence of death, they asked Pilate to have him killed. [29]When they had carried out everything that was written about him, they took him down from the tree and laid him in a tomb. [30]But God raised him from the dead; [31]and for many days he appeared to those who came up with him from Galilee to Jerusalem, and they are now his witnesses to the people. [32]And we bring you the good news that what God promised to our ancestors [33]he has fulfilled for us, their children, by raising Jesus; as also it is written in the second psalm,

'You are my Son;
    today I have begotten you.'

[34]As to his raising him from the dead, no more to return to corruption, he has spoken in this way,

'I will give you the holy promises
    made to David.'

[35]Therefore he has also said in another psalm,

'You will not let your Holy One
    experience corruption.'

19 καὶ καθελὼν ἔθνη ἑπτὰ ἐν γῇ Χανάαν κατεκληρονόμησεν τὴν γῆν αὐτῶν 20 ὡς ἔτεσιν τετρακοσίοις καὶ πεντήκοντα. καὶ μετὰ ταῦτα ἔδωκεν κριτὰς ἕως Σαμουὴλ [τοῦ] προφήτου. 21 κἀκεῖθεν ᾐτήσαντο βασιλέα καὶ ἔδωκεν αὐτοῖς ὁ θεὸς τὸν Σαοὺλ υἱὸν Κίς, ἄνδρα ἐκ φυλῆς Βενιαμίν, ἔτη τεσσεράκοντα, 22 καὶ μεταστήσας αὐτὸν ἤγειρεν τὸν Δαυὶδ αὐτοῖς εἰς βασιλέα ᾧ καὶ εἶπεν μαρτυρήσας, Εὗρον Δαυὶδ τὸν τοῦ Ἰεσσαί, ἄνδρα κατὰ τὴν καρδίαν μου, ὃς ποιήσει πάντα τὰ θελήματά μου. 23 τούτου ὁ θεὸς ἀπὸ τοῦ σπέρματος κατ' ἐπαγγελίαν ἤγαγεν τῷ Ἰσραὴλ σωτῆρα Ἰησοῦν, 24 προκηρύξαντος Ἰωάννου πρὸ προσώπου τῆς εἰσόδου αὐτοῦ βάπτισμα μετανοίας παντὶ τῷ λαῷ Ἰσραήλ. 25 ὡς δὲ ἐπλήρου Ἰωάννης τὸν δρόμον, ἔλεγεν, Τί ἐμὲ ὑπονοεῖτε εἶναι; οὐκ εἰμὶ ἐγώ· ἀλλ' ἰδοὺ ἔρχεται μετ' ἐμὲ οὗ οὐκ εἰμὶ ἄξιος τὸ ὑπόδημα τῶν ποδῶν λῦσαι.

26 Ἄνδρες ἀδελφοί, υἱοὶ γένους Ἀβραὰμ καὶ οἱ ἐν ὑμῖν φοβούμενοι τὸν θεόν, ἡμῖν[c] ὁ λόγος τῆς σωτηρίας ταύτης ἐξαπεστάλη. 27 οἱ γὰρ κατοικοῦντες ἐν Ἰερουσαλὴμ καὶ οἱ ἄρχοντες αὐτῶν τοῦτον ἀγνοήσαντες καὶ τὰς φωνὰς τῶν προφητῶν τὰς κατὰ πᾶν σάββατον ἀναγινωσκομένας κρίναντες ἐπλήρωσαν, 28 καὶ μηδεμίαν αἰτίαν θανάτου εὑρόντες ᾐτήσαντο Πιλᾶτον ἀναιρεθῆναι αὐτόν. 29 ὡς δὲ ἐτέλεσαν πάντα τὰ περὶ αὐτοῦ γεγραμμένα, καθελόντες ἀπὸ τοῦ ξύλου ἔθηκαν εἰς μνημεῖον. 30 ὁ δὲ θεὸς ἤγειρεν αὐτὸν ἐκ νεκρῶν, 31 ὃς ὤφθη ἐπὶ ἡμέρας πλείους τοῖς συναναβᾶσιν αὐτῷ ἀπὸ τῆς Γαλιλαίας εἰς Ἰερουσαλήμ, οἵτινες [νῦν] εἰσιν μάρτυρες αὐτοῦ πρὸς τὸν λαόν. 32 καὶ ἡμεῖς ὑμᾶς εὐαγγελιζόμεθα τὴν πρὸς τοὺς πατέρας ἐπαγγελίαν γενομένην, 33 ὅτι ταύτην ὁ θεὸς ἐκπεπλήρωκεν τοῖς τέκνοις [αὐτῶν] ἡμῖν ἀναστήσας Ἰησοῦν ὡς καὶ ἐν τῷ ψαλμῷ γέγραπται τῷ δευτέρῳ,

Υἱός μου εἶ σύ,
    ἐγὼ σήμερον γεγέννηκά σε.

34 ὅτι δὲ ἀνέστησεν αὐτὸν ἐκ νεκρῶν μηκέτι μέλλοντα ὑποστρέφειν εἰς διαφθοράν, οὕτως εἴρηκεν ὅτι

Δώσω ὑμῖν τὰ ὅσια Δαυὶδ τὰ πιστά. 35 διότι καὶ ἐν ἑτέρῳ λέγει,

Οὐ δώσεις τὸν ὅσιόν σου ἰδεῖν διαφθοράν.

desert, [19]he overthrew seven nations in Canaan and gave their land to his people as their inheritance. [20]All this took about 450 years.

"After this, God gave them judges until the time of Samuel the prophet. [21]Then the people asked for a king, and he gave them Saul son of Kish, of the tribe of Benjamin, who ruled forty years. [22]After removing Saul, he made David their king. He testified concerning him: 'I have found David son of Jesse a man after my own heart; he will do everything I want him to do.'

[23]"From this man's descendants God has brought to Israel the Savior Jesus, as he promised. [24]Before the coming of Jesus, John preached repentance and baptism to all the people of Israel. [25]As John was completing his work, he said: 'Who do you think I am? I am not that one. No, but he is coming after me, whose sandals I am not worthy to untie.'

[26]"Brothers, children of Abraham, and you God-fearing Gentiles, it is to us that this message of salvation has been sent. [27]The people of Jerusalem and their rulers did not recognize Jesus, yet in condemning him they fulfilled the words of the prophets that are read every Sabbath. [28]Though they found no proper ground for a death sentence, they asked Pilate to have him executed. [29]When they had carried out all that was written about him, they took him down from the tree and laid him in a tomb. [30]But God raised him from the dead, [31]and for many days he was seen by those who had traveled with him from Galilee to Jerusalem. They are now his witnesses to our people.

[32]"We tell you the good news: What God promised our fathers [33]he has fulfilled for us, their children, by raising up Jesus. As it is written in the second Psalm:

" 'You are my Son;
    today I have become your Father.'[b'c]

[34]The fact that God raised him from the dead, never to decay, is stated in these words:

" 'I will give you the holy and sure
    blessings promised to David.'[d]

[35]So it is stated elsewhere:

" 'You will not let your Holy One see
    decay.'[e]

---

[n] Gk *untie the sandals*   [o] Other ancient authorities read *you*

[c]26 NRSV note o ὑμῖν

[b]33 Or *have begotten you*   [c]33 Psalm 2:7   [d]34 Isaiah 55:3
[e]35 Psalm 16:10

NRSV

36For David, after he had served the purpose of God in his own generation, died,p was laid beside his ancestors, and experienced corruption; 37but he whom God raised up experienced no corruption. 38Let it be known to you therefore, my brothers, that through this man forgiveness of sins is proclaimed to you; 39by this Jesusq everyone who believes is set free from all those sinsr from which you could not be freed by the law of Moses. 40Beware, therefore, that what the prophets said does not happen to you:

41 'Look, you scoffers!
      Be amazed and perish,
      for in your days I am doing a work,
      a work that you will never believe,
         even if someone tells you.' "

42 As Paul and Barnabass were going out, the people urged them to speak about these things again the next sabbath. 43When the meeting of the synagogue broke up, many Jews and devout converts to Judaism followed Paul and Barnabas, who spoke to them and urged them to continue in the grace of God.

44 The next sabbath almost the whole city gathered to hear the word of the Lord.t 45But when the Jews saw the crowds, they were filled with jealousy; and blaspheming, they contradicted what was spoken by Paul. 46Then both Paul and Barnabas spoke out boldly, saying, "It was necessary that the word of God should be spoken first to you. Since you reject it and judge yourselves to be unworthy of eternal life, we are now turning to the Gentiles. 47For so the Lord has commanded us, saying,

'I have set you to be a light for the
      Gentiles,
   so that you may bring salvation to
      the ends of the earth.' "

48 When the Gentiles heard this, they were glad and praised the word of the Lord; and as many as had been destined for eternal life became believers. 49Thus the word of the Lord spread throughout the region. 50But the Jews incited the devout women of high standing and the leading men of the city, and stirred up persecution against Paul and Barnabas, and drove them out of their region. 51So they shook the dust off their feet in protest against them, and went to Iconium. 52And the disciples were filled with joy and with the Holy Spirit.

Greek

36 Δαυὶδ μὲν γὰρ ἰδίᾳ γενεᾷ ὑπηρετήσας τῇ τοῦ θεοῦ βουλῇ ἐκοιμήθη καὶ προσετέθη πρὸς τοὺς πατέρας αὐτοῦ καὶ εἶδεν διαφθοράν· 37 ὃν δὲ ὁ θεὸς ἤγειρεν, οὐκ εἶδεν διαφθοράν. 38 γνωστὸν οὖν ἔστω ὑμῖν, ἄνδρες ἀδελφοί, ὅτι διὰ τούτου ὑμῖν ἄφεσις ἁμαρτιῶν καταγγέλλεται[,d καὶ] ἀπὸ πάντων ὧν οὐκ ἠδυνήθητε ἐν νόμῳ Μωϋσέως δικαιωθῆναι 39 ἐν τούτῳ πᾶς ὁ πιστεύων δικαιοῦται. 40 βλέπετε οὖν μὴ ἐπέλθῃ τὸ εἰρημένον ἐν τοῖς προφήταις,

41 Ἴδετε, οἱ καταφρονηταί,
   καὶ θαυμάσατε καὶ ἀφανίσθητε,
   ὅτι ἔργον ἐργάζομαι ἐγὼ ἐν ταῖς
      ἡμέραις ὑμῶν,
   ἔργον ὃ οὐ μὴ πιστεύσητε ἐάν
      τις ἐκδιηγῆται ὑμῖν.

42 Ἐξιόντων δὲ αὐτῶνe παρεκάλουν εἰς τὸ μεταξὺ σάββατον λαληθῆναι αὐτοῖς τὰ ῥήματα ταῦτα. 43 λυθείσης δὲ τῆς συναγωγῆς ἠκολούθησαν πολλοὶ τῶν Ἰουδαίων καὶ τῶν σεβομένων προσηλύτων τῷ Παύλῳ καὶ τῷ Βαρναβᾷ, οἵτινες προσλαλοῦντες αὐτοῖς ἔπειθον αὐτοὺς προσμένειν τῇ χάριτι τοῦ θεοῦ. 44 Τῷ δὲ ἐρχομένῳ σαββάτῳ σχεδὸν πᾶσα ἡ πόλις συνήχθη ἀκοῦσαι τὸν λόγον τοῦ κυρίουf. 45 ἰδόντες δὲ οἱ Ἰουδαῖοι τοὺς ὄχλους ἐπλήσθησαν ζήλου καὶ ἀντέλεγον τοῖς ὑπὸ Παύλου λαλουμένοις βλασφημοῦντες. 46 παρρησιασάμενοί τε ὁ Παῦλος καὶ ὁ Βαρναβᾶς εἶπαν, Ὑμῖν ἦν ἀναγκαῖον πρῶτον λαληθῆναι τὸν λόγον τοῦ θεοῦ· ἐπειδὴ ἀπωθεῖσθε αὐτὸν καὶ οὐκ ἀξίους κρίνετε ἑαυτοὺς τῆς αἰωνίου ζωῆς, ἰδοὺ στρεφόμεθα εἰς τὰ ἔθνη. 47 οὕτως γὰρ ἐντέταλται ἡμῖν ὁ κύριος,

Τέθεικά σε εἰς φῶς ἐθνῶν
   τοῦ εἶναί σε εἰς σωτηρίαν ἕως
      ἐσχάτου τῆς γῆς.

48 ἀκούοντα δὲ τὰ ἔθνη ἔχαιρον καὶ ἐδόξαζον τὸν λόγον τοῦ κυρίου καὶ ἐπίστευσαν ὅσοι ἦσαν τεταγμένοι εἰς ζωὴν αἰώνιον· 49 διεφέρετο δὲ ὁ λόγος τοῦ κυρίου δι' ὅλης τῆς χώρας. 50 οἱ δὲ Ἰουδαῖοι παρώτρυναν τὰς σεβομένας γυναῖκας τὰς εὐσχήμονας καὶ τοὺς πρώτους τῆς πόλεως καὶ ἐπήγειραν διωγμὸν ἐπὶ τὸν Παῦλον καὶ Βαρναβᾶν καὶ ἐξέβαλον αὐτοὺς ἀπὸ τῶν ὁρίων αὐτῶν. 51 οἱ δὲ ἐκτιναξάμενοι τὸν κονιορτὸν τῶν ποδῶν ἐπ' αὐτοὺς ἦλθον εἰς Ἰκόνιον, 52 οἵ τε μαθηταὶ ἐπληροῦντο χαρᾶς καὶ πνεύματος ἁγίου.

NIV

36"For when David had served God's purpose in his own generation, he fell asleep; he was buried with his fathers and his body decayed. 37But the one whom God raised from the dead did not see decay.
38"Therefore, my brothers, I want you to know that through Jesus the forgiveness of sins is proclaimed to you. 39Through him everyone who believes is justified from everything you could not be justified from by the law of Moses. 40Take care that what the prophets have said does not happen to you:

41" 'Look, you scoffers,
      wonder and perish,
   for I am going to do something in your
         days
      that you would never believe,
      even if someone told you.'f"

42As Paul and Barnabas were leaving the synagogue, the people invited them to speak further about these things on the next Sabbath. 43When the congregation was dismissed, many of the Jews and devout converts to Judaism followed Paul and Barnabas, who talked with them and urged them to continue in the grace of God.

44On the next Sabbath almost the whole city gathered to hear the word of the Lord. 45When the Jews saw the crowds, they were filled with jealousy and talked abusively against what Paul was saying.
46Then Paul and Barnabas answered them boldly: "We had to speak the word of God to you first. Since you reject it and do not consider yourselves worthy of eternal life, we now turn to the Gentiles. 47For this is what the Lord has commanded us:

" 'I have made youg a light for the
      Gentiles,
   that youg may bring salvation to the
      ends of the earth.'h"

48When the Gentiles heard this, they were glad and honored the word of the Lord; and all who were appointed for eternal life believed.
49The word of the Lord spread through the whole region. 50But the Jews incited the God-fearing women of high standing and the leading men of the city. They stirred up persecution against Paul and Barnabas, and expelled them from their region. 51So they shook the dust from their feet in protest against them and went to Iconium. 52And the disciples were filled with joy and with the Holy Spirit.

---

p Gk *fell asleep*   q Gk *this*   r Gk *all*   s Gk *they*   t Other ancient authorities read *God*

d38 NIV begins verse 39 after καταγγέλλεται.   e42 NIV text adds ἐκ τῆς συναγωγῆς   f44 NRSV note t θεοῦ

f41 Hab. 1:5   g47 The Greek is singular.   h47 Isaiah 49:6

NRSV

Paul and Barnabas in Iconium

14 The same thing occurred in Iconium, where Paul and Barnabas[s] went into the Jewish synagogue and spoke in such a way that a great number of both Jews and Greeks became believers. 2But the unbelieving Jews stirred up the Gentiles and poisoned their minds against the brothers. 3So they remained for a long time, speaking boldly for the Lord, who testified to the word of his grace by granting signs and wonders to be done through them. 4But the residents of the city were divided; some sided with the Jews, and some with the apostles. 5And when an attempt was made by both Gentiles and Jews, with their rulers, to mistreat them and to stone them, 6the apostles[s] learned of it and fled to Lystra and Derbe, cities of Lycaonia, and to the surrounding country; 7and there they continued proclaiming the good news.

Paul and Barnabas in Lystra and Derbe

8 In Lystra there was a man sitting who could not use his feet and had never walked, for he had been crippled from birth. 9He listened to Paul as he was speaking. And Paul, looking at him intently and seeing that he had faith to be healed, 10said in a loud voice, "Stand upright on your feet." And the man[u] sprang up and began to walk. 11When the crowds saw what Paul had done, they shouted in the Lycaonian language, "The gods have come down to us in human form!" 12Barnabas they called Zeus, and Paul they called Hermes, because he was the chief speaker. 13The priest of Zeus, whose temple was just outside the city,[v] brought oxen and garlands to the gates; he and the crowds wanted to offer sacrifice. 14When the apostles Barnabas and Paul heard of it, they tore their clothes and rushed out into the crowd, shouting, 15"Friends,[w] why are you doing this? We are mortals just like you, and we bring you good news, that you should turn from these worthless things to the living God, who made the heaven and the earth and the sea and all that is in them. 16In past generations he allowed all the nations to follow their own ways; 17yet he has not left himself without a witness in doing good—giving you rains from heaven and fruitful seasons, and filling you with food and your hearts with joy." 18Even with these words,

s Gk *they*   u Gk *he*   v Or *The priest of Zeus-Outside-the-City*   w Gk *Men*

Greek

14 Ἐγένετο δὲ ἐν Ἰκονίῳ κατὰ τὸ αὐτὸ εἰσελθεῖν αὐτοὺς εἰς τὴν συναγωγὴν τῶν Ἰουδαίων καὶ λαλῆσαι οὕτως ὥστε πιστεῦσαι Ἰουδαίων τε καὶ Ἑλλήνων πολὺ πλῆθος. 2 οἱ δὲ ἀπειθήσαντες Ἰουδαῖοι ἐπήγειραν καὶ ἐκάκωσαν τὰς ψυχὰς τῶν ἐθνῶν κατὰ τῶν ἀδελφῶν. 3 ἱκανὸν μὲν οὖν χρόνον διέτριψαν παρρησιαζόμενοι ἐπὶ τῷ κυρίῳ τῷ μαρτυροῦντι [ἐπὶ] τῷ λόγῳ τῆς χάριτος αὐτοῦ, διδόντι σημεῖα καὶ τέρατα γίνεσθαι διὰ τῶν χειρῶν αὐτῶν. 4 ἐσχίσθη δὲ τὸ πλῆθος τῆς πόλεως, καὶ οἱ μὲν ἦσαν σὺν τοῖς Ἰουδαίοις, οἱ δὲ σὺν τοῖς ἀποστόλοις. 5 ὡς δὲ ἐγένετο ὁρμὴ τῶν ἐθνῶν τε καὶ Ἰουδαίων σὺν τοῖς ἄρχουσιν αὐτῶν ὑβρίσαι καὶ λιθοβολῆσαι αὐτούς, 6 συνιδόντες κατέφυγον εἰς τὰς πόλεις τῆς Λυκαονίας Λύστραν καὶ Δέρβην καὶ τὴν περίχωρον, 7 κἀκεῖ εὐαγγελιζόμενοι ἦσαν.

8 Καί τις ἀνὴρ ἀδύνατος ἐν Λύστροις τοῖς ποσὶν ἐκάθητο, χωλὸς ἐκ κοιλίας μητρὸς αὐτοῦ ὃς οὐδέποτε περιεπάτησεν. 9 οὗτος ἤκουσεν τοῦ Παύλου λαλοῦντος· ὃς ἀτενίσας αὐτῷ καὶ ἰδὼν ὅτι ἔχει πίστιν τοῦ σωθῆναι, 10 εἶπεν μεγάλῃ φωνῇ, Ἀνάστηθι ἐπὶ τοὺς πόδας σου ὀρθός. καὶ ἥλατο καὶ περιεπάτει. 11 οἵ τε ὄχλοι ἰδόντες ὃ ἐποίησεν Παῦλος ἐπῆραν τὴν φωνὴν αὐτῶν Λυκαονιστὶ λέγοντες, Οἱ θεοὶ ὁμοιωθέντες ἀνθρώποις κατέβησαν πρὸς ἡμᾶς, 12 ἐκάλουν τε τὸν Βαρναβᾶν Δία, τὸν δὲ Παῦλον Ἑρμῆν, ἐπειδὴ αὐτὸς ἦν ὁ ἡγούμενος τοῦ λόγου. 13 ὅ τε ἱερεὺς τοῦ Διὸς τοῦ ὄντος πρὸ τῆς πόλεως ταύρους καὶ στέμματα ἐπὶ τοὺς πυλῶνας ἐνέγκας σὺν τοῖς ὄχλοις ἤθελεν θύειν. 14 ἀκούσαντες δὲ οἱ ἀπόστολοι Βαρναβᾶς καὶ Παῦλος διαρρήξαντες τὰ ἱμάτια αὐτῶν ἐξεπήδησαν εἰς τὸν ὄχλον κράζοντες 15 καὶ λέγοντες, Ἄνδρες, τί ταῦτα ποιεῖτε; καὶ ἡμεῖς ὁμοιοπαθεῖς ἐσμεν ὑμῖν ἄνθρωποι εὐαγγελιζόμενοι ὑμᾶς ἀπὸ τούτων τῶν ματαίων ἐπιστρέφειν ἐπὶ θεὸν ζῶντα, ὃς ἐποίησεν τὸν οὐρανὸν καὶ τὴν γῆν καὶ τὴν θάλασσαν καὶ πάντα τὰ ἐν αὐτοῖς· 16 ὃς ἐν ταῖς παρῳχημέναις γενεαῖς εἴασεν πάντα τὰ ἔθνη πορεύεσθαι ταῖς ὁδοῖς αὐτῶν· 17 καίτοι οὐκ ἀμάρτυρον αὐτὸν ἀφῆκεν ἀγαθουργῶν, οὐρανόθεν ὑμῖν ὑετοὺς διδοὺς καὶ καιροὺς καρποφόρους, ἐμπιπλῶν τροφῆς καὶ εὐφροσύνης τὰς καρδίας ὑμῶν. 18 καὶ ταῦτα λέγοντες

NIV

In Iconium

14 At Iconium Paul and Barnabas went as usual into the Jewish synagogue. There they spoke so effectively that a great number of Jews and Gentiles believed. 2But the Jews who refused to believe stirred up the Gentiles and poisoned their minds against the brothers. 3So Paul and Barnabas spent considerable time there, speaking boldly for the Lord, who confirmed the message of his grace by enabling them to do miraculous signs and wonders. 4The people of the city were divided; some sided with the Jews, others with the apostles. 5There was a plot afoot among the Gentiles and Jews, together with their leaders, to mistreat them and stone them. 6But they found out about it and fled to the Lycaonian cities of Lystra and Derbe and to the surrounding country, 7where they continued to preach the good news.

In Lystra and Derbe

8In Lystra there sat a man crippled in his feet, who was lame from birth and had never walked. 9He listened to Paul as he was speaking. Paul looked directly at him, saw that he had faith to be healed 10and called out, "Stand up on your feet!" At that, the man jumped up and began to walk.

11When the crowd saw what Paul had done, they shouted in the Lycaonian language, "The gods have come down to us in human form!" 12Barnabas they called Zeus, and Paul they called Hermes because he was the chief speaker. 13The priest of Zeus, whose temple was just outside the city, brought bulls and wreaths to the city gates because he and the crowd wanted to offer sacrifices to them.

14But when the apostles Barnabas and Paul heard of this, they tore their clothes and rushed out into the crowd, shouting: 15"Men, why are you doing this? We too are only men, human like you. We are bringing you good news, telling you to turn from these worthless things to the living God, who made heaven and earth and sea and everything in them. 16In the past, he let all nations go their own way. 17Yet he has not left himself without testimony: He has shown kindness by giving you rain from heaven and crops in their seasons; he provides you with plenty of food and fills your hearts with joy." 18Even they scarcely restrained the crowds from offering sacrifice to them.

19 But Jews came there from Antioch and Iconium and won over the crowds. Then they stoned Paul and dragged him out of the city, supposing that he was dead. 20But when the disciples surrounded him, he got up and went into the city. The next day he went on with Barnabas to Derbe.

The Return to Antioch in Syria

21 After they had proclaimed the good news to that city and had made many disciples, they returned to Lystra, then on to Iconium and Antioch. 22There they strengthened the souls of the disciples and encouraged them to continue in the faith, saying, "It is through many persecutions that we must enter the kingdom of God." 23And after they had appointed elders for them in each church, with prayer and fasting they entrusted them to the Lord in whom they had come to believe.

24 Then they passed through Pisidia and came to Pamphylia. 25When they had spoken the word in Perga, they went down to Attalia. 26From there they sailed back to Antioch, where they had been commended to the grace of God for the work[x] that they had completed. 27When they arrived, they called the church together and related all that God had done with them, and how he had opened a door of faith for the Gentiles. 28And they stayed there with the disciples for some time.

The Council at Jerusalem

15 Then certain individuals came down from Judea and were teaching the brothers, "Unless you are circumcised according to the custom of Moses, you cannot be saved." 2And after Paul and Barnabas had no small dissension and debate with them, Paul and Barnabas and some of the others were appointed to go up to Jerusalem to discuss this question with the apostles and the elders. 3So they were sent on their way by the church, and as they passed through both Phoenicia and Samaria, they reported the conversion of the Gentiles, and brought great joy to all the believers.[y] 4When they came to Jerusalem, they were welcomed by the church and the apostles and the elders, and they reported all that God had done with them. 5But some believers who belonged to the sect of the Pharisees stood up and said, "It

μόλις κατέπαυσαν τοὺς ὄχλους τοῦ μὴ θύειν αὐτοῖς.

19 Ἐπῆλθαν δὲ ἀπὸ Ἀντιοχείας καὶ Ἰκονίου Ἰουδαῖοι καὶ πείσαντες τοὺς ὄχλους καὶ λιθάσαντες τὸν Παῦλον ἔσυρον ἔξω τῆς πόλεως νομίζοντες αὐτὸν τεθνηκέναι. 20 κυκλωσάντων δὲ τῶν μαθητῶν αὐτὸν ἀναστὰς εἰσῆλθεν εἰς τὴν πόλιν. καὶ τῇ ἐπαύριον ἐξῆλθεν σὺν τῷ Βαρναβᾷ εἰς Δέρβην.

21 Εὐαγγελισάμενοί τε τὴν πόλιν ἐκείνην καὶ μαθητεύσαντες ἱκανοὺς ὑπέστρεψαν εἰς τὴν Λύστραν καὶ εἰς Ἰκόνιον καὶ εἰς Ἀντιόχειαν 22 ἐπιστηρίζοντες τὰς ψυχὰς τῶν μαθητῶν, παρακαλοῦντες ἐμμένειν τῇ πίστει καὶ ὅτι διὰ πολλῶν θλίψεων δεῖ ἡμᾶς εἰσελθεῖν εἰς τὴν βασιλείαν τοῦ θεοῦ. 23 χειροτονήσαντες δὲ αὐτοῖς κατ' ἐκκλησίαν πρεσβυτέρους, προσευξάμενοι μετὰ νηστειῶν παρέθεντο αὐτοὺς τῷ κυρίῳ εἰς ὃν πεπιστεύκεισαν. 24 καὶ διελθόντες τὴν Πισιδίαν ἦλθον εἰς τὴν Παμφυλίαν 25 καὶ λαλήσαντες ἐν Πέργῃ τὸν λόγον κατέβησαν εἰς Ἀττάλειαν 26 κἀκεῖθεν ἀπέπλευσαν εἰς Ἀντιόχειαν, ὅθεν ἦσαν παραδεδομένοι τῇ χάριτι τοῦ θεοῦ εἰς τὸ ἔργον ὃ ἐπλήρωσαν. 27 παραγενόμενοι δὲ καὶ συναγαγόντες τὴν ἐκκλησίαν ἀνήγγελλον ὅσα ἐποίησεν ὁ θεὸς μετ' αὐτῶν καὶ ὅτι ἤνοιξεν τοῖς ἔθνεσιν θύραν πίστεως. 28 διέτριβον δὲ χρόνον οὐκ ὀλίγον σὺν τοῖς μαθηταῖς.

15 Καί τινες κατελθόντες ἀπὸ τῆς Ἰουδαίας ἐδίδασκον τοὺς ἀδελφοὺς ὅτι Ἐὰν μὴ περιτμηθῆτε τῷ ἔθει τῷ Μωϋσέως, οὐ δύνασθε σωθῆναι. 2 γενομένης δὲ στάσεως καὶ ζητήσεως οὐκ ὀλίγης τῷ Παύλῳ καὶ τῷ Βαρναβᾷ πρὸς αὐτούς, ἔταξαν ἀναβαίνειν Παῦλον καὶ Βαρναβᾶν καί τινας ἄλλους ἐξ αὐτῶν πρὸς τοὺς ἀποστόλους καὶ πρεσβυτέρους εἰς Ἰερουσαλὴμ περὶ τοῦ ζητήματος τούτου. 3 Οἱ μὲν οὖν προπεμφθέντες ὑπὸ τῆς ἐκκλησίας διήρχοντο τήν τε Φοινίκην καὶ Σαμάρειαν ἐκδιηγούμενοι τὴν ἐπιστροφὴν τῶν ἐθνῶν καὶ ἐποίουν χαρὰν μεγάλην πᾶσιν τοῖς ἀδελφοῖς. 4 παραγενόμενοι δὲ εἰς Ἰερουσαλὴμ παρεδέχθησαν ἀπὸ τῆς ἐκκλησίας καὶ τῶν ἀποστόλων καὶ τῶν πρεσβυτέρων, ἀνήγγειλάν τε ὅσα ὁ θεὸς ἐποίησεν μετ' αὐτῶν. 5 ἐξανέστησαν δέ τινες τῶν ἀπὸ τῆς αἱρέσεως τῶν Φαρισαίων πεπιστευκότες λέγον-

with these words, they had difficulty keeping the crowd from sacrificing to them.

19Then some Jews came from Antioch and Iconium and won the crowd over. They stoned Paul and dragged him outside the city, thinking he was dead. 20But after the disciples had gathered around him, he got up and went back into the city. The next day he and Barnabas left for Derbe.

The Return to Antioch in Syria

21They preached the good news in that city and won a large number of disciples. Then they returned to Lystra, Iconium and Antioch, 22strengthening the disciples and encouraging them to remain true to the faith. "We must go through many hardships to enter the kingdom of God," they said. 23Paul and Barnabas appointed elders[a] for them in each church and, with prayer and fasting, committed them to the Lord, in whom they had put their trust. 24After going through Pisidia, they came into Pamphylia, 25and when they had preached the word in Perga, they went down to Attalia.

26From Attalia they sailed back to Antioch, where they had been committed to the grace of God for the work they had now completed. 27On arriving there, they gathered the church together and reported all that God had done through them and how he had opened the door of faith to the Gentiles. 28And they stayed there a long time with the disciples.

The Council at Jerusalem

15 Some men came down from Judea to Antioch and were teaching the brothers: "Unless you are circumcised, according to the custom taught by Moses, you cannot be saved." 2This brought Paul and Barnabas into sharp dispute and debate with them. So Paul and Barnabas were appointed, along with some other believers, to go up to Jerusalem to see the apostles and elders about this question. 3The church sent them on their way, and as they traveled through Phoenicia and Samaria, they told how the Gentiles had been converted. This news made all the brothers very glad. 4When they came to Jerusalem, they were welcomed by the church and the apostles and elders, to whom they reported everything God had done through them. 5Then some of the believers who belonged to the party of the Pharisees stood

---

x Or *committed in the grace of God to the work*   y Gk *brothers*

a23 Or *Barnabas ordained elders*; or *Barnabas had elders elected*

is necessary for them to be circumcised and ordered to keep the law of Moses."

6 The apostles and the elders met together to consider this matter. [7]After there had been much debate, Peter stood up and said to them, "My brothers,[z] you know that in the early days God made a choice among you, that I should be the one through whom the Gentiles would hear the message of the good news and become believers. [8]And God, who knows the human heart, testified to them by giving them the Holy Spirit, just as he did to us; [9]and in cleansing their hearts by faith he has made no distinction between them and us. [10]Now therefore why are you putting God to the test by placing on the neck of the disciples a yoke that neither our ancestors nor we have been able to bear? [11]On the contrary, we believe that we will be saved through the grace of the Lord Jesus, just as they will."

12 The whole assembly kept silence, and listened to Barnabas and Paul as they told of all the signs and wonders that God had done through them among the Gentiles. [13]After they finished speaking, James replied, "My brothers,[z] listen to me. [14]Simeon has related how God first looked favorably on the Gentiles, to take from among them a people for his name. [15]This agrees with the words of the prophets, as it is written,

16 'After this I will return,
     and I will rebuild the dwelling of
          David, which has fallen;
      from its ruins I will rebuild it,
          and I will set it up,
17 so that all other peoples may seek the
          Lord—
     even all the Gentiles over whom my
          name has been called.
      Thus says the Lord, who has been
          making these things [18]known
          from long ago.'[a]

[19]Therefore I have reached the decision that we should not trouble those Gentiles who are turning to God, [20]but we should write to them to abstain only from things polluted by idols and from fornication and from whatever has been strangled[b] and from blood. [21]For in every city, for generations past, Moses has had those who proclaim him, for he has been read aloud every sabbath in the synagogues."

τες ὅτι δεῖ περιτέμνειν αὐτοὺς παραγγέλλειν τε τηρεῖν τὸν νόμον Μωϋσέως.

6 Συνήχθησάν τε οἱ ἀπόστολοι καὶ οἱ πρεσβύτεροι ἰδεῖν περὶ τοῦ λόγου τούτου. **7** πολλῆς δὲ ζητήσεως γενομένης ἀναστὰς Πέτρος εἶπεν πρὸς αὐτούς, Ἄνδρες ἀδελφοί, ὑμεῖς ἐπίστασθε ὅτι ἀφ' ἡμερῶν ἀρχαίων ἐν ὑμῖν ἐξελέξατο ὁ θεὸς διὰ τοῦ στόματός μου ἀκοῦσαι τὰ ἔθνη τὸν λόγον τοῦ εὐαγγελίου καὶ πιστεῦσαι. **8** καὶ ὁ καρδιογνώστης θεὸς ἐμαρτύρησεν αὐτοῖς δοὺς[a] τὸ πνεῦμα τὸ ἅγιον καθὼς καὶ ἡμῖν **9** καὶ οὐθὲν διέκρινεν μεταξὺ ἡμῶν τε καὶ αὐτῶν τῇ πίστει καθαρίσας τὰς καρδίας αὐτῶν. **10** νῦν οὖν τί πειράζετε τὸν θεὸν ἐπιθεῖναι ζυγὸν ἐπὶ τὸν τράχηλον τῶν μαθητῶν ὃν οὔτε οἱ πατέρες ἡμῶν οὔτε ἡμεῖς ἰσχύσαμεν βαστάσαι; **11** ἀλλὰ διὰ τῆς χάριτος τοῦ κυρίου Ἰησοῦ πιστεύομεν σωθῆναι καθ' ὃν τρόπον κἀκεῖνοι.

12 Ἐσίγησεν δὲ πᾶν τὸ πλῆθος καὶ ἤκουον Βαρναβᾶ καὶ Παύλου ἐξηγουμένων ὅσα ἐποίησεν ὁ θεὸς σημεῖα καὶ τέρατα ἐν τοῖς ἔθνεσιν δι' αὐτῶν. **13** Μετὰ δὲ τὸ σιγῆσαι αὐτοὺς ἀπεκρίθη Ἰάκωβος λέγων, Ἄνδρες ἀδελφοί, ἀκούσατέ μου. **14** Συμεὼν ἐξηγήσατο καθὼς πρῶτον ὁ θεὸς ἐπεσκέψατο λαβεῖν ἐξ ἐθνῶν λαὸν τῷ ὀνόματι αὐτοῦ. **15** καὶ τούτῳ συμφωνοῦσιν οἱ λόγοι τῶν προφητῶν καθὼς γέγραπται,
16 Μετὰ ταῦτα ἀναστρέψω
     καὶ ἀνοικοδομήσω τὴν σκηνὴν
          Δαυὶδ τὴν πεπτωκυῖαν
     καὶ τὰ κατεσκαμμένα αὐτῆς
          ἀνοικοδομήσω
     καὶ ἀνορθώσω αὐτήν,
17 ὅπως ἂν ἐκζητήσωσιν οἱ κατάλοιποι
     τῶν ἀνθρώπων τὸν κύριον
     καὶ πάντα τὰ ἔθνη ἐφ' οὓς
          ἐπικέκληται τὸ ὄνομά μου
          ἐπ' αὐτούς,
     λέγει κύριος ποιῶν ταῦτα
18 γνωστὰ ἀπ' αἰῶνος[b].

19 διὸ ἐγὼ κρίνω μὴ παρενοχλεῖν τοῖς ἀπὸ τῶν ἐθνῶν ἐπιστρέφουσιν ἐπὶ τὸν θεόν, **20** ἀλλὰ ἐπιστεῖλαι αὐτοῖς τοῦ ἀπέχεσθαι τῶν ἀλισγημάτων τῶν εἰδώλων καὶ τῆς πορνείας καὶ τοῦ πνικτοῦ καὶ τοῦ αἵματος. **21** Μωϋσῆς γὰρ ἐκ γενεῶν ἀρχαίων κατὰ πόλιν τοὺς κηρύσσοντας αὐτὸν ἔχει ἐν ταῖς συναγωγαῖς κατὰ πᾶν σάββατον ἀναγινωσκόμενος.

up and said, "The Gentiles must be circumcised and required to obey the law of Moses."

[6]The apostles and elders met to consider this question. [7]After much discussion, Peter got up and addressed them: "Brothers, you know that some time ago God made a choice among you that the Gentiles might hear from my lips the message of the gospel and believe. [8]God, who knows the heart, showed that he accepted them by giving the Holy Spirit to them, just as he did to us. [9]He made no distinction between us and them, for he purified their hearts by faith. [10]Now then, why do you try to test God by putting on the necks of the disciples a yoke that neither we nor our fathers have been able to bear? [11]No! We believe it is through the grace of our Lord Jesus that we are saved, just as they are."

[12]The whole assembly became silent as they listened to Barnabas and Paul telling about the miraculous signs and wonders God had done among the Gentiles through them. [13]When they finished, James spoke up: "Brothers, listen to me. [14]Simon[a] has described to us how God at first showed his concern by taking from the Gentiles a people for himself. [15]The words of the prophets are in agreement with this, as it is written:

16" 'After this I will return
     and rebuild David's fallen tent.
    Its ruins I will rebuild,
     and I will restore it,
17that the remnant of men may seek the
          Lord,
     and all the Gentiles who bear my
          name,
     says the Lord, who does these things'[b]
18   that have been known for ages.[c]

[19]"It is my judgment, therefore, that we should not make it difficult for the Gentiles who are turning to God. [20]Instead we should write to them, telling them to abstain from food polluted by idols, from sexual immorality, from the meat of strangled animals and from blood. [21]For Moses has been preached in every city from the earliest times and is read in the synagogues on every Sabbath."

---

[z] Gk *Men, brothers*   [a] Other ancient authorities read *things.* [18]*Known to God from of old are all his works.'*
[b] Other ancient authorities lack *and from whatever has been strangled*

[a]8 NIV text adds αὐτοῖς †   [b]18 NIV note adds τῷ κυρίῳ τὸ ἔργον αὐτοῦ; NRSV note a adds ἐστιν τῷ θεῷ πάντα τὰ ἔργα αὐτοῦ

[a]14 Greek *Simeon*, a variant of *Simon*; that is, Peter
[b]17 Amos 9:11,12   [c]17,18 Some manuscripts *things'*— /
18*known to the Lord for ages is his work*

NRSV

The Council's Letter to Gentile Believers

22 Then the apostles and the elders, with the consent of the whole church, decided to choose men from among their members[c] and to send them to Antioch with Paul and Barnabas. They sent Judas called Barsabbas, and Silas, leaders among the brothers, 23with the following letter: "The brothers, both the apostles and the elders, to the believers[d] of Gentile origin in Antioch and Syria and Cilicia, greetings. 24Since we have heard that certain persons who have gone out from us, though with no instructions from us, have said things to disturb you and have unsettled your minds,[e] 25we have decided unanimously to choose representatives[f] and send them to you, along with our beloved Barnabas and Paul, 26who have risked their lives for the sake of our Lord Jesus Christ. 27We have therefore sent Judas and Silas, who themselves will tell you the same things by word of mouth. 28For it has seemed good to the Holy Spirit and to us to impose on you no further burden than these essentials: 29that you abstain from what has been sacrificed to idols and from blood and from what is strangled[g] and from fornication. If you keep yourselves from these, you will do well. Farewell."

30 So they were sent off and went down to Antioch. When they gathered the congregation together, they delivered the letter. 31When its members[h] read it, they rejoiced at the exhortation. 32Judas and Silas, who were themselves prophets, said much to encourage and strengthen the believers.[i] 33After they had been there for some time, they were sent off in peace by the believers[j] to those who had sent them.[j] 35But Paul and Barnabas remained in Antioch, and there, with many others, they taught and proclaimed the word of the Lord.

Paul and Barnabas Separate

36 After some days Paul said to Barnabas, "Come, let us return and visit the believers[i] in every city where we proclaimed the word of the Lord and see how they are doing." 37Barnabas wanted to take with them John called Mark. 38But Paul decided not to take with them one who had deserted

c Gk *from among them*   d Gk *brothers*   e Other ancient
authorities add *saying, 'You must be circumcised and keep
the law,'*   f Gk *men*   g Other ancient authorities lack *and
from what is strangled*   h Gk *When they*   i Gk *brothers*
j Other ancient authorities add verse 34, *But it seemed
good to Silas to remain there*

Greek

22 Τότε ἔδοξε τοῖς ἀποστόλοις καὶ τοῖς πρεσβυτέροις σὺν ὅλῃ τῇ ἐκκλησίᾳ ἐκλεξαμένους ἄνδρας ἐξ αὐτῶν πέμψαι εἰς Ἀντιόχειαν σὺν τῷ Παύλῳ καὶ Βαρναβᾷ, Ἰούδαν τὸν καλούμενον Βαρσαββᾶν καὶ Σιλᾶν, ἄνδρας ἡγουμένους ἐν τοῖς ἀδελφοῖς, 23 γράψαντες διὰ χειρὸς αὐτῶν, Οἱ ἀπόστολοι καὶ οἱ πρεσβύτεροι ἀδελφοὶ τοῖς κατὰ τὴν Ἀντιόχειαν καὶ Συρίαν καὶ Κιλικίαν ἀδελφοῖς τοῖς ἐξ ἐθνῶν χαίρειν. 24 Ἐπειδὴ ἠκούσαμεν ὅτι τινὲς ἐξ ἡμῶν [ἐξελθόντες] ἐτάραξαν ὑμᾶς λόγοις ἀνασκευάζοντες τὰς ψυχὰς ὑμῶν[c] οἷς οὐ διεστειλάμεθα, 25 ἔδοξεν ἡμῖν γενομένοις ὁμοθυμαδὸν ἐκλεξαμένοις ἄνδρας πέμψαι πρὸς ὑμᾶς σὺν τοῖς ἀγαπητοῖς ἡμῶν Βαρναβᾷ καὶ Παύλῳ, 26 ἀνθρώποις παραδεδωκόσι τὰς ψυχὰς αὐτῶν ὑπὲρ τοῦ ὀνόματος τοῦ κυρίου ἡμῶν Ἰησοῦ Χριστοῦ. 27 ἀπεστάλκαμεν οὖν Ἰούδαν καὶ Σιλᾶν καὶ αὐτοὺς διὰ λόγου ἀπαγγέλλοντας τὰ αὐτά. 28 ἔδοξεν γὰρ τῷ πνεύματι τῷ ἁγίῳ καὶ ἡμῖν μηδὲν πλέον ἐπιτίθεσθαι ὑμῖν βάρος πλὴν τούτων τῶν ἐπάναγκες, 29 ἀπέχεσθαι εἰδωλοθύτων καὶ αἵματος καὶ πνικτῶν καὶ πορνείας, ἐξ ὧν διατηροῦντες ἑαυτοὺς εὖ πράξετε. Ἔρρωσθε.

30 Οἱ μὲν οὖν ἀπολυθέντες κατῆλθον εἰς Ἀντιόχειαν, καὶ συναγαγόντες τὸ πλῆθος ἐπέδωκαν τὴν ἐπιστολήν. 31 ἀναγνόντες δὲ ἐχάρησαν ἐπὶ τῇ παρακλήσει. 32 Ἰούδας τε καὶ Σιλᾶς καὶ αὐτοὶ προφῆται ὄντες διὰ λόγου πολλοῦ παρεκάλεσαν τοὺς ἀδελφοὺς καὶ ἐπεστήριξαν, 33 ποιήσαντες δὲ χρόνον ἀπελύθησαν μετ' εἰρήνης ἀπὸ τῶν ἀδελφῶν πρὸς τοὺς ἀποστείλαντας αὐτούς.[d] 35 Παῦλος δὲ καὶ Βαρναβᾶς διέτριβον ἐν Ἀντιοχείᾳ διδάσκοντες καὶ εὐαγγελιζόμενοι μετὰ καὶ ἑτέρων πολλῶν τὸν λόγον τοῦ κυρίου.

36 Μετὰ δέ τινας ἡμέρας εἶπεν πρὸς Βαρναβᾶν Παῦλος, Ἐπιστρέψαντες δὴ ἐπισκεψώμεθα τοὺς ἀδελφοὺς κατὰ πόλιν πᾶσαν ἐν αἷς κατηγγείλαμεν τὸν λόγον τοῦ κυρίου πῶς ἔχουσιν. 37 Βαρναβᾶς δὲ ἐβούλετο συμπαραλαβεῖν καὶ τὸν Ἰωάννην τὸν καλούμενον Μᾶρκον· 38 Παῦλος δὲ ἠξίου, τὸν ἀποστάντα ἀπ' αὐτῶν ἀπὸ Παμφυλίας

c24 NRSV note e adds λέγοντες περιτέμνεσθαι καὶ
τηρεῖν τὸν νόμον   d33 NIV/NRSV notes add 34 ἔδοξε
δὲ τῷ Σιλᾷ ἐπιμεῖναι αὐτοῦ

NIV

The Council's Letter to Gentile Believers

22Then the apostles and elders, with the whole church, decided to choose some of their own men and send them to Antioch with Paul and Barnabas. They chose Judas (called Barsabbas) and Silas, two men who were leaders among the brothers. 23With them they sent the following letter:

The apostles and elders, your brothers,

To the Gentile believers in Antioch, Syria and Cilicia:

Greetings.

24We have heard that some went out from us without our authorization and disturbed you, troubling your minds by what they said. 25So we all agreed to choose some men and send them to you with our dear friends Barnabas and Paul— 26men who have risked their lives for the name of our Lord Jesus Christ. 27Therefore we are sending Judas and Silas to confirm by word of mouth what we are writing. 28It seemed good to the Holy Spirit and to us not to burden you with anything beyond the following requirements: 29You are to abstain from food sacrificed to idols, from blood, from the meat of strangled animals and from sexual immorality. You will do well to avoid these things.

Farewell.

30The men were sent off and went down to Antioch, where they gathered the church together and delivered the letter. 31The people read it and were glad for its encouraging message. 32Judas and Silas, who themselves were prophets, said much to encourage and strengthen the brothers. 33After spending some time there, they were sent off by the brothers with the blessing of peace to return to those who had sent them.[d] 35But Paul and Barnabas remained in Antioch, where they and many others taught and preached the word of the Lord.

Disagreement Between Paul and Barnabas

36Some time later Paul said to Barnabas, "Let us go back and visit the brothers in all the towns where we preached the word of the Lord and see how they are doing." 37Barnabas wanted to take John, also called Mark, with them, 38but Paul did not think it wise to take him, because he had deserted

NRSV

them in Pamphylia and had not accompanied them in the work. [39]The disagreement became so sharp that they parted company; Barnabas took Mark with him and sailed away to Cyprus. [40]But Paul chose Silas and set out, the believers[i] commending him to the grace of the Lord. [41]He went through Syria and Cilicia, strengthening the churches.

Timothy Joins Paul and Silas

16 Paul[k] went on also to Derbe and to Lystra, where there was a disciple named Timothy, the son of a Jewish woman who was a believer; but his father was a Greek. [2]He was well spoken of by the believers[i] in Lystra and Iconium. [3]Paul wanted Timothy to accompany him; and he took him and had him circumcised because of the Jews who were in those places, for they all knew that his father was a Greek. [4]As they went from town to town, they delivered to them for observance the decisions that had been reached by the apostles and elders who were in Jerusalem. [5]So the churches were strengthened in the faith and increased in numbers daily.

Paul's Vision of the Man of Macedonia

6 They went through the region of Phrygia and Galatia, having been forbidden by the Holy Spirit to speak the word in Asia. [7]When they had come opposite Mysia, they attempted to go into Bithynia, but the Spirit of Jesus did not allow them; [8]so, passing by Mysia, they went down to Troas. [9]During the night Paul had a vision: there stood a man of Macedonia pleading with him and saying, "Come over to Macedonia and help us." [10]When he had seen the vision, we immediately tried to cross over to Macedonia, being convinced that God had called us to proclaim the good news to them.

The Conversion of Lydia

11 We set sail from Troas and took a straight course to Samothrace, the following day to Neapolis, [12]and from there to Philippi, which is a leading city of the district[l] of Macedonia and a Roman colony. We remained in this city for some days. [13]On the sabbath day we went outside the gate by the river, where we supposed there was a place of prayer; and we sat down and spoke to the women who had gathered there. [14]A certain woman named

(Greek)

καὶ μὴ συνελθόντα αὐτοῖς εἰς τὸ ἔργον μὴ συμπαραλαμβάνειν τοῦτον. **39** ἐγένετο δὲ παροξυσμὸς ὥστε ἀποχωρισθῆναι αὐτοὺς ἀπ᾽ ἀλλήλων, τόν τε Βαρναβᾶν παραλαβόντα τὸν Μᾶρκον ἐκπλεῦσαι εἰς Κύπρον, **40** Παῦλος δὲ ἐπιλεξάμενος Σιλᾶν ἐξῆλθεν παραδοθεὶς τῇ χάριτι τοῦ κυρίου ὑπὸ τῶν ἀδελφῶν. **41** διήρχετο δὲ τὴν Συρίαν καὶ [τὴν] Κιλικίαν ἐπιστηρίζων τὰς ἐκκλησίας.

16 Κατήντησεν δὲ [καὶ] εἰς Δέρβην καὶ εἰς Λύστραν. καὶ ἰδοὺ μαθητής τις ἦν ἐκεῖ ὀνόματι Τιμόθεος, υἱὸς γυναικὸς Ἰουδαίας πιστῆς, πατρὸς δὲ Ἕλληνος, **2** ὃς ἐμαρτυρεῖτο ὑπὸ τῶν ἐν Λύστροις καὶ Ἰκονίῳ ἀδελφῶν. **3** τοῦτον ἠθέλησεν ὁ Παῦλος σὺν αὐτῷ ἐξελθεῖν, καὶ λαβὼν περιέτεμεν αὐτὸν διὰ τοὺς Ἰουδαίους τοὺς ὄντας ἐν τοῖς τόποις ἐκείνοις· ᾔδεισαν γὰρ ἅπαντες ὅτι Ἕλλην ὁ πατὴρ αὐτοῦ ὑπῆρχεν. **4** ὡς δὲ διεπορεύοντο τὰς πόλεις, παρεδίδοσαν αὐτοῖς φυλάσσειν τὰ δόγματα τὰ κεκριμένα ὑπὸ τῶν ἀποστόλων καὶ πρεσβυτέρων τῶν ἐν Ἱεροσολύμοις. **5** αἱ μὲν οὖν ἐκκλησίαι ἐστερεοῦντο τῇ πίστει καὶ ἐπερίσσευον τῷ ἀριθμῷ καθ᾽ ἡμέραν.

6 Διῆλθον δὲ τὴν Φρυγίαν καὶ Γαλατικὴν χώραν κωλυθέντες ὑπὸ τοῦ ἁγίου πνεύματος λαλῆσαι τὸν λόγον ἐν τῇ Ἀσίᾳ· **7** ἐλθόντες δὲ κατὰ τὴν Μυσίαν ἐπείραζον εἰς τὴν Βιθυνίαν πορευθῆναι, καὶ οὐκ εἴασεν αὐτοὺς τὸ πνεῦμα Ἰησοῦ· **8** παρελθόντες δὲ τὴν Μυσίαν κατέβησαν εἰς Τρῳάδα. **9** καὶ ὅραμα διὰ [τῆς] νυκτὸς τῷ Παύλῳ ὤφθη, ἀνὴρ Μακεδών τις ἦν ἑστὼς καὶ παρακαλῶν αὐτὸν καὶ λέγων, Διαβὰς εἰς Μακεδονίαν βοήθησον ἡμῖν. **10** ὡς δὲ τὸ ὅραμα εἶδεν, εὐθέως ἐζητήσαμεν ἐξελθεῖν εἰς Μακεδονίαν συμβιβάζοντες ὅτι προσκέκληται ἡμᾶς ὁ θεὸς εὐαγγελίσασθαι αὐτούς.

11 Ἀναχθέντες δὲ ἀπὸ Τρῳάδος εὐθυδρομήσαμεν εἰς Σαμοθρᾴκην, τῇ δὲ ἐπιούσῃ εἰς Νέαν Πόλιν **12** κἀκεῖθεν εἰς Φιλίππους, ἥτις ἐστὶν πρώτη[ς][a] μερίδος τῆς Μακεδονίας πόλις, κολωνία. ἦμεν δὲ ἐν ταύτῃ τῇ πόλει διατρίβοντες ἡμέρας τινάς. **13** τῇ τε ἡμέρᾳ τῶν σαββάτων ἐξήλθομεν ἔξω τῆς πύλης παρὰ ποταμὸν οὗ ἐνομίζομεν προσευχὴν εἶναι, καὶ καθίσαντες ἐλαλοῦμεν ταῖς συνελθούσαις γυναιξίν. **14** καί τις γυνὴ ὀνόματι Λυδία,

NIV

them in Pamphylia and had not continued with them in the work. [39]They had such a sharp disagreement that they parted company. Barnabas took Mark and sailed for Cyprus, [40]but Paul chose Silas and left, commended by the brothers to the grace of the Lord. [41]He went through Syria and Cilicia, strengthening the churches.

Timothy Joins Paul and Silas

16 He came to Derbe and then to Lystra, where a disciple named Timothy lived, whose mother was a Jewess and a believer, but whose father was a Greek. [2]The brothers at Lystra and Iconium spoke well of him. [3]Paul wanted to take him along on the journey, so he circumcised him because of the Jews who lived in that area, for they all knew that his father was a Greek. [4]As they traveled from town to town, they delivered the decisions reached by the apostles and elders in Jerusalem for the people to obey. [5]So the churches were strengthened in the faith and grew daily in numbers.

Paul's Vision of the Man of Macedonia

[6]Paul and his companions traveled throughout the region of Phrygia and Galatia, having been kept by the Holy Spirit from preaching the word in the province of Asia. [7]When they came to the border of Mysia, they tried to enter Bithynia, but the Spirit of Jesus would not allow them to. [8]So they passed by Mysia and went down to Troas. [9]During the night Paul had a vision of a man of Macedonia standing and begging him, "Come over to Macedonia and help us." [10]After Paul had seen the vision, we got ready at once to leave for Macedonia, concluding that God had called us to preach the gospel to them.

Lydia's Conversion in Philippi

[11]From Troas we put out to sea and sailed straight for Samothrace, and the next day on to Neapolis. [12]From there we traveled to Philippi, a Roman colony and the leading city of that district of Macedonia. And we stayed there several days.

[13]On the Sabbath we went outside the city gate to the river, where we expected to find a place of prayer. We sat down and began to speak to the women who had gathered there. [14]One of those listening was a woman named Lydia, a dealer in

---

[i] Gk *brothers*   [k] Gk *He*   [l] Other authorities read *a city of the first district*

[a] 12 NIV/NRSV texts read πρώτη τῆς μερίδος; NRSV note l πρώτης μερίδος τῆς

Lydia, a worshiper of God, was listening to us; she was from the city of Thyatira and a dealer in purple cloth. The Lord opened her heart to listen eagerly to what was said by Paul. 15When she and her household were baptized, she urged us, saying, "If you have judged me to be faithful to the Lord, come and stay at my home." And she prevailed upon us.

Paul and Silas in Prison

16 One day, as we were going to the place of prayer, we met a slave-girl who had a spirit of divination and brought her owners a great deal of money by fortune-telling. 17While she followed Paul and us, she would cry out, "These men are slaves of the Most High God, who proclaim to you[m] a way of salvation." 18She kept doing this for many days. But Paul, very much annoyed, turned and said to the spirit, "I order you in the name of Jesus Christ to come out of her." And it came out that very hour.

19 But when her owners saw that their hope of making money was gone, they seized Paul and Silas and dragged them into the marketplace before the authorities. 20When they had brought them before the magistrates, they said, "These men are disturbing our city; they are Jews 21and are advocating customs that are not lawful for us as Romans to adopt or observe." 22The crowd joined in attacking them, and the magistrates had them stripped of their clothing and ordered them to be beaten with rods. 23After they had given them a severe flogging, they threw them into prison and ordered the jailer to keep them securely. 24Following these instructions, he put them in the innermost cell and fastened their feet in the stocks.

25 About midnight Paul and Silas were praying and singing hymns to God, and the prisoners were listening to them. 26Suddenly there was an earthquake, so violent that the foundations of the prison were shaken; and immediately all the doors were opened and everyone's chains were unfastened. 27When the jailer woke up and saw the prison doors wide open, he drew his sword and was about to kill himself, since he supposed that the prisoners had escaped. 28But Paul shouted in a loud voice, "Do not harm yourself, for we are all here."

πορφυρόπωλις πόλεως Θυατείρων σεβομένη τὸν θεόν, ἤκουεν, ἧς ὁ κύριος διήνοιξεν τὴν καρδίαν προσέχειν τοῖς λαλουμένοις ὑπὸ τοῦ Παύλου. 15 ὡς δὲ ἐβαπτίσθη καὶ ὁ οἶκος αὐτῆς, παρεκάλεσεν λέγουσα, Εἰ κεκρίκατέ με πιστὴν τῷ κυρίῳ εἶναι, εἰσελθόντες εἰς τὸν οἶκόν μου μένετε· καὶ παρεβιάσατο ἡμᾶς.

16 Ἐγένετο δὲ πορευομένων ἡμῶν εἰς τὴν προσευχὴν παιδίσκην τινὰ ἔχουσαν πνεῦμα πύθωνα ὑπαντῆσαι ἡμῖν, ἥτις ἐργασίαν πολλὴν παρεῖχεν τοῖς κυρίοις αὐτῆς μαντευομένη. 17 αὕτη κατακολουθοῦσα τῷ Παύλῳ καὶ ἡμῖν ἔκραζεν λέγουσα, Οὗτοι οἱ ἄνθρωποι δοῦλοι τοῦ θεοῦ τοῦ ὑψίστου εἰσίν, οἵτινες καταγγέλλουσιν ὑμῖν[b] ὁδὸν σωτηρίας. 18 τοῦτο δὲ ἐποίει ἐπὶ πολλὰς ἡμέρας. διαπονηθεὶς δὲ Παῦλος καὶ ἐπιστρέψας τῷ πνεύματι εἶπεν, Παραγγέλλω σοι ἐν ὀνόματι Ἰησοῦ Χριστοῦ ἐξελθεῖν ἀπ' αὐτῆς· καὶ ἐξῆλθεν αὐτῇ τῇ ὥρᾳ. 19 ἰδόντες δὲ οἱ κύριοι αὐτῆς ὅτι ἐξῆλθεν ἡ ἐλπὶς τῆς ἐργασίας αὐτῶν, ἐπιλαβόμενοι τὸν Παῦλον καὶ τὸν Σιλᾶν εἵλκυσαν εἰς τὴν ἀγορὰν ἐπὶ τοὺς ἄρχοντας 20 καὶ προσαγαγόντες αὐτοὺς τοῖς στρατηγοῖς εἶπαν, Οὗτοι οἱ ἄνθρωποι ἐκταράσσουσιν ἡμῶν τὴν πόλιν, Ἰουδαῖοι ὑπάρχοντες, 21 καὶ καταγγέλλουσιν ἔθη ἃ οὐκ ἔξεστιν ἡμῖν παραδέχεσθαι οὐδὲ ποιεῖν Ῥωμαίοις οὖσιν. 22 καὶ συνεπέστη ὁ ὄχλος κατ' αὐτῶν καὶ οἱ στρατηγοὶ περιρήξαντες αὐτῶν τὰ ἱμάτια ἐκέλευον ῥαβδίζειν, 23 πολλάς τε ἐπιθέντες αὐτοῖς πληγὰς ἔβαλον εἰς φυλακὴν παραγγείλαντες τῷ δεσμοφύλακι ἀσφαλῶς τηρεῖν αὐτούς. 24 ὃς παραγγελίαν τοιαύτην λαβὼν ἔβαλεν αὐτοὺς εἰς τὴν ἐσωτέραν φυλακὴν καὶ τοὺς πόδας ἠσφαλίσατο αὐτῶν εἰς τὸ ξύλον.

25 Κατὰ δὲ τὸ μεσονύκτιον Παῦλος καὶ Σιλᾶς προσευχόμενοι ὕμνουν τὸν θεόν, ἐπηκροῶντο δὲ αὐτῶν οἱ δέσμιοι. 26 ἄφνω δὲ σεισμὸς ἐγένετο μέγας ὥστε σαλευθῆναι τὰ θεμέλια τοῦ δεσμωτηρίου· ἠνεῴχθησαν δὲ παραχρῆμα αἱ θύραι πᾶσαι καὶ πάντων τὰ δεσμὰ ἀνέθη. 27 ἔξυπνος δὲ γενόμενος ὁ δεσμοφύλαξ καὶ ἰδὼν ἀνεῳγμένας τὰς θύρας τῆς φυλακῆς, σπασάμενος [τὴν] μάχαιραν ἤμελλεν ἑαυτὸν ἀναιρεῖν νομίζων ἐκπεφευγέναι τοὺς δεσμίους. 28 ἐφώνησεν δὲ μεγάλῃ φωνῇ [ὁ] Παῦλος λέγων, Μηδὲν πράξῃς σεαυτῷ κακόν, ἅπαντες γάρ ἐσμεν

purple cloth from the city of Thyatira, who was a worshiper of God. The Lord opened her heart to respond to Paul's message. 15When she and the members of her household were baptized, she invited us to her home. "If you consider me a believer in the Lord," she said, "come and stay at my house." And she persuaded us.

Paul and Silas in Prison

16Once when we were going to the place of prayer, we were met by a slave girl who had a spirit by which she predicted the future. She earned a great deal of money for her owners by fortune-telling. 17This girl followed Paul and the rest of us, shouting, "These men are servants of the Most High God, who are telling you the way to be saved." 18She kept this up for many days. Finally Paul became so troubled that he turned around and said to the spirit, "In the name of Jesus Christ I command you to come out of her!" At that moment the spirit left her.

19When the owners of the slave girl realized that their hope of making money was gone, they seized Paul and Silas and dragged them into the marketplace to face the authorities. 20They brought them before the magistrates and said, "These men are Jews, and are throwing our city into an uproar 21by advocating customs unlawful for us Romans to accept or practice."

22The crowd joined in the attack against Paul and Silas, and the magistrates ordered them to be stripped and beaten. 23After they had been severely flogged, they were thrown into prison, and the jailer was commanded to guard them carefully. 24Upon receiving such orders, he put them in the inner cell and fastened their feet in the stocks.

25About midnight Paul and Silas were praying and singing hymns to God, and the other prisoners were listening to them. 26Suddenly there was such a violent earthquake that the foundations of the prison were shaken. At once all the prison doors flew open, and everybody's chains came loose. 27The jailer woke up, and when he saw the prison doors open, he drew his sword and was about to kill himself because he thought the prisoners had escaped. 28But Paul shouted, "Don't harm yourself! We are all here!"

---

[m] Other ancient authorities read *to us*   [b]17 NRSV note m ἡμῖν

29The jailer[n] called for lights, and rushing in, he fell down trembling before Paul and Silas. 30Then he brought them outside and said, "Sirs, what must I do to be saved?" 31They answered, "Believe on the Lord Jesus, and you will be saved, you and your household." 32They spoke the word of the Lord[o] to him and to all who were in his house. 33At the same hour of the night he took them and washed their wounds; then he and his entire family were baptized without delay. 34He brought them up into the house and set food before them; and he and his entire household rejoiced that he had become a believer in God.

35 When morning came, the magistrates sent the police, saying, "Let those men go." 36And the jailer reported the message to Paul, saying, "The magistrates sent word to let you go; therefore come out now and go in peace." 37But Paul replied, "They have beaten us in public, uncondemned, men who are Roman citizens, and have thrown us into prison; and now are they going to discharge us in secret? Certainly not! Let them come and take us out themselves." 38The police reported these words to the magistrates, and they were afraid when they heard that they were Roman citizens; 39so they came and apologized to them. And they took them out and asked them to leave the city. 40After leaving the prison they went to Lydia's home; and when they had seen and encouraged the brothers and sisters[p] there, they departed.

The Uproar in Thessalonica

17 After Paul and Silas[q] had passed through Amphipolis and Apollonia, they came to Thessalonica, where there was a synagogue of the Jews. 2And Paul went in, as was his custom, and on three sabbath days argued with them from the scriptures, 3explaining and proving that it was necessary for the Messiah[r] to suffer and to rise from the dead, and saying, "This is the Messiah,[r] Jesus whom I am proclaiming to you." 4Some of them were persuaded and joined Paul and Silas, as did a great many of the devout Greeks and not a few of the leading women. 5But the Jews became jealous, and with the help of some ruffians in the marketplaces they formed a mob and set the city in an uproar. While

ἐνθάδε. **29** αἰτήσας δὲ φῶτα εἰσεπή-δησεν καὶ ἔντρομος γενόμενος προσέ-πεσεν τῷ Παύλῳ καὶ [τῷ] Σιλᾷ **30** καὶ προαγαγὼν αὐτοὺς ἔξω ἔφη, Κύριοι, τί με δεῖ ποιεῖν ἵνα σωθῶ; **31** οἱ δὲ εἶπαν, Πίστευσον ἐπὶ τὸν κύριον Ἰησοῦν καὶ σωθήσῃ σὺ καὶ ὁ οἶκός σου. **32** καὶ ἐλάλησαν αὐτῷ τὸν λόγον τοῦ κυρίου[c] σὺν πᾶσιν τοῖς ἐν τῇ οἰκίᾳ αὐτοῦ. **33** καὶ παραλαβὼν αὐτοὺς ἐν ἐκείνῃ τῇ ὥρᾳ τῆς νυκτὸς ἔλουσεν ἀπὸ τῶν πληγῶν, καὶ ἐβαπτίσθη αὐτὸς καὶ οἱ αὐτοῦ πάντες παραχρῆμα, **34** ἀναγαγών τε αὐτοὺς εἰς τὸν οἶκον παρέθηκεν τράπεζαν καὶ ἠγαλλιάσατο πανοικεὶ πεπιστευκὼς τῷ θεῷ.

35 Ἡμέρας δὲ γενομένης ἀπέστειλαν οἱ στρατηγοὶ τοὺς ῥαβδούχους λέγον-τες, Ἀπόλυσον τοὺς ἀνθρώπους ἐκεί-νους. **36** ἀπήγγειλεν δὲ ὁ δεσμοφύλαξ τοὺς λόγους [τούτους] πρὸς τὸν Παῦλον ὅτι Ἀπέσταλκαν οἱ στρατηγοὶ ἵνα ἀπολυθῆτε· νῦν οὖν ἐξελθόντες πορεύ-εσθε ἐν εἰρήνῃ. **37** ὁ δὲ Παῦλος ἔφη πρὸς αὐτούς, Δείραντες ἡμᾶς δημοσίᾳ ἀκατακρίτους, ἀνθρώπους Ῥωμαίους ὑπάρχοντας, ἔβαλαν εἰς φυλακήν, καὶ νῦν λάθρα ἡμᾶς ἐκβάλλουσιν; οὐ γάρ, ἀλλὰ ἐλθόντες αὐτοὶ ἡμᾶς ἐξαγαγέτω-σαν. **38** ἀπήγγειλαν δὲ τοῖς στρατηγοῖς οἱ ῥαβδοῦχοι τὰ ῥήματα ταῦτα. ἐφοβήθησαν δὲ ἀκούσαντες ὅτι Ῥωμαῖοί εἰσιν, **39** καὶ ἐλθόντες παρεκάλεσαν αὐτούς, καὶ ἐξαγαγόντες ἠρώτων ἀπελθεῖν ἀπὸ τῆς πόλεως. **40** ἐξελθόντες δὲ ἀπὸ τῆς φυλακῆς εἰσῆλθον πρὸς τὴν Λυδίαν καὶ ἰδόντες παρεκάλεσαν τοὺς ἀδελφοὺς καὶ ἐξῆλθαν.

17 Διοδεύσαντες δὲ τὴν Ἀμφί-πολιν καὶ τὴν Ἀπολλωνίαν ἦλθον εἰς Θεσσαλονίκην ὅπου ἦν συναγωγὴ τῶν Ἰουδαίων. **2** κατὰ δὲ τὸ εἰωθὸς τῷ Παύλῳ εἰσῆλθεν πρὸς αὐτοὺς καὶ ἐπὶ σάββατα τρία διελέξατο αὐτοῖς ἀπὸ τῶν γραφῶν, **3** διανοίγων καὶ παρατιθέμενος ὅτι τὸν Χριστὸν ἔδει παθεῖν καὶ ἀναστῆναι ἐκ νεκρῶν καὶ ὅτι οὗτός ἐστιν ὁ Χριστὸς [ὁ] Ἰησοῦς ὃν ἐγὼ καταγγέλλω ὑμῖν. **4** καί τινες ἐξ αὐτῶν ἐπείσθησαν καὶ προσεκληρώ-θησαν τῷ Παύλῳ καὶ τῷ Σιλᾷ, τῶν τε σεβομένων Ἑλλήνων πλῆθος πολύ, γυναικῶν τε τῶν πρώτων οὐκ ὀλίγαι. **5** Ζηλώσαντες δὲ οἱ Ἰουδαῖοι καὶ προσ-λαβόμενοι τῶν ἀγοραίων ἄνδρας τινὰς πονηροὺς καὶ ὀχλοποιήσαντες ἐθορύβουν τὴν πόλιν καὶ ἐπιστάντες τῇ οἰκίᾳ

29The jailer called for lights, rushed in and fell trembling before Paul and Silas. 30He then brought them out and asked, "Sirs, what must I do to be saved?"

31They replied, "Believe in the Lord Jesus, and you will be saved—you and your household." 32Then they spoke the word of the Lord to him and to all the others in his house. 33At that hour of the night the jailer took them and washed their wounds; then immediately he and all his family were baptized. 34The jailer brought them into his house and set a meal before them; he was filled with joy because he had come to believe in God—he and his whole family.

35When it was daylight, the magistrates sent their officers to the jailer with the or-der: "Release those men." 36The jailer told Paul, "The magistrates have ordered that you and Silas be released. Now you can leave. Go in peace."

37But Paul said to the officers: "They beat us publicly without a trial, even though we are Roman citizens, and threw us into prison. And now do they want to get rid of us quietly? No! Let them come themselves and escort us out."

38The officers reported this to the magis-trates, and when they heard that Paul and Silas were Roman citizens, they were alarmed. 39They came to appease them and escorted them from the prison, requesting them to leave the city. 40After Paul and Silas came out of the prison, they went to Lydia's house, where they met with the brothers and encouraged them. Then they left.

In Thessalonica

17 When they had passed through Amphipolis and Apollonia, they came to Thessalonica, where there was a Jewish synagogue. 2As his custom was, Paul went into the synagogue, and on three Sabbath days he reasoned with them from the Scriptures, 3explaining and proving that the Christ[a] had to suffer and rise from the dead. "This Jesus I am proclaiming to you is the Christ,[a]" he said. 4Some of the Jews were persuaded and joined Paul and Silas, as did a large number of God-fearing Greeks and not a few prominent women.

5But the Jews were jealous; so they rounded up some bad characters from the marketplace, formed a mob and started a riot in the city. They rushed to Jason's house

they were searching for Paul and Silas to bring them out to the assembly, they attacked Jason's house. 6When they could not find them, they dragged Jason and some believers[s] before the city authorities,[t] shouting, "These people who have been turning the world upside down have come here also, 7and Jason has entertained them as guests. They are all acting contrary to the decrees of the emperor, saying that there is another king named Jesus." 8The people and the city officials were disturbed when they heard this, 9and after they had taken bail from Jason and the others, they let them go.

Paul and Silas in Beroea

10 That very night the believers[s] sent Paul and Silas off to Beroea; and when they arrived, they went to the Jewish synagogue. 11These Jews were more receptive than those in Thessalonica, for they welcomed the message very eagerly and examined the scriptures every day to see whether these things were so. 12Many of them therefore believed, including not a few Greek women and men of high standing. 13But when the Jews of Thessalonica learned that the word of God had been proclaimed by Paul in Beroea as well, they came there too, to stir up and incite the crowds. 14Then the believers[s] immediately sent Paul away to the coast, but Silas and Timothy remained behind. 15Those who conducted Paul brought him as far as Athens; and after receiving instructions to have Silas and Timothy join him as soon as possible, they left him.

Paul in Athens

16 While Paul was waiting for them in Athens, he was deeply distressed to see that the city was full of idols. 17So he argued in the synagogue with the Jews and the devout persons, and also in the marketplace[u] every day with those who happened to be there. 18Also some Epicurean and Stoic philosophers debated with him. Some said, "What does this babbler want to say?" Others said, "He seems to be a proclaimer of foreign divinities." (This was because he was telling the good news about Jesus and the resurrection.) 19So they took him and brought him to the Areopagus and asked him, "May we know what this new teaching is that you are presenting? 20It sounds rather strange to us, so we would

Ἰάσονος ἐζήτουν αὐτοὺς προαγαγεῖν εἰς τὸν δῆμον· 6 μὴ εὑρόντες δὲ αὐτοὺς ἔσυρον Ἰάσονα καί τινας ἀδελφοὺς ἐπὶ τοὺς πολιτάρχας βοῶντες ὅτι Οἱ τὴν οἰκουμένην ἀναστατώσαντες οὗτοι καὶ ἐνθάδε πάρεισιν, 7 οὓς ὑποδέδεκται Ἰάσων· καὶ οὗτοι πάντες ἀπέναντι τῶν δογμάτων Καίσαρος πράσσουσι βασιλέα ἕτερον λέγοντες εἶναι Ἰησοῦν. 8 ἐτάραξαν δὲ τὸν ὄχλον καὶ τοὺς πολιτάρχας ἀκούοντας ταῦτα, 9 καὶ λαβόντες τὸ ἱκανὸν παρὰ τοῦ Ἰάσονος καὶ τῶν λοιπῶν ἀπέλυσαν αὐτούς.

10 Οἱ δὲ ἀδελφοὶ εὐθέως διὰ νυκτὸς ἐξέπεμψαν τόν τε Παῦλον καὶ τὸν Σιλᾶν εἰς Βέροιαν, οἵτινες παραγενόμενοι εἰς τὴν συναγωγὴν τῶν Ἰουδαίων ἀπῄεσαν. 11 οὗτοι δὲ ἦσαν εὐγενέστεροι τῶν ἐν Θεσσαλονίκῃ, οἵτινες ἐδέξαντο τὸν λόγον μετὰ πάσης προθυμίας καθ᾽ ἡμέραν ἀνακρίνοντες τὰς γραφὰς εἰ ἔχοι ταῦτα οὕτως. 12 πολλοὶ μὲν οὖν ἐξ αὐτῶν ἐπίστευσαν καὶ τῶν Ἑλληνίδων γυναικῶν τῶν εὐσχημόνων καὶ ἀνδρῶν οὐκ ὀλίγοι. 13 Ὡς δὲ ἔγνωσαν οἱ ἀπὸ τῆς Θεσσαλονίκης Ἰουδαῖοι ὅτι καὶ ἐν τῇ Βεροίᾳ κατηγγέλη ὑπὸ τοῦ Παύλου ὁ λόγος τοῦ θεοῦ, ἦλθον κἀκεῖ σαλεύοντες καὶ ταράσσοντες τοὺς ὄχλους. 14 εὐθέως δὲ τότε τὸν Παῦλον ἐξαπέστειλαν οἱ ἀδελφοὶ πορεύεσθαι ἕως ἐπὶ τὴν θάλασσαν, ὑπέμεινάν τε ὅ τε Σιλᾶς καὶ ὁ Τιμόθεος ἐκεῖ. 15 οἱ δὲ καθιστάνοντες τὸν Παῦλον ἤγαγον ἕως Ἀθηνῶν, καὶ λαβόντες ἐντολὴν πρὸς τὸν Σιλᾶν καὶ τὸν Τιμόθεον ἵνα ὡς τάχιστα ἔλθωσιν πρὸς αὐτὸν ἐξῄεσαν.

16 Ἐν δὲ ταῖς Ἀθήναις ἐκδεχομένου αὐτοὺς τοῦ Παύλου παρωξύνετο τὸ πνεῦμα αὐτοῦ ἐν αὐτῷ θεωροῦντος κατείδωλον οὖσαν τὴν πόλιν. 17 διελέγετο μὲν οὖν ἐν τῇ συναγωγῇ τοῖς Ἰουδαίοις καὶ τοῖς σεβομένοις καὶ ἐν τῇ ἀγορᾷ κατὰ πᾶσαν ἡμέραν πρὸς τοὺς παρατυγχάνοντας. 18 τινὲς δὲ καὶ τῶν Ἐπικουρείων καὶ Στοϊκῶν φιλοσόφων συνέβαλλον αὐτῷ, καί τινες ἔλεγον, Τί ἂν θέλοι ὁ σπερμολόγος οὗτος λέγειν; οἱ δέ, Ξένων δαιμονίων δοκεῖ καταγγελεὺς εἶναι, ὅτι τὸν Ἰησοῦν καὶ τὴν ἀνάστασιν εὐηγγελίζετο. 19 ἐπιλαβόμενοί τε αὐτοῦ ἐπὶ τὸν Ἄρειον Πάγον ἤγαγον λέγοντες, Δυνάμεθα γνῶναι τίς ἡ καινὴ αὕτη ἡ ὑπὸ σοῦ λαλουμένη διδαχή; 20 ξενίζοντα γάρ τινα εἰσφέρεις εἰς τὰς ἀκοὰς

in search of Paul and Silas in order to bring them out to the crowd.[b] 6But when they did not find them, they dragged Jason and some other brothers before the city officials, shouting: "These men who have caused trouble all over the world have now come here, 7and Jason has welcomed them into his house. They are all defying Caesar's decrees, saying that there is another king, one called Jesus." 8When they heard this, the crowd and the city officials were thrown into turmoil. 9Then they made Jason and the others post bond and let them go.

In Berea

10As soon as it was night, the brothers sent Paul and Silas away to Berea. On arriving there, they went to the Jewish synagogue. 11Now the Bereans were of more noble character than the Thessalonians, for they received the message with great eagerness and examined the Scriptures every day to see if what Paul said was true. 12Many of the Jews believed, as did also a number of prominent Greek women and many Greek men.

13When the Jews in Thessalonica learned that Paul was preaching the word of God at Berea, they went there too, agitating the crowds and stirring them up. 14The brothers immediately sent Paul to the coast, but Silas and Timothy stayed at Berea. 15The men who escorted Paul brought him to Athens and then left with instructions for Silas and Timothy to join him as soon as possible.

In Athens

16While Paul was waiting for them in Athens, he was greatly distressed to see that the city was full of idols. 17So he reasoned in the synagogue with the Jews and the God-fearing Greeks, as well as in the marketplace day by day with those who happened to be there. 18A group of Epicurean and Stoic philosophers began to dispute with him. Some of them asked, "What is this babbler trying to say?" Others remarked, "He seems to be advocating foreign gods." They said this because Paul was preaching the good news about Jesus and the resurrection. 19Then they took him and brought him to a meeting of the Areopagus, where they said to him, "May we know what this new teaching is that you are presenting? 20You are bringing some strange ideas to our ears, and we

[s] Gk *brothers*   [t] Gk *politarchs*   [u] Or *civic center;* Gk *agora*

[b]5 Or *the assembly of the people*

like to know what it means." 21Now all the Athenians and the foreigners living there would spend their time in nothing but telling or hearing something new.

22 Then Paul stood in front of the Areopagus and said, "Athenians, I see how extremely religious you are in every way. 23For as I went through the city and looked carefully at the objects of your worship, I found among them an altar with the inscription, 'To an unknown god.' What therefore you worship as unknown, this I proclaim to you. 24The God who made the world and everything in it, he who is Lord of heaven and earth, does not live in shrines made by human hands, 25nor is he served by human hands, as though he needed anything, since he himself gives to all mortals life and breath and all things. 26From one ancestorv he made all nations to inhabit the whole earth, and he allotted the times of their existence and the boundaries of the places where they would live, 27so that they would search for Godw and perhaps grope for him and find him—though indeed he is not far from each one of us. 28For 'In him we live and move and have our being'; as even some of your own poets have said,

'For we too are his offspring.'

29Since we are God's offspring, we ought not to think that the deity is like gold, or silver, or stone, an image formed by the art and imagination of mortals. 30While God has overlooked the times of human ignorance, now he commands all people everywhere to repent, 31because he has fixed a day on which he will have the world judged in righteousness by a man whom he has appointed, and of this he has given assurance to all by raising him from the dead."

32 When they heard of the resurrection of the dead, some scoffed; but others said, "We will hear you again about this." 33At that point Paul left them. 34But some of them joined him and became believers, including Dionysius the Areopagite and a woman named Damaris, and others with them.

Paul in Corinth

18 After this Paulx left Athens and went to Corinth. 2There he found a Jew named Aquila, a native of Pontus, who had recently come from Italy with his wife Priscilla, because Claudius had

ἡμῶν· βουλόμεθα οὖν γνῶναι τίνα θέλει ταῦτα εἶναι. 21 Ἀθηναῖοι δὲ πάντες καὶ οἱ ἐπιδημοῦντες ξένοι εἰς οὐδὲν ἕτερον ηὐκαίρουν ἢ λέγειν τι ἢ ἀκούειν τι καινότερον.

22 Σταθεὶς δὲ [ὁ] Παῦλος ἐν μέσῳ τοῦ Ἀρείου Πάγου ἔφη, Ἄνδρες Ἀθηναῖοι, κατὰ πάντα ὡς δεισιδαιμονεστέρους ὑμᾶς θεωρῶ. 23 διερχόμενος γὰρ καὶ ἀναθεωρῶν τὰ σεβάσματα ὑμῶν εὗρον καὶ βωμὸν ἐν ᾧ ἐπεγέγραπτο, Ἀγνώστῳ θεῷ. ὃ οὖν ἀγνοοῦντες εὐσεβεῖτε, τοῦτο ἐγὼ καταγγέλλω ὑμῖν. 24 ὁ θεὸς ὁ ποιήσας τὸν κόσμον καὶ πάντα τὰ ἐν αὐτῷ, οὗτος οὐρανοῦ καὶ γῆς ὑπάρχων κύριος οὐκ ἐν χειροποιήτοις ναοῖς κατοικεῖ 25 οὐδὲ ὑπὸ χειρῶν ἀνθρωπίνων θεραπεύεται προσδεόμενός τινος, αὐτὸς διδοὺς πᾶσι ζωὴν καὶ πνοὴν καὶ τὰ πάντα· 26 ἐποίησέν τε ἐξ ἑνὸςa πᾶν ἔθνος ἀνθρώπων κατοικεῖν ἐπὶ παντὸς προσώπου τῆς γῆς, ὁρίσας προστεταγμένους καιροὺς καὶ τὰς ὁροθεσίας τῆς κατοικίας αὐτῶν 27 ζητεῖν τὸν θεόνb, εἰ ἄρα γε ψηλαφήσειαν αὐτὸν καὶ εὕροιεν, καί γε οὐ μακρὰν ἀπὸ ἑνὸς ἑκάστου ἡμῶν ὑπάρχοντα. 28 Ἐν αὐτῷ γὰρ ζῶμεν καὶ κινούμεθα καὶ ἐσμέν, ὡς καί τινες τῶν καθ' ὑμᾶς ποιητῶν εἰρήκασιν.

Τοῦ γὰρ καὶ γένος ἐσμέν.

29 γένος οὖν ὑπάρχοντες τοῦ θεοῦ οὐκ ὀφείλομεν νομίζειν χρυσῷ ἢ ἀργύρῳ ἢ λίθῳ, χαράγματι τέχνης καὶ ἐνθυμήσεως ἀνθρώπου, τὸ θεῖον εἶναι ὅμοιον. 30 τοὺς μὲν οὖν χρόνους τῆς ἀγνοίας ὑπεριδὼν ὁ θεός, τὰ νῦν παραγγέλλει τοῖς ἀνθρώποις πάντας πανταχοῦ μετανοεῖν, 31 καθότι ἔστησεν ἡμέραν ἐν ᾗ μέλλει κρίνειν τὴν οἰκουμένην ἐν δικαιοσύνῃ ἐν ἀνδρὶ ᾧ ὥρισεν, πίστιν παρασχὼν πᾶσιν ἀναστήσας αὐτὸν ἐκ νεκρῶν.

32 Ἀκούσαντες δὲ ἀνάστασιν νεκρῶν οἱ μὲν ἐχλεύαζον, οἱ δὲ εἶπαν, Ἀκουσόμεθά σου περὶ τούτου καὶ πάλιν. 33 οὕτως ὁ Παῦλος ἐξῆλθεν ἐκ μέσου αὐτῶν. 34 τινὲς δὲ ἄνδρες κολληθέντες αὐτῷ ἐπίστευσαν, ἐν οἷς καὶ Διονύσιος ὁ Ἀρεοπαγίτης καὶ γυνὴ ὀνόματι Δάμαρις καὶ ἕτεροι σὺν αὐτοῖς.

18 Μετὰ ταῦτα χωρισθεὶς ἐκ τῶν Ἀθηνῶν ἦλθεν εἰς Κόρινθον. 2 καὶ εὑρών τινα Ἰουδαῖον ὀνόματι Ἀκύλαν, Ποντικὸν τῷ γένει προσφάτως ἐληλυθότα ἀπὸ τῆς Ἰταλίας καὶ Πρίσκιλλαν γυναῖκα αὐτοῦ, διὰ τὸ

want to know what they mean." 21(All the Athenians and the foreigners who lived there spent their time doing nothing but talking about and listening to the latest ideas.)

22Paul then stood up in the meeting of the Areopagus and said: "Men of Athens! I see that in every way you are very religious. 23For as I walked around and looked carefully at your objects of worship, I even found an altar with this inscription: TO AN UNKNOWN GOD. Now what you worship as something unknown I am going to proclaim to you.

24"The God who made the world and everything in it is the Lord of heaven and earth and does not live in temples built by hands. 25And he is not served by human hands, as if he needed anything, because he himself gives all men life and breath and everything else. 26From one man he made every nation of men, that they should inhabit the whole earth; and he determined the times set for them and the exact places where they should live. 27God did this so that men would seek him and perhaps reach out for him and find him, though he is not far from each one of us. 28'For in him we live and move and have our being.' As some of your own poets have said, 'We are his offspring.'

29"Therefore since we are God's offspring, we should not think that the divine being is like gold or silver or stone—an image made by man's design and skill. 30In the past God overlooked such ignorance, but now he commands all people everywhere to repent. 31For he has set a day when he will judge the world with justice by the man he has appointed. He has given proof of this to all men by raising him from the dead."

32When they heard about the resurrection of the dead, some of them sneered, but others said, "We want to hear you again on this subject." 33At that, Paul left the Council. 34A few men became followers of Paul and believed. Among them was Dionysius, a member of the Areopagus, also a woman named Damaris, and a number of others.

In Corinth

18 After this, Paul left Athens and went to Corinth. 2There he met a Jew named Aquila, a native of Pontus, who had recently come from Italy with his wife Priscilla, because Claudius had ordered all

---

v Gk *From one*; other ancient authorities read *From one blood*   w Other ancient authorities read *the Lord*   x Gk *he*

a26 NRSV note v adds αἵματος   b27 NRSV note w κύριον

ordered all Jews to leave Rome. Paul[y] went to see them, 3and, because he was of the same trade, he stayed with them, and they worked together—by trade they were tentmakers. 4Every sabbath he would argue in the synagogue and would try to convince Jews and Greeks.

5 When Silas and Timothy arrived from Macedonia, Paul was occupied with proclaiming the word,[z] testifying to the Jews that the Messiah[a] was Jesus. 6When they opposed and reviled him, in protest he shook the dust from his clothes[b] and said to them, "Your blood be on your own heads! I am innocent. From now on I will go to the Gentiles." 7Then he left the synagogue[c] and went to the house of a man named Titius[d] Justus, a worshiper of God; his house was next door to the synagogue. 8Crispus, the official of the synagogue, became a believer in the Lord, together with all his household; and many of the Corinthians who heard Paul became believers and were baptized. 9One night the Lord said to Paul in a vision, "Do not be afraid, but speak and do not be silent; 10for I am with you, and no one will lay a hand on you to harm you, for there are many in this city who are my people." 11He stayed there a year and six months, teaching the word of God among them.

12 But when Gallio was proconsul of Achaia, the Jews made a united attack on Paul and brought him before the tribunal. 13They said, "This man is persuading people to worship God in ways that are contrary to the law." 14Just as Paul was about to speak, Gallio said to the Jews, "If it were a matter of crime or serious villainy, I would be justified in accepting the complaint of you Jews; 15but since it is a matter of questions about words and names and your own law, see to it yourselves; I do not wish to be a judge of these matters." 16And he dismissed them from the tribunal. 17Then all of them[e] seized Sosthenes, the official of the synagogue, and beat him in front of the tribunal. But Gallio paid no attention to any of these things.

Paul's Return to Antioch

18 After staying there for a considerable time, Paul said farewell to the believers[f] and sailed for Syria, accompanied by Priscilla and Aquila. At Cenchreae he had his hair cut, for he was under a vow. 19When

[y] Gk *He* [z] Gk *with the word* [a] Or *the Christ*
[b] Gk *reviled him, he shook out his clothes* [c] Gk *left there*
[d] Other ancient authorities read *Titus* [e] Other ancient authorities read *all the Greeks* [f] Gk *brothers*

διατεταχέναι Κλαύδιον χωρίζεσθαι πάντας τοὺς Ἰουδαίους ἀπὸ τῆς Ῥώμης, προσῆλθεν αὐτοῖς **3** *καὶ διὰ τὸ ὁμότεχνον εἶναι ἔμενεν παρ' αὐτοῖς, καὶ ἠργάζετο· ἦσαν γὰρ σκηνοποιοὶ τῇ τέχνῃ.* **4** *διελέγετο δὲ ἐν τῇ συναγωγῇ κατὰ πᾶν σάββατον ἔπειθέν τε Ἰουδαίους καὶ Ἕλληνας.*

5 *Ὡς δὲ κατῆλθον ἀπὸ τῆς Μακεδονίας ὅ τε Σιλᾶς καὶ ὁ Τιμόθεος, συνείχετο τῷ λόγῳ ὁ Παῦλος διαμαρτυρόμενος τοῖς Ἰουδαίοις εἶναι τὸν Χριστὸν Ἰησοῦν.* **6** *ἀντιτασσομένων δὲ αὐτῶν καὶ βλασφημούντων ἐκτιναξάμενος τὰ ἱμάτια εἶπεν πρὸς αὐτούς, Τὸ αἷμα ὑμῶν ἐπὶ τὴν κεφαλὴν ὑμῶν· καθαρὸς ἐγὼ ἀπὸ τοῦ νῦν εἰς τὰ ἔθνη πορεύσομαι.* **7** *καὶ μεταβὰς ἐκεῖθεν εἰσῆλθεν εἰς οἰκίαν τινὸς ὀνόματι Τιτίου*[a] *Ἰούστου σεβομένου τὸν θεόν, οὗ ἡ οἰκία ἦν συνομοροῦσα τῇ συναγωγῇ.* **8** *Κρίσπος δὲ ὁ ἀρχισυνάγωγος ἐπίστευσεν τῷ κυρίῳ σὺν ὅλῳ τῷ οἴκῳ αὐτοῦ, καὶ πολλοὶ τῶν Κορινθίων ἀκούοντες ἐπίστευον καὶ ἐβαπτίζοντο.* **9** *εἶπεν δὲ ὁ κύριος ἐν νυκτὶ δι' ὁράματος τῷ Παύλῳ, Μὴ φοβοῦ, ἀλλὰ λάλει καὶ μὴ σιωπήσῃς,* **10** *διότι ἐγώ εἰμι μετὰ σοῦ καὶ οὐδεὶς ἐπιθήσεταί σοι τοῦ κακῶσαί σε, διότι λαός ἐστί μοι πολὺς ἐν τῇ πόλει ταύτῃ.* **11** *Ἐκάθισεν δὲ ἐνιαυτὸν καὶ μῆνας ἓξ διδάσκων ἐν αὐτοῖς τὸν λόγον τοῦ θεοῦ.*

12 *Γαλλίωνος δὲ ἀνθυπάτου ὄντος τῆς Ἀχαΐας κατεπέστησαν ὁμοθυμαδὸν οἱ Ἰουδαῖοι τῷ Παύλῳ καὶ ἤγαγον αὐτὸν ἐπὶ τὸ βῆμα* **13** *λέγοντες ὅτι Παρὰ τὸν νόμον ἀναπείθει οὗτος τοὺς ἀνθρώπους σέβεσθαι τὸν θεόν.* **14** *μέλλοντος δὲ τοῦ Παύλου ἀνοίγειν τὸ στόμα εἶπεν ὁ Γαλλίων πρὸς τοὺς Ἰουδαίους, Εἰ μὲν ἦν ἀδίκημά τι ἢ ῥᾳδιούργημα πονηρόν, ὦ Ἰουδαῖοι, κατὰ λόγον ἂν ἀνεσχόμην ὑμῶν,* **15** *εἰ δὲ ζητήματά ἐστιν περὶ λόγου καὶ ὀνομάτων καὶ νόμου τοῦ καθ' ὑμᾶς, ὄψεσθε αὐτοί· κριτὴς ἐγὼ τούτων οὐ βούλομαι εἶναι.* **16** *καὶ ἀπήλασεν αὐτοὺς ἀπὸ τοῦ βήματος.* **17** *ἐπιλαβόμενοι δὲ πάντες*[b] *Σωσθένην τὸν ἀρχισυνάγωγον ἔτυπτον ἔμπροσθεν τοῦ βήματος· καὶ οὐδὲν τούτων τῷ Γαλλίωνι ἔμελεν.*

18 *Ὁ δὲ Παῦλος ἔτι προσμείνας ἡμέρας ἱκανὰς τοῖς ἀδελφοῖς ἀποταξάμενος ἐξέπλει εἰς τὴν Συρίαν, καὶ σὺν αὐτῷ Πρίσκιλλα καὶ Ἀκύλας, κειράμενος ἐν Κεγχρεαῖς τὴν κεφαλήν, εἶχεν γὰρ εὐχήν.* **19** *κατήντησαν δὲ εἰς*

[a]7 NRSV note d *Τίτου* [b]17 NRSV note e adds *οἱ Ἕλληνες*

the Jews to leave Rome. Paul went to see them, 3and because he was a tentmaker as they were, he stayed and worked with them. 4Every Sabbath he reasoned in the synagogue, trying to persuade Jews and Greeks.

5When Silas and Timothy came from Macedonia, Paul devoted himself exclusively to preaching, testifying to the Jews that Jesus was the Christ.[a] 6But when the Jews opposed Paul and became abusive, he shook out his clothes in protest and said to them, "Your blood be on your own heads! I am clear of my responsibility. From now on I will go to the Gentiles."

7Then Paul left the synagogue and went next door to the house of Titius Justus, a worshiper of God. 8Crispus, the synagogue ruler, and his entire household believed in the Lord; and many of the Corinthians who heard him believed and were baptized.

9One night the Lord spoke to Paul in a vision: "Do not be afraid; keep on speaking, do not be silent. 10For I am with you, and no one is going to attack and harm you, because I have many people in this city." 11So Paul stayed for a year and a half, teaching them the word of God.

12While Gallio was proconsul of Achaia, the Jews made a united attack on Paul and brought him into court. 13"This man," they charged, "is persuading the people to worship God in ways contrary to the law."

14Just as Paul was about to speak, Gallio said to the Jews, "If you Jews were making a complaint about some misdemeanor or serious crime, it would be reasonable for me to listen to you. 15But since it involves questions about words and names and your own law—settle the matter yourselves. I will not be a judge of such things." 16So he had them ejected from the court. 17Then they all turned on Sosthenes the synagogue ruler and beat him in front of the court. But Gallio showed no concern whatever.

Priscilla, Aquila and Apollos

18Paul stayed on in Corinth for some time. Then he left the brothers and sailed for Syria, accompanied by Priscilla and Aquila. Before he sailed, he had his hair cut off at Cenchrea because of a vow he had taken.

[a]5 Or *Messiah;* also in verse 28

they reached Ephesus, he left them there, but first he himself went into the synagogue and had a discussion with the Jews. [20]When they asked him to stay longer, he declined; [21]but on taking leave of them, he said, "I[g] will return to you, if God wills." Then he set sail from Ephesus.

22 When he had landed at Caesarea, he went up to Jerusalem[h] and greeted the church, and then went down to Antioch. [23]After spending some time there he departed and went from place to place through the region of Galatia[i] and Phrygia, strengthening all the disciples.

Ministry of Apollos

24 Now there came to Ephesus a Jew named Apollos, a native of Alexandria. He was an eloquent man, well-versed in the scriptures. [25]He had been instructed in the Way of the Lord; and he spoke with burning enthusiasm and taught accurately the things concerning Jesus, though he knew only the baptism of John. [26]He began to speak boldly in the synagogue; but when Priscilla and Aquila heard him, they took him aside and explained the Way of God to him more accurately. [27]And when he wished to cross over to Achaia, the believers[j] encouraged him and wrote to the disciples to welcome him. On his arrival he greatly helped those who through grace had become believers, [28]for he powerfully refuted the Jews in public, showing by the scriptures that the Messiah[k] is Jesus.

Paul in Ephesus

19 While Apollos was in Corinth, Paul passed through the interior regions and came to Ephesus, where he found some disciples. [2]He said to them, "Did you receive the Holy Spirit when you became believers?" They replied, "No, we have not even heard that there is a Holy Spirit." [3]Then he said, "Into what then were you baptized?" They answered, "Into John's baptism." [4]Paul said, "John baptized with the baptism of repentance, telling the people to believe in the one who was to come after him, that is, in Jesus." [5]On hearing this, they were baptized in the name of the Lord Jesus. [6]When Paul had laid his hands on them, the Holy Spirit came upon them, and they spoke in tongues and prophesied— [7]altogether there were about twelve of them.

Ἔφεσον, κἀκείνους κατέλιπεν αὐτοῦ, αὐτὸς δὲ εἰσελθὼν εἰς τὴν συναγωγὴν διελέξατο τοῖς Ἰουδαίοις. **20** ἐρωτώντων δὲ αὐτῶν ἐπὶ πλείονα χρόνον μεῖναι οὐκ ἐπένευσεν, **21** ἀλλὰ ἀποταξάμενος καὶ εἰπών,[c] Πάλιν ἀνακάμψω πρὸς ὑμᾶς τοῦ θεοῦ θέλοντος, ἀνήχθη ἀπὸ τῆς Ἐφέσου, **22** καὶ κατελθὼν εἰς Καισάρειαν, ἀναβὰς καὶ ἀσπασάμενος τὴν ἐκκλησίαν κατέβη εἰς Ἀντιόχειαν. **23** καὶ ποιήσας χρόνον τινὰ ἐξῆλθεν διερχόμενος καθεξῆς τὴν Γαλατικὴν χώραν καὶ Φρυγίαν, ἐπιστηρίζων πάντας τοὺς μαθητάς.

24 Ἰουδαῖος δέ τις Ἀπολλῶς ὀνόματι, Ἀλεξανδρεὺς τῷ γένει, ἀνὴρ λόγιος, κατήντησεν εἰς Ἔφεσον, δυνατὸς ὢν ἐν ταῖς γραφαῖς. **25** οὗτος ἦν κατηχημένος τὴν ὁδὸν τοῦ κυρίου καὶ ζέων τῷ πνεύματι ἐλάλει καὶ ἐδίδασκεν ἀκριβῶς τὰ περὶ τοῦ Ἰησοῦ, ἐπιστάμενος μόνον τὸ βάπτισμα Ἰωάννου· **26** οὗτός τε ἤρξατο παρρησιάζεσθαι ἐν τῇ συναγωγῇ. ἀκούσαντες δὲ αὐτοῦ Πρίσκιλλα καὶ Ἀκύλας προσελάβοντο αὐτὸν καὶ ἀκριβέστερον αὐτῷ ἐξέθεντο τὴν ὁδὸν [τοῦ θεοῦ]. **27** βουλομένου δὲ αὐτοῦ διελθεῖν εἰς τὴν Ἀχαΐαν, προτρεψάμενοι οἱ ἀδελφοὶ ἔγραψαν τοῖς μαθηταῖς ἀποδέξασθαι αὐτόν, ὃς παραγενόμενος συνεβάλετο πολὺ τοῖς πεπιστευκόσιν διὰ τῆς χάριτος· **28** εὐτόνως γὰρ τοῖς Ἰουδαίοις διακατηλέγχετο δημοσίᾳ ἐπιδεικνὺς διὰ τῶν γραφῶν εἶναι τὸν Χριστὸν Ἰησοῦν.

19 Ἐγένετο δὲ ἐν τῷ τὸν Ἀπολλῶ εἶναι ἐν Κορίνθῳ Παῦλον διελθόντα τὰ ἀνωτερικὰ μέρη [κατ]ελθεῖν εἰς Ἔφεσον καὶ εὑρεῖν τινας μαθητὰς **2** εἶπέν τε πρὸς αὐτούς, Εἰ πνεῦμα ἅγιον ἐλάβετε πιστεύσαντες; οἱ δὲ πρὸς αὐτόν, Ἀλλ᾽ οὐδ᾽ εἰ πνεῦμα ἅγιον ἔστιν ἠκούσαμεν. **3** εἶπέν τε, Εἰς τί οὖν ἐβαπτίσθητε; οἱ δὲ εἶπαν, Εἰς τὸ Ἰωάννου βάπτισμα. **4** εἶπεν δὲ Παῦλος, Ἰωάννης ἐβάπτισεν βάπτισμα μετανοίας τῷ λαῷ λέγων εἰς τὸν ἐρχόμενον μετ᾽ αὐτὸν ἵνα πιστεύσωσιν, τοῦτ᾽ ἔστιν εἰς τὸν Ἰησοῦν. **5** ἀκούσαντες δὲ ἐβαπτίσθησαν εἰς τὸ ὄνομα τοῦ κυρίου Ἰησοῦ, **6** καὶ ἐπιθέντος αὐτοῖς τοῦ Παύλου [τὰς] χεῖρας ἦλθε τὸ πνεῦμα τὸ ἅγιον ἐπ᾽ αὐτούς, ἐλάλουν τε γλώσσαις καὶ ἐπροφήτευον. **7** ἦσαν δὲ οἱ πάντες ἄνδρες ὡσεὶ δώδεκα.

[19]They arrived at Ephesus, where Paul left Priscilla and Aquila. He himself went into the synagogue and reasoned with the Jews. [20]When they asked him to spend more time with them, he declined. [21]But as he left, he promised, "I will come back if it is God's will." Then he set sail from Ephesus. [22]When he landed at Caesarea, he went up and greeted the church and then went down to Antioch.

[23]After spending some time in Antioch, Paul set out from there and traveled from place to place throughout the region of Galatia and Phrygia, strengthening all the disciples.

[24]Meanwhile a Jew named Apollos, a native of Alexandria, came to Ephesus. He was a learned man, with a thorough knowledge of the Scriptures. [25]He had been instructed in the way of the Lord, and he spoke with great fervor[b] and taught about Jesus accurately, though he knew only the baptism of John. [26]He began to speak boldly in the synagogue. When Priscilla and Aquila heard him, they invited him to their home and explained to him the way of God more adequately.

[27]When Apollos wanted to go to Achaia, the brothers encouraged him and wrote to the disciples there to welcome him. On arriving, he was a great help to those who by grace had believed. [28]For he vigorously refuted the Jews in public debate, proving from the Scriptures that Jesus was the Christ.

Paul in Ephesus

19 While Apollos was at Corinth, Paul took the road through the interior and arrived at Ephesus. There he found some disciples [2]and asked them, "Did you receive the Holy Spirit when[a] you believed?"

They answered, "No, we have not even heard that there is a Holy Spirit."

[3]So Paul asked, "Then what baptism did you receive?"

"John's baptism," they replied.

[4]Paul said, "John's baptism was a baptism of repentance. He told the people to believe in the one coming after him, that is, in Jesus." [5]On hearing this, they were baptized into[b] the name of the Lord Jesus. [6]When Paul placed his hands on them, the Holy Spirit came on them, and they spoke in tongues[c] and prophesied. [7]There were about twelve men in all.

---

[g] Other ancient authorities read *I must at all costs keep the approaching festival in Jerusalem, but I*   [h] Gk *went up*   [i] Gk *the Galatian region*   [j] Gk *brothers*   [k] Or *the Christ*

[c]21 NRSV note g adds Δεῖ με πάντως τὴν ἑορτὴν τὴν ἐρχομένην ποιῆσαι εἰς Ἱεροσόλυμα

[b]25 Or *with fervor in the Spirit*   [a]2 Or *after*   [b]5 Or *in*   [c]6 Or *other languages*

8 He entered the synagogue and for three months spoke out boldly, and argued persuasively about the kingdom of God. 9When some stubbornly refused to believe and spoke evil of the Way before the congregation, he left them, taking the disciples with him, and argued daily in the lecture hall of Tyrannus.[l] 10This continued for two years, so that all the residents of Asia, both Jews and Greeks, heard the word of the Lord.

The Sons of Sceva

11 God did extraordinary miracles through Paul, 12so that when the handkerchiefs or aprons that had touched his skin were brought to the sick, their diseases left them, and the evil spirits came out of them. 13Then some itinerant Jewish exorcists tried to use the name of the Lord Jesus over those who had evil spirits, saying, "I adjure you by the Jesus whom Paul proclaims." 14Seven sons of a Jewish high priest named Sceva were doing this. 15But the evil spirit said to them in reply, "Jesus I know, and Paul I know; but who are you?" 16Then the man with the evil spirit leaped on them, mastered them all, and so overpowered them that they fled out of the house naked and wounded. 17When this became known to all residents of Ephesus, both Jews and Greeks, everyone was awestruck; and the name of the Lord Jesus was praised. 18Also many of those who became believers confessed and disclosed their practices. 19A number of those who practiced magic collected their books and burned them publicly; when the value of these books[m] was calculated, it was found to come to fifty thousand silver coins. 20So the word of the Lord grew mightily and prevailed.

The Riot in Ephesus

21 Now after these things had been accomplished, Paul resolved in the Spirit to go through Macedonia and Achaia, and then to go on to Jerusalem. He said, "After I have gone there, I must also see Rome." 22So he sent two of his helpers, Timothy

8 Εἰσελθὼν δὲ εἰς τὴν συναγωγὴν ἐπαρρησιάζετο ἐπὶ μῆνας τρεῖς διαλεγόμενος καὶ πείθων [τὰ] περὶ τῆς βασιλείας τοῦ θεοῦ. 9 ὡς δέ τινες ἐσκληρύνοντο καὶ ἠπείθουν κακολογοῦντες τὴν ὁδὸν ἐνώπιον τοῦ πλήθους, ἀποστὰς ἀπ' αὐτῶν ἀφώρισεν τοὺς μαθητὰς καθ' ἡμέραν διαλεγόμενος ἐν τῇ σχολῇ Τυράννου[a]. 10 τοῦτο δὲ ἐγένετο ἐπὶ ἔτη δύο, ὥστε πάντας τοὺς κατοικοῦντας τὴν Ἀσίαν ἀκοῦσαι τὸν λόγον τοῦ κυρίου, Ἰουδαίους τε καὶ Ἕλληνας.

11 Δυνάμεις τε οὐ τὰς τυχούσας ὁ θεὸς ἐποίει διὰ τῶν χειρῶν Παύλου, 12 ὥστε καὶ ἐπὶ τοὺς ἀσθενοῦντας ἀποφέρεσθαι ἀπὸ τοῦ χρωτὸς αὐτοῦ σουδάρια ἢ σιμικίνθια καὶ ἀπαλλάσσεσθαι ἀπ' αὐτῶν τὰς νόσους, τά τε πνεύματα τὰ πονηρὰ ἐκπορεύεσθαι. 13 ἐπεχείρησαν δέ τινες καὶ τῶν περιερχομένων Ἰουδαίων ἐξορκιστῶν ὀνομάζειν ἐπὶ τοὺς ἔχοντας τὰ πνεύματα τὰ πονηρὰ τὸ ὄνομα τοῦ κυρίου Ἰησοῦ λέγοντες, Ὁρκίζω ὑμᾶς τὸν Ἰησοῦν ὃν Παῦλος κηρύσσει. 14 ἦσαν δέ τινος Σκευᾶ Ἰουδαίου ἀρχιερέως ἑπτὰ υἱοὶ τοῦτο ποιοῦντες. 15 ἀποκριθὲν δὲ τὸ πνεῦμα τὸ πονηρὸν εἶπεν αὐτοῖς, Τὸν [μὲν] Ἰησοῦν γινώσκω καὶ τὸν Παῦλον ἐπίσταμαι, ὑμεῖς δὲ τίνες ἐστέ; 16 καὶ ἐφαλόμενος ὁ ἄνθρωπος ἐπ' αὐτοὺς ἐν ᾧ ἦν τὸ πνεῦμα τὸ πονηρόν, κατακυριεύσας ἀμφοτέρων ἴσχυσεν κατ' αὐτῶν ὥστε γυμνοὺς καὶ τετραυματισμένους ἐκφυγεῖν ἐκ τοῦ οἴκου ἐκείνου. 17 τοῦτο δὲ ἐγένετο γνωστὸν πᾶσιν Ἰουδαίοις τε καὶ Ἕλλησιν τοῖς κατοικοῦσιν τὴν Ἔφεσον καὶ ἐπέπεσεν φόβος ἐπὶ πάντας αὐτοὺς καὶ ἐμεγαλύνετο τὸ ὄνομα τοῦ κυρίου Ἰησοῦ. 18 πολλοί τε τῶν πεπιστευκότων ἤρχοντο ἐξομολογούμενοι καὶ ἀναγγέλλοντες τὰς πράξεις αὐτῶν. 19 ἱκανοὶ δὲ τῶν τὰ περίεργα πραξάντων συνενέγκαντες τὰς βίβλους κατέκαιον ἐνώπιον πάντων, καὶ συνεψήφισαν τὰς τιμὰς αὐτῶν καὶ εὗρον ἀργυρίου μυριάδας πέντε. 20 Οὕτως κατὰ κράτος τοῦ κυρίου ὁ λόγος ηὔξανεν καὶ ἴσχυεν.

21 Ὡς δὲ ἐπληρώθη ταῦτα, ἔθετο ὁ Παῦλος ἐν τῷ πνεύματι διελθὼν τὴν Μακεδονίαν καὶ Ἀχαΐαν πορεύεσθαι εἰς Ἱεροσόλυμα εἰπὼν ὅτι Μετὰ τὸ γενέσθαι με ἐκεῖ δεῖ με καὶ Ῥώμην ἰδεῖν. 22 ἀποστείλας δὲ εἰς τὴν

8Paul entered the synagogue and spoke boldly there for three months, arguing persuasively about the kingdom of God. 9But some of them became obstinate; they refused to believe and publicly maligned the Way. So Paul left them. He took the disciples with him and had discussions daily in the lecture hall of Tyrannus. 10This went on for two years, so that all the Jews and Greeks who lived in the province of Asia heard the word of the Lord.

11God did extraordinary miracles through Paul, 12so that even handkerchiefs and aprons that had touched him were taken to the sick, and their illnesses were cured and the evil spirits left them.

13Some Jews who went around driving out evil spirits tried to invoke the name of the Lord Jesus over those who were demon-possessed. They would say, "In the name of Jesus, whom Paul preaches, I command you to come out." 14Seven sons of Sceva, a Jewish chief priest, were doing this. 15[One day] the evil spirit answered them, "Jesus I know, and I know about Paul, but who are you?" 16Then the man who had the evil spirit jumped on them and overpowered them all. He gave them such a beating that they ran out of the house naked and bleeding.

17When this became known to the Jews and Greeks living in Ephesus, they were all seized with fear, and the name of the Lord Jesus was held in high honor. 18Many of those who believed now came and openly confessed their evil deeds. 19A number who had practiced sorcery brought their scrolls together and burned them publicly. When they calculated the value of the scrolls, the total came to fifty thousand drachmas.[d] 20In this way the word of the Lord spread widely and grew in power.

21After all this had happened, Paul decided to go to Jerusalem, passing through Macedonia and Achaia. "After I have been there," he said, "I must visit Rome also." 22He sent two of his helpers, Timothy and

---

[l] Other ancient authorities read of a certain Tyrannus, from eleven o'clock in the morning to four in the afternoon
[m] Gk them

[a]9 NRSV note l adds τινὸς ἀπὸ ὥρας πέμπτης ἕως δεκάτης

[d]19 A drachma was a silver coin worth about a day's wages.

NRSV

and Erastus, to Macedonia, while he himself stayed for some time longer in Asia.

23 About that time no little disturbance broke out concerning the Way. 24A man named Demetrius, a silversmith who made silver shrines of Artemis, brought no little business to the artisans. 25These he gathered together, with the workers of the same trade, and said, "Men, you know that we get our wealth from this business. 26You also see and hear that not only in Ephesus but in almost the whole of Asia this Paul has persuaded and drawn away a considerable number of people by saying that gods made with hands are not gods. 27And there is danger not only that this trade of ours may come into disrepute but also that the temple of the great goddess Artemis will be scorned, and she will be deprived of her majesty that brought all Asia and the world to worship her."

28 When they heard this, they were enraged and shouted, "Great is Artemis of the Ephesians!" 29The city was filled with the confusion; and people[m] rushed together to the theater, dragging with them Gaius and Aristarchus, Macedonians who were Paul's travel companions. 30Paul wished to go into the crowd, but the disciples would not let him; 31even some officials of the province of Asia,[o] who were friendly to him, sent him a message urging him not to venture into the theater. 32Meanwhile, some were shouting one thing, some another; for the assembly was in confusion, and most of them did not know why they had come together. 33Some of the crowd gave instructions to Alexander, whom the Jews had pushed forward. And Alexander motioned for silence and tried to make a defense before the people. 34But when they recognized that he was a Jew, for about two hours all of them shouted in unison, "Great is Artemis of the Ephesians!" 35But when the town clerk had quieted the crowd, he said, "Citizens of Ephesus, who is there that does not know that the city of the Ephesians is the temple keeper of the great Artemis and of the statue that fell from heaven?[p] 36Since these things cannot be denied, you ought to be quiet and do nothing rash. 37You have brought these men here who are neither temple robbers nor blasphemers of our[q] goddess. 38If therefore Demetrius and the

Greek

Μακεδονίαν δύο τῶν διακονούντων αὐτῷ, Τιμόθεον καὶ Ἔραστον, αὐτὸς ἐπέσχεν χρόνον εἰς τὴν Ἀσίαν.

23 Ἐγένετο δὲ κατὰ τὸν καιρὸν ἐκεῖνον τάραχος οὐκ ὀλίγος περὶ τῆς ὁδοῦ. 24 Δημήτριος γάρ τις ὀνόματι, ἀργυροκόπος, ποιῶν ναοὺς ἀργυροῦς Ἀρτέμιδος παρείχετο τοῖς τεχνίταις οὐκ ὀλίγην ἐργασίαν, 25 οὓς συναθροίσας καὶ τοὺς περὶ τὰ τοιαῦτα ἐργάτας εἶπεν, Ἄνδρες, ἐπίστασθε ὅτι ἐκ ταύτης τῆς ἐργασίας ἡ εὐπορία ἡμῖν ἐστιν 26 καὶ θεωρεῖτε καὶ ἀκούετε ὅτι οὐ μόνον Ἐφέσου ἀλλὰ σχεδὸν πάσης τῆς Ἀσίας ὁ Παῦλος οὗτος πείσας μετέστησεν ἱκανὸν ὄχλον λέγων ὅτι οὐκ εἰσὶν θεοὶ οἱ διὰ χειρῶν γινόμενοι. 27 οὐ μόνον δὲ τοῦτο κινδυνεύει ἡμῖν τὸ μέρος εἰς ἀπελεγμὸν ἐλθεῖν ἀλλὰ καὶ τὸ τῆς μεγάλης θεᾶς Ἀρτέμιδος ἱερὸν εἰς οὐθὲν λογισθῆναι, μέλλειν τε καὶ καθαιρεῖσθαι τῆς μεγαλειότητος αὐτῆς ἣν ὅλη ἡ Ἀσία καὶ ἡ οἰκουμένη σέβεται.

28 Ἀκούσαντες δὲ καὶ γενόμενοι πλήρεις θυμοῦ ἔκραζον λέγοντες, Μεγάλη ἡ Ἄρτεμις Ἐφεσίων. 29 καὶ ἐπλήσθη ἡ πόλις τῆς συγχύσεως, ὥρμησάν τε ὁμοθυμαδὸν εἰς τὸ θέατρον συναρπάσαντες Γάϊον καὶ Ἀρίσταρχον Μακεδόνας, συνεκδήμους Παύλου. 30 Παύλου δὲ βουλομένου εἰσελθεῖν εἰς τὸν δῆμον οὐκ εἴων αὐτὸν οἱ μαθηταί· 31 τινὲς δὲ καὶ τῶν Ἀσιαρχῶν, ὄντες αὐτῷ φίλοι, πέμψαντες πρὸς αὐτὸν παρεκάλουν μὴ δοῦναι ἑαυτὸν εἰς τὸ θέατρον. 32 ἄλλοι μὲν οὖν ἄλλο τι ἔκραζον· ἦν γὰρ ἡ ἐκκλησία συγκεχυμένη καὶ οἱ πλείους οὐκ ᾔδεισαν τίνος ἕνεκα συνεληλύθεισαν. 33 ἐκ δὲ τοῦ ὄχλου συνεβίβασαν Ἀλέξανδρον, προβαλόντων αὐτὸν τῶν Ἰουδαίων· ὁ δὲ Ἀλέξανδρος κατασείσας τὴν χεῖρα ἤθελεν ἀπολογεῖσθαι τῷ δήμῳ. 34 ἐπιγνόντες δὲ ὅτι Ἰουδαῖός ἐστιν, φωνὴ ἐγένετο μία ἐκ πάντων ὡς ἐπὶ ὥρας δύο κραζόντων, Μεγάλη ἡ Ἄρτεμις Ἐφεσίων. 35 καταστείλας δὲ ὁ γραμματεὺς τὸν ὄχλον φησίν, Ἄνδρες Ἐφέσιοι, τίς γάρ ἐστιν ἀνθρώπων ὃς οὐ γινώσκει τὴν Ἐφεσίων πόλιν νεωκόρον οὖσαν τῆς μεγάλης Ἀρτέμιδος καὶ τοῦ διοπετοῦς; 36 ἀναντιρρήτων οὖν ὄντων τούτων δέον ἐστὶν ὑμᾶς κατεσταλμένους ὑπάρχειν καὶ μηδὲν προπετὲς πράσσειν. 37 ἠγάγετε γὰρ τοὺς ἄνδρας τούτους οὔτε ἱεροσύλους οὔτε βλασφημοῦντας τὴν θεὸν ἡμῶν[b].

NIV

Erastus, to Macedonia, while he stayed in the province of Asia a little longer.

The Riot in Ephesus

23About that time there arose a great disturbance about the Way. 24A silversmith named Demetrius, who made silver shrines of Artemis, brought in no little business for the craftsmen. 25He called them together, along with the workmen in related trades, and said: "Men, you know we receive a good income from this business. 26And you see and hear how this fellow Paul has convinced and led astray large numbers of people here in Ephesus and in practically the whole province of Asia. He says that man-made gods are no gods at all. 27There is danger not only that our trade will lose its good name, but also that the temple of the great goddess Artemis will be discredited, and the goddess herself, who is worshiped throughout the province of Asia and the world, will be robbed of her divine majesty."

28When they heard this, they were furious and began shouting: "Great is Artemis of the Ephesians!" 29Soon the whole city was in an uproar. The people seized Gaius and Aristarchus, Paul's traveling companions from Macedonia, and rushed as one man into the theater. 30Paul wanted to appear before the crowd, but the disciples would not let him. 31Even some of the officials of the province, friends of Paul, sent him a message begging him not to venture into the theater.

32The assembly was in confusion: Some were shouting one thing, some another. Most of the people did not even know why they were there. 33The Jews pushed Alexander to the front, and some of the crowd shouted instructions to him. He motioned for silence in order to make a defense before the people. 34But when they realized he was a Jew, they all shouted in unison for about two hours: "Great is Artemis of the Ephesians!"

35The city clerk quieted the crowd and said: "Men of Ephesus, doesn't all the world know that the city of Ephesus is the guardian of the temple of the great Artemis and of her image, which fell from heaven? 36Therefore, since these facts are undeniable, you ought to be quiet and not do anything rash. 37You have brought these men here, though they have neither robbed temples nor blasphemed our goddess. 38If,

---

artisans with him have a complaint against anyone, the courts are open, and there are proconsuls; let them bring charges there against one another. [39]If there is anything further[r] you want to know, it must be settled in the regular assembly. [40]For we are in danger of being charged with rioting today, since there is no cause that we can give to justify this commotion." [41]When he had said this, he dismissed the assembly.

Paul Goes to Macedonia and Greece

20 After the uproar had ceased, Paul sent for the disciples; and after encouraging them and saying farewell, he left for Macedonia. [2]When he had gone through those regions and had given the believers[s] much encouragement, he came to Greece, [3]where he stayed for three months. He was about to set sail for Syria when a plot was made against him by the Jews, and so he decided to return through Macedonia. [4]He was accompanied by Sopater son of Pyrrhus from Beroea, by Aristarchus and Secundus from Thessalonica, by Gaius from Derbe, and by Timothy, as well as by Tychicus and Trophimus from Asia. [5]They went ahead and were waiting for us in Troas; [6]but we sailed from Philippi after the days of Unleavened Bread, and in five days we joined them in Troas, where we stayed for seven days.

Paul's Farewell Visit to Troas

7 On the first day of the week, when we met to break bread, Paul was holding a discussion with them; since he intended to leave the next day, he continued speaking until midnight. [8]There were many lamps in the room upstairs where we were meeting. [9]A young man named Eutychus, who was sitting in the window, began to sink off into a deep sleep while Paul talked still longer. Overcome by sleep, he fell to the ground three floors below and was picked up dead. [10]But Paul went down, and bending over him took him in his arms, and said, "Do not be alarmed, for his life is in him." [11]Then Paul went upstairs, and after he had broken bread and eaten, he continued to converse with them until dawn; then he left. [12]Meanwhile they had taken the boy away alive and were not a little comforted.

The Voyage from Troas to Miletus

13 We went ahead to the ship and set sail

38 εἰ μὲν οὖν Δημήτριος καὶ οἱ σὺν αὐτῷ τεχνῖται ἔχουσι πρός τινα λόγον, ἀγοραῖοι ἄγονται καὶ ἀνθύπατοί εἰσιν, ἐγκαλείτωσαν ἀλλήλοις. **39** εἰ δέ τι περαιτέρω[c] ἐπιζητεῖτε, ἐν τῇ ἐννόμῳ ἐκκλησίᾳ ἐπιλυθήσεται. **40** καὶ γὰρ κινδυνεύομεν ἐγκαλεῖσθαι στάσεως περὶ τῆς σήμερον, μηδενὸς αἰτίου ὑπάρχοντος περὶ οὗ [οὐ] δυνησόμεθα ἀποδοῦναι λόγον περὶ τῆς συστροφῆς ταύτης.[d] καὶ ταῦτα εἰπὼν ἀπέλυσεν τὴν ἐκκλησίαν.

20 Μετὰ δὲ τὸ παύσασθαι τὸν θόρυβον μεταπεμψάμενος ὁ Παῦλος τοὺς μαθητὰς καὶ παρακαλέσας, ἀσπασάμενος ἐξῆλθεν πορεύεσθαι εἰς Μακεδονίαν. **2** διελθὼν δὲ τὰ μέρη ἐκεῖνα καὶ παρακαλέσας αὐτοὺς λόγῳ πολλῷ ἦλθεν εἰς τὴν Ἑλλάδα **3** ποιήσας τε μῆνας τρεῖς· γενομένης ἐπιβουλῆς αὐτῷ ὑπὸ τῶν Ἰουδαίων μέλλοντι ἀνάγεσθαι εἰς τὴν Συρίαν, ἐγένετο γνώμης τοῦ ὑποστρέφειν διὰ Μακεδονίας. **4** συνείπετο δὲ αὐτῷ Σώπατρος Πύρρου Βεροιαῖος, Θεσσαλονικέων δὲ Ἀρίσταρχος καὶ Σεκοῦνδος, καὶ Γάϊος Δερβαῖος καὶ Τιμόθεος, Ἀσιανοὶ δὲ Τυχικὸς καὶ Τρόφιμος. **5** οὗτοι δὲ προελθόντες ἔμενον ἡμᾶς ἐν Τρῳάδι, **6** ἡμεῖς δὲ ἐξεπλεύσαμεν μετὰ τὰς ἡμέρας τῶν ἀζύμων ἀπὸ Φιλίππων καὶ ἤλθομεν πρὸς αὐτοὺς εἰς τὴν Τρῳάδα ἄχρι ἡμερῶν πέντε, ὅπου διετρίψαμεν ἡμέρας ἑπτά.

7 Ἐν δὲ τῇ μιᾷ τῶν σαββάτων συνηγμένων ἡμῶν κλάσαι ἄρτον, ὁ Παῦλος διελέγετο αὐτοῖς μέλλων ἐξιέναι τῇ ἐπαύριον, παρέτεινέν τε τὸν λόγον μέχρι μεσονυκτίου. **8** ἦσαν δὲ λαμπάδες ἱκαναὶ ἐν τῷ ὑπερῴῳ οὗ ἦμεν συνηγμένοι. **9** καθεζόμενος δέ τις νεανίας ὀνόματι Εὔτυχος ἐπὶ τῆς θυρίδος, καταφερόμενος ὕπνῳ βαθεῖ διαλεγομένου τοῦ Παύλου ἐπὶ πλεῖον, κατενεχθεὶς ἀπὸ τοῦ ὕπνου ἔπεσεν ἀπὸ τοῦ τριστέγου κάτω καὶ ἤρθη νεκρός. **10** καταβὰς δὲ ὁ Παῦλος ἐπέπεσεν αὐτῷ καὶ συμπεριλαβὼν εἶπεν, Μὴ θορυβεῖσθε, ἡ γὰρ ψυχὴ αὐτοῦ ἐν αὐτῷ ἐστιν. **11** ἀναβὰς δὲ καὶ κλάσας τὸν ἄρτον καὶ γευσάμενος ἐφ᾽ ἱκανόν τε ὁμιλήσας ἄχρι αὐγῆς, οὕτως ἐξῆλθεν. **12** ἤγαγον δὲ τὸν παῖδα ζῶντα καὶ παρεκλήθησαν οὐ μετρίως.

13 Ἡμεῖς δὲ προελθόντες ἐπὶ τὸ πλοῖον ἀνήχθημεν ἐπὶ τὴν Ἀσσον

then, Demetrius and his fellow craftsmen have a grievance against anybody, the courts are open and there are proconsuls. They can press charges. [39]If there is anything further you want to bring up, it must be settled in a legal assembly. [40]As it is, we are in danger of being charged with rioting because of today's events. In that case we would not be able to account for this commotion, since there is no reason for it." [41]After he had said this, he dismissed the assembly.

Through Macedonia and Greece

20 When the uproar had ended, Paul sent for the disciples and, after encouraging them, said good-by and set out for Macedonia. [2]He traveled through that area, speaking many words of encouragement to the people, and finally arrived in Greece, [3]where he stayed three months. Because the Jews made a plot against him just as he was about to sail for Syria, he decided to go back through Macedonia. [4]He was accompanied by Sopater son of Pyrrhus from Berea, Aristarchus and Secundus from Thessalonica, Gaius from Derbe, Timothy also, and Tychicus and Trophimus from the province of Asia. [5]These men went on ahead and waited for us at Troas. [6]But we sailed from Philippi after the Feast of Unleavened Bread, and five days later joined the others at Troas, where we stayed seven days.

Eutychus Raised From the Dead at Troas

[7]On the first day of the week we came together to break bread. Paul spoke to the people and, because he intended to leave the next day, kept on talking until midnight. [8]There were many lamps in the upstairs room where we were meeting. [9]Seated in a window was a young man named Eutychus, who was sinking into a deep sleep as Paul talked on and on. When he was sound asleep, he fell to the ground from the third story and was picked up dead. [10]Paul went down, threw himself on the young man and put his arms around him. "Don't be alarmed," he said. "He's alive!" [11]Then he went upstairs again and broke bread and ate. After talking until daylight, he left. [12]The people took the young man home alive and were greatly comforted.

Paul's Farewell to the Ephesian Elders

[13]We went on ahead to the ship and sailed

---

[r] Other ancient authorities read *about other matters*
[s] Gk *given them*

[c]39 NRSV note r περὶ ἑτέρων   [d]39 NIV/NRSV divide verse 40, starting verse 41 after ταύτης.

NRSV

for Assos, intending to take Paul on board there; for he had made this arrangement, intending to go by land himself. 14When he met us in Assos, we took him on board and went to Mitylene. 15We sailed from there, and on the following day we arrived opposite Chios. The next day we touched at Samos, and[t] the day after that we came to Miletus. 16For Paul had decided to sail past Ephesus, so that he might not have to spend time in Asia; he was eager to be in Jerusalem, if possible, on the day of Pentecost.

Paul Speaks to the Ephesian Elders

17 From Miletus he sent a message to Ephesus, asking the elders of the church to meet him. 18When they came to him, he said to them:

"You yourselves know how I lived among you the entire time from the first day that I set foot in Asia, 19serving the Lord with all humility and with tears, enduring the trials that came to me through the plots of the Jews. 20I did not shrink from doing anything helpful, proclaiming the message to you and teaching you publicly and from house to house, 21as I testified to both Jews and Greeks about repentance toward God and faith toward our Lord Jesus. 22And now, as a captive to the Spirit,[u] I am on my way to Jerusalem, not knowing what will happen to me there, 23except that the Holy Spirit testifies to me in every city that imprisonment and persecutions are waiting for me. 24But I do not count my life of any value to myself, if only I may finish my course and the ministry that I received from the Lord Jesus, to testify to the good news of God's grace.

25 "And now I know that none of you, among whom I have gone about proclaiming the kingdom, will ever see my face again. 26Therefore I declare to you this day that I am not responsible for the blood of any of you, 27for I did not shrink from declaring to you the whole purpose of God. 28Keep watch over yourselves and over all the flock, of which the Holy Spirit has made you overseers, to shepherd the church of God[v] that he obtained with the blood of his own Son.[w] 29I know that after I have gone, savage wolves will come in among

Greek

ἐκεῖθεν μέλλοντες ἀναλαμβάνειν τὸν Παῦλον· οὕτως γὰρ διατεταγμένος ἦν μέλλων αὐτὸς πεζεύειν. 14 ὡς δὲ συνέβαλλεν ἡμῖν εἰς τὴν Ἆσσον, ἀναλαβόντες αὐτὸν ἤλθομεν εἰς Μιτυλήνην, 15 κἀκεῖθεν ἀποπλεύσαντες τῇ ἐπιούσῃ κατηντήσαμεν ἄντικρυς Χίου, τῇ δὲ ἑτέρᾳ παρεβάλομεν εἰς Σάμον, τῇ δὲ[a] ἐχομένῃ ἤλθομεν εἰς Μίλητον. 16 κεκρίκει γὰρ ὁ Παῦλος παραπλεῦσαι τὴν Ἔφεσον, ὅπως μὴ γένηται αὐτῷ χρονοτριβῆσαι ἐν τῇ Ἀσίᾳ· ἔσπευδεν γὰρ εἰ δυνατὸν εἴη αὐτῷ τὴν ἡμέραν τῆς πεντηκοστῆς γενέσθαι εἰς Ἱεροσόλυμα.

17 Ἀπὸ δὲ τῆς Μιλήτου πέμψας εἰς Ἔφεσον μετεκαλέσατο τοὺς πρεσβυτέρους τῆς ἐκκλησίας. 18 ὡς δὲ παρεγένοντο πρὸς αὐτὸν εἶπεν αὐτοῖς, Ὑμεῖς ἐπίστασθε, ἀπὸ πρώτης ἡμέρας ἀφ᾽ ἧς ἐπέβην εἰς τὴν Ἀσίαν, πῶς μεθ᾽ ὑμῶν τὸν πάντα χρόνον ἐγενόμην, 19 δουλεύων τῷ κυρίῳ μετὰ πάσης ταπεινοφροσύνης καὶ δακρύων καὶ πειρασμῶν τῶν συμβάντων μοι ἐν ταῖς ἐπιβουλαῖς τῶν Ἰουδαίων, 20 ὡς οὐδὲν ὑπεστειλάμην τῶν συμφερόντων τοῦ μὴ ἀναγγεῖλαι ὑμῖν καὶ διδάξαι ὑμᾶς δημοσίᾳ καὶ κατ᾽ οἴκους, 21 διαμαρτυρόμενος Ἰουδαίοις τε καὶ Ἕλλησιν τὴν εἰς θεὸν μετάνοιαν καὶ πίστιν εἰς τὸν κύριον ἡμῶν Ἰησοῦν. 22 καὶ νῦν ἰδοὺ δεδεμένος ἐγὼ τῷ πνεύματι πορεύομαι εἰς Ἱερουσαλὴμ τὰ ἐν αὐτῇ συναντήσοντά μοι μὴ εἰδώς, 23 πλὴν ὅτι τὸ πνεῦμα τὸ ἅγιον κατὰ πόλιν διαμαρτύρεταί μοι λέγον ὅτι δεσμὰ καὶ θλίψεις με μένουσιν. 24 ἀλλ᾽ οὐδενὸς λόγου ποιοῦμαι τὴν ψυχὴν τιμίαν ἐμαυτῷ ὡς τελειῶσαι τὸν δρόμον μου καὶ τὴν διακονίαν ἣν ἔλαβον παρὰ τοῦ κυρίου Ἰησοῦ, διαμαρτύρασθαι τὸ εὐαγγέλιον τῆς χάριτος τοῦ θεοῦ.   ·

25 Καὶ νῦν ἰδοὺ ἐγὼ οἶδα ὅτι οὐκέτι ὄψεσθε τὸ πρόσωπόν μου ὑμεῖς πάντες ἐν οἷς διῆλθον κηρύσσων τὴν βασιλείαν. 26 διότι μαρτύρομαι ὑμῖν ἐν τῇ σήμερον ἡμέρᾳ ὅτι καθαρός εἰμι ἀπὸ τοῦ αἵματος πάντων· 27 οὐ γὰρ ὑπεστειλάμην τοῦ μὴ ἀναγγεῖλαι πᾶσαν τὴν βουλὴν τοῦ θεοῦ ὑμῖν. 28 προσέχετε ἑαυτοῖς καὶ παντὶ τῷ ποιμνίῳ, ἐν ᾧ ὑμᾶς τὸ πνεῦμα τὸ ἅγιον ἔθετο ἐπισκόπους ποιμαίνειν τὴν ἐκκλησίαν τοῦ θεοῦ[b], ἣν περιεποιήσατο διὰ τοῦ αἵματος τοῦ ἰδίου. 29 ἐγὼ οἶδα ὅτι εἰσελεύσονται μετὰ τὴν ἄφιξίν μου λύκοι βαρεῖς εἰς

NIV

for Assos, where we were going to take Paul aboard. He had made this arrangement because he was going there on foot. 14When he met us at Assos, we took him aboard and went on to Mitylene. 15The next day we set sail from there and arrived off Kios. The day after that we crossed over to Samos, and on the following day arrived at Miletus. 16Paul had decided to sail past Ephesus to avoid spending time in the province of Asia, for he was in a hurry to reach Jerusalem, if possible, by the day of Pentecost.

17From Miletus, Paul sent to Ephesus for the elders of the church. 18When they arrived, he said to them: "You know how I lived the whole time I was with you, from the first day I came into the province of Asia. 19I served the Lord with great humility and with tears, although I was severely tested by the plots of the Jews. 20You know that I have not hesitated to preach anything that would be helpful to you but have taught you publicly and from house to house. 21I have declared to both Jews and Greeks that they must turn to God in repentance and have faith in our Lord Jesus.

22"And now, compelled by the Spirit, I am going to Jerusalem, not knowing what will happen to me there. 23I only know that in every city the Holy Spirit warns me that prison and hardships are facing me. 24However, I consider my life worth nothing to me, if only I may finish the race and complete the task the Lord Jesus has given me—the task of testifying to the gospel of God's grace.

25"Now I know that none of you among whom I have gone about preaching the kingdom will ever see me again. 26Therefore, I declare to you today that I am innocent of the blood of all men. 27For I have not hesitated to proclaim to you the whole will of God. 28Keep watch over yourselves and all the flock of which the Holy Spirit has made you overseers.[a] Be shepherds of the church of God,[b] which he bought with his own blood. 29I know that after I leave, savage wolves will come in among you

---

[t]Other ancient authorities add *after remaining at Trogyllium* [u]Or *And now, bound in the spirit* [v]Other ancient authorities read *of the Lord* [w]Or *with his own blood*; Gk *with the blood of his Own*

[a]15 NRSV note t adds καὶ μείναντως ἐν Τρωγυλ(λ)ίῳ τῇ in place of τῇ δὲ [b]28 NIV/NRSV notes κυρίου

[a]28 Traditionally *bishops* [b]28 Many manuscripts *of the Lord*

you, not sparing the flock. ³⁰Some even from your own group will come distorting the truth in order to entice the disciples to follow them. ³¹Therefore be alert, remembering that for three years I did not cease night or day to warn everyone with tears. ³²And now I commend you to God and to the message of his grace, a message that is able to build you up and to give you the inheritance among all who are sanctified. ³³I coveted no one's silver or gold or clothing. ³⁴You know for yourselves that I worked with my own hands to support myself and my companions. ³⁵In all this I have given you an example that by such work we must support the weak, remembering the words of the Lord Jesus, for he himself said, 'It is more blessed to give than to receive.' "

36 When he had finished speaking, he knelt down with them all and prayed. ³⁷There was much weeping among them all; they embraced Paul and kissed him, ³⁸grieving especially because of what he had said, that they would not see him again. Then they brought him to the ship.

Paul's Journey to Jerusalem

21 When we had parted from them and set sail, we came by a straight course to Cos, and the next day to Rhodes, and from there to Patara.ˣ ²When we found a ship bound for Phoenicia, we went on board and set sail. ³We came in sight of Cyprus; and leaving it on our left, we sailed to Syria and landed at Tyre, because the ship was to unload its cargo there. ⁴We looked up the disciples and stayed there for seven days. Through the Spirit they told Paul not to go on to Jerusalem. ⁵When our days there were ended, we left and proceeded on our journey; and all of them, with wives and children, escorted us outside the city. There we knelt down on the beach and prayed ⁶and said farewell to one another. Then we went on board the ship, and they returned home.

7 When we had finishedʸ the voyage from Tyre, we arrived at Ptolemais; and we greeted the believersᶻ and stayed with them for one day. ⁸The next day we left and

ὑμᾶς μὴ φειδόμενοι τοῦ ποιμνίου, **30** καὶ ἐξ ὑμῶν αὐτῶν ἀναστήσονται ἄνδρες λαλοῦντες διεστραμμένα τοῦ ἀποσπᾶν τοὺς μαθητὰς ὀπίσω αὐτῶν. **31** διὸ γρηγορεῖτε μνημονεύοντες ὅτι τριετίαν νύκτα καὶ ἡμέραν οὐκ ἐπαυσάμην μετὰ δακρύων νουθετῶν ἕνα ἕκαστον. **32** καὶ τὰ νῦν παρατίθεμαι ὑμᾶς τῷ θεῷ καὶ τῷ λόγῳ τῆς χάριτος αὐτοῦ, τῷ δυναμένῳ οἰκοδομῆσαι καὶ δοῦναι τὴν κληρονομίαν ἐν τοῖς ἡγιασμένοις πᾶσιν. **33** ἀργυρίου ἢ χρυσίου ἢ ἱματισμοῦ οὐδενὸς ἐπεθύμησα· **34** αὐτοὶ γινώσκετε ὅτι ταῖς χρείαις μου καὶ τοῖς οὖσιν μετ' ἐμοῦ ὑπηρέτησαν αἱ χεῖρες αὗται. **35** πάντα ὑπέδειξα ὑμῖν ὅτι οὕτως κοπιῶντας δεῖ ἀντιλαμβάνεσθαι τῶν ἀσθενούντων, μνημονεύειν τε τῶν λόγων τοῦ κυρίου Ἰησοῦ ὅτι αὐτὸς εἶπεν, Μακάριόν ἐστιν μᾶλλον διδόναι ἢ λαμβάνειν.

36 Καὶ ταῦτα εἰπὼν θεὶς τὰ γόνατα αὐτοῦ σὺν πᾶσιν αὐτοῖς προσηύξατο. **37** ἱκανὸς δὲ κλαυθμὸς ἐγένετο πάντων καὶ ἐπιπεσόντες ἐπὶ τὸν τράχηλον τοῦ Παύλου κατεφίλουν αὐτόν, **38** ὀδυνώμενοι μάλιστα ἐπὶ τῷ λόγῳ ᾧ εἰρήκει, ὅτι οὐκέτι μέλλουσιν τὸ πρόσωπον αὐτοῦ θεωρεῖν. προέπεμπον δὲ αὐτὸν εἰς τὸ πλοῖον.

21 Ὡς δὲ ἐγένετο ἀναχθῆναι ἡμᾶς ἀποσπασθέντας ἀπ' αὐτῶν, εὐθυδρομήσαντες ἤλθομεν εἰς τὴν Κῶ, τῇ δὲ ἑξῆς εἰς τὴν Ῥόδον κἀκεῖθεν εἰς Πάταραª, **2** καὶ εὑρόντες πλοῖον διαπερῶν εἰς Φοινίκην ἐπιβάντες ἀνήχθημεν. **3** ἀναφάναντες δὲ τὴν Κύπρον καὶ καταλιπόντες αὐτὴν εὐώνυμον ἐπλέομεν εἰς Συρίαν καὶ κατήλθομεν εἰς Τύρον· ἐκεῖσε γὰρ τὸ πλοῖον ἦν ἀποφορτιζόμενον τὸν γόμον. **4** ἀνευρόντες δὲ τοὺς μαθητὰς ἐπεμείναμεν αὐτοῦ ἡμέρας ἑπτά, οἵτινες τῷ Παύλῳ ἔλεγον διὰ τοῦ πνεύματος μὴ ἐπιβαίνειν εἰς Ἱεροσόλυμα. **5** ὅτε δὲ ἐγένετο ἡμᾶς ἐξαρτίσαι τὰς ἡμέρας, ἐξελθόντες ἐπορευόμεθα προπεμπόντων ἡμᾶς πάντων σὺν γυναιξὶ καὶ τέκνοις ἕως ἔξω τῆς πόλεως, καὶ θέντες τὰ γόνατα ἐπὶ τὸν αἰγιαλὸν προσευξάμενοι **6** ἀπησπασάμεθα ἀλλήλους καὶ ἀνέβημεν εἰς τὸ πλοῖον, ἐκεῖνοι δὲ ὑπέστρεψαν εἰς τὰ ἴδια.

7 Ἡμεῖς δὲ τὸν πλοῦν διανύσαντες ἀπὸ Τύρου κατηντήσαμεν εἰς Πτολεμαΐδα καὶ ἀσπασάμενοι τοὺς ἀδελφοὺς ἐμείναμεν ἡμέραν μίαν παρ' αὐτοῖς. **8** τῇ δὲ ἐπαύριον ἐξελθόντες ἤλθομεν

and will not spare the flock. ³⁰Even from your own number men will arise and distort the truth in order to draw away disciples after them. ³¹So be on your guard! Remember that for three years I never stopped warning each of you night and day with tears.

³²"Now I commit you to God and to the word of his grace, which can build you up and give you an inheritance among all those who are sanctified. ³³I have not coveted anyone's silver or gold or clothing. ³⁴You yourselves know that these hands of mine have supplied my own needs and the needs of my companions. ³⁵In everything I did, I showed you that by this kind of hard work we must help the weak, remembering the words the Lord Jesus himself said: 'It is more blessed to give than to receive.' "

³⁶When he had said this, he knelt down with all of them and prayed. ³⁷They all wept as they embraced him and kissed him. ³⁸What grieved them most was his statement that they would never see his face again. Then they accompanied him to the ship.

On to Jerusalem

21 After we had torn ourselves away from them, we put out to sea and sailed straight to Cos. The next day we went to Rhodes and from there to Patara. ²We found a ship crossing over to Phoenicia, went on board and set sail. ³After sighting Cyprus and passing to the south of it, we sailed on to Syria. We landed at Tyre, where our ship was to unload its cargo. ⁴Finding the disciples there, we stayed with them seven days. Through the Spirit they urged Paul not to go on to Jerusalem. ⁵But when our time was up, we left and continued on our way. All the disciples and their wives and children accompanied us out of the city, and there on the beach we knelt to pray. ⁶After saying good-by to each other, we went aboard the ship, and they returned home.

⁷We continued our voyage from Tyre and landed at Ptolemais, where we greeted the brothers and stayed with them for a day. ⁸Leaving the next day, we reached

---

ˣ Other ancient authorities add *and Myra*   ʸ Or *continued*
ᶻ Gk *brothers*

ª1 NRSV note x adds καὶ Μύρα

came to Caesarea; and we went into the house of Philip the evangelist, one of the seven, and stayed with him. [9]He had four unmarried daughters[a] who had the gift of prophecy. [10]While we were staying there for several days, a prophet named Agabus came down from Judea. [11]He came to us and took Paul's belt, bound his own feet and hands with it, and said, "Thus says the Holy Spirit, 'This is the way the Jews in Jerusalem will bind the man who owns this belt and will hand him over to the Gentiles.' " [12]When we heard this, we and the people there urged him not to go up to Jerusalem. [13]Then Paul answered, "What are you doing, weeping and breaking my heart? For I am ready not only to be bound but even to die in Jerusalem for the name of the Lord Jesus." [14]Since he would not be persuaded, we remained silent except to say, "The Lord's will be done."

15 After these days we got ready and started to go up to Jerusalem. [16]Some of the disciples from Caesarea also came along and brought us to the house of Mnason of Cyprus, an early disciple, with whom we were to stay.

Paul Visits James at Jerusalem

17 When we arrived in Jerusalem, the brothers welcomed us warmly. [18]The next day Paul went with us to visit James; and all the elders were present. [19]After greeting them, he related one by one the things that God had done among the Gentiles through his ministry. [20]When they heard it, they praised God. Then they said to him, "You see, brother, how many thousands of believers there are among the Jews, and they are all zealous for the law. [21]They have been told about you that you teach all the Jews living among the Gentiles to forsake Moses, and that you tell them not to circumcise their children or observe the customs. [22]What then is to be done? They will certainly hear that you have come. [23]So do what we tell you. We have four men who are under a vow. [24]Join these men, go through the rite of purification with them, and pay for the shaving of their heads. Thus all will know that there is nothing in what they have been told

εἰς Καισάρειαν καὶ εἰσελθόντες εἰς τὸν οἶκον Φιλίππου τοῦ εὐαγγελιστοῦ, ὄντος ἐκ τῶν ἑπτά, ἐμείναμεν παρ' αὐτῷ 9 τούτῳ δὲ ἦσαν θυγατέρες τέσσαρες παρθένοι προφητεύουσαι. 10 ἐπιμενόντων δὲ ἡμέρας πλείους κατῆλθέν τις ἀπὸ τῆς Ἰουδαίας προφήτης ὀνόματι Ἄγαβος, 11 καὶ ἐλθὼν πρὸς ἡμᾶς καὶ ἄρας τὴν ζώνην τοῦ Παύλου, δήσας ἑαυτοῦ τοὺς πόδας καὶ τὰς χεῖρας εἶπεν, Τάδε λέγει τὸ πνεῦμα τὸ ἅγιον, Τὸν ἄνδρα οὗ ἐστιν ἡ ζώνη αὕτη, οὕτως δήσουσιν ἐν Ἰερουσαλὴμ οἱ Ἰουδαῖοι καὶ παραδώσουσιν εἰς χεῖρας ἐθνῶν. 12 ὡς δὲ ἠκούσαμεν ταῦτα, παρεκαλοῦμεν ἡμεῖς τε καὶ οἱ ἐντόπιοι τοῦ μὴ ἀναβαίνειν αὐτὸν εἰς Ἰερουσαλήμ. 13 τότε ἀπεκρίθη ὁ Παῦλος, Τί ποιεῖτε κλαίοντες καὶ συνθρύπτοντές μου τὴν καρδίαν; ἐγὼ γὰρ οὐ μόνον δεθῆναι ἀλλὰ καὶ ἀποθανεῖν εἰς Ἰερουσαλὴμ ἑτοίμως ἔχω ὑπὲρ τοῦ ὀνόματος τοῦ κυρίου Ἰησοῦ. 14 μὴ πειθομένου δὲ αὐτοῦ ἡσυχάσαμεν εἰπόντες, Τοῦ κυρίου τὸ θέλημα γινέσθω.

15 Μετὰ δὲ τὰς ἡμέρας ταύτας ἐπισκευασάμενοι ἀνεβαίνομεν εἰς Ἰεροσόλυμα· 16 συνῆλθον δὲ καὶ τῶν μαθητῶν ἀπὸ Καισαρείας σὺν ἡμῖν, ἄγοντες παρ' ᾧ ξενισθῶμεν Μνάσωνί τινι Κυπρίῳ, ἀρχαίῳ μαθητῇ.

17 Γενομένων δὲ ἡμῶν εἰς Ἰεροσόλυμα ἀσμένως ἀπεδέξαντο ἡμᾶς οἱ ἀδελφοί. 18 τῇ δὲ ἐπιούσῃ εἰσῄει ὁ Παῦλος σὺν ἡμῖν πρὸς Ἰάκωβον, πάντες τε παρεγένοντο οἱ πρεσβύτεροι. 19 καὶ ἀσπασάμενος αὐτοὺς ἐξηγεῖτο καθ' ἓν ἕκαστον, ὧν ἐποίησεν ὁ θεὸς ἐν τοῖς ἔθνεσιν διὰ τῆς διακονίας αὐτοῦ. 20 οἱ δὲ ἀκούσαντες ἐδόξαζον τὸν θεὸν εἶπόν τε αὐτῷ, Θεωρεῖς, ἀδελφέ, πόσαι μυριάδες εἰσὶν ἐν τοῖς Ἰουδαίοις τῶν πεπιστευκότων καὶ πάντες ζηλωταὶ τοῦ νόμου ὑπάρχουσιν· 21 κατηχήθησαν δὲ περὶ σοῦ ὅτι ἀποστασίαν διδάσκεις ἀπὸ Μωϋσέως τοὺς κατὰ τὰ ἔθνη πάντας Ἰουδαίους λέγων μὴ περιτέμνειν αὐτοὺς τὰ τέκνα μηδὲ τοῖς ἔθεσιν περιπατεῖν. 22 τί οὖν ἐστιν; πάντως ἀκούσονται ὅτι ἐλήλυθας. 23 τοῦτο οὖν ποίησον ὅ σοι λέγομεν· εἰσὶν ἡμῖν ἄνδρες τέσσαρες εὐχὴν ἔχοντες ἐφ' ἑαυτῶν. 24 τούτους παραλαβὼν ἁγνίσθητι σὺν αὐτοῖς καὶ δαπάνησον ἐπ' αὐτοῖς ἵνα ξυρήσονται τὴν κεφαλήν, καὶ γνώσονται πάντες ὅτι ὧν κατήχηνται περὶ σοῦ οὐδέν

Caesarea and stayed at the house of Philip the evangelist, one of the Seven. [9]He had four unmarried daughters who prophesied.

[10]After we had been there a number of days, a prophet named Agabus came down from Judea. [11]Coming over to us, he took Paul's belt, tied his own hands and feet with it and said, "The Holy Spirit says, 'In this way the Jews of Jerusalem will bind the owner of this belt and will hand him over to the Gentiles.' "

[12]When we heard this, we and the people there pleaded with Paul not to go up to Jerusalem. [13]Then Paul answered, "Why are you weeping and breaking my heart? I am ready not only to be bound, but also to die in Jerusalem for the name of the Lord Jesus." [14]When he would not be dissuaded, we gave up and said, "The Lord's will be done."

[15]After this, we got ready and went up to Jerusalem. [16]Some of the disciples from Caesarea accompanied us and brought us to the home of Mnason, where we were to stay. He was a man from Cyprus and one of the early disciples.

Paul's Arrival at Jerusalem

[17]When we arrived at Jerusalem, the brothers received us warmly. [18]The next day Paul and the rest of us went to see James, and all the elders were present. [19]Paul greeted them and reported in detail what God had done among the Gentiles through his ministry.

[20]When they heard this, they praised God. Then they said to Paul: "You see, brother, how many thousands of Jews have believed, and all of them are zealous for the law. [21]They have been informed that you teach all the Jews who live among the Gentiles to turn away from Moses, telling them not to circumcise their children or live according to our customs. [22]What shall we do? They will certainly hear that you have come, [23]so do what we tell you. There are four men with us who have made a vow. [24]Take these men, join in their purification rites and pay their expenses, so that they can have their heads shaved. Then everybody will know there is no truth in these reports about you, but that you

---

[a] Gk four daughters, virgins,

about you, but that you yourself observe and guard the law. 25But as for the Gentiles who have become believers, we have sent a letter with our judgment that they should abstain from what has been sacrificed to idols and from blood and from what is strangled[b] and from fornication." 26Then Paul took the men, and the next day, having purified himself, he entered the temple with them, making public the completion of the days of purification when the sacrifice would be made for each of them.

Paul Arrested in the Temple

27 When the seven days were almost completed, the Jews from Asia, who had seen him in the temple, stirred up the whole crowd. They seized him, 28shouting, "Fellow Israelites, help! This is the man who is teaching everyone everywhere against our people, our law, and this place; more than that, he has actually brought Greeks into the temple and has defiled this holy place." 29For they had previously seen Trophimus the Ephesian with him in the city, and they supposed that Paul had brought him into the temple. 30Then all the city was aroused, and the people rushed together. They seized Paul and dragged him out of the temple, and immediately the doors were shut. 31While they were trying to kill him, word came to the tribune of the cohort that all Jerusalem was in an uproar. 32Immediately he took soldiers and centurions and ran down to them. When they saw the tribune and the soldiers, they stopped beating Paul. 33Then the tribune came, arrested him, and ordered him to be bound with two chains; he inquired who he was and what he had done. 34Some in the crowd shouted one thing, some another; and as he could not learn the facts because of the uproar, he ordered him to be brought into the barracks. 35When Paul[c] came to the steps, the violence of the mob was so great that he had to be carried by the soldiers. 36The crowd that followed kept shouting, "Away with him!"

Paul Defends Himself

37 Just as Paul was about to be brought into the barracks, he said to the tribune, "May I say something to you?" The tribune[d] replied, "Do you know Greek? 38Then you are not the Egyptian who recently stirred up a revolt and led the four

ἐστιν ἀλλὰ στοιχεῖς καὶ αὐτὸς φυλάσσων τὸν νόμον. 25 περὶ δὲ τῶν πεπιστευκότων ἐθνῶν ἡμεῖς ἐπεστείλαμεν κρίναντες φυλάσσεσθαι αὐτοὺς τό τε εἰδωλόθυτον καὶ αἷμα καὶ πνικτὸν καὶ πορνείαν. 26 τότε ὁ Παῦλος παραλαβὼν τοὺς ἄνδρας τῇ ἐχομένῃ ἡμέρᾳ σὺν αὐτοῖς ἁγνισθείς, εἰσήει εἰς τὸ ἱερὸν διαγγέλλων τὴν ἐκπλήρωσιν τῶν ἡμερῶν τοῦ ἁγνισμοῦ ἕως οὗ προσηνέχθη ὑπὲρ ἑνὸς ἑκάστου αὐτῶν ἡ προσφορά.

27 Ὡς δὲ ἔμελλον αἱ ἑπτὰ ἡμέραι συντελεῖσθαι, οἱ ἀπὸ τῆς Ἀσίας Ἰουδαῖοι θεασάμενοι αὐτὸν ἐν τῷ ἱερῷ συνέχεον πάντα τὸν ὄχλον καὶ ἐπέβαλον ἐπ' αὐτὸν τὰς χεῖρας 28 κράζοντες, Ἄνδρες Ἰσραηλῖται, βοηθεῖτε· οὗτός ἐστιν ὁ ἄνθρωπος ὁ κατὰ τοῦ λαοῦ καὶ τοῦ νόμου καὶ τοῦ τόπου τούτου πάντας πανταχῇ διδάσκων, ἔτι τε καὶ Ἕλληνας εἰσήγαγεν εἰς τὸ ἱερὸν καὶ κεκοίνωκεν τὸν ἅγιον τόπον τοῦτον. 29 ἦσαν γὰρ προεωρακότες Τρόφιμον τὸν Ἐφέσιον ἐν τῇ πόλει σὺν αὐτῷ, ὃν ἐνόμιζον ὅτι εἰς τὸ ἱερὸν εἰσήγαγεν ὁ Παῦλος. 30 ἐκινήθη τε ἡ πόλις ὅλη καὶ ἐγένετο συνδρομὴ τοῦ λαοῦ, καὶ ἐπιλαβόμενοι τοῦ Παύλου εἷλκον αὐτὸν ἔξω τοῦ ἱεροῦ καὶ εὐθέως ἐκλείσθησαν αἱ θύραι. 31 ζητούντων τε αὐτὸν ἀποκτεῖναι ἀνέβη φάσις τῷ χιλιάρχῳ τῆς σπείρης ὅτι ὅλη συγχύννεται Ἰερουσαλήμ. 32 ὃς ἐξαυτῆς παραλαβὼν στρατιώτας καὶ ἑκατοντάρχας κατέδραμεν ἐπ' αὐτούς, οἱ δὲ ἰδόντες τὸν χιλίαρχον καὶ τοὺς στρατιώτας ἐπαύσαντο τύπτοντες τὸν Παῦλον. 33 τότε ἐγγίσας ὁ χιλίαρχος ἐπελάβετο αὐτοῦ καὶ ἐκέλευσεν δεθῆναι ἁλύσεσι δυσί, καὶ ἐπυνθάνετο τίς εἴη καὶ τί ἐστιν πεποιηκώς. 34 ἄλλοι δὲ ἄλλο τι ἐπεφώνουν ἐν τῷ ὄχλῳ. μὴ δυναμένου δὲ αὐτοῦ γνῶναι τὸ ἀσφαλὲς διὰ τὸν θόρυβον ἐκέλευσεν ἄγεσθαι αὐτὸν εἰς τὴν παρεμβολήν. 35 ὅτε δὲ ἐγένετο ἐπὶ τοὺς ἀναβαθμούς, συνέβη βαστάζεσθαι αὐτὸν ὑπὸ τῶν στρατιωτῶν διὰ τὴν βίαν τοῦ ὄχλου, 36 ἠκολούθει γὰρ τὸ πλῆθος τοῦ λαοῦ κράζοντες, Αἶρε αὐτόν.

37 Μέλλων τε εἰσάγεσθαι εἰς τὴν παρεμβολὴν ὁ Παῦλος λέγει τῷ χιλιάρχῳ, Εἰ ἔξεστίν μοι εἰπεῖν τι πρὸς σέ; ὁ δὲ ἔφη, Ἑλληνιστὶ γινώσκεις; 38 οὐκ ἄρα σὺ εἶ ὁ Αἰγύπτιος ὁ πρὸ τούτων τῶν ἡμερῶν ἀναστατώσας καὶ ἐξαγαγὼν εἰς τὴν ἔρημον τοὺς τετρακισχιλίους ἄνδρας τῶν σικαρίων;

yourself are living in obedience to the law. 25As for the Gentile believers, we have written to them our decision that they should abstain from food sacrificed to idols, from blood, from the meat of strangled animals and from sexual immorality."

26The next day Paul took the men and purified himself along with them. Then he went to the temple to give notice of the date when the days of purification would end and the offering would be made for each of them.

Paul Arrested

27When the seven days were nearly over, some Jews from the province of Asia saw Paul at the temple. They stirred up the whole crowd and seized him, 28shouting, "Men of Israel, help us! This is the man who teaches all men everywhere against our people and our law and this place. And besides, he has brought Greeks into the temple area and defiled this holy place." 29(They had previously seen Trophimus the Ephesian in the city with Paul and assumed that Paul had brought him into the temple area.)

30The whole city was aroused, and the people came running from all directions. Seizing Paul, they dragged him from the temple, and immediately the gates were shut. 31While they were trying to kill him, news reached the commander of the Roman troops that the whole city of Jerusalem was in an uproar. 32He at once took some officers and soldiers and ran down to the crowd. When the rioters saw the commander and his soldiers, they stopped beating Paul.

33The commander came up and arrested him and ordered him to be bound with two chains. Then he asked who he was and what he had done. 34Some in the crowd shouted one thing and some another, and since the commander could not get at the truth because of the uproar, he ordered that Paul be taken into the barracks. 35When Paul reached the steps, the violence of the mob was so great he had to be carried by the soldiers. 36The crowd that followed kept shouting, "Away with him!"

Paul Speaks to the Crowd

37As the soldiers were about to take Paul into the barracks, he asked the commander, "May I say something to you?"

"Do you speak Greek?" he replied. 38"Aren't you the Egyptian who started a revolt and led four thousand terrorists out

---

b Other ancient authorities lack *and from what is strangled*
c Gk *he*   d Gk *He*

thousand assassins out into the wilderness?" [39]Paul replied, "I am a Jew, from Tarsus in Cilicia, a citizen of an important city; I beg you, let me speak to the people." [40]When he had given him permission, Paul stood on the steps and motioned to the people for silence; and when there was a great hush, he addressed them in the Hebrew[e] language, saying:

22 "Brothers and fathers, listen to the defense that I now make before you."

[2] When they heard him addressing them in Hebrew,[e] they became even more quiet. Then he said:

[3] "I am a Jew, born in Tarsus in Cilicia, but brought up in this city at the feet of Gamaliel, educated strictly according to our ancestral law, being zealous for God, just as all of you are today. [4]I persecuted this Way up to the point of death by binding both men and women and putting them in prison, [5]as the high priest and the whole council of elders can testify about me. From them I also received letters to the brothers in Damascus, and I went there in order to bind those who were there and to bring them back to Jerusalem for punishment.

Paul Tells of His Conversion

[6] "While I was on my way and approaching Damascus, about noon a great light from heaven suddenly shone about me. [7]I fell to the ground and heard a voice saying to me, 'Saul, Saul, why are you persecuting me?' [8]I answered, 'Who are you, Lord?' Then he said to me, 'I am Jesus of Nazareth[f] whom you are persecuting.' [9]Now those who were with me saw the light but did not hear the voice of the one who was speaking to me. [10]I asked, 'What am I to do, Lord?' The Lord said to me, 'Get up and go to Damascus; there you will be told everything that has been assigned to you to do.' [11]Since I could not see because of the brightness of that light, those who were with me took my hand and led me to Damascus.

[12] "A certain Ananias, who was a devout man according to the law and well spoken of by all the Jews living there, [13]came to me; and standing beside me, he said, 'Brother Saul, regain your sight!' In that very hour I regained my sight and saw him. [14]Then he said, 'The God of our ancestors has chosen you to know his will, to see the Righteous One and to hear his

---

[39] εἶπεν δὲ ὁ Παῦλος, Ἐγὼ ἄνθρωπος μέν εἰμι Ἰουδαῖος, Ταρσεὺς τῆς Κιλικίας, οὐκ ἀσήμου πόλεως πολίτης· δέομαι δέ σου, ἐπίτρεψόν μοι λαλῆσαι πρὸς τὸν λαόν. [40] ἐπιτρέψαντος δὲ αὐτοῦ ὁ Παῦλος ἑστὼς ἐπὶ τῶν ἀναβαθμῶν κατέσεισεν τῇ χειρὶ τῷ λαῷ. πολλῆς δὲ σιγῆς γενομένης προσεφώνησεν τῇ Ἑβραΐδι διαλέκτῳ λέγων,

22 Ἄνδρες ἀδελφοὶ καὶ πατέρες, ἀκούσατέ μου τῆς πρὸς ὑμᾶς νυνὶ ἀπολογίας. [2] ἀκούσαντες δὲ ὅτι τῇ Ἑβραΐδι διαλέκτῳ προσεφώνει αὐτοῖς, μᾶλλον παρέσχον ἡσυχίαν. καὶ φησίν, [3] Ἐγώ εἰμι ἀνὴρ Ἰουδαῖος, γεγεννημένος ἐν Ταρσῷ τῆς Κιλικίας, ἀνατεθραμμένος δὲ ἐν τῇ πόλει ταύτῃ, παρὰ τοὺς πόδας Γαμαλιὴλ πεπαιδευμένος κατὰ ἀκρίβειαν τοῦ πατρῴου νόμου, ζηλωτὴς ὑπάρχων τοῦ θεοῦ καθὼς πάντες ὑμεῖς ἐστε σήμερον· [4] ὃς ταύτην τὴν ὁδὸν ἐδίωξα ἄχρι θανάτου δεσμεύων καὶ παραδιδοὺς εἰς φυλακὰς ἄνδρας τε καὶ γυναῖκας, [5] ὡς καὶ ὁ ἀρχιερεὺς μαρτυρεῖ μοι καὶ πᾶν τὸ πρεσβυτέριον, παρ᾽ ὧν καὶ ἐπιστολὰς δεξάμενος πρὸς τοὺς ἀδελφοὺς εἰς Δαμασκὸν ἐπορευόμην, ἄξων καὶ τοὺς ἐκεῖσε ὄντας δεδεμένους εἰς Ἰερουσαλὴμ ἵνα τιμωρηθῶσιν.

[6] Ἐγένετο δέ μοι πορευομένῳ καὶ ἐγγίζοντι τῇ Δαμασκῷ περὶ μεσημβρίαν ἐξαίφνης ἐκ τοῦ οὐρανοῦ περιαστράψαι φῶς ἱκανὸν περὶ ἐμέ, [7] ἔπεσά τε εἰς τὸ ἔδαφος καὶ ἤκουσα φωνῆς λεγούσης μοι, Σαοὺλ Σαούλ, τί με διώκεις; [8] ἐγὼ δὲ ἀπεκρίθην, Τίς εἶ, κύριε; εἶπέν τε πρός με, Ἐγώ εἰμι Ἰησοῦς ὁ Ναζωραῖος, ὃν σὺ διώκεις. [9] οἱ δὲ σὺν ἐμοὶ ὄντες τὸ μὲν φῶς ἐθεάσαντο τὴν δὲ φωνὴν οὐκ ἤκουσαν τοῦ λαλοῦντός μοι. [10] εἶπον δέ, Τί ποιήσω, κύριε; ὁ δὲ κύριος εἶπεν πρός με, Ἀναστὰς πορεύου εἰς Δαμασκὸν κἀκεῖ σοι λαληθήσεται περὶ πάντων ὧν τέτακταί σοι ποιῆσαι. [11] ὡς δὲ οὐκ ἐνέβλεπον ἀπὸ τῆς δόξης τοῦ φωτὸς ἐκείνου, χειραγωγούμενος ὑπὸ τῶν συνόντων μοι ἦλθον εἰς Δαμασκόν.

[12] Ἀνανίας δέ τις, ἀνὴρ εὐλαβὴς κατὰ τὸν νόμον, μαρτυρούμενος ὑπὸ πάντων τῶν κατοικούντων Ἰουδαίων, [13] ἐλθὼν πρός με[a] καὶ ἐπιστὰς εἶπέν μοι, Σαοὺλ ἀδελφέ, ἀνάβλεψον. κἀγὼ αὐτῇ τῇ ὥρᾳ ἀνέβλεψα εἰς αὐτόν. [14] ὁ δὲ εἶπεν, Ὁ θεὸς τῶν πατέρων ἡμῶν προεχειρίσατό σε γνῶναι τὸ θέλημα αὐτοῦ καὶ ἰδεῖν τὸν δίκαιον καὶ ἀκοῦσαι

---

into the desert some time ago?" [39]Paul answered, "I am a Jew, from Tarsus in Cilicia, a citizen of no ordinary city. Please let me speak to the people." [40]Having received the commander's permission, Paul stood on the steps and motioned to the crowd. When they were all silent, he said to them in Aramaic[a]:

22 "Brothers and fathers, listen now to my defense."

[2]When they heard him speak to them in Aramaic, they became very quiet.

Then Paul said: [3]"I am a Jew, born in Tarsus of Cilicia, but brought up in this city. Under Gamaliel I was thoroughly trained in the law of our fathers and was just as zealous for God as any of you are today. [4]I persecuted the followers of this Way to their death, arresting both men and women and throwing them into prison, [5]as also the high priest and all the Council can testify. I even obtained letters from them to their brothers in Damascus, and went there to bring these people as prisoners to Jerusalem to be punished.

[6]"About noon as I came near Damascus, suddenly a bright light from heaven flashed around me. [7]I fell to the ground and heard a voice say to me, 'Saul! Saul! Why do you persecute me?'

[8]" 'Who are you, Lord?' I asked.

" 'I am Jesus of Nazareth, whom you are persecuting,' he replied. [9]My companions saw the light, but they did not understand the voice of him who was speaking to me.

[10]" 'What shall I do, Lord?' I asked.

" 'Get up,' the Lord said, 'and go into Damascus. There you will be told all that you have been assigned to do.' [11]My companions led me by the hand into Damascus, because the brilliance of the light had blinded me.

[12]"A man named Ananias came to see me. He was a devout observer of the law and highly respected by all the Jews living there. [13]He stood beside me and said, 'Brother Saul, receive your sight!' And at that very moment I was able to see him.

[14]"Then he said: 'The God of our fathers has chosen you to know his will and to see the Righteous One and to hear words from

---

[e] That is, *Aramaic*   [f] Gk *the Nazorean*   [a] 13 NIV begins verse 13 after με   [a] 40 Or possibly *Hebrew*; also in 22:2

own voice; ¹⁵for you will be his witness to all the world of what you have seen and heard. ¹⁶And now why do you delay? Get up, be baptized, and have your sins washed away, calling on his name.'

Paul Sent to the Gentiles

17 "After I had returned to Jerusalem and while I was praying in the temple, I fell into a trance ¹⁸and saw Jesus^g saying to me, 'Hurry and get out of Jerusalem quickly, because they will not accept your testimony about me.' ¹⁹And I said, 'Lord, they themselves know that in every synagogue I imprisoned and beat those who believed in you. ²⁰And while the blood of your witness Stephen was shed, I myself was standing by, approving and keeping the coats of those who killed him.' ²¹Then he said to me, 'Go, for I will send you far away to the Gentiles.' "

Paul and the Roman Tribune

22 Up to this point they listened to him, but then they shouted, "Away with such a fellow from the earth! For he should not be allowed to live." ²³And while they were shouting, throwing off their cloaks, and tossing dust into the air, ²⁴the tribune directed that he was to be brought into the barracks, and ordered him to be examined by flogging, to find out the reason for this outcry against him. ²⁵But when they had tied him up with thongs,^h Paul said to the centurion who was standing by, "Is it legal for you to flog a Roman citizen who is uncondemned?" ²⁶When the centurion heard that, he went to the tribune and said to him, "What are you about to do? This man is a Roman citizen." ²⁷The tribune came and asked Paul,^g "Tell me, are you a Roman citizen?" And he said, "Yes." ²⁸The tribune answered, "It cost me a large sum of money to get my citizenship." Paul said, "But I was born a citizen." ²⁹Immediately those who were about to examine him drew back from him; and the tribune also was afraid, for he realized that Paul was a Roman citizen and that he had bound him.

Paul before the Council

30 Since he wanted to find out what Paulⁱ was being accused of by the Jews, the next day he released him and ordered the chief priests and the entire council to meet. He

φωνὴν ἐκ τοῦ στόματος αὐτοῦ, **15** ὅτι ἔσῃ μάρτυς αὐτῷ πρὸς πάντας ἀνθρώπους ὧν ἑώρακας καὶ ἤκουσας. **16** καὶ νῦν τί μέλλεις; ἀναστὰς βάπτισαι καὶ ἀπόλουσαι τὰς ἁμαρτίας σου ἐπικαλεσάμενος τὸ ὄνομα αὐτοῦ.

17 Ἐγένετο δέ μοι ὑποστρέψαντι εἰς Ἰερουσαλὴμ καὶ προσευχομένου μου ἐν τῷ ἱερῷ γενέσθαι με ἐν ἐκστάσει **18** καὶ ἰδεῖν αὐτὸν λέγοντά μοι, Σπεῦσον καὶ ἔξελθε ἐν τάχει ἐξ Ἰερουσαλήμ, διότι οὐ παραδέξονταί σου μαρτυρίαν περὶ ἐμοῦ. **19** κἀγὼ εἶπον, Κύριε, αὐτοὶ ἐπίστανται ὅτι ἐγὼ ἤμην φυλακίζων καὶ δέρων κατὰ τὰς συναγωγὰς τοὺς πιστεύοντας ἐπὶ σέ, **20** καὶ ὅτε ἐξεχύννετο τὸ αἷμα Στεφάνου τοῦ μάρτυρός σου, καὶ αὐτὸς ἤμην ἐφεστὼς καὶ συνευδοκῶν καὶ φυλάσσων τὰ ἱμάτια τῶν ἀναιρούντων αὐτόν. **21** καὶ εἶπεν πρός με, Πορεύου, ὅτι ἐγὼ εἰς ἔθνη μακρὰν ἐξαποστελῶ σε.

22 Ἤκουον δὲ αὐτοῦ ἄχρι τούτου τοῦ λόγου καὶ ἐπῆραν τὴν φωνὴν αὐτῶν λέγοντες, Αἶρε ἀπὸ τῆς γῆς τὸν τοιοῦτον, οὐ γὰρ καθῆκεν αὐτὸν ζῆν. **23** κραυγαζόντων τε αὐτῶν καὶ ῥιπτούντων τὰ ἱμάτια καὶ κονιορτὸν βαλλόντων εἰς τὸν ἀέρα, **24** ἐκέλευσεν ὁ χιλίαρχος εἰσάγεσθαι αὐτὸν εἰς τὴν παρεμβολήν, εἴπας μάστιξιν ἀνετάζεσθαι αὐτὸν ἵνα ἐπιγνῷ δι᾽ ἣν αἰτίαν οὕτως ἐπεφώνουν αὐτῷ. **25** ὡς δὲ προέτειναν αὐτὸν τοῖς ἱμᾶσιν, εἶπεν πρὸς τὸν ἑστῶτα ἑκατόνταρχον ὁ Παῦλος, Εἰ ἄνθρωπον Ῥωμαῖον καὶ ἀκατάκριτον ἔξεστιν ὑμῖν μαστίζειν; **26** ἀκούσας δὲ ὁ ἑκατοντάρχης προσελθὼν τῷ χιλιάρχῳ ἀπήγγειλεν λέγων, Τί μέλλεις ποιεῖν; ὁ γὰρ ἄνθρωπος οὗτος Ῥωμαῖός ἐστιν. **27** προσελθὼν δὲ ὁ χιλίαρχος εἶπεν αὐτῷ, Λέγε μοι, σὺ Ῥωμαῖος εἶ; ὁ δὲ ἔφη, Ναί. **28** ἀπεκρίθη δὲ ὁ χιλίαρχος, Ἐγὼ πολλοῦ κεφαλαίου τὴν πολιτείαν ταύτην ἐκτησάμην. ὁ δὲ Παῦλος ἔφη, Ἐγὼ δὲ καὶ γεγέννημαι. **29** εὐθέως οὖν ἀπέστησαν ἀπ᾽ αὐτοῦ οἱ μέλλοντες αὐτὸν ἀνετάζειν, καὶ ὁ χιλίαρχος δὲ ἐφοβήθη ἐπιγνοὺς ὅτι Ῥωμαῖός ἐστιν καὶ ὅτι αὐτὸν ἦν δεδεκώς.

30 Τῇ δὲ ἐπαύριον βουλόμενος γνῶναι τὸ ἀσφαλές, τὸ τί κατηγορεῖται ὑπὸ τῶν Ἰουδαίων, ἔλυσεν αὐτὸν καὶ ἐκέλευσεν συνελθεῖν τοὺς ἀρχιερεῖς καὶ πᾶν τὸ συνέδριον, καὶ καταγαγὼν

his mouth. ¹⁵You will be his witness to all men of what you have seen and heard. ¹⁶And now what are you waiting for? Get up, be baptized and wash your sins away, calling on his name.'

¹⁷"When I returned to Jerusalem and was praying at the temple, I fell into a trance ¹⁸and saw the Lord speaking. 'Quick!' he said to me. 'Leave Jerusalem immediately, because they will not accept your testimony about me.'

¹⁹" 'Lord,' I replied, 'these men know that I went from one synagogue to another to imprison and beat those who believe in you. ²⁰And when the blood of your martyr^a Stephen was shed, I stood there giving my approval and guarding the clothes of those who were killing him.'

²¹"Then the Lord said to me, 'Go; I will send you far away to the Gentiles.' "

Paul the Roman Citizen

²²The crowd listened to Paul until he said this. Then they raised their voices and shouted, "Rid the earth of him! He's not fit to live!"

²³As they were shouting and throwing off their cloaks and flinging dust into the air, ²⁴the commander ordered Paul to be taken into the barracks. He directed that he be flogged and questioned in order to find out why the people were shouting at him like this. ²⁵As they stretched him out to flog him, Paul said to the centurion standing there, "Is it legal for you to flog a Roman citizen who hasn't even been found guilty?"

²⁶When the centurion heard this, he went to the commander and reported it. "What are you going to do?" he asked. "This man is a Roman citizen."

²⁷The commander went to Paul and asked, "Tell me, are you a Roman citizen?"

"Yes, I am," he answered.

²⁸Then the commander said, "I had to pay a big price for my citizenship."

"But I was born a citizen," Paul replied.

²⁹Those who were about to question him withdrew immediately. The commander himself was alarmed when he realized that he had put Paul, a Roman citizen, in chains.

Before the Sanhedrin

³⁰The next day, since the commander wanted to find out exactly why Paul was being accused by the Jews, he released him and ordered the chief priests and all the Sanhedrin to assemble. Then he brought

---

^g Gk *him*   ^h Or *up for the lashes*   ^a20 Or *witness*

brought Paul down and had him stand before them.

23 While Paul was looking intently at the council he said, "Brothers,[j] up to this day I have lived my life with a clear conscience before God." [2]Then the high priest Ananias ordered those standing near him to strike him on the mouth. [3]At this Paul said to him, "God will strike you, you whitewashed wall! Are you sitting there to judge me according to the law, and yet in violation of the law you order me to be struck?" [4]Those standing nearby said, "Do you dare to insult God's high priest?" [5]And Paul said, "I did not realize, brothers, that he was high priest; for it is written, 'You shall not speak evil of a leader of your people.' "

6 When Paul noticed that some were Sadducees and others were Pharisees, he called out in the council, "Brothers, I am a Pharisee, a son of Pharisees. I am on trial concerning the hope of the resurrection[k] of the dead." [7]When he said this, a dissension began between the Pharisees and the Sadducees, and the assembly was divided. [8](The Sadducees say that there is no resurrection, or angel, or spirit; but the Pharisees acknowledge all three.) [9]Then a great clamor arose, and certain scribes of the Pharisees' group stood up and contended, "We find nothing wrong with this man. What if a spirit or an angel has spoken to him?" [10]When the dissension became violent, the tribune, fearing that they would tear Paul to pieces, ordered the soldiers to go down, take him by force, and bring him into the barracks.

11 That night the Lord stood near him and said, "Keep up your courage! For just as you have testified for me in Jerusalem, so you must bear witness also in Rome."

The Plot to Kill Paul

12 In the morning the Jews joined in a conspiracy and bound themselves by an oath neither to eat nor drink until they had killed Paul. [13]There were more than forty who joined in this conspiracy. [14]They went to the chief priests and elders and said, "We have strictly bound ourselves by an oath to taste no food until we have killed Paul. [15]Now then, you and the council must notify the tribune to bring him down to you, on the pretext that you want to make a more thorough examination of his case.

τὸν Παῦλον ἔστησεν εἰς αὐτούς.

23 ἀτενίσας δὲ ὁ Παῦλος τῷ συνεδρίῳ εἶπεν, Ἄνδρες ἀδελφοί, ἐγὼ πάσῃ συνειδήσει ἀγαθῇ πεπολίτευμαι τῷ θεῷ ἄχρι ταύτης τῆς ἡμέρας. 2 ὁ δὲ ἀρχιερεὺς Ἁνανίας ἐπέταξεν τοῖς παρεστῶσιν αὐτῷ τύπτειν αὐτοῦ τὸ στόμα. 3 τότε ὁ Παῦλος πρὸς αὐτὸν εἶπεν, Τύπτειν σε μέλλει ὁ θεός, τοῖχε κεκονιαμένε· καὶ σὺ κάθῃ κρίνων με κατὰ τὸν νόμον καὶ παρανομῶν κελεύεις με τύπτεσθαι; 4 οἱ δὲ παρεστῶτες εἶπαν, Τὸν ἀρχιερέα τοῦ θεοῦ λοιδορεῖς; 5 ἔφη τε ὁ Παῦλος, Οὐκ ᾔδειν, ἀδελφοί, ὅτι ἐστὶν ἀρχιερεύς· γέγραπται γὰρ ὅτι **Ἄρχοντα τοῦ λαοῦ σου οὐκ ἐρεῖς κακῶς.**

6 Γνοὺς δὲ ὁ Παῦλος ὅτι τὸ ἓν μέρος ἐστὶν Σαδδουκαίων τὸ δὲ ἕτερον Φαρισαίων ἔκραζεν ἐν τῷ συνεδρίῳ, Ἄνδρες ἀδελφοί, ἐγὼ Φαρισαῖός εἰμι, υἱὸς Φαρισαίων, περὶ ἐλπίδος καὶ ἀναστάσεως νεκρῶν [ἐγὼ] κρίνομαι. 7 τοῦτο δὲ αὐτοῦ εἰπόντος ἐγένετο στάσις τῶν Φαρισαίων καὶ Σαδδουκαίων καὶ ἐσχίσθη τὸ πλῆθος. 8 Σαδδουκαῖοι μὲν γὰρ λέγουσιν μὴ εἶναι ἀνάστασιν μήτε ἄγγελον μήτε πνεῦμα, Φαρισαῖοι δὲ ὁμολογοῦσιν τὰ ἀμφότερα. 9 ἐγένετο δὲ κραυγὴ μεγάλη, καὶ ἀναστάντες τινὲς τῶν γραμματέων τοῦ μέρους τῶν Φαρισαίων διεμάχοντο λέγοντες, Οὐδὲν κακὸν εὑρίσκομεν ἐν τῷ ἀνθρώπῳ τούτῳ· εἰ δὲ πνεῦμα ἐλάλησεν αὐτῷ ἢ ἄγγελος; 10 Πολλῆς δὲ γινομένης στάσεως φοβηθεὶς ὁ χιλίαρχος μὴ διασπασθῇ ὁ Παῦλος ὑπ' αὐτῶν ἐκέλευσεν τὸ στράτευμα καταβὰν ἁρπάσαι αὐτὸν ἐκ μέσου αὐτῶν ἄγειν τε εἰς τὴν παρεμβολήν.

11 Τῇ δὲ ἐπιούσῃ νυκτὶ ἐπιστὰς αὐτῷ ὁ κύριος εἶπεν, Θάρσει· ὡς γὰρ διεμαρτύρω τὰ περὶ ἐμοῦ εἰς Ἰερουσαλήμ, οὕτω σε δεῖ καὶ εἰς Ῥώμην μαρτυρῆσαι.

12 Γενομένης δὲ ἡμέρας ποιήσαντες συστροφὴν οἱ Ἰουδαῖοι ἀνεθεμάτισαν ἑαυτοὺς λέγοντες μήτε φαγεῖν μήτε πίειν ἕως οὗ ἀποκτείνωσιν τὸν Παῦλον, 13 ἦσαν δὲ πλείους τεσσεράκοντα οἱ ταύτην τὴν συνωμοσίαν ποιησάμενοι, 14 οἵτινες προσελθόντες τοῖς ἀρχιερεῦσιν καὶ τοῖς πρεσβυτέροις εἶπαν, Ἀναθέματι ἀνεθεματίσαμεν ἑαυτοὺς μηδενὸς γεύσασθαι ἕως οὗ ἀποκτείνωμεν τὸν Παῦλον. 15 νῦν οὖν ὑμεῖς ἐμφανίσατε τῷ χιλιάρχῳ σὺν τῷ συνεδρίῳ ὅπως καταγάγῃ αὐτὸν εἰς ὑμᾶς ὡς μέλλοντας διαγινώσκειν

Paul and had him stand before them.

23 Paul looked straight at the Sanhedrin and said, "My brothers, I have fulfilled my duty to God in all good conscience to this day." [2]At this the high priest Ananias ordered those standing near Paul to strike him on the mouth. [3]Then Paul said to him, "God will strike you, you whitewashed wall! You sit there to judge me according to the law, yet you yourself violate the law by commanding that I be struck!"

[4]Those who were standing near Paul said, "You dare to insult God's high priest?"

[5]Paul replied, "Brothers, I did not realize that he was the high priest; for it is written: 'Do not speak evil about the ruler of your people.'[a]"

[6]Then Paul, knowing that some of them were Sadducees and the others Pharisees, called out in the Sanhedrin, "My brothers, I am a Pharisee, the son of a Pharisee. I stand on trial because of my hope in the resurrection of the dead." [7]When he said this, a dispute broke out between the Pharisees and the Sadducees, and the assembly was divided. [8](The Sadducees say that there is no resurrection, and that there are neither angels nor spirits, but the Pharisees acknowledge them all.)

[9]There was a great uproar, and some of the teachers of the law who were Pharisees stood up and argued vigorously. "We find nothing wrong with this man," they said. "What if a spirit or an angel has spoken to him?" [10]The dispute became so violent that the commander was afraid Paul would be torn to pieces by them. He ordered the troops to go down and take him away from them by force and bring him into the barracks.

[11]The following night the Lord stood near Paul and said, "Take courage! As you have testified about me in Jerusalem, so you must also testify in Rome."

The Plot to Kill Paul

[12]The next morning the Jews formed a conspiracy and bound themselves with an oath not to eat or drink until they had killed Paul. [13]More than forty men were involved in this plot. [14]They went to the chief priests and elders and said, "We have taken a solemn oath not to eat anything until we have killed Paul. [15]Now then, you and the Sanhedrin petition the commander to bring him before you on the pretext of wanting more accurate information about

[j]Gk *Men, brothers* [k]Gk *concerning hope and resurrection*   [a]5 Exodus 22:28

And we are ready to do away with him before he arrives."

16 Now the son of Paul's sister heard about the ambush; so he went and gained entrance to the barracks and told Paul. [17]Paul called one of the centurions and said, "Take this young man to the tribune, for he has something to report to him." [18]So he took him, brought him to the tribune, and said, "The prisoner Paul called me and asked me to bring this young man to you; he has something to tell you." [19]The tribune took him by the hand, drew him aside privately, and asked, "What is it that you have to report to me?" [20]He answered, "The Jews have agreed to ask you to bring Paul down to the council tomorrow, as though they were going to inquire more thoroughly into his case. [21]But do not be persuaded by them, for more than forty of their men are lying in ambush for him. They have bound themselves by an oath neither to eat nor drink until they kill him. They are ready now and are waiting for your consent." [22]So the tribune dismissed the young man, ordering him, "Tell no one that you have informed me of this."

Paul Sent to Felix the Governor

23 Then he summoned two of the centurions and said, "Get ready to leave by nine o'clock tonight for Caesarea with two hundred soldiers, seventy horsemen, and two hundred spearmen. [24]Also provide mounts for Paul to ride, and take him safely to Felix the governor." [25]He wrote a letter to this effect:

26 "Claudius Lysias to his Excellency the governor Felix, greetings. [27]This man was seized by the Jews and was about to be killed by them, but when I had learned that he was a Roman citizen, I came with the guard and rescued him. [28]Since I wanted to know the charge for which they accused him, I had him brought to their council. [29]I found that he was accused concerning questions of their law, but was charged with nothing deserving death or imprisonment. [30]When I was informed that there would be a plot against the man, I sent him to you at once, ordering his accusers also to state before you what they have against him.[l]"

ἀκριβέστερον τὰ περὶ αὐτοῦ· ἡμεῖς δὲ πρὸ τοῦ ἐγγίσαι αὐτὸν ἕτοιμοί ἐσμεν τοῦ ἀνελεῖν αὐτόν. 16 Ἀκούσας δὲ ὁ υἱὸς τῆς ἀδελφῆς Παύλου τὴν ἐνέδραν, παραγενόμενος καὶ εἰσελθὼν εἰς τὴν παρεμβολὴν ἀπήγγειλεν τῷ Παύλῳ. 17 προσκαλεσάμενος δὲ ὁ Παῦλος ἕνα τῶν ἑκατονταρχῶν ἔφη, Τὸν νεανίαν τοῦτον ἀπάγαγε πρὸς τὸν χιλίαρχον, ἔχει γὰρ ἀπαγγεῖλαί τι αὐτῷ. 18 ὁ μὲν οὖν παραλαβὼν αὐτὸν ἤγαγεν πρὸς τὸν χιλίαρχον καὶ φησίν, Ὁ δέσμιος Παῦλος προσκαλεσάμενός με ἠρώτησεν τοῦτον τὸν νεανίσκον ἀγαγεῖν πρὸς σὲ ἔχοντά τι λαλῆσαί σοι. 19 ἐπιλαβόμενος δὲ τῆς χειρὸς αὐτοῦ ὁ χιλίαρχος καὶ ἀναχωρήσας κατ' ἰδίαν ἐπυνθάνετο, Τί ἐστιν ὃ ἔχεις ἀπαγγεῖλαί μοι; 20 εἶπεν δὲ ὅτι Οἱ Ἰουδαῖοι συνέθεντο τοῦ ἐρωτῆσαί σε ὅπως αὔριον τὸν Παῦλον καταγάγῃς εἰς τὸ συνέδριον ὡς μέλλον τι ἀκριβέστερον πυνθάνεσθαι περὶ αὐτοῦ. 21 σὺ οὖν μὴ πεισθῇς αὐτοῖς· ἐνεδρεύουσιν γὰρ αὐτὸν ἐξ αὐτῶν ἄνδρες πλείους τεσσεράκοντα, οἵτινες ἀνεθεμάτισαν ἑαυτοὺς μήτε φαγεῖν μήτε πιεῖν ἕως οὗ ἀνέλωσιν αὐτόν, καὶ νῦν εἰσιν ἕτοιμοι προσδεχόμενοι τὴν ἀπὸ σοῦ ἐπαγγελίαν. 22 ὁ μὲν οὖν χιλίαρχος ἀπέλυσε τὸν νεανίσκον παραγγείλας μηδενὶ ἐκλαλῆσαι ὅτι ταῦτα ἐνεφάνισας πρός με.

23 Καὶ προσκαλεσάμενος δύο [τινὰς] τῶν ἑκατονταρχῶν εἶπεν, Ἑτοιμάσατε στρατιώτας διακοσίους, ὅπως πορευθῶσιν ἕως Καισαρείας, καὶ ἱππεῖς ἑβδομήκοντα καὶ δεξιολάβους διακοσίους ἀπὸ τρίτης ὥρας τῆς νυκτός, 24 κτήνη τε παραστῆσαι ἵνα ἐπιβιβάσαντες τὸν Παῦλον διασώσωσι πρὸς Φήλικα τὸν ἡγεμόνα, 25 γράψας ἐπιστολὴν ἔχουσαν τὸν τύπον τοῦτον· 26 Κλαύδιος Λυσίας τῷ κρατίστῳ ἡγεμόνι Φήλικι χαίρειν. 27 Τὸν ἄνδρα τοῦτον συλλημφθέντα ὑπὸ τῶν Ἰουδαίων καὶ μέλλοντα ἀναιρεῖσθαι ὑπ' αὐτῶν ἐπιστὰς σὺν τῷ στρατεύματι ἐξειλάμην μαθὼν ὅτι Ῥωμαῖός ἐστιν. 28 βουλόμενός τε ἐπιγνῶναι τὴν αἰτίαν δι' ἣν ἐνεκάλουν αὐτῷ, κατήγαγον εἰς τὸ συνέδριον αὐτῶν 29 ὃν εὗρον ἐγκαλούμενον περὶ ζητημάτων τοῦ νόμου αὐτῶν, μηδὲν δὲ ἄξιον θανάτου ἢ δεσμῶν ἔχοντα ἔγκλημα. 30 μηνυθείσης δέ μοι ἐπιβουλῆς εἰς τὸν ἄνδρα ἔσεσθαι ἐξαυτῆς ἔπεμψα πρὸς σὲ παραγγείλας καὶ τοῖς κατηγόροις λέγειν [τὰ] πρὸς αὐτὸν ἐπὶ σοῦ.[a]

his case. We are ready to kill him before he gets here."

[16]But when the son of Paul's sister heard of this plot, he went into the barracks and told Paul.

[17]Then Paul called one of the centurions and said, "Take this young man to the commander; he has something to tell him." [18]So he took him to the commander.

The centurion said, "Paul, the prisoner, sent for me and asked me to bring this young man to you because he has something to tell you."

[19]The commander took the young man by the hand, drew him aside and asked, "What is it you want to tell me?"

[20]He said: "The Jews have agreed to ask you to bring Paul before the Sanhedrin tomorrow on the pretext of wanting more accurate information about him. [21]Don't give in to them, because more than forty of them are waiting in ambush for him. They have taken an oath not to eat or drink until they have killed him. They are ready now, waiting for your consent to their request."

[22]The commander dismissed the young man and cautioned him, "Don't tell anyone that you have reported this to me."

Paul Transferred to Caesarea

[23]Then he called two of his centurions and ordered them, "Get ready a detachment of two hundred soldiers, seventy horsemen and two hundred spearmen[b] to go to Caesarea at nine tonight. [24]Provide mounts for Paul so that he may be taken safely to Governor Felix."

[25]He wrote a letter as follows:

[26]Claudius Lysias,

To His Excellency, Governor Felix:

Greetings.

[27]This man was seized by the Jews and they were about to kill him, but I came with my troops and rescued him, for I had learned that he is a Roman citizen. [28]I wanted to know why they were accusing him, so I brought him to their Sanhedrin. [29]I found that the accusation had to do with questions about their law, but there was no charge against him that deserved death or imprisonment. [30]When I was informed of a plot to be carried out against the man, I sent him to you at once. I also ordered his accusers to present to you their case against him.

---

[l]Other ancient authorities add *Farewell*

[a]30 NRSV note l adds ἔρρωσο or ἔρρωσθε

[b]23 The meaning of the Greek for this word is uncertain.

31 So the soldiers, according to their instructions, took Paul and brought him during the night to Antipatris. 32The next day they let the horsemen go on with him, while they returned to the barracks. 33When they came to Caesarea and delivered the letter to the governor, they presented Paul also before him. 34On reading the letter, he asked what province he belonged to, and when he learned that he was from Cilicia, 35he said, "I will give you a hearing when your accusers arrive." Then he ordered that he be kept under guard in Herod's headquarters.m

Paul before Felix at Caesarea

24 Five days later the high priest Ananias came down with some elders and an attorney, a certain Tertullus, and they reported their case against Paul to the governor. 2When Pauln had been summoned, Tertullus began to accuse him, saying:

"Your Excellency,o because of you we have long enjoyed peace, and reforms have been made for this people because of your foresight. 3We welcome this in every way and everywhere with utmost gratitude. 4But, to detain you no further, I beg you to hear us briefly with your customary graciousness. 5We have, in fact, found this man a pestilent fellow, an agitator among all the Jews throughout the world, and a ringleader of the sect of the Nazarenes.p 6He even tried to profane the temple, and so we seized him.q 8By examining him yourself you will be able to learn from him concerning everything of which we accuse him."

9 The Jews also joined in the charge by asserting that all this was true.

Paul's Defense before Felix

10 When the governor motioned to him to speak, Paul replied:

"I cheerfully make my defense, knowing that for many years you have been a judge over this nation. 11As you can find out, it is not more than twelve days since I went up to worship in Jerusalem. 12They did not find me disputing with anyone in the temple or stirring up a crowd either in the synagogues or throughout the city. 13Neither can they prove to you the charge that they now bring against me. 14But this I

31 Οἱ μὲν οὖν στρατιῶται κατὰ τὸ διατεταγμένον αὐτοῖς ἀναλαβόντες τὸν Παῦλον ἤγαγον διὰ νυκτὸς εἰς τὴν Ἀντιπατρίδα, **32** τῇ δὲ ἐπαύριον ἐάσαντες τοὺς ἱππεῖς ἀπέρχεσθαι σὺν αὐτῷ ὑπέστρεψαν εἰς τὴν παρεμβολήν· **33** οἵτινες εἰσελθόντες εἰς τὴν Καισάρειαν καὶ ἀναδόντες τὴν ἐπιστολὴν τῷ ἡγεμόνι παρέστησαν καὶ τὸν Παῦλον αὐτῷ. **34** ἀναγνοὺς δὲ καὶ ἐπερωτήσας ἐκ ποίας ἐπαρχείας ἐστίν, καὶ πυθόμενος ὅτι ἀπὸ Κιλικίας, **35** Διακούσομαί σου, ἔφη, ὅταν καὶ οἱ κατήγοροί σου παραγένωνται· κελεύσας ἐν τῷ πραιτωρίῳ τοῦ Ἡρῴδου φυλάσσεσθαι αὐτόν.

24 Μετὰ δὲ πέντε ἡμέρας κατέβη ὁ ἀρχιερεὺς Ἀνανίας μετὰ πρεσβυτέρων τινῶν καὶ ῥήτορος Τερτύλλου τινός, οἵτινες ἐνεφάνισαν τῷ ἡγεμόνι κατὰ τοῦ Παύλου. 2 κληθέντος δὲ αὐτοῦ ἤρξατο κατηγορεῖν ὁ Τέρτυλλος λέγων, Πολλῆς εἰρήνης τυγχάνοντες διὰ σοῦ καὶ διορθωμάτων γινομένων τῷ ἔθνει τούτῳ διὰ τῆς σῆς προνοίας, 3 πάντῃ τε καὶ πανταχοῦ ἀποδεχόμεθα, κράτιστε Φῆλιξ, μετὰ πάσης εὐχαριστίας. 4 ἵνα δὲ μὴ ἐπὶ πλεῖόν σε ἐγκόπτω, παρακαλῶ ἀκοῦσαί σε ἡμῶν συντόμως τῇ σῇ ἐπιεικείᾳ. 5 εὑρόντες γὰρ τὸν ἄνδρα τοῦτον λοιμὸν καὶ κινοῦντα στάσεις πᾶσιν τοῖς Ἰουδαίοις τοῖς κατὰ τὴν οἰκουμένην πρωτοστάτην τε τῆς τῶν Ναζωραίων αἱρέσεως, 6 ὃς καὶ τὸ ἱερὸν ἐπείρασεν βεβηλῶσαι ὃν καὶ ἐκρατήσαμεν,a 8 παρ' οὗ δυνήσῃ αὐτὸς ἀνακρίνας περὶ πάντων τούτων ἐπιγνῶναι ὧν ἡμεῖς κατηγοροῦμεν αὐτοῦ. 9 συνεπέθεντο δὲ καὶ οἱ Ἰουδαῖοι φάσκοντες ταῦτα οὕτως ἔχειν.

10 Ἀπεκρίθη τε ὁ Παῦλος νεύσαντος αὐτῷ τοῦ ἡγεμόνος λέγειν, Ἐκ πολλῶν ἐτῶν ὄντα σε κριτὴν τῷ ἔθνει τούτῳ ἐπιστάμενος εὐθύμως τὰ περὶ ἐμαυτοῦ ἀπολογοῦμαι, 11 δυναμένου σου ἐπιγνῶναι ὅτι οὐ πλείους εἰσίν μοι ἡμέραι δώδεκα ἀφ' ἧς ἀνέβην προσκυνήσων εἰς Ἰερουσαλήμ. 12 καὶ οὔτε ἐν τῷ ἱερῷ εὗρόν με πρός τινα διαλεγόμενον ἢ ἐπίστασιν ποιοῦντα ὄχλου οὔτε ἐν ταῖς συναγωγαῖς οὔτε κατὰ τὴν πόλιν, 13 οὐδὲ παραστῆσαι δύνανταί σοι περὶ ὧν νυνὶ κατηγοροῦσίν μου. 14 ὁμολογῶ

31So the soldiers, carrying out their orders, took Paul with them during the night and brought him as far as Antipatris. 32The next day they let the cavalry go on with him, while they returned to the barracks. 33When the cavalry arrived in Caesarea, they delivered the letter to the governor and handed Paul over to him. 34The governor read the letter and asked what province he was from. Learning that he was from Cilicia, 35he said, "I will hear your case when your accusers get here." Then he ordered that Paul be kept under guard in Herod's palace.

The Trial Before Felix

24 Five days later the high priest Ananias went down to Caesarea with some of the elders and a lawyer named Tertullus, and they brought their charges against Paul before the governor. 2When Paul was called in, Tertullus presented his case before Felix: "We have enjoyed a long period of peace under you, and your foresight has brought about reforms in this nation. 3Everywhere and in every way, most excellent Felix, we acknowledge this with profound gratitude. 4But in order not to weary you further, I would request that you be kind enough to hear us briefly.

5"We have found this man to be a troublemaker, stirring up riots among the Jews all over the world. He is a ringleader of the Nazarene sect 6and even tried to desecrate the temple; so we seized him. 8Bya examining him yourself you will be able to learn the truth about all these charges we are bringing against him."

9The Jews joined in the accusation, asserting that these things were true.

10When the governor motioned for him to speak, Paul replied: "I know that for a number of years you have been a judge over this nation; so I gladly make my defense. 11You can easily verify that no more than twelve days ago I went up to Jerusalem to worship. 12My accusers did not find me arguing with anyone at the temple, or stirring up a crowd in the synagogues or anywhere else in the city. 13And they cannot prove to you the charges they are now making against me. 14However, I admit

---

m Gk *praetorium*   n Gk *he*   o Gk lacks *Your Excellency*
p Gk *Nazoreans*   q Other ancient authorities add *and we would have judged him according to our law.* 7But the chief captain Lysias came and with great violence took him out of our hands,* 8commanding his accusers to come before you.*

a6 NIV/NRSV notes add καὶ κατὰ τὸν ἡμέτερον νόμον ἠθελήσαμεν κρῖναι. 7 παρελθὼν δὲ Λυσίας ὁ χιλίαρχος μετὰ πολλῆς βίας ἐκ τῶν χειρῶν ἡμῶν ἀπήγαγε, 8 κελεύσας τοὺς κατηγόρους αὐτοῦ ἔρχεσθαι ἐπὶ σέ.

a6-8 Some manuscripts *him and wanted to judge him according to our law.* 7But the commander, Lysias, came and with the use of much force snatched him from our hands 8and ordered his accusers to come before you. By* admit to you, that according to the Way, which they call a sect, I worship the God of our ancestors, believing everything laid down according to the law or written in the prophets. [15]I have a hope in God—a hope that they themselves also accept— that there will be a resurrection of both[r] the righteous and the unrighteous. [16]Therefore I do my best always to have a clear conscience toward God and all people. [17]Now after some years I came to bring alms to my nation and to offer sacrifices. [18]While I was doing this, they found me in the temple, completing the rite of purification, without any crowd or disturbance. [19]But there were some Jews from Asia— they ought to be here before you to make an accusation, if they have anything against me. [20]Or let these men here tell what crime they had found when I stood before the council, [21]unless it was this one sentence that I called out while standing before them, 'It is about the resurrection of the dead that I am on trial before you today.' "

22 But Felix, who was rather well informed about the Way, adjourned the hearing with the comment, "When Lysias the tribune comes down, I will decide your case." [23]Then he ordered the centurion to keep him in custody, but to let him have some liberty and not to prevent any of his friends from taking care of his needs.

Paul Held in Custody

24 Some days later when Felix came with his wife Drusilla, who was Jewish, he sent for Paul and heard him speak concerning faith in Christ Jesus. [25]And as he discussed justice, self-control, and the coming judgment, Felix became frightened and said, "Go away for the present; when I have an opportunity, I will send for you." [26]At the same time he hoped that money would be given him by Paul, and for that reason he used to send for him very often and converse with him.

27 After two years had passed, Felix was succeeded by Porcius Festus; and since he wanted to grant the Jews a favor, Felix left Paul in prison.

Paul Appeals to the Emperor

25 Three days after Festus had arrived in the province, he went up from Caesarea to Jerusalem [2]where the chief priests and the leaders of the Jews gave him a report against Paul. They appealed to him [3]and requested, as a favor

[r] Other ancient authorities read *of the dead, both of*

δὲ τοῦτό σοι ὅτι κατὰ τὴν ὁδὸν ἣν λέγουσιν αἵρεσιν, οὕτως λατρεύω τῷ πατρῴῳ θεῷ πιστεύων πᾶσι τοῖς κατὰ τὸν νόμον καὶ τοῖς ἐν τοῖς προφήταις γεγραμμένοις, **15** ἐλπίδα ἔχων εἰς τὸν θεὸν ἣν καὶ αὐτοὶ οὗτοι προσδέχονται, ἀνάστασιν μέλλειν ἔσεσθαι[b] δικαίων τε καὶ ἀδίκων. **16** ἐν τούτῳ καὶ αὐτὸς ἀσκῶ ἀπρόσκοπον συνείδησιν ἔχειν πρὸς τὸν θεὸν καὶ τοὺς ἀνθρώπους διὰ παντός. **17** δι' ἐτῶν δὲ πλειόνων ἐλεημοσύνας ποιήσων εἰς τὸ ἔθνος μου παρεγενόμην καὶ προσφοράς, **18** ἐν αἷς εὗρόν με ἡγνισμένον ἐν τῷ ἱερῷ οὐ μετὰ ὄχλου οὐδὲ μετὰ θορύβου, **19** τινὲς δὲ ἀπὸ τῆς Ἀσίας Ἰουδαῖοι, οὓς ἔδει ἐπὶ σοῦ παρεῖναι καὶ κατηγορεῖν εἴ τι ἔχοιεν πρὸς ἐμέ. **20** ἢ αὐτοὶ οὗτοι εἰπάτωσαν τί εὗρον ἀδίκημα στάντος μου ἐπὶ τοῦ συνεδρίου, **21** ἢ περὶ μιᾶς ταύτης φωνῆς ἧς ἐκέκραξα ἐν αὐτοῖς ἑστὼς ὅτι Περὶ ἀναστάσεως νεκρῶν ἐγὼ κρίνομαι σήμερον ἐφ' ὑμῶν.

22 Ἀνεβάλετο δὲ αὐτοὺς ὁ Φῆλιξ, ἀκριβέστερον εἰδὼς τὰ περὶ τῆς ὁδοῦ εἴπας, Ὅταν Λυσίας ὁ χιλίαρχος καταβῇ, διαγνώσομαι τὰ καθ' ὑμᾶς· **23** διαταξάμενος τῷ ἑκατοντάρχῃ τηρεῖσθαι αὐτὸν ἔχειν τε ἄνεσιν καὶ μηδένα κωλύειν τῶν ἰδίων αὐτοῦ ὑπηρετεῖν αὐτῷ.

24 Μετὰ δὲ ἡμέρας τινὰς παραγενόμενος ὁ Φῆλιξ σὺν Δρουσίλλῃ τῇ ἰδίᾳ γυναικὶ οὔσῃ Ἰουδαίᾳ μετεπέμψατο τὸν Παῦλον καὶ ἤκουσεν αὐτοῦ περὶ τῆς εἰς Χριστὸν Ἰησοῦν πίστεως. **25** διαλεγομένου δὲ αὐτοῦ περὶ δικαιοσύνης καὶ ἐγκρατείας καὶ τοῦ κρίματος τοῦ μέλλοντος, ἔμφοβος γενόμενος ὁ Φῆλιξ ἀπεκρίθη, Τὸ νῦν ἔχον πορεύου, καιρὸν δὲ μεταλαβὼν μετακαλέσομαί σε, **26** ἅμα καὶ ἐλπίζων ὅτι χρήματα δοθήσεται αὐτῷ ὑπὸ τοῦ Παύλου· διὸ καὶ πυκνότερον αὐτὸν μεταπεμπόμενος ὡμίλει αὐτῷ.

27 Διετίας δὲ πληρωθείσης ἔλαβεν διάδοχον ὁ Φῆλιξ Πόρκιον Φῆστον, θέλων τε χάριτα καταθέσθαι τοῖς Ἰουδαίοις ὁ Φῆλιξ κατέλιπε τὸν Παῦλον δεδεμένον.

25 Φῆστος οὖν ἐπιβὰς τῇ ἐπαρχείᾳ μετὰ τρεῖς ἡμέρας ἀνέβη εἰς Ἱεροσόλυμα ἀπὸ Καισαρείας, **2** ἐνεφάνισάν τε αὐτῷ οἱ ἀρχιερεῖς καὶ οἱ πρῶτοι τῶν Ἰουδαίων κατὰ τοῦ Παύλου[a] καὶ παρεκάλουν αὐτὸν **3** αἰτούμενοι

that I worship the God of our fathers as a follower of the Way, which they call a sect. I believe everything that agrees with the Law and that is written in the Prophets, [15]and I have the same hope in God as these men, that there will be a resurrection of both the righteous and the wicked. [16]So I strive always to keep my conscience clear before God and man.

[17]"After an absence of several years, I came to Jerusalem to bring my people gifts for the poor and to present offerings. [18]I was ceremonially clean when they found me in the temple courts doing this. There was no crowd with me, nor was I involved in any disturbance. [19]But there are some Jews from the province of Asia, who ought to be here before you and bring charges if they have anything against me. [20]Or these who are here should state what crime they found in me when I stood before the Sanhedrin— [21]unless it was this one thing I shouted as I stood in their presence: 'It is concerning the resurrection of the dead that I am on trial before you today.' "

[22]Then Felix, who was well acquainted with the Way, adjourned the proceedings. "When Lysias the commander comes," he said, "I will decide your case." [23]He ordered the centurion to keep Paul under guard but to give him some freedom and permit his friends to take care of his needs.

[24]Several days later Felix came with his wife Drusilla, who was a Jewess. He sent for Paul and listened to him as he spoke about faith in Christ Jesus. [25]As Paul discoursed on righteousness, self-control and the judgment to come, Felix was afraid and said, "That's enough for now! You may leave. When I find it convenient, I will send for you." [26]At the same time he was hoping that Paul would offer him a bribe, so he sent for him frequently and talked with him.

[27]When two years had passed, Felix was succeeded by Porcius Festus, but because Felix wanted to grant a favor to the Jews, he left Paul in prison.

The Trial Before Festus

25 Three days after arriving in the province, Festus went up from Caesarea to Jerusalem, [2]where the chief priests and Jewish leaders appeared before him and presented the charges against Paul. [3]They urgently requested Festus, as

[b]15 NRSV note r adds νεκρῶν †   [a]2 NIV begins verse 3 after Παῦλον

to them against Paul,ˢ to have him transferred to Jerusalem. They were, in fact, planning an ambush to kill him along the way. 4Festus replied that Paul was being kept at Caesarea, and that he himself intended to go there shortly. 5"So," he said, "let those of you who have the authority come down with me, and if there is anything wrong about the man, let them accuse him."

6 After he had stayed among them not more than eight or ten days, he went down to Caesarea; the next day he took his seat on the tribunal and ordered Paul to be brought. 7When he arrived, the Jews who had gone down from Jerusalem surrounded him, bringing many serious charges against him, which they could not prove. 8Paul said in his defense, "I have in no way committed an offense against the law of the Jews, or against the temple, or against the emperor." 9But Festus, wishing to do the Jews a favor, asked Paul, "Do you wish to go up to Jerusalem and be tried there before me on these charges?" 10Paul said, "I am appealing to the emperor's tribunal; this is where I should be tried. I have done no wrong to the Jews, as you very well know. 11Now if I am in the wrong and have committed something for which I deserve to die, I am not trying to escape death; but if there is nothing to their charges against me, no one can turn me over to them. I appeal to the emperor." 12Then Festus, after he had conferred with his council, replied, "You have appealed to the emperor; to the emperor you will go."

Festus Consults King Agrippa

13 After several days had passed, King Agrippa and Bernice arrived at Caesarea to welcome Festus. 14Since they were staying there several days, Festus laid Paul's case before the king, saying, "There is a man here who was left in prison by Felix. 15When I was in Jerusalem, the chief priests and the elders of the Jews informed me about him and asked for a sentence against him. 16I told them that it was not the custom of the Romans to hand over anyone before the accused had met the accusers face to face and had been given an opportunity to make a defense against the charge. 17So when they met here, I lost no time, but on the next day took my seat on the tribunal and ordered the man to be

χάριν κατ' αὐτοῦ ὅπως μεταπέμψηται αὐτὸν εἰς Ἰερουσαλήμ, ἐνέδραν ποιοῦντες ἀνελεῖν αὐτὸν κατὰ τὴν ὁδόν. 4 ὁ μὲν οὖν Φῆστος ἀπεκρίθη τηρεῖσθαι τὸν Παῦλον εἰς Καισάρειαν, ἑαυτὸν δὲ μέλλειν ἐν τάχει ἐκπορεύεσθαι· 5 Οἱ οὖν ἐν ὑμῖν, φησίν, δυνατοὶ συγκαταβάντες εἴ τί ἐστιν ἐν τῷ ἀνδρὶ ἄτοπον κατηγορείτωσαν αὐτοῦ.

6 Διατρίψας δὲ ἐν αὐτοῖς ἡμέρας οὐ πλείουςᵇ ὀκτὼ ἢ δέκα, καταβὰς εἰς Καισάρειαν, τῇ ἐπαύριον καθίσας ἐπὶ τοῦ βήματος ἐκέλευσεν τὸν Παῦλον ἀχθῆναι. 7 παραγενομένου δὲ αὐτοῦ περιέστησαν αὐτὸν οἱ ἀπὸ Ἰεροσολύμων καταβεβηκότες Ἰουδαῖοι πολλὰ καὶ βαρέα αἰτιώματα καταφέροντες ἃ οὐκ ἴσχυον ἀποδεῖξαι, 8 τοῦ Παύλου ἀπολογουμένου ὅτι Οὔτε εἰς τὸν νόμον τῶν Ἰουδαίων οὔτε εἰς τὸ ἱερὸν οὔτε εἰς Καίσαρά τι ἥμαρτον. 9 ὁ Φῆστος δὲ θέλων τοῖς Ἰουδαίοις χάριν καταθέσθαι ἀποκριθεὶς τῷ Παύλῳ εἶπεν, Θέλεις εἰς Ἰεροσόλυμα ἀναβὰς ἐκεῖ περὶ τούτων κριθῆναι ἐπ' ἐμοῦ; 10 εἶπεν δὲ ὁ Παῦλος, Ἐπὶ τοῦ βήματος Καίσαρος ἑστώς εἰμι, οὗ με δεῖ κρίνεσθαι. Ἰουδαίους οὐδὲν ἠδίκησα ὡς καὶ σὺ κάλλιον ἐπιγινώσκεις. 11 εἰ μὲν οὖν ἀδικῶ καὶ ἄξιον θανάτου πέπραχά τι, οὐ παραιτοῦμαι τὸ ἀποθανεῖν· εἰ δὲ οὐδέν ἐστιν ὧν οὗτοι κατηγοροῦσίν μου, οὐδείς με δύναται αὐτοῖς χαρίσασθαι· Καίσαρα ἐπικαλοῦμαι. 12 τότε ὁ Φῆστος συλλαλήσας μετὰ τοῦ συμβουλίου ἀπεκρίθη, Καίσαρα ἐπικέκλησαι, ἐπὶ Καίσαρα πορεύσῃ.

13 Ἡμερῶν δὲ διαγενομένων τινῶν Ἀγρίππας ὁ βασιλεὺς καὶ Βερνίκη κατήντησαν εἰς Καισάρειαν ἀσπασάμενοι τὸν Φῆστον. 14 ὡς δὲ πλείους ἡμέρας διέτριβον ἐκεῖ, ὁ Φῆστος τῷ βασιλεῖ ἀνέθετο τὰ κατὰ τὸν Παῦλον λέγων, Ἀνήρ τίς ἐστιν καταλελειμμένος ὑπὸ Φήλικος δέσμιος, 15 περὶ οὗ γενομένου μου εἰς Ἰεροσόλυμα ἐνεφάνισαν οἱ ἀρχιερεῖς καὶ οἱ πρεσβύτεροι τῶν Ἰουδαίων αἰτούμενοι κατ' αὐτοῦ καταδίκην. 16 πρὸς οὓς ἀπεκρίθην ὅτι οὐκ ἔστιν ἔθος Ῥωμαίοις χαρίζεσθαί τινα ἄνθρωπον πρὶν ἢ ὁ κατηγορούμενος κατὰ πρόσωπον ἔχοι τοὺς κατηγόρους τόπον τε ἀπολογίας λάβοι περὶ τοῦ ἐγκλήματος. 17 συνελθόντων οὖν [αὐτῶν] ἐνθάδε ἀναβολὴν μηδεμίαν ποιησάμενος τῇ ἑξῆς καθίσας ἐπὶ τοῦ βήματος ἐκέλευσα ἀχθῆναι

a favor to them, to have Paul transferred to Jerusalem, for they were preparing an ambush to kill him along the way. 4Festus answered, "Paul is being held at Caesarea, and I myself am going there soon. 5Let some of your leaders come with me and press charges against the man there, if he has done anything wrong."

6After spending eight or ten days with them, he went down to Caesarea, and the next day he convened the court and ordered that Paul be brought before him. 7When Paul appeared, the Jews who had come down from Jerusalem stood around him, bringing many serious charges against him, which they could not prove.

8Then Paul made his defense: "I have done nothing wrong against the law of the Jews or against the temple or against Caesar."

9Festus, wishing to do the Jews a favor, said to Paul, "Are you willing to go up to Jerusalem and stand trial before me there on these charges?"

10Paul answered: "I am now standing before Caesar's court, where I ought to be tried. I have not done any wrong to the Jews, as you yourself know very well. 11If, however, I am guilty of doing anything deserving death, I do not refuse to die. But if the charges brought against me by these Jews are not true, no one has the right to hand me over to them. I appeal to Caesar!"

12After Festus had conferred with his council, he declared: "You have appealed to Caesar. To Caesar you will go!"

Festus Consults King Agrippa

13A few days later King Agrippa and Bernice arrived at Caesarea to pay their respects to Festus. 14Since they were spending many days there, Festus discussed Paul's case with the king. He said: "There is a man here whom Felix left as a prisoner. 15When I went to Jerusalem, the chief priests and elders of the Jews brought charges against him and asked that he be condemned.

16"I told them that it is not the Roman custom to hand over any man before he has faced his accusers and has had an opportunity to defend himself against their charges. 17When they came here with me, I did not delay the case, but convened the court the next day and ordered the man to

---

ˢGk *him*   ᵇ6 NIV text omits οὐ πλείους †

brought. [18]When the accusers stood up, they did not charge him with any of the crimes[t] that I was expecting. [19]Instead they had certain points of disagreement with him about their own religion and about a certain Jesus, who had died, but whom Paul asserted to be alive. [20]Since I was at a loss how to investigate these questions, I asked whether he wished to go to Jerusalem and be tried there on these charges.[u] [21]But when Paul had appealed to be kept in custody for the decision of his Imperial Majesty, I ordered him to be held until I could send him to the emperor." [22]Agrippa said to Festus, "I would like to hear the man myself." "Tomorrow," he said, "you will hear him."

Paul Brought before Agrippa

23 So on the next day Agrippa and Bernice came with great pomp, and they entered the audience hall with the military tribunes and the prominent men of the city. Then Festus gave the order and Paul was brought in. [24]And Festus said, "King Agrippa and all here present with us, you see this man about whom the whole Jewish community petitioned me, both in Jerusalem and here, shouting that he ought not to live any longer. [25]But I found that he had done nothing deserving death; and when he appealed to his Imperial Majesty, I decided to send him. [26]But I have nothing definite to write to our sovereign about him. Therefore I have brought him before all of you, and especially before you, King Agrippa, so that, after we have examined him, I may have something to write— [27]for it seems to me unreasonable to send a prisoner without indicating the charges against him."

Paul Defends Himself before Agrippa

26 Agrippa said to Paul, "You have permission to speak for yourself." Then Paul stretched out his hand and began to defend himself:

2 "I consider myself fortunate that it is before you, King Agrippa, I am to make my defense today against all the accusations of the Jews, [3]because you are especially familiar with all the customs and controversies of the Jews; therefore I beg of you to listen to me patiently.

4 "All the Jews know my way of life from my youth, a life spent from the beginning among my own people and in Jerusalem. [5]They have known for a long

τὸν ἄνδρα· 18 περὶ οὗ σταθέντες οἱ κατήγοροι οὐδεμίαν αἰτίαν ἔφερον ὧν ἐγὼ ὑπενόουν πονηρῶν[c], 19 ζητήματα δέ τινα περὶ τῆς ἰδίας δεισιδαιμονίας εἶχον πρὸς αὐτὸν καὶ περί τινος Ἰησοῦ τεθνηκότος ὃν ἔφασκεν ὁ Παῦλος ζῆν. 20 ἀπορούμενος δὲ ἐγὼ τὴν περὶ τούτων ζήτησιν ἔλεγον εἰ βούλοιτο πορεύεσθαι εἰς Ἱεροσόλυμα κἀκεῖ κρίνεσθαι περὶ τούτων. 21 τοῦ δὲ Παύλου ἐπικαλεσαμένου τηρηθῆναι αὐτὸν εἰς τὴν τοῦ Σεβαστοῦ διάγνωσιν, ἐκέλευσα τηρεῖσθαι αὐτὸν ἕως οὗ ἀναπέμψω αὐτὸν πρὸς Καίσαρα. 22 Ἀγρίππας δὲ πρὸς τὸν Φῆστον, Ἐβουλόμην καὶ αὐτὸς τοῦ ἀνθρώπου ἀκοῦσαι. Αὔριον, φησίν, ἀκούσῃ αὐτοῦ.

23 Τῇ οὖν ἐπαύριον ἐλθόντος τοῦ Ἀγρίππα καὶ τῆς Βερνίκης μετὰ πολλῆς φαντασίας καὶ εἰσελθόντων εἰς τὸ ἀκροατήριον σύν τε χιλιάρχοις καὶ ἀνδράσιν τοῖς κατ' ἐξοχὴν τῆς πόλεως καὶ κελεύσαντος τοῦ Φήστου ἤχθη ὁ Παῦλος. 24 καί φησιν ὁ Φῆστος, Ἀγρίππα βασιλεῦ καὶ πάντες οἱ συμπαρόντες ἡμῖν ἄνδρες, θεωρεῖτε τοῦτον περὶ οὗ ἅπαν τὸ πλῆθος τῶν Ἰουδαίων ἐνέτυχόν μοι ἔν τε Ἱεροσολύμοις καὶ ἐνθάδε βοῶντες μὴ δεῖν αὐτὸν ζῆν μηκέτι. 25 ἐγὼ δὲ κατελαβόμην μηδὲν ἄξιον αὐτὸν θανάτου πεπραχέναι, αὐτοῦ δὲ τούτου ἐπικαλεσαμένου τὸν Σεβαστὸν ἔκρινα πέμπειν. 26 περὶ οὗ ἀσφαλές τι γράψαι τῷ κυρίῳ οὐκ ἔχω, διὸ προήγαγον αὐτὸν ἐφ' ὑμῶν καὶ μάλιστα ἐπὶ σοῦ, βασιλεῦ Ἀγρίππα, ὅπως τῆς ἀνακρίσεως γενομένης σχῶ τί γράψω· 27 ἄλογον γάρ μοι δοκεῖ πέμποντα δέσμιον μὴ καὶ τὰς κατ' αὐτοῦ αἰτίας σημᾶναι.

26 Ἀγρίππας δὲ πρὸς τὸν Παῦλον ἔφη, Ἐπιτρέπεταί σοι περὶ σεαυτοῦ λέγειν. τότε ὁ Παῦλος ἐκτείνας τὴν χεῖρα ἀπελογεῖτο, 2 Περὶ πάντων ὧν ἐγκαλοῦμαι ὑπὸ Ἰουδαίων, βασιλεῦ Ἀγρίππα, ἥγημαι ἐμαυτὸν μακάριον ἐπὶ σοῦ μέλλων σήμερον ἀπολογεῖσθαι 3 μάλιστα γνώστην ὄντα σε πάντων τῶν κατὰ Ἰουδαίους ἐθῶν τε καὶ ζητημάτων, διὸ δέομαι μακροθύμως ἀκοῦσαί μου. 4 Τὴν μὲν οὖν βίωσίν μου [τὴν] ἐκ νεότητος τὴν ἀπ' ἀρχῆς γενομένην ἐν τῷ ἔθνει μου ἔν τε Ἱεροσολύμοις ἴσασι πάντες [οἱ] Ἰουδαῖοι 5 προγινώσκοντές με ἄνωθεν,

be brought in. [18]When his accusers got up to speak, they did not charge him with any of the crimes I had expected. [19]Instead, they had some points of dispute with him about their own religion and about a dead man named Jesus who Paul claimed was alive. [20]I was at a loss how to investigate such matters; so I asked if he would be willing to go to Jerusalem and stand trial there on these charges. [21]When Paul made his appeal to be held over for the Emperor's decision, I ordered him held until I could send him to Caesar."

[22]Then Agrippa said to Festus, "I would like to hear this man myself."

He replied, "Tomorrow you will hear him."

Paul Before Agrippa

[23]The next day Agrippa and Bernice came with great pomp and entered the audience room with the high ranking officers and the leading men of the city. At the command of Festus, Paul was brought in. [24]Festus said: "King Agrippa, and all who are present with us, you see this man! The whole Jewish community has petitioned me about him in Jerusalem and here in Caesarea, shouting that he ought not to live any longer. [25]I found he had done nothing deserving of death, but because he made his appeal to the Emperor I decided to send him to Rome. [26]But I have nothing definite to write to His Majesty about him. Therefore I have brought him before all of you, and especially before you, King Agrippa, so that as a result of this investigation I may have something to write. [27]For I think it is unreasonable to send on a prisoner without specifying the charges against him."

26 Then Agrippa said to Paul, "You have permission to speak for yourself."

So Paul motioned with his hand and began his defense: [2]"King Agrippa, I consider myself fortunate to stand before you today as I make my defense against all the accusations of the Jews, [3]and especially so because you are well acquainted with all the Jewish customs and controversies. Therefore, I beg you to listen to me patiently.

[4]"The Jews all know the way I have lived ever since I was a child, from the beginning of my life in my own country, and also in Jerusalem. [5]They have known me

---

[t] Other ancient authorities read *with anything*
[u] Gk *on them*

[c]18 NRSV note t omits πονηρῶν

time, if they are willing to testify, that I have belonged to the strictest sect of our religion and lived as a Pharisee. 6And now I stand here on trial on account of my hope in the promise made by God to our ancestors, 7a promise that our twelve tribes hope to attain, as they earnestly worship day and night. It is for this hope, your Excellency,v that I am accused by Jews! 8Why is it thought incredible by any of you that God raises the dead?

9 "Indeed, I myself was convinced that I ought to do many things against the name of Jesus of Nazareth.w 10And that is what I did in Jerusalem; with authority received from the chief priests, I not only locked up many of the saints in prison, but I also cast my vote against them when they were being condemned to death. 11By punishing them often in all the synagogues I tried to force them to blaspheme; and since I was so furiously enraged at them, I pursued them even to foreign cities.

Paul Tells of His Conversion

12 "With this in mind, I was traveling to Damascus with the authority and commission of the chief priests, 13when at midday along the road, your Excellency,v I saw a light from heaven, brighter than the sun, shining around me and my companions. 14When we had all fallen to the ground, I heard a voice saying to me in the Hebrewy language, 'Saul, Saul, why are you persecuting me? It hurts you to kick against the goads.' 15I asked, 'Who are you, Lord?' The Lord answered, 'I am Jesus whom you are persecuting. 16But get up and stand on your feet; for I have appeared to you for this purpose, to appoint you to serve and testify to the things in which you have seen mez and to those in which I will appear to you. 17I will rescue you from your people and from the Gentiles—to whom I am sending you 18to open their eyes so that they may turn from darkness to light and from the power of Satan to God, so that they may receive forgiveness of sins and a place among those who are sanctified by faith in me.'

Paul Tells of His Preaching

19 "After that, King Agrippa, I was not disobedient to the heavenly vision, 20but declared first to those in Damascus, then in Jerusalem and throughout the countryside of Judea, and also to the Gentiles, that

ἐὰν θέλωσι μαρτυρεῖν, ὅτι κατὰ τὴν ἀκριβεστάτην αἵρεσιν τῆς ἡμετέρας θρησκείας ἔζησα Φαρισαῖος. 6 καὶ νῦν ἐπ' ἐλπίδι τῆς εἰς τοὺς πατέρας ἡμῶν ἐπαγγελίας γενομένης ὑπὸ τοῦ θεοῦ ἕστηκα κρινόμενος, 7 εἰς ἣν τὸ δωδεκάφυλον ἡμῶν ἐν ἐκτενείᾳ νύκτα καὶ ἡμέραν λατρεῦον ἐλπίζει καταντῆσαι, περὶ ἧς ἐλπίδος ἐγκαλοῦμαι ὑπὸ Ἰουδαίων, βασιλεῦ. 8 τί ἄπιστον κρίνεται παρ' ὑμῖν εἰ ὁ θεὸς νεκροὺς ἐγείρει; 9 ἐγὼ μὲν οὖν ἔδοξα ἐμαυτῷ πρὸς τὸ ὄνομα Ἰησοῦ τοῦ Ναζωραίου δεῖν πολλὰ ἐναντία πρᾶξαι, 10 ὃ καὶ ἐποίησα ἐν Ἱεροσολύμοις, καὶ πολλούς τε τῶν ἁγίων ἐγὼ ἐν φυλακαῖς κατέκλεισα τὴν παρὰ τῶν ἀρχιερέων ἐξουσίαν λαβὼν ἀναιρουμένων τε αὐτῶν κατήνεγκα ψῆφον. 11 καὶ κατὰ πάσας τὰς συναγωγὰς πολλάκις τιμωρῶν αὐτοὺς ἠνάγκαζον βλασφημεῖν περισσῶς τε ἐμμαινόμενος αὐτοῖς ἐδίωκον ἕως καὶ εἰς τὰς ἔξω πόλεις.

12 Ἐν οἷς πορευόμενος εἰς τὴν Δαμασκὸν μετ' ἐξουσίας καὶ ἐπιτροπῆς τῆς τῶν ἀρχιερέων 13 ἡμέρας μέσης κατὰ τὴν ὁδὸν εἶδον, βασιλεῦ, οὐρανόθεν ὑπὲρ τὴν λαμπρότητα τοῦ ἡλίου περιλάμψαν με φῶς καὶ τοὺς σὺν ἐμοὶ πορευομένους. 14 πάντων τε καταπεσόντων ἡμῶν εἰς τὴν γῆν ἤκουσα φωνὴν λέγουσαν πρός με τῇ Ἑβραΐδι διαλέκτῳ, Σαοὺλ Σαούλ, τί με διώκεις; σκληρόν σοι πρὸς κέντρα λακτίζειν. 15 ἐγὼ δὲ εἶπα, Τίς εἶ, κύριε; ὁ δὲ κύριος εἶπεν, Ἐγώ εἰμι Ἰησοῦς ὃν σὺ διώκεις. 16 ἀλλὰ ἀνάστηθι καὶ στῆθι ἐπὶ τοὺς πόδας σου· εἰς τοῦτο γὰρ ὤφθην σοι, προχειρίσασθαί σε ὑπηρέτην καὶ μάρτυρα ὧν τε εἶδές [με]a ὧν τε ὀφθήσομαί σοι, 17 ἐξαιρούμενός σε ἐκ τοῦ λαοῦ καὶ ἐκ τῶν ἐθνῶν εἰς οὓς ἐγὼ ἀποστέλλω σε 18 ἀνοῖξαι ὀφθαλμοὺς αὐτῶν, τοῦ ἐπιστρέψαι ἀπὸ σκότους εἰς φῶς καὶ τῆς ἐξουσίας τοῦ Σατανᾶ ἐπὶ τὸν θεόν, τοῦ λαβεῖν αὐτοὺς ἄφεσιν ἁμαρτιῶν καὶ κλῆρον ἐν τοῖς ἡγιασμένοις πίστει τῇ εἰς ἐμέ.

19 Ὅθεν, βασιλεῦ Ἀγρίππα, οὐκ ἐγενόμην ἀπειθὴς τῇ οὐρανίῳ ὀπτασίᾳ 20 ἀλλὰ τοῖς ἐν Δαμασκῷ πρῶτόν τε καὶ Ἱεροσολύμοις, πᾶσάν τε τὴν χώραν τῆς Ἰουδαίας καὶ τοῖς ἔθνεσιν ἀπήγγελ-

for a long time and can testify, if they are willing, that according to the strictest sect of our religion, I lived as a Pharisee. 6And now it is because of my hope in what God has promised our fathers that I am on trial today. 7This is the promise our twelve tribes are hoping to see fulfilled as they earnestly serve God day and night. O king, it is because of this hope that the Jews are accusing me. 8Why should any of you consider it incredible that God raises the dead?

9"I too was convinced that I ought to do all that was possible to oppose the name of Jesus of Nazareth. 10And that is just what I did in Jerusalem. On the authority of the chief priests I put many of the saints in prison, and when they were put to death, I cast my vote against them. 11Many a time I went from one synagogue to another to have them punished, and I tried to force them to blaspheme. In my obsession against them, I even went to foreign cities to persecute them.

12"On one of these journeys I was going to Damascus with the authority and commission of the chief priests. 13About noon, O king, as I was on the road, I saw a light from heaven, brighter than the sun, blazing around me and my companions. 14We all fell to the ground, and I heard a voice saying to me in Aramaic,a 'Saul, Saul, why do you persecute me? It is hard for you to kick against the goads.'

15"Then I asked, 'Who are you, Lord?'

" 'I am Jesus, whom you are persecuting,' the Lord replied. 16'Now get up and stand on your feet. I have appeared to you to appoint you as a servant and as a witness of what you have seen of me and what I will show you. 17I will rescue you from your own people and from the Gentiles. I am sending you to them 18to open their eyes and turn them from darkness to light, and from the power of Satan to God, so that they may receive forgiveness of sins and a place among those who are sanctified by faith in me.'

19"So then, King Agrippa, I was not disobedient to the vision from heaven. 20First to those in Damascus, then to those in Jerusalem and in all Judea, and to the Gentiles also, I preached that they should

---

v Gk *O king*   w Gk *the Nazorean*   y That is, *Aramaic*
z Other ancient authorities read *the things that you have seen*

a16 NRSV note z omits με

a14 Or *Hebrew*

they should repent and turn to God and do deeds consistent with repentance. 21For this reason the Jews seized me in the temple and tried to kill me. 22To this day I have had help from God, and so I stand here, testifying to both small and great, saying nothing but what the prophets and Moses said would take place: 23that the Messiah[a] must suffer, and that, by being the first to rise from the dead, he would proclaim light both to our people and to the Gentiles."

Paul Appeals to Agrippa to Believe

24 While he was making this defense, Festus exclaimed, "You are out of your mind, Paul! Too much learning is driving you insane!" 25But Paul said, "I am not out of my mind, most excellent Festus, but I am speaking the sober truth. 26Indeed the king knows about these things, and to him I speak freely; for I am certain that none of these things has escaped his notice, for this was not done in a corner. 27King Agrippa, do you believe the prophets? I know that you believe." 28Agrippa said to Paul, "Are you so quickly persuading me to become a Christian?"[b] 29Paul replied, "Whether quickly or not, I pray to God that not only you but also all who are listening to me today might become such as I am—except for these chains."

30 Then the king got up, and with him the governor and Bernice and those who had been seated with them; 31and as they were leaving, they said to one another, "This man is doing nothing to deserve death or imprisonment." 32Agrippa said to Festus, "This man could have been set free if he had not appealed to the emperor."

Paul Sails for Rome

27 When it was decided that we were to sail for Italy, they transferred Paul and some other prisoners to a centurion of the Augustan Cohort, named Julius. 2Embarking on a ship of Adramyttium that was about to set sail to the ports along the coast of Asia, we put to sea, accompanied by Aristarchus, a Macedonian from Thessalonica. 3The next day we put in at Sidon; and Julius treated Paul kindly, and allowed him to go to his friends to be cared for. 4Putting out to sea from there, we sailed

λον μετανοεῖν καὶ ἐπιστρέφειν ἐπὶ τὸν θεόν, ἄξια τῆς μετανοίας ἔργα πράσσοντας. 21 ἕνεκα τούτων με Ἰουδαῖοι συλλαβόμενοι [ὄντα] ἐν τῷ ἱερῷ ἐπειρῶντο διαχειρίσασθαι. 22 ἐπικουρίας οὖν τυχὼν τῆς ἀπὸ τοῦ θεοῦ ἄχρι τῆς ἡμέρας ταύτης ἕστηκα μαρτυρόμενος μικρῷ τε καὶ μεγάλῳ οὐδὲν ἐκτὸς λέγων ὧν τε οἱ προφῆται ἐλάλησαν μελλόντων γίνεσθαι καὶ Μωϋσῆς, 23 εἰ παθητὸς ὁ Χριστός, εἰ πρῶτος ἐξ ἀναστάσεως νεκρῶν φῶς μέλλει καταγγέλλειν τῷ τε λαῷ καὶ τοῖς ἔθνεσιν.

24 Ταῦτα δὲ αὐτοῦ ἀπολογουμένου ὁ Φῆστος μεγάλῃ τῇ φωνῇ φησιν, Μαίνῃ, Παῦλε· τὰ πολλά σε γράμματα εἰς μανίαν περιτρέπει. 25 ὁ δὲ Παῦλος, Οὐ μαίνομαι, φησίν, κράτιστε Φῆστε, ἀλλὰ ἀληθείας καὶ σωφροσύνης ῥήματα ἀποφθέγγομαι. 26 ἐπίσταται γὰρ περὶ τούτων ὁ βασιλεὺς πρὸς ὃν καὶ παρρησιαζόμενος λαλῶ, λανθάνειν γὰρ αὐτὸν [τι] τούτων οὐ πείθομαι οὐθέν· οὐ γάρ ἐστιν ἐν γωνίᾳ πεπραγμένον τοῦτο. 27 πιστεύεις, βασιλεῦ Ἀγρίππα, τοῖς προφήταις; οἶδα ὅτι πιστεύεις. 28 ὁ δὲ Ἀγρίππας πρὸς τὸν Παῦλον, Ἐν ὀλίγῳ με πείθεις Χριστιανὸν ποιῆσαι. 29 ὁ δὲ Παῦλος, Εὐξαίμην ἂν τῷ θεῷ καὶ ἐν ὀλίγῳ καὶ ἐν μεγάλῳ οὐ μόνον σὲ ἀλλὰ καὶ πάντας τοὺς ἀκούοντάς μου σήμερον γενέσθαι τοιούτους ὁποῖος καὶ ἐγώ εἰμι παρεκτὸς τῶν δεσμῶν τούτων.

30 Ἀνέστη τε ὁ βασιλεὺς καὶ ὁ ἡγεμὼν ἥ τε Βερνίκη καὶ οἱ συγκαθήμενοι αὐτοῖς, 31 καὶ ἀναχωρήσαντες ἐλάλουν πρὸς ἀλλήλους λέγοντες ὅτι Οὐδὲν θανάτου ἢ δεσμῶν ἄξιον [τι] πράσσει ὁ ἄνθρωπος οὗτος. 32 Ἀγρίππας δὲ τῷ Φήστῳ ἔφη, Ἀπολελύσθαι ἐδύνατο ὁ ἄνθρωπος οὗτος εἰ μὴ ἐπεκέκλητο Καίσαρα.

27 Ὡς δὲ ἐκρίθη τοῦ ἀποπλεῖν ἡμᾶς εἰς τὴν Ἰταλίαν, παρεδίδουν τόν τε Παῦλον καί τινας ἑτέρους δεσμώτας ἑκατοντάρχῃ ὀνόματι Ἰουλίῳ σπείρης Σεβαστῆς. 2 ἐπιβάντες δὲ πλοίῳ Ἀδραμυττηνῷ μέλλοντι πλεῖν εἰς τοὺς κατὰ τὴν Ἀσίαν τόπους ἀνήχθημεν ὄντος σὺν ἡμῖν Ἀριστάρχου Μακεδόνος Θεσσαλονικέως. 3 τῇ τε ἑτέρᾳ κατήχθημεν εἰς Σιδῶνα, φιλανθρώπως τε ὁ Ἰούλιος τῷ Παύλῳ χρησάμενος ἐπέτρεψεν πρὸς τοὺς φίλους πορευθέντι ἐπιμελείας τυχεῖν. 4 κἀκεῖθεν ἀναχθέντες ὑπεπλεύσαμεν

repent and turn to God and prove their repentance by their deeds. 21That is why the Jews seized me in the temple courts and tried to kill me. 22But I have had God's help to this very day, and so I stand here and testify to small and great alike. I am saying nothing beyond what the prophets and Moses said would happen— 23that the Christ[b] would suffer and, as the first to rise from the dead, would proclaim light to his own people and to the Gentiles."

24At this point Festus interrupted Paul's defense. "You are out of your mind, Paul!" he shouted. "Your great learning is driving you insane."

25"I am not insane, most excellent Festus," Paul replied. "What I am saying is true and reasonable. 26The king is familiar with these things, and I can speak freely to him. I am convinced that none of this has escaped his notice, because it was not done in a corner. 27King Agrippa, do you believe the prophets? I know you do."

28Then Agrippa said to Paul, "Do you think that in such a short time you can persuade me to be a Christian?"

29Paul replied, "Short time or long—I pray God that not only you but all who are listening to me today may become what I am, except for these chains."

30The king rose, and with him the governor and Bernice and those sitting with them. 31They left the room, and while talking with one another, they said, "This man is not doing anything that deserves death or imprisonment."

32Agrippa said to Festus, "This man could have been set free if he had not appealed to Caesar."

Paul Sails for Rome

27 When it was decided that we would sail for Italy, Paul and some other prisoners were handed over to a centurion named Julius, who belonged to the Imperial Regiment. 2We boarded a ship from Adramyttium about to sail for ports along the coast of the province of Asia, and we put out to sea. Aristarchus, a Macedonian from Thessalonica, was with us.

3The next day we landed at Sidon; and Julius, in kindness to Paul, allowed him to go to his friends so they might provide for his needs. 4From there we put out to sea

---

[a] Or the Christ   [b] Or Quickly you will persuade me to play the Christian

[b]23 Or Messiah

under the lee of Cyprus, because the winds were against us. 5After we had sailed across the sea that is off Cilicia and Pamphylia, we came to Myra in Lycia. 6There the centurion found an Alexandrian ship bound for Italy and put us on board. 7We sailed slowly for a number of days and arrived with difficulty off Cnidus, and as the wind was against us, we sailed under the lee of Crete off Salmone. 8Sailing past it with difficulty, we came to a place called Fair Havens, near the city of Lasea.

9 Since much time had been lost and sailing was now dangerous, because even the Fast had already gone by, Paul advised them, 10saying, "Sirs, I can see that the voyage will be with danger and much heavy loss, not only of the cargo and the ship, but also of our lives." 11But the centurion paid more attention to the pilot and to the owner of the ship than to what Paul said. 12Since the harbor was not suitable for spending the winter, the majority was in favor of putting to sea from there, on the chance that somehow they could reach Phoenix, where they could spend the winter. It was a harbor of Crete, facing southwest and northwest.

The Storm at Sea

13 When a moderate south wind began to blow, they thought they could achieve their purpose; so they weighed anchor and began to sail past Crete, close to the shore. 14But soon a violent wind, called the northeaster, rushed down from Crete.c 15Since the ship was caught and could not be turned head-on into the wind, we gave way to it and were driven. 16By running under the lee of a small island called Caudad we were scarcely able to get the ship's boat under control. 17After hoisting it up they took measurese to undergird the ship; then, fearing that they would run on the Syrtis, they lowered the sea anchor and so were driven. 18We were being pounded by the storm so violently that on the next day they began to throw the cargo overboard, 19and on the third day with their own hands they threw the ship's tackle overboard. 20When neither sun nor stars appeared for many days, and no small tempest raged, all hope of our being saved was at last abandoned.

21 Since they had been without food for a long time, Paul then stood up among

τὴν Κύπρον διὰ τὸ τοὺς ἀνέμους εἶναι ἐναντίους, 5 τό τε πέλαγος τὸ κατὰ τὴν Κιλικίαν καὶ Παμφυλίαν διαπλεύσαντες κατήλθομεν εἰς Μύρα τῆς Λυκίας. 6 κἀκεῖ εὑρὼν ὁ ἑκατοντάρχης πλοῖον Ἀλεξανδρῖνον πλέον εἰς τὴν Ἰταλίαν ἐνεβίβασεν ἡμᾶς εἰς αὐτό. 7 ἐν ἱκαναῖς δὲ ἡμέραις βραδυπλοοῦντες καὶ μόλις γενόμενοι κατὰ τὴν Κνίδον, μὴ προσεῶντος ἡμᾶς τοῦ ἀνέμου ὑπεπλεύσαμεν τὴν Κρήτην κατὰ Σαλμώνην, 8 μόλις τε παραλεγόμενοι αὐτὴν ἤλθομεν εἰς τόπον τινὰ καλούμενον Καλοὺς Λιμένας ᾧ ἐγγὺς πόλις ἦν Λασαία.

9 Ἱκανοῦ δὲ χρόνου διαγενομένου καὶ ὄντος ἤδη ἐπισφαλοῦς τοῦ πλοὸς διὰ τὸ καὶ τὴν νηστείαν ἤδη παρεληλυθέναι παρῄνει ὁ Παῦλος 10 λέγων αὐτοῖς, Ἄνδρες, θεωρῶ ὅτι μετὰ ὕβρεως καὶ πολλῆς ζημίας οὐ μόνον τοῦ φορτίου καὶ τοῦ πλοίου ἀλλὰ καὶ τῶν ψυχῶν ἡμῶν μέλλειν ἔσεσθαι τὸν πλοῦν. 11 ὁ δὲ ἑκατοντάρχης τῷ κυβερνήτῃ καὶ τῷ ναυκλήρῳ μᾶλλον ἐπείθετο ἢ τοῖς ὑπὸ Παύλου λεγομένοις. 12 ἀνευθέτου δὲ τοῦ λιμένος ὑπάρχοντος πρὸς παραχειμασίαν οἱ πλείονες ἔθεντο βουλὴν ἀναχθῆναι ἐκεῖθεν, εἴ πως δύναιντο καταντήσαντες εἰς Φοίνικα παραχειμάσαι λιμένα τῆς Κρήτης βλέποντα κατὰ λίβα καὶ κατὰ χῶρον.

13 Ὑπονεύσαντος δὲ νότου δόξαντες τῆς προθέσεως κεκρατηκέναι, ἄραντες ἆσσον παρελέγοντο τὴν Κρήτην. 14 μετ' οὐ πολὺ δὲ ἔβαλεν κατ' αὐτῆς ἄνεμος τυφωνικὸς ὁ καλούμενος Εὐρακύλων· 15 συναρπασθέντος δὲ τοῦ πλοίου καὶ μὴ δυναμένου ἀντοφθαλμεῖν τῷ ἀνέμῳ ἐπιδόντες ἐφερόμεθα. 16 νησίον δέ τι ὑποδραμόντες καλούμενον Καῦδαa ἰσχύσαμεν μόλις περικρατεῖς γενέσθαι τῆς σκάφης, 17 ἣν ἄραντες βοηθείαις ἐχρῶντο ὑποζωννύντες τὸ πλοῖον, φοβούμενοί τε μὴ εἰς τὴν Σύρτιν ἐκπέσωσιν, χαλάσαντες τὸ σκεῦος, οὕτως ἐφέροντο. 18 σφοδρῶς δὲ χειμαζομένων ἡμῶν τῇ ἑξῆς ἐκβολὴν ἐποιοῦντο 19 καὶ τῇ τρίτῃ αὐτόχειρες τὴν σκευὴν τοῦ πλοίου ἔρριψαν. 20 μήτε δὲ ἡλίου μήτε ἄστρων ἐπιφαινόντων ἐπὶ πλείονας ἡμέρας, χειμῶνός τε οὐκ ὀλίγου ἐπικειμένου, λοιπὸν περιῃρεῖτο ἐλπὶς πᾶσα τοῦ σῴζεσθαι ἡμᾶς.

21 Πολλῆς τε ἀσιτίας ὑπαρχούσης τότε σταθεὶς ὁ Παῦλος ἐν μέσῳ αὐτῶν

again and passed to the lee of Cyprus because the winds were against us. 5When we had sailed across the open sea off the coast of Cilicia and Pamphylia, we landed at Myra in Lycia. 6There the centurion found an Alexandrian ship sailing for Italy and put us on board. 7We made slow headway for many days and had difficulty arriving off Cnidus. When the wind did not allow us to hold our course, we sailed to the lee of Crete, opposite Salmone. 8We moved along the coast with difficulty and came to a place called Fair Havens, near the town of Lasea.

9Much time had been lost, and sailing had already become dangerous because by now it was after the Fast.a So Paul warned them, 10"Men, I can see that our voyage is going to be disastrous and bring great loss to ship and cargo, and to our own lives also." 11But the centurion, instead of listening to what Paul said, followed the advice of the pilot and of the owner of the ship. 12Since the harbor was unsuitable to winter in, the majority decided that we should sail on, hoping to reach Phoenix and winter there. This was a harbor in Crete, facing both southwest and northwest.

The Storm

13When a gentle south wind began to blow, they thought they had obtained what they wanted; so they weighed anchor and sailed along the shore of Crete. 14Before very long, a wind of hurricane force, called the "northeaster," swept down from the island. 15The ship was caught by the storm and could not head into the wind; so we gave way to it and were driven along. 16As we passed to the lee of a small island called Cauda, we were hardly able to make the lifeboat secure. 17When the men had hoisted it aboard, they passed ropes under the ship itself to hold it together. Fearing that they would run aground on the sandbars of Syrtis, they lowered the sea anchor and let the ship be driven along. 18We took such a violent battering from the storm that the next day they began to throw the cargo overboard. 19On the third day, they threw the ship's tackle overboard with their own hands. 20When neither sun nor stars appeared for many days and the storm continued raging, we finally gave up all hope of being saved.

21After the men had gone a long time without food, Paul stood up before them

---

c Gk it   d Other ancient authorities read *Clauda*
e Gk *helps*

a16 NRSV note d Καῦδα

a9 That is, the Day of Atonement (Yom Kippur)

them and said, "Men, you should have listened to me and not have set sail from Crete and thereby avoided this damage and loss. 22I urge you now to keep up your courage, for there will be no loss of life among you, but only of the ship. 23For last night there stood by me an angel of the God to whom I belong and whom I worship, 24and he said, 'Do not be afraid, Paul; you must stand before the emperor; and indeed, God has granted safety to all those who are sailing with you.' 25So keep up your courage, men, for I have faith in God that it will be exactly as I have been told. 26But we will have to run aground on some island."

27 When the fourteenth night had come, as we were drifting across the sea of Adria, about midnight the sailors suspected that they were nearing land. 28So they took soundings and found twenty fathoms; a little farther on they took soundings again and found fifteen fathoms. 29Fearing that we might run on the rocks, they let down four anchors from the stern and prayed for day to come. 30But when the sailors tried to escape from the ship and had lowered the boat into the sea, on the pretext of putting out anchors from the bow, 31Paul said to the centurion and the soldiers, "Unless these men stay in the ship, you cannot be saved." 32Then the soldiers cut away the ropes of the boat and set it adrift.

33 Just before daybreak, Paul urged all of them to take some food, saying, "Today is the fourteenth day that you have been in suspense and remaining without food, having eaten nothing. 34Therefore I urge you to take some food, for it will help you survive; for none of you will lose a hair from your heads." 35After he had said this, he took bread; and giving thanks to God in the presence of all, he broke it and began to eat. 36Then all of them were encouraged and took food for themselves. 37(We were in all two hundred seventy-six[f] persons in the ship.) 38After they had satisfied their hunger, they lightened the ship by throwing the wheat into the sea.

The Shipwreck

39 In the morning they did not recognize the land, but they noticed a bay with a beach, on which they planned to run the

εἶπεν, Ἔδει μέν, ὦ ἄνδρες, πειθαρχή- σαντάς μοι μὴ ἀνάγεσθαι ἀπὸ τῆς Κρήτης κερδῆσαί τε τὴν ὕβριν ταύτην καὶ τὴν ζημίαν. 22 καὶ τὰ νῦν παραινῶ ὑμᾶς εὐθυμεῖν· ἀποβολὴ γὰρ ψυχῆς οὐδεμία ἔσται ἐξ ὑμῶν πλὴν τοῦ πλοίου. 23 παρέστη γάρ μοι ταύτῃ τῇ νυκτὶ τοῦ θεοῦ, οὗ εἰμι [ἐγώ] ᾧ καὶ λατρεύω, ἄγγελος 24 λέγων, Μὴ φοβοῦ, Παῦλε, Καίσαρί σε δεῖ παραστῆναι, καὶ ἰδοὺ κεχάρισταί σοι ὁ θεὸς πάντας τοὺς πλέοντας μετὰ σοῦ. 25 διὸ εὐθυμεῖτε, ἄνδρες· πιστεύω γὰρ τῷ θεῷ ὅτι οὕτως ἔσται καθ' ὃν τρόπον λελάληταί μοι. 26 εἰς νῆσον δέ τινα δεῖ ἡμᾶς ἐκπεσεῖν.

27 Ὡς δὲ τεσσαρεσκαιδεκάτη νὺξ ἐγένετο διαφερομένων ἡμῶν ἐν τῷ Ἀδρίᾳ, κατὰ μέσον τῆς νυκτὸς ὑπενόουν οἱ ναῦται προσάγειν τινὰ αὐτοῖς χώραν. 28 καὶ βολίσαντες εὗρον ὀργυιὰς εἴκοσι, βραχὺ δὲ διαστήσαντες καὶ πάλιν βολίσαντες εὗρον ὀργυιὰς δεκαπέντε· 29 φοβούμενοί τε μή που κατὰ τραχεῖς τόπους ἐκπέσωμεν, ἐκ πρύμνης ῥίψαντες ἀγκύρας τέσσαρας ηὔχοντο ἡμέραν γενέσθαι. 30 τῶν δὲ ναυτῶν ζητούντων φυγεῖν ἐκ τοῦ πλοίου καὶ χαλασάντων τὴν σκάφην εἰς τὴν θάλασσαν προφάσει ὡς ἐκ πρῴρης ἀγκύρας μελλόντων ἐκτείνειν, 31 εἶπεν ὁ Παῦλος τῷ ἑκατοντάρχῃ καὶ τοῖς στρατιώταις, Ἐὰν μὴ οὗτοι μείνωσιν ἐν τῷ πλοίῳ, ὑμεῖς σωθῆναι οὐ δύνασθε. 32 τότε ἀπέκοψαν οἱ στρατιῶται τὰ σχοινία τῆς σκάφης καὶ εἴασαν αὐτὴν ἐκπεσεῖν.

33 Ἄχρι δὲ οὗ ἡμέρα ἤμελλεν γίνεσθαι, παρεκάλει ὁ Παῦλος ἅπαντας μεταλαβεῖν τροφῆς λέγων, Τεσσαρεσ- καιδεκάτην σήμερον ἡμέραν προσ- δοκῶντες ἄσιτοι διατελεῖτε μηθὲν προσλαβόμενοι. 34 διὸ παρακαλῶ ὑμᾶς μεταλαβεῖν τροφῆς· τοῦτο γὰρ πρὸς τῆς ὑμετέρας σωτηρίας ὑπάρχει, οὐδενὸς γὰρ ὑμῶν θρὶξ ἀπὸ τῆς κεφαλῆς ἀπολεῖται. 35 εἴπας δὲ ταῦτα καὶ λαβὼν ἄρτον εὐχαρίστησεν τῷ θεῷ ἐνώπιον πάντων καὶ κλάσας ἤρξατο ἐσθίειν. 36 εὔθυμοι δὲ γενόμενοι πάντες καὶ αὐτοὶ προσελάβοντο τροφῆς. 37 ἤμεθα δὲ αἱ πᾶσαι ψυχαὶ ἐν τῷ πλοίῳ διακόσιαι[b] ἑβδομήκοντα ἕξ. 38 κορεσ- θέντες δὲ τροφῆς ἐκούφιζον τὸ πλοῖον ἐκβαλλόμενοι τὸν σῖτον εἰς τὴν θάλασσαν.

39 Ὅτε δὲ ἡμέρα ἐγένετο, τὴν γῆν οὐκ ἐπεγίνωσκον, κόλπον δέ τινα κατενόουν ἔχοντα αἰγιαλὸν εἰς ὃν

and said: "Men, you should have taken my advice not to sail from Crete; then you would have spared yourselves this damage and loss. 22But now I urge you to keep up your courage, because not one of you will be lost; only the ship will be destroyed. 23Last night an angel of the God whose I am and whom I serve stood beside me 24and said, 'Do not be afraid, Paul. You must stand trial before Caesar; and God has graciously given you the lives of all who sail with you.' 25So keep up your courage, men, for I have faith in God that it will happen just as he told me. 26Nevertheless, we must run aground on some island."

The Shipwreck

27On the fourteenth night we were still being driven across the Adriatic[b] Sea, when about midnight the sailors sensed they were approaching land. 28They took soundings and found that the water was a hundred and twenty feet[c] deep. A short time later they took soundings again and found it was ninety feet[d] deep. 29Fearing that we would be dashed against the rocks, they dropped four anchors from the stern and prayed for daylight. 30In an attempt to escape from the ship, the sailors let the lifeboat down into the sea, pretending they were going to lower some anchors from the bow. 31Then Paul said to the centurion and the soldiers, "Unless these men stay with the ship, you cannot be saved." 32So the soldiers cut the ropes that held the lifeboat and let it fall away.

33Just before dawn Paul urged them all to eat. "For the last fourteen days," he said, "you have been in constant suspense and have gone without food—you haven't eaten anything. 34Now I urge you to take some food. You need it to survive. Not one of you will lose a single hair from his head." 35After he said this, he took some bread and gave thanks to God in front of them all. Then he broke it and began to eat. 36They were all encouraged and ate some food themselves. 37Altogether there were 276 of us on board. 38When they had eaten as much as they wanted, they lightened the ship by throwing the grain into the sea.

39When daylight came, they did not recognize the land, but they saw a bay with a sandy beach, where they decided to run

[f] Other ancient authorities read seventy-six; others, about seventy-six

[b]37 NRSV note f omits διακόσιαι or reads ὡς in its place

[b]27 In ancient times the name referred to an area extending well south of Italy.   [c]28 Greek twenty orguias (about 37 meters)   [d]28 Greek fifteen orguias (about 27 meters)

ship ashore, if they could. ⁴⁰So they cast off the anchors and left them in the sea. At the same time they loosened the ropes that tied the steering-oars; then hoisting the foresail to the wind, they made for the beach. ⁴¹But striking a reef,ᵍ they ran the ship aground; the bow stuck and remained immovable, but the stern was being broken up by the force of the waves. ⁴²The soldiers' plan was to kill the prisoners, so that none might swim away and escape; ⁴³but the centurion, wishing to save Paul, kept them from carrying out their plan. He ordered those who could swim to jump overboard first and make for the land, ⁴⁴and the rest to follow, some on planks and others on pieces of the ship. And so it was that all were brought safely to land.

Paul on the Island of Malta

28 After we had reached safety, we then learned that the island was called Malta. ²The natives showed us unusual kindness. Since it had begun to rain and was cold, they kindled a fire and welcomed all of us around it. ³Paul had gathered a bundle of brushwood and was putting it on the fire, when a viper, driven out by the heat, fastened itself on his hand. ⁴When the natives saw the creature hanging from his hand, they said to one another, "This man must be a murderer; though he has escaped from the sea, justice has not allowed him to live." ⁵He, however, shook off the creature into the fire and suffered no harm. ⁶They were expecting him to swell up or drop dead, but after they had waited a long time and saw that nothing unusual had happened to him, they changed their minds and began to say that he was a god.

7 Now in the neighborhood of that place were lands belonging to the leading man of the island, named Publius, who received us and entertained us hospitably for three days. ⁸It so happened that the father of Publius lay sick in bed with fever and dysentery. Paul visited him and cured him by praying and putting his hands on him. ⁹After this happened, the rest of the people on the island who had diseases also came and were cured. ¹⁰They bestowed many honors on us, and when we were about to

ἐβουλεύοντο εἰ δύναιντο ἐξῶσαι τὸ πλοῖον. **40** καὶ τὰς ἀγκύρας περιελόντες εἴων εἰς τὴν θάλασσαν, ἅμα ἀνέντες τὰς ζευκτηρίας τῶν πηδαλίων καὶ ἐπάραντες τὸν ἀρτέμωνα τῇ πνεούσῃ κατεῖχον εἰς τὸν αἰγιαλόν. **41** περιπεσόντες δὲ εἰς τόπον διθάλασσον ἐπέκειλαν τὴν ναῦν καὶ ἡ μὲν πρῷρα ἐρείσασα ἔμεινεν ἀσάλευτος, ἡ δὲ πρύμνα ἐλύετο ὑπὸ τῆς βίας [τῶν κυμάτων]. **42** τῶν δὲ στρατιωτῶν βουλὴ ἐγένετο ἵνα τοὺς δεσμώτας ἀποκτείνωσιν, μή τις ἐκκολυμβήσας διαφύγῃ. **43** ὁ δὲ ἑκατοντάρχης βουλόμενος διασῶσαι τὸν Παῦλον ἐκώλυσεν αὐτοὺς τοῦ βουλήματος, ἐκέλευσέν τε τοὺς δυναμένους κολυμβᾶν ἀπορίψαντας πρώτους ἐπὶ τὴν γῆν ἐξιέναι **44** καὶ τοὺς λοιποὺς οὓς μὲν ἐπὶ σανίσιν, οὓς δὲ ἐπί τινων τῶν ἀπὸ τοῦ πλοίου. καὶ οὕτως ἐγένετο πάντας διασωθῆναι ἐπὶ τὴν γῆν.

28 Καὶ διασωθέντες τότε ἐπέγνωμεν ὅτι Μελίτη ἡ νῆσος καλεῖται. **2** οἵ τε βάρβαροι παρεῖχον οὐ τὴν τυχοῦσαν φιλανθρωπίαν ἡμῖν, ἅψαντες γὰρ πυρὰν προσελάβοντο πάντας ἡμᾶς διὰ τὸν ὑετὸν τὸν ἐφεστῶτα καὶ διὰ τὸ ψῦχος. **3** συστρέψαντος δὲ τοῦ Παύλου φρυγάνων τι πλῆθος καὶ ἐπιθέντος ἐπὶ τὴν πυράν, ἔχιδνα ἀπὸ τῆς θέρμης ἐξελθοῦσα καθῆψεν τῆς χειρὸς αὐτοῦ. **4** ὡς δὲ εἶδον οἱ βάρβαροι κρεμάμενον τὸ θηρίον ἐκ τῆς χειρὸς αὐτοῦ, πρὸς ἀλλήλους ἔλεγον, Πάντως φονεύς ἐστιν ὁ ἄνθρωπος οὗτος ὃν διασωθέντα ἐκ τῆς θαλάσσης ἡ δίκη ζῆν οὐκ εἴασεν. **5** ὁ μὲν οὖν ἀποτινάξας τὸ θηρίον εἰς τὸ πῦρ ἔπαθεν οὐδὲν κακόν, **6** οἱ δὲ προσεδόκων αὐτὸν μέλλειν πίμπρασθαι ἢ καταπίπτειν ἄφνω νεκρόν. ἐπὶ πολὺ δὲ αὐτῶν προσδοκώντων καὶ θεωρούντων μηδὲν ἄτοπον εἰς αὐτὸν γινόμενον μεταβαλόμενοι ἔλεγον αὐτὸν εἶναι θεόν. **7** Ἐν δὲ τοῖς περὶ τὸν τόπον ἐκεῖνον ὑπῆρχεν χωρία τῷ πρώτῳ τῆς νήσου ὀνόματι Ποπλίῳ, ὃς ἀναδεξάμενος ἡμᾶς τρεῖς ἡμέρας φιλοφρόνως ἐξένισεν. **8** ἐγένετο δὲ τὸν πατέρα τοῦ Ποπλίου πυρετοῖς καὶ δυσεντερίῳ συνεχόμενον κατακεῖσθαι, πρὸς ὃν ὁ Παῦλος εἰσελθὼν καὶ προσευξάμενος ἐπιθεὶς τὰς χεῖρας αὐτῷ ἰάσατο αὐτόν. **9** τούτου δὲ γενομένου καὶ οἱ λοιποὶ οἱ ἐν τῇ νήσῳ ἔχοντες ἀσθενείας προσήρχοντο καὶ ἐθεραπεύοντο, **10** οἳ καὶ πολλαῖς τιμαῖς ἐτίμησαν ἡμᾶς καὶ ἀναγομένοις

the ship aground if they could. ⁴⁰Cutting loose the anchors, they left them in the sea and at the same time untied the ropes that held the rudders. Then they hoisted the foresail to the wind and made for the beach. ⁴¹But the ship struck a sandbar and ran aground. The bow stuck fast and would not move, and the stern was broken to pieces by the pounding of the surf. ⁴²The soldiers planned to kill the prisoners to prevent any of them from swimming away and escaping. ⁴³But the centurion wanted to spare Paul's life and kept them from carrying out their plan. He ordered those who could swim to jump overboard first and get to land. ⁴⁴The rest were to get there on planks or on pieces of the ship. In this way everyone reached land in safety.

Ashore on Malta

28 Once safely on shore, we found out that the island was called Malta. ²The islanders showed us unusual kindness. They built a fire and welcomed us all because it was raining and cold. ³Paul gathered a pile of brushwood and, as he put it on the fire, a viper, driven out by the heat, fastened itself on his hand. ⁴When the islanders saw the snake hanging from his hand, they said to each other, "This man must be a murderer; for though he escaped from the sea, Justice has not allowed him to live." ⁵But Paul shook the snake off into the fire and suffered no ill effects. ⁶The people expected him to swell up or suddenly fall dead, but after waiting a long time and seeing nothing unusual happen to him, they changed their minds and said he was a god.

⁷There was an estate nearby that belonged to Publius, the chief official of the island. He welcomed us to his home and for three days entertained us hospitably. ⁸His father was sick in bed, suffering from fever and dysentery. Paul went in to see him and, after prayer, placed his hands on him and healed him. ⁹When this had happened, the rest of the sick on the island came and were cured. ¹⁰They honored us in many ways and when we were ready to

---

ᵍ Gk *place of two seas*

sail, they put on board all the provisions we needed.

Paul Arrives at Rome

11 Three months later we set sail on a ship that had wintered at the island, an Alexandrian ship with the Twin Brothers as its figurehead. 12We put in at Syracuse and stayed there for three days; 13then we weighed anchor and came to Rhegium. After one day there a south wind sprang up, and on the second day we came to Puteoli. 14There we found believers[h] and were invited to stay with them for seven days. And so we came to Rome. 15The believers[h] from there, when they heard of us, came as far as the Forum of Appius and Three Taverns to meet us. On seeing them, Paul thanked God and took courage.

16 When we came into Rome, Paul was allowed to live by himself, with the soldier who was guarding him.

Paul and Jewish Leaders in Rome

17 Three days later he called together the local leaders of the Jews. When they had assembled, he said to them, "Brothers, though I had done nothing against our people or the customs of our ancestors, yet I was arrested in Jerusalem and handed over to the Romans. 18When they had examined me, the Romans[i] wanted to release me, because there was no reason for the death penalty in my case. 19But when the Jews objected, I was compelled to appeal to the emperor—even though I had no charge to bring against my nation. 20For this reason therefore I have asked to see you and speak with you,[j] since it is for the sake of the hope of Israel that I am bound with this chain." 21They replied, "We have received no letters from Judea about you, and none of the brothers coming here has reported or spoken anything evil about you. 22But we would like to hear from you what you think, for with regard to this sect we know that everywhere it is spoken against."

Paul Preaches in Rome

23 After they had set a day to meet with him, they came to him at his lodgings in great numbers. From morning until evening he explained the matter to them, testifying to the kingdom of God and trying to convince them about Jesus both from

---

ἐπέθεντο τὰ πρὸς τὰς χρείας.

11 Μετὰ δὲ τρεῖς μῆνας ἀνήχθημεν ἐν πλοίῳ παρακεχειμακότι ἐν τῇ νήσῳ, Ἀλεξανδρίνῳ, παρασήμῳ Διοσκούροις. **12** καὶ καταχθέντες εἰς Συρακούσας ἐπεμείναμεν ἡμέρας τρεῖς, **13** ὅθεν περιελόντες κατηντήσαμεν εἰς Ῥήγιον. καὶ μετὰ μίαν ἡμέραν ἐπιγενομένου νότου δευτεραῖοι ἤλθομεν εἰς Ποτιόλους, **14** οὗ εὑρόντες ἀδελφοὺς παρεκλήθημεν παρ' αὐτοῖς ἐπιμεῖναι ἡμέρας ἑπτά· καὶ οὕτως εἰς τὴν Ῥώμην ἤλθαμεν. **15** κἀκεῖθεν οἱ ἀδελφοὶ ἀκούσαντες τὰ περὶ ἡμῶν ἦλθαν εἰς ἀπάντησιν ἡμῖν ἄχρι Ἀππίου Φόρου καὶ Τριῶν Ταβερνῶν, οὓς ἰδὼν ὁ Παῦλος εὐχαριστήσας τῷ θεῷ ἔλαβε θάρσος.

16 Ὅτε δὲ εἰσήλθομεν εἰς Ῥώμην, ἐπετράπη τῷ Παύλῳ μένειν καθ' ἑαυτὸν σὺν τῷ φυλάσσοντι αὐτὸν στρατιώτῃ.

17 Ἐγένετο δὲ μετὰ ἡμέρας τρεῖς συγκαλέσασθαι αὐτὸν τοὺς ὄντας τῶν Ἰουδαίων πρώτους· συνελθόντων δὲ αὐτῶν ἔλεγεν πρὸς αὐτούς, Ἐγώ, ἄνδρες ἀδελφοί, οὐδὲν ἐναντίον ποιήσας τῷ λαῷ ἢ τοῖς ἔθεσι τοῖς πατρῴοις δέσμιος ἐξ Ἱεροσολύμων παρεδόθην εἰς τὰς χεῖρας τῶν Ῥωμαίων, **18** οἵτινες ἀνακρίναντές με ἐβούλοντο ἀπολῦσαι διὰ τὸ μηδεμίαν αἰτίαν θανάτου ὑπάρχειν ἐν ἐμοί. **19** ἀντιλεγόντων δὲ τῶν Ἰουδαίων ἠναγκάσθην ἐπικαλέσασθαι Καίσαρα οὐχ ὡς τοῦ ἔθνους μου ἔχων τι κατηγορεῖν. **20** διὰ ταύτην οὖν τὴν αἰτίαν παρεκάλεσα ὑμᾶς ἰδεῖν καὶ προσλαλῆσαι, ἕνεκεν γὰρ τῆς ἐλπίδος τοῦ Ἰσραὴλ τὴν ἅλυσιν ταύτην περίκειμαι. **21** οἱ δὲ πρὸς αὐτὸν εἶπαν, Ἡμεῖς οὔτε γράμματα περὶ σοῦ ἐδεξάμεθα ἀπὸ τῆς Ἰουδαίας οὔτε παραγενόμενός τις τῶν ἀδελφῶν ἀπήγγειλεν ἢ ἐλάλησέν τι περὶ σοῦ πονηρόν. **22** ἀξιοῦμεν δὲ παρὰ σοῦ ἀκοῦσαι ἃ φρονεῖς, περὶ μὲν γὰρ τῆς αἱρέσεως ταύτης γνωστὸν ἡμῖν ἐστιν ὅτι πανταχοῦ ἀντιλέγεται.

23 Ταξάμενοι δὲ αὐτῷ ἡμέραν ἦλθον πρὸς αὐτὸν εἰς τὴν ξενίαν πλείονες οἷς ἐξετίθετο διαμαρτυρόμενος τὴν βασιλείαν τοῦ θεοῦ, πείθων τε αὐτοὺς περὶ τοῦ Ἰησοῦ ἀπό τε τοῦ νόμου

---

sail, they furnished us with the supplies we needed.

Arrival at Rome

11After three months we put out to sea in a ship that had wintered in the island. It was an Alexandrian ship with the figurehead of the twin gods Castor and Pollux. 12We put in at Syracuse and stayed there three days. 13From there we set sail and arrived at Rhegium. The next day the south wind came up, and on the following day we reached Puteoli. 14There we found some brothers who invited us to spend a week with them. And so we came to Rome. 15The brothers there had heard that we were coming, and they traveled as far as the Forum of Appius and the Three Taverns to meet us. At the sight of these men Paul thanked God and was encouraged. 16When we got to Rome, Paul was allowed to live by himself, with a soldier to guard him.

Paul Preaches at Rome Under Guard

17Three days later he called together the leaders of the Jews. When they had assembled, Paul said to them: "My brothers, although I have done nothing against our people or against the customs of our ancestors, I was arrested in Jerusalem and handed over to the Romans. 18They examined me and wanted to release me, because I was not guilty of any crime deserving death. 19But when the Jews objected, I was compelled to appeal to Caesar—not that I had any charge to bring against my own people. 20For this reason I have asked to see you and talk with you. It is because of the hope of Israel that I am bound with this chain."

21They replied, "We have not received any letters from Judea concerning you, and none of the brothers who have come from there has reported or said anything bad about you. 22But we want to hear what your views are, for we know that people everywhere are talking against this sect."

23They arranged to meet Paul on a certain day, and came in even larger numbers to the place where he was staying. From morning till evening he explained and declared to them the kingdom of God and tried to convince them about Jesus from

---

[h] Gk brothers   [i] Gk they   [j] Or I have asked you to see me and speak with me

the law of Moses and from the prophets. ²⁴Some were convinced by what he had said, while others refused to believe. ²⁵So they disagreed with each other; and as they were leaving, Paul made one further statement: "The Holy Spirit was right in saying to your ancestors through the prophet Isaiah,

²⁶ 'Go to this people and say,
      You will indeed listen, but never
         understand,
      and you will indeed look, but never
         perceive.
²⁷ For this people's heart has grown dull,
      and their ears are hard of hearing,
         and they have shut their eyes;
      so that they might not look with
         their eyes,
      and listen with their ears,
      and understand with their heart and
         turn—
      and I would heal them.'

²⁸Let it be known to you then that this salvation of God has been sent to the Gentiles; they will listen."^k

30 He lived there two whole years at his own expense^l and welcomed all who came to him, ³¹proclaiming the kingdom of God and teaching about the Lord Jesus Christ with all boldness and without hindrance.

Μωϋσέως καὶ τῶν προφητῶν, ἀπὸ πρωῒ ἕως ἑσπέρας. **24** καὶ οἱ μὲν ἐπείθοντο τοῖς λεγομένοις, οἱ δὲ ἠπίστουν· **25** ἀσύμφωνοι δὲ ὄντες πρὸς ἀλλήλους ἀπελύοντο εἰπόντος τοῦ Παύλου ῥῆμα ἕν, ὅτι Καλῶς τὸ πνεῦμα τὸ ἅγιον ἐλάλησεν διὰ Ἠσαΐου τοῦ προφήτου πρὸς τοὺς πατέρας ὑμῶν **26** λέγων,

    Πορεύθητι πρὸς τὸν λαὸν τοῦτον
       καὶ εἰπόν,
    Ἀκοῇ ἀκούσετε καὶ οὐ μὴ συνῆτε
       καὶ βλέποντες βλέψετε καὶ οὐ
          μὴ ἴδητε·
27 ἐπαχύνθη γὰρ ἡ καρδία τοῦ λαοῦ
       τούτου
    καὶ τοῖς ὠσὶν βαρέως ἤκουσαν
       καὶ τοὺς ὀφθαλμοὺς αὐτῶν
          ἐκάμμυσαν·
    μήποτε ἴδωσιν τοῖς ὀφθαλμοῖς
       καὶ τοῖς ὠσὶν ἀκούσωσιν
    καὶ τῇ καρδίᾳ συνῶσιν καὶ
       ἐπιστρέψωσιν,
    καὶ ἰάσομαι αὐτούς.

28 γνωστὸν οὖν ἔστω ὑμῖν ὅτι τοῖς ἔθνεσιν ἀπεστάλη τοῦτο τὸ σωτήριον τοῦ θεοῦ· αὐτοὶ καὶ ἀκούσονται.^a

30 Ἐνέμεινεν δὲ διετίαν ὅλην ἐν ἰδίῳ μισθώματι καὶ ἀπεδέχετο πάντας τοὺς εἰσπορευομένους πρὸς αὐτόν, **31** κηρύσσων τὴν βασιλείαν τοῦ θεοῦ καὶ διδάσκων τὰ περὶ τοῦ κυρίου Ἰησοῦ Χριστοῦ μετὰ πάσης παρρησίας ἀκωλύτως.

---

the Law of Moses and from the Prophets. ²⁴Some were convinced by what he said, but others would not believe. ²⁵They disagreed among themselves and began to leave after Paul had made this final statement: "The Holy Spirit spoke the truth to your forefathers when he said through Isaiah the prophet:

²⁶" 'Go to this people and say,
    "You will be ever hearing but never
        understanding;
    you will be ever seeing but never
        perceiving."
²⁷For this people's heart has become
        calloused;
    they hardly hear with their ears,
    and they have closed their eyes.
Otherwise they might see with their
        eyes,
    hear with their ears,
    understand with their hearts
and turn, and I would heal them.'^a

²⁸"Therefore I want you to know that God's salvation has been sent to the Gentiles, and they will listen!"^b

³⁰For two whole years Paul stayed there in his own rented house and welcomed all who came to see him. ³¹Boldly and without hindrance he preached the kingdom of God and taught about the Lord Jesus Christ.

---

^k Other ancient authorities add verse 29, *And when he had said these words, the Jews departed, arguing vigorously among themselves*   ^l*Or in his own hired dwelling*

^a28 NIV/NRSV notes add 29 καὶ ταῦτα αὐτοῦ εἰπόντος ἀπῆλθον οἱ Ἰουδαῖοι, πολλὴν ἔχοντες ἐν ἑαυτοῖς συζήτησιν.

^a27 Isaiah 6:9,10   ^b28 Some manuscripts *listen!"* ²⁹*After he said this, the Jews left, arguing vigorously among themselves.*

NRSV

Salutation

1 Paul, a servant[a] of Jesus Christ, called to be an apostle, set apart for the gospel of God, [2]which he promised beforehand through his prophets in the holy scriptures, [3]the gospel concerning his Son, who was descended from David according to the flesh [4]and was declared to be Son of God with power according to the spirit[b] of holiness by resurrection from the dead, Jesus Christ our Lord, [5]through whom we have received grace and apostleship to bring about the obedience of faith among all the Gentiles for the sake of his name, [6]including yourselves who are called to belong to Jesus Christ,

7 To all God's beloved in Rome, who are called to be saints:

Grace to you and peace from God our Father and the Lord Jesus Christ.

Prayer of Thanksgiving

8 First, I thank my God through Jesus Christ for all of you, because your faith is proclaimed throughout the world. [9]For God, whom I serve with my spirit by announcing the gospel[c] of his Son, is my witness that without ceasing I remember you always in my prayers, [10]asking that by God's will I may somehow at last succeed in coming to you. [11]For I am longing to see you so that I may share with you some spiritual gift to strengthen you—[12]or rather so that we may be mutually encouraged by each other's faith, both yours and mine. [13]I want you to know, brothers and sisters,[d] that I have often intended to come to you (but thus far have been prevented), in order that I may reap some harvest among you as I have among the rest of the Gentiles. [14]I am a debtor both to Greeks and to barbarians, both to the wise and to the foolish [15]—hence my eagerness to proclaim the gospel to you also who are in Rome.

The Power of the Gospel

16 For I am not ashamed of the gospel; it is the power of God for salvation to everyone who has faith, to the Jew first and also to the Greek. [17]For in it the righteousness of God is revealed through faith for faith; as it is written, "The one who is righteous will live by faith."[e]

ΠΡΟΣ ΡΩΜΑΙΟΥΣ

1 Παῦλος δοῦλος Χριστοῦ Ἰησοῦ, κλητὸς ἀπόστολος ἀφωρισμένος εἰς εὐαγγέλιον θεοῦ, **2** ὃ προεπηγγείλατο διὰ τῶν προφητῶν αὐτοῦ ἐν γραφαῖς ἁγίαις **3** περὶ τοῦ υἱοῦ αὐτοῦ τοῦ γενομένου ἐκ σπέρματος Δαυὶδ κατὰ σάρκα, **4** τοῦ ὁρισθέντος υἱοῦ θεοῦ ἐν δυνάμει κατὰ πνεῦμα ἁγιωσύνης ἐξ ἀναστάσεως νεκρῶν, Ἰησοῦ Χριστοῦ τοῦ κυρίου ἡμῶν, **5** δι᾽ οὗ ἐλάβομεν χάριν καὶ ἀποστολὴν εἰς ὑπακοὴν πίστεως ἐν πᾶσιν τοῖς ἔθνεσιν ὑπὲρ τοῦ ὀνόματος αὐτοῦ, **6** ἐν οἷς ἐστε καὶ ὑμεῖς κλητοὶ Ἰησοῦ Χριστοῦ, **7** πᾶσιν τοῖς οὖσιν ἐν Ῥώμῃ ἀγαπητοῖς θεοῦ, κλητοῖς ἁγίοις, χάρις ὑμῖν καὶ εἰρήνη ἀπὸ θεοῦ πατρὸς ἡμῶν καὶ κυρίου Ἰησοῦ Χριστοῦ.

8 Πρῶτον μὲν εὐχαριστῶ τῷ θεῷ μου διὰ Ἰησοῦ Χριστοῦ περὶ πάντων ὑμῶν ὅτι ἡ πίστις ὑμῶν καταγγέλλεται ἐν ὅλῳ τῷ κόσμῳ. **9** μάρτυς γάρ μού ἐστιν ὁ θεός, ᾧ λατρεύω ἐν τῷ πνεύματί μου ἐν τῷ εὐαγγελίῳ τοῦ υἱοῦ αὐτοῦ, ὡς ἀδιαλείπτως μνείαν ὑμῶν ποιοῦμαι **10** πάντοτε ἐπὶ τῶν προσευχῶν μου δεόμενος εἴ πως ἤδη ποτὲ εὐοδωθήσομαι ἐν τῷ θελήματι τοῦ θεοῦ ἐλθεῖν πρὸς ὑμᾶς. **11** ἐπιποθῶ γὰρ ἰδεῖν ὑμᾶς, ἵνα τι μεταδῶ χάρισμα ὑμῖν πνευματικὸν εἰς τὸ στηριχθῆναι ὑμᾶς, **12** τοῦτο δέ ἐστιν συμπαρακληθῆναι ἐν ὑμῖν διὰ τῆς ἐν ἀλλήλοις πίστεως ὑμῶν τε καὶ ἐμοῦ. **13** οὐ θέλω δὲ ὑμᾶς ἀγνοεῖν, ἀδελφοί, ὅτι πολλάκις προεθέμην ἐλθεῖν πρὸς ὑμᾶς, καὶ ἐκωλύθην ἄχρι τοῦ δεῦρο, ἵνα τινὰ καρπὸν σχῶ καὶ ἐν ὑμῖν καθὼς καὶ ἐν τοῖς λοιποῖς ἔθνεσιν. **14** Ἕλλησίν τε καὶ βαρβάροις, σοφοῖς τε καὶ ἀνοήτοις ὀφειλέτης εἰμί, **15** οὕτως τὸ κατ᾽ ἐμὲ πρόθυμον καὶ ὑμῖν τοῖς ἐν Ῥώμῃ εὐαγγελίσασθαι.

16 Οὐ γὰρ ἐπαισχύνομαι τὸ εὐαγγέλιον, δύναμις γὰρ θεοῦ ἐστιν εἰς σωτηρίαν παντὶ τῷ πιστεύοντι, Ἰουδαίῳ τε πρῶτον καὶ Ἕλληνι. **17** δικαιοσύνη γὰρ θεοῦ ἐν αὐτῷ ἀποκαλύπτεται ἐκ πίστεως εἰς πίστιν, καθὼς γέγραπται, Ὁ δὲ δίκαιος ἐκ πίστεως ζήσεται.

NIV

1 Paul, a servant of Christ Jesus, called to be an apostle and set apart for the gospel of God— [2]the gospel he promised beforehand through his prophets in the Holy Scriptures [3]regarding his Son, who as to his human nature was a descendant of David, [4]and who through the Spirit[a] of holiness was declared with power to be the Son of God[b] by his resurrection from the dead: Jesus Christ our Lord. [5]Through him and for his name's sake, we received grace and apostleship to call people from among all the Gentiles to the obedience that comes from faith. [6]And you also are among those who are called to belong to Jesus Christ.

[7]To all in Rome who are loved by God and called to be saints:

Grace and peace to you from God our Father and from the Lord Jesus Christ.

Paul's Longing to Visit Rome

[8]First, I thank my God through Jesus Christ for all of you, because your faith is being reported all over the world. [9]God, whom I serve with my whole heart in preaching the gospel of his Son, is my witness how constantly I remember you [10]in my prayers at all times; and I pray that now at last by God's will the way may be opened for me to come to you.

[11]I long to see you so that I may impart to you some spiritual gift to make you strong— [12]that is, that you and I may be mutually encouraged by each other's faith. [13]I do not want you to be unaware, brothers, that I planned many times to come to you (but have been prevented from doing so until now) in order that I might have a harvest among you, just as I have had among the other Gentiles.

[14]I am obligated both to Greeks and non-Greeks, both to the wise and the foolish. [15]That is why I am so eager to preach the gospel also to you who are at Rome.

[16]I am not ashamed of the gospel, because it is the power of God for the salvation of everyone who believes: first for the Jew, then for the Gentile. [17]For in the gospel a righteousness from God is revealed, a righteousness that is by faith from first to last,[c] just as it is written: "The righteous will live by faith."[d]

---

[a] Gk *slave*   [b] Or *Spirit*   [c] Gk *my spirit in the gospel*
[d] Gk *brothers*   [e] Or *The one who is righteous through faith will live*

[a]4 Or *who as to his spirit*   [b]4 Or *was appointed to be the Son of God with power*   [c]17 Or *is from faith to faith*
[d]17 Hab. 2:4

The Guilt of Humankind

18 For the wrath of God is revealed from heaven against all ungodliness and wickedness of those who by their wickedness suppress the truth. [19]For what can be known about God is plain to them, because God has shown it to them. [20]Ever since the creation of the world his eternal power and divine nature, invisible though they are, have been understood and seen through the things he has made. So they are without excuse; [21]for though they knew God, they did not honor him as God or give thanks to him, but they became futile in their thinking, and their senseless minds were darkened. [22]Claiming to be wise, they became fools; [23]and they exchanged the glory of the immortal God for images resembling a mortal human being or birds or four-footed animals or reptiles.

24 Therefore God gave them up in the lusts of their hearts to impurity, to the degrading of their bodies among themselves, [25]because they exchanged the truth about God for a lie and worshiped and served the creature rather than the Creator, who is blessed forever! Amen.

26 For this reason God gave them up to degrading passions. Their women exchanged natural intercourse for unnatural, [27]and in the same way also the men, giving up natural intercourse with women, were consumed with passion for one another. Men committed shameless acts with men and received in their own persons the due penalty for their error.

28 And since they did not see fit to acknowledge God, God gave them up to a debased mind and to things that should not be done. [29]They were filled with every kind of wickedness, evil, covetousness, malice. Full of envy, murder, strife, deceit, craftiness, they are gossips, [30]slanderers, God-haters,[f] insolent, haughty, boastful, inventors of evil, rebellious toward parents, [31]foolish, faithless, heartless, ruthless. [32]They know God's decree, that those who practice such things deserve to die—yet they not only do them but even applaud others who practice them.

The Righteous Judgment of God

2 Therefore you have no excuse, whoever you are, when you judge others; for in passing judgment on another you

[f] Or *God-hated*

---

18 Ἀποκαλύπτεται γὰρ ὀργὴ θεοῦ ἀπ᾽ οὐρανοῦ ἐπὶ πᾶσαν ἀσέβειαν καὶ ἀδικίαν ἀνθρώπων τῶν τὴν ἀλήθειαν ἐν ἀδικίᾳ κατεχόντων, **19** διότι τὸ γνωστὸν τοῦ θεοῦ φανερόν ἐστιν ἐν αὐτοῖς· ὁ θεὸς γὰρ αὐτοῖς ἐφανέρωσεν. **20** τὰ γὰρ ἀόρατα αὐτοῦ ἀπὸ κτίσεως κόσμου τοῖς ποιήμασιν νοούμενα καθορᾶται, ἥ τε ἀΐδιος αὐτοῦ δύναμις καὶ θειότης, εἰς τὸ εἶναι αὐτοὺς ἀναπολογήτους, **21** διότι γνόντες τὸν θεὸν οὐχ ὡς θεὸν ἐδόξασαν ἢ ηὐχαρίστησαν, ἀλλ᾽ ἐματαιώθησαν ἐν τοῖς διαλογισμοῖς αὐτῶν καὶ ἐσκοτίσθη ἡ ἀσύνετος αὐτῶν καρδία. **22** φάσκοντες εἶναι σοφοὶ ἐμωράνθησαν **23** καὶ ἤλλαξαν τὴν δόξαν τοῦ ἀφθάρτου θεοῦ ἐν ὁμοιώματι εἰκόνος φθαρτοῦ ἀνθρώπου καὶ πετεινῶν καὶ τετραπόδων καὶ ἑρπετῶν.

24 Διὸ παρέδωκεν αὐτοὺς ὁ θεὸς ἐν ταῖς ἐπιθυμίαις τῶν καρδιῶν αὐτῶν εἰς ἀκαθαρσίαν τοῦ ἀτιμάζεσθαι τὰ σώματα αὐτῶν ἐν αὐτοῖς· **25** οἵτινες μετήλλαξαν τὴν ἀλήθειαν τοῦ θεοῦ ἐν τῷ ψεύδει καὶ ἐσεβάσθησαν καὶ ἐλάτρευσαν τῇ κτίσει παρὰ τὸν κτίσαντα, ὅς ἐστιν εὐλογητὸς εἰς τοὺς αἰῶνας, ἀμήν. **26** διὰ τοῦτο παρέδωκεν αὐτοὺς ὁ θεὸς εἰς πάθη ἀτιμίας, αἵ τε γὰρ θήλειαι αὐτῶν μετήλλαξαν τὴν φυσικὴν χρῆσιν εἰς τὴν παρὰ φύσιν, **27** ὁμοίως τε καὶ οἱ ἄρσενες ἀφέντες τὴν φυσικὴν χρῆσιν τῆς θηλείας ἐξεκαύθησαν ἐν τῇ ὀρέξει αὐτῶν εἰς ἀλλήλους, ἄρσενες ἐν ἄρσεσιν τὴν ἀσχημοσύνην κατεργαζόμενοι καὶ τὴν ἀντιμισθίαν ἣν ἔδει τῆς πλάνης αὐτῶν ἐν ἑαυτοῖς ἀπολαμβάνοντες. **28** καὶ καθὼς οὐκ ἐδοκίμασαν τὸν θεὸν ἔχειν ἐν ἐπιγνώσει, παρέδωκεν αὐτοὺς ὁ θεὸς εἰς ἀδόκιμον νοῦν, ποιεῖν τὰ μὴ καθήκοντα, **29** πεπληρωμένους πάσῃ ἀδικίᾳ πονηρίᾳ πλεονεξίᾳ κακίᾳ, μεστοὺς φθόνου φόνου ἔριδος δόλου κακοηθείας, ψιθυριστὰς **30** καταλάλους θεοστυγεῖς ὑβριστὰς ὑπερηφάνους ἀλαζόνας, ἐφευρετὰς κακῶν, γονεῦσιν ἀπειθεῖς, **31** ἀσυνέτους ἀσυνθέτους ἀστόργους ἀνελεήμονας· **32** οἵτινες τὸ δικαίωμα τοῦ θεοῦ ἐπιγνόντες ὅτι οἱ τὰ τοιαῦτα πράσσοντες ἄξιοι θανάτου εἰσίν, οὐ μόνον αὐτὰ ποιοῦσιν ἀλλὰ καὶ συνευδοκοῦσιν τοῖς πράσσουσιν.

2 Διὸ ἀναπολόγητος εἶ, ὦ ἄνθρωπε πᾶς ὁ κρίνων· ἐν ᾧ γὰρ κρίνεις

God's Wrath Against Mankind

[18]The wrath of God is being revealed from heaven against all the godlessness and wickedness of men who suppress the truth by their wickedness, [19]since what may be known about God is plain to them, because God has made it plain to them. [20]For since the creation of the world God's invisible qualities—his eternal power and divine nature—have been clearly seen, being understood from what has been made, so that men are without excuse.

[21]For although they knew God, they neither glorified him as God nor gave thanks to him, but their thinking became futile and their foolish hearts were darkened. [22]Although they claimed to be wise, they became fools [23]and exchanged the glory of the immortal God for images made to look like mortal man and birds and animals and reptiles.

[24]Therefore God gave them over in the sinful desires of their hearts to sexual impurity for the degrading of their bodies with one another. [25]They exchanged the truth of God for a lie, and worshiped and served created things rather than the Creator—who is forever praised. Amen.

[26]Because of this, God gave them over to shameful lusts. Even their women exchanged natural relations for unnatural ones. [27]In the same way the men also abandoned natural relations with women and were inflamed with lust for one another. Men committed indecent acts with other men, and received in themselves the due penalty for their perversion.

[28]Furthermore, since they did not think it worthwhile to retain the knowledge of God, he gave them over to a depraved mind, to do what ought not to be done. [29]They have become filled with every kind of wickedness, evil, greed and depravity. They are full of envy, murder, strife, deceit and malice. They are gossips, [30]slanderers, God-haters, insolent, arrogant and boastful; they invent ways of doing evil; they disobey their parents; [31]they are senseless, faithless, heartless, ruthless. [32]Although they know God's righteous decree that those who do such things deserve death, they not only continue to do these very things but also approve of those who practice them.

God's Righteous Judgment

2 You, therefore, have no excuse, you who pass judgment on someone else, for at whatever point you judge the other,

condemn yourself, because you, the judge, are doing the very same things. [2]You say,[g] "We know that God's judgment on those who do such things is in accordance with truth." [3]Do you imagine, whoever you are, that when you judge those who do such things and yet do them yourself, you will escape the judgment of God? [4]Or do you despise the riches of his kindness and forbearance and patience? Do you not realize that God's kindness is meant to lead you to repentance? [5]But by your hard and impenitent heart you are storing up wrath for yourself on the day of wrath, when God's righteous judgment will be revealed. [6]For he will repay according to each one's deeds: [7]to those who by patiently doing good seek for glory and honor and immortality, he will give eternal life; [8]while for those who are self-seeking and who obey not the truth but wickedness, there will be wrath and fury. [9]There will be anguish and distress for everyone who does evil, the Jew first and also the Greek, [10]but glory and honor and peace for everyone who does good, the Jew first and also the Greek. [11]For God shows no partiality.

12 All who have sinned apart from the law will also perish apart from the law, and all who have sinned under the law will be judged by the law. [13]For it is not the hearers of the law who are righteous in God's sight, but the doers of the law who will be justified. [14]When Gentiles, who do not possess the law, do instinctively what the law requires, these, though not having the law, are a law to themselves. [15]They show that what the law requires is written on their hearts, to which their own conscience also bears witness; and their conflicting thoughts will accuse or perhaps excuse them [16]on the day when, according to my gospel, God, through Jesus Christ, will judge the secret thoughts of all.

The Jews and the Law

17 But if you call yourself a Jew and rely on the law and boast of your relation to God [18]and know his will and determine what is best because you are instructed in the law, [19]and if you are sure that you are a guide to the blind, a light to those who are in darkness, [20]a corrector of the foolish, a teacher of children, having in the law the embodiment of knowledge and truth,

τὸν ἕτερον, σεαυτὸν κατακρίνεις, τὰ γὰρ αὐτὰ πράσσεις ὁ κρίνων. **2** οἴδαμεν δὲ ὅτι τὸ κρίμα τοῦ θεοῦ ἐστιν κατὰ ἀλήθειαν ἐπὶ τοὺς τὰ τοιαῦτα πράσσοντας. **3** λογίζῃ δὲ τοῦτο, ὦ ἄνθρωπε ὁ κρίνων τοὺς τὰ τοιαῦτα πράσσοντας καὶ ποιῶν αὐτά, ὅτι σὺ ἐκφεύξῃ τὸ κρίμα τοῦ θεοῦ; **4** ἢ τοῦ πλούτου τῆς χρηστότητος αὐτοῦ καὶ τῆς ἀνοχῆς καὶ τῆς μακροθυμίας καταφρονεῖς, ἀγνοῶν ὅτι τὸ χρηστὸν τοῦ θεοῦ εἰς μετάνοιάν σε ἄγει; **5** κατὰ δὲ τὴν σκληρότητά σου καὶ ἀμετανόητον καρδίαν θησαυρίζεις σεαυτῷ ὀργὴν ἐν ἡμέρᾳ ὀργῆς καὶ ἀποκαλύψεως δικαιοκρισίας τοῦ θεοῦ **6** ὃς ἀποδώσει ἑκάστῳ κατὰ τὰ ἔργα αὐτοῦ· **7** τοῖς μὲν καθ᾽ ὑπομονὴν ἔργου ἀγαθοῦ δόξαν καὶ τιμὴν καὶ ἀφθαρσίαν ζητοῦσιν ζωὴν αἰώνιον, **8** τοῖς δὲ ἐξ ἐριθείας καὶ ἀπειθοῦσι τῇ ἀληθείᾳ πειθομένοις δὲ τῇ ἀδικίᾳ ὀργὴ καὶ θυμός. **9** θλῖψις καὶ στενοχωρία ἐπὶ πᾶσαν ψυχὴν ἀνθρώπου τοῦ κατεργαζομένου τὸ κακόν, Ἰουδαίου τε πρῶτον καὶ Ἕλληνος· **10** δόξα δὲ καὶ τιμὴ καὶ εἰρήνη παντὶ τῷ ἐργαζομένῳ τὸ ἀγαθόν, Ἰουδαίῳ τε πρῶτον καὶ Ἕλληνι· **11** οὐ γάρ ἐστιν προσωπολημψία παρὰ τῷ θεῷ. **12** ὅσοι γὰρ ἀνόμως ἥμαρτον, ἀνόμως καὶ ἀπολοῦνται, καὶ ὅσοι ἐν νόμῳ ἥμαρτον, διὰ νόμου κριθήσονται· **13** οὐ γὰρ οἱ ἀκροαταὶ νόμου δίκαιοι παρὰ [τῷ] θεῷ, ἀλλ᾽ οἱ ποιηταὶ νόμου δικαιωθήσονται. **14** ὅταν γὰρ ἔθνη τὰ μὴ νόμον ἔχοντα φύσει τὰ τοῦ νόμου ποιῶσιν, οὗτοι νόμον μὴ ἔχοντες ἑαυτοῖς εἰσιν νόμος· **15** οἵτινες ἐνδείκνυνται τὸ ἔργον τοῦ νόμου γραπτὸν ἐν ταῖς καρδίαις αὐτῶν, συμμαρτυρούσης αὐτῶν τῆς συνειδήσεως καὶ μεταξὺ ἀλλήλων τῶν λογισμῶν κατηγορούντων ἢ καὶ ἀπολογουμένων, **16** ἐν ἡμέρᾳ ὅτε κρίνει ὁ θεὸς τὰ κρυπτὰ τῶν ἀνθρώπων κατὰ τὸ εὐαγγέλιόν μου διὰ Χριστοῦ Ἰησοῦ[a].

17 Εἰ δὲ σὺ Ἰουδαῖος ἐπονομάζῃ καὶ ἐπαναπαύῃ νόμῳ καὶ καυχᾶσαι ἐν θεῷ **18** καὶ γινώσκεις τὸ θέλημα καὶ δοκιμάζεις τὰ διαφέροντα κατηχούμενος ἐκ τοῦ νόμου, **19** πέποιθάς τε σεαυτὸν ὁδηγὸν εἶναι τυφλῶν, φῶς τῶν ἐν σκότει, **20** παιδευτὴν ἀφρόνων, διδάσκαλον νηπίων, ἔχοντα τὴν μόρφωσιν τῆς γνώσεως καὶ τῆς ἀληθείας ἐν

you are condemning yourself, because you who pass judgment do the same things. [2]Now we know that God's judgment against those who do such things is based on truth. [3]So when you, a mere man, pass judgment on them and yet do the same things, do you think you will escape God's judgment? [4]Or do you show contempt for the riches of his kindness, tolerance and patience, not realizing that God's kindness leads you toward repentance?

[5]But because of your stubbornness and your unrepentant heart, you are storing up wrath against yourself for the day of God's wrath, when his righteous judgment will be revealed. [6]God "will give to each person according to what he has done."[a] [7]To those who by persistence in doing good seek glory, honor and immortality, he will give eternal life. [8]But for those who are self-seeking and who reject the truth and follow evil, there will be wrath and anger. [9]There will be trouble and distress for every human being who does evil: first for the Jew, then for the Gentile; [10]but glory, honor and peace for everyone who does good: first for the Jew, then for the Gentile. [11]For God does not show favoritism.

[12]All who sin apart from the law will also perish apart from the law, and all who sin under the law will be judged by the law. [13]For it is not those who hear the law who are righteous in God's sight, but it is those who obey the law who will be declared righteous. [14](Indeed, when Gentiles, who do not have the law, do by nature things required by the law, they are a law for themselves, even though they do not have the law, [15]since they show that the requirements of the law are written on their hearts, their consciences also bearing witness, and their thoughts now accusing, now even defending them.) [16]This will take place on the day when God will judge men's secrets through Jesus Christ, as my gospel declares.

The Jews and the Law

[17]Now you, if you call yourself a Jew; if you rely on the law and brag about your relationship to God; [18]if you know his will and approve of what is superior because you are instructed by the law; [19]if you are convinced that you are a guide for the blind, a light for those who are in the dark, [20]an instructor of the foolish, a teacher of infants, because you have in the law the embodiment of knowledge and truth—

NRSV

[21]you, then, that teach others, will you not teach yourself? While you preach against stealing, do you steal? [22]You that forbid adultery, do you commit adultery? You that abhor idols, do you rob temples? [23]You that boast in the law, do you dishonor God by breaking the law? [24]For, as it is written, "The name of God is blasphemed among the Gentiles because of you."

25 Circumcision indeed is of value if you obey the law; but if you break the law, your circumcision has become uncircumcision. [26]So, if those who are uncircumcised keep the requirements of the law, will not their uncircumcision be regarded as circumcision? [27]Then those who are physically uncircumcised but keep the law will condemn you that have the written code and circumcision but break the law. [28]For a person is not a Jew who is one outwardly, nor is true circumcision something external and physical. [29]Rather, a person is a Jew who is one inwardly, and real circumcision is a matter of the heart—it is spiritual and not literal. Such a person receives praise not from others but from God.

3 Then what advantage has the Jew? Or what is the value of circumcision? [2]Much, in every way. For in the first place the Jews[h] were entrusted with the oracles of God. [3]What if some were unfaithful? Will their faithlessness nullify the faithfulness of God? [4]By no means! Although everyone is a liar, let God be proved true, as it is written,

"So that you may be justified in your words,
    and prevail in your judging."[i]

[5]But if our injustice serves to confirm the justice of God, what should we say? That God is unjust to inflict wrath on us? (I speak in a human way.) [6]By no means! For then how could God judge the world? [7]But if through my falsehood God's truthfulness abounds to his glory, why am I still being condemned as a sinner? [8]And why not say (as some people slander us by saying that we say), "Let us do evil so that good may come"? Their condemnation is deserved!

Greek

τῷ νόμῳ· **21** ὁ οὖν διδάσκων ἕτερον σεαυτὸν οὐ διδάσκεις; ὁ κηρύσσων μὴ κλέπτειν κλέπτεις; **22** ὁ λέγων μὴ μοιχεύειν μοιχεύεις; ὁ βδελυσσόμενος τὰ εἴδωλα ἱεροσυλεῖς; **23** ὃς ἐν νόμῳ καυχᾶσαι, διὰ τῆς παραβάσεως τοῦ νόμου τὸν θεὸν ἀτιμάζεις· **24** τὸ γὰρ ὄνομα τοῦ θεοῦ δι᾽ ὑμᾶς βλασφημεῖται ἐν τοῖς ἔθνεσιν, καθὼς γέγραπται. **25** περιτομὴ μὲν γὰρ ὠφελεῖ ἐὰν νόμον πράσσῃς· ἐὰν δὲ παραβάτης νόμου ᾖς, ἡ περιτομή σου ἀκροβυστία γέγονεν. **26** ἐὰν οὖν ἡ ἀκροβυστία τὰ δικαιώματα τοῦ νόμου φυλάσσῃ, οὐχ ἡ ἀκροβυστία αὐτοῦ εἰς περιτομὴν λογισθήσεται; **27** καὶ κρινεῖ ἡ ἐκ φύσεως ἀκροβυστία τὸν νόμον τελοῦσα σὲ τὸν διὰ γράμματος καὶ περιτομῆς παραβάτην νόμου. **28** οὐ γὰρ ὁ ἐν τῷ φανερῷ Ἰουδαῖός ἐστιν οὐδὲ ἡ ἐν τῷ φανερῷ ἐν σαρκὶ περιτομή, **29** ἀλλ᾽ ὁ ἐν τῷ κρυπτῷ Ἰουδαῖος, καὶ περιτομὴ καρδίας ἐν πνεύματι οὐ γράμματι, οὗ ὁ ἔπαινος οὐκ ἐξ ἀνθρώπων ἀλλ᾽ ἐκ τοῦ θεοῦ.

3 Τί οὖν τὸ περισσὸν τοῦ Ἰουδαίου ἢ τίς ἡ ὠφέλεια τῆς περιτομῆς; **2** πολὺ κατὰ πάντα τρόπον. πρῶτον μὲν [γὰρ] ὅτι ἐπιστεύθησαν τὰ λόγια τοῦ θεοῦ. **3** τί γάρ; εἰ ἠπίστησάν τινες, μὴ ἡ ἀπιστία αὐτῶν τὴν πίστιν τοῦ θεοῦ καταργήσει; **4** μὴ γένοιτο· γινέσθω δὲ ὁ θεὸς ἀληθής, πᾶς δὲ ἄνθρωπος ψεύστης, καθὼς γέγραπται,

Ὅπως ἂν δικαιωθῇς ἐν τοῖς λόγοις σου
    καὶ νικήσεις ἐν τῷ κρίνεσθαί σε.

5 εἰ δὲ ἡ ἀδικία ἡμῶν θεοῦ δικαιοσύνην συνίστησιν, τί ἐροῦμεν; μὴ ἄδικος ὁ θεὸς ὁ ἐπιφέρων τὴν ὀργήν; κατὰ ἄνθρωπον λέγω. **6** μὴ γένοιτο· ἐπεὶ πῶς κρινεῖ ὁ θεὸς τὸν κόσμον; **7** εἰ δὲ ἡ ἀλήθεια τοῦ θεοῦ ἐν τῷ ἐμῷ ψεύσματι ἐπερίσσευσεν εἰς τὴν δόξαν αὐτοῦ, τί ἔτι κἀγὼ ὡς ἁμαρτωλὸς κρίνομαι; **8** καὶ μὴ καθὼς βλασφημούμεθα καὶ καθώς φασίν τινες ἡμᾶς λέγειν ὅτι Ποιήσωμεν τὰ κακά, ἵνα ἔλθῃ τὰ ἀγαθά; ὧν τὸ κρίμα ἔνδικόν ἐστιν.

NIV

[21]you, then, who teach others, do you not teach yourself? You who preach against stealing, do you steal? [22]You who say that people should not commit adultery, do you commit adultery? You who abhor idols, do you rob temples? [23]You who brag about the law, do you dishonor God by breaking the law? [24]As it is written: "God's name is blasphemed among the Gentiles because of you."[b]

[25]Circumcision has value if you observe the law, but if you break the law, you have become as though you had not been circumcised. [26]If those who are not circumcised keep the law's requirements, will they not be regarded as though they were circumcised? [27]The one who is not circumcised physically and yet obeys the law will condemn you who, even though you have the[c] written code and circumcision, are a lawbreaker.

[28]A man is not a Jew if he is only one outwardly, nor is circumcision merely outward and physical. [29]No, a man is a Jew if he is one inwardly; and circumcision is circumcision of the heart, by the Spirit, not by the written code. Such a man's praise is not from men, but from God.

God's Faithfulness

3 What advantage, then, is there in being a Jew, or what value is there in circumcision? [2]Much in every way! First of all, they have been entrusted with the very words of God.

[3]What if some did not have faith? Will their lack of faith nullify God's faithfulness? [4]Not at all! Let God be true, and every man a liar. As it is written:

"So that you may be proved right when you speak
    and prevail when you judge."[a]

[5]But if our unrighteousness brings out God's righteousness more clearly, what shall we say? That God is unjust in bringing his wrath on us? (I am using a human argument.) [6]Certainly not! If that were so, how could God judge the world? [7]Someone might argue, "If my falsehood enhances God's truthfulness and so increases his glory, why am I still condemned as a sinner?" [8]Why not say—as we are being slanderously reported as saying and as some claim that we say—"Let us do evil that good may result"? Their condemnation is deserved.

---

[h] Gk *they*   [i] Gk *when you are being judged*

[b]24 Isaiah 52:5; Ezek. 36:22   [c]27 Or *who, by means of a*   [a]4 Psalm 51:4

None Is Righteous

9 What then? Are we any better off?[i] No, not at all; for we have already charged that all, both Jews and Greeks, are under the power of sin, [10]as it is written:

"There is no one who is righteous, not even one;

[11]   there is no one who has understanding,
        there is no one who seeks God.

[12] All have turned aside, together they have become worthless;
        there is no one who shows kindness, there is not even one."

[13] "Their throats are opened graves; they use their tongues to deceive."
"The venom of vipers is under their lips."

[14]   "Their mouths are full of cursing and bitterness."

[15] "Their feet are swift to shed blood;

[16]   ruin and misery are in their paths,

[17]   and the way of peace they have not known."

[18]   "There is no fear of God before their eyes."

19 Now we know that whatever the law says, it speaks to those who are under the law, so that every mouth may be silenced, and the whole world may be held accountable to God. [20]For "no human being will be justified in his sight" by deeds prescribed by the law, for through the law comes the knowledge of sin.

Righteousness through Faith

21 But now, apart from law, the righteousness of God has been disclosed, and is attested by the law and the prophets, [22]the righteousness of God through faith in Jesus Christ[k] for all who believe. For there is no distinction, [23]since all have sinned and fall short of the glory of God; [24]they are now justified by his grace as a gift, through the redemption that is in Christ Jesus, [25]whom God put forward as a sacrifice of atonement[l] by his blood, effective through faith. He did this to show his righteousness, because in his divine forbearance he had passed over the sins previously committed; [26]it was to prove at the present time that he himself is righteous and that he justifies the one who has faith in Jesus.[m]

27 Then what becomes of boasting? It is excluded. By what law? By that of works?

[i] Or at any disadvantage? [k] Or through the faith of Jesus Christ [l] Or a place of atonement [m] Or who has the faith of Jesus

---

9 Τί οὖν; προεχόμεθα; οὐ πάντως· προῃτιασάμεθα γὰρ Ἰουδαίους τε καὶ Ἕλληνας πάντας ὑφ' ἁμαρτίαν εἶναι, 10 καθὼς γέγραπται ὅτι

Οὐκ ἔστιν δίκαιος οὐδὲ εἷς,

11   οὐκ ἔστιν ὁ συνίων,
     οὐκ ἔστιν ὁ ἐκζητῶν τὸν θεόν.

12 πάντες ἐξέκλιναν ἅμα ἠχρεώθησαν·
     οὐκ ἔστιν ὁ ποιῶν χρηστότητα,
     [οὐκ ἔστιν] ἕως ἑνός.

13 τάφος ἀνεῳγμένος ὁ λάρυγξ αὐτῶν,
     ταῖς γλώσσαις αὐτῶν ἐδολιοῦσαν,
     ἰὸς ἀσπίδων ὑπὸ τὰ χείλη αὐτῶν·

14   ὧν τὸ στόμα ἀρᾶς καὶ πικρίας γέμει,

15 ὀξεῖς οἱ πόδες αὐτῶν ἐκχέαι αἷμα,

16   σύντριμμα καὶ ταλαιπωρία ἐν ταῖς ὁδοῖς αὐτῶν,

17 καὶ ὁδὸν εἰρήνης οὐκ ἔγνωσαν.

18   οὐκ ἔστιν φόβος θεοῦ ἀπέναντι τῶν ὀφθαλμῶν αὐτῶν.

19 Οἴδαμεν δὲ ὅτι ὅσα ὁ νόμος λέγει τοῖς ἐν τῷ νόμῳ λαλεῖ, ἵνα πᾶν στόμα φραγῇ καὶ ὑπόδικος γένηται πᾶς ὁ κόσμος τῷ θεῷ· 20 διότι ἐξ ἔργων νόμου οὐ δικαιωθήσεται πᾶσα σὰρξ ἐνώπιον αὐτοῦ, διὰ γὰρ νόμου ἐπίγνωσις ἁμαρτίας.

21 Νυνὶ δὲ χωρὶς νόμου δικαιοσύνη θεοῦ πεφανέρωται μαρτυρουμένη ὑπὸ τοῦ νόμου καὶ τῶν προφητῶν, 22 δικαιοσύνη δὲ θεοῦ διὰ πίστεως Ἰησοῦ Χριστοῦ εἰς πάντας τοὺς πιστεύοντας. οὐ γάρ ἐστιν διαστολή, 23 πάντες γὰρ ἥμαρτον καὶ ὑστεροῦνται τῆς δόξης τοῦ θεοῦ 24 δικαιούμενοι δωρεὰν τῇ αὐτοῦ χάριτι διὰ τῆς ἀπολυτρώσεως τῆς ἐν Χριστῷ Ἰησοῦ· 25 ὃν προέθετο ὁ θεὸς ἱλαστήριον διὰ [τῆς] πίστεως ἐν τῷ αὐτοῦ αἵματι εἰς ἔνδειξιν τῆς δικαιοσύνης αὐτοῦ διὰ τὴν πάρεσιν τῶν προγεγονότων ἁμαρτημάτων 26 ἐν τῇ ἀνοχῇ τοῦ θεοῦ,[a] πρὸς τὴν ἔνδειξιν τῆς δικαιοσύνης αὐτοῦ ἐν τῷ νῦν καιρῷ, εἰς τὸ εἶναι αὐτὸν δίκαιον καὶ δικαιοῦντα τὸν ἐκ πίστεως Ἰησοῦ.

27 Ποῦ οὖν ἡ καύχησις; ἐξεκλείσθη. διὰ ποίου νόμου; τῶν ἔργων; οὐχί,

[a]26 NIV/NRSV begin verse 26 after θεοῦ.

No One Is Righteous

[9]What shall we conclude then? Are we any better[b]? Not at all! We have already made the charge that Jews and Gentiles alike are all under sin. [10]As it is written:

"There is no one righteous, not even one;

[11] there is no one who understands,
      no one who seeks God.

[12]All have turned away,
      they have together become worthless;
there is no one who does good,
      not even one."[c]

[13]"Their throats are open graves;
      their tongues practice deceit."[d]
"The poison of vipers is on their lips."[e]

[14] "Their mouths are full of cursing and bitterness."[f]

[15]"Their feet are swift to shed blood;

[16] ruin and misery mark their ways,

[17]and the way of peace they do not know."[g]

[18] "There is no fear of God before their eyes."[h]

[19]Now we know that whatever the law says, it says to those who are under the law, so that every mouth may be silenced and the whole world held accountable to God. [20]Therefore no one will be declared righteous in his sight by observing the law; rather, through the law we become conscious of sin.

Righteousness Through Faith

[21]But now a righteousness from God, apart from law, has been made known, to which the Law and the Prophets testify. [22]This righteousness from God comes through faith in Jesus Christ to all who believe. There is no difference, [23]for all have sinned and fall short of the glory of God, [24]and are justified freely by his grace through the redemption that came by Christ Jesus. [25]God presented him as a sacrifice of atonement,[i] through faith in his blood. He did this to demonstrate his justice, because in his forbearance he had left the sins committed beforehand unpunished— [26]he did it to demonstrate his justice at the present time, so as to be just and the one who justifies those who have faith in Jesus.

[27]Where, then, is boasting? It is excluded. On what principle? On that of observing

[b]9 Or worse   [c]12 Psalms 14:1-3; 53:1-3; Eccles. 7:20
[d]13 Psalm 5:9   [e]13 Psalm 140:3   [f]14 Psalm 10:7
[g]17 Isaiah 59:7,8   [h]18 Psalm 36:1   [i]25 Or as the one who would turn aside his wrath, taking away sin

No, but by the law of faith. [28]For we hold that a person is justified by faith apart from works prescribed by the law. [29]Or is God the God of Jews only? Is he not the God of Gentiles also? Yes, of Gentiles also, [30]since God is one; and he will justify the circumcised on the ground of faith and the uncircumcised through that same faith. [31]Do we then overthrow the law by this faith? By no means! On the contrary, we uphold the law.

The Example of Abraham

4 What then are we to say was gained by[n] Abraham, our ancestor according to the flesh? [2]For if Abraham was justified by works, he has something to boast about, but not before God. [3]For what does the scripture say? "Abraham believed God, and it was reckoned to him as righteousness." [4]Now to one who works, wages are not reckoned as a gift but as something due. [5]But to one without works trusts him who justifies the ungodly, such faith is reckoned as righteousness. [6]So also David speaks of the blessedness of those to whom God reckons righteousness apart from works:

[7] "Blessed are those whose iniquities
     are forgiven,
    and whose sins are covered;
[8]   blessed is the one against whom the
     Lord will not reckon sin."

[9] Is this blessedness, then, pronounced only on the circumcised, or also on the uncircumcised? We say, "Faith was reckoned to Abraham as righteousness." [10]How then was it reckoned to him? Was it before or after he had been circumcised? It was not after, but before he was circumcised. [11]He received the sign of circumcision as a seal of the righteousness that he had by faith while he was still uncircumcised. The purpose was to make him the ancestor of all who believe without being circumcised and who thus have righteousness reckoned to them, [12]and likewise the ancestor of the circumcised who are not only circumcised but who also follow the example of the faith that our ancestor Abraham had before he was circumcised.

God's Promise Realized through Faith

[13] For the promise that he would inherit the world did not come to Abraham or to his descendants through the law but through the righteousness of faith. [14]If it is the adherents of the law who are to be the

---

ἀλλὰ διὰ νόμου πίστεως. **28** λογιζόμεθα γὰρ δικαιοῦσθαι πίστει ἄνθρωπον χωρὶς ἔργων νόμου. **29** ἢ Ἰουδαίων ὁ θεὸς μόνον; οὐχὶ καὶ ἐθνῶν; ναὶ καὶ ἐθνῶν, **30** εἴπερ εἷς ὁ θεὸς ὃς δικαιώσει περιτομὴν ἐκ πίστεως καὶ ἀκροβυστίαν διὰ τῆς πίστεως. **31** νόμον οὖν καταργοῦμεν διὰ τῆς πίστεως; μὴ γένοιτο· ἀλλὰ νόμον ἱστάνομεν.

4 Τί οὖν ἐροῦμεν εὑρηκέναι[a] Ἀβραὰμ τὸν προπάτορα ἡμῶν κατὰ σάρκα; **2** εἰ γὰρ Ἀβραὰμ ἐξ ἔργων ἐδικαιώθη, ἔχει καύχημα, ἀλλ' οὐ πρὸς θεόν. **3** τί γὰρ ἡ γραφὴ λέγει; Ἐπίστευσεν δὲ Ἀβραὰμ τῷ θεῷ καὶ ἐλογίσθη αὐτῷ εἰς δικαιοσύνην. **4** τῷ δὲ ἐργαζομένῳ ὁ μισθὸς οὐ λογίζεται κατὰ χάριν ἀλλὰ κατὰ ὀφείλημα, **5** τῷ δὲ μὴ ἐργαζομένῳ πιστεύοντι δὲ ἐπὶ τὸν δικαιοῦντα τὸν ἀσεβῆ λογίζεται ἡ πίστις αὐτοῦ εἰς δικαιοσύνην· **6** καθάπερ καὶ Δαυὶδ λέγει τὸν μακαρισμὸν τοῦ ἀνθρώπου ᾧ ὁ θεὸς λογίζεται δικαιοσύνην χωρὶς ἔργων,

7 Μακάριοι ὧν ἀφέθησαν αἱ ἀνομίαι καὶ ὧν ἐπεκαλύφθησαν αἱ ἁμαρτίαι·

8 μακάριος ἀνὴρ οὗ οὐ μὴ λογίσηται κύριος ἁμαρτίαν.

9 ὁ μακαρισμὸς οὖν οὗτος ἐπὶ τὴν περιτομὴν ἢ καὶ ἐπὶ τὴν ἀκροβυστίαν; λέγομεν γάρ, Ἐλογίσθη τῷ Ἀβραὰμ ἡ πίστις εἰς δικαιοσύνην. **10** πῶς οὖν ἐλογίσθη; ἐν περιτομῇ ὄντι ἢ ἐν ἀκροβυστίᾳ; οὐκ ἐν περιτομῇ ἀλλ' ἐν ἀκροβυστίᾳ· **11** καὶ σημεῖον ἔλαβεν περιτομῆς σφραγῖδα τῆς δικαιοσύνης τῆς πίστεως τῆς ἐν τῇ ἀκροβυστίᾳ, εἰς τὸ εἶναι αὐτὸν πατέρα πάντων τῶν πιστευόντων δι' ἀκροβυστίας, εἰς τὸ λογισθῆναι [καὶ][b] αὐτοῖς [τὴν] δικαιοσύνην, **12** καὶ πατέρα περιτομῆς τοῖς οὐκ ἐκ περιτομῆς μόνον ἀλλὰ καὶ τοῖς στοιχοῦσιν τοῖς ἴχνεσιν τῆς ἐν ἀκροβυστίᾳ πίστεως τοῦ πατρὸς ἡμῶν Ἀβραάμ.

13 Οὐ γὰρ διὰ νόμου ἡ ἐπαγγελία τῷ Ἀβραὰμ ἢ τῷ σπέρματι αὐτοῦ, τὸ κληρονόμον αὐτὸν εἶναι κόσμου, ἀλλὰ διὰ δικαιοσύνης πίστεως. **14** εἰ γὰρ οἱ ἐκ νόμου κληρονόμοι, κεκένωται ἡ

---

the law? No, but on that of faith. [28]For we maintain that a man is justified by faith apart from observing the law. [29]Is God the God of Jews only? Is he not the God of Gentiles too? Yes, of Gentiles too, [30]since there is only one God, who will justify the circumcised by faith and the uncircumcised through that same faith. [31]Do we, then, nullify the law by this faith? Not at all! Rather, we uphold the law.

Abraham Justified by Faith

4 What then shall we say that Abraham, our forefather, discovered in this matter? [2]If, in fact, Abraham was justified by works, he had something to boast about— but not before God. [3]What does the Scripture say? "Abraham believed God, and it was credited to him as righteousness."[a]

[4]Now when a man works, his wages are not credited to him as a gift, but as an obligation. [5]However, to the man who does not work but trusts God who justifies the wicked, his faith is credited as righteousness. [6]David says the same thing when he speaks of the blessedness of the man to whom God credits righteousness apart from works:

[7]"Blessed are they
    whose transgressions are forgiven,
    whose sins are covered.
[8]Blessed is the man
    whose sin the Lord will never count
     against him."[b]

[9]Is this blessedness only for the circumcised, or also for the uncircumcised? We have been saying that Abraham's faith was credited to him as righteousness. [10]Under what circumstances was it credited? Was it after he was circumcised, or before? It was not after, but before! [11]And he received the sign of circumcision, a seal of the righteousness that he had by faith while he was still uncircumcised. So then, he is the father of all who believe but have not been circumcised, in order that righteousness might be credited to them. [12]And he is also the father of the circumcised who not only are circumcised but who also walk in the footsteps of the faith that our father Abraham had before he was circumcised.

[13]It was not through law that Abraham and his offspring received the promise that he would be heir of the world, but through the righteousness that comes by faith. [14]For if those who live by law are heirs, faith has

---

heirs, faith is null and the promise is void. [15]For the law brings wrath; but where there is no law, neither is there violation.

16 For this reason it depends on faith, in order that the promise may rest on grace and be guaranteed to all his descendants, not only to those who are the adherents of the law but also to those who share the faith of Abraham (for he is the father of all of us, [17]as it is written, "I have made you the father of many nations")—in the presence of the God in whom he believed, who gives life to the dead and calls into existence the things that do not exist. [18]Hoping against hope, he believed that he would become "the father of many nations," according to what was said, "So numerous shall your descendants be." [19]He did not weaken in faith when he considered his own body, which was already[o] as good as dead (for he was about a hundred years old), or when he considered the barrenness of Sarah's womb. [20]No distrust made him waver concerning the promise of God, but he grew strong in his faith as he gave glory to God, [21]being fully convinced that God was able to do what he had promised. [22]Therefore his faith[p] "was reckoned to him as righteousness." [23]Now the words, "it was reckoned to him," were written not for his sake alone, [24]but for ours also. It will be reckoned to us who believe in him who raised Jesus our Lord from the dead, [25]who was handed over to death for our trespasses and was raised for our justification.

Results of Justification

5 Therefore, since we are justified by faith, we[q] have peace with God through our Lord Jesus Christ, [2]through whom we have obtained access[r] to this grace in which we stand; and we[s] boast in our hope of sharing the glory of God. [3]And not only that, but we[s] also boast in our sufferings, knowing that suffering produces endurance, [4]and endurance produces character, and character produces hope, [5]and hope does not disappoint us, because God's love has been poured into our hearts through the Holy Spirit that has been given to us.

6 For while we were still weak, at the right time Christ died for the ungodly. [7]Indeed, rarely will anyone die for a righteous person—though perhaps for a good person someone might actually dare to die.

πίστις καὶ κατήργηται ἡ ἐπαγγελία·
15 ὁ γὰρ νόμος ὀργὴν κατεργάζεται·
οὗ δὲ οὐκ ἔστιν νόμος οὐδὲ παράβασις.
16 διὰ τοῦτο ἐκ πίστεως, ἵνα κατὰ
χάριν, εἰς τὸ εἶναι βεβαίαν τὴν
ἐπαγγελίαν παντὶ τῷ σπέρματι, οὐ τῷ
ἐκ τοῦ νόμου μόνον ἀλλὰ καὶ τῷ ἐκ
πίστεως Ἀβραάμ, ὅς ἐστιν πατὴρ
πάντων ἡμῶν, 17 καθὼς γέγραπται ὅτι
Πατέρα πολλῶν ἐθνῶν τέθεικά σε,
κατέναντι οὗ ἐπίστευσεν θεοῦ τοῦ ζῳ-
οποιοῦντος τοὺς νεκροὺς καὶ καλοῦντος
τὰ μὴ ὄντα ὡς ὄντα· 18 ὃς παρ' ἐλπίδα
ἐπ' ἐλπίδι ἐπίστευσεν εἰς τὸ γενέσθαι
αὐτὸν **πατέρα πολλῶν ἐθνῶν** κατὰ τὸ
εἰρημένον, **Οὕτως ἔσται τὸ σπέρμα
σου,** 19 καὶ μὴ ἀσθενήσας τῇ πίστει
κατενόησεν τὸ ἑαυτοῦ σῶμα [ἤδη][c]
νενεκρωμένον, ἑκατονταετής που
ὑπάρχων, καὶ τὴν νέκρωσιν τῆς μήτρας
Σάρρας· 20 εἰς δὲ τὴν ἐπαγγελίαν τοῦ
θεοῦ οὐ διεκρίθη τῇ ἀπιστίᾳ ἀλλ'
ἐνεδυναμώθη τῇ πίστει, δοὺς δόξαν
τῷ θεῷ 21 καὶ πληροφορηθεὶς ὅτι ὃ
ἐπήγγελται δυνατός ἐστιν καὶ ποιῆσαι.
22 διὸ [καὶ] ἐλογίσθη αὐτῷ εἰς δικαιοσύνην. 23 Οὐκ ἐγράφη δὲ δι' αὐτὸν
μόνον ὅτι ἐλογίσθη αὐτῷ 24 ἀλλὰ καὶ
δι' ἡμᾶς, οἷς μέλλει λογίζεσθαι, τοῖς
πιστεύουσιν ἐπὶ τὸν ἐγείραντα Ἰησοῦν
τὸν κύριον ἡμῶν ἐκ νεκρῶν, 25 ὃς
παρεδόθη διὰ τὰ παραπτώματα ἡμῶν
καὶ ἠγέρθη διὰ τὴν δικαίωσιν ἡμῶν.

5 Δικαιωθέντες οὖν ἐκ πίστεως
εἰρήνην ἔχομεν[a] πρὸς τὸν θεὸν
διὰ τοῦ κυρίου ἡμῶν Ἰησοῦ Χριστοῦ
2 δι' οὗ καὶ τὴν προσαγωγὴν ἐσχήκαμεν
[τῇ πίστει][b] εἰς τὴν χάριν ταύτην ἐν
ᾗ ἑστήκαμεν καὶ καυχώμεθα ἐπ' ἐλπίδι
τῆς δόξης τοῦ θεοῦ. 3 οὐ μόνον δέ,
ἀλλὰ καὶ καυχώμεθα ἐν ταῖς θλίψεσιν,
εἰδότες ὅτι ἡ θλῖψις ὑπομονὴν κατεργάζεται, 4 ἡ δὲ ὑπομονὴ δοκιμήν, ἡ δὲ
δοκιμὴ ἐλπίδα. 5 ἡ δὲ ἐλπὶς οὐ
καταισχύνει, ὅτι ἡ ἀγάπη τοῦ θεοῦ
ἐκκέχυται ἐν ταῖς καρδίαις ἡμῶν διὰ
πνεύματος ἁγίου τοῦ δοθέντος ἡμῖν.
6 ἔτι γὰρ Χριστὸς ὄντων ἡμῶν ἀσθενῶν
ἔτι κατὰ καιρὸν ὑπὲρ ἀσεβῶν ἀπέθανεν.
7 μόλις γὰρ ὑπὲρ δικαίου τις ἀποθα-
νεῖται· ὑπὲρ γὰρ τοῦ ἀγαθοῦ τάχα τις
καὶ τολμᾷ ἀποθανεῖν· 8 συνίστησιν δὲ

---

no value and the promise is worthless, [15]because law brings wrath. And where there is no law there is no transgression.

[16]Therefore, the promise comes by faith, so that it may be by grace and may be guaranteed to all Abraham's offspring—not only to those who are of the law but also to those who are of the faith of Abraham. He is the father of us all. [17]As it is written: "I have made you a father of many nations."[c] He is our father in the sight of God, in whom he believed—the God who gives life to the dead and calls things that are not as though they were.

[18]Against all hope, Abraham in hope believed and so became the father of many nations, just as it had been said to him, "So shall your offspring be."[d] [19]Without weakening in his faith, he faced the fact that his body was as good as dead—since he was about a hundred years old—and that Sarah's womb was also dead. [20]Yet he did not waver through unbelief regarding the promise of God, but was strengthened in his faith and gave glory to God, [21]being fully persuaded that God had power to do what he had promised. [22]This is why it was credited to him as righteousness." [23]The words "it was credited to him" were written not for him alone, [24]but also for us, to whom God will credit righteousness—for us who believe in him who raised Jesus our Lord from the dead. [25]He was delivered over to death for our sins and was raised to life for our justification.

Peace and Joy

5 Therefore, since we have been justified through faith, we[a] have peace with God through our Lord Jesus Christ, [2]through whom we have gained access by faith into this grace in which we now stand. And we[a] rejoice in the hope of the glory of God. [3]Not only so, but we[a] also rejoice in our sufferings, because we know that suffering produces perseverance; [4]perseverance, character; and character, hope. [5]And hope does not disappoint us, because God has poured out his love into our hearts by the Holy Spirit, whom he has given us.

[6]You see, at just the right time, when we were still powerless, Christ died for the ungodly. [7]Very rarely will anyone die for a righteous man, though for a good man someone might possibly dare to die. [8]But

---

o Other ancient authorities lack *already*   p Gk *Therefore it*
q Other ancient authorities read *let us*   r Other ancient
authorities add *by faith*   s Or *let us*

c19 NRSV note o omits ἤδη   a1 NRSV note q ἔχωμεν
b2 NRSV text omits τῇ πίστει; NRSV note r as UBS

c17 Gen. 17:5   d18 Gen. 15:5   a1,2,3 Or *let us*

8But God proves his love for us in that while we still were sinners Christ died for us. 9Much more surely then, now that we have been justified by his blood, will we be saved through him from the wrath of God.t 10For if while we were enemies, we were reconciled to God through the death of his Son, much more surely, having been reconciled, will we be saved by his life! 11But more than that, we even boast in God through our Lord Jesus Christ, through whom we have now received reconciliation.

Adam and Christ

12 Therefore, just as sin came into the world through one man, and death came through sin, and so death spread to all because all have sinned— 13sin was indeed in the world before the law, but sin is not reckoned when there is no law. 14Yet death exercised dominion from Adam to Moses, even over those whose sins were not like the transgression of Adam, who is a type of the one who was to come.

15 But the free gift is not like the trespass. For if the many died through the one man's trespass, much more surely have the grace of God and the free gift in the grace of the one man, Jesus Christ, abounded for the many. 16And the free gift is not like the effect of the one man's sin. For the judgment following one trespass brought condemnation, but the free gift following many trespasses brings justification. 17If, because of the one man's trespass, death exercised dominion through that one, much more surely will those who receive the abundance of grace and the free gift of righteousness exercise dominion in life through the one man, Jesus Christ.

18 Therefore just as one man's trespass led to condemnation for all, so one man's act of righteousness leads to justification and life for all. 19For just as by the one man's disobedience the many were made sinners, so by the one man's obedience the many will be made righteous. 20But law came in, with the result that the trespass multiplied; but where sin increased, grace abounded all the more, 21so that, just as sin exercised dominion in death, so grace might also exercise dominion through justificationu leading to eternal life through Jesus Christ our Lord.

τὴν ἑαυτοῦ ἀγάπην εἰς ἡμᾶς ὁ θεός, ὅτι ἔτι ἁμαρτωλῶν ὄντων ἡμῶν Χριστὸς ὑπὲρ ἡμῶν ἀπέθανεν. 9 πολλῷ οὖν μᾶλλον δικαιωθέντες νῦν ἐν τῷ αἵματι αὐτοῦ σωθησόμεθα δι' αὐτοῦ ἀπὸ τῆς ὀργῆς. 10 εἰ γὰρ ἐχθροὶ ὄντες κατηλλάγημεν τῷ θεῷ διὰ τοῦ θανάτου τοῦ υἱοῦ αὐτοῦ, πολλῷ μᾶλλον καταλλαγέντες σωθησόμεθα ἐν τῇ ζωῇ αὐτοῦ· 11 οὐ μόνον δέ, ἀλλὰ καὶ καυχώμενοι ἐν τῷ θεῷ διὰ τοῦ κυρίου ἡμῶν Ἰησοῦ Χριστοῦ δι' οὗ νῦν τὴν καταλλαγὴν ἐλάβομεν.

12 Διὰ τοῦτο ὥσπερ δι' ἑνὸς ἀνθρώπου ἡ ἁμαρτία εἰς τὸν κόσμον εἰσῆλθεν καὶ διὰ τῆς ἁμαρτίας ὁ θάνατος, καὶ οὕτως εἰς πάντας ἀνθρώπους ὁ θάνατος διῆλθεν, ἐφ' ᾧ πάντες ἥμαρτον· 13 ἄχρι γὰρ νόμου ἁμαρτία ἦν ἐν κόσμῳ, ἁμαρτία δὲ οὐκ ἐλλογεῖται μὴ ὄντος νόμου, 14 ἀλλὰ ἐβασίλευσεν ὁ θάνατος ἀπὸ Ἀδὰμ μέχρι Μωϋσέως καὶ ἐπὶ τοὺς μὴ ἁμαρτήσαντας ἐπὶ τῷ ὁμοιώματι τῆς παραβάσεως Ἀδὰμ ὅς ἐστιν τύπος τοῦ μέλλοντος.

15 Ἀλλ' οὐχ ὡς τὸ παράπτωμα, οὕτως καὶ τὸ χάρισμα· εἰ γὰρ τῷ τοῦ ἑνὸς παραπτώματι οἱ πολλοὶ ἀπέθανον, πολλῷ μᾶλλον ἡ χάρις τοῦ θεοῦ καὶ ἡ δωρεὰ ἐν χάριτι τῇ τοῦ ἑνὸς ἀνθρώπου Ἰησοῦ Χριστοῦ εἰς τοὺς πολλοὺς ἐπερίσσευσεν. 16 καὶ οὐχ ὡς δι' ἑνὸς ἁμαρτήσαντος τὸ δώρημα· τὸ μὲν γὰρ κρίμα ἐξ ἑνὸς εἰς κατάκριμα, τὸ δὲ χάρισμα ἐκ πολλῶν παραπτωμάτων εἰς δικαίωμα. 17 εἰ γὰρ τῷ τοῦ ἑνὸς παραπτώματι ὁ θάνατος ἐβασίλευσεν διὰ τοῦ ἑνός, πολλῷ μᾶλλον οἱ τὴν περισσείαν τῆς χάριτος καὶ τῆς δωρεᾶς τῆς δικαιοσύνης λαμβάνοντες ἐν ζωῇ βασιλεύσουσιν διὰ τοῦ ἑνὸς Ἰησοῦ Χριστοῦ. 18 Ἄρα οὖν ὡς δι' ἑνὸς παραπτώματος εἰς πάντας ἀνθρώπους εἰς κατάκριμα, οὕτως καὶ δι' ἑνὸς δικαιώματος εἰς πάντας ἀνθρώπους εἰς δικαίωσιν ζωῆς· 19 ὥσπερ γὰρ διὰ τῆς παρακοῆς τοῦ ἑνὸς ἀνθρώπου ἁμαρτωλοὶ κατεστάθησαν οἱ πολλοί, οὕτως καὶ διὰ τῆς ὑπακοῆς τοῦ ἑνὸς δίκαιοι κατασταθήσονται οἱ πολλοί. 20 νόμος δὲ παρεισῆλθεν, ἵνα πλεονάσῃ τὸ παράπτωμα· οὗ δὲ ἐπλεόνασεν ἡ ἁμαρτία, ὑπερεπερίσσευσεν ἡ χάρις, 21 ἵνα ὥσπερ ἐβασίλευσεν ἡ ἁμαρτία ἐν τῷ θανάτῳ, οὕτως καὶ ἡ χάρις βασιλεύσῃ διὰ δικαιοσύνης εἰς ζωὴν αἰώνιον διὰ Ἰησοῦ Χριστοῦ τοῦ κυρίου ἡμῶν.

God demonstrates his own love for us in this: While we were still sinners, Christ died for us.

9Since we have now been justified by his blood, how much more shall we be saved from God's wrath through him! 10For if, when we were God's enemies, we were reconciled to him through the death of his Son, how much more, having been reconciled, shall we be saved through his life! 11Not only is this so, but we also rejoice in God through our Lord Jesus Christ, through whom we have now received reconciliation.

Death Through Adam, Life Through Christ

12Therefore, just as sin entered the world through one man, and death through sin, and in this way death came to all men, because all sinned— 13for before the law was given, sin was in the world. But sin is not taken into account when there is no law. 14Nevertheless, death reigned from the time of Adam to the time of Moses, even over those who did not sin by breaking a command, as did Adam, who was a pattern of the one to come.

15But the gift is not like the trespass. For if the many died by the trespass of the one man, how much more did God's grace and the gift that came by the grace of the one man, Jesus Christ, overflow to the many! 16Again, the gift of God is not like the result of the one man's sin: The judgment followed one sin and brought condemnation, but the gift followed many trespasses and brought justification. 17For if, by the trespass of the one man, death reigned through that one man, how much more will those who receive God's abundant provision of grace and of the gift of righteousness reign in life through the one man, Jesus Christ.

18Consequently, just as the result of one trespass was condemnation for all men, so also the result of one act of righteousness was justification that brings life for all men. 19For just as through the disobedience of the one man the many were made sinners, so also through the obedience of the one man the many will be made righteous.

20The law was added so that the trespass might increase. But where sin increased, grace increased all the more, 21so that, just as sin reigned in death, so also grace might reign through righteousness to bring eternal life through Jesus Christ our Lord.

---

tGk *the wrath*   uOr *righteousness*

Dying and Rising with Christ

6 What then are we to say? Should we continue in sin in order that grace may abound? [2]By no means! How can we who died to sin go on living in it? [3]Do you not know that all of us who have been baptized into Christ Jesus were baptized into his death? [4]Therefore we have been buried with him by baptism into death, so that, just as Christ was raised from the dead by the glory of the Father, so we too might walk in newness of life.

5 For if we have been united with him in a death like his, we will certainly be united with him in a resurrection like his. [6]We know that our old self was crucified with him so that the body of sin might be destroyed, and we might no longer be enslaved to sin. [7]For whoever has died is freed from sin. [8]But if we have died with Christ, we believe that we will also live with him. [9]We know that Christ, being raised from the dead, will never die again; death no longer has dominion over him. [10]The death he died, he died to sin, once for all; but the life he lives, he lives to God. [11]So you also must consider yourselves dead to sin and alive to God in Christ Jesus.

12 Therefore, do not let sin exercise dominion in your mortal bodies, to make you obey their passions. [13]No longer present your members to sin as instruments[v] of wickedness, but present yourselves to God as those who have been brought from death to life, and present your members to God as instruments[v] of righteousness. [14]For sin will have no dominion over you, since you are not under law but under grace.

Slaves of Righteousness

15 What then? Should we sin because we are not under law but under grace? By no means! [16]Do you not know that if you present yourselves to anyone as obedient slaves, you are slaves of the one whom you obey, either of sin, which leads to death, or of obedience, which leads to righteousness? [17]But thanks be to God that you, having once been slaves of sin, have become obedient from the heart to the form of teaching to which you were entrusted, [18]and that you, having been set free from sin, have become slaves of righteousness. [19]I am speaking in human terms because of your natural limitations.[w] For just as

6 Τί οὖν ἐροῦμεν; ἐπιμένωμεν τῇ ἁμαρτίᾳ, ἵνα ἡ χάρις πλεονάσῃ; [2]μὴ γένοιτο. οἵτινες ἀπεθάνομεν τῇ ἁμαρτίᾳ, πῶς ἔτι ζήσομεν ἐν αὐτῇ; [3]ἢ ἀγνοεῖτε ὅτι, ὅσοι ἐβαπτίσθημεν εἰς Χριστὸν Ἰησοῦν, εἰς τὸν θάνατον αὐτοῦ ἐβαπτίσθημεν; [4]συνετάφημεν οὖν αὐτῷ διὰ τοῦ βαπτίσματος εἰς τὸν θάνατον, ἵνα ὥσπερ ἠγέρθη Χριστὸς ἐκ νεκρῶν διὰ τῆς δόξης τοῦ πατρός, οὕτως καὶ ἡμεῖς ἐν καινότητι ζωῆς περιπατήσωμεν. [5]εἰ γὰρ σύμφυτοι γεγόναμεν τῷ ὁμοιώματι τοῦ θανάτου αὐτοῦ, ἀλλὰ καὶ τῆς ἀναστάσεως ἐσόμεθα· [6]τοῦτο γινώσκοντες ὅτι ὁ παλαιὸς ἡμῶν ἄνθρωπος συνεσταυρώθη, ἵνα καταργηθῇ τὸ σῶμα τῆς ἁμαρτίας, τοῦ μηκέτι δουλεύειν ἡμᾶς τῇ ἁμαρτίᾳ· [7]ὁ γὰρ ἀποθανὼν δεδικαίωται ἀπὸ τῆς ἁμαρτίας. [8]εἰ δὲ ἀπεθάνομεν σὺν Χριστῷ, πιστεύομεν ὅτι καὶ συζήσομεν αὐτῷ, [9]εἰδότες ὅτι Χριστὸς ἐγερθεὶς ἐκ νεκρῶν οὐκέτι ἀποθνῄσκει, θάνατος αὐτοῦ οὐκέτι κυριεύει. [10]ὃ γὰρ ἀπέθανεν, τῇ ἁμαρτίᾳ ἀπέθανεν ἐφάπαξ· ὃ δὲ ζῇ, ζῇ τῷ θεῷ. [11]οὕτως καὶ ὑμεῖς λογίζεσθε ἑαυτοὺς [εἶναι][a] νεκροὺς μὲν τῇ ἁμαρτίᾳ ζῶντας δὲ τῷ θεῷ ἐν Χριστῷ Ἰησοῦ.

[12]Μὴ οὖν βασιλευέτω ἡ ἁμαρτία ἐν τῷ θνητῷ ὑμῶν σώματι εἰς τὸ ὑπακούειν ταῖς ἐπιθυμίαις αὐτοῦ, [13]μηδὲ παριστάνετε τὰ μέλη ὑμῶν ὅπλα ἀδικίας τῇ ἁμαρτίᾳ, ἀλλὰ παραστήσατε ἑαυτοὺς τῷ θεῷ ὡσεὶ ἐκ νεκρῶν ζῶντας καὶ τὰ μέλη ὑμῶν ὅπλα δικαιοσύνης τῷ θεῷ. [14]ἁμαρτία γὰρ ὑμῶν οὐ κυριεύσει· οὐ γάρ ἐστε ὑπὸ νόμον ἀλλὰ ὑπὸ χάριν.

[15]Τί οὖν; ἁμαρτήσωμεν, ὅτι οὐκ ἐσμὲν ὑπὸ νόμον ἀλλὰ ὑπὸ χάριν; μὴ γένοιτο. [16]οὐκ οἴδατε ὅτι ᾧ παριστάνετε ἑαυτοὺς δούλους εἰς ὑπακοήν, δοῦλοί ἐστε ᾧ ὑπακούετε, ἤτοι ἁμαρτίας εἰς θάνατον ἢ ὑπακοῆς εἰς δικαιοσύνην; [17]χάρις δὲ τῷ θεῷ ὅτι ἦτε δοῦλοι τῆς ἁμαρτίας ὑπηκούσατε δὲ ἐκ καρδίας εἰς ὃν παρεδόθητε τύπον διδαχῆς, [18]ἐλευθερωθέντες δὲ ἀπὸ τῆς ἁμαρτίας ἐδουλώθητε τῇ δικαιοσύνῃ. [19]ἀνθρώπινον λέγω διὰ τὴν ἀσθένειαν τῆς σαρκὸς ὑμῶν. ὥσπερ γὰρ παρεστήσατε

Dead to Sin, Alive in Christ

6 What shall we say, then? Shall we go on sinning so that grace may increase? [2]By no means! We died to sin; how can we live in it any longer? [3]Or don't you know that all of us who were baptized into Christ Jesus were baptized into his death? [4]We were therefore buried with him through baptism into death in order that, just as Christ was raised from the dead through the glory of the Father, we too may live a new life.

[5]If we have been united with him like this in his death, we will certainly also be united with him in his resurrection. [6]For we know that our old self was crucified with him so that the body of sin might be done away with,[a] that we should no longer be slaves to sin— [7]because anyone who has died has been freed from sin.

[8]Now if we died with Christ, we believe that we will also live with him. [9]For we know that since Christ was raised from the dead, he cannot die again; death no longer has mastery over him. [10]The death he died, he died to sin once for all; but the life he lives, he lives to God.

[11]In the same way, count yourselves dead to sin but alive to God in Christ Jesus. [12]Therefore do not let sin reign in your mortal body so that you obey its evil desires. [13]Do not offer the parts of your body to sin, as instruments of wickedness, but rather offer yourselves to God, as those who have been brought from death to life; and offer the parts of your body to him as instruments of righteousness. [14]For sin shall not be your master, because you are not under law, but under grace.

Slaves to Righteousness

[15]What then? Shall we sin because we are not under law but under grace? By no means! [16]Don't you know that when you offer yourselves to someone to obey him as slaves, you are slaves to the one whom you obey—whether you are slaves to sin, which leads to death, or to obedience, which leads to righteousness? [17]But thanks be to God that, though you used to be slaves to sin, you wholeheartedly obeyed the form of teaching to which you were entrusted. [18]You have been set free from sin and have become slaves to righteousness.

[19]I put this in human terms because you are weak in your natural selves. Just as

---

[v] Or *weapons*   [w] Gk *the weakness of your flesh*   [a]11 NIV text omits εἶναι †   [a]6 Or *be rendered powerless*

you once presented your members as slaves to impurity and to greater and greater iniquity, so now present your members as slaves to righteousness for sanctification.

20 When you were slaves of sin, you were free in regard to righteousness. 21So what advantage did you then get from the things of which you now are ashamed? The end of those things is death. 22But now that you have been freed from sin and enslaved to God, the advantage you get is sanctification. The end is eternal life. 23For the wages of sin is death, but the free gift of God is eternal life in Christ Jesus our Lord.

An Analogy from Marriage

7 Do you not know, brothers and sisters[x]—for I am speaking to those who know the law—that the law is binding on a person only during that person's lifetime? 2Thus a married woman is bound by the law to her husband as long as he lives; but if her husband dies, she is discharged from the law concerning the husband. 3Accordingly, she will be called an adulteress if she lives with another man while her husband is alive. But if her husband dies, she is free from that law, and if she marries another man, she is not an adulteress.

4 In the same way, my friends,[x] you have died to the law through the body of Christ, so that you may belong to another, to him who has been raised from the dead in order that we may bear fruit for God. 5While we were living in the flesh, our sinful passions, aroused by the law, were at work in our members to bear fruit for death. 6But now we are discharged from the law, dead to that which held us captive, so that we are slaves not under the old written code but in the new life of the Spirit.

The Law and Sin

7 What then should we say? That the law is sin? By no means! Yet, if it had not been for the law, I would not have known sin. I would not have known what it is to covet if the law had not said, "You shall not covet." 8But sin, seizing an opportunity in the commandment, produced in me all kinds of covetousness. Apart from the law sin lies dead. 9I was once alive apart from the law, but when the commandment came, sin revived 10and I died, and the very

τὰ μέλη ὑμῶν δοῦλα τῇ ἀκαθαρσίᾳ καὶ τῇ ἀνομίᾳ εἰς τὴν ἀνομίαν, οὕτως νῦν παραστήσατε τὰ μέλη ὑμῶν δοῦλα τῇ δικαιοσύνῃ εἰς ἁγιασμόν. 20 ὅτε γὰρ δοῦλοι ἦτε τῆς ἁμαρτίας, ἐλεύθεροι ἦτε τῇ δικαιοσύνῃ. 21 τίνα οὖν καρπὸν εἴχετε τότε; ἐφ᾽ οἷς νῦν ἐπαισχύνεσθε, τὸ γὰρ τέλος ἐκείνων θάνατος. 22 νυνὶ δὲ ἐλευθερωθέντες ἀπὸ τῆς ἁμαρτίας δουλωθέντες δὲ τῷ θεῷ ἔχετε τὸν καρπὸν ὑμῶν εἰς ἁγιασμόν, τὸ δὲ τέλος ζωὴν αἰώνιον. 23 τὰ γὰρ ὀψώνια τῆς ἁμαρτίας θάνατος, τὸ δὲ χάρισμα τοῦ θεοῦ ζωὴ αἰώνιος ἐν Χριστῷ Ἰησοῦ τῷ κυρίῳ ἡμῶν.

7 Ἢ ἀγνοεῖτε, ἀδελφοί, γινώσκουσιν γὰρ νόμον λαλῶ, ὅτι ὁ νόμος κυριεύει τοῦ ἀνθρώπου ἐφ᾽ ὅσον χρόνον ζῇ; 2 ἡ γὰρ ὕπανδρος γυνὴ τῷ ζῶντι ἀνδρὶ δέδεται νόμῳ· ἐὰν δὲ ἀποθάνη ὁ ἀνήρ, κατήργηται ἀπὸ τοῦ νόμου τοῦ ἀνδρός. 3 ἄρα οὖν ζῶντος τοῦ ἀνδρὸς μοιχαλὶς χρηματίσει ἐὰν γένηται ἀνδρὶ ἑτέρῳ· ἐὰν δὲ ἀποθάνη ὁ ἀνήρ, ἐλευθέρα ἐστὶν ἀπὸ τοῦ νόμου, τοῦ μὴ εἶναι αὐτὴν μοιχαλίδα γενομένην ἀνδρὶ ἑτέρῳ. 4 ὥστε, ἀδελφοί μου, καὶ ὑμεῖς ἐθανατώθητε τῷ νόμῳ διὰ τοῦ σώματος τοῦ Χριστοῦ, εἰς τὸ γενέσθαι ὑμᾶς ἑτέρῳ, τῷ ἐκ νεκρῶν ἐγερθέντι, ἵνα καρποφορήσωμεν τῷ θεῷ. 5 ὅτε γὰρ ἦμεν ἐν τῇ σαρκί, τὰ παθήματα τῶν ἁμαρτιῶν τὰ διὰ τοῦ νόμου ἐνηργεῖτο ἐν τοῖς μέλεσιν ἡμῶν, εἰς τὸ καρποφορῆσαι τῷ θανάτῳ· 6 νυνὶ δὲ κατηργήθημεν ἀπὸ τοῦ νόμου ἀποθανόντες ἐν ᾧ κατειχόμεθα, ὥστε δουλεύειν ἡμᾶς ἐν καινότητι πνεύματος καὶ οὐ παλαιότητι γράμματος.

7 Τί οὖν ἐροῦμεν; ὁ νόμος ἁμαρτία; μὴ γένοιτο· ἀλλὰ τὴν ἁμαρτίαν οὐκ ἔγνων εἰ μὴ διὰ νόμου· τήν τε γὰρ ἐπιθυμίαν οὐκ ᾔδειν εἰ μὴ ὁ νόμος ἔλεγεν, Οὐκ ἐπιθυμήσεις. 8 ἀφορμὴν δὲ λαβοῦσα ἡ ἁμαρτία διὰ τῆς ἐντολῆς κατειργάσατο ἐν ἐμοὶ πᾶσαν ἐπιθυμίαν· χωρὶς γὰρ νόμου ἁμαρτία νεκρά. 9 ἐγὼ δὲ ἔζων χωρὶς νόμου ποτέ, ἐλθούσης δὲ τῆς ἐντολῆς ἡ ἁμαρτία ἀνέζησεν, 10 ἐγὼ δὲ ἀπέθανον[a] καὶ εὑρέθη μοι ἡ

you used to offer the parts of your body in slavery to impurity and to ever-increasing wickedness, so now offer them in slavery to righteousness leading to holiness. 20When you were slaves to sin, you were free from the control of righteousness. 21What benefit did you reap at that time from the things you are now ashamed of? Those things result in death! 22But now that you have been set free from sin and have become slaves to God, the benefit you reap leads to holiness, and the result is eternal life. 23For the wages of sin is death, but the gift of God is eternal life in[b] Christ Jesus our Lord.

An Illustration From Marriage

7 Do you not know, brothers—for I am speaking to men who know the law—that the law has authority over a man only as long as he lives? 2For example, by law a married woman is bound to her husband as long as he is alive, but if her husband dies, she is released from the law of marriage. 3So then, if she marries another man while her husband is still alive, she is called an adulteress. But if her husband dies, she is released from that law and is not an adulteress, even though she marries another man.

4So, my brothers, you also died to the law through the body of Christ, that you might belong to another, to him who was raised from the dead, in order that we might bear fruit to God. 5For when we were controlled by the sinful nature,[a] the sinful passions aroused by the law were at work in our bodies, so that we bore fruit for death. 6But now, by dying to what once bound us, we have been released from the law so that we serve in the new way of the Spirit, and not in the old way of the written code.

Struggling With Sin

7What shall we say, then? Is the law sin? Certainly not! Indeed I would not have known what sin was except through the law. For I would not have known what coveting really was if the law had not said, "Do not covet."[b] 8But sin, seizing the opportunity afforded by the commandment, produced in me every kind of covetous desire. For apart from law, sin is dead. 9Once I was alive apart from law; but when the commandment came, sin sprang to life and I died. 10I found that the very

---

     a10 NIV begins verse 10 after ἀπέθανον   b23 Or *through*; a5 Or *the flesh*; also in verse 25
b7 Exodus 20:17; Deut. 5:21

commandment that promised life proved to be death to me. ¹¹For sin, seizing an opportunity in the commandment, deceived me and through it killed me. ¹²So the law is holy, and the commandment is holy and just and good.

13 Did what is good, then, bring death to me? By no means! It was sin, working death in me through what is good, in order that sin might be shown to be sin, and through the commandment might become sinful beyond measure.

The Inner Conflict

14 For we know that the law is spiritual; but I am of the flesh, sold into slavery under sin.ʸ ¹⁵I do not understand my own actions. For I do not do what I want, but I do the very thing I hate. ¹⁶Now if I do what I do not want, I agree that the law is good. ¹⁷But in fact it is no longer I that do it, but sin that dwells within me. ¹⁸For I know that nothing good dwells within me, that is, in my flesh. I can will what is right, but I cannot do it. ¹⁹For I do not do the good I want, but the evil I do not want is what I do. ²⁰Now if I do what I do not want, it is no longer I that do it, but sin that dwells within me.

21 So I find it to be a law that when I want to do what is good, evil lies close at hand. ²²For I delight in the law of God in my inmost self, ²³but I see in my members another law at war with the law of my mind, making me captive to the law of sin that dwells in my members. ²⁴Wretched man that I am! Who will rescue me from this body of death? ²⁵Thanks be to God through Jesus Christ our Lord!

So then, with my mind I am a slave to the law of God, but with my flesh I am a slave to the law of sin.

Life in the Spirit

8 There is therefore now no condemnation for those who are in Christ Jesus. ²For the law of the Spiritᶻ of life in Christ Jesus has set youᵃ free from the law of sin and of death. ³For God has done what the law, weakened by the flesh, could not do: by sending his own Son in the likeness of sinful flesh, and to deal with sin,ᵇ he condemned sin in the flesh, ⁴so that the just requirement of the law might be fulfilled

ἐντολὴ ἡ εἰς ζωήν, αὕτη εἰς θάνατον· 11 ἡ γὰρ ἁμαρτία ἀφορμὴν λαβοῦσα διὰ τῆς ἐντολῆς ἐξηπάτησέν με καὶ δι' αὐτῆς ἀπέκτεινεν. 12 ὥστε ὁ μὲν νόμος ἅγιος καὶ ἡ ἐντολὴ ἁγία καὶ δικαία καὶ ἀγαθή.

13 Τὸ οὖν ἀγαθὸν ἐμοὶ ἐγένετο θάνατος; μὴ γένοιτο· ἀλλὰ ἡ ἁμαρτία, ἵνα φανῇ ἁμαρτία, διὰ τοῦ ἀγαθοῦ μοι κατεργαζομένη θάνατον, ἵνα γένηται καθ' ὑπερβολὴν ἁμαρτωλὸς ἡ ἁμαρτία διὰ τῆς ἐντολῆς. 14 οἴδαμεν γὰρ ὅτι ὁ νόμος πνευματικός ἐστιν, ἐγὼ δὲ σάρκινός εἰμι πεπραμένος ὑπὸ τὴν ἁμαρτίαν. 15 ὃ γὰρ κατεργάζομαι οὐ γινώσκω· οὐ γὰρ ὃ θέλω τοῦτο πράσσω, ἀλλ' ὃ μισῶ τοῦτο ποιῶ. 16 εἰ δὲ ὃ οὐ θέλω τοῦτο ποιῶ, σύμφημι τῷ νόμῳ ὅτι καλός. 17 νυνὶ δὲ οὐκέτι ἐγὼ κατεργάζομαι αὐτὸ ἀλλὰ ἡ οἰκοῦσα ἐν ἐμοὶ ἁμαρτία. 18 οἶδα γὰρ ὅτι οὐκ οἰκεῖ ἐν ἐμοί, τοῦτ' ἔστιν ἐν τῇ σαρκί μου, ἀγαθόν· τὸ γὰρ θέλειν παράκειταί μοι, τὸ δὲ κατεργάζεσθαι τὸ καλὸν οὔ· 19 οὐ γὰρ ὃ θέλω ποιῶ ἀγαθόν, ἀλλὰ ὃ οὐ θέλω κακὸν τοῦτο πράσσω. 20 εἰ δὲ ὃ οὐ θέλω [ἐγὼ] τοῦτο ποιῶ, οὐκέτι ἐγὼ κατεργάζομαι αὐτὸ ἀλλὰ ἡ οἰκοῦσα ἐν ἐμοὶ ἁμαρτία. 21 Εὑρίσκω ἄρα τὸν νόμον, τῷ θέλοντι ἐμοὶ ποιεῖν τὸ καλόν, ὅτι ἐμοὶ τὸ κακὸν παράκειται· 22 συνήδομαι γὰρ τῷ νόμῳ τοῦ θεοῦ κατὰ τὸν ἔσω ἄνθρωπον, 23 βλέπω δὲ ἕτερον νόμον ἐν τοῖς μέλεσίν μου ἀντιστρατευόμενον τῷ νόμῳ τοῦ νοός μου καὶ αἰχμαλωτίζοντά με ἐν τῷ νόμῳ τῆς ἁμαρτίας τῷ ὄντι ἐν τοῖς μέλεσίν μου. 24 ταλαίπωρος ἐγὼ ἄνθρωπος· τίς με ῥύσεται ἐκ τοῦ σώματος τοῦ θανάτου τούτου; 25 χάρις δὲ τῷ θεῷ διὰ Ἰησοῦ Χριστοῦ τοῦ κυρίου ἡμῶν. ἄρα οὖν αὐτὸς ἐγὼ τῷ μὲν νοῒ δουλεύω νόμῳ θεοῦ τῇ δὲ σαρκὶ νόμῳ ἁμαρτίας.

8 Οὐδὲν ἄρα νῦν κατάκριμα τοῖς ἐν Χριστῷ Ἰησοῦᵃ. 2 ὁ γὰρ νόμος τοῦ πνεύματος τῆς ζωῆς ἐν Χριστῷ Ἰησοῦ ἠλευθέρωσέν σεᵇ ἀπὸ τοῦ νόμου τῆς ἁμαρτίας καὶ τοῦ θανάτου. 3 τὸ γὰρ ἀδύνατον τοῦ νόμου ἐν ᾧ ἠσθένει διὰ τῆς σαρκός, ὁ θεὸς τὸν ἑαυτοῦ υἱὸν πέμψας ἐν ὁμοιώματι σαρκὸς ἁμαρτίας καὶ περὶ ἁμαρτίας κατέκρινεν τὴν ἁμαρτίαν ἐν τῇ σαρκί, 4 ἵνα τὸ δικαίωμα τοῦ νόμου πληρωθῇ ἐν ἡμῖν

commandment that was intended to bring life actually brought death. ¹¹For sin, seizing the opportunity afforded by the commandment, deceived me, and through the commandment put me to death. ¹²So then, the law is holy, and the commandment is holy, righteous and good.

¹³Did that which is good, then, become death to me? By no means! But in order that sin might be recognized as sin, it produced death in me through what was good, so that through the commandment sin might become utterly sinful.

¹⁴We know that the law is spiritual; but I am unspiritual, sold as a slave to sin. ¹⁵I do not understand what I do. For what I want to do I do not do, but what I hate I do. ¹⁶And if I do what I do not want to do, I agree that the law is good. ¹⁷As it is, it is no longer I myself who do it, but it is sin living in me. ¹⁸I know that nothing good lives in me, that is, in my sinful nature.ᶜ For I have the desire to do what is good, but I cannot carry it out. ¹⁹For what I do is not the good I want to do; no, the evil I do not want to do—this I keep on doing. ²⁰Now if I do what I do not want to do, it is no longer I who do it, but it is sin living in me that does it.

²¹So I find this law at work: When I want to do good, evil is right there with me. ²²For in my inner being I delight in God's law; ²³but I see another law at work in the members of my body, waging war against the law of my mind and making me a prisoner of the law of sin at work within my members. ²⁴What a wretched man I am! Who will rescue me from this body of death? ²⁵Thanks be to God—through Jesus Christ our Lord!

So then, I myself in my mind am a slave to God's law, but in the sinful nature a slave to the law of sin.

Life Through the Spirit

8 Therefore, there is now no condemnation for those who are in Christ Jesus,ᵃ ²because through Christ Jesus the law of the Spirit of life set me free from the law of sin and death. ³For what the law was powerless to do in that it was weakened by the sinful nature,ᵇ God did by sending his own Son in the likeness of sinful man to be a sin offering.ᶜ And so he condemned sin in sinful man,ᵈ ⁴in order that the righteous requirements of the law might be fully met

---

ʸ Gk *sold under sin*   ᶻ Or *spirit*   ᵃ Here the Greek word *you* is singular number; other ancient authorities read *me* or *us*   ᵇ Or *and as a sin offering*

ᵃ1 NIV note adds μὴ κατὰ σάρκα περιπατοῦσιν ἀλλὰ κατὰ πνεῦμα   ᵇ2 NIV text με; NRSV note a με or ἡμᾶς

ᶜ18 Or *my flesh*   ᵃ1 Some later manuscripts *Jesus, who do not live according to the sinful nature but according to the Spirit,*   ᵇ3 Or *the flesh; also in verses 4, 5, 8, 9, 12 and 13*   ᶜ3 Or *man, for sin*   ᵈ3 Or *in the flesh*

NRSV

in us, who walk not according to the flesh but according to the Spirit.[z] [5]For those who live according to the flesh set their minds on the things of the flesh, but those who live according to the Spirit[z] set their minds on the things of the Spirit.[z] [6]To set the mind on the flesh is death, but to set the mind on the Spirit[z] is life and peace. [7]For this reason the mind that is set on the flesh is hostile to God; it does not submit to God's law—indeed it cannot, [8]and those who are in the flesh cannot please God.

9 But you are not in the flesh; you are in the Spirit,[z] since the Spirit of God dwells in you. Anyone who does not have the Spirit of Christ does not belong to him. [10]But if Christ is in you, though the body is dead because of sin, the Spirit[z] is life because of righteousness. [11]If the Spirit of him who raised Jesus from the dead dwells in you, he who raised Christ[c] from the dead will give life to your mortal bodies also through[d] his Spirit that dwells in you.

12 So then, brothers and sisters,[e] we are debtors, not to the flesh, to live according to the flesh— [13]for if you live according to the flesh, you will die; but if by the Spirit you put to death the deeds of the body, you will live. [14]For all who are led by the Spirit of God are children of God. [15]For you did not receive a spirit of slavery to fall back into fear, but you have received a spirit of adoption. When we cry, "Abba![f] Father!" [16]it is that very Spirit bearing witness[g] with our spirit that we are children of God, [17]and if children, then heirs, heirs of God and joint heirs with Christ— if, in fact, we suffer with him so that we may also be glorified with him.

Future Glory

18 I consider that the sufferings of this present time are not worth comparing with the glory about to be revealed to us. [19]For the creation waits with eager longing for the revealing of the children of God; [20]for the creation was subjected to futility, not of its own will but by the will of the one who subjected it, in hope [21]that the creation itself will be set free from its bondage to decay and will obtain the freedom of the glory of the children of God. [22]We

[Greek]

τοῖς μὴ κατὰ σάρκα περιπατοῦσιν ἀλλὰ κατὰ πνεῦμα. **5** οἱ γὰρ κατὰ σάρκα ὄντες τὰ τῆς σαρκὸς φρονοῦσιν, οἱ δὲ κατὰ πνεῦμα τὰ τοῦ πνεύματος. **6** τὸ γὰρ φρόνημα τῆς σαρκὸς θάνατος, τὸ δὲ φρόνημα τοῦ πνεύματος ζωὴ καὶ εἰρήνη· **7** διότι τὸ φρόνημα τῆς σαρκὸς ἔχθρα εἰς θεόν, τῷ γὰρ νόμῳ τοῦ θεοῦ οὐχ ὑποτάσσεται, οὐδὲ γὰρ δύναται· **8** οἱ δὲ ἐν σαρκὶ ὄντες θεῷ ἀρέσαι οὐ δύνανται. **9** ὑμεῖς δὲ οὐκ ἐστὲ ἐν σαρκὶ ἀλλὰ ἐν πνεύματι, εἴπερ πνεῦμα θεοῦ οἰκεῖ ἐν ὑμῖν. εἰ δέ τις πνεῦμα Χριστοῦ οὐκ ἔχει, οὗτος οὐκ ἔστιν αὐτοῦ. **10** εἰ δὲ Χριστὸς ἐν ὑμῖν, τὸ μὲν σῶμα νεκρὸν διὰ ἁμαρτίαν τὸ δὲ πνεῦμα ζωὴ διὰ δικαιοσύνην. **11** εἰ δὲ τὸ πνεῦμα τοῦ ἐγείραντος τὸν Ἰησοῦν ἐκ νεκρῶν οἰκεῖ ἐν ὑμῖν, ὁ ἐγείρας Χριστὸν[c] ἐκ νεκρῶν ζωοποιήσει καὶ τὰ θνητὰ σώματα ὑμῶν διὰ τοῦ ἐνοικοῦντος αὐτοῦ πνεύματος[d] ἐν ὑμῖν.

12 Ἄρα οὖν, ἀδελφοί, ὀφειλέται ἐσμὲν οὐ τῇ σαρκὶ τοῦ κατὰ σάρκα ζῆν, **13** εἰ γὰρ κατὰ σάρκα ζῆτε, μέλλετε ἀποθνῄσκειν· εἰ δὲ πνεύματι τὰς πράξεις τοῦ σώματος θανατοῦτε, ζήσεσθε. **14** ὅσοι γὰρ πνεύματι θεοῦ ἄγονται, οὗτοι υἱοὶ θεοῦ εἰσιν. **15** οὐ γὰρ ἐλάβετε πνεῦμα δουλείας πάλιν εἰς φόβον ἀλλὰ ἐλάβετε πνεῦμα υἱοθεσίας ἐν ᾧ κράζομεν, Αββα ὁ πατήρ. **16** αὐτὸ τὸ πνεῦμα συμμαρτυρεῖ τῷ πνεύματι ἡμῶν ὅτι ἐσμὲν τέκνα θεοῦ. **17** εἰ δὲ τέκνα, καὶ κληρονόμοι· κληρονόμοι μὲν θεοῦ, συγκληρονόμοι δὲ Χριστοῦ, εἴπερ συμπάσχομεν ἵνα καὶ συνδοξασθῶμεν.

18 Λογίζομαι γὰρ ὅτι οὐκ ἄξια τὰ παθήματα τοῦ νῦν καιροῦ πρὸς τὴν μέλλουσαν δόξαν ἀποκαλυφθῆναι εἰς ἡμᾶς. **19** ἡ γὰρ ἀποκαραδοκία τῆς κτίσεως τὴν ἀποκάλυψιν τῶν υἱῶν τοῦ θεοῦ ἀπεκδέχεται. **20** τῇ γὰρ ματαιότητι ἡ κτίσις ὑπετάγη, οὐχ ἑκοῦσα ἀλλὰ διὰ τὸν ὑποτάξαντα, ἐφ᾽ ἑλπίδι **21** ὅτι καὶ αὐτὴ ἡ κτίσις ἐλευθερωθήσεται ἀπὸ τῆς δουλείας τῆς φθορᾶς εἰς τὴν ἐλευθερίαν τῆς δόξης τῶν τέκνων τοῦ θεοῦ. **22** οἴδαμεν γὰρ ὅτι

NIV

in us, who do not live according to the sinful nature but according to the Spirit.

[5]Those who live according to the sinful nature have their minds set on what that nature desires; but those who live in accordance with the Spirit have their minds set on what the Spirit desires. [6]The mind of sinful man[e] is death, but the mind controlled by the Spirit is life and peace; [7]the sinful mind[f] is hostile to God. It does not submit to God's law, nor can it do so. [8]Those controlled by the sinful nature cannot please God.

[9]You, however, are controlled not by the sinful nature but by the Spirit, if the Spirit of God lives in you. And if anyone does not have the Spirit of Christ, he does not belong to Christ. [10]But if Christ is in you, your body is dead because of sin, yet your spirit is alive because of righteousness. [11]And if the Spirit of him who raised Jesus from the dead is living in you, he who raised Christ from the dead will also give life to your mortal bodies through his Spirit, who lives in you.

[12]Therefore, brothers, we have an obligation—but it is not to the sinful nature, to live according to it. [13]For if you live according to the sinful nature, you will die; but if by the Spirit you put to death the misdeeds of the body, you will live, [14]because those who are led by the Spirit of God are sons of God. [15]For you did not receive a spirit that makes you a slave again to fear, but you received the Spirit of sonship.[g] And by him we cry, "Abba,[h] Father." [16]The Spirit himself testifies with our spirit that we are God's children. [17]Now if we are children, then we are heirs—heirs of God and co-heirs with Christ, if indeed we share in his sufferings in order that we may also share in his glory.

Future Glory

[18]I consider that our present sufferings are not worth comparing with the glory that will be revealed in us. [19]The creation waits in eager expectation for the sons of God to be revealed. [20]For the creation was subjected to frustration, not by its own choice, but by the will of the one who subjected it, in hope [21]that[i] the creation itself will be liberated from its bondage to decay and brought into the glorious freedom of the children of God.

[z] Or *spirit*   [c] Other ancient authorities read *the Christ* or *Christ Jesus* or *Jesus Christ*   [d] Other ancient authorities read *on account of*   [e] Gk *brothers*   [f] Aramaic for *Father* [g] Or [15]*a spirit of adoption, by which we cry,* "*Abba! Father!*" [16]*The Spirit itself bears witness*

[c]11 NRSV note c reads τὸν Χριστὸν or Χριστὸν Ἰησοῦν (before or after ἐκ νεκρῶν) or Ἰησοῦν Χριστόν † [d]11 NRSV note d τὸ ἐνοικοῦν αὐτοῦ πνεῦμα †

[e]6 Or *mind set on the flesh*   [f]7 Or *the mind set on the flesh* [g]15 Or *adoption*   [h]15 Aramaic for *Father*   [i]20,21 Or *subjected it in hope.* [21]*For*

know that the whole creation has been groaning in labor pains until now; 23and not only the creation, but we ourselves, who have the first fruits of the Spirit, groan inwardly while we wait for adoption, the redemption of our bodies. 24For inh hope we were saved. Now hope that is seen is not hope. For who hopesi for what is seen? 25But if we hope for what we do not see, we wait for it with patience.

26 Likewise the Spirit helps us in our weakness; for we do not know how to pray as we ought, but that very Spirit intercedesj with sighs too deep for words. 27And God,k who searches the heart, knows what is the mind of the Spirit, because the Spiritl intercedes for the saints according to the will of God.m

28 We know that all things work together for goodn for those who love God, who are called according to his purpose. 29For those whom he foreknew he also predestined to be conformed to the image of his Son, in order that he might be the firstborn within a large family.o 30And those whom he predestined he also called; and those whom he called he also justified; and those whom he justified he also glorified.

God's Love in Christ Jesus

31 What then are we to say about these things? If God is for us, who is against us? 32He who did not withhold his own Son, but gave him up for all of us, will he not with him also give us everything else? 33Who will bring any charge against God's elect? It is God who justifies. 34Who is to condemn? It is Christ Jesus, who died, yes, who was raised, who is at the right hand of God, who indeed intercedes for us.p 35Who will separate us from the love of Christ? Will hardship, or distress, or persecution, or famine, or nakedness, or peril, or sword? 36As it is written,

"For your sake we are being killed all day long;
    we are accounted as sheep to be slaughtered."

37No, in all these things we are more than conquerors through him who loved us. 38For I am convinced that neither death, nor life, nor angels, nor rulers, nor things

πᾶσα ἡ κτίσις συστενάζει καὶ συνωδίνει ἄχρι τοῦ νῦν· 23 οὐ μόνον δέ, ἀλλὰ καὶ αὐτοὶe τὴν ἀπαρχὴν τοῦ πνεύματος ἔχοντες, ἡμεῖς καὶ αὐτοὶ ἐν ἑαυτοῖς στενάζομεν υἱοθεσίαν ἀπεκδεχόμενοι, τὴν ἀπολύτρωσιν τοῦ σώματος ἡμῶν. 24 τῇ γὰρ ἐλπίδι ἐσώθημεν· ἐλπὶς δὲ βλεπομένη οὐκ ἔστιν ἐλπίς· ὃ γὰρ βλέπει τίς ἐλπίζειf; 25 εἰ δὲ ὃ οὐ βλέπομεν ἐλπίζομεν, δι' ὑπομονῆς ἀπεκδεχόμεθα.

26 Ὡσαύτως δὲ καὶ τὸ πνεῦμα συναντιλαμβάνεται τῇ ἀσθενείᾳ ἡμῶν· τὸ γὰρ τί προσευξώμεθα καθὸ δεῖ οὐκ οἴδαμεν, ἀλλὰ αὐτὸ τὸ πνεῦμα ὑπερεντυγχάνειg στεναγμοῖς ἀλαλήτοις· 27 ὁ δὲ ἐραυνῶν τὰς καρδίας οἶδεν τί τὸ φρόνημα τοῦ πνεύματος, ὅτι κατὰ θεὸν ἐντυγχάνει ὑπὲρ ἁγίων. 28 οἴδαμεν δὲ ὅτι τοῖς ἀγαπῶσιν τὸν θεὸν πάντα συνεργεῖh εἰς ἀγαθόν, τοῖς κατὰ πρόθεσιν κλητοῖς οὖσιν. 29 ὅτι οὓς προέγνω, καὶ προώρισεν συμμόρφους τῆς εἰκόνος τοῦ υἱοῦ αὐτοῦ, εἰς τὸ εἶναι αὐτὸν πρωτότοκον ἐν πολλοῖς ἀδελφοῖς· 30 οὓς δὲ προώρισεν, τούτους καὶ ἐκάλεσεν· καὶ οὓς ἐκάλεσεν, τούτους καὶ ἐδικαίωσεν· οὓς δὲ ἐδικαίωσεν, τούτους καὶ ἐδόξασεν.

31 Τί οὖν ἐροῦμεν πρὸς ταῦτα; εἰ ὁ θεὸς ὑπὲρ ἡμῶν, τίς καθ' ἡμῶν; 32 ὅς γε τοῦ ἰδίου υἱοῦ οὐκ ἐφείσατο ἀλλὰ ὑπὲρ ἡμῶν πάντων παρέδωκεν αὐτόν, πῶς οὐχὶ καὶ σὺν αὐτῷ τὰ πάντα ἡμῖν χαρίσεται; 33 τίς ἐγκαλέσει κατὰ ἐκλεκτῶν θεοῦ; θεὸς ὁ δικαιῶν· 34 τίς ὁ κατακρινῶν; Χριστὸς [Ἰησοῦς] ὁ ἀποθανών, μᾶλλον δὲ ἐγερθείς, ὃς καί ἐστιν ἐν δεξιᾷ τοῦ θεοῦ, ὃς καὶ ἐντυγχάνει ὑπὲρ ἡμῶν. 35 τίς ἡμᾶς χωρίσει ἀπὸ τῆς ἀγάπης τοῦ Χριστοῦ; θλῖψις ἢ στενοχωρία ἢ διωγμὸς ἢ λιμὸς ἢ γυμνότης ἢ κίνδυνος ἢ μάχαιρα; 36 καθὼς γέγραπται ὅτι

Ἕνεκεν σοῦ θανατούμεθα ὅλην τὴν ἡμέραν,
ἐλογίσθημεν ὡς πρόβατα σφαγῆς.
37 ἀλλ' ἐν τούτοις πᾶσιν ὑπερνικῶμεν διὰ τοῦ ἀγαπήσαντος ἡμᾶς. 38 πέπεισμαι γὰρ ὅτι οὔτε θάνατος οὔτε ζωὴ οὔτε ἄγγελοι οὔτε ἀρχαὶ οὔτε ἐνεστῶτα

22We know that the whole creation has been groaning as in the pains of childbirth right up to the present time. 23Not only so, but we ourselves, who have the firstfruits of the Spirit, groan inwardly as we wait eagerly for our adoption as sons, the redemption of our bodies. 24For in this hope we were saved. But hope that is seen is no hope at all. Who hopes for what he already has? 25But if we hope for what we do not yet have, we wait for it patiently.

26In the same way, the Spirit helps us in our weakness. We do not know what we ought to pray for, but the Spirit himself intercedes for us with groans that words cannot express. 27And he who searches our hearts knows the mind of the Spirit, because the Spirit intercedes for the saints in accordance with God's will.

More Than Conquerors

28And we know that in all things God works for the good of those who love him,j whok have been called according to his purpose. 29For those God foreknew he also predestined to be conformed to the likeness of his Son, that he might be the firstborn among many brothers. 30And those he predestined, he also called; those he called, he also justified; those he justified, he also glorified.

31What, then, shall we say in response to this? If God is for us, who can be against us? 32He who did not spare his own Son, but gave him up for us all—how will he not also, along with him, graciously give us all things? 33Who will bring any charge against those whom God has chosen? It is God who justifies. 34Who is he that condemns? Christ Jesus, who died—more than that, who was raised to life—is at the right hand of God and is also interceding for us. 35Who shall separate us from the love of Christ? Shall trouble or hardship or persecution or famine or nakedness or danger or sword? 36As it is written:

"For your sake we face death all day long;
    we are considered as sheep to be slaughtered."l

37No, in all these things we are more than conquerors through him who loved us. 38For I am convinced that neither death nor life, neither angels nor demons,m

---

h Or by i Other ancient authorities read awaits j Other ancient authorities add for us k Gk the one l Gk he or it m Gk according to God n Other ancient authorities read God makes all things work together for good, or in all things God works for good o Gk among many brothers p Or Is it Christ Jesus . . . for us?

e23 NIV text omits καὶ αὐτοὶ † f24 NRSV note i ὑπομένει g26 NIV text and NRSV note j adds ὑπὲρ ἡμῶν h28 NIV text and NRSV note n add ὁ θεός; NIV note and NRSV text as UBS

j28 Some manuscripts And we know that all things work together for good to those who love God k28 Or works together with those who love him to bring about what is good—with those who l36 Psalm 44:22 m38 Or nor heavenly rulers

present, nor things to come, nor powers, [39]nor height, nor depth, nor anything else in all creation, will be able to separate us from the love of God in Christ Jesus our Lord.

God's Election of Israel

9 I am speaking the truth in Christ—I am not lying; my conscience confirms it by the Holy Spirit— [2]I have great sorrow and unceasing anguish in my heart. [3]For I could wish that I myself were accursed and cut off from Christ for the sake of my own people,[q] my kindred according to the flesh. [4]They are Israelites, and to them belong the adoption, the glory, the covenants, the giving of the law, the worship, and the promises; [5]to them belong the patriarchs, and from them, according to the flesh, comes the Messiah,[r] who is over all, God blessed forever.[s] Amen.

6 It is not as though the word of God had failed. For not all Israelites truly belong to Israel, [7]and not all of Abraham's children are his true descendants; but "It is through Isaac that descendants shall be named for you." [8]This means that it is not the children of the flesh who are the children of God, but the children of the promise are counted as descendants. [9]For this is what the promise said, "About this time I will return and Sarah shall have a son." [10]Nor is that all; something similar happened to Rebecca when she had conceived children by one husband, our ancestor Isaac. [11]Even before they had been born or had done anything good or bad (so that God's purpose of election might continue, [12]not by works but by his call) she was told, "The elder shall serve the younger." [13]As it is written,

"I have loved Jacob,
 but I have hated Esau."

14 What then are we to say? Is there injustice on God's part? By no means! [15]For he says to Moses,

"I will have mercy on whom I have mercy,
 and I will have compassion on whom I have compassion."

[16]So it depends not on human will or exertion, but on God who shows mercy. [17]For the scripture says to Pharaoh, "I have raised you up for the very purpose of showing my power in you, so that my name may be proclaimed in all the earth." [18]So then he

---

οὔτε μέλλοντα οὔτε δυνάμεις [39] οὔτε ὕψωμα οὔτε βάθος οὔτε τις κτίσις ἑτέρα δυνήσεται ἡμᾶς χωρίσαι ἀπὸ τῆς ἀγάπης τοῦ θεοῦ τῆς ἐν Χριστῷ Ἰησοῦ τῷ κυρίῳ ἡμῶν.

9 Ἀλήθειαν λέγω ἐν Χριστῷ, οὐ ψεύδομαι, συμμαρτυρούσης μοι τῆς συνειδήσεώς μου ἐν πνεύματι ἁγίῳ, 2 ὅτι λύπη μοί ἐστιν μεγάλη καὶ ἀδιάλειπτος ὀδύνη τῇ καρδίᾳ μου. 3 ηὐχόμην γὰρ ἀνάθεμα εἶναι αὐτὸς ἐγὼ ἀπὸ τοῦ Χριστοῦ ὑπὲρ τῶν ἀδελφῶν μου τῶν συγγενῶν μου κατὰ σάρκα, 4 οἵτινές εἰσιν Ἰσραηλῖται, ὧν ἡ υἱοθεσία καὶ ἡ δόξα καὶ αἱ διαθῆκαι καὶ ἡ νομοθεσία καὶ ἡ λατρεία καὶ αἱ ἐπαγγελίαι, 5 ὧν οἱ πατέρες καὶ ἐξ ὧν ὁ Χριστὸς τὸ κατὰ σάρκα, ὁ ὢν ἐπὶ πάντων θεὸς εὐλογητὸς εἰς τοὺς αἰῶνας, ἀμήν.

6 Οὐχ οἷον δὲ ὅτι ἐκπέπτωκεν ὁ λόγος τοῦ θεοῦ. οὐ γὰρ πάντες οἱ ἐξ Ἰσραὴλ οὗτοι Ἰσραήλ· 7 οὐδ᾽ ὅτι εἰσὶν σπέρμα Ἀβραὰμ πάντες τέκνα, ἀλλ᾽, Ἐν Ἰσαὰκ κληθήσεταί σοι σπέρμα. 8 τοῦτ᾽ ἔστιν, οὐ τὰ τέκνα τῆς σαρκὸς ταῦτα τέκνα τοῦ θεοῦ ἀλλὰ τὰ τέκνα τῆς ἐπαγγελίας λογίζεται εἰς σπέρμα. 9 ἐπαγγελίας γὰρ ὁ λόγος οὗτος, Κατὰ τὸν καιρὸν τοῦτον ἐλεύσομαι καὶ ἔσται τῇ Σάρρᾳ υἱός. 10 οὐ μόνον δέ, ἀλλὰ καὶ Ῥεβέκκα ἐξ ἑνὸς κοίτην ἔχουσα, Ἰσαὰκ τοῦ πατρὸς ἡμῶν· 11 μήπω γὰρ γεννηθέντων μηδὲ πραξάντων τι ἀγαθὸν ἢ φαῦλον, ἵνα ἡ κατ᾽ ἐκλογὴν πρόθεσις τοῦ θεοῦ μένῃ, 12 οὐκ ἐξ ἔργων ἀλλ᾽ ἐκ τοῦ καλοῦντος, ἐρρέθη αὐτῇ ὅτι Ὁ μείζων δουλεύσει τῷ ἐλάσσονι, 13 καθὼς γέγραπται,

Τὸν Ἰακὼβ ἠγάπησα,
 τὸν δὲ Ἠσαῦ ἐμίσησα.

14 Τί οὖν ἐροῦμεν; μὴ ἀδικία παρὰ τῷ θεῷ; μὴ γένοιτο. 15 τῷ Μωϋσεῖ γὰρ λέγει,

Ἐλεήσω ὃν ἂν ἐλεῶ
 καὶ οἰκτιρήσω ὃν ἂν οἰκτίρω.

16 ἄρα οὖν οὐ τοῦ θέλοντος οὐδὲ τοῦ τρέχοντος ἀλλὰ τοῦ ἐλεῶντος θεοῦ. 17 λέγει γὰρ ἡ γραφὴ τῷ Φαραὼ ὅτι Εἰς αὐτὸ τοῦτο ἐξήγειρά σε ὅπως ἐνδείξωμαι ἐν σοὶ τὴν δύναμίν μου καὶ ὅπως διαγγελῇ τὸ ὄνομά μου ἐν πάσῃ τῇ γῇ. 18 ἄρα οὖν ὃν θέλει ἐλεεῖ,

---

neither the present nor the future, nor any powers, [39]neither height nor depth, nor anything else in all creation, will be able to separate us from the love of God that is in Christ Jesus our Lord.

God's Sovereign Choice

9 I speak the truth in Christ—I am not lying, my conscience confirms it in the Holy Spirit— [2]I have great sorrow and unceasing anguish in my heart. [3]For I could wish that I myself were cursed and cut off from Christ for the sake of my brothers, those of my own race, [4]the people of Israel. Theirs is the adoption as sons; theirs the divine glory, the covenants, the receiving of the law, the temple worship and the promises. [5]Theirs are the patriarchs, and from them is traced the human ancestry of Christ, who is God over all, forever praised![a] Amen.

[6]It is not as though God's word had failed. For not all who are descended from Israel are Israel. [7]Nor because they are his descendants are they all Abraham's children. On the contrary, "It is through Isaac that your offspring will be reckoned."[b] [8]In other words, it is not the natural children who are God's children, but it is the children of the promise who are regarded as Abraham's offspring. [9]For this was how the promise was stated: "At the appointed time I will return, and Sarah will have a son."[c]

[10]Not only that, but Rebekah's children had one and the same father, our father Isaac. [11]Yet, before the twins were born or had done anything good or bad—in order that God's purpose in election might stand: [12]not by works but by him who calls—she was told, "The older will serve the younger."[d] [13]Just as it is written: "Jacob I loved, but Esau I hated."[e]

[14]What then shall we say? Is God unjust? Not at all! [15]For he says to Moses,

"I will have mercy on whom I have mercy,
 and I will have compassion on whom I have compassion."[f]

[16]It does not, therefore, depend on man's desire or effort, but on God's mercy. [17]For the Scripture says to Pharaoh: "I raised you up for this very purpose, that I might display my power in you and that my name might be proclaimed in all the earth."[g]

---

has mercy on whomever he chooses, and he hardens the heart of whomever he chooses.

God's Wrath and Mercy

19 You will say to me then, "Why then does he still find fault? For who can resist his will?" 20But who indeed are you, a human being, to argue with God? Will what is molded say to the one who molds it, "Why have you made me like this?" 21Has the potter no right over the clay, to make out of the same lump one object for special use and another for ordinary use? 22What if God, desiring to show his wrath and to make known his power, has endured with much patience the objects of wrath that are made for destruction; 23and what if he has done so in order to make known the riches of his glory for the objects of mercy, which he has prepared beforehand for glory— 24including us whom he has called, not from the Jews only but also from the Gentiles? 25As indeed he says in Hosea,

"Those who were not my people I will
    call 'my people,'
    and her who was not beloved I will
    call 'beloved.' "
26 "And in the very place where it was
    said to them, 'You are not my
    people,'
    there they shall be called children of
    the living God."

27 And Isaiah cries out concerning Israel, "Though the number of the children of Israel were like the sand of the sea, only a remnant of them will be saved; 28for the Lord will execute his sentence on the earth quickly and decisively."t 29And as Isaiah predicted,

"If the Lord of hosts had not left
    survivorsu to us,
    we would have fared like Sodom
    and been made like Gomorrah."

Israel's Unbelief

30 What then are we to say? Gentiles, who did not strive for righteousness, have attained it, that is, righteousness through faith; 31but Israel, who did strive for the righteousness that is based on the law, did not succeed in fulfilling that law. 32Why not? Because they did not strive for it on the basis of faith, but as if it were based on works. They have stumbled over the

19 Ἐρεῖς μοι οὖν, Τί [οὖν] ἔτι μέμφεται; τῷ γὰρ βουλήματι αὐτοῦ τίς ἀνθέστηκεν; 20 ὦ ἄνθρωπε, μενοῦνγε σὺ τίς εἶ ὁ ἀνταποκρινόμενος τῷ θεῷ; μὴ ἐρεῖ τὸ πλάσμα τῷ πλάσαντι, Τί με ἐποίησας οὕτως; 21 ἢ οὐκ ἔχει ἐξουσίαν ὁ κεραμεὺς τοῦ πηλοῦ ἐκ τοῦ αὐτοῦ φυράματος ποιῆσαι ὃ μὲν εἰς τιμὴν σκεῦος ὃ δὲ εἰς ἀτιμίαν; 22 εἰ δὲ θέλων ὁ θεὸς ἐνδείξασθαι τὴν ὀργὴν καὶ γνωρίσαι τὸ δυνατὸν αὐτοῦ ἤνεγκεν ἐν πολλῇ μακροθυμίᾳ σκεύη ὀργῆς κατηρτισμένα εἰς ἀπώλειαν, 23 καὶ ἵνα γνωρίσῃ τὸν πλοῦτον τῆς δόξης αὐτοῦ ἐπὶ σκεύη ἐλέους ἃ προητοίμασεν εἰς δόξαν; 24 οὓς καὶ ἐκάλεσεν ἡμᾶς οὐ μόνον ἐξ Ἰουδαίων ἀλλὰ καὶ ἐξ ἐθνῶν, 25 ὡς καὶ ἐν τῷ Ὡσηὲ λέγει,

Καλέσω τὸν οὐ λαόν μου λαόν μου
    καὶ τὴν οὐκ ἠγαπημένην
    ἠγαπημένην·
26 καὶ ἔσται ἐν τῷ τόπῳ οὗ ἐρρέθη
    αὐτοῖς, Οὐ λαός μου ὑμεῖς,
    ἐκεῖ κληθήσονται υἱοὶ θεοῦ
    ζῶντος.

27 Ἡσαΐας δὲ κράζει ὑπὲρ τοῦ Ἰσραήλ, Ἐὰν ᾖ ὁ ἀριθμὸς τῶν υἱῶν Ἰσραὴλ ὡς ἡ ἄμμος τῆς θαλάσσης, τὸ ὑπόλειμμα σωθήσεται· 28 λόγον γὰρ συντελῶν καὶ συντέμνωνa ποιήσει κύριος ἐπὶ τῆς γῆς. 29 καὶ καθὼς προείρηκεν Ἡσαΐας,

Εἰ μὴ κύριος Σαβαὼθ ἐγκατέλιπεν
    ἡμῖν σπέρμα,
    ὡς Σόδομα ἂν ἐγενήθημεν
    καὶ ὡς Γόμορρα ἂν ὡμοιώθημεν.

30 Τί οὖν ἐροῦμεν; ὅτι ἔθνη τὰ μὴ διώκοντα δικαιοσύνην κατέλαβεν δικαιοσύνην, δικαιοσύνην δὲ τὴν ἐκ πίστεως. 31 Ἰσραὴλ δὲ διώκων νόμον δικαιοσύνης εἰς νόμον οὐκ ἔφθασεν. 32 διὰ τί; ὅτι οὐκ ἐκ πίστεως ἀλλ᾽ ὡς ἐξ ἔργων·

18Therefore God has mercy on whom he wants to have mercy, and he hardens whom he wants to harden.

19One of you will say to me: "Then why does God still blame us? For who resists his will?" 20But who are you, O man, to talk back to God? "Shall what is formed say to him who formed it, 'Why did you make me like this?' "h 21Does not the potter have the right to make out of the same lump of clay some pottery for noble purposes and some for common use?

22What if God, choosing to show his wrath and make his power known, bore with great patience the objects of his wrath—prepared for destruction? 23What if he did this to make the riches of his glory known to the objects of his mercy, whom he prepared in advance for glory— 24even us, whom he also called, not only from the Jews but also from the Gentiles? 25As he says in Hosea:

"I will call them 'my people' who are
    not my people;
    and I will call her 'my loved one' who
    is not my loved one,"i
26and,

"It will happen that in the very place
    where it was said to them,
    'You are not my people,'
    they will be called 'sons of the living
    God.' "j

27Isaiah cries out concerning Israel:

"Though the number of the Israelites be
    like the sand by the sea,
    only the remnant will be saved.
28For the Lord will carry out
    his sentence on earth with speed and
    finality."k

29It is just as Isaiah said previously:

"Unless the Lord Almighty
    had left us descendants,
    we would have become like Sodom,
    we would have been like Gomorrah."l

Israel's Unbelief

30What then shall we say? That the Gentiles, who did not pursue righteousness, have obtained it, a righteousness that is by faith; 31but Israel, who pursued a law of righteousness, has not attained it. 32Why not? Because they pursued it not by faith but as if it were by works. They stumbled

---

t Other ancient authorities read *for he will finish his work and cut it short in righteousness, because the Lord will make the sentence shortened on the earth*   u Or *descendants; Gk seed*

a28 NRSV note t adds ἐν δικαιοσύνῃ ὅτι λόγον συντετμημένον

h20 Isaiah 29:16; 45:9   i25 Hosea 2:23   j26 Hosea 1:10
k28 Isaiah 10:22,23   l29 Isaiah 1:9

NRSV

stumbling stone, [33]as it is written,

"See, I am laying in Zion a stone that
    will make people stumble, a rock
    that will make them fall,
and whoever believes in him[v] will
    not be put to shame."

10 Brothers and sisters,[w] my heart's desire and prayer to God for them is that they may be saved. [2]I can testify that they have a zeal for God, but it is not enlightened. [3]For, being ignorant of the righteousness that comes from God, and seeking to establish their own, they have not submitted to God's righteousness. [4]For Christ is the end of the law so that there may be righteousness for everyone who believes.

Salvation Is for All

[5] Moses writes concerning the righteousness that comes from the law, that "the person who does these things will live by them." [6]But the righteousness that comes from faith says, "Do not say in your heart, 'Who will ascend into heaven?' " (that is, to bring Christ down) [7]or 'Who will descend into the abyss?' " (that is, to bring Christ up from the dead). [8]But what does it say?

"The word is near you,
    on your lips and in your heart"
(that is, the word of faith that we proclaim); [9]because[x] if you confess with your lips that Jesus is Lord and believe in your heart that God raised him from the dead, you will be saved. [10]For one believes with the heart and so is justified, and one confesses with the mouth and so is saved. [11]The scripture says, "No one who believes in him will be put to shame." [12]For there is no distinction between Jew and Greek; the same Lord is Lord of all and is generous to all who call on him. [13]For, "Everyone who calls on the name of the Lord shall be saved."

[14] But how are they to call on one in whom they have not believed? And how are they to believe in one of whom they have never heard? And how are they to hear without someone to proclaim him? [15]And how are they to proclaim him unless they are sent? As it is written, "How beautiful are the feet of those who bring good news!" [16]But not all have obeyed the good news;[y] for Isaiah says, "Lord, who has believed our message?" [17]So faith

Greek

προσέκοψαν τῷ λίθῳ τοῦ προσκόμματος, 33 καθὼς γέγραπται,

᾽Ιδοὺ τίθημι ἐν Σιὼν λίθον
    προσκόμματος καὶ πέτραν
    σκανδάλου,
καὶ ὁ πιστεύων ἐπ᾽ αὐτῷ οὐ
    καταισχυνθήσεται.

10 ᾽Αδελφοί, ἡ μὲν εὐδοκία τῆς ἐμῆς καρδίας καὶ ἡ δέησις πρὸς τὸν θεὸν ὑπὲρ αὐτῶν εἰς σωτηρίαν. 2 μαρτυρῶ γὰρ αὐτοῖς ὅτι ζῆλον θεοῦ ἔχουσιν ἀλλ᾽ οὐ κατ᾽ ἐπίγνωσιν· 3 ἀγνοοῦντες γὰρ τὴν τοῦ θεοῦ δικαιοσύνην καὶ τὴν ἰδίαν [δικαιοσύνην] ζητοῦντες στῆσαι, τῇ δικαιοσύνῃ τοῦ θεοῦ οὐχ ὑπετάγησαν· 4 τέλος γὰρ νόμου Χριστὸς εἰς δικαιοσύνην παντὶ τῷ πιστεύοντι.

5 Μωϋσῆς γὰρ γράφει τὴν δικαιοσύνην τὴν ἐκ [τοῦ] νόμου ὅτι ὁ ποιήσας αὐτὰ ἄνθρωπος ζήσεται ἐν αὐτοῖς. 6 ἡ δὲ ἐκ πίστεως δικαιοσύνη οὕτως λέγει, Μὴ εἴπῃς ἐν τῇ καρδίᾳ σου, Τίς ἀναβήσεται εἰς τὸν οὐρανόν; τοῦτ᾽ ἔστιν Χριστὸν καταγαγεῖν· 7 ἤ, Τίς καταβήσεται εἰς τὴν ἄβυσσον; τοῦτ᾽ ἔστιν Χριστὸν ἐκ νεκρῶν ἀναγαγεῖν. 8 ἀλλὰ τί λέγει;

᾽Εγγύς σου τὸ ῥῆμά ἐστιν
    ἐν τῷ στόματί σου καὶ ἐν τῇ
    καρδίᾳ σου,
τοῦτ᾽ ἔστιν τὸ ῥῆμα τῆς πίστεως ὃ κηρύσσομεν. 9 ὅτι ἐὰν ὁμολογήσῃς ἐν τῷ στόματί σου κύριον ᾽Ιησοῦν καὶ πιστεύσῃς ἐν τῇ καρδίᾳ σου ὅτι ὁ θεὸς αὐτὸν ἤγειρεν ἐκ νεκρῶν, σωθήσῃ· 10 καρδίᾳ γὰρ πιστεύεται εἰς δικαιοσύνην, στόματι δὲ ὁμολογεῖται εἰς σωτηρίαν. 11 λέγει γὰρ ἡ γραφή, Πᾶς ὁ πιστεύων ἐπ᾽ αὐτῷ οὐ καταισχυνθήσεται. 12 οὐ γάρ ἐστιν διαστολὴ ᾽Ιουδαίου τε καὶ ῞Ελληνος, ὁ γὰρ αὐτὸς κύριος πάντων, πλουτῶν εἰς πάντας τοὺς ἐπικαλουμένους αὐτόν· 13 Πᾶς γὰρ ὃς ἂν ἐπικαλέσηται τὸ ὄνομα κυρίου σωθήσεται.

14 Πῶς οὖν ἐπικαλέσωνται εἰς ὃν οὐκ ἐπίστευσαν; πῶς δὲ πιστεύσωσιν οὗ οὐκ ἤκουσαν; πῶς δὲ ἀκούσωσιν χωρὶς κηρύσσοντος; 15 πῶς δὲ κηρύξωσιν ἐὰν μὴ ἀποσταλῶσιν; καθὼς γέγραπται, ῾Ως ὡραῖοι οἱ πόδες τῶν εὐαγγελιζομένων [τὰ] ἀγαθά. 16 ᾽Αλλ᾽ οὐ πάντες ὑπήκουσαν τῷ εὐαγγελίῳ. ῾Ησαΐας γὰρ λέγει, Κύριε, τίς ἐπίστευσεν τῇ ἀκοῇ ἡμῶν; 17 ἄρα ἡ πίστις ἐξ

NIV

over the "stumbling stone." [33]As it is written:

"See, I lay in Zion a stone that causes
    men to stumble
and a rock that makes them fall,
and the one who trusts in him will
    never be put to shame."[m]

10 Brothers, my heart's desire and prayer to God for the Israelites is that they may be saved. [2]For I can testify about them that they are zealous for God, but their zeal is not based on knowledge. [3]Since they did not know the righteousness that comes from God and sought to establish their own, they did not submit to God's righteousness. [4]Christ is the end of the law so that there may be righteousness for everyone who believes.

[5]Moses describes in this way the righteousness that is by the law: "The man who does these things will live by them."[a] [6]But the righteousness that is by faith says: "Do not say in your heart, 'Who will ascend into heaven?'"[b] (that is, to bring Christ down) [7]"or 'Who will descend into the deep?'"[c] (that is, to bring Christ up from the dead). [8]But what does it say? "The word is near you; it is in your mouth and in your heart,"[d] that is, the word of faith we are proclaiming: [9]That if you confess with your mouth, "Jesus is Lord," and believe in your heart that God raised him from the dead, you will be saved. [10]For it is with your heart that you believe and are justified, and it is with your mouth that you confess and are saved. [11]As the Scripture says, "Anyone who trusts in him will never be put to shame."[e] [12]For there is no difference between Jew and Gentile—the same Lord is Lord of all and richly blesses all who call on him, [13]for, "Everyone who calls on the name of the Lord will be saved."[f]

[14]How, then, can they call on the one they have not believed in? And how can they believe in the one of whom they have not heard? And how can they hear without someone preaching to them? [15]And how can they preach unless they are sent? As it is written, "How beautiful are the feet of those who bring good news!"[g]

[16]But not all the Israelites accepted the good news. For Isaiah says, "Lord, who has believed our message?"[h] [17]Consequently, faith comes from hearing the

---

v Or *trusts in it*   w Gk *Brothers*   x Or *namely, that*
y Or *gospel*

*m*33 Isaiah 8:14; 28:16   *a*5 Lev. 18:5   *b*6 Deut. 30:12
*c*7 Deut. 30:13   *d*8 Deut. 30:14   *e*11 Isaiah 28:16
*f*13 Joel 2:32   *g*15 Isaiah 52:7   *h*16 Isaiah 53:1

comes from what is heard, and what is heard comes through the word of Christ.[z]

18 But I ask, have they not heard? Indeed they have; for

"Their voice has gone out to all the
    earth,
and their words to the ends of the
    world."

[19]Again I ask, did Israel not understand? First Moses says,

"I will make you jealous of those who
    are not a nation;
with a foolish nation I will make
    you angry."

[20]Then Isaiah is so bold as to say,

"I have been found by those who did
    not seek me;
I have shown myself to those who
    did not ask for me."

[21]But of Israel he says, "All day long I have held out my hands to a disobedient and contrary people."

Israel's Rejection Is Not Final

11 I ask, then, has God rejected his people? By no means! I myself am an Israelite, a descendant of Abraham, a member of the tribe of Benjamin. [2]God has not rejected his people whom he foreknew. Do you not know what the scripture says of Elijah, how he pleads with God against Israel? [3]"Lord, they have killed your prophets, they have demolished your altars; I alone am left, and they are seeking my life." [4]But what is the divine reply to him? "I have kept for myself seven thousand who have not bowed the knee to Baal." [5]So too at the present time there is a remnant, chosen by grace. [6]But if it is by grace, it is no longer on the basis of works, otherwise grace would no longer be grace.[a]

7 What then? Israel failed to obtain what it was seeking. The elect obtained it, but the rest were hardened, [8]as it is written,

"God gave them a sluggish spirit,
    eyes that would not see
and ears that would not hear,
down to this very day."

[9]And David says,

"Let their table become a snare and a
    trap,

ἀκοῆς, ἡ δὲ ἀκοὴ διὰ ῥήματος Χριστοῦ[a]. 18 ἀλλὰ λέγω, μὴ οὐκ ἤκουσαν; μενοῦνγε,

Εἰς πᾶσαν τὴν γῆν ἐξῆλθεν ὁ
    φθόγγος αὐτῶν
καὶ εἰς τὰ πέρατα τῆς οἰκουμένης
    τὰ ῥήματα αὐτῶν.

19 ἀλλὰ λέγω, μὴ Ἰσραὴλ οὐκ ἔγνω; πρῶτος Μωϋσῆς λέγει,

Ἐγὼ παραζηλώσω ὑμᾶς ἐπ' οὐκ
    ἔθνει,
ἐπ' ἔθνει ἀσυνέτῳ παροργιῶ ὑμᾶς.

20 Ἡσαΐας δὲ ἀποτολμᾷ καὶ λέγει,

Εὑρέθην [ἐν] τοῖς ἐμὲ μὴ ζητοῦσιν,
ἐμφανὴς ἐγενόμην τοῖς ἐμὲ μὴ
    ἐπερωτῶσιν.

21 πρὸς δὲ τὸν Ἰσραὴλ λέγει, Ὅλην τὴν ἡμέραν ἐξεπέτασα τὰς χεῖράς μου πρὸς λαὸν ἀπειθοῦντα καὶ ἀντιλέγοντα.

11 Λέγω οὖν, μὴ ἀπώσατο ὁ θεὸς τὸν λαὸν αὐτοῦ; μὴ γένοιτο· καὶ γὰρ ἐγὼ Ἰσραηλίτης εἰμί, ἐκ σπέρματος Ἀβραάμ, φυλῆς Βενιαμίν. 2 οὐκ ἀπώσατο ὁ θεὸς τὸν λαὸν αὐτοῦ ὃν προέγνω. ἢ οὐκ οἴδατε ἐν Ἠλίᾳ τί λέγει ἡ γραφή, ὡς ἐντυγχάνει τῷ θεῷ κατὰ τοῦ Ἰσραήλ; 3 Κύριε, τοὺς προφήτας σου ἀπέκτειναν, τὰ θυσιαστήριά σου κατέσκαψαν, κἀγὼ ὑπελείφθην μόνος καὶ ζητοῦσιν τὴν ψυχήν μου. 4 ἀλλὰ τί λέγει αὐτῷ ὁ χρηματισμός; Κατέλιπον ἐμαυτῷ ἑπτακισχιλίους ἄνδρας, οἵτινες οὐκ ἔκαμψαν γόνυ τῇ Βάαλ. 5 οὕτως οὖν καὶ ἐν τῷ νῦν καιρῷ λεῖμμα κατ' ἐκλογὴν χάριτος γέγονεν· 6 εἰ δὲ χάριτι, οὐκέτι ἐξ ἔργων, ἐπεὶ ἡ χάρις οὐκέτι γίνεται χάρις[a]. 7 τί οὖν; ὃ ἐπιζητεῖ Ἰσραήλ, τοῦτο οὐκ ἐπέτυχεν, ἡ δὲ ἐκλογὴ ἐπέτυχεν· οἱ δὲ λοιποὶ ἐπωρώθησαν, 8 καθὼς γέγραπται,

Ἔδωκεν αὐτοῖς ὁ θεὸς πνεῦμα
    κατανύξεως,
ὀφθαλμοὺς τοῦ μὴ βλέπειν
καὶ ὦτα τοῦ μὴ ἀκούειν,
ἕως τῆς σήμερον ἡμέρας.

9 καὶ Δαυὶδ λέγει,

Γενηθήτω ἡ τράπεζα αὐτῶν εἰς
    παγίδα καὶ εἰς θήραν

---

message, and the message is heard through the word of Christ. [18]But I ask: Did they not hear? Of course they did:

"Their voice has gone out into all the
    earth,
their words to the ends of the world."[i]

[19]Again I ask: Did Israel not understand? First, Moses says,

"I will make you envious by those who
    are not a nation;
I will make you angry by a nation
    that has no understanding."[j]

[20]And Isaiah boldly says,

"I was found by those who did not seek
    me;
I revealed myself to those who did
    not ask for me."[k]

[21]But concerning Israel he says,

"All day long I have held out my hands
    to a disobedient and obstinate people."[l]

The Remnant of Israel

11 I ask then: Did God reject his people? By no means! I am an Israelite myself, a descendant of Abraham, from the tribe of Benjamin. [2]God did not reject his people, whom he foreknew. Don't you know what the Scripture says in the passage about Elijah—how he appealed to God against Israel: [3]"Lord, they have killed your prophets and torn down your altars; I am the only one left, and they are trying to kill me"[a]? [4]And what was God's answer to him? "I have reserved for myself seven thousand who have not bowed the knee to Baal."[b] [5]So too, at the present time there is a remnant chosen by grace. [6]And if by grace, then it is no longer by works; if it were, grace would no longer be grace.[c]

[7]What then? What Israel sought so earnestly it did not obtain, but the elect did. The others were hardened, [8]as it is written:

"God gave them a spirit of stupor,
    eyes so that they could not see
and ears so that they could not hear,
to this very day."[d]

[9]And David says:

"May their table become a snare and a
    trap,

---

z Or *about Christ*; other ancient authorities read *of God*
a Other ancient authorities add *But if it is by works, it is no longer on the basis of grace, otherwise work would no longer be work*

a17 NRSV note z θεοῦ   a6 NIV/NRSV notes add εἰ δὲ ἐξ ἔργων, οὐκέτι ἐστὶ χάρις, ἐπεὶ τὸ ἔργον οὐκέτι ἐστὶν ἔργον.

*i*18 Psalm 19:4   *j*19 Deut. 32:21   *k*20 Isaiah 65:1
*l*21 Isaiah 65:2   *a*3 1 Kings 19:10,14   *b*4 1 Kings 19:18
*c*6 Some manuscripts *by grace. But if by works, then it is no longer grace; if it were, work would no longer be work.*
*d*8 Deut. 29:4; Isaiah 29:10

a stumbling block and a retribution
for them;
10 let their eyes be darkened so that they
cannot see,
and keep their backs forever bent."

The Salvation of the Gentiles

11 So I ask, have they stumbled so as to fall? By no means! But through their stumbling[b] salvation has come to the Gentiles, so as to make Israel[c] jealous. 12Now if their stumbling[b] means riches for the world, and if their defeat means riches for Gentiles, how much more will their full inclusion mean!

13 Now I am speaking to you Gentiles. Inasmuch then as I am an apostle to the Gentiles, I glorify my ministry 14in order to make my own people[d] jealous, and thus save some of them. 15For if their rejection is the reconciliation of the world, what will their acceptance be but life from the dead! 16If the part of the dough offered as first fruits is holy, then the whole batch is holy; and if the root is holy, then the branches also are holy.

17 But if some of the branches were broken off, and you, a wild olive shoot, were grafted in their place to share the rich root[e] of the olive tree, 18do not boast over the branches. If you do boast, remember that it is not you that support the root, but the root that supports you. 19You will say, "Branches were broken off so that I might be grafted in." 20That is true. They were broken off because of their unbelief, but you stand only through faith. So do not become proud, but stand in awe. 21For if God did not spare the natural branches, perhaps he will not spare you.[f] 22Note then the kindness and the severity of God: severity toward those who have fallen, but God's kindness toward you, provided you continue in his kindness; otherwise you also will be cut off. 23And even those of Israel,[g] if they do not persist in unbelief, will be grafted in, for God has the power to graft them in again. 24For if you have been cut from what is by nature a wild olive tree and grafted, contrary to nature, into a cultivated olive tree, how much more will these natural branches be grafted back into their own olive tree.

All Israel Will Be Saved

25 So that you may not claim to be wiser

καὶ εἰς σκάνδαλον καὶ εἰς
ἀνταπόδομα αὐτοῖς,
10 σκοτισθήτωσαν οἱ ὀφθαλμοὶ αὐτῶν
τοῦ μὴ βλέπειν
καὶ τὸν νῶτον αὐτῶν διὰ
παντὸς σύγκαμψον.

11 Λέγω οὖν, μὴ ἔπταισαν ἵνα πέσωσιν; μὴ γένοιτο· ἀλλὰ τῷ αὐτῶν παραπτώματι ἡ σωτηρία τοῖς ἔθνεσιν εἰς τὸ παραζηλῶσαι αὐτούς. 12 εἰ δὲ τὸ παράπτωμα αὐτῶν πλοῦτος κόσμου καὶ τὸ ἥττημα αὐτῶν πλοῦτος ἐθνῶν, πόσῳ μᾶλλον τὸ πλήρωμα αὐτῶν.
13 Ὑμῖν δὲ λέγω τοῖς ἔθνεσιν· ἐφ' ὅσον μὲν οὖν εἰμι ἐγὼ ἐθνῶν ἀπόστολος, τὴν διακονίαν μου δοξάζω, 14 εἴ πως παραζηλώσω μου τὴν σάρκα καὶ σώσω τινὰς ἐξ αὐτῶν. 15 εἰ γὰρ ἡ ἀποβολὴ αὐτῶν καταλλαγὴ κόσμου, τίς ἡ πρόσλημψις εἰ μὴ ζωὴ ἐκ νεκρῶν; 16 εἰ δὲ ἡ ἀπαρχὴ ἁγία, καὶ τὸ φύραμα· καὶ εἰ ἡ ῥίζα ἁγία, καὶ οἱ κλάδοι.
17 Εἰ δέ τινες τῶν κλάδων ἐξεκλάσθησαν, σὺ δὲ ἀγριέλαιος ὢν ἐνεκεντρίσθης ἐν αὐτοῖς καὶ συγκοινωνὸς τῆς ῥίζης[b] τῆς πιότητος τῆς ἐλαίας ἐγένου, 18 μὴ κατακαυχῶ τῶν κλάδων· εἰ δὲ κατακαυχᾶσαι οὐ σὺ τὴν ῥίζαν βαστάζεις ἀλλὰ ἡ ῥίζα σέ. 19 ἐρεῖς οὖν, Ἐξεκλάσθησαν κλάδοι ἵνα ἐγὼ ἐγκεντρισθῶ. 20 καλῶς· τῇ ἀπιστίᾳ ἐξεκλάσθησαν, σὺ δὲ τῇ πίστει ἕστηκας. μὴ ὑψηλὰ φρόνει ἀλλὰ φοβοῦ· 21 εἰ γὰρ ὁ θεὸς τῶν κατὰ φύσιν κλάδων οὐκ ἐφείσατο, [μή πως][c] οὐδὲ σοῦ φείσεται. 22 ἴδε οὖν χρηστότητα καὶ ἀποτομίαν θεοῦ· ἐπὶ μὲν τοὺς πεσόντας ἀποτομία, ἐπὶ δὲ σὲ χρηστότης θεοῦ, ἐὰν ἐπιμένῃς τῇ χρηστότητι, ἐπεὶ καὶ σὺ ἐκκοπήσῃ. 23 κἀκεῖνοι δέ, ἐὰν μὴ ἐπιμένωσιν τῇ ἀπιστίᾳ, ἐγκεντρισθήσονται· δυνατὸς γάρ ἐστιν ὁ θεὸς πάλιν ἐγκεντρίσαι αὐτούς. 24 εἰ γὰρ σὺ ἐκ τῆς κατὰ φύσιν ἐξεκόπης ἀγριελαίου καὶ παρὰ φύσιν ἐνεκεντρίσθης εἰς καλλιέλαιον, πόσῳ μᾶλλον οὗτοι οἱ κατὰ φύσιν ἐγκεντρισθήσονται τῇ ἰδίᾳ ἐλαίᾳ.
25 Οὐ γὰρ θέλω ὑμᾶς ἀγνοεῖν, ἀδελφοί, τὸ μυστήριον τοῦτο, ἵνα μὴ ἦτε [παρ']

a stumbling block and a retribution
for them.
10May their eyes be darkened so they
cannot see,
and their backs be bent forever."[e]

Ingrafted Branches

11Again I ask: Did they stumble so as to fall beyond recovery? Not at all! Rather, because of their transgression, salvation has come to the Gentiles to make Israel envious. 12But if their transgression means riches for the world, and their loss means riches for the Gentiles, how much greater riches will their fullness bring!

13I am talking to you Gentiles. Inasmuch as I am the apostle to the Gentiles, I make much of my ministry 14in the hope that I may somehow arouse my own people to envy and save some of them. 15For if their rejection is the reconciliation of the world, what will their acceptance be but life from the dead? 16If the part of the dough offered as firstfruits is holy, then the whole batch is holy; if the root is holy, so are the branches.

17If some of the branches have been broken off, and you, though a wild olive shoot, have been grafted in among the others and now share in the nourishing sap from the olive root, 18do not boast over those branches. If you do, consider this: You do not support the root, but the root supports you. 19You will say then, "Branches were broken off so that I could be grafted in." 20Granted. But they were broken off because of unbelief, and you stand by faith. Do not be arrogant, but be afraid. 21For if God did not spare the natural branches, he will not spare you either.

22Consider therefore the kindness and sternness of God: sternness to those who fell, but kindness to you, provided that you continue in his kindness. Otherwise, you also will be cut off. 23And if they do not persist in unbelief, they will be grafted in, for God is able to graft them in again. 24After all, if you were cut out of an olive tree that is wild by nature, and contrary to nature were grafted into a cultivated olive tree, how much more readily will these, the natural branches, be grafted into their own olive tree!

All Israel Will Be Saved

25I do not want you to be ignorant of this mystery, brothers, so that you may not be

---

[b] Gk *transgression*   [c] Gk *them*   [b] Gk *transgression*
[e] Other ancient authorities read *the richness*   [f] Other
ancient authorities read *neither will he spare you*
[g] Gk lacks *of Israel*

[b]17 NRSV note e omits τῆς ῥίζης   [c]21 NIV text and
NRSV note f omit μή πως

[e]10 Psalm 69:22,23

than you are, brothers and sisters,[h] I want you to understand this mystery: a hardening has come upon part of Israel, until the full number of the Gentiles has come in. 26And so all Israel will be saved; as it is written,

> "Out of Zion will come the Deliverer;
>   he will banish ungodliness from
>   Jacob."

27 "And this is my covenant with them,
  when I take away their sins."

28As regards the gospel they are enemies of God[i] for your sake; but as regards election they are beloved, for the sake of their ancestors; 29for the gifts and the calling of God are irrevocable. 30Just as you were once disobedient to God but have now received mercy because of their disobedience, 31so they have now been disobedient in order that, by the mercy shown to you, they too may now[j] receive mercy. 32For God has imprisoned all in disobedience so that he may be merciful to all.

33 O the depth of the riches and wisdom and knowledge of God! How unsearchable are his judgments and how inscrutable his ways!

34 "For who has known the mind of the
    Lord?
  Or who has been his counselor?"
35 "Or who has given a gift to him,
  to receive a gift in return?"

36For from him and through him and to him are all things. To him be the glory forever. Amen.

The New Life in Christ

12 I appeal to you therefore, brothers and sisters,[h] by the mercies of God, to present your bodies as a living sacrifice, holy and acceptable to God, which is your spiritual[l] worship. 2Do not be conformed to this world,[m] but be transformed by the renewing of your minds, so that you may discern what is the will of God—what is good and acceptable and perfect.[n]

3 For by the grace given to me I say to everyone among you not to think of yourself more highly than you ought to think, but to think with sober judgment, each according to the measure of faith that God has assigned. 4For as in one body we have many members, and not all the members have the same function, 5so we, who are

---

ἑαυτοῖς φρόνιμοι, ὅτι πώρωσις ἀπὸ μέρους τῷ Ἰσραὴλ γέγονεν ἄχρις οὗ τὸ πλήρωμα τῶν ἐθνῶν εἰσέλθῃ 26 καὶ οὕτως πᾶς Ἰσραὴλ σωθήσεται, καθὼς γέγραπται,

> Ἥξει ἐκ Σιὼν ὁ ῥυόμενος,
> ἀποστρέψει ἀσεβείας ἀπὸ
>   Ἰακώβ.
27 καὶ αὕτη αὐτοῖς ἡ παρ᾽ ἐμοῦ
  διαθήκη,
> ὅταν ἀφέλωμαι τὰς ἁμαρτίας
>   αὐτῶν.

28 κατὰ μὲν τὸ εὐαγγέλιον ἐχθροὶ δι᾽ ὑμᾶς, κατὰ δὲ τὴν ἐκλογὴν ἀγαπητοὶ διὰ τοὺς πατέρας· 29 ἀμεταμέλητα γὰρ τὰ χαρίσματα καὶ ἡ κλῆσις τοῦ θεοῦ. 30 ὥσπερ γὰρ ὑμεῖς ποτε ἠπειθήσατε τῷ θεῷ, νῦν δὲ ἠλεήθητε τῇ τούτων ἀπειθείᾳ, 31 οὕτως καὶ οὗτοι νῦν ἠπείθησαν τῷ ὑμετέρῳ ἐλέει, ἵνα καὶ αὐτοὶ [νῦν] ἐλεηθῶσιν. 32 συνέκλεισεν γὰρ ὁ θεὸς τοὺς πάντας εἰς ἀπείθειαν, ἵνα τοὺς πάντας ἐλεήσῃ.

33 Ὦ βάθος πλούτου καὶ σοφίας καὶ γνώσεως θεοῦ· ὡς ἀνεξεραύνητα τὰ κρίματα αὐτοῦ καὶ ἀνεξιχνίαστοι αἱ ὁδοὶ αὐτοῦ.

34 Τίς γὰρ ἔγνω νοῦν κυρίου;
  ἢ τίς σύμβουλος αὐτοῦ ἐγένετο;
35 ἢ τίς προέδωκεν αὐτῷ,
  καὶ ἀνταποδοθήσεται αὐτῷ;
36 ὅτι ἐξ αὐτοῦ καὶ δι᾽ αὐτοῦ καὶ εἰς αὐτὸν τὰ πάντα· αὐτῷ ἡ δόξα εἰς τοὺς αἰῶνας, ἀμήν.

12 Παρακαλῶ οὖν ὑμᾶς, ἀδελφοί, διὰ τῶν οἰκτιρμῶν τοῦ θεοῦ παραστῆσαι τὰ σώματα ὑμῶν θυσίαν ζῶσαν ἁγίαν εὐάρεστον τῷ θεῷ, τὴν λογικὴν λατρείαν ὑμῶν· 2 καὶ μὴ συσχηματίζεσθε τῷ αἰῶνι τούτῳ, ἀλλὰ μεταμορφοῦσθε τῇ ἀνακαινώσει τοῦ νοὸς εἰς τὸ δοκιμάζειν ὑμᾶς τί τὸ θέλημα τοῦ θεοῦ, τὸ ἀγαθὸν καὶ εὐάρεστον καὶ τέλειον.

3 Λέγω γὰρ διὰ τῆς χάριτος τῆς δοθείσης μοι παντὶ τῷ ὄντι ἐν ὑμῖν μὴ ὑπερφρονεῖν παρ᾽ ὃ δεῖ φρονεῖν ἀλλὰ φρονεῖν εἰς τὸ σωφρονεῖν, ἑκάστῳ ὡς ὁ θεὸς ἐμέρισεν μέτρον πίστεως. 4 καθάπερ γὰρ ἐν ἑνὶ σώματι πολλὰ μέλη ἔχομεν, τὰ δὲ μέλη πάντα οὐ τὴν αὐτὴν ἔχει πρᾶξιν, 5 οὕτως οἱ πολλοὶ

---

conceited: Israel has experienced a hardening in part until the full number of the Gentiles has come in. 26And so all Israel will be saved, as it is written:

> "The deliverer will come from Zion;
>   he will turn godlessness away from
>   Jacob.
27And this is[f] my covenant with them
>   when I take away their sins."[g]

28As far as the gospel is concerned, they are enemies on your account; but as far as election is concerned, they are loved on account of the patriarchs, 29for God's gifts and his call are irrevocable. 30Just as you who were at one time disobedient to God have now received mercy as a result of their disobedience, 31so they too have now become disobedient in order that they too may now[h] receive mercy as a result of God's mercy to you. 32For God has bound all men over to disobedience so that he may have mercy on them all.

Doxology

33Oh, the depth of the riches of the
    wisdom and[i] knowledge of God!
  How unsearchable his judgments,
  and his paths beyond tracing out!
34"Who has known the mind of the Lord?
  Or who has been his counselor?"[j]
35"Who has ever given to God,
  that God should repay him?"[k]
36For from him and through him and to
    him are all things.
  To him be the glory forever! Amen.

Living Sacrifices

12 Therefore, I urge you, brothers, in view of God's mercy, to offer your bodies as living sacrifices, holy and pleasing to God—this is your spiritual[a] act of worship. 2Do not conform any longer to the pattern of this world, but be transformed by the renewing of your mind. Then you will be able to test and approve what God's will is—his good, pleasing and perfect will.

3For by the grace given me I say to every one of you: Do not think of yourself more highly than you ought, but rather think of yourself with sober judgment, in accordance with the measure of faith God has given you. 4Just as each of us has one body with many members, and these members do not all have the same function, 5so in

---

[h] Gk *brothers*   [i] Gk lacks *of God*   [j] Other ancient authorities lack *now*   [l] Or *reasonable*   [m] Gk *age*
[n] Or *what is the good and acceptable and perfect will of God*

[f]27 Or *will be*   [g]27 Isaiah 59:20,21; 27:9; Jer. 31:33,34
[h]31 Some manuscripts do not have *now*.   [i]33 Or *riches and the wisdom and the*   [j]34 Isaiah 40:13   [k]35 Job 41:11
[a]1 Or *reasonable*

many, are one body in Christ, and individually we are members one of another. [6]We have gifts that differ according to the grace given to us: prophecy, in proportion to faith; [7]ministry, in ministering; the teacher, in teaching; [8]the exhorter, in exhortation; the giver, in generosity; the leader, in diligence; the compassionate, in cheerfulness.

Marks of the True Christian

9 Let love be genuine; hate what is evil, hold fast to what is good; [10]love one another with mutual affection; outdo one another in showing honor. [11]Do not lag in zeal, be ardent in spirit, serve the Lord.[o] [12]Rejoice in hope, be patient in suffering, persevere in prayer. [13]Contribute to the needs of the saints; extend hospitality to strangers.

14 Bless those who persecute you; bless and do not curse them. [15]Rejoice with those who rejoice, weep with those who weep. [16]Live in harmony with one another; do not be haughty, but associate with the lowly;[p] do not claim to be wiser than you are. [17]Do not repay anyone evil for evil, but take thought for what is noble in the sight of all. [18]If it is possible, so far as it depends on you, live peaceably with all. [19]Beloved, never avenge yourselves, but leave room for the wrath of God;[q] for it is written, "Vengeance is mine, I will repay, says the Lord." [20]No, "if your enemies are hungry, feed them; if they are thirsty, give them something to drink; for by doing this you will heap burning coals on their heads." [21]Do not be overcome by evil, but overcome evil with good.

Being Subject to Authorities

13 Let every person be subject to the governing authorities; for there is no authority except from God, and those authorities that exist have been instituted by God. [2]Therefore whoever resists authority resists what God has appointed, and those who resist will incur judgment. [3]For rulers are not a terror to good conduct,

ἐν σῶμά ἐσμεν ἐν Χριστῷ, τὸ δὲ καθ᾽ εἷς ἀλλήλων μέλη. **6** ἔχοντες δὲ χαρίσματα κατὰ τὴν χάριν τὴν δοθεῖσαν ἡμῖν διάφορα, εἴτε προφητείαν κατὰ τὴν ἀναλογίαν τῆς πίστεως, **7** εἴτε διακονίαν ἐν τῇ διακονίᾳ, εἴτε ὁ διδάσκων ἐν τῇ διδασκαλίᾳ, **8** εἴτε ὁ παρακαλῶν ἐν τῇ παρακλήσει· ὁ μεταδιδοὺς ἐν ἁπλότητι, ὁ προϊστάμενος ἐν σπουδῇ, ὁ ἐλεῶν ἐν ἱλαρότητι.

9 Ἡ ἀγάπη ἀνυπόκριτος. ἀποστυγοῦντες τὸ πονηρόν, κολλώμενοι τῷ ἀγαθῷ, **10** τῇ φιλαδελφίᾳ εἰς ἀλλήλους φιλόστοργοι, τῇ τιμῇ ἀλλήλους προηγούμενοι, **11** τῇ σπουδῇ μὴ ὀκνηροί, τῷ πνεύματι ζέοντες, τῷ κυρίῳ[a] δουλεύοντες, **12** τῇ ἐλπίδι χαίροντες, τῇ θλίψει ὑπομένοντες, τῇ προσευχῇ προσκαρτεροῦντες, **13** ταῖς χρείαις τῶν ἁγίων κοινωνοῦντες, τὴν φιλοξενίαν διώκοντες. **14** εὐλογεῖτε τοὺς διώκοντας [ὑμᾶς], εὐλογεῖτε καὶ μὴ καταρᾶσθε. **15** χαίρειν μετὰ χαιρόντων, κλαίειν μετὰ κλαιόντων. **16** τὸ αὐτὸ εἰς ἀλλήλους φρονοῦντες, μὴ τὰ ὑψηλὰ φρονοῦντες ἀλλὰ τοῖς ταπεινοῖς συναπαγόμενοι. μὴ γίνεσθε φρόνιμοι παρ᾽ ἑαυτοῖς. **17** μηδενὶ κακὸν ἀντὶ κακοῦ ἀποδιδόντες, προνοούμενοι καλὰ ἐνώπιον πάντων ἀνθρώπων· **18** εἰ δυνατὸν τὸ ἐξ ὑμῶν, μετὰ πάντων ἀνθρώπων εἰρηνεύοντες· **19** μὴ ἑαυτοὺς ἐκδικοῦντες, ἀγαπητοί, ἀλλὰ δότε τόπον τῇ ὀργῇ, γέγραπται γάρ, Ἐμοὶ ἐκδίκησις, ἐγὼ ἀνταποδώσω, λέγει κύριος. **20** ἀλλὰ ἐὰν πεινᾷ ὁ ἐχθρός σου, ψώμιζε αὐτόν· ἐὰν διψᾷ, πότιζε αὐτόν· τοῦτο γὰρ ποιῶν ἄνθρακας πυρὸς σωρεύσεις ἐπὶ τὴν κεφαλὴν αὐτοῦ. **21** μὴ νικῶ ὑπὸ τοῦ κακοῦ ἀλλὰ νίκα ἐν τῷ ἀγαθῷ τὸ κακόν.

13 Πᾶσα ψυχὴ ἐξουσίαις ὑπερεχούσαις ὑποτασσέσθω. οὐ γὰρ ἔστιν ἐξουσία εἰ μὴ ὑπὸ θεοῦ, αἱ δὲ οὖσαι ὑπὸ θεοῦ τεταγμέναι εἰσίν. **2** ὥστε ὁ ἀντιτασσόμενος τῇ ἐξουσίᾳ τῇ τοῦ θεοῦ διαταγῇ ἀνθέστηκεν, οἱ δὲ ἀνθεστηκότες ἑαυτοῖς κρίμα λήμψονται. **3** οἱ γὰρ ἄρχοντες οὐκ εἰσὶν φόβος

Christ we who are many form one body, and each member belongs to all the others. [6]We have different gifts, according to the grace given us. If a man's gift is prophesying, let him use it in proportion to his[b] faith. [7]If it is serving, let him serve; if it is teaching, let him teach; [8]if it is encouraging, let him encourage; if it is contributing to the needs of others, let him give generously; if it is leadership, let him govern diligently; if it is showing mercy, let him do it cheerfully.

Love

[9]Love must be sincere. Hate what is evil; cling to what is good. [10]Be devoted to one another in brotherly love. Honor one another above yourselves. [11]Never be lacking in zeal, but keep your spiritual fervor, serving the Lord. [12]Be joyful in hope, patient in affliction, faithful in prayer. [13]Share with God's people who are in need. Practice hospitality.

[14]Bless those who persecute you; bless and do not curse. [15]Rejoice with those who rejoice; mourn with those who mourn. [16]Live in harmony with one another. Do not be proud, but be willing to associate with people of low position.[c] Do not be conceited.

[17]Do not repay anyone evil for evil. Be careful to do what is right in the eyes of everybody. [18]If it is possible, as far as it depends on you, live at peace with everyone. [19]Do not take revenge, my friends, but leave room for God's wrath, for it is written: "It is mine to avenge; I will repay,"[d] says the Lord. [20]On the contrary:

"If your enemy is hungry, feed him;
  if he is thirsty, give him something to
    drink.
In doing this, you will heap burning
  coals on his head."[e]

[21]Do not be overcome by evil, but overcome evil with good.

Submission to the Authorities

13 Everyone must submit himself to the governing authorities, for there is no authority except that which God has established. The authorities that exist have been established by God. [2]Consequently, he who rebels against the authority is rebelling against what God has instituted, and those who do so will bring judgment on themselves. [3]For rulers hold

---

[o] Other ancient authorities read *serve the opportune time*
[p] Or *give yourselves to humble tasks*   [q] Gk *the wrath*

[a]11 NRSV note ο καιρῷ

[b]6 Or *in agreement with the*   [c]16 Or *willing to do menial work*   [d]19 Deut. 32:35   [e]20 Prov. 25:21,22

but to bad. Do you wish to have no fear of the authority? Then do what is good, and you will receive its approval;[r] 4for it is God's servant for your good. But if you do what is wrong, you should be afraid, for the authority[r] does not bear the sword in vain! It is the servant of God to execute wrath on the wrongdoer. 5Therefore one must be subject, not only because of wrath but also because of conscience. 6For the same reason you also pay taxes, for the authorities are God's servants, busy with this very thing. 7Pay to all what is due them—taxes to whom taxes are due, revenue to whom revenue is due, respect to whom respect is due, honor to whom honor is due.

Love for One Another

8 Owe no one anything, except to love one another; for the one who loves another has fulfilled the law. 9The commandments, "You shall not commit adultery; You shall not murder; You shall not steal; You shall not covet"; and any other commandment, are summed up in this word, "Love your neighbor as yourself." 10Love does no wrong to a neighbor; therefore, love is the fulfilling of the law.

An Urgent Appeal

11 Besides this, you know what time it is, how it is now the moment for you to wake from sleep. For salvation is nearer to us now than when we became believers; 12the night is far gone, the day is near. Let us then lay aside the works of darkness and put on the armor of light; 13let us live honorably as in the day, not in reveling and drunkenness, not in debauchery and licentiousness, not in quarreling and jealousy. 14Instead, put on the Lord Jesus Christ, and make no provision for the flesh, to gratify its desires.

Do Not Judge Another

14 Welcome those who are weak in faith,[s] but not for the purpose of quarreling over opinions. 2Some believe in eating anything, while the weak eat only vegetables. 3Those who eat must not despise those who abstain, and those who abstain must not pass judgment on those who eat; for God has welcomed them. 4Who are you to pass judgment on servants

τῷ ἀγαθῷ ἔργῳ ἀλλὰ τῷ κακῷ. θέλεις δὲ μὴ φοβεῖσθαι τὴν ἐξουσίαν· τὸ ἀγαθὸν ποίει, καὶ ἕξεις ἔπαινον ἐξ αὐτῆς· **4** θεοῦ γὰρ διάκονός ἐστιν σοὶ εἰς τὸ ἀγαθόν. ἐὰν δὲ τὸ κακὸν ποιῇς, φοβοῦ· οὐ γὰρ εἰκῇ τὴν μάχαιραν φορεῖ· θεοῦ γὰρ διάκονός ἐστιν ἔκδικος εἰς ὀργὴν τῷ τὸ κακὸν πράσσοντι. **5** διὸ ἀνάγκη ὑποτάσσεσθαι, οὐ μόνον διὰ τὴν ὀργὴν ἀλλὰ καὶ διὰ τὴν συνείδησιν. **6** διὰ τοῦτο γὰρ καὶ φόρους τελεῖτε· λειτουργοὶ γὰρ θεοῦ εἰσιν εἰς αὐτὸ τοῦτο προσκαρτεροῦντες. **7** ἀπόδοτε πᾶσιν τὰς ὀφειλάς, τῷ τὸν φόρον τὸν φόρον, τῷ τὸ τέλος τὸ τέλος, τῷ τὸν φόβον τὸν φόβον, τῷ τὴν τιμὴν τὴν τιμήν.

8 Μηδενὶ μηδὲν ὀφείλετε εἰ μὴ τὸ ἀλλήλους ἀγαπᾶν· ὁ γὰρ ἀγαπῶν τὸν ἕτερον νόμον πεπλήρωκεν. **9** τὸ γὰρ **Οὐ μοιχεύσεις, Οὐ φονεύσεις, Οὐ κλέψεις, Οὐκ ἐπιθυμήσεις,** καὶ εἴ τις ἑτέρα ἐντολή, ἐν τῷ λόγῳ τούτῳ ἀνακεφαλαιοῦται [ἐν τῷ][a] **Ἀγαπήσεις τὸν πλησίον σου ὡς σεαυτόν. 10** ἡ ἀγάπη τῷ πλησίον κακὸν οὐκ ἐργάζεται· πλήρωμα οὖν νόμου ἡ ἀγάπη.

11 Καὶ τοῦτο εἰδότες τὸν καιρόν, ὅτι ὥρα ἤδη ὑμᾶς ἐξ ὕπνου ἐγερθῆναι, νῦν γὰρ ἐγγύτερον ἡμῶν ἡ σωτηρία ἢ ὅτε ἐπιστεύσαμεν. **12** ἡ νὺξ προέκοψεν, ἡ δὲ ἡμέρα ἤγγικεν. ἀποθώμεθα οὖν τὰ ἔργα τοῦ σκότους, ἐνδυσώμεθα [δὲ] τὰ ὅπλα τοῦ φωτός. **13** ὡς ἐν ἡμέρᾳ εὐσχημόνως περιπατήσωμεν, μὴ κώμοις καὶ μέθαις, μὴ κοίταις καὶ ἀσελγείαις, μὴ ἔριδι καὶ ζήλῳ, **14** ἀλλὰ ἐνδύσασθε τὸν κύριον Ἰησοῦν Χριστὸν καὶ τῆς σαρκὸς πρόνοιαν μὴ ποιεῖσθε εἰς ἐπιθυμίας.

14 Τὸν δὲ ἀσθενοῦντα τῇ πίστει προσλαμβάνεσθε, μὴ εἰς διακρίσεις διαλογισμῶν. **2** ὃς μὲν πιστεύει φαγεῖν πάντα, ὁ δὲ ἀσθενῶν λάχανα ἐσθίει. **3** ὁ ἐσθίων τὸν μὴ ἐσθίοντα μὴ ἐξουθενείτω, ὁ δὲ μὴ ἐσθίων τὸν ἐσθίοντα μὴ κρινέτω, ὁ θεὸς γὰρ αὐτὸν προσελάβετο. **4** σὺ τίς εἶ ὁ κρίνων

no terror for those who do right, but for those who do wrong. Do you want to be free from fear of the one in authority? Then do what is right and he will commend you. 4For he is God's servant to do you good. But if you do wrong, be afraid, for he does not bear the sword for nothing. He is God's servant, an agent of wrath to bring punishment on the wrongdoer. 5Therefore, it is necessary to submit to the authorities, not only because of possible punishment but also because of conscience.

6This is also why you pay taxes, for the authorities are God's servants, who give their full time to governing. 7Give everyone what you owe him: If you owe taxes, pay taxes; if revenue, then revenue; if respect, then respect; if honor, then honor.

Love, for the Day is Near

8Let no debt remain outstanding, except the continuing debt to love one another, for he who loves his fellowman has fulfilled the law. 9The commandments, "Do not commit adultery," "Do not murder," "Do not steal," "Do not covet,"[a] and whatever other commandment there may be, are summed up in this one rule: "Love your neighbor as yourself."[b] 10Love does no harm to its neighbor. Therefore love is the fulfillment of the law.

11And do this, understanding the present time. The hour has come for you to wake up from your slumber, because our salvation is nearer now than when we first believed. 12The night is nearly over; the day is almost here. So let us put aside the deeds of darkness and put on the armor of light. 13Let us behave decently, as in the daytime, not in orgies and drunkenness, not in sexual immorality and debauchery, not in dissension and jealousy. 14Rather, clothe yourselves with the Lord Jesus Christ, and do not think about how to gratify the desires of the sinful nature.[c]

The Weak and the Strong

14 Accept him whose faith is weak, without passing judgment on disputable matters. 2One man's faith allows him to eat everything, but another man, whose faith is weak, eats only vegetables. 3The man who eats everything must not look down on him who does not, and the man who does not eat everything must not condemn the man who does, for God has accepted him. 4Who are you to judge

---

NRSV

of another? It is before their own lord that they stand or fall. And they will be upheld, for the Lord[t] is able to make them stand.

5 Some judge one day to be better than another, while others judge all days to be alike. Let all be fully convinced in their own minds. 6Those who observe the day, observe it in honor of the Lord. Also those who eat, eat in honor of the Lord, since they give thanks to God; while those who abstain, abstain in honor of the Lord and give thanks to God.

7 We do not live to ourselves, and we do not die to ourselves. 8If we live, we live to the Lord, and if we die, we die to the Lord; so then, whether we live or whether we die, we are the Lord's. 9For to this end Christ died and lived again, so that he might be Lord of both the dead and the living.

10 Why do you pass judgment on your brother or sister?[u] Or you, why do you despise your brother or sister?[u] For we will all stand before the judgment seat of God.[v] 11For it is written,

"As I live, says the Lord, every knee
    shall bow to me,
and every tongue shall give praise
    to[w] God."

12So then, each of us will be accountable to God.[x]

Do Not Make Another Stumble

13 Let us therefore no longer pass judgment on one another, but resolve instead never to put a stumbling block or hindrance in the way of another.[y] 14I know and am persuaded in the Lord Jesus that nothing is unclean in itself; but it is unclean for anyone who thinks it unclean. 15If your brother or sister[u] is being injured by what you eat, you are no longer walking in love. Do not let what you eat cause the ruin of one for whom Christ died. 16So do not let your good be spoken of as evil. 17For the kingdom of God is not food and drink but righteousness and peace and joy in the Holy Spirit. 18The one who thus serves Christ is acceptable to God and has human approval. 19Let us then pursue what makes for peace and for mutual upbuilding. 20Do not, for the sake of food, destroy the work of God. Everything is indeed clean, but it is wrong for you to make others fall by what you eat; 21it is good not

NIV

someone else's servant? To his own master he stands or falls. And he will stand, for the Lord is able to make him stand.

5One man considers one day more sacred than another; another man considers every day alike. Each one should be fully convinced in his own mind. 6He who regards one day as special, does so to the Lord. He who eats meat, eats to the Lord, for he gives thanks to God; and he who abstains, does so to the Lord and gives thanks to God. 7For none of us lives to himself alone and none of us dies to himself alone. 8If we live, we live to the Lord; and if we die, we die to the Lord. So, whether we live or die, we belong to the Lord.

9For this very reason, Christ died and returned to life so that he might be the Lord of both the dead and the living. 10You, then, why do you judge your brother? Or why do you look down on your brother? For we will all stand before God's judgment seat. 11It is written:

" 'As surely as I live,' says the Lord,
'every knee will bow before me;
    every tongue will confess to God.' "[a]

12So then, each of us will give an account of himself to God.

13Therefore let us stop passing judgment on one another. Instead, make up your mind not to put any stumbling block or obstacle in your brother's way. 14As one who is in the Lord Jesus, I am fully convinced that no food[b] is unclean in itself. But if anyone regards something as unclean, then for him it is unclean. 15If your brother is distressed because of what you eat, you are no longer acting in love. Do not by your eating destroy your brother for whom Christ died. 16Do not allow what you consider good to be spoken of as evil. 17For the kingdom of God is not a matter of eating and drinking, but of righteousness, peace and joy in the Holy Spirit, 18because anyone who serves Christ in this way is pleasing to God and approved by men.

19Let us therefore make every effort to do what leads to peace and to mutual edification. 20Do not destroy the work of God for the sake of food. All food is clean, but it is wrong for a man to eat anything that causes someone else to stumble. 21It is better not to eat meat or drink wine or to

---

[t] Other ancient authorities read *for God*   [u] Gk *brother*
[v] Other ancient authorities read *of Christ*   [w] Or *confess*
[x] Other ancient authorities lack *to God*   [y] Gk *of a brother*

[a]4 NRSV note t θεός   [b]5 NIV text omits γάρ
[c]10 NRSV note v Χριστοῦ

[a]11 Isaiah 45:23   [b]14 Or *that nothing*

NRSV

to eat meat or drink wine or do anything that make your brother or sister[z] stumble.[a] [22]The faith that you have, have as your own conviction before God. Blessed are those who have no reason to condemn themselves because of what they approve. [23]But those who have doubts are condemned if they eat, because they do not act from faith;[b] for whatever does not proceed from faith[b] is sin.[c]

Please Others, Not Yourselves

15 We who are strong ought to put up with the failings of the weak, and not to please ourselves. [2]Each of us must please our neighbor for the good purpose of building up the neighbor. [3]For Christ did not please himself; but, as it is written, "The insults of those who insult you have fallen on me." [4]For whatever was written in former days was written for our instruction, so that by steadfastness and by the encouragement of the scriptures we might have hope. [5]May the God of steadfastness and encouragement grant you to live in harmony with one another, in accordance with Christ Jesus, [6]so that together you may with one voice glorify the God and Father of our Lord Jesus Christ.

The Gospel for Jews and Gentiles Alike

[7] Welcome one another, therefore, just as Christ has welcomed you, for the glory of God. [8]For I tell you that Christ has become a servant of the circumcised on behalf of the truth of God in order that he might confirm the promises given to the patriarchs, [9]and in order that the Gentiles might glorify God for his mercy. As it is written,

"Therefore I will confess[d] you among
     the Gentiles,
   and sing praises to your name";
[10]and again he says,
"Rejoice, O Gentiles, with his people";
[11]and again,
"Praise the Lord, all you Gentiles,
   and let all the peoples praise him";
[12]and again Isaiah says,
"The root of Jesse shall come,
   the one who rises to rule the Gentiles;
   in him the Gentiles shall hope."
[13]May the God of hope fill you with all joy and peace in believing, so that you may abound in hope by the power of the Holy Spirit.

z Gk *brother*   a Other ancient authorities add *or be upset or be weakened*   b Or *conviction*   c Other authorities, some ancient, add here 16.25-27   d Or *thank*

Greek

μηδὲ πιεῖν οἶνον μηδὲ ἐν ᾧ ὁ ἀδελφός σου προσκόπτει[d]. **22** σὺ πίστιν [ἣν] ἔχεις κατὰ σεαυτὸν ἔχε ἐνώπιον τοῦ θεοῦ. μακάριος ὁ μὴ κρίνων ἑαυτὸν ἐν ᾧ δοκιμάζει· **23** ὁ δὲ διακρινόμενος ἐὰν φάγῃ κατακέκριται, ὅτι οὐκ ἐκ πίστεως· πᾶν δὲ ὃ οὐκ ἐκ πίστεως ἁμαρτία ἐστίν.

15 Ὀφείλομεν δὲ ἡμεῖς οἱ δυνατοὶ τὰ ἀσθενήματα τῶν ἀδυνάτων βαστάζειν καὶ μὴ ἑαυτοῖς ἀρέσκειν. **2** ἕκαστος ἡμῶν τῷ πλησίον ἀρεσκέτω εἰς τὸ ἀγαθὸν πρὸς οἰκοδομήν· **3** καὶ γὰρ ὁ Χριστὸς οὐχ ἑαυτῷ ἤρεσεν· ἀλλὰ καθὼς γέγραπται, **Οἱ ὀνειδισμοὶ τῶν ὀνειδιζόντων σε ἐπέπεσαν ἐπ' ἐμέ.** **4** ὅσα γὰρ προεγράφη, εἰς τὴν ἡμετέραν διδασκαλίαν ἐγράφη, ἵνα διὰ τῆς ὑπομονῆς καὶ διὰ τῆς παρακλήσεως τῶν γραφῶν τὴν ἐλπίδα ἔχωμεν. **5** ὁ δὲ θεὸς τῆς ὑπομονῆς καὶ τῆς παρακλήσεως δῴη ὑμῖν τὸ αὐτὸ φρονεῖν ἐν ἀλλήλοις κατὰ Χριστὸν Ἰησοῦν, **6** ἵνα ὁμοθυμαδὸν ἐν ἑνὶ στόματι δοξάζητε τὸν θεὸν καὶ πατέρα τοῦ κυρίου ἡμῶν Ἰησοῦ Χριστοῦ.

7 Διὸ προσλαμβάνεσθε ἀλλήλους, καθὼς καὶ ὁ Χριστὸς προσελάβετο ὑμᾶς εἰς δόξαν τοῦ θεοῦ. **8** λέγω γὰρ Χριστὸν διάκονον γεγενῆσθαι περιτομῆς ὑπὲρ ἀληθείας θεοῦ, εἰς τὸ βεβαιῶσαι τὰς ἐπαγγελίας τῶν πατέρων, **9** τὰ δὲ ἔθνη ὑπὲρ ἐλέους δοξάσαι τὸν θεόν, καθὼς γέγραπται,

**Διὰ τοῦτο ἐξομολογήσομαί σοι ἐν
     ἔθνεσιν
   καὶ τῷ ὀνόματί σου ψαλῶ.**
10 καὶ πάλιν λέγει,
**Εὐφράνθητε, ἔθνη, μετὰ τοῦ λαοῦ
     αὐτοῦ.**
11 καὶ πάλιν,
**Αἰνεῖτε, πάντα τὰ ἔθνη, τὸν κύριον
   καὶ ἐπαινεσάτωσαν αὐτὸν
     πάντες οἱ λαοί.**
12 καὶ πάλιν Ἠσαΐας λέγει,
**Ἔσται ἡ ῥίζα τοῦ Ἰεσσαὶ
   καὶ ὁ ἀνιστάμενος ἄρχειν ἐθνῶν,
   ἐπ' αὐτῷ ἔθνη ἐλπιοῦσιν.**
13 ὁ δὲ θεὸς τῆς ἐλπίδος πληρώσαι ὑμᾶς πάσης χαρᾶς καὶ εἰρήνης ἐν τῷ πιστεύειν, εἰς τὸ περισσεύειν ὑμᾶς ἐν τῇ ἐλπίδι ἐν δυνάμει πνεύματος ἁγίου.

d21 NRSV note a adds ἢ σκανδαλίζεται ἢ ἀσθενεῖ

NIV

do anything else that will cause your brother to fall.

[22]So whatever you believe about these things keep between yourself and God. Blessed is the man who does not condemn himself by what he approves. [23]But the man who has doubts is condemned if he eats, because his eating is not from faith; and everything that does not come from faith is sin.

15 We who are strong ought to bear with the failings of the weak and not to please ourselves. [2]Each of us should please his neighbor for his good, to build him up. [3]For even Christ did not please himself but, as it is written: "The insults of those who insult you have fallen on me."[a] [4]For everything that was written in the past was written to teach us, so that through endurance and the encouragement of the Scriptures we might have hope.

[5]May the God who gives endurance and encouragement give you a spirit of unity among yourselves as you follow Christ Jesus, [6]so that with one heart and mouth you may glorify the God and Father of our Lord Jesus Christ.

[7]Accept one another, then, just as Christ accepted you, in order to bring praise to God. [8]For I tell you that Christ has become a servant of the Jews[b] on behalf of God's truth, to confirm the promises made to the patriarchs [9]so that the Gentiles may glorify God for his mercy, as it is written:

"Therefore I will praise you among the
     Gentiles;
   I will sing hymns to your name."[c]

[10]Again, it says,

"Rejoice, O Gentiles, with his people."[d]

[11]And again,

"Praise the Lord, all you Gentiles,
   and sing praises to him, all you
     peoples."[e]

[12]And again, Isaiah says,

"The Root of Jesse will spring up,
   one who will arise to rule over the
     nations;
   the Gentiles will hope in him."[f]

[13]May the God of hope fill you with all joy and peace as you trust in him, so that you may overflow with hope by the power of the Holy Spirit.

a3 Psalm 69:9   b8 Greek *circumcision*   c9 2 Samuel 22:50; Psalm 18:49   d10 Deut. 32:43   e11 Psalm 117:1   f12 Isaiah 11:10

NRSV

Paul's Reason for Writing So Boldly

14 I myself feel confident about you, my brothers and sisters,[e] that you yourselves are full of goodness, filled with all knowledge, and able to instruct one another. [15]Nevertheless on some points I have written to you rather boldly by way of reminder, because of the grace given me by God [16]to be a minister of Christ Jesus to the Gentiles in the priestly service of the gospel of God, so that the offering of the Gentiles may be acceptable, sanctified by the Holy Spirit. [17]In Christ Jesus, then, I have reason to boast of my work for God. [18]For I will not venture to speak of anything except what Christ has accomplished[f] through me to win obedience from the Gentiles, by word and deed, [19]by the power of signs and wonders, by the power of the Spirit of God,[g] so that from Jerusalem and as far around as Illyricum I have fully proclaimed the good news[h] of Christ. [20]Thus I make it my ambition to proclaim the good news,[h] not where Christ has already been named, so that I do not build on someone else's foundation, [21]but as it is written,

"Those who have never been told of
     him shall see,
and those who have never heard of
     him shall understand."

Paul's Plan to Visit Rome

22 This is the reason that I have so often been hindered from coming to you. [23]But now, with no further place for me in these regions, I desire, as I have for many years, to come to you [24]when I go to Spain. For I do hope to see you on my journey and to be sent on by you, once I have enjoyed your company for a little while. [25]At present, however, I am going to Jerusalem in a ministry to the saints; [26]for Macedonia and Achaia have been pleased to share their resources with the poor among the saints at Jerusalem. [27]They were pleased to do this, and indeed they owe it to them; for if the Gentiles have come to share in their spiritual blessings, they ought also to be of service to them in material things. [28]So, when I have completed this, and have delivered to them what has been collected,[i] I will set out by way of you to Spain; [29]and I know that when I come to you, I will come in the fullness of the blessing[j] of Christ.

14 Πέπεισμαι δέ, ἀδελφοί μου, καὶ αὐτὸς ἐγὼ περὶ ὑμῶν ὅτι καὶ αὐτοὶ μεστοί ἐστε ἀγαθωσύνης, πεπληρωμένοι πάσης [τῆς] γνώσεως, δυνάμενοι καὶ ἀλλήλους νουθετεῖν. 15 τολμηρότερον δὲ ἔγραψα ὑμῖν ἀπὸ μέρους ὡς ἐπαναμιμνῄσκων ὑμᾶς διὰ τὴν χάριν τὴν δοθεῖσάν μοι ὑπὸ τοῦ θεοῦ 16 εἰς τὸ εἶναί με λειτουργὸν Χριστοῦ Ἰησοῦ εἰς τὰ ἔθνη, ἱερουργοῦντα τὸ εὐαγγέλιον τοῦ θεοῦ, ἵνα γένηται ἡ προσφορὰ τῶν ἐθνῶν εὐπρόσδεκτος, ἡγιασμένη ἐν πνεύματι ἁγίῳ. 17 ἔχω οὖν [τὴν] καύχησιν ἐν Χριστῷ Ἰησοῦ τὰ πρὸς τὸν θεόν· 18 οὐ γὰρ τολμήσω τι λαλεῖν ὧν οὐ κατειργάσατο Χριστὸς δι' ἐμοῦ εἰς ὑπακοὴν ἐθνῶν, λόγῳ καὶ ἔργῳ, 19 ἐν δυνάμει σημείων καὶ τεράτων, ἐν δυνάμει πνεύματος [θεοῦ]ᵃ· ὥστε με ἀπὸ Ἰερουσαλὴμ καὶ κύκλῳ μέχρι τοῦ Ἰλλυρικοῦ πεπληρωκέναι τὸ εὐαγγέλιον τοῦ Χριστοῦ, 20 οὕτως δὲ φιλοτιμούμενον εὐαγγελίζεσθαι οὐχ ὅπου ὠνομάσθη Χριστός, ἵνα μὴ ἐπ' ἀλλότριον θεμέλιον οἰκοδομῶ, 21 ἀλλὰ καθὼς γέγραπται,

Οἷς οὐκ ἀνηγγέλη περὶ αὐτοῦ
     ὄψονται,
καὶ οἳ οὐκ ἀκηκόασιν συνήσουσιν.

22 Διὸ καὶ ἐνεκοπτόμην τὰ πολλὰ τοῦ ἐλθεῖν πρὸς ὑμᾶς· 23 νυνὶ δὲ μηκέτι τόπον ἔχων ἐν τοῖς κλίμασι τούτοις, ἐπιποθίαν δὲ ἔχων τοῦ ἐλθεῖν πρὸς ὑμᾶς ἀπὸ πολλῶν ἐτῶν, 24 ὡς ἂν πορεύωμαι εἰς τὴν Σπανίαν· ἐλπίζω γὰρ διαπορευόμενος θεάσασθαι ὑμᾶς καὶ ὑφ' ὑμῶν προπεμφθῆναι ἐκεῖ ἐὰν ὑμῶν πρῶτον ἀπὸ μέρους ἐμπλησθῶ. 25 νυνὶ δὲ πορεύομαι εἰς Ἰερουσαλὴμ διακονῶν τοῖς ἁγίοις. 26 εὐδόκησαν γὰρ Μακεδονία καὶ Ἀχαΐα κοινωνίαν τινὰ ποιήσασθαι εἰς τοὺς πτωχοὺς τῶν ἁγίων τῶν ἐν Ἰερουσαλήμ. 27 εὐδόκησαν γὰρ καὶ ὀφειλέται εἰσὶν αὐτῶν· εἰ γὰρ τοῖς πνευματικοῖς αὐτῶν ἐκοινώνησαν τὰ ἔθνη, ὀφείλουσιν καὶ ἐν τοῖς σαρκικοῖς λειτουργῆσαι αὐτοῖς. 28 τοῦτο οὖν ἐπιτελέσας καὶ σφραγισάμενος αὐτοῖς τὸν καρπὸν τοῦτον, ἀπελεύσομαι δι' ὑμῶν εἰς Σπανίαν· 29 οἶδα δὲ ὅτι ἐρχόμενος πρὸς ὑμᾶς ἐν πληρώματι εὐλογίας[b] Χριστοῦ ἐλεύσομαι.

NIV

Paul the Minister to the Gentiles

[14]I myself am convinced, my brothers, that you yourselves are full of goodness, complete in knowledge and competent to instruct one another. [15]I have written you quite boldly on some points, as if to remind you of them again, because of the grace God gave me [16]to be a minister of Christ Jesus to the Gentiles with the priestly duty of proclaiming the gospel of God, so that the Gentiles might become an offering acceptable to God, sanctified by the Holy Spirit.

[17]Therefore I glory in Christ Jesus in my service to God. [18]I will not venture to speak of anything except what Christ has accomplished through me in leading the Gentiles to obey God by what I have said and done— [19]by the power of signs and miracles, through the power of the Spirit. So from Jerusalem all the way around to Illyricum, I have fully proclaimed the gospel of Christ. [20]It has always been my ambition to preach the gospel where Christ was not known, so that I would not be building on someone else's foundation. [21]Rather, as it is written:

"Those who were not told about him
     will see,
and those who have not heard will
     understand."[g]

[22]This is why I have often been hindered from coming to you.

Paul's Plan to Visit Rome

[23]But now that there is no more place for me to work in these regions, and since I have been longing for many years to see you, [24]I plan to do so when I go to Spain. I hope to visit you while passing through and to have you assist me on my journey there, after I have enjoyed your company for a while. [25]Now, however, I am on my way to Jerusalem in the service of the saints there. [26]For Macedonia and Achaia were pleased to make a contribution for the poor among the saints in Jerusalem. [27]They were pleased to do it, and indeed they owe it to them. For if the Gentiles have shared in the Jews' spiritual blessings, they owe it to the Jews to share with them their material blessings. [28]So after I have completed this task and have made sure that they have received this fruit, I will go to Spain and visit you on the way. [29]I know that when I come to you, I will come in the full measure of the blessing of Christ.

---

e Gk *brothers*   f Gk *speak of those things that Christ has not accomplished*   g Other ancient authorities read *of the Spirit or of the Holy Spirit*   h Or *gospel*   i Gk *have sealed to them this fruit*   j Other ancient authorities add *of the gospel*

a 19 NIV text omits θεοῦ; NRSV note g omits θεοῦ or reads ἁγίου in its place   b 29 NRSV note j adds τοῦ εὐαγγελίου τοῦ

g 21 Isaiah 52:15

30 I appeal to you, brothers and sisters,[k] by our Lord Jesus Christ and by the love of the Spirit, to join me in earnest prayer to God on my behalf, 31that I may be rescued from the unbelievers in Judea, and that my ministry[l] to Jerusalem may be acceptable to the saints, 32so that by God's will I may come to you with joy and be refreshed in your company. 33The God of peace be with all of you.[m] Amen.

Personal Greetings

16 I commend to you our sister Phoebe, a deacon[n] of the church at Cenchreae, 2so that you may welcome her in the Lord as is fitting for the saints, and help her in whatever she may require from you, for she has been a benefactor of many and of myself as well.

3 Greet Prisca and Aquila, who work with me in Christ Jesus, 4and who risked their necks for my life, to whom not only I give thanks, but also all the churches of the Gentiles. 5Greet also the church in their house. Greet my beloved Epaenetus, who was the first convert[o] in Asia for Christ. 6Greet Mary, who has worked very hard among you. 7Greet Andronicus and Junia,[p] my relatives[q] who were in prison with me; they are prominent among the apostles, and they were in Christ before I was. 8Greet Ampliatus, my beloved in the Lord. 9Greet Urbanus, our co-worker in Christ, and my beloved Stachys. 10Greet Apelles, who is approved in Christ. Greet those who belong to the family of Aristobulus. 11Greet my relative[r] Herodion. Greet those in the Lord who belong to the family of Narcissus. 12Greet those workers in the Lord, Tryphaena and Tryphosa. Greet the beloved Persis, who has worked hard in the Lord. 13Greet Rufus, chosen in the Lord; and greet his mother—a mother to me also. 14Greet Asyncritus, Phlegon, Hermes,

---

30 Παρακαλῶ δὲ ὑμᾶς[, ἀδελφοί,] διὰ τοῦ κυρίου ἡμῶν Ἰησοῦ Χριστοῦ καὶ διὰ τῆς ἀγάπης τοῦ πνεύματος συναγωνίσασθαί μοι ἐν ταῖς προσευχαῖς ὑπὲρ ἐμοῦ πρὸς τὸν θεόν, **31** ἵνα ῥυσθῶ ἀπὸ τῶν ἀπειθούντων ἐν τῇ Ἰουδαίᾳ καὶ ἡ διακονία[c] μου ἡ εἰς Ἰερουσαλὴμ εὐπρόσδεκτος τοῖς ἁγίοις γένηται, **32** ἵνα ἐν χαρᾷ ἐλθὼν πρὸς ὑμᾶς διὰ θελήματος θεοῦ συναναπαύσωμαι ὑμῖν. **33** ὁ δὲ θεὸς τῆς εἰρήνης μετὰ πάντων ὑμῶν, ἀμήν.

16 Συνίστημι δὲ ὑμῖν Φοίβην τὴν ἀδελφὴν ἡμῶν, οὖσαν [καὶ] διάκονον τῆς ἐκκλησίας τῆς ἐν Κεγχρεαῖς, **2** ἵνα αὐτὴν προσδέξησθε ἐν κυρίῳ ἀξίως τῶν ἁγίων καὶ παραστῆτε αὐτῇ ἐν ᾧ ἂν ὑμῶν χρῄζῃ πράγματι· καὶ γὰρ αὐτὴ προστάτις πολλῶν ἐγενήθη καὶ ἐμοῦ αὐτοῦ.

3 Ἀσπάσασθε Πρίσκαν καὶ Ἀκύλαν τοὺς συνεργούς μου ἐν Χριστῷ Ἰησοῦ, **4** οἵτινες ὑπὲρ τῆς ψυχῆς μου τὸν ἑαυτῶν τράχηλον ὑπέθηκαν, οἷς οὐκ ἐγὼ μόνος εὐχαριστῶ ἀλλὰ καὶ πᾶσαι αἱ ἐκκλησίαι τῶν ἐθνῶν, **5** καὶ τὴν κατ᾽ οἶκον αὐτῶν ἐκκλησίαν. ἀσπάσασθε Ἐπαίνετον τὸν ἀγαπητόν μου, ὅς ἐστιν ἀπαρχὴ τῆς Ἀσίας εἰς Χριστόν. **6** ἀσπάσασθε Μαρίαν, ἥτις πολλὰ ἐκοπίασεν εἰς ὑμᾶς. **7** ἀσπάσασθε Ἀνδρόνικον καὶ Ἰουνιᾶν[a] τοὺς συγγενεῖς μου καὶ συναιχμαλώτους μου, οἵτινές εἰσιν ἐπίσημοι ἐν τοῖς ἀποστόλοις, οἳ καὶ πρὸ ἐμοῦ γέγοναν ἐν Χριστῷ. **8** ἀσπάσασθε Ἀμπλιᾶτον τὸν ἀγαπητόν μου ἐν κυρίῳ. **9** ἀσπάσασθε Οὐρβανὸν τὸν συνεργὸν ἡμῶν ἐν Χριστῷ καὶ Στάχυν τὸν ἀγαπητόν μου. **10** ἀσπάσασθε Ἀπελλῆν τὸν δόκιμον ἐν Χριστῷ. ἀσπάσασθε τοὺς ἐκ τῶν Ἀριστοβούλου. **11** ἀσπάσασθε Ἡρῳδίωνα τὸν συγγενῆ μου. ἀσπάσασθε τοὺς ἐκ τῶν Ναρκίσσου τοὺς ὄντας ἐν κυρίῳ. **12** ἀσπάσασθε Τρύφαιναν καὶ Τρυφῶσαν τὰς κοπιώσας ἐν κυρίῳ. ἀσπάσασθε Περσίδα τὴν ἀγαπητήν, ἥτις πολλὰ ἐκοπίασεν ἐν κυρίῳ. **13** ἀσπάσασθε Ροῦφον τὸν ἐκλεκτὸν ἐν κυρίῳ καὶ τὴν μητέρα αὐτοῦ καὶ ἐμοῦ. **14** ἀσπάσασθε Ἀσύγκριτον, Φλέγοντα, Ἑρμῆν, Πατροβᾶν, Ἑρμᾶν,

---

30I urge you, brothers, by our Lord Jesus Christ and by the love of the Spirit, to join me in my struggle by praying to God for me. 31Pray that I may be rescued from the unbelievers in Judea and that my service in Jerusalem may be acceptable to the saints there, 32so that by God's will I may come to you with joy and together with you be refreshed. 33The God of peace be with you all. Amen.

Personal Greetings

16 I commend to you our sister Phoebe, a servant[a] of the church in Cenchrea. 2I ask you to receive her in the Lord in a way worthy of the saints and to give her any help she may need from you, for she has been a great help to many people, including me.

3Greet Priscilla[b] and Aquila, my fellow workers in Christ Jesus. 4They risked their lives for me. Not only I but all the churches of the Gentiles are grateful to them.

5Greet also the church that meets at their house.

Greet my dear friend Epenetus, who was the first convert to Christ in the province of Asia.

6Greet Mary, who worked very hard for you.

7Greet Andronicus and Junias, my relatives who have been in prison with me. They are outstanding among the apostles, and they were in Christ before I was.

8Greet Ampliatus, whom I love in the Lord.

9Greet Urbanus, our fellow worker in Christ, and my dear friend Stachys.

10Greet Apelles, tested and approved in Christ.

Greet those who belong to the household of Aristobulus.

11Greet Herodion, my relative.

Greet those in the household of Narcissus who are in the Lord.

12Greet Tryphena and Tryphosa, those women who work hard in the Lord.

Greet my dear friend Persis, another woman who has worked very hard in the Lord.

13Greet Rufus, chosen in the Lord, and his mother, who has been a mother to me, too.

14Greet Asyncritus, Phlegon, Hermes,

---

k Gk *brothers*   l Other ancient authorities read *my bringing of a gift*   m One ancient authority adds 16.25-27 here   n Or *minister*   o Gk *first fruits*   p Or *Junias*; other ancient authorities read *Julia*   q Or *compatriots*   r Or *compatriot*

c31 NRSV note l δωροφορία   a7 NRSV text Ἰουνίαν (feminine); NRSV note p Ἰουνιᾶν (masculine) or Ἰουλίαν

a1 Or *deaconess*   b3 Greek *Prisca*, a variant of *Priscilla*

Patrobas, Hermas, and the brothers and sisters[s] who are with them. [15]Greet Philologus, Julia, Nereus and his sister, and Olympas, and all the saints who are with them. [16]Greet one another with a holy kiss. All the churches of Christ greet you.

Final Instructions

[17] I urge you, brothers and sisters,[s] to keep an eye on those who cause dissensions and offenses, in opposition to the teaching that you have learned; avoid them. [18]For such people do not serve our Lord Christ, but their own appetites,[t] and by smooth talk and flattery they deceive the hearts of the simple-minded. [19]For while your obedience is known to all, so that I rejoice over you, I want you to be wise in what is good and guileless in what is evil. [20]The God of peace will shortly crush Satan under your feet. The grace of our Lord Jesus Christ be with you.[u]

[21] Timothy, my co-worker, greets you; so do Lucius and Jason and Sosipater, my relatives.[v]

[22] I Tertius, the writer of this letter, greet you in the Lord.[w]

[23] Gaius, who is host to me and to the whole church, greets you. Erastus, the city treasurer, and our brother Quartus, greet you.[x]

Final Doxology

[25] Now to God[y] who is able to strengthen you according to my gospel and the proclamation of Jesus Christ, according to the revelation of the mystery that was kept secret for long ages [26]but is now disclosed, and through the prophetic writings is made known to all the Gentiles, according to the command of the eternal God, to bring about the obedience of faith— [27]to the only wise God, through Jesus Christ, to whom[z] be the glory forever! Amen.[a]

καὶ τοὺς σὺν αὐτοῖς ἀδελφούς. 15 ἀσπάσασθε Φιλόλογον καὶ Ἰουλίαν, Νηρέα καὶ τὴν ἀδελφὴν αὐτοῦ, καὶ Ὀλυμπᾶν καὶ τοὺς σὺν αὐτοῖς πάντας ἁγίους. 16 Ἀσπάσασθε ἀλλήλους ἐν φιλήματι ἁγίῳ. Ἀσπάζονται ὑμᾶς αἱ ἐκκλησίαι πᾶσαι τοῦ Χριστοῦ.

17 Παρακαλῶ δὲ ὑμᾶς, ἀδελφοί, σκοπεῖν τοὺς τὰς διχοστασίας καὶ τὰ σκάνδαλα παρὰ τὴν διδαχὴν ἣν ὑμεῖς ἐμάθετε ποιοῦντας, καὶ ἐκκλίνετε ἀπ' αὐτῶν· 18 οἱ γὰρ τοιοῦτοι τῷ κυρίῳ ἡμῶν Χριστῷ οὐ δουλεύουσιν ἀλλὰ τῇ ἑαυτῶν κοιλίᾳ, καὶ διὰ τῆς χρηστολογίας καὶ εὐλογίας ἐξαπατῶσιν τὰς καρδίας τῶν ἀκάκων. 19 ἡ γὰρ ὑμῶν ὑπακοὴ εἰς πάντας ἀφίκετο· ἐφ' ὑμῖν οὖν χαίρω, θέλω δὲ ὑμᾶς σοφοὺς εἶναι εἰς τὸ ἀγαθόν, ἀκεραίους δὲ εἰς τὸ κακόν. 20 ὁ δὲ θεὸς τῆς εἰρήνης συντρίψει τὸν Σατανᾶν ὑπὸ τοὺς πόδας ὑμῶν ἐν τάχει. ἡ χάρις τοῦ κυρίου ἡμῶν Ἰησοῦ μεθ' ὑμῶν.

21 Ἀσπάζεται ὑμᾶς Τιμόθεος ὁ συνεργός μου, καὶ Λούκιος καὶ Ἰάσων καὶ Σωσίπατρος οἱ συγγενεῖς μου. 22 ἀσπάζομαι ὑμᾶς ἐγὼ Τέρτιος ὁ γράψας τὴν ἐπιστολὴν ἐν κυρίῳ. 23 ἀσπάζεται ὑμᾶς Γάϊος ὁ ξένος μου καὶ ὅλης τῆς ἐκκλησίας. ἀσπάζεται ὑμᾶς Ἔραστος ὁ οἰκονόμος τῆς πόλεως καὶ Κούαρτος ὁ ἀδελφός.[b]

[25 Τῷ δὲ δυναμένῳ ὑμᾶς στηρίξαι κατὰ τὸ εὐαγγέλιόν μου καὶ τὸ κήρυγμα Ἰησοῦ Χριστοῦ, κατὰ ἀποκάλυψιν μυστηρίου χρόνοις αἰωνίοις σεσιγημένου, 26 φανερωθέντος δὲ νῦν διά τε γραφῶν προφητικῶν κατ' ἐπιταγὴν τοῦ αἰωνίου θεοῦ εἰς ὑπακοὴν πίστεως εἰς πάντα τὰ ἔθνη γνωρισθέντος, 27 μόνῳ σοφῷ θεῷ, διὰ Ἰησοῦ Χριστοῦ, ᾧ ἡ δόξα εἰς τοὺς αἰῶνας, ἀμήν.]

Patrobas, Hermas and the brothers with them. [15]Greet Philologus, Julia, Nereus and his sister, and Olympas and all the saints with them. [16]Greet one another with a holy kiss.

All the churches of Christ send greetings.

[17]I urge you, brothers, to watch out for those who cause divisions and put obstacles in your way that are contrary to the teaching you have learned. Keep away from them. [18]For such people are not serving our Lord Christ, but their own appetites. By smooth talk and flattery they deceive the minds of naive people. [19]Everyone has heard about your obedience, so I am full of joy over you; but I want you to be wise about what is good, and innocent about what is evil. [20]The God of peace will soon crush Satan under your feet.

The grace of our Lord Jesus be with you. [21]Timothy, my fellow worker, sends his greetings to you, as do Lucius, Jason and Sosipater, my relatives. [22]I, Tertius, who wrote down this letter, greet you in the Lord. [23]Gaius, whose hospitality I and the whole church here enjoy, sends you his greetings.

Erastus, who is the city's director of public works, and our brother Quartus send you their greetings.[c] [25]Now to him who is able to establish you by my gospel and the proclamation of Jesus Christ, according to the revelation of the mystery hidden for long ages past, [26]but now revealed and made known through the prophetic writings by the command of the eternal God, so that all nations might believe and obey him— [27]to the only wise God be glory forever through Jesus Christ! Amen.

---

[s] Gk *brothers*   [t] Gk *their own belly*   [u] Other ancient authorities lack this sentence   [v] Or *compatriots*   [w] Or *I Tertius, writing this letter in the Lord, greet you*   [x] Other ancient authorities add verse 24, *The grace of our Lord Jesus Christ be with all of you. Amen.*   [y] Gk *the one*   [z] Other ancient authorities lack *to whom*. The verse then reads, *to the only wise God be the glory through Jesus Christ forever. Amen.*   [a] Other ancient authorities lack 16.25-27 or include it after 14.23 or 15.33; others put verse 24 after verse 27

[b]23 NIV/NRSV notes add 24 ἡ χάρις τοῦ κυρίου ἡμῶν Ἰησοῦ Χριστοῦ μετὰ πάντων ὑμῶν. ἀμήν.

[c]23 Some manuscripts *their greetings.* [24]*May the grace of our Lord Jesus Christ be with all of you. Amen.*

NRSV

Salutation

1 Paul, called to be an apostle of Christ Jesus by the will of God, and our brother Sosthenes,

2 To the church of God that is in Corinth, to those who are sanctified in Christ Jesus, called to be saints, together with all those who in every place call on the name of our Lord Jesus Christ, both their Lord[a] and ours:

3 Grace to you and peace from God our Father and the Lord Jesus Christ.

4 I give thanks to my[b] God always for you because of the grace of God that has been given you in Christ Jesus, [5]for in every way you have been enriched in him, in speech and knowledge of every kind— [6]just as the testimony of[c] Christ has been strengthened among you— [7]so that you are not lacking in any spiritual gift as you wait for the revealing of our Lord Jesus Christ. [8]He will also strengthen you to the end, so that you may be blameless on the day of our Lord Jesus Christ. [9]God is faithful; by him you were called into the fellowship of his Son, Jesus Christ our Lord.

Divisions in the Church

10 Now I appeal to you, brothers and sisters,[d] by the name of our Lord Jesus Christ, that all of you be in agreement and that there be no divisions among you, but that you be united in the same mind and the same purpose. [11]For it has been reported to me by Chloe's people that there are quarrels among you, my brothers and sisters.[e] [12]What I mean is that each of you says, "I belong to Paul," or "I belong to Apollos," or "I belong to Cephas," or "I belong to Christ." [13]Has Christ been divided? Was Paul crucified for you? Or were you baptized in the name of Paul? [14]I thank God[f] that I baptized none of you except Crispus and Gaius, [15]so that no one can say that you were baptized in my name. [16](I did baptize also the household of Stephanas; beyond that, I do not know whether I baptized anyone else.) [17]For Christ did not send me to baptize but to proclaim the gospel, and not with eloquent wisdom, so that the cross of Christ might not be emptied of its power.

Christ the Power and Wisdom of God

18 For the message about the cross is foolishness to those who are perishing, but to us who are being saved it is the power

a Gk *theirs*   b Other ancient authorities lack *my*   c Or *to*   d Gk *brothers*   e Gk *my brothers*

ΠΡΟΣ ΚΟΡΙΝΘΙΟΥΣ Α

1 Παῦλος κλητὸς ἀπόστολος Χριστοῦ Ἰησοῦ διὰ θελήματος θεοῦ καὶ Σωσθένης ὁ ἀδελφὸς **2** τῇ ἐκκλησίᾳ τοῦ θεοῦ τῇ οὔσῃ ἐν Κορίνθῳ, ἡγιασμένοις ἐν Χριστῷ Ἰησοῦ, κλητοῖς ἁγίοις, σὺν πᾶσιν τοῖς ἐπικαλουμένοις τὸ ὄνομα τοῦ κυρίου ἡμῶν Ἰησοῦ Χριστοῦ ἐν παντὶ τόπῳ, αὐτῶν καὶ ἡμῶν· **3** χάρις ὑμῖν καὶ εἰρήνη ἀπὸ θεοῦ πατρὸς ἡμῶν καὶ κυρίου Ἰησοῦ Χριστοῦ.

4 Εὐχαριστῶ τῷ θεῷ μου πάντοτε περὶ ὑμῶν ἐπὶ τῇ χάριτι τοῦ θεοῦ τῇ δοθείσῃ ὑμῖν ἐν Χριστῷ Ἰησοῦ, **5** ὅτι ἐν παντὶ ἐπλουτίσθητε ἐν αὐτῷ, ἐν παντὶ λόγῳ καὶ πάσῃ γνώσει, **6** καθὼς τὸ μαρτύριον τοῦ Χριστοῦ ἐβεβαιώθη ἐν ὑμῖν, **7** ὥστε ὑμᾶς μὴ ὑστερεῖσθαι ἐν μηδενὶ χαρίσματι ἀπεκδεχομένους τὴν ἀποκάλυψιν τοῦ κυρίου ἡμῶν Ἰησοῦ Χριστοῦ· **8** ὃς καὶ βεβαιώσει ὑμᾶς ἕως τέλους ἀνεγκλήτους ἐν τῇ ἡμέρᾳ τοῦ κυρίου ἡμῶν Ἰησοῦ [Χριστοῦ]. **9** πιστὸς ὁ θεός, δι᾽ οὗ ἐκλήθητε εἰς κοινωνίαν τοῦ υἱοῦ αὐτοῦ Ἰησοῦ Χριστοῦ τοῦ κυρίου ἡμῶν.

10 Παρακαλῶ δὲ ὑμᾶς, ἀδελφοί, διὰ τοῦ ὀνόματος τοῦ κυρίου ἡμῶν Ἰησοῦ Χριστοῦ, ἵνα τὸ αὐτὸ λέγητε πάντες καὶ μὴ ᾖ ἐν ὑμῖν σχίσματα, ἦτε δὲ κατηρτισμένοι ἐν τῷ αὐτῷ νοῒ καὶ ἐν τῇ αὐτῇ γνώμῃ. **11** ἐδηλώθη γάρ μοι περὶ ὑμῶν, ἀδελφοί μου, ὑπὸ τῶν Χλόης ὅτι ἔριδες ἐν ὑμῖν εἰσιν. **12** λέγω δὲ τοῦτο ὅτι ἕκαστος ὑμῶν λέγει, Ἐγὼ μέν εἰμι Παύλου, Ἐγὼ δὲ Ἀπολλῶ, Ἐγὼ δὲ Κηφᾶ, Ἐγὼ δὲ Χριστοῦ. **13** μεμέρισται ὁ Χριστός; μὴ Παῦλος ἐσταυρώθη ὑπὲρ ὑμῶν, ἢ εἰς τὸ ὄνομα Παύλου ἐβαπτίσθητε; **14** εὐχαριστῶ [τῷ θεῷ][a] ὅτι οὐδένα ὑμῶν ἐβάπτισα εἰ μὴ Κρίσπον καὶ Γάιον, **15** ἵνα μή τις εἴπῃ ὅτι εἰς τὸ ἐμὸν ὄνομα ἐβαπτίσθητε. **16** ἐβάπτισα δὲ καὶ τὸν Στεφανᾶ οἶκον, λοιπὸν οὐκ οἶδα εἴ τινα ἄλλον ἐβάπτισα. **17** οὐ γὰρ ἀπέστειλέν με Χριστὸς βαπτίζειν ἀλλὰ εὐαγγελίζεσθαι, οὐκ ἐν σοφίᾳ λόγου, ἵνα μὴ κενωθῇ ὁ σταυρὸς τοῦ Χριστοῦ.

18 Ὁ λόγος γὰρ ὁ τοῦ σταυροῦ τοῖς μὲν ἀπολλυμένοις μωρία ἐστίν, τοῖς δὲ σῳζομένοις ἡμῖν δύναμις θεοῦ ἐστιν.

a14 NIV text and NRSV note f omit τῷ θεῷ

NIV

1 Paul, called to be an apostle of Christ Jesus by the will of God, and our brother Sosthenes,

[2]To the church of God in Corinth, to those sanctified in Christ Jesus and called to be holy, together with all those everywhere who call on the name of our Lord Jesus Christ—their Lord and ours:

[3]Grace and peace to you from God our Father and the Lord Jesus Christ.

Thanksgiving

[4]I always thank God for you because of his grace given you in Christ Jesus. [5]For in him you have been enriched in every way—in all your speaking and in all your knowledge— [6]because our testimony about Christ was confirmed in you. [7]Therefore you do not lack any spiritual gift as you eagerly wait for our Lord Jesus Christ to be revealed. [8]He will keep you strong to the end, so that you will be blameless on the day of our Lord Jesus Christ. [9]God, who has called you into fellowship with his Son Jesus Christ our Lord, is faithful.

Divisions in the Church

[10]I appeal to you, brothers, in the name of our Lord Jesus Christ, that all of you agree with one another so that there may be no divisions among you and that you may be perfectly united in mind and thought. [11]My brothers, some from Chloe's household have informed me that there are quarrels among you. [12]What I mean is this: One of you says, "I follow Paul"; another, "I follow Apollos"; another, "I follow Cephas[a]"; still another, "I follow Christ."

[13]Is Christ divided? Was Paul crucified for you? Were you baptized into[b] the name of Paul? [14]I am thankful that I did not baptize any of you except Crispus and Gaius, [15]so no one can say that you were baptized into my name. [16](Yes, I also baptized the household of Stephanas; beyond that, I don't remember if I baptized anyone else.) [17]For Christ did not send me to baptize, but to preach the gospel—not with words of human wisdom, lest the cross of Christ be emptied of its power.

Christ the Wisdom and Power of God

[18]For the message of the cross is foolishness to those who are perishing, but to us who are being saved it is the power of

a12 That is, Peter   b13 Or *in*; also in verse 15

NRSV

of God. [19]For it is written,

"I will destroy the wisdom of the wise,
and the discernment of the
discerning I will thwart."

[20]Where is the one who is wise? Where is the scribe? Where is the debater of this age? Has not God made foolish the wisdom of the world? [21]For since, in the wisdom of God, the world did not know God through wisdom, God decided, through the foolishness of our proclamation, to save those who believe. [22]For Jews demand signs and Greeks desire wisdom, [23]but we proclaim Christ crucified, a stumbling block to Jews and foolishness to Gentiles, [24]but to those who are the called, both Jews and Greeks, Christ the power of God and the wisdom of God. [25]For God's foolishness is wiser than human wisdom, and God's weakness is stronger than human strength.

[26] Consider your own call, brothers and sisters:[d] not many of you were wise by human standards,[g] not many were powerful, not many were of noble birth. [27]But God chose what is foolish in the world to shame the wise; God chose what is weak in the world to shame the strong; [28]God chose what is low and despised in the world, things that are not, to reduce to nothing things that are, [29]so that no one[h] might boast in the presence of God. [30]He is the source of your life in Christ Jesus, who became for us wisdom from God, and righteousness and sanctification and redemption, [31]in order that, as it is written, "Let the one who boasts, boast in[i] the Lord."

Proclaiming Christ Crucified

2 When I came to you, brothers and sisters,[d] I did not come proclaiming the mystery[j] of God to you in lofty words or wisdom. [2]For I decided to know nothing among you except Jesus Christ, and him crucified. [3]And I came to you in weakness and in fear and in much trembling. [4]My speech and my proclamation were not with plausible words of wisdom,[k] but with a demonstration of the Spirit and of power, [5]so that your faith might rest not on human wisdom but on the power of God.

The True Wisdom of God

6 Yet among the mature we do speak wisdom, though it is not a wisdom of this

[d] Gk *brothers*   [f] Other ancient authorities read *I am thankful*   [g] Gk *according to the flesh*   [h] Gk *no flesh*   [i] Or *of*   [j] Other ancient authorities read *testimony*   [k] Other ancient authorities read *the persuasiveness of wisdom*

Greek

19 γέγραπται γάρ,

Ἀπολῶ τὴν σοφίαν τῶν σοφῶν
καὶ τὴν σύνεσιν τῶν συνετῶν
ἀθετήσω.

20 ποῦ σοφός; ποῦ γραμματεύς; ποῦ συζητητὴς τοῦ αἰῶνος τούτου; οὐχὶ ἐμώρανεν ὁ θεὸς τὴν σοφίαν τοῦ κόσμου; 21 ἐπειδὴ γὰρ ἐν τῇ σοφίᾳ τοῦ θεοῦ οὐκ ἔγνω ὁ κόσμος διὰ τῆς σοφίας τὸν θεόν, εὐδόκησεν ὁ θεὸς διὰ τῆς μωρίας τοῦ κηρύγματος σῶσαι τοὺς πιστεύοντας· 22 ἐπειδὴ καὶ Ἰουδαῖοι σημεῖα αἰτοῦσιν καὶ Ἕλληνες σοφίαν ζητοῦσιν, 23 ἡμεῖς δὲ κηρύσσομεν Χριστὸν ἐσταυρωμένον, Ἰουδαίοις μὲν σκάνδαλον, ἔθνεσιν δὲ μωρίαν, 24 αὐτοῖς δὲ τοῖς κλητοῖς, Ἰουδαίοις τε καὶ Ἕλλησιν, Χριστὸν θεοῦ δύναμιν καὶ θεοῦ σοφίαν· 25 ὅτι τὸ μωρὸν τοῦ θεοῦ σοφώτερον τῶν ἀνθρώπων ἐστὶν καὶ τὸ ἀσθενὲς τοῦ θεοῦ ἰσχυρότερον τῶν ἀνθρώπων.

26 Βλέπετε γὰρ τὴν κλῆσιν ὑμῶν, ἀδελφοί, ὅτι οὐ πολλοὶ σοφοὶ κατὰ σάρκα, οὐ πολλοὶ δυνατοί, οὐ πολλοὶ εὐγενεῖς· 27 ἀλλὰ τὰ μωρὰ τοῦ κόσμου ἐξελέξατο ὁ θεός, ἵνα καταισχύνῃ τοὺς σοφούς, καὶ τὰ ἀσθενῆ τοῦ κόσμου ἐξελέξατο ὁ θεός, ἵνα καταισχύνῃ τὰ ἰσχυρά, 28 καὶ τὰ ἀγενῆ τοῦ κόσμου καὶ τὰ ἐξουθενημένα ἐξελέξατο ὁ θεός, τὰ μὴ ὄντα, ἵνα τὰ ὄντα καταργήσῃ, 29 ὅπως μὴ καυχήσηται πᾶσα σὰρξ ἐνώπιον τοῦ θεοῦ. 30 ἐξ αὐτοῦ δὲ ὑμεῖς ἐστε ἐν Χριστῷ Ἰησοῦ, ὃς ἐγενήθη σοφία ἡμῖν ἀπὸ θεοῦ, δικαιοσύνη τε καὶ ἁγιασμὸς καὶ ἀπολύτρωσις, 31 ἵνα καθὼς γέγραπται, Ὁ καυχώμενος ἐν κυρίῳ καυχάσθω.

2 Κἀγὼ ἐλθὼν πρὸς ὑμᾶς, ἀδελφοί, ἦλθον οὐ καθ' ὑπεροχὴν λόγου ἢ σοφίας καταγγέλλων ὑμῖν τὸ μυστήριον[a] τοῦ θεοῦ. 2 οὐ γὰρ ἔκρινά τι εἰδέναι ἐν ὑμῖν εἰ μὴ Ἰησοῦν Χριστὸν καὶ τοῦτον ἐσταυρωμένον. 3 κἀγὼ ἐν ἀσθενείᾳ καὶ ἐν φόβῳ καὶ ἐν τρόμῳ πολλῷ ἐγενόμην πρὸς ὑμᾶς, 4 καὶ ὁ λόγος μου καὶ τὸ κήρυγμά μου οὐκ ἐν πειθοῖ[ς] σοφίας [λόγοις][b] ἀλλ' ἐν ἀποδείξει πνεύματος καὶ δυνάμεως, 5 ἵνα ἡ πίστις ὑμῶν μὴ ᾖ ἐν σοφίᾳ ἀνθρώπων ἀλλ' ἐν δυνάμει θεοῦ.

6 Σοφίαν δὲ λαλοῦμεν ἐν τοῖς τελείοις, σοφίαν δὲ οὐ τοῦ αἰῶνος τούτου οὐδὲ

[a]1 NIV text and NRSV note j μαρτύριον; NIV note and NRSV text as UBS   [b]4 NRSV note k omits λόγοις

NIV

God. [19]For it is written:

"I will destroy the wisdom of the wise;
the intelligence of the intelligent I will
frustrate."[c]

[20]Where is the wise man? Where is the scholar? Where is the philosopher of this age? Has not God made foolish the wisdom of the world? [21]For since in the wisdom of God the world through its wisdom did not know him, God was pleased through the foolishness of what was preached to save those who believe. [22]Jews demand miraculous signs and Greeks look for wisdom, [23]but we preach Christ crucified: a stumbling block to Jews and foolishness to Gentiles, [24]but to those whom God has called, both Jews and Greeks, Christ the power of God and the wisdom of God. [25]For the foolishness of God is wiser than man's wisdom, and the weakness of God is stronger than man's strength.

[26]Brothers, think of what you were when you were called. Not many of you were wise by human standards; not many were influential; not many were of noble birth. [27]But God chose the foolish things of the world to shame the wise; God chose the weak things of the world to shame the strong. [28]He chose the lowly things of this world and the despised things—and the things that are not—to nullify the things that are, [29]so that no one may boast before him. [30]It is because of him that you are in Christ Jesus, who has become for us wisdom from God—that is, our righteousness, holiness and redemption. [31]Therefore, as it is written: "Let him who boasts boast in the Lord."[d]

2 When I came to you, brothers, I did not come with eloquence or superior wisdom as I proclaimed to you the testimony about God.[a] [2]For I resolved to know nothing while I was with you except Jesus Christ and him crucified. [3]I came to you in weakness and fear, and with much trembling. [4]My message and my preaching were not with wise and persuasive words, but with a demonstration of the Spirit's power, [5]so that your faith might not rest on men's wisdom, but on God's power.

Wisdom From the Spirit

[6]We do, however, speak a message of wisdom among the mature, but not the wisdom of this age or of the rulers of this

[c]19 Isaiah 29:14   [d]31 Jer. 9:24   [a]1 Some manuscripts *as I proclaimed to you God's mystery*

NRSV

age or of the rulers of this age, who are doomed to perish. [7]But we speak God's wisdom, secret and hidden, which God decreed before the ages for our glory. [8]None of the rulers of this age understood this; for if they had, they would not have crucified the Lord of glory. [9]But, as it is written,

"What no eye has seen, nor ear heard,
nor the human heart conceived,
what God has prepared for those who love him"—

[10]these things God has revealed to us through the Spirit; for the Spirit searches everything, even the depths of God. [11]For what human being knows what is truly human except the human spirit that is within? So also no one comprehends what is truly God's except the Spirit of God. [12]Now we have received not the spirit of the world, but the Spirit that is from God, so that we may understand the gifts bestowed on us by God. [13]And we speak of these things in words not taught by human wisdom but taught by the Spirit, interpreting spiritual things to those who are spiritual.[l]

14 Those who are unspiritual[m] do not receive the gifts of God's Spirit, for they are foolishness to them, and they are unable to understand them because they are spiritually discerned. [15]Those who are spiritual discern all things, and they are themselves subject to no one else's scrutiny.
[16] "For who has known the mind of the Lord
so as to instruct him?"
But we have the mind of Christ.

On Divisions in the Corinthian Church

3 And so, brothers and sisters,[n] I could not speak to you as spiritual people, but rather as people of the flesh, as infants in Christ. [2]I fed you with milk, not solid food, for you were not ready for solid food. Even now you are still not ready, [3]for you are still of the flesh. For as long as there is jealousy and quarreling among you, are you not of the flesh, and behaving according to human inclinations? [4]For when one says, "I belong to Paul," and another, "I belong to Apollos," are you not merely human?

5 What then is Apollos? What is Paul? Servants through whom you came to believe, as the Lord assigned to each. [6]I

[l]Or *interpreting spiritual things in spiritual language,* or *comparing spiritual things with spiritual*   [m]Or *natural*   [n]Gk *brothers*

NIV

age, who are coming to nothing. [7]No, we speak of God's secret wisdom, a wisdom that has been hidden and that God destined for our glory before time began. [8]None of the rulers of this age understood it, for if they had, they would not have crucified the Lord of glory. [9]However, as it is written:

"No eye has seen,
no ear has heard,
no mind has conceived
what God has prepared for those who love him"[b]—

[10]but God has revealed it to us by his Spirit. The Spirit searches all things, even the deep things of God. [11]For who among men knows the thoughts of a man except the man's spirit within him? In the same way no one knows the thoughts of God except the Spirit of God. [12]We have not received the spirit of the world but the Spirit who is from God, that we may understand what God has freely given us. [13]This is what we speak, not in words taught us by human wisdom but in words taught by the Spirit, expressing spiritual truths in spiritual words.[c] [14]The man without the Spirit does not accept the things that come from the Spirit of God, for they are foolishness to him, and he cannot understand them, because they are spiritually discerned. [15]The spiritual man makes judgments about all things, but he himself is not subject to any man's judgment:

[16]"For who has known the mind of the Lord
that he may instruct him?"[d]

But we have the mind of Christ.

On Divisions in the Church

3 Brothers, I could not address you as spiritual but as worldly—mere infants in Christ. [2]I gave you milk, not solid food, for you were not yet ready for it. Indeed, you are still not ready. [3]You are still worldly. For since there is jealousy and quarreling among you, are you not worldly? Are you not acting like mere men? [4]For when one says, "I follow Paul," and another, "I follow Apollos," are you not mere men?

[5]What, after all, is Apollos? And what is Paul? Only servants, through whom you came to believe—as the Lord has assigned to each his task. [6]I planted the seed, Apollos

[b]9 Isaiah 64:4   [c]13 Or *Spirit, interpreting spiritual truths to spiritual men*   [d]16 Isaiah 40:13

NRSV

planted, Apollos watered, but God gave the growth. 7So neither the one who plants nor the one who waters is anything, but only God who gives the growth. 8The one who plants and the one who waters have a common purpose, and each will receive wages according to the labor of each. 9For we are God's servants, working together; you are God's field, God's building.

10 According to the grace of God given to me, like a skilled master builder I laid a foundation, and someone else is building on it. Each builder must choose with care how to build on it. 11For no one can lay any foundation other than the one that has been laid; that foundation is Jesus Christ. 12Now if anyone builds on the foundation with gold, silver, precious stones, wood, hay, straw— 13the work of each builder will become visible, for the Day will disclose it, because it will be revealed with fire, and the fire will test what sort of work each has done. 14If what has been built on the foundation survives, the builder will receive a reward. 15If the work is burned up, the builder will suffer loss; the builder will be saved, but only as through fire.

16 Do you not know that you are God's temple and that God's Spirit dwells in you?o 17If anyone destroys God's temple, God will destroy that person. For God's temple is holy, and you are that temple.

18 Do not deceive yourselves. If you think that you are wise in this age, you should become fools so that you may become wise. 19For the wisdom of this world is foolishness with God. For it is written,

"He catches the wise in their craftiness,"
20and again,

"The Lord knows the thoughts of the wise,
that they are futile."

21So let no one boast about human leaders. For all things are yours, 22whether Paul or Apollos or Cephas or the world or life or death or the present or the future—all belong to you, 23and you belong to Christ, and Christ belongs to God.

The Ministry of the Apostles

4 Think of us in this way, as servants of Christ and stewards of God's mysteries. 2Moreover, it is required of stewards that they be found trustworthy. 3But with me it is a very small thing that I should be judged by you or by any human court. I do not even judge myself. 4I am not aware of anything against myself, but I am not

o In verses 16 and 17 the Greek word for *you* is plural

NIV

watered it, but God made it grow. 7So neither he who plants nor he who waters is anything, but only God, who makes things grow. 8The man who plants and the man who waters have one purpose, and each will be rewarded according to his own labor. 9For we are God's fellow workers; you are God's field, God's building.

10By the grace God has given me, I laid a foundation as an expert builder, and someone else is building on it. But each one should be careful how he builds. 11For no one can lay any foundation other than the one already laid, which is Jesus Christ. 12If any man builds on this foundation using gold, silver, costly stones, wood, hay or straw, 13his work will be shown for what it is, because the Day will bring it to light. It will be revealed with fire, and the fire will test the quality of each man's work. 14If what he has built survives, he will receive his reward. 15If it is burned up, he will suffer loss; he himself will be saved, but only as one escaping through the flames.

16Don't you know that you yourselves are God's temple and that God's Spirit lives in you? 17If anyone destroys God's temple, God will destroy him; for God's temple is sacred, and you are that temple.

18Do not deceive yourselves. If any one of you thinks he is wise by the standards of this age, he should become a "fool" so that he may become wise. 19For the wisdom of this world is foolishness in God's sight. As it is written: "He catches the wise in their craftiness"[a]; 20and again, "The Lord knows that the thoughts of the wise are futile."[b] 21So then, no more boasting about men! All things are yours, 22whether Paul or Apollos or Cephas[c] or the world or life or death or the present or the future—all are yours, 23and you are of Christ, and Christ is of God.

Apostles of Christ

4 So then, men ought to regard us as servants of Christ and as those entrusted with the secret things of God. 2Now it is required that those who have been given a trust must prove faithful. 3I care very little if I am judged by you or by any human court; indeed, I do not even judge myself. 4My conscience is clear, but that does not make me innocent. It is the Lord

a19 Job 5:13　b20 Psalm 94:11　c22 That is, Peter

thereby acquitted. It is the Lord who judges me. [5]Therefore do not pronounce judgment before the time, before the Lord comes, who will bring to light the things now hidden in darkness and will disclose the purposes of the heart. Then each one will receive commendation from God.

6 I have applied all this to Apollos and myself for your benefit, brothers and sisters,[P] so that you may learn through us the meaning of the saying, "Nothing beyond what is written," so that none of you will be puffed up in favor of one against another. [7]For who sees anything different in you?[q] What do you have that you did not receive? And if you received it, why do you boast as if it were not a gift?

8 Already you have all you want! Already you have become rich! Quite apart from us you have become kings! Indeed, I wish that you had become kings, so that we might be kings with you! [9]For I think that God has exhibited us apostles as last of all, as though sentenced to death, because we have become a spectacle to the world, to angels and to mortals. [10]We are fools for the sake of Christ, but you are wise in Christ. We are weak, but you are strong. You are held in honor, but we in disrepute. [11]To the present hour we are hungry and thirsty, we are poorly clothed and beaten and homeless, [12]and we grow weary from the work of our own hands. When reviled, we bless; when persecuted, we endure; [13]when slandered, we speak kindly. We have become like the rubbish of the world, the dregs of all things, to this very day.

Fatherly Admonition

14 I am not writing this to make you ashamed, but to admonish you as my beloved children. [15]For though you might have ten thousand guardians in Christ, you do not have many fathers. Indeed, in Christ Jesus I became your father through the gospel. [16]I appeal to you, then, be imitators of me. [17]For this reason I sent[r] you Timothy, who is my beloved and faithful child in the Lord, to remind you of my ways in Christ Jesus, as I teach them everywhere in every church. [18]But some of you, thinking that I am not coming to you, have become arrogant. [19]But I will come to you soon, if the Lord wills, and I will find out not the talk of these arrogant people but their power. [20]For the kingdom of God

ἀνακρίνων με κύριός ἐστιν. **5** ὥστε μὴ πρὸ καιροῦ τι κρίνετε ἕως ἂν ἔλθη ὁ κύριος, ὃς καὶ φωτίσει τὰ κρυπτὰ τοῦ σκότους καὶ φανερώσει τὰς βουλὰς τῶν καρδιῶν· καὶ τότε ὁ ἔπαινος γενήσεται ἑκάστῳ ἀπὸ τοῦ θεοῦ.

6 Ταῦτα δέ, ἀδελφοί, μετεσχημάτισα εἰς ἐμαυτὸν καὶ Ἀπολλῶν δι᾿ ὑμᾶς, ἵνα ἐν ἡμῖν μάθητε τὸ Μὴ ὑπὲρ ἃ γέγραπται, ἵνα μὴ εἷς ὑπὲρ τοῦ ἑνὸς φυσιοῦσθε κατὰ τοῦ ἑτέρου. **7** τίς γὰρ σε διακρίνει; τί δὲ ἔχεις ὃ οὐκ ἔλαβες; εἰ δὲ καὶ ἔλαβες, τί καυχᾶσαι ὡς μὴ λαβών; **8** ἤδη κεκορεσμένοι ἐστέ, ἤδη ἐπλουτήσατε, χωρὶς ἡμῶν ἐβασιλεύσατε· καὶ ὄφελόν γε ἐβασιλεύσατε, ἵνα καὶ ἡμεῖς ὑμῖν συμβασιλεύσωμεν. **9** δοκῶ γάρ,[a] ὁ θεὸς ἡμᾶς τοὺς ἀποστόλους ἐσχάτους ἀπέδειξεν ὡς ἐπιθανατίους, ὅτι θέατρον ἐγενήθημεν τῷ κόσμῳ καὶ ἀγγέλοις καὶ ἀνθρώποις. **10** ἡμεῖς μωροὶ διὰ Χριστόν, ὑμεῖς δὲ φρόνιμοι ἐν Χριστῷ· ἡμεῖς ἀσθενεῖς, ὑμεῖς δὲ ἰσχυροί· ὑμεῖς ἔνδοξοι, ἡμεῖς δὲ ἄτιμοι. **11** ἄχρι τῆς ἄρτι ὥρας καὶ πεινῶμεν καὶ διψῶμεν καὶ γυμνιτεύομεν καὶ κολαφιζόμεθα καὶ ἀστατοῦμεν **12** καὶ κοπιῶμεν ἐργαζόμενοι ταῖς ἰδίαις χερσίν· λοιδορούμενοι εὐλογοῦμεν, διωκόμενοι ἀνεχόμεθα, **13** δυσφημούμενοι παρακαλοῦμεν· ὡς περικαθάρματα τοῦ κόσμου ἐγενήθημεν, πάντων περίψημα ἕως ἄρτι.

14 Οὐκ ἐντρέπων ὑμᾶς γράφω ταῦτα ἀλλ᾿ ὡς τέκνα μου ἀγαπητὰ νουθετῶ[ν]. **15** ἐὰν γὰρ μυρίους παιδαγωγοὺς ἔχητε ἐν Χριστῷ ἀλλ᾿ οὐ πολλοὺς πατέρας· ἐν γὰρ Χριστῷ Ἰησοῦ διὰ τοῦ εὐαγγελίου ἐγὼ ὑμᾶς ἐγέννησα. **16** παρακαλῶ οὖν ὑμᾶς, μιμηταί μου γίνεσθε. **17** διὰ τοῦτο ἔπεμψα ὑμῖν Τιμόθεον, ὅς ἐστίν μου τέκνον ἀγαπητὸν καὶ πιστὸν ἐν κυρίῳ, ὃς ὑμᾶς ἀναμνήσει τὰς ὁδούς μου τὰς ἐν Χριστῷ [Ἰησοῦ], καθὼς πανταχοῦ ἐν πάσῃ ἐκκλησίᾳ διδάσκω. **18** ὡς μὴ ἐρχομένου δέ μου πρὸς ὑμᾶς ἐφυσιώθησάν τινες· **19** ἐλεύσομαι δὲ ταχέως πρὸς ὑμᾶς ἐὰν ὁ κύριος θελήσῃ, καὶ γνώσομαι οὐ τὸν λόγον τῶν πεφυσιωμένων ἀλλὰ τὴν δύναμιν· **20** οὐ γὰρ ἐν λόγῳ ἡ βασιλεία τοῦ θεοῦ ἀλλ᾿

who judges me. [5]Therefore judge nothing before the appointed time; wait till the Lord comes. He will bring to light what is hidden in darkness and will expose the motives of men's hearts. At that time each will receive his praise from God.

[6]Now, brothers, I have applied these things to myself and Apollos for your benefit, so that you may learn from us the meaning of the saying, "Do not go beyond what is written." Then you will not take pride in one man over against another. [7]For who makes you different from anyone else? What do you have that you did not receive? And if you did receive it, why do you boast as though you did not?

[8]Already you have all you want! Already you have become rich! You have become kings—and that without us! How I wish that you really had become kings so that we might be kings with you! [9]For it seems to me that God has put us apostles on display at the end of the procession, like men condemned to die in the arena. We have been made a spectacle to the whole universe, to angels as well as to men. [10]We are fools for Christ, but you are so wise in Christ! We are weak, but you are strong! You are honored, we are dishonored! [11]To this very hour we go hungry and thirsty, we are in rags, we are brutally treated, we are homeless. [12]We work hard with our own hands. When we are cursed, we bless; when we are persecuted, we endure it; [13]when we are slandered, we answer kindly. Up to this moment we have become the scum of the earth, the refuse of the world.

[14]I am not writing this to shame you, but to warn you, as my dear children. [15]Even though you have ten thousand guardians in Christ, you do not have many fathers, for in Christ Jesus I became your father through the gospel. [16]Therefore I urge you to imitate me. [17]For this reason I am sending to you Timothy, my son whom I love, who is faithful in the Lord. He will remind you of my way of life in Christ Jesus, which agrees with what I teach everywhere in every church.

[18]Some of you have become arrogant, as if I were not coming to you. [19]But I will come to you very soon, if the Lord is willing, and then I will find out not only how these arrogant people are talking, but what power they have. [20]For the kingdom of God is not a matter of talk but of power.

[P] Gk *brothers*   [q] Or *Who makes you different from another?*
[r] Or *am sending*

[a]9 NIV text adds ὅτι †

depends not on talk but on power. 21What would you prefer? Am I to come to you with a stick, or with love in a spirit of gentleness?

Sexual Immorality Defiles the Church

5 It is actually reported that there is sexual immorality among you, and of a kind that is not found even among pagans; for a man is living with his father's wife. 2And you are arrogant! Should you not rather have mourned, so that he who has done this would have been removed from among you?

3 For though absent in body, I am present in spirit; and as if present I have already pronounced judgment 4in the name of the Lord Jesus on the man who has done such a thing.s When you are assembled, and my spirit is present with the power of our Lord Jesus, 5you are to hand this man over to Satan for the destruction of the flesh, so that his spirit may be saved in the day of the Lord.t

6 Your boasting is not a good thing. Do you not know that a little yeast leavens the whole batch of dough? 7Clean out the old yeast so that you may be a new batch, as you really are unleavened. For our paschal lamb, Christ, has been sacrificed. 8Therefore, let us celebrate the festival, not with the old yeast, the yeast of malice and evil, but with the unleavened bread of sincerity and truth.

Sexual Immorality Must Be Judged

9 I wrote to you in my letter not to associate with sexually immoral persons— 10not at all meaning the immoral of this world, or the greedy and robbers, or idolaters, since you would then need to go out of the world. 11But now I am writing to you not to associate with anyone who bears the name of brother or sisteru who is sexually immoral or greedy, or is an idolater, reviler, drunkard, or robber. Do not even eat with such a one. 12For what have I to do with judging those outside? Is it not those who are inside that you are to judge? 13God will judge those outside. "Drive out the wicked person from among you."

Lawsuits among Believers

6 When any of you has a grievance against another, do you dare to take it to court before the unrighteous, instead of taking it before the saints? 2Do you not

ἐν δυνάμει. 21 τί θέλετε; ἐν ῥάβδῳ ἔλθω πρὸς ὑμᾶς ἢ ἐν ἀγάπῃ πνεύματί τε πραΰτητος;

5 Ὅλως ἀκούεται ἐν ὑμῖν πορνεία, καὶ τοιαύτη πορνεία ἥτις οὐδὲ ἐν τοῖς ἔθνεσιν, ὥστε γυναῖκά τινα τοῦ πατρὸς ἔχειν. 2 καὶ ὑμεῖς πεφυσιωμένοι ἐστὲ καὶ οὐχὶ μᾶλλον ἐπενθήσατε, ἵνα ἀρθῇ ἐκ μέσου ὑμῶν ὁ τὸ ἔργον τοῦτο πράξας; 3 ἐγὼ μὲν γάρ, ἀπὼν τῷ σώματι παρὼν δὲ τῷ πνεύματι, ἤδη κέκρικα ὡς παρὼν τὸν οὕτως τοῦτο κατεργα-σάμενον· 4 ἐν τῷ ὀνόματι τοῦ κυρίου [ἡμῶν] Ἰησοῦ συναχθέντων ὑμῶν καὶ τοῦ ἐμοῦ πνεύματος σὺν τῇ δυνάμει τοῦ κυρίου ἡμῶν Ἰησοῦ, 5 παραδοῦναι τὸν τοιοῦτον τῷ Σατανᾷ εἰς ὄλεθρον τῆς σαρκός, ἵνα τὸ πνεῦμα σωθῇ ἐν τῇ ἡμέρᾳ τοῦ κυρίουa. 6 Οὐ καλὸν τὸ καύχημα ὑμῶν. οὐκ οἴδατε ὅτι μικρὰ ζύμη ὅλον τὸ φύραμα ζυμοῖ; 7 ἐκκαθά-ρατε τὴν παλαιὰν ζύμην, ἵνα ἦτε νέον φύραμα, καθὼς ἐστε ἄζυμοι· καὶ γὰρ τὸ πάσχα ἡμῶν ἐτύθη Χριστός. 8 ὥστε ἑορτάζωμεν μὴ ἐν ζύμῃ παλαιᾷ μηδὲ ἐν ζύμῃ κακίας καὶ πονηρίας ἀλλ᾽ ἐν ἀζύμοις εἰλικρινείας καὶ ἀληθείας.

9 Ἔγραψα ὑμῖν ἐν τῇ ἐπιστολῇ μὴ συναναμίγνυσθαι πόρνοις, 10 οὐ πάντως τοῖς πόρνοις τοῦ κόσμου τούτου ἢ τοῖς πλεονέκταις καὶ ἅρπαξιν ἢ εἰδωλολάτραις, ἐπεὶ ὠφείλετε ἄρα ἐκ τοῦ κόσμου ἐξελθεῖν. 11 νῦν δὲ ἔγραψα ὑμῖν μὴ συναναμίγνυσθαι ἐάν τις ἀδελφὸς ὀνομαζόμενος ἢ πόρνος ἢ πλεονέκτης ἢ εἰδωλολάτρης ἢ λοίδορος ἢ μέθυσος ἢ ἅρπαξ, τῷ τοιούτῳ μηδὲ συνεσθίειν. 12 τί γάρ μοι τοὺς ἔξω κρίνειν; οὐχὶ τοὺς ἔσω ὑμεῖς κρίνετε; 13 τοὺς δὲ ἔξω ὁ θεὸς κρινεῖ. ἐξάρατε τὸν πονηρὸν ἐξ ὑμῶν αὐτῶν.

6 Τολμᾷ τις ὑμῶν πρᾶγμα ἔχων πρὸς τὸν ἕτερον κρίνεσθαι ἐπὶ τῶν ἀδίκων καὶ οὐχὶ ἐπὶ τῶν ἁγίων; 2 ἢ οὐκ οἴδατε ὅτι οἱ ἅγιοι τὸν κόσμον

21What do you prefer? Shall I come to you with a whip, or in love and with a gentle spirit?

Expel the Immoral Brother!

5 It is actually reported that there is sexual immorality among you, and of a kind that does not occur even among pagans: A man has his father's wife. 2And you are proud! Shouldn't you rather have been filled with grief and have put out of your fellowship the man who did this? 3Even though I am not physically present, I am with you in spirit. And I have already passed judgment on the one who did this, just as if I were present. 4When you are assembled in the name of our Lord Jesus and I am with you in spirit, and the power of our Lord Jesus is present, 5hand this man over to Satan, so that the sinful naturea may be destroyed and his spirit saved on the day of the Lord.

6Your boasting is not good. Don't you know that a little yeast works through the whole batch of dough? 7Get rid of the old yeast that you may be a new batch without yeast—as you really are. For Christ, our Passover lamb, has been sacrificed. 8Therefore let us keep the Festival, not with the old yeast, the yeast of malice and wickedness, but with bread without yeast, the bread of sincerity and truth.

9I have written you in my letter not to associate with sexually immoral people— 10not at all meaning the people of this world who are immoral, or the greedy and swindlers, or idolaters. In that case you would have to leave this world. 11But now I am writing you that you must not associate with anyone who calls himself a brother but is sexually immoral or greedy, an idolater or a slanderer, a drunkard or a swindler. With such a man do not even eat.

12What business is it of mine to judge those outside the church? Are you not to judge those inside? 13God will judge those outside. "Expel the wicked man from among you."b

Lawsuits Among Believers

6 If any of you has a dispute with another, dare he take it before the ungodly for judgment instead of before the saints? 2Do you not know that the saints

---

s Or on the man who has done such a thing in the name of the Lord Jesus   t Other ancient authorities add Jesus
u Gk brother

a5 NRSV note t adds Ἰησοῦ

a5 Or that his body; or that the flesh   b13 Deut. 17:7; 19:19; 21:21; 22:21,24; 24:7

know that the saints will judge the world? And if the world is to be judged by you, are you incompetent to try trivial cases? [3]Do you not know that we are to judge angels—to say nothing of ordinary matters? [4]If you have ordinary cases, then, do you appoint as judges those who have no standing in the church? [5]I say this to your shame. Can it be that there is no one among you wise enough to decide between one believer[u] and another, [6]but a believer[u] goes to court against a believer[u]—and before unbelievers at that?

7 In fact, to have lawsuits at all with one another is already a defeat for you. Why not rather be wronged? Why not rather be defrauded? [8]But you yourselves wrong and defraud—and believers[v] at that.

9 Do you not know that wrongdoers will not inherit the kingdom of God? Do not be deceived! Fornicators, idolaters, adulterers, male prostitutes, sodomites, [10]thieves, the greedy, drunkards, revilers, robbers—none of these will inherit the kingdom of God. [11]And this is what some of you used to be. But you were washed, you were sanctified, you were justified in the name of the Lord Jesus Christ and in the Spirit of our God.

Glorify God in Body and Spirit

12 "All things are lawful for me," but not all things are beneficial. "All things are lawful for me," but I will not be dominated by anything. [13]"Food is meant for the stomach and the stomach for food,"[w] and God will destroy both one and the other. The body is meant not for fornication but for the Lord, and the Lord for the body. [14]And God raised the Lord and will also raise us by his power. [15]Do you not know that your bodies are members of Christ? Should I therefore take the members of Christ and make them members of a prostitute? Never! [16]Do you not know that whoever is united to a prostitute becomes one body with her? For it is said, "The two shall be one flesh." [17]But anyone united to the Lord becomes one spirit with him. [18]Shun fornication! Every sin that a person commits is outside the body; but the fornicator sins against the body itself. [19]Or do you not know that your body is a temple[x] of the Holy Spirit within you,

κρινοῦσιν· καὶ εἰ ἐν ὑμῖν κρίνεται ὁ κόσμος, ἀνάξιοί ἐστε κριτηρίων ἐλαχί-στων; 3 οὐκ οἴδατε ὅτι ἀγγέλους κρινοῦμεν, μήτιγε βιωτικά; 4 βιωτικὰ μὲν οὖν κριτήρια ἐὰν ἔχητε, τοὺς ἐξουθενημένους ἐν τῇ ἐκκλησίᾳ, τούτους καθίζετε; 5 πρὸς ἐντροπὴν ὑμῖν λέγω. οὕτως οὐκ ἔνι ἐν ὑμῖν οὐδεὶς σοφός, ὃς δυνήσεται διακρῖναι ἀνὰ μέσον τοῦ ἀδελφοῦ αὐτοῦ; 6 ἀλλὰ ἀδελφὸς μετὰ ἀδελφοῦ κρίνεται καὶ τοῦτο ἐπὶ ἀπίστων; 7 ἤδη μὲν [οὖν][a] ὅλως ἥττημα ὑμῖν ἐστιν ὅτι κρίματα ἔχετε μεθ' ἑαυτῶν. διὰ τί οὐχὶ μᾶλλον ἀδικεῖσθε; διὰ τί οὐχὶ μᾶλλον ἀποστερεῖσθε; 8 ἀλλὰ ὑμεῖς ἀδικεῖτε καὶ ἀποστερεῖτε, καὶ τοῦτο ἀδελφούς. 9 ἢ οὐκ οἴδατε ὅτι ἄδικοι θεοῦ βασιλείαν οὐ κληρονομήσουσιν; μὴ πλανᾶσθε· οὔτε πόρνοι οὔτε εἰδωλολάτραι οὔτε μοιχοὶ οὔτε μαλακοὶ οὔτε ἀρσενοκοῖται 10 οὔτε κλέπται οὔτε πλεονέκται, οὐ μέθυσοι, οὐ λοίδοροι, οὐχ ἅρπαγες βασιλείαν θεοῦ κληρονομήσουσιν. 11 καὶ ταῦτά τινες ἦτε· ἀλλὰ ἀπελούσασθε, ἀλλὰ ἡγιάσθη-τε, ἀλλὰ ἐδικαιώθητε ἐν τῷ ὀνόματι τοῦ κυρίου Ἰησοῦ Χριστοῦ καὶ ἐν τῷ πνεύματι τοῦ θεοῦ ἡμῶν.

12 Πάντα μοι ἔξεστιν ἀλλ᾽ οὐ πάντα συμφέρει· πάντα μοι ἔξεστιν ἀλλ᾽ οὐκ ἐγὼ ἐξουσιασθήσομαι ὑπό τινος. 13 τὰ βρώματα τῇ κοιλίᾳ καὶ ἡ κοιλία τοῖς βρώμασιν, ὁ δὲ θεὸς καὶ ταύτην καὶ ταῦτα καταργήσει. τὸ δὲ σῶμα οὐ τῇ πορνείᾳ ἀλλὰ τῷ κυρίῳ, καὶ ὁ κύριος τῷ σώματι· 14 ὁ δὲ θεὸς καὶ τὸν κύριον ἤγειρεν καὶ ἡμᾶς ἐξεγερεῖ διὰ τῆς δυνάμεως αὐτοῦ. 15 οὐκ οἴδατε ὅτι τὰ σώματα ὑμῶν μέλη Χριστοῦ ἐστιν; ἄρας οὖν τὰ μέλη τοῦ Χριστοῦ ποιήσω πόρνης μέλη; μὴ γένοιτο. 16 [ἢ] οὐκ οἴδατε ὅτι ὁ κολλώμενος τῇ πόρνῃ ἓν σῶμά ἐστιν; Ἔσονται γάρ, φησίν, οἱ δύο εἰς σάρκα μίαν. 17 ὁ δὲ κολλώ-μενος τῷ κυρίῳ ἓν πνεῦμά ἐστιν. 18 φεύγετε τὴν πορνείαν. πᾶν ἁμάρ-τημα ὃ ἐὰν ποιήσῃ ἄνθρωπος ἐκτὸς τοῦ σώματός ἐστιν· ὁ δὲ πορνεύων εἰς τὸ ἴδιον σῶμα ἁμαρτάνει. 19 ἢ οὐκ οἴδατε ὅτι τὸ σῶμα ὑμῶν ναὸς τοῦ ἐν ὑμῖν ἁγίου πνεύματός ἐστιν οὗ ἔχετε

will judge the world? And if you are to judge the world, are you not competent to judge trivial cases? [3]Do you not know that we will judge angels? How much more the things of this life! [4]Therefore, if you have disputes about such matters, appoint as judges even men of little account in the church![a] [5]I say this to shame you. Is it possible that there is nobody among you wise enough to judge a dispute between believers? [6]But instead, one brother goes to law against another—and this in front of unbelievers!

[7]The very fact that you have lawsuits among you means you have been completely defeated already. Why not rather be wronged? Why not rather be cheated? [8]Instead, you yourselves cheat and do wrong, and you do this to your brothers.

[9]Do you not know that the wicked will not inherit the kingdom of God? Do not be deceived: Neither the sexually immoral nor idolaters nor adulterers nor male prostitutes nor homosexual offenders [10]nor thieves nor the greedy nor drunkards nor slanderers nor swindlers will inherit the kingdom of God. [11]And that is what some of you were. But you were washed, you were sanctified, you were justified in the name of the Lord Jesus Christ and by the Spirit of our God.

Sexual Immorality

[12]"Everything is permissible for me"— but not everything is beneficial. "Everything is permissible for me"—but I will not be mastered by anything. [13]"Food for the stomach and the stomach for food"— but God will destroy them both. The body is not meant for sexual immorality, but for the Lord, and the Lord for the body. [14]By his power God raised the Lord from the dead, and he will raise us also. [15]Do you not know that your bodies are members of Christ himself? Shall I then take the members of Christ and unite them with a prostitute? Never! [16]Do you not know that he who unites himself with a prostitute is one with her in body? For it is said, "The two will become one flesh."[b] [17]But he who unites himself with the Lord is one with him in spirit.

[18]Flee from sexual immorality. All other sins a man commits are outside his body, but he who sins sexually sins against his own body. [19]Do you not know that your body is a temple of the Holy Spirit, who is

---

[a]7 NIV text omits οὖν †

[a]4 Or matters, do you appoint as judges men of little account in the church?   [b]16 Gen. 2:24

which you have from God, and that you are not your own? [20]For you were bought with a price; therefore glorify God in your body.

Directions concerning Marriage

7 Now concerning the matters about which you wrote: "It is well for a man not to touch a woman." [2]But because of cases of sexual immorality, each man should have his own wife and each woman her own husband. [3]The husband should give to his wife her conjugal rights, and likewise the wife to her husband. [4]For the wife does not have authority over her own body, but the husband does; likewise the husband does not have authority over his own body, but the wife does. [5]Do not deprive one another except perhaps by agreement for a set time, to devote yourselves to prayer, and then come together again, so that Satan may not tempt you because of your lack of self-control. [6]This I say by way of concession, not of command. [7]I wish that all were as I myself am. But each has a particular gift from God, one having one kind and another a different kind.

[8] To the unmarried and the widows I say that it is well for them to remain unmarried as I am. [9]But if they are not practicing self-control, they should marry. For it is better to marry than to be aflame with passion.

[10] To the married I give this command—not I but the Lord—that the wife should not separate from her husband [11](but if she does separate, let her remain unmarried or else be reconciled to her husband), and that the husband should not divorce his wife.

[12] To the rest I say—I and not the Lord—that if any believer[y] has a wife who is an unbeliever, and she consents to live with him, he should not divorce her. [13]And if any woman has a husband who is an unbeliever, and he consents to live with her, she should not divorce him. [14]For the unbelieving husband is made holy through his wife, and the unbelieving wife is made holy through her husband. Otherwise, your children would be unclean, but as it is, they are holy. [15]But if the unbelieving partner separates, let it be so; in such a case the brother or sister is not bound. It is to peace that God has called you.[z] [16]Wife, for all you know, you might save your husband. Husband, for all you know, you might save your wife.

ἀπὸ θεοῦ, καὶ οὐκ ἐστὲ ἑαυτῶν; [20] ἠγοράσθητε γὰρ τιμῆς· δοξάσατε δὴ τὸν θεὸν ἐν τῷ σώματι ὑμῶν.

7 Περὶ δὲ ὧν ἐγράψατε, καλὸν ἀνθρώπῳ γυναικὸς μὴ ἅπτεσθαι· [2] διὰ δὲ τὰς πορνείας ἕκαστος τὴν ἑαυτοῦ γυναῖκα ἐχέτω καὶ ἑκάστη τὸν ἴδιον ἄνδρα ἐχέτω. [3] τῇ γυναικὶ ὁ ἀνὴρ τὴν ὀφειλὴν ἀποδιδότω, ὁμοίως δὲ καὶ ἡ γυνὴ τῷ ἀνδρί. [4] ἡ γυνὴ τοῦ ἰδίου σώματος οὐκ ἐξουσιάζει ἀλλὰ ὁ ἀνήρ, ὁμοίως δὲ καὶ ὁ ἀνὴρ τοῦ ἰδίου σώματος οὐκ ἐξουσιάζει ἀλλὰ ἡ γυνή. [5] μὴ ἀποστερεῖτε ἀλλήλους, εἰ μήτι ἂν ἐκ συμφώνου πρὸς καιρόν, ἵνα σχολάσητε τῇ προσευχῇ καὶ πάλιν ἐπὶ τὸ αὐτὸ ἦτε, ἵνα μὴ πειράζῃ ὑμᾶς ὁ Σατανᾶς διὰ τὴν ἀκρασίαν ὑμῶν. [6] τοῦτο δὲ λέγω κατὰ συγγνώμην οὐ κατ᾽ ἐπιταγήν. [7] θέλω δὲ πάντας ἀνθρώπους εἶναι ὡς καὶ ἐμαυτόν· ἀλλὰ ἕκαστος ἴδιον ἔχει χάρισμα ἐκ θεοῦ, ὁ μὲν οὕτως, ὁ δὲ οὕτως.

[8] Λέγω δὲ τοῖς ἀγάμοις καὶ ταῖς χήραις, καλὸν αὐτοῖς ἐὰν μείνωσιν ὡς κἀγώ· [9] εἰ δὲ οὐκ ἐγκρατεύονται, γαμησάτωσαν, κρεῖττον γάρ ἐστιν γαμῆσαι ἢ πυροῦσθαι. [10] τοῖς δὲ γεγαμηκόσιν παραγγέλλω, οὐκ ἐγὼ ἀλλὰ ὁ κύριος, γυναῖκα ἀπὸ ἀνδρὸς μὴ χωρισθῆναι, [11] – ἐὰν δὲ καὶ χωρισθῇ, μενέτω ἄγαμος ἢ τῷ ἀνδρὶ καταλλαγήτω, – καὶ ἄνδρα γυναῖκα μὴ ἀφιέναι. [12] Τοῖς δὲ λοιποῖς λέγω ἐγώ οὐχ ὁ κύριος· εἴ τις ἀδελφὸς γυναῖκα ἔχει ἄπιστον καὶ αὕτη συνευδοκεῖ οἰκεῖν μετ᾽ αὐτοῦ, μὴ ἀφιέτω αὐτήν· [13] καὶ γυνὴ εἴ τις ἔχει ἄνδρα ἄπιστον καὶ οὗτος συνευδοκεῖ οἰκεῖν μετ᾽ αὐτῆς, μὴ ἀφιέτω τὸν ἄνδρα. [14] ἡγίασται γὰρ ὁ ἀνὴρ ὁ ἄπιστος ἐν τῇ γυναικὶ καὶ ἡγίασται ἡ γυνὴ ἡ ἄπιστος ἐν τῷ ἀδελφῷ· ἐπεὶ ἄρα τὰ τέκνα ὑμῶν ἀκάθαρτά ἐστιν, νῦν δὲ ἅγιά ἐστιν. [15] εἰ δὲ ὁ ἄπιστος χωρίζεται, χωριζέσθω· οὐ δεδούλωται ὁ ἀδελφὸς ἢ ἡ ἀδελφὴ ἐν τοῖς τοιούτοις· ἐν δὲ εἰρήνῃ κέκληκεν ὑμᾶς[a] ὁ θεός. [16] τί γὰρ οἶδας, γύναι, εἰ τὸν ἄνδρα σώσεις; ἢ τί οἶδας, ἄνερ, εἰ τὴν γυναῖκα σώσεις;

---

in you, whom you have received from God? You are not your own; [20]you were bought at a price. Therefore honor God with your body.

Marriage

7 Now for the matters you wrote about: It is good for a man not to marry.[a] [2]But since there is so much immorality, each man should have his own wife, and each woman her own husband. [3]The husband should fulfill his marital duty to his wife, and likewise the wife to her husband. [4]The wife's body does not belong to her alone but also to her husband. In the same way, the husband's body does not belong to him alone but also to his wife. [5]Do not deprive each other except by mutual consent and for a time, so that you may devote yourselves to prayer. Then come together again so that Satan will not tempt you because of your lack of self-control. [6]I say this as a concession, not as a command. [7]I wish that all men were as I am. But each man has his own gift from God; one has this gift, another has that.

[8]Now to the unmarried and the widows I say: It is good for them to stay unmarried, as I am. [9]But if they cannot control themselves, they should marry, for it is better to marry than to burn with passion.

[10]To the married I give this command (not I, but the Lord): A wife must not separate from her husband. [11]But if she does, she must remain unmarried or else be reconciled to her husband. And a husband must not divorce his wife.

[12]To the rest I say this (I, not the Lord): If any brother has a wife who is not a believer and she is willing to live with him, he must not divorce her. [13]And if a woman has a husband who is not a believer and he is willing to live with her, she must not divorce him. [14]For the unbelieving husband has been sanctified through his wife, and the unbelieving wife has been sanctified through her believing husband. Otherwise your children would be unclean, but as it is, they are holy.

[15]But if the unbeliever leaves, let him do so. A believing man or woman is not bound in such circumstances; God has called us to live in peace. [16]How do you know, wife, whether you will save your husband? Or, how do you know, husband, whether you will save your wife?

---

[y] Gk *brother*   [z] Other ancient authorities read *us*

[a]15 NIV text and NRSV note z *ἡμᾶς*

[a]1 Or "It is good for a man not to have sexual relations with a woman."

NRSV

The Life That the Lord Has Assigned

17 However that may be, let each of you lead the life that the Lord has assigned, to which God called you. This is my rule in all the churches. 18Was anyone at the time of his call already circumcised? Let him not seek to remove the marks of circumcision. Was anyone at the time of his call uncircumcised? Let him not seek circumcision. 19Circumcision is nothing, and uncircumcision is nothing; but obeying the commandments of God is everything. 20Let each of you remain in the condition in which you were called.

21 Were you a slave when called? Do not be concerned about it. Even if you can gain your freedom, make use of your present condition now more than ever.ᵃ 22For whoever was called in the Lord as a slave is a freed person belonging to the Lord, just as whoever was free when called is a slave of Christ. 23You were bought with a price; do not become slaves of human masters. 24In whatever condition you were called, brothers and sisters,ᵇ there remain with God.

The Unmarried and the Widows

25 Now concerning virgins, I have no command of the Lord, but I give my opinion as one who by the Lord's mercy is trustworthy. 26I think that, in view of the impendingᶜ crisis, it is well for you to remain as you are. 27Are you bound to a wife? Do not seek to be free. Are you free from a wife? Do not seek a wife. 28But if you marry, you do not sin, and if a virgin marries, she does not sin. Yet those who marry will experience distress in this life,ᵈ and I would spare you that. 29I mean, brothers and sisters,ᵇ the appointed time has grown short; from now on, let even those who have wives be as though they had none, 30and those who mourn as though they were not mourning, and those who rejoice as though they were not rejoicing, and those who buy as though they had no possessions, 31and those who deal with the world as though they had no dealings with it. For the present form of this world is passing away.

32 I want you to be free from anxieties. The unmarried man is anxious about the affairs of the Lord, how to please the Lord; 33but the married man is anxious about the affairs of the world, how to please his wife, 34and his interests are divided. And the unmarried woman and the virgin are

Greek

17 Εἰ μὴ ἑκάστῳ ὡς ἐμέρισεν ὁ κύριος, ἕκαστον ὡς κέκληκεν ὁ θεός, οὕτως περιπατείτω. καὶ οὕτως ἐν ταῖς ἐκκλησίαις πάσαις διατάσσομαι. **18** περιτετμημένος τις ἐκλήθη, μὴ ἐπισπάσθω· ἐν ἀκροβυστίᾳ κέκληταί τις, μὴ περιτεμνέσθω. **19** ἡ περιτομὴ οὐδέν ἐστιν καὶ ἡ ἀκροβυστία οὐδέν ἐστιν, ἀλλὰ τήρησις ἐντολῶν θεοῦ. **20** ἕκαστος ἐν τῇ κλήσει ᾗ ἐκλήθη, ἐν ταύτῃ μενέτω. **21** δοῦλος ἐκλήθης, μή σοι μελέτω· ἀλλ᾽ εἰ καὶ δύνασαι ἐλεύθερος γενέσθαι, μᾶλλον χρῆσαι. **22** ὁ γὰρ ἐν κυρίῳ κληθεὶς δοῦλος ἀπελεύθερος κυρίου ἐστίν, ὁμοίως ὁ ἐλεύθερος κληθεὶς δοῦλός ἐστιν Χριστοῦ. **23** τιμῆς ἠγοράσθητε· μὴ γίνεσθε δοῦλοι ἀνθρώπων. **24** ἕκαστος ἐν ᾧ ἐκλήθη, ἀδελφοί, ἐν τούτῳ μενέτω παρὰ θεῷ.

25 Περὶ δὲ τῶν παρθένων ἐπιταγὴν κυρίου οὐκ ἔχω, γνώμην δὲ δίδωμι ὡς ἠλεημένος ὑπὸ κυρίου πιστὸς εἶναι. **26** Νομίζω οὖν τοῦτο καλὸν ὑπάρχειν διὰ τὴν ἐνεστῶσαν ἀνάγκην, ὅτι καλὸν ἀνθρώπῳ τὸ οὕτως εἶναι. **27** δέδεσαι γυναικί, μὴ ζήτει λύσιν· λέλυσαι ἀπὸ γυναικός, μὴ ζήτει γυναῖκα. **28** ἐὰν δὲ καὶ γαμήσῃς, οὐχ ἥμαρτες, καὶ ἐὰν γήμῃ ἡ παρθένος, οὐχ ἥμαρτεν· θλῖψιν δὲ τῇ σαρκὶ ἕξουσιν οἱ τοιοῦτοι, ἐγὼ δὲ ὑμῶν φείδομαι. **29** τοῦτο δέ φημι, ἀδελφοί, ὁ καιρὸς συνεσταλμένος ἐστίν· τὸ λοιπόν, ἵνα καὶ οἱ ἔχοντες γυναῖκας ὡς μὴ ἔχοντες ὦσιν **30** καὶ οἱ κλαίοντες ὡς μὴ κλαίοντες καὶ οἱ χαίροντες ὡς μὴ χαίροντες καὶ οἱ ἀγοράζοντες ὡς μὴ κατέχοντες, **31** καὶ οἱ χρώμενοι τὸν κόσμον ὡς μὴ καταχρώμενοι· παράγει γὰρ τὸ σχῆμα τοῦ κόσμου τούτου. **32** θέλω δὲ ὑμᾶς ἀμερίμνους εἶναι. ὁ ἄγαμος μεριμνᾷ τὰ τοῦ κυρίου, πῶς ἀρέσῃ τῷ κυρίῳ· **33** ὁ δὲ γαμήσας μεριμνᾷ τὰ τοῦ κόσμου, πῶς ἀρέσῃ τῇ γυναικί, **34** καὶ μεμέρισται. καὶ ἡ γυνὴ ἡ ἄγαμος καὶ ἡ παρθένος μεριμνᾷ τὰ

NIV

17Nevertheless, each one should retain the place in life that the Lord assigned to him and to which God has called him. This is the rule I lay down in all the churches. 18Was a man already circumcised when he was called? He should not become uncircumcised. Was a man uncircumcised when he was called? He should not be circumcised. 19Circumcision is nothing and uncircumcision is nothing. Keeping God's commands is what counts. 20Each one should remain in the situation which he was in when God called him. 21Were you a slave when you were called? Don't let it trouble you—although if you can gain your freedom, do so. 22For he who was a slave when he was called by the Lord is the Lord's freedman; similarly, he who was a free man when he was called is Christ's slave. 23You were bought at a price; do not become slaves of men. 24Brothers, each man, as responsible to God, should remain in the situation God called him to.

25Now about virgins: I have no command from the Lord, but I give a judgment as one who by the Lord's mercy is trustworthy. 26Because of the present crisis, I think that it is good for you to remain as you are. 27Are you married? Do not seek a divorce. Are you unmarried? Do not look for a wife. 28But if you do marry, you have not sinned; and if a virgin marries, she has not sinned. But those who marry will face many troubles in this life, and I want to spare you this.

29What I mean, brothers, is that the time is short. From now on those who have wives should live as if they had none; 30those who mourn, as if they did not; those who are happy, as if they were not; those who buy something, as if it were not theirs to keep; 31those who use the things of the world, as if not engrossed in them. For this world in its present form is passing away.

32I would like you to be free from concern. An unmarried man is concerned about the Lord's affairs—how he can please the Lord. 33But a married man is concerned about the affairs of this world—how he can please his wife— 34and his interests are divided. An unmarried woman or virgin is concerned about the Lord's affairs:

ᵃ Or *avail yourself of the opportunity*   ᵇ Gk *brothers*
ᶜ Or *present*   ᵈ Gk *in the flesh*

anxious about the affairs of the Lord, so that they may be holy in body and spirit; but the married woman is anxious about the affairs of the world, how to please her husband. [35]I say this for your own benefit, not to put any restraint upon you, but to promote good order and unhindered devotion to the Lord.

36 If anyone thinks that he is not behaving properly toward his fiancée,[e] if his passions are strong, and so it has to be, let him marry as he wishes; it is no sin. Let them marry. [37]But if someone stands firm in his resolve, being under no necessity but having his own desire under control, and has determined in his own mind to keep her as his fiancée,[e] he will do well. [38]So then, he who marries his fiancée[e] does well; and he who refrains from marriage will do better.

39 A wife is bound as long as her husband lives. But if the husband dies,[f] she is free to marry anyone she wishes, only in the Lord. [40]But in my judgment she is more blessed if she remains as she is. And I think that I too have the Spirit of God.

Food Offered to Idols

8 Now concerning food sacrificed to idols: we know that "all of us possess knowledge." Knowledge puffs up, but love builds up. [2]Anyone who claims to know something does not yet have the necessary knowledge; [3]but anyone who loves God is known by him.

4 Hence, as to the eating of food offered to idols, we know that "no idol in the world really exists," and that "there is no God but one." [5]Indeed, even though there may be so-called gods in heaven or on earth— as in fact there are many gods and many lords— [6]yet for us there is one God, the Father, from whom are all things and for whom we exist, and one Lord, Jesus Christ, through whom are all things and through whom we exist.

7 It is not everyone, however, who has this knowledge. Since some have become so accustomed to idols until now, they still think of the food they eat as food offered

τοῦ κυρίου, ἵνα ᾖ ἁγία καὶ τῷ σώματι καὶ τῷ πνεύματι· ἡ δὲ γαμήσασα μεριμνᾷ τὰ τοῦ κόσμου, πῶς ἀρέσῃ τῷ ἀνδρί. **35** τοῦτο δὲ πρὸς τὸ ὑμῶν αὐτῶν σύμφορον λέγω, οὐχ ἵνα βρόχον ὑμῖν ἐπιβάλω ἀλλὰ πρὸς τὸ εὔσχημον καὶ εὐπάρεδρον τῷ κυρίῳ ἀπερισπάστως.

36 Εἰ δέ τις ἀσχημονεῖν ἐπὶ τὴν παρθένον αὐτοῦ νομίζει, ἐὰν ᾖ ὑπέρ- ακμος καὶ οὕτως ὀφείλει γίνεσθαι, ὃ θέλει ποιείτω, οὐχ ἁμαρτάνει, γαμεί- τωσαν. **37** ὃς δὲ ἕστηκεν ἐν τῇ καρδίᾳ αὐτοῦ ἑδραῖος μὴ ἔχων ἀνάγκην, ἐξουσίαν δὲ ἔχει περὶ τοῦ ἰδίου θελήματος καὶ τοῦτο κέκρικεν ἐν τῇ ἰδίᾳ καρδίᾳ, τηρεῖν τὴν ἑαυτοῦ παρθένον, καλῶς ποιήσει. **38** ὥστε καὶ ὁ γαμίζων τὴν ἑαυτοῦ παρθένον καλῶς ποιεῖ καὶ ὁ μὴ γαμίζων κρεῖσσον ποιήσει.

39 Γυνὴ δέδεται ἐφ᾽ ὅσον χρόνον ζῇ ὁ ἀνὴρ αὐτῆς· ἐὰν δὲ κοιμηθῇ ὁ ἀνήρ, ἐλευθέρα ἐστὶν ᾧ θέλει γαμηθῆναι, μόνον ἐν κυρίῳ. **40** μακαριωτέρα δέ ἐστιν ἐὰν οὕτως μείνῃ, κατὰ τὴν ἐμὴν γνώμην· δοκῶ δὲ κἀγὼ πνεῦμα θεοῦ ἔχειν.

8 Περὶ δὲ τῶν εἰδωλοθύτων, οἴδαμεν ὅτι πάντες γνῶσιν ἔχομεν. ἡ γνῶσις φυσιοῖ, ἡ δὲ ἀγάπη οἰκοδομεῖ· **2** εἴ τις δοκεῖ ἐγνωκέναι τι, οὔπω ἔγνω καθὼς δεῖ γνῶναι· **3** εἰ δέ τις ἀγαπᾷ τὸν θεόν, οὗτος ἔγνωσται ὑπ᾽ αὐτοῦ. **4** Περὶ τῆς βρώσεως οὖν τῶν εἰδωλοθύτων, οἴδαμεν ὅτι οὐδὲν εἴδωλον ἐν κόσμῳ καὶ ὅτι οὐδεὶς θεὸς εἰ μὴ εἷς. **5** καὶ γὰρ εἴπερ εἰσὶν λεγόμενοι θεοὶ εἴτε ἐν οὐρανῷ εἴτε ἐπὶ γῆς, ὥσπερ εἰσὶν θεοὶ πολλοὶ καὶ κύριοι πολλοί, **6** ἀλλ᾽ ἡμῖν εἷς θεὸς ὁ πατὴρ ἐξ οὗ τὰ πάντα καὶ ἡμεῖς εἰς αὐτόν, καὶ εἷς κύριος Ἰησοῦς Χριστὸς δι᾽ οὗ τὰ πάντα καὶ ἡμεῖς δι᾽ αὐτοῦ.

7 Ἀλλ᾽ οὐκ ἐν πᾶσιν ἡ γνῶσις· τινὲς δὲ τῇ συνηθείᾳ ἕως ἄρτι τοῦ εἰδώλου ὡς εἰδωλόθυτον ἐσθίουσιν, καὶ ἡ

Her aim is to be devoted to the Lord in both body and spirit. But a married woman is concerned about the affairs of this world—how she can please her husband. [35]I am saying this for your own good, not to restrict you, but that you may live in a right way in undivided devotion to the Lord.

[36]If anyone thinks he is acting improperly toward the virgin he is engaged to, and if she is getting along in years and he feels he ought to marry, he should do as he wants. He is not sinning. They should get married. [37]But the man who has settled the matter in his own mind, who is under no compulsion but has control over his own will, and who has made up his mind not to marry the virgin—this man also does the right thing. [38]So then, he who marries the virgin does right, but he who does not marry her does even better.[b]

[39]A woman is bound to her husband as long as he lives. But if her husband dies, she is free to marry anyone she wishes, but he must belong to the Lord. [40]In my judgment, she is happier if she stays as she is— and I think that I too have the Spirit of God.

Food Sacrificed to Idols

8 Now about food sacrificed to idols: We know that we all possess knowledge.[a] Knowledge puffs up, but love builds up. [2]The man who thinks he knows something does not yet know as he ought to know. [3]But the man who loves God is known by God.

[4]So then, about eating food sacrificed to idols: We know that an idol is nothing at all in the world and that there is no God but one. [5]For even if there are so-called gods, whether in heaven or on earth (as indeed there are many "gods" and many "lords"), [6]yet for us there is but one God, the Father, from whom all things came and for whom we live; and there is but one Lord, Jesus Christ, through whom all things came and through whom we live.

[7]But not everyone knows this. Some people are still so accustomed to idols that when they eat such food they think of it as

[b]36-38 Or [36]*If anyone thinks he is not treating his daughter properly, and if she is getting along in years, and he feels she ought to marry, he should do as he wants. He is not sinning. He should let her get married. [37]But the man who has settled the matter in his own mind, who is under no compulsion but has control over his own will, and who has made up his mind to keep the virgin unmarried—this man also does the right thing. [38]So then, he who gives his virgin in marriage does right, but he who does not give her in marriage does even better.* [a]1 Or "We all possess knowledge," as you say

to an idol; and their conscience, being weak, is defiled. 8"Food will not bring us close to God."g We are no worse off if we do not eat, and no better off if we do. 9But take care that this liberty of yours does not somehow become a stumbling block to the weak. 10For if others see you, who possess knowledge, eating in the temple of an idol, might they not, since their conscience is weak, be encouraged to the point of eating food sacrificed to idols? 11So by your knowledge those weak believers for whom Christ died are destroyed.h 12But when you thus sin against members of your family,i and wound their conscience when it is weak, you sin against Christ. 13Therefore, if food is a cause of their falling,j I will never eat meat, so that I may not cause one of themk to fall.

The Rights of an Apostle

9 Am I not free? Am I not an apostle? Have I not seen Jesus our Lord? Are you not my work in the Lord? 2If I am not an apostle to others, at least I am to you; for you are the seal of my apostleship in the Lord.

3 This is my defense to those who would examine me. 4Do we not have the right to our food and drink? 5Do we not have the right to be accompanied by a believing wife,l as do the other apostles and the brothers of the Lord and Cephas? 6Or is it only Barnabas and I who have no right to refrain from working for a living? 7Who at any time pays the expenses for doing military service? Who plants a vineyard and does not eat any of its fruit? Or who tends a flock and does not get any of its milk?

8 Do I say this on human authority? Does not the law also say the same? 9For it is written in the law of Moses, "You shall not muzzle an ox while it is treading out the grain." Is it for oxen that God is concerned? 10Or does he not speak entirely for our sake? It was indeed written for our sake, for whoever plows should plow in hope and whoever threshes should thresh in hope of a share in the crop. 11If we have sown spiritual good among you, is it too much if we reap your material benefits? 12If others share this rightful claim on you, do not we still more?

Nevertheless, we have not made use of this right, but we endure anything rather

συνείδησις αὐτῶν ἀσθενὴς οὖσα μολύνεται. 8 βρῶμα δὲ ἡμᾶς οὐ παραστήσει τῷ θεῷ· οὔτε ἐὰν μὴ φάγωμεν ὑστερούμεθα, οὔτε ἐὰν φάγωμεν περισσεύομεν. 9 βλέπετε δὲ μή πως ἡ ἐξουσία ὑμῶν αὕτη πρόσκομμα γένηται τοῖς ἀσθενέσιν. 10 ἐὰν γάρ τις ἴδῃ σὲ τὸν ἔχοντα γνῶσιν ἐν εἰδωλείῳ κατακείμενον, οὐχὶ ἡ συνείδησις αὐτοῦ ἀσθενοῦς ὄντος οἰκοδομηθήσεται εἰς τὸ τὰ εἰδωλόθυτα ἐσθίειν; 11 ἀπόλλυται γὰρ ὁ ἀσθενῶν ἐν τῇ σῇ γνώσει, ὁ ἀδελφὸς δι᾽ ὃν Χριστὸς ἀπέθανεν. 12 οὕτως δὲ ἁμαρτάνοντες εἰς τοὺς ἀδελφοὺς καὶ τύπτοντες αὐτῶν τὴν συνείδησιν ἀσθενοῦσαν εἰς Χριστὸν ἁμαρτάνετε. 13 διόπερ εἰ βρῶμα σκανδαλίζει τὸν ἀδελφόν μου, οὐ μὴ φάγω κρέα εἰς τὸν αἰῶνα, ἵνα μὴ τὸν ἀδελφόν μου σκανδαλίσω.

9 Οὐκ εἰμὶ ἐλεύθερος; οὐκ εἰμὶ ἀπόστολος; οὐχὶ Ἰησοῦν τὸν κύριον ἡμῶν ἑώρακα; οὐ τὸ ἔργον μου ὑμεῖς ἐστε ἐν κυρίῳ; 2 εἰ ἄλλοις οὐκ εἰμὶ ἀπόστολος, ἀλλά γε ὑμῖν εἰμι· ἡ γὰρ σφραγίς μου τῆς ἀποστολῆς ὑμεῖς ἐστε ἐν κυρίῳ.

3 Ἡ ἐμὴ ἀπολογία τοῖς ἐμὲ ἀνακρίνουσίν ἐστιν αὕτη. 4 μὴ οὐκ ἔχομεν ἐξουσίαν φαγεῖν καὶ πεῖν; 5 μὴ οὐκ ἔχομεν ἐξουσίαν ἀδελφὴν γυναῖκα περιάγειν ὡς καὶ οἱ λοιποὶ ἀπόστολοι καὶ οἱ ἀδελφοὶ τοῦ κυρίου καὶ Κηφᾶς; 6 ἢ μόνος ἐγὼ καὶ Βαρναβᾶς οὐκ ἔχομεν ἐξουσίαν μὴ ἐργάζεσθαι; 7 τίς στρατεύεται ἰδίοις ὀψωνίοις ποτέ; τίς φυτεύει ἀμπελῶνα καὶ τὸν καρπὸν αὐτοῦ οὐκ ἐσθίει; ἢ τίς ποιμαίνει ποίμνην καὶ ἐκ τοῦ γάλακτος τῆς ποίμνης οὐκ ἐσθίει; 8 Μὴ κατὰ ἄνθρωπον ταῦτα λαλῶ ἢ καὶ ὁ νόμος ταῦτα οὐ λέγει; 9 ἐν γὰρ τῷ Μωϋσέως νόμῳ γέγραπται, Οὐ κημώσεις βοῦν ἀλοῶντα. μὴ τῶν βοῶν μέλει τῷ θεῷ 10 ἢ δι᾽ ἡμᾶς πάντως λέγει; δι᾽ ἡμᾶς γὰρ ἐγράφη ὅτι ὀφείλει ἐπ᾽ ἐλπίδι ὁ ἀροτριῶν ἀροτριᾶν καὶ ὁ ἀλοῶν ἐπ᾽ ἐλπίδι τοῦ μετέχειν. 11 εἰ ἡμεῖς ὑμῖν τὰ πνευματικὰ ἐσπείραμεν, μέγα εἰ ἡμεῖς ὑμῶν τὰ σαρκικὰ θερίσομεν; 12 εἰ ἄλλοι τῆς ὑμῶν ἐξουσίας μετέχουσιν, οὐ μᾶλλον ἡμεῖς;

Ἀλλ᾽ οὐκ ἐχρησάμεθα τῇ ἐξουσίᾳ ταύτῃ, ἀλλὰ πάντα στέγομεν, ἵνα μὴ

having been sacrificed to an idol, and since their conscience is weak, it is defiled. 8But food does not bring us near to God; we are no worse if we do not eat, and no better if we do.

9Be careful, however, that the exercise of your freedom does not become a stumbling block to the weak. 10For if anyone with a weak conscience sees you who have this knowledge eating in an idol's temple, won't he be emboldened to eat what has been sacrificed to idols? 11So this weak brother, for whom Christ died, is destroyed by your knowledge. 12When you sin against your brothers in this way and wound their weak conscience, you sin against Christ. 13Therefore, if what I eat causes my brother to fall into sin, I will never eat meat again, so that I will not cause him to fall.

The Rights of an Apostle

9 Am I not free? Am I not an apostle? Have I not seen Jesus our Lord? Are you not the result of my work in the Lord? 2Even though I may not be an apostle to others, surely I am to you! For you are the seal of my apostleship in the Lord.

3This is my defense to those who sit in judgment on me. 4Don't we have the right to food and drink? 5Don't we have the right to take a believing wife along with us, as do the other apostles and the Lord's brothers and Cephasa? 6Or is it only I and Barnabas who must work for a living?

7Who serves as a soldier at his own expense? Who plants a vineyard and does not eat of its grapes? Who tends a flock and does not drink of the milk? 8Do I say this merely from a human point of view? Doesn't the Law say the same thing? 9For it is written in the Law of Moses: "Do not muzzle an ox while it is treading out the grain."b Is it about oxen that God is concerned? 10Surely he says this for us, doesn't he? Yes, this was written for us, because when the plowman plows and the thresher threshes, they ought to do so in the hope of sharing in the harvest. 11If we have sown spiritual seed among you, is it too much if we reap a material harvest from you? 12If others have this right of support from you, shouldn't we have it all the more?

But we did not use this right. On the contrary, we put up with anything rather

---

g The quotation may extend to the end of the verse
h Gk *the weak brother . . . is destroyed*   i Gk *against the brothers*   j Gk *my brother's falling*   k Gk *cause my brother to fall*
l Gk *a sister as wife*

than put an obstacle in the way of the gospel of Christ. 13Do you not know that those who are employed in the temple service get their food from the temple, and those who serve at the altar share in what is sacrificed on the altar? 14In the same way, the Lord commanded that those who proclaim the gospel should get their living by the gospel.

15 But I have made no use of any of these rights, nor am I writing this so that they may be applied in my case. Indeed, I would rather die than that—no one will deprive me of my ground for boasting! 16If I proclaim the gospel, this gives me no ground for boasting, for an obligation is laid on me, and woe to me if I do not proclaim the gospel! 17For if I do this of my own will, I have a reward; but if not of my own will, I am entrusted with a commission. 18What then is my reward? Just this: that in my proclamation I may make the gospel free of charge, so as not to make full use of my rights in the gospel.

19 For though I am free with respect to all, I have made myself a slave to all, so that I might win more of them. 20To the Jews I became as a Jew, in order to win Jews. To those under the law I became as one under the law (though I myself am not under the law) so that I might win those under the law. 21To those outside the law I became as one outside the law (though I am not free from God's law but am under Christ's law) so that I might win those outside the law. 22To the weak I became weak, so that I might win the weak. I have become all things to all people, that I might by all means save some. 23I do it all for the sake of the gospel, so that I may share in its blessings.

24 Do you not know that in a race the runners all compete, but only one receives the prize? Run in such a way that you may win it. 25Athletes exercise self-control in all things; they do it to receive a perishable wreath, but we an imperishable one. 26So I do not run aimlessly, nor do I box as though beating the air; 27but I punish my body and enslave it, so that after proclaiming to others I myself should not be disqualified.

Warnings from Israel's History

10 I do not want you to be unaware, brothers and sisters,[m] that our ancestors were all under the cloud, and all passed through the sea, 2and all were baptized into Moses in the cloud and in the

m Gk *brothers*

τινα ἐγκοπὴν δῶμεν τῷ εὐαγγελίῳ τοῦ Χριστοῦ. **13** οὐκ οἴδατε ὅτι οἱ τὰ ἱερὰ ἐργαζόμενοι [τὰ] ἐκ τοῦ ἱεροῦ ἐσθίουσιν, οἱ τῷ θυσιαστηρίῳ παρεδρεύοντες τῷ θυσιαστηρίῳ συμμερίζονται; **14** οὕτως καὶ ὁ κύριος διέταξεν τοῖς τὸ εὐαγγέλιον καταγγέλλουσιν ἐκ τοῦ εὐαγγελίου ζῆν. **15** ἐγὼ δὲ οὐ κέχρημαι οὐδενὶ τούτων. οὐκ ἔγραψα δὲ ταῦτα, ἵνα οὕτως γένηται ἐν ἐμοί· καλὸν γάρ μοι μᾶλλον ἀποθανεῖν ἤ – τὸ καύχημά μου οὐδεὶς κενώσει. **16** ἐὰν γὰρ εὐαγγελίζωμαι, οὐκ ἔστιν μοι καύχημα· ἀνάγκη γάρ μοι ἐπίκειται· οὐαὶ γάρ μοί ἐστιν ἐὰν μὴ εὐαγγελίσωμαι. **17** εἰ γὰρ ἑκὼν τοῦτο πράσσω, μισθὸν ἔχω· εἰ δὲ ἄκων, οἰκονομίαν πεπίστευμαι· **18** τίς οὖν μού ἐστιν ὁ μισθός; ἵνα εὐαγγελιζόμενος ἀδάπανον θήσω τὸ εὐαγγέλιον εἰς τὸ μὴ καταχρήσασθαι τῇ ἐξουσίᾳ μου ἐν τῷ εὐαγγελίῳ.

19 Ἐλεύθερος γὰρ ὢν ἐκ πάντων πᾶσιν ἐμαυτὸν ἐδούλωσα, ἵνα τοὺς πλείονας κερδήσω· **20** καὶ ἐγενόμην τοῖς Ἰουδαίοις ὡς Ἰουδαῖος, ἵνα Ἰουδαίους κερδήσω· τοῖς ὑπὸ νόμον ὡς ὑπὸ νόμον, μὴ ὢν αὐτὸς ὑπὸ νόμον, ἵνα τοὺς ὑπὸ νόμον κερδήσω· **21** τοῖς ἀνόμοις ὡς ἄνομος, μὴ ὢν ἄνομος θεοῦ ἀλλ' ἔννομος Χριστοῦ, ἵνα κερδάνω τοὺς ἀνόμους· **22** ἐγενόμην τοῖς ἀσθενέσιν ἀσθενής, ἵνα τοὺς ἀσθενεῖς κερδήσω· τοῖς πᾶσιν γέγονα πάντα, ἵνα πάντως τινὰς σώσω. **23** πάντα δὲ ποιῶ διὰ τὸ εὐαγγέλιον, ἵνα συγκοινωνὸς αὐτοῦ γένωμαι.

24 Οὐκ οἴδατε ὅτι οἱ ἐν σταδίῳ τρέχοντες πάντες μὲν τρέχουσιν, εἷς δὲ λαμβάνει τὸ βραβεῖον; οὕτως τρέχετε ἵνα καταλάβητε. **25** πᾶς δὲ ὁ ἀγωνιζόμενος πάντα ἐγκρατεύεται, ἐκεῖνοι μὲν οὖν ἵνα φθαρτὸν στέφανον λάβωσιν, ἡμεῖς δὲ ἄφθαρτον. **26** ἐγὼ τοίνυν οὕτως τρέχω ὡς οὐκ ἀδήλως, οὕτως πυκτεύω ὡς οὐκ ἀέρα δέρων· **27** ἀλλὰ ὑπωπιάζω μου τὸ σῶμα καὶ δουλαγωγῶ, μή πως ἄλλοις κηρύξας αὐτὸς ἀδόκιμος γένωμαι.

10 Οὐ θέλω γὰρ ὑμᾶς ἀγνοεῖν, ἀδελφοί, ὅτι οἱ πατέρες ἡμῶν πάντες ὑπὸ τὴν νεφέλην ἦσαν καὶ πάντες διὰ τῆς θαλάσσης διῆλθον **2** καὶ πάντες εἰς τὸν Μωϋσῆν ἐβαπτίσθησαν ἐν τῇ νεφέλῃ καὶ ἐν τῇ θαλάσσῃ **3** καὶ

than hinder the gospel of Christ. 13Don't you know that those who work in the temple get their food from the temple, and those who serve at the altar share in what is offered on the altar? 14In the same way, the Lord has commanded that those who preach the gospel should receive their living from the gospel.

15But I have not used any of these rights. And I am not writing this in the hope that you will do such things for me. I would rather die than have anyone deprive me of this boast. 16Yet when I preach the gospel, I cannot boast, for I am compelled to preach. Woe to me if I do not preach the gospel! 17If I preach voluntarily, I have a reward; if not voluntarily, I am simply discharging the trust committed to me. 18What then is my reward? Just this: that in preaching the gospel I may offer it free of charge, and so not make use of my rights in preaching it.

19Though I am free and belong to no man, I make myself a slave to everyone, to win as many as possible. 20To the Jews I became like a Jew, to win the Jews. To those under the law I became like one under the law (though I myself am not under the law), so as to win those under the law. 21To those not having the law I became like one not having the law (though I am not free from God's law but am under Christ's law), so as to win those not having the law. 22To the weak I became weak, to win the weak. I have become all things to all men so that by all possible means I might save some. 23I do all this for the sake of the gospel, that I may share in its blessings.

24Do you not know that in a race all the runners run, but only one gets the prize? Run in such a way as to get the prize. 25Everyone who competes in the games goes into strict training. They do it to get a crown that will not last; but we do it to get a crown that will last forever. 26Therefore I do not run like a man running aimlessly; I do not fight like a man beating the air. 27No, I beat my body and make it my slave so that after I have preached to others, I myself will not be disqualified for the prize.

Warnings From Israel's History

10 For I do not want you to be ignorant of the fact, brothers, that our forefathers were all under the cloud and that they all passed through the sea. 2They were all baptized into Moses in the cloud sea, [3]and all ate the same spiritual food, [4]and all drank the same spiritual drink. For they drank from the spiritual rock that followed them, and the rock was Christ. [5]Nevertheless, God was not pleased with most of them, and they were struck down in the wilderness.

6 Now these things occurred as examples for us, so that we might not desire evil as they did. [7]Do not become idolaters as some of them did; as it is written, "The people sat down to eat and drink, and they rose up to play." [8]We must not indulge in sexual immorality as some of them did, and twenty-three thousand fell in a single day. [9]We must not put Christ[n] to the test, as some of them did, and were destroyed by serpents. [10]And do not complain as some of them did, and were destroyed by the destroyer. [11]These things happened to them to serve as an example, and they were written down to instruct us, on whom the ends of the ages have come. [12]So if you think you are standing, watch out that you do not fall. [13]No testing has overtaken you that is not common to everyone. God is faithful, and he will not let you be tested beyond your strength, but with the testing he will also provide the way out so that you may be able to endure it.

14 Therefore, my dear friends,[o] flee from the worship of idols. [15]I speak as to sensible people; judge for yourselves what I say. [16]The cup of blessing that we bless, is it not a sharing in the blood of Christ? The bread that we break, is it not a sharing in the body of Christ? [17]Because there is one bread, we who are many are one body, for we all partake of the one bread. [18]Consider the people of Israel;[p] are not those who eat the sacrifices partners in the altar? [19]What do I imply then? That food sacrificed to idols is anything, or that an idol is anything? [20]No, I imply that what pagans sacrifice, they sacrifice to demons and not to God. I do not want you to be partners with demons. [21]You cannot drink the cup of the Lord and the cup of demons. You cannot partake of the table of the Lord and the table of demons. [22]Or are we provoking the Lord to jealousy? Are we stronger than he?

Do All to the Glory of God

23 "All things are lawful," but not all

πάντες τὸ αὐτὸ πνευματικὸν βρῶμα ἔφαγον 4 καὶ πάντες τὸ αὐτὸ πνευματικὸν ἔπιον πόμα· ἔπινον γὰρ ἐκ πνευματικῆς ἀκολουθούσης πέτρας, ἡ πέτρα δὲ ἦν ὁ Χριστός. 5 ἀλλ' οὐκ ἐν τοῖς πλείοσιν αὐτῶν εὐδόκησεν ὁ θεός, κατεστρώθησαν γὰρ ἐν τῇ ἐρήμῳ. 6 ταῦτα δὲ τύποι ἡμῶν ἐγενήθησαν, εἰς τὸ μὴ εἶναι ἡμᾶς ἐπιθυμητὰς κακῶν, καθὼς κἀκεῖνοι ἐπεθύμησαν. 7 μηδὲ εἰδωλολάτραι γίνεσθε καθώς τινες αὐτῶν, ὥσπερ γέγραπται, Ἐκάθισεν ὁ λαὸς φαγεῖν καὶ πεῖν καὶ ἀνέστησαν παίζειν. 8 μηδὲ πορνεύωμεν, καθὼς τινες αὐτῶν ἐπόρνευσαν καὶ ἔπεσαν μιᾷ ἡμέρᾳ εἴκοσι τρεῖς χιλιάδες. 9 μηδὲ ἐκπειράζωμεν τὸν Χριστόν[a], καθὼς τινες αὐτῶν ἐπείρασαν καὶ ὑπὸ τῶν ὄφεων ἀπώλλυντο. 10 μηδὲ γογγύζετε, καθάπερ τινὲς αὐτῶν ἐγόγγυσαν καὶ ἀπώλοντο ὑπὸ τοῦ ὀλοθρευτοῦ. 11 ταῦτα δὲ τυπικῶς συνέβαινεν ἐκείνοις, ἐγράφη δὲ πρὸς νουθεσίαν ἡμῶν, εἰς οὓς τὰ τέλη τῶν αἰώνων κατήντηκεν. 12 ὥστε ὁ δοκῶν ἑστάναι βλεπέτω μὴ πέσῃ. 13 πειρασμὸς ὑμᾶς οὐκ εἴληφεν εἰ μὴ ἀνθρώπινος· πιστὸς δὲ ὁ θεός, ὃς οὐκ ἐάσει ὑμᾶς πειρασθῆναι ὑπὲρ ὃ δύνασθε ἀλλὰ ποιήσει σὺν τῷ πειρασμῷ καὶ τὴν ἔκβασιν τοῦ δύνασθαι ὑπενεγκεῖν.

14 Διόπερ, ἀγαπητοί μου, φεύγετε ἀπὸ τῆς εἰδωλολατρίας. 15 ὡς φρονίμοις λέγω· κρίνατε ὑμεῖς ὅ φημι. 16 τὸ ποτήριον τῆς εὐλογίας ὃ εὐλογοῦμεν, οὐχὶ κοινωνία ἐστὶν τοῦ αἵματος τοῦ Χριστοῦ; τὸν ἄρτον ὃν κλῶμεν, οὐχὶ κοινωνία τοῦ σώματος τοῦ Χριστοῦ ἐστιν; 17 ὅτι εἷς ἄρτος, ἓν σῶμα οἱ πολλοί ἐσμεν, οἱ γὰρ πάντες ἐκ τοῦ ἑνὸς ἄρτου μετέχομεν. 18 βλέπετε τὸν Ἰσραὴλ κατὰ σάρκα· οὐχ οἱ ἐσθίοντες τὰς θυσίας κοινωνοὶ τοῦ θυσιαστηρίου εἰσίν; 19 τί οὖν φημι; ὅτι εἰδωλόθυτόν τί ἐστιν ἢ ὅτι εἰδωλόν τί ἐστιν; 20 ἀλλ' ὅτι ἃ θύουσιν, δαιμονίοις καὶ οὐ θεῷ [θύουσιν][b]· οὐ θέλω δὲ ὑμᾶς κοινωνοὺς τῶν δαιμονίων γίνεσθαι. 21 οὐ δύνασθε ποτήριον κυρίου πίνειν καὶ ποτήριον δαιμονίων, οὐ δύνασθε τραπέζης κυρίου μετέχειν καὶ τραπέζης δαιμονίων. 22 ἢ παραζηλοῦμεν τὸν κύριον; μὴ ἰσχυρότεροι αὐτοῦ ἐσμεν;

23 Πάντα ἔξεστιν ἀλλ' οὐ πάντα

and in the sea. [3]They all ate the same spiritual food [4]and drank the same spiritual drink; for they drank from the spiritual rock that accompanied them, and that rock was Christ. [5]Nevertheless, God was not pleased with most of them; their bodies were scattered over the desert.

[6]Now these things occurred as examples[a] to keep us from setting our hearts on evil things as they did. [7]Do not be idolaters, as some of them were; as it is written: "The people sat down to eat and drink and got up to indulge in pagan revelry."[b] [8]We should not commit sexual immorality, as some of them did—and in one day twenty-three thousand of them died. [9]We should not test the Lord, as some of them did—and were killed by snakes. [10]And do not grumble, as some of them did—and were killed by the destroying angel.

[11]These things happened to them as examples and were written down as warnings for us, on whom the fulfillment of the ages has come. [12]So, if you think you are standing firm, be careful that you don't fall! [13]No temptation has seized you except what is common to man. And God is faithful; he will not let you be tempted beyond what you can bear. But when you are tempted, he will also provide a way out so that you can stand up under it.

Idol Feasts and the Lord's Supper

[14]Therefore, my dear friends, flee from idolatry. [15]I speak to sensible people; judge for yourselves what I say. [16]Is not the cup of thanksgiving for which we give thanks a participation in the blood of Christ? And is not the bread that we break a participation in the body of Christ? [17]Because there is one loaf, we, who are many, are one body, for we all partake of the one loaf.

[18]Consider the people of Israel: Do not those who eat the sacrifices participate in the altar? [19]Do I mean then that a sacrifice offered to an idol is anything, or that an idol is anything? [20]No, but the sacrifices of pagans are offered to demons, not to God, and I do not want you to be participants with demons. [21]You cannot drink the cup of the Lord and the cup of demons too; you cannot have a part in both the Lord's table and the table of demons. [22]Are we trying to arouse the Lord's jealousy? Are we stronger than he?

The Believer's Freedom

[23]"Everything is permissible"—but not

things are beneficial. "All things are lawful," but not all things build up. 24Do not seek your own advantage, but that of the other. 25Eat whatever is sold in the meat market without raising any question on the ground of conscience, 26for "the earth and its fullness are the Lord's." 27If an unbeliever invites you to a meal and you are disposed to go, eat whatever is set before you without raising any question on the ground of conscience. 28But if someone says to you, "This has been offered in sacrifice," then do not eat it, out of consideration for the one who informed you, and for the sake of conscience— 29I mean the other's conscience, not your own. For why should my liberty be subject to the judgment of someone else's conscience? 30If I partake with thankfulness, why should I be denounced because of that for which I give thanks?

31 So, whether you eat or drink, or whatever you do, do everything for the glory of God. 32Give no offense to Jews or to Greeks or to the church of God, 33just as I try to please everyone in everything I do, not seeking my own advantage, but that of many, so that they may be saved.

11 1Be imitators of me, as I am of Christ.

Head Coverings

2 I commend you because you remember me in everything and maintain the traditions just as I handed them on to you. 3But I want you to understand that Christ is the head of every man, and the husband[q] is the head of his wife,[r] and God is the head of Christ. 4Any man who prays or prophesies with something on his head disgraces his head, 5but any woman who prays or prophesies with her head unveiled disgraces her head—it is one and the same thing as having her head shaved. 6For if a woman will not veil herself, then she should cut off her hair; but if it is disgraceful for a woman to have her hair cut off or to be shaved, she should wear a veil. 7For a man ought not to have his head veiled, since he is the image and reflection[s] of God; but woman is the reflection[s] of man. 8Indeed, man was not made from woman,

συμφέρει· πάντα ἔξεστιν ἀλλ' οὐ πάντα οἰκοδομεῖ. **24** *μηδεὶς τὸ ἑαυτοῦ ζητείτω ἀλλὰ τὸ τοῦ ἑτέρου.* **25** *Πᾶν τὸ ἐν μακέλλῳ πωλούμενον ἐσθίετε μηδὲν ἀνακρίνοντες διὰ τὴν συνείδησιν·* **26 τοῦ κυρίου** *γὰρ* **ἡ γῆ καὶ τὸ πλήρωμα αὐτῆς.** **27** *εἴ τις καλεῖ ὑμᾶς τῶν ἀπίστων καὶ θέλετε πορεύεσθαι, πᾶν τὸ παρατιθέμενον ὑμῖν ἐσθίετε μηδὲν ἀνακρίνοντες διὰ τὴν συνείδησιν.* **28** *ἐὰν δέ τις ὑμῖν εἴπῃ, Τοῦτο ἱερόθυτόν ἐστιν, μὴ ἐσθίετε δι' ἐκεῖνον τὸν μηνύσαντα καὶ τὴν συνείδησιν·*[c] **29** *συνείδησιν δὲ λέγω οὐχὶ τὴν ἑαυτοῦ ἀλλὰ τὴν τοῦ ἑτέρου. ἱνατί γὰρ ἡ ἐλευθερία μου κρίνεται ὑπὸ ἄλλης συνειδήσεως;* **30** *εἰ ἐγὼ χάριτι μετέχω, τί βλασφημοῦμαι ὑπὲρ οὗ ἐγὼ εὐχαριστῶ;* **31** *εἴτε οὖν ἐσθίετε εἴτε πίνετε εἴτε τι ποιεῖτε, πάντα εἰς δόξαν θεοῦ ποιεῖτε.* **32** *ἀπρόσκοποι καὶ Ἰουδαίοις γίνεσθε καὶ Ἕλλησιν καὶ τῇ ἐκκλησίᾳ τοῦ θεοῦ,* **33** *καθὼς κἀγὼ πάντα πᾶσιν ἀρέσκω μὴ ζητῶν τὸ ἐμαυτοῦ σύμφορον ἀλλὰ τὸ τῶν πολλῶν, ἵνα σωθῶσιν.*

11 *μιμηταί μου γίνεσθε καθὼς κἀγὼ Χριστοῦ.*

2 *Ἐπαινῶ δὲ ὑμᾶς ὅτι πάντα μου μέμνησθε καί, καθὼς παρέδωκα ὑμῖν, τὰς παραδόσεις κατέχετε.* **3** *θέλω δὲ ὑμᾶς εἰδέναι ὅτι παντὸς ἀνδρὸς ἡ κεφαλὴ ὁ Χριστός ἐστιν, κεφαλὴ δὲ γυναικὸς ὁ ἀνήρ, κεφαλὴ δὲ τοῦ Χριστοῦ ὁ θεός.* **4** *πᾶς ἀνὴρ προσευχόμενος ἢ προφητεύων κατὰ κεφαλῆς ἔχων καταισχύνει τὴν κεφαλὴν αὐτοῦ.* **5** *πᾶσα δὲ γυνὴ προσευχομένη ἢ προφητεύουσα ἀκατακαλύπτῳ τῇ κεφαλῇ καταισχύνει τὴν κεφαλὴν αὐτῆς· ἓν γάρ ἐστιν καὶ τὸ αὐτὸ τῇ ἐξυρημένῃ.* **6** *εἰ γὰρ οὐ κατακαλύπτεται γυνή, καὶ κειράσθω· εἰ δὲ αἰσχρὸν γυναικὶ τὸ κείρασθαι ἢ ξυρᾶσθαι, κατακαλυπτέσθω.* **7** *ἀνὴρ μὲν γὰρ οὐκ ὀφείλει κατακαλύπτεσθαι τὴν κεφαλὴν εἰκὼν καὶ δόξα θεοῦ ὑπάρχων· ἡ γυνὴ δὲ δόξα ἀνδρός ἐστιν.* **8** *οὐ γάρ ἐστιν ἀνὴρ ἐκ γυναικὸς ἀλλὰ γυνὴ ἐξ*

everything is beneficial. "Everything is permissible"—but not everything is constructive. 24Nobody should seek his own good, but the good of others.

25Eat anything sold in the meat market without raising questions of conscience, 26for, "The earth is the Lord's, and everything in it."[c]

27If some unbeliever invites you to a meal and you want to go, eat whatever is put before you without raising questions of conscience. 28But if anyone says to you, "This has been offered in sacrifice," then do not eat it, both for the sake of the man who told you and for conscience' sake[d]— 29the other man's conscience, I mean, not yours. For why should my freedom be judged by another's conscience? 30If I take part in the meal with thankfulness, why am I denounced because of something I thank God for?

31So whether you eat or drink or whatever you do, do it all for the glory of God. 32Do not cause anyone to stumble, whether Jews, Greeks or the church of God— 33even as I try to please everybody in every way. For I am not seeking my own good but the good of many, so that they may be saved.

11 1Follow my example, as I follow the example of Christ.

Propriety in Worship

2I praise you for remembering me in everything and for holding to the teachings,[a] just as I passed them on to you.

3Now I want you to realize that the head of every man is Christ, and the head of the woman is man, and the head of Christ is God. 4Every man who prays or prophesies with his head covered dishonors his head. 5And every woman who prays or prophesies with her head uncovered dishonors her head—it is just as though her head were shaved. 6If a woman does not cover her head, she should have her hair cut off; and if it is a disgrace for a woman to have her hair cut or shaved off, she should cover her head. 7A man ought not to cover his head,[b] since he is the image and glory of God; but the woman is the glory of man. 8For man did not come from woman, but

[q] The same Greek word means *man* or *husband*
[r] Or *head of the woman* [s] Or *glory*

[c]28 NIV note adds *τοῦ γὰρ κυρίου ἡ γῆ καὶ τὸ πλήρωμα αὐτῆς*

[c]26 Psalm 24:1 [d]28 Some manuscripts *conscience' sake, for "the earth is the Lord's and everything in it"* [a]2 Or *traditions* [b]4-7 Or *4Every man who prays or prophesies with long hair dishonors his head. 5And every woman who prays or prophesies with no covering ⌞of hair⌟ on her head dishonors her head—she is just like one of the "shorn women." 6If a woman has no covering, let her be for now with short hair, but since it is a disgrace for a woman to have her hair shorn or shaved, she should grow it again. 7A man ought not to have long hair*

but woman from man. [9]Neither was man created for the sake of woman, but woman for the sake of man. [10]For this reason a woman ought to have a symbol of[t] authority on her head,[u] because of the angels. [11]Nevertheless, in the Lord woman is not independent of man or man independent of woman. [12]For just as woman came from man, so man comes through woman; but all things come from God. [13]Judge for yourselves: is it proper for a woman to pray to God with her head unveiled? [14]Does not nature itself teach you that if a man wears long hair, it is degrading to him, [15]but if a woman has long hair, it is her glory? For her hair is given to her for a covering. [16]But if anyone is disposed to be contentious—we have no such custom, nor do the churches of God.

Abuses at the Lord's Supper

17 Now in the following instructions I do not commend you, because when you come together it is not for the better but for the worse. [18]For, to begin with, when you come together as a church, I hear that there are divisions among you; and to some extent I believe it. [19]Indeed, there have to be factions among you, for only so will it become clear who among you are genuine. [20]When you come together, it is not really to eat the Lord's supper. [21]For when the time comes to eat, each of you goes ahead with your own supper, and one goes hungry and another becomes drunk. [22]What! Do you not have homes to eat and drink in? Or do you show contempt for the church of God and humiliate those who have nothing? What should I say to you? Should I commend you? In this matter I do not commend you!

The Institution of the Lord's Supper

23 For I received from the Lord what I also handed on to you, that the Lord Jesus on the night when he was betrayed took a loaf of bread, [24]and when he had given thanks, he broke it and said, "This is my body that is for[v] you. Do this in remembrance of me." [25]In the same way he took the cup also, after supper, saying, "This cup is the new covenant in my blood. Do this, as often as you drink it, in remembrance of me." [26]For as often as you eat this bread and drink the cup, you proclaim the Lord's death until he comes.

ἀνδρός· **9** καὶ γὰρ οὐκ ἐκτίσθη ἀνὴρ διὰ τὴν γυναῖκα, ἀλλὰ γυνὴ διὰ τὸν ἄνδρα. **10** διὰ τοῦτο ὀφείλει ἡ γυνὴ ἐξουσίαν ἔχειν ἐπὶ τῆς κεφαλῆς διὰ τοὺς ἀγγέλους. **11** πλὴν οὔτε γυνὴ χωρὶς ἀνδρὸς οὔτε ἀνὴρ χωρὶς γυναικὸς ἐν κυρίῳ· **12** ὥσπερ γὰρ ἡ γυνὴ ἐκ τοῦ ἀνδρός, οὕτως καὶ ὁ ἀνὴρ διὰ τῆς γυναικός· τὰ δὲ πάντα ἐκ τοῦ θεοῦ. **13** ἐν ὑμῖν αὐτοῖς κρίνατε· πρέπον ἐστὶν γυναῖκα ἀκατακάλυπτον τῷ θεῷ προσεύχεσθαι; **14** οὐδὲ ἡ φύσις αὐτὴ διδάσκει ὑμᾶς ὅτι ἀνὴρ μὲν ἐὰν κομᾷ ἀτιμία αὐτῷ ἐστιν, **15** γυνὴ δὲ ἐὰν κομᾷ δόξα αὐτῇ ἐστιν; ὅτι ἡ κόμη ἀντὶ περιβολαίου δέδοται [αὐτῇ]. **16** Εἰ δέ τις δοκεῖ φιλόνεικος εἶναι, ἡμεῖς τοιαύτην συνήθειαν οὐκ ἔχομεν οὐδὲ αἱ ἐκκλησίαι τοῦ θεοῦ.

17 Τοῦτο δὲ παραγγέλλων οὐκ ἐπαινῶ ὅτι οὐκ εἰς τὸ κρεῖσσον ἀλλὰ εἰς τὸ ἧσσον συνέρχεσθε. **18** πρῶτον μὲν γὰρ συνερχομένων ὑμῶν ἐν ἐκκλησίᾳ ἀκούω σχίσματα ἐν ὑμῖν ὑπάρχειν καὶ μέρος τι πιστεύω. **19** δεῖ γὰρ καὶ αἱρέσεις ἐν ὑμῖν εἶναι, ἵνα [καὶ] οἱ δόκιμοι φανεροὶ γένωνται ἐν ὑμῖν. **20** Συνερχομένων οὖν ὑμῶν ἐπὶ τὸ αὐτὸ οὐκ ἔστιν κυριακὸν δεῖπνον φαγεῖν· **21** ἕκαστος γὰρ τὸ ἴδιον δεῖπνον προλαμβάνει ἐν τῷ φαγεῖν, καὶ ὃς μὲν πεινᾷ ὃς δὲ μεθύει. **22** μὴ γὰρ οἰκίας οὐκ ἔχετε εἰς τὸ ἐσθίειν καὶ πίνειν; ἢ τῆς ἐκκλησίας τοῦ θεοῦ καταφρονεῖτε, καὶ καταισχύνετε τοὺς μὴ ἔχοντας; τί εἴπω ὑμῖν; ἐπαινέσω ὑμᾶς; ἐν τούτῳ οὐκ ἐπαινῶ. **23** Ἐγὼ γὰρ παρέλαβον ἀπὸ τοῦ κυρίου, ὃ καὶ παρέδωκα ὑμῖν, ὅτι ὁ κύριος Ἰησοῦς ἐν τῇ νυκτὶ ᾗ παρεδίδετο ἔλαβεν ἄρτον **24** καὶ εὐχαριστήσας ἔκλασεν καὶ εἶπεν, Τοῦτό μού ἐστιν τὸ σῶμα τὸ ὑπὲρ ὑμῶν[a]· τοῦτο ποιεῖτε εἰς τὴν ἐμὴν ἀνάμνησιν. **25** ὡσαύτως καὶ τὸ ποτήριον μετὰ τὸ δειπνῆσαι λέγων, Τοῦτο τὸ ποτήριον ἡ καινὴ διαθήκη ἐστὶν ἐν τῷ ἐμῷ αἵματι· τοῦτο ποιεῖτε, ὁσάκις ἐὰν πίνητε, εἰς τὴν ἐμὴν ἀνάμνησιν. **26** ὁσάκις γὰρ ἐὰν ἐσθίητε τὸν ἄρτον τοῦτον καὶ τὸ ποτήριον πίνητε, τὸν θάνατον τοῦ κυρίου καταγγέλλετε ἄχρις οὗ ἔλθῃ.

woman from man; [9]neither was man created for woman, but woman for man. [10]For this reason, and because of the angels, the woman ought to have a sign of authority on her head.

[11]In the Lord, however, woman is not independent of man, nor is man independent of woman. [12]For as woman came from man, so also man is born of woman. But everything comes from God. [13]Judge for yourselves: Is it proper for a woman to pray to God with her head uncovered? [14]Does not the very nature of things teach you that if a man has long hair, it is a disgrace to him, [15]but that if a woman has long hair, it is her glory? For long hair is given to her as a covering. [16]If anyone wants to be contentious about this, we have no other practice—nor do the churches of God.

The Lord's Supper

[17]In the following directives I have no praise for you, for your meetings do more harm than good. [18]In the first place, I hear that when you come together as a church, there are divisions among you, and to some extent I believe it. [19]No doubt there have to be differences among you to show which of you have God's approval. [20]When you come together, it is not the Lord's Supper you eat, [21]for as you eat, each of you goes ahead without waiting for anybody else. One remains hungry, another gets drunk. [22]Don't you have homes to eat and drink in? Or do you despise the church of God and humiliate those who have nothing? What shall I say to you? Shall I praise you for this? Certainly not!

[23]For I received from the Lord what I also passed on to you: The Lord Jesus, on the night he was betrayed, took bread, [24]and when he had given thanks, he broke it and said, "This is my body, which is for you; do this in remembrance of me." [25]In the same way, after supper he took the cup, saying, "This cup is the new covenant in my blood; do this, whenever you drink it, in remembrance of me." [26]For whenever you eat this bread and drink this cup, you proclaim the Lord's death until he comes.

---

[t]Gk lacks *a symbol of*   [u]Or *have freedom of choice regarding her head*   [v]Other ancient authorities read *is broken for*

[a]24 NRSV note v adds κλώμενον

Partaking of the Supper Unworthily

27 Whoever, therefore, eats the bread or drinks the cup of the Lord in an unworthy manner will be answerable for the body and blood of the Lord. 28Examine yourselves, and only then eat of the bread and drink of the cup. 29For all who eat and drinkw without discerning the body,x eat and drink judgment against themselves. 30For this reason many of you are weak and ill, and some have died.y 31But if we judged ourselves, we would not be judged. 32But when we are judged by the Lord, we are disciplinedz so that we may not be condemned along with the world.

33 So then, my brothers and sisters,a when you come together to eat, wait for one another. 34If you are hungry, eat at home, so that when you come together, it will not be for your condemnation. About the other things I will give instructions when I come.

Spiritual Gifts

12 Now concerning spiritual gifts,b brothers and sisters,a I do not want you to be uninformed. 2You know that when you were pagans, you were enticed and led astray to idols that could not speak. 3Therefore I want you to understand that no one speaking by the Spirit of God ever says "Let Jesus be cursed!" and no one can say "Jesus is Lord" except by the Holy Spirit.

4 Now there are varieties of gifts, but the same Spirit; 5and there are varieties of services, but the same Lord; 6and there are varieties of activities, but it is the same God who activates all of them in everyone. 7To each is given the manifestation of the Spirit for the common good. 8To one is given through the Spirit the utterance of wisdom, and to another the utterance of knowledge according to the same Spirit, 9to another faith by the same Spirit, to another gifts of healing by the one Spirit, 10to another the working of miracles, to another prophecy, to another the discernment of spirits, to another various kinds of tongues, to another the interpretation of tongues. 11All these are activated by one and the same Spirit, who allots to each one individually just as the Spirit chooses.

One Body with Many Members

12 For just as the body is one and has many members, and all the members of

27 Ὥστε ὃς ἂν ἐσθίῃ τὸν ἄρτον ἢ πίνῃ τὸ ποτήριον τοῦ κυρίου ἀναξίως, ἔνοχος ἔσται τοῦ σώματος καὶ τοῦ αἵματος τοῦ κυρίου. 28 δοκιμαζέτω δὲ ἄνθρωπος ἑαυτὸν καὶ οὕτως ἐκ τοῦ ἄρτου ἐσθιέτω καὶ ἐκ τοῦ ποτηρίου πινέτω· 29 ὁ γὰρ ἐσθίων καὶ πίνωνb κρίμα ἑαυτῷ ἐσθίει καὶ πίνει μὴ διακρίνων τὸ σῶμαc. 30 διὰ τοῦτο ἐν ὑμῖν πολλοὶ ἀσθενεῖς καὶ ἄρρωστοι καὶ κοιμῶνται ἱκανοί. 31 εἰ δὲ ἑαυτοὺς διεκρίνομεν, οὐκ ἂν ἐκρινόμεθα· 32 κρινόμενοι δὲ ὑπὸ [τοῦ] κυρίου παιδευόμεθα, ἵνα μὴ σὺν τῷ κόσμῳ κατακριθῶμεν. 33 ὥστε, ἀδελφοί μου, συνερχόμενοι εἰς τὸ φαγεῖν ἀλλήλους ἐκδέχεσθε. 34 εἴ τις πεινᾷ, ἐν οἴκῳ ἐσθιέτω, ἵνα μὴ εἰς κρίμα συνέρχησθε. Τὰ δὲ λοιπὰ ὡς ἂν ἔλθω διατάξομαι.

12 Περὶ δὲ τῶν πνευματικῶν, ἀδελφοί, οὐ θέλω ὑμᾶς ἀγνοεῖν. 2 Οἴδατε ὅτι ὅτε ἔθνη ἦτε πρὸς τὰ εἴδωλα τὰ ἄφωνα ὡς ἂν ἤγεσθε ἀπαγόμενοι. 3 διὸ γνωρίζω ὑμῖν ὅτι οὐδεὶς ἐν πνεύματι θεοῦ λαλῶν λέγει, Ἀνάθεμα Ἰησοῦς, καὶ οὐδεὶς δύναται εἰπεῖν, Κύριος Ἰησοῦς, εἰ μὴ ἐν πνεύματι ἁγίῳ.

4 Διαιρέσεις δὲ χαρισμάτων εἰσίν, τὸ δὲ αὐτὸ πνεῦμα· 5 καὶ διαιρέσεις διακονιῶν εἰσιν, καὶ ὁ αὐτὸς κύριος· 6 καὶ διαιρέσεις ἐνεργημάτων εἰσίν, ὁ δὲ αὐτὸς θεὸς ὁ ἐνεργῶν τὰ πάντα ἐν πᾶσιν. 7 ἑκάστῳ δὲ δίδοται ἡ φανέρωσις τοῦ πνεύματος πρὸς τὸ συμφέρον. 8 ᾧ μὲν γὰρ διὰ τοῦ πνεύματος δίδοται λόγος σοφίας, ἄλλῳ δὲ λόγος γνώσεως κατὰ τὸ αὐτὸ πνεῦμα, 9 ἑτέρῳ πίστις ἐν τῷ αὐτῷ πνεύματι, ἄλλῳ δὲ χαρίσματα ἰαμάτων ἐν τῷ ἑνὶ πνεύματι, 10 ἄλλῳ δὲ ἐνεργήματα δυνάμεων, ἄλλῳ [δὲ] προφητεία, ἄλλῳ [δὲ] διακρίσεις πνευμάτων, ἑτέρῳ γένη γλωσσῶν, ἄλλῳ δὲ ἑρμηνεία γλωσσῶν· 11 πάντα δὲ ταῦτα ἐνεργεῖ τὸ ἓν καὶ τὸ αὐτὸ πνεῦμα διαιροῦν ἰδίᾳ ἑκάστῳ καθὼς βούλεται.

12 Καθάπερ γὰρ τὸ σῶμα ἕν ἐστιν καὶ μέλη πολλὰ ἔχει, πάντα δὲ τὰ

27Therefore, whoever eats the bread or drinks the cup of the Lord in an unworthy manner will be guilty of sinning against the body and blood of the Lord. 28A man ought to examine himself before he eats of the bread and drinks of the cup. 29For anyone who eats and drinks without recognizing the body of the Lord eats and drinks judgment on himself. 30That is why many among you are weak and sick, and a number of you have fallen asleep. 31But if we judged ourselves, we would not come under judgment. 32When we are judged by the Lord, we are being disciplined so that we will not be condemned with the world.

33So then, my brothers, when you come together to eat, wait for each other. 34If anyone is hungry, he should eat at home, so that when you meet together it may not result in judgment.

And when I come I will give further directions.

Spiritual Gifts

12 Now about spiritual gifts, brothers, I do not want you to be ignorant. 2You know that when you were pagans, somehow or other you were influenced and led astray to mute idols. 3Therefore I tell you that no one who is speaking by the Spirit of God says, "Jesus be cursed," and no one can say, "Jesus is Lord," except by the Holy Spirit.

4There are different kinds of gifts, but the same Spirit. 5There are different kinds of service, but the same Lord. 6There are different kinds of working, but the same God works all of them in all men.

7Now to each one the manifestation of the Spirit is given for the common good. 8To one there is given through the Spirit the message of wisdom, to another the message of knowledge by means of the same Spirit, 9to another faith by the same Spirit, to another gifts of healing by that one Spirit, 10to another miraculous powers, to another prophecy, to another distinguishing between spirits, to another speaking in different kinds of tongues,a and to still another the interpretation of tongues.b 11All these are the work of one and the same Spirit, and he gives them to each one, just as he determines.

One Body, Many Parts

12The body is a unit, though it is made up of many parts; and though all its parts

---

wOther ancient authorities add *in an unworthy manner,*
xOther ancient authorities read *the Lord's body*
yGk *fallen asleep* zOr *When we are judged, we are being disciplined by the Lord* aGk *brothers* bOr *spiritual persons*

b29 NRSV note w adds ἀναξίως c29 NIV text and NRSV note x add τοῦ κυρίου

a10 Or *languages;* also in verse 28 b10 Or *languages;* also in verse 28

the body, though many, are one body, so it is with Christ. ¹³For in the one Spirit we were all baptized into one body—Jews or Greeks, slaves or free—and we were all made to drink of one Spirit.

14 Indeed, the body does not consist of one member but of many. ¹⁵If the foot would say, "Because I am not a hand, I do not belong to the body," that would not make it any less a part of the body. ¹⁶And if the ear would say, "Because I am not an eye, I do not belong to the body," that would not make it any less a part of the body. ¹⁷If the whole body were an eye, where would the hearing be? If the whole body were hearing, where would the sense of smell be? ¹⁸But as it is, God arranged the members in the body, each one of them, as he chose. ¹⁹If all were a single member, where would the body be? ²⁰As it is, there are many members, yet one body. ²¹The eye cannot say to the hand, "I have no need of you," nor again the head to the feet, "I have no need of you." ²²On the contrary, the members of the body that seem to be weaker are indispensable, ²³and those members of the body that we think less honorable we clothe with greater honor, and our less respectable members are treated with greater respect; ²⁴whereas our more respectable members do not need this. But God has so arranged the body, giving the greater honor to the inferior member, ²⁵that there may be no dissension within the body, but the members may have the same care for one another. ²⁶If one member suffers, all suffer together with it; if one member is honored, all rejoice together with it.

27 Now you are the body of Christ and individually members of it. ²⁸And God has appointed in the church first apostles, second prophets, third teachers; then deeds of power, then gifts of healing, forms of assistance, forms of leadership, various kinds of tongues. ²⁹Are all apostles? Are all prophets? Are all teachers? Do all work miracles? ³⁰Do all possess gifts of healing? Do all speak in tongues? Do all interpret? ³¹But strive for the greater gifts. And I will show you a still more excellent way.

μέλη τοῦ σώματος πολλὰ ὄντα ἕν ἐστιν σῶμα, οὕτως καὶ ὁ Χριστός· **13** καὶ γὰρ ἐν ἑνὶ πνεύματι ἡμεῖς πάντες εἰς ἓν σῶμα ἐβαπτίσθημεν, εἴτε Ἰουδαῖοι εἴτε Ἕλληνες εἴτε δοῦλοι εἴτε ἐλεύθεροι, καὶ πάντες ἓν πνεῦμα ἐποτίσθημεν. **14** καὶ γὰρ τὸ σῶμα οὐκ ἔστιν ἓν μέλος ἀλλὰ πολλά. **15** ἐὰν εἴπῃ ὁ πούς, Ὅτι οὐκ εἰμὶ χείρ, οὐκ εἰμὶ ἐκ τοῦ σώματος, οὐ παρὰ τοῦτο οὐκ ἔστιν ἐκ τοῦ σώματος· **16** καὶ ἐὰν εἴπῃ τὸ οὖς, Ὅτι οὐκ εἰμὶ ὀφθαλμός, οὐκ εἰμὶ ἐκ τοῦ σώματος, οὐ παρὰ τοῦτο οὐκ ἔστιν ἐκ τοῦ σώματος· **17** εἰ ὅλον τὸ σῶμα ὀφθαλμός, ποῦ ἡ ἀκοή; εἰ ὅλον ἀκοή, ποῦ ἡ ὄσφρησις; **18** νυνὶ δὲ ὁ θεὸς ἔθετο τὰ μέλη, ἓν ἕκαστον αὐτῶν ἐν τῷ σώματι καθὼς ἠθέλησεν. **19** εἰ δὲ ἦν τὰ πάντα ἓν μέλος, ποῦ τὸ σῶμα; **20** νῦν δὲ πολλὰ μὲν μέλη, ἓν δὲ σῶμα. **21** οὐ δύναται δὲ ὁ ὀφθαλμὸς εἰπεῖν τῇ χειρί, Χρείαν σου οὐκ ἔχω, ἢ πάλιν ἡ κεφαλὴ τοῖς ποσίν, Χρείαν ὑμῶν οὐκ ἔχω· **22** ἀλλὰ πολλῷ μᾶλλον τὰ δοκοῦντα μέλη τοῦ σώματος ἀσθενέστερα ὑπάρχειν ἀναγκαῖά ἐστιν, **23** καὶ ἃ δοκοῦμεν ἀτιμότερα εἶναι τοῦ σώματος τούτοις τιμὴν περισσοτέραν περιτίθεμεν, καὶ τὰ ἀσχήμονα ἡμῶν εὐσχημοσύνην περισσοτέραν ἔχει, **24** τὰ δὲ εὐσχήμονα ἡμῶν οὐ χρείαν ἔχειª. ἀλλὰ ὁ θεὸς συνεκέρασεν τὸ σῶμα τῷ ὑστερουμένῳ περισσοτέραν δοὺς τιμήν, **25** ἵνα μὴ ᾖ σχίσμα ἐν τῷ σώματι ἀλλὰ τὸ αὐτὸ ὑπὲρ ἀλλήλων μεριμνῶσιν τὰ μέλη. **26** καὶ εἴτε πάσχει ἓν μέλος, συμπάσχει πάντα τὰ μέλη· εἴτε δοξάζεται [ἓν] μέλος, συγχαίρει πάντα τὰ μέλη.

27 Ὑμεῖς δέ ἐστε σῶμα Χριστοῦ καὶ μέλη ἐκ μέρους. **28** καὶ οὓς μὲν ἔθετο ὁ θεὸς ἐν τῇ ἐκκλησίᾳ πρῶτον ἀποστόλους, δεύτερον προφήτας, τρίτον διδασκάλους, ἔπειτα δυνάμεις, ἔπειτα χαρίσματα ἰαμάτων, ἀντιλήμψεις, κυβερνήσεις, γένη γλωσσῶν. **29** μὴ πάντες ἀπόστολοι; μὴ πάντες προφῆται; μὴ πάντες διδάσκαλοι; μὴ πάντες δυνάμεις; **30** μὴ πάντες χαρίσματα ἔχουσιν ἰαμάτων; μὴ πάντες γλώσσαις λαλοῦσιν; μὴ πάντες διερμηνεύουσιν; **31** ζηλοῦτε δὲ τὰ χαρίσματα τὰ μείζονα.

Καὶ ἔτι καθ' ὑπερβολὴν ὁδὸν ὑμῖν

are many, they form one body. So it is with Christ. ¹³For we were all baptized by[c] one Spirit into one body—whether Jews or Greeks, slave or free—and we were all given the one Spirit to drink.

¹⁴Now the body is not made up of one part but of many. ¹⁵If the foot should say, "Because I am not a hand, I do not belong to the body," it would not for that reason cease to be part of the body. ¹⁶And if the ear should say, "Because I am not an eye, I do not belong to the body," it would not for that reason cease to be part of the body. ¹⁷If the whole body were an eye, where would the sense of hearing be? If the whole body were an ear, where would the sense of smell be? ¹⁸But in fact God has arranged the parts in the body, every one of them, just as he wanted them to be. ¹⁹If they were all one part, where would the body be? ²⁰As it is, there are many parts, but one body.

²¹The eye cannot say to the hand, "I don't need you!" And the head cannot say to the feet, "I don't need you!" ²²On the contrary, those parts of the body that seem to be weaker are indispensable, ²³and the parts that we think are less honorable we treat with special honor. And the parts that are unpresentable are treated with special modesty, ²⁴while our presentable parts need no special treatment. But God has combined the members of the body and has given greater honor to the parts that lacked it, ²⁵so that there should be no division in the body, but that its parts should have equal concern for each other. ²⁶If one part suffers, every part suffers with it; if one part is honored, every part rejoices with it.

²⁷Now you are the body of Christ, and each one of you is a part of it. ²⁸And in the church God has appointed first of all apostles, second prophets, third teachers, then workers of miracles, also those having gifts of healing, those able to help others, those with gifts of administration, and those speaking in different kinds of tongues. ²⁹Are all apostles? Are all prophets? Are all teachers? Do all work miracles? ³⁰Do all have gifts of healing? Do all speak in tongues[d]? Do all interpret? ³¹But eagerly desire[e] the greater gifts.

Love

And now I will show you the most excellent way.

ª24 NIV text adds τιμῆς †

[c]13 Or with; or in   [d]30 Or other languages   [e]31 Or But you are eagerly desiring

The Gift of Love

13 If I speak in the tongues of mortals and of angels, but do not have love, I am a noisy gong or a clanging cymbal. [2]And if I have prophetic powers, and understand all mysteries and all knowledge, and if I have all faith, so as to remove mountains, but do not have love, I am nothing. [3]If I give away all my possessions, and if I hand over my body so that I may boast,[c] but do not have love, I gain nothing.

4 Love is patient; love is kind; love is not envious or boastful or arrogant [5]or rude. It does not insist on its own way; it is not irritable or resentful; [6]it does not rejoice in wrongdoing, but rejoices in the truth. [7]It bears all things, believes all things, hopes all things, endures all things.

8 Love never ends. But as for prophecies, they will come to an end; as for tongues, they will cease; as for knowledge, it will come to an end. [9]For we know only in part, and we prophesy only in part; [10]but when the complete comes, the partial will come to an end. [11]When I was a child, I spoke like a child, I thought like a child, I reasoned like a child; when I became an adult, I put an end to childish ways. [12]For now we see in a mirror, dimly,[d] but then we will see face to face. Now I know only in part; then I will know fully, even as I have been fully known. [13]And now faith, hope, and love abide, these three; and the greatest of these is love.

Gifts of Prophecy and Tongues

14 Pursue love and strive for the spiritual gifts, and especially that you may prophesy. [2]For those who speak in a tongue do not speak to other people but to God; for nobody understands them, since they are speaking mysteries in the Spirit. [3]On the other hand, those who prophesy speak to other people for their upbuilding and encouragement and consolation. [4]Those who speak in a tongue build up themselves, but those who prophesy build up the church. [5]Now I would like all of you to speak in tongues, but even more to prophesy. One who prophesies is greater than one who speaks in tongues, unless someone interprets, so that the church may be built up.

6 Now, brothers and sisters,[e] if I come to you speaking in tongues, how will I benefit you unless I speak to you in some

13 δείκνυμι. 1 Ἐὰν ταῖς γλώσσαις τῶν ἀνθρώπων λαλῶ καὶ τῶν ἀγγέλων, ἀγάπην δὲ μὴ ἔχω, γέγονα χαλκὸς ἠχῶν ἢ κύμβαλον ἀλαλάζον. 2 καὶ ἐὰν ἔχω προφητείαν καὶ εἰδῶ τὰ μυστήρια πάντα καὶ πᾶσαν τὴν γνῶσιν καὶ ἐὰν ἔχω πᾶσαν τὴν πίστιν ὥστε ὄρη μεθιστάναι, ἀγάπην δὲ μὴ ἔχω, οὐθέν εἰμι. 3 κἂν ψωμίσω πάντα τὰ ὑπάρχοντά μου καὶ ἐὰν παραδῶ τὸ σῶμά μου ἵνα καυχήσωμαι, ἀγάπην δὲ μὴ ἔχω, οὐδὲν ὠφελοῦμαι.

4 Ἡ ἀγάπη μακροθυμεῖ, χρηστεύεται ἡ ἀγάπη, οὐ ζηλοῖ, [ἡ ἀγάπη] οὐ περπερεύεται, οὐ φυσιοῦται, 5 οὐκ ἀσχημονεῖ, οὐ ζητεῖ τὰ ἑαυτῆς, οὐ παροξύνεται, οὐ λογίζεται τὸ κακόν, 6 οὐ χαίρει ἐπὶ τῇ ἀδικίᾳ, συγχαίρει δὲ τῇ ἀληθείᾳ· 7 πάντα στέγει, πάντα πιστεύει, πάντα ἐλπίζει, πάντα ὑπομένει.

8 Ἡ ἀγάπη οὐδέποτε πίπτει· εἴτε δὲ προφητεῖαι, καταργηθήσονται· εἴτε γλῶσσαι, παύσονται· εἴτε γνῶσις, καταργηθήσεται. 9 ἐκ μέρους γὰρ γινώσκομεν καὶ ἐκ μέρους προφητεύομεν· 10 ὅταν δὲ ἔλθῃ τὸ τέλειον, τὸ ἐκ μέρους καταργηθήσεται. 11 ὅτε ἤμην νήπιος, ἐλάλουν ὡς νήπιος, ἐφρόνουν ὡς νήπιος, ἐλογιζόμην ὡς νήπιος· ὅτε γέγονα ἀνήρ, κατήργηκα τὰ τοῦ νηπίου. 12 βλέπομεν γὰρ ἄρτι δι᾽ ἐσόπτρου ἐν αἰνίγματι, τότε δὲ πρόσωπον πρὸς πρόσωπον· ἄρτι γινώσκω ἐκ μέρους, τότε δὲ ἐπιγνώσομαι καθὼς καὶ ἐπεγνώσθην. 13 νυνὶ δὲ μένει πίστις, ἐλπίς, ἀγάπη, τὰ τρία ταῦτα· μείζων δὲ τούτων ἡ ἀγάπη.

14 Διώκετε τὴν ἀγάπην, ζηλοῦτε δὲ τὰ πνευματικά, μᾶλλον δὲ ἵνα προφητεύητε. 2 ὁ γὰρ λαλῶν γλώσσῃ οὐκ ἀνθρώποις λαλεῖ ἀλλὰ θεῷ· οὐδεὶς γὰρ ἀκούει, πνεύματι δὲ λαλεῖ μυστήρια· 3 ὁ δὲ προφητεύων ἀνθρώποις λαλεῖ οἰκοδομὴν καὶ παράκλησιν καὶ παραμυθίαν. 4 ὁ λαλῶν γλώσσῃ ἑαυτὸν οἰκοδομεῖ· ὁ δὲ προφητεύων ἐκκλησίαν οἰκοδομεῖ. 5 θέλω δὲ πάντας ὑμᾶς λαλεῖν γλώσσαις, μᾶλλον δὲ ἵνα προφητεύητε· μείζων δὲ ὁ προφητεύων ἢ ὁ λαλῶν γλώσσαις ἐκτὸς εἰ μὴ διερμηνεύῃ, ἵνα ἡ ἐκκλησία οἰκοδομὴν λάβῃ.

6 Νῦν δέ, ἀδελφοί, ἐὰν ἔλθω πρὸς ὑμᾶς γλώσσαις λαλῶν, τί ὑμᾶς ὠφελήσω ἐὰν μὴ ὑμῖν λαλήσω ἢ ἐν ἀποκαλύψει

13 If I speak in the tongues[a] of men and of angels, but have not love, I am only a resounding gong or a clanging cymbal. [2]If I have the gift of prophecy and can fathom all mysteries and all knowledge, and if I have a faith that can move mountains, but have not love, I am nothing. [3]If I give all I possess to the poor and surrender my body to the flames,[b] but have not love, I gain nothing.

[4]Love is patient, love is kind. It does not envy, it does not boast, it is not proud. [5]It is not rude, it is not self-seeking, it is not easily angered, it keeps no record of wrongs. [6]Love does not delight in evil but rejoices with the truth. [7]It always protects, always trusts, always hopes, always perseveres.

[8]Love never fails. But where there are prophecies, they will cease; where there are tongues, they will be stilled; where there is knowledge, it will pass away. [9]For we know in part and we prophesy in part, [10]but when perfection comes, the imperfect disappears. [11]When I was a child, I talked like a child, I thought like a child, I reasoned like a child. When I became a man, I put childish ways behind me. [12]Now we see but a poor reflection as in a mirror; then we shall see face to face. Now I know in part; then I shall know fully, even as I am fully known.

[13]And now these three remain: faith, hope and love. But the greatest of these is love.

Gifts of Prophecy and Tongues

14 Follow the way of love and eagerly desire spiritual gifts, especially the gift of prophecy. [2]For anyone who speaks in a tongue[a] does not speak to men but to God. Indeed, no one understands him; he utters mysteries with his spirit.[b] [3]But everyone who prophesies speaks to men for their strengthening, encouragement and comfort. [4]He who speaks in a tongue edifies himself, but he who prophesies edifies the church. [5]I would like every one of you to speak in tongues,[c] but I would rather have you prophesy. He who prophesies is greater than one who speaks in tongues,[c] unless he interprets, so that the church may be edified.

[6]Now, brothers, if I come to you and speak in tongues, what good will I be to you, unless I bring you some revelation or

---

[c]Other ancient authorities read *body to be burned*
[d]Gk *in a riddle* [e]Gk *brothers*

[a]3 NIV text and NRSV note c καυθήσομαι; NIV note and NRSV text as UBS

[a]1 Or *languages* [b]3 Some early manuscripts *body that I may boast* [a]2 Or *another language*; also in verses 4, 13, 14, 19, 26 and 27 [b]2 Or *by the Spirit* [c]5 Or *other languages*; also in verses 6, 18, 22, 23 and 39

revelation or knowledge or prophecy or teaching? 7It is the same way with lifeless instruments that produce sound, such as the flute or the harp. If they do not give distinct notes, how will anyone know what is being played? 8And if the bugle gives an indistinct sound, who will get ready for battle? 9So with yourselves; if in a tongue you utter speech that is not intelligible, how will anyone know what is being said? For you will be speaking into the air. 10There are doubtless many different kinds of sounds in the world, and nothing is without sound. 11If then I do not know the meaning of a sound, I will be a foreigner to the speaker and the speaker a foreigner to me. 12So with yourselves; since you are eager for spiritual gifts, strive to excel in them for building up the church.

13 Therefore, one who speaks in a tongue should pray for the power to interpret. 14For if I pray in a tongue, my spirit prays but my mind is unproductive. 15What should I do then? I will pray with the spirit, but I will pray with the mind also; I will sing praise with the spirit, but I will sing praise with the mind also. 16Otherwise, if you say a blessing with the spirit, how can anyone in the position of an outsider say the "Amen" to your thanksgiving, since the outsider does not know what you are saying? 17For you may give thanks well enough, but the other person is not built up. 18I thank God that I speak in tongues more than all of you; 19nevertheless, in church I would rather speak five words with my mind, in order to instruct others also, than ten thousand words in a tongue.

20 Brothers and sisters,e do not be children in your thinking; rather, be infants in evil, but in thinking be adults. 21In the law it is written,

"By people of strange tongues
 and by the lips of foreigners
I will speak to this people;
 yet even then they will not listen to
 me,"

says the Lord. 22Tongues, then, are a sign not for believers but for unbelievers, while prophecy is not for unbelievers but for believers. 23If, therefore, the whole church comes together and all speak in tongues, and outsiders or unbelievers enter, will they not say that you are out of your mind? 24But if all prophesy, an unbeliever or

e Gk brothers

ἢ ἐν γνώσει ἢ ἐν προφητείᾳ ἢ [ἐν] διδαχῇ; 7 ὅμως τὰ ἄψυχα φωνὴν διδόντα, εἴτε αὐλὸς εἴτε κιθάρα, ἐὰν διαστολὴν τοῖς φθόγγοις μὴ δῷ, πῶς γνωσθήσεται τὸ αὐλούμενον ἢ τὸ κιθαριζόμενον; 8 καὶ γὰρ ἐὰν ἄδηλον σάλπιγξ φωνὴν δῷ, τίς παρασκευάσεται εἰς πόλεμον; 9 οὕτως καὶ ὑμεῖς διὰ τῆς γλώσσης ἐὰν μὴ εὔσημον λόγον δῶτε, πῶς γνωσθήσεται τὸ λαλούμενον; ἔσεσθε γὰρ εἰς ἀέρα λαλοῦντες. 10 τοσαῦτα εἰ τύχοι γένη φωνῶν εἰσιν ἐν κόσμῳ καὶ οὐδὲν ἄφωνον· 11 ἐὰν οὖν μὴ εἰδῶ τὴν δύναμιν τῆς φωνῆς, ἔσομαι τῷ λαλοῦντι βάρβαρος καὶ ὁ λαλῶν ἐν ἐμοὶ βάρβαρος. 12 οὕτως καὶ ὑμεῖς, ἐπεὶ ζηλωταί ἐστε πνευμάτων, πρὸς τὴν οἰκοδομὴν τῆς ἐκκλησίας ζητεῖτε ἵνα περισσεύητε. 13 διὸ ὁ λαλῶν γλώσσῃ προσευχέσθω ἵνα διερμηνεύῃ. 14 ἐὰν [γὰρ] προσεύχωμαι γλώσσῃ, τὸ πνεῦμά μου προσεύχεται, ὁ δὲ νοῦς μου ἄκαρπός ἐστιν. 15 τί οὖν ἐστιν; προσεύξομαι τῷ πνεύματι, προσεύξομαι δὲ καὶ τῷ νοΐ· ψαλῶ τῷ πνεύματι, ψαλῶ δὲ καὶ τῷ νοΐ. 16 ἐπεὶ ἐὰν εὐλογῇς [ἐν] πνεύματι, ὁ ἀναπληρῶν τὸν τόπον τοῦ ἰδιώτου πῶς ἐρεῖ τὸ Ἀμήν ἐπὶ τῇ σῇ εὐχαριστίᾳ; ἐπειδὴ τί λέγεις οὐκ οἶδεν· 17 σὺ μὲν γὰρ καλῶς εὐχαριστεῖς ἀλλ᾿ ὁ ἕτερος οὐκ οἰκοδομεῖται. 18 εὐχαριστῶ τῷ θεῷ, πάντων ὑμῶν μᾶλλον γλώσσαις λαλῶ· 19 ἀλλὰ ἐν ἐκκλησίᾳ θέλω πέντε λόγους τῷ νοΐ μου λαλῆσαι, ἵνα καὶ ἄλλους κατηχήσω, ἢ μυρίους λόγους ἐν γλώσσῃ.

20 Ἀδελφοί, μὴ παιδία γίνεσθε ταῖς φρεσὶν ἀλλὰ τῇ κακίᾳ νηπιάζετε, ταῖς δὲ φρεσὶν τέλειοι γίνεσθε. 21 ἐν τῷ νόμῳ γέγραπται ὅτι

Ἐν ἑτερογλώσσοις
 καὶ ἐν χείλεσιν ἑτέρων
λαλήσω τῷ λαῷ τούτῳ
 καὶ οὐδ᾿ οὕτως εἰσακούσονταί μου,
λέγει κύριος. 22 ὥστε αἱ γλῶσσαι εἰς σημεῖόν εἰσιν οὐ τοῖς πιστεύουσιν ἀλλὰ τοῖς ἀπίστοις, ἡ δὲ προφητεία οὐ τοῖς ἀπίστοις ἀλλὰ τοῖς πιστεύουσιν. 23 Ἐὰν οὖν συνέλθῃ ἡ ἐκκλησία ὅλη ἐπὶ τὸ αὐτὸ καὶ πάντες λαλῶσιν γλώσσαις, εἰσέλθωσιν δὲ ἰδιῶται ἢ ἄπιστοι, οὐκ ἐροῦσιν ὅτι μαίνεσθε; 24 ἐὰν δὲ πάντες προφητεύωσιν, εἰσέλθῃ δέ τις ἄπιστος ἢ ἰδιώτης,

---

knowledge or prophecy or word of instruction? 7Even in the case of lifeless things that make sounds, such as the flute or harp, how will anyone know what tune is being played unless there is a distinction in the notes? 8Again, if the trumpet does not sound a clear call, who will get ready for battle? 9So it is with you. Unless you speak intelligible words with your tongue, how will anyone know what you are saying? You will just be speaking into the air. 10Undoubtedly there are all sorts of languages in the world, yet none of them is without meaning. 11If then I do not grasp the meaning of what someone is saying, I am a foreigner to the speaker, and he is a foreigner to me. 12So it is with you. Since you are eager to have spiritual gifts, try to excel in gifts that build up the church.

13For this reason anyone who speaks in a tongue should pray that he may interpret what he says. 14For if I pray in a tongue, my spirit prays, but my mind is unfruitful. 15So what shall I do? I will pray with my spirit, but I will also pray with my mind; I will sing with my spirit, but I will also sing with my mind. 16If you are praising God with your spirit, how can one who finds himself among those who do not understandd say "Amen" to your thanksgiving, since he does not know what you are saying? 17You may be giving thanks well enough, but the other man is not edified.

18I thank God that I speak in tongues more than all of you. 19But in the church I would rather speak five intelligible words to instruct others than ten thousand words in a tongue.

20Brothers, stop thinking like children. In regard to evil be infants, but in your thinking be adults. 21In the Law it is written:

"Through men of strange tongues
 and through the lips of foreigners
I will speak to this people,
 but even then they will not listen to
 me,"e

says the Lord.

22Tongues, then, are a sign, not for believers but for unbelievers; prophecy, however, is for believers, not for unbelievers. 23So if the whole church comes together and everyone speaks in tongues, and some who do not understandf or some unbelievers come in, will they not say that you are out of your mind? 24But if an unbeliever or someone who does not understandg comes

d16 Or among the inquirers   e21 Isaiah 28:11,12
f23 Or some inquirers   g24 Or or some inquirer

NRSV

outsider who enters is reproved by all and called to account by all. 25After the secrets of the unbeliever's heart are disclosed, that person will bow down before God and worship him, declaring, "God is really among you."

Orderly Worship

26 What should be done then, my friends?f When you come together, each one has a hymn, a lesson, a revelation, a tongue, or an interpretation. Let all things be done for building up. 27If anyone speaks in a tongue, let there be only two or at most three, and each in turn; and let one interpret. 28But if there is no one to interpret, let them be silent in church and speak to themselves and to God. 29Let two or three prophets speak, and let the others weigh what is said. 30If a revelation is made to someone else sitting nearby, let the first person be silent. 31For you can all prophesy one by one, so that all may learn and all be encouraged. 32And the spirits of prophets are subject to the prophets, 33for God is a God not of disorder but of peace.

(As in all the churches of the saints, 34women should be silent in the churches. For they are not permitted to speak, but should be subordinate, as the law also says. 35If there is anything they desire to know, let them ask their husbands at home. For it is shameful for a woman to speak in church.g 36Or did the word of God originate with you? Or are you the only ones it has reached?)

37 Anyone who claims to be a prophet, or to have spiritual powers, must acknowledge that what I am writing to you is a command of the Lord. 38Anyone who does not recognize this is not to be recognized. 39So, my friends,h be eager to prophesy, and do not forbid speaking in tongues; 40but all things should be done decently and in order.

The Resurrection of Christ

15 Now I would remind you, brothers and sisters,f of the good newsi that I proclaimed to you, which you in turn received, in which also you stand, 2through which also you are being saved, if you hold firmly to the message that I proclaimed to you—unless you have come to believe in vain.

Greek

ἐλέγχεται ὑπὸ πάντων, ἀνακρίνεται ὑπὸ πάντων, 25 τὰ κρυπτὰ τῆς καρδίας αὐτοῦ φανερὰ γίνεται, καὶ οὕτως πεσὼν ἐπὶ πρόσωπον προσκυνήσει τῷ θεῷ ἀπαγγέλλων ὅτι Ὄντως ὁ θεὸς ἐν ὑμῖν ἐστιν.

26 Τί οὖν ἐστιν, ἀδελφοί; ὅταν συνέρχησθε, ἕκαστος ψαλμὸν ἔχει, διδαχὴν ἔχει, ἀποκάλυψιν ἔχει, γλῶσσαν ἔχει, ἑρμηνείαν ἔχει· πάντα πρὸς οἰκοδομὴν γινέσθω. 27 εἴτε γλώσσῃ τις λαλεῖ, κατὰ δύο ἢ τὸ πλεῖστον τρεῖς καὶ ἀνὰ μέρος, καὶ εἷς διερμηνευέτω· 28 ἐὰν δὲ μὴ ᾖ διερμηνευτής, σιγάτω ἐν ἐκκλησίᾳ, ἑαυτῷ δὲ λαλείτω καὶ τῷ θεῷ. 29 προφῆται δὲ δύο ἢ τρεῖς λαλείτωσαν καὶ οἱ ἄλλοι διακρινέτωσαν· 30 ἐὰν δὲ ἄλλῳ ἀποκαλυφθῇ καθημένῳ, ὁ πρῶτος σιγάτω. 31 δύνασθε γὰρ καθ' ἕνα πάντες προφητεύειν, ἵνα πάντες μανθάνωσιν καὶ πάντες παρακαλῶνται. 32 καὶ πνεύματα προφητῶν προφήταις ὑποτάσσεται, 33 οὐ γάρ ἐστιν ἀκαταστασίας ὁ θεὸς ἀλλὰ εἰρήνης.

Ὡς ἐν πάσαις ταῖς ἐκκλησίαις τῶν ἁγίων 34 αἱ γυναῖκες ἐν ταῖς ἐκκλησίαις σιγάτωσαν· οὐ γὰρ ἐπιτρέπεται αὐταῖς λαλεῖν, ἀλλὰ ὑποτασσέσθωσαν, καθὼς καὶ ὁ νόμος λέγει. 35 εἰ δέ τι μαθεῖν θέλουσιν, ἐν οἴκῳ τοὺς ἰδίους ἄνδρας ἐπερωτάτωσαν· αἰσχρὸν γάρ ἐστιν γυναικὶ λαλεῖν ἐν ἐκκλησίᾳ. 36 ἢ ἀφ' ὑμῶν ὁ λόγος τοῦ θεοῦ ἐξῆλθεν, ἢ εἰς ὑμᾶς μόνους κατήντησεν;

37 Εἴ τις δοκεῖ προφήτης εἶναι ἢ πνευματικός, ἐπιγινωσκέτω ἃ γράφω ὑμῖν ὅτι κυρίου ἐστὶν ἐντολή· 38 εἰ δέ τις ἀγνοεῖ, ἀγνοεῖταιa. 39 ὥστε, ἀδελφοί [μου], ζηλοῦτε τὸ προφητεύειν καὶ τὸ λαλεῖν μὴ κωλύετε γλώσσαις· 40 πάντα δὲ εὐσχημόνως καὶ κατὰ τάξιν γινέσθω.

15 Γνωρίζω δὲ ὑμῖν, ἀδελφοί, τὸ εὐαγγέλιον ὃ εὐηγγελισάμην ὑμῖν, ὃ καὶ παρελάβετε, ἐν ᾧ καὶ ἑστήκατε, 2 δι' οὗ καὶ σῴζεσθε, τίνι λόγῳ εὐηγγελισάμην ὑμῖν εἰ κατέχετε, ἐκτὸς εἰ μὴ εἰκῇ ἐπιστεύσατε.

NIV

in while everybody is prophesying, he will be convinced by all that he is a sinner and will be judged by all, 25and the secrets of his heart will be laid bare. So he will fall down and worship God, exclaiming, "God is really among you!"

Orderly Worship

26What then shall we say, brothers? When you come together, everyone has a hymn, or a word of instruction, a revelation, a tongue or an interpretation. All of these must be done for the strengthening of the church. 27If anyone speaks in a tongue, two—or at the most three—should speak, one at a time, and someone must interpret. 28If there is no interpreter, the speaker should keep quiet in the church and speak to himself and God.

29Two or three prophets should speak, and the others should weigh carefully what is said. 30And if a revelation comes to someone who is sitting down, the first speaker should stop. 31For you can all prophesy in turn so that everyone may be instructed and encouraged. 32The spirits of prophets are subject to the control of prophets. 33For God is not a God of disorder but of peace.

As in all the congregations of the saints, 34women should remain silent in the churches. They are not allowed to speak, but must be in submission, as the Law says. 35If they want to inquire about something, they should ask their own husbands at home; for it is disgraceful for a woman to speak in the church.

36Did the word of God originate with you? Or are you the only people it has reached? 37If anybody thinks he is a prophet or spiritually gifted, let him acknowledge that what I am writing to you is the Lord's command. 38If he ignores this, he himself will be ignored.h

39Therefore, my brothers, be eager to prophesy, and do not forbid speaking in tongues. 40But everything should be done in a fitting and orderly way.

The Resurrection of Christ

15 Now, brothers, I want to remind you of the gospel I preached to you, which you received and on which you have taken your stand. 2By this gospel you are saved, if you hold firmly to the word I preached to you. Otherwise, you have believed in vain.

---

fGk brothers   gOther ancient authorities put verses 34-35 after verse 40   hGk my brothers   iOr gospel

a38 NIVnote ἀγνοείτω

h38 Some manuscripts If he is ignorant of this, let him be ignorant

3 For I handed on to you as of first importance what I in turn had received: that Christ died for our sins in accordance with the scriptures, [4]and that he was buried, and that he was raised on the third day in accordance with the scriptures, [5]and that he appeared to Cephas, then to the twelve. [6]Then he appeared to more than five hundred brothers and sisters[j] at one time, most of whom are still alive, though some have died.[k] [7]Then he appeared to James, then to all the apostles. [8]Last of all, as to one untimely born, he appeared also to me. [9]For I am the least of the apostles, unfit to be called an apostle, because I persecuted the church of God. [10]But by the grace of God I am what I am, and his grace toward me has not been in vain. On the contrary, I worked harder than any of them—though it was not I, but the grace of God that is with me. [11]Whether then it was I or they, so we proclaim and so you have come to believe.

The Resurrection of the Dead

12 Now if Christ is proclaimed as raised from the dead, how can some of you say there is no resurrection of the dead? [13]If there is no resurrection of the dead, then Christ has not been raised; [14]and if Christ has not been raised, then our proclamation has been in vain and your faith has been in vain. [15]We are even found to be misrepresenting God, because we testified of God that he raised Christ—whom he did not raise if it is true that the dead are not raised. [16]For if the dead are not raised, then Christ has not been raised. [17]If Christ has not been raised, your faith is futile and you are still in your sins. [18]Then those also who have died[k] in Christ have perished. [19]If for this life only we have hoped in Christ, we are of all people most to be pitied.

20 But in fact Christ has been raised from the dead, the first fruits of those who have died.[k] [21]For since death came through a human being, the resurrection of the dead has also come through a human being; [22]for as all die in Adam, so all will be made alive in Christ. [23]But each in his own order: Christ the first fruits, then at his coming those who belong to Christ. [24]Then comes the end,[l] when he hands over the kingdom to God the Father, after he has destroyed every ruler and every authority and power. [25]For he must reign until he has put all his enemies under his feet. [26]The

[j] Gk brothers [k] Gk fallen asleep [l] Or Then come the rest

3 παρέδωκα γὰρ ὑμῖν ἐν πρώτοις, ὃ καὶ παρέλαβον, ὅτι Χριστὸς ἀπέθανεν ὑπὲρ τῶν ἁμαρτιῶν ἡμῶν κατὰ τὰς γραφὰς 4 καὶ ὅτι ἐτάφη καὶ ὅτι ἐγήγερται τῇ ἡμέρᾳ τῇ τρίτῃ κατὰ τὰς γραφὰς 5 καὶ ὅτι ὤφθη Κηφᾷ εἶτα τοῖς δώδεκα· 6 ἔπειτα ὤφθη ἐπάνω πεντακοσίοις ἀδελφοῖς ἐφάπαξ, ἐξ ὧν οἱ πλείονες μένουσιν ἕως ἄρτι, τινὲς δὲ ἐκοιμήθησαν· 7 ἔπειτα ὤφθη Ἰακώβῳ εἶτα τοῖς ἀποστόλοις πᾶσιν· 8 ἔσχατον δὲ πάντων ὡσπερεὶ τῷ ἐκτρώματι ὤφθη κἀμοί. 9 Ἐγὼ γάρ εἰμι ὁ ἐλάχιστος τῶν ἀποστόλων ὃς οὐκ εἰμὶ ἱκανὸς καλεῖσθαι ἀπόστολος, διότι ἐδίωξα τὴν ἐκκλησίαν τοῦ θεοῦ· 10 χάριτι δὲ θεοῦ εἰμι ὅ εἰμι, καὶ ἡ χάρις αὐτοῦ ἡ εἰς ἐμὲ οὐ κενὴ ἐγενήθη, ἀλλὰ περισσότερον αὐτῶν πάντων ἐκοπίασα, οὐκ ἐγὼ δὲ ἀλλὰ ἡ χάρις τοῦ θεοῦ [ἡ] σὺν ἐμοί. 11 εἴτε οὖν ἐγὼ εἴτε ἐκεῖνοι, οὕτως κηρύσσομεν καὶ οὕτως ἐπιστεύσατε.

12 Εἰ δὲ Χριστὸς κηρύσσεται ὅτι ἐκ νεκρῶν ἐγήγερται, πῶς λέγουσιν ἐν ὑμῖν τινες ὅτι ἀνάστασις νεκρῶν οὐκ ἔστιν; 13 εἰ δὲ ἀνάστασις νεκρῶν οὐκ ἔστιν, οὐδὲ Χριστὸς ἐγήγερται· 14 εἰ δὲ Χριστὸς οὐκ ἐγήγερται, κενὸν ἄρα [καὶ] τὸ κήρυγμα ἡμῶν, κενὴ καὶ ἡ πίστις ὑμῶν· 15 εὑρισκόμεθα δὲ καὶ ψευδομάρτυρες τοῦ θεοῦ, ὅτι ἐμαρτυρήσαμεν κατὰ τοῦ θεοῦ ὅτι ἤγειρεν τὸν Χριστόν, ὃν οὐκ ἤγειρεν εἴπερ ἄρα νεκροὶ οὐκ ἐγείρονται. 16 εἰ γὰρ νεκροὶ οὐκ ἐγείρονται, οὐδὲ Χριστὸς ἐγήγερται· 17 εἰ δὲ Χριστὸς οὐκ ἐγήγερται, ματαία ἡ πίστις ὑμῶν, ἔτι ἐστὲ ἐν ταῖς ἁμαρτίαις ὑμῶν, 18 ἄρα καὶ οἱ κοιμηθέντες ἐν Χριστῷ ἀπώλοντο. 19 εἰ ἐν τῇ ζωῇ ταύτῃ ἐν Χριστῷ ἠλπικότες ἐσμὲν μόνον, ἐλεεινότεροι πάντων ἀνθρώπων ἐσμέν.

20 Νυνὶ δὲ Χριστὸς ἐγήγερται ἐκ νεκρῶν ἀπαρχὴ τῶν κεκοιμημένων. 21 ἐπειδὴ γὰρ δι᾽ ἀνθρώπου θάνατος, καὶ δι᾽ ἀνθρώπου ἀνάστασις νεκρῶν. 22 ὥσπερ γὰρ ἐν τῷ Ἀδὰμ πάντες ἀποθνῄσκουσιν, οὕτως καὶ ἐν τῷ Χριστῷ πάντες ζῳοποιηθήσονται. 23 ἕκαστος δὲ ἐν τῷ ἰδίῳ τάγματι· ἀπαρχὴ Χριστός, ἔπειτα οἱ τοῦ Χριστοῦ ἐν τῇ παρουσίᾳ αὐτοῦ, 24 εἶτα τὸ τέλος, ὅταν παραδιδῷ τὴν βασιλείαν τῷ θεῷ καὶ πατρί, ὅταν καταργήσῃ πᾶσαν ἀρχὴν καὶ πᾶσαν ἐξουσίαν καὶ δύναμιν. 25 δεῖ γὰρ αὐτὸν βασιλεύειν ἄχρι οὗ θῇ πάντας τοὺς ἐχθροὺς ὑπὸ τοὺς πόδας αὐτοῦ. 26 ἔσχατος ἐχθρὸς καταργεῖται ὁ

[3]For what I received I passed on to you as of first importance[a]: that Christ died for our sins according to the Scriptures, [4]that he was buried, that he was raised on the third day according to the Scriptures, [5]and that he appeared to Peter,[b] and then to the Twelve. [6]After that, he appeared to more than five hundred of the brothers at the same time, most of whom are still living, though some have fallen asleep. [7]Then he appeared to James, then to all the apostles, [8]and last of all he appeared to me also, as to one abnormally born.

[9]For I am the least of the apostles and do not even deserve to be called an apostle, because I persecuted the church of God. [10]But by the grace of God I am what I am, and his grace to me was not without effect. No, I worked harder than all of them—yet not I, but the grace of God that was with me. [11]Whether, then, it was I or they, this is what we preach, and this is what you believed.

The Resurrection of the Dead

[12]But if it is preached that Christ has been raised from the dead, how can some of you say that there is no resurrection of the dead? [13]If there is no resurrection of the dead, then not even Christ has been raised. [14]And if Christ has not been raised, our preaching is useless and so is your faith. [15]More than that, we are then found to be false witnesses about God, for we have testified about God that he raised Christ from the dead. But he did not raise him if in fact the dead are not raised. [16]For if the dead are not raised, then Christ has not been raised either. [17]And if Christ has not been raised, your faith is futile; you are still in your sins. [18]Then those also who have fallen asleep in Christ are lost. [19]If only for this life we have hope in Christ, we are to be pitied more than all men.

[20]But Christ has indeed been raised from the dead, the firstfruits of those who have fallen asleep. [21]For since death came through a man, the resurrection of the dead comes also through a man. [22]For as in Adam all die, so in Christ all will be made alive. [23]But each in his own turn: Christ, the firstfruits; then, when he comes, those who belong to him. [24]Then the end will come, when he hands over the kingdom to God the Father after he has destroyed all dominion, authority and power. [25]For he must reign until he has put all his enemies under his feet. [26]The last enemy to be

[a]3 Or you at the first [b]5 Greek Cephas

last enemy to be destroyed is death. [27]For "God[m] has put all things in subjection under his feet." But when it says, "All things are put in subjection," it is plain that this does not include the one who put all things in subjection under him. [28]When all things are subjected to him, then the Son himself will also be subjected to the one who put all things in subjection under him, so that God may be all in all.

[29] Otherwise, what will those people do who receive baptism on behalf of the dead? If the dead are not raised at all, why are people baptized on their behalf?

[30] And why are we putting ourselves in danger every hour? [31]I die every day! That is as certain, brothers and sisters,[n] as my boasting of you—a boast that I make in Christ Jesus our Lord. [32]If with merely human hopes I fought with wild animals at Ephesus, what would I have gained by it? If the dead are not raised,

"Let us eat and drink,
    for tomorrow we die."

[33]Do not be deceived:

"Bad company ruins good morals."

[34]Come to a sober and right mind, and sin no more; for some people have no knowledge of God. I say this to your shame.

The Resurrection Body

[35] But someone will ask, "How are the dead raised? With what kind of body do they come?" [36]Fool! What you sow does not come to life unless it dies. [37]And as for what you sow, you do not sow the body that is to be, but a bare seed, perhaps of wheat or of some other grain. [38]But God gives it a body as he has chosen, and to each kind of seed its own body. [39]Not all flesh is alike, but there is one flesh for human beings, another for animals, another for birds, and another for fish. [40]There are both heavenly bodies and earthly bodies, but the glory of the heavenly is one thing, and that of the earthly is another. [41]There is one glory of the sun, and another glory of the moon, and another glory of the stars; indeed, star differs from star in glory.

[42] So it is with the resurrection of the dead. What is sown is perishable, what is raised is imperishable. [43]It is sown in dishonor, it is raised in glory. It is sown in weakness, it is raised in power. [44]It is sown a physical body, it is raised a spiritual body. If there is a physical body, there is also a spiritual body. [45]Thus it is written, "The

---

θάνατος· **27** πάντα γὰρ ὑπέταξεν ὑπὸ τοὺς πόδας αὐτοῦ. ὅταν δὲ εἴπῃ ὅτι πάντα ὑποτέτακται, δῆλον ὅτι ἐκτὸς τοῦ ὑποτάξαντος αὐτῷ τὰ πάντα. **28** ὅταν δὲ ὑποταγῇ αὐτῷ τὰ πάντα, τότε [καὶ][a] αὐτὸς ὁ υἱὸς ὑποταγήσεται τῷ ὑποτάξαντι αὐτῷ τὰ πάντα, ἵνα ᾖ ὁ θεὸς [τὰ][b] πάντα ἐν πᾶσιν.

29 Ἐπεὶ τί ποιήσουσιν οἱ βαπτιζόμενοι ὑπὲρ τῶν νεκρῶν; εἰ ὅλως νεκροὶ οὐκ ἐγείρονται, τί καὶ βαπτίζονται ὑπὲρ αὐτῶν; **30** τί καὶ ἡμεῖς κινδυνεύομεν πᾶσαν ὥραν; **31** καθ᾽ ἡμέραν ἀποθνῄσκω, νὴ τὴν ὑμετέραν καύχησιν, [ἀδελφοί,] ἣν ἔχω ἐν Χριστῷ Ἰησοῦ τῷ κυρίῳ ἡμῶν. **32** εἰ κατὰ ἄνθρωπον ἐθηριομάχησα ἐν Ἐφέσῳ, τί μοι τὸ ὄφελος; εἰ νεκροὶ οὐκ ἐγείρονται,

Φάγωμεν καὶ πίωμεν,
    αὔριον γὰρ ἀποθνῄσκομεν.

33 μὴ πλανᾶσθε·
    Φθείρουσιν ἤθη χρηστὰ ὁμιλίαι
    κακαί.

34 ἐκνήψατε δικαίως καὶ μὴ ἁμαρτάνετε, ἀγνωσίαν γὰρ θεοῦ τινες ἔχουσιν, πρὸς ἐντροπὴν ὑμῖν λαλῶ.

35 Ἀλλὰ ἐρεῖ τις, Πῶς ἐγείρονται οἱ νεκροί; ποίῳ δὲ σώματι ἔρχονται; **36** ἄφρων, σὺ ὃ σπείρεις, οὐ ζῳοποιεῖται ἐὰν μὴ ἀποθάνῃ· **37** καὶ ὃ σπείρεις, οὐ τὸ σῶμα τὸ γενησόμενον σπείρεις ἀλλὰ γυμνὸν κόκκον εἰ τύχοι σίτου ἤ τινος τῶν λοιπῶν· **38** ὁ δὲ θεὸς δίδωσιν αὐτῷ σῶμα καθὼς ἠθέλησεν, καὶ ἑκάστῳ τῶν σπερμάτων ἴδιον σῶμα. **39** οὐ πᾶσα σὰρξ ἡ αὐτὴ σὰρξ ἀλλὰ ἄλλη μὲν ἀνθρώπων, ἄλλη δὲ σὰρξ κτηνῶν, ἄλλη δὲ σὰρξ πτηνῶν, ἄλλη δὲ ἰχθύων. **40** καὶ σώματα ἐπουράνια, καὶ σώματα ἐπίγεια· ἀλλὰ ἑτέρα μὲν ἡ τῶν ἐπουρανίων δόξα, ἑτέρα δὲ ἡ τῶν ἐπιγείων. **41** ἄλλη δόξα ἡλίου, καὶ ἄλλη δόξα σελήνης, καὶ ἄλλη δόξα ἀστέρων· ἀστὴρ γὰρ ἀστέρος διαφέρει ἐν δόξῃ.

42 Οὕτως καὶ ἡ ἀνάστασις τῶν νεκρῶν. σπείρεται ἐν φθορᾷ, ἐγείρεται ἐν ἀφθαρσίᾳ· **43** σπείρεται ἐν ἀτιμίᾳ, ἐγείρεται ἐν δόξῃ· σπείρεται ἐν ἀσθενείᾳ, ἐγείρεται ἐν δυνάμει· **44** σπείρεται σῶμα ψυχικόν, ἐγείρεται σῶμα πνευματικόν. εἰ ἔστιν σῶμα ψυχικόν, ἔστιν καὶ πνευματικόν. **45** οὕτως καὶ γέγραπται, Ἐγένετο ὁ

---

destroyed is death. [27]For he "has put everything under his feet."[c] Now when it says that "everything" has been put under him, it is clear that this does not include God himself, who put everything under Christ. [28]When he has done this, then the Son himself will be made subject to him who put everything under him, so that God may be all in all.

[29]Now if there is no resurrection, what will those do who are baptized for the dead? If the dead are not raised at all, why are people baptized for them? [30]And as for us, why do we endanger ourselves every hour? [31]I die every day—I mean that, brothers—just as surely as I glory over you in Christ Jesus our Lord. [32]If I fought wild beasts in Ephesus for merely human reasons, what have I gained? If the dead are not raised,

"Let us eat and drink,
    for tomorrow we die."[d]

[33]Do not be misled: "Bad company corrupts good character." [34]Come back to your senses as you ought, and stop sinning; for there are some who are ignorant of God— I say this to your shame.

The Resurrection Body

[35]But someone may ask, "How are the dead raised? With what kind of body will they come?" [36]How foolish! What you sow does not come to life unless it dies. [37]When you sow, you do not plant the body that will be, but just a seed, perhaps of wheat or of something else. [38]But God gives it a body as he has determined, and to each kind of seed he gives its own body. [39]All flesh is not the same: Men have one kind of flesh, animals have another, birds another and fish another. [40]There are also heavenly bodies and there are earthly bodies; but the splendor of the heavenly bodies is one kind, and the splendor of the earthly bodies is another. [41]The sun has one kind of splendor, the moon another and the stars another; and star differs from star in splendor.

[42]So will it be with the resurrection of the dead. The body that is sown is perishable, it is raised imperishable; [43]it is sown in dishonor, it is raised in glory; it is sown in weakness, it is raised in power; [44]it is sown a natural body, it is raised a spiritual body.

If there is a natural body, there is also a spiritual body. [45]So it is written: "The first

---

[m] Gk *he*   [n] Gk *brothers*   [a]28 NIV text omits καί †   [b]28 NIV text omits τά †   [c]27 Psalm 8:6   [d]32 Isaiah 22:13

first man, Adam, became a living being";
the last Adam became a life-giving spirit.
[46]But it is not the spiritual that is first, but
the physical, and then the spiritual. [47]The
first man was from the earth, a man of
dust; the second man is[o] from heaven. [48]As
was the man of dust, so are those who are
of the dust; and as is the man of heaven, so
are those who are of heaven. [49]Just as we
have borne the image of the man of dust,
we will[p] also bear the image of the man of
heaven.

50 What I am saying, brothers and
sisters,[n] is this: flesh and blood cannot inherit the kingdom of God, nor does the
perishable inherit the imperishable. [51]Lis-
ten, I will tell you a mystery! We will not
all die,[q] but we will all be changed, [52]in a
moment, in the twinkling of an eye, at the
last trumpet. For the trumpet will sound,
and the dead will be raised imperishable,
and we will be changed. [53]For this perishable body must put on imperishability, and
this mortal body must put on immortality.
[54]When this perishable body puts on imperishability, and this mortal body puts
on immortality, then the saying that is written will be fulfilled:

"Death has been swallowed up in
victory."
55   "Where, O death, is your victory?
Where, O death, is your sting?"

[56]The sting of death is sin, and the power
of sin is the law. [57]But thanks be to God,
who gives us the victory through our Lord
Jesus Christ.

58 Therefore, my beloved,[r] be steadfast,
immovable, always excelling in the work
of the Lord, because you know that in the
Lord your labor is not in vain.

The Collection for the Saints

16 Now concerning the collection for
the saints: you should follow the
directions I gave to the churches of Galatia.
[2]On the first day of every week, each of
you is to put aside and save whatever extra you earn, so that collections need not
be taken when I come. [3]And when I arrive,
I will send any whom you approve with
letters to take your gift to Jerusalem. [4]If it
seems advisable that I should go also, they
will accompany me.

Plans for Travel

5 I will visit you after passing through

πρῶτος **ἄνθρωπος** Ἀδὰμ **εἰς ψυχὴν**
ζῶσαν, ὁ ἔσχατος Ἀδὰμ εἰς πνεῦμα
ζῳοποιοῦν. **46** ἀλλ' οὐ πρῶτον τὸ
πνευματικὸν ἀλλὰ τὸ ψυχικόν, ἔπειτα
τὸ πνευματικόν. **47** ὁ πρῶτος ἄνθρωπος
ἐκ γῆς χοϊκός, ὁ δεύτερος ἄνθρωπος[c]
ἐξ οὐρανοῦ. **48** οἷος ὁ χοϊκός, τοιοῦτοι
καὶ οἱ χοϊκοί, καὶ οἷος ὁ ἐπουράνιος,
τοιοῦτοι καὶ οἱ ἐπουράνιοι· **49** καὶ καθὼς
ἐφορέσαμεν τὴν εἰκόνα τοῦ χοϊκοῦ,
φορέσομεν[d] καὶ τὴν εἰκόνα τοῦ
ἐπουρανίου.

50 Τοῦτο δέ φημι, ἀδελφοί, ὅτι σὰρξ
καὶ αἷμα βασιλείαν θεοῦ κληρονομῆσαι
οὐ δύναται οὐδὲ ἡ φθορὰ τὴν ἀφθαρσίαν
κληρονομεῖ. **51** ἰδοὺ μυστήριον ὑμῖν
λέγω· πάντες οὐ κοιμηθησόμεθα, πάντες
δὲ ἀλλαγησόμεθα, **52** ἐν ἀτόμῳ, ἐν
ῥιπῇ ὀφθαλμοῦ, ἐν τῇ ἐσχάτῃ σάλπιγγι·
σαλπίσει γὰρ καὶ οἱ νεκροὶ ἐγερθήσονται ἄφθαρτοι καὶ ἡμεῖς ἀλλαγησόμεθα. **53** δεῖ γὰρ τὸ φθαρτὸν τοῦτο
ἐνδύσασθαι ἀφθαρσίαν καὶ τὸ θνητὸν
τοῦτο ἐνδύσασθαι ἀθανασίαν. **54** ὅταν
δὲ τὸ φθαρτὸν τοῦτο ἐνδύσηται ἀφθαρσίαν καὶ τὸ θνητὸν τοῦτο ἐνδύσηται
ἀθανασίαν, τότε γενήσεται ὁ λόγος ὁ
γεγραμμένος,

Κατεπόθη ὁ θάνατος εἰς νῖκος.
55 ποῦ σου, θάνατε, τὸ νῖκος;

ποῦ σου, θάνατε, τὸ κέντρον;

56 τὸ δὲ κέντρον τοῦ θανάτου ἡ
ἁμαρτία, ἡ δὲ δύναμις τῆς ἁμαρτίας ὁ
νόμος· **57** τῷ δὲ θεῷ χάρις τῷ διδόντι
ἡμῖν τὸ νῖκος διὰ τοῦ κυρίου ἡμῶν
Ἰησοῦ Χριστοῦ. **58** Ὥστε, ἀδελφοί μου
ἀγαπητοί, ἑδραῖοι γίνεσθε, ἀμετα-
κίνητοι, περισσεύοντες ἐν τῷ ἔργῳ
τοῦ κυρίου πάντοτε, εἰδότες ὅτι ὁ
κόπος ὑμῶν οὐκ ἔστιν κενὸς ἐν κυρίῳ.

16 Περὶ δὲ τῆς λογείας τῆς εἰς
τοὺς ἁγίους ὥσπερ διέταξα
ταῖς ἐκκλησίαις τῆς Γαλατίας, οὕτως
καὶ ὑμεῖς ποιήσατε. **2** κατὰ μίαν
σαββάτου ἕκαστος ὑμῶν παρ' ἑαυτῷ
τιθέτω θησαυρίζων ὅ τι ἐὰν εὐοδῶται,
ἵνα μὴ ὅταν ἔλθω τότε λογεῖαι γίνωνται.
3 ὅταν δὲ παραγένωμαι, οὓς ἐὰν
δοκιμάσητε, δι' ἐπιστολῶν τούτους
πέμψω ἀπενεγκεῖν τὴν χάριν ὑμῶν εἰς
Ἰερουσαλήμ. **4** ἐὰν δὲ ἄξιον ᾖ τοῦ
κἀμὲ πορεύεσθαι, σὺν ἐμοὶ πορεύσονται.

5 Ἐλεύσομαι δὲ πρὸς ὑμᾶς ὅταν

man Adam became a living being"[e]; the
last Adam, a life-giving spirit. [46]The spiritual did not come first, but the natural,
and after that the spiritual. [47]The first man
was of the dust of the earth, the second
man from heaven. [48]As was the earthly
man, so are those who are of the earth; and
as is the man from heaven, so also are
those who are of heaven. [49]And just as we
have borne the likeness of the earthly man,
so shall we[f] bear the likeness of the man
from heaven.

[50]I declare to you, brothers, that flesh
and blood cannot inherit the kingdom of
God, nor does the perishable inherit the
imperishable. [51]Listen, I tell you a mystery: We will not all sleep, but we will all
be changed— [52]in a flash, in the twinkling
of an eye, at the last trumpet. For the trumpet will sound, the dead will be raised
imperishable, and we will be changed.
[53]For the perishable must clothe itself with
the imperishable, and the mortal with immortality. [54]When the perishable has been
clothed with the imperishable, and the
mortal with immortality, then the saying
that is written will come true: "Death has
been swallowed up in victory."[g]

[55]"Where, O death, is your victory?
Where, O death, is your sting?"[h]

[56]The sting of death is sin, and the power
of sin is the law. [57]But thanks be to God!
He gives us the victory through our Lord
Jesus Christ.

[58]Therefore, my dear brothers, stand firm.
Let nothing move you. Always give yourselves fully to the work of the Lord, because you know that your labor in the
Lord is not in vain.

The Collection for God's People

16 Now about the collection for
God's people: Do what I told the
Galatian churches to do. [2]On the first day
of every week, each one of you should set
aside a sum of money in keeping with his
income, saving it up, so that when I come
no collections will have to be made. [3]Then,
when I arrive, I will give letters of introduction to the men you approve and send
them with your gift to Jerusalem. [4]If it
seems advisable for me to go also, they
will accompany me.

Personal Requests

[5]After I go through Macedonia, I will

---

n Gk *brothers*   o Other ancient authorities add *the Lord*
p Other ancient authorities read *let us*   q Gk *fall asleep*
r Gk *beloved brothers*

c47 NRSV note o adds ὁ κύριος   d49 NIV/NRSV notes
φορέσωμεν

e45 Gen. 2:7   f49 Some early manuscripts *so let us*   g54
Isaiah 25:8   h55 Hosea 13:14

Macedonia—for I intend to pass through Macedonia— [6]and perhaps I will stay with you or even spend the winter, so that you may send me on my way, wherever I go. [7]I do not want to see you now just in passing, for I hope to spend some time with you, if the Lord permits. [8]But I will stay in Ephesus until Pentecost, [9]for a wide door for effective work has opened to me, and there are many adversaries.

[10]If Timothy comes, see that he has nothing to fear among you, for he is doing the work of the Lord just as I am; [11]therefore let no one despise him. Send him on his way in peace, so that he may come to me; for I am expecting him with the brothers.

[12]Now concerning our brother Apollos, I strongly urged him to visit you with the other brothers, but he was not at all willing[s] to come now. He will come when he has the opportunity.

Final Messages and Greetings

[13]Keep alert, stand firm in your faith, be courageous, be strong. [14]Let all that you do be done in love.

[15]Now, brothers and sisters,[t] you know that members of the household of Stephanas were the first converts in Achaia, and they have devoted themselves to the service of the saints; [16]I urge you to put yourselves at the service of such people, and of everyone who works and toils with them. [17]I rejoice at the coming of Stephanas and Fortunatus and Achaicus, because they have made up for your absence; [18]for they refreshed my spirit as well as yours. So give recognition to such persons.

[19]The churches of Asia send greetings. Aquila and Prisca, together with the church in their house, greet you warmly in the Lord. [20]All the brothers and sisters[t] send greetings. Greet one another with a holy kiss.

[21]I, Paul, write this greeting with my own hand. [22]Let anyone be accursed who has no love for the Lord. Our Lord, come![u] [23]The grace of the Lord Jesus be with you. [24]My love be with all of you in Christ Jesus.[v]

Μακεδονίαν διέλθω· Μακεδονίαν γὰρ διέρχομαι, **6** πρὸς ὑμᾶς δὲ τυχὸν παραμενῶ ἢ καὶ παραχειμάσω, ἵνα ὑμεῖς με προπέμψητε οὗ ἐὰν πορεύωμαι. **7** οὐ θέλω γὰρ ὑμᾶς ἄρτι ἐν παρόδῳ ἰδεῖν, ἐλπίζω γὰρ χρόνον τινὰ ἐπιμεῖναι πρὸς ὑμᾶς ἐὰν ὁ κύριος ἐπιτρέψῃ. **8** ἐπιμενῶ δὲ ἐν Ἐφέσῳ ἕως τῆς πεντηκοστῆς· **9** θύρα γάρ μοι ἀνέῳγεν μεγάλη καὶ ἐνεργής, καὶ ἀντικείμενοι πολλοί.

10 Ἐὰν δὲ ἔλθῃ Τιμόθεος, βλέπετε, ἵνα ἀφόβως γένηται πρὸς ὑμᾶς· τὸ γὰρ ἔργον κυρίου ἐργάζεται ὡς κἀγώ· **11** μή τις οὖν αὐτὸν ἐξουθενήσῃ. προπέμψατε δὲ αὐτὸν ἐν εἰρήνῃ, ἵνα ἔλθῃ πρός με· ἐκδέχομαι γὰρ αὐτὸν μετὰ τῶν ἀδελφῶν.

12 Περὶ δὲ Ἀπολλῶ τοῦ ἀδελφοῦ, πολλὰ παρεκάλεσα αὐτόν, ἵνα ἔλθῃ πρὸς ὑμᾶς μετὰ τῶν ἀδελφῶν· καὶ πάντως οὐκ ἦν θέλημα ἵνα νῦν ἔλθῃ· ἐλεύσεται δὲ ὅταν εὐκαιρήσῃ.

13 Γρηγορεῖτε, στήκετε ἐν τῇ πίστει, ἀνδρίζεσθε, κραταιοῦσθε. **14** πάντα ὑμῶν ἐν ἀγάπῃ γινέσθω.

15 Παρακαλῶ δὲ ὑμᾶς, ἀδελφοί· οἴδατε τὴν οἰκίαν Στεφανᾶ, ὅτι ἐστὶν ἀπαρχὴ τῆς Ἀχαΐας καὶ εἰς διακονίαν τοῖς ἁγίοις ἔταξαν ἑαυτούς· **16** ἵνα καὶ ὑμεῖς ὑποτάσσησθε τοῖς τοιούτοις καὶ παντὶ τῷ συνεργοῦντι καὶ κοπιῶντι. **17** χαίρω δὲ ἐπὶ τῇ παρουσίᾳ Στεφανᾶ καὶ Φορτουνάτου καὶ Ἀχαϊκοῦ, ὅτι τὸ ὑμέτερον ὑστέρημα οὗτοι ἀνεπλήρωσαν· **18** ἀνέπαυσαν γὰρ τὸ ἐμὸν πνεῦμα καὶ τὸ ὑμῶν. ἐπιγινώσκετε οὖν τοὺς τοιούτους.

19 Ἀσπάζονται ὑμᾶς αἱ ἐκκλησίαι τῆς Ἀσίας. ἀσπάζεται ὑμᾶς ἐν κυρίῳ πολλὰ Ἀκύλας καὶ Πρίσκα σὺν τῇ κατ᾽ οἶκον αὐτῶν ἐκκλησίᾳ. **20** ἀσπάζονται ὑμᾶς οἱ ἀδελφοὶ πάντες. Ἀσπάσασθε ἀλλήλους ἐν φιλήματι ἁγίῳ. **21** Ὁ ἀσπασμὸς τῇ ἐμῇ χειρὶ Παύλου. **22** εἴ τις οὐ φιλεῖ τὸν κύριον, ἤτω ἀνάθεμα. Μαρανα θα. **23** ἡ χάρις τοῦ κυρίου Ἰησοῦ μεθ᾽ ὑμῶν. **24** ἡ ἀγάπη μου μετὰ πάντων ὑμῶν ἐν Χριστῷ Ἰησοῦ.[a]

---

come to you—for I will be going through Macedonia. [6]Perhaps I will stay with you awhile, or even spend the winter, so that you can help me on my journey, wherever I go. [7]I do not want to see you now and make only a passing visit; I hope to spend some time with you, if the Lord permits. [8]But I will stay on at Ephesus until Pentecost, [9]because a great door for effective work has opened to me, and there are many who oppose me.

[10]If Timothy comes, see to it that he has nothing to fear while he is with you, for he is carrying on the work of the Lord, just as I am. [11]No one, then, should refuse to accept him. Send him on his way in peace so that he may return to me. I am expecting him along with the brothers.

[12]Now about our brother Apollos: I strongly urged him to go to you with the brothers. He was quite unwilling to go now, but he will go when he has the opportunity.

[13]Be on your guard; stand firm in the faith; be men of courage; be strong. [14]Do everything in love.

[15]You know that the household of Stephanas were the first converts in Achaia, and they have devoted themselves to the service of the saints. I urge you, brothers, [16]to submit to such as these and to everyone who joins in the work, and labors at it. [17]I was glad when Stephanas, Fortunatus and Achaicus arrived, because they have supplied what was lacking from you. [18]For they refreshed my spirit and yours also. Such men deserve recognition.

Final Greetings

[19]The churches in the province of Asia send you greetings. Aquila and Priscilla[a] greet you warmly in the Lord, and so does the church that meets at their house. [20]All the brothers here send you greetings. Greet one another with a holy kiss.

[21]I, Paul, write this greeting in my own hand.

[22]If anyone does not love the Lord—a curse be on him. Come, O Lord[b]!

[23]The grace of the Lord Jesus be with you.

[24]My love to all of you in Christ Jesus. Amen.[c]

---

[s] Or *it was not at all God's will for him*   [t] Gk *brothers*
[t] Gk *brothers*   [u] Gk *Marana tha.* These Aramaic words can also be read *Maran atha*, meaning *Our Lord has come*   [v] Other ancient authorities add *Amen*

[a]24 NIV text and NRSV note v add ἀμήν.; NIV note and NRSV text as UBS

[a]19 Greek *Prisca*, a variant of *Priscilla*   [b]22 In Aramaic the expression *Come, O Lord* is *Marana tha.*   [c]24 Some manuscripts do not have *Amen.*

NRSV

Salutation

1 Paul, an apostle of Christ Jesus by the will of God, and Timothy our brother,

To the church of God that is in Corinth, including all the saints throughout Achaia:

2 Grace to you and peace from God our Father and the Lord Jesus Christ.

Paul's Thanksgiving after Affliction

3 Blessed be the God and Father of our Lord Jesus Christ, the Father of mercies and the God of all consolation, 4who consoles us in all our affliction, so that we may be able to console those who are in any affliction with the consolation with which we ourselves are consoled by God. 5For just as the sufferings of Christ are abundant for us, so also our consolation is abundant through Christ. 6If we are being afflicted, it is for your consolation and salvation; if we are being consoled, it is for your consolation, which you experience when you patiently endure the same sufferings that we are also suffering. 7Our hope for you is unshaken; for we know that as you share in our sufferings, so also you share in our consolation.

8 We do not want you to be unaware, brothers and sisters,[a] of the affliction we experienced in Asia; for we were so utterly, unbearably crushed that we despaired of life itself. 9Indeed, we felt that we had received the sentence of death so that we would rely not on ourselves but on God who raises the dead. 10He who rescued us from so deadly a peril will continue to rescue us; on him we have set our hope that he will rescue us again, 11as you also join in helping us by your prayers, so that many will give thanks on our[b] behalf for the blessing granted us through the prayers of many.

The Postponement of Paul's Visit

12 Indeed, this is our boast, the testimony of our conscience: we have behaved in the world with frankness[c] and godly sincerity, not by earthly wisdom but by the grace of God—and all the more toward you. 13For we write you nothing other than what you can read and also understand; I hope you will understand until the end— 14as you have already understood us in part—that on the day of the Lord Jesus we are your boast even as you are our boast.

ΠΡΟΣ ΚΟΡΙΝΘΙΟΥΣ Β

1 Παῦλος ἀπόστολος Χριστοῦ Ἰησοῦ διὰ θελήματος θεοῦ καὶ Τιμόθεος ὁ ἀδελφὸς τῇ ἐκκλησίᾳ τοῦ θεοῦ τῇ οὔσῃ ἐν Κορίνθῳ σὺν τοῖς ἁγίοις πᾶσιν τοῖς οὖσιν ἐν ὅλῃ τῇ Ἀχαΐᾳ, 2 χάρις ὑμῖν καὶ εἰρήνη ἀπὸ θεοῦ πατρὸς ἡμῶν καὶ κυρίου Ἰησοῦ Χριστοῦ.

3 Εὐλογητὸς ὁ θεὸς καὶ πατὴρ τοῦ κυρίου ἡμῶν Ἰησοῦ Χριστοῦ, ὁ πατὴρ τῶν οἰκτιρμῶν καὶ θεὸς πάσης παρακλήσεως, 4 ὁ παρακαλῶν ἡμᾶς ἐπὶ πάσῃ τῇ θλίψει ἡμῶν εἰς τὸ δύνασθαι ἡμᾶς παρακαλεῖν τοὺς ἐν πάσῃ θλίψει διὰ τῆς παρακλήσεως ἧς παρακαλούμεθα αὐτοὶ ὑπὸ τοῦ θεοῦ. 5 ὅτι καθὼς περισσεύει τὰ παθήματα τοῦ Χριστοῦ εἰς ἡμᾶς, οὕτως διὰ τοῦ Χριστοῦ περισσεύει καὶ ἡ παράκλησις ἡμῶν. 6 εἴτε δὲ θλιβόμεθα, ὑπὲρ τῆς ὑμῶν παρακλήσεως καὶ σωτηρίας· εἴτε παρακαλούμεθα, ὑπὲρ τῆς ὑμῶν παρακλήσεως τῆς ἐνεργουμένης ἐν ὑπομονῇ τῶν αὐτῶν παθημάτων ὧν καὶ ἡμεῖς πάσχομεν. 7 καὶ ἡ ἐλπὶς ἡμῶν βεβαία ὑπὲρ ὑμῶν εἰδότες ὅτι ὡς κοινωνοί ἐστε τῶν παθημάτων, οὕτως καὶ τῆς παρακλήσεως.

8 Οὐ γὰρ θέλομεν ὑμᾶς ἀγνοεῖν, ἀδελφοί, ὑπὲρ τῆς θλίψεως ἡμῶν τῆς γενομένης ἐν τῇ Ἀσίᾳ, ὅτι καθ' ὑπερβολὴν ὑπὲρ δύναμιν ἐβαρήθημεν ὥστε ἐξαπορηθῆναι ἡμᾶς καὶ τοῦ ζῆν· 9 ἀλλὰ αὐτοὶ ἐν ἑαυτοῖς τὸ ἀπόκριμα τοῦ θανάτου ἐσχήκαμεν, ἵνα μὴ πεποιθότες ὦμεν ἐφ' ἑαυτοῖς ἀλλ' ἐπὶ τῷ θεῷ τῷ ἐγείροντι τοὺς νεκρούς· 10 ὃς ἐκ τηλικούτου θανάτου ἐρρύσατο ἡμᾶς καὶ ῥύσεται, εἰς ὃν ἠλπίκαμεν [ὅτι] καὶ ἔτι ῥύσεται, 11 συνυπουργούντων καὶ ὑμῶν ὑπὲρ ἡμῶν τῇ δεήσει, ἵνα ἐκ πολλῶν προσώπων τὸ εἰς ἡμᾶς χάρισμα διὰ πολλῶν εὐχαριστηθῇ ὑπὲρ ἡμῶν[a].

12 Ἡ γὰρ καύχησις ἡμῶν αὕτη ἐστίν, τὸ μαρτύριον τῆς συνειδήσεως ἡμῶν, ὅτι ἐν ἁπλότητι[b] καὶ εἰλικρινείᾳ τοῦ θεοῦ, [καὶ][c] οὐκ ἐν σοφίᾳ σαρκικῇ ἀλλ' ἐν χάριτι θεοῦ, ἀνεστράφημεν ἐν τῷ κόσμῳ, περισσοτέρως δὲ πρὸς ὑμᾶς. 13 οὐ γὰρ ἄλλα γράφομεν ὑμῖν ἀλλ' ἢ ἃ ἀναγινώσκετε ἢ καὶ ἐπιγινώσκετε· ἐλπίζω δὲ ὅτι[d] ἕως τέλους ἐπιγνώσεσθε, 14 καθὼς καὶ ἐπέγνωτε ἡμᾶς ἀπὸ μέρους, ὅτι καύχημα ὑμῶν ἐσμεν καθάπερ καὶ ὑμεῖς ἡμῶν ἐν τῇ ἡμέρᾳ

NIV

1 Paul, an apostle of Christ Jesus by the will of God, and Timothy our brother,

To the church of God in Corinth, together with all the saints throughout Achaia:

2Grace and peace to you from God our Father and the Lord Jesus Christ.

The God of All Comfort

3Praise be to the God and Father of our Lord Jesus Christ, the Father of compassion and the God of all comfort, 4who comforts us in all our troubles, so that we can comfort those in any trouble with the comfort we ourselves have received from God. 5For just as the sufferings of Christ flow over into our lives, so also through Christ our comfort overflows. 6If we are distressed, it is for your comfort and salvation; if we are comforted, it is for your comfort, which produces in you patient endurance of the same sufferings we suffer. 7And our hope for you is firm, because we know that just as you share in our sufferings, so also you share in our comfort.

8We do not want you to be uninformed, brothers, about the hardships we suffered in the province of Asia. We were under great pressure, far beyond our ability to endure, so that we despaired even of life. 9Indeed, in our hearts we felt the sentence of death. But this happened that we might not rely on ourselves but on God, who raises the dead. 10He has delivered us from such a deadly peril, and he will deliver us. On him we have set our hope that he will continue to deliver us, 11as you help us by your prayers. Then many will give thanks on our[a] behalf for the gracious favor granted us in answer to the prayers of many.

Paul's Change of Plans

12Now this is our boast: Our conscience testifies that we have conducted ourselves in the world, and especially in our relations with you, in the holiness and sincerity that are from God. We have done so not according to worldly wisdom but according to God's grace. 13For we do not write you anything you cannot read or understand. And I hope that, 14as you have understood us in part, you will come to understand fully that you can boast of us just as we will boast of you in the day of

NRSV

15 Since I was sure of this, I wanted to come to you first, so that you might have a double favor;[d] 16I wanted to visit you on my way to Macedonia, and to come back to you from Macedonia and have you send me on to Judea. 17Was I vacillating when I wanted to do this? Do I make my plans according to ordinary human standards,[e] ready to say "Yes, yes" and "No, no" at the same time? 18As surely as God is faithful, our word to you has not been "Yes and No." 19For the Son of God, Jesus Christ, whom we proclaimed among you, Silvanus and Timothy and I, was not "Yes and No"; but in him it is always "Yes." 20For in him every one of God's promises is a "Yes." For this reason it is through him that we say the "Amen," to the glory of God. 21But it is God who establishes us with you in Christ and has anointed us, 22by putting his seal on us and giving us his Spirit in our hearts as a first installment.

23 But I call on God as witness against me: it was to spare you that I did not come again to Corinth. 24I do not mean to imply that we lord it over your faith; rather, we are workers with you for your joy, because you stand firm in the faith. 1So I made up my mind not to make you another painful visit. 2For if I cause you pain, who is there to make me glad but the one whom I have pained? 3And I wrote as I did, so that when I came, I might not suffer pain from those who should have made me rejoice; for I am confident about all of you, that my joy would be the joy of all of you. 4For I wrote you out of much distress and anguish of heart and with many tears, not to cause you pain, but to let you know the abundant love that I have for you.

Forgiveness for the Offender

5 But if anyone has caused pain, he has caused it not to me, but to some extent—not to exaggerate it—to all of you. 6This punishment by the majority is enough for such a person; 7so now instead you should forgive and console him, so that he may not be overwhelmed by excessive sorrow. 8So I urge you to reaffirm your love for him. 9I wrote for this reason: to test you and to know whether you are obedient in everything. 10Anyone whom you forgive, I also forgive. What I have forgiven, if I have forgiven anything, has been for your

[Greek]

τοῦ κυρίου [ἡμῶν][e] Ἰησοῦ.

15 Καὶ ταύτῃ τῇ πεποιθήσει ἐβουλόμην πρότερον πρὸς ὑμᾶς ἐλθεῖν, ἵνα δευτέραν χάριν[f] σχῆτε, 16 καὶ δι᾽ ὑμῶν διελθεῖν εἰς Μακεδονίαν καὶ πάλιν ἀπὸ Μακεδονίας ἐλθεῖν πρὸς ὑμᾶς καὶ ὑφ᾽ ὑμῶν προπεμφθῆναι εἰς τὴν Ἰουδαίαν. 17 τοῦτο οὖν βουλόμενος μήτι ἄρα τῇ ἐλαφρίᾳ ἐχρησάμην; ἢ ἃ βουλεύομαι κατὰ σάρκα βουλεύομαι, ἵνα ᾖ παρ᾽ ἐμοὶ τὸ Ναὶ ναὶ καὶ τὸ Οὒ οὔ; 18 πιστὸς δὲ ὁ θεὸς ὅτι ὁ λόγος ἡμῶν ὁ πρὸς ὑμᾶς οὐκ ἔστιν Ναὶ καὶ Οὔ. 19 ὁ τοῦ θεοῦ γὰρ υἱὸς Ἰησοῦς Χριστὸς ὁ ἐν ὑμῖν δι᾽ ἡμῶν κηρυχθείς, δι᾽ ἐμοῦ καὶ Σιλουανοῦ καὶ Τιμοθέου, οὐκ ἐγένετο Ναὶ καὶ Οὒ ἀλλὰ Ναὶ ἐν αὐτῷ γέγονεν. 20 ὅσαι γὰρ ἐπαγγελίαι θεοῦ, ἐν αὐτῷ τὸ Ναί· διὸ καὶ δι᾽ αὐτοῦ τὸ Ἀμὴν τῷ θεῷ πρὸς δόξαν δι᾽ ἡμῶν. 21 ὁ δὲ βεβαιῶν ἡμᾶς σὺν ὑμῖν εἰς Χριστὸν καὶ χρίσας ἡμᾶς θεός, 22 ὁ καὶ σφραγισάμενος ἡμᾶς καὶ δοὺς τὸν ἀρραβῶνα τοῦ πνεύματος ἐν ταῖς καρδίαις ἡμῶν.

23 Ἐγὼ δὲ μάρτυρα τὸν θεὸν ἐπικαλοῦμαι ἐπὶ τὴν ἐμὴν ψυχήν, ὅτι φειδόμενος ὑμῶν οὐκέτι ἦλθον εἰς Κόρινθον. 24 οὐχ ὅτι κυριεύομεν ὑμῶν τῆς πίστεως ἀλλὰ συνεργοί ἐσμεν τῆς χαρᾶς ὑμῶν· τῇ γὰρ πίστει ἑστήκατε. 1 ἔκρινα γὰρ ἐμαυτῷ τοῦτο τὸ μὴ πάλιν ἐν λύπῃ πρὸς ὑμᾶς ἐλθεῖν. 2 εἰ γὰρ ἐγὼ λυπῶ ὑμᾶς, καὶ τίς ὁ εὐφραίνων με εἰ μὴ ὁ λυπούμενος ἐξ ἐμοῦ; 3 καὶ ἔγραψα τοῦτο αὐτό, ἵνα μὴ ἐλθὼν λύπην σχῶ ἀφ᾽ ὧν ἔδει με χαίρειν, πεποιθὼς ἐπὶ πάντας ὑμᾶς ὅτι ἡ ἐμὴ χαρὰ πάντων ὑμῶν ἐστιν. 4 ἐκ γὰρ πολλῆς θλίψεως καὶ συνοχῆς καρδίας ἔγραψα ὑμῖν διὰ πολλῶν δακρύων, οὐχ ἵνα λυπηθῆτε ἀλλὰ τὴν ἀγάπην ἵνα γνῶτε ἣν ἔχω περισσοτέρως εἰς ὑμᾶς.

5 Εἰ δέ τις λελύπηκεν, οὐκ ἐμὲ λελύπηκεν, ἀλλὰ ἀπὸ μέρους, ἵνα μὴ ἐπιβαρῶ, πάντας ὑμᾶς. 6 ἱκανὸν τῷ τοιούτῳ ἡ ἐπιτιμία αὕτη ἡ ὑπὸ τῶν πλειόνων, 7 ὥστε τοὐναντίον μᾶλλον ὑμᾶς χαρίσασθαι καὶ παρακαλέσαι, μή πως τῇ περισσοτέρᾳ λύπῃ καταποθῇ ὁ τοιοῦτος. 8 διὸ παρακαλῶ ὑμᾶς κυρῶσαι εἰς αὐτὸν ἀγάπην· 9 εἰς τοῦτο γὰρ καὶ ἔγραψα, ἵνα γνῶ τὴν δοκιμὴν ὑμῶν, εἰ εἰς πάντα ὑπήκοοί ἐστε. 10 ᾧ δέ τι χαρίζεσθε, κἀγώ· καὶ γὰρ ἐγὼ ὃ κεχάρισμαι, εἴ τι κεχάρισμαι, δι᾽ ὑμᾶς

NIV

the Lord Jesus.

15Because I was confident of this, I planned to visit you first so that you might benefit twice. 16I planned to visit you on my way to Macedonia and to come back to you from Macedonia, and then to have you send me on my way to Judea. 17When I planned this, did I do it lightly? Or do I make my plans in a worldly manner so that in the same breath I say, "Yes, yes" and "No, no"?

18But as surely as God is faithful, our message to you is not "Yes" and "No." 19For the Son of God, Jesus Christ, who was preached among you by me and Silas[b] and Timothy, was not "Yes" and "No," but in him it has always been "Yes." 20For no matter how many promises God has made, they are "Yes" in Christ. And so through him the "Amen" is spoken by us to the glory of God. 21Now it is God who makes both us and you stand firm in Christ. He anointed us, 22set his seal of ownership on us, and put his Spirit in our hearts as a deposit, guaranteeing what is to come.

23I call God as my witness that it was in order to spare you that I did not return to Corinth. 24Not that we lord it over your faith, but we work with you for your joy, because it is by faith you stand firm. 1So I made up my mind that I would not make another painful visit to you. 2For if I grieve you, who is left to make me glad but you whom I have grieved? 3I wrote as I did so that when I came I should not be distressed by those who ought to make me rejoice. I had confidence in all of you, that you would all share my joy. 4For I wrote you out of great distress and anguish of heart and with many tears, not to grieve you but to let you know the depth of my love for you.

Forgiveness for the Sinner

5If anyone has caused grief, he has not so much grieved me as he has grieved all of you, to some extent—not to put it too severely. 6The punishment inflicted on him by the majority is sufficient for him. 7Now instead, you ought to forgive and comfort him, so that he will not be overwhelmed by excessive sorrow. 8I urge you, therefore, to reaffirm your love for him. 9The reason I wrote you was to see if you would stand the test and be obedient in everything. 10If you forgive anyone, I also forgive him. And what I have forgiven—if there was anything to forgive—I have forgiven

---

[d] Other ancient authorities read *pleasure*   [e] Gk *according to the flesh*

[e]14 NIV/NRSV texts omit ἡμῶν   [f]15 NRSV note d χαράν

[b]19 Greek *Silvanus*, a variant of *Silas*

sake in the presence of Christ. [11]And we do this so that we may not be outwitted by Satan; for we are not ignorant of his designs.

Paul's Anxiety in Troas

12 When I came to Troas to proclaim the good news of Christ, a door was opened for me in the Lord; [13]but my mind could not rest because I did not find my brother Titus there. So I said farewell to them and went on to Macedonia.

14 But thanks be to God, who in Christ always leads us in triumphal procession, and through us spreads in every place the fragrance that comes from knowing him. [15]For we are the aroma of Christ to God among those who are being saved and among those who are perishing; [16]to the one a fragrance from death to death, to the other a fragrance from life to life. Who is sufficient for these things? [17]For we are not peddlers of God's word like so many;[f] but in Christ we speak as persons of sincerity, as persons sent from God and standing in his presence.

Ministers of the New Covenant

3 Are we beginning to commend ourselves again? Surely we do not need, as some do, letters of recommendation to you or from you, do we? [2]You yourselves are our letter, written on our[g] hearts, to be known and read by all; [3]and you show that you are a letter of Christ, prepared by us, written not with ink but with the Spirit of the living God, not on tablets of stone but on tablets of human hearts.

4 Such is the confidence that we have through Christ toward God. [5]Not that we are competent of ourselves to claim anything as coming from us; our competence is from God, [6]who has made us competent to be ministers of a new covenant, not of letter but of spirit; for the letter kills, but the Spirit gives life.

7 Now if the ministry of death, chiseled in letters on stone tablets,[h] came in glory so that the people of Israel could not gaze at Moses' face because of the glory of his face, a glory now set aside, [8]how much more will the ministry of the Spirit come in glory? [9]For if there was glory in the ministry of condemnation, much more does the ministry of justification abound in glory! [10]Indeed, what once had glory has lost its glory because of the greater

ἐν προσώπῳ Χριστοῦ, 11 ἵνα μὴ πλεονεκτηθῶμεν ὑπὸ τοῦ Σατανᾶ· οὐ γὰρ αὐτοῦ τὰ νοήματα ἀγνοοῦμεν.

12 Ἐλθὼν δὲ εἰς τὴν Τρῳάδα εἰς τὸ εὐαγγέλιον τοῦ Χριστοῦ καὶ θύρας μοι ἀνεῳγμένης ἐν κυρίῳ, 13 οὐκ ἔσχηκα ἄνεσιν τῷ πνεύματί μου τῷ μὴ εὑρεῖν με Τίτον τὸν ἀδελφόν μου, ἀλλὰ ἀποταξάμενος αὐτοῖς ἐξῆλθον εἰς Μακεδονίαν.

14 Τῷ δὲ θεῷ χάρις τῷ πάντοτε θριαμβεύοντι ἡμᾶς ἐν τῷ Χριστῷ καὶ τὴν ὀσμὴν τῆς γνώσεως αὐτοῦ φανεροῦντι δι᾽ ἡμῶν ἐν παντὶ τόπῳ· 15 ὅτι Χριστοῦ εὐωδία ἐσμὲν τῷ θεῷ ἐν τοῖς σῳζομένοις καὶ ἐν τοῖς ἀπολλυμένοις, 16 οἷς μὲν ὀσμὴ ἐκ θανάτου εἰς θάνατον, οἷς δὲ ὀσμὴ ἐκ ζωῆς εἰς ζωήν. καὶ πρὸς ταῦτα τίς ἱκανός; 17 οὐ γάρ ἐσμεν ὡς οἱ πολλοὶ[a] καπηλεύοντες τὸν λόγον τοῦ θεοῦ, ἀλλ᾽ ὡς ἐξ εἰλικρινείας, ἀλλ᾽ ὡς ἐκ θεοῦ κατέναντι θεοῦ ἐν Χριστῷ λαλοῦμεν.

3 Ἀρχόμεθα πάλιν ἑαυτοὺς συνιστάνειν; ἢ μὴ χρῄζομεν ὥς τινες συστατικῶν ἐπιστολῶν πρὸς ὑμᾶς ἢ ἐξ ὑμῶν; 2 ἡ ἐπιστολὴ ἡμῶν ὑμεῖς ἐστε, ἐγγεγραμμένη ἐν ταῖς καρδίαις ἡμῶν[a], γινωσκομένη καὶ ἀναγινωσκομένη ὑπὸ πάντων ἀνθρώπων, 3 φανερούμενοι ὅτι ἐστὲ ἐπιστολὴ Χριστοῦ διακονηθεῖσα ὑφ᾽ ἡμῶν, ἐγγεγραμμένη οὐ μέλανι ἀλλὰ πνεύματι θεοῦ ζῶντος, οὐκ ἐν πλαξὶν λιθίναις ἀλλ᾽ ἐν πλαξὶν καρδίαις σαρκίναις.

4 Πεποίθησιν δὲ τοιαύτην ἔχομεν διὰ τοῦ Χριστοῦ πρὸς τὸν θεόν. 5 οὐχ ὅτι ἀφ᾽ ἑαυτῶν ἱκανοί ἐσμεν λογίσασθαί τι ὡς ἐξ ἑαυτῶν, ἀλλ᾽ ἡ ἱκανότης ἡμῶν ἐκ τοῦ θεοῦ, 6 ὃς καὶ ἱκάνωσεν ἡμᾶς διακόνους καινῆς διαθήκης, οὐ γράμματος ἀλλὰ πνεύματος· τὸ γὰρ γράμμα ἀποκτέννει, τὸ δὲ πνεῦμα ζῳοποιεῖ.

7 Εἰ δὲ ἡ διακονία τοῦ θανάτου ἐν γράμμασιν ἐντετυπωμένη λίθοις ἐγενήθη ἐν δόξῃ, ὥστε μὴ δύνασθαι ἀτενίσαι τοὺς υἱοὺς Ἰσραὴλ εἰς τὸ πρόσωπον Μωϋσέως διὰ τὴν δόξαν τοῦ προσώπου αὐτοῦ τὴν καταργουμένην, 8 πῶς οὐχὶ μᾶλλον ἡ διακονία τοῦ πνεύματος ἔσται ἐν δόξῃ; 9 εἰ γὰρ τῇ διακονίᾳ τῆς κατακρίσεως δόξα, πολλῷ μᾶλλον περισσεύει ἡ διακονία τῆς δικαιοσύνης δόξῃ. 10 καὶ γὰρ οὐ δεδόξασται τὸ δεδοξασμένον ἐν τούτῳ τῷ μέρει

in the sight of Christ for your sake, [11]in order that Satan might not outwit us. For we are not unaware of his schemes.

Ministers of the New Covenant

[12]Now when I went to Troas to preach the gospel of Christ and found that the Lord had opened a door for me, [13]I still had no peace of mind, because I did not find my brother Titus there. So I said goodby to them and went on to Macedonia.

[14]But thanks be to God, who always leads us in triumphal procession in Christ and through us spreads everywhere the fragrance of the knowledge of him. [15]For we are to God the aroma of Christ among those who are being saved and those who are perishing. [16]To the one we are the smell of death; to the other, the fragrance of life. And who is equal to such a task? [17]Unlike so many, we do not peddle the word of God for profit. On the contrary, in Christ we speak before God with sincerity, like men sent from God.

3 Are we beginning to commend ourselves again? Or do we need, like some people, letters of recommendation to you or from you? [2]You yourselves are our letter, written on our hearts, known and read by everybody. [3]You show that you are a letter from Christ, the result of our ministry, written not with ink but with the Spirit of the living God, not on tablets of stone but on tablets of human hearts.

[4]Such confidence as this is ours through Christ before God. [5]Not that we are competent in ourselves to claim anything for ourselves, but our competence comes from God. [6]He has made us competent as ministers of a new covenant—not of the letter but of the Spirit; for the letter kills, but the Spirit gives life.

The Glory of the New Covenant

[7]Now if the ministry that brought death, which was engraved in letters on stone, came with glory, so that the Israelites could not look steadily at the face of Moses because of its glory, fading though it was, [8]will not the ministry of the Spirit be even more glorious? [9]If the ministry that condemns men is glorious, how much more glorious is the ministry that brings righteousness! [10]For what was glorious has no glory now in comparison with the sur-

---

glory; [11]for if what was set aside came through glory, much more has the permanent come in glory!

12 Since, then, we have such a hope, we act with great boldness, [13]not like Moses, who put a veil over his face to keep the people of Israel from gazing at the end of the glory that[i] was being set aside. [14]But their minds were hardened. Indeed, to this very day, when they hear the reading of the old covenant, that same veil is still there, since only in Christ is it set aside. [15]Indeed, to this very day whenever Moses is read, a veil lies over their minds; [16]but when one turns to the Lord, the veil is removed. [17]Now the Lord is the Spirit, and where the Spirit of the Lord is, there is freedom. [18]And all of us, with unveiled faces, seeing the glory of the Lord as though reflected in a mirror, are being transformed into the same image from one degree of glory to another; for this comes from the Lord, the Spirit.

Treasure in Clay Jars

4 Therefore, since it is by God's mercy that we are engaged in this ministry, we do not lose heart. [2]We have renounced the shameful things that one hides; we refuse to practice cunning or to falsify God's word; but by the open statement of the truth we commend ourselves to the conscience of everyone in the sight of God. [3]And even if our gospel is veiled, it is veiled to those who are perishing. [4]In their case the god of this world has blinded the minds of the unbelievers, to keep them from seeing the light of the gospel of the glory of Christ, who is the image of God. [5]For we do not proclaim ourselves; we proclaim Jesus Christ as Lord and ourselves as your slaves for Jesus' sake. [6]For it is the God who said, "Let light shine out of darkness," who has shone in our hearts to give the light of the knowledge of the glory of God in the face of Jesus Christ.

7 But we have this treasure in clay jars, so that it may be made clear that this extraordinary power belongs to God and does not come from us. [8]We are afflicted in every way, but not crushed; perplexed, but not driven to despair; [9]persecuted, but not forsaken; struck down, but not destroyed; [10]always carrying in the body the death of Jesus, so that the life of Jesus may

εἵνεκεν τῆς ὑπερβαλλούσης δόξης. 11 εἰ γὰρ τὸ καταργούμενον διὰ δόξης, πολλῷ μᾶλλον τὸ μένον ἐν δόξῃ.

12 Ἔχοντες οὖν τοιαύτην ἐλπίδα πολλῇ παρρησίᾳ χρώμεθα 13 καὶ οὐ καθάπερ Μωϋσῆς ἐτίθει κάλυμμα ἐπὶ τὸ πρόσωπον αὐτοῦ πρὸς τὸ μὴ ἀτενίσαι τοὺς υἱοὺς Ἰσραὴλ εἰς τὸ τέλος τοῦ καταργουμένου. 14 ἀλλὰ ἐπωρώθη τὰ νοήματα αὐτῶν. ἄχρι γὰρ τῆς σήμερον ἡμέρας τὸ αὐτὸ κάλυμμα ἐπὶ τῇ ἀναγνώσει τῆς παλαιᾶς διαθήκης μένει, μὴ ἀνακαλυπτόμενον ὅτι ἐν Χριστῷ καταργεῖται· 15 ἀλλ' ἕως σήμερον ἡνίκα ἂν ἀναγινώσκηται Μωϋσῆς, κάλυμμα ἐπὶ τὴν καρδίαν αὐτῶν κεῖται· 16 ἡνίκα δὲ ἐὰν ἐπιστρέψῃ πρὸς κύριον, περιαιρεῖται τὸ κάλυμμα. 17 ὁ δὲ κύριος τὸ πνεῦμά ἐστιν· οὗ δὲ τὸ πνεῦμα κυρίου, ἐλευθερία. 18 ἡμεῖς δὲ πάντες ἀνακεκαλυμμένῳ προσώπῳ τὴν δόξαν κυρίου κατοπτριζόμενοι τὴν αὐτὴν εἰκόνα μεταμορφούμεθα ἀπὸ δόξης εἰς δόξαν καθάπερ ἀπὸ κυρίου πνεύματος.

4 Διὰ τοῦτο, ἔχοντες τὴν διακονίαν ταύτην καθὼς ἠλεήθημεν, οὐκ ἐγκακοῦμεν 2 ἀλλὰ ἀπειπάμεθα τὰ κρυπτὰ τῆς αἰσχύνης, μὴ περιπατοῦντες ἐν πανουργίᾳ μηδὲ δολοῦντες τὸν λόγον τοῦ θεοῦ ἀλλὰ τῇ φανερώσει τῆς ἀληθείας συνιστάνοντες ἑαυτοὺς πρὸς πᾶσαν συνείδησιν ἀνθρώπων ἐνώπιον τοῦ θεοῦ. 3 εἰ δὲ καὶ ἔστιν κεκαλυμμένον τὸ εὐαγγέλιον ἡμῶν, ἐν τοῖς ἀπολλυμένοις ἐστὶν κεκαλυμμένον, 4 ἐν οἷς ὁ θεὸς τοῦ αἰῶνος τούτου ἐτύφλωσεν τὰ νοήματα τῶν ἀπίστων εἰς τὸ μὴ αὐγάσαι τὸν φωτισμὸν τοῦ εὐαγγελίου τῆς δόξης τοῦ Χριστοῦ, ὅς ἐστιν εἰκὼν τοῦ θεοῦ. 5 οὐ γὰρ ἑαυτοὺς κηρύσσομεν ἀλλὰ Ἰησοῦν Χριστὸν κύριον, ἑαυτοὺς δὲ δούλους ὑμῶν διὰ Ἰησοῦν. 6 ὅτι ὁ θεὸς ὁ εἰπών, Ἐκ σκότους φῶς λάμψει, ὃς ἔλαμψεν ἐν ταῖς καρδίαις ἡμῶν πρὸς φωτισμὸν τῆς γνώσεως τῆς δόξης τοῦ θεοῦ ἐν προσώπῳ [Ἰησοῦ][a] Χριστοῦ.

7 Ἔχομεν δὲ τὸν θησαυρὸν τοῦτον ἐν ὀστρακίνοις σκεύεσιν, ἵνα ἡ ὑπερβολὴ τῆς δυνάμεως ᾖ τοῦ θεοῦ καὶ μὴ ἐξ ἡμῶν· 8 ἐν παντὶ θλιβόμενοι ἀλλ' οὐ στενοχωρούμενοι, ἀπορούμενοι ἀλλ' οὐκ ἐξαπορούμενοι, 9 διωκόμενοι ἀλλ' οὐκ ἐγκαταλειπόμενοι, καταβαλλόμενοι ἀλλ' οὐκ ἀπολλύμενοι, 10 πάντοτε τὴν νέκρωσιν τοῦ Ἰησοῦ ἐν τῷ σώματι περιφέροντες, ἵνα καὶ ἡ ζωὴ τοῦ Ἰησοῦ

passing glory. [11]And if what was fading away came with glory, how much greater is the glory of that which lasts!

[12]Therefore, since we have such a hope, we are very bold. [13]We are not like Moses, who would put a veil over his face to keep the Israelites from gazing at it while the radiance was fading away. [14]But their minds were made dull, for to this day the same veil remains when the old covenant is read. It has not been removed, because only in Christ is it taken away. [15]Even to this day when Moses is read, a veil covers their hearts. [16]But whenever anyone turns to the Lord, the veil is taken away. [17]Now the Lord is the Spirit, and where the Spirit of the Lord is, there is freedom. [18]And we, who with unveiled faces all reflect[a] the Lord's glory, are being transformed into his likeness with ever-increasing glory, which comes from the Lord, who is the Spirit.

Treasures in Jars of Clay

4 Therefore, since through God's mercy we have this ministry, we do not lose heart. [2]Rather, we have renounced secret and shameful ways; we do not use deception, nor do we distort the word of God. On the contrary, by setting forth the truth plainly we commend ourselves to every man's conscience in the sight of God. [3]And even if our gospel is veiled, it is veiled to those who are perishing. [4]The god of this age has blinded the minds of unbelievers, so that they cannot see the light of the gospel of the glory of Christ, who is the image of God. [5]For we do not preach ourselves, but Jesus Christ as Lord, and ourselves as your servants for Jesus' sake. [6]For God, who said, "Let light shine out of darkness,"[a] made his light shine in our hearts to give us the light of the knowledge of the glory of God in the face of Christ.

[7]But we have this treasure in jars of clay to show that this all-surpassing power is from God and not from us. [8]We are hard pressed on every side, but not crushed; perplexed, but not in despair; [9]persecuted, but not abandoned; struck down, but not destroyed. [10]We always carry around in our body the death of Jesus, so that the life

---

also be made visible in our bodies. [11]For while we live, we are always being given up to death for Jesus' sake, so that the life of Jesus may be made visible in our mortal flesh. [12]So death is at work in us, but life in you.

13 But just as we have the same spirit of faith that is in accordance with scripture—"I believed, and so I spoke"—we also believe, and so we speak, [14]because we know that the one who raised the Lord Jesus will raise us also with Jesus, and will bring us with you into his presence. [15]Yes, everything is for your sake, so that grace, as it extends to more and more people, may increase thanksgiving, to the glory of God.

Living by Faith

16 So we do not lose heart. Even though our outer nature is wasting away, our inner nature is being renewed day by day. [17]For this slight momentary affliction is preparing us for an eternal weight of glory beyond all measure, [18]because we look not at what can be seen but at what cannot be seen; for what can be seen is temporary, but what cannot be seen is eternal.

5 For we know that if the earthly tent we live in is destroyed, we have a building from God, a house not made with hands, eternal in the heavens. [2]For in this tent we groan, longing to be clothed with our heavenly dwelling— [3]if indeed, when we have taken it off[j] we will not be found naked. [4]For while we are still in this tent, we groan under our burden, because we wish not to be unclothed but to be further clothed, so that what is mortal may be swallowed up by life. [5]He who has prepared us for this very thing is God, who has given us the Spirit as a guarantee.

6 So we are always confident; even though we know that while we are at home in the body we are away from the Lord—[7]for we walk by faith, not by sight. [8]Yes, we do have confidence, and we would rather be away from the body and at home with the Lord. [9]So whether we are at home or away, we make it our aim to please him. [10]For all of us must appear before the judgment seat of Christ, so that each may receive recompense for what has been done in the body, whether good or evil.

The Ministry of Reconciliation

11 Therefore, knowing the fear of the Lord, we try to persuade others; but we

ἐν τῷ σώματι ἡμῶν φανερωθῇ. 11 ἀεὶ γὰρ ἡμεῖς οἱ ζῶντες εἰς θάνατον παραδιδόμεθα διὰ Ἰησοῦν, ἵνα καὶ ἡ ζωὴ τοῦ Ἰησοῦ φανερωθῇ ἐν τῇ θνητῇ σαρκὶ ἡμῶν. 12 ὥστε ὁ θάνατος ἐν ἡμῖν ἐνεργεῖται, ἡ δὲ ζωὴ ἐν ὑμῖν. 13 ἔχοντες δὲ τὸ αὐτὸ πνεῦμα τῆς πίστεως κατὰ τὸ γεγραμμένον, Ἐπίστευσα, διὸ ἐλάλησα, καὶ ἡμεῖς πιστεύομεν, διὸ καὶ λαλοῦμεν, 14 εἰδότες ὅτι ὁ ἐγείρας τὸν κύριον Ἰησοῦν καὶ ἡμᾶς σὺν Ἰησοῦ ἐγερεῖ καὶ παραστήσει σὺν ὑμῖν. 15 τὰ γὰρ πάντα δι᾽ ὑμᾶς, ἵνα ἡ χάρις πλεονάσασα διὰ τῶν πλειόνων τὴν εὐχαριστίαν περισσεύσῃ εἰς τὴν δόξαν τοῦ θεοῦ.

16 Διὸ οὐκ ἐγκακοῦμεν, ἀλλ᾽ εἰ καὶ ὁ ἔξω ἡμῶν ἄνθρωπος διαφθείρεται, ἀλλ᾽ ὁ ἔσω ἡμῶν ἀνακαινοῦται ἡμέρα καὶ ἡμέρα. 17 τὸ γὰρ παραυτίκα ἐλαφρὸν τῆς θλίψεως ἡμῶν καθ᾽ ὑπερβολὴν εἰς ὑπερβολὴν αἰώνιον βάρος δόξης κατεργάζεται ἡμῖν, 18 μὴ σκοπούντων ἡμῶν τὰ βλεπόμενα ἀλλὰ τὰ μὴ βλεπόμενα· τὰ γὰρ βλεπόμενα πρόσκαιρα, τὰ δὲ μὴ βλεπόμενα αἰώνια.

5 Οἴδαμεν γὰρ ὅτι ἐὰν ἡ ἐπίγειος ἡμῶν οἰκία τοῦ σκήνους καταλυθῇ, οἰκοδομὴν ἐκ θεοῦ ἔχομεν, οἰκίαν ἀχειροποίητον αἰώνιον ἐν τοῖς οὐρανοῖς. 2 καὶ γὰρ ἐν τούτῳ στενάζομεν τὸ οἰκητήριον ἡμῶν τὸ ἐξ οὐρανοῦ ἐπενδύσασθαι ἐπιποθοῦντες, 3 εἴ γε καὶ ἐκδυσάμενοι[a] οὐ γυμνοὶ εὑρεθησόμεθα. 4 καὶ γὰρ οἱ ὄντες ἐν τῷ σκήνει στενάζομεν βαρούμενοι, ἐφ᾽ ᾧ οὐ θέλομεν ἐκδύσασθαι ἀλλ᾽ ἐπενδύσασθαι, ἵνα καταποθῇ τὸ θνητὸν ὑπὸ τῆς ζωῆς. 5 ὁ δὲ κατεργασάμενος ἡμᾶς εἰς αὐτὸ τοῦτο θεός, ὁ δοὺς ἡμῖν τὸν ἀρραβῶνα τοῦ πνεύματος.

6 Θαρροῦντες οὖν πάντοτε καὶ εἰδότες ὅτι ἐνδημοῦντες ἐν τῷ σώματι ἐκδημοῦμεν ἀπὸ τοῦ κυρίου· 7 διὰ πίστεως γὰρ περιπατοῦμεν, οὐ διὰ εἴδους· 8 θαρροῦμεν δὲ καὶ εὐδοκοῦμεν μᾶλλον ἐκδημῆσαι ἐκ τοῦ σώματος καὶ ἐνδημῆσαι πρὸς τὸν κύριον. 9 διὸ καὶ φιλοτιμούμεθα, εἴτε ἐνδημοῦντες εἴτε ἐκδημοῦντες, εὐάρεστοι αὐτῷ εἶναι. 10 τοὺς γὰρ πάντας ἡμᾶς φανερωθῆναι δεῖ ἔμπροσθεν τοῦ βήματος τοῦ Χριστοῦ, ἵνα κομίσηται ἕκαστος τὰ διὰ τοῦ σώματος πρὸς ἃ ἔπραξεν, εἴτε ἀγαθὸν εἴτε φαῦλον.

11 Εἰδότες οὖν τὸν φόβον τοῦ κυρίου ἀνθρώπους πείθομεν, θεῷ δὲ πεφανερώ-

of Jesus may also be revealed in our body. [11]For we who are alive are always being given over to death for Jesus' sake, so that his life may be revealed in our mortal body. [12]So then, death is at work in us, but life is at work in you.

[13]It is written: "I believed; therefore I have spoken."[b] With that same spirit of faith we also believe and therefore speak, [14]because we know that the one who raised the Lord Jesus from the dead will also raise us with Jesus and present us with you in his presence. [15]All this is for your benefit, so that the grace that is reaching more and more people may cause thanksgiving to overflow to the glory of God.

[16]Therefore we do not lose heart. Though outwardly we are wasting away, yet inwardly we are being renewed day by day. [17]For our light and momentary troubles are achieving for us an eternal glory that far outweighs them all. [18]So we fix our eyes not on what is seen, but on what is unseen. For what is seen is temporary, but what is unseen is eternal.

Our Heavenly Dwelling

5 Now we know that if the earthly tent we live in is destroyed, we have a building from God, an eternal house in heaven, not built by human hands. [2]Meanwhile we groan, longing to be clothed with our heavenly dwelling, [3]because when we are clothed, we will not be found naked. [4]For while we are in this tent, we groan and are burdened, because we do not wish to be unclothed but to be clothed with our heavenly dwelling, so that what is mortal may be swallowed up by life. [5]Now it is God who has made us for this very purpose and has given us the Spirit as a deposit, guaranteeing what is to come.

[6]Therefore we are always confident and know that as long as we are at home in the body we are away from the Lord. [7]We live by faith, not by sight. [8]We are confident, I say, and would prefer to be away from the body and at home with the Lord. [9]So we make it our goal to please him, whether we are at home in the body or away from it. [10]For we must all appear before the judgment seat of Christ, that each one may receive what is due him for the things done while in the body, whether good or bad.

The Ministry of Reconciliation

[11]Since, then, we know what it is to fear the Lord, we try to persuade men. What

---

ourselves are well known to God, and I hope that we are also well known to your consciences. 12We are not commending ourselves to you again, but giving you an opportunity to boast about us, so that you may be able to answer those who boast in outward appearance and not in the heart. 13For if we are beside ourselves, it is for God; if we are in our right mind, it is for you. 14For the love of Christ urges us on, because we are convinced that one has died for all; therefore all have died. 15And he died for all, so that those who live might live no longer for themselves, but for him who died and was raised for them.

16 From now on, therefore, we regard no one from a human point of view;[k] even though we once knew Christ from a human point of view,[k] we know him no longer in that way. 17So if anyone is in Christ, there is a new creation: everything old has passed away; see, everything has become new! 18All this is from God, who reconciled us to himself through Christ, and has given us the ministry of reconciliation; 19that is, in Christ God was reconciling the world to himself,[l] not counting their trespasses against them, and entrusting the message of reconciliation to us. 20So we are ambassadors for Christ, since God is making his appeal through us; we entreat you on behalf of Christ, be reconciled to God. 21For our sake he made him to be sin who knew no sin, so that in him we might become the righteousness of God.

6 As we work together with him,[m] we urge you also not to accept the grace of God in vain. 2For he says,

"At an acceptable time I have listened
    to you,
  and on a day of salvation I have
    helped you."

See, now is the acceptable time; see, now is the day of salvation! 3We are putting no obstacle in anyone's way, so that no fault may be found with our ministry, 4but as servants of God we have commended ourselves in every way: through great endurance, in afflictions, hardships, calamities, 5beatings, imprisonments, riots, labors, sleepless nights, hunger; 6by purity, knowledge, patience, kindness, holiness of spirit, genuine love, 7truthful speech, and the power of God; with the weapons of righteousness for the right hand and for the left; 8in honor and dishonor, in ill repute

μεθα· ἐλπίζω δὲ καὶ ἐν ταῖς συνειδήσεσιν ὑμῶν πεφανερῶσθαι. 12 οὐ πάλιν ἑαυτοὺς συνιστάνομεν ὑμῖν ἀλλὰ ἀφορμὴν διδόντες ὑμῖν καυχήματος ὑπὲρ ἡμῶν, ἵνα ἔχητε πρὸς τοὺς ἐν προσώπῳ καυχωμένους καὶ μὴ ἐν καρδίᾳ. 13 εἴτε γὰρ ἐξέστημεν, θεῷ· εἴτε σωφρονοῦμεν, ὑμῖν. 14 ἡ γὰρ ἀγάπη τοῦ Χριστοῦ συνέχει ἡμᾶς, κρίναντας τοῦτο, ὅτι εἷς ὑπὲρ πάντων ἀπέθανεν, ἄρα οἱ πάντες ἀπέθανον· 15 καὶ ὑπὲρ πάντων ἀπέθανεν, ἵνα οἱ ζῶντες μηκέτι ἑαυτοῖς ζῶσιν ἀλλὰ τῷ ὑπὲρ αὐτῶν ἀποθανόντι καὶ ἐγερθέντι.

16 Ὥστε ἡμεῖς ἀπὸ τοῦ νῦν οὐδένα οἴδαμεν κατὰ σάρκα· εἰ καὶ ἐγνώκαμεν κατὰ σάρκα Χριστόν, ἀλλὰ νῦν οὐκέτι γινώσκομεν. 17 ὥστε εἴ τις ἐν Χριστῷ, καινὴ κτίσις· τὰ ἀρχαῖα παρῆλθεν, ἰδοὺ γέγονεν καινά· 18 τὰ δὲ πάντα ἐκ τοῦ θεοῦ τοῦ καταλλάξαντος ἡμᾶς ἑαυτῷ διὰ Χριστοῦ καὶ δόντος ἡμῖν τὴν διακονίαν τῆς καταλλαγῆς, 19 ὡς ὅτι θεὸς ἦν ἐν Χριστῷ κόσμον καταλλάσσων ἑαυτῷ, μὴ λογιζόμενος αὐτοῖς τὰ παραπτώματα αὐτῶν καὶ θέμενος ἐν ἡμῖν τὸν λόγον τῆς καταλλαγῆς. 20 ὑπὲρ Χριστοῦ οὖν πρεσβεύομεν ὡς τοῦ θεοῦ παρακαλοῦντος δι' ἡμῶν· δεόμεθα ὑπὲρ Χριστοῦ, καταλλάγητε τῷ θεῷ. 21 τὸν μὴ γνόντα ἁμαρτίαν ὑπὲρ ἡμῶν ἁμαρτίαν ἐποίησεν, ἵνα ἡμεῖς γενώμεθα δικαιοσύνη θεοῦ ἐν αὐτῷ.

6 Συνεργοῦντες δὲ καὶ παρακαλοῦμεν μὴ εἰς κενὸν τὴν χάριν τοῦ θεοῦ δέξασθαι ὑμᾶς· 2 λέγει γάρ,

Καιρῷ δεκτῷ ἐπήκουσά σου
καὶ ἐν ἡμέρᾳ σωτηρίας ἐβοήθησά
    σοι.

ἰδοὺ νῦν καιρὸς εὐπρόσδεκτος, ἰδοὺ νῦν ἡμέρα σωτηρίας· 3 μηδεμίαν ἐν μηδενὶ διδόντες προσκοπήν, ἵνα μὴ μωμηθῇ ἡ διακονία, 4 ἀλλ' ἐν παντὶ συνιστάντες ἑαυτοὺς ὡς θεοῦ διάκονοι, ἐν ὑπομονῇ πολλῇ, ἐν θλίψεσιν, ἐν ἀνάγκαις, ἐν στενοχωρίαις, 5 ἐν πληγαῖς, ἐν φυλακαῖς, ἐν ἀκαταστασίαις, ἐν κόποις, ἐν ἀγρυπνίαις, ἐν νηστείαις, 6 ἐν ἁγνότητι, ἐν γνώσει, ἐν μακροθυμίᾳ, ἐν χρηστότητι, ἐν πνεύματι ἁγίῳ, ἐν ἀγάπῃ ἀνυποκρίτῳ, 7 ἐν λόγῳ ἀληθείας, ἐν δυνάμει θεοῦ· διὰ τῶν ὅπλων τῆς δικαιοσύνης τῶν δεξιῶν καὶ ἀριστερῶν, 8 διὰ δόξης καὶ ἀτιμίας, διὰ δυσφημίας καὶ εὐφημίας·

we are is plain to God, and I hope it is also plain to your conscience. 12We are not trying to commend ourselves to you again, but are giving you an opportunity to take pride in us, so that you can answer those who take pride in what is seen rather than in what is in the heart. 13If we are out of our mind, it is for the sake of God; if we are in our right mind, it is for you. 14For Christ's love compels us, because we are convinced that one died for all, and therefore all died. 15And he died for all, that those who live should no longer live for themselves but for him who died for them and was raised again.

16So from now on we regard no one from a worldly point of view. Though we once regarded Christ in this way, we do so no longer. 17Therefore, if anyone is in Christ, he is a new creation; the old has gone, the new has come! 18All this is from God, who reconciled us to himself through Christ and gave us the ministry of reconciliation: 19that God was reconciling the world to himself in Christ, not counting men's sins against them. And he has committed to us the message of reconciliation. 20We are therefore Christ's ambassadors, as though God were making his appeal through us. We implore you on Christ's behalf: Be reconciled to God. 21God made him who had no sin to be sin[a] for us, so that in him we might become the righteousness of God.

6 As God's fellow workers we urge you not to receive God's grace in vain. 2For he says,

"In the time of my favor I heard you,
  and in the day of salvation I helped
    you."[a]

I tell you, now is the time of God's favor, now is the day of salvation.

Paul's Hardships

3We put no stumbling block in anyone's path, so that our ministry will not be discredited. 4Rather, as servants of God we commend ourselves in every way: in great endurance; in troubles, hardships and distresses; 5in beatings, imprisonments and riots; in hard work, sleepless nights and hunger; 6in purity, understanding, patience and kindness; in the Holy Spirit and in sincere love; 7in truthful speech and in the power of God; with weapons of righteousness in the right hand and in the left; 8through glory and dishonor, bad report

---

[k] Gk *according to the flesh* [l] Or *God was in Christ reconciling the world to himself* [m] Gk *As we work together*   [a]21 Or *be a sin offering* [a]2 Isaiah 49:8

NRSV

and good repute. We are treated as impostors, and yet are true; [9]as unknown, and yet are well known; as dying, and see—we are alive; as punished, and yet not killed; [10]as sorrowful, yet always rejoicing; as poor, yet making many rich; as having nothing, and yet possessing everything.

11 We have spoken frankly to you Corinthians; our heart is wide open to you. [12]There is no restriction in our affections, but only in yours. [13]In return—I speak as to children—open wide your hearts also.

The Temple of the Living God

14 Do not be mismatched with unbelievers. For what partnership is there between righteousness and lawlessness? Or what fellowship is there between light and darkness? [15]What agreement does Christ have with Beliar? Or what does a believer share with an unbeliever? [16]What agreement has the temple of God with idols? For we[n] are the temple of the living God; as God said,

"I will live in them and walk among
      them,
   and I will be their God,
   and they shall be my people.
[17] Therefore come out from them,
   and be separate from them, says the
      Lord,
   and touch nothing unclean;
      then I will welcome you,
[18] and I will be your father,
   and you shall be my sons and
      daughters,
   says the Lord Almighty."

7 Since we have these promises, beloved, let us cleanse ourselves from every defilement of body and of spirit, making holiness perfect in the fear of God.

Paul's Joy at the Church's Repentance

2 Make room in your hearts[o] for us; we have wronged no one, we have corrupted no one, we have taken advantage of no one. [3]I do not say this to condemn you, for I said before that you are in our hearts, to die together and to live together. [4]I often boast about you; I have great pride in you; I am filled with consolation; I am overjoyed in all our affliction.

5 For even when we came into Macedonia, our bodies had no rest, but we were afflicted in every way—disputes without

Greek

ὡς πλάνοι καὶ ἀληθεῖς, 9 ὡς ἀγνοούμενοι καὶ ἐπιγινωσκόμενοι, ὡς ἀποθνῄσκοντες καὶ ἰδοὺ ζῶμεν, ὡς παιδευόμενοι καὶ μὴ θανατούμενοι, 10 ὡς λυπούμενοι ἀεὶ δὲ χαίροντες, ὡς πτωχοὶ πολλοὺς δὲ πλουτίζοντες, ὡς μηδὲν ἔχοντες καὶ πάντα κατέχοντες.

11 Τὸ στόμα ἡμῶν ἀνέῳγεν πρὸς ὑμᾶς, Κορίνθιοι, ἡ καρδία ἡμῶν πεπλάτυνται· 12 οὐ στενοχωρεῖσθε ἐν ἡμῖν, στενοχωρεῖσθε δὲ ἐν τοῖς σπλάγχνοις ὑμῶν· 13 τὴν δὲ αὐτὴν ἀντιμισθίαν, ὡς τέκνοις λέγω, πλατύνθητε καὶ ὑμεῖς.

14 Μὴ γίνεσθε ἑτεροζυγοῦντες ἀπίστοις· τίς γὰρ μετοχὴ δικαιοσύνῃ καὶ ἀνομίᾳ ἢ τίς κοινωνία φωτὶ πρὸς σκότος; 15 τίς δὲ συμφώνησις Χριστοῦ πρὸς Βελιάρ, ἢ τίς μερὶς πιστῷ μετὰ ἀπίστου; 16 τίς δὲ συγκατάθεσις ναῷ θεοῦ μετὰ εἰδώλων; ἡμεῖς[a] γὰρ ναὸς θεοῦ ἐσμεν ζῶντος, καθὼς εἶπεν ὁ θεὸς ὅτι

Ἐνοικήσω ἐν αὐτοῖς καὶ ἐμπεριπατήσω
   καὶ ἔσομαι αὐτῶν θεὸς
   καὶ αὐτοὶ ἔσονταί μου λαός.
17 διὸ ἐξέλθατε ἐκ μέσου αὐτῶν
   καὶ ἀφορίσθητε, λέγει κύριος,
   καὶ ἀκαθάρτου μὴ ἅπτεσθε·
   κἀγὼ εἰσδέξομαι ὑμᾶς
18 καὶ ἔσομαι ὑμῖν εἰς πατέρα
   καὶ ὑμεῖς ἔσεσθέ μοι εἰς υἱοὺς
   καὶ θυγατέρας,
   λέγει κύριος παντοκράτωρ.

7 ταύτας οὖν ἔχοντες τὰς ἐπαγγελίας, ἀγαπητοί, καθαρίσωμεν ἑαυτοὺς ἀπὸ παντὸς μολυσμοῦ σαρκὸς καὶ πνεύματος, ἐπιτελοῦντες ἁγιωσύνην ἐν φόβῳ θεοῦ.

2 Χωρήσατε ἡμᾶς· οὐδένα ἠδικήσαμεν, οὐδένα ἐφθείραμεν, οὐδένα ἐπλεονεκτήσαμεν. 3 πρὸς κατάκρισιν οὐ λέγω· προείρηκα γὰρ ὅτι ἐν ταῖς καρδίαις ἡμῶν ἐστε εἰς τὸ συναποθανεῖν καὶ συζῆν. 4 πολλή μοι παρρησία πρὸς ὑμᾶς, πολλή μοι καύχησις ὑπὲρ ὑμῶν· πεπλήρωμαι τῇ παρακλήσει, ὑπερπερισσεύομαι τῇ χαρᾷ ἐπὶ πάσῃ τῇ θλίψει ἡμῶν.

5 Καὶ γὰρ ἐλθόντων ἡμῶν εἰς Μακεδονίαν οὐδεμίαν ἔσχηκεν ἄνεσιν ἡ σὰρξ ἡμῶν ἀλλ' ἐν παντὶ θλιβόμενοι·

NIV

and good report; genuine, yet regarded as impostors; [9]known, yet regarded as unknown; dying, and yet we live on; beaten, and yet not killed; [10]sorrowful, yet always rejoicing; poor, yet making many rich; having nothing, and yet possessing everything.

[11]We have spoken freely to you, Corinthians, and opened wide our hearts to you. [12]We are not withholding our affection from you, but you are withholding yours from us. [13]As a fair exchange—I speak as to my children—open wide your hearts also.

Do Not Be Yoked With Unbelievers

[14]Do not be yoked together with unbelievers. For what do righteousness and wickedness have in common? Or what fellowship can light have with darkness? [15]What harmony is there between Christ and Belial[b]? What does a believer have in common with an unbeliever? [16]What agreement is there between the temple of God and idols? For we are the temple of the living God. As God has said: "I will live with them and walk among them, and I will be their God, and they will be my people."[c]

[17]"Therefore come out from them
   and be separate,
                     says the Lord.
Touch no unclean thing,
   and I will receive you."[d]
[18]"I will be a Father to you,
   and you will be my sons and
      daughters,
                 says the Lord Almighty."[e]

7 Since we have these promises, dear friends, let us purify ourselves from everything that contaminates body and spirit, perfecting holiness out of reverence for God.

Paul's Joy

[2]Make room for us in your hearts. We have wronged no one, we have corrupted no one, we have exploited no one. [3]I do not say this to condemn you; I have said before that you have such a place in our hearts that we would live or die with you. [4]I have great confidence in you; I take great pride in you. I am greatly encouraged; in all our troubles my joy knows no bounds.

[5]For when we came into Macedonia, this body of ours had no rest, but we were harassed at every turn—conflicts on the

---

[n] Other ancient authorities read *you*   [o] Gk lacks *in your hearts*

[a]16 NRSV note n ὑμεῖς γὰρ ναὸς θεοῦ ἐστε

[b]15 Greek *Beliar*, a variant of *Belial*   [c]16 Lev. 26:12; Jer. 32:38; Ezek. 37:27   [d]17 Isaiah 52:11; Ezek. 20:34,41   [e]18 2 Samuel 7:14; 7:8

and fears within. 6But God, who consoles
the downcast, consoled us by the arrival of
Titus, 7and not only by his coming, but
also by the consolation with which he was
consoled about you, as he told us of your
longing, your mourning, your zeal for me,
so that I rejoiced still more. 8For even if I
made you sorry with my letter, I do not
regret it (though I did regret it, for I see
that I grieved you with that letter, though
only briefly). 9Now I rejoice, not because
you were grieved, but because your grief
led to repentance; for you felt a godly grief,
so that you were not harmed in any way
by us. 10For godly grief produces a repentance that leads to salvation and brings no
regret, but worldly grief produces death.
11For see what earnestness this godly grief
has produced in you, what eagerness to
clear yourselves, what indignation, what
alarm, what longing, what zeal, what punishment! At every point you have proved
yourselves guiltless in the matter. 12So although I wrote to you, it was not on account of the one who did the wrong, nor
on account of the one who was wronged,
but in order that your zeal for us might be
made known to you before God. 13In this
we find comfort.

In addition to our own consolation, we
rejoiced still more at the joy of Titus, because his mind has been set at rest by all of
you. 14For if I have been somewhat boastful about you to him, I was not disgraced;
but just as everything we said to you was
true, so our boasting to Titus has proved
true as well. 15And his heart goes out all
the more to you, as he remembers the obedience of all of you, and how you welcomed him with fear and trembling. 16I
rejoice, because I have complete confidence
in you.

Encouragement to Be Generous

8 We want you to know, brothers and
sisters,[p] about the grace of God that
has been granted to the churches of Macedonia; 2for during a severe ordeal of affliction, their abundant joy and their extreme
poverty have overflowed in a wealth of
generosity on their part. 3For, as I can testify, they voluntarily gave according to
their means, and even beyond their means,
4begging us earnestly for the privilege[q] of
sharing in this ministry to the saints—5and
this, not merely as we expected; they gave
themselves first to the Lord and, by the

[p] Gk *brothers* [q] Gk *grace*

ἔξωθεν μάχαι, ἔσωθεν φόβοι. **6** ἀλλ᾽ ὁ
παρακαλῶν τοὺς ταπεινοὺς παρεκάλεσεν ἡμᾶς ὁ θεὸς ἐν τῇ παρουσίᾳ
Τίτου, **7** οὐ μόνον δὲ ἐν τῇ παρουσίᾳ
αὐτοῦ ἀλλὰ καὶ ἐν τῇ παρακλήσει ᾗ
παρεκλήθη ἐφ᾽ ὑμῖν, ἀναγγέλλων ἡμῖν
τὴν ὑμῶν ἐπιπόθησιν, τὸν ὑμῶν ὀδυρμόν,
τὸν ὑμῶν ζῆλον ὑπὲρ ἐμοῦ ὥστε με
μᾶλλον χαρῆναι. **8** ὅτι εἰ καὶ ἐλύπησα
ὑμᾶς ἐν τῇ ἐπιστολῇ, οὐ μεταμέλομαι·
εἰ καὶ μετεμελόμην, βλέπω [γὰρ] ὅτι ἡ
ἐπιστολὴ ἐκείνη εἰ καὶ πρὸς ὥραν
ἐλύπησεν ὑμᾶς, **9** νῦν χαίρω, οὐχ ὅτι
ἐλυπήθητε ἀλλ᾽ ὅτι ἐλυπήθητε εἰς
μετάνοιαν· ἐλυπήθητε γὰρ κατὰ θεόν,
ἵνα ἐν μηδενὶ ζημιωθῆτε ἐξ ἡμῶν. **10** ἡ
γὰρ κατὰ θεὸν λύπη μετάνοιαν εἰς
σωτηρίαν ἀμεταμέλητον ἐργάζεται· ἡ
δὲ τοῦ κόσμου λύπη θάνατον κατεργάζεται. **11** ἰδοὺ γὰρ αὐτὸ τοῦτο τὸ κατὰ
θεὸν λυπηθῆναι πόσην κατειργάσατο
ὑμῖν σπουδήν, ἀλλὰ ἀπολογίαν, ἀλλὰ
ἀγανάκτησιν, ἀλλὰ φόβον, ἀλλὰ ἐπιπόθησιν, ἀλλὰ ζῆλον, ἀλλὰ ἐκδίκησιν. ἐν
παντὶ συνεστήσατε ἑαυτοὺς ἁγνοὺς
εἶναι τῷ πράγματι. **12** ἄρα εἰ καὶ
ἔγραψα ὑμῖν, οὐχ ἕνεκεν τοῦ ἀδικήσαν-
τος οὐδὲ ἕνεκεν τοῦ ἀδικηθέντος ἀλλ᾽
ἕνεκεν τοῦ φανερωθῆναι τὴν σπουδὴν
ὑμῶν τὴν ὑπὲρ ἡμῶν πρὸς ὑμᾶς ἐνώπιον
τοῦ θεοῦ. **13** διὰ τοῦτο παρακεκλήμεθα.

Ἐπὶ δὲ τῇ παρακλήσει ἡμῶν περισσοτέρως μᾶλλον ἐχάρημεν ἐπὶ τῇ χαρᾷ
Τίτου, ὅτι ἀναπέπαυται τὸ πνεῦμα
αὐτοῦ ἀπὸ πάντων ὑμῶν· **14** ὅτι εἴ τι
αὐτῷ ὑπὲρ ὑμῶν κεκαύχημαι, οὐ κατῃ-
σχύνθην, ἀλλ᾽ ὡς πάντα ἐν ἀληθείᾳ
ἐλαλήσαμεν ὑμῖν, οὕτως καὶ ἡ καύχησις
ἡμῶν ἡ ἐπὶ Τίτου ἀλήθεια ἐγενήθη.
15 καὶ τὰ σπλάγχνα αὐτοῦ περισσοτέρως εἰς ὑμᾶς ἐστιν ἀναμιμνῃσκομένου
τὴν πάντων ὑμῶν ὑπακοήν, ὡς μετὰ
φόβου καὶ τρόμου ἐδέξασθε αὐτόν.
16 χαίρω ὅτι ἐν παντὶ θαρρῶ ἐν ὑμῖν.

8 Γνωρίζομεν δὲ ὑμῖν, ἀδελφοί, τὴν
χάριν τοῦ θεοῦ τὴν δεδομένην ἐν
ταῖς ἐκκλησίαις τῆς Μακεδονίας, **2** ὅτι
ἐν πολλῇ δοκιμῇ θλίψεως ἡ περισσεία
τῆς χαρᾶς αὐτῶν καὶ ἡ κατὰ βάθους
πτωχεία αὐτῶν ἐπερίσσευσεν εἰς τὸ
πλοῦτος τῆς ἁπλότητος αὐτῶν· **3** ὅτι
κατὰ δύναμιν, μαρτυρῶ, καὶ παρὰ
δύναμιν, αὐθαίρετοι **4** μετὰ πολλῆς
παρακλήσεως δεόμενοι ἡμῶν τὴν χάριν
καὶ τὴν κοινωνίαν τῆς διακονίας τῆς
εἰς τοὺς ἁγίους, **5** καὶ οὐ καθὼς
ἠλπίσαμεν ἀλλ᾽ ἑαυτοὺς ἔδωκαν πρῶτον

outside, fears within. 6But God, who comforts the downcast, comforted us by the
coming of Titus, 7and not only by his coming but also by the comfort you had given
him. He told us about your longing for
me, your deep sorrow, your ardent concern for me, so that my joy was greater
than ever.

8Even if I caused you sorrow by my letter, I do not regret it. Though I did regret
it—I see that my letter hurt you, but only
for a little while— 9yet now I am happy,
not because you were made sorry, but because your sorrow led you to repentance.
For you became sorrowful as God intended
and so were not harmed in any way by us.
10Godly sorrow brings repentance that
leads to salvation and leaves no regret, but
worldly sorrow brings death. 11See what
this godly sorrow has produced in you:
what earnestness, what eagerness to clear
yourselves, what indignation, what alarm,
what longing, what concern, what readiness to see justice done. At every point
you have proved yourselves to be innocent in this matter. 12So even though I wrote
to you, it was not on account of the one
who did the wrong or of the injured party,
but rather that before God you could see
for yourselves how devoted to us you are.
13By all this we are encouraged.

In addition to our own encouragement,
we were especially delighted to see how
happy Titus was, because his spirit has
been refreshed by all of you. 14I had boasted
to him about you, and you have not em-
barrassed me. But just as everything we
said to you was true, so our boasting about
you to Titus has proved to be true as well.
15And his affection for you is all the greater
when he remembers that you were all obedient, receiving him with fear and trembling. 16I am glad I can have complete confidence in you.

Generosity Encouraged

8 And now, brothers, we want you to
know about the grace that God has
given the Macedonian churches. 2Out of
the most severe trial, their overflowing joy
and their extreme poverty welled up in
rich generosity. 3For I testify that they gave
as much as they were able, and even beyond their ability. Entirely on their own,
4they urgently pleaded with us for the
privilege of sharing in this service to the
saints. 5And they did not do as we expected, but they gave themselves first to

will of God, to us, [6]so that we might urge Titus that, as he had already made a beginning, so he should also complete this generous undertaking[r] among you. [7]Now as you excel in everything—in faith, in speech, in knowledge, in utmost eagerness, and in our love for you[s]—so we want you to excel also in this generous undertaking.[r]

8 I do not say this as a command, but I am testing the genuineness of your love against the earnestness of others. [9]For you know the generous act[t] of our Lord Jesus Christ, that though he was rich, yet for your sakes he became poor, so that by his poverty you might become rich. [10]And in this matter I am giving my advice: it is appropriate for you who began last year not only to do something but even to desire to do something— [11]now finish doing it, so that your eagerness may be matched by completing it according to your means. [12]For if the eagerness is there, the gift is acceptable according to what one has— not according to what one does not have. [13]I do not mean that there should be relief for others and pressure on you, but it is a question of a fair balance between [14]your present abundance and their need, so that their abundance may be for your need, in order that there may be a fair balance. [15]As it is written,

"The one who had much did not have
    too much,
and the one who had little did not
    have too little."

Commendation of Titus

16 But thanks be to God who put in the heart of Titus the same eagerness for you that I myself have. [17]For he not only accepted our appeal, but since he is more eager than ever, he is going to you of his own accord. [18]With him we are sending the brother who is famous among all the churches for his proclaiming the good news;[u] [19]and not only that, but he has also been appointed by the churches to travel with us while we are administering this generous undertaking[r] for the glory of the Lord himself[v] and to show our goodwill. [20]We intend that no one should blame us about this generous gift that we are administering, [21]for we intend to do what is right not only in the Lord's sight but also in the sight of others. [22]And with them we are sending our brother whom we have

τῷ κυρίῳ καὶ ἡμῖν διὰ θελήματος θεοῦ **6** εἰς τὸ παρακαλέσαι ἡμᾶς Τίτον, ἵνα καθὼς προενήρξατο οὕτως καὶ ἐπιτελέσῃ εἰς ὑμᾶς καὶ τὴν χάριν ταύτην. **7** ἀλλ᾽ ὥσπερ ἐν παντὶ περισσεύετε, πίστει καὶ λόγῳ καὶ γνώσει καὶ πάσῃ σπουδῇ καὶ τῇ ἐξ ἡμῶν ἐν ὑμῖν[a] ἀγάπῃ, ἵνα καὶ ἐν ταύτῃ τῇ χάριτι περισσεύητε.

8 Οὐ κατ᾽ ἐπιταγὴν λέγω ἀλλὰ διὰ τῆς ἑτέρων σπουδῆς καὶ τὸ τῆς ὑμετέρας ἀγάπης γνήσιον δοκιμάζων· **9** γινώσκετε γὰρ τὴν χάριν τοῦ κυρίου ἡμῶν Ἰησοῦ Χριστοῦ, ὅτι δι᾽ ὑμᾶς ἐπτώχευσεν πλούσιος ὤν, ἵνα ὑμεῖς τῇ ἐκείνου πτωχείᾳ πλουτήσητε. **10** καὶ γνώμην ἐν τούτῳ δίδωμι· τοῦτο γὰρ ὑμῖν συμφέρει, οἵτινες οὐ μόνον τὸ ποιῆσαι ἀλλὰ καὶ τὸ θέλειν προενήρξασθε ἀπὸ πέρυσι· **11** νυνὶ δὲ καὶ τὸ ποιῆσαι ἐπιτελέσατε, ὅπως καθάπερ ἡ προθυμία τοῦ θέλειν, οὕτως καὶ τὸ ἐπιτελέσαι ἐκ τοῦ ἔχειν. **12** εἰ γὰρ ἡ προθυμία πρόκειται, καθὸ ἐὰν ἔχῃ εὐπρόσδεκτος, οὐ καθὸ οὐκ ἔχει. **13** οὐ γὰρ ἵνα ἄλλοις ἄνεσις, ὑμῖν θλῖψις, ἀλλ᾽ ἐξ ἰσότητος· **14** ἐν τῷ νῦν καιρῷ τὸ ὑμῶν περίσσευμα εἰς τὸ ἐκείνων ὑστέρημα, ἵνα καὶ τὸ ἐκείνων περίσσευμα γένηται εἰς τὸ ὑμῶν ὑστέρημα, ὅπως γένηται ἰσότης, **15** καθὼς γέγραπται,

Ὁ τὸ πολὺ οὐκ ἐπλεόνασεν,
    καὶ ὁ τὸ ὀλίγον οὐκ ἠλαττόνησεν.

16 Χάρις δὲ τῷ θεῷ τῷ δόντι τὴν αὐτὴν σπουδὴν ὑπὲρ ὑμῶν ἐν τῇ καρδίᾳ Τίτου, **17** ὅτι τὴν μὲν παράκλησιν ἐδέξατο, σπουδαιότερος δὲ ὑπάρχων αὐθαίρετος ἐξῆλθεν πρὸς ὑμᾶς. **18** συνεπέμψαμεν δὲ μετ᾽ αὐτοῦ τὸν ἀδελφὸν οὗ ὁ ἔπαινος ἐν τῷ εὐαγγελίῳ διὰ πασῶν τῶν ἐκκλησιῶν, **19** οὐ μόνον δέ, ἀλλὰ καὶ χειροτονηθεὶς ὑπὸ τῶν ἐκκλησιῶν συνέκδημος ἡμῶν σὺν τῇ χάριτι ταύτῃ τῇ διακονουμένῃ ὑφ᾽ ἡμῶν πρὸς τὴν [αὐτοῦ] τοῦ κυρίου δόξαν καὶ προθυμίαν ἡμῶν, **20** στελλόμενοι τοῦτο, μή τις ἡμᾶς μωμήσηται ἐν τῇ ἁδρότητι ταύτῃ τῇ διακονουμένῃ ὑφ᾽ ἡμῶν· **21** προνοοῦμεν γὰρ καλὰ οὐ μόνον ἐνώπιον κυρίου ἀλλὰ καὶ ἐνώπιον ἀνθρώπων. **22** συνεπέμψαμεν δὲ αὐτοῖς τὸν ἀδελφὸν ἡμῶν ὃν ἐδοκιμάσαμεν ἐν

the Lord and then to us in keeping with God's will. [6]So we urged Titus, since he had earlier made a beginning, to bring also to completion this act of grace on your part. [7]But just as you excel in everything— in faith, in speech, in knowledge, in complete earnestness and in your love for us[a]— see that you also excel in this grace of giving.

[8]I am not commanding you, but I want to test the sincerity of your love by comparing it with the earnestness of others. [9]For you know the grace of our Lord Jesus Christ, that though he was rich, yet for your sakes he became poor, so that you through his poverty might become rich.

[10]And here is my advice about what is best for you in this matter: Last year you were the first not only to give but also to have the desire to do so. [11]Now finish the work, so that your eager willingness to do it may be matched by your completion of it, according to your means. [12]For if the willingness is there, the gift is acceptable according to what one has, not according to what he does not have.

[13]Our desire is not that others might be relieved while you are hard pressed, but that there might be equality. [14]At the present time your plenty will supply what they need, so that in turn their plenty will supply what you need. Then there will be equality, [15]as it is written: "He who gathered much did not have too much, and he who gathered little did not have too little."[b]

Titus Sent to Corinth

[16]I thank God, who put into the heart of Titus the same concern I have for you. [17]For Titus not only welcomed our appeal, but he is coming to you with much enthusiasm and on his own initiative. [18]And we are sending along with him the brother who is praised by all the churches for his service to the gospel. [19]What is more, he was chosen by the churches to accompany us as we carry the offering, which we administer in order to honor the Lord himself and to show our eagerness to help. [20]We want to avoid any criticism of the way we administer this liberal gift. [21]For we are taking pains to do what is right, not only in the eyes of the Lord but also in the eyes of men.

[22]In addition, we are sending with them our brother who has often proved to us in

[r] Gk *this grace*   [s] Other ancient authorities read *your love for us*   [t] Gk *the grace*   [u] Or *the gospel*   [v] Other ancient authorities lack *himself*

[a]7 NIV text and NRSV note s ἐξ ὑμῶν ἐν ἡμῖν; NIV note and NRSV text as UBS

[a]7 Some manuscripts *in our love for you*   [b]15 Exodus 16:18

NRSV

often tested and found eager in many matters, but who is now more eager than ever because of his great confidence in you. 23As for Titus, he is my partner and co-worker in your service; as for our brothers, they are messengers[x] of the churches, the glory of Christ. 24Therefore openly before the churches, show them the proof of your love and of our reason for boasting about you.

The Collection for Christians at Jerusalem

9 Now it is not necessary for me to write you about the ministry to the saints, 2for I know your eagerness, which is the subject of my boasting about you to the people of Macedonia, saying that Achaia has been ready since last year; and your zeal has stirred up most of them. 3But I am sending the brothers in order that our boasting about you may not prove to have been empty in this case, so that you may be ready, as I said you would be; 4otherwise, if some Macedonians come with me and find that you are not ready, we would be humiliated—to say nothing of you—in this undertaking.[y] 5So I thought it necessary to urge the brothers to go on ahead to you, and arrange in advance for this bountiful gift that you have promised, so that it may be ready as a voluntary gift and not as an extortion.

6 The point is this: the one who sows sparingly will also reap sparingly, and the one who sows bountifully will also reap bountifully. 7Each of you must give as you have made up your mind, not reluctantly or under compulsion, for God loves a cheerful giver. 8And God is able to provide you with every blessing in abundance, so that by always having enough of everything, you may share abundantly in every good work. 9As it is written,

"He scatters abroad, he gives to the
　　poor;
　　his righteousness[z] endures forever."

10He who supplies seed to the sower and bread for food will supply and multiply your seed for sowing and increase the harvest of your righteousness.[z] 11You will be enriched in every way for your great generosity, which will produce thanksgiving to God through us; 12for the rendering of this ministry not only supplies the needs of the saints but also overflows with many thanksgivings to God. 13Through the test-

Greek

πολλοῖς πολλάκις σπουδαῖον ὄντα, νυνὶ δὲ πολὺ σπουδαιότερον πεποιθήσει πολλῇ τῇ εἰς ὑμᾶς. 23 εἴτε ὑπὲρ Τίτου, κοινωνὸς ἐμὸς καὶ εἰς ὑμᾶς συνεργός· εἴτε ἀδελφοὶ ἡμῶν, ἀπόστολοι ἐκκλησιῶν, δόξα Χριστοῦ. 24 τὴν οὖν ἔνδειξιν τῆς ἀγάπης ὑμῶν καὶ ἡμῶν καυχήσεως ὑπὲρ ὑμῶν εἰς αὐτοὺς ἐνδεικνύμενοι εἰς πρόσωπον τῶν ἐκκλησιῶν.

9 Περὶ μὲν γὰρ τῆς διακονίας τῆς εἰς τοὺς ἁγίους περισσόν μοί ἐστιν τὸ γράφειν ὑμῖν· 2 οἶδα γὰρ τὴν προθυμίαν ὑμῶν ἣν ὑπὲρ ὑμῶν καυχῶμαι Μακεδόσιν, ὅτι Ἀχαΐα παρεσκεύασται ἀπὸ πέρυσι, καὶ τὸ ὑμῶν ζῆλος ἠρέθισεν τοὺς πλείονας. 3 ἔπεμψα δὲ τοὺς ἀδελφούς, ἵνα μὴ τὸ καύχημα ἡμῶν τὸ ὑπὲρ ὑμῶν κενωθῇ ἐν τῷ μέρει τούτῳ, ἵνα καθὼς ἔλεγον παρεσκευασμένοι ἦτε, 4 μή πως ἐὰν ἔλθωσιν σὺν ἐμοὶ Μακεδόνες καὶ εὕρωσιν ὑμᾶς ἀπαρασκευάστους καταισχυνθῶμεν ἡμεῖς, ἵνα μὴ λέγω ὑμεῖς, ἐν τῇ ὑποστάσει ταύτῃ. 5 ἀναγκαῖον οὖν ἡγησάμην παρακαλέσαι τοὺς ἀδελφούς, ἵνα προέλθωσιν εἰς ὑμᾶς καὶ προκαταρτίσωσιν τὴν προεπηγγελμένην εὐλογίαν ὑμῶν, ταύτην ἑτοίμην εἶναι οὕτως ὡς εὐλογίαν καὶ μὴ ὡς πλεονεξίαν.

6 Τοῦτο δέ, ὁ σπείρων φειδομένως φειδομένως καὶ θερίσει, καὶ ὁ σπείρων ἐπ᾽ εὐλογίαις ἐπ᾽ εὐλογίαις καὶ θερίσει. 7 ἕκαστος καθὼς προῄρηται τῇ καρδίᾳ, μὴ ἐκ λύπης ἢ ἐξ ἀνάγκης· ἱλαρὸν γὰρ δότην ἀγαπᾷ ὁ θεός. 8 δυνατεῖ δὲ ὁ θεὸς πᾶσαν χάριν περισσεῦσαι εἰς ὑμᾶς, ἵνα ἐν παντὶ πάντοτε πᾶσαν αὐτάρκειαν ἔχοντες περισσεύητε εἰς πᾶν ἔργον ἀγαθόν, 9 καθὼς γέγραπται,

Ἐσκόρπισεν, ἔδωκεν τοῖς πένησιν,
ἡ δικαιοσύνη αὐτοῦ μένει εἰς
τὸν αἰῶνα.

10 ὁ δὲ ἐπιχορηγῶν σπόρον τῷ σπείροντι καὶ ἄρτον εἰς βρῶσιν χορηγήσει καὶ πληθυνεῖ τὸν σπόρον ὑμῶν καὶ αὐξήσει τὰ γενήματα τῆς δικαιοσύνης ὑμῶν· 11 ἐν παντὶ πλουτιζόμενοι εἰς πᾶσαν ἁπλότητα, ἥτις κατεργάζεται δι᾽ ἡμῶν εὐχαριστίαν τῷ θεῷ· 12 ὅτι ἡ διακονία τῆς λειτουργίας ταύτης οὐ μόνον ἐστὶν προσαναπληροῦσα τὰ ὑστερήματα τῶν ἁγίων, ἀλλὰ καὶ περισσεύουσα διὰ πολλῶν εὐχαριστιῶν τῷ θεῷ· 13 διὰ τῆς δοκιμῆς τῆς διακονίας

NIV

many ways that he is zealous, and now even more so because of his great confidence in you. 23As for Titus, he is my partner and fellow worker among you; as for our brothers, they are representatives of the churches and an honor to Christ. 24Therefore show these men the proof of your love and the reason for our pride in you, so that the churches can see it.

9 There is no need for me to write to you about this service to the saints. 2For I know your eagerness to help, and I have been boasting about it to the Macedonians, telling them that since last year you in Achaia were ready to give; and your enthusiasm has stirred most of them to action. 3But I am sending the brothers in order that our boasting about you in this matter should not prove hollow, but that you may be ready, as I said you would be. 4For if any Macedonians come with me and find you unprepared, we—not to say anything about you—would be ashamed of having been so confident. 5So I thought it necessary to urge the brothers to visit you in advance and finish the arrangements for the generous gift you had promised. Then it will be ready as a generous gift, not as one grudgingly given.

Sowing Generously

6Remember this: Whoever sows sparingly will also reap sparingly, and whoever sows generously will also reap generously. 7Each man should give what he has decided in his heart to give, not reluctantly or under compulsion, for God loves a cheerful giver. 8And God is able to make all grace abound to you, so that in all things at all times, having all that you need, you will abound in every good work. 9As it is written:

"He has scattered abroad his gifts to the
　　poor;
　　his righteousness endures forever."[a]

10Now he who supplies seed to the sower and bread for food will also supply and increase your store of seed and will enlarge the harvest of your righteousness. 11You will be made rich in every way so that you can be generous on every occasion, and through us your generosity will result in thanksgiving to God.

12This service that you perform is not only supplying the needs of God's people but is also overflowing in many expressions of thanks to God. 13Because of the

---

ing of this ministry you glorify God by your obedience to the confession of the gospel of Christ and by the generosity of your sharing with them and with all others, [14]while they long for you and pray for you because of the surpassing grace of God that he has given you. [15]Thanks be to God for his indescribable gift!

Paul Defends His Ministry

10 I myself, Paul, appeal to you by the meekness and gentleness of Christ—I who am humble when face to face with you, but bold toward you when I am away!— [2]I ask that when I am present I need not show boldness by daring to oppose those who think we are acting according to human standards.[a] [3]Indeed, we live as human beings,[b] but we do not wage war according to human standards;[a] [4]for the weapons of our warfare are not merely human,[c] but they have divine power to destroy strongholds. We destroy arguments [5]and every proud obstacle raised up against the knowledge of God, and we take every thought captive to obey Christ. [6]We are ready to punish every disobedience when your obedience is complete.

7 Look at what is before your eyes. If you are confident that you belong to Christ, remind yourself of this, that just as you belong to Christ, so also do we. [8]Now, even if I boast a little too much of our authority, which the Lord gave for building you up and not for tearing you down, I will not be ashamed of it. [9]I do not want to seem as though I am trying to frighten you with my letters. [10]For they say, "His letters are weighty and strong, but his bodily presence is weak, and his speech contemptible." [11]Let such people understand that what we say by letter when absent, we will also do when present.

12 We do not dare to classify or compare ourselves with some of those who commend themselves. But when they measure themselves by one another, and compare themselves with one another, they do not show good sense. [13]We, however, will not boast beyond limits, but will keep within the field that God has assigned to us, to reach out even as far as you. [14]For we were not overstepping our limits when we reached you; we were the first to come all

ταύτης δοξάζοντες τὸν θεὸν ἐπὶ τῇ ὑποταγῇ τῆς ὁμολογίας ὑμῶν εἰς τὸ εὐαγγέλιον τοῦ Χριστοῦ καὶ ἁπλότητι τῆς κοινωνίας εἰς αὐτοὺς καὶ εἰς πάντας, **14** καὶ αὐτῶν δεήσει ὑπὲρ ὑμῶν ἐπιποθούντων ὑμᾶς διὰ τὴν ὑπερβάλλουσαν χάριν τοῦ θεοῦ ἐφ' ὑμῖν. **15** χάρις τῷ θεῷ ἐπὶ τῇ ἀνεκδιηγήτῳ αὐτοῦ δωρεᾷ.

10 Αὐτὸς δὲ ἐγὼ Παῦλος παρακαλῶ ὑμᾶς διὰ τῆς πραΰτητος καὶ ἐπιεικείας τοῦ Χριστοῦ, ὃς κατὰ πρόσωπον μὲν ταπεινὸς ἐν ὑμῖν, ἀπὼν δὲ θαρρῶ εἰς ὑμᾶς· **2** δέομαι δὲ τὸ μὴ παρὼν θαρρῆσαι τῇ πεποιθήσει ᾗ λογίζομαι τολμῆσαι ἐπί τινας τοὺς λογιζομένους ἡμᾶς ὡς κατὰ σάρκα περιπατοῦντας. **3** ἐν σαρκὶ γὰρ περιπατοῦντες οὐ κατὰ σάρκα στρατευόμεθα, **4** τὰ γὰρ ὅπλα τῆς στρατείας ἡμῶν οὐ σαρκικὰ ἀλλὰ δυνατὰ τῷ θεῷ πρὸς καθαίρεσιν ὀχυρωμάτων,[a] λογισμοὺς καθαιροῦντες **5** καὶ πᾶν ὕψωμα ἐπαιρόμενον κατὰ τῆς γνώσεως τοῦ θεοῦ, καὶ αἰχμαλωτίζοντες πᾶν νόημα εἰς τὴν ὑπακοὴν τοῦ Χριστοῦ, **6** καὶ ἐν ἑτοίμῳ ἔχοντες ἐκδικῆσαι πᾶσαν παρακοήν, ὅταν πληρωθῇ ὑμῶν ἡ ὑπακοή.

7 Τὰ κατὰ πρόσωπον βλέπετε. εἴ τις πέποιθεν ἑαυτῷ Χριστοῦ εἶναι, τοῦτο λογιζέσθω πάλιν ἐφ' ἑαυτοῦ, ὅτι καθὼς αὐτὸς Χριστοῦ, οὕτως καὶ ἡμεῖς. **8** ἐάν [τε] γὰρ περισσότερόν τι καυχήσωμαι περὶ τῆς ἐξουσίας ἡμῶν ἧς ἔδωκεν ὁ κύριος εἰς οἰκοδομὴν καὶ οὐκ εἰς καθαίρεσιν ὑμῶν, οὐκ αἰσχυνθήσομαι. **9** ἵνα μὴ δόξω ὡς ἂν ἐκφοβεῖν ὑμᾶς διὰ τῶν ἐπιστολῶν· **10** ὅτι, Αἱ ἐπιστολαὶ μέν, φησίν, βαρεῖαι καὶ ἰσχυραί, ἡ δὲ παρουσία τοῦ σώματος ἀσθενὴς καὶ ὁ λόγος ἐξουθενημένος. **11** τοῦτο λογιζέσθω ὁ τοιοῦτος, ὅτι οἷοί ἐσμεν τῷ λόγῳ δι' ἐπιστολῶν ἀπόντες, τοιοῦτοι καὶ παρόντες τῷ ἔργῳ.

12 Οὐ γὰρ τολμῶμεν ἐγκρῖναι ἢ συγκρῖναι ἑαυτούς τισιν τῶν ἑαυτοὺς συνιστανόντων, ἀλλὰ αὐτοὶ ἐν ἑαυτοῖς ἑαυτοὺς μετροῦντες καὶ συγκρίνοντες ἑαυτοὺς ἑαυτοῖς οὐ συνιᾶσιν. **13** ἡμεῖς δὲ οὐκ εἰς τὰ ἄμετρα καυχησόμεθα ἀλλὰ κατὰ τὸ μέτρον τοῦ κανόνος οὗ ἐμέρισεν ἡμῖν ὁ θεὸς μέτρου, ἐφικέσθαι ἄχρι καὶ ὑμῶν. **14** οὐ γὰρ ὡς μὴ ἐφικνούμενοι εἰς ὑμᾶς ὑπερεκτείνομεν ἑαυτούς, ἄχρι γὰρ καὶ ὑμῶν ἐφθάσαμεν

service by which you have proved yourselves, men will praise God for the obedience that accompanies your confession of the gospel of Christ, and for your generosity in sharing with them and with everyone else. [14]And in their prayers for you their hearts will go out to you, because of the surpassing grace God has given you. [15]Thanks be to God for his indescribable gift!

Paul's Defense of His Ministry

10 By the meekness and gentleness of Christ, I appeal to you—I, Paul, who am "timid" when face to face with you, but "bold" when away! [2]I beg you that when I come I may not have to be as bold as I expect to be toward some people who think that we live by the standards of this world. [3]For though we live in the world, we do not wage war as the world does. [4]The weapons we fight with are not the weapons of the world. On the contrary, they have divine power to demolish strongholds. [5]We demolish arguments and every pretension that sets itself up against the knowledge of God, and we take captive every thought to make it obedient to Christ. [6]And we will be ready to punish every act of disobedience, once your obedience is complete.

[7]You are looking only on the surface of things.[a] If anyone is confident that he belongs to Christ, he should consider again that we belong to Christ just as much as he. [8]For even if I boast somewhat freely about the authority the Lord gave us for building you up rather than pulling you down, I will not be ashamed of it. [9]I do not want to seem to be trying to frighten you with my letters. [10]For some say, "His letters are weighty and forceful, but in person he is unimpressive and his speaking amounts to nothing." [11]Such people should realize that what we are in our letters when we are absent, we will be in our actions when we are present.

[12]We do not dare to classify or compare ourselves with some who commend themselves. When they measure themselves by themselves and compare themselves with themselves, they are not wise. [13]We, however, will not boast beyond proper limits, but will confine our boasting to the field God has assigned to us, a field that reaches even to you. [14]We are not going too far in our boasting, as would be the case if we had not come to you, for we did get as far

---

[a] Gk *according to the flesh* [b] Gk *in the flesh* [c] Gk *fleshly*

[a]4 NIV begins verse 5 after ὀχυρωμάτων.

[a]7 Or *Look at the obvious facts*

the way to you with the good news[d] of Christ. [15]We do not boast beyond limits, that is, in the labors of others; but our hope is that, as your faith increases, our sphere of action among you may be greatly enlarged, [16]so that we may proclaim the good news[d] in lands beyond you, without boasting of work already done in someone else's sphere of action. [17]"Let the one who boasts, boast in the Lord." [18]For it is not those who commend themselves that are approved, but those whom the Lord commends.

Paul and the False Apostles

11 I wish you would bear with me in a little foolishness. Do bear with me! [2]I feel a divine jealousy for you, for I promised you in marriage to one husband, to present you as a chaste virgin to Christ. [3]But I am afraid that as the serpent deceived Eve by its cunning, your thoughts will be led astray from a sincere and pure[e] devotion to Christ. [4]For if someone comes and proclaims another Jesus than the one we proclaimed, or if you receive a different spirit from the one you received, or a different gospel from the one you accepted, you submit to it readily enough. [5]I think that I am not in the least inferior to these super-apostles. [6]I may be untrained in speech, but not in knowledge; certainly in every way and in all things we have made this evident to you.

7 Did I commit a sin by humbling myself so that you might be exalted, because I proclaimed God's good news[f] to you free of charge? [8]I robbed other churches by accepting support from them in order to serve you. [9]And when I was with you and was in need, I did not burden anyone, for my needs were supplied by the friends[g] who came from Macedonia. So I refrained and will continue to refrain from burdening you in any way. [10]As the truth of Christ is in me, this boast of mine will not be silenced in the regions of Achaia. [11]And why? Because I do not love you? God knows I do!

12 And what I do I will also continue to do, in order to deny an opportunity to those who want an opportunity to be recognized as our equals in what they boast

ἐν τῷ εὐαγγελίῳ τοῦ Χριστοῦ, **15** οὐκ εἰς τὰ ἄμετρα καυχώμενοι ἐν ἀλλοτρίοις κόποις, ἐλπίδα δὲ ἔχοντες αὐξανομένης τῆς πίστεως ὑμῶν ἐν ὑμῖν μεγαλυνθῆναι κατὰ τὸν κανόνα ἡμῶν εἰς περισσείαν **16** εἰς τὰ ὑπερέκεινα ὑμῶν εὐαγγελί- σασθαι, οὐκ ἐν ἀλλοτρίῳ κανόνι εἰς τὰ ἕτοιμα καυχήσασθαι. **17** Ὁ δὲ **καυχώ- μενος ἐν κυρίῳ καυχάσθω** · **18** οὐ γὰρ ὁ ἑαυτὸν συνιστάνων, ἐκεῖνός ἐστιν δόκιμος, ἀλλὰ ὃν ὁ κύριος συνίστησιν.

11 Ὄφελον ἀνείχεσθέ μου μικρόν τι ἀφροσύνης· ἀλλὰ καὶ ἀνέχεσ- θέ μου. **2** ζηλῶ γὰρ ὑμᾶς θεοῦ ζήλῳ, ἡρμοσάμην γὰρ ὑμᾶς ἑνὶ ἀνδρὶ παρθένον ἁγνὴν παραστῆσαι τῷ Χριστῷ· **3** φοβοῦ- μαι δὲ μή πως, ὡς ὁ ὄφις ἐξηπάτησεν Εὕαν ἐν τῇ πανουργίᾳ αὐτοῦ, φθαρῇ τὰ νοήματα ὑμῶν ἀπὸ τῆς ἁπλότητος [καὶ τῆς ἁγνότητος] τῆς εἰς τὸν Χριστόν. **4** εἰ μὲν γὰρ ὁ ἐρχόμενος ἄλλον Ἰησοῦν κηρύσσει ὃν οὐκ ἐκηρύξα- μεν, ἢ πνεῦμα ἕτερον λαμβάνετε ὃ οὐκ ἐλάβετε, ἢ εὐαγγέλιον ἕτερον ὃ οὐκ ἐδέξασθε, καλῶς ἀνέχεσθε. **5** λογίζομαι γὰρ μηδὲν ὑστερηκέναι τῶν ὑπερλίαν ἀποστόλων. **6** εἰ δὲ καὶ ἰδιώτης τῷ λόγῳ, ἀλλ᾽ οὐ τῇ γνώσει, ἀλλ᾽ ἐν παντὶ φανερώσαντες ἐν πᾶσιν εἰς ὑμᾶς.

7 Ἢ ἁμαρτίαν ἐποίησα ἐμαυτὸν ταπεινῶν ἵνα ὑμεῖς ὑψωθῆτε, ὅτι δωρεὰν τὸ τοῦ θεοῦ εὐαγγέλιον εὐηγγελισάμην ὑμῖν; **8** ἄλλας ἐκκλησίας ἐσύλησα λαβὼν ὀψώνιον πρὸς τὴν ὑμῶν διακονίαν, **9** καὶ παρὼν πρὸς ὑμᾶς καὶ ὑστερηθεὶς οὐ κατενάρκησα οὐθενός· τὸ γὰρ ὑστέρημά μου προσανεπλήρωσαν οἱ ἀδελφοὶ ἐλθόντες ἀπὸ Μακεδονίας, καὶ ἐν παντὶ ἀβαρῆ ἐμαυτὸν ὑμῖν ἐτήρησα καὶ τηρήσω. **10** ἔστιν ἀλήθεια Χριστοῦ ἐν ἐμοὶ ὅτι ἡ καύχησις αὕτη οὐ φραγήσεται εἰς ἐμὲ ἐν τοῖς κλίμασιν τῆς Ἀχαΐας· **11** διὰ τί; ὅτι οὐκ ἀγαπῶ ὑμᾶς; ὁ θεὸς οἶδεν.

12 Ὃ δὲ ποιῶ, καὶ ποιήσω, ἵνα ἐκκόψω τὴν ἀφορμὴν τῶν θελόντων ἀφορμήν, ἵνα ἐν ᾧ καυχῶνται εὑρεθῶσιν καθὼς

as you with the gospel of Christ. [15]Neither do we go beyond our limits by boasting of work done by others.[b] Our hope is that, as your faith continues to grow, our area of activity among you will greatly expand, [16]so that we can preach the gospel in the regions beyond you. For we do not want to boast about work already done in another man's territory. [17]But, "Let him who boasts boast in the Lord."[c] [18]For it is not the one who commends himself who is approved, but the one whom the Lord commends.

Paul and the False Apostles

11 I hope you will put up with a little of my foolishness; but you are already doing that. [2]I am jealous for you with a godly jealousy. I promised you to one husband, to Christ, so that I might present you as a pure virgin to him. [3]But I am afraid that just as Eve was deceived by the serpent's cunning, your minds may somehow be led astray from your sincere and pure devotion to Christ. [4]For if someone comes to you and preaches a Jesus other than the Jesus we preached, or if you receive a different spirit from the one you received, or a different gospel from the one you accepted, you put up with it easily enough. [5]But I do not think I am in the least inferior to those "super-apostles." [6]I may not be a trained speaker, but I do have knowledge. We have made this perfectly clear to you in every way.

[7]Was it a sin for me to lower myself in order to elevate you by preaching the gospel of God to you free of charge? [8]I robbed other churches by receiving support from them so as to serve you. [9]And when I was with you and needed something, I was not a burden to anyone, for the brothers who came from Macedonia supplied what I needed. I have kept myself from being a burden to you in any way, and will continue to do so. [10]As surely as the truth of Christ is in me, nobody in the regions of Achaia will stop this boasting of mine. [11]Why? Because I do not love you? God knows I do! [12]And I will keep on doing what I am doing in order to cut the ground from under those who want an opportunity to be considered equal with us in the things they boast about.

---

[d] Or *the gospel*   [e] Other ancient authorities lack *and pure*
[f] Gk *the gospel of God*   [g] Gk *brothers*

[b]13-15 Or [13]*We, however, will not boast about things that cannot be measured, but we will boast according to the standard of measurement that the God of measure has assigned us—a measurement that relates even to you.* [14] . . . .
[15]*Neither do we boast about things that cannot be measured in regard to the work done by others.*   [c]17 Jer. 9:24

about. ¹³For such boasters are false apostles, deceitful workers, disguising themselves as apostles of Christ. ¹⁴And no wonder! Even Satan disguises himself as an angel of light. ¹⁵So it is not strange if his ministers also disguise themselves as ministers of righteousness. Their end will match their deeds.

Paul's Sufferings as an Apostle

16 I repeat, let no one think that I am a fool; but if you do, then accept me as a fool, so that I too may boast a little. ¹⁷What I am saying in regard to this boastful confidence, I am saying not with the Lord's authority, but as a fool;¹⁸since many boast according to human standards,ʰ I will also boast. ¹⁹For you gladly put up with fools, being wise yourselves! ²⁰For you put up with it when someone makes slaves of you, or preys upon you, or takes advantage of you, or puts on airs, or gives you a slap in the face. ²¹To my shame, I must say, we were too weak for that!

But whatever anyone dares to boast of— I am speaking as a fool—I also dare to boast of that. ²²Are they Hebrews? So am I. Are they Israelites? So am I. Are they descendants of Abraham? So am I. ²³Are they ministers of Christ? I am talking like a madman—I am a better one: with far greater labors, far more imprisonments, with countless floggings, and often near death. ²⁴Five times I have received from the Jews the forty lashes minus one. ²⁵Three times I was beaten with rods. Once I received a stoning. Three times I was shipwrecked; for a night and a day I was adrift at sea; ²⁶on frequent journeys, in danger from rivers, danger from bandits, danger from my own people, danger from Gentiles, danger in the city, danger in the wilderness, danger at sea, danger from false brothers and sisters;ⁱ ²⁷in toil and hardship, through many a sleepless night, hungry and thirsty, often without food, cold and naked. ²⁸And, besides other things, I am under daily pressure because of my anxiety for all the churches. ²⁹Who is weak, and I am not weak? Who is made to stumble, and I am not indignant?

30 If I must boast, I will boast of the things that show my weakness. ³¹The God and Father of the Lord Jesus (blessed be he forever!) knows that I do not lie. ³²In Damascus, the governorʲ under King Aretas guarded the city of Damascus in

καὶ ἡμεῖς. **13** οἱ γὰρ τοιοῦτοι ψευδαπόστολοι, ἐργάται δόλιοι, μετασχηματιζόμενοι εἰς ἀποστόλους Χριστοῦ. **14** καὶ οὐ θαῦμα· αὐτὸς γὰρ ὁ Σατανᾶς μετασχηματίζεται εἰς ἄγγελον φωτός. **15** οὐ μέγα οὖν εἰ καὶ οἱ διάκονοι αὐτοῦ μετασχηματίζονται ὡς διάκονοι δικαιοσύνης· ὧν τὸ τέλος ἔσται κατὰ τὰ ἔργα αὐτῶν.

16 Πάλιν λέγω, μή τίς με δόξῃ ἄφρονα εἶναι· εἰ δὲ μή γε, κἂν ὡς ἄφρονα δέξασθέ με, ἵνα κἀγὼ μικρόν τι καυχήσωμαι. **17** ὃ λαλῶ, οὐ κατὰ κύριον λαλῶ ἀλλ᾿ ὡς ἐν ἀφροσύνῃ, ἐν ταύτῃ τῇ ὑποστάσει τῆς καυχήσεως. **18** ἐπεὶ πολλοὶ καυχῶνται κατὰ σάρκα, κἀγὼ καυχήσομαι. **19** ἡδέως γὰρ ἀνέχεσθε τῶν ἀφρόνων φρόνιμοι ὄντες· **20** ἀνέχεσθε γὰρ εἴ τις ὑμᾶς καταδουλοῖ, εἴ τις κατεσθίει, εἴ τις λαμβάνει, εἴ τις ἐπαίρεται, εἴ τις εἰς πρόσωπον ὑμᾶς δέρει. **21** κατὰ ἀτιμίαν λέγω, ὡς ὅτι ἡμεῖς ἠσθενήκαμεν. ἐν ᾧ δ᾿ ἄν τις τολμᾷ, ἐν ἀφροσύνῃ λέγω, τολμῶ κἀγώ. **22** Ἑβραῖοί εἰσιν; κἀγώ. Ἰσραηλῖταί εἰσιν; κἀγώ. σπέρμα Ἀβραάμ εἰσιν; κἀγώ. **23** διάκονοι Χριστοῦ εἰσιν; παραφρονῶν λαλῶ, ὑπὲρ ἐγώ· ἐν κόποις περισσοτέρως, ἐν φυλακαῖς περισσοτέρως, ἐν πληγαῖς ὑπερβαλλόντως, ἐν θανάτοις πολλάκις. **24** ὑπὸ Ἰουδαίων πεντάκις τεσσεράκοντα παρὰ μίαν ἔλαβον, **25** τρὶς ἐραβδίσθην, ἅπαξ ἐλιθάσθην, τρὶς ἐναυάγησα, νυχθήμερον ἐν τῷ βυθῷ πεποίηκα· **26** ὁδοιπορίαις πολλάκις, κινδύνοις ποταμῶν, κινδύνοις λῃστῶν, κινδύνοις ἐκ γένους, κινδύνοις ἐξ ἐθνῶν, κινδύνοις ἐν πόλει, κινδύνοις ἐν ἐρημίᾳ, κινδύνοις ἐν θαλάσσῃ, κινδύνοις ἐν ψευδαδέλφοις, **27** κόπῳ καὶ μόχθῳ, ἐν ἀγρυπνίαις πολλάκις, ἐν λιμῷ καὶ δίψει, ἐν νηστείαις πολλάκις, ἐν ψύχει καὶ γυμνότητι· **28** χωρὶς τῶν παρεκτὸς ἡ ἐπίστασίς μοι ἡ καθ᾿ ἡμέραν, ἡ μέριμνα πασῶν τῶν ἐκκλησιῶν. **29** τίς ἀσθενεῖ καὶ οὐκ ἀσθενῶ; τίς σκανδαλίζεται καὶ οὐκ ἐγὼ πυροῦμαι;

30 Εἰ καυχᾶσθαι δεῖ, τὰ τῆς ἀσθενείας μου καυχήσομαι. **31** ὁ θεὸς καὶ πατὴρ τοῦ κυρίου Ἰησοῦ οἶδεν, ὁ ὢν εὐλογητὸς εἰς τοὺς αἰῶνας, ὅτι οὐ ψεύδομαι. **32** ἐν Δαμασκῷ ὁ ἐθνάρχης Ἀρέτα τοῦ βασιλέως ἐφρούρει τὴν πόλιν

¹³For such men are false apostles, deceitful workmen, masquerading as apostles of Christ. ¹⁴And no wonder, for Satan himself masquerades as an angel of light. ¹⁵It is not surprising, then, if his servants masquerade as servants of righteousness. Their end will be what their actions deserve.

Paul Boasts About His Sufferings

¹⁶I repeat: Let no one take me for a fool. But if you do, then receive me just as you would a fool, so that I may do a little boasting. ¹⁷In this self-confident boasting I am not talking as the Lord would, but as a fool. ¹⁸Since many are boasting in the way the world does, I too will boast. ¹⁹You gladly put up with fools since you are so wise! ²⁰In fact, you even put up with anyone who enslaves you or exploits you or takes advantage of you or pushes himself forward or slaps you in the face. ²¹To my shame I admit that we were too weak for that!

What anyone else dares to boast about— I am speaking as a fool—I also dare to boast about. ²²Are they Hebrews? So am I. Are they Israelites? So am I. Are they Abraham's descendants? So am I. ²³Are they servants of Christ? (I am out of my mind to talk like this.) I am more. I have worked much harder, been in prison more frequently, been flogged more severely, and been exposed to death again and again. ²⁴Five times I received from the Jews the forty lashes minus one. ²⁵Three times I was beaten with rods, once I was stoned, three times I was shipwrecked, I spent a night and a day in the open sea, ²⁶I have been constantly on the move. I have been in danger from rivers, in danger from bandits, in danger from my own countrymen, in danger from Gentiles; in danger in the city, in danger in the country, in danger at sea; and in danger from false brothers. ²⁷I have labored and toiled and have often gone without sleep; I have known hunger and thirst and have often gone without food; I have been cold and naked. ²⁸Besides everything else, I face daily the pressure of my concern for all the churches. ²⁹Who is weak, and I do not feel weak? Who is led into sin, and I do not inwardly burn?

³⁰If I must boast, I will boast of the things that show my weakness. ³¹The God and Father of the Lord Jesus, who is to be praised forever, knows that I am not lying. ³²In Damascus the governor under King Aretas had the city of the Damascenes

order to[k] seize me, [33]but I was let down in a basket through a window in the wall,[l] and escaped from his hands.

Paul's Visions and Revelations

12 It is necessary to boast; nothing is to be gained by it, but I will go on to visions and revelations of the Lord. [2]I know a person in Christ who fourteen years ago was caught up to the third heaven—whether in the body or out of the body I do not know; God knows. [3]And I know that such a person—whether in the body or out of the body I do not know; God knows—[4]was caught up into Paradise and heard things that are not to be told, that no mortal is permitted to repeat. [5]On behalf of such a one I will boast, but on my own behalf I will not boast, except of my weaknesses. [6]But if I wish to boast, I will not be a fool, for I will be speaking the truth. But I refrain from it, so that no one may think better of me than what is seen in me or heard from me, [7]even considering the exceptional character of the revelations. Therefore, to keep[m] me from being too elated, a thorn was given me in the flesh, a messenger of Satan to torment me, to keep me from being too elated.[n] [8]Three times I appealed to the Lord about this, that it would leave me, [9]but he said to me, "My grace is sufficient for you, for power[o] is made perfect in weakness." So, I will boast all the more gladly of my weaknesses, so that the power of Christ may dwell in me. [10]Therefore I am content with weaknesses, insults, hardships, persecutions, and calamities for the sake of Christ; for whenever I am weak, then I am strong.

Paul's Concern for the Corinthian Church

11 I have been a fool! You forced me to it. Indeed you should have been the ones commending me, for I am not at all inferior to these super-apostles, even though I am nothing. [12]The signs of a true apostle were performed among you with utmost patience, signs and wonders and mighty works. [13]How have you been worse off than the other churches, except that I myself did not burden you? Forgive me this wrong!

14 Here I am, ready to come to you this third time. And I will not be a burden, because I do not want what is yours but you; for children ought not to lay up for

Δαμασκηνῶν πιάσαι με[a], **33** καὶ διὰ θυρίδος ἐν σαργάνη ἐχαλάσθην διὰ τοῦ τείχους καὶ ἐξέφυγον τὰς χεῖρας αὐτοῦ.

12 Καυχᾶσθαι δεῖ, οὐ συμφέρον μέν, ἐλεύσομαι δὲ εἰς ὀπτασίας καὶ ἀποκαλύψεις κυρίου. **2** οἶδα ἄνθρωπον ἐν Χριστῷ πρὸ ἐτῶν δεκατεσσάρων, εἴτε ἐν σώματι οὐκ οἶδα, εἴτε ἐκτὸς τοῦ σώματος οὐκ οἶδα, ὁ θεὸς οἶδεν, ἁρπαγέντα τὸν τοιοῦτον ἕως τρίτου οὐρανοῦ. **3** καὶ οἶδα τὸν τοιοῦτον ἄνθρωπον, εἴτε ἐν σώματι εἴτε χωρὶς τοῦ σώματος οὐκ οἶδα, ὁ θεὸς οἶδεν, **4** ὅτι ἡρπάγη εἰς τὸν παράδεισον καὶ ἤκουσεν ἄρρητα ῥήματα ἃ οὐκ ἐξὸν ἀνθρώπῳ λαλῆσαι. **5** ὑπὲρ τοῦ τοιούτου καυχήσομαι, ὑπὲρ δὲ ἐμαυτοῦ οὐ καυχήσομαι εἰ μὴ ἐν ταῖς ἀσθενείαις. **6** ἐὰν γὰρ θελήσω καυχήσασθαι, οὐκ ἔσομαι ἄφρων, ἀλήθειαν γὰρ ἐρῶ· φείδομαι δέ, μή τις εἰς ἐμὲ λογίσηται ὑπὲρ ὃ βλέπει με ἢ ἀκούει [τι] ἐξ ἐμοῦ **7** καὶ τῇ ὑπερβολῇ τῶν ἀποκαλύψεων. διὸ[a] ἵνα μὴ ὑπεραίρωμαι, ἐδόθη μοι σκόλοψ τῇ σαρκί, ἄγγελος Σατανᾶ, ἵνα με κολαφίζη, ἵνα μὴ ὑπεραίρωμαι. **8** ὑπὲρ τούτου τρὶς τὸν κύριον παρεκάλεσα ἵνα ἀποστῇ ἀπ᾽ ἐμοῦ. **9** καὶ εἴρηκέν μοι, Ἀρκεῖ σοι ἡ χάρις μου, ἡ γὰρ δύναμις[b] ἐν ἀσθενείᾳ τελεῖται. ἥδιστα οὖν μᾶλλον καυχήσομαι ἐν ταῖς ἀσθενείαις μου, ἵνα ἐπισκηνώση ἐπ᾽ ἐμὲ ἡ δύναμις τοῦ Χριστοῦ. **10** διὸ εὐδοκῶ ἐν ἀσθενείαις, ἐν ὕβρεσιν, ἐν ἀνάγκαις, ἐν διωγμοῖς καὶ στενοχωρίαις, ὑπὲρ Χριστοῦ· ὅταν γὰρ ἀσθενῶ, τότε δυνατός εἰμι.

11 Γέγονα ἄφρων, ὑμεῖς με ἠναγκάσατε. ἐγὼ γὰρ ὤφειλον ὑφ᾽ ὑμῶν συνίστασθαι· οὐδὲν γὰρ ὑστέρησα τῶν ὑπερλίαν ἀποστόλων εἰ καὶ οὐδέν εἰμι. **12** τὰ μὲν σημεῖα τοῦ ἀποστόλου κατειργάσθη ἐν ὑμῖν ἐν πάση ὑπομονῇ, σημείοις τε καὶ τέρασιν καὶ δυνάμεσιν. **13** τί γάρ ἐστιν ὃ ἡσσώθητε ὑπὲρ τὰς λοιπὰς ἐκκλησίας, εἰ μὴ ὅτι αὐτὸς ἐγὼ οὐ κατενάρκησα ὑμῶν; χαρίσασθέ μοι τὴν ἀδικίαν ταύτην. **14** Ἰδοὺ τρίτον τοῦτο ἑτοίμως ἔχω ἐλθεῖν πρὸς ὑμᾶς, καὶ οὐ καταναρκήσω· οὐ γὰρ ζητῶ τὰ ὑμῶν ἀλλὰ ὑμᾶς. οὐ γὰρ ὀφείλει τὰ τέκνα τοῖς γονεῦσιν θησαυρίζειν ἀλλὰ

guarded in order to arrest me. [33]But I was lowered in a basket from a window in the wall and slipped through his hands.

Paul's Vision and His Thorn

12 I must go on boasting. Although there is nothing to be gained, I will go on to visions and revelations from the Lord. [2]I know a man in Christ who fourteen years ago was caught up to the third heaven. Whether it was in the body or out of the body I do not know—God knows. [3]And I know that this man—whether in the body or apart from the body I do not know, but God knows—[4]was caught up to paradise. He heard inexpressible things, things that man is not permitted to tell. [5]I will boast about a man like that, but I will not boast about myself, except about my weaknesses. [6]Even if I should choose to boast, I would not be a fool, because I would be speaking the truth. But I refrain, so no one will think more of me than is warranted by what I do or say.

[7]To keep me from becoming conceited because of these surpassingly great revelations, there was given me a thorn in my flesh, a messenger of Satan, to torment me. [8]Three times I pleaded with the Lord to take it away from me. [9]But he said to me, "My grace is sufficient for you, for my power is made perfect in weakness." Therefore I will boast all the more gladly about my weaknesses, so that Christ's power may rest on me. [10]That is why, for Christ's sake, I delight in weaknesses, in insults, in hardships, in persecutions, in difficulties. For when I am weak, then I am strong.

Paul's Concern for the Corinthians

[11]I have made a fool of myself, but you drove me to it. I ought to have been commended by you, for I am not in the least inferior to the "super-apostles," even though I am nothing. [12]The things that mark an apostle—signs, wonders and miracles—were done among you with great perseverance. [13]How were you inferior to the other churches, except that I was never a burden to you? Forgive me this wrong!

[14]Now I am ready to visit you for the third time, and I will not be a burden to you, because what I want is not your possessions but you. After all, children should not have to save up for their parents, but

[k] Other ancient authorities read *and wanted to*   [l] Gk *through the wall*   [m] Other ancient authorities read *To keep*   [n] Other ancient authorities lack *to keep me from being too elated*   [o] Other ancient authorities read *my power*

[a]32 NRSV note k adds θέλων before or after πιάσαι με
[a]7 NRSV note m omits διὸ   [b]9 NRSV note o adds μου

their parents, but parents for their children. [15]I will most gladly spend and be spent for you. If I love you more, am I to be loved less? [16]Let it be assumed that I did not burden you. Nevertheless (you say) since I was crafty, I took you in by deceit. [17]Did I take advantage of you through any of those whom I sent to you? [18]I urged Titus to go, and sent the brother with him. Titus did not take advantage of you, did he? Did we not conduct ourselves with the same spirit? Did we not take the same steps?

19 Have you been thinking all along that we have been defending ourselves before you? We are speaking in Christ before God. Everything we do, beloved, is for the sake of building you up. [20]For I fear that when I come, I may find you not as I wish, and that you may find me not as you wish; I fear that there may perhaps be quarreling, jealousy, anger, selfishness, slander, gossip, conceit, and disorder. [21]I fear that when I come again, my God may humble me before you, and that I may have to mourn over many who previously sinned and have not repented of the impurity, sexual immorality, and licentiousness that they have practiced.

Further Warning

13 This is the third time I am coming to you. "Any charge must be sustained by the evidence of two or three witnesses." [2]I warned those who sinned previously and all the others, and I warn them now while absent, as I did when present on my second visit, that if I come again, I will not be lenient— [3]since you desire proof that Christ is speaking in me. He is not weak in dealing with you, but is powerful in you. [4]For he was crucified in weakness, but lives by the power of God. For we are weak in him,[p] but in dealing with you we will live with him by the power of God.

5 Examine yourselves to see whether you are living in the faith. Test yourselves. Do you not realize that Jesus Christ is in you?— unless, indeed, you fail to meet the test! [6]I hope you will find out that we have not failed. [7]But we pray to God that you may not do anything wrong—not that we may appear to have met the test, but that you may do what is right, though we may seem to have failed. [8]For we cannot do anything against the truth, but only for the truth.

οἱ γονεῖς τοῖς τέκνοις. **15** ἐγὼ δὲ ἥδιστα δαπανήσω καὶ ἐκδαπανηθήσομαι ὑπὲρ τῶν ψυχῶν ὑμῶν. εἰ περισσοτέρως ὑμᾶς ἀγαπῶ[ν], ἧσσον ἀγαπῶμαι; **16** ἔστω δέ, ἐγὼ οὐ κατεβάρησα ὑμᾶς· ἀλλὰ ὑπάρχων πανοῦργος δόλῳ ὑμᾶς ἔλαβον. **17** μή τινα ὧν ἀπέσταλκα πρὸς ὑμᾶς, δι᾽ αὐτοῦ ἐπλεονέκτησα ὑμᾶς; **18** παρεκάλεσα Τίτον καὶ συναπέστειλα τὸν ἀδελφόν· μήτι ἐπλεονέκτησεν ὑμᾶς Τίτος; οὐ τῷ αὐτῷ πνεύματι περιεπατή-σαμεν; οὐ τοῖς αὐτοῖς ἴχνεσιν;

19 Πάλαι δοκεῖτε ὅτι ὑμῖν ἀπολογού-μεθα. κατέναντι θεοῦ ἐν Χριστῷ λαλοῦμεν· τὰ δὲ πάντα, ἀγαπητοί, ὑπὲρ τῆς ὑμῶν οἰκοδομῆς. **20** φοβοῦμαι γὰρ μή πως ἐλθὼν οὐχ οἵους θέλω εὕρω ὑμᾶς κἀγὼ εὑρεθῶ ὑμῖν οἷον οὐ θέλετε· μή πως ἔρις, ζῆλος, θυμοί, ἐριθεῖαι, καταλαλιαί, ψιθυρισμοί, φυσιώσεις, ἀκαταστασίαι· **21** μὴ πάλιν ἐλθόντος μου ταπεινώσῃ με ὁ θεός μου πρὸς ὑμᾶς καὶ πενθήσω πολλοὺς τῶν προημαρτηκότων καὶ μὴ μετανοη-σάντων ἐπὶ τῇ ἀκαθαρσίᾳ καὶ πορνείᾳ καὶ ἀσελγείᾳ ᾗ ἔπραξαν.

13 Τρίτον τοῦτο ἔρχομαι πρὸς ὑμᾶς· ἐπὶ στόματος δύο μαρτύ-ρων καὶ τριῶν σταθήσεται πᾶν ῥῆμα. **2** προείρηκα καὶ προλέγω, ὡς παρὼν τὸ δεύτερον καὶ ἀπὼν νῦν, τοῖς προημαρτη-κόσιν καὶ τοῖς λοιποῖς πᾶσιν, ὅτι ἐὰν ἔλθω εἰς τὸ πάλιν οὐ φείσομαι, **3** ἐπεὶ δοκιμὴν ζητεῖτε τοῦ ἐν ἐμοὶ λαλοῦντος Χριστοῦ, ὃς εἰς ὑμᾶς οὐκ ἀσθενεῖ ἀλλὰ δυνατεῖ ἐν ὑμῖν. **4** καὶ γὰρ ἐσταυρώθη ἐξ ἀσθενείας, ἀλλὰ ζῇ ἐκ δυνάμεως θεοῦ. καὶ γὰρ ἡμεῖς ἀσθε-νοῦμεν ἐν[a] αὐτῷ, ἀλλὰ ζήσομεν σὺν αὐτῷ ἐκ δυνάμεως θεοῦ εἰς ὑμᾶς.

5 Ἑαυτοὺς πειράζετε εἰ ἐστὲ ἐν τῇ πίστει, ἑαυτοὺς δοκιμάζετε· ἢ οὐκ ἐπιγινώσκετε ἑαυτοὺς ὅτι Ἰησοῦς Χριστὸς ἐν ὑμῖν; εἰ μήτι ἀδόκιμοί ἐστε. **6** ἐλπίζω δὲ ὅτι γνώσεσθε ὅτι ἡμεῖς οὐκ ἐσμὲν ἀδόκιμοι. **7** εὐχόμεθα δὲ πρὸς τὸν θεὸν μὴ ποιῆσαι ὑμᾶς κακὸν μηδέν, οὐχ ἵνα ἡμεῖς δόκιμοι φανῶμεν, ἀλλ᾽ ἵνα ὑμεῖς τὸ καλὸν ποιῆτε, ἡμεῖς δὲ ὡς ἀδόκιμοι ὦμεν. **8** οὐ γὰρ δυνάμεθά τι κατὰ τῆς ἀληθείας ἀλλὰ ὑπὲρ τῆς ἀληθείας. **9** χαίρομεν

parents for their children. [15]So I will very gladly spend for you everything I have and expend myself as well. If I love you more, will you love me less? [16]Be that as it may, I have not been a burden to you. Yet, crafty fellow that I am, I caught you by trickery! [17]Did I exploit you through any of the men I sent you? [18]I urged Titus to go to you and I sent our brother with him. Titus did not exploit you, did he? Did we not act in the same spirit and follow the same course?

[19]Have you been thinking all along that we have been defending ourselves to you? We have been speaking in the sight of God as those in Christ; and everything we do, dear friends, is for your strengthening. [20]For I am afraid that when I come I may not find you as I want you to be, and you may not find me as you want me to be. I fear that there may be quarreling, jealousy, outbursts of anger, factions, slander, gossip, arrogance and disorder. [21]I am afraid that when I come again my God will humble me before you, and I will be grieved over many who have sinned earlier and have not repented of the impurity, sexual sin and debauchery in which they have indulged.

Final Warnings

13 This will be my third visit to you. "Every matter must be established by the testimony of two or three witnesses."[a] [2]I already gave you a warning when I was with you the second time. I now repeat it while absent: On my return I will not spare those who sinned earlier or any of the others, [3]since you are demanding proof that Christ is speaking through me. He is not weak in dealing with you, but is powerful among you. [4]For to be sure, he was crucified in weakness, yet he lives by God's power. Likewise, we are weak in him, yet by God's power we will live with him to serve you.

[5]Examine yourselves to see whether you are in the faith; test yourselves. Do you not realize that Christ Jesus is in you—unless, of course, you fail the test? [6]And I trust that you will discover that we have not failed the test. [7]Now we pray to God that you will not do anything wrong. Not that people will see that we have stood the test but that you will do what is right even though we may seem to have failed. [8]For we cannot do anything against the truth,

9For we rejoice when we are weak and you are strong. This is what we pray for, that you may become perfect. 10So I write these things while I am away from you, so that when I come, I may not have to be severe in using the authority that the Lord has given me for building up and not for tearing down.

Final Greetings and Benediction

11 Finally, brothers and sisters,q farewell.r Put things in order, listen to my appeal,s agree with one another, live in peace; and the God of love and peace will be with you. 12Greet one another with a holy kiss. All the saints greet you.

13 The grace of the Lord Jesus Christ, the love of God, and the communion oft the Holy Spirit be with all of you.

γὰρ ὅταν ἡμεῖς ἀσθενῶμεν, ὑμεῖς δὲ δυνατοὶ ἦτε· τοῦτο καὶ εὐχόμεθα, τὴν ὑμῶν κατάρτισιν. 10 διὰ τοῦτο ταῦτα ἀπὼν γράφω, ἵνα παρὼν μὴ ἀποτόμως χρήσωμαι κατὰ τὴν ἐξουσίαν ἣν ὁ κύριος ἔδωκέν μοι εἰς οἰκοδομὴν καὶ οὐκ εἰς καθαίρεσιν.

11 Λοιπόν, ἀδελφοί, χαίρετε, καταρτί-ζεσθε, παρακαλεῖσθε, τὸ αὐτὸ φρονεῖτε, εἰρηνεύετε, καὶ ὁ θεὸς τῆς ἀγάπης καὶ εἰρήνης ἔσται μεθ' ὑμῶν. 12 ἀσπάσασθε ἀλλήλους ἐν ἁγίῳ φιλήματι.b ἀσπάζονται ὑμᾶς οἱ ἅγιοι πάντες.

13b Ἡ χάρις τοῦ κυρίου Ἰησοῦ Χριστοῦ καὶ ἡ ἀγάπη τοῦ θεοῦ καὶ ἡ κοινωνία τοῦ ἁγίου πνεύματος μετὰ πάντων ὑμῶν.

but only for the truth. 9We are glad whenever we are weak but you are strong; and our prayer is for your perfection. 10This is why I write these things when I am absent, that when I come I may not have to be harsh in my use of authority—the authority the Lord gave me for building you up, not for tearing you down.

Final Greetings

11Finally, brothers, good-by. Aim for perfection, listen to my appeal, be of one mind, live in peace. And the God of love and peace will be with you.

12Greet one another with a holy kiss. 13All the saints send their greetings.

14May the grace of the Lord Jesus Christ, and the love of God, and the fellowship of the Holy Spirit be with you all.

q Gk *brothers*　r Or *rejoice*　s Or *encourage one another*
t Or *and the sharing in*

b12 NIV begins verse 13 after φιλήματι and numbers verse 13 as 14

NRSV

Salutation

1 Paul an apostle—sent neither by human commission nor from human authorities, but through Jesus Christ and God the Father, who raised him from the dead— ²and all the members of God's family[a] who are with me,

To the churches of Galatia:

3 Grace to you and peace from God our Father and the Lord Jesus Christ, ⁴who gave himself for our sins to set us free from the present evil age, according to the will of our God and Father, ⁵to whom be the glory forever and ever. Amen.

There Is No Other Gospel

6 I am astonished that you are so quickly deserting the one who called you in the grace of Christ and are turning to a different gospel— ⁷not that there is another gospel, but there are some who are confusing you and want to pervert the gospel of Christ. ⁸But even if we or an angel[b] from heaven should proclaim to you a gospel contrary to what we proclaimed to you, let that one be accursed! ⁹As we have said before, so now I repeat, if anyone proclaims to you a gospel contrary to what you received, let that one be accursed!

10 Am I now seeking human approval, or God's approval? Or am I trying to please people? If I were still pleasing people, I would not be a servant[c] of Christ.

Paul's Vindication of His Apostleship

11 For I want you to know, brothers and sisters,[d] that the gospel that was proclaimed by me is not of human origin; ¹²for I did not receive it from a human source, nor was I taught it, but I received it through a revelation of Jesus Christ.

13 You have heard, no doubt, of my earlier life in Judaism. I was violently persecuting the church of God and was trying to destroy it. ¹⁴I advanced in Judaism beyond many among my people of the same age, for I was far more zealous for the traditions of my ancestors. ¹⁵But when God, who had set me apart before I was born and called me through his grace, was pleased ¹⁶to reveal his Son to me,[e] so that I might proclaim him among the Gentiles, I did not confer with any human being, ¹⁷nor did I go up to Jerusalem to those who were already apostles before me, but I went away at once into Arabia, and afterwards I returned to Damascus.

ΠΡΟΣ ΓΑΛΑΤΑΣ

1 Παῦλος ἀπόστολος οὐκ ἀπ᾽ ἀνθρώπων οὐδὲ δι᾽ ἀνθρώπου ἀλλὰ διὰ Ἰησοῦ Χριστοῦ καὶ θεοῦ πατρὸς τοῦ ἐγείραντος αὐτὸν ἐκ νεκρῶν, 2 καὶ οἱ σὺν ἐμοὶ πάντες ἀδελφοὶ ταῖς ἐκκλησίαις τῆς Γαλατίας, 3 χάρις ὑμῖν καὶ εἰρήνη ἀπὸ θεοῦ πατρὸς ἡμῶν καὶ κυρίου Ἰησοῦ Χριστοῦ 4 τοῦ δόντος ἑαυτὸν ὑπὲρ τῶν ἁμαρτιῶν ἡμῶν, ὅπως ἐξέληται ἡμᾶς ἐκ τοῦ αἰῶνος τοῦ ἐνεστῶτος πονηροῦ κατὰ τὸ θέλημα τοῦ θεοῦ καὶ πατρὸς ἡμῶν, 5 ᾧ ἡ δόξα εἰς τοὺς αἰῶνας τῶν αἰώνων, ἀμήν.

6 Θαυμάζω ὅτι οὕτως ταχέως μετατίθεσθε ἀπὸ τοῦ καλέσαντος ὑμᾶς ἐν χάριτι [Χριστοῦ] εἰς ἕτερον εὐαγγέλιον, 7 ὃ οὐκ ἔστιν ἄλλο, εἰ μή τινές εἰσιν οἱ ταράσσοντες ὑμᾶς καὶ θέλοντες μεταστρέψαι τὸ εὐαγγέλιον τοῦ Χριστοῦ. 8 ἀλλὰ καὶ ἐὰν ἡμεῖς ἢ ἄγγελος ἐξ οὐρανοῦ εὐαγγελίζηται [ὑμῖν][a] παρ᾽ ὃ εὐηγγελισάμεθα ὑμῖν, ἀνάθεμα ἔστω. 9 ὡς προειρήκαμεν καὶ ἄρτι πάλιν λέγω, εἴ τις ὑμᾶς εὐαγγελίζεται παρ᾽ ὃ παρελάβετε, ἀνάθεμα ἔστω.

10 Ἄρτι γὰρ ἀνθρώπους πείθω ἢ τὸν θεόν; ἢ ζητῶ ἀνθρώποις ἀρέσκειν; εἰ ἔτι ἀνθρώποις ἤρεσκον, Χριστοῦ δοῦλος οὐκ ἂν ἤμην.

11 Γνωρίζω γὰρ ὑμῖν, ἀδελφοί, τὸ εὐαγγέλιον τὸ εὐαγγελισθὲν ὑπ᾽ ἐμοῦ ὅτι οὐκ ἔστιν κατὰ ἄνθρωπον· 12 οὐδὲ γὰρ ἐγὼ παρὰ ἀνθρώπου παρέλαβον αὐτὸ οὔτε ἐδιδάχθην ἀλλὰ δι᾽ ἀποκαλύψεως Ἰησοῦ Χριστοῦ.

13 Ἠκούσατε γὰρ τὴν ἐμὴν ἀναστροφήν ποτε ἐν τῷ Ἰουδαϊσμῷ, ὅτι καθ᾽ ὑπερβολὴν ἐδίωκον τὴν ἐκκλησίαν τοῦ θεοῦ καὶ ἐπόρθουν αὐτήν, 14 καὶ προέκοπτον ἐν τῷ Ἰουδαϊσμῷ ὑπὲρ πολλοὺς συνηλικιώτας ἐν τῷ γένει μου, περισσοτέρως ζηλωτὴς ὑπάρχων τῶν πατρικῶν μου παραδόσεων. 15 ὅτε δὲ εὐδόκησεν [ὁ θεὸς] ὁ ἀφορίσας με ἐκ κοιλίας μητρός μου καὶ καλέσας διὰ τῆς χάριτος αὐτοῦ 16 ἀποκαλύψαι τὸν υἱὸν αὐτοῦ ἐν ἐμοί, ἵνα εὐαγγελίζωμαι αὐτὸν ἐν τοῖς ἔθνεσιν, εὐθέως οὐ προσανεθέμην σαρκὶ καὶ αἵματι 17 οὐδὲ ἀνῆλθον εἰς Ἱεροσόλυμα πρὸς τοὺς πρὸ ἐμοῦ ἀποστόλους, ἀλλὰ ἀπῆλθον εἰς Ἀραβίαν καὶ πάλιν ὑπέστρεψα εἰς Δαμασκόν.

NIV

1 Paul, an apostle—sent not from men nor by man, but by Jesus Christ and God the Father, who raised him from the dead— ²and all the brothers with me,

To the churches in Galatia:

³Grace and peace to you from God our Father and the Lord Jesus Christ, ⁴who gave himself for our sins to rescue us from the present evil age, according to the will of our God and Father, ⁵to whom be glory for ever and ever. Amen.

No Other Gospel

⁶I am astonished that you are so quickly deserting the one who called you by the grace of Christ and are turning to a different gospel— ⁷which is really no gospel at all. Evidently some people are throwing you into confusion and are trying to pervert the gospel of Christ. ⁸But even if we or an angel from heaven should preach a gospel other than the one we preached to you, let him be eternally condemned! ⁹As we have already said, so now I say again: If anybody is preaching to you a gospel other than what you accepted, let him be eternally condemned!

¹⁰Am I now trying to win the approval of men, or of God? Or am I trying to please men? If I were still trying to please men, I would not be a servant of Christ.

Paul Called by God

¹¹I want you to know, brothers, that the gospel I preached is not something that man made up. ¹²I did not receive it from any man, nor was I taught it; rather, I received it by revelation from Jesus Christ.

¹³For you have heard of my previous way of life in Judaism, how intensely I persecuted the church of God and tried to destroy it. ¹⁴I was advancing in Judaism beyond many Jews of my own age and was extremely zealous for the traditions of my fathers. ¹⁵But when God, who set me apart from birth[a] and called me by his grace, was pleased ¹⁶to reveal his Son in me so that I might preach him among the Gentiles, I did not consult any man, ¹⁷nor did I go up to Jerusalem to see those who were apostles before I was, but I went immediately into Arabia and later returned to Damascus.

---

18 Then after three years I did go up to Jerusalem to visit Cephas and stayed with him fifteen days; 19but I did not see any other apostle except James the Lord's brother. 20In what I am writing to you, before God, I do not lie! 21Then I went into the regions of Syria and Cilicia, 22and I was still unknown by sight to the churches of Judea that are in Christ; 23they only heard it said, "The one who formerly was persecuting us is now proclaiming the faith he once tried to destroy." 24And they glorified God because of me.

Paul and the Other Apostles

2 Then after fourteen years I went up again to Jerusalem with Barnabas, taking Titus along with me. 2I went up in response to a revelation. Then I laid before them (though only in a private meeting with the acknowledged leaders) the gospel that I proclaim among the Gentiles, in order to make sure that I was not running, or had not run, in vain. 3But even Titus, who was with me, was not compelled to be circumcised, though he was a Greek. 4But because of false believers[f] secretly brought in, who slipped in to spy on the freedom we have in Christ Jesus, so that they might enslave us— 5we did not submit to them even for a moment, so that the truth of the gospel might always remain with you. 6And from those who were supposed to be acknowledged leaders (what they actually were makes no difference to me; God shows no partiality)—those leaders contributed nothing to me. 7On the contrary, when they saw that I had been entrusted with the gospel for the uncircumcised, just as Peter had been entrusted with the gospel for the circumcised 8(for he who worked through Peter making him an apostle to the circumcised also worked through me in sending me to the Gentiles), 9and when James and Cephas and John, who were acknowledged pillars, recognized the grace that had been given to me, they gave to Barnabas and me the right hand of fellowship, agreeing that we should go to the Gentiles and they to the circumcised. 10They asked only one thing, that we remember the poor, which was actually what I was[g] eager to do.

Paul Rebukes Peter at Antioch

11 But when Cephas came to Antioch, I opposed him to his face, because he stood self-condemned; 12for until certain people

[f] Gk *false brothers* [g] Or *had been*

18 Ἔπειτα μετὰ ἔτη τρία ἀνῆλθον εἰς Ἱεροσόλυμα ἱστορῆσαι Κηφᾶν καὶ ἐπέμεινα πρὸς αὐτὸν ἡμέρας δεκαπέντε, 19 ἕτερον δὲ τῶν ἀποστόλων οὐκ εἶδον εἰ μὴ Ἰάκωβον τὸν ἀδελφὸν τοῦ κυρίου. 20 ἃ δὲ γράφω ὑμῖν, ἰδοὺ ἐνώπιον τοῦ θεοῦ ὅτι οὐ ψεύδομαι. 21 ἔπειτα ἦλθον εἰς τὰ κλίματα τῆς Συρίας καὶ τῆς Κιλικίας· 22 ἤμην δὲ ἀγνοούμενος τῷ προσώπῳ ταῖς ἐκκλησίαις τῆς Ἰουδαίας ταῖς ἐν Χριστῷ. 23 μόνον δὲ ἀκούοντες ἦσαν ὅτι Ὁ διώκων ἡμᾶς ποτε νῦν εὐαγγελίζεται τὴν πίστιν ἥν ποτε ἐπόρθει. 24 καὶ ἐδόξαζον ἐν ἐμοὶ τὸν θεόν.

2 Ἔπειτα διὰ δεκατεσσάρων ἐτῶν πάλιν ἀνέβην εἰς Ἱεροσόλυμα μετὰ Βαρναβᾶ συμπαραλαβὼν καὶ Τίτον· 2 ἀνέβην δὲ κατὰ ἀποκάλυψιν· καὶ ἀνεθέμην αὐτοῖς τὸ εὐαγγέλιον ὃ κηρύσσω ἐν τοῖς ἔθνεσιν, κατ᾽ ἰδίαν δὲ τοῖς δοκοῦσιν, μή πως εἰς κενὸν τρέχω ἢ ἔδραμον. 3 ἀλλ᾽ οὐδὲ Τίτος ὁ σὺν ἐμοί, Ἕλλην ὤν, ἠναγκάσθη περιτμηθῆναι· 4 διὰ δὲ τοὺς παρεισάκτους ψευδαδέλφους, οἵτινες παρεισῆλθον κατασκοπῆσαι τὴν ἐλευθερίαν ἡμῶν ἣν ἔχομεν ἐν Χριστῷ Ἰησοῦ, ἵνα ἡμᾶς καταδουλώσουσιν, 5 οἷς οὐδὲ πρὸς ὥραν εἴξαμεν τῇ ὑποταγῇ, ἵνα ἡ ἀλήθεια τοῦ εὐαγγελίου διαμείνῃ πρὸς ὑμᾶς. 6 ἀπὸ δὲ τῶν δοκούντων εἶναί τι,—ὁποῖοί ποτε ἦσαν οὐδέν μοι διαφέρει· πρόσωπον [ὁ] θεὸς ἀνθρώπου οὐ λαμβάνει – ἐμοὶ γὰρ οἱ δοκοῦντες οὐδὲν προσανέθεντο, 7 ἀλλὰ τοὐναντίον ἰδόντες ὅτι πεπίστευμαι τὸ εὐαγγέλιον τῆς ἀκροβυστίας καθὼς Πέτρος τῆς περιτομῆς, 8 ὁ γὰρ ἐνεργήσας Πέτρῳ εἰς ἀποστολὴν τῆς περιτομῆς ἐνήργησεν καὶ ἐμοὶ εἰς τὰ ἔθνη, 9 καὶ γνόντες τὴν χάριν τὴν δοθεῖσάν μοι, Ἰάκωβος καὶ Κηφᾶς καὶ Ἰωάννης, οἱ δοκοῦντες στῦλοι εἶναι, δεξιὰς ἔδωκαν ἐμοὶ καὶ Βαρναβᾷ κοινωνίας, ἵνα ἡμεῖς εἰς τὰ ἔθνη, αὐτοὶ δὲ εἰς τὴν περιτομήν· 10 μόνον τῶν πτωχῶν ἵνα μνημονεύωμεν, ὃ καὶ ἐσπούδασα αὐτὸ τοῦτο ποιῆσαι. 11 Ὅτε δὲ ἦλθεν Κηφᾶς εἰς Ἀντιόχειαν, κατὰ πρόσωπον αὐτῷ ἀντέστην, ὅτι κατεγνωσμένος ἦν. 12 πρὸ τοῦ γὰρ

18Then after three years, I went up to Jerusalem to get acquainted with Peter[b] and stayed with him fifteen days. 19I saw none of the other apostles—only James, the Lord's brother. 20I assure you before God that what I am writing you is no lie. 21Later I went to Syria and Cilicia. 22I was personally unknown to the churches of Judea that are in Christ. 23They only heard the report: "The man who formerly persecuted us is now preaching the faith he once tried to destroy." 24And they praised God because of me.

Paul Accepted by the Apostles

2 Fourteen years later I went up again to Jerusalem, this time with Barnabas. I took Titus along also. 2I went in response to a revelation and set before them the gospel that I preach among the Gentiles. But I did this privately to those who seemed to be leaders, for fear that I was running or had run my race in vain. 3Yet not even Titus, who was with me, was compelled to be circumcised, even though he was a Greek. 4This matter arose because some false brothers had infiltrated our ranks to spy on the freedom we have in Christ Jesus and to make us slaves. 5We did not give in to them for a moment, so that the truth of the gospel might remain with you.

6As for those who seemed to be important—whatever they were makes no difference to me; God does not judge by external appearance—those men added nothing to my message. 7On the contrary, they saw that I had been entrusted with the task of preaching the gospel to the Gentiles,[a] just as Peter had been to the Jews.[b] 8For God, who was at work in the ministry of Peter as an apostle to the Jews, was also at work in my ministry as an apostle to the Gentiles. 9James, Peter[c] and John, those reputed to be pillars, gave me and Barnabas the right hand of fellowship when they recognized the grace given to me. They agreed that we should go to the Gentiles, and they to the Jews. 10All they asked was that we should continue to remember the poor, the very thing I was eager to do.

Paul Opposes Peter

11When Peter came to Antioch, I opposed him to his face, because he was clearly in the wrong. 12Before certain men came from

[b]18 Greek *Cephas* [a]7 Greek *uncircumcised* [b]7 Greek *circumcised*; also in verses 8 and 9 [c]9 Greek *Cephas*; also in verses 11 and 14

came from James, he used to eat with the Gentiles. But after they came, he drew back and kept himself separate for fear of the circumcision faction. 13And the other Jews joined him in this hypocrisy, so that even Barnabas was led astray by their hypocrisy. 14But when I saw that they were not acting consistently with the truth of the gospel, I said to Cephas before them all, "If you, though a Jew, live like a Gentile and not like a Jew, how can you compel the Gentiles to live like Jews?"h

Jews and Gentiles Are Saved by Faith

15 We ourselves are Jews by birth and not Gentile sinners; 16yet we know that a person is justifiedi not by the works of the law but through faith in Jesus Christ.j And we have come to believe in Christ Jesus, so that we might be justified by faith in Christ,k and not by doing the works of the law, because no one will be justified by the works of the law. 17But if, in our effort to be justified in Christ, we ourselves have been found to be sinners, is Christ then a servant of sin? Certainly not! 18But if I build up again the very things that I once tore down, then I demonstrate that I am a transgressor. 19For through the law I died to the law, so that I might live to God. I have been crucified with Christ; 20and it is no longer I who live, but it is Christ who lives in me. And the life I now live in the flesh I live by faith in the Son of God,l who loved me and gave himself for me. 21I do not nullify the grace of God; for if justificationm comes through the law, then Christ died for nothing.

Law or Faith

3 You foolish Galatians! Who has bewitched you? It was before your eyes that Jesus Christ was publicly exhibited as crucified! 2The only thing I want to learn from you is this: Did you receive the Spirit by doing the works of the law or by believing what you heard? 3Are you so foolish? Having started with the Spirit, are you now ending with the flesh? 4Did you experience so much for nothing?—if it really was for nothing. 5Well then, does Godn supply you with the Spirit and work miracles among you by your doing the works of the law, or by your believing what you heard?

ἐλθεῖν τινας ἀπὸ Ἰακώβου μετὰ τῶν ἐθνῶν συνήσθιεν· ὅτε δὲ ἦλθον, ὑπέστελλεν καὶ ἀφώριζεν ἑαυτὸν φοβούμενος τοὺς ἐκ περιτομῆς. 13 καὶ συνυπεκρίθησαν αὐτῷ [καὶ]a οἱ λοιποὶ Ἰουδαῖοι, ὥστε καὶ Βαρναβᾶς συναπήχθη αὐτῶν τῇ ὑποκρίσει. 14 ἀλλ᾽ ὅτε εἶδον ὅτι οὐκ ὀρθοποδοῦσιν πρὸς τὴν ἀλήθειαν τοῦ εὐαγγελίου, εἶπον τῷ Κηφᾷ ἔμπροσθεν πάντων, Εἰ σὺ Ἰουδαῖος ὑπάρχων ἐθνικῶς καὶ οὐχὶ Ἰουδαϊκῶς ζῇς, πῶς τὰ ἔθνη ἀναγκάζεις Ἰουδαΐζειν;

15 Ἡμεῖς φύσει Ἰουδαῖοι καὶ οὐκ ἐξ ἐθνῶν ἁμαρτωλοί· 16 εἰδότες [δὲ] ὅτι οὐ δικαιοῦται ἄνθρωπος ἐξ ἔργων νόμου ἐὰν μὴ διὰ πίστεως Ἰησοῦ Χριστοῦ, καὶ ἡμεῖς εἰς Χριστὸν Ἰησοῦν ἐπιστεύσαμεν, ἵνα δικαιωθῶμεν ἐκ πίστεως Χριστοῦ καὶ οὐκ ἐξ ἔργων νόμου, ὅτι ἐξ ἔργων νόμου οὐ δικαιωθήσεται πᾶσα σάρξ. 17 εἰ δὲ ζητοῦντες δικαιωθῆναι ἐν Χριστῷ εὑρέθημεν καὶ αὐτοὶ ἁμαρτωλοί, ἆρα Χριστὸς ἁμαρτίας διάκονος; μὴ γένοιτο. 18 εἰ γὰρ ἃ κατέλυσα ταῦτα πάλιν οἰκοδομῶ, παραβάτην ἐμαυτὸν συνιστάνω. 19 ἐγὼ γὰρ διὰ νόμου νόμῳ ἀπέθανον, ἵνα θεῷ ζήσω.b Χριστῷ συνεσταύρωμαι· 20 ζῶ δὲ οὐκέτι ἐγώ, ζῇ δὲ ἐν ἐμοὶ Χριστός· ὃ δὲ νῦν ζῶ ἐν σαρκί, ἐν πίστει ζῶ τῇ τοῦ υἱοῦ τοῦ θεοῦ τοῦ ἀγαπήσαντός με καὶ παραδόντος ἑαυτὸν ὑπὲρ ἐμοῦ. 21 οὐκ ἀθετῶ τὴν χάριν τοῦ θεοῦ· εἰ γὰρ διὰ νόμου δικαιοσύνη, ἄρα Χριστὸς δωρεὰν ἀπέθανεν.

3 Ὦ ἀνόητοι Γαλάται, τίς ὑμᾶς ἐβάσκανεν, οἷς κατ᾽ ὀφθαλμοὺς Ἰησοῦς Χριστὸς προεγράφη ἐσταυρωμένος; 2 τοῦτο μόνον θέλω μαθεῖν ἀφ᾽ ὑμῶν· ἐξ ἔργων νόμου τὸ πνεῦμα ἐλάβετε ἢ ἐξ ἀκοῆς πίστεως; 3 οὕτως ἀνόητοί ἐστε, ἐναρξάμενοι πνεύματι νῦν σαρκὶ ἐπιτελεῖσθε; 4 τοσαῦτα ἐπάθετε εἰκῆ; εἴ γε καὶ εἰκῆ. 5 ὁ οὖν ἐπιχορηγῶν ὑμῖν τὸ πνεῦμα καὶ ἐνεργῶν δυνάμεις ἐν ὑμῖν, ἐξ ἔργων νόμου ἢ ἐξ ἀκοῆς πίστεως; 6 καθὼς Ἀβραὰμ

James, he used to eat with the Gentiles. But when they arrived, he began to draw back and separate himself from the Gentiles because he was afraid of those who belonged to the circumcision group. 13The other Jews joined him in his hypocrisy, so that by their hypocrisy even Barnabas was led astray.

14When I saw that they were not acting in line with the truth of the gospel, I said to Peter in front of them all, "You are a Jew, yet you live like a Gentile and not like a Jew. How is it, then, that you force Gentiles to follow Jewish customs?"

15"We who are Jews by birth and not 'Gentile sinners' 16know that a man is not justified by observing the law, but by faith in Jesus Christ. So we, too, have put our faith in Christ Jesus that we may be justified by faith in Christ and not by observing the law, because by observing the law no one will be justified.

17"If, while we seek to be justified in Christ, it becomes evident that we ourselves are sinners, does that mean that Christ promotes sin? Absolutely not! 18If I rebuild what I destroyed, I prove that I am a lawbreaker. 19For through the law I died to the law so that I might live for God. 20I have been crucified with Christ and I no longer live, but Christ lives in me. The life I live in the body, I live by faith in the Son of God, who loved me and gave himself for me. 21I do not set aside the grace of God, for if righteousness could be gained through the law, Christ died for nothing!"d

Faith or Observance of the Law

3 You foolish Galatians! Who has bewitched you? Before your very eyes Jesus Christ was clearly portrayed as crucified. 2I would like to learn just one thing from you: Did you receive the Spirit by observing the law, or by believing what you heard? 3Are you so foolish? After beginning with the Spirit, are you now trying to attain your goal by human effort? 4Have you suffered so much for nothing— if it really was for nothing? 5Does God give you his Spirit and work miracles among you because you observe the law, or because you believe what you heard?

---

h Some interpreters hold that the quotation extends into the following paragraph i Or *reckoned as righteous;* and so elsewhere j Or *the faith of Jesus Christ* k Or *the faith of Christ* l Or *by the faith of the Son of God* m Or *righteousness* n Gk *he*

a13 NIV text omits καὶ † b19 NIV begins verse 20 after ζήσω.

d21 Some interpreters end the quotation after verse 14.

6 Just as Abraham "believed God, and it was reckoned to him as righteousness," [7]so, you see, those who believe are the descendants of Abraham. [8]And the scripture, foreseeing that God would justify the Gentiles by faith, declared the gospel beforehand to Abraham, saying, "All the Gentiles shall be blessed in you." [9]For this reason, those who believe are blessed with Abraham who believed.

10 For all who rely on the works of the law are under a curse; for it is written, "Cursed is everyone who does not observe and obey all the things written in the book of the law." [11]Now it is evident that no one is justified before God by the law; for "The one who is righteous will live by faith."[o] [12]But the law does not rest on faith; on the contrary, "Whoever does the works of the law[p] will live by them." [13]Christ redeemed us from the curse of the law by becoming a curse for us—for it is written, "Cursed is everyone who hangs on a tree"— [14]in order that in Christ Jesus the blessing of Abraham might come to the Gentiles, so that we might receive the promise of the Spirit through faith.

The Promise to Abraham

15 Brothers and sisters,[q] I give an example from daily life: once a person's will[r] has been ratified, no one adds to it or annuls it. [16]Now the promises were made to Abraham and to his offspring;[s] it does not say, "And to offsprings,"[t] as of many; but it says, "And to your offspring,"[s] that is, to one person, who is Christ. [17]My point is this: the law, which came four hundred thirty years later, does not annul a covenant previously ratified by God, so as to nullify the promise. [18]For if the inheritance comes from the law, it no longer comes from the promise; but God granted it to Abraham through the promise.

The Purpose of the Law

19 Why then the law? It was added because of transgressions, until the offspring[s] would come to whom the promise had been made; and it was ordained through angels by a mediator. [20]Now a mediator involves more than one party; but God is one.

21 Is the law then opposed to the promises of God? Certainly not! For if a law had been given that could make alive, then

---

ἐπίστευσεν τῷ θεῷ, καὶ ἐλογίσθη αὐτῷ εἰς δικαιοσύνην.

7 Γινώσκετε ἄρα ὅτι οἱ ἐκ πίστεως, οὗτοι υἱοί εἰσιν Ἀβραάμ. **8** προϊδοῦσα δὲ ἡ γραφὴ ὅτι ἐκ πίστεως δικαιοῖ τὰ ἔθνη ὁ θεός, προευηγγελίσατο τῷ Ἀβραὰμ ὅτι Ἐνευλογηθήσονται ἐν σοὶ πάντα τὰ ἔθνη· **9** ὥστε οἱ ἐκ πίστεως εὐλογοῦνται σὺν τῷ πιστῷ Ἀβραάμ. **10** ὅσοι γὰρ ἐξ ἔργων νόμου εἰσίν, ὑπὸ κατάραν εἰσίν· γέγραπται γὰρ ὅτι Ἐπικατάρατος πᾶς ὃς οὐκ ἐμμένει πᾶσιν τοῖς γεγραμμένοις ἐν τῷ βιβλίῳ τοῦ νόμου τοῦ ποιῆσαι αὐτά. **11** ὅτι δὲ ἐν νόμῳ οὐδεὶς δικαιοῦται παρὰ τῷ θεῷ δῆλον, ὅτι Ὁ δίκαιος ἐκ πίστεως ζήσεται· **12** ὁ δὲ νόμος οὐκ ἔστιν ἐκ πίστεως, ἀλλ᾽ Ὁ ποιήσας αὐτὰ ζήσεται ἐν αὐτοῖς. **13** Χριστὸς ἡμᾶς ἐξηγόρασεν ἐκ τῆς κατάρας τοῦ νόμου γενόμενος ὑπὲρ ἡμῶν κατάρα, ὅτι γέγραπται, Ἐπικατάρατος πᾶς ὁ κρεμάμενος ἐπὶ ξύλου, **14** ἵνα εἰς τὰ ἔθνη ἡ εὐλογία τοῦ Ἀβραὰμ γένηται ἐν Χριστῷ Ἰησοῦ, ἵνα τὴν ἐπαγγελίαν τοῦ πνεύματος λάβωμεν διὰ τῆς πίστεως.

15 Ἀδελφοί, κατὰ ἄνθρωπον λέγω· ὅμως ἀνθρώπου κεκυρωμένην διαθήκην οὐδεὶς ἀθετεῖ ἢ ἐπιδιατάσσεται. **16** τῷ δὲ Ἀβραὰμ ἐρρέθησαν αἱ ἐπαγγελίαι καὶ τῷ σπέρματι αὐτοῦ. οὐ λέγει, Καὶ τοῖς σπέρμασιν, ὡς ἐπὶ πολλῶν ἀλλ᾽ ὡς ἐφ᾽ ἑνός, Καὶ τῷ σπέρματί σου, ὅς ἐστιν Χριστός. **17** τοῦτο δὲ λέγω· διαθήκην προκεκυρωμένην ὑπὸ τοῦ θεοῦ ὁ μετὰ τετρακόσια καὶ τριάκοντα ἔτη γεγονὼς νόμος οὐκ ἀκυροῖ εἰς τὸ καταργῆσαι τὴν ἐπαγγελίαν. **18** εἰ γὰρ ἐκ νόμου ἡ κληρονομία, οὐκέτι ἐξ ἐπαγγελίας· τῷ δὲ Ἀβραὰμ δι᾽ ἐπαγγελίας κεχάρισται ὁ θεός. **19** Τί οὖν ὁ νόμος; τῶν παραβάσεων χάριν προσετέθη, ἄχρις οὗ ἔλθῃ τὸ σπέρμα ᾧ ἐπήγγελται, διαταγεὶς δι᾽ ἀγγέλων ἐν χειρὶ μεσίτου. **20** ὁ δὲ μεσίτης ἑνὸς οὐκ ἔστιν, ὁ δὲ θεὸς εἷς ἐστιν.

21 Ὁ οὖν νόμος κατὰ τῶν ἐπαγγελιῶν [τοῦ θεοῦ]; μὴ γένοιτο. εἰ γὰρ ἐδόθη νόμος ὁ δυνάμενος ζῳοποιῆσαι, ὄντως

---

[6]Consider Abraham: "He believed God, and it was credited to him as righteousness."[a] [7]Understand, then, that those who believe are children of Abraham. [8]The Scripture foresaw that God would justify the Gentiles by faith, and announced the gospel in advance to Abraham: "All nations will be blessed through you."[b] [9]So those who have faith are blessed along with Abraham, the man of faith.

[10]All who rely on observing the law are under a curse, for it is written: "Cursed is everyone who does not continue to do everything written in the Book of the Law."[c] [11]Clearly no one is justified before God by the law, because, "The righteous will live by faith."[d] [12]The law is not based on faith; on the contrary, "The man who does these things will live by them."[e] [13]Christ redeemed us from the curse of the law by becoming a curse for us, for it is written: "Cursed is everyone who is hung on a tree."[f] [14]He redeemed us in order that the blessing given to Abraham might come to the Gentiles through Christ Jesus, so that by faith we might receive the promise of the Spirit.

The Law and the Promise

[15]Brothers, let me take an example from everyday life. Just as no one can set aside or add to a human covenant that has been duly established, so it is in this case. [16]The promises were spoken to Abraham and to his seed. The Scripture does not say "and to seeds," meaning many people, but "and to your seed,"[g] meaning one person, who is Christ. [17]What I mean is this: The law, introduced 430 years later, does not set aside the covenant previously established by God and thus do away with the promise. [18]For if the inheritance depends on the law, then it no longer depends on a promise; but God in his grace gave it to Abraham through a promise.

[19]What, then, was the purpose of the law? It was added because of transgressions until the Seed to whom the promise referred had come. The law was put into effect through angels by a mediator. [20]A mediator, however, does not represent just one party; but God is one.

[21]Is the law, therefore, opposed to the promises of God? Absolutely not! For if a law had been given that could impart life,

---

[o] Or *The one who is righteous through faith will live*
[p] Gk *does them*   [q] Gk *Brothers*   [r] Or *covenant* (as in verse 17)   [s] Gk *seed*   [t] Gk *seeds*

[a]6 Gen. 15:6   [b]8 Gen. 12:3; 18:18; 22:18   [c]10 Deut. 27:26   [d]11 Hab. 2:4   [e]12 Lev. 18:5   [f]13 Deut. 21:23   [g]16 Gen. 12:7; 13:15; 24:7

righteousness would indeed come through the law. 22But the scripture has imprisoned all things under the power of sin, so that what was promised through faith in Jesus Christ[v] might be given to those who believe.

23 Now before faith came, we were imprisoned and guarded under the law until faith would be revealed. 24Therefore the law was our disciplinarian until Christ came, so that we might be justified by faith. 25But now that faith has come, we are no longer subject to a disciplinarian, 26for in Christ Jesus you are all children of God through faith. 27As many of you as were baptized into Christ have clothed yourselves with Christ. 28There is no longer Jew or Greek, there is no longer slave or free, there is no longer male and female; for all of you are one in Christ Jesus. 29And if you belong to Christ, then you are Abraham's offspring,[u] heirs according to the promise.

4 My point is this: heirs, as long as they are minors, are no better than slaves, though they are the owners of all the property; 2but they remain under guardians and trustees until the date set by the father. 3So with us; while we were minors, we were enslaved to the elemental spirits[w] of the world. 4But when the fullness of time had come, God sent his Son, born of a woman, born under the law, 5in order to redeem those who were under the law, so that we might receive adoption as children. 6And because you are children, God has sent the Spirit of his Son into our[x] hearts, crying, "Abba![y] Father!" 7So you are no longer a slave but a child, and if a child then also an heir, through God.[z]

Paul Reproves the Galatians

8 Formerly, when you did not know God, you were enslaved to beings that by nature are not gods. 9Now, however, that you have come to know God, or rather to be known by God, how can you turn back again to the weak and beggarly elemental spirits?[a] How can you want to be enslaved to them again? 10You are observing special days, and months, and seasons, and years. 11I am afraid that my work for you may have been wasted.

12 Friends,[b] I beg you, become as I am, for I also have become as you are. You

ἐκ νόμου ἂν ἦν ἡ δικαιοσύνη· 22 ἀλλὰ συνέκλεισεν ἡ γραφὴ τὰ πάντα ὑπὸ ἁμαρτίαν, ἵνα ἡ ἐπαγγελία ἐκ πίστεως Ἰησοῦ Χριστοῦ δοθῇ τοῖς πιστεύουσιν.

23 Πρὸ τοῦ δὲ ἐλθεῖν τὴν πίστιν ὑπὸ νόμον ἐφρουρούμεθα συγκλειόμενοι εἰς τὴν μέλλουσαν πίστιν ἀποκαλυφθῆναι, 24 ὥστε ὁ νόμος παιδαγωγὸς ἡμῶν γέγονεν εἰς Χριστόν, ἵνα ἐκ πίστεως δικαιωθῶμεν· 25 ἐλθούσης δὲ τῆς πίστεως οὐκέτι ὑπὸ παιδαγωγόν ἐσμεν. 26 Πάντες γὰρ υἱοὶ θεοῦ ἐστε διὰ τῆς πίστεως ἐν Χριστῷ Ἰησοῦ· 27 ὅσοι γὰρ εἰς Χριστὸν ἐβαπτίσθητε, Χριστὸν ἐνεδύσασθε. 28 οὐκ ἔνι Ἰουδαῖος οὐδὲ Ἕλλην, οὐκ ἔνι δοῦλος οὐδὲ ἐλεύθερος, οὐκ ἔνι ἄρσεν καὶ θῆλυ· πάντες γὰρ ὑμεῖς εἷς ἐστε ἐν Χριστῷ Ἰησοῦ. 29 εἰ δὲ ὑμεῖς Χριστοῦ, ἄρα τοῦ Ἀβραὰμ σπέρμα ἐστέ, κατ' ἐπαγγελίαν κληρονόμοι.

4 Λέγω δέ, ἐφ' ὅσον χρόνον ὁ κληρονόμος νήπιός ἐστιν, οὐδὲν διαφέρει δούλου κύριος πάντων ὤν, 2 ἀλλὰ ὑπὸ ἐπιτρόπους ἐστὶν καὶ οἰκονόμους ἄχρι τῆς προθεσμίας τοῦ πατρός. 3 οὕτως καὶ ἡμεῖς, ὅτε ἦμεν νήπιοι, ὑπὸ τὰ στοιχεῖα τοῦ κόσμου ἤμεθα δεδουλωμένοι· 4 ὅτε δὲ ἦλθεν τὸ πλήρωμα τοῦ χρόνου, ἐξαπέστειλεν ὁ θεὸς τὸν υἱὸν αὐτοῦ, γενόμενον ἐκ γυναικός, γενόμενον ὑπὸ νόμον, 5 ἵνα τοὺς ὑπὸ νόμον ἐξαγοράσῃ, ἵνα τὴν υἱοθεσίαν ἀπολάβωμεν. 6 Ὅτι δέ ἐστε υἱοί, ἐξαπέστειλεν ὁ θεὸς τὸ πνεῦμα τοῦ υἱοῦ αὐτοῦ εἰς τὰς καρδίας ἡμῶν[a] κρᾶζον, Αββα ὁ πατήρ. 7 ὥστε οὐκέτι εἶ δοῦλος ἀλλὰ υἱός· εἰ δὲ υἱός, καὶ κληρονόμος διὰ θεοῦ[b].

8 Ἀλλὰ τότε μὲν οὐκ εἰδότες θεὸν ἐδουλεύσατε τοῖς φύσει μὴ οὖσιν θεοῖς· 9 νῦν δὲ γνόντες θεόν, μᾶλλον δὲ γνωσθέντες ὑπὸ θεοῦ, πῶς ἐπιστρέφετε πάλιν ἐπὶ τὰ ἀσθενῆ καὶ πτωχὰ στοιχεῖα οἷς πάλιν ἄνωθεν δουλεύειν θέλετε; 10 ἡμέρας παρατηρεῖσθε καὶ μῆνας καὶ καιροὺς καὶ ἐνιαυτούς, 11 φοβοῦμαι ὑμᾶς μή πως εἰκῆ κεκοπίακα εἰς ὑμᾶς.

12 Γίνεσθε ὡς ἐγώ, ὅτι κἀγὼ ὡς ὑμεῖς, ἀδελφοί, δέομαι ὑμῶν. οὐδέν με

then righteousness would certainly have come by the law. 22But the Scripture declares that the whole world is a prisoner of sin, so that what was promised, being given through faith in Jesus Christ, might be given to those who believe.

23Before this faith came, we were held prisoners by the law, locked up until faith should be revealed. 24So the law was put in charge to lead us to Christ[h] that we might be justified by faith. 25Now that faith has come, we are no longer under the supervision of the law.

Sons of God

26You are all sons of God through faith in Christ Jesus, 27for all of you who were baptized into Christ have clothed yourselves with Christ. 28There is neither Jew nor Greek, slave nor free, male nor female, for you are all one in Christ Jesus. 29If you belong to Christ, then you are Abraham's seed, and heirs according to the promise.

4 What I am saying is that as long as the heir is a child, he is no different from a slave, although he owns the whole estate. 2He is subject to guardians and trustees until the time set by his father. 3So also, when we were children, we were in slavery under the basic principles of the world. 4But when the time had fully come, God sent his Son, born of a woman, born under law, 5to redeem those under law, that we might receive the full rights of sons. 6Because you are sons, God sent the Spirit of his Son into our hearts, the Spirit who calls out, "*Abba,[a]* Father." 7So you are no longer a slave, but a son; and since you are a son, God has made you also an heir.

Paul's Concern for the Galatians

8Formerly, when you did not know God, you were slaves to those who by nature are not gods. 9But now that you know God—or rather are known by God—how is it that you are turning back to those weak and miserable principles? Do you wish to be enslaved by them all over again? 10You are observing special days and months and seasons and years! 11I fear for you, that somehow I have wasted my efforts on you.

12I plead with you, brothers, become like me, for I became like you. You have done

---

u Gk seed   v Or through the faith of Jesus Christ   w Or the rudiments   x Other ancient authorities read your   y Aramaic for Father   z Other ancient authorities read an heir of God through Christ   a Or beggarly rudiments   b Gk Brothers

a6 NRSV note x ὑμῶν   b7 NRSV note z κληρονόμος θεοῦ διὰ Χριστοῦ

h24 Or charge until Christ came   a6 Aramaic for Father

have done me no wrong. ¹³You know that it was because of a physical infirmity that I first announced the gospel to you; ¹⁴though my condition put you to the test, you did not scorn or despise me, but welcomed me as an angel of God, as Christ Jesus. ¹⁵What has become of the goodwill you felt? For I testify that, had it been possible, you would have torn out your eyes and given them to me. ¹⁶Have I now become your enemy by telling you the truth? ¹⁷They make much of you, but for no good purpose; they want to exclude you, so that you may make much of them. ¹⁸It is good to be made much of for a good purpose at all times, and not only when I am present with you. ¹⁹My little children, for whom I am again in the pain of childbirth until Christ is formed in you, ²⁰I wish I were present with you now and could change my tone, for I am perplexed about you.

The Allegory of Hagar and Sarah

21 Tell me, you who desire to be subject to the law, will you not listen to the law? ²²For it is written that Abraham had two sons, one by a slave woman and the other by a free woman. ²³One, the child of the slave, was born according to the flesh; the other, the child of the free woman, was born through the promise. ²⁴Now this is an allegory: these women are two covenants. One woman, in fact, is Hagar, from Mount Sinai, bearing children for slavery. ²⁵Now Hagar is Mount Sinai in Arabia[c] and corresponds to the present Jerusalem, for she is in slavery with her children. ²⁶But the other woman corresponds to the Jerusalem above; she is free, and she is our mother. ²⁷For it is written,

"Rejoice, you childless one, you who
    bear no children,
  burst into song and shout, you who
    endure no birth pangs;
  for the children of the desolate woman
    are more numerous
    than the children of the one who is
    married."

²⁸Now you,[d] my friends,[e] are children of the promise, like Isaac. ²⁹But just as at that time the child who was born according to the flesh persecuted the child who was born according to the Spirit, so it is now also. ³⁰But what does the scripture say? "Drive out the slave and her child; for the

ἠδικήσατε· 13 οἴδατε δὲ ὅτι δι' ἀσθένειαν τῆς σαρκὸς εὐηγγελισάμην ὑμῖν τὸ πρότερον, 14 καὶ τὸν πειρασμὸν ὑμῶν ἐν τῇ σαρκί μου οὐκ ἐξουθενήσατε οὐδὲ ἐξεπτύσατε, ἀλλὰ ὡς ἄγγελον θεοῦ ἐδέξασθέ με, ὡς Χριστὸν Ἰησοῦν. 15 ποῦ οὖν ὁ μακαρισμὸς ὑμῶν; μαρτυρῶ γὰρ ὑμῖν ὅτι εἰ δυνατὸν τοὺς ὀφθαλμοὺς ὑμῶν ἐξορύξαντες ἐδώκατέ μοι. 16 ὥστε ἐχθρὸς ὑμῶν γέγονα ἀληθεύων ὑμῖν; 17 ζηλοῦσιν ὑμᾶς οὐ καλῶς, ἀλλὰ ἐκκλεῖσαι ὑμᾶς θέλουσιν, ἵνα αὐτοὺς ζηλοῦτε· 18 καλὸν δὲ ζηλοῦσθαι ἐν καλῷ πάντοτε καὶ μὴ μόνον ἐν τῷ παρεῖναί με πρὸς ὑμᾶς. 19 τέκνα μου, οὓς πάλιν ὠδίνω μέχρις οὗ μορφωθῇ Χριστὸς ἐν ὑμῖν· 20 ἤθελον δὲ παρεῖναι πρὸς ὑμᾶς ἄρτι καὶ ἀλλάξαι τὴν φωνήν μου, ὅτι ἀποροῦμαι ἐν ὑμῖν.

21 Λέγετέ μοι, οἱ ὑπὸ νόμον θέλοντες εἶναι, τὸν νόμον οὐκ ἀκούετε; 22 γέγραπται γὰρ ὅτι Ἀβραὰμ δύο υἱοὺς ἔσχεν, ἕνα ἐκ τῆς παιδίσκης καὶ ἕνα ἐκ τῆς ἐλευθέρας. 23 ἀλλ' ὁ μὲν ἐκ τῆς παιδίσκης κατὰ σάρκα γεγέννηται, ὁ δὲ ἐκ τῆς ἐλευθέρας δι' ἐπαγγελίας. 24 ἅτινά ἐστιν ἀλληγορούμενα· αὗται γάρ εἰσιν δύο διαθῆκαι, μία μὲν ἀπὸ ὄρους Σινᾶ εἰς δουλείαν γεννῶσα, ἥτις ἐστὶν Ἁγάρ. 25 τὸ δὲ Ἁγὰρ Σινᾶ[c] ὄρος ἐστὶν ἐν τῇ Ἀραβίᾳ· συστοιχεῖ δὲ τῇ νῦν Ἰερουσαλήμ, δουλεύει γὰρ μετὰ τῶν τέκνων αὐτῆς. 26 ἡ δὲ ἄνω Ἰερουσαλὴμ ἐλευθέρα ἐστίν, ἥτις ἐστὶν μήτηρ ἡμῶν· 27 γέγραπται γάρ,

Εὐφράνθητι, στεῖρα ἡ οὐ τίκτουσα,
  ῥῆξον καὶ βόησον, ἡ οὐκ ὠδίνουσα·
  ὅτι πολλὰ τὰ τέκνα τῆς ἐρήμου
    μᾶλλον ἢ τῆς ἐχούσης τὸν
    ἄνδρα.

28 ὑμεῖς[d] δέ, ἀδελφοί, κατὰ Ἰσαὰκ ἐπαγγελίας τέκνα ἐστέ[d]. 29 ἀλλ' ὥσπερ τότε ὁ κατὰ σάρκα γεννηθεὶς ἐδίωκεν τὸν κατὰ πνεῦμα, οὕτως καὶ νῦν. 30 ἀλλὰ τί λέγει ἡ γραφή; Ἔκβαλε τὴν παιδίσκην καὶ τὸν υἱὸν αὐτῆς· οὐ

me no wrong. ¹³As you know, it was because of an illness that I first preached the gospel to you. ¹⁴Even though my illness was a trial to you, you did not treat me with contempt or scorn. Instead, you welcomed me as if I were an angel of God, as if I were Christ Jesus himself. ¹⁵What has happened to all your joy? I can testify that, if you could have done so, you would have torn out your eyes and given them to me. ¹⁶Have I now become your enemy by telling you the truth?

¹⁷Those people are zealous to win you over, but for no good. What they want is to alienate you ⌊from us⌋, so that you may be zealous for them. ¹⁸It is fine to be zealous, provided the purpose is good, and to be so always and not just when I am with you. ¹⁹My dear children, for whom I am again in the pains of childbirth until Christ is formed in you, ²⁰how I wish I could be with you now and change my tone, because I am perplexed about you!

Hagar and Sarah

²¹Tell me, you who want to be under the law, are you not aware of what the law says? ²²For it is written that Abraham had two sons, one by the slave woman and the other by the free woman. ²³His son by the slave woman was born in the ordinary way; but his son by the free woman was born as the result of a promise.

²⁴These things may be taken figuratively, for the women represent two covenants. One covenant is from Mount Sinai and bears children who are to be slaves: This is Hagar. ²⁵Now Hagar stands for Mount Sinai in Arabia and corresponds to the present city of Jerusalem, because she is in slavery with her children. ²⁶But the Jerusalem that is above is free, and she is our mother. ²⁷For it is written:

"Be glad, O barren woman,
  who bears no children;
  break forth and cry aloud,
  you who have no labor pains;
  because more are the children of the
    desolate woman
  than of her who has a husband."[b]

²⁸Now you, brothers, like Isaac, are children of promise. ²⁹At that time the son born in the ordinary way persecuted the son born by the power of the Spirit. It is the same now. ³⁰But what does the Scripture say? "Get rid of the slave woman and her son, for the slave woman's son will

---

[c] Other ancient authorities read *For Sinai is a mountain in Arabia*   [d] Other ancient authorities read *we*
[e] Gk *brothers*

[c]25 NRSV note c *γὰρ Σινᾶ*   [d]28 NRSV note d *ἡμεῖς ... ἐσμέν.*

[b]27 Isaiah 54:1

child of the slave will not share the inheritance with the child of the free woman." [31]So then, friends,[e] we are children, not of the slave but of the free woman.

5 [1]For freedom Christ has set us free. Stand firm, therefore, and do not submit again to a yoke of slavery.

The Nature of Christian Freedom

[2]Listen! I, Paul, am telling you that if you let yourselves be circumcised, Christ will be of no benefit to you. [3]Once again I testify to every man who lets himself be circumcised that he is obliged to obey the entire law. [4]You who want to be justified by the law have cut yourselves off from Christ; you have fallen away from grace. [5]For through the Spirit, by faith, we eagerly wait for the hope of righteousness. [6]For in Christ Jesus neither circumcision nor uncircumcision counts for anything; the only thing that counts is faith working[f] through love.

[7]You were running well; who prevented you from obeying the truth? [8]Such persuasion does not come from the one who calls you. [9]A little yeast leavens the whole batch of dough. [10]I am confident about you in the Lord that you will not think otherwise. But whoever it is that is confusing you will pay the penalty. [11]But my friends,[e] why am I still being persecuted if I am still preaching circumcision? In that case the offense of the cross has been removed. [12]I wish those who unsettle you would castrate themselves!

[13]For you were called to freedom, brothers and sisters;[e] only do not use your freedom as an opportunity for self-indulgence,[g] but through love become slaves to one another. [14]For the whole law is summed up in a single commandment, "You shall love your neighbor as yourself." [15]If, however, you bite and devour one another, take care that you are not consumed by one another.

The Works of the Flesh

[16]Live by the Spirit, I say, and do not gratify the desires of the flesh. [17]For what the flesh desires is opposed to the Spirit, and what the Spirit desires is opposed to the flesh; for these are opposed to each other, to prevent you from doing what you want. [18]But if you are led by the Spirit, you are not subject to the law. [19]Now the

---

γὰρ μὴ κληρονομήσει ὁ υἱὸς τῆς παιδίσκης μετὰ τοῦ υἱοῦ τῆς ἐλευθέρας. 31 διό, ἀδελφοί, οὐκ ἐσμὲν παιδίσκης τέκνα ἀλλὰ τῆς ἐλευθέρας.

5 τῇ ἐλευθερίᾳ ἡμᾶς Χριστὸς ἠλευθέρωσεν· στήκετε οὖν καὶ μὴ πάλιν ζυγῷ δουλείας ἐνέχεσθε.

2 Ἴδε ἐγὼ Παῦλος λέγω ὑμῖν ὅτι ἐὰν περιτέμνησθε, Χριστὸς ὑμᾶς οὐδὲν ὠφελήσει. 3 μαρτύρομαι δὲ πάλιν παντὶ ἀνθρώπῳ περιτεμνομένῳ ὅτι ὀφειλέτης ἐστὶν ὅλον τὸν νόμον ποιῆσαι. 4 κατηργήθητε ἀπὸ Χριστοῦ, οἵτινες ἐν νόμῳ δικαιοῦσθε, τῆς χάριτος ἐξεπέσατε. 5 ἡμεῖς γὰρ πνεύματι ἐκ πίστεως ἐλπίδα δικαιοσύνης ἀπεκδεχόμεθα. 6 ἐν γὰρ Χριστῷ Ἰησοῦ οὔτε περιτομή τι ἰσχύει οὔτε ἀκροβυστία ἀλλὰ πίστις δι᾽ ἀγάπης ἐνεργουμένη.

7 Ἐτρέχετε καλῶς· τίς ὑμᾶς ἐνέκοψεν [τῇ] ἀληθείᾳ μὴ πείθεσθαι; 8 ἡ πεισμονὴ οὐκ ἐκ τοῦ καλοῦντος ὑμᾶς. 9 μικρὰ ζύμη ὅλον τὸ φύραμα ζυμοῖ. 10 ἐγὼ πέποιθα εἰς ὑμᾶς ἐν κυρίῳ ὅτι οὐδὲν ἄλλο φρονήσετε· ὁ δὲ ταράσσων ὑμᾶς βαστάσει τὸ κρίμα, ὅστις ἐὰν ᾖ. 11 ἐγὼ δέ, ἀδελφοί, εἰ περιτομὴν ἔτι κηρύσσω, τί ἔτι διώκομαι; ἄρα κατήργηται τὸ σκάνδαλον τοῦ σταυροῦ. 12 ὄφελον καὶ ἀποκόψονται οἱ ἀναστατοῦντες ὑμᾶς.

13 Ὑμεῖς γὰρ ἐπ᾽ ἐλευθερίᾳ ἐκλήθητε, ἀδελφοί· μόνον μὴ τὴν ἐλευθερίαν εἰς ἀφορμὴν τῇ σαρκί, ἀλλὰ διὰ τῆς ἀγάπης δουλεύετε ἀλλήλοις. 14 ὁ γὰρ πᾶς νόμος ἐν ἑνὶ λόγῳ πεπλήρωται, ἐν τῷ Ἀγαπήσεις τὸν πλησίον σου ὡς σεαυτόν. 15 εἰ δὲ ἀλλήλους δάκνετε καὶ κατεσθίετε, βλέπετε μὴ ὑπ᾽ ἀλλήλων ἀναλωθῆτε.

16 Λέγω δέ, πνεύματι περιπατεῖτε καὶ ἐπιθυμίαν σαρκὸς οὐ μὴ τελέσητε. 17 ἡ γὰρ σὰρξ ἐπιθυμεῖ κατὰ τοῦ πνεύματος, τὸ δὲ πνεῦμα κατὰ τῆς σαρκός, ταῦτα γὰρ ἀλλήλοις ἀντίκειται, ἵνα μὴ ἃ ἐὰν θέλητε ταῦτα ποιῆτε. 18 εἰ δὲ πνεύματι ἄγεσθε, οὐκ ἐστὲ ὑπὸ νόμον. 19 φανερὰ δέ ἐστιν τὰ

---

never share in the inheritance with the free woman's son."[c] [31]Therefore, brothers, we are not children of the slave woman, but of the free woman.

Freedom in Christ

5 It is for freedom that Christ has set us free. Stand firm, then, and do not let yourselves be burdened again by a yoke of slavery.

[2]Mark my words! I, Paul, tell you that if you let yourselves be circumcised, Christ will be of no value to you at all. [3]Again I declare to every man who lets himself be circumcised that he is obligated to obey the whole law. [4]You who are trying to be justified by law have been alienated from Christ; you have fallen away from grace. [5]But by faith we eagerly await through the Spirit the righteousness for which we hope. [6]For in Christ Jesus neither circumcision nor uncircumcision has any value. The only thing that counts is faith expressing itself through love.

[7]You were running a good race. Who cut in on you and kept you from obeying the truth? [8]That kind of persuasion does not come from the one who calls you. [9]"A little yeast works through the whole batch of dough." [10]I am confident in the Lord that you will take no other view. The one who is throwing you into confusion will pay the penalty, whoever he may be. [11]Brothers, if I am still preaching circumcision, why am I still being persecuted? In that case the offense of the cross has been abolished. [12]As for those agitators, I wish they would go the whole way and emasculate themselves!

[13]You, my brothers, were called to be free. But do not use your freedom to indulge the sinful nature[a]; rather, serve one another in love. [14]The entire law is summed up in a single command: "Love your neighbor as yourself."[b] [15]If you keep on biting and devouring each other, watch out or you will be destroyed by each other.

Life by the Spirit

[16]So I say, live by the Spirit, and you will not gratify the desires of the sinful nature. [17]For the sinful nature desires what is contrary to the Spirit, and the Spirit what is contrary to the sinful nature. They are in conflict with each other, so that you do not do what you want. [18]But if you are led by the Spirit, you are not under law.

---

[e] Gk brothers   [f] Or made effective   [g] Gk the flesh

[c]30 Gen. 21:10   [a]13 Or the flesh; also in verses 16, 17, 19 and 24   [b]14 Lev. 19:18

works of the flesh are obvious: fornication, impurity, licentiousness, 20idolatry, sorcery, enmities, strife, jealousy, anger, quarrels, dissensions, factions, 21envy,h drunkenness, carousing, and things like these. I am warning you, as I warned you before: those who do such things will not inherit the kingdom of God.

The Fruit of the Spirit

22 By contrast, the fruit of the Spirit is love, joy, peace, patience, kindness, generosity, faithfulness, 23gentleness, and self-control. There is no law against such things. 24And those who belong to Christ Jesus have crucified the flesh with its passions and desires. 25If we live by the Spirit, let us also be guided by the Spirit. 26Let us not become conceited, competing against one another, envying one another.

Bear One Another's Burdens

6 My friends,i if anyone is detected in a transgression, you who have received the Spirit should restore such a one in a spirit of gentleness. Take care that you yourselves are not tempted. 2Bear one another's burdens, and in this way you will fulfillj the law of Christ. 3For if those who are nothing think they are something, they deceive themselves. 4All must test their own work; then that work, rather than their neighbor's work, will become a cause for pride. 5For all must carry their own loads.

6 Those who are taught the word must share in all good things with their teacher.

7 Do not be deceived; God is not mocked, for you reap whatever you sow. 8If you sow to your own flesh, you will reap corruption from the flesh; but if you sow to the Spirit, you will reap eternal life from the Spirit. 9So let us not grow weary in doing what is right, for we will reap at harvest time, if we do not give up. 10So then, whenever we have an opportunity, let us work for the good of all, and especially for those of the family of faith.

Final Admonitions and Benediction

11 See what large letters I make when I am writing in my own hand! 12It is those who want to make a good showing in the flesh that try to compel you to be circumcised—only that they may not be persecuted for the cross of Christ. 13Even the

ἔργα τῆς σαρκός, ἅτινά ἐστιν πορνεία, ἀκαθαρσία, ἀσέλγεια, 20 εἰδωλολατρία, φαρμακεία, ἔχθραι, ἔρις, ζῆλος, θυμοί, ἐριθεῖαι, διχοστασίαι, αἱρέσεις, 21 φθόνοιa, μέθαι, κῶμοι καὶ τὰ ὅμοια τούτοις, ἅ προλέγω ὑμῖν καθὼς προεῖπον ὅτι οἱ τὰ τοιαῦτα πράσσοντες βασιλείαν θεοῦ οὐ κληρονομήσουσιν.

22 Ὁ δὲ καρπὸς τοῦ πνεύματός ἐστιν ἀγάπη χαρὰ εἰρήνη, μακροθυμία χρηστότης ἀγαθωσύνη, πίστις 23 πραΰτης ἐγκράτεια· κατὰ τῶν τοιούτων οὐκ ἔστιν νόμος. 24 οἱ δὲ τοῦ Χριστοῦ [Ἰησοῦ] τὴν σάρκα ἐσταύρωσαν σὺν τοῖς παθήμασιν καὶ ταῖς ἐπιθυμίαις. 25 εἰ ζῶμεν πνεύματι, πνεύματι καὶ στοιχῶμεν. 26 μὴ γινώμεθα κενόδοξοι, ἀλλήλους προκαλούμενοι, ἀλλήλοις φθονοῦντες.

6 Ἀδελφοί, ἐὰν καὶ προλημφθῇ ἄνθρωπος ἔν τινι παραπτώματι, ὑμεῖς οἱ πνευματικοὶ καταρτίζετε τὸν τοιοῦτον ἐν πνεύματι πραΰτητος, σκοπῶν σεαυτὸν μὴ καὶ σὺ πειρασθῇς. 2 Ἀλλήλων τὰ βάρη βαστάζετε καὶ οὕτως ἀναπληρώσετεa τὸν νόμον τοῦ Χριστοῦ. 3 εἰ γὰρ δοκεῖ τις εἶναί τι μηδὲν ὤν, φρεναπατᾷ ἑαυτόν. 4 τὸ δὲ ἔργον ἑαυτοῦ δοκιμαζέτω ἕκαστος, καὶ τότε εἰς ἑαυτὸν μόνον τὸ καύχημα ἕξει καὶ οὐκ εἰς τὸν ἕτερον· 5 ἕκαστος γὰρ τὸ ἴδιον φορτίον βαστάσει. 6 Κοινωνείτω δὲ ὁ κατηχούμενος τὸν λόγον τῷ κατηχοῦντι ἐν πᾶσιν ἀγαθοῖς. 7 Μὴ πλανᾶσθε, θεὸς οὐ μυκτηρίζεται. ὃ γὰρ ἐὰν σπείρῃ ἄνθρωπος, τοῦτο καὶ θερίσει· 8 ὅτι ὁ σπείρων εἰς τὴν σάρκα ἑαυτοῦ ἐκ τῆς σαρκὸς θερίσει φθοράν, ὁ δὲ σπείρων εἰς τὸ πνεῦμα ἐκ τοῦ πνεύματος θερίσει ζωὴν αἰώνιον. 9 τὸ δὲ καλὸν ποιοῦντες μὴ ἐγκακῶμεν, καιρῷ γὰρ ἰδίῳ θερίσομεν μὴ ἐκλυόμενοι. 10 ἄρα οὖν ὡς καιρὸν ἔχομεν, ἐργαζώμεθα τὸ ἀγαθὸν πρὸς πάντας, μάλιστα δὲ πρὸς τοὺς οἰκείους τῆς πίστεως.

11 Ἴδετε πηλίκοις ὑμῖν γράμμασιν ἔγραψα τῇ ἐμῇ χειρί. 12 ὅσοι θέλουσιν εὐπροσωπῆσαι ἐν σαρκί, οὗτοι ἀναγκάζουσιν ὑμᾶς περιτέμνεσθαι, μόνον ἵνα τῷ σταυρῷ τοῦ Χριστοῦ μὴ διώκωνται.

19The acts of the sinful nature are obvious: sexual immorality, impurity and debauchery;20idolatry and witchcraft; hatred, discord, jealousy, fits of rage, selfish ambition, dissensions, factions 21and envy; drunkenness, orgies, and the like. I warn you, as I did before, that those who live like this will not inherit the kingdom of God.

22But the fruit of the Spirit is love, joy, peace, patience, kindness, goodness, faithfulness, 23gentleness and self-control. Against such things there is no law. 24Those who belong to Christ Jesus have crucified the sinful nature with its passions and desires. 25Since we live by the Spirit, let us keep in step with the Spirit. 26Let us not become conceited, provoking and envying each other.

Doing Good to All

6 Brothers, if someone is caught in a sin, you who are spiritual should restore him gently. But watch yourself, or you also may be tempted. 2Carry each other's burdens, and in this way you will fulfill the law of Christ. 3If anyone thinks he is something when he is nothing, he deceives himself. 4Each one should test his own actions. Then he can take pride in himself, without comparing himself to somebody else, 5for each one should carry his own load.

6Anyone who receives instruction in the word must share all good things with his instructor.

7Do not be deceived: God cannot be mocked. A man reaps what he sows. 8The one who sows to please his sinful nature, from that naturea will reap destruction; the one who sows to please the Spirit, from the Spirit will reap eternal life. 9Let us not become weary in doing good, for at the proper time we will reap a harvest if we do not give up. 10Therefore, as we have opportunity, let us do good to all people, especially to those who belong to the family of believers.

Not Circumcision but a New Creation

11See what large letters I use as I write to you with my own hand!

12Those who want to make a good impression outwardly are trying to compel you to be circumcised. The only reason they do this is to avoid being persecuted for the cross of Christ. 13Not even those

---

h Other ancient authorities add *murder* i Gk *Brothers*
j Other ancient authorities read *in this way fulfill*

a21 NRSV note h adds φόνοι a2 NRSV note j ἀναπληρώσατε

a8 Or *his flesh, from the flesh*

circumcised do not themselves obey the law, but they want you to be circumcised so that they may boast about your flesh. [14]May I never boast of anything except the cross of our Lord Jesus Christ, by which[k] the world has been crucified to me, and I to the world. [15]For[l] neither circumcision nor uncircumcision is anything; but a new creation is everything! [16]As for those who will follow this rule—peace be upon them, and mercy, and upon the Israel of God.

[17] From now on, let no one make trouble for me; for I carry the marks of Jesus branded on my body.

[18] May the grace of our Lord Jesus Christ be with your spirit, brothers and sisters.[m] Amen.

13 οὐδὲ γὰρ οἱ περιτεμνόμενοι αὐτοὶ νόμον φυλάσσουσιν ἀλλὰ θέλουσιν ὑμᾶς περιτέμνεσθαι, ἵνα ἐν τῇ ὑμετέρᾳ σαρκὶ καυχήσωνται. **14** ἐμοὶ δὲ μὴ γένοιτο καυχᾶσθαι εἰ μὴ ἐν τῷ σταυρῷ τοῦ κυρίου ἡμῶν Ἰησοῦ Χριστοῦ, δι' οὗ ἐμοὶ κόσμος ἐσταύρωται κἀγὼ κόσμῳ. **15** οὔτε γὰρ[b] περιτομή τί ἐστιν οὔτε ἀκροβυστία ἀλλὰ καινὴ κτίσις. **16** καὶ ὅσοι τῷ κανόνι τούτῳ στοιχήσουσιν, εἰρήνη ἐπ' αὐτοὺς καὶ ἔλεος καὶ ἐπὶ τὸν Ἰσραὴλ τοῦ θεοῦ.

17 Τοῦ λοιποῦ κόπους μοι μηδεὶς παρεχέτω· ἐγὼ γὰρ τὰ στίγματα τοῦ Ἰησοῦ ἐν τῷ σώματί μου βαστάζω.

18 Ἡ χάρις τοῦ κυρίου ἡμῶν Ἰησοῦ Χριστοῦ μετὰ τοῦ πνεύματος ὑμῶν, ἀδελφοί· ἀμήν.

who are circumcised obey the law, yet they want you to be circumcised that they may boast about your flesh. [14]May I never boast except in the cross of our Lord Jesus Christ, through which[b] the world has been crucified to me, and I to the world. [15]Neither circumcision nor uncircumcision means anything; what counts is a new creation. [16]Peace and mercy to all who follow this rule, even to the Israel of God.

[17]Finally, let no one cause me trouble, for I bear on my body the marks of Jesus.

[18]The grace of our Lord Jesus Christ be with your spirit, brothers. Amen.

---

[k] Or *through whom*   [l] Other ancient authorities add *in Christ Jesus*   [m] Gk *brothers*   [b]15 NRSV note l ἐν γὰρ Χριστῷ Ἰησοῦ οὔτε   [b]14 Or *whom*

NRSV

Salutation

1 Paul, an apostle of Christ Jesus by the will of God,

To the saints who are in Ephesus and are faithful[a] in Christ Jesus:

2 Grace to you and peace from God our Father and the Lord Jesus Christ.

Spiritual Blessings in Christ

3 Blessed be the God and Father of our Lord Jesus Christ, who has blessed us in Christ with every spiritual blessing in the heavenly places, [4]just as he chose us in Christ[b] before the foundation of the world to be holy and blameless before him in love. [5]He destined us for adoption as his children through Jesus Christ, according to the good pleasure of his will, [6]to the praise of his glorious grace that he freely bestowed on us in the Beloved. [7]In him we have redemption through his blood, the forgiveness of our trespasses, according to the riches of his grace [8]that he lavished on us. With all wisdom and insight [9]he has made known to us the mystery of his will, according to his good pleasure that he set forth in Christ, [10]as a plan for the fullness of time, to gather up all things in him, things in heaven and things on earth. [11]In Christ we have also obtained an inheritance,[c] having been destined according to the purpose of him who accomplishes all things according to his counsel and will, [12]so that we, who were the first to set our hope on Christ, might live for the praise of his glory. [13]In him you also, when you had heard the word of truth, the gospel of your salvation, and had believed in him, were marked with the seal of the promised Holy Spirit; [14]this[d] is the pledge of our inheritance toward redemption as God's own people, to the praise of his glory.

Paul's Prayer

15 I have heard of your faith in the Lord Jesus and your love[e] toward all the saints, and for this reason [16]I do not cease to give thanks for you as I remember you in my prayers. [17]I pray that the God of our Lord Jesus Christ, the Father of glory, may give you a spirit of wisdom and revelation as you come to know him, [18]so that, with the

ΠΡΟΣ ΕΦΕΣΙΟΥΣ

1 Παῦλος ἀπόστολος Χριστοῦ Ἰησοῦ διὰ θελήματος θεοῦ τοῖς ἁγίοις τοῖς οὖσιν [ἐν Ἐφέσῳ] καὶ πιστοῖς ἐν Χριστῷ Ἰησοῦ, **2** χάρις ὑμῖν καὶ εἰρήνη ἀπὸ θεοῦ πατρὸς ἡμῶν καὶ κυρίου Ἰησοῦ Χριστοῦ.

3 Εὐλογητὸς ὁ θεὸς καὶ πατὴρ τοῦ κυρίου ἡμῶν Ἰησοῦ Χριστοῦ, ὁ εὐλογήσας ἡμᾶς ἐν πάσῃ εὐλογίᾳ πνευματικῇ ἐν τοῖς ἐπουρανίοις ἐν Χριστῷ, **4** καθὼς ἐξελέξατο ἡμᾶς ἐν αὐτῷ πρὸ καταβολῆς κόσμου εἶναι ἡμᾶς ἁγίους καὶ ἀμώμους κατενώπιον αὐτοῦ ἐν ἀγάπῃ, **5** προορίσας ἡμᾶς εἰς υἱοθεσίαν διὰ Ἰησοῦ Χριστοῦ εἰς αὐτόν, κατὰ τὴν εὐδοκίαν τοῦ θελήματος αὐτοῦ, **6** εἰς ἔπαινον δόξης τῆς χάριτος αὐτοῦ ἧς ἐχαρίτωσεν ἡμᾶς ἐν τῷ ἠγαπημένῳ. **7** ἐν ᾧ ἔχομεν τὴν ἀπολύτρωσιν διὰ τοῦ αἵματος αὐτοῦ, τὴν ἄφεσιν τῶν παραπτωμάτων, κατὰ τὸ πλοῦτος τῆς χάριτος αὐτοῦ **8** ἧς ἐπερίσσευσεν εἰς ἡμᾶς, ἐν πάσῃ σοφίᾳ καὶ φρονήσει, **9** γνωρίσας ἡμῖν τὸ μυστήριον τοῦ θελήματος αὐτοῦ, κατὰ τὴν εὐδοκίαν αὐτοῦ ἣν προέθετο ἐν αὐτῷ **10** εἰς οἰκονομίαν τοῦ πληρώματος τῶν καιρῶν, ἀνακεφαλαιώσασθαι τὰ πάντα ἐν τῷ Χριστῷ, τὰ ἐπὶ τοῖς οὐρανοῖς καὶ τὰ ἐπὶ τῆς γῆς ἐν αὐτῷ. **11** ἐν ᾧ καὶ ἐκληρώθημεν προορισθέντες κατὰ πρόθεσιν τοῦ τὰ πάντα ἐνεργοῦντος κατὰ τὴν βουλὴν τοῦ θελήματος αὐτοῦ **12** εἰς τὸ εἶναι ἡμᾶς εἰς ἔπαινον δόξης αὐτοῦ τοὺς προηλπικότας ἐν τῷ Χριστῷ. **13** ἐν ᾧ καὶ ὑμεῖς ἀκούσαντες τὸν λόγον τῆς ἀληθείας, τὸ εὐαγγέλιον τῆς σωτηρίας ὑμῶν, ἐν ᾧ καὶ πιστεύσαντες ἐσφραγίσθητε τῷ πνεύματι τῆς ἐπαγγελίας τῷ ἁγίῳ, **14** ὅ[a] ἐστιν ἀρραβὼν τῆς κληρονομίας ἡμῶν, εἰς ἀπολύτρωσιν τῆς περιποιήσεως, εἰς ἔπαινον τῆς δόξης αὐτοῦ.

15 Διὰ τοῦτο κἀγὼ ἀκούσας τὴν καθ' ὑμᾶς πίστιν ἐν τῷ κυρίῳ Ἰησοῦ καὶ τὴν ἀγάπην τὴν εἰς πάντας τοὺς ἁγίους **16** οὐ παύομαι εὐχαριστῶν ὑπὲρ ὑμῶν μνείαν ποιούμενος ἐπὶ τῶν προσευχῶν μου, **17** ἵνα ὁ θεὸς τοῦ κυρίου ἡμῶν Ἰησοῦ Χριστοῦ, ὁ πατὴρ τῆς δόξης, δώῃ ὑμῖν πνεῦμα σοφίας καὶ ἀποκαλύψεως ἐν ἐπιγνώσει αὐτοῦ.

NIV

1 Paul, an apostle of Christ Jesus by the will of God,

To the saints in Ephesus,[a] the faithful[b] in Christ Jesus:

[2]Grace and peace to you from God our Father and the Lord Jesus Christ.

Spiritual Blessings in Christ

[3]Praise be to the God and Father of our Lord Jesus Christ, who has blessed us in the heavenly realms with every spiritual blessing in Christ. [4]For he chose us in him before the creation of the world to be holy and blameless in his sight. In love [5]he[c] predestined us to be adopted as his sons through Jesus Christ, in accordance with his pleasure and will— [6]to the praise of his glorious grace, which he has freely given us in the One he loves. [7]In him we have redemption through his blood, the forgiveness of sins, in accordance with the riches of God's grace [8]that he lavished on us with all wisdom and understanding. [9]And he[d] made known to us the mystery of his will according to his good pleasure, which he purposed in Christ, [10]to be put into effect when the times will have reached their fulfillment—to bring all things in heaven and on earth together under one head, even Christ.

[11]In him we were also chosen,[e] having been predestined according to the plan of him who works out everything in conformity with the purpose of his will, [12]in order that we, who were the first to hope in Christ, might be for the praise of his glory. [13]And you also were included in Christ when you heard the word of truth, the gospel of your salvation. Having believed, you were marked in him with a seal, the promised Holy Spirit, [14]who is a deposit guaranteeing our inheritance until the redemption of those who are God's possession—to the praise of his glory.

Thanksgiving and Prayer

[15]For this reason, ever since I heard about your faith in the Lord Jesus and your love for all the saints, [16]I have not stopped giving thanks for you, remembering you in my prayers. [17]I keep asking that the God of our Lord Jesus Christ, the glorious Father, may give you the Spirit[f] of wisdom and revelation, so that you may know him

---

eyes of your heart enlightened, you may know what is the hope to which he has called you, what are the riches of his glorious inheritance among the saints, 19and what is the immeasurable greatness of his power for us who believe, according to the working of his great power. 20Godf put this power to work in Christ when he raised him from the dead and seated him at his right hand in the heavenly places, 21far above all rule and authority and power and dominion, and above every name that is named, not only in this age but also in the age to come. 22And he has put all things under his feet and has made him the head over all things for the church, 23which is his body, the fullness of him who fills all in all.

From Death to Life

2 You were dead through the trespasses and sins 2in which you once lived, following the course of this world, following the ruler of the power of the air, the spirit that is now at work among those who are disobedient. 3All of us once lived among them in the passions of our flesh, following the desires of flesh and senses, and we were by nature children of wrath, like everyone else. 4But God, who is rich in mercy, out of the great love with which he loved us 5even when we were dead through our trespasses, made us alive together with Christg—by grace you have been saved— 6and raised us up with him and seated us with him in the heavenly places in Christ Jesus, 7so that in the ages to come he might show the immeasurable riches of his grace in kindness toward us in Christ Jesus. 8For by grace you have been saved through faith, and this is not your own doing; it is the gift of God— 9not the result of works, so that no one may boast. 10For we are what he has made us, created in Christ Jesus for good works, which God prepared beforehand to be our way of life.

One in Christ

11 So then, remember that at one time you Gentiles by birth,h called "the uncircumcision" by those who are called "the circumcision"—a physical circumcision made in the flesh by human hands— 12remember that you were at that time without Christ, being aliens from the commonwealth of Israel, and strangers to the

f Gk He   g Other ancient authorities read *in Christ*
h Gk *in the flesh*

---

18 πεφωτισμένους τοὺς ὀφθαλμοὺς τῆς καρδίας [ὑμῶν] εἰς τὸ εἰδέναι ὑμᾶς τίς ἐστιν ἡ ἐλπὶς τῆς κλήσεως αὐτοῦ, τίς ὁ πλοῦτος τῆς δόξης τῆς κληρονομίας αὐτοῦ ἐν τοῖς ἁγίοις, 19 καὶ τί τὸ ὑπερβάλλον μέγεθος τῆς δυνάμεως αὐτοῦ εἰς ἡμᾶς τοὺς πιστεύοντας κατὰ τὴν ἐνέργειαν τοῦ κράτους τῆς ἰσχύος αὐτοῦ. 20 ἣν ἐνήργησεν ἐν τῷ Χριστῷ ἐγείρας αὐτὸν ἐκ νεκρῶν καὶ καθίσας ἐν δεξιᾷ αὐτοῦ ἐν τοῖς ἐπουρανίοις 21 ὑπεράνω πάσης ἀρχῆς καὶ ἐξουσίας καὶ δυνάμεως καὶ κυριότητος καὶ παντὸς ὀνόματος ὀνομαζομένου, οὐ μόνον ἐν τῷ αἰῶνι τούτῳ ἀλλὰ καὶ ἐν τῷ μέλλοντι· 22 καὶ πάντα ὑπέταξεν ὑπὸ τοὺς πόδας αὐτοῦ καὶ αὐτὸν ἔδωκεν κεφαλὴν ὑπὲρ πάντα τῇ ἐκκλησίᾳ, 23 ἥτις ἐστὶν τὸ σῶμα αὐτοῦ, τὸ πλήρωμα τοῦ τὰ πάντα ἐν πᾶσιν πληρουμένου.

2 Καὶ ὑμᾶς ὄντας νεκροὺς τοῖς παραπτώμασιν καὶ ταῖς ἁμαρτίαις ὑμῶν, 2 ἐν αἷς ποτε περιεπατήσατε κατὰ τὸν αἰῶνα τοῦ κόσμου τούτου, κατὰ τὸν ἄρχοντα τῆς ἐξουσίας τοῦ ἀέρος, τοῦ πνεύματος τοῦ νῦν ἐνεργοῦντος ἐν τοῖς υἱοῖς τῆς ἀπειθείας· 3 ἐν οἷς καὶ ἡμεῖς πάντες ἀνεστράφημέν ποτε ἐν ταῖς ἐπιθυμίαις τῆς σαρκὸς ἡμῶν ποιοῦντες τὰ θελήματα τῆς σαρκὸς καὶ τῶν διανοιῶν, καὶ ἤμεθα τέκνα φύσει ὀργῆς ὡς καὶ οἱ λοιποί· 4 ὁ δὲ θεὸς πλούσιος ὢν ἐν ἐλέει, διὰ τὴν πολλὴν ἀγάπην αὐτοῦ ἣν ἠγάπησεν ἡμᾶς, 5 καὶ ὄντας ἡμᾶς νεκροὺς τοῖς παραπτώμασιν συνεζωοποίησενa τῷ Χριστῷ, – χάριτί ἐστε σεσωσμένοι – 6 καὶ συνήγειρεν καὶ συνεκάθισεν ἐν τοῖς ἐπουρανίοις ἐν Χριστῷ Ἰησοῦ, 7 ἵνα ἐνδείξηται ἐν τοῖς αἰῶσιν τοῖς ἐπερχομένοις τὸ ὑπερβάλλον πλοῦτος τῆς χάριτος αὐτοῦ ἐν χρηστότητι ἐφ᾽ ἡμᾶς ἐν Χριστῷ Ἰησοῦ. 8 τῇ γὰρ χάριτί ἐστε σεσωσμένοι διὰ πίστεως· καὶ τοῦτο οὐκ ἐξ ὑμῶν, θεοῦ τὸ δῶρον· 9 οὐκ ἐξ ἔργων, ἵνα μή τις καυχήσηται. 10 αὐτοῦ γάρ ἐσμεν ποίημα, κτισθέντες ἐν Χριστῷ Ἰησοῦ ἐπὶ ἔργοις ἀγαθοῖς οἷς προητοίμασεν ὁ θεός, ἵνα ἐν αὐτοῖς περιπατήσωμεν.

11 Διὸ μνημονεύετε ὅτι ποτὲ ὑμεῖς τὰ ἔθνη ἐν σαρκί, οἱ λεγόμενοι ἀκροβυστία ὑπὸ τῆς λεγομένης περιτομῆς ἐν σαρκὶ χειροποιήτου, 12 ὅτι ἦτε τῷ καιρῷ ἐκείνῳ χωρὶς Χριστοῦ, ἀπηλλοτριωμένοι τῆς πολιτείας τοῦ Ἰσραὴλ καὶ ξένοι τῶν διαθηκῶν τῆς

a5 NRSV note g adds ἐν

---

better. 18I pray also that the eyes of your heart may be enlightened in order that you may know the hope to which he has called you, the riches of his glorious inheritance in the saints, 19and his incomparably great power for us who believe. That power is like the working of his mighty strength, 20which he exerted in Christ when he raised him from the dead and seated him at his right hand in the heavenly realms, 21far above all rule and authority, power and dominion, and every title that can be given, not only in the present age but also in the one to come. 22And God placed all things under his feet and appointed him to be head over everything for the church, 23which is his body, the fullness of him who fills everything in every way.

Made Alive in Christ

2 As for you, you were dead in your transgressions and sins, 2in which you used to live when you followed the ways of this world and of the ruler of the kingdom of the air, the spirit who is now at work in those who are disobedient. 3All of us also lived among them at one time, gratifying the cravings of our sinful naturea and following its desires and thoughts. Like the rest, we were by nature objects of wrath. 4But because of his great love for us, God, who is rich in mercy, 5made us alive with Christ even when we were dead in transgressions—it is by grace you have been saved. 6And God raised us up with Christ and seated us with him in the heavenly realms in Christ Jesus, 7in order that in the coming ages he might show the incomparable riches of his grace, expressed in his kindness to us in Christ Jesus. 8For it is by grace you have been saved, through faith—and this not from yourselves, it is the gift of God— 9not by works, so that no one can boast. 10For we are God's workmanship, created in Christ Jesus to do good works, which God prepared in advance for us to do.

One in Christ

11Therefore, remember that formerly you who are Gentiles by birth and called "uncircumcised" by those who call themselves "the circumcision" (that done in the body by the hands of men)— 12remember that at that time you were separate from Christ, excluded from citizenship in Israel and foreigners to the covenants of the promise,

a3 Or *our flesh*

covenants of promise, having no hope and without God in the world. 13But now in Christ Jesus you who once were far off have been brought near by the blood of Christ. 14For he is our peace; in his flesh he has made both groups into one and has broken down the dividing wall, that is, the hostility between us. 15He has abolished the law with its commandments and ordinances, that he might create in himself one new humanity in place of the two, thus making peace, 16and might reconcile both groups to God in one bodyⁱ through the cross, thus putting to death that hostility through it.ʲ 17So he came and proclaimed peace to you who were far off and peace to those who were near; 18for through him both of us have access in one Spirit to the Father. 19So then you are no longer strangers and aliens, but you are citizens with the saints and also members of the household of God, 20built upon the foundation of the apostles and prophets, with Christ Jesus himself as the cornerstone.ᵏ 21In him the whole structure is joined together and grows into a holy temple in the Lord; 22in whom you also are built together spirituallyˡ into a dwelling place for God.

Paul's Ministry to the Gentiles

3 This is the reason that I Paul am a prisoner forᵐ Christ Jesus for the sake of you Gentiles— 2for surely you have already heard of the commission of God's grace that was given me for you, 3and how the mystery was made known to me by revelation, as I wrote above in a few words, 4a reading of which will enable you to perceive my understanding of the mystery of Christ. 5In former generations this mysteryⁿ was not made known to humankind, as it has now been revealed to his holy apostles and prophets by the Spirit: 6that is, the Gentiles have become fellow heirs, members of the same body, and sharers in the promise in Christ Jesus through the gospel.

7 Of this gospel I have become a servant according to the gift of God's grace that was given me by the working of his power. 8Although I am the very least of all the saints, this grace was given to me to bring to the Gentiles the news of the boundless riches of Christ, 9and to make everyone seeᵒ what is the plan of the mystery hidden for ages inᵖ God who created all things;

ἐπαγγελίας, ἐλπίδα μὴ ἔχοντες καὶ ἄθεοι ἐν τῷ κόσμῳ. 13 νυνὶ δὲ ἐν Χριστῷ Ἰησοῦ ὑμεῖς οἵ ποτε ὄντες μακρὰν ἐγενήθητε ἐγγὺς ἐν τῷ αἵματι τοῦ Χριστοῦ.

14 Αὐτὸς γάρ ἐστιν ἡ εἰρήνη ἡμῶν, ὁ ποιήσας τὰ ἀμφότερα ἓν καὶ τὸ μεσότοιχον τοῦ φραγμοῦ λύσας, τὴν ἔχθρανᵇ ἐν τῇ σαρκὶ αὐτοῦ, 15 τὸν νόμον τῶν ἐντολῶν ἐν δόγμασιν καταργήσας, ἵνα τοὺς δύο κτίσῃ ἐν αὐτῷᶜ εἰς ἕνα καινὸν ἄνθρωπον ποιῶν εἰρήνην 16 καὶ ἀποκαταλλάξῃ τοὺς ἀμφοτέρους ἐν ἑνὶ σώματι τῷ θεῷ διὰ τοῦ σταυροῦ, ἀποκτείνας τὴν ἔχθραν ἐν αὐτῷ. 17 καὶ ἐλθὼν εὐηγγελίσατο εἰρήνην ὑμῖν τοῖς μακρὰν καὶ εἰρήνην τοῖς ἐγγύς· 18 ὅτι δι᾽ αὐτοῦ ἔχομεν τὴν προσαγωγὴν οἱ ἀμφότεροι ἐν ἑνὶ πνεύματι πρὸς τὸν πατέρα. 19 ἄρα οὖν οὐκέτι ἐστὲ ξένοι καὶ πάροικοι ἀλλὰ ἐστὲ συμπολῖται τῶν ἁγίων καὶ οἰκεῖοι τοῦ θεοῦ, 20 ἐποικοδομηθέντες ἐπὶ τῷ θεμελίῳ τῶν ἀποστόλων καὶ προφητῶν, ὄντος ἀκρογωνιαίου αὐτοῦ Χριστοῦ Ἰησοῦ, 21 ἐν ᾧ πᾶσαᵈ οἰκοδομὴ συναρμολογουμένη αὔξει εἰς ναὸν ἅγιον ἐν κυρίῳ, 22 ἐν ᾧ καὶ ὑμεῖς συνοικοδομεῖσθε εἰς κατοικητήριον τοῦ θεοῦ ἐν πνεύματι.

3 Τούτου χάριν ἐγὼ Παῦλος ὁ δέσμιος τοῦ Χριστοῦ [Ἰησοῦ] ὑπὲρ ὑμῶν τῶν ἐθνῶν— 2 εἴ γε ἠκούσατε τὴν οἰκονομίαν τῆς χάριτος τοῦ θεοῦ τῆς δοθείσης μοι εἰς ὑμᾶς, 3 [ὅτι] κατὰ ἀποκάλυψιν ἐγνωρίσθη μοι τὸ μυστήριον, καθὼς προέγραψα ἐν ὀλίγῳ, 4 πρὸς ὃ δύνασθε ἀναγινώσκοντες νοῆσαι τὴν σύνεσίν μου ἐν τῷ μυστηρίῳ τοῦ Χριστοῦ, 5 ὃ ἑτέραις γενεαῖς οὐκ ἐγνωρίσθη τοῖς υἱοῖς τῶν ἀνθρώπων ὡς νῦν ἀπεκαλύφθη τοῖς ἁγίοις ἀποστόλοις αὐτοῦ καὶ προφήταις ἐν πνεύματι, 6 εἶναι τὰ ἔθνη συγκληρονόμα καὶ σύσσωμα καὶ συμμέτοχα τῆς ἐπαγγελίας ἐν Χριστῷ Ἰησοῦ διὰ τοῦ εὐαγγελίου, 7 οὗ ἐγενήθην διάκονος κατὰ τὴν δωρεὰν τῆς χάριτος τοῦ θεοῦ τῆς δοθείσης μοι κατὰ τὴν ἐνέργειαν τῆς δυνάμεως αὐτοῦ. 8 ἐμοὶ τῷ ἐλαχιστοτέρῳ πάντων ἁγίων ἐδόθη ἡ χάρις αὕτη, τοῖς ἔθνεσιν εὐαγγελίσασθαι τὸ ἀνεξιχνίαστον πλοῦτος τοῦ Χριστοῦ 9 καὶ φωτίσαι [πάντας]ᵃ τίς ἡ οἰκονομία τοῦ μυστηρίου τοῦ ἀποκεκρυμμένου ἀπὸ τῶν αἰώνων ἐν τῷ θεῷ τῷ τὰ πάντα κτίσαντι, 10 ἵνα γνωρισθῇ

without hope and without God in the world. 13But now in Christ Jesus you who once were far away have been brought near through the blood of Christ.

14For he himself is our peace, who has made the two one and has destroyed the barrier, the dividing wall of hostility, 15by abolishing in his flesh the law with its commandments and regulations. His purpose was to create in himself one new man out of the two, thus making peace, 16and in this one body to reconcile both of them to God through the cross, by which he put to death their hostility. 17He came and preached peace to you who were far away and peace to those who were near. 18For through him we both have access to the Father by one Spirit.

19Consequently, you are no longer foreigners and aliens, but fellow citizens with God's people and members of God's household, 20built on the foundation of the apostles and prophets, with Christ Jesus himself as the chief cornerstone. 21In him the whole building is joined together and rises to become a holy temple in the Lord. 22And in him you too are being built together to become a dwelling in which God lives by his Spirit.

Paul the Preacher to the Gentiles

3 For this reason I, Paul, the prisoner of Christ Jesus for the sake of you Gentiles—

2Surely you have heard about the administration of God's grace that was given to me for you, 3that is, the mystery made known to me by revelation, as I have already written briefly. 4In reading this, then, you will be able to understand my insight into the mystery of Christ, 5which was not made known to men in other generations as it has now been revealed by the Spirit to God's holy apostles and prophets. 6This mystery is that through the gospel the Gentiles are heirs together with Israel, members together of one body, and sharers together in the promise in Christ Jesus.

7I became a servant of this gospel by the gift of God's grace given me through the working of his power. 8Although I am less than the least of all God's people, this grace was given me: to preach to the Gentiles the unsearchable riches of Christ, 9and to make plain to everyone the administration of this mystery, which for ages past was kept hidden in God, who created all things.

ⁱOr *reconcile both of us in one body for God* ʲOr *in him, or in himself* ᵏOr *keystone* ˡGk *in the Spirit* ᵐOr *of* ⁿGk *it* ᵒOther ancient authorities read *to bring to light* ᵖOr *by*

ᵇ14 NIV begins verse 15 after ἔχθραν ᶜ15 NIV text ἑαυτῷ † ᵈ21 NIV text adds ἡ ᵃ9 NRSV note o omits πάντας

[10]so that through the church the wisdom of God in its rich variety might now be made known to the rulers and authorities in the heavenly places. [11]This was in accordance with the eternal purpose that he has carried out in Christ Jesus our Lord, [12]in whom we have access to God in boldness and confidence through faith in him.[q] [13]I pray therefore that you[r] may not lose heart over my sufferings for you; they are your glory.

Prayer for the Readers

[14]For this reason I bow my knees before the Father,[s] [15]from whom every family[t] in heaven and on earth takes its name. [16]I pray that, according to the riches of his glory, he may grant that you may be strengthened in your inner being with power through his Spirit, [17]and that Christ may dwell in your hearts through faith, as you are being rooted and grounded in love. [18]I pray that you may have the power to comprehend, with all the saints, what is the breadth and length and height and depth, [19]and to know the love of Christ that surpasses knowledge, so that you may be filled with all the fullness of God.

[20]Now to him who by the power at work within us is able to accomplish abundantly far more than all we can ask or imagine, [21]to him be glory in the church and in Christ Jesus to all generations, forever and ever. Amen.

Unity in the Body of Christ

4 I therefore, the prisoner in the Lord, beg you to lead a life worthy of the calling to which you have been called, [2]with all humility and gentleness, with patience, bearing with one another in love, [3]making every effort to maintain the unity of the Spirit in the bond of peace. [4]There is one body and one Spirit, just as you were called to the one hope of your calling, [5]one Lord, one faith, one baptism, [6]one God and Father of all, who is above all and through all and in all.

[7]But each of us was given grace according to the measure of Christ's gift. [8]Therefore it is said,

"When he ascended on high he made
    captivity itself a captive;
he gave gifts to his people."

[9](When it says, "He ascended," what does it mean but that he had also descended[u]

νῦν ταῖς ἀρχαῖς καὶ ταῖς ἐξουσίαις ἐν τοῖς ἐπουρανίοις διὰ τῆς ἐκκλησίας ἡ πολυποίκιλος σοφία τοῦ θεοῦ, **11** κατὰ πρόθεσιν τῶν αἰώνων ἣν ἐποίησεν ἐν τῷ Χριστῷ Ἰησοῦ τῷ κυρίῳ ἡμῶν, **12** ἐν ᾧ ἔχομεν τὴν παρρησίαν καὶ προσαγωγὴν ἐν πεποιθήσει διὰ τῆς πίστεως αὐτοῦ. **13** διὸ αἰτοῦμαι μὴ ἐγκακεῖν ἐν ταῖς θλίψεσίν μου ὑπὲρ ὑμῶν, ἥτις ἐστὶν δόξα ὑμῶν.

14 Τούτου χάριν κάμπτω τὰ γόνατά μου πρὸς τὸν πατέρα[b], **15** ἐξ οὗ πᾶσα πατριὰ ἐν οὐρανοῖς καὶ ἐπὶ γῆς ὀνομάζεται, **16** ἵνα δῷ ὑμῖν κατὰ τὸ πλοῦτος τῆς δόξης αὐτοῦ δυνάμει κραταιωθῆναι διὰ τοῦ πνεύματος αὐτοῦ εἰς τὸν ἔσω ἄνθρωπον, **17** κατοικῆσαι τὸν Χριστὸν διὰ τῆς πίστεως ἐν ταῖς καρδίαις ὑμῶν, ἐν ἀγάπῃ ἐρριζωμένοι καὶ τεθεμελιωμένοι, **18** ἵνα ἐξισχύσητε καταλαβέσθαι σὺν πᾶσιν τοῖς ἁγίοις τί τὸ πλάτος καὶ μῆκος καὶ ὕψος καὶ βάθος, **19** γνῶναί τε τὴν ὑπερβάλλουσαν τῆς γνώσεως ἀγάπην τοῦ Χριστοῦ, ἵνα πληρωθῆτε εἰς πᾶν τὸ πλήρωμα τοῦ θεοῦ.

20 Τῷ δὲ δυναμένῳ ὑπὲρ πάντα ποιῆσαι ὑπερεκπερισσοῦ ὧν αἰτούμεθα ἢ νοοῦμεν κατὰ τὴν δύναμιν τὴν ἐνεργουμένην ἐν ἡμῖν, **21** αὐτῷ ἡ δόξα ἐν τῇ ἐκκλησίᾳ καὶ ἐν Χριστῷ Ἰησοῦ εἰς πάσας τὰς γενεὰς τοῦ αἰῶνος τῶν αἰώνων, ἀμήν.

4 Παρακαλῶ οὖν ὑμᾶς ἐγὼ ὁ δέσμιος ἐν κυρίῳ ἀξίως περιπατῆσαι τῆς κλήσεως ἧς ἐκλήθητε, **2** μετὰ πάσης ταπεινοφροσύνης καὶ πραΰτητος, μετὰ μακροθυμίας, ἀνεχόμενοι ἀλλήλων ἐν ἀγάπῃ, **3** σπουδάζοντες τηρεῖν τὴν ἑνότητα τοῦ πνεύματος ἐν τῷ συνδέσμῳ τῆς εἰρήνης· **4** ἓν σῶμα καὶ ἓν πνεῦμα, καθὼς καὶ ἐκλήθητε ἐν μιᾷ ἐλπίδι τῆς κλήσεως ὑμῶν· **5** εἷς κύριος, μία πίστις, ἓν βάπτισμα, **6** εἷς θεὸς καὶ πατὴρ πάντων, ὁ ἐπὶ πάντων καὶ διὰ πάντων καὶ ἐν πᾶσιν.

7 Ἑνὶ δὲ ἑκάστῳ ἡμῶν ἐδόθη ἡ χάρις κατὰ τὸ μέτρον τῆς δωρεᾶς τοῦ Χριστοῦ. **8** διὸ λέγει,

Ἀναβὰς εἰς ὕψος ᾐχμαλώτευσεν αἰχμαλωσίαν,
ἔδωκεν δόματα τοῖς ἀνθρώποις.

9 τὸ δὲ Ἀνέβη τί ἐστιν, εἰ μὴ ὅτι καὶ κατέβη[a] εἰς τὰ κατώτερα [μέρη]

[10]His intent was that now, through the church, the manifold wisdom of God should be made known to the rulers and authorities in the heavenly realms, [11]according to his eternal purpose which he accomplished in Christ Jesus our Lord. [12]In him and through faith in him we may approach God with freedom and confidence. [13]I ask you, therefore, not to be discouraged because of my sufferings for you, which are your glory.

A Prayer for the Ephesians

[14]For this reason I kneel before the Father, [15]from whom his whole family[a] in heaven and on earth derives its name. [16]I pray that out of his glorious riches he may strengthen you with power through his Spirit in your inner being, [17]so that Christ may dwell in your hearts through faith. And I pray that you, being rooted and established in love, [18]may have power, together with all the saints, to grasp how wide and long and high and deep is the love of Christ, [19]and to know this love that surpasses knowledge—that you may be filled to the measure of all the fullness of God.

[20]Now to him who is able to do immeasurably more than all we ask or imagine, according to his power that is at work within us, [21]to him be glory in the church and in Christ Jesus throughout all generations, for ever and ever! Amen.

Unity in the Body of Christ

4 As a prisoner for the Lord, then, I urge you to live a life worthy of the calling you have received. [2]Be completely humble and gentle; be patient, bearing with one another in love. [3]Make every effort to keep the unity of the Spirit through the bond of peace. [4]There is one body and one Spirit— just as you were called to one hope when you were called— [5]one Lord, one faith, one baptism; [6]one God and Father of all, who is over all and through all and in all.

[7]But to each one of us grace has been given as Christ apportioned it. [8]This is why it[a] says:

"When he ascended on high,
    he led captives in his train
    and gave gifts to men."[b]

[9](What does "he ascended" mean except that he also descended to the lower, earthly

---

[q] Or *the faith of him*   [r] Or *I*   [s] Other ancient authorities add *of our Lord Jesus Christ*   [t] Gk *fatherhood*   [u] Other ancient authorities add *first*

[b]14 NRSV note s adds τοῦ κυρίου ἡμῶν Ἰησοῦ Χριστοῦ
[a]9 NRSV note u adds πρῶτον

[a]15 Or *whom all fatherhood*   [a]8 Or *God*   [b]8 Psalm 68:18

NRSV

into the lower parts of the earth? [10]He who descended is the same one who ascended far above all the heavens, so that he might fill all things.) [11]The gifts he gave were that some would be apostles, some prophets, some evangelists, some pastors and teachers, [12]to equip the saints for the work of ministry, for building up the body of Christ, [13]until all of us come to the unity of the faith and of the knowledge of the Son of God, to maturity, to the measure of the full stature of Christ. [14]We must no longer be children, tossed to and fro and blown about by every wind of doctrine, by people's trickery, by their craftiness in deceitful scheming. [15]But speaking the truth in love, we must grow up in every way into him who is the head, into Christ, [16]from whom the whole body, joined and knit together by every ligament with which it is equipped, as each part is working properly, promotes the body's growth in building itself up in love.

The Old Life and the New

17 Now this I affirm and insist on in the Lord: you must no longer live as the Gentiles live, in the futility of their minds. [18]They are darkened in their understanding, alienated from the life of God because of their ignorance and hardness of heart. [19]They have lost all sensitivity and have abandoned themselves to licentiousness, greedy to practice every kind of impurity. [20]That is not the way you learned Christ! [21]For surely you have heard about him and were taught in him, as truth is in Jesus. [22]You were taught to put away your former way of life, your old self, corrupt and deluded by its lusts, [23]and to be renewed in the spirit of your minds, [24]and to clothe yourselves with the new self, created according to the likeness of God in true righteousness and holiness.

Rules for the New Life

25 So then, putting away falsehood, let all of us speak the truth to our neighbors, for we are members of one another. [26]Be angry but do not sin; do not let the sun go down on your anger, [27]and do not make room for the devil. [28]Thieves must give up stealing; rather let them labor and work honestly with their own hands, so as to have something to share with the needy.

Greek

τῆς γῆς; **10** ὁ καταβὰς αὐτός ἐστιν καὶ ὁ ἀναβὰς ὑπεράνω πάντων τῶν οὐρανῶν, ἵνα πληρώσῃ τὰ πάντα. **11** καὶ αὐτὸς ἔδωκεν τοὺς μὲν ἀποστόλους, τοὺς δὲ προφήτας, τοὺς δὲ εὐαγγελιστάς, τοὺς δὲ ποιμένας καὶ διδασκάλους, **12** πρὸς τὸν καταρτισμὸν τῶν ἁγίων εἰς ἔργον διακονίας, εἰς οἰκοδομὴν τοῦ σώματος τοῦ Χριστοῦ, **13** μέχρι καταντήσωμεν οἱ πάντες εἰς τὴν ἑνότητα τῆς πίστεως καὶ τῆς ἐπιγνώσεως τοῦ υἱοῦ τοῦ θεοῦ, εἰς ἄνδρα τέλειον, εἰς μέτρον ἡλικίας τοῦ πληρώματος τοῦ Χριστοῦ, **14** ἵνα μηκέτι ὦμεν νήπιοι, κλυδωνιζόμενοι καὶ περιφερόμενοι παντὶ ἀνέμῳ τῆς διδασκαλίας ἐν τῇ κυβείᾳ τῶν ἀνθρώπων, ἐν πανουργίᾳ πρὸς τὴν μεθοδείαν τῆς πλάνης, **15** ἀληθεύοντες δὲ ἐν ἀγάπῃ αὐξήσωμεν εἰς αὐτὸν τὰ πάντα, ὅς ἐστιν ἡ κεφαλή, Χριστός, **16** ἐξ οὗ πᾶν τὸ σῶμα συναρμολογούμενον καὶ συμβιβαζόμενον διὰ πάσης ἁφῆς τῆς ἐπιχορηγίας κατ' ἐνέργειαν ἐν μέτρῳ ἑνὸς ἑκάστου μέρους τὴν αὔξησιν τοῦ σώματος ποιεῖται εἰς οἰκοδομὴν ἑαυτοῦ ἐν ἀγάπῃ.

17 Τοῦτο οὖν λέγω καὶ μαρτύρομαι ἐν κυρίῳ, μηκέτι ὑμᾶς περιπατεῖν, καθὼς καὶ τὰ ἔθνη περιπατεῖ ἐν ματαιότητι τοῦ νοὸς αὐτῶν, **18** ἐσκοτωμένοι τῇ διανοίᾳ ὄντες, ἀπηλλοτριωμένοι τῆς ζωῆς τοῦ θεοῦ διὰ τὴν ἄγνοιαν τὴν οὖσαν ἐν αὐτοῖς, διὰ τὴν πώρωσιν τῆς καρδίας αὐτῶν, **19** οἵτινες ἀπηλγηκότες ἑαυτοὺς παρέδωκαν τῇ ἀσελγείᾳ εἰς ἐργασίαν ἀκαθαρσίας πάσης ἐν πλεονεξίᾳ. **20** ὑμεῖς δὲ οὐχ οὕτως ἐμάθετε τὸν Χριστόν, **21** εἴ γε αὐτὸν ἠκούσατε καὶ ἐν αὐτῷ ἐδιδάχθητε, καθώς ἐστιν ἀλήθεια ἐν τῷ Ἰησοῦ, **22** ἀποθέσθαι ὑμᾶς κατὰ τὴν προτέραν ἀναστροφὴν τὸν παλαιὸν ἄνθρωπον τὸν φθειρόμενον κατὰ τὰς ἐπιθυμίας τῆς ἀπάτης, **23** ἀνανεοῦσθαι δὲ τῷ πνεύματι τοῦ νοὸς ὑμῶν **24** καὶ ἐνδύσασθαι τὸν καινὸν ἄνθρωπον τὸν κατὰ θεὸν κτισθέντα ἐν δικαιοσύνῃ καὶ ὁσιότητι τῆς ἀληθείας.

25 Διὸ ἀποθέμενοι τὸ ψεῦδος **λαλεῖτε ἀλήθειαν ἕκαστος μετὰ τοῦ πλησίον αὐτοῦ,** ὅτι ἐσμὲν ἀλλήλων μέλη. **26 ὀργίζεσθε καὶ μὴ ἁμαρτάνετε·** ὁ ἥλιος μὴ ἐπιδυέτω ἐπὶ [τῷ] παροργισμῷ ὑμῶν, **27** μηδὲ δίδοτε τόπον τῷ διαβόλῳ. **28** ὁ κλέπτων μηκέτι κλεπτέτω, μᾶλλον δὲ κοπιάτω ἐργαζόμενος ταῖς [ἰδίαις] χερσὶν τὸ ἀγαθόν, ἵνα ἔχῃ μεταδιδόναι τῷ χρείαν ἔχοντι. **29** πᾶς λόγος σαπρὸς

NIV

regions[c]? [10]He who descended is the very one who ascended higher than all the heavens, in order to fill the whole universe.) [11]It was he who gave some to be apostles, some to be prophets, some to be evangelists, and some to be pastors and teachers, [12]to prepare God's people for works of service, so that the body of Christ may be built up [13]until we all reach unity in the faith and in the knowledge of the Son of God and become mature, attaining to the whole measure of the fullness of Christ.

[14]Then we will no longer be infants, tossed back and forth by the waves, and blown here and there by every wind of teaching and by the cunning and craftiness of men in their deceitful scheming. [15]Instead, speaking the truth in love, we will in all things grow up into him who is the Head, that is, Christ. [16]From him the whole body, joined and held together by every supporting ligament, grows and builds itself up in love, as each part does its work.

Living as Children of Light

[17]So I tell you this, and insist on it in the Lord, that you must no longer live as the Gentiles do, in the futility of their thinking. [18]They are darkened in their understanding and separated from the life of God because of the ignorance that is in them due to the hardening of their hearts. [19]Having lost all sensitivity, they have given themselves over to sensuality so as to indulge in every kind of impurity, with a continual lust for more.

[20]You, however, did not come to know Christ that way. [21]Surely you heard of him and were taught in him in accordance with the truth that is in Jesus. [22]You were taught, with regard to your former way of life, to put off your old self, which is being corrupted by its deceitful desires; [23]to be made new in the attitude of your minds; [24]and to put on the new self, created to be like God in true righteousness and holiness.

[25]Therefore each of you must put off falsehood and speak truthfully to his neighbor, for we are all members of one body. [26]"In your anger do not sin"[d]: Do not let the sun go down while you are still angry, [27]and do not give the devil a foothold. [28]He who has been stealing must steal no longer, but must work, doing something useful with his own hands, that he may have something to share with those in need.

29Let no evil talk come out of your mouths, but only what is useful for building up,v as there is need, so that your words may give grace to those who hear. 30And do not grieve the Holy Spirit of God, with which you were marked with a seal for the day of redemption. 31Put away from you all bitterness and wrath and anger and wrangling and slander, together with all malice, 32and be kind to one another, tenderhearted, forgiving one another, as God in Christ has forgiven you.w 1Therefore be imitators of God, as beloved children, 2and live in love, as Christ loved usx and gave himself up for us, a fragrant offering and sacrifice to God.

Renounce Pagan Ways

3 But fornication and impurity of any kind, or greed, must not even be mentioned among you, as is proper among saints. 4Entirely out of place is obscene, silly, and vulgar talk; but instead, let there be thanksgiving. 5Be sure of this, that no fornicator or impure person, or one who is greedy (that is, an idolater), has any inheritance in the kingdom of Christ and of God.

6 Let no one deceive you with empty words, for because of these things the wrath of God comes on those who are disobedient. 7Therefore do not be associated with them. 8For once you were darkness, but now in the Lord you are light. Live as children of light— 9for the fruit of the light is found in all that is good and right and true. 10Try to find out what is pleasing to the Lord. 11Take no part in the unfruitful works of darkness, but instead expose them. 12For it is shameful even to mention what such people do secretly; 13but everything exposed by the light becomes visible, 14for everything that becomes visible is light. Therefore it says,

"Sleeper, awake!
Rise from the dead,
and Christ will shine on you."

15 Be careful then how you live, not as unwise people but as wise, 16making the most of the time, because the days are evil. 17So do not be foolish, but understand what the will of the Lord is. 18Do not get drunk with wine, for that is debauchery; but be filled with the Spirit, 19as you sing psalms and hymns and spiritual songs among yourselves, singing and making melody to

ἐκ τοῦ στόματος ὑμῶν μὴ ἐκπορευέσθω, ἀλλὰ εἴ τις ἀγαθὸς πρὸς οἰκοδομὴν τῆς χρείαςb, ἵνα δῷ χάριν τοῖς ἀκούουσιν. 30 καὶ μὴ λυπεῖτε τὸ πνεῦμα τὸ ἅγιον τοῦ θεοῦ, ἐν ᾧ ἐσφραγίσθητε εἰς ἡμέραν ἀπολυτρώσεως. 31 πᾶσα πικρία καὶ θυμὸς καὶ ὀργὴ καὶ κραυγὴ καὶ βλασφημία ἀρθήτω ἀφ᾽ ὑμῶν σὺν πάσῃ κακίᾳ. 32 γίνεσθε [δὲ] εἰς ἀλλήλους χρηστοί, εὔσπλαγχνοι, χαριζόμενοι ἑαυτοῖς, καθὼς καὶ ὁ θεὸς ἐν Χριστῷ ἐχαρίσατο ὑμῖνc. 1 γίνεσθε οὖν μιμηταὶ τοῦ θεοῦ ὡς τέκνα ἀγαπητὰ 2 καὶ περιπατεῖτε ἐν ἀγάπῃ, καθὼς καὶ ὁ Χριστὸς ἠγάπησεν ἡμᾶςa καὶ παρέδωκεν ἑαυτὸν ὑπὲρ ἡμῶν προσφορὰν καὶ θυσίαν τῷ θεῷ εἰς ὀσμὴν εὐωδίας. 3 πορνεία δὲ καὶ ἀκαθαρσία πᾶσα ἢ πλεονεξία μηδὲ ὀνομαζέσθω ἐν ὑμῖν, καθὼς πρέπει ἁγίοις, 4 καὶ αἰσχρότης καὶ μωρολογία ἢ εὐτραπελία, ἃ οὐκ ἀνῆκεν, ἀλλὰ μᾶλλον εὐχαριστία. 5 τοῦτο γὰρ ἴστε γινώσκοντες, ὅτι πᾶς πόρνος ἢ ἀκάθαρτος ἢ πλεονέκτης, ὅ ἐστιν εἰδωλολάτρης, οὐκ ἔχει κληρονομίαν ἐν τῇ βασιλείᾳ τοῦ Χριστοῦ καὶ θεοῦ.

6 Μηδεὶς ὑμᾶς ἀπατάτω κενοῖς λόγοις· διὰ ταῦτα γὰρ ἔρχεται ἡ ὀργὴ τοῦ θεοῦ ἐπὶ τοὺς υἱοὺς τῆς ἀπειθείας. 7 μὴ οὖν γίνεσθε συμμέτοχοι αὐτῶν· 8 ἦτε γάρ ποτε σκότος, νῦν δὲ φῶς ἐν κυρίῳ· ὡς τέκνα φωτὸς περιπατεῖτε 9 – ὁ γὰρ καρπὸς τοῦ φωτὸς ἐν πάσῃ ἀγαθωσύνῃ καὶ δικαιοσύνῃ καὶ ἀληθείᾳ – 10 δοκιμάζοντες τί ἐστιν εὐάρεστον τῷ κυρίῳ, 11 καὶ μὴ συγκοινωνεῖτε τοῖς ἔργοις τοῖς ἀκάρποις τοῦ σκότους, μᾶλλον δὲ καὶ ἐλέγχετε. 12 τὰ γὰρ κρυφῇ γινόμενα ὑπ᾽ αὐτῶν αἰσχρόν ἐστιν καὶ λέγειν, 13 τὰ δὲ πάντα ἐλεγχόμενα ὑπὸ τοῦ φωτὸς φανεροῦται, 14 πᾶν γὰρ τὸ φανερούμενον φῶς ἐστιν. διὸ λέγει,

Ἔγειρε, ὁ καθεύδων,
καὶ ἀνάστα ἐκ τῶν νεκρῶν,
καὶ ἐπιφαύσει σοι ὁ Χριστός.

15 Βλέπετε οὖν ἀκριβῶς πῶς περιπατεῖτε μὴ ὡς ἄσοφοι ἀλλ᾽ ὡς σοφοί, 16 ἐξαγοραζόμενοι τὸν καιρόν, ὅτι αἱ ἡμέραι πονηραί εἰσιν. 17 διὰ τοῦτο μὴ γίνεσθε ἄφρονες, ἀλλὰ συνίετε τί τὸ θέλημα τοῦ κυρίου. 18 καὶ μὴ μεθύσκεσθε οἴνῳ, ἐν ᾧ ἐστιν ἀσωτία, ἀλλὰ πληροῦσθε ἐν πνεύματι, 19 λαλοῦντες ἑαυτοῖς [ἐν] ψαλμοῖς καὶ ὕμνοις καὶ ᾠδαῖς πνευματικαῖς, ᾄδοντες καὶ

29Do not let any unwholesome talk come out of your mouths, but only what is helpful for building others up according to their needs, that it may benefit those who listen. 30And do not grieve the Holy Spirit of God, with whom you were sealed for the day of redemption. 31Get rid of all bitterness, rage and anger, brawling and slander, along with every form of malice. 32Be kind and compassionate to one another, forgiving each other, just as in Christ God forgave you.

Be imitators of God, therefore, as dearly loved children 2and live a life of love, just as Christ loved us and gave himself up for us as a fragrant offering and sacrifice to God.

3But among you there must not be even a hint of sexual immorality, or of any kind of impurity, or of greed, because these are improper for God's holy people. 4Nor should there be obscenity, foolish talk or coarse joking, which are out of place, but rather thanksgiving. 5For of this you can be sure: No immoral, impure or greedy person—such a man is an idolater—has any inheritance in the kingdom of Christ and of God.a 6Let no one deceive you with empty words, for because of such things God's wrath comes on those who are disobedient. 7Therefore do not be partners with them.

8For you were once darkness, but now you are light in the Lord. Live as children of light 9(for the fruit of the light consists in all goodness, righteousness and truth) 10and find out what pleases the Lord. 11Have nothing to do with the fruitless deeds of darkness, but rather expose them. 12For it is shameful even to mention what the disobedient do in secret. 13But everything exposed by the light becomes visible, 14for it is light that makes everything visible. This is why it is said:

"Wake up, O sleeper,
rise from the dead,
and Christ will shine on you."

15Be very careful, then, how you live— not as unwise but as wise, 16making the most of every opportunity, because the days are evil. 17Therefore do not be foolish, but understand what the Lord's will is. 18Do not get drunk on wine, which leads to debauchery. Instead, be filled with the Spirit. 19Speak to one another with psalms, hymns and spiritual songs. Sing and make

---

v Other ancient authorities read *building up faith*
w Other ancient authorities read *us*   x Other ancient authorities read *you*

b29 NRSV note v πίστεως   c32 NRSV note w ἡμῖν
a2 NRSV note x ὑμᾶς

a5 Or *kingdom of the Christ and God*

the Lord in your hearts, 20giving thanks to God the Father at all times and for everything in the name of our Lord Jesus Christ.

The Christian Household

21 Be subject to one another out of reverence for Christ.

22 Wives, be subject to your husbands as you are to the Lord. 23For the husband is the head of the wife just as Christ is the head of the church, the body of which he is the Savior. 24Just as the church is subject to Christ, so also wives ought to be, in everything, to their husbands.

25 Husbands, love your wives, just as Christ loved the church and gave himself up for her, 26in order to make her holy by cleansing her with the washing of water by the word, 27so as to present the church to himself in splendor, without a spot or wrinkle or anything of the kind—yes, so that she may be holy and without blemish. 28In the same way, husbands should love their wives as they do their own bodies. He who loves his wife loves himself. 29For no one ever hates his own body, but he nourishes and tenderly cares for it, just as Christ does for the church, 30because we are members of his body.y 31"For this reason a man will leave his father and mother and be joined to his wife, and the two will become one flesh." 32This is a great mystery, and I am applying it to Christ and the church. 33Each of you, however, should love his wife as himself, and a wife should respect her husband.

Children and Parents

6 Children, obey your parents in the Lord,z for this is right. 2"Honor your father and mother"—this is the first commandment with a promise: 3"so that it may be well with you and you may live long on the earth."

4 And, fathers, do not provoke your children to anger, but bring them up in the discipline and instruction of the Lord.

Slaves and Masters

5 Slaves, obey your earthly masters with fear and trembling, in singleness of heart, as you obey Christ; 6not only while being watched, and in order to please them, but as slaves of Christ, doing the will of God from the heart. 7Render service with enthusiasm, as to the Lord and not to men and women,8knowing that whatever good

ψάλλοντες τῇ καρδίᾳ ὑμῶν τῷ κυρίῳ, **20** εὐχαριστοῦντες πάντοτε ὑπὲρ πάντων ἐν ὀνόματι τοῦ κυρίου ἡμῶν Ἰησοῦ Χριστοῦ τῷ θεῷ καὶ πατρί.

21 ὑποτασσόμενοι ἀλλήλοις ἐν φόβῳ Χριστοῦ, **22** Αἱ γυναῖκες τοῖς ἰδίοις ἀνδράσιν ὡς τῷ κυρίῳ, **23** ὅτι ἀνήρ ἐστιν κεφαλὴ τῆς γυναικὸς ὡς καὶ ὁ Χριστὸς κεφαλὴ τῆς ἐκκλησίας, αὐτὸς σωτὴρ τοῦ σώματος· **24** ἀλλὰ ὡς ἡ ἐκκλησία ὑποτάσσεται τῷ Χριστῷ, οὕτως καὶ αἱ γυναῖκες τοῖς ἀνδράσιν ἐν παντί. **25** Οἱ ἄνδρες, ἀγαπᾶτε τὰς γυναῖκας, καθὼς καὶ ὁ Χριστὸς ἠγάπησεν τὴν ἐκκλησίαν καὶ ἑαυτὸν παρέδωκεν ὑπὲρ αὐτῆς, **26** ἵνα αὐτὴν ἁγιάσῃ καθαρίσας τῷ λουτρῷ τοῦ ὕδατος ἐν ῥήματι, **27** ἵνα παραστήσῃ αὐτὸς ἑαυτῷ ἔνδοξον τὴν ἐκκλησίαν, μὴ ἔχουσαν σπίλον ἢ ῥυτίδα ἤ τι τῶν τοιούτων, ἀλλ' ἵνα ᾖ ἁγία καὶ ἄμωμος. **28** οὕτως ὀφείλουσιν [καὶ] οἱ ἄνδρες ἀγαπᾶν τὰς ἑαυτῶν γυναῖκας ὡς τὰ ἑαυτῶν σώματα. ὁ ἀγαπῶν τὴν ἑαυτοῦ γυναῖκα ἑαυτὸν ἀγαπᾷ. **29** οὐδεὶς γάρ ποτε τὴν ἑαυτοῦ σάρκα ἐμίσησεν ἀλλὰ ἐκτρέφει καὶ θάλπει αὐτήν, καθὼς καὶ ὁ Χριστὸς τὴν ἐκκλησίαν, **30** ὅτι μέλη ἐσμὲν τοῦ σώματος αὐτοῦb. **31** ἀντὶ τούτου καταλείψει ἄνθρωπος [τὸν] πατέρα καὶ [τὴν] μητέρα καὶ προσκολληθήσεται πρὸς τὴν γυναῖκα αὐτοῦ, καὶ ἔσονται οἱ δύο εἰς σάρκα μίαν. **32** τὸ μυστήριον τοῦτο μέγα ἐστίν· ἐγὼ δὲ λέγω εἰς Χριστὸν καὶ εἰς τὴν ἐκκλησίαν. **33** πλὴν καὶ ὑμεῖς οἱ καθ' ἕνα, ἕκαστος τὴν ἑαυτοῦ γυναῖκα οὕτως ἀγαπάτω ὡς ἑαυτόν, ἡ δὲ γυνὴ ἵνα φοβῆται τὸν ἄνδρα.

6 Τὰ τέκνα, ὑπακούετε τοῖς γονεῦσιν ὑμῶν [ἐν κυρίῳ]· τοῦτο γάρ ἐστιν δίκαιον. **2** τίμα τὸν πατέρα σου καὶ τὴν μητέρα, ἥτις ἐστὶν ἐντολὴ πρώτη ἐν ἐπαγγελίᾳ, **3** ἵνα εὖ σοι γένηται καὶ ἔσῃ μακροχρόνιος ἐπὶ τῆς γῆς. **4** Καὶ οἱ πατέρες, μὴ παροργίζετε τὰ τέκνα ὑμῶν ἀλλὰ ἐκτρέφετε αὐτὰ ἐν παιδείᾳ καὶ νουθεσίᾳ κυρίου.

5 Οἱ δοῦλοι, ὑπακούετε τοῖς κατὰ σάρκα κυρίοις μετὰ φόβου καὶ τρόμου ἐν ἁπλότητι τῆς καρδίας ὑμῶν ὡς τῷ Χριστῷ, **6** μὴ κατ' ὀφθαλμοδουλίαν ὡς ἀνθρωπάρεσκοι ἀλλ' ὡς δοῦλοι Χριστοῦ ποιοῦντες τὸ θέλημα τοῦ θεοῦ ἐκ ψυχῆς, **7** μετ' εὐνοίας δουλεύοντες ὡς τῷ κυρίῳ καὶ οὐκ ἀνθρώποις, **8** εἰδότες

music in your heart to the Lord, 20always giving thanks to God the Father for everything, in the name of our Lord Jesus Christ.

21Submit to one another out of reverence for Christ.

Wives and Husbands

22Wives, submit to your husbands as to the Lord. 23For the husband is the head of the wife as Christ is the head of the church, his body, of which he is the Savior. 24Now as the church submits to Christ, so also wives should submit to their husbands in everything.

25Husbands, love your wives, just as Christ loved the church and gave himself up for her 26to make her holy, cleansingb her by the washing with water through the word, 27and to present her to himself as a radiant church, without stain or wrinkle or any other blemish, but holy and blameless. 28In this same way, husbands ought to love their wives as their own bodies. He who loves his wife loves himself. 29After all, no one ever hated his own body, but he feeds and cares for it, just as Christ does the church— 30for we are members of his body. 31"For this reason a man will leave his father and mother and be united to his wife, and the two will become one flesh."c 32This is a profound mystery—but I am talking about Christ and the church. 33However, each one of you also must love his wife as he loves himself, and the wife must respect her husband.

Children and Parents

6 Children, obey your parents in the Lord, for this is right. 2"Honor your father and mother"—which is the first commandment with a promise— 3"that it may go well with you and that you may enjoy long life on the earth."a

4Fathers, do not exasperate your children; instead, bring them up in the training and instruction of the Lord.

Slaves and Masters

5Slaves, obey your earthly masters with respect and fear, and with sincerity of heart, just as you would obey Christ. 6Obey them not only to win their favor when their eye is on you, but like slaves of Christ, doing the will of God from your heart. 7Serve wholeheartedly, as if you were serving the Lord, not men, 8because you know that

---

y Other ancient authorities add *of his flesh and of his bones*   z Other ancient authorities lack *in the Lord*

b30 NRSV note y ἐκ τῆς σαρκὸς αὐτοῦ καὶ ἐκ τῶν ὀστέων αὐτοῦ

b26 Or *having cleansed*   c31 Gen. 2:24   a3 Deut. 5:16

we do, we will receive the same again from the Lord, whether we are slaves or free.

9 And, masters, do the same to them. Stop threatening them, for you know that both of you have the same Master in heaven, and with him there is no partiality.

The Whole Armor of God

10 Finally, be strong in the Lord and in the strength of his power. [11]Put on the whole armor of God, so that you may be able to stand against the wiles of the devil. [12]For our[a] struggle is not against enemies of blood and flesh, but against the rulers, against the authorities, against the cosmic powers of this present darkness, against the spiritual forces of evil in the heavenly places. [13]Therefore take up the whole armor of God, so that you may be able to withstand on that evil day, and having done everything, to stand firm. [14]Stand therefore, and fasten the belt of truth around your waist, and put on the breastplate of righteousness. [15]As shoes for your feet put on whatever will make you ready to proclaim the gospel of peace. [16]With all of these,[b] take the shield of faith, with which you will be able to quench all the flaming arrows of the evil one. [17]Take the helmet of salvation, and the sword of the Spirit, which is the word of God.

18 Pray in the Spirit at all times in every prayer and supplication. To that end keep alert and always persevere in supplication for all the saints. [19]Pray also for me, so that when I speak, a message may be given to me to make known with boldness the mystery of the gospel,[c] [20]for which I am an ambassador in chains. Pray that I may declare it boldly, as I must speak.

Personal Matters and Benediction

21 So that you also may know how I am and what I am doing, Tychicus will tell you everything. He is a dear brother and a faithful minister in the Lord. [22]I am sending him to you for this very purpose, to let you know how we are, and to encourage your hearts.

23 Peace be to the whole community,[d] and love with faith, from God the Father and the Lord Jesus Christ. [24]Grace be with all who have an undying love for our Lord Jesus Christ.[e]

ὅτι ἕκαστος ἐάν τι ποιήσῃ ἀγαθόν, τοῦτο κομίσεται παρὰ κυρίου εἴτε δοῦλος εἴτε ἐλεύθερος. 9 Καὶ οἱ κύριοι, τὰ αὐτὰ ποιεῖτε πρὸς αὐτούς, ἀνιέντες τὴν ἀπειλήν, εἰδότες ὅτι καὶ αὐτῶν καὶ ὑμῶν ὁ κύριός ἐστιν ἐν οὐρανοῖς καὶ προσωπολημψία οὐκ ἔστιν παρ' αὐτῷ.

10 Τοῦ λοιποῦ, ἐνδυναμοῦσθε ἐν κυρίῳ καὶ ἐν τῷ κράτει τῆς ἰσχύος αὐτοῦ. 11 ἐνδύσασθε τὴν πανοπλίαν τοῦ θεοῦ πρὸς τὸ δύνασθαι ὑμᾶς στῆναι πρὸς τὰς μεθοδείας τοῦ διαβόλου· 12 ὅτι οὐκ ἔστιν ἡμῖν[a] ἡ πάλη πρὸς αἷμα καὶ σάρκα, ἀλλὰ πρὸς τὰς ἀρχάς, πρὸς τὰς ἐξουσίας, πρὸς τοὺς κοσμοκράτορας τοῦ σκότους τούτου, πρὸς τὰ πνευματικὰ τῆς πονηρίας ἐν τοῖς ἐπουρανίοις. 13 διὰ τοῦτο ἀναλάβετε τὴν πανοπλίαν τοῦ θεοῦ, ἵνα δυνηθῆτε ἀντιστῆναι ἐν τῇ ἡμέρᾳ τῇ πονηρᾷ καὶ ἅπαντα κατεργασάμενοι στῆναι. 14 στῆτε οὖν περιζωσάμενοι τὴν ὀσφὺν ὑμῶν ἐν ἀληθείᾳ καὶ ἐνδυσάμενοι τὸν θώρακα τῆς δικαιοσύνης 15 καὶ ὑποδησάμενοι τοὺς πόδας ἐν ἑτοιμασίᾳ τοῦ εὐαγγελίου τῆς εἰρήνης, 16 ἐν πᾶσιν ἀναλαβόντες τὸν θυρεὸν τῆς πίστεως, ἐν ᾧ δυνήσεσθε πάντα τὰ βέλη τοῦ πονηροῦ [τὰ] πεπυρωμένα σβέσαι· 17 καὶ τὴν περικεφαλαίαν τοῦ σωτηρίου δέξασθε καὶ τὴν μάχαιραν τοῦ πνεύματος, ὅ ἐστιν ῥῆμα θεοῦ. 18 διὰ πάσης προσευχῆς καὶ δεήσεως προσευχόμενοι ἐν παντὶ καιρῷ ἐν πνεύματι, καὶ εἰς αὐτὸ ἀγρυπνοῦντες ἐν πάσῃ προσκαρτερήσει καὶ δεήσει περὶ πάντων τῶν ἁγίων 19 καὶ ὑπὲρ ἐμοῦ, ἵνα μοι δοθῇ λόγος ἐν ἀνοίξει τοῦ στόματός μου, ἐν παρρησίᾳ γνωρίσαι τὸ μυστήριον τοῦ εὐαγγελίου, 20 ὑπὲρ οὗ πρεσβεύω ἐν ἁλύσει, ἵνα ἐν αὐτῷ παρρησιάσωμαι ὡς δεῖ με λαλῆσαι.

21 Ἵνα δὲ εἰδῆτε καὶ ὑμεῖς τὰ κατ' ἐμέ, τί πράσσω, πάντα γνωρίσει ὑμῖν Τυχικὸς ὁ ἀγαπητὸς ἀδελφὸς καὶ πιστὸς διάκονος ἐν κυρίῳ, 22 ὃν ἔπεμψα πρὸς ὑμᾶς εἰς αὐτὸ τοῦτο, ἵνα γνῶτε τὰ περὶ ἡμῶν καὶ παρακαλέσῃ τὰς καρδίας ὑμῶν.

23 Εἰρήνη τοῖς ἀδελφοῖς καὶ ἀγάπη μετὰ πίστεως ἀπὸ θεοῦ πατρὸς καὶ κυρίου Ἰησοῦ Χριστοῦ. 24 ἡ χάρις μετὰ πάντων τῶν ἀγαπώντων τὸν κύριον ἡμῶν Ἰησοῦν Χριστὸν ἐν ἀφθαρσίᾳ.[b]

the Lord will reward everyone for whatever good he does, whether he is slave or free.

[9]And masters, treat your slaves in the same way. Do not threaten them, since you know that he who is both their Master and yours is in heaven, and there is no favoritism with him.

The Armor of God

[10]Finally, be strong in the Lord and in his mighty power. [11]Put on the full armor of God so that you can take your stand against the devil's schemes. [12]For our struggle is not against flesh and blood, but against the rulers, against the authorities, against the powers of this dark world and against the spiritual forces of evil in the heavenly realms. [13]Therefore put on the full armor of God, so that when the day of evil comes, you may be able to stand your ground, and after you have done everything, to stand. [14]Stand firm then, with the belt of truth buckled around your waist, with the breastplate of righteousness in place, [15]and with your feet fitted with the readiness that comes from the gospel of peace. [16]In addition to all this, take up the shield of faith, with which you can extinguish all the flaming arrows of the evil one. [17]Take the helmet of salvation and the sword of the Spirit, which is the word of God. [18]And pray in the Spirit on all occasions with all kinds of prayers and requests. With this in mind, be alert and always keep on praying for all the saints.

[19]Pray also for me, that whenever I open my mouth, words may be given me so that I will fearlessly make known the mystery of the gospel, [20]for which I am an ambassador in chains. Pray that I may declare it fearlessly, as I should.

Final Greetings

[21]Tychicus, the dear brother and faithful servant in the Lord, will tell you everything, so that you also may know how I am and what I am doing. [22]I am sending him to you for this very purpose, that you may know how we are, and that he may encourage you.

[23]Peace to the brothers, and love with faith from God the Father and the Lord Jesus Christ. [24]Grace to all who love our Lord Jesus Christ with an undying love.

---

[a] Other ancient authorities read *your*   [b] Or *In all circumstances*   [c] Other ancient authorities lack *of the gospel*   [d] Gk *to the brothers*   [e] Other ancient authorities add *Amen*

[a]12 NRSV note a ὑμῖν   [b]24 NRSV note e adds ἀμήν.

NRSV

Salutation

1 Paul and Timothy, servants[a] of Christ Jesus,

To all the saints in Christ Jesus who are in Philippi, with the bishops[b] and deacons:[c] 2 Grace to you and peace from God our Father and the Lord Jesus Christ.

Paul's Prayer for the Philippians

3 I thank my God every time I remember you, [4]constantly praying with joy in every one of my prayers for all of you, [5]because of your sharing in the gospel from the first day until now. [6]I am confident of this, that the one who began a good work among you will bring it to completion by the day of Jesus Christ. [7]It is right for me to think this way about all of you, because you hold me in your heart,[d] for all of you share in God's grace[e] with me, both in my imprisonment and in the defense and confirmation of the gospel. [8]For God is my witness, how I long for all of you with the compassion of Christ Jesus. [9]And this is my prayer, that your love may overflow more and more with knowledge and full insight [10]to help you to determine what is best, so that in the day of Christ you may be pure and blameless, [11]having produced the harvest of righteousness that comes through Jesus Christ for the glory and praise of God.

Paul's Present Circumstances

12 I want you to know, beloved,[f] that what has happened to me has actually helped to spread the gospel, [13]so that it has become known throughout the whole imperial guard[g] and to everyone else that my imprisonment is for Christ; [14]and most of the brothers and sisters,[f] having been made confident in the Lord by my imprisonment, dare to speak the word[h] with greater boldness and without fear.

15 Some proclaim Christ from envy and rivalry, but others from goodwill. [16]These proclaim Christ out of love, knowing that I have been put here for the defense of the gospel; [17]the others proclaim Christ out of selfish ambition, not sincerely but intending to increase my suffering in my imprisonment. [18]What does it matter? Just this, that Christ is proclaimed in every way, whether out of false motives or true; and in that I rejoice.

Yes, and I will continue to rejoice, [19]for I

ΠΡΟΣ ΦΙΛΙΠΠΗΣΙΟΥΣ

1 Παῦλος καὶ Τιμόθεος δοῦλοι Χριστοῦ Ἰησοῦ πᾶσιν τοῖς ἁγίοις ἐν Χριστῷ Ἰησοῦ τοῖς οὖσιν ἐν Φιλίπποις σὺν ἐπισκόποις καὶ διακόνοις, **2** χάρις ὑμῖν καὶ εἰρήνη ἀπὸ θεοῦ πατρὸς ἡμῶν καὶ κυρίου Ἰησοῦ Χριστοῦ.

3 Εὐχαριστῶ τῷ θεῷ μου ἐπὶ πάσῃ τῇ μνείᾳ ὑμῶν **4** πάντοτε ἐν πάσῃ δεήσει μου ὑπὲρ πάντων ὑμῶν, μετὰ χαρᾶς τὴν δέησιν ποιούμενος, **5** ἐπὶ τῇ κοινωνίᾳ ὑμῶν εἰς τὸ εὐαγγέλιον ἀπὸ τῆς πρώτης ἡμέρας ἄχρι τοῦ νῦν, **6** πεποιθὼς αὐτὸ τοῦτο, ὅτι ὁ ἐναρξάμενος ἐν ὑμῖν ἔργον ἀγαθὸν ἐπιτελέσει ἄχρι ἡμέρας Χριστοῦ Ἰησοῦ· **7** καθώς ἐστιν δίκαιον ἐμοὶ τοῦτο φρονεῖν ὑπὲρ πάντων ὑμῶν διὰ τὸ ἔχειν με ἐν τῇ καρδίᾳ ὑμᾶς, ἔν τε τοῖς δεσμοῖς μου καὶ ἐν τῇ ἀπολογίᾳ καὶ βεβαιώσει τοῦ εὐαγγελίου συγκοινωνούς μου τῆς χάριτος πάντας ὑμᾶς ὄντας. **8** μάρτυς γάρ μου ὁ θεὸς ὡς ἐπιποθῶ πάντας ὑμᾶς ἐν σπλάγχνοις Χριστοῦ Ἰησοῦ. **9** καὶ τοῦτο προσεύχομαι, ἵνα ἡ ἀγάπη ὑμῶν ἔτι μᾶλλον καὶ μᾶλλον περισσεύῃ ἐν ἐπιγνώσει καὶ πάσῃ αἰσθήσει **10** εἰς τὸ δοκιμάζειν ὑμᾶς τὰ διαφέροντα, ἵνα ἦτε εἰλικρινεῖς καὶ ἀπρόσκοποι εἰς ἡμέραν Χριστοῦ, **11** πεπληρωμένοι καρπὸν δικαιοσύνης τὸν διὰ Ἰησοῦ Χριστοῦ εἰς δόξαν καὶ ἔπαινον θεοῦ.

12 Γινώσκειν δὲ ὑμᾶς βούλομαι, ἀδελφοί, ὅτι τὰ κατ' ἐμὲ μᾶλλον εἰς προκοπὴν τοῦ εὐαγγελίου ἐλήλυθεν, **13** ὥστε τοὺς δεσμούς μου φανεροὺς ἐν Χριστῷ γενέσθαι ἐν ὅλῳ τῷ πραιτωρίῳ καὶ τοῖς λοιποῖς πᾶσιν, **14** καὶ τοὺς πλείονας τῶν ἀδελφῶν ἐν κυρίῳ πεποιθότας τοῖς δεσμοῖς μου περισσοτέρως τολμᾶν ἀφόβως τὸν λόγον[a] λαλεῖν. **15** Τινὲς μὲν καὶ διὰ φθόνον καὶ ἔριν, τινὲς δὲ καὶ δι᾽ εὐδοκίαν τὸν Χριστὸν κηρύσσουσιν· **16** οἱ μὲν ἐξ ἀγάπης, εἰδότες ὅτι εἰς ἀπολογίαν τοῦ εὐαγγελίου κεῖμαι, **17** οἱ δὲ ἐξ ἐριθείας τὸν Χριστὸν καταγγέλλουσιν, οὐχ ἁγνῶς, οἰόμενοι θλῖψιν ἐγείρειν τοῖς δεσμοῖς μου. **18** τί γάρ; πλὴν ὅτι παντὶ τρόπῳ, εἴτε προφάσει εἴτε ἀληθείᾳ, Χριστὸς καταγγέλλεται, καὶ ἐν τούτῳ χαίρω. ἀλλὰ καὶ χαρήσομαι,

NIV

1 Paul and Timothy, servants of Christ Jesus,

To all the saints in Christ Jesus at Philippi, together with the overseers[a] and deacons:

[2]Grace and peace to you from God our Father and the Lord Jesus Christ.

Thanksgiving and Prayer

[3]I thank my God every time I remember you. [4]In all my prayers for all of you, I always pray with joy [5]because of your partnership in the gospel from the first day until now, [6]being confident of this, that he who began a good work in you will carry it on to completion until the day of Christ Jesus.

[7]It is right for me to feel this way about all of you, since I have you in my heart; for whether I am in chains or defending and confirming the gospel, all of you share in God's grace with me. [8]God can testify how I long for all of you with the affection of Christ Jesus.

[9]And this is my prayer: that your love may abound more and more in knowledge and depth of insight, [10]so that you may be able to discern what is best and may be pure and blameless until the day of Christ, [11]filled with the fruit of righteousness that comes through Jesus Christ—to the glory and praise of God.

Paul's Chains Advance the Gospel

[12]Now I want you to know, brothers, that what has happened to me has really served to advance the gospel. [13]As a result, it has become clear throughout the whole palace guard[b] and to everyone else that I am in chains for Christ. [14]Because of my chains, most of the brothers in the Lord have been encouraged to speak the word of God more courageously and fearlessly.

[15]It is true that some preach Christ out of envy and rivalry, but others out of goodwill. [16]The latter do so in love, knowing that I am put here for the defense of the gospel. [17]The former preach Christ out of selfish ambition, not sincerely, supposing that they can stir up trouble for me while I am in chains.[c] [18]But what does it matter? The important thing is that in every way, whether from false motives or true, Christ is preached. And because of this I rejoice.

Yes, and I will continue to rejoice, [19]for I

---

a Gk *slaves*   b Or *overseers*   c Or *overseers and helpers*
d Or *because I hold you in my heart*   e Gk *in grace*
f Gk *brothers*   g Gk *whole praetorium*   h Other ancient authorities read *word of God*

a14 NIV text and NRSV note h add τοῦ θεοῦ

a1 Traditionally *bishops*   b13 Or *whole palace*
c16,17 Some late manuscripts have verses 16 and 17 in reverse order.

know that through your prayers and the help of the Spirit of Jesus Christ this will turn out for my deliverance. 20It is my eager expectation and hope that I will not be put to shame in any way, but that by my speaking with all boldness, Christ will be exalted now as always in my body, whether by life or by death. 21For to me, living is Christ and dying is gain. 22If I am to live in the flesh, that means fruitful labor for me; and I do not know which I prefer. 23I am hard pressed between the two: my desire is to depart and be with Christ, for that is far better; 24but to remain in the flesh is more necessary for you. 25Since I am convinced of this, I know that I will remain and continue with all of you for your progress and joy in faith, 26so that I may share abundantly in your boasting in Christ Jesus when I come to you again.

27 Only, live your life in a manner worthy of the gospel of Christ, so that, whether I come and see you or am absent and hear about you, I will know that you are standing firm in one spirit, striving side by side with one mind for the faith of the gospel, 28and are in no way intimidated by your opponents. For them this is evidence of their destruction, but of your salvation. And this is God's doing. 29For he has graciously granted you the privilege not only of believing in Christ, but of suffering for him as well— 30since you are having the same struggle that you saw I had and now hear that I still have.

Imitating Christ's Humility

2 If then there is any encouragement in Christ, any consolation from love, any sharing in the Spirit, any compassion and sympathy, 2make my joy complete: be of the same mind, having the same love, being in full accord and of one mind. 3Do nothing from selfish ambition or conceit, but in humility regard others as better than yourselves. 4Let each of you look not to your own interests, but to the interests of others. 5Let the same mind be in you that was[i] in Christ Jesus,

6   who, though he was in the form of God,
       did not regard equality with God
       as something to be exploited,
7   but emptied himself,
       taking the form of a slave,

19 οἶδα γὰρ ὅτι τοῦτό μοι ἀποβήσεται εἰς σωτηρίαν διὰ τῆς ὑμῶν δεήσεως καὶ ἐπιχορηγίας τοῦ πνεύματος Ἰησοῦ Χριστοῦ 20 κατὰ τὴν ἀποκαραδοκίαν καὶ ἐλπίδα μου, ὅτι ἐν οὐδενὶ αἰσχυνθήσομαι ἀλλ᾽ ἐν πάσῃ παρρησίᾳ ὡς πάντοτε καὶ νῦν μεγαλυνθήσεται Χριστὸς ἐν τῷ σώματί μου, εἴτε διὰ ζωῆς εἴτε διὰ θανάτου. 21 ἐμοὶ γὰρ τὸ ζῆν Χριστὸς καὶ τὸ ἀποθανεῖν κέρδος. 22 εἰ δὲ τὸ ζῆν ἐν σαρκί, τοῦτό μοι καρπὸς ἔργου, καὶ τί αἱρήσομαι οὐ γνωρίζω. 23 συνέχομαι δὲ ἐκ τῶν δύο, τὴν ἐπιθυμίαν ἔχων εἰς τὸ ἀναλῦσαι καὶ σὺν Χριστῷ εἶναι, πολλῷ [γὰρ] μᾶλλον κρεῖσσον· 24 τὸ δὲ ἐπιμένειν [ἐν] τῇ σαρκὶ ἀναγκαιότερον δι᾽ ὑμᾶς. 25 καὶ τοῦτο πεποιθὼς οἶδα ὅτι μενῶ καὶ παραμενῶ πᾶσιν ὑμῖν εἰς τὴν ὑμῶν προκοπὴν καὶ χαρὰν τῆς πίστεως, 26 ἵνα τὸ καύχημα ὑμῶν περισσεύῃ ἐν Χριστῷ Ἰησοῦ ἐν ἐμοὶ διὰ τῆς ἐμῆς παρουσίας πάλιν πρὸς ὑμᾶς.

27 Μόνον ἀξίως τοῦ εὐαγγελίου τοῦ Χριστοῦ πολιτεύεσθε, ἵνα εἴτε ἐλθὼν καὶ ἰδὼν ὑμᾶς εἴτε ἀπὼν ἀκούω τὰ περὶ ὑμῶν, ὅτι στήκετε ἐν ἑνὶ πνεύματι, μιᾷ ψυχῇ συναθλοῦντες τῇ πίστει τοῦ εὐαγγελίου 28 καὶ μὴ πτυρόμενοι ἐν μηδενὶ ὑπὸ τῶν ἀντικειμένων, ἥτις ἐστὶν αὐτοῖς ἔνδειξις ἀπωλείας, ὑμῶν δὲ σωτηρίας, καὶ τοῦτο ἀπὸ θεοῦ· 29 ὅτι ὑμῖν ἐχαρίσθη τὸ ὑπὲρ Χριστοῦ, οὐ μόνον τὸ εἰς αὐτὸν πιστεύειν ἀλλὰ καὶ τὸ ὑπὲρ αὐτοῦ πάσχειν, 30 τὸν αὐτὸν ἀγῶνα ἔχοντες, οἷον εἴδετε ἐν ἐμοὶ καὶ νῦν ἀκούετε ἐν ἐμοί.

2 Εἴ τις οὖν παράκλησις ἐν Χριστῷ, εἴ τι παραμύθιον ἀγάπης, εἴ τις κοινωνία πνεύματος, εἴ τις σπλάγχνα καὶ οἰκτιρμοί, 2 πληρώσατέ μου τὴν χαρὰν ἵνα τὸ αὐτὸ φρονῆτε, τὴν αὐτὴν ἀγάπην ἔχοντες, σύμψυχοι, τὸ ἓν φρονοῦντες, 3 μηδὲν κατ᾽ ἐριθείαν μηδὲ κατὰ κενοδοξίαν ἀλλὰ τῇ ταπεινοφροσύνῃ ἀλλήλους ἡγούμενοι ὑπερέχοντας ἑαυτῶν, 4 μὴ τὰ ἑαυτῶν ἕκαστος σκοποῦντες ἀλλὰ [καὶ] τὰ ἑτέρων ἕκαστοι. 5 τοῦτο φρονεῖτε ἐν ὑμῖν ὃ καὶ ἐν Χριστῷ Ἰησοῦ, 6 ὃς ἐν μορφῇ θεοῦ ὑπάρχων οὐχ ἁρπαγμὸν ἡγήσατο τὸ εἶναι ἴσα θεῷ, 7 ἀλλὰ ἑαυτὸν ἐκένωσεν μορφὴν δούλου λαβών, ἐν ὁμοιώματι

know that through your prayers and the help given by the Spirit of Jesus Christ, what has happened to me will turn out for my deliverance.[d] 20I eagerly expect and hope that I will in no way be ashamed, but will have sufficient courage so that now as always Christ will be exalted in my body, whether by life or by death. 21For to me, to live is Christ and to die is gain. 22If I am to go on living in the body, this will mean fruitful labor for me. Yet what shall I choose? I do not know! 23I am torn between the two: I desire to depart and be with Christ, which is better by far; 24but it is more necessary for you that I remain in the body. 25Convinced of this, I know that I will remain, and I will continue with all of you for your progress and joy in the faith, 26so that through my being with you again your joy in Christ Jesus will overflow on account of me.

27Whatever happens, conduct yourselves in a manner worthy of the gospel of Christ. Then, whether I come and see you or only hear about you in my absence, I will know that you stand firm in one spirit, contending as one man for the faith of the gospel 28without being frightened in any way by those who oppose you. This is a sign to them that they will be destroyed, but that you will be saved—and that by God. 29For it has been granted to you on behalf of Christ not only to believe on him, but also to suffer for him, 30since you are going through the same struggle you saw I had, and now hear that I still have.

Imitating Christ's Humility

2 If you have any encouragement from being united with Christ, if any comfort from his love, if any fellowship with the Spirit, if any tenderness and compassion, 2then make my joy complete by being like-minded, having the same love, being one in spirit and purpose. 3Do nothing out of selfish ambition or vain conceit, but in humility consider others better than yourselves. 4Each of you should look not only to your own interests, but also to the interests of others.

5Your attitude should be the same as that of Christ Jesus:

6Who, being in very nature[a] God,
    did not consider equality with God
    something to be grasped,
7but made himself nothing,
    taking the very nature[b] of a servant,

NRSV

being born in human likeness.
And being found in human form,
8   he humbled himself
and became obedient to the point of
death—
even death on a cross.

9   Therefore God also highly exalted him
and gave him the name
that is above every name,
10   so that at the name of Jesus
every knee should bend,
in heaven and on earth and under
the earth,
11   and every tongue should confess
that Jesus Christ is Lord,
to the glory of God the Father.

Shining as Lights in the World

12 Therefore, my beloved, just as you have always obeyed me, not only in my presence, but much more now in my absence, work out your own salvation with fear and trembling; 13for it is God who is at work in you, enabling you both to will and to work for his good pleasure.

14 Do all things without murmuring and arguing, 15so that you may be blameless and innocent, children of God without blemish in the midst of a crooked and perverse generation, in which you shine like stars in the world. 16It is by your holding fast to the word of life that I can boast on the day of Christ that I did not run in vain or labor in vain. 17But even if I am being poured out as a libation over the sacrifice and the offering of your faith, I am glad and rejoice with all of you— 18and in the same way you also must be glad and rejoice with me.

Timothy and Epaphroditus

19 I hope in the Lord Jesus to send Timothy to you soon, so that I may be cheered by news of you. 20I have no one like him who will be genuinely concerned for your welfare. 21All of them are seeking their own interests, not those of Jesus Christ. 22But Timothy's^j worth you know, how like a son with a father he has served with me in the work of the gospel. 23I hope therefore to send him as soon as I see how things go with me; 24and I trust in the Lord that I will also come soon.

25 Still, I think it necessary to send to you Epaphroditus—my brother and co-worker and fellow soldier, your messenger^k and minister to my need; 26for he has

(Greek)

ἀνθρώπων γενόμενος·^a καὶ σχήματι εὑρεθεὶς ὡς ἄνθρωπος 8 ἐταπείνωσεν ἑαυτὸν γενόμενος ὑπήκοος μέχρι θανάτου, θανάτου δὲ σταυροῦ. 9 διὸ καὶ ὁ θεὸς αὐτὸν ὑπερύψωσεν καὶ ἐχαρίσατο αὐτῷ τὸ ὄνομα τὸ ὑπὲρ πᾶν ὄνομα, 10 ἵνα ἐν τῷ ὀνόματι Ἰησοῦ πᾶν γόνυ κάμψῃ ἐπουρανίων καὶ ἐπιγείων καὶ καταχθονίων 11 καὶ πᾶσα γλῶσσα ἐξομολογήσηται ὅτι κύριος Ἰησοῦς Χριστὸς εἰς δόξαν θεοῦ πατρός.

12 Ὥστε, ἀγαπητοί μου, καθὼς πάν-τοτε ὑπηκούσατε, μὴ ὡς ἐν τῇ παρουσίᾳ μου μόνον ἀλλὰ νῦν πολλῷ μᾶλλον ἐν τῇ ἀπουσίᾳ μου, μετὰ φόβου καὶ τρόμου τὴν ἑαυτῶν σωτηρίαν κατεργάζεσθε· 13 θεὸς γάρ ἐστιν ὁ ἐνεργῶν ἐν ὑμῖν καὶ τὸ θέλειν καὶ τὸ ἐνεργεῖν ὑπὲρ τῆς εὐδοκίας. 14 πάντα ποιεῖτε χωρὶς γογγυσμῶν καὶ διαλογισμῶν, 15 ἵνα γένησθε ἄμεμπτοι καὶ ἀκέραιοι, τέκνα θεοῦ ἄμωμα μέσον γενεᾶς σκολιᾶς καὶ διεστραμμένης, ἐν οἷς φαίνεσθε ὡς φωστῆρες ἐν κόσμῳ, 16 λόγον ζωῆς ἐπέχοντες, εἰς καύχημα ἐμοὶ εἰς ἡμέραν Χριστοῦ, ὅτι οὐκ εἰς κενὸν ἔδραμον οὐδὲ εἰς κενὸν ἐκοπίασα. 17 ἀλλὰ εἰ καὶ σπένδομαι ἐπὶ τῇ θυσίᾳ καὶ λει-τουργίᾳ τῆς πίστεως ὑμῶν, χαίρω καὶ συγχαίρω πᾶσιν ὑμῖν· 18 τὸ δὲ αὐτὸ καὶ ὑμεῖς χαίρετε καὶ συγχαίρετέ μοι.

19 Ἐλπίζω δὲ ἐν κυρίῳ Ἰησοῦ Τιμόθεον ταχέως πέμψαι ὑμῖν, ἵνα κἀγὼ εὐψυχῶ γνοὺς τὰ περὶ ὑμῶν. 20 οὐδένα γὰρ ἔχω ἰσόψυχον, ὅστις γνησίως τὰ περὶ ὑμῶν μεριμνήσει· 21 οἱ πάντες γὰρ τὰ ἑαυτῶν ζητοῦσιν, οὐ τὰ Ἰησοῦ Χριστοῦ. 22 τὴν δὲ δοκιμὴν αὐτοῦ γινώσκετε, ὅτι ὡς πατρὶ τέκνον σὺν ἐμοὶ ἐδούλευσεν εἰς τὸ εὐαγγέλιον. 23 τοῦτον μὲν οὖν ἐλπίζω πέμψαι ὡς ἂν ἀφίδω τὰ περὶ ἐμὲ ἐξαυτῆς· 24 πέποιθα δὲ ἐν κυρίῳ ὅτι καὶ αὐτὸς ταχέως ἐλεύσομαι.

25 Ἀναγκαῖον δὲ ἡγησάμην Ἐπαφρό-διτον τὸν ἀδελφὸν καὶ συνεργὸν καὶ συστρατιώτην μου, ὑμῶν δὲ ἀπόστολον καὶ λειτουργὸν τῆς χρείας μου, πέμψαι πρὸς ὑμᾶς, 26 ἐπειδὴ ἐπιποθῶν ἦν

NIV

being made in human likeness.
8And being found in appearance as a man,
he humbled himself
and became obedient to death—
even death on a cross!
9Therefore God exalted him to the
highest place
and gave him the name that is above
every name,
10that at the name of Jesus every knee
should bow,
in heaven and on earth and under the
earth,
11and every tongue confess that Jesus
Christ is Lord,
to the glory of God the Father.

Shining as Stars

12Therefore, my dear friends, as you have always obeyed—not only in my presence, but now much more in my absence—continue to work out your salvation with fear and trembling, 13for it is God who works in you to will and to act according to his good purpose.

14Do everything without complaining or arguing, 15so that you may become blameless and pure, children of God without fault in a crooked and depraved generation, in which you shine like stars in the universe 16as you hold out^c the word of life—in order that I may boast on the day of Christ that I did not run or labor for nothing. 17But even if I am being poured out like a drink offering on the sacrifice and service coming from your faith, I am glad and rejoice with all of you. 18So you too should be glad and rejoice with me.

Timothy and Epaphroditus

19I hope in the Lord Jesus to send Timothy to you soon, that I also may be cheered when I receive news about you. 20I have no one else like him, who takes a genuine interest in your welfare. 21For everyone looks out for his own interests, not those of Jesus Christ. 22But you know that Timothy has proved himself, because as a son with his father he has served with me in the work of the gospel. 23I hope, therefore, to send him as soon as I see how things go with me. 24And I am confident in the Lord that I myself will come soon.

25But I think it is necessary to send back to you Epaphroditus, my brother, fellow worker and fellow soldier, who is also your messenger, whom you sent to take care of my needs. 26For he longs for all of you and

---

^jGk *his*   ^kGk *apostle*   ^a7 NIV begins verse 8 after γενόμενος·   ^c16 Or *hold on to*

been longing for[l] all of you, and has been distressed because you heard that he was ill. [27]He was indeed so ill that he nearly died. But God had mercy on him, and not only on him but on me also, so that I would not have one sorrow after another. [28]I am the more eager to send him, therefore, in order that you may rejoice at seeing him again, and that I may be less anxious. [29]Welcome him then in the Lord with all joy, and honor such people, [30]because he came close to death for the work of Christ,[m] risking his life to make up for those services that you could not give me.

3 Finally, my brothers and sisters,[n] rejoice[o] in the Lord.

Breaking with the Past

To write the same things to you is not troublesome to me, and for you it is a safeguard.

2 Beware of the dogs, beware of the evil workers, beware of those who mutilate the flesh![p] [3]For it is we who are the circumcision, who worship in the Spirit of God[q] and boast in Christ Jesus and have no confidence in the flesh— [4]even though I, too, have reason for confidence in the flesh.

If anyone else has reason to be confident in the flesh, I have more: [5]circumcised on the eighth day, a member of the people of Israel, of the tribe of Benjamin, a Hebrew born of Hebrews; as to the law, a Pharisee; [6]as to zeal, a persecutor of the church; as to righteousness under the law, blameless.

7 Yet whatever gains I had, these I have come to regard as loss because of Christ. [8]More than that, I regard everything as loss because of the surpassing value of knowing Christ Jesus my Lord. For his sake I have suffered the loss of all things, and I regard them as rubbish, in order that I may gain Christ [9]and be found in him, not having a righteousness of my own that comes from the law, but one that comes through faith in Christ,[r] the righteousness from God based on faith. [10]I want to know Christ[s] and the power of his resurrection and the sharing of his sufferings by becoming like him in his death, [11]if somehow I may attain the resurrection from the dead.

πάντας ὑμᾶς[b] καὶ ἀδημονῶν, διότι ἠκούσατε ὅτι ἠσθένησεν. 27 καὶ γὰρ ἠσθένησεν παραπλήσιον θανάτῳ· ἀλλὰ ὁ θεὸς ἠλέησεν αὐτόν, οὐκ αὐτὸν δὲ μόνον ἀλλὰ καὶ ἐμέ, ἵνα μὴ λύπην ἐπὶ λύπην σχῶ. 28 σπουδαιοτέρως οὖν ἔπεμψα αὐτόν, ἵνα ἰδόντες αὐτὸν πάλιν χαρῆτε κἀγὼ ἀλυπότερος ὦ. 29 προσδέχεσθε οὖν αὐτὸν ἐν κυρίῳ μετὰ πάσης χαρᾶς καὶ τοὺς τοιούτους ἐντίμους ἔχετε, 30 ὅτι διὰ τὸ ἔργον Χριστοῦ[c] μέχρι θανάτου ἤγγισεν παραβολευσάμενος τῇ ψυχῇ, ἵνα ἀναπληρώσῃ τὸ ὑμῶν ὑστέρημα τῆς πρός με λειτουργίας.

3 Τὸ λοιπόν, ἀδελφοί μου, χαίρετε ἐν κυρίῳ. τὰ αὐτὰ γράφειν ὑμῖν ἐμοὶ μὲν οὐκ ὀκνηρόν, ὑμῖν δὲ ἀσφαλές. 2 Βλέπετε τοὺς κύνας, βλέπετε τοὺς κακοὺς ἐργάτας, βλέπετε τὴν κατατομήν. 3 ἡμεῖς γάρ ἐσμεν ἡ περιτομή, οἱ πνεύματι θεοῦ[a] λατρεύοντες καὶ καυχώμενοι ἐν Χριστῷ Ἰησοῦ καὶ οὐκ ἐν σαρκὶ πεποιθότες, 4 καίπερ ἐγὼ ἔχων πεποίθησιν καὶ ἐν σαρκί. εἴ τις δοκεῖ ἄλλος πεποιθέναι ἐν σαρκί, ἐγὼ μᾶλλον· 5 περιτομῇ ὀκταήμερος, ἐκ γένους Ἰσραήλ, φυλῆς Βενιαμίν, Ἑβραῖος ἐξ Ἑβραίων, κατὰ νόμον Φαρισαῖος, 6 κατὰ ζῆλος διώκων τὴν ἐκκλησίαν, κατὰ δικαιοσύνην τὴν ἐν νόμῳ γενόμενος ἄμεμπτος. 7 [ἀλλὰ] ἅτινα ἦν μοι κέρδη, ταῦτα ἥγημαι διὰ τὸν Χριστὸν ζημίαν. 8 ἀλλὰ μενοῦνγε καὶ ἡγοῦμαι πάντα ζημίαν εἶναι διὰ τὸ ὑπερέχον τῆς γνώσεως Χριστοῦ Ἰησοῦ τοῦ κυρίου μου, δι᾽ ὃν τὰ πάντα ἐζημιώθην, καὶ ἡγοῦμαι σκύβαλα, ἵνα Χριστὸν κερδήσω 9 καὶ εὑρεθῶ ἐν αὐτῷ, μὴ ἔχων ἐμὴν δικαιοσύνην τὴν ἐκ νόμου ἀλλὰ τὴν διὰ πίστεως Χριστοῦ, τὴν ἐκ θεοῦ δικαιοσύνην ἐπὶ τῇ πίστει, 10 τοῦ γνῶναι αὐτὸν καὶ τὴν δύναμιν τῆς ἀναστάσεως αὐτοῦ καὶ [τὴν] κοινωνίαν [τῶν] παθημάτων αὐτοῦ, συμμορφιζόμενος τῷ θανάτῳ αὐτοῦ, 11 εἴ πως καταντήσω εἰς τὴν ἐξανάστασιν τὴν ἐκ νεκρῶν.

is distressed because you heard he was ill. [27]Indeed he was ill, and almost died. But God had mercy on him, and not on him only but also on me, to spare me sorrow upon sorrow. [28]Therefore I am all the more eager to send him, so that when you see him again you may be glad and I may have less anxiety. [29]Welcome him in the Lord with great joy, and honor men like him, [30]because he almost died for the work of Christ, risking his life to make up for the help you could not give me.

No Confidence in the Flesh

3 Finally, my brothers, rejoice in the Lord! It is no trouble for me to write the same things to you again, and it is a safeguard for you.

[2]Watch out for those dogs, those men who do evil, those mutilators of the flesh. [3]For it is we who are the circumcision, we who worship by the Spirit of God, who glory in Christ Jesus, and who put no confidence in the flesh— [4]though I myself have reasons for such confidence.

If anyone else thinks he has reasons to put confidence in the flesh, I have more: [5]circumcised on the eighth day, of the people of Israel, of the tribe of Benjamin, a Hebrew of Hebrews; in regard to the law, a Pharisee; [6]as for zeal, persecuting the church; as for legalistic righteousness, faultless.

[7]But whatever was to my profit I now consider loss for the sake of Christ. [8]What is more, I consider everything a loss compared to the surpassing greatness of knowing Christ Jesus my Lord, for whose sake I have lost all things. I consider them rubbish, that I may gain Christ [9]and be found in him, not having a righteousness of my own that comes from the law, but that which is through faith in Christ—the righteousness that comes from God and is by faith. [10]I want to know Christ and the power of his resurrection and the fellowship of sharing in his sufferings, becoming like him in his death, [11]and so, somehow, to attain to the resurrection from the dead.

---

[l] Other ancient authorities read *longing to see*   [m] Other ancient authorities read *of the Lord*   [n] Gk *my brothers*   [o] Or *farewell*   [p] Gk *the mutilation*   [q] Other ancient authorities read *worship God in spirit*   [r] Or *through the faith of Christ*   [s] Gk *him*

[b]26 NRSV note l adds ἰδεῖν   [c]30 NRSV note m κυρίου
[a]3 NRSV note q θεῷ

NRSV

Pressing toward the Goal

12 Not that I have already obtained this or have already reached the goal;[t] but I press on to make it my own, because Christ Jesus has made me his own. 13Beloved,[u] I do not consider that I have made it my own;[v] but this one thing I do: forgetting what lies behind and straining forward to what lies ahead, 14I press on toward the goal for the prize of the heavenly[w] call of God in Christ Jesus. 15Let those of us then who are mature be of the same mind; and if you think differently about anything, this too God will reveal to you. 16Only let us hold fast to what we have attained.

17 Brothers and sisters,[u] join in imitating me, and observe those who live according to the example you have in us. 18For many live as enemies of the cross of Christ; I have often told you of them, and now I tell you even with tears. 19Their end is destruction; their god is the belly; and their glory is in their shame; their minds are set on earthly things. 20But our citizenship[x] is in heaven, and it is from there that we are expecting a Savior, the Lord Jesus Christ. 21He will transform the body of our humiliation[y] that it may be conformed to the body of his glory,[z] by the power that also enables him to make all things subject to himself. ¹Therefore, my brothers and sisters,[a] whom I love and long for, my joy and crown, stand firm in the Lord in this way, my beloved.

Exhortations

2 I urge Euodia and I urge Syntyche to be of the same mind in the Lord. 3Yes, and I ask you also, my loyal companion,[b] help these women, for they have struggled beside me in the work of the gospel, together with Clement and the rest of my co-workers, whose names are in the book of life.

4 Rejoice[c] in the Lord always; again I will say, Rejoice.[c] 5Let your gentleness be known to everyone. The Lord is near. 6Do not worry about anything, but in everything by prayer and supplication with thanksgiving let your requests be made known to God. 7And the peace of God, which surpasses all understanding, will guard your hearts and your minds in Christ Jesus.

8 Finally, beloved,[d] whatever is true,

NIV

Pressing on Toward the Goal

12Not that I have already obtained all this, or have already been made perfect, but I press on to take hold of that for which Christ Jesus took hold of me. 13Brothers, I do not consider myself yet to have taken hold of it. But one thing I do: Forgetting what is behind and straining toward what is ahead, 14I press on toward the goal to win the prize for which God has called me heavenward in Christ Jesus.

15All of us who are mature should take such a view of things. And if on some point you think differently, that too God will make clear to you. 16Only let us live up to what we have already attained.

17Join with others in following my example, brothers, and take note of those who live according to the pattern we gave you. 18For, as I have often told you before and now say again even with tears, many live as enemies of the cross of Christ. 19Their destiny is destruction, their god is their stomach, and their glory is in their shame. Their mind is on earthly things. 20But our citizenship is in heaven. And we eagerly await a Savior from there, the Lord Jesus Christ, 21who, by the power that enables him to bring everything under his control, will transform our lowly bodies so that they will be like his glorious body.

Therefore, my brothers, you whom I love and long for, my joy and crown, that is how you should stand firm in the Lord, dear friends!

Exhortations

2I plead with Euodia and I plead with Syntyche to agree with each other in the Lord. 3Yes, and I ask you, loyal yokefellow,[a] help these women who have contended at my side in the cause of the gospel, along with Clement and the rest of my fellow workers, whose names are in the book of life.

4Rejoice in the Lord always. I will say it again: Rejoice! 5Let your gentleness be evident to all. The Lord is near. 6Do not be anxious about anything, but in everything, by prayer and petition, with thanksgiving, present your requests to God. 7And the peace of God, which transcends all understanding, will guard your hearts and your minds in Christ Jesus.

8Finally, brothers, whatever is true, what-

t Or have already been made perfect   u Gk Brothers
v Other ancient authorities read my own yet
w Gk upward   x Or commonwealth   y Or our humble
bodies   z Or his glorious body   a Gk my brothers   b Or
loyal Syzygus   c Or Farewell   d Gk brothers

b13 NIV text and NRSV note v οὔπω

a3 Or loyal Syzygus

whatever is honorable, whatever is just, whatever is pure, whatever is pleasing, whatever is commendable, if there is any excellence and if there is anything worthy of praise, think about[e] these things. [9]Keep on doing the things that you have learned and received and heard and seen in me, and the God of peace will be with you.

Acknowledgment of the Philippians' Gift

10 I rejoice[f] in the Lord greatly that now at last you have revived your concern for me; indeed, you were concerned for me, but had no opportunity to show it.[g] [11]Not that I am referring to being in need; for I have learned to be content with whatever I have. [12]I know what it is to have little, and I know what it is to have plenty. In any and all circumstances I have learned the secret of being well-fed and of going hungry, of having plenty and of being in need. [13]I can do all things through him who strengthens me. [14]In any case, it was kind of you to share my distress.

15 You Philippians indeed know that in the early days of the gospel, when I left Macedonia, no church shared with me in the matter of giving and receiving, except you alone. [16]For even when I was in Thessalonica, you sent me help for my needs more than once. [17]Not that I seek the gift, but I seek the profit that accumulates to your account. [18]I have been paid in full and have more than enough; I am fully satisfied, now that I have received from Epaphroditus the gifts you sent, a fragrant offering, a sacrifice acceptable and pleasing to God. [19]And my God will fully satisfy every need of yours according to his riches in glory in Christ Jesus. [20]To our God and Father be glory forever and ever. Amen.

Final Greetings and Benediction

21 Greet every saint in Christ Jesus. The friends[h] who are with me greet you. [22]All the saints greet you, especially those of the emperor's household.

23 The grace of the Lord Jesus Christ be with your spirit.[i]

ὅσα σεμνά, ὅσα δίκαια, ὅσα ἁγνά, ὅσα προσφιλῆ, ὅσα εὔφημα, εἴ τις ἀρετὴ καὶ εἴ τις ἔπαινος, ταῦτα λογίζεσθε· 9 ἃ καὶ ἐμάθετε καὶ παρελάβετε καὶ ἠκούσατε καὶ εἴδετε ἐν ἐμοί, ταῦτα πράσσετε· καὶ ὁ θεὸς τῆς εἰρήνης ἔσται μεθ᾽ ὑμῶν.

10 Ἐχάρην δὲ ἐν κυρίῳ μεγάλως ὅτι ἤδη ποτὲ ἀνεθάλετε τὸ ὑπὲρ ἐμοῦ φρονεῖν, ἐφ᾽ ᾧ καὶ ἐφρονεῖτε, ἠκαιρεῖσθε δέ. 11 οὐχ ὅτι καθ᾽ ὑστέρησιν λέγω, ἐγὼ γὰρ ἔμαθον ἐν οἷς εἰμι αὐτάρκης εἶναι. 12 οἶδα καὶ ταπεινοῦσθαι, οἶδα καὶ περισσεύειν· ἐν παντὶ καὶ ἐν πᾶσιν μεμύημαι, καὶ χορτάζεσθαι καὶ πεινᾶν καὶ περισσεύειν καὶ ὑστερεῖσθαι· 13 πάντα ἰσχύω ἐν τῷ ἐνδυναμοῦντί με. 14 πλὴν καλῶς ἐποιήσατε συγκοινωνήσαντές μου τῇ θλίψει.

15 Οἴδατε δὲ καὶ ὑμεῖς, Φιλιππήσιοι, ὅτι ἐν ἀρχῇ τοῦ εὐαγγελίου, ὅτε ἐξῆλθον ἀπὸ Μακεδονίας, οὐδεμία μοι ἐκκλησία ἐκοινώνησεν εἰς λόγον δόσεως καὶ λήμψεως εἰ μὴ ὑμεῖς μόνοι, 16 ὅτι καὶ ἐν Θεσσαλονίκῃ καὶ ἅπαξ καὶ δὶς εἰς τὴν χρείαν μοι ἐπέμψατε. 17 οὐχ ὅτι ἐπιζητῶ τὸ δόμα, ἀλλὰ ἐπιζητῶ τὸν καρπὸν τὸν πλεονάζοντα εἰς λόγον ὑμῶν. 18 ἀπέχω δὲ πάντα καὶ περισσεύω· πεπλήρωμαι δεξάμενος παρὰ Ἐπαφροδίτου τὰ παρ᾽ ὑμῶν, ὀσμὴν εὐωδίας, θυσίαν δεκτήν, εὐάρεστον τῷ θεῷ. 19 ὁ δὲ θεός μου πληρώσει πᾶσαν χρείαν ὑμῶν κατὰ τὸ πλοῦτος αὐτοῦ ἐν δόξῃ ἐν Χριστῷ Ἰησοῦ. 20 τῷ δὲ θεῷ καὶ πατρὶ ἡμῶν ἡ δόξα εἰς τοὺς αἰῶνας τῶν αἰώνων, ἀμήν.

21 Ἀσπάσασθε πάντα ἅγιον ἐν Χριστῷ Ἰησοῦ. ἀσπάζονται ὑμᾶς οἱ σὺν ἐμοὶ ἀδελφοί. 22 ἀσπάζονται ὑμᾶς πάντες οἱ ἅγιοι, μάλιστα δὲ οἱ ἐκ τῆς Καίσαρος οἰκίας. 23 ἡ χάρις τοῦ κυρίου Ἰησοῦ Χριστοῦ μετὰ τοῦ πνεύματος ὑμῶν.

---

ever is noble, whatever is right, whatever is pure, whatever is lovely, whatever is admirable—if anything is excellent or praiseworthy—think about such things. [9]Whatever you have learned or received or heard from me, or seen in me—put it into practice. And the God of peace will be with you.

Thanks for Their Gifts

[10]I rejoice greatly in the Lord that at last you have renewed your concern for me. Indeed, you have been concerned, but you had no opportunity to show it. [11]I am not saying this because I am in need, for I have learned to be content whatever the circumstances. [12]I know what it is to be in need, and I know what it is to have plenty. I have learned the secret of being content in any and every situation, whether well fed or hungry, whether living in plenty or in want. [13]I can do everything through him who gives me strength.

[14]Yet it was good of you to share in my troubles. [15]Moreover, as you Philippians know, in the early days of your acquaintance with the gospel, when I set out from Macedonia, not one church shared with me in the matter of giving and receiving, except you only; [16]for even when I was in Thessalonica, you sent me aid again and again when I was in need. [17]Not that I am looking for a gift, but I am looking for what may be credited to your account. [18]I have received full payment and even more; I am amply supplied, now that I have received from Epaphroditus the gifts you sent. They are a fragrant offering, an acceptable sacrifice, pleasing to God. [19]And my God will meet all your needs according to his glorious riches in Christ Jesus.

[20]To our God and Father be glory for ever and ever. Amen.

Final Greetings

[21]Greet all the saints in Christ Jesus. The brothers who are with me send greetings. [22]All the saints send you greetings, especially those who belong to Caesar's household.

[23]The grace of the Lord Jesus Christ be with your spirit. Amen.[b]

NRSV

Salutation

1 Paul, an apostle of Christ Jesus by the will of God, and Timothy our brother, 2 To the saints and faithful brothers and sisters[a] in Christ in Colossae:

Grace to you and peace from God our Father.

Paul Thanks God for the Colossians

3 In our prayers for you we always thank God, the Father of our Lord Jesus Christ, [4]for we have heard of your faith in Christ Jesus and of the love that you have for all the saints, [5]because of the hope laid up for you in heaven. You have heard of this hope before in the word of the truth, the gospel [6]that has come to you. Just as it is bearing fruit and growing in the whole world, so it has been bearing fruit among yourselves from the day you heard it and truly comprehended the grace of God. [7]This you learned from Epaphras, our beloved fellow servant.[b] He is a faithful minister of Christ on your[c] behalf, [8]and he has made known to us your love in the Spirit.

9 For this reason, since the day we heard it, we have not ceased praying for you and asking that you may be filled with the knowledge of God's[d] will in all spiritual wisdom and understanding, [10]so that you may lead lives worthy of the Lord, fully pleasing to him, as you bear fruit in every good work and as you grow in the knowledge of God. [11]May you be made strong with all the strength that comes from his glorious power, and may you be prepared to endure everything with patience, while joyfully [12]giving thanks to the Father, who has enabled[e] you[f] to share in the inheritance of the saints in the light. [13]He has rescued us from the power of darkness and transferred us into the kingdom of his beloved Son, [14]in whom we have redemption, the forgiveness of sins.[g]

The Supremacy of Christ

15 He is the image of the invisible God, the firstborn of all creation; [16]for in[h] him all things in heaven and on earth were created, things visible and invisible, whether thrones or dominions or rulers or powers—all things have been created through him and for him. [17]He himself is

ΠΡΟΣ ΚΟΛΟΣΣΑΕΙΣ

1 Παῦλος ἀπόστολος Χριστοῦ Ἰησοῦ διὰ θελήματος θεοῦ καὶ Τιμόθεος ὁ ἀδελφὸς **2** τοῖς ἐν Κολοσσαῖς ἁγίοις καὶ πιστοῖς ἀδελφοῖς ἐν Χριστῷ, χάρις ὑμῖν καὶ εἰρήνη ἀπὸ θεοῦ πατρὸς ἡμῶν[a]. **3** Εὐχαριστοῦμεν τῷ θεῷ πατρὶ τοῦ κυρίου ἡμῶν Ἰησοῦ Χριστοῦ πάντοτε περὶ ὑμῶν προσευχόμενοι, **4** ἀκούσαντες τὴν πίστιν ὑμῶν ἐν Χριστῷ Ἰησοῦ καὶ τὴν ἀγάπην ἣν ἔχετε εἰς πάντας τοὺς ἁγίους **5** διὰ τὴν ἐλπίδα τὴν ἀποκειμένην ὑμῖν ἐν τοῖς οὐρανοῖς, ἣν προηκούσατε ἐν τῷ λόγῳ τῆς ἀληθείας τοῦ εὐαγγελίου **6** τοῦ παρόντος εἰς ὑμᾶς, καθὼς καὶ ἐν παντὶ τῷ κόσμῳ ἐστὶν καρποφορούμενον καὶ αὐξανόμενον καθὼς καὶ ἐν ὑμῖν, ἀφ᾽ ἧς ἡμέρας ἠκούσατε καὶ ἐπέγνωτε τὴν χάριν τοῦ θεοῦ ἐν ἀληθείᾳ· **7** καθὼς ἐμάθετε ἀπὸ Ἐπαφρᾶ τοῦ ἀγαπητοῦ συνδούλου ἡμῶν, ὅς ἐστιν πιστὸς ὑπὲρ ὑμῶν[b] διάκονος τοῦ Χριστοῦ, **8** ὁ καὶ δηλώσας ἡμῖν τὴν ὑμῶν ἀγάπην ἐν πνεύματι. **9** Διὰ τοῦτο καὶ ἡμεῖς, ἀφ᾽ ἧς ἡμέρας ἠκούσαμεν, οὐ παυόμεθα ὑπὲρ ὑμῶν προσευχόμενοι καὶ αἰτούμενοι, ἵνα πληρωθῆτε τὴν ἐπίγνωσιν τοῦ θελήματος αὐτοῦ ἐν πάσῃ σοφίᾳ καὶ συνέσει πνευματικῇ, **10** περιπατῆσαι ἀξίως τοῦ κυρίου εἰς πᾶσαν ἀρεσκείαν, ἐν παντὶ ἔργῳ ἀγαθῷ καρποφοροῦντες καὶ αὐξανόμενοι τῇ ἐπιγνώσει τοῦ θεοῦ, **11** ἐν πάσῃ δυνάμει δυναμούμενοι κατὰ τὸ κράτος τῆς δόξης αὐτοῦ εἰς πᾶσαν ὑπομονὴν καὶ μακροθυμίαν. μετὰ χαρᾶς **12** εὐχαριστοῦντες τῷ πατρὶ τῷ ἱκανώσαντι[c] ὑμᾶς[d] εἰς τὴν μερίδα τοῦ κλήρου τῶν ἁγίων ἐν τῷ φωτί· **13** ὃς ἐρρύσατο ἡμᾶς ἐκ τῆς ἐξουσίας τοῦ σκότους καὶ μετέστησεν εἰς τὴν βασιλείαν τοῦ υἱοῦ τῆς ἀγάπης αὐτοῦ, **14** ἐν ᾧ ἔχομεν τὴν ἀπολύτρωσιν[e], τὴν ἄφεσιν τῶν ἁμαρτιῶν· **15** ὅς ἐστιν εἰκὼν τοῦ θεοῦ τοῦ ἀοράτου, πρωτότοκος πάσης κτίσεως, **16** ὅτι ἐν αὐτῷ ἐκτίσθη τὰ πάντα ἐν τοῖς οὐρανοῖς καὶ ἐπὶ τῆς γῆς, τὰ ὁρατὰ καὶ τὰ ἀόρατα, εἴτε θρόνοι εἴτε κυριότητες εἴτε ἀρχαὶ εἴτε ἐξουσίαι· τὰ πάντα δι᾽ αὐτοῦ καὶ εἰς αὐτὸν ἔκτισται· **17** καὶ αὐτός ἐστιν

NIV

1 Paul, an apostle of Christ Jesus by the will of God, and Timothy our brother,

[2]To the holy and faithful[a] brothers in Christ at Colosse:

Grace and peace to you from God our Father.[b]

Thanksgiving and Prayer

[3]We always thank God, the Father of our Lord Jesus Christ, when we pray for you, [4]because we have heard of your faith in Christ Jesus and of the love you have for all the saints— [5]the faith and love that spring from the hope that is stored up for you in heaven and that you have already heard about in the word of truth, the gospel [6]that has come to you. All over the world this gospel is bearing fruit and growing, just as it has been doing among you since the day you heard it and understood God's grace in all its truth. [7]You learned it from Epaphras, our dear fellow servant, who is a faithful minister of Christ on our[c] behalf, [8]and who also told us of your love in the Spirit.

[9]For this reason, since the day we heard about you, we have not stopped praying for you and asking God to fill you with the knowledge of his will through all spiritual wisdom and understanding. [10]And we pray this in order that you may live a life worthy of the Lord and may please him in every way: bearing fruit in every good work, growing in the knowledge of God, [11]being strengthened with all power according to his glorious might so that you may have great endurance and patience, and joyfully [12]giving thanks to the Father, who has qualified you[d] to share in the inheritance of the saints in the kingdom of light. [13]For he has rescued us from the dominion of darkness and brought us into the kingdom of the Son he loves, [14]in whom we have redemption,[e] the forgiveness of sins.

The Supremacy of Christ

[15]He is the image of the invisible God, the firstborn over all creation. [16]For by him all things were created: things in heaven and on earth, visible and invisible, whether thrones or powers or rulers or authorities; all things were created by him

---

[a] Gk *brothers*   [b] Gk *slave*   [c] Other ancient authorities read *our*   [d] Gk *his*   [e] Other ancient authorities read *called*   [f] Other ancient authorities read *us*   [g] Other ancient authorities add *through his blood*   [h] Or *by*

[a]2 NIV note adds καὶ κυρίου Ἰησοῦ Χριστοῦ
[b]7 NIV text and NRSV note c ἡμῶν; NIV note and NRSV text as UBS   [c]12 NRSV note e καλέσαντι
[d]12 NIV/NRSV notes ἡμᾶς   [e]14 NIV/NRSV notes add διὰ τοῦ αἵματος αὐτοῦ

[a]2 Or *believing*   [b]2 Some manuscripts *Father and the Lord Jesus Christ*   [c]7 Some manuscripts *your*   [d]12 Some manuscripts *us*   [e]14 A few late manuscripts *redemption through his blood*

before all things, and in[h] him all things hold together. [18]He is the head of the body, the church; he is the beginning, the firstborn from the dead, so that he might come to have first place in everything. [19]For in him all the fullness of God was pleased to dwell, [20]and through him God was pleased to reconcile to himself all things, whether on earth or in heaven, by making peace through the blood of his cross.

21 And you who were once estranged and hostile in mind, doing evil deeds, [22]he has now reconciled[i] in his fleshly body[j] through death, so as to present you holy and blameless and irreproachable before him— [23]provided that you continue securely established and steadfast in the faith, without shifting from the hope promised by the gospel that you heard, which has been proclaimed to every creature under heaven. I, Paul, became a servant of this gospel.

Paul's Interest in the Colossians

24 I am now rejoicing in my sufferings for your sake, and in my flesh I am completing what is lacking in Christ's afflictions for the sake of his body, that is, the church. [25]I became its servant according to God's commission that was given to me for you, to make the word of God fully known, [26]the mystery that has been hidden throughout the ages and generations but has now been revealed to his saints. [27]To them God chose to make known how great among the Gentiles are the riches of the glory of this mystery, which is Christ in you, the hope of glory. [28]It is he whom we proclaim, warning everyone and teaching everyone in all wisdom, so that we may present everyone mature in Christ. [29]For this I toil and struggle with all the energy that he powerfully inspires within me.

2 For I want you to know how much I am struggling for you, and for those in Laodicea, and for all who have not seen me face to face. [2]I want their hearts to be encouraged and united in love, so that they may have all the riches of assured understanding and have the knowledge of God's mystery, that is, Christ himself,[k] [3]in whom

πρὸ πάντων καὶ τὰ πάντα ἐν αὐτῷ συνέστηκεν, **18** καὶ αὐτός ἐστιν ἡ κεφαλὴ τοῦ σώματος τῆς ἐκκλησίας· ὅς ἐστιν ἀρχή, πρωτότοκος ἐκ τῶν νεκρῶν, ἵνα γένηται ἐν πᾶσιν αὐτὸς πρωτεύων, **19** ὅτι ἐν αὐτῷ εὐδόκησεν πᾶν τὸ πλήρωμα κατοικῆσαι **20** καὶ δι᾽ αὐτοῦ ἀποκαταλλάξαι τὰ πάντα εἰς αὐτόν, εἰρηνοποιήσας διὰ τοῦ αἵματος τοῦ σταυροῦ αὐτοῦ, [δι᾽ αὐτοῦ][f] εἴτε τὰ ἐπὶ τῆς γῆς εἴτε τὰ ἐν τοῖς οὐρανοῖς.

21 Καὶ ὑμᾶς ποτε ὄντας ἀπηλλοτριωμένους καὶ ἐχθροὺς τῇ διανοίᾳ ἐν τοῖς ἔργοις τοῖς πονηροῖς, **22** νυνὶ δὲ ἀποκατήλλαξεν[g] ἐν τῷ σώματι τῆς σαρκὸς αὐτοῦ διὰ τοῦ θανάτου παραστῆσαι ὑμᾶς ἁγίους καὶ ἀμώμους καὶ ἀνεγκλήτους κατενώπιον αὐτοῦ, **23** εἴ γε ἐπιμένετε τῇ πίστει τεθεμελιωμένοι καὶ ἑδραῖοι καὶ μὴ μετακινούμενοι ἀπὸ τῆς ἐλπίδος τοῦ εὐαγγελίου οὗ ἠκούσατε, τοῦ κηρυχθέντος ἐν πάσῃ κτίσει τῇ ὑπὸ τὸν οὐρανόν, οὗ ἐγενόμην ἐγὼ Παῦλος διάκονος.

24 Νῦν χαίρω ἐν τοῖς παθήμασιν ὑπὲρ ὑμῶν καὶ ἀνταναπληρῶ τὰ ὑστερήματα τῶν θλίψεων τοῦ Χριστοῦ ἐν τῇ σαρκί μου ὑπὲρ τοῦ σώματος αὐτοῦ, ὅ ἐστιν ἡ ἐκκλησία, **25** ἧς ἐγενόμην ἐγὼ διάκονος κατὰ τὴν οἰκονομίαν τοῦ θεοῦ τὴν δοθεῖσάν μοι εἰς ὑμᾶς πληρῶσαι τὸν λόγον τοῦ θεοῦ, **26** τὸ μυστήριον τὸ ἀποκεκρυμμένον ἀπὸ τῶν αἰώνων καὶ ἀπὸ τῶν γενεῶν – νῦν δὲ ἐφανερώθη τοῖς ἁγίοις αὐτοῦ, **27** οἷς ἠθέλησεν ὁ θεὸς γνωρίσαι τί τὸ πλοῦτος τῆς δόξης τοῦ μυστηρίου τούτου ἐν τοῖς ἔθνεσιν, ὅ ἐστιν Χριστὸς ἐν ὑμῖν, ἡ ἐλπὶς τῆς δόξης· **28** ὃν ἡμεῖς καταγγέλλομεν νουθετοῦντες πάντα ἄνθρωπον καὶ διδάσκοντες πάντα ἄνθρωπον ἐν πάσῃ σοφίᾳ, ἵνα παραστήσωμεν πάντα ἄνθρωπον τέλειον ἐν Χριστῷ· **29** εἰς ὃ καὶ κοπιῶ ἀγωνιζόμενος κατὰ τὴν ἐνέργειαν αὐτοῦ τὴν ἐνεργουμένην ἐν ἐμοὶ ἐν δυνάμει.

2 Θέλω γὰρ ὑμᾶς εἰδέναι ἡλίκον ἀγῶνα ἔχω ὑπὲρ ὑμῶν καὶ τῶν ἐν Λαοδικείᾳ καὶ ὅσοι οὐχ ἑόρακαν τὸ πρόσωπόν μου ἐν σαρκί, **2** ἵνα παρακληθῶσιν αἱ καρδίαι αὐτῶν συμβιβασθέντες ἐν ἀγάπῃ καὶ εἰς πᾶν πλοῦτος τῆς πληροφορίας τῆς συνέσεως, εἰς ἐπίγνωσιν τοῦ μυστηρίου τοῦ θεοῦ, Χριστοῦ[a], **3** ἐν ᾧ εἰσιν πάντες οἱ

and for him. [17]He is before all things, and in him all things hold together. [18]And he is the head of the body, the church; he is the beginning and the firstborn from among the dead, so that in everything he might have the supremacy. [19]For God was pleased to have all his fullness dwell in him, [20]and through him to reconcile to himself all things, whether things on earth or things in heaven, by making peace through his blood, shed on the cross.

[21]Once you were alienated from God and were enemies in your minds because of[f] your evil behavior. [22]But now he has reconciled you by Christ's physical body through death to present you holy in his sight, without blemish and free from accusation— [23]if you continue in your faith, established and firm, not moved from the hope held out in the gospel. This is the gospel that you heard and that has been proclaimed to every creature under heaven, and of which I, Paul, have become a servant.

Paul's Labor for the Church

[24]Now I rejoice in what was suffered for you, and I fill up in my flesh what is still lacking in regard to Christ's afflictions, for the sake of his body, which is the church. [25]I have become its servant by the commission God gave me to present to you the word of God in its fullness— [26]the mystery that has been kept hidden for ages and generations, but is now disclosed to the saints. [27]To them God has chosen to make known among the Gentiles the glorious riches of this mystery, which is Christ in you, the hope of glory.

[28]We proclaim him, admonishing and teaching everyone with all wisdom, so that we may present everyone perfect in Christ. [29]To this end I labor, struggling with all his energy, which so powerfully works in me.

2 I want you to know how much I am struggling for you and for those at Laodicea, and for all who have not met me personally. [2]My purpose is that they may be encouraged in heart and united in love, so that they may have the full riches of complete understanding, in order that they may know the mystery of God, namely, Christ, [3]in whom are hidden all the

[h] Or *by* [i] Other ancient authorities read *you have now been reconciled* [j] Gk *in the body of his flesh* [k] Other ancient authorities read *of the mystery of God, both of the Father and of Christ*

[f]20 NIV text omits δι᾽ αὐτοῦ [g]22 NRSV note i ἀποκατηλλάγητε [a]2 NRSV note k θεοῦ καὶ πατρὸς καὶ τοῦ Χριστοῦ

[f]21 Or *minds, as shown by*

are hidden all the treasures of wisdom and knowledge. [4]I am saying this so that no one may deceive you with plausible arguments. [5]For though I am absent in body, yet I am with you in spirit, and I rejoice to see your morale and the firmness of your faith in Christ.

Fullness of Life in Christ

6 As you therefore have received Christ Jesus the Lord, continue to live your lives[l] in him, [7]rooted and built up in him and established in the faith, just as you were taught, abounding in thanksgiving.

8 See to it that no one takes you captive through philosophy and empty deceit, according to human tradition, according to the elemental spirits of the universe,[m] and not according to Christ. [9]For in him the whole fullness of deity dwells bodily, [10]and you have come to fullness in him, who is the head of every ruler and authority. [11]In him also you were circumcised with a spiritual circumcision,[n] by putting off the body of the flesh in the circumcision of Christ; [12]when you were buried with him in baptism, you were also raised with him through faith in the power of God, who raised him from the dead. [13]And when you were dead in trespasses and the uncircumcision of your flesh, God[o] made you[p] alive together with him, when he forgave us all our trespasses, [14]erasing the record that stood against us with its legal demands. He set this aside, nailing it to the cross. [15]He disarmed[q] the rulers and authorities and made a public example of them, triumphing over them in it.

16 Therefore do not let anyone condemn you in matters of food and drink or of observing festivals, new moons, or sabbaths. [17]These are only a shadow of what is to come, but the substance belongs to Christ. [18]Do not let anyone disqualify you, insisting on self-abasement and worship of angels, dwelling[r] on visions,[s] puffed up without cause by a human way of thinking,[t] [19]and not holding fast to the head, from whom the whole body, nourished and held together by its ligaments and sinews, grows with a growth that is from God.

θησαυροὶ τῆς σοφίας καὶ γνώσεως ἀπόκρυφοι. **4** Τοῦτο λέγω, ἵνα μηδεὶς ὑμᾶς παραλογίζηται ἐν πιθανολογίᾳ. **5** εἰ γὰρ καὶ τῇ σαρκὶ ἄπειμι, ἀλλὰ τῷ πνεύματι σὺν ὑμῖν εἰμι, χαίρων καὶ βλέπων ὑμῶν τὴν τάξιν καὶ τὸ στερέωμα τῆς εἰς Χριστὸν πίστεως ὑμῶν.

6 Ὡς οὖν παρελάβετε τὸν Χριστὸν Ἰησοῦν τὸν κύριον, ἐν αὐτῷ περιπατεῖτε, **7** ἐρριζωμένοι καὶ ἐποικοδομούμενοι ἐν αὐτῷ καὶ βεβαιούμενοι τῇ πίστει καθὼς ἐδιδάχθητε, περισσεύοντες ἐν εὐχαριστίᾳ. **8** βλέπετε μή τις ὑμᾶς ἔσται ὁ συλαγωγῶν διὰ τῆς φιλοσοφίας καὶ κενῆς ἀπάτης κατὰ τὴν παράδοσιν τῶν ἀνθρώπων, κατὰ τὰ στοιχεῖα τοῦ κόσμου καὶ οὐ κατὰ Χριστόν· **9** ὅτι ἐν αὐτῷ κατοικεῖ πᾶν τὸ πλήρωμα τῆς θεότητος σωματικῶς, **10** καὶ ἐστὲ ἐν αὐτῷ πεπληρωμένοι, ὅς ἐστιν ἡ κεφαλὴ πάσης ἀρχῆς καὶ ἐξουσίας. **11** ἐν ᾧ καὶ περιετμήθητε περιτομῇ ἀχειροποιήτῳ ἐν τῇ ἀπεκδύσει τοῦ σώματος τῆς σαρκός, ἐν τῇ περιτομῇ τοῦ Χριστοῦ, **12** συνταφέντες αὐτῷ ἐν τῷ βαπτισμῷ, ἐν ᾧ καὶ συνηγέρθητε διὰ τῆς πίστεως τῆς ἐνεργείας τοῦ θεοῦ τοῦ ἐγείραντος αὐτὸν ἐκ νεκρῶν· **13** καὶ ὑμᾶς νεκροὺς ὄντας [ἐν] τοῖς παραπτώμασιν καὶ τῇ ἀκροβυστίᾳ τῆς σαρκὸς ὑμῶν, συνεζωοποίησεν ὑμᾶς[b] σὺν αὐτῷ, χαρισάμενος ἡμῖν πάντα τὰ παραπτώματα. **14** ἐξαλείψας τὸ καθ' ἡμῶν χειρόγραφον τοῖς δόγμασιν ὃ ἦν ὑπεναντίον ἡμῖν, καὶ αὐτὸ ἦρκεν ἐκ τοῦ μέσου προσηλώσας αὐτὸ τῷ σταυρῷ· **15** ἀπεκδυσάμενος τὰς ἀρχὰς καὶ τὰς ἐξουσίας ἐδειγμάτισεν ἐν παρρησίᾳ, θριαμβεύσας αὐτοὺς ἐν αὐτῷ.

16 Μὴ οὖν τις ὑμᾶς κρινέτω ἐν βρώσει καὶ ἐν πόσει ἢ ἐν μέρει ἑορτῆς ἢ νεομηνίας ἢ σαββάτων· **17** ἅ ἐστιν σκιὰ τῶν μελλόντων, τὸ δὲ σῶμα τοῦ Χριστοῦ. **18** μηδεὶς ὑμᾶς καταβραβευέτω θέλων ἐν ταπεινοφροσύνῃ καὶ θρησκείᾳ τῶν ἀγγέλων, ἃ[c] ἑόρακεν ἐμβατεύων, εἰκῇ φυσιούμενος ὑπὸ τοῦ νοὸς τῆς σαρκὸς αὐτοῦ, **19** καὶ οὐ κρατῶν τὴν κεφαλήν, ἐξ οὗ πᾶν τὸ σῶμα διὰ τῶν ἁφῶν καὶ συνδέσμων ἐπιχορηγούμενον καὶ συμβιβαζόμενον αὔξει τὴν αὔξησιν τοῦ θεοῦ.

treasures of wisdom and knowledge. [4]I tell you this so that no one may deceive you by fine-sounding arguments. [5]For though I am absent from you in body, I am present with you in spirit and delight to see how orderly you are and how firm your faith in Christ is.

Freedom From Human Regulations Through Life With Christ

[6]So then, just as you received Christ Jesus as Lord, continue to live in him, [7]rooted and built up in him, strengthened in the faith as you were taught, and overflowing with thankfulness.

[8]See to it that no one takes you captive through hollow and deceptive philosophy, which depends on human tradition and the basic principles of this world rather than on Christ.

[9]For in Christ all the fullness of the Deity lives in bodily form, [10]and you have been given fullness in Christ, who is the head over every power and authority. [11]In him you were also circumcised, in the putting off of the sinful nature,[a] not with a circumcision done by the hands of men but with the circumcision done by Christ, [12]having been buried with him in baptism and raised with him through your faith in the power of God, who raised him from the dead.

[13]When you were dead in your sins and in the uncircumcision of your sinful nature,[b] God made you[c] alive with Christ. He forgave us all our sins, [14]having canceled the written code, with its regulations, that was against us and that stood opposed to us; he took it away, nailing it to the cross. [15]And having disarmed the powers and authorities, he made a public spectacle of them, triumphing over them by the cross.[d]

[16]Therefore do not let anyone judge you by what you eat or drink, or with regard to a religious festival, a New Moon celebration or a Sabbath day. [17]These are a shadow of the things that were to come; the reality, however, is found in Christ. [18]Do not let anyone who delights in false humility and the worship of angels disqualify you for the prize. Such a person goes into great detail about what he has seen, and his unspiritual mind puffs him up with idle notions. [19]He has lost connection with the Head, from whom the whole body, supported and held together by its ligaments and sinews, grows as God causes it to grow.

---

[l]Gk *to walk*   [m]Or *the rudiments of the world*   [n]Gk *a circumcision made without hands*   [o]Gk *he*   [p]Other ancient authorities read *made us*; others, *made*   [q]Or *divested himself of*   [r]Other ancient authorities read *not dwelling*   [s]Meaning of Gk uncertain   [t]Gk *by the mind of his flesh*

[b]13 NIV note ἡμᾶς; NRSV note p ἡμᾶς or omit ὑμᾶς   [c]18 NRSV note r adds μή

[a]11 Or *the flesh*   [b]13 Or *your flesh*   [c]13 Some manuscripts *us*   [d]15 Or *them in him*

Warnings against False Teachers

20 If with Christ you died to the elemental spirits of the universe,[m] why do you live as if you still belonged to the world? Why do you submit to regulations, 21"Do not handle, Do not taste, Do not touch"? 22All these regulations refer to things that perish with use; they are simply human commands and teachings. 23These have indeed an appearance of wisdom in promoting self-imposed piety, humility, and severe treatment of the body, but they are of no value in checking self-indulgence.[u]

The New Life in Christ

3 So if you have been raised with Christ, seek the things that are above, where Christ is, seated at the right hand of God. 2Set your minds on things that are above, not on things that are on earth, 3for you have died, and your life is hidden with Christ in God. 4When Christ who is your[v] life is revealed, then you also will be revealed with him in glory.

5 Put to death, therefore, whatever in you is earthly: fornication, impurity, passion, evil desire, and greed (which is idolatry). 6On account of these the wrath of God is coming on those who are disobedient.[w] 7These are the ways you also once followed, when you were living that life.[x] 8But now you must get rid of all such things—anger, wrath, malice, slander, and abusive[y] language from your mouth. 9Do not lie to one another, seeing that you have stripped off the old self with its practices 10and have clothed yourselves with the new self, which is being renewed in knowledge according to the image of its creator. 11In that renewal[z] there is no longer Greek and Jew, circumcised and uncircumcised, barbarian, Scythian, slave and free; but Christ is all and in all!

12 As God's chosen ones, holy and beloved, clothe yourselves with compassion, kindness, humility, meekness, and patience. 13Bear with one another and, if anyone has a complaint against another, forgive each other; just as the Lord[a] has forgiven you, so you also must forgive. 14Above all, clothe yourselves with love, which binds everything together in perfect harmony. 15And let the peace of Christ rule in your hearts, to which indeed you

---

20 Εἰ ἀπεθάνετε σὺν Χριστῷ ἀπὸ τῶν στοιχείων τοῦ κόσμου, τί ὡς ζῶντες ἐν κόσμῳ δογματίζεσθε; 21 Μὴ ἅψῃ μηδὲ γεύσῃ μηδὲ θίγῃς, 22 ἅ ἐστιν πάντα εἰς φθορὰν τῇ ἀποχρήσει, κατὰ τὰ ἐντάλματα καὶ διδασκαλίας τῶν ἀνθρώπων, 23 ἅτινά ἐστιν λόγον μὲν ἔχοντα σοφίας ἐν ἐθελοθρησκίᾳ καὶ ταπεινοφροσύνῃ [καὶ] ἀφειδίᾳ σώματος, οὐκ ἐν τιμῇ τινι πρὸς πλησμονὴν τῆς σαρκός.

3 Εἰ οὖν συνηγέρθητε τῷ Χριστῷ, τὰ ἄνω ζητεῖτε, οὗ ὁ Χριστός ἐστιν ἐν δεξιᾷ τοῦ θεοῦ καθήμενος· 2 τὰ ἄνω φρονεῖτε, μὴ τὰ ἐπὶ τῆς γῆς. 3 ἀπεθάνετε γὰρ καὶ ἡ ζωὴ ὑμῶν κέκρυπται σὺν τῷ Χριστῷ ἐν τῷ θεῷ· 4 ὅταν ὁ Χριστὸς φανερωθῇ, ἡ ζωὴ ὑμῶν[a], τότε καὶ ὑμεῖς σὺν αὐτῷ φανερωθήσεσθε ἐν δόξῃ.

5 Νεκρώσατε οὖν τὰ μέλη[b] τὰ ἐπὶ τῆς γῆς, πορνείαν ἀκαθαρσίαν πάθος ἐπιθυμίαν κακήν, καὶ τὴν πλεονεξίαν, ἥτις ἐστὶν εἰδωλολατρία, 6 δι᾽ ἃ ἔρχεται ἡ ὀργὴ τοῦ θεοῦ [ἐπὶ τοὺς υἱοὺς τῆς ἀπειθείας][c]. 7 ἐν οἷς καὶ ὑμεῖς περιεπατήσατέ ποτε, ὅτε ἐζῆτε ἐν τούτοις· 8 νυνὶ δὲ ἀπόθεσθε καὶ ὑμεῖς τὰ πάντα, ὀργήν, θυμόν, κακίαν, βλασφημίαν, αἰσχρολογίαν ἐκ τοῦ στόματος ὑμῶν· 9 μὴ ψεύδεσθε εἰς ἀλλήλους, ἀπεκδυσάμενοι τὸν παλαιὸν ἄνθρωπον σὺν ταῖς πράξεσιν αὐτοῦ 10 καὶ ἐνδυσάμενοι τὸν νέον τὸν ἀνακαινούμενον εἰς ἐπίγνωσιν κατ᾽ εἰκόνα τοῦ κτίσαντος αὐτόν, 11 ὅπου οὐκ ἔνι Ἕλλην καὶ Ἰουδαῖος, περιτομὴ καὶ ἀκροβυστία, βάρβαρος, Σκύθης, δοῦλος, ἐλεύθερος, ἀλλὰ [τὰ] πάντα καὶ ἐν πᾶσιν Χριστός.

12 Ἐνδύσασθε οὖν, ὡς ἐκλεκτοὶ τοῦ θεοῦ ἅγιοι καὶ ἠγαπημένοι, σπλάγχνα οἰκτιρμοῦ χρηστότητα ταπεινοφροσύνην πραΰτητα μακροθυμίαν, 13 ἀνεχόμενοι ἀλλήλων καὶ χαριζόμενοι ἑαυτοῖς ἐάν τις πρός τινα ἔχῃ μομφήν· καθὼς καὶ ὁ κύριος[d] ἐχαρίσατο ὑμῖν, οὕτως καὶ ὑμεῖς· 14 ἐπὶ πᾶσιν δὲ τούτοις τὴν ἀγάπην, ὅ ἐστιν σύνδεσμος τῆς τελειότητος. 15 καὶ ἡ εἰρήνη τοῦ Χριστοῦ βραβευέτω ἐν ταῖς καρδίαις ὑμῶν, εἰς ἣν καὶ ἐκλήθητε ἐν ἑνὶ

20Since you died with Christ to the basic principles of this world, why, as though you still belonged to it, do you submit to its rules: 21"Do not handle! Do not taste! Do not touch!"? 22These are all destined to perish with use, because they are based on human commands and teachings. 23Such regulations indeed have an appearance of wisdom, with their self-imposed worship, their false humility and their harsh treatment of the body, but they lack any value in restraining sensual indulgence.

Rules for Holy Living

3 Since, then, you have been raised with Christ, set your hearts on things above, where Christ is seated at the right hand of God. 2Set your minds on things above, not on earthly things. 3For you died, and your life is now hidden with Christ in God. 4When Christ, who is your[a] life, appears, then you also will appear with him in glory.

5Put to death, therefore, whatever belongs to your earthly nature: sexual immorality, impurity, lust, evil desires and greed, which is idolatry. 6Because of these, the wrath of God is coming.[b] 7You used to walk in these ways, in the life you once lived. 8But now you must rid yourselves of all such things as these: anger, rage, malice, slander, and filthy language from your lips. 9Do not lie to each other, since you have taken off your old self with its practices 10and have put on the new self, which is being renewed in knowledge in the image of its Creator. 11Here there is no Greek or Jew, circumcised or uncircumcised, barbarian, Scythian, slave or free, but Christ is all, and is in all.

12Therefore, as God's chosen people, holy and dearly loved, clothe yourselves with compassion, kindness, humility, gentleness and patience. 13Bear with each other and forgive whatever grievances you may have against one another. Forgive as the Lord forgave you. 14And over all these virtues put on love, which binds them all together in perfect unity.

15Let the peace of Christ rule in your hearts, since as members of one body you

---

m Or the rudiments of the world   u Or are of no value, serving only to indulge the flesh   v Other authorities read our
w Other ancient authorities lack on those who are disobedient (Gk the children of disobedience)   x Or living among such people   y Or filthy   z Gk its creator, 11where
a Other ancient authorities read just as Christ

a4 NIV/NRSV notes ἡμῶν   b5 NIV text adds ὑμῶν †
c6 NIV text and NRSV note w omit ἐπὶ τοὺς υἱοὺς τῆς ἀπειθείας; NIV note and NRSV text as UBS
d13 NRSV note a Χριστός

a4 Some manuscripts our   b6 Some early manuscripts coming on those who are disobedient

were called in the one body. And be thankful. [16]Let the word of Christ[b] dwell in you richly; teach and admonish one another in all wisdom; and with gratitude in your hearts sing psalms, hymns, and spiritual songs to God.[c] [17]And whatever you do, in word or deed, do everything in the name of the Lord Jesus, giving thanks to God the Father through him.

Rules for Christian Households

18 Wives, be subject to your husbands, as is fitting in the Lord. [19]Husbands, love your wives and never treat them harshly.

20 Children, obey your parents in everything, for this is your acceptable duty in the Lord. [21]Fathers, do not provoke your children, or they may lose heart. [22]Slaves, obey your earthly masters[d] in everything, not only while being watched and in order to please them, but wholeheartedly, fearing the Lord.[d] [23]Whatever your task, put yourselves into it, as done for the Lord and not for your masters,[e] [24]since you know that from the Lord you will receive the inheritance as your reward; you serve[f] the Lord Christ. [25]For the wrongdoer will be paid back for whatever wrong has been done, and there is no partiality. [4] [1]Masters, treat your slaves justly and fairly, for you know that you also have a Master in heaven.

Further Instructions

2 Devote yourselves to prayer, keeping alert in it with thanksgiving. [3]At the same time pray for us as well that God will open to us a door for the word, that we may declare the mystery of Christ, for which I am in prison, [4]so that I may reveal it clearly, as I should.

5 Conduct yourselves wisely toward outsiders, making the most of the time.[g] [6]Let your speech always be gracious, seasoned with salt, so that you may know how you ought to answer everyone.

Final Greetings and Benediction

7 Tychicus will tell you all the news about me; he is a beloved brother, a faithful minister, and a fellow servant[h] in the Lord. [8]I have sent him to you for this very purpose, so that you may know how we are[i] and that he may encourage your hearts;

σώματι· καὶ εὐχάριστοι γίνεσθε. **16** ὁ λόγος τοῦ Χριστοῦ[e] ἐνοικείτω ἐν ὑμῖν πλουσίως, ἐν πάσῃ σοφίᾳ διδάσκοντες καὶ νουθετοῦντες ἑαυτούς, ψαλμοῖς ὕμνοις ᾠδαῖς πνευματικαῖς ἐν [τῇ] χάριτι ᾄδοντες ἐν ταῖς καρδίαις ὑμῶν τῷ θεῷ[f]· **17** καὶ πᾶν ὅ τι ἐὰν ποιῆτε ἐν λόγῳ ἢ ἐν ἔργῳ, πάντα ἐν ὀνόματι κυρίου Ἰησοῦ, εὐχαριστοῦντες τῷ θεῷ πατρὶ δι’ αὐτοῦ.

18 Αἱ γυναῖκες, ὑποτάσσεσθε τοῖς ἀνδράσιν ὡς ἀνῆκεν ἐν κυρίῳ. **19** Οἱ ἄνδρες, ἀγαπᾶτε τὰς γυναῖκας καὶ μὴ πικραίνεσθε πρὸς αὐτάς.

20 Τὰ τέκνα, ὑπακούετε τοῖς γονεῦσιν κατὰ πάντα, τοῦτο γὰρ εὐάρεστόν ἐστιν ἐν κυρίῳ. **21** Οἱ πατέρες, μὴ ἐρεθίζετε τὰ τέκνα ὑμῶν, ἵνα μὴ ἀθυμῶσιν.

22 Οἱ δοῦλοι, ὑπακούετε κατὰ πάντα τοῖς κατὰ σάρκα κυρίοις, μὴ ἐν ὀφθαλμοδουλίᾳ ὡς ἀνθρωπάρεσκοι, ἀλλ’ ἐν ἁπλότητι καρδίας φοβούμενοι τὸν κύριον. **23** ὃ ἐὰν ποιῆτε, ἐκ ψυχῆς ἐργάζεσθε ὡς τῷ κυρίῳ καὶ οὐκ ἀνθρώποις, **24** εἰδότες ὅτι ἀπὸ κυρίου ἀπολήμψεσθε τὴν ἀνταπόδοσιν τῆς κληρονομίας. τῷ κυρίῳ Χριστῷ δουλεύετε· **25** ὁ γὰρ ἀδικῶν κομίσεται ὃ ἠδίκησεν, καὶ οὐκ ἔστιν προσωπολημψία. [4] **1** Οἱ κύριοι, τὸ δίκαιον καὶ τὴν ἰσότητα τοῖς δούλοις παρέχεσθε, εἰδότες ὅτι καὶ ὑμεῖς ἔχετε κύριον ἐν οὐρανῷ.

2 Τῇ προσευχῇ προσκαρτερεῖτε, γρηγοροῦντες ἐν αὐτῇ ἐν εὐχαριστίᾳ, **3** προσευχόμενοι ἅμα καὶ περὶ ἡμῶν, ἵνα ὁ θεὸς ἀνοίξῃ ἡμῖν θύραν τοῦ λόγου λαλῆσαι τὸ μυστήριον τοῦ Χριστοῦ, δι’ ὃ καὶ δέδεμαι, **4** ἵνα φανερώσω αὐτὸ ὡς δεῖ με λαλῆσαι. **5** Ἐν σοφίᾳ περιπατεῖτε πρὸς τοὺς ἔξω τὸν καιρὸν ἐξαγοραζόμενοι. **6** ὁ λόγος ὑμῶν πάντοτε ἐν χάριτι, ἅλατι ἠρτυμένος, εἰδέναι πῶς δεῖ ὑμᾶς ἑνὶ ἑκάστῳ ἀποκρίνεσθαι.

7 Τὰ κατ’ ἐμὲ πάντα γνωρίσει ὑμῖν Τυχικὸς ὁ ἀγαπητὸς ἀδελφὸς καὶ πιστὸς διάκονος καὶ σύνδουλος ἐν κυρίῳ, **8** ὃν ἔπεμψα πρὸς ὑμᾶς εἰς αὐτὸ τοῦτο, ἵνα γνῶτε τὰ περὶ ἡμῶν[a] καὶ παρακαλέσῃ τὰς καρδίας ὑμῶν,

were called to peace. And be thankful. [16]Let the word of Christ dwell in you richly as you teach and admonish one another with all wisdom, and as you sing psalms, hymns and spiritual songs with gratitude in your hearts to God. [17]And whatever you do, whether in word or deed, do it all in the name of the Lord Jesus, giving thanks to God the Father through him.

Rules for Christian Households

[18]Wives, submit to your husbands, as is fitting in the Lord.

[19]Husbands, love your wives and do not be harsh with them.

[20]Children, obey your parents in everything, for this pleases the Lord.

[21]Fathers, do not embitter your children, or they will become discouraged.

[22]Slaves, obey your earthly masters in everything; and do it, not only when their eye is on you and to win their favor, but with sincerity of heart and reverence for the Lord. [23]Whatever you do, work at it with all your heart, as working for the Lord, not for men, [24]since you know that you will receive an inheritance from the Lord as a reward. It is the Lord Christ you are serving. [25]Anyone who does wrong will be repaid for his wrong, and there is no favoritism. [4] Masters, provide your slaves with what is right and fair, because you know that you also have a Master in heaven.

Further Instructions

[2]Devote yourselves to prayer, being watchful and thankful. [3]And pray for us, too, that God may open a door for our message, so that we may proclaim the mystery of Christ, for which I am in chains. [4]Pray that I may proclaim it clearly, as I should. [5]Be wise in the way you act toward outsiders; make the most of every opportunity. [6]Let your conversation be always full of grace, seasoned with salt, so that you may know how to answer everyone.

Final Greetings

[7]Tychicus will tell you all the news about me. He is a dear brother, a faithful minister and fellow servant in the Lord. [8]I am sending him to you for the express purpose that you may know about our[a] circumstances and that he may encourage

---

b Other ancient authorities read *of God,* or *of the Lord*
c Other ancient authorities read *to the Lord*   d In Greek the same word is used for *master* and *Lord*   e Gk *not for men*   f Or *you are slaves of,* or *be slaves of*   g Or *opportunity*   h Gk *slave*   i Other authorities read *that I may know how you are*

e16 NRSV note b *θεοῦ* or *κυρίου*   f16 NRSV note c *κυρίῳ*
a8 NIV note *γνῷ τὰ περὶ ὑμῶν*; NRSV note i *γνῷ τὰ περὶ ὑμῶν*

a8 Some manuscripts *that he may know about your*

9he is coming with Onesimus, the faithful and beloved brother, who is one of you. They will tell you about everything here.

10 Aristarchus my fellow prisoner greets you, as does Mark the cousin of Barnabas, concerning whom you have received instructions—if he comes to you, welcome him. 11And Jesus who is called Justus greets you. These are the only ones of the circumcision among my co-workers for the kingdom of God, and they have been a comfort to me. 12Epaphras, who is one of you, a servanth of Christ Jesus, greets you. He is always wrestling in his prayers on your behalf, so that you may stand mature and fully assured in everything that God wills. 13For I testify for him that he has worked hard for you and for those in Laodicea and in Hierapolis. 14Luke, the beloved physician, and Demas greet you. 15Give my greetings to the brothers and sistersj in Laodicea, and to Nympha and the church in her house. 16And when this letter has been read among you, have it read also in the church of the Laodiceans; and see that you read also the letter from Laodicea. 17And say to Archippus, "See that you complete the task that you have received in the Lord."

18 I, Paul, write this greeting with my own hand. Remember my chains. Grace be with you.k

9 σὺν Ὀνησίμῳ τῷ πιστῷ καὶ ἀγαπητῷ ἀδελφῷ, ὅς ἐστιν ἐξ ὑμῶν· πάντα ὑμῖν γνωρίσουσιν τὰ ὧδε.

10 Ἀσπάζεται ὑμᾶς Ἀρίσταρχος ὁ συναιχμάλωτός μου καὶ Μᾶρκος ὁ ἀνεψιὸς Βαρναβᾶ (περὶ οὗ ἐλάβετε ἐντολάς, ἐὰν ἔλθῃ πρὸς ὑμᾶς, δέξασθε αὐτόν) 11 καὶ Ἰησοῦς ὁ λεγόμενος Ἰοῦστος, οἱ ὄντες ἐκ περιτομῆς, οὗτοι μόνοι συνεργοὶ εἰς τὴν βασιλείαν τοῦ θεοῦ, οἵτινες ἐγενήθησάν μοι παρηγορία. 12 ἀσπάζεται ὑμᾶς Ἐπαφρᾶς ὁ ἐξ ὑμῶν, δοῦλος Χριστοῦ [Ἰησοῦ], πάντοτε ἀγωνιζόμενος ὑπὲρ ὑμῶν ἐν ταῖς προσευχαῖς, ἵνα σταθῆτε τέλειοι καὶ πεπληροφορημένοι ἐν παντὶ θελήματι τοῦ θεοῦ. 13 μαρτυρῶ γὰρ αὐτῷ ὅτι ἔχει πολὺν πόνον ὑπὲρ ὑμῶν καὶ τῶν ἐν Λαοδικείᾳ καὶ τῶν ἐν Ἱεραπόλει. 14 ἀσπάζεται ὑμᾶς Λουκᾶς ὁ ἰατρὸς ὁ ἀγαπητὸς καὶ Δημᾶς. 15 Ἀσπάσασθε τοὺς ἐν Λαοδικείᾳ ἀδελφοὺς καὶ Νύμφαν καὶ τὴν κατ' οἶκον αὐτῆς ἐκκλησίαν. 16 καὶ ὅταν ἀναγνωσθῇ παρ' ὑμῖν ἡ ἐπιστολή, ποιήσατε ἵνα καὶ ἐν τῇ Λαοδικέων ἐκκλησίᾳ ἀναγνωσθῇ, καὶ τὴν ἐκ Λαοδικείας ἵνα καὶ ὑμεῖς ἀναγνῶτε. 17 καὶ εἴπατε Ἀρχίππῳ, Βλέπε τὴν διακονίαν ἣν παρέλαβες ἐν κυρίῳ, ἵνα αὐτὴν πληροῖς.

18 Ὁ ἀσπασμὸς τῇ ἐμῇ χειρὶ Παύλου. μνημονεύετέ μου τῶν δεσμῶν. ἡ χάρις μεθ' ὑμῶν.b

your hearts. 9He is coming with Onesimus, our faithful and dear brother, who is one of you. They will tell you everything that is happening here.

10My fellow prisoner Aristarchus sends you his greetings, as does Mark, the cousin of Barnabas. (You have received instructions about him; if he comes to you, welcome him.) 11Jesus, who is called Justus, also sends greetings. These are the only Jews among my fellow workers for the kingdom of God, and they have proved a comfort to me. 12Epaphras, who is one of you and a servant of Christ Jesus, sends greetings. He is always wrestling in prayer for you, that you may stand firm in all the will of God, mature and fully assured. 13I vouch for him that he is working hard for you and for those at Laodicea and Hierapolis. 14Our dear friend Luke, the doctor, and Demas send greetings. 15Give my greetings to the brothers at Laodicea, and to Nympha and the church in her house.

16After this letter has been read to you, see that it is also read in the church of the Laodiceans and that you in turn read the letter from Laodicea.

17Tell Archippus: "See to it that you complete the work you have received in the Lord."

18I, Paul, write this greeting in my own hand. Remember my chains. Grace be with you.

---

h Gk slave   i Gk brothers   k Other ancient authorities add Amen

b18 NRSV note k adds ἀμήν.

NRSV

Salutation

1 Paul, Silvanus, and Timothy,

To the church of the Thessalonians in God the Father and the Lord Jesus Christ: Grace to you and peace.

The Thessalonians' Faith and Example

2 We always give thanks to God for all of you and mention you in our prayers, constantly [3]remembering before our God and Father your work of faith and labor of love and steadfastness of hope in our Lord Jesus Christ. [4]For we know, brothers and sisters[a] beloved by God, that he has chosen you, [5]because our message of the gospel came to you not in word only, but also in power and in the Holy Spirit and with full conviction; just as you know what kind of persons we proved to be among you for your sake. [6]And you became imitators of us and of the Lord, for in spite of persecution you received the word with joy inspired by the Holy Spirit, [7]so that you became an example to all the believers in Macedonia and in Achaia. [8]For the word of the Lord has sounded forth from you not only in Macedonia and Achaia, but in every place your faith in God has become known, so that we have no need to speak about it. [9]For the people of those regions[b] report about us what kind of welcome we had among you, and how you turned to God from idols, to serve a living and true God, [10]and to wait for his Son from heaven, whom he raised from the dead—Jesus, who rescues us from the wrath that is coming.

Paul's Ministry in Thessalonica

2 You yourselves know, brothers and sisters,[c] that our coming to you was not in vain, [2]but though we had already suffered and been shamefully mistreated at Philippi, as you know, we had courage in our God to declare to you the gospel of God in spite of great opposition. [3]For our appeal does not spring from deceit or impure motives or trickery, [4]but just as we have been approved by God to be entrusted with the message of the gospel, even so we speak, not to please mortals, but to please God who tests our hearts. [5]As you know and as God is our witness, we never came with words of flattery or with a pretext for greed; [6]nor did we seek praise from mortals, whether from you or from others,

ΠΡΟΣ ΘΕΣΣΑΛΟΝΙΚΕΙΣ Α

1 Παῦλος καὶ Σιλουανὸς καὶ Τιμόθεος τῇ ἐκκλησίᾳ Θεσσαλονικέων ἐν θεῷ πατρὶ καὶ κυρίῳ Ἰησοῦ Χριστῷ, χάρις ὑμῖν καὶ εἰρήνη[a].

2 Εὐχαριστοῦμεν τῷ θεῷ πάντοτε περὶ πάντων ὑμῶν μνείαν ποιούμενοι ἐπὶ τῶν προσευχῶν ἡμῶν,[b] ἀδιαλείπτως 3 μνημονεύοντες ὑμῶν τοῦ ἔργου τῆς πίστεως καὶ τοῦ κόπου τῆς ἀγάπης καὶ τῆς ὑπομονῆς τῆς ἐλπίδος τοῦ κυρίου ἡμῶν Ἰησοῦ Χριστοῦ ἔμπροσθεν τοῦ θεοῦ καὶ πατρὸς ἡμῶν, 4 εἰδότες, ἀδελφοὶ ἠγαπημένοι ὑπὸ [τοῦ] θεοῦ, τὴν ἐκλογὴν ὑμῶν, 5 ὅτι τὸ εὐαγγέλιον ἡμῶν οὐκ ἐγενήθη εἰς ὑμᾶς ἐν λόγῳ μόνον ἀλλὰ καὶ ἐν δυνάμει καὶ ἐν πνεύματι ἁγίῳ καὶ [ἐν] πληροφορίᾳ πολλῇ, καθὼς οἴδατε οἷοι ἐγενήθημεν [ἐν] ὑμῖν δι᾽ ὑμᾶς. 6 καὶ ὑμεῖς μιμηταὶ ἡμῶν ἐγενήθητε καὶ τοῦ κυρίου, δεξάμενοι τὸν λόγον ἐν θλίψει πολλῇ μετὰ χαρᾶς πνεύματος ἁγίου, 7 ὥστε γενέσθαι ὑμᾶς τύπον πᾶσιν τοῖς πιστεύουσιν ἐν τῇ Μακεδονίᾳ καὶ ἐν τῇ Ἀχαΐᾳ. 8 ἀφ᾽ ὑμῶν γὰρ ἐξήχηται ὁ λόγος τοῦ κυρίου οὐ μόνον ἐν τῇ Μακεδονίᾳ καὶ [ἐν τῇ] Ἀχαΐᾳ, ἀλλ᾽ ἐν παντὶ τόπῳ ἡ πίστις ὑμῶν ἡ πρὸς τὸν θεὸν ἐξελήλυθεν, ὥστε μὴ χρείαν ἔχειν ἡμᾶς λαλεῖν τι. 9 αὐτοὶ γὰρ περὶ ἡμῶν ἀπαγγέλλουσιν ὁποίαν εἴσοδον ἔσχομεν πρὸς ὑμᾶς, καὶ πῶς ἐπεστρέψατε πρὸς τὸν θεὸν ἀπὸ τῶν εἰδώλων δουλεύειν θεῷ ζῶντι καὶ ἀληθινῷ 10 καὶ ἀναμένειν τὸν υἱὸν αὐτοῦ ἐκ τῶν οὐρανῶν, ὃν ἤγειρεν ἐκ [τῶν] νεκρῶν, Ἰησοῦν τὸν ῥυόμενον ἡμᾶς ἐκ τῆς ὀργῆς τῆς ἐρχομένης.

2 Αὐτοὶ γὰρ οἴδατε, ἀδελφοί, τὴν εἴσοδον ἡμῶν τὴν πρὸς ὑμᾶς ὅτι οὐ κενὴ γέγονεν, 2 ἀλλὰ προπαθόντες καὶ ὑβρισθέντες, καθὼς οἴδατε, ἐν Φιλίπποις ἐπαρρησιασάμεθα ἐν τῷ θεῷ ἡμῶν λαλῆσαι πρὸς ὑμᾶς τὸ εὐαγγέλιον τοῦ θεοῦ ἐν πολλῷ ἀγῶνι. 3 ἡ γὰρ παράκλησις ἡμῶν οὐκ ἐκ πλάνης οὐδὲ ἐξ ἀκαθαρσίας οὐδὲ ἐν δόλῳ, 4 ἀλλὰ καθὼς δεδοκιμάσμεθα ὑπὸ τοῦ θεοῦ πιστευθῆναι τὸ εὐαγγέλιον, οὕτως λαλοῦμεν, οὐχ ὡς ἀνθρώποις ἀρέσκοντες ἀλλὰ θεῷ τῷ δοκιμάζοντι τὰς καρδίας ἡμῶν. 5 οὔτε γάρ ποτε ἐν λόγῳ κολακείας ἐγενήθημεν, καθὼς οἴδατε, οὔτε ἐν προφάσει πλεονεξίας, θεὸς μάρτυς, 6 οὔτε ζητοῦντες ἐξ ἀνθρώπων δόξαν οὔτε ἀφ᾽ ὑμῶν οὔτε ἀπ᾽ ἄλλων,

NIV

1 Paul, Silas[a] and Timothy,

To the church of the Thessalonians in God the Father and the Lord Jesus Christ:

Grace and peace to you.[b]

Thanksgiving for the Thessalonians' Faith

[2]We always thank God for all of you, mentioning you in our prayers. [3]We continually remember before our God and Father your work produced by faith, your labor prompted by love, and your endurance inspired by hope in our Lord Jesus Christ.

[4]For we know, brothers loved by God, that he has chosen you, [5]because our gospel came to you not simply with words, but also with power, with the Holy Spirit and with deep conviction. You know how we lived among you for your sake. [6]You became imitators of us and of the Lord; in spite of severe suffering, you welcomed the message with the joy given by the Holy Spirit. [7]And so you became a model to all the believers in Macedonia and Achaia. [8]The Lord's message rang out from you not only in Macedonia and Achaia—your faith in God has become known everywhere. Therefore we do not need to say anything about it, [9]for they themselves report what kind of reception you gave us. They tell how you turned to God from idols to serve the living and true God, [10]and to wait for his Son from heaven, whom he raised from the dead—Jesus, who rescues us from the coming wrath.

Paul's Ministry in Thessalonica

2 You know, brothers, that our visit to you was not a failure. [2]We had previously suffered and been insulted in Philippi, as you know, but with the help of our God we dared to tell you his gospel in spite of strong opposition. [3]For the appeal we make does not spring from error or impure motives, nor are we trying to trick you. [4]On the contrary, we speak as men approved by God to be entrusted with the gospel. We are not trying to please men but God, who tests our hearts. [5]You know we never used flattery, nor did we put on a mask to cover up greed—God is our witness. [6]We were not looking for praise from men, not from you or anyone else.

---

a Gk brothers   b Gk For they

a1 NIV note adds ἀπὸ θεοῦ πατρὸς καὶ κυρίου Ἰησοῦ Χριστοῦ   b2 NIV begins verse 3 after ἡμῶν.

a1 Greek *Silvanus*, a variant of *Silas*   b1 Some early manuscripts *you from God our Father and the Lord Jesus Christ*

7though we might have made demands as apostles of Christ. But we were gentle[d] among you, like a nurse tenderly caring for her own children. 8So deeply do we care for you that we are determined to share with you not only the gospel of God but also our own selves, because you have become very dear to us.

9 You remember our labor and toil, brothers and sisters;[c] we worked night and day, so that we might not burden any of you while we proclaimed to you the gospel of God. 10You are witnesses, and God also, how pure, upright, and blameless our conduct was toward you believers. 11As you know, we dealt with each one of you like a father with his children, 12urging and encouraging you and pleading that you lead a life worthy of God, who calls you into his own kingdom and glory.

13 We also constantly give thanks to God for this, that when you received the word of God that you heard from us, you accepted it not as a human word but as what it really is, God's word, which is also at work in you believers. 14For you, brothers and sisters,[c] became imitators of the churches of God in Christ Jesus that are in Judea, for you suffered the same things from your own compatriots as they did from the Jews, 15who killed both the Lord Jesus and the prophets,[e] and drove us out; they displease God and oppose everyone 16by hindering us from speaking to the Gentiles so that they may be saved. Thus they have constantly been filling up the measure of their sins; but God's wrath has overtaken them at last.[f]

Paul's Desire to Visit the Thessalonians Again

17 As for us, brothers and sisters,[c] when, for a short time, we were made orphans by being separated from you—in person, not in heart—we longed with great eagerness to see you face to face. 18For we wanted to come to you—certainly I, Paul, wanted to again and again—but Satan blocked our way. 19For what is our hope or joy or crown of boasting before our Lord Jesus at his coming? Is it not you? 20Yes, you are our glory and joy!

3 Therefore when we could bear it no longer, we decided to be left alone in Athens; 2and we sent Timothy, our brother

7 δυνάμενοι ἐν βάρει εἶναι ὡς Χριστοῦ ἀπόστολοι.[a] ἀλλὰ ἐγενήθημεν νήπιοι[b] ἐν μέσῳ ὑμῶν, ὡς ἐὰν τροφὸς θάλπῃ τὰ ἑαυτῆς τέκνα, 8 οὕτως ὁμειρόμενοι ὑμῶν εὐδοκοῦμεν μεταδοῦναι ὑμῖν οὐ μόνον τὸ εὐαγγέλιον τοῦ θεοῦ ἀλλὰ καὶ τὰς ἑαυτῶν ψυχάς, διότι ἀγαπητοὶ ἡμῖν ἐγενήθητε. 9 μνημονεύετε γάρ, ἀδελφοί, τὸν κόπον ἡμῶν καὶ τὸν μόχθον· νυκτὸς καὶ ἡμέρας ἐργαζόμενοι πρὸς τὸ μὴ ἐπιβαρῆσαί τινα ὑμῶν ἐκηρύξαμεν εἰς ὑμᾶς τὸ εὐαγγέλιον τοῦ θεοῦ. 10 ὑμεῖς μάρτυρες καὶ ὁ θεός, ὡς ὁσίως καὶ δικαίως καὶ ἀμέμπτως ὑμῖν τοῖς πιστεύουσιν ἐγενήθημεν, 11 καθάπερ οἴδατε, ὡς ἕνα ἕκαστον ὑμῶν ὡς πατὴρ τέκνα ἑαυτοῦ 12 παρακαλοῦντες ὑμᾶς καὶ παραμυθούμενοι καὶ μαρτυρόμενοι εἰς τὸ περιπατεῖν ὑμᾶς ἀξίως τοῦ θεοῦ τοῦ καλοῦντος ὑμᾶς εἰς τὴν ἑαυτοῦ βασιλείαν καὶ δόξαν.

13 Καὶ διὰ τοῦτο καὶ ἡμεῖς εὐχαριστοῦμεν τῷ θεῷ ἀδιαλείπτως, ὅτι παραλαβόντες λόγον ἀκοῆς παρ' ἡμῶν τοῦ θεοῦ ἐδέξασθε οὐ λόγον ἀνθρώπων ἀλλὰ καθὼς ἐστιν ἀληθῶς λόγον θεοῦ, ὃς καὶ ἐνεργεῖται ἐν ὑμῖν τοῖς πιστεύουσιν. 14 ὑμεῖς γὰρ μιμηταὶ ἐγενήθητε, ἀδελφοί, τῶν ἐκκλησιῶν τοῦ θεοῦ τῶν οὐσῶν ἐν τῇ Ἰουδαίᾳ ἐν Χριστῷ Ἰησοῦ, ὅτι τὰ αὐτὰ ἐπάθετε καὶ ὑμεῖς ὑπὸ τῶν ἰδίων συμφυλετῶν καθὼς καὶ αὐτοὶ ὑπὸ τῶν Ἰουδαίων, 15 τῶν καὶ τὸν κύριον ἀποκτεινάντων Ἰησοῦν καὶ τοὺς[c] προφήτας καὶ ἡμᾶς ἐκδιωξάντων καὶ θεῷ μὴ ἀρεσκόντων καὶ πᾶσιν ἀνθρώποις ἐναντίων, 16 κωλυόντων ἡμᾶς τοῖς ἔθνεσιν λαλῆσαι ἵνα σωθῶσιν, εἰς τὸ ἀναπληρῶσαι αὐτῶν τὰς ἁμαρτίας πάντοτε. ἔφθασεν δὲ ἐπ' αὐτοὺς ἡ ὀργὴ[d] εἰς τέλος.

17 Ἡμεῖς δέ, ἀδελφοί, ἀπορφανισθέντες ἀφ' ὑμῶν πρὸς καιρὸν ὥρας, προσώπῳ οὐ καρδίᾳ, περισσοτέρως ἐσπουδάσαμεν τὸ πρόσωπον ὑμῶν ἰδεῖν ἐν πολλῇ ἐπιθυμίᾳ. 18 διότι ἠθελήσαμεν ἐλθεῖν πρὸς ὑμᾶς, ἐγὼ μὲν Παῦλος καὶ ἅπαξ καὶ δίς, καὶ ἐνέκοψεν ἡμᾶς ὁ Σατανᾶς. 19 τίς γὰρ ἡμῶν ἐλπὶς ἢ χαρὰ ἢ στέφανος καυχήσεως – ἢ οὐχὶ καὶ ὑμεῖς – ἔμπροσθεν τοῦ κυρίου ἡμῶν Ἰησοῦ ἐν τῇ αὐτοῦ παρουσίᾳ; 20 ὑμεῖς γάρ ἐστε ἡ δόξα ἡμῶν καὶ ἡ χαρά.

3 Διὸ μηκέτι στέγοντες εὐδοκήσαμεν καταλειφθῆναι ἐν Ἀθήναις

As apostles of Christ we could have been a burden to you, 7but we were gentle among you, like a mother caring for her little children. 8We loved you so much that we were delighted to share with you not only the gospel of God but our lives as well, because you had become so dear to us. 9Surely you remember, brothers, our toil and hardship; we worked night and day in order not to be a burden to anyone while we preached the gospel of God to you.

10You are witnesses, and so is God, of how holy, righteous and blameless we were among you who believed. 11For you know that we dealt with each of you as a father deals with his own children, 12encouraging, comforting and urging you to live lives worthy of God, who calls you into his kingdom and glory.

13And we also thank God continually because, when you received the word of God, which you heard from us, you accepted it not as the word of men, but as it actually is, the word of God, which is at work in you who believe. 14For you, brothers, became imitators of God's churches in Judea, which are in Christ Jesus: You suffered from your own countrymen the same things those churches suffered from the Jews, 15who killed the Lord Jesus and the prophets and also drove us out. They displease God and are hostile to all men 16in their effort to keep us from speaking to the Gentiles so that they may be saved. In this way they always heap up their sins to the limit. The wrath of God has come upon them at last.[a]

Paul's Longing to See the Thessalonians

17But, brothers, when we were torn away from you for a short time (in person, not in thought), out of our intense longing we made every effort to see you. 18For we wanted to come to you—certainly I, Paul, did, again and again—but Satan stopped us. 19For what is our hope, our joy, or the crown in which we will glory in the presence of our Lord Jesus when he comes? Is it not you? 20Indeed, you are our glory and joy.

3 So when we could stand it no longer, we thought it best to be left by ourselves in Athens. 2We sent Timothy, who

---

[c] Gk *brothers* [d] Other ancient authorities read *infants*
[e] Other ancient authorities read *their own prophets*
[f] Or *completely* or *forever*

[a]7 NIV begins verse 7 after ἀπόστολοι. [b]7 NIV/NRSV texts ἤπιοι; NRSV note d as UBS [c]15 NRSV note e adds ἰδίους [d]16 NIV text adds τοῦ θεοῦ

[a]16 Or *them fully*

NRSV

and co-worker for God in proclaiming[g] the gospel of Christ, to strengthen and encourage you for the sake of your faith, [3]so that no one would be shaken by these persecutions. Indeed, you yourselves know that this is what we are destined for. [4]In fact, when we were with you, we told you beforehand that we were to suffer persecution; so it turned out, as you know. [5]For this reason, when I could bear it no longer, I sent to find out about your faith; I was afraid that somehow the tempter had tempted you and that our labor had been in vain.

Timothy's Encouraging Report

6 But Timothy has just now come to us from you, and has brought us the good news of your faith and love. He has told us also that you always remember us kindly and long to see us—just as we long to see you. [7]For this reason, brothers and sisters,[h] during all our distress and persecution we have been encouraged about you through your faith. [8]For we now live, if you continue to stand firm in the Lord. [9]How can we thank God enough for you in return for all the joy that we feel before our God because of you? [10]Night and day we pray most earnestly that we may see you face to face and restore whatever is lacking in your faith.

11 Now may our God and Father himself and our Lord Jesus direct our way to you. [12]And may the Lord make you increase and abound in love for one another and for all, just as we abound in love for you. [13]And may he so strengthen your hearts in holiness that you may be blameless before our God and Father at the coming of our Lord Jesus with all his saints.

A Life Pleasing to God

4 Finally, brothers and sisters,[h] we ask and urge you in the Lord Jesus that, as you learned from us how you ought to live and to please God (as, in fact, you are doing), you should do so more and more. [2]For you know what instructions we gave you through the Lord Jesus. [3]For this is the will of God, your sanctification: that you abstain from fornication; [4]that each one of you know how to control your own body[i] in holiness and honor, [5]not with lustful

NIV

is our brother and God's fellow worker[a] in spreading the gospel of Christ, to strengthen and encourage you in your faith, [3]so that no one would be unsettled by these trials. You know quite well that we were destined for them. [4]In fact, when we were with you, we kept telling you that we would be persecuted. And it turned out that way, as you well know. [5]For this reason, when I could stand it no longer, I sent to find out about your faith. I was afraid that in some way the tempter might have tempted you and our efforts might have been useless.

Timothy's Encouraging Report

[6]But Timothy has just now come to us from you and has brought good news about your faith and love. He has told us that you always have pleasant memories of us and that you long to see us, just as we also long to see you. [7]Therefore, brothers, in all our distress and persecution we were encouraged about you because of your faith. [8]For now we really live, since you are standing firm in the Lord. [9]How can we thank God enough for you in return for all the joy we have in the presence of our God because of you? [10]Night and day we pray most earnestly that we may see you again and supply what is lacking in your faith.

[11]Now may our God and Father himself and our Lord Jesus clear the way for us to come to you. [12]May the Lord make your love increase and overflow for each other and for everyone else, just as ours does for you. [13]May he strengthen your hearts so that you will be blameless and holy in the presence of our God and Father when our Lord Jesus comes with all his holy ones.

Living to Please God

4 Finally, brothers, we instructed you how to live in order to please God, as in fact you are living. Now we ask you and urge you in the Lord Jesus to do this more and more. [2]For you know what instructions we gave you by the authority of the Lord Jesus. [3]It is God's will that you should be sanctified: that you should avoid sexual immorality; [4]that each of you should learn to control his own body[a] in a way that is holy and honorable, [5]not in passionate lust like

g Gk lacks *proclaiming*   h Gk *brothers*   i Or *how to take a wife for himself*

a2 NIV note omits τοῦ θεοῦ or reads διάκονον in place of συνεργόν   b13 NIV/NRSV texts omit ἀμήν

a2 Some manuscripts *brother and fellow worker*; other manuscripts *brother and God's servant*   a4 Or *learn to live with his own wife*; or *learn to acquire a wife*

NRSV

passion, like the Gentiles who do not know God; [6]that no one wrong or exploit a brother or sister[j] in this matter, because the Lord is an avenger in all these things, just as we have already told you beforehand and solemnly warned you. [7]For God did not call us to impurity but in holiness. [8]Therefore whoever rejects this rejects not human authority but God, who also gives his Holy Spirit to you.

9 Now concerning love of the brothers and sisters,[h] you do not need to have anyone write to you, for you yourselves have been taught by God to love one another; [10]and indeed you do love all the brothers and sisters[h] throughout Macedonia. But we urge you, beloved,[h] to do so more and more, [11]to aspire to live quietly, to mind your own affairs, and to work with your hands, as we directed you, [12]so that you may behave properly toward outsiders and be dependent on no one.

The Coming of the Lord

13 But we do not want you to be uninformed, brothers and sisters,[h] about those who have died,[k] so that you may not grieve as others do who have no hope. [14]For since we believe that Jesus died and rose again, even so, through Jesus, God will bring with him those who have died.[k] [15]For this we declare to you by the word of the Lord, that we who are alive, who are left until the coming of the Lord, will by no means precede those who have died.[k] [16]For the Lord himself, with a cry of command, with the archangel's call and with the sound of God's trumpet, will descend from heaven, and the dead in Christ will rise first. [17]Then we who are alive, who are left, will be caught up in the clouds together with them to meet the Lord in the air; and so we will be with the Lord forever. [18]Therefore encourage one another with these words.

5 Now concerning the times and the seasons, brothers and sisters,[h] you do not need to have anything written to you. [2]For you yourselves know very well that the day of the Lord will come like a thief in the night. [3]When they say, "There is peace and security," then sudden destruction will come upon them, as labor pains come upon a pregnant woman, and there will be no escape! [4]But you, beloved,[h] are not in darkness, for that day to surprise you like a thief; [5]for you are all children of light and

1 Thessalonians (Greek)

τὰ ἔθνη τὰ μὴ εἰδότα τὸν θεόν, 6 τὸ μὴ ὑπερβαίνειν καὶ πλεονεκτεῖν ἐν τῷ πράγματι τὸν ἀδελφὸν αὐτοῦ, διότι ἔκδικος κύριος περὶ πάντων τούτων, καθὼς καὶ προείπαμεν ὑμῖν καὶ διεμαρτυράμεθα. 7 οὐ γὰρ ἐκάλεσεν ἡμᾶς ὁ θεὸς ἐπὶ ἀκαθαρσίᾳ ἀλλ᾽ ἐν ἁγιασμῷ. 8 τοιγαροῦν ὁ ἀθετῶν οὐκ ἄνθρωπον ἀθετεῖ ἀλλὰ τὸν θεὸν τὸν [καὶ] διδόντα τὸ πνεῦμα αὐτοῦ τὸ ἅγιον εἰς ὑμᾶς.

9 Περὶ δὲ τῆς φιλαδελφίας οὐ χρείαν ἔχετε γράφειν ὑμῖν, αὐτοὶ γὰρ ὑμεῖς θεοδίδακτοί ἐστε εἰς τὸ ἀγαπᾶν ἀλλήλους, 10 καὶ γὰρ ποιεῖτε αὐτὸ εἰς πάντας τοὺς ἀδελφοὺς [τοὺς] ἐν ὅλῃ τῇ Μακεδονίᾳ. παρακαλοῦμεν δὲ ὑμᾶς, ἀδελφοί, περισσεύειν μᾶλλον 11 καὶ φιλοτιμεῖσθαι ἡσυχάζειν καὶ πράσσειν τὰ ἴδια καὶ ἐργάζεσθαι ταῖς [ἰδίαις] [a] χερσὶν ὑμῶν, καθὼς ὑμῖν παρηγγείλαμεν, 12 ἵνα περιπατῆτε εὐσχημόνως πρὸς τοὺς ἔξω καὶ μηδενὸς χρείαν ἔχητε.

13 Οὐ θέλομεν δὲ ὑμᾶς ἀγνοεῖν, ἀδελφοί, περὶ τῶν κοιμωμένων, ἵνα μὴ λυπῆσθε καθὼς καὶ οἱ λοιποὶ οἱ μὴ ἔχοντες ἐλπίδα. 14 εἰ γὰρ πιστεύομεν ὅτι Ἰησοῦς ἀπέθανεν καὶ ἀνέστη, οὕτως καὶ ὁ θεὸς τοὺς κοιμηθέντας διὰ τοῦ Ἰησοῦ ἄξει σὺν αὐτῷ.

15 Τοῦτο γὰρ ὑμῖν λέγομεν ἐν λόγῳ κυρίου, ὅτι ἡμεῖς οἱ ζῶντες οἱ περιλειπόμενοι εἰς τὴν παρουσίαν τοῦ κυρίου οὐ μὴ φθάσωμεν τοὺς κοιμηθέντας· 16 ὅτι αὐτὸς ὁ κύριος ἐν κελεύσματι, ἐν φωνῇ ἀρχαγγέλου καὶ ἐν σάλπιγγι θεοῦ, καταβήσεται ἀπ᾽ οὐρανοῦ καὶ οἱ νεκροὶ ἐν Χριστῷ ἀναστήσονται πρῶτον, 17 ἔπειτα ἡμεῖς οἱ ζῶντες οἱ περιλειπόμενοι ἅμα σὺν αὐτοῖς ἁρπαγησόμεθα ἐν νεφέλαις εἰς ἀπάντησιν τοῦ κυρίου εἰς ἀέρα· καὶ οὕτως πάντοτε σὺν κυρίῳ ἐσόμεθα. 18 Ὥστε παρακαλεῖτε ἀλλήλους ἐν τοῖς λόγοις τούτοις.

5 Περὶ δὲ τῶν χρόνων καὶ τῶν καιρῶν, ἀδελφοί, οὐ χρείαν ἔχετε ὑμῖν γράφεσθαι, 2 αὐτοὶ γὰρ ἀκριβῶς οἴδατε ὅτι ἡμέρα κυρίου ὡς κλέπτης ἐν νυκτὶ οὕτως ἔρχεται. 3 ὅταν λέγωσιν, Εἰρήνη καὶ ἀσφάλεια, τότε αἰφνίδιος αὐτοῖς ἐφίσταται ὄλεθρος ὥσπερ ἡ ὠδὶν τῇ ἐν γαστρὶ ἐχούσῃ, καὶ οὐ μὴ ἐκφύγωσιν. 4 ὑμεῖς δέ, ἀδελφοί, οὐκ ἐστὲ ἐν σκότει, ἵνα ἡ ἡμέρα ὑμᾶς ὡς κλέπτης καταλάβῃ· 5 πάντες γὰρ ὑμεῖς

NIV

the heathen, who do not know God; [6]and that in this matter no one should wrong his brother or take advantage of him. The Lord will punish men for all such sins, as we have already told you and warned you. [7]For God did not call us to be impure, but to live a holy life. [8]Therefore, he who rejects this instruction does not reject man but God, who gives you his Holy Spirit.

[9]Now about brotherly love we do not need to write to you, for you yourselves have been taught by God to love each other. [10]And in fact, you do love all the brothers throughout Macedonia. Yet we urge you, brothers, to do so more and more.

[11]Make it your ambition to lead a quiet life, to mind your own business and to work with your hands, just as we told you, [12]so that your daily life may win the respect of outsiders and so that you will not be dependent on anybody.

The Coming of the Lord

[13]Brothers, we do not want you to be ignorant about those who fall asleep, or to grieve like the rest of men, who have no hope. [14]We believe that Jesus died and rose again and so we believe that God will bring with Jesus those who have fallen asleep in him. [15]According to the Lord's own word, we tell you that we who are still alive, who are left till the coming of the Lord, will certainly not precede those who have fallen asleep. [16]For the Lord himself will come down from heaven, with a loud command, with the voice of the archangel and with the trumpet call of God, and the dead in Christ will rise first. [17]After that, we who are still alive and are left will be caught up together with them in the clouds to meet the Lord in the air. And so we will be with the Lord forever. [18]Therefore encourage each other with these words.

5 Now, brothers, about times and dates we do not need to write to you, [2]for you know very well that the day of the Lord will come like a thief in the night. [3]While people are saying, "Peace and safety," destruction will come on them suddenly, as labor pains on a pregnant woman, and they will not escape.

[4]But you, brothers, are not in darkness so that this day should surprise you like a thief. [5]You are all sons of the light and

---

[h] Gk brothers [j] Gk brother [k] Gk fallen asleep

[a]11 NIV text omits ἰδίαις

children of the day; we are not of the night or of darkness. ⁶So then let us not fall asleep as others do, but let us keep awake and be sober; ⁷for those who sleep sleep at night, and those who are drunk get drunk at night. ⁸But since we belong to the day, let us be sober, and put on the breastplate of faith and love, and for a helmet the hope of salvation. ⁹For God has destined us not for wrath but for obtaining salvation through our Lord Jesus Christ, ¹⁰who died for us, so that whether we are awake or asleep we may live with him. ¹¹Therefore encourage one another and build up each other, as indeed you are doing.

Final Exhortations, Greetings, and Benediction

12 But we appeal to you, brothers and sisters,[l] to respect those who labor among you, and have charge of you in the Lord and admonish you; ¹³esteem them very highly in love because of their work. Be at peace among yourselves. ¹⁴And we urge you, beloved,[l] to admonish the idlers, encourage the faint hearted, help the weak, be patient with all of them. ¹⁵See that none of you repays evil for evil, but always seek to do good to one another and to all. ¹⁶Rejoice always, ¹⁷pray without ceasing, ¹⁸give thanks in all circumstances; for this is the will of God in Christ Jesus for you. ¹⁹Do not quench the Spirit. ²⁰Do not despise the words of prophets,[m] ²¹but test everything; hold fast to what is good; ²²abstain from every form of evil.

23 May the God of peace himself sanctify you entirely; and may your spirit and soul and body be kept sound[n] and blameless at the coming of our Lord Jesus Christ. ²⁴The one who calls you is faithful, and he will do this.

25 Beloved,[o] pray for us.

26 Greet all the brothers and sisters[l] with a holy kiss. ²⁷I solemnly command you by the Lord that this letter be read to all of them.[p]

28 The grace of our Lord Jesus Christ be with you.[q]

υἱοὶ φωτός ἐστε καὶ υἱοὶ ἡμέρας. οὐκ ἐσμὲν νυκτὸς οὐδὲ σκότους· **6** ἄρα οὖν μὴ καθεύδωμεν ὡς οἱ λοιποὶ ἀλλὰ γρηγορῶμεν καὶ νήφωμεν. **7** οἱ γὰρ καθεύδοντες νυκτὸς καθεύδουσιν καὶ οἱ μεθυσκόμενοι νυκτὸς μεθύουσιν· **8** ἡμεῖς δὲ ἡμέρας ὄντες νήφωμεν ἐνδυσάμενοι θώρακα πίστεως καὶ ἀγάπης καὶ περικεφαλαίαν ἐλπίδα σωτηρίας· **9** ὅτι οὐκ ἔθετο ἡμᾶς ὁ θεὸς εἰς ὀργὴν ἀλλὰ εἰς περιποίησιν σωτηρίας διὰ τοῦ κυρίου ἡμῶν Ἰησοῦ Χριστοῦ **10** τοῦ ἀποθανόντος ὑπὲρ ἡμῶν, ἵνα εἴτε γρηγορῶμεν εἴτε καθεύδωμεν ἅμα σὺν αὐτῷ ζήσωμεν. **11** Διὸ παρακαλεῖτε ἀλλήλους καὶ οἰκοδομεῖτε εἷς τὸν ἕνα, καθὼς καὶ ποιεῖτε.

12 Ἐρωτῶμεν δὲ ὑμᾶς, ἀδελφοί, εἰδέναι τοὺς κοπιῶντας ἐν ὑμῖν καὶ προϊσταμένους ὑμῶν ἐν κυρίῳ καὶ νουθετοῦντας ὑμᾶς **13** καὶ ἡγεῖσθαι αὐτοὺς ὑπερεκπερισσοῦ ἐν ἀγάπῃ διὰ τὸ ἔργον αὐτῶν. εἰρηνεύετε ἐν ἑαυτοῖς. **14** παρακαλοῦμεν δὲ ὑμᾶς, ἀδελφοί, νουθετεῖτε τοὺς ἀτάκτους, παραμυθεῖσθε τοὺς ὀλιγοψύχους, ἀντέχεσθε τῶν ἀσθενῶν, μακροθυμεῖτε πρὸς πάντας. **15** ὁρᾶτε μή τις κακὸν ἀντὶ κακοῦ τινι ἀποδῷ, ἀλλὰ πάντοτε τὸ ἀγαθὸν διώκετε [καὶ] εἰς ἀλλήλους καὶ εἰς πάντας.

16 Πάντοτε χαίρετε, **17** ἀδιαλείπτως προσεύχεσθε, **18** ἐν παντὶ εὐχαριστεῖτε· τοῦτο γὰρ θέλημα θεοῦ ἐν Χριστῷ Ἰησοῦ εἰς ὑμᾶς. **19** τὸ πνεῦμα μὴ σβέννυτε, **20** προφητείας μὴ ἐξουθενεῖτε, **21** πάντα δὲ δοκιμάζετε, τὸ καλὸν κατέχετε, **22** ἀπὸ παντὸς εἴδους πονηροῦ ἀπέχεσθε.

23 Αὐτὸς δὲ ὁ θεὸς τῆς εἰρήνης ἁγιάσαι ὑμᾶς ὁλοτελεῖς, καὶ ὁλόκληρον ὑμῶν τὸ πνεῦμα καὶ ἡ ψυχὴ καὶ τὸ σῶμα ἀμέμπτως ἐν τῇ παρουσίᾳ τοῦ κυρίου ἡμῶν Ἰησοῦ Χριστοῦ τηρηθείη. **24** πιστὸς ὁ καλῶν ὑμᾶς, ὃς καὶ ποιήσει. **25** Ἀδελφοί, προσεύχεσθε [καὶ] περὶ ἡμῶν.

26 Ἀσπάσασθε τοὺς ἀδελφοὺς πάντας ἐν φιλήματι ἁγίῳ. **27** Ἐνορκίζω ὑμᾶς τὸν κύριον ἀναγνωσθῆναι τὴν ἐπιστολὴν πᾶσιν τοῖς ἀδελφοῖς.

28 Ἡ χάρις τοῦ κυρίου ἡμῶν Ἰησοῦ Χριστοῦ μεθ' ὑμῶν.[a]

sons of the day. We do not belong to the night or to the darkness. ⁶So then, let us not be like others, who are asleep, but let us be alert and self-controlled. ⁷For those who sleep, sleep at night, and those who get drunk, get drunk at night. ⁸But since we belong to the day, let us be self-controlled, putting on faith and love as a breastplate, and the hope of salvation as a helmet. ⁹For God did not appoint us to suffer wrath but to receive salvation through our Lord Jesus Christ. ¹⁰He died for us so that, whether we are awake or asleep, we may live together with him. ¹¹Therefore encourage one another and build each other up, just as in fact you are doing.

Final Instructions

¹²Now we ask you, brothers, to respect those who work hard among you, who are over you in the Lord and who admonish you. ¹³Hold them in the highest regard in love because of their work. Live in peace with each other. ¹⁴And we urge you, brothers, warn those who are idle, encourage the timid, help the weak, be patient with everyone. ¹⁵Make sure that nobody pays back wrong for wrong, but always try to be kind to each other and to everyone else.

¹⁶Be joyful always; ¹⁷pray continually; ¹⁸give thanks in all circumstances, for this is God's will for you in Christ Jesus.

¹⁹Do not put out the Spirit's fire; ²⁰do not treat prophecies with contempt. ²¹Test everything. Hold on to the good. ²²Avoid every kind of evil.

²³May God himself, the God of peace, sanctify you through and through. May your whole spirit, soul and body be kept blameless at the coming of our Lord Jesus Christ. ²⁴The one who calls you is faithful and he will do it.

²⁵Brothers, pray for us. ²⁶Greet all the brothers with a holy kiss. ²⁷I charge you before the Lord to have this letter read to all the brothers.

²⁸The grace of our Lord Jesus Christ be with you.

---

[l] Gk *brothers* [m] Gk *despise prophecies* [n] Or *complete*
[o] Gk *Brothers* [p] Gk *to all the brothers* [q] Other ancient authorities add *Amen*

[a]28 NRSV note q adds ἀμήν

NRSV

Salutation

1 Paul, Silvanus, and Timothy,
To the church of the Thessalonians in God our Father and the Lord Jesus Christ: 2 Grace to you and peace from God our[a] Father and the Lord Jesus Christ.

Thanksgiving

3 We must always give thanks to God for you, brothers and sisters,[b] as is right, because your faith is growing abundantly, and the love of everyone of you for one another is increasing. 4Therefore we ourselves boast of you among the churches of God for your steadfastness and faith during all your persecutions and the afflictions that you are enduring.

The Judgment at Christ's Coming

5 This is evidence of the righteous judgment of God, and is intended to make you worthy of the kingdom of God, for which you are also suffering. 6For it is indeed just of God to repay with affliction those who afflict you, 7and to give relief to the afflicted as well as to us, when the Lord Jesus is revealed from heaven with his mighty angels 8in flaming fire, inflicting vengeance on those who do not know God and on those who do not obey the gospel of our Lord Jesus. 9These will suffer the punishment of eternal destruction, separated from the presence of the Lord and from the glory of his might, 10when he comes to be glorified by his saints and to be marveled at on that day among all who have believed, because our testimony to you was believed. 11To this end we always pray for you, asking that our God will make you worthy of his call and will fulfill by his power every good resolve and work of faith, 12so that the name of our Lord Jesus may be glorified in you, and you in him, according to the grace of our God and the Lord Jesus Christ.

The Man of Lawlessness

2 As to the coming of our Lord Jesus Christ and our being gathered together to him, we beg you, brothers and sisters,[b] 2not to be quickly shaken in mind or alarmed, either by spirit or by word or by letter, as though from us, to the effect that the day of the Lord is already here. 3Let no one deceive you in any way; for that day will not come unless the rebellion

ΠΡΟΣ ΘΕΣΣΑΛΟΝΙΚΕΙΣ Β

1 Παῦλος καὶ Σιλουανὸς καὶ Τιμόθεος τῇ ἐκκλησίᾳ Θεσσαλονικέων ἐν θεῷ πατρὶ ἡμῶν καὶ κυρίῳ Ἰησοῦ Χριστῷ, **2** χάρις ὑμῖν καὶ εἰρήνη ἀπὸ θεοῦ πατρὸς [ἡμῶν][a] καὶ κυρίου Ἰησοῦ Χριστοῦ.

3 Εὐχαριστεῖν ὀφείλομεν τῷ θεῷ πάντοτε περὶ ὑμῶν, ἀδελφοί, καθὼς ἄξιόν ἐστιν, ὅτι ὑπεραυξάνει ἡ πίστις ὑμῶν καὶ πλεονάζει ἡ ἀγάπη ἑνὸς ἑκάστου πάντων ὑμῶν εἰς ἀλλήλους, **4** ὥστε αὐτοὺς ἡμᾶς ἐν ὑμῖν ἐγκαυχᾶσθαι ἐν ταῖς ἐκκλησίαις τοῦ θεοῦ ὑπὲρ τῆς ὑπομονῆς ὑμῶν καὶ πίστεως ἐν πᾶσιν τοῖς διωγμοῖς ὑμῶν καὶ ταῖς θλίψεσιν αἷς ἀνέχεσθε, **5** ἔνδειγμα τῆς δικαίας κρίσεως τοῦ θεοῦ εἰς τὸ καταξιωθῆναι ὑμᾶς τῆς βασιλείας τοῦ θεοῦ, ὑπὲρ ἧς καὶ πάσχετε, **6** εἴπερ δίκαιον παρὰ θεῷ ἀνταποδοῦναι τοῖς θλίβουσιν ὑμᾶς θλῖψιν **7** καὶ ὑμῖν τοῖς θλιβομένοις ἄνεσιν μεθ' ἡμῶν, ἐν τῇ ἀποκαλύψει τοῦ κυρίου Ἰησοῦ ἀπ' οὐρανοῦ μετ' ἀγγέλων δυνάμεως αὐτοῦ **8** ἐν πυρὶ φλογός,[b] διδόντος ἐκδίκησιν τοῖς μὴ εἰδόσιν θεὸν καὶ τοῖς μὴ ὑπακούουσιν τῷ εὐαγγελίῳ τοῦ κυρίου ἡμῶν Ἰησοῦ, **9** οἵτινες δίκην τίσουσιν ὄλεθρον αἰώνιον ἀπὸ προσώπου τοῦ κυρίου καὶ ἀπὸ τῆς δόξης τῆς ἰσχύος αὐτοῦ, **10** ὅταν ἔλθῃ ἐνδοξασθῆναι ἐν τοῖς ἁγίοις αὐτοῦ καὶ θαυμασθῆναι ἐν πᾶσιν τοῖς πιστεύσασιν, ὅτι ἐπιστεύθη τὸ μαρτύριον ἡμῶν ἐφ' ὑμᾶς, ἐν τῇ ἡμέρᾳ ἐκείνῃ. **11** εἰς ὃ καὶ προσευχόμεθα πάντοτε περὶ ὑμῶν, ἵνα ὑμᾶς ἀξιώσῃ τῆς κλήσεως ὁ θεὸς ἡμῶν καὶ πληρώσῃ πᾶσαν εὐδοκίαν ἀγαθωσύνης καὶ ἔργον πίστεως ἐν δυνάμει, **12** ὅπως ἐνδοξασθῇ τὸ ὄνομα τοῦ κυρίου ἡμῶν Ἰησοῦ ἐν ὑμῖν, καὶ ὑμεῖς ἐν αὐτῷ, κατὰ τὴν χάριν τοῦ θεοῦ ἡμῶν καὶ κυρίου Ἰησοῦ Χριστοῦ.

2 Ἐρωτῶμεν δὲ ὑμᾶς, ἀδελφοί, ὑπὲρ τῆς παρουσίας τοῦ κυρίου ἡμῶν Ἰησοῦ Χριστοῦ καὶ ἡμῶν ἐπισυναγωγῆς ἐπ' αὐτὸν **2** εἰς τὸ μὴ ταχέως σαλευθῆναι ὑμᾶς ἀπὸ τοῦ νοὸς μηδὲ θροεῖσθαι, μήτε διὰ πνεύματος μήτε διὰ λόγου μήτε δι' ἐπιστολῆς ὡς δι' ἡμῶν, ὡς ὅτι ἐνέστηκεν ἡ ἡμέρα τοῦ κυρίου· **3** μή τις ὑμᾶς ἐξαπατήσῃ κατὰ μηδένα τρόπον. ὅτι ἐὰν μὴ ἔλθῃ ἡ ἀποστασία

NIV

1 Paul, Silas[a] and Timothy,

To the church of the Thessalonians in God our Father and the Lord Jesus Christ:

2Grace and peace to you from God the Father and the Lord Jesus Christ.

Thanksgiving and Prayer

3We ought always to thank God for you, brothers, and rightly so, because your faith is growing more and more, and the love every one of you has for each other is increasing. 4Therefore, among God's churches we boast about your perseverance and faith in all the persecutions and trials you are enduring.

5All this is evidence that God's judgment is right, and as a result you will be counted worthy of the kingdom of God, for which you are suffering. 6God is just: He will pay back trouble to those who trouble you 7and give relief to you who are troubled, and to us as well. This will happen when the Lord Jesus is revealed from heaven in blazing fire with his powerful angels. 8He will punish those who do not know God and do not obey the gospel of our Lord Jesus. 9They will be punished with everlasting destruction and shut out from the presence of the Lord and from the majesty of his power 10on the day he comes to be glorified in his holy people and to be marveled at among all those who have believed. This includes you, because you believed our testimony to you.

11With this in mind, we constantly pray for you, that our God may count you worthy of his calling, and that by his power he may fulfill every good purpose of yours and every act prompted by your faith. 12We pray this so that the name of our Lord Jesus may be glorified in you, and you in him, according to the grace of our God and the Lord Jesus Christ.[b]

The Man of Lawlessness

2 Concerning the coming of our Lord Jesus Christ and our being gathered to him, we ask you, brothers, 2not to become easily unsettled or alarmed by some prophecy, report or letter supposed to have come from us, saying that the day of the Lord has already come. 3Don't let anyone deceive you in any way, for [that day will not come] until the rebellion occurs and

---

a Other ancient authorities read *the*   b Gk *brothers*

a2 NIV text and NRSV note a omit ἡμῶν.   b8 NIV begins verse 8 after φλογός.

a1 Greek *Silvanus*, a variant of *Silas*   b12 Or *God and Lord, Jesus Christ*

comes first and the lawless one[c] is revealed, the one destined for destruction.[d] [4]He opposes and exalts himself above every so-called god or object of worship, so that he takes his seat in the temple of God, declaring himself to be God. [5]Do you not remember that I told you these things when I was still with you? [6]And you know what is now restraining him, so that he may be revealed when his time comes. [7]For the mystery of lawlessness is already at work, but only until the one who now restrains it is removed. [8]And then the lawless one will be revealed, whom the Lord Jesus[e] will destroy[f] with the breath of his mouth, annihilating him by the manifestation of his coming. [9]The coming of the lawless one is apparent in the working of Satan, who uses all power, signs, lying wonders, [10]and every kind of wicked deception for those who are perishing, because they refused to love the truth and so be saved. [11]For this reason God sends them a powerful delusion, leading them to believe what is false, [12]so that all who have not believed the truth but took pleasure in unrighteousness will be condemned.

Chosen for Salvation

13 But we must always give thanks to God for you, brothers and sisters[g] beloved by the Lord, because God chose you as the first fruits[h] for salvation through sanctification by the Spirit and through belief in the truth. [14]For this purpose he called you through our proclamation of the good news,[i] so that you may obtain the glory of our Lord Jesus Christ. [15]So then, brothers and sisters,[g] stand firm and hold fast to the traditions that you were taught by us, either by word of mouth or by our letter.

16 Now may our Lord Jesus Christ himself and God our Father, who loved us and through grace gave us eternal comfort and good hope, [17]comfort your hearts and strengthen them in every good work and word.

Request for Prayer

3 Finally, brothers and sisters,[g] pray for us, so that the word of the Lord may spread rapidly and be glorified everywhere, just as it is among you, [2]and that we may be rescued from wicked and evil people; for not all have faith. [3]But the Lord

---

πρῶτον καὶ ἀποκαλυφθῇ ὁ ἄνθρωπος τῆς ἀνομίας[a], ὁ υἱὸς τῆς ἀπωλείας, 4 ὁ ἀντικείμενος καὶ ὑπεραιρόμενος ἐπὶ πάντα λεγόμενον θεὸν ἢ σέβασμα, ὥστε αὐτὸν εἰς τὸν ναὸν τοῦ θεοῦ καθίσαι ἀποδεικνύντα ἑαυτὸν ὅτι ἔστιν θεός. 5 Οὐ μνημονεύετε ὅτι ἔτι ὢν πρὸς ὑμᾶς ταῦτα ἔλεγον ὑμῖν; 6 καὶ νῦν τὸ κατέχον οἴδατε εἰς τὸ ἀποκαλυφθῆναι αὐτὸν ἐν τῷ ἑαυτοῦ καιρῷ. 7 τὸ γὰρ μυστήριον ἤδη ἐνεργεῖται τῆς ἀνομίας· μόνον ὁ κατέχων ἄρτι ἕως ἐκ μέσου γένηται. 8 καὶ τότε ἀποκαλυφθήσεται ὁ ἄνομος, ὃν ὁ κύριος [Ἰησοῦς] ἀνελεῖ[b] τῷ πνεύματι τοῦ στόματος αὐτοῦ καὶ καταργήσει τῇ ἐπιφανείᾳ τῆς παρουσίας αὐτοῦ, 9 οὗ ἐστιν ἡ παρουσία κατ᾽ ἐνέργειαν τοῦ Σατανᾶ ἐν πάσῃ δυνάμει καὶ σημείοις καὶ τέρασιν ψεύδους 10 καὶ ἐν πάσῃ ἀπάτῃ ἀδικίας τοῖς ἀπολλυμένοις, ἀνθ᾽ ὧν τὴν ἀγάπην τῆς ἀληθείας οὐκ ἐδέξαντο εἰς τὸ σωθῆναι αὐτούς. 11 καὶ διὰ τοῦτο πέμπει αὐτοῖς ὁ θεὸς ἐνέργειαν πλάνης εἰς τὸ πιστεῦσαι αὐτοὺς τῷ ψεύδει, 12 ἵνα κριθῶσιν πάντες οἱ μὴ πιστεύσαντες τῇ ἀληθείᾳ ἀλλὰ εὐδοκήσαντες τῇ ἀδικίᾳ.

13 Ἡμεῖς δὲ ὀφείλομεν εὐχαριστεῖν τῷ θεῷ πάντοτε περὶ ὑμῶν, ἀδελφοὶ ἠγαπημένοι ὑπὸ κυρίου, ὅτι εἵλατο ὑμᾶς ὁ θεὸς ἀπαρχὴν[c] εἰς σωτηρίαν ἐν ἁγιασμῷ πνεύματος καὶ πίστει ἀληθείας, 14 εἰς ὃ [καὶ] ἐκάλεσεν ὑμᾶς διὰ τοῦ εὐαγγελίου ἡμῶν εἰς περιποίησιν δόξης τοῦ κυρίου ἡμῶν Ἰησοῦ Χριστοῦ. 15 ἄρα οὖν, ἀδελφοί, στήκετε, καὶ κρατεῖτε τὰς παραδόσεις ἃς ἐδιδάχθητε εἴτε διὰ λόγου εἴτε δι᾽ ἐπιστολῆς ἡμῶν. 16 Αὐτὸς δὲ ὁ κύριος ἡμῶν Ἰησοῦς Χριστὸς καὶ [ὁ] θεὸς ὁ πατὴρ ἡμῶν ὁ ἀγαπήσας ἡμᾶς καὶ δοὺς παράκλησιν αἰωνίαν καὶ ἐλπίδα ἀγαθὴν ἐν χάριτι, 17 παρακαλέσαι ὑμῶν τὰς καρδίας καὶ στηρίξαι ἐν παντὶ ἔργῳ καὶ λόγῳ ἀγαθῷ.

3 Τὸ λοιπὸν προσεύχεσθε, ἀδελφοί, περὶ ἡμῶν, ἵνα ὁ λόγος τοῦ κυρίου τρέχῃ καὶ δοξάζηται καθὼς καὶ πρὸς ὑμᾶς, 2 καὶ ἵνα ῥυσθῶμεν ἀπὸ τῶν ἀτόπων καὶ πονηρῶν ἀνθρώπων· οὐ γὰρ πάντων ἡ πίστις. 3 πιστὸς δέ

---

the man of lawlessness[a] is revealed, the man doomed to destruction. [4]He will oppose and will exalt himself over everything that is called God or is worshiped, so that he sets himself up in God's temple, proclaiming himself to be God.

[5]Don't you remember that when I was with you I used to tell you these things? [6]And now you know what is holding him back, so that he may be revealed at the proper time. [7]For the secret power of lawlessness is already at work; but the one who now holds it back will continue to do so till he is taken out of the way. [8]And then the lawless one will be revealed, whom the Lord Jesus will overthrow with the breath of his mouth and destroy by the splendor of his coming. [9]The coming of the lawless one will be in accordance with the work of Satan displayed in all kinds of counterfeit miracles, signs and wonders, [10]and in every sort of evil that deceives those who are perishing. They perish because they refused to love the truth and so be saved. [11]For this reason God sends them a powerful delusion so that they will believe the lie [12]and so that all will be condemned who have not believed the truth but have delighted in wickedness.

Stand Firm

[13]But we ought always to thank God for you, brothers loved by the Lord, because from the beginning God chose you[b] to be saved through the sanctifying work of the Spirit and through belief in the truth. [14]He called you to this through our gospel, that you might share in the glory of our Lord Jesus Christ. [15]So then, brothers, stand firm and hold to the teachings[c] we passed on to you, whether by word of mouth or by letter.

[16]May our Lord Jesus Christ himself and God our Father, who loved us and by his grace gave us eternal encouragement and good hope, [17]encourage your hearts and strengthen you in every good deed and word.

Request for Prayer

3 Finally, brothers, pray for us that the message of the Lord may spread rapidly and be honored, just as it was with you. [2]And pray that we may be delivered from wicked and evil men, for not everyone has faith. [3]But the Lord is faithful, and

---

[c] Gk *the man of lawlessness*; other ancient authorities read *the man of sin*   [d] Gk *the son of destruction*   [e] Other ancient authorities lack *Jesus*   [f] Other ancient authorities read *consume*   [g] Gk *brothers*   [h] Other ancient authorities read *from the beginning*   [i] Or *through our gospel*

[a] 3 NIV/NRSV notes ἁμαρτίας †   [b] 8 NRSV note f ἀναλώσει †   [c] 13 NIV text and NRSV note h ἀπ᾽ ἀρχῆς; NIV note and NRSV text as UBS

[a] 3 Some manuscripts *sin*   [b] 13 Some manuscripts *because God chose you as his firstfruits*   [c] 15 Or *traditions*

NRSV

is faithful; he will strengthen you and guard you from the evil one.ʲ 4And we have confidence in the Lord concerning you, that you are doing and will go on doing the things that we command. 5May the Lord direct your hearts to the love of God and to the steadfastness of Christ.

Warning against Idleness

6 Now we command you, beloved,ᵍ in the name of our Lord Jesus Christ, to keep away from believers who areᵏ living in idleness and not according to the tradition that theyˡ received from us. 7For you yourselves know how you ought to imitate us; we were not idle when we were with you, 8and we did not eat anyone's bread without paying for it; but with toil and labor we worked night and day, so that we might not burden any of you. 9This was not because we do not have that right, but in order to give you an example to imitate. 10For even when we were with you, we gave you this command: Anyone unwilling to work should not eat. 11For we hear that some of you are living in idleness, mere busybodies, not doing any work. 12Now such persons we command and exhort in the Lord Jesus Christ to do their work quietly and to earn their own living. 13Brothers and sisters,ᵐ do not be weary in doing what is right.

14 Take note of those who do not obey what we say in this letter; have nothing to do with them, so that they may be ashamed. 15Do not regard them as enemies, but warn them as believers.ⁿ

Final Greetings and Benediction

16 Now may the Lord of peace himself give you peace at all times in all ways. The Lord be with all of you.

17 I, Paul, write this greeting with my own hand. This is the mark in every letter of mine; it is the way I write. 18The grace of our Lord Jesus Christ be with all of you.ᵒ

NIV

he will strengthen and protect you from the evil one. 4We have confidence in the Lord that you are doing and will continue to do the things we command. 5May the Lord direct your hearts into God's love and Christ's perseverance.

Warning Against Idleness

6In the name of the Lord Jesus Christ, we command you, brothers, to keep away from every brother who is idle and does not live according to the teachingᵃ you received from us. 7For you yourselves know how you ought to follow our example. We were not idle when we were with you, 8nor did we eat anyone's food without paying for it. On the contrary, we worked night and day, laboring and toiling so that we would not be a burden to any of you. 9We did this, not because we do not have the right to such help, but in order to make ourselves a model for you to follow. 10For even when we were with you, we gave you this rule: "If a man will not work, he shall not eat."

11We hear that some among you are idle. They are not busy; they are busybodies. 12Such people we command and urge in the Lord Jesus Christ to settle down and earn the bread they eat. 13And as for you, brothers, never tire of doing what is right.

14If anyone does not obey our instruction in this letter, take special note of him. Do not associate with him, in order that he may feel ashamed. 15Yet do not regard him as an enemy, but warn him as a brother.

Final Greetings

16Now may the Lord of peace himself give you peace at all times and in every way. The Lord be with all of you.

17I, Paul, write this greeting in my own hand, which is the distinguishing mark in all my letters. This is how I write.

18The grace of our Lord Jesus Christ be with you all.

ᵍ Gk brothers ʲOr from evil ᵏGk from every brother who is ˡOther ancient authorities read you ᵐGk Brothers ⁿGk a brother ᵒOther ancient authorities add Amen

ᵃ6 NIV text omits ἡμῶν † ᵇ6 NIV text and NRSV note l παρελάβετε ᶜ18 NRSV note o adds ἀμήν.

ᵃ6 Or tradition

NRSV

Salutation

1 Paul, an apostle of Christ Jesus by the command of God our Savior and of Christ Jesus our hope,

2 To Timothy, my loyal child in the faith: Grace, mercy, and peace from God the Father and Christ Jesus our Lord.

Warning against False Teachers

3 I urge you, as I did when I was on my way to Macedonia, to remain in Ephesus so that you may instruct certain people not to teach any different doctrine, [4]and not to occupy themselves with myths and endless genealogies that promote speculations rather than the divine training[a] that is known by faith. [5]But the aim of such instruction is love that comes from a pure heart, a good conscience, and sincere faith. [6]Some people have deviated from these and turned to meaningless talk, [7]desiring to be teachers of the law, without understanding either what they are saying or the things about which they make assertions.

8 Now we know that the law is good, if one uses it legitimately. [9]This means understanding that the law is laid down not for the innocent but for the lawless and disobedient, for the godless and sinful, for the unholy and profane, for those who kill their father or mother, for murderers, [10]fornicators, sodomites, slave traders, liars, perjurers, and whatever else is contrary to the sound teaching [11]that conforms to the glorious gospel of the blessed God, which he entrusted to me.

Gratitude for Mercy

12 I am grateful to Christ Jesus our Lord, who has strengthened me, because he judged me faithful and appointed me to his service, [13]even though I was formerly a blasphemer, a persecutor, and a man of violence. But I received mercy because I had acted ignorantly in unbelief, [14]and the grace of our Lord overflowed for me with the faith and love that are in Christ Jesus. [15]The saying is sure and worthy of full acceptance, that Christ Jesus came into the world to save sinners—of whom I am the foremost. [16]But for that very reason I received mercy, so that in me, as the foremost, Jesus Christ might display the utmost patience, making me an example to those who would come to believe in him for eternal life. [17]To the King of the ages, immortal, invisible, the only God, be honor

ΠΡΟΣ ΤΙΜΟΘΕΟΝ Α

1 Παῦλος ἀπόστολος Χριστοῦ Ἰησοῦ κατ᾽ ἐπιταγὴν θεοῦ σωτῆρος ἡμῶν καὶ Χριστοῦ Ἰησοῦ τῆς ἐλπίδος ἡμῶν **2** Τιμοθέῳ γνησίῳ τέκνῳ ἐν πίστει, χάρις ἔλεος εἰρήνη ἀπὸ θεοῦ πατρὸς καὶ Χριστοῦ Ἰησοῦ τοῦ κυρίου ἡμῶν.

3 Καθὼς παρεκάλεσά σε προσμεῖναι ἐν Ἐφέσῳ πορευόμενος εἰς Μακεδονίαν, ἵνα παραγγείλῃς τισὶν μὴ ἑτεροδιδασκαλεῖν **4** μηδὲ προσέχειν μύθοις καὶ γενεαλογίαις ἀπεράντοις, αἵτινες ἐκζητήσεις παρέχουσιν μᾶλλον ἢ οἰκονομίαν θεοῦ τὴν ἐν πίστει. **5** τὸ δὲ τέλος τῆς παραγγελίας ἐστὶν ἀγάπη ἐκ καθαρᾶς καρδίας καὶ συνειδήσεως ἀγαθῆς καὶ πίστεως ἀνυποκρίτου, **6** ὧν τινες ἀστοχήσαντες ἐξετράπησαν εἰς ματαιολογίαν **7** θέλοντες εἶναι νομοδιδάσκαλοι, μὴ νοοῦντες μήτε ἃ λέγουσιν μήτε περὶ τίνων διαβεβαιοῦνται.

8 Οἴδαμεν δὲ ὅτι καλὸς ὁ νόμος, ἐάν τις αὐτῷ νομίμως χρῆται, **9** εἰδὼς τοῦτο, ὅτι δικαίῳ νόμος οὐ κεῖται, ἀνόμοις δὲ καὶ ἀνυποτάκτοις, ἀσεβέσι καὶ ἁμαρτωλοῖς, ἀνοσίοις καὶ βεβήλοις, πατρολῴαις καὶ μητρολῴαις, ἀνδροφόνοις **10** πόρνοις ἀρσενοκοίταις ἀνδραποδισταῖς ψεύσταις ἐπιόρκοις, καὶ εἴ τι ἕτερον τῇ ὑγιαινούσῃ διδασκαλίᾳ ἀντίκειται **11** κατὰ τὸ εὐαγγέλιον τῆς δόξης τοῦ μακαρίου θεοῦ, ὃ ἐπιστεύθην ἐγώ.

12 Χάριν ἔχω τῷ ἐνδυναμώσαντί με Χριστῷ Ἰησοῦ τῷ κυρίῳ ἡμῶν, ὅτι πιστόν με ἡγήσατο θέμενος εἰς διακονίαν **13** τὸ πρότερον ὄντα βλάσφημον καὶ διώκτην καὶ ὑβριστήν, ἀλλὰ ἠλεήθην, ὅτι ἀγνοῶν ἐποίησα ἐν ἀπιστίᾳ· **14** ὑπερεπλεόνασεν δὲ ἡ χάρις τοῦ κυρίου ἡμῶν μετὰ πίστεως καὶ ἀγάπης τῆς ἐν Χριστῷ Ἰησοῦ. **15** πιστὸς ὁ λόγος καὶ πάσης ἀποδοχῆς ἄξιος, ὅτι Χριστὸς Ἰησοῦς ἦλθεν εἰς τὸν κόσμον ἁμαρτωλοὺς σῶσαι, ὧν πρῶτός εἰμι ἐγώ. **16** ἀλλὰ διὰ τοῦτο ἠλεήθην, ἵνα ἐν ἐμοὶ πρώτῳ ἐνδείξηται Χριστὸς Ἰησοῦς τὴν ἅπασαν μακροθυμίαν πρὸς ὑποτύπωσιν τῶν μελλόντων πιστεύειν ἐπ᾽ αὐτῷ εἰς ζωὴν αἰώνιον. **17** τῷ δὲ βασιλεῖ τῶν αἰώνων, ἀφθάρτῳ ἀοράτῳ μόνῳ θεῷ, τιμὴ καὶ δόξα εἰς τοὺς

NIV

1 Paul, an apostle of Christ Jesus by the command of God our Savior and of Christ Jesus our hope,

[2]To Timothy my true son in the faith:

Grace, mercy and peace from God the Father and Christ Jesus our Lord.

Warning Against False Teachers of the Law

[3]As I urged you when I went into Macedonia, stay there in Ephesus so that you may command certain men not to teach false doctrines any longer [4]nor to devote themselves to myths and endless genealogies. These promote controversies rather than God's work—which is by faith. [5]The goal of this command is love, which comes from a pure heart and a good conscience and a sincere faith. [6]Some have wandered away from these and turned to meaningless talk. [7]They want to be teachers of the law, but they do not know what they are talking about or what they so confidently affirm.

[8]We know that the law is good if one uses it properly. [9]We also know that law[a] is made not for the righteous but for lawbreakers and rebels, the ungodly and sinful, the unholy and irreligious; for those who kill their fathers or mothers, for murderers, [10]for adulterers and perverts, for slave traders and liars and perjurers—and for whatever else is contrary to the sound doctrine [11]that conforms to the glorious gospel of the blessed God, which he entrusted to me.

The Lord's Grace to Paul

[12]I thank Christ Jesus our Lord, who has given me strength, that he considered me faithful, appointing me to his service. [13]Even though I was once a blasphemer and a persecutor and a violent man, I was shown mercy because I acted in ignorance and unbelief. [14]The grace of our Lord was poured out on me abundantly, along with the faith and love that are in Christ Jesus. [15]Here is a trustworthy saying that deserves full acceptance: Christ Jesus came into the world to save sinners—of whom I am the worst. [16]But for that very reason I was shown mercy so that in me, the worst of sinners, Christ Jesus might display his unlimited patience as an example for those who would believe on him and receive eternal life. [17]Now to the King eternal, immortal, invisible, the only God, be honor

---

and glory forever and ever.[b] Amen.

18 I am giving you these instructions, Timothy, my child, in accordance with the prophecies made earlier about you, so that by following them you may fight the good fight, [19]having faith and a good conscience. By rejecting conscience, certain persons have suffered shipwreck in the faith; [20]among them are Hymenaeus and Alexander, whom I have turned over to Satan, so that they may learn not to blaspheme.

Instructions concerning Prayer

2 First of all, then, I urge that supplications, prayers, intercessions, and thanksgivings be made for everyone, [2]for kings and all who are in high positions, so that we may lead a quiet and peaceable life in all godliness and dignity. [3]This is right and is acceptable in the sight of God our Savior, [4]who desires everyone to be saved and to come to the knowledge of the truth. [5]For

there is one God;
      there is also one mediator between
         God and humankind,
      Christ Jesus, himself human,
[6]   who gave himself a ransom for all

—this was attested at the right time. [7]For this I was appointed a herald and an apostle (I am telling the truth,[c] I am not lying), a teacher of the Gentiles in faith and truth.

8 I desire, then, that in every place the men should pray, lifting up holy hands without anger or argument; [9]also that the women should dress themselves modestly and decently in suitable clothing, not with their hair braided, or with gold, pearls, or expensive clothes, [10]but with good works, as is proper for women who profess reverence for God. [11]Let a woman[d] learn in silence with full submission. [12]I permit no woman[d] to teach or to have authority over a man;[e] she is to keep silent. [13]For Adam was formed first, then Eve; [14]and Adam was not deceived, but the woman was deceived and became a transgressor. [15]Yet she will be saved through childbearing, provided they continue in faith and love and holiness, with modesty.

Qualifications of Bishops

3 The saying is sure:[f] whoever aspires to the office of bishop[g] desires a noble task. [2]Now a bishop[h] must be above

αἰῶνας τῶν αἰώνων, ἀμήν.

18 Ταύτην τὴν παραγγελίαν παρατίθεμαί σοι, τέκνον Τιμόθεε, κατὰ τὰς προαγούσας ἐπὶ σὲ προφητείας, ἵνα στρατεύῃ ἐν αὐταῖς τὴν καλὴν στρατείαν 19 ἔχων πίστιν καὶ ἀγαθὴν συνείδησιν, ἥν τινες ἀπωσάμενοι περὶ τὴν πίστιν ἐναυάγησαν. 20 ὧν ἐστιν Ὑμέναιος καὶ Ἀλέξανδρος, οὓς παρέδωκα τῷ Σατανᾷ, ἵνα παιδευθῶσιν μὴ βλασφημεῖν.

2 Παρακαλῶ οὖν πρῶτον πάντων ποιεῖσθαι δεήσεις προσευχὰς ἐντεύξεις εὐχαριστίας ὑπὲρ πάντων ἀνθρώπων, 2 ὑπὲρ βασιλέων καὶ πάντων τῶν ἐν ὑπεροχῇ ὄντων, ἵνα ἤρεμον καὶ ἡσύχιον βίον διάγωμεν ἐν πάσῃ εὐσεβείᾳ καὶ σεμνότητι. 3 τοῦτο καλὸν καὶ ἀπόδεκτον ἐνώπιον τοῦ σωτῆρος ἡμῶν θεοῦ, 4 ὃς πάντας ἀνθρώπους θέλει σωθῆναι καὶ εἰς ἐπίγνωσιν ἀληθείας ἐλθεῖν. 5 εἷς γὰρ θεός, εἷς καὶ μεσίτης θεοῦ καὶ ἀνθρώπων, ἄνθρωπος Χριστὸς Ἰησοῦς, 6 ὁ δοὺς ἑαυτὸν ἀντίλυτρον ὑπὲρ πάντων, τὸ μαρτύριον καιροῖς ἰδίοις. 7 εἰς ὃ ἐτέθην ἐγὼ κῆρυξ καὶ ἀπόστολος, ἀλήθειαν λέγω[a] οὐ ψεύδομαι, διδάσκαλος ἐθνῶν ἐν πίστει καὶ ἀληθείᾳ.

8 Βούλομαι οὖν προσεύχεσθαι τοὺς ἄνδρας ἐν παντὶ τόπῳ ἐπαίροντας ὁσίους χεῖρας χωρὶς ὀργῆς καὶ διαλογισμοῦ. 9 ὡσαύτως [καὶ] γυναῖκας ἐν καταστολῇ κοσμίῳ μετὰ αἰδοῦς καὶ σωφροσύνης κοσμεῖν ἑαυτάς, μὴ ἐν πλέγμασιν καὶ χρυσίῳ ἢ μαργαρίταις ἢ ἱματισμῷ πολυτελεῖ, 10 ἀλλ᾽ ὃ πρέπει γυναιξὶν ἐπαγγελλομέναις θεοσέβειαν, δι᾽ ἔργων ἀγαθῶν. 11 γυνὴ ἐν ἡσυχίᾳ μανθανέτω ἐν πάσῃ ὑποταγῇ· 12 διδάσκειν δὲ γυναικὶ οὐκ ἐπιτρέπω οὐδὲ αὐθεντεῖν ἀνδρός, ἀλλ᾽ εἶναι ἐν ἡσυχίᾳ. 13 Ἀδὰμ γὰρ πρῶτος ἐπλάσθη, εἶτα Εὔα. 14 καὶ Ἀδὰμ οὐκ ἠπατήθη, ἡ δὲ γυνὴ ἐξαπατηθεῖσα ἐν παραβάσει γέγονεν· 15 σωθήσεται δὲ διὰ τῆς τεκνογονίας, ἐὰν μείνωσιν ἐν πίστει καὶ ἀγάπῃ καὶ ἁγιασμῷ μετὰ σωφροσύνης· 1 πιστὸς[a] ὁ λόγος.

3 Εἴ τις ἐπισκοπῆς ὀρέγεται, καλοῦ ἔργου ἐπιθυμεῖ. 2 δεῖ οὖν τὸν ἐπίσκοπον

and glory for ever and ever. Amen.

[18]Timothy, my son, I give you this instruction in keeping with the prophecies once made about you, so that by following them you may fight the good fight, [19]holding on to faith and a good conscience. Some have rejected these and so have shipwrecked their faith. [20]Among them are Hymenaeus and Alexander, whom I have handed over to Satan to be taught not to blaspheme.

Instructions on Worship

2 I urge, then, first of all, that requests, prayers, intercession and thanksgiving be made for everyone— [2]for kings and all those in authority, that we may live peaceful and quiet lives in all godliness and holiness. [3]This is good, and pleases God our Savior, [4]who wants all men to be saved and to come to a knowledge of the truth. [5]For there is one God and one mediator between God and men, the man Christ Jesus, [6]who gave himself as a ransom for all men—the testimony given in its proper time. [7]And for this purpose I was appointed a herald and an apostle—I am telling the truth, I am not lying—and a teacher of the true faith to the Gentiles.

[8]I want men everywhere to lift up holy hands in prayer, without anger or disputing.

[9]I also want women to dress modestly, with decency and propriety, not with braided hair or gold or pearls or expensive clothes, [10]but with good deeds, appropriate for women who profess to worship God.

[11]A woman should learn in quietness and full submission. [12]I do not permit a woman to teach or to have authority over a man; she must be silent. [13]For Adam was formed first, then Eve. [14]And Adam was not the one deceived; it was the woman who was deceived and became a sinner. [15]But women[a] will be saved[b] through childbearing—if they continue in faith, love and holiness with propriety.

Overseers and Deacons

3 Here is a trustworthy saying: If anyone sets his heart on being an overseer,[a] he desires a noble task. [2]Now the overseer must be above reproach, the

---

[b] Gk *to the ages of the ages*   [c] Other ancient authorities add *in Christ*   [d] Or *wife*   [d] Or *wife*   [e] Or *her husband*   [f] Some interpreters place these words at the end of the previous paragraph. Other ancient authorities read *The saying is commonly accepted*   [g] Or *overseer*   [h] Or *an overseer*

[a]7 NRSV note c adds ἐν Χριστῷ   [a]1 NRSV note f ἀνθρώπινος

[a]15 Greek *she*   [b]15 Or *restored*   [a]1 Traditionally *bishop*; also in verse 2

reproach, married only once,[i] temperate, sensible, respectable, hospitable, an apt teacher, [3]not a drunkard, not violent but gentle, not quarrelsome, and not a lover of money. [4]He must manage his own household well, keeping his children submissive and respectful in every way— [5]for if someone does not know how to manage his own household, how can he take care of God's church? [6]He must not be a recent convert, or he may be puffed up with conceit and fall into the condemnation of the devil. [7]Moreover, he must be well thought of by outsiders, so that he may not fall into disgrace and the snare of the devil.

Qualifications of Deacons

[8] Deacons likewise must be serious, not double-tongued, not indulging in much wine, not greedy for money; [9]they must hold fast to the mystery of the faith with a clear conscience. [10]And let them first be tested; then, if they prove themselves blameless, let them serve as deacons. [11]Women[j] likewise must be serious, not slanderers, but temperate, faithful in all things. [12]Let deacons be married only once,[k] and let them manage their children and their households well; [13]for those who serve well as deacons gain a good standing for themselves and great boldness in the faith that is in Christ Jesus.

The Mystery of Our Religion

[14] I hope to come to you soon, but I am writing these instructions to you so that, [15]if I am delayed, you may know how one ought to behave in the household of God, which is the church of the living God, the pillar and bulwark of the truth. [16]Without any doubt, the mystery of our religion is great:

He[l] was revealed in flesh,
    vindicated[m] in spirit,[n]
      seen by angels,
proclaimed among Gentiles,
    believed in throughout the world,
      taken up in glory.

False Asceticism

4 Now the Spirit expressly says that in later[o] times some will renounce the faith by paying attention to deceitful spirits and teachings of demons, [2]through the hypocrisy of liars whose consciences are seared with a hot iron. [3]They forbid

ἀνεπίλημπτον εἶναι, μιᾶς γυναικὸς ἄνδρα, νηφάλιον σώφρονα κόσμιον φιλόξενον διδακτικόν, 3 μὴ πάροινον μὴ πλήκτην, ἀλλὰ ἐπιεικῆ ἄμαχον ἀφιλάργυρον, 4 τοῦ ἰδίου οἴκου καλῶς προϊστάμενον, τέκνα ἔχοντα ἐν ὑποταγῇ, μετὰ πάσης σεμνότητος (5 εἰ δέ τις τοῦ ἰδίου οἴκου προστῆναι οὐκ οἶδεν, πῶς ἐκκλησίας θεοῦ ἐπιμελήσεται;), 6 μὴ νεόφυτον, ἵνα μὴ τυφωθεὶς εἰς κρίμα ἐμπέσῃ τοῦ διαβόλου. 7 δεῖ δὲ καὶ μαρτυρίαν καλὴν ἔχειν ἀπὸ τῶν ἔξωθεν, ἵνα μὴ εἰς ὀνειδισμὸν ἐμπέσῃ καὶ παγίδα τοῦ διαβόλου.

8 Διακόνους ὡσαύτως σεμνούς, μὴ διλόγους, μὴ οἴνῳ πολλῷ προσέχοντας, μὴ αἰσχροκερδεῖς, 9 ἔχοντας τὸ μυστήριον τῆς πίστεως ἐν καθαρᾷ συνειδήσει. 10 καὶ οὗτοι δὲ δοκιμαζέσθωσαν πρῶτον, εἶτα διακονείτωσαν ἀνέγκλητοι ὄντες. 11 γυναῖκας ὡσαύτως σεμνάς, μὴ διαβόλους, νηφαλίους, πιστὰς ἐν πᾶσιν. 12 διάκονοι ἔστωσαν μιᾶς γυναικὸς ἄνδρες, τέκνων καλῶς προϊστάμενοι καὶ τῶν ἰδίων οἴκων. 13 οἱ γὰρ καλῶς διακονήσαντες βαθμὸν ἑαυτοῖς καλὸν περιποιοῦνται καὶ πολλὴν παρρησίαν ἐν πίστει τῇ ἐν Χριστῷ Ἰησοῦ.

14 Ταῦτά σοι γράφω ἐλπίζων ἐλθεῖν πρὸς σὲ ἐν τάχει· 15 ἐὰν δὲ βραδύνω, ἵνα εἰδῇς πῶς δεῖ ἐν οἴκῳ θεοῦ ἀναστρέφεσθαι, ἥτις ἐστὶν ἐκκλησία θεοῦ ζῶντος, στῦλος καὶ ἑδραίωμα τῆς ἀληθείας. 16 καὶ ὁμολογουμένως μέγα ἐστὶν τὸ τῆς εὐσεβείας μυστήριον·

Ὃς[b] ἐφανερώθη ἐν σαρκί,
    ἐδικαιώθη ἐν πνεύματι,
    ὤφθη ἀγγέλοις,
ἐκηρύχθη ἐν ἔθνεσιν,
    ἐπιστεύθη ἐν κόσμῳ,
    ἀνελήμφθη ἐν δόξῃ.

4 Τὸ δὲ πνεῦμα ῥητῶς λέγει ὅτι ἐν ὑστέροις καιροῖς ἀποστήσονταί τινες τῆς πίστεως προσέχοντες πνεύμασιν πλάνοις καὶ διδασκαλίαις δαιμονίων, 2 ἐν ὑποκρίσει ψευδολόγων, κεκαυστηριασμένων τὴν ἰδίαν συνείδησιν, 3 κωλυόντων γαμεῖν, ἀπέχεσθαι

husband of but one wife, temperate, self-controlled, respectable, hospitable, able to teach, [3]not given to drunkenness, not violent but gentle, not quarrelsome, not a lover of money. [4]He must manage his own family well and see that his children obey him with proper respect. [5](If anyone does not know how to manage his own family, how can he take care of God's church?) [6]He must not be a recent convert, or he may become conceited and fall under the same judgment as the devil. [7]He must also have a good reputation with outsiders, so that he will not fall into disgrace and into the devil's trap.

[8]Deacons, likewise, are to be men worthy of respect, sincere, not indulging in much wine, and not pursuing dishonest gain. [9]They must keep hold of the deep truths of the faith with a clear conscience. [10]They must first be tested; and then if there is nothing against them, let them serve as deacons.

[11]In the same way, their wives[b] are to be women worthy of respect, not malicious talkers but temperate and trustworthy in everything.

[12]A deacon must be the husband of but one wife and must manage his children and his household well. [13]Those who have served well gain an excellent standing and great assurance in their faith in Christ Jesus.

[14]Although I hope to come to you soon, I am writing you these instructions so that, [15]if I am delayed, you will know how people ought to conduct themselves in God's household, which is the church of the living God, the pillar and foundation of the truth. [16]Beyond all question, the mystery of godliness is great:

He[c] appeared in a body,[d]
    was vindicated by the Spirit,
was seen by angels,
    was preached among the nations,
was believed on in the world,
    was taken up in glory.

Instructions to Timothy

4 The Spirit clearly says that in later times some will abandon the faith and follow deceiving spirits and things taught by demons. [2]Such teachings come through hypocritical liars, whose consciences have been seared as with a hot iron. [3]They forbid people to marry and order them to

marriage and demand abstinence from foods, which God created to be received with thanksgiving by those who believe and know the truth. [4]For everything created by God is good, and nothing is to be rejected, provided it is received with thanksgiving; [5]for it is sanctified by God's word and by prayer.

A Good Minister of Jesus Christ

6 If you put these instructions before the brothers and sisters,[p] you will be a good servant[q] of Christ Jesus, nourished on the words of the faith and of the sound teaching that you have followed. [7]Have nothing to do with profane myths and old wives' tales. Train yourself in godliness, [8]for, while physical training is of some value, godliness is valuable in every way, holding promise for both the present life and the life to come. [9]The saying is sure and worthy of full acceptance. [10]For to this end we toil and struggle,[r] because we have our hope set on the living God, who is the Savior of all people, especially of those who believe.

11 These are the things you must insist on and teach. [12]Let no one despise your youth, but set the believers an example in speech and conduct, in love, in faith, in purity. [13]Until I arrive, give attention to the public reading of scripture,[s] to exhorting, to teaching. [14]Do not neglect the gift that is in you, which was given to you through prophecy with the laying on of hands by the council of elders.[t] [15]Put these things into practice, devote yourself to them, so that all may see your progress. [16]Pay close attention to yourself and to your teaching; continue in these things, for in doing this you will save both yourself and your hearers.

Duties toward Believers

5 Do not speak harshly to an older man,[u] but speak to him as to a father, to younger men as brothers, [2]to older women as mothers, to younger women as sisters—with absolute purity.

3 Honor widows who are really widows. [4]If a widow has children or grandchildren, they should first learn their religious duty to their own family and make some repayment to their parents; for this is pleasing in God's sight. [5]The real widow, left alone, has set her hope on God and continues in

βρωμάτων, ἃ ὁ θεὸς ἔκτισεν εἰς μετάλημψιν μετὰ εὐχαριστίας τοῖς πιστοῖς καὶ ἐπεγνωκόσι τὴν ἀλήθειαν. 4 ὅτι πᾶν κτίσμα θεοῦ καλὸν καὶ οὐδὲν ἀπόβλητον μετὰ εὐχαριστίας λαμβανόμενον· 5 ἁγιάζεται γὰρ διὰ λόγου θεοῦ καὶ ἐντεύξεως.

6 Ταῦτα ὑποτιθέμενος τοῖς ἀδελφοῖς καλὸς ἔσῃ διάκονος Χριστοῦ Ἰησοῦ, ἐντρεφόμενος τοῖς λόγοις τῆς πίστεως καὶ τῆς καλῆς διδασκαλίας ᾗ παρηκολούθηκας· 7 τοὺς δὲ βεβήλους καὶ γραώδεις μύθους παραιτοῦ. γύμναζε δὲ σεαυτὸν πρὸς εὐσέβειαν· 8 ἡ γὰρ σωματικὴ γυμνασία πρὸς ὀλίγον ἐστὶν ὠφέλιμος, ἡ δὲ εὐσέβεια πρὸς πάντα ὠφέλιμός ἐστιν ἐπαγγελίαν ἔχουσα ζωῆς τῆς νῦν καὶ τῆς μελλούσης. 9 πιστὸς ὁ λόγος καὶ πάσης ἀποδοχῆς ἄξιος· 10 εἰς τοῦτο γὰρ κοπιῶμεν καὶ ἀγωνιζόμεθα[a], ὅτι ἠλπίκαμεν ἐπὶ θεῷ ζῶντι, ὅς ἐστιν σωτὴρ πάντων ἀνθρώπων μάλιστα πιστῶν.

11 Παράγγελλε ταῦτα καὶ δίδασκε. 12 μηδείς σου τῆς νεότητος καταφρονείτω, ἀλλὰ τύπος γίνου τῶν πιστῶν ἐν λόγῳ, ἐν ἀναστροφῇ, ἐν ἀγάπῃ, ἐν πίστει, ἐν ἁγνείᾳ. 13 ἕως ἔρχομαι πρόσεχε τῇ ἀναγνώσει, τῇ παρακλήσει, τῇ διδασκαλίᾳ. 14 μὴ ἀμέλει τοῦ ἐν σοὶ χαρίσματος, ὃ ἐδόθη σοι διὰ προφητείας μετὰ ἐπιθέσεως τῶν χειρῶν τοῦ πρεσβυτερίου. 15 ταῦτα μελέτα, ἐν τούτοις ἴσθι, ἵνα σου ἡ προκοπὴ φανερὰ ᾖ πᾶσιν. 16 ἔπεχε σεαυτῷ καὶ τῇ διδασκαλίᾳ, ἐπίμενε αὐτοῖς· τοῦτο γὰρ ποιῶν καὶ σεαυτὸν σώσεις καὶ τοὺς ἀκούοντάς σου.

5 Πρεσβυτέρῳ μὴ ἐπιπλήξῃς ἀλλὰ παρακάλει ὡς πατέρα, νεωτέρους ὡς ἀδελφούς, 2 πρεσβυτέρας ὡς μητέρας, νεωτέρας ὡς ἀδελφὰς ἐν πάσῃ ἁγνείᾳ.

3 Χήρας τίμα τὰς ὄντως χήρας. 4 εἰ δέ τις χήρα τέκνα ἢ ἔκγονα ἔχει, μανθανέτωσαν πρῶτον τὸν ἴδιον οἶκον εὐσεβεῖν καὶ ἀμοιβὰς ἀποδιδόναι τοῖς προγόνοις· τοῦτο γάρ ἐστιν ἀπόδεκτον ἐνώπιον τοῦ θεοῦ. 5 ἡ δὲ ὄντως χήρα καὶ μεμονωμένη ἤλπικεν ἐπὶ θεὸν καὶ

abstain from certain foods, which God created to be received with thanksgiving by those who believe and who know the truth. [4]For everything God created is good, and nothing is to be rejected if it is received with thanksgiving, [5]because it is consecrated by the word of God and prayer.

[6]If you point these things out to the brothers, you will be a good minister of Christ Jesus, brought up in the truths of the faith and of the good teaching that you have followed. [7]Have nothing to do with godless myths and old wives' tales; rather, train yourself to be godly. [8]For physical training is of some value, but godliness has value for all things, holding promise for both the present life and the life to come.

[9]This is a trustworthy saying that deserves full acceptance [10](and for this we labor and strive), that we have put our hope in the living God, who is the Savior of all men, and especially of those who believe.

[11]Command and teach these things. [12]Don't let anyone look down on you because you are young, but set an example for the believers in speech, in life, in love, in faith and in purity. [13]Until I come, devote yourself to the public reading of Scripture, to preaching and to teaching. [14]Do not neglect your gift, which was given you through a prophetic message when the body of elders laid their hands on you.

[15]Be diligent in these matters; give yourself wholly to them, so that everyone may see your progress. [16]Watch your life and doctrine closely. Persevere in them, because if you do, you will save both yourself and your hearers.

Advice About Widows, Elders and Slaves

5 Do not rebuke an older man harshly, but exhort him as if he were your father. Treat younger men as brothers, [2]older women as mothers, and younger women as sisters, with absolute purity.

[3]Give proper recognition to those widows who are really in need. [4]But if a widow has children or grandchildren, these should learn first of all to put their religion into practice by caring for their own family and so repaying their parents and grandparents, for this is pleasing to God. [5]The widow who is really in need and left all alone puts her hope in God and continues

---

p Gk brothers q Or deacon r Other ancient authorities read suffer reproach s Gk to the reading t Gk by the presbytery u Or an elder, or a presbyter

a 10 NRSV note r ὀνειδιζόμεθα

supplications and prayers night and day; 6but the widow[v] who lives for pleasure is dead even while she lives. 7Give these commands as well, so that they may be above reproach. 8And whoever does not provide for relatives, and especially for family members, has denied the faith and is worse than an unbeliever.

9 Let a widow be put on the list if she is not less than sixty years old and has been married only once;[w] 10she must be well attested for her good works, as one who has brought up children, shown hospitality, washed the saints' feet, helped the afflicted, and devoted herself to doing good in every way. 11But refuse to put younger widows on the list; for when their sensual desires alienate them from Christ, they want to marry, 12and so they incur condemnation for having violated their first pledge. 13Besides that, they learn to be idle, gadding about from house to house; and they are not merely idle, but also gossips and busybodies, saying what they should not say. 14So I would have younger widows marry, bear children, and manage their households, so as to give the adversary no occasion to revile us. 15For some have already turned away to follow Satan. 16If any believing woman[x] has relatives who are really widows, let her assist them; let the church not be burdened, so that it can assist those who are real widows.

17 Let the elders who rule well be considered worthy of double honor,[y] especially those who labor in preaching and teaching; 18for the scripture says, "You shall not muzzle an ox while it is treading out the grain," and, "The laborer deserves to be paid." 19Never accept any accusation against an elder except on the evidence of two or three witnesses. 20As for those who persist in sin, rebuke them in the presence of all, so that the rest also may stand in fear. 21In the presence of God and of Christ Jesus and of the elect angels, I warn you to keep these instructions without prejudice, doing nothing on the basis of partiality. 22Do not ordain[z] anyone hastily, and do not participate in the sins of others; keep yourself pure.

προσμένει ταῖς δεήσεσιν καὶ ταῖς προσευχαῖς νυκτὸς καὶ ἡμέρας, 6 ἡ δὲ σπαταλῶσα ζῶσα τέθνηκεν. 7 καὶ ταῦτα παράγγελλε, ἵνα ἀνεπίλημπτοι ὦσιν. 8 εἰ δέ τις τῶν ἰδίων καὶ μάλιστα οἰκείων οὐ προνοεῖ, τὴν πίστιν ἤρνηται καὶ ἔστιν ἀπίστου χείρων. 9 Χήρα καταλεγέσθω μὴ ἔλαττον ἐτῶν ἑξήκοντα γεγονυῖα, ἑνὸς ἀνδρὸς γυνή, 10 ἐν ἔργοις καλοῖς μαρτυρουμένη, εἰ ἐτεκνοτρόφησεν, εἰ ἐξενοδόχησεν, εἰ ἁγίων πόδας ἔνιψεν, εἰ θλιβομένοις ἐπήρκεσεν, εἰ παντὶ ἔργῳ ἀγαθῷ ἐπηκολούθησεν. 11 νεωτέρας δὲ χήρας παραιτοῦ· ὅταν γὰρ καταστρηνιάσωσιν τοῦ Χριστοῦ, γαμεῖν θέλουσιν 12 ἔχουσαι κρίμα ὅτι τὴν πρώτην πίστιν ἠθέτησαν· 13 ἅμα δὲ καὶ ἀργαὶ μανθάνουσιν περιερχόμεναι τὰς οἰκίας, οὐ μόνον δὲ ἀργαὶ ἀλλὰ καὶ φλύαροι καὶ περίεργοι, λαλοῦσαι τὰ μὴ δέοντα. 14 βούλομαι οὖν νεωτέρας γαμεῖν, τεκνογονεῖν, οἰκοδεσποτεῖν, μηδεμίαν ἀφορμὴν διδόναι τῷ ἀντικειμένῳ λοιδορίας χάριν· 15 ἤδη γάρ τινες ἐξετράπησαν ὀπίσω τοῦ Σατανᾶ. 16 εἴ τις πιστὴ[a] ἔχει χήρας, ἐπαρκείτω αὐταῖς καὶ μὴ βαρείσθω ἡ ἐκκλησία, ἵνα ταῖς ὄντως χήραις ἐπαρκέσῃ.

17 Οἱ καλῶς προεστῶτες πρεσβύτεροι διπλῆς τιμῆς ἀξιούσθωσαν, μάλιστα οἱ κοπιῶντες ἐν λόγῳ καὶ διδασκαλίᾳ. 18 λέγει γὰρ ἡ γραφή, Βοῦν ἀλοῶντα οὐ φιμώσεις, καί, Ἄξιος ὁ ἐργάτης τοῦ μισθοῦ αὐτοῦ. 19 κατὰ πρεσβυτέρου κατηγορίαν μὴ παραδέχου, ἐκτὸς εἰ μὴ ἐπὶ δύο ἢ τριῶν μαρτύρων. 20 τοὺς ἁμαρτάνοντας ἐνώπιον πάντων ἔλεγχε, ἵνα καὶ οἱ λοιποὶ φόβον ἔχωσιν. 21 Διαμαρτύρομαι ἐνώπιον τοῦ θεοῦ καὶ Χριστοῦ Ἰησοῦ καὶ τῶν ἐκλεκτῶν ἀγγέλων, ἵνα ταῦτα φυλάξῃς χωρὶς προκρίματος, μηδὲν ποιῶν κατὰ πρόσκλισιν. 22 Χεῖρας ταχέως μηδενὶ ἐπιτίθει μηδὲ κοινώνει ἁμαρτίαις ἀλλοτρίαις· σεαυτὸν ἁγνὸν τήρει.

night and day to pray and to ask God for help. 6But the widow who lives for pleasure is dead even while she lives. 7Give the people these instructions, too, so that no one may be open to blame. 8If anyone does not provide for his relatives, and especially for his immediate family, he has denied the faith and is worse than an unbeliever.

9No widow may be put on the list of widows unless she is over sixty, has been faithful to her husband,[a] 10and is well known for her good deeds, such as bringing up children, showing hospitality, washing the feet of the saints, helping those in trouble and devoting herself to all kinds of good deeds.

11As for younger widows, do not put them on such a list. For when their sensual desires overcome their dedication to Christ, they want to marry. 12Thus they bring judgment on themselves, because they have broken their first pledge. 13Besides, they get into the habit of being idle and going about from house to house. And not only do they become idlers, but also gossips and busybodies, saying things they ought not to. 14So I counsel younger widows to marry, to have children, to manage their homes and to give the enemy no opportunity for slander. 15Some have in fact already turned away to follow Satan.

16If any woman who is a believer has widows in her family, she should help them and not let the church be burdened with them, so that the church can help those widows who are really in need.

17The elders who direct the affairs of the church well are worthy of double honor, especially those whose work is preaching and teaching. 18For the Scripture says, "Do not muzzle the ox while it is treading out the grain,"[b] and "The worker deserves his wages."[c] 19Do not entertain an accusation against an elder unless it is brought by two or three witnesses. 20Those who sin are to be rebuked publicly, so that the others may take warning.

21I charge you, in the sight of God and Christ Jesus and the elect angels, to keep these instructions without partiality, and to do nothing out of favoritism.

22Do not be hasty in the laying on of hands, and do not share in the sins of others. Keep yourself pure.

---

v Gk she   w Gk the wife of one husband   x Other ancient authorities read believing man or woman; others, believing man   y Or compensation   z Gk Do not lay hands on

a16 NRSV note x πιστὸς ἢ πιστὴ or πιστὸς

a9 Or has had but one husband   b18 Deut. 25:4   c18 Luke 10:7

23 No longer drink only water, but take a little wine for the sake of your stomach and your frequent ailments.

24 The sins of some people are conspicuous and precede them to judgment, while the sins of others follow them there. 25So also good works are conspicuous; and even when they are not, they cannot remain hidden.

6 Let all who are under the yoke of slavery regard their masters as worthy of all honor, so that the name of God and the teaching may not be blasphemed. 2Those who have believing masters must not be disrespectful to them on the ground that they are members of the church;a rather they must serve them all the more, since those who benefit by their service are believers and beloved.b

False Teaching and True Riches

Teach and urge these duties. 3Whoever teaches otherwise and does not agree with the sound words of our Lord Jesus Christ and the teaching that is in accordance with godliness, 4is conceited, understanding nothing, and has a morbid craving for controversy and for disputes about words. From these come envy, dissension, slander, base suspicions, 5and wrangling among those who are depraved in mind and bereft of the truth, imagining that godliness is a means of gain.c 6Of course, there is great gain in godliness combined with contentment; 7for we brought nothing into the world, so thatd we can take nothing out of it; 8but if we have food and clothing, we will be content with these. 9But those who want to be rich fall into temptation and are trapped by many senseless and harmful desires that plunge people into ruin and destruction. 10For the love of money is a root of all kinds of evil, and in their eagerness to be rich some have wandered away from the faith and pierced themselves with many pains.

The Good Fight of Faith

11 But as for you, man of God, shun all this; pursue righteousness, godliness, faith, love, endurance, gentleness. 12Fight the good fight of the faith; take hold of the eternal life, to which you were called and for which you madee the good confession in the presence of many witnesses. 13In the

23 Μηκέτι ὑδροπότει, ἀλλὰ οἴνῳ ὀλίγῳ χρῶ διὰ τὸν στόμαχον καὶ τὰς πυκνάς σου ἀσθενείας.

24 Τινῶν ἀνθρώπων αἱ ἁμαρτίαι πρόδηλοί εἰσιν προάγουσαι εἰς κρίσιν, τισὶν δὲ καὶ ἐπακολουθοῦσιν· 25 ὡσαύτως καὶ τὰ ἔργα τὰ καλὰ πρόδηλα, καὶ τὰ ἄλλως ἔχοντα κρυβῆναι οὐ δύνανται.

6 Ὅσοι εἰσὶν ὑπὸ ζυγὸν δοῦλοι, τοὺς ἰδίους δεσπότας πάσης τιμῆς ἀξίους ἡγείσθωσαν, ἵνα μὴ τὸ ὄνομα τοῦ θεοῦ καὶ ἡ διδασκαλία βλασφημῆται. 2 οἱ δὲ πιστοὺς ἔχοντες δεσπότας μὴ καταφρονείτωσαν, ὅτι ἀδελφοί εἰσιν, ἀλλὰ μᾶλλον δουλευέτωσαν, ὅτι πιστοί εἰσιν καὶ ἀγαπητοὶ οἱ τῆς εὐεργεσίας ἀντιλαμβανόμενοι.

Ταῦτα δίδασκε καὶ παρακάλει. 3 εἴ τις ἑτεροδιδασκαλεῖ καὶ μὴ προσέρχεται ὑγιαίνουσιν λόγοις τοῖς τοῦ κυρίου ἡμῶν Ἰησοῦ Χριστοῦ καὶ τῇ κατ’ εὐσέβειαν διδασκαλίᾳ, 4 τετύφωται, μηδὲν ἐπιστάμενος, ἀλλὰ νοσῶν περὶ ζητήσεις καὶ λογομαχίας, ἐξ ὧν γίνεται φθόνος ἔρις βλασφημίαι, ὑπόνοιαι πονηραί, 5 διαπαρατριβαὶ διεφθαρμένων ἀνθρώπων τὸν νοῦν καὶ ἀπεστερημένων τῆς ἀληθείας, νομιζόντων πορισμὸν εἶναι τὴν εὐσέβειαν.ᵃ 6 ἔστιν δὲ πορισμὸς μέγας ἡ εὐσέβεια μετὰ αὐταρκείας· 7 οὐδὲν γὰρ εἰσηνέγκαμεν εἰς τὸν κόσμον,ᵇ ὅτι οὐδὲ ἐξενεγκεῖν τι δυνάμεθα· 8 ἔχοντες δὲ διατροφὰς καὶ σκεπάσματα, τούτοις ἀρκεσθησόμεθα. 9 οἱ δὲ βουλόμενοι πλουτεῖν ἐμπίπτουσιν εἰς πειρασμὸν καὶ παγίδα καὶ ἐπιθυμίας πολλὰς ἀνοήτους καὶ βλαβεράς, αἵτινες βυθίζουσιν τοὺς ἀνθρώπους εἰς ὄλεθρον καὶ ἀπώλειαν. 10 ῥίζα γὰρ πάντων τῶν κακῶν ἐστιν ἡ φιλαργυρία, ἧς τινες ὀρεγόμενοι ἀπεπλανήθησαν ἀπὸ τῆς πίστεως καὶ ἑαυτοὺς περιέπειραν ὀδύναις πολλαῖς.

11 Σὺ δέ, ὦ ἄνθρωπε θεοῦ, ταῦτα φεῦγε· δίωκε δὲ δικαιοσύνην εὐσέβειαν πίστιν, ἀγάπην ὑπομονὴν πραϋπαθίαν. 12 ἀγωνίζου τὸν καλὸν ἀγῶνα τῆς πίστεως, ἐπιλαβοῦ τῆς αἰωνίου ζωῆς, εἰς ἣν ἐκλήθης καὶ ὡμολόγησας τὴν καλὴν ὁμολογίαν ἐνώπιον πολλῶν μαρτύρων. 13 παραγγέλλω [σοι] ἐνώπιον

23Stop drinking only water, and use a little wine because of your stomach and your frequent illnesses.

24The sins of some men are obvious, reaching the place of judgment ahead of them; the sins of others trail behind them. 25In the same way, good deeds are obvious, and even those that are not cannot be hidden.

6 All who are under the yoke of slavery should consider their masters worthy of full respect, so that God's name and our teaching may not be slandered. 2Those who have believing masters are not to show less respect for them because they are brothers. Instead, they are to serve them even better, because those who benefit from their service are believers, and dear to them. These are the things you are to teach and urge on them.

Love of Money

3If anyone teaches false doctrines and does not agree to the sound instruction of our Lord Jesus Christ and to godly teaching, 4he is conceited and understands nothing. He has an unhealthy interest in controversies and quarrels about words that result in envy, strife, malicious talk, evil suspicions 5and constant friction between men of corrupt mind, who have been robbed of the truth and who think that godliness is a means to financial gain.

6But godliness with contentment is great gain. 7For we brought nothing into the world, and we can take nothing out of it. 8But if we have food and clothing, we will be content with that. 9People who want to get rich fall into temptation and a trap and into many foolish and harmful desires that plunge men into ruin and destruction. 10For the love of money is a root of all kinds of evil. Some people, eager for money, have wandered from the faith and pierced themselves with many griefs.

Paul's Charge to Timothy

11But you, man of God, flee from all this, and pursue righteousness, godliness, faith, love, endurance and gentleness. 12Fight the good fight of the faith. Take hold of the eternal life to which you were called when you made your good confession in the presence of many witnesses. 13In the sight of

---

a Gk *are brothers*   b Or *since they are believers and beloved, who devote themselves to good deeds*   c Other ancient authorities add *Withdraw yourself from such people*   d Other ancient authorities read *world—it is certain that*   e Gk *confessed*

a5 NRSV note c adds ἀφίστασο ἀπὸ τῶν τοιούτων
b7 NRSV note d adds δῆλον

presence of God, who gives life to all things, and of Christ Jesus, who in his testimony before Pontius Pilate made the good confession, I charge you [14]to keep the commandment without spot or blame until the manifestation of our Lord Jesus Christ, [15]which he will bring about at the right time—he who is the blessed and only Sovereign, the King of kings and Lord of lords. [16]It is he alone who has immortality and dwells in unapproachable light, whom no one has ever seen or can see; to him be honor and eternal dominion. Amen.

[17] As for those who in the present age are rich, command them not to be haughty, or to set their hopes on the uncertainty of riches, but rather on God who richly provides us with everything for our enjoyment. [18]They are to do good, to be rich in good works, generous, and ready to share, [19]thus storing up for themselves the treasure of a good foundation for the future, so that they may take hold of the life that really is life.

Personal Instructions and Benediction

[20] Timothy, guard what has been entrusted to you. Avoid the profane chatter and contradictions of what is falsely called knowledge; [21]by professing it some have missed the mark as regards the faith.

   Grace be with you.[f]

τοῦ θεοῦ τοῦ ζῳογονοῦντος τὰ πάντα καὶ Χριστοῦ Ἰησοῦ τοῦ μαρτυρήσαντος ἐπὶ Ποντίου Πιλάτου τὴν καλὴν ὁμολογίαν, **14** τηρῆσαί σε τὴν ἐντολὴν ἄσπιλον ἀνεπίλημπτον μέχρι τῆς ἐπιφανείας τοῦ κυρίου ἡμῶν Ἰησοῦ Χριστοῦ, **15** ἣν καιροῖς ἰδίοις δείξει ὁ μακάριος καὶ μόνος δυνάστης, ὁ βασιλεὺς τῶν βασιλευόντων καὶ κύριος τῶν κυριευόντων, **16** ὁ μόνος ἔχων ἀθανασίαν, φῶς οἰκῶν ἀπρόσιτον, ὃν εἶδεν οὐδεὶς ἀνθρώπων οὐδὲ ἰδεῖν δύναται· ᾧ τιμὴ καὶ κράτος αἰώνιον, ἀμήν.

17 Τοῖς πλουσίοις ἐν τῷ νῦν αἰῶνι παράγγελλε μὴ ὑψηλοφρονεῖν μηδὲ ἠλπικέναι ἐπὶ πλούτου ἀδηλότητι ἀλλ᾽ ἐπὶ θεῷ τῷ παρέχοντι ἡμῖν πάντα πλουσίως εἰς ἀπόλαυσιν, **18** ἀγαθοεργεῖν, πλουτεῖν ἐν ἔργοις καλοῖς, εὐμεταδότους εἶναι, κοινωνικούς, **19** ἀποθησαυρίζοντας ἑαυτοῖς θεμέλιον καλὸν εἰς τὸ μέλλον, ἵνα ἐπιλάβωνται τῆς ὄντως ζωῆς.

20 Ὦ Τιμόθεε, τὴν παραθήκην φύλαξον ἐκτρεπόμενος τὰς βεβήλους κενοφωνίας καὶ ἀντιθέσεις τῆς ψευδωνύμου γνώσεως, **21** ἥν τινες ἐπαγγελλόμενοι περὶ τὴν πίστιν ἠστόχησαν.

   Ἡ χάρις μεθ᾽ ὑμῶν.[c]

God, who gives life to everything, and of Christ Jesus, who while testifying before Pontius Pilate made the good confession, I charge you [14]to keep this command without spot or blame until the appearing of our Lord Jesus Christ, [15]which God will bring about in his own time—God, the blessed and only Ruler, the King of kings and Lord of lords, [16]who alone is immortal and who lives in unapproachable light, whom no one has seen or can see. To him be honor and might forever. Amen.

[17]Command those who are rich in this present world not to be arrogant nor to put their hope in wealth, which is so uncertain, but to put their hope in God, who richly provides us with everything for our enjoyment. [18]Command them to do good, to be rich in good deeds, and to be generous and willing to share. [19]In this way they will lay up treasure for themselves as a firm foundation for the coming age, so that they may take hold of the life that is truly life.

[20]Timothy, guard what has been entrusted to your care. Turn away from godless chatter and the opposing ideas of what is falsely called knowledge, [21]which some have professed and in so doing have wandered from the faith.

   Grace be with you.

---

[f]The Greek word for *you* here is plural; in other ancient authorities it is singular. Other ancient authorities add *Amen*

[c]21 NRSV note f reads μετὰ σοῦ and adds ἀμήν.

ΠΡΟΣ ΤΙΜΟΘΕΟΝ Β

NRSV

Salutation

1 Paul, an apostle of Christ Jesus by the will of God, for the sake of the promise of life that is in Christ Jesus,

2 To Timothy, my beloved child:

Grace, mercy, and peace from God the Father and Christ Jesus our Lord.

Thanksgiving and Encouragement

3 I am grateful to God—whom I worship with a clear conscience, as my ancestors did—when I remember you constantly in my prayers night and day. 4Recalling your tears, I long to see you so that I may be filled with joy. 5I am reminded of your sincere faith, a faith that lived first in your grandmother Lois and your mother Eunice and now, I am sure, lives in you. 6For this reason I remind you to rekindle the gift of God that is within you through the laying on of my hands; 7for God did not give us a spirit of cowardice, but rather a spirit of power and of love and of self-discipline.

8 Do not be ashamed, then, of the testimony about our Lord or of me his prisoner, but join with me in suffering for the gospel, relying on the power of God, 9who saved us and called us with a holy calling, not according to our works but according to his own purpose and grace. This grace was given to us in Christ Jesus before the ages began, 10but it has now been revealed through the appearing of our Savior Christ Jesus, who abolished death and brought life and immortality to light through the gospel. 11For this gospel I was appointed a herald and an apostle and a teacher,[a] 12and for this reason I suffer as I do. But I am not ashamed, for I know the one in whom I have put my trust, and I am sure that he is able to guard until that day what I have entrusted to him.[b] 13Hold to the standard of sound teaching that you have heard from me, in the faith and love that are in Christ Jesus. 14Guard the good treasure entrusted to you, with the help of the Holy Spirit living in us.

15 You are aware that all who are in Asia have turned away from me, including Phygelus and Hermogenes. 16May the Lord grant mercy to the household of Onesiphorus, because he often refreshed me and was not ashamed of my chain; 17when he arrived in Rome, he eagerly[c] searched for me and found me 18—may the Lord grant

Greek

1 Παῦλος ἀπόστολος Χριστοῦ Ἰησοῦ διὰ θελήματος θεοῦ κατ' ἐπαγγελίαν ζωῆς τῆς ἐν Χριστῷ Ἰησοῦ **2** Τιμοθέῳ ἀγαπητῷ τέκνῳ, χάρις ἔλεος εἰρήνη ἀπὸ θεοῦ πατρὸς καὶ Χριστοῦ Ἰησοῦ τοῦ κυρίου ἡμῶν.

3 Χάριν ἔχω τῷ θεῷ, ᾧ λατρεύω ἀπὸ προγόνων ἐν καθαρᾷ συνειδήσει, ὡς ἀδιάλειπτον ἔχω τὴν περὶ σοῦ μνείαν ἐν ταῖς δεήσεσίν μου νυκτὸς καὶ ἡμέρας, **4** ἐπιποθῶν σε ἰδεῖν, μεμνημένος σου τῶν δακρύων, ἵνα χαρᾶς πληρωθῶ, **5** ὑπόμνησιν λαβὼν τῆς ἐν σοὶ ἀνυποκρίτου πίστεως, ἥτις ἐνῴκησεν πρῶτον ἐν τῇ μάμμῃ σου Λωΐδι καὶ τῇ μητρί σου Εὐνίκῃ, πέπεισμαι δὲ ὅτι καὶ ἐν σοί. **6** δι' ἣν αἰτίαν ἀναμιμνῄσκω σε ἀναζωπυρεῖν τὸ χάρισμα τοῦ θεοῦ, ὅ ἐστιν ἐν σοὶ διὰ τῆς ἐπιθέσεως τῶν χειρῶν μου. **7** οὐ γὰρ ἔδωκεν ἡμῖν ὁ θεὸς πνεῦμα δειλίας ἀλλὰ δυνάμεως καὶ ἀγάπης καὶ σωφρονισμοῦ. **8** μὴ οὖν ἐπαισχυνθῇς τὸ μαρτύριον τοῦ κυρίου ἡμῶν μηδὲ ἐμὲ τὸν δέσμιον αὐτοῦ, ἀλλὰ συγκακοπάθησον τῷ εὐαγγελίῳ κατὰ δύναμιν θεοῦ, **9** τοῦ σώσαντος ἡμᾶς καὶ καλέσαντος κλήσει ἁγίᾳ, οὐ κατὰ τὰ ἔργα ἡμῶν ἀλλὰ κατὰ ἰδίαν πρόθεσιν καὶ χάριν, τὴν δοθεῖσαν ἡμῖν ἐν Χριστῷ Ἰησοῦ πρὸ χρόνων αἰωνίων, **10** φανερωθεῖσαν δὲ νῦν διὰ τῆς ἐπιφανείας τοῦ σωτῆρος ἡμῶν Χριστοῦ Ἰησοῦ, καταργήσαντος μὲν τὸν θάνατον φωτίσαντος δὲ ζωὴν καὶ ἀφθαρσίαν διὰ τοῦ εὐαγγελίου **11** εἰς ὃ ἐτέθην ἐγὼ κῆρυξ καὶ ἀπόστολος καὶ διδάσκαλος[a], **12** δι' ἣν αἰτίαν καὶ ταῦτα πάσχω· ἀλλ' οὐκ ἐπαισχύνομαι, οἶδα γὰρ ᾧ πεπίστευκα καὶ πέπεισμαι ὅτι δυνατός ἐστιν τὴν παραθήκην μου φυλάξαι εἰς ἐκείνην τὴν ἡμέραν. **13** ὑποτύπωσιν ἔχε ὑγιαινόντων λόγων ὧν παρ' ἐμοῦ ἤκουσας ἐν πίστει καὶ ἀγάπῃ τῇ ἐν Χριστῷ Ἰησοῦ· **14** τὴν καλὴν παραθήκην φύλαξον διὰ πνεύματος ἁγίου τοῦ ἐνοικοῦντος ἐν ἡμῖν.

15 Οἶδας τοῦτο, ὅτι ἀπεστράφησάν με πάντες οἱ ἐν τῇ Ἀσίᾳ, ὧν ἐστιν Φύγελος καὶ Ἑρμογένης. **16** δῴη ἔλεος ὁ κύριος τῷ Ὀνησιφόρου οἴκῳ, ὅτι πολλάκις με ἀνέψυξεν καὶ τὴν ἅλυσίν μου οὐκ ἐπαισχύνθη, **17** ἀλλὰ γενόμενος ἐν Ῥώμῃ σπουδαίως ἐζήτησέν με καὶ εὗρεν· **18** δῴη αὐτῷ ὁ κύριος εὑρεῖν

NIV

1 Paul, an apostle of Christ Jesus by the will of God, according to the promise of life that is in Christ Jesus,

2To Timothy, my dear son:

Grace, mercy and peace from God the Father and Christ Jesus our Lord.

Encouragement to Be Faithful

3I thank God, whom I serve, as my forefathers did, with a clear conscience, as night and day I constantly remember you in my prayers. 4Recalling your tears, I long to see you, so that I may be filled with joy. 5I have been reminded of your sincere faith, which first lived in your grandmother Lois and in your mother Eunice and, I am persuaded, now lives in you also. 6For this reason I remind you to fan into flame the gift of God, which is in you through the laying on of my hands. 7For God did not give us a spirit of timidity, but a spirit of power, of love and of self-discipline.

8So do not be ashamed to testify about our Lord, or ashamed of me his prisoner. But join with me in suffering for the gospel, by the power of God, 9who has saved us and called us to a holy life—not because of anything we have done but because of his own purpose and grace. This grace was given us in Christ Jesus before the beginning of time, 10but it has now been revealed through the appearing of our Savior, Christ Jesus, who has destroyed death and has brought life and immortality to light through the gospel. 11And of this gospel I was appointed a herald and an apostle and a teacher. 12That is why I am suffering as I am. Yet I am not ashamed, because I know whom I have believed, and am convinced that he is able to guard what I have entrusted to him for that day.

13What you heard from me, keep as the pattern of sound teaching, with faith and love in Christ Jesus. 14Guard the good deposit that was entrusted to you—guard it with the help of the Holy Spirit who lives in us.

15You know that everyone in the province of Asia has deserted me, including Phygelus and Hermogenes.

16May the Lord show mercy to the household of Onesiphorus, because he often refreshed me and was not ashamed of my chains. 17On the contrary, when he was in Rome, he searched hard for me until he found me. 18May the Lord grant that he

---

a11 NRSV note a adds ἐθνῶν

that he will find mercy from the Lord on that day! And you know very well how much service he rendered in Ephesus.

A Good Soldier of Christ Jesus

2 You then, my child, be strong in the grace that is in Christ Jesus; [2]and what you have heard from me through many witnesses entrust to faithful people who will be able to teach others as well. [3]Share in suffering like a good soldier of Christ Jesus. [4]No one serving in the army gets entangled in everyday affairs; the soldier's aim is to please the enlisting officer. [5]And in the case of an athlete, no one is crowned without competing according to the rules. [6]It is the farmer who does the work who ought to have the first share of the crops. [7]Think over what I say, for the Lord will give you understanding in all things.

8 Remember Jesus Christ, raised from the dead, a descendant of David—that is my gospel, [9]for which I suffer hardship, even to the point of being chained like a criminal. But the word of God is not chained. [10]Therefore I endure everything for the sake of the elect, so that they may also obtain the salvation that is in Christ Jesus, with eternal glory. [11]The saying is sure:

If we have died with him, we will also
    live with him;
[12] if we endure, we will also reign with
    him;
if we deny him, he will also deny us;
[13] if we are faithless, he remains
    faithful—
for he cannot deny himself.

A Worker Approved by God

14 Remind them of this, and warn them before God[d] that they are to avoid wrangling over words, which does no good but only ruins those who are listening. [15]Do your best to present yourself to God as one approved by him, a worker who has no need to be ashamed, rightly explaining the word of truth. [16]Avoid profane chatter, for it will lead people into more and more impiety, [17]and their talk will spread like gangrene. Among them are Hymenaeus and Philetus, [18]who have swerved from the truth by claiming that the resurrection has already taken place. They are upsetting the faith of some. [19]But God's firm foundation stands, bearing this inscription:

ἔλεος παρὰ κυρίου ἐν ἐκείνῃ τῇ ἡμέρᾳ. καὶ ὅσα ἐν Ἐφέσῳ διηκόνησεν, βέλτιον σὺ γινώσκεις.

2 Σὺ οὖν, τέκνον μου, ἐνδυναμοῦ ἐν τῇ χάριτι τῇ ἐν Χριστῷ Ἰησοῦ, 2 καὶ ἃ ἤκουσας παρ' ἐμοῦ διὰ πολλῶν μαρτύρων, ταῦτα παράθου πιστοῖς ἀνθρώποις, οἵτινες ἱκανοὶ ἔσονται καὶ ἑτέρους διδάξαι. 3 συγκακοπάθησον ὡς καλὸς στρατιώτης Χριστοῦ Ἰησοῦ. 4 οὐδεὶς στρατευόμενος ἐμπλέκεται ταῖς τοῦ βίου πραγματείαις, ἵνα τῷ στρατολογήσαντι ἀρέσῃ. 5 ἐὰν δὲ καὶ ἀθλῇ τις, οὐ στεφανοῦται ἐὰν μὴ νομίμως ἀθλήσῃ. 6 τὸν κοπιῶντα γεωργὸν δεῖ πρῶτον τῶν καρπῶν μεταλαμβάνειν. 7 νόει ὃ λέγω· δώσει γάρ σοι ὁ κύριος σύνεσιν ἐν πᾶσιν.

8 Μνημόνευε Ἰησοῦν Χριστὸν ἐγηγερμένον ἐκ νεκρῶν, ἐκ σπέρματος Δαυίδ, κατὰ τὸ εὐαγγέλιόν μου, 9 ἐν ᾧ κακοπαθῶ μέχρι δεσμῶν ὡς κακοῦργος, ἀλλὰ ὁ λόγος τοῦ θεοῦ οὐ δέδεται· 10 διὰ τοῦτο πάντα ὑπομένω διὰ τοὺς ἐκλεκτούς, ἵνα καὶ αὐτοὶ σωτηρίας τύχωσιν τῆς ἐν Χριστῷ Ἰησοῦ μετὰ δόξης αἰωνίου. 11 πιστὸς ὁ λόγος·
    εἰ γὰρ συναπεθάνομεν, καὶ
        συζήσομεν·
12 εἰ ὑπομένομεν, καὶ συμβασιλεύσομεν·
    εἰ ἀρνησόμεθα, κἀκεῖνος ἀρνήσεται
        ἡμᾶς·
13 εἰ ἀπιστοῦμεν, ἐκεῖνος πιστὸς μένει,
    ἀρνήσασθαι γὰρ ἑαυτὸν οὐ δύναται.

14 Ταῦτα ὑπομίμνῃσκε διαμαρτυρόμενος ἐνώπιον τοῦ θεοῦ[a] μὴ λογομαχεῖν, ἐπ' οὐδὲν χρήσιμον, ἐπὶ καταστροφῇ τῶν ἀκουόντων. 15 σπούδασον σεαυτὸν δόκιμον παραστῆσαι τῷ θεῷ, ἐργάτην ἀνεπαίσχυντον, ὀρθοτομοῦντα τὸν λόγον τῆς ἀληθείας. 16 τὰς δὲ βεβήλους κενοφωνίας περιΐστασο· ἐπὶ πλεῖον γὰρ προκόψουσιν ἀσεβείας 17 καὶ ὁ λόγος αὐτῶν ὡς γάγγραινα νομὴν ἕξει. ὧν ἐστιν Ὑμέναιος καὶ Φίλητος, 18 οἵτινες περὶ τὴν ἀλήθειαν ἠστόχησαν, λέγοντες [τὴν] ἀνάστασιν ἤδη γεγονέναι, καὶ ἀνατρέπουσιν τήν τινων πίστιν. 19 ὁ μέντοι στερεὸς θεμέλιος τοῦ θεοῦ ἕστηκεν, ἔχων τὴν σφραγῖδα

will find mercy from the Lord on that day! You know very well in how many ways he helped me in Ephesus.

2 You then, my son, be strong in the grace that is in Christ Jesus. [2]And the things you have heard me say in the presence of many witnesses entrust to reliable men who will also be qualified to teach others. [3]Endure hardship with us like a good soldier of Christ Jesus. [4]No one serving as a soldier gets involved in civilian affairs—he wants to please his commanding officer. [5]Similarly, if anyone competes as an athlete, he does not receive the victor's crown unless he competes according to the rules. [6]The hardworking farmer should be the first to receive a share of the crops. [7]Reflect on what I am saying, for the Lord will give you insight into all this.

[8]Remember Jesus Christ, raised from the dead, descended from David. This is my gospel, [9]for which I am suffering even to the point of being chained like a criminal. But God's word is not chained. [10]Therefore I endure everything for the sake of the elect, that they too may obtain the salvation that is in Christ Jesus, with eternal glory.

[11]Here is a trustworthy saying:

If we died with him,
    we will also live with him;
[12]if we endure,
    we will also reign with him.
If we disown him,
    he will also disown us;
[13]if we are faithless,
    he will remain faithful,
for he cannot disown himself.

A Workman Approved by God

[14]Keep reminding them of these things. Warn them before God against quarreling about words; it is of no value, and only ruins those who listen. [15]Do your best to present yourself to God as one approved, a workman who does not need to be ashamed and who correctly handles the word of truth. [16]Avoid godless chatter, because those who indulge in it will become more and more ungodly. [17]Their teaching will spread like gangrene. Among them are Hymenaeus and Philetus, [18]who have wandered away from the truth. They say that the resurrection has already taken place, and they destroy the faith of some. [19]Nevertheless, God's solid foundation stands firm, sealed with this inscription:

---

[d] Other ancient authorities read *the Lord*   [a]14 NRSV note d κυρίου

"The Lord knows those who are his," and, "Let everyone who calls on the name of the Lord turn away from wickedness."

20 In a large house there are utensils not only of gold and silver but also of wood and clay, some for special use, some for ordinary. 21All who cleanse themselves of the things I have mentioned[e] will become special utensils, dedicated and useful to the owner of the house, ready for every good work. 22Shun youthful passions and pursue righteousness, faith, love, and peace, along with those who call on the Lord from a pure heart. 23Have nothing to do with stupid and senseless controversies; you know that they breed quarrels. 24And the Lord's servant[f] must not be quarrelsome but kindly to everyone, an apt teacher, patient, 25correcting opponents with gentleness. God may perhaps grant that they will repent and come to know the truth, 26and that they may escape from the snare of the devil, having been held captive by him to do his will.[g]

Godlessness in the Last Days

3 You must understand this, that in the last days distressing times will come. 2For people will be lovers of themselves, lovers of money, boasters, arrogant, abusive, disobedient to their parents, ungrateful, unholy, 3inhuman, implacable, slanderers, profligates, brutes, haters of good, 4treacherous, reckless, swollen with conceit, lovers of pleasure rather than lovers of God, 5holding to the outward form of godliness but denying its power. Avoid them! 6For among them are those who make their way into households and captivate silly women, overwhelmed by their sins and swayed by all kinds of desires, 7who are always being instructed and can never arrive at a knowledge of the truth. 8As Jannes and Jambres opposed Moses, so these people, of corrupt mind and counterfeit faith, also oppose the truth. 9But they will not make much progress, because, as in the case of those two men,[h] their folly will become plain to everyone.

Paul's Charge to Timothy

10 Now you have observed my teaching, my conduct, my aim in life, my faith, my patience, my love, my steadfastness, 11my persecutions and suffering the things that happened to me in Antioch, Iconium, and

ταύτην· Ἔγνω κύριος τοὺς ὄντας αὐτοῦ, καί, Ἀποστήτω ἀπὸ ἀδικίας πᾶς ὁ ὀνομάζων τὸ ὄνομα κυρίου. 20 Ἐν μεγάλῃ δὲ οἰκίᾳ οὐκ ἔστιν μόνον σκεύη χρυσᾶ καὶ ἀργυρᾶ ἀλλὰ καὶ ξύλινα καὶ ὀστράκινα, καὶ ἃ μὲν εἰς τιμὴν ἃ δὲ εἰς ἀτιμίαν· 21 ἐὰν οὖν τις ἐκκαθάρῃ ἑαυτὸν ἀπὸ τούτων, ἔσται σκεῦος εἰς τιμήν, ἡγιασμένον, εὔχρηστον τῷ δεσπότῃ, εἰς πᾶν ἔργον ἀγαθὸν ἡτοιμασμένον. 22 τὰς δὲ νεωτερικὰς ἐπιθυμίας φεῦγε, δίωκε δὲ δικαιοσύνην πίστιν ἀγάπην εἰρήνην μετὰ τῶν ἐπικαλουμένων τὸν κύριον ἐκ καθαρᾶς καρδίας. 23 τὰς δὲ μωρὰς καὶ ἀπαιδεύτους ζητήσεις παραιτοῦ, εἰδὼς ὅτι γεννῶσιν μάχας· 24 δοῦλον δὲ κυρίου οὐ δεῖ μάχεσθαι ἀλλὰ ἤπιον εἶναι πρὸς πάντας, διδακτικόν, ἀνεξίκακον, 25 ἐν πραΰτητι παιδεύοντα τοὺς ἀντιδιατιθεμένους, μήποτε δώῃ αὐτοῖς ὁ θεὸς μετάνοιαν εἰς ἐπίγνωσιν ἀληθείας 26 καὶ ἀνανήψωσιν ἐκ τῆς τοῦ διαβόλου παγίδος, ἐζωγρημένοι ὑπ' αὐτοῦ εἰς τὸ ἐκείνου θέλημα.

3 Τοῦτο δὲ γίνωσκε, ὅτι ἐν ἐσχάταις ἡμέραις ἐνστήσονται καιροὶ χαλεποί· 2 ἔσονται γὰρ οἱ ἄνθρωποι φίλαυτοι φιλάργυροι ἀλαζόνες ὑπερήφανοι βλάσφημοι, γονεῦσιν ἀπειθεῖς, ἀχάριστοι ἀνόσιοι 3 ἄστοργοι ἄσπονδοι διάβολοι ἀκρατεῖς ἀνήμεροι ἀφιλάγαθοι 4 προδόται προπετεῖς τετυφωμένοι, φιλήδονοι μᾶλλον ἢ φιλόθεοι, 5 ἔχοντες μόρφωσιν εὐσεβείας τὴν δὲ δύναμιν αὐτῆς ἠρνημένοι· καὶ τούτους ἀποτρέπου. 6 ἐκ τούτων γάρ εἰσιν οἱ ἐνδύνοντες εἰς τὰς οἰκίας καὶ αἰχμαλωτίζοντες γυναικάρια σεσωρευμένα ἁμαρτίαις, ἀγόμενα ἐπιθυμίαις ποικίλαις, 7 πάντοτε μανθάνοντα καὶ μηδέποτε εἰς ἐπίγνωσιν ἀληθείας ἐλθεῖν δυνάμενα. 8 ὃν τρόπον δὲ Ἰάννης καὶ Ἰαμβρῆς ἀντέστησαν Μωϋσεῖ, οὕτως καὶ οὗτοι ἀνθίστανται τῇ ἀληθείᾳ, ἄνθρωποι κατεφθαρμένοι τὸν νοῦν, ἀδόκιμοι περὶ τὴν πίστιν. 9 ἀλλ' οὐ προκόψουσιν ἐπὶ πλεῖον· ἡ γὰρ ἄνοια αὐτῶν ἔκδηλος ἔσται πᾶσιν, ὡς καὶ ἡ ἐκείνων ἐγένετο.

10 Σὺ δὲ παρηκολούθησάς μου τῇ διδασκαλίᾳ, τῇ ἀγωγῇ, τῇ προθέσει, τῇ πίστει, τῇ μακροθυμίᾳ, τῇ ἀγάπῃ, τῇ ὑπομονῇ, 11 τοῖς διωγμοῖς, τοῖς παθήμασιν, οἷά μοι ἐγένετο ἐν Ἀντιοχείᾳ, ἐν Ἰκονίῳ, ἐν Λύστροις, οἵους

"The Lord knows those who are his,"[a] and, "Everyone who confesses the name of the Lord must turn away from wickedness."

20In a large house there are articles not only of gold and silver, but also of wood and clay; some are for noble purposes and some for ignoble. 21If a man cleanses himself from the latter, he will be an instrument for noble purposes, made holy, useful to the Master and prepared to do any good work.

22Flee the evil desires of youth, and pursue righteousness, faith, love and peace, along with those who call on the Lord out of a pure heart. 23Don't have anything to do with foolish and stupid arguments, because you know they produce quarrels. 24And the Lord's servant must not quarrel; instead, he must be kind to everyone, able to teach, not resentful. 25Those who oppose him he must gently instruct, in the hope that God will grant them repentance leading them to a knowledge of the truth, 26and that they will come to their senses and escape from the trap of the devil, who has taken them captive to do his will.

Godlessness in the Last Days

3 But mark this: There will be terrible times in the last days. 2People will be lovers of themselves, lovers of money, boastful, proud, abusive, disobedient to their parents, ungrateful, unholy, 3without love, unforgiving, slanderous, without self-control, brutal, not lovers of the good, 4treacherous, rash, conceited, lovers of pleasure rather than lovers of God— 5having a form of godliness but denying its power. Have nothing to do with them.

6They are the kind who worm their way into homes and gain control over weak-willed women, who are loaded down with sins and are swayed by all kinds of evil desires, 7always learning but never able to acknowledge the truth. 8Just as Jannes and Jambres opposed Moses, so also these men oppose the truth—men of depraved minds, who, as far as the faith is concerned, are rejected. 9But they will not get very far because, as in the case of those men, their folly will be clear to everyone.

Paul's Charge to Timothy

10You, however, know all about my teaching, my way of life, my purpose, faith, patience, love, endurance, 11persecutions, sufferings—what kinds of things happened to me in Antioch, Iconium and Lystra, the

---

e Gk of these things   f Gk slave   g Or by him, to do his (that is, God's) will   h Gk lacks two men

a19 Num. 16:5 (see Septuagint)

Lystra. What persecutions I endured! Yet the Lord rescued me from all of them. [12]Indeed, all who want to live a godly life in Christ Jesus will be persecuted. [13]But wicked people and impostors will go from bad to worse, deceiving others and being deceived. [14]But as for you, continue in what you have learned and firmly believed, knowing from whom you learned it, [15]and how from childhood you have known the sacred writings that are able to instruct you for salvation through faith in Christ Jesus. [16]All scripture is inspired by God and is[i] useful for teaching, for reproof, for correction, and for training in righteousness, [17]so that everyone who belongs to God may be proficient, equipped for every good work.

4 In the presence of God and of Christ Jesus, who is to judge the living and the dead, and in view of his appearing and his kingdom, I solemnly urge you: [2]proclaim the message; be persistent whether the time is favorable or unfavorable; convince, rebuke, and encourage, with the utmost patience in teaching. [3]For the time is coming when people will not put up with sound doctrine, but having itching ears, they will accumulate for themselves teachers to suit their own desires, [4]and will turn away from listening to the truth and wander away to myths. [5]As for you, always be sober, endure suffering, do the work of an evangelist, carry out your ministry fully.

6 As for me, I am already being poured out as a libation, and the time of my departure has come. [7]I have fought the good fight, I have finished the race, I have kept the faith. [8]From now on there is reserved for me the crown of righteousness, which the Lord, the righteous judge, will give me on that day, and not only to me but also to all who have longed for his appearing.

Personal Instructions

9 Do your best to come to me soon, [10]for Demas, in love with this present world, has deserted me and gone to Thessalonica; Crescens has gone to Galatia,[j] Titus to Dalmatia. [11]Only Luke is with me. Get Mark and bring him with you, for he is useful in my ministry. [12]I have sent Tychicus to Ephesus. [13]When you come, bring the cloak that I left with Carpus at Troas, also the books, and above all the parchments. [14]Alexander the coppersmith did

διωγμοὺς ὑπήνεγκα καὶ ἐκ πάντων με ἐρρύσατο ὁ κύριος. **12** καὶ πάντες δὲ οἱ θέλοντες εὐσεβῶς ζῆν ἐν Χριστῷ Ἰησοῦ διωχθήσονται. **13** πονηροὶ δὲ ἄνθρωποι καὶ γόητες προκόψουσιν ἐπὶ τὸ χεῖρον πλανῶντες καὶ πλανώμενοι. **14** σὺ δὲ μένε ἐν οἷς ἔμαθες καὶ ἐπιστώθης, εἰδὼς παρὰ τίνων ἔμαθες, **15** καὶ ὅτι ἀπὸ βρέφους [τὰ] ἱερὰ γράμματα οἶδας, τὰ δυνάμενά σε σοφίσαι εἰς σωτηρίαν διὰ πίστεως τῆς ἐν Χριστῷ Ἰησοῦ. **16** πᾶσα γραφὴ θεόπνευστος καὶ ὠφέλιμος πρὸς διδασκαλίαν, πρὸς ἐλεγμόν, πρὸς ἐπανόρθωσιν, πρὸς παιδείαν τὴν ἐν δικαιοσύνῃ, **17** ἵνα ἄρτιος ᾖ ὁ τοῦ θεοῦ ἄνθρωπος, πρὸς πᾶν ἔργον ἀγαθὸν ἐξηρτισμένος.

4 Διαμαρτύρομαι ἐνώπιον τοῦ θεοῦ καὶ Χριστοῦ Ἰησοῦ τοῦ μέλλοντος κρίνειν ζῶντας καὶ νεκρούς, καὶ τὴν ἐπιφάνειαν αὐτοῦ καὶ τὴν βασιλείαν αὐτοῦ· **2** κήρυξον τὸν λόγον, ἐπίστηθι εὐκαίρως ἀκαίρως, ἔλεγξον, ἐπιτίμησον, παρακάλεσον, ἐν πάσῃ μακροθυμίᾳ καὶ διδαχῇ. **3** ἔσται γὰρ καιρὸς ὅτε τῆς ὑγιαινούσης διδασκαλίας οὐκ ἀνέξονται ἀλλὰ κατὰ τὰς ἰδίας ἐπιθυμίας ἑαυτοῖς ἐπισωρεύσουσιν διδασκάλους κνηθόμενοι τὴν ἀκοὴν **4** καὶ ἀπὸ μὲν τῆς ἀληθείας τὴν ἀκοὴν ἀποστρέψουσιν, ἐπὶ δὲ τοὺς μύθους ἐκτραπήσονται. **5** σὺ δὲ νῆφε ἐν πᾶσιν, κακοπάθησον, ἔργον ποίησον εὐαγγελιστοῦ, τὴν διακονίαν σου πληροφόρησον.

6 Ἐγὼ γὰρ ἤδη σπένδομαι, καὶ ὁ καιρὸς τῆς ἀναλύσεώς μου ἐφέστηκεν. **7** τὸν καλὸν ἀγῶνα ἠγώνισμαι, τὸν δρόμον τετέλεκα, τὴν πίστιν τετήρηκα· **8** λοιπὸν ἀπόκειταί μοι ὁ τῆς δικαιοσύνης στέφανος, ὃν ἀποδώσει μοι ὁ κύριος ἐν ἐκείνῃ τῇ ἡμέρᾳ, ὁ δίκαιος κριτής, οὐ μόνον δὲ ἐμοὶ ἀλλὰ καὶ πᾶσι τοῖς ἠγαπηκόσι τὴν ἐπιφάνειαν αὐτοῦ.

9 Σπούδασον ἐλθεῖν πρός με ταχέως· **10** Δημᾶς γάρ με ἐγκατέλιπεν ἀγαπήσας τὸν νῦν αἰῶνα καὶ ἐπορεύθη εἰς Θεσσαλονίκην, Κρήσκης εἰς Γαλατίαν[a], Τίτος εἰς Δαλματίαν· **11** Λουκᾶς ἐστιν μόνος μετ' ἐμοῦ. Μᾶρκον ἀναλαβὼν ἄγε μετὰ σεαυτοῦ, ἔστιν γάρ μοι εὔχρηστος εἰς διακονίαν. **12** Τυχικὸν δὲ ἀπέστειλα εἰς Ἔφεσον. **13** τὸν φαιλόνην ὃν ἀπέλιπον ἐν Τρῳάδι παρὰ Κάρπῳ ἐρχόμενος φέρε, καὶ τὰ βιβλία μάλιστα τὰς μεμβράνας. **14** Ἀλέξανδρος ὁ

persecutions I endured. Yet the Lord rescued me from all of them. [12]In fact, everyone who wants to live a godly life in Christ Jesus will be persecuted, [13]while evil men and impostors will go from bad to worse, deceiving and being deceived. [14]But as for you, continue in what you have learned and have become convinced of, because you know those from whom you learned it, [15]and how from infancy you have known the holy Scriptures, which are able to make you wise for salvation through faith in Christ Jesus. [16]All Scripture is God-breathed and is useful for teaching, rebuking, correcting and training in righteousness, [17]so that the man of God may be thoroughly equipped for every good work.

4 In the presence of God and of Christ Jesus, who will judge the living and the dead, and in view of his appearing and his kingdom, I give you this charge: [2]Preach the Word; be prepared in season and out of season; correct, rebuke and encourage—with great patience and careful instruction. [3]For the time will come when men will not put up with sound doctrine. Instead, to suit their own desires, they will gather around them a great number of teachers to say what their itching ears want to hear. [4]They will turn their ears away from the truth and turn aside to myths. [5]But you, keep your head in all situations, endure hardship, do the work of an evangelist, discharge all the duties of your ministry.

[6]For I am already being poured out like a drink offering, and the time has come for my departure. [7]I have fought the good fight, I have finished the race, I have kept the faith. [8]Now there is in store for me the crown of righteousness, which the Lord, the righteous Judge, will award to me on that day—and not only to me, but also to all who have longed for his appearing.

Personal Remarks

[9]Do your best to come to me quickly, [10]for Demas, because he loved this world, has deserted me and has gone to Thessalonica. Crescens has gone to Galatia, and Titus to Dalmatia. [11]Only Luke is with me. Get Mark and bring him with you, because he is helpful to me in my ministry. [12]I sent Tychicus to Ephesus. [13]When you come, bring the cloak that I left with Carpus at Troas, and my scrolls, especially the parchments. [14]Alexander the metalworker did me a

i Or *Every scripture inspired by God is also*   j Other ancient authorities read *Gaul*   a 10 NRSV note j Γαλλίαν

me great harm; the Lord will pay him back for his deeds. [15]You also must beware of him, for he strongly opposed our message.

16 At my first defense no one came to my support, but all deserted me. May it not be counted against them! [17]But the Lord stood by me and gave me strength, so that through me the message might be fully proclaimed and all the Gentiles might hear it. So I was rescued from the lion's mouth. [18]The Lord will rescue me from every evil attack and save me for his heavenly kingdom. To him be the glory forever and ever. Amen.

Final Greetings and Benediction

19 Greet Prisca and Aquila, and the household of Onesiphorus. [20]Erastus remained in Corinth; Trophimus I left ill in Miletus. [21]Do your best to come before winter. Eubulus sends greetings to you, as do Pudens and Linus and Claudia and all the brothers and sisters.[k]

22 The Lord be with your spirit. Grace be with you.[l]

χαλκεὺς πολλά μοι κακὰ ἐνεδείξατο· ἀποδώσει αὐτῷ ὁ κύριος κατὰ τὰ ἔργα αὐτοῦ· 15 ὃν καὶ σὺ φυλάσσου, λίαν γὰρ ἀντέστη τοῖς ἡμετέροις λόγοις.

16 Ἐν τῇ πρώτῃ μου ἀπολογίᾳ οὐδείς μοι παρεγένετο, ἀλλὰ πάντες με ἐγκατέλιπον· μὴ αὐτοῖς λογισθείη· 17 ὁ δὲ κύριός μοι παρέστη καὶ ἐνεδυνά-μωσέν με, ἵνα δι' ἐμοῦ τὸ κήρυγμα πληροφορηθῇ καὶ ἀκούσωσιν πάντα τὰ ἔθνη, καὶ ἐρρύσθην ἐκ στόματος λέοντος. 18 ῥύσεταί με ὁ κύριος ἀπὸ παντὸς ἔργου πονηροῦ καὶ σώσει εἰς τὴν βασιλείαν αὐτοῦ τὴν ἐπουράνιον· ᾧ ἡ δόξα εἰς τοὺς αἰῶνας τῶν αἰώνων, ἀμήν.

19 Ἄσπασαι Πρίσκαν καὶ Ἀκύλαν καὶ τὸν Ὀνησιφόρου οἶκον. 20 Ἔραστος ἔμεινεν ἐν Κορίνθῳ, Τρόφιμον δὲ ἀπέλιπον ἐν Μιλήτῳ ἀσθενοῦντα. 21 Σπούδασον πρὸ χειμῶνος ἐλθεῖν. Ἀσπάζεταί σε Εὔβουλος καὶ Πούδης καὶ Λίνος καὶ Κλαυδία καὶ οἱ ἀδελφοὶ πάντες. 22 Ὁ κύριος μετὰ τοῦ πνεύμα-τός σου. ἡ χάρις μεθ' ὑμῶν.[b]

great deal of harm. The Lord will repay him for what he has done. [15]You too should be on your guard against him, because he strongly opposed our message.

[16]At my first defense, no one came to my support, but everyone deserted me. May it not be held against them. [17]But the Lord stood at my side and gave me strength, so that through me the message might be fully proclaimed and all the Gentiles might hear it. And I was delivered from the lion's mouth. [18]The Lord will rescue me from every evil attack and will bring me safely to his heavenly kingdom. To him be glory for ever and ever. Amen.

Final Greetings

[19]Greet Priscilla[a] and Aquila and the household of Onesiphorus. [20]Erastus stayed in Corinth, and I left Trophimus sick in Miletus. [21]Do your best to get here before winter. Eubulus greets you, and so do Pudens, Linus, Claudia and all the brothers.

[22]The Lord be with your spirit. Grace be with you.

---

k Gk all the brothers   l The Greek word for you here is plural. Other ancient authorities add Amen   b22 NRSV note l adds ἀμήν.   a19 Greek Prisca, a variant of Priscilla

Salutation

1 Paul, a servant[a] of God and an apostle of Jesus Christ, for the sake of the faith of God's elect and the knowledge of the truth that is in accordance with godliness, [2]in the hope of eternal life that God, who never lies, promised before the ages began— [3]in due time he revealed his word through the proclamation with which I have been entrusted by the command of God our Savior,

4 To Titus, my loyal child in the faith we share:

Grace[b] and peace from God the Father and Christ Jesus our Savior.

Titus in Crete

5 I left you behind in Crete for this reason, so that you should put in order what remained to be done, and should appoint elders in every town, as I directed you: [6]someone who is blameless, married only once,[c] whose children are believers, not accused of debauchery and not rebellious. [7]For a bishop,[d] as God's steward, must be blameless; he must not be arrogant or quick-tempered or addicted to wine or violent or greedy for gain; [8]but he must be hospitable, a lover of goodness, prudent, upright, devout, and self-controlled. [9]He must have a firm grasp of the word that is trustworthy in accordance with the teaching, so that he may be able both to preach with sound doctrine and to refute those who contradict it.

10 There are also many rebellious people, idle talkers and deceivers, especially those of the circumcision; [11]they must be silenced, since they are upsetting whole families by teaching for sordid gain what it is not right to teach. [12]It was one of them, their very own prophet, who said,

"Cretans are always liars, vicious
    brutes, lazy gluttons."

[13]That testimony is true. For this reason rebuke them sharply, so that they may become sound in the faith, [14]not paying attention to Jewish myths or to commandments of those who reject the truth. [15]To the pure all things are pure, but to the corrupt and unbelieving nothing is pure. Their very minds and consciences are corrupted. [16]They profess to know God, but they deny him by their actions. They are detestable, disobedient, unfit for any good work.

ΠΡΟΣ ΤΙΤΟΝ

1 Παῦλος δοῦλος θεοῦ, ἀπόστολος δὲ Ἰησοῦ Χριστοῦ κατὰ πίστιν ἐκλεκτῶν θεοῦ καὶ ἐπίγνωσιν ἀληθείας τῆς κατ᾽ εὐσέβειαν **2** ἐπ᾽ ἐλπίδι ζωῆς αἰωνίου, ἣν ἐπηγγείλατο ὁ ἀψευδὴς θεὸς πρὸ χρόνων αἰωνίων, **3** ἐφανέρωσεν δὲ καιροῖς ἰδίοις τὸν λόγον αὐτοῦ ἐν κηρύγματι, ὃ ἐπιστεύθην ἐγὼ κατ᾽ ἐπιταγὴν τοῦ σωτῆρος ἡμῶν θεοῦ, **4** Τίτῳ γνησίῳ τέκνῳ κατὰ κοινὴν πίστιν, χάρις καὶ[a] εἰρήνη ἀπὸ θεοῦ πατρὸς καὶ Χριστοῦ Ἰησοῦ τοῦ σωτῆρος ἡμῶν.

5 Τούτου χάριν ἀπέλιπόν σε ἐν Κρήτῃ, ἵνα τὰ λείποντα ἐπιδιορθώσῃ καὶ καταστήσῃς κατὰ πόλιν πρεσβυτέρους, ὡς ἐγώ σοι διεταξάμην, **6** εἴ τίς ἐστιν ἀνέγκλητος, μιᾶς γυναικὸς ἀνήρ, τέκνα ἔχων πιστά, μὴ ἐν κατηγορίᾳ ἀσωτίας ἢ ἀνυπότακτα. **7** δεῖ γὰρ τὸν ἐπίσκοπον ἀνέγκλητον εἶναι ὡς θεοῦ οἰκονόμον, μὴ αὐθάδη, μὴ ὀργίλον, μὴ πάροινον, μὴ πλήκτην, μὴ αἰσχροκερδῆ, **8** ἀλλὰ φιλόξενον φιλάγαθον σώφρονα δίκαιον ὅσιον ἐγκρατῆ, **9** ἀντεχόμενον τοῦ κατὰ τὴν διδαχὴν πιστοῦ λόγου, ἵνα δυνατὸς ᾖ καὶ παρακαλεῖν ἐν τῇ διδασκαλίᾳ τῇ ὑγιαινούσῃ καὶ τοὺς ἀντιλέγοντας ἐλέγχειν.

10 Εἰσὶν γὰρ πολλοὶ [καὶ][b] ἀνυπότακτοι, ματαιολόγοι καὶ φρεναπάται, μάλιστα οἱ ἐκ τῆς περιτομῆς, **11** οὓς δεῖ ἐπιστομίζειν, οἵτινες ὅλους οἴκους ἀνατρέπουσιν διδάσκοντες ἃ μὴ δεῖ αἰσχροῦ κέρδους χάριν. **12** εἶπέν τις ἐξ αὐτῶν ἴδιος αὐτῶν προφήτης,

Κρῆτες ἀεὶ ψεῦσται, κακὰ θηρία, γαστέρες ἀργαί.

13 ἡ μαρτυρία αὕτη ἐστὶν ἀληθής. δι᾽ ἣν αἰτίαν ἔλεγχε αὐτοὺς ἀποτόμως, ἵνα ὑγιαίνωσιν ἐν τῇ πίστει, **14** μὴ προσέχοντες Ἰουδαϊκοῖς μύθοις καὶ ἐντολαῖς ἀνθρώπων ἀποστρεφομένων τὴν ἀλήθειαν. **15** πάντα καθαρὰ τοῖς καθαροῖς· τοῖς δὲ μεμιαμμένοις καὶ ἀπίστοις οὐδὲν καθαρόν, ἀλλὰ μεμίανται αὐτῶν καὶ ὁ νοῦς καὶ ἡ συνείδησις. **16** θεὸν ὁμολογοῦσιν εἰδέναι, τοῖς δὲ ἔργοις ἀρνοῦνται, βδελυκτοὶ ὄντες καὶ ἀπειθεῖς καὶ πρὸς πᾶν ἔργον ἀγαθὸν ἀδόκιμοι.

NIV

1 Paul, a servant of God and an apostle of Jesus Christ for the faith of God's elect and the knowledge of the truth that leads to godliness— [2]a faith and knowledge resting on the hope of eternal life, which God, who does not lie, promised before the beginning of time, [3]and at his appointed season he brought his word to light through the preaching entrusted to me by the command of God our Savior,

[4]To Titus, my true son in our common faith:

Grace and peace from God the Father and Christ Jesus our Savior.

Titus' Task on Crete

[5]The reason I left you in Crete was that you might straighten out what was left unfinished and appoint[a] elders in every town, as I directed you. [6]An elder must be blameless, the husband of but one wife, a man whose children believe and are not open to the charge of being wild and disobedient. [7]Since an overseer[b] is entrusted with God's work, he must be blameless— not overbearing, not quick-tempered, not given to drunkenness, not violent, not pursuing dishonest gain. [8]Rather he must be hospitable, one who loves what is good, who is self-controlled, upright, holy and disciplined. [9]He must hold firmly to the trustworthy message as it has been taught, so that he can encourage others by sound doctrine and refute those who oppose it.

[10]For there are many rebellious people, mere talkers and deceivers, especially those of the circumcision group. [11]They must be silenced, because they are ruining whole households by teaching things they ought not to teach—and that for the sake of dishonest gain. [12]Even one of their own prophets has said, "Cretans are always liars, evil brutes, lazy gluttons." [13]This testimony is true. Therefore, rebuke them sharply, so that they will be sound in the faith [14]and will pay no attention to Jewish myths or to the commands of those who reject the truth. [15]To the pure, all things are pure, but to those who are corrupted and do not believe, nothing is pure. In fact, both their minds and consciences are corrupted. [16]They claim to know God, but by their actions they deny him. They are detestable, disobedient and unfit for doing anything good.

---

[a] Gk *slave*   [b] Other ancient authorities read *Grace, mercy*,   [c] Gk *husband of one wife*   [d] Or *an overseer*

[a]4 NRSV note b reads ἔλεος in place of καὶ   [b]10 NIV text omits καὶ

[a]5 Or *ordain*   [b]7 Traditionally *bishop*

NRSV

Teach Sound Doctrine

2 But as for you, teach what is consistent with sound doctrine. ²Tell the older men to be temperate, serious, prudent, and sound in faith, in love, and in endurance.

3 Likewise, tell the older women to be reverent in behavior, not to be slanderers or slaves to drink; they are to teach what is good, ⁴so that they may encourage the young women to love their husbands, to love their children, ⁵to be self-controlled, chaste, good managers of the household, kind, being submissive to their husbands, so that the word of God may not be discredited.

6 Likewise, urge the younger men to be self-controlled. ⁷Show yourself in all respects a model of good works, and in your teaching show integrity, gravity, ⁸and sound speech that cannot be censured; then any opponent will be put to shame, having nothing evil to say of us.

9 Tell slaves to be submissive to their masters and to give satisfaction in every respect; they are not to talk back, ¹⁰not to pilfer, but to show complete and perfect fidelity, so that in everything they may be an ornament to the doctrine of God our Savior.

11 For the grace of God has appeared, bringing salvation to all,ᵉ ¹²training us to renounce impiety and worldly passions, and in the present age to live lives that are self-controlled, upright, and godly, ¹³while we wait for the blessed hope and the manifestation of the glory of our great God and Savior,ᶠ Jesus Christ. ¹⁴He it is who gave himself for us that he might redeem us from all iniquity and purify for himself a people of his own who are zealous for good deeds.

15 Declare these things; exhort and reprove with all authority.ᵍ Let no one look down on you.

Maintain Good Deeds

3 Remind them to be subject to rulers and authorities, to be obedient, to be ready for every good work, ²to speak evil of no one, to avoid quarreling, to be gentle, and to show every courtesy to everyone. ³For we ourselves were once foolish, disobedient, led astray, slaves to various passions and pleasures, passing our days in malice and envy, despicable, hating one

Greek

2 Σὺ δὲ λάλει ἃ πρέπει τῇ ὑγιαινούσῃ διδασκαλίᾳ. **2** πρεσβύτας νηφαλίους εἶναι, σεμνούς, σώφρονας, ὑγιαίνοντας τῇ πίστει, τῇ ἀγάπῃ, τῇ ὑπομονῇ· **3** πρεσβύτιδας ὡσαύτως ἐν καταστήματι ἱεροπρεπεῖς, μὴ διαβόλους μηδὲ οἴνῳ πολλῷ δεδουλωμένας, καλοδιδασκάλους, **4** ἵνα σωφρονίζωσιν τὰς νέας φιλάνδρους εἶναι, φιλοτέκνους **5** σώφρονας ἁγνὰς οἰκουργούς ἀγαθάς, ὑποτασσομένας τοῖς ἰδίοις ἀνδράσιν, ἵνα μὴ ὁ λόγος τοῦ θεοῦ βλασφημῆται. **6** τοὺς νεωτέρους ὡσαύτως παρακάλει σωφρονεῖν **7** περὶ πάντα, σεαυτὸν παρεχόμενος τύπον καλῶν ἔργων, ἐν τῇ διδασκαλίᾳ ἀφθορίαν, σεμνότητα, **8** λόγον ὑγιῆ ἀκατάγνωστον, ἵνα ὁ ἐξ ἐναντίας ἐντραπῇ μηδὲν ἔχων λέγειν περὶ ἡμῶν φαῦλον. **9** δούλους ἰδίοις δεσπόταις ὑποτάσσεσθαι ἐν πᾶσιν, εὐαρέστους εἶναι, μὴ ἀντιλέγοντας, **10** μὴ νοσφιζομένους, ἀλλὰ πᾶσαν πίστιν ἐνδεικνυμένους ἀγαθήν, ἵνα τὴν διδασκαλίαν τὴν τοῦ σωτῆρος ἡμῶν θεοῦ κοσμῶσιν ἐν πᾶσιν.

11 Ἐπεφάνη γὰρ ἡ χάρις τοῦ θεοῦ σωτήριος πᾶσιν ἀνθρώποις **12** παιδεύουσα ἡμᾶς, ἵνα ἀρνησάμενοι τὴν ἀσέβειαν καὶ τὰς κοσμικὰς ἐπιθυμίας σωφρόνως καὶ δικαίως καὶ εὐσεβῶς ζήσωμεν ἐν τῷ νῦν αἰῶνι, **13** προσδεχόμενοι τὴν μακαρίαν ἐλπίδα καὶ ἐπιφάνειαν τῆς δόξης τοῦ μεγάλου θεοῦ καὶ σωτῆρος ἡμῶν Ἰησοῦ Χριστοῦ, **14** ὃς ἔδωκεν ἑαυτὸν ὑπὲρ ἡμῶν, ἵνα λυτρώσηται ἡμᾶς ἀπὸ πάσης ἀνομίας καὶ καθαρίσῃ ἑαυτῷ λαὸν περιούσιον, ζηλωτὴν καλῶν ἔργων. **15** Ταῦτα λάλει καὶ παρακάλει καὶ ἔλεγχε μετὰ πάσης ἐπιταγῆς· μηδείς σου περιφρονείτω.

3 Ὑπομίμνησκε αὐτοὺς ἀρχαῖς ἐξουσίαις ὑποτάσσεσθαι, πειθαρχεῖν, πρὸς πᾶν ἔργον ἀγαθὸν ἑτοίμους εἶναι, **2** μηδένα βλασφημεῖν, ἀμάχους εἶναι, ἐπιεικεῖς, πᾶσαν ἐνδεικνυμένους πραΰτητα πρὸς πάντας ἀνθρώπους. **3** Ἦμεν γάρ ποτε καὶ ἡμεῖς ἀνόητοι, ἀπειθεῖς, πλανώμενοι, δουλεύοντες ἐπιθυμίαις καὶ ἡδοναῖς ποικίλαις, ἐν κακίᾳ καὶ φθόνῳ διάγοντες, στυγητοί, μισοῦντες ἀλλήλους. **4** ὅτε δὲ ἡ

NIV

What Must Be Taught to Various Groups

2 You must teach what is in accord with sound doctrine. ²Teach the older men to be temperate, worthy of respect, self-controlled, and sound in faith, in love and in endurance.

³Likewise, teach the older women to be reverent in the way they live, not to be slanderers or addicted to much wine, but to teach what is good. ⁴Then they can train the younger women to love their husbands and children, ⁵to be self-controlled and pure, to be busy at home, to be kind, and to be subject to their husbands, so that no one will malign the word of God.

⁶Similarly, encourage the young men to be self-controlled. ⁷In everything set them an example by doing what is good. In your teaching show integrity, seriousness ⁸and soundness of speech that cannot be condemned, so that those who oppose you may be ashamed because they have nothing bad to say about us.

⁹Teach slaves to be subject to their masters in everything, to try to please them, not to talk back to them, ¹⁰and not to steal from them, but to show that they can be fully trusted, so that in every way they will make the teaching about God our Savior attractive.

¹¹For the grace of God that brings salvation has appeared to all men. ¹²It teaches us to say "No" to ungodliness and worldly passions, and to live self-controlled, upright and godly lives in this present age, ¹³while we wait for the blessed hope—the glorious appearing of our great God and Savior, Jesus Christ, ¹⁴who gave himself for us to redeem us from all wickedness and to purify for himself a people that are his very own, eager to do what is good.

¹⁵These, then, are the things you should teach. Encourage and rebuke with all authority. Do not let anyone despise you.

Doing What is Good

3 Remind the people to be subject to rulers and authorities, to be obedient, to be ready to do whatever is good, ²to slander no one, to be peaceable and considerate, and to show true humility toward all men.

³At one time we too were foolish, disobedient, deceived and enslaved by all kinds of passions and pleasures. We lived in malice and envy, being hated and hating one another. ⁴But when the kindness

another. [4]But when the goodness and loving kindness of God our Savior appeared, [5]he saved us, not because of any works of righteousness that we had done, but according to his mercy, through the water[h] of rebirth and renewal by the Holy Spirit. [6]This Spirit he poured out on us richly through Jesus Christ our Savior, [7]so that, having been justified by his grace, we might become heirs according to the hope of eternal life. [8]The saying is sure.

I desire that you insist on these things, so that those who have come to believe in God may be careful to devote themselves to good works; these things are excellent and profitable to everyone. [9]But avoid stupid controversies, genealogies, dissensions, and quarrels about the law, for they are unprofitable and worthless. [10]After a first and second admonition, have nothing more to do with anyone who causes divisions, [11]since you know that such a person is perverted and sinful, being self-condemned.

Final Messages and Benediction

12 When I send Artemas to you, or Tychicus, do your best to come to me at Nicopolis, for I have decided to spend the winter there. [13]Make every effort to send Zenas the lawyer and Apollos on their way, and see that they lack nothing. [14]And let people learn to devote themselves to good works in order to meet urgent needs, so that they may not be unproductive.

15 All who are with me send greetings to you. Greet those who love us in the faith. Grace be with all of you.[i]

χρηστότης καὶ ἡ φιλανθρωπία ἐπεφάνη τοῦ σωτῆρος ἡμῶν θεοῦ, **5** οὐκ ἐξ ἔργων τῶν ἐν δικαιοσύνῃ ἃ ἐποιήσαμεν ἡμεῖς ἀλλὰ κατὰ τὸ αὐτοῦ ἔλεος ἔσωσεν ἡμᾶς διὰ λουτροῦ παλιγγενεσίας καὶ ἀνακαινώσεως πνεύματος ἁγίου, **6** οὗ ἐξέχεεν ἐφ' ἡμᾶς πλουσίως διὰ Ἰησοῦ Χριστοῦ τοῦ σωτῆρος ἡμῶν, **7** ἵνα δικαιωθέντες τῇ ἐκείνου χάριτι κληρονόμοι γενηθῶμεν κατ' ἐλπίδα ζωῆς αἰωνίου.

8 Πιστὸς ὁ λόγος· καὶ περὶ τούτων βούλομαί σε διαβεβαιοῦσθαι, ἵνα φροντίζωσιν καλῶν ἔργων προΐστασθαι οἱ πεπιστευκότες θεῷ· ταῦτά ἐστιν καλὰ καὶ ὠφέλιμα τοῖς ἀνθρώποις. **9** μωρὰς δὲ ζητήσεις καὶ γενεαλογίας καὶ ἔρεις καὶ μάχας νομικὰς περιΐστασο· εἰσὶν γὰρ ἀνωφελεῖς καὶ μάταιοι. **10** αἱρετικὸν ἄνθρωπον μετὰ μίαν καὶ δευτέραν νουθεσίαν παραιτοῦ, **11** εἰδὼς ὅτι ἐξέστραπται ὁ τοιοῦτος καὶ ἁμαρτάνει ὢν αὐτοκατάκριτος.

12 Ὅταν πέμψω Ἀρτεμᾶν πρὸς σὲ ἢ Τυχικόν, σπούδασον ἐλθεῖν πρός με εἰς Νικόπολιν, ἐκεῖ γὰρ κέκρικα παραχειμάσαι. **13** Ζηνᾶν τὸν νομικὸν καὶ Ἀπολλὼν σπουδαίως πρόπεμψον, ἵνα μηδὲν αὐτοῖς λείπῃ. **14** μανθανέτωσαν δὲ καὶ οἱ ἡμέτεροι καλῶν ἔργων προΐστασθαι εἰς τὰς ἀναγκαίας χρείας, ἵνα μὴ ὦσιν ἄκαρποι.

15 Ἀσπάζονταί σε οἱ μετ' ἐμοῦ πάντες. Ἄσπασαι τοὺς φιλοῦντας ἡμᾶς ἐν πίστει. ἡ χάρις μετὰ πάντων ὑμῶν.[a]

and love of God our Savior appeared, [5]he saved us, not because of righteous things we had done, but because of his mercy. He saved us through the washing of rebirth and renewal by the Holy Spirit, [6]whom he poured out on us generously through Jesus Christ our Savior, [7]so that, having been justified by his grace, we might become heirs having the hope of eternal life. [8]This is a trustworthy saying. And I want you to stress these things, so that those who have trusted in God may be careful to devote themselves to doing what is good. These things are excellent and profitable for everyone.

[9]But avoid foolish controversies and genealogies and arguments and quarrels about the law, because these are unprofitable and useless. [10]Warn a divisive person once, and then warn him a second time. After that, have nothing to do with him. [11]You may be sure that such a man is warped and sinful; he is self-condemned.

Final Remarks

[12]As soon as I send Artemas or Tychicus to you, do your best to come to me at Nicopolis, because I have decided to winter there. [13]Do everything you can to help Zenas the lawyer and Apollos on their way and see that they have everything they need. [14]Our people must learn to devote themselves to doing what is good, in order that they may provide for daily necessities and not live unproductive lives.

[15]Everyone with me sends you greetings. Greet those who love us in the faith.

Grace be with you all.

NRSV

Salutation

1 Paul, a prisoner of Christ Jesus, and Timothy our brother,[a]

To Philemon our dear friend and co-worker, [2]to Apphia our sister,[b] to Archippus our fellow soldier, and to the church in your house:

3 Grace to you and peace from God our Father and the Lord Jesus Christ.

Philemon's Love and Faith

4 When I remember you[c] in my prayers, I always thank my God [5]because I hear of your love for all the saints and your faith toward the Lord Jesus. [6]I pray that the sharing of your faith may become effective when you perceive all the good that we[d] may do for Christ. [7]I have indeed received much joy and encouragement from your love, because the hearts of the saints have been refreshed through you, my brother.

Paul's Plea for Onesimus

8 For this reason, though I am bold enough in Christ to command you to do your duty, [9]yet I would rather appeal to you on the basis of love—and I, Paul, do this as an old man, and now also as a prisoner of Christ Jesus.[e] [10]I am appealing to you for my child, Onesimus, whose father I have become during my imprisonment. [11]Formerly he was useless to you, but now he is indeed useful[f] both to you and to me. [12]I am sending him, that is, my own heart, back to you. [13]I wanted to keep him with me, so that he might be of service to me in your place during my imprisonment for the gospel; [14]but I preferred to do nothing without your consent, in order that your good deed might be voluntary and not something forced. [15]Perhaps this is the reason he was separated from you for a while, so that you might have him back forever, [16]no longer as a slave but more than a slave, a beloved brother—especially to me but how much more to you, both in the flesh and in the Lord.

17 So if you consider me your partner, welcome him as you would welcome me. [18]If he has wronged you in any way, or owes you anything, charge that to my account. [19]I, Paul, am writing this with my own hand: I will repay it. I say nothing

ΠΡΟΣ ΦΙΛΗΜΟΝΑ

1 Παῦλος δέσμιος Χριστοῦ Ἰησοῦ καὶ Τιμόθεος ὁ ἀδελφὸς Φιλήμονι τῷ ἀγαπητῷ καὶ συνεργῷ ἡμῶν **2** καὶ Ἀπφίᾳ τῇ ἀδελφῇ καὶ Ἀρχίππῳ τῷ συστρατιώτῃ ἡμῶν καὶ τῇ κατ᾽ οἶκόν σου ἐκκλησίᾳ, **3** χάρις ὑμῖν καὶ εἰρήνη ἀπὸ θεοῦ πατρὸς ἡμῶν καὶ κυρίου Ἰησοῦ Χριστοῦ.

4 Εὐχαριστῶ τῷ θεῷ μου πάντοτε μνείαν σου ποιούμενος ἐπὶ τῶν προσευχῶν μου, **5** ἀκούων σου τὴν ἀγάπην καὶ τὴν πίστιν, ἣν ἔχεις πρὸς τὸν κύριον Ἰησοῦν καὶ εἰς πάντας τοὺς ἁγίους, **6** ὅπως ἡ κοινωνία τῆς πίστεώς σου ἐνεργὴς γένηται ἐν ἐπιγνώσει παντὸς ἀγαθοῦ τοῦ ἐν ἡμῖν[a] εἰς Χριστόν. **7** χαρὰν γὰρ πολλὴν ἔσχον καὶ παράκλησιν ἐπὶ τῇ ἀγάπῃ σου, ὅτι τὰ σπλάγχνα τῶν ἁγίων ἀναπέπαυται διὰ σοῦ, ἀδελφέ.

8 Διὸ πολλὴν ἐν Χριστῷ παρρησίαν ἔχων ἐπιτάσσειν σοι τὸ ἀνῆκον **9** διὰ τὴν ἀγάπην μᾶλλον παρακαλῶ, τοιοῦτος ὢν ὡς Παῦλος πρεσβύτης νυνὶ δὲ καὶ δέσμιος Χριστοῦ Ἰησοῦ· **10** παρακαλῶ σε περὶ τοῦ ἐμοῦ τέκνου, ὃν ἐγέννησα ἐν τοῖς δεσμοῖς, Ὀνήσιμον, **11** τόν ποτέ σοι ἄχρηστον νυνὶ δὲ [καὶ] σοὶ καὶ ἐμοὶ εὔχρηστον, **12** ὃν ἀνέπεμψά σοι, αὐτόν, τοῦτ᾽ ἔστιν τὰ ἐμὰ σπλάγχνα· **13** ὃν ἐγὼ ἐβουλόμην πρὸς ἐμαυτὸν κατέχειν, ἵνα ὑπὲρ σοῦ μοι διακονῇ ἐν τοῖς δεσμοῖς τοῦ εὐαγγελίου, **14** χωρὶς δὲ τῆς σῆς γνώμης οὐδὲν ἠθέλησα ποιῆσαι, ἵνα μὴ ὡς κατὰ ἀνάγκην τὸ ἀγαθόν σου ᾖ ἀλλὰ κατὰ ἑκούσιον. **15** τάχα γὰρ διὰ τοῦτο ἐχωρίσθη πρὸς ὥραν, ἵνα αἰώνιον αὐτὸν ἀπέχῃς, **16** οὐκέτι ὡς δοῦλον ἀλλὰ ὑπὲρ δοῦλον, ἀδελφὸν ἀγαπητόν, μάλιστα ἐμοί, πόσῳ δὲ μᾶλλον σοὶ καὶ ἐν σαρκὶ καὶ ἐν κυρίῳ.

17 Εἰ οὖν με ἔχεις κοινωνόν, προσλαβοῦ αὐτὸν ὡς ἐμέ. **18** εἰ δέ τι ἠδίκησέν σε ἢ ὀφείλει, τοῦτο ἐμοὶ ἐλλόγα. **19** ἐγὼ Παῦλος ἔγραψα τῇ ἐμῇ χειρί, ἐγὼ ἀποτίσω· ἵνα μὴ λέγω σοι ὅτι καὶ

NIV

[1]Paul, a prisoner of Christ Jesus, and Timothy our brother,

To Philemon our dear friend and fellow worker, [2]to Apphia our sister, to Archippus our fellow soldier and to the church that meets in your home:

[3]Grace to you and peace from God our Father and the Lord Jesus Christ.

Thanksgiving and Prayer

[4]I always thank my God as I remember you in my prayers, [5]because I hear about your faith in the Lord Jesus and your love for all the saints. [6]I pray that you may be active in sharing your faith, so that you will have a full understanding of every good thing we have in Christ. [7]Your love has given me great joy and encouragement, because you, brother, have refreshed the hearts of the saints.

Paul's Plea for Onesimus

[8]Therefore, although in Christ I could be bold and order you to do what you ought to do, [9]yet I appeal to you on the basis of love. I then, as Paul—an old man and now also a prisoner of Christ Jesus— [10]I appeal to you for my son Onesimus,[a] who became my son while I was in chains. [11]Formerly he was useless to you, but now he has become useful both to you and to me.

[12]I am sending him—who is my very heart—back to you. [13]I would have liked to keep him with me so that he could take your place in helping me while I am in chains for the gospel. [14]But I did not want to do anything without your consent, so that any favor you do will be spontaneous and not forced. [15]Perhaps the reason he was separated from you for a little while was that you might have him back for good— [16]no longer as a slave, but better than a slave, as a dear brother. He is very dear to me but even dearer to you, both as a man and as a brother in the Lord.

[17]So if you consider me a partner, welcome him as you would welcome me. [18]If he has done you any wrong or owes you anything, charge it to me. [19]I, Paul, am writing this with my own hand. I will pay it back—not to mention that you owe me

---

[a] Gk *the brother* [b] Gk *the sister* [c] From verse 4 through verse 21, *you* is singular [d] Other ancient authorities read *you* (plural) [e] Or *as an ambassador of Christ Jesus, and now also his prisoner* [f] The name Onesimus means *useful* or (compare verse 20) *beneficial*

[a]6 NRSV note d ὑμῖν

[a]10 Onesimus means *useful*.

about your owing me even your own self.
[20]Yes, brother, let me have this benefit from you in the Lord! Refresh my heart in Christ. [21]Confident of your obedience, I am writing to you, knowing that you will do even more than I say.

22 One thing more—prepare a guest room for me, for I am hoping through your prayers to be restored to you.

Final Greetings and Benediction

23 Epaphras, my fellow prisoner in Christ Jesus, sends greetings to you,[g] [24]and so do Mark, Aristarchus, Demas, and Luke, my fellow workers.

25 The grace of the Lord Jesus Christ be with your spirit.[h]

σεαυτόν μοι προσοφείλεις. **20** ναὶ ἀδελφέ, ἐγώ σου ὀναίμην ἐν κυρίῳ· ἀνάπαυσόν μου τὰ σπλάγχνα ἐν Χριστῷ. **21** Πεποιθὼς τῇ ὑπακοῇ σου ἔγραψά σοι, εἰδὼς ὅτι καὶ ὑπὲρ ἃ λέγω ποιήσεις. **22** ἅμα δὲ καὶ ἑτοίμαζέ μοι ξενίαν· ἐλπίζω γὰρ ὅτι διὰ τῶν προσευχῶν ὑμῶν χαρισθήσομαι ὑμῖν.

23 Ἀσπάζεταί σε Ἐπαφρᾶς ὁ συναιχμάλωτός μου ἐν Χριστῷ Ἰησοῦ, **24** Μᾶρκος, Ἀρίσταρχος, Δημᾶς, Λουκᾶς, οἱ συνεργοί μου. **25** Ἡ χάρις τοῦ κυρίου Ἰησοῦ Χριστοῦ μετὰ τοῦ πνεύματος ὑμῶν.[b]

your very self. [20]I do wish, brother, that I may have some benefit from you in the Lord; refresh my heart in Christ. [21]Confident of your obedience, I write to you, knowing that you will do even more than I ask.

[22]And one thing more: Prepare a guest room for me, because I hope to be restored to you in answer to your prayers.

[23]Epaphras, my fellow prisoner in Christ Jesus, sends you greetings. [24]And so do Mark, Aristarchus, Demas and Luke, my fellow workers.

[25]The grace of the Lord Jesus Christ be with your spirit.

[g] Here *you* is singular   [h] Other ancient authorities add *Amen*   [b]25 NRSV note h adds ἀμήν.

God Has Spoken by His Son

1 Long ago God spoke to our ancestors in many and various ways by the prophets, [2] but in these last days he has spoken to us by a Son,[a] whom he appointed heir of all things, through whom he also created the worlds. [3] He is the reflection of God's glory and the exact imprint of God's very being, and he sustains[b] all things by his powerful word. When he had made purification for sins, he sat down at the right hand of the Majesty on high, [4] having become as much superior to angels as the name he has inherited is more excellent than theirs.

The Son Is Superior to Angels

[5] For to which of the angels did God ever say,

"You are my Son;
   today I have begotten you"?

Or again,

"I will be his Father,
   and he will be my Son"?

[6] And again, when he brings the firstborn into the world, he says,

"Let all God's angels worship him."

[7] Of the angels he says,

"He makes his angels winds,
   and his servants flames of fire."

[8] But of the Son he says,

"Your throne, O God,[c] is forever and
      ever,
   and the righteous scepter is the
      scepter of your[d] kingdom.

[9] You have loved righteousness and
      hated wickedness;
   therefore God, your God, has anointed
      you
   with the oil of gladness beyond your
      companions."

[10] And,

"In the beginning, Lord, you founded
      the earth,
   and the heavens are the work of
      your hands;

[11] they will perish, but you remain;
   they will all wear out like clothing;

[12] like a cloak you will roll them up,
   and like clothing[e] they will be
      changed.
   But you are the same,
      and your years will never end."

ΠΡΟΣ ΕΒΡΑΙΟΥΣ

1 Πολυμερῶς καὶ πολυτρόπως πάλαι ὁ θεὸς λαλήσας τοῖς πατράσιν ἐν τοῖς προφήταις **2** ἐπ' ἐσχάτου τῶν ἡμερῶν τούτων ἐλάλησεν ἡμῖν ἐν υἱῷ, ὃν ἔθηκεν κληρονόμον πάντων, δι' οὗ καὶ ἐποίησεν τοὺς αἰῶνας· **3** ὃς ὢν ἀπαύγασμα τῆς δόξης καὶ χαρακτὴρ τῆς ὑποστάσεως αὐτοῦ, φέρων τε τὰ πάντα τῷ ῥήματι τῆς δυνάμεως αὐτοῦ, καθαρισμὸν τῶν ἁμαρτιῶν ποιησάμενος ἐκάθισεν ἐν δεξιᾷ τῆς μεγαλωσύνης ἐν ὑψηλοῖς, **4** τοσούτῳ κρείττων γενόμενος τῶν ἀγγέλων ὅσῳ διαφορώτερον παρ' αὐτοὺς κεκληρονόμηκεν ὄνομα.

5 Τίνι γὰρ εἶπέν ποτε τῶν ἀγγέλων,
Υἱός μου εἶ σύ,
   ἐγὼ σήμερον γεγέννηκά σε;
καὶ πάλιν,
Ἐγὼ ἔσομαι αὐτῷ εἰς πατέρα,
   καὶ αὐτὸς ἔσται μοι εἰς υἱόν;
6 ὅταν δὲ πάλιν εἰσαγάγῃ τὸν πρωτότοκον εἰς τὴν οἰκουμένην, λέγει,
Καὶ προσκυνησάτωσαν αὐτῷ
   πάντες ἄγγελοι θεοῦ.
7 καὶ πρὸς μὲν τοὺς ἀγγέλους λέγει,
Ὁ ποιῶν τοὺς ἀγγέλους αὐτοῦ
      πνεύματα
   καὶ τοὺς λειτουργοὺς αὐτοῦ
      πυρὸς φλόγα,
8 πρὸς δὲ τὸν υἱόν,
Ὁ θρόνος σου ὁ θεὸς εἰς τὸν
      αἰῶνα τοῦ αἰῶνος,
   καὶ ἡ ῥάβδος τῆς εὐθύτητος
      ῥάβδος τῆς βασιλείας σου[a].
9 ἠγάπησας δικαιοσύνην καὶ
      ἐμίσησας ἀνομίαν·
   διὰ τοῦτο ἔχρισέν σε ὁ θεὸς ὁ
      θεός σου
   ἔλαιον ἀγαλλιάσεως παρὰ τοὺς
      μετόχους σου.
10 καί,
Σὺ κατ' ἀρχάς, κύριε, τὴν γῆν
      ἐθεμελίωσας,
   καὶ ἔργα τῶν χειρῶν σού εἰσιν
      οἱ οὐρανοί·
11 αὐτοὶ ἀπολοῦνται, σὺ δὲ διαμένεις,
   καὶ πάντες ὡς ἱμάτιον παλαιωθήσονται,
12 καὶ ὡσεὶ περιβόλαιον ἑλίξεις
      αὐτούς,
   ὡς ἱμάτιον καὶ ἀλλαγήσονται·
   σὺ δὲ ὁ αὐτὸς εἶ
   καὶ τὰ ἔτη σου οὐκ ἐκλείψουσιν.

The Son Superior to Angels

1 In the past God spoke to our forefathers through the prophets at many times and in various ways, [2] but in these last days he has spoken to us by his Son, whom he appointed heir of all things, and through whom he made the universe. [3] The Son is the radiance of God's glory and the exact representation of his being, sustaining all things by his powerful word. After he had provided purification for sins, he sat down at the right hand of the Majesty in heaven. [4] So he became as much superior to the angels as the name he has inherited is superior to theirs.

[5] For to which of the angels did God ever say,

"You are my Son;
   today I have become your Father[a][b]?

Or again,

"I will be his Father,
   and he will be my Son"[c]?

[6] And again, when God brings his firstborn into the world, he says,

"Let all God's angels worship him."[d]

[7] In speaking of the angels he says,

"He makes his angels winds,
   his servants flames of fire."[e]

[8] But about the Son he says,

"Your throne, O God, will last for ever
      and ever,
   and righteousness will be the scepter
      of your kingdom.

[9] You have loved righteousness and
      hated wickedness;
   therefore God, your God, has set you
      above your companions
   by anointing you with the oil of joy."[f]

[10] He also says,

"In the beginning, O Lord, you laid the
      foundations of the earth,
   and the heavens are the work of your
      hands.

[11] They will perish, but you remain;
   they will all wear out like a garment.

[12] You will roll them up like a robe;
   like a garment they will be changed.
   But you remain the same,
      and your years will never end."[g]

---

a Or *the Son*   b Or *bears along*   c Or *God is your throne*
d Other ancient authorities read *his*   e Other ancient authorities lack *like clothing*

a8 NRSV note d αὐτοῦ

a5 Or *have begotten you*   b5 Psalm 2:7   c5 2 Samuel 7:14; 1 Chron. 17:13   d6 Deut. 32:43 (see Dead Sea Scrolls and Septuagint)   e7 Psalm 104:4   f9 Psalm 45:6,7
g12 Psalm 102:25-27

NRSV

13But to which of the angels has he ever said,

> "Sit at my right hand
> until I make your enemies a
> footstool for your feet"?

14Are not all angelsf spirits in the divine service, sent to serve for the sake of those who are to inherit salvation?

Warning to Pay Attention

2 Therefore we must pay greater attention to what we have heard, so that we do not drift away from it. 2For if the message declared through angels was valid, and every transgression or disobedience received a just penalty, 3how can we escape if we neglect so great a salvation? It was declared at first through the Lord, and it was attested to us by those who heard him, 4while God added his testimony by signs and wonders and various miracles, and by gifts of the Holy Spirit, distributed according to his will.

Exaltation through Abasement

5 Now Godg did not subject the coming world, about which we are speaking, to angels. 6But someone has testified somewhere,

> "What are human beings that you are
> mindful of them,h
> or mortals, that you care for them?i
> 7 You have made them for a little while
> lowerj than the angels;
> you have crowned them with glory
> and honor,k
> 8 subjecting all things under their feet."

Now in subjecting all things to them, Godg left nothing outside their control. As it is, we do not yet see everything in subjection to them, 9but we do see Jesus, who for a little while was made lowerl than the angels, now crowned with glory and honor because of the suffering of death, so that by the grace of Godm he might taste death for everyone.

10 It was fitting that God,g for whom and through whom all things exist, in bringing many children to glory, should make the pioneer of their salvation perfect through sufferings. 11For the one who sanctifies and those who are sanctified all have one Father.n For this reason Jesusg is not

[Greek]

13 πρὸς τίνα δὲ τῶν ἀγγέλων εἴρηκέν ποτε,

> Κάθου ἐκ δεξιῶν μου,
> ἕως ἂν θῶ τοὺς ἐχθρούς σου
> ὑποπόδιον τῶν ποδῶν σου;

14 οὐχὶ πάντες εἰσὶν λειτουργικὰ πνεύματα εἰς διακονίαν ἀποστελλόμενα διὰ τοὺς μέλλοντας κληρονομεῖν σωτηρίαν;

2 Διὰ τοῦτο δεῖ περισσοτέρως προσέχειν ἡμᾶς τοῖς ἀκουσθεῖσιν, μήποτε παραρυῶμεν. 2 εἰ γὰρ ὁ δι᾽ ἀγγέλων λαληθεὶς λόγος ἐγένετο βέβαιος καὶ πᾶσα παράβασις καὶ παρακοὴ ἔλαβεν ἔνδικον μισθαποδοσίαν, 3 πῶς ἡμεῖς ἐκφευξόμεθα τηλικαύτης ἀμελήσαντες σωτηρίας, ἥτις ἀρχὴν λαβοῦσα λαλεῖσθαι διὰ τοῦ κυρίου ὑπὸ τῶν ἀκουσάντων εἰς ἡμᾶς ἐβεβαιώθη, 4 συνεπιμαρτυροῦντος τοῦ θεοῦ σημείοις τε καὶ τέρασιν καὶ ποικίλαις δυνάμεσιν καὶ πνεύματος ἁγίου μερισμοῖς κατὰ τὴν αὐτοῦ θέλησιν;

5 Οὐ γὰρ ἀγγέλοις ὑπέταξεν τὴν οἰκουμένην τὴν μέλλουσαν, περὶ ἧς λαλοῦμεν. 6 διεμαρτύρατο δέ πού τις λέγων,

> Τί ἐστιν ἄνθρωπος ὅτι μιμνήσκη
> αὐτοῦ,
> ἢ υἱὸς ἀνθρώπου ὅτι ἐπισκέπτη
> αὐτόν;
> 7 ἠλάττωσας αὐτὸν βραχύ τι παρ᾽
> ἀγγέλους,
> δόξῃ καὶ τιμῇ ἐστεφάνωσας
> αὐτόνa,
> 8 πάντα ὑπέταξας ὑποκάτω τῶν
> ποδῶν αὐτοῦ.

ἐν τῷ γὰρ ὑποτάξαι [αὐτῷ] τὰ πάντα οὐδὲν ἀφῆκεν αὐτῷ ἀνυπότακτον. νῦν δὲ οὔπω ὁρῶμεν αὐτῷ τὰ πάντα ὑποτεταγμένα· 9 τὸν δὲ βραχύ τι παρ᾽ ἀγγέλους ἠλαττωμένον βλέπομεν Ἰησοῦν διὰ τὸ πάθημα τοῦ θανάτου δόξῃ καὶ τιμῇ ἐστεφανωμένον, ὅπως χάριτιb θεοῦ ὑπὲρ παντὸς γεύσηται θανάτου.

10 Ἔπρεπεν γὰρ αὐτῷ, δι᾽ ὃν τὰ πάντα καὶ δι᾽ οὗ τὰ πάντα, πολλοὺς υἱοὺς εἰς δόξαν ἀγαγόντα τὸν ἀρχηγὸν τῆς σωτηρίας αὐτῶν διὰ παθημάτων τελειῶσαι. 11 ὅ τε γὰρ ἁγιάζων καὶ οἱ ἁγιαζόμενοι ἐξ ἑνὸς πάντες· δι᾽ ἣν αἰτίαν οὐκ ἐπαισχύνεται ἀδελφοὺς

NIV

13To which of the angels did God ever say,

> "Sit at my right hand
> until I make your enemies
> a footstool for your feet"?h

14Are not all angels ministering spirits sent to serve those who will inherit salvation?

Warning to Pay Attention

2 We must pay more careful attention, therefore, to what we have heard, so that we do not drift away. 2For if the message spoken by angels was binding, and every violation and disobedience received its just punishment, 3how shall we escape if we ignore such a great salvation? This salvation, which was first announced by the Lord, was confirmed to us by those who heard him. 4God also testified to it by signs, wonders and various miracles, and gifts of the Holy Spirit distributed according to his will.

Jesus Made Like His Brothers

5It is not to angels that he has subjected the world to come, about which we are speaking. 6But there is a place where someone has testified:

> "What is man that you are mindful of
> him,
> the son of man that you care for him?
> 7You made him a littlea lower than the
> angels;
> you crowned him with glory and honor
> 8 and put everything under his feet."b

In putting everything under him, God left nothing that is not subject to him. Yet at present we do not see everything subject to him. 9But we see Jesus, who was made a little lower than the angels, now crowned with glory and honor because he suffered death, so that by the grace of God he might taste death for everyone.

10In bringing many sons to glory, it was fitting that God, for whom and through whom everything exists, should make the author of their salvation perfect through suffering. 11Both the one who makes men holy and those who are made holy are of the same family. So Jesus is not ashamed

---

f Gk all of them g Gk he h Gk What is man that you are mindful of him? i Gk or the son of man that you care for him? In the Hebrew of Psalm 8.4-6 both man and son of man refer to all humankind j Or them only a little lower k Other ancient authorities add and set them over the works of your hands l Or who was made a little lower m Other ancient authorities read apart from God n Gk are all of one

a7 NRSV note k adds καὶ κατέστησας αὐτὸν ἐπὶ τὰ ἔργα τῶν χειρῶν σου b9 NRSV note m χωρὶς

h13 Psalm 110:1 a7 Or him for a little while; also in verse 9 b8 Psalm 8:4-6

ashamed to call them brothers and sisters,P [12]saying,

> "I will proclaim your name to my
> brothers and sisters,P
> in the midst of the congregation I
> will praise you."

[13]And again,

> "I will put my trust in him."

And again,

> "Here am I and the children whom
> God has given me."

14 Since, therefore, the children share flesh and blood, he himself likewise shared the same things, so that through death he might destroy the one who has the power of death, that is, the devil, [15]and free those who all their lives were held in slavery by the fear of death. [16]For it is clear that he did not come to help angels, but the descendants of Abraham. [17]Therefore he had to become like his brothers and sistersP in every respect, so that he might be a merciful and faithful high priest in the service of God, to make a sacrifice of atonement for the sins of the people. [18]Because he himself was tested by what he suffered, he is able to help those who are being tested.

Moses a Servant, Christ a Son

3 Therefore, brothers and sisters,P holy partners in a heavenly calling, consider that Jesus, the apostle and high priest of our confession, [2]was faithful to the one who appointed him, just as Moses also "was faithful in allq God'sr house." [3]Yet Jesuss is worthy of more glory than Moses, just as the builder of a house has more honor than the house itself. [4](For every house is built by someone, but the builder of all things is God.) [5]Now Moses was faithful in all God'sr house as a servant, to testify to the things that would be spoken later. [6]Christ, however, was faithful over God'sr house as a son, and we are his house if we hold firmt the confidence and the pride that belong to hope.

Warning against Unbelief

7 Therefore, as the Holy Spirit says,
> "Today, if you hear his voice,
8   do not harden your hearts as in the
>   rebellion,
>   as on the day of testing in the
>   wilderness,
9   where your ancestors put me to the
>   test,

αὐτοὺς καλεῖν 12 λέγων,
> Ἀπαγγελῶ τὸ ὄνομά σου τοῖς
> ἀδελφοῖς μου,
> ἐν μέσῳ ἐκκλησίας ὑμνήσω σε,
13 καὶ πάλιν,
> Ἐγὼ ἔσομαι πεποιθὼς ἐπ᾽ αὐτῷ,
> καὶ πάλιν,
> Ἰδοὺ ἐγὼ καὶ τὰ παιδία ἅ μοι
> ἔδωκεν ὁ θεός.

14 ἐπεὶ οὖν τὰ παιδία κεκοινώνηκεν αἵματος καὶ σαρκός, καὶ αὐτὸς παραπλησίως μετέσχεν τῶν αὐτῶν, ἵνα διὰ τοῦ θανάτου καταργήσῃ τὸν τὸ κράτος ἔχοντα τοῦ θανάτου, τοῦτ᾽ ἔστιν τὸν διάβολον, 15 καὶ ἀπαλλάξῃ τούτους, ὅσοι φόβῳ θανάτου διὰ παντὸς τοῦ ζῆν ἔνοχοι ἦσαν δουλείας. 16 οὐ γὰρ δήπου ἀγγέλων ἐπιλαμβάνεται ἀλλὰ σπέρματος Ἀβραὰμ ἐπιλαμβάνεται. 17 ὅθεν ὤφειλεν κατὰ πάντα τοῖς ἀδελφοῖς ὁμοιωθῆναι, ἵνα ἐλεήμων γένηται καὶ πιστὸς ἀρχιερεὺς τὰ πρὸς τὸν θεὸν εἰς τὸ ἱλάσκεσθαι τὰς ἁμαρτίας τοῦ λαοῦ. 18 ἐν ᾧ γὰρ πέπονθεν αὐτὸς πειρασθείς, δύναται τοῖς πειραζομένοις βοηθῆσαι.

3 Ὅθεν, ἀδελφοὶ ἅγιοι, κλήσεως ἐπουρανίου μέτοχοι, κατανοήσατε τὸν ἀπόστολον καὶ ἀρχιερέα τῆς ὁμολογίας ἡμῶν Ἰησοῦν, 2 πιστὸν ὄντα τῷ ποιήσαντι αὐτὸν ὡς καὶ Μωϋσῆς ἐν [ὅλῳ] τῷ οἴκῳ αὐτοῦ. 3 πλείονος γὰρ οὗτος δόξης παρὰ Μωϋσῆν ἠξίωται, καθ᾽ ὅσον πλείονα τιμὴν ἔχει τοῦ οἴκου ὁ κατασκευάσας αὐτόν· 4 πᾶς γὰρ οἶκος κατασκευάζεται ὑπό τινος, ὁ δὲ πάντα κατασκευάσας θεός. 5 καὶ Μωϋσῆς μὲν πιστὸς ἐν ὅλῳ τῷ οἴκῳ αὐτοῦ ὡς θεράπων εἰς μαρτύριον τῶν λαληθησομένων, 6 Χριστὸς δὲ ὡς υἱὸς ἐπὶ τὸν οἶκον αὐτοῦ· οὗ οἶκός ἐσμεν ἡμεῖς, ἐάν[περ] τὴν παρρησίαν καὶ τὸ καύχημα τῆς ἐλπίδοςa κατάσχωμεν.

7 Διό, καθὼς λέγει τὸ πνεῦμα τὸ ἅγιον,
> Σήμερον ἐὰν τῆς φωνῆς αὐτοῦ
> ἀκούσητε,
8 μὴ σκληρύνητε τὰς καρδίας ὑμῶν
> ὡς ἐν τῷ παραπικρασμῷ
> κατὰ τὴν ἡμέραν τοῦ πειρασμοῦ
> ἐν τῇ ἐρήμῳ,
9 οὗ ἐπείρασαν οἱ πατέρες ὑμῶν ἐν
> δοκιμασίᾳ

to call them brothers. [12]He says,

> "I will declare your name to my
> brothers;
> in the presence of the congregation I
> will sing your praises."c

[13]And again,

> "I will put my trust in him."d

And again he says,

> "Here am I, and the children God has
> given me."e

[14]Since the children have flesh and blood, he too shared in their humanity so that by his death he might destroy him who holds the power of death—that is, the devil— [15]and free those who all their lives were held in slavery by their fear of death. [16]For surely it is not angels he helps, but Abraham's descendants. [17]For this reason he had to be made like his brothers in every way, in order that he might become a merciful and faithful high priest in service to God, and that he might make atonement forf the sins of the people. [18]Because he himself suffered when he was tempted, he is able to help those who are being tempted.

Jesus Greater Than Moses

3 Therefore, holy brothers, who share in the heavenly calling, fix your thoughts on Jesus, the apostle and high priest whom we confess. [2]He was faithful to the one who appointed him, just as Moses was faithful in all God's house. [3]Jesus has been found worthy of greater honor than Moses, just as the builder of a house has greater honor than the house itself. [4]For every house is built by someone, but God is the builder of everything. [5]Moses was faithful as a servant in all God's house, testifying to what would be said in the future. [6]But Christ is faithful as a son over God's house. And we are his house, if we hold on to our courage and the hope of which we boast.

Warning Against Unbelief

[7]So, as the Holy Spirit says:

> "Today, if you hear his voice,
8   do not harden your hearts
>   as you did in the rebellion,
>   during the time of testing in the desert,
> [9]where your fathers tested and tried me

P Gk *brothers*   q Other ancient authorities lack *all*
r Gk *his*   s Gk *this one*   t Other ancient authorities add
to the end

a6 NRSV note t adds μέχρι τέλους βεβαίαν

c12 Psalm 22:22   d13 Isaiah 8:17   e13 Isaiah 8:18   f17
Or *and that he might turn aside God's wrath, taking away*

though they had seen my works
    [10]for forty years.
Therefore I was angry with that
    generation,
and I said, 'They always go astray in
    their hearts,
and they have not known my ways.'
[11] As in my anger I swore,
    'They will not enter my rest.' "

[12]Take care, brothers and sisters,[p] that none of you may have an evil, unbelieving heart that turns away from the living God. [13]But exhort one another every day, as long as it is called "today," so that none of you may be hardened by the deceitfulness of sin. [14]For we have become partners of Christ, if only we hold our first confidence firm to the end. [15]As it is said,

    "Today, if you hear his voice,
    do not harden your hearts as in the
        rebellion."

[16]Now who were they who heard and yet were rebellious? Was it not all those who left Egypt under the leadership of Moses? [17]But with whom was he angry forty years? Was it not those who sinned, whose bodies fell in the wilderness? [18]And to whom did he swear that they would not enter his rest, if not to those who were disobedient? [19]So we see that they were unable to enter because of unbelief.

The Rest That God Promised

4 Therefore, while the promise of entering his rest is still open, let us take care that none of you should seem to have failed to reach it. [2]For indeed the good news came to us just as to them; but the message they heard did not benefit them, because they were not united by faith with those who listened.[u] [3]For we who have believed enter that rest, just as God[v] has said,

    "As in my anger I swore,
    'They shall not enter my rest,' "

though his works were finished at the foundation of the world. [4]For in one place it speaks about the seventh day as follows, "And God rested on the seventh day from all his works." [5]And again in this place it says, "They shall not enter my rest." [6]Since therefore it remains open for some to enter it, and those who formerly received the good news failed to enter because of dis-

---

καὶ εἶδον τὰ ἔργα μου
10 τεσσεράκοντα ἔτη· [b]
διὸ προσώχθισα τῇ γενεᾷ ταύτῃ
καὶ εἶπον, Ἀεὶ πλανῶνται τῇ
    καρδίᾳ,
αὐτοὶ δὲ οὐκ ἔγνωσαν τὰς
    ὁδούς μου,
11 ὡς ὤμοσα ἐν τῇ ὀργῇ μου·
Εἰ εἰσελεύσονται εἰς τὴν κατά-
    παυσίν μου.

12 Βλέπετε, ἀδελφοί, μήποτε ἔσται ἔν τινι ὑμῶν καρδία πονηρὰ ἀπιστίας ἐν τῷ ἀποστῆναι ἀπὸ θεοῦ ζῶντος, 13 ἀλλὰ παρακαλεῖτε ἑαυτοὺς καθ' ἑκάστην ἡμέραν, ἄχρις οὗ τὸ Σήμερον καλεῖται, ἵνα μὴ σκληρυνθῇ τις ἐξ ὑμῶν ἀπάτῃ τῆς ἁμαρτίας – 14 μέτοχοι γὰρ τοῦ Χριστοῦ γεγόναμεν, ἐάνπερ τὴν ἀρχὴν τῆς ὑποστάσεως μέχρι τέλους βεβαίαν κατάσχωμεν – 15 ἐν τῷ λέγεσθαι,

Σήμερον ἐὰν τῆς φωνῆς αὐτοῦ
    ἀκούσητε,
Μὴ σκληρύνητε τὰς καρδίας ὑμῶν
    ὡς ἐν τῷ παραπικρασμῷ.

16 τίνες γὰρ ἀκούσαντες παρεπίκραναν; ἀλλ' οὐ πάντες οἱ ἐξελθόντες ἐξ Αἰγύπτου διὰ Μωϋσέως; 17 τίσιν δὲ προσώχθισεν τεσσεράκοντα ἔτη; οὐχὶ τοῖς ἁμαρτήσασιν, ὧν τὰ κῶλα ἔπεσεν ἐν τῇ ἐρήμῳ; 18 τίσιν δὲ ὤμοσεν, μὴ εἰσελεύσεσθαι εἰς τὴν κατάπαυσιν αὐτοῦ εἰ μὴ τοῖς ἀπειθήσασιν; 19 καὶ βλέπομεν ὅτι οὐκ ἠδυνήθησαν εἰσελθεῖν δι' ἀπιστίαν.

4 Φοβηθῶμεν οὖν, μήποτε καταλειπομένης ἐπαγγελίας εἰσελθεῖν εἰς τὴν κατάπαυσιν αὐτοῦ δοκῇ τις ἐξ ὑμῶν ὑστερηκέναι. 2 καὶ γάρ ἐσμεν εὐηγγελισμένοι καθάπερ κἀκεῖνοι· ἀλλ' οὐκ ὠφέλησεν ὁ λόγος τῆς ἀκοῆς ἐκείνους μὴ συγκεκερασμένους[a] τῇ πίστει τοῖς ἀκούσασιν. 3 εἰσερχόμεθα γὰρ εἰς [τὴν] κατάπαυσιν οἱ πιστεύσαντες, καθὼς εἴρηκεν,

Ὡς ὤμοσα ἐν τῇ ὀργῇ μου,
Εἰ εἰσελεύσονται εἰς τὴν κατά-
    παυσίν μου,

καίτοι τῶν ἔργων ἀπὸ καταβολῆς κόσμου γενηθέντων. 4 εἴρηκεν γάρ που περὶ τῆς ἑβδόμης οὕτως, Καὶ κατέπαυσεν ὁ θεὸς ἐν τῇ ἡμέρᾳ τῇ ἑβδόμῃ ἀπὸ πάντων τῶν ἔργων αὐτοῦ, 5 καὶ ἐν τούτῳ πάλιν, Εἰ εἰσελεύσονται εἰς τὴν κατάπαυσίν μου. 6 ἐπεὶ οὖν ἀπολείπεται τινὰς εἰσελθεῖν εἰς αὐτήν, καὶ οἱ πρότερον εὐαγγελισθέντες οὐκ

---

and for forty years saw what I did.
[10]That is why I was angry with that
    generation,
and I said, 'Their hearts are always
    going astray,
and they have not known my ways.'
[11]So I declared on oath in my anger,
    'They shall never enter my rest.' "[a]

[12]See to it, brothers, that none of you has a sinful, unbelieving heart that turns away from the living God. [13]But encourage one another daily, as long as it is called Today, so that none of you may be hardened by sin's deceitfulness. [14]We have come to share in Christ if we hold firmly till the end the confidence we had at first. [15]As has just been said:

    "Today, if you hear his voice,
    do not harden your hearts
    as you did in the rebellion."[b]

[16]Who were they who heard and rebelled? Were they not all those Moses led out of Egypt? [17]And with whom was he angry for forty years? Was it not with those who sinned, whose bodies fell in the desert? [18]And to whom did God swear that they would never enter his rest if not to those who disobeyed[c]? [19]So we see that they were not able to enter, because of their unbelief.

A Sabbath-Rest for the People of God

4 Therefore, since the promise of entering his rest still stands, let us be careful that none of you be found to have fallen short of it. [2]For we also have had the gospel preached to us, just as they did; but the message they heard was of no value to them, because those who heard did not combine it with faith.[a] [3]Now we who have believed enter that rest, just as God has said,

    "So I declared on oath in my anger,
    'They shall never enter my rest.' "[b]

And yet his work has been finished since the creation of the world. [4]For somewhere he has spoken about the seventh day in these words: "And on the seventh day God rested from all his work."[c] [5]And again in the passage above he says, "They shall never enter my rest."

[6]It still remains that some will enter that rest, and those who formerly had the gospel preached to them did not go in, because of

---

[p] Gk *brothers*   [u] Other ancient authorities read *it did not meet with faith in those who listened*   [v] Gk *he*

[b]10 NIV begins verse 10 after ἔτη·   [a]2 NIV text and NRSV note u συγκεκ(ε)ρα(σ)μένος; NIV note and NRSV text as UBS

[a]11 Psalm 95:7-11   [b]15 Psalm 95:7,8   [c]18 Or *disbelieved*   [a]2 Many manuscripts *because they did not share in the faith of those who obeyed*   [b]3 Psalm 95:11; also in verse 5   [c]4 Gen. 2:2

obedience, 7again he sets a certain day—"today"—saying through David much later, in the words already quoted,

"Today, if you hear his voice,
    do not harden your hearts."

8For if Joshua had given them rest, God[v] would not speak later about another day. 9So then, a sabbath rest still remains for the people of God; 10for those who enter God's rest also cease from their labors as God did from his. 11Let us therefore make every effort to enter that rest, so that no one may fall through such disobedience as theirs.

12 Indeed, the word of God is living and active, sharper than any two-edged sword, piercing until it divides soul from spirit, joints from marrow; it is able to judge the thoughts and intentions of the heart. 13And before him no creature is hidden, but all are naked and laid bare to the eyes of the one to whom we must render an account.

Jesus the Great High Priest

14 Since, then, we have a great high priest who has passed through the heavens, Jesus, the Son of God, let us hold fast to our confession. 15For we do not have a high priest who is unable to sympathize with our weaknesses, but we have one who in every respect has been tested[w] as we are, yet without sin. 16Let us therefore approach the throne of grace with boldness, so that we may receive mercy and find grace to help in time of need.

5 Every high priest chosen from among mortals is put in charge of things pertaining to God on their behalf, to offer gifts and sacrifices for sins. 2He is able to deal gently with the ignorant and wayward, since he himself is subject to weakness; 3and because of this he must offer sacrifice for his own sins as well as for those of the people. 4And one does not presume to take this honor, but takes it only when called by God, just as Aaron was.

5 So also Christ did not glorify himself in becoming a high priest, but was appointed by the one who said to him,

"You are my Son,
    today I have begotten you";

6as he says also in another place,

εἰσῆλθον δι᾽ ἀπείθειαν, 7 πάλιν τινὰ ὁρίζει ἡμέραν, Σήμερον, ἐν Δαυὶδ λέγων μετὰ τοσοῦτον χρόνον, καθὼς προείρηται,

Σήμερον ἐὰν τῆς φωνῆς αὐτοῦ ἀκούσητε,

μὴ σκληρύνητε τὰς καρδίας ὑμῶν.

8 εἰ γὰρ αὐτοὺς Ἰησοῦς κατέπαυσεν, οὐκ ἂν περὶ ἄλλης ἐλάλει μετὰ ταῦτα ἡμέρας. 9 ἄρα ἀπολείπεται σαββατισμὸς τῷ λαῷ τοῦ θεοῦ. 10 ὁ γὰρ εἰσελθὼν εἰς τὴν κατάπαυσιν αὐτοῦ καὶ αὐτὸς κατέπαυσεν ἀπὸ τῶν ἔργων αὐτοῦ ὥσπερ ἀπὸ τῶν ἰδίων ὁ θεός. 11 σπουδάσωμεν οὖν εἰσελθεῖν εἰς ἐκείνην τὴν κατάπαυσιν, ἵνα μὴ ἐν τῷ αὐτῷ τις ὑποδείγματι πέσῃ τῆς ἀπειθείας.

12 Ζῶν γὰρ ὁ λόγος τοῦ θεοῦ καὶ ἐνεργὴς καὶ τομώτερος ὑπὲρ πᾶσαν μάχαιραν δίστομον καὶ διϊκνούμενος ἄχρι μερισμοῦ ψυχῆς καὶ πνεύματος, ἁρμῶν τε καὶ μυελῶν, καὶ κριτικὸς ἐνθυμήσεων καὶ ἐννοιῶν καρδίας· 13 καὶ οὐκ ἔστιν κτίσις ἀφανὴς ἐνώπιον αὐτοῦ, πάντα δὲ γυμνὰ καὶ τετραχηλισμένα τοῖς ὀφθαλμοῖς αὐτοῦ, πρὸς ὃν ἡμῖν ὁ λόγος.

14 Ἔχοντες οὖν ἀρχιερέα μέγαν διεληλυθότα τοὺς οὐρανούς, Ἰησοῦν τὸν υἱὸν τοῦ θεοῦ, κρατῶμεν τῆς ὁμολογίας. 15 οὐ γὰρ ἔχομεν ἀρχιερέα μὴ δυνάμενον συμπαθῆσαι ταῖς ἀσθενείαις ἡμῶν, πεπειρασμένον δὲ κατὰ πάντα καθ᾽ ὁμοιότητα χωρὶς ἁμαρτίας. 16 προσερχώμεθα οὖν μετὰ παρρησίας τῷ θρόνῳ τῆς χάριτος, ἵνα λάβωμεν ἔλεος καὶ χάριν εὕρωμεν εἰς εὔκαιρον βοήθειαν.

5 Πᾶς γὰρ ἀρχιερεὺς ἐξ ἀνθρώπων λαμβανόμενος ὑπὲρ ἀνθρώπων καθίσταται τὰ πρὸς τὸν θεόν, ἵνα προσφέρῃ δῶρά τε καὶ θυσίας ὑπὲρ ἁμαρτιῶν, 2 μετριοπαθεῖν δυνάμενος τοῖς ἀγνοοῦσιν καὶ πλανωμένοις, ἐπεὶ καὶ αὐτὸς περίκειται ἀσθένειαν 3 καὶ δι᾽ αὐτὴν ὀφείλει, καθὼς περὶ τοῦ λαοῦ, οὕτως καὶ περὶ αὐτοῦ προσφέρειν περὶ ἁμαρτιῶν. 4 καὶ οὐχ ἑαυτῷ τις λαμβάνει τὴν τιμὴν ἀλλὰ καλούμενος ὑπὸ τοῦ θεοῦ καθώσπερ καὶ Ἀαρών.

5 Οὕτως καὶ ὁ Χριστὸς οὐχ ἑαυτὸν ἐδόξασεν γενηθῆναι ἀρχιερέα ἀλλ᾽ ὁ λαλήσας πρὸς αὐτόν,

Υἱός μου εἶ σύ,
    ἐγὼ σήμερον γεγέννηκά σε·

6 καθὼς καὶ ἐν ἑτέρῳ λέγει,

---

their disobedience. 7Therefore God again set a certain day, calling it Today, when a long time later he spoke through David, as was said before:

"Today, if you hear his voice,
    do not harden your hearts."[d]

8For if Joshua had given them rest, God would not have spoken later about another day. 9There remains, then, a Sabbath-rest for the people of God; 10for anyone who enters God's rest also rests from his own work, just as God did from his. 11Let us, therefore, make every effort to enter that rest, so that no one will fall by following their example of disobedience.

12For the word of God is living and active. Sharper than any double-edged sword, it penetrates even to dividing soul and spirit, joints and marrow; it judges the thoughts and attitudes of the heart. 13Nothing in all creation is hidden from God's sight Everything is uncovered and laid bare before the eyes of him to whom we must give account.

Jesus the Great High Priest

14Therefore, since we have a great high priest who has gone through the heavens,[e] Jesus the Son of God, let us hold firmly to the faith we profess. 15For we do not have a high priest who is unable to sympathize with our weaknesses, but we have one who has been tempted in every way, just as we are—yet was without sin. 16Let us then approach the throne of grace with confidence, so that we may receive mercy and find grace to help us in our time of need.

5 Every high priest is selected from among men and is appointed to represent them in matters related to God, to offer gifts and sacrifices for sins. 2He is able to deal gently with those who are ignorant and are going astray, since he himself is subject to weakness. 3This is why he has to offer sacrifices for his own sins, as well as for the sins of the people.

4No one takes this honor upon himself; he must be called by God, just as Aaron was. 5So Christ also did not take upon himself the glory of becoming a high priest. But God said to him,

"You are my Son;
    today I have become your Father."[a][b]

6And he says in another place,

---

d7 Psalm 95:7,8   e14 Or *gone into heaven*   a5 Or *have begotten you*   b5 Psalm 2:7

NRSV

"You are a priest forever,
according to the order of Melchizedek."

7 In the days of his flesh, Jesus[v] offered up prayers and supplications, with loud cries and tears, to the one who was able to save him from death, and he was heard because of his reverent submission. 8Although he was a Son, he learned obedience through what he suffered; 9and having been made perfect, he became the source of eternal salvation for all who obey him, 10having been designated by God a high priest according to the order of Melchizedek.

Warning against Falling Away

11 About this[x] we have much to say that is hard to explain, since you have become dull in understanding. 12For though by this time you ought to be teachers, you need someone to teach you again the basic elements of the oracles of God. You need milk, not solid food; 13for everyone who lives on milk, being still an infant, is unskilled in the word of righteousness. 14But solid food is for the mature, for those whose faculties have been trained by practice to distinguish good from evil.

The Peril of Falling Away

6 Therefore let us go on toward perfection,[y] leaving behind the basic teaching about Christ, and not laying again the foundation: repentance from dead works and faith toward God, 2instruction about baptisms, laying on of hands, resurrection of the dead, and eternal judgment. 3And we will do[z] this, if God permits. 4For it is impossible to restore again to repentance those who have once been enlightened, and have tasted the heavenly gift, and have shared in the Holy Spirit, 5and have tasted the goodness of the word of God and the powers of the age to come, 6and then have fallen away, since on their own they are crucifying again the Son of God and are holding him up to contempt. 7Ground that drinks up the rain falling on it repeatedly, and that produces a crop useful to those for whom it is cultivated, receives a blessing from God. 8But if it produces thorns and thistles, it is worthless and on the verge of being cursed; its end is to be burned over.

9 Even though we speak in this way, beloved, we are confident of better things

Greek

Σὺ ἱερεὺς εἰς τὸν αἰῶνα
κατὰ τὴν τάξιν Μελχισέδεκ,

7 ὃς ἐν ταῖς ἡμέραις τῆς σαρκὸς αὐτοῦ δεήσεις τε καὶ ἱκετηρίας πρὸς τὸν δυνάμενον σῴζειν αὐτὸν ἐκ θανάτου μετὰ κραυγῆς ἰσχυρᾶς καὶ δακρύων προσενέγκας καὶ εἰσακουσθεὶς ἀπὸ τῆς εὐλαβείας, 8 καίπερ ὢν υἱός, ἔμαθεν ἀφ' ὧν ἔπαθεν τὴν ὑπακοήν, 9 καὶ τελειωθεὶς ἐγένετο πᾶσιν τοῖς ὑπακούουσιν αὐτῷ αἴτιος σωτηρίας αἰωνίου, 10 προσαγορευθεὶς ὑπὸ τοῦ θεοῦ ἀρχιερεὺς κατὰ τὴν τάξιν Μελχισέδεκ.

11 Περὶ οὗ πολὺς ἡμῖν ὁ λόγος καὶ δυσερμήνευτος λέγειν, ἐπεὶ νωθροὶ γεγόνατε ταῖς ἀκοαῖς. 12 καὶ γὰρ ὀφείλοντες εἶναι διδάσκαλοι διὰ τὸν χρόνον, πάλιν χρείαν ἔχετε τοῦ διδάσκειν ὑμᾶς τινὰ τὰ στοιχεῖα τῆς ἀρχῆς τῶν λογίων τοῦ θεοῦ καὶ γεγόνατε χρείαν ἔχοντες γάλακτος [καὶ] οὐ στερεᾶς τροφῆς. 13 πᾶς γὰρ ὁ μετέχων γάλακτος ἄπειρος λόγου δικαιοσύνης, νήπιος γάρ ἐστιν· 14 τελείων δέ ἐστιν ἡ στερεὰ τροφή, τῶν διὰ τὴν ἕξιν τὰ αἰσθητήρια γεγυμνασμένα ἐχόντων πρὸς διάκρισιν καλοῦ τε καὶ κακοῦ.

6 Διὸ ἀφέντες τὸν τῆς ἀρχῆς τοῦ Χριστοῦ λόγον ἐπὶ τὴν τελειότητα φερώμεθα, μὴ πάλιν θεμέλιον καταβαλλόμενοι μετανοίας ἀπὸ νεκρῶν ἔργων καὶ πίστεως ἐπὶ θεόν, 2 βαπτισμῶν διδαχῆς ἐπιθέσεώς τε χειρῶν, ἀναστάσεώς τε νεκρῶν καὶ κρίματος αἰωνίου. 3 καὶ τοῦτο ποιήσομεν[a], ἐάνπερ ἐπιτρέπῃ ὁ θεός. 4 Ἀδύνατον γὰρ τοὺς ἅπαξ φωτισθέντας, γευσαμένους τε τῆς δωρεᾶς τῆς ἐπουρανίου καὶ μετόχους γενηθέντας πνεύματος ἁγίου 5 καὶ καλὸν γευσαμένους θεοῦ ῥῆμα δυνάμεις τε μέλλοντος αἰῶνος 6 καὶ παραπεσόντας, πάλιν ἀνακαινίζειν εἰς μετάνοιαν, ἀνασταυροῦντας ἑαυτοῖς τὸν υἱὸν τοῦ θεοῦ καὶ παραδειγματίζοντας. 7 γῆ γὰρ ἡ πιοῦσα τὸν ἐπ' αὐτῆς ἐρχόμενον πολλάκις ὑετὸν καὶ τίκτουσα βοτάνην εὔθετον ἐκείνοις δι' οὓς καὶ γεωργεῖται, μεταλαμβάνει εὐλογίας ἀπὸ τοῦ θεοῦ· 8 ἐκφέρουσα δὲ ἀκάνθας καὶ τριβόλους, ἀδόκιμος καὶ κατάρας ἐγγύς, ἧς τὸ τέλος εἰς καῦσιν.

9 Πεπείσμεθα δὲ περὶ ὑμῶν, ἀγαπητοί,

NIV

"You are a priest forever,
in the order of Melchizedek."[c]

7During the days of Jesus' life on earth, he offered up prayers and petitions with loud cries and tears to the one who could save him from death, and he was heard because of his reverent submission. 8Although he was a son, he learned obedience from what he suffered 9and, once made perfect, he became the source of eternal salvation for all who obey him 10and was designated by God to be high priest in the order of Melchizedek.

Warning Against Falling Away

11We have much to say about this, but it is hard to explain because you are slow to learn. 12In fact, though by this time you ought to be teachers, you need someone to teach you the elementary truths of God's word all over again. You need milk, not solid food! 13Anyone who lives on milk, being still an infant, is not acquainted with the teaching about righteousness. 14But solid food is for the mature, who by constant use have trained themselves to distinguish good from evil.

6 Therefore let us leave the elementary teachings about Christ and go on to maturity, not laying again the foundation of repentance from acts that lead to death,[a] and of faith in God, 2instruction about baptisms, the laying on of hands, the resurrection of the dead, and eternal judgment. 3And God permitting, we will do so.

4It is impossible for those who have once been enlightened, who have tasted the heavenly gift, who have shared in the Holy Spirit, 5who have tasted the goodness of the word of God and the powers of the coming age, 6if they fall away, to be brought back to repentance, because[b] to their loss they are crucifying the Son of God all over again and subjecting him to public disgrace.

7Land that drinks in the rain often falling on it and that produces a crop useful to those for whom it is farmed receives the blessing of God. 8But land that produces thorns and thistles is worthless and is in danger of being cursed. In the end it will be burned.

9Even though we speak like this, dear friends, we are confident of better things

---

v Gk he   x Or him   y Or toward maturity   z Other ancient authorities read let us do

a3 NRSV note z ποιήσωμεν

c6 Psalm 110:4   a1 Or from useless rituals   b6 Or repentance while

in your case, things that belong to salvation. [10]For God is not unjust; he will not overlook your work and the love that you showed for his sake[a] in serving the saints, as you still do. [11]And we want each one of you to show the same diligence so as to realize the full assurance of hope to the very end, [12]so that you may not become sluggish, but imitators of those who through faith and patience inherit the promises.

The Certainty of God's Promise

13 When God made a promise to Abraham, because he had no one greater by whom to swear, he swore by himself, [14]saying, "I will surely bless you and multiply you." [15]And thus Abraham,[b] having patiently endured, obtained the promise. [16]Human beings, of course, swear by someone greater than themselves, and an oath given as confirmation puts an end to all dispute. [17]In the same way, when God desired to show even more clearly to the heirs of the promise the unchangeable character of his purpose, he guaranteed it by an oath, [18]so that through two unchangeable things, in which it is impossible that God would prove false, we who have taken refuge might be strongly encouraged to seize the hope set before us. [19]We have this hope, a sure and steadfast anchor of the soul, a hope that enters the inner shrine behind the curtain, [20]where Jesus, a forerunner on our behalf, has entered, having become a high priest forever according to the order of Melchizedek.

The Priestly Order of Melchizedek

7 This "King Melchizedek of Salem, priest of the Most High God, met Abraham as he was returning from defeating the kings and blessed him"; [2]and to him Abraham apportioned "one-tenth of everything." His name, in the first place, means "king of righteousness"; next he is also king of Salem, that is, "king of peace." [3]Without father, without mother, without genealogy, having neither beginning of days nor end of life, but resembling the Son of God, he remains a priest forever.

4 See how great he is! Even[c] Abraham the patriarch gave him a tenth of the spoils. [5]And those descendants of Levi who receive the priestly office have a commandment in the law to collect tithes[d] from the people, that is, from their kindred,[e] though

τὰ κρείσσονα καὶ ἐχόμενα σωτηρίας, εἰ καὶ οὕτως λαλοῦμεν. 10 οὐ γὰρ ἄδικος ὁ θεὸς ἐπιλαθέσθαι τοῦ ἔργου ὑμῶν καὶ τῆς ἀγάπης ἧς ἐνεδείξασθε εἰς τὸ ὄνομα αὐτοῦ, διακονήσαντες τοῖς ἁγίοις καὶ διακονοῦντες. 11 ἐπιθυμοῦμεν δὲ ἕκαστον ὑμῶν τὴν αὐτὴν ἐνδείκνυσθαι σπουδὴν πρὸς τὴν πληροφορίαν τῆς ἐλπίδος ἄχρι τέλους, 12 ἵνα μὴ νωθροὶ γένησθε, μιμηταὶ δὲ τῶν διὰ πίστεως καὶ μακροθυμίας κληρονομούντων τὰς ἐπαγγελίας.

13 Τῷ γὰρ Ἀβραὰμ ἐπαγγειλάμενος ὁ θεός, ἐπεὶ κατ᾽ οὐδενὸς εἶχεν μείζονος ὀμόσαι, **ὤμοσεν καθ᾽ ἑαυτοῦ** 14 λέγων, **Εἰ μὴν εὐλογῶν εὐλογήσω σε καὶ πληθύνων πληθυνῶ** σε· 15 καὶ οὕτως μακροθυμήσας ἐπέτυχεν τῆς ἐπαγγελίας. 16 ἄνθρωποι γὰρ κατὰ τοῦ μείζονος ὀμνύουσιν, καὶ πάσης αὐτοῖς ἀντιλογίας πέρας εἰς βεβαίωσιν ὁ ὅρκος· 17 ἐν ᾧ περισσότερον βουλόμενος ὁ θεὸς ἐπιδεῖξαι τοῖς κληρονόμοις τῆς ἐπαγγελίας τὸ ἀμετάθετον τῆς βουλῆς αὐτοῦ ἐμεσίτευσεν ὅρκῳ, 18 ἵνα διὰ δύο πραγμάτων ἀμεταθέτων, ἐν οἷς ἀδύνατον ψεύσασθαι [τὸν] θεόν, ἰσχυρὰν παράκλησιν ἔχωμεν οἱ καταφυγόντες κρατῆσαι τῆς προκειμένης ἐλπίδος· 19 ἣν ὡς ἄγκυραν ἔχομεν τῆς ψυχῆς ἀσφαλῆ τε καὶ βεβαίαν καὶ εἰσερχομένην εἰς τὸ ἐσώτερον τοῦ καταπετάσματος, 20 ὅπου πρόδρομος ὑπὲρ ἡμῶν εἰσῆλθεν Ἰησοῦς, κατὰ τὴν τάξιν Μελχισέδεκ ἀρχιερεὺς γενόμενος εἰς τὸν αἰῶνα.

7 Οὗτος γὰρ ὁ **Μελχισέδεκ, βασιλεὺς Σαλήμ,** ἱερεὺς τοῦ θεοῦ τοῦ **ὑψίστου,** ὁ **συναντήσας** Ἀβραὰμ **ὑποστρέφοντι ἀπὸ τῆς κοπῆς τῶν βασιλέων** καὶ **εὐλογήσας αὐτόν,** 2 ᾧ καὶ **δεκάτην ἀπὸ πάντων** ἐμέρισεν **Ἀβραάμ,** πρῶτον μὲν ἑρμηνευόμενος βασιλεὺς δικαιοσύνης ἔπειτα δὲ καὶ **βασιλεὺς Σαλήμ,** ὅ ἐστιν βασιλεὺς εἰρήνης, 3 ἀπάτωρ ἀμήτωρ ἀγενεαλόγητος, μήτε ἀρχὴν ἡμερῶν μήτε ζωῆς τέλος ἔχων, ἀφωμοιωμένος δὲ τῷ υἱῷ τοῦ θεοῦ, μένει ἱερεὺς εἰς τὸ διηνεκές.

4 Θεωρεῖτε δὲ πηλίκος οὗτος, ᾧ [καὶ] δεκάτην Ἀβραὰμ ἔδωκεν ἐκ τῶν ἀκροθινίων ὁ πατριάρχης. 5 καὶ οἱ μὲν ἐκ τῶν υἱῶν Λευὶ τὴν ἱερατείαν λαμβάνοντες ἐντολὴν ἔχουσιν ἀποδεκατοῦν τὸν λαὸν κατὰ τὸν νόμον, τοῦτ᾽ ἔστιν τοὺς ἀδελφοὺς αὐτῶν, καίπερ

in your case—things that accompany salvation. [10]God is not unjust; he will not forget your work and the love you have shown him as you have helped his people and continue to help them. [11]We want each of you to show this same diligence to the very end, in order to make your hope sure. [12]We do not want you to become lazy, but to imitate those who through faith and patience inherit what has been promised.

The Certainty of God's Promise

[13]When God made his promise to Abraham, since there was no one greater for him to swear by, he swore by himself, [14]saying, "I will surely bless you and give you many descendants."[c] [15]And so after waiting patiently, Abraham received what was promised.

[16]Men swear by someone greater than themselves, and the oath confirms what is said and puts an end to all argument. [17]Because God wanted to make the unchanging nature of his purpose very clear to the heirs of what was promised, he confirmed it with an oath. [18]God did this so that, by two unchangeable things in which it is impossible for God to lie, we who have fled to take hold of the hope offered to us may be greatly encouraged. [19]We have this hope as an anchor for the soul, firm and secure. It enters the inner sanctuary behind the curtain, [20]where Jesus, who went before us, has entered on our behalf. He has become a high priest forever, in the order of Melchizedek.

Melchizedek the Priest

7 This Melchizedek was king of Salem and priest of God Most High. He met Abraham returning from the defeat of the kings and blessed him, [2]and Abraham gave him a tenth of everything. First, his name means "king of righteousness"; then also, "king of Salem" means "king of peace." [3]Without father or mother, without genealogy, without beginning of days or end of life, like the Son of God he remains a priest forever.

[4]Just think how great he was: Even the patriarch Abraham gave him a tenth of the plunder! [5]Now the law requires the descendants of Levi who become priests to collect a tenth from the people—that is, their brothers—even though their brothers

---

a Gk for his name   b Gk he   c Other ancient authorities lack Even   d Or a tenth   e Gk brothers

c14 Gen. 22:17

these also are descended from Abraham. [6]But this man, who does not belong to their ancestry, collected tithes[d] from Abraham and blessed him who had received the promises. [7]It is beyond dispute that the inferior is blessed by the superior. [8]In the one case, tithes are received by those who are mortal; in the other, by one of whom it is testified that he lives. [9]One might even say that Levi himself, who receives tithes, paid tithes through Abraham, [10]for he was still in the loins of his ancestor when Melchizedek met him.

Another Priest, Like Melchizedek

11 Now if perfection had been attainable through the levitical priesthood—for the people received the law under this priesthood—what further need would there have been to speak of another priest arising according to the order of Melchizedek, rather than one according to the order of Aaron? [12]For when there is a change in the priesthood, there is necessarily a change in the law as well. [13]Now the one of whom these things are spoken belonged to another tribe, from which no one has ever served at the altar. [14]For it is evident that our Lord was descended from Judah, and in connection with that tribe Moses said nothing about priests.

15 It is even more obvious when another priest arises, resembling Melchizedek, [16]one who has become a priest, not through a legal requirement concerning physical descent, but through the power of an indestructible life. [17]For it is attested of him,

"You are a priest forever,
  according to the order of Melchizedek."

[18]There is, on the one hand, the abrogation of an earlier commandment because it was weak and ineffectual [19](for the law made nothing perfect); there is, on the other hand, the introduction of a better hope, through which we approach God.

20 This was confirmed with an oath; for others who became priests took their office without an oath, [21]but this one became a priest with an oath, because of the one who said to him,

"The Lord has sworn
  and will not change his mind,
  'You are a priest forever' "—
[22]accordingly Jesus has also become the guarantee of a better covenant.

23 Furthermore, the former priests were many in number, because they were

d Or a tenth

ἐξεληλυθότας ἐκ τῆς ὀσφύος Ἀβραάμ· **6** ὁ δὲ μὴ γενεαλογούμενος ἐξ αὐτῶν δεδεκάτωκεν Ἀβραὰμ καὶ τὸν ἔχοντα τὰς ἐπαγγελίας εὐλόγηκεν. **7** χωρὶς δὲ πάσης ἀντιλογίας τὸ ἔλαττον ὑπὸ τοῦ κρείττονος εὐλογεῖται. **8** καὶ ὧδε μὲν δεκάτας ἀποθνῄσκοντες ἄνθρωποι λαμβάνουσιν, ἐκεῖ δὲ μαρτυρούμενος ὅτι ζῇ. **9** καὶ ὡς ἔπος εἰπεῖν, δι᾽ Ἀβραὰμ καὶ Λευὶ ὁ δεκάτας λαμβάνων δεδεκάτωται· **10** ἔτι γὰρ ἐν τῇ ὀσφύϊ τοῦ πατρὸς ἦν ὅτε συνήντησεν αὐτῷ Μελχισέδεκ.

11 Εἰ μὲν οὖν τελείωσις διὰ τῆς Λευιτικῆς ἱερωσύνης ἦν, ὁ λαὸς γὰρ ἐπ᾽ αὐτῆς νενομοθέτηται, τίς ἔτι χρεία κατὰ τὴν τάξιν Μελχισέδεκ ἕτερον ἀνίστασθαι ἱερέα καὶ οὐ κατὰ τὴν τάξιν Ἀαρὼν λέγεσθαι; **12** μετατιθεμένης γὰρ τῆς ἱερωσύνης ἐξ ἀνάγκης καὶ νόμου μετάθεσις γίνεται. **13** ἐφ᾽ ὃν γὰρ λέγεται ταῦτα, φυλῆς ἑτέρας μετέσχηκεν, ἀφ᾽ ἧς οὐδεὶς προσέσχηκεν τῷ θυσιαστηρίῳ· **14** πρόδηλον γὰρ ὅτι ἐξ Ἰούδα ἀνατέταλκεν ὁ κύριος ἡμῶν, εἰς ἣν φυλὴν περὶ ἱερέων οὐδὲν Μωϋσῆς ἐλάλησεν. **15** καὶ περισσότερον ἔτι κατάδηλόν ἐστιν, εἰ κατὰ τὴν ὁμοιότητα Μελχισέδεκ ἀνίσταται ἱερεὺς ἕτερος, **16** ὃς οὐ κατὰ νόμον ἐντολῆς σαρκίνης γέγονεν ἀλλὰ κατὰ δύναμιν ζωῆς ἀκαταλύτου. **17** μαρτυρεῖται γὰρ ὅτι

Σὺ ἱερεὺς εἰς τὸν αἰῶνα
  κατὰ τὴν τάξιν Μελχισέδεκ.

18 ἀθέτησις μὲν γὰρ γίνεται προαγούσης ἐντολῆς διὰ τὸ αὐτῆς ἀσθενὲς καὶ ἀνωφελές – **19** οὐδὲν γὰρ ἐτελείωσεν ὁ νόμος – ἐπεισαγωγὴ δὲ κρείττονος ἐλπίδος δι᾽ ἧς ἐγγίζομεν τῷ θεῷ.

20 Καὶ καθ᾽ ὅσον οὐ χωρὶς ὁρκωμοσίας· οἱ μὲν γὰρ χωρὶς ὁρκωμοσίας εἰσὶν ἱερεῖς γεγονότες, **21** ὁ δὲ μετὰ ὁρκωμοσίας διὰ τοῦ λέγοντος πρὸς αὐτόν,

Ὤμοσεν κύριος
  καὶ οὐ μεταμεληθήσεται,
Σὺ ἱερεὺς εἰς τὸν αἰῶνα.

22 κατὰ τοσοῦτο [καὶ] κρείττονος διαθήκης γέγονεν ἔγγυος Ἰησοῦς. **23** καὶ οἱ μὲν πλείονές εἰσιν γεγονότες ἱερεῖς

are descended from Abraham. [6]This man, however, did not trace his descent from Levi, yet he collected a tenth from Abraham and blessed him who had the promises. [7]And without doubt the lesser person is blessed by the greater. [8]In the one case, the tenth is collected by men who die; but in the other case, by him who is declared to be living. [9]One might even say that Levi, who collects the tenth, paid the tenth through Abraham, [10]because when Melchizedek met Abraham, Levi was still in the body of his ancestor.

Jesus Like Melchizedek

[11]If perfection could have been attained through the Levitical priesthood (for on the basis of it the law was given to the people), why was there still need for another priest to come—one in the order of Melchizedek, not in the order of Aaron? [12]For when there is a change of the priesthood, there must also be a change of the law. [13]He of whom these things are said belonged to a different tribe, and no one from that tribe has ever served at the altar. [14]For it is clear that our Lord descended from Judah, and in regard to that tribe Moses said nothing about priests. [15]And what we have said is even more clear if another priest like Melchizedek appears, [16]one who has become a priest not on the basis of a regulation as to his ancestry but on the basis of the power of an indestructible life. [17]For it is declared:

"You are a priest forever,
  in the order of Melchizedek."[a]

[18]The former regulation is set aside because it was weak and useless [19](for the law made nothing perfect), and a better hope is introduced, by which we draw near to God.

[20]And it was not without an oath! Others became priests without any oath, [21]but he became a priest with an oath when God said to him:

"The Lord has sworn
  and will not change his mind:
'You are a priest forever.' "[a]

[22]Because of this oath, Jesus has become the guarantee of a better covenant.
[23]Now there have been many of those

a 17,21 Psalm 110:4

prevented by death from continuing in office; [24]but he holds his priesthood permanently, because he continues forever. [25]Consequently he is able for all time to save[f] those who approach God through him, since he always lives to make intercession for them.

26 For it was fitting that we should have such a high priest, holy, blameless, undefiled, separated from sinners, and exalted above the heavens. [27]Unlike the other[g] high priests, he has no need to offer sacrifices day after day, first for his own sins, and then for those of the people; this he did once for all when he offered himself. [28]For the law appoints as high priests those who are subject to weakness, but the word of the oath, which came later than the law, appoints a Son who has been made perfect forever.

Mediator of a Better Covenant

8 Now the main point in what we are saying is this: we have such a high priest, one who is seated at the right hand of the throne of the Majesty in the heavens, [2]a minister in the sanctuary and the true tent[h] that the Lord, and not any mortal, has set up. [3]For every high priest is appointed to offer gifts and sacrifices; hence it is necessary for this priest also to have something to offer. [4]Now if he were on earth, he would not be a priest at all, since there are priests who offer gifts according to the law. [5]They offer worship in a sanctuary that is a sketch and shadow of the heavenly one; for Moses, when he was about to erect the tent,[h] was warned, "See that you make everything according to the pattern that was shown you on the mountain." [6]But Jesus[i] has now obtained a more excellent ministry, and to that degree he is the mediator of a better covenant, which has been enacted through better promises. [7]For if that first covenant had been faultless, there would have been no need to look for a second one.

8 God[j] finds fault with them when he says:

"The days are surely coming, says the Lord,
　when I will establish a new
　　covenant with the house of Israel
　　and with the house of Judah;
[9]　not like the covenant that I made with
　　their ancestors,
　　on the day when I took them by the

διὰ τὸ θανάτῳ κωλύεσθαι παραμένειν· [24]ὁ δὲ διὰ τὸ μένειν αὐτὸν εἰς τὸν αἰῶνα ἀπαράβατον ἔχει τὴν ἱερωσύνην· [25]ὅθεν καὶ σῴζειν εἰς τὸ παντελὲς δύναται τοὺς προσερχομένους δι᾽ αὐτοῦ τῷ θεῷ, πάντοτε ζῶν εἰς τὸ ἐντυγχάνειν ὑπὲρ αὐτῶν.

[26]Τοιοῦτος γὰρ ἡμῖν καὶ ἔπρεπεν ἀρχιερεύς, ὅσιος ἄκακος ἀμίαντος, κεχωρισμένος ἀπὸ τῶν ἁμαρτωλῶν καὶ ὑψηλότερος τῶν οὐρανῶν γενόμενος, [27]ὃς οὐκ ἔχει καθ᾽ ἡμέραν ἀνάγκην, ὥσπερ οἱ ἀρχιερεῖς, πρότερον ὑπὲρ τῶν ἰδίων ἁμαρτιῶν θυσίας ἀναφέρειν ἔπειτα τῶν τοῦ λαοῦ· τοῦτο γὰρ ἐποίησεν ἐφάπαξ ἑαυτὸν ἀνενέγκας. [28]ὁ νόμος γὰρ ἀνθρώπους καθίστησιν ἀρχιερεῖς ἔχοντας ἀσθένειαν, ὁ λόγος δὲ τῆς ὁρκωμοσίας τῆς μετὰ τὸν νόμον υἱὸν εἰς τὸν αἰῶνα τετελειωμένον.

8 Κεφάλαιον δὲ ἐπὶ τοῖς λεγομένοις, τοιοῦτον ἔχομεν ἀρχιερέα, ὃς ἐκάθισεν ἐν δεξιᾷ τοῦ θρόνου τῆς μεγαλωσύνης ἐν τοῖς οὐρανοῖς, [2]τῶν ἁγίων λειτουργὸς καὶ τῆς σκηνῆς τῆς ἀληθινῆς, ἣν ἔπηξεν ὁ κύριος, οὐκ ἄνθρωπος. [3]πᾶς γὰρ ἀρχιερεὺς εἰς τὸ προσφέρειν δῶρά τε καὶ θυσίας καθίσταται· ὅθεν ἀναγκαῖον ἔχειν τι καὶ τοῦτον ὃ προσενέγκη. [4]εἰ μὲν οὖν ἦν ἐπὶ γῆς, οὐδ᾽ ἂν ἦν ἱερεύς, ὄντων τῶν προσφερόντων κατὰ νόμον τὰ δῶρα· [5]οἵτινες ὑποδείγματι καὶ σκιᾷ λατρεύουσιν τῶν ἐπουρανίων, καθὼς κεχρημάτισται Μωϋσῆς μέλλων ἐπιτελεῖν τὴν σκηνήν, Ὅρα γάρ φησίν, **ποιήσεις πάντα κατὰ τὸν τύπον τὸν δειχθέντα σοι ἐν τῷ ὄρει**· [6]νυν[ὶ] δὲ διαφορωτέρας τέτυχεν λειτουργίας, ὅσῳ καὶ κρείττονός ἐστιν διαθήκης μεσίτης, ἥτις ἐπὶ κρείττοσιν ἐπαγγελίαις νενομοθέτηται.

[7]Εἰ γὰρ ἡ πρώτη ἐκείνη ἦν ἄμεμπτος, οὐκ ἂν δευτέρας ἐζητεῖτο τόπος. [8]μεμφόμενος γὰρ αὐτοὺς[a] λέγει,

Ἰδοὺ ἡμέραι ἔρχονται, λέγει κύριος,
καὶ συντελέσω ἐπὶ τὸν οἶκον
　Ἰσραὴλ
καὶ ἐπὶ τὸν οἶκον Ἰούδα διαθήκην
　καινήν,
[9]οὐ κατὰ τὴν διαθήκην, ἣν ἐποίησα
　τοῖς πατράσιν αὐτῶν
ἐν ἡμέρα ἐπιλαβομένου μου τῆς

priests, since death prevented them from continuing in office; [24]but because Jesus lives forever, he has a permanent priesthood. [25]Therefore he is able to save completely[b] those who come to God through him, because he always lives to intercede for them.

[26]Such a high priest meets our need—one who is holy, blameless, pure, set apart from sinners, exalted above the heavens. [27]Unlike the other high priests, he does not need to offer sacrifices day after day, first for his own sins, and then for the sins of the people. He sacrificed for their sins once for all when he offered himself. [28]For the law appoints as high priests men who are weak; but the oath, which came after the law, appointed the Son, who has been made perfect forever.

The High Priest of a New Covenant

8 The point of what we are saying is this: We do have such a high priest, who sat down at the right hand of the throne of the Majesty in heaven, [2]and who serves in the sanctuary, the true tabernacle set up by the Lord, not by man.

[3]Every high priest is appointed to offer both gifts and sacrifices, and so it was necessary for this one also to have something to offer. [4]If he were on earth, he would not be a priest, for there are already men who offer the gifts prescribed by the law. [5]They serve at a sanctuary that is a copy and shadow of what is in heaven. This is why Moses was warned when he was about to build the tabernacle: "See to it that you make everything according to the pattern shown you on the mountain."[a] [6]But the ministry Jesus has received is as superior to theirs as the covenant of which he is mediator is superior to the old one, and it is founded on better promises.

[7]For if there had been nothing wrong with that first covenant, no place would have been sought for another. [8]But God found fault with the people and said[b]:

"The time is coming, declares the Lord,
　when I will make a new covenant
　with the house of Israel
　and with the house of Judah.
[9]It will not be like the covenant
　I made with their forefathers
　when I took them by the hand

---

[f] Or *able to save completely*　[g] Gk lacks *other*
[h] Or *tabernacle*　[i] Gk *he*　[j] Gk *He*

[a]8 NIV note αὐτοῖς

[b]25 Or *forever*　[a]5 Exodus 25:40　[b]8 Some manuscripts may be translated *fault and said to the people.*

NRSV

hand to lead them out of the land
of Egypt;
for they did not continue in my
covenant,
and so I had no concern for them,
says the Lord.

10 This is the covenant that I will make
with the house of Israel
after those days, says the Lord:
I will put my laws in their minds,
and write them on their hearts,
and I will be their God,
and they shall be my people.

11 And they shall not teach one another
or say to each other, 'Know the Lord,'
for they shall all know me,
from the least of them to the greatest.

12 For I will be merciful toward their
iniquities,
and I will remember their sins no
more."

13In speaking of "a new covenant," he has
made the first one obsolete. And what is
obsolete and growing old will soon disappear.

The Earthly and the Heavenly Sanctuaries

9 Now even the first covenant had regulations for worship and an earthly
sanctuary. 2For a tent[k] was constructed,
the first one, in which were the lampstand,
the table, and the bread of the Presence;[l]
this is called the Holy Place. 3Behind the
second curtain was a tent[k] called the Holy
of Holies. 4In it stood the golden altar of
incense and the ark of the covenant over-
laid on all sides with gold, in which there
were a golden urn holding the manna, and
Aaron's rod that budded, and the tablets
of the covenant; 5above it were the cherubim of glory overshadowing the mercy
seat.[m] Of these things we cannot speak
now in detail.

6 Such preparations having been made,
the priests go continually into the first tent[k]
to carry out their ritual duties; 7but only
the high priest goes into the second, and
he but once a year, and not without taking
the blood that he offers for himself and for
the sins committed unintentionally by the
people. 8By this the Holy Spirit indicates
that the way into the sanctuary has not yet
been disclosed as long as the first tent[k] is
still standing. 9This is a symbol[n] of the
present time, during which gifts and sacrifices are offered that cannot perfect the

[Greek]

χειρὸς αὐτῶν ἐξαγαγεῖν
αὐτοὺς ἐκ γῆς Αἰγύπτου,
ὅτι αὐτοὶ οὐκ ἐνέμειναν ἐν τῇ
διαθήκῃ μου,
κἀγὼ ἠμέλησα αὐτῶν, λέγει
κύριος·

10 ὅτι αὕτη ἡ διαθήκη, ἣν διαθήσομαι
τῷ οἴκῳ Ἰσραὴλ
μετὰ τὰς ἡμέρας ἐκείνας, λέγει
κύριος·
διδοὺς νόμους μου εἰς τὴν διάνοιαν
αὐτῶν
καὶ ἐπὶ καρδίας αὐτῶν ἐπιγράψω
αὐτούς,
καὶ ἔσομαι αὐτοῖς εἰς θεόν,
καὶ αὐτοὶ ἔσονταί μοι εἰς λαόν·

11 καὶ οὐ μὴ διδάξωσιν ἕκαστος τὸν
πολίτην αὐτοῦ
καὶ ἕκαστος τὸν ἀδελφὸν αὐτοῦ
λέγων, Γνῶθι τὸν κύριον,
ὅτι πάντες εἰδήσουσίν με
ἀπὸ μικροῦ ἕως μεγάλου αὐτῶν,

12 ὅτι ἵλεως ἔσομαι ταῖς ἀδικίαις
αὐτῶν
καὶ τῶν ἁμαρτιῶν αὐτῶν οὐ μὴ
μνησθῶ ἔτι.

13 ἐν τῷ λέγειν Καινὴν πεπαλαίωκεν
τὴν πρώτην· τὸ δὲ παλαιούμενον καὶ
γηράσκον ἐγγὺς ἀφανισμοῦ.

9 Εἶχε μὲν οὖν [καὶ] ἡ πρώτη
δικαιώματα τό τε ἅγιον
κοσμικόν. 2 σκηνὴ γὰρ κατεσκευάσθη
ἡ πρώτη ἐν ᾗ ἥ τε λυχνία καὶ ἡ
τράπεζα καὶ ἡ πρόθεσις τῶν ἄρτων,
ἥτις λέγεται Ἅγια· 3 μετὰ δὲ τὸ
δεύτερον καταπέτασμα σκηνὴ ἡ λεγομένη Ἅγια Ἁγίων, 4 χρυσοῦν ἔχουσα
θυμιατήριον καὶ τὴν κιβωτὸν τῆς
διαθήκης περικεκαλυμμένην πάντοθεν
χρυσίῳ, ἐν ᾗ στάμνος χρυσῆ ἔχουσα
τὸ μάννα καὶ ἡ ῥάβδος Ἀαρὼν ἡ
βλαστήσασα καὶ αἱ πλάκες τῆς διαθήκης, 5 ὑπεράνω δὲ αὐτῆς Χερουβὶν
δόξης κατασκιάζοντα τὸ ἱλαστήριον·
περὶ ὧν οὐκ ἔστιν νῦν λέγειν κατὰ
μέρος.

6 Τούτων δὲ οὕτως κατεσκευασμένων
εἰς μὲν τὴν πρώτην σκηνὴν διὰ παντὸς
εἰσίασιν οἱ ἱερεῖς τὰς λατρείας ἐπιτελοῦντες, 7 εἰς δὲ τὴν δευτέραν ἅπαξ
τοῦ ἐνιαυτοῦ μόνος ὁ ἀρχιερεύς, οὐ
χωρὶς αἵματος ὃ προσφέρει ὑπὲρ ἑαυτοῦ
καὶ τῶν τοῦ λαοῦ ἀγνοημάτων, 8 τοῦτο
δηλοῦντος τοῦ πνεύματος τοῦ ἁγίου,
μήπω πεφανερῶσθαι τὴν τῶν ἁγίων
ὁδὸν ἔτι τῆς πρώτης σκηνῆς ἐχούσης
στάσιν, 9 ἥτις παραβολὴ εἰς τὸν καιρὸν
τὸν ἐνεστηκότα, καθ' ἣν δῶρά τε καὶ
θυσίαι προσφέρονται μὴ δυνάμεναι κατὰ

NIV

to lead them out of Egypt,
because they did not remain faithful to
my covenant,
and I turned away from them,
declares the Lord.

10This is the covenant I will make with
the house of Israel
after that time, declares the Lord.
I will put my laws in their minds
and write them on their hearts.
I will be their God,
and they will be my people.

11No longer will a man teach his
neighbor,
or a man his brother, saying, 'Know
the Lord,'
because they will all know me,
from the least of them to the greatest.

12For I will forgive their wickedness
and will remember their sins no
more."[c]

13By calling this covenant "new," he has
made the first one obsolete; and what is
obsolete and aging will soon disappear.

Worship in the Earthly Tabernacle

9 Now the first covenant had regulations for worship and also an earthly
sanctuary. 2A tabernacle was set up. In its
first room were the lampstand, the table
and the consecrated bread; this was called
the Holy Place. 3Behind the second curtain
was a room called the Most Holy Place,
4which had the golden altar of incense and
the gold-covered ark of the covenant. This
ark contained the gold jar of manna,
Aaron's staff that had budded, and the
stone tablets of the covenant. 5Above the
ark were the cherubim of the Glory, overshadowing the atonement cover.[a] But we
cannot discuss these things in detail now.

6When everything had been arranged like
this, the priests entered regularly into the
outer room to carry on their ministry. 7But
only the high priest entered the inner room,
and that only once a year, and never without blood, which he offered for himself
and for the sins the people had committed
in ignorance. 8The Holy Spirit was showing by this that the way into the Most Holy
Place had not yet been disclosed as long as
the first tabernacle was still standing. 9This
is an illustration for the present time, indicating that the gifts and sacrifices being

---

k Or tabernacle   l Gk *the presentation of the loaves*
m Or *the place of atonement*   n Gk *parable*

c12 Jer. 31:31-34   a5 Traditionally *the mercy seat*

conscience of the worshiper, [10]but deal only with food and drink and various baptisms, regulations for the body imposed until the time comes to set things right.

11 But when Christ came as a high priest of the good things that have come,[o] then through the greater and perfect[p] tent[k] (not made with hands, that is, not of this creation), [12]he entered once for all into the Holy Place, not with the blood of goats and calves, but with his own blood, thus obtaining eternal redemption. [13]For if the blood of goats and bulls, with the sprinkling of the ashes of a heifer, sanctifies those who have been defiled so that their flesh is purified, [14]how much more will the blood of Christ, who through the eternal Spirit[q] offered himself without blemish to God, purify our[r] conscience from dead works to worship the living God!

15 For this reason he is the mediator of a new covenant, so that those who are called may receive the promised eternal inheritance, because a death has occurred that redeems them from the transgressions under the first covenant.[s] [16]Where a will[s] is involved, the death of the one who made it must be established. [17]For a will[s] takes effect only at death, since it is not in force as long as the one who made it is alive. [18]Hence not even the first covenant was inaugurated without blood. [19]For when every commandment had been told to all the people by Moses in accordance with the law, he took the blood of calves and goats,[t] with water and scarlet wool and hyssop, and sprinkled both the scroll itself and all the people, [20]saying, "This is the blood of the covenant that God has ordained for you." [21]And in the same way he sprinkled with the blood both the tent[k] and all the vessels used in worship. [22]Indeed, under the law almost everything is purified with blood, and without the shedding of blood there is no forgiveness of sins.

Christ's Sacrifice Takes Away Sin

23 Thus it was necessary for the sketches of the heavenly things to be purified with these rites, but the heavenly things themselves need better sacrifices than these. [24]For Christ did not enter a sanctuary made by human hands, a mere copy of the true

συνείδησιν τελειῶσαι τὸν λατρεύοντα, **10** μόνον ἐπὶ βρώμασιν καὶ πόμασιν καὶ διαφόροις βαπτισμοῖς, δικαιώματα σαρκὸς μέχρι καιροῦ διορθώσεως ἐπικείμενα.

11 Χριστὸς δὲ παραγενόμενος ἀρχιερεὺς τῶν γενομένων[a] ἀγαθῶν διὰ τῆς μείζονος καὶ τελειοτέρας σκηνῆς οὐ χειροποιήτου, τοῦτ' ἔστιν οὐ ταύτης τῆς κτίσεως, **12** οὐδὲ δι' αἵματος τράγων καὶ μόσχων διὰ δὲ τοῦ ἰδίου αἵματος εἰσῆλθεν ἐφάπαξ εἰς τὰ ἅγια αἰωνίαν λύτρωσιν εὑράμενος. **13** εἰ γὰρ τὸ αἷμα τράγων καὶ ταύρων καὶ σποδὸς δαμάλεως ῥαντίζουσα τοὺς κεκοινωμένους ἁγιάζει πρὸς τὴν τῆς σαρκὸς καθαρότητα, **14** πόσῳ μᾶλλον τὸ αἷμα τοῦ Χριστοῦ, ὃς διὰ πνεύματος αἰωνίου[b] ἑαυτὸν προσήνεγκεν ἄμωμον τῷ θεῷ, καθαριεῖ τὴν συνείδησιν ἡμῶν[c] ἀπὸ νεκρῶν ἔργων εἰς τὸ λατρεύειν θεῷ ζῶντι.

15 Καὶ διὰ τοῦτο διαθήκης καινῆς μεσίτης ἐστίν, ὅπως θανάτου γενομένου εἰς ἀπολύτρωσιν τῶν ἐπὶ τῇ πρώτῃ διαθήκῃ παραβάσεων τὴν ἐπαγγελίαν λάβωσιν οἱ κεκλημένοι τῆς αἰωνίου κληρονομίας. **16** ὅπου γὰρ διαθήκη, θάνατον ἀνάγκη φέρεσθαι τοῦ διαθεμένου· **17** διαθήκη γὰρ ἐπὶ νεκροῖς βεβαία, ἐπεὶ μήποτε ἰσχύει ὅτε ζῇ ὁ διαθέμενος. **18** ὅθεν οὐδὲ ἡ πρώτη χωρὶς αἵματος ἐγκεκαίνισται· **19** λαληθείσης γὰρ πάσης ἐντολῆς κατὰ τὸν νόμον ὑπὸ Μωϋσέως παντὶ τῷ λαῷ, λαβὼν τὸ αἷμα τῶν μόσχων [καὶ τῶν τράγων][d] μετὰ ὕδατος καὶ ἐρίου κοκκίνου καὶ ὑσσώπου αὐτό τε τὸ βιβλίον καὶ πάντα τὸν λαὸν ἐράντισεν **20** λέγων, Τοῦτο **τὸ αἷμα τῆς διαθήκης ἧς ἐνετείλατο πρὸς ὑμᾶς ὁ θεός.** **21** καὶ τὴν σκηνὴν δὲ καὶ πάντα τὰ σκεύη τῆς λειτουργίας τῷ αἵματι ὁμοίως ἐράντισεν. **22** καὶ σχεδὸν ἐν αἵματι πάντα καθαρίζεται κατὰ τὸν νόμον καὶ χωρὶς αἱματεκχυσίας οὐ γίνεται ἄφεσις.

23 Ἀνάγκη οὖν τὰ μὲν ὑποδείγματα τῶν ἐν τοῖς οὐρανοῖς τούτοις καθαρίζεσθαι, αὐτὰ δὲ τὰ ἐπουράνια κρείττοσιν θυσίαις παρὰ ταύτας. **24** οὐ γὰρ εἰς χειροποίητα εἰσῆλθεν ἅγια Χριστός, ἀντίτυπα τῶν ἀληθινῶν, ἀλλ' εἰς αὐτὸν

offered were not able to clear the conscience of the worshiper. [10]They are only a matter of food and drink and various ceremonial washings—external regulations applying until the time of the new order.

The Blood of Christ

[11]When Christ came as high priest of the good things that are already here,[b] he went through the greater and more perfect tabernacle that is not man-made, that is to say, not a part of this creation. [12]He did not enter by means of the blood of goats and calves; but he entered the Most Holy Place once for all by his own blood, having obtained eternal redemption. [13]The blood of goats and bulls and the ashes of a heifer sprinkled on those who are ceremonially unclean sanctify them so that they are outwardly clean. [14]How much more, then, will the blood of Christ, who through the eternal Spirit offered himself unblemished to God, cleanse our consciences from acts that lead to death,[c] so that we may serve the living God!

[15]For this reason Christ is the mediator of a new covenant, that those who are called may receive the promised eternal inheritance—now that he has died as a ransom to set them free from the sins committed under the first covenant.

[16]In the case of a will,[d] it is necessary to prove the death of the one who made it, [17]because a will is in force only when somebody has died; it never takes effect while the one who made it is living. [18]This is why even the first covenant was not put into effect without blood. [19]When Moses had proclaimed every commandment of the law to all the people, he took the blood of calves, together with water, scarlet wool and branches of hyssop, and sprinkled the scroll and all the people. [20]He said, "This is the blood of the covenant, which God has commanded you to keep."[e] [21]In the same way, he sprinkled with the blood both the tabernacle and everything used in its ceremonies. [22]In fact, the law requires that nearly everything be cleansed with blood, and without the shedding of blood there is no forgiveness.

[23]It was necessary, then, for the copies of the heavenly things to be purified with these sacrifices, but the heavenly things themselves with better sacrifices than these. [24]For Christ did not enter a man-made sanctuary that was only a copy of the true one;

---

k Or *tabernacle*   o Other ancient authorities read *good things to come*   p Gk *more perfect*   q Other ancient authorities read *Holy Spirit*   r Other ancient authorities read *your*   s The Greek word used here means both *covenant* and *will*   t Other ancient authorities lack *and goats*

a11 NIV/NRSV notes μελλόντων   b14 NRSV note q ἁγίου   c14 NRSV note r ὑμῶν   d19 NIV text and NRSV note t omit καὶ τῶν τράγων

b11 Some early manuscripts *are to come*   c14 Or *from useless rituals*   d16 Same Greek word as *covenant*; also in verse 17   e20 Exodus 24:8

one, but he entered into heaven itself, now to appear in the presence of God on our behalf. 25Nor was it to offer himself again and again, as the high priest enters the Holy Place year after year with blood that is not his own; 26for then he would have had to suffer again and again since the foundation of the world. But as it is, he has appeared once for all at the end of the age to remove sin by the sacrifice of himself. 27And just as it is appointed for mortals to die once, and after that the judgment, 28so Christ, having been offered once to bear the sins of many, will appear a second time, not to deal with sin, but to save those who are eagerly waiting for him.

Christ's Sacrifice Once for All

10 Since the law has only a shadow of the good things to come and not the true form of these realities, it[v] can never, by the same sacrifices that are continually offered year after year, make perfect those who approach. 2Otherwise, would they not have ceased being offered, since the worshipers, cleansed once for all, would no longer have any consciousness of sin? 3But in these sacrifices there is a reminder of sin year after year. 4For it is impossible for the blood of bulls and goats to take away sins. 5Consequently, when Christ[w] came into the world, he said,

"Sacrifices and offerings you have not
  desired,
  but a body you have prepared for
  me;
6 in burnt offerings and sin offerings
  you have taken no pleasure.
7 Then I said, 'See, God, I have come to
  do your will, O God'
  (in the scroll of the book[x] it is written
  of me)."

8When he said above, "You have neither desired nor taken pleasure in sacrifices and offerings and burnt offerings and sin offerings" (these are offered according to the law), 9then he added, "See, I have come to do your will." He abolishes the first in order to establish the second. 10And it is by God's will[y] that we have been sanctified through the offering of the body of Jesus Christ once for all.

11 And every priest stands day after day at his service, offering again and again the same sacrifices that can never take away sins. 12But when Christ[z] had offered for all time a single sacrifice for sins, "he sat down

τὸν οὐρανόν, νῦν ἐμφανισθῆναι τῷ προσώπῳ τοῦ θεοῦ ὑπὲρ ἡμῶν· **25** οὐδ' ἵνα πολλάκις προσφέρῃ ἑαυτόν, ὥσπερ ὁ ἀρχιερεὺς εἰσέρχεται εἰς τὰ ἅγια κατ' ἐνιαυτὸν ἐν αἵματι ἀλλοτρίῳ, **26** ἐπεὶ ἔδει αὐτὸν πολλάκις παθεῖν ἀπὸ καταβολῆς κόσμου· νυνὶ δὲ ἅπαξ ἐπὶ συντελείᾳ τῶν αἰώνων εἰς ἀθέτησιν [τῆς]e ἁμαρτίας διὰ τῆς θυσίας αὐτοῦ πεφανέρωται. **27** καὶ καθ' ὅσον ἀπόκειται τοῖς ἀνθρώποις ἅπαξ ἀποθανεῖν, μετὰ δὲ τοῦτο κρίσις, **28** οὕτως καὶ ὁ Χριστὸς ἅπαξ προσενεχθεὶς εἰς τὸ πολλῶν ἀνενεγκεῖν ἁμαρτίας, ἐκ δευτέρου χωρὶς ἁμαρτίας ὀφθήσεται τοῖς αὐτὸν ἀπεκδεχομένοις εἰς σωτηρίαν.

10 Σκιὰν γὰρ ἔχων ὁ νόμος τῶν μελλόντων ἀγαθῶν, οὐκ αὐτὴν τὴν εἰκόνα τῶν πραγμάτων, κατ' ἐνιαυτὸν ταῖς αὐταῖς θυσίαις ἃς προσφέρουσιν εἰς τὸ διηνεκὲς οὐδέποτε δύναταιa τοὺς προσερχομένους τελειῶσαι· **2** ἐπεὶ οὐκ ἂν ἐπαύσαντο προσφερόμεναι διὰ τὸ μηδεμίαν ἔχειν ἔτι συνείδησιν ἁμαρτιῶν τοὺς λατρεύοντας ἅπαξ κεκαθαρισμένους; **3** ἀλλ' ἐν αὐταῖς ἀνάμνησις ἁμαρτιῶν κατ' ἐνιαυτόν· **4** ἀδύνατον γὰρ αἷμα ταύρων καὶ τράγων ἀφαιρεῖν ἁμαρτίας.

5 Διὸ εἰσερχόμενος εἰς τὸν κόσμον λέγει,

Θυσίαν καὶ προσφορὰν οὐκ
  ἠθέλησας,
  σῶμα δὲ κατηρτίσω μοι·
6 ὁλοκαυτώματα καὶ περὶ ἁμαρτίας
  οὐκ εὐδόκησας.
7 τότε εἶπον,
  Ἰδοὺ ἥκω,
  ἐν κεφαλίδι βιβλίου γέγραπται
  περὶ ἐμοῦ,
  τοῦ ποιῆσαι ὁ θεὸς τὸ θέλημά
  σου.

8 ἀνώτερον λέγων ὅτι Θυσίας καὶ προσφορὰς καὶ ὁλοκαυτώματα καὶ περὶ ἁμαρτίας οὐκ ἠθέλησας οὐδὲ εὐδόκησας, αἵτινες κατὰ νόμον προσφέρονται, **9** τότε εἴρηκεν, Ἰδοὺ ἥκω τοῦ ποιῆσαι τὸ θέλημά σου. ἀναιρεῖ τὸ πρῶτον ἵνα τὸ δεύτερον στήσῃ, **10** ἐν ᾧ θελήματι ἡγιασμένοι ἐσμὲν διὰ τῆς προσφορᾶς τοῦ σώματος Ἰησοῦ Χριστοῦ ἐφάπαξ.

11 Καὶ πᾶς μὲν ἱερεὺς ἕστηκεν καθ' ἡμέραν λειτουργῶν καὶ τὰς αὐτὰς πολλάκις προσφέρων θυσίας, αἵτινες οὐδέποτε δύνανται περιελεῖν ἁμαρτίας, **12** οὗτος δὲ μίαν ὑπὲρ ἁμαρτιῶν προσενέγκας θυσίαν εἰς τὸ διηνεκὲς

he entered heaven itself, now to appear for us in God's presence. 25Nor did he enter heaven to offer himself again and again, the way the high priest enters the Most Holy Place every year with blood that is not his own. 26Then Christ would have had to suffer many times since the creation of the world. But now he has appeared once for all at the end of the ages to do away with sin by the sacrifice of himself. 27Just as man is destined to die once, and after that to face judgment, 28so Christ was sacrificed once to take away the sins of many people; and he will appear a second time, not to bear sin, but to bring salvation to those who are waiting for him.

Christ's Sacrifice Once for All

10 The law is only a shadow of the good things that are coming—not the realities themselves. For this reason it can never, by the same sacrifices repeated endlessly year after year, make perfect those who draw near to worship. 2If it could, would they not have stopped being offered? For the worshipers would have been cleansed once for all, and would no longer have felt guilty for their sins. 3But those sacrifices are an annual reminder of sins, 4because it is impossible for the blood of bulls and goats to take away sins.

5Therefore, when Christ came into the world, he said:

"Sacrifice and offering you did not
  desire,
  but a body you prepared for me;
6with burnt offerings and sin offerings
  you were not pleased.
7Then I said, 'Here I am—it is written
  about me in the scroll—
  I have come to do your will, O God.' "[a]

8First he said, "Sacrifices and offerings, burnt offerings and sin offerings you did not desire, nor were you pleased with them" (although the law required them to be made). 9Then he said, "Here I am, I have come to do your will." He sets aside the first to establish the second. 10And by that will, we have been made holy through the sacrifice of the body of Jesus Christ once for all.

11Day after day every priest stands and performs his religious duties; again and again he offers the same sacrifices, which can never take away sins. 12But when this priest had offered for all time one sacrifice

---

v Other ancient authorities read *they* w Gk *he* x Meaning of Gk uncertain y Gk *by that will* z Gk *this one*

e26 NIV text omits τῆς † a1 NRSV note v δύνανται

a7 Psalm 40:6-8 (see Septuagint)

at the right hand of God," 13and since then has been waiting "until his enemies would be made a footstool for his feet." 14For by a single offering he has perfected for all time those who are sanctified. 15And the Holy Spirit also testifies to us, for after saying,

16 "This is the covenant that I will make
      with them
      after those days, says the Lord:
   I will put my laws in their hearts,
      and I will write them on their minds,"

17he also adds,

   "I will remembera their sins and their
      lawless deeds no more."

18Where there is forgiveness of these, there is no longer any offering for sin.

A Call to Persevere

19 Therefore, my friends,b since we have confidence to enter the sanctuary by the blood of Jesus, 20by the new and living way that he opened for us through the curtain (that is, through his flesh), 21and since we have a great priest over the house of God, 22let us approach with a true heart in full assurance of faith, with our hearts sprinkled clean from an evil conscience and our bodies washed with pure water. 23Let us hold fast to the confession of our hope without wavering, for he who has promised is faithful. 24And let us consider how to provoke one another to love and good deeds, 25not neglecting to meet together, as is the habit of some, but encouraging one another, and all the more as you see the Day approaching.

26 For if we willfully persist in sin after having received the knowledge of the truth, there no longer remains a sacrifice for sins, 27but a fearful prospect of judgment, and a fury of fire that will consume the adversaries. 28Anyone who has violated the law of Moses dies without mercy "on the testimony of two or three witnesses." 29How much worse punishment do you think will be deserved by those who have spurned the Son of God, profaned the blood of the covenant by which they were sanctified, and outraged the Spirit of grace? 30For we know the one who said, "Vengeance is mine, I will repay." And again, "The Lord will judge his people." 31It is a fearful thing to fall into the hands of the living God.

ἐκάθισεν ἐν δεξιᾷ τοῦ θεοῦ, **13** τὸ λοιπὸν ἐκδεχόμενος ἕως τεθῶσιν οἱ ἐχθροὶ αὐτοῦ ὑποπόδιον τῶν ποδῶν αὐτοῦ. **14** μιᾷ γὰρ προσφορᾷ τετελείωκεν εἰς τὸ διηνεκὲς τοὺς ἁγιαζομένους.
15 Μαρτυρεῖ δὲ ἡμῖν καὶ τὸ πνεῦμα τὸ ἅγιον· μετὰ γὰρ τὸ εἰρηκέναι, **16** Αὕτη ἡ διαθήκη ἣν διαθήσομαι
      πρὸς αὐτοὺς
   μετὰ τὰς ἡμέρας ἐκείνας, λέγει
      κύριος·
   διδοὺς νόμους μου ἐπὶ καρδίας
      αὐτῶν
   καὶ ἐπὶ τὴν διάνοιαν αὐτῶν
      ἐπιγράψω αὐτούς,
17 bκαὶ τῶν ἁμαρτιῶν αὐτῶν καὶ τῶν
      ἀνομιῶν αὐτῶν
   οὐ μὴ μνησθήσομαι ἔτι.
18 ὅπου δὲ ἄφεσις τούτων, οὐκέτι προσφορὰ περὶ ἁμαρτίας.
19 Ἔχοντες οὖν, ἀδελφοί, παρρησίαν εἰς τὴν εἴσοδον τῶν ἁγίων ἐν τῷ αἵματι Ἰησοῦ, **20** ἣν ἐνεκαίνισεν ἡμῖν ὁδὸν πρόσφατον καὶ ζῶσαν διὰ τοῦ καταπετάσματος, τοῦτ᾽ ἔστιν τῆς σαρκὸς αὐτοῦ, **21** καὶ ἱερέα μέγαν ἐπὶ τὸν οἶκον τοῦ θεοῦ, **22** προσερχώμεθα μετὰ ἀληθινῆς καρδίας ἐν πληροφορίᾳ πίστεως ῥεραντισμένοι τὰς καρδίας ἀπὸ συνειδήσεως πονηρᾶς καὶ λελουσμένοι τὸ σῶμα ὕδατι καθαρῷ· **23** κατέχωμεν τὴν ὁμολογίαν τῆς ἐλπίδος ἀκλινῆ, πιστὸς γὰρ ὁ ἐπαγγειλάμενος, **24** καὶ κατανοῶμεν ἀλλήλους εἰς παροξυσμὸν ἀγάπης καὶ καλῶν ἔργων, **25** μὴ ἐγκαταλείποντες τὴν ἐπισυναγωγὴν ἑαυτῶν, καθὼς ἔθος τισίν, ἀλλὰ παρακαλοῦντες, καὶ τοσούτῳ μᾶλλον ὅσῳ βλέπετε ἐγγίζουσαν τὴν ἡμέραν.
26 Ἑκουσίως γὰρ ἁμαρτανόντων ἡμῶν μετὰ τὸ λαβεῖν τὴν ἐπίγνωσιν τῆς ἀληθείας, οὐκέτι περὶ ἁμαρτιῶν ἀπολείπεται θυσία, **27** φοβερὰ δέ τις ἐκδοχὴ κρίσεως καὶ πυρὸς ζῆλος ἐσθίειν μέλλοντος τοὺς ὑπεναντίους. **28** ἀθετήσας τις νόμον Μωϋσέως χωρὶς οἰκτιρμῶν ἐπὶ δυσὶν ἢ τρισὶν μάρτυσιν ἀποθνῄσκει· **29** πόσῳ δοκεῖτε χείρονος ἀξιωθήσεται τιμωρίας ὁ τὸν υἱὸν τοῦ θεοῦ καταπατήσας καὶ τὸ αἷμα τῆς διαθήκης κοινὸν ἡγησάμενος, ἐν ᾧ ἡγιάσθη, καὶ τὸ πνεῦμα τῆς χάριτος ἐνυβρίσας; **30** οἴδαμεν γὰρ τὸν εἰπόντα,
Ἐμοὶ ἐκδίκησις, ἐγὼ ἀνταποδώσω.
καὶ πάλιν,
Κρινεῖ κύριος τὸν λαὸν αὐτοῦ.
31 φοβερὸν τὸ ἐμπεσεῖν εἰς χεῖρας θεοῦ ζῶντος.

for sins, he sat down at the right hand of God. 13Since that time he waits for his enemies to be made his footstool, 14because by one sacrifice he has made perfect forever those who are being made holy.

15The Holy Spirit also testifies to us about this. First he says:

16"This is the covenant I will make with
      them
   after that time, says the Lord.
   I will put my laws in their hearts,
      and I will write them on their minds."b

17Then he adds:

   "Their sins and lawless acts
      I will remember no more."c

18And where these have been forgiven, there is no longer any sacrifice for sin.

A Call to Persevere

19Therefore, brothers, since we have confidence to enter the Most Holy Place by the blood of Jesus, 20by a new and living way opened for us through the curtain, that is, his body, 21and since we have a great priest over the house of God, 22let us draw near to God with a sincere heart in full assurance of faith, having our hearts sprinkled to cleanse us from a guilty conscience and having our bodies washed with pure water. 23Let us hold unswervingly to the hope we profess, for he who promised is faithful. 24And let us consider how we may spur one another on toward love and good deeds. 25Let us not give up meeting together, as some are in the habit of doing, but let us encourage one another—and all the more as you see the Day approaching.

26If we deliberately keep on sinning after we have received the knowledge of the truth, no sacrifice for sins is left, 27but only a fearful expectation of judgment and of raging fire that will consume the enemies of God. 28Anyone who rejected the law of Moses died without mercy on the testimony of two or three witnesses. 29How much more severely do you think a man deserves to be punished who has trampled the Son of God under foot, who has treated as an unholy thing the blood of the covenant that sanctified him, and who has insulted the Spirit of grace? 30For we know him who said, "It is mine to avenge; I will repay,"d and again, "The Lord will judge his people."e 31It is a dreadful thing to fall into the hands of the living God.

a Gk *on their minds and I will remember*   b Gk *Therefore, brothers*

b17 NIV text adds ὕστερον λέγει †

b16 Jer. 31:33   c17 Jer. 31:34   d30 Deut. 32:35
e30 Deut. 32:36; Psalm 135:14

32 But recall those earlier days when, after you had been enlightened, you endured a hard struggle with sufferings, [33]sometimes being publicly exposed to abuse and persecution, and sometimes being partners with those so treated. [34]For you had compassion for those who were in prison, and you cheerfully accepted the plundering of your possessions, knowing that you yourselves possessed something better and more lasting. [35]Do not, therefore, abandon that confidence of yours; it brings a great reward. [36]For you need endurance, so that when you have done the will of God, you may receive what was promised.

[37] For yet "in a very little while,
  the one who is coming will come
    and will not delay;
[38] but my righteous one will live by faith.
  My soul takes no pleasure in anyone
    who shrinks back."

[39]But we are not among those who shrink back and so are lost, but among those who have faith and so are saved.

The Meaning of Faith

11 Now faith is the assurance of things hoped for, the conviction of things not seen. [2]Indeed, by faith[c] our ancestors received approval. [3]By faith we understand that the worlds were prepared by the word of God, so that what is seen was made from things that are not visible.[d]

The Examples of Abel, Enoch, and Noah

4 By faith Abel offered to God a more acceptable[e] sacrifice than Cain's. Through this he received approval as righteous, God himself giving approval to his gifts; he died, but through his faith[f] he still speaks. [5]By faith Enoch was taken so that he did not experience death; and "he was not found, because God had taken him." For it was attested before he was taken away that "he had pleased God." [6]And without faith it is impossible to please God, for whoever would approach him must believe that he exists and that he rewards those who seek him. [7]By faith Noah, warned by God about events as yet unseen, respected the warning and built an ark to save his household; by this he condemned the world and became an heir to the righteousness that is in accordance with faith.

32 Ἀναμιμνῄσκεσθε δὲ τὰς πρότερον ἡμέρας, ἐν αἷς φωτισθέντες πολλὴν ἄθλησιν ὑπεμείνατε παθημάτων, **33** τοῦτο μὲν ὀνειδισμοῖς τε καὶ θλίψεσιν θεατριζόμενοι, τοῦτο δὲ κοινωνοὶ τῶν οὕτως ἀναστρεφομένων γενηθέντες. **34** καὶ γὰρ τοῖς δεσμίοις συνεπαθήσατε καὶ τὴν ἁρπαγὴν τῶν ὑπαρχόντων ὑμῶν μετὰ χαρᾶς προσεδέξασθε γινώσκοντες ἔχειν ἑαυτοὺς κρείττονα ὕπαρξιν καὶ μένουσαν. **35** μὴ ἀποβάλητε οὖν τὴν παρρησίαν ὑμῶν, ἥτις ἔχει μεγάλην μισθαποδοσίαν. **36** ὑπομονῆς γὰρ ἔχετε χρείαν ἵνα τὸ θέλημα τοῦ θεοῦ ποιήσαντες κομίσησθε τὴν ἐπαγγελίαν. **37** ἔτι γὰρ μικρὸν ὅσον ὅσον,

ὁ ἐρχόμενος ἥξει καὶ οὐ χρονίσει·
38 ὁ δὲ δίκαιός μου[a] ἐκ πίστεως
  ζήσεται,
καὶ ἐὰν ὑποστείληται,
  οὐκ εὐδοκεῖ ἡ ψυχή μου ἐν αὐτῷ.
39 ἡμεῖς δὲ οὐκ ἐσμὲν ὑποστολῆς εἰς ἀπώλειαν ἀλλὰ πίστεως εἰς περιποίησιν ψυχῆς.

11 Ἔστιν δὲ πίστις ἐλπιζομένων ὑπόστασις, πραγμάτων ἔλεγχος οὐ βλεπομένων. **2** ἐν ταύτῃ γὰρ ἐμαρτυρήθησαν οἱ πρεσβύτεροι.

3 Πίστει νοοῦμεν κατηρτίσθαι τοὺς αἰῶνας ῥήματι θεοῦ, εἰς τὸ μὴ ἐκ φαινομένων τὸ βλεπόμενον γεγονέναι.

4 Πίστει πλείονα θυσίαν Ἄβελ παρὰ Κάϊν προσήνεγκεν τῷ θεῷ, δι᾽ ἧς ἐμαρτυρήθη εἶναι δίκαιος, μαρτυροῦντος ἐπὶ τοῖς δώροις αὐτοῦ τοῦ θεοῦ, καὶ δι᾽ αὐτῆς ἀποθανὼν ἔτι λαλεῖ. **5** Πίστει Ἐνὼχ μετετέθη τοῦ μὴ ἰδεῖν θάνατον, καὶ οὐχ ηὑρίσκετο διότι μετέθηκεν αὐτὸν ὁ θεός. πρὸ γὰρ τῆς μεταθέσεως μεμαρτύρηται εὐαρεστηκέναι τῷ θεῷ· **6** χωρὶς δὲ πίστεως ἀδύνατον εὐαρεστῆσαι· πιστεῦσαι γὰρ δεῖ τὸν προσερχόμενον τῷ θεῷ ὅτι ἔστιν καὶ τοῖς ἐκζητοῦσιν αὐτὸν μισθαποδότης γίνεται. **7** Πίστει χρηματισθεὶς Νῶε περὶ τῶν μηδέπω βλεπομένων, εὐλαβηθεὶς κατεσκεύασεν κιβωτὸν εἰς σωτηρίαν τοῦ οἴκου αὐτοῦ δι᾽ ἧς κατέκρινεν τὸν κόσμον, καὶ τῆς κατὰ πίστιν δικαιοσύνης ἐγένετο κληρονόμος.

[32]Remember those earlier days after you had received the light, when you stood your ground in a great contest in the face of suffering. [33]Sometimes you were publicly exposed to insult and persecution; at other times you stood side by side with those who were so treated. [34]You sympathized with those in prison and joyfully accepted the confiscation of your property, because you knew that you yourselves had better and lasting possessions.

[35]So do not throw away your confidence; it will be richly rewarded. [36]You need to persevere so that when you have done the will of God, you will receive what he has promised. [37]For in just a very little while,

"He who is coming will come and will
  not delay.
[38] But my righteous one[f] will live by faith.
  And if he shrinks back,
    I will not be pleased with him."[g]

[39]But we are not of those who shrink back and are destroyed, but of those who believe and are saved.

By Faith

11 Now faith is being sure of what we hope for and certain of what we do not see. [2]This is what the ancients were commended for.

[3]By faith we understand that the universe was formed at God's command, so that what is seen was not made out of what was visible.

[4]By faith Abel offered God a better sacrifice than Cain did. By faith he was commended as a righteous man, when God spoke well of his offerings. And by faith he still speaks, even though he is dead.

[5]By faith Enoch was taken from this life, so that he did not experience death; he could not be found, because God had taken him away. For before he was taken, he was commended as one who pleased God. [6]And without faith it is impossible to please God, because anyone who comes to him must believe that he exists and that he rewards those who earnestly seek him.

[7]By faith Noah, when warned about things not yet seen, in holy fear built an ark to save his family. By his faith he condemned the world and became heir of the righteousness that comes by faith.

---

[c] Gk *by this*   [d] Or *was not made out of visible things*
[e] Gk *greater*   [f] Gk *through it*
    [c]38 NIV note omits μου †
[f]38 One early manuscript *But the righteous*
[g]38 Hab. 2:3,4

NRSV

The Faith of Abraham

8 By faith Abraham obeyed when he was called to set out for a place that he was to receive as an inheritance; and he set out, not knowing where he was going. 9By faith he stayed for a time in the land he had been promised, as in a foreign land, living in tents, as did Isaac and Jacob, who were heirs with him of the same promise. 10For he looked forward to the city that has foundations, whose architect and builder is God. 11By faith he received power of procreation, even though he was too old—and Sarah herself was barren—because he considered him faithful who had promised.g 12Therefore from one person, and this one as good as dead, descendants were born, "as many as the stars of heaven and as the innumerable grains of sand by the seashore."

13 All of these died in faith without having received the promises, but from a distance they saw and greeted them. They confessed that they were strangers and foreigners on the earth, 14for people who speak in this way make it clear that they are seeking a homeland. 15If they had been thinking of the land that they had left behind, they would have had opportunity to return. 16But as it is, they desire a better country, that is, a heavenly one. Therefore God is not ashamed to be called their God; indeed, he has prepared a city for them.

17 By faith Abraham, when put to the test, offered up Isaac. He who had received the promises was ready to offer up his only son, 18of whom he had been told, "It is through Isaac that descendants shall be named for you." 19He considered the fact that God is able even to raise someone from the dead—and figuratively speaking, he did receive him back. 20By faith Isaac invoked blessings for the future on Jacob and Esau. 21By faith Jacob, when dying, blessed each of the sons of Joseph, "bowing in worship over the top of his staff." 22By faith Joseph, at the end of his life, made mention of the exodus of the Israelites and gave instructions about his burial.h

The Faith of Moses

23 By faith Moses was hidden by his parents for three months after his birth, because they saw that the child was beautiful; and they were not afraid of the king's

Greek

8 Πίστει καλούμενος Ἀβραὰμ ὑπήκουσεν ἐξελθεῖν εἰς τόπον ὃν ἤμελλεν λαμβάνειν εἰς κληρονομίαν, καὶ ἐξῆλθεν μὴ ἐπιστάμενος ποῦ ἔρχεται. 9 Πίστει παρῴκησεν εἰς γῆν τῆς ἐπαγγελίας ὡς ἀλλοτρίαν ἐν σκηναῖς κατοικήσας μετὰ Ἰσαὰκ καὶ Ἰακὼβ τῶν συγκληρονόμων τῆς ἐπαγγελίας τῆς αὐτῆς· 10 ἐξεδέχετο γὰρ τὴν τοὺς θεμελίους ἔχουσαν πόλιν ἧς τεχνίτης καὶ δημιουργὸς ὁ θεός. 11 Πίστει καὶ αὐτὴ Σάρρα στεῖρα δύναμιν εἰς καταβολὴν σπέρματος ἔλαβεν καὶ παρὰ καιρὸν ἡλικίας, ἐπεὶ πιστὸν ἡγήσατο τὸν ἐπαγγειλάμενον. 12 διὸ καὶ ἀφ' ἑνὸς ἐγεννήθησαν, καὶ ταῦτα νενεκρωμένου, καθὼς τὰ ἄστρα τοῦ οὐρανοῦ τῷ πλήθει καὶ ὡς ἡ ἄμμος ἡ παρὰ τὸ χεῖλος τῆς θαλάσσης ἡ ἀναρίθμητος. 13 Κατὰ πίστιν ἀπέθανον οὗτοι πάντες, μὴ λαβόντες τὰς ἐπαγγελίας ἀλλὰ πόρρωθεν αὐτὰς ἰδόντες καὶ ἀσπασάμενοι καὶ ὁμολογήσαντες ὅτι ξένοι καὶ παρεπίδημοί εἰσιν ἐπὶ τῆς γῆς. 14 οἱ γὰρ τοιαῦτα λέγοντες ἐμφανίζουσιν ὅτι πατρίδα ἐπιζητοῦσιν. 15 καὶ εἰ μὲν ἐκείνης ἐμνημόνευον ἀφ' ἧς ἐξέβησαν, εἶχον ἂν καιρὸν ἀνακάμψαι· 16 νῦν δὲ κρείττονος ὀρέγονται, τοῦτ' ἔστιν ἐπουρανίου. διὸ οὐκ ἐπαισχύνεται αὐτοὺς ὁ θεὸς θεὸς ἐπικαλεῖσθαι αὐτῶν· ἡτοίμασεν γὰρ αὐτοῖς πόλιν. 17 Πίστει προσενήνοχεν Ἀβραὰμ τὸν Ἰσαὰκ πειραζόμενος καὶ τὸν μονογενῆ προσέφερεν, ὁ τὰς ἐπαγγελίας ἀναδεξάμενος, 18 πρὸς ὃν ἐλαλήθη ὅτι Ἐν **Ἰσαὰκ κληθήσεταί σοι σπέρμα,** 19 λογισάμενος ὅτι καὶ ἐκ νεκρῶν ἐγείρειν δυνατὸς ὁ θεός, ὅθεν αὐτὸν καὶ ἐν παραβολῇ ἐκομίσατο. 20 Πίστει καὶ περὶ μελλόντων εὐλόγησεν Ἰσαὰκ τὸν Ἰακὼβ καὶ τὸν Ἠσαῦ. 21 Πίστει Ἰακὼβ ἀποθνῄσκων ἕκαστον τῶν υἱῶν Ἰωσὴφ εὐλόγησεν καὶ **προσεκύνησεν ἐπὶ τὸ ἄκρον τῆς ῥάβδου αὐτοῦ.** 22 Πίστει Ἰωσὴφ τελευτῶν περὶ τῆς ἐξόδου τῶν υἱῶν Ἰσραὴλ ἐμνημόνευσεν καὶ περὶ τῶν ὀστέων αὐτοῦ ἐνετείλατο. 23 Πίστει Μωϋσῆς γεννηθεὶς ἐκρύβη τρίμηνον ὑπὸ τῶν πατέρων αὐτοῦ, διότι εἶδον ἀστεῖον τὸ παιδίον καὶ οὐκ ἐφοβήθησαν τὸ διάταγμα τοῦ

NIV

8By faith Abraham, when called to go to a place he would later receive as his inheritance, obeyed and went, even though he did not know where he was going. 9By faith he made his home in the promised land like a stranger in a foreign country; he lived in tents, as did Isaac and Jacob, who were heirs with him of the same promise. 10For he was looking forward to the city with foundations, whose architect and builder is God. 11By faith Abraham, even though he was past age—and Sarah herself was barren—was enabled to become a father because hea considered him faithful who had made the promise. 12And so from this one man, and he as good as dead, came descendants as numerous as the stars in the sky and as countless as the sand on the seashore.

13All these people were still living by faith when they died. They did not receive the things promised; they only saw them and welcomed them from a distance. And they admitted that they were aliens and strangers on earth. 14People who say such things show that they are looking for a country of their own. 15If they had been thinking of the country they had left, they would have had opportunity to return. 16Instead, they were longing for a better country—a heavenly one. Therefore God is not ashamed to be called their God, for he has prepared a city for them.

17By faith Abraham, when God tested him, offered Isaac as a sacrifice. He who had received the promises was about to sacrifice his one and only son, 18even though God had said to him, "It is through Isaac that your offspringb will be reckoned."c 19Abraham reasoned that God could raise the dead, and figuratively speaking, he did receive Isaac back from death.

20By faith Isaac blessed Jacob and Esau in regard to their future.

21By faith Jacob, when he was dying, blessed each of Joseph's sons, and worshiped as he leaned on the top of his staff.

22By faith Joseph, when his end was near, spoke about the exodus of the Israelites from Egypt and gave instructions about his bones.

23By faith Moses' parents hid him for three months after he was born, because they saw he was no ordinary child, and they were not afraid of the king's edict.

---

g Other ancient authorities read *By faith Sarah herself, though barren, received power to conceive, even when she was too old, because she considered him faithful who had promised.*   h Gk *his bones*

a11 Or *By faith even Sarah, who was past age, was enabled to bear children because she*   b18 Greek *seed*   c18 Gen. 21:12

NRSV

edit.[i] 24By faith Moses, when he was grown up, refused to be called a son of Pharaoh's daughter, 25choosing rather to share ill-treatment with the people of God than to enjoy the fleeting pleasures of sin. 26He considered abuse suffered for the Christ[j] to be greater wealth than the treasures of Egypt, for he was looking ahead to the reward. 27By faith he left Egypt, unafraid of the king's anger; for he persevered as though[k] he saw him who is invisible. 28By faith he kept the Passover and the sprinkling of blood, so that the destroyer of the firstborn would not touch the firstborn of Israel.[l]

The Faith of Other Israelite Heroes

29 By faith the people passed through the Red Sea as if it were dry land, but when the Egyptians attempted to do so they were drowned. 30By faith the walls of Jericho fell after they had been encircled for seven days. 31By faith Rahab the prostitute did not perish with those who were disobedient,[m] because she had received the spies in peace.

32 And what more should I say? For time would fail me to tell of Gideon, Barak, Samson, Jephthah, of David and Samuel and the prophets— 33who through faith conquered kingdoms, administered justice, obtained promises, shut the mouths of lions, 34quenched raging fire, escaped the edge of the sword, won strength out of weakness, became mighty in war, put foreign armies to flight. 35Women received their dead by resurrection. Others were tortured, refusing to accept release, in order to obtain a better resurrection. 36Others suffered mocking and flogging, and even chains and imprisonment. 37They were stoned to death, they were sawn in two,[n] they were killed by the sword; they went about in skins of sheep and goats, destitute, persecuted, tormented— 38of whom the world was not worthy. They wandered in deserts and mountains, and in caves and holes in the ground.

39 Yet all these, though they were commended for their faith, did not receive what was promised, 40since God had provided something better so that they would not, apart from us, be made perfect.

Greek

βασιλέως.ᵃ 24 Πίστει Μωϋσῆς μέγας γενόμενος ἠρνήσατο λέγεσθαι υἱὸς θυγατρὸς Φαραώ, 25 μᾶλλον ἑλόμενος συγκακουχεῖσθαι τῷ λαῷ τοῦ θεοῦ ἢ πρόσκαιρον ἔχειν ἁμαρτίας ἀπόλαυσιν. 26 μείζονα πλοῦτον ἡγησάμενος τῶν Αἰγύπτου θησαυρῶν τὸν ὀνειδισμὸν τοῦ Χριστοῦ· ἀπέβλεπεν γὰρ εἰς τὴν μισθαποδοσίαν. 27 Πίστει κατέλιπεν Αἴγυπτον μὴ φοβηθεὶς τὸν θυμὸν τοῦ βασιλέως· τὸν γὰρ ἀόρατον ὡς ὁρῶν ἐκαρτέρησεν. 28 Πίστει πεποίηκεν τὸ πάσχα καὶ τὴν πρόσχυσιν τοῦ αἵματος, ἵνα μὴ ὁ ὀλοθρεύων τὰ πρωτότοκα θίγῃ αὐτῶν. 29 Πίστει διέβησαν τὴν Ἐρυθρὰν Θάλασσαν ὡς διὰ ξηρᾶς γῆς, ἧς πεῖραν λαβόντες οἱ Αἰγύπτιοι κατεπόθησαν. 30 Πίστει τὰ τείχη Ἰεριχὼ ἔπεσαν κυκλωθέντα ἐπὶ ἑπτὰ ἡμέρας. 31 Πίστει Ῥαὰβ ἡ πόρνη οὐ συναπώλετο τοῖς ἀπειθήσασιν δεξαμένη τοὺς κατασκόπους μετ' εἰρήνης.

32 Καὶ τί ἔτι λέγω; ἐπιλείψει με γὰρ διηγούμενον ὁ χρόνος περὶ Γεδεών, Βαράκ, Σαμψών, Ἰεφθάε, Δαυίδ τε καὶ Σαμουὴλ καὶ τῶν προφητῶν, 33 οἳ διὰ πίστεως κατηγωνίσαντο βασιλείας, εἰργάσαντο δικαιοσύνην, ἐπέτυχον ἐπαγγελιῶν, ἔφραξαν στόματα λεόντων, 34 ἔσβεσαν δύναμιν πυρός, ἔφυγον στόματα μαχαίρης, ἐδυναμώθησαν ἀπὸ ἀσθενείας, ἐγενήθησαν ἰσχυροὶ ἐν πολέμῳ, παρεμβολὰς ἔκλιναν ἀλλοτρίων. 35 ἔλαβον γυναῖκες ἐξ ἀναστάσεως τοὺς νεκροὺς αὐτῶν· ἄλλοι δὲ ἐτυμπανίσθησαν οὐ προσδεξάμενοι τὴν ἀπολύτρωσιν, ἵνα κρείττονος ἀναστάσεως τύχωσιν· 36 ἕτεροι δὲ ἐμπαιγμῶν καὶ μαστίγων πεῖραν ἔλαβον, ἔτι δὲ δεσμῶν καὶ φυλακῆς· 37 ἐλιθάσθησαν, ἐπρίσθησαν,ᵇ ἐν φόνῳ μαχαίρης ἀπέθανον, περιῆλθον ἐν μηλωταῖς, ἐν αἰγείοις δέρμασιν, ὑστερούμενοι, θλιβόμενοι, κακουχούμενοι, 38 ὧν οὐκ ἦν ἄξιος ὁ κόσμος, ἐπὶ ἐρημίαις πλανώμενοι καὶ ὄρεσιν καὶ σπηλαίοις καὶ ταῖς ὀπαῖς τῆς γῆς. 39 Καὶ οὗτοι πάντες μαρτυρηθέντες διὰ τῆς πίστεως οὐκ ἐκομίσαντο τὴν ἐπαγγελίαν, 40 τοῦ θεοῦ περὶ ἡμῶν κρεῖττόν τι προβλεψαμένου, ἵνα μὴ χωρὶς ἡμῶν τελειωθῶσιν.

NIV

24By faith Moses, when he had grown up, refused to be known as the son of Pharaoh's daughter. 25He chose to be mistreated along with the people of God rather than to enjoy the pleasures of sin for a short time. 26He regarded disgrace for the sake of Christ as of greater value than the treasures of Egypt, because he was looking ahead to his reward. 27By faith he left Egypt, not fearing the king's anger; he persevered because he saw him who is invisible. 28By faith he kept the Passover and the sprinkling of blood, so that the destroyer of the firstborn would not touch the firstborn of Israel.

29By faith the people passed through the Red Sea[d] as on dry land; but when the Egyptians tried to do so, they were drowned.

30By faith the walls of Jericho fell, after the people had marched around them for seven days.

31By faith the prostitute Rahab, because she welcomed the spies, was not killed with those who were disobedient.[e]

32And what more shall I say? I do not have time to tell about Gideon, Barak, Samson, Jephthah, David, Samuel and the prophets, 33who through faith conquered kingdoms, administered justice, and gained what was promised; who shut the mouths of lions, 34quenched the fury of the flames, and escaped the edge of the sword; whose weakness was turned to strength; and who became powerful in battle and routed foreign armies. 35Women received back their dead, raised to life again. Others were tortured and refused to be released, so that they might gain a better resurrection. 36Some faced jeers and flogging, while still others were chained and put in prison. 37They were stoned[f]; they were sawed in two; they were put to death by the sword. They went about in sheepskins and goatskins, destitute, persecuted and mistreated— 38the world was not worthy of them. They wandered in deserts and mountains, and in caves and holes in the ground.

39These were all commended for their faith, yet none of them received what had been promised. 40God had planned something better for us so that only together with us would they be made perfect.

---

iOther ancient authorities add *By faith Moses, when he was grown up, killed the Egyptian, because he observed the humiliation of his people* (Gk *brothers*)   jOr *the Messiah* kOr *because*   lGk *would not touch them*   mOr *unbelieving* nOther ancient authorities add *they were tempted*

ᵃ23 NRSV note i adds Πίστει μέγας γενόμενος Μωϋσῆς ἀνεῖλεν τὸν Αἰγύπτιον κατανοῶν τὴν ταπείνωσιν τῶν ἀδελφῶν αὐτοῦ.   ᵇ37 NIV/NRSV notes add ἐπειράσθησαν before or after ἐπρίσθησαν

d29 That is, Sea of Reeds   e31 Or *unbelieving* f37 Some early manuscripts *stoned; they were put to the test;*

The Example of Jesus

12 Therefore, since we are surrounded by so great a cloud of witnesses,
let us also lay aside every weight and the
sin that clings so closely,[o] and let us run
with perseverance the race that is set before us, 2looking to Jesus the pioneer and
perfecter of our faith, who for the sake of[p]
the joy that was set before him endured
the cross, disregarding its shame, and has
taken his seat at the right hand of the throne
of God.

3 Consider him who endured such hostility against himself from sinners,[q] so that
you may not grow weary or lose heart. 4In
your struggle against sin you have not yet
resisted to the point of shedding your
blood. 5And you have forgotten the exhortation that addresses you as children—

"My child, do not regard lightly the
discipline of the Lord,
or lose heart when you are punished
by him;
6 for the Lord disciplines those whom
he loves,
and chastises every child whom he
accepts."

7Endure trials for the sake of discipline.
God is treating you as children; for what
child is there whom a parent does not discipline? 8If you do not have that discipline
in which all children share, then you are
illegitimate and not his children. 9More-
over, we had human parents to discipline
us, and we respected them. Should we not
be even more willing to be subject to the
Father of spirits and live? 10For they disciplined us for a short time as seemed best to
them, but he disciplines us for our good, in
order that we may share his holiness.
11Now, discipline always seems painful
rather than pleasant at the time, but later it
yields the peaceful fruit of righteousness
to those who have been trained by it.

12 Therefore lift your drooping hands
and strengthen your weak knees, 13and
make straight paths for your feet, so that
what is lame may not be put out of joint,
but rather be healed.

Warnings against Rejecting God's Grace

14 Pursue peace with everyone, and the
holiness without which no one will see the
Lord. 15See to it that no one fails to obtain
the grace of God; that no root of bitterness
springs up and causes trouble, and through

[o] Other ancient authorities read *sin that easily distracts*
[p] Or *who instead of* [q] Other ancient authorities read
such hostility from sinners against themselves

12 *Τοιγαροῦν καὶ ἡμεῖς τοσοῦτον
ἔχοντες περικείμενον ἡμῖν
νέφος μαρτύρων, ὄγκον ἀποθέμενοι
πάντα καὶ τὴν εὐπερίστατον*[a] *ἁμαρτίαν,
δι᾽ ὑπομονῆς τρέχωμεν τὸν προκείμενον
ἡμῖν ἀγῶνα* **2** *ἀφορῶντες εἰς τὸν τῆς
πίστεως ἀρχηγὸν καὶ τελειωτὴν Ἰησοῦν,
ὃς ἀντὶ τῆς προκειμένης αὐτῷ χαρᾶς
ὑπέμεινεν σταυρὸν αἰσχύνης κατα-
φρονήσας ἐν δεξιᾷ τε τοῦ θρόνου τοῦ
θεοῦ κεκάθικεν.* **3** *ἀναλογίσασθε γὰρ
τὸν τοιαύτην ὑπομεμενηκότα ὑπὸ τῶν
ἁμαρτωλῶν εἰς ἑαυτὸν*[b] *ἀντιλογίαν,
ἵνα μὴ κάμητε ταῖς ψυχαῖς ὑμῶν
ἐκλυόμενοι.*

4 *Οὔπω μέχρις αἵματος ἀντικατέστη-
τε πρὸς τὴν ἁμαρτίαν ἀνταγωνιζόμενοι.*
5 *καὶ ἐκλέλησθε τῆς παρακλήσεως, ἥτις
ὑμῖν ὡς υἱοῖς διαλέγεται,*

Υἱέ μου, μὴ ὀλιγώρει παιδείας
κυρίου
μηδὲ ἐκλύου ὑπ᾽ αὐτοῦ ἐλεγχό-
μενος·
6 ὃν γὰρ ἀγαπᾷ κύριος παιδεύει,
μαστιγοῖ δὲ πάντα υἱὸν ὃν
παραδέχεται.

7 *εἰς παιδείαν ὑπομένετε, ὡς υἱοῖς
ὑμῖν προσφέρεται ὁ θεός. τίς γὰρ υἱὸς
ὃν οὐ παιδεύει πατήρ;* **8** *εἰ δὲ χωρίς
ἐστε παιδείας ἧς μέτοχοι γεγόνασιν
πάντες, ἄρα νόθοι καὶ οὐχ υἱοί ἐστε.*
9 *εἶτα τοὺς μὲν τῆς σαρκὸς ἡμῶν
πατέρας εἴχομεν παιδευτὰς καὶ ἐνετρε-
πόμεθα· οὐ πολὺ [δὲ] μᾶλλον ὑποταγη-
σόμεθα τῷ πατρὶ τῶν πνευμάτων καὶ
ζήσομεν;* **10** *οἱ μὲν γὰρ πρὸς ὀλίγας
ἡμέρας κατὰ τὸ δοκοῦν αὐτοῖς ἐπαί-
δευον, ὁ δὲ ἐπὶ τὸ συμφέρον εἰς τὸ
μεταλαβεῖν τῆς ἁγιότητος αὐτοῦ.*
11 *πᾶσα δὲ παιδεία πρὸς μὲν τὸ παρὸν
οὐ δοκεῖ χαρᾶς εἶναι ἀλλὰ λύπης,
ὕστερον δὲ καρπὸν εἰρηνικὸν τοῖς δι᾽
αὐτῆς γεγυμνασμένοις ἀποδίδωσιν
δικαιοσύνης.*

12 *Διὸ τὰς παρειμένας χεῖρας καὶ
τὰ παραλελυμένα γόνατα ἀνορθώσατε,*
13 *καὶ τροχιὰς ὀρθὰς ποιεῖτε τοῖς
ποσὶν ὑμῶν, ἵνα μὴ τὸ χωλὸν ἐκτραπῇ,
ἰαθῇ δὲ μᾶλλον.*

14 *Εἰρήνην διώκετε μετὰ πάντων
καὶ τὸν ἁγιασμόν, οὗ χωρὶς οὐδεὶς
ὄψεται τὸν κύριον,* **15** *ἐπισκοποῦντες
μή τις ὑστερῶν ἀπὸ τῆς χάριτος τοῦ
θεοῦ, μή τις ῥίζα πικρίας ἄνω φύουσα
ἐνοχλῇ καὶ δι᾽ αὐτῆς μιανθῶσιν πολλοί,*

[a]1 NRSV note o *εὐπερίσπαστον* [b]3 NRSV note q *ἑαυτοὺς*

God Disciplines His Sons

12 Therefore, since we are surrounded by such a great cloud of witnesses, let us throw off everything that
hinders and the sin that so easily entangles,
and let us run with perseverance the race
marked out for us. 2Let us fix our eyes on
Jesus, the author and perfecter of our faith,
who for the joy set before him endured the
cross, scorning its shame, and sat down at
the right hand of the throne of God. 3Con-
sider him who endured such opposition
from sinful men, so that you will not grow
weary and lose heart.

4In your struggle against sin, you have
not yet resisted to the point of shedding
your blood. 5And you have forgotten that
word of encouragement that addresses you
as sons:

"My son, do not make light of the
Lord's discipline,
and do not lose heart when he rebukes
you,
6because the Lord disciplines those he
loves,
and he punishes everyone he accepts
as a son."[a]

7Endure hardship as discipline; God is
treating you as sons. For what son is not
disciplined by his father? 8If you are not
disciplined (and everyone undergoes discipline), then you are illegitimate children
and not true sons. 9Moreover, we have all
had human fathers who disciplined us and
we respected them for it. How much more
should we submit to the Father of our spirits and live! 10Our fathers disciplined us
for a little while as they thought best; but
God disciplines us for our good, that we
may share in his holiness. 11No discipline
seems pleasant at the time, but painful.
Later on, however, it produces a harvest of
righteousness and peace for those who
have been trained by it.

12Therefore, strengthen your feeble arms
and weak knees. 13"Make level paths for
your feet,"[b] so that the lame may not be
disabled, but rather healed.

Warning Against Refusing God

14Make every effort to live in peace with
all men and to be holy; without holiness
no one will see the Lord. 15See to it that no
one misses the grace of God and that no
bitter root grows up to cause trouble and

[a]6 Prov. 3:11,12 [b]13 Prov. 4:26

it many become defiled. [16]See to it that no one becomes like Esau, an immoral and godless person, who sold his birthright for a single meal. [17]You know that later, when he wanted to inherit the blessing, he was rejected, for he found no chance to repent,[r] even though he sought the blessing[s] with tears.

18 You have not come to something[t] that can be touched, a blazing fire, and darkness, and gloom, and a tempest, [19]and the sound of a trumpet, and a voice whose words made the hearers beg that not another word be spoken to them. [20](For they could not endure the order that was given, "If even an animal touches the mountain, it shall be stoned to death." [21]Indeed, so terrifying was the sight that Moses said, "I tremble with fear.") [22]But you have come to Mount Zion and to the city of the living God, the heavenly Jerusalem, and to innumerable angels in festal gathering, [23]and to the assembly[u] of the firstborn who are enrolled in heaven, and to God the judge of all, and to the spirits of the righteous made perfect, [24]and to Jesus, the mediator of a new covenant, and to the sprinkled blood that speaks a better word than the blood of Abel.

25 See that you do not refuse the one who is speaking; for if they did not escape when they refused the one who warned them on earth, how much less will we escape if we reject the one who warns from heaven! [26]At that time his voice shook the earth; but now he has promised, "Yet once more I will shake not only the earth but also the heaven." [27]This phrase, "Yet once more," indicates the removal of what is shaken—that is, created things—so that what cannot be shaken may remain. [28]Therefore, since we are receiving a kingdom that cannot be shaken, let us give thanks, by which we offer to God an acceptable worship with reverence and awe; [29]for indeed our God is a consuming fire.

Service Well-Pleasing to God

13 Let mutual love continue. [2]Do not neglect to show hospitality to strangers, for by doing that some have entertained angels without knowing it. [3]Remember those who are in prison, as though you were in prison with them; those who are being tortured, as though you yourselves were being tortured.[v] [4]Let marriage

16 μή τις πόρνος ἢ βέβηλος ὡς Ἠσαῦ, ὃς ἀντὶ βρώσεως μιᾶς ἀπέδετο τὰ πρωτοτόκια ἑαυτοῦ. 17 ἴστε γὰρ ὅτι καὶ μετέπειτα θέλων κληρονομῆσαι τὴν εὐλογίαν ἀπεδοκιμάσθη, μετανοίας γὰρ τόπον οὐχ εὗρεν καίπερ μετὰ δακρύων ἐκζητήσας αὐτήν.

18 Οὐ γὰρ προσεληλύθατε ψηλαφωμένῳ[c] καὶ κεκαυμένῳ πυρὶ καὶ γνόφῳ καὶ ζόφῳ καὶ θυέλλῃ 19 καὶ σάλπιγγος ἤχῳ καὶ φωνῇ ῥημάτων, ἧς οἱ ἀκούσαντες παρῃτήσαντο μὴ προστεθῆναι αὐτοῖς λόγον, 20 οὐκ ἔφερον γὰρ τὸ διαστελλόμενον, **Κἂν θηρίον θίγῃ τοῦ ὄρους, λιθοβοληθήσεται·** 21 καί, οὕτω φοβερὸν ἦν τὸ φανταζόμενον, Μωϋσῆς εἶπεν, **Ἔκφοβός εἰμι** καὶ ἔντρομος. 22 ἀλλὰ προσεληλύθατε Σιὼν ὄρει καὶ πόλει θεοῦ ζῶντος, Ἰερουσαλὴμ ἐπουρανίῳ, καὶ μυριάσιν ἀγγέλων, πανηγύρει 23 καὶ ἐκκλησίᾳ πρωτοτόκων ἀπογεγραμμένων ἐν οὐρανοῖς καὶ κριτῇ θεῷ πάντων καὶ πνεύμασι δικαίων τετελειωμένων 24 καὶ διαθήκης νέας μεσίτῃ Ἰησοῦ καὶ αἵματι ῥαντισμοῦ κρεῖττον λαλοῦντι παρὰ τὸν Ἄβελ.

25 Βλέπετε μὴ παραιτήσησθε τὸν λαλοῦντα· εἰ γὰρ ἐκεῖνοι οὐκ ἐξέφυγον ἐπὶ γῆς παραιτησάμενοι τὸν χρηματίζοντα, πολὺ μᾶλλον ἡμεῖς οἱ τὸν ἀπ᾽ οὐρανῶν ἀποστρεφόμενοι, 26 οὗ ἡ φωνὴ τὴν γῆν ἐσάλευσεν τότε, νῦν δὲ ἐπήγγελται λέγων, **Ἔτι ἅπαξ ἐγὼ σείσω** οὐ μόνον **τὴν γῆν** ἀλλὰ καὶ **τὸν οὐρανόν.** 27 τὸ δὲ Ἔτι ἅπαξ δηλοῖ [τὴν] τῶν σαλευομένων μετάθεσιν ὡς πεποιημένων, ἵνα μείνῃ τὰ μὴ σαλευόμενα. 28 Διὸ βασιλείαν ἀσάλευτον παραλαμβάνοντες ἔχωμεν χάριν, δι᾽ ἧς λατρεύωμεν εὐαρέστως τῷ θεῷ μετὰ εὐλαβείας καὶ δέους· 29 καὶ γὰρ ὁ θεὸς ἡμῶν πῦρ καταναλίσκον.

13 Ἡ φιλαδελφία μενέτω. 2 τῆς φιλοξενίας μὴ ἐπιλανθάνεσθε, διὰ ταύτης γὰρ ἔλαθόν τινες ξενίσαντες ἀγγέλους. 3 μιμνῄσκεσθε τῶν δεσμίων ὡς συνδεδεμένοι, τῶν κακουχουμένων ὡς καὶ αὐτοὶ ὄντες ἐν σώματι. 4 Τίμιος

defile many. [16]See that no one is sexually immoral, or is godless like Esau, who for a single meal sold his inheritance rights as the oldest son. [17]Afterward, as you know, when he wanted to inherit this blessing, he was rejected. He could bring about no change of mind, though he sought the blessing with tears.

[18]You have not come to a mountain that can be touched and that is burning with fire; to darkness, gloom and storm; [19]to a trumpet blast or to such a voice speaking words that those who heard it begged that no further word be spoken to them, [20]because they could not bear what was commanded: "If even an animal touches the mountain, it must be stoned."[c] [21]The sight was so terrifying that Moses said, "I am trembling with fear."[d]

[22]But you have come to Mount Zion, to the heavenly Jerusalem, the city of the living God. You have come to thousands upon thousands of angels in joyful assembly, [23]to the church of the firstborn, whose names are written in heaven. You have come to God, the judge of all men, to the spirits of righteous men made perfect, [24]to Jesus the mediator of a new covenant, and to the sprinkled blood that speaks a better word than the blood of Abel.

[25]See to it that you do not refuse him who speaks. If they did not escape when they refused him who warned them on earth, how much less will we, if we turn away from him who warns us from heaven? [26]At that time his voice shook the earth, but now he has promised, "Once more I will shake not only the earth but also the heavens."[e] [27]The words "once more" indicate the removing of what can be shaken—that is, created things—so that what cannot be shaken may remain.

[28]Therefore, since we are receiving a kingdom that cannot be shaken, let us be thankful, and so worship God acceptably with reverence and awe, [29]for our "God is a consuming fire."[f]

Concluding Exhortations

13 Keep on loving each other as brothers. [2]Do not forget to entertain strangers, for by so doing some people have entertained angels without knowing it. [3]Remember those in prison as if you were their fellow prisoners, and those who are mistreated as if you yourselves were suffering.

---

[r] Or *no chance to change his father's mind*   [s] Gk *it*   [t] Other ancient authorities read *a mountain*   [u] Or *angels, and to the festal gathering* [23]*and assembly*   [v] Gk *were in the body*

[c]18 NIV text and NRSV note t add ὄρει

[c]20 Exodus 19:12,13   [d]21 Deut. 9:19   [e]26 Haggai 2:6 [f]29 Deut. 4:24

be held in honor by all, and let the marriage bed be kept undefiled; for God will judge fornicators and adulterers. 5Keep your lives free from the love of money, and be content with what you have; for he has said, "I will never leave you or forsake you." 6So we can say with confidence,

"The Lord is my helper;
I will not be afraid.
What can anyone do to me?"

7 Remember your leaders, those who spoke the word of God to you; consider the outcome of their way of life, and imitate their faith. 8Jesus Christ is the same yesterday and today and forever. 9Do not be carried away by all kinds of strange teachings; for it is well for the heart to be strengthened by grace, not by regulations about food,w which have not benefited those who observe them. 10We have an altar from which those who officiate in the tentx have no right to eat. 11For the bodies of those animals whose blood is brought into the sanctuary by the high priest as a sacrifice for sin are burned outside the camp. 12Therefore Jesus also suffered outside the city gate in order to sanctify the people by his own blood. 13Let us then go to him outside the camp and bear the abuse he endured. 14For here we have no lasting city, but we are looking for the city that is to come. 15Through him, then, let us continually offer a sacrifice of praise to God, that is, the fruit of lips that confess his name. 16Do not neglect to do good and to share what you have, for such sacrifices are pleasing to God.

17 Obey your leaders and submit to them, for they are keeping watch over your souls and will give an account. Let them do this with joy and not with sighing—for that would be harmful to you.

18 Pray for us; we are sure that we have a clear conscience, desiring to act honorably in all things. 19I urge you all the more to do this, so that I may be restored to you very soon.

Benediction

20 Now may the God of peace, who brought back from the dead our Lord Jesus, the great shepherd of the sheep, by the blood of the eternal covenant, 21make you

---

ὁ γάμος ἐν πᾶσιν καὶ ἡ κοίτη ἀμίαντος, πόρνους γὰρ καὶ μοιχοὺς κρινεῖ ὁ θεός. 5 Ἀφιλάργυρος ὁ τρόπος, ἀρκούμενοι τοῖς παροῦσιν. αὐτὸς γὰρ εἴρηκεν, Οὐ μή σε ἀνῶ οὐδ᾽ οὐ μή σε ἐγκαταλίπω, 6 ὥστε θαρροῦντας ἡμᾶς λέγειν,

Κύριος ἐμοὶ βοηθός,

[καὶ] οὐ φοβηθήσομαι,

τί ποιήσει μοι ἄνθρωπος;

7 Μνημονεύετε τῶν ἡγουμένων ὑμῶν, οἵτινες ἐλάλησαν ὑμῖν τὸν λόγον τοῦ θεοῦ, ὧν ἀναθεωροῦντες τὴν ἔκβασιν τῆς ἀναστροφῆς μιμεῖσθε τὴν πίστιν. 8 Ἰησοῦς Χριστὸς ἐχθὲς καὶ σήμερον ὁ αὐτὸς καὶ εἰς τοὺς αἰῶνας. 9 διδαχαῖς ποικίλαις καὶ ξέναις μὴ παραφέρεσθε· καλὸν γὰρ χάριτι βεβαιοῦσθαι τὴν καρδίαν, οὐ βρώμασιν ἐν οἷς οὐκ ὠφελήθησαν οἱ περιπατοῦντες. 10 ἔχομεν θυσιαστήριον ἐξ οὗ φαγεῖν οὐκ ἔχουσιν ἐξουσίαν οἱ τῇ σκηνῇ λατρεύοντες. 11 ὧν γὰρ εἰσφέρεται ζῴων τὸ αἷμα περὶ ἁμαρτίας εἰς τὰ ἅγια διὰ τοῦ ἀρχιερέως, τούτων τὰ σώματα κατακαίεται ἔξω τῆς παρεμβολῆς. 12 διὸ καὶ Ἰησοῦς, ἵνα ἁγιάσῃ διὰ τοῦ ἰδίου αἵματος τὸν λαόν, ἔξω τῆς πύλης ἔπαθεν. 13 τοίνυν ἐξερχώμεθα πρὸς αὐτὸν ἔξω τῆς παρεμβολῆς τὸν ὀνειδισμὸν αὐτοῦ φέροντες· 14 οὐ γὰρ ἔχομεν ὧδε μένουσαν πόλιν ἀλλὰ τὴν μέλλουσαν ἐπιζητοῦμεν. 15 δι᾽ αὐτοῦ [οὖν] ἀναφέρωμεν θυσίαν αἰνέσεως διὰ παντὸς τῷ θεῷ, τοῦτ᾽ ἔστιν καρπὸν χειλέων ὁμολογούντων τῷ ὀνόματι αὐτοῦ. 16 τῆς δὲ εὐποιΐας καὶ κοινωνίας μὴ ἐπιλανθάνεσθε· τοιαύταις γὰρ θυσίαις εὐαρεστεῖται ὁ θεός.

17 Πείθεσθε τοῖς ἡγουμένοις ὑμῶν καὶ ὑπείκετε, αὐτοὶ γὰρ ἀγρυπνοῦσιν ὑπὲρ τῶν ψυχῶν ὑμῶν ὡς λόγον ἀποδώσοντες, ἵνα μετὰ χαρᾶς τοῦτο ποιῶσιν καὶ μὴ στενάζοντες· ἀλυσιτελὲς γὰρ ὑμῖν τοῦτο.

18 Προσεύχεσθε περὶ ἡμῶν· πειθόμεθα γὰρ ὅτι καλὴν συνείδησιν ἔχομεν, ἐν πᾶσιν καλῶς θέλοντες ἀναστρέφεσθαι. 19 περισσοτέρως δὲ παρακαλῶ τοῦτο ποιῆσαι, ἵνα τάχιον ἀποκατασταθῶ ὑμῖν.

20 Ὁ δὲ θεὸς τῆς εἰρήνης, ὁ ἀναγαγὼν ἐκ νεκρῶν τὸν ποιμένα τῶν προβάτων τὸν μέγαν ἐν αἵματι διαθήκης αἰωνίου, τὸν κύριον ἡμῶν Ἰησοῦν, 21 καταρτίσαι

4Marriage should be honored by all, and the marriage bed kept pure, for God will judge the adulterer and all the sexually immoral. 5Keep your lives free from the love of money and be content with what you have, because God has said,

"Never will I leave you;
never will I forsake you."a

6So we say with confidence,

"The Lord is my helper; I will not be afraid.
What can man do to me?"b

7Remember your leaders, who spoke the word of God to you. Consider the outcome of their way of life and imitate their faith. 8Jesus Christ is the same yesterday and today and forever.

9Do not be carried away by all kinds of strange teachings. It is good for our hearts to be strengthened by grace, not by ceremonial foods, which are of no value to those who eat them. 10We have an altar from which those who minister at the tabernacle have no right to eat.

11The high priest carries the blood of animals into the Most Holy Place as a sin offering, but the bodies are burned outside the camp. 12And so Jesus also suffered outside the city gate to make the people holy through his own blood. 13Let us, then, go to him outside the camp, bearing the disgrace he bore. 14For here we do not have an enduring city, but we are looking for the city that is to come.

15Through Jesus, therefore, let us continually offer to God a sacrifice of praise—the fruit of lips that confess his name. 16And do not forget to do good and to share with others, for with such sacrifices God is pleased.

17Obey your leaders and submit to their authority. They keep watch over you as men who must give an account. Obey them so that their work will be a joy, not a burden, for that would be of no advantage to you.

18Pray for us. We are sure that we have a clear conscience and desire to live honorably in every way. 19I particularly urge you to pray so that I may be restored to you soon.

20May the God of peace, who through the blood of the eternal covenant brought back from the dead our Lord Jesus, that great Shepherd of the sheep, 21equip you

---

w Gk *not by foods*   x Or *tabernacle*   a5 Deut. 31:6   b6 Psalm 118:6,7

complete in everything good so that you may do his will, working among us[y] that which is pleasing in his sight, through Jesus Christ, to whom be the glory forever and ever. Amen.

Final Exhortation and Greetings

22 I appeal to you, brothers and sisters,[z] bear with my word of exhortation, for I have written to you briefly. [23]I want you to know that our brother Timothy has been set free; and if he comes in time, he will be with me when I see you. [24]Greet all your leaders and all the saints. Those from Italy send you greetings. [25]Grace be with all of you.[a]

ὑμᾶς ἐν παντὶ ἀγαθῷ εἰς τὸ ποιῆσαι τὸ θέλημα αὐτοῦ, ποιῶν ἐν ἡμῖν[a] τὸ εὐάρεστον ἐνώπιον αὐτοῦ διὰ Ἰησοῦ Χριστοῦ, ᾧ ἡ δόξα εἰς τοὺς αἰῶνας [τῶν αἰώνων], ἀμήν.

22 Παρακαλῶ δὲ ὑμᾶς, ἀδελφοί, ἀνέχεσθε τοῦ λόγου τῆς παρακλήσεως, καὶ γὰρ διὰ βραχέων ἐπέστειλα ὑμῖν. **23** Γινώσκετε τὸν ἀδελφὸν ἡμῶν Τιμόθεον ἀπολελυμένον, μεθ᾽ οὗ ἐὰν τάχιον ἔρχηται ὄψομαι ὑμᾶς. **24** Ἀσπάσασθε πάντας τοὺς ἡγουμένους ὑμῶν καὶ πάντας τοὺς ἁγίους. ἀσπάζονται ὑμᾶς οἱ ἀπὸ τῆς Ἰταλίας. **25** ἡ χάρις μετὰ πάντων ὑμῶν.[b]

with everything good for doing his will, and may he work in us what is pleasing to him, through Jesus Christ, to whom be glory for ever and ever. Amen.

[22]Brothers, I urge you to bear with my word of exhortation, for I have written you only a short letter.

[23]I want you to know that our brother Timothy has been released. If he arrives soon, I will come with him to see you.

[24]Greet all your leaders and all God's people. Those from Italy send you their greetings.

[25]Grace be with you all.

y Other ancient authorities read *you*　z Gk *brothers*
a Other ancient authorities add *Amen*　　a21 NRSV note y ὑμῖν　b24 NRSV note a adds ἀμήν.

NRSV

Salutation

1 James, a servant[a] of God and of the Lord Jesus Christ,

To the twelve tribes in the Dispersion: Greetings.

Faith and Wisdom

2 My brothers and sisters,[b] whenever you face trials of any kind, consider it nothing but joy, 3because you know that the testing of your faith produces endurance; 4and let endurance have its full effect, so that you may be mature and complete, lacking in nothing.

5 If any of you is lacking in wisdom, ask God, who gives to all generously and ungrudgingly, and it will be given you. 6But ask in faith, never doubting, for the one who doubts is like a wave of the sea, driven and tossed by the wind; 7, 8for the doubter, being double-minded and unstable in every way, must not expect to receive anything from the Lord.

Poverty and Riches

9 Let the believer[c] who is lowly boast in being raised up, 10and the rich in being brought low, because the rich will disappear like a flower in the field. 11For the sun rises with its scorching heat and withers the field; its flower falls, and its beauty perishes. It is the same way with the rich; in the midst of a busy life, they will wither away.

Trial and Temptation

12 Blessed is anyone who endures temptation. Such a one has stood the test and will receive the crown of life that the Lord[d] has promised to those who love him. 13No one, when tempted, should say, "I am being tempted by God"; for God cannot be tempted by evil and he himself tempts no one. 14But one is tempted by one's own desire, being lured and enticed by it; 15then, when that desire has conceived, it gives birth to sin, and that sin, when it is fully grown, gives birth to death. 16Do not be deceived, my beloved.[e]

17 Every generous act of giving, with every perfect gift, is from above, coming down from the Father of lights, with whom there is no variation or shadow due to change.[f] 18In fulfillment of his own purpose he gave us birth by the word of truth,

ΙΑΚΩΒΟΥ

1 Ἰάκωβος θεοῦ καὶ κυρίου Ἰησοῦ Χριστοῦ δοῦλος ταῖς δώδεκα φυλαῖς ταῖς ἐν τῇ διασπορᾷ χαίρειν.

2 Πᾶσαν χαρὰν ἡγήσασθε, ἀδελφοί μου, ὅταν πειρασμοῖς περιπέσητε ποικίλοις, **3** γινώσκοντες ὅτι τὸ δοκίμιον ὑμῶν τῆς πίστεως κατεργάζεται ὑπομονήν. **4** ἡ δὲ ὑπομονὴ ἔργον τέλειον ἐχέτω, ἵνα ἦτε τέλειοι καὶ ὁλόκληροι ἐν μηδενὶ λειπόμενοι. **5** Εἰ δέ τις ὑμῶν λείπεται σοφίας, αἰτείτω παρὰ τοῦ διδόντος θεοῦ πᾶσιν ἁπλῶς καὶ μὴ ὀνειδίζοντος καὶ δοθήσεται αὐτῷ. **6** αἰτείτω δὲ ἐν πίστει μηδὲν διακρινόμενος· ὁ γὰρ διακρινόμενος ἔοικεν κλύδωνι θαλάσσης ἀνεμιζομένῳ καὶ ῥιπιζομένῳ. **7** μὴ γὰρ οἰέσθω ὁ ἄνθρωπος ἐκεῖνος ὅτι λήμψεταί τι παρὰ τοῦ κυρίου, **8** ἀνὴρ δίψυχος, ἀκατάστατος ἐν πάσαις ταῖς ὁδοῖς αὐτοῦ.

9 Καυχάσθω δὲ ὁ ἀδελφὸς ὁ ταπεινὸς ἐν τῷ ὕψει αὐτοῦ, **10** ὁ δὲ πλούσιος ἐν τῇ ταπεινώσει αὐτοῦ, ὅτι ὡς ἄνθος χόρτου παρελεύσεται. **11** ἀνέτειλεν γὰρ ὁ ἥλιος σὺν τῷ καύσωνι καὶ ἐξήρανεν τὸν χόρτον καὶ τὸ ἄνθος αὐτοῦ ἐξέπεσεν καὶ ἡ εὐπρέπεια τοῦ προσώπου αὐτοῦ ἀπώλετο· οὕτως καὶ ὁ πλούσιος ἐν ταῖς πορείαις αὐτοῦ μαρανθήσεται.

12 Μακάριος ἀνὴρ ὃς ὑπομένει πειρασμόν, ὅτι δόκιμος γενόμενος λήμψεται τὸν στέφανον τῆς ζωῆς ὃν ἐπηγγείλατο[a] τοῖς ἀγαπῶσιν αὐτόν. **13** μηδεὶς πειραζόμενος λεγέτω ὅτι Ἀπὸ θεοῦ πειράζομαι· ὁ γὰρ θεὸς ἀπείραστός ἐστιν κακῶν, πειράζει δὲ αὐτὸς οὐδένα. **14** ἕκαστος δὲ πειράζεται ὑπὸ τῆς ἰδίας ἐπιθυμίας ἐξελκόμενος καὶ δελεαζόμενος· **15** εἶτα ἡ ἐπιθυμία συλλαβοῦσα τίκτει ἁμαρτίαν, ἡ δὲ ἁμαρτία ἀποτελεσθεῖσα ἀποκύει θάνατον.

16 Μὴ πλανᾶσθε, ἀδελφοί μου ἀγαπητοί. **17** πᾶσα δόσις ἀγαθὴ καὶ πᾶν δώρημα τέλειον ἄνωθέν ἐστιν καταβαῖνον ἀπὸ τοῦ πατρὸς τῶν φώτων, παρ' ᾧ οὐκ ἔνι παραλλαγὴ ἢ τροπῆς ἀποσκίασμα[b]. **18** βουληθεὶς ἀπεκύησεν ἡμᾶς λόγῳ ἀληθείας εἰς τὸ εἶναι ἡμᾶς

NIV

1 James, a servant of God and of the Lord Jesus Christ,

To the twelve tribes scattered among the nations:

Greetings.

Trials and Temptations

2Consider it pure joy, my brothers, whenever you face trials of many kinds, 3because you know that the testing of your faith develops perseverance. 4Perseverance must finish its work so that you may be mature and complete, not lacking anything. 5If any of you lacks wisdom, he should ask God, who gives generously to all without finding fault, and it will be given to him. 6But when he asks, he must believe and not doubt, because he who doubts is like a wave of the sea, blown and tossed by the wind. 7That man should not think he will receive anything from the Lord; 8he is a double-minded man, unstable in all he does.

9The brother in humble circumstances ought to take pride in his high position. 10But the one who is rich should take pride in his low position, because he will pass away like a wild flower. 11For the sun rises with scorching heat and withers the plant; its blossom falls and its beauty is destroyed. In the same way, the rich man will fade away even while he goes about his business.

12Blessed is the man who perseveres under trial, because when he has stood the test, he will receive the crown of life that God has promised to those who love him. 13When tempted, no one should say, "God is tempting me." For God cannot be tempted by evil, nor does he tempt anyone; 14but each one is tempted when, by his own evil desire, he is dragged away and enticed. 15Then, after desire has conceived, it gives birth to sin; and sin, when it is full-grown, gives birth to death.

16Don't be deceived, my dear brothers. 17Every good and perfect gift is from above, coming down from the Father of the heavenly lights, who does not change like shifting shadows. 18He chose to give us birth through the word of truth, that we might

---

a Gk slave   b Gk brothers   c Gk brother   d Gk he; other ancient authorities read God   e Gk my beloved brothers
f Other ancient authorities read variation due to a shadow of turning

a12 NRSV note d adds ὁ θεός   b17 NRSV note f ἡ τροπῆς ἀποσκιάσματος

NRSV

so that we would become a kind of first fruits of his creatures.

Hearing and Doing the Word

19 You must understand this, my beloved:[e] let everyone be quick to listen, slow to speak, slow to anger; 20for your anger does not produce God's righteousness. 21Therefore rid yourselves of all sordidness and rank growth of wickedness, and welcome with meekness the implanted word that has the power to save your souls.

22 But be doers of the word, and not merely hearers who deceive themselves. 23For if any are hearers of the word and not doers, they are like those who look at themselves[g] in a mirror; 24for they look at themselves and, on going away, immediately forget what they were like. 25But those who look into the perfect law, the law of liberty, and persevere, being not hearers who forget but doers who act—they will be blessed in their doing.

26 If any think they are religious, and do not bridle their tongues but deceive their hearts, their religion is worthless. 27Religion that is pure and undefiled before God, the Father, is this: to care for orphans and widows in their distress, and to keep oneself unstained by the world.

Warning against Partiality

2 My brothers and sisters,[h] do you with your acts of favoritism really believe in our glorious Lord Jesus Christ?[i] 2For if a person with gold rings and in fine clothes comes into your assembly, and if a poor person in dirty clothes also comes in, 3and if you take notice of the one wearing the fine clothes and say, "Have a seat here, please," while to the one who is poor you say, "Stand there," or, "Sit at my feet,"[j] 4have you not made distinctions among yourselves, and become judges with evil thoughts? 5Listen, my beloved brothers and sisters.[k] Has not God chosen the poor in the world to be rich in faith and to be heirs of the kingdom that he has promised to those who love him? 6But you have dishonored the poor. Is it not the rich who oppress you? Is it not they who drag you into court? 7Is it not they who blaspheme the excellent name that was invoked over you?

Greek

ἀπαρχήν τινα τῶν αὐτοῦ κτισμάτων.

19 Ἴστε, ἀδελφοί μου ἀγαπητοί· ἔστω δὲ πᾶς ἄνθρωπος ταχὺς εἰς τὸ ἀκοῦσαι, βραδὺς εἰς τὸ λαλῆσαι, βραδὺς εἰς ὀργήν· 20 ὀργὴ γὰρ ἀνδρὸς δικαιοσύνην θεοῦ οὐκ ἐργάζεται. 21 διὸ ἀποθέμενοι πᾶσαν ῥυπαρίαν καὶ περισσείαν κακίας ἐν πραΰτητι, δέξασθε τὸν ἔμφυτον λόγον τὸν δυνάμενον σῶσαι τὰς ψυχὰς ὑμῶν.

22 Γίνεσθε δὲ ποιηταὶ λόγου καὶ μὴ μόνον ἀκροαταὶ παραλογιζόμενοι ἑαυτούς. 23 ὅτι εἴ τις ἀκροατὴς λόγου ἐστὶν καὶ οὐ ποιητής, οὗτος ἔοικεν ἀνδρὶ κατανοοῦντι τὸ πρόσωπον τῆς γενέσεως αὐτοῦ ἐν ἐσόπτρῳ· 24 κατενόησεν γὰρ ἑαυτὸν καὶ ἀπελήλυθεν καὶ εὐθέως ἐπελάθετο ὁποῖος ἦν. 25 ὁ δὲ παρακύψας εἰς νόμον τέλειον τὸν τῆς ἐλευθερίας καὶ παραμείνας, οὐκ ἀκροατὴς ἐπιλησμονῆς γενόμενος ἀλλὰ ποιητὴς ἔργου, οὗτος μακάριος ἐν τῇ ποιήσει αὐτοῦ ἔσται.

26 Εἴ τις δοκεῖ θρησκὸς εἶναι μὴ χαλιναγωγῶν γλῶσσαν αὐτοῦ ἀλλὰ ἀπατῶν καρδίαν αὐτοῦ, τούτου μάταιος ἡ θρησκεία. 27 θρησκεία καθαρὰ καὶ ἀμίαντος παρὰ τῷ θεῷ καὶ πατρὶ αὕτη ἐστίν, ἐπισκέπτεσθαι ὀρφανοὺς καὶ χήρας ἐν τῇ θλίψει αὐτῶν, ἄσπιλον ἑαυτὸν τηρεῖν ἀπὸ τοῦ κόσμου.

2 Ἀδελφοί μου, μὴ ἐν προσωπολημψίαις ἔχετε τὴν πίστιν τοῦ κυρίου ἡμῶν Ἰησοῦ Χριστοῦ τῆς δόξης. 2 ἐὰν γὰρ εἰσέλθῃ εἰς συναγωγὴν ὑμῶν ἀνὴρ χρυσοδακτύλιος ἐν ἐσθῆτι λαμπρᾷ, εἰσέλθῃ δὲ καὶ πτωχὸς ἐν ῥυπαρᾷ ἐσθῆτι, 3 ἐπιβλέψητε δὲ ἐπὶ τὸν φοροῦντα τὴν ἐσθῆτα τὴν λαμπρὰν καὶ εἴπητε, Σὺ κάθου ὧδε καλῶς, καὶ τῷ πτωχῷ εἴπητε, Σὺ στῆθι ἐκεῖ ἢ κάθου ὑπὸ τὸ ὑποπόδιόν μου, 4 οὐ διεκρίθητε ἐν ἑαυτοῖς καὶ ἐγένεσθε κριταὶ διαλογισμῶν πονηρῶν;

5 Ἀκούσατε, ἀδελφοί μου ἀγαπητοί· οὐχ ὁ θεὸς ἐξελέξατο τοὺς πτωχοὺς τῷ κόσμῳ πλουσίους ἐν πίστει καὶ κληρονόμους τῆς βασιλείας ἧς ἐπηγγείλατο τοῖς ἀγαπῶσιν αὐτόν; 6 ὑμεῖς δὲ ἠτιμάσατε τὸν πτωχόν. οὐχ οἱ πλούσιοι καταδυναστεύουσιν ὑμῶν καὶ αὐτοὶ ἕλκουσιν ὑμᾶς εἰς κριτήρια; 7 οὐκ αὐτοὶ βλασφημοῦσιν τὸ καλὸν ὄνομα τὸ ἐπικληθὲν ἐφ' ὑμᾶς; 8 εἰ μέντοι νόμον

NIV

be a kind of firstfruits of all he created.

Listening and Doing

19My dear brothers, take note of this: Everyone should be quick to listen, slow to speak and slow to become angry, 20for man's anger does not bring about the righteous life that God desires. 21Therefore, get rid of all moral filth and the evil that is so prevalent and humbly accept the word planted in you, which can save you.

22Do not merely listen to the word, and so deceive yourselves. Do what it says. 23Anyone who listens to the word but does not do what it says is like a man who looks at his face in a mirror 24and, after looking at himself, goes away and immediately forgets what he looks like. 25But the man who looks intently into the perfect law that gives freedom, and continues to do this, not forgetting what he has heard, but doing it—he will be blessed in what he does.

26If anyone considers himself religious and yet does not keep a tight rein on his tongue, he deceives himself and his religion is worthless. 27Religion that God our Father accepts as pure and faultless is this: to look after orphans and widows in their distress and to keep oneself from being polluted by the world.

Favoritism Forbidden

2 My brothers, as believers in our glorious Lord Jesus Christ, don't show favoritism. 2Suppose a man comes into your meeting wearing a gold ring and fine clothes, and a poor man in shabby clothes also comes in. 3If you show special attention to the man wearing fine clothes and say, "Here's a good seat for you," but say to the poor man, "You stand there" or "Sit on the floor by my feet," 4have you not discriminated among yourselves and become judges with evil thoughts?

5Listen, my dear brothers: Has not God chosen those who are poor in the eyes of the world to be rich in faith and to inherit the kingdom he promised those who love him? 6But you have insulted the poor. Is it not the rich who are exploiting you? Are they not the ones who are dragging you into court? 7Are they not the ones who are slandering the noble name of him to whom you belong?

---

e Gk *my beloved brothers* g Gk *at the face of his birth*
h Gk *My brothers* i Or *hold the faith of our glorious Lord Jesus Christ without acts of favoritism* j Gk *Sit under my footstool* k Gk *brothers*

8 You do well if you really fulfill the royal law according to the scripture, "You shall love your neighbor as yourself." [9]But if you show partiality, you commit sin and are convicted by the law as transgressors. [10]For whoever keeps the whole law but fails in one point has become accountable for all of it. [11]For the one who said, "You shall not commit adultery," also said, "You shall not murder." Now if you do not commit adultery but if you murder, you have become a transgressor of the law. [12]So speak and so act as those who are to be judged by the law of liberty. [13]For judgment will be without mercy to anyone who has shown no mercy; mercy triumphs over judgment.

Faith without Works Is Dead

14 What good is it, my brothers and sisters,[1] if you say you have faith but do not have works? Can faith save you? [15]If a brother or sister is naked and lacks daily food, [16]and one of you says to them, "Go in peace; keep warm and eat your fill," and yet you do not supply their bodily needs, what is the good of that? [17]So faith by itself, if it has no works, is dead.

18 But someone will say, "You have faith and I have works." Show me your faith apart from your works, and I by my works will show you my faith. [19]You believe that God is one; you do well. Even the demons believe—and shudder. [20]Do you want to be shown, you senseless person, that faith apart from works is barren? [21]Was not our ancestor Abraham justified by works when he offered his son Isaac on the altar? [22]You see that faith was active along with his works, and faith was brought to completion by the works. [23]Thus the scripture was fulfilled that says, "Abraham believed God, and it was reckoned to him as righteousness," and he was called the friend of God. [24]You see that a person is justified by works and not by faith alone. [25]Likewise, was not Rahab the prostitute also justified by works when she welcomed the messengers and sent them out by another road? [26]For just as the body without the spirit is dead, so faith without works is also dead.

τελεῖτε βασιλικὸν κατὰ τὴν γραφήν, Ἀγαπήσεις τὸν πλησίον σου ὡς σεαυτόν, καλῶς ποιεῖτε· 9 εἰ δὲ προσωπολημπτεῖτε, ἁμαρτίαν ἐργάζεσθε ἐλεγχόμενοι ὑπὸ τοῦ νόμου ὡς παραβάται. 10 ὅστις γὰρ ὅλον τὸν νόμον τηρήσῃ πταίσῃ δὲ ἐν ἑνί, γέγονεν πάντων ἔνοχος. 11 ὁ γὰρ εἰπών, Μὴ μοιχεύσῃς, εἶπεν καί, Μὴ φονεύσῃς· εἰ δὲ οὐ μοιχεύεις φονεύεις δέ, γέγονας παραβάτης νόμου. 12 οὕτως λαλεῖτε καὶ οὕτως ποιεῖτε ὡς διὰ νόμου ἐλευθερίας μέλλοντες κρίνεσθαι. 13 ἡ γὰρ κρίσις ἀνέλεος τῷ μὴ ποιήσαντι ἔλεος· κατακαυχᾶται ἔλεος κρίσεως.

14 Τί τὸ ὄφελος, ἀδελφοί μου, ἐὰν πίστιν λέγῃ τις ἔχειν ἔργα δὲ μὴ ἔχῃ; μὴ δύναται ἡ πίστις σῶσαι αὐτόν; 15 ἐὰν ἀδελφὸς ἢ ἀδελφὴ γυμνοὶ ὑπάρχωσιν καὶ λειπόμενοι τῆς ἐφημέρου τροφῆς 16 εἴπῃ δέ τις αὐτοῖς ἐξ ὑμῶν, Ὑπάγετε ἐν εἰρήνῃ, θερμαίνεσθε καὶ χορτάζεσθε, μὴ δῶτε δὲ αὐτοῖς τὰ ἐπιτήδεια τοῦ σώματος, τί τὸ ὄφελος; 17 οὕτως καὶ ἡ πίστις, ἐὰν μὴ ἔχῃ ἔργα, νεκρά ἐστιν καθ᾽ ἑαυτήν.

18 Ἀλλ᾽ ἐρεῖ τις, Σὺ πίστιν ἔχεις, κἀγὼ ἔργα ἔχω· δεῖξόν μοι τὴν πίστιν σου χωρὶς τῶν ἔργων, κἀγώ σοι δείξω ἐκ τῶν ἔργων μου τὴν πίστιν. 19 σὺ πιστεύεις ὅτι εἷς ἐστιν ὁ θεός, καλῶς ποιεῖς· καὶ τὰ δαιμόνια πιστεύουσιν καὶ φρίσσουσιν. 20 θέλεις δὲ γνῶναι, ὦ ἄνθρωπε κενέ, ὅτι ἡ πίστις χωρὶς τῶν ἔργων ἀργή[a] ἐστιν; 21 Ἀβραὰμ ὁ πατὴρ ἡμῶν οὐκ ἐξ ἔργων ἐδικαιώθη ἀνενέγκας Ἰσαὰκ τὸν υἱὸν αὐτοῦ ἐπὶ τὸ θυσιαστήριον; 22 βλέπεις ὅτι ἡ πίστις συνήργει τοῖς ἔργοις αὐτοῦ καὶ ἐκ τῶν ἔργων ἡ πίστις ἐτελειώθη, 23 καὶ ἐπληρώθη ἡ γραφὴ ἡ λέγουσα, Ἐπίστευσεν δὲ Ἀβραὰμ τῷ θεῷ, καὶ ἐλογίσθη αὐτῷ εἰς δικαιοσύνην καὶ φίλος θεοῦ ἐκλήθη. 24 ὁρᾶτε ὅτι ἐξ ἔργων δικαιοῦται ἄνθρωπος καὶ οὐκ ἐκ πίστεως μόνον. 25 ὁμοίως δὲ καὶ Ῥαὰβ ἡ πόρνη οὐκ ἐξ ἔργων ἐδικαιώθη ὑποδεξαμένη τοὺς ἀγγέλους καὶ ἑτέρα ὁδῷ ἐκβαλοῦσα; 26 ὥσπερ γὰρ τὸ σῶμα χωρὶς πνεύματος νεκρόν ἐστιν, οὕτως καὶ ἡ πίστις χωρὶς ἔργων νεκρά ἐστιν.

---

[8]If you really keep the royal law found in Scripture, "Love your neighbor as yourself,"[a] you are doing right. [9]But if you show favoritism, you sin and are convicted by the law as lawbreakers. [10]For whoever keeps the whole law and yet stumbles at just one point is guilty of breaking all of it. [11]For he who said, "Do not commit adultery,"[b] also said, "Do not murder."[c] If you do not commit adultery but do commit murder, you have become a lawbreaker. [12]Speak and act as those who are going to be judged by the law that gives freedom, [13]because judgment without mercy will be shown to anyone who has not been merciful. Mercy triumphs over judgment!

Faith and Deeds

[14]What good is it, my brothers, if a man claims to have faith but has no deeds? Can such faith save him? [15]Suppose a brother or sister is without clothes and daily food. [16]If one of you says to him, "Go, I wish you well; keep warm and well fed," but does nothing about his physical needs, what good is it? [17]In the same way, faith by itself, if it is not accompanied by action, is dead.

[18]But someone will say, "You have faith; I have deeds."

Show me your faith without deeds, and I will show you my faith by what I do. [19]You believe that there is one God. Good! Even the demons believe that—and shudder.

[20]You foolish man, do you want evidence that faith without deeds is useless[d]? [21]Was not our ancestor Abraham considered righteous for what he did when he offered his son Isaac on the altar? [22]You see that his faith and his actions were working together, and his faith was made complete by what he did. [23]And the scripture was fulfilled that says, "Abraham believed God, and it was credited to him as righteousness,"[e] and he was called God's friend. [24]You see that a person is justified by what he does and not by faith alone.

[25]In the same way, was not even Rahab the prostitute considered righteous for what she did when she gave lodging to the spies and sent them off in a different direction? [26]As the body without the spirit is dead, so faith without deeds is dead.

---

[1] Gk *brothers*

[a] 20 NIV note νεκρά

[a] 8 Lev. 19:18   [b] 11 Exodus 20:14; Deut. 5:18
[c] 11 Exodus 20:13; Deut. 5:17   [d] 20 Some early manuscripts *dead*   [e] 23 Gen. 15:6

Taming the Tongue

3 Not many of you should become teachers, my brothers and sisters,[1] for you know that we who teach will be judged with greater strictness. [2]For all of us make many mistakes. Anyone who makes no mistakes in speaking is perfect, able to keep the whole body in check with a bridle. [3]If we put bits into the mouths of horses to make them obey us, we guide their whole bodies. [4]Or look at ships: though they are so large that it takes strong winds to drive them, yet they are guided by a very small rudder wherever the will of the pilot directs. [5]So also the tongue is a small member, yet it boasts of great exploits.

How great a forest is set ablaze by a small fire! [6]And the tongue is a fire. The tongue is placed among our members as a world of iniquity; it stains the whole body, sets on fire the cycle of nature,[m] and is itself set on fire by hell.[n] [7]For every species of beast and bird, of reptile and sea creature, can be tamed and has been tamed by the human species, [8]but no one can tame the tongue—a restless evil, full of deadly poison. [9]With it we bless the Lord and Father, and with it we curse those who are made in the likeness of God. [10]From the same mouth come blessing and cursing. My brothers and sisters,[o] this ought not to be so. [11]Does a spring pour forth from the same opening both fresh and brackish water? [12]Can a fig tree, my brothers and sisters,[p] yield olives, or a grapevine figs? No more can salt water yield fresh.

Two Kinds of Wisdom

13 Who is wise and understanding among you? Show by your good life that your works are done with gentleness born of wisdom. [14]But if you have bitter envy and selfish ambition in your hearts, do not be boastful and false to the truth. [15]Such wisdom does not come down from above, but is earthly, unspiritual, devilish. [16]For where there is envy and selfish ambition, there will also be disorder and wickedness of every kind. [17]But the wisdom from above is first pure, then peaceable, gentle, willing to yield, full of mercy and good fruits, without a trace of partiality or hypocrisy. [18]And a harvest of righteousness is sown in peace for[q] those who make peace.

3 Μὴ πολλοὶ διδάσκαλοι γίνεσθε, ἀδελφοί μου, εἰδότες ὅτι μεῖζον κρίμα λημψόμεθα. 2 πολλὰ γὰρ πταίομεν ἅπαντες. εἴ τις ἐν λόγῳ οὐ πταίει, οὗτος τέλειος ἀνὴρ δυνατὸς χαλιναγωγῆσαι καὶ ὅλον τὸ σῶμα. 3 εἰ δὲ τῶν ἵππων τοὺς χαλινοὺς εἰς τὰ στόματα βάλλομεν εἰς τὸ πείθεσθαι αὐτοὺς ἡμῖν, καὶ ὅλον τὸ σῶμα αὐτῶν μετάγομεν. 4 ἰδοὺ καὶ τὰ πλοῖα τηλικαῦτα ὄντα καὶ ὑπὸ ἀνέμων σκληρῶν ἐλαυνόμενα, μετάγεται ὑπὸ ἐλαχίστου πηδαλίου ὅπου ἡ ὁρμὴ τοῦ εὐθύνοντος βούλεται, 5 οὕτως καὶ ἡ γλῶσσα μικρὸν μέλος ἐστὶν καὶ μεγάλα αὐχεῖ. Ἰδοὺ ἡλίκον πῦρ ἡλίκην ὕλην ἀνάπτει· 6 καὶ ἡ γλῶσσα πῦρ· ὁ κόσμος τῆς ἀδικίας ἡ γλῶσσα καθίσταται ἐν τοῖς μέλεσιν ἡμῶν, ἡ σπιλοῦσα ὅλον τὸ σῶμα καὶ φλογίζουσα τὸν τροχὸν τῆς γενέσεως καὶ φλογιζομένη ὑπὸ τῆς γεέννης. 7 πᾶσα γὰρ φύσις θηρίων τε καὶ πετεινῶν, ἑρπετῶν τε καὶ ἐναλίων δαμάζεται καὶ δεδάμασται τῇ φύσει τῇ ἀνθρωπίνῃ, 8 τὴν δὲ γλῶσσαν οὐδεὶς δαμάσαι δύναται ἀνθρώπων, ἀκατάστατον κακόν, μεστὴ ἰοῦ θανατηφόρου. 9 ἐν αὐτῇ εὐλογοῦμεν τὸν κύριον καὶ πατέρα καὶ ἐν αὐτῇ καταρώμεθα τοὺς ἀνθρώπους τοὺς καθ' ὁμοίωσιν θεοῦ γεγονότας, 10 ἐκ τοῦ αὐτοῦ στόματος ἐξέρχεται εὐλογία καὶ κατάρα. οὐ χρή, ἀδελφοί μου, ταῦτα οὕτως γίνεσθαι. 11 μήτι ἡ πηγὴ ἐκ τῆς αὐτῆς ὀπῆς βρύει τὸ γλυκὺ καὶ τὸ πικρόν; 12 μὴ δύναται, ἀδελφοί μου, συκῆ ἐλαίας ποιῆσαι ἢ ἄμπελος σῦκα; οὔτε ἁλυκὸν γλυκὺ ποιῆσαι ὕδωρ.

13 Τίς σοφὸς καὶ ἐπιστήμων ἐν ὑμῖν; δειξάτω ἐκ τῆς καλῆς ἀναστροφῆς τὰ ἔργα αὐτοῦ ἐν πραΰτητι σοφίας. 14 εἰ δὲ ζῆλον πικρὸν ἔχετε καὶ ἐριθείαν ἐν τῇ καρδίᾳ ὑμῶν, μὴ κατακαυχᾶσθε καὶ ψεύδεσθε κατὰ τῆς ἀληθείας. 15 οὐκ ἔστιν αὕτη ἡ σοφία ἄνωθεν κατερχομένη ἀλλὰ ἐπίγειος, ψυχική, δαιμονιώδης. 16 ὅπου γὰρ ζῆλος καὶ ἐριθεία, ἐκεῖ ἀκαταστασία καὶ πᾶν φαῦλον πρᾶγμα. 17 ἡ δὲ ἄνωθεν σοφία πρῶτον μὲν ἁγνή ἐστιν, ἔπειτα εἰρηνική, ἐπιεικής, εὐπειθής, μεστὴ ἐλέους καὶ καρπῶν ἀγαθῶν, ἀδιάκριτος, ἀνυπόκριτος. 18 καρπὸς δὲ δικαιοσύνης ἐν εἰρήνῃ σπείρεται τοῖς ποιοῦσιν εἰρήνην.

Taming the Tongue

3 Not many of you should presume to be teachers, my brothers, because you know that we who teach will be judged more strictly. [2]We all stumble in many ways. If anyone is never at fault in what he says, he is a perfect man, able to keep his whole body in check.

[3]When we put bits into the mouths of horses to make them obey us, we can turn the whole animal. [4]Or take ships as an example. Although they are so large and are driven by strong winds, they are steered by a very small rudder wherever the pilot wants to go. [5]Likewise the tongue is a small part of the body, but it makes great boasts. Consider what a great forest is set on fire by a small spark. [6]The tongue also is a fire, a world of evil among the parts of the body. It corrupts the whole person, sets the whole course of his life on fire, and is itself set on fire by hell.

[7]All kinds of animals, birds, reptiles and creatures of the sea are being tamed and have been tamed by man, [8]but no man can tame the tongue. It is a restless evil, full of deadly poison.

[9]With the tongue we praise our Lord and Father, and with it we curse men, who have been made in God's likeness. [10]Out of the same mouth come praise and cursing. My brothers, this should not be. [11]Can both fresh water and salt[a] water flow from the same spring? [12]My brothers, can a fig tree bear olives, or a grapevine bear figs? Neither can a salt spring produce fresh water.

Two Kinds of Wisdom

[13]Who is wise and understanding among you? Let him show it by his good life, by deeds done in the humility that comes from wisdom. [14]But if you harbor bitter envy and selfish ambition in your hearts, do not boast about it or deny the truth. [15]Such "wisdom" does not come down from heaven but is earthly, unspiritual, of the devil. [16]For where you have envy and selfish ambition, there you find disorder and every evil practice. [17]But the wisdom that comes from heaven is first of all pure; then peace-loving, considerate, submissive, full of mercy and good fruit, impartial and sincere. [18]Peacemakers who sow in peace raise a harvest of righteousness.

[1]Gk brothers   [m]Or wheel of birth   [n]Gk Gehenna
[o]Gk My brothers   [p]Gk my brothers   [q]Or by

[a]11 Greek bitter (see also verse 14)

NRSV

Friendship with the World

4 Those conflicts and disputes among you, where do they come from? Do they not come from your cravings that are at war within you? [2]You want something and do not have it; so you commit murder. And you covet[r] something and cannot obtain it; so you engage in disputes and conflicts. You do not have, because you do not ask. [3]You ask and do not receive, because you ask wrongly, in order to spend what you get on your pleasures. [4]Adulterers! Do you not know that friendship with the world is enmity with God? Therefore whoever wishes to be a friend of the world becomes an enemy of God. [5]Or do you suppose that it is for nothing that the scripture says, "God[s] yearns jealously for the spirit that he has made to dwell in us"? [6]But he gives all the more grace; therefore it says,

> "God opposes the proud,
> but gives grace to the humble."

[7]Submit yourselves therefore to God. Resist the devil, and he will flee from you. [8]Draw near to God, and he will draw near to you. Cleanse your hands, you sinners, and purify your hearts, you double-minded. [9]Lament and mourn and weep. Let your laughter be turned into mourning and your joy into dejection. [10]Humble yourselves before the Lord, and he will exalt you.

Warning against Judging Another

11 Do not speak evil against one another, brothers and sisters.[t] Whoever speaks evil against another or judges another, speaks evil against the law and judges the law; but if you judge the law, you are not a doer of the law but a judge. [12]There is one lawgiver and judge who is able to save and to destroy. So who, then, are you to judge your neighbor?

Boasting about Tomorrow

13 Come now, you who say, "Today or tomorrow we will go to such and such a town and spend a year there, doing business and making money." [14]Yet you do not even know what tomorrow will bring. What is your life? For you are a mist that appears for a little while and then vanishes. [15]Instead you ought to say, "If the Lord wishes, we will live and do this or that." [16]As it is, you boast in your arrogance; all such boasting is evil. [17]Anyone, then, who knows the right thing to do and fails to do it, commits sin.

[r] Or *you murder and you covet*   [s] Gk *He*   [t] Gk *brothers*

Greek

4 Πόθεν πόλεμοι καὶ πόθεν μάχαι ἐν ὑμῖν; οὐκ ἐντεῦθεν, ἐκ τῶν ἡδονῶν ὑμῶν τῶν στρατευομένων ἐν τοῖς μέλεσιν ὑμῶν; 2 ἐπιθυμεῖτε καὶ οὐκ ἔχετε, φονεύετε καὶ ζηλοῦτε καὶ οὐ δύνασθε ἐπιτυχεῖν, μάχεσθε καὶ πολεμεῖτε, οὐκ ἔχετε διὰ τὸ μὴ αἰτεῖσθαι ὑμᾶς, 3 αἰτεῖτε καὶ οὐ λαμβάνετε διότι κακῶς αἰτεῖσθε, ἵνα ἐν ταῖς ἡδοναῖς ὑμῶν δαπανήσητε. 4 μοιχαλίδες, οὐκ οἴδατε ὅτι ἡ φιλία τοῦ κόσμου ἔχθρα τοῦ θεοῦ ἐστιν; ὃς ἐὰν οὖν βουληθῇ φίλος εἶναι τοῦ κόσμου, ἐχθρὸς τοῦ θεοῦ καθίσταται. 5 ἢ δοκεῖτε ὅτι κενῶς ἡ γραφὴ λέγει, Πρὸς φθόνον ἐπιποθεῖ τὸ πνεῦμα ὃ κατῴκισεν ἐν ἡμῖν, 6 μείζονα δὲ δίδωσιν χάριν; διὸ λέγει,

Ὁ θεὸς ὑπερηφάνοις ἀντιτάσσεται, ταπεινοῖς δὲ δίδωσιν χάριν.

7 ὑποτάγητε οὖν τῷ θεῷ, ἀντίστητε δὲ τῷ διαβόλῳ καὶ φεύξεται ἀφ᾽ ὑμῶν, 8 ἐγγίσατε τῷ θεῷ καὶ ἐγγιεῖ ὑμῖν. καθαρίσατε χεῖρας, ἁμαρτωλοί, καὶ ἁγνίσατε καρδίας, δίψυχοι. 9 ταλαιπωρήσατε καὶ πενθήσατε καὶ κλαύσατε. ὁ γέλως ὑμῶν εἰς πένθος μετατραπήτω καὶ ἡ χαρὰ εἰς κατήφειαν. 10 ταπεινώθητε ἐνώπιον κυρίου καὶ ὑψώσει ὑμᾶς.

11 Μὴ καταλαλεῖτε ἀλλήλων, ἀδελφοί. ὁ καταλαλῶν ἀδελφοῦ ἢ κρίνων τὸν ἀδελφὸν αὐτοῦ καταλαλεῖ νόμου καὶ κρίνει νόμον· εἰ δὲ νόμον κρίνεις, οὐκ εἶ ποιητὴς νόμου ἀλλὰ κριτής. 12 εἷς ἐστιν [ὁ] νομοθέτης καὶ κριτὴς ὁ δυνάμενος σῶσαι καὶ ἀπολέσαι· σὺ δὲ τίς εἶ ὁ κρίνων τὸν πλησίον;

13 Ἄγε νῦν οἱ λέγοντες, Σήμερον ἢ αὔριον πορευσόμεθα εἰς τήνδε τὴν πόλιν καὶ ποιήσομεν ἐκεῖ ἐνιαυτὸν καὶ ἐμπορευσόμεθα καὶ κερδήσομεν· 14 οἵτινες οὐκ ἐπίστασθε τὸ τῆς αὔριον ποία ἡ ζωὴ ὑμῶν· ἀτμὶς γάρ ἐστε ἡ πρὸς ὀλίγον φαινομένη, ἔπειτα καὶ ἀφανιζομένη. 15 ἀντὶ τοῦ λέγειν ὑμᾶς, Ἐὰν ὁ κύριος θελήσῃ καὶ ζήσομεν καὶ ποιήσομεν τοῦτο ἢ ἐκεῖνο. 16 νῦν δὲ καυχᾶσθε ἐν ταῖς ἀλαζονείαις ὑμῶν· πᾶσα καύχησις τοιαύτη πονηρά ἐστιν. 17 εἰδότι οὖν καλὸν ποιεῖν καὶ μὴ ποιοῦντι, ἁμαρτία αὐτῷ ἐστιν.

NIV

Submit Yourselves to God

4 What causes fights and quarrels among you? Don't they come from your desires that battle within you? [2]You want something but don't get it. You kill and covet, but you cannot have what you want. You quarrel and fight. You do not have, because you do not ask God. [3]When you ask, you do not receive, because you ask with wrong motives, that you may spend what you get on your pleasures.

[4]You adulterous people, don't you know that friendship with the world is hatred toward God? Anyone who chooses to be a friend of the world becomes an enemy of God. [5]Or do you think Scripture says without reason that the spirit he caused to live in us envies intensely?[a] [6]But he gives us more grace. That is why Scripture says:

> "God opposes the proud
> but gives grace to the humble."[b]

[7]Submit yourselves, then, to God. Resist the devil, and he will flee from you. [8]Come near to God and he will come near to you. Wash your hands, you sinners, and purify your hearts, you double-minded. [9]Grieve, mourn and wail. Change your laughter to mourning and your joy to gloom. [10]Humble yourselves before the Lord, and he will lift you up.

[11]Brothers, do not slander one another. Anyone who speaks against his brother or judges him speaks against the law and judges it. When you judge the law, you are not keeping it, but sitting in judgment on it. [12]There is only one Lawgiver and Judge, the one who is able to save and destroy. But you—who are you to judge your neighbor?

Boasting About Tomorrow

[13]Now listen, you who say, "Today or tomorrow we will go to this or that city, spend a year there, carry on business and make money." [14]Why, you do not even know what will happen tomorrow. What is your life? You are a mist that appears for a little while and then vanishes. [15]Instead, you ought to say, "If it is the Lord's will, we will live and do this or that." [16]As it is, you boast and brag. All such boasting is evil. [17]Anyone, then, who knows the good he ought to do and doesn't do it, sins.

[a]5 Or *that God jealously longs for the spirit that he made to live in us*; or *that the Spirit he caused to live in us longs jealously*   [b]6 Prov. 3:34

NRSV

Warning to Rich Oppressors

5 Come now, you rich people, weep and wail for the miseries that are coming to you. [2]Your riches have rotted, and your clothes are moth-eaten. [3]Your gold and silver have rusted, and their rust will be evidence against you, and it will eat your flesh like fire. You have laid up treasure[u] for the last days. [4]Listen! The wages of the laborers who mowed your fields, which you kept back by fraud, cry out, and the cries of the harvesters have reached the ears of the Lord of hosts. [5]You have lived on the earth in luxury and in pleasure; you have fattened your hearts in a day of slaughter. [6]You have condemned and murdered the righteous one, who does not resist you.

Patience in Suffering

7 Be patient, therefore, beloved,[v] until the coming of the Lord. The farmer waits for the precious crop from the earth, being patient with it until it receives the early and the late rains. [8]You also must be patient. Strengthen your hearts, for the coming of the Lord is near.[w] [9]Beloved,[x] do not grumble against one another, so that you may not be judged. See, the Judge is standing at the doors! [10]As an example of suffering and patience, beloved,[v] take the prophets who spoke in the name of the Lord. [11]Indeed we call blessed those who showed endurance. You have heard of the endurance of Job, and you have seen the purpose of the Lord, how the Lord is compassionate and merciful.

12 Above all, my beloved,[v] do not swear, either by heaven or by earth or by any other oath, but let your "Yes" be yes and your "No" be no, so that you may not fall under condemnation.

The Prayer of Faith

13 Are any among you suffering? They should pray. Are any cheerful? They should sing songs of praise. [14]Are any among you sick? They should call for the elders of the church and have them pray over them, anointing them with oil in the name of the Lord. [15]The prayer of faith will save the sick, and the Lord will raise them up; and anyone who has committed sins will be forgiven. [16]Therefore confess your sins to one another, and pray for one another, so that you may be healed. The

Greek

5 Ἄγε νῦν οἱ πλούσιοι, κλαύσατε ὀλολύζοντες ἐπὶ ταῖς ταλαιπωρίαις ὑμῶν ταῖς ἐπερχομέναις. 2 ὁ πλοῦτος ὑμῶν σέσηπεν καὶ τὰ ἱμάτια ὑμῶν σητόβρωτα γέγονεν, 3 ὁ χρυσὸς ὑμῶν καὶ ὁ ἄργυρος κατίωται καὶ ὁ ἰὸς αὐτῶν εἰς μαρτύριον ὑμῖν ἔσται καὶ φάγεται τὰς σάρκας ὑμῶν ὡς πῦρ. ἐθησαυρίσατε ἐν ἐσχάταις ἡμέραις. 4 ἰδοὺ ὁ μισθὸς τῶν ἐργατῶν τῶν ἀμησάντων τὰς χώρας ὑμῶν ὁ ἀπεστερημένος ἀφ᾽ ὑμῶν κράζει, καὶ αἱ βοαὶ τῶν θερισάντων εἰς τὰ ὦτα κυρίου Σαβαὼθ εἰσελήλυθασιν. 5 ἐτρυφήσατε ἐπὶ τῆς γῆς καὶ ἐσπαταλήσατε, ἐθρέψατε τὰς καρδίας ὑμῶν ἐν ἡμέρᾳ σφαγῆς, 6 κατεδικάσατε, ἐφονεύσατε τὸν δίκαιον, οὐκ ἀντιτάσσεται ὑμῖν.

7 Μακροθυμήσατε οὖν, ἀδελφοί, ἕως τῆς παρουσίας τοῦ κυρίου. ἰδοὺ ὁ γεωργὸς ἐκδέχεται τὸν τίμιον καρπὸν τῆς γῆς μακροθυμῶν ἐπ᾽ αὐτῷ ἕως λάβῃ πρόϊμον καὶ ὄψιμον. 8 μακροθυμήσατε καὶ ὑμεῖς, στηρίξατε τὰς καρδίας ὑμῶν, ὅτι ἡ παρουσία τοῦ κυρίου ἤγγικεν. 9 μὴ στενάζετε, ἀδελφοί, κατ᾽ ἀλλήλων ἵνα μὴ κριθῆτε· ἰδοὺ ὁ κριτὴς πρὸ τῶν θυρῶν ἕστηκεν. 10 ὑπόδειγμα λάβετε, ἀδελφοί, τῆς κακοπαθείας καὶ τῆς μακροθυμίας τοὺς προφήτας οἳ ἐλάλησαν ἐν τῷ ὀνόματι κυρίου. 11 ἰδοὺ μακαρίζομεν τοὺς ὑπομείναντας· τὴν ὑπομονὴν Ἰὼβ ἠκούσατε καὶ τὸ τέλος κυρίου εἴδετε, ὅτι πολύσπλαγχνός ἐστιν ὁ κύριος καὶ οἰκτίρμων.

12 Πρὸ πάντων δέ, ἀδελφοί μου, μὴ ὀμνύετε μήτε τὸν οὐρανὸν μήτε τὴν γῆν μήτε ἄλλον τινὰ ὅρκον· ἤτω δὲ ὑμῶν τὸ Ναὶ ναὶ καὶ τὸ Οὒ οὔ, ἵνα μὴ ὑπὸ κρίσιν πέσητε.

13 Κακοπαθεῖ τις ἐν ὑμῖν, προσευχέσθω· εὐθυμεῖ τις, ψαλλέτω· 14 ἀσθενεῖ τις ἐν ὑμῖν, προσκαλεσάσθω τοὺς πρεσβυτέρους τῆς ἐκκλησίας καὶ προσευξάσθωσαν ἐπ᾽ αὐτὸν ἀλείψαντες [αὐτὸν] ἐλαίῳ ἐν τῷ ὀνόματι τοῦ κυρίου. 15 καὶ ἡ εὐχὴ τῆς πίστεως σώσει τὸν κάμνοντα καὶ ἐγερεῖ αὐτὸν ὁ κύριος· κἂν ἁμαρτίας ᾖ πεποιηκώς, ἀφεθήσεται αὐτῷ. 16 ἐξομολογεῖσθε οὖν ἀλλήλοις τὰς ἁμαρτίας καὶ εὔχεσθε ὑπὲρ ἀλλήλων ὅπως ἰαθῆτε. πολὺ ἰσχύει

NIV

Warning to Rich Oppressors

5 Now listen, you rich people, weep and wail because of the misery that is coming upon you. [2]Your wealth has rotted, and moths have eaten your clothes. [3]Your gold and silver are corroded. Their corrosion will testify against you and eat your flesh like fire. You have hoarded wealth in the last days. [4]Look! The wages you failed to pay the workmen who mowed your fields are crying out against you. The cries of the harvesters have reached the ears of the Lord Almighty. [5]You have lived on earth in luxury and self-indulgence. You have fattened yourselves in the day of slaughter.[a] [6]You have condemned and murdered innocent men, who were not opposing you.

Patience in Suffering

[7]Be patient, then, brothers, until the Lord's coming. See how the farmer waits for the land to yield its valuable crop and how patient he is for the autumn and spring rains. [8]You too, be patient and stand firm, because the Lord's coming is near. [9]Don't grumble against each other, brothers, or you will be judged. The Judge is standing at the door!

[10]Brothers, as an example of patience in the face of suffering, take the prophets who spoke in the name of the Lord. [11]As you know, we consider blessed those who have persevered. You have heard of Job's perseverance and have seen what the Lord finally brought about. The Lord is full of compassion and mercy.

[12]Above all, my brothers, do not swear—not by heaven or by earth or by anything else. Let your "Yes" be yes, and your "No," no, or you will be condemned.

The Prayer of Faith

[13]Is any one of you in trouble? He should pray. Is anyone happy? Let him sing songs of praise. [14]Is any one of you sick? He should call the elders of the church to pray over him and anoint him with oil in the name of the Lord. [15]And the prayer offered in faith will make the sick person well; the Lord will raise him up. If he has sinned, he will be forgiven. [16]Therefore confess your sins to each other and pray for each other so that you may be healed.

---

u Or will eat your flesh, since you have stored up fire
v Gk brothers   w Or is at hand   x Gk Brothers

a5 Or yourselves as in a day of feasting

prayer of the righteous is powerful and effective. [17]Elijah was a human being like us, and he prayed fervently that it might not rain, and for three years and six months it did not rain on the earth. [18]Then he prayed again, and the heaven gave rain and the earth yielded its harvest.

19 My brothers and sisters,[y] if anyone among you wanders from the truth and is brought back by another, [20]you should know that whoever brings back a sinner from wandering will save the sinner's[z] soul from death and will cover a multitude of sins.

δέησις δικαίου ἐνεργουμένη. **17** Ἠλίας ἄνθρωπος ἦν ὁμοιοπαθὴς ἡμῖν, καὶ προσευχῇ προσηύξατο τοῦ μὴ βρέξαι, καὶ οὐκ ἔβρεξεν ἐπὶ τῆς γῆς ἐνιαυτοὺς τρεῖς καὶ μῆνας ἕξ· **18** καὶ πάλιν προσηύξατο, καὶ ὁ οὐρανὸς ὑετὸν ἔδωκεν καὶ ἡ γῆ ἐβλάστησεν τὸν καρπὸν αὐτῆς.

19 Ἀδελφοί μου, ἐάν τις ἐν ὑμῖν πλανηθῇ ἀπὸ τῆς ἀληθείας καὶ ἐπιστρέψῃ τις αὐτόν, **20** γινωσκέτω ὅτι ὁ ἐπιστρέψας ἁμαρτωλὸν ἐκ πλάνης ὁδοῦ αὐτοῦ σώσει ψυχὴν αὐτοῦ ἐκ θανάτου καὶ καλύψει πλῆθος ἁμαρτιῶν.

The prayer of a righteous man is powerful and effective.

[17]Elijah was a man just like us. He prayed earnestly that it would not rain, and it did not rain on the land for three and a half years. [18]Again he prayed, and the heavens gave rain, and the earth produced its crops.

[19]My brothers, if one of you should wander from the truth and someone should bring him back, [20]remember this: Whoever turns a sinner from the error of his way will save him from death and cover over a multitude of sins.

---

[y] Gk *My brothers*   [z] Gk *his*

NRSV

Salutation

1 Peter, an apostle of Jesus Christ,
To the exiles of the Dispersion in Pontus, Galatia, Cappadocia, Asia, and Bithynia, [2]who have been chosen and destined by God the Father and sanctified by the Spirit to be obedient to Jesus Christ and to be sprinkled with his blood:

May grace and peace be yours in abundance.

A Living Hope

3 Blessed be the God and Father of our Lord Jesus Christ! By his great mercy he has given us a new birth into a living hope through the resurrection of Jesus Christ from the dead, [4]and into an inheritance that is imperishable, undefiled, and unfading, kept in heaven for you, [5]who are being protected by the power of God through faith for a salvation ready to be revealed in the last time. [6]In this you rejoice,[a] even if now for a little while you have had to suffer various trials, [7]so that the genuineness of your faith—being more precious than gold that, though perishable, is tested by fire—may be found to result in praise and glory and honor when Jesus Christ is revealed. [8]Although you have not seen[b] him, you love him; and even though you do not see him now, you believe in him and rejoice with an indescribable and glorious joy, [9]for you are receiving the outcome of your faith, the salvation of your souls.

10 Concerning this salvation, the prophets who prophesied of the grace that was to be yours made careful search and inquiry, [11]inquiring about the person or time that the Spirit of Christ within them indicated when it testified in advance to the sufferings destined for Christ and the subsequent glory. [12]It was revealed to them that they were serving not themselves but you, in regard to the things that have now been announced to you through those who brought you good news by the Holy Spirit sent from heaven—things into which angels long to look!

A Call to Holy Living

13 Therefore prepare your minds for action;[c] discipline yourselves; set all your hope on the grace that Jesus Christ will bring you when he is revealed. [14]Like obedient children, do not be conformed to the desires that you formerly had in ignorance.

---

a Or *Rejoice in this*   b Other ancient authorities read *known*   c Gk *gird up the loins of your mind*

ΠΕΤΡΟΥ Α

1 Πέτρος ἀπόστολος Ἰησοῦ Χριστοῦ ἐκλεκτοῖς παρεπιδήμοις διασπορᾶς Πόντου, Γαλατίας, Καππαδοκίας, Ἀσίας καὶ Βιθυνίας, **2** κατὰ πρόγνωσιν θεοῦ πατρὸς ἐν ἁγιασμῷ πνεύματος εἰς ὑπακοὴν καὶ ῥαντισμὸν αἵματος Ἰησοῦ Χριστοῦ, χάρις ὑμῖν καὶ εἰρήνη πληθυνθείη.

3 Εὐλογητὸς ὁ θεὸς καὶ πατὴρ τοῦ κυρίου ἡμῶν Ἰησοῦ Χριστοῦ, ὁ κατὰ τὸ πολὺ αὐτοῦ ἔλεος ἀναγεννήσας ἡμᾶς εἰς ἐλπίδα ζῶσαν δι᾿ ἀναστάσεως Ἰησοῦ Χριστοῦ ἐκ νεκρῶν, **4** εἰς κληρονομίαν ἄφθαρτον καὶ ἀμίαντον καὶ ἀμάραντον, τετηρημένην ἐν οὐρανοῖς εἰς ὑμᾶς **5** τοὺς ἐν δυνάμει θεοῦ φρουρουμένους διὰ πίστεως εἰς σωτηρίαν ἑτοίμην ἀποκαλυφθῆναι ἐν καιρῷ ἐσχάτῳ. **6** ἐν ᾧ ἀγαλλιᾶσθε, ὀλίγον ἄρτι εἰ δέον [ἐστὶν] λυπηθέντες ἐν ποικίλοις πειρασμοῖς, **7** ἵνα τὸ δοκίμιον ὑμῶν τῆς πίστεως πολυτιμότερον χρυσίου τοῦ ἀπολλυμένου διὰ πυρὸς δὲ δοκιμαζομένου, εὑρεθῇ εἰς ἔπαινον καὶ δόξαν καὶ τιμὴν ἐν ἀποκαλύψει Ἰησοῦ Χριστοῦ· **8** ὃν οὐκ ἰδόντες[a] ἀγαπᾶτε, εἰς ὃν ἄρτι μὴ ὁρῶντες πιστεύοντες δὲ ἀγαλλιᾶσθε χαρᾷ ἀνεκλαλήτῳ καὶ δεδοξασμένῃ **9** κομιζόμενοι τὸ τέλος τῆς πίστεως [ὑμῶν] σωτηρίαν ψυχῶν.

10 Περὶ ἧς σωτηρίας ἐξεζήτησαν καὶ ἐξηραύνησαν προφῆται οἱ περὶ τῆς εἰς ὑμᾶς χάριτος προφητεύσαντες, **11** ἐραυνῶντες εἰς τίνα ἢ ποῖον καιρὸν ἐδήλου τὸ ἐν αὐτοῖς πνεῦμα Χριστοῦ προμαρτυρόμενον τὰ εἰς Χριστὸν παθήματα καὶ τὰς μετὰ ταῦτα δόξας. **12** οἷς ἀπεκαλύφθη ὅτι οὐχ ἑαυτοῖς ὑμῖν δὲ διηκόνουν αὐτά, ἃ νῦν ἀνηγγέλη ὑμῖν διὰ τῶν εὐαγγελισαμένων ὑμᾶς [ἐν] πνεύματι ἁγίῳ ἀποσταλέντι ἀπ᾿ οὐρανοῦ, εἰς ἃ ἐπιθυμοῦσιν ἄγγελοι παρακύψαι.

13 Διὸ ἀναζωσάμενοι τὰς ὀσφύας τῆς διανοίας ὑμῶν νήφοντες τελείως ἐλπίσατε ἐπὶ τὴν φερομένην ὑμῖν χάριν ἐν ἀποκαλύψει Ἰησοῦ Χριστοῦ. **14** ὡς τέκνα ὑπακοῆς μὴ συσχηματιζόμενοι ταῖς πρότερον ἐν τῇ ἀγνοίᾳ ὑμῶν

---

a 8 NRSV note b εἰδότες

NIV

1 Peter, an apostle of Jesus Christ,

To God's elect, strangers in the world, scattered throughout Pontus, Galatia, Cappadocia, Asia and Bithynia, [2]who have been chosen according to the foreknowledge of God the Father, through the sanctifying work of the Spirit, for obedience to Jesus Christ and sprinkling by his blood:

Grace and peace be yours in abundance.

Praise to God for a Living Hope

[3]Praise be to the God and Father of our Lord Jesus Christ! In his great mercy he has given us new birth into a living hope through the resurrection of Jesus Christ from the dead, [4]and into an inheritance that can never perish, spoil or fade—kept in heaven for you, [5]who through faith are shielded by God's power until the coming of the salvation that is ready to be revealed in the last time. [6]In this you greatly rejoice, though now for a little while you may have had to suffer grief in all kinds of trials. [7]These have come so that your faith—of greater worth than gold, which perishes even though refined by fire—may be proved genuine and may result in praise, glory and honor when Jesus Christ is revealed. [8]Though you have not seen him, you love him; and even though you do not see him now, you believe in him and are filled with an inexpressible and glorious joy, [9]for you are receiving the goal of your faith, the salvation of your souls.

[10]Concerning this salvation, the prophets, who spoke of the grace that was to come to you, searched intently and with the greatest care, [11]trying to find out the time and circumstances to which the Spirit of Christ in them was pointing when he predicted the sufferings of Christ and the glories that would follow. [12]It was revealed to them that they were not serving themselves but you, when they spoke of the things that have now been told you by those who have preached the gospel to you by the Holy Spirit sent from heaven. Even angels long to look into these things.

Be Holy

[13]Therefore, prepare your minds for action; be self-controlled; set your hope fully on the grace to be given you when Jesus Christ is revealed. [14]As obedient children, do not conform to the evil desires you had when you lived in ignorance. [15]But just as

15Instead, as he who called you is holy, be holy yourselves in all your conduct; 16for it is written, "You shall be holy, for I am holy."

17 If you invoke as Father the one who judges all people impartially according to their deeds, live in reverent fear during the time of your exile. 18You know that you were ransomed from the futile ways inherited from your ancestors, not with perishable things like silver or gold, 19but with the precious blood of Christ, like that of a lamb without defect or blemish. 20He was destined before the foundation of the world, but was revealed at the end of the ages for your sake. 21Through him you have come to trust in God, who raised him from the dead and gave him glory, so that your faith and hope are set on God.

22 Now that you have purified your souls by your obedience to the truth[d] so that you have genuine mutual love, love one another deeply[e] from the heart.[f] 23You have been born anew, not of perishable but of imperishable seed, through the living and enduring word of God.[g] 24For

"All flesh is like grass
  and all its glory like the flower of
      grass.
The grass withers,
  and the flower falls,
25 but the word of the Lord endures
      forever."

That word is the good news that was announced to you.

The Living Stone and a Chosen People

2 Rid yourselves, therefore, of all malice, and all guile, insincerity, envy, and all slander. 2Like newborn infants, long for the pure, spiritual milk, so that by it you may grow into salvation— 3if indeed you have tasted that the Lord is good.

4 Come to him, a living stone, though rejected by mortals yet chosen and precious in God's sight, and 5like living stones, let yourselves be built[h] into a spiritual house, to be a holy priesthood, to offer spiritual sacrifices acceptable to God through Jesus Christ. 6For it stands in scripture:

"See, I am laying in Zion a stone,
  a cornerstone chosen and precious;
  and whoever believes in him[i] will not
      be put to shame."

ἐπιθυμίαις 15 ἀλλὰ κατὰ τὸν καλέσαντα ὑμᾶς ἅγιον καὶ αὐτοὶ ἅγιοι ἐν πάσῃ ἀναστροφῇ γενήθητε, 16 διότι γέγραπται [ὅτι] Ἅγιοι ἔσεσθε, ὅτι ἐγὼ ἅγιος [εἰμι].

17 Καὶ εἰ πατέρα ἐπικαλεῖσθε τὸν ἀπροσωπολήμπτως κρίνοντα κατὰ τὸ ἑκάστου ἔργον, ἐν φόβῳ τὸν τῆς παροικίας ὑμῶν χρόνον ἀναστράφητε, 18 εἰδότες ὅτι οὐ φθαρτοῖς, ἀργυρίῳ ἢ χρυσίῳ, ἐλυτρώθητε ἐκ τῆς ματαίας ὑμῶν ἀναστροφῆς πατροπαραδότου 19 ἀλλὰ τιμίῳ αἵματι ὡς ἀμνοῦ ἀμώμου καὶ ἀσπίλου Χριστοῦ, 20 προεγνωσμένου μὲν πρὸ καταβολῆς κόσμου φανερωθέντος δὲ ἐπ' ἐσχάτου τῶν χρόνων δι' ὑμᾶς 21 τοὺς δι' αὐτοῦ πιστοὺς εἰς θεὸν τὸν ἐγείραντα αὐτὸν ἐκ νεκρῶν καὶ δόξαν αὐτῷ δόντα, ὥστε τὴν πίστιν ὑμῶν καὶ ἐλπίδα εἶναι εἰς θεόν.

22 Τὰς ψυχὰς ὑμῶν ἡγνικότες ἐν τῇ ὑπακοῇ τῆς ἀληθείας[b] εἰς φιλαδελφίαν ἀνυπόκριτον, ἐκ [καθαρᾶς][c] καρδίας ἀλλήλους ἀγαπήσατε ἐκτενῶς 23 ἀναγεγεννημένοι οὐκ ἐκ σπορᾶς φθαρτῆς ἀλλὰ ἀφθάρτου διὰ λόγου ζῶντος θεοῦ καὶ μένοντος. 24 διότι

πᾶσα σὰρξ ὡς χόρτος
  καὶ πᾶσα δόξα αὐτῆς ὡς ἄνθος
      χόρτου·
ἐξηράνθη ὁ χόρτος
  καὶ τὸ ἄνθος ἐξέπεσεν·
25 τὸ δὲ ῥῆμα κυρίου μένει εἰς τὸν
      αἰῶνα.
τοῦτο δέ ἐστιν τὸ ῥῆμα τὸ εὐαγγελισθὲν εἰς ὑμᾶς.

2 Ἀποθέμενοι οὖν πᾶσαν κακίαν καὶ πάντα δόλον καὶ ὑποκρίσεις καὶ φθόνους καὶ πάσας καταλαλιάς, 2 ὡς ἀρτιγέννητα βρέφη τὸ λογικὸν ἄδολον γάλα ἐπιποθήσατε, ἵνα ἐν αὐτῷ αὐξηθῆτε εἰς σωτηρίαν, 3 εἰ ἐγεύσασθε ὅτι χρηστὸς ὁ κύριος. 4 πρὸς ὃν προσερχόμενοι λίθον ζῶντα ὑπὸ ἀνθρώπων μὲν ἀποδεδοκιμασμένον παρὰ δὲ θεῷ ἐκλεκτὸν ἔντιμον, 5 καὶ αὐτοὶ ὡς λίθοι ζῶντες οἰκοδομεῖσθε οἶκος πνευματικὸς εἰς ἱεράτευμα ἅγιον ἀνενέγκαι πνευματικὰς θυσίας εὐπροσδέκτους [τῷ] θεῷ διὰ Ἰησοῦ Χριστοῦ. 6 διότι περιέχει ἐν γραφῇ,

Ἰδοὺ τίθημι ἐν Σιὼν λίθον
ἀκρογωνιαῖον ἐκλεκτὸν ἔντιμον
καὶ ὁ πιστεύων ἐπ' αὐτῷ οὐ μὴ
      καταισχυνθῇ.

he who called you is holy, so be holy in all you do; 16for it is written: "Be holy, because I am holy."[a]

17Since you call on a Father who judges each man's work impartially, live your lives as strangers here in reverent fear. 18For you know that it was not with perishable things such as silver or gold that you were redeemed from the empty way of life handed down to you from your forefathers, 19but with the precious blood of Christ, a lamb without blemish or defect. 20He was chosen before the creation of the world, but was revealed in these last times for your sake. 21Through him you believe in God, who raised him from the dead and glorified him, and so your faith and hope are in God.

22Now that you have purified yourselves by obeying the truth so that you have sincere love for your brothers, love one another deeply, from the heart.[b] 23For you have been born again, not of perishable seed, but of imperishable, through the living and enduring word of God. 24For,

"All men are like grass,
  and all their glory is like the flowers
      of the field;
the grass withers and the flowers fall,
25 but the word of the Lord stands
      forever."[c]

And this is the word that was preached to you.

2 Therefore, rid yourselves of all malice and all deceit, hypocrisy, envy, and slander of every kind. 2Like newborn babies, crave pure spiritual milk, so that by it you may grow up in your salvation, 3now that you have tasted that the Lord is good.

The Living Stone and a Chosen People

4As you come to him, the living Stone— rejected by men but chosen by God and precious to him— 5you also, like living stones, are being built into a spiritual house to be a holy priesthood, offering spiritual sacrifices acceptable to God through Jesus Christ. 6For in Scripture it says:

"See, I lay a stone in Zion,
  a chosen and precious cornerstone,
  and the one who trusts in him
      will never be put to shame."[a]

---

d Other ancient authorities add *through the Spirit*
e Or *constantly* f Other ancient authorities read *a pure heart* g Or *through the word of the living and enduring God* h Or *you yourselves are being built* i Or *it*

b22 NRSV note d διὰ πνεύματος c22 NIV/NRSV texts omit καθαρᾶς; NIV/NRSV notes as UBS

a16 Lev. 11:44,45; 19:2; 20:7 b22 Some early manuscripts *from a pure heart* c25 Isaiah 40:6-8 a6 Isaiah 28:16

7To you then who believe, he is precious; but for those who do not believe,

> "The stone that the builders rejected
>> has become the very head of the corner,"

8and

> "A stone that makes them stumble,
>> and a rock that makes them fall."

They stumble because they disobey the word, as they were destined to do.

9 But you are a chosen race, a royal priesthood, a holy nation, God's own people,[j] in order that you may proclaim the mighty acts of him who called you out of darkness into his marvelous light.

10 Once you were not a people,
> but now you are God's people;
> once you had not received mercy,
> but now you have received mercy.

Live as Servants of God

11 Beloved, I urge you as aliens and exiles to abstain from the desires of the flesh that wage war against the soul. 12Conduct yourselves honorably among the Gentiles, so that, though they malign you as evildoers, they may see your honorable deeds and glorify God when he comes to judge.[k]

13 For the Lord's sake accept the authority of every human institution,[l] whether of the emperor as supreme, 14or of governors, as sent by him to punish those who do wrong and to praise those who do right. 15For it is God's will that by doing right you should silence the ignorance of the foolish. 16As servants[m] of God, live as free people, yet do not use your freedom as a pretext for evil. 17Honor everyone. Love the family of believers.[n] Fear God. Honor the emperor.

The Example of Christ's Suffering

18 Slaves, accept the authority of your masters with all deference, not only those who are kind and gentle but also those who are harsh. 19For it is a credit to you if, being aware of God, you endure pain while suffering unjustly. 20If you endure when you are beaten for doing wrong, what credit is that? But if you endure when you do right and suffer for it, you have God's approval. 21For to this you have been called, because Christ also suffered for you, leaving you an example, so that you should follow in his steps.

22 "He committed no sin,

---

7 ὑμῖν οὖν ἡ τιμὴ τοῖς πιστεύουσιν, ἀπιστοῦσιν δὲ

λίθος ὃν ἀπεδοκίμασαν οἱ οἰκοδομοῦντες,
οὗτος ἐγενήθη εἰς κεφαλὴν γωνίας

8 καὶ

λίθος προσκόμματος
καὶ πέτρα σκανδάλου·

οἳ προσκόπτουσιν τῷ λόγῳ ἀπειθοῦντες εἰς ὃ καὶ ἐτέθησαν.

9 Ὑμεῖς δὲ **γένος ἐκλεκτόν, βασίλειον ἱεράτευμα, ἔθνος ἅγιον, λαὸς εἰς περιποίησιν, ὅπως τὰς ἀρετὰς ἐξαγγείλητε** τοῦ ἐκ σκότους ὑμᾶς καλέσαντος εἰς τὸ θαυμαστὸν αὐτοῦ φῶς·

10 οἳ ποτε οὐ λαὸς
νῦν δὲ λαὸς θεοῦ,
οἱ οὐκ ἠλεημένοι
νῦν δὲ ἐλεηθέντες.

11 Ἀγαπητοί, παρακαλῶ ὡς παροίκους καὶ παρεπιδήμους ἀπέχεσθαι τῶν σαρκικῶν ἐπιθυμιῶν αἵτινες στρατεύονται κατὰ τῆς ψυχῆς· 12 τὴν ἀναστροφὴν ὑμῶν ἐν τοῖς ἔθνεσιν ἔχοντες καλήν, ἵνα, ἐν ᾧ καταλαλοῦσιν ὑμῶν ὡς κακοποιῶν ἐκ τῶν καλῶν ἔργων ἐποπτεύοντες δοξάσωσιν τὸν θεὸν ἐν ἡμέρᾳ ἐπισκοπῆς.

13 Ὑποτάγητε πάσῃ ἀνθρωπίνῃ κτίσει διὰ τὸν κύριον, εἴτε βασιλεῖ ὡς ὑπερέχοντι, 14 εἴτε ἡγεμόσιν ὡς δι' αὐτοῦ πεμπομένοις εἰς ἐκδίκησιν κακοποιῶν ἔπαινον δὲ ἀγαθοποιῶν· 15 ὅτι οὕτως ἐστὶν τὸ θέλημα τοῦ θεοῦ ἀγαθοποιοῦντας φιμοῦν τὴν τῶν ἀφρόνων ἀνθρώπων ἀγνωσίαν, 16 ὡς ἐλεύθεροι καὶ μὴ ὡς ἐπικάλυμμα ἔχοντες τῆς κακίας τὴν ἐλευθερίαν ἀλλ' ὡς θεοῦ δοῦλοι. 17 πάντας τιμήσατε, τὴν ἀδελφότητα ἀγαπᾶτε, τὸν θεὸν φοβεῖσθε, τὸν βασιλέα τιμᾶτε.

18 Οἱ οἰκέται ὑποτασσόμενοι ἐν παντὶ φόβῳ τοῖς δεσπόταις, οὐ μόνον τοῖς ἀγαθοῖς καὶ ἐπιεικέσιν ἀλλὰ καὶ τοῖς σκολιοῖς. 19 τοῦτο γὰρ χάρις εἰ διὰ συνείδησιν θεοῦ ὑποφέρει τις λύπας πάσχων ἀδίκως. 20 ποῖον γὰρ κλέος εἰ ἁμαρτάνοντες καὶ κολαφιζόμενοι ὑπομενεῖτε; ἀλλ' εἰ ἀγαθοποιοῦντες καὶ πάσχοντες ὑπομενεῖτε, τοῦτο χάρις παρὰ θεῷ. 21 εἰς τοῦτο γὰρ ἐκλήθητε, ὅτι καὶ Χριστὸς ἔπαθεν ὑπὲρ ὑμῶν ὑμῖν ὑπολιμπάνων ὑπογραμμὸν ἵνα ἐπακολουθήσητε τοῖς ἴχνεσιν αὐτοῦ.

22 ὃς ἁμαρτίαν οὐκ ἐποίησεν

7Now to you who believe, this stone is precious. But to those who do not believe,

> "The stone the builders rejected
>> has become the capstone,[b]"[c]

8and,

> "A stone that causes men to stumble
>> and a rock that makes them fall."[d]

They stumble because they disobey the message—which is also what they were destined for.

9But you are a chosen people, a royal priesthood, a holy nation, a people belonging to God, that you may declare the praises of him who called you out of darkness into his wonderful light. 10Once you were not a people, but now you are the people of God; once you had not received mercy, but now you have received mercy.

11Dear friends, I urge you, as aliens and strangers in the world, to abstain from sinful desires, which war against your soul. 12Live such good lives among the pagans that, though they accuse you of doing wrong, they may see your good deeds and glorify God on the day he visits us.

Submission to Rulers and Masters

13Submit yourselves for the Lord's sake to every authority instituted among men: whether to the king, as the supreme authority, 14or to governors, who are sent by him to punish those who do wrong and to commend those who do right. 15For it is God's will that by doing good you should silence the ignorant talk of foolish men. 16Live as free men, but do not use your freedom as a cover-up for evil; live as servants of God. 17Show proper respect to everyone: Love the brotherhood of believers, fear God, honor the king.

18Slaves, submit yourselves to your masters with all respect, not only to those who are good and considerate, but also to those who are harsh. 19For it is commendable if a man bears up under the pain of unjust suffering because he is conscious of God. 20But how is it to your credit if you receive a beating for doing wrong and endure it? But if you suffer for doing good and you endure it, this is commendable before God. 21To this you were called, because Christ suffered for you, leaving you an example, that you should follow in his steps.

22"He committed no sin,

---

[j] Gk *a people for his possession*   [k] Gk *God on the day of visitation*   [l] Or *every institution ordained for human beings*   [m] Gk *slaves*   [n] Gk *Love the brotherhood*

[b]7 Or *cornerstone*   [c]7 Psalm 118:22   [d]8 Isaiah 8:14

and no deceit was found in his
mouth."

23When he was abused, he did not return abuse; when he suffered, he did not threaten; but he entrusted himself to the one who judges justly. 24He himself bore our sins in his body on the cross,[o] so that, free from sins, we might live for righteousness; by his wounds[p] you have been healed. 25For you were going astray like sheep, but now you have returned to the shepherd and guardian of your souls.

Wives and Husbands

3 Wives, in the same way, accept the authority of your husbands, so that, even if some of them do not obey the word, they may be won over without a word by their wives' conduct, 2when they see the purity and reverence of your lives. 3Do not adorn yourselves outwardly by braiding your hair, and by wearing gold ornaments or fine clothing; 4rather, let your adornment be the inner self with the lasting beauty of a gentle and quiet spirit, which is very precious in God's sight. 5It was in this way long ago that the holy women who hoped in God used to adorn themselves by accepting the authority of their husbands. 6Thus Sarah obeyed Abraham and called him lord. You have become her daughters as long as you do what is good and never let fears alarm you.

7 Husbands, in the same way, show consideration for your wives in your life together, paying honor to the woman as the weaker sex,[q] since they too are also heirs of the gracious gift of life—so that nothing may hinder your prayers.

Suffering for Doing Right

8 Finally, all of you, have unity of spirit, sympathy, love for one another, a tender heart, and a humble mind. 9Do not repay evil for evil or abuse for abuse; but, on the contrary, repay with a blessing. It is for this that you were called—that you might inherit a blessing. 10For

"Those who desire life
and desire to see good days,
let them keep their tongues from evil
and their lips from speaking deceit;
11 let them turn away from evil and do
good;
let them seek peace and pursue it.
12 For the eyes of the Lord are on the
righteous,

[o] Or *carried up our sins in his body to the tree* [p] Gk *bruise*
[q] Gk *vessel*

οὐδὲ εὑρέθη δόλος ἐν τῷ
στόματι αὐτοῦ,

23 *ὃς λοιδορούμενος οὐκ ἀντελοιδόρει πάσχων οὐκ ἠπείλει, παρεδίδου δὲ τῷ κρίνοντι δικαίως·* **24** *ὃς τὰς ἁμαρτίας ἡμῶν αὐτὸς ἀνήνεγκεν ἐν τῷ σώματι αὐτοῦ ἐπὶ τὸ ξύλον, ἵνα ταῖς ἁμαρτίαις ἀπογενόμενοι τῇ δικαιοσύνῃ ζήσωμεν, οὗ τῷ μώλωπι ἰάθητε.* **25** *ἦτε γὰρ ὡς πρόβατα πλανώμενοι, ἀλλὰ ἐπεστράφητε νῦν ἐπὶ τὸν ποιμένα καὶ ἐπίσκοπον τῶν ψυχῶν ὑμῶν.*

3 *Ὁμοίως [αἱ] γυναῖκες, ὑποτασσόμεναι τοῖς ἰδίοις ἀνδράσιν, ἵνα καὶ εἴ τινες ἀπειθοῦσιν τῷ λόγῳ, διὰ τῆς τῶν γυναικῶν ἀναστροφῆς ἄνευ λόγου κερδηθήσονται,* **2** *ἐποπτεύσαντες τὴν ἐν φόβῳ ἁγνὴν ἀναστροφὴν ὑμῶν.* **3** *ὧν ἔστω οὐχ ὁ ἔξωθεν ἐμπλοκῆς τριχῶν καὶ περιθέσεως χρυσίων ἢ ἐνδύσεως ἱματίων κόσμος* **4** *ἀλλ' ὁ κρυπτὸς τῆς καρδίας ἄνθρωπος ἐν τῷ ἀφθάρτῳ τοῦ πραέως καὶ ἡσυχίου πνεύματος, ὅ ἐστιν ἐνώπιον τοῦ θεοῦ πολυτελές.* **5** *οὕτως γάρ ποτε καὶ αἱ ἅγιαι γυναῖκες αἱ ἐλπίζουσαι εἰς θεὸν ἐκόσμουν ἑαυτὰς ὑποτασσόμεναι τοῖς ἰδίοις ἀνδράσιν,* **6** *ὡς Σάρρα ὑπήκουσεν τῷ Ἀβραὰμ κύριον αὐτὸν καλοῦσα, ἧς ἐγενήθητε τέκνα ἀγαθοποιοῦσαι καὶ μὴ φοβούμεναι μηδεμίαν πτόησιν.*

7 *Οἱ ἄνδρες ὁμοίως, συνοικοῦντες κατὰ γνῶσιν ὡς ἀσθενεστέρῳ σκεύει τῷ γυναικείῳ, ἀπονέμοντες τιμὴν ὡς καὶ συγκληρονόμοις χάριτος ζωῆς εἰς τὸ μὴ ἐγκόπτεσθαι τὰς προσευχὰς ὑμῶν.*

8 *Τὸ δὲ τέλος πάντες ὁμόφρονες, συμπαθεῖς, φιλάδελφοι, εὔσπλαγχνοι, ταπεινόφρονες,* **9** *μὴ ἀποδιδόντες κακὸν ἀντὶ κακοῦ ἢ λοιδορίαν ἀντὶ λοιδορίας, τοὐναντίον δὲ εὐλογοῦντες ὅτι εἰς τοῦτο ἐκλήθητε ἵνα εὐλογίαν κληρονομήσητε.*

10 ὁ *γὰρ* θέλων ζωὴν ἀγαπᾶν
καὶ ἰδεῖν ἡμέρας ἀγαθὰς
παυσάτω τὴν γλῶσσαν ἀπὸ κακοῦ
καὶ χείλη τοῦ μὴ λαλῆσαι δόλον,
11 ἐκκλινάτω δὲ ἀπὸ κακοῦ καὶ
ποιησάτω ἀγαθόν,
ζητησάτω εἰρήνην καὶ διωξάτω
αὐτήν·
12 ὅτι ὀφθαλμοὶ κυρίου ἐπὶ δικαίους

and no deceit was found in his
mouth."[e]

23When they hurled their insults at him, he did not retaliate; when he suffered, he made no threats. Instead, he entrusted himself to him who judges justly. 24He himself bore our sins in his body on the tree, so that we might die to sins and live for righteousness; by his wounds you have been healed. 25For you were like sheep going astray, but now you have returned to the Shepherd and Overseer of your souls.

Wives and Husbands

3 Wives, in the same way be submissive to your husbands so that, if any of them do not believe the word, they may be won over without words by the behavior of their wives, 2when they see the purity and reverence of your lives. 3Your beauty should not come from outward adornment, such as braided hair and the wearing of gold jewelry and fine clothes. 4Instead, it should be that of your inner self, the unfading beauty of a gentle and quiet spirit, which is of great worth in God's sight. 5For this is the way the holy women of the past who put their hope in God used to make themselves beautiful. They were submissive to their own husbands, 6like Sarah, who obeyed Abraham and called him her master. You are her daughters if you do what is right and do not give way to fear.

7Husbands, in the same way be considerate as you live with your wives, and treat them with respect as the weaker partner and as heirs with you of the gracious gift of life, so that nothing will hinder your prayers.

Suffering for Doing Good

8Finally, all of you, live in harmony with one another; be sympathetic, love as brothers, be compassionate and humble. 9Do not repay evil with evil or insult with insult, but with blessing, because to this you were called so that you may inherit a blessing. 10For,

"Whoever would love life
and see good days
must keep his tongue from evil
and his lips from deceitful speech.
11He must turn from evil and do good;
he must seek peace and pursue it.
12For the eyes of the Lord are on the
righteous

[e]22 Isaiah 53:9

and his ears are open to their prayer.
But the face of the Lord is against
those who do evil."

13 Now who will harm you if you are eager to do what is good? [14]But even if you do suffer for doing what is right, you are blessed. Do not fear what they fear,[r] and do not be intimidated, [15]but in your hearts sanctify Christ as Lord. Always be ready to make your defense to anyone who demands from you an accounting for the hope that is in you; [16]yet do it with gentleness and reverence.[s] Keep your conscience clear, so that, when you are maligned, those who abuse you for your good conduct in Christ may be put to shame. [17]For it is better to suffer for doing good, if suffering should be God's will, than to suffer for doing evil. [18]For Christ also suffered[t] for sins once for all, the righteous for the unrighteous, in order to bring you[u] to God. He was put to death in the flesh, but made alive in the spirit, [19]in which also he went and made a proclamation to the spirits in prison, [20]who in former times did not obey, when God waited patiently in the days of Noah, during the building of the ark, in which a few, that is, eight persons, were saved through water. [21]And baptism, which this prefigured, now saves you—not as a removal of dirt from the body, but as an appeal to God for[v] a good conscience, through the resurrection of Jesus Christ, [22]who has gone into heaven and is at the right hand of God, with angels, authorities, and powers made subject to him.

Good Stewards of God's Grace

4 Since therefore Christ suffered in the flesh,[w] arm yourselves also with the same intention (for whoever has suffered in the flesh has finished with sin), [2]so as to live for the rest of your earthly life[x] no longer by human desires but by the will of God. [3]You have already spent enough time in doing what the Gentiles like to do, living in licentiousness, passions, drunkenness, revels, carousing, and lawless idolatry. [4]They are surprised that you no longer join them in the same excesses of dissipation, and so they blaspheme.[y] [5]But they will have to give an accounting to him who stands ready to judge the living and the dead. [6]For this is the reason the gospel was proclaimed even to the dead, so that,

καὶ ὦτα αὐτοῦ εἰς δέησιν αὐτῶν, πρόσωπον δὲ κυρίου ἐπὶ ποιοῦντας κακά.

13 Καὶ τίς ὁ κακώσων ὑμᾶς ἐὰν τοῦ ἀγαθοῦ ζηλωταὶ γένησθε; 14 ἀλλ᾽ εἰ καὶ πάσχοιτε διὰ δικαιοσύνην, μακάριοι. τὸν δὲ φόβον αὐτῶν μὴ φοβηθῆτε μηδὲ ταραχθῆτε, 15 κύριον δὲ τὸν Χριστὸν ἁγιάσατε ἐν ταῖς καρδίαις ὑμῶν, ἕτοιμοι ἀεὶ πρὸς ἀπολογίαν παντὶ τῷ αἰτοῦντι ὑμᾶς λόγον περὶ τῆς ἐν ὑμῖν ἐλπίδος, 16 ἀλλὰ μετὰ πραΰτητος καὶ φόβου,[a] συνείδησιν ἔχοντες ἀγαθήν, ἵνα ἐν ᾧ καταλαλεῖσθε καταισχυνθῶσιν οἱ ἐπηρεάζοντες ὑμῶν τὴν ἀγαθὴν ἐν Χριστῷ ἀναστροφήν. 17 κρεῖττον γὰρ ἀγαθοποιοῦντας, εἰ θέλοι τὸ θέλημα τοῦ θεοῦ, πάσχειν ἢ κακοποιοῦντας. 18 ὅτι καὶ Χριστὸς ἅπαξ περὶ ἁμαρτιῶν ἔπαθεν[b], δίκαιος ὑπὲρ ἀδίκων, ἵνα ὑμᾶς[c] προσαγάγῃ τῷ θεῷ θανατωθεὶς μὲν σαρκὶ ζῳοποιηθεὶς δὲ πνεύματι· 19 ἐν ᾧ καὶ τοῖς ἐν φυλακῇ πνεύμασιν πορευθεὶς ἐκήρυξεν, 20 ἀπειθήσασίν ποτε ὅτε ἀπεξεδέχετο ἡ τοῦ θεοῦ μακροθυμία ἐν ἡμέραις Νῶε κατασκευαζομένης κιβωτοῦ εἰς ἣν ὀλίγοι, τοῦτ᾽ ἔστιν ὀκτὼ ψυχαί, διεσώθησαν δι᾽ ὕδατος. 21 ὃ καὶ ὑμᾶς ἀντίτυπον νῦν σῴζει βάπτισμα, οὐ σαρκὸς ἀπόθεσις ῥύπου ἀλλὰ συνειδήσεως ἀγαθῆς ἐπερώτημα εἰς θεόν, δι᾽ ἀναστάσεως Ἰησοῦ Χριστοῦ, 22 ὅς ἐστιν ἐν δεξιᾷ [τοῦ] θεοῦ πορευθεὶς εἰς οὐρανὸν ὑποταγέντων αὐτῷ ἀγγέλων καὶ ἐξουσιῶν καὶ δυνάμεων.

4 Χριστοῦ οὖν παθόντος[a] σαρκὶ καὶ ὑμεῖς τὴν αὐτὴν ἔννοιαν ὁπλίσασθε, ὅτι ὁ παθὼν σαρκὶ πέπαυται ἁμαρτίας 2 εἰς τὸ μηκέτι ἀνθρώπων ἐπιθυμίαις ἀλλὰ θελήματι θεοῦ τὸν ἐπίλοιπον ἐν σαρκὶ βιῶσαι χρόνον. 3 ἀρκετὸς γὰρ ὁ παρεληλυθὼς χρόνος τὸ βούλημα τῶν ἐθνῶν κατειργάσθαι πεπορευμένους ἐν ἀσελγείαις, ἐπιθυμίαις, οἰνοφλυγίαις, κώμοις, πότοις καὶ ἀθεμίτοις εἰδωλολατρίαις. 4 ἐν ᾧ ξενίζονται μὴ συντρεχόντων ὑμῶν εἰς τὴν αὐτὴν τῆς ἀσωτίας ἀνάχυσιν βλασφημοῦντες, 5 οἳ ἀποδώσουσιν λόγον τῷ ἑτοίμως ἔχοντι κρῖναι ζῶντας καὶ νεκρούς. 6 εἰς τοῦτο γὰρ καὶ νεκροῖς εὐηγγελίσθη, ἵνα κριθῶσι μὲν κατὰ

and his ears are attentive to their
prayer,
but the face of the Lord is against those
who do evil."[a]

[13]Who is going to harm you if you are eager to do good? [14]But even if you should suffer for what is right, you are blessed. "Do not fear what they fear[b]; do not be frightened."[c] [15]But in your hearts set apart Christ as Lord. Always be prepared to give an answer to everyone who asks you to give the reason for the hope that you have. But do this with gentleness and respect, [16]keeping a clear conscience, so that those who speak maliciously against your good behavior in Christ may be ashamed of their slander. [17]It is better, if it is God's will, to suffer for doing good than for doing evil. [18]For Christ died for sins once for all, the righteous for the unrighteous, to bring you to God. He was put to death in the body but made alive by the Spirit, [19]through whom[d] also he went and preached to the spirits in prison [20]who disobeyed long ago when God waited patiently in the days of Noah while the ark was being built. In it only a few people, eight in all, were saved through water, [21]and this water symbolizes baptism that now saves you also—not the removal of dirt from the body but the pledge[e] of a good conscience toward God. It saves you by the resurrection of Jesus Christ, [22]who has gone into heaven and is at God's right hand—with angels, authorities and powers in submission to him.

Living for God

4 Therefore, since Christ suffered in his body, arm yourselves also with the same attitude, because he who has suffered in his body is done with sin. [2]As a result, he does not live the rest of his earthly life for evil human desires, but rather for the will of God. [3]For you have spent enough time in the past doing what pagans choose to do—living in debauchery, lust, drunkenness, orgies, carousing and detestable idolatry. [4]They think it strange that you do not plunge with them into the same flood of dissipation, and they heap abuse on you. [5]But they will have to give account to him who is ready to judge the living and the dead. [6]For this is the reason the gospel was preached even to those who are now dead, so that they might be judged

ʳGk *their fear* ˢOr *respect* ᵗOther ancient authorities read *died* ᵘOther ancient authorities read *us* ᵛOr *a pledge to God from* ʷOther ancient authorities add *for us*; others, *for you* ˣGk *rest of the time in the flesh* ʸOr *they malign you*

ᵃ16 NIV begins verse 16 after φόβου. ᵇ18 NIV text and NRSV note t ἀπέθανεν ᶜ18 NRSV note u ἡμᾶς ᵃ1 NRSV note w adds ὑπὲρ ἡμῶν or ὑπὲρ ὑμῶν

ᵃ12 Psalm 34:12-16 ᵇ14 Or *not fear their threats* ᶜ14 Isaiah 8:12 ᵈ18,19 Or *alive in the spirit,* [19]*through which* ᵉ21 Or *response*

though they had been judged in the flesh as everyone is judged, they might live in the spirit as God does.

7 The end of all things is near;[z] therefore be serious and discipline yourselves for the sake of your prayers. 8Above all, maintain constant love for one another, for love covers a multitude of sins. 9Be hospitable to one another without complaining. 10Like good stewards of the manifold grace of God, serve one another with whatever gift each of you has received. 11Whoever speaks must do so as one speaking the very words of God; whoever serves must do so with the strength that God supplies, so that God may be glorified in all things through Jesus Christ. To him belong the glory and the power forever and ever. Amen.

Suffering as a Christian

12 Beloved, do not be surprised at the fiery ordeal that is taking place among you to test you, as though something strange were happening to you. 13But rejoice insofar as you are sharing Christ's sufferings, so that you may also be glad and shout for joy when his glory is revealed. 14If you are reviled for the name of Christ, you are blessed, because the spirit of glory,[a] which is the Spirit of God, is resting on you.[b] 15But let none of you suffer as a murderer, a thief, a criminal, or even as a mischief maker. 16Yet if any of you suffers as a Christian, do not consider it a disgrace, but glorify God because you bear this name. 17For the time has come for judgment to begin with the household of God; if it begins with us, what will be the end for those who do not obey the gospel of God? 18And

"If it is hard for the righteous to be saved,
    what will become of the ungodly
    and the sinners?"

19Therefore, let those suffering in accordance with God's will entrust themselves to a faithful Creator, while continuing to do good.

Tending the Flock of God

5 Now as an elder myself and a witness of the sufferings of Christ, as well as one who shares in the glory to be revealed, I exhort the elders among you 2to tend the flock of God that is in your charge, exercising the oversight,[c] not under compulsion

7 Πάντων δὲ τὸ τέλος ἤγγικεν. σωφρονήσατε οὖν καὶ νήψατε εἰς προσευχάς· 8 πρὸ πάντων τὴν εἰς ἑαυτοὺς ἀγάπην ἐκτενῆ ἔχοντες, ὅτι ἀγάπη καλύπτει πλῆθος ἁμαρτιῶν. 9 φιλόξενοι εἰς ἀλλήλους ἄνευ γογγυσμοῦ· 10 ἕκαστος καθὼς ἔλαβεν χάρισμα εἰς ἑαυτοὺς αὐτὸ διακονοῦντες ὡς καλοὶ οἰκονόμοι ποικίλης χάριτος θεοῦ. 11 εἴ τις λαλεῖ, ὡς λόγια θεοῦ· εἴ τις διακονεῖ, ὡς ἐξ ἰσχύος ἧς χορηγεῖ ὁ θεός, ἵνα ἐν πᾶσιν δοξάζηται ὁ θεὸς διὰ Ἰησοῦ Χριστοῦ, ᾧ ἐστιν ἡ δόξα καὶ τὸ κράτος εἰς τοὺς αἰῶνας τῶν αἰώνων, ἀμήν.

12 Ἀγαπητοί, μὴ ξενίζεσθε τῇ ἐν ὑμῖν πυρώσει πρὸς πειρασμὸν ὑμῖν γινομένῃ ὡς ξένου ὑμῖν συμβαίνοντος, 13 ἀλλὰ καθὸ κοινωνεῖτε τοῖς τοῦ Χριστοῦ παθήμασιν χαίρετε, ἵνα καὶ ἐν τῇ ἀποκαλύψει τῆς δόξης αὐτοῦ χαρῆτε ἀγαλλιώμενοι. 14 εἰ ὀνειδίζεσθε ἐν ὀνόματι Χριστοῦ, μακάριοι, ὅτι τὸ τῆς δόξης[b] καὶ τὸ τοῦ θεοῦ πνεῦμα ἐφ' ὑμᾶς ἀναπαύεται[c]. 15 μὴ γάρ τις ὑμῶν πασχέτω ὡς φονεὺς ἢ κλέπτης ἢ κακοποιὸς ἢ ὡς ἀλλοτριεπίσκοπος· 16 εἰ δὲ ὡς Χριστιανός, μὴ αἰσχυνέσθω, δοξαζέτω δὲ τὸν θεὸν ἐν τῷ ὀνόματι τούτῳ. 17 ὅτι [ὁ] καιρὸς τοῦ ἄρξασθαι τὸ κρίμα ἀπὸ τοῦ οἴκου τοῦ θεοῦ· εἰ δὲ πρῶτον ἀφ' ἡμῶν, τί τὸ τέλος τῶν ἀπειθούντων τῷ τοῦ θεοῦ εὐαγγελίῳ;
18 καὶ εἰ ὁ δίκαιος μόλις σῴζεται,
    ὁ ἀσεβὴς καὶ ἁμαρτωλὸς ποῦ
    φανεῖται;
19 ὥστε καὶ οἱ πάσχοντες κατὰ τὸ θέλημα τοῦ θεοῦ πιστῷ κτίστῃ παρατιθέσθωσαν τὰς ψυχὰς αὐτῶν ἐν ἀγαθοποιίᾳ.

5 Πρεσβυτέρους οὖν ἐν ὑμῖν παρακαλῶ ὁ συμπρεσβύτερος καὶ μάρτυς τῶν τοῦ Χριστοῦ παθημάτων, ὁ καὶ τῆς μελλούσης ἀποκαλύπτεσθαι δόξης κοινωνός· 2 ποιμάνατε τὸ ἐν ὑμῖν ποίμνιον τοῦ θεοῦ [ἐπισκοποῦντες] μὴ ἀναγκαστῶς ἀλλὰ ἑκουσίως κατὰ θεόν,

according to men in regard to the body, but live according to God in regard to the spirit.

7The end of all things is near. Therefore be clear minded and self-controlled so that you can pray. 8Above all, love each other deeply, because love covers over a multitude of sins. 9Offer hospitality to one another without grumbling. 10Each one should use whatever gift he has received to serve others, faithfully administering God's grace in its various forms. 11If anyone speaks, he should do it as one speaking the very words of God. If anyone serves, he should do it with the strength God provides, so that in all things God may be praised through Jesus Christ. To him be the glory and the power for ever and ever. Amen.

Suffering for Being a Christian

12Dear friends, do not be surprised at the painful trial you are suffering, as though something strange were happening to you. 13But rejoice that you participate in the sufferings of Christ, so that you may be overjoyed when his glory is revealed. 14If you are insulted because of the name of Christ, you are blessed, for the Spirit of glory and of God rests on you. 15If you suffer, it should not be as a murderer or thief or any other kind of criminal, or even as a meddler. 16However, if you suffer as a Christian, do not be ashamed, but praise God that you bear that name. 17For it is time for judgment to begin with the family of God; and if it begins with us, what will the outcome be for those who do not obey the gospel of God? 18And,

"If it is hard for the righteous to be saved,
    what will become of the ungodly and
    the sinner?"[a]

19So then, those who suffer according to God's will should commit themselves to their faithful Creator and continue to do good.

To Elders and Young Men

5 To the elders among you, I appeal as a fellow elder, a witness of Christ's sufferings and one who also will share in the glory to be revealed: 2Be shepherds of God's flock that is under your care, serving as overseers—not because you must,

z Or is at hand   a Other ancient authorities add and of power   b Other ancient authorities add On their part he is blasphemed, but on your part he is glorified   c Other ancient authorities lack exercising the oversight

b14 NRSV note a adds καὶ δυνάμεως   c14 NRSV note b adds κατὰ μὲν αὐτοὺς βλασφημεῖται, κατὰ δὲ ὑμᾶς δοξάζεται

a18 Prov. 11:31

but willingly, as God would have you do it[d]—not for sordid gain but eagerly. [3]Do not lord it over those in your charge, but be examples to the flock. [4]And when the chief shepherd appears, you will win the crown of glory that never fades away. [5]In the same way, you who are younger must accept the authority of the elders.[e] And all of you must clothe yourselves with humility in your dealings with one another, for

"God opposes the proud,
    but gives grace to the humble."

[6]Humble yourselves therefore under the mighty hand of God, so that he may exalt you in due time. [7]Cast all your anxiety on him, because he cares for you. [8]Discipline yourselves, keep alert.[f] Like a roaring lion your adversary the devil prowls around, looking for someone to devour. [9]Resist him, steadfast in your faith, for you know that your brothers and sisters[g] in all the world are undergoing the same kinds of suffering. [10]And after you have suffered for a little while, the God of all grace, who has called you to his eternal glory in Christ, will himself restore, support, strengthen, and establish you. [11]To him be the power forever and ever. Amen.

Final Greetings and Benediction

[12] Through Silvanus, whom I consider a faithful brother, I have written this short letter to encourage you and to testify that this is the true grace of God. Stand fast in it. [13]Your sister church[h] in Babylon, chosen together with you, sends you greetings; and so does my son Mark. [14]Greet one another with a kiss of love.

Peace to all of you who are in Christ.[i]

μηδὲ αἰσχροκερδῶς ἀλλὰ προθύμως, [3] μηδ' ὡς κατακυριεύοντες τῶν κλήρων ἀλλὰ τύποι γινόμενοι τοῦ ποιμνίου· [4] καὶ φανερωθέντος τοῦ ἀρχιποίμενος κομιεῖσθε τὸν ἀμαράντινον τῆς δόξης στέφανον.

[5] Ὁμοίως, νεώτεροι, ὑποτάγητε πρεσβυτέροις· πάντες δὲ ἀλλήλοις τὴν ταπεινοφροσύνην ἐγκομβώσασθε, ὅτι

[Ὁ] θεὸς ὑπερηφάνοις
    ἀντιτάσσεται,
ταπεινοῖς δὲ δίδωσιν χάριν.

[6] Ταπεινώθητε οὖν ὑπὸ τὴν κραταιὰν χεῖρα τοῦ θεοῦ, ἵνα ὑμᾶς ὑψώσῃ ἐν καιρῷ, [7] πᾶσαν τὴν μέριμναν ὑμῶν ἐπιρίψαντες ἐπ' αὐτόν, ὅτι αὐτῷ μέλει περὶ ὑμῶν.

[8] Νήψατε, γρηγορήσατε. ὁ ἀντίδικος ὑμῶν διάβολος ὡς λέων ὠρυόμενος περιπατεῖ ζητῶν [τινα] καταπιεῖν· [9] ᾧ ἀντίστητε στερεοὶ τῇ πίστει εἰδότες τὰ αὐτὰ τῶν παθημάτων τῇ ἐν [τῷ] κόσμῳ ὑμῶν ἀδελφότητι ἐπιτελεῖσθαι. [10] Ὁ δὲ θεὸς πάσης χάριτος, ὁ καλέσας ὑμᾶς εἰς τὴν αἰώνιον αὐτοῦ δόξαν ἐν Χριστῷ [Ἰησοῦ][a], ὀλίγον παθόντας αὐτὸς καταρτίσει, στηρίξει, σθενώσει, θεμελιώσει. [11] αὐτῷ τὸ κράτος εἰς τοὺς αἰῶνας[b], ἀμήν.

[12] Διὰ Σιλουανοῦ ὑμῖν τοῦ πιστοῦ ἀδελφοῦ, ὡς λογίζομαι, δι' ὀλίγων ἔγραψα παρακαλῶν καὶ ἐπιμαρτυρῶν ταύτην εἶναι ἀληθῆ χάριν τοῦ θεοῦ εἰς ἣν στῆτε. [13] Ἀσπάζεται ὑμᾶς ἡ ἐν Βαβυλῶνι συνεκλεκτὴ καὶ Μᾶρκος ὁ υἱός μου. [14] ἀσπάσασθε ἀλλήλους ἐν φιλήματι ἀγάπης. εἰρήνη ὑμῖν πᾶσιν τοῖς ἐν Χριστῷ.[c]

but because you are willing, as God wants you to be; not greedy for money, but eager to serve; [3]not lording it over those entrusted to you, but being examples to the flock. [4]And when the Chief Shepherd appears, you will receive the crown of glory that will never fade away. [5]Young men, in the same way be submissive to those who are older. All of you, clothe yourselves with humility toward one another, because,

"God opposes the proud
    but gives grace to the humble."[a]

[6]Humble yourselves, therefore, under God's mighty hand, that he may lift you up in due time. [7]Cast all your anxiety on him because he cares for you. [8]Be self-controlled and alert. Your enemy the devil prowls around like a roaring lion looking for someone to devour. [9]Resist him, standing firm in the faith, because you know that your brothers throughout the world are undergoing the same kind of sufferings.

[10]And the God of all grace, who called you to his eternal glory in Christ, after you have suffered a little while, will himself restore you and make you strong, firm and steadfast. [11]To him be the power for ever and ever. Amen.

Final Greetings

[12]With the help of Silas,[b] whom I regard as a faithful brother, I have written to you briefly, encouraging you and testifying that this is the true grace of God. Stand fast in it.

[13]She who is in Babylon, chosen together with you, sends you her greetings, and so does my son Mark. [14]Greet one another with a kiss of love.

Peace to all of you who are in Christ.

[d] Other ancient authorities lack *as God would have you do it*   [e] Or *of those who are older*   [f] Or *be vigilant*   [g] Gk *your brotherhood*   [h] Gk *She who is*   [i] Other ancient authorities add *Amen*

[a]10 NIV/NRSV texts omit Ἰησοῦ   [b]11 NIV/NRSV texts add τῶν αἰώνων   [c]14 NRSV note i adds ἀμήν.   [a]5 Prov. 3:34   [b]12 Greek *Silvanus*, a variant of *Silas*

NRSV

Salutation

1 Simeon[a] Peter, a servant[b] and apostle of Jesus Christ,

To those who have received a faith as precious as ours through the righteousness of our God and Savior Jesus Christ:[c]

2 May grace and peace be yours in abundance in the knowledge of God and of Jesus our Lord.

The Christian's Call and Election

3 His divine power has given us everything needed for life and godliness, through the knowledge of him who called us by[d] his own glory and goodness. [4]Thus he has given us, through these things, his precious and very great promises, so that through them you may escape from the corruption that is in the world because of lust, and may become participants of the divine nature. [5]For this very reason, you must make every effort to support your faith with goodness, and goodness with knowledge, [6]and knowledge with self-control, and self-control with endurance, and endurance with godliness, [7]and godliness with mutual[e] affection, and mutual[e] affection with love. [8]For if these things are yours and are increasing among you, they keep you from being ineffective and unfruitful in the knowledge of our Lord Jesus Christ. [9]For anyone who lacks these things is nearsighted and blind, and is forgetful of the cleansing of past sins. [10]Therefore, brothers and sisters,[f] be all the more eager to confirm your call and election, for if you do this, you will never stumble. [11]For in this way, entry into the eternal kingdom of our Lord and Savior Jesus Christ will be richly provided for you.

12 Therefore I intend to keep on reminding you of these things, though you know them already and are established in the truth that has come to you. [13]I think it right, as long as I am in this body,[g] to refresh your memory, [14]since I know that my death[h] will come soon, as indeed our Lord Jesus Christ has made clear to me. [15]And I will make every effort so that after my departure you may be able at any time to recall these things.

Eyewitnesses of Christ's Glory

16 For we did not follow cleverly devised myths when we made known to you

ΠΕΤΡΟΥ Β

1 Συμεὼν[a] Πέτρος δοῦλος καὶ ἀπόστολος Ἰησοῦ Χριστοῦ τοῖς ἰσότιμον ἡμῖν λαχοῦσιν πίστιν ἐν δικαιοσύνῃ τοῦ θεοῦ ἡμῶν καὶ σωτῆρος Ἰησοῦ Χριστοῦ, 2 χάρις ὑμῖν καὶ εἰρήνη πληθυνθείη ἐν ἐπιγνώσει τοῦ θεοῦ καὶ Ἰησοῦ τοῦ κυρίου ἡμῶν.

3 Ὡς πάντα ἡμῖν τῆς θείας δυνάμεως αὐτοῦ τὰ πρὸς ζωὴν καὶ εὐσέβειαν δεδωρημένης διὰ τῆς ἐπιγνώσεως τοῦ καλέσαντος ἡμᾶς ἰδίᾳ δόξῃ καὶ ἀρετῇ[b], 4 δι᾽ ὧν τὰ τίμια καὶ μέγιστα ἡμῖν ἐπαγγέλματα δεδώρηται, ἵνα διὰ τούτων γένησθε θείας κοινωνοὶ φύσεως ἀποφυγόντες τῆς ἐν τῷ κόσμῳ ἐν ἐπιθυμίᾳ φθορᾶς. 5 καὶ αὐτὸ τοῦτο δὲ σπουδὴν πᾶσαν παρεισενέγκαντες ἐπιχορηγήσατε ἐν τῇ πίστει ὑμῶν τὴν ἀρετήν, ἐν δὲ τῇ ἀρετῇ τὴν γνῶσιν, 6 ἐν δὲ τῇ γνώσει τὴν ἐγκράτειαν, ἐν δὲ τῇ ἐγκρατείᾳ τὴν ὑπομονήν, ἐν δὲ τῇ ὑπομονῇ τὴν εὐσέβειαν, 7 ἐν δὲ τῇ εὐσεβείᾳ τὴν φιλαδελφίαν, ἐν δὲ τῇ φιλαδελφίᾳ τὴν ἀγάπην. 8 ταῦτα γὰρ ὑμῖν ὑπάρχοντα καὶ πλεονάζοντα οὐκ ἀργοὺς οὐδὲ ἀκάρπους καθίστησιν εἰς τὴν τοῦ κυρίου ἡμῶν Ἰησοῦ Χριστοῦ ἐπίγνωσιν· 9 ᾧ γὰρ μὴ πάρεστιν ταῦτα, τυφλός ἐστιν μυωπάζων, λήθην λαβὼν τοῦ καθαρισμοῦ τῶν πάλαι αὐτοῦ ἁμαρτιῶν. 10 διὸ μᾶλλον, ἀδελφοί, σπουδάσατε βεβαίαν ὑμῶν τὴν κλῆσιν καὶ ἐκλογὴν ποιεῖσθαι· ταῦτα γὰρ ποιοῦντες οὐ μὴ πταίσητέ ποτε. 11 οὕτως γὰρ πλουσίως ἐπιχορηγηθήσεται ὑμῖν ἡ εἴσοδος εἰς τὴν αἰώνιον βασιλείαν τοῦ κυρίου ἡμῶν καὶ σωτῆρος Ἰησοῦ Χριστοῦ.

12 Διὸ μελλήσω ἀεὶ ὑμᾶς ὑπομιμνῄσκειν περὶ τούτων καίπερ εἰδότας καὶ ἐστηριγμένους ἐν τῇ παρούσῃ ἀληθείᾳ. 13 δίκαιον δὲ ἡγοῦμαι, ἐφ᾽ ὅσον εἰμὶ ἐν τούτῳ τῷ σκηνώματι, διεγείρειν ὑμᾶς ἐν ὑπομνήσει, 14 εἰδὼς ὅτι ταχινή ἐστιν ἡ ἀπόθεσις τοῦ σκηνώματός μου καθὼς καὶ ὁ κύριος ἡμῶν Ἰησοῦς Χριστὸς ἐδήλωσέν μοι, 15 σπουδάσω δὲ καὶ ἑκάστοτε ἔχειν ὑμᾶς μετὰ τὴν ἐμὴν ἔξοδον τὴν τούτων μνήμην ποιεῖσθαι.

16 Οὐ γὰρ σεσοφισμένοις μύθοις ἐξακολουθήσαντες ἐγνωρίσαμεν ὑμῖν

NIV

1 Simon Peter, a servant and apostle of Jesus Christ,

To those who through the righteousness of our God and Savior Jesus Christ have received a faith as precious as ours:

[2]Grace and peace be yours in abundance through the knowledge of God and of Jesus our Lord.

Making One's Calling and Election Sure

[3]His divine power has given us everything we need for life and godliness through our knowledge of him who called us by his own glory and goodness. [4]Through these he has given us his very great and precious promises, so that through them you may participate in the divine nature and escape the corruption in the world caused by evil desires.

[5]For this very reason, make every effort to add to your faith goodness; and to goodness, knowledge; [6]and to knowledge, self-control; and to self-control, perseverance; and to perseverance, godliness; [7]and to godliness, brotherly kindness; and to brotherly kindness, love. [8]For if you possess these qualities in increasing measure, they will keep you from being ineffective and unproductive in your knowledge of our Lord Jesus Christ. [9]But if anyone does not have them, he is nearsighted and blind, and has forgotten that he has been cleansed from his past sins.

[10]Therefore, my brothers, be all the more eager to make your calling and election sure. For if you do these things, you will never fall, [11]and you will receive a rich welcome into the eternal kingdom of our Lord and Savior Jesus Christ.

Prophecy of Scripture

[12]So I will always remind you of these things, even though you know them and are firmly established in the truth you now have. [13]I think it is right to refresh your memory as long as I live in the tent of this body, [14]because I know that I will soon put it aside, as our Lord Jesus Christ has made clear to me. [15]And I will make every effort to see that after my departure you will always be able to remember these things.

[16]We did not follow cleverly invented stories when we told you about the power

---

[a] Other ancient authorities read *Simon* [b] Gk *slave*
[c] Or *of our God and the Savior Jesus Christ* [d] Other ancient
authorities read *through* [e] Gk *brotherly* [f] Gk *brothers*
[g] Gk *tent* [h] Gk *the putting off of my tent*

[a]1 NRSV note a Σίμων [b]3 NRSV note d διὰ δόξης καὶ ἀρετῆς

the power and coming of our Lord Jesus Christ, but we had been eyewitnesses of his majesty. [17]For he received honor and glory from God the Father when that voice was conveyed to him by the Majestic Glory, saying, "This is my Son, my Beloved,[i] with whom I am well pleased." [18]We ourselves heard this voice come from heaven, while we were with him on the holy mountain.

19 So we have the prophetic message more fully confirmed. You will do well to be attentive to this as to a lamp shining in a dark place, until the day dawns and the morning star rises in your hearts. [20]First of all you must understand this, that no prophecy of scripture is a matter of one's own interpretation, [21]because no prophecy ever came by human will, but men and women moved by the Holy Spirit spoke from God.[j]

False Prophets and Their Punishment

2 But false prophets also arose among the people, just as there will be false teachers among you, who will secretly bring in destructive opinions. They will even deny the Master who bought them— bringing swift destruction on themselves. [2]Even so, many will follow their licentious ways, and because of these teachers[k] the way of truth will be maligned. [3]And in their greed they will exploit you with deceptive words. Their condemnation, pronounced against them long ago, has not been idle, and their destruction is not asleep.

4 For if God did not spare the angels when they sinned, but cast them into hell[l] and committed them to chains[m] of deepest darkness to be kept until the judgment; [5]and if he did not spare the ancient world, even though he saved Noah, a herald of righteousness, with seven others, when he brought a flood on a world of the ungodly; [6]and if by turning the cities of Sodom and Gomorrah to ashes he condemned them to extinction[n] and made them an example of what is coming to the ungodly;[o] [7]and if he rescued Lot, a righteous man greatly distressed by the licentiousness of the lawless [8](for that righteous man, living among them day after day, was tormented in his righteous soul by their lawless deeds that he saw and heard), [9]then the Lord knows

τὴν τοῦ κυρίου ἡμῶν Ἰησοῦ Χριστοῦ δύναμιν καὶ παρουσίαν ἀλλ᾽ ἐπόπται γενηθέντες τῆς ἐκείνου μεγαλειότητος. **17** λαβὼν γὰρ παρὰ θεοῦ πατρὸς τιμὴν καὶ δόξαν φωνῆς ἐνεχθείσης αὐτῷ τοιᾶσδε ὑπὸ τῆς μεγαλοπρεποῦς δόξης, Ὁ υἱός μου ὁ ἀγαπητός μου[c] οὗτός ἐστιν εἰς ὃν ἐγὼ εὐδόκησα. **18** καὶ ταύτην τὴν φωνὴν ἡμεῖς ἠκούσαμεν ἐξ οὐρανοῦ ἐνεχθεῖσαν σὺν αὐτῷ ὄντες ἐν τῷ ἁγίῳ ὄρει. **19** καὶ ἔχομεν βεβαιότερον τὸν προφητικὸν λόγον, ᾧ καλῶς ποιεῖτε προσέχοντες ὡς λύχνῳ φαίνοντι ἐν αὐχμηρῷ τόπῳ, ἕως οὗ ἡμέρα διαυγάσῃ καὶ φωσφόρος ἀνατείλῃ ἐν ταῖς καρδίαις ὑμῶν, **20** τοῦτο πρῶτον γινώσκοντες ὅτι πᾶσα προφητεία γραφῆς ἰδίας ἐπιλύσεως οὐ γίνεται· **21** οὐ γὰρ θελήματι ἀνθρώπου ἠνέχθη προφητεία ποτέ, ἀλλὰ ὑπὸ πνεύματος ἁγίου[d] φερόμενοι ἐλάλησαν ἀπὸ θεοῦ ἄνθρωποι.

2 Ἐγένοντο δὲ καὶ ψευδοπροφῆται ἐν τῷ λαῷ, ὡς καὶ ἐν ὑμῖν ἔσονται ψευδοδιδάσκαλοι, οἵτινες παρεισάξουσιν αἱρέσεις ἀπωλείας καὶ τὸν ἀγοράσαντα αὐτοὺς δεσπότην ἀρνούμενοι, ἐπάγοντες ἑαυτοῖς ταχινὴν ἀπώλειαν, **2** καὶ πολλοὶ ἐξακολουθήσουσιν αὐτῶν ταῖς ἀσελγείαις δι᾽ οὓς ἡ ὁδὸς τῆς ἀληθείας βλασφημηθήσεται, **3** καὶ ἐν πλεονεξίᾳ πλαστοῖς λόγοις ὑμᾶς ἐμπορεύσονται, οἷς τὸ κρίμα ἔκπαλαι οὐκ ἀργεῖ καὶ ἡ ἀπώλεια αὐτῶν οὐ νυστάζει.

4 Εἰ γὰρ ὁ θεὸς ἀγγέλων ἁμαρτησάντων οὐκ ἐφείσατο ἀλλὰ σειραῖς[a] ζόφου ταρταρώσας παρέδωκεν εἰς κρίσιν τηρουμένους, **5** καὶ ἀρχαίου κόσμου οὐκ ἐφείσατο ἀλλὰ ὄγδοον Νῶε δικαιοσύνης κήρυκα ἐφύλαξεν κατακλυσμὸν κόσμῳ ἀσεβῶν ἐπάξας, **6** καὶ πόλεις Σοδόμων καὶ Γομόρρας τεφρώσας [καταστροφῇ][b] κατέκρινεν ὑπόδειγμα μελλόντων ἀσεβέ[σ]ιν[c] τεθεικώς, **7** καὶ δίκαιον Λὼτ καταπονούμενον ὑπὸ τῆς τῶν ἀθέσμων ἐν ἀσελγείᾳ ἀναστροφῆς ἐρρύσατο· **8** βλέμματι γὰρ καὶ ἀκοῇ ὁ δίκαιος ἐγκατοικῶν ἐν αὐτοῖς ἡμέραν ἐξ ἡμέρας ψυχὴν δικαίαν ἀνόμοις ἔργοις ἐβασάνιζεν· **9** οἶδεν κύριος

and coming of our Lord Jesus Christ, but we were eyewitnesses of his majesty. [17]For he received honor and glory from God the Father when the voice came to him from the Majestic Glory, saying, "This is my Son, whom I love; with him I am well pleased."[a] [18]We ourselves heard this voice that came from heaven when we were with him on the sacred mountain.

[19]And we have the word of the prophets made more certain, and you will do well to pay attention to it, as to a light shining in a dark place, until the day dawns and the morning star rises in your hearts. [20]Above all, you must understand that no prophecy of Scripture came about by the prophet's own interpretation. [21]For prophecy never had its origin in the will of man, but men spoke from God as they were carried along by the Holy Spirit.

False Teachers and Their Destruction

2 But there were also false prophets among the people, just as there will be false teachers among you. They will secretly introduce destructive heresies, even denying the sovereign Lord who bought them—bringing swift destruction on themselves. [2]Many will follow their shameful ways and will bring the way of truth into disrepute. [3]In their greed these teachers will exploit you with stories they have made up. Their condemnation has long been hanging over them, and their destruction has not been sleeping.

[4]For if God did not spare angels when they sinned, but sent them to hell,[a] putting them into gloomy dungeons[b] to be held for judgment; [5]if he did not spare the ancient world when he brought the flood on its ungodly people, but protected Noah, a preacher of righteousness, and seven others; [6]if he condemned the cities of Sodom and Gomorrah by burning them to ashes, and made them an example of what is going to happen to the ungodly; [7]and if he rescued Lot, a righteous man, who was distressed by the filthy lives of lawless men [8](for that righteous man, living among them day after day, was tormented in his righteous soul by the lawless deeds he saw and heard)— [9]if this is so, then the Lord

---

[i]Other ancient authorities read *my beloved Son*   [j]Other ancient authorities read *but moved by the Holy Spirit saints of God spoke*   [k]Gk *because of them*   [l]Gk *Tartaros*   [m]Other ancient authorities read *pits*   [n]Other authorities lack *to extinction*   [o]Other ancient authorities read *an example to those who were to be ungodly*

[c]17 NRSV note i omits μου   [d]21 NRSV note j ἅγιοι   [a]4 NIV text and NRSV note m σιροῖς; NIV note and NRSV text as UBS   [b]6 NIV text and NRSV note n omit καταστροφῇ   [c]6 NRSV note o ἀσεβεῖν

[a]17 Matt. 17:5; Mark 9:7; Luke 9:35   [a]4 Greek *Tartarus*   [b]4 Some manuscripts *into chains of darkness*

how to rescue the godly from trial, and to keep the unrighteous under punishment until the day of judgment [10]—especially those who indulge their flesh in depraved lust, and who despise authority.

Bold and willful, they are not afraid to slander the glorious ones,[p] [11]whereas angels, though greater in might and power, do not bring against them a slanderous judgment from the Lord.[q] [12]These people, however, are like irrational animals, mere creatures of instinct, born to be caught and killed. They slander what they do not understand, and when those creatures are destroyed,[r] they also will be destroyed, [13]suffering[s] the penalty for doing wrong. They count it a pleasure to revel in the daytime. They are blots and blemishes, reveling in their dissipation[t] while they feast with you. [14]They have eyes full of adultery, insatiable for sin. They entice unsteady souls. They have hearts trained in greed. Accursed children! [15]They have left the straight road and have gone astray, following the road of Balaam son of Bosor,[u] who loved the wages of doing wrong, [16]but was rebuked for his own transgression; a speechless donkey spoke with a human voice and restrained the prophet's madness.

[17] These are waterless springs and mists driven by a storm; for them the deepest darkness has been reserved. [18]For they speak bombastic nonsense, and with licentious desires of the flesh they entice people who have just[v] escaped from those who live in error. [19]They promise them freedom, but they themselves are slaves of corruption; for people are slaves to whatever masters them. [20]For if, after they have escaped the defilements of the world through the knowledge of our Lord and Savior Jesus Christ, they are again entangled in them and overpowered, the last state has become worse for them than the first. [21]For it would have been better for them never to have known the way of righteousness than, after knowing it, to turn back from the holy commandment that was passed on to them. [22]It has happened to them according to the true proverb,

"The dog turns back to its own vomit,"

εὐσεβεῖς ἐκ πειρασμοῦ ῥύεσθαι, ἀδίκους δὲ εἰς ἡμέραν κρίσεως κολαζομένους τηρεῖν, **10** μάλιστα δὲ τοὺς ὀπίσω σαρκὸς ἐν ἐπιθυμίᾳ μιασμοῦ πορευομένους καὶ κυριότητος καταφρονοῦντας.

Τολμηταὶ αὐθάδεις, δόξας οὐ τρέμουσιν βλασφημοῦντες, **11** ὅπου ἄγγελοι ἰσχύϊ καὶ δυνάμει μείζονες ὄντες οὐ φέρουσιν κατ᾽ αὐτῶν παρὰ κυρίου[d] βλάσφημον κρίσιν. **12** οὗτοι δὲ ὡς ἄλογα ζῷα γεγεννημένα φυσικὰ εἰς ἅλωσιν καὶ φθορὰν ἐν οἷς ἀγνοοῦσιν βλασφημοῦντες, ἐν τῇ φθορᾷ αὐτῶν καὶ φθαρήσονται **13** ἀδικούμενοι[e] μισθὸν ἀδικίας, ἡδονὴν ἡγούμενοι τὴν ἐν ἡμέρᾳ τρυφήν, σπίλοι καὶ μῶμοι ἐντρυφῶντες ἐν ταῖς ἀπάταις[f] αὐτῶν συνευωχούμενοι ὑμῖν, **14** ὀφθαλμοὺς ἔχοντες μεστοὺς μοιχαλίδος καὶ ἀκαταπαύστους ἁμαρτίας, δελεάζοντες ψυχὰς ἀστηρίκτους, καρδίαν γεγυμνασμένην πλεονεξίας ἔχοντες, κατάρας τέκνα· **15** καταλείποντες εὐθεῖαν ὁδὸν ἐπλανήθησαν, ἐξακολουθήσαντες τῇ ὁδῷ τοῦ Βαλαὰμ τοῦ Βοσόρ[g], ὃς μισθὸν ἀδικίας ἠγάπησεν **16** ἔλεγξιν δὲ ἔσχεν ἰδίας παρανομίας· ὑποζύγιον ἄφωνον ἐν ἀνθρώπου φωνῇ φθεγξάμενον ἐκώλυσεν τὴν τοῦ προφήτου παραφρονίαν.

17 Οὗτοί εἰσιν πηγαὶ ἄνυδροι καὶ ὁμίχλαι ὑπὸ λαίλαπος ἐλαυνόμεναι, οἷς ὁ ζόφος τοῦ σκότους τετήρηται. **18** ὑπέρογκα γὰρ ματαιότητος φθεγγόμενοι δελεάζουσιν ἐν ἐπιθυμίαις σαρκὸς ἀσελγείαις τοὺς ὀλίγως[h] ἀποφεύγοντας τοὺς ἐν πλάνῃ ἀναστρεφομένους, **19** ἐλευθερίαν αὐτοῖς ἐπαγγελλόμενοι, αὐτοὶ δοῦλοι ὑπάρχοντες τῆς φθορᾶς· ᾧ γάρ τις ἥττηται, τούτῳ δεδούλωται. **20** εἰ γὰρ ἀποφυγόντες τὰ μιάσματα τοῦ κόσμου ἐν ἐπιγνώσει τοῦ κυρίου [ἡμῶν] καὶ σωτῆρος Ἰησοῦ Χριστοῦ, τούτοις δὲ πάλιν ἐμπλακέντες ἡττῶνται, γέγονεν αὐτοῖς τὰ ἔσχατα χείρονα τῶν πρώτων. **21** κρεῖττον γὰρ ἦν αὐτοῖς μὴ ἐπεγνωκέναι τὴν ὁδὸν τῆς δικαιοσύνης ἢ ἐπιγνοῦσιν ὑποστρέψαι ἐκ τῆς παραδοθείσης αὐτοῖς ἁγίας ἐντολῆς. **22** συμβέβηκεν αὐτοῖς τὸ τῆς ἀληθοῦς παροιμίας.

Κύων ἐπιστρέψας ἐπὶ τὸ ἴδιον ἐξέραμα,

---

knows how to rescue godly men from trials and to hold the unrighteous for the day of judgment, while continuing their punishment.[c] [10]This is especially true of those who follow the corrupt desire of the sinful nature[d] and despise authority.

Bold and arrogant, these men are not afraid to slander celestial beings; [11]yet even angels, although they are stronger and more powerful, do not bring slanderous accusations against such beings in the presence of the Lord. [12]But these men blaspheme in matters they do not understand. They are like brute beasts, creatures of instinct, born only to be caught and destroyed, and like beasts they too will perish.

[13]They will be paid back with harm for the harm they have done. Their idea of pleasure is to carouse in broad daylight. They are blots and blemishes, reveling in their pleasures while they feast with you.[e] [14]With eyes full of adultery, they never stop sinning; they seduce the unstable; they are experts in greed—an accursed brood! [15]They have left the straight way and wandered off to follow the way of Balaam son of Beor, who loved the wages of wickedness. [16]But he was rebuked for his wrongdoing by a donkey—a beast without speech—who spoke with a man's voice and restrained the prophet's madness.

[17]These men are springs without water and mists driven by a storm. Blackest darkness is reserved for them. [18]For they mouth empty, boastful words and, by appealing to the lustful desires of sinful human nature, they entice people who are just escaping from those who live in error. [19]They promise them freedom, while they themselves are slaves of depravity—for a man is a slave to whatever has mastered him. [20]If they have escaped the corruption of the world by knowing our Lord and Savior Jesus Christ and are again entangled in it and overcome, they are worse off at the end than they were at the beginning. [21]It would have been better for them not to have known the way of righteousness, than to have known it and then to turn their backs on the sacred command that was passed on to them. [22]Of them the proverbs are true: "A dog returns to its vomit,"[f]

---

p Or *angels*; Gk *glories*   q Other ancient authorities read *before the Lord*; others lack the phrase   r Gk *in their destruction*   s Other ancient authorities read *receiving*   t Other ancient authorities read *love feasts*   u Other ancient authorities read *Beor*   v Other ancient authorities read *actually*

d11 NRSV note q reads παρὰ κυρίῳ or omits παρὰ κυρίου   e13 NRSV note s κομιούμενοι   f13 NIV/NRSV notes ἀγάπαις   g15 NIV text and NRSV note u Βεώρ   h18 NRSV note v ὄντως

c9 Or *unrighteous for punishment until the day of judgment*   d10 Or *the flesh*   e13 Some manuscripts *in their love feasts*   f22 Prov. 26:11

and,

> "The sow is washed only to wallow in
> the mud."

The Promise of the Lord's Coming

3 This is now, beloved, the second letter I am writing to you; in them I am trying to arouse your sincere intention by reminding you [2]that you should remember the words spoken in the past by the holy prophets, and the commandment of the Lord and Savior spoken through your apostles. [3]First of all you must understand this, that in the last days scoffers will come, scoffing and indulging their own lusts [4]and saying, "Where is the promise of his coming? For ever since our ancestors died,[w] all things continue as they were from the beginning of creation!" [5]They deliberately ignore this fact, that by the word of God heavens existed long ago and an earth was formed out of water and by means of water, [6]through which the world of that time was deluged with water and perished. [7]But by the same word the present heavens and earth have been reserved for fire, being kept until the day of judgment and destruction of the godless.

8 But do not ignore this one fact, beloved, that with the Lord one day is like a thousand years, and a thousand years are like one day. [9]The Lord is not slow about his promise, as some think of slowness, but is patient with you,[x] not wanting any to perish, but all to come to repentance. [10]But the day of the Lord will come like a thief, and then the heavens will pass away with a loud noise, and the elements will be dissolved with fire, and the earth and everything that is done on it will be disclosed.[y]

11 Since all these things are to be dissolved in this way, what sort of persons ought you to be in leading lives of holiness and godliness, [12]waiting for and hastening[z] the coming of the day of God, because of which the heavens will be set ablaze and dissolved, and the elements will melt with fire? [13]But, in accordance with his promise, we wait for new heavens and a new earth, where righteousness is at home.

Final Exhortation and Doxology

14 Therefore, beloved, while you are waiting for these things, strive to be found by him at peace, without spot or blemish;

καί,

> [ϒ]ς λουσαμένη εἰς κυλισμὸν
> βορβόρου.

3 Ταύτην ἤδη, ἀγαπητοί, δευτέραν ὑμῖν γράφω ἐπιστολήν ἐν αἷς διεγείρω ὑμῶν ἐν ὑπομνήσει τὴν εἰλικρινῆ διάνοιαν 2 μνησθῆναι τῶν προειρημένων ῥημάτων ὑπὸ τῶν ἁγίων προφητῶν καὶ τῆς τῶν ἀποστόλων ὑμῶν ἐντολῆς τοῦ κυρίου καὶ σωτῆρος. 3 τοῦτο πρῶτον γινώσκοντες ὅτι ἐλεύσονται ἐπ' ἐσχάτων τῶν ἡμερῶν [ἐν] ἐμπαιγμονῇ ἐμπαῖκται κατὰ τὰς ἰδίας ἐπιθυμίας αὐτῶν πορευόμενοι 4 καὶ λέγοντες, Ποῦ ἐστιν ἡ ἐπαγγελία τῆς παρουσίας αὐτοῦ; ἀφ' ἧς γὰρ οἱ πατέρες ἐκοιμήθησαν, πάντα οὕτως διαμένει ἀπ' ἀρχῆς κτίσεως. 5 λανθάνει γὰρ αὐτοὺς τοῦτο θέλοντας ὅτι οὐρανοὶ ἦσαν ἔκπαλαι καὶ γῆ ἐξ ὕδατος καὶ δι' ὕδατος συνεστῶσα τῷ τοῦ θεοῦ λόγῳ, 6 δι' ὧν ὁ τότε κόσμος ὕδατι κατακλυσθεὶς ἀπώλετο· 7 οἱ δὲ νῦν οὐρανοὶ καὶ ἡ γῆ τῷ αὐτῷ λόγῳ τεθησαυρισμένοι εἰσὶν πυρὶ τηρούμενοι εἰς ἡμέραν κρίσεως καὶ ἀπωλείας τῶν ἀσεβῶν ἀνθρώπων.

8 Ἕν δὲ τοῦτο μὴ λανθανέτω ὑμᾶς, ἀγαπητοί, ὅτι μία ἡμέρα παρὰ κυρίῳ ὡς χίλια ἔτη καὶ χίλια ἔτη ὡς ἡμέρα μία. 9 οὐ βραδύνει κύριος τῆς ἐπαγγελίας, ὥς τινες βραδύτητα ἡγοῦνται, ἀλλὰ μακροθυμεῖ εἰς[a] ὑμᾶς, μὴ βουλόμενός τινας ἀπολέσθαι ἀλλὰ πάντας εἰς μετάνοιαν χωρῆσαι. 10 Ἥξει δὲ ἡμέρα κυρίου ὡς κλέπτης, ἐν ᾗ οἱ οὐρανοὶ ῥοιζηδὸν παρελεύσονται στοιχεῖα δὲ καυσούμενα λυθήσεται καὶ γῆ καὶ τὰ ἐν αὐτῇ ἔργα εὑρεθήσεται[b]. 11 τούτων οὕτως πάντων λυομένων ποταποὺς δεῖ ὑπάρχειν [ὑμᾶς] ἐν ἁγίαις ἀναστροφαῖς καὶ εὐσεβείαις, 12 προσδοκῶντας καὶ σπεύδοντας τὴν παρουσίαν τῆς τοῦ θεοῦ ἡμέρας δι' ἣν οὐρανοὶ πυρούμενοι λυθήσονται καὶ στοιχεῖα καυσούμενα τήκεται. 13 καινοὺς δὲ οὐρανοὺς καὶ γῆν καινὴν κατὰ τὸ ἐπάγγελμα αὐτοῦ προσδοκῶμεν, ἐν οἷς δικαιοσύνη κατοικεῖ. 14 Διό, ἀγαπητοί, ταῦτα προσδοκῶντες σπουδάσατε ἄσπιλοι καὶ ἀμώμητοι αὐτῷ εὑρεθῆναι ἐν εἰρήνῃ 15 καὶ τὴν

---

and, "A sow that is washed goes back to her wallowing in the mud."

The Day of the Lord

3 Dear friends, this is now my second letter to you. I have written both of them as reminders to stimulate you to wholesome thinking. [2]I want you to recall the words spoken in the past by the holy prophets and the command given by our Lord and Savior through your apostles.

[3]First of all, you must understand that in the last days scoffers will come, scoffing and following their own evil desires. [4]They will say, "Where is this 'coming' he promised? Ever since our fathers died, everything goes on as it has since the beginning of creation." [5]But they deliberately forget that long ago by God's word the heavens existed and the earth was formed out of water and by water. [6]By these waters also the world of that time was deluged and destroyed. [7]By the same word the present heavens and earth are reserved for fire, being kept for the day of judgment and destruction of ungodly men.

[8]But do not forget this one thing, dear friends: With the Lord a day is like a thousand years, and a thousand years are like a day. [9]The Lord is not slow in keeping his promise, as some understand slowness. He is patient with you, not wanting anyone to perish, but everyone to come to repentance.

[10]But the day of the Lord will come like a thief. The heavens will disappear with a roar; the elements will be destroyed by fire, and the earth and everything in it will be laid bare.[a]

[11]Since everything will be destroyed in this way, what kind of people ought you to be? You ought to live holy and godly lives [12]as you look forward to the day of God and speed its coming.[b] That day will bring about the destruction of the heavens by fire, and the elements will melt in the heat. [13]But in keeping with his promise we are looking forward to a new heaven and a new earth, the home of righteousness.

[14]So then, dear friends, since you are looking forward to this, make every effort to be found spotless, blameless and at peace

---

w Gk *our fathers fell asleep*   x Other ancient authorities read *on your account*   y Other ancient authorities read *will be burned up*   z Or *earnestly desiring*

a9 NRSV note x δι'   b10 NIV/NRSV notes κατακαήσεται

a10 Some manuscripts *be burned up*   b12 Or *as you wait eagerly for the day of God to come*

[15]and regard the patience of our Lord as salvation. So also our beloved brother Paul wrote to you according to the wisdom given him, [16]speaking of this as he does in all his letters. There are some things in them hard to understand, which the ignorant and unstable twist to their own destruction, as they do the other scriptures. [17]You therefore, beloved, since you are forewarned, beware that you are not carried away with the error of the lawless and lose your own stability. [18]But grow in the grace and knowledge of our Lord and Savior Jesus Christ. To him be the glory both now and to the day of eternity. Amen.[a]

τοῦ κυρίου ἡμῶν μακροθυμίαν σωτηρίαν ἡγεῖσθε, καθὼς καὶ ὁ ἀγαπητὸς ἡμῶν ἀδελφὸς Παῦλος κατὰ τὴν δοθεῖσαν αὐτῷ σοφίαν ἔγραψεν ὑμῖν, **16** ὡς καὶ ἐν πάσαις ἐπιστολαῖς λαλῶν ἐν αὐταῖς περὶ τούτων, ἐν αἷς ἐστιν δυσνόητά τινα, ἃ οἱ ἀμαθεῖς καὶ ἀστήρικτοι στρεβλοῦσιν ὡς καὶ τὰς λοιπὰς γραφὰς πρὸς τὴν ἰδίαν αὐτῶν ἀπώλειαν. **17** Ὑμεῖς οὖν, ἀγαπητοί, προγινώσκοντες φυλάσσεσθε, ἵνα μὴ τῇ τῶν ἀθέσμων πλάνῃ συναπαχθέντες ἐκπέσητε τοῦ ἰδίου στηριγμοῦ, **18** αὐξάνετε δὲ ἐν χάριτι καὶ γνώσει τοῦ κυρίου ἡμῶν καὶ σωτῆρος Ἰησοῦ Χριστοῦ. αὐτῷ ἡ δόξα καὶ νῦν καὶ εἰς ἡμέραν αἰῶνος. [ἀμήν.]

with him. [15]Bear in mind that our Lord's patience means salvation, just as our dear brother Paul also wrote you with the wisdom that God gave him. [16]He writes the same way in all his letters, speaking in them of these matters. His letters contain some things that are hard to understand, which ignorant and unstable people distort, as they do the other Scriptures, to their own destruction.

[17]Therefore, dear friends, since you already know this, be on your guard so that you may not be carried away by the error of lawless men and fall from your secure position. [18]But grow in the grace and knowledge of our Lord and Savior Jesus Christ. To him be glory both now and forever! Amen.

NRSV

The Word of Life

1 We declare to you what was from the beginning, what we have heard, what we have seen with our eyes, what we have looked at and touched with our hands, concerning the word of life— [2]this life was revealed, and we have seen it and testify to it, and declare to you the eternal life that was with the Father and was revealed to us— [3]we declare to you what we have seen and heard so that you also may have fellowship with us; and truly our fellowship is with the Father and with his Son Jesus Christ. [4]We are writing these things so that our[a] joy may be complete.

God Is Light

[5] This is the message we have heard from him and proclaim to you, that God is light and in him there is no darkness at all. [6]If we say that we have fellowship with him while we are walking in darkness, we lie and do not do what is true; [7]but if we walk in the light as he himself is in the light, we have fellowship with one another, and the blood of Jesus his Son cleanses us from all sin. [8]If we say that we have no sin, we deceive ourselves, and the truth is not in us. [9]If we confess our sins, he who is faithful and just will forgive us our sins and cleanse us from all unrighteousness. [10]If we say that we have not sinned, we make him a liar, and his word is not in us.

Christ Our Advocate

2 My little children, I am writing these things to you so that you may not sin. But if anyone does sin, we have an advocate with the Father, Jesus Christ the righteous; [2]and he is the atoning sacrifice for our sins, and not for ours only but also for the sins of the whole world.

[3] Now by this we may be sure that we know him, if we obey his commandments. [4]Whoever says, "I have come to know him," but does not obey his commandments, is a liar, and in such a person the truth does not exist; [5]but whoever obeys his word, truly in this person the love of God has reached perfection. By this we may be sure that we are in him: [6]whoever says, "I abide in him," ought to walk just as he walked.

A New Commandment

[7] Beloved, I am writing you no new com-

ΙΩΑΝΝΟΥ Α

1 Ὃ ἦν ἀπ᾽ ἀρχῆς, ὃ ἀκηκόαμεν, ὃ ἑωράκαμεν τοῖς ὀφθαλμοῖς ἡμῶν, ὃ ἐθεασάμεθα καὶ αἱ χεῖρες ἡμῶν ἐψηλάφησαν περὶ τοῦ λόγου τῆς ζωῆς – **2** καὶ ἡ ζωὴ ἐφανερώθη, καὶ ἑωράκαμεν καὶ μαρτυροῦμεν καὶ ἀπαγγέλλομεν ὑμῖν τὴν ζωὴν τὴν αἰώνιον ἥτις ἦν πρὸς τὸν πατέρα καὶ ἐφανερώθη ἡμῖν – **3** ὃ ἑωράκαμεν καὶ ἀκηκόαμεν, ἀπαγγέλλομεν καὶ ὑμῖν, ἵνα καὶ ὑμεῖς κοινωνίαν ἔχητε μεθ᾽ ἡμῶν. καὶ ἡ κοινωνία δὲ ἡ ἡμετέρα μετὰ τοῦ πατρὸς καὶ μετὰ τοῦ υἱοῦ αὐτοῦ Ἰησοῦ Χριστοῦ. **4** καὶ ταῦτα γράφομεν ἡμεῖς, ἵνα ἡ χαρὰ ἡμῶν[a] ᾖ πεπληρωμένη.

5 Καὶ ἔστιν αὕτη ἡ ἀγγελία ἣν ἀκηκόαμεν ἀπ᾽ αὐτοῦ καὶ ἀναγγέλλομεν ὑμῖν, ὅτι ὁ θεὸς φῶς ἐστιν καὶ σκοτία ἐν αὐτῷ οὐκ ἔστιν οὐδεμία. **6** Ἐὰν εἴπωμεν ὅτι κοινωνίαν ἔχομεν μετ᾽ αὐτοῦ καὶ ἐν τῷ σκότει περιπατῶμεν, ψευδόμεθα καὶ οὐ ποιοῦμεν τὴν ἀλήθειαν· **7** ἐὰν δὲ ἐν τῷ φωτὶ περιπατῶμεν ὡς αὐτός ἐστιν ἐν τῷ φωτί, κοινωνίαν ἔχομεν μετ᾽ ἀλλήλων καὶ τὸ αἷμα Ἰησοῦ τοῦ υἱοῦ αὐτοῦ καθαρίζει ἡμᾶς ἀπὸ πάσης ἁμαρτίας. **8** ἐὰν εἴπωμεν ὅτι ἁμαρτίαν οὐκ ἔχομεν, ἑαυτοὺς πλανῶμεν καὶ ἡ ἀλήθεια οὐκ ἔστιν ἐν ἡμῖν. **9** ἐὰν ὁμολογῶμεν τὰς ἁμαρτίας ἡμῶν, πιστός ἐστιν καὶ δίκαιος, ἵνα ἀφῇ ἡμῖν τὰς ἁμαρτίας καὶ καθαρίσῃ ἡμᾶς ἀπὸ πάσης ἀδικίας. **10** ἐὰν εἴπωμεν ὅτι οὐχ ἡμαρτήκαμεν, ψεύστην ποιοῦμεν αὐτὸν καὶ ὁ λόγος αὐτοῦ οὐκ ἔστιν ἐν ἡμῖν.

2 Τεκνία μου, ταῦτα γράφω ὑμῖν ἵνα μὴ ἁμάρτητε. καὶ ἐάν τις ἁμάρτῃ, παράκλητον ἔχομεν πρὸς τὸν πατέρα Ἰησοῦν Χριστὸν δίκαιον· **2** καὶ αὐτὸς ἱλασμός ἐστιν περὶ τῶν ἁμαρτιῶν ἡμῶν, οὐ περὶ τῶν ἡμετέρων δὲ μόνον ἀλλὰ καὶ περὶ ὅλου τοῦ κόσμου. **3** Καὶ ἐν τούτῳ γινώσκομεν ὅτι ἐγνώκαμεν αὐτόν, ἐὰν τὰς ἐντολὰς αὐτοῦ τηρῶμεν. **4** ὁ λέγων ὅτι Ἔγνωκα αὐτὸν καὶ τὰς ἐντολὰς αὐτοῦ μὴ τηρῶν, ψεύστης ἐστὶν καὶ ἐν τούτῳ ἡ ἀλήθεια οὐκ ἔστιν· **5** ὃς δ᾽ ἂν τηρῇ αὐτοῦ τὸν λόγον, ἀληθῶς ἐν τούτῳ ἡ ἀγάπη τοῦ θεοῦ τετελείωται, ἐν τούτῳ γινώσκομεν ὅτι ἐν αὐτῷ ἐσμεν. **6** ὁ λέγων ἐν αὐτῷ μένειν ὀφείλει καθὼς ἐκεῖνος περιεπάτησεν καὶ αὐτὸς [οὕτως] περιπατεῖν.

7 Ἀγαπητοί, οὐκ ἐντολὴν καινὴν

NIV

The Word of Life

1 That which was from the beginning, which we have heard, which we have seen with our eyes, which we have looked at and our hands have touched—this we proclaim concerning the Word of life. [2]The life appeared; we have seen it and testify to it, and we proclaim to you the eternal life, which was with the Father and has appeared to us. [3]We proclaim to you what we have seen and heard, so that you also may have fellowship with us. And our fellowship is with the Father and with his Son, Jesus Christ. [4]We write this to make our[a] joy complete.

Walking in the Light

[5]This is the message we have heard from him and declare to you: God is light; in him there is no darkness at all. [6]If we claim to have fellowship with him yet walk in the darkness, we lie and do not live by the truth. [7]But if we walk in the light, as he is in the light, we have fellowship with one another, and the blood of Jesus, his Son, purifies us from all[b] sin.

[8]If we claim to be without sin, we deceive ourselves and the truth is not in us. [9]If we confess our sins, he is faithful and just and will forgive us our sins and purify us from all unrighteousness. [10]If we claim we have not sinned, we make him out to be a liar and his word has no place in our lives.

2 My dear children, I write this to you so that you will not sin. But if anybody does sin, we have one who speaks to the Father in our defense—Jesus Christ, the Righteous One. [2]He is the atoning sacrifice for our sins, and not only for ours but also for[a] the sins of the whole world.

[3]We know that we have come to know him if we obey his commands. [4]The man who says, "I know him," but does not do what he commands is a liar, and the truth is not in him. [5]But if anyone obeys his word, God's love[b] is truly made complete in him. This is how we know we are in him: [6]Whoever claims to live in him must walk as Jesus did.

[7]Dear friends, I am not writing you a

---

[a] Other ancient authorities read *your*

[a]4 NIV/NRSV notes ὑμῶν

[a]4 Some manuscripts *your*   [b]7 Or *every*   [a]2 Or *He is the one who turns aside God's wrath, taking away our sins, and not only ours but also*   [b]5 Or *word, love for God*

mandment, but an old commandment that you have had from the beginning; the old commandment is the word that you have heard. 8Yet I am writing you a new commandment that is true in him and in you, becauseᵇ the darkness is passing away and the true light is already shining. 9Whoever says, "I am in the light," while hating a brother or sister,ᶜ is still in the darkness. 10Whoever loves a brother or sisterᵈ lives in the light, and in such a personᵉ there is no cause for stumbling. 11But whoever hates another believerᶠ is in the darkness, walks in the darkness, and does not know the way to go, because the darkness has brought on blindness.

12 I am writing to you, little children,
　　because your sins are forgiven on
　　　　account of his name.
13 I am writing to you, fathers,
　　because you know him who is from
　　　　the beginning.
　I am writing to you, young people,
　　because you have conquered the
　　　　evil one.
14 I write to you, children,
　　because you know the Father.
　I write to you, fathers,
　　because you know him who is from
　　　　the beginning.
　I write to you, young people,
　　because you are strong
　　　and the word of God abides in you,
　　　　and you have overcome the evil
　　　　　one.

15 Do not love the world or the things in the world. The love of the Father is not in those who love the world; 16for all that is in the world—the desire of the flesh, the desire of the eyes, the pride in riches—comes not from the Father but from the world. 17And the world and its desireᵍ are passing away, but those who do the will of God live forever.

Warning against Antichrists

18 Children, it is the last hour! As you have heard that antichrist is coming, so now many antichrists have come. From this we know that it is the last hour. 19They went out from us, but they did not belong to us; for if they had belonged to us, they would have remained with us. But by going out they made it plain that none of them belongs to us. 20But you have been

γράφω ὑμῖν ἀλλ' ἐντολὴν παλαιὰν ἣν εἴχετε ἀπ' ἀρχῆς· ἡ ἐντολὴ ἡ παλαιά ἐστιν ὁ λόγος ὃν ἠκούσατε. 8 πάλιν ἐντολὴν καινὴν γράφω ὑμῖν, ὅ ἐστιν ἀληθὲς ἐν αὐτῷ καὶ ἐν ὑμῖν, ὅτι ἡ σκοτία παράγεται καὶ τὸ φῶς τὸ ἀληθινὸν ἤδη φαίνει. 9 ὁ λέγων ἐν τῷ φωτὶ εἶναι καὶ τὸν ἀδελφὸν αὐτοῦ μισῶν ἐν τῇ σκοτίᾳ ἐστὶν ἕως ἄρτι. 10 ὁ ἀγαπῶν τὸν ἀδελφὸν αὐτοῦ ἐν τῷ φωτὶ μένει καὶ σκάνδαλον ἐν αὐτῷ οὐκ ἔστιν· 11 ὁ δὲ μισῶν τὸν ἀδελφὸν αὐτοῦ ἐν τῇ σκοτίᾳ ἐστὶν καὶ ἐν τῇ σκοτίᾳ περιπατεῖ καὶ οὐκ οἶδεν ποῦ ὑπάγει, ὅτι ἡ σκοτία ἐτύφλωσεν τοὺς ὀφθαλμοὺς αὐτοῦ.

12 Γράφω ὑμῖν, τεκνία,
　ὅτι ἀφέωνται ὑμῖν αἱ ἁμαρτίαι
　　διὰ τὸ ὄνομα αὐτοῦ.
13 γράφω ὑμῖν, πατέρες,
　ὅτι ἐγνώκατε τὸν ἀπ' ἀρχῆς.
　γράφω ὑμῖν, νεανίσκοι,
　ὅτι νενικήκατε τὸν πονηρόν.
14 ἔγραψα ὑμῖν, παιδία,
　ὅτι ἐγνώκατε τὸν πατέρα.ᵃ
　ἔγραψα ὑμῖν, πατέρες,
　ὅτι ἐγνώκατε τὸν ἀπ' ἀρχῆς.
　ἔγραψα ὑμῖν, νεανίσκοι,
　ὅτι ἰσχυροί ἐστε
　καὶ ὁ λόγος τοῦ θεοῦ ἐν ὑμῖν
　　μένει καὶ νενικήκατε τὸν
　　πονηρόν.

15 Μὴ ἀγαπᾶτε τὸν κόσμον μηδὲ τὰ ἐν τῷ κόσμῳ. ἐάν τις ἀγαπᾷ τὸν κόσμον, οὐκ ἔστιν ἡ ἀγάπη τοῦ πατρὸς ἐν αὐτῷ· 16 ὅτι πᾶν τὸ ἐν τῷ κόσμῳ, ἡ ἐπιθυμία τῆς σαρκὸς καὶ ἡ ἐπιθυμία τῶν ὀφθαλμῶν καὶ ἡ ἀλαζονεία τοῦ βίου, οὐκ ἔστιν ἐκ τοῦ πατρὸς ἀλλ' ἐκ τοῦ κόσμου ἐστίν. 17 καὶ ὁ κόσμος παράγεται καὶ ἡ ἐπιθυμία αὐτοῦ, ὁ δὲ ποιῶν τὸ θέλημα τοῦ θεοῦ μένει εἰς τὸν αἰῶνα. 18 Παιδία, ἐσχάτη ὥρα ἐστίν, καὶ καθὼς ἠκούσατε ὅτι ἀντίχριστος ἔρχεται, καὶ νῦν ἀντίχριστοι πολλοὶ γεγόνασιν, ὅθεν γινώσκομεν ὅτι ἐσχάτη ὥρα ἐστίν. 19 ἐξ ἡμῶν ἐξῆλθαν ἀλλ' οὐκ ἦσαν ἐξ ἡμῶν· εἰ γὰρ ἐξ ἡμῶν ἦσαν, μεμενήκεισαν ἂν μεθ' ἡμῶν· ἀλλ' ἵνα φανερωθῶσιν ὅτι οὐκ εἰσὶν πάντες ἐξ ἡμῶν. 20 καὶ ὑμεῖς χρῖσμα

new command but an old one, which you have had since the beginning. This old command is the message you have heard. 8Yet I am writing you a new command; its truth is seen in him and you, because the darkness is passing and the true light is already shining.

9Anyone who claims to be in the light but hates his brother is still in the darkness. 10Whoever loves his brother lives in the light, and there is nothing in himᶜ to make him stumble. 11But whoever hates his brother is in the darkness and walks around in the darkness; he does not know where he is going, because the darkness has blinded him.

12I write to you, dear children,
　　because your sins have been forgiven
　　　　on account of his name.
13I write to you, fathers,
　　because you have known him who is
　　　from the beginning.
　I write to you, young men,
　　because you have overcome the evil
　　　one.
　I write to you, dear children,
　　because you have known the Father.
14I write to you, fathers,
　　because you have known him who is
　　　from the beginning.
　I write to you, young men,
　　because you are strong,
　　and the word of God lives in you,
　　and you have overcome the evil one.

Do Not Love the World

15Do not love the world or anything in the world. If anyone loves the world, the love of the Father is not in him. 16For everything in the world—the cravings of sinful man, the lust of his eyes and the boasting of what he has and does—comes not from the Father but from the world. 17The world and its desires pass away, but the man who does the will of God lives forever.

Warning Against Antichrists

18Dear children, this is the last hour; and as you have heard that the antichrist is coming, even now many antichrists have come. This is how we know it is the last hour. 19They went out from us, but they did not really belong to us. For if they had belonged to us, they would have remained with us; but their going showed that none of them belonged to us.

ᵇOr that   ᶜGk hating a brother   ᵈGk loves a brother
ᵉOr in it   ᶠGk hates a brother   ᵍOr the desire for it

ᵃ14 NIV begins verse 14 after πατέρα.

ᶜ10 Or it

anointed by the Holy One, and all of you have knowledge.[h] [21]I write to you, not because you do not know the truth, but because you know it, and you know that no lie comes from the truth. [22]Who is the liar but the one who denies that Jesus is the Christ?[i] This is the antichrist, the one who denies the Father and the Son. [23]No one who denies the Son has the Father; everyone who confesses the Son has the Father also. [24]Let what you heard from the beginning abide in you. If what you heard from the beginning abides in you, then you will abide in the Son and in the Father. [25]And this is what he has promised us,[j] eternal life.

[26] I write these things to you concerning those who would deceive you. [27]As for you, the anointing that you received from him abides in you, and so you do not need anyone to teach you. But as his anointing teaches you about all things, and is true and is not a lie, and just as it has taught you, abide in him.[k]

[28] And now, little children, abide in him, so that when he is revealed we may have confidence and not be put to shame before him at his coming.

Children of God

[29] If you know that he is righteous, you may be sure that everyone who does right has been born of him. [1]See what love the Father has given us, that we should be called children of God; and that is what we are. The reason the world does not know us is that it did not know him. [2]Beloved, we are God's children now; what we will be has not yet been revealed. What we do know is this: when he[k] is revealed, we will be like him, for we will see him as he is. [3]And all who have this hope in him purify themselves, just as he is pure.

[4] Everyone who commits sin is guilty of lawlessness; sin is lawlessness. [5]You know that he was revealed to take away sins, and in him there is no sin. [6]No one who abides in him sins; no one who sins has either seen him or known him. [7]Little children, let no one deceive you. Everyone who does what is right is righteous, just as he is righteous. [8]Everyone who commits sin is a child of the devil; for the devil has

[20]But you have an anointing from the Holy One, and all of you know the truth.[d] [21]I do not write to you because you do not know the truth, but because you do know it and because no lie comes from the truth. [22]Who is the liar? It is the man who denies that Jesus is the Christ. Such a man is the antichrist—he denies the Father and the Son. [23]No one who denies the Son has the Father; whoever acknowledges the Son has the Father also.

[24]See that what you have heard from the beginning remains in you. If it does, you also will remain in the Son and in the Father. [25]And this is what he promised us— even eternal life.

[26]I am writing these things to you about those who are trying to lead you astray. [27]As for you, the anointing you received from him remains in you, and you do not need anyone to teach you. But as his anointing teaches you about all things and as that anointing is real, not counterfeit—just as it has taught you, remain in him.

Children of God

[28]And now, dear children, continue in him, so that when he appears we may be confident and unashamed before him at his coming.

[29]If you know that he is righteous, you know that everyone who does what is right has been born of him. [1]How great is the love the Father has lavished on us, that we should be called children of God! And that is what we are! The reason the world does not know us is that it did not know him. [2]Dear friends, now we are children of God, and what we will be has not yet been made known. But we know that when he appears,[a] we shall be like him, for we shall see him as he is. [3]Everyone who has this hope in him purifies himself, just as he is pure.

[4]Everyone who sins breaks the law; in fact, sin is lawlessness. [5]But you know that he appeared so that he might take away our sins. And in him is no sin. [6]No one who lives in him keeps on sinning. No one who continues to sin has either seen him or known him.

[7]Dear children, do not let anyone lead you astray. He who does what is right is righteous, just as he is righteous. [8]He who does what is sinful is of the devil, because

[h] Other ancient authorities read *you know all things*
[i] Or *the Messiah* [j] Other ancient authorities read *you*
[k] Or *it*

[b]20 NIV/NRSV notes πάντα [c]25 NRSV note j ὑμῖν

[d]20 Some manuscripts *and you know all things*
[a]2 Or *when it is made known*

been sinning from the beginning. The Son of God was revealed for this purpose, to destroy the works of the devil. [9]Those who have been born of God do not sin, because God's seed abides in them;[1] they cannot sin, because they have been born of God. [10]The children of God and the children of the devil are revealed in this way: all who do not do what is right are not from God, nor are those who do not love their brothers and sisters.[m]

Love One Another

11 For this is the message you have heard from the beginning, that we should love one another. [12]We must not be like Cain who was from the evil one and murdered his brother. And why did he murder him? Because his own deeds were evil and his brother's righteous. [13]Do not be astonished, brothers and sisters,[n] that the world hates you. [14]We know that we have passed from death to life because we love one another. Whoever does not love abides in death. [15]All who hate a brother or sister[m] are murderers, and you know that murderers do not have eternal life abiding in them. [16]We know love by this, that he laid down his life for us—and we ought to lay down our lives for one another. [17]How does God's love abide in anyone who has the world's goods and sees a brother or sister[o] in need and yet refuses help?

18 Little children, let us love, not in word or speech, but in truth and action. [19]And by this we will know that we are from the truth and will reassure our hearts before him [20]whenever our hearts condemn us; for God is greater than our hearts, and he knows everything. [21]Beloved, if our hearts do not condemn us, we have boldness before God; [22]and we receive from him whatever we ask, because we obey his commandments and do what pleases him.

23 And this is his commandment, that we should believe in the name of his Son Jesus Christ and love one another, just as he has commanded us. [24]All who obey his commandments abide in him, and he abides in them. And by this we know that he abides in us, by the Spirit that he has given us.

Testing the Spirits

4 Beloved, do not believe every spirit, but test the spirits to see whether they

---

διάβολος ἁμαρτάνει. εἰς τοῦτο ἐφανερώθη ὁ υἱὸς τοῦ θεοῦ, ἵνα λύσῃ τὰ ἔργα τοῦ διαβόλου. 9 Πᾶς ὁ γεγεννημένος ἐκ τοῦ θεοῦ ἁμαρτίαν οὐ ποιεῖ, ὅτι σπέρμα αὐτοῦ ἐν αὐτῷ μένει, καὶ οὐ δύναται ἁμαρτάνειν, ὅτι ἐκ τοῦ θεοῦ γεγέννηται. 10 ἐν τούτῳ φανερά ἐστι τὰ τέκνα τοῦ θεοῦ καὶ τὰ τέκνα τοῦ διαβόλου· πᾶς ὁ μὴ ποιῶν δικαιοσύνην οὐκ ἔστιν ἐκ τοῦ θεοῦ, καὶ ὁ μὴ ἀγαπῶν τὸν ἀδελφὸν αὐτοῦ.

11 Ὅτι αὕτη ἐστὶν ἡ ἀγγελία ἣν ἠκούσατε ἀπ᾽ ἀρχῆς, ἵνα ἀγαπῶμεν ἀλλήλους, 12 οὐ καθὼς Κάϊν ἐκ τοῦ πονηροῦ ἦν καὶ ἔσφαξεν τὸν ἀδελφὸν αὐτοῦ· καὶ χάριν τίνος ἔσφαξεν αὐτόν; ὅτι τὰ ἔργα αὐτοῦ πονηρὰ ἦν τὰ δὲ τοῦ ἀδελφοῦ αὐτοῦ δίκαια. 13 [καὶ] μὴ θαυμάζετε, ἀδελφοί, εἰ μισεῖ ὑμᾶς ὁ κόσμος. 14 ἡμεῖς οἴδαμεν ὅτι μεταβεβήκαμεν ἐκ τοῦ θανάτου εἰς τὴν ζωήν, ὅτι ἀγαπῶμεν τοὺς ἀδελφούς· ὁ μὴ ἀγαπῶν μένει ἐν τῷ θανάτῳ. 15 πᾶς ὁ μισῶν τὸν ἀδελφὸν αὐτοῦ ἀνθρωποκτόνος ἐστίν, καὶ οἴδατε ὅτι πᾶς ἀνθρωποκτόνος οὐκ ἔχει ζωὴν αἰώνιον ἐν αὐτῷ μένουσαν. 16 ἐν τούτῳ ἐγνώκαμεν τὴν ἀγάπην, ὅτι ἐκεῖνος ὑπὲρ ἡμῶν τὴν ψυχὴν αὐτοῦ ἔθηκεν· καὶ ἡμεῖς ὀφείλομεν ὑπὲρ τῶν ἀδελφῶν τὰς ψυχὰς θεῖναι. 17 ὃς δ᾽ ἂν ἔχῃ τὸν βίον τοῦ κόσμου καὶ θεωρῇ τὸν ἀδελφὸν αὐτοῦ χρείαν ἔχοντα καὶ κλείσῃ τὰ σπλάγχνα αὐτοῦ ἀπ᾽ αὐτοῦ, πῶς ἡ ἀγάπη τοῦ θεοῦ μένει ἐν αὐτῷ; 18 Τεκνία, μὴ ἀγαπῶμεν λόγῳ μηδὲ τῇ γλώσσῃ ἀλλὰ ἐν ἔργῳ καὶ ἀληθείᾳ.

19 [Καὶ] ἐν τούτῳ γνωσόμεθα ὅτι ἐκ τῆς ἀληθείας ἐσμέν, καὶ ἔμπροσθεν αὐτοῦ πείσομεν τὴν καρδίαν ἡμῶν, 20 ὅτι ἐὰν καταγινώσκῃ ἡμῶν ἡ καρδία, ὅτι μείζων ἐστὶν ὁ θεὸς τῆς καρδίας ἡμῶν καὶ γινώσκει πάντα. 21 Ἀγαπητοί, ἐὰν ἡ καρδία [ἡμῶν] μὴ καταγινώσκῃ, παρρησίαν ἔχομεν πρὸς τὸν θεὸν 22 καὶ ὃ ἐὰν αἰτῶμεν λαμβάνομεν ἀπ᾽ αὐτοῦ, ὅτι τὰς ἐντολὰς αὐτοῦ τηροῦμεν καὶ τὰ ἀρεστὰ ἐνώπιον αὐτοῦ ποιοῦμεν. 23 καὶ αὕτη ἐστὶν ἡ ἐντολὴ αὐτοῦ, ἵνα πιστεύσωμεν τῷ ὀνόματι τοῦ υἱοῦ αὐτοῦ Ἰησοῦ Χριστοῦ καὶ ἀγαπῶμεν ἀλλήλους, καθὼς ἔδωκεν ἐντολὴν ἡμῖν. 24 καὶ ὁ τηρῶν τὰς ἐντολὰς αὐτοῦ ἐν αὐτῷ μένει καὶ αὐτὸς ἐν αὐτῷ· καὶ ἐν τούτῳ γινώσκομεν ὅτι μένει ἐν ἡμῖν, ἐκ τοῦ πνεύματος οὗ ἡμῖν ἔδωκεν.

4 Ἀγαπητοί, μὴ παντὶ πνεύματι πιστεύετε ἀλλὰ δοκιμάζετε τὰ

---

the devil has been sinning from the beginning. The reason the Son of God appeared was to destroy the devil's work. [9]No one who is born of God will continue to sin, because God's seed remains in him; he cannot go on sinning, because he has been born of God. [10]This is how we know who the children of God are and who the children of the devil are: Anyone who does not do what is right is not a child of God; nor is anyone who does not love his brother.

Love One Another

[11]This is the message you heard from the beginning: We should love one another. [12]Do not be like Cain, who belonged to the evil one and murdered his brother. And why did he murder him? Because his own actions were evil and his brother's were righteous. [13]Do not be surprised, my brothers, if the world hates you. [14]We know that we have passed from death to life, because we love our brothers. Anyone who does not love remains in death. [15]Anyone who hates his brother is a murderer, and you know that no murderer has eternal life in him.

[16]This is how we know what love is: Jesus Christ laid down his life for us. And we ought to lay down our lives for our brothers. [17]If anyone has material possessions and sees his brother in need but has no pity on him, how can the love of God be in him? [18]Dear children, let us not love with words or tongue but with actions and in truth. [19]This then is how we know that we belong to the truth, and how we set our hearts at rest in his presence [20]whenever our hearts condemn us. For God is greater than our hearts, and he knows everything.

[21]Dear friends, if our hearts do not condemn us, we have confidence before God [22]and receive from him anything we ask, because we obey his commands and do what pleases him. [23]And this is his command: to believe in the name of his Son, Jesus Christ, and to love one another as he commanded us. [24]Those who obey his commands live in him, and he in them. And this is how we know that he lives in us: We know it by the Spirit he gave us.

Test the Spirits

4 Dear friends, do not believe every spirit, but test the spirits to see

---

[1]Or *because the children of God abide in him*   [m]Gk *his brother*   [n]Gk *brothers*   [o]Gk *brother*

are from God; for many false prophets have gone out into the world. [2]By this you know the Spirit of God: every spirit that confesses that Jesus Christ has come in the flesh is from God, [3]and every spirit that does not confess Jesus[P] is not from God. And this is the spirit of the antichrist, of which you have heard that it is coming; and now it is already in the world. [4]Little children, you are from God, and have conquered them; for the one who is in you is greater than the one who is in the world. [5]They are from the world; therefore what they say is from the world, and the world listens to them. [6]We are from God. Whoever knows God listens to us, and whoever is not from God does not listen to us. From this we know the spirit of truth and the spirit of error.

God Is Love

7 Beloved, let us love one another, because love is from God; everyone who loves is born of God and knows God. [8]Whoever does not love does not know God, for God is love. [9]God's love was revealed among us in this way: God sent his only Son into the world so that we might live through him. [10]In this is love, not that we loved God but that he loved us and sent his Son to be the atoning sacrifice for our sins. [11]Beloved, since God loved us so much, we also ought to love one another. [12]No one has ever seen God; if we love one another, God lives in us, and his love is perfected in us.

13 By this we know that we abide in him and he in us, because he has given us of his Spirit. [14]And we have seen and do testify that the Father has sent his Son as the Savior of the world. [15]God abides in those who confess that Jesus is the Son of God, and they abide in God. [16]So we have known and believe the love that God has for us.

God is love, and those who abide in love abide in God, and God abides in them. [17]Love has been perfected among us in this: that we may have boldness on the day of judgment, because as he is, so are

πνεύματα εἰ ἐκ τοῦ θεοῦ ἐστιν, ὅτι πολλοὶ ψευδοπροφῆται ἐξεληλύθασιν εἰς τὸν κόσμον. **2** ἐν τούτῳ γινώσκετε τὸ πνεῦμα τοῦ θεοῦ· πᾶν πνεῦμα ὃ ὁμολογεῖ Ἰησοῦν Χριστὸν ἐν σαρκὶ ἐληλυθότα ἐκ τοῦ θεοῦ ἐστιν, **3** καὶ πᾶν πνεῦμα ὃ μὴ ὁμολογεῖ[a] τὸν Ἰησοῦν ἐκ τοῦ θεοῦ οὐκ ἔστιν· καὶ τοῦτό ἐστιν τὸ τοῦ ἀντιχρίστου, ὃ ἀκηκόατε ὅτι ἔρχεται, καὶ νῦν ἐν τῷ κόσμῳ ἐστὶν ἤδη. **4** ὑμεῖς ἐκ τοῦ θεοῦ ἐστε, τεκνία, καὶ νενικήκατε αὐτούς, ὅτι μείζων ἐστὶν ὁ ἐν ὑμῖν ἢ ὁ ἐν τῷ κόσμῳ. **5** αὐτοὶ ἐκ τοῦ κόσμου εἰσίν, διὰ τοῦτο ἐκ τοῦ κόσμου λαλοῦσιν καὶ ὁ κόσμος αὐτῶν ἀκούει. **6** ἡμεῖς ἐκ τοῦ θεοῦ ἐσμεν, ὁ γινώσκων τὸν θεὸν ἀκούει ἡμῶν, ὃς οὐκ ἔστιν ἐκ τοῦ θεοῦ οὐκ ἀκούει ἡμῶν. ἐκ τούτου γινώσκομεν τὸ πνεῦμα τῆς ἀληθείας καὶ τὸ πνεῦμα τῆς πλάνης.

7 Ἀγαπητοί, ἀγαπῶμεν ἀλλήλους, ὅτι ἡ ἀγάπη ἐκ τοῦ θεοῦ ἐστιν, καὶ πᾶς ὁ ἀγαπῶν ἐκ τοῦ θεοῦ γεγέννηται καὶ γινώσκει τὸν θεόν. **8** ὁ μὴ ἀγαπῶν οὐκ ἔγνω τὸν θεόν, ὅτι ὁ θεὸς ἀγάπη ἐστίν. **9** ἐν τούτῳ ἐφανερώθη ἡ ἀγάπη τοῦ θεοῦ ἐν ἡμῖν, ὅτι τὸν υἱὸν αὐτοῦ τὸν μονογενῆ ἀπέσταλκεν ὁ θεὸς εἰς τὸν κόσμον ἵνα ζήσωμεν δι' αὐτοῦ. **10** ἐν τούτῳ ἐστὶν ἡ ἀγάπη, οὐχ ὅτι ἡμεῖς ἠγαπήκαμεν τὸν θεὸν ἀλλ' ὅτι αὐτὸς ἠγάπησεν ἡμᾶς καὶ ἀπέστειλεν τὸν υἱὸν αὐτοῦ ἱλασμὸν περὶ τῶν ἁμαρτιῶν ἡμῶν. **11** Ἀγαπητοί, εἰ οὕτως ὁ θεὸς ἠγάπησεν ἡμᾶς, καὶ ἡμεῖς ὀφείλομεν ἀλλήλους ἀγαπᾶν. **12** θεὸν οὐδεὶς πώποτε τεθέαται. ἐὰν ἀγαπῶμεν ἀλλήλους, ὁ θεὸς ἐν ἡμῖν μένει καὶ ἡ ἀγάπη αὐτοῦ ἐν ἡμῖν τετελειωμένη ἐστίν.

13 Ἐν τούτῳ γινώσκομεν ὅτι ἐν αὐτῷ μένομεν καὶ αὐτὸς ἐν ἡμῖν, ὅτι ἐκ τοῦ πνεύματος αὐτοῦ δέδωκεν ἡμῖν. **14** καὶ ἡμεῖς τεθεάμεθα καὶ μαρτυροῦμεν ὅτι ὁ πατὴρ ἀπέσταλκεν τὸν υἱὸν σωτῆρα τοῦ κόσμου. **15** ὃς ἐὰν ὁμολογήσῃ ὅτι Ἰησοῦς ἐστιν ὁ υἱὸς τοῦ θεοῦ, ὁ θεὸς ἐν αὐτῷ μένει καὶ αὐτὸς ἐν τῷ θεῷ. **16** καὶ ἡμεῖς ἐγνώκαμεν καὶ πεπιστεύκαμεν τὴν ἀγάπην ἣν ἔχει ὁ θεὸς ἐν ἡμῖν.

Ὁ θεὸς ἀγάπη ἐστίν, καὶ ὁ μένων ἐν τῇ ἀγάπῃ ἐν τῷ θεῷ μένει καὶ ὁ θεὸς ἐν αὐτῷ μένει. **17** ἐν τούτῳ τετελείωται ἡ ἀγάπη μεθ' ἡμῶν, ἵνα παρρησίαν ἔχωμεν ἐν τῇ ἡμέρᾳ τῆς κρίσεως, ὅτι

whether they are from God, because many false prophets have gone out into the world. [2]This is how you can recognize the Spirit of God: Every spirit that acknowledges that Jesus Christ has come in the flesh is from God, [3]but every spirit that does not acknowledge Jesus is not from God. This is the spirit of the antichrist, which you have heard is coming and even now is already in the world.

[4]You, dear children, are from God and have overcome them, because the one who is in you is greater than the one who is in the world. [5]They are from the world and therefore speak from the viewpoint of the world, and the world listens to them. [6]We are from God, and whoever knows God listens to us; but whoever is not from God does not listen to us. This is how we recognize the Spirit[a] of truth and the spirit of falsehood.

God's Love and Ours

[7]Dear friends, let us love one another, for love comes from God. Everyone who loves has been born of God and knows God. [8]Whoever does not love does not know God, because God is love. [9]This is how God showed his love among us: He sent his one and only Son[b] into the world that we might live through him. [10]This is love: not that we loved God, but that he loved us and sent his Son as an atoning sacrifice for[c] our sins. [11]Dear friends, since God so loved us, we also ought to love one another. [12]No one has ever seen God; but if we love one another, God lives in us and his love is made complete in us.

[13]We know that we live in him and he in us, because he has given us of his Spirit. [14]And we have seen and testify that the Father has sent his Son to be the Savior of the world. [15]If anyone acknowledges that Jesus is the Son of God, God lives in him and he in God. [16]And so we know and rely on the love God has for us.

God is love. Whoever lives in love lives in God, and God in him. [17]In this way, love is made complete among us so that we will have confidence on the day of judg-

---

P Other ancient authorities read *does away with Jesus* (Gk *dissolves Jesus*)

a3 NRSV note q λύει

a6 Or *spirit*   b9 Or *his only begotten Son*   c10 Or *as the one who would turn aside his wrath, taking away*

we in this world. [18]There is no fear in love, but perfect love casts out fear; for fear has to do with punishment, and whoever fears has not reached perfection in love. [19]We love[q] because he first loved us. [20]Those who say, "I love God," and hate their brothers or sisters,[r] are liars; for those who do not love a brother or sister[s] whom they have seen, cannot love God whom they have not seen. [21]The commandment we have from him is this: those who love God must love their brothers and sisters[r] also.

Faith Conquers the World

5 Everyone who believes that Jesus is the Christ[t] has been born of God, and everyone who loves the parent loves the child. [2]By this we know that we love the children of God, when we love God and obey his commandments. [3]For the love of God is this, that we obey his commandments. And his commandments are not burdensome, [4]for whatever is born of God conquers the world. And this is the victory that conquers the world, our faith. [5]Who is it that conquers the world but the one who believes that Jesus is the Son of God?

Testimony concerning the Son of God

6 This is the one who came by water and blood, Jesus Christ, not with the water only but with the water and the blood. And the Spirit is the one that testifies, for the Spirit is the truth. [7]There are three that testify:[u] [8]the Spirit and the water and the blood, and these three agree. [9]If we receive human testimony, the testimony of God is greater; for this is the testimony of God that he has testified to his Son. [10]Those who believe in the Son of God have the testimony in their hearts. Those who do not believe in God[v] have made him a liar by not believing in the testimony that God has given concerning his Son. [11]And this is the testimony: God gave us eternal life, and this life is in his Son. [12]Whoever has the Son has life; whoever does not have the Son of God does not have life.

καθὼς ἐκεῖνός ἐστιν καὶ ἡμεῖς ἐσμεν ἐν τῷ κόσμῳ τούτῳ. **18** φόβος οὐκ ἔστιν ἐν τῇ ἀγάπῃ ἀλλ᾽ ἡ τελεία ἀγάπη ἔξω βάλλει τὸν φόβον, ὅτι ὁ φόβος κόλασιν ἔχει, ὁ δὲ φοβούμενος οὐ τετελείωται ἐν τῇ ἀγάπῃ. **19** ἡμεῖς ἀγαπῶμεν[b], ὅτι αὐτὸς πρῶτος ἠγάπησεν ἡμᾶς. **20** ἐάν τις εἴπῃ ὅτι Ἀγαπῶ τὸν θεὸν καὶ τὸν ἀδελφὸν αὐτοῦ μισῇ, ψεύστης ἐστίν· ὁ γὰρ μὴ ἀγαπῶν τὸν ἀδελφὸν αὐτοῦ ὃν ἑώρακεν, τὸν θεὸν ὃν οὐχ ἑώρακεν οὐ δύναται ἀγαπᾶν. **21** καὶ ταύτην τὴν ἐντολὴν ἔχομεν ἀπ᾽ αὐτοῦ, ἵνα ὁ ἀγαπῶν τὸν θεὸν ἀγαπᾷ καὶ τὸν ἀδελφὸν αὐτοῦ.

5 Πᾶς ὁ πιστεύων ὅτι Ἰησοῦς ἐστιν ὁ Χριστός, ἐκ τοῦ θεοῦ γεγέννηται, καὶ πᾶς ὁ ἀγαπῶν τὸν γεννήσαντα ἀγαπᾷ [καὶ] τὸν γεγεννημένον ἐξ αὐτοῦ. **2** ἐν τούτῳ γινώσκομεν ὅτι ἀγαπῶμεν τὰ τέκνα τοῦ θεοῦ, ὅταν τὸν θεὸν ἀγαπῶμεν καὶ τὰς ἐντολὰς αὐτοῦ ποιῶμεν. **3** αὕτη γάρ ἐστιν ἡ ἀγάπη τοῦ θεοῦ, ἵνα τὰς ἐντολὰς αὐτοῦ τηρῶμεν, καὶ αἱ ἐντολαὶ αὐτοῦ βαρεῖαι οὐκ εἰσίν. **4** ὅτι πᾶν τὸ γεγεννημένον ἐκ τοῦ θεοῦ νικᾷ τὸν κόσμον· καὶ αὕτη ἐστὶν ἡ νίκη ἡ νικήσασα τὸν κόσμον, ἡ πίστις ἡμῶν. **5** τίς [δέ] ἐστιν ὁ νικῶν τὸν κόσμον εἰ μὴ ὁ πιστεύων ὅτι Ἰησοῦς ἐστιν ὁ υἱὸς τοῦ θεοῦ;

6 Οὗτός ἐστιν ὁ ἐλθὼν δι᾽ ὕδατος καὶ αἵματος, Ἰησοῦς Χριστός, οὐκ ἐν τῷ ὕδατι μόνον ἀλλ᾽ ἐν τῷ ὕδατι καὶ ἐν τῷ αἵματι· καὶ τὸ πνεῦμά ἐστιν τὸ μαρτυροῦν, ὅτι τὸ πνεῦμά ἐστιν ἡ ἀλήθεια. **7** ὅτι τρεῖς εἰσιν οἱ μαρτυροῦντες[a], **8** τὸ πνεῦμα καὶ τὸ ὕδωρ καὶ τὸ αἷμα, καὶ οἱ τρεῖς εἰς τὸ ἕν εἰσιν. **9** εἰ τὴν μαρτυρίαν τῶν ἀνθρώπων λαμβάνομεν, ἡ μαρτυρία τοῦ θεοῦ μείζων ἐστίν· ὅτι αὕτη ἐστὶν ἡ μαρτυρία τοῦ θεοῦ ὅτι μεμαρτύρηκεν περὶ τοῦ υἱοῦ αὐτοῦ. **10** ὁ πιστεύων εἰς τὸν υἱὸν τοῦ θεοῦ ἔχει τὴν μαρτυρίαν ἐν ἑαυτῷ, ὁ μὴ πιστεύων τῷ θεῷ[b] ψεύστην πεποίηκεν αὐτόν, ὅτι οὐ πεπίστευκεν εἰς τὴν μαρτυρίαν ἣν μεμαρτύρηκεν ὁ θεὸς περὶ τοῦ υἱοῦ αὐτοῦ. **11** καὶ αὕτη ἐστὶν ἡ μαρτυρία, ὅτι ζωὴν αἰώνιον ἔδωκεν ἡμῖν ὁ θεός, καὶ αὕτη ἡ ζωὴ ἐν τῷ υἱῷ αὐτοῦ ἐστιν. **12** ὁ ἔχων τὸν υἱὸν ἔχει τὴν ζωήν· ὁ μὴ ἔχων τὸν υἱὸν τοῦ θεοῦ τὴν ζωὴν οὐκ ἔχει.

ment, because in this world we are like him. [18]There is no fear in love. But perfect love drives out fear, because fear has to do with punishment. The one who fears is not made perfect in love.

[19]We love because he first loved us. [20]If anyone says, "I love God," yet hates his brother, he is a liar. For anyone who does not love his brother, whom he has seen, cannot love God, whom he has not seen. [21]And he has given us this command: Whoever loves God must also love his brother.

Faith in the Son of God

5 Everyone who believes that Jesus is the Christ is born of God, and everyone who loves the father loves his child as well. [2]This is how we know that we love the children of God: by loving God and carrying out his commands. [3]This is love for God: to obey his commands. And his commands are not burdensome, [4]for everyone born of God overcomes the world. This is the victory that has overcome the world, even our faith. [5]Who is it that overcomes the world? Only he who believes that Jesus is the Son of God.

[6]This is the one who came by water and blood—Jesus Christ. He did not come by water only, but by water and blood. And it is the Spirit who testifies, because the Spirit is the truth. [7]For there are three that testify: [8]the[a] Spirit, the water and the blood; and the three are in agreement. [9]We accept man's testimony, but God's testimony is greater because it is the testimony of God, which he has given about his Son. [10]Anyone who believes in the Son of God has this testimony in his heart. Anyone who does not believe God has made him out to be a liar, because he has not believed the testimony God has given about his Son. [11]And this is the testimony: God has given us eternal life, and this life is in his Son. [12]He who has the Son has life; he who does not have the Son of God does not have life.

---

[q] Other ancient authorities add *him*; others add *God*
[r] Gk *brothers*   [s] Gk *brother*   [t] Or *the Messiah*   [u] A few other authorities read (with variations) [7]*There are three that testify in heaven, the Father, the Word, and the Holy Spirit, and these three are one.* [8]*And there are three that testify on earth:*   [v] Other ancient authorities read *in the Son*

[b]19 NRSV note q adds αὐτόν or τὸν θεόν
[a]7 NIV/NRSV notes add ἐν τῷ οὐρανῷ, ὁ πατὴρ ὁ λόγος καὶ τὸ ἅγιον πνεῦμα, καὶ οὗτοι οἱ τρεῖς ἕν εἰσιν.
8 καὶ τρεῖς εἰσιν οἱ μαρτυροῦντες ἐν τῇ γῇ,
[b]10 NRSV note v υἱῷ

[a]7,8 Late manuscripts of the Vulgate *testify in heaven: the Father, the Word and the Holy Spirit, and these three are one.* [8]*And there are three that testify on earth: the* (not found in any Greek manuscript before the sixteenth century)

Epilogue

13 I write these things to you who believe in the name of the Son of God, so that you may know that you have eternal life.

14 And this is the boldness we have in him, that if we ask anything according to his will, he hears us. 15And if we know that he hears us in whatever we ask, we know that we have obtained the requests made of him. 16If you see your brother or sister[w] committing what is not a mortal sin, you will ask, and God[x] will give life to such a one—to those whose sin is not mortal. There is sin that is mortal; I do not say that you should pray about that. 17All wrongdoing is sin, but there is sin that is not mortal.

18 We know that those who are born of God do not sin, but the one who was born of God protects them, and the evil one does not touch them. 19We know that we are God's children, and that the whole world lies under the power of the evil one. 20And we know that the Son of God has come and has given us understanding so that we may know him who is true;[y] and we are in him who is true, in his Son Jesus Christ. He is the true God and eternal life.

21 Little children, keep yourselves from idols.[z]

13 Ταῦτα ἔγραψα ὑμῖν ἵνα εἰδῆτε ὅτι ζωὴν ἔχετε αἰώνιον, τοῖς πιστεύουσιν εἰς τὸ ὄνομα τοῦ υἱοῦ τοῦ θεοῦ. **14** καὶ αὕτη ἐστὶν ἡ παρρησία ἣν ἔχομεν πρὸς αὐτὸν ὅτι ἐάν τι αἰτώμεθα κατὰ τὸ θέλημα αὐτοῦ ἀκούει ἡμῶν. **15** καὶ ἐὰν οἴδαμεν ὅτι ἀκούει ἡμῶν ὃ ἐὰν αἰτώμεθα, οἴδαμεν ὅτι ἔχομεν τὰ αἰτήματα ἃ ᾐτήκαμεν ἀπ᾽ αὐτοῦ. **16** Ἐάν τις ἴδῃ τὸν ἀδελφὸν αὐτοῦ ἁμαρτάνοντα ἁμαρτίαν μὴ πρὸς θάνατον, αἰτήσει καὶ δώσει αὐτῷ ζωήν, τοῖς ἁμαρτάνουσιν μὴ πρὸς θάνατον. ἔστιν ἁμαρτία πρὸς θάνατον· οὐ περὶ ἐκείνης λέγω ἵνα ἐρωτήσῃ. **17** πᾶσα ἀδικία ἁμαρτία ἐστίν, καὶ ἔστιν ἁμαρτία οὐ πρὸς θάνατον.

18 Οἴδαμεν ὅτι πᾶς ὁ γεγεννημένος ἐκ τοῦ θεοῦ οὐχ ἁμαρτάνει, ἀλλ᾽ ὁ γεννηθεὶς ἐκ τοῦ θεοῦ τηρεῖ αὐτὸν καὶ ὁ πονηρὸς οὐχ ἅπτεται αὐτοῦ. **19** οἴδαμεν ὅτι ἐκ τοῦ θεοῦ ἐσμεν καὶ ὁ κόσμος ὅλος ἐν τῷ πονηρῷ κεῖται. **20** οἴδαμεν δὲ ὅτι ὁ υἱὸς τοῦ θεοῦ ἥκει καὶ δέδωκεν ἡμῖν διάνοιαν ἵνα γινώσκωμεν τὸν ἀληθινόν[c], καὶ ἐσμὲν ἐν τῷ ἀληθινῷ, ἐν τῷ υἱῷ αὐτοῦ Ἰησοῦ Χριστῷ. οὗτός ἐστιν ὁ ἀληθινὸς θεὸς καὶ ζωὴ αἰώνιος. **21** Τεκνία, φυλάξατε ἑαυτὰ ἀπὸ τῶν εἰδώλων.[d]

Concluding Remarks

13I write these things to you who believe in the name of the Son of God so that you may know that you have eternal life. 14This is the confidence we have in approaching God: that if we ask anything according to his will, he hears us. 15And if we know that he hears us—whatever we ask—we know that we have what we asked of him.

16If anyone sees his brother commit a sin that does not lead to death, he should pray and God will give him life. I refer to those whose sin does not lead to death. There is a sin that leads to death. I am not saying that he should pray about that. 17All wrongdoing is sin, and there is sin that does not lead to death.

18We know that anyone born of God does not continue to sin; the one who was born of God keeps him safe, and the evil one cannot harm him. 19We know that we are children of God, and that the whole world is under the control of the evil one. 20We know also that the Son of God has come and has given us understanding, so that we may know him who is true. And we are in him who is true—even in his Son Jesus Christ. He is the true God and eternal life.

21Dear children, keep yourselves from idols.

---

[w] Gk *your brother*   [x] Gk *he*   [y] Other ancient authorities read *know the true God*   [z] Other ancient authorities add *Amen*

[c]20 NRSV note y adds *θεόν*   [d]21 NRSV note z adds *ἀμήν.*

ΙΩΑΝΝΟΥ Β

NRSV

Salutation

1 The elder to the elect lady and her children, whom I love in the truth, and not only I but also all who know the truth, [2]because of the truth that abides in us and will be with us forever:

3 Grace, mercy, and peace will be with us from God the Father and from[a] Jesus Christ, the Father's Son, in truth and love.

Truth and Love

4 I was overjoyed to find some of your children walking in the truth, just as we have been commanded by the Father. [5]But now, dear lady, I ask you, not as though I were writing you a new commandment, but one we have had from the beginning, let us love one another. [6]And this is love, that we walk according to his commandments; this is the commandment just as you have heard it from the beginning—you must walk in it.

7 Many deceivers have gone out into the world, those who do not confess that Jesus Christ has come in the flesh; any such person is the deceiver and the antichrist! [8]Be on your guard, so that you do not lose what we[b] have worked for, but may receive a full reward. [9]Everyone who does not abide in the teaching of Christ, but goes beyond it, does not have God; whoever abides in the teaching has both the Father and the Son. [10]Do not receive into the house or welcome anyone who comes to you and does not bring this teaching; [11]for to welcome is to participate in the evil deeds of such a person.

Final Greetings

12 Although I have much to write to you, I would rather not use paper and ink; instead I hope to come to you and talk with you face to face, so that our joy may be complete.

13 The children of your elect sister send you their greetings.[c]

Greek

1 Ὁ πρεσβύτερος ἐκλεκτῇ κυρίᾳ καὶ τοῖς τέκνοις αὐτῆς, οὓς ἐγὼ ἀγαπῶ ἐν ἀληθείᾳ, καὶ οὐκ ἐγὼ μόνος ἀλλὰ καὶ πάντες οἱ ἐγνωκότες τὴν ἀλήθειαν, 2 διὰ τὴν ἀλήθειαν τὴν μένουσαν ἐν ἡμῖν καὶ μεθ᾽ ἡμῶν ἔσται εἰς τὸν αἰῶνα. 3 ἔσται μεθ᾽ ἡμῶν χάρις ἔλεος εἰρήνη παρὰ θεοῦ πατρός καὶ παρὰ[a] Ἰησοῦ Χριστοῦ τοῦ υἱοῦ τοῦ πατρὸς ἐν ἀληθείᾳ καὶ ἀγάπῃ.

4 Ἐχάρην λίαν ὅτι εὕρηκα ἐκ τῶν τέκνων σου περιπατοῦντας ἐν ἀληθείᾳ, καθὼς ἐντολὴν ἐλάβομεν παρὰ τοῦ πατρός. 5 καὶ νῦν ἐρωτῶ σε, κυρία, οὐχ ὡς ἐντολὴν καινὴν γράφων σοι ἀλλὰ ἣν εἴχομεν ἀπ᾽ ἀρχῆς, ἵνα ἀγαπῶμεν ἀλλήλους. 6 καὶ αὕτη ἐστὶν ἡ ἀγάπη, ἵνα περιπατῶμεν κατὰ τὰς ἐντολὰς αὐτοῦ· αὕτη ἡ ἐντολή ἐστιν, καθὼς ἠκούσατε ἀπ᾽ ἀρχῆς, ἵνα ἐν αὐτῇ περιπατῆτε. 7 ὅτι πολλοὶ πλάνοι ἐξῆλθον εἰς τὸν κόσμον, οἱ μὴ ὁμολογοῦντες Ἰησοῦν Χριστὸν ἐρχόμενον ἐν σαρκί· οὗτός ἐστιν ὁ πλάνος καὶ ὁ ἀντίχριστος. 8 βλέπετε ἑαυτούς, ἵνα μὴ ἀπολέσητε ἃ εἰργασάμεθα[b] ἀλλὰ μισθὸν πλήρη ἀπολάβητε. 9 πᾶς ὁ προάγων καὶ μὴ μένων ἐν τῇ διδαχῇ τοῦ Χριστοῦ θεὸν οὐκ ἔχει· ὁ μένων ἐν τῇ διδαχῇ, οὗτος καὶ τὸν πατέρα καὶ τὸν υἱὸν ἔχει. 10 εἴ τις ἔρχεται πρὸς ὑμᾶς καὶ ταύτην τὴν διδαχὴν οὐ φέρει, μὴ λαμβάνετε αὐτὸν εἰς οἰκίαν καὶ χαίρειν αὐτῷ μὴ λέγετε· 11 ὁ λέγων γὰρ αὐτῷ χαίρειν κοινωνεῖ τοῖς ἔργοις αὐτοῦ τοῖς πονηροῖς.

12 Πολλὰ ἔχων ὑμῖν γράφειν οὐκ ἐβουλήθην διὰ χάρτου καὶ μέλανος, ἀλλὰ ἐλπίζω γενέσθαι πρὸς ὑμᾶς καὶ στόμα πρὸς στόμα λαλῆσαι, ἵνα ἡ χαρὰ ἡμῶν πεπληρωμένη ᾖ. 13 Ἀσπάζεταί σε τὰ τέκνα τῆς ἀδελφῆς σου τῆς ἐκλεκτῆς.[c]

NIV

[1]The elder,

To the chosen lady and her children, whom I love in the truth—and not I only, but also all who know the truth— [2]because of the truth, which lives in us and will be with us forever:

[3]Grace, mercy and peace from God the Father and from Jesus Christ, the Father's Son, will be with us in truth and love.

[4]It has given me great joy to find some of your children walking in the truth, just as the Father commanded us. [5]And now, dear lady, I am not writing you a new command but one we have had from the beginning. I ask that we love one another. [6]And this is love: that we walk in obedience to his commands. As you have heard from the beginning, his command is that you walk in love.

[7]Many deceivers, who do not acknowledge Jesus Christ as coming in the flesh, have gone out into the world. Any such person is the deceiver and the antichrist. [8]Watch out that you do not lose what you have worked for, but that you may be rewarded fully. [9]Anyone who runs ahead and does not continue in the teaching of Christ does not have God; whoever continues in the teaching has both the Father and the Son. [10]If anyone comes to you and does not bring this teaching, do not take him into your house or welcome him. [11]Anyone who welcomes him shares in his wicked work.

[12]I have much to write to you, but I do not want to use paper and ink. Instead, I hope to visit you and talk with you face to face, so that our joy may be complete.

[13]The children of your chosen sister send their greetings.

---

[a] Other ancient authorities add *the Lord*   [b] Other ancient authorities read *you*   [c] Other ancient authorities add *Amen*

[a]3 NRSV note a adds κυρίου   [b]8 NIV text and NRSV note b εἰργάσασθε   [c]13 NRSV note c adds ἀμήν.

Salutation

1 The elder to the beloved Gaius, whom I love in truth.

Gaius Commended for His Hospitality

2 Beloved, I pray that all may go well with you and that you may be in good health, just as it is well with your soul. ³I was overjoyed when some of the friends[a] arrived and testified to your faithfulness to the truth, namely how you walk in the truth. ⁴I have no greater joy than this, to hear that my children are walking in the truth.

5 Beloved, you do faithfully whatever you do for the friends,[a] even though they are strangers to you; ⁶they have testified to your love before the church. You will do well to send them on in a manner worthy of God; ⁷for they began their journey for the sake of Christ,[b] accepting no support from non-believers.[c] ⁸Therefore we ought to support such people, so that we may become co-workers with the truth.

Diotrephes and Demetrius

9 I have written something to the church; but Diotrephes, who likes to put himself first, does not acknowledge our authority. ¹⁰So if I come, I will call attention to what he is doing in spreading false charges against us. And not content with those charges, he refuses to welcome the friends,[a] and even prevents those who want to do so and expels them from the church.

11 Beloved, do not imitate what is evil but imitate what is good. Whoever does good is from God; whoever does evil has not seen God. ¹²Everyone has testified favorably about Demetrius, and so has the truth itself. We also testify for him,[d] and you know that our testimony is true.

Final Greetings

13 I have much to write to you, but I would rather not write with pen and ink; ¹⁴instead I hope to see you soon, and we will talk together face to face.

15 Peace to you. The friends send you their greetings. Greet the friends there, each by name.

ΙΩΑΝΝΟΥ Γ

1 Ὁ πρεσβύτερος Γαΐῳ τῷ ἀγαπητῷ, ὃν ἐγὼ ἀγαπῶ ἐν ἀληθείᾳ.

2 Ἀγαπητέ, περὶ πάντων εὔχομαί σε εὐοδοῦσθαι καὶ ὑγιαίνειν, καθὼς εὐοδοῦταί σου ἡ ψυχή. 3 ἐχάρην γὰρ λίαν ἐρχομένων ἀδελφῶν καὶ μαρτυρούντων σου τῇ ἀληθείᾳ, καθὼς σὺ ἐν ἀληθείᾳ περιπατεῖς. 4 μειζοτέραν τούτων οὐκ ἔχω χαράν, ἵνα ἀκούω τὰ ἐμὰ τέκνα ἐν τῇ ἀληθείᾳ περιπατοῦντα.

5 Ἀγαπητέ, πιστὸν ποιεῖς ὃ ἐὰν ἐργάσῃ εἰς τοὺς ἀδελφοὺς καὶ τοῦτο ξένους, 6 οἳ ἐμαρτύρησάν σου τῇ ἀγάπῃ ἐνώπιον ἐκκλησίας, οὓς καλῶς ποιήσεις προπέμψας ἀξίως τοῦ θεοῦ· 7 ὑπὲρ γὰρ τοῦ ὀνόματος ἐξῆλθον μηδὲν λαμβάνοντες ἀπὸ τῶν ἐθνικῶν. 8 ἡμεῖς οὖν ὀφείλομεν ὑπολαμβάνειν τοὺς τοιούτους, ἵνα συνεργοὶ γινώμεθα τῇ ἀληθείᾳ.

9 Ἔγραψά τι τῇ ἐκκλησίᾳ· ἀλλ' ὁ φιλοπρωτεύων αὐτῶν Διοτρέφης οὐκ ἐπιδέχεται ἡμᾶς. 10 διὰ τοῦτο, ἐὰν ἔλθω, ὑπομνήσω αὐτοῦ τὰ ἔργα ἃ ποιεῖ λόγοις πονηροῖς φλυαρῶν ἡμᾶς, καὶ μὴ ἀρκούμενος ἐπὶ τούτοις οὔτε αὐτὸς ἐπιδέχεται τοὺς ἀδελφοὺς καὶ τοὺς βουλομένους κωλύει καὶ ἐκ τῆς ἐκκλησίας ἐκβάλλει.

11 Ἀγαπητέ, μὴ μιμοῦ τὸ κακὸν ἀλλὰ τὸ ἀγαθόν. ὁ ἀγαθοποιῶν ἐκ τοῦ θεοῦ ἐστιν· ὁ κακοποιῶν οὐχ ἑώρακεν τὸν θεόν. 12 Δημητρίῳ μεμαρτύρηται ὑπὸ πάντων καὶ ὑπὸ αὐτῆς τῆς ἀληθείας· καὶ ἡμεῖς δὲ μαρτυροῦμεν, καὶ οἶδας ὅτι ἡ μαρτυρία ἡμῶν ἀληθής ἐστιν.

13 Πολλὰ εἶχον γράψαι σοι ἀλλ' οὐ θέλω διὰ μέλανος καὶ καλάμου σοι γράφειν· 14 ἐλπίζω δὲ εὐθέως σε ἰδεῖν, καὶ στόμα πρὸς στόμα λαλήσομεν. 15[a] εἰρήνη σοι. ἀσπάζονταί σε οἱ φίλοι. ἀσπάζου τοὺς φίλους κατ' ὄνομα.

¹The elder,

To my dear friend Gaius, whom I love in the truth.

²Dear friend, I pray that you may enjoy good health and that all may go well with you, even as your soul is getting along well. ³It gave me great joy to have some brothers come and tell about your faithfulness to the truth and how you continue to walk in the truth. ⁴I have no greater joy than to hear that my children are walking in the truth.

⁵Dear friend, you are faithful in what you are doing for the brothers, even though they are strangers to you. ⁶They have told the church about your love. You will do well to send them on their way in a manner worthy of God. ⁷It was for the sake of the Name that they went out, receiving no help from the pagans. ⁸We ought therefore to show hospitality to such men so that we may work together for the truth.

⁹I wrote to the church, but Diotrephes, who loves to be first, will have nothing to do with us. ¹⁰So if I come, I will call attention to what he is doing, gossiping maliciously about us. Not satisfied with that, he refuses to welcome the brothers. He also stops those who want to do so and puts them out of the church.

¹¹Dear friend, do not imitate what is evil but what is good. Anyone who does what is good is from God. Anyone who does what is evil has not seen God. ¹²Demetrius is well spoken of by everyone—and even by the truth itself. We also speak well of him, and you know that our testimony is true.

¹³I have much to write you, but I do not want to do so with pen and ink. ¹⁴I hope to see you soon, and we will talk face to face.

Peace to you. The friends here send their greetings. Greet the friends there by name.

---

[a] Gk *brothers*   [b] Gk *for the sake of the name*
[c] Gk *the Gentiles*   [d] Gk lacks *for him*

[a]15 NIV does not use verse number 15, but includes all the text of verse 15 in verse 14

NRSV

Salutation

1 Jude,[a] a servant[b] of Jesus Christ and brother of James,

To those who are called, who are beloved[c] in[d] God the Father and kept safe for[d] Jesus Christ:

2 May mercy, peace, and love be yours in abundance.

Occasion of the Letter

3 Beloved, while eagerly preparing to write to you about the salvation we share, I find it necessary to write and appeal to you to contend for the faith that was once for all entrusted to the saints. [4]For certain intruders have stolen in among you, people who long ago were designated for this condemnation as ungodly, who pervert the grace of our God into licentiousness and deny our only Master and Lord, Jesus Christ.[e]

Judgment on False Teachers

5 Now I desire to remind you, though you are fully informed, that the Lord, who once for all saved[f] a people out of the land of Egypt, afterward destroyed those who did not believe. [6]And the angels who did not keep their own position, but left their proper dwelling, he has kept in eternal chains in deepest darkness for the judgment of the great Day. [7]Likewise, Sodom and Gomorrah and the surrounding cities, which, in the same manner as they, indulged in sexual immorality and pursued unnatural lust,[g] serve as an example by undergoing a punishment of eternal fire.

8 Yet in the same way these dreamers also defile the flesh, reject authority, and slander the glorious ones.[h] [9]But when the archangel Michael contended with the devil and disputed about the body of Moses, he did not dare to bring a condemnation of slander[i] against him, but said, "The Lord rebuke you!" [10]But these people slander whatever they do not understand, and they are destroyed by those things that, like irrational animals, they know by instinct. [11]Woe to them! For they go the way of Cain, and abandon themselves to Balaam's error for the sake of gain, and perish in Korah's rebellion. [12]These are blemishes[j] on your love-feasts, while they

ΙΟΥΔΑ

1 Ἰούδας Ἰησοῦ Χριστοῦ δοῦλος, ἀδελφὸς δὲ Ἰακώβου, τοῖς ἐν θεῷ πατρὶ ἠγαπημένοις[a] καὶ Ἰησοῦ Χριστῷ τετηρημένοις κλητοῖς· 2 ἔλεος ὑμῖν καὶ εἰρήνη καὶ ἀγάπη πληθυνθείη.

3 Ἀγαπητοί, πᾶσαν σπουδὴν ποιούμενος γράφειν ὑμῖν περὶ τῆς κοινῆς ἡμῶν σωτηρίας ἀνάγκην ἔσχον γράψαι ὑμῖν παρακαλῶν ἐπαγωνίζεσθαι τῇ ἅπαξ παραδοθείσῃ τοῖς ἁγίοις πίστει. 4 παρεισέδυσαν γάρ τινες ἄνθρωποι, οἱ πάλαι προγεγραμμένοι εἰς τοῦτο τὸ κρίμα, ἀσεβεῖς, τὴν τοῦ θεοῦ ἡμῶν χάριτα μετατιθέντες εἰς ἀσέλγειαν καὶ τὸν μόνον δεσπότην καὶ κύριον ἡμῶν Ἰησοῦν Χριστὸν ἀρνούμενοι.

5 Ὑπομνῆσαι δὲ ὑμᾶς βούλομαι, εἰδότας [ὑμᾶς] πάντα ὅτι [ὁ] κύριος[b] ἅπαξ λαὸν ἐκ γῆς Αἰγύπτου σώσας τὸ δεύτερον τοὺς μὴ πιστεύσαντας ἀπώλεσεν, 6 ἀγγέλους τε τοὺς μὴ τηρήσαντας τὴν ἑαυτῶν ἀρχὴν ἀλλὰ ἀπολιπόντας τὸ ἴδιον οἰκητήριον εἰς κρίσιν μεγάλης ἡμέρας δεσμοῖς ἀϊδίοις ὑπὸ ζόφον τετήρηκεν, 7 ὡς Σόδομα καὶ Γόμορρα καὶ αἱ περὶ αὐτὰς πόλεις τὸν ὅμοιον τρόπον τούτοις ἐκπορνεύσασαι καὶ ἀπελθοῦσαι ὀπίσω σαρκὸς ἑτέρας, πρόκεινται δεῖγμα πυρὸς αἰωνίου δίκην ὑπέχουσαι.

8 Ὁμοίως μέντοι καὶ οὗτοι ἐνυπνιαζόμενοι σάρκα μὲν μιαίνουσιν κυριότητα δὲ ἀθετοῦσιν δόξας δὲ βλασφημοῦσιν. 9 ὁ δὲ Μιχαὴλ ὁ ἀρχάγγελος, ὅτε τῷ διαβόλῳ διακρινόμενος διελέγετο περὶ τοῦ Μωϋσέως σώματος, οὐκ ἐτόλμησεν κρίσιν ἐπενεγκεῖν βλασφημίας ἀλλὰ εἶπεν, Ἐπιτιμήσαι σοι κύριος. 10 οὗτοι δὲ ὅσα μὲν οὐκ οἴδασιν βλασφημοῦσιν, ὅσα δὲ φυσικῶς ὡς τὰ ἄλογα ζῷα ἐπίστανται, ἐν τούτοις φθείρονται. 11 οὐαὶ αὐτοῖς, ὅτι τῇ ὁδῷ τοῦ Κάϊν ἐπορεύθησαν καὶ τῇ πλάνῃ τοῦ Βαλαὰμ μισθοῦ ἐξεχύθησαν καὶ τῇ ἀντιλογίᾳ τοῦ Κόρε ἀπώλοντο. 12 οὗτοί εἰσιν οἱ ἐν ταῖς ἀγάπαις ὑμῶν σπιλάδες

NIV

[1]Jude, a servant of Jesus Christ and a brother of James,

To those who have been called, who are loved by God the Father and kept by[a] Jesus Christ:

[2]Mercy, peace and love be yours in abundance.

The Sin and Doom of Godless Men

[3]Dear friends, although I was very eager to write to you about the salvation we share, I felt I had to write and urge you to contend for the faith that was once for all entrusted to the saints. [4]For certain men whose condemnation was written about[b] long ago have secretly slipped in among you. They are godless men, who change the grace of our God into a license for immorality and deny Jesus Christ our only Sovereign and Lord.

[5]Though you already know all this, I want to remind you that the Lord[c] delivered his people out of Egypt, but later destroyed those who did not believe. [6]And the angels who did not keep their positions of authority but abandoned their own home—these he has kept in darkness, bound with everlasting chains for judgment on the great Day. [7]In a similar way, Sodom and Gomorrah and the surrounding towns gave themselves up to sexual immorality and perversion. They serve as an example of those who suffer the punishment of eternal fire.

[8]In the very same way, these dreamers pollute their own bodies, reject authority and slander celestial beings. [9]But even the archangel Michael, when he was disputing with the devil about the body of Moses, did not dare to bring a slanderous accusation against him, but said, "The Lord rebuke you!" [10]Yet these men speak abusively against whatever they do not understand; and what things they do understand by instinct, like unreasoning animals—these are the very things that destroy them.

[11]Woe to them! They have taken the way of Cain; they have rushed for profit into Balaam's error; they have been destroyed in Korah's rebellion.

[12]These men are blemishes at your love

---

a Gk *Judas*   b Gk *slave*   c Other ancient authorities read *sanctified*   d Or *by*   e Or *the only Master and our Lord Jesus Christ*   f Other ancient authorities read *though you were once for all fully informed, that Jesus (or Joshua) who saved*   g Gk *went after other flesh*   h Or *angels*; Gk *glories*   i Or *condemnation for blasphemy*   j Or *reefs*

[a]1 NRSV note c ἠγασμένοις   [b]5 NIV note Ἰησοῦς; NRSV note f ἅπαξ πάντα, ὅτι Ἰησοῦς

[a]1 Or *for; or in*   [b]4 Or *men who were marked out for condemnation*   [c]5 Some early manuscripts *Jesus*

feast with you without fear, feeding themselves.[k] They are waterless clouds carried along by the winds; autumn trees without fruit, twice dead, uprooted; [13]wild waves of the sea, casting up the foam of their own shame; wandering stars, for whom the deepest darkness has been reserved forever.

[14] It was also about these that Enoch, in the seventh generation from Adam, prophesied, saying, "See, the Lord is coming[l] with ten thousands of his holy ones, [15]to execute judgment on all, and to convict everyone of all the deeds of ungodliness that they have committed in such an ungodly way, and of all the harsh things that ungodly sinners have spoken against him." [16]These are grumblers and malcontents; they indulge their own lusts; they are bombastic in speech, flattering people to their own advantage.

Warnings and Exhortations

[17] But you, beloved, must remember the predictions of the apostles of our Lord Jesus Christ; [18]for they said to you, "In the last time there will be scoffers, indulging their own ungodly lusts." [19]It is these worldly people, devoid of the Spirit, who are causing divisions. [20]But you, beloved, build yourselves up on your most holy faith; pray in the Holy Spirit; [21]keep yourselves in the love of God; look forward to the mercy of our Lord Jesus Christ that leads to[m] eternal life. [22]And have mercy on some who are wavering; [23]save others by snatching them out of the fire; and have mercy on still others with fear, hating even the tunic defiled by their bodies.[n]

Benediction

[24] Now to him who is able to keep you from falling, and to make you stand without blemish in the presence of his glory with rejoicing, [25]to the only God our Savior, through Jesus Christ our Lord, be glory, majesty, power, and authority, before all time and now and forever. Amen.

συνευωχούμενοι ἀφόβως, ἑαυτοὺς ποιμαίνοντες, νεφέλαι ἄνυδροι ὑπὸ ἀνέμων παραφερόμεναι, δένδρα φθινοπωρινὰ ἄκαρπα δὶς ἀποθανόντα ἐκριζωθέντα, 13 κύματα ἄγρια θαλάσσης ἐπαφρίζοντα τὰς ἑαυτῶν αἰσχύνας, ἀστέρες πλανῆται οἷς ὁ ζόφος τοῦ σκότους εἰς αἰῶνα τετήρηται. 14 Προεφήτευσεν δὲ καὶ τούτοις ἕβδομος ἀπὸ Ἀδὰμ Ἑνὼχ λέγων, Ἰδοὺ ἦλθεν κύριος ἐν ἁγίαις μυριάσιν αὐτοῦ 15 ποιῆσαι κρίσιν κατὰ πάντων καὶ ἐλέγξαι πᾶσαν ψυχὴν[c] περὶ πάντων τῶν ἔργων ἀσεβείας αὐτῶν ὧν ἠσέβησαν καὶ περὶ πάντων τῶν σκληρῶν ὧν ἐλάλησαν κατ' αὐτοῦ ἁμαρτωλοὶ ἀσεβεῖς. 16 Οὗτοί εἰσιν γογγυσταὶ μεμψίμοιροι κατὰ τὰς ἐπιθυμίας ἑαυτῶν πορευόμενοι, καὶ τὸ στόμα αὐτῶν λαλεῖ ὑπέρογκα, θαυμάζοντες πρόσωπα ὠφελείας χάριν. 17 Ὑμεῖς δέ, ἀγαπητοί, μνήσθητε τῶν ῥημάτων τῶν προειρημένων ὑπὸ τῶν ἀποστόλων τοῦ κυρίου ἡμῶν Ἰησοῦ Χριστοῦ 18 ὅτι ἔλεγον ὑμῖν [ὅτι] Ἐπ' ἐσχάτου [τοῦ] χρόνου ἔσονται ἐμπαῖκται κατὰ τὰς ἑαυτῶν ἐπιθυμίας πορευόμενοι τῶν ἀσεβειῶν. 19 Οὗτοί εἰσιν οἱ ἀποδιορίζοντες, ψυχικοί, πνεῦμα μὴ ἔχοντες. 20 ὑμεῖς δέ, ἀγαπητοί, ἐποικοδομοῦντες ἑαυτοὺς τῇ ἁγιωτάτῃ ὑμῶν πίστει, ἐν πνεύματι ἁγίῳ προσευχόμενοι, 21 ἑαυτοὺς ἐν ἀγάπῃ θεοῦ τηρήσατε προσδεχόμενοι τὸ ἔλεος τοῦ κυρίου ἡμῶν Ἰησοῦ Χριστοῦ εἰς ζωὴν αἰώνιον. 22 καὶ οὓς μὲν ἐλεᾶτε διακρινομένους, 23 οὓς δὲ σῴζετε ἐκ πυρὸς ἁρπάζοντες, οὓς δὲ ἐλεᾶτε ἐν φόβῳ μισοῦντες καὶ τὸν ἀπὸ τῆς σαρκὸς ἐσπιλωμένον χιτῶνα. 24 Τῷ δὲ δυναμένῳ φυλάξαι ὑμᾶς ἀπταίστους καὶ στῆσαι κατενώπιον τῆς δόξης αὐτοῦ ἀμώμους ἐν ἀγαλλιάσει, 25 μόνῳ θεῷ σωτῆρι ἡμῶν διὰ Ἰησοῦ Χριστοῦ τοῦ κυρίου ἡμῶν δόξα μεγαλωσύνη κράτος καὶ ἐξουσία πρὸ παντὸς τοῦ αἰῶνος καὶ νῦν καὶ εἰς πάντας τοὺς αἰῶνας, ἀμήν.

feasts, eating with you without the slightest qualm—shepherds who feed only themselves. They are clouds without rain, blown along by the wind; autumn trees, without fruit and uprooted—twice dead. [13]They are wild waves of the sea, foaming up their shame; wandering stars, for whom blackest darkness has been reserved forever.

[14]Enoch, the seventh from Adam, prophesied about these men: "See, the Lord is coming with thousands upon thousands of his holy ones [15]to judge everyone, and to convict all the ungodly of all the ungodly acts they have done in the ungodly way, and of all the harsh words ungodly sinners have spoken against him." [16]These men are grumblers and faultfinders; they follow their own evil desires; they boast about themselves and flatter others for their own advantage.

A Call to Persevere

[17]But, dear friends, remember what the apostles of our Lord Jesus Christ foretold. [18]They said to you, "In the last times there will be scoffers who will follow their own ungodly desires." [19]These are the men who divide you, who follow mere natural instincts and do not have the Spirit.

[20]But you, dear friends, build yourselves up in your most holy faith and pray in the Holy Spirit. [21]Keep yourselves in God's love as you wait for the mercy of our Lord Jesus Christ to bring you to eternal life.

[22]Be merciful to those who doubt; [23]snatch others from the fire and save them; to others show mercy, mixed with fear—hating even the clothing stained by corrupted flesh.

Doxology

[24]To him who is able to keep you from falling and to present you before his glorious presence without fault and with great joy— [25]to the only God our Savior be glory, majesty, power and authority, through Jesus Christ our Lord, before all ages, now and forevermore! Amen.

---

[k] Or *without fear. They are shepherds who care only for themselves* [l] Gk *came* [m] Gk *Christ to* [n] Gk *by the flesh.* The Greek text of verses 22-23 is uncertain at several points

[c]15 NIV text πάντας τοὺς ἀσεβεῖς †

NRSV

Introduction and Salutation

1 The revelation of Jesus Christ, which God gave him to show his servants[a] what must soon take place; he made[b] it known by sending his angel to his servant[c] John, 2who testified to the word of God and to the testimony of Jesus Christ, even to all that he saw.

3 Blessed is the one who reads aloud the words of the prophecy, and blessed are those who hear and who keep what is written in it; for the time is near.

4 John to the seven churches that are in Asia:

Grace to you and peace from him who is and who was and who is to come, and from the seven spirits who are before his throne, 5and from Jesus Christ, the faithful witness, the firstborn of the dead, and the ruler of the kings of the earth.

To him who loves us and freed[d] us from our sins by his blood, 6and made[e] us to be a kingdom, priests serving[f] his God and Father, to him be glory and dominion forever and ever. Amen.

7 Look! He is coming with the clouds;
      every eye will see him,
   even those who pierced him;
      and on his account all the tribes of
         the earth will wail.
So it is to be. Amen.

8 "I am the Alpha and the Omega," says the Lord God, who is and who was and who is to come, the Almighty.

A Vision of Christ

9 I, John, your brother who share with you in Jesus the persecution and the kingdom and the patient endurance, was on the island called Patmos because of the word of God and the testimony of Jesus.[g] 10I was in the spirit[h] on the Lord's day, and I heard behind me a loud voice like a trumpet 11saying, "Write in a book what you see and send it to the seven churches, to Ephesus, to Smyrna, to Pergamum, to Thyatira, to Sardis, to Philadelphia, and to Laodicea."

12 Then I turned to see whose voice it was that spoke to me, and on turning I saw seven golden lampstands, 13and in the midst of the lampstands I saw one like the Son of Man, clothed with a long robe and

ΑΠΟΚΑΛΥΨΙΣ ΙΩΑΝΝΟΥ

1 Ἀποκάλυψις Ἰησοῦ Χριστοῦ ἣν ἔδωκεν αὐτῷ ὁ θεὸς δεῖξαι τοῖς δούλοις αὐτοῦ ἃ δεῖ γενέσθαι ἐν τάχει, καὶ ἐσήμανεν ἀποστείλας διὰ τοῦ ἀγγέλου αὐτοῦ τῷ δούλῳ αὐτοῦ Ἰωάννῃ, **2** ὃς ἐμαρτύρησεν τὸν λόγον τοῦ θεοῦ καὶ τὴν μαρτυρίαν Ἰησοῦ Χριστοῦ ὅσα εἶδεν. **3** μακάριος ὁ ἀναγινώσκων καὶ οἱ ἀκούοντες τοὺς λόγους τῆς προφητείας καὶ τηροῦντες τὰ ἐν αὐτῇ γεγραμμένα, ὁ γὰρ καιρὸς ἐγγύς.

4 Ἰωάννης ταῖς ἑπτὰ ἐκκλησίαις ταῖς ἐν τῇ Ἀσίᾳ· χάρις ὑμῖν καὶ εἰρήνη ἀπὸ ὁ ὢν καὶ ὁ ἦν καὶ ὁ ἐρχόμενος καὶ ἀπὸ τῶν ἑπτὰ πνευμάτων ἃ ἐνώπιον τοῦ θρόνου αὐτοῦ **5** καὶ ἀπὸ Ἰησοῦ Χριστοῦ, ὁ μάρτυς, ὁ πιστός, ὁ πρωτότοκος τῶν νεκρῶν καὶ ὁ ἄρχων τῶν βασιλέων τῆς γῆς.

Τῷ ἀγαπῶντι ἡμᾶς καὶ λύσαντι ἡμᾶς ἐκ[a] τῶν ἁμαρτιῶν ἡμῶν ἐν τῷ αἵματι αὐτοῦ, **6** καὶ ἐποίησεν ἡμᾶς βασιλείαν, ἱερεῖς τῷ θεῷ καὶ πατρὶ αὐτοῦ, αὐτῷ ἡ δόξα καὶ τὸ κράτος εἰς τοὺς αἰῶνας [τῶν αἰώνων]· ἀμήν.

7 Ἰδοὺ ἔρχεται μετὰ τῶν νεφελῶν, καὶ ὄψεται αὐτὸν πᾶς ὀφθαλμὸς καὶ οἵτινες αὐτὸν ἐξεκέντησαν, καὶ κόψονται ἐπ' αὐτὸν πᾶσαι αἱ φυλαὶ τῆς γῆς.

ναί, ἀμήν.

8 Ἐγώ εἰμι τὸ Ἄλφα καὶ τὸ Ὦ, λέγει κύριος ὁ θεός, ὁ ὢν καὶ ὁ ἦν καὶ ὁ ἐρχόμενος, ὁ παντοκράτωρ.

9 Ἐγὼ Ἰωάννης, ὁ ἀδελφὸς ὑμῶν καὶ συγκοινωνὸς ἐν τῇ θλίψει καὶ βασιλείᾳ καὶ ὑπομονῇ ἐν Ἰησοῦ, ἐγενόμην ἐν τῇ νήσῳ τῇ καλουμένῃ Πάτμῳ διὰ τὸν λόγον τοῦ θεοῦ καὶ τὴν μαρτυρίαν Ἰησοῦ. **10** ἐγενόμην ἐν πνεύματι ἐν τῇ κυριακῇ ἡμέρᾳ καὶ ἤκουσα ὀπίσω μου φωνὴν μεγάλην ὡς σάλπιγγος **11** λεγούσης, Ὃ βλέπεις γράψον εἰς βιβλίον καὶ πέμψον ταῖς ἑπτὰ ἐκκλησίαις, εἰς Ἔφεσον καὶ εἰς Σμύρναν καὶ εἰς Πέργαμον καὶ εἰς Θυάτειρα καὶ εἰς Σάρδεις καὶ εἰς Φιλαδέλφειαν καὶ εἰς Λαοδίκειαν.

12 Καὶ ἐπέστρεψα βλέπειν τὴν φωνὴν ἥτις ἐλάλει μετ' ἐμοῦ, καὶ ἐπιστρέψας εἶδον ἑπτὰ λυχνίας χρυσᾶς **13** καὶ ἐν μέσῳ τῶν λυχνιῶν ὅμοιον υἱὸν ἀνθρώπου ἐνδεδυμένον ποδήρη καὶ περιεζωσμένον

NIV

Prologue

1 The revelation of Jesus Christ, which God gave him to show his servants what must soon take place. He made it known by sending his angel to his servant John, 2who testifies to everything he saw— that is, the word of God and the testimony of Jesus Christ. 3Blessed is the one who reads the words of this prophecy, and blessed are those who hear it and take to heart what is written in it, because the time is near.

Greetings and Doxology

4John,

To the seven churches in the province of Asia:

Grace and peace to you from him who is, and who was, and who is to come, and from the seven spirits[a] before his throne, 5and from Jesus Christ, who is the faithful witness, the firstborn from the dead, and the ruler of the kings of the earth.

To him who loves us and has freed us from our sins by his blood, 6and has made us to be a kingdom and priests to serve his God and Father—to him be glory and power for ever and ever! Amen.

7Look, he is coming with the clouds,
   and every eye will see him,
even those who pierced him;
   and all the peoples of the earth will
      mourn because of him.
                    So shall it be! Amen.

8"I am the Alpha and the Omega," says the Lord God, "who is, and who was, and who is to come, the Almighty."

One Like a Son of Man

9I, John, your brother and companion in the suffering and kingdom and patient endurance that are ours in Jesus, was on the island of Patmos because of the word of God and the testimony of Jesus. 10On the Lord's Day I was in the Spirit, and I heard behind me a loud voice like a trumpet, 11which said: "Write on a scroll what you see and send it to the seven churches: to Ephesus, Smyrna, Pergamum, Thyatira, Sardis, Philadelphia and Laodicea."

12I turned around to see the voice that was speaking to me. And when I turned I saw seven golden lampstands, 13and among the lampstands was someone "like a son of man,"[b] dressed in a robe reaching down to his feet and with a golden sash

---

a Gk *slaves*   b Gk *and he made*   c Gk *slave*   d Other ancient authorities read *washed*   e Gk *and he made*
f Gk *priests to*   g Or *testimony to Jesus*   h Or *in the Spirit*

a5 NRSV note d λύσαντι ἡμᾶς ἀπό

a4 Or *the sevenfold Spirit*   b13 Daniel 7:13

with a golden sash across his chest. [14]His head and his hair were white as white wool, white as snow; his eyes were like a flame of fire, [15]his feet were like burnished bronze, refined as in a furnace, and his voice was like the sound of many waters. [16]In his right hand he held seven stars, and from his mouth came a sharp, two-edged sword, and his face was like the sun shining with full force.

17 When I saw him, I fell at his feet as though dead. But he placed his right hand on me, saying, "Do not be afraid; I am the first and the last, [18]and the living one. I was dead, and see, I am alive forever and ever; and I have the keys of Death and of Hades. [19]Now write what you have seen, what is, and what is to take place after this. [20]As for the mystery of the seven stars that you saw in my right hand, and the seven golden lampstands: the seven stars are the angels of the seven churches, and the seven lampstands are the seven churches.

The Message to Ephesus

2 "To the angel of the church in Ephesus write: These are the words of him who holds the seven stars in his right hand, who walks among the seven golden lampstands:

2 "I know your works, your toil and your patient endurance. I know that you cannot tolerate evildoers; you have tested those who claim to be apostles but are not, and have found them to be false. [3]I also know that you are enduring patiently and bearing up for the sake of my name, and that you have not grown weary. [4]But I have this against you, that you have abandoned the love you had at first. [5]Remember then from what you have fallen; repent, and do the works you did at first. If not, I will come to you and remove your lampstand from its place, unless you repent. [6]Yet this is to your credit: you hate the works of the Nicolaitans, which I also hate. [7]Let anyone who has an ear listen to what the Spirit is saying to the churches. To everyone who conquers, I will give permission to eat from the tree of life that is in the paradise of God.

The Message to Smyrna

8 "And to the angel of the church in

πρὸς τοῖς μαστοῖς ζώνην χρυσᾶν. **14** ἡ δὲ κεφαλὴ αὐτοῦ καὶ αἱ τρίχες λευκαὶ ὡς ἔριον λευκὸν ὡς χιὼν καὶ οἱ ὀφθαλμοὶ αὐτοῦ ὡς φλὸξ πυρός **15** καὶ οἱ πόδες αὐτοῦ ὅμοιοι χαλκολιβάνῳ ὡς ἐν καμίνῳ πεπυρωμένης καὶ ἡ φωνὴ αὐτοῦ ὡς φωνὴ ὑδάτων πολλῶν, **16** καὶ ἔχων ἐν τῇ δεξιᾷ χειρὶ αὐτοῦ ἀστέρας ἑπτὰ καὶ ἐκ τοῦ στόματος αὐτοῦ ῥομφαία δίστομος ὀξεῖα ἐκπορευομένη καὶ ἡ ὄψις αὐτοῦ ὡς ὁ ἥλιος φαίνει ἐν τῇ δυνάμει αὐτοῦ.

17 Καὶ ὅτε εἶδον αὐτόν, ἔπεσα πρὸς τοὺς πόδας αὐτοῦ ὡς νεκρός, καὶ ἔθηκεν τὴν δεξιὰν αὐτοῦ ἐπ' ἐμὲ λέγων, Μὴ φοβοῦ· ἐγώ εἰμι ὁ πρῶτος καὶ ὁ ἔσχατος **18** καὶ ὁ ζῶν, καὶ ἐγενόμην νεκρὸς καὶ ἰδοὺ ζῶν εἰμι εἰς τοὺς αἰῶνας τῶν αἰώνων καὶ ἔχω τὰς κλεῖς τοῦ θανάτου καὶ τοῦ ᾅδου. **19** γράψον οὖν ἃ εἶδες καὶ ἃ εἰσὶν καὶ ἃ μέλλει γενέσθαι μετὰ ταῦτα. **20** τὸ μυστήριον τῶν ἑπτὰ ἀστέρων οὓς εἶδες ἐπὶ τῆς δεξιᾶς μου καὶ τὰς ἑπτὰ λυχνίας τὰς χρυσᾶς· οἱ ἑπτὰ ἀστέρες ἄγγελοι τῶν ἑπτὰ ἐκκλησιῶν εἰσιν καὶ αἱ λυχνίαι αἱ ἑπτὰ ἑπτὰ ἐκκλησίαι εἰσίν.

2 Τῷ ἀγγέλῳ τῆς ἐν Ἐφέσῳ ἐκκλησίας γράψον·

Τάδε λέγει ὁ κρατῶν τοὺς ἑπτὰ ἀστέρας ἐν τῇ δεξιᾷ αὐτοῦ, ὁ περιπατῶν ἐν μέσῳ τῶν ἑπτὰ λυχνιῶν τῶν χρυσῶν· **2** Οἶδα τὰ ἔργα σου καὶ τὸν κόπον καὶ τὴν ὑπομονήν σου καὶ ὅτι οὐ δύνῃ βαστάσαι κακούς, καὶ ἐπείρασας τοὺς λέγοντας ἑαυτοὺς ἀποστόλους καὶ οὐκ εἰσὶν καὶ εὗρες αὐτοὺς ψευδεῖς, **3** καὶ ὑπομονὴν ἔχεις καὶ ἐβάστασας διὰ τὸ ὄνομά μου καὶ οὐ κεκοπίακες. **4** ἀλλὰ ἔχω κατὰ σοῦ ὅτι τὴν ἀγάπην σου τὴν πρώτην ἀφῆκες. **5** μνημόνευε οὖν πόθεν πέπτωκας καὶ μετανόησον καὶ τὰ πρῶτα ἔργα ποίησον· εἰ δὲ μή, ἔρχομαί σοι καὶ κινήσω τὴν λυχνίαν σου ἐκ τοῦ τόπου αὐτῆς, ἐὰν μὴ μετανοήσῃς. **6** ἀλλὰ τοῦτο ἔχεις, ὅτι μισεῖς τὰ ἔργα τῶν Νικολαϊτῶν ἃ κἀγὼ μισῶ. **7** ὁ ἔχων οὖς ἀκουσάτω τί τὸ πνεῦμα λέγει ταῖς ἐκκλησίαις. τῷ νικῶντι δώσω αὐτῷ φαγεῖν ἐκ τοῦ ξύλου τῆς ζωῆς, ὅ ἐστιν ἐν τῷ παραδείσῳ τοῦ θεοῦ.

8 Καὶ τῷ ἀγγέλῳ τῆς ἐν Σμύρνῃ ἐκκλησίας γράψον·

around his chest. [14]His head and hair were white like wool, as white as snow, and his eyes were like blazing fire. [15]His feet were like bronze glowing in a furnace, and his voice was like the sound of rushing waters. [16]In his right hand he held seven stars, and out of his mouth came a sharp double-edged sword. His face was like the sun shining in all its brilliance.

[17]When I saw him, I fell at his feet as though dead. Then he placed his right hand on me and said: "Do not be afraid. I am the First and the Last. [18]I am the Living One; I was dead, and behold I am alive for ever and ever! And I hold the keys of death and Hades.

[19]"Write, therefore, what you have seen, what is now and what will take place later. [20]The mystery of the seven stars that you saw in my right hand and of the seven golden lampstands is this: The seven stars are the angels[c] of the seven churches, and the seven lampstands are the seven churches.

To the Church in Ephesus

2 "To the angel[a] of the church in Ephesus write:

These are the words of him who holds the seven stars in his right hand and walks among the seven golden lampstands: [2]I know your deeds, your hard work and your perseverance. I know that you cannot tolerate wicked men, that you have tested those who claim to be apostles but are not, and have found them false. [3]You have persevered and have endured hardships for my name, and have not grown weary.

[4]Yet I hold this against you: You have forsaken your first love. [5]Remember the height from which you have fallen! Repent and do the things you did at first. If you do not repent, I will come to you and remove your lampstand from its place. [6]But you have this in your favor: You hate the practices of the Nicolaitans, which I also hate.

[7]He who has an ear, let him hear what the Spirit says to the churches. To him who overcomes, I will give the right to eat from the tree of life, which is in the paradise of God.

To the Church in Smyrna

[8]"To the angel of the church in Smyrna write:

---

[c]20 Or *messengers*   [a]1 Or *messenger*; also in verses 8, 12 and 18

Smyrna write: These are the words of the first and the last, who was dead and came to life:

9 "I know your affliction and your poverty, even though you are rich. I know the slander on the part of those who say that they are Jews and are not, but are a synagogue of Satan. 10Do not fear what you are about to suffer. Beware, the devil is about to throw some of you into prison so that you may be tested, and for ten days you will have affliction. Be faithful until death, and I will give you the crown of life. 11Let anyone who has an ear listen to what the Spirit is saying to the churches. Whoever conquers will not be harmed by the second death.

The Message to Pergamum

12 "And to the angel of the church in Pergamum write: These are the words of him who has the sharp two-edged sword:

13 "I know where you are living, where Satan's throne is. Yet you are holding fast to my name, and you did not deny your faith in me[i] even in the days of Antipas my witness, my faithful one, who was killed among you, where Satan lives. 14But I have a few things against you: you have some there who hold to the teaching of Balaam, who taught Balak to put a stumbling block before the people of Israel, so that they would eat food sacrificed to idols and practice fornication. 15So you also have some who hold to the teaching of the Nicolaitans. 16Repent then. If not, I will come to you soon and make war against them with the sword of my mouth. 17Let anyone who has an ear listen to what the Spirit is saying to the churches. To everyone who conquers I will give some of the hidden manna, and I will give a white stone, and on the white stone is written a new name that no one knows except the one who receives it.

The Message to Thyatira

18 "And to the angel of the church in Thyatira write: These are the words of the Son of God, who has eyes like a flame of fire, and whose feet are like burnished bronze:

19 "I know your works—your love, faith, service, and patient endurance. I know that your last works are greater than the first.

Τάδε λέγει ὁ πρῶτος καὶ ὁ ἔσχατος, ὃς ἐγένετο νεκρὸς καὶ ἔζησεν· 9 Οἶδά σου τὴν θλῖψιν καὶ τὴν πτωχείαν, ἀλλὰ πλούσιος εἶ, καὶ τὴν βλασφημίαν ἐκ τῶν λεγόντων Ἰουδαίους εἶναι ἑαυτοὺς καὶ οὐκ εἰσὶν ἀλλὰ συναγωγὴ τοῦ Σατανᾶ. 10 μηδὲν φοβοῦ ἃ μέλλεις πάσχειν. ἰδοὺ μέλλει βάλλειν ὁ διάβολος ἐξ ὑμῶν εἰς φυλακὴν ἵνα πειρασθῆτε καὶ ἕξετε θλῖψιν ἡμερῶν δέκα. γίνου πιστὸς ἄχρι θανάτου, καὶ δώσω σοι τὸν στέφανον τῆς ζωῆς. 11 ὁ ἔχων οὖς ἀκουσάτω τί τὸ πνεῦμα λέγει ταῖς ἐκκλησίαις. ὁ νικῶν οὐ μὴ ἀδικηθῇ ἐκ τοῦ θανάτου τοῦ δευτέρου.

12 Καὶ τῷ ἀγγέλῳ τῆς ἐν Περγάμῳ ἐκκλησίας γράψον·

Τάδε λέγει ὁ ἔχων τὴν ῥομφαίαν τὴν δίστομον τὴν ὀξεῖαν· 13 Οἶδα ποῦ κατοικεῖς, ὅπου ὁ θρόνος τοῦ Σατανᾶ, καὶ κρατεῖς τὸ ὄνομά μου καὶ οὐκ ἠρνήσω τὴν πίστιν μου καὶ ἐν ταῖς ἡμέραις Ἀντιπᾶς ὁ μάρτυς μου ὁ πιστός μου, ὃς ἀπεκτάνθη παρ' ὑμῖν, ὅπου ὁ Σατανᾶς κατοικεῖ. 14 ἀλλ' ἔχω κατὰ σοῦ ὀλίγα ὅτι ἔχεις ἐκεῖ κρατοῦντας τὴν διδαχὴν Βαλαάμ, ὃς ἐδίδασκεν τῷ Βαλὰκ βαλεῖν σκάνδαλον ἐνώπιον τῶν υἱῶν Ἰσραὴλ φαγεῖν εἰδωλόθυτα καὶ πορνεῦσαι. 15 οὕτως ἔχεις καὶ σὺ κρατοῦντας τὴν διδαχὴν [τῶν] Νικολαϊτῶν ὁμοίως. 16 μετανόησον οὖν· εἰ δὲ μή, ἔρχομαί σοι ταχὺ καὶ πολεμήσω μετ' αὐτῶν ἐν τῇ ῥομφαίᾳ τοῦ στόματός μου. 17 ὁ ἔχων οὖς ἀκουσάτω τί τὸ πνεῦμα λέγει ταῖς ἐκκλησίαις. τῷ νικῶντι δώσω αὐτῷ τοῦ μάννα τοῦ κεκρυμμένου καὶ δώσω αὐτῷ ψῆφον λευκήν, καὶ ἐπὶ τὴν ψῆφον ὄνομα καινὸν γεγραμμένον ὃ οὐδεὶς οἶδεν εἰ μὴ ὁ λαμβάνων.

18 Καὶ τῷ ἀγγέλῳ τῆς ἐν Θυατείροις ἐκκλησίας γράψον·

Τάδε λέγει ὁ υἱὸς τοῦ θεοῦ, ὁ ἔχων τοὺς ὀφθαλμοὺς αὐτοῦ ὡς φλόγα πυρὸς καὶ οἱ πόδες αὐτοῦ ὅμοιοι χαλκολιβάνῳ· 19 Οἶδά σου τὰ ἔργα καὶ τὴν ἀγάπην καὶ τὴν πίστιν καὶ τὴν διακονίαν καὶ τὴν ὑπομονήν σου, καὶ τὰ ἔργα σου τὰ ἔσχατα πλείονα τῶν πρώτων. 20 ἀλλὰ

These are the words of him who is the First and the Last, who died and came to life again. 9I know your afflictions and your poverty—yet you are rich! I know the slander of those who say they are Jews and are not, but are a synagogue of Satan. 10Do not be afraid of what you are about to suffer. I tell you, the devil will put some of you in prison to test you, and you will suffer persecution for ten days. Be faithful, even to the point of death, and I will give you the crown of life.

11He who has an ear, let him hear what the Spirit says to the churches. He who overcomes will not be hurt at all by the second death.

To the Church in Pergamum

12"To the angel of the church in Pergamum write:

These are the words of him who has the sharp, double-edged sword. 13I know where you live—where Satan has his throne. Yet you remain true to my name. You did not renounce your faith in me, even in the days of Antipas, my faithful witness, who was put to death in your city—where Satan lives.

14Nevertheless, I have a few things against you: You have people there who hold to the teaching of Balaam, who taught Balak to entice the Israelites to sin by eating food sacrificed to idols and by committing sexual immorality. 15Likewise you also have those who hold to the teaching of the Nicolaitans. 16Repent therefore! Otherwise, I will soon come to you and will fight against them with the sword of my mouth.

17He who has an ear, let him hear what the Spirit says to the churches. To him who overcomes, I will give some of the hidden manna. I will also give him a white stone with a new name written on it, known only to him who receives it.

To the Church in Thyatira

18"To the angel of the church in Thyatira write:

These are the words of the Son of God, whose eyes are like blazing fire and whose feet are like burnished bronze. 19I know your deeds, your love and faith, your service and perseverance, and that you are now doing more than you did at first.

---

i Or deny my faith

²⁰But I have this against you: you tolerate that woman Jezebel, who calls herself a prophet and is teaching and beguiling my servants^j to practice fornication and to eat food sacrificed to idols. ²¹I gave her time to repent, but she refuses to repent of her fornication. ²²Beware, I am throwing her on a bed, and those who commit adultery with her I am throwing into great distress, unless they repent of her doings; ²³and I will strike her children dead. And all the churches will know that I am the one who searches minds and hearts, and I will give to each of you as your works deserve. ²⁴But to the rest of you in Thyatira, who do not hold this teaching, who have not learned what some call 'the deep things of Satan,' to you I say, I do not lay on you any other burden; ²⁵only hold fast to what you have until I come. ²⁶To everyone who conquers and continues to do my works to the end,

I will give authority over the nations;
²⁷   to rule^k them with an iron rod,
    as when clay pots are shattered—
²⁸even as I also received authority from my Father. To the one who conquers I will also give the morning star. ²⁹Let anyone who has an ear listen to what the Spirit is saying to the churches.

The Message to Sardis

3 "And to the angel of the church in Sardis write: These are the words of him who has the seven spirits of God and the seven stars:

"I know your works; you have a name of being alive, but you are dead. ²Wake up, and strengthen what remains and is on the point of death, for I have not found your works perfect in the sight of my God. ³Remember then what you received and heard; obey it, and repent. If you do not wake up, I will come like a thief, and you will not know at what hour I will come to you. ⁴Yet you have still a few persons in Sardis who have not soiled their clothes; they will walk with me, dressed in white, for they are worthy. ⁵If you conquer, you will be clothed like them in white robes, and I will not blot your name out of the book of life;

ἔχω κατὰ σοῦ ὅτι ἀφεῖς τὴν γυναῖκα Ἰεζάβελ, ἡ λέγουσα ἑαυτὴν προφῆτιν καὶ διδάσκει καὶ πλανᾷ τοὺς ἐμοὺς δούλους πορνεῦσαι καὶ φαγεῖν εἰδωλόθυτα. **21** καὶ ἔδωκα αὐτῇ χρόνον ἵνα μετανοήσῃ, καὶ οὐ θέλει μετανοῆσαι ἐκ τῆς πορνείας αὐτῆς. **22** ἰδοὺ βάλλω αὐτὴν εἰς κλίνην καὶ τοὺς μοιχεύοντας μετ᾽ αὐτῆς εἰς θλῖψιν μεγάλην, ἐὰν μὴ μετανοήσωσιν ἐκ τῶν ἔργων αὐτῆς, **23** καὶ τὰ τέκνα αὐτῆς ἀποκτενῶ ἐν θανάτῳ. καὶ γνώσονται πᾶσαι αἱ ἐκκλησίαι ὅτι ἐγώ εἰμι ὁ ἐραυνῶν νεφροὺς καὶ καρδίας, καὶ δώσω ὑμῖν ἑκάστῳ κατὰ τὰ ἔργα ὑμῶν. **24** ὑμῖν δὲ λέγω τοῖς λοιποῖς τοῖς ἐν Θυατείροις, ὅσοι οὐκ ἔχουσιν τὴν διδαχὴν ταύτην, οἵτινες οὐκ ἔγνωσαν τὰ βαθέα τοῦ Σατανᾶ ὡς λέγουσιν· οὐ βάλλω ἐφ᾽ ὑμᾶς ἄλλο βάρος, **25** πλὴν ὃ ἔχετε κρατήσατε ἄχρι[ς] οὗ ἂν ἥξω. **26** καὶ ὁ νικῶν καὶ ὁ τηρῶν ἄχρι τέλους τὰ ἔργα μου,

δώσω αὐτῷ ἐξουσίαν ἐπὶ τῶν ἐθνῶν
27 καὶ ποιμανεῖ αὐτοὺς ἐν ῥάβδῳ σιδηρᾷ
    ὡς τὰ σκεύη τὰ κεραμικὰ
      συντρίβεται,
28 ὡς κἀγὼ εἴληφα παρὰ τοῦ πατρός μου,^a καὶ δώσω αὐτῷ τὸν ἀστέρα τὸν πρωϊνόν. **29** ὁ ἔχων οὖς ἀκουσάτω τί τὸ πνεῦμα λέγει ταῖς ἐκκλησίαις.

3 Καὶ τῷ ἀγγέλῳ τῆς ἐν Σάρδεσιν ἐκκλησίας γράψον·

Τάδε λέγει ὁ ἔχων τὰ ἑπτὰ πνεύματα τοῦ θεοῦ καὶ τοὺς ἑπτὰ ἀστέρας· Οἶδά σου τὰ ἔργα ὅτι ὄνομα ἔχεις ὅτι ζῇς, καὶ νεκρὸς εἶ. **2** γίνου γρηγορῶν καὶ στήρισον τὰ λοιπὰ ἃ ἔμελλον ἀποθανεῖν, οὐ γὰρ εὕρηκά σου τὰ ἔργα πεπληρωμένα ἐνώπιον τοῦ θεοῦ μου. **3** μνημόνευε οὖν πῶς εἴληφας καὶ ἤκουσας καὶ τήρει καὶ μετανόησον. ἐὰν οὖν μὴ γρηγορήσῃς, ἥξω ὡς κλέπτης, καὶ οὐ μὴ γνῷς ποίαν ὥραν ἥξω ἐπὶ σέ. **4** ἀλλὰ ἔχεις ὀλίγα ὀνόματα ἐν Σάρδεσιν ἃ οὐκ ἐμόλυναν τὰ ἱμάτια αὐτῶν, καὶ περιπατήσουσιν μετ᾽ ἐμοῦ ἐν λευκοῖς, ὅτι ἄξιοί εἰσιν. **5** ὁ νικῶν οὕτως περιβαλεῖται ἐν ἱματίοις λευκοῖς καὶ οὐ μὴ ἐξαλείψω τὸ ὄνομα αὐτοῦ ἐκ

²⁰Nevertheless, I have this against you: You tolerate that woman Jezebel, who calls herself a prophetess. By her teaching she misleads my servants into sexual immorality and the eating of food sacrificed to idols. ²¹I have given her time to repent of her immorality, but she is unwilling. ²²So I will cast her on a bed of suffering, and I will make those who commit adultery with her suffer intensely, unless they repent of her ways. ²³I will strike her children dead. Then all the churches will know that I am he who searches hearts and minds, and I will repay each of you according to your deeds. ²⁴Now I say to the rest of you in Thyatira, to you who do not hold to her teaching and have not learned Satan's so-called deep secrets (I will not impose any other burden on you): ²⁵Only hold on to what you have until I come.

²⁶To him who overcomes and does my will to the end, I will give authority over the nations—

²⁷'He will rule them with an iron scepter;
   he will dash them to pieces like pottery'^b—

just as I have received authority from my Father. ²⁸I will also give him the morning star. ²⁹He who has an ear, let him hear what the Spirit says to the churches.

To the Church in Sardis

3 "To the angel^a of the church in Sardis write:

These are the words of him who holds the seven spirits^b of God and the seven stars. I know your deeds; you have a reputation of being alive, but you are dead. ²Wake up! Strengthen what remains and is about to die, for I have not found your deeds complete in the sight of my God. ³Remember, therefore, what you have received and heard; obey it, and repent. But if you do not wake up, I will come like a thief, and you will not know at what time I will come to you.

⁴Yet you have a few people in Sardis who have not soiled their clothes. They will walk with me, dressed in white, for they are worthy. ⁵He who overcomes will, like them, be dressed in white. I will never blot out his name

---

I will confess your name before my Father and before his angels. 6Let anyone who has an ear listen to what the Spirit is saying to the churches.

The Message to Philadelphia

7 "And to the angel of the church in Philadelphia write:

These are the words of the holy one,
the true one,
who has the key of David,
who opens and no one will shut,
who shuts and no one opens:

8 "I know your works. Look, I have set before you an open door, which no one is able to shut. I know that you have but little power, and yet you have kept my word and have not denied my name. 9I will make those of the synagogue of Satan who say that they are Jews and are not, but are lying—I will make them come and bow down before your feet, and they will learn that I have loved you. 10Because you have kept my word of patient endurance, I will keep you from the hour of trial that is coming on the whole world to test the inhabitants of the earth. 11I am coming soon; hold fast to what you have, so that no one may seize your crown. 12If you conquer, I will make you a pillar in the temple of my God; you will never go out of it. I will write on you the name of my God, and the name of the city of my God, the new Jerusalem that comes down from my God out of heaven, and my own new name. 13Let anyone who has an ear listen to what the Spirit is saying to the churches.

The Message to Laodicea

14 "And to the angel of the church in Laodicea write: The words of the Amen, the faithful and true witness, the origin[1] of God's creation:

15 "I know your works; you are neither cold nor hot. I wish that you were either cold or hot. 16So, because you are lukewarm, and neither cold nor hot, I am about to spit you out of my mouth. 17For you say, 'I am rich, I have prospered, and I need nothing.' You do not realize that you are wretched, pitiable, poor, blind, and naked. 18Therefore I counsel you to buy from me gold refined by fire so that you may be rich; and white robes to clothe you

---

[1]Or beginning

τῆς βίβλου τῆς ζωῆς καὶ ὁμολογήσω τὸ ὄνομα αὐτοῦ ἐνώπιον τοῦ πατρός μου καὶ ἐνώπιον τῶν ἀγγέλων αὐτοῦ. **6** ὁ ἔχων οὖς ἀκουσάτω τί τὸ πνεῦμα λέγει ταῖς ἐκκλησίαις.

7 Καὶ τῷ ἀγγέλῳ τῆς ἐν Φιλαδελφείᾳ ἐκκλησίας γράψον·

Τάδε λέγει ὁ ἅγιος, ὁ ἀληθινός,
ὁ ἔχων τὴν κλεῖν Δαυίδ,
ὁ ἀνοίγων καὶ οὐδεὶς κλείσει
καὶ κλείων καὶ οὐδεὶς ἀνοίγει·

8 Οἶδά σου τὰ ἔργα, ἰδοὺ δέδωκα ἐνώπιόν σου θύραν ἠνεῳγμένην, ἣν οὐδεὶς δύναται κλεῖσαι αὐτήν, ὅτι μικρὰν ἔχεις δύναμιν καὶ ἐτήρησάς μου τὸν λόγον καὶ οὐκ ἠρνήσω τὸ ὄνομά μου. **9** ἰδοὺ διδῶ ἐκ τῆς συναγωγῆς τοῦ Σατανᾶ τῶν λεγόντων ἑαυτοὺς Ἰουδαίους εἶναι, καὶ οὐκ εἰσὶν ἀλλὰ ψεύδονται. ἰδοὺ ποιήσω αὐτοὺς ἵνα ἥξουσιν καὶ προσκυνήσουσιν ἐνώπιον τῶν ποδῶν σου καὶ γνῶσιν ὅτι ἐγὼ ἠγάπησά σε. **10** ὅτι ἐτήρησας τὸν λόγον τῆς ὑπομονῆς μου, κἀγώ σε τηρήσω ἐκ τῆς ὥρας τοῦ πειρασμοῦ τῆς μελλούσης ἔρχεσθαι ἐπὶ τῆς οἰκουμένης ὅλης πειράσαι τοὺς κατοικοῦντας ἐπὶ τῆς γῆς. **11** ἔρχομαι ταχύ· κράτει ὃ ἔχεις, ἵνα μηδεὶς λάβῃ τὸν στέφανόν σου. **12** ὁ νικῶν ποιήσω αὐτὸν στῦλον ἐν τῷ ναῷ τοῦ θεοῦ μου καὶ ἔξω οὐ μὴ ἐξέλθῃ ἔτι καὶ γράψω ἐπ' αὐτὸν τὸ ὄνομα τοῦ θεοῦ μου καὶ τὸ ὄνομα τῆς πόλεως τοῦ θεοῦ μου, τῆς καινῆς Ἰερουσαλὴμ ἡ καταβαίνουσα ἐκ τοῦ οὐρανοῦ ἀπὸ τοῦ θεοῦ μου, καὶ τὸ ὄνομά μου τὸ καινόν. **13** ὁ ἔχων οὖς ἀκουσάτω τί τὸ πνεῦμα λέγει ταῖς ἐκκλησίαις.

14 Καὶ τῷ ἀγγέλῳ τῆς ἐν Λαοδικείᾳ ἐκκλησίας γράψον·

Τάδε λέγει ὁ Ἀμήν, ὁ μάρτυς ὁ πιστὸς καὶ ἀληθινός, ἡ ἀρχὴ τῆς κτίσεως τοῦ θεοῦ· **15** Οἶδά σου τὰ ἔργα ὅτι οὔτε ψυχρὸς εἶ οὔτε ζεστός. ὄφελον ψυχρὸς ἦς ἢ ζεστός. **16** οὕτως ὅτι χλιαρὸς εἶ καὶ οὔτε ζεστὸς οὔτε ψυχρός, μέλλω σε ἐμέσαι ἐκ τοῦ στόματός μου. **17** ὅτι λέγεις ὅτι Πλούσιός εἰμι καὶ πεπλούτηκα καὶ οὐδὲν χρείαν ἔχω, καὶ οὐκ οἶδας ὅτι σὺ εἶ ὁ ταλαίπωρος καὶ ἐλεεινὸς καὶ πτωχὸς καὶ τυφλὸς καὶ γυμνός, **18** συμβουλεύω σοι ἀγοράσαι παρ' ἐμοῦ χρυσίον πεπυρωμένον ἐκ πυρὸς ἵνα πλουτήσῃς, καὶ ἱμάτια λευκὰ ἵνα

---

from the book of life, but will acknowledge his name before my Father and his angels. 6He who has an ear, let him hear what the Spirit says to the churches.

To the Church in Philadelphia

7"To the angel of the church in Philadelphia write:

These are the words of him who is holy and true, who holds the key of David. What he opens no one can shut, and what he shuts no one can open. 8I know your deeds. See, I have placed before you an open door that no one can shut. I know that you have little strength, yet you have kept my word and have not denied my name. 9I will make those who are of the synagogue of Satan, who claim to be Jews though they are not, but are liars—I will make them come and fall down at your feet and acknowledge that I have loved you. 10Since you have kept my command to endure patiently, I will also keep you from the hour of trial that is going to come upon the whole world to test those who live on the earth.

11I am coming soon. Hold on to what you have, so that no one will take your crown. 12Him who overcomes I will make a pillar in the temple of my God. Never again will he leave it. I will write on him the name of my God and the name of the city of my God, the new Jerusalem, which is coming down out of heaven from my God; and I will also write on him my new name. 13He who has an ear, let him hear what the Spirit says to the churches.

To the Church in Laodicea

14"To the angel of the church in Laodicea write:

These are the words of the Amen, the faithful and true witness, the ruler of God's creation. 15I know your deeds, that you are neither cold nor hot. I wish you were either one or the other! 16So, because you are lukewarm—neither hot nor cold—I am about to spit you out of my mouth. 17You say, 'I am rich; I have acquired wealth and do not need a thing.' But you do not realize that you are wretched, pitiful, poor, blind and naked. 18I counsel you to buy from me gold refined in the fire, so you can become rich; and white clothes to wear, and to keep the shame of your nakedness from being seen; and salve to anoint your eyes so that you may see. [19]I reprove and discipline those whom I love. Be earnest, therefore, and repent. [20]Listen! I am standing at the door, knocking; if you hear my voice and open the door, I will come in to you and eat with you, and you with me. [21]To the one who conquers I will give a place with me on my throne, just as I myself conquered and sat down with my Father on his throne. [22]Let anyone who has an ear listen to what the Spirit is saying to the churches."

The Heavenly Worship

4 After this I looked, and there in heaven a door stood open! And the first voice, which I had heard speaking to me like a trumpet, said, "Come up here, and I will show you what must take place after this." [2]At once I was in the spirit,[m] and there in heaven stood a throne, with one seated on the throne! [3]And the one seated there looks like jasper and carnelian, and around the throne is a rainbow that looks like an emerald. [4]Around the throne are twenty-four thrones, and seated on the thrones are twenty-four elders, dressed in white robes, with golden crowns on their heads. [5]Coming from the throne are flashes of lightning, and rumblings and peals of thunder, and in front of the throne burn seven flaming torches, which are the seven spirits of God; [6]and in front of the throne there is something like a sea of glass, like crystal.

Around the throne, and on each side of the throne, are four living creatures, full of eyes in front and behind: [7]the first living creature like a lion, the second living creature like an ox, the third living creature with a face like a human face, and the fourth living creature like a flying eagle. [8]And the four living creatures, each of them with six wings, are full of eyes all around and inside. Day and night without ceasing they sing,

"Holy, holy, holy,
the Lord God the Almighty,
who was and is and is to come."

[9]And whenever the living creatures give glory and honor and thanks to the one who is seated on the throne, who lives forever and ever, [10]the twenty-four elders fall before the one who is seated on the throne and worship the one who lives

ᵐ Or *in the Spirit*

περιβάλῃ καὶ μὴ φανερωθῇ ἡ αἰσχύνη τῆς γυμνότητός σου, καὶ κολλ[ο]ύριον ἐγχρῖσαι τοὺς ὀφθαλμούς σου ἵνα βλέπῃς. **19** ἐγὼ ὅσους ἐὰν φιλῶ ἐλέγχω καὶ παιδεύω· ζήλευε οὖν καὶ μετανόησον. **20** ἰδοὺ ἔστηκα ἐπὶ τὴν θύραν καὶ κρούω· ἐάν τις ἀκούσῃ τῆς φωνῆς μου καὶ ἀνοίξῃ τὴν θύραν, [καὶ] εἰσελεύσομαι πρὸς αὐτὸν καὶ δειπνήσω μετ᾽ αὐτοῦ καὶ αὐτὸς μετ᾽ ἐμοῦ. **21** ὁ νικῶν δώσω αὐτῷ καθίσαι μετ᾽ ἐμοῦ ἐν τῷ θρόνῳ μου, ὡς κἀγὼ ἐνίκησα καὶ ἐκάθισα μετὰ τοῦ πατρός μου ἐν τῷ θρόνῳ αὐτοῦ. **22** ὁ ἔχων οὖς ἀκουσάτω τί τὸ πνεῦμα λέγει ταῖς ἐκκλησίαις.

4 Μετὰ ταῦτα εἶδον, καὶ ἰδοὺ θύρα ἠνεῳγμένη ἐν τῷ οὐρανῷ, καὶ ἡ φωνὴ ἡ πρώτη ἣν ἤκουσα ὡς σάλπιγγος λαλούσης μετ᾽ ἐμοῦ λέγων, Ἀνάβα ὧδε, καὶ δείξω σοι ἃ δεῖ γενέσθαι μετὰ ταῦτα. **2** εὐθέως ἐγενόμην ἐν πνεύματι, καὶ ἰδοὺ θρόνος ἔκειτο ἐν τῷ οὐρανῷ, καὶ ἐπὶ τὸν θρόνον καθήμενος, **3** καὶ ὁ καθήμενος ὅμοιος ὁράσει λίθῳ ἰάσπιδι καὶ σαρδίῳ, καὶ ἶρις κυκλόθεν τοῦ θρόνου ὅμοιος ὁράσει σμαραγδίνῳ. **4** καὶ κυκλόθεν τοῦ θρόνου θρόνους εἴκοσι τέσσαρες, καὶ ἐπὶ τοὺς θρόνους εἴκοσι τέσσαρας πρεσβυτέρους καθημένους περιβεβλημένους ἐν ἱματίοις λευκοῖς καὶ ἐπὶ τὰς κεφαλὰς αὐτῶν στεφάνους χρυσοῦς. **5** καὶ ἐκ τοῦ θρόνου ἐκπορεύονται ἀστραπαὶ καὶ φωναὶ καὶ βρονταί, καὶ ἑπτὰ λαμπάδες πυρὸς καιόμεναι ἐνώπιον τοῦ θρόνου, ἅ εἰσιν τὰ ἑπτὰ πνεύματα τοῦ θεοῦ, **6** καὶ ἐνώπιον τοῦ θρόνου ὡς θάλασσα ὑαλίνη ὁμοία κρυστάλλῳ.

Καὶ ἐν μέσῳ τοῦ θρόνου καὶ κύκλῳ τοῦ θρόνου τέσσαρα ζῷα γέμοντα ὀφθαλμῶν ἔμπροσθεν καὶ ὄπισθεν. **7** καὶ τὸ ζῷον τὸ πρῶτον ὅμοιον λέοντι καὶ τὸ δεύτερον ζῷον ὅμοιον μόσχῳ καὶ τὸ τρίτον ζῷον ἔχων τὸ πρόσωπον ὡς ἀνθρώπου καὶ τὸ τέταρτον ζῷον ὅμοιον ἀετῷ πετομένῳ. **8** καὶ τὰ τέσσαρα ζῷα, ἓν καθ᾽ ἓν αὐτῶν ἔχων ἀνὰ πτέρυγας ἕξ, κυκλόθεν καὶ ἔσωθεν γέμουσιν ὀφθαλμῶν, καὶ ἀνάπαυσιν οὐκ ἔχουσιν ἡμέρας καὶ νυκτὸς λέγοντες,

Ἅγιος ἅγιος ἅγιος
κύριος ὁ θεὸς ὁ παντοκράτωρ,
ὁ ἦν καὶ ὁ ὢν καὶ ὁ ἐρχόμενος.

9 καὶ ὅταν δώσουσιν τὰ ζῷα δόξαν καὶ τιμὴν καὶ εὐχαριστίαν τῷ καθημένῳ ἐπὶ τῷ θρόνῳ τῷ ζῶντι εἰς τοὺς αἰῶνας τῶν αἰώνων, **10** πεσοῦνται οἱ εἴκοσι τέσσαρες πρεσβύτεροι ἐνώπιον τοῦ καθημένου ἐπὶ τοῦ θρόνου καὶ

so you can cover your shameful nakedness; and salve to put on your eyes, so you can see.

[19]Those whom I love I rebuke and discipline. So be earnest, and repent. [20]Here I am! I stand at the door and knock. If anyone hears my voice and opens the door, I will come in and eat with him, and he with me.

[21]To him who overcomes, I will give the right to sit with me on my throne, just as I overcame and sat down with my Father on his throne. [22]He who has an ear, let him hear what the Spirit says to the churches."

The Throne in Heaven

4 After this I looked, and there before me was a door standing open in heaven. And the voice I had first heard speaking to me like a trumpet said, "Come up here, and I will show you what must take place after this." [2]At once I was in the Spirit, and there before me was a throne in heaven with someone sitting on it. [3]And the one who sat there had the appearance of jasper and carnelian. A rainbow, resembling an emerald, encircled the throne. [4]Surrounding the throne were twenty-four other thrones, and seated on them were twenty-four elders. They were dressed in white and had crowns of gold on their heads. [5]From the throne came flashes of lightning, rumblings and peals of thunder. Before the throne, seven lamps were blazing. These are the seven spirits[a] of God. [6]Also before the throne there was what looked like a sea of glass, clear as crystal.

In the center, around the throne, were four living creatures, and they were covered with eyes, in front and in back. [7]The first living creature was like a lion, the second was like an ox, the third had a face like a man, the fourth was like a flying eagle. [8]Each of the four living creatures had six wings and was covered with eyes all around, even under his wings. Day and night they never stop saying:

"Holy, holy, holy
is the Lord God Almighty,
who was, and is, and is to come."

[9]Whenever the living creatures give glory, honor and thanks to him who sits on the throne and who lives for ever and ever, [10]the twenty-four elders fall down before him who sits on the throne, and worship

ᵃ5,6 Or *the sevenfold Spirit*

forever and ever; they cast their crowns before the throne, singing,

11 "You are worthy, our Lord and God,
    to receive glory and honor and power,
    for you created all things,
    and by your will they existed and
        were created."

The Scroll and the Lamb

5 Then I saw in the right hand of the one seated on the throne a scroll written on the inside and on the back, sealed[n] with seven seals; [2]and I saw a mighty angel proclaiming with a loud voice, "Who is worthy to open the scroll and break its seals?" [3]And no one in heaven or on earth or under the earth was able to open the scroll or to look into it. [4]And I began to weep bitterly because no one was found worthy to open the scroll or to look into it. [5]Then one of the elders said to me, "Do not weep. See, the Lion of the tribe of Judah, the Root of David, has conquered, so that he can open the scroll and its seven seals."

6 Then I saw between the throne and the four living creatures and among the elders a Lamb standing as if it had been slaughtered, having seven horns and seven eyes, which are the seven spirits of God sent out into all the earth. [7]He went and took the scroll from the right hand of the one who was seated on the throne. [8]When he had taken the scroll, the four living creatures and the twenty-four elders fell before the Lamb, each holding a harp and golden bowls full of incense, which are the prayers of the saints. [9]They sing a new song:

"You are worthy to take the scroll
    and to open its seals,
for you were slaughtered and by your
        blood you ransomed for God
    saints from[o] every tribe and
        language and people and nation;
10 you have made them to be a kingdom
        and priests serving[p] our God,
    and they will reign on earth."

11 Then I looked, and I heard the voice of many angels surrounding the throne and the living creatures and the elders; they numbered myriads of myriads and thousands of thousands, [12]singing with full voice,

προσκυνήσουσιν τῷ ζῶντι εἰς τοὺς
αἰῶνας τῶν αἰώνων καὶ βαλοῦσιν τοὺς
στεφάνους αὐτῶν ἐνώπιον τοῦ θρόνου
λέγοντες,
11 Ἄξιος εἶ, ὁ κύριος καὶ ὁ θεὸς
        ἡμῶν,
    λαβεῖν τὴν δόξαν καὶ τὴν τιμὴν
        καὶ τὴν δύναμιν,
    ὅτι σὺ ἔκτισας τὰ πάντα
    καὶ διὰ τὸ θέλημά σου ἦσαν καὶ
        ἐκτίσθησαν.

5 Καὶ εἶδον ἐπὶ τὴν δεξιὰν τοῦ καθημένου ἐπὶ τοῦ θρόνου βιβλίον γεγραμμένον ἔσωθεν καὶ ὄπισθεν κατεσφραγισμένον σφραγῖσιν ἑπτά. 2 καὶ εἶδον ἄγγελον ἰσχυρὸν κηρύσσοντα ἐν φωνῇ μεγάλῃ, Τίς ἄξιος ἀνοῖξαι τὸ βιβλίον καὶ λῦσαι τὰς σφραγῖδας αὐτοῦ; 3 καὶ οὐδεὶς ἐδύνατο ἐν τῷ οὐρανῷ οὐδὲ ἐπὶ τῆς γῆς οὐδὲ ὑποκάτω τῆς γῆς ἀνοῖξαι τὸ βιβλίον οὔτε βλέπειν αὐτό. 4 καὶ ἔκλαιον πολύ, ὅτι οὐδεὶς ἄξιος εὑρέθη ἀνοῖξαι τὸ βιβλίον οὔτε βλέπειν αὐτό. 5 καὶ εἷς ἐκ τῶν πρεσβυτέρων λέγει μοι, Μὴ κλαῖε, ἰδοὺ ἐνίκησεν ὁ λέων ὁ ἐκ τῆς φυλῆς Ἰούδα, ἡ ῥίζα Δαυίδ, ἀνοῖξαι τὸ βιβλίον καὶ τὰς ἑπτὰ σφραγῖδας αὐτοῦ.

6 Καὶ εἶδον ἐν μέσῳ τοῦ θρόνου καὶ τῶν τεσσάρων ζῴων καὶ ἐν μέσῳ τῶν πρεσβυτέρων ἀρνίον ἑστηκὸς ὡς ἐσφαγμένον ἔχων κέρατα ἑπτὰ καὶ ὀφθαλμοὺς ἑπτὰ οἵ εἰσιν τὰ [ἑπτὰ] πνεύματα τοῦ θεοῦ ἀπεσταλμένοι εἰς πᾶσαν τὴν γῆν. 7 καὶ ἦλθεν καὶ εἴληφεν ἐκ τῆς δεξιᾶς τοῦ καθημένου ἐπὶ τοῦ θρόνου. 8 καὶ ὅτε ἔλαβεν τὸ βιβλίον, τὰ τέσσαρα ζῷα καὶ οἱ εἴκοσι τέσσαρες πρεσβύτεροι ἔπεσαν ἐνώπιον τοῦ ἀρνίου ἔχοντες ἕκαστος κιθάραν καὶ φιάλας χρυσᾶς γεμούσας θυμιαμάτων, αἵ εἰσιν αἱ προσευχαὶ τῶν ἁγίων, 9 καὶ ᾄδουσιν ᾠδὴν καινὴν λέγοντες,

Ἄξιος εἶ λαβεῖν τὸ βιβλίον
    καὶ ἀνοῖξαι τὰς σφραγῖδας αὐτοῦ,
    ὅτι ἐσφάγης καὶ ἠγόρασας τῷ θεῷ
        ἐν τῷ αἵματί σου
    ἐκ πάσης φυλῆς καὶ γλώσσης
        καὶ λαοῦ καὶ ἔθνους
10 καὶ ἐποίησας αὐτοὺς τῷ θεῷ ἡμῶν
        βασιλείαν καὶ ἱερεῖς,
    καὶ βασιλεύσουσιν ἐπὶ τῆς γῆς.

11 Καὶ εἶδον, καὶ ἤκουσα φωνὴν ἀγγέλων πολλῶν κύκλῳ τοῦ θρόνου καὶ τῶν ζῴων καὶ τῶν πρεσβυτέρων, καὶ ἦν ὁ ἀριθμὸς αὐτῶν μυριάδες μυριάδων καὶ χιλιάδες χιλιάδων 12 λέγοντες φωνῇ μεγάλῃ,

him who lives for ever and ever. They lay their crowns before the throne and say:

[11]"You are worthy, our Lord and God,
    to receive glory and honor and power,
    for you created all things,
    and by your will they were created
        and have their being."

The Scroll and the Lamb

5 Then I saw in the right hand of him who sat on the throne a scroll with writing on both sides and sealed with seven seals. [2]And I saw a mighty angel proclaiming in a loud voice, "Who is worthy to break the seals and open the scroll?" [3]But no one in heaven or on earth or under the earth could open the scroll or even look inside it. [4]I wept and wept because no one was found who was worthy to open the scroll or look inside. [5]Then one of the elders said to me, "Do not weep! See, the Lion of the tribe of Judah, the Root of David, has triumphed. He is able to open the scroll and its seven seals."

[6]Then I saw a Lamb, looking as if it had been slain, standing in the center of the throne, encircled by the four living creatures and the elders. He had seven horns and seven eyes, which are the seven spirits[a] of God sent out into all the earth. [7]He came and took the scroll from the right hand of him who sat on the throne. [8]And when he had taken it, the four living creatures and the twenty-four elders fell down before the Lamb. Each one had a harp and they were holding golden bowls full of incense, which are the prayers of the saints. [9]And they sang a new song:

"You are worthy to take the scroll
    and to open its seals,
because you were slain,
    and with your blood you purchased
        men for God
    from every tribe and language and
        people and nation.
[10]You have made them to be a kingdom
        and priests to serve our God,
    and they will reign on the earth."

[11]Then I looked and heard the voice of many angels, numbering thousands upon thousands, and ten thousand times ten thousand. They encircled the throne and the living creatures and the elders. [12]In a loud voice they sang:

"Worthy is the Lamb that was
slaughtered
to receive power and wealth and
wisdom and might
and honor and glory and blessing!"

¹³Then I heard every creature in heaven and on earth and under the earth and in the sea, and all that is in them, singing,

"To the one seated on the throne and
to the Lamb
be blessing and honor and glory and
might
forever and ever!"

¹⁴And the four living creatures said, "Amen!" And the elders fell down and worshiped.

The Seven Seals

6 Then I saw the Lamb open one of the seven seals, and I heard one of the four living creatures call out, as with a voice of thunder, "Come!"[q] ²I looked, and there was a white horse! Its rider had a bow; a crown was given to him, and he came out conquering and to conquer.

3 When he opened the second seal, I heard the second living creature call out, "Come!"[q] ⁴And out came[r] another horse, bright red; its rider was permitted to take peace from the earth, so that people would slaughter one another; and he was given a great sword.

5 When he opened the third seal, I heard the third living creature call out, "Come!"[q] I looked, and there was a black horse! Its rider held a pair of scales in his hand, ⁶and I heard what seemed to be a voice in the midst of the four living creatures saying, "A quart of wheat for a day's pay,[s] and three quarts of barley for a day's pay,[s] but do not damage the olive oil and the wine!"

7 When he opened the fourth seal, I heard the voice of the fourth living creature call out, "Come!"[q] ⁸I looked and there was a pale green horse! Its rider's name was Death, and Hades followed with him; they were given authority over a fourth of the earth, to kill with sword, famine, and pestilence, and by the wild animals of the earth.

9 When he opened the fifth seal, I saw under the altar the souls of those who had been slaughtered for the word of God and for the testimony they had given; ¹⁰they cried out with a loud voice, "Sovereign Lord, holy and true, how long will it be

---

Ἄξιόν ἐστιν τὸ ἀρνίον τὸ
ἐσφαγμένον λαβεῖν
τὴν δύναμιν καὶ πλοῦτον καὶ
σοφίαν καὶ ἰσχὺν
καὶ τιμὴν καὶ δόξαν καὶ εὐλογίαν.

13 καὶ πᾶν κτίσμα ὃ ἐν τῷ οὐρανῷ καὶ ἐπὶ τῆς γῆς καὶ ὑποκάτω τῆς γῆς καὶ ἐπὶ τῆς θαλάσσης καὶ τὰ ἐν αὐτοῖς πάντα ἤκουσα λέγοντας,

Τῷ καθημένῳ ἐπὶ τῷ θρόνῳ καὶ
τῷ ἀρνίῳ
ἡ εὐλογία καὶ ἡ τιμὴ καὶ ἡ δόξα
καὶ τὸ κράτος
εἰς τοὺς αἰῶνας τῶν αἰώνων.

14 καὶ τὰ τέσσαρα ζῷα ἔλεγον, Ἀμήν. καὶ οἱ πρεσβύτεροι ἔπεσαν καὶ προσεκύνησαν.

6 Καὶ εἶδον ὅτε ἤνοιξεν τὸ ἀρνίον μίαν ἐκ τῶν ἑπτὰ σφραγίδων, καὶ ἤκουσα ἑνὸς ἐκ τῶν τεσσάρων ζῴων λέγοντος ὡς φωνὴ βροντῆς, Ἔρχου. **2** καὶ εἶδον, καὶ ἰδοὺ ἵππος λευκός, καὶ ὁ καθήμενος ἐπ᾽ αὐτὸν ἔχων τόξον καὶ ἐδόθη αὐτῷ στέφανος καὶ ἐξῆλθεν νικῶν καὶ ἵνα νικήσῃ.

3 Καὶ ὅτε ἤνοιξεν τὴν σφραγῖδα τὴν δευτέραν, ἤκουσα τοῦ δευτέρου ζῴου λέγοντος, Ἔρχου. **4** καὶ ἐξῆλθεν ἄλλος ἵππος πυρρός, καὶ τῷ καθημένῳ ἐπ᾽ αὐτὸν ἐδόθη αὐτῷ λαβεῖν τὴν εἰρήνην ἐκ τῆς γῆς καὶ ἵνα ἀλλήλους σφάξουσιν καὶ ἐδόθη αὐτῷ μάχαιρα μεγάλη.

5 Καὶ ὅτε ἤνοιξεν τὴν σφραγῖδα τὴν τρίτην, ἤκουσα τοῦ τρίτου ζῴου λέγοντος, Ἔρχου. καὶ εἶδον, καὶ ἰδοὺ ἵππος μέλας, καὶ ὁ καθήμενος ἐπ᾽ αὐτὸν ἔχων ζυγὸν ἐν τῇ χειρὶ αὐτοῦ. **6** καὶ ἤκουσα ὡς φωνὴν ἐν μέσῳ τῶν τεσσάρων ζῴων λέγουσαν, Χοῖνιξ σίτου δηναρίου καὶ τρεῖς χοίνικες κριθῶν δηναρίου, καὶ τὸ ἔλαιον καὶ τὸν οἶνον μὴ ἀδικήσῃς.

7 Καὶ ὅτε ἤνοιξεν τὴν σφραγῖδα τὴν τετάρτην, ἤκουσα φωνὴν τοῦ τετάρτου ζῴου λέγοντος, Ἔρχου. **8** καὶ εἶδον, καὶ ἰδοὺ ἵππος χλωρός, καὶ ὁ καθήμενος ἐπάνω αὐτοῦ ὄνομα αὐτῷ [ὁ] Θάνατος, καὶ ὁ ᾅδης ἠκολούθει μετ᾽ αὐτοῦ καὶ ἐδόθη αὐτοῖς ἐξουσία ἐπὶ τὸ τέταρτον τῆς γῆς ἀποκτεῖναι ἐν ῥομφαίᾳ καὶ ἐν λιμῷ καὶ ἐν θανάτῳ καὶ ὑπὸ τῶν θηρίων τῆς γῆς.

9 Καὶ ὅτε ἤνοιξεν τὴν πέμπτην σφραγῖδα, εἶδον ὑποκάτω τοῦ θυσιαστηρίου τὰς ψυχὰς τῶν ἐσφαγμένων διὰ τὸν λόγον τοῦ θεοῦ καὶ διὰ τὴν μαρτυρίαν ἣν εἶχον. **10** καὶ ἔκραξαν φωνῇ μεγάλῃ λέγοντες, Ἕως πότε, ὁ δεσπότης ὁ ἅγιος καὶ ἀληθινός, οὐ κρίνεις καὶ

"Worthy is the Lamb, who was slain,
to receive power and wealth and
wisdom and strength
and honor and glory and praise!"

¹³Then I heard every creature in heaven and on earth and under the earth and on the sea, and all that is in them, singing:

"To him who sits on the throne and to
the Lamb
be praise and honor and glory and power,
for ever and ever!"

¹⁴The four living creatures said, "Amen," and the elders fell down and worshiped.

The Seals

6 I watched as the Lamb opened the first of the seven seals. Then I heard one of the four living creatures say in a voice like thunder, "Come!" ²I looked, and there before me was a white horse! Its rider held a bow, and he was given a crown, and he rode out as a conqueror bent on conquest.

³When the Lamb opened the second seal, I heard the second living creature say, "Come!" ⁴Then another horse came out, a fiery red one. Its rider was given power to take peace from the earth and to make men slay each other. To him was given a large sword.

⁵When the Lamb opened the third seal, I heard the third living creature say, "Come!" I looked, and there before me was a black horse! Its rider was holding a pair of scales in his hand. ⁶Then I heard what sounded like a voice among the four living creatures, saying, "A quart[a] of wheat for a day's wages,[b] and three quarts of barley for a day's wages,[b] and do not damage the oil and the wine!"

⁷When the Lamb opened the fourth seal, I heard the voice of the fourth living creature say, "Come!" ⁸I looked, and there before me was a pale horse! Its rider was named Death, and Hades was following close behind him. They were given power over a fourth of the earth to kill by sword, famine and plague, and by the wild beasts of the earth.

⁹When he opened the fifth seal, I saw under the altar the souls of those who had been slain because of the word of God and the testimony they had maintained. ¹⁰They called out in a loud voice, "How long, Sovereign Lord, holy and true, until you

---

^q Or "Go!"   ^r Or went   ^s Gk *a denarius*

^a6 Greek *a choinix* (probably about a liter)   ^b6 Greek *a denarius*

before you judge and avenge our blood on the inhabitants of the earth?" [11]They were each given a white robe and told to rest a little longer, until the number would be complete both of their fellow servants[t] and of their brothers and sisters,[u] who were soon to be killed as they themselves had been killed.

12 When he opened the sixth seal, I looked, and there came a great earthquake; the sun became black as sackcloth, the full moon became like blood, [13]and the stars of the sky fell to the earth as the fig tree drops its winter fruit when shaken by a gale. [14]The sky vanished like a scroll rolling itself up, and every mountain and island was removed from its place. [15]Then the kings of the earth and the magnates and the generals and the rich and the powerful, and everyone, slave and free, hid in the caves and among the rocks of the mountains, [16]calling to the mountains and rocks, "Fall on us and hide us from the face of the one seated on the throne and from the wrath of the Lamb; [17]for the great day of their wrath has come, and who is able to stand?"

The 144,000 of Israel Sealed

7 After this I saw four angels standing at the four corners of the earth, holding back the four winds of the earth so that no wind could blow on earth or sea or against any tree. [2]I saw another angel ascending from the rising of the sun, having the seal of the living God, and he called with a loud voice to the four angels who had been given power to damage earth and sea, [3]saying, "Do not damage the earth or the sea or the trees, until we have marked the servants[t] of our God with a seal on their foreheads."

4 And I heard the number of those who were sealed, one hundred forty-four thousand, sealed out of every tribe of the people of Israel:

5 From the tribe of Judah twelve
    thousand sealed,
  from the tribe of Reuben twelve
    thousand,
  from the tribe of Gad twelve thousand,
6 from the tribe of Asher twelve
    thousand,
  from the tribe of Naphtali twelve
    thousand,
  from the tribe of Manasseh twelve
    thousand,

ἐκδικεῖς τὸ αἷμα ἡμῶν ἐκ τῶν κατοικούντων ἐπὶ τῆς γῆς; 11 καὶ ἐδόθη αὐτοῖς ἑκάστῳ στολὴ λευκὴ καὶ ἐρρέθη αὐτοῖς ἵνα ἀναπαύσονται ἔτι χρόνον μικρόν, ἕως πληρωθῶσιν καὶ οἱ σύνδουλοι αὐτῶν καὶ οἱ ἀδελφοὶ αὐτῶν οἱ μέλλοντες ἀποκτέννεσθαι ὡς καὶ αὐτοί.

12 Καὶ εἶδον ὅτε ἤνοιξεν τὴν σφραγῖδα τὴν ἕκτην, καὶ σεισμὸς μέγας ἐγένετο καὶ ὁ ἥλιος ἐγένετο μέλας ὡς σάκκος τρίχινος καὶ ἡ σελήνη ὅλη ἐγένετο ὡς αἷμα 13 καὶ οἱ ἀστέρες τοῦ οὐρανοῦ ἔπεσαν εἰς τὴν γῆν, ὡς συκῆ βάλλει τοὺς ὀλύνθους αὐτῆς ὑπὸ ἀνέμου μεγάλου σειομένη, 14 καὶ ὁ οὐρανὸς ἀπεχωρίσθη ὡς βιβλίον ἑλισσόμενον καὶ πᾶν ὄρος καὶ νῆσος ἐκ τῶν τόπων αὐτῶν ἐκινήθησαν. 15 καὶ οἱ βασιλεῖς τῆς γῆς καὶ οἱ μεγιστᾶνες καὶ οἱ χιλίαρχοι καὶ οἱ πλούσιοι καὶ οἱ ἰσχυροὶ καὶ πᾶς δοῦλος καὶ ἐλεύθερος ἔκρυψαν ἑαυτοὺς εἰς τὰ σπήλαια καὶ εἰς τὰς πέτρας τῶν ὀρέων 16 καὶ λέγουσιν τοῖς ὄρεσιν καὶ ταῖς πέτραις, Πέσετε ἐφ᾽ ἡμᾶς καὶ κρύψατε ἡμᾶς ἀπὸ προσώπου τοῦ καθημένου ἐπὶ τοῦ θρόνου καὶ ἀπὸ τῆς ὀργῆς τοῦ ἀρνίου, 17 ὅτι ἦλθεν ἡ ἡμέρα ἡ μεγάλη τῆς ὀργῆς αὐτῶν, καὶ τίς δύναται σταθῆναι;

7 Μετὰ τοῦτο εἶδον τέσσαρας ἀγγέλους ἑστῶτας ἐπὶ τὰς τέσσαρας γωνίας τῆς γῆς, κρατοῦντας τοὺς τέσσαρας ἀνέμους τῆς γῆς ἵνα μὴ πνέῃ ἄνεμος ἐπὶ τῆς γῆς μήτε ἐπὶ τῆς θαλάσσης μήτε ἐπὶ πᾶν δένδρον. 2 καὶ εἶδον ἄλλον ἄγγελον ἀναβαίνοντα ἀπὸ ἀνατολῆς ἡλίου ἔχοντα σφραγῖδα θεοῦ ζῶντος, καὶ ἔκραξεν φωνῇ μεγάλῃ τοῖς τέσσαρσιν ἀγγέλοις οἷς ἐδόθη αὐτοῖς ἀδικῆσαι τὴν γῆν καὶ τὴν θάλασσαν 3 λέγων, Μὴ ἀδικήσητε τὴν γῆν μήτε τὴν θάλασσαν μήτε τὰ δένδρα, ἄχρι σφραγίσωμεν τοὺς δούλους τοῦ θεοῦ ἡμῶν ἐπὶ τῶν μετώπων αὐτῶν. 4 καὶ ἤκουσα τὸν ἀριθμὸν τῶν ἐσφραγισμένων, ἑκατὸν τεσσεράκοντα τέσσαρες χιλιάδες, ἐσφραγισμένοι ἐκ πάσης φυλῆς υἱῶν Ἰσραήλ·

5 ἐκ φυλῆς Ἰούδα δώδεκα χιλιάδες
    ἐσφραγισμένοι,
  ἐκ φυλῆς Ῥουβὴν δώδεκα χιλιάδες,
  ἐκ φυλῆς Γὰδ δώδεκα χιλιάδες,
6 ἐκ φυλῆς Ἀσὴρ δώδεκα χιλιάδες,
  ἐκ φυλῆς Νεφθαλὶμ δώδεκα χιλιάδες,
  ἐκ φυλῆς Μανασσῆ δώδεκα χιλιάδες,

judge the inhabitants of the earth and avenge our blood?" [11]Then each of them was given a white robe, and they were told to wait a little longer, until the number of their fellow servants and brothers who were to be killed as they had been was completed.

[12]I watched as he opened the sixth seal. There was a great earthquake. The sun turned black like sackcloth made of goat hair, the whole moon turned blood red, [13]and the stars in the sky fell to earth, as late figs drop from a fig tree when shaken by a strong wind. [14]The sky receded like a scroll, rolling up, and every mountain and island was removed from its place.

[15]Then the kings of the earth, the princes, the generals, the rich, the mighty, and every slave and every free man hid in caves and among the rocks of the mountains. [16]They called to the mountains and the rocks, "Fall on us and hide us from the face of him who sits on the throne and from the wrath of the Lamb! [17]For the great day of their wrath has come, and who can stand?"

144,000 Sealed

7 After this I saw four angels standing at the four corners of the earth, holding back the four winds of the earth to prevent any wind from blowing on the land or on the sea or on any tree. [2]Then I saw another angel coming up from the east, having the seal of the living God. He called out in a loud voice to the four angels who had been given power to harm the land and the sea: [3]"Do not harm the land or the sea or the trees until we put a seal on the foreheads of the servants of our God." [4]Then I heard the number of those who were sealed: 144,000 from all the tribes of Israel.

[5]From the tribe of Judah 12,000 were
    sealed,
  from the tribe of Reuben 12,000,
  from the tribe of Gad 12,000,
[6]from the tribe of Asher 12,000,
  from the tribe of Naphtali 12,000,
  from the tribe of Manasseh 12,000,

NRSV

7 from the tribe of Simeon twelve
thousand,
from the tribe of Levi twelve thousand,
from the tribe of Issachar twelve
thousand,
8 from the tribe of Zebulun twelve
thousand,
from the tribe of Joseph twelve
thousand,
from the tribe of Benjamin twelve
thousand sealed.

The Multitude from Every Nation

9 After this I looked, and there was a
great multitude that no one could count,
from every nation, from all tribes and
peoples and languages, standing before the
throne and before the Lamb, robed in
white, with palm branches in their hands.
10They cried out in a loud voice, saying,

"Salvation belongs to our God who is
seated on the throne, and to the
Lamb!"

11And all the angels stood around the
throne and around the elders and the four
living creatures, and they fell on their faces
before the throne and worshiped God,
12singing,

"Amen! Blessing and glory and
wisdom
and thanksgiving and honor
and power and might
be to our God forever and ever! Amen."

13 Then one of the elders addressed me,
saying, "Who are these, robed in white,
and where have they come from?" 14I said
to him, "Sir, you are the one that knows."
Then he said to me, "These are they who
have come out of the great ordeal; they
have washed their robes and made them
white in the blood of the Lamb.

15 For this reason they are before the
throne of God,
and worship him day and night
within his temple,
and the one who is seated on the
throne will shelter them.
16 They will hunger no more, and thirst
no more;
the sun will not strike them,
nor any scorching heat;
17 for the Lamb at the center of the
throne will be their shepherd,
and he will guide them to springs of
the water of life,
and God will wipe away every tear
from their eyes."

Greek

7 ἐκ φυλῆς Συμεὼν δώδεκα χιλιάδες,
ἐκ φυλῆς Λευὶ δώδεκα χιλιάδες,
ἐκ φυλῆς Ἰσσαχὰρ δώδεκα
χιλιάδες,
8 ἐκ φυλῆς Ζαβουλὼν δώδεκα
χιλιάδες,
ἐκ φυλῆς Ἰωσὴφ δώδεκα χιλιάδες,
ἐκ φυλῆς Βενιαμὶν δώδεκα
χιλιάδες ἐσφραγισμένοι.
9 Μετὰ ταῦτα εἶδον, καὶ ἰδοὺ ὄχλος
πολύς, ὃν ἀριθμῆσαι αὐτὸν οὐδεὶς
ἐδύνατο, ἐκ παντὸς ἔθνους καὶ φυλῶν
καὶ λαῶν καὶ γλωσσῶν ἑστῶτες ἐνώπιον
τοῦ θρόνου καὶ ἐνώπιον τοῦ ἀρνίου
περιβεβλημένους στολὰς λευκὰς καὶ
φοίνικες ἐν ταῖς χερσὶν αὐτῶν, **10** καὶ
κράζουσιν φωνῇ μεγάλῃ λέγοντες,
Ἡ σωτηρία τῷ θεῷ ἡμῶν τῷ καθημένῳ ἐπὶ τῷ θρόνῳ καὶ τῷ ἀρνίῳ.
11 καὶ πάντες οἱ ἄγγελοι εἱστήκεισαν
κύκλῳ τοῦ θρόνου καὶ τῶν πρεσβυτέρων
καὶ τῶν τεσσάρων ζῴων καὶ ἔπεσαν
ἐνώπιον τοῦ θρόνου ἐπὶ τὰ πρόσωπα
αὐτῶν καὶ προσεκύνησαν τῷ θεῷ
12 λέγοντες,
Ἀμήν, ἡ εὐλογία καὶ ἡ δόξα
καὶ ἡ σοφία καὶ ἡ εὐχαριστία
καὶ ἡ τιμὴ καὶ ἡ δύναμις
καὶ ἡ ἰσχὺς τῷ θεῷ ἡμῶν
εἰς τοὺς αἰῶνας τῶν αἰώνων·
ἀμήν.
13 Καὶ ἀπεκρίθη εἷς ἐκ τῶν πρεσβυτέρων λέγων μοι, Οὗτοι οἱ περιβεβλημένοι τὰς στολὰς τὰς λευκὰς τίνες
εἰσὶν καὶ πόθεν ἦλθον; **14** καὶ εἴρηκα
αὐτῷ, Κύριέ μου, σὺ οἶδας. καὶ εἶπέν
μοι, Οὗτοί εἰσιν οἱ ἐρχόμενοι ἐκ τῆς
θλίψεως τῆς μεγάλης καὶ ἔπλυναν τὰς
στολὰς αὐτῶν καὶ ἐλεύκαναν αὐτὰς ἐν
τῷ αἵματι τοῦ ἀρνίου.
15 διὰ τοῦτό εἰσιν ἐνώπιον τοῦ
θρόνου τοῦ θεοῦ
καὶ λατρεύουσιν αὐτῷ ἡμέρας
καὶ νυκτὸς ἐν τῷ ναῷ αὐτοῦ,
καὶ ὁ καθήμενος ἐπὶ τοῦ θρόνου
σκηνώσει ἐπ' αὐτούς.
16 οὐ πεινάσουσιν ἔτι οὐδὲ διψήσουσιν
ἔτι
οὐδὲ μὴ πέσῃ ἐπ' αὐτοὺς ὁ ἥλιος
οὐδὲ πᾶν καῦμα,
17 ὅτι τὸ ἀρνίον τὸ ἀνὰ μέσον τοῦ
θρόνου ποιμανεῖ αὐτοὺς
καὶ ὁδηγήσει αὐτοὺς ἐπὶ ζωῆς
πηγὰς ὑδάτων,
καὶ ἐξαλείψει ὁ θεὸς πᾶν δάκρυον
ἐκ τῶν ὀφθαλμῶν αὐτῶν.

NIV

7from the tribe of Simeon 12,000,
from the tribe of Levi 12,000,
from the tribe of Issachar 12,000,
8from the tribe of Zebulun 12,000,
from the tribe of Joseph 12,000,
from the tribe of Benjamin 12,000.

The Great Multitude in White Robes

9After this I looked and there before me
was a great multitude that no one could
count, from every nation, tribe, people and
language, standing before the throne and
in front of the Lamb. They were wearing
white robes and were holding palm
branches in their hands. 10And they cried
out in a loud voice:

"Salvation belongs to our God,
who sits on the throne,
and to the Lamb."

11All the angels were standing around the
throne and around the elders and the four
living creatures. They fell down on their
faces before the throne and worshiped God,
12saying:

"Amen!
Praise and glory
and wisdom and thanks and honor
and power and strength
be to our God for ever and ever.
Amen!"

13Then one of the elders asked me, "These
in white robes—who are they, and where
did they come from?"
14I answered, "Sir, you know."
And he said, "These are they who have
come out of the great tribulation; they have
washed their robes and made them white
in the blood of the Lamb. 15Therefore,

"they are before the throne of God
and serve him day and night in his
temple;
and he who sits on the throne will
spread his tent over them.
16Never again will they hunger;
never again will they thirst.
The sun will not beat upon them,
nor any scorching heat.
17For the Lamb at the center of the throne
will be their shepherd;
he will lead them to springs of living
water.
And God will wipe away every tear
from their eyes."

NRSV

The Seventh Seal and the Golden Censer

8 When the Lamb opened the seventh seal, there was silence in heaven for about half an hour. ²And I saw the seven angels who stand before God, and seven trumpets were given to them.

3 Another angel with a golden censer came and stood at the altar; he was given a great quantity of incense to offer with the prayers of all the saints on the golden altar that is before the throne. ⁴And the smoke of the incense, with the prayers of the saints, rose before God from the hand of the angel. ⁵Then the angel took the censer and filled it with fire from the altar and threw it on the earth; and there were peals of thunder, rumblings, flashes of lightning, and an earthquake.

The Seven Trumpets

6 Now the seven angels who had the seven trumpets made ready to blow them.

7 The first angel blew his trumpet, and there came hail and fire, mixed with blood, and they were hurled to the earth; and a third of the earth was burned up, and a third of the trees were burned up, and all green grass was burned up.

8 The second angel blew his trumpet, and something like a great mountain, burning with fire, was thrown into the sea. ⁹A third of the sea became blood, a third of the living creatures in the sea died, and a third of the ships were destroyed.

10 The third angel blew his trumpet, and a great star fell from heaven, blazing like a torch, and it fell on a third of the rivers and on the springs of water. ¹¹The name of the star is Wormwood. A third of the waters became wormwood, and many died from the water, because it was made bitter.

12 The fourth angel blew his trumpet, and a third of the sun was struck, and a third of the moon, and a third of the stars, so that a third of their light was darkened; a third of the day was kept from shining, and likewise the night.

13 Then I looked, and I heard an eagle crying with a loud voice as it flew in midheaven, "Woe, woe, woe to the inhabitants of the earth, at the blasts of the other trumpets that the three angels are about to blow!"

Greek

8 Καὶ ὅταν ἤνοιξεν τὴν σφραγῖδα τὴν ἑβδόμην, ἐγένετο σιγὴ ἐν τῷ οὐρανῷ ὡς ἡμιώριον. **2** καὶ εἶδον τοὺς ἑπτὰ ἀγγέλους οἳ ἐνώπιον τοῦ θεοῦ ἑστήκασιν, καὶ ἐδόθησαν αὐτοῖς ἑπτὰ σάλπιγγες.

3 Καὶ ἄλλος ἄγγελος ἦλθεν καὶ ἐστάθη ἐπὶ τοῦ θυσιαστηρίου ἔχων λιβανωτὸν χρυσοῦν, καὶ ἐδόθη αὐτῷ θυμιάματα πολλά, ἵνα δώσει ταῖς προσευχαῖς τῶν ἁγίων πάντων ἐπὶ τὸ θυσιαστήριον τὸ χρυσοῦν τὸ ἐνώπιον τοῦ θρόνου. **4** καὶ ἀνέβη ὁ καπνὸς τῶν θυμιαμάτων ταῖς προσευχαῖς τῶν ἁγίων ἐκ χειρὸς τοῦ ἀγγέλου ἐνώπιον τοῦ θεοῦ. **5** καὶ εἴληφεν ὁ ἄγγελος τὸν λιβανωτὸν καὶ ἐγέμισεν αὐτὸν ἐκ τοῦ πυρὸς τοῦ θυσιαστηρίου καὶ ἔβαλεν εἰς τὴν γῆν, καὶ ἐγένοντο βρονταὶ καὶ φωναὶ καὶ ἀστραπαὶ καὶ σεισμός.

6 Καὶ οἱ ἑπτὰ ἄγγελοι οἱ ἔχοντες τὰς ἑπτὰ σάλπιγγας ἡτοίμασαν αὐτοὺς ἵνα σαλπίσωσιν.

7 Καὶ ὁ πρῶτος ἐσάλπισεν· καὶ ἐγένετο χάλαζα καὶ πῦρ μεμιγμένα ἐν αἵματι καὶ ἐβλήθη εἰς τὴν γῆν, καὶ τὸ τρίτον τῆς γῆς κατεκάη καὶ τὸ τρίτον τῶν δένδρων κατεκάη καὶ πᾶς χόρτος χλωρὸς κατεκάη.

8 Καὶ ὁ δεύτερος ἄγγελος ἐσάλπισεν· καὶ ὡς ὄρος μέγα πυρὶ καιόμενον ἐβλήθη εἰς τὴν θάλασσαν, καὶ ἐγένετο τὸ τρίτον τῆς θαλάσσης αἷμα **9** καὶ ἀπέθανεν τὸ τρίτον τῶν κτισμάτων τῶν ἐν τῇ θαλάσσῃ τὰ ἔχοντα ψυχὰς καὶ τὸ τρίτον τῶν πλοίων διεφθάρησαν.

10 Καὶ ὁ τρίτος ἄγγελος ἐσάλπισεν· καὶ ἔπεσεν ἐκ τοῦ οὐρανοῦ ἀστὴρ μέγας καιόμενος ὡς λαμπὰς καὶ ἔπεσεν ἐπὶ τὸ τρίτον τῶν ποταμῶν καὶ ἐπὶ τὰς πηγὰς τῶν ὑδάτων, **11** καὶ τὸ ὄνομα τοῦ ἀστέρος λέγεται ὁ Ἄψινθος, καὶ ἐγένετο τὸ τρίτον τῶν ὑδάτων εἰς ἄψινθον καὶ πολλοὶ τῶν ἀνθρώπων ἀπέθανον ἐκ τῶν ὑδάτων ὅτι ἐπικράνθησαν.

12 Καὶ ὁ τέταρτος ἄγγελος ἐσάλπισεν· καὶ ἐπλήγη τὸ τρίτον τοῦ ἡλίου καὶ τὸ τρίτον τῆς σελήνης καὶ τὸ τρίτον τῶν ἀστέρων, ἵνα σκοτισθῇ τὸ τρίτον αὐτῶν καὶ ἡ ἡμέρα μὴ φάνῃ τὸ τρίτον αὐτῆς καὶ ἡ νὺξ ὁμοίως.

13 Καὶ εἶδον, καὶ ἤκουσα ἑνὸς ἀετοῦ πετομένου ἐν μεσουρανήματι λέγοντος φωνῇ μεγάλῃ, Οὐαὶ οὐαὶ οὐαὶ τοὺς κατοικοῦντας ἐπὶ τῆς γῆς ἐκ τῶν λοιπῶν φωνῶν τῆς σάλπιγγος τῶν τριῶν ἀγγέλων τῶν μελλόντων σαλπίζειν.

NIV

The Seventh Seal and the Golden Censer

8 When he opened the seventh seal, there was silence in heaven for about half an hour.

²And I saw the seven angels who stand before God, and to them were given seven trumpets.

³Another angel, who had a golden censer, came and stood at the altar. He was given much incense to offer, with the prayers of all the saints, on the golden altar before the throne. ⁴The smoke of the incense, together with the prayers of the saints, went up before God from the angel's hand. ⁵Then the angel took the censer, filled it with fire from the altar, and hurled it on the earth; and there came peals of thunder, rumblings, flashes of lightning and an earthquake.

The Trumpets

⁶Then the seven angels who had the seven trumpets prepared to sound them.

⁷The first angel sounded his trumpet, and there came hail and fire mixed with blood, and it was hurled down upon the earth. A third of the earth was burned up, a third of the trees were burned up, and all the green grass was burned up.

⁸The second angel sounded his trumpet, and something like a huge mountain, all ablaze, was thrown into the sea. A third of the sea turned into blood, ⁹a third of the living creatures in the sea died, and a third of the ships were destroyed.

¹⁰The third angel sounded his trumpet, and a great star, blazing like a torch, fell from the sky on a third of the rivers and on the springs of water— ¹¹the name of the star is Wormwood.[a] A third of the waters turned bitter, and many people died from the waters that had become bitter.

¹²The fourth angel sounded his trumpet, and a third of the sun was struck, a third of the moon, and a third of the stars, so that a third of them turned dark. A third of the day was without light, and also a third of the night.

¹³As I watched, I heard an eagle that was flying in midair call out in a loud voice: "Woe! Woe! Woe to the inhabitants of the earth, because of the trumpet blasts about to be sounded by the other three angels!"

NRSV

9 And the fifth angel blew his trumpet, and I saw a star that had fallen from heaven to earth, and he was given the key to the shaft of the bottomless pit; ²he opened the shaft of the bottomless pit, and from the shaft rose smoke like the smoke of a great furnace, and the sun and the air were darkened with the smoke from the shaft. ³Then from the smoke came locusts on the earth, and they were given authority like the authority of scorpions of the earth. ⁴They were told not to damage the grass of the earth or any green growth or any tree, but only those people who do not have the seal of God on their foreheads. ⁵They were allowed to torture them for five months, but not to kill them, and their torture was like the torture of a scorpion when it stings someone. ⁶And in those days people will seek death but will not find it; they will long to die, but death will flee from them.

7 In appearance the locusts were like horses equipped for battle. On their heads were what looked like crowns of gold; their faces were like human faces, ⁸their hair like women's hair, and their teeth like lions' teeth; ⁹they had scales like iron breastplates, and the noise of their wings was like the noise of many chariots with horses rushing into battle. ¹⁰They have tails like scorpions, with stingers, and in their tails is their power to harm people for five months. ¹¹They have as king over them the angel of the bottomless pit; his name in Hebrew is Abaddon,ʷ and in Greek he is called Apollyon.ˣ

12 The first woe has passed. There are still two woes to come.

13 Then the sixth angel blew his trumpet, and I heard a voice from the fourʸ horns of the golden altar before God, ¹⁴saying to the sixth angel who had the trumpet, "Release the four angels who are bound at the great river Euphrates." ¹⁵So the four angels were released, who had been held ready for the hour, the day, the month, and the year, to kill a third of humankind. ¹⁶The number of the troops of

[Greek column]

9 Καὶ ὁ πέμπτος ἄγγελος ἐσάλπισεν· καὶ εἶδον ἀστέρα ἐκ τοῦ οὐρανοῦ πεπτωκότα εἰς τὴν γῆν, καὶ ἐδόθη αὐτῷ ἡ κλεὶς τοῦ φρέατος τῆς ἀβύσσου 2 καὶ ἤνοιξεν τὸ φρέαρ τῆς ἀβύσσου, καὶ ἀνέβη καπνὸς ἐκ τοῦ φρέατος ὡς καπνὸς καμίνου μεγάλης, καὶ ἐσκοτώθη ὁ ἥλιος καὶ ὁ ἀὴρ ἐκ τοῦ καπνοῦ τοῦ φρέατος. 3 καὶ ἐκ τοῦ καπνοῦ ἐξῆλθον ἀκρίδες εἰς τὴν γῆν, καὶ ἐδόθη αὐταῖς ἐξουσία ὡς ἔχουσιν ἐξουσίαν οἱ σκορπίοι τῆς γῆς. 4 καὶ ἐρρέθη αὐταῖς ἵνα μὴ ἀδικήσουσιν τὸν χόρτον τῆς γῆς οὐδὲ πᾶν χλωρὸν οὐδὲ πᾶν δένδρον, εἰ μὴ τοὺς ἀνθρώπους οἵτινες οὐκ ἔχουσι τὴν σφραγῖδα τοῦ θεοῦ ἐπὶ τῶν μετώπων. 5 καὶ ἐδόθη αὐτοῖς ἵνα μὴ ἀποκτείνωσιν αὐτούς, ἀλλ' ἵνα βασανισθήσονται μῆνας πέντε, καὶ ὁ βασανισμὸς αὐτῶν ὡς βασανισμὸς σκορπίου ὅταν παίσῃ ἄνθρωπον. 6 καὶ ἐν ταῖς ἡμέραις ἐκείναις ζητήσουσιν οἱ ἄνθρωποι τὸν θάνατον καὶ οὐ μὴ εὑρήσουσιν αὐτόν, καὶ ἐπιθυμήσουσιν ἀποθανεῖν καὶ φεύγει ὁ θάνατος ἀπ' αὐτῶν.

7 Καὶ τὰ ὁμοιώματα τῶν ἀκρίδων ὅμοια ἵπποις ἡτοιμασμένοις εἰς πόλεμον, καὶ ἐπὶ τὰς κεφαλὰς αὐτῶν ὡς στέφανοι ὅμοιοι χρυσῷ, καὶ τὰ πρόσωπα αὐτῶν ὡς πρόσωπα ἀνθρώπων, 8 καὶ εἶχον τρίχας ὡς τρίχας γυναικῶν, καὶ οἱ ὀδόντες αὐτῶν ὡς λεόντων ἦσαν, 9 καὶ εἶχον θώρακας ὡς θώρακας σιδηροῦς, καὶ ἡ φωνὴ τῶν πτερύγων αὐτῶν ὡς φωνὴ ἁρμάτων ἵππων πολλῶν τρεχόντων εἰς πόλεμον, 10 καὶ ἔχουσιν οὐρὰς ὁμοίας σκορπίοις καὶ κέντρα, καὶ ἐν ταῖς οὐραῖς αὐτῶν ἡ ἐξουσία αὐτῶν ἀδικῆσαι τοὺς ἀνθρώπους μῆνας πέντε, 11 ἔχουσιν ἐπ' αὐτῶν βασιλέα τὸν ἄγγελον τῆς ἀβύσσου, ὄνομα αὐτῷ Ἑβραϊστὶ Ἀβαδδών, καὶ ἐν τῇ Ἑλληνικῇ ὄνομα ἔχει Ἀπολλύων.

12 Ἡ οὐαὶ ἡ μία ἀπῆλθεν· ἰδοὺ ἔρχεται ἔτι δύο οὐαὶ μετὰ ταῦτα.

13 Καὶ ὁ ἕκτος ἄγγελος ἐσάλπισεν· καὶ ἤκουσα φωνὴν μίαν ἐκ τῶν [τεσσάρων]ᵃ κεράτων τοῦ θυσιαστηρίου τοῦ χρυσοῦ τοῦ ἐνώπιον τοῦ θεοῦ, 14 λέγοντα τῷ ἕκτῳ ἀγγέλῳ, ὁ ἔχων τὴν σάλπιγγα, Λῦσον τοὺς τέσσαρας ἀγγέλους τοὺς δεδεμένους ἐπὶ τῷ ποταμῷ τῷ μεγάλῳ Εὐφράτῃ. 15 καὶ ἐλύθησαν οἱ τέσσαρες ἄγγελοι οἱ ἡτοιμασμένοι εἰς τὴν ὥραν καὶ ἡμέραν καὶ μῆνα καὶ ἐνιαυτόν, ἵνα ἀποκτείνωσιν τὸ τρίτον τῶν ἀνθρώπων. 16 καὶ ὁ ἀριθμὸς τῶν στρατευμάτων τοῦ

NIV

9 The fifth angel sounded his trumpet, and I saw a star that had fallen from the sky to the earth. The star was given the key to the shaft of the Abyss. ²When he opened the Abyss, smoke rose from it like the smoke from a gigantic furnace. The sun and sky were darkened by the smoke from the Abyss. ³And out of the smoke locusts came down upon the earth and were given power like that of scorpions of the earth. ⁴They were told not to harm the grass of the earth or any plant or tree, but only those people who did not have the seal of God on their foreheads. ⁵They were not given power to kill them, but only to torture them for five months. And the agony they suffered was like that of the sting of a scorpion when it strikes a man. ⁶During those days men will seek death, but will not find it; they will long to die, but death will elude them.

⁷The locusts looked like horses prepared for battle. On their heads they wore something like crowns of gold, and their faces resembled human faces. ⁸Their hair was like women's hair, and their teeth were like lions' teeth. ⁹They had breastplates like breastplates of iron, and the sound of their wings was like the thundering of many horses and chariots rushing into battle. ¹⁰They had tails and stings like scorpions, and in their tails they had power to torment people for five months. ¹¹They had as king over them the angel of the Abyss, whose name in Hebrew is Abaddon, and in Greek, Apollyon.ᵃ

¹²The first woe is past; two other woes are yet to come.

¹³The sixth angel sounded his trumpet, and I heard a voice coming from the hornsᵇ of the golden altar that is before God. ¹⁴It said to the sixth angel who had the trumpet, "Release the four angels who are bound at the great river Euphrates." ¹⁵And the four angels who had been kept ready for this very hour and day and month and year were released to kill a third of mankind. ¹⁶The number of the mounted troops

---

ʷ That is, *Destruction*   ˣ That is, *Destroyer*   ʸ Other ancient authorities lack *four*

ᵃ13 NIV text and NRSV note y omit τεσσάρων

ᵃ11 *Abaddon* and *Apollyon* mean *Destroyer*.   ᵇ13 That is, projections

cavalry was two hundred million; I heard their number. [17]And this was how I saw the horses in my vision: the riders wore breastplates the color of fire and of sapphire[z] and of sulfur; the heads of the horses were like lions' heads, and fire and smoke and sulfur came out of their mouths. [18]By these three plagues a third of humankind was killed, by the fire and smoke and sulfur coming out of their mouths. [19]For the power of the horses is in their mouths and in their tails; their tails are like serpents, having heads; and with them they inflict harm.

20 The rest of humankind, who were not killed by these plagues, did not repent of the works of their hands or give up worshiping demons and idols of gold and silver and bronze and stone and wood, which cannot see or hear or walk. [21]And they did not repent of their murders or their sorceries or their fornication or their thefts.

The Angel with the Little Scroll

10 And I saw another mighty angel coming down from heaven, wrapped in a cloud, with a rainbow over his head; his face was like the sun, and his legs like pillars of fire. [2]He held a little scroll open in his hand. Setting his right foot on the sea and his left foot on the land, [3]he gave a great shout, like a lion roaring. And when he shouted, the seven thunders sounded. [4]And when the seven thunders had sounded, I was about to write, but I heard a voice from heaven saying, "Seal up what the seven thunders have said, and do not write it down." [5]Then the angel whom I saw standing on the sea and the land

raised his right hand to heaven
[6]   and swore by him who lives forever and ever,
who created heaven and what is in it, the earth and what is in it, and the sea and what is in it: "There will be no more delay, [7]but in the days when the seventh angel is to blow his trumpet, the mystery of God will be fulfilled, as he announced to his

ἱππικοῦ δισμυριάδες μυριάδων, ἤκουσα τὸν ἀριθμὸν αὐτῶν. **17** καὶ οὕτως εἶδον τοὺς ἵππους ἐν τῇ ὁράσει καὶ τοὺς καθημένους ἐπ᾽ αὐτῶν, ἔχοντας θώρακας πυρίνους καὶ ὑακινθίνους καὶ θειώδεις, καὶ αἱ κεφαλαὶ τῶν ἵππων ὡς κεφαλαὶ λεόντων, καὶ ἐκ τῶν στομάτων αὐτῶν ἐκπορεύεται πῦρ καὶ καπνὸς καὶ θεῖον. **18** ἀπὸ τῶν τριῶν πληγῶν τούτων ἀπεκτάνθησαν τὸ τρίτον τῶν ἀνθρώπων, ἐκ τοῦ πυρὸς καὶ τοῦ καπνοῦ καὶ τοῦ θείου τοῦ ἐκπορευομένου ἐκ τῶν στομάτων αὐτῶν. **19** ἡ γὰρ ἐξουσία τῶν ἵππων ἐν τῷ στόματι αὐτῶν ἐστιν καὶ ἐν ταῖς οὐραῖς αὐτῶν, αἱ γὰρ οὐραὶ αὐτῶν ὅμοιαι ὄφεσιν, ἔχουσαι κεφαλὰς καὶ ἐν αὐταῖς ἀδικοῦσιν.

20 Καὶ οἱ λοιποὶ τῶν ἀνθρώπων, οἳ οὐκ ἀπεκτάνθησαν ἐν ταῖς πληγαῖς ταύταις, οὐδὲ μετενόησαν ἐκ τῶν ἔργων τῶν χειρῶν αὐτῶν, ἵνα μὴ προσκυνήσουσιν τὰ δαιμόνια καὶ τὰ εἴδωλα τὰ χρυσᾶ καὶ τὰ ἀργυρᾶ καὶ τὰ χαλκᾶ καὶ τὰ λίθινα καὶ τὰ ξύλινα, ἃ οὔτε βλέπειν δύνανται οὔτε ἀκούειν οὔτε περιπατεῖν, **21** καὶ οὐ μετενόησαν ἐκ τῶν φόνων αὐτῶν οὔτε ἐκ τῶν φαρμάκων αὐτῶν οὔτε ἐκ τῆς πορνείας αὐτῶν οὔτε ἐκ τῶν κλεμμάτων αὐτῶν.

10 Καὶ εἶδον ἄλλον ἄγγελον ἰσχυρὸν καταβαίνοντα ἐκ τοῦ οὐρανοῦ περιβεβλημένον νεφέλην, καὶ ἡ ἶρις ἐπὶ τῆς κεφαλῆς αὐτοῦ καὶ τὸ πρόσωπον αὐτοῦ ὡς ὁ ἥλιος καὶ οἱ πόδες αὐτοῦ ὡς στῦλοι πυρός, **2** καὶ ἔχων ἐν τῇ χειρὶ αὐτοῦ βιβλαρίδιον ἠνεῳγμένον. καὶ ἔθηκεν τὸν πόδα αὐτοῦ τὸν δεξιὸν ἐπὶ τῆς θαλάσσης, τὸν δὲ εὐώνυμον ἐπὶ τῆς γῆς, **3** καὶ ἔκραξεν φωνῇ μεγάλῃ ὥσπερ λέων μυκᾶται. καὶ ὅτε ἔκραξεν, ἐλάλησαν αἱ ἑπτὰ βρονταὶ τὰς ἑαυτῶν φωνάς. **4** καὶ ὅτε ἐλάλησαν αἱ ἑπτὰ βρονταί, ἤμελλον γράφειν, καὶ ἤκουσα φωνὴν ἐκ τοῦ οὐρανοῦ λέγουσαν, Σφράγισον ἃ ἐλάλησαν αἱ ἑπτὰ βρονταί, καὶ μὴ αὐτὰ γράψῃς. **5** Καὶ ὁ ἄγγελος, ὃν εἶδον ἑστῶτα ἐπὶ τῆς θαλάσσης καὶ ἐπὶ τῆς γῆς,

ἦρεν τὴν χεῖρα αὐτοῦ τὴν δεξιὰν εἰς τὸν οὐρανὸν
6   καὶ ὤμοσεν ἐν τῷ ζῶντι εἰς τοὺς αἰῶνας τῶν αἰώνων,
ὃς ἔκτισεν τὸν οὐρανὸν καὶ τὰ ἐν αὐτῷ καὶ τὴν γῆν καὶ τὰ ἐν αὐτῇ καὶ τὴν θάλασσαν καὶ τὰ ἐν αὐτῇ, ὅτι χρόνος οὐκέτι ἔσται, **7** ἀλλ᾽ ἐν ταῖς ἡμέραις τῆς φωνῆς τοῦ ἑβδόμου ἀγγέλου, ὅταν μέλλῃ σαλπίζειν, καὶ ἐτελέσθη τὸ μυστήριον τοῦ θεοῦ, ὡς

was two hundred million. I heard their number.

[17]The horses and riders I saw in my vision looked like this: Their breastplates were fiery red, dark blue, and yellow as sulfur. The heads of the horses resembled the heads of lions, and out of their mouths came fire, smoke and sulfur. [18]A third of mankind was killed by the three plagues of fire, smoke and sulfur that came out of their mouths. [19]The power of the horses was in their mouths and in their tails; for their tails were like snakes, having heads with which they inflict injury.

[20]The rest of mankind that were not killed by these plagues still did not repent of the work of their hands; they did not stop worshiping demons, and idols of gold, silver, bronze, stone and wood—idols that cannot see or hear or walk. [21]Nor did they repent of their murders, their magic arts, their sexual immorality or their thefts.

The Angel and the Little Scroll

10 Then I saw another mighty angel coming down from heaven. He was robed in a cloud, with a rainbow above his head; his face was like the sun, and his legs were like fiery pillars. [2]He was holding a little scroll, which lay open in his hand. He planted his right foot on the sea and his left foot on the land, [3]and he gave a loud shout like the roar of a lion. When he shouted, the voices of the seven thunders spoke. [4]And when the seven thunders spoke, I was about to write; but I heard a voice from heaven say, "Seal up what the seven thunders have said and do not write it down."

[5]Then the angel I had seen standing on the sea and on the land raised his right hand to heaven. [6]And he swore by him who lives for ever and ever, who created the heavens and all that is in them, the earth and all that is in it, and the sea and all that is in it, and said, "There will be no more delay! [7]But in the days when the seventh angel is about to sound his trumpet, the mystery of God will be accom-

servants[a] the prophets."

8 Then the voice that I had heard from heaven spoke to me again, saying, "Go, take the scroll that is open in the hand of the angel who is standing on the sea and on the land." [9]So I went to the angel and told him to give me the little scroll; and he said to me, "Take it, and eat; it will be bitter to your stomach, but sweet as honey in your mouth." [10]So I took the little scroll from the hand of the angel and ate it; it was sweet as honey in my mouth, but when I had eaten it, my stomach was made bitter.

11 Then they said to me, "You must prophesy again about many peoples and nations and languages and kings."

The Two Witnesses

11 Then I was given a measuring rod like a staff, and I was told, "Come and measure the temple of God and the altar and those who worship there, [2]but do not measure the court outside the temple; leave that out, for it is given over to the nations, and they will trample over the holy city for forty-two months. [3]And I will grant my two witnesses authority to prophesy for one thousand two hundred sixty days, wearing sackcloth."

4 These are the two olive trees and the two lampstands that stand before the Lord of the earth. [5]And if anyone wants to harm them, fire pours from their mouth and consumes their foes; anyone who wants to harm them must be killed in this manner. [6]They have authority to shut the sky, so that no rain may fall during the days of their prophesying, and they have authority over the waters to turn them into blood, and to strike the earth with every kind of plague, as often as they desire.

7 When they have finished their testimony, the beast that comes up from the bottomless pit will make war on them and conquer them and kill them, [8]and their dead bodies will lie in the street of the great city that is prophetically[b] called Sodom and Egypt, where also their Lord was crucified. [9]For three and a half days members of the peoples and tribes and languages and nations will gaze at their dead bodies and refuse to let them be placed in a tomb; [10]and the inhabitants of

εὐηγγέλισεν τοὺς ἑαυτοῦ δούλους τοὺς προφήτας.

[8] Καὶ ἡ φωνὴ ἣν ἤκουσα ἐκ τοῦ οὐρανοῦ πάλιν λαλοῦσαν μετ᾽ ἐμοῦ καὶ λέγουσαν, Ὕπαγε λάβε τὸ βιβλίον τὸ ἠνεῳγμένον ἐν τῇ χειρὶ τοῦ ἀγγέλου τοῦ ἑστῶτος ἐπὶ τῆς θαλάσσης καὶ ἐπὶ τῆς γῆς. [9] καὶ ἀπῆλθα πρὸς τὸν ἄγγελον λέγων αὐτῷ δοῦναί μοι τὸ βιβλαρίδιον. καὶ λέγει μοι, Λάβε καὶ κατάφαγε αὐτό, καὶ πικρανεῖ σου τὴν κοιλίαν, ἀλλ᾽ ἐν τῷ στόματί σου ἔσται γλυκὺ ὡς μέλι. [10] καὶ ἔλαβον τὸ βιβλαρίδιον ἐκ τῆς χειρὸς τοῦ ἀγγέλου καὶ κατέφαγον αὐτό, καὶ ἦν ἐν τῷ στόματί μου ὡς μέλι γλυκὺ καὶ ὅτε ἔφαγον αὐτό, ἐπικράνθη ἡ κοιλία μου. [11] καὶ λέγουσίν μοι, Δεῖ σε πάλιν προφητεῦσαι ἐπὶ λαοῖς καὶ ἔθνεσιν καὶ γλώσσαις καὶ βασιλεῦσιν πολλοῖς.

11 Καὶ ἐδόθη μοι κάλαμος ὅμοιος ῥάβδῳ, λέγων, Ἔγειρε καὶ μέτρησον τὸν ναὸν τοῦ θεοῦ καὶ τὸ θυσιαστήριον καὶ τοὺς προσκυνοῦντας ἐν αὐτῷ. [2] καὶ τὴν αὐλὴν τὴν ἔξωθεν τοῦ ναοῦ ἔκβαλε ἔξωθεν καὶ μὴ αὐτὴν μετρήσῃς, ὅτι ἐδόθη τοῖς ἔθνεσιν, καὶ τὴν πόλιν τὴν ἁγίαν πατήσουσιν μῆνας τεσσεράκοντα [καὶ] δύο. [3] καὶ δώσω τοῖς δυσὶν μάρτυσίν μου καὶ προφητεύσουσιν ἡμέρας χιλίας διακοσίας ἑξήκοντα περιβεβλημένοι σάκκους. [4] οὗτοί εἰσιν αἱ δύο ἐλαῖαι καὶ αἱ δύο λυχνίαι αἱ ἐνώπιον τοῦ κυρίου τῆς γῆς ἑστῶτες. [5] καὶ εἴ τις αὐτοὺς θέλει ἀδικῆσαι πῦρ ἐκπορεύεται ἐκ τοῦ στόματος αὐτῶν καὶ κατεσθίει τοὺς ἐχθροὺς αὐτῶν· καὶ εἴ τις θελήσῃ αὐτοὺς ἀδικῆσαι, οὕτως δεῖ αὐτὸν ἀποκτανθῆναι. [6] οὗτοι ἔχουσιν τὴν ἐξουσίαν κλεῖσαι τὸν οὐρανόν, ἵνα μὴ ὑετὸς βρέχῃ τὰς ἡμέρας τῆς προφητείας αὐτῶν, καὶ ἐξουσίαν ἔχουσιν ἐπὶ τῶν ὑδάτων στρέφειν αὐτὰ εἰς αἷμα καὶ πατάξαι τὴν γῆν ἐν πάσῃ πληγῇ ὁσάκις ἐὰν θελήσωσιν. [7] καὶ ὅταν τελέσωσιν τὴν μαρτυρίαν αὐτῶν, τὸ θηρίον τὸ ἀναβαῖνον ἐκ τῆς ἀβύσσου ποιήσει μετ᾽ αὐτῶν πόλεμον καὶ νικήσει αὐτοὺς καὶ ἀποκτενεῖ αὐτούς. [8] καὶ τὸ πτῶμα αὐτῶν ἐπὶ τῆς πλατείας τῆς πόλεως τῆς μεγάλης, ἥτις καλεῖται πνευματικῶς Σόδομα καὶ Αἴγυπτος, ὅπου καὶ ὁ κύριος αὐτῶν ἐσταυρώθη. [9] καὶ βλέπουσιν ἐκ τῶν λαῶν καὶ φυλῶν καὶ γλωσσῶν καὶ ἐθνῶν τὸ πτῶμα αὐτῶν ἡμέρας τρεῖς καὶ ἥμισυ καὶ τὰ πτώματα αὐτῶν οὐκ ἀφίουσιν τεθῆναι εἰς μνῆμα. [10] καὶ οἱ κατοικοῦντες ἐπὶ

plished, just as he announced to his servants the prophets."

[8]Then the voice that I had heard from heaven spoke to me once more: "Go, take the scroll that lies open in the hand of the angel who is standing on the sea and on the land."

[9]So I went to the angel and asked him to give me the little scroll. He said to me, "Take it and eat it. It will turn your stomach sour, but in your mouth it will be as sweet as honey." [10]I took the little scroll from the angel's hand and ate it. It tasted as sweet as honey in my mouth, but when I had eaten it, my stomach turned sour. [11]Then I was told, "You must prophesy again about many peoples, nations, languages and kings."

The Two Witnesses

11 I was given a reed like a measuring rod and was told, "Go and measure the temple of God and the altar, and count the worshipers there. [2]But exclude the outer court; do not measure it, because it has been given to the Gentiles. They will trample on the holy city for 42 months. [3]And I will give power to my two witnesses, and they will prophesy for 1,260 days, clothed in sackcloth." [4]These are the two olive trees and the two lampstands that stand before the Lord of the earth. [5]If anyone tries to harm them, fire comes from their mouths and devours their enemies. This is how anyone who wants to harm them must die. [6]These men have power to shut up the sky so that it will not rain during the time they are prophesying; and they have power to turn the waters into blood and to strike the earth with every kind of plague as often as they want.

[7]Now when they have finished their testimony, the beast that comes up from the Abyss will attack them, and overpower and kill them. [8]Their bodies will lie in the street of the great city, which is figuratively called Sodom and Egypt, where also their Lord was crucified. [9]For three and a half days men from every people, tribe, language and nation will gaze on their bodies and refuse them burial. [10]The inhabitants of the earth will gloat over them

---

the earth will gloat over them and celebrate and exchange presents, because these two prophets had been a torment to the inhabitants of the earth.

11 But after the three and a half days, the breath[c] of life from God entered them, and they stood on their feet, and those who saw them were terrified. 12Then they[d] heard a loud voice from heaven saying to them, "Come up here!" And they went up to heaven in a cloud while their enemies watched them. 13At that moment there was a great earthquake, and a tenth of the city fell; seven thousand people were killed in the earthquake, and the rest were terrified and gave glory to the God of heaven.

14 The second woe has passed. The third woe is coming very soon.

The Seventh Trumpet

15 Then the seventh angel blew his trumpet, and there were loud voices in heaven, saying,

"The kingdom of the world has
    become the kingdom of our Lord
    and of his Messiah,[e]
and he will reign forever and ever."

16 Then the twenty-four elders who sit on their thrones before God fell on their faces and worshiped God, 17singing,

"We give you thanks, Lord God
    Almighty,
who are and who were,
for you have taken your great power
    and begun to reign.
18 The nations raged,
    but your wrath has come,
    and the time for judging the dead,
for rewarding your servants,[f] the
        prophets
    and saints and all who fear your
        name,
    both small and great,
and for destroying those who destroy
    the earth."

19 Then God's temple in heaven was opened, and the ark of his covenant was seen within his temple; and there were flashes of lightning, rumblings, peals of thunder, an earthquake, and heavy hail.

τῆς γῆς χαίρουσιν ἐπ᾽ αὐτοῖς καὶ εὐφραίνονται καὶ δῶρα πέμψουσιν ἀλλήλοις, ὅτι οὗτοι οἱ δύο προφῆται ἐβασάνισαν τοὺς κατοικοῦντας ἐπὶ τῆς γῆς. **11** καὶ μετὰ τὰς τρεῖς ἡμέρας καὶ ἥμισυ πνεῦμα ζωῆς ἐκ τοῦ θεοῦ εἰσῆλθεν ἐν αὐτοῖς, καὶ ἔστησαν ἐπὶ τοὺς πόδας αὐτῶν, καὶ φόβος μέγας ἐπέπεσεν ἐπὶ τοὺς θεωροῦντας αὐτούς. **12** καὶ ἤκουσαν[a] φωνῆς μεγάλης ἐκ τοῦ οὐρανοῦ λεγούσης αὐτοῖς, Ἀνάβατε ὧδε. καὶ ἀνέβησαν εἰς τὸν οὐρανὸν ἐν τῇ νεφέλῃ, καὶ ἐθεώρησαν αὐτοὺς οἱ ἐχθροὶ αὐτῶν. **13** Καὶ ἐν ἐκείνῃ τῇ ὥρᾳ ἐγένετο σεισμὸς μέγας καὶ τὸ δέκατον τῆς πόλεως ἔπεσεν καὶ ἀπεκτάνθησαν ἐν τῷ σεισμῷ ὀνόματα ἀνθρώπων χιλιάδες ἑπτὰ καὶ οἱ λοιποὶ ἔμφοβοι ἐγένοντο καὶ ἔδωκαν δόξαν τῷ θεῷ τοῦ οὐρανοῦ.

14 Ἡ οὐαὶ ἡ δευτέρα ἀπῆλθεν· ἰδοὺ ἡ οὐαὶ ἡ τρίτη ἔρχεται ταχύ.

15 Καὶ ὁ ἕβδομος ἄγγελος ἐσάλπισεν· καὶ ἐγένοντο φωναὶ μεγάλαι ἐν τῷ οὐρανῷ λέγοντες,
    Ἐγένετο ἡ βασιλεία τοῦ κόσμου
        τοῦ κυρίου ἡμῶν
    καὶ τοῦ Χριστοῦ αὐτοῦ,
    καὶ βασιλεύσει εἰς τοὺς αἰῶνας
        τῶν αἰώνων.

16 καὶ οἱ εἴκοσι τέσσαρες πρεσβύτεροι [οἱ] ἐνώπιον τοῦ θεοῦ καθήμενοι ἐπὶ τοὺς θρόνους αὐτῶν ἔπεσαν ἐπὶ τὰ πρόσωπα αὐτῶν καὶ προσεκύνησαν τῷ θεῷ **17** λέγοντες,
    Εὐχαριστοῦμέν σοι, κύριε ὁ θεὸς ὁ
        παντοκράτωρ,
    ὁ ὢν καὶ ὁ ἦν,
    ὅτι εἴληφας τὴν δύναμίν σου τὴν
        μεγάλην
    καὶ ἐβασίλευσας.
18 καὶ τὰ ἔθνη ὠργίσθησαν,
    καὶ ἦλθεν ἡ ὀργή σου
    καὶ ὁ καιρὸς τῶν νεκρῶν κριθῆναι
    καὶ δοῦναι τὸν μισθὸν τοῖς
        δούλοις σου τοῖς προφήταις
    καὶ τοῖς ἁγίοις καὶ τοῖς
        φοβουμένοις τὸ ὄνομά σου,
    τοὺς μικροὺς καὶ τοὺς μεγάλους,
    καὶ διαφθεῖραι τοὺς διαφθείροντας
        τὴν γῆν.

19 καὶ ἠνοίγη ὁ ναὸς τοῦ θεοῦ ὁ ἐν τῷ οὐρανῷ καὶ ὤφθη ἡ κιβωτὸς τῆς διαθήκης αὐτοῦ ἐν τῷ ναῷ αὐτοῦ, καὶ ἐγένοντο ἀστραπαὶ καὶ φωναὶ καὶ βρονταὶ καὶ σεισμὸς καὶ χάλαζα μεγάλη.

and will celebrate by sending each other gifts, because these two prophets had tormented those who live on the earth.

11But after the three and a half days a breath of life from God entered them, and they stood on their feet, and terror struck those who saw them. 12Then they heard a loud voice from heaven saying to them, "Come up here." And they went up to heaven in a cloud, while their enemies looked on.

13At that very hour there was a severe earthquake and a tenth of the city collapsed. Seven thousand people were killed in the earthquake, and the survivors were terrified and gave glory to the God of heaven.

14The second woe has passed; the third woe is coming soon.

The Seventh Trumpet

15The seventh angel sounded his trumpet, and there were loud voices in heaven, which said:

"The kingdom of the world has become
    the kingdom of our Lord and of
    his Christ,
and he will reign for ever and ever."

16And the twenty-four elders, who were seated on their thrones before God, fell on their faces and worshiped God, 17saying:

"We give thanks to you, Lord God
    Almighty,
the One who is and who was,
because you have taken your great power
    and have begun to reign.
18The nations were angry;
    and your wrath has come.
The time has come for judging the dead,
    and for rewarding your servants the
        prophets
and your saints and those who
    reverence your name,
    both small and great—
and for destroying those who destroy
    the earth."

19Then God's temple in heaven was opened, and within his temple was seen the ark of his covenant. And there came flashes of lightning, rumblings, peals of thunder, an earthquake and a great hailstorm.

---

[c] Or *the spirit*   [d] Other ancient authorities read *I*
[e] Gk *Christ*   [f] Gk *slaves*

[a]12 NRSV note d ἤκουσα

NRSV

The Woman and the Dragon

12 A great portent appeared in heaven: a woman clothed with the sun, with the moon under her feet, and on her head a crown of twelve stars. ²She was pregnant and was crying out in birth pangs, in the agony of giving birth. ³Then another portent appeared in heaven: a great red dragon, with seven heads and ten horns, and seven diadems on his heads. ⁴His tail swept down a third of the stars of heaven and threw them to the earth. Then the dragon stood before the woman who was about to bear a child, so that he might devour her child as soon as it was born. ⁵And she gave birth to a son, a male child, who is to ruleg all the nations with a rod of iron. But her child was snatched away and taken to God and to his throne; ⁶and the woman fled into the wilderness, where she has a place prepared by God, so that there she can be nourished for one thousand two hundred sixty days.

Michael Defeats the Dragon

7 And war broke out in heaven; Michael and his angels fought against the dragon. The dragon and his angels fought back, ⁸but they were defeated, and there was no longer any place for them in heaven. ⁹The great dragon was thrown down, that ancient serpent, who is called the Devil and Satan, the deceiver of the whole world—he was thrown down to the earth, and his angels were thrown down with him.

10 Then I heard a loud voice in heaven, proclaiming,

"Now have come the salvation and
   the power
  and the kingdom of our God
  and the authority of his Messiah,ʰ
for the accuser of our comradesⁱ has
   been thrown down,
  who accuses them day and night
  before our God.

11 But they have conquered him by the
   blood of the Lamb
  and by the word of their testimony,
for they did not cling to life even in
  the face of death.

12 Rejoice then, you heavens
  and those who dwell in them!
But woe to the earth and the sea,
  for the devil has come down to you
  with great wrath,
   because he knows that his time is
   short!"

---

12 Καὶ σημεῖον μέγα ὤφθη ἐν τῷ οὐρανῷ, γυνὴ περιβεβλημένη τὸν ἥλιον, καὶ ἡ σελήνη ὑποκάτω τῶν ποδῶν αὐτῆς καὶ ἐπὶ τῆς κεφαλῆς αὐτῆς στέφανος ἀστέρων δώδεκα, **2** καὶ ἐν γαστρὶ ἔχουσα, καὶ κράζει ὠδίνουσα καὶ βασανιζομένη τεκεῖν. **3** καὶ ὤφθη ἄλλο σημεῖον ἐν τῷ οὐρανῷ, καὶ ἰδοὺ δράκων μέγας πυρρὸς ἔχων κεφαλὰς ἑπτὰ καὶ κέρατα δέκα καὶ ἐπὶ τὰς κεφαλὰς αὐτοῦ ἑπτὰ διαδήματα, **4** καὶ ἡ οὐρὰ αὐτοῦ σύρει τὸ τρίτον τῶν ἀστέρων τοῦ οὐρανοῦ καὶ ἔβαλεν αὐτοὺς εἰς τὴν γῆν. καὶ ὁ δράκων ἕστηκεν ἐνώπιον τῆς γυναικὸς τῆς μελλούσης τεκεῖν, ἵνα ὅταν τέκῃ τὸ τέκνον αὐτῆς καταφάγῃ. **5** καὶ ἔτεκεν υἱὸν ἄρσεν, ὃς μέλλει ποιμαίνειν πάντα τὰ ἔθνη ἐν ῥάβδῳ σιδηρᾷ. καὶ ἡρπάσθη τὸ τέκνον αὐτῆς πρὸς τὸν θεὸν καὶ πρὸς τὸν θρόνον αὐτοῦ. **6** καὶ ἡ γυνὴ ἔφυγεν εἰς τὴν ἔρημον, ὅπου ἔχει ἐκεῖ τόπον ἡτοιμασμένον ἀπὸ τοῦ θεοῦ, ἵνα ἐκεῖ τρέφωσιν αὐτὴν ἡμέρας χιλίας διακοσίας ἑξήκοντα.

7 Καὶ ἐγένετο πόλεμος ἐν τῷ οὐρανῷ, ὁ Μιχαὴλ καὶ οἱ ἄγγελοι αὐτοῦ τοῦ πολεμῆσαι μετὰ τοῦ δράκοντος. καὶ ὁ δράκων ἐπολέμησεν καὶ οἱ ἄγγελοι αὐτοῦ, **8** καὶ οὐκ ἴσχυσεν οὐδὲ τόπος εὑρέθη αὐτῶν ἔτι ἐν τῷ οὐρανῷ. **9** καὶ ἐβλήθη ὁ δράκων ὁ μέγας, ὁ ὄφις ὁ ἀρχαῖος, ὁ καλούμενος Διάβολος καὶ ὁ Σατανᾶς, ὁ πλανῶν τὴν οἰκουμένην ὅλην, ἐβλήθη εἰς τὴν γῆν, καὶ οἱ ἄγγελοι αὐτοῦ μετ' αὐτοῦ ἐβλήθησαν. **10** καὶ ἤκουσα φωνὴν μεγάλην ἐν τῷ οὐρανῷ λέγουσαν,

Ἄρτι ἐγένετο ἡ σωτηρία καὶ ἡ
   δύναμις
  καὶ ἡ βασιλεία τοῦ θεοῦ ἡμῶν
  καὶ ἡ ἐξουσία τοῦ Χριστοῦ αὐτοῦ,
ὅτι ἐβλήθη ὁ κατήγωρ τῶν ἀδελφῶν
   ἡμῶν,
  ὁ κατηγορῶν αὐτοὺς ἐνώπιον τοῦ
   θεοῦ ἡμῶν ἡμέρας καὶ νυκτός.

11 καὶ αὐτοὶ ἐνίκησαν αὐτὸν διὰ τὸ
   αἷμα τοῦ ἀρνίου
  καὶ διὰ τὸν λόγον τῆς μαρτυρίας
   αὐτῶν
  καὶ οὐκ ἠγάπησαν τὴν ψυχὴν
   αὐτῶν ἄχρι θανάτου.

12 διὰ τοῦτο εὐφραίνεσθε, [οἱ] οὐρανοὶ καὶ οἱ ἐν αὐτοῖς σκηνοῦντες. οὐαὶ τὴν γῆν καὶ τὴν θάλασσαν, ὅτι κατέβη ὁ διάβολος πρὸς ὑμᾶς ἔχων θυμὸν μέγαν, εἰδὼς ὅτι ὀλίγον καιρὸν ἔχει.

NIV

The Woman and the Dragon

12 A great and wondrous sign appeared in heaven: a woman clothed with the sun, with the moon under her feet and a crown of twelve stars on her head. ²She was pregnant and cried out in pain as she was about to give birth. ³Then another sign appeared in heaven: an enormous red dragon with seven heads and ten horns and seven crowns on his heads. ⁴His tail swept a third of the stars out of the sky and flung them to the earth. The dragon stood in front of the woman who was about to give birth, so that he might devour her child the moment it was born. ⁵She gave birth to a son, a male child, who will rule all the nations with an iron scepter. And her child was snatched up to God and to his throne. ⁶The woman fled into the desert to a place prepared for her by God, where she might be taken care of for 1,260 days.

7And there was war in heaven. Michael and his angels fought against the dragon, and the dragon and his angels fought back. ⁸But he was not strong enough, and they lost their place in heaven. ⁹The great dragon was hurled down—that ancient serpent called the devil, or Satan, who leads the whole world astray. He was hurled to the earth, and his angels with him.

10Then I heard a loud voice in heaven say:

"Now have come the salvation and the
   power and the kingdom of our
   God,
  and the authority of his Christ.
For the accuser of our brothers,
  who accuses them before our God
   day and night,
  has been hurled down.

11They overcame him
  by the blood of the Lamb
  and by the word of their testimony;
they did not love their lives so much
  as to shrink from death.

12Therefore rejoice, you heavens
  and you who dwell in them!
But woe to the earth and the sea,
  because the devil has gone down to
   you!
He is filled with fury,
  because he knows that his time is
   short."

---

g Or *to shepherd*   h Gk *Christ*   i Gk *brothers*

NRSV

The Dragon Fights Again on Earth

13 So when the dragon saw that he had been thrown down to the earth, he pursued[j] the woman who had given birth to the male child. 14But the woman was given the two wings of the great eagle, so that she could fly from the serpent into the wilderness, to her place where she is nourished for a time, and times, and half a time. 15Then from his mouth the serpent poured water like a river after the woman, to sweep her away with the flood. 16But the earth came to the help of the woman; it opened its mouth and swallowed the river that the dragon had poured from his mouth. 17Then the dragon was angry with the woman, and went off to make war on the rest of her children, those who keep the commandments of God and hold the testimony of Jesus.

The First Beast

18 Then the dragon[k] took his stand on the sand of the seashore. 1And I saw a beast rising out of the sea, having ten horns and seven heads; and on its horns were ten diadems, and on its heads were blasphemous names. 2And the beast that I saw was like a leopard, its feet were like a bear's, and its mouth was like a lion's mouth. And the dragon gave it his power and his throne and great authority. 3One of its heads seemed to have received a death-blow, but its mortal wound[l] had been healed. In amazement the whole earth followed the beast. 4They worshiped the dragon, for he had given his authority to the beast, and they worshiped the beast, saying, "Who is like the beast, and who can fight against it?"

5 The beast was given a mouth uttering haughty and blasphemous words, and it was allowed to exercise authority for forty-two months. 6It opened its mouth to utter blasphemies against God, blaspheming his name and his dwelling, that is, those who dwell in heaven. 7Also it was allowed to make war on the saints and to conquer them.[m] It was given authority over every tribe and people and language and nation, 8and all the inhabitants of the earth will worship it, everyone whose name has not been written from the foundation of the world in the book of life of the Lamb that

Greek Text

13 Καὶ ὅτε εἶδεν ὁ δράκων ὅτι ἐβλήθη εἰς τὴν γῆν, ἐδίωξεν τὴν γυναῖκα ἥτις ἔτεκεν τὸν ἄρσενα. 14 καὶ ἐδόθησαν τῇ γυναικὶ αἱ δύο πτέρυγες τοῦ ἀετοῦ τοῦ μεγάλου, ἵνα πέτηται εἰς τὴν ἔρημον εἰς τὸν τόπον αὐτῆς, ὅπου τρέφεται ἐκεῖ καιρὸν καὶ καιροὺς καὶ ἥμισυ καιροῦ ἀπὸ προσώπου τοῦ ὄφεως. 15 καὶ ἔβαλεν ὁ ὄφις ἐκ τοῦ στόματος αὐτοῦ ὀπίσω τῆς γυναικὸς ὕδωρ ὡς ποταμόν, ἵνα αὐτὴν ποταμοφόρητον ποιήσῃ. 16 καὶ ἐβοήθησεν ἡ γῆ τῇ γυναικὶ καὶ ἤνοιξεν ἡ γῆ τὸ στόμα αὐτῆς καὶ κατέπιεν τὸν ποταμὸν ὃν ἔβαλεν ὁ δράκων ἐκ τοῦ στόματος αὐτοῦ. 17 καὶ ὠργίσθη ὁ δράκων ἐπὶ τῇ γυναικὶ καὶ ἀπῆλθεν ποιῆσαι πόλεμον μετὰ τῶν λοιπῶν τοῦ σπέρματος αὐτῆς τῶν τηρούντων τὰς ἐντολὰς τοῦ θεοῦ καὶ ἐχόντων τὴν μαρτυρίαν Ἰησοῦ.[a] 18 καὶ ἐστάθη[b] ἐπὶ τὴν ἄμμον τῆς θαλάσσης.

13 Καὶ εἶδον ἐκ τῆς θαλάσσης θηρίον ἀναβαῖνον, ἔχον κέρατα δέκα καὶ κεφαλὰς ἑπτὰ καὶ ἐπὶ τῶν κεράτων αὐτοῦ δέκα διαδήματα καὶ ἐπὶ τὰς κεφαλὰς αὐτοῦ ὀνόμα[τα][a] βλασφημίας. 2 καὶ τὸ θηρίον ὃ εἶδον ἦν ὅμοιον παρδάλει καὶ οἱ πόδες αὐτοῦ ὡς ἄρκου καὶ τὸ στόμα αὐτοῦ ὡς στόμα λέοντος. καὶ ἔδωκεν αὐτῷ ὁ δράκων τὴν δύναμιν αὐτοῦ καὶ τὸν θρόνον αὐτοῦ καὶ ἐξουσίαν μεγάλην. 3 καὶ μίαν ἐκ τῶν κεφαλῶν αὐτοῦ ὡς ἐσφαγμένην εἰς θάνατον, καὶ ἡ πληγὴ τοῦ θανάτου αὐτοῦ ἐθεραπεύθη. καὶ ἐθαυμάσθη ὅλη ἡ γῆ ὀπίσω τοῦ θηρίου 4 καὶ προσεκύνησαν τῷ δράκοντι, ὅτι ἔδωκεν τὴν ἐξουσίαν τῷ θηρίῳ, καὶ προσεκύνησαν τῷ θηρίῳ λέγοντες, Τίς ὅμοιος τῷ θηρίῳ καὶ τίς δύναται πολεμῆσαι μετ' αὐτοῦ;

5 Καὶ ἐδόθη αὐτῷ στόμα λαλοῦν μεγάλα καὶ βλασφημίας καὶ ἐδόθη αὐτῷ ἐξουσία ποιῆσαι μῆνας τεσσεράκοντα [καὶ] δύο. 6 καὶ ἤνοιξεν τὸ στόμα αὐτοῦ εἰς βλασφημίας πρὸς τὸν θεὸν βλασφημῆσαι τὸ ὄνομα αὐτοῦ καὶ τὴν σκηνὴν αὐτοῦ, τοὺς ἐν τῷ οὐρανῷ σκηνοῦντας. 7 καὶ ἐδόθη αὐτῷ ποιῆσαι πόλεμον μετὰ τῶν ἁγίων καὶ νικῆσαι αὐτούς, καὶ ἐδόθη αὐτῷ ἐξουσία ἐπὶ πᾶσαν φυλὴν καὶ λαὸν καὶ γλῶσσαν καὶ ἔθνος. 8 καὶ προσκυνήσουσιν αὐτὸν πάντες οἱ κατοικοῦντες ἐπὶ τῆς γῆς, οὗ οὐ γέγραπται τὸ ὄνομα αὐτοῦ ἐν τῷ βιβλίῳ τῆς ζωῆς τοῦ ἀρνίου τοῦ

NIV

13When the dragon saw that he had been hurled to the earth, he pursued the woman who had given birth to the male child. 14The woman was given the two wings of a great eagle, so that she might fly to the place prepared for her in the desert, where she would be taken care of for a time, times and half a time, out of the serpent's reach. 15Then from his mouth the serpent spewed water like a river, to overtake the woman and sweep her away with the torrent. 16But the earth helped the woman by opening its mouth and swallowing the river that the dragon had spewed out of his mouth. 17Then the dragon was enraged at the woman and went off to make war against the rest of her offspring—those who obey God's commandments and hold to the testimony of Jesus. 1And the dragon[a] stood on the shore of the sea.

The Beast out of the Sea

And I saw a beast coming out of the sea. He had ten horns and seven heads, with ten crowns on his horns, and on each head a blasphemous name. 2The beast I saw resembled a leopard, but had feet like those of a bear and a mouth like that of a lion. The dragon gave the beast his power and his throne and great authority. 3One of the heads of the beast seemed to have had a fatal wound, but the fatal wound had been healed. The whole world was astonished and followed the beast. 4Men worshiped the dragon because he had given authority to the beast, and they also worshiped the beast and asked, "Who is like the beast? Who can make war against him?"

5The beast was given a mouth to utter proud words and blasphemies and to exercise his authority for forty-two months. 6He opened his mouth to blaspheme God, and to slander his name and his dwelling place and those who live in heaven. 7He was given power to make war against the saints and to conquer them. And he was given authority over every tribe, people, language and nation. 8All inhabitants of the earth will worship the beast—all whose names have not been written in the book of life belonging to the Lamb that was slain

---

j Or persecuted   k Gk Then he; other ancient authorities read Then I stood   l Gk the plague of its death   m Other ancient authorities lack this sentence

a17 NIV begins 13:1 after Ἰησοῦ.   b18 NIV note (13:1a) and NRSV note k ἐστάθην   a1 NIV text ὄνομα

a1 Some late manuscripts And I

was slaughtered.[n]

9 Let anyone who has an ear listen:

10 If you are to be taken captive,
   into captivity you go;
   if you kill with the sword,
   with the sword you must be killed.

Here is a call for the endurance and faith of the saints.

The Second Beast

11 Then I saw another beast that rose out of the earth; it had two horns like a lamb and it spoke like a dragon. 12It exercises all the authority of the first beast on its behalf, and it makes the earth and its inhabitants worship the first beast, whose mortal wound[o] had been healed. 13It performs great signs, even making fire come down from heaven to earth in the sight of all; 14and by the signs that it is allowed to perform on behalf of the beast, it deceives the inhabitants of earth, telling them to make an image for the beast that had been wounded by the sword[p] and yet lived; 15and it was allowed to give breath[q] to the image of the beast so that the image of the beast could even speak and cause those who would not worship the image of the beast to be killed. 16Also it causes all, both small and great, both rich and poor, both free and slave, to be marked on the right hand or the forehead, 17so that no one can buy or sell who does not have the mark, that is, the name of the beast or the number of its name. 18This calls for wisdom: let anyone with understanding calculate the number of the beast, for it is the number of a person. Its number is six hundred sixty-six.[r]

The Lamb and the 144,000

14 Then I looked, and there was the Lamb, standing on Mount Zion! And with him were one hundred forty-four thousand who had his name and his Father's name written on their foreheads. 2And I heard a voice from heaven like the sound of many waters and like the sound of loud thunder; the voice I heard was like the sound of harpists playing on their harps, 3and they sing a new song before the throne and before the four living creatures and before the elders. No one could

---

ἐσφαγμένου ἀπὸ καταβολῆς κόσμου.

9 Εἴ τις ἔχει οὖς ἀκουσάτω.

10 εἴ τις εἰς αἰχμαλωσίαν,
   εἰς αἰχμαλωσίαν ὑπάγει·
   εἴ τις ἐν μαχαίρῃ ἀποκτανθῆναι[b]
   αὐτὸν ἐν μαχαίρῃ ἀποκτανθῆναι.
Ὧδέ ἐστιν ἡ ὑπομονὴ καὶ ἡ πίστις τῶν ἁγίων.

11 Καὶ εἶδον ἄλλο θηρίον ἀναβαῖνον ἐκ τῆς γῆς, καὶ εἶχεν κέρατα δύο ὅμοια ἀρνίῳ καὶ ἐλάλει ὡς δράκων. 12 καὶ τὴν ἐξουσίαν τοῦ πρώτου θηρίου πᾶσαν ποιεῖ ἐνώπιον αὐτοῦ, καὶ ποιεῖ τὴν γῆν καὶ τοὺς ἐν αὐτῇ κατοικοῦντας ἵνα προσκυνήσουσιν τὸ θηρίον τὸ πρῶτον, οὗ ἐθεραπεύθη ἡ πληγὴ τοῦ θανάτου αὐτοῦ. 13 καὶ ποιεῖ σημεῖα μεγάλα, ἵνα καὶ πῦρ ποιῇ ἐκ τοῦ οὐρανοῦ καταβαίνειν εἰς τὴν γῆν ἐνώπιον τῶν ἀνθρώπων, 14 καὶ πλανᾷ τοὺς κατοικοῦντας ἐπὶ τῆς γῆς διὰ τὰ σημεῖα ἃ ἐδόθη αὐτῷ ποιῆσαι ἐνώπιον τοῦ θηρίου, λέγων τοῖς κατοικοῦσιν ἐπὶ τῆς γῆς ποιῆσαι εἰκόνα τῷ θηρίῳ, ὃς ἔχει τὴν πληγὴν τῆς μαχαίρης καὶ ἔζησεν. 15 καὶ ἐδόθη αὐτῷ δοῦναι πνεῦμα τῇ εἰκόνι τοῦ θηρίου, ἵνα καὶ λαλήσῃ ἡ εἰκὼν τοῦ θηρίου καὶ ποιήσῃ [ἵνα] ὅσοι ἐὰν μὴ προσκυνήσωσιν τῇ εἰκόνι τοῦ θηρίου ἀποκτανθῶσιν. 16 καὶ ποιεῖ πάντας, τοὺς μικροὺς καὶ τοὺς μεγάλους, καὶ τοὺς πλουσίους καὶ τοὺς πτωχούς, καὶ τοὺς ἐλευθέρους καὶ τοὺς δούλους, ἵνα δῶσιν αὐτοῖς χάραγμα ἐπὶ τῆς χειρὸς αὐτῶν τῆς δεξιᾶς ἢ ἐπὶ τὸ μέτωπον αὐτῶν 17 καὶ ἵνα μή τις δύνηται ἀγοράσαι ἢ πωλῆσαι εἰ μὴ ὁ ἔχων τὸ χάραγμα τὸ ὄνομα τοῦ θηρίου ἢ τὸν ἀριθμὸν τοῦ ὀνόματος αὐτοῦ. 18 Ὧδε ἡ σοφία ἐστίν. ὁ ἔχων νοῦν ψηφισάτω τὸν ἀριθμὸν τοῦ θηρίου, ἀριθμὸς γὰρ ἀνθρώπου ἐστίν, καὶ ὁ ἀριθμὸς αὐτοῦ ἑξακόσιοι ἑξήκοντα[c] ἕξ.

14 Καὶ εἶδον, καὶ ἰδοὺ τὸ ἀρνίον ἑστὸς ἐπὶ τὸ ὄρος Σιὼν καὶ μετ' αὐτοῦ ἑκατὸν τεσσεράκοντα τέσσαρες χιλιάδες ἔχουσαι τὸ ὄνομα αὐτοῦ καὶ τὸ ὄνομα τοῦ πατρὸς αὐτοῦ γεγραμμένον ἐπὶ τῶν μετώπων αὐτῶν. 2 καὶ ἤκουσα φωνὴν ἐκ τοῦ οὐρανοῦ ὡς φωνὴν ὑδάτων πολλῶν καὶ ὡς φωνὴν βροντῆς μεγάλης, καὶ ἡ φωνὴ ἣν ἤκουσα ὡς κιθαρῳδῶν κιθαριζόντων ἐν ταῖς κιθάραις αὐτῶν. 3 καὶ ᾄδουσιν [ὡς][a] ᾠδὴν καινὴν ἐνώπιον τοῦ θρόνου καὶ ἐνώπιον τῶν τεσσάρων ζῴων καὶ τῶν πρεσβυτέρων, καὶ οὐδεὶς ἐδύνατο μαθεῖν

---

from the creation of the world.[b]

9He who has an ear, let him hear.

10If anyone is to go into captivity,
   into captivity he will go.
   If anyone is to be killed[c] with the sword,
   with the sword he will be killed.

This calls for patient endurance and faithfulness on the part of the saints.

The Beast out of the Earth

11Then I saw another beast, coming out of the earth. He had two horns like a lamb, but he spoke like a dragon. 12He exercised all the authority of the first beast on his behalf, and made the earth and its inhabitants worship the first beast, whose fatal wound had been healed. 13And he performed great and miraculous signs, even causing fire to come down from heaven to earth in full view of men. 14Because of the signs he was given power to do on behalf of the first beast, he deceived the inhabitants of the earth. He ordered them to set up an image in honor of the beast who was wounded by the sword and yet lived. 15He was given power to give breath to the image of the first beast, so that it could speak and cause all who refused to worship the image to be killed. 16He also forced everyone, small and great, rich and poor, free and slave, to receive a mark on his right hand or on his forehead, 17so that no one could buy or sell unless he had the mark, which is the name of the beast or the number of his name.

18This calls for wisdom. If anyone has insight, let him calculate the number of the beast, for it is man's number. His number is 666.

The Lamb and the 144,000

14 Then I looked, and there before me was the Lamb, standing on Mount Zion, and with him 144,000 who had his name and his Father's name written on their foreheads. 2And I heard a sound from heaven like the roar of rushing waters and like a loud peal of thunder. The sound I heard was like that of harpists playing their harps. 3And they sang a new song before the throne and before the four living creatures and the elders. No one

---

learn that song except the one hundred forty-four thousand who have been redeemed from the earth. [4]It is these who have not defiled themselves with women, for they are virgins; these follow the Lamb wherever he goes. They have been redeemed from humankind as first fruits for God and the Lamb, [5]and in their mouth no lie was found; they are blameless.

The Messages of the Three Angels

6 Then I saw another angel flying in midheaven, with an eternal gospel to proclaim to those who live[s] on the earth—to every nation and tribe and language and people. [7]He said in a loud voice, "Fear God and give him glory, for the hour of his judgment has come; and worship him who made heaven and earth, the sea and the springs of water."

8 Then another angel, a second, followed, saying, "Fallen, fallen is Babylon the great! She has made all nations drink of the wine of the wrath of her fornication."

9 Then another angel, a third, followed them, crying with a loud voice, "Those who worship the beast and its image, and receive a mark on their foreheads or on their hands, [10]they will also drink the wine of God's wrath, poured unmixed into the cup of his anger, and they will be tormented with fire and sulfur in the presence of the holy angels and in the presence of the Lamb. [11]And the smoke of their torment goes up forever and ever. There is no rest day or night for those who worship the beast and its image and for anyone who receives the mark of its name."

12 Here is a call for the endurance of the saints, those who keep the commandments of God and hold fast to the faith of[t] Jesus.

13 And I heard a voice from heaven saying, "Write this: Blessed are the dead who from now on die in the Lord." "Yes," says the Spirit, "they will rest from their labors, for their deeds follow them."

Reaping the Earth's Harvest

14 Then I looked, and there was a white cloud, and seated on the cloud was one like the Son of Man, with a golden crown on his head, and a sharp sickle in his hand! [15]Another angel came out of the temple, calling with a loud voice to the one who sat on the cloud, "Use your sickle and reap,

---

τὴν ᾠδὴν εἰ μὴ αἱ ἑκατὸν τεσσεράκοντα τέσσαρες χιλιάδες, οἱ ἠγορασμένοι ἀπὸ τῆς γῆς. 4 οὗτοί εἰσιν οἳ μετὰ γυναικῶν οὐκ ἐμολύνθησαν, παρθένοι γάρ εἰσιν, οὗτοι οἱ ἀκολουθοῦντες τῷ ἀρνίῳ ὅπου ἂν ὑπάγῃ. οὗτοι ἠγοράσθησαν ἀπὸ τῶν ἀνθρώπων ἀπαρχὴ τῷ θεῷ καὶ τῷ ἀρνίῳ, 5 καὶ ἐν τῷ στόματι αὐτῶν οὐχ εὑρέθη ψεῦδος, ἄμωμοί εἰσιν.

6 Καὶ εἶδον ἄλλον ἄγγελον πετόμενον ἐν μεσουρανήματι, ἔχοντα εὐαγγέλιον αἰώνιον εὐαγγελίσαι ἐπὶ τοὺς καθημένους ἐπὶ τῆς γῆς καὶ ἐπὶ πᾶν ἔθνος καὶ φυλὴν καὶ γλῶσσαν καὶ λαόν, 7 λέγων ἐν φωνῇ μεγάλῃ, Φοβήθητε τὸν θεὸν καὶ δότε αὐτῷ δόξαν, ὅτι ἦλθεν ἡ ὥρα τῆς κρίσεως αὐτοῦ, καὶ προσκυνήσατε τῷ ποιήσαντι τὸν οὐρανὸν καὶ τὴν γῆν καὶ θάλασσαν καὶ πηγὰς ὑδάτων.

8 Καὶ ἄλλος ἄγγελος δεύτερος ἠκολούθησεν λέγων, Ἔπεσεν ἔπεσεν Βαβυλὼν ἡ μεγάλη ἣ ἐκ τοῦ οἴνου τοῦ θυμοῦ τῆς πορνείας αὐτῆς πεπότικεν πάντα τὰ ἔθνη.

9 Καὶ ἄλλος ἄγγελος τρίτος ἠκολούθησεν αὐτοῖς λέγων ἐν φωνῇ μεγάλῃ, Εἴ τις προσκυνεῖ τὸ θηρίον καὶ τὴν εἰκόνα αὐτοῦ καὶ λαμβάνει χάραγμα ἐπὶ τοῦ μετώπου αὐτοῦ ἢ ἐπὶ τὴν χεῖρα αὐτοῦ, 10 καὶ αὐτὸς πίεται ἐκ τοῦ οἴνου τοῦ θυμοῦ τοῦ θεοῦ τοῦ κεκερασμένου ἀκράτου ἐν τῷ ποτηρίῳ τῆς ὀργῆς αὐτοῦ καὶ βασανισθήσεται ἐν πυρὶ καὶ θείῳ ἐνώπιον ἀγγέλων ἁγίων καὶ ἐνώπιον τοῦ ἀρνίου. 11 καὶ ὁ καπνὸς τοῦ βασανισμοῦ αὐτῶν εἰς αἰῶνας αἰώνων ἀναβαίνει, καὶ οὐκ ἔχουσιν ἀνάπαυσιν ἡμέρας καὶ νυκτὸς οἱ προσκυνοῦντες τὸ θηρίον καὶ τὴν εἰκόνα αὐτοῦ καὶ εἴ τις λαμβάνει τὸ χάραγμα τοῦ ὀνόματος αὐτοῦ. 12 Ὧδε ἡ ὑπομονὴ τῶν ἁγίων ἐστίν, οἱ τηροῦντες τὰς ἐντολὰς τοῦ θεοῦ καὶ τὴν πίστιν Ἰησοῦ.

13 Καὶ ἤκουσα φωνῆς ἐκ τοῦ οὐρανοῦ λεγούσης, Γράψον· Μακάριοι οἱ νεκροὶ οἱ ἐν κυρίῳ ἀποθνῄσκοντες ἀπ' ἄρτι. ναί, λέγει τὸ πνεῦμα, ἵνα ἀναπαήσονται ἐκ τῶν κόπων αὐτῶν, τὰ γὰρ ἔργα αὐτῶν ἀκολουθεῖ μετ' αὐτῶν.

14 Καὶ εἶδον, καὶ ἰδοὺ νεφέλη λευκή, καὶ ἐπὶ τὴν νεφέλην καθήμενον ὅμοιον υἱὸν ἀνθρώπου, ἔχων ἐπὶ τῆς κεφαλῆς αὐτοῦ στέφανον χρυσοῦν καὶ ἐν τῇ χειρὶ αὐτοῦ δρέπανον ὀξύ. 15 καὶ ἄλλος ἄγγελος ἐξῆλθεν ἐκ τοῦ ναοῦ κράζων ἐν φωνῇ μεγάλῃ τῷ καθημένῳ ἐπὶ τῆς νεφέλης, Πέμψον τὸ δρέπανόν σου καὶ

---

could learn the song except the 144,000 who had been redeemed from the earth. [4]These are those who did not defile themselves with women, for they kept themselves pure. They follow the Lamb wherever he goes. They were purchased from among men and offered as firstfruits to God and the Lamb. [5]No lie was found in their mouths; they are blameless.

The Three Angels

[6]Then I saw another angel flying in midair, and he had the eternal gospel to proclaim to those who live on the earth—to every nation, tribe, language and people. [7]He said in a loud voice, "Fear God and give him glory, because the hour of his judgment has come. Worship him who made the heavens, the earth, the sea and the springs of water."

[8]A second angel followed and said, "Fallen! Fallen is Babylon the Great, which made all the nations drink the maddening wine of her adulteries."

[9]A third angel followed them and said in a loud voice: "If anyone worships the beast and his image and receives his mark on the forehead or on the hand, [10]he, too, will drink of the wine of God's fury, which has been poured full strength into the cup of his wrath. He will be tormented with burning sulfur in the presence of the holy angels and of the Lamb. [11]And the smoke of their torment rises for ever and ever. There is no rest day or night for those who worship the beast and his image, or for anyone who receives the mark of his name." [12]This calls for patient endurance on the part of the saints who obey God's commandments and remain faithful to Jesus.

[13]Then I heard a voice from heaven say, "Write: Blessed are the dead who die in the Lord from now on."

"Yes," says the Spirit, "they will rest from their labor, for their deeds will follow them."

The Harvest of the Earth

[14]I looked, and there before me was a white cloud, and seated on the cloud was one "like a son of man"[a] with a crown of gold on his head and a sharp sickle in his hand. [15]Then another angel came out of the temple and called in a loud voice to him who was sitting on the cloud, "Take your sickle and reap, because the time to

---

[s] Gk sit   [t] Or to their faith in

[a]14 Daniel 7:13

for the hour to reap has come, because the harvest of the earth is fully ripe." [16]So the one who sat on the cloud swung his sickle over the earth, and the earth was reaped.

[17] Then another angel came out of the temple in heaven, and he too had a sharp sickle. [18]Then another angel came out from the altar, the angel who has authority over fire, and he called with a loud voice to him who had the sharp sickle, "Use your sharp sickle and gather the clusters of the vine of the earth, for its grapes are ripe." [19]So the angel swung his sickle over the earth and gathered the vintage of the earth, and he threw it into the great wine press of the wrath of God. [20]And the wine press was trodden outside the city, and blood flowed from the wine press, as high as a horse's bridle, for a distance of about two hundred miles.[u]

The Angels with the Seven Last Plagues

15 Then I saw another portent in heaven, great and amazing: seven angels with seven plagues, which are the last, for with them the wrath of God is ended.

[2] And I saw what appeared to be a sea of glass mixed with fire, and those who had conquered the beast and its image and the number of its name, standing beside the sea of glass with harps of God in their hands. [3]And they sing the song of Moses, the servant[v] of God, and the song of the Lamb:

"Great and amazing are your deeds,
   Lord God the Almighty!
Just and true are your ways,
   King of the nations![w]
[4] Lord, who will not fear
   and glorify your name?
For you alone are holy.
   All nations will come
   and worship before you,
for your judgments have been
   revealed."

[5] After this I looked, and the temple of the tent[x] of witness in heaven was opened, [6]and out of the temple came the seven angels with the seven plagues, robed in pure bright linen,[y] with golden sashes across their chests. [7]Then one of the four living creatures gave the seven angels seven golden bowls full of the wrath of

θέρισον, ὅτι ἦλθεν ἡ ὥρα θερίσαι, ὅτι ἐξηράνθη ὁ θερισμὸς τῆς γῆς. **16** καὶ ἔβαλεν ὁ καθήμενος ἐπὶ τῆς νεφέλης τὸ δρέπανον αὐτοῦ ἐπὶ τὴν γῆν καὶ ἐθερίσθη ἡ γῆ.

17 Καὶ ἄλλος ἄγγελος ἐξῆλθεν ἐκ τοῦ ναοῦ τοῦ ἐν τῷ οὐρανῷ ἔχων καὶ αὐτὸς δρέπανον ὀξύ. **18** Καὶ ἄλλος ἄγγελος [ἐξῆλθεν] ἐκ τοῦ θυσιαστηρίου [ὁ] ἔχων ἐξουσίαν ἐπὶ τοῦ πυρός, καὶ ἐφώνησεν φωνῇ μεγάλῃ τῷ ἔχοντι τὸ δρέπανον τὸ ὀξὺ λέγων, Πέμψον σου τὸ δρέπανον τὸ ὀξὺ καὶ τρύγησον τοὺς βότρυας τῆς ἀμπέλου τῆς γῆς, ὅτι ἤκμασαν αἱ σταφυλαὶ αὐτῆς. **19** καὶ ἔβαλεν ὁ ἄγγελος τὸ δρέπανον αὐτοῦ εἰς τὴν γῆν καὶ ἐτρύγησεν τὴν ἄμπελον τῆς γῆς καὶ ἔβαλεν εἰς τὴν ληνὸν τοῦ θυμοῦ τοῦ θεοῦ τὸν μέγαν. **20** καὶ ἐπατήθη ἡ ληνὸς ἔξωθεν τῆς πόλεως καὶ ἐξῆλθεν αἷμα ἐκ τῆς ληνοῦ ἄχρι τῶν χαλινῶν τῶν ἵππων ἀπὸ σταδίων χιλίων ἑξακοσίων.

15 Καὶ εἶδον ἄλλο σημεῖον ἐν τῷ οὐρανῷ μέγα καὶ θαυμαστόν, ἀγγέλους ἑπτὰ ἔχοντας πληγὰς ἑπτὰ τὰς ἐσχάτας, ὅτι ἐν αὐταῖς ἐτελέσθη ὁ θυμὸς τοῦ θεοῦ.

2 Καὶ εἶδον ὡς θάλασσαν ὑαλίνην μεμιγμένην πυρὶ καὶ τοὺς νικῶντας ἐκ τοῦ θηρίου καὶ ἐκ τῆς εἰκόνος αὐτοῦ καὶ ἐκ τοῦ ἀριθμοῦ τοῦ ὀνόματος αὐτοῦ ἑστῶτας ἐπὶ τὴν θάλασσαν τὴν ὑαλίνην ἔχοντας κιθάρας τοῦ θεοῦ. **3** καὶ ᾄδουσιν τὴν ᾠδὴν Μωϋσέως τοῦ δούλου τοῦ θεοῦ καὶ τὴν ᾠδὴν τοῦ ἀρνίου λέγοντες,

Μεγάλα καὶ θαυμαστὰ τὰ ἔργα σου,
   κύριε ὁ θεὸς ὁ παντοκράτωρ·
δίκαιαι καὶ ἀληθιναὶ αἱ ὁδοί σου,
   ὁ βασιλεὺς τῶν ἐθνῶν[a]·
4 τίς οὐ μὴ φοβηθῇ, κύριε,
   καὶ δοξάσει τὸ ὄνομά σου;
ὅτι μόνος ὅσιος,
   ὅτι πάντα τὰ ἔθνη ἥξουσιν
   καὶ προσκυνήσουσιν ἐνώπιόν σου,
ὅτι τὰ δικαιώματά σου ἐφανερώ-
   θησαν.

5 Καὶ μετὰ ταῦτα εἶδον, καὶ ἠνοίγη ὁ ναὸς τῆς σκηνῆς τοῦ μαρτυρίου ἐν τῷ οὐρανῷ, **6** καὶ ἐξῆλθον οἱ ἑπτὰ ἄγγελοι [οἱ] ἔχοντες τὰς ἑπτὰ πληγὰς ἐκ τοῦ ναοῦ ἐνδεδυμένοι λίνον[b] καθαρὸν λαμπρὸν καὶ περιεζωσμένοι περὶ τὰ στήθη ζώνας χρυσᾶς. **7** καὶ ἓν ἐκ τῶν τεσσάρων ζῴων ἔδωκεν τοῖς ἑπτὰ ἀγγέλοις ἑπτὰ φιάλας χρυσᾶς γεμούσας

reap has come, for the harvest of the earth is ripe." [16]So he who was seated on the cloud swung his sickle over the earth, and the earth was harvested.

[17]Another angel came out of the temple in heaven, and he too had a sharp sickle. [18]Still another angel, who had charge of the fire, came from the altar and called in a loud voice to him who had the sharp sickle, "Take your sharp sickle and gather the clusters of grapes from the earth's vine, because its grapes are ripe." [19]The angel swung his sickle on the earth, gathered its grapes and threw them into the great winepress of God's wrath. [20]They were trampled in the winepress outside the city, and blood flowed out of the press, rising as high as the horses' bridles for a distance of 1,600 stadia.[b]

Seven Angels With Seven Plagues

15 I saw in heaven another great and marvelous sign: seven angels with the seven last plagues—last, because with them God's wrath is completed. [2]And I saw what looked like a sea of glass mixed with fire and, standing beside the sea, those who had been victorious over the beast and his image and over the number of his name. They held harps given them by God [3]and sang the song of Moses the servant of God and the song of the Lamb:

"Great and marvelous are your deeds,
   Lord God Almighty.
Just and true are your ways,
   King of the ages.
[4]Who will not fear you, O Lord,
   and bring glory to your name?
For you alone are holy.
All nations will come
   and worship before you,
for your righteous acts have been
   revealed."

[5]After this I looked and in heaven the temple, that is, the tabernacle of the Testimony, was opened. [6]Out of the temple came the seven angels with the seven plagues. They were dressed in clean, shining linen and wore golden sashes around their chests. [7]Then one of the four living creatures gave to the seven angels seven golden bowls filled with the wrath of God,

---

[u] Gk *one thousand six hundred stadia*   [v] Gk *slave*
[w] Other ancient authorities read *the ages*   [x] Or *tabernacle*
[y] Other ancient authorities read *stone*

[a]3 NIV text and NRSV note w αἰώνων
[b]6 NRSV note y λίθον

[b]20 That is, about 180 miles (about 300 kilometers)

God, who lives forever and ever; 8and the temple was filled with smoke from the glory of God and from his power, and no one could enter the temple until the seven plagues of the seven angels were ended.

The Bowls of God's Wrath

16 Then I heard a loud voice from the temple telling the seven angels, "Go and pour out on the earth the seven bowls of the wrath of God."

2 So the first angel went and poured his bowl on the earth, and a foul and painful sore came on those who had the mark of the beast and who worshiped its image.

3 The second angel poured his bowl into the sea, and it became like the blood of a corpse, and every living thing in the sea died.

4 The third angel poured his bowl into the rivers and the springs of water, and they became blood. 5And I heard the angel of the waters say,

"You are just, O Holy One, who are
     and were,
   for you have judged these things;
6 because they shed the blood of saints
     and prophets,
   you have given them blood to drink.
   It is what they deserve!"

7And I heard the altar respond,

"Yes, O Lord God, the Almighty,
   your judgments are true and just!"

8 The fourth angel poured his bowl on the sun, and it was allowed to scorch them with fire; 9they were scorched by the fierce heat, but they cursed the name of God, who had authority over these plagues, and they did not repent and give him glory.

10 The fifth angel poured his bowl on the throne of the beast, and its kingdom was plunged into darkness; people gnawed their tongues in agony, 11and cursed the God of heaven because of their pains and sores, and they did not repent of their deeds.

12 The sixth angel poured his bowl on the great river Euphrates, and its water was dried up in order to prepare the way for the kings from the east. 13And I saw

---

τοῦ θυμοῦ τοῦ θεοῦ τοῦ ζῶντος εἰς τοὺς αἰῶνας τῶν αἰώνων. **8** καὶ ἐγεμίσθη ὁ ναὸς καπνοῦ ἐκ τῆς δόξης τοῦ θεοῦ καὶ ἐκ τῆς δυνάμεως αὐτοῦ, καὶ οὐδεὶς ἐδύνατο εἰσελθεῖν εἰς τὸν ναὸν ἄχρι τελεσθῶσιν αἱ ἑπτὰ πληγαὶ τῶν ἑπτὰ ἀγγέλων.

16 Καὶ ἤκουσα μεγάλης φωνῆς ἐκ τοῦ ναοῦ λεγούσης τοῖς ἑπτὰ ἀγγέλοις, Ὑπάγετε καὶ ἐκχέετε τὰς ἑπτὰ φιάλας τοῦ θυμοῦ τοῦ θεοῦ εἰς τὴν γῆν.

2 Καὶ ἀπῆλθεν ὁ πρῶτος καὶ ἐξέχεεν τὴν φιάλην αὐτοῦ εἰς τὴν γῆν, καὶ ἐγένετο ἕλκος κακὸν καὶ πονηρὸν ἐπὶ τοὺς ἀνθρώπους τοὺς ἔχοντας τὸ χάραγμα τοῦ θηρίου καὶ τοὺς προσκυνοῦντας τῇ εἰκόνι αὐτοῦ.

3 Καὶ ὁ δεύτερος ἐξέχεεν τὴν φιάλην αὐτοῦ εἰς τὴν θάλασσαν, καὶ ἐγένετο αἷμα ὡς νεκροῦ, καὶ πᾶσα ψυχὴ ζωῆς ἀπέθανεν τὰ ἐν τῇ θαλάσσῃ.

4 Καὶ ὁ τρίτος ἐξέχεεν τὴν φιάλην αὐτοῦ εἰς τοὺς ποταμοὺς καὶ τὰς πηγὰς τῶν ὑδάτων, καὶ ἐγένετο αἷμα. **5** καὶ ἤκουσα τοῦ ἀγγέλου τῶν ὑδάτων λέγοντος,

Δίκαιος εἶ, ὁ ὢν καὶ ὁ ἦν, ὁ ὅσιος,
   ὅτι ταῦτα ἔκρινας,
6 ὅτι αἷμα ἁγίων καὶ προφητῶν
     ἐξέχεαν
   καὶ αἷμα αὐτοῖς [δ]έδωκας πιεῖν,
   ἄξιοί εἰσιν.

7 καὶ ἤκουσα τοῦ θυσιαστηρίου λέγοντος,

Ναί κύριε ὁ θεὸς ὁ παντοκράτωρ,
   ἀληθιναὶ καὶ δίκαιαι αἱ κρίσεις
     σου.

8 Καὶ ὁ τέταρτος ἐξέχεεν τὴν φιάλην αὐτοῦ ἐπὶ τὸν ἥλιον, καὶ ἐδόθη αὐτῷ καυματίσαι τοὺς ἀνθρώπους ἐν πυρί. **9** καὶ ἐκαυματίσθησαν οἱ ἄνθρωποι καῦμα μέγα καὶ ἐβλασφήμησαν τὸ ὄνομα τοῦ θεοῦ τοῦ ἔχοντος τὴν ἐξουσίαν ἐπὶ τὰς πληγὰς ταύτας καὶ οὐ μετενόησαν δοῦναι αὐτῷ δόξαν.

10 Καὶ ὁ πέμπτος ἐξέχεεν τὴν φιάλην αὐτοῦ ἐπὶ τὸν θρόνον τοῦ θηρίου, καὶ ἐγένετο ἡ βασιλεία αὐτοῦ ἐσκοτωμένη, καὶ ἐμασῶντο τὰς γλώσσας αὐτῶν ἐκ τοῦ πόνου, **11** καὶ ἐβλασφήμησαν τὸν θεὸν τοῦ οὐρανοῦ ἐκ τῶν πόνων αὐτῶν καὶ ἐκ τῶν ἑλκῶν αὐτῶν καὶ οὐ μετενόησαν ἐκ τῶν ἔργων αὐτῶν.

12 Καὶ ὁ ἕκτος ἐξέχεεν τὴν φιάλην αὐτοῦ ἐπὶ τὸν ποταμὸν τὸν μέγαν τὸν Εὐφράτην, καὶ ἐξηράνθη τὸ ὕδωρ αὐτοῦ, ἵνα ἑτοιμασθῇ ἡ ὁδὸς τῶν βασιλέων τῶν ἀπὸ ἀνατολῆς ἡλίου. **13** Καὶ εἶδον

---

who lives for ever and ever. 8And the temple was filled with smoke from the glory of God and from his power, and no one could enter the temple until the seven plagues of the seven angels were completed.

The Seven Bowls of God's Wrath

16 Then I heard a loud voice from the temple saying to the seven angels, "Go, pour out the seven bowls of God's wrath on the earth."

2The first angel went and poured out his bowl on the land, and ugly and painful sores broke out on the people who had the mark of the beast and worshiped his image.

3The second angel poured out his bowl on the sea, and it turned into blood like that of a dead man, and every living thing in the sea died.

4The third angel poured out his bowl on the rivers and springs of water, and they became blood. 5Then I heard the angel in charge of the waters say:

"You are just in these judgments,
   you who are and who were, the Holy
     One,
   because you have so judged;
6for they have shed the blood of your
     saints and prophets,
   and you have given them blood to
     drink as they deserve."

7And I heard the altar respond:

"Yes, Lord God Almighty,
   true and just are your judgments."

8The fourth angel poured out his bowl on the sun, and the sun was given power to scorch people with fire. 9They were seared by the intense heat and they cursed the name of God, who had control over these plagues, but they refused to repent and glorify him.

10The fifth angel poured out his bowl on the throne of the beast, and his kingdom was plunged into darkness. Men gnawed their tongues in agony 11and cursed the God of heaven because of their pains and their sores, but they refused to repent of what they had done.

12The sixth angel poured out his bowl on the great river Euphrates, and its water was dried up to prepare the way for the kings from the East. 13Then I saw three

three foul spirits like frogs coming from the mouth of the dragon, from the mouth of the beast, and from the mouth of the false prophet. 14These are demonic spirits, performing signs, who go abroad to the kings of the whole world, to assemble them for battle on the great day of God the Almighty. 15("See, I am coming like a thief! Blessed is the one who stays awake and is clothed,z not going about naked and exposed to shame.") 16And they assembled them at the place that in Hebrew is called Harmagedon.

17 The seventh angel poured his bowl into the air, and a loud voice came out of the temple, from the throne, saying, "It is done!" 18And there came flashes of lightning, rumblings, peals of thunder, and a violent earthquake, such as had not occurred since people were upon the earth, so violent was that earthquake. 19The great city was split into three parts, and the cities of the nations fell. God remembered great Babylon and gave her the wine-cup of the fury of his wrath. 20And every island fled away, and no mountains were to be found; 21and huge hailstones, each weighing about a hundred pounds,a dropped from heaven on people, until they cursed God for the plague of the hail, so fearful was that plague.

The Great Whore and the Beast

17 Then one of the seven angels who had the seven bowls came and said to me, "Come, I will show you the judgment of the great whore who is seated on many waters, 2with whom the kings of the earth have committed fornication, and with the wine of whose fornication the inhabitants of the earth have become drunk." 3So he carried me away in the spiritb into a wilderness, and I saw a woman sitting on a scarlet beast that was full of blasphemous names, and it had seven heads and ten horns. 4The woman was clothed in purple and scarlet, and adorned with gold and jewels and pearls, holding in her hand a golden cup full of abominations and the impurities of her fornication; 5and on her forehead was written a name, a mystery: "Babylon the great, mother of whores and of earth's abominations." 6And I saw that

ἐκ τοῦ στόματος τοῦ δράκοντος καὶ ἐκ τοῦ στόματος τοῦ θηρίου καὶ ἐκ τοῦ στόματος τοῦ ψευδοπροφήτου πνεύματα τρία ἀκάθαρτα ὡς βάτραχοι· **14** εἰσὶν γὰρ πνεύματα δαιμονίων ποιοῦντα σημεῖα, ἃ ἐκπορεύεται ἐπὶ τοὺς βασιλεῖς τῆς οἰκουμένης ὅλης συναγαγεῖν αὐτοὺς εἰς τὸν πόλεμον τῆς ἡμέρας τῆς μεγάλης τοῦ θεοῦ τοῦ παντοκράτορος. **15** Ἰδοὺ ἔρχομαι ὡς κλέπτης. μακάριος ὁ γρηγορῶν καὶ τηρῶν τὰ ἱμάτια αὐτοῦ, ἵνα μὴ γυμνὸς περιπατῇ καὶ βλέπωσιν τὴν ἀσχημοσύνην αὐτοῦ. **16** καὶ συνήγαγεν αὐτοὺς εἰς τὸν τόπον τὸν καλούμενον Ἑβραϊστὶ Ἁρμαγεδών.

17 Καὶ ὁ ἕβδομος ἐξέχεεν τὴν φιάλην αὐτοῦ ἐπὶ τὸν ἀέρα, καὶ ἐξῆλθεν φωνὴ μεγάλη ἐκ τοῦ ναοῦ ἀπὸ τοῦ θρόνου λέγουσα, Γέγονεν. **18** καὶ ἐγένοντο ἀστραπαὶ καὶ φωναὶ καὶ βρονταὶ καὶ σεισμὸς ἐγένετο μέγας, οἷος οὐκ ἐγένετο ἀφ᾽ οὗ ἄνθρωπος ἐγένετο ἐπὶ τῆς γῆς τηλικοῦτος σεισμὸς οὕτω μέγας. **19** καὶ ἐγένετο ἡ πόλις ἡ μεγάλη εἰς τρία μέρη καὶ αἱ πόλεις τῶν ἐθνῶν ἔπεσαν. καὶ Βαβυλὼν ἡ μεγάλη ἐμνήσθη ἐνώπιον τοῦ θεοῦ δοῦναι αὐτῇ τὸ ποτήριον τοῦ οἴνου τοῦ θυμοῦ τῆς ὀργῆς αὐτοῦ. **20** καὶ πᾶσα νῆσος ἔφυγεν καὶ ὄρη οὐχ εὑρέθησαν. **21** καὶ χάλαζα μεγάλη ὡς ταλαντιαία καταβαίνει ἐκ τοῦ οὐρανοῦ ἐπὶ τοὺς ἀνθρώπους, καὶ ἐβλασφήμησαν οἱ ἄνθρωποι τὸν θεὸν ἐκ τῆς πληγῆς τῆς χαλάζης, ὅτι μεγάλη ἐστὶν ἡ πληγὴ αὐτῆς σφόδρα.

17 Καὶ ἦλθεν εἷς ἐκ τῶν ἑπτὰ ἀγγέλων τῶν ἐχόντων τὰς ἑπτὰ φιάλας καὶ ἐλάλησεν μετ᾽ ἐμοῦ λέγων, Δεῦρο, δείξω σοι τὸ κρίμα τῆς πόρνης τῆς μεγάλης τῆς καθημένης ἐπὶ ὑδάτων πολλῶν, **2** μεθ᾽ ἧς ἐπόρνευσαν οἱ βασιλεῖς τῆς γῆς καὶ ἐμεθύσθησαν οἱ κατοικοῦντες τὴν γῆν ἐκ τοῦ οἴνου τῆς πορνείας αὐτῆς **3** καὶ ἀπήνεγκέν με εἰς ἔρημον ἐν πνεύματι. καὶ εἶδον γυναῖκα καθημένην ἐπὶ θηρίον κόκκινον, γέμον[τα] ὀνόματα βλασφημίας, ἔχων κεφαλὰς ἑπτὰ καὶ κέρατα δέκα. **4** καὶ ἡ γυνὴ ἦν περιβεβλημένη πορφυροῦν καὶ κόκκινον καὶ κεχρυσωμένη χρυσίῳ καὶ λίθῳ τιμίῳ καὶ μαργαρίταις, ἔχουσα ποτήριον χρυσοῦν ἐν τῇ χειρὶ αὐτῆς γέμον βδελυγμάτων καὶ τὰ ἀκάθαρτα τῆς πορνείας αὐτῆς **5** καὶ ἐπὶ τὸ μέτωπον αὐτῆς ὄνομα γεγραμμένον, μυστήριον, Βαβυλὼν ἡ μεγάλη, ἡ μήτηρ τῶν πορνῶν καὶ τῶν βδελυγμάτων τῆς

evila spirits that looked like frogs; they came out of the mouth of the dragon, out of the mouth of the beast and out of the mouth of the false prophet. 14They are spirits of demons performing miraculous signs, and they go out to the kings of the whole world, to gather them for the battle on the great day of God Almighty.

15"Behold, I come like a thief! Blessed is he who stays awake and keeps his clothes with him, so that he may not go naked and be shamefully exposed."

16Then they gathered the kings together to the place that in Hebrew is called Armageddon.

17The seventh angel poured out his bowl into the air, and out of the temple came a loud voice from the throne, saying, "It is done!" 18Then there came flashes of lightning, rumblings, peals of thunder and a severe earthquake. No earthquake like it has ever occurred since man has been on earth, so tremendous was the quake. 19The great city split into three parts, and the cities of the nations collapsed. God remembered Babylon the Great and gave her the cup filled with the wine of the fury of his wrath. 20Every island fled away and the mountains could not be found. 21From the sky huge hailstones of about a hundred pounds each fell upon men. And they cursed God on account of the plague of hail, because the plague was so terrible.

The Woman on the Beast

17 One of the seven angels who had the seven bowls came and said to me, "Come, I will show you the punishment of the great prostitute, who sits on many waters. 2With her the kings of the earth committed adultery and the inhabitants of the earth were intoxicated with the wine of her adulteries."

3Then the angel carried me away in the Spirit into a desert. There I saw a woman sitting on a scarlet beast that was covered with blasphemous names and had seven heads and ten horns. 4The woman was dressed in purple and scarlet, and was glittering with gold, precious stones and pearls. She held a golden cup in her hand, filled with abominable things and the filth of her adulteries. 5This title was written on her forehead:

MYSTERY

BABYLON THE GREAT

THE MOTHER OF PROSTITUTES

AND OF THE ABOMINATIONS OF THE EARTH.

z Gk *and keeps his robes*   a Gk *weighing about a talent*
b Or *in the Spirit*

a13 Greek *unclean*

the woman was drunk with the blood of the saints and the blood of the witnesses to Jesus.

When I saw her, I was greatly amazed. 7But the angel said to me, "Why are you so amazed? I will tell you the mystery of the woman, and of the beast with seven heads and ten horns that carries her. 8The beast that you saw was, and is not, and is about to ascend from the bottomless pit and go to destruction. And the inhabitants of the earth, whose names have not been written in the book of life from the foundation of the world, will be amazed when they see the beast, because it was and is not and is to come.

9 "This calls for a mind that has wisdom: the seven heads are seven mountains on which the woman is seated; also, they are seven kings, 10of whom five have fallen, one is living, and the other has not yet come; and when he comes, he must remain only a little while. 11As for the beast that was and is not, it is an eighth but it belongs to the seven, and it goes to destruction. 12And the ten horns that you saw are ten kings who have not yet received a kingdom, but they are to receive authority as kings for one hour, together with the beast. 13These are united in yielding their power and authority to the beast; 14they will make war on the Lamb, and the Lamb will conquer them, for he is Lord of lords and King of kings, and those with him are called and chosen and faithful."

15 And he said to me, "The waters that you saw, where the whore is seated, are peoples and multitudes and nations and languages. 16And the ten horns that you saw, they and the beast will hate the whore; they will make her desolate and naked; they will devour her flesh and burn her up with fire. 17For God has put it into their hearts to carry out his purpose by agreeing to give their kingdom to the beast, until the words of God will be fulfilled. 18The woman you saw is the great city that rules over the kings of the earth."

The Fal! of Babylon

18 After this I saw another angel coming down from heaven, having great authority; and the earth was made bright with his splendor. 2He called out with a mighty voice,

γῆς. **6** καὶ εἶδον τὴν γυναῖκα μεθύουσαν ἐκ τοῦ αἵματος τῶν ἁγίων καὶ ἐκ τοῦ αἵματος τῶν μαρτύρων Ἰησοῦ.

Καὶ ἐθαύμασα ἰδὼν αὐτὴν θαῦμα μέγα. **7** καὶ εἶπέν μοι ὁ ἄγγελος, Διὰ τί ἐθαύμασας; ἐγὼ ἐρῶ σοι τὸ μυστήριον τῆς γυναικὸς καὶ τοῦ θηρίου τοῦ βαστάζοντος αὐτὴν τοῦ ἔχοντος τὰς ἑπτὰ κεφαλὰς καὶ τὰ δέκα κέρατα. **8** τὸ θηρίον ὃ εἶδες ἦν καὶ οὐκ ἔστιν καὶ μέλλει ἀναβαίνειν ἐκ τῆς ἀβύσσου καὶ εἰς ἀπώλειαν ὑπάγει, καὶ θαυμασθήσονται οἱ κατοικοῦντες ἐπὶ τῆς γῆς, ὧν οὐ γέγραπται τὸ ὄνομα ἐπὶ τὸ βιβλίον τῆς ζωῆς ἀπὸ καταβολῆς κόσμου, βλεπόντων τὸ θηρίον ὅτι ἦν καὶ οὐκ ἔστιν καὶ παρέσται **9** ὧδε ὁ νοῦς ὁ ἔχων σοφίαν. αἱ ἑπτὰ κεφαλαὶ ἑπτὰ ὄρη εἰσίν, ὅπου ἡ γυνὴ κάθηται ἐπ' αὐτῶν.[a] καὶ βασιλεῖς ἑπτά εἰσιν· **10** οἱ πέντε ἔπεσαν, ὁ εἷς ἔστιν, ὁ ἄλλος οὔπω ἦλθεν, καὶ ὅταν ἔλθῃ ὀλίγον αὐτὸν δεῖ μεῖναι. **11** καὶ τὸ θηρίον ὃ ἦν καὶ οὐκ ἔστιν καὶ αὐτὸς ὄγδοός ἐστιν καὶ ἐκ τῶν ἑπτά ἐστιν, καὶ εἰς ἀπώλειαν ὑπάγει. **12** καὶ τὰ δέκα κέρατα ἃ εἶδες δέκα βασιλεῖς εἰσιν, οἵτινες βασιλείαν οὔπω ἔλαβον, ἀλλὰ ἐξουσίαν ὡς βασιλεῖς μίαν ὥραν λαμβάνουσιν μετὰ τοῦ θηρίου. **13** οὗτοι μίαν γνώμην ἔχουσιν καὶ τὴν δύναμιν καὶ ἐξουσίαν αὐτῶν τῷ θηρίῳ διδόασιν. **14** οὗτοι μετὰ τοῦ ἀρνίου πολεμήσουσιν καὶ τὸ ἀρνίον νικήσει αὐτούς, ὅτι κύριος κυρίων ἐστὶν καὶ βασιλεὺς βασιλέων καὶ οἱ μετ' αὐτοῦ κλητοὶ καὶ ἐκλεκτοὶ καὶ πιστοί.

15 Καὶ λέγει μοι, Τὰ ὕδατα ἃ εἶδες οὗ ἡ πόρνη κάθηται, λαοὶ καὶ ὄχλοι εἰσὶν καὶ ἔθνη καὶ γλῶσσαι. **16** καὶ τὰ δέκα κέρατα ἃ εἶδες καὶ τὸ θηρίον οὗτοι μισήσουσιν τὴν πόρνην καὶ ἠρημωμένην ποιήσουσιν αὐτὴν καὶ γυμνὴν καὶ τὰς σάρκας αὐτῆς φάγονται καὶ αὐτὴν κατακαύσουσιν ἐν πυρί. **17** ὁ γὰρ θεὸς ἔδωκεν εἰς τὰς καρδίας αὐτῶν ποιῆσαι τὴν γνώμην αὐτοῦ καὶ ποιῆσαι μίαν γνώμην καὶ δοῦναι τὴν βασιλείαν αὐτῶν τῷ θηρίῳ ἄχρι τελεσθήσονται οἱ λόγοι τοῦ θεοῦ. **18** καὶ ἡ γυνὴ ἣν εἶδες ἔστιν ἡ πόλις ἡ μεγάλη ἡ ἔχουσα βασιλείαν ἐπὶ τῶν βασιλέων τῆς γῆς.

18 Μετὰ ταῦτα εἶδον ἄλλον ἄγγελον καταβαίνοντα ἐκ τοῦ οὐρανοῦ ἔχοντα ἐξουσίαν μεγάλην, καὶ ἡ γῆ ἐφωτίσθη ἐκ τῆς δόξης αὐτοῦ. **2** καὶ ἔκραξεν ἐν ἰσχυρᾷ φωνῇ λέγων,

6I saw that the woman was drunk with the blood of the saints, the blood of those who bore testimony to Jesus.

When I saw her, I was greatly astonished. 7Then the angel said to me: "Why are you astonished? I will explain to you the mystery of the woman and of the beast she rides, which has the seven heads and ten horns. 8The beast, which you saw, once was, now is not, and will come up out of the Abyss and go to his destruction. The inhabitants of the earth whose names have not been written in the book of life from the creation of the world will be astonished when they see the beast, because he once was, now is not, and yet will come.

9"This calls for a mind with wisdom. The seven heads are seven hills on which the woman sits. 10They are also seven kings. Five have fallen, one is, the other has not yet come; but when he does come, he must remain for a little while. 11The beast who once was, and now is not, is an eighth king. He belongs to the seven and is going to his destruction.

12"The ten horns you saw are ten kings who have not yet received a kingdom, but who for one hour will receive authority as kings along with the beast. 13They have one purpose and will give their power and authority to the beast. 14They will make war against the Lamb, but the Lamb will overcome them because he is Lord of lords and King of kings—and with him will be his called, chosen and faithful followers."

15Then the angel said to me, "The waters you saw, where the prostitute sits, are peoples, multitudes, nations and languages. 16The beast and the ten horns you saw will hate the prostitute. They will bring her to ruin and leave her naked; they will eat her flesh and burn her with fire. 17For God has put it into their hearts to accomplish his purpose by agreeing to give the beast their power to rule, until God's words are fulfilled. 18The woman you saw is the great city that rules over the kings of the earth."

The Fall of Babylon

18 After this I saw another angel coming down from heaven. He had great authority, and the earth was illuminated by his splendor. 2With a mighty voice he shouted:

[a]9 NIV begins verse 10 after αὐτῶν.

NRSV

"Fallen, fallen is Babylon the great!
　It has become a dwelling place of
　　demons,
　a haunt of every foul spirit,
　a haunt of every foul bird,
　a haunt of every foul and hateful
　　beast.c
3 For all the nations have drunkd
　of the wine of the wrath of her
　　fornication,
　and the kings of the earth have
　　committed fornication with her,
　and the merchants of the earth have
　　grown rich from the powere of
　　her luxury."

4 Then I heard another voice from heaven
saying,
　"Come out of her, my people,
　　so that you do not take part in her
　　　sins,
　and so that you do not share
　　in her plagues;
5 　for her sins are heaped high as heaven,
　　and God has remembered her
　　　iniquities.
6 　Render to her as she herself has
　　rendered,
　　and repay her double for her deeds;
　　mix a double draught for her in the
　　　cup she mixed.
7 　As she glorified herself and lived
　　luxuriously,
　　so give her a like measure of
　　　torment and grief.
　Since in her heart she says,
　'I rule as a queen;
　I am no widow,
　　and I will never see grief,'
8 　therefore her plagues will come in a
　　single day—
　　pestilence and mourning and
　　　famine—
　and she will be burned with fire;
　　for mighty is the Lord God who
　　　judges her."

9 And the kings of the earth, who committed fornication and lived in luxury with
her, will weep and wail over her when
they see the smoke of her burning; 10they
will stand far off, in fear of her torment,
and say,
　"Alas, alas, the great city,
　　Babylon, the mighty city!
　For in one hour your judgment has
　　come."

Greek

Ἔπεσεν ἔπεσεν Βαβυλὼν ἡ μεγάλη,
　καὶ ἐγένετο κατοικητήριον
　　δαιμονίων
　καὶ φυλακὴ παντὸς πνεύματος
　　ἀκαθάρτου
　καὶ φυλακὴ παντὸς ὀρνέου
　　ἀκαθάρτου
　[καὶ φυλακὴ παντὸς θηρίου
　　ἀκαθάρτου]a καὶ μεμισημένου,
3 ὅτι ἐκ τοῦ οἴνου τοῦ θυμοῦ τῆς
　　πορνείας αὐτῆς
　πέπωκανb πάντα τὰ ἔθνη
　καὶ οἱ βασιλεῖς τῆς γῆς μετ᾽
　　αὐτῆς ἐπόρνευσαν
　καὶ οἱ ἔμποροι τῆς γῆς ἐκ τῆς
　　δυνάμεως τοῦ στρήνους αὐτῆς
　　ἐπλούτησαν.
4 Καὶ ἤκουσα ἄλλην φωνὴν ἐκ τοῦ
　οὐρανοῦ λέγουσαν,
　Ἐξέλθατε ὁ λαός μου ἐξ αὐτῆς
　ἵνα μὴ συγκοινωνήσητε ταῖς
　　ἁμαρτίαις αὐτῆς,
　καὶ ἐκ τῶν πληγῶν αὐτῆς
　ἵνα μὴ λάβητε,
5 ὅτι ἐκολλήθησαν αὐτῆς αἱ ἁμαρτίαι
　ἄχρι τοῦ οὐρανοῦ
　καὶ ἐμνημόνευσεν ὁ θεὸς τὰ
　　ἀδικήματα αὐτῆς.
6 ἀπόδοτε αὐτῇ ὡς καὶ αὐτὴ ἀπέδωκεν
　καὶ διπλώσατε τὰ διπλᾶ κατὰ τὰ
　　ἔργα αὐτῆς,
　ἐν τῷ ποτηρίῳ ᾧ ἐκέρασεν
　　κεράσατε αὐτῇ διπλοῦν,
7 ὅσα ἐδόξασεν αὐτὴν καὶ
　　ἐστρηνίασεν,
　τοσοῦτον δότε αὐτῇ βασανισμὸν
　　καὶ πένθος.
　ὅτι ἐν τῇ καρδίᾳ αὐτῆς λέγει ὅτι
　Κάθημαι βασίλισσα
　καὶ χήρα οὐκ εἰμὶ
　καὶ πένθος οὐ μὴ ἴδω.
8 διὰ τοῦτο ἐν μιᾷ ἡμέρᾳ ἥξουσιν
　αἱ πληγαὶ αὐτῆς,
　θάνατος καὶ πένθος καὶ λιμός,
　καὶ ἐν πυρὶ κατακαυθήσεται,
　ὅτι ἰσχυρὸς κύριος ὁ θεὸς ὁ
　　κρίνας αὐτήν.
9 Καὶ κλαύσουσιν καὶ κόψονται ἐπ᾽
αὐτὴν οἱ βασιλεῖς τῆς γῆς οἱ μετ᾽
αὐτῆς πορνεύσαντες καὶ στρηνιάσαν-
τες, ὅταν βλέπωσιν τὸν καπνὸν τῆς
πυρώσεως αὐτῆς, 10 ἀπὸ μακρόθεν
ἑστηκότες διὰ τὸν φόβον τοῦ βασανισμοῦ αὐτῆς λέγοντες,
　Οὐαὶ οὐαί, ἡ πόλις ἡ μεγάλη,
　Βαβυλὼν ἡ πόλις ἡ ἰσχυρά,
　ὅτι μιᾷ ὥρᾳ ἦλθεν ἡ κρίσις σου.

NIV

"Fallen! Fallen is Babylon the Great!
　She has become a home for demons
and a haunt for every evila spirit,
　a haunt for every unclean and
　　detestable bird.
3For all the nations have drunk
　the maddening wine of her adulteries.
The kings of the earth committed
　adultery with her,
　and the merchants of the earth grew
　　rich from her excessive luxuries."

4Then I heard another voice from heaven
say:

　"Come out of her, my people,
　　so that you will not share in her sins,
　　so that you will not receive any of her
　　　plagues;
5for her sins are piled up to heaven,
　and God has remembered her crimes.
6Give back to her as she has given;
　pay her back double for what she has
　　done.
　Mix her a double portion from her
　　own cup.
7Give her as much torture and grief
　as the glory and luxury she gave
　　herself.
In her heart she boasts,
　'I sit as queen; I am not a widow,
　and I will never mourn.'
8Therefore in one day her plagues will
　overtake her:
　death, mourning and famine.
She will be consumed by fire,
　for mighty is the Lord God who
　　judges her.

9"When the kings of the earth who committed adultery with her and shared her
luxury see the smoke of her burning, they
will weep and mourn over her. 10Terrified
at her torment, they will stand far off and
cry:

　" 'Woe! Woe, O great city,
　O Babylon, city of power!
　In one hour your doom has come!'

---

c Other ancient authorities lack the words *a haunt of
every foul beast* and attach the words *and hateful* to the
previous line so as to read *a haunt of every foul and
hateful bird*.　d Other ancient authorities read *she has
made all nations drink*　e Or *resources*

b2 NIV text and NRSV note c omit καὶ φυλακὴ παντὸς
θηρίου ἀκαθάρτου　c3 NRSV note d πεπότικεν

a2 Greek *unclean*

11 And the merchants of the earth weep and mourn for her, since no one buys their cargo anymore, 12cargo of gold, silver, jewels and pearls, fine linen, purple, silk and scarlet, all kinds of scented wood, all articles of ivory, all articles of costly wood, bronze, iron, and marble; 13cinnamon, spice, incense, myrrh, frankincense, wine, olive oil, choice flour and wheat, cattle and sheep, horses and chariots, slaves— and human lives.f

14 "The fruit for which your soul longed
    has gone from you,
 and all your dainties and your
    splendor
 are lost to you,
    never to be found again!"

15The merchants of these wares, who gained wealth from her, will stand far off, in fear of her torment, weeping and mourning aloud,

16 "Alas, alas, the great city,
    clothed in fine linen,
      in purple and scarlet,
    adorned with gold,
      with jewels, and with pearls!

17 For in one hour all this wealth has
      been laid waste!"

And all shipmasters and seafarers, sailors and all whose trade is on the sea, stood far off 18and cried out as they saw the smoke of her burning,

 "What city was like the great city?"

19And they threw dust on their heads, as they wept and mourned, crying out,

 "Alas, alas, the great city,
    where all who had ships at sea
    grew rich by her wealth!
 For in one hour she has been laid waste.

20 Rejoice over her, O heaven,
    you saints and apostles and
      prophets!
 For God has given judgment for you
    against her."

21 Then a mighty angel took up a stone like a great millstone and threw it into the sea, saying,

 "With such violence Babylon the great
    city
 will be thrown down,
    and will be found no more;

---

11 Καὶ οἱ ἔμποροι τῆς γῆς κλαίουσιν καὶ πενθοῦσιν ἐπ' αὐτήν, ὅτι τὸν γόμον αὐτῶν οὐδεὶς ἀγοράζει οὐκέτι **12** γόμον χρυσοῦ καὶ ἀργύρου καὶ λίθου τιμίου καὶ μαργαριτῶν καὶ βυσσίνου καὶ πορφύρας καὶ σιρικοῦ καὶ κοκκίνου, καὶ πᾶν ξύλον θύϊνον καὶ πᾶν σκεῦος ἐλεφάντινον καὶ πᾶν σκεῦος ἐκ ξύλου τιμιωτάτου καὶ χαλκοῦ καὶ σιδήρου καὶ μαρμάρου, **13** καὶ κιννάμωμον καὶ ἄμωμον καὶ θυμιάματα καὶ μύρον καὶ λίβανον καὶ οἶνον καὶ ἔλαιον καὶ σεμίδαλιν καὶ σῖτον καὶ κτήνη καὶ πρόβατα, καὶ ἵππων καὶ ῥεδῶν καὶ σωμάτων, καὶ ψυχὰς ἀνθρώπων.

14 καὶ ἡ ὀπώρα σου τῆς ἐπιθυμίας
      τῆς ψυχῆς
   ἀπῆλθεν ἀπὸ σοῦ,
   καὶ πάντα τὰ λιπαρὰ καὶ τὰ λαμπρὰ
   ἀπώλετο ἀπὸ σοῦ
   καὶ οὐκέτι οὐ μὴ αὐτὰ εὑρήσουσιν.

15 οἱ ἔμποροι τούτων οἱ πλουτήσαντες ἀπ' αὐτῆς ἀπὸ μακρόθεν στήσονται διὰ τὸν φόβον τοῦ βασανισμοῦ αὐτῆς κλαίοντες καὶ πενθοῦντες **16** λέγοντες,

   Οὐαὶ οὐαί, ἡ πόλις ἡ μεγάλη,
   ἡ περιβεβλημένη βύσσινον
   καὶ πορφυροῦν καὶ κόκκινον
   καὶ κεχρυσωμένη [ἐν] χρυσίῳ
   καὶ λίθῳ τιμίῳ καὶ μαργαρίτῃ,

17 ὅτι μιᾷ ὥρᾳ ἠρημώθη ὁ τοσοῦτος πλοῦτος.

   Καὶ πᾶς κυβερνήτης καὶ πᾶς ὁ ἐπὶ τόπον πλέων καὶ ναῦται καὶ ὅσοι τὴν θάλασσαν ἐργάζονται, ἀπὸ μακρόθεν ἔστησαν **18** καὶ ἔκραζον βλέποντες τὸν καπνὸν τῆς πυρώσεως αὐτῆς λέγοντες, Τίς ὁμοία τῇ πόλει τῇ μεγάλῃ; **19** καὶ ἔβαλον χοῦν ἐπὶ τὰς κεφαλὰς αὐτῶν καὶ ἔκραζον κλαίοντες καὶ πενθοῦντες λέγοντες,

   Οὐαὶ οὐαί, ἡ πόλις ἡ μεγάλη,
   ἐν ᾗ ἐπλούτησαν πάντες οἱ
      ἔχοντες τὰ πλοῖα
   ἐν τῇ θαλάσσῃ ἐκ τῆς τιμιότητος
      αὐτῆς,
   ὅτι μιᾷ ὥρᾳ ἠρημώθη.

20 Εὐφραίνου ἐπ' αὐτῇ, οὐρανὲ
   καὶ οἱ ἅγιοι καὶ οἱ ἀπόστολοι
      καὶ οἱ προφῆται,
   ὅτι ἔκρινεν ὁ θεὸς τὸ κρίμα ὑμῶν
      ἐξ αὐτῆς.

21 Καὶ ἦρεν εἷς ἄγγελος ἰσχυρὸς λίθον ὡς μύλινον μέγαν καὶ ἔβαλεν εἰς τὴν θάλασσαν λέγων,

   Οὕτως ὁρμήματι βληθήσεται
   Βαβυλὼν ἡ μεγάλη πόλις
   καὶ οὐ μὴ εὑρεθῇ ἔτι.

11"The merchants of the earth will weep and mourn over her because no one buys their cargoes any more—12cargoes of gold, silver, precious stones and pearls; fine linen, purple, silk and scarlet cloth; every sort of citron wood, and articles of every kind made of ivory, costly wood, bronze, iron and marble; 13cargoes of cinnamon and spice, of incense, myrrh and frankincense, of wine and olive oil, of fine flour and wheat; cattle and sheep; horses and carriages; and bodies and souls of men.

14"They will say, 'The fruit you longed for is gone from you. All your riches and splendor have vanished, never to be recovered.' 15The merchants who sold these things and gained their wealth from her will stand far off, terrified at her torment. They will weep and mourn 16and cry out:

 " 'Woe! Woe, O great city,
    dressed in fine linen, purple and
      scarlet,
    and glittering with gold, precious
      stones and pearls!

17In one hour such great wealth has been
      brought to ruin!'

"Every sea captain, and all who travel by ship, the sailors, and all who earn their living from the sea, will stand far off. 18When they see the smoke of her burning, they will exclaim, 'Was there ever a city like this great city?' 19They will throw dust on their heads, and with weeping and mourning cry out:

 " 'Woe! Woe, O great city,
    where all who had ships on the sea
      became rich through her wealth!
 In one hour she has been brought to ruin!

20Rejoice over her, O heaven!
    Rejoice, saints and apostles and
      prophets!
 God has judged her for the way she
      treated you.' "

21Then a mighty angel picked up a boulder the size of a large millstone and threw it into the sea, and said:

 "With such violence
    the great city of Babylon will be thrown
      down,
    never to be found again.

---

f Or chariots, and human bodies and souls

NRSV

22 and the sound of harpists and minstrels
    and of flutists and trumpeters
  will be heard in you no more;
and an artisan of any trade
  will be found in you no more;
and the sound of the millstone
  will be heard in you no more;
23 and the light of a lamp
  will shine in you no more;
and the voice of bridegroom and bride
  will be heard in you no more;
for your merchants were the magnates
    of the earth,
and all nations were deceived by your
    sorcery.
24 And in you[g] was found the blood of
    prophets and of saints,
  and of all who have been slaughtered
    on earth."

The Rejoicing in Heaven

19 After this I heard what seemed to
be the loud voice of a great multitude in heaven, saying,
  "Hallelujah!
  Salvation and glory and power to our
    God,
2   for his judgments are true and just;
he has judged the great whore
  who corrupted the earth with her
    fornication,
and he has avenged on her the blood
    of his servants."[h]
3 Once more they said,
  "Hallelujah!
  The smoke goes up from her forever
    and ever."
4 And the twenty-four elders and the four
living creatures fell down and worshiped
God who is seated on the throne, saying,
  "Amen. Hallelujah!"
  5 And from the throne came a voice saying,
  "Praise our God,
    all you his servants,[h]
  and all who fear him,
    small and great."
6 Then I heard what seemed to be the voice
of a great multitude, like the sound of many
waters and like the sound of mighty thunderpeals, crying out,
  "Hallelujah!
  For the Lord our God
    the Almighty reigns.
7   Let us rejoice and exult

Greek

22 καὶ φωνὴ κιθαρῳδῶν καὶ μουσικῶν
    καὶ αὐλητῶν καὶ σαλπιστῶν
  οὐ μὴ ἀκουσθῇ ἐν σοὶ ἔτι,
καὶ πᾶς τεχνίτης πάσης τέχνης
  οὐ μὴ εὑρεθῇ ἐν σοὶ ἔτι,
καὶ φωνὴ μύλου
  οὐ μὴ ἀκουσθῇ ἐν σοὶ ἔτι,
23 καὶ φῶς λύχνου
  οὐ μὴ φάνῃ ἐν σοὶ ἔτι,
καὶ φωνὴ νυμφίου καὶ νύμφης
  οὐ μὴ ἀκουσθῇ ἐν σοὶ ἔτι·
ὅτι οἱ ἔμποροί σου ἦσαν οἱ
    μεγιστᾶνες τῆς γῆς,
ὅτι ἐν τῇ φαρμακείᾳ σου
    ἐπλανήθησαν πάντα τὰ ἔθνη,
24 καὶ ἐν αὐτῇ αἷμα προφητῶν καὶ
    ἁγίων εὑρέθη
  καὶ πάντων τῶν ἐσφαγμένων ἐπὶ
    τῆς γῆς.

19 Μετὰ ταῦτα ἤκουσα ὡς φωνὴν
μεγάλην ὄχλου πολλοῦ ἐν τῷ
οὐρανῷ λεγόντων,
  Ἁλληλουϊά·
  ἡ σωτηρία καὶ ἡ δόξα καὶ ἡ δύναμις
    τοῦ θεοῦ ἡμῶν,
2   ὅτι ἀληθιναὶ καὶ δίκαιαι αἱ κρίσεις
    αὐτοῦ·
  ὅτι ἔκρινεν τὴν πόρνην τὴν μεγάλην
    ἥτις ἔφθειρεν τὴν γῆν ἐν τῇ
    πορνείᾳ αὐτῆς,
  καὶ ἐξεδίκησεν τὸ αἷμα τῶν δούλων
    αὐτοῦ
  ἐκ χειρὸς αὐτῆς.
3 καὶ δεύτερον εἴρηκαν,
  Ἁλληλουϊά·
  καὶ ὁ καπνὸς αὐτῆς ἀναβαίνει εἰς
    τοὺς αἰῶνας τῶν αἰώνων.
4 καὶ ἔπεσαν οἱ πρεσβύτεροι οἱ εἴκοσι
τέσσαρες καὶ τὰ τέσσαρα ζῷα καὶ
προσεκύνησαν τῷ θεῷ τῷ καθημένῳ
ἐπὶ τῷ θρόνῳ λέγοντες,
  Ἀμὴν Ἁλληλουϊά,
  5 Καὶ φωνὴ ἀπὸ τοῦ θρόνου ἐξῆλθεν
λέγουσα,
  Αἰνεῖτε τῷ θεῷ ἡμῶν
    πάντες οἱ δοῦλοι αὐτοῦ
  [καὶ] οἱ φοβούμενοι αὐτόν,
  οἱ μικροὶ καὶ οἱ μεγάλοι.
6 καὶ ἤκουσα ὡς φωνὴν ὄχλου πολλοῦ
καὶ ὡς φωνὴν ὑδάτων πολλῶν καὶ ὡς
φωνὴν βροντῶν ἰσχυρῶν λεγόντων,
  Ἁλληλουϊά,
  ὅτι ἐβασίλευσεν κύριος
  ὁ θεὸς [ἡμῶν] ὁ παντοκράτωρ.
7 χαίρωμεν καὶ ἀγαλλιῶμεν

NIV

22 The music of harpists and musicians,
    flute players and trumpeters,
  will never be heard in you again.
No workman of any trade
  will ever be found in you again.
The sound of a millstone
  will never be heard in you again.
23 The light of a lamp
  will never shine in you again.
The voice of bridegroom and bride
  will never be heard in you again.
Your merchants were the world's great
    men.
By your magic spell all the nations
    were led astray.
24 In her was found the blood of prophets
    and of the saints,
  and of all who have been killed on the
    earth."

Hallelujah!

19 After this I heard what sounded
like the roar of a great multitude in heaven shouting:

  "Hallelujah!
  Salvation and glory and power belong
    to our God,
2   for true and just are his judgments.
He has condemned the great prostitute
  who corrupted the earth by her
    adulteries.
He has avenged on her the blood of his
    servants."

3 And again they shouted:

  "Hallelujah!
  The smoke from her goes up for ever
    and ever."

4 The twenty-four elders and the four living creatures fell down and worshiped God, who was seated on the throne. And they cried:

  "Amen, Hallelujah!"

5 Then a voice came from the throne, saying:

  "Praise our God,
    all you his servants,
  you who fear him,
    both small and great!"

6 Then I heard what sounded like a great multitude, like the roar of rushing waters and like loud peals of thunder, shouting:

  "Hallelujah!
  For our Lord God Almighty reigns.
7 Let us rejoice and be glad

g Gk *her*   h Gk *slaves*

NRSV (left column)

and give him the glory,
  for the marriage of the Lamb has come,
    and his bride has made herself ready;
8 to her it has been granted to be clothed
    with fine linen, bright and pure"—
for the fine linen is the righteous deeds of
the saints.

9 And the angel said[i] to me, "Write this:
Blessed are those who are invited to the
marriage supper of the Lamb." And he
said to me, "These are true words of God."
[10]Then I fell down at his feet to worship
him, but he said to me, "You must not do
that! I am a fellow servant[j] with you and
your comrades[k] who hold the testimony
of Jesus.[l] Worship God! For the testimony
of Jesus[l] is the spirit of prophecy."

The Rider on the White Horse

11 Then I saw heaven opened, and there
was a white horse! Its rider is called Faithful and True, and in righteousness he
judges and makes war. [12]His eyes are like
a flame of fire, and on his head are many
diadems; and he has a name inscribed that
no one knows but himself. [13]He is clothed
in a robe dipped in[m] blood, and his name
is called The Word of God. [14]And the
armies of heaven, wearing fine linen, white
and pure, were following him on white
horses. [15]From his mouth comes a sharp
sword with which to strike down the nations, and he will rule[n] them with a rod of
iron; he will tread the wine press of the
fury of the wrath of God the Almighty.
[16]On his robe and on his thigh he has a
name inscribed, "King of kings and Lord
of lords."

The Beast and Its Armies Defeated

17 Then I saw an angel standing in the
sun, and with a loud voice he called to all
the birds that fly in midheaven, "Come,
gather for the great supper of God, [18]to eat
the flesh of kings, the flesh of captains, the
flesh of the mighty, the flesh of horses and
their riders—flesh of all, both free and
slave, both small and great." [19]Then I saw
the beast and the kings of the earth with
their armies gathered to make war against
the rider on the horse and against his army.
[20]And the beast was captured, and with it

Greek (center column)

καὶ δώσωμεν τὴν δόξαν αὐτῷ,
ὅτι ἦλθεν ὁ γάμος τοῦ ἀρνίου
καὶ ἡ γυνὴ αὐτοῦ ἡτοίμασεν ἑαυτὴν
8 καὶ ἐδόθη αὐτῇ ἵνα περιβάληται
βύσσινον λαμπρὸν καθαρόν·
τὸ γὰρ βύσσινον τὰ δικαιώματα
τῶν ἁγίων ἐστίν.

9 Καὶ λέγει μοι, Γράψον· Μακάριοι
οἱ εἰς τὸ δεῖπνον τοῦ γάμου τοῦ
ἀρνίου κεκλημένοι. καὶ λέγει μοι, Οὗτοι
οἱ λόγοι ἀληθινοὶ τοῦ θεοῦ εἰσιν. 10 καὶ
ἔπεσα ἔμπροσθεν τῶν ποδῶν αὐτοῦ
προσκυνῆσαι αὐτῷ. καὶ λέγει μοι, Ὅρα
μή· σύνδουλός σού εἰμι καὶ τῶν ἀδελφῶν
σου τῶν ἐχόντων τὴν μαρτυρίαν Ἰησοῦ·
τῷ θεῷ προσκύνησον. ἡ γὰρ μαρτυρία
Ἰησοῦ ἐστιν τὸ πνεῦμα τῆς προφητείας.
11 Καὶ εἶδον τὸν οὐρανὸν ἠνεῳγμένον,
καὶ ἰδοὺ ἵππος λευκὸς καὶ ὁ καθήμενος
ἐπ' αὐτὸν [καλούμενος] πιστὸς καὶ
ἀληθινός, καὶ ἐν δικαιοσύνῃ κρίνει καὶ
πολεμεῖ. 12 οἱ δὲ ὀφθαλμοὶ αὐτοῦ [ὡς]
φλὸξ πυρός, καὶ ἐπὶ τὴν κεφαλὴν αὐτοῦ
διαδήματα πολλά, ἔχων ὄνομα γεγραμμένον ὃ οὐδεὶς οἶδεν εἰ μὴ αὐτός,
13 καὶ περιβεβλημένος ἱμάτιον βεβαμ-
μένον[a] αἵματι, καὶ κέκληται τὸ ὄνομα
αὐτοῦ ὁ λόγος τοῦ θεοῦ. 14 καὶ τὰ
στρατεύματα [τὰ] ἐν τῷ οὐρανῷ
ἠκολούθει αὐτῷ ἐφ' ἵπποις λευκοῖς,
ἐνδεδυμένοι βύσσινον λευκὸν καθαρόν.
15 καὶ ἐκ τοῦ στόματος αὐτοῦ ἐκπορεύεται ῥομφαία ὀξεῖα, ἵνα ἐν αὐτῇ πατάξῃ
τὰ ἔθνη, καὶ αὐτὸς ποιμανεῖ αὐτοὺς
ἐν ῥάβδῳ σιδηρᾷ, καὶ αὐτὸς πατεῖ τὴν
ληνὸν τοῦ οἴνου τοῦ θυμοῦ τῆς ὀργῆς
τοῦ θεοῦ τοῦ παντοκράτορος. 16 καὶ
ἔχει ἐπὶ τὸ ἱμάτιον καὶ ἐπὶ τὸν μηρὸν
αὐτοῦ ὄνομα γεγραμμένον· Βασιλεὺς
βασιλέων καὶ κύριος κυρίων.
17 Καὶ εἶδον ἕνα ἄγγελον ἑστῶτα ἐν
τῷ ἡλίῳ καὶ ἔκραξεν [ἐν] φωνῇ μεγάλῃ
λέγων πᾶσιν τοῖς ὀρνέοις τοῖς πετο-
μένοις ἐν μεσουρανήματι, Δεῦτε
συνάχθητε εἰς τὸ δεῖπνον τὸ μέγα τοῦ
θεοῦ 18 ἵνα φάγητε σάρκας βασιλέων
καὶ σάρκας χιλιάρχων καὶ σάρκας
ἰσχυρῶν καὶ σάρκας ἵππων καὶ τῶν
καθημένων ἐπ' αὐτῶν καὶ σάρκας
πάντων ἐλευθέρων τε καὶ δούλων καὶ
μικρῶν καὶ μεγάλων. 19 Καὶ εἶδον τὸ
θηρίον καὶ τοὺς βασιλεῖς τῆς γῆς καὶ
τὰ στρατεύματα αὐτῶν συνηγμένα
ποιῆσαι τὸν πόλεμον μετὰ τοῦ καθημένου ἐπὶ τοῦ ἵππου καὶ μετὰ τοῦ
στρατεύματος αὐτοῦ. 20 καὶ ἐπιάσθη
τὸ θηρίον καὶ μετ' αὐτοῦ ὁ ψευδο-

NIV (right column)

and give him glory!
  For the wedding of the Lamb has come,
    and his bride has made herself ready.
[8]Fine linen, bright and clean,
    was given her to wear."
(Fine linen stands for the righteous acts of
the saints.)

[9]Then the angel said to me, "Write:
'Blessed are those who are invited to the
wedding supper of the Lamb!' " And he
added, "These are the true words of God."

[10]At this I fell at his feet to worship him.
But he said to me, "Do not do it! I am a
fellow servant with you and with your
brothers who hold to the testimony of Jesus.
Worship God! For the testimony of Jesus is
the spirit of prophecy."

The Rider on the White Horse

[11]I saw heaven standing open and there
before me was a white horse, whose rider
is called Faithful and True. With justice he
judges and makes war. [12]His eyes are like
blazing fire, and on his head are many
crowns. He has a name written on him
that no one knows but he himself. [13]He is
dressed in a robe dipped in blood, and his
name is the Word of God. [14]The armies of
heaven were following him, riding on
white horses and dressed in fine linen,
white and clean. [15]Out of his mouth comes
a sharp sword with which to strike down
the nations. "He will rule them with an
iron scepter."[a] He treads the winepress of
the fury of the wrath of God Almighty.
[16]On his robe and on his thigh he has this
name written:

KING OF KINGS AND LORD OF LORDS.

[17]And I saw an angel standing in the sun,
who cried in a loud voice to all the birds
flying in midair, "Come, gather together
for the great supper of God, [18]so that you
may eat the flesh of kings, generals, and
mighty men, of horses and their riders,
and the flesh of all people, free and slave,
small and great."

[19]Then I saw the beast and the kings of
the earth and their armies gathered together to make war against the rider on
the horse and his army. [20]But the beast
was captured, and with him the false

---

[i]Gk *he said* [j]Gk *slave* [k]Gk *brothers* [l]Or *to Jesus*
[m]Other ancient authorities read *sprinkled with*
[n]Or *will shepherd*   [a]13 NRSV note m ἐρραντισμένον   [a]15 Psalm 2:9

the false prophet who had performed in its presence the signs by which he deceived those who had received the mark of the beast and those who worshiped its image. These two were thrown alive into the lake of fire that burns with sulfur. 21And the rest were killed by the sword of the rider on the horse, the sword that came from his mouth; and all the birds were gorged with their flesh.

The Thousand Years

20 Then I saw an angel coming down from heaven, holding in his hand the key to the bottomless pit and a great chain. 2He seized the dragon, that ancient serpent, who is the Devil and Satan, and bound him for a thousand years, 3and threw him into the pit, and locked and sealed it over him, so that he would deceive the nations no more, until the thousand years were ended. After that he must be let out for a little while.

4 Then I saw thrones, and those seated on them were given authority to judge. I also saw the souls of those who had been beheaded for their testimony to Jesus[o] and for the word of God. They had not worshiped the beast or its image and had not received its mark on their foreheads or their hands. They came to life and reigned with Christ a thousand years. 5(The rest of the dead did not come to life until the thousand years were ended.) This is the first resurrection. 6Blessed and holy are those who share in the first resurrection. Over these the second death has no power, but they will be priests of God and of Christ, and they will reign with him a thousand years.

Satan's Doom

7 When the thousand years are ended, Satan will be released from his prison 8and will come out to deceive the nations at the four corners of the earth, Gog and Magog, in order to gather them for battle; they are as numerous as the sands of the sea. 9They marched up over the breadth of the earth and surrounded the camp of the saints and the beloved city. And fire came down from heaven[p] and consumed them. 10And the devil who had deceived them was thrown into the lake of fire and sulfur, where the beast and the false prophet were,

προφήτης ὁ ποιήσας τὰ σημεῖα ἐνώπιον αὐτοῦ, ἐν οἷς ἐπλάνησεν τοὺς λαβόντας τὸ χάραγμα τοῦ θηρίου καὶ τοὺς προσκυνοῦντας τῇ εἰκόνι αὐτοῦ· ζῶντες ἐβλήθησαν οἱ δύο εἰς τὴν λίμνην τοῦ πυρὸς τῆς καιομένης ἐν θείῳ. 21 καὶ οἱ λοιποὶ ἀπεκτάνθησαν ἐν τῇ ῥομφαίᾳ τοῦ καθημένου ἐπὶ τοῦ ἵππου τῇ ἐξελθούσῃ ἐκ τοῦ στόματος αὐτοῦ, καὶ πάντα τὰ ὄρνεα ἐχορτάσθησαν ἐκ τῶν σαρκῶν αὐτῶν.

20 Καὶ εἶδον ἄγγελον καταβαίνοντα ἐκ τοῦ οὐρανοῦ ἔχοντα τὴν κλεῖν τῆς ἀβύσσου καὶ ἄλυσιν μεγάλην ἐπὶ τὴν χεῖρα αὐτοῦ. 2 καὶ ἐκράτησεν τὸν δράκοντα, ὁ ὄφις ὁ ἀρχαῖος, ὅς ἐστιν Διάβολος καὶ ὁ Σατανᾶς, καὶ ἔδησεν αὐτὸν χίλια ἔτη 3 καὶ ἔβαλεν αὐτὸν εἰς τὴν ἄβυσσον καὶ ἔκλεισεν καὶ ἐσφράγισεν ἐπάνω αὐτοῦ, ἵνα μὴ πλανήσῃ ἔτι τὰ ἔθνη ἄχρι τελεσθῇ τὰ χίλια ἔτη. μετὰ ταῦτα δεῖ λυθῆναι αὐτὸν μικρὸν χρόνον.

4 Καὶ εἶδον θρόνους καὶ ἐκάθισαν ἐπ᾽ αὐτοὺς καὶ κρίμα ἐδόθη αὐτοῖς, καὶ τὰς ψυχὰς τῶν πεπελεκισμένων διὰ τὴν μαρτυρίαν Ἰησοῦ καὶ διὰ τὸν λόγον τοῦ θεοῦ καὶ οἵτινες οὐ προσεκύνησαν τὸ θηρίον οὐδὲ τὴν εἰκόνα αὐτοῦ καὶ οὐκ ἔλαβον τὸ χάραγμα ἐπὶ τὸ μέτωπον καὶ ἐπὶ τὴν χεῖρα αὐτῶν. καὶ ἔζησαν καὶ ἐβασίλευσαν μετὰ τοῦ Χριστοῦ χίλια ἔτη. 5 οἱ λοιποὶ τῶν νεκρῶν οὐκ ἔζησαν ἄχρι τελεσθῇ τὰ χίλια ἔτη. αὕτη ἡ ἀνάστασις ἡ πρώτη. 6 μακάριος καὶ ἅγιος ὁ ἔχων μέρος ἐν τῇ ἀναστάσει τῇ πρώτῃ· ἐπὶ τούτων ὁ δεύτερος θάνατος οὐκ ἔχει ἐξουσίαν, ἀλλ᾽ ἔσονται ἱερεῖς τοῦ θεοῦ καὶ τοῦ Χριστοῦ καὶ βασιλεύσουσιν μετ᾽ αὐτοῦ [τὰ] χίλια ἔτη.

7 Καὶ ὅταν τελεσθῇ τὰ χίλια ἔτη, λυθήσεται ὁ Σατανᾶς ἐκ τῆς φυλακῆς αὐτοῦ 8 καὶ ἐξελεύσεται πλανῆσαι τὰ ἔθνη τὰ ἐν ταῖς τέσσαρσιν γωνίαις τῆς γῆς, τὸν Γὼγ καὶ Μαγώγ, συναγαγεῖν αὐτοὺς εἰς τὸν πόλεμον, ὧν ὁ ἀριθμὸς αὐτῶν ὡς ἡ ἄμμος τῆς θαλάσσης. 9 καὶ ἀνέβησαν ἐπὶ τὸ πλάτος τῆς γῆς καὶ ἐκύκλευσαν τὴν παρεμβολὴν τῶν ἁγίων καὶ τὴν πόλιν τὴν ἠγαπημένην, καὶ κατέβη πῦρ ἐκ τοῦ οὐρανοῦ[a] καὶ κατέφαγεν αὐτούς. 10 καὶ ὁ διάβολος ὁ πλανῶν αὐτοὺς ἐβλήθη εἰς τὴν λίμνην τοῦ πυρὸς καὶ θείου ὅπου καὶ τὸ θηρίον καὶ ὁ ψευδοπροφήτης, καὶ βασανισθήσονται

prophet who had performed the miraculous signs on his behalf. With these signs he had deluded those who had received the mark of the beast and worshiped his image. The two of them were thrown alive into the fiery lake of burning sulfur. 21The rest of them were killed with the sword that came out of the mouth of the rider on the horse, and all the birds gorged themselves on their flesh.

The Thousand Years

20 And I saw an angel coming down out of heaven, having the key to the Abyss and holding in his hand a great chain. 2He seized the dragon, that ancient serpent, who is the devil, or Satan, and bound him for a thousand years. 3He threw him into the Abyss, and locked and sealed it over him, to keep him from deceiving the nations anymore until the thousand years were ended. After that, he must be set free for a short time.

4I saw thrones on which were seated those who had been given authority to judge. And I saw the souls of those who had been beheaded because of their testimony for Jesus and because of the word of God. They had not worshiped the beast or his image and had not received his mark on their foreheads or their hands. They came to life and reigned with Christ a thousand years. 5(The rest of the dead did not come to life until the thousand years were ended.) This is the first resurrection. 6Blessed and holy are those who have part in the first resurrection. The second death has no power over them, but they will be priests of God and of Christ and will reign with him for a thousand years.

Satan's Doom

7When the thousand years are over, Satan will be released from his prison 8and will go out to deceive the nations in the four corners of the earth—Gog and Magog—to gather them for battle. In number they are like the sand on the seashore. 9They marched across the breadth of the earth and surrounded the camp of God's people, the city he loves. But fire came down from heaven and devoured them. 10And the devil, who deceived them, was thrown into the lake of burning sulfur, where the beast and the false prophet had been thrown. They will be tormented day

---

[o] Or *for the testimony of Jesus* [p] Other ancient authorities read *from God, out of heaven*, or *out of heaven from God*

[a]9 NRSV note p adds ἀπὸ τοῦ θεοῦ before or after ἐκ τοῦ οὐρανοῦ

and they will be tormented day and night forever and ever.

The Dead Are Judged

11 Then I saw a great white throne and the one who sat on it; the earth and the heaven fled from his presence, and no place was found for them. 12And I saw the dead, great and small, standing before the throne, and books were opened. Also another book was opened, the book of life. And the dead were judged according to their works, as recorded in the books. 13And the sea gave up the dead that were in it, Death and Hades gave up the dead that were in them, and all were judged according to what they had done. 14Then Death and Hades were thrown into the lake of fire. This is the second death, the lake of fire; 15and anyone whose name was not found written in the book of life was thrown into the lake of fire.

The New Heaven and the New Earth

21 Then I saw a new heaven and a new earth; for the first heaven and the first earth had passed away, and the sea was no more. 2And I saw the holy city, the new Jerusalem, coming down out of heaven from God, prepared as a bride adorned for her husband. 3And I heard a loud voice from the throne saying,

"See, the home q of God is among
        mortals.
He will dwell r with them;
they will be his peoples, s
and God himself will be with them; t
4 he will wipe every tear from their eyes.
Death will be no more;
mourning and crying and pain will be
        no more,
for the first things have passed away."

5 And the one who was seated on the throne said, "See, I am making all things new." Also he said, "Write this, for these words are trustworthy and true." 6Then he said to me, "It is done! I am the Alpha and the Omega, the beginning and the end. To the thirsty I will give water as a gift from the spring of the water of life. 7Those who conquer will inherit these things, and I will be their God and they will be my children. 8But as for the cowardly, the faithless, u the polluted, the murderers, the fornicators, the sorcerers, the idolaters, and

ἡμέρας καὶ νυκτὸς εἰς τοὺς αἰῶνας τῶν αἰώνων.

11 Καὶ εἶδον θρόνον μέγαν λευκὸν καὶ τὸν καθήμενον ἐπ' αὐτόν, οὗ ἀπὸ τοῦ προσώπου ἔφυγεν ἡ γῆ καὶ ὁ οὐρανὸς καὶ τόπος οὐχ εὑρέθη αὐτοῖς. 12 καὶ εἶδον τοὺς νεκρούς, τοὺς μεγάλους καὶ τοὺς μικρούς, ἑστῶτας ἐνώπιον τοῦ θρόνου. καὶ βιβλία ἠνοίχθησαν, καὶ ἄλλο βιβλίον ἠνοίχθη, ὅ ἐστιν τῆς ζωῆς, καὶ ἐκρίθησαν οἱ νεκροὶ ἐκ τῶν γεγραμμένων ἐν τοῖς βιβλίοις κατὰ τὰ ἔργα αὐτῶν. 13 καὶ ἔδωκεν ἡ θάλασσα τοὺς νεκροὺς τοὺς ἐν αὐτῇ καὶ ὁ θάνατος καὶ ὁ ᾅδης ἔδωκαν τοὺς νεκροὺς τοὺς ἐν αὐτοῖς, καὶ ἐκρίθησαν ἕκαστος κατὰ τὰ ἔργα αὐτῶν. 14 καὶ ὁ θάνατος καὶ ὁ ᾅδης ἐβλήθησαν εἰς τὴν λίμνην τοῦ πυρός. οὗτος ὁ θάνατος ὁ δεύτερός ἐστιν, ἡ λίμνη τοῦ πυρός. 15 καὶ εἴ τις οὐχ εὑρέθη ἐν τῇ βίβλῳ τῆς ζωῆς γεγραμμένος, ἐβλήθη εἰς τὴν λίμνην τοῦ πυρός.

21 Καὶ εἶδον οὐρανὸν καινὸν καὶ γῆν καινήν. ὁ γὰρ πρῶτος οὐρανὸς καὶ ἡ πρώτη γῆ ἀπῆλθαν καὶ ἡ θάλασσα οὐκ ἔστιν ἔτι. 2 καὶ τὴν πόλιν τὴν ἁγίαν Ἰερουσαλὴμ καινὴν εἶδον καταβαίνουσαν ἐκ τοῦ οὐρανοῦ ἀπὸ τοῦ θεοῦ ἡτοιμασμένην ὡς νύμφην κεκοσμημένην τῷ ἀνδρὶ αὐτῆς. 3 καὶ ἤκουσα φωνῆς μεγάλης ἐκ τοῦ θρόνου λεγούσης, Ἰδοὺ ἡ σκηνὴ τοῦ θεοῦ μετὰ τῶν ἀνθρώπων, καὶ σκηνώσει μετ' αὐτῶν, καὶ αὐτοὶ λαοὶ a αὐτοῦ ἔσονται, καὶ αὐτὸς ὁ θεὸς μετ' αὐτῶν ἔσται [αὐτῶν θεός], b 4 καὶ ἐξαλείψει πᾶν δάκρυον ἐκ τῶν ὀφθαλμῶν αὐτῶν, καὶ ὁ θάνατος οὐκ ἔσται ἔτι οὔτε πένθος οὔτε κραυγὴ οὔτε πόνος οὐκ ἔσται ἔτι, [ὅτι] τὰ πρῶτα ἀπῆλθαν.

5 Καὶ εἶπεν ὁ καθήμενος ἐπὶ τῷ θρόνῳ, Ἰδοὺ καινὰ ποιῶ πάντα, καὶ λέγει, Γράψον, ὅτι οὗτοι οἱ λόγοι πιστοὶ καὶ ἀληθινοί εἰσιν. 6 καὶ εἶπέν μοι, Γέγοναν. ἐγώ [εἰμι] τὸ Ἄλφα καὶ τὸ Ὦ, ἡ ἀρχὴ καὶ τὸ τέλος. ἐγὼ τῷ διψῶντι δώσω ἐκ τῆς πηγῆς τοῦ ὕδατος τῆς ζωῆς δωρεάν. 7 ὁ νικῶν κληρονομήσει ταῦτα καὶ ἔσομαι αὐτῷ θεὸς καὶ αὐτὸς ἔσται μοι υἱός. 8 τοῖς δὲ δειλοῖς καὶ ἀπίστοις καὶ ἐβδελυγμένοις καὶ φονεῦσιν καὶ πόρνοις καὶ φαρμάκοις καὶ εἰδωλολάτραις καὶ πᾶσιν τοῖς ψευδέσιν τὸ μέρος αὐτῶν ἐν τῇ λίμνη

and night for ever and ever.

The Dead Are Judged

11Then I saw a great white throne and him who was seated on it. Earth and sky fled from his presence, and there was no place for them. 12And I saw the dead, great and small, standing before the throne, and books were opened. Another book was opened, which is the book of life. The dead were judged according to what they had done as recorded in the books. 13The sea gave up the dead that were in it, and death and Hades gave up the dead that were in them, and each person was judged according to what he had done. 14Then death and Hades were thrown into the lake of fire. The lake of fire is the second death. 15If anyone's name was not found written in the book of life, he was thrown into the lake of fire.

The New Jerusalem

21 Then I saw a new heaven and a new earth, for the first heaven and the first earth had passed away, and there was no longer any sea. 2I saw the Holy City, the new Jerusalem, coming down out of heaven from God, prepared as a bride beautifully dressed for her husband. 3And I heard a loud voice from the throne saying, "Now the dwelling of God is with men, and he will live with them. They will be his people, and God himself will be with them and be their God. 4He will wipe every tear from their eyes. There will be no more death or mourning or crying or pain, for the old order of things has passed away."

5He who was seated on the throne said, "I am making everything new!" Then he said, "Write this down, for these words are trustworthy and true."

6He said to me: "It is done. I am the Alpha and the Omega, the Beginning and the End. To him who is thirsty I will give to drink without cost from the spring of the water of life. 7He who overcomes will inherit all this, and I will be his God and he will be my son. 8But the cowardly, the unbelieving, the vile, the murderers, the sexually immoral, those who practice magic arts, the idolaters and all liars—their place will be in the fiery lake of burning

---

q Gk the tabernacle r will tabernacle s Other ancient authorities read people t Other ancient authorities add and be their God u Or the unbelieving

a3 NRSV note s λαός b3 NRSV text omits αὐτῶν θεός; NRSV note t as UBS

all liars, their place will be in the lake that burns with fire and sulfur, which is the second death."

Vision of the New Jerusalem

9 Then one of the seven angels who had the seven bowls full of the seven last plagues came and said to me, "Come, I will show you the bride, the wife of the Lamb." [10]And in the spirit[v] he carried me away to a great, high mountain and showed me the holy city Jerusalem coming down out of heaven from God. [11]It has the glory of God and a radiance like a very rare jewel, like jasper, clear as crystal. [12]It has a great, high wall with twelve gates, and at the gates twelve angels, and on the gates are inscribed the names of the twelve tribes of the Israelites; [13]on the east three gates, on the north three gates, on the south three gates, and on the west three gates. [14]And the wall of the city has twelve foundations, and on them are the twelve names of the twelve apostles of the Lamb.

15 The angel[w] who talked to me had a measuring rod of gold to measure the city and its gates and walls. [16]The city lies foursquare, its length the same as its width; and he measured the city with his rod, fifteen hundred miles;[x] its length and width and height are equal. [17]He also measured its wall, one hundred forty-four cubits[y] by human measurement, which the angel was using. [18]The wall is built of jasper, while the city is pure gold, clear as glass. [19]The foundations of the wall of the city are adorned with every jewel; the first was jasper, the second sapphire, the third agate, the fourth emerald, [20]the fifth onyx, the sixth carnelian, the seventh chrysolite, the eighth beryl, the ninth topaz, the tenth chrysoprase, the eleventh jacinth, the twelfth amethyst. [21]And the twelve gates are twelve pearls, each of the gates is a single pearl, and the street of the city is pure gold, transparent as glass.

22 I saw no temple in the city, for its temple is the Lord God the Almighty and the Lamb. [23]And the city has no need of

τῇ καιομένῃ πυρὶ καὶ θείῳ, ὅ ἐστιν ὁ θάνατος ὁ δεύτερος.

9 Καὶ ἦλθεν εἷς ἐκ τῶν ἑπτὰ ἀγγέλων τῶν ἐχόντων τὰς ἑπτὰ φιάλας τῶν γεμόντων τῶν ἑπτὰ πληγῶν τῶν ἐσχάτων καὶ ἐλάλησεν μετ᾽ ἐμοῦ λέγων, Δεῦρο, δείξω σοι τὴν νύμφην τὴν γυναῖκα τοῦ ἀρνίου. **10** καὶ ἀπήνεγκέν με ἐν πνεύματι ἐπὶ ὄρος μέγα καὶ ὑψηλόν, καὶ ἔδειξέν μοι τὴν πόλιν τὴν ἁγίαν Ἰερουσαλὴμ καταβαίνουσαν ἐκ τοῦ οὐρανοῦ ἀπὸ τοῦ θεοῦ **11** ἔχουσαν τὴν δόξαν τοῦ θεοῦ, ὁ φωστὴρ αὐτῆς ὅμοιος λίθῳ τιμιωτάτῳ ὡς λίθῳ ἰάσπιδι κρυσταλλίζοντι. **12** ἔχουσα τεῖχος μέγα καὶ ὑψηλόν, ἔχουσα πυλῶνας δώδεκα καὶ ἐπὶ τοῖς πυλῶσιν ἀγγέλους δώδεκα καὶ ὀνόματα ἐπιγεγραμμένα, ἅ ἐστιν [τὰ ὀνόματα] τῶν δώδεκα φυλῶν υἱῶν Ἰσραήλ· **13** ἀπὸ ἀνατολῆς πυλῶνες τρεῖς καὶ ἀπὸ βορρᾶ πυλῶνες τρεῖς καὶ ἀπὸ νότου πυλῶνες τρεῖς καὶ ἀπὸ δυσμῶν πυλῶνες τρεῖς. **14** καὶ τὸ τεῖχος τῆς πόλεως ἔχων θεμελίους δώδεκα καὶ ἐπ᾽ αὐτῶν δώδεκα ὀνόματα τῶν δώδεκα ἀποστόλων τοῦ ἀρνίου.

15 Καὶ ὁ λαλῶν μετ᾽ ἐμοῦ εἶχεν μέτρον κάλαμον χρυσοῦν, ἵνα μετρήσῃ τὴν πόλιν καὶ τοὺς πυλῶνας αὐτῆς καὶ τὸ τεῖχος αὐτῆς. **16** καὶ ἡ πόλις τετράγωνος κεῖται καὶ τὸ μῆκος αὐτῆς ὅσον [καὶ] τὸ πλάτος. καὶ ἐμέτρησεν τὴν πόλιν τῷ καλάμῳ ἐπὶ σταδίων δώδεκα χιλιάδων, τὸ μῆκος καὶ τὸ πλάτος καὶ τὸ ὕψος αὐτῆς ἴσα ἐστίν. **17** καὶ ἐμέτρησεν τὸ τεῖχος αὐτῆς ἑκατὸν τεσσεράκοντα τεσσάρων πηχῶν μέτρον ἀνθρώπου, ὅ ἐστιν ἀγγέλου. **18** καὶ ἡ ἐνδώμησις τοῦ τείχους αὐτῆς ἴασπις καὶ ἡ πόλις χρυσίον καθαρὸν ὅμοιον ὑάλῳ καθαρῷ. **19** οἱ θεμέλιοι τοῦ τείχους τῆς πόλεως παντὶ λίθῳ τιμίῳ κεκοσμημένοι· ὁ θεμέλιος ὁ πρῶτος ἴασπις, ὁ δεύτερος σάπφιρος, ὁ τρίτος χαλκηδών, ὁ τέταρτος σμάραγδος, **20** ὁ πέμπτος σαρδόνυξ, ὁ ἕκτος σάρδιον, ὁ ἕβδομος χρυσόλιθος, ὁ ὄγδοος βήρυλλος, ὁ ἔνατος τοπάζιον, ὁ δέκατος χρυσόπρασος, ὁ ἑνδέκατος ὑάκινθος, ὁ δωδέκατος ἀμέθυστος. **21** καὶ οἱ δώδεκα πυλῶνες δώδεκα μαργαρῖται, ἀνὰ εἷς ἕκαστος τῶν πυλώνων ἦν ἐξ ἑνὸς μαργαρίτου. καὶ ἡ πλατεῖα τῆς πόλεως χρυσίον καθαρὸν ὡς ὕαλος διαυγής.

22 Καὶ ναὸν οὐκ εἶδον ἐν αὐτῇ, ὁ γὰρ κύριος ὁ θεὸς ὁ παντοκράτωρ ναὸς αὐτῆς ἐστιν καὶ τὸ ἀρνίον. **23** καὶ ἡ πόλις οὐ χρείαν ἔχει τοῦ ἡλίου οὐδὲ

sulfur. This is the second death."

[9]One of the seven angels who had the seven bowls full of the seven last plagues came and said to me, "Come, I will show you the bride, the wife of the Lamb." [10]And he carried me away in the Spirit to a mountain great and high, and showed me the Holy City, Jerusalem, coming down out of heaven from God. [11]It shone with the glory of God, and its brilliance was like that of a very precious jewel, like a jasper, clear as crystal. [12]It had a great, high wall with twelve gates, and with twelve angels at the gates. On the gates were written the names of the twelve tribes of Israel. [13]There were three gates on the east, three on the north, three on the south and three on the west. [14]The wall of the city had twelve foundations, and on them were the names of the twelve apostles of the Lamb.

[15]The angel who talked with me had a measuring rod of gold to measure the city, its gates and its walls. [16]The city was laid out like a square, as long as it was wide. He measured the city with the rod and found it to be 12,000 stadia[a] in length, and as wide and high as it is long. [17]He measured its wall and it was 144 cubits[b] thick,[c] by man's measurement, which the angel was using. [18]The wall was made of jasper, and the city of pure gold, as pure as glass. [19]The foundations of the city walls were decorated with every kind of precious stone. The first foundation was jasper, the second sapphire, the third chalcedony, the fourth emerald, [20]the fifth sardonyx, the sixth carnelian, the seventh chrysolite, the eighth beryl, the ninth topaz, the tenth chrysoprase, the eleventh jacinth, and the twelfth amethyst.[d] [21]The twelve gates were twelve pearls, each gate made of a single pearl. The great street of the city was of pure gold, like transparent glass.

[22]I did not see a temple in the city, because the Lord God Almighty and the Lamb are its temple. [23]The city does not need the sun or the moon to shine on it, for

---

[v] Or *in the Spirit*   [w] Gk *He*   [x] Gk *twelve thousand stadia*
[y] That is, almost seventy-five yards

[a]16 That is, about 1,400 miles (about 2,200 kilometers)
[b]17 That is, about 200 feet (about 65 meters)   [c]17 Or *high*   [d]20 The precise identification of some of these precious stones is uncertain.

sun or moon to shine on it, for the glory of God is its light, and its lamp is the Lamb. 24The nations will walk by its light, and the kings of the earth will bring their glory into it. 25Its gates will never be shut by day—and there will be no night there. 26People will bring into it the glory and the honor of the nations. 27But nothing unclean will enter it, nor anyone who practices abomination or falsehood, but only those who are written in the Lamb's book of life.

The River of Life

22 Then the angelz showed me the river of the water of life, bright as crystal, flowing from the throne of God and of the Lamb 2through the middle of the street of the city. On either side of the river is the tree of lifea with its twelve kinds of fruit, producing its fruit each month; and the leaves of the tree are for the healing of the nations. 3Nothing accursed will be found there any more. But the throne of God and of the Lamb will be in it, and his servantsb will worship him; 4they will see his face, and his name will be on their foreheads. 5And there will be no more night; they need no light of lamp or sun, for the Lord God will be their light, and they will reign forever and ever.

6 And he said to me, "These words are trustworthy and true, for the Lord, the God of the spirits of the prophets, has sent his angel to show his servantsb what must soon take place."

7 "See, I am coming soon! Blessed is the one who keeps the words of the prophecy of this book."

Epilogue and Benediction

8 I, John, am the one who heard and saw these things. And when I heard and saw them, I fell down to worship at the feet of the angel who showed them to me; 9but he said to me, "You must not do that! I am a fellow servantc with you and your comradesd the prophets, and with those who keep the words of this book. Worship God!"

10 And he said to me, "Do not seal up the words of the prophecy of this book, for the time is near. 11Let the evildoer still do evil, and the filthy still be filthy, and the righteous still do right, and the holy still be

τῆς σελήνης ἵνα φαίνωσιν αὐτῇ, ἡ γὰρ δόξα τοῦ θεοῦ ἐφώτισεν αὐτήν, καὶ ὁ λύχνος αὐτῆς τὸ ἀρνίον. 24 καὶ περιπατήσουσιν τὰ ἔθνη διὰ τοῦ φωτὸς αὐτῆς, καὶ οἱ βασιλεῖς τῆς γῆς φέρουσιν τὴν δόξαν αὐτῶν εἰς αὐτήν, 25 καὶ οἱ πυλῶνες αὐτῆς οὐ μὴ κλεισθῶσιν ἡμέρας, νὺξ γὰρ οὐκ ἔσται ἐκεῖ, 26 καὶ οἴσουσιν τὴν δόξαν καὶ τὴν τιμὴν τῶν ἐθνῶν εἰς αὐτήν. 27 καὶ οὐ μὴ εἰσέλθῃ εἰς αὐτὴν πᾶν κοινὸν καὶ [ὁ] ποιῶν βδέλυγμα καὶ ψεῦδος εἰ μὴ οἱ γεγραμμένοι ἐν τῷ βιβλίῳ τῆς ζωῆς τοῦ ἀρνίου.

22 Καὶ ἔδειξέν μοι ποταμὸν ὕδατος ζωῆς λαμπρὸν ὡς κρύσταλλον, ἐκπορευόμενον ἐκ τοῦ θρόνου τοῦ θεοῦ καὶ τοῦ ἀρνίου. 2 ἐν μέσῳ τῆς πλατείας αὐτῆς καὶ τοῦ ποταμοῦ ἐντεῦθεν καὶ ἐκεῖθεν ξύλον ζωῆς ποιοῦν καρποὺς δώδεκα, κατὰ μῆνα ἕκαστον ἀποδιδοῦν τὸν καρπὸν αὐτοῦ, καὶ τὰ φύλλα τοῦ ξύλου εἰς θεραπείαν τῶν ἐθνῶν. 3 καὶ πᾶν κατάθεμα οὐκ ἔσται ἔτι. καὶ ὁ θρόνος τοῦ θεοῦ καὶ τοῦ ἀρνίου ἐν αὐτῇ ἔσται, καὶ οἱ δοῦλοι αὐτοῦ λατρεύσουσιν αὐτῷ 4 καὶ ὄψονται τὸ πρόσωπον αὐτοῦ, καὶ τὸ ὄνομα αὐτοῦ ἐπὶ τῶν μετώπων αὐτῶν. 5 καὶ νὺξ οὐκ ἔσται ἔτι καὶ οὐκ ἔχουσιν χρείαν φωτὸς λύχνου καὶ φωτὸς ἡλίου, ὅτι κύριος ὁ θεὸς φωτίσει ἐπ᾽ αὐτούς, καὶ βασιλεύσουσιν εἰς τοὺς αἰῶνας τῶν αἰώνων.

6 Καὶ εἶπέν μοι, Οὗτοι οἱ λόγοι πιστοὶ καὶ ἀληθινοί, καὶ ὁ κύριος ὁ θεὸς τῶν πνευμάτων τῶν προφητῶν ἀπέστειλεν τὸν ἄγγελον αὐτοῦ δεῖξαι τοῖς δούλοις αὐτοῦ ἃ δεῖ γενέσθαι ἐν τάχει. 7 καὶ ἰδοὺ ἔρχομαι ταχύ. μακάριος ὁ τηρῶν τοὺς λόγους τῆς προφητείας τοῦ βιβλίου τούτου.

8 Κἀγὼ Ἰωάννης ὁ ἀκούων καὶ βλέπων ταῦτα. καὶ ὅτε ἤκουσα καὶ ἔβλεψα, ἔπεσα προσκυνῆσαι ἔμπροσθεν τῶν ποδῶν τοῦ ἀγγέλου τοῦ δεικνύοντός μοι ταῦτα. 9 καὶ λέγει μοι, Ὅρα μή· σύνδουλός σού εἰμι καὶ τῶν ἀδελφῶν σου τῶν προφητῶν καὶ τῶν τηρούντων τοὺς λόγους τοῦ βιβλίου τούτου· τῷ θεῷ προσκύνησον. 10 καὶ λέγει μοι, Μὴ σφραγίσῃς τοὺς λόγους τῆς προφητείας τοῦ βιβλίου τούτου, ὁ καιρὸς γὰρ ἐγγύς ἐστιν. 11 ὁ ἀδικῶν ἀδικησάτω ἔτι καὶ ὁ ῥυπαρὸς ῥυπανθήτω ἔτι, καὶ ὁ δίκαιος δικαιοσύνην ποιησάτω ἔτι καὶ ὁ ἅγιος ἁγιασθήτω ἔτι.

the glory of God gives it light, and the Lamb is its lamp. 24The nations will walk by its light, and the kings of the earth will bring their splendor into it. 25On no day will its gates ever be shut, for there will be no night there. 26The glory and honor of the nations will be brought into it. 27Nothing impure will ever enter it, nor will anyone who does what is shameful or deceitful, but only those whose names are written in the Lamb's book of life.

The River of Life

22 Then the angel showed me the river of the water of life, as clear as crystal, flowing from the throne of God and of the Lamb 2down the middle of the great street of the city. On each side of the river stood the tree of life, bearing twelve crops of fruit, yielding its fruit every month. And the leaves of the tree are for the healing of the nations. 3No longer will there be any curse. The throne of God and of the Lamb will be in the city, and his servants will serve him. 4They will see his face, and his name will be on their foreheads. 5There will be no more night. They will not need the light of a lamp or the light of the sun, for the Lord God will give them light. And they will reign for ever and ever.

6The angel said to me, "These words are trustworthy and true. The Lord, the God of the spirits of the prophets, sent his angel to show his servants the things that must soon take place."

Jesus Is Coming

7"Behold, I am coming soon! Blessed is he who keeps the words of the prophecy in this book."

8I, John, am the one who heard and saw these things. And when I had heard and seen them, I fell down to worship at the feet of the angel who had been showing them to me. 9But he said to me, "Do not do it! I am a fellow servant with you and with your brothers the prophets and of all who keep the words of this book. Worship God!"

10Then he told me, "Do not seal up the words of the prophecy of this book, because the time is near. 11Let him who does wrong continue to do wrong; let him who is vile continue to be vile; let him who does right continue to do right; and let him who is holy continue to be holy."

---

z Gk he   a Or the Lamb. 2In the middle of the street of the city, and on either side of the river, is the tree of life   b Gk slaves   c Gk slave   d Gk brothers

holy."

12 "See, I am coming soon; my reward is with me, to repay according to everyone's work. [13]I am the Alpha and the Omega, the first and the last, the beginning and the end."

14 Blessed are those who wash their robes,[e] so that they will have the right to the tree of life and may enter the city by the gates. [15]Outside are the dogs and sorcerers and fornicators and murderers and idolaters, and everyone who loves and practices falsehood.

16 "It is I, Jesus, who sent my angel to you with this testimony for the churches. I am the root and the descendant of David, the bright morning star."

[17] The Spirit and the bride say, "Come."
    And let everyone who hears say,
        "Come."
    And let everyone who is thirsty come.
    Let anyone who wishes take the water
        of life as a gift.

18 I warn everyone who hears the words of the prophecy of this book: if anyone adds to them, God will add to that person the plagues described in this book; [19]if anyone takes away from the words of the book of this prophecy, God will take away that person's share in the tree of life and in the holy city, which are described in this book.

20 The one who testifies to these things says, "Surely I am coming soon."

    Amen. Come, Lord Jesus!

21 The grace of the Lord Jesus be with all the saints. Amen.[f]

12 Ἰδοὺ ἔρχομαι ταχύ, καὶ ὁ μισθός μου μετ᾽ ἐμοῦ ἀποδοῦναι ἑκάστῳ ὡς τὸ ἔργον ἐστὶν αὐτοῦ. 13 ἐγὼ τὸ Ἄλφα καὶ τὸ Ὦ, ὁ πρῶτος καὶ ὁ ἔσχατος, ἡ ἀρχὴ καὶ τὸ τέλος.

14 Μακάριοι οἱ πλύνοντες τὰς στολὰς αὐτῶν[a], ἵνα ἔσται ἡ ἐξουσία αὐτῶν ἐπὶ τὸ ξύλον τῆς ζωῆς καὶ τοῖς πυλῶσιν εἰσέλθωσιν εἰς τὴν πόλιν. 15 ἔξω οἱ κύνες καὶ οἱ φάρμακοι καὶ οἱ πόρνοι καὶ οἱ φονεῖς καὶ οἱ εἰδωλολάτραι καὶ πᾶς φιλῶν καὶ ποιῶν ψεῦδος.

16 Ἐγὼ Ἰησοῦς ἔπεμψα τὸν ἄγγελόν μου μαρτυρῆσαι ὑμῖν ταῦτα ἐπὶ ταῖς ἐκκλησίαις. ἐγώ εἰμι ἡ ῥίζα καὶ τὸ γένος Δαυίδ, ὁ ἀστὴρ ὁ λαμπρὸς ὁ πρωϊνός. 17 Καὶ τὸ πνεῦμα καὶ ἡ νύμφη λέγουσιν, Ἔρχου. καὶ ὁ ἀκούων εἰπάτω, Ἔρχου. καὶ ὁ διψῶν ἐρχέσθω, ὁ θέλων λαβέτω ὕδωρ ζωῆς δωρεάν.

18 Μαρτυρῶ ἐγὼ παντὶ τῷ ἀκούοντι τοὺς λόγους τῆς προφητείας τοῦ βιβλίου τούτου· ἐάν τις ἐπιθῇ ἐπ᾽ αὐτά, ἐπιθήσει ὁ θεὸς ἐπ᾽ αὐτὸν τὰς πληγὰς τὰς γεγραμμένας ἐν τῷ βιβλίῳ τούτῳ, 19 καὶ ἐάν τις ἀφέλῃ ἀπὸ τῶν λόγων τοῦ βιβλίου τῆς προφητείας ταύτης, ἀφελεῖ ὁ θεὸς τὸ μέρος αὐτοῦ ἀπὸ τοῦ ξύλου τῆς ζωῆς καὶ ἐκ τῆς πόλεως τῆς ἁγίας τῶν γεγραμμένων ἐν τῷ βιβλίῳ τούτῳ.

20 Λέγει ὁ μαρτυρῶν ταῦτα, Ναί, ἔρχομαι ταχύ. Ἀμήν, ἔρχου κύριε Ἰησοῦ.

21 Ἡ χάρις τοῦ κυρίου Ἰησοῦ μετὰ πάντων[b].

[12]"Behold, I am coming soon! My reward is with me, and I will give to everyone according to what he has done. [13]I am the Alpha and the Omega, the First and the Last, the Beginning and the End.

[14]"Blessed are those who wash their robes, that they may have the right to the tree of life and may go through the gates into the city. [15]Outside are the dogs, those who practice magic arts, the sexually immoral, the murderers, the idolaters and everyone who loves and practices falsehood.

[16]"I, Jesus, have sent my angel to give you[a] this testimony for the churches. I am the Root and the Offspring of David, and the bright Morning Star."

[17]The Spirit and the bride say, "Come!" And let him who hears say, "Come!" Whoever is thirsty, let him come; and whoever wishes, let him take the free gift of the water of life.

[18]I warn everyone who hears the words of the prophecy of this book: If anyone adds anything to them, God will add to him the plagues described in this book. [19]And if anyone takes words away from this book of prophecy, God will take away from him his share in the tree of life and in the holy city, which are described in this book.

[20]He who testifies to these things says, "Yes, I am coming soon."

    Amen. Come, Lord Jesus.

[21]The grace of the Lord Jesus be with God's people. Amen.

---

[e] Other ancient authorities read *do his commandments*
[f] Other ancient authorities lack *all*; others lack *the saints*; others lack *Amen*

[a]14 NRSV note e ποιοῦντες τὰς ἐντολὰς αὐτοῦ
[b]21 NIV text omits πάντων; NIV/NRSV texts add τῶν ἁγίων. ἀμήν.

[a]16 The Greek is plural.

COLOPHON

The Greek New Testament © 1966, 1993 Deutsche Bibelgesellschaft

The New Revised Standard Version Bible © 1989
Division of Christian Education of the National Council of the
Churches of Christ in the United States of America

The Holy Bible, New International Version © 1973, 1978, 1984
International Bible Society

The Greek text was extracted from the Portland Index,
created by John R. Kohlenberger III and Edward M. Goodrick.
It was compared to machine readable copies of UBS[3] and NA[26]
from Hermeneutika Bible Research Software and
Logos Bible Software using SuperC and Compare.

The Greek text was preformatted in MicroSoft® Word for Windows™.
The English texts were preformatted in WordPerfect Office™ Editor 3.0
and WordPerfect™ 5.1.

The Greek New Testament With UBS[4], NRSV and NIV
was typeset with Aldus® PageMaker® 5.0 for Windows™
running under MicroSoft® Windows™ 3.1.
The English font is Palatino.
The Greek font is Graeca™
© 1986-1993 The Payne Loving Trust.
This Postscript font is available from
Linguist's Software, Inc.
P.O. Box 580
Edmonds, WA 98020-0580

Formatting, editing and typesetting were done on
AST Bravo 4/33 and AST Premium Exec 386SX/20 computers.

The Greek New Testament With UBS[4], NRSV and NIV
was designed and edited by
John R. Kohlenberger III and Ed M. van der Maas
and typeset by John R. Kohlenberger III.